Collins
ENGLISH
DICTIONARY
& THESAURUS

Published by Collins
An imprint of HarperCollins Publishers
Westerhill Road
Bishopbriggs
Glasgow G64 2QT

Paperback Sixth Edition 2020
ISBN 978-0-00-830941-1

Essential Second Edition 2020
ISBN 978-0-00-830940-4

10 9 8 7 6 5 4 3 2 1

www.collinsdictionary.com

Typeset by Davidson Publishing Solutions

Printed and bound in Great Britain by
CPI Group (UK) Ltd, Croydon, CR0 4YY

A catalogue record for this book is available
from the British Library.

If you would like to comment on any aspect
of this book, please contact us at the given
address or online.
E-mail: dictionaries@harpercollins.co.uk
facebook.com/collinsdictionary
@collinsdict

Acknowledgements
We would like to thank those authors
and publishers who kindly gave
permission for copyright material to
be used in the Collins Corpus. We would
also like to thank Times Newspapers Ltd
for providing valuable data.

MIX
Paper from
responsible sources
FSC™ C007454

FSC
www.fsc.org

This book is produced from independently certified FSC™ paper
to ensure responsible forest management.

For more information visit: www.harpercollins.co.uk/green

Contents

Using this dictionary & thesaurus

Dictionary content

Main entry words   printed in large bold type, eg
abbey

All main entry words, including abbreviations and combining forms, in one alphabetical sequence, eg
abbot
abbreviate
ABC¹
ABC²
abdicate

Variant spellings   shown in full, eg
adrenalin *or* **adrenaline**

Note: where the spellings **-ize** and **-ization** are used at the end of a word, the alternative forms **-ise** and **-isation** are equally acceptable.

Pronunciations   given in brackets for words that are difficult or confusing; the word is respelt as it is pronounced, with the stressed syllable in bold type, eg
antipodes (an-**tip**-pod-deez)

Parts of speech   shown in italics as an abbreviation, eg
ablaze *adj*

When a word can be used as more than one part of speech, the change of part of speech is shown after an arrow, eg
adept *adj* 1 proficient in something requiring skill ▶ *n* 2 a person skilled in something

Parts of speech may be combined for words, eg
awash *adv, adj* washed over by water

Irregular parts	or confusing forms of verbs, nouns, adjectives, and adverbs shown in bold type, eg **begin** *vb* -ginning, -gan, -gun **regret** *vb* -gretting, -gretted **anniversary** *n, pl* -ries **angry** *adj* -grier, -griest **well** *adv* better, best
Meanings	separated by numbers, eg **absorb** *vb* **1** to soak up a liquid **2** to engage the interest of someone **3** to receive the force of an impact ...
Phrases and idioms	are included in the meanings of the main entry word, eg **hand** ... **22 keep one's hand in** to continue to practise something **23 (near) at hand** very close **24 on hand** close by; available
Related words	shown in the same paragraph as the main entry word, eg **absurd** *adj* obviously senseless or illogical; ridiculous **absurdity** *n* **absurdly** *adv* *Note*: where the meaning of a related word is not given, it may be understood from the main entry word, or from another related word.
Usage labels	give information about, for example, the country or subject field in which a word is used, or how formal or informal it is, eg **avocation** *n* **1** *Brit, Austral & NZ old-fashioned* a person's regular job **2** *formal* a hobby

Thesaurus content

Alternatives   given in roman, eg

> **actually** *adv* = really, in fact, indeed, truly, literally, genuinely, in reality, in truth

Sense numbers   and/or parts of speech match the alternative words with the meanings in the dictionary entry above, eg

collide *vb* **-liding, -lided 1** to crash together violently **2** to conflict or disagree

> **collide** *vb* **1** = crash, clash, meet head-on, come into collision **2** = conflict, clash, be incompatible, be at variance

Where no numbers are shown, the alternatives relate to the various senses of an entry, or of a part of speech, eg

> **laden** *adj* = loaded, burdened, full, charged, weighed down, encumbered

Opposites   given after the list of alternatives and are introduced by a 'does not equal' sign (≠), eg

> **abundance** *n* **1** = plenty, bounty, exuberance, profusion, plethora, affluence, fullness, fruitfulness; ≠ shortage

Usage labels   give information about, for example, the region in which a word or phrase is used, or how formal or informal it is, eg

> **leader** *n* **1** = principal, president, head, chief, boss (*informal*), director, manager, chairperson, sherang (*Austral, NZ*); ≠ follower

Abbreviations used in this dictionary & thesaurus

adj	adjective	*masc*	masculine
adv	adverb	*maths*	mathematics
archaeol	archaeology	*med*	medicine
archit	architecture	*meteorol*	meteorology
astrol	astrology	*myth*	mythology
astron	astronomy	*n*	noun
Austral	Australian	N	North(ern)
bacteriol	bacteriology	*naut*	nautical
biochem	biochemistry	NZ	New Zealand
biol	biology	*ornithol*	ornithology
Brit	Britain, British	*pathol*	pathology
Canad	Canadian	*pharmacol*	pharmacology
cap	capital (letter)	*physiol*	physiology
chem	chemistry	*pl*	plural
conj	conjunction	*prep*	preposition
E	East(ern)	*pron*	pronoun
econ	economics	*psychol*	psychology
esp.	especially	RC	Roman Catholic
etc.	et cetera	S	South(ern)
fem	feminine	*Scot*	Scottish
foll.	followed	*sing*	singular
geog	geography	*sociol*	sociology
geol	geology	*theol*	theology
geom	geometry	US	United States
interj	interjection	*vb*	verb
kg	kilogram(s)	W	West(ern)
km	kilometre(s)	*zool*	zoology

Aa

a or **A** *n*, *pl* **a's**, **A's** or **As** 1 the first letter of the
English alphabet 2 **from A to B** from one place
to another: *I just want a car that takes me from A to B*
3 **from A to Z** from start to finish

a *adj* (*indefinite article*) 1 used preceding a singular
count noun that has not been mentioned before:
a book; a great shame 2 used preceding a noun or
adjective of quantity: *a litre of wine; a great amount
has been written; I swim a lot and walk much more*
3 each or every; per: *I saw him once a week for six
weeks*

A 1 *music* the sixth note of the scale of C major
2 ampere(s) 3 atomic: *an A-bomb*

AA 1 Alcoholics Anonymous 2 (in Britain and
South Africa) Automobile Association

aardvark *n* a S African anteater with long ears
and snout

AB 1 able-bodied seaman 2 Alberta

aback *adv* **taken aback** startled or disconcerted

abacus (ab-a-cuss) *n* a counting device
consisting of a frame holding beads on metal
rods

abalone (ab-a-**lone**-ee) *n* an edible sea creature
with a shell lined with mother-of-pearl

abandon *vb* 1 to desert or leave: *he had already
abandoned his first wife* 2 to give up completely: *did
you abandon all attempts at contact with the boy?* 3 to
give oneself over completely to an emotion ▸ *n*
4 **with abandon** uninhibitedly and without
restraint › **abandonment** *n*

> **abandon** *vb* 1 = leave, strand, ditch (*slang*),
> forsake, run out on, desert, dump 2 = stop, give
> up, halt, pack in (*Brit informal*), discontinue,
> leave off; ≠ continue

abandoned *adj* 1 no longer used or occupied:
four people were found dead in an abandoned vehicle
2 wild and uninhibited: *that fluffy abandoned laugh*

abase *vb* **abasing, abased** › **abase oneself** to
make oneself humble › **abasement** *n*

abashed *adj* embarrassed and ashamed

abate *vb* **abating, abated** to make or become
less strong: *the tension has abated in recent months*
› **abatement** *n*

abattoir (ab-a-**twahr**) *n* a slaughterhouse

abbess *n* the nun in charge of a convent

abbey *n* 1 a church associated with a
community of monks or nuns 2 a community
of monks or nuns 3 a building inhabited by
monks or nuns

> **abbey** *n* 3 = monastery, convent, priory,
> nunnery, friary

abbot *n* the head of an abbey of monks

abbreviate *vb* **-ating, -ated** 1 to shorten a word
by leaving out some letters 2 to cut short
› **abbreviation** *n*

ABC¹ *n* 1 the alphabet 2 an alphabetical guide
3 the basics of something

ABC² Australian Broadcasting Corporation

abdicate *vb* **-cating, -cated** 1 to give up the
throne formally 2 to give up one's
responsibilities › **abdication** *n*

abdomen *n* the part of the body that contains
the stomach and intestines › **abdominal** *adj*

abduct *vb* to remove (a person) by force; kidnap
› **abduction** *n* › **abductor** *n*

> **abduct** *vb* = kidnap, seize, carry off, snatch
> (*slang*)

aberrant *adj* not normal, accurate, or correct:
aberrant behaviour

aberration *n* 1 a sudden change from what is
normal, accurate, or correct 2 a brief lapse in
control of one's thoughts or feelings: *he suddenly
had a mental aberration*

abet *vb* **abetting, abetted** to help or encourage
in wrongdoing

abeyance *n* **in abeyance** put aside temporarily

abhor *vb* **-horring, -horred** to detest utterly

abhorrent *adj* hateful or disgusting
› **abhorrence** *n*

abide *vb* 1 to tolerate: *I can't abide stupid people* 2 to
last or exist for a long time: *regions of the world
where conflict abides* 3 **abide by** to act in
accordance with: *we must abide by the findings of the
report* 4 *archaic* to live

> **abide** *vb* 1 = tolerate, suffer, accept, bear,
> endure, put up with, take, stand 3 **abide by
> something** = obey, follow, agree to, carry out,
> observe, fulfil, act on, comply with

abiding *adj* lasting for ever: *an abiding interest in
history*

> **abiding** *adj* = enduring, lasting, continuing,
> permanent, persistent, everlasting; ≠ brief

ability *n*, *pl* **-ties** 1 possession of the necessary
skill or power to do something 2 great skill or
competence: *his ability as a speaker was legendary*

> **ability** *n* 1 = capability, potential, competence,
> proficiency; ≠ inability 2 = skill, talent,
> expertise, competence, aptitude, proficiency,
> cleverness

abject *adj* 1 utterly miserable: *his mother grew
up in abject poverty* 2 lacking all self-respect
› **abjectly** *adv*

abjure *vb* **-juring, -jured** to renounce or deny
under oath › **abjuration** *n*

ablaze *adj* 1 on fire 2 brightly illuminated:
the sky was ablaze with the stars shining bright
3 emotionally aroused: *his eyes were ablaze with
anger*

able *adj* 1 having the necessary power, skill, or

a

opportunity to do something **2** capable or talented

able _adj_ **2** = capable, qualified, efficient, accomplished, competent, skilful, proficient; ≠ incapable

able-bodied _adj_ strong and healthy
ablutions _pl n_ the act of washing: _after the nightly ablutions, I settled down to read_
ably _adv_ competently or skilfully
abnormal _adj_ differing from the usual or typical > **abnormality** _n_ > **abnormally** _adv_

abnormal _adj_ = unusual, different, odd, strange, extraordinary, remarkable, exceptional, peculiar; ≠ normal

aboard _adv, adj, prep_ on, in, onto, or into (a ship, plane, or train)
abode _n_ one's home
abolish _vb_ to do away with (laws, regulations, or customs)

abolish _vb_ = do away with, end, destroy, eliminate, cancel, get rid of, ditch (_slang_), throw out; ≠ establish

abolition _n_ **1** the act of doing away with something: _the abolition of the death penalty_ **2 Abolition** the ending of slavery > **abolitionist** _n, adj_

abolition _n_ **1** = eradication, ending, end, destruction, wiping out, elimination, cancellation, termination

abominable _adj_ very bad or unpleasant: _I think that what is being done here is utterly abominable_ > **abominably** _adv_
abominable snowman _n_ a large creature, like a man or an ape, that is said to live in the Himalayas
aboriginal _adj_ existing in a place from the earliest known period
Aboriginal _adj_ of or relating to the peoples who inhabited Australia before the arrival of European settlers
Aborigine _n_ _sometimes offensive_ a member or descendant of any of the peoples who were already living in Australia before the arrival of European settlers
abort _vb_ **1** (of a pregnancy) to end before the fetus is viable **2** to perform an abortion on a pregnant woman **3** to end a plan or process before completion

abort _vb_ **1** = terminate, **3** = stop, end, finish, check, arrest, halt, cease, axe (_informal_)

abortion _n_ **1** an operation to end pregnancy **2** the premature ending of a pregnancy when a fetus is expelled from the womb before it can live independently **3** the failure of a mission or project > **abortionist** _n_

abortion _n_ **1** = termination, deliberate miscarriage

abortive _adj_ failing to achieve its purpose
abound _vb_ **1** to exist in large numbers **2 abound in** to have a large number of

abound _vb_ **1** = be plentiful, thrive, flourish, be numerous, proliferate, be abundant, be thick on the ground

about _prep_ **1** relating to or concerning **2** near to **3** carried on: _I haven't any money about me_ **4** on every side of ▸ _adv_ **5** near in number, time, or degree; approximately **6** nearby **7** here and there: _there were some fifteen other people scattered about on the first floor_ **8** all around; on every side **9** in or to the opposite direction **10** in rotation: _turn and turn about_ **11** used to indicate understatement: _it's about time somebody told the truth on that subject_ **12 about to** on the point of; intending to: _she was about to get in the car_ **13 not about to** determined not to: _we're not about to help her out_ ▸ _adj_ **14** active: _he was off the premises well before anyone was up and about_

about _prep_ **1** = regarding, on, concerning, dealing with, referring to, relating to, as regards **2** = near, around, close to, nearby, beside, adjacent to, in the neighbourhood of ▸ _adv_ **5** = approximately, around, almost, nearly, approaching, close to, roughly, just about

about-turn _or US_ **about-face** _n_ **1** a complete change of opinion or direction **2** a reversal of the direction in which one is facing
above _prep_ **1** higher than; over **2** greater than in quantity or degree: _above average_ **3** superior to or higher than in quality, rank, or ability **4** too high-minded for: _she considered herself above the task of working_ **5** too respected for; beyond: _his fleet was above suspicion_ **6** too difficult to be understood by: _a discussion that was way above my head_ **7** louder or higher than (other noise) **8** in preference to **9 above all** most of all; especially ▸ _adv_ **10** in or to a higher place: _the hills above_ **11** in a previous place (in something written or printed) **12** higher in rank or position ▸ _n_ **13 the above** something previously mentioned ▸ _adj_ **14** appearing in a previous place (in something written or printed): _for a copy of the free brochure write to the above address_

above _prep_ **1** = over, upon, beyond, on top of, exceeding, higher than; ≠ under **3** = senior to, over, ahead of, in charge of, higher than, superior to, more powerful than

above board _adj_ completely honest and open
abracadabra _n_ a word used by conjurors when performing a magic trick
abrasion _n_ **1** a scraped area on the skin; graze **2** _geog_ the erosion of rock by rock fragments scratching and scraping it
abrasive _adj_ **1** rude and unpleasant in manner **2** tending to rub or scrape; rough ▸ _n_ **3** a substance used for cleaning, smoothing, or polishing

abreast *adj* **1** alongside each other and facing in the same direction: *the two cars were abreast* **2 abreast of** up to date with

abridge *vb* **abridging**, **abridged** to shorten a written work by taking out parts > **abridgment** *or* **abridgement** *n*

abroad *adv* **1** to or in a foreign country **2** generally known or felt: *there is a new spirit abroad*

> **abroad** *adv* **1** = overseas, out of the country, in foreign lands

abrogate *vb* **-gating, -gated** to cancel (a law or an agreement) formally > **abrogation** *n*

abrupt *adj* **1** sudden or unexpected: *an abrupt departure* **2** rather rude in speech or manner > **abruptly** *adv* > **abruptness** *n*

> **abrupt** *adj* **1** = sudden, unexpected, rapid, surprising, quick, rash, precipitate; ≠ slow **2** = curt, brief, short, rude, impatient, terse, gruff, succinct; ≠ polite

abs *pl n* abdominal muscles

abscess (ab-sess) *n* **1** a swelling containing pus as a result of inflammation ▸ *vb* **2** to form a swelling containing pus > **abscessed** *adj*

abscond *vb* to run away unexpectedly

abseil (ab-sale) *vb* **1** to go down a steep drop by a rope fastened at the top and tied around one's body ▸ *n* **2** an instance of abseiling

absence *n* **1** the state of being away **2** the time during which a person or thing is away **3** the fact of being without something

> **absence** *n* **2** = time off, leave, break, vacation, recess, truancy, absenteeism, nonattendance **3** = lack, deficiency, omission, scarcity, want, need, shortage, dearth

absent *adj* **1** not present in a place or situation **2** lacking **3** not paying attention ▸ *vb* **4 absent oneself** to stay away > **absently** *adv*

> **absent** *adj* **1** = away, missing, gone, elsewhere, unavailable, nonexistent; ≠ present **3** = absent-minded, blank, vague, distracted, vacant, preoccupied, oblivious, inattentive; ≠ alert ▸ *vb* **absent oneself** = stay away, withdraw, keep away, play truant

absentee *n* a person who should be present but is not

absenteeism *n* persistent absence from work or school

absent-minded *adj* inattentive or forgetful > **absent-mindedly** *adv*

absinthe *n* a strong, green, alcoholic drink, originally containing wormwood

absolute *adj* **1** total and complete: *he ordered an immediate and absolute ceasefire* **2** with unrestricted power and authority: *she has absolute control with fifty per cent of the shares* **3** undoubted or certain: *I was telling the absolute truth* **4** not dependent on or relative to anything else **5** pure; unmixed: *absolute alcohol* ▸ *n* **6** a principle or rule believed to be unfailingly correct **7 the Absolute** *philosophy* that which is totally unconditioned, perfect, or complete

> **absolute** *adj* **1** = complete, total, perfect, pure, sheer, utter, outright, thorough **2** = supreme, sovereign, unlimited, ultimate, full, unconditional, unrestricted, pre-eminent

absolutely *adv* **1** completely or perfectly ▸ *interj* **2** yes indeed, certainly

> **absolutely** *adv* = completely, totally, perfectly, fully, entirely, altogether, wholly, utterly; ≠ somewhat

absolution *n* *Christianity* a formal forgiveness of sin pronounced by a priest

absolutism *n* a political system in which a monarch or dictator has unrestricted power

absolve *vb* **-solving, -solved** to declare to be free from blame or sin

absorb *vb* **1** to soak up a liquid **2** to engage the interest of someone **3** to receive the force of an impact **4** *physics* to take in radiant energy and retain it **5** to take in or incorporate: *the country absorbed almost one million refugees* > **absorbent** *adj* > **absorbency** *n* > **absorbing** *adj*

> **absorb** *vb* **1** = soak up, suck up, receive, digest, imbibe **2** = engross, involve, engage, fascinate, rivet, captivate

absorption *n* **1** the process of absorbing something or the state of being absorbed **2** *physiol* the process by which nutrients enter the tissues of an animal or a plant > **absorptive** *adj*

> **absorption** *n* **1** = immersion, involvement, concentration, fascination, preoccupation, intentness **2** = soaking up, consumption, digestion, sucking up

abstain *vb* **1** (usually foll. by *from*) to choose not to do or partake of something: *you will be asked to abstain from food prior to your general anaesthetic* **2** to choose not to vote > **abstainer** *n*

abstemious (ab-steem-ee-uss) *adj* taking very little alcohol or food > **abstemiously** *adv* > **abstemiousness** *n*

abstention *n* **1** the formal act of not voting **2** the act of abstaining from something, such as drinking alcohol

abstinence *n* the practice of choosing not to do something one would like > **abstinent** *adj*

abstract *adj* **1** referring to ideas or qualities rather than material objects: *an abstract noun* **2** not applied or practical; theoretical: *he was frustrated by the highly abstract mathematics being taught* **3** of art in which the subject is represented by shapes and patterns rather than by a realistic likeness ▸ *n* **4** a summary **5** an abstract painting or sculpture **6** an abstract word or idea **7 in the abstract** without referring to specific circumstances ▸ *vb* **8** to summarize **9** to remove or extract

a

abstract *adj* **2** = theoretical, general, academic, speculative, indefinite, hypothetical, notional, abstruse; ≠ actual ▸ *n* **4** = summary, résumé, outline, digest, epitome, rundown, synopsis, précis; ≠ expansion ▸ *vb* **9** = extract, draw, pull, remove, separate, withdraw, isolate, pull out; ≠ add

abstracted *adj* lost in thought; preoccupied > **abstractedly** *adv*

abstraction *n* **1** a general idea rather than a specific example: *these absurd philosophical abstractions continued to bother him* **2** the quality of being abstract or abstracted

abstruse *adj* not easy to understand

absurd *adj* obviously senseless or illogical; ridiculous > **absurdity** *n* > **absurdly** *adv*

absurd *adj* = ridiculous, crazy (*informal*), silly, foolish, ludicrous, unreasonable, irrational, senseless; ≠ sensible

abundance *n* **1** a great amount **2** degree of plentifulness **3 in abundance** in great amounts: *they had fish and fruit in abundance* > **abundant** *adj*

abundance *n* **1** = plenty, bounty, exuberance, profusion, plethora, affluence, fullness, fruitfulness; ≠ shortage

abundantly *adv* **1** very: *he made his disagreement with the prime minister abundantly clear* **2** plentifully; in abundance

abuse *n* **1** prolonged ill-treatment of or violence towards someone: *child abuse* **2** insulting comments **3** improper use: *an abuse of power* ▸ *vb* **abusing, abused 4** to take advantage of dishonestly: *these two ministers had abused their position for financial gain* **5** to ill-treat violently or sexually **6** to speak insultingly or cruelly to > **abuser** *n*

abuse *n* **1** = maltreatment, damage, injury, hurt, harm, manhandling, ill-treatment **2** = insults, blame, slights, put-downs, censure, reproach, scolding, defamation **3** = misuse, misapplication, exploitation ▸ *vb* **5** = ill-treat, damage, hurt, injure, harm, molest, maltreat, knock about *or* around; ≠ care for **6** = insult, offend, curse, put down, malign, scold, disparage, castigate; ≠ praise

abusive *adj* **1** rude or insulting: *he was alleged to have used abusive language towards spectators* **2** involving cruelty and ill-treatment: *an abusive relationship* > **abusively** *adv*

abusive *adj* **1** = insulting, offensive, rude, degrading, scathing, contemptuous, disparaging, scurrilous; ≠ complimentary

abut *vb* **abutting, abutted** to be next to or touching

abysmal *adj informal* extremely bad > **abysmally** *adv*

abyss *n* **1** a very deep hole in the ground **2** a frightening or threatening situation: *the abyss of revolution and war ahead*

AC 1 alternating current **2** athletic club

a/c 1 account **2** account current

acacia (a-kay-sha) *n* a shrub or tree with small yellow or white flowers

academic *adj* **1** relating to a college or university **2** (of pupils) having an aptitude for study **3** relating to studies such as languages and pure science rather than technical or professional studies **4** of theoretical interest only: *the argument is academic* ▸ *n* **5** a member of the teaching or research staff of a college or university > **academically** *adv*

academic *adj* **1** = scholastic, educational **4** = theoretical, abstract, speculative, hypothetical, impractical, notional, conjectural ▸ *n* = scholar, intellectual, don, master, professor, fellow, lecturer, tutor, acca (*Austral slang*)

academy *n, pl* **-mies 1** a society for the advancement of literature, art, or science **2** a school for training in a particular skill: *sixteen hundred students would also spend their first year at the military academy* **3** a secondary school

acanthus *n* **1** a plant with large spiny leaves and spikes of white or purplish flowers **2** a carved ornament based on the leaves of the acanthus plant

ACAS (in Britain) Advisory Conciliation and Arbitration Service

ACC (in New Zealand) Accident Compensation Corporation

accede *vb* **-ceding, -ceded** > **accede to 1** to agree to **2** to take up (an office or position): *he acceded to the throne after his Irish exile*

accelerate *vb* **-ating, -ated 1** to move or cause to move more quickly **2** to cause to happen sooner than expected

accelerate *vb* **1** = increase, grow, advance, extend, expand, raise, swell, enlarge; ≠ fall **2** = expedite, further, speed up, hasten; ≠ delay

acceleration *n* **1** the act of increasing speed **2** the rate of increase of speed or the rate of change of velocity

acceleration *n* **1** = hastening, hurrying, stepping up (*informal*), speeding up, quickening

accelerator *n* **1** a pedal in a motor vehicle that is pressed to increase speed **2** *physics* a machine for increasing the speed and energy of charged particles

accent *n* **1** the distinctive style of pronunciation of a person or group from a particular area, country, or social background **2** a mark used in writing to indicate the prominence of a syllable or the way a vowel is pronounced **3** particular emphasis: *there will be an accent on sport and many will enjoy rowing* **4** the stress on a syllable or musical note ▸ *vb* **5** to lay particular emphasis on

accent *n* **1** = pronunciation, tone, articulation, inflection, brogue, intonation, diction, modulation ▸ *vb* = emphasize, stress, highlight, underline, underscore, accentuate

accentuate *vb* **-ating, -ated** to stress or emphasize › **accentuation** *n*

accept *vb* **1** to take or receive something offered **2** to agree to **3** to consider something as true **4** to tolerate or resign oneself to **5** to take on the responsibilities of: *he asked if I would become his assistant and I accepted that position* **6** to receive someone into a community or group **7** to receive something as adequate or valid

accept *vb* **1** = receive, take, gain, pick up, secure, collect, get, obtain **3** = acknowledge, believe, allow, admit, approve, recognize, yield, concede

acceptable *adj* **1** able to be endured; tolerable: *in war killing is acceptable* **2** good enough; adequate: *he found the article acceptable* › **acceptability** *n* › **acceptably** *adv*

acceptable *adj* **2** = satisfactory, fair, all right, suitable, sufficient, good enough, adequate, tolerable; ≠ unsatisfactory

acceptance *n* **1** the act of accepting something **2** favourable reception **3** belief or agreement

acceptance *n* **1** = accepting, taking, receiving, obtaining, acquiring, reception, receipt

access *n* **1** a means of approaching or entering a place **2** the condition of allowing entry, for example entry to a building by wheelchairs or prams **3** the right or opportunity to use something or enter a place: *the bourgeoisie gained access to political power* **4** the opportunity or right to see or approach someone: *I have access to the children every second weekend* ▸ *vb* **5** to obtain (information) from a computer

access *n* **1** = entrance, road, approach, entry, path, gate, opening, passage **3** = admission, entry, passage

accessible *adj* **1** easy to approach, enter, or use **2** easy to understand: *the most accessible opera by Wagner* › **accessibility** *n*

accessible *adj* **1** = handy, near, nearby, at hand, within reach, reachable, achievable; ≠ inaccessible

accession *n* the act of taking up an office or position: *the 40th anniversary of her accession to the throne*

accessory *n, pl* **-ries 1** a supplementary part or object **2** a small item, such as a bag or belt, worn or carried by someone to complete his or her outfit **3** a person who is involved in a crime but who was not present when it took place

accessory *n* **1** = extra, addition, supplement, attachment, adjunct, appendage **3** = accomplice, partner, ally, associate, assistant, helper, colleague, collaborator

accident *n* **1** an unpleasant event that causes damage, injury, or death **2** an unforeseen event or one without apparent cause: *they had met in town by accident*

accident *n* **1** = crash, smash, wreck, collision **2** = chance, fortune, luck, fate, hazard, coincidence, fluke, fortuity

accidental *adj* **1** occurring by chance or unintentionally ▸ *n* **2** *music* a symbol denoting a sharp, flat, or natural that is not a part of the key signature › **accidentally** *adv*

accidental *adj* = unintentional, unexpected, incidental, unforeseen, unplanned; ≠ deliberate

acclaim *vb* **1** to applaud or praise: *the highly acclaimed children's TV series* **2** to acknowledge publicly: *he was immediately acclaimed the new prime minister* ▸ *n* **3** an enthusiastic expression of approval

acclaim *vb* **1** = praise, celebrate, honour, cheer, admire, hail, applaud, compliment ▸ *n* = praise, honour, celebration, approval, tribute, applause, kudos, commendation; ≠ criticism

acclamation *n* **1** an enthusiastic reception or display of approval **2** *Canad* an instance of being elected without opposition **3 by acclamation** by a majority without a ballot

acclimatize *or* **-tise** *vb* **-tizing, -tized** *or* **-tising, -tised** to adapt to a new climate or environment › **acclimatization** *or* **-tisation** *n*

accolade *n* **1** an award, praise, or honour **2** a touch on the shoulder with a sword conferring a knighthood

accommodate *vb* **-dating, -dated 1** to provide with lodgings **2** to have room for **3** to do a favour for **4** to adjust or become adjusted; to adapt

accommodate *vb* **1** = house, put up, take in, lodge, shelter, entertain, cater for **3** = help, support, aid, assist, cooperate with, abet, lend a hand to **4** = adapt, fit, settle, alter, adjust, modify, comply, reconcile

accommodating *adj* willing to help; obliging

accommodating *adj* = obliging, willing, kind, friendly, helpful, polite, cooperative, agreeable; ≠ unhelpful

accommodation *n* a place in which to sleep, live, or work

accommodation *n* = housing, homes, houses, board, quarters, digs (*Brit informal*), shelter, lodging(s)

accompaniment n 1 something that accompanies something else 2 music a supporting part for an instrument, a band, or an orchestra

> **accompaniment** n 1 = supplement, extra, addition, companion, accessory, complement, decoration, adjunct 2 = backing music, backing, support, obbligato

accompanist n a person who plays a musical accompaniment

accompany vb -nies, -nying, -nied 1 to go with (someone) 2 to happen or exist at the same time as 3 to provide a musical accompaniment for

> **accompany** vb 1 = go with, lead, partner, guide, attend, conduct, escort, shepherd 2 = occur with, belong to, come with, supplement, go together with, follow

accomplice n a person who helps someone else commit a crime

accomplish vb 1 to manage to do; achieve: most infants accomplish it immediately 2 to complete

> **accomplish** vb = realize, produce, effect, finish, complete, manage, achieve, perform; ≠ fail

accomplished adj 1 expert or proficient: an accomplished liar 2 successfully completed

> **accomplished** adj 1 = skilled, able, professional, expert, masterly, talented, gifted, polished; ≠ unskilled

accomplishment n 1 the successful completion of something 2 something successfully completed 3 (often pl) personal abilities or skills

> **accomplishment** n 1 = accomplishing, finishing, carrying out, conclusion, bringing about, execution, completion, fulfilment 2 = achievement, feat, act, stroke, triumph, coup, exploit, deed

accord n 1 agreement or harmony 2 a formal agreement between groups or nations: the Paris peace accords 3 of one's own accord voluntarily or willingly 4 with one accord unanimously ▶ vb 5 to grant: she was at last accorded her true status 6 accord with to fit in with or be consistent with

> **accord** n 1 = sympathy, agreement, harmony, unison, rapport, conformity; ≠ conflict 2 = treaty, contract, agreement, arrangement, settlement, pact, deal (informal) ▶ vb 6 accord with something = agree with, match, coincide with, fit with, correspond with, conform with, tally with, harmonize with

accordance n in accordance with conforming to or according to: food is prepared in accordance with Jewish laws

according adv 1 according to A as stated by: according to her, they were once engaged B in conformity with: work hours varied according to the tides 2 according as depending on whether

accordingly adv 1 in an appropriate manner 2 consequently

> **accordingly** adv 1 = appropriately, correspondingly, properly, suitably, fitly 2 = consequently, so, thus, therefore, hence, subsequently, in consequence, ergo

accordion n a box-shaped musical instrument played by moving the two sides apart and together, and pressing a keyboard or buttons to produce the notes > **accordionist** n

accost vb to approach, stop, and speak to (someone) rudely or aggressively

account n 1 a report or description 2 an arrangement for a financial institution to look after one's money 3 a statement of financial transactions with the resulting balance 4 part or behalf: I am sorry that you suffered on my account 5 call someone to account to demand an explanation from someone 6 give a good or bad account of oneself to perform well or fail to perform well 7 of no account of little importance or value 8 on account of because of 9 take account of or take into account to take into consideration; allow for ▶ vb 10 to consider as: the evening was accounted a major step forward by all concerned

> **account** n 1 = description, report, story, statement, version, tale, explanation, narrative ▶ vb = consider, rate, value, judge, estimate, think, count, reckon

accountable adj responsible to someone or for some action > **accountability** n

> **accountable** adj = answerable, subject, responsible, obliged, liable, amenable, obligated, chargeable

accountant n a person who maintains and audits business accounts > **accountancy** n

> **accountant** n = auditor, book-keeper, bean counter (informal)

accounting n the skill or practice of maintaining and auditing business accounts

accoutrements (ak-koo-tra-ments) or US **accouterments** (ak-koo-ter-ments) pl n clothing and equipment for a particular activity

accredit vb 1 to give official recognition to 2 to send (a diplomat) with official credentials to a particular country 3 to certify as meeting required standards 4 to attribute (a quality or an action) to (a person) > **accreditation** n

accretion (ak-kree-shun) n 1 a gradual increase in size, through growth or addition 2 something added, such as an extra layer

accrue vb -cruing, -crued 1 (of money or interest) to increase gradually over a period of time **2 accrue to** to fall naturally to: *some advantage must accrue to the weaker party* ⊳ **accrual** *n*

accumulate *vb* **-lating, -lated** to gather together in an increasing quantity; collect ⊳ **accumulative** *adj*

> **accumulate** *vb* = build up, increase, be stored, collect, gather, pile up, amass, hoard; ≠ disperse

accumulation *n* **1** something that has been collected **2** the collecting together of things

> **accumulation** *n* **1** = collection, increase, stock, store, mass, build-up, pile, stack **2** = growth, collection, gathering, build-up

accumulator *n* **1** *Brit & Austral* a rechargeable device for storing electrical energy **2** *Brit horse racing* a collective bet on successive races, with both stake and winnings being carried forward to accumulate progressively

accuracy *n* faithful representation of the truth: *care is taken to ensure the accuracy of the content*

> **accuracy** *n* = exactness, precision, fidelity, authenticity, correctness, closeness, veracity, truthfulness; ≠ inaccuracy

accurate *adj* faithfully representing the truth: *all the information was accurate* ⊳ **accurately** *adv*

> **accurate** *adj* = correct, true, exact, spot-on (*Brit informal*)

accursed (a-**curse**-id) *adj* **1** under a curse **2** hateful or detestable

accusation *n* **1** an allegation that a person is guilty of some wrongdoing **2** a formal charge brought against a person ⊳ **accusatory** *adj*

> **accusation** *n* **2** = charge, complaint, allegation, indictment, recrimination, denunciation, incrimination

accusative *n grammar* a grammatical case in some languages that identifies the direct object of a verb

accuse *vb* **-cusing, -cused** to charge a person with wrongdoing ⊳ **accuser** *n* ⊳ **accusing** *adj* ⊳ **accusingly** *adv*

> **accuse** *vb* = charge with, indict for, impeach for, censure with, incriminate for; ≠ absolve

accused *n* **the accused** *law* the defendant appearing on a criminal charge

accustom *vb* **accustom oneself to** to become familiar with or used to from habit or experience

accustomed *adj* **1** usual or customary: *he parked his motorcycle in its accustomed place* **2 accustomed to A** used to **B** in the habit of

> **accustomed** *adj* **1** = usual, established, expected, common, standard, traditional, normal, regular; ≠ unusual

ace *n* **1** a playing card with one symbol on it

2 *informal* an expert: *an American stock car ace* **3** *tennis* a winning serve that the opponent fails to reach **4** a fighter pilot who has destroyed several enemy aircraft ▸ *adj* **5** *informal* superb or excellent: *an ace skateboarder*

> **ace** *n* **2** = expert, star, champion, authority, professional, master, specialist, guru ▸ *adj* = great (*informal*), brilliant, fine, wonderful, excellent, outstanding, superb, fantastic (*informal*), booshit (*Austral slang*), exo (*Austral slang*), sik (*Austral slang*), ka pai (*NZ*), rad (*informal*), phat (*slang*), schmick (*Austral informal*)

acerbic (ass-**sir**-bik) *adj* harsh or bitter: *an acerbic critic*

acerbity *n, pl* **-ties 1** bitter speech or temper **2** bitterness of taste

acetate (**ass**-it-tate) *n* **1** *chem* any salt or ester of acetic acid **2** *Also:* **acetate rayon** a synthetic textile fibre made from cellulose acetate

acetic (ass-**see**-tik) *adj chem* of, containing, or producing acetic acid or vinegar

acetic acid *n chem* a strong-smelling colourless liquid used to make vinegar

acetone (**ass**-it-tone) *n chem* a strong-smelling colourless liquid used as a solvent for paints and lacquers

acetylene (ass-**set**-ill-een) *n chem* a colourless soluble flammable gas used in welding metals

ache *vb* **aching, ached 1** to feel or be the source of a continuous dull pain **2** to suffer mental anguish ▸ *n* **3** a continuous dull pain

> **ache** *vb* **1** = hurt, suffer, burn, pain, smart, sting, pound, throb ▸ *n* = pain, discomfort, suffering, hurt, throbbing, irritation, tenderness, pounding

achieve *vb* **achieving, achieved** to gain by hard work or effort ⊳ **achiever** *n*

> **achieve** *vb* = accomplish, fulfil, complete, gain, perform, do, get, carry out

achievement *n* **1** something that has been accomplished by hard work, ability, or heroism **2** the successful completion of something

> **achievement** *n* **1** = accomplishment, effort, feat, deed, stroke, triumph, coup, exploit

Achilles heel (ak-**kill**-eez) *n* a small but fatal weakness

Achilles tendon *n* the fibrous cord that connects the muscles of the calf to the heel bone

achromatic *adj* **1** without colour **2** refracting light without breaking it up into its component colours **3** *music* involving no sharps or flats ⊳ **achromatically** *adv*

acid *n* **1** *chem* one of a class of compounds, corrosive and sour when dissolved in water, that combine with a base to form a salt **2** *slang* LSD **3** a sour-tasting substance ▸ *adj* **4** *chem* of, containing acid **5** sharp or sour in taste **6** sharp in speech or manner ⊳ **acidly** *adv*

a

acid adj **5** = sour, tart, pungent, acerbic, acrid, vinegary; ≠ sweet **6** = sharp, cutting, biting, bitter, harsh, barbed, caustic, vitriolic; ≠ kindly

Acid House or **Acid** n a type of funk-based, electronically edited dance music of the late 1980s, which has hypnotic sound effects and which is associated with the use of the drug ecstasy

acidic adj containing acid

acidify vb **-fies, -fying, -fied** to convert into acid ▷ **acidification** n

acidity n **1** the quality of being acid **2** the amount of acid in a solution

acid rain n rain containing pollutants released into the atmosphere by burning coal or oil

acid test n a rigorous and conclusive test of worth or value

acknowledge vb **-edging, -edged 1** to recognize or admit the truth of a statement **2** to show recognition of a person by a greeting or glance **3** to make known that a message or letter has been received **4** to express gratitude for (a favour or compliment)

acknowledge vb **1** = admit, own up to, allow, accept, reveal, grant, declare, recognize; ≠ deny **2** = greet, address, notice, recognize, salute, accost; ≠ snub **3** = reply to, answer, notice, recognize, respond to, react to, retort to; ≠ ignore

acknowledgment or **acknowledgement** n **1** the act of acknowledging something or someone **2** something done or given as an expression of gratitude

acme (ak-mee) n the highest point of achievement or excellence

acne (ak-nee) n a skin disease in which pus-filled spots form on the face

acolyte n **1** a follower or attendant **2** Christianity a person who assists a priest

aconite n **1** a poisonous plant with hoodlike flowers **2** dried aconite root, used as a narcotic

acorn n the fruit of the oak tree, consisting of a smooth nut in a cuplike base

acoustic adj **1** of sound, hearing, or acoustics **2** (of a musical instrument) without electronic amplification **3** designed to absorb sound: acoustic tiles ▷ **acoustically** adv

acoustics n **1** the scientific study of sound ▶ pl n **2** the characteristics of a room or auditorium determining how well sound can be heard within it

acquaint vb **acquaint with** to make (someone) familiar with

acquaintance n **1** a person whom one knows slightly **2** slight knowledge of a person or subject **3** make the acquaintance of to come into social contact with **4** the people one knows: an actress of my acquaintance

acquaintance n **1** = associate, contact, ally, colleague, comrade; ≠ intimate **2** = relationship, connection, fellowship, familiarity; ≠ unfamiliarity

acquainted adj **1** on terms of familiarity but not intimacy **2** acquainted with familiar with: she became acquainted with the classics of Chinese literature

acquiesce (ak-wee-ess) vb **-escing, -esced** to agree to what someone wants ▷ **acquiescence** n ▷ **acquiescent** adj

acquire vb **-quiring, -quired** to get or develop (something such as an object, trait, or ability) ▷ **acquirement** n

acquire vb = get, win, buy, receive, gain, earn, secure, collect; ≠ lose

acquisition n **1** something acquired, often to add to a collection **2** the act of acquiring something

acquisition n **1** = purchase, buy, investment, property, gain, prize, asset, possession **2** = acquiring, gaining, procurement, attainment

acquisitive adj eager to gain material possessions ▷ **acquisitively** adv ▷ **acquisitiveness** n

acquit vb **-quitting, -quitted 1** to pronounce someone not guilty: he's been acquitted of negligence **2** to behave in a particular way: she acquitted herself well in the meeting ▷ **acquittal** n

acquit vb **1** = clear, free, release, excuse, discharge, liberate, vindicate; ≠ find guilty

acre n **1** a unit of area equal to 4840 square yards (4046.86 square metres) **2** acres informal a large amount: acres of skin

acreage (ake-er-rij) n land area in acres

acrid (ak-rid) adj **1** unpleasantly strong-smelling **2** sharp in speech or manner ▷ **acridity** n ▷ **acridly** adv

acrimony n bitterness and resentment felt about something ▷ **acrimonious** adj

acrobat n an entertainer who performs gymnastic feats requiring skill, agility, and balance ▷ **acrobatic** adj ▷ **acrobatically** adv

acrobatics pl n the skills or feats of an acrobat

acronym n a word made from the initial letters of other words, for example UNESCO for the United Nations Educational, Scientific, and Cultural Organization

across prep **1** from one side to the other side of **2** on or at the other side of ▶ adv **3** from one side to the other **4** on or to the other side

acrostic n a number of lines of writing, such as a poem, in which the first or last letters form a word or proverb

acrylic adj **1** made of acrylic ▶ n **2** a man-made fibre used for clothes and blankets **3** a kind of paint made from acrylic acid

acrylic acid n *chem* a strong-smelling colourless corrosive liquid

act n **1** something done **2** a formal decision reached or law passed by a law-making body: *an act of parliament* **3** a major division of a play or opera **4** a short performance, such as a sketch or dance **5** a pretended attitude: *she appeared calm but it was just an act* **6** **get in on the act** *informal* to become involved in something in order to share the benefit **7** **get one's act together** *informal* to organize oneself ▸ vb **8** to do something **9** to perform (a part or role) in a play, film, or broadcast **10** to present (a play) on stage **11** **act for** to be a substitute for: *Mr Lewis was acting for the head of the department* **12** **act as** to serve the function of: *she is acting as my bodyguard* **13** to behave: *she acts as though she really hates you* **14** to behave in an unnatural way

> **act** n **1** = deed, action, performance, achievement, undertaking, exploit, feat, accomplishment **2** = law, bill, measure, resolution, decree, statute, ordinance, enactment **4** = performance, show, turn, production, routine (*informal*), presentation, gig (*informal*), sketch **5** = pretence, show, front, performance, display, attitude, pose, posture ▸ vb **8** = do something, perform, function **9** = perform, mimic

ACT Australian Capital Territory

acting n **1** the art of an actor ▸ adj **2** temporarily performing the duties of: *the acting president has declared a state of emergency*

> **acting** n = performance, playing, performing, theatre, portrayal, impersonation, characterization, stagecraft ▸ adj = temporary, substitute, interim, provisional, surrogate, stopgap, pro tem

actinium n *chem* a radioactive element of the actinide series, occurring as a decay product of uranium. Symbol: **Ac**

action n **1** doing something for a particular purpose **2** something done on a particular occasion **3** a lawsuit **4** movement during some physical activity **5** the operating mechanism in a gun or machine **6** the way in which something operates or works **7** *slang* the main activity in a place **8** the events that form the plot of a story or play **9** activity, force, or energy **10** a minor battle **11** **actions** behaviour **12** **out of action** not functioning

> **action** n **1** = deed, act, performance, achievement, exploit, feat, accomplishment **2** = measure, act, manoeuvre **3** = lawsuit, case, trial, suit, proceeding, dispute, prosecution, litigation **9** = energy, activity, spirit, force, vitality, vigour, liveliness, vim **10** = battle, fight, conflict, clash, contest, encounter, combat, engagement

actionable adj *law* giving grounds for legal action

action replay n the rerunning of a small section of a television film or tape, for example of a sporting event

activate vb **-vating, -vated 1** to make something active **2** *physics* to make something radioactive **3** *chem* to increase the rate of a reaction › **activation** n

> **activate** vb **1** = start, move, initiate, rouse, mobilize, set in motion, galvanize; ≠ stop

active adj **1** busy and energetic **2** energetically involved in or working hard for: *active in the peace movement* **3** happening now and energetically: *the plan is under active discussion* **4** functioning or causing a reaction: *the active ingredient is held within the capsule* **5** (of a volcano) erupting periodically **6** *grammar* denoting a form of a verb used to indicate that the subject is performing the action, for example *kicked* in *The boy kicked the football* ▸ n **7** *grammar* the active form of a verb › **actively** adv

> **active** adj **1** = energetic, quick, alert, dynamic, lively, vigorous, animated, forceful; ≠ inactive

activist n a person who works energetically to achieve political or social goals › **activism** n

> **activist** n = militant, partisan

activity n **1** the state of being active **2** lively movement **3** pl **-ties** any specific action or pursuit: *he was engaged in political activities abroad*

> **activity** n **1** = action, labour, movement, energy, exercise, spirit, motion, bustle; ≠ inaction **3** = pursuit, project, scheme, pleasure, interest, hobby, pastime

act of God n *law* a sudden occurrence caused by natural forces, such as a flood

actor n a person who acts in a play, film, or broadcast

> **actor** n = performer, player, Thespian, luvvie (*informal*)

actress n a female actor

actual adj existing in reality or as a matter of fact

actuality n, pl **-ties** reality

actually adv as an actual fact; really

> **actually** adv = really, in fact, indeed, truly, literally, genuinely, in reality, in truth

actuary n, pl **-aries** a person qualified to calculate commercial risks and probabilities involving uncertain future events, esp. in such contexts as life assurance › **actuarial** adj

actuate vb **-ating, -ated 1** to start up a mechanical device **2** to motivate someone

acuity (ak-kew-it-ee) n keenness of vision or thought

acumen (ak-yew-men) n the ability to make good decisions

a

acupuncture *n* a medical treatment involving the insertion of needles at various parts of the body to stimulate the nerve impulses
> **acupuncturist** *n*

acute *adj* **1** severe or intense: *acute staff shortages* **2** penetrating in perception or insight **3** sensitive or keen: *it was amazing how acute your hearing got in the bush* **4** (of a disease) sudden and severe **5** *maths* (of an angle) of less than 90° ▸ *n* **6** an accent (´) over a vowel in some languages, which indicates that the vowel is pronounced in a particular way > **acutely** *adv* > **acuteness** *n*

> **acute** *adj* **2** = perceptive, sharp, keen, smart, sensitive, clever, astute, insightful; ≠ slow **4** = serious, important, dangerous, critical, crucial (*informal*), severe, grave, urgent

ad *n informal* an advertisement
AD (indicating years numbered from the supposed year of the birth of Christ) in the year of the Lord
adage (ad-ij) *n* a traditional saying that is generally accepted as being true
adagio (ad-dahj-yo) *music* ▸ *adv* **1** slowly ▸ *n, pl* **-gios** **2** a movement or piece to be performed slowly
adamant *adj* unshakable in determination or purpose > **adamantly** *adv*

> **adamant** *adj* = determined, firm, fixed, stubborn, uncompromising, resolute, unbending, obdurate; ≠ flexible

Adam's apple *n* the projecting lump of thyroid cartilage at the front of a person's neck
adapt *vb* **1** to adjust (something or oneself) to different conditions **2** to change something to suit a new purpose > **adaptable** *adj* > **adaptability** *n*

> **adapt** *vb* **1** = adjust, change, alter, modify, accommodate, conform, acclimatize **2** = convert, change, transform, alter, modify, tailor, remodel

adaptation *n* **1** something that is produced by adapting something else: *a TV adaptation of a Victorian novel* **2** the act of adapting

> **adaptation** *n* **1** = conversion, change, variation, adjustment, transformation, modification, alteration **2** = acclimatization, naturalization, familiarization

adaptor *or* **adapter** *n* **1** a device used to connect several electrical appliances to a single socket **2** any device for connecting two parts of different sizes or types
add *vb* **1** to combine (numbers or quantities) so as to make a larger number or quantity **2** to join something to something else so as to increase its size, effect, or scope: *these new rules will add an extra burden on already overworked officials* **3** to say or write something further **4 add in** to include

> **add** *vb* **1** = count up, total, reckon, compute, add up, tot up; ≠ take away

addendum *n, pl* **-da** something added on, esp. an appendix to a book or magazine
adder *n* a small poisonous snake with a black zigzag pattern along the back
addict *n* **1** a person who is unable to stop taking narcotic drugs **2** *informal* a person who is devoted to something: *he's a telly addict* > **addictive** *adj*

> **addict** *n* **2** = fan, lover, nut (*slang*), follower, enthusiast, admirer, buff (*informal*), junkie (*informal*)

addicted *adj* **1** dependent on a narcotic drug **2** *informal* devoted to something: *I'm a news freak and addicted to radio news* > **addiction** *n*

> **addicted** *adj* **1** = hooked (*informal*), dependent

addition *n* **1** the act of adding **2** a person or thing that is added **3** a mathematical operation in which the total of two or more numbers or quantities is calculated **4 in addition (to)** besides; as well (as) > **additional** *adj* > **additionally** *adv*

> **addition** *n* **1** = inclusion, adding, increasing, extension, attachment, insertion, incorporation, augmentation; ≠ removal **2** = extra, supplement, increase, gain, bonus, extension, accessory, additive **3** = counting up, totalling, adding up, computation, totting up; ≠ subtraction **4 in addition to** = as well as, along with, on top of, besides, to boot, additionally, over and above, to say nothing of

additive *n* any substance added to something, such as food, to improve it or prevent deterioration
addled *adj* **1** confused or unable to think clearly **2** (of eggs) rotten
address *n* **1** the place at which someone lives **2** the conventional form by which the location of a building is described **3** a formal speech **4** *computers* **a** a number giving the location of a piece of stored information **b** a series of characters that represents a location on the internet ▸ *vb* **5** to mark (a letter or parcel) with an address **6** to speak to **7** to direct one's attention to (a problem or an issue) **8 address oneself to a** to speak or write to **b** to apply oneself to: *we have got to address ourselves properly to this problem*

> **address** *n* **2** = location, home, place, house, point, position, situation, site **3** = speech, talk, lecture, discourse, sermon, dissertation, homily, oration ▸ *vb* **6** = speak to, talk to, greet, hail, approach, converse with, korero (*NZ*)

addressee *n* a person to whom a letter or parcel is addressed
adduce *vb* **-ducing, -duced** to mention something as evidence

adenoidal *adj* having a nasal voice or impaired breathing because of enlarged adenoids

adenoids (ad-in-oidz) *pl n* a mass of tissue at the back of the throat

adept *adj* **1** proficient in something requiring skill ▸ *n* **2** a person skilled in something › **adeptness** *n*

> **adept** *adj* = skilful, able, skilled, expert, practised, accomplished, versed, proficient; ≠ unskilled ▸ *n* = expert, master, genius, hotshot (*informal*), dab hand (*Brit informal*)

adequate *adj* just enough in amount or just good enough in quality › **adequacy** *n* › **adequately** *adv*

> **adequate** *adj* = passable, acceptable, average, fair, satisfactory, competent, mediocre, so-so (*informal*); ≠ inadequate

adhere *vb* **-hering, -hered 1** to stick to **2** to act according to (a rule or agreement) **3** to be a loyal supporter of (something)

adherent *n* **1** a supporter or follower ▸ *adj* **2** sticking or attached › **adherence** *n*

adhesion *n* **1** the quality or condition of sticking together **2** *pathol* the joining together of two structures or parts of the body that are normally separate, for example after surgery

adhesive *n* **1** a substance used for sticking things together ▸ *adj* **2** able or designed to stick to things

ad hoc *adj, adv* for a particular purpose only

adieu (a-dew) *interj, n, pl* **adieux** *or* **adieus** (a-**dewz**) goodbye

ad infinitum *adv* endlessly: *we would not be able to sustain the currency ad infinitum*

adipose *adj* of or containing fat; fatty: *adipose tissue*

adj. adjective

adjacent *adj* **1** near or next: *the schools were adjacent but there were separate doors* **2** *geom* (of a side of a right-angled triangle) lying between a specified angle and the right angle

> **adjacent** *adj* **1** = adjoining, neighbouring, nearby; ≠ far away

adjective *n* a word that adds information about a noun or pronoun › **adjectival** *adj*

adjoin *vb* to be next to and joined onto › **adjoining** *adj*

> **adjoin** *vb* = connect with *or* to, join, link with, touch on, border on

adjourn *vb* **1** to close a court at the end of a session **2** to postpone or be postponed temporarily **3** *informal* to go elsewhere: *can we adjourn to the dining room?* › **adjournment** *n*

> **adjourn** *vb* **2** = postpone, delay, suspend, interrupt, put off, defer, discontinue; ≠ continue

adjudge *vb* **-judging, -judged** to declare someone to be something specified: *my wife was adjudged to be the guilty party*

adjudicate *vb* **-cating, -cated 1** to give a formal decision on a dispute **2** to serve as a judge, for example in a competition › **adjudication** *n* › **adjudicator** *n*

adjunct *n* **1** something added that is not essential **2** a person who is subordinate to another

adjure *vb* **-juring, -jured 1** to command someone to do something **2** to appeal earnestly to someone › **adjuration** *n*

adjust *vb* **1** to adapt to a new environment **2** to alter slightly, so as to be accurate or suitable **3** *insurance* to determine the amount payable in settlement of a claim › **adjustable** *adj* › **adjuster** *n*

> **adjust** *vb* **1** = adapt, change, alter, accustom, conform **2** = modify, alter, adapt

adjustment *n* **1** a slight alteration **2** the act of adjusting

> **adjustment** *n* **1** = alteration, change, tuning, repair, conversion, modifying, adaptation, modification **2** = acclimatization, orientation, change, regulation, amendment, adaptation, revision, modification

adjutant (**aj**-oo-tant) *n* an officer in an army who acts as administrative assistant to a superior

ad-lib *vb* **-libbing, -libbed 1** to improvise a speech or piece of music without preparation ▸ *adj* **2** improvised: *ad-lib studio chat* ▸ *n* **3** an improvised remark ▸ *adv* **ad lib 4** spontaneously or freely

Adm. Admiral

admin *n informal* administration

administer *vb* **1** to manage (an organization or estate) **2** to organize and put into practice: *anyone can learn to administer the test procedure* **3** to give medicine to someone **4** to supervise the taking of (an oath)

> **administer** *vb* **1** = manage, run, control, direct, handle, conduct, command, govern **2** = execute, give, provide, apply, perform, carry out, impose, implement

administrate *vb* **-trating, -trated** to manage an organization

administration *n* **1** management of the affairs of an organization **2** the people who administer an organization **3** a government: *the first non-communist administration in the country's history* **4** the act of administering something, such as medicine or an oath › **administrative** *adj*

> **administration** *n* **1** = management, government, running, control, handling, direction, conduct, application **2** = directors, board, executive(s), employers **3** = government, leadership, regime

a

administrator n a person who administers an organization or estate

> **administrator** n = manager, head, official, director, executive, boss (informal), governor, supervisor

admirable (ad-mer-a-bl) adj deserving or inspiring admiration: *the boldness of the undertaking is admirable* > **admirably** adv

> **admirable** adj = praiseworthy, good, great (informal), fine, wonderful, excellent, brilliant, outstanding, booshit (Austral slang), exo (Austral slang), sik (Austral slang), ka pai (NZ), rad (informal), phat (slang), schmick (Austral informal); ≠ deplorable

admiral n 1 Also called: **admiral of the fleet** a naval officer of the highest rank 2 any of various brightly coloured butterflies

Admiralty n Brit the former government department in charge of the Royal Navy

admire vb -miring, -mired to respect and approve of (a person or thing) > **admiration** n > **admirer** n > **admiring** adj > **admiringly** adv

> **admire** vb = respect, value, prize, honour, praise, appreciate, esteem, approve of; ≠ despise

admissible adj law allowed to be brought as evidence in court

admission n 1 permission or the right to enter 2 permission to join an organization 3 the price charged for entrance 4 a confession: *she was, by her own admission, not educated*

> **admission** n 1, 2 = admittance, access, entry, introduction, entrance, acceptance, initiation, entrée 4 = confession, declaration, revelation, allowance, disclosure, acknowledgement, unburdening, divulgence

admit vb -mitting, -mitted 1 to confess or acknowledge (a crime or mistake) 2 to concede (the truth of something) 3 to allow (someone) to enter 4 to take (someone) in to a hospital for treatment: *he was admitted for tests* 5 **admit to** to allow someone to participate in something 6 **admit of** to allow for: *these rules admit of no violation*

> **admit** vb 1 = confess, confide, own up, come clean (informal) 2 = allow, agree, accept, reveal, grant, declare, acknowledge, recognize; ≠ deny 3 = let in, allow, receive, accept, introduce, take in, initiate, give access to; ≠ keep out

admittance n 1 the right to enter 2 the act of entering a place

admittedly adv it must be agreed: *my research is admittedly incomplete*

admixture n 1 a mixture 2 an ingredient

admonish vb to reprimand sternly > **admonition** n > **admonitory** adj

ad nauseam (ad naw-zee-am) adv to a boring or sickening extent: *she went on and on ad nauseam about her divorce*

ado n fuss: *without further ado*

adobe (ad-oh-bee) n 1 a sun-dried brick 2 the claylike material from which such bricks are made 3 a building made of such bricks

adolescence n the period between puberty and adulthood

> **adolescence** n = teens, youth, minority, boyhood, girlhood

adolescent adj 1 of or relating to adolescence 2 informal (of behaviour) immature ▸ n 3 an adolescent person

> **adolescent** adj 1 = young, junior, teenage, juvenile, youthful, childish, immature, boyish 2 = immature, young, teen (informal) ▸ n = teenager, girl, boy, kid (informal), youth, lad, minor, young man, young woman

adopt vb 1 law to take someone else's child as one's own 2 to choose (a plan or method) 3 to choose (a country or name) to be one's own > **adoptee** n > **adopter** n > **adoption** n

> **adopt** vb 1 = take in, raise, nurse, parent, rear, foster, bring up, take care of; ≠ abandon

adoptive adj 1 acquired or related by adoption: *an adoptive father* 2 of or relating to adoption

adorable adj very attractive; lovable

adore vb **adoring, adored** 1 to love intensely or deeply 2 informal to like very much: *I adore being in the country* 3 to worship a god with religious rites > **adoration** n > **adoring** adj > **adoringly** adv

> **adore** vb 1 = love, honour, admire, worship, esteem, cherish, revere, dote on; ≠ hate

adorn vb to decorate; increase the beauty of > **adornment** n

> **adorn** vb = decorate, array, embellish, festoon

adrenal (ad-reen-al) adj anatomy 1 on or near the kidneys 2 of or relating to the adrenal glands

adrenal glands pl n anatomy two endocrine glands covering the upper surface of the kidneys

adrenalin or **adrenaline** n biochem a hormone secreted by the adrenal gland in response to stress. It increases heart rate, pulse rate, and blood pressure

adrift adj, adv 1 drifting 2 without a clear purpose 3 informal off course, wrong: *it was obvious that something had gone adrift*

> **adrift** adj, adv 1 = drifting, afloat, unmoored, unanchored 2 = aimless, goalless, directionless, purposeless 3 = wrong, astray, off course, amiss, off target, wide of the mark

adroit adj quick and skilful in how one behaves or thinks > **adroitly** adv > **adroitness** n

adsorb vb (of a gas or vapour) to condense and form a thin film on a surface > **adsorbent** adj > **adsorption** n

adulation n uncritical admiration

adult n 1 a mature fully grown person, animal, or plant ▸ adj 2 having reached maturity; fully developed 3 suitable for or typical of adult people: she had very adult features 4 sexually explicit: adult films > **adulthood** n

> **adult** n = grown-up, mature person, person of mature age, grown or grown-up person, man or woman ▸ adj 2 = fully grown, mature, grown-up, of age, ripe, fully fledged, fully developed, full grown

adulterate vb -ating, -ated to spoil something by adding inferior material > **adulteration** n

adulterer or fem **adulteress** n a person who has committed adultery

adultery n, pl -teries sexual unfaithfulness of a husband or wife > **adulterous** adj

adv. adverb

advance vb -vancing, -vanced 1 to go or bring forward 2 to make progress: this student has advanced in reading and writing 3 to further a cause: an association founded to advance the interests of ex-soldiers 4 **advance on** to move towards someone in a threatening manner 5 to present an idea for consideration 6 to lend a sum of money ▸ n 7 a forward movement 8 improvement or progress: the greatest advance in modern medicine 9 a loan of money 10 a payment made before it is legally due 11 an increase in price: any advance on fifty pounds? 12 **in advance** beforehand: you have to pay in advance 13 **in advance of** ahead of in time or development ▸ adj 14 done or happening before an event: advance warning

> **advance** vb 1, 2 = progress, proceed, come forward, make inroads, make headway; ≠ retreat 5 = suggest, offer, present, propose, advocate, submit, prescribe, put forward; ≠ withhold 6 = lend, loan, supply on credit; ≠ withhold payment ▸ n 8 = improvement, development, gain, growth, breakthrough, step, headway, inroads 10 = down payment, credit, fee, deposit, retainer, prepayment, loan 12 **in advance** = beforehand, earlier, ahead, previously ▸ adj = prior, early, beforehand

advanced adj 1 at a late stage in development 2 not elementary: he was taking the advanced class in economics

> **advanced** adj 1 = sophisticated, foremost, modern, revolutionary, up-to-date, higher, leading, recent; ≠ backward

advancement n promotion in rank or status

> **advancement** n = promotion, rise, gain, progress, improvement, betterment, preferment

advantage n 1 a more favourable position or state 2 benefit or profit: they could make this work to their advantage 3 tennis the point scored after deuce 4 **take advantage of** A to use a person unfairly B to use an opportunity 5 **to advantage** to good effect: her hair was shaped to display her features to advantage

> **advantage** n 1 = lead, sway, dominance, precedence 2 = benefit, help, profit, favour; ≠ disadvantage

advantageous adj likely to bring benefits > **advantageously** adv

Advent n Christianity the season that includes the four Sundays before Christmas

Adventist n a member of a Christian group that believes in the imminent return of Christ

adventitious adj added or appearing accidentally

adventure n 1 a risky undertaking, the ending of which is uncertain: our African adventure 2 exciting or unexpected events

> **adventure** n 1 = venture, experience, incident, enterprise, undertaking, exploit, occurrence, caper

adventurer or fem **adventuress** n 1 a person who seeks money or power by unscrupulous means 2 a person who seeks adventure

adventurous adj daring or enterprising

> **adventurous** adj = daring, enterprising, bold, reckless, intrepid, daredevil; ≠ cautious

adverb n a word that modifies a sentence, verb, adverb, or adjective, for example easily, very, and happily in They could easily envy the very happily married couple > **adverbial** adj

adversary (ad-verse-er-ree) n, pl -saries an opponent in a fight, disagreement, or sporting contest

> **adversary** n = opponent, rival, enemy, competitor, foe (formal, literary), contestant, antagonist; ≠ ally

adverse adj 1 unfavourable to one's interests: adverse effects 2 antagonistic or hostile > **adversely** adv

> **adverse** adj 1 = harmful, damaging, negative, destructive, detrimental, hurtful, injurious, inopportune; ≠ beneficial 2 = negative, opposing, hostile, contrary, dissenting, unsympathetic, ill-disposed

adversity n, pl -ties very difficult or hard circumstances

advert n informal an advertisement

> **advert** n = advertisement, notice, commercial, ad (informal), announcement, poster, plug (informal), blurb, banner ad

advertise vb -tising, -tised 1 to present or praise (goods or a service) to the public, in order

a

to encourage sales **2** to make (a vacancy, an event, or an article for sale) publicly known ▷ **advertiser** *n* ▷ **advertising** *n*

advertise *vb* **1** = publicize, promote, plug (*informal*), announce, inform, hype, notify, tout

advertisement *n* any public announcement designed to sell goods or publicize an event

advertisement *n* = advert (*Brit*), notice, commercial, ad (*informal*), announcement, poster, plug (*informal*), blurb

advice *n* **1** recommendation as to an appropriate choice of action **2** formal notification of facts

advice *n* **1** = guidance, help, opinion, direction, suggestion, instruction, counsel, counselling

advisable *adj* sensible and likely to achieve the desired result ▷ **advisability** *n*

advise *vb* **-vising, -vised 1** to offer advice to **2** to inform or notify ▷ **adviser** *or* **advisor** *n*

advise *vb* **1** = recommend, suggest, urge, counsel, advocate, caution, prescribe, commend **2** = notify, tell, report, announce, warn, declare, inform, acquaint

advised *adj* thought-out: *ill-advised*
advisedly (ad-**vize**-id-lee) *adv* deliberately; after careful consideration: *I use the word advisedly*
advisory *adj* **1** able to offer advice ▸ *n, pl* **-ries 2** a statement giving advice or a warning **3** a person or organization that gives advice: *the Prime Minister's media advisory*

advisory *adj* = advising, helping, recommending, counselling, consultative

advocaat *n* a liqueur with a raw egg base
advocacy *n* active support of a cause or course of action
advocate *vb* **-cating, -cated 1** to recommend a course of action publicly ▸ *n* **2** a person who upholds or defends a cause or course of action **3** a person who speaks on behalf of another in a court of law **4** *Scots law* a barrister

advocate *vb* = recommend, support, champion, encourage, propose, promote, advise, endorse; ≠ oppose ▸ *n* **2** = supporter, spokesman *or* woman *or* person, champion, defender, campaigner, promoter, counsellor, proponent **3** = lawyer, attorney, solicitor, counsel, barrister

adze *or US* **adz** *n* a tool with a blade at right angles to the handle, used for shaping timber
aegis (**ee**-jiss) *n* **under the aegis of** with the sponsorship or protection of
aeolian harp (ee-**oh**-lee-an) *n* a musical instrument that produces sounds when the wind passes over its strings

aeon *or US* **eon** (**ee**-on) *n* **1** an immeasurably long period of time **2** the longest division of geological time
aerate *vb* **-ating, -ated** to put gas into a liquid, for example when making a fizzy drink ▷ **aeration** *n*
aerial *n* **1** the metal pole or wire on a television or radio which transmits or receives signals ▸ *adj* **2** in, from, or operating in the air **3** extending high into the air **4** of or relating to aircraft
aerial top dressing *n* spreading of fertilizer from an aeroplane onto remote areas
aerobatics *n* spectacular manoeuvres, such as loops or rolls, performed by aircraft
aerobic *adj* designed for or relating to aerobics: *aerobic exercise*
aerobics *n* exercises to increase the amount of oxygen in the blood and strengthen the heart and lungs
aerodrome *n* a small airport
aerodynamics *n* the study of how air flows around moving objects ▷ **aerodynamic** *adj* ▷ **aerodynamicist** *n*
aerofoil *n* a part of an aircraft, such as the wing, designed to give lift in flight
aerogram *n* an airmail letter on a single sheet of light paper that seals to form an envelope
aeronautics *n* the study or practice of flight through the air ▷ **aeronautical** *adj*
aeroplane *or US & Canad* **airplane** *n* a heavier-than-air powered flying vehicle with fixed wings
aerosol *n* a small metal pressurized can from which a substance can be dispensed in a fine spray
aerospace *n* **1** the earth's atmosphere and space beyond ▸ *adj* **2** of rockets or space vehicles: *the aerospace industry*
aesthete *or US* **esthete** (**eess**-theet) *n* a person who has or who pretends to have a highly developed appreciation of beauty
aesthetic *or US* **esthetic** (iss-**thet**-ik) *adj* **1** relating to the appreciation of art and beauty ▸ *n* **2** a principle or set of principles relating to the appreciation of art and beauty ▷ **aesthetically** *or US* **esthetically** *adv* ▷ **aestheticism** *or US* **estheticism** *n*
aesthetics *or US* **esthetics** *n* **1** the branch of philosophy concerned with the study of the concepts of beauty and taste **2** the study of the rules and principles of art
aether *n* same as **ether** (senses 2, 3)
aetiology (ee-tee-ol-a-jee) *n* same as **etiology**
afar *n* **from afar** from or at a great distance
affable *adj* showing warmth and friendliness ▷ **affability** *n* ▷ **affably** *adv*
affair *n* **1** an event or happening: *the Watergate affair* **2** a sexual relationship outside marriage **3** a thing to be done or attended to: *your choice of career is your own affair* **4** something previously specified: *lunch was a subdued affair*

affair n **1** = matter, business, happening, event, activity, incident, episode, topic **2** = relationship, romance, intrigue, fling, liaison, flirtation, amour, dalliance

affect¹ vb **1** to influence (someone or something): *the very difficult conditions continued to affect our performance* **2** (of pain or disease) to attack: *the virus can spread to affect the heart muscle* **3** to move someone emotionally: *the experience has affected him deeply*

affect vb **1** = influence, concern, alter, change, manipulate, act on, bear upon, impinge upon **3** = emotionally move, touch, upset, overcome, stir, disturb, perturb

affect² vb **1** to put on a show of: *she affects a certain disinterest* **2** to wear or use by preference: *he likes to be called Captain John and affects a nautical cap*

affect vb **1** = put on, assume, adopt, pretend, imitate, simulate, contrive, aspire to

affectation n an attitude or manner put on to impress others

affected adj **1** behaving or speaking in a manner put on to impress others **2** pretended: *an affected indifference*

affected adj = pretended, artificial, contrived, put-on, mannered, unnatural, feigned, insincere; ≠ genuine

affection n **1** fondness or tenderness for a person or thing **2 affections** feelings of love; emotions: *I was angry with her for playing with their affections*

affection n **1** = fondness, liking, feeling, love, care, warmth, attachment, goodwill, aroha (NZ)

affectionate adj having or displaying tenderness, affection, or warmth
> **affectionately** adv

affectionate adj = fond, loving, kind, caring, friendly, attached, devoted, tender; ≠ cool

affianced (af-**fie**-anst) adj old-fashioned engaged to be married

affidavit (af-fid-**dave**-it) n law a written statement made under oath

affiliate vb **-ating, -ated 1** (of a group) to link up with a larger group ▸ n **2** a person or organization that is affiliated with another
> **affiliation** n

affiliate vb = associate, unite, join, link, ally, combine, incorporate, amalgamate

affinity n, pl **-ties 1** a feeling of closeness to and understanding of a person **2** a close similarity in appearance, structure, or quality **3** a chemical attraction

affinity n **1** = attraction, liking, leaning, sympathy, inclination, rapport, fondness, partiality, aroha (NZ); ≠ hostility

2 = similarity, relationship, connection, correspondence, analogy, resemblance, closeness, likeness; ≠ difference

affirm vb **1** to declare to be true **2** to state clearly one's support for (an idea or belief)
> **affirmation** n

affirm vb **1** = declare, state, maintain, swear, assert, testify, pronounce, certify; ≠ deny **2** = confirm, prove, endorse, ratify, verify, validate, bear out, substantiate; ≠ refute

affirmative adj **1** indicating agreement: *an affirmative answer* ▸ n **2** a word or phrase indicating agreement, such as *yes*

affirmative adj = agreeing, confirming, positive, approving, consenting, favourable, concurring, assenting; ≠ negative

affix vb **1** to attach or fasten ▸ n **2** a word or syllable added to a word to produce a derived or inflected form, such as -ment in establishment

afflict vb to cause someone suffering or unhappiness

afflict vb = torment, trouble, pain, hurt, distress, plague, grieve, harass

affliction n **1** something that causes physical or mental suffering **2** a condition of great distress or suffering

affluent adj having plenty of money
> **affluence** n

affluent adj = wealthy, rich, prosperous, loaded (slang), well-off, opulent, well-heeled (informal), well-to-do, minted (Brit slang); ≠ poor

afford vb **1 can afford** to be able to do or spare something without risking financial difficulties or undesirable consequences: *she can't afford to be choosy* **2** to give or supply: *afford me an opportunity to judge for myself* > **affordable** adj
> **affordability** n

afford vb **2** = give, offer, provide, produce, supply, yield, render

afforest vb to plant trees on > **afforestation** n

affray n Brit, Austral & NZ a noisy fight in a public place

affront n **1** a deliberate insult ▸ vb **2** to hurt someone's pride or dignity

Afghan adj **1** of Afghanistan ▸ n **2** a person from Afghanistan **3** the language of Afghanistan

Afghan hound n a large slim dog with long silky hair

aficionado (af-fish-yo-**nah**-do) n, pl **-dos** an enthusiastic fan of a sport or interest

afield adv **far afield** far away: *they used to travel as far afield as Hungary*

aflame adv, adj **1** in flames **2** deeply aroused: *his face was aflame with self-contempt and embarrassment*

a

afloat *adj* **1** floating **2** free of debt: *his goal is to keep the company afloat* **3** aboard ship ▸ *adv* **4** floating **5** free of debt **6** aboard ship; at sea

afoot *adj, adv* happening; in operation: *I had no suspicion of what was afoot*

aforementioned *adj* mentioned before

aforesaid *adj* referred to previously

aforethought *adj* premeditated: *malice aforethought*

afraid *adj* **1** feeling fear or apprehension **2** regretful: *I'm afraid I lost my temper*

> **afraid** *adj* **1** = scared, frightened, nervous, terrified, shaken, startled, fearful, cowardly; ≠ unafraid **2** = sorry, apologetic, regretful, sad, distressed, unhappy; ≠ pleased

afresh *adv* once more

African *adj* **1** of Africa ▸ *n* **2** a person from Africa

African violet *n* a flowering house plant with pink or purple flowers and hairy leaves

Afrikaans *n* one of the official languages of South Africa, descended from Dutch

Afrikaner *n* a White South African whose native language is Afrikaans

Afro- *combining form* indicating Africa or African: *Afro-Caribbean*

aft *adv, adj* at or towards the rear of a ship or aircraft

after *prep* **1** following in time or place **2** in pursuit of: *he was after my mother's jewellery* **3** concerning: *she asked after Laura* **4** considering: *you seem all right after what happened last night* **5** next in excellence or importance to **6** in imitation of; in the manner of **7** in accordance with: *a man after his own heart* **8** with the same name as: *the street is named after the designer of the church* **9** US past (the hour of): *fifteen after twelve* **10** **after all** **A** in spite of everything: *I was, after all, a suspect* **B** in spite of expectations or efforts **11** **after you** please go before me ▸ *adv* **12** at a later time; afterwards ▸ *conj* **13** at a time later than the time when: *she arrived after the reading had begun* ▸ *adj* **14** *naut* further aft: *the after cabin*

> **after** *prep* **1** = at the end of, following, subsequent to; ≠ before ▸ *adv* = following, later, next, succeeding, afterwards, subsequently, thereafter

afterbirth *n* the placenta and fetal membranes expelled from the mother's womb after childbirth

aftercare *n* **1** the help and support given to a person discharged from a hospital or prison **2** the regular care required to keep something in good condition

aftereffect *n* any result occurring some time after its cause

afterglow *n* **1** the glow left after the source of a light has disappeared, for example after sunset **2** a pleasant feeling remaining after an enjoyable experience

afterlife *n* life after death

aftermath *n* effects or results of an event considered collectively: *the aftermath of the weekend violence*

> **aftermath** *n* = effects, results, wake, consequences, outcome, sequel, end result, upshot

afternoon *n* the period between noon and evening

afters *n informal* the sweet course of a meal

aftershave *n* a scented lotion applied to a man's face after shaving

afterthought *n* **1** something thought of after the opportunity to use it has passed **2** an addition to something already completed

afterwards *or* **afterward** *adv* later

Ag *chem* silver

again *adv* **1** another or a second time: *I want to look at that atlas again* **2** once more in a previously experienced state or condition: *he pictured her again as she used to be* **3** in addition to the original amount: *twice as much again* **4** on the other hand **5** moreover or furthermore: *she is talented and, again, hard-working* **6** **again and again** continually or repeatedly

> **again** *adv* **1, 2** = once more, another time, anew, afresh **5** = also, in addition, moreover, besides, furthermore

against *prep* **1** standing or leaning beside: *she leaned against a tree* **2** opposed to or in disagreement with **3** in contrast to: *his complexion was a sickly white against the black stubble of his beard* **4** coming in contact with: *rain rattled against the window* **5** having an unfavourable effect on: *the system works against you when you don't have money* **6** as a protection from: *a safeguard against bacteria* **7** in exchange for or in return for: *the dollar has gained very slightly against the yen* **8** **as against** as opposed to; as compared with

> **against** *prep* **1, 4** = beside, on, up against, in contact with, abutting **2** = opposed to, anti (*informal*), hostile to, in opposition to, averse to, opposite to **3** = in opposition to, resisting, versus, counter to, in the opposite direction of

agape *adj* **1** (of the mouth) wide open **2** (of a person) very surprised

agaric *n* any fungus with gills on the underside of the cap, such as a mushroom

agate (ag-git) *n* a hard semiprecious form of quartz with striped colouring

age *n* **1** the length of time that a person or thing has existed **2** a period or state of human life **3** the latter part of human life **4** a period of history marked by some feature **5** **ages** *informal* a long time **6** **come of age** to become legally responsible for one's actions (usually at 18 years) ▸ *vb* **ageing** *or* **aging**, **aged** **7** to become old: *skin type changes as one ages* **8** to appear or cause to appear older: *the years had not aged her in any way*

age *n* 1 = years, days, generation, lifetime, length of existence 3 = old age, experience, maturity, seniority, majority, senility, decline, advancing years; ≠ youth 4 = time, day(s), period, generation, era, epoch ▶ *vb* 7 = grow old, decline, weather, fade, deteriorate, wither 8 = mature, season, condition, soften, mellow, ripen

aged *adj* 1 (**ay**-jid) advanced in years; old 2 (rhymes with **raged**) being at the age of: *a girl aged thirteen*

aged *adj* 1 = old, getting on, grey, ancient, antique, elderly, antiquated; ≠ young

ageing *or* **aging** *n* 1 the fact or process of growing old ▶ *adj* 2 becoming or appearing older
ageless *adj* 1 apparently never growing old 2 seeming to have existed for ever; eternal: *an ageless profession*
agency *n, pl* -**cies** 1 an organization providing a specific service: *an advertising agency* 2 the business or functions of an agent 3 action or power by which something happens: *the intervention of a human agency in the sequence of events*

agency *n* 1 = business, company, office, firm, department, organization, enterprise, establishment 3 = medium, means, activity, vehicle, instrument, mechanism

agenda *n* 1 a schedule or list of items to be attended to, for example at a meeting 2 *US & Canad* an appointment diary with room for storing addresses, telephone numbers, etc.

agenda *n* 1 = programme, list, plan, schedule, diary, calendar, timetable

agent *n* 1 a person who arranges business for other people, esp. for actors or singers 2 a spy 3 a substance which causes change in other substances: *an emulsifying agent* 4 someone or something which causes an effect: *the agent of change*

agent *n* 1 = representative, rep (*informal*), negotiator, envoy, surrogate, go-between 3 = force, means, power, cause, instrument 4 = author, worker, vehicle, instrument, operator, performer, catalyst, doer

agent provocateur (azh-on prov-vok-at-**tur**) *n, pl* **agents provocateurs** (azh-on prov-vok-at-**tur**) a person employed by the authorities to tempt people to commit illegal acts and so be discredited or punished
age-old *adj* very old; ancient
agglomeration *n* a confused mass or cluster
aggrandize *or* -**dise** *vb* -**dizing**, -**dized** *or* -**dising**, -**dised** to make greater in size, power, or rank > **aggrandizement** *or* -**disement** *n*
aggravate *vb* -**vating**, -**vated** 1 to make (a disease, situation, or problem) worse 2 *informal* to annoy > **aggravating** *adj* > **aggravation** *n*

aggravate *vb* 1 = make worse, exaggerate, intensify, worsen, exacerbate, magnify, inflame, increase; ≠ improve 2 = annoy, bother, provoke, irritate, nettle, get on your nerves (*informal*); ≠ please

aggregate *n* 1 an amount or total formed from separate units 2 *geol* a rock, such as granite, consisting of a mixture of minerals 3 the sand and stone mixed with cement and water to make concrete ▶ *adj* 4 formed of separate units collected into a whole ▶ *vb* -**gating**, -**gated** 5 to combine or be combined into a whole 6 to amount to (a particular number) > **aggregation** *n*

aggregate *n* 1 = total, body, whole, amount, collection, cluster, mass, sum, combination ▶ *adj* = collective, mixed, combined, collected, accumulated, composite, cumulative ▶ *vb* 5 = combine, mix, collect, assemble, heap, accumulate, pile, amass

aggression *n* 1 violent and hostile behaviour 2 an unprovoked attack > **aggressor** *n*

aggression *n* 1 = hostility, malice, antagonism, antipathy, ill will, belligerence, destructiveness, pugnacity 2 = attack, campaign, injury, assault, raid, invasion, offensive, onslaught

aggressive *adj* 1 full of anger or hostility 2 forceful or determined: *an aggressive sales technique* > **aggressively** *adv* > **aggressiveness** *n*

aggressive *adj* 1 = hostile, offensive, destructive, belligerent, unfriendly, contrary, antagonistic, pugnacious, aggro (*Austral, NZ*), aggers (*Austral slang*), biffo (*Austral slang*); ≠ friendly 2 = forceful, powerful, convincing, effective, enterprising, dynamic, bold, militant; ≠ submissive

aggrieved *adj* upset and angry
aggro *slang* ▶ *n* 1 *Brit, Austral & NZ* aggressive behaviour ▶ *adj* 2 *Austral* angry and aggressive
aghast *adj* overcome with amazement or horror
agile *adj* 1 quick in movement; nimble 2 mentally quick or acute > **agility** *n*
agitate *vb* -**tating**, -**tated** 1 to excite, disturb, or trouble 2 to shake or stir (a liquid) 3 to attempt to stir up public opinion for or against something > **agitated** *adj* > **agitatedly** *adv* > **agitation** *n* > **agitator** *n*

agitate *vb* 1 = upset, worry, trouble, excite, distract, unnerve, disconcert, fluster; ≠ calm 2 = stir, beat, shake, disturb, toss, rouse

aglow *adj* glowing
AGM annual general meeting
agnostic *n* 1 a person who believes that it is impossible to know whether God exists 2 a person who claims that the answer to some specific question cannot be known with certainty ▶ *adj* 3 of or relating to agnostics > **agnosticism** *n*

a

ago *adv* in the past: *fifty years ago*

agog *adj* eager or curious: *Marcia would be agog to hear his news*

agonize *or* **-nise** *vb* **-nizing, -nized** *or* **-nising, -nised** **1** to worry greatly **2** to suffer agony > **agonizing** *or* **-nising** *adj* > **agonizingly** *or* **-nisingly** *adv*

agony *n, pl* **-nies** acute physical or mental pain

> **agony** *n* = suffering, pain, distress, misery, torture, discomfort, torment, hardship

agony aunt *n* a person who replies to readers' letters in an agony column

agony column *n* a newspaper or magazine feature offering advice on readers' personal problems

agoraphobia *n* a pathological fear of being in public places > **agoraphobic** *adj, n*

agrarian *adj* of or relating to land or agriculture > **agrarianism** *n*

agree *vb* **agreeing, agreed** **1** to be of the same opinion **2** to give assent; consent **3** to be consistent **4** **agree on** to reach a joint decision about: *the ministers agreed on a strategy* **5** **agree with** to be agreeable or suitable to (one's health or appearance): *you look good – your new job must agree with you* **6** to concede: *they agreed that the price they were asking was too high* **7** *grammar* to be the same in number, gender, and case as a connected word

> **agree** *vb* **1** = concur, be as one, sympathize, assent, see eye to eye, be of the same opinion; ≠ disagree **3** = correspond, match, coincide, tally, conform **5 agree with someone** = suit, get on with, befit

agreeable *adj* **1** pleasant and enjoyable **2** prepared to consent: *I cannot say that she was agreeable to the project but she was resigned* > **agreeably** *adv*

agreement *n* **1** the act or state of agreeing **2** a legally enforceable contract

> **agreement** *n* **1** = concurrence, harmony, compliance, union, agreeing, consent, unison, assent; ≠ disagreement **2** = treaty, contract, arrangement, alliance, deal (*informal*), understanding, settlement, bargain

agriculture *n* the rearing of crops and livestock; farming > **agricultural** *adj* > **agriculturalist** *n*

> **agriculture** *n* = farming, culture, cultivation, husbandry, tillage

agronomy (ag-ron-om-mee) *n* the science of land cultivation, soil management, and crop production > **agronomist** *n*

aground *adv* onto the bottom of shallow water: *they felt a jolt as the ship ran aground*

ague (aig-yew) *n* **1** *old-fashioned* malarial fever with shivering **2** a fit of shivering

ahead *adv* **1** at or in the front; before **2** forwards: *go straight ahead* **3** **get ahead** to achieve success: *I was young and hungry to get ahead* ▸ *adj* **4** in a leading position: *he is ahead in the polls*

> **ahead** *adv* **1, 2** = in front, in advance, towards the front, frontwards

ahoy *interj naut* a shout made to call a ship or to attract attention

AI **1** artificial insemination **2** artificial intelligence

aid *n* **1** money, equipment, or services provided for people in need; assistance **2** a person or device that helps or assists ▸ *vb* **3** to help financially or in other ways

> **aid** *n* **1** = help, backing, support, benefit, favour, relief, promotion, assistance; ≠ hindrance ▸ *vb* = help, support, serve, sustain, assist, avail, subsidize, be of service to; ≠ hinder

aide *n* an assistant: *a senior aide to the Prime Minister*

> **aide** *n* = assistant, supporter, attendant, helper, right-hand man *or* woman *or* person, second

aide-de-camp (aid-de-kom) *n, pl* **aides-de-camp** (aid-de-kom) a military officer serving as personal assistant to a senior

AIDS acquired immunodeficiency syndrome: a viral disease that destroys the body's ability to fight infection

AIH artificial insemination by husband

ail *vb literary* **1** to trouble or afflict **2** to feel unwell

aileron (ale-er-on) *n* a hinged flap on the back of an aircraft wing which controls rolling

ailing *adj* unwell or unsuccessful over a long period: *an ailing company*

> **ailing** *adj* = weak, failing, poor, flawed, unstable, unsatisfactory, deficient

ailment *n* a slight illness

> **ailment** *n* = illness, disease, complaint, disorder, sickness, affliction, malady, infirmity

aim *vb* **1** to point (a weapon or missile) or direct (a blow or remark) at a particular person or object **2** to propose or intend: *they aim to provide full and equal rights to all groups* ▸ *n* **3** the action of directing something at an object **4** intention or purpose **5** **take aim** to point a weapon or missile at a person or object

> **aim** *vb* **1** = point ▸ *n* **4** = intention, point, plan, goal, design, target, purpose, desire

aimless *adj* having no purpose or direction > **aimlessly** *adv*

ain't *not standard* am not, is not, are not, have not, or has not: *it ain't fair*

air *n* **1** the mixture of gases that forms the earth's atmosphere. It consists chiefly of nitrogen, oxygen, argon, and carbon dioxide

2 the space above and around the earth; sky. Related adjective: **aerial** 3 a distinctive quality, appearance, or manner: *I thought he had an air of elegance and celebrity about him* 4 a simple tune 5 transportation in aircraft: *I went off to Italy by air and train* 6 **in the air** in circulation; current: *a sense of expectation is in the air* 7 **into thin air** leaving no trace behind 8 **on the air** in the act of broadcasting on radio or television 9 **up in the air** uncertain ▸ *vb* 10 to make known publicly: *these issues will be aired at a ministerial meeting* 11 to expose to air to dry or ventilate 12 (of a television or radio programme) to be broadcast

> **air** *n* **1, 2** = atmosphere, sky, heavens, aerosphere **3** = manner, appearance, look, aspect, atmosphere, mood, impression, aura **4** = tune, song, theme, melody, strain, lay, aria ▸ *vb* **10** = publicize, reveal, exhibit, voice, express, display, circulate, make public

airbag *n* a safety device in a car, consisting of a bag that inflates automatically in an accident to protect the driver or passenger

airborne *adj* 1 carried by air 2 (of aircraft) flying; in the air

> **airborne** *adj* **2** = flying, floating, in the air, hovering, gliding, in flight, on the wing

airbrush *n* 1 an atomizer which sprays paint by means of compressed air ▸ *vb* 2 to paint using an airbrush 3 to improve the image of (a person or thing) by hiding defects beneath a bland exterior

air conditioning *n* a system for controlling the temperature and humidity of the air in a building > **air-conditioned** *adj* > **air conditioner** *n*

aircraft *n*, *pl* **-craft** any machine capable of flying, such as a glider or aeroplane

aircraft carrier *n* a warship with a long flat deck for the launching and landing of aircraft

airfield *n* a place where aircraft can land and take off

air force *n* the branch of a nation's armed services that is responsible for air warfare

air gun *n* a gun fired by means of compressed air

air hostess *n* chiefly Brit old-fashioned a female flight attendant on an airline

airily *adv* in a light-hearted and casual manner

airing *n* 1 exposure to air or warmth for drying or ventilation 2 exposure to public debate: *both these notions got an airing during the campaign*

> **airing** *n* **1** = ventilation, drying, freshening, aeration **2** = exposure, display, expression, publicity, vent, utterance, dissemination

airless *adj* lacking fresh air; stuffy

airlift *n* 1 the transportation by air of troops or cargo when other routes are blocked ▸ *vb* 2 to transport by an airlift

airline *n* an organization that provides scheduled flights for passengers or cargo

airliner *n* a large passenger aircraft

airlock *n* 1 a bubble of air blocking the flow of liquid in a pipe 2 an airtight chamber between places that do not have the same air pressure, such as in a spacecraft or submarine

airmail *n* 1 the system of sending mail by aircraft 2 mail sent by aircraft

airman *or fem* **airwoman** *n*, *pl* **-men** *or* **-women** a person serving in an air force

airplane *n* US & Canad an aeroplane

> **airplane** *n* = plane, aircraft, jet, aeroplane, airliner

airplay *n* the broadcast performances of a record on radio

airport *n* a landing and taking-off area for civil aircraft, with facilities for aircraft maintenance and passenger arrival and departure

air raid *n* an attack by enemy aircraft in which bombs are dropped

airship *n* a lighter-than-air self-propelled aircraft

airspace *n* the atmosphere above a particular country, regarded as its territory

airstrip *n* a cleared area for the landing and taking-off of aircraft

airtight *adj* 1 sealed so that air cannot enter 2 having no weak points: *your reasoning is airtight and your evidence sound*

airworthy *adj* (of an aircraft) safe to fly > **airworthiness** *n*

airy *adj* **airier**, **airiest** 1 spacious and well ventilated 2 light-hearted and casual 3 having little basis in reality; fanciful: *airy assurances*

aisle (rhymes with *mile*) *n* a passageway separating seating areas in a church, theatre, or train, or separating rows of shelves in a supermarket

> **aisle** *n* = passageway, path, lane, passage, corridor, alley, gangway

ajar *adj*, *adv* (of a door) slightly open

aka also known as

akimbo *adv* (**with**) **arms akimbo** with hands on hips and elbows turned outwards

akin *adj* **akin to** similar or very close to: *the technique is akin to impressionist painting*

alabaster *n* a kind of white stone used for making statues and vases

à la carte *adj*, *adv* (of a menu) having dishes individually priced

alacrity *n* speed or eagerness: *I accepted the invitation with alacrity*

à la mode *adj* fashionable

alarm *n* 1 fear aroused by awareness of danger 2 a noise warning of danger: *there had been no time to put on life jackets or to sound the alarm* 3 a device that transmits a warning 4 short for **alarm clock** ▸ *vb* 5 to fill with fear 6 to fit or activate a burglar alarm on (a house, car, etc.) > **alarming** *adj*

a

alarm n 1 = fear, panic, anxiety, fright, apprehension, nervousness, consternation, trepidation (formal); ≠ calmness 2, 3 = danger signal, warning, bell, alert, siren, alarm bell, hooter, distress signal ▸ vb 5 = frighten, scare, panic, distress, startle, dismay, daunt, unnerve; ≠ calm

alarm clock n a clock that sounds at a set time to wake a person up

alarmist n 1 a person who alarms others needlessly ▸ adj 2 causing needless alarm

alas adv 1 unfortunately or regrettably: the answer, alas, is that they cannot get any for the moment ▸ interj 2 old-fashioned an exclamation of grief or alarm

albatross n 1 a large sea bird with very long wings 2 golf a score of three strokes under par for a hole

albeit conj even though: these effects occur, albeit to a lesser degree

albino n, pl -nos a person or animal with white or almost white hair and skin and pinkish eyes > **albinism** n

album n 1 a book with blank pages, for keeping photographs or stamps in 2 a collection of recordings released as a single item

albumen n 1 egg white 2 biochem same as **albumin**

albumin or **albumen** n biochem a water-soluble protein found in blood plasma, egg white, milk, and muscle

alchemy n a medieval form of chemistry concerned with trying to change base metals into gold and to find an elixir to prolong life indefinitely > **alchemist** n

alcohol n 1 a colourless flammable liquid present in intoxicating drinks 2 intoxicating drinks generally

alcoholic n 1 a person who is addicted to alcohol ▸ adj 2 of or relating to alcohol

alcoholic n = drinker, drunkard, drunk, inebriate, tippler, lush (slang), wino (informal), toper (literary) ▸ adj = intoxicating, hard, strong, stiff, brewed, fermented, distilled

alcoholism n a condition in which dependence on alcohol harms a person's health and everyday life

alcopop n informal an alcoholic drink that tastes like a soft drink

alcove n a recess in the wall of a room

aldehyde n chem any organic compound containing the group –CHO, derived from alcohol by oxidation

alder n a tree with toothed leaves and conelike fruits, often found in damp places

alderman n, pl -men 1 (formerly, in England and Wales) a senior member of a local council, elected by other councillors 2 (in the US, Canada and Australia) a member of the governing body of a city

ale n 1 a beer fermented in an open vessel using yeasts that rise to the top of the brew 2 (formerly) an alcoholic drink that is unflavoured by hops 3 Brit another word for **beer**

alert adj 1 watchful and attentive 2 **alert to** aware of ▸ n 3 a warning or the period during which a warning remains in effect 4 **on the alert** watchful ▸ vb 5 to warn of danger 6 to make aware of a fact > **alertness** n

alert adj 1 = attentive, awake, vigilant, watchful, on the lookout, circumspect, observant, on guard; ≠ careless ▸ vb 5 = warn, signal, inform, alarm, notify, tip off, forewarn; ≠ lull

A level n 1 Brit the advanced level of a subject taken for the General Certificate of Education 2 a pass in a subject at A level

alfalfa n a plant widely used for feeding farm animals

alfresco adj, adv in the open air

algae (al-jee) pl n, sing alga (al-ga) plants which grow in water or moist ground, and which have no true stems, roots, or leaves

algebra n a branch of mathematics in which symbols are used to represent numbers > **algebraic** adj

ALGOL n an early computer programming language designed for mathematical and scientific purposes

algorithm n a logical arithmetical or computational procedure for solving problems

alias adv 1 also known as: Iris florentina, alias orris root ▸ n, pl -ases 2 a false name

alibi n, pl -bis 1 law a plea of being somewhere else when a crime was committed 2 informal an excuse ▸ vb -biing, -bied 3 to provide someone with an alibi

alien adj 1 foreign 2 from another world 3 **alien to** repugnant or opposed to: these methods are alien to the world of politics ▸ n 4 a person who is a citizen of a country other than the one in which he or she lives 5 a being from another world 6 a person who does not seem to fit in with his or her environment

alien adj 1 = foreign, strange, imported, unknown, exotic, unfamiliar ▸ n 4 = foreigner, incomer, immigrant, stranger, outsider, newcomer, asylum seeker; ≠ citizen

alienate vb -ating, -ated 1 to cause (a friend) to become unfriendly or hostile 2 to cause (someone) to feel that he or she does not belong somewhere 3 law to transfer the ownership of property to another person > **alienation** n

alienate vb 1 = antagonize, anger, annoy, offend, irritate, hassle (informal), estrange, hack off (informal)

alight¹ vb **alighting, alighted** or **alit 1** to step out of a vehicle or off a horse: we alighted on Vladivostok *station* **2** to land: *we saw thirty goldfinches alighting on the ledge*

alight *vb* **1** = get off, descend, get down, disembark, dismount **2** = land, light, settle, come down, descend, perch, touch down, come to rest; ≠ take off

alight² *adj, adv* **1** on fire **2** illuminated: *the lamp on the desk was alight*

alight *adj, adv* **2** = lit up, bright, brilliant, shining, illuminated, fiery

align (a-line) *vb* **1** to bring (a person or group) into agreement with the policy of another **2** to place (two objects) in a particular position in relation to each other > **alignment** *n*

align *vb* **2** = line up, order, range, regulate, straighten, even up

alike *adj* **1** similar: *they were thought to be very alike* ▸ *adv* **2** in the same way: *they even dressed alike* **3** considered together: *players and spectators alike*

alike *adj* = similar, close, the same, parallel, resembling, identical, corresponding, akin; ≠ different ▸ *adv* **2** = similarly, identically, equally, uniformly, correspondingly, analogously; ≠ differently

alimentary *adj* of or relating to nutrition
alimentary canal *n* the tubular passage in the body through which food is passed and digested
alimony *n law* an allowance paid under a court order by one spouse to another after separation
A-line *adj* (of a skirt) slightly flared
aliquot *adj maths* denoting or belonging to an exact divisor of a number
alive *adj* **1** living; having life **2** in existence: *he said that he would keep the company alive, no matter what* **3** lively **4** alive to aware of **5** alive with swarming with: *the rocky shoreline was alive with birds*

alive *adj* **1** = living, breathing, animate, subsisting, existing, functioning, in the land of the living (*informal*); ≠ dead **2** = in existence, existing, functioning, active, operative, in force, on-going, prevalent; ≠ inoperative **3** = lively, active, vital, alert, energetic, animated, agile, perky; ≠ dull

alkali (alk-a-lie) *n chem* a substance that combines with acid and neutralizes it to form a salt
alkaline *adj chem* having the properties of or containing an alkali > **alkalinity** *n*
alkaloid *n chem* any of a group of organic compounds containing nitrogen. Many are poisonous and some are used as drugs
all *determiner* **1** the whole quantity or number (of): *all the banks agree; we're all to blame* **2** every one of a class: *almost all animals sneeze* ▸ *adj* **3** the greatest possible: *in all seriousness* **4** any whatever:

I'm leaving out all question of motive for the time being **5 all along** since the beginning **6 all but** nearly **7 all in all** everything considered **8 all over A** finished **B** everywhere in or on: *we send them all over the world* **C** *informal* typically: *that's him all over* **9 all the** so much (more or less) than otherwise: *the need for new drugs is all the more important* **10 at all** used for emphasis: *my throat's no better at all* **11 be all for** *informal* to be strongly in favour of **12 for all** in spite of: *for all his cynicism, he's at heart a closet idealist* **13 in all** altogether: *there were five in all* ▸ *adv* **14** (in scores of games) each: *the score was two all* ▸ *n* **15 give one's all** to make the greatest possible effort

all *determiner* **1** = the whole amount, everything, the total, the aggregate, the totality, the sum total, the entirety, the entire amount **2** = every, each, every single, every one of, each and every ▸ *adj* **3** = complete, greatest, full, total, perfect, entire, utter

Allah *n* the name of God in Islam
allay *vb* to reduce (fear, doubt, or anger)
allegation *n* an unproved assertion or accusation

allegation *n* = claim, charge, statement, declaration, accusation, assertion, affirmation

allege *vb* **-leging, -leged** to state without proof

allege *vb* = claim, charge, challenge, state, maintain, declare, assert, uphold; ≠ deny

alleged *adj* stated but not proved: *the spot where the alleged crime took place* > **allegedly** (al-lej-id-lee) *adv*

alleged *adj* = claimed, supposed, declared, assumed, so-called, apparent, stated, described

allegiance *n* loyalty or dedication to a person, cause, or belief

allegiance *n* = loyalty, devotion, fidelity, obedience, constancy, faithfulness; ≠ disloyalty

allegory *n, pl* **-ries** a story, poem, or picture with an underlying meaning as well as the literal one > **allegorical** *adj* > **allegorize** or **-rise** *vb*
allegretto *music* ▸ *adv* **1** fairly quickly or briskly ▸ *n, pl* **-tos** **2** a piece or passage to be performed fairly quickly or briskly
allegro *music* ▸ *adv* **1** in a brisk lively manner ▸ *n, pl* **-gros** **2** a piece or passage to be performed in a brisk lively manner
alleluia *interj* praise the Lord!
allergen (al-ler-jen) *n* a substance capable of causing an allergic reaction > **allergenic** *adj*
allergic *adj* **1** having or caused by an allergy **2 allergic to** *informal* having a strong dislike of: *father and son seemed to have been allergic to each other from the start*

allergic *adj* **1** = sensitive, affected, susceptible, hypersensitive

allergy *n, pl* **-gies 1** extreme sensitivity to a substance such as a food or pollen, which causes the body to react to any contact with it **2** *informal* a strong dislike for something

> **allergy** *n* **1** = sensitivity, reaction, susceptibility, antipathy, hypersensitivity, sensitiveness

alleviate *vb* **-ating, -ated** to lessen (pain or suffering) › **alleviation** *n*

> **alleviate** *vb* = ease, reduce, relieve, moderate, soothe, lessen, lighten, allay

alley *n* **1** a narrow passage between or behind buildings **2** **A** a building containing lanes for tenpin bowling **B** a long narrow wooden lane down which the ball is rolled in tenpin bowling **3** a path in a garden, often lined with trees

> **alley** *n* **1** = passage, walk, lane, pathway, alleyway, passageway, backstreet

alliance *n* **1** the state of being allied **2** a formal relationship between two or more countries or political parties to work together **3** the countries or parties involved

> **alliance** *n* **2** = union, league, association, agreement, marriage, connection, combination, coalition; ≠ division

allied *adj* **1** united by a common aim or common characteristics: *the allied areas of telepathy and clairvoyance* **2** **Allied** relating to the countries that fought against Germany and Japan in the Second World War: *the Allied bombing of German cities*

> **allied** *adj* **1** = united, linked, related, combined, integrated, affiliated, cooperating, in league

alligator *n* a large reptile of the southern US, similar to the crocodile but with a shorter broader snout

all in *adj* *informal* exhausted **2** (of wrestling) with no style forbidden › *adv* **3** with all expenses included

alliteration *n* the use of the same sound at the start of words occurring together, as in *round the rugged rock the ragged rascal ran* › **alliterative** *adj*

allocate *vb* **-cating, -cated** to assign to someone or for a particular purpose › **allocation** *n*

> **allocate** *vb* = assign, grant, distribute, designate, set aside, earmark, give out, consign

allot *vb* **-lotting, -lotted** to assign as a share or for a particular purpose

allotment *n* **1** *Brit* a small piece of land rented by a person to grow vegetables on **2** a portion allotted **3** distribution

allotrope *n* *chem* any of two or more physical forms in which an element can exist

allow *vb* **1** to permit someone to do something **2** to set aside: *I allowed plenty of time* **3** to

acknowledge (a point or claim) **4** **allow for** to take into account › **allowable** *adj*

> **allow** *vb* **1** = permit, approve, enable, sanction, endure, license, tolerate, authorize; ≠ prohibit **2** = give, provide, grant, spare, devote, assign, allocate, set aside **3** = acknowledge, accept, admit, grant, recognize, yield, concede, confess **4** **allow for something** = take into account, consider, plan for, accommodate, provide for, make provision for, make allowances for, make concessions for

allowance *n* **1** an amount of money given at regular intervals **2** (in Britain) an amount of a person's income that is not subject to income tax **3** **make allowances for** **A** to treat or judge someone less severely because he or she has special problems **B** to take into account in one's plans

> **allowance** *n* **1** = pocket money, grant, fee, payment, ration, handout, remittance

alloy *n* **1** a mixture of two or more metals ► *vb* **2** to mix metals in order to obtain a substance with a desired property

all right *adj* **1** acceptable or satisfactory: *is everything all right?* **2** safe: *I'm going to check if he's all right* ► *interj* **3** an expression of approval or agreement ► *adv* **4** satisfactorily **5** safely **6** without doubt: *it was her all right*

> **all right** *adj* **1** = satisfactory, O.K. *or* okay (*informal*), average, fair, sufficient, standard, acceptable, good enough; ≠ unsatisfactory **2** = well, O.K. *or* okay (*informal*), whole (*archaic*), sound, fit, safe, healthy, unharmed; ≠ ill

all-rounder *n* a person with many skills and abilities

allspice *n* a spice used in cooking, which comes from the berries of a tropical American tree

allude *vb* **-luding, -luded** › **allude to** to refer indirectly to

allure *n* attractiveness or appeal

alluring *adj* extremely attractive

allusion *n* an indirect reference

alluvial *adj* **1** of or relating to alluvium ► *n* **2** same as **alluvium**

alluvium *n, pl* **-via** a fertile soil consisting of mud, silt, and sand deposited by flowing water

ally *n, pl* **-lies 1** a country, person, or group with an agreement to support another ► *vb* **-lies, -lying, -lied 2** **ally oneself with** to agree to support another country, person, or group

> **ally** *n* = partner, friend, colleague, associate, mate (*informal*), comrade, helper, collaborator, cobber (*Austral, NZ old-fashioned, informal*), E hoa (*NZ*); ≠ opponent ► *vb* **ally oneself with something or someone** = unite with, associate with, unify, collaborate with, join forces with, band together with

alma mater *n* the school, college, or university that one attended

almanac *n* a yearly calendar with detailed information on matters like anniversaries and phases of the moon

almighty *adj* 1 having power over everything 2 *informal* very great: *there was an almighty bang* ▸ *n* 3 **the Almighty** God

almond *n* an edible oval nut with a yellowish-brown shell, which grows on a small tree

almoner *n Brit* a former name for a hospital social worker

almost *adv* very nearly

> **almost** *adv* = nearly, about, close to, virtually, practically, roughly, just about, not quite

alms (ahmz) *pl n old-fashioned* donations of money or goods to poor people

aloe *n* 1 a plant with fleshy spiny leaves 2 **aloes** a bitter drug made from aloe leaves

aloft *adv* 1 in the air 2 *naut* in the rigging of a ship

alone *adj* 1 without anyone or anything else ▸ *adv* 2 without anyone or anything else 3 **leave someone** *or* **something alone** to refrain from annoying someone or interfering with something 4 **let alone** not to mention: *it looked inconceivable that he could run again, let alone be elected*

> **alone** *adj* = solitary, isolated, separate, apart, by yourself, unaccompanied, on your tod (*slang*); ≠ accompanied ▸ *adv* 2 = solely, only, individually, singly, exclusively, uniquely; ≠ with help

along *prep* 1 over part or all of the length of: *we were going along the railway tracks* ▸ *adv* 2 moving forward: *they were roaring along at 40mph* 3 in company with another or others: *let them go along for the ride* 4 **along with** together with: *I'm including the good days along with the bad*

alongside *prep* 1 close beside ▸ *adv* 2 near the side of something

aloof *adj* distant or haughty in manner

alopecia (al-loh-**pee**-sha) *n* loss of hair, usually due to illness

aloud *adv* in an audible voice

> **aloud** *adv* = out loud, clearly, plainly, distinctly, audibly, intelligibly

alpaca *n* 1 a South American mammal related to the llama, with dark shaggy hair 2 wool or cloth made from this hair

alpenstock *n* a strong stick with an iron tip used by hikers and mountain climbers

alpha *n* 1 the first letter in the Greek alphabet (A, α) 2 *Brit* the highest grade in an examination or for a piece of academic work 3 **alpha and omega** the first and last

alphabet *n* a set of letters in fixed conventional order, used in a writing system

alphabetical *adj* in the conventional order of the letters of an alphabet > **alphabetically** *adv*

alphabetize *or* **-ise** *vb* **-izing, -ized** *or* **-ising, -ised** to put in alphabetical order > **alphabetization** *or* **-isation** *n*

alpine *adj* 1 of high mountains 2 **Alpine** of the Alps ▸ *n* 3 a plant grown on or native to mountains

already *adv* 1 before the present time 2 before an implied or expected time

> **already** *adv* = before now, before, previously, at present, by now, by then, even now, just now

alright *adj, interj, adv not standard* same as **all right**

Alsatian *n* a large wolflike dog

also *adv* in addition; too

> **also** *adv* = and, too, further, in addition, as well, moreover, besides, furthermore

also-ran *n* a loser in a race, competition, or election

alt *combining form* alternative: *alt rock*

altar *n* 1 the table used for Communion in Christian churches 2 a raised structure on which sacrifices are offered and religious rites performed

altarpiece *n* a painting or a decorated screen set above and behind the altar in a Christian church

alter *vb* to make or become different; change

> **alter** *vb* = modify, change, reform, vary, transform, adjust, adapt, revise

alteration *n* a change or modification

altercation *n* a noisy argument

alter ego *n* 1 a hidden side to one's personality 2 a very close friend

alternate *vb* **-nating, -nated** 1 to occur by turns 2 to interchange regularly or in succession ▸ *adj* 3 occurring by turns 4 every second (one) of a series: *alternate days* 5 being a second choice > **alternately** *adv* > **alternation** *n*

> **alternate** *vb* 1 = interchange, change, fluctuate, take turns, oscillate, chop and change 2 = intersperse, interchange, exchange, swap, stagger, rotate ▸ *adj* 3 = alternating, interchanging, every other, rotating, every second, sequential

alternating current *n* an electric current that reverses direction at frequent regular intervals

alternative *n* 1 a possibility of choice between two or more things 2 either or any of such choices ▸ *adj* 3 presenting a choice between two or more possibilities 4 of a lifestyle, etc. that is less conventional or materialistic than is usual > **alternatively** *adv*

> **alternative** *n* = substitute, choice, other, option, preference, recourse

alternator *n* an electrical machine that generates an alternating current

although *conj* in spite of the fact that

a

although conj = though, while, even if, even though, whilst, albeit, despite the fact that, notwithstanding

altimeter (al-tim-it-er) n an instrument that measures altitude

altitude n height, esp. above sea level

alto n, pl **-tos 1** short for **contralto 2** the highest adult male voice **3** a singer with an alto voice **4** a musical instrument, for instance a saxophone, that is the second or third highest in its family ▸ adj **5** denoting such an instrument, singer, or voice: an alto flute

altogether adv **1** completely: an altogether different message **2** on the whole: this is not altogether a bad thing **3** in total: altogether, 25 aircraft took part ▸ n **4 in the altogether** informal naked

altogether adv **1** = absolutely, quite, completely, totally, perfectly, fully, thoroughly, wholly; ≠ partially **2** = on the whole, generally, mostly, in general, collectively, all things considered, on average, for the most part **3** = in total, in all, all told, taken together, in sum, everything included

altruism n unselfish concern for the welfare of others > **altruist** n > **altruistic** adj

aluminium or US & Canad **aluminum** n chem a light malleable silvery-white metallic element that does not rust. Symbol: **Al**

alumnus (al-lumm-nuss) or fem **alumna** (al-lumm-na) n, pl **-ni** (-nie) or **-nae** (-nee) chiefly US & Canad a graduate of a school or college

always adv **1** without exception: she was always at the top of her form in school work **2** continually: you're always shouting or whining **3** in any case: they're all adults, they can always say no

always adv **1** = habitually, regularly, every time, consistently, invariably, perpetually, without exception, customarily; ≠ seldom **2** = continually, constantly, all the time, forever, repeatedly, persistently, perpetually, incessantly

alyssum n a garden plant with clusters of small white flowers

am vb (with "I" as subject) a form of the present tense of **be**

AM 1 amplitude modulation **2** (in Britain) Member of the National Assembly for Wales

a.m. before noon

amalgam n **1** a blend or combination **2** an alloy of mercury with another metal: dental amalgam

amalgamate vb **-mating, -mated 1** to combine or unite **2** to alloy (a metal) with mercury > **amalgamation** n

amandla (a-mand-la) n S African a political slogan calling for power to the Black population

amanuensis (am-man-yew-en-siss) n, pl **-ses** (-seez) a person who copies manuscripts or takes dictation

amaranth n **1** poetic an imaginary flower that never fades **2** a lily-like plant with small green, red, or purple flowers

amaryllis n a lily-like plant with large red or white flowers and a long stalk

amass vb to accumulate or collect: the desire to amass wealth

amass vb = collect, gather, assemble, compile, accumulate, pile up, hoard

amateur n **1** a person who engages in a sport or other activity as a pastime rather than as a profession **2** a person unskilled in a subject or activity ▸ adj **3** doing something out of interest, not for money **4** amateurish > **amateurism** n

amateur n **1** = nonprofessional, outsider, layperson, layman or woman, dilettante, non-specialist, dabbler

amateurish adj lacking skill

amatory adj of or relating to romantic or sexual love

amaze vb **amazing, amazed** to fill with surprise; astonish > **amazement** n > **amazing** adj > **amazingly** adv

amaze vb = astonish, surprise, shock, stun, alarm, stagger, startle, bewilder

Amazon n **1** a strong and powerful woman **2** Greek myth one of a race of women warriors of Scythia > **Amazonian** adj

ambassador n **1** a diplomat of the highest rank, sent to another country as permanent representative of his or her own country **2** a representative or messenger: he saw himself as an ambassador for the game > **ambassadorial** adj

ambassador n **1** = representative, minister, agent, deputy, diplomat, envoy, consul, attaché

amber n **1** a yellow translucent fossilized resin, used in jewellery ▸ adj **2** brownish-yellow

ambergris (am-ber-greece) n a waxy substance secreted by the sperm whale, which is used in making perfumes

ambidextrous adj able to use both hands with equal ease

ambience or **ambiance** n the atmosphere of a place

ambient adj **1** surrounding: low ambient temperatures **2** creating a relaxing atmosphere: ambient music

ambiguity n, pl **-ties 1** the possibility of interpreting an expression in more than one way **2** an ambiguous situation or expression: the ambiguities of feminine identity

ambiguity n **1** = vagueness, doubt, uncertainty, obscurity, equivocation, dubiousness

ambiguous adj having more than one possible interpretation > **ambiguously** adv

ambiguous *adj* = unclear, obscure, vague, dubious, enigmatic, indefinite, inconclusive, indeterminate; ≠ clear

ambit *n* limits or boundary

ambition *n* **1** strong desire for success **2** something so desired; a goal

ambition *n* **1** = enterprise, longing, drive, spirit, desire, passion, enthusiasm, striving **2** = goal, hope, dream, target, aim, wish, purpose, desire

ambitious *adj* **1** having a strong desire for success **2** requiring great effort or ability: *ambitious plans*

ambitious *adj* **1** = enterprising, spirited, daring, eager, intent, enthusiastic, hopeful, striving; ≠ unambitious

ambivalence (am-biv-a-lenss) *n* the state of feeling two conflicting emotions at the same time > **ambivalent** *adj*

amble *vb* **-bling, -bled 1** to walk at a leisurely pace ▸ *n* **2** a leisurely walk or pace

ambrosia *n* **1** something delightful to taste or smell **2** *classical myth* the food of the gods

ambulance *n* a motor vehicle designed to carry sick or injured people

ambush *n* **1** the act of waiting in a concealed position to make a surprise attack **2** an attack from such a position ▸ *vb* **3** to attack suddenly from a concealed position

ambush *n* **2** = trap, snare, lure, waylaying ▸ *vb* = trap, attack, surprise, deceive, dupe, ensnare, waylay, bushwhack (US)

ameliorate (am-meal-yor-rate) *vb* **-rating, -rated** to make (something) better > **amelioration** *n*

amen *interj* so be it: used at the end of a prayer

amenable (a-mean-a-bl) *adj* likely or willing to cooperate

amend *vb* to make small changes to something such as a piece of writing or a contract, in order to improve it: *he has amended the basic design*

amend *vb* = change, improve, reform, fix, correct, repair, edit, alter

amendment *n* an improvement or correction

amendment *n* = addition, change, adjustment, attachment, adaptation, revision, modification, alteration

amends *pl n* **make amends for** to compensate for some injury or insult

amenity *n, pl* **-ties** a useful or enjoyable feature: *all kinds of amenities including horse riding and golf*

amenity *n* = facility, service, advantage, comfort, convenience

American *adj* **1** of the United States of America or the American continent ▸ *n* **2** a person from the United States of America or the American continent

Americanism *n* an expression or custom that is characteristic of the people of the United States

Americano *n, pl* **-nos** espresso coffee diluted with hot water

amethyst (am-myth-ist) *n* **1** a purple or violet variety of quartz used as a gemstone ▸ *adj* **2** purple or violet

amiable *adj* having a pleasant nature; friendly > **amiability** *n* > **amiably** *adv*

amicable *adj* characterized by friendliness: *ideally the parting should be amicable* > **amicability** *n* > **amicably** *adv*

amid *or* **amidst** *prep* in the middle of; among

amid *or* **amidst** *prep* = in the middle of, among, surrounded by, amongst, in the midst of, in the thick of

amidships *adv* *naut* at, near, or towards the centre of a ship

amino acid (am-mean-oh) *n* *chem* any of a group of organic compounds containing the amino group, $-NH_2$, and one or more carboxyl groups, $-COOH$, esp. one that is a component of protein

amiss *adv* **1** wrongly or badly: *anxious not to tread amiss* **2 take something amiss** to be offended by something ▸ *adj* **3** wrong or faulty

amity *n* *formal* friendship

ammeter *n* an instrument for measuring an electric current in amperes

ammonia *n* **1** a colourless strong-smelling gas containing hydrogen and nitrogen **2** a solution of this in water

ammonite *n* the fossilized spiral shell of an extinct sea creature

ammunition *n* **1** bullets, bombs, and shells that can be fired from or as a weapon **2** facts that can be used in an argument

ammunition *n* **1** = munitions, rounds, shot, shells, powder, explosives, armaments

amnesia *n* a partial or total loss of memory > **amnesiac** *adj, n*

amnesty *n, pl* **-ties 1** a general pardon for offences against a government **2** a period during which a law is suspended, to allow people to confess to crime or give up weapons without fear of prosecution

amnesty *n* **1** = general pardon, mercy, pardoning, immunity, forgiveness, reprieve, remission, clemency

amniocentesis *n, pl* **-ses** removal of amniotic fluid from the womb of a pregnant woman in order to detect possible abnormalities in the fetus

amniotic fluid *n* the fluid surrounding the fetus in the womb

a

amoeba *or US* **ameba** (am-mee-ba) *n, pl* **-bae** (-bee) *or* **-bas** a microscopic single-cell creature that is able to change its shape

amok *or* **amuck** *adv* **run amok** to run about in a violent frenzy

among *or* **amongst** *prep* **1** in the midst of: *she decided to dwell among the Greeks* **2** in the group, class, or number of: *he is among the top trainers* **3** to each of: *the stakes should be divided among the players* **4** with one another within a group: *sort it out among yourselves*

> **among** *or* **amongst** *prep* **1** = in the midst of, with, together with, in the middle of, amid, surrounded by, amidst, in the thick of **2** = in the group of, one of, part of, included in, in the company of, in the class of, in the number of **3** = between, to

amoral (aim-mor-ral) *adj* without moral standards or principles › **amorality** *n*

amorous *adj* feeling, displaying, or relating to sexual love or desire

amorphous *adj* **1** lacking a definite shape **2** of no recognizable character or type

amortize *or* **-tise** *vb* **-tizing, -tized** *or* **-tising, -tised** *finance* to pay off (a debt) gradually by periodic transfers to a sinking fund

amount *n* **1** extent or quantity ▸ *vb* **2** **amount to** to be equal or add up to

> **amount** *n* = quantity, measure, size, supply, mass, volume, capacity, extent ▸ *vb* **amount to something** = add up to, mean, total, equal, constitute, comprise, be equivalent to

amour *n* a secret love affair

amp *n* **1** an ampere **2** *informal* an amplifier

ampere (am-pair) *n* the basic unit of electric current

ampersand *n* the character &, meaning *and*

amphetamine (am-fet-am-mean) *n* a drug used as a stimulant

amphibian *n* **1** an animal, such as a newt, frog, or toad, that lives on land but breeds in water **2** a vehicle that can travel on both water and land

amphibious *adj* **1** living or operating both on land and in or on water **2** relating to a military attack launched from the sea against a shore

amphitheatre *or US* **amphitheater** *n* a circular or oval building without a roof, in which tiers of seats rise from a central open arena

amphora (am-for-ra) *n, pl* **-phorae** (-for-ree) an ancient Greek or Roman jar with two handles and a narrow neck

ample *adj* **1** more than sufficient: *there is already ample evidence* **2** large: *ample helpings of stewed pomegranates and pears*

> **ample** *adj* **1** = plenty of, generous, lavish, abundant, plentiful, expansive, copious, profuse; ≠ insufficient **2** = large, full, extensive, generous, abundant, bountiful

amplifier *n* an electronic device used to increase the strength of a current or sound signal

amplify *vb* **-fies, -fying, -fied 1** *electronics* to increase the strength of (a current or sound signal) **2** to explain in more detail **3** to increase the size, extent, or effect of › **amplification** *n*

amplitude *n* **1** greatness of extent **2** *physics* the maximum displacement from the zero or mean position of a wave or oscillation

amply *adv* fully or generously: *she was amply rewarded for it*

> **amply** *adv* = fully, completely, richly, generously, abundantly, profusely, copiously; ≠ insufficiently

ampoule *or US* **ampule** *n* *med* a small glass container in which liquids for injection are sealed

amputate *vb* **-tating, -tated** to cut off (a limb or part of a limb) for medical reasons › **amputation** *n*

amuck *adv* same as **amok**

amulet *n* a trinket or jewel worn as a protection against evil

amuse *vb* **amusing, amused 1** to cause to laugh or smile **2** to entertain or keep interested › **amusing** *adj* › **amusingly** *adv*

> **amuse** *vb* **1** = entertain, please, delight, charm, cheer, tickle; ≠ bore **2** = occupy, interest, involve, engage, entertain, absorb, engross

amusement *n* **1** the state of being amused **2** something that amuses or entertains someone

> **amusement** *n* **1** = enjoyment, entertainment, cheer, mirth, merriment; ≠ boredom **2** = pastime, game, sport, joke, entertainment, hobby, recreation, diversion

an *adj* (*indefinite article*) same as **a**: used before an initial vowel sound: *an old man; an hour*

anabolic steroid *n* a synthetic steroid hormone used to stimulate muscle and bone growth

anachronism (an-nak-kron-iz-zum) *n* **1** the representation of something in a historical context in which it could not have occurred or existed **2** a person or thing that seems to belong to another time › **anachronistic** *adj*

anaconda *n* a large S American snake which squeezes its prey to death

anaemia *or US* **anemia** (an-neem-ee-a) *n* a deficiency of red blood cells or their haemoglobin content, resulting in paleness and lack of energy

anaemic *or US* **anemic** *adj* **1** having anaemia **2** pale and sickly-looking **3** lacking vitality

anaesthesia *or US* **anesthesia** (an-niss-theez-ee-a) *n* loss of bodily feeling caused by disease or accident or by drugs such as ether: called **general anaesthesia** when consciousness is lost and **local anaesthesia** when only a specific area of the body is involved

anaesthetic or US **anesthetic** (an-niss-thet-ik) n **1** a substance that causes anaesthesia ▸ adj **2** causing anaesthesia

> **anaesthetic** or **anesthetic** n = painkiller, narcotic, sedative, opiate, anodyne, analgesic, soporific ▸ adj = pain-killing, dulling, numbing, sedative, deadening, anodyne, analgesic, soporific

anaesthetist (an-neess-thet-ist) n Brit a doctor who administers anaesthetics

anaesthetize, anaesthetise or US **anesthetize** vb **-tizing, -tized** or **-tising, -tised** to cause to feel no pain by administering an anaesthetic

anagram n a word or phrase made by rearranging the letters of another word or phrase

anal (ain-al) adj of or relating to the anus

analgesia n the absence of pain

analgesic (an-nal-jeez-ik) n **1** a drug that relieves pain ▸ adj **2** pain-relieving: an analgesic balm

analog n same as **analogue**

analogous adj similar in some respects

analogue or US **analog** n **1** a physical object or quantity used to measure or represent another quantity **2** something that is analogous to something else ▸ adj **3** displaying information by means of a dial: analogue speedometers

analogy n, pl **-gies 1** a similarity, usually in a limited number of features **2** a comparison made to show such a similarity › **analogical** adj

> **analogy** n = similarity, relation, comparison, parallel, correspondence, resemblance, correlation, likeness

analyse or US **-lyze** (an-nal-lize) vb **-lysing, -lysed** or **-lyzing, -lyzed 1** to examine (something) in detail in order to discover its meaning or essential features **2** to break (something) down into its components **3** to psychoanalyse (someone)

> **analyse** or **-lyze** vb **1, 3** = examine, test, study, research, survey, investigate, evaluate, inspect **2** = break down, separate, divide, resolve, dissect, think through

analysis (an-nal-liss-iss) n, pl **-ses** (-seez) **1** the separation of a whole into its parts for study or interpretation **2** a statement of the results of this **3** short for **psychoanalysis**

> **analysis** n **1** = examination, test, inquiry, investigation, interpretation, breakdown, scanning, evaluation

analyst n **1** a person who is skilled in analysis **2** a psychoanalyst

analytical or **analytic** adj relating to or using analysis › **analytically** adv

anarchism n a doctrine advocating the abolition of government and its replacement by a social system based on voluntary cooperation

anarchist n **1** a person who advocates anarchism **2** a person who causes disorder or upheaval > **anarchistic** adj

anarchy (an-ark-ee) n **1** general lawlessness and disorder **2** the absence of government > **anarchic** adj

> **anarchy** n **1** = lawlessness, revolution, riot, disorder, confusion, chaos, disorganization; ≠ order

anathema (an-nath-im-a) n a detested person or thing: the very colour was anathema to her

anatomist n an expert in anatomy

anatomy n, pl **-mies 1** the science of the physical structure of animals and plants **2** the structure of an animal or plant **3** informal a person's body: the male anatomy **4** a detailed analysis: an anatomy of the massacre > **anatomical** adj > **anatomically** adv

> **anatomy** n **2** = structure, build, make-up, frame, framework, composition **4** = examination, study, division, inquiry, investigation, analysis, dissection

ANC African National Congress

ancestor n **1** a person in former times from whom one is descended **2** a forerunner: the immediate ancestor of rock and roll is rhythm and blues

> **ancestor** n **1** = forefather, predecessor, precursor, forerunner, forebear, antecedent, tupuna or tipuna (NZ); ≠ descendant

ancestral adj of or inherited from ancestors

ancestry n, pl **-tries 1** family descent: of Japanese ancestry **2** origin or roots: a vehicle whose ancestry dated back to the 1950s

anchor n **1** a hooked device attached to a boat by a cable and dropped overboard to fasten the boat to the sea bottom **2** a source of stability or security: a spiritual anchor **3** anchors slang the brakes of a motor vehicle: he rammed on the anchors ▸ vb **4** to use an anchor to hold (a boat) in one place **5** to fasten securely: we anchored his wheelchair to a rock

anchorage n a place where boats can be anchored

anchorite n a person who chooses to live in isolation for religious reasons

anchorman or **anchorwoman** n, pl **-men** or **-women 1** a broadcaster in a central studio, who links up and presents items from outside camera units and reporters in other studios **2** the last person to compete in a relay team

anchovy (an-chov-ee) n, pl **-vies** a small marine food fish with a salty taste

ancient adj **1** dating from very long ago **2** very old **3** of the far past, esp. before the collapse of the Western Roman Empire (476 AD)

▸ *n* **4 ancients** people who lived very long ago, such as the Romans and Greeks

ancient *adj* **1** = classical, old, former, past, bygone, primordial, primeval, olden **2** = very old, aged, antique, archaic, timeworn

ancillary *adj* **1** supporting the main work of an organization: *hospital ancillary workers* **2** used as an extra or supplement: *I had a small ancillary sleeping tent*

and *conj* **1** in addition to: *plants and birds* **2** as a consequence: *she fell downstairs and broke her neck* **3** afterwards: *she excused herself and left* **4** used for emphasis or to indicate repetition or continuity: *they called again and again* **5** used to express a contrast between instances of something: *there are jobs and jobs* **6** *informal* used in place of *to* in infinitives after verbs such as *try, go,* and *come*: *come and see us again*

and *conj* **1** = also, including, along with, together with, in addition to, as well as

andante (an-dan-tay) *music* ▸ *adv* **1** moderately slowly ▸ *n* **2** a passage or piece to be performed moderately slowly

andiron *n* either of a pair of metal stands for supporting logs in a fireplace

androgynous *adj* having both male and female characteristics

android *n* a robot resembling a human being

anecdote *n* a short amusing account of an incident > **anecdotal** *adj*

anecdote *n* = story, tale, sketch, short story, yarn (*informal*), reminiscence, urban myth, urban legend

anemia *n US* same as **anaemia**

anemometer *n* an instrument for recording wind speed

anemone (an-nem-on-ee) *n* a flowering plant with white, purple, or red flowers

aneroid barometer *n* a device for measuring air pressure, consisting of a partially evacuated chamber, in which variations in pressure cause a pointer on the lid to move

aneurysm *or* **aneurism** (an-new-riz-zum) *n med* a permanent swelling of a blood vessel

anew *adv* **1** once more **2** in a different way

angel *n* **1** a spiritual being believed to be an attendant or messenger of God **2** a conventional representation of an angel as a human being with wings **3** *informal* a person who is kind, pure, or beautiful **4** *informal* an investor in a theatrical production

angel *n* **1, 2** = divine messenger, cherub, archangel, seraph **3** = dear, beauty, saint, treasure, darling, jewel, gem, paragon

angelic *adj* **1** very kind, pure, or beautiful **2** of or relating to angels > **angelically** *adv*

angelica (an-jell-ik-a) *n* a plant whose candied stalks are used in cookery

Angelus (an-jell-uss) *n RC Church* **1** prayers recited in the morning, at midday, and in the evening **2** the bell signalling the times of these prayers

anger *n* **1** a feeling of extreme annoyance or displeasure ▸ *vb* **2** to make (someone) angry

anger *n* = rage, outrage, temper, fury, resentment, wrath, annoyance, ire;
≠ calmness ▸ *vb* = enrage, outrage, annoy, infuriate, incense, gall, madden, exasperate;
≠ soothe

angina (an-jine-a) *or* **angina pectoris** (peck-tor-riss) *n* a sudden intense pain in the chest caused by a momentary lack of adequate blood supply to the heart muscle

angle¹ *n* **1** the space between or shape formed by two straight lines or surfaces that meet **2** the divergence between two such lines or surfaces, measured in degrees **3** a recess or corner **4** point of view ▸ *vb* **-gling, -gled 5** to move in or place at an angle **6** to write (an article) from a particular point of view

angle *n* **1, 2** = gradient, bank, slope, incline, inclination **3** = intersection, point, edge, corner, bend, elbow, crook, nook **4** = point of view, position, approach, direction, aspect, perspective, outlook, viewpoint

angle² *vb* **-gling, -gled 1** to fish with a hook and line **2 angle for** to try to get by hinting: *he's just angling for sympathy*

angler *n* a person who fishes with a hook and line

Anglican *adj* **1** of or relating to the Church of England ▸ *n* **2** a member of the Anglican Church > **Anglicanism** *n*

anglicize *or* **-cise** *vb* **-cizing, -cized** *or* **-cising, -cised** to make or become English in outlook or form

angling *n* the art or sport of fishing with a hook and line

Anglo- *combining form* English or British: *the history of Anglo-German relations*

Anglo-Saxon *n* **1** a member of any of the West Germanic tribes that settled in Britain from the 5th century AD **2** any White person whose native language is English **3** *informal* plain, blunt, and often rude English ▸ *adj* **4** of the Anglo-Saxons or the Old English language **5** of the White Protestant culture of Britain and the US

angora *n* **1** a variety of goat, cat, or rabbit with long silky hair **2** the hair of the angora goat or rabbit **3** cloth made from this hair

Angostura Bitters *pl n trademark* a bitter tonic, used as a flavouring in alcoholic drinks

angry *adj* **-grier, -griest 1** feeling or expressing annoyance or rage **2** severely inflamed: *he had angry welts on his forehead* **3** dark and stormy: *angry waves* > **angrily** *adv*

angry *adj* **1** = furious, cross, mad (*informal*), outraged, annoyed, infuriated, incensed, enraged, tooshie (*Austral slang*), off the air (*Austral slang*), aerated; ≠ calm

angst *n* a feeling of anxiety

angst *n* = anxiety, worry, unease, apprehension; ≠ peace of mind

angstrom *n* a unit of length equal to 10^{-10} metre, used to measure wavelengths

anguish *n* great mental pain

anguish *n* = suffering, pain, distress, grief, misery, agony, torment, sorrow

anguished *adj* feeling or showing great mental pain: *anguished cries*

angular *adj* **1** lean and bony: *his angular face* **2** having an angle or angles **3** measured by an angle: *angular momentum* > **angularity** *n*

anhydrous *adj chem* containing no water

aniline *n chem* a colourless oily poisonous liquid, obtained from coal tar and used for making dyes, plastics, and explosives

animal *n* **1** *zool* any living being that is capable of voluntary movement and possesses specialized sense organs **2** any living being other than a human being **3** any living being with four legs **4** a cruel or coarse person **5** *facetious* a person or thing: *there's no such animal* ▸ *adj* **6** of or from animals **7** of or relating to physical needs or desires

animal *n* **1, 2, 3** = creature, beast, brute **4** = brute, devil, monster, savage, beast, villain, barbarian ▸ *adj* **7** = physical, gross, bodily, sensual, carnal, brutish, bestial, animalistic

animate *vb* **-mating, -mated 1** to give life to **2** to make lively **3** to produce (a story) as an animated cartoon ▸ *adj* **4** having life

animate *vb* **2** = enliven, excite, inspire, move, fire, stimulate, energize, kindle; ≠ inhibit ▸ *adj* = living, live, moving, alive, breathing, alive and kicking

animated *adj* **1** interesting and lively **2** (of a cartoon) made by using animation > **animatedly** *adv*

animated *adj* **1** = lively, spirited, excited, enthusiastic, passionate, energetic, ebullient, vivacious; ≠ listless

animation *n* **1** the techniques used in the production of animated cartoons **2** an animated cartoon **3** liveliness and enthusiasm: *there's an animation in her that is new*

animation *n* **3** = liveliness, energy, spirit, passion, enthusiasm, excitement, verve, zest

animator *n* a person who makes animated cartoons

animism *n* the belief that natural objects possess souls > **animist** *n, adj* > **animistic** *adj*

animosity *n, pl* **-ties** a powerful dislike or hostility

animus *n* intense dislike; hatred

anion (an-eye-on) *n* an ion with negative charge > **anionic** *adj*

anise (an-niss) *n* a Mediterranean plant with liquorice-flavoured seeds

aniseed *n* the liquorice-flavoured seeds of the anise plant, used for flavouring

ankle *n* **1** the joint connecting the leg and the foot **2** the part of the leg just above the foot

anklet *n* an ornamental chain worn round the ankle

annals *pl n* **1** yearly records of events **2** regular reports of the work of a society or other organization > **annalist** *n*

anneal *vb* to toughen (glass or metal) by heat treatment

annelid *n* a worm with a segmented body, such as the earthworm

annex *vb* **1** to seize (territory) by conquest or occupation **2** to take without permission **3** to join or add (something) to something larger > **annexation** *n*

annexe *or esp US* **annex** *n* **1** an extension to a main building **2** a building used as an addition to a main one nearby

annihilate *vb* **-lating, -lated 1** to destroy (a place or a group of people) completely **2** *informal* to defeat totally in an argument or a contest > **annihilation** *n*

anniversary *n, pl* **-ries 1** the date on which an event, such as a wedding, occurred in some previous year **2** the celebration of this

anno Domini *adv* in the year of our Lord

annotate *vb* **-tating, -tated** to add critical or explanatory notes to a written work > **annotation** *n*

announce *vb* **-nouncing, -nounced 1** to make known publicly **2** to proclaim **3** to declare the arrival of (a person) **4** to be a sign of: *snowdrops announced the arrival of spring* > **announcement** *n*

announce *vb* **1, 2** = make known, tell, report, reveal, declare, advertise, broadcast, disclose, post, tweet; ≠ keep secret

announcer *n* a person who introduces programmes on radio or television

annoy *vb* **1** to irritate or displease **2** to harass sexually > **annoyance** *n* > **annoying** *adj*

annoy *vb* **1** = irritate, trouble, anger, bother, disturb, plague, hassle (*informal*), madden, hack you off (*informal*); ≠ soothe

annual *adj* **1** occurring or done once a year: *the union's annual conference* **2** lasting for a year: *the annual subscription* ▸ *n* **3** a plant that completes its life cycle in one year **4** a book published once every year > **annually** *adv*

annual adj 1 = once a year, yearly
2 = yearlong, yearly

annuity n, pl -ties a fixed sum payable at specified intervals over a period

annul vb -nulling, -nulled to declare (a contract or marriage) invalid

annular (an-new-lar) adj ring-shaped

annulment n the formal declaration that a contract or marriage is invalid

Annunciation n Christianity the Annunciation A the announcement by the angel Gabriel to the Virgin Mary of her conception of Christ B the festival commemorating this, on March 25 (Lady Day)

anode n electronics the positive electrode in an electrolytic cell or in an electronic valve

anodize or -**dise** vb -dizing, -dized or -dising, -dised chem to coat (a metal) with a protective oxide film by electrolysis

anodyne n 1 something that relieves pain or distress ▸ adj 2 bland or dull 3 capable of relieving pain or distress

anoint vb to smear with oil as a sign of consecration

anomalous adj different from the normal or usual order or type

anomaly (an-nom-a-lee) n, pl -lies something that deviates from the normal; an irregularity

anomaly n = irregularity, exception, abnormality, inconsistency, eccentricity, oddity, peculiarity, incongruity

anon adv old-fashioned or informal soon: you shall see him anon

anon. anonymous

anonymous adj 1 by someone whose name is unknown or withheld: an anonymous letter 2 having no known name: an anonymous writer 3 lacking distinguishing characteristics: an anonymous little town 4 Anonymous of an organization that helps applicants who remain anonymous: Alcoholics Anonymous > **anonymously** adv > **anonymity** n

anonymous adj 1 = unsigned, uncredited, unattributed; ≠ signed 2 = unnamed, unknown, unidentified, nameless, unacknowledged, incognito; ≠ identified

anorak n 1 a waterproof hip-length jacket with a hood 2 Brit informal a socially inept person with a hobby considered to be boring·

anorexia or **anorexia nervosa** n a mental health condition characterized by fear of gaining weight, often leading to refusal of food > **anorexic** adj, n

another adj 1 one more: they don't have the right to demand another chance 2 different: you'll have to find another excuse ▸ pron 3 one more: help yourself to another 4 a different one: one way or another

answer vb 1 to reply or respond (to) by word or act 2 to be responsible (to a person) 3 to reply correctly to (a question) 4 to respond or react: a dog that answers to the name of Pugg 5 to meet the requirements of 6 to give a defence of (a charge) ▸ n 7 a reply to a question, request, letter, or article 8 a solution to a problem 9 a reaction or response

answer vb 1 = reply, explain, respond, resolve, react, return, retort; ≠ ask ▸ n 7, 9 = reply, response, reaction, explanation, comeback, retort, return, defence; ≠ question 8 = solution, resolution, explanation

answerable adj answerable for or to responsible for or accountable to

answering machine n a device for answering a telephone automatically and recording messages

ant n a small, often wingless, insect, living in highly organized colonies

antacid chem ▸ n 1 a substance used to treat acidity in the stomach ▸ adj 2 having the properties of this substance

antagonism n openly expressed hostility

antagonist n an opponent or adversary > **antagonistic** adj

antagonize or -**nise** vb -nizing, -nized or -nising, -nised to arouse hostility in: it was not prudent to antagonize a hired killer

Antarctic n 1 the Antarctic the area around the South Pole ▸ adj 2 of this region

ante n 1 the stake put up before the deal in poker by the players 2 informal a sum of money representing a person's share 3 up the ante informal to increase the costs or risks involved in an action ▸ vb -teing, -ted or -teed 4 to place (one's stake) in poker 5 ante up informal to pay

ante- prefix before in time or position: antediluvian; antechamber

anteater n a mammal with a long snout used for eating termites

antecedent n 1 an event or circumstance that happens or exists before another 2 grammar a word or phrase to which a relative pronoun, such as who, refers 3 antecedents a person's ancestors and past history ▸ adj 4 preceding in time or order

antedate vb -dating, -dated 1 to be or occur at an earlier date than 2 to give (something) a date that is earlier than the actual date

antediluvian adj 1 belonging to the ages before the biblical Flood 2 old-fashioned

antelope n, pl -lopes or -lope any of a group of graceful deerlike mammals of Africa and Asia, which have long legs and horns

antenatal adj before birth; during pregnancy: an antenatal clinic

antenna n 1 pl -nae one of a pair of mobile feelers on the heads of insects, lobsters, and certain other creatures 2 pl -nas an aerial: TV antennas

anterior adj 1 at or towards the front 2 earlier

anteroom n a small room leading into a larger room, often used as a waiting room

anthem *n* **1** a song of loyalty or devotion: *a national anthem* **2** a piece of music for a choir, usually set to words from the Bible

> **anthem** *n* = song of praise, carol, chant, hymn, psalm, paean, chorale, canticle

anther *n botany* the part of the stamen of a flower which contains the pollen

ant hill *n* a mound of soil built by ants around the entrance to their nest

anthology *n, pl* **-gies** a collection of poems or other literary pieces by various authors > **anthologist** *n*

> **anthology** *n* = collection, selection, treasury, compilation, compendium, miscellany

anthracite *n* a hard coal that burns slowly with little smoke or flame but intense heat

anthrax *n* a dangerous infectious disease of cattle and sheep, which can be passed to humans

anthropoid *adj* **1** resembling a human being ▸ *n* **2** an ape, such as the chimpanzee, that resembles a human being

anthropology *n* the study of human origins, institutions, and beliefs > **anthropological** *adj* > **anthropologist** *n*

anthropomorphism *n* the attribution of human form or personality to a god, animal, or object > **anthropomorphic** *adj*

anti- *prefix* **1** against or opposed to: *antiwar* **2** opposite to: *anticlimax* **3** counteracting or neutralizing: *antifreeze*

anti-aircraft *adj* for defence against aircraft attack

antibiotic *n* **1** a chemical substance capable of destroying bacteria ▸ *adj* **2** of or relating to antibiotics

antibody *n, pl* **-bodies** a protein produced in the blood which destroys bacteria

anticipate *vb* **-pating, -pated** **1** to foresee and act in advance of: *he anticipated some probing questions* **2** to look forward to **3** to make use of (something, such as one's salary) before receiving it **4** to mention (part of a story) before its proper time > **anticipatory** *adj*

> **anticipate** *vb* **1** = expect, predict, prepare for, hope for, envisage, foresee, bank on, foretell **2** = await, look forward to, count the hours until

anticipation *n* the act of anticipating; expectation, premonition, or foresight: *smiling in happy anticipation*

> **anticipation** *n* = expectancy, expectation, foresight, premonition, prescience, forethought

anticlimax *n* a disappointing conclusion to a series of events > **anticlimactic** *adj*

anticlockwise *adv, adj* in the opposite direction to the rotation of the hands of a clock

antics *pl n* absurd acts or postures

> **antics** *pl n* = clowning, tricks, mischief, pranks, escapades, playfulness, horseplay, tomfoolery

anticyclone *n meteorol* an area of moving air of high pressure in which the winds rotate outwards

antidote *n* **1** *med* a substance that counteracts a poison **2** anything that counteracts a harmful condition: *exercise may be a good antidote to insomnia*

antifreeze *n* a liquid added to water to lower its freezing point, used in the radiator of a motor vehicle to prevent freezing

antigen (an-tee-jen) *n* a substance, usually a toxin, that causes the body to produce antibodies

antihero *n, pl* **-roes** a central character in a novel, play, or film, who lacks the traditional heroic virtues

antihistamine *n* a drug that neutralizes the effects of histamine, used in the treatment of allergies

antimacassar *n* a cloth put over the back of a chair to prevent it getting dirty

antimony (an-tim-mon-ee) *n chem* a silvery-white metallic element that is added to alloys to increase their strength. Symbol: **Sb**

antipasto *n, pl* **-tos** an appetizer in an Italian meal

antipathy (an-tip-a-thee) *n* a feeling of strong dislike or hostility > **antipathetic** *adj*

antiperspirant *n* a substance applied to the skin to reduce or prevent perspiration

antiphon *n* a hymn sung in alternate parts by two groups of singers

antipodes (an-tip-pod-deez) *pl n* **1** any two places that are situated diametrically opposite one another on the earth's surface **2** **the Antipodes** *Brit* Australia and New Zealand > **antipodean** *adj*

antipyretic *adj* **1** reducing fever ▸ *n* **2** a drug that reduces fever

antiquarian *adj* **1** collecting or dealing with antiquities or rare books ▸ *n* **2** an antiquary

antiquary *n, pl* **-quaries** a person who collects, deals in, or studies antiques or ancient works of art

antiquated *adj* obsolete or old-fashioned

antique *n* **1** a decorative object or piece of furniture, of an earlier period, that is valued for its beauty, workmanship, and age ▸ *adj* **2** made in an earlier period **3** *informal* old-fashioned

> **antique** *n* = period piece, relic, bygone, heirloom, collector's item, museum piece ▸ *adj* **2** = vintage, classic, antiquarian, olden

antiquity *n, pl* **-ties** **1** great age **2** the far distant past **3** **antiquities** objects dating from ancient times

antiracism *n* the policy of challenging racism or promoting racial tolerance > **antiracist** *n, adj*

antirrhinum *n* a two-lipped flower of various colours, such as the snapdragon

anti-Semitic *adj* discriminating against Jews > **anti-Semite** *n* > **anti-Semitism** *n*

antiseptic *adj* **1** preventing infection by killing germs ▶ *n* **2** an antiseptic substance

antisocial *adj* **1** avoiding the company of other people **2** (of behaviour) annoying or harmful to other people

antistatic *adj* reducing the effects of static electricity

antithesis (an-tith-iss-iss) *n*, *pl* **-ses** (-seez) **1** the exact opposite **2** *rhetoric* the placing together of contrasting ideas or words to produce an effect of balance, such as *where gods command, mere mortals must obey* > **antithetical** *adj*

antitoxin *n* an antibody that acts against a toxin > **antitoxic** *adj*

antitrust *adj US, Austral & S African* (of laws) opposing business monopolies

antivirus *adj* **1** relating to software designed to protect computer files from viruses ▶ *n* **2** such a piece of software

antler *n* one of a pair of branched horns on the heads of male deer

antonym *n* a word that means the opposite of another

anus (ain-uss) *n* the opening at the end of the alimentary canal, through which faeces are discharged

anvil *n* a heavy iron block on which metals are hammered into particular shapes

anxiety *n*, *pl* **-ties 1** a state of uneasiness about what may happen **2** eagerness: *she was uneasy with his mixture of diffidence and anxiety to please* **3** *psychol* a state of intense worry

> **anxiety** *n* **1** = uneasiness, concern, worry, doubt, tension, angst, apprehension, misgiving; ≠ confidence

anxious *adj* **1** worried and tense: *he was anxious about the enormity of the task ahead* **2** causing anxiety: *an anxious time* **3** intensely desiring: *both sides were anxious for a deal* > **anxiously** *adv*

> **anxious** *adj* **1, 2** = uneasy, concerned, worried, troubled, nervous, uncomfortable, tense, fearful; ≠ confident **3** = eager, keen, intent, yearning, impatient, itching, desirous; ≠ reluctant

any *determiner* **1** one, some, or several, no matter how much or what kind: *the jar opener fits over the top of any bottle or jar*; *have you left me any?* **2** even the smallest amount or even one: *we can't answer any questions*; *don't give her any* **3** whatever or whichever: *police may board any bus or train* **4** an indefinite or unlimited amount or number: *he would sign cheques for any amount of money* ▶ *adv* **5** to even the smallest extent: *the outcome wouldn't have been any different*

anybody *pron* same as **anyone**

anyhow *adv* same as **anyway**

anyone *pron* **1** any person: *is anyone there?* **2** a person of any importance: *is he anyone?*

anything *pron* **1** any object, event, or action whatever: *they'll do anything to please you* ▶ *adv* **2** in any way: *it is not a computer nor anything like a computer* **3** **anything but** not at all: *the result is anything but simple*

anyway *adv* **1** at any rate; nevertheless **2** in any manner **3** carelessly

anywhere *adv* **1** in, at, or to any place **2** **get anywhere** to be successful: *we will not get anywhere by being negative*

Anzac *n* (in the First World War) a soldier serving with the Australian and New Zealand Army Corps

Anzac Day April 25, a public holiday in Australia and New Zealand commemorating the Anzac landing at Gallipoli in 1915

AOB (on the agenda for a meeting) any other business

aorta (eh-or-ta) *n* the main artery of the body, which carries oxygen-rich blood from the heart

apace *adv literary* quickly: *repairs to the grid continued apace*

apart *adj, adv* **1** to or in pieces: *he took a couple of cars apart and rebuilt them* **2** separate in time, place, or position: *my father and myself stood slightly apart from them* **3** individual or distinct: *a nation apart* **4** not being taken into account: *early timing difficulties apart, they encountered few problems* **5** **apart from** other than: *apart from searching the house there is little more we can do*

> **apart** *adj, adv* **1** = to pieces, to bits, asunder (*literary*) **2** = away from each other, distant from each other **5** **apart from** = except for, excepting, other than, excluding, besides, not including, aside from, but

apartheid *n* (formerly) the official government policy of racial segregation in South Africa

apartment *n* **1** any room in a building, usually one of several forming a suite, used as living accommodation **2** *chiefly US & Canad* a set of rooms forming a home within a building usually incorporating other similar homes. Also called (*Brit*): **flat**

> **apartment** *n* **1** = rooms, quarters, accommodation, living quarters **2** = flat, room, suite, penthouse, duplex (*US, Canad*), crib, bachelor apartment (*Canad*)

apathy *n* lack of interest or enthusiasm > **apathetic** *adj*

> **apathy** *n* = lack of interest, indifference, inertia, coolness, passivity, nonchalance, torpor, unconcern; ≠ interest

apatosaurus *n* a very large plant-eating four-footed dinosaur that had a long neck and long tail

ape *n* **1** an animal, such as a chimpanzee or gorilla, which is closely related to human beings and the monkeys, and which has no tail **2** a stupid, clumsy, or ugly man ▸ *vb* **aping, aped 3** to imitate › **apelike** *adj*

aperient (ap-**peer**-ee-ent) *med* ▸ *adj* **1** having a mild laxative effect ▸ *n* **2** a mild laxative

aperitif (ap-per-rit-**teef**) *n* an alcoholic drink taken before a meal

aperture *n* **1** a hole or opening **2** an opening in a camera or telescope that controls the amount of light entering it

apex *n* the highest point

APEX Advance Purchase Excursion: a reduced fare for journeys by air or rail booked a specified period in advance

aphasia *n* a disorder of the central nervous system that affects the ability to use and understand words

aphid (**eh**-fid) *or* **aphis** (**eh**-fiss) *n, pl* **aphids** *or* **aphides** (**eh**-fid-deez) a small insect which feeds by sucking the juices from plants

aphorism *n* a short clever saying expressing a general truth

aphrodisiac (af-roh-**diz**-zee-ak) *n* **1** a substance that arouses sexual desire ▸ *adj* **2** arousing sexual desire

apiary (**ape**-yar-ee) *n, pl* **-aries** a place where bees are kept › **apiarist** *n*

apiculture *n* the breeding and care of bees › **apiculturist** *n*

apiece *adv* each: *they had another cocktail apiece and then went down to dinner*

> **apiece** *adv* = each, individually, separately, for each, to each, respectively, from each; ≠ all together

aplomb (ap-**plom**) *n* calm self-possession

apocalypse *n* **1** the end of the world **2** an event of great destructive violence › **apocalyptic** *adj*

Apocalypse *n* **the Apocalypse** *Bible* the Book of Revelation, the last book of the New Testament

Apocrypha (ap-**pok**-rif-fa) *pl n* **the Apocrypha** the 14 books included as an appendix to the Old Testament, which are not accepted as part of the Hebrew scriptures

apocryphal *adj* of questionable authenticity: *the paranoid and clearly apocryphal story*

apogee (**ap**-oh-jee) *n* **1** *astron* the point in its orbit around the earth when the moon or a satellite is farthest from the earth **2** the highest point: *the concept found its apogee in Renaissance Italy*

apologetic *adj* showing or expressing regret › **apologetically** *adv*

apologetics *n* the branch of theology concerned with the reasoned defence of Christianity

apologist *n* a person who offers a formal defence of a cause

apologize *or* **-gise** *vb* **-gizing, -gized** *or* **-gising, -gised** to say that one is sorry for some wrongdoing

> **apologize** *or* **-gise** *vb* = say sorry, express regret, ask forgiveness, make an apology, beg pardon

apology *n, pl* **-gies 1** an expression of regret for some wrongdoing **2 an apology for** a poor example of: *an apology for a manager*

> **apology** *n* **1** = regret, explanation, excuse, confession **2 an apology for something or someone** = mockery of, excuse for, imitation of, caricature of, travesty of, poor substitute for

apoplectic *adj* **1** of apoplexy **2** *informal* furious

apoplexy *n* *med* a stroke

apostasy (ap-**poss**-stass-ee) *n, pl* **-sies** abandonment of one's religious faith, political party, or cause

apostate *n* **1** a person who has abandoned his or her religion, political party, or cause ▸ *adj* **2** guilty of apostasy

a posteriori (eh poss-steer-ee-**or**-rye) *adj logic* involving reasoning from effect to cause

apostle *n* **1** *Christianity* one of the twelve disciples chosen by Christ to preach his gospel **2** an ardent supporter of a cause or movement

apostolic (ap-poss-**stoll**-ik) *adj* **1** of or relating to the Apostles or their teachings **2** of or relating to the pope

apostrophe (ap-poss-**trof**-fee) *n* the punctuation mark (') used to indicate the omission of a letter or letters, such as *he's* for *he has* or *he is*, and to form the possessive, as in *John's father*

apothecary *n, pl* **-caries** *old-fashioned* a chemist

apotheosis (ap-poth-ee-oh-**siss**) *n, pl* **-ses** (-seez) **1** *Christianity* a perfect example of elitism **2** elevation to the rank of a god

app *n* a computer program designed for a particular purpose, esp. one for use on a mobile device

appal *or US* **appall** *vb* **-palling, -palled** to fill with horror; terrify

> **appal** *or* **appall** *vb* = horrify, shock, alarm, frighten, outrage, disgust, dishearten, revolt

appalling *adj* **1** causing dismay, horror, or revulsion **2** very bad › **appallingly** *adv*

> **appalling** *adj* **1** = horrifying, shocking (*informal*), alarming, awful, terrifying, horrible, dreadful, fearful (*informal*); ≠ reassuring **2** = awful, dreadful, horrendous

apparatus *n* **1** a collection of equipment used for a particular purpose **2** any complicated device, system, or organization: *the whole apparatus of law enforcement*

> **apparatus** *n* **1** = equipment, tackle, gear, device, tools, mechanism, machinery, appliance **2** = organization, system, network, structure, bureaucracy, hierarchy, setup (*informal*), chain of command

apparel (ap-**par**-rel) *n* *old-fashioned* clothing

apparent *adj* **1** readily seen or understood; obvious **2** seeming as opposed to real: *he frowned in apparent bewilderment* › **apparently** *adv*

apparent *adj* **1** = obvious, marked, visible, evident, distinct, manifest, noticeable, unmistakable; ≠ unclear **2** = seeming, outward, superficial, ostensible; ≠ actual

apparition *n* a ghost or ghostlike figure

appeal *vb* **1** to make an earnest request **2 appeal to** to attract, please, or interest **3** *law* to apply to a higher court to review (a case or issue decided by a lower court) **4** to resort to a higher authority to change a decision **5** to call on in support of an earnest request: *he appealed for volunteers to help in relief work* **6** *cricket* to request the umpire to declare a batsman out ▸ *n* **7** an earnest request for money or help **8** the power to attract, please, or interest people **9** *law* a request for a review of a lower court's decision by a higher court **10** an application to a higher authority to change a decision that has been made **11** *cricket* a request to the umpire to declare the batsman out

appeal *vb* **1, 5** = plead, ask, request, pray, beg, entreat; ≠ refuse **2 appeal to someone** = attract, interest, draw (*informal*), please, charm, fascinate, tempt, lure ▸ *n* **7** = plea, call, application, request, prayer, petition, overture, entreaty; ≠ refusal **8** = attraction, charm, fascination, beauty, allure; ≠ repulsiveness

appealing *adj* attractive or pleasing

appealing *adj* = attractive, engaging, charming, desirable, alluring, winsome; ≠ repellent

appear *vb* **1** to come into sight **2** to seem: *it appears that no one survived the crash* **3** to come into existence: *a rash and small sores appeared around the shoulder and neck* **4** to perform: *she hadn't appeared in a film for almost fifty years* **5** to be present in court before a magistrate or judge: *two men have appeared in court in London charged with conspiracy* **6** to be published or become available: *both books appeared in 1934*

appear *vb* **1** = come into view, emerge, occur, surface, come out, turn up, be present, show up (*informal*); ≠ disappear **2** = look (like *or* as if), seem, occur, look to be, come across as, strike you as

appearance *n* **1** a sudden or unexpected arrival of someone or something at a place **2** the introduction or invention of something: *the appearance of smartphones* **3** an act or instance of appearing: *it will be her fiftieth appearance for her country* **4** the way a person or thing looks: *I spotted a man of extraordinary appearance* **5 keep up appearances** to maintain the public impression of wellbeing or normality **6 put in an appearance** to attend an event briefly **7 to all appearances** apparently: *to all appearances they seemed enthralled by what she was saying*

appearance *n* **1, 2** = arrival, presence, introduction, emergence **4** = look, form, figure, looks, manner, expression, demeanour, mien (*literary*)

appease *vb* **-peasing, -peased 1** to pacify (someone) by yielding to his or her demands **2** to satisfy or relieve (a feeling) ▸ **appeasement** *n*

appease *vb* **1** = pacify, satisfy, calm, soothe, quiet, placate, mollify, conciliate; ≠ anger **2** = ease, calm, relieve, soothe, alleviate, allay

appellant *law* ▸ *n* a person who appeals to a higher court to review the decision of a lower court

appellation *n formal* a name or title

append *vb formal* to add as a supplement: *a series of notes appended to his translation of the poems*

appendage *n* a secondary part attached to a main part

appendicitis *n* inflammation of the appendix, causing abdominal pain

appendix (ap-pen-dix) *n, pl* **-dices** (-diss-seez) *or* **-dixes 1** separate additional material at the end of a book **2** *anatomy* a short thin tube, closed at one end and attached to the large intestine at the other end

appendix *n* **1** = supplement, postscript, adjunct, appendage, addendum, addition

appertain *vb* **appertain to** to belong to, relate to, or be connected with

appetite *n* **1** a desire for food or drink **2** a liking or willingness: *he had an insatiable appetite for publicity*

appetite *n* **1** = hunger **2** = desire, liking, longing, demand, taste, passion, stomach, hunger; ≠ distaste

appetizer *or* **-iser** *n* a small amount of food or drink taken at the start of a meal to stimulate the appetite

appetizing *or* **-ising** *adj* stimulating the appetite; looking or smelling delicious

applaud *vb* **1** to show approval of by clapping one's hands **2** to express approval of: *we applaud her determination and ambition*

applaud *vb* **1** = clap, encourage, praise, cheer, acclaim; ≠ boo **2** = praise, celebrate, approve, acclaim, compliment, salute, commend, extol; ≠ criticize

applause *n* appreciation shown by clapping one's hands

applause *n* = ovation, praise, cheers, approval, clapping, accolade, big hand

apple *n* **1** a round firm fruit with red, yellow, or green skin and crisp whitish flesh, that grows on trees **2 apple of one's eye** a person that one loves very much

appliance *n* a machine or device that has a specific function

> **appliance** *n* = device, machine, tool, instrument, implement, mechanism, apparatus, gadget

applicable *adj* appropriate or relevant

> **applicable** *adj* = appropriate, fitting, useful, suitable, relevant, apt, pertinent; ≠ inappropriate

applicant *n* a person who applies for something, such as a job or grant

> **applicant** *n* = candidate, claimant, inquirer

application *n* **1** a formal request, for example for a job **2** the act of applying something to a particular use: *you can make practical application of this knowledge to everyday living* **3** concentrated effort: *success would depend on their talent and application* **4** the act of putting something, such as a lotion or paint, onto a surface **5** Also called: **application programme** a computer program designed for a particular purpose

> **application** *n* **1** = request, claim, appeal, inquiry, petition, requisition **3** = effort, work, industry, trouble, struggle, pains, commitment, hard work

applied *adj* put to practical use: *applied mathematics*

appliqué (ap-**plee**-kay) *n* a kind of decoration in which one material is cut out and sewn or fixed onto another

apply *vb* **-plies, -plying, -plied** **1** to make a formal request for something, such as a job or a loan **2** to put to practical use: *he applied his calligrapher's skill* **3** to put onto a surface: *the hand lotion should be applied whenever possible throughout the day* **4** to be relevant or appropriate: *he had been involved in research applied to flying wing aircraft* **5** apply oneself to concentrate one's efforts or faculties

> **apply** *vb* **1** = request, appeal, put in, petition, inquire, claim, requisition **2** = use, exercise, carry out, employ, implement, practise, exert, enact **3** = put on, work in, cover with, lay on, paint on, spread on, rub in, smear on **4** = be relevant, relate, refer, be fitting, be appropriate, fit, pertain, be applicable **5** apply oneself = work hard, concentrate, try, commit yourself, buckle down (*informal*), devote yourself, be diligent, dedicate yourself

appoint *vb* **1** to assign officially to a job or position **2** to fix or decide (a time or place for an event) **3** to equip or furnish: *it was a beautifully appointed room with rows and rows of books* > **appointee** *n*

> **appoint** *vb* **1** = assign, name, choose, commission, select, elect, delegate, nominate; ≠ fire **2** = decide, set, choose, establish, fix, arrange, assign, designate; ≠ cancel

appointment *n* **1** an arrangement to meet a person **2** the act of placing someone in a job or position **3** the person appointed **4** the job or position to which a person is appointed **5** appointments fixtures or fittings

> **appointment** *n* **1** = meeting, interview, date, arrangement, engagement, fixture, rendezvous, assignation **2** = selection, naming, election, choice, nomination, assignment **4** = job, office, position, post, situation, place, employment, assignment

apportion *vb* to divide out in shares

apposite *adj* suitable or appropriate: *an apposite saying*

apposition *n* a grammatical construction in which a noun or group of words is placed after another to modify its meaning, for example *my friend the mayor*

appraisal *n* an assessment of the worth or quality of a person or thing

> **appraisal** *n* = assessment, opinion, estimate, judgment, evaluation, estimation

appraise *vb* **-praising, -praised** to assess the worth, value, or quality of

appreciable *adj* enough to be noticed; significant > **appreciably** *adv*

appreciate *vb* **-ating, -ated** **1** to value highly: *we appreciate his music but can't afford £400 a seat* **2** to be aware of and understand: *I can fully appreciate how desperate you must feel* **3** to feel grateful for: *we do appreciate all you do for us* **4** to increase in value

> **appreciate** *vb* **1** = enjoy, like, value, respect, prize, admire, treasure, rate highly; ≠ scorn **2** = be aware of, understand, realize, recognize, perceive, take account of, be sensitive to, sympathize with; ≠ be unaware of **3** = be grateful for, be obliged for, be thankful for, give thanks for, be indebted for, be in debt for, be appreciative of; ≠ be ungrateful for **4** = increase, rise, grow, gain, improve, enhance, soar; ≠ fall

appreciation *n* **1** gratitude **2** awareness and understanding of a problem or difficulty **3** sensitive recognition of good qualities, as in art **4** an increase in value

> **appreciation** *n* **1** = gratitude, thanks, recognition, obligation, acknowledgment, indebtedness, thankfulness, gratefulness; ≠ ingratitude **2** = awareness, understanding, recognition, perception, sympathy, consciousness, sensitivity, realization; ≠ ignorance **3** = admiration, enjoyment **4** = increase, rise, gain, growth, improvement, escalation, enhancement; ≠ fall

appreciative *adj* feeling or expressing appreciation > **appreciatively** *adv*

apprehend *vb* **1** to arrest and take into custody **2** to grasp (something) mentally; understand

apprehension n **1** anxiety or dread **2** the act of arresting **3** understanding

> **apprehension** n **1** = anxiety, concern, fear, worry, alarm, suspicion, dread, trepidation (*formal*); ≠ confidence **2** = arrest, catching, capture, taking, seizure; ≠ release **3** = awareness, understanding, perception, grasp, comprehension; ≠ incomprehension

apprehensive adj fearful or anxious about the future

apprentice n **1** someone who works for a skilled person for a fixed period in order to learn his or her trade ▸ vb **-ticing, -ticed 2** to take or place as an apprentice › **apprenticeship** n

> **apprentice** n = trainee, student, pupil, novice, beginner, learner, probationer; ≠ master

apprise or **-prize** vb **-prising, -prised** or **-prizing, -prized** to make aware: *I needed to apprise the students of the dangers that may be involved*

appro n **on appro** informal on approval

approach vb **1** to come close or closer to **2** to make a proposal or suggestion to **3** to begin to deal with (a matter) ▸ n **4** the act of coming close or closer **5** a proposal or suggestion made to a person **6** the way or means of reaching a place; access **7** a way of dealing with a matter **8** an approximation **9** the course followed by an aircraft preparing for landing › **approachable** adj

> **approach** vb **1** = move towards, reach, near, come close, come near, draw near **2** = make a proposal to, speak to, apply to, appeal to, proposition, solicit, sound out, make overtures to **3** = set about, tackle, undertake, embark on, get down to, launch into, begin work on, commence on ▸ n **4** = advance, coming, nearing, appearance, arrival, drawing near **5** = proposal, offer, appeal, advance, application, invitation, proposition, overture **6** = access, way, drive, road, passage, entrance, avenue, passageway **7** = way, means, style, method, technique, manner

approach road n a smaller road leading into a major road

approbation n approval

appropriate adj **1** right or suitable ▸ vb **-ating, -ated 2** to take for one's own use without permission **3** to put (money) aside for a particular purpose › **appropriately** adv › **appropriateness** n

> **appropriate** adj = suitable, fitting, relevant, to the point, apt, pertinent, befitting, well-suited; ≠ unsuitable ▸ vb **2** = seize, claim, acquire, confiscate, usurp, impound, commandeer, take possession of; ≠ relinquish **3** = allocate, allow, budget, devote, assign, designate, set aside, earmark; ≠ withhold

appropriation n **1** the act of putting money aside for a particular purpose **2** money put aside for a particular purpose

approval n **1** consent **2** a favourable opinion **3 on approval** (of articles for sale) with an option to be returned without payment if unsatisfactory: *each volume in the collection will be sent to you on approval*

> **approval** n **1, 2** = consent, agreement, sanction, blessing, permission, recommendation, endorsement, assent

approve vb **-proving, -proved 1 approve of** to consider fair, good, or right **2** to authorize or agree to

> **approve** vb **1 approve of something or someone** = favour, like, respect, praise, admire, commend, have a good opinion of, regard highly **2** = agree to, allow, pass, recommend, permit, sanction, endorse, authorize; ≠ veto

approx. approximate or approximately

approximate adj **1** almost but not quite exact ▸ vb **-mating, -mated 2 approximate to** ʌ to come close to ʙ to be almost the same as › **approximately** adv › **approximation** n

appurtenances pl n minor or additional features or possessions

Apr. April

après-ski (ap-ray-skee) n social activities after a day's skiing

apricot n **1** a yellowish-orange juicy fruit which resembles a small peach ▸ adj **2** yellowish-orange

April n the fourth month of the year

April fool n a victim of a practical joke played on April 1 (**April Fools' Day** or **All Fools' Day**)

a priori (eh pry-or-rye) adj logic involving reasoning from cause to effect

apron n **1** a garment worn over the front of the body to protect one's clothes **2** a hard-surfaced area at an airport or hangar for manoeuvring and loading aircraft **3** the part of a stage extending in front of the curtain **4 tied to someone's apron strings** dependent on or dominated by someone

apropos (ap-prop-poh) adj **1** appropriate ▸ adv **2** by the way; incidentally **3 apropos of** with regard to

apse n an arched or domed recess at the east end of a church

apt adj **1** having a specified tendency: *they are apt to bend the rules* **2** suitable or appropriate **3** quick to learn: *she was turning out to be a more apt pupil than he had expected* › **aptly** adv › **aptness** n

> **apt** adj **1** = inclined, likely, ready, disposed, prone, liable, given, predisposed **2** = appropriate, fitting, suitable, relevant, to the point, pertinent; ≠ inappropriate **3** = gifted, skilled, quick, talented, sharp, capable, smart, clever; ≠ slow

aptitude *n* natural tendency or ability

aqualung *n* an apparatus for breathing underwater, consisting of a mouthpiece attached to air cylinders

aquamarine *n* **1** a clear greenish-blue gemstone ▸ *adj* **2** greenish-blue

aquaplane *n* **1** a board on which a person stands to be towed by a motorboat for sport ▸ *vb* **-planing, -planed 2** to ride on an aquaplane **3** (of a motor vehicle) to skim uncontrollably on a thin film of water

aquarium *n, pl* **aquariums** or **aquaria 1** a tank in which fish and other underwater creatures are kept **2** a building containing such tanks

aquatic *adj* **1** growing or living in water **2** *sport* performed in or on water ▸ *n* **3** an aquatic animal or plant **4 aquatics** water sports

aquatint *n* a print like a watercolour, produced by etching copper with acid

aqua vitae (ak-wa **vee**-tie) *n old-fashioned* brandy

aqueduct *n* a structure, often a bridge, that carries water across a valley or river

aqueous *adj* **1** of, like, or containing water **2** produced by the action of water

aquiline *adj* **1** (of a nose) curved like an eagle's beak **2** of or like an eagle

Arab *n* **1** a member of a Semitic people originally from Arabia ▸ *adj* **2** of the Arabs

arabesque (ar-ab-**besk**) *n* **1** a ballet position in which one leg is raised behind and the arms are extended **2** *arts* an elaborate design of intertwined leaves, flowers, and scrolls **3** an ornate piece of music

Arabian *adj* **1** of Arabia or the Arabs ▸ *n* **2** same as **Arab**

Arabic *n* **1** the language of the Arabs ▸ *adj* **2** of this language, the Arabs, or Arabia

arable *adj* (of land) suitable for growing crops on

arachnid (ar-**rak**-nid) *n* an eight-legged insect-like creature, such as a spider, scorpion, or tick

Aran *adj* (of knitwear) knitted in a complicated pattern traditional to the Aran Islands off the west coast of Ireland

arbiter *n* **1** a person empowered to judge in a dispute **2** a person with influential opinions about something: *the customer must be the ultimate arbiter of quality*

arbitrary *adj* **1** not done according to any plan or for any particular reason **2** without consideration for the wishes of others: *the arbitrary power of the king* > **arbitrarily** *adv*

> **arbitrary** *adj* **1** = random, chance, subjective, inconsistent, erratic, personal, whimsical, capricious; ≠ logical

arbitrate *vb* **-trating, -trated** to settle (a dispute) by arbitration > **arbitrator** *n*

arbitration *n* the hearing and settlement of a dispute by an impartial referee chosen by both sides

> **arbitration** *n* = decision, settlement, judgment, determination, adjudication

arbor¹ *n US* same as **arbour**

arbor² *n* a revolving shaft or axle in a machine

arboreal (ahr-**bore**-ee-al) *adj* **1** of or resembling a tree **2** living in or among trees

arboretum (ahr-bore-**ee**-tum) *n, pl* **-ta** (-ta) a botanical garden where rare trees or shrubs are cultivated

arboriculture *n* the cultivation of trees or shrubs

arbour or *US* **arbor** *n* a shelter in a garden shaded by trees or climbing plants

arc *n* **1** something curved in shape **2** *maths* a section of a circle or other curve **3** *electronics* a stream of very bright light that forms when an electric current flows across a small gap between two electrodes ▸ *vb* **4** to form an arc

> **arc** *n* **1** = curve, bend, bow, arch, crescent, half-moon

arcade *n* **1** a covered passageway lined with shops **2** a set of arches and their supporting columns

> **arcade** *n* **2** = gallery, cloister, portico, colonnade

arcane *adj* very mysterious

arch¹ *n* **1** a curved structure that spans an opening or supports a bridge or roof **2** something curved **3** the curved lower part of the foot ▸ *vb* **4** to form an arch

> **arch** *n* **1** = archway, curve, dome, span, vault **2** = curve, bend, bow, crook, arc, hunch, sweep, hump ▸ *vb* = curve, bridge, bend, bow, span, arc

arch² *adj* **1** knowing or superior **2** coyly playful: *she gave him an arch smile* > **archly** *adv*

> **arch** *adj* **2** = playful, sly, mischievous, saucy, pert, roguish, frolicsome, waggish

arch- or **archi-** *combining form* chief or principal: *archbishop; archenemy*

archaeology or **archeology** *n* the study of ancient cultures by the scientific analysis of physical remains > **archaeological** or **archeological** *adj* > **archaeologist** or **archeologist** *n*

archaic (ark-**kay**-ik) *adj* **1** of a much earlier period **2** out of date or old-fashioned **3** (of a word or phrase) no longer in everyday use > **archaically** *adv*

archaism (ark-**kay**-iz-zum) *n* an archaic word or style > **archaistic** *adj*

archangel (ark-ain-jell) *n* an angel of the highest rank

archbishop *n* a bishop of the highest rank

archdeacon *n* a church official ranking just below a bishop > **archdeaconry** *n*

archdiocese *n* the diocese of an archbishop

archer *n* a person who shoots with a bow and arrow

archery *n* the art or sport of shooting with a bow and arrow

archetype (ark-ee-type) *n* **1** a perfect or typical specimen **2** an original model; prototype > **archetypal** *adj*

archipelago (ark-ee-pel-a-go) *n*, *pl* -**gos** **1** a group of islands **2** a sea full of small islands

architect *n* **1** a person qualified to design and supervise the construction of buildings **2** any planner or creator: *you will be the architect of your own future*

> **architect** *n* **1** = designer, planner, draughtsman *or* woman *or* person, master builder

architecture *n* **1** the style in which a building is designed and built: *Gothic architecture* **2** the science of designing and constructing buildings **3** the structure or design of anything: *computer architecture* > **architectural** *adj*

> **architecture** *n* **1** = construction, design, style **2** = design, planning, building, construction **3** = structure, design, shape, make-up, construction, framework, layout, anatomy

architrave (ark-ee-trave) *n archit* **1** a beam that rests on top of columns **2** a moulding around a doorway or window opening

archive (ark-ive) *n* **1** a place where records or documents are kept **2** **archives** a collection of records or documents **3** *computers* data moved to a disk or directory for long-term storage ▸ *vb* **4** to store in an archive > **archival** *adj*

> **archive** *n* **1** = record office, museum, registry, repository **2** = records, papers, accounts, rolls, documents, files, deeds, chronicles

archivist (ark-iv-ist) *n* a person in charge of archives

archway *n* a passageway under an arch

arctic *adj informal* very cold; freezing

> **arctic** *adj* = freezing, cold, frozen, icy, chilly, glacial, frigid

Arctic *n* **1 the Arctic** the area around the North Pole ▸ *adj* **2** of this region

> **Arctic** *adj* = polar, far-northern, hyperborean

ardent *adj* **1** passionate **2** intensely enthusiastic > **ardently** *adv*

> **ardent** *adj* **1** = passionate, intense, impassioned, emotional, lusty, amorous, hot-blooded; ≠ cold **2** = enthusiastic, keen, eager, avid, zealous; ≠ indifferent

ardour *or US* **ardor** *n* **1** emotional warmth; passion **2** intense enthusiasm

arduous *adj* difficult to accomplish; strenuous

are[1] *vb* the plural form of the present tense of **be**: used as the singular form with *you*

are[2] *n* a unit of measure equal to one hundred square metres

area *n* **1** a section, part, or region **2** a part having a specified function: *reception area* **3** the size of a two-dimensional surface **4** a subject field: *the area of literature* **5** a sunken area giving access to a basement **6** any flat, curved, or irregular expanse of a surface **7** range or scope

> **area** *n* **1, 2** = part, section, sector, portion **4** = realm, part, department (*informal*), field, province, sphere, domain

arena *n* **1** a seated enclosure where sports events take place **2** the area of an ancient Roman amphitheatre where gladiators fought **3** a sphere of intense activity: *the political arena*

> **arena** *n* **1** = ring, ground, field, theatre, bowl, pitch, stadium, enclosure **3** = scene (*informal*), world, area, stage, field, sector, territory, province

aren't are not

areola *n*, *pl* -**lae** *or* -**las** a small circular area, such as the coloured ring around the human nipple

argon *n chem* an unreactive odourless element of the rare gas series, forming almost 1 per cent of the atmosphere. Symbol: **Ar**

argot (ahr-go) *n* slang or jargon peculiar to a particular group

argue *vb* -**guing**, -**gued** **1** to try to prove by presenting reasons **2** to debate **3** to quarrel **4** to persuade: *we argued her out of going* **5** to suggest: *her looks argue despair* > **arguable** *adj* > **arguably** *adv*

> **argue** *vb* **1** = claim, reason, challenge, insist, maintain, allege, assert, uphold **2** = discuss, debate, dispute **3** = quarrel, fight, row, clash, dispute, disagree, squabble, bicker

argument *n* **1** a quarrel **2** a discussion **3** a point presented to support or oppose a proposition

> **argument** *n* **1** = quarrel, fight, row, clash, dispute, controversy, disagreement, feud; ≠ agreement **2** = debate, questioning, claim, discussion, dispute, issue, controversy, plea, assertion **3** = reason, case, reasoning, ground(s), defence, logic, polemic, dialectic

argumentation *n* the process of reasoning methodically

argumentative *adj* likely to argue

argy-bargy *or* **argie-bargie** *n*, *pl* -**bargies** *Brit informal* a squabbling argument

aria (ah-ree-a) *n* an elaborate song for solo voice in an opera or choral work

arid *adj* **1** having little or no rain **2** uninteresting > **aridity** *n*

aright *adv* correctly or properly

arise *vb* **arising**, **arose**, **arisen** **1** to come into being: *the opportunity for action did not arise*

2 to come into notice: *people can seek answers to their problems as and when they arise* **3** **arise from** to happen as a result of **4** *old-fashioned* to get or stand up

> **arise** *vb* **1, 2** = happen, start, begin, follow, result, develop, emerge, occur **4** = get to your feet, get up, rise, stand up, spring up, leap up

aristocracy *n, pl* **-cies 1** a class of people of high social rank **2** government by this class **3** a group of people considered to be outstanding in a particular sphere of activity

aristocrat *n* a member of the aristocracy

aristocratic *adj* **1** of the aristocracy **2** grand or elegant

> **aristocratic** *adj* **1** = upper-class, lordly, titled, elite, gentlemanly, noble, patrician, blue-blooded; ≠ common

arithmetic *n* **1** the branch of mathematics concerned with numerical calculations, such as addition, subtraction, multiplication, and division **2** calculations involving numerical operations **3** knowledge of or skill in arithmetic: *even simple arithmetic was beyond him* ▸ *adj also* **arithmetical 4** of or using arithmetic > **arithmetically** *adv* > **arithmetician** *n*

ark *n Bible* the boat built by Noah, which survived the Flood

Ark *n Judaism* **1** Also called: **Holy Ark** the cupboard in a synagogue in which the Torah scrolls are kept **2** Also called: **Ark of the Covenant** a chest containing the laws of the Jewish religion, regarded as the most sacred symbol of God's presence among the Hebrew people

arm¹ *n* **1** (in humans, apes, and monkeys) either of the upper limbs from the shoulder to the wrist **2** the sleeve of a garment **3** the side of a chair on which one's arm can rest **4** a subdivision or section of an organization: *the London-based arm of a Swiss bank* **5** something resembling an arm in appearance or function: *the arm of a record player* **6** power or authority: *the long arm of the law* **7** **arm in arm** with arms linked **8** **at arm's length** at a distance **9** **with open arms** with warmth and hospitality

> **arm** *n* **1** = upper limb, limb, appendage

arm² *vb* **1** to supply with weapons **2** to prepare (an explosive device) for use **3** to provide (a person or thing) with something that strengthens or protects: *you will be armed with all the information you will ever need* ▸ See also **arms** > **armed** *adj*

armada *n* **1** a large number of ships **2** **the Armada** the great fleet sent by Spain against England in 1588

armadillo *n, pl* **-los** a small S American burrowing mammal covered in strong bony plates

Armageddon *n* **1** *New Testament* the final battle between good and evil at the end of the world

2 a catastrophic and extremely destructive conflict

armament *n* **1** **armaments** the weapon equipment of a military vehicle, ship, or aircraft **2** preparation for war

armature *n* **1** a revolving structure in an electric motor or generator, wound with the coils that carry the current **2** *sculpture* a framework to support the clay or other material used in modelling

armchair *n* **1** an upholstered chair with side supports for the arms ▸ *adj* **2** taking no active part: *we are, on the whole, a nation of armchair athletes*

armful *n* as much as can be held in the arms: *armfuls of lovely flowers*

armhole *n* the opening in a piece of clothing through which the arm passes

armistice (arm-miss-stiss) *n* an agreement between opposing armies to stop fighting

armour *or US* **armor** *n* **1** metal clothing worn by medieval warriors for protection in battle **2** *military* armoured fighting vehicles in general **3** the protective metal plates on a tank or warship **4** protective covering, such as the shell of certain animals **5** a quality or attitude that gives protection ▸ *vb* **6** to equip or cover with armour

> **armour** *or* **armor** *n* **1, 3, 4** = protection, covering, shield, sheathing, armour plate, chain mail, protective covering

armourer *or US* **armorer** *n* **1** a person who makes or mends arms and armour **2** a person in charge of small arms in a military unit

armoury *or US* **armory** *n, pl* **-mouries** *or* **-mories 1** a secure storage place for weapons **2** military supplies **3** resources on which to draw: *modern medicine has a large armoury of drugs for the treatment of illness*

armpit *n* **1** the hollow beneath the arm where it joins the shoulder **2** *slang* an extremely unpleasant place: *the armpit of the Mediterranean*

arms *pl n* **1** weapons collectively **2** military exploits: *prowess in arms* **3** the heraldic symbols of a family or state **4** **take up arms** to prepare to fight **5** **under arms** armed and prepared for war **6** **up in arms** prepared to protest strongly

army *n, pl* **-mies 1** the military land forces of a nation **2** a large number of people or animals

> **army** *n* **1** = soldiers, military, troops, armed force, legions, infantry, military force, land force **2** = vast number, host, gang, mob, flock, array, legion, swarm

aroma *n* **1** a distinctive pleasant smell **2** a subtle pervasive quality or atmosphere

> **aroma** *n* **1** = scent, smell, perfume, fragrance, bouquet, savour, odour, redolence

aromatherapy *n* the use of fragrant essential oils as a treatment in alternative medicine, often to relieve tension

aromatic *adj* **1** having a distinctive pleasant smell **2** *chem* (of an organic compound) having an unsaturated ring of atoms, usually six carbon atoms ▸ *n* **3** something, such as a plant or drug, that gives off a fragrant smell

arose *vb* the past tense of **arise**

around *prep* **1** situated at various points in: *cameramen were positioned around the auditorium* **2** from place to place in: *he had spent twenty-five minutes driving around Amsterdam* **3** somewhere in or near **4** approximately in: *around 1980* ▸ *adv* **5** in all directions from a point of reference: *there wasn't a house for miles around* **6** in the vicinity, esp. restlessly but idly: *I couldn't hang around too long* **7** in no particular place or direction: *a few tropical fish tanks dotted around* **8** *informal* present in some unknown or unspecified place **9** *informal* available: *these laptops have been around for several years* **10 have been around** *informal* to have gained considerable experience of a worldly or social nature

> **around** *prep* **1** = surrounding, about, enclosing, encompassing, framing, encircling, on all sides of, on every side of **4** = approximately, about, nearly, close to, roughly, just about, in the region of, circa ▸ *adv* **5**, **7** = everywhere, about, throughout, all over, here and there, on all sides, in all directions, to and fro

arouse *vb* **arousing**, **aroused** **1** to produce (a reaction, emotion, or response) **2** to awaken from sleep > **arousal** *n*

> **arouse** *vb* **1** = stimulate, encourage, inspire, prompt, spur, provoke, rouse, stir up; ≠ quell **2** = awaken, wake up, rouse, waken

arpeggio (arp-pej-ee-oh) *n*, *pl* **-gios** a chord whose notes are played or sung in rapid succession

arraign (ar-rain) *vb* **1** to bring (a prisoner) before a court to answer a charge **2** to accuse > **arraignment** *n*

arrange *vb* **-ranging**, **-ranged** **1** to plan in advance: *my parents had arranged a surprise party* **2** to arrive at an agreement: *they had arranged to go to the cinema* **3** to put into a proper or systematic order **4** to adapt (a musical composition) for performance in a certain way

> **arrange** *vb* **1** = plan, agree, prepare, determine, organize, construct, devise, contrive, jack up (NZ *informal*) **3** = put in order, group, order, sort, position, line up, organize, classify, jack up (NZ *informal*); ≠ disorganize **4** = adapt, score, orchestrate, harmonize, instrument

arrangement *n* **1** a preparation or plan made for an event: *travel arrangements* **2** an agreement or a plan to do something **3** a thing composed of various ordered parts: *a flower arrangement* **4** the form in which things are arranged **5** an adaptation of a piece of music for performance in a different way

> **arrangement** *n* **1** = plan, planning, provision, preparation **2** = agreement, contract, settlement, appointment, compromise, deal (*informal*), pact, compact **3**, **4** = display, system, structure, organization, exhibition, presentation, classification, alignment **5** = adaptation, score, version, interpretation, instrumentation, orchestration, harmonization

arrant *adj* utter or downright: *that's the most arrant nonsense I've ever heard*

arras *n* a tapestry wall-hanging

array *n* **1** an impressive display or collection **2** an orderly arrangement, such as of troops in battle order **3** *computers* a data structure in which elements may be located by index numbers **4** *poetic* rich clothing ▸ *vb* **5** to arrange in order **6** to dress in rich clothing

> **array** *n* **1** = arrangement, show, supply, display, collection, exhibition, line-up, mixture **4** = clothing, dress, clothes, garments, apparel (*old-fashioned*), attire, finery, regalia ▸ *vb* **5** = arrange, show, group, present, range, display, parade, exhibit **6** = dress, clothe, deck, decorate, adorn, festoon, attire

arrears *pl n* **1** money owed **2 in arrears** late in paying a debt

arrest *vb* **1** to take (a person) into custody **2** to slow or stop the development of **3** to catch and hold (one's attention) ▸ *n* **4** the act of taking a person into custody **5 under arrest** being held in custody by the police **6** the slowing or stopping of something: *a cardiac arrest*

> **arrest** *vb* **1** = capture, catch, nick (*slang, chiefly Brit*), seize, detain, apprehend, take prisoner; ≠ release **2** = stop, end, limit, block, slow, delay, interrupt, suppress; ≠ speed up **3** = fascinate, hold, occupy, engage, grip, absorb, entrance, intrigue ▸ *n* **4** = capture, bust (*informal*), detention, seizure; ≠ release **6** = stoppage, suppression, obstruction, blockage, hindrance; ≠ acceleration

arresting *adj* attracting attention; striking

> **arresting** *adj* = striking, surprising, engaging, stunning (*informal*), impressive, outstanding, remarkable, noticeable; ≠ unremarkable

arrival *n* **1** the act of arriving **2** a person or thing that has just arrived **3** *informal* a recently born baby

> **arrival** *n* **1** = appearance, coming, arriving, entrance, advent, materialization **2** = newcomer, incomer, visitor, caller, entrant

arrive *vb* **-riving**, **-rived** **1** to reach a place or destination **2 arrive at** to come to (a conclusion, idea, or decision) **3** to occur: *the crisis he predicted then has now arrived* **4** *informal* to be born **5** *informal* to attain success

> **arrive** *vb* **1** = come, appear, turn up, show up (*informal*), draw near; ≠ depart **3** = occur, happen, take place **5** = succeed, make it (*informal*), triumph, do well, thrive, flourish, be successful, make good

arrogant *adj* having an exaggerated opinion of one's own importance or ability > **arrogance** *n* > **arrogantly** *adv*

> **arrogant** *adj* = conceited, proud, cocky, overbearing, haughty, scornful, egotistical, disdainful; ≠ modest

arrogate *vb* **-gating, -gated** to claim or seize without justification > **arrogation** *n*
arrow *n* **1** a long slender pointed weapon, with feathers at one end, that is shot from a bow **2** an arrow-shaped sign or symbol used to show the direction to a place

> **arrow** *n* **1** = dart, flight, bolt, shaft (*archaic*), quarrel **2** = pointer, indicator, marker

arrowhead *n* the pointed tip of an arrow
arrowroot *n* an easily digestible starch obtained from the root of a West Indian plant
arse *or US & Canad* **ass** *n vulgar slang* the buttocks or anus
arsehole *or US & Canad* **asshole** *n vulgar slang* **1** the anus **2** a stupid or annoying person
arsenal *n* **1** a building in which arms and ammunition are made or stored **2** a store of anything regarded as weapons: *this new weapon in the medical arsenal*

> **arsenal** *n* **1** = armoury, storehouse, ammunition dump, arms depot, ordnance depot **2** = store, supply, stockpile

arsenic *n* **1** a toxic metalloid element. Symbol: **As 2** a nontechnical name for **arsenic trioxide**, a highly poisonous compound used as a rat poison and insecticide ▸ *adj also* **arsenical 3** of or containing arsenic
arson *n* the crime of intentionally setting fire to property > **arsonist** *n*
art *n* **1** the creation of works of beauty or other special significance **2** works of art collectively **3** human creativity as distinguished from nature **4** skill: *she was still new to the art of bargaining* **5** any branch of the visual arts, esp. painting **6 get something down to a fine art** to become proficient at something through practice

> **art** *n* **1, 5** = artwork, style of art, fine art, creativity **4** = skill, craft, expertise, competence, mastery, ingenuity, virtuosity, cleverness

artefact *or* **artifact** *n* something made by human beings, such as a tool or a work of art
arterial *adj* **1** of or affecting an artery **2** being a major route: *an arterial road*

arteriosclerosis (art-ear-ee-oh-skler-oh-siss) *n* thickening and loss of elasticity of the walls of the arteries. Nontechnical name: **hardening of the arteries**
artery *n, pl* **-teries 1** any of the tubes that carry oxygenated blood from the heart to various parts of the body **2** a major road or means of communication
artesian well (art-teez-yan) *n* a well receiving water from a higher altitude, so the water is forced to flow upwards
Artex *n trademark Brit* a type of coating for walls and ceilings that gives a textured finish
artful *adj* **1** cunning **2** skilful in achieving a desired end > **artfully** *adv*
arthritis *n* inflammation of a joint or joints, causing pain and stiffness > **arthritic** *adj, n*
arthropod *n* a creature, such as an insect or a spider, which has jointed legs and a hard case on its body
artic *n Brit informal* an articulated lorry
artichoke *n* **1** Also called: **globe artichoke** the flower head of a thistle-like plant, cooked as a vegetable **2** same as **Jerusalem artichoke**
article *n* **1** a written composition in a magazine or newspaper **2** an item or object **3** a clause in a written document **4** *grammar* any of the words *a, an,* or *the*

> **article** *n* **1** = feature, story, paper, piece, item, creation, essay, composition **2** = thing, piece, unit, item, object, device, tool, implement **3** = clause, point, part, section, item, passage, portion, paragraph

articled *adj* bound by a written contract, such as one that governs a period of training: *an articled clerk*
articulate *adj* **1** able to express oneself fluently and coherently **2** distinct, clear, or definite: *his amiable and articulate campaign attracted support* **3** *zool* possessing joints ▸ *vb* **-lating, -lated 4** to speak clearly and distinctly **5** to express coherently in words > **articulately** *adv*

> **articulate** *adj* **1, 2** = expressive, clear, coherent, fluent, eloquent, lucid; ≠ incoherent ▸ *vb* **4** = pronounce, say, talk, speak, voice, utter, enunciate **5** = express, say, state, word, declare, phrase, communicate, utter

articulated lorry *n* a large lorry in two separate sections connected by a pivoted bar
articulation *n* **1** the expressing of an idea in words **2** the process of articulating a speech sound or the sound so produced **3** a being jointed together **4** *zool* a joint between bones or arthropod segments
artifice *n* **1** a clever trick **2** skill or cleverness
artificer (art-tiff-iss-er) *n* a skilled craftsman
artificial *adj* **1** man-made; not occurring naturally **2** made in imitation of a natural product: *artificial flavourings* **3** not sincere > **artificiality** *n* > **artificially** *adv*

a

artificial *adj* **1**, **2** = synthetic, manufactured, plastic (*slang*), man-made, non-natural; ≠ authentic **3** = insincere, forced, affected, phoney or phony (*informal*), false, contrived, unnatural, feigned; ≠ genuine

artificial insemination *n* introduction of semen into the womb by means other than sexual intercourse

artificial intelligence *n* the branch of computer science aiming to produce machines which can imitate intelligent human behaviour

artificial respiration *n* any method of restarting a person's breathing after it has stopped

artillery *n* **1** large-calibre guns **2** military units specializing in the use of such guns

artillery *n* **1** = big guns, battery, cannon, ordnance, gunnery

artisan *n* a skilled worker; craftsperson
> **artisanal** *adj*

artist *n* **1** a person who produces works of art such as paintings or sculpture **2** a person who is skilled at something **3** same as **artiste** > **artistic** *adj* > **artistically** *adv*

artiste *n* a professional entertainer such as a singer or dancer

artistry *n* **1** artistic ability **2** great skill

artless *adj* **1** free from deceit or cunning: *artless generosity* **2** natural or unpretentious
> **artlessly** *adv*

arty *adj* **artier**, **artiest** *informal* having an affected interest in art > **artiness** *n*

arum lily *n* a plant with a white funnel-shaped leaf surrounding a yellow spike of flowers

as *conj* **1** while or when: *he arrived just as the band finished the song* **2** in the way that: *they had talked and laughed as only the best of friends can* **3** that which; what: *George did as he was asked* **4** (of) which fact or event (referring to the previous statement): *to become wise, as we all know, is not easy* **5 as it were** in a way; in a manner of speaking: *he was, as it were, on probation* **6** since; seeing that **7** for instance ▸ *adv, conj* **8** used to indicate amount or extent in comparisons: *he was as fat as his mum and dad* ▸ *prep* **9** in the role of; being: *my task, as his physician, is to do the best that I can* **10 as for** *or* **to** with reference to **11 as if** *or* **though** as it would be if: *she felt as if she had been run over by a bulldozer* **12 as (it) is** in the existing state of affairs

as *conj* **1** = when, while, just as, at the time that **2** = in the way that, like, in the manner that **6** = since, because, seeing that, considering that, on account of the fact that ▸ *prep* **9** = in the role of, being, under the name of, in the character of

ASA (in Britain) **1** Amateur Swimming Association **2** Advertising Standards Authority

asafoetida *n* a strong-smelling plant resin used as a spice in Eastern cookery

a.s.a.p. as soon as possible

asbestos *n* a fibrous mineral which does not burn, formerly widely used as a heat-resistant material

asbestosis *n* inflammation of the lungs resulting from inhalation of asbestos fibre

ascend *vb* **1** to go or move up **2** to slope upwards **3 ascend the throne** to become king or queen

ascendancy *or* **ascendance** *n* the condition of being dominant: *when hardliners were in the ascendancy last winter*

ascendant *or* **ascendent** *adj* **1** dominant or influential ▸ *n* **2** *astrol* the sign of the zodiac that is rising on the eastern horizon at a particular moment **3 in the ascendant** increasing in power or influence

ascension *n* the act of ascending

ascent *n* **1** the act of ascending **2** an upward slope

ascertain *vb* to find out definitely
> **ascertainment** *n*

ascetic (ass-**set**-tik) *n* **1** a person who abstains from worldly comforts and pleasures ▸ *adj* **2** rigidly abstinent and self-denying

ascorbic acid (ass-**core**-bik) *n* a vitamin that occurs in citrus fruits, tomatoes, and green vegetables, and which prevents and cures scurvy. Also called: **vitamin C**

ascribe *vb* **-cribing**, **-cribed 1** to attribute, as to a particular origin: *headaches which may be ascribed to stress* **2** to consider that (a particular quality) is possessed by something or someone: *specific human qualities are ascribed to each of the four elements*
> **ascription** *n*

aseptic (eh-**sep**-tik) *adj* free from harmful bacteria

asexual (eh-**sex**-yew-al) *adj* **1** having no apparent sex or sex organs **2** (of reproduction) not involving sexual activity **3** (of a person) not sexually attracted to other people > **asexually** *adv*

ash[1] *n* **1** the powdery substance formed when something is burnt **2** fine particles of lava thrown out by an erupting volcano

ash[2] *n* a tree with grey bark and winged seeds

ashamed *adj* **1** overcome with shame or remorse **2** unwilling through fear of humiliation or shame: *she'd be ashamed to admit to jealousy*

ashamed *adj* **1** = embarrassed, sorry, guilty, distressed, humiliated, self-conscious, red-faced, mortified; ≠ proud **2** = reluctant, embarrassed

ashen *adj* pale with shock

ashlar *or* **ashler** *n* **1** a square block of cut stone for use in building **2** a thin dressed stone used to face a wall

ashore *adv* towards or on land

ashore *adv* = on land, on the beach, on the shore, aground, to the shore, on dry land, shorewards, landwards

ashram *n* a religious retreat where a Hindu holy man lives

ashtray *n* a dish for tobacco ash and cigarette ends

Ash Wednesday *n* the first day of Lent, named from the Christian custom of sprinkling ashes on penitents' heads

Asian *adj* 1 of Asia 2 *Brit* of the Indian subcontinent ▸ *n* 3 a person from Asia 4 *Brit* a person from the Indian subcontinent or a descendant of one

Asian pear *n* an apple-shaped pear with crisp juicy flesh

Asiatic *adj* Asian

aside *adv* 1 to one side 2 out of other people's hearing: *her mother took her aside for a serious talk* 3 out of mind: *she pushed aside her fears of being beaten or killed* 4 into reserve: *a certain amount must also be put aside for defence and government* ▸ *n* 5 a remark not meant to be heard by everyone present 6 a remark that is not connected with the subject being discussed

> **aside** *adv* 1, 2, 3 = to one side, separately, apart, beside, out of the way, on one side, to the side ▸ *n* 5 = interpolation, parenthesis

asinine (ass-in-nine) *adj* 1 obstinate or stupid 2 of or like an ass

ask *vb* 1 to say or write (something) in a form that requires an answer: *I asked him his name; 'do you think we'll have trouble landing?' he asked* 2 to make a request or demand: *the chairman asked for a show of hands* 3 to invite 4 to inquire about: *I pretended to be lost and asked for directions* 5 to expect: *is that too much to ask?*

> **ask** *vb* 1 = inquire, question, quiz, query, interrogate; ≠ answer 3 = invite, bid, summon

askance (ass-kanss) *adv* **look askance at A** to look at with an oblique glance **B** to regard with suspicion

askew *adv, adj* towards one side; crooked

aslant *adv* 1 at a slant ▸ *prep* 2 slanting across

asleep *adj* 1 in or into a state of sleep 2 (of limbs) numb 3 *informal* not listening or paying attention

> **asleep** *adj* 1 = sleeping, napping, dormant, dozing, slumbering, snoozing (*informal*), fast asleep, sound asleep

AS level *n* 1 *Brit* the advanced subsidiary level of a subject taken for the General Certificate of Education, having a smaller content than the advanced level 2 a pass in a subject at AS level

asp *n* a small viper of S Europe

asparagus *n* the young shoots of a plant of the lily family, which can be cooked and eaten

aspect *n* 1 a distinct feature or element in a problem or situation 2 a position facing a particular direction: *the room's east-facing aspect* 3 appearance or look: *a room with a somewhat gloomy aspect*

> **aspect** *n* 1 = feature, side, factor, angle, characteristic, facet 2 = position, view, situation, scene, prospect, point of view, outlook 3 = appearance, look, air, condition, quality, bearing, attitude, cast

aspen *n* a poplar tree whose leaves quiver in the wind

Asperger syndrome *or* **Asperger's syndrome** *n* a form of autism in which the person affected has limited but obsessive interests

asperity (ass-per-rit-ee) *n, pl* **-ties** roughness or sharpness of temper

aspersion *n* **cast aspersions on** to make disparaging or malicious remarks about

asphalt *n* 1 a black tarlike substance used in road-surfacing and roofing materials ▸ *vb* 2 to cover with asphalt

asphodel *n* a plant with clusters of yellow or white flowers

asphyxia (ass-fix-ee-a) *n* unconsciousness or death caused by lack of oxygen

asphyxiate *vb* **-ating, -ated** to smother or suffocate > **asphyxiation** *n*

aspic *n* a savoury jelly based on meat or fish stock, used as a mould for meat or vegetables

aspidistra *n* a house plant with long tapered evergreen leaves

aspirant *n* a person who aspires, such as to a powerful position

aspirate *phonetics* ▸ *vb* **-rating, -rated** 1 to pronounce (a word or syllable) with an initial *h* ▸ *n* 2 the sound represented in English and several other languages as *h*

aspiration *n* 1 a strong desire or aim 2 *phonetics* the pronunciation of an aspirated consonant > **aspirational** *adj*

> **aspiration** *n* 1 = aim, plan, hope, goal, dream, wish, desire, objective

aspire *vb* **-piring, -pired** to yearn for something or hope to do or be something: *it struck him as bizarre that somebody could aspire to be a dental technician* > **aspiring** *adj*

aspirin *n, pl* **-rin** *or* **-rins** 1 a drug used to relieve pain and fever 2 a tablet of aspirin

ass *n* 1 a mammal resembling the horse but with longer ears 2 a foolish person

> **ass** *n* 1 = donkey, moke (*slang*) 2 = fool, idiot, twit (*informal, chiefly Brit*), oaf, jackass, blockhead, dorba *or* dorb (*Austral slang*)

assagai *n* same as **assegai**

assail *vb* 1 to attack violently 2 to criticize strongly 3 to disturb: *he was assailed by a dizzy sensation* > **assailant** *n*

assassin *n* a murderer of a prominent person

> **assassin** *n* = murderer, killer, slayer, liquidator, executioner, hitman *or* woman (*slang*), hatchet man *or* woman *or* person (*slang*)

a

assassinate *vb* **-nating, -nated** to murder (a prominent person) > **assassination** *n*

> **assassinate** *vb* = murder, kill, eliminate (*slang*), take out (*slang*), terminate, hit (*slang*), slay, liquidate

assault *n* **1** a violent attack, either physical or verbal ▶ *vb* **2** to attack violently

> **assault** *n* = attack, raid, invasion, charge, offensive, onslaught, foray; ≠ defence ▶ *vb* = strike, attack, beat, knock, bang, slap, smack, thump

assault course *n* an obstacle course designed to give soldiers practice in negotiating hazards

assay *vb* **1** to analyse (a substance, such as gold) to find out how pure it is ▶ *n* **2** an analysis of the purity of an ore or precious metal

assegai *or* **assagai** *n, pl* **-gais** a sharp light spear used in southern Africa

assemblage *n* **1** a collection or group of things **2** the act of assembling

assemble *vb* **-bling, -bled** **1** to collect or gather together **2** to put together the parts of (a machine)

> **assemble** *vb* **1** = gather, meet, collect, rally, come together, muster, congregate; ≠ scatter **2** = put together, join, set up, build up, connect, construct, piece together, fabricate; ≠ take apart

assembly *n, pl* **-blies** **1** a number of people gathered together for a meeting **2** a group of people who meet regularly to make decisions or laws for a particular region or country: *the National Assembly for Wales* **3** the act of assembling

> **assembly** *n* **1** = gathering, group, meeting, council, conference, crowd, congress, collection, hui (NZ), runanga (NZ) **3** = putting together, setting up, construction, building up, connecting, piecing together

assembly line *n* a sequence of machines and workers in a factory assembling a product

assent *n* **1** agreement, consent ▶ *vb* **2** to agree

assert *vb* **1** to state or declare **2** to insist upon (one's rights, etc.) **3 assert oneself** to speak and act forcefully

> **assert** *vb* **1** = state, argue, maintain, declare, swear, pronounce, affirm, profess; ≠ deny **2** = insist upon, stress, defend, uphold, put forward, press, stand up for; ≠ retract **3 assert oneself** = be forceful, put your foot down (*informal*), put yourself forward, make your presence felt, exert your influence

assertion *n* **1** a positive statement, usually made without evidence **2** the act of asserting

> **assertion** *n* **1** = statement, claim, declaration, pronouncement **2** = insistence, stressing, maintenance

assertive *adj* confident and direct in dealing with others > **assertively** *adv* > **assertiveness** *n*

> **assertive** *adj* = confident, positive, aggressive, forceful, emphatic, insistent, feisty (*informal*), pushy (*informal*); ≠ meek

assess *vb* **1** to judge the worth or importance of **2** to estimate the value of (income or property) for taxation purposes > **assessment** *n*

> **assess** *vb* **1** = judge, estimate, analyse, evaluate, rate, value, check out, weigh up **2** = evaluate, rate, tax, value, estimate, fix, impose, levy

assessor *n* **1** a person who values property for taxation or insurance purposes **2** a person with technical expertise called in to advise a court **3** a person who evaluates the merits of something

asset *n* **1** a thing or person that is valuable or useful **2** any property owned by a person or company

> **asset** *n* **1** = benefit, help, service, aid, advantage, strength, resource, attraction; ≠ disadvantage

asseverate *vb* **-ating, -ated** *formal* to declare solemnly > **asseveration** *n*

assiduous *adj* **1** hard-working **2** done with care > **assiduity** *n* > **assiduously** *adv*

assign *vb* **1** to select (someone) for a post or task **2** to give a task or duty (to someone) **3** to attribute to a specified cause **4** to set apart (a place or time) for a particular function or event: *to assign a day for the meeting* **5** *law* to transfer (one's right, interest, or title to property) to someone else

> **assign** *vb* **1** = select for, post, commission, elect, appoint, delegate, nominate, name **2** = give, set, grant, allocate, give out, consign, allot, apportion **3** = attribute, credit, put down, set down, ascribe, accredit

assignation (ass-sig-nay-shun) *n* a secret arrangement to meet, esp. one between lovers

assignment *n* **1** something that has been assigned, such as a task **2** the act of assigning **3** *law* the transfer to another person of a right, interest, or title to property

> **assignment** *n* **1** = task, job, position, post, commission, exercise, responsibility, duty

assimilate *vb* **-lating, -lated** **1** to learn and understand (information) thoroughly **2** to adjust or become adjusted: *they became assimilated to German culture* **3** to absorb (food) > **assimilable** *adj* > **assimilation** *n*

assist *vb* **1** to give help or support ▶ *n* **2** *sport* a pass by a player which enables another player to score a goal

> **assist** *vb* = help, support, aid, cooperate with, abet, lend a helping hand to

assistance *n* help or support

> **assistance** *n* = help, backing, support, aid, cooperation, helping hand; ≠ hindrance

assistant *n* **1** a helper or subordinate ▸ *adj* **2** junior or deputy: *assistant manager*

> **assistant** *n* = helper, ally, colleague, supporter, aide, second, attendant, accomplice

assizes *pl n Brit* (formerly in England and Wales) the sessions of the principal court in each county

associate *vb* **-ating, -ated 1** to connect in the mind **2** to mix socially: *addicts are driven to associate with criminals* **3 be associated** or **associate oneself with** to be involved with (a group) because of shared views: *she had long been associated with the far right* ▸ *n* **4** a partner in business **5** a companion or friend ▸ *adj* **6** having partial rights or subordinate status: *an associate member* **7** joined with in business: *an associate director*

> **associate** *vb* **1** = connect, link, ally, identify, join, combine, attach, fasten; ≠ separate **2** = socialize, mix, accompany, mingle, consort, hobnob; ≠ avoid ▸ *n* = partner, friend, ally, colleague, mate (*informal*), companion, comrade, affiliate, cobber (*Austral, NZ old-fashioned, informal*), E hoa (*NZ*)

association *n* **1** a group of people with a common interest **2** the act of associating or the state of being associated **3** friendship: *their association still had to remain a secret* **4** a mental connection of ideas or feelings: *the place contained associations for her*

> **association** *n* **1** = group, club, society, league, band, set, pack, collection, social network (*computers*) **2** = connection, union, joining, pairing, combination, mixture, blend, juxtaposition

assonance *n* the rhyming of vowel sounds but not consonants, as in *time* and *light*

assorted *adj* **1** consisting of various kinds mixed together **2** matched: *an ill-assorted childless couple*

> **assorted** *adj* **1** = various, different, mixed, varied, diverse, miscellaneous, sundry, motley; ≠ similar

assortment *n* a collection of various things or sorts

assuage (ass-**wage**) *vb* **-suaging, -suaged** to relieve (grief, pain, or thirst)

assume *vb* **-suming, -sumed 1** to take to be true without proof **2** to undertake or take on: *every general staff officer was able to assume control of the army* **3** to make a pretence of: *the man had assumed a debonair attitude* **4** to take on: *her eyes assumed a scared haunted look*

assume *vb* **1** = presume, think, believe, expect, suppose, imagine, fancy, take for granted; ≠ know **2** = take on, accept, shoulder, take over, put on, enter upon **3** = simulate, affect, adopt, put on, imitate, mimic, feign, impersonate

assumption *n* **1** something that is taken for granted **2** the act of assuming power or possession

> **assumption** *n* **1** = presumption, belief, guess, hypothesis, inference, conjecture, surmise, supposition **2** = taking on, managing, handling, shouldering, putting on, taking up, takeover, acquisition

assurance *n* **1** a statement or assertion intended to inspire confidence **2** feeling of confidence; certainty **3** insurance that provides for events that are certain to happen, such as death

> **assurance** *n* **1** = promise, statement, guarantee, commitment, pledge, vow, declaration, assertion; ≠ lie **2** = confidence, conviction, certainty, self-confidence, poise, faith, nerve, aplomb; ≠ self-doubt

assure *vb* **-suring, -sured 1** to promise or guarantee **2** to convince: *they assured me that they had not seen the document* **3** to make (something) certain **4** *chiefly Brit* to insure against loss of life

> **assure** *vb* **1** = promise to, pledge to, vow to, guarantee to, swear to, confirm to, certify to, give your word to **2** = convince, encourage, persuade, satisfy, comfort, reassure, hearten, embolden **3** = make certain, ensure, confirm, guarantee, secure, make sure, complete, seal

assured *adj* **1** confident or self-assured **2** certain to happen **3** *chiefly Brit* insured > **assuredly** (a-**sure**-id-lee) *adv*

> **assured** *adj* **1** = confident, certain, positive, poised, fearless, self-confident, self-assured, dauntless; ≠ self-conscious **2** = certain, sure, ensured, confirmed, settled, guaranteed, fixed, secure, nailed-on (*slang*); ≠ doubtful

astatine *n chem* a radioactive element occurring naturally in minute amounts or artificially produced by bombarding bismuth with alpha particles. Symbol: **At**

aster *n* a plant with white, blue, purple, or pink daisy-like flowers

asterisk *n* **1** a star-shaped character (*) used in printing or writing to indicate a footnote, etc. ▸ *vb* **2** to mark with an asterisk

astern *adv, adj naut* **1** at or towards the stern of a ship **2** backwards **3** behind a vessel

asteroid *n* any of the small planets that orbit the sun between Mars and Jupiter

asthma (ass-ma) *n* an illness causing difficulty in breathing > **asthmatic** *adj, n*

a

astigmatism (eh-**stig**-mat-tiz-zum) n a defect of a lens, esp. of the eye, causing it not to focus properly

astir adj 1 out of bed 2 in motion

astonish vb to surprise greatly > **astonishing** adj > **astonishment** n

> **astonish** vb = amaze, surprise, stun, stagger, bewilder, astound, daze, confound

astound vb to overwhelm with amazement > **astounding** adj

astrakhan n 1 a fur made of the dark curly fleece of lambs from Astrakhan in Russia 2 a cloth resembling this

astral adj 1 relating to or resembling the stars 2 of the spirit world

astray adj, adv out of the right or expected way

astride adj 1 with a leg on either side 2 with legs far apart ▸ prep 3 with a leg on either side of

astringent adj 1 causing contraction of body tissue 2 checking the flow of blood from a cut 3 severe or harsh ▸ n 4 an astringent drug or lotion > **astringency** n

astrolabe n an instrument formerly used to measure the altitude of stars and planets

astrology n the study of the alleged influence of the stars, planets, sun, and moon on human affairs > **astrologer** or **astrologist** n > **astrological** adj

astronaut n a person trained for travelling in space

astronautics n the science and technology of space flight > **astronautical** adj

astronomical or **astronomic** adj 1 enormously large 2 of astronomy > **astronomically** adv

astronomy n the scientific study of heavenly bodies > **astronomer** n

astrophysics n the study of the physical and chemical properties of celestial bodies > **astrophysical** adj > **astrophysicist** n

Astroturf n trademark a brand of artificial grass

astute adj quick to notice or understand > **astutely** adv > **astuteness** n

> **astute** adj = intelligent, sharp, clever, subtle, shrewd, cunning, canny, perceptive; ≠ stupid

asunder adv, adj literary into parts or pieces; apart

asylum n 1 refuge granted to a political refugee from a foreign country 2 (formerly) a psychiatric hospital

> **asylum** n 1 = refuge, haven, safety, protection, preserve, shelter, retreat, harbour 2 = psychiatric hospital, hospital, institution

asymmetry n lack of symmetry > **asymmetric** or **asymmetrical** adj

asymptote (ass-im-tote) n a straight line that is closely approached but never met by a curve > **asymptotic** adj

at prep 1 indicating location or position: she had planted a vegetable garden at the back 2 towards; in the direction of: she was staring at the wall behind him 3 indicating position in time: we arrived at 12.30 4 engaged in: the innocent laughter of children at play 5 during the passing of: she works at night as a nurse's aide 6 for; in exchange for: crude oil is selling at its lowest price since September 7 indicating the object of an emotion: I'm angry at you because you were rude to me

atavism (at-a-viz-zum) n 1 the recurrence of primitive characteristics that were present in distant ancestors but not in more recent ones 2 reversion to a former type > **atavistic** adj

ate vb the past tense of **eat**

atheism (aith-ee-iz-zum) n the belief that there is no God > **atheist** n

atherosclerosis n, pl -ses a disease in which deposits of fat cause the walls of the arteries to thicken > **atherosclerotic** adj

athlete n 1 a person trained to compete in sports or exercises 2 chiefly Brit a competitor in track-and-field events

> **athlete** n 1 = sportsperson, player, runner, competitor, sportsman, contestant, gymnast, sportswoman

athletic adj 1 physically fit or strong 2 of or for an athlete or athletics > **athletically** adv > **athleticism** n

> **athletic** adj 1 = fit, strong, powerful, healthy, active, trim, strapping, energetic; ≠ feeble

athletics pl n Brit & Austral track-and-field events

> **athletics** pl n = sports, games, races, exercises, contests, sporting events, gymnastics, track and field events

athwart prep 1 across ▸ adv 2 transversely; from one side to another

atlas n a book of maps

atmosphere n 1 the mass of gases surrounding the earth or any other heavenly body 2 the air in a particular place 3 a pervasive feeling or mood: the atmosphere was tense 4 a unit of pressure equal to the normal pressure of the air at sea level > **atmospheric** adj > **atmospherically** adv

> **atmosphere** n 1 = air, sky, heavens, aerosphere 3 = feeling, character, environment, spirit, surroundings, tone, mood, climate

atmospherics pl n radio interference caused by electrical disturbance in the atmosphere

atoll n a circular coral reef surrounding a lagoon

atom n 1 A the smallest quantity of an element which can take part in a chemical reaction B this entity as a source of nuclear energy 2 a very small amount

> **atom** n 2 = particle, bit, spot, trace, molecule, dot, speck

atom bomb *n* same as **atomic bomb**

atomic *adj* **1** of or using atomic bombs or atomic energy **2** of atoms > **atomically** *adv*

atomic bomb *or* **atom bomb** *n* a type of bomb in which the energy is provided by nuclear fission

atomic energy *n* same as **nuclear energy**

atomic number *n* the number of protons in the nucleus of an atom of an element

atomic weight *n* the ratio of the average mass per atom of an element to one twelfth of the mass of an atom of carbon-12

atomize *or* **-ise** *vb* **-izing, -ized** *or* **-ising, -ised** **1** to separate into free atoms **2** to reduce to fine particles or spray **3** to destroy by nuclear weapons

atomizer *or* **-iser** *n* a device for reducing a liquid to a fine spray

atonal (eh-tone-al) *adj* (of music) not written in an established key > **atonality** *n*

atone *vb* **atoning, atoned** to make amends (for a sin, crime, or wrongdoing)

atonement *n* **1** something done to make amends for wrongdoing **2** *Christian theol* the reconciliation of humankind with God through the sacrificial death of Christ

atop *prep* on top of

atrium *n, pl* **atria 1** *anatomy* the upper chamber of each half of the heart **2** a central hall that extends through several storeys in a modern building **3** the open main court of an ancient Roman house > **atrial** *adj*

atrocious *adj* **1** extremely cruel or wicked **2** horrifying or shocking **3** *informal* very bad > **atrociously** *adv*

atrocity *n* **1** behaviour that is wicked or cruel **2** *pl* **-ties** an act of extreme cruelty

> **atrocity** *n* **1** = cruelty, horror, brutality, savagery, wickedness, barbarity, viciousness, fiendishness **2** = act of cruelty, crime, horror, evil, outrage, abomination

atrophy (at-trof-fee) *n, pl* **-phies 1** a wasting away of a physical organ or part **2** a failure to grow ▸ *vb* **-phies, -phying, -phied 3** to waste away

attach *vb* **1** to join, fasten, or connect **2** to attribute or ascribe: *he attaches particular importance to the proposed sale* **3 attach oneself** *or* **be attached to** to become associated with or join

> **attach** *vb* **1** = affix, stick, secure, add, join, couple, link, tie; ≠ detach **2** = ascribe, connect, attribute, assign, associate

attaché (at-tash-shay) *n* a specialist attached to a diplomatic mission

attaché case *n* a flat rectangular briefcase for carrying papers

attached *adj* **1** married, engaged, or in an exclusive sexual relationship **2 attached to** fond of

> **attached** *adj* **1** = spoken for, married, partnered, engaged, accompanied **2 attached to** = fond of, devoted to, affectionate towards, full of regard for

attachment *n* **1** affection or regard for **2** an accessory that can be fitted to a device to change what it can do **3** a computer file sent with an email message

> **attachment** *n* **1** = fondness, liking, feeling, relationship, regard, attraction, affection, affinity, aroha (NZ); ≠ aversion **2** = accessory, fitting, extra, component, extension, supplement, fixture, accoutrement

attack *vb* **1** to launch a physical assault (against) **2** to criticize vehemently **3** to set about (a job or problem) with vigour **4** to affect adversely: *BSE attacks the animal's brain* **5** to take the initiative in a game or sport ▸ *n* **6** the act of attacking **7** any sudden appearance of a disease or symptoms: *a bad attack of mumps* > **attacker** *n*

> **attack** *vb* **1** = assault, strike (at), mug (*informal*), ambush, tear into, set upon, lay into (*informal*); ≠ defend **2** = criticize, blame, abuse, condemn, knock (*informal*), put down, slate (*informal*), have a go (at) (*informal*) ▸ *n* **6** = assault, charge, campaign, strike, raid, invasion, offensive, blitz; ≠ defence **7** = bout, fit, stroke, seizure, spasm, convulsion, paroxysm

attain *vb* **1** to manage to do or get (something): *the country attained economic growth* **2** to reach > **attainable** *adj*

> **attain** *vb* **1** = obtain, get, reach, complete, gain, achieve, acquire, fulfil **2** = reach, achieve, acquire, accomplish

attainment *n* an achievement or the act of achieving something

attar *n* a perfume made from damask roses

attempt *vb* **1** to make an effort (to do or achieve something); try ▸ *n* **2** an endeavour to achieve something; effort **3 attempt on someone's life** an attack on someone with the intention to kill

> **attempt** *vb* = try, seek, aim, struggle, venture, undertake, strive, endeavour ▸ *n* **2** = try, go (*informal*), shot (*informal*), effort, trial, bid, crack (*informal*), stab (*informal*)

attend *vb* **1** to be present at (an event) **2** to go regularly to a school, college, etc. **3** to look after: *the actors lounged in their canvas chairs, attended by sycophants* **4** to pay attention **5 attend to** to apply oneself to: *I've a few things I must attend to*

> **attend** *vb* **1** = be present, go to, visit, frequent, haunt, appear at, turn up at, patronize; ≠ be absent **4** = pay attention, listen, hear, mark, note, observe, heed, pay heed; ≠ ignore **5 attend to something** = apply yourself to, concentrate on, look after, take care of, see to, get to work on, devote yourself to, occupy yourself with

a

attendance *n* 1 the act of attending 2 the number of people present 3 regularity in attending

> **attendance** *n* 1 = presence, being there, attending, appearance 2 = turnout, audience, gate, congregation, house, crowd, throng, number present

attendant *n* 1 a person who assists, guides, or provides a service ▸ *adj* 2 associated: *nuclear power and its attendant dangers* 3 being in attendance

> **attendant** *n* = assistant, guard, servant, companion, aide, escort, follower, helper ▸ *adj* 2 = accompanying, related, associated, accessory, consequent, resultant, concomitant

attention *n* 1 concentrated direction of the mind 2 consideration, notice, or observation 3 detailed care or treatment 4 the alert position in military drill 5 **attentions** acts of courtesy: *the attentions of men seemed to embarrass her*

> **attention** *n* 1 = thinking, thought, mind, consideration, scrutiny, heed, deliberation, intentness 2 = awareness, regard, notice, recognition, consideration, observation, consciousness; ≠ inattention 3 = care, support, concern, treatment, looking after, succour, ministration

attentive *adj* 1 paying close attention 2 considerately helpful: *at society parties he is attentive to his wife* > **attentively** *adv* > **attentiveness** *n*

attenuated *adj* 1 weakened 2 thin and extended > **attenuation** *n*

attest *vb* 1 to affirm or prove the truth of 2 to bear witness to (an act or event) > **attestation** *n*

attic *n* a space or room within the roof of a house

> **attic** *n* = loft, garret, roof space

attire *n* clothes, esp. fine or formal ones

attired *adj* dressed in a specified way

attitude *n* 1 the way a person thinks and behaves 2 a position of the body 3 *informal* a hostile manner 4 the orientation of an aircraft or spacecraft in relation to some plane or direction

> **attitude** *n* 1 = opinion, view, position, approach, mood, perspective, point of view, stance 2 = position, bearing, pose, stance, carriage, posture

attorney *n* 1 a person legally appointed to act for another 2 *US* a lawyer

attract *vb* 1 to arouse the interest or admiration of 2 (of a magnet) to draw (something) closer by exerting a force on it

> **attract** *vb* 1 = allure, draw, persuade, charm, appeal to, win over, tempt, lure (*informal*); ≠ repel 2 = pull (*informal*), draw, magnetize

attraction *n* 1 the act or quality of attracting 2 an interesting or desirable feature: *the attractions of working abroad* 3 an object or place that people visit for interest: *this carefully preserved tourist attraction* 4 (of a magnet) a force by which one object attracts another

> **attraction** *n* 1, 2 = appeal, pull (*informal*), charm, lure, temptation, fascination, allure, magnetism 4 = pull, magnetism

attractive *adj* appealing to the senses or mind > **attractively** *adv* > **attractiveness** *n*

> **attractive** *adj* = seductive, charming, tempting, pretty, fair, inviting, lovely, pleasant, hot (*informal*), fit (*Brit informal*), lush (*slang*); ≠ unattractive

attribute *vb* **-uting, -uted** 1 **attribute to** to regard as belonging to or produced by: *a play attributed to William Shakespeare* ▸ *n* 2 a quality or feature belonging to or representative of a person or thing > **attributable** *adj* > **attribution** *n*

> **attribute** *vb* = ascribe, credit, refer, trace, assign, charge, allocate, put down ▸ *n* = quality, feature, property, character, element, aspect, characteristic, distinction

attributive *adj grammar* (of an adjective) coming before the noun modified

attrition *n* constant wearing down to weaken or destroy: *a war of attrition*

attune *vb* **-tuning, -tuned** to adjust or accustom (a person or thing)

atypical (eh-**tip**-ik-kl) *adj* not typical > **atypically** *adv*

Au *chem* gold

aubergine (**oh**-bur-zheen) *n Brit* the dark purple fruit of a tropical plant, cooked and eaten as a vegetable

aubrietia (aw-**bree**-sha) *n* a trailing purple-flowered rock plant

auburn *adj* (of hair) reddish-brown

auction *n* 1 a public sale at which articles are sold to the highest bidder ▸ *vb* 2 to sell by auction

auctioneer *n* a person who conducts an auction

audacious *adj* 1 recklessly bold or daring 2 impudent or presumptuous > **audacity** *n*

audible *adj* loud enough to be heard > **audibility** *n* > **audibly** *adv*

audience *n* 1 a group of spectators or listeners at a concert or play 2 the people reached by a book, film, or radio or television programme 3 a formal interview

> **audience** *n* 1 = spectators, company, crowd, gathering, gallery, assembly, viewers, listeners 3 = interview, meeting, hearing, exchange, reception, consultation

audio *adj* **1** of or relating to sound or hearing **2** of or for the transmission or reproduction of sound

audiovisual *adj* involving both hearing and sight: *audiovisual teaching aids*

audit *n* **1** an official inspection of business accounts, conducted by an independent qualified accountant **2** any thoroughgoing assessment or review: *an audit of their lifestyle* ▸ *vb* **auditing, audited 3** to examine (business accounts) officially

audition *n* **1** a test of a performer's or musician's ability for a particular role or job ▸ *vb* **2** to test or be tested in an audition

auditor *n* a person qualified to audit accounts

auditorium *n, pl* **-toriums** *or* **-toria 1** the area of a concert hall or theatre in which the audience sits **2** *US & Canad* a building for public meetings

auditory *adj* of or relating to hearing

au fait (oh **fay**) *adj* **1** (usually foll. by *with*) fully informed (about) **2** expert

Aug. August

auger *n* a pointed tool for boring holes

aught *pron old-fashioned or literary* anything whatever: *for aught I know*

augment *vb* to make or become greater in number or strength ▸ **augmentation** *n*

au gratin (oh **grat**-tan) *adj* cooked with a topping of breadcrumbs and sometimes cheese

augur *vb* to be a good or bad sign of future events: *a double fault on the opening point did not augur well*

augury *n* **1** the foretelling of the future **2** *pl* **-ries** an omen

august *adj* dignified and imposing

August *n* the eighth month of the year

auk *n* a northern sea bird with a heavy body, short wings, and black-and-white plumage

aunt *n* **1** a sister of one's father or mother **2** the wife of one's uncle **3** a child's term of address for a female friend of the parents

auntie *or* **aunty** *n, pl* **-ies** *informal* an aunt

Aunt Sally *n, pl* **-lies 1** a figure used in fairgrounds as a target **2** any target for insults or criticism

au pair *n* a young foreign person, typically a woman, who helps with childcare or housework in return for board and lodging

aura *n, pl* **auras** *or* **aurae 1** a distinctive air or quality associated with a person or thing **2** any invisible emanation

> **aura** *n* **1** = air, feeling, quality, atmosphere, tone, mood, ambience

aural *adj* of or using the ears or hearing > **aurally** *adv*

aureole *or* **aureola** *n* **1** a ring of light surrounding the head of a figure represented as holy; halo **2** the sun's corona, visible as a faint halo during eclipses

au revoir (oh riv-**vwahr**) *interj* goodbye

auricle *n* **1** the upper chamber of the heart **2** the outer part of the ear > **auricular** *adj*

aurora *n, pl* **-ras** *or* **-rae 1** an atmospheric phenomenon of bands of light sometimes seen in the polar regions **2** *poetic* the dawn

aurora australis *n* the aurora seen around the South Pole

aurora borealis *n* the aurora seen around the North Pole

auscultation *n* the listening to of the internal sounds of the body, usually with a stethoscope, to help with medical diagnosis

auspices (aw-**spiss**-siz) *pl n* **under the auspices of** with the support and approval of

auspicious *adj* showing the signs of future success

Aussie *n, adj informal* Australian

austere *adj* **1** stern or severe: *his austere and serious attitude to events* **2** self-disciplined or ascetic: *an extraordinarily austere and puritanical organization* **3** severely simple or plain: *the austere backdrop of grey*

austerity *n, pl* **-ties 1** the state of being austere **2** reduced availability of luxuries and consumer goods

> **austerity** *n* **1** = plainness, simplicity, starkness

Australasian *adj* of Australia, New Zealand, and neighbouring islands

Australia Day *n* a public holiday in Australia on January 26

Australian *adj* **1** of Australia ▸ *n* **2** a person from Australia

autarchy (aw-**tar**-kee) *n, pl* **-chies** absolute power or autocracy

autarky (aw-**tar**-kee) *n, pl* **-kies** a policy of economic self-sufficiency

authentic *adj* **1** of undisputed origin or authorship; genuine **2** reliable or accurate **3** *music* using period instruments, scores, and playing techniques > **authentically** *adv* > **authenticity** *n*

> **authentic** *adj* **1** = real, pure, genuine, valid, undisputed, lawful, bona fide, dinkum (*Austral, NZ informal*), true-to-life, live; ≠ fake **2** = accurate, legitimate, authoritative

authenticate *vb* **-cating, -cated** to establish as genuine > **authentication** *n*

author *n* **1** a person who writes a book, article, or other written work **2** an originator or creator

> **author** *n* **1** = writer, composer, novelist, hack, creator, scribbler, scribe, wordsmith **2** = creator, father, producer, designer, founder, architect, inventor, originator

authoritarian *adj* **1** insisting on strict obedience to authority ▸ *n* **2** a person who insists on strict obedience to authority > **authoritarianism** *n*

authoritarian adj = strict, severe, autocratic, dictatorial, dogmatic, tyrannical, doctrinaire; ≠ lenient ▸ n = disciplinarian, dictator, tyrant, despot, autocrat, absolutist

authoritative adj 1 recognized as being reliable: *the authoritative book on Shakespeare* 2 possessing authority; official > **authoritatively** adv

authoritative adj 1 = reliable, accurate, valid, authentic, definitive, dependable, trustworthy; ≠ unreliable 2 = commanding, masterly, imposing, assertive, imperious, self-assured; ≠ timid

authority n, pl **-ties** 1 the power to command, control, or judge others 2 a person or group with this power: *a third escapee turned himself in to the authorities* 3 a decision-making organization or government department: *the local authority* 4 an expert in a particular field 5 official permission: *she had no authority to negotiate* 6 a position that has the power to command, control, or judge others: *people in authority* 7 **on good authority** from reliable evidence 8 confidence resulting from expertise

authority n 1 = prerogative, influence, power, control, weight, direction, command, licence, mana (NZ) 2, 3 = powers that be, government, police, officials, the state, management, administration, the system 4 = expert, specialist, professional, master, guru, virtuoso, connoisseur, fundi (S African) 6 = command, power, control, rule, management, direction, mastery

authorize or **-ise** vb **-izing, -ized** or **-ising, -ised** 1 to give authority to 2 to give official permission for > **authorization** or **-isation** n

authorize or **-ise** vb 1 = empower, commission, enable, entitle, mandate, accredit, give authority to 2 = permit, allow, grant, approve, sanction, license, warrant, consent to; ≠ forbid

authorship n 1 the origin or originator of a written work or plan 2 the profession of writing

autism n *psychiatry* a developmental condition characterized by difficulties in responding to and communicating with other people > **autistic** adj

auto- or sometimes before a vowel **aut-** combining form 1 self; of or by the same one: *autobiography* 2 self-propelling: *automobile*

autobiography n, pl **-phies** an account of a person's life written by that person > **autobiographer** n > **autobiographical** adj

autocracy n, pl **-cies** government by an individual with unrestricted authority

autocrat n 1 a ruler with absolute authority 2 a dictatorial person > **autocratic** adj > **autocratically** adv

autocross n a sport in which cars race over a circuit of rough grass

Autocue n *trademark* an electronic television prompting device displaying a speaker's script, unseen by the audience

autogiro or **autogyro** n, pl **-ros** a self-propelled aircraft resembling a helicopter but with an unpowered rotor

autograph n 1 a handwritten signature of a famous person ▸ vb 2 to write one's signature on or in

automat n US a vending machine

automate vb **-mating, -mated** to make (a manufacturing process) automatic

automatic adj 1 (of a device or mechanism) able to activate or regulate itself 2 (of a process) performed by automatic equipment 3 done without conscious thought 4 (of a firearm) utilizing some of the force of each explosion to reload and fire continuously 5 occurring as a necessary consequence: *the certificate itself carries no automatic legal benefits* ▸ n 6 an automatic firearm 7 a motor vehicle with automatic transmission > **automatically** adv

automatic adj 1, 2 = mechanical, automated, mechanized, push-button, self-propelling; ≠ done by hand 3 = involuntary, natural, unconscious, mechanical, spontaneous, reflex, instinctive, unwilled; ≠ conscious

automation n the use of automatic, often electronic, methods to control industrial processes

automaton n, pl **-tons** or **-ta** 1 a mechanical device operating under its own power 2 a person who acts mechanically

automobile n US & Canad a car

autonomous adj 1 having self-government 2 independent of others

autonomous adj = self-ruling, free, independent, sovereign, self-sufficient, self-governing, self-determining

autonomy n, pl **-mies** 1 the right or state of self-government 2 freedom to determine one's own actions and behaviour

autonomy n = independence, freedom, sovereignty, self-determination, self-government, self-rule, self-sufficiency, home rule, rangatiratanga (NZ); ≠ dependency

autopsy n, pl **-sies** examination of a corpse to determine the cause of death

autosuggestion n a process in which a person unconsciously supplies the means of influencing his or her own behaviour or beliefs

autumn n 1 the season of the year between summer and winter 2 a period of late maturity followed by a decline > **autumnal** adj

auxiliary adj 1 secondary or supplementary 2 supporting ▸ n, pl **-ries** 3 a person or thing that supports or supplements

auxiliary verb *n* a verb used to indicate the tense, voice, or mood of another verb, such as *will* in *I will go*

avail *vb* **1** to be of use, advantage, or assistance (to) **2 avail oneself of** to make use of ▸ *n* **3** use or advantage: *to no avail*

available *adj* **1** obtainable or accessible **2** able to be contacted and willing to talk: *a spokesman insisted she was not available for comment* > **availability** *n* > **availably** *adv*

> **available** *adj* **1** = accessible, ready, to hand, handy, at hand, free, to be had, achievable; ≠ in use

avalanche *n* **1** a fall of large masses of snow and ice down a mountain **2** a sudden or overwhelming quantity of anything

> **avalanche** *n* **1** = snow-slide, landslide, landslip **2** = large amount, barrage, torrent, deluge, inundation

avant-garde (av-ong-**gard**) *n* **1** those artists, writers, or musicians whose techniques and ideas are in advance of those generally accepted ▸ *adj* **2** using ideas or techniques in advance of those generally accepted

> **avant-garde** *adj* = progressive, pioneering, experimental, innovative, unconventional, ground-breaking; ≠ conservative

avarice (**av**-a-riss) *n* extreme greed for wealth > **avaricious** *adj*

avast *interj naut* stop! cease!

avatar *n* **1** *Hinduism* the appearance of a god in human or animal form **2** a movable image that represents a person in a virtual environment, such as an online role-playing game

Ave. avenue

avenge *vb* **avenging**, **avenged** to inflict a punishment in retaliation for (harm done) or on behalf of (the person harmed) > **avenger** *n*

avenue *n* **1** a wide street **2** a road bordered by two rows of trees **3** a line of approach: *the United States was exhausting every avenue to achieve a diplomatic solution*

> **avenue** *n* **1** = street, way, course, drive, road, approach, route, path

aver (av-**vur**) *vb* **averring**, **averred** to state to be true > **averment** *n*

average *n* **1** the typical or normal amount or quality **2** the result obtained by adding the numbers or quantities in a set and dividing the total by the number of members in the set **3 on average** usually or typically ▸ *adj* **4** usual or typical **5** calculated as an average **6** mediocre or inferior ▸ *vb* **-aging, -aged 7** to calculate or estimate the average of **8** to amount to or be on average

> **average** *n* **1, 2** = standard, normal, usual, par, mode, mean, medium, norm **3 on average** = usually, generally, normally, typically, for the most part, as a rule ▸ *adj* **4** = usual, standard, general, normal, regular, ordinary, typical, commonplace; ≠ unusual **5** = mean, middle, medium, intermediate, median ▸ *vb* **8** = make on average, be on average, even out to, do on average, balance out to

averse *adj* opposed: *he's not averse to publicity, of the right kind*

aversion *n* **1** extreme dislike or disinclination **2** a person or thing that arouses this

avert *vb* **1** to turn away: *he had to avert his eyes* **2** to ward off: *a final attempt to avert war*

> **avert** *vb* **1** = turn away, turn aside **2** = ward off, avoid, prevent, frustrate, fend off, preclude, stave off, forestall, deflect

avian (**aiv**-ee-an) *adj* of or like a bird: *the treatment of avian diseases*

avian flu *n* another name for **bird flu**

aviary *n, pl* **aviaries** a large enclosure in which birds are kept

aviation *n* the art or science of flying aircraft

aviator *or fem* **aviatrix** *n old-fashioned* the pilot of an aircraft

avid *adj* **1** very keen or enthusiastic: *she is an avid football fan* **2** eager: *avid for economic development* > **avidity** *n* > **avidly** *adv*

avocado *n, pl* **-dos** a pear-shaped tropical fruit with a leathery green skin and greenish-yellow flesh

avocation *n* **1** *Brit, Austral & NZ old-fashioned* a person's regular job **2** *formal* a hobby

avocet *n* a long-legged shore bird with a long slender upward-curving bill

avoid *vb* **1** to refrain from doing **2** to prevent from happening **3** to keep out of the way of > **avoidable** *adj* > **avoidably** *adv* > **avoidance** *n*

> **avoid** *vb* **1** = refrain from, bypass, dodge, eschew, escape, duck (out of) (*informal*), fight shy of, shirk from **2** = prevent, stop, frustrate, hamper, foil, inhibit, avert, thwart **3** = keep away from, dodge, shun, evade, steer clear of, bypass

avoirdupois *or* **avoirdupois weight** (av-er-de-**poise**) *n* a system of weights based on the pound, which contains 16 ounces

avow *vb* **1** to state or affirm **2** to admit openly > **avowal** *n* > **avowed** *adj* > **avowedly** (a-**vow**-id-lee) *adv*

avuncular *adj* (of a man) friendly, helpful, and caring towards someone younger

await *vb* **1** to wait for **2** to be in store for

> **await** *vb* **1** = wait for, expect, look for, look forward to, anticipate, stay for **2** = be in store for, wait for, be ready for, lie in wait for, be in readiness for

awake *adj* **1** not sleeping **2** alert or aware: *awake to the danger* ▸ *vb* **awaking**, **awoke** *or* **awaked**, **awoken** *or* **awaked 3** to emerge or rouse from sleep **4** to become or cause to become alert

a

awake *adj* **1** = not sleeping, sleepless, wide-awake, aware, conscious, aroused, awakened, restless; ≠ asleep ▸ *vb* **3** = wake up, come to, wake, stir, awaken, rouse **4** = alert, stimulate, provoke, revive, arouse, stir up, kindle

awaken *vb* **1** to awake **2** to cause to be aware of: *anxieties awakened by reunification*

award *vb* **1** to give (something) for merit **2** *law* to declare to be entitled, such as by decision of a court ▸ *n* **3** something awarded, such as a prize ▸ *n* **4** *law* the decision of an arbitrator or court

award *vb* **1** = present with, give, grant, hand out, confer, endow, bestow **2** = grant, give, confer ▸ *n* **3** = prize, gift, trophy, decoration, grant, bonsela (*S African*), koha (NZ)

aware *adj* **1 aware of** knowing about: *he's at least aware of the problem* **2** informed: *they are becoming more politically aware every day* > **awareness** *n*

aware *adj* **2** = informed, enlightened, knowledgeable, learned, expert, versed, up to date, in the picture; ≠ ignorant

awash *adv, adj* washed over by water

away *adv* **1** from a particular place: *I saw them walk away and felt absolutely desolated* **2** in or to another, a usual, or a proper place: *he decided to put the car away in the garage* **3** at a distance: *keep away from the windows* **4** out of existence: *the pillars rotted away* **5** indicating motion or distance from a normal or proper place: *the girl shook her head and looked away* **6** continuously: *he continued to scribble away* ▸ *adj* **7** not present: *she had been away from home for years* **8** distant: *the castle was farther away than he had thought* **9** *sport* played on an opponent's ground

away *adv* **1** = off, elsewhere, abroad, hence, from here **3** = at a distance, far, apart, remote, isolated **6** = continuously, repeatedly, relentlessly, incessantly, interminably, unremittingly, uninterruptedly ▸ *adj* **7** = absent, out, gone, elsewhere, abroad, not here, not present, on vacation

awe *n* **1** wonder and respect mixed with dread ▸ *vb* **awing, awed 2** to inspire with reverence or dread

awe *n* = wonder, fear, respect, reverence, horror, terror, dread, admiration; ≠ contempt ▸ *vb* = impress, amaze, stun, frighten, terrify, astonish, horrify, intimidate

awesome *adj* **1** inspiring or displaying awe **2** *slang* excellent or outstanding

awesome *adj* **1** = awe-inspiring, amazing, stunning (*informal*), impressive, astonishing, formidable, intimidating, breathtaking

awestruck *adj* overcome or filled with awe

awful *adj* **1** very bad or unpleasant **2** *informal* considerable or great: *that's an awful lot of money, isn't it?* **3** *obsolete* inspiring reverence or dread ▸ *adv* **4** *not standard* very: *I'm working awful hard on my lines*

awfully *adv* **1** in an unpleasant way **2** *informal* very: *we were both awfully busy*

awfully *adv* **1** = badly, woefully, dreadfully, disgracefully, wretchedly, unforgivably, reprehensibly **2** = very, extremely, terribly, exceptionally, greatly, immensely, exceedingly, dreadfully

awhile *adv* for a brief period

awkward *adj* **1** clumsy or ungainly **2** embarrassed: *he was awkward and nervous around girls* **3** difficult to deal with: *the lawyer was in an awkward situation* **4** difficult to use or handle: *it was small but heavy enough to make it awkward to carry* **5** embarrassing: *there were several moments of awkward silence* > **awkwardly** *adv* > **awkwardness** *n*

awkward *adj* **1** = clumsy, lumbering, bumbling, unwieldy, ponderous, ungainly, gauche, gawky, unco (*Austral slang*); ≠ graceful **4** = inconvenient, difficult, troublesome, cumbersome, unwieldy, unmanageable, clunky (*informal*); ≠ convenient **5** = embarrassing, difficult, sensitive, delicate, uncomfortable, humiliating, disconcerting, inconvenient, barro (*Austral slang*); ≠ comfortable

awl *n* a pointed hand tool for piercing wood, leather, etc.

awning *n* a canvas roof supported by a frame to give protection against the weather

awoke *vb* a past tense and (now rare or dialectal) past participle of **awake**

awoken *vb* a past participle of **awake**

AWOL (eh-woll) *adj military* absent without leave but without intending to desert

awry (a-rye) *adv, adj* **1** with a twist to one side; askew: *my neck was really awry after the journey* **2** amiss or faulty: *if a gear gets stuck, the whole system goes awry*

axe *or US* **ax** *n, pl* **axes 1** a hand tool with one side of its head sharpened to a cutting edge, used for felling trees and splitting timber **2 an axe to grind** a favourite topic one wishes to promote **3** *informal* a severe cut in spending or in the number of staff employed ▸ *vb* **axing, axed 4** *informal* to dismiss (employees), restrict (expenditure), or terminate (a project)

axe *or* **ax** *n* **1** = hatchet, chopper, tomahawk, cleaver, adze ▸ *vb* = abandon, end, eliminate, cancel, scrap, cut back, terminate, dispense with

axial *adj* **1** forming or of an axis **2** in, on, or along an axis > **axially** *adv*

axil *n* the angle where the stalk of a leaf joins a stem

axiom *n* **1** a generally accepted principle **2** a self-evident statement

axiomatic *adj* **1** containing axioms **2** self-evident or obvious > **axiomatically** *adv*

axis (ax-iss) *n, pl* **axes** (ax-eez) **1** a real or imaginary line about which a body can rotate or about which an object or geometrical construction is symmetrical **2** one of two or three reference lines used in coordinate geometry to locate a point in a plane or in space

> **axis** *n* **1** = pivot, shaft, axle, spindle, centre line

axle *n* a shaft on which a wheel or pair of wheels revolves

axolotl *n* an aquatic salamander of N America

ayatollah *n* one of a class of Islamic religious leaders in Iran

aye *or* **ay** *interj* **1** *Brit, Austral & NZ* yes ▸ *n* **2** an affirmative vote or voter

azalea (az-**zale**-ya) *n* a garden shrub grown for its showy flowers

azimuth *n* **1** the arc of the sky between the zenith and the horizon **2** *surveying* the horizontal angle of a bearing measured clockwise from the north

Aztec *n* **1** a member of a Mexican Indian race who established a great empire, overthrown by the Spanish in the early 16th century **2** the language of the Aztecs ▸ *adj* **3** of the Aztecs or their language

azure *n* **1** the deep blue colour of a clear blue sky **2** *poetic* a clear blue sky ▸ *adj* **3** deep blue

BA 1 Bachelor of Arts **2** British Airways

baa *vb* **baaing, baaed 1** (of a sheep) to make a characteristic bleating sound ▸ *n* **2** the cry made by a sheep

baas *n S African offensive* a boss

babble *vb* **-bling, -bled 1** to talk in a quick, foolish, or muddled way **2** to make meaningless sounds: *children first gurgle and babble at random* **3** to disclose secrets carelessly **4** *literary* (of streams) to make a low murmuring sound ▸ *n* **5** muddled or foolish speech **6** a murmuring sound > **babbler** *n* > **babbling** *n*

babe *n* **1** a baby **2 babe in arms** *informal* a naive or inexperienced person **3** *informal* an attractive person, esp. a young woman

babel (**babe**-el) *n* **1** a confusion of noises or voices **2** a scene of noise and confusion

baboon *n* a medium-sized monkey with a long face, large teeth, and a fairly long tail

baby *n, pl* **-bies 1** a newborn child **2** the youngest or smallest of a family or group **3** a recently born animal **4** an immature person **5** *slang* a sweetheart **6** a project of personal concern **7 be left holding the baby** to be left with a responsibility ▸ *adj* **8** comparatively small of its type: *baby carrots* ▸ *vb* **-bies, -bying, -bied 9** to treat like a baby > **babyhood** *n* > **babyish** *adj*

> **baby** *n* **1** = child, infant, babe, bairn (*Scot, N English*), newborn child, babe in arms, ankle biter (*Austral slang*), tacker (*Austral slang*) ▸ *adj* = small, little, minute, tiny, mini, wee, miniature, petite

baby-sit *vb* **-sitting, -sat** to act or work as a baby-sitter > **baby-sitting** *n, adj*

baby-sitter *n* a person who takes care of a child while the parents are out

baccarat (**back**-a-rah) *n* a card game in which two or more punters gamble against the banker

bacchanalian (back-a-**nail**-ee-an) *adj literary* (of a party) unrestrained and involving a great deal of drinking and sometimes sexual activity

bach (batch) *NZ* ▸ *n* **1** a small holiday cottage ▸ *vb* **2** to look after oneself when one's spouse is away

bachelor *n* **1** an unmarried man **2** a person who holds a first degree from a university or college > **bachelorhood** *n*

bacillus (bass-**ill**-luss) *n, pl* **-li** (-lie) a rod-shaped bacterium, esp. one causing disease

b

back *n* **1** the rear part of the human body, from the neck to the pelvis **2** the spinal column **3** the part or side of an object opposite the front **4** the part of anything less often seen or used **5** *ball games* a defensive player or position **6 at the back of one's mind** not in one's conscious thoughts **7 behind someone's back** secretly or deceitfully **8 put** *or* **get someone's back up** to annoy someone **9 turn one's back on someone** to refuse to help someone ▶ *vb* **10** to move or cause to move backwards **11** to provide money for (a person or enterprise) **12** to bet on the success of: *to back a horse* **13** to provide (a pop singer) with a musical accompaniment **14** (foll. by *on* or *onto*) to have the back facing (towards): *his garden backs onto a school* **15** (of the wind) to change direction anticlockwise ▶ *adj* **16** situated behind: *back garden* **17** owing from an earlier date: *back rent* **18** remote: *a back road* ▶ *adv* **19** at, to, or towards the rear **20** to or towards the original starting point or condition: *I went back home* **21** in reply or retaliation: *to hit someone back* **22** in concealment or reserve: *to keep something back* **23 back and forth** to and fro **24 back to front** **A** in reverse **B** in disorder

> **back** *n* **2** = spine, backbone, vertebrae, spinal column, vertebral column **3** = rear; ≠ front **4** = reverse, rear, other side, wrong side, underside, flip side ▶ *vb* **11** = subsidize, help, support, sponsor, assist ▶ *adj* **16** = rear; ≠ front

backbencher *n* a Member of Parliament who does not hold office in the government or opposition

backbite *vb* **-biting, -bit, -bitten** *or* **-bit** to talk spitefully about an absent person > **backbiter** *n*

backbone *n* **1** the spinal column **2** strength of character **3** the part of something that gives it strength: *they formed the backbone of the regiment*

> **backbone** *n* **1** = spinal column, spine, vertebrae, vertebral column **2** = strength of character, character, resolution, nerve, daring, courage, determination, pluck

backchat *n informal* impudent replies

backcloth *n* a painted curtain at the back of a stage set. Also called: **backdrop**

backdate *vb* **-dating, -dated** to make (a document or arrangement) effective from a date earlier than its completion

backer *n* a person who gives financial or other support

> **backer** *n* = supporter, second, angel (*informal*), patron, promoter, subscriber, helper, benefactor

backfire *vb* **-firing, -fired 1** (of a plan or scheme) to fail to have the desired effect **2** (of an internal-combustion engine) to make a loud noise as a result of an explosion of unburnt gases in the exhaust system

> **backfire** *vb* **1** = fail, founder, flop (*informal*), rebound, boomerang, miscarry, misfire

backgammon *n* a game for two people played on a board with pieces moved according to throws of the dice

background *n* **1** the events or circumstances that help to explain something **2** a person's social class, education, or experience **3** the part of a scene furthest from the viewer **4** an inconspicuous position: *in the background* **5** the space behind the chief figures or objects in a picture

> **background** *n* **1** = circumstances, history, conditions, situation, atmosphere, environment, framework, ambience **2** = upbringing, history, culture, environment, tradition, circumstances

backhand *tennis & squash etc.* ▶ *adj* **1** (of a stroke) made from across the body with the back of the hand facing the direction of the stroke ▶ *n* **2** a backhand stroke

backhanded *adj* **1** (of a blow or shot) performed with the arm moving from across the body **2** ambiguous or implying criticism: *a backhanded compliment*

backhander *n* **1** *slang* a bribe **2** a backhanded stroke or blow

backing *n* **1** support **2** something that forms or strengthens the back of something **3** musical accompaniment for a pop singer

> **backing** *n* **1** = support, encouragement, endorsement, moral support

backlash *n* **1** a sudden and adverse reaction **2** a recoil between interacting badly fitting parts in machinery

> **backlash** *n* **1** = reaction, response, resistance, retaliation, repercussion, counterblast, counteraction

backlog *n* an accumulation of things to be dealt with

backpack *n* **1** a rucksack ▶ *vb* **2** to go hiking or travelling with a backpack > **backpacker** *n*

backside *n informal* the buttocks

backslide *vb* **-sliding, -slid** to relapse into former bad habits or vices > **backslider** *n*

backstage *adv* **1** behind the stage in a theatre ▶ *adj* **2** situated backstage

backstop *n* **1** *sport* a screen or fence to prevent balls leaving the playing area **2** a system that will come into effect if no other arrangement is made

backstroke *n swimming* a stroke performed on the back, using backward circular strokes of each arm

backtrack *vb* **1** to go back along the same route one has just travelled **2** to retract or reverse one's opinion or policy

back up *vb* **1** to support **2** *computers* to make a copy of (a data file), esp. as a security copy **3** (of traffic) to become jammed behind an obstruction ▸ *n* **backup 4** support or reinforcement **5** a reserve or substitute ▸ *adj* **backup 6** able to be substituted: *a backup copy*

backward *adj* **1** directed towards the rear **2** *sometimes offensive* slow in physical or material development **3** reluctant or bashful ▸ *adv* **4** same as **backwards** > **backwardness** *n*

> **backward** *adj* **2** = slow, behind, underdeveloped

backwards *or* **backward** *adv* **1** towards the rear **2** with the back foremost **3** in the reverse of the usual direction **4** into a worse state: *the Gothic novel's been going backwards since Radcliffe* **5 bend over backwards** *informal* to make a special effort to please someone

> **backwards** *or* **backward** *adv* **1, 2** = towards the rear, behind you, in reverse, rearwards

backwash *n* **1** water washed backwards by the motion of oars or a ship **2** an unpleasant aftereffect of an event or situation

backwater *n* **1** an isolated or backward place or condition **2** a body of stagnant water connected to a river

backwoods *pl n* **1** any remote, sparsely populated place **2** partially cleared, sparsely populated forests > **backwoodsman** *n*

bacon *n* **1** meat from the back and sides of a pig, dried, salted, and often smoked **2 bring home the bacon** *informal* **A** to achieve success **B** to provide material support

BACS Bankers' Automated Clearing System: a method of making payments directly to a creditor's bank

bacteria *pl n*, *sing* **-rium** a large group of microorganisms, many of which cause disease > **bacterial** *adj*

> **bacteria** *pl n* = microorganisms, viruses, bugs (*slang*), germs, microbes, pathogens, bacilli

bacteriology *n* the study of bacteria > **bacteriologist** *n*

bad *adj* **worse**, **worst 1** not good; of poor quality **2** lacking skill or talent: *I'm so bad at that sort of thing* **3** harmful: *smoking is bad for you* **4** evil or immoral **5** naughty or mischievous **6** rotten or decayed: *a bad egg* **7** severe: *a bad headache* **8** incorrect or faulty: *bad grammar* **9** sorry or upset: *I feel bad about saying no* **10** unfavourable or distressing: *bad news* **11** offensive or unpleasant: *bad language* **12** not valid: *a bad cheque* **13** not recoverable: *a bad debt* **14 badder**, **baddest** *slang* good; excellent **15 not bad** *or* **not so bad** *informal* fairly good **16 too bad** *informal* (often used dismissively) regrettable ▸ *n* **17** unfortunate or unpleasant events: *you've got to take the good with the bad* ▸ *adv* **18** *not standard* badly: *to want something bad* > **badness** *n*

bad *adj* **1, 3** = harmful, damaging, dangerous, destructive, unhealthy, detrimental, hurtful, ruinous; ≠ beneficial **2** = incompetent, poor, useless (*informal*), incapable, unfit, inexpert **4** = wicked, criminal, evil, corrupt, immoral, sinful, depraved; ≠ virtuous **5** = naughty, defiant, wayward, mischievous, wicked, unruly, impish, undisciplined; ≠ well-behaved **6** = rotten, off, rank, sour, rancid, mouldy, putrid, festy (*Austral slang*) **10** = unfavourable, distressing, unfortunate, grim, unpleasant, gloomy, adverse

bade *or* **bad** *vb* a past tense of **bid**

badge *n* **1** a distinguishing emblem or mark worn to show membership or achievement **2** any revealing feature or mark

> **badge** *n* **1** = image, brand, stamp, identification, crest, emblem, insignia **2** = mark, sign, token

badger *n* **1** a stocky burrowing mammal with a black and white striped head ▸ *vb* **2** to pester or harass

> **badger** *vb* = pester, harry, bother, bug (*informal*), bully, plague, hound, harass

badinage (**bad**-in-nahzh) *n* playful and witty conversation

badly *adv* **worse**, **worst 1** poorly; inadequately **2** unfavourably: *our plan worked out badly* **3** severely: *badly damaged* **4** very much: *he badly needed to improve his image* **5 badly off** poor

> **badly** *adv* **1** = poorly, incorrectly, carelessly, inadequately, imperfectly, ineptly; ≠ well **2** = unfavourably, unsuccessfully **3** = severely, greatly, deeply, seriously, desperately, intensely, exceedingly

badminton *n* a game played with rackets and a shuttlecock which is hit back and forth across a high net

Bafana Bafana (bah-**fan**-na) *pl n S African* the South African national soccer team

baffle *vb* **-fling**, **-fled 1** to perplex ▸ *n* **2** a mechanical device to limit or regulate the flow of fluid, light, or sound > **bafflement** *n* > **baffling** *adj*

> **baffle** *vb* = puzzle, confuse, stump, bewilder, confound, perplex, mystify, flummox; ≠ explain

bag *n* **1** a flexible container with an opening at one end **2** the contents of such a container **3** a piece of luggage **4** a handbag **5** a loose fold of skin under the eyes **6** any sac in the body of an animal **7** *derogatory slang* an ugly or bad-tempered woman: *an old bag* **8** the amount of game taken by a hunter **9 in the bag** *slang* assured of succeeding ▸ *vb* **bagging**, **bagged 10** to put into a bag **11** to bulge or cause to bulge **12** to capture or kill, as in hunting **13** *informal* to succeed in securing: *he bagged the best chair*

b

bag n **1** = sack, container, sac, receptacle ► vb **12** = catch, kill, shoot, capture, acquire, trap **13** = get, land (informal), score (slang), capture, acquire, procure

bagatelle n **1** something of little value **2** a board game in which balls are struck into holes **3** a short piece of music

bagel (bay-gl) n a hard ring-shaped bread roll

baggage n **1** suitcases packed for a journey **2** an army's portable equipment **3** informal previous knowledge or experience that may have an influence in new circumstances: cultural baggage

baggage n **1** = luggage, things, cases, bags, equipment, gear, suitcases, belongings

baggy adj **-gier, -giest** (of clothes) hanging loosely > **bagginess** n

baggy adj = loose, slack, bulging, sagging, sloppy, floppy, roomy, ill-fitting; ≠ tight

bagpipes pl n a musical wind instrument in which sounds are produced in reed pipes by air from an inflated bag

bail¹ law ► n **1** a sum of money deposited with the court as security for a person's reappearance in court **2** the person giving such security **3** **jump bail** to fail to reappear in court after bail has been paid **4** **stand** or **go bail** to act as surety for someone ► vb **5** (foll. by out) to obtain the release of (a person) from custody by depositing money with the court

bail n **1** = security, bond, guarantee, pledge, warranty, surety

bail² or **bale** vb **bail out** to remove water from (a boat)

bail³ n **1** cricket either of two small wooden bars across the tops of the stumps **2** a partition between stalls in a stable or barn **3** Austral & NZ a framework in a cow shed used to secure the head of a cow during milking **4** a movable bar on a typewriter that holds the paper against the roller

bailey n the outermost wall or court of a castle

bailiff n **1** Brit a sheriff's officer who serves writs and summonses **2** the agent of a landlord or landowner

bairn n Scot & N English a child

bait n **1** something edible fixed to a hook or in a trap to attract fish or animals **2** an enticement ► vb **3** to put a piece of food on or in (a hook or trap) **4** to persecute or tease **5** to set dogs upon (a bear or badger)

bait n **2** = lure, attraction, incentive, carrot (informal), temptation, snare, inducement, decoy ► vb **4** = tease, annoy, irritate, bother, mock, wind up (Brit slang), hound, torment

baize n a feltlike woollen fabric, usually green, which is used for the tops of billiard and card tables

bake vb **baking, baked 1** to cook by dry heat in an oven **2** to cook bread, pastry, or cakes **3** to make or become hardened by heat **4** informal to be extremely hot

bakeoff n a baking competition

baker n a person who makes or sells bread, cakes, etc.

baker's dozen n thirteen

bakery n, pl **-eries** a place where bread, cakes, etc. are made or sold

baking powder n a powdered mixture that contains sodium bicarbonate and cream of tartar: used in baking as a raising agent

bakkie (buck-ee) n S African a small truck with an enclosed cab and an open goods area at the back

bakkie n = truck, pick-up, van, lorry, pick-up truck

Balaclava or **Balaclava helmet** n a close-fitting woollen hood that covers the ears and neck

balalaika n a Russian musical instrument with a triangular body and three strings

balance n **1** stability of mind or body: lose one's balance **2** a state of being in balance **3** harmony in the parts of a whole **4** the power to influence or control: the balance of power **5** something that remains: the balance of what you owe **6** accounting **A** the matching of debit and credit totals in an account **B** a difference between such totals **7** a weighing device **8** **in the balance** in an undecided condition **9** **on balance** after weighing up all the factors ► vb **-ancing, -anced 10** to weigh in or as if in a balance **11** to be or come into equilibrium **12** to bring into or hold in equilibrium **13** to compare the relative weight or importance of **14** to arrange so as to create a state of harmony **15** accounting to compare or equalize the credit and debit totals of (an account)

balance n **1** = equilibrium, stability, steadiness, evenness; ≠ instability **2** = stability, equanimity, steadiness **5, 6B** = remainder, rest, difference, surplus, residue ► vb **10, 13** = weigh, consider, compare, estimate, contrast, assess, evaluate, set against **12** = stabilize, level, steady; ≠ overbalance **15** = calculate, total, determine, estimate, settle, count, square, reckon

balcony n, pl **-nies 1** a platform projecting from a building with a balustrade along its outer edge, often with access from a door **2** an upper tier of seats in a theatre or cinema

balcony n **1** = terrace, veranda **2** = upper circle, gods, gallery

bald adj **1** having no hair or fur, esp. of a person having no hair on the scalp **2** lacking natural covering **3** plain or blunt: the bald facts **4** (of a tyre) having a worn tread > **baldly** adv > **baldness** n

bald *adj* **1** = hairless, depilated, baldheaded **3** = plain, direct, frank, straightforward, blunt, rude, forthright, unadorned

balderdash *n* stupid or illogical talk

balding *adj* becoming bald

bale¹ *n* **1** a large bundle of hay or goods bound by ropes or wires for storage or transportation ▸ *vb* **baling, baled** **2** to make (hay) or put (goods) into a bale or bales

bale² *vb* **baling, baled** same as **bail²**

baleful *adj* harmful, menacing, or vindictive > **balefully** *adv*

balk *or* **baulk** *vb* **1** to stop short: *the horse balked at the jump* **2** to recoil: *France balked at the parliament having a veto* **3** to thwart, check, or foil: *he was balked in his plans*

Balkan *adj* of any of the countries of the Balkan Peninsula in SE Europe, between the Adriatic and Aegean Seas

ball¹ *n* **1** a spherical or nearly spherical mass: *a ball of wool* **2** a round or roundish object used in various games **3** a single delivery of the ball in a game **4** any more or less rounded part of the body: *the ball of the foot* **5** **have the ball at one's feet** to have the chance of doing something **6** **on the ball** *informal* alert; informed **7** **play ball** *informal* to cooperate **8** **set** *or* **keep the ball rolling** to initiate or maintain the progress of an action, discussion, or project ▸ *vb* **9** to form into a ball

ball *n* **1** = sphere, drop, globe, pellet, orb, globule, spheroid

ball² *n* **1** a lavish or formal social function for dancing **2** **have a ball** *informal* to have a very enjoyable time

ballad *n* **1** a narrative song or poem often with a chorus that is repeated **2** a slow sentimental song

ballast *n* **1** a substance, such as sand, used to stabilize a ship when it is not carrying cargo **2** crushed rock used for the foundation of a road or railway track ▸ *vb* **3** to give stability or weight to

ball cock *n* a device consisting of a floating ball and valve for regulating the flow of liquid into a tank or cistern

ballerina *n* a female ballet dancer

ballet *n* **1** a classical style of expressive dancing based on precise conventional steps **2** a theatrical representation of a story performed by ballet dancers > **balletic** *adj*

ballistic missile *n* a launched weapon which is guided automatically in flight but falls freely at its target

ballistics *n* the study of the flight of projectiles, often in relation to firearms > **ballistic** *adj*

balloon *n* **1** an inflatable rubber bag used as a plaything or party decoration **2** a large bag inflated with a lighter-than-air gas, designed to rise and float in the atmosphere with a basket for carrying passengers **3** an outline containing the words or thoughts of a character in a cartoon ▸ *vb* **4** to fly in a balloon **5** to swell or increase rapidly in size: *the cost of health care has ballooned* > **balloonist** *n*

balloon *vb* **5** = expand, rise, increase, swell, blow up, inflate, bulge, billow

ballot *n* **1** the practice of selecting a representative or course of action by voting **2** the number of votes cast in an election **3** the actual vote or paper indicating a person's choice ▸ *vb* **-loting, -loted** **4** to vote or ask for a vote from: *we balloted the members on this issue* **5** to vote for or decide on something by ballot

ballot *n* **1** = vote, election, voting, poll, polling, referendum, show of hands

ballpoint *or* **ballpoint pen** *n* a pen which has a small ball bearing as a writing point

ballroom *n* a large hall for dancing

ballyhoo *n informal* unnecessary or exaggerated fuss

balm *n* **1** an aromatic substance obtained from certain tropical trees and used for healing and soothing **2** something comforting or soothing: *her calmness was like a balm to my troubled mind* **3** an aromatic herb, lemon balm

balmy *adj* **balmier, balmiest** **1** (of weather) mild and pleasant **2** same as **barmy**

baloney *or* **boloney** *n informal* nonsense

balsa (bawl-sa) *n* **1** a tree of tropical America which yields light wood **2** Also: **balsawood** the light wood of this tree, used for making rafts, models, etc.

balsam *n* **1** an aromatic resin obtained from various trees and shrubs and used in medicines and perfumes **2** any plant yielding balsam **3** a flowering plant, such as busy lizzie

baluster *n* a set of posts supporting a rail

balustrade *n* an ornamental rail supported by a set of posts

bamboo *n* a tall treelike tropical grass with hollow stems which are used to make canes, furniture, etc.

bamboozle *vb* **-zling, -zled** *informal* **1** to cheat; mislead **2** to confuse > **bamboozlement** *n*

BAME Black, Asian, and minority ethnic

ban *vb* **banning, banned** **1** to prohibit or forbid officially ▸ *n* **2** an official prohibition

ban *vb* = prohibit, bar, block, veto, forbid, boycott, outlaw, banish; ≠ permit ▸ *n* = prohibition, restriction, veto, boycott, embargo, injunction, taboo, disqualification, rahui (NZ), restraining order (US law); ≠ permission

banal (ban-nahl) *adj* lacking originality > **banality** *n*

banana *n* a crescent-shaped fruit that grows on a tropical or subtropical treelike plant

band¹ *n* **1** a group of musicians playing together, esp. on brass or percussion instruments **2** a group of people having a common purpose: *a band of revolutionaries* ▸ *vb* **3** (foll. by *together*) to unite

> **band** *n* **1** = ensemble, group, orchestra, combo **2** = gang, company, group, party, team, body, crowd, pack

band² *n* **1** a strip of some material, used to hold objects together: *a rubber band* **2** a strip of fabric used as an ornament or to reinforce clothing **3** a stripe of contrasting colour or texture **4** a driving belt in machinery **5** *physics* a range of frequencies or wavelengths between two limits ▸ *vb* **6** to fasten or mark with a band

> **band** *n* **2** = headband, strip, ribbon

bandage *n* **1** a piece of material used to dress a wound or wrap an injured limb ▸ *vb* **-daging, -daged 2** to cover or wrap with a bandage

> **bandage** *n* = dressing, plaster, compress, gauze ▸ *vb* = dress, cover, bind, swathe

bandanna or **bandana** *n* a large brightly-coloured handkerchief or neckerchief

B & B bed and breakfast

bandicoot *n* **1** an Australian marsupial with a long pointed muzzle and a long tail **2 bandicoot rat** any of three burrowing rats of S and SE Asia

bandit *n* a robber, esp. a member of an armed gang > **banditry** *n*

> **bandit** *n* = robber, outlaw, raider, plunderer, mugger (*informal*), looter, highwayman or woman, desperado

bandolier *n* a shoulder belt with small pockets for cartridges

bandsman *n, pl* **-men** a player in a musical band

bandstand *n* a roofed outdoor platform for a band

bandwagon *n* **jump** or **climb on the bandwagon** to join a popular party or movement that seems assured of success

bandwidth *n* the range of frequencies used for transmitting electronic information

bandy *adj* **-dier, -diest 1** Also: **bandy-legged** having legs curved outwards at the knees **2** (of legs) curved outwards at the knees ▸ *vb* **-dies, -dying, -died 3** to exchange (words), sometimes in a heated manner **4 bandy about** to use (a name, term, etc.) frequently

bane *n* a person or thing that causes misery or distress: *the bane of my life* > **baneful** *adj*

bang *n* **1** a short loud explosive noise, such as the report of a gun **2** a hard blow or loud knock **3** *vulgar slang* an act of sexual intercourse **4 with a bang** successfully: *the party went with a bang* ▸ *vb* **5** to hit or knock, esp. with a loud noise **6** to close (a door) noisily **7** to make or cause to make a loud noise, as of an explosion **8** *vulgar slang* to have sexual intercourse with ▸ *adv* **9** with a sudden impact: *the car drove bang into a lamppost* **10** precisely: *bang in the middle*

bang *n* **1** = explosion, pop, clash, crack, blast, slam, discharge, thump **2** = blow, knock, stroke, punch, bump, sock (*slang*), smack, thump ▸ *vb* **5** = hit, strike, knock, belt (*informal*), slam, thump, clatter, beat or knock seven bells out of (*informal*) **7** = resound, boom, explode, thunder, thump, clang ▸ *adv* **10** = exactly, straight, square, squarely, precisely, slap, smack (*informal*), plumb (*informal*)

banger *n* **1** *Brit & Austral informal* an old decrepit car **2** *slang* a sausage **3** a firework that explodes loudly

bangle *n* a bracelet worn round the arm or sometimes round the ankle

banish *vb* **1** to send into exile **2** to drive away: *it's the only way to banish weeds from the garden* > **banishment** *n*

> **banish** *vb* **1** = expel, exile, outlaw, deport; ≠ admit **2** = get rid of, remove

banisters or **bannisters** *pl n* the railing and supporting balusters on a staircase

banjo *n, pl* **-jos** or **-joes** a stringed musical instrument with a long neck and a circular drumlike body > **banjoist** *n*

bank¹ *n* **1** an institution offering services, such as the safekeeping and lending of money at interest **2** the building used by such an institution **3** the funds held by a banker or dealer in some gambling games **4** any supply, store, or reserve: *a data bank* ▸ *vb* **5** to deposit (cash or a cheque) in a bank **6** to transact business with a bank ▸ See also **bank on**

> **bank** *n* **1** = financial institution, repository, depository **4** = store, fund, stock, source, supply, reserve, pool, reservoir ▸ *vb* **5** = deposit, keep, save

bank² *n* **1** a long raised mass, esp. of earth **2** a slope, as of a hill **3** the sloping side and ground on either side of a river ▸ *vb* **4** to form into a bank or mound **5** to cover (a fire) with ashes and fuel so that it will burn slowly **6** (of an aircraft) to tip to one side in turning

> **bank** *n* **2** = mound, banking, rise, hill, mass, pile, heap, ridge, kopje or koppie (*S African*) **3** = side, edge, margin, shore, brink ▸ *vb* **6** = tilt, tip, pitch, heel, slope, incline, slant, cant

bank³ *n* **1** an arrangement of similar objects in a row or in tiers ▸ *vb* **2** to arrange in a bank

> **bank** *n* = row, group, line, range, series, file, rank, sequence

banker *n* **1** a person who owns or manages a bank **2** the keeper of the bank in various gambling games

banking *n* the business engaged in by a bank

banknote *n* a piece of paper money issued by a central bank

bank on *vb* to rely on

bankrupt *n* **1** a person, declared by a court to be unable to pay his or her debts, whose property is sold and the proceeds distributed among the creditors **2** a person no longer having a particular quality: *a spiritual bankrupt* ▸ *adj* **3** declared insolvent **4** financially ruined **5** no longer having a particular quality: *morally bankrupt* ▸ *vb* **6** to make bankrupt › **bankruptcy** *n*

> **bankrupt** *adj* **3, 4** = insolvent, broke (*informal*), ruined, wiped out (*informal*), impoverished, in the red, destitute, gone bust (*informal*); ≠ solvent

banksia *n* an Australian evergreen tree or shrub

banner *n* **1** a long strip of material displaying a slogan, advertisement, etc. **2** a placard carried in a demonstration **3** Also called: **banner headline** a large headline in a newspaper extending across the page **4** an advertisement, often animated, that extends across the width of a web page

> **banner** *n* **1** = flag, standard, colours, pennant, ensign, streamer **2** = placard

banns *pl n* the public announcement of an intended marriage

banquet *n* **1** an elaborate formal dinner often followed by speeches ▸ *vb* **-queting, -queted** **2** to hold or take part in a banquet

> **banquet** *n* = feast, spread (*informal*), dinner, meal, revel, repast, hakari (*NZ*)

banshee *n* (in Irish folklore) a female spirit whose wailing warns of a coming death

bantam *n* **1** a small breed of domestic fowl **2** a small but aggressive person

bantamweight *n* a professional boxer weighing up to 118 pounds (53.5 kg) or an amateur weighing up to 119 pounds (54 kg)

banter *vb* **1** to tease jokingly ▸ *n* **2** teasing or joking conversation

Bantu *n* **1** a group of languages of Africa **2** *pl* **-tu** or **-tus** *offensive* a Black speaker of a Bantu language ▸ *adj* **3** of the Bantu languages

baobab (bay-oh-bab) *n* an African tree with a massive grey trunk, short angular branches, and large pulpy fruit

baptism *n* a Christian religious rite in which a person is immersed in or sprinkled with water as a sign of being cleansed from sin and accepted as a member of the Church › **baptismal** *adj*

Baptist *n* **1** a member of a Protestant denomination that believes in the necessity of adult baptism by immersion **2 the Baptist** John the Baptist ▸ *adj* **3** of the Baptist Church

baptize *or* **-tise** *vb* **-tizing, -tized** *or* **-tising, -tised** **1** *Christianity* to immerse (a person) in water or sprinkle water on (him or her) as part of the rite of baptism **2** to give a name to

bar¹ *n* **1** a rigid usually straight length of metal, wood, etc. used as a barrier or structural part **2** a solid usually rectangular block of any material: *a bar of soap* **3** anything that obstructs or prevents: *a bar to mobility* **4** a counter or room where alcoholic drinks are served **5** a narrow band or stripe, as of colour or light **6** a heating element in an electric fire **7** See **Bar** **8** the place in a court of law where the accused stands during trial **9** *music* a group of beats that is repeated with a consistent rhythm throughout a piece of music **10** *football etc.* same as **crossbar** **11** *heraldry* a narrow horizontal line across a shield **12 behind bars** in prison ▸ *vb* **barring, barred** **13** to secure with a bar: *to bar the door* **14** to obstruct: *the fallen tree barred the road* **15** to exclude: *he was barred from membership of the club* **16** to mark with a bar or bars ▸ *prep* **17** except for

> **bar** *n* **1** = rod, staff, stick, stake, rail, pole, paling, shaft **3** = obstacle, block, barrier, hurdle, hitch, barricade, snag, deterrent; ≠ aid **4** = public house, pub (*informal, chiefly Brit*), counter, inn, saloon, tavern, canteen, watering hole (*facetious slang*), beer parlour (*Canad*) ▸ *vb* **13** = lock, block, secure, attach, bolt, blockade, barricade, fortify **14** = block, restrict, restrain, hamper, thwart, hinder, obstruct, impede **15** = exclude, ban, forbid, prohibit, keep out of, disallow, shut out of, blackball; ≠ admit

bar² *n* a unit of pressure equal to 10^5 newtons per square metre

Bar *n* **1 the Bar** barristers collectively **2 be called to the Bar** *Brit* to become a barrister

barb *n* **1** a cutting remark **2** a point facing in the opposite direction to the main point of a fish-hook, harpoon, etc. **3** a beardlike growth, hair, or projection ▸ *vb* **4** to provide with a barb or barbs › **barbed** *adj*

barbarian *n* **1** a member of a primitive or uncivilized people **2** a coarse or vicious person ▸ *adj* **3** uncivilized or brutal

> **barbarian** *n* **2** = lout, yahoo, bigot, philistine, hoon (*Austral, NZ informal*), cougan (*Austral slang*), scozza (*Austral slang*), bogan (*Austral slang*), boor, vulgarian

barbaric *adj* primitive or brutal

barbarism *n* **1** a brutal, coarse, or ignorant act **2** the condition of being backward, coarse, or ignorant **3** a substandard word or expression

barbarity *n, pl* **-ties** **1** the state of being barbaric or barbarous **2** a vicious act

barbarous *adj* **1** uncivilized: *a barbarous and uninhabitable jungle* **2** brutal or cruel: *the barbarous tortures inflicted on them*

barbecue *n* **1** a grill on which food is cooked over hot charcoal, usually out of doors **2** food cooked over hot charcoal, usually out of doors **3** a party or picnic at which barbecued food is served ▸ *vb* **-cuing, -cued** **4** to cook on a grill, usually over charcoal

b

b

barbed wire *n* strong wire with sharp points protruding at close intervals

barber *n* a person whose business is cutting men's hair and shaving beards

barbiturate *n* a derivative of barbituric acid used in medicine as a sedative

bar code *n* an arrangement of numbers and parallel lines on a package, which can be electronically scanned at a checkout to give the price of the goods

bard *n* 1 *archaic or literary* a poet 2 **A** (formerly) an ancient Celtic poet **B** a poet who wins a verse competition at a Welsh eisteddfod 3 **the Bard** William Shakespeare, English playwright and poet

bare *adj* 1 unclothed: used esp. of a part of the body 2 without the natural, conventional, or usual covering: *bare trees* 3 lacking appropriate furnishings, etc.: *a bare room* 4 simple: *the bare facts* 5 just sufficient: *the bare minimum* ▸ *vb* **baring, bared** 6 to uncover > **bareness** *n*

> **bare** *adj* 1 = naked, nude, stripped, uncovered, undressed, unclothed, unclad, without a stitch on (*informal*); ≠ dressed 2 = simple, spare, stark, austere, spartan, unadorned, unembellished, unornamented, bare-bones; ≠ adorned 4 = plain, simple, basic, obvious, sheer, patent, evident, stark

bareback *adj, adv* (of horse-riding) without a saddle

bare-faced *or* **barefaced** *adj* obvious or shameless: *a bare-faced lie*

barefoot *or* **barefooted** *adj, adv* with the feet uncovered

barely *adv* 1 only just: *barely enough* 2 scantily: *barely furnished*

> **barely** *adv* 1 = only just, just, hardly, scarcely, at a push; ≠ completely

bargain *n* 1 an agreement establishing what each party will give, receive, or perform in a transaction 2 something acquired or received in such an agreement 3 something bought or offered at a low price 4 **drive a hard bargain** to forcefully pursue one's own profit in a transaction 5 **into the bargain** besides ▸ *vb* 6 to negotiate the terms of an agreement or transaction

> **bargain** *n* 1 = agreement, deal (*informal*), promise, contract, arrangement, settlement, pledge, pact 3 = good buy, discount purchase, good deal, steal (*informal*), snip (*informal*), giveaway, cheap purchase ▸ *vb* = negotiate, deal, contract, mediate, covenant, stipulate, transact, cut a deal

bargain for *vb* to anticipate

barge *n* 1 a flat-bottomed boat, used for transporting freight, esp. on canals 2 a boat, often decorated, used in pageants, etc. ▸ *vb* **barging, barged** *informal* 3 (foll. by *into*) to bump into 4 to push one's way violently 5 (foll. by *into* or *in*) to interrupt rudely: *he barged into our conversation*

> **barge** *n* 1 = canal boat, lighter, narrow boat, flatboat

barista (bar-ee-sta) *n* a person who makes and sells coffee in a coffee bar

baritone *n* 1 the second lowest adult male voice 2 a singer with such a voice

barium (bare-ee-um) *n* *chem* a soft silvery-white metallic chemical element. Symbol: **Ba**

bark[1] *n* 1 the loud harsh cry of a dog or certain other animals ▸ *vb* 2 (of a dog or other animal) to make its typical cry 3 to shout in an angry tone: *he barked an order* 4 **bark up the wrong tree** *informal* to misdirect one's attention or efforts

> **bark** *n* = yap, bay, howl, snarl, growl, yelp, woof ▸ *vb* 2 = yap, bay, howl, snarl, growl, yelp, woof

bark[2] *n* 1 an outer protective layer of dead corklike cells on the trunks of trees ▸ *vb* 2 to scrape or rub off (skin), as in an injury 3 to remove the bark from (a tree)

> **bark** *n* = covering, casing, cover, skin, layer, crust, cortex (*anatomy, botany*), rind

barley *n* 1 a tall grasslike plant with dense bristly flower spikes, widely cultivated for grain 2 the grain of this grass used in making beer and whisky and for soups

barman *n, pl* **-men** a man who serves in a pub

barmy *adj* **-mier, -miest** *slang* foolish or slightly crazy: *a barmy idea*

barn *n* a large farm outbuilding, chiefly for storing grain, but also for livestock

barnacle *n* a marine shellfish that lives attached to rocks, ship bottoms, etc. > **barnacled** *adj*

barney *n* *informal* a noisy fight or argument

barometer *n* an instrument for measuring atmospheric pressure, used to determine weather or altitude changes > **barometric** *adj*

baron *n* 1 a member of the lowest rank of nobility in the British Isles 2 a powerful business owner or financier: *a press baron* > **baronial** *adj*

baroness *n* 1 a woman holding the rank of baron 2 the wife or widow of a baron

baronet *n* a commoner who holds the lowest hereditary British title > **baronetcy** *n*

baroque (bar-rock) *n* 1 a highly ornate style of architecture and art, popular in Europe from the late 16th to the early 18th century 2 a highly ornamented 17th-century style of music ▸ *adj* 3 ornate in style

barque (bark) *n* 1 a sailing ship, esp. one with three masts 2 *poetic* any boat

barrack[1] *vb* to house (soldiers) in barracks

barrack[2] *vb* 1 *Brit, Austral & NZ informal* to criticize loudly or shout against (a team or speaker)

b

2 *Austral & NZ* (foll. by *for*) to shout encouragement for (a team)

barracks *pl n* **1** a building or group of buildings used to accommodate military personnel **2** a large and bleak building

> **barracks** *pl n* **1** = camp, quarters, garrison, encampment, billet

barracuda (bar-rack-**kew**-da) *n*, *pl* **-da** *or* **-das** a tropical fish which feeds on other fishes

barrage (bar-**rahzh**) *n* **1** a continuous delivery of questions, complaints, etc. **2** *military* the continuous firing of artillery over a wide area **3** a construction built across a river to control the water level

> **barrage** *n* **1** = torrent, mass, burst, stream, hail, spate, onslaught, deluge
> **2** = bombardment, attack, bombing, assault, shelling, battery, volley, blitz

barramundi *n* an edible Australian fish

barrel *n* **1** a cylindrical container, usually with rounded sides and flat ends, and held together by metal hoops **2** a unit of capacity of varying amount in different industries **3** the tube through which the bullet of a firearm is fired **4 over a barrel** *informal* powerless ▸ *vb* **-relling, -relled** *or US* **-reling, -reled 5** to put into a barrel or barrels

barrel organ *n* a musical instrument played by turning a handle

barren *adj* **1** incapable of producing offspring **2** unable to support the growth of crops, fruit, etc.: *barren land* **3** unprofitable or unsuccessful: *the team has had a barren season* **4** dull ▸ **barrenness** *n*

> **barren** *adj* **1** = infertile, sterile, unproductive

barricade *n* **1** a barrier, esp. one erected hastily for defence ▸ *vb* **-cading, -caded 2** to erect a barricade across (an entrance)

> **barricade** *n* = barrier, wall, fence, blockade, obstruction, rampart, bulwark, palisade ▸ *vb* = bar, block, defend, secure, lock, bolt, blockade, fortify

barrier *n* **1** anything that blocks a way or separates, such as a gate **2** anything that prevents progress: *a barrier of distrust* **3** anything that separates or hinders union: *a language barrier*

> **barrier** *n* **1** = barricade, wall, bar, fence, boundary, obstacle, blockade, obstruction

barring *prep* unless something occurs; except for

barrister *n* a lawyer who is qualified to plead in the higher courts

barrow¹ *n* **1** same as **wheelbarrow 2** a handcart used by street traders

barrow² *n* a heap of earth placed over a prehistoric tomb

bartender *n* a person who serves drinks behind a bar

barter *vb* **1** to trade goods or services in exchange

for other goods or services, rather than for money ▸ *n* **2** trade by the exchange of goods

basalt (**bass**-awlt) *n* a dark volcanic rock
> **basaltic** *adj*

base¹ *n* **1** the bottom or supporting part of anything **2** the fundamental principle or part: *agriculture was the economic base of the city's growth* **3** a centre of operations, organization, or supply **4** a starting point: *the new discovery became the base for further research* **5** the main ingredient of a mixture: *to use rice as a base in cookery* **6** *chem* a compound that combines with an acid to form a salt **7** the lower side or face of a geometric construction **8** *maths* the number of units in a counting system that is equivalent to one in the next higher counting place: *10 is the base of the decimal system* **9** a starting or finishing point in any of various games ▸ *vb* **basing, based 10** (foll. by *on* or *upon*) to use as a basis for **11** (foll. by *at* or *in*) to station, post, or place

> **base** *n* **1** = bottom, floor, lowest part; ≠ top **2** = foundation, institution, organization, establishment, starting point **3** = centre, post, station, camp, settlement, headquarters ▸ *vb* **10** = ground, found, build, establish, depend, construct, derive, hinge **11** = place, set, post, station, establish, locate, install

base² *adj* **1** dishonourable or immoral: *base motives* **2** of inferior quality or value: *a base coin* **3** debased; counterfeit: *base currency*

> **base** *adj* **1** = dishonourable, evil, disgraceful, shameful, immoral, wicked, sordid, despicable, scungy (*Austral, NZ*); ≠ honourable

baseball *n* **1** a team game in which the object is to score runs by batting the ball and running round all four bases **2** the ball used in this game

baseless *adj* not based on fact

basement *n* a partly or wholly underground storey of a building

bash *informal* ▸ *vb* **1** to strike violently or crushingly **2** (foll. by *into*) to crash into ▸ *n* **3** a heavy blow **4 have a bash** *informal* to make an attempt

> **bash** *vb* **1** = hit, beat, strike, knock, smash, belt (*informal*), slap, sock (*slang*)

bashful *adj* shy or modest ▸ **bashfully** *adv*

basic *adj* **1** of or forming a base or basis **2** elementary or simple: *a few basic facts* **3** excluding additions or extras: *basic pay* **4** *chem* of or containing a base ▸ *n* **5 basics** fundamental principles, facts, etc. ▸ **basically** *adv*

> **basic** *adj* **1** = fundamental, main, essential, primary, vital, principal, cardinal, elementary; ≠ secondary **2** = plain, simple, classic, unfussy, unembellished, bare-bones, lo-fi ▸ *n* = essentials, principles, fundamentals, nuts and bolts (*informal*), nitty-gritty (*informal*), rudiments, brass tacks (*informal*)

b

BASIC *n* a computer programming language that uses common English terms

basil *n* an aromatic herb used for seasoning food

basilica *n* **1** a Roman building, used for public administration, which is rectangular with two aisles and a rounded end **2** a Christian church of similar design

basilisk *n* (in classical legend) a serpent that could kill by its breath or glance

basin *n* **1** a round wide container open at the top **2** the amount a basin will hold **3** a washbasin or sink **4** any partially enclosed area of water where ships or boats may be moored **5** the catchment area of a particular river **6** a depression in the earth's surface

basis *n*, *pl* **bases 1** something that underlies, supports, or is essential to an idea, belief, etc. **2** a principle on which something depends

> **basis** *n* = foundation, support, base, ground, footing, bottom, groundwork

bask *vb* (foll. by *in*) **1** to lie in or be exposed (to pleasant warmth or sunshine) **2** to enjoy (approval or favourable conditions)

> **bask** *vb* **1** = lie, relax, lounge, sprawl, loaf, lie about, swim in, sunbathe, outspan (*S African*)

basket *n* **1** a container made of interwoven strips of wood or cane **2** the amount a basket will hold **3** *basketball* **A** the high horizontal hoop through which a player must throw the ball to score points **B** a point scored in this way

basketball *n* a team game in which points are scored by throwing the ball through a high horizontal hoop

basketwork *n* same as **wickerwork**

basque *n* a tight-fitting bodice

Basque *n* **1** a member of a people living in the W Pyrenees in France and Spain **2** the language of the Basques ▸ *adj* **3** of the Basques

bas-relief *n* sculpture in which the figures project slightly from the background

bass¹ (base) *n* **1** the lowest adult male voice **2** a singer with such a voice **3** *informal* same as **double bass** ▸ *adj* **4** of the lowest range of musical notes: *the system is engineered to give good bass sound from very small speakers* **5** denoting a musical instrument that is lowest or second lowest in pitch in its family: *bass trombone* **6** of or relating to a bass guitar or double bass: *the band is unusual in that it has two bass players* **7** of or written for a singer with the lowest adult male voice: *the bass soloist in next week's performance of Handel's 'Messiah'*

> **bass** *adj* **4, 5, 7** = deep, low, resonant, sonorous, low-pitched, deep-toned

bass² (rhymes with **gas**) *n* **1** any of various Australian freshwater and sea fish **2** a European spiny-finned freshwater fish

basset hound *n* a smooth-haired dog with short legs and long ears

bassoon *n* a woodwind instrument that produces a range of low sounds > **bassoonist** *n*

bastard *n* **1** *informal, derogatory* an obnoxious or despicable person **2** *old-fashioned or offensive* a person born of parents not married to each other **3** *informal* something extremely difficult or unpleasant ▸ *adj* **4** *old-fashioned or offensive* illegitimate by birth **5** counterfeit; spurious > **bastardy** *n*

baste¹ *vb* **basting, basted** to sew with loose temporary stitches

baste² *vb* **basting, basted** to moisten (meat) during cooking with hot fat

bastion *n* **1** a projecting part of a fortification **2** a thing or person regarded as defending a principle or way of life: *a bastion of anti-communism*

bat¹ *n* **1** any of various types of club used to hit the ball in certain sports **2** *cricket* a batsman **3 off one's own bat A** of one's own accord **B** by one's own unaided efforts ▸ *vb* **batting, batted 4** to strike with or as if with a bat **5** *cricket etc.* to take a turn at batting

bat² *n* **1** a nocturnal mouselike flying animal with leathery wings **2 blind as a bat** having extremely poor eyesight

batch *n* **1** a group of similar objects or people dispatched or dealt with at the same time **2** the bread, cakes, etc. produced at one baking ▸ *vb* **3** to group (items) for efficient processing

> **batch** *n* **1** = group, set, lot, crowd, pack, collection, quantity, bunch

bated *adj* **with bated breath** in suspense or fear

bath *n* **1** a large container in which to wash the body **2** the act of washing in such a container **3** the amount of water in a bath **4 baths** a public swimming pool **5 A** a liquid in which something is immersed as part of a chemical process, such as developing photographs **B** the vessel containing such a liquid ▸ *vb* **6** *Brit* to wash in a bath

> **bath** *n* **2** = wash, cleaning, shower, soak, cleansing, scrub, scrubbing, douche ▸ *vb* = clean, wash, shower, soak, cleanse, scrub, bathe, rinse

Bath chair *n* *old-fashioned* a wheelchair for invalids

bathe *vb* **bathing, bathed 1** to swim in open water for pleasure **2** to apply liquid to (the skin or a wound) in order to cleanse or soothe **3** *chiefly US & Canad* to wash in a bath **4** to spread over: *bathed in moonlight* ▸ *n* **5** *Brit* a swim in open water > **bather** *n*

> **bathe** *vb* **1** = swim **2** = cleanse, clean, wash, soak, rinse **3** = wash, clean, bath, shower, soak, cleanse, scrub, rinse **4** = cover, flood, steep, engulf, immerse, overrun, suffuse, wash over

bathos (bay-thoss) *n* a sudden ludicrous descent from exalted to ordinary matters in speech or writing > **bathetic** *adj*

bathroom *n* **1** a room with a bath or shower, washbasin, and toilet **2** *US & Canad* a toilet

batik (bat-teek) *n* **A** a process of printing fabric in which areas not to be dyed are covered by wax **B** fabric printed in this way

batman *n*, *pl* **-men** an officer's servant in the armed forces

baton *n* **1** a thin stick used by the conductor of an orchestra or choir **2** *athletics* a short bar transferred from one runner to another in a relay race **3** a police officer's truncheon **4** a short stick or something shaped like one

> **baton** *n* **4** = stick, club, staff, pole, rod, crook, cane, mace, mere (NZ), patu (NZ)

batsman *n*, *pl* **-men** *cricket etc.* a player who bats or specializes in batting

battalion *n* a military unit comprised of three or more companies

batten *n* **1** a strip of wood used to strengthen something or make it secure **2** a strip of wood used for holding a tarpaulin in place over a hatch on a ship ▸ *vb* **3** to strengthen or fasten with battens

batter¹ *vb* **1** to hit repeatedly **2** to damage or injure, as by blows, heavy wear, etc. **3** to subject (someone, usually a close relative) to repeated physical violence > **battered** *adj* > **batterer** *n* > **battering** *n*

> **batter** *vb* = beat, hit, strike, knock, bang, thrash, pound, buffet

batter² *n* a mixture of flour, eggs, and milk, used in cooking

battering ram *n* (esp. formerly) a large beam used to break down fortifications

battery *n*, *pl* **-teries** **1** two or more primary cells connected to provide a source of electric current **2** a number of similar things occurring together: *a battery of questions* **3** *criminal law* unlawful beating or wounding of a person **4** *chiefly Brit* a series of cages for intensive rearing of poultry **5** a fortified structure on which artillery is mounted ▸ *adj* **6** kept in a series of cages for intensive rearing: *battery hens*

battle *n* **1** a fight between large armed forces **2** conflict or struggle ▸ *vb* **-tling**, **-tled** **3** to fight in or as if in military combat: *shop stewards battling to improve conditions at work* **4** to struggle: *she battled through the crowd*

> **battle** *n* **1** = fight, attack, action, struggle, conflict, clash, encounter, combat, biffo (*Austral slang*), boilover (*Austral*); ≠ peace **2** = campaign, drive, movement, push (*informal*), struggle ▸ *vb* **3** = wrestle, war, fight, argue, dispute, grapple, clamour, lock horns **4** = struggle, work, labour, strain, strive, toil, go all out (*informal*), give it your best shot (*informal*)

battle-axe *n* **1** *informal*, *derogatory* a domineering woman **2** (formerly) a large broad-headed axe

battlement *n* a wall with gaps, originally for firing through

battleship *n* a large heavily armoured warship

batty *adj* **-tier**, **-tiest** *slang* **1** slightly crazy **2** eccentric: *a batty scientist*

> **batty** *adj* = eccentric, odd, peculiar, potty (*Brit informal*)

b

bauble *n* **1** a trinket of little value **2** a small round ornament hung from a branch of a Christmas tree

bauera *n* small evergreen Australian shrub

baulk *vb*, *n* same as **balk**

bauxite *n* a claylike substance that is the chief source of aluminium

bawdy *adj* **bawdier**, **bawdiest** (of language, writing, etc.) containing humorous references to sex > **bawdily** *adv* > **bawdiness** *n*

bawl *vb* **1** to cry noisily **2** to shout loudly ▸ *n* **3** a loud shout or cry > **bawling** *n*

bay¹ *n* a stretch of shoreline that curves inwards

> **bay** *n* = inlet, sound, gulf, creek, cove, fjord, bight, natural harbour

bay² *n* **1** a recess in a wall **2** an area set aside for a particular purpose: *a sick bay; a loading bay* **3** an area off a road in which vehicles may park or unload **4** a compartment in an aircraft: *the bomb bay*

> **bay** *n* **1** = recess, opening, corner, niche, compartment, nook, alcove

bay³ *n* **1** a deep howl of a hound or wolf **2 at bay A** forced to turn and face attackers: *the stag at bay* **B** at a safe distance: *to keep his mind blank and his despair at bay* ▸ *vb* **3** to howl in deep prolonged tones

> **bay** *n* **1** = cry, roar, bark, howl, wail, growl, bellow, clamour ▸ *vb* = howl, cry, roar, bark, wail, growl, bellow, clamour

bay⁴ *n* **1** a Mediterranean laurel tree with glossy aromatic leaves **2 bays** a wreath of bay leaves

bay⁵ *adj* **1** reddish-brown ▸ *n* **2** a reddish-brown horse

bay leaf *n* the dried leaf of a laurel, used for flavouring in cooking

bayonet *n* **1** a blade that can be attached to the end of a rifle and used as a weapon ▸ *vb* **-neting**, **-neted** *or* **-netting**, **-netted** **2** to stab or kill with a bayonet

bazaar *n* **1** a sale, esp. one in aid of charity **2** (esp. in Arab countries) a market area, esp. a street of small stalls

> **bazaar** *n* **1** = fair, fête, gala, bring-and-buy **2** = market, exchange, fair, marketplace

bazooka *n* a portable rocket launcher that fires a projectile capable of piercing armour

BBC British Broadcasting Corporation

BC **1** (indicating years numbered back from the supposed year of the birth of Christ) before Christ **2** British Columbia

BCE (used, esp. by non-Christians, in numbering years BC) before Common Era

BCG *trademark* Bacillus Calmette-Guérin (antituberculosis vaccine)

be *vb present sing 1st person* **am**, *2nd person* **are**, *3rd person* **is**, *present pl* **are**, *past sing 1st person* **was**, *2nd person* **were**, *3rd person* **was**, *past pl* **were**, *present participle* **being**, *past participle* **been** **1** to exist; live: *I think, therefore I am* **2** to pay a visit; go: *have you been to Spain?* **3** to take place: *my birthday was last Thursday* **4** used as a linking verb between the subject of a sentence and its complement: *Shamin is a musician; honey is sweet; the dance is on Saturday* **5** forms the progressive present tense: *the man is running* **6** forms the passive voice of all transitive verbs: *a good film is being shown on television tomorrow* **7** expresses intention, expectation, or obligation: *the president is to arrive at 9.30*

> **be** *vb* **1** = be alive, live, exist, survive, breathe, be present, endure

beach *n* **1** an area of sand or pebbles sloping down to the sea or a lake ▸ *vb* **2** to run or haul (a boat) onto a beach

> **beach** *n* = shore, coast, sands, seaside, water's edge, seashore

beachhead *n military* an area of shore captured by an attacking army, on which troops and equipment are landed

beacon *n* **1** a signal fire or light on a hill or tower, used formerly as a warning of invasion **2** a lighthouse **3** a radio or other signal marking a flight course in air navigation

> **beacon** *n* **1** = signal, sign, beam, flare, bonfire **2** = lighthouse, watchtower

bead *n* **1** a small pierced piece of glass, wood, or plastic that may be strung with others to form a necklace, rosary, etc. **2** a small drop of moisture **3** a small metal knob acting as the sight of a firearm ▸ *vb* **4** to decorate with beads > **beaded** *adj*

> **bead** *n* **2** = drop, tear, bubble, pearl, dot, drip, blob, droplet

beading *n* a narrow rounded strip of moulding used for edging furniture

beady *adj* **beadier**, **beadiest** small, round, and glittering: *beady eyes*

beagle *n* a small hound with a smooth coat, short legs, and drooping ears

beak¹ *n* **1** the projecting horny jaws of a bird **2** *slang* a person's nose > **beaky** *adj*

beak² *n Brit, Austral & NZ slang* a judge, magistrate, or headmaster

beaker *n* **1** a tall drinking cup **2** a lipped glass container used in laboratories

beam *n* **1** a broad smile **2** a ray of light **3** a narrow flow of electromagnetic radiation or particles: *an electron beam* **4** a long thick piece of wood, metal, etc. used in building **5** the central shaft of a plough to which all the main parts are attached **6** the breadth of a ship at its widest part **7 off (the) beam** *informal* mistaken or irrelevant ▸ *vb* **8** to smile broadly **9** to send out or radiate **10** to divert or aim (a radio signal, light, etc.) in a certain direction: *the concert was beamed live from Geneva*

> **beam** *n* **1** = smile, grin **2** = ray, flash, stream, glow, streak, shaft, gleam, glint **4** = rafter, support, timber, spar, plank, girder, joist ▸ *vb* **8** = smile, grin **9** = radiate, flash, shine, glow, glitter, glare, gleam **10** = transmit, show, air, broadcast, cable, send out, relay, televise, stream

bean *n* **1** the seed or pod of various climbing plants, eaten as a vegetable **2** any of various beanlike seeds, such as coffee **3 full of beans** *informal* full of energy and vitality **4 not have a bean** *slang* to be without money

beanie *n Brit, Austral & NZ* a close-fitting woollen hat

bear¹ *vb* **bearing**, **bore**, **borne** **1** to support or hold up **2** to bring: *to bear gifts* **3** to accept the responsibility of: *to bear a heavier burden of taxation* **4** to give birth to **5** to produce by natural growth: *to bear fruit* **6** to tolerate or endure **7** to stand up to; sustain: *his story does not bear scrutiny* **8** to hold in the mind: *to bear a grudge* **9** to show or be marked with: *he still bears the scars* **10** to have, be, or stand in (relation or comparison): *her account bears no relation to the facts* **11** to move in a specified direction: *bear left* **12 bring to bear** to bring into effect

> **bear** *vb* **1** = support, shoulder, sustain, endure, uphold, withstand; ≠ give up **2** = carry, take, move, bring, transfer, conduct, transport, haul; ≠ put down **4** = give birth to, produce, deliver, breed, bring forth, beget (*old-fashioned*) **5** = produce, generate, yield, bring forth **6** = suffer, experience, go through, sustain, stomach, endure, brook, abide **8** = exhibit, hold, maintain **9** = display, have, show, hold, carry, possess

bear² *n, pl* **bears** *or* **bear** **1** a large heavily-built mammal with a long shaggy coat **2** a bearlike animal, such as the koala **3** an ill-mannered person **4** *Stock Exchange* a person who sells shares in anticipation of falling prices to make a profit on repurchase **5 like a bear with a sore head** *informal* bad-tempered, irritable

bearable *adj* endurable; tolerable

beard *n* **1** the hair growing on the lower parts of a man's face **2** any similar growth in animals ▸ *vb* **3** to oppose boldly: *I bearded my formidable employer in her den* > **bearded** *adj*

bearer *n* **1** a person or thing that carries, presents, or upholds something **2** a person who presents a note or bill for payment

> **bearer** *n* **1** = agent, carrier, courier, herald, envoy, messenger, conveyor, emissary

bearing n **1** (foll. by on or upon) relevance to: it has no bearing on this problem **2** a part of a machine supporting another part, and usually reducing friction **3** the act of producing fruit or young **4** a person's general social conduct **5** the angular direction of a point measured from a known position **6** the position, as of a ship, fixed with reference to two or more known points **7 bearings** a sense of one's relative position: I lost my bearings in the dark **8** heraldry a device on a heraldic shield

> **bearing** n **1** = relevance, relation, application, connection, import, reference, significance, pertinence; ≠ irrelevance **4** = manner, attitude, conduct, aspect, behaviour, posture, demeanour, deportment **7** = way, course, position, situation, track, aim, direction, location

bear out vb to show to be truthful: the witness will bear me out

> **bear out** vb bear something out = support, prove, confirm, justify, endorse, uphold, substantiate, corroborate

bearskin n **1** the pelt of a bear **2** a tall fur helmet worn by certain British Army regiments

beast n **1** a large wild animal **2** a brutal or uncivilized person **3** savage nature or characteristics: the beast in people

> **beast** n **1** = animal, creature, brute **2** = brute, monster, savage, barbarian, fiend, swine, ogre, sadist

beastly adj **-lier, -liest** informal unpleasant; disagreeable

> **beastly** adj = unpleasant, mean, awful, nasty, rotten (informal), horrid (informal), disagreeable; ≠ pleasant

beat vb **beating, beat, beaten** or **beat 1** to strike with a series of violent blows **2** to move (wings) up and down **3** to throb rhythmically **4** cookery to stir or whisk vigorously **5** to shape (metal) by repeated blows **6** music to indicate (time) by one's hand or a baton **7** to produce (a sound) by striking a drum **8** to overcome or defeat: he was determined to beat his illness **9** to form (a path or track) by repeated use **10** to arrive, achieve, or finish before (someone or something): she beat her team mate fair and square **11** (foll. by back, down or off etc.) to drive, push, or thrust **12** to scour (woodlands or undergrowth) to rouse game for shooting **13** slang to puzzle or baffle: it beats me ▸ n **14** a stroke or blow **15** the sound made by a stroke or blow **16** a regular throb **17** an assigned route, as of a police officer **18** the basic rhythmic unit in a piece of music **19** pop or rock music characterized by a heavy rhythmic beat ▸ adj **20** slang totally exhausted ▸ See also **beat up** > **beating** n

beat vb **1** = batter, hit, strike, knock, pound, smack, thrash, thump **2** = flap, thrash, flutter, wag **3** = throb, thump, pound, quake, vibrate, pulsate, palpitate **7** = hit, strike, bang **8** = defeat, outdo, trounce, overcome, crush, overwhelm, conquer, surpass ▸ n **16** = throb, pounding, pulse, thumping, vibration, pulsating, palpitation **17** = route, way, course, rounds, path, circuit

beatbox n **1** a drum machine ▸ vb **2** to simulate percussion instruments with the voice, esp. in hip-hop music > **beatboxing** n

beatific adj literary **1** displaying great happiness **2** having a divine aura

beatify (bee-at-if-fie) vb **-fies, -fying, -fied 1** RC Church to declare (a deceased person) to be among the blessed in heaven: the first step towards canonization **2** to make extremely happy > **beatification** n

Beatitude n Christianity any of the blessings on the poor, meek, etc. in the Sermon on the Mount

beat up informal ▸ vb **1** to inflict severe physical damage on (someone) by striking or kicking repeatedly ▸ n **2** Austral & NZ a small matter deliberately exaggerated ▸ adj **beat-up 3** dilapidated

> **beat up** vb beat someone up = assault, attack, batter, thrash, set about, set upon, lay into (informal), beat the living daylights out of (informal)

beau (boh) n, pl **beaux** or **beaus** (bohz) **1** chiefly US a boyfriend **2** a man who is greatly concerned with his appearance

Beaufort scale n meteorol a scale for measuring wind speeds, ranging from 0 (calm) to 12 (hurricane)

beautician n a person who works in a beauty salon

beautiful adj **1** very attractive to look at **2** highly enjoyable; very pleasant > **beautifully** adv

> **beautiful** adj **1** = attractive, pretty, lovely, charming, tempting, pleasant, handsome, fetching (informal), hot (informal), fit (Brit informal); ≠ ugly

beautify vb **-fies, -fying, -fied** to make beautiful > **beautification** n

beauty n, pl **-ties 1** the combination of all the qualities of a person or thing that delight the senses and mind **2** a very attractive woman **3** informal an outstanding example of its kind **4** informal an advantageous feature: the beauty of this job is the short hours

> **beauty** n **1** = attractiveness, charm, grace, glamour, elegance, loveliness, handsomeness, comeliness (old-fashioned); ≠ ugliness **2** = good-looker, lovely (slang), belle, stunner (informal), beaut (Austral, NZ slang)

b

beaver *n* **1** a large amphibious rodent with soft brown fur, a broad flat tail, and webbed hind feet **2** its fur **3** a tall hat made of this fur ▸ *vb* **4 beaver away** to work very hard and steadily

becalmed *adj* (of a sailing ship) motionless through lack of wind

became *vb* the past tense of **become**

because *conj* **1** on account of the fact that: *because it's so cold we'll go home* **2 because of** on account of: *I lost my job because of her*

> **because** *conj* **1** = since, as, in that **2 because of** = as a result of, on account of, by reason of, thanks to, owing to

beck¹ *n* **at someone's beck and call** having to be constantly available to do as someone asks

beck² *n* (in N England) a stream

beckon *vb* **1** to summon with a gesture **2** to lure: *fame beckoned*

> **beckon** *vb* **1** = gesture, sign, wave, indicate, signal, nod, motion, summon

become *vb* **-coming, -came, -come 1** to come to be: *she became Prime Minister in 2016* **2** (foll. by *of*) to happen to: *what became of him?* **3** to suit: *that dress becomes you*

> **become** *vb* **1** = come to be, develop into, be transformed into, grow into, change into, alter to, mature into, ripen into **3** = suit, fit, enhance, flatter, embellish, set off

becoming *adj* suitable or appropriate: *his conduct was not becoming to the rank of officer*

> **becoming** *adj* = appropriate, seemly, fitting, suitable, proper, worthy, in keeping, compatible; ≠ inappropriate

bed *n* **1** a piece of furniture on which to sleep **2** a plot of ground in which plants are grown **3** the bottom of a river, lake, or sea **4** any underlying structure or part **5** a layer of rock **6 get out of bed on the wrong side** *informal* to begin the day in a bad mood **7 go to bed with** to have sexual intercourse with ▸ *vb* **bedding, bedded 8** (foll. by *down*) to go to or put into a place to sleep or rest **9** to have sexual intercourse with **10** to place firmly into position: *the poles were bedded in concrete* **11** *geol* to form or be arranged in a distinct layer **12** to plant in a bed of soil

> **bed** *n* **1** = bedstead, couch, berth, cot, divan **2** = plot, area, row, strip, patch, ground, land, garden **4** = base, footing, basis, bottom, foundation, underpinning, groundwork, bedrock

bedding *n* **1** bedclothes, sometimes with a mattress **2** litter, such as straw, for animals **3** the distinct layered deposits of rocks

bedevil (bid-**dev**-ill) *vb* **-illing, -illed** or US **-iling, -iled 1** to harass or torment **2** to throw into confusion ▸ **bedevilment** *n*

bedlam *n* a noisy confused situation

bedpan *n* a shallow container used as a toilet by people who are not well enough to leave bed

bedraggled *adj* with hair or clothing that is untidy, wet, or dirty

bedridden *adj* unable to leave bed because of illness

bedrock *n* **1** the solid rock beneath the surface soil **2** basic principles or facts

bedroom *n* **1** a room used for sleeping ▸ *adj* **2** containing references to sex: *a bedroom comedy*

bedsit or **bedsitter** *n* a furnished sitting room with a bed

bee¹ *n* **1** a four-winged insect that collects nectar and pollen to make honey and wax **2 have a bee in one's bonnet** to be obsessed with an idea

bee² *n* a social gathering to carry out a communal task: *quilting bee*

beech *n* **1** a tree with smooth greyish bark **2** the hard wood of this tree

beef *n* **1** the flesh of a cow, bull, or ox **2** *slang* a complaint ▸ *vb* **3** *slang* to complain

beefburger *n* a flat fried or grilled cake of minced beef; hamburger

beefeater *n* a yeoman warder of the Tower of London

beefy *adj* **beefier, beefiest 1** *informal* muscular **2** like beef ▸ **beefiness** *n*

beehive *n* a structure in which bees are housed

been *vb* the past participle of **be**

beep *n* **1** a high-pitched sound, like that of a car horn or some electronic devices ▸ *vb* **2** to make or cause to make such a noise

beer *n* **1** an alcoholic drink brewed from malt, sugar, hops, and water **2** a glass, can, or bottle containing this drink

beery *adj* **beerier, beeriest** smelling or tasting of beer

beeswax *n* **1** a wax produced by honeybees for making honeycombs **2** this wax after refining, used in polishes, etc.

beet *n* a plant with an edible root and leaves, such as the sugar beet and beetroot

beetle *n* **1** an insect with a hard wing-case closed over its back for protection ▸ *vb* **-tling, -tled 2** (foll. by *along* or *off* etc.) *informal* to scuttle or scurry

beetroot *n* a variety of the beet plant with a dark red root that may be eaten as a vegetable, in salads, or pickled

befall *vb* **-falling, -fell, -fallen** *archaic* or *literary* to happen to

befit *vb* **-fitting, -fitted** to be appropriate to or suitable for ▸ **befitting** *adj*

before *conj* **1** earlier than the time when **2** rather than: *she'll resign before she agrees to it* ▸ *prep* **3** preceding in space or time; in front of; ahead of: *they stood before the altar* **4** in the presence of: *to be brought before a judge* **5** in preference to: *to put friendship before money* ▸ *adv* **6** previously **7** in front

before *prep* **3** = earlier than, ahead of, prior to, in advance of; ≠ after **4** = in the presence of, in front of ▸ *adv* **6** = previously, earlier, sooner, in advance, formerly; ≠ after

beforehand *adj, adv* early; in advance

beforehand *adj, adv* = in advance, before, earlier, already, sooner, ahead, previously, in anticipation

befriend *vb* to become a friend to

beg *vb* **begging, begged** **1** to ask for money or food in the street **2** to ask formally, humbly, or earnestly: *I beg forgiveness*; *I beg to differ* **3** **beg the question A** to put forward an argument that assumes the very point it is supposed to establish, or that depends on some other questionable assumption **B** *not standard* to suggest that a question needs to be asked **4** **go begging** to be unwanted or unused

beg *vb* **1** = scrounge (*informal*), bum (*informal*), touch (someone) for (*slang*), cadge, sponge on (someone) for, freeload (*slang*), seek charity, solicit charity; ≠ give **2** = implore, plead with, beseech, request, petition, solicit, entreat

began *vb* the past tense of **begin**

beget *vb* **-getting, -got** or **-gat, -gotten** or **-got** *old-fashioned* **1** to cause or create: *repetition begets boredom* **2** to father

beggar *n* **1** a person who lives by begging **2** *chiefly Brit* a fellow: *lucky beggar!* ▸ *vb* **3** **beggar description** to be impossible to describe ▸ **beggarly** *adj*

beggar *n* **1** = vagrant (*old-fashioned*), tramp (*old-fashioned*), bum (*informal*), derelict (*old-fashioned*), drifter, down-and-out, pauper (*old-fashioned*), bag lady, derro (*Austral slang*)

begin *vb* **-ginning, -gan, -gun** **1** to start (something) **2** to bring or come into being **3** to start to say or speak **4** to have the least capacity to do something: *it doesn't even begin to address the problem* ▸ **beginner** *n*

begin *vb* **1** = start, commence, proceed; ≠ stop **2** = come into existence, start, appear, emerge, arise, originate, come into being **3** = start talking, start, initiate, commence

beginning *n* **1** a start **2** **beginnings** an early part or stage **3** the place where or time when something starts **4** an origin; source

beginning *n* **1** = start, opening, birth, origin, outset, onset, initiation, inauguration; ≠ end **3** = outset, start, opening, birth, onset, commencement

begonia *n* a tropical plant with ornamental leaves and waxy flowers

begrudge *vb* **-grudging, -grudged** **1** to envy (someone) the possession of something **2** to give or allow unwillingly: *he begrudged her an apology*

beguile (big-*gile*) *vb* **-guiling, -guiled** to charm (someone) into doing something he or she would not normally do

beguiling *adj* charming, often in a deceptive way

begun *vb* the past participle of **begin**

behalf *n* **on** or *US & Canad* **in behalf of** in the interest of or for the benefit of

behave *vb* **-having, -haved** **1** to act or function in a particular way **2** to conduct oneself in a particular way: *the baby behaved very well* **3** to conduct oneself properly

behave *vb* **2** = act **3** = be well-behaved, mind your manners, keep your nose clean, act correctly, conduct yourself properly; ≠ misbehave

behaviour or *US* **behavior** *n* **1** manner of behaving **2** *psychol* the response of an organism to a stimulus ▸ **behavioural** or *US* **behavioral** *adj*

behaviour or **behavior** *n* **1** = conduct, ways, actions, bearing, attitude, manner, manners, demeanour

behead *vb* to remove the head from

beheld *vb* the past of **behold**

behest *n* an order or earnest request: *I came at her behest*

behind *prep* **1** in or to a position further back than **2** in the past in relation to: *I want to leave the past behind me* **3** late according to: *running behind schedule* **4** concerning the circumstances surrounding: *the reasons behind his departure* **5** supporting: *I'm right behind you in your application* ▸ *adv* **6** in or to a position further back **7** remaining after someone's departure: *she left her books behind* **8** in arrears: *to fall behind with payments* ▸ *adj* **9** in a position further back ▸ *n* **10** *informal* the buttocks

behind *prep* **1** = at the rear of, at the back of, at the heels of **3** = later than, after **4** = causing, responsible for, initiating, at the bottom of, instigating **5** = supporting, for, backing, on the side of, in agreement with ▸ *adv* **6** = after, next, following, afterwards, subsequently, in the wake (of); ≠ in advance of **8** = overdue, in debt, in arrears, behindhand ▸ *adj* = after, next, following, afterwards, subsequently, in the wake (of); ≠ in advance of ▸ *n* = bottom (*informal*), butt (*informal*), buttocks, posterior

behold *vb* **-holding, -held** *archaic* or *literary* to look (at); observe ▸ **beholder** *n*

beholden *adj* indebted; obliged: *I am beholden to you*

behove *vb* **-hoving, -hoved** *archaic* to be necessary or fitting for: *it behoves me to warn you*

beige *adj* pale creamy-brown

being *n* **1** the state or fact of existing **2** essential nature; self **3** something that exists or is thought to exist: *a being from outer space* **4** a human being

being n 1 = life, reality; ≠ nonexistence 2 = soul, spirit, substance, creature, essence, organism, entity 3, 4 = individual, creature, human being, living thing

belabour or US **belabor** vb to attack verbally or physically

belated adj late or too late: *belated greetings* > **belatedly** adv

belch vb 1 to expel wind from the stomach noisily through the mouth 2 to expel or be expelled forcefully: *smoke belching from factory chimneys* ▸ n 3 an act of belching

beleaguered adj 1 struggling against difficulties or criticism: *the country's beleaguered health system* 2 besieged by an enemy: *a ship bringing food to the beleaguered capital of Monrovia*

beleaguered adj 1 = harassed, troubled, plagued, hassled (*informal*), badgered, persecuted, pestered, vexed 2 = besieged, surrounded, blockaded, beset, encircled, assailed, hemmed in

belfry n, pl **-fries** 1 the part of a tower or steeple in which bells are hung 2 a tower or steeple

belgium sausage n Austral & NZ a large smooth bland sausage

belie vb **-lying, -lied** 1 to show to be untrue: *the facts belied the theory* 2 to misrepresent: *the score belied the closeness of the match* 3 to fail to justify: *the promises were soon belied*

belief n 1 trust or confidence: *belief in the free market* 2 opinion; conviction: *it's my firm belief* 3 a principle, etc. accepted as true, often without proof 4 religious faith

belief n 1 = trust, confidence, conviction; ≠ disbelief 2 = opinion, feeling, idea, impression, assessment, notion, judgment, point of view 3 = faith, principles, doctrine, ideology, creed, dogma, tenet, credo

believe vb **-lieving, -lieved** 1 to accept as true or real: *I believe God exists* 2 to think, assume, or suppose: *I believe you know my father* 3 to accept the statement or opinion of (a person) as true 4 to have religious faith 5 **believe in** to be convinced of the truth or existence of: *I don't believe in ghosts* > **believable** adj > **believer** n

believe vb 1, 3 = accept, trust, credit, depend on, rely on, have faith in, swear by, be certain of; ≠ disbelieve 2 = think, judge, suppose, estimate, imagine, assume, gather, reckon

belittle vb **-tling, -tled** to treat (something or someone) as having little value or importance

bell n 1 a hollow, usually metal, cup-shaped instrument that emits a ringing sound when struck 2 the sound made by such an instrument 3 an electrical device that rings or buzzes as a signal 4 something shaped like a bell 5 *Brit slang* a telephone call 6 **ring a bell** to sound familiar; recall to the mind something previously experienced

belladonna n 1 a drug obtained from deadly nightshade 2 same as **deadly nightshade**

belle n a beautiful woman, esp. the most attractive woman at a function: *the belle of the ball*

bellicose adj warlike; aggressive

belligerence n the act or quality of being belligerent or warlike

belligerent adj 1 marked by readiness to fight 2 relating to or engaged in war ▸ n 3 a person or country engaged in war

bellow vb 1 to make a loud deep cry like that of a bull 2 to shout in anger ▸ n 3 the characteristic noise of a bull 4 a loud deep roar

bellow vb 1 = shout, cry (out), scream, roar, yell, howl, shriek, bawl ▸ n 4 = shout, cry, scream, roar, yell, howl, shriek, bawl

bellows n 1 a device consisting of an air chamber with flexible sides that is used to create and direct a stream of air 2 a flexible corrugated part, such as that connecting the lens system of some cameras to the body

belly n, pl **-lies** 1 the part of the body of a vertebrate containing the intestines and other organs 2 the stomach 3 the front, lower, or inner part of something 4 **go belly up** informal to die, fail, or end ▸ vb **-lies, -lying, -lied** 5 to swell out; bulge

belly n 1, 2 = stomach, insides (*informal*), gut, abdomen, tummy (*informal*), paunch, potbelly, corporation (*informal*), puku (NZ)

bellyful n 1 slang more than one can tolerate 2 as much as one wants or can eat

belong vb 1 (foll. by to) to be the property of 2 (foll. by to) to be bound to (a person, organization, etc.) by ties of affection, association, membership, etc.: *the nations concerned belonged to NATO* 3 (foll. by to, under or with etc.) to be classified with: *it belongs to a different class of comets* 4 (foll. by to) to be a part of: *this lid belongs to that tin* 5 to have a proper or usual place 6 informal to be acceptable, esp. socially

belong vb 4 = go with, fit into, be part of, relate to, be connected with, pertain to

belongings pl n the things that a person owns or has with him or her

belongings pl n = possessions, goods, things, effects, property, stuff, gear, paraphernalia

beloved adj 1 dearly loved ▸ n 2 a person who is dearly loved

beloved adj = dear, loved, valued, prized, admired, treasured, precious, darling

below prep 1 at or to a position lower than; under 2 less than 3 unworthy of; beneath ▸ adv 4 at or to a lower position 5 at a later place in something written 6 archaic on earth or in hell

below *prep* **1** = under, underneath, lower than **2** = less than, lower than ▸ *adv* **4** = lower, down, under, beneath, underneath

belt *n* **1** a band of leather or cloth worn around the waist **2** an area where a specific thing is found; zone: *a belt of high pressure* **3** same as **seat belt 4** a band of flexible material between rotating shafts or pulleys to transfer motion or transmit goods: *a fan belt; a conveyer belt* **5** *informal* a sharp blow **6 below the belt** *informal* unscrupulous or cowardly **7 tighten one's belt** to reduce expenditure **8 under one's belt** as part of one's experience: *he had a string of successes under his belt* ▸ *vb* **9** to fasten with or as if with a belt **10** to hit with a belt **11** *slang* to give (someone) a sharp blow **12** (foll. by *along*) *slang* to move very fast

belt *n* **1** = waistband, band, sash, girdle, girth, cummerbund **2** = zone, area, region, section, district, stretch, strip, layer **4** = conveyor belt, band, loop, fan belt, drive belt

bemoan *vb* to lament: *he's always bemoaning his fate*
bemused *adj* puzzled or confused

bemused *adj* = puzzled, confused, baffled, at sea, bewildered, muddled, perplexed, mystified

bench *n* **1** a long seat for more than one person **2 the bench A** a judge or magistrate sitting in court **B** judges or magistrates collectively **3** a long and strong worktable

bench *n* **1** = seat, stall, pew **2 the bench** = court, judges, magistrates, tribunal, judiciary, courtroom **3** = worktable, stand, table, counter, trestle table, workbench

benchmark *n* **1** a mark on a fixed object, used as a reference point in surveying **2** a criterion by which to measure something: *the speech was a benchmark of his commitment*

benchmark *n* **2** = reference point, gauge, yardstick, measure, level, standard, model, par

bend *vb* **bending, bent 1** to form a curve **2** to turn from a particular direction: *the road bends right* **3** (often foll. by *down* etc.) to incline the body **4** to submit: *to bend before public opinion* **5** to turn or direct (one's eyes, steps, or attention) **6 bend someone's ear** *informal* to complain (to someone) for a long time **7 bend the rules** *informal* to ignore or change rules to suit oneself ▸ *n* **8** a curved part **9** the act of bending **10 round the bend** *Brit slang* foolish or silly > **bendy** *adj*

bend *vb* **1** = twist, turn, wind, lean, hook, bow, curve, arch ▸ *n* **8** = curve, turn, corner, twist, angle, bow, loop, arc

beneath *prep* **1** below; under **2** too trivial for: *beneath his dignity* ▸ *adv* **3** below; underneath

beneath *prep* **1** = under, below, underneath, lower than; ≠ over **2** = unworthy of, unfitting for, unsuitable for, inappropriate for, unbefitting ▸ *adv* = underneath, below, in a lower place

Benedictine *n* **1** a monk or nun of the Christian order of Saint Benedict **2** a liqueur first made by Benedictine monks ▸ *adj* **3** of Saint Benedict or his order

benediction *n* **1** a prayer for divine blessing **2** a Roman Catholic service in which the congregation is blessed with the sacrament > **benedictory** *adj*

benefaction *n* **1** the act of doing good, particularly donating to charity **2** the donation or help given

benefactor *or fem* **benefactress** *n* a person who supports a person or institution by giving money

beneficent (bin-**eff**-iss-ent) *adj* charitable; generous > **beneficence** *n*
beneficial *adj* helpful or advantageous

beneficial *adj* = favourable, useful, valuable, helpful, profitable, benign, wholesome, advantageous; ≠ harmful

beneficiary *n, pl* **-ciaries 1** a person who gains or benefits **2** *law* a person entitled to receive funds or property under a trust, will, etc.

beneficiary *n* **1** = recipient, receiver, payee **2** = heir, inheritor

benefit *n* **1** something that improves or promotes **2** advantage or sake: *I'm doing this for your benefit* **3** a payment made by an institution or government to a person who is ill, unemployed, etc. **4** a theatrical performance or sports event to raise money for a charity ▸ *vb* **-fiting, -fited** *or US* **-fitting, -fitted 5** to do or receive good; profit

benefit *n* **1, 3** = good, help, profit, favour; ≠ harm **2** = advantage, aid, favour, assistance ▸ *vb* = profit from, make the most of, gain from, do well out of, reap benefits from, turn to your advantage; ≠ harm

benevolence *n* **1** inclination to do good **2** an act of kindness > **benevolent** *adj*
benighted *adj* lacking cultural, moral, or intellectual enlightenment
benign (bin-**nine**) *adj* **1** showing kindliness **2** favourable: *a stroke of benign fate* **3** *pathol* (of a tumour, etc.) able to be controlled > **benignly** *adv*

benign *adj* **1** = benevolent, kind, kindly, warm, friendly, obliging, sympathetic, compassionate; ≠ unkind **3** = harmless, innocent, innocuous, curable, inoffensive, remediable; ≠ malignant

bent *adj* **1** not straight; curved **2** *slang* **A** dishonest; corrupt: *bent officials* **B** *Brit & Austral* *offensive slang* homosexual **3 bent on** determined to pursue (a course of action) ▸ **4** personal inclination or aptitude: *he had a strong practical bent in his nature*

> **bent** *adj* **1** = misshapen, twisted, angled, bowed, curved, arched, crooked, distorted; ≠ straight **3 bent on** = intent on, set on, fixed on, predisposed to, resolved on, insistent on ▸ *n* = inclination, ability, leaning, tendency, preference, penchant, propensity, aptitude

bento *or* **bento box** *n* a thin box, made of plastic or lacquered wood, divided into compartments, which contain small separate dishes comprising a Japanese meal, esp. lunch

benzene *n* a flammable poisonous liquid used as a solvent, insecticide, etc.

bequeath *vb* **1** *law* to dispose of (property) as in a will **2** to hand down: *the author bequeaths no solutions*

> **bequeath** *vb* **1** = leave, will, give, grant, hand down, endow, bestow, entrust **2** = give, accord, grant, afford, yield, lend, pass on, confer

bequest *n* **1** the act of gifting money or property in a will **2** money or property that has been gifted in a will

berate *vb* **-rating, -rated** to scold harshly

bereaved *adj* having recently lost a close relative or friend through death
> **bereavement** *n*

bereft *adj* (foll. by *of*) deprived: *a government bereft of ideas*

beret (ber-ray) *n* a round flat close-fitting brimless cap

berg¹ *n* short for **iceberg**

berg² *n* S African a mountain

bergamot *n* **1** a small Asian tree with sour pear-shaped fruit **2 essence of bergamot** a fragrant essential oil from the fruit rind of this plant, used in perfumery

beri-beri *n* a disease caused by a dietary deficiency of thiamine (vitamin B_1)

berk *or* **burk** *n* Brit, Austral & NZ slang a stupid person; fool

berm *n* NZ a narrow grass strip between the road and the footpath in a residential area

berry *n, pl* **-ries** a small round fruit that grows on bushes or trees and is often edible

berserk *adj* **go berserk** to become violent or destructive

berth *n* **1** a bunk in a ship or train **2** *naut* a place assigned to a ship at a mooring **3** *naut* sufficient room for a ship to manoeuvre **4 give a wide berth to** to keep clear of ▸ *vb* **5** *naut* to dock (a ship) **6** to provide with a sleeping place **7** *naut* to pick up a mooring in an anchorage

> **berth** *n* **1** = bunk, bed, hammock, billet **2** = anchorage, haven, port, harbour, dock, pier, wharf, quay ▸ *vb* **5** = anchor, land, dock, moor, tie up, drop anchor

beryl *n* a transparent hard mineral, used as a source of beryllium and as a gemstone

beryllium *n* a toxic silvery-white metallic element. Symbol: **Be**

beseech *vb* **-seeching, -sought** *or* **-seeched** to ask earnestly; beg

beset *vb* **-setting, -set** **1** to trouble or harass constantly **2** to surround or attack from all sides

beside *prep* **1** next to; at, by, or to the side of **2** as compared with **3** away from: *beside the point* **4 beside oneself** overwhelmed; overwrought: *beside oneself with grief* ▸ *adv* **5** at, by, to, or along the side of something or someone

> **beside** *prep* **1** = next to, near, close to, neighbouring, alongside, adjacent to, at the side of, abreast of **4 beside oneself** = distraught, desperate, distressed, frantic, frenzied, unhinged, overwrought

besides *adv* **1** in addition ▸ *prep* **2** apart from; even considering ▸ *conj* **3** anyway; moreover

> **besides** *adv* = also, too, further, otherwise, in addition, as well, moreover, furthermore ▸ *prep* = apart from, barring, excepting, other than, excluding, as well (as), in addition to, over and above

besiege *vb* **-sieging, -sieged** **1** to surround with military forces to bring about surrender **2** to hem in **3** to overwhelm, as with requests

> **besiege** *vb* **1, 2** = surround, enclose, blockade, encircle, hem in, shut in, lay siege to **3** = harass, harry, plague, hound, hassle (*informal*), badger, pester

besotted *adj* **1** having an irrational passion for a person or thing **2** stupefied with alcohol

besought *vb* a past of **beseech**

bespeak *vb* **-speaking, -spoke, -spoken** *or* **-spoke** **1** to indicate or suggest: *imitation bespeaks admiration* **2** to engage or ask for in advance: *she was bespoke to a family in the town*

bespoke *adj* chiefly Brit **1** (esp. of a suit) made to the customer's specifications **2** making or selling such suits: *a bespoke tailor*

best *adj* **1** the superlative of **good 2** most excellent of a particular group, category, etc. **3** most suitable, desirable, etc. ▸ *adv* **4** the superlative of **well¹ 5** in a manner surpassing all others; most attractively, etc. ▸ *n* **6 the best** the most outstanding or excellent person, thing, or group in a category **7** the utmost effort: *I did my best* **8** a person's finest clothes **9 at best A** in the most favourable interpretation **B** under the most favourable conditions **10 for the best A** for an ultimately good outcome **B** with good intentions **11 get the best of** to defeat or outwit **12 make the best of** to cope as well as possible with ▸ *vb* **13** to defeat

best adj **2** = finest, leading, supreme, principal, foremost, pre-eminent, unsurpassed, most accomplished ▸ adv **5** = most highly, most fully, most deeply ▸ n **6 the best** = the finest, the pick, the flower, the cream, the elite, the crème de la crème

bestial adj **1** brutal or savage **2** of or relating to a beast

bestiality n, pl **-ties 1** brutal behaviour, character, or action **2** sexual activity between a person and an animal

bestir vb **-stirring, -stirred** to cause (oneself) to become active

best man n the male attendant of the bridegroom at a wedding

bestow vb to present (a gift) or confer (an honour) > **bestowal** n

bestow vb = present, give, award, grant, commit, hand out, lavish, impart; ≠ obtain

bestride vb **-striding, -strode, -stridden** to have or put a leg on either side of

bestseller n a book or other product that has sold in great numbers > **bestselling** adj

bet n **1** the act of staking a sum of money or other stake on the outcome of an event **2** the stake risked **3** a course of action: your best bet is to go by train **4** informal an opinion: my bet is that you've been up to no good ▸ vb **betting, bet** or **betted 5** to make or place a bet with (someone) **6** to stake (money, etc.) in a bet **7** informal to predict (a certain outcome): I bet she doesn't turn up **8 you bet** informal of course

bet n **1** = gamble, risk, stake, venture, speculation, flutter (informal), punt (chiefly Brit), wager ▸ vb **6** = gamble, chance, stake, venture, hazard, speculate, wager, risk money

betel (bee-tl) n an Asian climbing plant, the leaves and nuts of which can be chewed

bête noire (bet nwahr) n, pl **bêtes noires** a person or thing that one particularly dislikes or dreads

betide vb **-tiding, -tided** to happen or happen to: woe betide us if we're not ready on time

betoken vb to indicate; signify

betray vb **1** to hand over or expose (one's nation, friend, etc.) treacherously to an enemy **2** to disclose (a secret or confidence) treacherously **3** to reveal unintentionally: his singing voice betrays his origins > **betrayal** n > **betrayer** n

betray vb **1** = be disloyal to, dob in (Austral slang), double-cross (informal), stab in the back, be unfaithful to, inform on or against **2** = give away, reveal, expose, disclose, uncover, divulge, unmask, let slip

betrothed old-fashioned ▸ adj **1** engaged to be married ▸ n **2** the person to whom one is engaged

better adj **1** the comparative of **good 2** more excellent than others **3** more suitable, attractive, etc. **4** improved or fully recovered in health **5 the better part of** a large part of ▸ adv **6** the comparative of **well¹ 7** in a more excellent manner **8** in or to a greater degree **9 better off** in more favourable circumstances, esp. financially **10 had better** would be sensible, etc. to: I had better be off ▸ n **11 the better** something that is the more excellent, useful, etc. of two such things **12 betters** people who are one's superiors, esp. in social standing **13 get the better of** to defeat or outwit ▸ vb **14** to improve upon

better adj **2, 3** = superior, finer, higher-quality, surpassing, preferable, more desirable; ≠ inferior **4** = well, stronger, recovering, cured, fully recovered, on the mend (informal); ≠ worse ▸ adv **7** = in a more excellent manner, more effectively, more attractively, more advantageously, more competently, in a superior way; ≠ worse **8** = to a greater degree, more completely, more thoroughly

between prep **1** at a point intermediate to two other points in space, time, etc. **2** in combination; together: between them, they saved enough money to buy a car **3** confined to: between you and me **4** indicating a linking relation or comparison **5** indicating alternatives, strictly only two alternatives ▸ adv also **in between 6** between one specified thing and another

between prep **1** = amidst, among, mid, in the middle of, betwixt

betwixt prep, adv **1** archaic between **2 betwixt and between** in an intermediate or indecisive position

bevel n **1** a slanting edge ▸ vb **-elling, -elled** or US **-eling, -eled 2** to be inclined; slope **3** to cut a bevel on (a piece of timber, etc.)

beverage n any drink other than water

beverage n = drink, liquid, liquor, refreshment

bevy n, pl **bevies** a flock; a group

bewail vb to express great sorrow over; lament

beware vb **-waring, -wared** (often foll. by of) to be wary (of); be on one's guard (against)

beware vb = be careful, look out, watch out, be wary, be cautious, take heed, guard against something

bewilder vb to confuse utterly; puzzle > **bewildering** adj > **bewilderment** n

bewilder vb = confound, confuse, puzzle, baffle, perplex, mystify, flummox, bemuse

bewitch vb **1** to attract and fascinate **2** to cast a spell over > **bewitching** adj

beyond prep **1** at or to a point on the other side of: beyond those hills **2** outside the limits or scope of ▸ adv **3** at or to the other or far side of something **4** outside the limits of something ▸ n **5 the beyond** the unknown, esp. life after death

> **beyond** prep **1** = on the other side of **2** = past

b

BF or **bf 1** best friend **2** boyfriend

bi- combining form **1** having two: bifocal **2** occurring or lasting for two: biennial **3** on both sides, directions, etc.: bilateral **4** occurring twice during: biweekly **5** chem **A** denoting a compound containing two identical cyclical hydrocarbon systems: biphenyl **B** indicating an acid salt of a dibasic acid: sodium bicarbonate

biannual adj occurring twice a year
> **biannually** adv

bias n **1** mental tendency, esp. prejudice **2** a diagonal cut across the weave of a fabric **3** bowls a bulge or weight inside one side of a bowl that causes it to roll in a curve ▸ vb **-asing, -ased** or **-assing, -assed 4** to cause to have a bias; prejudice > **biased** or **biassed** adj

> **bias** n **1** = prejudice, leaning, tendency, inclination, favouritism, partiality; ≠ impartiality ▸ vb = influence, colour, weight, prejudice, distort, sway, warp, slant

bib n **1** a piece of cloth or plastic worn to protect a very young child's clothes while eating **2** the upper front part of some aprons, dungarees, etc.

Bible n **1 the Bible** the sacred writings of the Christian religion, comprising the Old and New Testaments **2** a book regarded as authoritative: this guide has long been regarded as the hill walkers' bible > **biblical** adj

bibliography n, pl **-phies 1** a list of books on a subject or by a particular author **2** a list of sources used in a book, etc. **3** the study of the history, etc. of literary material
> **bibliographer** n

bibliophile n a person who collects or is fond of books

bibulous adj literary addicted to alcohol

bicarbonate n a salt of carbonic acid

bicarbonate of soda n sodium bicarbonate used as medicine or a raising agent in baking

bicentenary or US **bicentennial** adj **1** marking a 200th anniversary ▸ n, pl **-naries 2** a 200th anniversary

biceps n, pl **-ceps** anatomy a muscle with two origins, esp. the muscle that flexes the forearm

bicker vb to argue over petty matters; squabble

bicycle n **1** a vehicle with a metal frame and two wheels, one behind the other, pedalled by the rider ▸ vb **-cling, -cled 2** to ride a bicycle

bid vb **bidding, bad, bade** or **bid, bidden** or **bid 1** to offer (an amount) in an attempt to buy something **2** to say (a greeting): to bid farewell **3** to order: do as you are bid! **4** bridge etc. to declare how many tricks one expects to make ▸ n **5 A** an

offer of a specified amount **B** the price offered **6 A** the quoting by a seller of a price **B** the price quoted **7** an attempt, esp. to attain power **8** bridge etc. the number of tricks a player undertakes to make > **bidder** n

> **bid** vb **1** = make an offer, offer, propose, submit, tender, proffer **2** = wish, say, call, tell, greet **3** = tell, ask, order, require, direct, command, instruct ▸ n **5** = offer, price, amount, advance, proposal, sum, tender **7** = attempt, try, effort, go (informal), shot (informal), stab (informal), crack (informal)

biddable adj obedient

bidding n **1** an order or command: she had done his bidding **2** an invitation; summons: he knew to knock and wait for bidding before he entered **3** the bids in an auction, card game, etc.

> **bidding** n **1** = order, request, command, instruction, summons, beck and call

biddy-bid or **biddy-biddy** n, pl **-bids** or **-biddies** NZ a low-growing plant with hooked burrs

bide vb **biding, bided** or **bode, bided 1** archaic or dialect to remain **2 bide one's time** to wait patiently for an opportunity

bidet (bee-day) n a small low basin for washing the genital area

biennial adj **1** occurring every two years ▸ n **2** a plant that completes its life cycle in two years

bier n a stand on which a corpse or a coffin rests before burial

bifocals pl n a pair of spectacles with bifocal lenses

big adj **bigger, biggest 1** of great or considerable size, weight, number, or capacity **2** having great significance; important **3** important through having power, wealth, etc. **4 A** elder: my big brother **B** grown-up **5** generous: that's very big of you **6** extravagant; boastful **7 too big for one's boots** conceited; unduly self-confident **8** in an advanced stage of pregnancy: big with child **9 in a big way** in a very grand or enthusiastic way ▸ adv informal **10** boastfully; pretentiously: he talks big **11** on a grand scale: think big

> **big** adj **1** = large, great, huge, massive, vast, enormous, substantial, extensive, supersize; ≠ small **2** = important, significant, urgent, far-reaching; ≠ unimportant **3** = powerful, important, prominent, dominant, influential, eminent, skookum (Canad) **4** = grown-up, adult, grown, mature, elder, full-grown **5** = generous, good, noble, gracious, benevolent, altruistic, unselfish, magnanimous

bigamy n the crime of marrying a person while still legally married to someone else > **bigamist** n > **bigamous** adj

bighead n informal a conceited person > **big-headed** adj

bigot _n_ a person who is intolerant, esp. regarding religion, politics, or race > **bigoted** _adj_ > **bigotry** _n_

big shot _n informal_ an important person

bijou (bee-zhoo) _n, pl_ **-joux** (-zhooz) **1** something small and delicately worked ▸ _adj_ **2** small but tasteful: _a bijou residence_

bike _n informal_ a bicycle or motorcycle

bikini _n_ a woman's brief two-piece swimming costume

bilateral _adj_ affecting or undertaken by two parties; mutual

bilberry _n, pl_ **-ries** a blue or blackish edible berry that grows on a shrub

bilby _n, pl_ **-bies** an Australian marsupial with long pointed ears and grey fur

bile _n_ **1** a greenish fluid secreted by the liver to aid digestion of fats **2** irritability or peevishness

bilge _n_ **1** _informal_ nonsense **2** _naut_ the bottom of a ship's hull **3** the dirty water that collects in a ship's bilge

bilingual _adj_ **1** able to speak two languages **2** expressed in two languages > **bilingualism** _n_

bilious _adj_ **1** nauseous; sick: _a bilious attack_ **2** _informal_ bad-tempered; irritable: _the regime's most persistent and bilious critic_ **3** (of a colour) harsh and offensive

bill¹ _n_ **1** a statement of money owed for goods or services supplied **2** a draft of a proposed new law presented to a law-making body **3** a printed notice or advertisement **4** _US & Canad_ a piece of paper money; note **5** any list of items, events, etc., such as a theatre programme ▸ _vb_ **6** to send or present an account for payment to (a person) **7** to advertise by posters **8** to schedule as a future programme: _next week they will discuss what are billed as new ideas for economic reform_ **9** **fit** or **fill the bill** _informal_ to be suitable or adequate

> **bill** _n_ **1** = charges, rate, costs, score, account, statement, reckoning, expense **2** = act of parliament, measure, proposal, piece of legislation, projected law **3** = advertisement, notice, poster, leaflet, bulletin, circular, handout, placard **5** = list, listing, programme, card, schedule, agenda, catalogue, inventory ▸ _vb_ **6** = charge, debit, invoice, send a statement to, send an invoice to **7** = advertise, post, announce, promote, plug (_informal_), tout, publicize, give advance notice of

bill² _n_ **1** the projecting jaws of a bird; beak ▸ _vb_ **2** **bill and coo** (of lovers) to kiss and whisper amorously

> **bill** _n_ = beak, nib, neb (_archaic, dialect_), mandible

billabong _n Austral_ a pool in the bed of a stream with an interrupted water flow

billboard _n_ a hoarding

billet _vb_ **-leting, -leted 1** to assign a lodging to (a soldier) ▸ _n_ **2** accommodation, esp. for a soldier, in civilian lodgings **3** _Austral & NZ_ a person who is billeted

billet-doux (bill-ee-doo) _n, pl_ **billets-doux** (bill-ee-dooz) _old-fashioned or humorous_ a love letter

billhook _n_ a tool with a hooked blade, used for chopping, etc.

billiards _n_ a game in which a long cue is used to propel balls on a table

billion _n, pl_ **-lions** _or_ **-lion 1** one thousand million: 1 000 000 000 or 10^9 **2** (in Britain, originally) one million million: 1 000 000 000 000 or 10^{12} **3** (often _pl_) _informal_ an extremely large but unspecified number: _billions of dollars_ > **billionth** _adj, n_

billow _n_ **1** a large sea wave **2** a swelling or surging mass, as of smoke or sound ▸ _vb_ **3** to rise up or swell out > **billowing** _adj, n_ > **billowy** _adj_

billy _or_ **billycan** _n, pl_ **-lies** _or_ **-lycans** a metal can or pot for boiling water, etc. over a campfire

biltong _n S African_ strips of meat dried and cured in the sun

bimbo _n, pl_ **-bos** _informal, offensive_ an attractive but empty-headed young woman

bin _n_ **1** a container for rubbish, etc. **2** a large container for storing something in bulk, such as coal, grain, or bottled wine ▸ _vb_ **binning, binned 3** to put in a rubbish bin: _I bin my junk mail without reading it_

binary (bine-a-ree) _adj_ **1** composed of two parts **2** _maths & computers_ of or expressed in a system with two as its base **3** _chem_ containing atoms of two different elements ▸ _n, pl_ **-ries 4** something composed of two parts

bind _vb_ **binding, bound 1** to make secure, such as with a rope **2** to unite with emotional ties or commitment **3** to place (someone) under legal or moral obligation **4** to place under certain constraints: _bound by the rules_ **5** to stick together or cause to stick: _egg binds fat and flour_ **6** to enclose and fasten (the pages of a book) between covers **7** to provide (a garment) with an edging **8** (foll. by _up_) to bandage ▸ _n_ **9** _informal_ a difficult or annoying situation

> **bind** _vb_ **1** = tie, join, stick, secure, wrap, knot, strap, lash; ≠ untie **3** = oblige, make, force, require, engage, compel, constrain, necessitate ▸ _n_ = nuisance, inconvenience, hassle (_informal_), drag (_informal_), spot (_informal_), difficulty, bore, dilemma, uphill (_S African_)

binder _n_ **1** a firm cover for holding loose sheets of paper together **2** a person who binds books **3** something used to fasten or tie, such as rope or twine **4** _obsolete_ a machine for cutting and binding grain into sheaves

binding _n_ **1** anything that binds or fastens **2** the covering of a book ▸ _adj_ **3** imposing an obligation or duty

> **binding** _adj_ = compulsory, necessary, mandatory, obligatory, irrevocable, unalterable, indissoluble; ≠ optional

bindweed _n_ a plant that twines around a support

binge *n informal* **1** a bout of excessive eating or drinking **2** excessive indulgence in anything

> **binge** *n* **1** = bout, spell, fling, feast, stint, spree, orgy, bender (*informal*)

bingo *n* a gambling game in which numbers called out are covered by players on their individual cards. The first to cover a given arrangement is the winner

binoculars *pl n* an optical instrument for use with both eyes, consisting of two small telescopes joined together

binomial *n* **1** a mathematical expression consisting of two terms, such as $3x + 2y$ ▸ *adj* **2** referring to two names or terms

bio- *combining form* **1** indicating life or living organisms: *biogenesis* **2** indicating a human life or career: *biography*

biochemistry *n* the study of the chemical compounds, reactions, etc. occurring in living organisms > **biochemical** *adj* > **biochemist** *n*

biodegradable *adj* (of sewage and packaging) capable of being decomposed by natural means > **biodegradability** *n*

biodiesel *n* a biofuel intended for use in diesel engines

biodiversity *n* the existence of a wide variety of plant and animal species in their natural environments

biofuel *n* fuel derived from renewable biological resources

biography *n, pl* **-phies 1** an account of a person's life by another person **2** such accounts collectively > **biographer** *n* > **biographical** *adj*

> **biography** *n* **1** = life story, life, record, account, profile, memoir, CV, curriculum vitae

biological *adj* **1** of or relating to biology **2** (of a detergent) containing enzymes that remove natural stains, such as blood or grass > **biologically** *adv*

biology *n* the study of living organisms > **biologist** *n*

biometric *adj* relating to the analysis of biological data using mathematical and statistical methods, esp. for purposes of identification: *biometric passport*

bionic *adj* **1** of or relating to bionics **2** (in science fiction) having physical functions augmented by electronic equipment

biopsy *n, pl* **-sies** examination of tissue from a living body to determine the cause or extent of a disease

biosphere *n* the part of the earth's surface and atmosphere inhabited by living things

biotechnology *n* the use of microorganisms, such as cells or bacteria, in industry and technology

bioterrorism *n* the use of viruses, bacteria, etc. by terrorists > **bioterrorist** *n*

biped (**bye-ped**) *n* **1** any animal with two feet ▸ *adj also* **bipedal 2** having two feet

biplane *n* an aeroplane with two sets of wings, one above the other

bipolar *adj* **1** having two poles **2** having two extremes **3** *psychiatry* having bipolar disorder > **bipolarity** *n*

bipolar disorder *n psychiatry* a condition characterized by an alternation between extreme euphoria and deep depression

birch *n* **1** a tree with thin peeling bark and hard close-grained wood **2 the birch** a bundle of birch twigs or a birch rod used, esp. formerly, for flogging offenders ▸ *vb* **3** to flog with the birch

bird *n* **1** a two-legged creature with feathers and wings, which lays eggs and can usually fly. Related adjective: **avian 2** *Brit slang, sometimes offensive* a girl or young woman **3** *informal* a person: *he's a rare bird* **4 a bird in the hand** something definite or certain **5 birds of a feather** people with the same ideas or interests **6 kill two birds with one stone** to accomplish two things with one action

> **bird** *n* **1** = feathered friend, fowl, songbird

bird flu *n* a form of influenza occurring in poultry caused by a virus capable of spreading to humans

birdie *n* **1** *informal* a bird **2** *golf* a score of one stroke under par for a hole

biretta *n* *RC Church* a stiff square clerical cap

Biro *n, pl* **-ros** *trademark* a kind of ballpoint pen

birth *n* **1** the process of bearing young; childbirth **2** the act of being born **3** the beginning of something; origin **4** ancestry: *of noble birth* **5 give birth to A** to bear (offspring) **B** to produce or originate (an idea, plan, etc.)

> **birth** *n* **1** = childbirth, delivery, nativity, parturition; ≠ death **4** = ancestry, stock, blood, background, breeding, pedigree, lineage, parentage

birth control *n* limitation of child-bearing by means of contraception

birthday *n* **1** an anniversary of the day of one's birth **2** the day on which a person was born

birthmark *n* a blemish on the skin formed before birth

birthright *n* privileges or possessions that a person has or is believed to be entitled to as soon as he or she is born

biscuit *n* **1** a small flat dry sweet or plain cake **2** porcelain that has been fired but not glazed ▸ *adj* **3** pale brown or yellowish-grey

bisect *vb* **1** *maths* to divide into two equal parts **2** to cut or split into two > **bisection** *n*

bisexual *adj* **1** sexually or romantically attracted by both men and women **2** showing characteristics of both sexes ▸ *n* **3** a bisexual person > **bisexuality** *n*

bishop *n* **1** a member of the clergy having spiritual and administrative powers over a diocese **2** a chess piece capable of moving diagonally

bishopric *n* the see, diocese, or office of a bishop

bismuth *n chem* a brittle pinkish-white metallic element. Some compounds are used in alloys and in medicine. Symbol: **Bi**

bison *n*, *pl* **-son** an animal of the cattle family with a massive head, shaggy forequarters, and a humped back

bisque *n* a thick rich soup made from shellfish

bistro *n*, *pl* **-tros** a small restaurant

bit¹ *n* **1** a small piece, portion, or quantity **2** a short time or distance **3 a bit** rather; somewhat: *a bit stupid* **4 a bit of** rather: *a bit of a fool* **5 bit by bit** gradually **6 do one's bit** to make one's expected contribution

> **bit** *n* **1** = slice, fragment, crumb, morsel

bit² *n* **1** a metal mouthpiece on a bridle for controlling a horse **2** a cutting or drilling tool, part, or head in a brace, drill, etc.

> **bit** *n* **1** = curb, check, brake, restraint, snaffle

bit³ *vb* the past tense of **bite**

bit⁴ *n maths & computers* **1** a single digit of binary notation, represented either by 0 or by 1 **2** the smallest unit of information, indicating the presence or absence of a single feature

bitch *n* **1** a female dog, fox, or wolf **2** *derogatory slang* a malicious or spiteful woman **3** *informal* a difficult situation or problem ▸ *vb* **4** *informal* to complain; grumble

bitchy *adj* **bitchier**, **bitchiest** *informal* spiteful or malicious ▸ **bitchiness** *n*

bite *vb* **biting**, **bit**, **bitten 1** to grip, cut off, or tear with the teeth or jaws **2** (of animals or insects) to injure by puncturing (the skin) with the teeth or fangs **3** (of corrosive material) to eat away or into **4** to smart or cause to smart; sting **5** *angling* (of a fish) to take the bait or lure **6** to take firm hold of or act effectively upon: *turn the screw till it bites the wood* **7** *slang* to annoy or worry: *what's biting her?* ▸ *n* **8** the act of biting **9** a thing or amount bitten off **10** a wound or sting inflicted by biting **11** *angling* an attempt by a fish to take the bait or lure **12** a snack **13** a stinging or smarting sensation ▸ **biter** *n*

> **bite** *vb* **1, 2** = nip, cut, tear, wound, snap, pierce, pinch, chew ▸ *n* **10** = wound, sting, pinch, nip, prick **12** = snack, food, piece, taste, refreshment, mouthful, titbit

biting *adj* **1** piercing; keen: *a biting wind* **2** sarcastic; incisive

> **biting** *adj* **1** = piercing, cutting, sharp, frozen, harsh, penetrating, arctic (*informal*), icy **2** = sarcastic, cutting, stinging, scathing, acrimonious, incisive, virulent, caustic

bitter *adj* **1** having an unpalatable harsh taste, as the peel of an orange **2** showing or caused by hostility or resentment **3** difficult to accept: *a bitter blow* **4** sarcastic: *bitter words* **5** bitingly cold: *a bitter night* ▸ *n* **6** *Brit* beer with a slightly bitter taste ▸ **bitterly** *adv* ▸ **bitterness** *n*

> **bitter** *adj* **1** = sour, sharp, acid, harsh, tart, astringent, acrid, unsweetened; ≠ sweet **2** = resentful, angry, offended, sour, sore, acrimonious, sullen, miffed (*informal*); ≠ happy **5** = freezing, biting, severe, intense, raw, fierce, chill, stinging; ≠ mild

bittern *n* a large wading marsh bird with a booming call

bitumen *n* a sticky or solid substance that occurs naturally in asphalt and tar and is used in road surfacing ▸ **bituminous** *adj*

bivalve *n* **1** a sea creature, such as an oyster or mussel, that has a shell consisting of two hinged valves and breathes through gills ▸ *adj* **2** of these molluscs

bivouac *n* **1** a temporary camp, as used by soldiers or mountaineers ▸ *vb* **-acking**, **-acked 2** to make a temporary camp

bizarre *adj* odd or unusual, esp. in an interesting or amusing way

> **bizarre** *adj* = strange, unusual, extraordinary, fantastic, weird, peculiar, eccentric, ludicrous, daggy (*Austral*, *NZ informal*); ≠ normal

blab *vb* **blabbing**, **blabbed** to divulge (secrets) indiscreetly

black *adj* **1** having no hue, owing to the absorption of all or almost all light; of the colour of coal **2** without light **3** without hope; gloomy: *the future looked black* **4** dirty or soiled **5** angry or resentful: *black looks* **6** unpleasant in a cynical or macabre manner: *black comedy* **7** (of coffee or tea) without milk or cream **8** wicked or harmful: *a black lie* ▸ *n* **9** the darkest colour; the colour of coal **10** a dye or pigment producing this colour **11** black clothing, worn esp. in mourning: *she was in black, as though in mourning* **12** complete darkness: *the black of the night* **13 in the black** in credit or without debt ▸ *vb* **14** same as **blacken 15** to polish (shoes or boots) with blacking **16** *Brit*, *Austral & NZ* (of trade unionists) to organize a boycott of (specified goods, work, etc.) ▸ See also **blackout** ▸ **blackness** *n* ▸ **blackish** *adj*

> **black** *adj* **1** = dark, raven, ebony, sable, jet, dusky, pitch-black, swarthy; ≠ light **3** = gloomy, sad, depressing, grim, bleak, hopeless, dismal, ominous; ≠ happy **5** = angry, cross, furious, hostile, sour, menacing, moody, resentful; ≠ happy **8** = wicked, bad, evil, corrupt, vicious, immoral, depraved, villainous; ≠ good

Black *adj* **1** (of a person) belonging to a race of people with dark skins **2** of or relating to a Black person or Black people ▸ *n* **3** *sometimes offensive* a member of a race of people with dark skins

blackball¹ *vb* **1** to vote against **2** to exclude (someone) from a group, etc.

b

blackball² n NZ a hard boiled sweet with black-and-white stripes

blackberry n, pl -ries a small blackish edible fruit that grows on a woody bush with thorny stems. Also called: **bramble**

BlackBerry n, pl -ries trademark a brand of smartphone

blackbird n a common European thrush, the male of which has black plumage and a yellow bill

blackboard n a hard or rigid surface made of a smooth usually dark substance, used for writing or drawing on with chalk, esp. in teaching

blackcurrant n a very small blackish edible fruit that grows in bunches on a bush

blacken vb 1 to make or become black or dirty 2 to damage (someone's reputation); discredit: they planned to blacken my father's name

blackguard (blag-gard) n an unprincipled contemptible person

blackhead n 1 a black-tipped plug of fatty matter clogging a pore of the skin 2 a bird with black plumage on the head

blackleg n Brit 1 a person who continues to work or does another's job during a strike ▸ vb -legging, -legged 2 to refuse to join a strike

blacklist n 1 a list of people or organizations considered untrustworthy or disloyal ▸ vb 2 to put (someone) on a blacklist

black magic n magic used for evil purposes

blackmail n 1 the act of attempting to obtain money by threatening to reveal shameful information 2 the use of unfair pressure in an attempt to influence someone ▸ vb 3 to obtain or attempt to obtain money by intimidation 4 to attempt to influence (a person) by unfair pressure > **blackmailer** n

> **blackmail** n = threat, intimidation, ransom, extortion, hush money (slang) ▸ vb = threaten, squeeze, compel, intimidate, coerce, dragoon, extort, hold to ransom

black market n a place or a system for buying or selling goods or currencies illegally, esp. in violation of controls or rationing > **black marketeer** n

blackout n 1 (in wartime) the putting out or hiding of all lights as a precaution against a night air attack 2 a momentary loss of consciousness, vision, or memory 3 a temporary electrical power failure 4 the prevention of information broadcasts: a news blackout ▸ vb **black out** 5 to put out (lights) 6 to lose vision, consciousness, or memory temporarily 7 to stop (news, a television programme, etc.) from being broadcast

black sheep n a person who is regarded as a disgrace or failure by his or her family or peer group

blacksmith n a person who works iron with a furnace, anvil, and hammer

black spot n 1 a place on a road where accidents frequently occur 2 an area where a particular situation is exceptionally bad: an unemployment black spot

bladder n 1 anatomy a membranous sac, usually containing liquid, esp. the urinary bladder 2 a hollow bag made of leather, etc. which becomes round when filled with air or liquid 3 a hollow saclike part in certain plants, such as seaweed > **bladdery** adj

blade n 1 the part of a sharp weapon, tool, or knife, that forms the cutting edge 2 the thin flattish part of a propeller, oar, or fan 3 the flattened part of a leaf, sepal, or petal 4 the long narrow leaf of a grass or related plant

blame vb **blaming, blamed** 1 to consider (someone) responsible for: I blame her for the failure 2 (foll. by on) to put responsibility for (something) on (someone): she blames the failure on me 3 **be to blame** to be at fault ▸ n 4 responsibility for something that is wrong: they must take the blame for the failure 5 an expression of condemnation: analysts lay the blame on party activists > **blamable** or **blameable** adj > **blameless** adj

> **blame** vb 1 = hold responsible, accuse, denounce, indict, impeach, incriminate, impute; ≠ absolve 2 = attribute to, credit to, assign to, put down to, impute to ▸ n 4 = responsibility, liability, accountability, onus, culpability, answerability; ≠ praise

blameworthy adj deserving blame > **blameworthiness** n

blanch vb 1 to whiten 2 to become pale, as with sickness or fear 3 to prepare (meat or vegetables) by plunging them in boiling water 4 to cause (celery, chicory, etc.) to grow white from lack of light

blancmange (blam-monzh) n a jelly-like dessert of milk, stiffened usually with cornflour

bland adj 1 dull and uninteresting: the bland predictability of the film 2 (of food, drink, etc.) flavourless 3 smooth in manner: he looked at his visitor with a bland smile > **blandly** adv

> **bland** adj 1 = dull, boring, plain, flat, dreary, run-of-the-mill, uninspiring, humdrum; ≠ exciting 2 = tasteless, insipid, flavourless, thin

blandishments pl n flattery intended to coax or cajole

blank adj 1 (of a writing surface) not written on 2 (of a form, etc.) with spaces left for details to be filled in 3 without ornament or break: a blank wall 4 empty or void: a blank space 5 showing no interest or expression: a blank look 6 lacking ideas or inspiration: his mind went blank ▸ n 7 an empty space 8 an empty space for writing in 9 the condition of not understanding: my mind went a complete blank 10 a mark, often a dash, in place of a word 11 **draw a blank** to get no results from something ▸ vb 12 (foll. by out) to cross out, blot, or obscure **13 blank something out** to refuse to think about something; clear something from one's mind **14** *slang* to ignore: *the crowd blanked her for the first four numbers* ▸ **blankly** *adv*

> **blank** *adj* **1, 2, 3, 4** = unmarked, white, clear, clean, empty, plain, bare, void; ≠ marked **5** = expressionless, empty, vague, vacant, deadpan, impassive, poker-faced (*informal*); ≠ expressive ▸ *n* **7, 8** = empty space, space, gap **9** = void, vacuum, vacancy, emptiness, nothingness

blanket *n* **1** a large piece of thick cloth for use as a bed covering **2** a concealing cover, as of smoke, leaves, or snow ▸ *adj* **3** applying to or covering a wide group or variety of people, conditions, situations, etc.: *a blanket ban on all supporters travelling to away matches* ▸ *vb* **-keting, -keted 4** to cover as if with a blanket **5** to cover a wide area of; give blanket coverage to

> **blanket** *n* **1** = cover, rug, coverlet **2** = covering, sheet, coat, layer, carpet, cloak, mantle, thickness ▸ *vb* **4** = coat, cover, hide, mask, conceal, obscure, cloak

blank verse *n* unrhymed verse

blare *vb* **blaring, blared 1** to sound loudly and harshly **2** to proclaim loudly: *the newspaper headlines blared the news* ▸ *n* **3** a loud harsh noise

blarney *n* flattering talk

blasé (blah-**zay**) *adj* indifferent or bored, esp. through familiarity

blaspheme *vb* **-pheming, -phemed 1** to speak disrespectfully of (God or sacred things) **2** to utter curses ▸ **blasphemer** *n*

blasphemy *n, pl* **-mies** behaviour or language that shows disrespect for God or sacred things ▸ **blasphemous** *adj*

blast *n* **1** an explosion, such as that caused by dynamite **2** the charge used in a single explosion **3** a sudden strong gust of wind or air **4** a sudden loud sound, such as that made by a trumpet **5** a violent verbal outburst, esp. critical **6** *slang* a very enjoyable or thrilling experience: *the party was a blast* **7 at full blast** at maximum speed, volume, etc. ▸ *interj* **8** *slang* an exclamation of annoyance ▸ *vb* **9** to blow up (a rock, tunnel, etc.) with explosives **10** to make or cause to make a loud harsh noise **11** to criticize severely

> **blast** *n* **1** = explosion, crash, burst, discharge, eruption, detonation **3** = gust, rush, storm, breeze, puff, gale, tempest (*literary*), squall **4** = blare, blow, scream, trumpet, wail, resound, clamour, toot ▸ *vb* **9** = blow up, bomb, destroy, burst, ruin, break up, explode

blastoff *n* **1** the launching of a rocket under its own power ▸ *vb* **blast off 2** (of a rocket) to be launched

blatant (**blay**-tant) *adj* **1** glaringly obvious: *a blatant lie* **2** offensively noticeable: *their blatant disregard for my feelings* ▸ **blatantly** *adv*

blatant *adj* **1** = obvious, clear, plain, evident, glaring, manifest, noticeable, conspicuous; ≠ subtle

blaze[1] *n* **1** a strong fire or flame **2** a very bright light or glare **3** an outburst (of passion, patriotism, etc.) ▸ *vb* **blazing, blazed 4** to burn fiercely **5** to shine brightly **6** to become stirred, as with anger or excitement **7 blaze away** to shoot continuously

> **blaze** *n* **1** = inferno, fire, flames, bonfire, combustion, conflagration **2** = flash, glow, glitter, flare, glare, gleam, brilliance, radiance ▸ *vb* **4** = burn, glow, flare, be on fire, go up in flames, be ablaze, fire, flame **5** = shine, flash, beam, glow, flare, glare, gleam, radiate

blaze[2] *n* **1** a mark, usually indicating a path, made on a tree **2** a light-coloured marking on the face of an animal ▸ *vb* **blazing, blazed 3** to mark (a tree, path, etc.) with a blaze **4 blaze a trail** to explore new territories, areas of knowledge, etc.

blazer *n* a fairly lightweight jacket, often in the colours of a sports club, school, etc.

blazon *vb* **1** to proclaim publicly: *the newspaper photographs were blazoned on the front pages* **2** *heraldry* to describe or colour (heraldic arms) conventionally ▸ *n* **3** *heraldry* a coat of arms

bleach *vb* **1** to make or become white or colourless by exposure to sunlight, or by the action of chemical agents ▸ *n* **2** a bleaching agent

> **bleach** *vb* = lighten, wash out, blanch, whiten

bleak *adj* **1** exposed and barren **2** cold and raw **3** offering little hope; dismal: *a bleak future* ▸ **bleakly** *adv* ▸ **bleakness** *n*

> **bleak** *adj* **1** = exposed, empty, bare, barren, desolate, windswept, weather-beaten, unsheltered; ≠ sheltered **2** = stormy, severe, rough, harsh, tempestuous, intemperate **3** = dismal, dark, depressing, grim, discouraging, gloomy, hopeless, dreary; ≠ cheerful

bleary *adj* **blearier, bleariest 1** with eyes dimmed, by tears or tiredness: *a few bleary hacks* **2** indistinct or unclear ▸ **blearily** *adv*

bleat *vb* **1** (of a sheep, goat, or calf) to utter its plaintive cry **2** to whine ▸ *n* **3** the characteristic cry of sheep, goats, and calves **4** a weak complaint or whine

bleed *vb* **bleeding, bled 1** to lose or emit blood **2** to remove or draw blood from (a person or animal) **3** (of plants) to exude (sap or resin), esp. from a cut **4** *informal* to obtain money, etc. from (someone), esp. by extortion **5** to draw liquid or gas from (a container or enclosed system) **6 my heart bleeds for you** I am sorry for you: often used ironically

b

bleed *vb* **1** = lose blood, flow, gush, spurt, shed blood **4** = extort, milk, squeeze, drain, exhaust, fleece

bleep *n* **1** a short high-pitched signal made by an electronic device **2** same as **bleeper** ▸ *vb* **3** to make a bleeping signal **4** to call (someone) by means of a bleeper

bleeper *n* a small portable radio receiver that makes a bleeping signal

blemish *n* **1** a defect; flaw; stain ▸ *vb* **2** to spoil or tarnish

blench *vb* to shy away, as in fear

blend *vb* **1** to mix or mingle (components) **2** to mix (different varieties of tea, whisky, etc.) **3** to look good together; harmonize **4** (esp. of colours) to shade gradually into each other ▸ *n* **5** a mixture produced by blending

blend *vb* **1** = mix, join, combine, compound, merge, unite, mingle, amalgamate **3** = go well, match, fit, suit, go with, correspond, complement, coordinate ▸ *n* = mixture, mix, combination, compound, brew, union, synthesis, alloy

blender *n* an electrical kitchen appliance for pureeing vegetables, etc.

bless *vb* **blessing**, **blessed** *or* **blest** **1** to make holy by means of a religious rite **2** to give honour or glory to (a person or thing) as holy **3** to call upon God to protect **4** to worship or adore (God) **5 be blessed with** to be endowed with: *she is blessed with immense energy* **6 bless me!** an exclamation of surprise **7 bless you!** said to a person who has just sneezed

bless *vb* **1, 3** = sanctify, dedicate, ordain, exalt, anoint, consecrate, hallow; ≠ curse

blessed *adj* **1** made holy **2** RC Church (of a person) beatified by the pope **3** bringing great happiness or good fortune: *he was blessed with good looks* **4** euphemistic damned: *I'm blessed if I know*

blessed *adj* **1** = holy, sacred, divine, adored, revered, hallowed, sanctified, beatified

blessing *n* **1** the act of invoking divine protection or aid **2** approval; good wishes **3** a happy event

blessing *n* **1** = benediction, grace, dedication, thanksgiving, invocation, commendation, consecration, benison; ≠ curse **2** = approval, backing, support, agreement, favour, sanction, permission, leave; ≠ disapproval

blether *Scot* ▸ *vb* **1** to speak foolishly at length ▸ *n* **2** foolish talk **3** a person who blethers

blew *vb* the past tense of **blow**¹

blight *n* **1** a person or thing that spoils or prevents growth **2** any plant disease characterized by withering and shrivelling without rotting **3** a fungus or insect that causes

blight in plants **4** an ugly urban district ▸ *vb* **5** to cause to suffer a blight **6** to frustrate or disappoint: *blighted love* **7** to destroy: *the event blighted her life*

blight *n* **1** = curse, suffering, evil, corruption, pollution, plague (*informal*), hardship, woe; ≠ blessing **2, 3** = disease, pest, fungus, mildew, infestation, pestilence, canker ▸ *vb* **5** = frustrate, destroy, ruin, crush, mar, dash, wreck, spoil, crool *or* cruel (*Austral slang*)

blighter *n Brit, Austral & NZ informal* a despicable or irritating person or thing

blimp *n* **1** a small nonrigid airship **2** *films* a soundproof cover fixed over a camera during shooting

blind *adj* **1** unable to see **2** unable or unwilling to understand: *she is blind to his faults* **3** not determined by reason: *blind hatred* **4** acting or performed without control or preparation **5** done without being able to see, relying on instruments for information **6** hidden from sight: *a blind corner* **7** closed at one end: *a blind alley* **8** completely lacking awareness or consciousness: *a blind stupor* **9** having no openings: *a blind wall* ▸ *adv* **10** without being able to see ahead or using only instruments: *flying blind* **11** without adequate information: *we bought the house blind* **12 blind drunk** *informal* very drunk ▸ *vb* **13** to deprive of sight permanently or temporarily **14** to deprive of good sense, reason, or judgment **15** to darken; conceal **16** to overwhelm by showing detailed knowledge: *he tried to blind us with science* ▸ *n* **17** a shade for a window **18** any obstruction or hindrance to sight, light, or air **19** a person, action, or thing that serves to deceive or conceal the truth ▸ **blinding** *adj* ▸ **blindly** *adv* ▸ **blindness** *n*

blind *adj* **1** = sightless, unsighted, unseeing, visionless; ≠ sighted **2** = unaware of, unconscious of, ignorant of, indifferent to, insensitive to, oblivious of, unconcerned about, inconsiderate of; ≠ aware **3** = unquestioning, prejudiced, wholesale, indiscriminate, uncritical, unreasoning, undiscriminating

blindfold *vb* **1** to prevent (a person or animal) from seeing by covering the eyes ▸ *n* **2** a piece of cloth used to cover the eyes ▸ *adj, adv* **3** having the eyes covered with a cloth

blink *vb* **1** to close and immediately reopen (the eyes), usually involuntarily **2** to shine intermittently or unsteadily ▸ *n* **3** the act or an instance of blinking **4** a glance; glimpse **5 on the blink** *slang* not working properly

blink *vb* **1** = flutter, wink, bat **2** = flash, flicker, wink, shimmer, twinkle, glimmer ▸ *n* **5 on the blink** = not working (properly), faulty, defective, playing up, out of action, malfunctioning, out of order

blinkers *pl n Brit & Austral* leather side pieces attached to a horse's bridle to prevent sideways vision

blip *n* **1** a repetitive sound, such as the kind produced by an electronic device **2** the spot of light on a radar screen indicating the position of an object **3** a temporary irregularity in the performance of something

bliss *n* **1** perfect happiness; serene joy **2** the joy of heaven > **blissful** *adj* > **blissfully** *adv*

> **bliss** *n* **1** = joy, ecstasy, euphoria, rapture, nirvana, felicity, gladness, blissfulness; ≠ misery **2** = beatitude, blessedness

blister *n* **1** a small bubble on the skin filled with a watery fluid **2** a swelling containing air or liquid, such as on a painted surface ▶ *vb* **3** to have or cause to have blisters **4** to attack verbally with great scorn > **blistering** *adj*

> **blister** *n* **1** = sore, boil, swelling, cyst, pimple, carbuncle, pustule

blithe *adj* **1** heedless; casual and indifferent **2** very happy or cheerful > **blithely** *adv*

blitz *n* **1** a violent and sustained attack by enemy aircraft **2** any intensive attack or concerted effort ▶ *vb* **3** to attack suddenly and intensively

> **blitz** *n* **1** = attack, strike, assault, raid, offensive, onslaught, bombardment, bombing campaign

blizzard *n* a blinding storm of wind and snow

bloat *vb* **1** to cause to swell, as with a liquid or air **2** to cause to be puffed up, as with conceit **3** to cure (fish, esp. herring) by half drying in smoke > **bloated** *adj*

bloater *n Brit* a herring that has been salted in brine, smoked, and cured

blob *n* **1** a soft mass or drop **2** a spot of colour, ink, etc. **3** an indistinct or shapeless form or object

bloc *n* a group of people or countries combined by a common interest

> **bloc** *n* = group, union, league, alliance, coalition, axis

block *n* **1** a large solid piece of wood, stone, etc. **2** such a piece on which particular tasks may be done, as chopping, cutting, etc. **3** a large building of offices, flats, etc. **4** a group of buildings in a city bounded by intersecting streets on each side **5** an obstruction or hindrance: *a writer with a block* **6** one of a set of wooden or plastic cubes as a child's toy **7** *slang* a person's head **8** a piece of wood, metal, etc. engraved for printing **9** a casing housing one or more freely rotating pulleys **10** a quantity considered as a single unit ▶ *vb* **11** to obstruct or impede by introducing an obstacle: *lorry drivers had blocked the routes to Paris* **12** to impede, retard, or prevent (an action or procedure) **13** to stamp

(a title or design) on (a book cover, etc.) **14** *cricket* to play (a ball) defensively > **blockage** *n*

> **block** *n* **1** = piece, bar, mass, brick, lump, chunk, hunk, ingot **5** = obstruction, bar, barrier, obstacle, impediment, hindrance ▶ *vb* **11** = obstruct, close, stop, plug, choke, clog, stop up, bung up (*informal*); ≠ clear

blockade *n* **1** *military* the closing off of a port or region to prevent the passage of goods ▶ *vb* **-ading, -aded 2** to impose a blockade on

> **blockade** *n* = stoppage, block, barrier, restriction, obstacle, barricade, obstruction, impediment

blockhead *n* a stupid person > **blockheaded** *adj*

blockie *n Austral* an owner of a small property, esp. a farm

block letter *n* a plain capital letter. Also called: **block capital**

blog *n* **1** a journal written online and accessible to users of the internet. Full name: **weblog** ▶ *vb* **blogging, blogged 2** to write a blog > **blogger** *n* > **blogging** *n*

blogosphere *n informal* a collective term for the weblogs on the internet

bloke *n Brit, Austral & NZ informal* a man > **blokeish** *or* **blokey** *adj*

> **bloke** *n* = man, person, individual, character (*informal*), guy (*informal*), fellow (*old-fashioned*), chap

blonde *or masc* **blond** *adj* **1** (of hair) fair **2** (of a person) having fair hair and a light complexion ▶ *n* **3** a person having light-coloured hair and skin > **blondeness** *or masc* **blondness** *n*

> **blonde** *or* **blond** *adj* **1** = fair, light, flaxen **2** = fair-haired, golden-haired, tow-headed

blood *n* **1** a reddish fluid in vertebrates that is pumped by the heart through the arteries and veins. Related adjective: **haemal 2** bloodshed, esp. when resulting in murder: *they were responsible for the spilling of blood throughout the country* **3** lifeblood **4** relationship through being of the same family, race, or kind; kinship **5 the blood** royal or noble descent: *a prince of the blood* **6 flesh and blood A** near kindred or kinship, esp. that between a parent and child **B** human nature: *it's more than flesh and blood can stand* **7 in one's blood** as a natural or inherited characteristic **8** newcomers viewed as an invigorating force: *new blood* **9 in cold blood** showing no passion; ruthlessly **10 make one's blood boil** to cause one to be angry or indignant **11 make one's blood run cold** to fill one with horror ▶ *vb* **12** *hunting* to cause (young hounds) to taste the blood of a freshly killed quarry **13** to initiate (a person) to war or hunting

> **blood** *n* **1** = lifeblood, gore, vital fluid **4** = family, relations, birth, descent, extraction, ancestry, lineage, kinship

blood bath *n* a massacre

bloodhound *n* a large hound, formerly used in tracking and police work

bloodless *adj* 1 without blood: *bloodless surgery* 2 conducted without violence: *a bloodless coup* 3 anaemic-looking; pale 4 lacking vitality; lifeless: *the bloodless ambience of supermarkets*

bloodshed *n* slaughter; killing

> **bloodshed** *n* = killing, murder, massacre, slaughter, slaying, carnage, butchery, blood-letting

bloodshot *adj* (of an eye) inflamed

blood sport *n* any sport involving the killing of an animal

bloodstream *n* the flow of blood through the vessels of a living body

bloodsucker *n* 1 an animal that sucks blood, esp. a leech 2 *informal* a person who preys upon another person, esp. by extorting money

bloodthirsty *adj* **-thirstier, -thirstiest** taking pleasure in bloodshed or violence

bloody *adj* **bloodier, bloodiest** 1 covered with blood 2 marked by much killing and bloodshed: *a bloody war* 3 cruel or murderous: *a bloody tyrant* ▸ *adj, adv* 4 *slang* extreme or extremely: *a bloody fool; a bloody good idea* ▸ *vb* **bloodies, bloodying, bloodied** 5 to stain with blood

> **bloody** *adj* 1 = bloodstained, raw, bleeding, blood-soaked, blood-spattered 3 = cruel, fierce, savage, brutal, vicious, ferocious, cut-throat, warlike

bloody-minded *adj Brit & NZ informal* deliberately obstructive and unhelpful

bloom *n* 1 a blossom on a flowering plant 2 the state or period when flowers open 3 a healthy or flourishing condition; prime 4 a youthful or healthy glow 5 a fine whitish coating on the surface of fruits or leaves ▸ *vb* 6 (of flowers) to open 7 to bear flowers 8 to flourish or grow 9 to be in a healthy, glowing condition

> **bloom** *n* 1 = flower, bud, blossom 3 = prime, flower, beauty, height, peak, flourishing, heyday, zenith 4 = glow, freshness, lustre, radiance; ≠ pallor ▸ *vb* 6 = flower, blossom, open, bud; ≠ wither 8 = succeed, flourish, thrive, prosper, fare well; ≠ fail

bloomer *n Brit informal* a stupid mistake; blunder

bloomers *pl n* 1 *informal* women's baggy knickers 2 (formerly) loose trousers gathered at the knee, worn by women

blossom *n* 1 the flower or flowers of a plant, esp. producing edible fruit 2 the period of flowering ▸ *vb* 3 (of plants) to flower 4 to come to a promising stage

> **blossom** *n* 1 = flower, bloom, bud, efflorescence, floret ▸ *vb* 3 = flower, bloom, bud 4 = succeed, progress, thrive, flourish, prosper

blot *n* 1 a stain or spot, esp. of ink 2 something that spoils 3 a stain on one's character ▸ *vb* **blotting, blotted** 4 to stain or spot 5 to cause a blemish in or on: *he blotted his copybook by missing a penalty* 6 to soak up (excess ink, etc.) by using blotting paper 7 **blot out** A to darken or hide completely: *the mist blotted out the sea* B to block from one's mind: *to blot out the memories*

blotch *n* 1 an irregular spot or discoloration 2 to become or cause to become marked by such discoloration > **blotchy** *adj*

blotter *n* a sheet of blotting paper

blotting paper *n* a soft absorbent paper, used for soaking up surplus ink

blotto *adj Brit, Austral & NZ slang* extremely drunk

blouse *n* 1 a woman's shirtlike garment 2 a waist-length belted jacket worn by soldiers ▸ *vb* **blousing, bloused** 3 to hang or cause to hang in full loose folds

blow¹ *vb* **blowing, blew, blown** 1 (of a current of air, the wind, etc.) to be or cause to be in motion 2 to move or be carried by or as if by wind 3 to expel (air, etc.) through the mouth or nose 4 to breathe hard; pant 5 to inflate with air or the breath 6 (of wind, etc.) to make a roaring sound 7 to cause (a musical instrument) to sound by forcing air into it 8 (often foll. by *up* or *in* etc.) to explode, break, or disintegrate completely 9 *electronics* (of a fuse or valve) to burn out because of excessive current 10 to shape (glass, etc.) by forcing air or gas through the material when molten 11 *slang* to spend (money) freely 12 *slang* to use (an opportunity) ineffectively 13 *slang* to expose or betray (a secret) 14 *past participle* **blowed** *informal* same as **damn** 15 **blow hot and cold** *informal* to keep changing one's attitude towards someone or something 16 **blow one's top** *informal* to lose one's temper ▸ *n* 17 the act or an instance of blowing 18 the sound produced by blowing 19 a blast of air or wind 20 *Brit slang* cannabis ▸ See also **blow out** *etc.*

> **blow** *vb* 2 = be carried, flutter 3 = exhale, breathe, pant, puff 7 = play, sound, pipe, trumpet, blare, toot 8 **blow up** = explode, burst, shatter, erupt, detonate

blow² *n* 1 a powerful or heavy stroke with the fist, a weapon, etc. 2 a sudden setback: *the scheme was dealt a blow by the introduction of martial law* 3 an attacking action: *a blow for freedom* 4 **come to blows** A to fight B to result in a fight

> **blow** *n* 1 = knock, stroke, punch, bang, sock (*slang*), smack, thump, clout (*informal*) 2 = setback, shock, disaster, reverse, disappointment, catastrophe, misfortune, bombshell

blow-dry *vb* **-dries, -drying, -dried** 1 to style (the hair) while drying it with a hand-held hair dryer ▸ *n* 2 this method of styling hair

blower n **1** a mechanical device, such as a fan, that blows **2** *informal* a telephone

blowie n *Austral informal* a bluebottle

blown vb a past participle of **blow¹**

blow out vb **1** (of a flame) to extinguish or be extinguished **2** (of a tyre) to puncture suddenly **3** (of an oil or gas well) to lose oil or gas in an uncontrolled manner ▸ n **blowout 4** a sudden burst in a tyre **5** the uncontrolled escape of oil or gas from a well **6** *slang* a large filling meal **7** *Austral* a sudden large increase

blowsy *adj* **blowsier**, **blowsiest 1** (of a woman) untidy in appearance **2** (of a woman) ruddy in complexion

blow up vb **1** to explode or cause to explode **2** to inflate with air **3** to increase the importance of (something): *an affair blown up out of all proportion* **4** *informal* to lose one's temper **5** *informal* to reprimand (someone) **6** *informal* to enlarge (a photograph) **7** to come into existence with sudden force: *a crisis had blown up* ▸ n **blow-up 8** *informal* an enlarged photograph

> **blow up** vb **1 blow something up** = explode, bomb, blast, detonate, blow sky-high **2 blow something up** = inflate, pump up, fill, expand, swell, enlarge, puff up, distend **4** = lose your temper, rage, erupt, see red (*informal*), become angry, hit the roof (*informal*), fly off the handle (*informal*), go crook (*Austral, NZ slang*), blow your top **6 blow something up** = magnify, increase, extend, expand, widen, broaden, amplify

blowy *adj* **blowier**, **blowiest** windy

blubber n **1** the fatty tissue of aquatic mammals such as the whale **2** *informal* flabby body fat ▸ vb **3** to sob without restraint

bludge *Austral & NZ informal* ▸ vb **bludging**, **bludged 1** (foll. by *on*) to scrounge from **2** to evade work ▸ n **3** a very easy task › **bludger** n

> **bludge** vb **2** = slack, skive (*Brit informal*), idle, shirk

bludgeon n **1** a stout heavy club, typically thicker at one end ▸ vb **2** to hit as if with a bludgeon **3** to force; bully; coerce

blue n **1** the colour of a clear unclouded sky **2** anything blue, such as blue clothing or blue paint: *she is clothed in blue* **3** a sportsperson who represents or has represented Oxford or Cambridge University **4** *Brit informal* a Tory **5** *Austral & NZ slang* an argument or fight **6** Also: **bluey** *Austral & NZ slang* a court summons **7** *Austral & NZ informal* a mistake **8 out of the blue** unexpectedly ▸ *adj* **bluer**, **bluest 9** of the colour blue; of the colour of a clear unclouded sky **10** (of the flesh) having a purple tinge from cold **11** depressed or unhappy **12** pornographic: *blue movies* ▸ vb **blueing** or **bluing**, **blued 13** to make or become blue or bluer **14** *old-fashioned, informal* to spend extravagantly or wastefully: *I consoled myself by blueing my royalty cheque* › **blueness** n

> **blue** *adj* **11** = depressed, low, sad, unhappy, melancholy, dejected, despondent, downcast; ≠ happy

bluebell n a woodland plant with blue bell-shaped flowers

bluebottle n **1** a large fly with a dark-blue body; blowfly **2** *Austral & NZ informal* a Portuguese man-of-war

blue-collar *adj* denoting manual industrial workers

blue heeler n *Austral & NZ informal* a dog that controls cattle by biting their heels

blueprint n **1** an original description of a plan or idea that explains how it is expected to work **2** a photographic print of plans, technical drawings, etc. consisting of white lines on a blue background

> **blueprint** n **1** = scheme, plan, design, system, programme, proposal, strategy, pattern **2** = plan, scheme, pattern, draft, outline, sketch

bluetongue n an Australian lizard with a blue tongue

Bluetooth n *trademark* a short-range radio technology that allows wireless communication between computers, mobile phones, etc.

bluff¹ vb **1** to pretend to be confident in order to influence (someone) ▸ n **2** deliberate deception to create the impression of a strong position **3 call someone's bluff** to challenge someone to give proof of his or her claims

> **bluff** vb = deceive, trick, fool, pretend, cheat, con, fake, mislead ▸ n **2** = deception, fraud, sham, pretence, deceit, bravado, bluster, humbug

bluff² n **1** a steep promontory, bank, or cliff **2** *Canad* a clump of trees on the prairie; copse ▸ *adj* **3** good-naturedly frank and hearty

> **bluff** n **1** = precipice, bank, peak, cliff, ridge, crag, escarpment, promontory ▸ *adj* = hearty, open, blunt, outspoken, genial, ebullient, jovial, plain-spoken; ≠ tactful

bluish or **blueish** *adj* slightly blue

blunder n **1** a stupid or clumsy mistake ▸ vb **2** to make stupid or clumsy mistakes **3** to act clumsily; stumble › **blundering** n, adj

> **blunder** n = mistake, slip, fault, error, oversight, gaffe, slip-up (*informal*), indiscretion, barry or Barry Crocker (*Austral slang*); ≠ correctness ▸ vb **2** = make a mistake, blow it (*slang*), err, slip up (*informal*), foul up, put your foot in it (*informal*); ≠ be correct **3** = stumble, fall, reel, stagger, lurch

blunderbuss n an obsolete gun with wide barrel and flared muzzle

blunt *adj* **1** (esp. of a knife) lacking sharpness **2** not having a sharp edge or point: *a blunt*

b

instrument **3** (of people, manner of speaking, etc.) straightforward and uncomplicated ▸ *vb* **4** to make less sharp **5** to diminish the sensitivity or perception of: *prison life has blunted his mind* ▹ **bluntly** *adv*

> **blunt** *adj* **1, 2** = dull, rounded, dulled, edgeless, unsharpened; ≠ sharp **3** = frank, forthright, straightforward, rude, outspoken, bluff, brusque, plain-spoken; ≠ tactful

blur *vb* **blurring, blurred 1** to make or become vague or less distinct **2** to smear or smudge **3** to make (the judgment, memory, or perception) less clear; dim ▸ *n* **4** something vague, hazy, or indistinct **5** a smear or smudge ▹ **blurred** *adj* ▹ **blurry** *adj*

> **blur** *vb* **1** = become indistinct, become vague, become hazy, become fuzzy ▸ *n* **4** = haze, confusion, fog, obscurity, indistinctness

blurb *n* a promotional description, such as on the jackets of books

blurt *vb* (foll. by *out*) to utter suddenly and involuntarily

blush *vb* **1** to become suddenly red in the face, esp. from embarrassment or shame ▸ *n* **2** a sudden reddening of the face, esp. from embarrassment or shame **3** a rosy glow **4** same as **rosé**

> **blush** *vb* = turn red, colour, glow, flush, redden, go red (as a beetroot), turn scarlet; ≠ turn pale ▸ *n* **3** = reddening, colour, glow, flush, pink tinge, rosiness, ruddiness, rosy tint

bluster *vb* **1** to speak loudly or in a bullying way **2** (of the wind) to be gusty ▸ *n* **3** empty threats or protests ▹ **blustery** *adj*

BMA British Medical Association

BMI body mass index: an index used to indicate whether or not a person is a healthy weight for his or her height

BO 1 *informal* body odour **2** box office

boa *n* **1** a large nonvenomous snake of Central and South America that kills its prey by constriction **2** a long thin scarf of feathers or fur

boab (boh-ab) *n Austral informal* short for **baobab**

boa constrictor *n* a very large snake of tropical America and the West Indies that kills its prey by constriction

boar *n* **1** an uncastrated male pig **2** a wild pig

board *n* **1** a long wide flat piece of sawn timber **2** a smaller flat piece of rigid material for a specific purpose: *ironing board* **3** **A** a group of people who officially administer a company, trust, etc. **B** any other official group, such as examiners or interviewers **4** a person's meals, provided regularly for money **5** stiff cardboard or similar material, used for the outside covers of a book **6** a flat thin rectangular sheet of composite material, such as chipboard **7** *naut*

the side of a ship **8** a portable surface for indoor games such as chess or backgammon **9 go by the board** *informal* to be in disuse, neglected, or lost **10 on board** on or in a ship, aeroplane, etc. ▸ *vb* **11** to go aboard (a train or other vehicle) **12** to attack (a ship) by forcing one's way aboard **13** (foll. by *up* or *in* etc.) to cover with boards **14** to receive meals and lodging in return for money **15 board out** to arrange for (someone, esp. a child) to receive food and lodging away from home **16** (in ice hockey and box lacrosse) to bodycheck an opponent against the boards

> **board** *n* **1** = plank, panel, timber, slat, piece of timber **3B** = council, directors, committee, congress, advisers, panel, assembly, trustees **4** = meals, provisions, victuals, daily meals ▸ *vb* **11** = get on, enter, mount, embark; ≠ get off

boarder *n Brit* a pupil who lives at school during term time

boarding house *n* a private house that provides accommodation and meals for paying guests

boardroom *n* a room where the board of directors of a company meets

boast *vb* **1** to speak in excessively proud terms of one's possessions, talents, etc. **2** to possess (something to be proud of): *a team which boasts five current world record holders* ▸ *n* **3** a bragging statement **4** something that is bragged about: *this proved to be a false boast*

> **boast** *vb* **1** = brag, crow, vaunt, talk big (*slang*), blow your own trumpet, show off, be proud of, congratulate yourself on, skite (*Austral, NZ informal*); ≠ cover up **2** = possess, exhibit

boastful *adj* tending to boast

boat *n* **1** a small vessel propelled by oars, paddle, sails, or motor **2** *informal* a ship **3 in the same boat** sharing the same problems **4 miss the boat** to lose an opportunity **5 rock the boat** *informal* to cause a disturbance in the existing situation ▸ *vb* **6** to travel or go in a boat, esp. as recreation

boater *n* a stiff straw hat with a straight brim and flat crown

boating *n* rowing, sailing, or cruising in boats as a form of recreation

boatswain (boh-sn) *n naut* same as **bosun**

bob¹ *vb* **bobbing, bobbed 1** to move or cause to move up and down repeatedly, such as while floating in water **2** to move or cause to move with a short abrupt movement, esp. of the head **3 bob up** to appear or emerge suddenly ▸ *n* **4** a short abrupt movement, as of the head

> **bob** *vb* **1** = bounce, duck, hop, oscillate

bob² *n* **1** a hairstyle in which the hair is cut short evenly all round the head **2** a dangling weight on a pendulum or plumb line ▸ *vb* **bobbing, bobbed 3** to cut (the hair) in a bob

bobbin *n* a reel on which thread or yarn is wound

bobble *n* **1** a tufted ball, usually woollen, that is used for decoration ▸ *vb* **-bling, -bled 2** (of a ball) to bounce erratically because of an uneven playing surface

bobby *n, pl* **-bies** *Brit informal* a British police officer

bobotie (ba-**boot**-ee) *n S African* a traditional Cape dish of curried minced meat

bobsleigh *n* **1** a sledge for racing down a steeply banked ice-covered run ▸ *vb* **2** to ride on a bobsleigh

bode *vb* **boding, boded** to be an omen of (good or ill); portend

bodice *n* **1** the upper part of a dress, from the shoulder to the waist **2** a tight-fitting corset worn laced over a blouse, or (formerly) as a woman's undergarment

bodily *adj* **1** relating to the human body ▸ *adv* **2** by taking hold of the body: *he threw him bodily from the platform* **3** in person; in the flesh

> **bodily** *adj* = physical, material, actual, substantial (*formal*), tangible, corporal, carnal, corporeal

bodkin *n* a blunt large-eyed needle

body *n, pl* **bodies 1** the entire physical structure of an animal or human. Related adjective: **corporal 2** the trunk or torso **3** a corpse **4** a group regarded as a single entity: *a local voluntary body* **5** the main part of anything: *the body of a car* **6** a separate mass of water or land **7** the flesh as opposed to the spirit **8** fullness in the appearance of the hair **9** the characteristic full quality of certain wines **10** *informal* a person: *all the important bodies from the council were present* **11** a woman's one-piece undergarment **12 keep body and soul together** to manage to survive

> **body** *n* **1** = physique, build, form, figure, shape, frame, constitution **2** = torso, trunk **3** = corpse, dead body, remains, carcass, cadaver, stiff (*slang*) **4** = organization, company, group, society, association, band, congress, institution **5** = main part, matter, material, mass, substance, bulk, essence **6** = expanse, mass

bodyguard *n* a person or group of people employed to protect someone

body mass index *n*

bodywork *n* the external shell of a motor vehicle

Boer *n* a descendant of any of the Dutch or Huguenot colonists who settled in South Africa

boerewors (boor-a-vorss) *n S African* a traditional home-made farmer's sausage

boffin *n* *old-fashioned, informal* a scientist or expert

bog *n* **1** a wet spongy area of land **2** *slang* a toilet > **boggy** *adj* > **bogginess** *n*

> **bog** *n* **1** = marsh, swamp, slough, wetlands, fen, mire, quagmire, morass, pakihi (*NZ*), muskeg (*Canad*)

bog down *vb* **bogging, bogged** to impede physically or mentally

bogey *or* **bogy** *n* **1** an evil or mischievous spirit **2** something that worries or annoys **3** *golf* a score of one stroke over par on a hole **4** *slang* a piece of dried mucus from the nose

> **bogey** *or* **bogy** *n* **2** = bugbear, bête noire, horror, nightmare, bugaboo

boggle *vb* **-gling, -gled 1** to be surprised, confused, or alarmed: *the mind boggles at the idea* **2** to hesitate or be evasive when confronted with a problem

bogie *or* **bogy** *n* an assembly of wheels forming a pivoted support at either end of a railway coach

bogus (**boh**-guss) *adj* not genuine

> **bogus** *adj* = fake, false, artificial, forged, imitation, sham, fraudulent, counterfeit; ≠ genuine

bogy *n, pl* **-gies** same as **bogey** *or* **bogie**

bohemian *n* **1** a person, esp. an artist or writer, who lives an unconventional life ▸ *adj* **2** unconventional in appearance, behaviour, etc. > **bohemianism** *n*

boil¹ *vb* **1** to change or cause to change from a liquid to a vapour so rapidly that bubbles of vapour are formed in the liquid **2** to reach or cause to reach boiling point **3** to cook or be cooked by the process of boiling **4** to bubble and be agitated like something boiling: *the sea was boiling* **5** to be extremely angry ▸ *n* **6** the state or action of boiling

> **boil** *vb* **4** = simmer, bubble, foam, seethe, fizz, froth, effervesce

boil² *n* a red painful swelling with a hard pus-filled core caused by infection of the skin

> **boil** *n* = pustule, gathering (*informal*), swelling, blister, carbuncle

boiler *n* **1** a closed vessel in which water is heated to provide steam to drive machinery **2** a domestic device to provide hot water, esp. for central heating

boilerplate *n* a standard text, esp. for a contract or letter, that can be modified to cover different situations

boisterous *adj* **1** noisy and lively; unruly **2** (of the sea, etc.) turbulent or stormy

bold *adj* **1** courageous, confident, and fearless **2** immodest or impudent: *she gave him a bold look* **3** *Irish* (of a child) naughty; badly behaved **4** standing out distinctly; conspicuous: *a figure carved in bold relief* > **boldly** *adv* > **boldness** *n*

> **bold** *adj* **1** = fearless, enterprising, brave, daring, heroic, adventurous, courageous, audacious; ≠ timid **2** = impudent, forward, confident, rude, cheeky, feisty (*informal*), brazen, shameless, insolent; ≠ shy

bole *n* the trunk of a tree

bolero *n, pl* **-ros 1** a Spanish dance, usually in triple time **2** music for this dance **3** a short open jacket not reaching the waist

bollard *n* **1** *Brit & Austral* a small post marking a kerb or traffic island or barring cars from entering **2** a strong wooden or metal post on a wharf, quay, etc., used for securing mooring lines

Bolshevik *n* **1** (formerly) a Russian Communist **2** any Communist **3** *informal, derogatory* any political radical, esp. a revolutionary > **Bolshevism** *n* > **Bolshevist** *adj, n*

bolshie or **bolshy** *Brit & NZ informal* ▸ *adj* **1** difficult to manage; rebellious **2** politically radical or left-wing ▸ *n, pl* **-shies 3** any political radical

bolster *vb* **1** to support or strengthen: *the government were unwilling to bolster sterling* ▸ *n* **2** a long narrow pillow **3** any pad or support

> **bolster** *vb* = support, help, boost, strengthen, reinforce, shore up, augment

bolt *n* **1** a bar that can be slid into a socket to lock a door, gate, etc. **2** a metal rod or pin that has a head and a screw thread to take a nut **3** a flash (of lightning) **4** a sudden movement, esp. in order to escape **5** an arrow, esp. for a crossbow **6 a bolt from the blue** a sudden, unexpected, and usually unwelcome event **7 shoot one's bolt** to exhaust one's efforts ▸ *vb* **8** to run away suddenly **9** to secure or lock with or as if with a bolt **10** to attach firmly (one thing to another) by means of a nut and bolt **11** to eat hurriedly: *bolting your food may lead to indigestion* **12** (of a horse) to run away without control **13** (of vegetables) to produce flowers and seeds too soon ▸ *adv* **14 bolt upright** stiff and rigid

> **bolt** *n* **1** = bar, catch, lock, latch, fastener, sliding bar **2** = pin, rod, peg, rivet ▸ *vb* **9** = lock, close, bar, secure, fasten, latch **11** = gobble, stuff, wolf, cram, gorge, devour, gulp, guzzle

bolt hole *n* a place of escape

bomb *n* **1** a hollow projectile containing explosive, incendiary, or other destructive substance **2** an object in which an explosive device has been planted: *a car bomb* **3** *chiefly Brit slang* a large sum of money: *it cost a bomb* **4** *slang* a disastrous failure: *the new play was a total bomb* **5 like a bomb** *informal* with great speed or success **6 the bomb** a hydrogen or an atom bomb considered as the ultimate destructive weapon ▸ *vb* **7** to attack with a bomb or bombs; drop bombs (on) **8** (foll. by *along*) *informal* to move or drive very quickly **9** *slang* to fail disastrously ▸ See also **bomb out** > **bombing** *n*

> **bomb** *n* **1** = explosive, mine, shell, missile, device, rocket, grenade, torpedo ▸ *vb* **7** = blow up, attack, destroy, assault, shell, blitz, bombard, torpedo

bombard *vb* **1** to attack with concentrated artillery fire or bombs **2** to attack persistently **3** to attack verbally, esp. with questions **4** *physics* to direct high-energy particles or photons against (atoms, nuclei, etc.) > **bombardment** *n*

> **bombard** *vb* **1** = bomb, shell, blitz, open fire, strafe, fire upon **2** = attack, assault, besiege, beset, assail

bombast *n* pompous and flowery language > **bombastic** *adj*

bomber *n* **1** a military aircraft designed to carry out bombing missions **2** a person who plants bombs

bomb out *vb informal* to fail disastrously

bombshell *n* a shocking or unwelcome surprise

bona fide (bone-a **fide**-ee) *adj* **1** genuine: *a bona fide manuscript* **2** undertaken in good faith: *a bona fide agreement*

bonanza *n* **1** sudden and unexpected luck or wealth **2** *US & Canad* a mine or vein rich in ore

bond *n* **1** something that binds, fastens, or holds together **2** something that brings or holds people together; tie: *a bond of friendship* **3 bonds** something that restrains or imprisons **4** a written or spoken agreement, esp. a promise: *a marriage bond* **5** *chem* a means by which atoms are combined in a molecule **6** *finance* a certificate of debt issued in order to raise funds **7** *S African* the conditional pledging of property, esp. a house, as security for the repayment of a loan **8** *law* a written acknowledgment of an obligation to pay a sum or to perform a contract **9 in bond** *commerce* securely stored until duty is paid ▸ *vb* **10** to hold or be held together; bind **11** to form a friendship **12** to put or hold (goods) in bond

> **bond** *n* **1** = fastening, tie, chain, cord, shackle, fetter, manacle **2** = tie, union, coupling, link, association, relation, connection, alliance **4** = agreement, word, promise, contract, guarantee, pledge, obligation, covenant ▸ *vb* **10** = fix, hold, bind, connect, glue, stick, paste, fasten **11** = form friendships, connect

bondage *n* **1** a sexual practice in which one partner is tied or chained up **2** slavery **3** subjection to some influence or duty

bonded *adj* **1** *finance* consisting of, secured by, or operating under a bond or bonds **2** *commerce* in bond

bone *n* **1** any of the various structures that make up the skeleton in most vertebrates **2** the porous rigid tissue of which these parts are made **3** something consisting of bone or a bonelike substance **4 bones** the human skeleton **5** a thin strip of plastic, etc. used to stiffen corsets and brassieres **6 close to** or **near the bone** risqué or indecent **7 have a bone to pick** to have grounds for a quarrel **8 make no bones about A** to be direct and candid about **B** to have no scruples about **9 the bare bones** the essentials ▸ vb **boning**, **boned** 10 to remove the bones from (meat for cooking, etc.) 11 to stiffen (a corset, etc.) by inserting bones ▸ **boneless** adj

bone-dry adj informal completely dry

bone-idle adj extremely lazy

bonfire n a large outdoor fire

bongo n, pl -**gos** or -**goes** a small bucket-shaped drum, usually one of a pair, played by beating with the fingers

bonhomie (bon-om-mee) n exuberant friendliness

bonito (ba-nee-toh) n, pl -**os** 1 a small tunny-like marine food fish 2 a related fish, whose flesh is dried and flaked and used in Japanese cookery

bonk vb informal 1 to have sexual intercourse 2 to hit ▸ **bonking** n

bonnet n 1 Brit the hinged metal cover over a motor vehicle's engine 2 any of various hats tied with ribbons under the chin 3 (in Scotland) a soft cloth cap

bonny adj -**nier**, -**niest** 1 Scot & N English dialect beautiful: a bonny lass 2 good or fine

bonsai n, pl -**sai** an ornamental tree or shrub grown in a small shallow pot in order to stunt its growth

bonus n something given, paid, or received above what is due or expected

> **bonus** n = extra, prize, gift, reward, premium, dividend

bony adj **bonier**, **boniest** 1 resembling or consisting of bone 2 thin 3 having many bones

boo interj 1 a shout uttered to express dissatisfaction or contempt 2 an exclamation uttered to startle someone ▸ vb **booing**, **booed** 3 to shout 'boo' at (someone or something) as an expression of disapproval

boob slang ▸ n 1 Brit, Austral & NZ an embarrassing mistake; blunder 2 a female breast 3 Austral a prison ▸ vb 4 Brit, Austral & NZ to make a blunder

boobook (boo-book) n a small spotted Australian brown owl

booby n, pl -**bies** 1 old-fashioned an ignorant or foolish person 2 a tropical marine bird related to the gannet

booby prize n a mock prize given to the person with the lowest score in a competition

booby trap n 1 a hidden explosive device primed so as to be set off by an unsuspecting victim 2 a trap for an unsuspecting person, esp. one intended as a practical joke

boogie vb -**gieing**, -**gied** slang to dance to fast pop music

book n 1 a number of printed pages bound together along one edge and protected by covers 2 a written work or composition, such as a novel 3 a number of sheets of paper bound together: an account book 4 **books** a record of the transactions of a business or society 5 the libretto of an opera or musical 6 a major division of a written composition, such as of a long novel or of the Bible 7 a number of tickets, stamps, etc. fastened together along one edge 8 a record of betting transactions 9 **a closed book** a subject that is beyond comprehension: art remains a closed book to him 10 **bring to book** to reprimand or require (someone) to give an explanation of his or her conduct 11 **by the book** according to the rules 12 **in someone's good** or **bad books** regarded by someone with favour or disfavour 13 **throw the book at someone** A to charge someone with every relevant offence B to inflict the most severe punishment on someone ▸ vb 14 to reserve (a place, passage, etc.) or engage the services of (someone) in advance 15 (of a police officer) to take the name and address of (a person) for an alleged offence with a view to prosecution 16 (of a football referee) to take the name of (a player) who has broken the rules seriously

> **book** n 1, 2 = work, title, volume, publication, tract, tome, e-book or ebook, blook
> 3 = notebook, album, journal, diary, pad, notepad, exercise book, jotter ▸ vb 14 = reserve, schedule, engage, organize, charter, arrange for, make reservations, e-book or ebook

bookie n informal short for **bookmaker**

book-keeping n the skill or occupation of systematically recording business transactions ▸ **book-keeper** n

booklet n a thin book with paper covers

> **booklet** n = brochure, leaflet, hand-out, pamphlet, folder, mailshot, handbill

bookmaker n a person who as an occupation accepts bets, esp. on horse racing ▸ **bookmaking** n

bookmark n 1 a strip of some material put between the pages of a book to mark a place 2 an identifier put on a website that enables the user to return to it quickly and easily ▸ vb 3 to identify and store (a website) so that one can return to it quickly and easily

bookworm n 1 a person devoted to reading 2 a small insect that feeds on the binding paste of books

boom[1] vb 1 to make a loud deep echoing sound 2 to prosper vigorously and rapidly: business boomed ▸ n 3 a loud deep echoing sound 4 a period of high economic growth

> **boom** vb 1 = bang, roll, crash, blast, explode, roar, thunder, rumble 2 = increase, flourish, grow, develop, expand, strengthen, swell, thrive; ≠ fall ▸ n 3 = bang, crash, clash, blast, burst, explosion, roar, thunder 4 = expansion, increase, development, growth, jump, boost, improvement, upsurge; ≠ decline

boom[2] n 1 naut a spar to which the foot of a sail is fastened to control its position 2 a pole carrying an overhead microphone and projected over a film or television set 3 a barrier across a waterway

b

boomer n *Austral* a large male kangaroo

boomerang n **1** a curved wooden missile of Australian Aborigines which can be made to return to the thrower **2** an action or statement that recoils on its originator ▸ vb **3** (of a plan) to recoil unexpectedly, harming its originator

boon n something extremely useful, helpful, or beneficial

> **boon** n = benefit, blessing, godsend, gift

boongary (boong-gar-ree) n a tree kangaroo of NE Queensland, Australia

boor n an ill-mannered, clumsy, or insensitive person > **boorish** adj

boost n **1** encouragement or help: *a boost to morale* **2** an upward thrust or push **3** an increase or rise ▸ vb **4** to encourage or improve: *to boost morale* **5** to cause to rise; increase: *we significantly boosted our market share* **6** to advertise on a big scale

> **boost** n **1** = encouragement, help **3** = rise, increase, jump, addition, improvement, expansion, upsurge, upturn; ≠ fall ▸ vb **5** = increase, develop, raise, expand, add to, heighten, enlarge, amplify; ≠ decrease

booster n **1** a supplementary injection of a vaccine given to ensure that the first injection will remain effective **2** a radio-frequency amplifier to strengthen signals **3** the first stage of a multistage rocket

boot¹ n **1** an outer covering for the foot that extends above the ankle **2** *Brit* an enclosed compartment of a car for holding luggage **3** *informal* a kick: *he gave the door a boot* **4** **lick someone's boots** to behave flatteringly towards someone **5** **put the boot in** *slang* **A** to kick a person when already down **B** to finish something off with unnecessary brutality **6** **the boot** *slang* dismissal from employment ▸ vb **7** to kick **8** to start up (a computer) **9** **boot out** *informal* **A** to eject forcibly **B** to dismiss from employment

> **boot** vb **7** = kick, punt, put the boot in(to) (*slang*), drop-kick

boot² n **to boot** as well; in addition

boot camp n a centre for juvenile offenders, with strict discipline and hard physical exercise

bootee n a soft boot for a baby, esp. a knitted one

booth n, pl **booths** **1** a small partially enclosed cubicle **2** a stall, esp. a temporary one at a fair or market

bootleg vb **-legging, -legged** **1** to make, carry, or sell (illicit goods, esp. alcohol) ▸ adj **2** produced, distributed, or sold illicitly ▸ n **3** something that is produced, distributed, or sold illicitly > **bootlegger** n

booty n, pl **-ties** any valuable article or articles obtained as plunder

booze *informal* ▸ n **1** alcoholic drink ▸ vb **boozing, boozed** **2** to drink alcohol, esp. in excess > **boozy** adj

booze bus n *Austral & NZ informal* a mobile police unit used to conduct drug and alcohol tests on drivers

boozer n *informal* **1** a person who is fond of drinking **2** *Brit, Austral & NZ* a bar or pub

booze-up n *Brit, Austral & NZ slang* a drinking spree

bop n **1** a form of jazz with complex rhythms and harmonies ▸ vb **bopping, bopped** **2** *informal* to dance to pop music > **bopper** n

bora n *Austral* an Aboriginal ceremony

borax n a white mineral in crystalline form used in making glass, soap, etc.

border n **1** the dividing line between political or geographic regions **2** a band or margin around or along the edge of something **3** a design around the edge of something **4** a narrow strip of ground planted with flowers or shrubs: *a herbaceous border* ▸ vb **5** to provide with a border **6** **A** to be adjacent to; lie along the boundary of **B** to be nearly the same as; verge on: *a story that borders on the unbelievable*

> **border** n **1** = frontier, line, limit, bounds, boundary, perimeter, borderline **2, 3** = edge, margin, verge (*Brit*), rim ▸ vb **5** = edge, bound, decorate, trim, fringe, rim, hem

bore¹ vb **boring, bored** **1** to produce (a hole) with a drill, etc. **2** to produce (a tunnel, mine shaft, etc.) by drilling ▸ n **3** a hole or tunnel in the ground drilled in search of minerals, oil, etc. **4** **A** the hollow of a gun barrel **B** the diameter of this hollow; calibre

> **bore** vb = drill, mine, sink, tunnel, pierce, penetrate, burrow, puncture

bore² vb **boring, bored** **1** to tire or make weary by being dull, repetitious, or uninteresting ▸ n **2** a dull or repetitious person, activity, or state > **bored** adj > **boring** adj

> **bore** vb = tire, fatigue, weary, wear out, jade, be tedious, pall on, send to sleep; ≠ excite ▸ n = nuisance, pain (*informal*), yawn (*informal*), anorak (*informal*)

bore³ n a high wave moving up a narrow estuary, caused by the tide

bore⁴ vb the past tense of **bear¹**

boredom n the state of being bored

> **boredom** n = tedium, apathy, weariness, monotony, sameness, ennui (*literary*), flatness, world-weariness; ≠ excitement

boree (baw-ree) n *Austral* same as **myall**

born vb **1** a past participle of **bear¹** **2** **not have been born yesterday** not to be gullible or foolish ▸ adj **3** possessing certain qualities from birth: *a born musician* **4** being in a particular social status at birth: *ignobly born*

borne vb a past participle of **bear¹**

boron n *chem* a hard almost colourless crystalline metalloid element that is used in hardening steel. Symbol: **B**

boronia *n* an Australian aromatic flowering shrub

borough *n* **1** a town, esp. (in Britain) one that forms the constituency of an MP or that was originally incorporated by royal charter **2** any of the constituent divisions of Greater London or New York City

borrow *vb* **1** to obtain (something, such as money) on the understanding that it will be returned to the lender **2** to adopt (ideas, words, etc.) from another source ▸ **borrower** *n* ▸ **borrowing** *n*

> **borrow** *vb* **1** = take on loan, touch (someone) for (*slang*), scrounge (*informal*), cadge, use temporarily; ≠ lend **2** = steal, take, copy, adopt, pinch (*informal*)

borscht *or* **borsch** *n* a Russian soup based on beetroot

borstal *n* (formerly, in Britain) a prison for offenders aged 15 to 21

borzoi *n* a tall dog with a narrow head and a long coat

bosh *n Brit, Austral & NZ informal* meaningless talk or opinions; nonsense

Bosnian *adj* **1** from Bosnia ▸ *n* **2** a person from Bosnia

bosom *n* **1** the chest or breast of a person, esp. the female breasts **2** a protective centre or part: *the bosom of the family* **3** the breast considered as the seat of emotions ▸ *adj* **4** very dear: *a bosom friend*

boss¹ *informal* ▸ *n* **1** a person in charge of or employing others ▸ *vb* **2** to employ, supervise, or be in charge of **3** **boss around** *or* **about** to be domineering or overbearing towards

> **boss** *n* = manager, head, leader, director, chief, master, employer, supervisor, sherang (*Austral, NZ*) ▸ *vb* **3** **boss someone around** = order around, dominate, bully, oppress, push around (*slang*)

boss² *n* a raised knob or stud, esp. an ornamental one on a vault, shield, etc.

bossy *adj* **bossier, bossiest** *informal* domineering, overbearing, or authoritarian ▸ **bossiness** *n*

bosun *or* **boatswain** (boh-sn) *n* an officer who is responsible for the maintenance of a ship and its equipment

bot *n* a computer program that carries out tasks for other programs or users

botany *n, pl* **-nies** the study of plants, including their classification, structure, etc. ▸ **botanical** *or* **botanic** *adj* ▸ **botanist** *n*

botch *vb* **1** to spoil through clumsiness or ineptitude **2** to repair badly or clumsily ▸ *n also* **botch-up 3** a badly done piece of work or repair

both *adj* **1** two considered together: *both parents were killed during the war* ▸ *pron* **2** two considered together: *both are to blame* ▸ *conj* **3** not just one but also the other of two (people or things): *both she and her sister enjoyed the show*

bother *vb* **1** to take the time or trouble: *don't bother to come with me* **2** to give annoyance, pain, or trouble to **3** to trouble (a person) by repeatedly disturbing; pester ▸ *n* **4** a state of worry, trouble, or confusion **5** a person or thing that causes fuss, trouble, or annoyance **6** *informal* a disturbance or fight: *a spot of bother* ▸ *interj* **7** *Brit, Austral & NZ* an exclamation of slight annoyance

> **bother** *vb* **2** = trouble, concern, worry, alarm, disturb, disconcert, perturb **3** = pester, plague, harass, hassle (*informal*), inconvenience; ≠ help ▸ *n* **4** = trouble, problem, worry, difficulty, fuss, irritation, hassle (*informal*), nuisance, uphill (*S African*); ≠ help

bothersome *adj* causing bother

Botox *n trademark* **1** a preparation of botulinum toxin used to treat muscle spasm and to remove wrinkles ▸ *vb* **2** to apply Botox to (a person or a part of the body)

bottle *n* **1** a container, often of glass and usually cylindrical with a narrow neck, for holding liquids **2** the amount such a container will hold **3** *Brit slang* courage; nerve: *you don't have the bottle* **4** **the bottle** *informal* drinking of alcohol, esp. to excess ▸ *vb* **-tling, -tled** **5** to put or place in a bottle or bottles ▸ See also **bottle up**

bottleneck *n* **1** a narrow stretch of road or a junction at which traffic is or may be held up **2** something that holds up progress

bottle shop *n Austral & NZ* a shop licensed to sell alcohol for drinking elsewhere

> **bottle shop** *n* = off-licence (*Brit*), liquor store (*US, Canad*), bottle store (*S African*), package store (*US, Canad*), offie *or* offy (*Brit informal*)

bottle store *n S African* a shop licensed to sell alcohol for drinking elsewhere

> **bottle store** *n* = off-licence (*Brit*), liquor store (*US, Canad*), bottle shop (*Austral, NZ*), package store (*US, Canad*), offie *or* offy (*Brit informal*)

bottle tree *n* an Australian tree with a bottle-shaped swollen trunk

bottle up *vb* to restrain (powerful emotion)

bottom *n* **1** the lowest, deepest, or farthest removed part of a thing: *the bottom of a hill* **2** the least important or successful position: *the bottom of a class* **3** the ground underneath a sea, lake, or river **4** the underneath part of a thing **5** the buttocks **6** **at bottom** in reality; basically **7** **be at the bottom of** to be the ultimate cause of **8** **get to the bottom of** to discover the real truth about ▸ *adj* **9** lowest or last

> **bottom** *n* **1** = lowest part, base, foot, bed, floor, foundation, depths; ≠ top **4** = underside, sole, underneath, lower side **5** = buttocks, behind (*informal*), rear, backside, rump, seat, posterior ▸ *adj* = lowest, last; ≠ higher

b

bottomless *adj* 1 unlimited; inexhaustible: *bottomless resources* 2 very deep: *bottomless valleys*

botulism *n* severe food poisoning resulting from the toxin **botulin**, produced in imperfectly preserved food

boudoir (boo-dwahr) *n* a woman's bedroom or private sitting room

bougainvillea *n* a tropical climbing plant with flowers surrounded by showy red or purple bracts

bough *n* any of the main branches of a tree

bought *vb* the past of **buy**

boulder *n* a smooth rounded mass of rock shaped by erosion

boulevard *n* a wide usually tree-lined road in a city

bounce *vb* **bouncing, bounced** 1 (of a ball, etc.) to rebound from an impact 2 to cause (a ball, etc.) to hit a solid surface and spring back 3 to move or cause to move suddenly; spring: *I bounced down the stairs* 4 *slang* (of a bank) to send (a cheque) back or (of a cheque) to be sent back unredeemed because of lack of funds in the account ▸ *n* 5 the action of rebounding from an impact 6 a leap or jump 7 springiness 8 *informal* vitality; vigour 9 *informal* a temporary increase or rise: *a sales bounce* ▸ **bouncy** *adj*

> **bounce** *vb* 1 = rebound, recoil, ricochet 3 = bound, spring, jump, leap, skip, gambol ▸ *n* 7 = springiness, give, spring, resilience, elasticity, recoil 8 = life, go (*informal*), energy, zip (*informal*), vigour, exuberance, dynamism, vivacity

bouncer *n* 1 *slang* a person employed at a nightclub, etc. to prevent unwanted people from entering and to eject drunks or troublemakers 2 *cricket* a ball bowled so that it bounces high on pitching

bouncing *adj* vigorous and robust: *a bouncing baby*

bound¹ *vb* 1 the past of **bind** ▸ *adj* 2 tied as if with a rope 3 restricted or confined: *housebound* 4 certain: *it's bound to happen* 5 compelled or obliged: *they agreed to be bound by the board's recommendations* 6 (of a book) secured within a cover or binding 7 **bound up with** closely or inextricably linked with

> **bound** *adj* 2 = tied, fixed, secured, attached, tied up, fastened, pinioned 4 = certain, sure, fated, doomed, destined 5 = compelled, obliged, forced, committed, pledged, constrained, beholden, duty-bound

bound² *vb* 1 to move forwards by leaps or jumps 2 to bounce; spring away from an impact ▸ *n* 3 a jump upwards or forwards 4 a bounce, as of a ball

> **bound** *vb* = leap, bob, spring, jump, bounce, skip, vault ▸ *n* 3 = leap, bob, spring, jump, bounce, hurdle, skip, vault

bound³ *vb* 1 to place restrictions on; limit: *bounded by tradition* 2 to form a boundary of ▸ **boundless** *adj*

> **bound** *vb* 1 = limit, restrict, confine, restrain, circumscribe 2 = surround, confine, enclose, encircle, hem in, demarcate

bound⁴ *adj* going or intending to go towards: *homeward bound*

boundary *n, pl* **-ries** 1 something that indicates the farthest limit, such as of an area 2 *cricket* A the marked limit of the playing area B a stroke that hits the ball beyond this limit, scoring four or six runs

> **boundary** *n* 1 = frontier, edge, border, barrier, margin, brink

bountiful *or* **bounteous** *adj literary* 1 plentiful; ample: *a bountiful harvest* 2 giving freely; generous

bounty *n, pl* **-ties** 1 *literary* generosity; liberality 2 something provided in generous amounts: *nature's bounty* 3 a reward or premium by a government

bouquet *n* 1 a bunch of flowers, esp. a large carefully arranged one 2 the aroma of wine

> **bouquet** *n* 1 = bunch of flowers, spray, garland, wreath, posy, buttonhole, corsage, nosegay 2 = aroma, smell, scent, perfume, fragrance, savour, odour, redolence

bourbon (bur-bn) *n* a whiskey distilled, chiefly in the US, from maize

bourgeois (boor-zhwah) *often derogatory* ▸ *adj* 1 characteristic of or comprising the middle class 2 conservative or materialistic in outlook 3 (in Marxist thought) dominated by capitalism ▸ *n, pl* **-geois** 4 a member of the middle class, esp. one regarded as being conservative and materialistic

> **bourgeois** *adj* 1, 2 = middle-class, traditional, conventional, materialistic, hidebound

bout *n* 1 A a period of time spent doing something, such as drinking alcohol B a period of illness: *a bad bout of flu* 2 a boxing, wrestling, or fencing match

> **bout** *n* 1A = period, term, fit, spell, turn, interval 2 = fight, match, competition, struggle, contest, set-to (*informal*), encounter, engagement

boutique *n* a small shop, esp. one that sells fashionable clothes

boutique hotel *n* a small, high-quality, fashionable hotel

bovine *adj* 1 of or relating to cattle 2 dull, sluggish, or ugly

bow¹ (rhymes with **cow**) *vb* 1 to lower (one's head) or bend (one's knee or body) as a sign of respect, greeting, agreement, or shame 2 to comply or accept: *bow to the inevitable*

3 bow and scrape to behave in a slavish manner ▸ *n* **4** a lowering or bending of the head or body as a mark of respect, etc. **5 take a bow** to acknowledge applause

> **bow** *vb* **1** = bend, bob, nod, stoop, droop, genuflect ▸ *n* **4** = bending, bob, nod, obeisance, kowtow, genuflection

bow² (rhymes with **know**) *n* **1** a decorative knot usually having two loops and two loose ends **2** a long stick across which are stretched strands of horsehair, used for playing a violin, viola, cello, etc. **3** a weapon for shooting arrows, consisting of an arch of flexible wood, plastic, etc. bent by a string fastened at each end **4** something that is curved, bent, or arched ▸ *vb* **5** to form or cause to form a curve or curves

bow³ (rhymes with **cow**) *n* **1** *chiefly naut* the front end or part of a vessel **2** *rowing* the oarsman at the bow

> **bow** *n* **1** = prow, head, stem, fore, beak

bowdlerize *or* **-ise** *vb* **-izing, -ized** *or* **-ising, -ised** to remove passages or words regarded as indecent from (a play, novel, etc.)
> **bowdlerization** *or* **-isation** *n*

bowel *n* **1** an intestine, esp. the large intestine in humans **2 bowels** entrails **3 bowels** the innermost part: *the bowels of the earth*

> **bowel** *n* **2** = guts, insides (*informal*), intestines, innards (*informal*), entrails, viscera, vitals **3** = depths, hold, inside (*informal*), deep, interior, core, belly

bower *n* a shady leafy shelter in a wood or garden
bowerbird *n* a brightly coloured songbird of Australia and New Guinea
bowl¹ *n* **1** a round container open at the top, used for holding liquid or serving food **2** the amount a bowl will hold **3** the hollow part of an object, esp. of a spoon or tobacco pipe

> **bowl** *n* **1** = basin, plate, dish, vessel

bowl² *n* **1 A** a wooden ball used in the game of bowls **B** a large heavy ball with holes for gripping used in the game of bowling ▸ *vb* **2** to roll smoothly or cause to roll smoothly along the ground **3** *cricket* **A** to send (a ball) from one's hand towards the batsman **B** Also: **bowl out** to dismiss (a batsman) by delivering a ball that breaks his wicket **4** to play bowls **5 bowl along** to move easily and rapidly, as in a car

> **bowl** *vb* **3A** = throw, hurl, launch, cast, pitch, toss, fling, chuck (*informal*)

bow-legged *adj* having legs that curve outwards at the knees
bowler¹ *n* **1** a person who bowls in cricket **2** a player at the game of bowls
bowler² *n* a stiff felt hat with a rounded crown and narrow curved brim

bowling *n* **1** a game in which a heavy ball is rolled down a long narrow alley at a group of wooden pins **2** *cricket* the act of delivering the ball to the batsman
box¹ *n* **1** a container with a firm base and sides and sometimes a removable or hinged lid **2** the contents of such a container **3** a separate compartment for a small group of people, as in a theatre **4** a compartment for a horse in a stable or a vehicle **5** a section of printed matter on a page, enclosed by lines or a border **6** a central agency to which mail is addressed and from which it is collected or redistributed: *a post-office box* **7 the box** *Brit informal* television ▸ *vb* **8** to put into a box > **boxlike** *adj*

> **box** *n* **1** = container, case, chest, trunk, pack, package, carton, casket ▸ *vb* = pack, package, wrap, encase, bundle up

box² *vb* **1** to fight (an opponent) in a boxing match **2** to engage in boxing **3** to hit (esp. a person's ears) with the fist ▸ *n* **4** a punch with the fist, esp. on the ear

> **box** *vb* **2** = fight, spar, exchange blows

box³ *n* a slow-growing evergreen tree or shrub with small shiny leaves
boxer *n* **1** a person who boxes **2** a medium-sized dog with smooth hair and a short nose

> **boxer** *n* **1** = fighter, pugilist, prizefighter

boxer shorts *or* **boxers** *pl n* men's underpants shaped like shorts but with a front opening
boxing *n* the act, art, or profession of fighting with the fists
box jellyfish *n* a highly venomous jellyfish with a cuboid body that lives in Australian tropical waters
box office *n* **1** an office at a theatre, cinema, etc. where tickets are sold **2** the public appeal of an actor or production ▸ *adj* **box-office** **3** relating to the sales at the box office: *a box-office success*
box set *n* **1** a collection of items of the same type, packaged together for sale in a presentation box **2** a set of episodes of a television series made available to watch or listen to at the same time
boy *n* **1** a male child **2** a man regarded as immature or inexperienced **3** *S African offensive* a Black male servant > **boyhood** *n* > **boyish** *adj*

> **boy** *n* **1** = lad, kid (*informal*), youth, fellow (*old-fashioned*), youngster, schoolboy, junior, stripling

boycott *vb* **1** to refuse to deal with (an organization or country) as a protest against its actions or policy ▸ *n* **2** an instance or the use of boycotting

> **boycott** *vb* = embargo, reject, snub, black; ≠ support

b

boyfriend *n* a male friend with whom a person is romantically or sexually involved

> **boyfriend** *n* = sweetheart, man, lover, beloved, admirer, suitor, beau (*old-fashioned*), date

bra *n* an undergarment for covering and supporting the breasts

braaivleis (brye-flayss) *S African* ▸ *n* 1 a grill on which food is cooked over hot charcoal, usually outdoors 2 an outdoor party at which food like this is served ▸ *vb* 3 to cook (food) in this way. Also: **braai**

brace *n* 1 something that steadies, binds, or holds up another thing 2 a beam or prop, used to stiffen a framework 3 a hand tool for drilling holes 4 a pair, esp. of game birds 5 either of a pair of characters, { }, used for connecting lines of printing or writing ▸ *vb* **bracing, braced** 6 to steady or prepare (oneself) before an impact 7 to provide, strengthen, or fit with a brace

> **brace** *n* 1 = support, stay, prop, bolster, bracket, reinforcement, strut, truss ▸ *vb* 6 = steady, support, secure, stabilize 7 = support, strengthen, steady, reinforce, bolster, fortify, buttress

bracelet *n* an ornamental chain or band worn around the arm or wrist

bracing *adj* refreshing: *the bracing climate*

> **bracing** *adj* = refreshing, fresh, stimulating, crisp, brisk, exhilarating, invigorating; ≠ tiring

bracken *n* 1 a fern with large fronds 2 a clump of these ferns

bracket *n* 1 a pair of characters, [ ], ( ), or { }, used to enclose a section of writing or printing 2 a group or category falling within certain defined limits: *the lower income bracket* 3 an L-shaped or other support fixed to a wall to hold a shelf, etc. ▸ *vb* **-eting, -eted** 4 to put (written or printed matter) in brackets 5 to group or class together

brackish *adj* (of water) slightly salty

bract *n* a leaf, usually small and scaly, growing at the base of a flower

brag *vb* **bragging, bragged** 1 to speak arrogantly and boastfully ▸ *n* 2 boastful talk or behaviour 3 a card game similar to poker

braggart *n* a person who boasts loudly or exaggeratedly

braid *vb* 1 to interweave (hair, thread, etc.) 2 to decorate with an ornamental trim or border ▸ *n* 3 a length of hair that has been braided 4 narrow ornamental tape of woven silk, wool, etc. ▸ **braiding** *n*

Braille *n* a system of writing for blind people consisting of raised dots interpreted by touch

brain *n* 1 the soft mass of nervous tissue within the skull of vertebrates that controls and coordinates the nervous system 2 (*often pl*) *informal* intellectual ability: *he's got brains* 3 *informal* an intelligent person 4 **on the brain** *informal* constantly in mind: *I had that song on the brain* 5 **the brains** *informal* a person who plans and organizes something: *the brains behind the bid* ▸ *vb* 6 *slang* to hit (someone) hard on the head

> **brain** *n* 2 = intelligence, understanding, sense, intellect

brainchild *n informal* an idea or plan produced by creative thought

brainfood *n* any foodstuff containing nutrients thought to promote brain function

brainless *adj* stupid or foolish

brainwash *vb* to cause (a person) to alter his or her beliefs, by methods based on isolation, sleeplessness, etc. ▸ **brainwashing** *n*

brainwave *n informal* a sudden idea or inspiration

brainy *adj* **brainier, brainiest** *informal* clever; intelligent

braise *vb* **braising, braised** to cook (food) slowly in a closed pan with a small amount of liquid

brake *n* 1 a device for slowing or stopping a vehicle 2 something that slows down or stops progress: *he put a brake on my enthusiasm* ▸ *vb* **braking, braked** 3 to slow down or cause to slow down, by or as if by using a brake

> **brake** *n* 2 = control, check, curb, restraint, constraint, rein ▸ *vb* = slow, decelerate, reduce speed

bramble *n* 1 a prickly plant or shrub such as the blackberry 2 *Scot, N English & NZ* a blackberry ▸ **brambly** *adj*

bran *n* husks of cereal grain separated from the flour

branch *n* 1 a secondary woody stem extending from the trunk or main branch of a tree 2 one of a number of shops, offices, or groups that belongs to a central organization: *she was transferred to their Japanese branch* 3 a subdivision or subsidiary section of something larger or more complex: *branches of learning* ▸ *vb* 4 to divide, then develop in different directions ▸ **branchlike** *adj*

> **branch** *n* 1 = bough, shoot, arm, spray, limb, sprig, offshoot 2 = office, department, unit, wing, chapter, bureau 3 = division, part, section, subdivision, subsection

branch out *vb* to expand or extend one's interests

brand *n* 1 a particular product or a characteristic that identifies a particular producer 2 a trade name or trademark 3 a particular kind or variety 4 an identifying mark made, usually by burning, on the skin of animals as a proof of ownership 5 an iron used for branding animals 6 a mark of disgrace 7 *archaic or poetic* a flaming torch ▸ *vb* 8 to label, burn, or mark with or as if with a brand 9 to label (someone): *he was branded a war criminal*

brand n 1 = trademark ▸ vb 8 = mark, burn, label, stamp, scar 9 = stigmatize, mark, expose, denounce, disgrace, discredit, censure

brandish vb to wave (a weapon, etc.) in a triumphant or threatening way

brand-new adj absolutely new

brandy n, pl **-dies** an alcoholic spirit distilled from wine

brash adj 1 tastelessly or offensively loud, or showy: brash modernization 2 impudent or bold: I thought it was very brash of her to ask me > **brashness** n

> **brash** adj 2 = bold, rude, cocky, pushy (informal), brazen, impertinent, insolent, impudent; ≠ timid

brass n 1 an alloy of copper and zinc 2 an object, ornament, or utensil made of brass 3 **A** the large family of wind instruments including the trumpet, trombone, etc. made of brass **B** instruments of this family forming a section in an orchestra 4 same as **top brass** 5 N English dialect money 6 Brit an engraved brass memorial tablet in a church 7 informal bold self-confidence; nerve

brasserie n a bar or restaurant serving drinks and cheap meals

brassiere n same as **bra**

brassy adj **brassier**, **brassiest** 1 brazen or flashy 2 like brass, esp. in colour 3 (of sound) harsh and strident

brat n a child, esp. one who is unruly

bravado n an outward display of self-confidence

brave adj 1 having or displaying courage, resolution, or daring 2 fine; splendid: a brave sight ▸ n 3 old-fashioned a warrior of a Native American tribe of N America ▸ vb **braving**, **braved** 4 to confront with resolution or courage: she braved the 21 miles of Lake Tahoe > **bravery** n

> **brave** adj 1 = courageous, daring, bold, heroic, adventurous, fearless, resolute, audacious; ≠ timid ▸ vb = confront, face, suffer, tackle, endure, defy, withstand, stand up to; ≠ give in to

bravo interj 1 well done! ▸ n 2 pl **-vos** a cry of 'bravo' 3 pl **-voes** or **-vos** a hired killer or assassin

brawl n 1 a loud disagreement or fight ▸ vb 2 to quarrel or fight noisily

> **brawl** n = fight, clash, fray, skirmish, scuffle, punch-up (Brit informal), fracas, altercation, biffo (Austral slang) ▸ vb = fight, scrap (informal), wrestle, tussle, scuffle

brawn n 1 strong well-developed muscles 2 physical strength 3 Brit & NZ a seasoned jellied loaf made from the head of a pig > **brawny** adj

bray vb 1 (of a donkey) to utter its characteristic loud harsh sound 2 to utter something with a loud harsh sound ▸ n 3 the loud harsh sound uttered by a donkey 4 a similar loud sound

brazen adj 1 shameless and bold 2 made of or resembling brass 3 having a ringing metallic sound ▸ vb 4 **brazen it out** to face and overcome a difficult or embarrassing situation boldly or shamelessly > **brazenly** adv

brazier (bray-zee-er) n a portable metal container for burning charcoal or coal

breach n 1 a breaking of a promise, obligation, etc. 2 any serious disagreement or separation 3 a crack, break, or gap ▸ vb 4 to break (a promise, law, etc.) 5 to break through or make an opening or hole in

> **breach** n 1 = nonobservance, abuse, violation, infringement, trespass, transgression, contravention, infraction; ≠ compliance 3 = opening, crack, split, gap, rift, rupture, cleft, fissure

bread n 1 a food made from a dough of flour or meal mixed with water or milk, usually raised with yeast and then baked 2 necessary food 3 slang money ▸ vb 4 to cover (food) with breadcrumbs before cooking

> **bread** n 2 = food, fare, kai (NZ informal), nourishment, sustenance 3 = money, cash, dough (slang)

breadth n 1 the extent or measurement of something from side to side 2 openness and lack of restriction, esp. of viewpoint or interest; liberality

> **breadth** n 1 = extent, range, scale, scope, compass, expanse

breadwinner n a person supporting a family with his or her earnings

break vb **breaking**, **broke**, **broken** 1 to separate or become separated into two or more pieces 2 to damage or become damaged so as not to work 3 to burst or cut the surface of (skin) 4 to fracture (a bone) in (a limb, etc.) 5 to fail to observe (an agreement, promise, or law): they broke their promise 6 to reveal or be revealed: she broke the news gently 7 (foll. by with) to separate oneself from 8 to discontinue or become discontinued: to break a journey 9 to bring or come to an end: the winter weather broke at last 10 to weaken or overwhelm or be weakened or overwhelmed, as in spirit: he felt his life was broken by his illness 11 to cut through or penetrate: silence broken by shouts 12 to improve on or surpass: she broke three world records 13 (often foll. by in) to accustom (a horse) to the bridle and saddle, to being ridden, etc. 14 (foll. by of) to cause (a person) to give up (a habit): this cure will break you of smoking 15 to weaken the impact or force of: this net will break his fall 16 to decipher: to break a code 17 to lose the order of: to break ranks 18 to reduce to poverty or the state of bankruptcy 19 to come into being: light broke over the mountains 20 (foll. by

b

into) **A** to burst into (song, laughter, etc.) **B** to change to (a faster pace) **21** to open with explosives: *to break a safe* **22 A** (of waves) to strike violently against **B** (of waves) to collapse into foam or surf **23** *snooker* to scatter the balls at the start of a game **24** *boxing & wrestling* (of two fighters) to separate from a clinch **25** (of the male voice) to undergo a change in register, quality, and range at puberty **26** to interrupt the flow of current in (an electrical circuit) **27 break camp** to pack up and leave a camp **28 break even** to make neither a profit nor a loss **29 break the mould** to make a change that breaks an established habit or pattern ▸ *n* **30** the act or result of breaking; fracture **31** a brief rest **32** a sudden rush, esp. to escape: *they made a sudden break for freedom* **33** any sudden interruption in a continuous action **34** *Brit & NZ* a short period between classes at school **35** a (short) holiday **36** *informal* a fortunate opportunity, esp. to prove oneself **37** *informal* a piece of good or bad luck **38** *billiards & snooker* a series of successful shots during one turn **39** *snooker* the opening shot that scatters the placed balls **40** a discontinuity in an electrical circuit **41 break of day** the dawn ▸ See also **break down** *etc.* ▸ **breakable** *adj*

> **break** *vb* **1** = shatter, separate, destroy, crack, snap, smash, crush, fragment; ≠ repair **3** = burst, tear, split **4** = fracture, crack, smash **5** = disobey, breach, defy, violate, disregard, flout, infringe, contravene (*formal*); ≠ obey **6** = reveal, tell, announce, declare, disclose, proclaim, make known **9** = stop, cut, suspend, interrupt, cut short, discontinue **10** = weaken, undermine, tame, subdue, demoralize, dispirit **12** = beat, top, better, exceed, go beyond, excel, surpass, outstrip ▸ *n* **30** = fracture, opening, tear, hole, split, crack, gap, fissure **35** = holiday, leave, vacation, time off, recess, awayday, schoolie (*Austral*), accumulated day off or ADO (*Austral*) **36** = stroke of luck, chance, opportunity, advantage, fortune, opening

breakage *n* **1** the act or result of breaking **2** compensation or allowance for goods damaged while in use, transit, etc.

break down *vb* **1** to cease to function; become ineffective **2** to give way to strong emotion or tears **3** to crush or destroy **4** to have a nervous breakdown **5** to separate into component parts: *with exercise the body breaks down fat to use as fuel* **6** to separate or cause to separate into simpler chemical elements; decompose **7** to analyse or be subjected to analysis ▸ *n* **breakdown 8** an act or instance of breaking down; collapse **9** same as **nervous breakdown 10** an analysis of something into its parts

breaker *n* **1** a large sea wave with a white crest or one that breaks into foam on the shore **2** a Citizens' Band radio operator

breakfast *n* **1** the first meal of the day ▸ *vb* **2** to eat breakfast

breakneck *adj* (of speed or pace) excessively fast and dangerous

break off *vb* **1** to sever or detach **2** to end (a relationship or association) **3** to stop abruptly

> **break off** *vb* **1 break something off** = detach, separate, divide, cut off, pull off, sever, part, remove

break out *vb* **1** to begin or arise suddenly: *fighting broke out between the two factions* **2** to make an escape, esp. from prison **3 break out in** to erupt in (a rash or spots) ▸ *n* **break-out 4** an escape, esp. from prison

> **break out** *vb* **1** = begin, start, happen, occur, arise, set in, commence, spring up

break through *vb* **1** to penetrate **2** to achieve success after lengthy efforts ▸ *n* **breakthrough 3** a significant development or discovery

> **break through** *n* **breakthrough** = development, advance, progress, discovery, find, invention, step forward, leap forwards

break up *vb* **1** to separate or cause to separate **2** to put an end to (a relationship) or (of a relationship) to come to an end **3** to dissolve or cause to dissolve: *the meeting broke up at noon* **4** *Brit* (of a school) to close for the holidays ▸ *n* **break-up 5** a separation or disintegration

> **break up** *vb* **2** = split up, separate, part, divorce **3** = finish, be suspended, adjourn

breakwater *n* a massive wall built out into the sea to protect a shore or harbour from the force of waves

bream *n, pl* **bream 1** a freshwater fish covered with silvery scales **2** a food fish of European seas **3** a food fish of Australasian seas

breast *n* **1** either of the two soft fleshy milk-secreting glands on a woman's chest **2** the front part of the body from the neck to the abdomen; chest **3** the corresponding part in certain other mammals **4** the source of human emotions **5** the part of a garment that covers the breast **6 make a clean breast of something** to divulge truths about oneself ▸ *vb literary* **7** to reach the summit of: *breasting the mountain top* **8** to confront boldly; face: *breast the storm*

> **breast** *n* **1** = bosom, boob (*slang*), booby (*slang*), tit (*vulgar slang*)

breastbone *n* same as **sternum**

breaststroke *n* a swimming stroke in which the arms are extended in front of the head and swept back on either side

breath *n* **1** the taking in and letting out of air during breathing **2** a single instance of this **3** the air taken in or let out during breathing **4** the vapour, heat, or odour of air breathed out **5** a slight gust of air **6** a short pause or rest

7 a suggestion or slight evidence; suspicion: *trembling at the least breath of scandal* **8** a whisper or soft sound **9 catch one's breath A** to rest until breathing is normal **B** to stop breathing momentarily from excitement, fear, etc. **10 out of breath** gasping for air after exertion **11 save one's breath** to avoid useless talk **12 take someone's breath away** to overwhelm someone with surprise, etc. **13 under one's breath** in a quiet voice or whisper

> **breath** *n* **2** = inhalation, breathing, pant, gasp, gulp, wheeze, exhalation, respiration

Breathalyser *or* **-lyzer** *n Brit trademark* a device for estimating the amount of alcohol in the breath > **breathalyse** *or* **-lyze** *vb*

breathe *vb* **breathing**, **breathed** **1** to take in oxygen and give out carbon dioxide; respire **2** to exist; be alive **3** to rest to regain breath or composure **4** (esp. of air) to blow lightly **5** to exhale or emit: *the dragon breathed fire* **6** to impart; instil: *a change that breathed new life into Polish industry* **7** to speak softly; whisper **8 breathe again** *or* **freely** *or* **easily** to feel relief **9 breathe one's last** to die

> **breathe** *vb* **1** = inhale and exhale, pant, gasp, puff, gulp, wheeze, respire, draw in breath **7** = inhalation, breathing, pant, gasp, gulp, wheeze, exhalation, respiration

breather *n informal* a short pause for rest

breathing *n* **1** the passage of air into and out of the lungs to supply the body with oxygen **2** the sound this makes

breathless *adj* **1** out of breath; gasping, etc. **2** holding one's breath or having it taken away by excitement, etc. **3** (esp. of the atmosphere) motionless and stifling > **breathlessness** *n*

> **breathless** *adj* **1** = out of breath, panting, gasping, gulping, wheezing, short-winded **2** = excited, curious, eager, enthusiastic, impatient, on tenterhooks, in suspense

breathtaking *adj* causing awe or excitement

> **breathtaking** *adj* = amazing, exciting, stunning (*informal*), impressive, thrilling, magnificent, astonishing, sensational

bred *vb* the past of **breed**

breech *n* **1** the buttocks **2** the part of a firearm behind the barrel

breeches *pl n* trousers extending to the knee or just below, worn for riding, etc.

breed *vb* **breeding**, **bred** **1** to produce new or improved strains of (domestic animals and plants) **2** to produce or cause to produce by mating **3** to bear (offspring) **4** to bring up; raise: *she was city bred* **5** to produce or be produced: *the agreement bred confidence between the two* ▸ *n* **6** a group of animals, esp. domestic animals, within a species, that have certain clearly defined characteristics **7** a kind, sort, or

group: *he was a gentleman, a breed not greatly admired* **8** a lineage or race > **breeder** *n*

> **breed** *vb* **1** = rear, tend, keep, raise, maintain, farm, look after, care for **2, 3** = reproduce, multiply, propagate, procreate (*formal*), produce offspring, bear young, bring forth young **5** = produce, cause, create, generate, bring about, arouse, give rise to, stir up ▸ *n* **6** = variety, race, stock, type, species, strain, pedigree **7** = kind, sort, type, variety, brand, stamp

breeding *n* **1** the process of producing plants or animals by controlled methods of reproduction **2** the process of bearing offspring **3** the result of good upbringing or training

> **breeding** *n* **3** = refinement, culture, taste, manners, polish, courtesy, sophistication, cultivation

breeze *n* **1** a gentle or light wind **2** *informal* an easy task ▸ *vb* **breezing**, **breezed** **3** to move quickly or casually: *he breezed into the room*

> **breeze** *n* **1** = light wind, air, draught, gust, waft, zephyr, breath of wind, current of air ▸ *vb* = sweep, move briskly, pass, sail, hurry, glide, flit

breezy *adj* **breezier**, **breeziest** **1** fresh; windy **2** casual or carefree

brethren *pl n archaic* a plural of **brother**

Breton *adj* **1** of Brittany ▸ *n* **2** a person from Brittany **3** the Celtic language of Brittany

brevity *n* **1** a short duration; brief time **2** lack of verbosity

brew *vb* **1** to make (beer, ale, etc.) from malt and other ingredients by steeping, boiling, and fermentation **2** to prepare (a drink, such as tea) by infusing **3** to devise or plan: *to brew a plot* **4** to be in the process of being brewed **5** to be about to happen or forming: *a rebellion was brewing* ▸ *n* **6** a beverage produced by brewing, esp. tea or beer **7** an instance of brewing: *last year's brew* > **brewer** *n*

> **brew** *vb* **1** = make, ferment **2** = boil, make, soak, steep, stew, infuse **5** = start, develop, gather, foment ▸ *n* **6** = drink, preparation, mixture, blend, liquor, beverage, infusion, concoction

brewery *n, pl* **-eries** a place where beer, ale, etc. is brewed

Brexit *n* the withdrawal of the United Kingdom from the European Union

briar¹ *or* **brier** *n* **1** a shrub of S Europe, with a hard woody root (**briarroot**) **2** a tobacco pipe made from this root

briar² *n* same as **briar¹**

bribe *vb* **bribing**, **bribed** **1** to promise, offer, or give something, often illegally, to (a person) to receive services or gain influence ▸ *n* **2** a reward, such as money or favour, given or offered for this purpose > **bribery** *n*

b

bribe vb = buy off, reward, pay off (*informal*), corrupt, suborn, grease the palm or hand of (*slang*) ▸ n = inducement, pay-off (*informal*), sweetener (*slang*), kickback, backhander (*slang*), enticement, allurement

bric-a-brac n miscellaneous small ornamental objects

brick n 1 a rectangular block of baked or dried clay, used in building construction 2 the material used to make such blocks 3 any rectangular block: *a brick of ice cream* 4 bricks collectively 5 *informal* a reliable, trustworthy, or helpful person 6 **drop a brick** *Brit & NZ informal* to make a tactless or indiscreet remark ▸ vb 7 (foll. by *in*, *up* or *over*) to construct, line, pave, fill, or wall up with bricks: *they bricked up access to the historic pillar*

bricklayer n a person who builds with bricks

bridal adj of a bride or a wedding

bride n a woman who has just been or is about to be married

bridegroom n a man who has just been or is about to be married

bridesmaid n a girl or woman who attends a bride at her wedding

bridge¹ n 1 a structure that provides a way over a railway, river, etc. 2 a platform from which a ship is piloted and navigated 3 the hard ridge at the upper part of the nose 4 a dental plate containing artificial teeth that is secured to natural teeth 5 a piece of wood supporting the strings of a violin, guitar, etc. ▸ vb **bridging**, **bridged** 6 to build or provide a bridge over (something) 7 to connect or reduce the distance between: *talks aimed at bridging the gap between the two sides*

bridge n 1 = arch, span, viaduct, flyover, overpass, fixed link (*Canad*) ▸ vb 6 = span, cross 7 = reconcile, resolve

bridge² n a card game for four players, based on whist, in which the trump suit is decided by bidding between the players

bridgehead n *military* a fortified or defensive position at the end of a bridge nearest to the enemy

bridle n 1 headgear for controlling a horse, consisting of straps and a bit and reins 2 something that curbs or restrains ▸ vb **-dling**, **-dled** 3 to show anger or indignation: *he bridled at the suggestion that he should resign* 4 to put a bridle on (a horse) 5 to restrain; curb

bridle path n a path suitable for riding or leading horses

Brie (bree) n a soft creamy white cheese

brief adj 1 short in duration 2 short in length or extent; scanty: *a brief bikini* 3 terse or concise ▸ n 4 a condensed statement or written synopsis 5 *law* a document containing all the facts and points of law of a case by which a solicitor instructs a barrister to represent a client

6 *RC Church* a papal letter that is less formal than a bull 7 Also called: **briefing** instructions 8 **hold a brief for** to argue for; champion 9 **in brief** in short; to sum up ▸ vb 10 to prepare or instruct (someone) by giving a summary of relevant facts 11 *English law* ᴀ to instruct (a barrister) by brief ʙ to retain (a barrister) as counsel > **briefly** adv

brief adj 1 = short, quick, fleeting, swift, short-lived, momentary, ephemeral, transitory; ≠ long ▸ n 4 = summary, résumé, outline, sketch, abstract, digest, epitome, rundown ▸ vb 10 = inform, prime, prepare, advise, fill in (*informal*), instruct, put in the picture (*informal*), keep (someone) posted

briefcase n a flat portable case for carrying papers, books, etc.

brier¹ or **briar** n any of various thorny shrubs or other plants, such as the sweetbrier

brier² n same as **briar¹**

brig n *naut* a two-masted square-rigged ship

brigade n 1 a military formation smaller than a division and usually commanded by a brigadier 2 a group of people organized for a certain task: *a rescue brigade*

brigade n 1 = corps, company, force, unit, division, troop, squad, team 2 = group, band, squad, organization

brigadier n a senior officer in an army, usually commanding a brigade

brigalow n *Austral* a type of acacia tree

brigand n a bandit, esp. a member of a gang operating in mountainous areas

brigantine n a two-masted sailing ship

bright adj 1 emitting or reflecting much light; shining 2 (of colours) intense or vivid 3 full of promise: *a bright future* 4 lively or cheerful 5 quick-witted or clever ▸ adv 6 brightly: *the light burned bright in his office* > **brightly** adv > **brightness** n

bright adj 1 = shining, glowing, dazzling, gleaming, shimmering, radiant, luminous, lustrous 2 = vivid, rich, brilliant, glowing, colourful 5 = clever, smart, ingenious

brighten vb 1 to make or become bright or brighter 2 to make or become cheerful

brighten vb 1 = light up, shine, glow, gleam, lighten; ≠ dim

brilliance or **brilliancy** n 1 great brightness 2 excellence in physical or mental ability 3 splendour

brilliance or **brilliancy** n 1 = brightness, intensity, sparkle, dazzle, lustre, radiance, luminosity, vividness; ≠ darkness 2 = cleverness, talent, wisdom, distinction, genius, excellence, greatness, inventiveness; ≠ stupidity 3 = splendour, glamour, grandeur, magnificence, éclat, illustriousness

brilliant *adj* **1** shining with light; sparkling **2** (of a colour) vivid **3** splendid; magnificent: *a brilliant show* **4** of outstanding intelligence or intellect ▸ *n* **5** a diamond cut with many facets to increase its sparkle

> **brilliant** *adj* **1** = bright, shining, intense, sparkling, glittering, dazzling, vivid, radiant; ≠ dark **3** = splendid, famous, celebrated, outstanding, superb, magnificent, glorious, notable **4** = intelligent, sharp, intellectual, clever, profound, penetrating, inventive, perspicacious (*formal*); ≠ stupid

brim *n* **1** the upper rim of a cup, bowl, etc. **2** a projecting edge of a hat ▸ *vb* **brimming**, **brimmed 3** to be full to the brim: *he saw the tears that brimmed in her eyes* > **brimless** *adj*

> **brim** *n* **1** = rim, edge, border, lip, margin, verge (*Brit*), brink ▸ *vb* = be full, spill, well over, run over

brimstone *n obsolete* sulphur

brine *n* **1** a strong solution of salt and water, used for pickling **2** *literary* the sea or its water

bring *vb* **bringing**, **brought 1** to carry, convey, or take (something or someone) to a designated place or person **2** to cause to happen: *responsibility brings maturity* **3** to cause to come to mind: *it brought back memories* **4** to cause to be in a certain state, position, etc.: *the punch brought him to his knees* **5** to make (oneself): *she couldn't bring herself to do it* **6** to sell for: *the painting brought a large sum* **7** *law* **A** to institute (proceedings, charges, etc.) **B** to put (evidence, etc.) before a tribunal ▸ See also **bring about**

> **bring** *vb* **1** = take, guide, conduct, escort **2, 4** = cause, produce, create, effect, occasion (*formal*), result in, contribute to, inflict

bring about *vb* to cause to happen: *a late harvest brought about by bad weather*

> **bring about** *vb* **bring something about** = cause, produce, create, effect, achieve, generate, accomplish, give rise to

bring off *vb* to succeed in achieving (something difficult)

> **bring off** *vb* **bring something off** = accomplish, achieve, perform, succeed, execute, pull off, carry off

bring out *vb* **1** to produce, publish, or have (a book) published **2** to expose, reveal, or cause to be seen: *he brought out the best in me* **3** to cause (a person) to become covered with (a rash, spots, etc.)

bring up *vb* **1** to care for and train (a child); rear **2** to raise (a subject) for discussion; mention **3** to vomit (food)

> **bring up** *vb* **1 bring someone up** = rear, raise, support, train, develop, teach, breed, foster **2 bring something up** = mention, raise, introduce, point out, refer to, allude to, broach

brinjal *n S African & Indian* a dark purple tropical fruit, cooked and eaten as a vegetable

brink *n* **1** the edge or border of a steep place **2** the land at the edge of a body of water **3 on the brink of** very near; on the point of: *on the brink of disaster*

> **brink** *n* **1, 2** = edge, limit, border, lip, margin, boundary, skirt, frontier

briny *adj* **brinier**, **briniest 1** of or like brine; salty ▸ *n* **2 the briny** *informal* the sea

brisk *adj* **1** lively and quick; vigorous: *brisk trade* **2** invigorating or sharp: *brisk weather* **3** practical and businesslike: *his manner was brisk* > **briskly** *adv*

> **brisk** *adj* **1** = quick, lively, energetic, active, vigorous, bustling, sprightly, spry; ≠ slow **2** = short, brief, blunt, abrupt, terse, gruff, brusque, monosyllabic

brisket *n* beef from the breast of a cow

bristle *n* **1** any short stiff hair, such as on a pig's back **2** something resembling these hairs: *toothbrush bristle* ▸ *vb* **-tling**, **-tled 3** to stand up or cause to stand up like bristles **4** to show anger or indignation: *she bristled at the suggestion* **5** to be thickly covered or set: *the hedges bristled with blossom* > **bristly** *adj*

> **bristle** *n* **1** = hair, spine, thorn, whisker, barb, stubble, prickle ▸ *vb* **3** = stand up, rise, stand on end **4** = be angry, rage, seethe, flare up, bridle, see red

Brit *n informal* a British person

British *adj* **1** of Britain or the British Commonwealth **2** denoting the English language as spoken and written in Britain ▸ *pl n* **3 the British** the people of Britain

Briton *n* **1** a native or inhabitant of Britain **2** *history* any of the early Celtic inhabitants of S Britain

brittle *adj* **1** easily cracked or broken; fragile **2** curt or irritable: *a brittle reply* **3** hard or sharp in quality: *a brittle laugh* > **brittly** *adv*

> **brittle** *adj* **1** = fragile, delicate, crisp, crumbling, frail, crumbly, breakable, friable; ≠ tough

broach *vb* **1** to initiate or introduce (a topic) for discussion **2** to tap or pierce (a container) to draw off (a liquid) **3** to open in order to begin to use ▸ *n* **4** a spit for roasting meat

broad *adj* **1** having great breadth or width **2** of vast extent: *broad plains* **3** not detailed; general **4** clear and open: *broad daylight* **5** obvious: *broad hints* **6** tolerant: *a broad view* **7** extensive: *broad support* **8** vulgar or coarse **9** strongly marked: *he spoke broad Australian English* ▸ *n* **10** *chiefly US & Canad slang, sometimes offensive* a woman **11 the Broads** in East Anglia, a group of shallow lakes connected by a network of rivers > **broadly** *adv*

b

broad *adj* **1** = wide, large, ample, generous, expansive **2** = large, huge, vast, extensive, ample, spacious, expansive, roomy; ≠ narrow **3** = general, loose, vague, approximate, indefinite, ill-defined, inexact, unspecific **7** = full, general, comprehensive, complete, wide, sweeping, wide-ranging, thorough

broadband *n* a telecommunications technique that uses a wide range of frequencies to allow messages to be sent simultaneously

broad bean *n* the large edible flattened seed of a Eurasian bean plant

broadcast *n* **1** a transmission or programme on radio or television ▸ *vb* **-casting**, **-cast** *or* **-casted** **2** to transmit (announcements or programmes) on radio or television **3** to take part in a radio or television programme **4** to make widely known throughout an area: *to broadcast news* **5** to scatter (seed, etc.) ▸ **broadcaster** *n* ▸ **broadcasting** *n*

broadcast *n* = transmission, show, programme, telecast, podcast, webcast, vodcast, mobcast ▸ *vb* **2** = transmit, show, air, radio, cable, beam, send out, relay, stream, podcast, open-line (*Canad*) **4** = make public, report, announce, publish, spread, advertise, proclaim, circulate

broaden *vb* to make or become broad or broader; widen

broaden *vb* = expand, increase, develop, spread, extend, stretch, swell, supplement; ≠ restrict

broad-minded *adj* **1** tolerant of opposing viewpoints; liberal **2** not easily shocked

broadside *n* **1** a strong or abusive verbal or written attack **2** *naval* the simultaneous firing of all the guns on one side of a ship **3** *naut* the entire side of a ship ▸ *adv* **4** with a broader side facing an object

brocade *n* **1** a rich fabric woven with a raised design ▸ *vb* **-cading**, **-caded** **2** to weave with such a design

broccoli *n* a variety of cabbage with greenish flower heads

brochure *n* a pamphlet or booklet, esp. one containing introductory information or advertising

brochure *n* = booklet, advertisement, leaflet, hand-out, circular, pamphlet, folder, mailshot

broekies (brook-eez) *pl n S African informal* underpants

broekies *pl n* = underpants, pants (*Brit*), briefs, drawers, knickers, panties, boxer shorts, Y-fronts (*trademark*), underdaks (*Austral slang*)

brogue[1] *n* a sturdy walking shoe, often with ornamental perforations

brogue[2] *n* a broad gentle-sounding dialectal accent, esp. that used by the Irish in speaking English

broil *vb* same as **grill** (sense 1)

broke *vb* **1** the past tense of **break** ▸ *adj* **2** *informal* having no money

broke *adj* = penniless, short, ruined, bust (*informal*), bankrupt, impoverished, in the red, insolvent; ≠ rich

broken *vb* **1** the past participle of **break** ▸ *adj* **2** fractured, smashed, or splintered **3** interrupted; disturbed: *broken sleep* **4** not functioning **5** (of a promise or contract) violated; infringed **6** (of the speech of a foreigner) imperfectly spoken: *broken English* **7** Also: **broken-in** made tame by training **8** exhausted or weakened, as through ill-health or misfortune

broken *adj* **2** = smashed, burst, shattered, fragmented, fractured, severed, ruptured, separated **3** = interrupted, incomplete, erratic, intermittent, fragmentary, spasmodic, discontinuous **4** = defective, not working, imperfect, out of order, on the blink (*slang*), kaput (*informal*) **6** = imperfect, halting, hesitating, stammering, disjointed

brokenhearted *adj* overwhelmed by grief or disappointment

broker *n* **1** an agent who buys or sells goods, securities, etc.: *an insurance broker* **2** a person who deals in second-hand goods

broker *n* = dealer, agent, trader, supplier, merchant, negotiator, mediator, intermediary

brolga *n* a large grey Australian crane with a trumpeting call. Also called: **native companion**

brolly *n*, *pl* **-lies** *Brit, Austral & NZ informal* an umbrella

bromance *n informal* a close, non-sexual friendship between two men

bromide *n* **1** *chem* any compound of bromine with another element or radical **2** a dose of sodium or potassium bromide given as a sedative **3** a boring, meaningless, or obvious remark

bromine *n chem* a dark red liquid chemical element that gives off a pungent vapour. Symbol: **Br**

bronchial *adj* of or relating to both of the bronchi or the smaller tubes into which they divide

bronchitis *n* inflammation of the bronchial tubes, causing coughing and difficulty in breathing

bronchus (bronk-uss) *n*, *pl* **bronchi** (bronk-eye) either of the two main branches of the windpipe

bronco *n*, *pl* **-cos** (in the US and Canada) a wild or partially tamed horse

brontosaurus *n* a former name for **apatosaurus**

bronze *n* **1** an alloy of copper and smaller proportions of tin **2** a statue, medal, or other object made of bronze ▸ *adj* **3** made of or resembling bronze **4** yellowish-brown ▸ *vb* **bronzing, bronzed 5** (esp. of the skin) to make or become brown; tan

> **bronze** *adj* **4** = yellowish-brown, reddish-brown, copper, tan, rust, chestnut, brownish

Bronze Age *n* a phase of human culture, lasting in Britain from about 2000 to 500 BC during which weapons and tools were made of bronze

brooch *n* an ornament with a hinged pin and catch, worn fastened to clothing

brood *n* **1** a number of young animals, esp. birds, produced at one hatching **2** all the children in a family: *often used jokingly* ▸ *vb* **3** (of a bird) to sit on or hatch eggs **4** to think long and unhappily about something: *he brooded on his failure to avert the confrontation* > **brooding** *n, adj*

> **brood** *n* **1** = offspring, issue, clutch, litter, progeny **2** = children, family, nearest and dearest, flesh and blood, ainga (*NZ*) ▸ *vb* **4** = think, obsess, muse, ponder, agonize, mull over, mope, ruminate

broody *adj* **broodier, broodiest 1** moody; introspective **2** (of poultry) wishing to sit on or hatch eggs **3** *informal* (of a woman) wishing to have a baby

brook¹ *n* a natural freshwater stream

> **brook** *n* = stream, burn (*Scot, N English*), rivulet, beck, watercourse, rill

brook² *vb* to bear; tolerate: *she would brook no opposition*

broom *n* **1** a type of long-handled sweeping brush **2** a yellow-flowered shrub **3 a new broom** a newly appointed official, etc., eager to make radical changes

broomstick *n* the long handle of a broom

broth *n* a soup made by boiling meat, vegetables, etc. in water

brothel *n* a house where men pay to have sexual intercourse with prostitutes

brother *n* **1** a man or boy with the same parents as another person. Related adjective: **fraternal 2** a man belonging to the same group, trade union, etc. as another or others; fellow member **3** comrade; friend **4** *Christianity* a member of a male religious order

> **brother** *n* **1** = male sibling **4** = monk, cleric, friar, religious

brotherhood *n* **1** fellowship **2** an association, such as a trade union **3** the state of being a brother

brother-in-law *n, pl* **brothers-in-law 1** the brother of one's wife or husband **2** the husband of one's sibling

brotherly *adj* of or like a brother, esp. in showing loyalty and affection

> **brotherly** *adj* = fraternal, friendly, neighbourly, sympathetic, affectionate, benevolent, kind, amicable

brought *vb* the past of **bring**

brow *n* **1** the part of the face from the eyes to the hairline; forehead **2** same as **eyebrow 3** the jutting top of a hill

browbeat *vb* **-beating, -beat, -beaten** to frighten (someone) with threats

brown *adj* **1** of the colour of wood or the earth **2** (of bread) made from wheatmeal or wholemeal flour **3** deeply tanned ▸ *n* **4** the colour of wood or the earth **5** anything brown, such as brown paint or brown clothing: *clad in brown* ▸ *vb* **6** to make or become brown or browner, for example as a result of cooking > **brownish** *adj*

> **brown** *adj* **1** = brunette, bay, coffee, chocolate, chestnut, hazel, dun, auburn **3** = tanned, bronze, tan, sunburnt ▸ *vb* = fry, cook, grill, sear, sauté

browned-off *adj informal, chiefly Brit* thoroughly bored and depressed

Brownie Guide *or* **Brownie** *n* a member of the junior branch of the Guides

browse *vb* **browsing, browsed 1** to look through (a book or articles for sale) in a casual leisurely manner **2** *computers* to read hypertext, esp. on the internet **3** (of deer, goats, etc.) to feed upon vegetation by continual nibbling ▸ *n* **4** an instance of browsing

> **browse** *vb* **1** = skim, scan, glance at, survey, look through, look round, dip into, leaf through **3** = graze, eat, feed, nibble

browser *n computers* a software package that enables a user to read hypertext, esp. on the internet

bruise *vb* **bruising, bruised 1** to injure (body tissue) without breaking the skin, usually with discoloration, or (of body tissue) to be injured in this way **2** to hurt (someone's feelings) **3** to damage (fruit) ▸ *n* **4** a bodily injury without a break in the skin, usually with discoloration

> **bruise** *vb* **1** = hurt, injure, mark **3** = damage, mark, mar, discolour ▸ *n* = discoloration, mark, injury, blemish, contusion (*formal*)

bruiser *n informal* a strong tough person, esp. a boxer or a bully

brumby *n, pl* **-bies** *Austral* **1** a wild horse **2** an unruly person

brunch *n* a meal eaten late in the morning, combining breakfast with lunch

brunette *n* a woman with dark brown hair

brunt *n* the main force or shock of a blow, attack, etc.: *the town bore the brunt of the earthquake*

brush[1] *n* **1** a device made of bristles, hairs, wires, etc. set into a firm back or handle: used to apply paint, groom the hair, etc. **2** the act of brushing **3** a brief encounter, esp. an unfriendly one **4** the bushy tail of a fox **5** an electric conductor, esp. one made of carbon, that conveys current between stationary and rotating parts of a generator, motor, etc. ▸ *vb* **6** to clean, scrub, or paint with a brush **7** to apply or remove with a brush or brushing movement **8** to touch lightly and briefly ▸ See also **brush off**, **brush up**

> **brush** *n* **1** = broom, sweeper, besom **3** = encounter, meeting, confrontation, rendezvous ▸ *vb* **6** = clean, wash, polish, buff **8** = touch, sweep, kiss, stroke, glance, flick, scrape, graze

brush[2] *n* a thick growth of shrubs and small trees; scrub

> **brush** *n* = shrubs, bushes, scrub, undergrowth, thicket, copse, brushwood

brush off *slang* ▸ *vb* **1** to dismiss and ignore (a person), esp. curtly ▸ *n* **brushoff 2 give someone the brushoff** to reject someone

> **brush off** *vb* **brush someone off** = ignore, reject, dismiss, snub, disregard, scorn, disdain, spurn

brush turkey *n* a bird of New Guinea and Australia resembling the domestic fowl, with black plumage

brush up *vb* **1** (often foll. by *on*) to refresh one's knowledge or memory of (a subject) ▸ *n* **brush-up 2** *Brit* the act of tidying one's appearance: *have a wash and brush-up*

> **brush up** *vb* **brush something up or brush up on something** = revise, study, go over, cram, polish up, read up on, relearn, bone up on (*informal*)

brusque *adj* blunt or curt in manner or speech > **brusquely** *adv* > **brusqueness** *n*

Brussels sprout *n* a vegetable like a tiny cabbage

brutal *adj* **1** cruel; vicious; savage **2** harsh or severe **3** extremely honest or frank in speech or manner > **brutality** *n* > **brutally** *adv*

> **brutal** *adj* **1** = cruel, savage, vicious, ruthless, callous, sadistic, heartless, inhuman; ≠ kind **2** = harsh, tough, severe, rough, rude, indifferent, insensitive, callous; ≠ sensitive

brutalize *or* **-ise** *vb* **-izing**, **-ized** *or* **-ising**, **-ised** **1** to make or become brutal **2** to treat (someone) brutally > **brutalization** *or* **-isation** *n*

brute *n* **1** a brutal person **2** any animal that is not a human; beast ▸ *adj* **3** wholly instinctive or physical, like that of an animal: *cricket is not a game of brute force* **4** without reason or intelligence **5** coarse and grossly sensual

brutish *adj* **1** of or resembling a brute; animal **2** coarse; cruel; stupid

BSc Bachelor of Science

BSE bovine spongiform encephalopathy: a fatal virus disease of cattle

BST British Summer Time

BTW by the way

bubble *n* **1** a small globule of air or a gas in a liquid or a solid **2** a thin film of liquid forming a ball around air or a gas: *a soap bubble* **3** a dome, esp. a transparent glass or plastic one **4** an unreliable scheme or enterprise ▸ *vb* **-bling**, **-bled 5** to form bubbles **6** to move or flow with a gurgling sound **7 bubble over** to express an emotion freely: *she was bubbling over with excitement*

> **bubble** *n* **1** = air ball, drop, bead, blister, blob, droplet, globule ▸ *vb* **5** = foam, fizz, froth, percolate, effervesce **6** = gurgle, splash, murmur, trickle, ripple, babble, burble, lap

bubbly *adj* **-blier**, **-bliest 1** lively; animated; excited **2** full of or resembling bubbles ▸ *n* **3** *informal* champagne

> **bubbly** *adj* **1** = lively, happy, excited, animated, merry, bouncy, elated, sparky **2** = frothy, sparkling, fizzy, effervescent, carbonated, foamy

bubonic plague *n* an acute infectious disease characterized by the formation of buboes

buccaneer *n* a pirate, esp. in the Caribbean in the 17th and 18th centuries

buck[1] *n* **1** the male of the goat, hare, kangaroo, rabbit, and reindeer **2** *archaic* a spirited young man **3** the act of bucking ▸ *vb* **4** (of a horse or other animal) to jump vertically, with legs stiff and back arched **5** (of a horse, etc.) to throw (its rider) by bucking **6** *informal* to resist or oppose obstinately: *bucking the system* ▸ See also **buck up**

buck[2] *n US, Canad, Austral & NZ informal* a dollar

buck[3] *n* **pass the buck** *informal* to shift blame or responsibility onto another

bucket *n* **1** an open-topped cylindrical container with a handle **2** the amount a bucket will hold **3** a bucket-like part of a machine, such as the scoop on a mechanical shovel **4 kick the bucket** *slang* to die ▸ *vb* **-eting**, **-eted 5** (often foll. by *down*) (of rain) to fall very heavily

bucket list *n informal* a list of things one wants to experience before one dies

buckle *n* **1** a clasp for fastening together two loose ends, esp. of a belt or strap ▸ *vb* **-ling**, **-led 2** to fasten or be fastened with a buckle **3** to bend or cause to bend out of shape, esp. as a result of pressure or heat

> **buckle** *n* = fastener, catch, clip, clasp, hasp ▸ *vb* **2** = fasten, close, secure, hook, clasp **3** = distort, bend, warp, crumple, contort

buckle down *vb* to apply oneself with determination

buckshee *adj Brit slang* without charge; free

buckteeth pl n projecting upper front teeth
> **buck-toothed** adj

buck up vb informal **1** to make or become more cheerful or confident **2** to make haste

buckwheat n **1** a type of small black seed used as animal fodder and in making flour **2** the flour obtained from such seeds

bucolic (byew-koll-ik) adj **1** of the countryside or country life; rustic **2** of or relating to shepherds; pastoral ▸ n **3** a pastoral poem

bud n **1** a swelling on the stem of a plant that develops into a flower or leaf **2** a partially opened flower: rosebud **3** any small budlike outgrowth: taste buds **4** **nip something in the bud** to put an end to something in its initial stages ▸ vb **budding, budded** **5** (of plants and some animals) to produce buds **6** horticulture to graft (a bud) from one plant onto another

> **bud** n **1** = shoot, branch, sprout, sprig, offshoot ▸ vb **5** = shoot, branch, sprout, sprig, offshoot

Buddhism n a religion founded by the Buddha that teaches that all suffering can be brought to an end by overcoming greed, hatred, and delusion > **Buddhist** n, adj

budding adj beginning to develop or grow: a budding actor

> **budding** adj = developing, beginning, growing, promising, potential, burgeoning, fledgling, embryonic

buddleia n a shrub which has long spikes of purple flowers

buddy n, pl **-dies** **1** chiefly US & Canad informal a friend **2** a volunteer who helps and supports a person with a chronic illness ▸ vb **-dies, -dying, -died** **3** to act as a buddy to (a person with a chronic illness)

budge vb **budging, budged** **1** to move slightly: he refuses to budge off that chair **2** to change or cause to change opinions: nothing would budge her from this idea

> **budge** vb **1** = move, stir

budgerigar n a small cage bird bred in many different-coloured varieties

budget n **1** a plan of expected income and expenditure over a specified period **2** the total amount of money allocated for a specific purpose during a specified period ▸ adj **3** inexpensive: a budget hotel ▸ vb **-eting, -eted** **4** to enter or provide for in a budget **5** to plan the expenditure of (money or time) > **budgetary** adj

> **budget** n **2** = allowance, means, funds, income, finances, resources, allocation ▸ vb **5** = plan, estimate, allocate, cost, ration, apportion

budgie n informal same as **budgerigar**

buff¹ n **1** a soft thick flexible undyed leather **2** a cloth or pad of material used for polishing **3** **in the buff** informal completely naked ▸ adj **4** dull yellowish-brown **5** informal physically fit and attractive ▸ vb **6** to clean or polish (a metal, floor, shoes, etc.) with a buff

> **buff** adj **4** = fawn, tan, beige, yellowish, straw-coloured, sand-coloured, yellowish-brown ▸ vb = polish, smooth, brush, shine, rub, wax, brighten, burnish

buff² n informal an expert on or devotee of a given subject: an opera buff

> **buff** n = expert, fan, addict, enthusiast, admirer, devotee, connoisseur, aficionado, fundi (S African)

buffalo n, pl **-loes** or **-lo** **1** a type of cattle with upward-curving horns **2** same as **water buffalo** **3** US & Canad a bison

buffer n **1** one of a pair of spring-loaded steel pads at the ends of railway vehicles and railway tracks that reduces shock on impact **2** a person or thing that lessens shock or protects from damaging impact, circumstances, etc. **3** chem **A** a substance added to a solution to resist changes in its acidity or alkalinity **B** Also called: **buffer solution** a solution containing such a substance **4** computers a memory device for temporarily storing data ▸ vb **5** to cushion; provide a buffer for **6** computers to store (data) temporarily in a buffer

> **buffer** n **2** = safeguard, screen, shield, cushion, intermediary, bulwark

buffet¹ (boof-fay, buff-ay) n **1** a counter where light refreshments are served **2** a meal at which guests help themselves from a number of dishes

> **buffet** n **1** = snack bar, café, cafeteria, brasserie, refreshment counter **2** = smorgasbord

buffet² (buff-it) vb **-feting, -feted** **1** to knock against or about; batter: the ship was buffeted by strong winds **2** to hit, esp. with the fist ▸ n **3** a blow, esp. with the fist

buffoon n a person who amuses others by silly behaviour > **buffoonery** n

bug n **1** any of various insects having piercing and sucking mouthparts **2** chiefly US & Canad any insect **3** informal a minor illness caused by a germ or virus **4** informal a small error, esp. in a computer or computer program **5** informal an obsessive idea or hobby **6** informal a concealed microphone used for recording conversations in spying **7** Austral a flattish edible shellfish ▸ vb **bugging, bugged** informal **8** to irritate or upset (someone) **9** to conceal a microphone in (a room or telephone)

> **bug** n **3** = illness, disease, virus, infection, disorder, sickness, ailment, affliction ▸ vb **8** = annoy, bother, disturb, irritate, hassle (informal), pester, vex, get on your nerves (informal) **9** = tap, eavesdrop, listen in on

b

bugbear _n_ a thing that causes obsessive anxiety

bugger _n_ **1** _slang_ a person or thing considered to be unpleasant or difficult **2** _slang_ a humorous or affectionate term for someone: _a friendly little bugger_ **3** _offensive_ a person who practises anal intercourse ▶ _vb_ **4** _slang_ to tire; weary **5** _offensive_ to practise anal intercourse with ▶ _interj_ **6** _slang_ an exclamation of annoyance or disappointment

buggery _n_ anal intercourse

bugle _music_ ▶ _n_ **1** a brass instrument used chiefly for military calls ▶ _vb_ **-gling, -gled 2** to play or sound (on) a bugle > **bugler** _n_

build _vb_ **building, built 1** to make or construct by joining parts or materials: _more than 100 bypasses have been built in the past decade_ **2** to establish and develop: _it took ten years to build the business_ **3** to make in a particular way or for a particular purpose: _she's built for speed, not stamina_ **4** (often foll. by _up_) to increase in intensity ▶ _n_ **5** physical form, figure, or proportions: _he has an athletic build_

> **build** _vb_ **1** = construct, make, raise, put up, assemble, erect, fabricate, form; ≠ demolish ▶ _n_ = physique, form, body, figure, shape, structure, frame

builder _n_ a person who constructs houses and other buildings

building _n_ **1** a structure, such as a house, with a roof and walls **2** the business of building houses, etc.

> **building** _n_ = structure, house, construction, dwelling (_formal, literary_), erection (_formal_), edifice, domicile

building society _n_ (in the UK) a cooperative banking enterprise where money can be invested and mortgage loans made available. Since 1986 they have been empowered to offer banking services

built _vb_ the past of **build**

built-up _adj_ **1** having many buildings: _a built-up area_ **2** increased by the addition of parts: _built-up heels_

bulb _n_ **1** same as **light bulb 2** the onion-shaped base of the stem of some plants, which sends down roots **3** a plant, such as a daffodil, which grows from a bulb **4** any bulb-shaped thing > **bulbous** _adj_

bulge _n_ **1** a swelling or an outward curve on a normally flat surface **2** a sudden increase in number, esp. of population ▶ _vb_ **bulging, bulged 3** to swell outwards > **bulging** _adj_

> **bulge** _n_ **1** = lump, swelling, bump, projection, hump, protuberance, protrusion; ≠ hollow **2** = increase, rise, boost, surge, intensification ▶ _vb_ = swell out, project, expand, stick out, protrude, puff out, distend

bulimia _or_ **bulimia nervosa** _n_ a mental health condition characterized by a compulsion to purge oneself of the food one has eaten > **bulimic** _adj, n_

bulk _n_ **1** volume or size, esp. when great **2** the main part: _he spends the bulk of his time abroad_ **3** a large body, esp. of a person **4** the part of food which passes unabsorbed through the digestive system **5 in bulk** in large quantities: _how frequently do you buy food in bulk for your family?_ ▶ _vb_ **6 bulk large** to be or seem important or prominent

> **bulk** _n_ **1** = size, volume, dimensions, magnitude, substance, immensity, largeness **2** = majority, mass, most, body, best part, lion's share, better part, preponderance

bulkhead _n_ any upright partition in a ship or aeroplane

bulky _adj_ **bulkier, bulkiest** very large and massive, esp. so as to be unwieldy > **bulkiness** _n_

bull¹ _n_ **1** a male of domestic cattle, esp. one that is sexually mature **2** the male of various other animals including the elephant and whale **3** a very large, strong, or aggressive person **4** _Stock Exchange_ a speculator who buys in anticipation of rising prices in order to make a profit on resale **5** _chiefly Brit_ same as **bull's-eye** (senses 1, 2) **6 like a bull in a china shop** clumsy **7 take the bull by the horns** to face and tackle a difficulty without shirking

bull² _n_ a ludicrously self-contradictory or nonsensical statement

bull³ _n_ a formal document issued by the pope

bulldog _n_ a thickset dog with a broad head and a muscular body

bulldoze _vb_ **-dozing, -dozed 1** to move, demolish, or flatten with a bulldozer **2** _informal_ to coerce (someone) into doing something by intimidation

bulldozer _n_ a powerful tractor fitted with caterpillar tracks and a blade at the front, used for moving earth

bullet _n_ a small metallic missile used as the projectile of a gun or rifle

> **bullet** _n_ = projectile, ball, shot, missile, slug, pellet

bulletin _n_ **1** a broadcast summary of the news **2** an official statement on a matter of public interest **3** a periodical published by an organization for its members

> **bulletin** _n_ **1, 2** = report, account, statement, message, communication, announcement, dispatch, communiqué

bullet point _n_ one of a series of important items for discussion or action in a document, usually marked by a square or round symbol

bullfight _n_ a public show, popular in Spain, in which a matador baits and usually kills a bull in an arena > **bullfighter** _n_ > **bullfighting** _n_

bullion _n_ gold or silver in the form of bars and ingots

bullock n a gelded bull; steer

bull's-eye n 1 the small central disc of a target or a dartboard 2 a shot hitting this 3 informal something that exactly achieves its aim 4 a peppermint-flavoured boiled sweet 5 a small circular window 6 a thick disc of glass set into a ship's deck, etc. to admit light 7 the glass boss at the centre of a sheet of blown glass 8 A a convex lens used as a condenser B a lamp or lantern containing such a lens

bully n, pl -lies 1 a person who repeatedly hurts, persecutes, or intimidates other people ▸ vb -lies, -lying, -lied 2 to hurt, intimidate, or persecute (another person) ▸ interj 3 **bully for you** informal well done! bravo!: now usually used sarcastically

bully n = persecutor, tough, oppressor, tormentor, bully boy, browbeater, coercer, ruffian ▸ vb = persecute, intimidate, torment, oppress, pick on, victimize, terrorize, push around (slang)

bulrush n 1 a tall reedlike marsh plant with brown spiky flowers 2 Bible same as **papyrus** (sense 1)

bulwark n 1 a wall or similar structure used as a fortification; rampart 2 a person or thing acting as a defence

bum[1] n Brit, Austral & NZ slang the buttocks or anus

bum[2] informal ▸ n 1 a disreputable loafer or idler 2 a tramp; hobo ▸ vb **bumming, bummed** 3 to get by begging; cadge: to bum a lift 4 **bum around** to spend time to no good purpose; loaf ▸ adj 5 of poor quality; useless: he hit a bum note

bumble vb -bling, -bled 1 to speak or do in a clumsy, muddled, or inefficient way 2 to move in a clumsy or unsteady way > **bumbling** adj, n

bumblebee n a large hairy bee

bumf or **bumph** n Brit, Austral & NZ 1 official documents or forms 2 slang toilet paper

bump vb 1 to knock or strike (someone or something) with a jolt 2 to travel or proceed in jerks and jolts 3 to hurt by knocking ▸ n 4 an impact; knock; jolt; collision 5 a dull thud from an impact or collision 6 a lump on the body caused by a blow 7 a raised uneven part, such as on a road surface ▸ See also **bump off** > **bumpy** adj

bump vb 2 = jerk, shake, bounce, rattle, jog, lurch, jolt ▸ n 4 = knock, blow, impact, collision, thump 6 = lump, swelling, bulge, hump, nodule, protuberance, contusion (formal)

bumper[1] n a horizontal bar attached to the front and rear of a vehicle to protect against damage from impact

bumper[2] n 1 a glass or tankard, filled to the brim, esp. as a toast 2 an unusually large or fine example of something ▸ adj 3 unusually large, fine, or abundant: a bumper crop

bumper adj = exceptional, excellent, exo (Austral slang), massive, jumbo (informal), abundant, whopping (informal), bountiful

bumph n same as **bumf**

bumpkin n an awkward simple rustic person: a country bumpkin

bump off vb slang to murder (someone)

bumptious adj offensively self-assertive or conceited

bun n 1 a small sweetened bread roll, often containing currants or spices 2 a small round cake 3 a hairstyle in which long hair is gathered into a bun shape at the back of the head

bunch n 1 a number of things growing, fastened, or grouped together: a bunch of grapes; a bunch of keys 2 a collection; group: a bunch of queries 3 a group or company: a bunch of cowards ▸ vb 4 (sometimes foll. by together or up) to group or be grouped into a bunch

bunch n 1 = bouquet, sheaf 3 = group, band, crowd, party, team, gathering, gang, flock ▸ vb **bunch together or up** = group, mass, collect, assemble, cluster, huddle

bundle n 1 a number of things or a quantity of material gathered or loosely bound together: a bundle of sticks 2 something wrapped or tied for carrying; package 3 a number of different items sold as a single package 4 biol a collection of strands of specialized tissue such as nerve fibres 5 botany a strand of conducting tissue within plants ▸ vb -dling, -dled 6 (foll. by out, off or into etc.) to cause (someone) to go, esp. roughly or unceremoniously: she bundled them unceremoniously out into the garden 7 to push or throw (something), esp. in a quick untidy way: the soiled items were bundled into a black plastic bag 8 to sell (different items) together as a single package

bundle n 1 = bunch, group, collection, mass, pile, stack, heap, batch ▸ vb 6 = push, thrust, shove, throw, rush, hurry, jostle, hustle

bundle up vb to make (something) into a bundle or bundles

bung n 1 a stopper, esp. of cork or rubber, used to close something such as a cask or flask ▸ vb 2 (foll. by up) informal to close or seal (something) with or as if with a bung 3 Brit, Austral & NZ slang to throw (something) somewhere in a careless manner; sling

bungalow n a one-storey house

bungee jumping or **bungy jumping** n a sport in which a person jumps from a high bridge, tower, etc., to which he or she is connected by a rubber rope

bungle vb -gling, -gled 1 to spoil (an operation) through clumsiness or incompetence; botch ▸ n 2 a clumsy or unsuccessful performance; blunder > **bungler** n > **bungling** adj, n

bungle *vb* = mess up, blow (*slang*), ruin, spoil, blunder, botch, make a mess of, muff, crool *or* cruel (*Austral slang*); ≠ accomplish

bunion *n* an inflamed swelling of the first joint of the big toe

bunk[1] *n* **1** a narrow shelflike bed fixed along a wall, esp. in a caravan or ship **2** same as **bunk bed**

bunk[2] *n informal* same as **bunkum**

bunk[3] *n* **do a bunk 1** *Brit, Austral & NZ slang* to make a hurried and secret departure **2** *chiefly NZ & S African* to be absent without permission

bunk bed *n* one of a pair of beds constructed one above the other to save space

bunker *n* **1** an obstacle on a golf course, usually a sand-filled hollow bordered by a ridge **2** an underground shelter **3** a large storage container for coal, etc.

bunkum *n* empty talk; nonsense

bunny *n, pl* **-nies** a child's word for **rabbit**

Bunsen burner *n* a gas burner consisting of a metal tube with an adjustable air valve at the base

bunting *n* decorative flags, pennants, and streamers

bunya *n* a tall dome-shaped Australian coniferous tree

bunyip *n Austral* a legendary monster said to live in swamps and lakes

buoy *n* **1** a brightly coloured floating object anchored to the sea bed for marking moorings, navigable channels, or obstructions in the water ▸ *vb* **2** (foll. by *up*) to prevent from sinking: *the life belt buoyed him up* **3** to raise the spirits of; hearten: *exports are on the increase, buoyed by a weak dollar* **4** *naut* to mark (a channel or obstruction) with a buoy or buoys

buoy *n* = float, guide, signal, marker, beacon

buoyant *adj* **1** able to float in or rise to the surface of a liquid **2** (of a liquid or gas) able to keep a body afloat **3** thriving: *a buoyant economy* **4** cheerful or resilient > **buoyancy** *n*

buoyant *adj* **1** = floating, light **4** = cheerful, happy, upbeat (*informal*), carefree, jaunty, chirpy (*informal*), light-hearted; ≠ gloomy

bur *or* **burr** *n* **1** a seed case or flower head with hooks or prickles **2** any plant that produces burs

burble *vb* **-bling, -bled 1** to make or utter with a bubbling sound; gurgle **2** to talk quickly and excitedly

burden[1] *n* **1** something that is carried; load **2** something that is difficult to bear. ▸ Related adjective: **onerous** ▸ *vb* **3** to put or impose a burden on; load **4** to weigh down; oppress > **burdensome** *adj*

burden *n* **1** = load, weight, cargo, freight, consignment, encumbrance **2** = trouble, worry, weight, responsibility, strain, affliction, onus, millstone ▸ *vb* = weigh down, worry, load, tax, bother, handicap, oppress, inconvenience

burden[2] *n* **1** a line of words recurring at the end of each verse of a song **2** the theme of a speech, book, etc.

bureau (**byew-roe**) *n, pl* **-reaus** *or* **-reaux** (-rose) **1** an office or agency, esp. one providing services for the public **2** *US* a government department **3** *chiefly Brit* a writing desk with pigeonholes and drawers against which the writing surface can be closed when not in use **4** *US* a chest of drawers

bureau *n* **1** = office, department, section, branch, station, unit, division, subdivision **3** = desk, writing desk

bureaucracy *n, pl* **-cies 1** a rigid system of administration based upon organization into bureaus, division of labour, a hierarchy of authority, etc. **2** government by such a system **3** government officials collectively **4** any administration in which action is impeded by unnecessary official procedures

bureaucracy *n* **1, 2, 3** = government, officials, authorities, administration, the system, civil service, corridors of power **4** = red tape, regulations, officialdom

bureaucrat *n* **1** an official in a bureaucracy **2** an official who adheres rigidly to bureaucracy > **bureaucratic** *adj*

bureaucrat *n* **1** = official, officer, administrator, civil servant, public servant, functionary, mandarin

bureau de change *n* a place where foreign currencies can be exchanged

burgeon *vb* to develop or grow rapidly; flourish

burgh *n* (in Scotland until 1975) a town with a degree of self-government

burglar *n* a person who illegally enters a property to commit a crime

burglar *n* = housebreaker, thief, robber, pilferer, filcher, cat burglar, sneak thief

burglary *n, pl* **-ries** the crime of entering a building as a trespasser to commit theft or another offence

burglary *n* = breaking and entering, housebreaking, break-in, home invasion (*Austral, NZ*)

burgle *vb* **-gling, -gled** to break into (a house, shop, etc.)

Burgundy *n* **1** a red or white wine produced in the Burgundy region, around Dijon in France ▸ *adj* **burgundy 2** dark purplish-red

burial *n* the burying of a dead body

burial *n* = funeral, interment, obsequies, entombment, exequies

burlesque *n* **1** an artistic work, esp. literary or dramatic, satirizing a subject by caricaturing it **2** *US & Canad theatre* a bawdy comedy show of the late 19th and early 20th centuries ▸ *adj* **3** of or characteristic of a burlesque

burly *adj* **-lier, -liest** large and thick of build; sturdy

burn¹ *vb* **burning, burnt** *or* **burned** **1** to be or set on fire **2** to destroy or be destroyed by fire **3** to damage, injure, or mark by heat: *he burnt his hand* **4** to die or put to death by fire **5** to be or feel hot: *my forehead is burning* **6** to smart or cause to smart: *brandy burns your throat* **7** to feel strong emotion, esp. anger or passion **8** to use for the purposes of light, heat, or power: *to burn coal* **9** to form by or as if by fire: *to burn a hole* **10** to char or become charred: *the toast is burning* **11** to copy information onto (a compact disc) **12 burn one's bridges** *or* **boats** to commit oneself to a particular course of action with no possibility of turning back **13 burn one's fingers** to suffer from having meddled or interfered ▸ *n* **14** an injury caused by exposure to heat, electrical, chemical, or radioactive agents **15** a mark caused by burning

> **burn** *vb* **1** = be on fire, blaze, be ablaze, smoke, flame, glow, flare, go up in flames **2** = set on fire, light, ignite, kindle, incinerate **7** = be passionate, be aroused, be inflamed **10** = scorch, toast, sear, char, singe

burn² *n Scot & N English* a small stream

burning *adj* **1** intense; passionate **2** urgent; crucial: *a burning problem*

> **burning** *adj* **1** = intense, passionate, eager, ardent, fervent, impassioned, vehement; ≠ mild **2** = crucial (*informal*), important, pressing, significant, essential, vital, critical, acute

burnish *vb* to make or become shiny or smooth by friction; polish

burp *n* **1** *informal* a belch ▸ *vb* **2** *informal* to belch **3** to cause (a baby) to belch

burr *n* **1** the soft trilling sound given to the letter (r) in some English dialects **2** a whirring or humming sound **3** a rough edge left on metal or paper after cutting **4** a small hand-operated drill

burrawang *n* an Australian plant with fern-like flowers and an edible nut

burrow *n* **1** a hole dug in the ground by a rabbit or other small animal ▸ *vb* **2** to dig (a tunnel or hole) in, through, or under ground **3** to move through a place by or as if by digging **4** to delve deeply: *he burrowed into his coat pocket* **5** to live in or as if in a burrow

> **burrow** *n* = hole, shelter, tunnel, den, lair, retreat ▸ *vb* **2** = dig, tunnel, excavate **4** = delve, search, probe, ferret, rummage, forage, fossick (*Austral, NZ*)

bursar *n* a treasurer of a school, college, or university

bursary *n, pl* **-ries** **1** a scholarship or grant awarded esp. in Scottish and New Zealand schools and universities **2** *NZ* a state examination for senior pupils at secondary school

burst *vb* **bursting, burst** **1** to break or cause to break open or apart suddenly and noisily; explode **2** to come or go suddenly and forcibly: *he burst into the room* **3** to be full to the point of breaking open: *bursting at the seams* **4** (foll. by *into*) to give vent to (something) suddenly or loudly: *she burst into song* ▸ *n* **5** an instance of breaking open suddenly; explosion **6** a break; breach: *there was a burst in the pipe* **7** a sudden increase of effort; spurt: *a burst of speed* **8** a sudden and violent occurrence or outbreak: *a burst of applause*

> **burst** *vb* **1** = explode, blow up, break, split, crack, shatter, puncture, rupture **2** = rush, run, break, break out, erupt, spout, gush forth ▸ *n* **5** = explosion, crack, blast, bang, discharge **7** = rush, surge, outburst, outburst, spate, gush, torrent, spurt

bury *vb* **buries, burying, buried** **1** to place (a corpse) in a grave **2** to place (something) in the earth and cover it with soil **3** to cover (something) from sight; hide **4** to occupy (oneself) with deep concentration: *he buried himself in his work* **5** to dismiss (a feeling) from the mind: *they decided to bury any hard feelings*

> **bury** *vb* **1** = inter, lay to rest, entomb, consign to the grave, inhume; ≠ dig up **3** = hide, cover, conceal, stash (*informal*), secrete, stow away; ≠ uncover **5** = forget

bus *n* **1** a large motor vehicle designed to carry passengers between stopping places along a regular route **2** *informal* a car or aircraft that is old and shaky **3** *electronics & computers* an electrical conductor used to make a common connection between several circuits ▸ *vb* **bussing, bussed** *or* **busing, bused** **4** to travel or transport by bus **5** *chiefly US & Canad* to transport (children) by bus from one area to another in order to create racially integrated schools

busby *n, pl* **-bies** a tall fur helmet worn by certain British soldiers

bush *n* **1** a dense woody plant, smaller than a tree, with many branches; shrub **2** a dense cluster of such shrubs; thicket **3** something resembling a bush, esp. in density: *a bush of hair* **4 the bush** an uncultivated area covered with trees or shrubs in Australia, Africa, New Zealand, and Canada **5** *Canad* an area on a farm on which timber is grown and cut **6 beat about the bush** to avoid the point at issue

> **bush** *n* **1, 2** = shrub, plant, hedge, thicket, shrubbery **4 the bush** = the wilds, brush, scrub, woodland, backwoods, scrubland

bushbaby *n, pl* **-babies** a small agile tree-living mammal with large eyes and a long tail

bushel *n Brit* an obsolete unit of dry or liquid measure equal to 8 gallons (36.4 litres)

bushfire *n* an uncontrolled scrub or forest fire
bushy *adj* **bushier, bushiest 1** (of hair) thick and shaggy **2** covered or overgrown with bushes
business *n* **1** the purchase and sale of goods and services **2** a commercial or industrial establishment **3** a trade or profession **4** commercial activity: *the two countries should do business with each other* **5** proper or rightful concern or responsibility: *mind your own business* **6** an affair; matter: *it's a dreadful business* **7** serious work or activity: *get down to business* **8** a difficult or complicated matter: *it's a business trying to see him* **9 mean business** to be in earnest

> **business** *n* **1, 4** = trade, selling, industry, manufacturing, commerce, dealings **2** = establishment, company, firm, concern, organization, corporation, venture, enterprise **3** = profession, work, job, line, trade, career, function, employment **5, 6** = concern, affair

businesslike *adj* efficient and methodical
businessman *or fem* **businesswoman** *n, pl* **-men** *or* **-women** a person engaged in commercial or industrial business, usually an owner or executive

> **businessman** *or* **businesswoman** *n* = executive, director, manager, merchant, capitalist, administrator, entrepreneur, tycoon

busker *n* a person who entertains for money in streets, stations, etc. > **busk** *vb*
bust[1] *n* **1** a woman's bosom **2** a sculpture of the head, shoulders, and upper chest of a person

> **bust** *n* **1** = bosom, breasts, chest, front

bust[2] *informal* ► *vb* **busting, busted** *or* **bust 1** to burst or break **2** (of the police) to raid or search (a place) or arrest (someone) **3** *US & Canad* to demote in military rank ► *adj* **4** broken **5 go bust** to become bankrupt

> **bust** *vb* **1** = break, smash, split, burst, shatter, fracture, rupture **2** = arrest, catch, raid ► *adj* **5 go bust** = go bankrupt, fail, be ruined, become insolvent

bustard *n* a bird with long strong legs, a heavy body, a long neck, and speckled plumage
bustle[1] *vb* **-tling, -tled 1** (often foll. by *about*) to hurry with a great show of energy or activity ► *n* **2** energetic and noisy activity > **bustling** *adj*

> **bustle** *vb* = hurry, rush, fuss, hasten, scuttle, scurry, scamper; ≠ idle ► *n* = activity, to-do, stir, excitement, fuss, flurry, commotion, ado; ≠ inactivity

bustle[2] *n* a cushion or framework worn by women in the late 19th century at the back in order to expand the skirt
busy *adj* **busier, busiest 1** actively or fully engaged; occupied **2** crowded with or characterized by activity **3** (of a telephone line) in use; engaged ► *vb* **busies, busying, busied 4** to make or keep (someone, esp. oneself) busy; occupy > **busily** *adv*

> **busy** *adj* **1** = active, industrious, rushed off your feet; ≠ idle **2** = hectic, full, exacting, energetic ► *vb* **busy yourself** = occupy yourself, be engrossed, immerse yourself, involve yourself, absorb yourself, employ yourself, engage yourself

busybody *n, pl* **-bodies** a meddlesome, prying, or officious person
but *conj* **1** contrary to expectation: *he cut his hand but didn't cry* **2** in contrast; on the contrary: *I like seafood but my husband doesn't* **3** other than: *we can't do anything but wait* **4** without it happening: *we never go out but it rains* ► *prep* **5** except: *they saved all but one* **6 but for** were it not for: *but for you, we couldn't have managed* ► *adv* **7** only: *I can but try; he was but a child* ► *n* **8** an objection: *ifs and buts*

> **but** *conj* **2** = however, still, yet, nevertheless ► *prep* **5** = except (for), save, bar, barring, excepting, excluding, with the exception of ► *adv* = only, just, simply, merely

butane (byew-tane) *n* a colourless gas used in the manufacture of rubber and fuels
butch *adj slang* (of a woman or man) markedly or aggressively masculine
butcher *n* **1** a person who sells meat **2** a person who kills animals for meat **3** a brutal murderer ► *vb* **4** to kill and prepare (animals) for meat **5** to kill (people) at random or brutally **6** to make a mess of; botch

> **butcher** *n* **3** = murderer, killer, slaughterer, slayer, destroyer, executioner, cut-throat, exterminator ► *vb* **4** = slaughter, prepare, carve, cut up, dress, cut, clean, joint **5** = kill, slaughter, massacre, destroy, cut down, assassinate, slay (*archaic, literary*), liquidate

butcherbird *n* an Australian magpie that impales its prey on thorns
butchery *n, pl* **-eries 1** senseless slaughter **2** the business of a butcher
butler *n* the head manservant of a household, in charge of the wines, table, etc.
butt[1] *n* **1** the thicker or blunt end of something, such as the stock of a rifle **2** the unused end of a cigarette or cigar; stub **3** *chiefly US & Canad slang* the buttocks

> **butt** *n* **1** = end, handle, shaft, stock, shank, hilt, haft **2** = stub, tip, leftover, fag end (*informal*)

butt[2] *n* **1** a person or thing that is the target of ridicule or teasing **2** *shooting & archery* **a** a mound of earth behind the target **b butts** the target range

> **butt** *n* **1** = target, victim, dupe, laughing stock, Aunt Sally

butt³ *vb* **1** to strike (something or someone) with the head or horns **2** (foll. by *in* or *into*) to intrude, esp. into a conversation; interfere ▸ *n* **3** a blow with the head or horns

> **butt** *vb* **1** = knock, push, bump, thrust, ram, shove, poke, prod **2 butt in** = interrupt, cut in, break in, chip in (*informal*)

butt⁴ *n* a large cask for collecting or storing liquids

> **butt** *n* = cask, barrel

butter *n* **1** an edible fatty yellow solid made from cream by churning **2** any substance with a butter-like consistency, such as peanut butter ▸ *vb* **3** to put butter on or in (something) ▸ See also **butter up** ▷ **buttery** *adj*

butter bean *n* a large pale flat edible bean

buttercup *n* a small bright yellow flower

butterfingers *n informal* a person who drops things by mistake or fails to catch things

butterfly *n*, *pl* **-flies** **1** an insect with a slender body and brightly coloured wings **2** a swimming stroke in which the arms are plunged forward together in large circular movements **3** a person who never settles with one interest or occupation for long

buttermilk *n* the sourish liquid remaining after the butter has been separated from milk

butterscotch *n* a hard brittle toffee made with butter, brown sugar, etc.

butter up *vb* to flatter

buttery *n*, *pl* **-teries** *Brit* (in some universities) a room in which food and drink are sold to students

buttock *n* **1** either of the two large fleshy masses that form the human rump **2** the corresponding part in some mammals

button *n* **1** a disc or knob of plastic, wood, etc., attached to a garment, which fastens two surfaces together by passing through a buttonhole **2** a small disc that operates a door bell or machine when pressed **3** a small round object, such as a sweet or badge ▸ *vb* **4** to fasten (a garment) with a button or buttons

buttonhole *n* **1** a slit in a garment through which a button is passed to fasten two surfaces together **2** a flower worn pinned to the lapel or in the buttonhole ▸ *vb* **-holing, -holed** **3** to detain (a person) in conversation

buttress *n* **1** a construction, usually of brick or stone, built to support a wall **2** any support or prop ▸ *vb* **3** to support (a wall) with a buttress **4** to support or sustain: *his observations are buttressed by the most recent scholarly research*

buxom *adj* (of a woman) healthily plump, attractive, and full-bosomed

buy *vb* **buying, bought** **1** to acquire (something) by paying a sum of money for it; purchase **2** to be capable of purchasing: *money can't buy love* **3** to acquire by any exchange or sacrifice: *the rise in interest rates was just to buy time until the weekend*

4 to bribe (someone) **5** *slang* to accept (something) as true **6** (foll. by *into*) to purchase shares of (a company) ▸ *n* **7** a purchase: *a good buy*

> **buy** *vb* **1** = purchase, get, pay for, obtain, acquire, invest in, shop for, procure; ≠ sell ▸ *n* = purchase, deal (*informal*), bargain, acquisition, steal (*informal*), snip (*informal*), giveaway

buyer *n* **1** a person who buys; customer **2** a person employed to buy merchandise for a shop or factory

buzz *n* **1** a rapidly vibrating humming sound, such as of a bee **2** a low sound, such as of many voices in conversation **3** *informal* a telephone call **4** *informal* a sense of excitement ▸ *vb* **5** to make a vibrating sound like that of a prolonged *z* **6** (of a place) to be filled with an air of excitement: *the city buzzed with the news* **7** to summon (someone) with a buzzer **8** *informal* to fly an aircraft very low over (people, buildings, or another aircraft) **9 buzz about** *or* **around** to move around quickly and busily

buzzard *n* a bird of prey with broad wings and tail and a soaring flight

buzzer *n* an electronic device that produces a buzzing sound as a signal

buzz word *n informal* a word, originally from a particular jargon, which becomes a popular vogue word

by *prep* **1** used to indicate the performer of the action of a passive verb: *seeds eaten by the birds* **2** used to indicate the person responsible for a creative work: *three songs by Britten* **3** via; through: *enter by the back door* **4** used to indicate a means used: *he frightened her by hiding behind the door* **5** beside; next to; near: *a tree by the stream* **6** passing the position of; past: *I drove by the place where she works* **7** not later than; before: *return the books by Tuesday* **8** used to indicate extent: *it is hotter by five degrees* **9** multiplied by: *four by three equals twelve* **10** during the passing of: *by night* **11** placed between measurements of the various dimensions of something: *a plank fourteen inches by seven* ▸ *adv* **12** near: *the house is close by* **13** away; aside: *he put some money by each week* **14** passing a point near something; past: *he drove by*

> **by** *prep* **1, 2** = through, through the agency of **3** = via, over, by way of **5, 6** = near, past, along, close to, closest to, neighbouring, next to, beside ▸ *adv* **12** = nearby, close, handy, at hand, within reach

bye *or* **bye-bye** *interj informal* goodbye

by-election *or* **bye-election** *n* an election held during the life of a parliament to fill a vacant seat

bygone *adj* past; former: *a bygone age*

bylaw *or* **bye-law** *n* a rule made by a local authority

BYO *or* **BYOG** *n Austral & NZ* an unlicensed restaurant at which diners may bring their own alcoholic drink

bypass *n* **1** a main road built to avoid a city **2** a secondary pipe, channel, or appliance through which the flow of a substance, such as gas or electricity, is redirected **3** a surgical operation in which the blood flow is redirected away from a diseased or blocked part of the heart ▸ *vb* **4** to go around or avoid (a city, obstruction, problem, etc.) **5** to proceed without reference to (regulations or a superior); get round; avoid

> **bypass** *vb* **4** = get round, avoid **5** = go round, circumvent, depart from, deviate from, pass round, detour round; ≠ cross

by-product *n* **1** a secondary or incidental product of a manufacturing process **2** a side effect

byre *n Brit* a shelter for cows

bystander *n* a person present but not involved; onlooker; spectator

byte *n computers* a group of bits processed as one unit of data

byway *n* a secondary or side road, esp. in the country

byword *n* **1** a person or thing regarded as a perfect example of something: *their name is a byword for quality* **2** a common saying; proverb

Cc

C 1 centi- **2** *cricket* caught **3** cubic **4** the speed of light in free space

C 1 *music* the first note of a major scale containing no sharps or flats (**C major**) **2** *chem* carbon **3** Celsius **4** centigrade **5** century: C20 **6** coulomb **7** the Roman numeral for 100 **8** a high-level computer programming language

c. (used preceding a date) about: *c. 1800*

cab *n* **1** a taxi **2** the enclosed driver's compartment of a lorry, bus, or train

> **cab** *n* **1** = taxi, minicab, taxicab, hackney carriage

cabal (kab-**bal**) *n* **1** a small group of political plotters **2** a secret plot or conspiracy

cabaret (kab-a-ray) *n* **1** a floor show of dancing and singing at a nightclub or restaurant **2** a place providing such entertainment

cabbage *n* **1** a vegetable with a large head of green or reddish-purple leaves **2** *informal, offensive* a person who is unable to move or think, as a result of brain damage

cabbage tree *n NZ* a palm-like tree with a bare trunk and spiky leaves

cabbie *or* **cabby** *n, pl* **-bies** *informal* a taxi driver

caber *n Scot* a heavy section of trimmed tree trunk tossed in competition at Highland games

cabin *n* **1** a room used as living quarters in a ship or boat **2** a small simple dwelling: *a log cabin* **3** the enclosed part of an aircraft in which the passengers or crew sit

> **cabin** *n* **1** = room, berth, quarters, compartment **2** = hut, shed, cottage, lodge, shack, chalet, shanty, whare (NZ)

cabin cruiser *n* a motorboat with a cabin

cabinet *n* a piece of furniture containing shelves, cupboards, or drawers for storage or display: *a filing cabinet; a cocktail cabinet*

> **cabinet** *n* = cupboard, case, locker, dresser, closet (US), press, chiffonier

Cabinet *n* a committee of senior government ministers or advisers to a president

> **Cabinet** *n* = council, committee, administration, ministry, assembly, board

cabinet-maker *n* a person who makes fine furniture ▸ **cabinet-making** *n*

cable *n* **1** a strong thick rope of twisted hemp or wire **2** a bundle of wires covered with plastic or rubber that conducts electricity **3** a telegram sent abroad by submarine cable or telephone line **4** Also called: **cable stitch** a knitted design which resembles a twisted rope **5** short for **cable television** ▸ vb **-bling, -bled 6** to send (someone) a message by cable

cable car n a vehicle that is pulled up a steep slope by a moving cable

cable television n a television service in which the subscriber's television is connected to a central receiver by cable

caboodle n **the whole caboodle** informal the whole lot

cabriolet (kab-ree-oh-lay) n a small two-wheeled horse-drawn carriage with a folding hood

cacao (kak-kah-oh) n a tropical American tree with seed pods (**cacao beans**) from which cocoa and chocolate are prepared

cache (kash) n a hidden store of weapons, provisions, or treasure

cachet (kash-shay) n prestige or distinction: *a Mercedes carries a certain cachet*

cack-handed adj informal clumsy: *I open cans in a very cack-handed way*

cackle vb **-ling, -led 1** to laugh shrilly **2** (of a hen) to squawk with shrill broken notes ▸ n **3** the sound of cackling > **cackling** adj

cacophony (kak-koff-on-ee) n harsh discordant sound: *a cacophony of barking* > **cacophonous** adj

cactus n, pl **-tuses** or **-ti** a thick fleshy desert plant with spines but no leaves

cad n old-fashioned, informal a man who behaves dishonourably > **caddish** adj

> **cad** n = scoundrel (slang), rat (informal), bounder (Brit old-fashioned slang), rotter (slang, chiefly Brit), heel, wrong 'un (slang)

cadaver (kad-dav-ver) n med a corpse

cadaverous adj pale, thin, and haggard

caddie n **1** a person who carries a golfer's clubs ▸ vb **-dying, -died 2** to act as a caddie

caddis fly n an insect whose larva (the **caddis worm**) lives underwater in a protective case of silk, sand, and stones

caddy n, pl **-dies** chiefly Brit a small container for tea

cadence (kade-enss) n **1** the rise and fall in the pitch of the voice **2** the close of a musical phrase

cadenza n a complex solo passage in a piece of music

cadet n a young person training for the armed forces or the police

cadge vb **cadging, cadged** informal to get (something) from someone by taking advantage of his or her generosity > **cadger** n

cadmium n chem a bluish-white metallic element found in zinc ores and used in electroplating and alloys. Symbol: **Cd**

cadre (kah-der) n a small group of people selected and trained to form the core of a political organization or military unit

caecum or US **cecum** (seek-um) n, pl **-ca** (-ka) the pouch at the beginning of the large intestine

Caesar (seez-ar) n **1** a Roman emperor **2** any emperor or dictator **3** short for **Caesar salad**

Caesarean section n surgical incision into the womb in order to deliver a baby

Caesar salad n a salad of lettuce, cheese, and croutons with a dressing of olive oil, garlic, and lemon juice

caesium or US **cesium** n chem a silvery-white metallic element used in photocells. Symbol: **Cs**

café n **1** a small or inexpensive restaurant that serves drinks and snacks or light meals **2** S African a corner shop

> **café** n **1** = snack bar, restaurant, cafeteria, coffee shop, brasserie, coffee bar, tearoom, lunchroom

cafeteria n a self-service restaurant

caffeine n a stimulant found in tea, coffee, and cocoa

caftan n same as **kaftan**

cage n **1** an enclosure made of bars or wires, for keeping birds or animals in **2** the enclosed platform of a lift in a mine ▸ vb **caging, caged 3** to confine in a cage > **caged** adj

> **cage** n **1** = enclosure, pen, coop, hutch, pound

cagey adj **cagier, cagiest** informal reluctant to go into details; wary: *he is cagey about what he paid for the business* > **cagily** adv

cagoule (kag-gool) n Brit a lightweight hooded waterproof jacket

cahoots pl n **in cahoots** informal conspiring together: *the loan sharks were in cahoots with the home-improvement companies*

cairn n a mound of stones erected as a memorial or marker

cajole vb **-joling, -joled** to persuade by flattery; coax: *he allowed himself to be cajoled into staying on* > **cajolery** n

cake n **1** a sweet food baked from a mixture of flour, sugar, eggs, etc. **2** a flat compact mass of something: *a cake of soap* **3** **have one's cake and eat it** to enjoy both of two incompatible alternatives **4** **piece of cake** informal something that is easy to do **5** **sell like hot cakes** informal to be sold very quickly: *commercial novels sell like hot cakes* ▸ vb **caking, caked 6** to form into a hardened mass or crust: *her hair was caked with grease and dust*

> **cake** n **2** = block, bar, slab, lump, cube, loaf, mass

cakewalk n informal a task that is easy to accomplish

calamine n a pink powder consisting chiefly of zinc oxide, used to make soothing skin lotions and ointments

calamitous adj resulting in or from disaster: *the country's calamitous economic decline*

calamity *n, pl* **-ties** a disaster or misfortune

calcify *vb* **-fies, -fying, -fied** to harden by the depositing of calcium salts › **calcification** *n*

calcium *n chem* a soft silvery-white metallic element found in bones, teeth, limestone, and chalk. Symbol: **Ca**

calculable *adj* able to be computed or estimated

calculate *vb* **-lating, -lated** **1** to solve or find out by a mathematical procedure or by reasoning **2** to aim to have a particular effect: *this ad campaign is calculated to offend*

calculating *adj* selfishly scheming

> **calculating** *adj* = scheming, sharp, shrewd, cunning, sly, devious, manipulative, crafty; ≠ direct

calculation *n* **1** the act or result of calculating **2** selfish scheming: *there was an element of calculation in her insistence on arriving after dark*

> **calculation** *n* **1** = computation, working out, reckoning, estimate, forecast, judgment, result, answer **2** = planning, intention, deliberation, foresight, contrivance, forethought, premeditation

calculator *n* a small electronic device for doing mathematical calculations

calculus *n* **1** the branch of mathematics dealing with infinitesimal changes to a variable number or quantity **2** *pl* **-li** *pathol* same as **stone** (sense 7)

Caledonian *adj* Scottish

calendar *n* **1** a chart showing a year divided up into months, weeks, and days **2** a system for determining the beginning, length, and divisions of years: *the Jewish calendar* **3** a schedule of events or appointments: *concerts were an important part of the social calendar of the Venetian nobility*

calendula *n* a plant with orange-and-yellow rayed flowers

calf¹ *n, pl* **calves** a young cow, bull, elephant, whale, or seal

calf² *n, pl* **calves** the back of the leg between the ankle and the knee

calibrate *vb* **-brating, -brated** to mark the scale or check the accuracy of (a measuring instrument) › **calibration** *n*

calibre *or US* **caliber** (**kal-lib-ber**) *n* **1** a person's ability or worth: *a poet of Wordsworth's calibre* **2** the diameter of the bore of a gun or of a shell or bullet

> **calibre** *or* **caliber** *n* **1** = worth, quality, ability, talent, capacity, merit, distinction, stature **2** = diameter, bore, gauge, measure

calico *n* a white or unbleached cotton fabric

caliph *n Islam* the title of the successors of Mohammed as rulers of the Islamic world

call *vb* **1** to name: *a town called Eyemouth* **2** to describe (someone or something) as being: *they called him a Hitler* **3** to speak loudly so as to attract attention **4** to telephone: *he left a message for Lynch to call him* **5** to summon: *a doctor must be called immediately* **6** to pay someone a visit: *the social worker called and she didn't answer the door* **7** to arrange: *the meeting was called for the lunch hour* **8** **call someone's bluff** See **bluff¹** (sense 3) ▸ *n* **9** a cry or shout **10** the cry made by a bird or animal **11** a communication by telephone **12** a short visit: *I paid a call on an old friend* **13** a summons or invitation: *the police and fire brigade continued to respond to calls* **14** need, demand, or desire: *a call for economic sanctions* **15** allure or fascination: *the call of the open road* **16** **on call** available when summoned: *there's a doctor on call in town* ▸ See also **call for** › **caller** *n*

> **call** *vb* **1** = name, entitle, dub, designate, term, style, label, describe as **3** = cry, shout, scream, yell, whoop; ≠ whisper **4** = phone, telephone, ring (up) (*informal, chiefly Brit*), Skype (*trademark*), video call ▸ *n* **9** = cry, shout, scream, yell, whoop; ≠ whisper **11** = telephone call, bell (*informal*), phone call, buzz (*informal*), ring (*informal*), video call, Skype (*trademark*) **12** = visit **13** = request, order, demand, appeal, notice, command, invitation, plea **14** = need, cause, reason, grounds, occasion, excuse, justification **15** = attraction, pull (*informal*), appeal, lure, allure, magnetism

call box *n* a soundproof enclosure for a public telephone

call centre *n Brit, Austral & NZ* an office where staff carry out an organization's telephone transactions

call for *vb* **1** to require: *appendicitis calls for removal of the appendix* **2** to come and fetch

> **call for** *vb* **1 call for something** = require, need, involve, demand, occasion, entail, necessitate

calligraphy *n* beautiful handwriting › **calligrapher** *n* › **calligraphic** *adj*

calling *n* **1** a strong urge to follow a particular profession or occupation, esp. a caring one **2** a profession or occupation, esp. a caring one

> **calling** *n* **2** = profession, trade, career, mission, vocation, life's work

calliper *or US* **caliper** *n* **1** a metal splint for supporting the leg **2** a measuring instrument consisting of two steel legs hinged together

callisthenics *or* **calisthenics** *n* light exercises designed to promote general fitness › **callisthenic** *or* **calisthenic** *adj*

call off *vb* **1** to cancel or abandon: *the strike has now been called off* **2** to order (a dog or a person) to stop attacking someone

callous *adj* showing no concern for other people's feelings › **callously** *adv* › **callousness** *n*

calloused *adj* covered in calluses

callow *adj* young and inexperienced: *a callow youth*

call up vb **1** to summon for active military service **2** to cause one to remember ▸ n **call-up** **3** a general order to report for military service

callus n, pl **-luses** an area of hard or thickened skin on the hand or foot

calm adj **1** not showing or not feeling agitation or excitement **2** not ruffled by the wind: *a flat calm sea* **3** (of weather) windless ▸ n **4** a peaceful state ▸ vb **5** (often foll. by *down*) to make or become calm > **calmly** adv > **calmness** n

> **calm** adj **1** = cool, relaxed, composed, sedate, collected, dispassionate, unemotional, self-possessed, chilled (*informal*); ≠ excited **2, 3** = still, quiet, smooth, mild, serene, tranquil, balmy, windless; ≠ rough ▸ n = peacefulness, peace, serenity ▸ vb = soothe, quiet, relax, appease, still, allay, assuage, quieten; ≠ excite

calorie n **1** a unit of measure for the energy value of food **2** Also: **small calorie** the quantity of heat required to raise the temperature of 1 gram of water by 1°C

calorific adj of calories or heat

calumny n, pl **-nies** a false or malicious statement; slander

calve vb **calving**, **calved** to give birth to a calf

calypso n, pl **-sos** a West Indian song with improvised topical lyrics

calyx (kale-ix) n, pl **calyxes** or **calyces** (kal-iss-seez) the outer leaves that protect the developing bud of a flower

cam n a part of an engine that converts a circular motion into a to-and-fro motion

camaraderie n familiarity and trust between friends

camber n a slight upward curve to the centre of a road surface

cambric n a fine white linen fabric

camcorder n a combined portable video camera and recorder

came vb the past tense of **come**

camel n either of two humped mammals, the dromedary and Bactrian camel, that can survive long periods without food or water in desert regions

camellia (kam-meal-ya) n an ornamental shrub with glossy leaves and white, pink, or red flowers

Camembert (kam-mem-bare) n a soft creamy cheese

cameo n, pl **cameos** **1** a brooch or ring with a profile head carved in relief **2** a small but important part in a film or play played by a well-known actor

camera n **1** a piece of equipment used for taking photographs, video, or film **2 in camera** in private

cameraman n, pl **-men** a person who operates a camera for television or cinema

camera phone n a mobile phone incorporating a digital camera

camiknickers pl n Brit a woman's undergarment consisting of knickers attached to a camisole top

camisole n a bodice-like garment with shoulder straps

camomile or **chamomile** (kam-mo-mile) n a sweet-smelling plant used to make herbal tea

camouflage (kam-moo-flahzh) n **1** the use of natural surroundings or artificial aids to conceal or disguise something ▸ vb **-flaging**, **-flaged** **2** to conceal by camouflage

> **camouflage** n = protective colouring ▸ vb = disguise, cover, screen, hide, mask, conceal, obscure, veil; ≠ reveal

camp[1] n **1** a place where people stay in tents **2** a collection of huts and other buildings used as temporary lodgings for military troops or for prisoners of war **3** a group that supports a particular doctrine: *the socialist camp* ▸ vb **4** to stay in a camp > **camper** n > **camping** n

> **camp** n **1** = camp site, tents, encampment, camping ground **2** = bivouac, cantonment (*military*)

camp[2] informal ▸ adj **1** effeminate; affected in mannerisms or dress **2** consciously artificial, vulgar, or mannered ▸ vb **3 camp it up** to behave in a camp manner

> **camp** adj **1** = effeminate **2** = affected, mannered, artificial, posturing, ostentatious

campaign n **1** a series of coordinated activities designed to achieve a goal **2** military a number of operations aimed at achieving a single objective ▸ vb **3** to take part in a campaign: *he paid tribute to all those who'd campaigned for his release* > **campaigner** n

> **campaign** n **1** = drive, appeal, movement, push (*informal*), offensive, crusade **2** = operation, drive, attack, movement, push, offensive, expedition, crusade

campanology n the art of ringing bells > **campanologist** n

campanula n a plant with blue or white bell-shaped flowers

camphor n a sweet-smelling crystalline substance obtained from the wood of the **camphor tree**, which is used medicinally and in mothballs

campion n a red, pink, or white European wild flower

campus n, pl **-puses** the grounds and buildings of a university or college

camshaft n a part of an engine consisting of a rod to which cams are attached

can[1] vb, past tense **could** **1** be able to: *make sure he can breathe easily* **2** be allowed to: *you can swim in the large pool*

can[2] n **1** a metal container, usually sealed, for food or liquids ▸ vb **canning**, **canned** **2** to put (something) into a can

Canadian *adj* **1** of Canada ▶ *n* **2** a person from Canada

canal *n* **1** an artificial waterway constructed for navigation or irrigation **2** a passage or duct in a person's body: *the alimentary canal*

> **canal** *n* **1** = waterway, channel, passage, conduit, duct, watercourse

canapé (kan-nap-pay) *n* a small piece of bread or toast spread with a savoury topping

canary *n, pl* **-naries** a small yellow songbird often kept as a pet

canasta *n* a card game like rummy, played with two packs of cards

cancan *n* a lively high-kicking dance performed by a female group

cancel *vb* **-celling, -celled** *or US* **-celing, -celed** **1** to stop (something that has been arranged) from taking place **2** to mark (a cheque or stamp) with an official stamp to prevent further use **3 cancel out** to make ineffective by having the opposite effect: *economic vulnerability cancels out any possible political gain* > **cancellation** *n*

> **cancel** *vb* **1** = call off, drop, forget about **3 cancel something out** = counterbalance, offset, make up for, compensate for, neutralize, nullify, balance out

cancer *n* **1** a serious disease resulting from a malignant growth or tumour, caused by abnormal and uncontrolled cell division **2** a malignant growth or tumour **3** an evil influence that spreads dangerously: *their country would remain a cancer of instability* > **cancerous** *adj*

> **cancer** *n* **2** = growth, tumour, malignancy **3** = evil, corruption, sickness, pestilence

candela (kan-dee-la) *n* the SI unit of luminous intensity (the amount of light a source gives off in a given direction)

candelabrum *or* **candelabra** *n, pl* **-bra, -brums** *or* **-bras** a large branched holder for candles or overhead lights

candid *adj* honest and straightforward in speech or behaviour > **candidly** *adv*

candidate *n* **1** a person seeking a job or position **2** a person taking an examination **3** a person or thing regarded as suitable or likely for a particular fate or position: *someone who smokes, drinks, or eats too much is a candidate for heart disease* > **candidacy** *or* **candidature** *n*

> **candidate** *n* **1** = contender, competitor, applicant, nominee, entrant, claimant, contestant, runner

candied *adj* coated with or cooked in sugar: *candied peel*

candle *n* **1** a stick or block of wax or tallow surrounding a wick, which is burned to produce light **2 burn the candle at both ends** to exhaust oneself by doing too much

candlestick *or* **candleholder** *n* a holder for a candle

candlewick *n* cotton with a tufted pattern, used to make bedspreads and dressing gowns

candour *or US* **candor** *n* honesty and straightforwardness of speech or behaviour

candy *n, pl* **-dies** *chiefly US & Canad* a sweet or sweets

candyfloss *n Brit* a light fluffy mass of spun sugar, held on a stick

candy-striped *adj* having narrow coloured stripes on a white background

cane *n* **1** the long flexible stems of the bamboo or any similar plant **2** strips of such stems, woven to make wickerwork **3** a bamboo stem tied to a garden plant to support it **4** a flexible rod used to beat someone **5** a slender walking stick ▶ *vb* **caning, caned 6** to beat with a cane

cane toad *n* a large toad used to control insects and other pests of sugar cane plantations

canine (kay-nine) *adj* **1** of or like a dog ▶ *n* **2** a sharp-pointed tooth between the incisors and the molars

canister *n* a metal container for dry food

canker *n* **1** an ulceration or ulcerous disease **2** something evil that spreads and corrupts

cannabis *n* a drug obtained from the dried leaves and flowers of the hemp plant

> **cannabis** *n* = marijuana, pot (*slang*), green (*slang*), dope (*slang*), grass (*slang*), hemp, dagga (*S African*)

canned *adj* **1** preserved in a can **2** *informal* recorded in advance: *canned carols*

cannelloni *or* **canneloni** *pl n* tubular pieces of pasta filled with meat or cheese

cannery *n, pl* **-neries** a place where foods are canned

cannibal *n* **1** a person who eats human flesh **2** an animal that eats the flesh of other animals of its kind > **cannibalism** *n*

cannibalize *or* **-ise** *vb* **-izing, -ized** *or* **-ising, -ised** to use parts from (one machine or vehicle) to repair another

cannon *n, pl* **-nons** *or* **-non 1** a large gun consisting of a metal tube mounted on a carriage, formerly used in battles **2** an automatic aircraft gun **3** *billiards* a shot in which the cue ball strikes two balls successively ▶ *vb* **4 cannon into** to collide with

> **cannon** *n* **1** = gun, big gun, field gun, mortar

cannonade *n* continuous heavy gunfire

cannonball *n* a heavy metal ball fired from a cannon

cannot *vb* can not

canny *adj* **-nier, -niest** shrewd or cautious > **cannily** *adv*

canoe *n* a light narrow open boat, propelled by one or more paddles > **canoeist** *n*

canoeing *n* the sport of rowing or racing in a canoe

canon¹ n a priest serving in a cathedral

canon² n 1 *Christianity* a Church decree regulating morals or religious practices 2 a general rule or standard: *the Marx-Engels canon* 3 a list of the works of an author that are accepted as authentic: *the Yeats canon* 4 a piece of music in which a melody in one part is taken up in one or more other parts successively

> **canon** n 2 = rule, standard, principle, regulation, formula, criterion, dictate, statute 3 = list, index, catalogue, roll

canonical adj 1 conforming with canon law 2 included in a canon of writings

canonize or **-ise** vb **-izing, -ized** or **-ising, -ised** RC Church to declare (a dead person) to be a saint > **canonization** or **-isation** n

canoodle vb **-dling, -dled** slang to kiss and cuddle

canopied adj covered with a canopy: *canopied niches*

canopy n, pl **-pies** 1 an ornamental awning above a bed or throne 2 a rooflike covering over an altar, niche, or door 3 any large or wide covering: *the thick forest canopy* 4 the part of a parachute that opens out 5 the transparent hood of an aircraft cockpit

> **canopy** n 1, 2 = awning, covering, shade, sunshade

cant¹ n 1 insincere talk concerning religion or morals 2 specialized vocabulary of a particular group, such as thieves or lawyers ▸ vb 3 to use cant: *canting hypocrites*

cant² n 1 a tilted position ▸ vb 2 to tilt or overturn: *the engine was canted to one side*

can't vb can not

cantaloupe or **cantaloup** n Brit a kind of melon with sweet-tasting orange flesh

cantankerous adj quarrelsome or bad-tempered

cantata (kan-tah-ta) n a musical setting of a text, consisting of arias, duets, and choruses

canteen n 1 a restaurant attached to a workplace or school 2 a box containing a set of cutlery

canter n 1 a gait of horses that is faster than a trot but slower than a gallop ▸ vb 2 (of a horse) to move at a canter

canticle n a short hymn with words from the Bible

cantilever n a beam or girder fixed at one end only

canto (kan-toe) n, pl **-tos** a main division of a long poem

canton n a political division of a country, such as Switzerland

cantor n Judaism a man employed to lead synagogue services

canvas n 1 a heavy cloth of cotton, hemp, or jute, used to make tents and sails and for painting on in oils 2 an oil painting done on

canvas 3 **under canvas** in a tent: *sleeping under canvas*

canvass vb 1 to try to persuade (people) to vote for a particular candidate or party in an election 2 to find out the opinions of (people) by conducting a survey ▸ n 3 the activity of canvassing > **canvasser** n > **canvassing** n

canyon n a deep narrow steep-sided valley

canyoning n the sport of travelling down a river situated in a canyon by a variety of means including scrambling, swimming, and abseiling

cap n 1 a soft close-fitting covering for the head 2 sport a cap given to someone selected for a national team 3 a small flat lid: *petrol cap* 4 a small amount of explosive enclosed in paper and used in a toy gun 5 a contraceptive device placed over the mouth of the womb 6 an upper financial limit 7 **cap in hand** humbly ▸ vb **capping, capped** 8 to cover or top with something: *a thick cover of snow capped the cars* 9 sport to select (a player) for a national team: *Australia's most capped player* 10 to impose an upper level on (a tax): *charge capping* 11 informal to outdo or excel: *capping anecdote with anecdote*

> **cap** vb 8 = top, crown 11 = beat, top, better, exceed, eclipse, surpass, transcend, outstrip

capability n, pl **-ties** the ability or skill to do something

> **capability** n = ability, means, power, potential, capacity, qualification(s), competence, proficiency; ≠ inability

capable adj 1 having the ability or skill to do something: *a side capable of winning the championship* 2 competent and efficient: *capable high achievers* > **capably** adv

> **capable** adj 1 = able, suited; ≠ incapable 2 = accomplished, qualified, talented, gifted, efficient, competent, proficient; ≠ incompetent

capacious adj having a large capacity or area

capacitance n physics 1 the ability of a capacitor to store electrical charge 2 a measure of this

capacitor n physics a device for storing a charge of electricity

capacity n, pl **-ties** 1 the ability to contain, absorb, or hold something 2 the maximum amount something can contain or absorb: *filled to capacity* 3 the ability to do something: *his capacity to elicit great loyalty* 4 a position or function: *acting in an official capacity* 5 the maximum output of which an industry or factory is capable: *the refinery had a capacity of three hundred thousand barrels a day* 6 physics same as **capacitance** ▸ adj 7 of the maximum amount or number possible: *a capacity crowd*

> **capacity** n 1 = size, room, range, space, volume, extent, dimensions, scope 3 = ability, facility, gift, genius, capability, aptitude, aptness, competence or competency 4 = function, position, role, post, office

caparisoned (kap-**par**-riss-sond) *adj* (esp. of a horse) magnificently decorated or dressed

cape¹ *n* a short sleeveless cloak

cape² *n* a large piece of land that juts out into the sea

> **cape** *n* = headland, point, head, peninsula, promontory

caper *n* **1** a high-spirited escapade ▸ *vb* **2** to skip about light-heartedly

capercaillie *or* **capercailzie** (kap-per-**kale**-yee) *n* a large black European woodland grouse

capers *pl n* the pickled flower buds of a Mediterranean shrub, used in making sauces

capillary (kap-**pill**-a-ree) *n, pl* **-laries 1** *anatomy* one of the very fine blood vessels linking the arteries and the veins ▸ *adj* **2** (of a tube) having a fine bore **3** *anatomy* of the capillaries

capital¹ *n* **1** the chief city of a country, where the government meets **2** the total wealth owned or used in business by an individual or group **3** wealth used to produce more wealth by investment **4 make capital out of** to gain advantage from: *to make political capital out of the hostage situation* **5** a capital letter ▸ *adj* **6** *law* involving or punishable by death: *a capital offence* **7** denoting the large letter used as the initial letter in a sentence, personal name, or place name **8** *Brit, Austral & NZ old-fashioned* excellent or first-rate: *a capital dinner*

> **capital** *n* **2, 3** = money, funds, investment(s), cash, finances, resources, assets, wealth ▸ *adj* **8** = first-rate, fine, excellent, superb

capital² *n* the top part of a column or pillar

capitalism *n* an economic system based on the private ownership of industry

> **capitalism** *n* = private enterprise, free enterprise, private ownership, laissez faire *or* laisser faire

capitalist *adj* **1** based on or supporting capitalism: *capitalist countries* ▸ *n* **2** a supporter of capitalism **3** a person who owns a business > **capitalistic** *adj*

capitalize *or* **-ise** *vb* **-izing, -ized** *or* **-ising, -ised 1 capitalize on** to take advantage of: *to capitalize on the available opportunities* **2** to write or print (words) in capital letters **3** to convert (debt or earnings) into capital stock > **capitalization** *or* **-isation** *n*

capitation *n* a tax of a fixed amount per person

capitulate *vb* **-lating, -lated** to surrender under agreed conditions > **capitulation** *n*

capon (**kay**-pon) *n* a castrated cock fowl fattened for eating

cappuccino (kap-poo-**cheen**-oh) *n, pl* **-nos** coffee with steamed milk, usually sprinkled with powdered chocolate

caprice (kap-**reess**) *n* **1** a sudden change of attitude or behaviour **2** a tendency to have such changes

capricious *adj* having a tendency to sudden unpredictable changes of attitude or behaviour > **capriciously** *adv*

capsicum *n* a kind of pepper used as a vegetable or ground to produce a spice

capsize *vb* **-sizing, -sized** (of a boat) to overturn accidentally

capstan *n* a vertical rotating cylinder round which a ship's rope or cable is wound

capsule *n* **1** a soluble gelatine case containing a dose of medicine **2** *botany* a plant's seed case that opens when ripe **3** *anatomy* a membrane or sac surrounding an organ or part ▸ *adj* **4** very concise: *capsule courses*

> **capsule** *n* **1** = pill, tablet, lozenge **2** = pod, case, shell, vessel, sheath, receptacle, seed case

captain *n* **1** the person in charge of a ship, boat, or civil aircraft **2** a middle-ranking naval officer **3** a junior officer in the army **4** the leader of a team or group ▸ *vb* **5** to be captain of > **captaincy** *n*

> **captain** *n* **1** = commander, skipper **4** = leader, boss, master, skipper, head, chief

captcha *n* a test designed to determine whether a computer user is a person or a machine

caption *n* **1** a title, brief explanation, or comment accompanying a picture or cartoon ▸ *vb* **2** to provide with a caption

captious *adj* tending to make trivial criticisms

captivate *vb* **-vating, -vated** to attract and hold the attention of; enchant > **captivating** *adj*

> **captivate** *vb* = charm, attract, fascinate, entrance, enchant, enthral, beguile, allure; ≠ repel

captive *n* **1** a person who is kept in confinement ▸ *adj* **2** kept in confinement **3** (of an audience) unable to leave

> **captive** *n* = prisoner, hostage, convict, prisoner of war, detainee, internee ▸ *adj* **2** = confined, caged, imprisoned, locked up, enslaved, incarcerated, ensnared, subjugated

captivity *n* the state of being kept in confinement

> **captivity** *n* = confinement, custody, detention, imprisonment, incarceration, internment

captor *n* a person who captures a person or animal

capture *vb* **-turing, -tured 1** to take by force **2** to succeed in representing (something elusive) in words, pictures, or music: *today's newspapers capture the mood of the nation* **3** *physics* (of an atomic nucleus) to acquire (an additional particle) ▸ *n* **4** the act of capturing or the state of being captured

capture vb **1** = catch, arrest, take, bag, secure, seize, collar (informal), apprehend; ≠ release ▸ n = arrest, catching, trapping, imprisonment, seizure, apprehension, taking, taking captive

car n **1** a motorized road vehicle designed to carry a small number of people **2** the passenger compartment of a cable car, airship, lift, or balloon **3** US & Canad a railway carriage

car n **1** = vehicle, motor, wheels (informal), auto (US), automobile, jalopy (informal), motor car, machine **3** = (railway) carriage, coach, cable car, dining car, sleeping car, buffet car, van

carafe (kar-raff) n a wide-mouthed bottle for water or wine

caramel n **1** a chewy sweet made from sugar and milk **2** burnt sugar, used for colouring and flavouring food

caramelize or **-ise** vb **-izing, -ized** or **-ising, -ised** to turn into caramel

carapace n the thick hard upper shell of tortoises and crustaceans

carat n **1** a unit of weight of precious stones, equal to 0.20 grams **2** a measure of the purity of gold in an alloy, expressed as the number of parts of gold in 24 parts of the alloy

caravan n **1** a large enclosed vehicle designed to be pulled by a car or horse and equipped to be lived in **2** (in some Eastern countries) a company of traders or other travellers journeying together

caraway n a Eurasian plant with seeds that are used as a spice in cooking

carb n informal short for **carbohydrate**

carbide n chem a compound of carbon with a metal

carbine n a type of light rifle

carbohydrate n any of a large group of energy-producing compounds, including sugars and starches, that contain carbon, hydrogen, and oxygen

carbolic acid n a disinfectant derived from coal tar

carbon n **1** a nonmetallic element occurring in three forms: charcoal, graphite, and diamond: present in all organic compounds. Symbol: **C 2** short for **carbon paper** or **carbon copy**

carbonate n a salt or ester of carbonic acid

carbonated adj (of a drink) containing carbon dioxide; fizzy

carbon copy n **1** a duplicate obtained by using carbon paper **2** informal a person or thing that is identical or very similar to another

carbon dioxide n a colourless odourless incombustible gas formed during breathing, and used in fire extinguishers and in making fizzy drinks

carbon footprint n a measure of the amount of carbon dioxide released into the atmosphere through a single endeavour or through the activities of a person, company, etc. over a given period

carbonic acid n a weak acid formed when carbon dioxide combines with water

carbonize or **-ise** vb **-izing, -ized** or **-ising, -ised 1** to turn into carbon as a result of partial burning **2** to coat (a substance) with carbon > **carbonization** or **-isation** n

carbon-neutral adj not affecting the overall volume of carbon dioxide in the atmosphere

carbon offset n a compensatory measure made by an individual or company for carbon emissions, such as tree planting

carbon paper n a thin sheet of paper coated on one side with a dark waxy pigment, containing carbon, used to make a duplicate of something as it is typed or written

Carborundum n trademark an abrasive material consisting of silicon carbide

carbuncle n a large painful swelling under the skin like a boil

carburettor or US & Canad **carburetor** n a device in an internal-combustion engine that mixes petrol with air and regulates the intake of the mixture into the engine

carcass or **carcase** n **1** the dead body of an animal **2** informal a person's body: ask that person to move his carcass

carcinogen n a substance that produces cancer > **carcinogenic** adj

carcinoma n, pl **-mas** or **-mata** a malignant tumour

card n **1** a piece of stiff paper or thin cardboard used for reference, identification, or sending greetings or messages: a business card; a Christmas card **2** one of a set of small pieces of cardboard, marked with figures or symbols, used for playing games or for fortune-telling **3** a small rectangle of stiff plastic used for identification or for making financial transactions: a library card; a charge card **4** old-fashioned, informal a witty or eccentric person

cardamom n a spice that is obtained from the seeds of a tropical plant

cardboard n a thin stiff board made from paper pulp

cardholder n a person who owns a credit or debit card

cardiac adj of or relating to the heart

cardigan n a knitted jacket

cardinal n **1** any of the high-ranking clergymen of the Roman Catholic Church who elect the pope and act as his chief counsellors ▸ adj **2** fundamentally important; principal

cardinal adj = principal, first, leading, chief, main, central, key, essential; ≠ secondary

cardinal number n a number denoting quantity but not order in a group, for example one, two, or three

cardinal points pl n the four main points of the compass: north, south, east, and west

cardiogram n an electrocardiogram. See **electrocardiograph**

cardiograph *n* an electrocardiograph
> **cardiographer** *n* > **cardiography** *n*

cardiology *n* the branch of medicine dealing with the heart and its diseases > **cardiologist** *n*

cardiovascular *adj* of or relating to the heart and the blood vessels

cardsharp *or* **cardsharper** *n* a professional card player who cheats

care *vb* **caring, cared 1** to be worried or concerned: *he does not care what people think about him* **2** to like (to do something): *anybody care to go out?* **3 care for A** to look after or provide for: *it is still largely women who care for dependent family members* **B** to like or be fond of: *he did not care for his concentration to be disturbed; I don't suppose you could ever care for me seriously* **4 I couldn't care less** I am completely indifferent ▸ *n* **5** careful or serious attention; caution: *treat all raw meat with extreme care to avoid food poisoning* **6** protection or charge: *the children are now in the care of a state orphanage* **7** trouble or worry: *his mind turned towards money cares* **8 care of** (written on envelopes) at the address of **9 in** *or* **into care** *Brit & NZ* (of a child) made the legal responsibility of a local authority or the state by order of a court **10 take care** to be careful **11 take care of** to look after: *women have to take greater care of themselves during pregnancy*

> **care** *vb* **1** = be concerned, mind, bother, be interested, be bothered, give a damn, concern yourself **3A care for someone** = look after, mind, tend, attend, nurse, minister to, watch over **3B care for something or someone** = like, enjoy, take to, relish, be fond of, be keen on, be partial to ▸ *n* **5** = caution, attention, pains, consideration, heed, prudence, vigilance, forethought; ≠ carelessness **6** = custody, keeping, control, charge, management, protection, supervision, guardianship **7** = worry, concern, pressure, trouble, responsibility, stress, anxiety, disquiet; ≠ pleasure

careen *vb* to tilt over to one side

career *n* **1** the series of jobs in a profession or occupation that a person has through his or her life: *a career in child psychology* **2** the part of a person's life spent in a particular occupation or type of work: *a school career punctuated with exams* ▸ *vb* **3** to rush in an uncontrolled way ▸ *adj* **4** having chosen to dedicate his or her life to a particular occupation: *a career soldier*

> **career** *n* **1** = occupation, calling, employment, pursuit, vocation, livelihood, life's work ▸ *vb* = rush, race, speed, tear, dash, barrel (along) (*informal*), bolt, hurtle

careerist *n* a person who seeks to advance his or her career by any means possible > **careerism** *n*

carefree *adj* without worry or responsibility

careful *adj* **1** cautious in attitude or action **2** very exact and thorough > **carefully** *adv* > **carefulness** *n*

careful *adj* **1** = cautious, scrupulous, circumspect, chary, thoughtful, discreet; ≠ careless **2** = thorough, full, particular, precise, intensive, in-depth, meticulous, conscientious; ≠ casual

careless *adj* **1** done or acting with insufficient attention **2** unconcerned in attitude or action > **carelessly** *adv* > **carelessness** *n*

> **careless** *adj* **1** = slapdash, irresponsible, sloppy (*informal*), cavalier, offhand, neglectful, slipshod, lackadaisical; ≠ careful **2** = nonchalant, casual, offhand, artless, unstudied; ≠ careful

caress *n* **1** a gentle affectionate touch or embrace ▸ *vb* **2** to touch gently and affectionately

caret (kar-ret) *n* a symbol (⁁) indicating a place in written or printed matter where something is to be inserted

caretaker *n* **1** a person employed to look after a place or thing ▸ *adj* **2** performing the duties of an office temporarily: *a caretaker administration*

> **caretaker** *n* = warden, keeper, porter (*Brit*), superintendent (*US*), curator, custodian, watchman, janitor

careworn *adj* showing signs of stress or worry

cargo *n, pl* **-goes** *or esp US* **-gos** goods carried by a ship, aircraft, or other vehicle

> **cargo** *n* = load, goods, contents, shipment, freight, merchandise, baggage, consignment

cargo pants *or* **cargo trousers** *pl n* loose trousers with a large external pocket on the side of each leg

caribou *n, pl* **-bou** *or* **-bous** a large North American reindeer

caricature *n* **1** a drawing or description of a person which exaggerates characteristic features for comic effect **2** a description or explanation of something that is so exaggerated or over-simplified that it is difficult to take seriously: *the classic caricature of the henpecked husband* ▸ *vb* **-turing, -tured 3** to make a caricature of

> **caricature** *n* = parody, cartoon, distortion, satire, send-up (*Brit informal*), travesty, takeoff (*informal*), lampoon ▸ *vb* = parody, take off (*informal*), mock, distort, mimic, send up (*Brit informal*), lampoon

caries (care-reez) *n* tooth decay

carillon (kar-rill-yon) *n* **1** a set of bells hung in a tower and played either from a keyboard or mechanically **2** a tune played on such bells

cark *vb* **cark it** *Austral & NZ slang* to die

carmine *adj* vivid red

carnage *n* extensive slaughter of people

> **carnage** *n* = slaughter, murder, massacre, holocaust, havoc, bloodshed, shambles, mass murder

carnal *adj* of a sexual or sensual nature: *carnal knowledge* ▷ **carnality** *n*

carnation *n* a cultivated plant with clove-scented white, pink, or red flowers

carnival *n* **1** a festive period with processions, music, and dancing in the street **2** a travelling funfair

> **carnival** *n* **1** = festival, fair, fête, celebration, gala, jubilee, jamboree, revelry

carnivore (car-niv-vore) *n* **1** a meat-eating animal **2** *informal* an aggressively ambitious person ▷ **carnivorous** (car-niv-or-uss) *adj*

carob *n* the pod of a Mediterranean tree, used as a chocolate substitute

carol *n* **1** a joyful religious song sung at Christmas ▸ *vb* **-olling, -olled** *or US* **-oling, -oled** **2** to sing carols **3** to sing joyfully

> **carol** *n* = song, hymn, Christmas song

carotid (kar-rot-id) *n* **1** either of the two arteries that supply blood to the head and neck ▸ *adj* **2** of either of these arteries

carouse *vb* **-rousing, -roused** to have a merry drinking party: *carousing with friends*

carousel (kar-roo-**sell**) *n* **1** a revolving conveyor for luggage at an airport or for slides for a projector **2** *US & Canad* a merry-go-round

carp¹ *n, pl* **carp** *or* **carps** a large freshwater food fish

carp² *vb* to complain or find fault ▷ **carping** *adj, n*

> **carp** *vb* = find fault, complain, criticize, reproach, quibble, cavil, pick holes, nit-pick (*informal*); ≠ praise

car park *n* an area or building reserved for parking cars

carpel *n* the female reproductive organ of a flowering plant

carpenter *n* a person who makes or repairs wooden structures

> **carpenter** *n* = joiner, cabinet-maker, woodworker

carpentry *n* the skill or work of a carpenter

carpet *n* **1** a heavy fabric for covering floors **2** a covering like a carpet: *a carpet of leaves* **3** **on the carpet** *informal* being or about to be reprimanded **4** **sweep something under the carpet** to conceal or keep silent about something that one does not want to be discovered ▸ *vb* **-peting, -peted** **5** to cover with a carpet or a covering like a carpet

carpet snake *n* a large nonvenomous Australian snake with a carpet-like pattern on its back

carpus *n, pl* **-pi** the set of eight bones of the human wrist

carriage *n* **1** *Brit, Austral & NZ* one of the sections of a train for passengers **2** the way a person holds and moves his or her head and body **3** a four-wheeled horse-drawn passenger vehicle **4** the moving part of a machine, such as a typewriter, that supports and shifts another part **5** the charge made for conveying goods

> **carriage** *n* **2** = bearing, posture, gait, deportment, air **3** = vehicle, coach, trap, gig, cab, wagon, hackney, conveyance (*old-fashioned*)

carriageway *n* **1** *Brit* the part of a road along which traffic passes in one direction: *the westbound carriageway of the M4* **2** *NZ* the part of a road used by vehicles

carrier *n* **1** a person, vehicle, or organization that carries something: *armoured personnel carriers* **2** a person or animal that, without suffering from a disease, is capable of transmitting it to others **3** short for **aircraft carrier**

carrier pigeon *n* a homing pigeon used for carrying messages

carrion *n* dead and rotting flesh

carrot *n* **1** a long tapering orange root vegetable **2** something offered as an incentive

carroty *adj* (of hair) reddish-orange

carry *vb* **-ries, -rying, -ried** **1** to take from one place to another **2** to have with one habitually, for example in one's pocket or handbag: *to carry a donor card* **3** to transmit or be transmitted: *to carry disease* **4** to have as a factor or result: *the offence carries a maximum penalty of seven years in prison* **5** to be pregnant with: *she is carrying her third child* **6** to hold (one's head or body) in a specified manner: *she walked out, carrying her head high* **7** to secure the adoption of (a bill or motion): *the resolution was carried by fewer than twenty votes* **8** (of a newspaper or television or radio station) to include in the contents: *several papers carried front-page pictures of the Russian president* **9** *maths* to transfer (a number) from one column of figures to the next **10** to travel a certain distance or reach a specified point: *his faint voice carried no farther than the front few rows* **11** **carry the can** *informal* to take all the blame for something

> **carry** *vb* **1** = convey, take, move, bring, bear, transfer, conduct, transport **3** = transmit, transfer, spread, pass on

carry on *vb* **1** to continue: *we'll carry on exactly where we left off* **2** to do, run, or take part in: *the vast trade carried on in the city* **3** *informal* to cause a fuss: *I don't want to carry on and make a big scene* ▸ *n* **carry-on** **4** *informal, chiefly Brit* a fuss

> **carry on** *vb* **1** = continue, last, endure, persist, keep going, persevere, crack on (*informal*) **3** = make a fuss, misbehave, create (*slang*), raise Cain ▸ *n* **carry-on** = fuss, disturbance, racket, commotion

carry out *vb* **1** to follow (an order or instruction) **2** to accomplish (a task): *to carry out repairs*

> **carry out** *vb* **carry something out** = perform, effect, achieve, realize, implement, fulfil, accomplish, execute

C

cart n **1** an open horse-drawn vehicle, usually with two wheels, used to carry goods or passengers **2** any small vehicle that is pulled or pushed by hand ▸ vb **3** to carry, usually with some effort: *men carted bricks and tiles and wooden boards*

carte blanche n complete authority: *she's got carte blanche to redecorate*

cartel n an association of competing firms formed in order to fix prices

carthorse n a large heavily built horse kept for pulling carts or for farm work

cartilage (kar-till-ij) n a strong flexible tissue forming part of the skeleton ▸ **cartilaginous** adj

cartography n the art of making maps or charts ▸ **cartographer** n ▸ **cartographic** adj

carton n **1** a cardboard box or container **2** a container of waxed paper in which drinks are sold

> **carton** n **1** = box, case, pack, package, container

cartoon n **1** a humorous or satirical drawing in a newspaper or magazine **2** a film produced by photographing a series of gradually changing drawings, which give the illusion of movement when the series is projected rapidly ▸ **cartoonist** n

> **cartoon** n **1** = drawing, parody, satire, caricature, comic strip, takeoff (*informal*), lampoon, sketch **2** = animation, animated film, animated cartoon

cartridge n **1** a metal casing containing an explosive charge and bullet for a gun **2** the part of the pick-up of a record player that converts the movements of the stylus into electrical signals **3** a sealed container of film or tape, or ink for a printer or pen

cartridge paper n a type of heavy rough drawing paper

cartwheel n **1** a sideways somersault supported by the hands with legs outstretched **2** the large spoked wheel of a cart

carve vb **carving, carved 1** to cut in order to form something: *carving wood* **2** to form (something) by cutting: *the statue which was carved by Michelangelo* **3** to slice (cooked meat) ▸ **carver** n

> **carve** vb **1** = sculpt, cut, chip, whittle, chisel, hew (*old-fashioned*), fashion **2** = etch, engrave

carving n a figure or design produced by carving stone or wood

caryatid (kar-ree-**at**-id) n a supporting column in the shape of a female figure

Casanova n a promiscuous man

casbah n the citadel of a North African city

cascade n **1** a waterfall or series of waterfalls over rocks **2** something flowing or falling like a waterfall: *a cascade of luxuriant hair* ▸ vb **-cading, -caded 3** to flow or fall in a cascade: *rays of sunshine cascaded down*

> **cascade** n **1** = waterfall, falls, torrent, flood, shower, fountain, avalanche, deluge ▸ vb = flow, fall, flood, pour, plunge, surge, spill, tumble

case[1] n **1** a single instance or example of something: *cases of teenage pregnancies* **2** a matter for discussion: *the case before the Ethics Committee* **3** a specific condition or state of affairs: *a sudden-death play-off in the case of a draw* **4** a set of arguments supporting an action or cause: *I put my case before them* **5** a person or problem dealt with by a doctor, social worker, or solicitor **6** **A** an action or lawsuit: *a rape case* **B** the evidence offered in court to support a claim: *he will try to show that the case against his client is largely circumstantial* **7** grammar a form of a noun, pronoun, or adjective showing its relation to other words in the sentence: *the accusative case* **8** informal an amusingly eccentric person **9 in any case** no matter what **10 in case** so as to allow for the possibility that: *the President has ordered a medical team to stand by in case hostages are released* **11 in case of** in the event of: *in case of a future conflict*

> **case** n **1** = instance, example, occasion, specimen, occurrence **2, 3** = situation, event, circumstance(s), state, position, condition, context, contingency **6A** = lawsuit, trial, suit, proceedings, dispute, action

case[2] n **1** a container, such as a box or chest **2** a suitcase **3** a protective outer covering ▸ vb **casing, cased 4** slang to inspect carefully (a place one plans to rob)

> **case** n **1** = cabinet, box, chest, holder **2** = suitcase, bag, grip, holdall, portmanteau, valise **3** = covering, casing, shell, jacket, envelope, capsule, sheath, wrapper

case-hardened adj having been made callous by experience: *a case-hardened senior policewoman*

casement n a window that is hinged on one side

case-sensitive adj distinguishing between upper-case and lower-case letters: *your password is case-sensitive*

cash n **1** money in the form of banknotes and coins **2** informal money: *strapped for cash* ▸ adj **3** of, for, or paid in cash: *cash hand-outs* ▸ vb **4** to obtain or pay banknotes or coins for (a cheque or postal order) ▸ See also **cash in on** ▸ **cashless** adj

> **cash** n = money, funds, notes, currency, silver, brass (N English dialect), dough (slang), coinage

cashew n an edible kidney-shaped nut

cashier[1] n a person responsible for handling cash in a bank, shop, or other business

cashier[2] vb to dismiss with dishonour from the armed forces

cash in on vb informal to gain profit or advantage from: *trying to cash in on the dispute*

cashmere *n* a very fine soft wool obtained from goats

cash register *n* a till that has a mechanism for displaying and adding the prices of the goods sold

casing *n* a protective case or covering

casino *n, pl* **-nos** a public building or room where gambling games are played

cask *n* **1** a strong barrel used to hold alcoholic drink **2** *Austral* a cubic carton containing wine, with a tap for dispensing

casket *n* **1** a small box for valuables **2** *US* a coffin

cassava *n* a starch obtained from the root of a tropical American plant, used to make tapioca

casserole *n* **1** a covered dish in which food is cooked slowly, usually in an oven, and served **2** a dish cooked and served in this way: *beef casserole* ▸ *vb* **-roling, -roled 3** to cook in a casserole

cassette *n* a plastic case containing a reel of film or magnetic tape

cassock *n* an ankle-length garment, usually black, worn by some Christian priests

cassowary *n, pl* **-waries** a large flightless bird of Australia and New Guinea

cast *n* **1** the actors in a play collectively **2** ᴀ an object made of material that has been shaped, while molten, by a mould ʙ the mould used to shape such an object **3** *surgery* a rigid casing made of plaster of Paris for immobilizing broken bones while they heal **4** a sort, kind, or style: *people of an academic cast of mind* **5** a slight squint in the eye ▸ *vb* **casting, cast 6** to select (an actor) to play a part in a play or film **7** to give or deposit (a vote) **8** to express (doubts or aspersions) **9** to cause to appear: *a shadow cast by the grandstand; the gloom cast by the recession* **10** ᴀ to shape (molten material) by pouring it into a mould ʙ to make (an object) by such a process **11** to throw (a fishing line) into the water **12** to throw with force: *cast into a bonfire* **13** to direct (a glance): *he cast his eye over the horse-chestnut trees* **14** to roll or throw (a dice) **15 cast aside** to abandon or reject: *cast aside by her lover* **16 cast a spell** ᴀ to perform magic ʙ to have an irresistible influence

> **cast** *n* **1** = actors, company, players, characters, troupe, dramatis personae **4** = type, sort, kind, style, stamp ▸ *vb* **6** = choose, name, pick, select, appoint, assign, allot **9** = give out, spread, deposit, shed, distribute, scatter, emit, radiate **10** = mould, set, found, form, model, shape **12, 14** = throw, launch, pitch, toss, thrust, hurl, fling, sling **13** = bestow, give, level, direct

castanets *pl n* a musical instrument, used by Spanish dancers, consisting of curved pieces of hollow wood, held between the fingers and thumb and clicked together

castaway *n* a person who has been shipwrecked

caste *n* **1** any of the four major hereditary classes into which Hindu society is divided **2** social rank

> **caste** *n* = class, order, rank, status, stratum, social order

castellated *adj* having turrets and battlements, like a castle

caster sugar *n* finely ground white sugar

castigate *vb* **-gating, -gated** to find fault with or reprimand (a person) harshly > **castigation** *n*

casting vote *n* the deciding vote used by the chairperson of a meeting when an equal number of votes are cast on each side

castle *n* **1** a large fortified building or set of buildings, often built as a residence for a ruler or nobleman in medieval Europe **2** same as **rook²**

> **castle** *n* **1** = fortress, keep, palace, tower, chateau, stronghold, citadel

cast-off *adj* **1** discarded because no longer wanted or needed: *cast-off clothing* ▸ *n* **2** a person or thing that has been discarded because no longer wanted or needed ▸ *vb* **cast off 3** to discard (something no longer wanted or needed) **4** to untie a ship from a dock **5** to knot and remove (a row of stitches, esp. the final row) from the needle in knitting

castor *n* a small swivelling wheel fixed to a piece of furniture to enable it to be moved easily in any direction

castor oil *n* an oil obtained from the seeds of an Indian plant, used as a lubricant and purgative

castrate *vb* **-trating, -trated 1** to remove the testicles of **2** to deprive of vigour or masculinity > **castration** *n*

casual *adj* **1** being or seeming careless or nonchalant: *she was casual about security* **2** occasional or irregular: *casual workers* **3** shallow or superficial: *casual relationships* **4** for informal wear: *a casual jacket* **5** happening by chance or without planning: *a casual comment* ▸ *n* **6** an occasional worker > **casually** *adv*

> **casual** *adj* **1** = careless, relaxed, unconcerned, blasé, offhand, nonchalant, lackadaisical; ≠ serious **4** = informal, leisure, sporty, non-dressy; ≠ formal **5** = chance, unexpected, random, accidental, incidental; ≠ planned

casualty *n, pl* **-ties 1** a person who is killed or injured in an accident or war **2** the hospital department where victims of accidents are given emergency treatment **3** a person or thing that has suffered as the result of a particular event or circumstance: *583 job losses with significant casualties among public-sector employees*

> **casualty** *n* **1** = fatality, death, loss, wounded **3** = victim, sufferer

casuarina (kass-yew-a-**reen**-a) *n* an Australian tree with jointed green branches

casuistry *n* reasoning that is misleading or oversubtle › **casuist** *n*

cat *n* **1** a small domesticated mammal with thick soft fur and whiskers **2** a wild animal related to the cat, such as the lynx, lion, or tiger. Related adjective: **feline 3 let the cat out of the bag** to disclose a secret **4 raining cats and dogs** raining very heavily **5 set the cat among the pigeons** to stir up trouble › **catlike** *adj*

> **cat** *n* **1** = feline, pussy (*informal*), moggy (*slang*), puss (*informal*), ballarat (*Austral informal*), tabby

cataclysm (kat-a-kliz-zum) *n* **1** a violent upheaval of a social, political, or military nature: *the cataclysm of the Second World War* **2** a disaster such as an earthquake or a flood › **cataclysmic** *adj*

catacombs (kat-a-koomz) *pl n* an underground burial place consisting of tunnels with side recesses for tombs

catafalque (kat-a-falk) *n* a raised platform on which a body lies in state before or during a funeral

catalepsy *n* a trancelike state in which the body is rigid › **cataleptic** *adj*

catalogue *or US* **catalog** *n* **1** a book containing details of items for sale **2** a list of all the books of a library **3** a list of events, qualities, or things considered as a group: *a catalogue of killings* ▸ *vb* **-loguing, -logued** *or* **-loging, -loged 4** to enter (an item) in a catalogue **5** to list a series of (events, qualities, or things): *the report catalogues two decades of human-rights violations* › **cataloguer** *n*

> **catalogue** *or* **catalog** *n* **1, 2** = list, record, schedule, index, register, directory, inventory, gazetteer ▸ *vb* **4** = list, file, index, register, classify, inventory, tabulate, alphabetize

catalyse *or US* **-lyze** *vb* **-lysing, -lysed** *or* **-lyzing, -lyzed** to influence (a chemical reaction) by catalysis

catalysis *n* acceleration of a chemical reaction by the action of a catalyst › **catalytic** *adj*

catalyst *n* **1** a substance that speeds up a chemical reaction without itself undergoing any permanent chemical change **2** a person or thing that causes an important change to take place: *a catalyst for peace*

catamaran *n* a boat with twin parallel hulls

catapult *n* **1** a Y-shaped device with a loop of elastic fastened to the ends of the prongs, used by children for firing stones **2** a device used to launch aircraft from a warship ▸ *vb* **3** to shoot forwards or upwards violently: *traffic catapulted forward with a roar* **4** to cause (someone) suddenly to be in a particular situation: *catapulted to stardom*

cataract *n* **1** *pathol* **A** a condition in which the lens of the eye becomes partially or totally opaque **B** the opaque area **2** a large waterfall

catarrh (kat-tar) *n* excessive mucus in the nose and throat, often experienced during or following a cold › **catarrhal** *adj*

catastrophe (kat-ass-trof-fee) *n* a great and sudden disaster or misfortune › **catastrophic** *adj*

> **catastrophe** *n* = disaster, tragedy, calamity, cataclysm, trouble, adversity, fiasco

catcall *n* a shrill whistle or cry of disapproval or derision

catch *vb* **catching, caught 1** to seize and hold **2** to capture (a person or a fish or animal) **3** to surprise in an act: *two boys were caught stealing* **4** to reach (a bus, train, or plane) in time to board it **5** to see or hear: *you'll have to be quick if you want to catch her DJ-ing* **6** to be infected with (an illness) **7** to entangle or become entangled **8** to attract (someone's attention, imagination, or interest) **9** to comprehend or make out: *you have to work hard to catch his tone and meaning* **10** to reproduce (a quality) accurately in a work of art **11** (of a fire) to start burning **12** *cricket* to dismiss (a batsman) by catching a ball struck by him or her before it touches the ground **13 catch at A** to attempt to grasp **B** to take advantage of (an opportunity) **14 catch it** *informal* to be punished ▸ *n* **15** a device such as a hook, for fastening a door, window, or box **16** the total number of fish caught **17** *informal* a concealed or unforeseen drawback **18** an emotional break in the voice **19** *informal* a person considered worth having as a husband or wife **20** *cricket* the act of catching a ball struck by a batsman before it touches the ground, resulting in him or her being out ▸ See also **catch on, catch out, catch up**

> **catch** *vb* **1** = seize, get, grab, snatch; ≠ release **2** = capture, arrest, trap, seize, snare, apprehend, ensnare, entrap; ≠ free **3** = discover, surprise, find out, expose, detect, catch in the act, take unawares **6** = contract, get, develop, suffer from, incur, succumb to, go down with; ≠ escape ▸ *n* **15** = fastener, clip, bolt, latch, clasp **17** = drawback, trick, trap, disadvantage, hitch, snag, stumbling block, fly in the ointment; ≠ advantage

catchcry *n, pl* **-cries** *Austral* a well-known, frequently used phrase, esp one associated with a particular group

catching *adj* infectious

> **catching** *adj* = infectious, contagious, transferable, communicable, transmittable; ≠ non-infectious

catchment area *n* **1** the area of land draining into a river, basin, or reservoir **2** the area served by a particular school or hospital

catch on *vb informal* **1** to become popular or fashionable **2** to understand: *I was slow to catch on to what she was trying to tell me*

catch on vb **1** = become popular, take off, become trendy, come into fashion **2** = understand, see, find out, grasp, see through, comprehend, twig (*Brit informal*), get the picture

catch out vb *informal, chiefly Brit* to trap (someone) in an error or a lie

catch phrase n a well-known phrase or slogan associated with a particular entertainer or other celebrity

catch up vb **1 be caught up in** to be unwillingly or accidentally involved in: *hundreds of civilians have been caught up in the clashes* **2 catch up on** or **with** to bring (something) up to date: *he had a lot of paperwork to catch up on* **3 catch up with** to reach or pass (someone or something): *she ran to catch up with him* ▸ n **catch-up 4** a meeting held in order to bring someone up to date with developments **5** a facility for watching a television programme after it has been broadcast **6 play catch-up** *informal* to attempt to match a standard set by another person or organization

catchword n a well-known and frequently used phrase or slogan

catchy adj **catchier**, **catchiest** (of a tune) pleasant and easily remembered

catechism (kat-tik-kiz-zum) n instruction on the doctrine of a Christian Church by a series of questions and answers

categorical or **categoric** adj absolutely clear and certain: *he was categorical in his denial* > **categorically** adv

categorize or **-rise** vb **-rizing, -rized** or **-rising, -rised** to put in a category > **categorization** or **-risation** n

category n, pl **-ries** a class or group of things or people with some quality or qualities in common

category n = class, grouping, heading, sort, department, type, division, section

cater vb **1** to provide what is needed or wanted: *operating theatres can cater for open-heart surgery* **2** to provide food or services: *chef is pleased to cater for vegetarians and vegans*

caterer n a person whose job is to provide food for social events such as parties and weddings

caterpillar n **1** the wormlike larva of a butterfly or moth **2** *trademark* Also: **caterpillar track** an endless track, driven by cogged wheels, used to propel a heavy vehicle such as a bulldozer

caterwaul vb **1** to make a yowling noise like a cat ▸ n **2** such a noise

catfish n, pl **-fish** or **-fishes** a freshwater fish with whisker-like barbels around the mouth

catgut n a strong cord made from dried animals' intestines, used to string musical instruments and sports rackets

catharsis (kath-thar-siss) n **1** the relief of strong suppressed emotions, for example through drama or psychoanalysis **2** evacuation of the bowels, esp. with the use of a laxative

cathartic adj **1** causing catharsis ▸ n **2** a drug that causes catharsis

cathedral n the principal church of a diocese

Catherine wheel n a firework that rotates, producing sparks and coloured flame

catheter (kath-it-er) n a slender flexible tube inserted into a body cavity to drain fluid

cathode n *electronics* the negative electrode in an electrolytic cell or in an electronic valve or tube

cathode rays pl n a stream of electrons emitted from the surface of a cathode in a valve

catholic adj (of tastes or interests) covering a wide range

Catholic *Christianity* ▸ adj **1** of the Roman Catholic Church ▸ n **2** a member of the Roman Catholic Church > **Catholicism** n

cation (kat-eye-on) n a positively charged ion

catkin n a drooping flower spike found on trees such as the birch, hazel, and willow

catnap n **1** a short sleep or doze ▸ vb **-napping, -napped 2** to sleep or doze for a short time or intermittently

Catseyes pl n *trademark Brit, Austral & NZ* glass reflectors set into the road at intervals to indicate traffic lanes by reflecting light from vehicles' headlights

cat's paw n a person used by someone else to do unpleasant things for him or her

cattle pl n domesticated cows and bulls. Related adjective: **bovine**

cattle pl n = cows, stock, beasts, livestock, bovines

catty adj **-tier, -tiest** *informal* spiteful: *her remarks were amusing and only slightly catty* > **cattiness** n

catwalk n **1** a narrow pathway over the stage of a theatre or along a bridge **2** a narrow platform where models display clothes in a fashion show

Caucasian or **Caucasoid** adj **1** of the predominantly light-skinned supposed racial group of humankind ▸ n **2** a member of this group

caucus n, pl **-cuses 1** a local committee or faction of a political party **2** a political meeting to decide future plans **3** *NZ* a formal meeting of all MPs of one party

caught vb the past of **catch**

cauldron or **caldron** n a large pot used for boiling

cauliflower n a vegetable with a large head of white flower buds surrounded by green leaves

caulk vb to fill in (cracks) with paste or some other material

causal adj of or being a cause: *a causal connection* > **causally** adv

causation or **causality** n **1** the production of an effect by a cause **2** the relationship of cause and effect

cause n **1** something that produces a particular effect **2** grounds for action; justification: *there is cause for concern* **3** an aim or principle which an individual or group is interested in and supports: *the Socialist cause* ▸ *vb* **causing**, **caused 4** to be the cause of › **causeless** *adj*

cause *n* **1** = origin, source, spring, agent, maker, producer, root, beginning; ≠ result **2** = reason, call, need, grounds, basis, incentive, motive, motivation **3** = aim, movement, principle, ideal, enterprise ▸ *vb* = produce, create, lead to, result in, generate, induce, bring about, give rise to; ≠ prevent

cause célèbre (kawz sill-**leb**-ra) *n*, *pl* **causes célèbres** (**kawz** sill-**leb**-raz) a controversial legal case, issue, or person

causeway *n* a raised path or road across water or marshland

caustic *adj* **1** capable of burning or corroding by chemical action: *caustic soda* **2** bitter and sarcastic: *caustic critics* ▸ *n* **3** *chem* a caustic substance › **caustically** *adv*

cauterize *or* **-ise** *vb* **-izing**, **-ized** *or* **-ising**, **-ised** to burn (a wound) with heat or a caustic agent to prevent infection › **cauterization** *or* **-isation** *n*

caution *n* **1** care or prudence, esp. in the face of danger **2** warning: *a word of caution* **3** *law*, *chiefly Brit* a formal warning given to a person suspected of an offence ▸ *vb* **4** to warn or advise: *he cautioned against an abrupt turnaround* › **cautionary** *adj*

caution *n* **1** = care, discretion, heed, prudence, vigilance, alertness, forethought, circumspection; ≠ carelessness **3** = reprimand, warning, injunction, admonition ▸ *vb* = warn, urge, advise, alert, tip off, forewarn

cautious *adj* showing or having caution › **cautiously** *adv*

cautious *adj* = careful, guarded, wary, tentative, prudent, judicious, circumspect, cagey (*informal*); ≠ careless

cavalcade *n* a procession of people on horseback or in cars

cavalier *adj* **1** showing haughty disregard; offhand ▸ *n* **2** *old-fashioned* a gallant or courtly gentleman

Cavalier *n* a supporter of Charles I during the English Civil War

cavalry *n* the part of an army originally mounted on horseback, but now often using fast armoured vehicles › **cavalryman** *n*

cavalry *n* = horsemen, horse, mounted troops; ≠ infantrymen

cave *n* a hollow in the side of a hill or cliff, or underground

cave = hollow, cavern, grotto, den, cavity

caveat (**kav**-vee-at) *n* **1** *law* a formal notice requesting the court not to take a certain action without warning the person lodging the caveat **2** a caution

cave in *vb* **1** to collapse inwards **2** *informal* to yield completely under pressure: *the government caved in to the revolutionaries' demands* ▸ *n* **cave-in 3** the sudden collapse of a roof or piece of ground

caveman *n*, *pl* **-men 1** a prehistoric cave dweller **2** *informal* a man who is primitive or brutal in behaviour

cavern *n* a large cave

cavernous *adj* like a cavern in vastness, depth, or hollowness: *the cavernous building*

caviar *or* **caviare** *n* the salted roe of the sturgeon, regarded as a delicacy and usually served as an appetizer

cavil *vb* **-illing**, **-illed** *or US* **-iling**, **-iled 1** to raise annoying petty objections ▸ *n* **2** a petty objection

caving *n* the sport of climbing in and exploring caves › **caver** *n*

cavity *n*, *pl* **-ties 1** a hollow space **2** *dentistry* a decayed area on a tooth

cavity *n* **1** = hollow, hole, gap, pit, dent, crater

cavort *vb* to skip about; caper

caw *n* **1** the cry of a crow, rook, or raven ▸ *vb* **2** to make this cry

cayenne pepper *or* **cayenne** *n* a very hot red spice made from the dried seeds of capsicums

cayman *or* **caiman** *n*, *pl* **-mans** a tropical American reptile similar to an alligator

CB 1 Citizens' Band **2** Commander of the Order of the Bath

CBE Commander of the Order of the British Empire (a Brit. title)

CBI Confederation of British Industry

cc *or* **c.c. 1** carbon copy **2** (in South Africa) closed corporation **3** cubic centimetre

CD compact disc

CD-ROM compact disc read-only memory: a compact disc used with a computer system as a read-only optical disc

CE (used, esp. by non-Christians, in numbering years AD) Common Era

cease *vb* **ceasing**, **ceased 1** to bring or come to an end ▸ *n* **2 without cease** without stopping

cease *vb* = stop, end, finish, come to an end; ≠ start

ceasefire *n* a temporary period of truce

ceaseless *adj* without stopping › **ceaselessly** *adv*

cedar *n* **1** a coniferous tree with needle-like evergreen leaves and barrel-shaped cones **2** the sweet-smelling wood of this tree

cede *vb* **ceding**, **ceded** to transfer or surrender (territory or legal rights)

cedilla *n* a character (˛) placed underneath a *c*, esp. in French or Portuguese, indicating that it is to be pronounced (s), not (k)

ceilidh (**kay**-lee) *n* an informal social gathering in Scotland or Ireland with folk music and country dancing

ceiling *n* **1** the inner upper surface of a room

2 an upper limit set on something such as a payment or salary **3** the upper altitude to which an aircraft can climb

celandine *n* a wild plant with yellow flowers

celebrant *n* a person who performs or takes part in a religious ceremony

celebrate *vb* **-brating, -brated 1** to hold festivities: *let's celebrate!* **2** to hold festivities to mark (a happy event, birthday, or anniversary) **3** to perform (a solemn or religious ceremony) **4** to praise publicly: *the novel is justly celebrated as a masterpiece* > **celebration** *n* > **celebratory** *adj*

> **celebrate** *vb* **1** = rejoice, party, enjoy yourself, carouse, live it up (*informal*), make merry, put the flags out, kill the fatted calf **3** = perform, observe, preside over, officiate at, solemnize

celebrated *adj* well known: *the celebrated musician*

> **celebrated** *adj* = renowned, popular, famous, distinguished, well-known, prominent, acclaimed, notable; ≠ unknown

celebrity *n, pl* **-ties 1** a famous person **2** the state of being famous

> **celebrity** *n* **1** = personality, star, superstar, big name, dignitary, luminary, big shot (*informal*), V.I.P.; ≠ nobody **2** = fame, reputation, distinction, prestige, prominence, stardom, renown, repute; ≠ obscurity

celeriac (sill-**ler**-ree-ak) *n* a variety of celery with a large turnip-like root

celerity (sill-**ler**-rit-tee) *n formal* swiftness

celery *n* a vegetable with long green crisp edible stalks

celestial *adj* **1** heavenly or divine: *celestial music* **2** of or relating to the sky or space: *celestial objects such as pulsars and quasars*

celibate *adj* **1** unmarried or abstaining from sex, esp. because of a religious vow of chastity ▸ *n* **2** a celibate person > **celibacy** *n*

cell *n* **1** *biol* the smallest unit of an organism that is able to function independently **2** a small simple room in a prison, convent, or monastery **3** any small compartment, such as a cell of a honeycomb **4** a small group operating as the core of a larger organization: *Communist cells* **5** a device that produces electrical energy by chemical action **6** *US & Canad* a cellular phone

> **cell** *n* **2** = room, chamber, lock-up, compartment, cavity, cubicle, dungeon, stall **4** = unit, group, section, core, nucleus, caucus, coterie

cellar *n* **1** an underground room, usually used for storage **2** a place where wine is stored **3** a stock of bottled wines

cello (**chell**-oh) *n, pl* **-los** a large low-pitched musical instrument of the violin family, held between the knees and played with a bow > **cellist** *n*

Cellophane *n trademark* a thin transparent material made from cellulose that is used as a protective wrapping, esp. for food

cellular *adj* **1** of, consisting of, or resembling a cell or cells: *cellular changes* **2** woven with an open texture: *cellular blankets* **3** designed for or using cellular radio: *cellular phones*

cellulite *n* fat deposits under the skin alleged to resist dieting

celluloid *n* **1** a kind of plastic made from cellulose nitrate and camphor, used to make toys and, formerly, photographic film **2** the cinema or films generally: *a Shakespeare play committed to celluloid*

cellulose *n* the main constituent of plant cell walls, used in making paper, rayon, and plastics

Celsius *adj* denoting a measurement on the Celsius scale

Celt (kelt) *n* **1** a person from Scotland, Ireland, Wales, Cornwall, or Brittany **2** a member of a people who inhabited Britain, Gaul, and Spain in pre-Roman times

Celtic (**kel**-tik, **sel**-tik) *n* **1** a group of languages that includes Gaelic, Welsh, and Breton ▸ *adj* **2** of the Celts or the Celtic languages

cement *n* **1** **A** a fine grey powder made of limestone and clay, mixed with water and sand to make mortar or concrete **B** mortar or concrete **2** something that unites, binds, or joins things or people: *bone cement*; *the cement of fear and hatred of the Left* **3** *dentistry* a material used for filling teeth ▸ *vb* **4** to join, bind, or cover with cement **5** to make (a relationship) stronger: *this would cement a firm alliance between the army and rebels*

> **cement** *n* **1** = mortar, plaster, paste **2** = sealant, glue, gum, adhesive ▸ *vb* **4** = stick, join, bond, attach, seal, glue, plaster, weld

cemetery *n, pl* **-teries** a place where dead people are buried: *a military cemetery*

> **cemetery** *n* = graveyard, churchyard, burial ground, necropolis, God's acre

cenotaph *n* a monument honouring soldiers who died in a war

censer *n* a container for burning incense

censor *n* **1** a person authorized to examine films, letters, or publications, in order to ban or cut anything considered obscene or objectionable ▸ *vb* **2** to ban or cut portions of (a film, letter, or publication)

> **censor** *vb* = expurgate, cut, blue-pencil, bowdlerize

censorious *adj* harshly critical

censorship *n* the practice or policy of censoring films, letters, or publications

censure *n* **1** severe disapproval ▸ *vb* **-suring, -sured 2** to criticize (someone or something) severely

C

censure n = disapproval, criticism, blame, condemnation, rebuke, reprimand, reproach, stick (slang); ≠ approval ▸ vb = criticize, blame, condemn, denounce, rebuke, reprimand, reproach, scold, damn; ≠ applaud

census n, pl **-suses** an official periodic count of a population including such information as sex, age, and occupation

cent n a monetary unit worth one hundredth of the main unit of currency in many countries

centaur n Greek myth a creature with the head, arms, and torso of a man, and the lower body and legs of a horse

centenarian n a person who is at least 100 years old

centenary (sen-teen-a-ree) n, pl **-naries** chiefly Brit a 100th anniversary or the celebration of one. US equivalent: **centennial**

center n, vb US same as **centre**

centi- prefix **1** denoting one hundredth: centimetre **2** denoting one hundred: centipede

centigrade adj same as **Celsius**

centigram or **centigramme** n one hundredth of a gram

centilitre or US **centiliter** n a measure of volume equivalent to one hundredth of a litre

centimetre or US **centimeter** n a unit of length equal to one hundredth of a metre

centipede n a small wormlike creature with many legs

central adj **1** of, at, or forming the centre of something: eastern and central parts of the country **2** main or principal: a central issue > **centrally** adv > **centrality** n

central adj **1** = inner, middle, mid, interior; ≠ outer **2** = main, central, chief, key, essential, primary, principal, fundamental, focal; ≠ minor

central heating n a system for heating a building by means of radiators or air vents connected to a central source of heat > **centrally heated** adj

centralism n the principle of bringing a country or an organization under central control > **centralist** adj

centralize or **-ise** vb **-izing, -ized** or **-ising, -ised** to bring (a country or an organization) under central control > **centralization** or **-isation** n

central reservation n Brit & NZ the strip that separates the two sides of a motorway or dual carriageway

centre or US **center** n **1** the middle point or part of something **2** a place where a specified activity takes place: a shopping centre **3** a person or thing that is a focus of interest: the centre of a long-running dispute **4** a place of activity or influence: the parliament building was the centre of resistance **5** a political party or group that favours moderation **6** sport a player who plays in the middle of the field rather than on a wing ▸ vb

-tring, -tred or US **-tering, -tered 7** to put in the centre of something **8 centre on** to have as a centre or main theme: the summit is expected to centre on expanding the role of the UN

centre or **center** n **1** = middle, heart, focus, core, nucleus, hub, pivot, kernel; ≠ edge ▸ vb **8 centre on something or someone** = focus, concentrate, cluster, revolve, converge

centrifugal (sent-riff-few-gl) adj **1** moving or tending to move away from a centre **2** of or operated by centrifugal force: centrifugal extractors

centrifuge n a machine that separates substances by the action of centrifugal force

centripetal (sent-rip-it-al) adj moving or tending to move towards a centre

centrist n a person who holds moderate political views

centurion n (in ancient Rome) the officer in command of a century

century n, pl **-ries 1** a period of 100 years **2** a score of 100 runs in cricket **3** (in ancient Rome) a unit of foot soldiers, originally consisting of 100 men

CEO chief executive officer

cephalopod (seff-a-loh-pod) n a sea mollusc with a head and tentacles, such as the octopus

ceramic n **1** a hard brittle material made by heating clay to a very high temperature **2** an object made of this material ▸ adj **3** made of ceramic: ceramic tiles

cereal n **1** any grass that produces an edible grain, such as oat, wheat, or rice **2** the grain produced by such a plant **3** a breakfast food made from this grain, usually eaten mixed with milk

cerebral (serr-rib-ral) adj **1** of the brain: a cerebral haemorrhage **2** involving intelligence rather than emotions or instinct: the cerebral joys of the literary world

cerebrum (serr-rib-rum) n, pl **-brums** or **-bra** (-bra) the main part of the human brain, associated with thought, emotion, and personality

ceremonial adj **1** of ceremony or ritual ▸ n **2** a system of formal rites; ritual > **ceremonially** adv

ceremonial adj = formal, public, official, ritual, stately, solemn, liturgical, courtly; ≠ informal ▸ n = ritual, ceremony, rite, formality, solemnity

ceremonious adj excessively polite or formal > **ceremoniously** adv

ceremony n, pl **-nies 1** a formal act or ritual performed for a special occasion: a wedding ceremony **2** formally polite behaviour **3 stand on ceremony** to insist on or act with excessive formality

ceremony n **1** = ritual, service, rite, observance, commemoration, solemnities **2** = formality, ceremonial, propriety, decorum

cerise (ser-reess) *adj* cherry-red

certain *adj* 1 positive and confident about something: *he was certain they would agree* 2 definitely known: *it is by no means certain the tomb still exists* 3 sure or bound: *the cuts are certain to go ahead* 4 some but not much: *a certain amount* 5 particular: *certain aspects* 6 named but not known: *a running commentary by a certain Mr Fox* 7 **for certain** without doubt

> **certain** *adj* 1 = sure, convinced, positive, confident, satisfied, assured; ≠ unsure 2 = known, true, positive, conclusive, unequivocal, undeniable, irrefutable, unquestionable, nailed-on (*slang*); ≠ doubtful 3 = bound, sure, fated, destined; ≠ unlikely

certainly *adv* without doubt: *he will certainly be back*

> **certainly** *adv* = definitely, surely, truly, undoubtedly, without doubt, undeniably, indisputably, assuredly

certainty *n* 1 the condition of being certain 2 *pl* **-ties** something established as inevitable

> **certainty** *n* 1 = confidence, trust, faith, conviction, assurance, sureness, positiveness; ≠ doubt 2 = inevitability; ≠ uncertainty

certifiable *adj* considered to be legally insane

certificate *n* an official document stating the details of something such as birth, death, or completion of an academic course

> **certificate** *n* = document, licence, warrant, voucher, diploma, testimonial, authorization, credential(s)

certify *vb* **-fies, -fying, -fied** 1 to confirm or attest to 2 to guarantee (that certain required standards have been met) 3 to declare legally insane > **certification** *n*

> **certify** *vb* 1, 2 = confirm, declare, guarantee, assure, testify, verify, validate, attest

certitude *n formal* confidence or certainty

cervix *n, pl* **cervixes** *or* **cervices** 1 the lower part of the womb that extends into the vagina 2 *anatomy* the neck > **cervical** *adj*

cesium *n* US same as **caesium**

cessation *n* an ending or pause: *a cessation of hostilities*

cesspool *or* **cesspit** *n* a covered tank or pit for collecting and storing sewage or waste water

cetacean (sit-**tay**-shun) *n* a sea creature such as a whale or dolphin, which belongs to a family of fish-shaped mammals and breathes through a blowhole

cf compare

CFC chlorofluorocarbon

CGI computer-generated image(s)

ch. 1 chapter 2 church

chafe *vb* **chafing, chafed** 1 to make sore or worn by rubbing 2 to be annoyed or impatient: *she chafes against the restrictions of her small-town community*

chaff[1] *n* 1 grain husks separated from the seeds during threshing 2 something of little worth; rubbish: *you had to be a very perceptive listener to sort the wheat from the chaff of his discourse*

chaff[2] *vb* to tease good-naturedly

chaffinch *n* a small European songbird with black-and-white wings and, in the male, a reddish body and blue-grey head

chagrin (**shag**-grin) *n* a feeling of annoyance and disappointment

chagrined *adj* annoyed and disappointed

chain *n* 1 a flexible length of metal links, used for fastening, binding, or connecting, or in jewellery 2 **chains** anything that restricts or restrains someone: *bound by the chains of duty* 3 a series of connected facts or events 4 a number of establishments, such as hotels or shops, that have the same owner or management 5 *chem* a number of atoms or groups bonded together so that the resulting molecule, ion, or radical resembles a chain 6 a row of mountains or islands ▸ *vb* 7 to restrict, fasten, or bind with or as if with a chain: *the demonstrators chained themselves to railings*

> **chain** *n* 1 = tether, coupling, link, bond, shackle, fetter, manacle 3 = series, set, train, string, sequence, succession, progression ▸ *vb* = bind, confine, restrain, handcuff, shackle, tether, fetter, manacle

chain reaction *n* 1 a series of events, each of which causes the next 2 a chemical or nuclear reaction in which the product of one step triggers the following step

chain-smoke *vb* **-smoking, -smoked** to smoke continuously, lighting one cigarette from the preceding one > **chain smoker** *n*

chair *n* 1 a seat with a back and four legs, for one person to sit on 2 an official position of authority or the person holding it: *the chair of the Security Council* 3 a professorship 4 **in the chair** presiding over a meeting 5 **the chair** *informal* the electric chair ▸ *vb* 6 to preside over (a meeting)

chairlift *n* a series of chairs suspended from a moving cable for carrying people up a slope

chairman *or fem* **chairwoman** *n, pl* **-men** *or* **-women** a person who is in charge of a company's board of directors or a meeting > **chairmanship** *n*

> **chairman** *or* **chairwoman** *n* = director, president, chief, executive, chairperson, chair

chaise (shaze) *n* a light horse-drawn carriage with two wheels

chaise longue (long) *n, pl* **chaise longues** *or* **chaises longues** a couch with a back and a single armrest

chalcedony (kal-**sed**-don-ee) *n, pl* **-nies** a form of quartz composed of very fine crystals, often greyish or blue in colour

chalet *n* **1** a type of Swiss wooden house with a steeply sloping roof **2** a similar house used as a ski lodge or holiday home

chalice (**chal-liss**) *n* **1** *poetic* a drinking cup or goblet **2** *Christianity* a gold or silver goblet containing the wine at communion

chalk *n* **1** a soft white rock consisting of calcium carbonate **2** a piece of chalk, either white or coloured, for writing and drawing on blackboards **3 as different as chalk and cheese** *informal* totally different **4 not by a long chalk** *informal* by no means: *you haven't finished by a long chalk* ▸ *vb* **5** to draw or mark with chalk > **chalky** *adj*

challenge *n* **1** a demanding or stimulating situation **2** a call to engage in a contest, fight, or argument **3** a questioning of a statement or fact **4** a demand by a sentry for identification or a password **5** *law* a formal objection to a juror ▸ *vb* **-lenging, -lenged** **6** to invite or call (someone) to take part in a contest, fight, or argument **7** to call (a decision or action) into question **8** to order (a person) to stop and be identified **9** *law* to make a formal objection to (a juror) > **challenger** *n* > **challenging** *adj*

> **challenge** *n* **1** = test, trial, opposition, confrontation, ultimatum **2** = dare, provocation, wero (NZ) ▸ *vb* **6** = dare, invite, defy, throw down the gauntlet **7** = dispute, question, tackle, confront, defy, object to, disagree with, take issue with

challenged *adj* disabled or disadvantaged as specified: *physically challenged performers*

chamber *n* **1** a meeting hall, usually one used for a legislative or judicial assembly **2** a room equipped for a particular purpose: *a decompression chamber* **3** a legislative or judicial assembly: *the Senate, the upper chamber of Canada's parliament* **4** old-fashioned or poetic a room in a house, esp. a bedroom **5** a compartment or cavity: *the heart chambers* **6** a compartment for a cartridge or shell in a gun

> **chamber** *n* **1** = hall, room **2, 4** = room, bedroom, enclosure, cubicle **3** = council, assembly, legislature, legislative body **5** = compartment

chamberlain *n* *history* an officer who managed the household of a king or nobleman

chambermaid *n* a woman employed to clean bedrooms in a hotel

chamber music *n* classical music to be performed by a small group of musicians

chamber pot *n* a bowl for urine, formerly used in bedrooms

chameleon (**kam-meal-yon**) *n* a small lizard with long legs that is able to change colour to blend in with its surroundings

chamfer (**cham-fer**) *n* **1** a bevelled surface at an edge or corner ▸ *vb* **2** to cut a chamfer on or in

chamois *n, pl* **-ois** **1** (**sham-wah**) a small mountain antelope of Europe and SW Asia **2** (**sham-ee**) a soft suede leather made from the skin of this animal or from sheep or goats **3** (**sham-ee**) *Also:* **chamois leather, shammy, chammy** a piece of such leather or similar material, used for cleaning and polishing

chamomile (**kam-mo-mile**) *n* same as **camomile**

champ¹ *vb* **1** to chew noisily **2 champ at the bit** *informal* to be restless or impatient to do something

champ² *n informal* short for **champion** (sense 1)

champagne *n* **1** a white sparkling wine produced around Reims and Épernay, France ▸ *adj* **2** denoting a luxurious lifestyle: *a champagne capitalist*

champion *n* **1** a person, plant, or animal that has defeated all others in a competition: *the Olympic 100 metres champion* **2** someone who defends a person or cause: *a champion of the downtrodden* ▸ *vb* **3** to support: *he unceasingly championed equal rights and opportunities* ▸ *adj* **4** *N English dialect* excellent > **championship** *n*

> **champion** *n* **1** = winner, hero, victor, conqueror, title holder **2** = defender, guardian, patron, backer, protector, upholder ▸ *vb* = support, back, defend, promote, advocate, fight for, uphold, espouse

chance *n* **1** the extent to which something is likely to happen; probability **2** an opportunity or occasion to do something: *a chance to escape rural poverty* **3** a risk or gamble: *the government is not in the mood to take any more chances* **4** the unknown and unpredictable element that causes something to happen in one way rather than another: *in Buddhism there is no such thing as chance or coincidence* **5 by chance** without planning: *by chance she met an old school friend* **6 on the off chance** acting on the slight possibility: *he had called on the agents on the off chance that he might learn something of value* ▸ *vb* **chancing, chanced** **7** to risk or hazard: *a few picnickers chanced the perilous footpath* **8** to do something without planning to: *I chanced to look down* **9 chance on** or **upon** to discover by accident: *I chanced upon a copy of this book*

> **chance** *n* **1** = probability, odds, possibility, prospect, likelihood; ≠ certainty **2** = opportunity, opening, occasion, time **3** = risk, speculation, gamble, hazard **4** = accident, fortune, luck, fate, destiny, coincidence, providence; ≠ design ▸ *vb* **7** = risk, try, stake, venture, gamble, hazard, wager

chancel *n* the part of a church containing the altar and choir

chancellor *n* **1** the head of government in several European countries **2** *US* the president of a university **3** *Brit, Austral & Canad* the honorary head of a university > **chancellorship** *n*

Chancery n (in England) the Lord Chancellor's court, a division of the High Court of Justice

chancy adj **chancier**, **chanciest** informal uncertain or risky

chandelier (shan-dill-**eer**) n an ornamental hanging light with branches and holders for several candles or bulbs

chandler n a dealer in a specified trade or merchandise: a ship's chandler > **chandlery** n

change n 1 the fact of becoming different 2 variety or novelty: they wanted to print some good news for a change 3 a different set, esp. of clothes 4 money exchanged for its equivalent in a larger denomination or in a different currency 5 the balance of money when the amount paid is larger than the amount due 6 coins of a small denomination ▸ vb **changing**, **changed** 7 to make or become different 8 to replace with or exchange for another: the Swedish Communist Party changed its name to the Left Party 9 to give and receive (something) in return: slaves and masters changed places 10 to give or receive (money) in exchange for its equivalent sum in a smaller denomination or different currency 11 to put on other clothes 12 to get off one bus, train, or airliner, and onto another: there's no direct train, so you'll need to change at York > **changeless** adj

change n 1 = alteration, innovation, transformation, modification, mutation, metamorphosis, difference, revolution 2 = variety, break (informal), departure, variation, novelty, diversion (Brit); ≠ monotony 3 = exchange, trade, conversion, swap, substitution, interchange ▸ vb 7 = alter, reform, transform, adjust, revise, modify, reorganize, restyle; ≠ keep 8, 9 = exchange, trade, replace, substitute, swap, interchange

changeable adj changing often > **changeability** n

changeling n a child believed to have been exchanged by fairies for the parents' real child

channel n 1 a band of radio frequencies assigned for the broadcasting of a radio or television signal 2 a path for an electrical signal or computer data 3 a means of access or communication: reports coming through diplomatic channels 4 a broad strait connecting two areas of sea 5 the bed or course of a river, stream, or canal 6 a navigable course through an area of water 7 a groove ▸ vb **-nelling**, **-nelled** or US **-neling**, **-neled** 8 to direct or convey through a channel or channels: tunnels that channel the pilgrims into the area; to channel funds abroad

channel n 3 = means, way, course, approach, medium, route, path, avenue 4, 5, 6 = strait, sound, route, passage, canal, waterway 7 = duct, artery, groove, gutter, furrow, conduit ▸ vb = direct, guide, conduct, transmit, convey

chant vb 1 to repeat (a slogan) over and over 2 to sing or recite (a psalm) ▸ n 3 a rhythmic or repetitious slogan repeated over and over, usually by more than one person 4 a religious song with a short simple melody in which several words or syllables are sung on one note

chant vb 2 = sing, chorus, recite, intone, carol ▸ n 4 = song, carol, chorus, melody, psalm

chanter n the pipe on a set of bagpipes on which the melody is played

chaos n complete disorder or confusion > **chaotic** adj > **chaotically** adv

chaos n = disorder, confusion, mayhem, havoc (informal), anarchy, lawlessness, pandemonium, bedlam, tumult; ≠ orderliness

chap n informal a man or boy

chap n = fellow (old-fashioned), man, person, individual, character, guy (informal), bloke (Brit informal)

chapati or **chapatti** n (in Indian cookery) a kind of flat thin unleavened bread

chapel n 1 a place of worship with its own altar, in a church or cathedral 2 a similar place of worship in a large house or institution 3 (in England and Wales) a Nonconformist place of worship 4 (in Scotland) a Roman Catholic church 5 the members of a trade union in a newspaper office, printing house, or publishing firm

chaperone (shap-per-rone) n 1 an older person who accompanies and supervises a young person or young people on social occasions ▸ vb **-oning**, **-oned** 2 to act as a chaperone to

chaplain n a member of the Christian clergy attached to a chapel, military body, or institution > **chaplaincy** n

chaplet n a garland worn on the head

chapped adj (of the skin) raw and cracked, through exposure to cold

chapter n 1 a division of a book 2 a period in a life or history: the latest chapter in the long and complex tale of British brewing 3 a sequence of events: a chapter of accidents 4 a branch of some societies or clubs 5 a group of the canons of a cathedral 6 **chapter and verse** exact authority for an action or statement

chapter n 1 = section, part, stage, division, episode, topic, segment, instalment 2 = period, time, stage, phase

char¹ vb **charring**, **charred** to blacken by partial burning

char² Brit informal ▸ n 1 short for **charwoman** ▸ vb **charring**, **charred** 2 to clean other people's houses as a job

char³ n Brit old-fashioned slang tea

charabanc (shar-rab-bang) n Brit obsolete a coach for sightseeing

character n 1 the combination of qualities distinguishing an individual person, group of people, or place: the unique charm and character of this historic town **2** a distinguishing quality or characteristic: *bodily movements of a deliberate character* **3** reputation, esp. good reputation: *a man of my Dad's character and standing in the community* **4** an attractively unusual or interesting quality: *the little town was full of life and character* **5** a person represented in a play, film, or story **6** an unusual or amusing person: *quite a character* **7** *informal* a person: *a flamboyant character* **8** a single letter, numeral, or symbol used in writing or printing **9 in** or **out of character** typical or not typical of the apparent character of a person › **characterless** *adj*

> **character** *n* **1** = personality, nature, attributes, temperament, complexion, disposition **2** = nature, kind, quality, calibre **3** = reputation, honour, integrity, good name, rectitude **5** = role, part, persona **6** = eccentric, card (*informal*), original, oddball (*informal*) **8** = symbol, mark, sign, letter, figure, device, rune, hieroglyph

characteristic *n* **1** a distinguishing feature or quality **2** *maths* the integral part of a logarithm: *the characteristic of 2.4771 is 2* ▸ *adj* **3** typical or representative of someone or something: *the prime minister fought with characteristic passion* › **characteristically** *adv*

> **characteristic** *n* **1** = feature, mark, quality, property, attribute, faculty, trait, quirk ▸ *adj* = typical, special, individual, representative, distinguishing, distinctive, peculiar, singular; ≠ rare

characterization or **-isation** *n* **1** the description or portrayal of a person by an actor or writer: *a novel full of rich characterization and complex plotting* **2** the act or an instance of characterizing

characterize or **-ise** *vb* **-izing**, **-ized** or **-ising**, **-ised 1** to be a characteristic of: *the violence that characterized the demonstrations* **2** to describe: *we have made what I would characterize as outstanding progress*

> **characterize** or **-ise** *vb* **1** = distinguish, mark, identify, brand, stamp, typify

charade (shar-**rahd**) *n* an absurd pretence

charcoal *n* **1** a black form of carbon made by partially burning wood or other organic matter **2** a stick of this used for drawing **3** a drawing done in charcoal ▸ *adj* **4** Also: **charcoal-grey** very dark grey

charge *vb* **charging**, **charged 1** to ask (an amount of money) as a price **2** to enter a debit against a person's account for (a purchase) **3** to accuse (someone) formally of a crime in a court of law **4** to make a rush at or sudden attack upon **5** to fill (a glass) **6** to cause (an accumulator or capacitor) to take and store electricity **7** to fill or saturate with liquid or gas: *old mine workings charged with foul gas* **8** to fill with a feeling or

mood: *the emotionally charged atmosphere* **9** *formal* to command or assign: *the president has charged his foreign minister with trying to open talks* ▸ *n* **10** a price charged for something; cost **11** a formal accusation of a crime in a court of law **12** an onrush or attack **13** custody or guardianship: *in the charge of the police* **14** a person or thing committed to someone's care: *a nanny reported the father of one of her charges to social workers* **15 A** a cartridge or shell **B** the explosive required to fire a gun **16** *physics* **A** the attribute of matter responsible for all electrical phenomena, existing in two forms, positive and negative **B** the total amount of electricity stored in a capacitor or an accumulator **17 in charge of** in control of and responsible for: *in charge of defence and foreign affairs*

> **charge** *vb* **3** = accuse, indict, impeach, incriminate, arraign; ≠ acquit **4** = attack, assault, assail; ≠ retreat **7, 8** = fill, load ▸ *n* **10** = price, rate, cost, amount, payment, expense, toll, expenditure **11** = accusation, allegation, indictment, imputation; ≠ acquittal **12** = attack, rush, assault, onset, onslaught, stampede, sortie; ≠ retreat **13** = care, trust, responsibility, custody, safekeeping **14** = duty, office, responsibility, remit

chargeable *adj* **1** liable to be taxed or charged **2** liable to result in a legal charge

chargé d'affaires (shar-zhay daf-**fair**) *n*, *pl* **chargés d'affaires** (shar-zhay daf-**fair**) **1** the temporary head of a diplomatic mission in the absence of the ambassador or minister **2** the head of a small or unimportant diplomatic mission

charger *n* **1** a device for charging a battery **2** (in the Middle Ages) a warhorse

chariot *n* a two-wheeled horse-drawn vehicle used in ancient times for wars and races

charioteer *n* a chariot driver

charisma (kar-**rizz**-ma) *n* the quality or power of an individual to attract, influence, or inspire people › **charismatic** (kar-rizz-**mat**-ik) *adj*

> **charisma** *n* = charm, appeal, personality, attraction, lure, allure, magnetism, force of personality, mojo (*slang*)

charitable *adj* **1** kind or lenient in one's attitude towards others **2** of or for charity: *a charitable organization* › **charitably** *adv*

> **charitable** *adj* **1** = kind, understanding, forgiving, sympathetic, favourable, tolerant, indulgent, lenient; ≠ unkind **2** = benevolent, liberal, generous, lavish, philanthropic, bountiful, beneficent; ≠ mean

charity *n* **1** *pl* **-ties** an organization set up to provide help to those in need **2** the giving of help, such as money or food, to those in need **3** help given to those in need; alms **4** a kindly attitude towards people

charity *n* **1** = charitable organization, fund, movement, trust, endowment **2, 3** = donations, help, relief, gift, contributions, assistance, hand-out, philanthropy, koha (NZ); ≠ meanness **4** = kindness, humanity, goodwill, compassion, generosity, indulgence, altruism, benevolence, aroha (NZ); ≠ ill will

charlady *n*, *pl* **-ladies** *Brit* same as **charwoman**

charlatan (shar-lat-tan) *n* a person who claims expertise that he or she does not have

charleston *n* a lively dance of the 1920s

charm *n* **1** the quality of attracting, fascinating, or delighting people **2** a trinket worn on a bracelet **3** a small object worn for supposed magical powers **4** a magic spell ▶ *vb* **5** to attract, fascinate, or delight **6** to influence or obtain by personal charm: *you can easily be charmed into changing your mind* **7** to protect as if by magic: *a charmed life* ▶ **charmer** *n* ▶ **charmless** *adj*

> **charm** *n* **1** = attraction, appeal, fascination, allure, magnetism; ≠ repulsiveness **2** = trinket **3** = talisman, amulet, fetish **4** = spell, magic, enchantment, sorcery, makutu (NZ) ▶ *vb* **5** = attract, delight, fascinate, entrance, win over, enchant, captivate, beguile; ≠ repel **6** = persuade, seduce, coax, beguile, sweet-talk (*informal*)

charming *adj* delightful or attractive > **charmingly** *adv*

> **charming** *adj* = attractive, pleasing, appealing, fetching (*informal*), delightful, cute, seductive, captivating; ≠ unpleasant

charnel house *n* (formerly) a building or vault for the bones of the dead

chart *n* **1** a graph, table, or sheet of information in the form of a diagram **2** a map of the sea or the stars **3 the charts** *informal* the weekly lists of the bestselling pop records or the most popular videos ▶ *vb* **4** to plot the course of **5** to make a chart of **6** to appear in the pop charts

> **chart** *n* **1** = table, diagram, blueprint, graph, plan, map ▶ *vb* **4** = monitor, follow, record, note, document, register, trace, outline **5** = plot, map out, delineate, sketch, draft, tabulate

charter *n* **1** a formal document granting or demanding certain rights or liberties: *a children's charter* **2** the fundamental principles of an organization: *the UN Charter* **3** the hire or lease of transportation for private use ▶ *vb* **4** to lease or hire by charter **5** to grant a charter to

> **charter** *n* **1** = document, contract, permit, licence, deed, prerogative **2** = constitution, laws, rules, code ▶ *vb* **4** = hire, commission, employ, rent, lease **5** = authorize, permit, sanction, entitle, license, empower, give authority

chartered accountant *n* an accountant who has passed the examinations of the Institute of Chartered Accountants

chartreuse (shar-truhz) *n* a green or yellow liqueur made from herbs

charwoman *n*, *pl* **-women** *Brit* a woman whose job is to clean other people's houses

chary (chair-ee) *adj* **charier**, **chariest** wary or careful: *chary of interfering*

chase¹ *vb* **chasing**, **chased** **1** to pursue (a person or animal) persistently or quickly **2** to force (a person or animal) to leave a place **3** *informal* to court (someone) in an unsubtle manner **4** *informal* to rush or run: *chasing around the world* **5** *informal* to pursue (something or someone) energetically in order to obtain results or information ▶ *n* **6** the act or an instance of chasing a person or animal

> **chase** *vb* **1** = pursue, follow, track, hunt, run after, course **2** = drive away, drive, expel, hound, send away, send packing, put to flight **4** = rush, run, race, shoot, fly, speed, dash, bolt ▶ *n* = pursuit, race, hunt, hunting

chase² *vb* **chasing**, **chased** to engrave or emboss (metal)

chaser *n* a drink drunk after another of a different kind, for example beer after whisky

chasm (kaz-zum) *n* **1** a very deep crack in the ground **2** a wide difference in interests or feelings: *a deep chasm separating science from politics*

chassis (shass-ee) *n*, *pl* **chassis** (shass-eez) the steel frame, wheels, and mechanical parts of a vehicle

chaste *adj* **1** abstaining from sex outside marriage or from all sexual intercourse **2** (of conduct or speech) pure, decent, or modest: *a chaste kiss on the forehead* **3** simple in style: *chaste furniture* > **chastely** *adv* > **chastity** *n*

chasten (chase-en) *vb* to subdue (someone) by criticism

chastise *vb* **-tising**, **-tised** **1** to scold severely **2** *old-fashioned* to punish by beating > **chastisement** *n*

chat *n* **1** an informal conversation **2** the activity of exchanging short messages using a computer or mobile phone ▶ *vb* **chatting**, **chatted** **3** to have an informal conversation **4** to exchange short messages using a computer or mobile phone

> **chat** *n* **1** = talk, tête-à-tête, conversation, gossip, heart-to-heart, natter, blather, blether (*Scot*), korero (NZ) ▶ *vb* **3** = talk, gossip, jaw (*slang*), natter, blather, blether (*Scot*)

chateau (shat-toe) *n*, *pl* **-teaux** (-toe) *or* **-teaus** a French country house or castle

chatelaine (shat-tell-lane) *n* (formerly) the mistress of a large house or castle

chatroom *n* a site on the internet where several connected users can exchange messages in real time

C

chattels *pl n old-fashioned* possessions

chatter *vb* **1** to speak quickly and continuously about unimportant things **2** (of birds or monkeys) to make rapid repetitive high-pitched noises **3** (of the teeth) to click together rapidly through cold or fear ▸ *n* **4** idle talk or gossip **5** the high-pitched repetitive noise made by a bird or monkey

> **chatter** *vb* **1** = prattle, chat, rabbit on (*Brit informal*), babble, gab (*informal*), natter, blather, schmooze (*slang*) ▸ *n* **4** = prattle, chat, gossip, babble, gab (*informal*), natter, blather, blether (*Scot*)

chatterbox *n informal* a person who talks a great deal, usually about unimportant things

chatty *adj* **-tier, -tiest 1** (of a person) fond of friendly, informal conversation; talkative **2** (of a letter) informal and friendly; gossipy

chauffeur *or fem* **chauffeuse** *n* **1** a person employed to drive a car for someone ▸ *vb* **2** to act as driver for (someone)

chauvinism (**show**-vin-iz-zum) *n* an irrational belief that one's own country, race, group, or sex is superior: *male chauvinism* > **chauvinist** *n, adj* > **chauvinistic** *adj*

chav *n Brit slang, derogatory* a young working-class person who dresses in casual sports clothes

cheap *adj* **1** costing relatively little; inexpensive **2** of poor quality; shoddy: *planks of cheap, splintery pine* **3** not valued highly; not worth much: *promises are cheap* **4** *informal* mean or despicable: *a cheap jibe* ▸ *n* **5 on the cheap** *Brit informal* at a low cost ▸ *adv* **6** at a low cost > **cheaply** *adv* > **cheapness** *n*

> **cheap** *adj* **1** = inexpensive, reduced, keen, reasonable, bargain, low-priced, low-cost, cut-price; ≠ expensive **2** = inferior, poor, worthless, second-rate, shoddy, tawdry, tatty (*Brit*), trashy, bodger *or* bodgie (*Austral slang*); ≠ good **4** = despicable, mean, contemptible, scungy (*Austral, NZ*); ≠ decent

cheapen *vb* **1** to lower the reputation of; degrade **2** to reduce the price of

cheapskate *n informal* a miserly person

cheat *vb* **1** to defraud: *he cheated her out of millions* **2** to act dishonestly in order to gain some advantage or profit **3 cheat on** *informal* to be unfaithful to (one's spouse or lover) ▸ *n* **4** a person who cheats **5** a fraud or deception

> **cheat** *vb* **1** = deceive, trick, fool, con (*informal*), mislead, rip off (*slang*), fleece, defraud, scam (*slang*) ▸ *n* **4** = deceiver, sharper, shark, charlatan, trickster, conman *or* woman (*informal*), con artist (*informal*), double-crosser (*informal*), swindler, rorter (*Austral slang*), rogue trader

check *vb* **1** to examine, investigate, or make an inquiry into **2** to slow the growth or progress of **3** to stop abruptly **4** to correspond or agree: *that all checks with our data here* ▸ *n* **5** a test to ensure accuracy or progress **6** a means to ensure against fraud or error **7** a break in progress; stoppage **8** *US* same as **cheque 9** *chiefly US & Canad* the bill in a restaurant **10** a pattern of squares or crossed lines **11** a single square in such a pattern **12** *chess* the state or position of a king under direct attack **13 in check** under control or restraint ▸ *interj* **14** *chiefly US & Canad* an expression of agreement ▸ See also **check in, check out** *etc.*

> **check** *vb* **1** = examine, test, study, look at, research, investigate, monitor, vet, parse; ≠ overlook **2** = stop, limit, delay, halt, restrain, inhibit, hinder, obstruct; ≠ further ▸ *n* **5** = examination, test, research, investigation, inspection, scrutiny, once-over (*informal*) **6** = control, limitation, restraint, constraint, obstacle, curb, obstruction, stoppage

checkered *adj US & Canad* same as **chequered**

check in *vb* **1 A** to register one's arrival at a hotel or airport **B** to register the arrival of (guests or passengers) at a hotel or airport ▸ *n* **check-in 2 A** the formal registration of arrival at a hotel or airport **B** the place where one registers one's arrival at a hotel or airport

checkmate *n* **1** *chess* the winning position in which an opponent's king is under attack and unable to escape **2** utter defeat ▸ *vb* **-mating, -mated 3** *chess* to place the king of (one's opponent) in checkmate **4** to thwart or defeat

check out *vb* **1** to pay the bill and leave a hotel **2** to investigate, examine, or look at: *he asked if he could check out the old man's theory; start the evening off by checking out one of the bars in the city* ▸ *n* **checkout 3** a counter in a supermarket, where customers pay

checkup *n* a thorough examination to see if a person or thing is in good condition

Cheddar *n* a firm orange or yellowy-white cheese

cheek *n* **1** either side of the face below the eye **2** *informal* impudence, boldness, or lack of respect **3** *informal* a buttock **4 cheek by jowl** close together **5 turn the other cheek** to refuse to retaliate ▸ *vb* **6** *Brit, Austral & NZ informal* to speak or behave disrespectfully to someone

> **cheek** *n* **2** = impudence, nerve (*informal*), disrespect, audacity, lip (*slang*), temerity, chutzpah (*US, Canad informal*), insolence

cheekbone *n* the bone at the top of the cheek, just below the eye

cheeky *adj* **cheekier, cheekiest** disrespectful; impudent > **cheekily** *adv* > **cheekiness** *n*

> **cheeky** *adj* = impudent, rude, forward, insulting, saucy, audacious, pert, disrespectful; ≠ respectful

cheep *n* **1** the short weak high-pitched cry of a young bird ▸ *vb* **2** to utter a cheep

cheer vb **1** to applaud or encourage with shouts
2 cheer up to make or become happy or hopeful;
comfort or be comforted ▸ n **3** a shout of
applause or encouragement **4** a feeling of
cheerfulness: *the news brought little cheer*

> **cheer** vb **1** = applaud, hail, acclaim, clap;
> ≠ boo **2 cheer someone up** = comfort,
> encourage, hearten, enliven, gladden, gee up,
> jolly along (*informal*) ▸ n **3** = applause, ovation

cheerful adj **1** having a happy disposition
2 pleasantly bright: *a cheerful colour*
3 ungrudging: *a cheerful giver* > **cheerfully** adv
> **cheerfulness** n

> **cheerful** adj **1** = happy, optimistic,
> enthusiastic, jolly, merry, upbeat (*informal*),
> buoyant, cheery; ≠ sad **2** = pleasant; ≠ gloomy

cheerio interj **1** informal a farewell greeting ▸ n
2 Austral & NZ a small red cocktail sausage
cheerless adj dreary or gloomy
cheery adj **cheerier**, **cheeriest** cheerful
> **cheerily** adv
cheese n **1** a food made from coagulated milk
curd **2** a block of this
cheeseburger n a hamburger with a slice of
cheese melted on top of it
cheesecake n **1** a dessert with a biscuit-crumb
base covered with a sweet cream-cheese
mixture and sometimes with a fruit topping
2 slang magazine photographs of naked or
scantily dressed women
cheesecloth n a light, loosely woven cotton
cloth
cheesed off adj Brit, Austral & NZ slang bored,
disgusted, or angry
cheesy adj **cheesier**, **cheesiest** like cheese
2 informal (of a smile) broad but possibly
insincere **3** informal in poor taste: *a cheesy game
show*
cheetah n a large fast-running wild cat of
Africa and SW Asia, which has a light brown
coat with black spots
chef n a cook, usually the head cook, in a
restaurant or hotel
chef-d'oeuvre (shay-durv) n, pl **chefs-d'oeuvre**
(shay-durv) a masterpiece
chemical n **1** any substance used in or resulting
from a reaction involving changes to atoms or
molecules ▸ adj **2** of or used in chemistry **3** of,
made from, or using chemicals: *a chemical additive
found in many foods* > **chemically** adv

> **chemical** n = compound, drug, substance,
> synthetic substance, potion

chemise (shem-meez) n an old-fashioned
loose-fitting slip or dress
chemist n **1** Brit, Austral & NZ a shop selling
medicines and cosmetics **2** Brit, Austral & NZ a
qualified dispenser of prescribed medicines
3 a specialist in chemistry

> **chemist** n **2** = pharmacist, apothecary
> (*obsolete*), dispenser

chemistry n the branch of science concerned
with the composition, properties, and reactions
of substances
chemo n informal short for **chemotherapy**
chemotherapy (kee-moh-ther-a-pee) n the
treatment of disease, often cancer, by means of
chemicals
chenille (shen-neel) n **1** a thick soft tufty yarn
2 a fabric made of this
cheque or US **check** n a written order to
someone's bank to pay money from his or her
account to the person to whom the cheque is
made out
cheque card n Brit a plastic card issued by a
bank guaranteeing payment of a customer's
cheques
chequered or US **checkered** adj **1** marked by
varied fortunes: *a chequered career* **2** marked with
alternating squares of colour
chequers or US **checkers** n the game of
draughts
cherish vb **1** to cling to (an idea or feeling):
cherished notions **2** to care for

> **cherish** vb **1** = cling to, prize, treasure, hold
> dear, cleave to; ≠ despise **2** = care for, love,
> support, comfort, look after, shelter, nurture,
> hold dear; ≠ neglect

cheroot (sher-root) n a cigar with both ends
cut off squarely
cherry n, pl **-ries 1** a small round soft fruit with
red or blackish skin and a hard stone **2** the tree
on which this fruit grows ▸ adj **3** deep red
cherub n, pl **cherubs** or (for sense 1) **cherubim**
1 Christianity an angel, often represented as a
winged child **2** an innocent or sweet child
> **cherubic** (chair-roo-bik) adj
chervil n an aniseed-flavoured herb
chess n a game of skill for two players using a
board marked with squares on which chessmen
are moved, with the object of checkmating the
opponent's king
chessman n, pl **-men** a piece used in chess
chest n **1** the front of the body, from the neck to
the waist **2 get something off one's chest**
informal to unburden oneself of worries or secrets
by talking about them **3** a heavy box for storage
or shipping: *a tea chest*

> **chest** n **1** = breast, front **3** = box, case, trunk,
> crate, coffer, casket, strongbox

chesterfield n **1** a large couch with high
padded sides and back **2** Canad any sofa or couch
chestnut n **1** a reddish-brown edible nut **2** the
tree that this nut grows on **3** a horse of a
reddish-brown colour **4** informal an old or stale
joke ▸ adj **5** dark reddish-brown: *chestnut hair*
chest of drawers n a piece of furniture
consisting of a set of drawers in a frame

C

chevron (**shev**-ron) *n* a V-shaped pattern, such as those worn on the sleeve of a military uniform to indicate rank

chew *vb* **1** to work the jaws and teeth in order to grind (food) ▸ *n* **2** the act of chewing **3** something that is chewed, such as a sweet or a piece of tobacco

> **chew** *vb* = munch, bite, grind, champ, crunch, gnaw, chomp, masticate

chewing gum *n* a flavoured gum which is chewed but not swallowed

chewy *adj* **chewier**, **chewiest** of a consistency requiring a lot of chewing

chianti (kee-**ant**-ee) *n* a dry red wine produced in Tuscany, Italy

chiaroscuro (kee-ah-roh-**skew**-roh) *n*, *pl* **-ros** the distribution of light and shade in a picture

chic (sheek) *adj* **1** stylish or elegant ▸ *n* **2** stylishness or elegance

> **chic** *adj* = stylish, smart, elegant, fashionable, trendy (*Brit informal*), schmick (*Austral informal*); ≠ unfashionable

chicane (shik-**kane**) *n* an obstacle placed on a motor-racing circuit to slow the cars down

chicanery *n* trickery or deception

chick *n* **1** a baby bird, esp. a domestic fowl **2** *slang, sometimes offensive* a young woman

chicken *n* **1** a domestic fowl bred for its flesh or eggs **2** the flesh of this bird used for food **3** *slang* a coward ▸ *adj* **4** *slang* cowardly

chicken feed *n slang* a trifling amount of money

chicken out *vb informal* to fail to do something through cowardice

chickenpox *n* an infectious viral disease, usually affecting children, which produces an itchy rash

chickpea *n* an edible hard yellow pealike seed

chickweed *n* a common garden weed with small white flowers

chicory *n* **1** a plant grown for its leaves, which are used in salads, and for its roots **2** the root of this plant, roasted, dried, and used as a coffee substitute

chide *vb* **chiding**, **chided** *or* **chid** *old-fashioned* to rebuke or scold

chief *n* **1** the head of a group or body of people **2** the head of a tribe ▸ *adj* **3** most important: *the chief suspects* **4** highest in rank: *the Chief Constable*

> **chief** *n* **1** = head, leader, director, manager, boss (*informal*), captain, master, governor, ariki (*NZ*), sherang (*Austral*, *NZ*); ≠ subordinate ▸ *adj* **3** = primary, highest, leading, main, prime, key, premier, supreme; ≠ minor

chiefly *adv* **1** especially or essentially **2** mainly or mostly

> **chiefly** *adv* **1** = especially, essentially, principally, primarily, above all **2** = mainly, largely, usually, mostly, in general, on the whole, predominantly, in the main

chieftain *n* the leader of a tribe or clan

chiffon (shif-**fon**) *n* a fine see-through fabric of silk or nylon

chignon (**sheen**-yon) *n* a roll or knot of long hair pinned up at the back of the head

chihuahua (chee-**wah**-wah) *n* a tiny short-haired dog, originally from Mexico

chilblain *n* an inflammation of the fingers or toes, caused by exposure to cold

child *n*, *pl* **children** **1** a young human being; boy or girl **2** a son or daughter. Related adjective: **filial 3** a childish or immature person **4** the product of an influence or environment: *a child of the Army* **5** **with child** *old-fashioned* pregnant > **childless** *adj* > **childlessness** *n*

> **child** *n* **1** = youngster, baby, kid (*informal*), infant, babe, juvenile, toddler, tot, littlie (*Austral informal*), ankle-biter (*Austral*, *US slang*), tacker (*Austral slang*) **2** = offspring

childbirth *n* the act of giving birth to a child. Related adjective: **natal**

> **childbirth** *n* = child-bearing, labour, delivery, lying-in, confinement, parturition

childhood *n* the time or condition of being a child

> **childhood** *n* = youth, minority, infancy, schooldays, immaturity, boyhood *or* girlhood

childish *adj* **1** immature or silly: *childish fighting over who did what* **2** of or like a child: *childish illnesses*

> **childish** *adj* **1** = immature, juvenile, foolish, infantile, puerile; ≠ mature **2** = youthful, young, boyish *or* girlish

childlike *adj* like a child, for example in being innocent or trustful

child's play *n informal* something that is easy to do

chill *n* **1** a feverish cold **2** a moderate coldness **3** a feeling of coldness resulting from a cold or damp environment or from sudden fear ▸ *vb* **4** to make (something) cool or cold: *chilled white wine* **5** to cause (someone) to feel cold or frightened **6** *informal* to relax or calm oneself ▸ *adj* **7** unpleasantly cold: *chill winds* > **chilling** *adj* > **chillingly** *adv*

> **chill** *n* **2** = coldness, bite, nip, sharpness, coolness, rawness, crispness, frigidity **3** = shiver, frisson ▸ *vb* **4** = cool, refrigerate, freeze ▸ *adj* = chilly, biting, sharp, freezing, raw, bleak, wintry

chilli *or* **chili** *n* **1** *pl* **chillies** *or* **chilies** the small red or green hot-tasting pod of a type of capsicum, used in cookery, often in powdered form **2** short for **chilli con carne**

chilli con carne *n* a highly seasoned Mexican dish of meat, onions, beans, and chilli powder

chilly *adj* **-lier**, **-liest** **1** feeling or causing to feel moderately cold **2** without warmth; unfriendly: *a chilly reception*

chilly adj **1** = cool, fresh, sharp, crisp, penetrating, brisk, draughty, nippy; ≠ warm **2** = unfriendly, hostile, unsympathetic, frigid, unresponsive, unwelcoming; ≠ friendly

chime n **1** the musical ringing sound made by a bell or clock ▸ vb **chiming, chimed 2** (of a bell) to make a clear musical ringing sound **3** (of a clock) to indicate (the time) by chiming

chimera (kime-**meer**-a) n **1** a wild and unrealistic dream or idea **2** Greek myth a fire-breathing monster with the head of a lion, body of a goat, and tail of a serpent

chimney n a hollow vertical structure that carries smoke or steam away from a fire or engine

chimney sweep n a person who cleans soot from chimneys

chimp n informal short for **chimpanzee**

chimpanzee n an intelligent small black ape of central W Africa

chin n the front part of the face below the mouth

china[1] n **1** ceramic ware of a type originally from China **2** dishes or ornamental objects made of china

china n = pottery, ceramics, ware, porcelain, crockery, tableware, service

china[2] n Brit & S African informal a friend or companion

china n = friend, pal (informal), mate (informal), buddy (informal), companion, best friend, intimate, comrade, cobber (Austral, NZ old-fashioned, informal), E hoa (NZ)

chinchilla n **1** a small S American rodent bred in captivity for its soft silvery-grey fur **2** the fur of this animal

chine n **1** a cut of meat including part of the backbone ▸ vb **chining, chined 2** to cut (meat) along the backbone

Chinese adj **1** of China ▸ n **2** pl -**nese** a person from China or a descendant of one **3** any of the languages of China

chink[1] n a small narrow opening: a chink of light

chink[2] vb **1** to make a light ringing sound ▸ n **2** a light ringing sound

chintz n a printed patterned cotton fabric with a glazed finish, used for curtains and chair coverings

chinwag n Brit, Austral & NZ informal a chat

chip n **1** a thin strip of potato fried in deep fat **2** US, Canad, Austral & NZ a potato crisp **3** electronics a tiny wafer of semiconductor material, such as silicon, processed to form an integrated circuit **4** a counter used to represent money in gambling games **5** a small piece removed by chopping, cutting, or breaking **6** a mark left where a small piece has been broken off something **7 chip off the old block** informal a person who resembles one of his or her parents in personality **8 have a chip on one's shoulder** informal to be resentful or bear a grudge **9 when the chips are down** informal at a time of crisis ▸ vb **chipping, chipped 10** to break small pieces from

chip n **4** = counter, disc, token **5** = fragment, shaving, wafer, sliver, shard **6** = scratch, nick, notch ▸ vb = nick, damage, gash

chip and PIN n a system for authorizing credit- or debit-card payment requiring the purchaser to enter a personal identification number

chipboard n thin rigid board made of compressed wood particles

chip in vb informal **1** to contribute to a common fund **2** to interrupt with a remark

chipmunk n a squirrel-like striped burrowing rodent of North America and Asia

chiropody (kir-**rop**-pod-ee) n the treatment of minor foot complaints like corns > **chiropodist** n

chiropractic (kire-oh-**prak**-tik) n a system of treating bodily disorders by manipulation of the spine > **chiropractor** n

chirp vb **1** (of some birds and insects) to make a short high-pitched sound **2** Brit, Austral & NZ to speak in a lively fashion ▸ n **3** a chirping sound

chirpy adj **chirpier, chirpiest** informal lively and cheerful > **chirpiness** n

chirrup vb **1** (of some birds) to chirp repeatedly ▸ n **2** a chirruping sound

chisel n **1** a metal tool with a sharp end for shaping wood or stone ▸ vb -**elling, -elled** or US -**eling, -eled 2** to carve or form with a chisel

chit n a short official note, such as a memorandum, requisition, or receipt. Also: **chitty**

chitchat n chat or gossip

chitterlings pl n the intestines of a pig or other animal prepared as food

chivalrous adj gallant or courteous > **chivalrously** adv

chivalry n **1** courteous behaviour, esp. by men towards women **2** the medieval system and principles of knighthood > **chivalric** adj

chives pl n the long slender hollow leaves of a small Eurasian plant, used in cooking for their onion-like flavour

chivvy vb -**vies, -vying, -vied** Brit to harass or nag

chlamydia (klam-**mid**-ee-a) n a sexually transmitted disease caused by a parasitic bacterium

chloride n chem **1** any compound of chlorine and another element and radical **2** any salt or ester of hydrochloric acid

chlorinate vb -**ating, -ated 1** to disinfect (water) with chlorine **2** chem to combine or treat (a substance) with chlorine: chlorinated hydrocarbons > **chlorination** n

chlorine n a poisonous strong-smelling greenish-yellow gaseous element, used in water purification and as a disinfectant, and,

C

combined with sodium, to make common salt. Symbol: **Cl**

chlorofluorocarbon n chem any of various gaseous compounds of carbon, hydrogen, chlorine, and fluorine, used as refrigerants and aerosol propellants, some of which break down the ozone in the atmosphere

chloroform n a sweet-smelling liquid, used as a solvent and cleansing agent, and formerly as an anaesthetic

chlorophyll or US **chlorophyl** n the green colouring matter of plants, which enables them to convert sunlight into energy

chock n 1 a block or wedge of wood used to prevent the sliding or rolling of a heavy object ▸ vb 2 to fit with or secure by a chock

chock-full adj completely full

chocolate n 1 a food made from roasted ground cacao seeds, usually sweetened and flavoured 2 a sweet or drink made from this ▸ adj 3 deep brown > **chocolaty** adj

choice n 1 the act of choosing or selecting 2 the opportunity or power of choosing: parental choice 3 a person or thing chosen or that may be chosen: the president's choice as the new head of the CIA 4 an alternative action or possibility: they had no choice but to accept 5 a range from which to select: a choice of weapons ▸ adj 6 of high quality: choice government jobs 7 carefully chosen: a few choice words 8 vulgar: choice language

> **choice** n 1, 2, 3 = selection, preference, pick 4 = option, say, alternative ▸ 5 = range, variety, selection, assortment ▸ adj 6 = best, prime, select, excellent, exclusive, elite, booshit (Austral slang), exo (Austral slang), sik (Austral slang), rad (informal), phat (slang), schmick (Austral informal)

choir n 1 an organized group of singers, such as in a church or school 2 the part of a church, in front of the altar, occupied by the choir

choke vb **choking, choked** 1 to hinder or stop the breathing of (a person or animal) by strangling or smothering 2 to have trouble in breathing, swallowing, or speaking 3 to block or clog up: the old narrow streets become choked to a standstill 4 to hinder the growth of: weeds would outgrow and choke the rice crop ▸ n 5 a device in a vehicle's engine that enriches the petrol-air mixture by reducing the air supply

> **choke** vb 1 = strangle, throttle, asphyxiate 2 = suffocate, stifle, smother, overpower, asphyxiate 3, 4 = block, clog, obstruct, bung, constrict, congest, stop, bar

choke back vb to suppress (tears or anger)

choker n a tight-fitting necklace

cholera (kol-ler-a) n a serious infectious disease causing severe diarrhoea and stomach cramps, caught from contaminated water or food

choleric adj bad-tempered

cholesterol (kol-lest-er-oll) n a fatty alcohol

found in all animal fats, tissues, and fluids, an excess of which is thought to contribute to heart and artery disease

chomp vb to chew (food) noisily

chook n informal, chiefly Austral & NZ a hen or chicken

choose vb **choosing, chose, chosen** 1 to select (a person, thing, or course of action) from a number of alternatives 2 to like or please: when she did choose to reveal her secret, the group were initially hushed 3 to consider it desirable or proper: I don't choose to read that sort of book

> **choose** vb 1 = pick, prefer, select, elect, adopt, opt for, designate, settle upon; ≠ reject 2, 3 = wish, want

choosy adj **choosier, choosiest** informal fussy; hard to please

chop[1] vb **chopping, chopped** 1 (often foll. by down or off) to cut (something) with a blow from an axe or other sharp tool 2 to cut into pieces 3 boxing & karate to hit (an opponent) with a short sharp blow 4 Brit, Austral & NZ informal to dispense with or reduce 5 sport to hit (a ball) sharply downwards ▸ n 6 a cutting blow 7 a slice of mutton, lamb, or pork, usually including a rib 8 sport a sharp downward blow or stroke 9 **the chop** slang dismissal from employment

> **chop** vb 1 = cut, fell, hack, sever, cleave, hew, lop

chop[2] vb **chopping, chopped** 1 **chop and change** to change one's mind repeatedly 2 **chop logic** to use excessively subtle or involved argument

chopper n 1 informal a helicopter 2 chiefly Brit a small hand axe 3 a butcher's cleaver 4 a type of bicycle or motorcycle with very high handlebars 5 NZ a child's bicycle

choppy adj **-pier, -piest** (of the sea) fairly rough > **choppiness** n

chops pl n Brit, Austral & NZ informal 1 the jaws or cheeks 2 **lick one's chops** to anticipate something with pleasure

chopsticks pl n a pair of thin sticks of ivory, wood, or plastic, used for eating Chinese or other East Asian food

chop suey n a Chinese-style dish of chopped meat, bean sprouts, and other vegetables in a sauce

choral adj of or for a choir

chorale (kor-**rahl**) n 1 a slow stately hymn tune 2 chiefly US a choir or chorus

chord[1] n 1 maths a straight line connecting two points on a curve 2 anatomy same as **cord** 3 **strike** or **touch a chord** to bring about an emotional response, usually of sympathy

chord[2] n the simultaneous sounding of three or more musical notes

chore n 1 a small routine task 2 an unpleasant task

chore *n* = task, job, duty, burden, hassle (*informal*), errand

choreograph *vb* to compose the steps and dances for (a piece of music or ballet)

choreography *n* **1** the composition of steps and movements for ballet and other dancing **2** the steps and movements of a ballet or dance > **choreographer** *n* > **choreographic** *adj*

chorister *n* a singer in a church choir

chortle *vb* **-tling, -tled 1** to chuckle with amusement ▸ *n* **2** an amused chuckle

chorus *n, pl* **-ruses 1** a large choir **2** a piece of music to be sung by a large choir **3** a part of a song repeated after each verse **4** something expressed by many people at once: *a chorus of boos* **5** the noise made by a group of birds or small animals: *the dawn chorus* **6** a group of singers or dancers who perform together in a show **7** (in ancient Greece) a group of actors who commented on the action of a play **8** (in Elizabethan drama) the actor who spoke the prologue and epilogue **9 in chorus** in unison ▸ *vb* **10** to sing or say together

chorus *n* **1, 6** = choir, singers, ensemble, vocalists, choristers **2, 3** = refrain, response **9 in chorus** = in unison, as one, all together, in concert, in harmony, in accord, with one voice

chose *vb* the past tense of **choose**

chosen *vb* **1** the past participle of **choose** ▸ *adj* **2** selected for some special quality: *the chosen one*

choux pastry (shoo) *n* a very light pastry made with eggs

chow *n* **1** a thick-coated dog with a curled tail, originally from China **2** *informal* food

chowder *n* a thick soup containing clams or fish

chow mein *n* a Chinese-American dish consisting of chopped meat or vegetables fried with noodles

Christ *n* **1** Jesus of Nazareth (Jesus Christ), regarded by Christians as the Messiah of Old Testament prophecies **2** the Messiah of Old Testament prophecies **3** an image or picture of Christ ▸ *interj* **4** *taboo slang* an oath expressing annoyance or surprise

christen *vb* **1** same as **baptize 2** to give a name to (a person or thing) **3** *informal* to use for the first time > **christening** *n*

christen *vb* **2** = baptize, name

Christendom *n* all Christian people or countries

Christian *n* **1** a person who believes in and follows Jesus Christ **2** *informal* a person who displays the virtues of kindness and mercy encouraged in the teachings of Jesus Christ ▸ *adj* **3** of Jesus Christ, Christians, or Christianity **4** kind or good

Christianity *n* **1** the religion based on the life and teachings of Christ **2** Christian beliefs or practices **3** same as **Christendom**

Christian name *n* a personal name formally given to Christians at baptism: loosely used to mean a person's first name

Christian Science *n* the religious system founded by Mary Baker Eddy (1866), which emphasizes spiritual regeneration and healing through prayer > **Christian Scientist** *n*

Christmas *n* **1 A** a Christian festival commemorating the birth of Christ, held by most Churches to have occurred on December 25 **B** Also: **Christmas Day** December 25, as a day of secular celebrations when gifts and greetings are exchanged ▸ *adj* **2** connected with or taking place at the time of year when this festival is celebrated: *the Christmas holidays* > **Christmassy** *adj*

Christmas *n* **1A** = the festive season, Noël, Xmas (*informal*), Yule (*archaic*), Yuletide (*archaic*)

Christmas Eve *n* the evening or the whole day before Christmas Day

Christmas tree *n* an evergreen tree or an imitation of one, decorated as part of Christmas celebrations

chromatic *adj* **1** of or in colour or colours **2** *music* **A** involving the sharpening or flattening of notes or the use of such notes **B** of the chromatic scale > **chromatically** *adv*

chromatography *n* the technique of separating and analysing the components of a mixture of liquids or gases by slowly passing it through an adsorbing material

chrome *n* **1** same as **chromium 2** anything plated with chromium ▸ *vb* **chroming, chromed 3** to plate with chromium

chromium *n* *chem* a hard grey metallic element, used in steel alloys and electroplating to increase hardness and corrosion resistance. Symbol: **Cr**

chromosome *n* any of the microscopic rod-shaped structures that appear in a cell nucleus during cell division, consisting of units (genes) that are responsible for the transmission of hereditary characteristics

chronic *adj* **1** (of a disease) developing slowly or lasting for a long time **2** (of a bad habit or bad behaviour) having continued for a long time; habitual: *chronic drug addiction* **3** very serious or severe: *chronic food shortages* **4** Brit, Austral & NZ *informal* very bad: *the play was chronic* > **chronically** *adv*

chronicle *n* **1** a record of events in chronological order ▸ *vb* **-cling, -cled 2** to record in or as if in a chronicle > **chronicler** *n*

chronicle *n* = record, story, history, account, register, journal, diary, narrative, blog ▸ *vb* = record, tell, report, enter, relate, register, recount, set down

chronological *adj* **1** (of a sequence of events) arranged in order of occurrence **2** relating to chronology > **chronologically** *adv*

chronology *n, pl* **-gies** **1** the arrangement of dates or events in order of occurrence **2** the determining of the proper sequence of past events **3** a table of events arranged in order of occurrence ▸ **chronologist** *n*

chronometer *n* a timepiece designed to be accurate in all conditions

chrysalis (kriss-a-liss) *n* an insect in the stage between larva and adult, when it is in a cocoon

chrysanthemum *n* a garden plant with large round flowers made up of many petals

chub *n, pl* **chub** *or* **chubs** a common freshwater game fish of the carp family with a dark greenish body

chubby *adj* **-bier, -biest** plump and round ▸ **chubbiness** *n*

chuck[1] *vb* **1** *informal* to throw carelessly **2** *informal* (sometimes foll. by *in* or *up*) to give up; reject: *he chucked in his job* **3** to pat (someone) affectionately under the chin **4** *Austral & NZ informal* to vomit ▸ *n* **5** a throw or toss **6** a pat under the chin

> **chuck** *vb* **1** = throw, cast, pitch, toss, hurl, fling, sling (*informal*), heave **2** = give up *or* over, leave, abandon, cease, resign from, pack in **4** = vomit, throw up (*informal*), spew, heave (*slang*), puke (*slang*), barf (*US slang*), chunder (*slang, chiefly Austral*)

chuck[2] *n* **1** Also: **chuck steak** a cut of beef from the neck to the shoulder blade **2** a device that holds a workpiece in a lathe or a tool in a drill

chuckle *vb* **-ling, -led** **1** to laugh softly or to oneself ▸ *n* **2** a partly suppressed laugh

> **chuckle** *vb* = laugh, giggle, snigger, chortle, titter ▸ *n* = laugh, giggle, snigger, chortle, titter

chuffed *adj informal* pleased or delighted: *I suppose you're feeling pretty chuffed*

chug *n* **1** a short dull sound like the noise of an engine ▸ *vb* **chugging, chugged** **2** (esp. of an engine) to operate or move with this sound: *lorries chug past*

chukka *or* **chukker** *n polo* a period of continuous play, usually 7¹/₂ minutes

chum *n* **1** *informal* a close friend ▸ *vb* **chumming, chummed** **2 chum up with** to form a close friendship with

> **chum** *n* = friend, mate (*informal*), pal (*informal*), companion, comrade, crony, cobber (*Austral, NZ old-fashioned, informal*), E hoa (*NZ*)

chummy *adj* **-mier, -miest** *informal* friendly ▸ **chummily** *adv* ▸ **chumminess** *n*

chump *n* **1** *informal* a stupid person **2** a thick piece of meat

chunder *vb slang, chiefly Austral* to vomit

chunk *n* **1** a thick solid piece of something **2** a considerable amount

> **chunk** *n* **1** = piece, block, mass, portion, lump, slab, hunk, nugget

chunky *adj* **chunkier, chunkiest** **1** thick and short **2** containing thick pieces **3** *chiefly Brit* (of clothes, esp. knitwear) made of thick bulky material ▸ **chunkiness** *n*

church *n* **1** a building for public Christian worship **2** religious services held in a church **3** a particular Christian denomination **4** Christians collectively **5** the clergy as distinguished from the laity **6 Church** institutional religion as a political or social force: *conflict between Church and State*

churchgoer *n* a person who attends church regularly

churchwarden *n* **1** *Church of England & Episcopal Church* a lay assistant of a parish priest **2** an old-fashioned long-stemmed tobacco pipe made of clay

churchyard *n* the grounds round a church, used as a graveyard

churlish *adj* surly and rude

churn *n* **1** a machine in which cream is shaken to make butter **2** a large container for milk ▸ *vb* **3** to stir (milk or cream) vigorously in order to make butter **4** to move about violently: *a hot tub of churning water*

> **churn** *vb* **3** = stir up, beat, disturb, swirl, agitate **4** = swirl, toss

churn out *vb informal* to produce (something) rapidly and in large numbers

chute[1] (shoot) *n* a steep sloping channel or passage down which things may be dropped

chute[2] *n informal* short for **parachute**

chutney *n* a pickle of Indian origin, made from fruit, vinegar, spices, and sugar: *mango chutney*

CIA Central Intelligence Agency; a US bureau responsible for espionage and intelligence activities

cicada (sik-kah-da) *n* a large broad insect, found in hot countries, that makes a high-pitched drone

cicatrix (sik-a-trix) *n, pl* **cicatrices** (sik-a-**trice**-eez) the tissue that forms in a wound during healing; scar

CID (in Britain) Criminal Investigation Department; the detective division of a police force

cider *n* an alcoholic drink made from fermented apple juice

cigar *n* a tube-like roll of cured tobacco leaves for smoking

cigarette *n* a thin roll of shredded tobacco in thin paper, for smoking

cinch (sinch) *n* **1** *informal* an easy task **2** *slang* a certainty

cinder *n* **1** a piece of material that will not burn, left after burning coal or wood **2 cinders** ashes

cinema *n* **1** a place designed for showing films **2 the cinema** **A** the art or business of making films **B** films collectively ▸ **cinematic** *adj*

cinema *n* 1 = pictures, movies, picture-house, flicks (*slang*) 2**a** = films, pictures, movies, the big screen (*informal*), motion pictures, the silver screen

cinematography *n* the technique of making films: *he won an Oscar for his stunning cinematography* > **cinematographer** *n* > **cinematographic** *adj*

cineraria *n* a garden plant with daisy-like flowers

cinnamon *n* the spice obtained from the aromatic bark of a tropical Asian tree

cipher *or* **cypher** (**sife**-er) *n* 1 a method of secret writing using substitution of letters according to a key 2 a secret message 3 the key to a secret message 4 a person or thing of no importance 5 *obsolete* the numeral zero ▸ *vb* 6 to put (a message) into secret writing

circa (**sir**-ka) *prep* (used with a date) approximately; about: *circa 1788*

circle *n* 1 a curved line surrounding a central point, every point of the line being the same distance from the centre 2 the figure enclosed by such a curve 3 something formed or arranged in the shape of a circle: *they ran round in little circles* 4 a group of people sharing an interest, activity, or upbringing: *his judgment is well respected in diplomatic circles* 5 *theatre* the section of seats above the main level of the auditorium 6 a process or chain of events or parts that forms a connected whole; cycle 7 **come full circle** to arrive back at one's starting point ▸ *vb* **-cling, -cled** 8 to move in a circle (around) 9 to enclose in a circle

circle *n* 1, 2, 3 = ring, disc, hoop, halo 4 = group, company, set, club, society, clique, coterie ▸ *vb* 8 = wheel, spiral 9 = go round, ring, surround, enclose, envelop, encircle, circumscribe, circumnavigate

circlet *n* a small circle or ring, esp. a circular ornament worn on the head

circuit *n* 1 a complete route or course, esp. one that is circular or that lies around an object 2 a complete path through which an electric current can flow 3 **a** a periodical journey around an area, as made by judges or salespeople **b** the places visited on such a journey 4 a motor-racing track 5 *sport* a series of tournaments in which the same players regularly take part: *the professional golf circuit* 6 a number of theatres or cinemas under one management

circuit *n* 1 = lap, tour, revolution, orbit 3 = course, tour, track, route, journey 4 = racetrack, course, track, racecourse

circuitous (sir-**kew**-it-uss) *adj* indirect and lengthy: *a circuitous route*

circuitry (sir-**kit**-tree) *n* 1 the design of an electrical circuit 2 the system of circuits used in an electronic device

circular *adj* 1 of or in the shape of a circle

2 travelling in a circle 3 (of an argument) not valid because a statement is used to prove the conclusion and the conclusion to prove the statement 4 (of letters or announcements) intended for general distribution ▸ *n* 5 a letter or advertisement sent to a large number of people at the same time > **circularity** *n*

circular *adj* 1 = round, ring-shaped 2 = circuitous, cyclical, orbital ▸ *n* = advertisement, notice, ad (*informal*), announcement, advert (*Brit*), press release

circulate *vb* **-lating, -lated** 1 to send, go, or pass from place to place or person to person: *rumours were circulating that he was about to resign* 2 to move through a circuit or system, returning to the starting point: *regular exercise keeps the blood circulating around the body* 3 to move around the guests at a party, talking to different people: *it wasn't like her not to circulate among all the guests* > **circulatory** *adj*

circulate *vb* 1 = spread, issue, publish, broadcast, distribute, publicize, disseminate, promulgate 2 = flow, revolve, rotate, radiate

circulation *n* 1 the flow of blood from the heart through the arteries, and then back through the veins to the heart, where the cycle is renewed 2 the number of copies of a newspaper or magazine that are sold 3 the distribution of newspapers or magazines 4 sending or moving around: *the circulation of air* 5 **in circulation** **a** (of currency) being used by the public **b** (of people) active in a social or business context

circulation *n* 1 = bloodstream, blood flow 2 = distribution, currency, readership 3 = spread, distribution, transmission, dissemination 4 = flow, circling, motion, rotation

circumcise *vb* **-cising, -cised** 1 to remove the foreskin of (a male) 2 to cut or remove the clitoris of (a female) 3 to perform such an operation as a religious rite on (someone) > **circumcision** *n*

circumference *n* 1 the boundary of a specific area or figure, esp. of a circle 2 the distance round this > **circumferential** *adj*

circumflex *n* a mark (^) placed over a vowel to show that it is pronounced in a particular way, for instance as a long vowel in French

circumlocution *n* 1 an indirect way of saying something 2 an indirect expression > **circumlocutory** *adj*

circumnavigate *vb* **-gating, -gated** to sail, fly, or walk right around > **circumnavigation** *n*

circumscribe *vb* **-scribing, -scribed** 1 *formal* to limit or restrict within certain boundaries: *the President's powers are circumscribed by the Constitution* 2 *geom* to draw a geometric figure around (another figure) so that the two are in contact but do not intersect > **circumscription** *n*

circumspect *adj* cautious and careful not to take risks > **circumspection** *n* > **circumspectly** *adv*

circumstance *n* **1** an occurrence or condition that accompanies or influences a person or event **2** unplanned events and situations which cannot be controlled: *a victim of circumstance* **3 pomp and circumstance** formal display or ceremony **4 under** *or* **in no circumstances** in no case; never **5 under the circumstances** because of conditions

> **circumstance** *n* **1** = condition, situation, contingency, state of affairs, lie of the land **2** = chance, the times, accident, fortune, luck, fate, destiny, providence

circumstantial *adj* **1** (of evidence) strongly suggesting something but not proving it **2** fully detailed

circumvent *vb formal* **1** to avoid or get round (a rule, restriction, etc.) **2** to outwit (a person) > **circumvention** *n*

circus *n, pl* **-cuses 1** a travelling company of entertainers such as acrobats, clowns, trapeze artists, and trained animals **2** a public performance given by such a company **3** *Brit* an open place in a town where several streets meet **4** *informal* a hectic or well-published situation: *her second marriage turned into a media circus* **5** (in ancient Rome) an open-air stadium for chariot races or public games **6** a travelling group of professional sportspeople: *the Formula One circus*

cirrhosis (sir-roh-siss) *n* a chronic progressive disease of the liver, often caused by drinking too much alcohol

cirrus *n, pl* **-ri 1** a thin wispy cloud found at high altitudes **2** a plant tendril **3** a slender tentacle in certain sea creatures

cis *adj* short for **cisgender**

cisgender *adj* having a gender identity that fully corresponds to the gender assigned to one at birth

cistern *n* **1** a water tank, esp. one which holds water for flushing a toilet **2** an underground reservoir

citadel *n* a fortress in a city

citation *n* **1** an official commendation or award, esp. for bravery **2** the quoting of a book or author **3** a quotation

cite *vb* **citing, cited 1** to quote or refer to (a passage, book, or author) **2** to bring forward as proof **3** to summon to appear before a court of law **4** to mention or commend (someone) for outstanding bravery **5** to enumerate: *the president cited the wonders of the American family*

> **cite** *vb* **1, 2** = quote, name, advance, mention, extract, specify, allude to, enumerate

citizen *n* **1** a native or naturalized member of a state or nation **2** an inhabitant of a city or town

> **citizen** *n* = inhabitant, resident, dweller, denizen, subject, townsman *or* woman *or* person

Citizens' Band *n* a range of radio frequencies for use by the public for private communication

citizenship *n* the condition or status of a citizen, with its rights and duties

citric acid *n* a weak acid found especially in citrus fruits and used as a flavouring (E330)

citrus fruit *n* a juicy, sharp-tasting fruit such as an orange, lemon, or lime

city *n, pl* **cities 1** any large town **2** (in Britain) a town that has received this title from the Crown **3** the people of a city collectively **4** (in the US and Canada) a large town with its own government established by charter from the state or provincial government

> **city** *n* **1** = town, metropolis, municipality, conurbation

City *n* **the City** *Brit* **1** the area in central London in which the United Kingdom's major financial business is transacted **2** the various financial institutions in this area

civet (siv-vit) *n* **1** a spotted catlike mammal of Africa and S Asia **2** the musky fluid produced by this animal, used in perfumes

civic *adj* of a city or citizens > **civically** *adv*

> **civic** *adj* = public, municipal, communal, urban, local

civics *n* the study of the rights and responsibilities of citizenship

civil *adj* **1** of or occurring within the state or between citizens: *civil unrest* **2** of or relating to the citizen as an individual: *civil rights* **3** not part of the military, legal, or religious structures of a country: *civil aviation* **4** polite or courteous: *he seemed very civil and listened politely* > **civilly** *adv*

> **civil** *adj* **1** = civic, political, domestic, municipal; ≠ state **4** = polite, obliging, courteous, considerate, affable, well-mannered; ≠ rude

civilian *n* **1** a person who is not a member of the armed forces or police ▸ *adj* **2** not relating to the armed forces or police: *civilian clothes*

civility *n, pl* **-ties 1** polite or courteous behaviour **2 civilities** polite words or actions

civilization *or* **-lisation** *n* **1** the total culture and way of life of a particular people, nation, region, or period **2** a human society that has a complex cultural, political, and legal organization **3** the races collectively who have achieved such a state **4** cities or populated areas, as contrasted with sparsely inhabited areas **5** intellectual, cultural, and moral refinement

> **civilization** *or* **-lisation** *n* **2** = society, people, community, nation, polity **5** = culture, development, education, progress, enlightenment, sophistication, advancement, cultivation

civilize or **-lise** vb **-lizing**, **-lized** or **-lising**, **-lised**
1 to bring out of barbarism into a state of
civilization **2** to refine, educate, or enlighten
> **civilized** or **-lised** adj

> **civilize** or **-lise** vb = cultivate, educate, refine,
> tame, enlighten, sophisticate

civil servant n a member of the civil service
civil service n the service responsible for the
public administration of the government of a
country
civil war n war between people of the same
country
civvies pl n Brit, Austral & NZ slang civilian clothes
as opposed to uniform
clack n **1** the sound made by two hard objects
striking each other ▶ vb **2** to make this sound
clad vb a past of **clothe**
cladding n **1** the material used to cover the
outside of a building **2** a protective metal
coating attached to another metal
claim vb **1** to assert as a fact: he had claimed to be too
ill to return **2** to demand as a right or as one's
property: you can claim housing benefit to help pay your
rent **3** to call for or need: this problem claims our
attention **4** to cause the death of: violence which has
claimed at least fifty lives **5** to succeed in obtaining;
win: she claimed her fifth European tour victory with a
closing round of 64 ▶ n **6** an assertion of something
as true or real **7** an assertion of a right; a
demand for something as due **8** a right or just
title to something: a claim to fame **9** anything
that is claimed, such as a piece of land staked
out by a miner **10 A** a demand for payment in
connection with an insurance policy **B** the sum
of money demanded > **claimant** n

> **claim** vb **1** = assert, insist, maintain, allege,
> uphold, profess **3** = demand, call for, ask for,
> insist on ▶ n **6** = assertion, statement,
> allegation, declaration, pretension,
> affirmation, protestation (formal) **7** = demand,
> application, request, petition, call **8** = right,
> title, entitlement

clairvoyance n the alleged power of
perceiving things beyond the natural range of
the senses
clairvoyant n **1** a person claiming to have the
power to foretell future events ▶ adj **2** of or
possessing clairvoyance
clam n an edible shellfish with a hinged shell
clamber vb **1** to climb awkwardly, using hands
and feet ▶ n **2** a climb performed in this manner
clammy adj **-mier**, **-miest** unpleasantly moist
and sticky > **clammily** adv > **clamminess** n
clamour or US **clamor** n **1** a loud protest **2** a
loud and persistent noise or outcry ▶ vb
3 clamour for to demand noisily **4** to make a
loud noise or outcry > **clamorous** adj

> **clamour** or **clamor** n **2** = noise, shouting,
> racket, outcry, din, uproar, commotion, hubbub

clamp n **1** a mechanical device with movable
jaws for holding things together tightly **2** See
wheel clamp ▶ vb **3** to fix or fasten with a clamp
4 to immobilize (a car) by means of a wheel clamp

> **clamp** n **1** = vice, press, grip, bracket, fastener
> ▶ vb **3** = fasten, fix, secure, brace, make fast

clan n **1** a group of families with a common
surname and a common ancestor, esp. among
Scottish Highlanders **2** an extended family
related by ancestry or marriage: America's leading
political clan, the Kennedys **3** a group of people with
common characteristics, aims, or interests
> **clansman** or fem **clanswoman** n

> **clan** n **1, 2** = family, group, society, tribe,
> fraternity (US, Canad), brotherhood, ainga (NZ),
> ngai or ngati (NZ) **3** = group, set, circle, gang,
> faction, coterie, cabal

clandestine adj formal secret and concealed: a
base for clandestine activities > **clandestinely** adv
clang vb **1** to make a loud ringing noise, as
metal does when it is struck ▶ n **2** a ringing
metallic noise
clanger n **drop a clanger** informal to make a very
noticeable mistake
clangour or US **clangor** n a loud continuous
clanging sound > **clangorous** adj
clank n **1** an abrupt harsh metallic sound ▶ vb
2 to make such a sound
clannish adj (of a group) tending to exclude
outsiders: the villagers can be very clannish
clap¹ vb **clapping**, **clapped** **1** to applaud by
striking the palms of one's hands sharply
together **2** to place or put quickly or forcibly: in
former times he would have been clapped in irons or shot
3 to strike (a person) lightly with an open hand
as in greeting **4** to make a sharp abrupt sound
like two objects being struck together **5 clap
eyes on** informal to catch sight of ▶ n **6** the act or
sound of clapping **7** a sharp abrupt sound, esp.
of thunder **8** a light blow

> **clap** vb **1** = applaud, cheer, acclaim; ≠ boo

clap² n slang gonorrhoea
clapped out adj informal worn out; dilapidated
clapper n **1** a small piece of metal hanging
inside a bell, which causes it to sound when
struck against the side **2 like the clappers** Brit
informal extremely quickly: he left, pedalling like the
clappers
clapperboard n a pair of hinged boards
clapped together during film shooting to help
in synchronizing sound and picture
claptrap n informal foolish or pretentious talk:
pseudo-intellectual claptrap
claret (klar-rit) n **1** a dry red wine, esp. one from
Bordeaux ▶ adj **2** purplish-red
clarify vb **-fies**, **-fying**, **-fied** **1** to make or become
clear or easy to understand **2** to make or become
free of impurities, esp. by heating: clarified butter
> **clarification** n

C

clarify *vb* 1 = explain, interpret, illuminate, clear up, simplify, make plain, elucidate, throw *or* shed light on

clarinet *n* a keyed woodwind instrument with a single reed > **clarinettist** *n*

clarion *n* 1 an obsolete high-pitched trumpet 2 its sound

clarion call *n* strong encouragement to do something

clarity *n* clearness

clarity *n* = clearness, precision, simplicity, transparency, lucidity, straightforwardness; ≠ obscurity

clash *vb* 1 to come into conflict 2 to be incompatible 3 (of dates or events) to coincide 4 (of colours or styles) to look ugly or incompatible together: *patterned fabrics which combine seemingly clashing shades to great effect* 5 to make a loud harsh sound, esp. by striking together ▸ *n* 6 a collision or conflict 7 a loud harsh noise

clash *vb* 1 = conflict, grapple, wrangle, lock horns, cross swords, war, feud, quarrel 2 = disagree, conflict, vary, counter, differ, contradict, diverge, run counter to 4 = not go, jar, not match 5 = crash, bang, rattle, jar, clatter, jangle, clang, clank ▸ *n* 6 = conflict, fight, brush, confrontation, collision, showdown (*informal*), boilover (*Austral*)

clasp *n* 1 a fastening, such as a catch or hook, for holding things together 2 a firm grasp or embrace ▸ *vb* 3 to grasp or embrace tightly 4 to fasten together with a clasp

clasp *n* 1 = fastening, catch, grip, hook, pin, clip, buckle, brooch 2 = grasp, hold, grip, embrace, hug ▸ *vb* 3 = grasp, hold, press, grip, seize, squeeze, embrace, clutch

class *n* 1 a group of people sharing a similar social and economic position 2 the system of dividing society into such groups 3 a group of people or things sharing a common characteristic 4 **A** a group of pupils or students who are taught together **B** a meeting of a group of students for tuition 5 a standard of quality or attainment: *second class* 6 *informal* excellence or elegance, esp. in dress, design, or behaviour: *a full-bodied red wine with real class* 7 *biol* one of the groups into which a phylum is divided, containing one or more orders 8 **in a class of its own** *or* **in a class by oneself** without an equal for ability, talent, etc. ▸ *adj* 9 *informal* excellent, skilful, or stylish: *a class act* ▸ *vb* 10 to place in a class

class *n* 3, 7 = group, set, division, rank ▸ *vb* = classify, group, rate, rank, brand, label, grade, designate

classic *adj* 1 serving as a standard or model of its kind; typical: *it is a classic symptom of iron*

deficiency 2 of lasting interest or significance because of excellence: *the classic work on Central America* 3 characterized by simplicity and purity of form: *a classic suit* ▸ *n* 4 an author, artist, or work of art of the highest excellence 5 a creation or work considered as definitive

classic *adj* 1 = typical, standard, model, regular, usual, ideal, characteristic, definitive, dinki-di (*Austral informal*) 2 = masterly, best, finest, world-class, consummate, first-rate; ≠ second-rate ▸ *n* = standard, masterpiece, prototype, paradigm, exemplar, model

classical *adj* 1 of or in a restrained conservative style: *it had been built in the 18th century in a severely classical style* 2 *music* **A** in a style or from a period marked by stability of form, intellectualism, and restraint **B** denoting serious art or music in general 3 of or influenced by ancient Greek and Roman culture 4 of the form of a language historically used for formal and literary purposes: *classical Chinese* 5 (of an education) based on the humanities and the study of Latin and Greek > **classically** *adv*

classicism *n* 1 an artistic style based on Greek and Roman models, showing emotional restraint and regularity of form 2 knowledge of the culture of ancient Greece and Rome > **classicist** *n*

classification *n* 1 placing things systematically in categories 2 a division or category in a classifying system > **classificatory** *adj*

classification *n* 1 = categorization, grading, taxonomy, sorting, analysis, arrangement, profiling 2 = class, grouping, heading, sort, department, type, division, section

classify *vb* **-fies, -fying, -fied** 1 to arrange or order by classes 2 *government* to declare (information) to be officially secret > **classifiable** *adj*

classify *vb* 1 = categorize, sort, rank, arrange, grade, catalogue, pigeonhole, tabulate

classy *adj* **classier, classiest** *informal* stylish and sophisticated > **classiness** *n*

classy *adj* = high-class, exclusive, superior, elegant, stylish, posh (*informal, chiefly Brit*), up-market, top-drawer, schmick (*Austral informal*)

clatter *vb* 1 to make a rattling noise, as when hard objects hit each other ▸ *n* 2 a rattling sound or noise

clause *n* 1 a section of a legal document such as a will or contract 2 *grammar* a group of words, consisting of a subject and a predicate including a finite verb, that does not necessarily constitute a sentence > **clausal** *adj*

clause *n* 1 = section, condition, article, chapter, passage, part, paragraph

claustrophobia *n* an abnormal fear of being in a confined space > **claustrophobic** *adj*

clavichord *n* an early keyboard instrument with a very soft tone

clavicle *n* either of the two bones connecting the shoulder blades with the upper part of the breastbone; the collarbone

claw *n* **1** a curved pointed nail on the foot of birds, some reptiles, and certain mammals **2** a similar part in some invertebrates, such as a crab's pincer ▸ *vb* **3** to scrape, tear, or dig with claws or nails: *she clawed his face with her fingernails* **4** to achieve (something) only after overcoming great difficulties: *he clawed his way to power and wealth; settlers attempting to claw a living from the desert*

> **claw** *n* **1** = nail, talon **2** = pincer ▸ *vb* **3** = scratch, tear, dig, rip, scrape, maul, mangulate (*Austral slang*), lacerate

clay *n* **1** a very fine-grained earth, soft when moist and hardening when baked, used to make bricks and pottery **2** earth or mud **3** *poetic* the material of the human body > **clayey, clayish** *or* **claylike** *adj*

claymore *n* a large two-edged broadsword used formerly by Scottish Highlanders

clay pigeon *n* a disc of baked clay hurled into the air from a machine as a target for shooting

clean *adj* **1** free from dirt or impurities: *clean water* **2** habitually hygienic and neat **3** morally sound: *clean living* **4** without objectionable language or obscenity: *good clean fun* **5** without anything in it or on it: *a clean sheet of paper* **6** causing little contamination or pollution: *rape seed oil may provide a clean alternative to petrol* **7** recently washed; fresh **8** thorough or complete: *a clean break with the past* **9** skilful and done without fumbling; dexterous: *a clean catch* **10** *sport* played fairly and without fouls **11** free from dishonesty or corruption: *clean government* **12** simple and streamlined in design: *the clean lines and colourful simplicity of these ceramics* **13** (esp. of a driving licence) showing or having no record of offences **14** *slang* **A** innocent **B** not carrying illegal drugs, weapons, etc. ▸ *vb* **15** to make or become free of dirt: *he wanted to help me clean the room* ▸ *adv* **16** in a clean way **17** *not standard* completely: *she clean forgot to face the camera* **18** **come clean** *informal* to make a revelation or confession ▸ *n* **19** the act or an instance of cleaning: *the fridge could do with a clean*

> **clean** *adj* **1, 6** = hygienic, fresh, sterile, pure, purified, antiseptic, sterilized, uncontaminated; ≠ contaminated **3, 4, 11** = moral, good, pure, decent, innocent, respectable, upright, honourable; ≠ immoral **7** = spotless, fresh, immaculate, impeccable, flawless, unblemished, unsullied; ≠ dirty **8** = complete, final, whole, total, perfect, entire, decisive, thorough ▸ *vb* = cleanse, wash, scrub, rinse, launder, scour, purify, disinfect; ≠ dirty

cleaner *n* **1** a person, device, or substance that removes dirt **2** a shop or firm that provides a dry-cleaning service **3** **take someone to the cleaners** *informal* to rob or defraud someone

cleanly (kleen-lee) *adv* **1** easily or smoothly **2** in a fair manner ▸ *adj* (klen-lee) **-lier, -liest** **3** habitually clean or neat > **cleanliness** *n*

cleanse *vb* **cleansing, cleansed** **1** to remove dirt from **2** to remove evil or guilt from > **cleanser** *n*

> **cleanse** *vb* **1** = clean, wash, scrub, rinse, scour **2** = absolve, clear, purge, purify

clean technology *n* techniques that minimize the damage caused to the environment as a result of manufacturing processes

clear *adj* **1** free from doubt or confusion: *clear instructions* **2** certain in the mind; sure: *I am still not clear about what they can and cannot do* **3** easy to see or hear; distinct **4** perceptive; alert: *clear thinking* **5** evident or obvious: *it is not clear how she died* **6** transparent: *clear glass doors* **7** free from darkness or obscurity; bright **8** (of sounds or the voice) not harsh or hoarse **9** even and pure in tone or colour **10** free of obstruction; open: *a clear path runs under the trees* **11** (of weather) free from dullness or clouds **12** without blemish or defect: *a clear skin* **13** free of suspicion, guilt, or blame: *a clear conscience* **14** (of money) without deduction; net **15** free from debt or obligation **16** without qualification or limitation; complete: *a clear lead* ▸ *adv* **17** in a clear or distinct manner **18** completely **19** **clear of** out of the way of: *once we were clear of the harbour we headed east* ▸ *n* **20** **in the clear** free of suspicion, guilt, or blame ▸ *vb* **21** to free from doubt or confusion **22** to rid of objects or obstructions **23** to make or form (a path) by removing obstructions **24** to move or pass by or over without contact: *he cleared the fence easily* **25** to make or become free from darkness or obscurity **26** to rid (one's throat) of phlegm **27** **A** (of the weather) to become free from dullness, fog, or rain **B** (of mist or fog) to disappear **28** (of a cheque) to pass through one's bank and be charged against one's account **29** to free from impurity or blemish **30** to obtain or give (clearance) **31** to prove (someone) innocent of a crime or mistake **32** to permit (someone) to see or handle classified information **33** to make or gain (money) as profit **34** to discharge or settle (a debt) **35** **clear the air** to sort out a misunderstanding ▸ See also **clear off** etc. > **clearly** *adv*

> **clear** *adj* **1** = comprehensible, explicit, understandable; ≠ confused **2** = certain, sure, convinced, positive, satisfied, resolved, definite, decided; ≠ confused **3** = distinct; ≠ indistinct **5** = obvious, plain, apparent, evident, distinct, pronounced, manifest, blatant; ≠ ambiguous **6** = transparent, see-through, translucent, crystalline, glassy,

limpid, pellucid; ≠ opaque **7, 11** = bright, fine, fair, shining, sunny, luminous, cloudless, light; ≠ cloudy **10** = unobstructed, open, free, empty, unhindered, unimpeded; ≠ blocked **12, 13** = untroubled, clean, pure, innocent, immaculate, unblemished, untarnished ▸ *vb* **22, 23** = unblock, free, loosen, extricate, open, disentangle **24** = pass over, jump, leap, vault, miss **25, 27** = brighten, break up, lighten **29** = remove, clean, wipe, cleanse, tidy (up), sweep away **31** = absolve, acquit, vindicate, exonerate; ≠ blame

clearance *n* **1** the act of clearing: *slum clearance* **2** permission for a vehicle or passengers to proceed **3** official permission to have access to secret information or areas **4** space between two parts in motion

clearing *n* an area with few or no trees or shrubs in wooded or overgrown land

clear off *vb informal* to go away: often used as a command

clear out *vb* **1** to remove and sort the contents of (a room or container) **2** *informal* to go away: often used as a command ▸ *n* **clear-out 3** an act of clearing someone or something out

clearway *n Brit & Austral* a stretch of road on which motorists may stop only in an emergency

cleat *n* **1** a wedge-shaped block attached to a structure to act as a support **2** a piece of wood or iron with two projecting ends round which ropes are fastened

cleavage *n* **1** the space between a woman's breasts, as revealed by a low-cut dress **2** a division or split **3** (of crystals) the act of splitting or the tendency to split along definite planes so as to make smooth surfaces

cleave¹ *vb* **cleaving, cleft, cleaved** *or* **clove, cleft, cleaved** *or* **cloven 1** to split apart: *cleave the stone along the fissures* **2** to make by or as if by cutting: *a two-lane highway that cleaved its way through the northern extremities of the Everglades*

cleave² *vb* **cleaving, cleaved** to cling or stick: *a farmhouse cleaved to the hill*

cleaver *n* a heavy knife with a square blade, used for chopping meat

clef *n music* a symbol placed at the beginning of each stave indicating the pitch of the music written after it

cleft *n* **1** a narrow opening in a rock **2** an indentation or split ▸ *adj* **3 in a cleft stick** in a very difficult position ▸ *vb* **4** a past of **cleave¹**

clematis *n* a climbing plant grown for its large colourful flowers

clemency *n* mercy

clement *adj* **1** (of the weather) mild **2** merciful

clementine *n* a citrus fruit resembling a tangerine

clench *vb* **1** to close or squeeze together (the teeth or a fist) tightly **2** to grasp or grip firmly ▸ *n* **3** a firm grasp or grip

clerestory (**clear-store-ee**) *n, pl* **-ries** a row of windows in the upper part of the wall of the nave of a church above the roof of the aisle ▸ **clerestoried** *adj*

clergy *n, pl* **-gies** priests and religious ministers as a group, esp. in the Christian Church

clergy *n* = priesthood, ministry, clerics, clergymen *or* women, churchmen *or* women, the cloth, holy orders

clergyman *or fem* **clergywoman** *n, pl* **-men** *or* **-women** a member of the clergy

cleric *n* a member of the clergy

clerical *adj* **1** of clerks or office work: *a clerical job* **2** of or associated with the clergy: *a Lebanese clerical leader*

clerk *n* **1** an employee in an office, bank, or court who keeps records, files, and accounts **2** *US & Canad* a hotel receptionist **3** *archaic* a scholar ▸ *vb* **4** to work as a clerk ▸ **clerkship** *n*

clever *adj* **1** displaying sharp intelligence or mental alertness **2** skilful with one's hands **3** smart in a superficial way **4** *Brit informal* sly or cunning ▸ **cleverly** *adv* ▸ **cleverness** *n*

clever *adj* **1** = intelligent, bright, talented, gifted, smart, knowledgeable, quick-witted; ≠ stupid **2** = skilful, talented, gifted; ≠ inept **4** = shrewd, bright (*informal*), ingenious, resourceful, canny; ≠ unimaginative

clianthus *n* a plant of Australia and New Zealand with clusters of ornamental scarlet flowers

cliché (**klee-shay**) *n* an expression or idea that is no longer effective because of overuse ▸ **clichéd** *or* **cliché'd** *adj*

cliché *n* = platitude, stereotype, commonplace, banality, truism, hackneyed phrase

click *n* **1** a short light often metallic sound ▸ *vb* **2** to make a clicking sound: *cameras clicked and whirred* **3** Also: **click on** *computers* to press and release (a button on a mouse) or select (a particular function) by pressing and releasing a button on a mouse **4** *informal* to become suddenly clear: *it wasn't until I saw the photograph that everything clicked into place* **5** *slang* (of two people) to get on well together: *I met him at a dinner party and we clicked straight away* **6** *slang* to be a great success: *the film cost so much that if it hadn't clicked at the box office we'd have been totally wiped out*

client *n* **1** someone who uses the services of a professional person or organization **2** a customer **3** *computers* a program or work station that requests data from a server

client *n* **1, 2** = customer, consumer, buyer, patron, shopper, patient

clientele (**klee-on-tell**) *n* customers or clients collectively

cliff *n* a steep rock face, esp. along the seashore

cliff *n* = rock face, overhang, crag, precipice, escarpment, scar, bluff

cliffhanger *n* a film, game, etc. which is exciting and full of suspense because its outcome is uncertain > **cliffhanging** *adj*

climate *n* **1** the typical weather conditions of an area **2** an area with a particular kind of climate **3** a prevailing trend: *the current economic climate* > **climatic** *adj* > **climatically** *adv*

climate *n* **1, 2** = weather, temperature

climax *n* **1** the most intense or highest point of an experience or of a series of events: *a striking climax to the year's efforts to promote tourism* **2** a decisive moment in a dramatic or other work: *the film has a climax set atop a gale-swept lighthouse* **3** an orgasm ▸ *vb* **4** to reach or bring to a climax > **climactic** *adj*

climax *n* **1** = culmination, top, summit, height, highlight, peak, high point, zenith

climb *vb* **1** to go up or ascend (stairs, a mountain, etc.) **2** to move or go with difficulty: *she climbed through a window* **3** to rise to a higher point or intensity: *I grew increasingly delirious as my temperature climbed* **4** to increase in value or amount: *the number could eventually climb to half-a-million* **5** to ascend in social position: *he climbed the ranks of the organization* **6** (of plants) to grow upwards by twining, using tendrils or suckers **7** to incline or slope upwards: *the road climbed up through the foothills* **8 climb into** *informal* to put on or get into: *I climbed into the van* ▸ *n* **9** the act or an instance of climbing **10** a place or thing to be climbed, esp. a route in mountaineering > **climbable** *adj* > **climber** *n* > **climbing** *n, adj*

climb *vb* **1** = ascend, scale, mount, go up, clamber, shin up **2** = clamber, descend, scramble, dismount **3** = rise, go up, soar, ascend, fly up

climb down *vb* **1** to retreat (from an opinion or position) ▸ *n* **climb-down 2** a retreat from an opinion or position

clime *n poetic* a region or its climate

clinch *vb* **1** to settle (an argument or agreement) decisively **2** to secure (a nail) by bending the protruding point over **3** to engage in a clinch, as in boxing or wrestling ▸ *n* **4** the act of clinching **5** *boxing & wrestling* a movement in which one or both competitors hold on to the other to avoid punches or regain wind **6** *slang* a lovers' embrace

clinch *vb* **1** = secure, close, confirm, conclude, seal, sew up (*informal*), close out, set the seal on

clincher *n informal* something decisive, such as a fact, argument, or point scored

cling *vb* **clinging, clung 1** (often foll. by *to*) to hold fast or stick closely (to something) **2** to be emotionally overdependent on **3** to continue to do or believe in: *he clings to the belief that people are capable of change* > **clinging** or **clingy** *adj*

cling *vb* **1** = clutch, grip, embrace, grasp, hug, hold on to, clasp

clingfilm *n Brit* a thin polythene material used for wrapping food

clinic *n* **1** a place in which outpatients are given medical treatment or advice **2** a similar place staffed by specialist physicians or surgeons: *I have an antenatal clinic on Friday afternoon* **3** *Brit & NZ* a private hospital or nursing home **4** the teaching of medicine to students at the bedside

clinical *adj* **1** of or relating to the observation and treatment of patients directly: *clinical trials of a new drug* **2** of or relating to a clinic **3** logical and unemotional: *they have a somewhat clinical attitude to their children's upbringing* **4** (of a room or buildings) plain, simple, and usually unattractive > **clinically** *adv*

clinical *adj* **3** = unemotional, cold, scientific, objective, detached, analytic, impersonal, dispassionate

clink[1] *vb* **1** to make a light sharp metallic sound ▸ *n* **2** such a sound

clink[2] *n slang* prison

clinker *n* the fused coal left over in a fire or furnace

clinker-built *adj* (of a boat or ship) with a hull made from overlapping planks

clip[1] *vb* **clipping, clipped 1** to cut or trim with scissors or shears **2** to remove a short section from (a film or newspaper) **3** *Brit & Austral* to punch a hole in (something, esp. a ticket) **4** *informal* to strike with a sharp, often slanting, blow **5** to shorten (a word) **6** *slang* to obtain (money) by cheating ▸ *n* **7** the act of clipping **8** a short extract from a film **9** something that has been clipped **10** *informal* a sharp, often slanting, blow: *a clip on the ear* **11** *informal* speed: *proceeding at a smart clip* **12** *Austral & NZ* the total quantity of wool shorn, as in one place or season

clip *vb* **1** = trim, cut, crop, prune, shorten, shear, snip, pare **4** = smack, strike, knock, punch, thump, clout (*informal*), cuff, whack ▸ *n* **10** = smack, strike, knock, punch, thump, clout (*informal*), cuff, whack

clip[2] *n* **1** a device for attaching or holding things together **2** an article of jewellery that can be clipped onto a dress or hat ▸ *vb* **clipping, clipped 3** to attach or hold together with a clip

clip *vb* = attach, fix, secure, connect, pin, staple, fasten, hold

clipboard *n* **1** a portable writing board with a clip at the top for holding paper **2** *computers* a temporary storage area for holding text or graphics that have been cut or copied from a document

clipper *n* a fast commercial sailing ship

clippers *pl n* a tool used for clipping and cutting

clipping *n* something cut out, esp. an article from a newspaper

clique (kleek) *n* a small exclusive group of friends or associates ▷ **cliquey, cliquy** or **cliquish** *adj*

clitoris (klit-or-riss) *n* a small sexually sensitive organ at the front of the vulva ▷ **clitoral** *adj*

cloak *n* 1 a loose sleeveless outer garment, fastened at the throat and falling straight from the shoulders 2 something that covers or conceals ▸ *vb* 3 to hide or disguise 4 to cover with or as if with a cloak

> **cloak** *n* 1 = cape, coat, wrap, mantle (*archaic*) 2 = covering, layer, blanket, shroud ▸ *vb* 3 = hide, cover, screen, mask, disguise, conceal, obscure, veil 4 = cover, coat, wrap, blanket, shroud, envelop

cloakroom *n* 1 a room in which coats may be left temporarily 2 *Brit euphemistic* a toilet

clobber¹ *vb informal* 1 to batter 2 to defeat utterly 3 to criticize severely

clobber² *n Brit, Austral & NZ informal* personal belongings, such as clothes

cloche (klosh) *n* 1 *Brit, Austral & NZ* a small glass or plastic cover for protecting young plants 2 a woman's close-fitting hat

clock *n* 1 a device for showing the time, either through pointers that revolve over a numbered dial, or through a display of figures 2 a device with a dial for recording or measuring 3 the downy head of a dandelion that has gone to seed 4 *informal* same as **speedometer** or **mileometer** 5 *Brit slang* the face 6 **round the clock** all day and all night ▸ *vb* 7 to record (time) with a stopwatch, esp. in the calculation of speed 8 *Brit, Austral & NZ slang* to strike, esp. on the face or head 9 *informal* to turn back the mileometer on (a car) illegally so that its mileage appears less 10 *Brit slang* to see or notice

clock in *or* **clock on** *vb* to register one's arrival at work on an automatic time recorder

clock out *or* **clock off** *vb* to register one's departure from work on an automatic time recorder

clock up *vb* to record or reach (a total): *he has now clocked up over 500 games for the club*

clockwise *adv, adj* in the direction in which the hands of a clock rotate

clockwork *n* 1 a mechanism similar to that of a spring-driven clock, as in a wind-up toy 2 **like clockwork** with complete regularity and precision

clod *n* 1 a lump of earth or clay 2 *Brit, Austral & NZ* a dull or stupid person ▷ **cloddish** *adj*

clog *vb* **clogging, clogged** 1 to obstruct or become obstructed with thick or sticky matter 2 to encumber 3 to stick in a mass ▸ *n* 4 a wooden or wooden-soled shoe

clog *vb* 1 = obstruct, block, jam, hinder, impede, congest

cloister *n* 1 a covered pillared walkway within a religious building 2 a place of religious seclusion, such as a monastery ▸ *vb* 3 to confine or seclude in or as if in a monastery

cloistered *adj* sheltered or protected

clone *n* 1 a group of organisms or cells of the same genetic constitution that have been reproduced asexually from a single plant or animal 2 *informal* a person who closely resembles another 3 *slang* a mobile phone that has been given the electronic identity of an existing mobile phone, so that calls made on it are charged to that owner ▸ *vb* **cloning, cloned** 4 to produce as a clone 5 *informal* to produce near copies of (a person) 6 *slang* to give (a mobile phone) the electronic identity of an existing mobile phone so that calls made on it are charged to that owner ▷ **cloning** *n*

close¹ *vb* **closing, closed** 1 to shut: *he lay back and closed his eyes* 2 to bar, obstruct, or fill up (an entrance, a hole, etc.): *the blockades had closed major roads, railways, and border crossings* 3 to cease or cause to cease giving service: *both stores closed at 9 p.m.*; *the Shipping Company closed its offices in Bangkok* 4 to end; terminate: *'Never,' she said, so firmly that it closed the subject* 5 (of agreements or deals) to complete or be completed successfully 6 to come closer (to): *she was still in second place but closing fast on the leader* 7 to take hold: *his small fingers closed around the coin* 8 *Stock Exchange* to have a value at the end of a day's trading, as specified: *the pound closed four-and-a-half cents higher* 9 to join the ends or edges of something: *to close a circuit* ▸ *n* 10 the act of closing 11 the end or conclusion: *the close of play* 12 (rhymes with **dose**) *Brit* a courtyard or quadrangle enclosed by buildings 13 *Scot* the entry from the street to a tenement building

> **close** *vb* 1 = shut, lock, fasten, secure; ≠ open 2 = block up, bar, seal; ≠ open 3 = shut down, finish, cease 4 = end, finish, complete, conclude, wind up, terminate; ≠ begin 5 = clinch, confirm, secure, conclude, seal, sew up (*informal*), set the seal on 7 = come together, join, connect; ≠ separate ▸ *n* 11 = end, ending, finish, conclusion, completion, finale, culmination, denouement

close² *adj* 1 near in space or time 2 intimate: *we were such close friends in those days* 3 near in relationship: *she seems to have had no close relatives* 4 careful, strict, or searching: *their research will not stand up to close scrutiny* 5 having the parts near together: *a close formation* 6 near to the surface; short: *an NCO's haircut, cropped close on top, shaved clean at sides and back* 7 almost equal: *a close game* 8 not deviating or varying greatly from something: *a close resemblance* 9 confined or enclosed 10 oppressive, heavy, or airless: *damp,* close weather **11** strictly guarded: *he had been placed in close arrest* **12** secretive or reticent **13** miserly; not generous **14** restricted as to public admission or membership ▸ *adv* **15** closely; tightly **16** near or in proximity > **closely** *adv* > **closeness** *n*

close *adj* **1** = near, neighbouring, nearby, handy, adjacent, adjoining, cheek by jowl; ≠ far **2** = intimate, loving, familiar, thick (*informal*), attached, devoted, confidential, inseparable; ≠ distant **4** = careful, detailed, intense, minute, thorough, rigorous, painstaking **7** = even, level, neck and neck, fifty-fifty (*informal*), evenly matched **8** = noticeable, marked, strong, distinct, pronounced **9, 10** = stifling, oppressive, suffocating, stuffy, humid, sweltering, airless, muggy; ≠ airy ▸ *adv* **16** = imminent, near, impending, at hand, nigh; ≠ far away

closed shop *n Brit, Austral & NZ* (formerly) a place of work in which all workers had to belong to a particular trade union

close season *n* **1** the period of the year when it is illegal to kill certain game or fish **2** *sport* the period of the year when there is no domestic competition

close shave *n informal* a narrow escape

closet *n* **1** *US & Austral* a small cupboard **2** a small private room **3** short for **water closet 4 in the closet** *informal* not openly acknowledging the fact that one is homosexual ▸ *adj* **5** private or secret: *a closet fan of horror films* ▸ *vb* **-eting, -eted 6** to shut away in private, esp. in order to talk: *he was closeted with the President*

close-up *n* **1** a photograph or film or television shot taken at close range **2** a detailed or intimate view or examination ▸ *vb* **close up 3** to shut entirely: *every other shop front seemed to be closed up* **4** to draw together: *the ranks closed up and marched on* **5** (of wounds) to heal completely

closure *n* **1** the act of closing or the state of being closed **2** something that closes or shuts **3** a procedure by which a debate may be stopped and an immediate vote taken **4** *chiefly US* **A** a resolution of a significant event or relationship in a person's life **B** the sense of contentment experienced after such a resolution

clot *n* **1** a soft thick lump formed from liquid **2** *informal* a stupid person ▸ *vb* **clotting, clotted 3** to form soft thick lumps

cloth *n, pl* **cloths 1** a fabric formed by weaving, felting, or knitting fibres **2** a piece of such fabric used for a particular purpose **3 the cloth** the clergy

cloth *n* **1** = fabric, material, textiles

clothe *vb* **clothing, clothed** or **clad 1** to put clothes on **2** to provide with clothes **3** to cover or envelop (something) so as to change its appearance: *a small valley clothed in thick woodland*

clothe *vb* **1, 2** = dress, array, robe, drape, swathe, attire, fit out, garb; ≠ undress

clothes *pl n* articles of dress

clothes *pl n* = clothing, wear, dress, gear (*informal*), outfit, costume, wardrobe, garments

clothing *n* **1** garments collectively **2** something that covers or clothes

clothing *n* **1** = clothes, wear, dress, gear (*informal*), outfit, costume, wardrobe, garments

cloud *n* **1** a mass of water or ice particles visible in the sky **2** a floating mass of smoke, dust, etc. **3** a large number of insects or other small animals in flight **4** something that darkens, threatens, or carries gloom **5 in the clouds** not in contact with reality **6 on cloud nine** *informal* elated; very happy **7 the cloud** a network of remote computers that can be accessed via the internet on a temporary basis **8 under a cloud A** under reproach or suspicion **B** in a state of gloom or bad temper ▸ *vb* **9** to make or become more difficult to see through: *my glasses kept clouding up; mud clouded the water* **10** to confuse or impair: *her judgment was no longer clouded by alcohol* **11** to make or become gloomy or depressed: *bereavement clouded the last years of his life* > **cloudless** *adj*

cloud *n* **1** = mist, haze, vapour, murk, gloom ▸ *vb* **9** = darken, dim, be overshadowed **10** = confuse, distort, impair, muddle, disorient

cloudburst *n* a heavy fall of rain

cloud computing *n* a system in which services stored on the internet are accessible to users on a temporary basis

cloudy *adj* **cloudier, cloudiest 1** covered with cloud or clouds **2** (of liquids) opaque or muddy **3** confused or unclear > **cloudily** *adv* > **cloudiness** *n*

clout *n* **1** *informal* a fairly hard blow **2** power or influence ▸ *vb* **3** *informal* to hit hard

clout *n* **1** = thump, blow, punch, slap, sock (*slang*), wallop (*informal*) **2** = influence, power, authority, pull (*informal*), weight, prestige, mana (*NZ*) ▸ *vb* = hit, strike, punch, slap, sock (*slang*), smack, thump, clobber (*slang*)

clove[1] *n* a dried closed flower bud of a tropical tree, used as a spice

clove[2] *n* a segment of a bulb of garlic

clove[3] *vb* a past tense of **cleave**[1]

clove hitch *n* a knot used to fasten a rope to a spar or a larger rope

cloven *vb* **1** a past participle of **cleave**[1] ▸ *adj* **2** split or divided

cloven hoof or **cloven foot** *n* the divided hoof of a pig, goat, cow, or deer

clover *n* **1** a plant with three-lobed leaves and dense flower heads **2 in clover** *informal* in ease or luxury

clown n 1 a comic entertainer, usually bizarrely dressed and made up, appearing in the circus 2 an amusing person 3 a clumsy rude person ▸ vb 4 to behave foolishly 5 to perform as a clown › **clownish** adj

> **clown** n 1 = comedian, fool, harlequin, jester, buffoon 2 = joker, comic, prankster ▸ vb 4 = play the fool, mess about, jest, act the fool

club n 1 a group or association of people with common aims or interests 2 the building used by such a group 3 a stout stick used as a weapon 4 a stick or bat used to strike the ball in various sports, esp. golf 5 an establishment where people go to drink and dance, esp. late in the evening 6 a building in which members go to meet, dine, read, etc. 7 chiefly Brit an organization, esp. in a shop, set up as a means of saving 8 a playing card marked with one or more black trefoil symbols ▸ vb **clubbing, clubbed** 9 to beat with a club 10 **club together** to combine resources or efforts for a common purpose

> **club** n 1 = association, company, group, union, society, lodge, guild, fraternity (US, Canad) 3 = stick, bat, bludgeon, truncheon (Brit), cosh (Brit), cudgel ▸ vb 9 = beat, strike, hammer (informal), batter, bash, bludgeon, pummel, cosh (Brit)

cluck n 1 the low clicking noise made by a hen ▸ vb 2 (of a hen) to make a clicking sound 3 to express (a feeling) by making a similar sound: the landlady was clucking feverishly behind them

clue n 1 something that helps to solve a problem or unravel a mystery 2 **not have a clue** A to be completely baffled B to be ignorant or incompetent

> **clue** n 1 = indication, lead, sign, evidence, suggestion, trace, hint, suspicion

clueless adj slang helpless or stupid

clump n 1 a small group of things or people together 2 a dull heavy tread ▸ vb 3 to walk or tread heavily 4 to form into clumps › **clumpy** adj

> **clump** n 1 = cluster, group, bunch, bundle ▸ vb 3 = stomp, thump, lumber, tramp, plod, thud

clumsy adj **-sier, -siest** 1 lacking in skill or physical coordination: an extraordinarily clumsy player 2 badly made or done 3 said or done without thought or tact: I took the clumsy hint and left › **clumsily** adv › **clumsiness** n

> **clumsy** adj 1 = awkward, lumbering, bumbling, ponderous, ungainly, gauche, gawky, uncoordinated, unco (Austral slang); ≠ skilful

clung vb the past of **cling**

clunk n 1 a dull metallic sound ▸ vb 2 to make such a sound

cluster n 1 a number of things growing, fastened, or occurring close together 2 a number of people or things grouped together ▸ vb 3 to gather or be gathered in clusters

> **cluster** n = gathering, group, collection, bunch (informal), knot, clump, assemblage, aggregate ▸ vb = gather, group, collect, bunch, assemble, flock, huddle

clutch¹ vb 1 to seize with or as if with hands or claws 2 to grasp or hold firmly 3 **clutch at** to attempt to get hold or possession of ▸ n 4 a device that enables two revolving shafts to be joined or disconnected, esp. one that transmits the drive from the engine to the gearbox in a vehicle 5 the pedal that operates the clutch in a car 6 a firm grasp 7 **clutches** A hands or claws in the act of clutching: a photo of a red salmon escaping the clutches of a bear cub B power or control: rescued from the clutches of the Gestapo

> **clutch** vb 1 = seize, catch, grab, grasp, snatch 2 = hold, grip, embrace, grasp, cling to, clasp ▸ n 7 = power, hands, control, grip, possession, grasp, custody, sway

clutch² n 1 a set of eggs laid at the same time 2 a group, bunch, or cluster: a clutch of gloomy economic reports

clutter vb 1 to scatter objects about (a place) in an untidy manner ▸ n 2 an untidy heap or mass of objects 3 a state of untidiness

> **clutter** vb = litter, scatter, strew, mess up; ≠ tidy ▸ n 3 = untidiness, mess, disorder, confusion, litter, muddle, disarray, jumble; ≠ order

cm centimetre

CO 1 Colorado 2 Commanding Officer

Co. or **co.** 1 Company 2 **and co.** informal and the rest of them: Harold and co.

co- prefix 1 together; joint or jointly: coproduction 2 indicating partnership or equality: co-star; copilot 3 to the same or a similar degree: coextend 4 (in mathematics and astronomy) of the complement of an angle: cosecant

c/o 1 care of 2 accounting carried over

coach n 1 a large comfortable single-decker bus used for sightseeing or long-distance travel 2 a railway carriage 3 a large four-wheeled enclosed carriage, usually horse-drawn 4 a trainer or instructor: the coach of the Mexican national team 5 a tutor who prepares students for examinations ▸ vb 6 to train or teach › **coaching** n

> **coach** n 1, 3 = bus, charabanc 4, 5 = instructor, teacher, trainer, tutor, handler ▸ vb = instruct, train, prepare, exercise, drill, tutor

coagulate (koh-ag-yew-late) vb **-lating, -lated** to change from a liquid into a soft semisolid mass; clot › **coagulant** n › **coagulation** n

coal *n* **1** a compact black or dark brown rock consisting largely of carbon formed from partially decomposed vegetation: a fuel and a source of coke, coal gas, and coal tar **2** one or more lumps of coal **3 coals to Newcastle** something supplied to a place where it is already plentiful

coalesce (koh-a-less) *vb* **-lescing, -lesced** to unite or come together in one body or mass > **coalescence** *n* > **coalescent** *adj*

coalfield *n* an area rich in deposits of coal

coalition (koh-a-lish-un) *n* a temporary alliance, esp. between political parties

> **coalition** *n* = alliance, union, association, combination, merger, conjunction, bloc, confederation

coarse *adj* **1** rough in texture or structure **2** unrefined or indecent: *coarse humour* **3** of inferior quality > **coarsely** *adv* > **coarseness** *n*

> **coarse** *adj* **1** = rough, crude, unfinished, homespun, impure, unrefined, unprocessed, unpolished; ≠ smooth **2** = vulgar, rude, indecent, improper, earthy, smutty, ribald, indelicate

coarse fish *n Brit* a freshwater fish that is not of the salmon family > **coarse fishing** *n*

coarsen *vb* to make or become coarse

coast *n* **1** the place where the land meets the sea **2 the coast is clear** *informal* the obstacles or dangers are gone ► *vb* **3** to move by momentum or force of gravity, without the use of power **4** to proceed without great effort: *they coasted to a 31–9 win in the pairs* > **coastal** *adj*

> **coast** *n* **1** = shore, border, beach, seaside, coastline, seaboard ► *vb* **3** = cruise, sail, drift, taxi, glide, freewheel

coaster *n* **1** a small mat placed under a bottle or glass to protect a table **2** *Brit* a small ship used for coastal trade

coastguard *n* **1** an organization which aids shipping, saves lives at sea, and prevents smuggling **2** a member of such an organization

coastline *n* the outline of a coast

coat *n* **1** an outer garment with sleeves, covering the body from the shoulders to below the waist **2** the hair, wool, or fur of an animal **3** any layer that covers a surface ► *vb* **4** to cover with a layer

> **coat** *n* **2** = fur, hair, skin, hide, wool, fleece, pelt **3** = layer, covering, coating, overlay ► *vb* = cover, spread, plaster, smear

coat hanger *n* a curved piece of wood, wire, or plastic, fitted with a hook and used to hang up clothes

coating *n* a layer or film spread over a surface: *a thick coating of breadcrumbs*

coat of arms *n* the heraldic emblem of a family or organization

coax *vb* **1** to persuade (someone) gently **2** to obtain (something) by gentle coaxing **3** to work on (something) carefully and patiently so as to make it function as desired: *I watched him coax the last few drops of beer out of his glass*

> **coax** *vb* **1** = persuade, cajole, talk into, wheedle, sweet-talk (*informal*), prevail upon, entice, allure; ≠ bully

coaxial (koh-ax-ee-al) *adj* **1** *electronics* (of a cable) transmitting by means of two concentric conductors separated by an insulator **2** having a common axis

cob *n* **1** a male swan **2** a thickset type of horse **3** the stalk of an ear of maize **4** *Brit & Austral* a round loaf of bread **5** *Brit* a hazel tree or hazelnut

cobalt *n chem* a brittle hard silvery-white metallic element used in alloys. Symbol: **Co**

cobber *n Austral & NZ informal* a friend

> **cobber** *n* = friend, pal (*informal*), mate (*informal*), buddy (*informal*), china (*Brit, S African informal*), best friend, intimate, comrade, E hoa (*NZ*)

cobble *n* a cobblestone

cobbler *n* a person who makes or mends shoes

cobblestone *n* a rounded stone used for paving

cobble together *vb* **-bling, -bled** to put together clumsily: *a coalition cobbled together from parties with widely differing aims*

cobia (koh-bee-a) *n* a large dark-striped game fish of tropical and subtropical seas

cobra *n* a highly venomous hooded snake of tropical Africa and Asia

cobweb *n* **1** a web spun by certain spiders **2** a single thread of such a web > **cobwebbed** *adj* > **cobwebby** *adj*

cocaine *n* an addictive drug derived from coca leaves, used as a narcotic and local anaesthetic

coccyx (kok-six) *n, pl* **coccyges** (kok-sije-eez) *anatomy* a small triangular bone at the base of the spine in human beings and some apes > **coccygeal** *adj*

cochineal *n* a scarlet dye obtained from a Mexican insect, used for colouring food

cock *n* **1** a male bird, esp. of domestic fowl **2** a stopcock **3** *vulgar slang* a penis **4** the hammer of a gun **5** *Brit informal* friend: used as a term of address ► *vb* **6** to draw back the hammer of (a gun) so that it is ready to fire **7** to lift and turn (part of the body) in a particular direction

cockade *n* a feather or rosette worn on the hat as a badge

cock-a-hoop *adj Brit, Austral & NZ* in very high spirits

cock-and-bull story *n informal* an obviously improbable story, esp. one used as an excuse

cockatiel *n* a crested Australian parrot with a greyish-brown and yellow plumage

cockatoo *n, pl* **-toos** a light-coloured crested parrot of Australia and E Asia

cockerel *n* a young domestic cock, less than a year old

cocker spaniel *n* a small spaniel

cockeyed *adj informal* **1** crooked or askew **2** foolish or absurd **3** cross-eyed

cockie *or* **cocky** *n, pl* **-kies** *Austral & NZ informal* a cockatoo

cockle *n* **1** an edible bivalve shellfish **2** its shell **3 warm the cockles of one's heart** to make one feel happy

cockney *n* **1** a native of London, esp. of its East End **2** the urban dialect of London or its East End ▸ *adj* **3** characteristic of cockneys or their dialect

cockpit *n* **1** the compartment in an aircraft for the pilot and crew **2** the driver's compartment in a racing car **3** *naut* a space in a small vessel containing the wheel and tiller **4** the site of many battles or conflicts: *the south of the country is a cockpit of conflicting interests* **5** an enclosure used for cockfights

cockroach *n* a beetle-like insect that is a household pest

cocksure *adj* overconfident or arrogant

cocktail *n* **1** a mixed alcoholic drink **2** an appetizer of seafood or mixed fruits **3** any combination of diverse elements: *Central America was a cocktail of death, poverty, and destruction*

> **cocktail** *n* **3** = mixture, combination, compound, blend, mix

cocky *adj* **cockier**, **cockiest** excessively proud of oneself > **cockily** *adv* > **cockiness** *n*

cocoa *or* **cacao** *n* **1** a powder made by roasting and grinding cocoa beans **2** a hot or cold drink made from cocoa powder

coconut *n* **1** the fruit of a type of palm tree (**coconut palm**), which has a thick fibrous oval husk and a thin hard shell enclosing edible white flesh. The hollow centre is filled with a milky fluid (**coconut milk**) **2** the flesh of the coconut

cocoon *n* **1** a silky protective covering produced by a silkworm or other insect larva, in which the pupa develops **2** a protective covering ▸ *vb* **3** to wrap in or protect as if in a cocoon

cod *n, pl* **cod** *or* **cods** a large food fish

COD cash (in the US, collect) on delivery

coda (**kode**-a) *n music* the final part of a musical movement or work

coddle *vb* **-dling, -dled 1** to pamper or overprotect **2** to cook (eggs) in water just below boiling point

code *n* **1** a system of letters, symbols, or prearranged signals, by which information can be communicated secretly or briefly **2** a set of principles or rules: *a code of practice* **3** a system of letters or digits used for identification purposes: *area code; tax code* ▸ *vb* **coding, coded 4** to translate or arrange into a code **5** to write computer programs

> **code** *n* **1** = cipher, cryptograph **2** = principles, rules, manners, custom, convention, ethics, maxim, etiquette, kawa (NZ), tikanga (NZ)

codeine (**kode**-een) *n* a drug made mainly from morphine, used as a painkiller and sedative

codex (**koh**-dex) *n, pl* **-dices** (-diss-seez) a volume of manuscripts of an ancient text

codger *n Brit, Austral & NZ informal* an old man

codicil (**cod**-iss-ill) *n law* an addition to a will

codify (**kode**-if-fie) *vb* **-fies, -fying, -fied** to organize or collect together (rules or procedures) systematically > **codification** *n*

coeducation *n* the education of boys and girls together > **coeducational** *adj*

coefficient *n* **1** *maths* a number or constant placed before and multiplying another quantity: *the coefficient of the term 3xyz is 3* **2** *physics* a number or constant used to calculate the behaviour of a given substance under specified conditions

coelacanth (**seel**-a-kanth) *n* a primitive marine fish, thought to be extinct until a living specimen was discovered in 1938

coeliac disease (**seel**-ee-ak) *n* a disease which makes the digestion of food difficult

coerce (koh-**urss**) *vb* **-ercing, -erced** to compel or force > **coercion** *n*

coercive *adj* using force or authority to make a person do something against his or her will

coeval (koh-**eev**-al) *adj* **1** contemporary ▸ *n* **2** a contemporary > **coevally** *adv*

coexist *vb* **1** to exist together at the same time or in the same place **2** to exist together in peace despite differences > **coexistence** *n* > **coexistent** *adj*

C of E Church of England

coffee *n* **1** a drink made from the roasted and ground seeds of a tall tropical shrub **2** Also called: **coffee beans** the beanlike seeds of this shrub **3** the shrub yielding these seeds ▸ *adj* **4** medium-brown

coffee bar *n* a café; snack bar

coffee table *n* a small low table

coffer *n* **1** a chest for storing valuables **2 coffers** a store of money **3** an ornamental sunken panel in a ceiling or dome

coffin *n* a box in which a corpse is buried or cremated

cog *n* **1** one of the teeth on the rim of a gearwheel **2** a gearwheel, esp. a small one **3** an unimportant person in a large organization or process

cogent (**koh**-jent) *adj* forcefully convincing > **cogency** *n*

cogitate (**koj**-it-tate) *vb* **-tating, -tated** to think deeply about (something) > **cogitation** *n* > **cogitative** *adj*

cognac (**kon**-yak) *n* high-quality French brandy

cognate *adj* **1** derived from a common original form: *cognate languages* **2** related to or descended from a common ancestor ▸ *n* **3** a cognate word or language **4** a relative > **cognation** *n*

cognition *n formal* 1 the processes of getting knowledge, including perception, intuition, and reasoning 2 the results of such a process > **cognitive** *adj*

cognizance *or* **cognisance** *n formal* 1 knowledge or understanding 2 **take cognizance of** to take notice of 3 the range or scope of knowledge or understanding > **cognizant** *or* **cognisant** *adj*

cognoscenti (kon-yo-shen-tee) *pl n, sing* **-te** (-tee) connoisseurs

cohabit *vb* to live together as a couple without being married > **cohabitation** *n*

cohere *vb* **-hering, -hered** 1 to hold or stick firmly together 2 to be logically connected or consistent

coherent *adj* 1 logical and consistent 2 capable of intelligible speech 3 cohering or sticking together 4 *physics* (of two or more waves) having the same frequency and a constant fixed phase difference > **coherence** *n*

> **coherent** *adj* 1 = consistent, reasoned, organized, rational, logical, meaningful, systematic, orderly; ≠ inconsistent 2 = articulate, lucid, comprehensible, intelligible; ≠ unintelligible

cohesion *n* 1 sticking together 2 *physics* the force that holds together the atoms or molecules in a solid or liquid > **cohesive** *adj*

cohort *n* 1 a band of associates 2 a tenth part of an ancient Roman Legion

coiffeur (kwah-fur) *or fem* **coiffeuse** (kwah-furz) *n* a hairdresser

coiffure (kwah-fyoor) *n* a hairstyle

coil *vb* 1 to wind or be wound into loops 2 to move in a winding course ▸ *n* 3 something wound in a connected series of loops 4 a single loop of such a series 5 a contraceptive device in the shape of a coil, inserted in the womb 6 an electrical conductor wound into a spiral, to provide inductance

> **coil** *vb* 1 = wind, twist, curl, loop, spiral, twine 2 = curl, wind, twist, snake, loop, twine, wreathe

coin *n* 1 a metal disc used as money 2 metal currency collectively ▸ *vb* 3 to invent (a new word or phrase) 4 to make or stamp (coins) 5 **coin it in** *or* **coin money** *informal* to make money rapidly

> **coin** *n* 2 = money, change, cash, silver, copper, specie, kembla (*Austral slang*) ▸ *vb* 3 = invent, create, make up, forge, originate, fabricate

coinage *n* 1 coins collectively 2 the currency of a country 3 a newly invented word or phrase 4 the act of coining

coincide *vb* **-ciding, -cided** 1 to happen at the same time 2 to agree or correspond exactly: *what she had said coincided exactly with his own thinking* 3 to occupy the same place in space

> **coincide** *vb* 1 = occur simultaneously, coexist, synchronize, be concurrent 2 = agree, match, accord, square, correspond, tally, concur, harmonize; ≠ disagree

coincidence *n* 1 a chance occurrence of simultaneous or apparently connected events 2 a coinciding

> **coincidence** *n* 1 = chance, accident, luck, fluke, stroke of luck, happy accident

coincident *adj* 1 having the same position in space or time 2 **coincident with** in exact agreement with

coincidental *adj* resulting from coincidence; not intentional > **coincidentally** *adv*

coir *n* coconut fibre, used in making rope and matting

coitus (koh-it-uss) *or* **coition** (koh-ish-un) *n* sexual intercourse > **coital** *adj*

coke¹ *n* 1 a solid fuel left after gas has been distilled from coal ▸ *vb* **coking, coked** 2 to become or convert into coke

coke² *n slang* cocaine

col *n* the lowest point of a ridge connecting two mountain peaks

cola *n* 1 a soft drink flavoured with an extract from the nuts of a tropical tree 2 the W African tree whose nuts contain this extract

colander *n* a bowl with a perforated bottom for straining or rinsing foods

cold *adj* 1 low in temperature: *the cold March wind; cans of cold beer* 2 not hot enough: *eat your food before it gets cold!* 3 lacking in affection or enthusiasm 4 not affected by emotion: *the cold truth* 5 dead 6 (of a trail or scent in hunting) faint 7 (of a colour) giving the impression of coldness 8 *slang* unconscious 9 *informal* (of a seeker) far from the object of a search 10 denoting the contacting of potential customers without previously approaching them to establish their interest: *cold mailing* 11 **cold comfort** little or no comfort 12 **have** *or* **get cold feet** to be or become fearful or reluctant 13 **in cold blood** deliberately and without mercy 14 **leave someone cold** *informal* to fail to excite or impress someone 15 **throw cold water on** *informal* to discourage ▸ *n* 16 the absence of heat 17 a viral infection of the nose and throat characterized by catarrh and sneezing 18 the sensation caused by loss or lack of heat 19 **(out) in the cold** *informal* neglected or ignored ▸ *adv* 20 *informal* unrehearsed or unprepared: *he played his part cold* > **coldly** *adv* > **coldness** *n*

> **cold** *adj* 1 = chilly, freezing, bleak, arctic (*informal*), icy, frosty, wintry, frigid; ≠ hot 3 = distant, reserved, indifferent, aloof, frigid, undemonstrative, standoffish; ≠ emotional ▸ *n* 16 = coldness, chill, frigidity, frostiness, iciness

cold-blooded *adj* 1 callous or cruel 2 *zool* (of all animals except birds and mammals) having a body temperature that varies according to the temperature of the surroundings

cold cream n a creamy preparation used for softening and cleansing the skin

cold war n a state of political hostility between two countries without actual warfare

coleslaw n a salad dish of shredded raw cabbage in a dressing

coley n Brit an edible fish with white or grey flesh

colic n severe pains in the stomach and bowels > **colicky** adj

colitis (koh-**lie**-tiss) n inflammation of the colon, usually causing diarrhoea and lower abdominal pain

collaborate vb -rating, -rated 1 to work with another or others on a joint project 2 to cooperate with an enemy invader > **collaboration** n > **collaborative** adj > **collaborator** n

> **collaborate** vb 1 = work together, team up, join forces, cooperate, play ball (informal), participate 2 = conspire, cooperate, collude, fraternize

collage (kol-**lahzh**) n 1 an art form in which various materials or objects are glued onto a surface to make a picture 2 a picture made in this way 3 a work, such as a piece of music, created by combining unrelated styles > **collagist** n

collapse vb -lapsing, -lapsed 1 to fall down or cave in suddenly 2 to fail completely: a package holiday company which collapsed last year 3 to fall down from lack of strength, exhaustion, or illness: he collapsed with an asthma attack 4 to sit down and rest because of tiredness or lack of energy: she collapsed in front of the telly when she got home 5 to fold compactly, esp. for storage ▸ n 6 the act of falling down or falling to pieces 7 a sudden failure or breakdown

> **collapse** vb 1 = fall down, fall, give way, subside, cave in, crumple, fall apart at the seams 2 = fail, fold, founder, break down, fall through, come to nothing, go belly-up (informal) ▸ n 6 = falling down, ruin, falling apart, cave-in, disintegration, subsidence 7 = failure, slump, breakdown, flop (informal), downfall

collapsible adj able to be folded up for storage

collar n 1 the part of a garment round the neck 2 a band of leather, rope, or metal placed around an animal's neck 3 biol a ringlike marking around the neck of a bird or animal 4 a cut of meat, esp. bacon, from the neck of an animal 5 a ring or band around a pipe, rod, or shaft ▸ vb Brit, Austral & NZ informal 6 to seize; arrest 7 to catch in order to speak to 8 to take for oneself

> **collar** vb 6 = seize, catch, arrest, grab, capture, nail (informal), nab (informal), apprehend

collarbone n same as **clavicle**

collate vb -lating, -lated 1 to examine and compare carefully 2 to gather together and put in order > **collator** n

collateral n 1 security pledged for the repayment of a loan 2 a person, animal, or plant descended from the same ancestor as another but through a different line ▸ adj 3 descended from a common ancestor but through different lines 4 additional but subordinate: a spokeswoman said that there was no collateral information to dispute the assurances the government had been given 5 situated or running side by side: collateral ridges of mountains

collation n 1 the act or result of collating 2 formal a light meal

colleague n a fellow worker, esp. in a profession

> **colleague** n = fellow worker, partner, ally, associate, assistant, team-mate, comrade, helper, co-worker

collect[1] vb 1 to gather together or be gathered together 2 to gather (objects, such as stamps) as a hobby or for study 3 to go to a place to fetch (a person or thing) 4 to receive payments of (taxes, dues, or contributions) 5 to regain control of (oneself or one's emotions)

> **collect** vb 1, 2 = gather, save, assemble, heap, accumulate, amass, stockpile, hoard; ≠ scatter

collect[2] n Christianity a short prayer said during certain church services

collected adj 1 calm and self-controlled 2 brought together into one book or set of books: the collected works of Dickens

> **collected** adj = calm, cool, composed, poised, serene, unperturbed, unruffled, self-possessed, chilled (informal); ≠ nervous

collection n 1 things collected or accumulated 2 a group of people 3 the act or process of collecting 4 a selection of clothes usually presented by a particular designer 5 a sum of money collected, as in church 6 a regular removal of letters from a postbox

> **collection** n 1 = accumulation, set, store, mass, pile, heap, stockpile, hoard, aggregate 2 = group, company, crowd, assembly, cluster, assortment 3 = gathering 5 = contribution, donation, alms

collective adj 1 done by or characteristic of individuals acting as a group: the army's collective wisdom regarding peacekeeping ▸ n 2 a group of people working together on an enterprise and sharing the benefits from it > **collectively** adv

> **collective** adj = joint, united, shared, combined, corporate, unified; ≠ individual

collector n 1 a person who collects objects as a hobby 2 a person employed to collect debts, rents, or tickets

colleen *n Irish* a girl

college *n* **1** an institution of higher or further education that is not a university **2** a self-governing section of certain universities **3** *Brit & NZ* a name given to some secondary schools **4** an organized body of people with specific rights and duties: *the president is elected by an electoral college* **5** a body organized within a particular profession, concerned with regulating standards **6** the staff and students of a college

collegiate *adj* **1** of a college or college students **2** (of a university) composed of various colleges

collide *vb* **-liding, -lided 1** to crash together violently **2** to conflict or disagree

> **collide** *vb* **1** = crash, clash, meet head-on, come into collision **2** = conflict, clash, be incompatible, be at variance

collie *n* a silky-haired dog used for herding sheep and cattle

collier *n chiefly Brit* a coal miner **2** a ship designed to carry coal

colliery *n, pl* **-lieries** *chiefly Brit* a coal mine and its buildings

collision *n* **1** a violent crash between moving objects **2** the conflict of opposed ideas or wishes

> **collision** *n* **1** = crash, impact, accident, smash, bump, pile-up (*informal*), prang (*informal*) **2** = conflict, opposition, clash, encounter, disagreement, incompatibility

collocate *vb* **-cating, -cated** (of words) to occur together regularly > **collocation** *n*

colloid *n* a mixture of particles of one substance suspended in a different substance > **colloidal** *adj*

colloquial *adj* suitable for informal speech or writing > **colloquially** *adv*

colloquialism *n* **1** a colloquial word or phrase **2** the use of colloquial words and phrases

collude *vb* **-luding, -luded** to cooperate secretly or dishonestly with someone

collusion *n* secret or illegal agreement or cooperation > **collusive** *adj*

collywobbles *pl n slang* **1** an intense feeling of nervousness **2** an upset stomach

cologne *n* a perfumed toilet water

colon¹ *n, pl* **-lons** the punctuation mark (:) used before an explanation or an example, a list, or an extended quotation

colon² *n, pl* **-lons** *or* **-la** the part of the large intestine connected to the rectum > **colonic** *adj*

colonel *n* a senior commissioned officer in the army or air force > **colonelcy** *n*

colonial *adj* **1** of or inhabiting a colony or colonies **2** of a style of architecture popular in North America in the 17th and 18th centuries: *a colonial mansion* **3** of a style of architecture popular in Australia when it was a colony of Britain ▸ *n* **4** an inhabitant of a colony

colonialism *n* the practice of establishing colonies to extend a state's control over other peoples or territories > **colonialist** *n, adj*

colonist *n* a settler in or inhabitant of a colony

colonize *or* **-nise** *vb* **-nizing, -nized** *or* **-nising, -nised 1** to establish a colony in (an area) **2** to settle in (an area) as colonists > **colonization** *or* **-nisation** *n*

colonnade *n* a row of evenly spaced columns, usually supporting a roof > **colonnaded** *adj*

colony *n, pl* **-nies 1** a group of people who settle in a new country but remain under the rule of their homeland **2** the territory occupied by such a settlement **3** a group of people with the same nationality or interests, forming a community in a particular place: *an artists' colony* **4** *zool* a group of the same type of animal or plant living or growing together **5** *bacteriol* a group of microorganisms when grown on a culture medium

> **colony** *n* **2** = settlement, territory, province, possession, dependency, outpost, dominion, satellite state

color *n, vb US* same as **colour**

Colorado beetle *n* a black-and-yellow beetle that is a serious pest of potatoes

coloration *or* **colouration** *n* arrangement of colours: *a red coloration of the eyes*

colossal *adj* **1** very large in size: *the turbulent rivers and colossal mountains of New Zealand* **2** very serious or significant: *a colossal legal blunder*

colossus *n, pl* **-si** *or* **-suses 1** a very large statue **2** a huge or important person or thing

colostomy *n, pl* **-mies** an operation to form an opening from the colon onto the surface of the body, for emptying the bowel

colour *or US* **color** *n* **1** a property of things that results from the particular wavelengths of light which they reflect or give out, producing a sensation in the eye **2** a colour, such as a red or green, that possesses hue, as opposed to black, white, or grey **3** a substance, such as a dye, that gives colour **4** the skin complexion of a person **5** the use of all the colours in painting, drawing, or photography **6** the distinctive tone of a musical sound **7** details which give vividness or authenticity: *I walked the streets and absorbed the local colour* **8** semblance or pretext: *under colour of* **9** of colour *chiefly US* not of White or European heritage ▸ *vb* **10** to apply colour to (something) **11** to influence or distort: *anger coloured her judgment* **12** to become red in the face, esp. when embarrassed or annoyed **13** to give a convincing appearance to: *he coloured his account of what had happened*

> **colour** *or* **color** *n* **2** = hue, tone, shade, tint, colourway **3** = paint, stain, dye, tint, pigment, colorant ▸ *vb* **12** = blush, flush, redden

colour-blind *adj* **1** unable to distinguish between certain colours, esp. red and green **2** not discriminating on grounds of skin colour: *colour-blind policies* > **colour blindness** *n*

coloured *or US* **colored** *adj* **1** having a colour or colours other than black or white: *coloured glass bottles; a peach-coloured outfit with matching hat* **2** *old-fashioned, offensive* (of a person) not White

Coloured *or US* **Colored** *S African* ▸ *n* **1** a person of racially mixed parentage or descent ▸ *adj* **2** of mixed White and non-White parentage

colourful *or US* **colorful** *adj* **1** with bright or richly varied colours **2** vivid or distinctive in character

> **colourful** *or* **colorful** *adj* **1** = bright, brilliant, psychedelic, variegated, multicoloured; ≠ drab **2** = interesting, rich, graphic, lively, distinctive, vivid, picturesque; ≠ boring

colourless *or US* **colorless** *adj* **1** without colour: *a colourless gas* **2** dull and uninteresting: *a colourless personality* **3** grey or pallid in tone or hue: *a watery sun hung low in the colourless sky*

colt *n* **1** a young male horse or pony **2** *sport* a young and inexperienced player

columbine *n* a plant that has brightly coloured flowers with five spurred petals

column *n* **1** an upright pillar usually having a cylindrical shaft, a base, and a capital **2** a form or structure in the shape of a column: *a column of smoke* **3** a vertical division of a page of text, esp. in a newspaper or dictionary **4** a regular feature in a paper: *a cookery column* **5** a vertical arrangement of numbers **6** *military* a narrow formation in which individuals or units follow one behind the other › **columnar** *adj*

> **column** *n* **1** = pillar, support, post, shaft, upright, obelisk **6** = line, row, file, rank, procession, cavalcade

columnist *n* a journalist who writes a regular feature in a newspaper

coma *n* a state of unconsciousness from which a person cannot be aroused, caused by injury, disease, or drugs

> **coma** *n* = unconsciousness, trance, oblivion, stupor

comatose *adj* **1** in a coma **2** sound asleep

comb *n* **1** a toothed instrument for disentangling or arranging hair **2** a tool or machine that cleans and straightens wool or cotton **3** a fleshy serrated crest on the head of a domestic fowl **4** a honeycomb ▸ *vb* **5** to use a comb on **6** to search with great care: *police combed the streets for the missing girl*

> **comb** *vb* **5** = untangle, arrange, groom, dress **6** = search, hunt through, rake, sift, scour, rummage, ransack, forage, fossick (*Austral, NZ*)

combat *n* **1** a fight or struggle ▸ *vb* **-bating, -bated** **2** to fight: *a coordinated approach to combating the growing drugs problem* › **combative** *adj*

combat *n* = fight, war, action, battle, conflict, engagement, warfare, skirmish; ≠ peace ▸ *vb* = fight, oppose, resist, defy, withstand, do battle with; ≠ support

combatant *n* **1** a person taking part in a combat ▸ *adj* **2** engaged in or ready for combat

combat trousers *or* **combats** *pl n* loose casual trousers with large pockets on the sides of the legs

combination *n* **1** the act of combining or state of being combined **2** people or things combined **3** the set of numbers or letters that opens a combination lock **4** a motorcycle with a sidecar **5** *maths* an arrangement of the members of a set into specified groups without regard to order in the group

> **combination** *n* **1** = association, union, alliance, coalition, federation, consortium, syndicate, confederation **2** = mixture, mix, blend, composite, amalgamation, coalescence

combine *vb* **-bining, -bined** **1** to join together **2** to form a chemical compound ▸ *n* **3** an association of people or firms for a common purpose **4** short for **combine harvester**

> **combine** *vb* **1** = join together, link, connect, integrate, merge, amalgamate; ≠ split up **2** = amalgamate, mix, blend, integrate, merge; ≠ separate

combine harvester *n* a machine used to reap and thresh grain in one process

combustible *adj* capable of igniting and burning easily

combustion *n* **1** the process of burning **2** a chemical reaction in which a substance combines with oxygen to produce heat and light

come *vb* **coming, came, come** **1** to move towards a place considered near to the speaker or hearer: *come and see me as soon as you can* **2** to arrive or reach: *turn left and continue until you come to a cattle-grid; he came to Britain in the 1920s* **3** to occur: *Christmas comes but once a year* **4** to happen as a result: *no good will come of this* **5** to occur to the mind: *the truth suddenly came to me* **6** to reach a specified point, state, or situation: *a dull brown dress that came down to my ankles; he'd come to a decision* **7** to be produced: *it also comes in other colours* **8 come from** to be or have been a resident or native (of): *my mother comes from Greenock* **9** to become: *it was like a dream come true* **10** *slang* to have an orgasm **11** *Brit & NZ informal* to play the part of: *don't come the innocent with me* **12** (*subjunctive use*) when a specified time arrives: *come next August* **13 as ... as they come** the most characteristic example of a type: *he's an arrogant swine and as devious as they come* **14 come again?** *informal* what did you say? **15 come to light** to be revealed ▸ *interj* **16** an exclamation expressing annoyance or impatience: *come now!* ▸ See also **come across** *etc.*

come *vb* 1 = approach, near, advance, move towards, draw near 2, 6 = reach, extend 3, 4 = happen, fall, occur, take place, come about, come to pass 7 = be available, be made, be offered, be produced, be on offer

come across *vb* 1 to meet or find by accident 2 to communicate the intended meaning or impression 3 **come across to** to give a certain impression

come across *vb* 1 **come across someone** = meet, encounter, run into, bump into (*informal*) 3 **come across as something or someone** = seem, look, seem to be, appear to be, give the impression of being

comeback *n informal* 1 a return to a former position or status 2 a response or retaliation ▸ *vb* **come back** 3 to return, esp. to the memory 4 to become fashionable again

comeback *n* 1 = return, revival, rebound, resurgence, rally, recovery, triumph 2 = response, reply, retort, retaliation, riposte, rejoinder

comedian *or fem* **comedienne** *n* 1 an entertainer who tells jokes 2 a person who performs in comedy

comedian *or* **comedienne** *n* = comic, wit, clown, funny man *or* woman, humorist, wag, joker, jester, dag (*NZ informal*)

comedown *n* 1 a decline in status or prosperity 2 *informal* a disappointment ▸ *vb* **come down** 3 (of prices) to become lower 4 to reach a decision: *a 1989 court ruling came down in favour of three councils who wanted Sunday trading banned* 5 to be handed down by tradition or inheritance 6 **come down in the world** to lose status or prosperity 7 **come down on** to reprimand sharply 8 **come down to** to amount to: *at the end the case came down to the one simple issue* 9 **come down with** to begin to suffer from (illness)

comedy *n, pl* **-dies** 1 a humorous film, play, or broadcast 2 such works as a genre 3 the humorous aspect of life or of events 4 (in classical literature) a play that ends happily

comedy *n* 2 = humour, fun, joking, farce, jesting, hilarity; ≠ seriousness

comely *adj* **-lier, -liest** *old-fashioned* good-looking > **comeliness** *n*

comestibles *pl n* food

comet *n* a heavenly body that travels round the sun, leaving a long bright trail behind it

comeuppance *n informal* deserved punishment

comfit *n* a sugar-coated sweet

comfort *n* 1 a state of physical ease or well-being 2 relief from suffering or grief 3 a person or thing that brings ease 4 **comforts** things that make life easier or more pleasant: *the comforts of home* ▸ *vb* 5 to soothe or console

6 to bring physical ease to > **comforting** *adj*

comfort *n* 1 = ease, luxury, wellbeing, opulence 2 = consolation, succour, help, support, relief, compensation; ≠ annoyance ▸ *vb* 5 = console, reassure, soothe, hearten, commiserate with; ≠ distress

comfortable *adj* 1 giving comfort; relaxing 2 free from trouble or pain 3 *informal* well-off financially 4 not afraid or embarrassed: *he was not comfortable expressing sympathy* > **comfortably** *adv*

comfortable *adj* 1 = pleasant, homely, relaxing, cosy, agreeable, restful; ≠ unpleasant 2 = at ease, happy, at home, contented, relaxed, serene; ≠ uncomfortable 3 = well-off, prosperous, affluent, well-to-do, comfortably-off, in clover (*informal*)

comforter *n* 1 a person or thing that comforts 2 a baby's dummy 3 *Brit* a woollen scarf

comfrey *n* a tall plant with bell-shaped blue, purple, or white flowers

comfy *adj* **-fier, -fiest** *informal* comfortable

comic *adj* 1 humorous; funny 2 of or relating to comedy ▸ *n* 3 a comedian 4 a magazine containing comic strips

comic *adj* 1 = funny, amusing, witty, humorous, farcical, comical, droll, jocular; ≠ sad ▸ *n* 3 = comedian, funny man *or* woman, humorist, wit, clown, wag, jester, dag (*NZ informal*), buffoon

comical *adj* causing amusement, often because of being ludicrous or ridiculous: *an enthusiasm comical to behold* > **comically** *adv*

comma *n* the punctuation mark (,) indicating a slight pause and used when there is a list of items or to separate the parts of a sentence

command *vb* 1 to order or compel 2 to have authority over 3 to deserve and get: *a public figure who commands almost universal respect* 4 to look down over: *the house commands a magnificent view of the sea and the islands* ▸ *n* 5 an authoritative instruction that something must be done 6 the authority to command 7 knowledge; control: *a fluent command of French* 8 a military or naval unit with a specific function 9 *computers* a part of a program consisting of a coded instruction to the computer to perform a specified function

command *vb* 1 = order, tell, charge (*formal*), demand, require, direct, bid, compel; ≠ beg 2 = have authority over, lead, head, control, rule, manage, handle, dominate; ≠ be subordinate to ▸ *n* 5 = order, demand, instruction, dictate, requirement, decree, directive, ultimatum, commandment 6 = management, power, control, charge, authority, supervision 7 = domination, control, rule, mastery, power, government

commandant *n* an officer in charge of a place or group of people

commandeer *vb* **1** to seize for military use **2** to take as if by right: *he commandeered the one waiting taxi outside the station*

commander *n* **1** an officer in command of a military group or operation **2** a middle-ranking naval officer **3** a high-ranking member of some orders of knights

> **commander** *n* = leader, chief, officer, boss, head, captain, ruler, sherang (*Austral, NZ*)

commander-in-chief *n*, *pl* **commanders-in-chief** the supreme commander of a nation's armed forces

commandment *n* a divine command, esp. one of the Ten Commandments in the Old Testament

commando *n*, *pl* **-dos** *or* **-does** **A** a military unit trained to make swift raids in enemy territory **B** a member of such a unit

commemorate *vb* **-rating, -rated** to honour or keep alive the memory of: *a series of events to commemorate the end of the Second World War* > **commemoration** *n* > **commemorative** *adj*

> **commemorate** *vb* = celebrate, remember, honour, recognize, salute, pay tribute to, immortalize; ≠ ignore

commence *vb* **-mencing, -menced** to begin

> **commence** *vb* = embark on, start, open, begin, initiate, originate, instigate, enter upon; ≠ stop

commencement *n* **1** the beginning; start **2** *US & Canad* a graduation ceremony

commend *vb* **1** to praise in a formal manner: *the judge commended her bravery* **2** to recommend: *he commended the scheme warmly* **3** to entrust: *I commend my child to your care* > **commendable** *adj* > **commendation** *n*

> **commend** *vb* **1** = praise, acclaim, applaud, compliment, extol, approve, speak highly of; ≠ criticize **2** = recommend, suggest, approve, advocate, endorse

commensurable *adj* **1** measurable by the same standards **2** *maths* **A** having a common factor **B** having units of the same dimensions and being related by whole numbers > **commensurability** *n*

commensurate *adj* **1** corresponding in degree, size, or value **2** commensurable

comment *n* **1** a remark, criticism, or observation **2** a situation or event that expresses some feeling: *a sad comment on the nature of many relationships* **3** talk or gossip **4** a note explaining or criticizing a passage in a text **5 no comment** I decline to say anything about the matter ▸ *vb* **6** to remark or express an opinion

> **comment** *n* **1** = remark, statement, observation **4** = note, explanation, illustration, commentary, exposition, annotation, elucidation ▸ *vb* = remark, say, note, mention, point out, observe, utter

commentary *n*, *pl* **-taries** **1** a spoken accompaniment to an event, broadcast, or film **2** a series of explanatory notes on a subject

> **commentary** *n* = narration, report, review, explanation, description, voice-over

commentate *vb* **-tating, -tated** to act as a commentator

commentator *n* **1** a person who provides a spoken commentary for a broadcast, esp. of a sporting event **2** an expert who reports on and analyses a particular subject

> **commentator** *n* **1** = reporter, special correspondent, sportscaster **2** = critic, interpreter, annotator

commerce *n* **1** the buying and selling of goods and services **2** *literary* social relations

commercial *adj* **1** of or engaged in commerce: *commercial exploitation of sport* **2** sponsored or paid for by an advertiser: *commercial radio* **3** having profit as the main aim: *this is a more commercial, accessible album than its predecessor* ▸ *n* **4** a radio or television advertisement

> **commercial** *adj* **1** = mercantile, trading **3** = materialistic, mercenary, profit-making

commercialize *or* **-ise** *vb* **-izing, -ized** *or* **-ising, -ised** **1** to make commercial **2** to exploit for profit, esp. at the expense of quality > **commercialization** *or* **-isation** *n*

commiserate *vb* **-ating, -ated** (usually foll. by *with*) to express sympathy or pity (for) > **commiseration** *n*

commissar *n* (formerly) an official responsible for political education in Communist countries

commissariat *n* a military department in charge of food supplies

commission *n* **1** an order for a piece of work, esp. a work of art or a piece of writing **2** a duty given to a person or group to perform **3** the fee or percentage paid to a salesperson for each sale made **4** a group of people appointed to perform certain duties: *a new parliamentary commission on defence* **5** the act of committing a sin or crime **6** *military* the rank or authority officially given to an officer **7** authority to perform certain duties **8 in** *or* **out of commission** in *or* not in working order ▸ *vb* **9** to place an order for: *a report commissioned by the United Nations*; *a new work commissioned by the BBC Symphony Orchestra* **10** *military* to give a commission to **11** to prepare (a ship) for active service **12** to grant authority to

> **commission** *n* **2** = duty, task, mission, mandate, errand **3** = fee, cut (*informal*), percentage, royalties, rake-off (*slang*) **4** = committee, board, representatives, commissioners, delegation, deputation ▸ *vb* **9** = appoint, order, contract, select, engage, delegate, nominate, authorize

commissionaire *n chiefly Brit* a uniformed doorman at a hotel, theatre, or cinema

commissioner *n* **1** an appointed official in a government department or other organization **2** a member of a commission

commit *vb* **-mitting, -mitted 1** to perform (a crime or error) **2** to hand over or allocate: *a marked reluctance to commit new money to business* **3** to pledge to a cause or a course of action **4** to send (someone) to prison or hospital **5 commit to memory** to memorize **6 commit to paper** to write down

> **commit** *vb* **1** = do, perform, carry out, execute, enact, perpetrate

commitment *n* **1** dedication to a cause or principle **2** an obligation, responsibility, or promise that restricts freedom of action **3** the act of committing or state of being committed

> **commitment** *n* **1** = dedication, loyalty, devotion **2** = responsibility, tie, duty, obligation, liability, engagement

committal *n* the official consignment of a person to a prison or psychiatric hospital

committee *n* a group of people appointed to perform a specified service or function

commode *n* **1** a chair with a hinged flap concealing a chamber pot **2** a chest of drawers

commodious *adj* with plenty of space

commodity *n, pl* **-ties** something that can be bought or sold

commodore *n* **1** *Brit* a senior commissioned officer in the navy **2** the president of a yacht club

common *adj* **1** frequently encountered: *a fairly common plant; this disease is most common in kittens and young cats* **2** widespread among people in general: *common practice* **3** belonging to two or more people: *we share common interests* **4** belonging to the whole community: *common property* **5** low-class, vulgar, or coarse **6** *maths* belonging to two or more: *the lowest common denominator* **7** not belonging to the upper classes: *the common people* **8 common or garden** *informal* ordinary ▸ *n* **9** a piece of open land belonging to all the members of a community **10 in common** shared, in joint use > **commonly** *adv*

> **common** *adj* **1** = usual, standard, regular, ordinary, familiar, conventional, routine, frequent; ≠ rare **2** = popular, general, accepted, standard, routine, widespread, universal, prevailing **3** = shared, collective **4** = collective, public, community, social, communal; ≠ personal **5** = vulgar, inferior, coarse, plebeian; ≠ refined **7** = ordinary, average, typical, dinki-di (*Austral informal*); ≠ important

commoner *n* a person who does not belong to the nobility

Common Market *n* a former name for **European Union**

commonplace *adj* **1** so common or frequent as not to be worth commenting on: *foreign holidays have now become commonplace* **2** dull or unoriginal: *a commonplace observation* ▸ *n* **3** a cliché **4** an ordinary thing

> **commonplace** *adj* = everyday, common, ordinary, widespread, mundane, banal, run-of-the-mill, humdrum; ≠ rare ▸ *n* **3** = cliché, platitude, banality, truism

common sense *n* **1** good practical understanding ▸ *adj* **common-sense 2** inspired by or displaying this

> **common sense** *n* = good sense, sound judgment, level-headedness, prudence, gumption (*Brit informal*), horse sense, native intelligence, wit

commonwealth *n* the people of a state or nation viewed politically

Commonwealth *n* **the Commonwealth A** Official name: **the Commonwealth of Nations** an association of sovereign states that are or at some time have been ruled by Britain **B** the official title of the federated states of Australia

commotion *n* noisy disturbance

communal *adj* **1** belonging to or used by a community as a whole **2** of a commune > **communally** *adv*

> **communal** *adj* **1** = public, shared, general, joint, collective; ≠ private

commune[1] *n* **1** a group of people living together and sharing possessions and responsibilities **2** the smallest district of local government in Belgium, France, Italy, and Switzerland

> **commune** *n* **1** = community, collective, cooperative, kibbutz

commune[2] *vb* **-muning, -muned** > **commune with A** to experience strong emotion for: *communing with nature* **B** to talk intimately with

communicable *adj* **1** capable of being communicated **2** (of a disease) capable of being passed on easily

communicant *n Christianity* a person who receives Communion

communicate *vb* **-cating, -cated 1** to exchange (thoughts) or make known (information or feelings) by speech, writing, or other means **2** (usually foll. by *to*) to transmit (to): *the reaction of the rapturous audience communicated itself to the performers* **3** to have a sympathetic mutual understanding **4** *Christianity* to receive Communion > **communicator** *n* > **communicative** *adj*

> **communicate** *vb* **1** = contact, talk, speak, make contact, get in contact, email *or* e-mail, text, message; ≠ keep secret **2** = pass on, transfer, spread, transmit

C

communicating *adj* making or having a direct connection from one room to another: *the suite is made up of three communicating rooms; the communicating door*

communication *n* **1** the exchange of information, ideas, or feelings **2** something communicated, such as a message **3 communications** means of travelling or sending messages

> **communication** *n* **1** = contact, conversation, correspondence, link, relations **2** = message, news, report, word, information, statement, announcement, disclosure, email *or* e-mail, text

communion *n* **1** a sharing of thoughts, emotions, or beliefs **2 communion with** strong feelings for: *private communion with nature* **3** a religious group with shared beliefs and practices: *the Anglican communion*

Communion *n Christianity* **1** a ritual commemorating Christ's Last Supper by the consecration of bread and wine **2** the consecrated bread and wine. Also called: **Holy Communion**

communiqué (kom-mune-ik-kay) *n* an official announcement

communism *n* the belief that private ownership should be abolished and all work and property should be shared by the community > **communist** *n, adj*

> **communism** *n* = socialism, Marxism, collectivism, Bolshevism, state socialism

Communism *n* **1** a political movement based upon the writings of Karl Marx that advocates communism **2** the political and social system established in countries with a ruling Communist Party > **Communist** *n, adj*

community *n, pl* **-ties 1** all the people living in one district **2** a group of people with shared origins or interests: *the local Jewish community* **3** a group of countries with common interests in common **4** the public; society **5** a group of interdependent plants and animals inhabiting the same region

> **community** *n* **1, 4** = society, people, public, residents, commonwealth, general public, populace, state

community centre *n* a building used by a community for social gatherings or activities

commutator *n* a device used to change alternating electric current into direct current

commute *vb* **-muting, -muted 1** to travel some distance regularly between one's home and one's place of work **2** *law* to reduce (a sentence) to one less severe **3** to substitute **4** to pay (an annuity or pension) at one time, instead of in instalments ▸ *n* **5** a journey made by commuting > **commutable** *adj* > **commutation** *n*

commuter *n* a person who regularly travels a considerable distance to work

> **commuter** *n* = daily traveller, passenger, suburbanite

compact[1] *adj* **1** closely packed together **2** neatly fitted into a restricted space **3** concise; brief ▸ *vb* **4** to pack closely together ▸ *n* **5** a small flat case containing a mirror and face powder > **compactly** *adv* > **compactness** *n*

> **compact** *adj* **1** = closely packed, solid, thick, dense, compressed, condensed, pressed together; ≠ loose **3** = concise, brief, to the point, succinct, terse; ≠ lengthy

compact[2] *n* a contract or agreement

> **compact** *n* = agreement, deal (*informal*), understanding, contract, bond, arrangement, treaty, bargain

compact disc *n* a small digital audio disc on which the sound is read by an optical laser system

companion *n* **1** a person who associates with or accompanies someone: *a travelling companion* **2** (esp. formerly) a woman paid to live or travel with another woman **3** a guidebook or handbook **4** one of a pair > **companionship** *n*

> **companion** *n* **1** = friend, partner, ally, colleague, associate, mate (*informal*), comrade, accomplice, plus-one (*informal*), cobber (*Austral, NZ old-fashioned, informal*) **2** = assistant, aide, escort, attendant

companionable *adj* friendly and pleasant to be with > **companionably** *adv*

companionway *n* a ladder from one deck to another in a ship

company *n, pl* **-nies 1** a business organization **2** a group of actors **3** a small unit of troops **4** the officers and crew of a ship **5** the fact of being with someone: *I enjoy her company* **6** a number of people gathered together **7** a guest or guests **8** a person's associates **9 keep someone company** to accompany someone **10 part company** to disagree or separate

> **company** *n* **1** = business, firm, association, corporation, partnership, establishment, syndicate, house **2, 6** = group, set, community, band, crowd, collection, gathering, assembly **3** = troop, unit, squad, team **5** = companionship, society (*old-fashioned*), presence, fellowship **7** = guests, party, visitors, callers

comparable *adj* **1** worthy of comparison **2** able to be compared (with) > **comparability** *n*

> **comparable** *adj* **1** = similar, related, alike, corresponding, akin, analogous, of a piece, cognate **2** = equal, equivalent, on a par, tantamount, a match, proportionate, commensurate, as good; ≠ unequal

comparative *adj* **1** relative: *despite the importance of his discoveries, he died in comparative poverty* **2** involving comparison: *comparative religion* **3** *grammar* the form of an adjective or adverb that indicates that the quality denoted is possessed to a greater extent. In English the comparative is marked by the suffix *-er* or the word *more* ▸ *n* **4** the comparative form of an adjective or adverb > **comparatively** *adv*

> **comparative** *adj* **1** = relative, qualified, by comparison

compare *vb* **-paring, -pared 1** to examine in order to observe resemblances or differences: *the survey compared the health of three groups of children* **2 compare to** to declare to be like: *one ambulance driver compared the carnage to an air crash* **3** (usually foll. by *with*) to resemble: *his storytelling compares with the likes of Le Carré* **4** to bear a specified relation when examined: *this full-flavoured white wine compares favourably with more expensive French wines* **5 compare notes** to exchange opinions ▸ *n* **6 beyond compare** without equal

> **compare** *vb* **1** = contrast, balance, weigh, set against, juxtapose **2 compare to something** = liken to, parallel, identify with, equate to, correlate to, mention in the same breath as

comparison *n* **1** a comparing or being compared **2** likeness or similarity: *there is no comparison at all between her and Catherine* **3** *grammar* the positive, comparative, and superlative forms of an adjective or adverb **4 in comparison to** or **with** compared to **5 bear** or **stand comparison with** to be able to be compared with (something else), esp. favourably: *his half-dozen best novels can stand comparison with anyone's*

> **comparison** *n* **1** = contrast, distinction, differentiation, juxtaposition **2** = similarity, analogy, resemblance, correlation, likeness, comparability

compartment *n* **1** one of the sections into which a railway carriage is sometimes divided **2** a separate section: *filing the information away in some compartment of his mind* **3** a small storage space: *the ice-making compartment of the fridge*

> **compartment** *n* **1** = section, carriage, berth **3** = bay, booth, locker, niche, cubicle, alcove, pigeonhole, cubbyhole

compass *n* **1** an instrument for finding direction, with a magnetized needle which points to magnetic north **2** limits or range: *within the compass of a normal-sized book such a comprehensive survey is not possible* **3 compasses** an instrument used for drawing circles or measuring distances, that consists of two arms, joined at one end

> **compass** *n* **2** = range, field, area, reach, scope, limit, extent, boundary

compassion *n* a feeling of distress and pity for the suffering or misfortune of another

> **compassion** *n* = sympathy, understanding, pity, humanity, mercy, sorrow, kindness, tenderness, aroha (NZ); ≠ indifference

compassionate *adj* showing or having compassion > **compassionately** *adv*

> **compassionate** *adj* = sympathetic, understanding, pitying, humanitarian, charitable, humane, benevolent, merciful; ≠ uncaring

compatible *adj* **1** able to exist together harmoniously **2** consistent: *his evidence is fully compatible with the other data* **3** (of pieces of equipment) capable of being used together > **compatibility** *n*

> **compatible** *adj* **1** = like-minded, harmonious, in harmony; ≠ incompatible **2** = consistent, in keeping, congruous; ≠ inappropriate

compatriot *n* a fellow countryman or countrywoman

compel *vb* **-pelling, -pelled 1** to force (to be or do something) **2** to obtain by force: *his performance compelled attention*

> **compel** *vb* **1** = force, make, railroad (*informal*), oblige, constrain, coerce, impel, dragoon

compendious *adj* brief but comprehensive

compendium *n, pl* **-diums** *or* **-dia 1** *Brit* a selection of different table games in one container **2** a concise but comprehensive summary

compensate *vb* **-sating, -sated 1** to make amends to (someone), esp. for loss or injury **2** to cancel out the effects of (something): *the car's nifty handling fails to compensate for its many flaws* **3** to serve as compensation for (injury or loss) > **compensatory** *adj*

> **compensate** *vb* **1** = recompense, repay, refund, reimburse, remunerate (*formal*), make good **2** = balance, cancel (out), offset, make up for, redress, counteract, counterbalance **3** = make amends for, make up for, atone for, pay for, do penance for, cancel out, make reparation for

compensation *n* **1** payment made as reparation for loss or injury **2** the act of making amends for something

> **compensation** *n* **1** = reparation, damages, recompense, remuneration, restitution, reimbursement **2** = recompense, amends, reparation, restitution, atonement

compere *Brit, Austral & NZ* ▸ *n* **1** a person who introduces a stage, radio, or television show ▸ *vb* **-pering, -pered 2** to be the compere of

compete vb **-peting, -peted 1** to take part in (a contest or competition) **2** to strive (to achieve something or to be successful): *able to compete on the international market*

> **compete** vb **1** = take part, participate, be in the running, be a competitor, be a contestant, play **2** = contend, fight, vie, challenge, struggle, contest, strive

competence or **competency** n **1** the ability to do something well or effectively **2** a sufficient income to live on **3** the state of being legally competent or qualified

> **competence** or **competency** n **1, 3** = ability, skill, talent, capacity, expertise, proficiency, capability; ≠ incompetence

competent adj **1** having sufficient skill or knowledge: *he was a very competent engineer* **2** suitable or sufficient for the purpose: *it was a competent performance, but hardly a remarkable one* **3** having valid legal authority: *lawful detention after conviction by a competent court* > **competently** adv

> **competent** adj **1** = able, skilled, capable, proficient; ≠ incompetent **3** = fit, qualified, suitable, adequate; ≠ unqualified

competition n **1** the act of competing; rivalry: *competition for places was keen* **2** an event in which people compete **3** the opposition offered by competitors **4** people against whom one competes

> **competition** n **1** = rivalry, opposition, struggle, strife **2** = contest, event, championship, tournament, head-to-head **3, 4** = opposition, field, rivals, challengers

competitive adj **1** involving rivalry: *the increasingly competitive computer industry* **2** characterized by an urge to compete: *her naturally competitive spirit* **3** of good enough value to be successful against commercial rivals: *we offer worldwide flights at competitive prices* > **competitiveness** n

> **competitive** adj **1** = cut-throat, aggressive, fierce, ruthless, relentless, antagonistic, dog-eat-dog **2** = ambitious, pushing, opposing, aggressive, vying, contentious, combative

competitor n a person, team, or firm that competes

> **competitor** n = rival, adversary, antagonist

compile vb **-piling, -piled 1** to collect and arrange (information) from various sources **2** *computers* to convert (commands for a computer) from the language used by the person using it into machine code suitable for the computer, using a compiler > **compilation** n

> **compile** vb **1** = put together, collect, gather, organize, accumulate, marshal, garner, amass

compiler n **1** a person who compiles information **2** a computer program that converts a high-level programming language into the machine language used by a computer

complacency n extreme self-satisfaction > **complacent** adj > **complacently** adv

> **complacency** n = smugness, satisfaction, contentment, self-congratulation, self-satisfaction

complain vb **1** to express resentment or displeasure **2 complain of** to state that one is suffering from (a pain or illness): *she complained of breathing trouble and chest pains* **3** to make a formal protest: *he complained to the police about his rowdy neighbours*

> **complain** vb **1** = find fault, moan (*informal*), grumble, whinge (*informal*), carp, groan, lament, whine, nit-pick (*informal*)

complainant n *law* a plaintiff

complaint n **1** the act of complaining **2** a reason for complaining **3** a mild illness **4** a formal protest

> **complaint** n **1, 2** = grumble, criticism, moan, lament, grievance, grouse, gripe (*informal*) **3** = disorder, problem, disease, upset, illness, sickness, ailment, affliction **4** = protest, objection, grievance, charge

complaisant (kom-**play**-zant) adj willing to please or oblige > **complaisance** n

complement n **1** a person or thing that completes something **2** a complete amount or number: *a full complement of staff nurses and care assistants* **3** the officers and crew needed to operate a ship **4** *grammar* a word or words added to the verb to complete the meaning of the predicate in a sentence, as *a fool* in *He is a fool* or *that he would come* in *I hoped that he would come* **5** *maths* the angle that when added to a specified angle produces a right angle ▶ vb **6** to complete or form a complement to

> **complement** n **1** = accompaniment, companion, accessory, completion, finishing touch, rounding-off, adjunct, supplement **2** = total, capacity, quota, aggregate, contingent, entirety ▶ vb = enhance, complete, improve, boost, crown, add to, set off, heighten

complementary adj **1** forming a complete or balanced whole **2** forming a complement

> **complementary** adj = matching, companion, corresponding, compatible, reciprocal, interrelating, interdependent, harmonizing; ≠ incompatible

complete adj **1** thorough; absolute: *it was a complete shambles* **2** perfect in quality or kind: *he is the complete modern footballer* **3** finished **4** having all the necessary parts **5 complete with** having as an extra feature or part: *a mansion complete with swimming pool* ▸ *vb* **-pleting, -pleted 6** to finish **7** to make whole or perfect > **completely** *adv* > **completeness** *n* > **completion** *n*

> **complete** *adj* **1, 2** = total, perfect, absolute, utter, outright, thorough, consummate, out-and-out **3** = finished, done, ended, achieved, concluded, fulfilled, accomplished; ≠ unfinished **4** = entire, full, whole, intact, unbroken, faultless; ≠ incomplete ▸ *vb* **6** = finish, conclude, end, close, settle, wrap up (*informal*), finalize; ≠ start **7** = perfect, finish off, round off, crown; ≠ spoil

complex *adj* **1** made up of interconnected parts **2** intricate or complicated **3** *maths* of or involving complex numbers ▸ *n* **4** a whole made up of related parts: *a leisure complex including a gymnasium, squash courts, and a 20-metre swimming pool* **5** *psychoanalysis* a group of unconscious feelings that influences a person's behaviour **6** *informal* an obsession or phobia: *I have never had a complex about my height*

> **complex** *adj* **1** = compound, multiple, composite, manifold (*formal*), heterogeneous, multifarious **2** = complicated, difficult, involved, elaborate, tangled, intricate, tortuous, convoluted; ≠ simple ▸ *n* **4** = structure, system, scheme, network, organization, aggregate, composite **6** = obsession, preoccupation, phobia, fixation, fixed idea, idée fixe (*French*)

complexion *n* **1** the colour and general appearance of the skin of a person's face **2** character or nature: *the political complexion of the government*

> **complexion** *n* **1** = skin, colour, colouring, hue, skin tone, pigmentation **2** = nature, character, make-up

complexity *n, pl* **-ties 1** the state or quality of being intricate or complex **2** something complicated

> **complexity** *n* = complication, involvement, intricacy, entanglement

compliance *n* **1** complying **2** a tendency to do what others want > **compliant** *adj*
complicate *vb* **-cating, -cated** to make or become complex or difficult to deal with

> **complicate** *vb* = make difficult, confuse, muddle, entangle, involve; ≠ simplify

complication *n* **1** something that makes a situation more difficult to deal with: *an added complication is the growing concern for the environment* **2** a medical condition arising as a consequence of another

> **complication** *n* **1** = problem, difficulty, obstacle, drawback, snag, uphill (*S African*)

complicit *adj* involved with others in an undesirable or illegal activity: *the government was complicit in abuses of human rights*
complicity *n, pl* **-ties** the fact of being an accomplice in a crime
compliment *n* **1** an expression of praise **2 compliments** formal greetings ▸ *vb* **3** to express admiration for

> **compliment** *n* **1** = praise, honour, tribute, bouquet, flattery, eulogy; ≠ criticism **2** = greetings, regards, respects, good wishes, salutation; ≠ insult ▸ *vb* = praise, flatter, salute, congratulate, pay tribute to, commend, extol, wax lyrical about; ≠ criticize

complimentary *adj* **1** expressing praise **2** free of charge: *a complimentary drink*

> **complimentary** *adj* **1** = flattering, approving, appreciative, congratulatory, commendatory; ≠ critical **2** = free, donated, courtesy, honorary, on the house, gratuitous, gratis

compline *n* last service of the day in the Roman Catholic Church
comply *vb* **-plies, -plying, -plied** to act in accordance (with a rule, order, or request)

> **comply** *vb* = obey, follow, observe, submit to, conform to, adhere to, abide by, acquiesce with; ≠ defy

component *n* **1** a constituent part or feature of a whole **2** *maths* one of a set of two or more vectors whose resultant is a given vector ▸ *adj* **3** forming or functioning as a part or feature: *over 60 component parts*

> **component** *n* **1** = part, piece, unit, item, element, ingredient, constituent ▸ *adj* = constituent, inherent, intrinsic

comport *vb formal* **1 comport oneself** to behave in a specified way **2 comport with** to suit or be appropriate to > **comportment** *n*
compose *vb* **-posing, -posed 1** to put together or make up **2** to be the component elements of **3** to create (a musical or literary work) **4 compose oneself** to calm (oneself) **5** to arrange artistically **6** *printing* to set up (type)

> **compose** *vb* **1** = arrange, make up, construct, put together, order, organize **3** = create, write, produce, invent, devise, contrive **4 compose oneself** = calm yourself, control yourself, collect yourself, pull yourself together

composer *n* a person who writes music
composite *adj* **1** made up of separate parts **2** (of a plant) with flower heads made up of many small flowers, such as the dandelion **3** *maths* capable of being factorized: *a composite function* ▸ *n* **4** something composed of separate parts **5** a composite plant

composition *n* **1** the act of putting together or composing **2** something composed **3** the things or parts which make up a whole **4** a work of music, art, or literature **5** the harmonious arrangement of the parts of a work of art **6** a written exercise; an essay **7** *printing* the act or technique of setting up type

> **composition** *n* **1** = production, creation, making, fashioning, formation, putting together, compilation, formulation **3** = design, structure, make-up, organization, arrangement, formation, layout, configuration **4** = creation, work, piece, production, opus, masterpiece **6** = essay, exercise, treatise, literary work

compositor *n* a person who arranges type for printing

compos mentis *adj* sane

compost *n* **1** a mixture of decaying plants and manure, used as a fertilizer **2** soil mixed with fertilizer, used for growing plants ▸ *vb* **3** to make (vegetable matter) into compost

composure *n* the state of being calm or unworried

compote *n* fruit stewed with sugar or in a syrup

compound[1] *n* **1** *chem* a substance that contains atoms of two or more chemical elements held together by chemical bonds **2** any combination of two or more parts, features, or qualities **3** a word formed from two existing words or combining forms ▸ *vb* **4** to combine so as to create a compound **5** to make by combining parts or features: *the film's score is compounded from surging strings, a heavenly chorus, and jazzy saxophones* **6** to intensify by an added element: *the problems of undertaking relief work are compounded by continuing civil war* **7** *law* to agree not to prosecute in return for payment: *to compound a crime* ▸ *adj* **8** composed of two or more parts or elements **9** *music* with a time in which the number of beats per bar is a multiple of three: *such tunes are usually in a form of compound time, for example six-four*
> **compoundable** *adj*

> **compound** *n* **2** = combination, mixture, blend, composite, fusion, synthesis, alloy, medley; ≠ element ▸ *vb* **4** = combine, unite, mix, blend, synthesize, amalgamate, intermingle; ≠ divide **6** = intensify, add to, complicate, worsen, heighten, exacerbate, aggravate, magnify; ≠ lessen ▸ *adj* **8** = complex, multiple, composite, intricate; ≠ simple

compound[2] *n* a fenced enclosure containing buildings, such as a camp for prisoners of war

comprehend *vb* **1** to understand **2** to include
> **comprehensible** *adj*

> **comprehend** *vb* **1** = understand, see, take in, perceive, grasp, conceive, make out, fathom; ≠ misunderstand

comprehension *n* **1** understanding **2** inclusion

comprehension *n* **1** = understanding, grasp, conception, realization, intelligence, perception, discernment; ≠ incomprehension

comprehensive *adj* **1** of broad scope or content **2** (of car insurance) providing protection against most risks, including third-party liability, fire, theft, and damage **3** *Brit* of the comprehensive school system ▸ *n* **4** *Brit* a comprehensive school

> **comprehensive** *adj* **1** = broad, full, complete, blanket, thorough, inclusive, exhaustive, all-inclusive; ≠ limited

comprehensive school *n* *Brit* a secondary school for children of all abilities

compress *vb* **1** to squeeze together **2** to condense ▸ *n* **3** a cloth or pad applied firmly to some part of the body to cool inflammation or relieve pain

> **compress** *vb* **1** = squeeze, crush, squash, press **2** = condense, contract, concentrate, shorten, abbreviate, zip

compression *n* **1** the act of compressing **2** the reduction in volume and increase in pressure of the fuel mixture in an internal-combustion engine before ignition

compressor *n* a device that compresses a gas

comprise *vb* **-prising, -prised 1** to be made up of: *the group comprised six French diplomats, five Italians, and three Bulgarians* **2** to form or make up: *women comprised 57 per cent of all employees*

> **comprise** *vb* **1** = be composed of, include, contain, consist of, take in, embrace, encompass **2** = make up, form, constitute, compose

compromise (kom-prom-mize) *n* **1** settlement of a dispute by concessions on each side: *everyone pleaded for compromise; the compromise was only reached after hours of hard bargaining* **2** the terms of such a settlement **3** something midway between different things ▸ *vb* **-mising, -mised 4** to settle (a dispute) by making concessions **5** to put (oneself or another person) in a dishonourable position ▸ *adj* **6** being, or having the nature of, a compromise: *a compromise solution*
> **compromising** *adj*

> **compromise** *n* **1** = give-and-take, agreement, settlement, accommodation, concession, adjustment, trade-off; ≠ disagreement ▸ *vb* **4** = meet halfway, concede, make concessions, give and take, strike a balance, strike a happy medium, go fifty-fifty (*informal*); ≠ disagree **5** = undermine, expose, embarrass, weaken, prejudice, discredit, jeopardize, dishonour; ≠ support

comptroller *n* a financial controller

compulsion *n* **1** an irresistible urge to perform some action **2** compelling or being compelled

compulsive *adj* 1 resulting from or acting from a compulsion 2 irresistible or absorbing > **compulsively** *adv*

compulsive *adj* 1 = obsessive, confirmed, chronic, persistent, addictive, uncontrollable, incurable, inveterate 2 = irresistible, overwhelming, compelling, urgent, uncontrollable, driving

compulsory *adj* required by regulations or laws

compulsory *adj* = obligatory, forced, required, binding, mandatory, imperative, requisite, de rigueur (*French*); ≠ voluntary

compunction *n* a feeling of guilt or regret

computation *n* a calculation involving numbers or quantities > **computational** *adj*

compute *vb* **-puting**, **-puted** to calculate (an answer or result), often by using a computer

compute *vb* = calculate, total, count, reckon, figure out, add up, tally, enumerate

computer *n* an electronic device that processes data according to a set of instructions

computerize *or* **-ise** *vb* **-izing**, **-ized** *or* **-ising**, **-ised** 1 to equip with a computer 2 to control or perform (operations) by means of a computer > **computerization** *or* **-isation** *n*

comrade *n* 1 a fellow member of a union or a socialist political party 2 a companion > **comradely** *adj* > **comradeship** *n*

comrade *n* 2 = companion, friend, partner, ally, colleague, associate, fellow, co-worker, blood (*Brit slang*), cobber (*Austral, NZ old-fashioned, informal*)

con¹ *informal* ▸ *n* 1 same as **confidence trick** ▸ *vb* **conning**, **conned** 2 to swindle or defraud

con *vb* = swindle, trick, cheat, rip off (*slang*), deceive, defraud, dupe, hoodwink, scam (*slang*)

con² *n* See **pros and cons**

concatenation *n* *formal* a series of linked events

concave *adj* curving inwards like the inside surface of a ball > **concavity** *n*

conceal *vb* 1 to cover and hide 2 to keep secret > **concealment** *n*

conceal *vb* 1 = hide, bury, cover, screen, disguise, obscure, camouflage; ≠ reveal 2 = keep secret, hide, disguise, mask, suppress, veil; ≠ show

concede *vb* **-ceding**, **-ceded** 1 to admit (something) as true or correct 2 to give up or grant (something, such as a right) 3 to acknowledge defeat in (a contest or argument)

concede *vb* 1 = admit, allow, accept, acknowledge, own, grant, confess; ≠ deny 2 = give up, yield, hand over, surrender, relinquish, cede; ≠ conquer

conceit *n* 1 an excessively high opinion of oneself 2 *literary* a far-fetched or clever comparison

conceited *adj* having an excessively high opinion of oneself > **conceitedness** *n*

conceivable *adj* capable of being understood, believed, or imagined > **conceivably** *adv*

conceive *vb* **-ceiving**, **-ceived** 1 to imagine or think 2 to consider in a certain way: *we must do what we conceive to be right* 3 to form in the mind 4 to become pregnant

conceive *vb* 1, 2 = imagine, envisage, comprehend, visualize, think, believe, suppose, fancy 3 = think up, create, design, devise, formulate, contrive 4 = become pregnant, get pregnant, become impregnated

concentrate *vb* **-trating**, **-trated** 1 to focus all one's attention, thoughts, or efforts on something: *she tried hard to concentrate, but her mind kept flashing back to the previous night* 2 to bring or come together in large numbers or amounts in one place: *a flawed system that concentrates power in the hands of the few* 3 to make (a liquid) stronger by removing water from it ▸ *n* 4 a concentrated substance > **concentrated** *adj*

concentrate *vb* 1 = focus your attention, focus, pay attention, be engrossed, apply yourself; ≠ pay no attention 2 = focus, centre, converge, bring to bear; ≠ scatter

concentration *n* 1 intense mental application 2 the act of concentrating 3 something that is concentrated 4 the amount or proportion of a substance in a mixture or solution

concentration *n* 1 = attention, application, absorption, single-mindedness, intentness; ≠ inattention 2 = focusing, centring, consolidation, convergence, bringing to bear, intensification, centralization 3 = convergence, collection, mass, cluster, accumulation, aggregation; ≠ scattering

concentration camp *n* a prison camp for civilian prisoners, as in Nazi Germany

concentric *adj* having the same centre: *concentric circles*

concept *n* an abstract or general idea: *one of the basic concepts of quantum theory*

concept *n* = idea, view, image, theory, notion, conception, hypothesis, abstraction

conception *n* 1 a notion, idea, or plan 2 the fertilization of an egg by a sperm in the Fallopian tube followed by implantation in the womb 3 origin or beginning: *the gap between the conception of an invention and its production*

conception *n* 1 = idea, plan, design, image, concept, notion 2 = impregnation, insemination, fertilization, germination

conceptual *adj* of or based on concepts

conceptualize or **-ise** vb **-izing, -ized** or **-ising, -ised** to form a concept or idea of > **conceptualization** or **-isation** n

concern n 1 anxiety or worry: *the current concern over teenage pregnancies* 2 something that is of interest or importance to a person 3 regard or interest: *a scrupulous concern for client confidentiality* 4 a business or firm ▶ vb 5 to worry or make anxious 6 to involve or interest: *he had converted the building into flats without concerning himself with the niceties of planning permission* 7 to be relevant or important to

> **concern** n 1 = worry, care, anxiety 2 = affair, issue, matter, consideration 3 = care, interest, attentiveness 4 = company, business, firm, organization, corporation, enterprise, establishment ▶ vb 5 = worry, trouble, bother, disturb, distress, disquiet, perturb, make anxious 6 = be about, cover, deal with, go into, relate to, have to do with 7 = be relevant to, involve, affect, regard, apply to, bear on, have something to do with, pertain to

concerned adj 1 interested or involved: *I have spoken to the person concerned and she has no recollection of saying such a thing* 2 worried or anxious: *we are increasingly concerned for her safety*

> **concerned** adj 1 = involved, interested, active, mixed up, implicated, privy to 2 = worried, troubled, upset, bothered, disturbed, anxious, distressed, uneasy; ≠ indifferent

concerning prep about; regarding

> **concerning** prep = regarding, about, re, touching, respecting, relating to, on the subject of, with reference to

concert n 1 a performance of music by players or singers in front of an audience 2 **in concert** A working together B (of musicians or singers) performing live

concerted adj decided or planned by mutual agreement: *a concerted effort*

concertina n 1 a small musical instrument similar to an accordion ▶ vb **-naing, -naed** 2 to collapse or fold up like a concertina

concerto (kon-**chair**-toe) n, pl **-tos** or **-ti** (-tee) a large-scale composition for an orchestra and one or more soloists

concession n 1 any grant of rights, land, or property by a government, local authority, or company 2 a reduction in price for a certain category of person: *fare concessions for senior citizens* 3 the act of yielding or conceding 4 something conceded 5 *Canad* a land subdivision in a township survey > **concessionary** adj

> **concession** n 1 = privilege, right, permit, licence, entitlement, indulgence, prerogative 2 = reduction, saving, grant, discount, allowance 3 = surrender, yielding, conceding, renunciation, relinquishment 4 = compromise, agreement, settlement, accommodation, adjustment, trade-off, give-and-take

conch n, pl **conchs** or **conches** 1 a marine mollusc with a large brightly coloured spiral shell 2 its shell

concierge (kon-see-**airzh**) n (esp. in France) a caretaker in a block of flats

conciliate vb **-ating, -ated** to try to end a disagreement with or pacify (someone) > **conciliator** n

conciliation n 1 the act of conciliating 2 a method of helping the parties in a dispute to reach agreement, esp. divorcing or separating couples to part amicably

conciliatory adj intended to end a disagreement

concise adj brief and to the point > **concisely** adv > **conciseness** or **concision** n

conclave n 1 a secret meeting 2 *RC Church* a private meeting of cardinals to elect a new pope

conclude vb **-cluding, -cluded** 1 to decide by reasoning: *a police investigation concluded that no crime had been committed* 2 to come or bring to an end: *the festival concludes on December 19th* 3 to arrange or settle finally: *officials have refused to comment on the failure to conclude an agreement*

> **conclude** vb 1 = decide, judge, assume, gather, work out, infer, deduce, surmise 2 = come to an end, end, close, finish, wind up; ≠ begin 3 = accomplish, effect, bring about, carry out, pull off

conclusion n 1 a final decision, opinion, or judgment based on reasoning: *the obvious conclusion is that something is being covered up* 2 end or ending 3 outcome or result: *if you take that strategy to its logical conclusion you end up with communism* 4 **in conclusion** finally 5 **jump to conclusions** to come to a conclusion too quickly, without sufficient thought or evidence

> **conclusion** n 1 = decision, opinion, conviction, verdict, judgment, deduction, inference 2 = end, ending, close, finish, completion, finale, termination, bitter end 3 = outcome, result, upshot, consequence, culmination, end result

conclusive adj putting an end to doubt: *there is no conclusive proof of this* > **conclusively** adv

concoct vb 1 to make by combining different ingredients 2 to invent or make up (a story or plan) > **concoction** n

concomitant adj 1 existing or along with (something else): *the concomitant health gains* ▶ n 2 something that is concomitant

concord n 1 agreement or harmony 2 peaceful relations between nations 3 *music* a harmonious combination of musical notes > **concordant** adj

concordance n 1 a state of harmony or agreement 2 an alphabetical list of words in a text, with the context and often the meaning

concourse n 1 a large open space in a public place, where people can meet: *a crowded concourse at Heathrow Airport* 2 a crowd

concrete n 1 a building material made of cement, sand, stone, and water that hardens to a stonelike mass ▸ vb **-creting, -creted** 2 to cover with concrete ▸ adj 3 made of concrete 4 specific as opposed to general 5 relating to things that can be perceived by the senses, as opposed to abstractions

> **concrete** adj 4 = specific, precise, explicit, definite, clear-cut, unequivocal; ≠ vague 5 = real, material, actual, substantial (*formal*), sensible, tangible, factual; ≠ abstract

concubine (kon-kew-bine) n 1 *archaic* a woman cohabiting with a man 2 a secondary wife in polygamous societies › **concubinage** n

concupiscence (kon-kew-piss-enss) n *formal* strong sexual desire › **concupiscent** adj

concur vb **-curring, -curred** to agree; be in accord

concurrence n 1 agreement 2 simultaneous occurrence

concurrent adj 1 taking place at the same time or place 2 meeting at, approaching, or having a common point: *concurrent lines* 3 in agreement › **concurrently** adv

concussion n 1 a brain injury caused by a blow or fall, usually resulting in loss of consciousness 2 violent shaking

condemn vb 1 to express strong disapproval of 2 to pronounce sentence on in a court of law 3 to force into a particular state: *a system that condemns most of our youngsters to failure* 4 to judge or declare (something) unfit for use 5 to indicate the guilt of: *everything the man had said condemned him, morally if not technically* › **condemnation** n › **condemnatory** adj

> **condemn** vb 1 = denounce, damn, criticize, disapprove, censure, reprove, upbraid, blame; ≠ approve 2 = sentence, convict, damn, doom, pass sentence on; ≠ acquit

condensation n 1 anything that has condensed from a vapour, esp. on a window 2 the act of condensing, or the state of being condensed

condense vb **-densing, -densed** 1 to express in fewer words 2 to increase the density of; concentrate 3 to change from a gas to a liquid or solid

condenser n 1 an apparatus for reducing gases to their liquid or solid form by the removal of heat 2 same as **capacitor** 3 a lens that concentrates light

condescend vb 1 to behave patronizingly towards (one's supposed inferiors) 2 to do something as if it were beneath one's dignity › **condescending** adj › **condescension** n

condiment n any seasoning for food, such as salt, pepper, or sauces

condition n 1 a particular state of being: *the human condition; the van is in very poor condition* 2 **conditions** circumstances: *worsening weather conditions; the government pledged to improve living and working conditions* 3 a necessary requirement for something else to happen: *food is a necessary condition for survival* 4 a restriction or a qualification 5 a term of an agreement: *the conditions of the lease are set out* 6 state of physical fitness, esp. good health: *she is in a serious condition in hospital; out of condition* 7 an ailment: *a heart condition* 8 **on condition that** provided that ▸ vb 9 to accustom or alter the reaction of (a person or animal) to a particular stimulus or situation 10 to treat with a conditioner 11 to make fit or healthy 12 to influence or determine the form that something takes: *he argued that the failure of Latin American industry was conditioned by international economic structures* › **conditioning** n, adj

> **condition** n 1 = state, order, shape, nick (*Brit informal*), trim 2 = circumstances, situation, environment, surroundings, way of life, milieu 3, 4, 5 = requirement, terms, rider, restriction, qualification, limitation, prerequisite, proviso 6 = health, shape, fitness, trim, form, kilter, state of health, fettle 7 = ailment, problem, complaint, weakness, malady, infirmity ▸ vb 9 = train, teach, adapt, accustom

conditional adj 1 depending on other factors 2 *grammar* expressing a condition on which something else depends, for example 'If he comes' is a conditional clause in the sentence 'If he comes I shall go'

> **conditional** adj 1 = dependent, limited, qualified, contingent, provisional, with reservations; ≠ unconditional

conditioner n a thick liquid used when washing to make hair or clothes feel softer

condo n, pl **-dos** *US & Canad informal* a condominium building or apartment

condolence n sympathy expressed for someone in grief or pain › **condole** vb

condom n a rubber sheath worn on the penis or in the vagina during sexual intercourse to prevent conception or infection

condominium n, pl **-ums** 1 *Austral, US & Canad* A an apartment building in which each apartment is individually owned B an apartment in such a building 2 joint rule of a state by two or more other states

condone vb **-doning, -doned** to overlook or forgive (an offence or wrongdoing)

> **condone** vb = overlook, excuse, forgive, pardon, turn a blind eye to, look the other way, make allowance for, let pass; ≠ condemn

condor n a very large rare S American vulture

conducive adj (often foll. by to) likely to lead to or produce (a result)

conduct n 1 behaviour 2 the management or handling of an activity or business ▸ vb 3 to carry out: *the police are conducting an investigation into the affair* 4 **conduct oneself** to behave (oneself) 5 to control (an orchestra or choir) by the movements of the hands or a baton 6 to accompany and guide (people or a party): *a conducted tour* 7 to transmit (heat or electricity)

> **conduct** n 1 = behaviour, ways, bearing, attitude, manners, demeanour, deportment 2 = management, running, control, handling, administration, direction, organization, guidance ▸ vb 3 = carry out, run, control, manage, direct, handle, organize, administer 4 **conduct oneself** = behave yourself, act, carry yourself, acquit yourself, deport yourself, comport yourself 6 = accompany, lead, escort, guide, steer, convey, usher

conduction n the transmission of heat or electricity

conductivity n the property of transmitting heat, electricity, or sound

conductor n 1 a person who conducts an orchestra or choir 2 an official on a bus who collects fares 3 *US, Canad & NZ* a railway official in charge of a train 4 something that conducts electricity or heat > **conductress** *fem n*

conduit (kon-dew-it) n 1 a route or system for transferring things from one place to another: *a conduit for sending money to the United States* 2 a channel or tube for carrying a fluid or electrical cables 3 a means of access or communication

cone n 1 a geometric solid consisting of a circular or oval base, tapering to a point 2 a cone-shaped wafer shell used to contain ice cream 3 the scaly fruit of a conifer tree 4 *Brit, Austral & NZ* a plastic cone used as a temporary traffic marker on roads 5 a type of cell in the retina, sensitive to colour and bright light

coney n same as **cony**

confab n *informal* a conversation

confabulation n *formal* a conversation

confection n 1 any sweet food, such as a cake or a sweet 2 *old-fashioned* an elaborate piece of clothing

confectioner n a person who makes or sells confectionery

confectionery n, pl **-eries** 1 sweets and chocolates collectively: *a drop in confectionery sales* 2 the art or business of a confectioner

confederacy n, pl **-cies** a union of states or people joined for a common purpose > **confederal** adj

confederate n 1 a state or individual that is part of a confederacy 2 an accomplice or conspirator ▸ adj 3 united; allied ▸ vb **-ating, -ated** 4 to unite in a confederacy

confederation n 1 a union or alliance of states or groups 2 confederating or being confederated 3 a federation

confer vb **-ferring, -ferred** 1 to discuss together 2 to grant or give: *the power conferred by wealth* > **conferment** n > **conferrable** adj

> **confer** vb 1 = discuss, talk, consult, deliberate, discourse, converse 2 = grant, give, present, accord, award, hand out, bestow

conference n a meeting for formal consultation or discussion

> **conference** n = meeting, congress, discussion, convention, forum, consultation, seminar, symposium, hui (NZ)

confess vb 1 to admit (a fault or crime) 2 to admit to be true, esp. reluctantly 3 *Christianity* to declare (one's sins) to God or to a priest, so as to obtain forgiveness

> **confess** vb 1 = admit, acknowledge, disclose, confide, own up, come clean (*informal*), divulge; ≠ cover up 2 = declare, allow, reveal, confirm, concede, assert, affirm, profess

confession n 1 something confessed 2 an admission of one's faults, sins, or crimes 3 **confession of faith** a formal public statement of religious beliefs

> **confession** n 1, 2 = admission, revelation, disclosure, acknowledgment, exposure, unbosoming

confessional n 1 *Christianity* a small room or enclosed stall in a church where a priest hears confessions ▸ adj 2 of or suited to a confession

confessor n 1 *Christianity* a priest who hears confessions and gives spiritual advice 2 *history* a person who demonstrates their Christian religious faith by the holiness of their life: *Edward the Confessor*

confetti n small pieces of coloured paper thrown at weddings

confidant or fem **confidante** n a person to whom private matters are confided

> **confidant** or **confidante** n = close friend, familiar, intimate, crony, alter ego, bosom friend

confide vb **-fiding, -fided** 1 **confide in** to tell (something to someone) in confidence 2 *formal* to entrust into another's keeping

confidence n 1 trust in a person or thing 2 belief in one's own abilities 3 trust or a trustful relationship: *she won first the confidence, then the admiration, of her bosses* 4 something confided, such as a secret 5 **in confidence** as a secret

> **confidence** n 1 = trust, belief, faith, dependence, reliance, credence; ≠ distrust 2 = self-assurance, courage, assurance, aplomb, boldness, self-possession, nerve; ≠ shyness 5 **in confidence** = in secrecy, privately, confidentially, between you and me (and the gatepost), (just) between ourselves

confidence trick *n* a swindle in which the swindler gains the victim's trust in order to cheat him or her

confident *adj* **1** having or showing certainty: *we are now confident that this technique works* **2** sure of oneself > **confidently** *adv*

> **confident** *adj* **1** = certain, sure, convinced, positive, secure, satisfied, counting on; ≠ unsure **2** = self-assured, positive, assured, bold, assertive, self-confident, self-reliant, sure of yourself; ≠ insecure

confidential *adj* **1** spoken or given in confidence **2** entrusted with another's secret affairs: *a confidential secretary* **3** suggestive of intimacy: *a halting, confidential manner* > **confidentiality** *n* > **confidentially** *adv*

> **confidential** *adj* **1** = secret, private, intimate, classified, privy (*archaic*), off the record, hush-hush (*informal*), closed or closed source (*computers*), protected (*computers*) **3** = secretive, low, soft, hushed

configuration *n* **1** the arrangement of the parts of something **2** the form or outline of such an arrangement

configure *vb* **-guring, -gured** *computers* to set up (a piece of hardware or software) so that it is ready for use

confine *vb* **-fining, -fined 1** to keep within bounds **2** to restrict the free movement of: *a nasty dose of flu which confined her to bed for days* ▶ *n* **3 confines** boundaries or limits

> **confine** *vb* **1** = imprison, enclose, shut up, intern, incarcerate, hem in, keep, cage **2** = restrict, limit ▶ *n* = limits, bounds, boundaries, compass, precincts, circumference, edge

confinement *n* **1** being confined **2** the period of childbirth

confirm *vb* **1** to prove to be true or valid **2** to reaffirm (something), so as to make (it) more definite: *she confirmed that she is about to resign as leader of the council* **3** to strengthen: *this cruise confirmed my first impressions of the boat's performance* **4** to formally make valid **5** *Christianity* to administer the rite of confirmation to

> **confirm** *vb* **1** = prove, support, establish, back up, verify, validate, bear out, substantiate **3** = strengthen, establish, fix, secure, reinforce, fortify **4** = ratify, establish, sanction, endorse, authorize

confirmation *n* **1** the act of confirming **2** something that confirms **3** a rite in several Christian churches that admits a baptized person to full church membership

> **confirmation** *n* **1** = affirmation, approval, acceptance, endorsement, ratification, assent, agreement; ≠ disapproval **2** = proof, evidence, testimony, verification, ratification, validation, corroboration, authentication; ≠ repudiation

confirmed *adj* long-established in a habit or condition: *a confirmed bachelor*

> **confirmed** *adj* = long-established, seasoned, chronic, hardened, habitual, ingrained, inveterate, dyed-in-the-wool

confiscate *vb* **-cating, -cated** to seize (property) by authority > **confiscation** *n*

> **confiscate** *vb* = seize, appropriate, impound, commandeer, sequester; ≠ give back

conflagration *n* a large destructive fire

conflate *vb* **-flating, -flated** to combine or blend into a whole > **conflation** *n*

conflict *n* **1** opposition between ideas or interests **2** a struggle or battle ▶ *vb* **3** to be incompatible > **conflicting** *adj*

> **conflict** *n* **1** = dispute, difference, opposition, hostility, disagreement, friction, strife, fighting, cyberwar; ≠ agreement **2** = battle, war, fight, clash, contest, encounter, combat, strife, boilover (*Austral*); ≠ peace ▶ *vb* = be incompatible, clash, differ, disagree, collide, be at variance; ≠ agree

confluence *n* **1** a place where rivers flow into one another **2** a gathering > **confluent** *adj*

conform *vb* **1** to comply with accepted standards, rules, or customs **2** (usually foll. by *with*) to be like or in accordance with: *people tend to absorb ideas that conform with their existing beliefs, and reject those that do not*

> **conform** *vb* **1** = fit in, follow, adjust, adapt, comply, obey, fall in, toe the line **2** = fulfil, meet, match, suit, satisfy, agree with, obey, abide by

conformist *adj* **1 A** (of a person) behaving or thinking like most other people rather than in an original or unconventional way: *a shy and conformist type of boy* **B** (of an organization or society) expecting everyone to behave in the same way: *the school was a dull, conformist place for staff and students alike* ▶ *n* **2** a person who behaves or thinks like most other people rather than in an original or unconventional way

conformity *n, pl* **-ities 1** compliance in actions or behaviour with certain accepted rules, customs, or standards **2** likeness

confound *vb* **1** to astound or bewilder **2** to fail to distinguish between **3 confound it!** damn it!

> **confound** *vb* **1** = bewilder, baffle, confuse, astound, perplex, mystify, flummox, dumbfound

confounded *adj* **1** *informal* damned: *what a confounded nuisance!* **2** bewildered; confused: *her silent, utterly confounded daughter*

confront *vb* **1** (of a problem or task) to present itself to **2** to meet face to face in hostility or defiance **3** to present (someone) with something, esp. in order to accuse or criticize: *she finally confronted him with her suspicions*

confront *vb* **1** = trouble, face, perturb, bedevil **2, 3** = challenge, face, oppose, tackle, encounter, defy, stand up to, accost; ≠ evade

confrontation *n* a serious argument or fight

confrontation *n* = conflict, fight, contest, set-to (*informal*), encounter, showdown (*informal*), head-to-head, boilover (*Austral*)

confuse *vb* **-fusing, -fused 1** to fail to distinguish between (one thing and another) **2** to perplex or disconcert **3** to make unclear: *he confused his talk with irrelevant detail* **4** to throw into disorder › **confusing** *adj* › **confusingly** *adv*

confuse *vb* **1** = mix up with, take for, muddle with **2** = bewilder, puzzle, baffle, perplex, mystify, fluster, faze, flummox **3** = obscure, cloud, make more difficult

confusion *n* **1** mistaking one person or thing for another **2** bewilderment **3** lack of clarity **4** disorder

confusion *n* **2** = bewilderment, doubt, uncertainty; ≠ enlightenment **4** = disorder, chaos, turmoil, upheaval, muddle, shambles, commotion; ≠ order

confute *vb* **-futing, -futed** to prove to be wrong › **confutation** *n*

conga *n* **1** a Latin American dance performed by a number of people in single file **2** a large single-headed drum played with the hands ▸ *vb* **-gaing, -gaed 3** to dance the conga

congeal *vb* to change from a liquid to a semisolid state

congenial *adj* **1** friendly, pleasant, or agreeable: *she found the Botanic Gardens a most congenial place for strolling* **2** having a similar disposition or tastes › **congeniality** *n*

congenital *adj* (of an abnormal condition) existing at birth but not inherited: *congenital heart disease* › **congenitally** *adv*

conger *n* a large sea eel

congested *adj* **1** crowded to excess **2** clogged or blocked › **congestion** *n*

conglomerate *n* **1** a large corporation made up of many different companies **2** a thing composed of several different elements **3** a type of rock consisting of rounded pebbles or fragments held together by silica or clay ▸ *vb* **-ating, -ated 4** to form into a mass ▸ *adj* **5** made up of several different elements **6** (of rock) consisting of rounded pebbles or fragments held together by silica or clay › **conglomeration** *n*

congratulate *vb* **-lating, -lated 1** to express one's pleasure to (a person) at his or her success or good fortune **2 congratulate oneself** to consider oneself clever or fortunate (as a result of): *she congratulated herself on her own business acumen* › **congratulatory** *adj*

congratulate *vb* **1** = compliment, pat on the back, wish joy to

congratulations *pl n, interj* expressions of pleasure or joy on another's success or good fortune

congratulations *pl n, interj* = good wishes, greetings, compliments, best wishes, felicitations

congregate *vb* **-gating, -gated** to collect together in or as a crowd

congregation *n* a group of worshippers › **congregational** *adj*

congregation *n* = parishioners, brethren, crowd, assembly, flock, fellowship, multitude, throng

Congregationalism *n* a system of Protestant church government in which each church is self-governing › **Congregationalist** *adj, n*

congress *n* a formal meeting of representatives for discussion › **congressional** *adj*

congress *n* = meeting, council, conference, assembly, convention, conclave, hui (NZ), runanga (NZ)

Congress *n* the federal legislature of the US, consisting of the House of Representatives and the Senate › **Congressional** *adj* › **Congressman** *or fem* **Congresswoman** *n*

congruent *adj* **1** agreeing or corresponding **2** *geom* identical in shape and size: *congruent triangles* › **congruence** *n*

conical *adj* in the shape of a cone

conifer *n* a tree or shrub bearing cones and evergreen leaves, such as the fir or larch › **coniferous** *adj*

conjecture *n* **1** the formation of conclusions from incomplete evidence **2** a guess ▸ *vb* **-turing, -tured 3** to form (an opinion or conclusion) from incomplete evidence › **conjectural** *adj*

conjoined twins *pl n* twins born joined together at some part of the body

conjugal (kon-jew-gal) *adj* of marriage: *conjugal rights*

conjugate *vb* (kon-jew-gate) **-gating, -gated 1** *grammar* to give the inflections of (a verb) **2** (of a verb) to undergo inflection according to a specific set of rules **3** *formal* to combine: *a country in which conjugating Marxism with Christianity has actually been tried* ▸ *n* (kon-jew-git) **4** *formal* something formed by conjugation: *haemoglobin is a conjugate of a protein with an iron-containing pigment*

conjugation *n* **1** *grammar* **a** inflection of a verb for person, number, tense, voice, and mood **b** the complete set of the inflections of a given verb **2** a joining

conjunction *n* **1** joining together **2** simultaneous occurrence of events **3** a word or group of words that connects words, phrases, or clauses; for example *and, if,* and *but* **4** *astron* the apparent nearness of two heavenly bodies to each other › **conjunctional** *adj*

conjunctiva *n, pl* **-vas** *or* **-vae** the delicate mucous membrane that covers the eyeball and inner eyelid > **conjunctival** *adj*

conjunctivitis *n* inflammation of the conjunctiva

conjure *vb* **-juring, -jured 1** to make (something) appear, as if by magic **2** to perform tricks that appear to be magic **3** to summon (a spirit or demon) by magic **4** *formal or literary* to appeal earnestly to: *I conjure you by all which you profess: answer me!* > **conjuring** *n*

> **conjure** *vb* **1** = produce, generate, bring about, give rise to, make, create, effect, produce as if by magic

conjure up *vb* **1** to create an image in the mind: *the name Versailles conjures up a past of sumptuous grandeur* **2** to produce as if from nowhere: *he conjured up a fabulous opening goal*

> **conjure up** *vb* **1 conjure something up** = bring to mind, recall, evoke, re-create, recollect

conjuror *or* **conjurer** *n* a person who performs magic tricks for people's entertainment

conk *Brit, Austral & NZ slang* ▸ *n* **1** the head or nose ▸ *vb* **2** to strike (someone) on the head or nose

conker *n* same as **horse chestnut** (sense 2)

conk out *vb informal* **1** (of a machine or car) to break down **2** to become tired or fall asleep suddenly

connect *vb* **1** to link or be linked: *high blood pressure is closely connected to heart disease* **2** to put into telephone communication with **3** (of two public vehicles) to have the arrival of one timed to occur just before the departure of the other, for the convenience of passengers **4** to associate in the mind: *he had always connected sex with violence and attacks rather than loving and concern* **5** to relate by birth or marriage: *she was distantly connected with the Wedgwood family* > **connective** *adj*

> **connect** *vb* **1** = link, join, couple, attach, fasten, affix, unite; ≠ separate **4** = associate, join, link, identify, lump together

connection *or* **connexion** *n* **1** a relationship or association **2** a link or bond **3** a link between two components in an electric circuit **4 A** an opportunity to transfer from one public vehicle to another **B** the vehicle scheduled to provide such an opportunity **5** an influential acquaintance **6** a relative **7** logical sequence in thought or expression **8** a telephone link **9** *slang* a supplier of illegal drugs, such as heroin **10 in connection with** with reference to: *a number of people have been arrested in connection with the explosion*

> **connection** *or* **connexion** *n* **1** = association, relationship, link, bond, relevance, tie-in **2** = link, coupling, junction, fastening, tie, portal (*computers*), USB port **5, 6** = contact, friend, ally, associate, acquaintance

conning tower *n* the raised observation tower containing the periscope on a submarine

connivance *n* encouragement or permission of wrongdoing

connive *vb* **-niving, -nived 1 connive at** to allow or encourage (wrongdoing) by ignoring it **2** to conspire

connoisseur (kon-noss-**sir**) *n* a person with special knowledge of the arts, food, or drink

connotation *n* an additional meaning or association implied by a word: *the German term carries a connotation of elitism* > **connote** *vb*

connubial (kon-**new**-bee-al) *adj formal* of marriage: *connubial bliss*

conquer *vb* **1** to defeat (an opponent or opponents) **2** to overcome (a difficulty or feeling) **3** to gain possession of (a place) by force or war > **conquering** *adj* > **conqueror** *n*

> **conquer** *vb* **1** = defeat, overcome, overthrow, beat, master, crush, overpower, quell; ≠ lose to **2** = overcome, beat, defeat, master, overpower **3** = seize, obtain, acquire, occupy, overrun, annex, win

conquest *n* **1** the act of conquering **2** a person or thing that has been conquered **3** a person whose affections have been won

> **conquest** *n* **1** = takeover, coup, invasion, occupation, annexation, subjugation

conscience *n* **1** the sense of right and wrong that governs a person's thoughts and actions **2** a feeling of guilt: *he showed no hint of conscience over the suffering he had inflicted* **3 in (all) conscience** in fairness **4 on one's conscience** causing feelings of guilt

> **conscience** *n* **1** = principles, scruples, moral sense, sense of right and wrong, still small voice **2** = guilt, shame, regret, remorse, contrition, self-reproach

conscientious *adj* **1** painstaking or thorough in one's work **2** governed by conscience > **conscientiously** *adv* > **conscientiousness** *n*

conscientious objector *n* a person who refuses to serve in the armed forces on moral or religious grounds

conscious *adj* **1** alert and awake **2** aware of one's surroundings and of oneself **3** aware (of something): *he was conscious of a need to urinate* **4** deliberate or intentional: *a conscious attempt* **5** of the part of the mind that is aware of a person's self, surroundings, and thoughts, and that to a certain extent determines choices of action ▸ *n* **6** the conscious part of the mind > **consciously** *adv* > **consciousness** *n*

> **conscious** *adj* **1, 2** = awake, wide-awake, sentient, alive; ≠ asleep **3** = aware of, alert to, responsive to, sensible of; ≠ unaware **4** = deliberate, knowing, studied, calculated, self-conscious, intentional, wilful, premeditated; ≠ unintentional

conscript n 1 a person who is enrolled for compulsory military service ▶ vb 2 to enrol (someone) for compulsory military service

conscription n compulsory military service

consecrate vb **-crating, -crated** 1 to make or declare sacred or for religious use 2 to devote or dedicate (something) to a specific purpose 3 *Christianity* to sanctify (bread and wine) to be received as the body and blood of Christ > **consecration** n

consecutive adj following in order without interruption: *three consecutive nights of rioting* > **consecutively** adv

> **consecutive** adj = successive, running, succeeding, in turn, uninterrupted, sequential, in sequence

consensus n general or widespread agreement

> **consensus** n = agreement, general agreement, unanimity, common consent, unity, harmony, assent, concord, kotahitanga (NZ)

consent n 1 agreement, permission, or approval 2 **age of consent** the age at which sexual intercourse is permitted by law ▶ vb 3 to permit or agree (to) > **consenting** adj

> **consent** n 1 = agreement, sanction, approval, go-ahead (informal), permission, compliance, assent, acquiescence; ≠ refusal ▶ vb = agree, approve, permit, concur, assent, acquiesce; ≠ refuse

consequence n 1 a logical result or effect 2 significance or importance: *we said little of consequence to each other; my opinion is of little consequence* 3 **in consequence** as a result 4 **take the consequences** to accept whatever results from one's actions

> **consequence** n 1 = result, effect, outcome, repercussion, issue, sequel, end result, upshot 2 = importance, concern, moment, value, account, weight, import (formal), significance

consequent adj 1 following as an effect 2 following as a logical conclusion

consequential adj 1 important or significant 2 following as a result

consequently adv as a result; therefore

> **consequently** adv = as a result, thus, therefore, hence, subsequently, accordingly, for that reason, thence

conservancy n environmental conservation

conservation n 1 protection and careful management of the environment and natural resources 2 protection from change, loss, or injury 3 *physics* the principle that the quantity of a specified aspect of a system, such as momentum or charge, remains constant > **conservationist** n

conservation n 1 = preservation, saving, protection, maintenance, safeguarding, upkeep, guardianship, safekeeping 2 = economy, saving, thrift, husbandry

conservative adj 1 favouring the preservation of established customs and values, and opposing change 2 moderate or cautious: *a conservative estimate* 3 conventional in style: *people in this area are conservative in their tastes* ▶ n 4 a conservative person > **conservatism** n

> **conservative** adj 1, 3 = traditional, conventional, cautious, sober, reactionary, die-hard, hidebound; ≠ radical ▶ n = traditionalist, reactionary, die-hard, stick-in-the-mud (informal); ≠ radical

Conservative adj 1 of or supporting the Conservative Party, the major right-wing political party in Britain, which believes in private enterprise and capitalism 2 of or supporting a similar right-wing party in other countries ▶ n 3 a supporter or member of the Conservative Party

conservatoire (kon-serv-a-twahr) n a school of music

conservatory n, pl **-tories** 1 a greenhouse attached to a house 2 a conservatoire

conserve vb **-serving, -served** 1 to protect from harm, decay, or loss 2 to preserve (fruit or other food) with sugar ▶ n 3 fruit preserved by cooking in sugar

> **conserve** vb 1 = save, husband, take care of, hoard, store up, use sparingly; ≠ waste

consider vb 1 to be of the opinion that 2 to think carefully about (a problem or decision) 3 to bear in mind: *Corsica is well worth considering for those seeking a peaceful holiday in beautiful surroundings* 4 to have regard for or care about: *you must try to consider other people's feelings more* 5 to discuss (something) in order to make a decision 6 to look at: *he considered her and she forced herself to sit calmly under his gaze*

> **consider** vb 1 = think, see, believe, rate, judge, suppose, deem, view as 2 = think about, reflect on, weigh, contemplate, deliberate, ponder, meditate, ruminate 3, 4 = bear in mind, remember, respect, think about, take into account, reckon with, take into consideration, make allowance for

considerable adj 1 large enough to reckon with: *a considerable number of people* 2 a lot of: *he was in considerable pain* > **considerably** adv

> **considerable** adj 1 = large, goodly, great, marked, substantial, noticeable, plentiful, appreciable; ≠ small

considerate adj thoughtful towards other people

consideration n 1 careful thought 2 a fact to be taken into account when making a decision

3 thoughtfulness for other people **4** payment for a service **5 take into consideration** to bear in mind **6 under consideration** being currently discussed

> **consideration** n **1** = thought, review, analysis, examination, reflection, scrutiny, deliberation **2** = factor, point, issue, concern, element, aspect **3** = thoughtfulness, concern, respect, kindness, tact, considerateness **4** = payment, fee, reward, remuneration, recompense, tip

considering conj, prep **1** = taking (a specified fact) into account: considering the mileage the car had done, it was lasting well ▸ adv **2** informal taking into account the circumstances: it's not bad considering

> **considering** conj, prep = taking into account, in the light of, bearing in mind, in view of, keeping in mind, taking into consideration

consign vb **1** to give into the care or charge of **2** to put irrevocably: those events have been consigned to history **3** to put (in a specified place or situation): only a few months ago such demands would have consigned the student leaders to prisons and labour camps **4** to address or deliver (goods): a cargo of oil drilling equipment consigned to Saudi Arabia > **consignee** n > **consignor** n

consignment n **1** a shipment of goods **2** the act or an instance of consigning: the goods are sent to Hong Kong for onward consignment to customers in the area

consist vb **1 consist of** to be made up of: a match consists of seven games **2 consist in** to have as its main or only part: their religion consists only in going to church

> **consist** vb **1 consist of something** = be made up of, include, contain, incorporate, amount to, comprise, be composed of **2 consist in something** = lie in, involve, reside in, be expressed by, subsist in, be found or contained in

consistency n, pl **-encies 1** degree of thickness or smoothness **2** being consistent

> **consistency** n **1** = texture, density, thickness, firmness, viscosity, compactness **2** = agreement, regularity, uniformity, constancy, steadiness, steadfastness, evenness

consistent adj **1** holding to the same principles **2** in agreement > **consistently** adv

> **consistent** adj **1** = steady, even, regular, stable, constant, persistent, dependable, unchanging; ≠ erratic **2** = compatible, agreeing, in keeping, harmonious, in harmony, consonant, in accord, congruous; ≠ incompatible

consolation n **1** a person or thing that is a comfort in a time of sadness or distress **2** a consoling or being consoled

consolation n = comfort, help, support, relief, cheer, encouragement, solace, succour

console[1] vb **-soling, -soled** to comfort (someone) in sadness or distress > **consolable** adj

> **console** vb = comfort, cheer, soothe, support, encourage, calm, succour, express sympathy for; ≠ distress

console[2] n **1** a panel of controls for electronic equipment **2** a cabinet for a television or audio equipment **3** an ornamental bracket used to support a wall fixture **4** the desklike case of an organ, containing the pedals, stops, and keys

consolidate vb **-dating, -dated 1** to make or become stronger or more stable **2** to combine into a whole > **consolidation** n > **consolidator** n

> **consolidate** vb **1** = strengthen, secure, reinforce, fortify, stabilize **2** = combine, unite, join, merge, unify, amalgamate, federate

consommé (kon-**som**-may) n a thin clear meat soup

consonance n formal agreement or harmony

consonant n **1 A** a speech sound made by partially or completely blocking the breath streams, for example b or f **B** a letter representing this ▸ adj **2 consonant with** in keeping or agreement with: an individualistic style of religion, more consonant with liberal society **3** harmonious: this highly dissonant chord is followed by a more consonant one

consort vb **1 consort with** to keep company with ▸ n **2** a husband or wife of a reigning monarch **3** a small group of voices or instruments

consortium n, pl **-tia** an association of business firms

conspectus n formal a survey or summary

conspicuous adj **1** clearly visible **2** noteworthy or striking: conspicuous bravery > **conspicuously** adv

> **conspicuous** adj **1** = obvious, clear, patent, evident, noticeable, blatant, salient; ≠ inconspicuous

conspiracy n, pl **-cies 1** a secret plan to carry out an illegal or harmful act **2** the act of making such plans

> **conspiracy** n = plot, scheme, intrigue, collusion, machination

conspire vb **-spiring, -spired 1** to plan a crime together in secret **2** to act together as if by design: the weather and the recession conspired to hit wine production and sales > **conspirator** n > **conspiratorial** adj

> **conspire** vb **1** = plot, scheme, intrigue, manoeuvre, contrive, machinate, plan **2** = work together, combine, contribute, cooperate, concur, tend

constable n a police officer of the lowest rank

constabulary *n, pl* **-laries** *chiefly Brit* the police force of an area

constant *adj* **1** continuous: *she has endured constant criticism, mockery, and humiliation* **2** unchanging: *the average speed of the winds remained constant over this period* **3** faithful ▸ *n* **4** *maths & physics* a quantity or number which remains invariable: *the velocity of light is a constant* **5** something that is unchanging > **constancy** *n* > **constantly** *adv*

> **constant** *adj* **1** = continuous, sustained, perpetual, interminable, unrelenting, incessant, ceaseless, nonstop; ≠ occasional **2** = unchanging, even, fixed, permanent, stable, steady, uniform, invariable; ≠ changing **3** = faithful, true, devoted, loyal, stalwart, staunch, trustworthy, trusty; ≠ undependable

constellation *n* **1** a group of stars which form a pattern and are given a name **2** a group of people or things: *the constellation of favourable circumstances*

consternation *n* a feeling of anxiety or dismay

constipated *adj* unable to empty one's bowels

constipation *n* a condition in which emptying one's bowels is difficult

constituency *n, pl* **-cies** **1** the area represented by a Member of Parliament **2** the voters in such an area

constituent *n* **1** a person living in an MP's constituency **2** a component part ▸ *adj* **3** forming part of a whole: *the constituent parts of the universe* **4** having the power to make or change a constitution of a state: *a constituent assembly*

> **constituent** *n* **1** = voter, elector, member of the electorate **2** = component, element, ingredient, part, unit, factor ▸ *adj* **3** = component, basic, essential, integral, elemental

constitute *vb* **-tuting, -tuted** **1** to form or make up: *the amazing range of crags that constitute the Eglwyseg Mountains* **2** to set up (an institution) formally

> **constitute** *vb* **1** = make up, form, compose, comprise

constitution *n* **1** the principles on which a state is governed **2** **the Constitution** (in certain countries) the statute embodying such principles **3** a person's state of health **4** the make-up or structure of something: *changes in the very constitution of society*

> **constitution** *n* **3** = state of health, build, body, frame, physique, physical condition **4** = structure, form, nature, make-up, composition, character, disposition

constitutional *adj* **1** of a constitution **2** authorized by or in accordance with the Constitution of a nation: *constitutional monarchy* **3** inherent in the nature of a person or thing: *a constitutional sensitivity to cold* ▸ *n* **4** a regular walk taken for the good of one's health > **constitutionally** *adv*

> **constitutional** *adj* **1, 2** = legitimate, official, legal, chartered, statutory, vested

constrain *vb* **1** to compel or force: *he felt constrained to apologize* **2** to limit, restrict, or inhibit: *the mobility of workers is constrained by the serious housing shortage*

> **constrain** *vb* **1** = force, bind, compel, oblige, necessitate, coerce, impel, pressurize **2** = restrict, confine, curb, restrain, constrict, straiten, check

constraint *n* **1** something that limits a person's freedom of action **2** repression of natural feelings **3** a forced unnatural manner

> **constraint** *n* **1** = restriction, limitation, curb, rein, deterrent, hindrance, check

constrict *vb* **1** to make smaller or narrower by squeezing **2** to limit or restrict > **constrictive** *adj*

constriction *n* **1** a feeling of tightness in some part of the body, such as the chest **2** a narrowing **3** something that constricts

constrictor *n* **1** a snake that coils around and squeezes its prey to kill it **2** a muscle that contracts an opening

construct *vb* **1** to build or put together **2** *geom* to draw (a figure) to specified requirements **3** to compose (an argument or sentence) ▸ *n* **4** a complex idea resulting from the combination of simpler ideas **5** something formulated or built systematically > **constructor** *n*

> **construct** *vb* **1** = build, make, form, create, fashion, shape, manufacture, assemble; ≠ demolish **3** = create, make, form, compose, put together

construction *n* **1** the act of constructing or manner in which a thing is constructed **2** something that has been constructed **3** the business or work of building houses or other structures **4** *formal* an interpretation: *the financial markets will put the worst possible construction on any piece of news which might affect them* **5** *grammar* the way in which words are arranged in a sentence, clause, or phrase > **constructional** *adj*

> **construction** *n* **1** = building, creation, composition **4** = interpretation, reading, explanation, rendering, inference

constructive *adj* **1** useful and helpful: *constructive criticism* **2** *law* deduced by inference; not openly expressed > **constructively** *adv*

> **constructive** *adj* **1** = helpful, positive, useful, practical, valuable, productive; ≠ unproductive

construe vb **-struing, -strued 1** to interpret the meaning of (something): *her indifference was construed as rudeness* **2** to analyse the grammatical structure of (a sentence) **3** to combine (words) grammatically **4** *old-fashioned* to translate literally

consul n **1** an official representing a state in a foreign country **2** one of the two chief magistrates in ancient Rome > **consular** adj > **consulship** n

consulate n **1** the workplace and official home of a consul **2** the position or period of office of a consul

consult vb **1** to ask advice from or discuss matters with (someone): *he never consults his wife about what he's about to do* **2** to refer to for information: *she consulted the map again*

> **consult** vb **1** = ask, refer to, turn to, take counsel, pick (someone's) brains, question **2** = refer to, check in, look in

consultant n **1** a specialist doctor with a senior position in a hospital **2** a specialist who gives expert professional advice > **consultancy** n

> **consultant** n **2** = specialist, adviser, counsellor, authority

consultation n **1** the act of consulting **2** a meeting for discussion or the seeking of advice > **consultative** adj

> **consultation** n **1** = discussion, talk, council, conference, dialogue **2** = meeting, interview, session, appointment, examination, deliberation, hearing

consume vb **-suming, -sumed 1** to eat or drink **2** to use up **3** to destroy: *the ship blew up and was consumed by flames* **4** to obsess: *he was consumed with jealousy over the ending of their affair* > **consumable** adj > **consuming** adj

> **consume** vb **1** = eat, swallow, devour, put away, gobble (up), eat up **2** = use up, spend, waste, absorb, exhaust, squander, dissipate, expend **3** = destroy, devastate, demolish (*facetious*), ravage, annihilate, lay waste **4** = obsess, dominate, absorb, preoccupy, eat up, monopolize, engross

consumer n a person who buys goods or uses services

> **consumer** n = buyer, customer, user, shopper, purchaser

consummate vb (kon-sum-mate) **-mating, -mated 1** to make (a marriage) legal by sexual intercourse **2** to complete or fulfil ▸ adj (kon-**sum**-mit) **3** supremely skilled: *a consummate craftsman* **4** complete or extreme: *consummate skill*; *consummate ignorance* > **consummation** n

consumption n **1** the quantity of something consumed or used: *for such a powerful car, fuel consumption is modest* **2** the act of eating or

drinking something: *this meat is unfit for human consumption* **3** *econ* purchase of goods and services for personal use **4** *old-fashioned* tuberculosis of the lungs

> **consumption** n **1** = using up, use, loss, waste, expenditure, exhaustion, depletion, dissipation **4** = tuberculosis, T.B.

consumptive adj **1** wasteful or destructive **2** of tuberculosis of the lungs ▸ n **3** a person with tuberculosis of the lungs

cont. continued

contact n **1** the state or act of communication: *the airport lost contact with the plane shortly before the crash* **2** the state or act of touching: *rugby is a game of hard physical contact* **3** an acquaintance who might be useful in business **4** a connection between two electrical conductors in a circuit **5** a person who has been exposed to a contagious disease ▸ vb **6** to come or be in communication or touch with > **contactless** adj

> **contact** n **1** = communication, link, association, connection, correspondence **2** = touch, contiguity **3** = connection, colleague, associate, liaison, acquaintance, confederate ▸ vb = get or be in touch with, call, reach, approach, write to, speak to, communicate with, email or e-mail, text, message

contact lens n a small lens placed on the eyeball to correct defective vision

contagion n **1** the passing on of disease by contact **2** a contagious disease **3** a corrupting influence that tends to spread

contagious adj **1** (of a disease) capable of being passed on by contact **2** (of a person) capable of passing on a transmissible disease **3** spreading from person to person: *contagious enthusiasm*

contain vb **1** to hold or be capable of holding: *the bag contained a selection of men's clothing* **2** to have as one of its ingredients or constituents: *tea and coffee both contain appreciable amounts of caffeine* **3** to consist of: *the book contains 13 very different and largely separate chapters* **4** to check or restrain (feelings or behaviour) **5** to prevent from spreading or going beyond fixed limits: *the blockade was too weak to contain the French fleet* > **containable** adj

> **contain** vb **1** = hold, incorporate, accommodate, enclose, have capacity for **2, 3** = include, consist of, embrace, comprise, embody, comprehend **4, 5** = restrain, control, hold in, curb, suppress, hold back, stifle, repress

container n **1** an object used to hold or store things in **2** a large standard-sized box for transporting cargo by lorry or ship

> **container** n **1** = holder, vessel, repository, receptacle

C

containment *n* the prevention of the spread of something harmful

contaminate *vb* **-nating, -nated** 1 to make impure; pollute 2 to make radioactive
> **contaminant** *n* > **contamination** *n*

> **contaminate** *vb* 1 = pollute, infect, stain, corrupt, taint, defile, adulterate, befoul; ≠ purify

contemplate *vb* **-plating, -plated** 1 to think deeply about 2 to consider as a possibility 3 to look at thoughtfully 4 to meditate
> **contemplation** *n*

> **contemplate** *vb* 1 = think about, consider, ponder, reflect upon, ruminate (upon), muse over, deliberate over 2 = consider, plan, think of, intend, envisage, foresee 3 = look at, examine, inspect, gaze at, eye up, view, study, regard

contemplative *adj* 1 of or given to contemplation ▶ *n* 2 a person dedicated to religious contemplation

contemporaneous *adj* happening at the same time > **contemporaneity** *n*

contemporary *adj* 1 existing or occurring at the present time 2 living or occurring in the same period 3 modern in style or fashion 4 of approximately the same age ▶ *n, pl* **-raries** 5 a person or thing living at the same time or of approximately the same age as another

> **contemporary** *adj* 1, 3 = modern, recent, current, up-to-date, present-day, à la mode, newfangled, present; ≠ old-fashioned 2, 4 = coexisting, concurrent, contemporaneous ▶ *n* = peer, fellow, equal

contempt *n* 1 scorn 2 **hold in contempt** to scorn or despise 3 deliberate disrespect for the authority of a court of law: *contempt of court*

> **contempt** *n* 1 = scorn, disdain, mockery, derision, disrespect, disregard; ≠ respect

contemptible *adj* deserving to be despised or hated: *a contemptible lack of courage*

contemptuous *adj* showing or feeling strong dislike or disrespect > **contemptuously** *adv*

contend *vb* 1 **contend with** to deal with 2 to assert 3 to compete or fight 4 to argue earnestly > **contender** *n*

> **contend** *vb* 2 = argue, hold, maintain, allege, assert, affirm 3 = compete, fight, struggle, clash, contest, strive, vie, jostle

content¹ *n* 1 **contents** everything inside a container 2 **contents** a list of chapters at the front of a book 3 the meaning or substance of a piece of writing, often as distinguished from its style or form 4 the information presented on a website 5 the amount of a substance contained in a mixture: *the water vapour content of the atmosphere*

> **content** *n* 1 = constituents, elements, load, ingredients 3 = subject matter, material, theme, substance, essence, gist 5 = amount, measure, size, load, volume, capacity

content² *adj* 1 satisfied with things as they are 2 willing to accept a situation or a proposed course of action ▶ *vb* 3 to satisfy (oneself or another person) ▶ *n* 4 peace of mind
> **contentment** *n*

> **content** *adj* 1 = satisfied, happy, pleased, contented, comfortable, fulfilled, at ease, gratified ▶ *n* = satisfaction, ease, pleasure, comfort, peace of mind, gratification, contentment

contented *adj* satisfied with one's situation or life > **contentedly** *adv* > **contentedness** *n*

> **contented** *adj* = satisfied, happy, pleased, content, comfortable, glad, thankful, gratified; ≠ discontented

contention *n* 1 disagreement or dispute 2 a point asserted in argument 3 **bone of contention** a point of dispute

contentious *adj* 1 causing disagreement 2 tending to quarrel > **contentiousness** *n*

> **contentious** *adj* 2 = argumentative, wrangling, bickering, quarrelsome, querulous, cavilling, disputatious, captious

contest *n* 1 a game or match in which people or teams compete 2 a struggle for power or control ▶ *vb* 3 to dispute: *he has said he will not contest the verdict* 4 to take part in (a contest or struggle for power): *all parties which meet the legal requirements will be allowed to contest the election*
> **contestable** *adj*

> **contest** *n* 1 = competition, game, match, trial, tournament 2 = struggle, fight, battle, conflict, dispute, controversy, combat ▶ *vb* 3 = oppose, question, challenge, argue, debate, dispute, object to, call in *or* into question 4 = compete in, take part in, fight in, go in for, contend for, vie in

contestant *n* a person who takes part in a contest

> **contestant** *n* = competitor, candidate, participant, contender, entrant, player

context *n* 1 the circumstances relevant to an event or fact 2 the words before and after a word or passage in a piece of writing that contribute to its meaning: *taken out of context, lines like these sound ridiculous, but, as part of a scrupulously written play, they are just right* > **contextual** *adj*

> **context** *n* 1 = circumstances, conditions, situation, ambience 2 = frame of reference, background, framework, relation, connection

contiguous *adj formal* very near or touching

continent[1] *n* one of the earth's large landmasses (Asia, Australia, Africa, Europe, North and South America, and Antarctica) > **continental** *adj*

continent[2] *adj* 1 able to control one's bladder and bowels 2 sexually restrained > **continence** *n*

Continent *n* **the Continent** the mainland of Europe as distinct from the British Isles > **Continental** *adj*

continental breakfast *n* a light breakfast of coffee and rolls

contingency *n, pl* **-cies** 1 an unknown or unforeseen future event or condition 2 something dependent on a possible future event

> **contingency** *n* = possibility, happening, chance, event, incident, accident, emergency, eventuality

contingent *n* 1 a group of people with a common interest, that represents a larger group: *a contingent of European scientists* 2 a military group that is part of a larger force: *the force includes a contingent of the Foreign Legion* ▸ *adj* 3 (foll. by *on* or *upon*) dependent on (something uncertain) 4 happening by chance

continual *adj* 1 occurring without interruption 2 recurring frequently > **continually** *adv*

> **continual** *adj* 1 = constant, interminable, incessant, unremitting; ≠ erratic 2 = frequent, regular, repeated, recurrent; ≠ occasional

continuance *n* 1 the act of continuing 2 duration

continuation *n* 1 the act of continuing 2 a part or thing added, such as a sequel 3 a renewal of an interrupted action or process

> **continuation** *n* 1 = continuing, lasting, carrying on, keeping up, endurance, perpetuation, prolongation 2 = addition, extension, supplement, sequel, resumption, postscript

continue *vb* **-tinuing, -tinued** 1 to remain or cause to remain in a particular condition or place 2 to carry on (doing something): *we continued kissing; heavy fighting continued until Thursday afternoon* 3 to resume after an interruption: *we'll continue after lunch* 4 to go on to a further place: *the road continues on up the hill*

> **continue** *vb* 1 = remain, last, stay, survive, carry on, live on, endure, persist; ≠ quit 2 = keep on, go on, maintain, sustain, carry on, persist in, persevere, stick at; ≠ stop 3 = resume, return to, take up again, proceed, carry on, recommence, pick up where you left off; ≠ stop 4 = go on, progress, proceed, carry on, keep going, crack on (*informal*)

continuity *n, pl* **-ties** 1 a smooth development or sequence 2 the arrangement of scenes in a film so that they follow each other logically and without breaks

> **continuity** *n* 1 = cohesion, flow, connection, sequence, succession, progression

continuo *n, pl* **-tinuos** *music* a continuous bass accompaniment played usually on a keyboard instrument

continuous *adj* 1 without end: *a continuous process* 2 not having any breaks or gaps in it: *a continuous line of boats; continuous rain* > **continuously** *adv*

> **continuous** *adj* 2 = constant, extended, prolonged, unbroken, uninterrupted, unceasing; ≠ occasional

continuum *n, pl* **-tinua** *or* **-tinuums** a continuous series or whole, no part of which is noticeably different from the parts immediately next to it, although the ends or extremes of it are very different from each other: *the continuum from minor misbehaviour to major crime*

contort *vb* to twist or bend out of shape > **contortion** *n*

contortionist *n* a performer who contorts his or her body to entertain others

contour *n* 1 an outline 2 same as **contour line** ▸ *vb* 3 to shape so as to form or follow the contour of something

contour line *n* a line on a map or chart joining points of equal height or depth

contra- *prefix* 1 against or contrasting: *contraceptive* 2 (in music) lower in pitch: *contrabass*

contraband *n* 1 smuggled goods ▸ *adj* 2 (of goods) smuggled

contraception *n* the deliberate use of artificial or natural means to prevent pregnancy

contraceptive *n* 1 a device, such as a condom, that is used to prevent pregnancy ▸ *adj* 2 providing or relating to contraception: *the contraceptive pill*

contract *n* 1 a formal agreement between two or more parties 2 a document setting out a formal agreement ▸ *vb* 3 to make a formal agreement with (a person or company) to do or deliver (something) 4 to enter into (a relationship or marriage) formally: *to contract a marriage without the approval of one's guardian* 5 to make or become smaller, narrower, or shorter 6 to become affected by (an illness) 7 to draw (muscles) together or (of muscles) to be drawn together 8 to shorten (a word or phrase) by omitting letters or syllables, usually indicated in writing by an apostrophe > **contractible** *adj*

> **contract** *n* 1 = agreement, commitment, arrangement, settlement, bargain, pact, covenant ▸ *vb* 3 = agree, negotiate, pledge, bargain, undertake, come to terms, covenant, make a deal; ≠ refuse 5 = constrict, confine, tighten, shorten, compress, condense, shrivel; ≠ increase 6 = catch, get, develop, acquire, incur, be infected with, go down with, be afflicted with; ≠ avoid 7 = tighten, narrow, shorten; ≠ stretch

contraction *n* **1** a contracting or being contracted **2** a shortening of a word or group of words, often marked by an apostrophe, for example *I've come* for *I have come* **3 contractions** *med* temporary shortening and tensing of the uterus during pregnancy and labour

> **contraction** *n* **1** = tightening, narrowing, shortening, constricting, shrinkage **2** = abbreviation, reduction, shortening, compression

contractor *n* a person or firm that supplies materials or labour for other companies
contractual *adj* of or in the nature of a contract
contradict *vb* **1** to declare the opposite of (a statement) to be true **2** (of a fact or statement) to suggest that (another fact or statement) is wrong > **contradiction** *n*

> **contradict** *vb* **1** = negate, deny, rebut, controvert; ≠ confirm **2** = dispute, deny, challenge, belie, fly in the face of, be at variance with

contradictory *adj* (of facts or statements) inconsistent

> **contradictory** *adj* = inconsistent, conflicting, opposed, opposite, contrary, incompatible, paradoxical

contraflow *n* a flow of road traffic going alongside but in an opposite direction to the usual flow
contralto *n*, *pl* **-tos** *or* **-ti** **1** the lowest female voice **2** a singer with such a voice
contraption *n informal* a strange-looking device or gadget
contrapuntal *adj music* of or in counterpoint
contrariwise *adv* **1** from a contrasting point of view **2** in the opposite way
contrary *n*, *pl* **-ries 1 on** *or* **to the contrary** in opposition to what has just been said or implied ▸ *adj* **2** opposed; completely different: *a contrary view, based on equally good information* **3** perverse; obstinate **4** (of the wind) unfavourable ▸ *adv* **contrary to 5** in opposition or contrast to: *contrary to popular belief* **6** in conflict with: *contrary to nature* > **contrariness** *n*

> **contrary** *adj* **2** = opposite, different, opposed, clashing, counter, reverse, adverse, contradictory; ≠ in agreement **3** = perverse, difficult, awkward, intractable, obstinate, stroppy (*Brit slang*), cantankerous, disobliging; ≠ cooperative

contrast *n* **1** a difference which is clearly seen when two things are compared **2** a person or thing showing differences when compared with another **3** the degree of difference between the colours in a photograph or television picture ▸ *vb* **4** to compare or be compared in order to show the differences between (things): *he contrasts that society with*

contemporary America **5 contrast with** to be very different from: *her speed of reaction contrasted with her husband's vagueness* > **contrasting** *adj*

> **contrast** *n* **1** = difference, opposition, comparison, distinction, foil, disparity, divergence, dissimilarity ▸ *vb* **4** = differentiate, compare, oppose, distinguish, set in opposition

contravene *vb* **-vening, -vened** *formal* to break (a rule or law) > **contravention** *n*
contretemps (kon-tra-tahn) *n*, *pl* **-temps** an embarrassing minor disagreement
contribute *vb* **-buting, -buted** (often foll. by *to*) **1** to give (support or money) for a common purpose or fund **2** to supply (ideas or opinions) **3 contribute to** to be partly responsible for: *his own unconvincing play contributed to his defeat* **4** to write (an article) for a publication > **contribution** *n* > **contributory** *adj* > **contributor** *n*

> **contribute** *vb* **1** = give, provide, supply, donate, subscribe, chip in (*informal*), bestow **3 contribute to something** = be partly responsible for, lead to, be instrumental in, be conducive to, help

contrite *adj* full of guilt or regret > **contritely** *adv* > **contrition** *n*
contrivance *n* **1** an ingenious device **2** an elaborate or deceitful plan **3** the act or power of contriving
contrive *vb* **-triving, -trived 1** to make happen: *he had already contrived the murder of King Alexander* **2** to devise or construct ingeniously: *he contrived a plausible reason to fly back to London; he contrived a hook from a bent nail*

> **contrive** *vb* = devise, plan, fabricate, create, design, scheme, manufacture, plot

contrived *adj* obviously planned or artificial
control *n* **1** power to direct something: *the province is mostly under guerrilla control* **2** a curb or check: *import controls* **3 controls** instruments used to operate a machine **4** a standard of comparison used in an experiment **5** an experiment used to verify another by having all aspects identical except for the one that is being tested ▸ *vb* **-trolling, -trolled 6** to have power over: *the gland which controls the body's metabolic rate* **7** to limit or restrain: *he could not control his jealousy* **8** to regulate or operate (a machine) **9** to restrict the authorized supply of (certain drugs) > **controllable** *adj*

> **control** *n* **1** = power, authority, management, command, guidance, supervision, supremacy, charge **2** = restraint, check, regulation, brake, limitation, curb **3** = instruments, dash, dials, console, dashboard, control panel ▸ *vb* **6** = have power over, manage, direct, handle, command, govern, administer, supervise **7** = restrain, limit, check, contain, curb, hold back, subdue, repress

controller *n* **1** a person who is in charge **2** a person in charge of the financial aspects of a business

controversy *n, pl* **-sies** argument or debate concerning a matter about which there is strong disagreement > **controversial** *adj*

> **controversy** *n* = argument, debate, row, dispute, quarrel, squabble, wrangling, altercation

contumely (kon-tume-mill-ee) *n, pl* **-lies** *literary* **1** scornful or insulting treatment **2** a humiliating insult

contusion *n formal* a bruise > **contuse** *vb*

conundrum *n* **1** a puzzling question or problem **2** a riddle whose answer contains a pun

conurbation *n* a large heavily populated urban area formed by the growth and merging of towns

convalesce *vb* **-lescing, -lesced** to recover health after an illness or operation

convalescence *n* **1** gradual return to health after illness or an operation **2** the period during which such recovery occurs > **convalescent** *n, adj*

convection *n* the transmission of heat caused by movement of molecules from cool regions to warmer regions of lower density

convector *n* a heating device which gives out hot air

convene *vb* **-vening, -vened** to gather or summon for a formal meeting

> **convene** *vb* = call, gather, assemble, summon, bring together, convoke (*formal*)

convener *or* **convenor** *n* a person who calls or chairs a meeting: *the shop stewards' convener at the factory* > **convenership** *or* **convenorship** *n*

convenience *n* **1** the quality of being suitable or convenient **2 at your convenience** at a time suitable to you **3** an object that is useful: *a house with every modern convenience* **4** *euphemistic, chiefly Brit* a public toilet

> **convenience** *n* **1** = suitability, fitness, appropriateness; ≠ uselessness **3** = appliance, facility, comfort, amenity, labour-saving device, help

convenient *adj* **1** suitable or opportune **2** easy to use **3** nearby > **conveniently** *adv*

> **convenient** *adj* **1** = suitable, fit, handy, satisfactory **2** = useful, practical, handy, serviceable, labour-saving; ≠ useless **3** = nearby, available, accessible, handy, at hand, within reach, close at hand, just round the corner; ≠ inaccessible

convent *n* **1** a building where nuns live **2** a school in which the teachers are nuns **3** a community of nuns

convention *n* **1** the established view of what is thought to be proper behaviour **2** an accepted rule or method: *a convention used by printers*

3 a formal agreement or contract between people and nations **4** a large formal assembly of a group with common interests

> **convention** *n* **1, 2** = custom, practice, tradition, code, usage, protocol, etiquette, propriety, kawa (NZ), tikanga (NZ) **3** = agreement, contract, treaty, bargain, pact, protocol **4** = assembly, meeting, council, conference, congress, convocation (*formal*), hui (NZ), runanga (NZ)

conventional *adj* **1** following the accepted customs and lacking originality **2** established by accepted usage or general agreement **3** (of weapons or warfare) not nuclear > **conventionally** *adv*

> **conventional** *adj* **1** = traditional, accepted, orthodox, customary; ≠ unconventional **2** = ordinary, standard, normal, regular, usual

conventionality *n, pl* **-ties** **1** the quality of being conventional **2** something conventional

converge *vb* **-verging, -verged** **1** to move towards or meet at the same point **2** (of opinions or effects) to move towards a shared conclusion or result > **convergence** *n* > **convergent** *adj*

> **converge** *vb* = come together, meet, join, combine, gather, merge, coincide, intersect

conversant *adj* **conversant with** having knowledge or experience of

conversation *n* informal talk between two or more people

> **conversation** *n* = talk, discussion, dialogue, tête-à-tête, conference, chat, gossip, discourse, korero (NZ)

conversational *adj* **1** of or used in conversation: *conversational French* **2** resembling informal spoken language: *the author's easy, conversational style*

conversationalist *n* a person with a specified ability at conversation: *a brilliant conversationalist*

converse¹ *vb* **-versing, -versed** to have a conversation

converse² *adj* **1** reversed or opposite ▸ *n* **2** a statement or idea that is the opposite of another > **conversely** *adv*

conversion *n* **1** a change or adaptation **2** *maths* a calculation in which a weight, volume, or distance is worked out in a different system of measurement: *the conversion from Fahrenheit to Celsius* **3** a change to another belief or religion **4** *rugby* a score made after a try by kicking the ball over the crossbar from a place kick

> **conversion** *n* **1** = adaptation, reconstruction, modification, alteration, remodelling, reorganization

convert *vb* **1** to change or adapt **2** to cause (someone) to change in opinion or belief **3** to

change (a measurement) from one system of units to another **4** to change (money) into a different currency **5** *rugby* to make a conversion after (a try) ▸ *n* **6** a person who has been converted to another belief or religion
▸ **converter** *or* **convertor** *n*

> **convert** *vb* **1** = adapt, modify, remodel, reorganize, customize, restyle **2** = reform, convince, proselytize ▸ *n* = neophyte (*formal*), disciple, proselyte

convertible *adj* **1** capable of being converted **2** *finance* (of a currency) freely exchangeable into other currencies ▸ *n* **3** a car with a folding or removable roof

convex *adj* curving outwards like the outside surface of a ball ▸ **convexity** *n*

convey *vb* **1** to communicate (information) **2** to carry or transport from one place to another **3** (of a channel or path) to transfer or transmit **4** *law* to transfer (the title to property)
▸ **conveyable** *adj* ▸ **conveyor** *n*

> **convey** *vb* **1** = communicate, impart, reveal, relate, disclose, make known, tell **2** = carry, transport, move, bring, bear, conduct, fetch

conveyance *n* **1** *old-fashioned* a vehicle **2** *law* **A** a transfer of the legal title to property **B** the document effecting such a transfer **3** the act of conveying: *the conveyance of cycles on peak hour trains*
▸ **conveyancer** *n*

conveyancing *n* the branch of law dealing with the transfer of ownership of property

conveyor belt *n* an endless moving belt driven by rollers and used to transport objects, esp. in a factory

convict *vb* **1** to declare (someone) guilty of an offence ▸ *n* **2** a person serving a prison sentence

> **convict** *vb* = find guilty, sentence, condemn, imprison, pronounce guilty ▸ *n* = prisoner, criminal, lag (*slang*), felon, jailbird

conviction *n* **1** a firmly held belief or opinion **2** an instance of being found guilty of a crime: *he had several convictions for petty theft* **3** a convincing or being convinced **4 carry conviction** to be convincing

> **conviction** *n* **1** = belief, view, opinion, principle, faith, persuasion, creed, tenet, kaupapa (NZ) **3** = certainty, confidence, assurance, firmness, certitude

convince *vb* **-vincing, -vinced** to persuade by argument or evidence ▸ **convinced** *adj*
▸ **convincible** *adj* ▸ **convincing** *adj*
▸ **convincingly** *adv*

> **convince** *vb* = assure, persuade, satisfy, reassure

convivial *adj* sociable or lively: *a convivial atmosphere; convivial company* ▸ **conviviality** *n*

convocation *n formal* a large formal meeting

convoke *vb* **-voking, -voked** *formal* to call together

convoluted *adj* **1** coiled or twisted **2** (of an argument or sentence) complex and difficult to understand

convolution *n* **1** a coil or twist **2** an intricate or confused matter or condition **3** a convex fold in the surface of the brain

convolvulus *n*, *pl* **-luses** *or* **-li** a twining plant with funnel-shaped flowers and triangular leaves

convoy *n* a group of vehicles or ships travelling together

convulse *vb* **-vulsing, -vulsed** **1** to shake or agitate violently **2** (of muscles) to undergo violent spasms **3** *informal* to be overcome (with laughter or rage) **4** to disrupt the normal running of: *student riots have convulsed India*
▸ **convulsive** *adj*

convulsion *n* **1** a violent muscular spasm **2** a violent upheaval **3 convulsions** *informal* uncontrollable laughter: *I was in convulsions*

cony *or* **coney** *n*, *pl* **-nies** *or* **-neys** *Brit* **1** a rabbit **2** rabbit fur

coo *vb* **cooing, cooed** **1** (of a dove or pigeon) to make a soft murmuring sound **2 bill and coo** to murmur softly or lovingly ▸ *n* **3** a cooing sound ▸ *interj* **4** *Brit slang* an exclamation of surprise or amazement ▸ **cooing** *adj*, *n*

cooee *interj* **1** *Brit, Austral & NZ* a call used to attract attention **2** *Austral & NZ* **within cooee** within calling distance: *the school was within cooee of our house*

cook *vb* **1** to prepare (food) by heating or (of food) to be prepared in this way **2** *slang* to alter or falsify (figures or accounts): *she had cooked the books* ▸ *n* **3** a person who prepares food for eating
▸ See also **cook up**

cooker *n* **1** *chiefly Brit* an apparatus for cooking heated by gas or electricity **2** *Brit* an apple suitable for cooking but not for eating raw

cookery *n* the art or practice of cooking. Related adjective: **culinary**

cookie *n*, *pl* **cookies** **1** *US & Canad* a biscuit **2 that's the way the cookie crumbles** *informal* that is how things inevitably are **3** *informal* a person: *a real tough cookie* **4** *computers* a piece of data downloaded from a website to a user's computer, allowing the user to be identified on future visits to the website

cook up *vb* to invent (a story or scheme)

cool *adj* **1** moderately cold: *it should be served cool, even chilled* **2** comfortably free of heat: *it was one of the few cool days that summer* **3** calm and unemotional: *a cool head* **4** indifferent or unfriendly: *the idea met with a cool response* **5** calmly impudent **6** *informal* (of a large sum of money) without exaggeration: *a cool million* **7** *informal* sophisticated or elegant **8** (of a colour) having violet, blue, or green predominating **9** *informal* excellent; marvellous ▸ *vb* **10** to make or become cooler **11** to calm down ▸ *n* **12** coolness:

in the cool of the evening **13** *slang* calmness; composure: *he lost his cool and wantonly kicked the ball away* ▸ **coolly** *adv* ▸ **coolness** *n*

cool *adj* **1** = cold, chilled, refreshing, chilly, nippy; ≠ warm **3** = calm, collected, relaxed, composed, sedate, self-controlled, unruffled, unemotional, chilled (*informal*); ≠ agitated **4** = unfriendly, distant, indifferent, aloof, lukewarm, offhand, unenthusiastic, unwelcoming; ≠ friendly ▸ *vb* **10** = lose heat, cool off; ≠ warm (up) ▸ *n* **12** = coldness, chill, coolness **13** = calmness, control, temper, composure, self-control, poise, self-discipline, self-possession

coolant *n* a fluid used to cool machinery while it is working

cool drink *n S African* a soft drink

cooler *n* a container for making or keeping things cool

coolibah *n* an Australian eucalypt that grows beside rivers

coolie *n old-fashioned, offensive* an unskilled E Asian labourer

coomb *or* **coombe** *n* a short valley or deep hollow

coon *n* **1** *informal* short for **raccoon 2** *offensive slang* a Black person of African origin or a member of an Australian Aboriginal people **3** *S African offensive* a person of mixed race

coop[1] *n* **1** a cage or pen for poultry or small animals ▸ *vb* **2 coop up** to confine in a restricted place

coop[2] *or* **co-op** (koh-op) *n Brit, Austral & NZ* a cooperative society or a shop run by a cooperative society

cooper *n* a person who makes or repairs barrels or casks

cooperate *or* **co-operate** *vb* **1** to work or act together **2** to assist or be willing to assist ▸ **cooperation** *or* **co-operation** *n*

cooperate *or* **co-operate** *vb* **1** = work together, collaborate, coordinate, join forces, conspire, pull together, pool resources, combine your efforts; ≠ conflict

cooperative *or* **co-operative** *adj* **1** willing to cooperate **2** (of an enterprise or farm) owned and managed collectively ▸ *n* **3** a cooperative organization

cooperative *or* **co-operative** *adj* **1** = helpful, obliging, accommodating, supportive, responsive, onside (*informal*) **2** = shared, joint, combined, collective, collaborative

coopt *or* **co-opt** (koh-opt) *vb* to add (someone) to a group by the agreement of the existing members

coordinate *or* **co-ordinate** *vb* **-nating, -nated 1** to bring together and cause to work together efficiently ▸ *n* **2** *maths* any of a set of numbers

defining the location of a point with reference to a system of axes ▸ *adj* **3** of or involving coordination **4** of or involving the use of coordinates: *coordinate geometry* ▸ **coordination** *or* **co-ordination** *n* ▸ **coordinator** *or* **co-ordinator** *n*

coot *n* **1** a small black water bird **2** *Brit, Austral & NZ* a foolish person

cop *slang* ▸ *n* **1** a police officer **2 not much cop** of little value or worth ▸ *vb* **copping, copped 3** to take or seize **4 cop it** to get into trouble or be punished: *he copped it after he was spotted driving a car without a seat belt* ▸ See also **cop out**

cope[1] *vb* **coping, coped 1** to deal successfully (with): *well-nourished people cope better with stress* **2** to tolerate or endure: *the ability to cope with his pain*

cope *vb* = manage, get by (*informal*), struggle through, survive, carry on, make the grade, hold your own

cope[2] *n* a large ceremonial cloak worn by some Christian priests

coping *n* a layer of rounded or sloping bricks on the top of a wall

copious (kope-ee-uss) *adj* existing or produced in large quantities ▸ **copiously** *adv*

cop out *slang* ▸ *vb* **1** to avoid taking responsibility or committing oneself ▸ *n* **cop-out 2** a way or an instance of avoiding responsibility or commitment

copper[1] *n* **1** a soft reddish metallic element, used in such alloys as brass and bronze. Symbol: **Cu 2** *informal* any copper or bronze coin **3** *chiefly Brit* a large metal container used to boil water ▸ *adj* **4** reddish-brown

copper[2] *n Brit slang* a police officer

copper-bottomed *adj* financially reliable

copperplate *n* **1** an elegant handwriting style **2** a polished copper plate engraved for printing **3** a print taken from such a plate

coppice *n* a small group of trees or bushes growing close together

copra *n* the dried oil-yielding kernel of the coconut

copse *n* same as **coppice**

copulate *vb* **-lating, -lated** to have sexual intercourse ▸ **copulation** *n*

copy *n, pl* **copies 1** a thing made to look exactly like another **2** a single specimen of a book, magazine, or record of which there are many others exactly the same: *my copy of 'Death on the Nile'* **3** written material for printing **4** the text of an advertisement **5** *journalism informal* suitable material for an article: *disasters are always good copy* ▸ *vb* **copies, copying, copied 6** to make a copy (of) **7** to act or try to be like another

copy *n* **1** = reproduction, duplicate, replica, imitation, forgery, counterfeit, likeness, facsimile; ≠ original ▸ *vb* **6** = reproduce, replicate, duplicate, transcribe, counterfeit; ≠ create **7** = imitate, act like, emulate, behave like, follow, repeat, mirror, ape

copyright *n* **1** the exclusive legal right to reproduce and control an original literary, musical, or artistic work ▸ *vb* **2** to take out a copyright on ▸ *adj* **3** protected by copyright

copywriter *n* a person employed to write advertising copy

coquette *n* a woman who flirts > **coquetry** *n* > **coquettish** *adj*

coracle *n* a small round boat made of wicker covered with skins

coral *n* **1** the stony substance formed by the skeletons of marine animals called polyps, often forming an island or reef **2** any of the polyps whose skeletons form coral ▸ *adj* **3** orange-pink

cor anglais *n, pl* **cors anglais** *music* an alto woodwind instrument of the oboe family

cord *n* **1** string or thin rope made of twisted strands **2** *anatomy* a structure in the body resembling a rope: *the vocal cords* **3** a ribbed fabric like corduroy **4** *US, Canad, Austral & NZ* an electrical flex **5** a unit for measuring cut wood, equal to 128 cubic feet ▸ *adj* **6** (of fabric) ribbed

> **cord** *n* **1** = rope, line, string, twine

corded *adj* **1** tied or fastened with cord **2** (of a fabric) ribbed: *white corded silk* **3** (of muscles) standing out like cords

cordial *adj* **1** warm and friendly: *a cordial atmosphere* **2** heartfelt or sincere: *I developed a cordial dislike for the place* ▸ *n* **3** a drink with a fruit base: *lime cordial* > **cordially** *adv*

cordiality *n* warmth of feeling

cordite *n* a smokeless explosive used in guns and bombs

cordon *n* **1** a chain of police, soldiers, or vehicles guarding an area **2** an ornamental braid or ribbon **3** *horticulture* a fruit tree trained to grow as a single stem bearing fruit ▸ *vb* **4** **cordon off** to put or form a cordon round

> **cordon** *n* **1** = chain, line, ring, barrier, picket line ▸ *vb* **cordon something off** = surround, isolate, close off, fence off, separate, enclose, picket, encircle

cordon bleu (**bluh**) *adj* (of cookery or cooks) of the highest standard: *a cordon bleu chef*

corduroy *n* a heavy cotton fabric with a velvety ribbed surface

core *n* **1** the central part of certain fleshy fruits, containing the seeds **2** the central or essential part of something: *the historic core of the city* **3** a piece of magnetic soft iron inside an electromagnet or transformer **4** *geol* the central part of the earth **5** a cylindrical sample of rock or soil, obtained by the use of a hollow drill **6** *physics* the region of a nuclear reactor containing the fissionable material **7** the main internal memory of a computer ▸ *vb* **coring**, **cored 8** to remove the core from (fruit)

> **core** *n* **2** = heart, essence, nucleus, kernel, crux, gist, nub, pith

corella *n* a white Australian cockatoo

co-respondent *n* a person with whom someone being sued for divorce is claimed to have committed adultery

corgi *n* a short-legged sturdy dog

coriander *n* a European plant, cultivated for its aromatic seeds and leaves, used in flavouring foods

cork *n* **1** the thick light porous outer bark of a Mediterranean oak **2** a piece of cork used as a stopper **3** *botany* the outer bark of a woody plant ▸ *vb* **4** to stop up (a bottle) with a cork

corkage *n* a charge made at a restaurant for serving wine bought elsewhere

corkscrew *n* **1** a device for pulling corks from bottles, usually consisting of a pointed metal spiral attached to a handle ▸ *adj* **2** like a corkscrew in shape ▸ *vb* **3** to move in a spiral or zigzag course

corm *n* the scaly bulblike underground stem of certain plants

cormorant *n* a large dark-coloured long-necked sea bird

corn[1] *n* **1** a cereal plant such as wheat, oats, or barley **2** the grain of such plants **3** *US, Canad, Austral & NZ* maize **4** *slang* something unoriginal or oversentimental

corn[2] *n* a painful hardening of the skin around a central point in the foot, caused by pressure

cornea (**korn-ee-a**) *n* the transparent membrane covering the eyeball > **corneal** *adj*

corned beef *n* cooked beef preserved in salt

corner *n* **1** the place or angle formed by the meeting of two converging lines or surfaces **2** the space within the angle formed, as in a room **3** the place where two streets meet **4** a sharp bend in a road **5** a remote place: *far-flung corners of the world* **6** any secluded or private place **7** *sport* a free kick or shot taken from the corner of the field **8 cut corners** to take the shortest or easiest way at the expense of high standards **9 turn the corner** to pass the critical point of an illness or a difficult time ▸ *adj* **10** on or in a corner: *a corner seat* ▸ *vb* **11** to force (a person or animal) into a difficult or inescapable position **12** (of a vehicle or its driver) to turn a corner **13** to obtain a monopoly of

> **corner** *n* **1** = angle, joint, crook **4** = bend, curve **5** = space, hideaway, nook, hide-out ▸ *vb* **11** = trap, catch, run to earth **13** = monopolize, take over, dominate, control, hog (*slang*), engross

cornerstone *n* **1** an indispensable part or basis: *the food we eat is one of the cornerstones of good health* **2** a stone at the corner of a wall

cornet *n* **1** a brass instrument of the trumpet family **2** *Brit* a cone-shaped ice-cream wafer > **cornetist** *n*

cornflakes *pl n* a breakfast cereal made from toasted maize

cornflour n 1 a fine maize flour, used for thickening sauces 2 NZ a fine wheat flour
cornflower n a small plant with blue flowers
cornice (korn-iss) n 1 a decorative moulding round the top of a wall or building 2 archit the projecting mouldings at the top of a column
Cornish adj 1 of Cornwall ▸ n 2 a Celtic language of Cornwall, extinct by 1800 ▸ pl n 3 **the Cornish** the people of Cornwall
Cornish pasty n a pastry case with a filling of meat and vegetables
cornucopia (korn-yew-kope-ee-a) n 1 a great abundance: a cornucopia of rewards 2 a symbol of plenty, consisting of a horn overflowing with fruit and flowers
corny adj **cornier, corniest** slang unoriginal or oversentimental
corolla n the petals of a flower collectively
corollary (kor-oll-a-ree) n, pl **-laries** 1 a proposition that follows directly from another that has been proved 2 a natural consequence
corona (kor-rone-a) n, pl **-nas** or **-nae** (-nee) 1 a circle of light around a luminous body, usually the moon 2 the outermost part of the sun's atmosphere, visible as a faint halo during a total eclipse 3 a long cigar with blunt ends 4 botany a crownlike part of some flowers on top of the seed or on the inner side of the corolla 5 physics an electrical glow appearing around the surface of a charged conductor
coronary (kor-ron-a-ree) adj 1 anatomy of the arteries that supply blood to the heart ▸ n, pl **-naries** 2 a coronary thrombosis
coronary thrombosis n a condition where the blood flow to the heart is blocked by a clot in a coronary artery
coronation n the ceremony of crowning a monarch
coronavirus n a type of airborne virus accounting for 10–30% of all colds
coroner n a public official responsible for the investigation of violent, sudden, or suspicious deaths
coronet n 1 a small crown worn by princes or peers 2 a band of jewels worn as a headdress
corpora pl n the plural of **corpus**
corporal[1] n a noncommissioned officer in an army
corporal[2] adj of the body
corporal punishment n physical punishment, such as caning
corporate adj 1 relating to business corporations: corporate finance 2 shared by a group 3 forming a corporation; incorporated
corporation n 1 a large business or company 2 a city or town council 3 informal a large paunch ▸ **corporative** adj

> **corporation** n 1 = business, company, concern, firm, society, association, organization, enterprise 2 = town council, council, municipal authorities, civic authorities

corporeal (kore-pore-ee-al) adj of the physical world rather than the spiritual
corps (kore) n, pl **corps** 1 a military unit with a specific function: medical corps 2 an organized body of people: the diplomatic corps

> **corps** n = team, unit, regiment, detachment, company, band, division, troop

corpse n a dead body, esp. of a human being

> **corpse** n = body, remains, carcass, cadaver, stiff (slang)

corpulent adj fat or plump > **corpulence** n
corpus n, pl **-pora** a collection of writings, such as one by a single author or on a specific topic: the corpus of Marxist theory
corpuscle n a red blood cell (see **erythrocyte**) or white blood cell (see **leucocyte**) > **corpuscular** adj
corral US & Canad ▸ n 1 an enclosure for cattle or horses ▸ vb **-ralling, -ralled** 2 to put in a corral
correct adj 1 free from error; true: the correct answer 2 in conformity with accepted standards: in most cultures there is a strong sense of correct sexual conduct ▸ vb 3 to make free from or put right errors 4 to indicate the errors in (something) 5 to rebuke or punish in order to improve: I stand corrected 6 to make conform to a standard > **correctly** adv > **correctness** n

> **correct** adj 1 = accurate, right, true, exact, precise, flawless, faultless, O.K. or okay (informal); ≠ inaccurate 2 = right, standard, appropriate, acceptable, proper, precise; ≠ inappropriate ▸ vb 3 = rectify, remedy, redress, right, reform, cure, adjust, amend; ≠ spoil 5 = rebuke, discipline, reprimand, chide, admonish, chastise, chasten, reprove; ≠ praise

correction n 1 an act or instance of correcting 2 an alteration correcting something: corrections to the second proofs 3 a reproof or punishment > **correctional** adj

> **correction** n 1, 2 = rectification, improvement, amendment, adjustment, modification, alteration, emendation 3 = punishment, discipline, reformation, admonition, chastisement, reproof, castigation

corrective adj intended to put right something that is wrong: corrective action
correlate vb **-lating, -lated** 1 to place or be placed in a mutual relationship: water consumption is closely correlated to the number of people living in a house ▸ n 2 either of two things mutually related > **correlation** n
correspond vb 1 to be consistent or compatible (with) 2 to be similar (to) 3 to communicate (with) by letter > **corresponding** adj > **correspondingly** adv

C

correspond vb 1 = be consistent, match, agree, accord, fit, square, tally, conform; ≠ differ 3 = communicate, write, keep in touch, exchange letters, email or e-mail, text

correspondence n 1 communication by letters 2 the letters exchanged in this way 3 relationship or similarity

correspondence n 1 = communication, writing, contact 2 = letters, post, mail 3 = relation, match, agreement, comparison, harmony, coincidence, similarity, correlation

correspondent n 1 a person who communicates by letter 2 a person employed by a newspaper or news service to report on a special subject or from a foreign country

correspondent n 1 = letter writer, pen friend or pen pal 2 = reporter, journalist, contributor, hack

corridor n 1 a passage in a building or a train 2 a strip of land or airspace that provides access through the territory of a foreign country 3 **corridors of power** the higher levels of government or the Civil Service

corridor n 1 = passage, alley, aisle, hallway, passageway

corrigendum (kor-rij-end-um) n, pl **-da** (-da) 1 an error to be corrected 2 a slip of paper inserted into a book after printing, listing corrections

corroborate vb **-rating, -rated** to support (a fact or opinion) by giving proof > **corroboration** n > **corroborative** adj

corroboree n Austral 1 an Aboriginal gathering or dance of festive or warlike character 2 informal any noisy gathering

corrode vb **-roding, -roded** 1 to eat away or be eaten away by chemical action or rusting 2 to destroy gradually: *rumours corroding the public's affection for the royal family*

corrosion n 1 the process by which something, esp. a metal, is corroded 2 the result of corrosion > **corrosive** adj

corrugate vb **-gating, -gated** to fold into alternate grooves and ridges

corrupt adj 1 open to or involving bribery or other dishonest practices: *corrupt practices* 2 morally depraved 3 (of a text or data) made unreliable by errors or alterations ▶ vb 4 to make corrupt > **corruptive** adj

corrupt adj 1 = dishonest, bent (slang), crooked (informal), fraudulent, unscrupulous, venal, unprincipled; ≠ honest 2 = depraved, vicious, degenerate, debased, profligate, dissolute 3 = distorted, doctored, altered, falsified ▶ vb = deprave, pervert, subvert, debauch; ≠ reform

corruptible adj capable of being corrupted

corruption n 1 dishonesty and illegal behaviour 2 the act of corrupting morally or sexually 3 the process of rotting or decaying 4 an unintentional or unauthorized alteration in a text or data 5 an altered form of a word

corruption n 1 = dishonesty, fraud, bribery, extortion, venality, shady dealings (informal) 2 = depravity, vice, evil, perversion, decadence, wickedness, immorality 4 = distortion, doctoring, falsification

corsage (kore-**sahzh**) n a small bouquet worn on the bodice of a dress

corsair n 1 a pirate 2 a pirate ship 3 a privateer

corset n 1 a close-fitting undergarment worn to shape the torso 2 a similar garment worn to support and protect the back > **corsetry** n

cortege (kore-**tayzh**) n a funeral procession

cortex (kore-tex) n, pl **-tices** (-tiss-seez) anatomy the outer layer of the brain or some other internal organ > **cortical** adj

cortisone n a steroid hormone used in treating rheumatoid arthritis, allergies, and skin diseases

corundum n a hard mineral used as an abrasive, of which the ruby and white sapphire are precious forms

coruscate vb **-cating, -cated** formal to emit flashes of light; sparkle > **coruscating** adj > **coruscation** n

corvette n a lightly armed escort warship

cos cosine

cosh chiefly Brit ▶ n 1 a heavy blunt weapon, often made of hard rubber ▶ vb 2 to hit on the head with a cosh

cosine (koh-sine) n (in trigonometry) the ratio of the length of the adjacent side to that of the hypotenuse in a right-angled triangle

cosmetic n 1 anything applied to the face or body in order to improve the appearance ▶ adj 2 done or used to improve the appearance of the face or body 3 improving in appearance only: *glossy brochures are part of a cosmetic exercise*

cosmetic adj 3 = superficial, surface, nonessential

cosmic adj 1 of or relating to the whole universe: *the cosmic order* 2 occurring in or coming from outer space: *cosmic dust*

cosmic adj 1 = universal, general, overarching 2 = extraterrestrial, stellar

cosmology n the study of the origin and nature of the universe > **cosmological** adj > **cosmologist** n

cosmonaut n the Russian name for an astronaut

cosmopolitan adj 1 composed of people or elements from many different countries or cultures 2 having lived and travelled in many countries 3 sophisticated and cultured ▶ n 4 a cosmopolitan person > **cosmopolitanism** n

cosmopolitan *adj* **3** = sophisticated, cultured, refined, cultivated, urbane, well-travelled, worldly-wise; ≠ unsophisticated

cosmos *n* the universe considered as an ordered system

Cossack *n* **1** a member of a S Russian people, famous as horsemen and dancers ▸ *adj* **2** of the Cossacks: *a Cossack dance*

cosset *vb* **-seting, -seted** to pamper or pet

cost *n* **1** the amount of money, time, or energy required to obtain or produce something **2** suffering or sacrifice: *these were crucial truths which rugby never grasped, to its cost* **3** the amount paid for a commodity by its seller: *to sell at cost* **4 costs** *law* the expenses of a lawsuit **5 at all costs** regardless of any cost or effort involved **6 at the cost of** at the expense of losing: *they eventually triumphed, but at the cost of many lives* ▸ *vb* **costing, cost 7** to be obtained or obtainable in exchange for: *calls cost 45p a minute* **8** to involve the loss or sacrifice of: *a fall which almost cost him his life* **9 costing, costed** to estimate the cost of producing (something)

cost *n* **1** = price, worth, expense, charge, damage (*informal*), amount, payment, outlay **2** = loss, suffering, damage, injury, penalty, hurt, expense, harm ▸ *vb* **7** = sell at, come to, set (someone) back (*informal*), be priced at, command a price of **8** = lose, deprive of, cheat of

costermonger *n Brit* a person who sells fruit and vegetables from a barrow in the street

costly *adj* **-lier, -liest 1** expensive **2** involving great loss or sacrifice: *a bitter and costly war* > **costliness** *n*

costly *adj* **1** = expensive, dear, stiff, steep (*informal*), highly-priced, exorbitant, extortionate; ≠ inexpensive **2** = damaging, disastrous, harmful, catastrophic, loss-making, ruinous, deleterious (*formal*)

costume *n* **1** a style of dressing, including all the clothes and accessories, typical of a particular country or period **2** the clothes worn by an actor or performer: *a jester's costume* ▸ *vb* **-tuming, -tumed 3** to provide with a costume: *she was costumed by many of the great Hollywood designers* > **costumed** *adj*

costume *n* = outfit, dress, clothing, uniform, ensemble, livery, apparel (*old-fashioned*), attire

costume jewellery *n* inexpensive but attractive jewellery

costumier *n* a maker or supplier of theatrical or fancy dress costumes

cosy *or US* **cozy** *adj* **-sier, -siest** *or US* **-zier, -ziest 1** warm and snug **2** intimate and friendly: *a cosy chat* ▸ *n, pl* **-sies** *or US* **-zies 3** a cover for keeping things warm: *a tea cosy* > **cosiness** *or US* **coziness** *n*

cosy *or* **cozy** *adj* **1** = snug, warm, comfortable, sheltered, comfy (*informal*), tucked up **2** = intimate, friendly, informal

cot *n* **1** a bed with high sides for a baby or very young child **2** a small portable bed

cot death *n* the unexplained sudden death of a baby while asleep

cote *or* **cot** *n* a small shelter for birds or animals

coterie (kote-er-ee) *n* a small exclusive group of friends or people with common interests

cotoneaster (kot-tone-ee-**ass**-ter) *n* a garden shrub with red berries

cottage *n* a small simple house, usually in the country > **cottager** *n*

cottage *n* = cabin, lodge, hut, shack, chalet, whare (*NZ*)

cottage cheese *n* a mild soft white cheese made from skimmed milk curds

cottage industry *n* a craft industry in which employees work at home

cottage pie *n* a dish of minced meat topped with mashed potato

cotter *n machinery* a bolt or wedge that is used to secure parts of machinery

cotton *n* **1** the soft white downy fibre surrounding the seeds of a plant grown in warm climates, used to make cloth and thread **2** cloth or thread made from cotton fibres > **cottony** *adj*

cotton wool *n chiefly Brit* absorbent fluffy cotton, used for surgical dressings and to apply creams to the skin

cotyledon (kot-ill-ee-don) *n* the first leaf produced by a plant embryo

couch *n* **1** a piece of upholstered furniture for seating more than one person **2** a bed on which patients of a doctor or a psychoanalyst lie during examination or treatment ▸ *vb* **3** to express in a particular style of language: *a proclamation couched in splendidly archaic phraseology* **4** *archaic* (of an animal) to crouch, as when preparing to leap

couchette (koo-**shett**) *n* a bed converted from seats on a train or ship

couch grass *n* a grassy weed which spreads quickly

couch potato *n slang* a physically lazy person, esp. one who spends most of the day in front of the television

cougan *n Austral slang* a drunk and rowdy person

cougar (koo-gar) *n* same as **puma**

cough *vb* **1** to expel air abruptly and noisily from the lungs **2** (of an engine or other machine) to make a sound similar to this ▸ *n* **3** an act or sound of coughing **4** an illness which causes frequent coughing

cough *vb* **1** = clear your throat, bark, hack (*informal*) ▸ *n* **3** = frog or tickle in your throat, bark, hack (*informal*)

could *vb* **1** used to make the past tense of **can**[1]

C

2 used to make the subjunctive mood of **can**[1], esp. in polite requests or conditional sentences: *could I have a word with you, please?* **3** used to indicate the suggestion of a course of action: *we could make a fortune from selling players, but that would not be in the long-term interests of the club* **4** used to indicate a possibility: *it could simply be a spelling mistake*

couldn't could not

coulomb (koo-lom) *n* the SI unit of electric charge

coulter (kole-ter) *n* a vertical blade on a plough in front of the ploughshare

council *n* **1** a group meeting for discussion or consultation **2** a legislative or advisory body: *the United Nations Security Council* **3** *Brit* the local governing authority of a town or county **4** *Austral* the local governing authority of a district or shire ▸ *adj* **5** of or provided by a local council: *a council house*

> **council** *n* **1** = committee, governing body, board **2** = governing body, parliament, congress, cabinet, panel, assembly, convention, conference, runanga (NZ)

councillor *or US* **councilor** *n* a member of a council

council tax *n* (in Britain) a tax based on the relative value of property, levied to fund local council services

counsel *n* **1** advice or guidance **2** discussion or consultation: *when it was over they took counsel of their consciences* **3** a barrister or group of barristers who conduct cases in court and advise on legal matters ▸ *vb* **-selling**, **-selled** *or US* **-seling**, **-seled** **4** to give advice or guidance to **5** to recommend or urge > **counselling** *or US* **counseling** *n*

> **counsel** *n* **1** = advice, information, warning, direction, suggestion, recommendation, guidance **3** = legal adviser, lawyer, attorney, solicitor, advocate, barrister ▸ *vb* **5** = advise, recommend, advocate, warn, urge, instruct, exhort (*formal*)

counsellor *or US* **counselor** *n* **1** an adviser **2** *US* a lawyer who conducts cases in court

count[1] *vb* **1** to say numbers in ascending order up to and including: *count from one to ten* **2** to add up or check (each thing in a group) in order to find the total: *she counted the money she had left* **3** to be important: *it's the thought that counts* **4** to consider: *she can count herself lucky* **5** to take into account or include: *the time he'd spent in prison on remand counted towards his sentence* **6** **not counting** excluding **7** *music* to keep time by counting beats ▸ *n* **8** the act of counting **9** the number reached by counting: *a high pollen count* **10** *law* one of a number of charges **11** **keep** *or* **lose count** to keep or fail to keep an accurate record of items or events **12** **out for the count** unconscious ▸ See also **countdown** *etc.* > **countable** *adj*

count[2] *vb* **2** = add (up), total, reckon (up), tot up, calculate, compute, tally, number **3** = matter, be important, carry weight, tell, rate, weigh, signify (*informal*) **4** = consider, judge, regard, deem, think of, rate, look upon **5** = include, number among, take into account *or* consideration

count[2] *n* a middle-ranking European nobleman

countdown *n* the act of counting backwards to zero to time exactly an operation such as the launching of a rocket

countenance *n* **1** *literary* the face or facial expression ▸ *vb* **-nancing**, **-nanced** **2** to support or tolerate

counter[1] *n* **1** a long flat surface in a bank or shop, on which business is transacted **2** a small flat disc used in board games **3** **under the counter** (of the sale of goods) illegal

counter[2] *vb* **1** to oppose or act against ▸ *adv* **2** in an opposite or opposing direction or manner ▸ *n* **3** an opposing action

> **counter** *vb* = oppose, meet, block, resist, parry, deflect, repel, rebuff ▸ *adv* = opposite to, against, versus, conversely, in defiance of, at variance with, contrariwise; ≠ in accordance with

counter- *prefix* **1** against or opposite: *counterattack* **2** complementary or corresponding: *counterpart*

counteract *vb* to act against or neutralize > **counteraction** *n* > **counteractive** *adj*

counterattack *n* **1** an attack in response to an attack ▸ *vb* **2** to make a counterattack (against)

counterbalance *n* **1** a weight or influence that balances or neutralizes another ▸ *vb* **-ancing**, **-anced** **2** to act as a counterbalance to

counterblast *n* an aggressive response to a verbal attack

counterfeit *adj* **1** made in imitation of something genuine with the intent to deceive or defraud: *counterfeit currency* **2** pretended: *counterfeit friendship* ▸ *n* **3** an imitation designed to deceive or defraud ▸ *vb* **4** to make a fraudulent imitation of **5** to feign: *surprise is an easy emotion to counterfeit*

counterfoil *n Brit* the part of a cheque or receipt kept as a record

countermand *vb* to cancel (a previous order)

counterpane *n* a bed covering

counterpart *n* **1** a person or thing complementary to or corresponding to another **2** a duplicate of a legal document

> **counterpart** *n* **1** = opposite number, equal, twin, equivalent, match, fellow, mate

counterpoint *n* **1** the harmonious combining of two or more parts or melodies **2** a melody or part combined in this way ▸ *vb* **3** to set in contrast

counterpoise *vb* **-poising, -poised** to oppose with something of equal weight or effect: *counterpoising humour and horror*

counterproductive *adj* having an effect opposite to the one intended

countersign *vb* **1** to sign (a document already signed by another) as confirmation ▸ *n* **2** the signature so written

countersink *vb* **-sinking, -sank, -sunk** to drive (a screw) into a shaped hole so that its head is below the surface

countertenor *n* **1** an adult male voice with an alto range **2** a singer with such a voice

counterterrorism *n* activities intended to prevent terrorist acts or to eradicate terrorist groups > **counterterrorist** *adj*

countess *n* **1** a woman holding the rank of count or earl **2** the wife or widow of a count or earl

countless *adj* too many to count

> **countless** *adj* = innumerable, legion, infinite, myriad, untold, limitless, incalculable, immeasurable; ≠ limited

count on *vb* to rely or depend on

> **count on** *vb* **count on something or someone** = depend on, trust, rely on, bank on, take for granted, lean on, reckon on, take on trust

countrified *adj* having an appearance or manner associated with the countryside rather than a town

country *n*, *pl* **-tries 1** an area distinguished by its people, culture, language, or government **2** the territory of a nation or state **3** the people of a nation or state **4** the part of the land that is away from cities or industrial areas **5** a person's native land **6** same as **country and western 7 across country** not keeping to roads **8 go to the country** *Brit & NZ* to dissolve Parliament and hold a general election

> **country** *n* **1** = nation, state, land, commonwealth, kingdom, realm, people **3** = people, community, nation, society, citizens, inhabitants, populace, public **4** = countryside, provinces, sticks (*informal*), farmland, outback (*Austral, NZ*), green belt, backwoods, bush (*NZ, S African*); ≠ town

country and western *or* **country music** *n* popular music based on American White folk music

countryman *or fem* **countrywoman** *n*, *pl* **-men** *or* **-women 1** a person from one's own country **2** *Brit, Austral & NZ* a person who lives in the country

countryside *n* land away from the cities

> **countryside** *n* = country, rural areas, outback (*Austral, NZ*), green belt, sticks (*informal*)

county *n*, *pl* **-ties 1** (in some countries) a division of a country ▸ *adj* **2** *Brit informal* upper-class

> **county** *n* = province, district, shire

coup (koo) *n* **1** a brilliant and successful action **2** a coup d'état

> **coup** *n* **1** = masterstroke, feat, stunt, action, exploit, manoeuvre, deed, accomplishment

coup de grâce (koo de grahss) *n*, *pl* **coups de grâce** (koo de grahss) a final or decisive action

coup d'état (koo day-tah) *n*, *pl* **coups d'état** (kooz day-tah) a sudden violent or illegal overthrow of a government

coupé (koo-pay) *n* a sports car with two doors and a sloping fixed roof

couple *n* **1** two people who are married, living together, or having a sexual relationship **2** two partners in a dance or game **3 a couple of A** a pair of: *a couple of guys* **B** *informal* a few: *a couple of weeks* ▸ *pron* **4 a couple A** two **B** *informal* a few: *give him a couple* ▸ *vb* **-pling, -pled 5** to connect or link: *an ingrained sense of shame, coupled with a fear of ridicule* **6** *literary* to have sexual intercourse

> **couple** *n* **2** = pair, two, brace, duo, twosome

couplet *n* two successive lines of verse, usually rhyming and of the same metre

coupling *n* a device for connecting things, such as railway cars or trucks

coupon *n* **1** a piece of paper entitling the holder to a discount or free gift **2** a detachable slip that can be used as a commercial order form **3** *Brit* a detachable entry form for a competition

> **coupon** *n* **1, 2** = slip, ticket, certificate, token, voucher, card

courage *n* **1** the ability to face danger or pain without fear **2 the courage of one's convictions** the confidence to act according to one's beliefs

> **courage** *n* **1** = bravery, nerve, resolution, daring, pluck, heroism, mettle, gallantry; ≠ cowardice

courageous *adj* showing courage > **courageously** *adv*

> **courageous** *adj* = brave, daring, bold, gritty, fearless, gallant, intrepid, valiant; ≠ cowardly

courgette *n* a type of small vegetable marrow

courier *n* **1** a person who looks after and guides travellers **2** a person paid to deliver urgent messages or parcels ▸ *vb* **3** to transport (a message or parcel) by courier

> **courier** *n* **1** = guide, representative, escort, conductor **2** = messenger, runner, carrier, bearer, envoy

course *n* **1** a complete series of lessons or lectures: *a training course* **2** a sequence of medical treatment prescribed for a period of time: *a course of antibiotics* **3** an onward movement in time or space: *during the course of his career he worked with many leading actors* **4** a route or direction taken: *the ships were blown off course by a gale* **5** the path or channel along which a river moves **6** an area on which a sport is played or a race is held: *a golf course* **7** any of the successive parts of a meal **8** a continuous, usually horizontal layer of building material, such as bricks or tiles, at one level in a building **9** a mode of conduct or action: *the safest course of action was to do nothing* **10** the natural development of a sequence of events: *allow the fever to run its course* **11** a period of time: *over the course of the last two years* **12 as a matter of course** as a natural or normal consequence or event **13 in the course of** in the process of **14 in due course** at the natural or appropriate time **15 of course A** (*adv*) as expected; naturally **B** (*interj*) certainly; definitely ▸ *vb* **coursing, coursed 16** (of a liquid) to run swiftly **17** to hunt with hounds that follow the quarry by sight and not scent

> **course** *n* **1** = classes, programme, schedule, lectures, curriculum **3** = progression, order, unfolding, development, movement, progress, flow, sequence **4, 5** = route, way, line, road, track, direction, path, passage **6** = racecourse, circuit **9** = procedure, plan, policy, programme, method, conduct, behaviour, manner **11** = period, time, duration, term, passing **15 of course** = naturally, certainly, obviously, definitely, undoubtedly, needless to say, without a doubt, indubitably ▸ *vb* **16** = run, flow, stream, gush, race, speed, surge **17** = hunt, follow, chase, pursue

court *n* **1** *law* **A** a judicial body that hears and makes decisions on legal cases **B** the room or building in which such a body meets **2** a marked area used for playing a racket game **3** an area of ground wholly or partly surrounded by walls or buildings **4** a name given to some short streets, blocks of flats, or large country houses as a part of their address: *Carlton Court* **5** the residence or retinue of a sovereign **6** any formal assembly held by a sovereign **7 go to court** to take legal action **8 hold court** to preside over a group of admirers **9 out of court** without a trial or legal case **10 pay court to** to give flattering attention to ▸ *vb* **11** to attempt to gain the love of **12** to pay attention to (someone) in order to gain favour **13** to try to obtain (something): *he has not courted controversy, but he has certainly attracted it* **14** to make oneself open to or vulnerable to: *courting disaster*

> **court** *n* **1** = law court, bar, bench, tribunal **5** = palace, hall, castle, manor ▸ *vb* **11** = woo, go (out) with, date, take out, run after, walk out with, set your cap at, step out with (*informal*) **12** = cultivate, seek, flatter, solicit, pander to, curry favour with, fawn upon **13** = invite, seek, attract, prompt, provoke, bring about, incite

courteous *adj* polite and considerate in manner > **courteously** *adv* > **courteousness** *n*

courtesan (kore-tiz-**zan**) *n history* a mistress or high-class prostitute

courtesy *n*, *pl* -**sies 1** politeness; good manners **2** a courteous act or remark **3 by courtesy of** with the consent of

> **courtesy** *n* **1** = politeness, good manners, civility, gallantry, graciousness, affability, urbanity **2** = favour, kindness, indulgence

courtier *n* an attendant at a royal court

courtly *adj* -**lier**, -**liest 1** ceremoniously polite **2** of or suitable for a royal court > **courtliness** *n*

court martial *n*, *pl* **court martials** *or* **courts martial 1** the trial of a member of the armed forces charged with breaking military law ▸ *vb* **court-martial**, -**tialling**, -**tialled** *or* US -**tialing**, -**tialed 2** to try by court martial

courtship *n* the courting of an intended spouse or mate

court shoe *n* a low-cut shoe for women, without laces or straps

courtyard *n* an open area of ground surrounded by walls or buildings

> **courtyard** *n* = yard, square, piazza, quadrangle, plaza, enclosure, cloister, quad (*informal*)

cousin *n* the child of one's aunt or uncle. Also called: **first cousin**

couture (koo-**toor**) *n* **1** high-fashion designing and dressmaking ▸ *adj* **2** relating to high fashion design and dressmaking: *couture clothes*

couturier *n* a person who designs fashion clothes for women

cove *n* a small bay or inlet

> **cove** *n* = bay, sound, inlet, anchorage

coven (**kuv**-ven) *n* a meeting of witches

covenant (**kuv**-ven-ant) *n* **1** *chiefly Brit* a formal agreement to make an annual payment to charity **2** *law* a formal sealed agreement **3** *Bible* God's promise to the Israelites and their commitment to worship him alone ▸ *vb* **4** to agree by a legal covenant > **covenanter** *n*

> **covenant** *n* **2** = promise, contract, agreement, commitment, arrangement, pledge, pact

Coventry *n* **send someone to Coventry** to punish someone by refusing to speak to him or her

cover *vb* **1** to place something over so as to protect or conceal **2** to put a garment on; clothe **3** to extend over or lie thickly on the surface of: *the ground was covered with dry leaves* **4** (sometimes foll. by *up*) to screen or conceal; hide from view **5** to travel over **6** to protect (an individual or group) by taking up a position from which fire may be returned if those being protected are fired upon **7** to keep a gun aimed at

8 A to insure against loss or risk **B** to provide for (loss or risk) by insurance **9** to include or deal with: *the course covers accounting, economics, statistics, law, and computer applications* **10** to act as reporter or photographer on (a news event) for a newspaper or magazine **11** (of a sum of money) to be enough to pay for (something) **12** *music* to record a cover version of **13** *sport* to guard or obstruct (an opponent, team-mate, or area) **14 cover for** to deputize for (a person) **15** (foll. by *for* or *up for*) to provide an alibi (for): *can my men count on your friends at City Hall to cover for us?* ▸ *n* **16** anything which covers **17** a blanket or bedspread **18** the outside of a book or magazine **19** a pretext or disguise: *he claimed UN resolutions were being used as a cover for planned American aggression* **20** an envelope or other postal wrapping: *under plain cover* **21** an individual table setting **22** insurance **23** a cover version **24 the covers** *cricket* the area roughly at right angles to the pitch on the off side and about halfway to the boundary **25 break cover** to come out from a shelter or hiding place **26 take cover** to make for a place of safety or shelter **27 under cover** protected or in secret > **covering** *adj, n*

> **cover** *vb* **1, 4** = conceal, hide, mask, disguise, obscure, veil, cloak, shroud; ≠ reveal
> **2** = clothe, dress, wrap, envelop; ≠ uncover
> **3** = overlay, blanket **5** = travel over, cross, traverse, pass through *or* over **6** = protect, guard, defend, shield **9** = consider, deal with, investigate, describe, tell of **10** = report on, write about, commentate on, relate, tell of, narrate, write up **11** = pay for, fund, provide for, offset, be enough for ▸ *n* **16** = covering, case, top, coating, envelope, lid, canopy, wrapper **17** = bedclothes, bedding, sheet, blanket, quilt, duvet, eiderdown **18** = jacket, case, wrapper **19** = disguise, front (*informal*), screen, mask, veil, facade, pretext, smoke screen **22** = insurance, protection, compensation, indemnity, reimbursement

coverage *n journalism* the amount of reporting given to a subject or event

covert *adj* **1** concealed or secret ▸ *n* **2** a thicket or woodland providing shelter for game **3** *ornithol* any of the small feathers on the wings and tail of a bird that surround the bases of the larger feathers > **covertly** *adv*

covet *vb* **-eting, -eted** to long to possess (something, esp. something belonging to another person)

> **covet** *vb* = long for, desire, envy, crave, aspire to, yearn for, lust after, set your heart on

covetous *adj* jealously longing to possess something > **covetously** *adv* > **covetousness** *n*

covey (kuv-vee) *n* **1** a small flock of grouse or partridge **2** a small group of people

cow[1] *n* **1** the mature female of cattle **2** the mature female of various other mammals, such as the elephant or whale **3** *not in technical use* any domestic species of cattle **4** *informal, offensive* a disagreeable woman

cow[2] *vb* to frighten or subdue with threats

coward *n* a person who is easily frightened and avoids dangerous or difficult situations > **cowardly** *adj*

> **coward** *n* = weakling, chicken (*slang*), wimp (*informal*), scaredy-cat (*informal*), yellow-belly (*slang*)

cowardice *n* lack of courage

cowboy *n* **1** (in the US and Canada) a ranch worker who herds and tends cattle, usually on horseback **2** a conventional character of Wild West folklore or films **3** *Brit, Austral & NZ informal* an irresponsible or unscrupulous worker or businessperson > **cowgirl** *fem n*

> **cowboy** *n* **1, 2** = cowhand, drover, rancher, stockman, cattleman, herdsman *or* woman (*Brit*), gaucho

cower *vb* to cringe or shrink in fear

cowl *n* **1** a loose hood **2** a monk's hooded robe **3** a cover fitted to a chimney to increase ventilation and prevent draughts > **cowled** *adj*

cowling *n* a streamlined detachable metal covering around an engine

cowrie *n, pl* **-ries** the glossy brightly-marked shell of a marine mollusc

cowslip *n* a European wild plant with yellow flowers

cox *n* **1** a coxswain ▸ *vb* **2** to act as coxswain of (a boat)

coxswain (kok-sn) *n* the person who steers a lifeboat or rowing boat

coy *adj* **1** affectedly shy and modest **2** unwilling to give information > **coyly** *adv* > **coyness** *n*

coyote (koy-ote-ee) *n, pl* **-otes** *or* **-ote** a small wolf of the deserts and prairies of North America

coypu *n, pl* **-pus** *or* **-pu** a beaver-like amphibious rodent, bred for its fur

cozen *vb literary* to cheat or trick > **cozenage** *n*

CPR cardiopulmonary resuscitation: a medical technique for reviving someone whose heart has stopped beating

CPU *computers* central processing unit

crab *n* **1** an edible shellfish with five pairs of legs, the first pair modified into pincers **2 catch a crab** *rowing* to make a stroke in which the oar misses the water or digs too deeply, causing the rower to fall backwards

crab apple *n* a kind of small sour apple

crabbed *adj* **1** (of handwriting) cramped and hard to read **2** bad-tempered

crabby *adj* **-bier, -biest** bad-tempered

crack *vb* **1** to break or split without complete separation of the parts **2** to break with a sudden sharp sound **3** to make or cause to make a sudden sharp sound: *the coachman cracked his whip* **4** (of the voice) to become harsh or change pitch suddenly **5** *informal* to fail or break down: *she had* *cracked under the strain of losing her job* **6** to yield or cease to resist: *he had cracked under torture* **7** to hit with a forceful or resounding blow **8** to break into or force open: *it'll take me longer if I have to crack the safe myself* **9** to solve or decipher (a code or problem) **10** *informal* to tell (a joke) **11** to break (a molecule) into smaller molecules or radicals by heat or catalysis as in the distillation of petroleum **12** to open (a bottle) for drinking **13 crack it** *informal* to achieve something ▸ *n* **14** a sudden sharp noise **15** a break or fracture without complete separation of the two parts **16** a narrow opening or fissure **17** *informal* a sharp blow **18 crack of dawn** daybreak **19** a broken or cracked tone of voice **20** *informal* an attempt **21** *informal* a gibe or joke **22** *slang* a highly addictive form of cocaine **23** *chiefly Irish informal* fun; informal entertainment **24 a fair crack of the whip** *informal* a fair chance or opportunity ▸ *adj* **25** *slang* first-class or excellent: *crack troops* ▸ See also **crack down**

> **crack** *vb* **1** = cleave, break **2** = snap, ring, crash, burst, explode, pop, detonate **5, 6** = break down, collapse, yield, give in, give way, succumb, lose control, be overcome **7** = hit, clip (*informal*), slap, smack, clout (*informal*), cuff, whack **9** = solve, work out, resolve, clear up, fathom, decipher, suss (out) (*slang*), get to the bottom of ▸ *n* **14** = snap, pop, crash, burst, explosion, clap, report **15, 16** = break, chink, gap, fracture, rift, cleft, crevice, fissure **17** = blow, slap, smack, clout (*informal*), cuff, whack, clip (*informal*) **21** = joke, dig, gag (*informal*), quip, jibe, wisecrack, witticism, funny remark ▸ *adj* = first-class, choice, excellent, ace (*informal*), elite, superior, world-class, first-rate

crack down *vb* **1 crack down on** to take severe measures against ▸ *n* **crackdown 2** severe or repressive measures

> **crack down** *n* **crackdown** = clampdown, crushing, repression, suppression

cracker *n* **1** a thin crisp unsweetened biscuit **2** a decorated cardboard tube, pulled apart with a bang, containing a paper hat and a joke or a toy **3** a small explosive firework **4** *slang* an excellent or notable thing or person
crackers *adj Brit & NZ slang* foolish or crazy
cracking *adj* **1 get cracking** *informal* to start doing something immediately **2 a cracking pace** *informal* a high speed ▸ *adv*, *adj* **3** *Brit informal* first-class: *five cracking good saves* ▸ *n* **4** the oil-refining process in which heavy oils are broken down into smaller molecules by heat or catalysis
crackle *vb* **-ling, -led 1** to make small sharp popping noises ▸ *n* **2** a crackling sound
> **crackly** *adj*
crackling *n* **1** a series of small sharp popping noises **2** the crisp browned skin of roast pork

crackpot *informal* ▸ *n* **1** an eccentric person ▸ *adj* **2** eccentric: *crackpot philosophies*
cradle *n* **1** a baby's bed on rockers **2** a place where something originates: *the cradle of civilization* **3** a supporting framework or structure **4** a platform or trolley in which workmen are suspended on the side of a building or ship ▸ *vb* **-dling, -dled 5** to hold gently as if in a cradle

> **cradle** *n* **1** = crib, cot, Moses basket, bassinet **2** = birthplace, beginning, source, spring, origin, fount, fountainhead, wellspring ▸ *vb* = hold, support, rock, nurse, nestle

craft *n* **1** an occupation requiring skill or manual dexterity **2** skill or ability **3** cunning or guile **4** *pl* **craft** a boat, ship, aircraft, or spacecraft ▸ *vb* **5** to make skilfully

> **craft** *n* **1** = occupation, work, business, trade, employment, pursuit, vocation, handicraft **2** = skill, art, ability, technique, know-how (*informal*), expertise, aptitude, artistry **4** = vessel, boat, ship, plane, aircraft, spacecraft

craftsman *or fem* **craftswoman** *n, pl* **-men** *or* **-women 1** a skilled worker **2** a skilled artist
> **craftsmanship** *n*

> **craftsman** *or* **craftswoman** *n* **1** = skilled worker, artisan, master, maker, wright, technician, smith, crafter

crafty *adj* **-tier, -tiest** skilled in deception
> **craftily** *adv* > **craftiness** *n*
crag *n* a steep rugged rock or peak > **craggy** *adj*
cram *vb* **cramming, crammed 1** to force (more people or things) into (a place) than it can hold **2** to eat or feed to excess **3** *chiefly Brit* to study hard just before an examination

> **cram** *vb* **1** = stuff, force, jam, shove, compress **3** = study, revise, swot (*informal*), bone up (*informal*), mug up (*slang*)

cramp¹ *n* **1** a sudden painful contraction of a muscle **2** temporary stiffness of a muscle group from overexertion: *writer's cramp* **3** severe stomach pain **4** a clamp for holding masonry or timber together ▸ *vb* **5** to affect with a cramp

> **cramp** *n* **1** = spasm, pain, ache, contraction, pang, stitch, convulsion, twinge

cramp² *vb* **1** to confine or restrict **2 cramp someone's style** *informal* to prevent someone from impressing another person or from behaving naturally: *shyness will cramp their style*

> **cramp** *vb* **1** = restrict, hamper, inhibit, hinder, handicap, constrain, obstruct, impede

crampon *n* a spiked iron plate strapped to a boot for climbing on ice
cranberry *n, pl* **-ries** a sour edible red berry
crane *n* **1** a machine for lifting and moving heavy objects, usually by suspending them from

a movable projecting arm **2** a large wading bird with a long neck and legs ▶ *vb* **craning, craned 3** to stretch out (the neck) in order to see something

crane fly *n* a fly with long legs, slender wings, and a narrow body

cranial *adj* of or relating to the skull

cranium *n, pl* **-niums** *or* **-nia** *anatomy* **1** the skull **2** the part of the skull that encloses the brain

crank *n* **1** a device for transmitting or converting motion, consisting of an arm projecting at right angles from a shaft **2** a handle incorporating a crank, used to start an engine or motor **3** *informal* an eccentric or odd person ▶ *vb* **4** to turn with a crank **5** to start (an engine) with a crank

crankshaft *n* a shaft with one or more cranks, to which the connecting rods are attached

cranky *adj* **-kier, -kiest** *informal* **1** eccentric **2** bad-tempered ⟩ **crankiness** *n*

cranny *n, pl* **-nies** a narrow opening

crape *n* same as **crepe**

craps *n* **1** a gambling game played with two dice **2 shoot craps** to play this game

crash *n* **1** a collision involving a vehicle or vehicles **2** a sudden descent of an aircraft as a result of which it crashes **3** a sudden loud noise **4** a breaking and falling to pieces **5** the sudden collapse of a business or stock exchange ▶ *vb* **6** to cause (a vehicle or aircraft) to collide with another vehicle, the ground, or some other object or (of vehicles or aircraft) to be involved in a collision **7** to make or cause to make a loud smashing noise **8** to drop with force and break into pieces with a loud noise **9** to break or smash into pieces with a loud noise **10** (of a business or stock exchange) to collapse or fail suddenly **11** to move violently or noisily **12** (of a computer system or program) to fail suddenly because of a malfunction **13** *Brit & Austral informal* to gate-crash ▶ *adj* **14** requiring or using great effort in order to achieve results quickly: *a crash course*

> **crash** *n* **1, 2** = collision, accident, smash, wreck, prang (*informal*), bump, pile-up (*informal*) **3** = smash, clash, boom, bang, thunder, racket, din, clatter **5** = collapse, failure, depression, ruin, downfall ▶ *vb* **8** = plunge, hurtle **10** = collapse, fail, go under, be ruined, go bust (*informal*), fold up, go to the wall, go belly up (*informal*) **11** = fall, plunge, topple, lurch, hurtle, overbalance, fall headlong

crash helmet *n* a helmet worn by motorcyclists to protect the head in case of a crash

crash-land *vb* (of an aircraft) to land in an emergency, causing damage ⟩ **crash-landing** *n*

crass *adj* stupid and insensitive: *the enquiry is crass and naive* ⟩ **crassly** *adv* ⟩ **crassness** *n*

crate *n* **1** a large container made of wooden slats, used for packing goods **2** *slang* an old car or aeroplane ▶ *vb* **crating, crated 3** to put in a crate ⟩ **crateful** *n*

> **crate** *n* **1** = container, case, box, packing case, tea chest

crater *n* **1** the bowl-shaped opening in a volcano or a geyser **2** a cavity made by the impact of a meteorite or an explosion **3** a roughly circular cavity on the surface of the moon and some planets ▶ *vb* **4** to make or form craters in (a surface, such as the ground) ⟩ **cratered** *adj*

> **crater** *n* **1, 2** = hollow, hole, depression, dip, cavity

cravat *n* a scarf worn round the neck instead of a tie

crave *vb* **craving, craved 1** to desire intensely: *a vulnerable, unhappy girl who craved affection* **2** *formal* to beg or plead for: *may I crave your lordship's indulgence?* ⟩ **craving** *n*

> **crave** *vb* **1** = long for, yearn for, hanker after, want, desire, hope for, covet, lust after **2** = beg, ask for, seek, petition, pray for, plead for, solicit, implore

craven *adj* **1** cowardly ▶ *n* **2** a coward

crawfish *n, pl* **-fish** *or* **-fishes** same as **crayfish**

crawl *vb* **1** to move on one's hands and knees **2** (of insects, worms, or snakes) to creep slowly **3** to move very slowly **4** to act in a servile manner **5** to be or feel as if covered with crawling creatures: *the kind of smile that made your hair stand on end and your flesh crawl* ▶ *n* **6** a slow creeping pace or motion **7** *swimming* a stroke in which the feet are kicked like paddles while each arm in turn reaches forward and pulls back through the water ⟩ **crawler** *n*

> **crawl** *vb* **1, 2, 3** = creep, slither, inch, wriggle, writhe, worm your way, advance slowly; ≠ run **4** = grovel, creep, humble yourself

crayfish *or esp US* **crawfish** *n, pl* **-fish** *or* **-fishes** an edible shellfish like a lobster

crayon *n* **1** a small stick or pencil of coloured wax or clay ▶ *vb* **2** to draw or colour with a crayon

craze *n* **1** a short-lived fashion or enthusiasm ▶ *vb* **crazing, crazed 2** to make mad **3** *ceramics & metallurgy* to develop or cause to develop fine cracks: *you must prevent the drill crazing the glazed surface of the tile*

> **craze** *n* = fad, fashion, trend, rage, enthusiasm, vogue, mania, infatuation

crazed *adj* **1** wild and uncontrolled in behaviour **2** (of porcelain) having fine cracks

crazy *adj* **-zier, -ziest** *informal* **1** ridiculous **2 crazy about** extremely fond of: *he was crazy about me* **3** extremely annoyed or upset **4** behaving in a wild way ⟩ **crazily** *adv* ⟩ **craziness** *n*

crazy adj 1 = ridiculous, absurd, foolish, ludicrous, senseless, preposterous, idiotic, nonsensical, porangi (NZ); ≠ sensible

crazy paving n Brit, Austral & NZ a form of paving on a path, made of irregular slabs of stone

creak vb 1 to make or move with a harsh squeaking sound ▸ n 2 a harsh squeaking sound > **creaky** adj > **creakiness** n

cream n 1 the fatty part of milk, which rises to the top 2 a cosmetic or medication that resembles cream in consistency 3 any of various foods resembling or containing cream 4 the best part of something 5 **cream sherry** a full-bodied sweet sherry ▸ adj 6 yellowish-white ▸ vb 7 to beat (foodstuffs) to a light creamy consistency 8 to remove the cream from (milk) 9 to prepare or cook (foodstuffs) with cream or milk 10 **cream off** to take away the best part of > **creamy** adj

cream n 2 = lotion, ointment, oil, essence, cosmetic, paste, emulsion, salve 4 = best, elite, prime, pick, flower, the crème de la crème ▸ adj = off-white, ivory, yellowish-white

cream cheese n a type of very rich soft white cheese

crease n 1 a line made by folding or pressing 2 a wrinkle or furrow, esp. on the face 3 cricket any of four lines near each wicket marking positions for the bowler or batsman ▸ vb **creasing, creased** 4 to make or become wrinkled or furrowed > **creasy** adj

crease n 1 = fold, line, ridge, groove, corrugation 2 = wrinkle, line, crow's-foot ▸ vb = crumple, rumple, fold, double up, corrugate

create vb -ating, -ated 1 to cause to come into existence 2 to be the cause of 3 to appoint to a new rank or position 4 Brit slang to make an angry fuss

create vb 1 = make, produce, invent, compose, devise, originate, formulate, spawn; ≠ destroy 2 = cause, lead to, occasion (formal), bring about 3 = appoint, make, establish, set up, invest, install, constitute

Creation n Christianity 1 God's act of bringing the universe into being 2 the universe as thus brought into being by God

Creation n 2 = universe, world, nature, cosmos

creationism n the doctrine that ascribes the origins of all things to God's acts of creation rather than to evolution > **creationist** n, adj

creative adj 1 having the ability to create 2 imaginative or inventive ▸ n 3 a creative person, esp. one who devises advertising campaigns > **creativity** n

creative adj 2 = imaginative, gifted, artistic, inventive, original, inspired, clever, ingenious

creator n a person who creates

creator n = maker, father, mother, parent, author, designer, architect, inventor, originator

creature n 1 an animal, bird, or fish 2 a person 3 a person or thing controlled by another

creature n 1 = living thing, being, animal, beast, brute 2 = person, man, woman, individual, soul, human being, mortal

crèche n 1 a day nursery for very young children 2 a supervised play area provided for young children for short periods

credence (kreed-enss) n belief in the truth or accuracy of a statement: the question is, how much credence to give to their accounts?

credentials pl n 1 something that entitles a person to credit or confidence 2 a document giving evidence of the bearer's identity or qualifications

credentials pl n 1 = qualifications, ability, skill, fitness, attribute, capability, eligibility, aptitude 2 = certification, document, reference(s), papers, licence, passport, testimonial, authorization

credible adj 1 capable of being believed; convincing: there is no credible evidence 2 trustworthy or reliable: the latest claim is the only one to involve a credible witness > **credibility** n

credible adj 1 = believable, possible, likely, reasonable, probable, plausible, conceivable, imaginable; ≠ unbelievable 2 = reliable, honest, dependable, trustworthy, sincere, trusty; ≠ unreliable

credit n 1 **A** the system of allowing customers to receive goods or services before payment **B** the time allowed for paying for such goods or services 2 a reputation for trustworthiness in paying debts 3 **A** the positive balance in a person's bank account **B** the sum of money that a bank makes available to a client in excess of any deposit 4 a sum of money or equivalent purchasing power, available for a person's use 5 accounting **A** acknowledgment of a sum of money by entry on the right-hand side of an account **B** an entry or total of entries on this side 6 praise or approval, as for an achievement or quality: you must give her credit for her perseverance 7 a person or thing who is a source of praise or approval: she is a credit to her family 8 influence or reputation based on the good opinion of others: he acquired credit within the community 9 belief or confidence in someone or something: this theory is now gaining credit among the scientific community 10 education **A** distinction awarded to an examination candidate obtaining good marks **B** certification that a section of an examination syllabus has been satisfactorily completed 11 **on credit** with payment to be made at a future date

▸ *vb* **-iting, -ited 12** *accounting* **A** to enter (an item) as a credit in an account **B** to acknowledge (a payer) by making such an entry **13 credit with** to give credit for: *credit us with some intelligence* **14** to believe

credit *n* **6** = praise, honour, recognition, approval, tribute, acclaim, acknowledgment, kudos **7** = source of satisfaction *or* pride, asset, honour, feather in your cap **8** = prestige, reputation, standing, position, influence, regard, status, esteem **9** = belief, trust, confidence, faith, reliance, credence ▸ *vb* **13 credit someone with something** = attribute to, assign to, ascribe to, impute to **14** = believe, rely on, have faith in, trust, accept

creditable *adj* deserving praise or honour
> **creditably** *adv*
credit card *n* a card issued by banks or shops, allowing the holder to buy on credit
credit crunch *n* a period during which there is a sudden reduction in the availability of credit from banks, mortgage lenders, etc.
creditor *n* a person or company to whom money is owed
credo *n*, *pl* **-dos** a creed
credulity *n* willingness to believe something on little evidence
credulous *adj* **1** too willing to believe: *he has convinced only a few credulous American intellectuals* **2** arising from or showing credulity: *credulous optimism*
creed *n* **1** a system of beliefs or principles **2** a formal statement of the essential parts of Christian belief

creed *n* **1** = belief, principles, doctrine, dogma, credo, catechism, articles of faith

creek *n* **1** a narrow inlet or bay **2** *US, Canad, Austral & NZ* a small stream or tributary **3 up the creek** *slang* in a difficult position

creek *n* **1** = inlet, bay, cove, bight, firth *or* frith (*Scot*) **2** = stream, brook, tributary, bayou, rivulet, watercourse, runnel

creel *n* a wickerwork basket used by fishermen
creep *vb* **creeping, crept 1** to move quietly and cautiously **2** to crawl with the body near to or touching the ground **3** to have the sensation of something crawling over the skin, from fear or disgust: *she makes my flesh creep* **4** (of plants) to grow along the ground or over rocks ▸ *n* **5** a creeping movement **6** *slang* an obnoxious or servile person

creep *vb* **1** = sneak, steal, tiptoe, slink, skulk, approach unnoticed ▸ *n* **6** = bootlicker (*informal*), sneak, sycophant, crawler (*slang*), toady

creeper *n* a plant, such as ivy, that grows by creeping
creepy *adj* **creepier, creepiest** *informal* causing a feeling of fear or disgust > **creepiness** *n*

cremate *vb* **-mating, -mated** to burn (a corpse) to ash > **cremation** *n*
crematorium *n*, *pl* **-riums** *or* **-ria** a building where corpses are cremated
crenellated *or US* **crenelated** *adj* having battlements > **crenellation** *or US* **crenelation** *n*
creole *n* **1** a language developed from a mixture of different languages which has become the main language of a place ▸ *adj* **2** of or relating to a creole
Creole *n* **1** (in the West Indies and Latin America) a native-born person of mixed European and African descent **2** (in the Gulf States of the US) a native-born person of French descent **3** the French creole spoken in the Gulf States ▸ *adj* **4** of or relating to any of these peoples: *Creole cooking*
creosote *n* **1** a thick dark liquid made from coal tar and used for preserving wood **2** a colourless liquid made from wood tar and used as an antiseptic ▸ *vb* **-soting, -soted 3** to treat with creosote
crepe (**krayp**) *n* **1** a thin light fabric with a crinkled texture **2** a very thin pancake, often folded around a filling **3** a type of rubber with a wrinkled surface, used for the soles of shoes
crepe paper *n* paper with a crinkled texture, used for decorations
crept *vb* the past of **creep**
crepuscular *adj* **1** of or like twilight **2** (of animals) active at twilight
crescendo (**krish-end-oh**) *n*, *pl* **-dos 1** a gradual increase in loudness **2** a musical passage that gradually gets louder ▸ *adv* **3** gradually getting louder
crescent *n* **1** the curved shape of the moon when in its first or last quarter **2** *chiefly Brit & NZ* a crescent-shaped street ▸ *adj* **3** crescent-shaped

crescent *n* **1** = meniscus, sickle, new moon

cress *n* a plant with strong-tasting leaves, used in salads and as a garnish
crest *n* **1** the top of a mountain, hill, or wave **2** a tuft or growth of feathers or skin on the top of a bird's or animal's head **3** a heraldic design or figure used on a coat of arms and elsewhere **4** an ornamental plume or emblem on top of a helmet ▸ *vb* **5** to come or rise to a high point **6** to lie at the top of **7** to reach the top of (a hill or wave) > **crested** *adj*

crest *n* **1** = top, summit, peak, ridge, highest point, pinnacle, apex, crown **2** = tuft, crown, comb, plume, mane **3** = emblem, badge, symbol, insignia, bearings, device

crestfallen *adj* disappointed or disheartened
cretin *n* **1** *offensive* a very stupid person **2** *not in technical use, old-fashioned* a person with learning difficulties and physical disabilities because of a thyroid deficiency > **cretinism** *n* > **cretinous** *adj*
crevasse *n* a deep open crack in a glacier
crevice *n* a narrow crack or gap in rock

crew n **1** the people who serve on or operate a ship, boat, or aircraft **2** a group of people working together: *a film crew* **3** *informal* any group of people ▶ vb **4** to serve as a crew member on a ship or boat

> **crew** n **1** = (ship's) company, hands, (ship's) complement **2** = team, squad, gang, corps, posse **3** = crowd, set, bunch (*informal*), band, pack, gang, mob, horde

crew cut n a closely cut haircut for men
crewel n a loosely twisted worsted yarn, used in embroidery > **crewelwork** n
crib n **1** a piece of writing stolen from elsewhere **2** a translation or list of answers used by students, often dishonestly **3** a baby's cradle **4** a rack or manger for fodder **5** a model of the manger scene at Bethlehem **6** short for **cribbage 7** NZ a small holiday house ▶ vb **cribbing, cribbed 8** to copy (someone's work) dishonestly **9** to confine in a small space
cribbage n a card game for two to four players, who each try to win a set number of points before the others
crib-wall n NZ a retaining wall built against an earth bank
crick *informal* ▶ n **1** a painful muscle spasm or cramp in the neck or back ▶ vb **2** to cause a crick in
cricket¹ n **1** a game played by two teams of eleven players using a ball, bats, and wickets **2** **not cricket** *informal* not fair play > **cricketer** n
cricket² n a jumping insect like a grasshopper, which produces a chirping sound by rubbing together its forewings
crime n **1** an act prohibited and punished by law **2** unlawful acts collectively **3** *informal* a disgraceful act: *it would be a crime to travel to Australia and not stop in Sydney*

> **crime** n **1** = offence, violation, trespass, felony, misdemeanour, misdeed, transgression, unlawful act **2** = lawbreaking, corruption, illegality, vice, misconduct, wrongdoing, e-crime *or* ecrime, cybercrime

criminal n **1** a person guilty of a crime ▶ adj **2** of or relating to crime or its punishment **3** *informal* senseless or disgraceful: *a criminal waste of money* > **criminally** adv > **criminality** n

> **criminal** n = lawbreaker, convict, offender, crook (*informal*), villain, culprit, sinner, felon, rorter (*Austral slang*), skelm (*S African*), rogue trader, perp (*US, Canad informal*) ▶ adj **2** = unlawful, illicit, lawless, wrong, illegal, corrupt, crooked (*informal*), immoral; ≠ lawful **3** = disgraceful, ridiculous, foolish, senseless, scandalous, preposterous, deplorable

criminology n the scientific study of crime > **criminologist** n
crimp vb **1** to fold or press into ridges **2** to curl (hair) tightly with curling tongs **3** *chiefly US*

informal to restrict or hinder: *a slowdown in the US economy could crimp some big Swedish concerns' profits* ▶ n **4** the act or result of crimping
crimson adj deep purplish-red
cringe vb **cringing, cringed 1** to shrink or flinch in fear: *he cringed and shrank against the wall* **2** to behave in a submissive or timid way: *an organization that tends to cringe before political authority* **3** *informal* to be very embarrassed: *I cringe every time I see that old photo of me* ▶ n **4** the act of cringing
crinkle vb **-kling, -kled 1** to become slightly creased or folded ▶ n **2** a crease or fold > **crinkly** adj
crinoline n a petticoat stiffened with hoops to make the skirt stand out
cripple n *offensive* **1** a person who is unable to walk or walk easily **2** a person who is or seems deficient in some way: *an emotional cripple* ▶ vb **-pling, -pled 3** to disable (a person or animal) **4** to damage (something) > **crippled** adj > **crippling** adj

> **cripple** vb **3** = disable, paralyse, lame, maim, incapacitate, weaken, hamstring **4** = damage, destroy, ruin, spoil, impair, put paid to, put out of action; ≠ help

crisis n, pl **-ses 1** a crucial stage or turning point in the course of anything **2** a time of extreme trouble or danger

> **crisis** n **1** = critical point, climax, height, crunch (*informal*), turning point, culmination, crux, moment of truth, tipping point **2** = emergency, plight, predicament, trouble, deep water, meltdown (*informal*), dire straits

crisp adj **1** fresh and firm: *a crisp green salad* **2** dry and brittle: *bake until crisp and golden brown* **3** clean and neat: *crisp white cotton* **4** (of weather) cold but invigorating: *a crisp autumn day* **5** clear and sharp: *the telescope is able to provide crisp images of distant galaxies* **6** lively or brisk: *the service is crisp and efficient* ▶ n **7** *Brit* a very thin slice of potato fried till crunchy ▶ vb **8** to make or become crisp > **crisply** adv > **crispness** n

> **crisp** adj **1, 2** = firm, crunchy, crispy, crumbly, fresh, brittle, unwilted; ≠ soft **3** = clean, smart, trim, neat, tidy, spruce, well-groomed, well-pressed **4** = bracing, fresh, refreshing, brisk, invigorating; ≠ warm

crispbread n a thin dry biscuit made of wheat or rye
crispy adj **crispier, crispiest** hard and crunchy > **crispiness** n
crisscross vb **1** to move in or mark with a crosswise pattern ▶ adj **2** (of lines) crossing one another in different directions
criterion n, pl **-ria** *or* **-rions** a standard by which something can be judged or decided

> **criterion** n = standard, test, rule, measure, principle, gauge, yardstick, touchstone

critic *n* 1 a professional judge of art, music, or literature 2 a person who finds fault and criticizes

> **critic** *n* 1 = judge, authority, expert, analyst, commentator, pundit, reviewer, connoisseur 2 = fault-finder, attacker, detractor, knocker (*informal*)

critical *adj* 1 very important or dangerous: *this was a critical moment in her career* 2 so seriously ill or injured as to be in danger of dying: *he is in a critical condition in hospital* 3 fault-finding or disparaging: *the article is highly critical of the government* 4 examining and judging analytically and without bias: *he submitted the plans to critical examination* 5 of a critic or criticism 6 *physics* denoting a constant value at which the properties of a system undergo an abrupt change: *the critical temperature above which the material loses its superconductivity* 7 (of a nuclear power station or reactor) having reached a state in which a nuclear chain reaction becomes self-sustaining > **critically** *adv*

> **critical** *adj* 1 = crucial, decisive, pressing, serious, vital, urgent, all-important, pivotal; ≠ unimportant 2 = grave, serious, acute, precarious; ≠ safe 3 = disparaging, disapproving, scathing, derogatory, nit-picking (*informal*), censorious, fault-finding, captious, nit-picky (*informal*); ≠ complimentary 4 = analytical, penetrating, discriminating, discerning, perceptive, judicious; ≠ undiscriminating

criticism *n* 1 fault-finding or censure 2 an analysis of a work of art or literature 3 the occupation of a critic 4 a work that sets out to analyse

> **criticism** *n* 1 = fault-finding, censure, disapproval, disparagement, stick (*slang*), flak (*informal*), bad press, character assassination 2 = analysis, assessment, judgment, commentary, evaluation, appreciation, appraisal, critique

criticize *or* **-cise** *vb* **-cizing, -cized** *or* **-cising, -cised** 1 to find fault with 2 to analyse (something)

> **criticize** *or* **-cise** *vb* 1 = find fault with, censure, disapprove of, knock (*informal*), condemn, carp, put down, slate (*informal*), nit-pick (*informal*); ≠ praise

critique *n* 1 a critical essay or commentary 2 the act or art of criticizing

croak *vb* 1 (of a frog or crow) to make a low hoarse cry 2 to utter or speak with a croak 3 *slang* to die ▸ *n* 4 a low hoarse sound > **croaky** *adj*

Croatian (kroh-ay-shun) *adj* 1 of Croatia ▸ *n* 2 a person from Croatia 3 the dialect of Serbo-Croat spoken in Croatia

crochet (kroh-shay) *vb* **-cheting, -cheted** 1 to make (a piece of needlework) by looping and intertwining thread with a hooked needle ▸ *n* 2 work made by crocheting

crock[1] *n* an earthenware pot or jar

crock[2] *n* **old crock** *Brit, Austral & NZ slang* a person or thing that is old or broken-down

crockery *n* china dishes or earthenware vessels collectively

crocodile *n* 1 a large amphibious tropical reptile with a tapering snout 2 *Brit, Austral & NZ informal* a line of people, esp. schoolchildren, walking two by two

crocodile tears *pl n* an insincere show of grief

crocus *n*, *pl* **-cuses** a plant with white, yellow, or purple flowers in spring

croft *n* a small farm worked by one family in Scotland > **crofter** *n* > **crofting** *adj, n*

croissant (krwah-son) *n* a flaky crescent-shaped bread roll

cromlech *n Brit* 1 a circle of prehistoric standing stones 2 *not in technical use* a dolmen

crone *n* a witchlike old woman

crony *n*, *pl* **-nies** a close friend

crook *n* 1 *informal* a dishonest person 2 a bent or curved place or thing: *she held the puppy in the crook of her arm* 3 a bishop's or shepherd's staff with a hooked end ▸ *adj* 4 *Austral & NZ informal* **A** ill **B** of poor quality **C** unpleasant; bad 5 **go (off) crook** *Austral & NZ informal* to lose one's temper 6 **go crook at** *or* **on** *Austral & NZ informal* to rebuke or upbraid ▸ *vb* 7 to bend or curve

> **crook** *n* 1 = criminal, rogue, cheat, thief, shark, villain, robber, racketeer, skelm (*S African*) ▸ *adj* 5 **go (off) crook** = lose your temper, be furious, rage, go mad, lose it (*informal*), crack up (*informal*), see red (*informal*), blow your top

crooked *adj* 1 bent or twisted 2 set at an angle 3 *informal* dishonest or illegal > **crookedly** *adv* > **crookedness** *n*

> **crooked** *adj* 1 = bent, twisted, curved, irregular, warped, out of shape, misshapen; ≠ straight 2 = at an angle, uneven, slanting, squint, awry, lopsided, askew, off-centre 3 = dishonest, criminal, illegal, corrupt, unlawful, shady (*informal*), fraudulent, bent (*slang*); ≠ honest

croon *vb* to sing, hum, or speak in a soft low tone > **crooner** *n*

crop *n* 1 a cultivated plant, such as a cereal, vegetable, or fruit plant 2 the season's total yield of farm produce 3 any group of things appearing at one time: *a remarkable crop of new Scottish plays* 4 the handle of a whip 5 a pouchlike part of the gullet of a bird, in which food is stored or prepared for digestion 6 a short cropped hairstyle ▸ *vb* **cropping, cropped** 7 to cut (something) very short 8 to produce or harvest as a crop 9 (of animals) to feed on (grass) **10** to clip part of (the ear or ears) of (an animal), esp. for identification ▸ See also **crop up**

> **crop** n **2** = yield, produce, gathering, fruits, harvest, vintage, reaping ▸ vb **7** = cut, trim, clip, prune, shear, snip, pare, lop **9** = graze, eat, browse, feed on, nibble

cropper n **come a cropper** informal **A** to fail completely **B** to fall heavily

crop up vb informal to occur or appear unexpectedly

> **crop up** vb = happen, appear, emerge, occur, arise, turn up, spring up

croquet (kroh-kay) n a game played on a lawn in which balls are hit through hoops

croquette (kroh-kett) n a fried cake of mashed potato, meat, or fish

crosier n same as **crozier**

cross vb **1** to move or go across (something): *she crossed the street to the gallery* **2** to meet and pass: *further south, the way is crossed by Brewer Street* **3** Brit & NZ to draw two parallel lines across (a cheque) and so make it payable only into a bank account **4** to mark with a cross or crosses **5** to cancel or delete with a cross or with lines: *she crossed out the first three words* **6** to place across or crosswise: *he sat down and crossed his legs* **7** to make the sign of the cross upon as a blessing **8** to annoy or anger (someone) by challenging or opposing their wishes and plans **9** to interbreed or cross-fertilize **10** football to pass (the ball) from a wing to the middle of the field **11** (of each of two letters or messages) to be sent before the other is received **12** (of telephone lines) to interfere with each other so that several callers are connected together at one time **13 cross one's fingers** to fold one finger across another in the hope of bringing good luck **14 cross one's heart** to promise by making the sign of a cross over one's heart **15 cross one's mind** to occur to one briefly or suddenly ▸ n **16** a structure, symbol, or mark consisting of two intersecting lines **17** an upright post with a bar across it, used in ancient times as a means of execution **18** a representation of the Cross on which Jesus Christ was executed as an emblem of Christianity **19** a symbol (×) used as a signature or error mark **20 the sign of the cross** a sign made with the hand by some Christians to represent the Cross **21** a medal or monument in the shape of a cross **22** the place in a town or village where a cross has been set up **23** biol **A** the process of crossing; hybridization **B** a hybrid **24** a mixture of two things **25** a hindrance or misfortune: *we've all got our own cross to bear* **26** football a pass of the ball from a wing to the middle of the field ▸ adj **27** angry **28** lying or placed across: *a cross beam* > **crossly** adv > **crossness** n

> **cross** vb **1** = go across, pass over, traverse, cut across, move across, travel across **2** = intersect, intertwine, crisscross **8** = oppose, interfere with, obstruct, block, resist, impede **9** = interbreed, mix, blend, cross-pollinate, crossbreed, hybridize, cross-fertilize, intercross ▸ n **18** = crucifix **24** = mixture, combination, blend, amalgam, amalgamation **25** = trouble, worry, trial, load, burden, grief, woe, misfortune ▸ adj **27** = angry, annoyed, put out, grumpy, short, ill-tempered, irascible, tooshie (*Austral slang*), in a bad mood, hoha (NZ); ≠ good-humoured

Cross n **the Cross A** the cross on which Jesus Christ was crucified **B** Christianity

crossbar n **1** a horizontal beam across a pair of goalposts **2** the horizontal bar on a man's bicycle

crossbow n a weapon consisting of a bow fixed across a wooden stock, which releases an arrow when the trigger is pulled

crossbreed vb **-breeding, -bred 1** to produce (a hybrid animal or plant) by crossing two different species ▸ n **2** a hybrid animal or plant

cross-country adj, adv **1** by way of open country or fields ▸ n **2** a long race held over open ground

cross-examine vb **-examining, -examined 1** law to question (a witness for the opposing side) in order to check his or her testimony **2** to question closely or relentlessly > **cross-examination** n > **cross-examiner** n

cross-eyed adj with one or both eyes turning inwards towards the nose

cross-fertilize or **-lise** vb **-lizing, -lized** or **-lising, -lised** to fertilize (an animal or plant) by fusion of male and female reproductive cells from different individuals of the same species > **cross-fertilization** or **-lisation** n

crossfire n **1** military gunfire crossing another line of fire **2** a lively exchange of ideas or opinions

crossing n **1** a place where a street, railway, or river may be crossed **2** the place where one thing crosses another **3** a journey across water

crossover n a combination of two different styles, esp. of music or fashion

cross-purposes pl n **at cross-purposes** misunderstanding each other in a discussion

cross-reference n **1** a reference within a text to another part of the text ▸ vb **-referencing, -referenced 2** to cross-refer

crossroads n **1** the point at which roads cross one another **2 at the crossroads** at the point at which an important choice has to be made

cross section n **1** maths a surface formed by cutting across a solid, usually at right angles to its longest axis **2** a random sample regarded as representative: *a cross section of society* > **cross-sectional** adj

crosswise or **crossways** adj, adv **1** across: *slice the celery crosswise* **2** in the shape of a cross

crossword puzzle or **crossword** n a puzzle in which vertically and horizontally crossing words suggested by clues are written into a grid of squares

crotch n 1 the forked part of the human body between the legs 2 the corresponding part of a pair of trousers or pants 3 any forked part formed by the joining of two things: *the crotch of the tree* > **crotched** adj

crotchet n music a note having the time value of a quarter of a semibreve

crotchety adj informal bad-tempered

crouch vb 1 to bend low with the legs and body pulled close together ▸ n 2 this position

> **crouch** vb = bend down, kneel, squat, stoop, bow, duck, hunch

croup[1] (kroop) n a throat disease of children, with a hoarse cough and laboured breathing

croup[2] (kroop) n the hindquarters of a horse

croupier (kroop-ee-ay) n a person who collects bets and pays out winnings at a gambling table

crouton n a small piece of fried or toasted bread served in soup

crow[1] n 1 a large black bird with a harsh call 2 **as the crow flies** in a straight line

crow[2] vb 1 past tense **crowed** or **crew** (of a cock) to utter a shrill squawking sound 2 to boast about one's superiority 3 (of a baby) to utter cries of pleasure ▸ n 4 a crowing sound

> **crow** vb 2 = gloat, triumph, boast, swagger, brag, exult, blow your own trumpet

crowbar n a heavy iron bar used as a lever

crowd n 1 a large number of things or people gathered together 2 a particular group of people: *we got to know a French crowd from Lyons* 3 **the crowd** the masses ▸ vb 4 to gather together in large numbers 5 to press together into a confined space 6 to fill or occupy fully 7 informal to make (someone) uncomfortable by coming too close > **crowded** adj

> **crowd** n 1 = multitude, mass, throng, army, host, pack, mob, swarm 2 = group, set, lot, circle, gang, bunch (informal), clique ▸ vb 4 = flock, mass, collect, gather, stream, surge, swarm, throng 5 = squeeze, pack, pile, bundle, cram 6 = congest, pack, cram

crowdsourcing n the use of many disparate people as contributors to a project, esp. via the internet

crown n 1 a monarch's ornamental headdress, usually made of gold and jewels 2 a wreath for the head, given as an honour 3 the highest or central point of something arched or curved: *the crown of the head* 4 **a** the enamel-covered part of a tooth projecting beyond the gum **b** a substitute crown, usually of gold or porcelain, fitted over a decayed or broken tooth 5 a former British coin worth 25 pence (five shillings) 6 the outstanding quality or achievement: *the last piece is the crown of the evening* ▸ vb 7 to put a crown on the head of (someone) to proclaim him or her monarch 8 to put on the top of 9 to reward 10 to form the topmost part of 11 to put the finishing touch to (a series of events): *she crowned a superb display with three goals* 12 to attach a crown to (a tooth) 13 Brit, Austral & NZ slang to hit over the head 14 draughts to promote (a draught) to a king by placing another draught on top of it

> **crown** n 1 = coronet, tiara, diadem (old-fashioned), circlet 2 = laurel wreath, trophy, prize, honour, garland, laurels, wreath 3 = high point, top, tip, summit, crest, pinnacle, apex ▸ vb 7 = install, honour, dignify, ordain, inaugurate 8,10 = top, cap, be on top of, surmount (formal) 11 = cap, finish, complete, perfect, round off, put the finishing touch to, be the climax or culmination of 13 = strike, belt (informal), bash, hit over the head, box, punch, cuff, biff (slang)

Crown n **the Crown** the power or institution of the monarchy

> **Crown** n **the Crown** = monarch, ruler, sovereign, emperor or empress, king or queen

crown court n a local criminal court in England and Wales

crown-of-thorns n a starfish with a spiny outer covering that feeds on living coral

crown prince n the male heir to a sovereign throne > **crown princess** n

crow's feet pl n wrinkles at the outer corners of the eye

crow's nest n a lookout platform fixed at the top of a ship's mast

crozier or **crosier** n a hooked staff carried by bishops as a symbol of office

crucial adj 1 of exceptional importance 2 Brit slang very good > **crucially** adv

> **crucial** adj 1 = vital, important, pressing, essential, urgent, momentous, high-priority

cruciate ligament n anatomy either of a pair of ligaments that cross each other in the knee

crucible n a pot in which metals or other substances are melted

crucifix n a model cross with a figure of Christ upon it

crucifixion n a method of execution by fastening to a cross, normally by the hands and feet

Crucifixion n Christianity 1 **the Crucifixion** the crucifying of Christ 2 a representation of this

cruciform adj shaped like a cross

crucify vb **-fies, -fying, -fied** 1 to put to death by crucifixion 2 to treat cruelly 3 slang to defeat or ridicule totally

crude adj 1 rough and simple: *crude farm implements* 2 tasteless or vulgar 3 in a natural or unrefined state > **crudely** adv > **crudity** or **crudeness** n

C

crude *adj* **1** = simple, rudimentary, basic, primitive, coarse, clumsy, rough-and-ready **2** = vulgar, dirty, rude, obscene, coarse, indecent, tasteless, smutty; ≠ tasteful **3** = unrefined, natural, raw, unprocessed; ≠ processed

cruel *adj* **1** deliberately causing pain without pity **2** causing pain or suffering ▷ **cruelly** *adv* ▷ **cruelty** *n*

cruel *adj* **1** = brutal, ruthless, callous, sadistic, inhumane, vicious, monstrous, unkind; ≠ kind **2** = bitter, ruthless, traumatic, grievous, unrelenting, merciless, pitiless

cruet *n* **1** a small container for pepper, salt, etc. at table **2** a set of such containers on a stand

cruise *n* **1** a sail taken for pleasure, stopping at various places ▷ *vb* **cruising, cruised 2** to sail about from place to place for pleasure **3** (of a vehicle, aircraft, or ship) to travel at a moderate and efficient speed **4** to proceed steadily or easily: *they cruised into the final of the qualifying competition*

cruise *n* = sail, voyage, boat trip, sea trip ▷ *vb* **2** = sail, coast, voyage **3** = travel along, coast, drift, keep a steady pace

cruise missile *n* a low-flying subsonic missile that is guided throughout its flight

cruiser *n* **1** a large fast warship armed with medium-calibre weapons **2** *Also called:* **cabin cruiser** a motorboat with a cabin

crumb *n* **1** a small fragment of bread or other dry food **2** a small bit or scrap: *a crumb of comfort*

crumb *n* **1** = bit, grain, fragment, shred, morsel **2** = morsel, scrap, shred, snippet, soupçon (*French*)

crumble *vb* **-bling, -bled 1** to break into crumbs or fragments **2** to fall apart or decay ▷ *n* **3** a baked pudding consisting of stewed fruit with a crumbly topping: *rhubarb crumble* ▷ **crumbly** *adj* ▷ **crumbliness** *n*

crumble *vb* **1** = crush, fragment, pulverize, pound, grind, powder, granulate **2** = disintegrate, collapse, deteriorate, decay, fall apart, degenerate, tumble down, go to pieces

crummy *adj* **-mier, -miest** *slang* **1** of very bad quality: *a crummy hotel* **2** unwell: *I felt really crummy*

crumpet *n* **1** a light soft yeast cake, eaten buttered **2** *chiefly Brit slang, sometimes offensive* attractive women collectively

crumple *vb* **-pling, -pled 1** to crush or become crushed into untidy wrinkles or creases **2** to collapse in an untidy heap: *her father lay crumpled on the floor* ▷ *n* **3** an untidy crease or wrinkle ▷ **crumply** *adj*

crumple *vb* **1** = crush, squash, screw up, scrumple **2** = collapse, sink, go down, fall

crunch *vb* **1** to bite or chew with a noisy crushing sound **2** to make a crisp or brittle sound ▷ *n* **3** a crunching sound **4 the crunch** *informal* the critical moment or situation ▷ **crunchy** *adj* ▷ **crunchiness** *n*

crunch *vb* **1** = chomp, champ, munch, chew noisily, grind ▷ *n* **4 the crunch** = critical point, test, crisis, emergency, crux, moment of truth

crupper *n* **1** a strap that passes from the back of a saddle under a horse's tail **2** the horse's rump

crusade *n* **1** any of the medieval military expeditions undertaken by European Christians to recapture the Holy Land from the Muslims **2** a vigorous campaign in favour of a cause ▷ *vb* **-sading, -saded 3** to take part in a crusade ▷ **crusader** *n*

crusade *n* **1** = holy war **2** = campaign, drive, movement, cause, push (*informal*) ▷ *vb* = campaign, fight, push, struggle, lobby, agitate, work

crush *vb* **1** to press or squeeze so as to injure, break, or put out of shape **2** to break or grind into small pieces **3** to control or subdue by force **4** to extract (liquid) by pressing: *crush the juice from a lemon* **5** to defeat or humiliate utterly **6** to crowd together ▷ *n* **7** a dense crowd **8** the act of crushing **9** *informal* an infatuation: *I had a teenage crush on my French teacher* **10** a drink made by crushing fruit: *orange crush*

crush *vb* **1, 2** = squash, break, squeeze, compress, press, pulverize **3** = overcome, overwhelm, put down, subdue, overpower, quash, quell, stamp out **5** = demoralize, depress, devastate, discourage, humble, put down (*slang*), humiliate, squash ▷ *n* **7** = crowd, mob, horde, throng, pack, mass, jam, huddle

crust *n* **1** the hard outer part of bread **2** the baked shell of a pie or tart **3** any hard outer layer: *a thin crust of snow* **4** the solid outer shell of the earth ▷ *vb* **5** to cover with or form a crust

crust *n* **3** = layer, covering, coating, skin, surface, shell

crustacean *n* **1** an animal with a hard outer shell and several pairs of legs, which usually lives in water, such as a crab or lobster ▷ *adj* **2** of crustaceans

crusty *adj* **crustier, crustiest 1** having a crust **2** rude or irritable ▷ **crustiness** *n*

crutch *n* **1** a long staff with a rest for the armpit, used to support the weight of the body **2** something that supports **3** *Brit* same as **crotch** (sense 1)

crux *n*, *pl* **cruxes** *or* **cruces** a crucial or decisive point

cry *vb* **cries, crying, cried 1** to shed tears **2** to make a loud vocal sound, usually to express pain or fear or to appeal for help **3** to utter loudly or shout **4** (of an animal or bird) to utter loud characteristic sounds **5 cry out for** to need urgently ▸ n, pl **cries** 6 a fit of weeping 7 the act or sound of crying 8 the characteristic utterance of an animal or bird 9 an urgent appeal: *a cry for help* 10 a public demand: *a cry for more law and order on the streets* 11 **a far cry from** something very different from 12 **in full cry** ▲ in eager pursuit ʙ in the middle of talking or doing something ▸ See also **cry off**

> **cry** vb 1 = weep, sob, shed tears, blubber, snivel; ≠ laugh 2, 3 = shout, scream, roar, yell, howl, call out, exclaim, shriek; ≠ whisper ▸ n 6 = weep, sob, bawl, blubber 7 = shout, call, scream, roar, yell, howl, shriek, bellow

cry off vb informal to withdraw from an arrangement

> **cry off** vb = back out, withdraw, quit, excuse yourself

cryogenics n the branch of physics concerned with very low temperatures and their effects > **cryogenic** adj

crypt n a vault or underground chamber, such as one beneath a church, used as a burial place

cryptic adj having a hidden or secret meaning; puzzling: *no-one knew what he meant by that cryptic remark* > **cryptically** adv

cryptography n the art of writing in and deciphering codes > **cryptographer** n > **cryptographic** adj

crystal n 1 a solid with a regular structure and symmetrical arrangement of faces 2 a single grain of a crystalline substance 3 a very clear and brilliant glass 4 something made of crystal 5 crystal glass articles collectively 6 *electronics* a crystalline element used in certain electronic devices, such as a detector or oscillator ▸ adj 7 bright and clear: *the crystal waters of the pool*

crystalline adj 1 of or like crystal or crystals 2 clear

crystallize, crystalize or **-ise** vb **-izing, -ized** or **-ising, -ised** 1 to make or become definite 2 to form into crystals 3 to preserve (fruit) in sugar > **crystallization, crystalization** or **-isation** n

cu. cubic

cub n 1 the young of certain mammals, such as the lion or bear 2 a young or inexperienced person ▸ vb **cubbing, cubbed** 3 to give birth to (cubs)

Cub n short for **Cub Scout**

cubbyhole n a small enclosed space or room

cube n 1 an object with six equal square faces 2 the product obtained by multiplying a number by itself twice: *the cube of 2 is 8* ▸ vb **cubing, cubed** 3 to find the cube of (a number) 4 to cut into cubes

cube root n the number or quantity whose cube is a given number or quantity: *2 is the cube root of 8*

cubic adj 1 ▲ having three dimensions ʙ having the same volume as a cube with length, width,

and depth each measuring the given unit: *a cubic metre* 2 having the shape of a cube 3 *maths* involving the cubes of numbers

cubicle n an enclosed part of a large room, screened for privacy

cubism n a style of art, begun in the early 20th century, in which objects are represented by geometrical shapes > **cubist** adj, n

Cub Scout or **Cub** n a member of a junior branch of the Scout Association

cuckold literary or old-fashioned ▸ n 1 a man whose spouse has been unfaithful to him ▸ vb 2 to make a cuckold of

cuckoo n, pl **cuckoos** 1 a migratory bird with a characteristic two-note call, noted for laying its eggs in the nests of other birds ▸ adj 2 informal foolish or mad

cucumber n 1 a long fruit with thin green rind and crisp white flesh, used in salads 2 **as cool as a cucumber** calm and self-possessed

cud n 1 partially digested food which a ruminant brings back into its mouth to chew again 2 **chew the cud** to think deeply

cuddle vb **-dling, -dled** 1 to hug or embrace fondly 2 **cuddle up** to lie close and snug ▸ n 3 a fond hug > **cuddly** adj

> **cuddle** vb 1 = hug, embrace, fondle, cosset 2 **cuddle up** = snuggle

cudgel n a short thick stick used as a weapon

cue¹ n 1 a signal to an actor or musician to begin speaking or playing 2 a signal or reminder 3 **on cue** at the right moment ▸ vb **cueing, cued** 4 to give a cue to

> **cue** n 2 = signal, sign, hint, prompt, reminder, suggestion

cue² n 1 a long tapering stick used to hit the balls in billiards, snooker, or pool ▸ vb **cueing, cued** 2 to hit (a ball) with a cue

cuff¹ n 1 the end of a sleeve 2 US, Canad, Austral & NZ a turn-up on trousers 3 **off the cuff** informal impromptu: *he delivers many speeches off the cuff*

cuff² Brit, Austral & NZ ▸ vb 1 to strike with an open hand ▸ n 2 a blow with an open hand

cuff link n one of a pair of decorative fastenings for shirt cuffs

cuisine (quiz-zeen) n 1 a style of cooking: *Italian cuisine* 2 the range of food served in a restaurant

cul-de-sac n, pl **culs-de-sac** or **cul-de-sacs** a road with one end blocked off

culinary adj of the kitchen or cookery

cull vb 1 to choose or gather 2 to remove or kill (the inferior or surplus animals) from a herd ▸ n 3 the act of culling

culminate vb **-nating, -nated** to reach the highest point or climax: *the parade culminated in a memorial service* > **culmination** n

> **culminate** vb = end up, close, finish, conclude, wind up, climax, come to a head, come to a climax

culottes *pl n* flared trousers cut to look like a skirt

culpable *adj* deserving blame ⊳ **culpability** *n*

culprit *n* the person guilty of an offence or misdeed

> **culprit** *n* = offender, criminal, felon, guilty party, wrongdoer, miscreant, evildoer, transgressor, perp (*US, Canad informal*)

cult *n* **1** a specific system of religious worship **2** a sect devoted to the beliefs of a cult **3** devoted attachment to a person, idea, or activity **4** a popular fashion: *the bungee-jumping cult* ▸ *adj* **5** very popular among a limited group of people: *a cult TV series*

> **cult** *n* **1, 2** = sect, faction, school, religion, clique, hauhau (NZ) **3** = obsession, worship, devotion, idolization **4** = craze, fashion, trend, fad

cultivate *vb* **-vating, -vated 1** to prepare (land) to grow crops **2** to grow (plants) **3** to develop or improve (something) by giving special attention to it: *he tried to cultivate a reputation for fairness* **4** to try to develop a friendship with (a person)

> **cultivate** *vb* **1, 2** = farm, work, plant, tend, till, plough **3** = develop, establish, foster **4** = court, seek out, run after, dance attendance upon

cultivated *adj* well-educated: *a civilized and cultivated man*

cultivation *n* **1** the act of cultivating **2** culture or refinement

culture *n* **1** the ideas, customs, and art of a particular society **2** a particular civilization at a particular period **3** a developed understanding of the arts **4** the cultivation and rearing of plants or animals **5** a growth of bacteria for study ▸ *vb* **-turing, -tured 6** to grow (bacteria) in a special medium ⊳ **cultural** *adj*

> **culture** *n* **1** = lifestyle, habit, way of life, mores **2** = civilization, society, customs, way of life **3** = refinement, education, enlightenment, sophistication, good taste, urbanity

cultured *adj* **1** showing good taste or manners **2** artificially grown or synthesized

> **cultured** *adj* **1** = refined, intellectual, educated, sophisticated, enlightened, well-informed, urbane, highbrow; ≠ uneducated

cultured pearl *n* a pearl artificially grown in an oyster shell

culvert *n* a drain or pipe that crosses under a road or railway

cumbersome *or* **cumbrous** *adj* **1** awkward because of size or shape **2** difficult because of complexity: *the cumbersome appeals procedure*

cumin *or* **cummin** *n* **1** the spicy-smelling seeds of a Mediterranean herb, used in cooking **2** the plant from which these seeds are obtained

cummerbund *n* a wide sash worn round the waist, esp. with a dinner jacket

cumulative (kew-myew-la-tiv) *adj* growing in amount, strength, or effect by small steps: *the cumulative effect of twelve years of war*

cumulus (kew-myew-luss) *n, pl* **-li** (-lie) a thick or billowing white or dark grey cloud

cuneiform (kew-nif-form) *n* **1** an ancient system of writing using wedge-shaped characters ▸ *adj* **2** written in cuneiform

cunjevoi *n Austral* **1** a plant of tropical Asia and Australia with small flowers, cultivated for its edible rhizome **2** a sea squirt

cunning *adj* **1** clever at deceiving **2** made with skill ▸ *n* **3** cleverness at deceiving **4** skill or ingenuity ▸ **cunningly** *adv*

> **cunning** *adj* **1** = crafty, sly, devious, artful, sharp, wily, Machiavellian, shifty (*informal*); ≠ frank **2** = ingenious, imaginative, sly, devious, artful, Machiavellian; ≠ clumsy ▸ *n* **3** = craftiness, guile, trickery, deviousness, artfulness, slyness; ≠ candour **4** = skill, subtlety, ingenuity, artifice, cleverness; ≠ clumsiness

cup *n* **1** a small bowl-shaped drinking container with a handle **2** the contents of a cup **3** something shaped like a cup: *a bra with padded cups* **4** a cup-shaped trophy awarded as a prize **5** a sporting contest in which a cup is awarded to the winner **6** a mixed drink with fruit juice or wine as a base: *claret cup* **7** one's lot in life: *his cup of bitterness was full to overflowing* **8 someone's cup of tea** *informal* someone's chosen or preferred thing ▸ *vb* **cupping, cupped 9** to form (the hands) into the shape of a cup **10** to hold in cupped hands

> **cup** *n* **1** = mug, goblet, chalice, teacup, beaker, bowl **4** = trophy

cupboard *n* a piece of furniture or a recess with a door, for storage

> **cupboard** *n* = cabinet, press

cupidity (kew-**pid**-it-ee) *n formal* strong desire for wealth or possessions

cupola (kew-pol-la) *n* **1** a domed roof or ceiling **2** a small dome on the top of a roof **3** an armoured revolving gun turret on a warship

cur *n* **1** a vicious mongrel dog **2** a contemptible person

curable *adj* capable of being cured ⊳ **curability** *n*

curaçao (kew-rah-so) *n* an orange-flavoured liqueur

curacy (kew-rah-see) *n, pl* **-cies** the work or position of a curate

curare (kew-rah-ree) *n* a poisonous resin obtained from a South American tree, used as a muscle relaxant in medicine

curate¹ (kyoor-it) *n* a member of the clergy who assists a vicar or parish priest

curate² (kew-**rate**) *vb* **1** to be the curator of (a museum or art gallery) **2** to organize, arrange, and present (a cultural event)

curative *adj* **1** able to cure ▸ *n* **2** something able to cure

curator *n* the person in charge of a museum or art gallery > **curatorial** *adj* > **curatorship** *n*

curb *n* **1** something that restrains or holds back **2** a horse's bit with an attached chain or strap, used to check the horse **3** a raised edge that strengthens or encloses ▸ *vb* **4** to control or restrain ▸ See also **kerb**

> **curb** *n* **1** = restraint, control, check, brake, limitation, rein, deterrent, bridle ▸ *vb* = restrain, control, check, restrict, suppress, inhibit, hinder, retard

curd *n* **1** coagulated milk, used in making cheese or as a food **2** any similar substance: *bean curd*

curdle *vb* **-dling, -dled** **1** to turn into curd; coagulate **2 make someone's blood curdle** to fill someone with horror

cure *vb* **curing, cured** **1** to get rid of (an ailment or problem) **2** to restore (someone) to health **3** to preserve (meat or fish) by salting or smoking **4** to preserve (leather or tobacco) by drying **5** to vulcanize (rubber) ▸ *n* **6** a restoration to health **7** medical treatment that restores health **8** a means of restoring health or improving a situation **9** a curacy

> **cure** *vb* **1** = make better, correct, heal, relieve, remedy, mend, ease **2** = restore to health, restore, heal **3, 4** = preserve, smoke, dry, salt, pickle ▸ *n* **7, 8** = remedy, treatment, antidote, panacea, nostrum

curette *or* **curet** *n* **1** a surgical instrument for scraping tissue from body cavities ▸ *vb* **-retting, -retted** **2** to scrape with a curette > **curettage** *n*

curfew *n* **1** a law which states that people must stay inside their houses after a specific time at night **2** the time set as a deadline by such a law **3** *history* the ringing of a bell at a fixed time, as a signal for putting out fires and lights

curie *n* the standard unit of radioactivity

curio (kew-ree-oh) *n, pl* **-rios** a rare or unusual thing valued as a collector's item

curiosity *n, pl* **-ties** **1** eagerness to know or find out **2** a rare or unusual thing

> **curiosity** *n* **1** = inquisitiveness, interest, prying, snooping (*informal*), nosiness (*informal*), infomania **2** = oddity, wonder, sight, phenomenon, spectacle, freak, novelty, rarity

curious *adj* **1** eager to learn or know **2** eager to find out private details **3** unusual or peculiar > **curiously** *adv*

curious *adj* **1, 2** = inquisitive, interested, questioning, searching, inquiring, meddling, prying, nosy (*informal*); ≠ uninterested **3** = strange, unusual, bizarre, odd, novel, rare, extraordinary, unexpected; ≠ ordinary

curl *vb* **1** to twist (hair) or (of hair) to grow in coils or ringlets **2** to twist into a spiral or curve **3** to play the game of curling **4 curl one's lip** to show contempt by raising a corner of the lip ▸ *n* **5** a coil of hair **6** a curved or spiral shape > **curly** *adj*

> **curl** *vb* **1** = crimp, wave, perm **2** = twirl, turn, bend, twist, curve, loop, spiral, coil ▸ *n* **5** = ringlet, lock **6** = twist, spiral, coil, kink, whorl

curlew *n* a large wading bird with a long downward-curving bill

curling *n* a game played on ice, in which heavy stones with handles are slid towards a target circle

curmudgeon *n* a bad-tempered or mean person > **curmudgeonly** *adj*

currajong *n* same as **kurrajong**

currant *n* **1** a small dried seedless raisin **2** a small round acid berry, such as the redcurrant

currawong *n* an Australian songbird

currency *n, pl* **-cies** **1** the system of money or the actual coins and banknotes in use in a particular country **2** general acceptance or use: *ideas that had gained currency during the early 1960s*

> **currency** *n* **1** = money, coinage, legal tender, notes, coins **2** = acceptance, popularity, circulation, vogue, prevalence

current *adj* **1** of the immediate present: *current affairs; the current economic climate* **2** most recent or up-to-date: *the current edition* **3** commonly accepted: *current thinking on this issue* **4** circulating and valid at present: *current coins* ▸ *n* **5** a flow of water or air in a particular direction **6** *physics* a flow or rate of flow of electric charge through a conductor **7** a general trend or drift: *two opposing currents of thought* > **currently** *adv*

> **current** *adj* **1, 2** = present, fashionable, up-to-date, contemporary, trendy (*Brit informal*), topical, present-day, in fashion, live; ≠ out-of-date **3** = prevalent, common, accepted, popular, widespread, customary, in circulation ▸ *n* **5** = flow, course, undertow, jet, stream, tide, progression, river **7** = mood, feeling, spirit, atmosphere, trend, tendency, undercurrent

curriculum *n, pl* **-la** *or* **-lums** **1** all the courses of study offered by a school or college **2** a course of study in one subject at a school or college: *the history curriculum* > **curricular** *adj*

curriculum vitae (vee-tie) *n, pl* **curricula vitae** an outline of someone's educational and professional history, prepared for job applications

curry[1] *n, pl* **-ries 1** a dish of Indian origin consisting of meat or vegetables in a hot spicy sauce **2** curry seasoning or sauce **3 curry powder** a mixture of spices for making curry ▸ *vb* **-ries, -rying, -ried 4** to prepare (food) with curry powder

curry[2] *vb* **-ries, -rying, -ried 1** to groom (a horse) **2** to dress (leather) after it has been tanned **3 curry favour** to ingratiate oneself with an important person

curse *vb* **cursing, cursed 1** to swear or swear at (someone) **2** to call on supernatural powers to bring harm to (someone or something) ▸ *n* **3** a profane or obscene expression, usually of anger **4** an appeal to a supernatural power for harm to come to a person **5** harm resulting from a curse **6** something that causes great trouble or harm **7 the curse** *informal* menstruation or a menstrual period

> **curse** *vb* **1** = swear, cuss (*informal*), blaspheme, take the Lord's name in vain ▸ *n* **3** = oath, obscenity, blasphemy, expletive, profanity, imprecation, swearword **4** = malediction, jinx, anathema, hoodoo (*informal*), excommunication **6** = affliction, plague (*informal*), scourge, trouble, torment, hardship, bane

cursed *adj* **1** under a curse **2 cursed with** having (something unfortunate or unwanted): *the player has been cursed with injuries this season*

> **cursed** *adj* **1** = under a curse, damned, doomed, jinxed, bedevilled, accursed, ill-fated

cursive *adj* **1** of handwriting or print in which letters are joined in a flowing style ▸ *n* **2** a cursive letter or printing type

cursor *n* **1** a movable shape, typically a flashing bar or underline, that shows a specific position on a computer screen **2** the sliding part of a slide rule or other measuring instrument

cursory *adj* hasty and usually superficial > **cursorily** *adv*

curt *adj* so blunt and brief as to be rude > **curtly** *adv* > **curtness** *n*

curtail *vb* **1** to cut short: *the opening round was curtailed by heavy rain* **2** to restrict: *a plan to curtail drinks advertising* > **curtailment** *n*

> **curtail** *vb* = reduce, diminish, decrease, dock, cut back, shorten, lessen, cut short

curtain *n* **1** a piece of material hung at an opening or window to shut out light or to provide privacy **2** a hanging cloth that conceals all or part of a theatre stage from the audience **3** the end of a scene or a performance in the theatre, marked by the fall or closing of the curtain **4** the rise or opening of the curtain at the start of a performance **5** something forming a barrier or screen: *a curtain of rain* ▸ *vb* **6** to shut off or conceal with a curtain **7** to provide with curtains

curtain *n* **1** = hanging, drape (*chiefly US*), portière

curtsy *or* **curtsey** *n, pl* **-sies** *or* **-seys 1** a woman's formal gesture of respect made by bending the knees and bowing the head ▸ *vb* **-sies, -sying, -sied** *or* **-seys, -seying, -seyed 2** to make a curtsy

curvaceous *adj informal* having a curved shapely body

curvature *n* the state or degree of being curved

curve *n* **1** a continuously bending line with no straight parts **2** something that curves or is curved **3** curvature **4** *maths* a system of points whose coordinates satisfy a given equation **5** a line representing data on a graph ▸ *vb* **curving, curved 6** to form into or move in a curve > **curvy** *adj*

> **curve** *n* **1** = bend, turn, loop, arc, curvature ▸ *vb* = bend, turn, wind, twist, arch, snake, arc, coil

curvilinear *adj* consisting of or bounded by a curved line

cuscus *n, pl* **-cuses** a large nocturnal possum of N Australia and New Guinea

cushion *n* **1** a bag filled with a soft material, used to make a seat more comfortable **2** something that provides comfort or absorbs shock **3** the resilient felt-covered rim of a billiard table ▸ *vb* **4** to protect from injury or shock **5** to lessen the effects of **6** to provide with cushions > **cushiony** *adj*

> **cushion** *n* **1** = pillow, pad, bolster, headrest, beanbag, hassock ▸ *vb* **4** = protect **5** = soften, dampen, muffle, mitigate, deaden, suppress, stifle

cushy *adj* **cushier, cushiest** *informal* easy: *a cushy job*

cusp *n* **1** a small point on the grinding or chewing surface of a tooth **2** a point where two curves meet **3** *astrol* any division between houses or signs of the zodiac **4** *astron* either of the points of a crescent moon **5 on the cusp** at the point of moving from one state into another: *on the cusp of middle age*

cuss *informal* ▸ *n* **1** a curse or oath **2** an annoying person ▸ *vb* **3** to swear or swear at

cussed (**kuss-id**) *adj informal* **1** obstinate: *the older she got the more cussed she became* **2** same as **cursed** > **cussedness** *n*

custard *n* **1** a sauce made of milk and sugar thickened with cornflour **2** a baked sweetened mixture of eggs and milk

custodian *n* the person in charge of a public building > **custodianship** *n*

custody *n, pl* **-dies 1** the act of keeping safe **2** imprisonment prior to being tried > **custodial** *adj*

> **custody** *n* **1** = care, charge, protection, supervision, safekeeping, keeping **2** = imprisonment, detention, confinement, incarceration

custom _n_ **1** a long-established activity, action, or festivity: _the custom of serving port after dinner_ **2** the long-established habits or traditions of a society **3** a usual practice or habit: _she held his hand more tightly than was her custom in public_ **4** regular use of a shop or business ▸ _adj_ **5** made to the specifications of an individual customer: _a custom car; custom-tailored suits_

> **custom** _n_ **1, 2** = tradition, practice, convention, ritual, policy, rule, usage, kaupapa (NZ) **3** = habit, way, practice, procedure, routine, wont **4** = customers, business, trade, patronage

customary _adj_ **1** usual **2** established by custom > **customarily** _adv_ > **customariness** _n_

> **customary** _adj_ **1** = usual, common, accepted, established, traditional, normal, ordinary, conventional; ≠ unusual **2** = accustomed, regular, usual

custom-built _or_ **-made** _adj_ made according to the specifications of an individual customer
customer _n_ **1** a person who buys goods or services **2** _informal_ a person with whom one has to deal: _a tricky customer_

> **customer** _n_ **1** = client, consumer, regular (_informal_), buyer, patron, shopper, purchaser

customize _or_ **-ise** _vb_ **-izing, -ized** _or_ **-ising, -ised** to make (something) according to a customer's individual requirements
cut _vb_ **cutting, cut** **1** to open up or penetrate (a person or thing) with a sharp instrument **2** (of a sharp instrument) to penetrate or open up (a person or thing) **3** to divide or be divided with or as if with a sharp instrument **4** to trim **5** to abridge or shorten **6** to reduce or restrict: _cut your intake of fried foods_ **7** to form or shape by cutting **8** to reap or mow **9** _sport_ to hit (the ball) so that it spins and swerves **10** to hurt the feelings of (a person): _her rudeness cut me to the core_ **11** _informal_ to pretend not to recognize **12** _informal_ to absent oneself from without permission: _he found the course boring, and was soon cutting classes_ **13** to stop (doing something): _cut the nonsense_ **14** to dilute or adulterate: _heroin cut with talcum powder_ **15** to make a sharp or sudden change in direction: _the path cuts to the right just after you pass the quarry_ **16** to grow (teeth) through the gums **17** _films_ **A** to call a halt to a shooting sequence **B cut to** to move quickly to (another scene) **18** _films_ to edit (film) **19** to switch off (a light or engine) **20** to make (a commercial recording): _he cut his first solo album in 1971_ **21** _cards_ **A** to divide (the pack) at random into two parts after shuffling **B** to pick cards from a spread pack to decide the dealer or who plays first **22 cut a dash** to make a stylish impression **23 cut a person dead** _informal_ to ignore a person completely **24 cut and run** _informal_ to escape quickly from a difficult situation **25 cut both ways** **A** to have both good

and bad effects **B** to serve both sides of an argument **26 cut it fine** _informal_ to allow little margin of time or space **27 cut no ice** _informal_ to fail to make an impression **28 cut one's teeth on** _informal_ to get experience from ▸ _n_ **29** the act of cutting **30** a stroke or incision made by cutting **31** a piece cut off **32** a channel or path cut or hollowed out **33** a reduction: _a pay cut_ **34** a deletion in a text, film, or play **35** _informal_ a portion or share **36** the style in which hair or a garment is cut **37** a direct route; short cut **38** _sport_ a stroke which makes the ball spin and swerve **39** _films_ an immediate transition from one shot to the next **40** _Brit_ a canal **41 a cut above** _informal_ superior to; better than ▸ _adj_ **42** made or shaped by cutting **43** reduced by cutting: _the shop has hundreds of suits, all at cut prices_ **44** adulterated or diluted **45 cut and dried** _informal_ settled in advance

> **cut** _vb_ **1, 2** = slit, score, slice, slash, pierce, penetrate **3** = chop, split, slice, dissect **4, 8** = clip, mow, trim, prune, snip, pare, lop **5** = abridge, edit, shorten, curtail, condense, abbreviate; ≠ extend **6** = reduce, lower, slim (down), diminish, slash, decrease, cut back, kennet (_Austral slang_), jeff (_Austral slang_); ≠ increase **7** = shape, carve, engrave, chisel, form, score, fashion, whittle **10** = hurt, wound, upset, sting, hurt someone's feelings **11** = ignore, avoid, slight, blank (_slang_), snub, spurn, cold-shoulder, turn your back on; ≠ greet **15** = cross, bisect ▸ _n_ **30** = incision, nick, stroke, slash, slit **33** = reduction, fall, lowering, slash, decrease, cutback **35** = share, piece, slice, percentage, portion **36** = style, look, fashion, shape

cutaneous (kew-tane-ee-uss) _adj_ of the skin
cute _adj_ **1** appealing or attractive **2** _informal_ clever or shrewd > **cuteness** _n_

> **cute** _adj_ **1** = appealing, sweet, attractive, engaging, charming, delightful, lovable, winsome

cuticle (kew-tik-kl) _n_ **1** hardened skin round the base of a fingernail or toenail **2** same as **epidermis**
cut in _vb_ **1** to interrupt **2** to move in front of another vehicle, leaving too little space
cutlass _n_ a curved one-edged sword formerly used by sailors
cutler _n_ a person who makes or sells cutlery
cutlery _n_ knives, forks, and spoons, used for eating
cutlet _n_ **1** a small piece of meat taken from the neck or ribs **2** a flat croquette of chopped meat or fish
cutter _n_ **1** a person or tool that cuts **2** a small fast boat
cut-throat _adj_ **1** fierce or ruthless in competition: _the cut-throat world of international finance_ **2** (of a card game) played by three people:

cut-throat poker ▸ *n* **3** a murderer **4** *Brit & NZ* a razor with a long blade that folds into its handle

cutting *n* **1** an article cut from a newspaper or magazine **2** a piece cut from a plant for rooting or grafting **3** a passage cut through high ground for a road or railway **4** the editing process of a film ▸ *adj* **5** (of a remark) likely to hurt the feelings **6** keen; piercing: *a cutting wind* **7** designed for cutting: *the hatchet's blade is largely stone, but its cutting edge is made of copper*

> **cutting** *adj* **5** = hurtful, wounding, bitter, malicious, scathing, acrimonious, barbed, sarcastic; ≠ kind

cuttlefish *n, pl* -**fish** *or* -**fishes** a flat squidlike mollusc which squirts an inky fluid when in danger

CV curriculum vitae

cwt hundredweight

cyanide *n* any of a number of highly poisonous substances containing a carbon-nitrogen group of atoms

cyber- *combining form* indicating computers: *cyberspace*

cyberattack *n* an attempt to cause damage or disruption by interfering with a computer system

cybercrime *n* crime committed by means of computers or the internet

cybernetics *n* the branch of science in which electronic and mechanical systems are studied and compared to biological systems > **cybernetic** *adj*

cyberspace *n* the hypothetical environment which contains all the data stored in computers

cyclamen (sik-la-men) *n* a plant with white, pink, or red flowers, with turned-back petals

cycle *vb* -**cling**, -**cled** **1** to ride a bicycle **2** to occur in cycles ▸ *n* **3** *Brit, Austral & NZ* a bicycle **4** *US* a motorcycle **5** a complete series of recurring events **6** the time taken or needed for one such series **7** a single complete movement in an electrical, electronic, or mechanical process **8** a set of plays, songs, or poems about a figure or event > **cycling** *n*

> **cycle** *n* **5, 7** = series of events, circle, revolution, rotation

cyclical *or* **cyclic** *adj* **1** occurring in cycles **2** *chem* (of an organic compound) containing a closed ring of atoms

cyclist *n* a person who rides a bicycle

cyclone *n* **1** a body of moving air below normal atmospheric pressure, which often brings rain **2** a violent tropical storm > **cyclonic** *adj*

cyclotron *n* an apparatus, used in atomic research, which accelerates charged particles by means of a strong vertical magnetic field

cygnet *n* a young swan

cylinder *n* **1** a solid or hollow body with circular equal ends and straight parallel sides **2** a container or other object shaped like a cylinder

3 the chamber in an internal-combustion engine within which the piston moves **4** the rotating mechanism of a revolver, containing cartridge chambers > **cylindrical** *adj*

cymbal *n* a percussion instrument consisting of a round brass plate which is struck against another or hit with a stick > **cymbalist** *n*

cynic (sin-ik) *n* a person who believes that people always act selfishly

> **cynic** *n* = sceptic, doubter, pessimist, misanthrope, misanthropist, scoffer

cynical *adj* **1** believing that people always act selfishly **2** sarcastic or sneering > **cynically** *adv*

> **cynical** *adj* **1** = unbelieving, sceptical, disillusioned, pessimistic, disbelieving, mistrustful; ≠ optimistic **2** = sceptical, mocking, pessimistic, scoffing, contemptuous, scornful, distrustful, derisive; ≠ trusting

cynicism *n* the attitude or beliefs of a cynic

> **cynicism** *n* = scepticism, pessimism, misanthropy

cynosure (sin-oh-zyure) *n literary* a centre of interest or attention

cypher (sife-er) *n, vb* same as **cipher**

cypress *n* **1** an evergreen tree with dark green leaves **2** the wood of this tree

Cypriot *adj* **1** of Cyprus ▸ *n* **2** a person from Cyprus **3** the dialect of Greek spoken in Cyprus

cyst (sist) *n* **1** *pathol* an abnormal membranous sac containing fluid or diseased matter **2** *anatomy* any normal sac in the body

cystitis (siss-tite-iss) *n* inflammation of the bladder, causing a desire to urinate frequently, accompanied by a burning sensation

cytology (site-ol-a-jee) *n* the study of plant and animal cells > **cytological** *adj* > **cytologically** *adv* > **cytologist** *n*

czar (zahr) *n* same as **tsar**

Czech *adj* **1** of the Czech Republic ▸ *n* **2** a person from the Czech Republic **3** the language of the Czech Republic

Dd

d 1 *physics* density **2** deci-

D 1 *music* the second note of the scale of C major **2** *chem* deuterium **3** the Roman numeral for 500

d. 1 *Brit & NZ* (before decimalization) penny *or* pennies **2** died **3** daughter

dab¹ *vb* **dabbing, dabbed 1** to pat lightly and quickly **2** to apply with short tapping strokes: *dabbing antiseptic on cuts* ▸ *n* **3** a small amount of something soft or moist **4** a light stroke or tap **5** **dabs** *slang, chiefly Brit* fingerprints

> **dab** *vb* **1** = pat, touch, tap **2** = apply, daub, stipple ▸ *n* **3** = spot (*Brit*), bit, drop, pat, smudge, speck **4** = touch, stroke, flick

dab² *n* a small European flatfish covered with rough toothed scales

dabble *vb* **-bling, -bled 1** to be involved in an activity in a superficial way: *she dabbles in right-wing politics* **2** to splash (one's toes or fingers) in water ▸ **dabbler** *n*

dab hand *n informal* a person who is particularly skilled at something: *a dab hand with a needle and thread*

dace *n, pl* **dace** *or* **daces** a European freshwater fish of the carp family

dachshund *n* a small dog with short legs and a long body

dad *or* **daddy** *n informal* father

daddy-longlegs *n informal* **1** a crane fly **2** a small web-spinning spider with long legs

dado (day-doe) *n, pl* **-does** *or* **-dos 1** the lower part of an interior wall, often separated by a rail, that is decorated differently from the upper part **2** *archit* the part of a pedestal between the base and the cornice

daffodil *n* **1** a spring plant with yellow trumpet-shaped flowers ▸ *adj* **2** brilliant yellow

daft *adj informal, chiefly Brit* **1** foolish or slightly crazy **2** **daft about** very enthusiastic about: *he's daft about football*

> **daft** *adj* **1** = stupid, crazy (*informal*), silly, foolish, idiotic, witless

dag *Austral & NZ* ▸ *n* **1** the dried dung on a sheep's rear **2** *informal* an amusing person ▸ *pl n* **3** **rattle one's dags** *informal* hurry up ▸ *vb* **4** to remove the dags from a sheep

> **dag** *n* **2** = joker, comic, wag, wit, comedian, clown, humorist, prankster ▸ *pl n* **rattle one's dags** = hurry up, get a move on, step on it (*informal*), get your skates on (*informal*), make haste

dagga (duhh-a) *n S African* a local name for marijuana

> **dagga** *n* = cannabis, marijuana, pot (*slang*), dope (*slang*), hash (*slang*), grass (*slang*), weed (*slang*), hemp

dagger *n* **1** a short knifelike weapon with a double-edged pointed blade **2** a character (†) used to indicate a cross-reference **3** **at daggers drawn** in a state of open hostility **4** **look daggers** to glare with hostility

daggy *adj* **-gier, -giest** *Austral & NZ informal* **1** untidy; dishevelled **2** eccentric

> **daggy** *adj* **1** = untidy, unkempt, dishevelled, tousled, disordered, messy, ruffled, scruffy, rumpled, bedraggled, ratty (*informal*), straggly, windblown, disarranged, mussed up (*informal*) **2** = eccentric, odd, strange, bizarre, weird, peculiar, abnormal, queer (*old-fashioned*), irregular, uncommon, quirky, singular, unconventional, idiosyncratic, off-the-wall (*slang*), outlandish, whimsical, rum (*Brit slang*), capricious, anomalous, freakish, aberrant, outré

daguerreotype (dag-gair-oh-type) *n* a type of early photograph produced on chemically treated silver

dahlia (day-lya) *n* a garden plant with showy flowers

daily *adj* **1** occurring every day or every weekday: *there have been daily airdrops of food, blankets, and water* **2** of or relating to a single day or to one day at a time: *her home help comes in on a daily basis; exercise has become part of our daily lives* ▸ *adv* **3** every day ▸ *n, pl* **-lies 4** *Brit & Austral* a daily newspaper **5** *Brit informal* a person employed to keep someone's house clean

> **daily** *adj* **1** = everyday, diurnal, quotidian ▸ *adv* = every day, day by day, once a day

dainty *adj* **-tier, -tiest 1** delicate, pretty, or elegant: *dainty little pink shoes* ▸ *n, pl* **-ties 2** *Brit* a small choice cake or sweet ▸ **daintily** *adv*

daiquiri (dak-eer-ee) *n, pl* **-ris** an iced drink containing rum, lime juice, and sugar

dairy *n, pl* **dairies 1** a company or shop that sells milk and milk products **2** a place where milk and cream are stored or made into butter and cheese **3** food containing milk or milk products: *I can't eat dairy* **4** *NZ* a small shop selling groceries and milk often outside normal trading hours ▸ *adj* **5** of milk or milk products: *dairy produce*

dais (day-iss) *n* a raised platform in a hall or meeting place used by a speaker

daisy *n, pl* **-sies** a small low-growing flower with a yellow centre and pinkish-white petals

Dalai Lama *n* the chief lama and (until 1959) ruler of Tibet

dale *n* an open valley

dalliance *n old-fashioned* flirtation

dally vb **-lies, -lying, -lied 1** old-fashioned to waste time or dawdle **2 dally with** to deal frivolously with: to dally with someone's affections

Dalmatian n a large dog with a smooth white coat and black spots

dam¹ n **1** a barrier built across a river to create a lake **2** a lake created by such a barrier ▸ vb **damming, dammed 3** to block up (a river) by a dam

> **dam** n **1** = barrier, wall, barrage, obstruction, embankment ▸ vb = block up, restrict, hold back, barricade, obstruct

dam² n the female parent of an animal such as a sheep or horse

damage vb **-aging, -aged 1** to harm or injure ▸ n **2** injury or harm caused to a person or thing **3** informal cost: what's the damage? > **damaging** adj

> **damage** vb = spoil, hurt, injure, harm, ruin, crush, devastate, wreck; ≠ fix ▸ n
> **2** = destruction, harm, loss, injury, suffering, hurt, ruin, devastation; ≠ improvement
> **3** = cost, price, charge, bill, amount, payment, expense, outlay

damask n a heavy fabric with a pattern woven into it, used for tablecloths, curtains, etc.

dame n slang a woman

Dame n (in Britain) the title of a woman who has been awarded the Order of the British Empire or another order of chivalry

> **Dame** n = lady, baroness, dowager, grande dame (French), noblewoman, peeress

damn interj **1** slang an exclamation of annoyance ▸ adv **2** slang Also: **damned** extremely ▸ adj **3** slang Also: **damned** extreme: a damn nuisance ▸ vb **4** to condemn as bad or worthless **5** to curse **6** (of God) to condemn to hell or eternal punishment **7** to prove (someone) guilty **8 damn with faint praise** to praise so unenthusiastically that the effect is condemnation ▸ n **9 not give a damn** informal not to care > **damning** adj

> **damn** vb **4** = criticize, condemn, blast, denounce, put down, censure; ≠ praise

damnable adj very unpleasant or annoying > **damnably** adv

damnation interj **1** an exclamation of anger ▸ n **2** theol eternal punishment

damned adj **1** condemned to hell ▸ adv, adj slang **2** extreme or extremely: a damned good try **3** used to indicate amazement or refusal: I'm damned if I'll do it!

damp adj **1** slightly wet ▸ n **2** slight wetness; moisture ▸ vb **3** to make slightly wet **4 damp down A** to reduce the intensity of (someone's emotions or reactions): they attempted to damp down protests **B** to reduce the flow of air to (a fire) to make it burn more slowly > **damply** adv > **dampness** n

damp adj = moist, wet, soggy, humid, dank, sopping, clammy, dewy; ≠ dry ▸ n = moisture, liquid, drizzle, dampness, wetness, dankness; ≠ dryness ▸ vb **3** = moisten, wet, soak, dampen, moisturize **4A damp something down** = curb, reduce, check, diminish, inhibit, stifle, allay, pour cold water on

dampen vb **1** to reduce the intensity of **2** to make damp

> **dampen** vb **1** = reduce, check, moderate, dull, restrain, stifle, lessen **2** = moisten, wet, spray, make damp

damper n **1 put a damper on** to produce a depressing or inhibiting effect on **2** a movable plate to regulate the draught in a stove or furnace **3** the pad in a piano or harpsichord that deadens the vibration of each string as its key is released **4** chiefly Austral & NZ any of various unleavened loaves and scones, typically cooked on an open fire

damsel n archaic or poetic a young woman

damson n a small blue-black edible plumlike fruit that grows on a tree

dance vb **dancing, danced 1** to move the feet and body rhythmically in time to music **2** to perform (a particular dance): to dance a tango **3** to skip or leap **4** to move in a rhythmic way: their reflection danced in the black waters **5 dance attendance on someone** to carry out someone's slightest wish in an overeager manner ▸ n **6** a social meeting arranged for dancing **7** a series of rhythmic steps and movements in time to music **8** a piece of music in the rhythm of a particular dance > **dancer** n > **dancing** n, adj

> **dance** vb **1** = prance, trip, hop, skip, sway, whirl, caper, jig **3** = caper, trip, spring, jump, bound, skip, frolic, cavort ▸ n **6** = ball, social, hop (informal), disco, knees-up (Brit informal), discotheque, B and S (Austral informal)

D and C n med dilatation of the cervix and curettage of the uterus: a minor operation to clear the womb or remove tissue for diagnosis

dandelion n a wild plant with yellow rayed flowers and deeply notched leaves

dander n **get one's dander up** Brit, Austral & NZ slang to become angry

dandified adj dressed like or resembling a dandy

dandle vb **-dling, -dled** to move (a young child) up and down on one's knee

dandruff n loose scales of dry dead skin shed from the scalp

dandy n, pl **-dies 1** a man who is greatly concerned with the elegance of his appearance ▸ adj **-dier, -diest 2** informal very good or fine

Dane n a person from Denmark

danger n **1** the possibility that someone may be injured or killed **2** someone or something that may cause injury or harm **3** a likelihood that something unpleasant will happen: *the danger of flooding*

> **danger** *n* **1** = jeopardy, vulnerability **2** = hazard, risk, threat, menace, peril, pitfall

dangerous *adj* likely or able to cause injury or harm › **dangerously** *adv*

> **dangerous** *adj* = perilous, risky, hazardous, vulnerable, insecure, unsafe, precarious, breakneck; ≠ safe

dangle *vb* **-gling, -gled** **1** to hang loosely **2** to display (something attractive) as an enticement

> **dangle** *vb* **1** = hang, swing, trail, sway, flap, hang down **2** = offer, flourish, brandish, flaunt

Danish *adj* **1** of Denmark › *n* **2** the language of Denmark
Danish blue *n* a white cheese with blue veins and a strong flavour
Danish pastry *n* a rich puff pastry filled with apple, almond paste, etc. and topped with icing
dank *adj* (esp. of cellars or caves) unpleasantly damp and chilly
dapper *adj* (of a man) neat in appearance and slight in build
dappled *adj* **1** marked with spots of a different colour; mottled **2** covered in patches of light and shadow
dapple-grey *n* a horse with a grey coat and darker-coloured spots
dare *vb* **daring, dared** **1** to be courageous enough to try (to do something) **2** to challenge (someone) to do something risky **3** **I dare say** **A** it is quite possible **B** probably › *n* **4** a challenge to do something risky

> **dare** *vb* **1** = risk doing, venture, presume, make bold (*archaic*), hazard doing **2** = challenge, provoke, defy, taunt, goad, throw down the gauntlet

daredevil *n* **1** a recklessly bold person › *adj* **2** recklessly bold or daring
daring *adj* **1** willing to do things that may be dangerous › *n* **2** the courage to do things that may be dangerous › **daringly** *adv*

> **daring** *adj* = brave, bold, adventurous, reckless, fearless, audacious, intrepid, daredevil; ≠ timid › *n* = bravery, nerve (*informal*), courage, spirit, bottle (*Brit slang*), pluck, audacity, boldness; ≠ timidity

dark *adj* **1** having little or no light **2** (of a colour) reflecting little light: *dark brown* **3** (of hair or skin) brown or black **4** (of thoughts or ideas) gloomy or sad **5** sinister or evil: *a dark deed* **6** sullen or angry: *a dark scowl* **7** secret or mysterious: *keep it dark* › *n* **8** absence of light; darkness **9** night or nightfall **10** **in the dark** in ignorance › **darkly** *adv* › **darkness** *n*

dark *adj* **1** = dim, murky, shady, shadowy, grey, dingy, unlit, poorly lit **3** = black, brunette, ebony, dark-skinned, sable, dusky, swarthy; ≠ fair **4** = gloomy, sad, grim, miserable, bleak, dismal, pessimistic, melancholy; ≠ cheerful **5** = evil, foul, sinister, vile, wicked, infernal (*informal*) **7** = secret, hidden, mysterious, concealed ▸ *n* **8** = darkness, shadows, gloom, dusk (*poetic*), obscurity, murk, dimness, semi-darkness **9** = night, twilight, evening, evo (*Austral slang*), dusk, night-time, nightfall

darken *vb* **1** to make or become dark or darker **2** to make gloomy, angry, or sad

> **darken** *vb* **1** = cloud, obscure, dim, overshadow, blacken; ≠ brighten

dark horse *n* a person who reveals little about himself or herself, esp. someone who has unexpected talents
darkroom *n* a darkened room in which photographic film is developed
darling *n* **1** a person very much loved: used as a term of address **2** a favourite: *the darling of the gossip columns* ▸ *adj* **3** beloved **4** pleasing: *a darling film*

> **darling** *n* **1** = beloved, love, dear, dearest, angel (*informal*), treasure, precious, sweetheart ▸ *adj* **3** = beloved, dear, treasured, precious, adored, cherished

darn[1] *vb* **1** to mend a hole in (a knitted garment) with a series of interwoven stitches ▸ *n* **2** a patch of darned work on a garment
darn[2] *interj, adj, adv, vb, n euphemistic* same as **damn**
dart *n* **1** a small narrow pointed missile that is thrown or shot, as in the game of darts **2** a sudden quick movement **3** a tapered tuck made in dressmaking ▸ *vb* **4** to move or throw swiftly and suddenly › **darting** *adj*

> **dart** *vb* = dash, run, race, shoot, fly, speed, spring, tear

Darwinism *or* **Darwinian theory** *n* the theory of the origin of animal and plant species by evolution › **Darwinian** *adj, n* › **Darwinist** *n, adj*
dash *vb* **1** to move hastily; rush **2** to hurl; crash: *deep-sea rollers dashing spray over jagged rocks* **3** to frustrate: *prospects for peace have been dashed* ▸ *n* **4** a sudden quick movement **5** a small amount: *a dash of milk* **6** a mixture of style and courage: *the commander's dash did not impress him* **7** the punctuation mark (—), used to indicate a change of subject **8** the symbol (–), used in combination with the symbol *dot* (.) in Morse code

> **dash** *vb* **1** = rush, run, race, shoot, fly, career, speed, tear; ≠ dawdle **2** = throw, cast, pitch, slam, toss, hurl, fling, chuck (*informal*) ▸ *n* **4** = rush, run, race, sprint, dart, spurt, sortie **5** = drop, little, bit, shot (*informal*), touch, spot (*Brit*), trace, hint; ≠ lot **6** = style, spirit, flair (*informal*), flourish, verve, panache, élan, brio

dashboard *n* the instrument panel in a car, boat, or aircraft

dashing *adj* stylish and attractive: *a splendidly dashing character*

> **dashing** *adj* = stylish, smart, elegant, flamboyant, sporty, jaunty, showy

dassie *n S African* a hyrax, esp. a rock hyrax

dastardly *adj old-fashioned* mean and cowardly

dasyure (dass-ee-your) *n* a small marsupial of Australia, New Guinea, and adjacent islands

data *n* 1 a series of observations, measurements, or facts; information 2 the numbers, digits, characters, and symbols operated on by a computer

> **data** *n* 1 = details, facts, figures, intelligence, statistics 2 = information

data capture *n* a process for converting information into a form that can be handled by a computer

data processing *n* a sequence of operations performed on data, esp. by a computer, in order to extract or interpret information

date¹ *n* 1 a specified day of the month 2 the particular day or year when an event happened 3 ᴀ an appointment, esp. with a person to whom one is romantically or sexually attached ʙ the person with whom the appointment is made 4 **to date** up to now ▸ *vb* **dating, dated** 5 to mark (a letter, cheque, etc.) with the date 6 to assign a date of occurrence or creation to 7 to reveal the age of: *that dress dates her* 8 to make or become old-fashioned: *it's the freshest look this year but may date quickly* 9 *informal, chiefly US & Canad* to be a boyfriend or girlfriend of 10 **date from** *or* **date back to** to have originated at (a specified time)

> **date** *n* 2 = time, stage, period 3ᴀ = appointment, meeting, arrangement, commitment, engagement, rendezvous, tryst, assignation 3ʙ = partner, escort, friend ▸ *vb* 6 = put a date on, assign a date to, fix the period of 8 = become dated, become old-fashioned 10 **date from** *or* **date back to** = come from, belong to, originate in, exist from, bear a date of

date² *n* the dark-brown, sweet-tasting fruit of the date palm

dated *adj* unfashionable; outmoded

> **dated** *adj* = old-fashioned, outdated, out of date, obsolete, unfashionable, outmoded, passé, old hat; ≠ modern

date palm *n* a tall palm grown in tropical regions for its fruit

dative *n grammar* the grammatical case in certain languages that expresses the indirect object

datum *n, pl* **-ta** a single piece of information usually in the form of a fact or statistic

daub *vb* 1 to smear (paint or mud) quickly or carelessly over a surface 2 to paint (a picture) clumsily or badly ▸ *n* 3 a crude or badly done painting: *a typical child's daub*

daughter *n* 1 a female child 2 a girl or woman who comes from a certain place or is connected with a certain thing: *a daughter of the church* ▸ *adj* 3 *biol* denoting a cell, chromosome, etc. produced by the division of one of its own kind 4 *physics* (of a nuclide) formed from another nuclide by radioactive decay > **daughterly** *adj*

daughter-in-law *n, pl* **daughters-in-law** the wife of one's son or daughter

daunting *adj* intimidating or worrying: *this project grows more daunting every day*

> **daunting** *adj* = intimidating, alarming, frightening, discouraging, unnerving, disconcerting, demoralizing, off-putting (*Brit informal*); ≠ reassuring

dauntless *adj* fearless; not discouraged

dauphin (daw-fin) *n* (formerly) the eldest son of the king of France

davenport *n* 1 *chiefly Brit* a writing desk with drawers at the side 2 *Austral, US & Canad* a large sofa

davit (dav-vit) *n* a crane, usually one of a pair, on the side of a ship for lowering or hoisting a lifeboat

dawdle *vb* **-dling, -dled** to walk slowly or lag behind

dawn *n* 1 daybreak 2 the beginning of something ▸ *vb* 3 to begin to grow light after the night 4 to begin to develop or appear 5 **dawn on** *or* **upon** to become apparent (to someone)

> **dawn** *n* 1 = daybreak, morning, sunrise, daylight, aurora (*poetic*), crack of dawn, sunup, cockcrow 2 = beginning, start, birth, rise, origin, emergence, advent, genesis ▸ *vb* 3 = grow light, break, brighten, lighten 4 = begin, start, rise, develop, emerge, unfold, originate 5 **dawn on someone** = hit, strike, occur to, register (*informal*), become apparent, come to mind, come into your head

day *n* 1 the period of 24 hours from one midnight to the next 2 the period of light between sunrise and sunset 3 the part of a day occupied with regular activity, esp. work 4 a period or point in time: *in days gone by; in Shakespeare's day* 5 a day of special observance: *Christmas Day* 6 a time of success or recognition: *his day will come* 7 **all in a day's work** part of one's normal activity 8 **at the end of the day** in the final reckoning 9 **call it a day** to stop work or other activity 10 **day in, day out** every day without changing 11 **that'll be the day** ᴀ that is most unlikely to happen ʙ I look forward to that. ▸ Related adjective: **diurnal**

day *n* **1** = twenty-four hours **2** = daytime, daylight **4** = time, age, era, period, epoch

daybreak *n* the time in the morning when light first appears

daycare *n* care that is provided during the working day for people who cannot look after themselves, such as young children or people who are ill

daydream *n* **1** a pleasant fantasy indulged in while awake ▸ *vb* **2** to indulge in idle fantasy > **daydreamer** *n*

daylight *n* **1** light from the sun **2** daytime **3** daybreak **4** **see daylight** to realize that the end of a difficult task is approaching

daylight *n* **1** = sunlight, sunshine, light of day

day release *n* Brit a system whereby workers go to college one day a week for vocational training

day-to-day *adj* routine; everyday

daze *vb* **dazing, dazed** **1** to cause to be in a state of confusion or shock ▸ *n* **2** a state of confusion or shock: *in a daze* > **dazed** *adj*

daze *vb* = stun, shock, paralyse, numb, stupefy, benumb ▸ *n* = shock, confusion, distraction, trance, bewilderment, stupor, trancelike state

dazzle *vb* **-zling, -zled** **1** to impress greatly: *she was dazzled by his wit* **2** to blind for a short time by sudden excessive light: *he passed two cars and they dazzled him with their headlights* ▸ *n* **3** bright light that dazzles > **dazzling** *adj* > **dazzlingly** *adv*

dazzle *vb* **1** = impress, amaze, overwhelm, astonish, overpower, bowl over (*informal*), take your breath away **2** = blind, confuse, daze, bedazzle

dB *or* **db** decibel(s)

DC **1** direct current **2** District of Columbia

DD Doctor of Divinity

D-day *n* the day selected for the start of some operation

DDT *n* dichlorodiphenyltrichloroethane; an insecticide, now banned in many countries

de- *prefix* **1** indicating removal: *dethrone* **2** indicating reversal: *declassify* **3** indicating departure from: *decamp*

deacon *n* Christianity **1** (in episcopal churches) an ordained minister ranking immediately below a priest **2** (in some Protestant churches) a lay official who assists the minister

dead *adj* **1** no longer alive **2** no longer in use or finished: *a dead language; a dead match* **3** unresponsive **4** (of a limb) numb **5** complete or absolute: *there was dead silence* **6** informal very tired **7** (of a place) lacking activity **8** *electronics* **A** drained of electric charge **B** not connected to a source of electric charge **9** *sport* (of a ball) out of play **10** **dead from the neck up** informal stupid **11** **dead to the world** informal fast asleep

▸ *n* **12** a period during which coldness or darkness is most intense: *the dead of winter* ▸ *adv* **13** informal extremely: *dead easy* **14** suddenly and abruptly: *stop dead* **15** **dead on** exactly right

dead *adj* **1** = deceased, departed (*euphemistic*), late, perished, extinct, defunct, passed away; ≠ alive **4** = numb, frozen, paralysed, insensitive, inert, deadened, immobilized, unfeeling **5** = total, complete, absolute, utter, outright, thorough, unqualified **6** = exhausted, tired, worn out, spent, done in (*informal*), all in (*slang*), drained, knackered (*slang*) ▸ *n* = middle, heart, depth, midst ▸ *adv* **13** = exactly, completely, totally, directly, fully, entirely, absolutely, thoroughly

deadbeat *n* informal a lazy or socially undesirable person

dead beat *adj* informal exhausted

deaden *vb* to make (something) less intense: *drugs deaden the pain; heavy curtains deadened the echo* > **deadening** *adj*

dead end *n* **1** a cul-de-sac **2** a situation in which further progress is impossible: *efforts to free the hostages had reached a dead end*

dead heat *n* a tie for first place between two or more participants in a race or contest

deadline *n* a time or date by which a job or task must be completed

deadline *n* = time limit, cutoff point, target date *or* time, limit

deadlock *n* a point in a dispute at which no agreement can be reached

deadlock *n* = impasse, stalemate, standstill, gridlock, standoff

deadlocked *adj* having reached a deadlock

deadly *adj* **-lier, -liest** **1** likely to cause death: *deadly poison* **2** informal extremely boring ▸ *adv*, *adj* **3** like or suggestive of death: *deadly pale* ▸ *adv* **4** extremely: *she was being deadly serious*

deadly *adj* **1** = lethal, fatal, deathly, dangerous, devastating, mortal, murderous, malignant **2** = boring, dull, tedious, flat, monotonous, uninteresting, mind-numbing, wearisome

deadly nightshade *n* a poisonous plant with purple bell-shaped flowers and black berries

deadpan *adj* **1** deliberately emotionless ▸ *adv* **2** in a deliberately emotionless manner

dead reckoning *n* a method of establishing one's position using the distance and direction travelled

dead set *adv* firmly decided: *he is dead set on leaving*

dead weight *n* **1** a heavy weight or load **2** the difference between the loaded and the unloaded weights of a ship

deaf *adj* **1** unable to hear **2** **deaf to** refusing to listen or take notice of > **deafness** *n*

d

deaf *adj* 1 = hard of hearing, without hearing, stone deaf

deafen *vb* to make deaf, esp. momentarily by a loud noise > **deafening** *adj*

deal¹ *n* 1 an agreement or transaction 2 a particular type of treatment received: *a fair deal* 3 a large amount: *the land alone is worth a good deal* 4 *cards* a player's turn to distribute the cards 5 **big deal** *slang* an important matter: often used sarcastically ▸ *vb* **dealing, dealt** (**delt**) 6 to inflict (a blow) on 7 *slang* to sell any illegal drug 8 **deal in** to engage in commercially 9 **deal out** to apportion or distribute ▸ See also **deal with**

> **deal** *n* 1 = agreement, understanding, contract, arrangement, bargain, transaction, pact 3 = amount, quantity, measure, degree, mass, volume, share, portion ▸ *vb* 8 **deal in something** = sell, trade in, stock, traffic in, buy and sell 9 **deal something out** = distribute, give, share, assign, allocate, dispense, allot, mete out

deal² *n* 1 a plank of softwood timber 2 the sawn wood of various coniferous trees

dealer *n* 1 a person or organization whose business involves buying and selling things 2 *slang* a person who sells illegal drugs 3 *cards* the person who distributes the cards

> **dealer** *n* 1 = trader, merchant, supplier, wholesaler, purveyor, tradesperson

dealings *pl n* business relations with a person or organization

deal with *vb* 1 to take action on: *he was not competent to deal with the legal aspects* 2 to be concerned with: *I do not wish to deal with specifics* 3 to do business with

> **deal with** *vb* 1 **deal with something or someone** = handle, manage, treat, cope with, take care of, see to, attend to, get to grips with 2 **deal with something** = be concerned with, involve, concern, touch, regard, apply to, bear on, pertain to

dean *n* 1 the chief administrative official of a college or university faculty 2 *chiefly Church of England* the chief administrator of a cathedral or collegiate church

deanery *n, pl* **-eries** 1 a place where a dean lives 2 the parishes presided over by a rural dean

dear *n* 1 (often used in direct address) someone regarded with affection ▸ *adj* 2 beloved; precious 3 highly priced 4 charging high prices 4 a form of address used at the beginning of a letter before the name of the recipient: *Dear Mr Anderson* 5 **dear to** important or close to ▸ *interj* 6 an exclamation of surprise or dismay: *oh dear, I've broken it* ▸ *adv* 7 dearly: *her errors have cost her dear* > **dearly** *adv*

dear *n* = darling, love, dearest, angel (*informal*), treasure, precious, beloved, loved one ▸ *adj* 2 = beloved, close, valued, favourite, prized, treasured, precious, intimate; ≠ hated 3 = expensive, costly, high-priced, pricey (*informal*), at a premium, overpriced, exorbitant

dearth (**dirth**) *n* an inadequate amount; scarcity

death *n* 1 the permanent end of life in a person or animal 2 an instance of this: *his sudden death* 3 ending or destruction 4 **at death's door** likely to die soon 5 **catch one's death (of cold)** *informal* to contract a severe cold 6 **like death warmed up** *informal* looking or feeling very ill or very tired 7 **put to death** to execute 8 **to death** A until dead B very much: *I had probably scared him to death*

> **death** *n* 1, 2 = dying, demise (*euphemistic*), end, passing, departure; ≠ birth 3 = destruction, finish, ruin, undoing, extinction, downfall; ≠ beginning

death duty *n* (in Britain) the former name for **inheritance tax**

deathly *adj* 1 resembling death: *a deathly pallor* 2 deadly

> **deathly** *adj* 1 = deathlike, white, pale, ghastly, wan, pallid, ashen

death's-head *n* a human skull or a picture of one used to represent death or danger

death trap *n* a place or vehicle considered very unsafe

deathwatch beetle *n* a beetle that bores into wood and produces a tapping sound

deb *n informal* a debutante

debacle (**day-bah-kl**) *n* something that ends in a disastrous failure, esp. because it has not been properly planned

> **debacle** *n* = disaster, catastrophe, fiasco

debar *vb* **-barring, -barred** to prevent (someone) from doing something

debase *vb* **-basing, -based** to lower in quality, character, or value > **debasement** *n*

debatable *adj* not absolutely certain: *her motives are highly debatable*

debate *n* 1 a discussion 2 a formal discussion, as in a parliament, in which opposing arguments are put forward ▸ *vb* **-bating, -bated** 3 to discuss (something) formally 4 to consider (possible courses of action)

> **debate** *n* 1 = discussion, talk, argument, dispute, analysis, conversation, controversy, dialogue ▸ *vb* 3 = discuss, question, talk about, argue about, dispute, examine, deliberate 4 = consider, reflect, think about, weigh, contemplate, deliberate, ponder, ruminate

debauch (**dib-bawch**) *vb* to make someone bad or corrupt, esp. sexually

debauched *adj* immoral; sexually corrupt

debauchery *n* excessive drunkenness or sexual activity

debenture *n* a long-term bond, bearing fixed interest and usually unsecured, issued by a company or governmental agency > **debentured** *adj*

debilitate *vb* **-tating, -tated** to make gradually weaker > **debilitating** *adj* > **debilitation** *n*

debility *n, pl* **-ties** a state of weakness, esp. caused by illness

debit *n* **1** the money, or a record of the money, withdrawn from a person's bank account **2** *accounting* **A** acknowledgment of a sum owing by entry on the left side of an account **B** an entry or the total of entries on this side ▸ *vb* **-iting, -ited 3** to charge (an account) with a debit: *they had debited our account* **4** *accounting* to record (an item) as a debit in an account

debonair *or* **debonnaire** *adj* (of a man) confident, charming, and well-dressed

debouch *vb* **1** (esp. of troops) to move into a more open space **2** (of a river, glacier, etc.) to flow into a larger area or body > **debouchment** *n*

debrief *vb* to interrogate (a soldier, diplomat, astronaut, etc.) on the completion of a mission > **debriefing** *n*

debris (deb-ree) *n* **1** fragments of something destroyed; rubble **2** a mass of loose stones and earth

> **debris** *n* **1** = remains, bits, waste, ruins, fragments, rubble, wreckage, detritus

debt *n* **1** a sum of money owed **2** **bad debt** a debt that is unlikely to be paid **3** **in debt** owing money **4** **in someone's debt** grateful to someone for his or her help: *I couldn't have managed without you – I'm in your debt*

> **debt** *n* **1** = debit, commitment, obligation, liability **3 in debt** = owing, liable, in the red (*informal*), in arrears

debtor *n* a person who owes money

> **debtor** *n* = borrower, mortgagor

debug *vb* **-bugging, -bugged** *informal* **1** to locate and remove defects in (a computer program) **2** to remove concealed microphones from (a room or telephone)

debunk *vb informal* to expose the falseness of: *many commonly held myths are debunked by the book* > **debunker** *n*

debut (day-byoo) *n* the first public appearance of a performer

> **debut** *n* = entrance, beginning, launch, introduction, first appearance

debutante (day-byoo-tont) *n* a young upper-class woman who is formally presented to society

Dec. December

decade *n* a period of ten years

decadence (deck-a-denss) *n* a decline in morality or culture > **decadent** *adj*

decaffeinated (dee-kaf-fin-ate-id) *adj* with the caffeine removed: *decaffeinated tea*

decagon *n geom* a figure with ten sides > **decagonal** *adj*

decahedron (deck-a-heed-ron) *n* a solid figure with ten plane faces > **decahedral** *adj*

decamp *vb* to leave secretly or suddenly

decant *vb* **1** to pour (a liquid, esp. wine) from one container to another **2** *chiefly Brit* to rehouse (people) while their homes are being renovated

decanter *n* a stoppered bottle into which a drink is poured for serving

decapitate *vb* **-tating, -tated** to behead > **decapitation** *n*

decathlon *n* an athletic contest in which each athlete competes in ten different events > **decathlete** *n*

decay *vb* **1** to decline gradually in health, prosperity, or quality **2** to rot or cause to rot **3** *physics* (of an atomic nucleus) to undergo radioactive disintegration ▸ *n* **4** the process of something rotting: *too much sugar can cause tooth decay* **5** the state brought about by this process **6** *physics* disintegration of a nucleus, occurring spontaneously or as a result of electron capture

> **decay** *vb* **1** = decline, diminish, crumble, deteriorate, fall off, dwindle, lessen, wane; ≠ grow **2** = rot, spoil, crumble, deteriorate, perish, decompose, moulder, go bad ▸ *n* **4** = rot, corruption, mould, blight, decomposition, gangrene, canker, caries

decease *n formal* death

deceased *formal* ▸ *adj* **1** dead ▸ *n* **2** a dead person: *the deceased*

> **deceased** *adj* = dead, late, departed (*euphemistic*), expired, defunct, lifeless

deceit *n* behaviour intended to deceive

deceitful *adj* full of deceit

deceive *vb* **-ceiving, -ceived 1** to mislead by lying **2** **deceive oneself** to refuse to acknowledge something one knows to be true **3** to be unfaithful to (one's sexual partner)

> **deceive** *vb* **1** = take in, trick, fool (*informal*), cheat, con (*informal*), mislead, dupe, swindle, scam (*slang*)

decelerate *vb* **-ating, -ated** to slow down > **deceleration** *n*

December *n* the twelfth month of the year

decency *n* conformity to the prevailing standards of what is right

> **decency** *n* = propriety, correctness, decorum, respectability, etiquette

decent *adj* **1** conforming to an acceptable standard or quality: *a decent living wage*; *she's made a few decent films* **2** polite or respectable: *he's a decent man* **3** fitting or proper: *that's the decent thing to do*

4 conforming to conventions of sexual behaviour **5** *informal* kind; generous: *she was pretty decent to me* > **decently** *adv*

> **decent** *adj* **1** = satisfactory, fair, all right, reasonable, sufficient, good enough, adequate, ample; ≠ unsatisfactory **2, 4** = respectable, pure, proper, modest, chaste, decorous **3** = proper, becoming, seemly, fitting, appropriate, suitable, respectable, befitting; ≠ improper **5** = good, kind, friendly, neighbourly, generous, helpful, obliging, accommodating

decentralize *or* **-ise** *vb* **-izing, -ized** *or* **-ising, -ised** to reorganize into smaller local units > **decentralization** *or* **-isation** *n*

deception *n* **1** the act of deceiving someone or the state of being deceived **2** something that deceives; trick

> **deception** *n* **1** = trickery, fraud, deceit, cunning, treachery, guile, legerdemain; ≠ honesty **2** = trick, lie, bluff, hoax, decoy, ruse, subterfuge, fastie (*Austral slang*)

deceptive *adj* likely or designed to deceive > **deceptively** *adv* > **deceptiveness** *n*

deci- *combining form* denoting one tenth: *decimetre*

decibel *n* a unit for comparing two power levels or measuring the intensity of a sound

decide *vb* **-ciding, -cided 1** to reach a decision: *we must decide on suitable action; he decided to stay on* **2** to cause to reach a decision **3** to settle (a question): *possible profits decided the issue* **4** to influence the outcome of (a contest) decisively: *the goal that decided the match came just before half-time*

> **decide** *vb* **1** = make a decision, make up your mind, reach *or* come to a decision, choose, determine, conclude; ≠ hesitate **3, 4** = settle, determine, resolve

decided *adj* **1** definite or noticeable: *a decided improvement* **2** strong and definite: *he has decided views on the matter* > **decidedly** *adv*

deciduous *adj* **1** (of a tree) shedding all leaves annually **2** (of antlers or teeth) being shed at the end of a period of growth

decimal *n* **1** a fraction written in the form of a dot followed by one or more numbers, for example .2 = $^2/_{10}$ ▸ *adj* **2** relating to or using powers of ten **3** expressed as a decimal

decimal currency *n* a system of currency in which the units are parts or powers of ten

decimal point *n* the dot between the unit and the fraction of a number in the decimal system

decimal system *n* a number system with a base of ten, in which numbers are expressed by combinations of the digits 0 to 9

decimate *vb* **-mating, -mated** to destroy or kill a large proportion of > **decimation** *n*

decipher *vb* **1** to make out the meaning of (something obscure or illegible) **2** to convert from code into plain text > **decipherable** *adj*

decision *n* **1** a choice or judgment made about something **2** the act of making up one's mind **3** the ability to make quick and definite decisions

> **decision** *n* **1** = judgment, finding, ruling, sentence, resolution, conclusion, verdict, decree **3** = decisiveness, purpose, resolution, resolve, determination, firmness, forcefulness, strength of mind *or* will

decisive *adj* **1** having great influence on the result of something: *the decisive goal was scored in the closing minutes* **2** having the ability to make quick decisions > **decisively** *adv* > **decisiveness** *n*

> **decisive** *adj* **1** = crucial, significant, critical, influential, momentous, conclusive, fateful; ≠ uncertain **2** = resolute, decided, firm, determined, forceful, incisive, trenchant, strong-minded; ≠ indecisive

deck *n* **1** an area of a ship that forms a floor, at any level **2** a similar area in a bus **3** *US & Austral* a pack of playing cards **4 clear the decks** *informal* to prepare for action, as by removing obstacles ▸ *vb* **5** *slang* to knock (a person) to the ground

deck chair *n* a folding chair with a wooden frame and a canvas seat

decking *n* a wooden deck or platform, esp. one in a garden for deck chairs, etc.

deck out *vb* to make more attractive by decorating: *the village was decked out in the blue-and-white flags*

declaim *vb* **1** to speak loudly and dramatically **2 declaim against** to protest against loudly and publicly > **declamation** *n* > **declamatory** *adj*

declaration *n* **1** a firm, emphatic statement **2** an official announcement or statement > **declaratory** *adj*

> **declaration** *n* **1** = affirmation, profession, assertion, revelation, disclosure, acknowledgment, protestation (*formal*), avowal **2** = announcement, proclamation, decree, notice, notification, edict, pronouncement

declare *vb* **-claring, -clared 1** to state firmly and forcefully **2** to announce publicly or officially: *a state of emergency has been declared* **3** to state officially that (someone or something) is as specified: *he was declared fit to play* **4** to acknowledge (dutiable goods or income) for tax purposes **5** *cards* to decide (the trump suit) by making the winning bid **6** *cricket* to bring an innings to an end before the last batsman is out **7 declare for** *or* **against** to state one's support or opposition for something

> **declare** *vb* **1** = state, claim, announce, voice, express, maintain, assert, proclaim **2** = make known, reveal, show, broadcast, confess, communicate, disclose

declension *n grammar* changes in the form of nouns, pronouns, or adjectives to show case, number, and gender

decline *vb* **-clining, -clined 1** to become smaller, weaker, or less important **2** to politely refuse to accept or do (something) **3** *grammar* to list the inflections of (a noun, pronoun, or adjective) ▸ *n* **4** a gradual weakening or loss

> **decline** *vb* **1** = fall, drop, lower, sink, fade, shrink, diminish, decrease; ≠ rise **2** = refuse, reject, turn down, avoid, spurn, abstain, say 'no'; ≠ accept ▸ *n* = depression, recession, slump, falling off, downturn, dwindling, lessening; ≠ rise

declivity *n, pl* **-ties** a downward slope > **declivitous** *adj*

declutch *vb* to disengage the clutch of a motor vehicle

decoct *vb* to extract the essence from (a substance) by boiling > **decoction** *n*

decode *vb* **-coding, -coded** to convert from code into ordinary language > **decoder** *n*

décolleté (day-kol-tay) *adj* **1** (of a woman's garment) low-cut ▸ *n* **2** a low-cut neckline

decommission *vb* to dismantle or remove from service (a nuclear reactor, weapon, ship, etc. which is no longer required)

decompose *vb* **-posing, -posed 1** to rot **2** to break up or separate into constituent parts > **decomposition** *n*

decompress *vb* **1** to free from pressure **2** to return (a diver) to normal atmospheric pressure > **decompression** *n*

decompression sickness *n* a disorder characterized by severe pain and difficulty in breathing caused by a sudden and sustained change in atmospheric pressure

decongestant *n* a drug that relieves nasal congestion

decontaminate *vb* **-nating, -nated** to make (a place or object) safe by removing poisons, radioactivity, etc. > **decontamination** *n*

decor (day-core) *n* a style or scheme of interior decoration and furnishings in a room or house

> **decor** *n* = decoration, colour scheme, ornamentation, furnishing style

decorate *vb* **-rating, -rated 1** to make more attractive by adding some ornament or colour **2** to paint or wallpaper **3** to confer a mark of distinction, esp. a medal, upon > **decorative** *adj* > **decorator** *n*

> **decorate** *vb* **1** = adorn, trim, embroider, ornament, embellish, festoon, beautify, grace **2** = do up, paper, paint, wallpaper, renovate (*informal*), furbish **3** = pin a medal on, cite, confer an honour on *or* upon

decoration *n* **1** an addition that makes something more attractive or ornate **2** the way in which a room or building is decorated **3** something, esp. a medal, conferred as a mark of honour

> **decoration** *n* **1** = ornament, trimmings, garnish, frill, bauble **2** = adornment, trimming, enhancement, elaboration, embellishment, ornamentation, beautification **3** = medal, award, star, ribbon, badge

decorous (deck-or-uss) *adj* polite, calm, and sensible in behaviour > **decorously** *adv* > **decorousness** *n*

decorum (dik-core-um) *n* polite and socially correct behaviour

decoy *n* **1** a person or thing used to lure someone into danger **2** an image of a bird or animal, used to lure game into a trap or within shooting range ▸ *vb* **3** to lure into danger by means of a decoy

decrease *vb* **-creasing, -creased 1** to make or become less in size, strength, or quantity ▸ *n* **2** a lessening; reduction **3** the amount by which something has been diminished > **decreasing** *adj* > **decreasingly** *adv*

> **decrease** *vb* = drop, decline, lessen, lower, shrink, diminish, dwindle, subside; ≠ increase ▸ *n* **2** = lessening, decline, reduction, loss, falling off, dwindling, contraction, cutback; ≠ growth

decree *n* **1** a law made by someone in authority **2** a judgment of a court ▸ *vb* **decreeing, decreed 3** to order by decree

> **decree** *n* **1** = law, order, ruling, act, command, statute, proclamation, edict **2** = judgment, finding, ruling, decision, verdict, arbitration ▸ *vb* = order, rule, command, demand, proclaim, prescribe, pronounce, ordain (*formal*)

decrepit *adj* weakened or worn out by age or long use > **decrepitude** *n*

decry *vb* **-cries, -crying, -cried** to express open disapproval of

decrypt *vb* **1** to decode (a message) with or without previous knowledge of its key **2** to make intelligible (a television or other signal) that has been deliberately distorted for transmission ▸ See also **encrypt** > **decryption** *n*

dedicate *vb* **-cating, -cated 1** to devote (oneself or one's time) wholly to a special purpose or cause **2** to inscribe or address (a book, piece of music, etc.) to someone as a token of affection or respect **3** to play (a record) on radio for someone as a greeting **4** to set apart for sacred uses

> **dedicate** *vb* **1** = devote, give, apply, commit, pledge, surrender, give over to **2** = offer, address, inscribe

dedicated *adj* **1** devoted to a particular purpose or cause **2** *computers* designed to fulfil one function

d

dedicated adj 1 = committed, devoted, enthusiastic, single-minded, zealous, purposeful, wholehearted; ≠ indifferent

dedication n 1 wholehearted devotion 2 an inscription in a book dedicating it to a person

dedication n 1 = commitment, loyalty, devotion, allegiance, adherence, single-mindedness, faithfulness, wholeheartedness; ≠ indifference 2 = inscription, message, address

deduce vb **-ducing, -duced** to reach (a conclusion) by reasoning from evidence; work out > **deducible** adj

deduct vb to subtract (a number, quantity, or part)

deduct vb = subtract, remove, take off, take away, reduce by, knock off (informal), decrease by; ≠ add

deduction n 1 the act or process of subtracting 2 something that is deducted 3 logic **A** a process of reasoning by which a conclusion necessarily follows from a set of general premises **B** a conclusion reached by this process > **deductive** adj

deduction n 1 = subtraction, reduction, concession 2 = discount, reduction, cut, concession, decrease, rebate, diminution 3**A** = reasoning, thinking, thought, analysis, logic 3**B** = conclusion, finding, verdict, judgment, assumption, inference

deed n 1 something that is done 2 a notable achievement 3 action as opposed to words 4 law a legal document, esp. one concerning the ownership of property

deed n 1, 2 = action, act, performance, achievement, exploit, feat 4 = document, title, contract

deem vb to judge or consider: common sense is deemed to be a virtue

deep adj 1 extending or situated far down from a surface: a deep ditch 2 extending or situated far inwards, backwards, or sideways 3 of a specified dimension downwards, inwards, or backwards: six metres deep 4 coming from or penetrating to a great depth 5 difficult to understand 6 of great intensity: deep doubts 7 **deep in** totally absorbed in: deep in conversation 8 (of a colour) intense or dark 9 low in pitch: a deep laugh 10 **go off the deep end** informal to lose one's temper 11 **in deep water** informal in a tricky position or in trouble ▶ n 12 any deep place on land or under water 13 **the deep A** poetic the ocean **B** cricket the area of the field relatively far from the pitch 14 the most profound, intense, or central part: the deep of winter ▶ adv 15 late: deep into the night 16 profoundly or intensely: deep down I was afraid it was all my fault > **deeply** adv

deep adj 1 = big, wide, broad, profound, yawning, bottomless, unfathomable; ≠ shallow 5 = secret, hidden, mysterious, obscure, abstract, esoteric, mystifying, arcane 6 = intense, great, serious (informal), acute, extreme, grave, profound, heartfelt; ≠ superficial 8 = dark, strong, rich, intense, vivid; ≠ light 9 = low, booming, bass, resonant, sonorous, low-pitched; ≠ high ▶ n 13**A the deep** = the ocean, the sea, the waves, the main, the high seas, the briny (informal)

deepen vb to make or become deeper or more intense

deepen vb = intensify, increase, grow, strengthen, reinforce, escalate, magnify

deepfake n a technique by which a digital image or video can be superimposed onto another, which maintains the appearance of an unedited image or video

deep-freeze n 1 same as **freezer** ▶ vb **-freezing, -froze, -frozen** 2 to freeze or keep in a deep-freeze

deer n, pl **deer** or **deers** a large hoofed mammal

deerstalker n a cloth hat with peaks at the front and back and earflaps

deface vb **-facing, -faced** to deliberately spoil the surface or appearance of > **defacement** n

de facto adv 1 in fact ▶ adj 2 existing in fact, whether legally recognized or not

de facto adv = in fact, really, actually, in effect, in reality ▶ adj = actual, real, existing

defame vb **-faming, -famed** to attack the good reputation of > **defamation** n > **defamatory** (dif-fam-a-tree) adj

default n 1 a failure to do something, esp. to meet a financial obligation or to appear in court 2 an instruction to a computer to select a particular option unless the user specifies otherwise 3 **by default** happening because something else has not happened: they gained a colony by default because no other European power wanted it 4 **in default of** in the absence of ▶ vb 5 to fail to fulfil an obligation, esp. to make payment when due > **defaulter** n

default n 1 = failure, neglect, deficiency, lapse, omission, dereliction ▶ vb = fail to pay, dodge, evade, neglect

defeat vb 1 to win a victory over 2 to thwart or frustrate: this accident has defeated all his hopes of winning ▶ n 3 the act of defeating or state of being defeated

defeat vb 1 = beat, crush, overwhelm, conquer, master, rout, trounce, vanquish; ≠ surrender 2 = frustrate, foil, thwart, ruin, baffle, confound, balk, get the better of ▶ n = conquest, beating, overthrow, rout; ≠ victory

defeatism n a ready acceptance or expectation of defeat > **defeatist** n, adj

defecate vb -cating, -cated to discharge waste from the body through the anus > **defecation** n

defect n 1 an imperfection or blemish ▶ vb 2 to desert one's country or cause to join the opposing forces > **defection** n > **defector** n

> **defect** n = deficiency, failing, fault, error, flaw, imperfection ▶ vb = desert, rebel, quit, revolt, change sides

defective adj imperfect or faulty: *defective hearing*

defence or US **defense** n 1 resistance against attack 2 something that provides such resistance 3 an argument or piece of writing in support of something that has been criticized or questioned 4 a country's military resources 5 law a defendant's denial of the truth of a charge 6 law the defendant and his or her legal advisers collectively 7 sport the players in a team whose function is to prevent the opposing team from scoring 8 **defences** fortifications > **defenceless** or US **defenseless** adj

> **defence** or **defense** n 1, 2 = protection, cover, security, guard, shelter, safeguard, immunity 3 = argument, explanation, excuse, plea, justification, vindication, rationalization 4 = armaments, weapons 5 = plea (*law*), testimony, denial, alibi, rebuttal 8 = shield, barricade, fortification, buttress, rampart, bulwark, fortified pa (NZ)

defend vb 1 to protect from harm or danger 2 to support in the face of criticism: *I spoke up to defend her* 3 to represent (a defendant) in court 4 to protect (a title or championship) against a challenge > **defender** n

> **defend** vb 1 = protect, cover, guard, screen, preserve, look after, shelter, shield 2 = support, champion, justify, endorse, uphold, vindicate, stand up for, speak up for

defendant n a person accused of a crime

> **defendant** n = accused, respondent, prisoner at the bar

defensible adj capable of being defended because believed to be right > **defensibility** n

defensive adj 1 intended for defence 2 guarding against criticism or exposure of one's failings: *he can be highly defensive and wary* ▶ n 3 **on the defensive** in a position of defence, as in being ready to reject criticism > **defensively** adv

> **defensive** adj 1 = protective, watchful, on the defensive, on guard 2 = oversensitive, uptight (*informal*)

defer[1] vb -ferring, -ferred to delay until a future time; postpone: *payment was deferred indefinitely* > **deferment** or **deferral** n

defer vb = postpone, delay, put off, suspend, shelve, hold over, procrastinate, put on ice (*informal*)

defer[2] vb -ferring, -ferred > **defer to** to submit to or comply with the wishes or judgments (of): *I defer to your superior knowledge*

deference n polite and respectful behaviour

deferential adj showing respect > **deferentially** adv

defiance n open resistance to authority or opposition > **defiant** adj

> **defiance** n = resistance, opposition, confrontation, contempt, disregard, disobedience, insolence, insubordination; ≠ obedience

defibrillator n med an apparatus for stopping fibrillation of the heart by application of an electric current

deficiency n, pl -cies 1 the state of being deficient 2 a lack or shortage

> **deficiency** n 1 = failing, fault, weakness, defect, flaw, drawback, shortcoming, imperfection 2 = lack, want, deficit, absence, shortage, scarcity, dearth; ≠ sufficiency

deficient adj 1 lacking something essential 2 inadequate in quantity or quality

deficit n the amount by which a sum is lower than that expected or required

> **deficit** n = shortfall, shortage, deficiency, loss, arrears

defile[1] vb -filing, -filed 1 to make foul or dirty 2 to make unfit for ceremonial use > **defilement** n

defile[2] n a narrow pass or gorge: *the sandy defile of Wadi Rum*

define vb -fining, -fined 1 to describe the nature of 2 to state precisely the meaning of 3 to show clearly the outline of: *the picture was sharp and cleanly defined* 4 to fix with precision; specify: *define one's duties* > **definable** adj

> **define** vb 1 = describe, interpret, characterize, explain, spell out, expound 3 = mark out, outline, limit, bound, delineate, circumscribe, demarcate 4 = establish, specify, designate

definite adj 1 firm, clear, and precise: *I have very definite views on this subject* 2 having precise limits or boundaries 3 known for certain: *it's definite that they have won* > **definitely** adv

> **definite** adj 1 = specific, exact, precise, clear, particular, fixed, black-and-white, cut-and-dried (*informal*); ≠ vague 3 = certain, decided, sure, settled, convinced, positive, confident, assured; ≠ uncertain

definition n 1 a statement of the meaning of a word or phrase 2 a description of the essential qualities of something 3 the quality of being clear and distinct 4 sharpness of outline

definition n 1 = description, interpretation, explanation, clarification, exposition, elucidation, statement of meaning
3, 4 = sharpness, focus, clarity, contrast, precision, distinctness

definitive adj 1 final and unable to be questioned or altered: a definitive verdict 2 most complete, or the best of its kind: the book was hailed as the definitive Dickens biography > **definitively** adv

definitive adj 1 = final, convincing, absolute, clinching, decisive, definite, conclusive, irrefutable 2 = authoritative, greatest, ultimate, reliable, exhaustive, superlative

deflate vb **-flating, -flated** 1 to collapse or cause to collapse through the release of gas 2 to take away the self-esteem or conceit from 3 to cause deflation of (an economy)

deflation n 1 econ a reduction in economic activity resulting in lower levels of output and investment 2 a feeling of sadness following excitement > **deflationary** adj

deflect vb to turn or cause to turn aside from a course > **deflection** n > **deflector** n

deflect vb = turn aside, bend

deflower vb literary to deprive (a woman) of her virginity

defoliate vb **-ating, -ated** to deprive (a plant) of its leaves > **defoliant** n > **defoliation** n

deforestation n the cutting down or destruction of forests

deform vb to put (something) out of shape or spoil its appearance

deformity n, pl **-ties** 1 pathol a distortion of an organ or part 2 the state of being deformed

defraud vb to cheat out of money, property, or a right to do something

defrost vb 1 to make or become free of frost or ice 2 to thaw (frozen food) by removing from a deep-freeze

deft adj quick and skilful in movement; dexterous > **deftly** adv > **deftness** n

defunct adj no longer existing or working properly

defuse or US sometimes **defuze** vb **-fusing, -fused** or **-fuzing, -fuzed** 1 to remove the fuse of (an explosive device) 2 to reduce the tension in (a difficult situation): I said it in a bid to defuse the situation

defy vb **-fies, -fying, -fied** 1 to resist openly and boldly 2 to elude in a baffling way: his actions defy explanation 3 formal to challenge (someone to do something)

defy vb 1 = resist, oppose, confront, brave, disregard, stand up to, spurn, flout

degenerate adj 1 having deteriorated to a lower mental, moral, or physical level ▸ n 2 a degenerate person ▸ vb **-ating, -ated** 3 to become degenerate > **degeneracy** n

degenerate adj = depraved, corrupt, low, perverted, immoral, decadent, debauched, dissolute ▸ vb = decline, slip, sink, decrease, deteriorate, worsen, decay, lapse

degeneration n 1 the process of degenerating 2 biol the loss of specialization or function by organisms

degrade vb **-grading, -graded** 1 to reduce to dishonour or disgrace 2 to reduce in status or quality 3 chem to decompose into atoms or smaller molecules > **degradation** n > **degrading** adj

degrade vb 1 = demean, disgrace, humiliate, shame, humble, discredit, debase, dishonour; ≠ ennoble

degree n 1 a stage in a scale of relative amount or intensity: this task involved a greater degree of responsibility 2 an academic award given by a university or college on successful completion of a course 3 grammar any of the forms of an adjective used to indicate relative amount or intensity 4 a unit of temperature. Symbol: ° 5 a measure of angle equal to one three-hundred-and-sixtieth of the circumference of a circle. Symbol: ° 6 a unit of latitude or longitude. Symbol: ° 7 **by degrees** little by little; gradually

degree n 1 = amount, stage, grade

dehumanize or **-ise** vb **-izing, -ized** or **-ising, -ised** 1 to deprive of the qualities thought of as being best in human beings, such as kindness 2 to make (an activity) mechanical or routine > **dehumanization** or **-isation** n

dehydrate vb **-drating, -drated** 1 to remove water from (food) in order to preserve it 2 **be dehydrated** (of a person) to be weak or ill through losing too much water from the body > **dehydration** n

de-ice vb **de-icing, de-iced** to free of ice > **de-icer** n

deify (day-if-fie) vb **-fies, -fying, -fied** to treat or worship (someone or something) as a god > **deification** n

deign (dane) vb to do something that one considers beneath one's dignity: she did not deign to reply

deity (day-it-ee) n, pl **-ties** 1 a god or goddess 2 the state of being divine

déjà vu (day-zhah voo) n a feeling of having experienced before something that is happening at the present moment

dejected adj in low spirits; downhearted > **dejectedly** adv > **dejection** n

de jure adv according to law

dekko n **have a dekko** Brit, Austral & NZ slang to have a look

delay vb 1 to put (something) off to a later time 2 to slow up or cause to be late 3 **a** to hesitate in doing something **b** to deliberately take longer than necessary to do something ▸ n 4 the act of delaying **5** a period of inactivity or waiting before something happens or continues

delay *vb* **1** = put off, suspend, postpone, shelve, defer, hold over **2** = hold up, detain, hold back, hinder, obstruct, impede, bog down, set back; ≠ speed (up) ▸ *n* **5** = hold-up, wait, setback, interruption, stoppage, impediment, hindrance

delectable *adj* delightful or very attractive
delectation *n formal* great pleasure and enjoyment
delegate *n* **1** a person chosen to represent others at a conference or meeting ▸ *vb* **-gating, -gated 2** to entrust (duties or powers) to another person **3** to appoint as a representative

delegate *n* = representative, agent, deputy, ambassador, commissioner, envoy, proxy, legate ▸ *vb* **2** = entrust, transfer, hand over, give, pass on, assign, consign, devolve **3** = appoint, commission, select, contract, engage, nominate, designate, mandate

delegation *n* **1** a group chosen to represent others **2** the act of delegating

delegation *n* **1** = deputation, envoys, contingent, commission, embassy, legation **2** = commissioning, assignment, devolution, committal

delete *vb* **-leting, -leted** to remove or cross out (something printed or written) > **deletion** *n*

delete *vb* = remove, cancel, erase, strike out, obliterate, efface, cross out, expunge (*formal*)

deleterious (del-lit-**eer**-ee-uss) *adj formal* harmful or injurious
deli *n informal* short for **delicatessen**
deliberate *adj* **1** carefully thought out in advance; intentional **2** careful and unhurried: *a deliberate gait* ▸ *vb* **-ating, -ated 3** to consider (something) deeply; think over > **deliberately** *adv* > **deliberative** *adj*

deliberate *adj* **1** = intentional, meant, planned, intended, conscious, calculated, wilful, purposeful; ≠ accidental **2** = careful, measured, slow, cautious, thoughtful, circumspect, methodical, unhurried; ≠ hurried ▸ *vb* = consider, think, ponder, discuss, debate, reflect, consult, weigh

deliberation *n* **1** careful consideration **2** calmness and absence of hurry **3 deliberations** formal discussions

deliberation *n* **1** = consideration, thought, reflection, calculation, meditation, forethought, circumspection **3** = discussion, talk, conference, debate, analysis, conversation, dialogue, consultation

delicacy *n, pl* **-cies 1** fine or subtle quality, construction, etc.: *delicacy of craftsmanship*
2 fragile or graceful beauty **3** something that is considered particularly nice to eat **4** frail health **5** refinement of feeling, manner, or appreciation: *the delicacy of the orchestra's playing* **6** need for careful or tactful treatment

delicacy *n* **1** = fragility, flimsiness **2** = daintiness, charm, grace, elegance, neatness, prettiness, slenderness, exquisiteness **3** = treat, luxury, savoury, dainty, morsel, titbit **5** = sensitivity, understanding, consideration, diplomacy, discretion, tact, thoughtfulness, sensitiveness **6** = difficulty

delicate *adj* **1** fine or subtle in quality or workmanship **2** having a fragile beauty **3** (of colour, smell, or taste) pleasantly subtle **4** easily damaged; fragile **5** precise or sensitive in action: *the delicate digestive system* **6** requiring tact: *a delicate matter* **7** showing consideration for the feelings of other people > **delicately** *adv*

delicate *adj* **1** = fine, elegant, exquisite, graceful **3** = subtle, fine, delicious, faint, refined, understated, dainty **4** = fragile, weak, frail, brittle, tender, flimsy, dainty, breakable **7** = diplomatic, sensitive, thoughtful, discreet, considerate, tactful; ≠ insensitive

delicatessen *n* a shop selling unusual or imported foods, often already cooked or prepared
delicious *adj* **1** very appealing to taste or smell **2** extremely enjoyable > **deliciously** *adv*

delicious *adj* **1** = delectable, tasty, choice, savoury, dainty, mouthwatering, scrumptious (*informal*), appetizing, lekker (*S African slang*), yummo (*Austral slang*); ≠ unpleasant

delight *n* **1** extreme pleasure **2** something or someone that causes this ▸ *vb* **3** to please greatly **4 delight in** to take great pleasure in > **delightful** *adj* > **delightfully** *adv*

delight *n* **1** = pleasure, joy, satisfaction, happiness, ecstasy, enjoyment, bliss, glee; ≠ displeasure ▸ *vb* **3** = please, satisfy, thrill, charm, cheer, amuse, enchant, gratify **4 delight in or take a delight in something or someone** = like, love, enjoy, appreciate, relish, savour, revel in, take pleasure in

delimit *vb* **-iting, -ited** to mark or lay down the limits of > **delimitation** *n*
delineate (dill-**lin**-ee-ate) *vb* **-ating, -ated 1** to show by drawing **2** to describe in words > **delineation** *n*
delinquent *n* **1** someone, esp. a young person, who breaks the law ▸ *adj* **2** repeatedly breaking the law > **delinquency** *n*
delirious *adj* **1** having delirium **2** wildly excited and happy > **deliriously** *adv*
delirium *n* **1** a state of excitement and mental confusion, often with hallucinations **2** violent excitement

deliver vb 1 to carry (goods or mail) to a destination 2 to hand over: *the tenants were asked to deliver up their keys* 3 to aid in the birth of (offspring) 4 to present (a lecture or speech) 5 to release or rescue (from captivity or danger) 6 to strike (a blow) suddenly 7 *informal* Also: **deliver the goods** to produce something promised > **deliverance** n

> **deliver** vb 1 = bring, carry, bear, transport, distribute, convey, cart 2 = hand over, commit, give up, yield, surrender, turn over, relinquish, make over 4 = give, read, present, announce, declare, utter 5 = release, free, save, rescue, loose, liberate, ransom, emancipate 6 = strike, give, deal, launch, direct, aim, administer, inflict

delivery n, pl **-eries** A the act of delivering goods or mail B something that is delivered 2 the act of giving birth to a baby 3 manner or style in public speaking: *her delivery was clear and humorous* 4 *cricket* the act or manner of bowling a ball 5 *S African* a semi-official slogan for the provision of services to previously disadvantaged communities

> **delivery** n 1A = handing over, transfer, distribution, transmission, dispatch, consignment, conveyance 1B = consignment, goods, shipment, batch 2 = childbirth, labour, confinement, parturition 3 = speech, utterance, articulation, intonation, elocution, enunciation

dell n *chiefly Brit* a small wooded hollow

Delphic adj obscure or ambiguous, like the ancient Greek oracle at Delphi

delphinium n, pl **-iums** or **-ia** a large garden plant with spikes of blue flowers

delta n 1 the fourth letter in the Greek alphabet (Δ, δ) 2 the flat area at the mouth of some rivers where the main stream splits up into several branches

delude vb **-luding, -luded** to make someone believe something that is not true

deluge (del-lyooj) n 1 a great flood of water 2 torrential rain 3 an overwhelming number ▸ vb **-uging, -uged** 4 to flood 5 to overwhelm

delusion n 1 a mistaken idea or belief 2 the state of being deluded > **delusive** adj > **delusory** adj

> **delusion** n 1 = misconception, mistaken idea, misapprehension, fancy, illusion, hallucination, fallacy, false impression

de luxe adj rich or sumptuous; superior in quality: *a de luxe hotel*

delve vb **delving, delved** 1 to research deeply or intensively (for information) 2 *old-fashioned* to dig

demagogue or US sometimes **demagog** n a political agitator who attempts to win support by appealing to the prejudice and passions of the mob > **demagogic** adj > **demagogy** n

demand vb 1 to request forcefully 2 to require as just, urgent, etc.: *the situation demands intervention* 3 to claim as a right ▸ n 4 a forceful request 5 something that requires special effort or sacrifice: *demands upon one's time* 6 *econ* willingness and ability to purchase goods and services 7 **in demand** sought after; popular 8 **on demand** as soon as requested: *the funds will be available on demand*

> **demand** vb 1 = request, ask (for), order, expect, claim, seek, insist on, exact 2 = require, want, need, involve, call for, entail, necessitate, cry out for; ≠ provide ▸ n 4 = request, order 6 = need, want, call, market, claim, requirement

demanding adj requiring a lot of skill, time, or effort: *a demanding relationship*

> **demanding** adj = difficult, trying, hard, taxing, wearing, challenging, tough, exacting; ≠ easy

demarcation n the act of establishing limits or boundaries, esp. between the work performed by members of different trade unions

demean vb 1 to undermine the status or dignity of (someone or something) 2 **demean oneself** to do something unworthy of one's status or character: *there is no doubt that he will lose face with the boss by having to demean himself in this way*

demeanour or US **demeanor** n the way a person behaves

demented adj 1 having dementia 2 acting strangely or foolishly > **dementedly** adv

dementia (dim-men-sha) n a state of serious mental deterioration

demerara sugar n brown crystallized cane sugar from the West Indies

demerit n 1 a fault or disadvantage 2 *US & Canad* a mark given against a student for failure or misconduct

demesne (dim-mane) n 1 land surrounding a house or manor 2 *property law* the possession of one's own property or land 3 a region or district; domain

demi- *combining form* 1 half: *demirelief* 2 of less than full size, status, or rank: *demigod*

demijohn n a large bottle with a short narrow neck, often encased in wickerwork

demilitarize or **-rise** vb **-rizing, -rized** or **-rising, -rised** to remove all military forces from (an area): *demilitarized zone* > **demilitarization** or **-risation** n

demimonde n 1 (esp. in the 19th century) a class of women considered to be outside respectable society because of promiscuity 2 any group considered not wholly respectable

demise n 1 the eventual failure of something originally successful 2 *euphemistic, formal* death 3 *property law* a transfer of an estate by lease ▸ vb **-mising, -mised** 4 *property law* to transfer for a limited period; lease

demise *n* **1** = failure, end, fall, defeat, collapse, ruin, breakdown, overthrow **2** = death, end, dying, passing, departure, decease

demo *n*, *pl* **-os** *informal* **1** short for **demonstration** (sense 1) **2** a demonstration record or tape

demob *vb* **-mobbing, -mobbed** *Brit, Austral & NZ informal* to demobilize

demobilize *or* **-lise** *vb* **-lizing, -lized** *or* **-lising, -lised** to release from the armed forces > **demobilization** *or* **-lisation** *n*

democracy *n*, *pl* **-cies** **1** a system of government or organization in which the citizens or members choose leaders or make other important decisions by voting **2** a country in which the citizens choose their government by voting

democracy *n* **1** = self-government, republic, commonwealth

democrat *n* a person who believes in democracy

Democrat *n* US a member or supporter of the Democratic Party, the more liberal of the two main political parties in the US > **Democratic** *adj*

Democrat *n* = left-winger

democratic *adj* of or relating to a country, organization, or system in which leaders are chosen or decisions are made by voting > **democratically** *adv*

democratic *adj* = self-governing, popular, representative, autonomous, populist, egalitarian

demographic *adj* **1** of or relating to population statistics ▸ *n* **2** a group of people within a population who share a particular characteristic: *the female demographic*

demography *n* the study of population statistics, such as births and deaths

demolish *vb* **1** to tear down or break up (buildings) **2** to put an end to; destroy: *I demolished her argument in seconds* **3** *facetious* to eat up: *he demolished the whole cake* > **demolisher** *n* > **demolition** *n*

demolish *vb* **1** = knock down, level, destroy, dismantle, flatten, tear down, bulldoze, raze; ≠ build **2** = destroy, wreck, overturn, overthrow, undo

demon *n* **1** an evil spirit **2** a person, obsession, etc. thought of as evil or persistently tormenting **3** a person extremely skilful in or devoted to a given activity: *a demon at pool* > **demonic** *adj*

demon *n* **1** = evil spirit, devil, fiend, goblin, ghoul, malignant spirit, atua (NZ), wairua (NZ) **3** = wizard, master, ace (*informal*), fiend (*informal*)

demoniac *or* **demoniacal** *adj* **1** appearing to be possessed by a devil **2** suggesting inner possession or inspiration: *the demoniac fire of genius* **3** frantic or frenzied: *demoniac activity* > **demoniacally** *adv*

demonology *n* the study of demons or demonic beliefs

demonstrable *adj* able to be proved > **demonstrably** *adv*

demonstrate *vb* **-strating, -strated** **1** to show or prove by reasoning or evidence **2** to display and explain the workings of (a machine, product, etc.) **3** to reveal the existence of: *the adult literacy campaign demonstrated the scale of educational deprivation* **4** to show support or opposition by public parades or rallies

demonstrate *vb* **1** = show, express, display, indicate, exhibit, manifest, flag up **2** = describe, show, explain, teach, illustrate **3** = prove, show, indicate, make clear, manifest, testify to, flag up **4** = march, protest, rally, object, parade, picket, remonstrate (*formal*), express disapproval, hikoi (NZ)

demonstration *n* **1** a march or public meeting to demonstrate opposition to something or support for something **2** an explanation, display, or experiment showing how something works **3** proof or evidence leading to proof

demonstration *n* **1** = march, protest, rally, sit-in, parade, picket, mass lobby, hikoi (NZ) **2** = display, show, performance, explanation, description, presentation, exposition **3** = indication, proof, testimony, confirmation, substantiation

demonstrative *adj* **1** tending to show one's feelings freely and openly **2** *grammar* denoting a word used to point out the person or thing referred to, such as *this* and *those* **3** **demonstrative of** giving proof of > **demonstratively** *adv*

demonstrator *n* **1** a person who demonstrates how a device or machine works **2** a person who takes part in a public demonstration

demoralize *or* **-ise** *vb* **-izing, -ized** *or* **-ising, -ised** to deprive (someone) of confidence or enthusiasm: *she had been demoralized and had just given up* > **demoralization** *or* **-isation** *n*

demote *vb* **-moting, -moted** to lower in rank or position > **demotion** *n*

demur *vb* **-murring, -murred** **1** to show reluctance; object ▸ *n* **2** **without demur** without objecting

demure *adj* quiet, reserved, and rather shy > **demurely** *adv* > **demureness** *n*

den *n* **1** the home of a wild animal; lair **2** *chiefly US* a small secluded room in a home, often used for a hobby **3** a place where people indulge in criminal or immoral activities: *a den of iniquity*

den *n* **1** = lair, hole, shelter, cave, haunt, cavern, hide-out **2** = study, retreat, sanctuary, hideaway, sanctum, cubbyhole

denationalize or **-ise** vb **-izing, -ized** or **-ising, -ised** to transfer (an industry or a service) from public to private ownership ▷ **denationalization** or **-isation** n

denature vb **-turing, -tured** 1 to change the nature of 2 to make (alcohol) unfit to drink by adding another substance

dene or **dean** n chiefly Brit a narrow wooded valley

denial n 1 a statement that something is not true 2 a rejection of a request 3 psychol a process by which painful thoughts are not permitted into the consciousness

> **denial** n 1 = negation, contradiction, dissent, retraction, repudiation; ≠ admission
> 2 = refusal, veto, rejection, prohibition, rebuff, repulse

denier (den-yer) n a unit of weight used to measure the fineness of silk and man-made fibres

denigrate vb **-grating, -grated** to criticize (someone or something) unfairly ▷ **denigration** n ▷ **denigrator** n

denim n 1 a hard-wearing cotton fabric used for jeans, skirts, etc. 2 **denims** jeans made of denim

denizen n 1 a person, animal, or plant that lives or grows in a particular place 2 an animal or plant established in a place to which it is not native

denominate vb **-nating, -nated** to give a specific name to; designate

denomination n 1 a group which has slightly different beliefs from other groups within the same faith 2 a unit in a system of weights, values, or measures: coins of small denomination have been withdrawn 3 a name given to a class or group; classification ▷ **denominational** adj

> **denomination** n 1 = religious group, belief, sect, persuasion, creed, school, hauhau (NZ)
> 2 = unit, value, size, grade

denominator n the number below the line in a fraction, as 8 in $^7/_8$

denote vb **-noting, -noted** 1 to be a sign or indication of: these contracts denote movement on the widest possible scale 2 (of a word or phrase) to have as a literal or obvious meaning ▷ **denotation** n

denouement (day-noo-mon) n the final outcome or solution in a play or other work

denounce vb **-nouncing, -nounced** 1 to condemn openly or vehemently 2 to give information against

> **denounce** vb 1 = condemn, attack, censure, revile, damn, vilify, stigmatize 2 = report, dob in (Austral slang)

dense adj 1 thickly crowded or closely packed 2 difficult to see through: dense clouds of smoke 3 informal stupid or dull 4 (of a film, book, etc.) difficult to follow or understand: the content should be neither too dense nor too abstract ▷ **densely** adv

dense adj 1 = thick, heavy, solid, compact, condensed, impenetrable, close-knit; ≠ thin 2 = heavy, thick, opaque, impenetrable 3 = stupid (informal), thick, dull, dumb (informal), dozy (Brit informal), stolid, dopey (informal), moronic; ≠ bright

density n, pl **-ties** 1 the degree to which something is filled or occupied: an average population density 2 physics a measure of the compactness of a substance, expressed as its mass per unit volume 3 a measure of a physical quantity per unit of length, area, or volume

> **density** n 1 = tightness, thickness, compactness, impenetrability, denseness
> 2 = mass, bulk, consistency, solidity

dent n 1 a hollow in the surface of something ▶ vb 2 to make a dent in

> **dent** n = hollow, chip, indentation, depression, impression, pit, dip, crater, ding (Austral, NZ obsolete, informal) ▶ vb = make a dent in, press in, gouge, hollow, push in

dental adj of or relating to the teeth or dentistry

dental floss n a waxed thread used to remove particles of food from between the teeth

dentine (den-teen) n the hard dense tissue that forms the bulk of a tooth

dentist n a person qualified to practise dentistry

dentistry n the branch of medicine concerned with the teeth and gums

denture n (often pl) a partial or full set of artificial teeth

denude vb **-nuding, -nuded** 1 to make bare; strip: the atrocious weather denuded the trees 2 geol to expose (rock) by the erosion of the layers above ▷ **denudation** n

denunciation n open condemnation; denouncing

deny vb **-nies, -nying, -nied** 1 to declare (a statement) to be untrue 2 to refuse to give or allow: we have been denied permission 3 to refuse to acknowledge: the baron denied his wicked son

> **deny** vb 1 = contradict, disagree with, rebuff, negate, rebut, refute; ≠ admit 2 = refuse, forbid, reject, rule out, turn down, prohibit, withhold, preclude; ≠ permit 3 = renounce, reject, retract, repudiate, disown, recant, disclaim

deodorant n a substance applied to the body to prevent or disguise the odour of perspiration

deodorize or **-ise** vb **-izing, -ized** or **-ising, -ised** to remove or disguise the odour of ▷ **deodorization** or **-isation** n

depart vb 1 to leave 2 to differ or deviate: to depart from the original concept

> **depart** vb 1 = leave, go, withdraw, retire, disappear, quit, retreat, exit, rack off (Austral, NZ slang); ≠ arrive 2 = deviate, vary, differ, stray, veer, swerve, diverge, digress

departed *adj euphemistic* dead

department *n* **1** a specialized division of a large business organization, hospital, university, etc. **2** a major subdivision of the administration of a government **3** an administrative division in several countries, such as France **4** *informal* a specialized sphere of activity: *wine-making is my wife's department* > **departmental** *adj*

> **department** *n* **1, 2** = section, office, unit, station, division, branch, bureau, subdivision

department store *n* a large shop divided into departments selling many kinds of goods

departure *n* **1** the act of departing **2** a divergence from previous custom, rule, etc. **3** a course of action or venture: *the album represents a new departure for them*

> **departure** *n* **1** = leaving, going, retirement, withdrawal, exit, going away, removal, exodus; ≠ arrival **2** = shift, change, difference, variation, innovation, novelty, deviation, divergence

depend *vb* **depend on A** to put trust (in); rely (on) **B** to be influenced or determined (by): *the answer depends on four main issues* **C** to rely (on) for income or support

> **depend** *vb* **1A** = count on, turn to, trust in, bank on, lean on, rely upon, reckon on **1B** = be determined by, be based on, be subject to, hang on, rest on, revolve around, hinge on, be subordinate to

dependable *adj* reliable and trustworthy > **dependability** *n* > **dependably** *adv*

dependant *n* a person who depends on another for financial support

dependence *n* **1** the state of relying on something in order to be able to survive or operate properly **2** reliance or trust: *they had a bond between them of mutual dependence and trust*

dependency *n, pl* **-cies 1** a territory subject to a state on which it does not border **2** *psychol* overreliance on another person or on a drug

dependent *adj* **1** depending on a person or thing for aid or support **2 dependent on** *or* **upon** influenced or conditioned by

> **dependent** *adj* **1** = reliant, vulnerable, helpless, powerless, weak, defenceless; ≠ independent **2** = determined by, depending on, subject to, influenced by, conditional on, contingent on

depict *vb* **1** to represent by drawing, painting, etc. **2** to describe in words > **depiction** *n*

> **depict** *vb* **1** = illustrate, portray, picture, paint, outline, draw, sketch, delineate **2** = describe, present, represent, outline, characterize

depilatory (dip-**pill**-a-tree) *adj* **1** able or serving to remove hair ▸ *n, pl* **-ries 2** a chemical used to remove hair

deplete *vb* **-pleting, -pleted 1** to use up (supplies or money) **2** to reduce in number > **depletion** *n*

> **deplete** *vb* **1** = use up, reduce, drain, exhaust, consume, empty, lessen, impoverish; ≠ increase

deplorable *adj* very bad or unpleasant > **deplorably** *adv*

deplore *vb* **-ploring, -plored** to express or feel strong disapproval of

> **deplore** *vb* = disapprove of, condemn, object to, denounce, censure, abhor, take a dim view of

deploy *vb* to organize (troops or resources) into a position ready for immediate and effective action > **deployment** *n*

> **deploy** *vb* = use, station, position, arrange, set out, utilize

depopulate *vb* **-lating, -lated** to cause to be reduced in population > **depopulation** *n*

deport *vb* **1** to remove forcibly from a country **2 deport oneself** to behave in a specified manner

> **deport** *vb* **1** = expel, exile, throw out, oust, banish, expatriate, extradite, evict

deportation *n* the act of expelling someone from a country

deportee *n* a person deported or awaiting deportation

deportment *n* the way in which a person moves and stands: *she had the manners and deportment of a great lady*

depose *vb* **-posing, -posed 1** to remove from an office or position of power **2** *law* to testify on oath

> **depose** *vb* **1** = oust, dismiss, displace, demote, dethrone, remove from office

deposit *vb* **-iting, -ited 1** to put down **2** to entrust (money or valuables) for safekeeping **3** to place (money) in a bank account or other savings account **4** to lay down naturally: *the river deposits silt* ▸ *n* **5** a sum of money placed in a bank account or other savings account **6** money given in part payment for goods or services **7** an amount of a substance left on a surface as a result of a chemical or geological process

> **deposit** *vb* **1** = put, place, lay, drop **2, 3** = store, keep, put, bank, lodge, entrust, consign ▸ *n* **6** = down payment, security, stake, pledge, instalment, retainer, part payment **7** = accumulation, mass, build-up, layer

depositary *n, pl* **-taries** a person or group to whom something is entrusted for safety

deposition *n* **1** *law* the sworn statement of a witness used in court in his or her absence **2** the act of deposing **3** the act of depositing **4** something deposited

depositor *n* a person who places or has money on deposit in a bank or similar organization: *panic-stricken depositors*

depository *n, pl* **-ries 1** a store where furniture, valuables, etc. can be kept for safety **2** same as **depositary**

depot (dep-oh) *n* **1** a place where goods and vehicles are kept when not in use **2** *US, Canad & NZ* a bus or railway station

> **depot** *n* **1** = arsenal, warehouse, storehouse, repository, depository **2** = bus station, station, garage, terminus

depraved *adj* morally bad; corrupt

depravity *n, pl* **-ties** moral corruption

deprecate *vb* **-cating, -cated** to express disapproval of > **deprecation** *n* > **deprecatory** *adj*

depreciate *vb* **-ating, -ated 1** to decline in value or price **2** to deride or criticize > **depreciatory** *adj*

depreciation *n* **1** *accounting* the reduction in value of a fixed asset through use, obsolescence, etc. **2** a decrease in the exchange value of a currency **3** the act or an instance of belittling

> **depreciation** *n* **2** = devaluation, fall, drop, depression, slump, deflation

depredation *n* plundering; pillage

depress *vb* **1** to make sad and gloomy **2** to lower (prices) **3** to push down > **depressing** *adj* > **depressingly** *adv*

> **depress** *vb* **1** = sadden, upset, distress, discourage, grieve, oppress, weigh down, make sad; ≠ cheer **2** = devalue, depreciate, cheapen **3** = press down, push, squeeze, lower, flatten, compress, push down

depressant *adj* **1** *med* able to reduce nervous or functional activity; sedative ▶ *n* **2** a depressant drug

depressed *adj* **1** (of a person) having depression **2** low in spirits; downcast **3** suffering from economic hardship, such as unemployment: *the current depressed conditions* **4** pressed down or flattened

> **depressed** *adj* **2** = sad, blue, unhappy, discouraged, fed up, mournful, dejected, despondent **3** = poverty-stricken, poor, deprived, disadvantaged, rundown, impoverished, needy **4** = sunken, hollow, recessed, indented, concave

depression *n* **1** a mental health condition in which a person has strong feelings of dejection and inadequacy **2** an economic condition in which there is substantial unemployment, low output and low investment; slump **3** *meteorol* a mass of air below normal atmospheric pressure, which often causes rain **4** a sunken place

> **depression** *n* **1** = despair, misery, sadness, the dumps (*informal*), the blues, melancholy, unhappiness, despondency **2** = recession, slump, economic decline, credit crunch, stagnation, inactivity, hard *or* bad times **4** = hollow, pit, dip, bowl, valley, dent, cavity, indentation

depressive *adj* **1** causing sadness and lack of energy **2** subject to periods of depression

deprive *vb* **-priving, -prived** > **deprive of** to prevent from having or enjoying > **deprivation** *n*

deprived *adj* lacking adequate living conditions, education, etc.: *deprived ghettos*

> **deprived** *adj* = poor, disadvantaged, needy, in need, lacking, bereft, destitute, down at heel; ≠ prosperous

dept department

depth *n* **1** the distance downwards, backwards, or inwards **2** intensity of emotion or feeling **3** the quality of having a high degree of knowledge, insight, and understanding **4** intensity of colour **5** lowness of pitch **6 depths A** a remote inaccessible region: *the depths of the forest* **B** the most severe part: *the depths of depression* **C** a low moral state **7 out of one's depth A** in water deeper than one is tall **B** beyond the range of one's competence or understanding

> **depth** *n* **1** = deepness, drop, measure, extent **3** = insight, wisdom, penetration, profundity, discernment, sagacity, astuteness, profoundness; ≠ superficiality

depth charge *n* a bomb used to attack submarines that explodes at a preset depth of water

deputation *n* a body of people appointed to represent others

depute *vb* **-puting, -puted** to appoint (someone) to act on one's behalf

deputize *or* **-tise** *vb* **-tizing, -tized** *or* **-tising, -tised** (usually foll. by *for*) to act as deputy

deputy *n, pl* **-ties** a person appointed to act on behalf of another

> **deputy** *n* = substitute, representative, delegate, lieutenant, proxy, surrogate, second-in-command, legate

derail *vb* to cause (a train or tram) to go off the rails > **derailment** *n*

deranged *adj* **1** behaving in a wild and uncontrolled way **2** in a state of disorder > **derangement** *n*

Derby *n, pl* **-bies 1 the Derby** an annual horse race for three-year-olds, run at Epsom Downs, Surrey **2 local derby** a sporting event between teams from the same area

deregulate *vb* **-lating, -lated** to remove regulations or controls from ▸ **deregulation** *n*

derelict *adj* **1** abandoned or unused and falling into ruins ▸ *n* **2** a social outcast or vagrant

> **derelict** *adj* = abandoned, deserted, ruined, neglected, discarded, forsaken, dilapidated ▸ *n* = vagrant, tramp (*old-fashioned*), outcast, drifter, down-and-out, bag lady, derro (*Austral slang*)

dereliction *n* **1** the state of being abandoned **2 dereliction of duty** wilful neglect of one's duty

deride *vb* **-riding, -rided** to speak of or treat with contempt or ridicule ▸ **derision** *n*

de rigueur (de rig-*gur*) *adj* required by fashion

derisive *adj* mocking or scornful ▸ **derisively** *adv*

derisory *adj* too small or inadequate to be considered seriously: *the shareholders have dismissed the offer as derisory*

derivation *n* the origin or descent of something, such as a word

derivative *adj* **1** based on other sources; not original ▸ *n* **2** a word, idea, etc. that is derived from another **3** *maths* the rate of change of one quantity with respect to another

derive *vb* **-riving, -rived** to draw or be drawn (from) in source or origin

dermatitis *n* inflammation of the skin

dermatology *n* the branch of medicine concerned with the skin ▸ **dermatologist** *n*

derogatory (dir-*rog*-a-tree) *adj* expressing or showing a low opinion of someone or something

derrick *n* **1** a simple crane that has lifting tackle slung from a boom **2** the framework erected over an oil well to enable drill tubes to be raised and lowered

derv *n Brit* diesel oil, when used for road transport

dervish *n* a member of a Muslim religious order noted for a frenzied, ecstatic, whirling dance

descant *n* **1** a tune played or sung above a basic melody ▸ *adj* **2** of the highest member in a family of musical instruments: *a descant clarinet*

descend *vb* **1** to move down (a slope, staircase, etc.) **2** to move or fall to a lower level, pitch, etc. **3 be descended from** to be connected by a blood relationship to **4 descend on** to visit unexpectedly **5 descend to** to stoop to (unworthy behaviour)

> **descend** *vb* **1** = go down, come down, walk down, move down, climb down **2** = fall, drop, sink, go down, plunge, dive, tumble, plummet; ≠ rise **3 be descended from** = originate from, derive from, spring from, proceed from, issue from

descendant *n* a person or animal descended from an individual, race, or species

descendent *adj* descending

descent *n* **1** the act of descending **2** a downward slope **3** a path or way leading downwards **4** derivation from an ancestor; family origin **5** a decline or degeneration

> **descent** *n* **1** = fall, drop, plunge, coming down, swoop **2, 3** = slope, drop, dip, incline, slant, declivity **4** = origin, extraction, ancestry, lineage, family tree, parentage, genealogy, derivation **5** = decline, deterioration, degeneration

describe *vb* **-scribing, -scribed 1** to give an account of (something or someone) in words **2** to trace the outline of (a circle, etc.)

> **describe** *vb* **1** = relate, tell, report, explain, express, recount, recite, narrate **2** = trace, draw, outline, mark out, delineate

description *n* **1** a statement or account that describes someone or something **2** the act of describing **3** sort, kind, or variety: *antiques of every description*

> **description** *n* **1** = account, report, explanation, representation, sketch, narrative, portrayal, depiction **2** = calling, naming, branding, labelling, dubbing, designation **3** = kind, sort, type, order, class, variety, brand, category

descriptive *adj* describing something: *it was a very descriptive account of the play* ▸ **descriptively** *adv*

descry *vb* **-scries, -scrying, -scried 1** to catch sight of **2** to discover by looking carefully

desecrate *vb* **-crating, -crated** to violate the sacred character of (an object or place) ▸ **desecration** *n*

desegregate *vb* **-gating, -gated** to end racial segregation in (a school or other public institution) ▸ **desegregation** *n*

deselect *vb* **1** to cancel (a highlighted selection of data) on a computer screen **2** *Brit politics* (of a constituency organization) to refuse to select (an MP) for re-election ▸ **deselection** *n*

desert¹ *n* a region that has little or no vegetation because of low rainfall

> **desert** *n* = wilderness, waste, wilds, wasteland

desert² *vb* **1** to abandon (a person or place) without intending to return **2** *chiefly military* to leave (a post or duty) with no intention of returning ▸ **deserted** *adj* ▸ **deserter** *n* ▸ **desertion** *n*

> **desert** *vb* **1** = abandon, leave, quit (*informal*), forsake; ≠ take care of **2** = abscond

deserts *pl n* **get one's just deserts** to get the punishment one deserves

deserve *vb* **-serving, -served** to be entitled to or worthy of

> **deserve** *vb* = merit, warrant, be entitled to, have a right to, rate, earn, justify, be worthy of

d

deserved _adj_ rightfully earned ▸ **deservedly** (diz-**zerv**-id-lee) _adv_

> **deserved** _adj_ = well-earned, fitting, due, earned, justified, merited, proper, warranted

deserving _adj_ worthy of a reward, help, or praise

> **deserving** _adj_ = worthy, righteous, commendable, laudable, praiseworthy, meritorious, estimable; ≠ undeserving

deshabille (day-zab-**beel**) _or_ **dishabille** _n_ the state of being partly dressed

desiccate _vb_ -**cating**, -**cated** to remove most of the water from; dry ▸ **desiccated** _adj_ ▸ **desiccation** _n_

> **desiccate** _vb_ = dry, drain, evaporate, dehydrate, parch, exsiccate

design _vb_ **1** to work out the structure or form of (something), by making a sketch or plans **2** to plan and make (something) artistically **3** to intend (something) for a specific purpose: _the move is designed to reduce travelling costs_ ▸ _n_ **4** a sketch, plan, or preliminary drawing **5** the arrangement or features of an artistic or decorative work: _he built it to his own design_ **6** a finished artistic or decorative creation **7** the art of designing **8** an intention; purpose **9 have designs on** to plot to gain possession of

> **design** _vb_ **1** = plan, draw, draft, trace, outline, devise, sketch, formulate **2** = create, plan, fashion, propose, invent, conceive, originate, fabricate **3** = intend, mean, plan, aim, purpose ▸ _n_ **4** = plan, drawing, model, scheme, draft, outline, sketch, blueprint **5** = pattern, form, style, shape, organization, arrangement, construction **8** = intention, end, aim, goal, target, purpose, object, objective

designate (**dez**-zig-nate) _vb_ -**nating**, -**nated** **1** to give a name to or describe as: _vessels sunk during battle are designated as war graves_ **2** to select (someone) for an office or duty; appoint ▸ _adj_ **3** appointed, but not yet in office: _a Prime Minister designate_

> **designate** _vb_ **1** = name, call, term, style, label, entitle, dub **2** = appoint, name, choose, commission, select, elect, delegate, nominate

designation _n_ **1** something that designates, such as a name **2** the act of designating

designedly (dee-**zine**-id-lee) _adv_ by intention

designer _n_ **1** a person who draws up original sketches or plans from which things are made ▸ _adj_ **2** designed by a well-known fashion designer: _a wardrobe full of designer clothes_ **3** having an appearance of fashionable trendiness: _designer stubble_

> **designer** _n_ = couturier

designing _adj_ cunning and scheming

desirable _adj_ **1** worth having or doing: _a desirable lifestyle_ **2** arousing sexual desire ▸ **desirability** _n_ ▸ **desirably** _adv_

> **desirable** _adj_ **1** = advantageous, useful, valuable, helpful, profitable, of service, convenient, worthwhile; ≠ disadvantageous **2** = attractive, appealing, pretty, fair, inviting, lovely, charming, sexy (_informal_); ≠ unattractive

desire _vb_ -**siring**, -**sired** **1** to want very much **2** _formal_ to request: _we desire your company at the wedding of our daughter_ ▸ _n_ **3** a wish or longing **4** sexual appetite **5** a person or thing that is desired

> **desire** _vb_ **1** = want, long for, crave, hope for, ache for, wish for, yearn for, thirst for ▸ _n_ **3** = wish, want, longing, hope, urge, aspiration, craving, thirst **4** = lust, passion, libido, appetite, lasciviousness

desist _vb_ to stop doing: _please desist from talking_

desk _n_ **1** a piece of furniture with a writing surface and usually drawers **2** a service counter in a public building, such as a hotel **3** the section of a newspaper or television station responsible for a particular subject: _the picture desk_

desktop _n_ **1** the main screen display on a personal computer **2** a personal computer that is small enough to use at a desk ▸ _adj_ **3** (esp. of a computer system) for use at a desk

desolate _adj_ **1** uninhabited and bleak **2** made uninhabitable; devastated **3** without friends, hope, or encouragement **4** gloomy or dismal; depressing ▸ _vb_ -**lating**, -**lated** **5** to deprive of inhabitants **6** to make barren; devastate **7** to make wretched or forlorn ▸ **desolately** _adv_ ▸ **desolateness** _n_

desolation _n_ **1** ruin or devastation **2** solitary misery; wretchedness

despair _n_ **1** total loss of hope ▸ _vb_ **2** to lose or give up hope: _we must not despair of finding a peaceful solution_

> **despair** _n_ = despondency, depression, misery, gloom, desperation, anguish, hopelessness, dejection ▸ _vb_ = lose hope, give up, lose heart

despatch _vb, n_ same as **dispatch**

desperado _n, pl_ -**does** _or_ -**dos** a reckless person ready to commit any violent illegal act

desperate _adj_ **1** willing to do anything to improve one's situation **2** (of an action) undertaken as a last resort **3** very grave: _in desperate agony_ **4** having a great need or desire: _I was desperate for a child_ ▸ **desperately** _adv_

> **desperate** _adj_ **2** = last-ditch, daring, furious, risky, frantic, audacious **3** = grave, pressing, serious, severe, extreme, urgent, drastic

desperation _n_ **1** desperate recklessness **2** the state of being desperate

desperation *n* 1 = recklessness, madness (*informal*), frenzy, impetuosity, rashness, foolhardiness 2 = misery, worry, trouble, despair, agony, anguish, unhappiness, hopelessness

despicable *adj* deserving contempt
> **despicably** *adv*

despise *vb* **-pising, -pised** to look down on with contempt

despise *vb* = look down on, loathe, scorn, detest, revile, abhor; ≠ admire

despite *prep* in spite of

despite *prep* = in spite of, in the face of, regardless of, even with, notwithstanding, in the teeth of, undeterred by

despoil *vb formal* to plunder > **despoliation** *n*
despondent *adj* dejected or depressed
> **despondency** *n* > **despondently** *adv*
despot *n* any person in power who acts tyrannically > **despotic** *adj* > **despotically** *adv*
despotism *n* 1 absolute or tyrannical government 2 tyrannical behaviour
dessert *n* the sweet course served at the end of a meal
dessertspoon *n* a spoon between a tablespoon and a teaspoon in size
destabilize *or* **-lise** *vb* **-lizing, -lized** *or* **-lising, -lised** to make or become unstable or less stable > **destabilization** *or* **-lisation** *n*
destination *n* the place to which someone or something is going

destination *n* = stop, station, haven, resting-place, terminus, journey's end

destined (**dess**-tinnd) *adj* 1 certain to be or do something: *the school is destined to close this summer* 2 heading towards a specific destination: *some of the oil was destined for Eastern Europe*

destined *adj* 1 = fated, meant, intended, certain, bound, doomed, predestined

destiny *n, pl* **-nies** 1 the future destined for a person or thing 2 the predetermined course of events 3 the power that predetermines the course of events

destiny *n* 1 = fate, fortune, lot, portion, doom, nemesis 3 = fortune, chance, karma, providence, kismet, predestination, divine will

destitute *adj* lacking the means to live; totally impoverished > **destitution** *n*
destroy *vb* 1 to ruin; demolish 2 to put an end to 3 to kill (an animal) 4 to crush or defeat

destroy *vb* 1 = ruin, crush, devastate, wreck, shatter, wipe out, demolish, eradicate 3 = slaughter, kill

destroyer *n* 1 a small heavily armed warship 2 a person or thing that destroys

destruction *n* 1 the act of destroying something or state of being destroyed 2 a cause of ruin

destruction *n* 1 = ruin, havoc, wreckage, demolition, devastation, annihilation

destructive *adj* 1 causing or capable of causing harm, damage, or injury 2 intended to discredit, esp. without positive suggestions or help: *destructive speeches against the platform* > **destructively** *adv*

destructive *adj* 1 = devastating, fatal, deadly, lethal, harmful, damaging, catastrophic, ruinous

desuetude (diss-**syoo**-it-tude) *n formal* the condition of not being in use
desultory (dez-zl-tree) *adj* 1 passing or jumping from one thing to another; disconnected: *desultory conversation* 2 occurring in a random way: *a desultory thought* > **desultorily** *adv*
detach *vb* 1 to disengage and separate 2 *military* to send (a regiment, officer, etc.) on a special assignment > **detachable** *adj*

detach *vb* 1 = separate, remove, divide, cut off, sever, disconnect, tear off, disengage; ≠ attach

detached *adj* 1 *Brit, Austral & S African* separate or standing apart: *a detached farmhouse* 2 showing no emotional involvement: *she continued to watch him in her grave and detached manner*

detached *adj* 1 = separate, disconnected, discrete, unconnected, undivided 2 = objective, neutral, impartial, reserved, impersonal, disinterested, unbiased, dispassionate; ≠ subjective

detachment *n* 1 the state of not being personally involved in something 2 *military* a small group of soldiers separated from the main group

detachment *n* 1 = indifference, fairness, neutrality, objectivity, impartiality, coolness, remoteness, nonchalance 2 = unit, party, force, body, squad, patrol, task force

detail *n* 1 an item that is considered separately 2 an item considered to be unimportant: *a mere detail* 3 treatment of individual parts: *the census provides a considerable amount of detail* 4 a small section of a work of art often enlarged to make the smaller features more distinct 5 *chiefly military* **A** personnel assigned a specific duty **B** the duty 6 **in detail** including all the important particulars ▸ *vb* 7 to list fully 8 *chiefly military* to select (personnel) for a specific duty

detail *n* 1 = point, fact, feature, particular, respect, factor, element, aspect 2 = fine point, particular, nicety, triviality 5A = party, force, body, duty, squad, assignment, fatigue, detachment ▸ *vb* 7 = list, relate, catalogue, recount, rehearse, recite, enumerate, itemize

detain vb 1 to delay (someone) 2 to force (someone) to stay: *the police detained him for questioning* > **detainee** n > **detainment** n

> **detain** vb 1 = delay, hold up, hamper, hinder, retard, impede, keep back, slow up or down 2 = hold, arrest, confine, restrain, imprison, intern, take prisoner, hold in custody

detect vb 1 to perceive or notice: *to detect a note of sarcasm* 2 to discover the existence or presence of: *to detect alcohol in the blood* > **detectable** adj > **detector** n

> **detect** vb 1 = notice, see, spot, note, identify, observe, recognize, perceive 2 = discover, find, uncover, track down, unmask

detection n 1 the act of noticing, discovering, or sensing something 2 the act or process of extracting information

detective n a police officer who investigates crimes

> **detective** n = investigator, cop (*slang*), private eye, sleuth, private investigator, gumshoe (*US slang, old-fashioned*)

detente (day-tont) n the easing of tension between nations

detention n 1 imprisonment, esp. of a suspect awaiting trial 2 a form of punishment in which a pupil is detained after school

> **detention** n 1 = imprisonment, custody, quarantine, confinement, incarceration; ≠ release

deter vb **-terring, -terred** to discourage or prevent someone from doing something by instilling fear or doubt in them

> **deter** vb = prevent, stop

detergent n 1 a chemical substance used for washing clothes, dishes, etc. ▸ adj 2 having cleansing power

deteriorate vb **-rating, -rated** to become worse > **deterioration** n

> **deteriorate** vb = decline, worsen, degenerate, slump, go downhill; ≠ improve

determinant adj 1 serving to determine or affect ▸ n 2 a factor that controls or influences what will happen 3 *maths* a square array of elements that represents the sum of certain products of these elements

determinate adj definitely limited or fixed

determination n 1 the condition of being determined; resoluteness 2 the act of making a decision

> **determination** n 1 = resolution, purpose, resolve, dedication, fortitude, persistence, tenacity, perseverance; ≠ indecision

determine vb **-mining, -mined** 1 to settle (an argument or a question) conclusively 2 to find

out the facts about (something): *the tests determined it was in fact cancer* 3 to fix in scope, extent, etc.: *to determine the degree of the problem* 4 to make a decision

> **determine** vb 1 = affect, decide, regulate, ordain (*formal*) 2, 3 = settle, learn, establish, discover, find out, work out, detect, verify 4 = decide, conclude, resolve, make up your mind

determined adj firmly decided > **determinedly** adv

> **determined** adj = resolute, firm, dogged, intent, persistent, persevering, single-minded, tenacious

determiner n *grammar* a word, such as a number, article, or personal pronoun, that determines the meaning of a noun phrase

determinism n the theory that human choice is not free, but is decided by past events > **determinist** n, adj

deterrent n 1 something that deters 2 a weapon or set of weapons held by one country to deter another country attacking ▸ adj 3 tending to deter > **deterrence** n

> **deterrent** n 1 = discouragement, obstacle, curb, restraint, impediment, check, hindrance, disincentive; ≠ incentive

detest vb to dislike intensely > **detestable** adj

detestation n intense hatred

dethrone vb **-throning, -throned** to remove from a throne or deprive of any high position > **dethronement** n

detonate vb **-nating, -nated** to make (an explosive device) explode or (of an explosive device) to explode > **detonation** n

detonator n a small amount of explosive or a device used to set off an explosion

detour n a deviation from a direct route or course of action

detox vb, n short for **detoxify** or **detoxification**

detoxify vb **-fies, -fying, -fied** to remove poison from > **detoxification** n

detract vb **detract from** to make (something) seem less good, valuable, or impressive: *I wouldn't want to detract from your triumph* > **detraction** n > **detractor** n

detriment n disadvantage or damage > **detrimental** adj > **detrimentally** adv

detritus (dit-trite-uss) n 1 a loose mass of stones and silt worn away from rocks 2 debris > **detrital** adj

de trop (de troh) adj unwanted or unwelcome: *I know when I'm de trop, so I'll leave you two together*

deuce (dyewss) n 1 *tennis* a tied score that requires one player to gain two successive points to win the game 2 a playing card or dice with two spots

deuterium n a stable isotope of hydrogen. Symbol: **D**, ^{2}**H**

Deutschmark (doytch-mark) or **Deutsche Mark** (doytch-a) n a former monetary unit of Germany

devalue vb **-valuing, -valued** 1 to reduce the exchange value of (a currency) 2 to reduce the value of (something or someone) > **devaluation** n

devastate vb **-tating, -tated** to damage (a place) severely or destroy it > **devastation** n

> **devastate** vb = destroy, ruin, sack, wreck, demolish, level, ravage, raze

devastated adj shocked and extremely upset > **devastating** adj > **devastatingly** adv

develop vb 1 to grow or bring to a later, more elaborate, or more advanced stage 2 to come or bring into existence: the country has developed a consumer society 3 to make or become gradually clearer or more widely known 4 to follow as a result of something: Cubism developed from attempts to give painting a more intellectual concept of form 5 to contract (an illness) 6 to improve the value or change the use of (land) 7 to exploit the natural resources of (a country or region) 8 photog to treat (a photographic plate or film) to produce a visible image

> **develop** vb 1 = grow, advance, progress, mature, evolve, flourish, ripen 2 = establish, set up, promote, generate, undertake, initiate, embark on, cultivate 3 = expand, extend, work out, elaborate, unfold, enlarge, broaden, amplify

developer n 1 a person who develops property 2 photog a chemical used to develop photographic film

developing country n a poor or nonindustrial country that is seeking to develop its resources by industrialization

development n 1 the process of growing or developing 2 the product of developing 3 an event or incident that changes a situation 4 an area of land that has been developed > **developmental** adj

> **development** n 1 = growth, increase, advance, progress, spread, expansion, evolution, enlargement 3 = event, happening, result, incident, improvement, evolution, unfolding, occurrence

deviant adj 1 deviating from what is considered acceptable behaviour ▶ n 2 a person whose behaviour deviates from what is considered to be acceptable > **deviance** n

> **deviant** adj = twisted, warped, perverted, sick (informal); ≠ normal ▶ n = misfit, pervert, freak

deviate vb **-ating, -ated** 1 to differ from others in belief or thought 2 to depart from one's usual or previous behaviour > **deviation** n

device n 1 a machine or tool used for a particular purpose 2 euphemistic a bomb 3 a scheme or plan 4 a design or emblem

5 **leave someone to his** or **her own devices** to leave someone alone to do as he or she wishes

> **device** n 1 = gadget, machine, tool, instrument, implement, appliance, apparatus, contraption (informal) 3 = ploy, scheme, plan, trick, manoeuvre, gambit, stratagem, wile

devil n 1 theol **the Devil** the chief spirit of evil and enemy of God 2 any evil spirit 3 a person regarded as wicked 4 a person: lucky devil 5 a person regarded as daring: be a devil! 6 informal something difficult or annoying 7 **between the devil and the deep blue sea** between equally undesirable alternatives 8 **give the devil his due** to acknowledge the talent or success of an unpleasant person 9 **talk of the devil!** used when an absent person who has been the subject of conversation arrives unexpectedly 10 **the devil** used as an exclamation to show surprise or annoyance: what the devil is she doing here? ▶ vb **-villing, -villed** or US **-viling, -viled** 11 to prepare (food) by coating with a highly flavoured spiced mixture 12 chiefly Brit to do routine literary work for a lawyer or author

> **devil** n 1 **the Devil** = Satan, Lucifer, Prince of Darkness, Mephistopheles, Evil One, Beelzebub, Old Nick (informal) 2 = evil spirit, demon, fiend, atua (NZ), wairua (NZ) 3 = brute, monster, beast, barbarian, fiend, terror, swine, ogre 4 = person, individual, soul, creature, thing, beggar

devilish adj 1 of or like a devil; fiendish ▶ adv, adj 2 informal, old-fashioned extreme or extremely: devilish good food > **devilishly** adv

devil-may-care adj happy-go-lucky; reckless

devilment n mischievous conduct

devilry n 1 reckless fun or mischief 2 wickedness

devil's advocate n a person who takes an opposing or unpopular point of view for the sake of argument

devious adj 1 insincere and dishonest 2 (of a route or course of action) indirect > **deviously** adv

devise vb **-vising, -vised** to work out (something) in one's mind

> **devise** vb = work out, design, construct, invent, conceive, formulate, contrive, dream up

devoid adj **devoid of** completely lacking in a particular quality: she was a woman totally devoid of humour

> **devoid** adj = lacking in, without, free from, wanting in, bereft of, empty of, deficient in

devolution n a transfer of authority from a central government to regional governments > **devolutionist** n, adj

d

devolve *vb* **-volving, -volved** to pass or cause to pass to a successor or substitute, as duties or power

devote *vb* **-voting, -voted** to apply or dedicate (one's time, money, or effort) to a particular purpose

> **devote** *vb* = dedicate, give, commit, apply, reserve, pledge, surrender, assign

devoted *adj* feeling or demonstrating loyalty or devotion: *he was clearly devoted to his family* > **devotedly** *adv*

> **devoted** *adj* = dedicated, committed, true, constant, loyal, faithful, ardent, staunch; ≠ disloyal

devotee (dev-vote-tee) *n* **1** a person fanatically enthusiastic about a subject or activity **2** a zealous follower of a religion

> **devotee** *n* **1** = enthusiast, fan, supporter, follower, admirer, buff (*informal*), fanatic, adherent, fanboy (*informal*), fangirl (*informal*)

devotion *n* **1** strong attachment to or affection for someone or something **2** religious zeal; piety **3 devotions** religious observance or prayers > **devotional** *adj*

> **devotion** *n* **1** = love, passion, affection, attachment, fondness; ≠ indifference **2** = worship, reverence, spirituality, holiness, piety, godliness, devoutness; ≠ irreverence **3** = prayers, religious observance, church service, divine office

devour *vb* **1** to eat up greedily **2** to engulf and destroy **3** to read avidly > **devouring** *adj*

> **devour** *vb* **1** = eat, consume, swallow, wolf, gulp, gobble, guzzle, polish off (*informal*) **3** = enjoy, take in, read compulsively *or* voraciously

devout *adj* **1** deeply religious **2** sincere; heartfelt: *a devout confession* > **devoutly** *adv*

> **devout** *adj* = religious, godly, pious, pure, holy, saintly, reverent; ≠ irreverent

dew *n* drops of water that form on the ground or on a cool surface at night from vapour in the air > **dewy** *adj*

dewlap *n* a loose fold of skin hanging under the throat in cattle, dogs, etc.

dexterity *n* **1** skill in using one's hands **2** mental quickness

dexterous *adj* possessing or done with dexterity > **dexterously** *adv*

dextrose *n* a glucose occurring in fruit, honey, and in the blood of animals

DI 1 *Brit* Detective Inspector **2** Donor Insemination: a method of making a woman pregnant by transferring sperm from a man other than her husband or regular partner using artificial means

diabetes (die-a-beet-eez) *n* a medical condition in which the body is unable to control the level of sugar in the blood

diabetic *n* **1** a person who has diabetes ▸ *adj* **2** of or having diabetes **3** suitable for people who have diabetes: *diabetic chocolate*

diabolic *adj* of the Devil; satanic

diabolical *adj* **1** *informal* unpleasant or annoying: *the weather was diabolical* **2** *informal* extreme: *diabolical cheek* **3** same as **diabolic** > **diabolically** *adv*

diabolism *n* **A** witchcraft or sorcery **B** worship of devils > **diabolist** *n*

diaconate *n* the position or period of office of a deacon > **diaconal** *adj*

diacritic *n* a sign placed above or below a character or letter to indicate phonetic value or stress

diadem *n old-fashioned* a small jewelled crown or headband, usually worn by royalty: *a gold diadem*

diaeresis *or esp US* **dieresis** (die-air-iss-iss) *n, pl* **-ses** (-seez) the mark (¨) placed over the second of two adjacent vowels to indicate that it is to be pronounced separately, as in naïve

diagnose *vb* **-nosing, -nosed** to determine by diagnosis

> **diagnose** *vb* = identify, determine, recognize, distinguish, interpret, pronounce, pinpoint

diagnosis (die-ag-no-siss) *n, pl* **-ses** (-seez) the discovery and identification of diseases from the examination of symptoms > **diagnostic** *adj*

> **diagnosis** *n* = identification, discovery, recognition, detection

diagonal *adj* **1** *maths* connecting any two vertices in a polygon that are not adjacent **2** slanting ▸ *n* **3** a diagonal line, plane, or pattern > **diagonally** *adv*

diagram *n* a sketch or plan showing the form or workings of something > **diagrammatic** *adj*

> **diagram** *n* = plan, figure, drawing, chart, representation, sketch, graph

dial *n* **1** the face of a clock or watch, marked with divisions representing units of time **2** the graduated disc on a measuring instrument **3** the control on a radio or television set used to change the station **4** a numbered disc on the front of some telephones ▸ *vb* **dialling, dialled** *or* *US* **dialing, dialed 5** to try to establish a telephone connection with (someone) by operating the dial or buttons on a telephone

dialect *n* a form of a language spoken in a particular geographical area > **dialectal** *adj*

dialectic *n* **1** logical debate by question and answer to resolve differences between two views **2** the art of logical argument > **dialectical** *adj*

dialogue *or US sometimes* **dialog** *n* **1** conversation between two people **2** a conversation in a literary or dramatic work **3** a discussion between representatives of two nations or groups

dialogue or **dialog** n 1 = conversation, discussion, communication, discourse 3 = discussion, conference, exchange, debate

dialysis (die-al-iss-iss) n, pl -ses (-seez) 1 med the filtering of blood through a semipermeable membrane to remove waste products 2 the separation of the particles in a solution by filtering through a semipermeable membrane > **dialyser** or US **-lyzer** n > **dialytic** adj

diamanté (die-a-man-tee) adj decorated with glittering bits of material, such as sequins

diameter n **A** a straight line through the centre of a circle or sphere **B** the length of such a line

diametric or **diametrical** adj 1 of or relating to a diameter 2 completely opposed: the diametric opposition of the two camps > **diametrically** adv

diamond n 1 a usually colourless exceptionally hard precious stone of crystallized carbon 2 geom a figure with four sides of equal length forming two acute and two obtuse angles 3 a playing card marked with one or more red diamond-shaped symbols 4 baseball the playing field ▸ adj 5 (of an anniversary) the sixtieth: diamond wedding

diaper n US & Canad a nappy

diaphanous (die-af-fan-uss) adj (of fabrics) fine and translucent

diaphragm (die-a-fram) n 1 anatomy the muscular partition that separates the abdominal cavity and chest cavity 2 same as **cap** (sense 5) 3 a device to control the amount of light entering an optical instrument 4 a thin vibrating disc which converts sound to electricity or vice versa, as in a microphone or loudspeaker

diarist n a person who writes a diary that is subsequently published

diarrhoea or esp US **diarrhea** (die-a-ree-a) n frequent discharge of abnormally liquid faeces

diary n, pl -ries 1 a book containing a record of daily events, appointments, or observations 2 a written record of daily events, appointments, or observations

diary n 1 = journal, chronicle, blog (informal) 2 = engagement book, appointment book, personal organizer

diatribe n a bitter critical attack

dibble n a small hand tool used to make holes in the ground for bulbs, seeds, or roots

dice n, pl **dice 1** a small cube, each of whose sides has a different number of spots (1 to 6), used in games of chance ▸ vb **dicing, diced 2** to cut (food) into small cubes 3 **dice with death** to take a risk

dicey adj **dicier, diciest** informal dangerous or tricky

dichotomy (die-kot-a-mee) n, pl -mies division into two opposed groups or parts > **dichotomous** adj

dicky¹ n, pl **dickies** informal a false shirt front

dicky² adj **dickier, dickiest** Brit & NZ informal shaky or weak: a dicky heart

dicky-bird n a child's word for a bird

dictate vb -tating, -tated 1 to say (words) aloud for another person to transcribe 2 to seek to impose one's will on others ▸ n 3 an authoritative command 4 a guiding principle: the dictates of reason

dictate vb 1 = speak, say, utter, read out ▸ n 3 = command, order, decree, demand, direction, injunction, fiat, edict 4 = principle, law, rule, standard, code, criterion, maxim

dictation n 1 the act of dictating words to be taken down in writing 2 the words dictated

dictator n 1 a ruler who has complete power 2 a person who behaves in a tyrannical manner > **dictatorship** n

dictator n = absolute ruler, tyrant, despot, oppressor, autocrat, absolutist, martinet

dictatorial adj 1 of or pertaining to a dictator 2 tyrannical; overbearing > **dictatorially** adv

diction n the manner of pronouncing words and sounds

dictionary n, pl -aries 1 **A** a book that consists of an alphabetical list of words with their meanings **B** a similar book giving equivalent words in two languages 2 a reference book listing terms and giving information about a particular subject

dictionary n 1, 2 = wordbook, vocabulary, glossary, lexicon

dictum n, pl -tums or -ta 1 a formal statement; pronouncement 2 a popular saying or maxim

did vb the past tense of **do**

didactic adj intended to teach or instruct people: an Impressionist work can be as didactic in its way as a sermon > **didactically** adv > **didacticism** n

diddle vb -dling, -dled informal to swindle > **diddler** n

didgeridoo n an Australian Aboriginal deep-toned wind instrument

didn't did not

die¹ vb **dying, died 1** (of a person, animal, or plant) to cease all biological activity permanently 2 (of something inanimate) to cease to exist 3 to lose strength, power, or energy by degrees 4 to stop working: the engine died 5 **be dying** to be eager (for something or to do something) 6 **be dying of** informal to be nearly overcome with (laughter, boredom, etc.) 7 **die hard** to change or disappear only slowly: old loyalties die hard 8 **to die for** informal highly desirable: a salary to die for

die vb 1 = pass away, expire, perish, croak (slang), give up the ghost, snuff it (slang), peg out (informal, rare), kick the bucket (slang), cark it (Austral, NZ slang); ≠ live 3 = dwindle, decline, sink, fade, diminish, decrease, decay, wither; ≠ increase 4 = stop, fail, halt, break down, run down, stop working, peter out, fizzle out

die² *n* **1** a shaped block used to cut or form metal **2** a casting mould **3** same as **dice** (sense 1) **4 the die is cast** an irrevocable decision has been taken

die-hard *or* **diehard** *n* a person who resists change

dieresis (die-air-iss-iss) *n*, *pl* **-ses** (-seez) same as **diaeresis**

diesel *n* **1** same as **diesel engine 2** a vehicle driven by a diesel engine **3** *informal* diesel oil

diesel engine *n* an internal-combustion engine in which oil is ignited by compression

diesel oil *or* **diesel fuel** *n* a fuel obtained from petroleum distillation, used in diesel engines

diet¹ *n* **1** the food that a person or animal regularly eats **2** a specific allowance or selection of food, to control weight or for health reasons: *a high-fibre diet* ▸ *vb* **3** to follow a special diet so as to lose weight ▸ *adj* **4** suitable for eating with a weight-reduction diet: *diet soft drinks* > **dietary** *adj* > **dieter** *n*

> **diet** *n* **1** = food, provisions, fare, rations, kai (NZ *informal*), nourishment, sustenance, victuals **2** = fast, regime, abstinence, regimen ▸ *vb* = food, provisions, fare, rations, kai (NZ *informal*), nourishment, sustenance, victuals

diet² *n* a legislative assembly in some countries

> **diet** *n* = council, meeting, parliament, congress, chamber, convention, legislature

dietary fibre *n* the roughage in fruits and vegetables that aids digestion

dietetic *adj* prepared for special dietary requirements

dietetics *n* the study of diet, nutrition, and the preparation of food

dietician *n* a person qualified to advise people about healthy eating

differ *vb* **1** to be dissimilar in quality, nature, or degree **2** to disagree

> **differ** *vb* **2** = disagree, clash, dispute, dissent; ≠ agree

difference *n* **1** the state or quality of being unlike **2** a disagreement or argument **3** the result of the subtraction of one number or quantity from another **4 make a difference** to have an effect **5 split the difference A** to compromise **B** to divide a remainder equally

> **difference** *n* **1** = dissimilarity, contrast, variation, change, variety, diversity, alteration, discrepancy; ≠ similarity **2** = disagreement, conflict, argument, clash, dispute, quarrel, contretemps; ≠ agreement **3** = remainder, rest, balance, remains, excess

different *adj* **1** partly or completely unlike **2** new or unusual **3** not identical or the same; other: *he wears a different tie every day* > **differently** *adv*

different *adj* **1** = dissimilar, opposed, contrasting, changed, unlike, altered, inconsistent, disparate **2** = unusual, special, strange, extraordinary, distinctive, peculiar, uncommon, singular

differential *adj* **1** of, relating to, or using a difference **2** *maths* involving differentials ▸ *n* **3** a factor that differentiates between two comparable things **4** *maths* a minute difference between values in a scale **5** *chiefly Brit* the difference between rates of pay for different types of labour, esp. within a company or industry

differential calculus *n* the branch of mathematics concerned with derivatives and differentials

differentiate *vb* **-ating, -ated 1** to perceive or show the difference (between) **2** to make (one thing) distinct from other such things **3** *maths* to determine the derivative of a function or variable > **differentiation** *n*

> **differentiate** *vb* **1** = distinguish, separate, discriminate, contrast, mark off, make a distinction, tell apart, set off *or* apart **2** = make different, separate, distinguish, characterize, single out, segregate, individualize, mark off

difficult *adj* **1** not easy to do, understand, or solve **2** not easily pleased or satisfied: *a difficult patient* **3** full of hardships or trials: *he had recently had a difficult time with his job as a self-employed builder*

> **difficult** *adj* **1** = hard, tough, taxing, demanding, challenging, exacting, formidable, uphill; ≠ easy **2** = troublesome, demanding, perverse, fussy, fastidious, hard to please, refractory, unaccommodating; ≠ cooperative

difficulty *n*, *pl* **-ties 1** the state or quality of being difficult **2** a task or problem that is hard to deal with **3** a troublesome or embarrassing situation: *in financial difficulties* **4** an objection or obstacle: *you're just making difficulties* **5** lack of ease; awkwardness: *she could run only with difficulty*

> **difficulty** *n* **2, 4** = problem, trouble, obstacle, hurdle, dilemma, complication, snag, uphill (S African) **5** = hardship, strain, awkwardness, strenuousness, arduousness, laboriousness

diffident *adj* lacking self-confidence; shy > **diffidence** *n* > **diffidently** *adv*

diffraction *n* **1** *physics* a deviation in the direction of a wave at the edge of an obstacle in its path **2** the formation of light and dark fringes by the passage of light through a small aperture

diffuse *vb* **-fusing, -fused 1** to spread over a wide area **2** *physics* to cause to undergo diffusion ▸ *adj* **3** spread out over a wide area **4** lacking conciseness > **diffuser** *n* > **diffusible** *adj*

diffusion *n* **1** the act of diffusing or the fact of being diffused; dispersion **2** *physics* the random thermal motion of atoms and molecules in gases, liquids, and some solids **3** *physics* the transmission or reflection of light, in which the radiation is scattered in many directions

dig *vb* **digging, dug** **1** to cut into, break up, and turn over or remove (earth), esp. with a spade **2** to excavate (a hole or tunnel) by digging, usually with an implement or (of animals) with claws **3** to obtain by digging: *dig out potatoes* **4** to find by effort or searching: *she dug out a torch from her bag* **5** *informal* to like or understand **6** (foll. by *in* or *into*) to thrust or jab ▸ *n* **7** the act of digging **8** an archaeological excavation **9** a thrust or poke **10** a cutting remark

> **dig** *vb* **1** = turn over **2** = hollow out, mine, quarry, excavate, scoop out **6** = poke, drive, push, stick, punch, stab, thrust, shove ▸ *n* **9** = poke, thrust, nudge, prod, jab, punch **10** = cutting remark, crack (*slang*), insult, taunt, sneer, jeer, barb, wisecrack (*informal*)

digest *vb* **1** to subject (food) to a process of digestion **2** to absorb mentally ▸ *n* **3** a shortened version of a book, report, or article > **digestible** *adj*

> **digest** *vb* **1** = ingest, absorb, incorporate, dissolve, assimilate **2** = take in, absorb, grasp, soak up ▸ *n* = summary, résumé, abstract, epitome, synopsis, précis, abridgment

digestion *n* **1** the process of breaking down food into easily absorbed substances **2** the body's system for doing this
digestive *adj* relating to digestion
digger *n* a machine used for excavation
digit (dij-it) *n* **1** a finger or toe **2** any numeral from 0 to 9
digital *adj* **1** displaying information as numbers rather than with a dial **2** representing data as a series of numerical values **3** of or possessing digits > **digitally** *adv*
digitalis *n* a drug made from foxglove leaves: used as a heart stimulant
dignify *vb* **-fies, -fying, -fied** **1** to add distinction to: *the meeting was dignified by the minister* **2** to add a semblance of dignity to by the use of a pretentious name or title: *she dignifies every plant with its Latin name*
dignitary *n, pl* **-taries** a person of high official position or rank
dignity *n, pl* **-ties** **1** serious, calm, and controlled behaviour or manner **2** the quality of being worthy of honour **3** sense of self-importance: *he considered the job beneath his dignity*

> **dignity** *n* **1** = decorum, gravity, majesty, grandeur, respectability, nobility, solemnity, courtliness **3** = self-importance, pride, self-esteem, self-respect

digress *vb* to depart from the main subject in speech or writing > **digression** *n*

dilapidated *adj* (of a building) having fallen into ruin > **dilapidation** *n*
dilate *vb* **-lating, -lated** to make or become wider or larger: *her eyes dilated in the dark* > **dilation** *or* **dilatation** *n*
dilatory (dill-a-tree) *adj* tending or intended to waste time > **dilatorily** *adv* > **dilatoriness** *n*
dildo *n, pl* **-dos** an object used as a substitute for an erect penis
dilemma *n* a situation offering a choice between two equally undesirable alternatives

> **dilemma** *n* = predicament, problem, difficulty, spot (*informal*), mess, puzzle, plight, quandary

dilettante (dill-it-tan-tee) *n, pl* **-tantes** *or* **-tanti** a person whose interest in a subject is superficial rather than serious > **dilettantism** *n*
diligent *adj* **1** careful and persevering in carrying out tasks or duties **2** carried out with care and perseverance: *a diligent approach to work* > **diligence** *n* > **diligently** *adv*
dill *n* a sweet-smelling herb used for flavouring
dilly-dally *vb* **-lies, -lying, -lied** *Brit, Austral & NZ informal* to dawdle or waste time
dilute *vb* **-luting, -luted** **1** to make (a liquid) less concentrated by adding water or another liquid **2** to make (someone's power, idea, or role) weaker or less effective: *socialists used their majority in parliament to dilute legislation crucial to developing a market economy* ▸ *adj* **3** *chem* (of a solution) having a low concentration > **dilution** *n*

> **dilute** *vb* **1** = water down, thin (out), weaken, adulterate, make thinner, cut (*informal*); ≠ condense **2** = reduce, weaken, diminish, temper, decrease, lessen, diffuse, mitigate; ≠ intensify

diluvian *or* **diluvial** *adj* of a flood, esp. the great Flood described in the Old Testament
dim *adj* **dimmer, dimmest** **1** badly lit **2** not clearly seen; faint: *a dim figure in the doorway* **3** not seeing clearly: *eyes dim with tears* **4** *informal* slow to understand **5** not clear in the mind; obscure: *a dim awareness* **6** lacking in brightness or lustre: *a dim colour* **7** **take a dim view of** to disapprove of ▸ *vb* **dimming, dimmed** **8** to become or cause to become dim **9** to cause to seem less bright **10** *US & Canad* same as **dip** (sense 4) > **dimly** *adv* > **dimness** *n*

> **dim** *adj* **1** = poorly lit, dark, gloomy, murky, shady, shadowy, dusky, tenebrous **2** = unclear, obscured, faint, blurred, fuzzy, shadowy, hazy, bleary; ≠ distinct **4** = stupid, thick, dull, dense, dumb (*informal*), daft (*informal*), dozy (*Brit informal*), obtuse; ≠ bright **6** = cloudy, grey, gloomy, dismal, overcast, leaden; ≠ bright ▸ *vb* **8** = grow *or* become faint, fade, dull, grow *or* become dim **9** = turn down, fade, dull

dime *n* a coin of the US and Canada worth ten cents

dimension *n* **1** an aspect or factor: *the attack brought a whole new dimension to the bombing campaign* **2 dimensions** scope or extent **3** (*often pl*) a measurement of the size of something in a particular direction ▷ **dimensional** *adj*

> **dimension** *n* **1** = aspect, side, feature, angle, facet **2** = extent, size

diminish *vb* **1** to make or become smaller, fewer, or less **2** *music* to decrease (a minor interval) by a semitone **3** to reduce in authority or status

> **diminish** *vb* **1** = decrease, decline, lessen, shrink, dwindle, wane, recede, subside; ≠ grow

diminuendo *music* ▸ *n, pl* **-dos 1 A** a gradual decrease in loudness **B** a passage which gradually decreases in loudness ▸ *adv* **2** gradually decreasing in loudness

diminution *n* reduction in size, volume, intensity, or importance

diminutive *adj* **1** very small; tiny **2** *grammar* **A** denoting an affix added to a word to convey the meaning *small* or *unimportant* or to express affection, as for example, the suffix *-ette* in French **B** denoting a word formed by the addition of a diminutive affix ▸ *n* **3** *grammar* a diminutive word or affix ▷ **diminutiveness** *n*

dimmer *n* **1** a device for dimming an electric light **2** *US* **A** a dipped headlight on a road vehicle **B** a parking light on a car

dimple *n* **1** a small natural dent on the cheeks or chin ▸ *vb* **-pling, -pled 2** to produce dimples by smiling

din *n* **1** a loud unpleasant confused noise ▸ *vb* **dinning, dinned 2 din something into someone** to instil something into someone by constant repetition

> **din** *n* = noise, row, racket, crash, clamour, clatter, uproar, commotion; ≠ silence

dinar (**dee-nahr**) *n* a monetary unit of various Balkan, Middle Eastern, and North African countries

dine *vb* **dining, dined 1** to eat dinner **2 dine on** *or* **off** to make one's meal of: *the guests dined on roast beef*

> **dine** *vb* **1** = eat, lunch, feast, sup

diner *n* **1** a person eating a meal in a restaurant **2** *chiefly US & Canad* a small cheap restaurant **3** short for **dining car**

ding *n informal* a small dent in a vehicle

ding-dong *n* **1** the sound of a bell **2** *Brit informal* a violent exchange of blows or words

dinghy (**ding-ee, ding-gee**) *n, pl* **-ghies** a small boat, powered by sail, oars, or outboard motor

dingo *n, pl* **-goes** an Australian native wild dog

dingy (**din-jee**) *adj* **-gier, -giest 1** *Brit, Austral & NZ* dull, neglected, and drab: *he waited in this dingy little outer office* **2** shabby and discoloured: *she was wearing dingy white overalls* ▷ **dinginess** *n*

dining car *n* a railway coach in which meals are served

dining room *n* a room where meals are eaten

dinkum *adj Austral & NZ informal* genuine or right: *a fair dinkum offer*

> **dinkum** *adj* = genuine, honest, natural, frank, sincere, candid, upfront (*informal*), artless

dinky *adj* **dinkier, dinkiest** *chiefly Brit informal* small and neat; dainty

dinky-di *adj Austral informal* typical

dinner *n* **1** the main meal of the day, eaten either in the evening or at midday **2** a formal social occasion at which an evening meal is served

> **dinner** *n* **1** = meal, main meal, spread (*informal*), repast **2** = banquet, feast, repast, hakari (NZ)

dinner jacket *n* a man's semiformal black evening jacket without tails

dinosaur *n* any of a large order of extinct prehistoric reptiles many of which were gigantic

dint *n* **by dint of** by means of: *by dint of their own efforts*

diocesan *adj* of or relating to a diocese

diocese (**die-a-siss**) *n* the district over which a bishop has control

diode *n* **1** a semiconductor device for converting alternating current to direct current **2** an electronic valve with two electrodes between which a current can flow only in one direction

dioptre *or US* **diopter** (**die-op-ter**) *n* a unit for measuring the refractive power of a lens

dioxide *n* an oxide containing two oxygen atoms per molecule

dip *vb* **dipping, dipped 1** to plunge or be plunged quickly or briefly into a liquid **2** to put one's hands into something, esp. to obtain an object: *she dipped into her handbag looking for change* **3** to slope downwards **4** to switch (car headlights) from the main to the lower beam **5** to undergo a slight decline, esp. temporarily: *sales dipped in November* **6** to immerse (farm animals) briefly in a chemical to rid them of insects **7** to lower or be lowered briefly: *she dipped her knee in a curtsy* ▸ *n* **8** the act of dipping **9** a brief swim **10** a liquid chemical in which farm animals are dipped **11** a depression, esp. in a landscape **12** a momentary sinking down **13** a creamy mixture into which pieces of food are dipped before being eaten ▸ See also **dip into**

> **dip** *vb* **1, 6** = plunge, immerse, bathe, duck, douse, dunk **3** = slope, drop (down), descend, fall, decline, sink, incline, drop away **7** = drop (down), fall, lower, sink, descend, subside ▸ *n* **8** = plunge, ducking, soaking, drenching, immersion, douche **11** = hollow, hole, depression, pit, basin, trough, concavity **12** = nod, drop, lowering, slump, sag

diphtheria (dif-**theer**-ree-a) *n* a contagious disease producing fever and difficulty in breathing and swallowing

diphthong *n* a vowel sound, occupying a single syllable, in which the speaker's tongue moves continuously from one position to another, as in the pronunciation of *a* in *late*

dip into *vb* **1** to draw upon: *he dipped into his savings* **2** to read passages at random from (a book or journal)

> **dip into** *vb* **2 dip into something** = sample, skim, glance at, browse, peruse, surf (*computers*)

diploma *n* a document conferring a qualification or recording successful completion of a course of study

diplomacy *n* **1** the conduct of the relations between nations by peaceful means **2** skill in the management of international relations **3** tact or skill in dealing with people

> **diplomacy** *n* **1** = statesmanship, statecraft, international negotiation **3** = tact, skill, sensitivity, craft, discretion, subtlety, delicacy, finesse; ≠ tactlessness

diplomat *n* an official, such as an ambassador, engaged in diplomacy

> **diplomat** *n* = official, ambassador, envoy, statesperson, consul, attaché, emissary, chargé d'affaires

diplomatic *adj* **1** of or relating to diplomacy **2** skilled in negotiating between nations **3** tactful in dealing with people > **diplomatically** *adv*

> **diplomatic** *adj* **1** = consular, official, foreign-office, ambassadorial, foreign-politic **3** = tactful, politic, sensitive, subtle, delicate, polite, discreet, prudent; ≠ tactless

dipper *n* **1** a ladle used for dipping **2** a songbird that inhabits fast-flowing streams

diprotodont (die-**pro**-toe-dont) *n* a marsupial with fewer than three upper incisor teeth on each side of the jaw

dipsomania *n* a compulsive desire to drink alcoholic beverages > **dipsomaniac** *n*, *adj*

diptych (**dip**-tik) *n* a painting on two hinged panels

dire *adj* disastrous, urgent, or terrible: *he was now in dire financial straits*

> **dire** *adj* = desperate, pressing, critical, terrible, crucial, extreme, awful, urgent

direct *adj* **1** shortest; straight: *a direct route* **2** without intervening people: *they secretly arranged direct links to their commanders* **3** honest; frank: *he was polite but very direct* **4** diametric: *the direct opposite* **5** in an unbroken line of descent: *a direct descendant* ▸ *adv* **6** directly; straight ▸ *vb* **7** to conduct or control the affairs of **8** to give orders with authority to (a person or group)

9 to tell (someone) the way to a place **10** to address (a letter, parcel, etc.) **11** to address (a look or remark) at someone: *the look she directed at him was one of unconcealed hatred* **12 a** to provide guidance to (actors, cameramen, etc.) in (a play or film) **b** to supervise the making or staging of (a film or play) > **directness** *n*

> **direct** *adj* **1** = quickest, shortest; ≠ circuitous **2** = first-hand, personal, immediate; ≠ indirect **3** = straightforward, open, straight, frank, blunt, honest, candid, forthright; ≠ indirect ▸ *adv* = non-stop, straight ▸ *vb* **7** = control, run, manage, lead, guide, handle, conduct, oversee **8** = order, command, instruct, charge (*formal*), demand, require, bid **9** = guide, show, lead, point the way, point in the direction of **10** = address, send, mail, route, label **11** = aim, point, level, train, focus

direct current *n* an electric current that flows in one direction only

direction *n* **1** the course or line along which a person or thing moves, points, or lies **2** management or guidance: *the campaign was successful under his direction* **3** the work of a stage or film director

> **direction** *n* **1** = way, course, line, road, track, bearing, route, path **2** = management, control, charge, administration, leadership, command, guidance, supervision

directional *adj* **1** of or showing direction **2** *electronics* (of an aerial) transmitting or receiving radio waves more effectively in some directions than in others

directive *n* an instruction; order

> **directive** *n* = order, ruling, regulation, command, instruction, decree, mandate, injunction

directly *adv* **1** in a direct manner **2** at once; without delay **3** immediately or very soon: *I'll do that directly* ▸ *conj* **4** as soon as: *we left directly the money arrived*

> **directly** *adv* **1** = straight, unswervingly, without deviation, by the shortest route, in a beeline **2** = at once, as soon as possible, straightaway, forthwith **3** = immediately, promptly, right away, straight away

direct message *n* (on a social network) a message that can be read only by one or more named recipients

director *n* **1** a person or thing that directs or controls **2** a member of the governing board of a business, trust, etc. **3** the person responsible for the artistic and technical aspects of the making of a film or television programme > **directorial** *adj* > **directorship** *n*

> **director** *n* **1, 2** = controller, head, leader, manager, chief, executive, governor, administrator, sherang (*Austral, NZ*)

d

directorate *n* **1** a board of directors **2** the position of director

directory *n, pl* **-ries 1** a book listing names, addresses, and telephone numbers of individuals or business companies **2** *computers* an area of a disk containing the names and locations of the files it currently holds

dirge *n* **1** a chant of lamentation for the dead **2** any mournful song

dirigible (dir-rij-jib-bl) *adj* **1** able to be steered ▶ *n* **2** same as **airship**

dirk *n* a dagger, formerly worn by Scottish Highlanders

dirndl *n* **1** a woman's dress with a full gathered skirt and fitted bodice **2** a gathered skirt of this kind

dirt *n* **1** any unclean substance, such as mud; filth **2** loose earth; soil **3** packed earth, cinders, etc., used to make a racetrack **4** obscene speech or writing **5** *informal* harmful gossip

> **dirt** *n* **1** = filth, muck, grime, dust, mud, impurity, kak (*S African vulgar slang*) **2** = soil, ground, earth, clay, turf, loam

dirt track *n* a racetrack made of packed earth or cinders

dirty *adj* **dirtier, dirtiest 1** covered or marked with dirt; filthy **2** causing one to become grimy: *a dirty job* **3** (of a colour) not clear and bright **4** unfair, dishonest, or unkind: *dirty tricks* **5** **A** obscene: *dirty jokes* **B** sexually clandestine: *a dirty weekend* **6** revealing dislike or anger: *a dirty look* **7** (of weather) rainy or stormy **8** **dirty work** unpleasant or illicit activity ▶ *n* **9** **do the dirty on** *informal* to behave meanly towards ▶ *vb* **dirties, dirtying, dirtied 10** to make dirty; soil > **dirtiness** *n*

> **dirty** *adj* **1** = filthy, soiled, grubby, foul, muddy, polluted, messy, grimy, festy (*Austral slang*); ≠ clean **4** = dishonest, illegal, unfair, cheating, crooked (*informal*), fraudulent, treacherous, unscrupulous; ≠ honest **5A** = obscene, indecent, blue (*old-fashioned*), offensive, filthy, pornographic, sleazy, lewd ▶ *vb* = soil, foul, stain, spoil, muddy, pollute, blacken, defile; ≠ clean

dis- *prefix* **1** indicating reversal: *disconnect* **2** indicating negation or lack: *dissimilar; disgrace* **3** indicating removal or release: *disembowel*

disability *n, pl* **-ties 1** a physical or mental condition or illness that restricts a person in his or her ability to move or use his or her senses **2** something that disables someone

> **disability** *n* **1** = condition, disorder, infirmity, handicap (*old-fashioned, offensive*)

disable *vb* **-abling, -abled 1** to cause a person to be restricted in his or her ability to move or use the senses **2** to switch off (a device or computer program) > **disablement** *n*

disabled *adj* having a physical or mental condition that restricts one's ability to move or use one's senses

> **disabled** *adj* = with a disability, paralysed, handicapped (*old-fashioned, offensive*)

disabuse *vb* **-abusing, -abused** to rid (someone) of a mistaken idea: *Krysia felt unable to disabuse him of his prejudices*

disadvantage *n* **1** an unfavourable or harmful circumstance **2** **at a disadvantage** in a less favourable position than other people: *he continued to insist that he was at a disadvantage at the hearings* > **disadvantageous** *adj*

> **disadvantage** *n* = drawback, trouble, handicap, nuisance, snag, inconvenience, downside; ≠ advantage

disadvantaged *adj* socially or economically deprived

disaffected *adj* having lost loyalty to or affection for someone or something; alienated: *three million disaffected voters* > **disaffection** *n*

disagree *vb* **-greeing, -greed 1** to have differing opinions or argue about (something) **2** to fail to correspond; conflict **3** to cause physical discomfort to: *curry disagrees with me*

> **disagree** *vb* **1** = differ (in opinion), argue, clash, dispute, dissent, quarrel, take issue with, cross swords; ≠ agree **3** = make ill, upset, sicken, trouble, hurt, bother, distress, discomfort

disagreeable *adj* **1** (of an incident or situation) unpleasant **2** (of a person) bad-tempered or disobliging > **disagreeably** *adv*

disagreement *n* **1** refusal or failure to agree **2** a difference between results, totals, etc. which shows that they cannot all be true **3** an argument

> **disagreement** *n* **3** = argument, row, conflict, clash, dispute, dissent, quarrel, squabble; ≠ agreement

disallow *vb* to reject as untrue or invalid; cancel

disappear *vb* **1** to cease to be visible; vanish **2** to go away or become lost, esp. without explanation **3** to cease to exist: *the pain has disappeared* > **disappearance** *n*

> **disappear** *vb* **1** = vanish, recede, evanesce (*formal*); ≠ appear **3** = cease, dissolve, evaporate, perish, die out, pass away, melt away, leave no trace

disappoint *vb* **1** to fail to meet the expectations or hopes of; let down **2** to prevent the fulfilment of (a plan, etc.); frustrate > **disappointed** *adj* > **disappointing** *adj*

> **disappoint** *vb* **1** = let down, dismay, fail, disillusion, dishearten, disenchant, dissatisfy, disgruntle

disappointment *n* **1** the feeling of being disappointed **2** a person or thing that disappoints

> **disappointment** *n* **1** = regret, discontent, dissatisfaction, disillusionment, chagrin, disenchantment, dejection, despondency **2** = letdown, blow, setback, misfortune, calamity, choker (*informal*)

disapprobation *n* disapproval
disapprove *vb* **-proving, -proved** to consider wrong or bad > **disapproval** *n* > **disapproving** *adj*

> **disapprove** *vb* = condemn, object to, dislike, deplore, frown on, take exception to, take a dim view of, find unacceptable; ≠ approve

disarm *vb* **1** to deprive of weapons **2** to win the confidence or affection of **3** (of a country) to decrease the size and capability of one's armed forces

> **disarm** *vb* **1, 3** = demilitarize, disband, demobilize, deactivate **2** = win over, persuade

disarmament *n* the reduction of fighting capability by a country

> **disarmament** *n* = arms reduction, demobilization, arms limitation, demilitarization, de-escalation

disarming *adj* removing hostility or suspicion > **disarmingly** *adv*

> **disarming** *adj* = charming, winning, irresistible, persuasive, likable *or* likeable

disarrange *vb* **-ranging, -ranged** to throw into disorder > **disarrangement** *n*
disarray *n* **1** confusion and lack of discipline **2** extreme untidiness ▸ *vb* **3** to throw into confusion

> **disarray** *n* **1** = confusion, disorder, indiscipline, disunity, disorganization, unruliness; ≠ order **2** = untidiness, mess, chaos, muddle, clutter, shambles, jumble, hotchpotch; ≠ tidiness

disaster *n* **1** an accident that causes great distress or destruction **2** something, such as a project, that fails or has been ruined > **disastrous** *adj* > **disastrously** *adv*

> **disaster** *n* **1** = catastrophe, trouble, tragedy, ruin, misfortune, adversity, calamity, cataclysm **2** = failure, mess, flop (*informal*), catastrophe, debacle, cock-up (*Brit slang*), washout (*informal*)

disavow *vb* to deny connection with or responsibility for (something) > **disavowal** *n*
disband *vb* to stop or cause to stop functioning as a unit or group > **disbandment** *n*
disbelieve *vb* **-lieving, -lieved 1** to reject (a person or statement) as being untruthful

2 disbelieve in to have no faith or belief in: *to disbelieve in the supernatural* > **disbelief** *n*
disburse *vb* **-bursing, -bursed** to pay out > **disbursement** *n*
disc *n* **1** a flat circular object **2** a sound recording made on such an object **3** *anatomy* a circular flat structure in the body, esp. between the vertebrae **4** *computers* same as **disk**
discard *vb* to get rid of (something or someone) as useless or undesirable

> **discard** *vb* = get rid of, drop, throw away *or* out, reject, abandon, dump (*informal*), dispose of, dispense with; ≠ keep

discern *vb* to see or be aware of (something) clearly > **discernible** *adj*
discerning *adj* having or showing good judgment > **discernment** *n*
discharge *vb* **-charging, -charged 1** to release or allow to go **2** to dismiss (someone) from duty or employment **3** to fire (a gun) **4** to cause to pour forth: *the scar was red and swollen and began to discharge pus* **5** to remove (the cargo) from a boat, etc.; unload **6** to meet the demands of (a duty or responsibility) **7** to relieve oneself of (a debt) **8** *physics* to take or supply electrical current from (a cell or battery) ▸ *n* **9** something that is discharged **10** dismissal or release from an office, job, etc. **11** a pouring out of a fluid; emission **12** *physics* a conduction of electricity through a gas

> **discharge** *vb* **1** = release, free, clear, liberate, pardon, allow to go, set free **2** = dismiss, sack (*informal*), fire (*informal*), remove, expel, discard, oust, cashier, kennet (*Austral slang*), jeff (*Austral slang*) **3** = fire, shoot, set off, explode, let off, detonate, let loose (*informal*) **4** = pour forth, release, leak, emit, dispense, ooze, exude, give off **6** = carry out, perform, fulfil, accomplish, do, effect, realize, observe **7** = pay, meet, clear, settle, square (up), honour, satisfy, relieve ▸ *n* **10** = dismissal, notice (*Brit*), removal, the boot (*slang*), expulsion, the sack (*informal*), the push (*slang*), marching orders (*informal*), ejection **11** = emission, ooze, secretion, excretion, pus, seepage, suppuration

disciple (diss-*sipe*-pl) *n* **1** a follower of the doctrines of a teacher **2** *Christianity* one of the personal followers of Christ during his earthly life

> **disciple** *n* **1** = follower, student, supporter, pupil, devotee, apostle, adherent; ≠ teacher **2** = apostle

disciplinarian *n* a person who practises strict discipline
disciplinary *adj* of or imposing discipline; corrective
discipline *n* **1** the practice of imposing strict rules of behaviour on other people **2** the ability to behave and work in a controlled manner

3 a particular area of academic study ▸ *vb* **-plining, -plined 4** to improve or attempt to improve the behaviour of (oneself or someone else) by training or rules **5** to punish

> **discipline** *n* **1** = control, authority, regulation, supervision, orderliness, strictness **2** = self-control, control, restraint, self-discipline, willpower, self-restraint, orderliness **3** = field of study, area, subject, theme, topic, course, curriculum, speciality ▸ *vb* **4** = train, educate **5** = punish, correct, reprimand, castigate, chastise, chasten, penalize, bring to book

disciplined *adj* able to behave and work in a controlled way

disc jockey *n* a person who announces and plays recorded pop records on a radio programme or at a disco

disclaim *vb* **1** to deny (responsibility for or knowledge of something) **2** to give up (any claim to)

disclaimer *n* a statement denying responsibility for or knowledge of something

disclose *vb* **-closing, -closed 1** to make (information) known **2** to allow to be seen: *she agreed to disclose the contents of the box* > **disclosure** *n*

> **disclose** *vb* **1** = make known, reveal, publish, relate, broadcast, confess, communicate, divulge; ≠ keep secret **2** = show, reveal, expose, unveil, uncover, lay bare, bring to light; ≠ hide

disco *n, pl* **-cos 1** a nightclub for dancing to amplified pop records **2** an occasion at which people dance to amplified pop records **3** mobile equipment for providing music for a disco

discolour *or US* **discolor** *vb* to change in colour; to fade or stain > **discoloration** *n*

discomfit *vb* **-fiting, -fited** to make uneasy or confused > **discomfiture** *n*

discomfort *n* **1** a mild pain **2** a feeling of worry or embarrassment **3 discomforts** conditions that cause physical uncomfortableness: *the physical discomforts of pregnancy*

> **discomfort** *n* **1** = pain, hurt, ache, throbbing, irritation, tenderness, pang, malaise; ≠ comfort **2** = uneasiness, worry, anxiety, doubt, distress, misgiving, qualms, trepidation (*formal*); ≠ reassurance

discommode *vb* **-moding, -moded** to cause inconvenience > **discommodious** *adj*

disconcert *vb* to disturb the confidence or self-possession of; upset, embarrass, or take aback > **disconcerting** *adj*

disconnect *vb* **1** to undo or break the connection between (two things) **2** to stop the supply of (gas or electricity to a building) ▸ *n* **3** a lack of connection; disconnection: *a disconnect between political discourse and the public* > **disconnection** *n*

disconnected *adj* (of speech or ideas) not logically connected

disconsolate *adj* sad beyond comfort > **disconsolately** *adv*

discontent *n* lack of contentment, as with one's condition or lot in life > **discontented** *adj* > **discontentedly** *adv*

> **discontent** *n* = dissatisfaction, unhappiness, displeasure, regret, envy, restlessness, uneasiness

discontinue *vb* **-nuing, -nued** to come or bring to an end; stop

discontinuous *adj* characterized by interruptions; intermittent > **discontinuity** *n*

discord *n* **1** lack of agreement or harmony between people **2** harsh confused sounds **3** a combination of musical notes that lacks harmony

discordant *adj* **1** at variance; disagreeing **2** harsh in sound; inharmonious > **discordance** *n*

discotheque *n* same as **disco**

discount *vb* **1** to leave (something) out of account as being unreliable, prejudiced, or irrelevant **2** to deduct (an amount or percentage) from the price of something ▸ *n* **3** a deduction from the full amount of a price **4 at a discount** below the regular price

> **discount** *vb* **1** = disregard, reject, ignore, overlook, discard, set aside, dispel, pass over ▸ *n* **3** = deduction, cut, reduction, concession, rebate

discourage *vb* **-raging, -raged 1** to deprive of the will or enthusiasm to persist in something **2** to oppose by expressing disapproval > **discouragement** *n* > **discouraging** *adj*

> **discourage** *vb* **1** = dishearten, depress, intimidate, overawe, demoralize, put a damper on, dispirit, deject; ≠ hearten **2** = put off, deter, prevent, dissuade, talk out of; ≠ encourage

discourse *n* **1** conversation **2** a formal treatment of a subject in speech or writing ▸ *vb* **-coursing, -coursed 3** to speak or write (about) at length

> **discourse** *n* **1** = conversation, talk, discussion, speech, communication, chat, dialogue **2** = speech, essay, lecture, sermon, treatise, dissertation, homily, oration, whaikorero (NZ)

discourteous *adj* showing bad manners; rude > **discourteously** *adv* > **discourtesy** *n*

discover *vb* **1** to be the first to find or find out about **2** to learn about for the first time **3** to find after study or search > **discoverer** *n*

> **discover** *vb* **2** = find out, learn, notice, realize, recognize, perceive, detect, uncover **3** = find, come across, uncover, unearth, turn up, dig up, come upon

discovery *n*, *pl* **-veries** 1 the act of discovering 2 a person, place, or thing that has been discovered

> **discovery** *n* 1 = finding out, news, revelation, disclosure, realization
> 2 = invention, launch, institution, pioneering, innovation, inauguration

discredit *vb* **-diting, -dited** 1 to damage the reputation of (someone) 2 to cause (an idea) to be disbelieved or distrusted ▸ *n* 3 something that causes disgrace > **discreditable** *adj*

> **discredit** *vb* 1 = disgrace, shame, smear, humiliate, taint, disparage, vilify, slander; ≠ honour 2 = dispute, question, challenge, deny, reject, discount, distrust, mistrust ▸ *n* = disgrace, scandal, shame, disrepute, stigma, ignominy, dishonour, ill-repute; ≠ honour

discreet *adj* 1 careful to avoid embarrassment when dealing with secret or private matters 2 unobtrusive: *there was a discreet entrance down a side alley* > **discreetly** *adv*

> **discreet** *adj* 1 = tactful, diplomatic, guarded, careful, cautious, wary, prudent, considerate; ≠ tactless

discrepancy *n*, *pl* **-cies** a conflict or variation between facts, figures, or claims > **discrepant** *adj*

> **discrepancy** *n* = disagreement, difference, variation, conflict, contradiction, inconsistency, disparity, divergence

discrete *adj* separate or distinct > **discreteness** *n*
discretion (diss-**kresh**-on) *n* 1 the quality of behaving so as to avoid social embarrassment or distress 2 freedom or authority to make judgments and to act as one sees fit: *at his discretion* > **discretionary** *adj*

> **discretion** *n* 1 = tact, consideration, caution, diplomacy, prudence, wariness, carefulness, judiciousness; ≠ tactlessness 2 = choice, will, pleasure, preference, inclination, volition

discriminate *vb* **-nating, -nated** 1 to make a distinction against or in favour of a particular person or group 2 to recognize or understand a difference: *to discriminate between right and wrong* > **discriminating** *adj*

> **discriminate** *vb* 2 = differentiate, distinguish, separate, tell the difference, draw a distinction

discrimination *n* 1 unfair treatment of a person, racial group, or minority 2 subtle appreciation in matters of taste 3 the ability to see fine distinctions

> **discrimination** *n* 1 = prejudice, bias, injustice, intolerance, bigotry, favouritism, unfairness 2 = discernment, taste, judgment, perception, subtlety, refinement

discriminatory *adj* based on prejudice
discursive *adj* passing from one topic to another
discus *n* *athletics* a disc-shaped object with a heavy middle, thrown by athletes
discuss *vb* 1 to consider (something) by talking it over 2 to treat (a subject) in speech or writing > **discussion** *n*

> **discuss** *vb* 1 = talk about, consider, debate, examine, argue about, deliberate about, converse about, confer about

disdain *n* 1 a feeling of superiority and dislike; contempt ▸ *vb* 2 to refuse or reject with disdain: *he disdained domestic conventions* > **disdainful** *adj* > **disdainfully** *adv*

> **disdain** *n* = contempt, scorn, arrogance, derision, haughtiness, superciliousness ▸ *vb* = scorn, reject, slight, disregard, spurn, deride, look down on, sneer at

disease *n* an unhealthy condition in a person, animal, or plant which is caused by bacteria or infection > **diseased** *adj*

> **disease** *n* = illness, condition, complaint, infection, disorder, sickness, ailment, affliction

disembark *vb* to land or cause to land from a ship, aircraft, or other vehicle > **disembarkation** *n*
disembodied *adj* 1 lacking a body 2 seeming not to be attached to or come from anyone > **disembodiment** *n*
disembowel *vb* **-elling, -elled** *or US* **-eling, -eled** to remove the entrails of > **disembowelment** *n*
disenchanted *adj* disappointed and disillusioned (with something) > **disenchantment** *n*
disenfranchise *vb* **-chising, -chised** to deprive (someone) of the right to vote or of other rights of citizenship
disengage *vb* **-gaging, -gaged** 1 to release from a connection 2 *military* to withdraw from close action > **disengagement** *n*
disentangle *vb* **-gling, -gled** 1 to release from entanglement or confusion 2 to unravel or work out > **disentanglement** *n*
disfavour *or US* **disfavor** *n* 1 disapproval or dislike 2 the state of being disapproved of or disliked
disfigure *vb* **-guring, -gured** to spoil the appearance or shape of > **disfigurement** *n*
disfranchise *vb* **-chising, -chised** same as **disenfranchise**
disgorge *vb* **-gorging, -gorged** 1 to vomit 2 to discharge (contents)
disgrace *n* 1 a condition of shame, loss of reputation, or dishonour 2 a shameful person or thing 3 exclusion from confidence or trust: *he was sent home in disgrace* ▸ *vb* **-gracing, -graced** 4 to bring shame upon (oneself or others) > **disgraceful** *adj* > **disgracefully** *adv*

disgrace n 1 = shame, degradation, disrepute, ignominy, dishonour, infamy, opprobrium, odium (formal); ≠ honour 2 = scandal, stain, stigma, blot, blemish ▶ vb = shame, humiliate, discredit, degrade, taint, sully, dishonour, bring shame upon; ≠ honour

disgruntled adj sulky or discontented: the disgruntled home supporters > **disgruntlement** n

disgruntled adj = discontented, dissatisfied, annoyed, irritated, put out, grumpy, vexed, displeased, hoha (NZ)

disguise vb **-guising, -guised** 1 to change the appearance or manner in order to conceal the identity of (someone or something) 2 to misrepresent (something) in order to obscure its actual nature or meaning ▶ n 3 a mask, costume, or manner that disguises 4 the state of being disguised > **disguised** adj

disguise vb 1 = hide, cover, conceal, screen, mask, suppress, withhold, veil ▶ n 3 = costume, mask, camouflage

disgust n 1 a great loathing or distaste ▶ vb 2 to sicken or fill with loathing > **disgusted** adj > **disgusting** adj

disgust vb = sicken, offend, revolt, put off, repel, nauseate; ≠ delight

dish n 1 a container used for holding or serving food, esp. an open shallow container 2 the food in a dish 3 a particular kind of food 4 short for **dish aerial** 5 informal an attractive person ▶ See also **dish out, dish up**

dish n 1, 2, 3 = food, fare, recipe

dishabille (diss-a-beel) n same as **deshabille**
dish aerial n a large disc-shaped aerial with a concave reflector, used to receive signals in radar, radio telescopes, and satellite broadcasting
dishcloth n a cloth for washing dishes
dishearten vb to weaken or destroy the hope, courage, or enthusiasm of > **disheartened** adj > **disheartening** adj
dishevelled or US **disheveled** adj (of a person's hair, clothes, or general appearance) disordered and untidy
dishonest adj not honest or fair > **dishonestly** adv > **dishonesty** n

dishonest adj = deceitful, corrupt, crooked (informal), lying, bent (slang), false, cheating, treacherous; ≠ honest

dishonour or US **dishonor** vb 1 to treat with disrespect 2 to refuse to pay (a cheque) ▶ n 3 a lack of honour or respect 4 a state of shame or disgrace 5 something that causes a loss of honour > **dishonourable** or US **dishonorable** adj > **dishonourably** or US **dishonorably** adv

dish out vb 1 to distribute 2 **dish it out** to inflict punishment
dish up vb to serve (food)
disillusion vb 1 to destroy the illusions or false ideas of (someone) ▶ n also **disillusionment** 2 the state of being disillusioned
disincentive n something that discourages someone from behaving or acting in a particular way
disinclined adj unwilling or reluctant > **disinclination** n
disinfect vb to rid of harmful germs by cleaning with a chemical substance > **disinfection** n
disinfectant n a substance that destroys harmful germs
disinformation n false information intended to mislead
disingenuous adj dishonest and insincere > **disingenuously** adv
disinherit vb **-iting, -ited** law to deprive (an heir) of inheritance > **disinheritance** n
disintegrate vb **-grating, -grated** 1 to lose cohesion; break up: the business disintegrated 2 (of an object) to break into fragments; shatter 3 physics **a** to undergo nuclear fission or include nuclear fission in **b** same as **decay** (sense 3) > **disintegration** n

disintegrate vb 2 = break up, crumble, fall apart, separate, shatter, splinter, break apart, go to pieces

disinter vb **-terring, -terred** 1 to dig up 2 to bring to light; expose
disinterested adj 1 free from bias; objective 2 feeling or showing a lack of interest; uninterested > **disinterest** n
disjointed adj having no coherence; disconnected: a disjointed conversation
disk n 1 chiefly US & Canad same as **disc** 2 computers a storage device, consisting of a stack of plates coated with a magnetic layer, which rotates rapidly as a single unit
dislike vb **-liking, -liked** 1 to consider unpleasant or disagreeable ▶ n 2 a feeling of not liking something or someone

dislike vb = hate, object to, loathe, despise, disapprove of, detest, recoil from, take a dim view of; ≠ like ▶ n = hatred, hostility, disapproval, distaste, animosity, aversion, displeasure, antipathy; ≠ liking

dislocate vb **-cating, -cated** 1 to displace (a bone or joint) from its normal position 2 to disrupt or shift out of place > **dislocation** n
dislodge vb **-lodging, -lodged** to remove (something) from a previously fixed position
disloyal adj not loyal; deserting one's allegiance or duty > **disloyalty** n
dismal adj 1 gloomy and depressing 2 informal of poor quality > **dismally** adv

dismal *adj* **1** = sad, gloomy, dark, depressing, discouraging, bleak, dreary, sombre; ≠ happy **2** = bad, awful, dreadful, rotten (*informal*), terrible, poor, dire, abysmal

dismantle *vb* **-tling, -tled 1** to take apart piece by piece **2** to cause (an organization or political system) to stop functioning by gradually reducing its power or purpose

> **dismantle** *vb* **1** = take apart, strip, demolish, disassemble, take to pieces *or* bits

dismay *vb* **1** to fill with alarm or depression ▸ *n* **2** a feeling of alarm or depression

> **dismay** *vb* = disappoint, upset, discourage, daunt, disillusion, let down, dishearten, dispirit ▸ *n* = alarm, fear, horror, anxiety, dread, apprehension, nervousness, consternation

dismember *vb* **1** to remove the limbs of **2** to cut to pieces > **dismemberment** *n*

dismiss *vb* **1** to remove (an employee) from a job **2** to allow (someone) to leave **3** to put out of one's mind; no longer think about **4** (of a judge) to state that (a case) will not be brought to trial **5** *cricket* to bowl out (a side) for a particular number of runs > **dismissal** *n* > **dismissive** *adj*

> **dismiss** *vb* **1** = sack (*informal*), fire (*informal*), remove (*informal*), axe (*informal*), expel, discharge, lay off, cashier, give (someone) notice, kennet (*Austral slang*), jeff (*Austral slang*) **2** = let go, free, release, discharge, dissolve, liberate, disperse, send away **3** = reject, disregard

dismount *vb* to get off a horse or bicycle

disobedient *adj* refusing to obey > **disobedience** *n*

disobey *vb* to neglect or refuse to obey (a person or an order)

> **disobey** *vb* = defy, ignore, rebel, disregard, refuse to obey

disobliging *adj* unwilling to help

disorder *n* **1** a state of untidiness and disorganization **2** public violence or rioting **3** an illness > **disordered** *adj*

> **disorder** *n* **1** = untidiness, mess, confusion, chaos, havoc (*informal*), muddle, clutter, shambles, disarray **2** = disturbance, riot, turmoil, unrest, uproar, commotion, unruliness, biffo (*Austral slang*) **3** = illness, disease, complaint, condition, sickness, ailment, affliction, malady

disorderly *adj* **1** untidy and disorganized **2** uncontrolled; unruly **3** *law* violating public peace

> **disorderly** *adj* **1** = untidy, confused, chaotic, messy, jumbled, shambolic (*informal*), disorganized, higgledy-piggledy (*informal*); ≠ tidy **2** = unruly, disruptive, rowdy, turbulent, tumultuous, lawless, riotous, ungovernable

disorganize *or* **-ise** *vb* **-izing, -ized** *or* **-ising, -ised** to disrupt the arrangement or system of > **disorganization** *or* **-isation** *n*

disorientate *or* **disorient** *vb* **-tating, -tated** *or* **-enting, -ented** to cause (someone) to lose his or her bearings > **disorientation** *n*

disown *vb* to deny any connection with (someone)

disparage *vb* **-aging, -aged** to speak contemptuously of > **disparagement** *n* > **disparaging** *adj*

disparate *adj* utterly different in kind > **disparity** *n*

dispassionate *adj* not influenced by emotion; objective > **dispassionately** *adv*

dispatch *or* **despatch** *vb* **1** to send off to a destination or to perform a task **2** to carry out (a duty or task) promptly **3** to murder ▸ *n* **4** an official communication or report, sent in haste **5** a report sent to a newspaper by a correspondent **6** murder **7** with dispatch quickly

> **dispatch** *or* **despatch** *vb* **1** = send, consign **2** = carry out, perform, fulfil, effect, finish, achieve, settle, dismiss **3** = kill, murder, destroy, execute, slaughter, assassinate, slay (*archaic, literary*), liquidate ▸ *n* **4, 5** = message, news, report, story, account, communication, bulletin, communiqué

dispatch rider *n Brit, Austral & NZ* a motorcyclist who carries dispatches

dispel *vb* **-pelling, -pelled** to disperse or drive away

> **dispel** *vb* = drive away, dismiss, eliminate, expel, disperse, banish, chase away

dispensable *adj* not essential; expendable

dispensary *n, pl* **-ries** a place where medicine is prepared and given out

dispensation *n* **1** the act of distributing or dispensing **2** *chiefly RC Church* permission to dispense with an obligation of church law **3** any exemption from an obligation **4** the ordering of life and events by God

dispense *vb* **-pensing, -pensed 1** to distribute in portions **2** to prepare and distribute (medicine) **3** to administer (the law, etc.) **4 dispense with** to do away with or manage without > **dispenser** *n*

> **dispense** *vb* **1** = distribute, assign, allocate, allot, dole out, share out, apportion, deal out **2** = prepare, measure, supply, mix **3** = administer, operate, carry out, implement, enforce, execute, apply, discharge **4 dispense with something or someone** = do away with, give up, cancel, abolish, brush aside, forgo, relinquish

dispensing optician *n* See **optician** (sense 2)

disperse *vb* **-persing, -persed 1** to scatter over a wide area **2** to leave or cause to leave a gathering:

police dispersed rioters **3** to separate (light) into its different wavelengths **4** to separate (particles) throughout a solid, liquid, or gas > **dispersal** or **dispersion** *n*

> **disperse** *vb* **1** = scatter, spread, distribute, strew, diffuse, disseminate, throw about **2** = break up, separate, scatter, dissolve, disband; ≠ gather

dispirit *vb* to make downhearted > **dispirited** *adj* > **dispiriting** *adj*

displace *vb* **-placing, -placed** **1** to move (something) from its usual place **2** to remove (someone) from a post or position of authority

> **displace** *vb* **1** = move, shift, disturb, budge, misplace

displaced person *n* a person forced from his or her home or country, esp. by war or revolution

displacement *n* **1** the act of displacing **2** *physics* the weight or volume of liquid displaced by an object submerged or floating in it **3** *maths* the distance measured in a particular direction from a reference point. Symbol: *s*

display *vb* **1** to show **2** to reveal or make evident: *to display anger* ▸ *n* **3** the act of exhibiting or displaying **4** something displayed **5** an exhibition **6** *electronics* a device capable of representing information visually, as on a screen **7** *zool* a pattern of behaviour by which an animal attracts attention while courting, defending its territory, etc.

> **display** *vb* **1** = show, present, exhibit, put on view; ≠ conceal **2** = expose, show, reveal, exhibit, uncover ▸ *n* **3** = proof, exhibition, demonstration, evidence, expression, illustration, revelation, testimony **4** = show, exhibition, parade, spectacle, pageant **5** = exhibition, show, demonstration, presentation, array

displease *vb* **-pleasing, -pleased** to annoy or offend (someone) > **displeasure** *n*

disport *vb* **disport oneself** to indulge oneself in pleasure

disposable *adj* **1** designed for disposal after use: *disposable cups* **2** available for use if needed: *disposable capital*

> **disposable** *adj* **1** = throwaway, nonreturnable **2** = available, expendable, consumable

disposal *n* **1** the act or means of getting rid of something **2** **at one's disposal** available for use

> **disposal** *n* **1** = throwing away, dumping (*informal*), scrapping, removal, discarding, jettisoning, ejection, riddance **2** **at one's disposal** = available, ready, to hand, accessible, handy, at hand, on tap (*informal*), expendable

dispose *vb* **-posing, -posed** **1** **dispose of** **A** to throw away **B** to give, sell, or transfer to another

C to deal with or settle: *I disposed of that problem right away* **D** to kill **2** to arrange or place in a particular way: *around them are disposed the moulded masks of witch doctors*

> **dispose** *vb* **1A** **dispose of something** = get rid of, destroy, dump (*informal*), scrap, discard, unload, jettison, throw out or away **1C** **dispose of something** = deal with, manage, treat, handle, settle, cope with, take care of, see to **1D** **dispose of someone** = kill, murder, destroy, execute, slaughter, assassinate, slay, liquidate **2** = arrange, put, place, group, order, distribute, array

disposed *adj* **1** willing or eager (to do something): *few would feel disposed to fault his judgment* **2** having an inclination as specified (towards someone or something): *my people aren't too well disposed towards defectors*

disposition *n* **1** a person's usual temperament **2** a tendency or habit **3** arrangement; layout

> **disposition** *n* **1** = character, nature, spirit, make-up, constitution, temper, temperament **2** = tendency, inclination, propensity, habit, leaning, bent, bias, proclivity (*formal*) **3** = arrangement, grouping, ordering, organization, distribution, placement

dispossess *vb* to deprive (someone) of (a possession) > **dispossessed** *adj* > **dispossession** *n*

disproportion *n* lack of proportion or equality

disproportionate *adj* out of proportion > **disproportionately** *adv*

disprove *vb* **-proving, -proved** to show (an assertion or claim) to be incorrect

dispute *n* **1** a disagreement between workers and their employer **2** an argument between two or more people **3** **beyond dispute** unable to be questioned or denied: *it's beyond dispute that tensions already existed between them* ▸ *vb* **-puting, -puted** **4** to argue or quarrel about (something) **5** to doubt the validity of **6** to fight over possession of > **disputation** *n* > **disputatious** *adj*

> **dispute** *n* **1** = disagreement, conflict, argument, dissent, altercation **2** = argument, row, clash, controversy, contention, feud, quarrel, squabble ▸ *vb* **5** = contest, question, challenge, deny, doubt, oppose, object to, contradict

disqualify *vb* **-fies, -fying, -fied** **1** to officially ban (someone) from doing something: *he was disqualified from driving for ten years* **2** to make ineligible, as for entry to an examination > **disqualification** *n*

> **disqualify** *vb* **1** = ban, rule out, prohibit, preclude, debar, declare ineligible

disquiet *n* **1** a feeling of anxiety or uneasiness ▸ *vb* **2** to make (someone) anxious > **disquieting** *adj* > **disquietude** *n*

disregard *vb* **1** to give little or no attention to; ignore ▸ *n* **2** lack of attention or respect

> **disregard** *vb* = ignore, discount, overlook, neglect, pass over, turn a blind eye to, make light of, pay no heed to; ≠ pay attention to ▸ *n* = ignoring, neglect, contempt, indifference, negligence, disdain, disrespect

disrepair *n* the condition of being worn out or in poor working order
disreputable *adj* having or causing a bad reputation > **disreputably** *adv*
disrepute *n* a loss or lack of good reputation
disrespect *n* contempt or lack of respect
> **disrespectful** *adj*
disrobe *vb* **-robing, -robed** *literary* to undress
disrupt *vb* to interrupt the progress of
> **disruption** *n* > **disruptive** *adj*

> **disrupt** *vb* = interrupt, stop, upset, hold up, interfere with, unsettle, obstruct, cut short

dissatisfied *adj* displeased or discontented
> **dissatisfaction** *n*

> **dissatisfied** *adj* = discontented, frustrated, unhappy, disappointed, fed up, disgruntled, displeased, unsatisfied; ≠ satisfied

dissect *vb* **1** to cut open (a corpse) to examine it **2** to examine critically and minutely: *the above conclusion causes one to dissect that policy more closely*
> **dissection** *n*
dissemble *vb* **-bling, -bled** to conceal one's real motives or emotions by pretence
> **dissembler** *n*
disseminate *vb* **-nating, -nated** to spread (information, ideas, etc.) widely
> **dissemination** *n*
dissension *n* disagreement and argument
dissent *vb* **1** to disagree **2** *Christianity* to reject the doctrines of an established church ▸ *n* **3** a disagreement **4** *Christianity* separation from an established church > **dissenter** *n*
> **dissenting** *adj*

> **dissent** *n* **3** = disagreement, opposition, protest, resistance, refusal, objection, discord, demur; ≠ assent

dissertation *n* **1** a written thesis, usually required for a higher degree **2** a long formal speech
disservice *n* a harmful action
dissident *n* **1** a person who disagrees with a government or a powerful organization ▸ *adj* **2** disagreeing or dissenting > **dissidence** *n*

> **dissident** *n* = protester, rebel, dissenter, demonstrator, agitator ▸ *adj* = dissenting, disagreeing, nonconformist, heterodox

dissimilar *adj* not alike; different
> **dissimilarity** *n*
dissimulate *vb* **-lating, -lated** to conceal one's real feelings by pretence > **dissimulation** *n*

dissipate *vb* **-pating, -pated** **1** to waste or squander **2** to scatter or break up
dissipated *adj* showing signs of overindulgence in alcohol or other physical pleasures
dissipation *n* **1** the process of dissipating **2** unrestrained indulgence in physical pleasures
dissociate *vb* **-ciating, -ciated** **1** dissociate oneself from to deny or break an association with (a person or organization) **2** to regard or treat as separate > **dissociation** *n*
dissolute *adj* leading an immoral life
dissolution *n* **1** the act of officially breaking up an organization or institution **2** the act of officially ending a formal agreement, such as a marriage **3** the formal ending of a meeting or assembly, such as a Parliament
dissolve *vb* **-solving, -solved** **1** to become or cause to become liquid; melt **2** to officially break up (an organization or institution) **3** to formally end: *the campaign started as soon as Parliament was dissolved last month* **4** to collapse emotionally: *she dissolved in loud tears* **5** *films & television* to fade out one scene and replace with another to make two scenes merge imperceptibly

> **dissolve** *vb* **1** = melt, soften, thaw, liquefy, deliquesce, **2, 3** = end, suspend, break up, wind up, terminate, discontinue, dismantle, disband

dissonance *n* a lack of agreement or harmony between things: *this dissonance of colours*
> **dissonant** *adj*
dissuade *vb* **-suading, -suaded** to deter (someone) by persuasion from doing something or believing in something > **dissuasion** *n*
distaff *n* the rod on which flax is wound for spinning
distaff side *n* the female side of a family
distance *n* **1** the space between two points or places **2** the state of being apart **3** a distant place **4** remoteness in manner **5 the distance** the most distant part of the visible scene **6 go the distance** **A** *boxing* to complete a bout without being knocked out **B** to complete an assigned task or responsibility **7 keep one's distance** to maintain a reserved attitude to another person ▸ *vb* **-tancing, -tanced** **8 distance oneself from** or **be distanced from** to separate oneself or be separated mentally from

> **distance** *n* **1** = space, length, extent, range, stretch, gap, interval, span **4** = aloofness, reserve, detachment, restraint, stiffness, coolness, coldness, standoffishness

distant *adj* **1** far-off; remote **2** far apart **3** separated by a specified distance: *five kilometres distant* **4** apart in relationship: *a distant cousin* **5** going to a faraway place **6** remote in manner; aloof **7** abstracted: *a distant look entered her eyes*
> **distantly** *adv*

d

distant *adj* 1 = far-off, far, remote, abroad, out-of-the-way, far-flung, faraway, outlying; ≠ close 6 = reserved, withdrawn, cool, remote, detached, aloof, unfriendly, reticent; ≠ friendly 7 = faraway, blank, vague, distracted, vacant, preoccupied, oblivious, absent-minded

distaste *n* a dislike of something offensive

distasteful *adj* unpleasant or offensive
> **distastefulness** *n*

distemper¹ *n* a highly contagious viral disease that can affect young dogs

distemper² *n* 1 paint mixed with water, glue, etc. which is used for painting walls ▸ *vb* 2 to paint with distemper

distend *vb* to expand by pressure from within; swell > **distensible** *adj* > **distension** *n*

distil *or US* **distill** *vb* **-tilling, -tilled** 1 to subject to or obtain by distillation 2 to give off (a substance) in drops 3 to extract the essence of

distillation *n* 1 the process of evaporating a liquid and condensing its vapour 2 *Also:* **distillate** a concentrated essence

distiller *n* a person or company that makes spirits

distillery *n, pl* **-eries** a place where alcoholic drinks are made by distillation

distinct *adj* 1 not the same; different: *these two areas produce wines with distinct characteristics* 2 clearly seen, heard, or recognized: *it is not possible to draw a distinct line between the two categories*; *there's a distinct smell of burning* 3 clear and definite: *there is a distinct possibility of rain* 4 obvious: *a distinct improvement* > **distinctly** *adv*

distinct *adj* 1 = different, individual, separate, discrete, unconnected; ≠ similar 2 = striking, dramatic, outstanding, noticeable, well-defined 3, 4 = definite, marked, clear, decided, obvious, evident, noticeable, conspicuous; ≠ vague

distinction *n* 1 the act of distinguishing or differentiating 2 a distinguishing feature 3 the state of being different or distinguishable 4 special honour, recognition, or fame 5 excellence of character 6 a symbol of honour or rank

distinction *n* 2 = feature, quality, characteristic, mark, individuality, peculiarity, distinctiveness, particularity 3 = difference, contrast, variation, differential, discrepancy, disparity, dissimilarity 4 = merit, honour, integrity, excellence, rectitude 5 = excellence, importance, fame, merit, prominence, greatness, eminence, repute

distinctive *adj* easily recognizable; characteristic
> **distinctively** *adv* > **distinctiveness** *n*

distinctive *adj* = characteristic, special, individual, unique, typical, peculiar, singular, idiosyncratic; ≠ ordinary

distinguish *vb* 1 to make, show, or recognize a difference: *I have tried to distinguish between fact and theory* 2 to be a distinctive feature of: *what distinguishes the good teenage reader from the less competent one?* 3 to make out by hearing, seeing, or tasting: *she listened but could distinguish nothing except the urgency of their discussion* 4 **distinguish oneself** to make oneself noteworthy
> **distinguishable** *adj* > **distinguishing** *adj*

distinguish *vb* 1 = differentiate, determine, separate, discriminate, decide, judge, ascertain, tell the difference 2 = characterize, mark, separate, single out, set apart 3 = make out, recognize, perceive, know, see, tell, pick out, discern

distinguished *adj* 1 dignified in appearance or behaviour 2 highly respected: *a distinguished historian*

distinguished *adj* 2 = eminent, noted, famous, celebrated, well-known, prominent, esteemed, acclaimed; ≠ unknown

distort *vb* 1 to alter or misrepresent (facts) 2 to twist out of shape; deform 3 *electronics* to reproduce or amplify (a signal) inaccurately
> **distorted** *adj* > **distortion** *n*

distort *vb* 1 = misrepresent, twist, bias, disguise, pervert, slant, colour, misinterpret 2 = deform, bend, twist, warp, buckle, mangle, mangulate (*Austral slang*), disfigure, contort

distract *vb* 1 to draw (a person or his or her attention) away from something 2 to amuse or entertain

distract *vb* 1 = divert, sidetrack, draw away, turn aside, lead astray, draw or lead away from 2 = amuse, occupy, entertain, beguile, engross

distracted *adj* unable to concentrate because one's mind is on other things

distracted *adj* = agitated, troubled, puzzled, at sea, perplexed, flustered, in a flap (*informal*)

distraction *n* 1 something that diverts the attention 2 something that serves as an entertainment 3 mental turmoil

distraction *n* 1 = disturbance, interference, diversion, interruption 2 = entertainment, recreation, amusement, diversion, pastime

distrait (diss-**tray**) *adj* absent-minded or abstracted

distraught (diss-**trawt**) *adj* upset or agitated

distraught *adj* = frantic, desperate, distressed, distracted, worked-up, agitated, overwrought, out of your mind

distress *n* 1 extreme unhappiness or worry 2 great physical pain 3 financial trouble 4 **in distress** in dire need of help ▸ *vb* 5 to upset badly > **distressing** *adj* > **distressingly** *adv*

distress n **1, 2** = suffering, pain, worry, grief, misery, torment, sorrow, heartache **3** = need, trouble, difficulties, poverty, hard times, hardship, misfortune, adversity ▸ vb = upset, worry, trouble, disturb, grieve, torment, harass, agitate

distressed adj **1** much troubled; upset **2** in great physical pain **3** in financial difficulties **4** (of furniture or fabric) having signs of ageing artificially applied

distressed adj **1** = upset, worried, troubled, distracted, tormented, distraught, agitated, wretched **3** = poverty-stricken, poor, impoverished, needy, destitute, indigent (formal), down at heel, straitened

distribute vb **-uting, -uted 1** to hand out or deliver (leaflets, mail, etc.) **2** to share (something) among the members of a particular group

distribute vb **1** = hand out, pass round **2** = share, deal, allocate, dispense, allot, dole out, apportion

distribution n **1** the delivering of leaflets, mail, etc. to individual people or organizations **2** the sharing out of something among a particular group **3** the arrangement or spread of anything over an area, space, or period of time: the unequal distribution of wealth **4** commerce the process of satisfying the demand for goods and services

distribution n **1** = delivery, mailing, transportation, handling **2** = sharing, division, assignment, rationing, allocation, allotment, apportionment **3** = spread, organization, arrangement, placement

distributive adj **1** of or relating to distribution **2** maths of the rule that the same result is produced when multiplication is performed on a set of numbers as when performed on the members of the set individually

distributor n **1** a wholesaler who distributes goods to retailers in a specific area **2** the device in a petrol engine that sends the electric current to the sparking plugs

district n **1** an area of land regarded as an administrative or geographical unit **2** an area which has recognizable or special features: an upper-class residential district

district n = area, region, sector, quarter, parish, neighbourhood, vicinity, locality

district court judge n Austral & NZ a judge presiding over a lower court

distrust vb **1** to regard as untrustworthy ▸ n **2** a feeling of suspicion or doubt ▸ **distrustful** adj

distrust vb = suspect, doubt, be wary of, mistrust, disbelieve, be suspicious of; ≠ trust ▸ n = suspicion, question, doubt, disbelief, scepticism, mistrust, misgiving, wariness; ≠ trust

disturb vb **1** to intrude on; interrupt **2** to upset or worry **3** to disarrange; muddle **4** to inconvenience ▸ **disturbing** adj ▸ **disturbingly** adv

disturb vb **1, 4** = interrupt, trouble, bother, plague, disrupt, interfere with, hassle, inconvenience **2** = upset, concern, worry, trouble, alarm, distress, unsettle, unnerve; ≠ calm **3** = muddle, disorder, mix up, mess up, jumble up, disarrange, muss (US, Canad)

disturbance n **1** an interruption or intrusion **2** an unruly outburst in public

disturbance n **1** = upset, bother, distraction, intrusion, interruption, annoyance **2** = disorder, fray, brawl, fracas, commotion, rumpus

disturbed adj psychiatry emotionally upset, troubled, or maladjusted

disturbed adj = unbalanced, troubled, disordered, unstable, neurotic, upset, deranged, maladjusted; ≠ balanced

disunite vb **-niting, -nited** to cause disagreement among ▸ **disunion** n ▸ **disunity** n

disuse n the state of being neglected or no longer used; neglect

disused adj no longer used

ditch n **1** a narrow channel dug in the earth for drainage or irrigation ▸ vb **2** slang to abandon or discard: she ditched her boyfriend last month

ditch n = channel, drain, trench, dyke, furrow, gully, moat, watercourse ▸ vb = get rid of, dump (informal), scrap, discard, dispose of, dispense with, jettison, throw out or overboard

dither vb **1** chiefly Brit & NZ to be uncertain or indecisive ▸ n **2** chiefly Brit a state of indecision or agitation ▸ **ditherer** n ▸ **dithery** adj

ditto n, pl **-tos 1** the above; the same: used in lists to avoid repetition, and represented by the mark (") placed under the thing repeated ▸ adv **2** in the same way

ditty n, pl **-ties** a short simple song or poem

diuretic (die-yoor-et-ik) n a drug that increases the flow of urine

diurnal (die-urn-al) adj **1** happening during the day or daily **2** (of animals) active during the day

diva n, pl **-vas** or **-ve** a distinguished female singer; prima donna

divan n **A** a low bed with a thick base under the mattress **B** a couch with no back or arms

dive vb **diving, dived** or US **dove, dived 1** to plunge headfirst into water **2** (of a submarine or diver) to submerge under water **3** (of a bird or aircraft) to fly in a steep nose-down descending path **4** to move quickly in a specified direction: he dived for the door **5** dive in or into **A** to put (one's hand) quickly and forcefully into **B** to start doing (something) enthusiastically ▸ n **6** a headlong plunge into water **7** the act of diving **8** a steep

d

nose-down descent of a bird or aircraft **9** *slang* a disreputable bar or club

> **dive** *vb* **1** = plunge, drop, duck, dip, descend, plummet **2** = go underwater **3** = nose-dive, plunge, crash, swoop, plummet ▸ *n* **6** = plunge, spring, jump, leap, lunge, nose dive

dive bomber *n* a military aircraft designed to release bombs on a target during a dive
> **dive-bomb** *vb*

diver *n* **1** a person who works or explores underwater **2** a person who dives for sport **3** a large diving bird of northern oceans with a straight pointed bill and webbed feet

diverge *vb* **-verging, -verged** **1** to separate and go in different directions **2** to be at variance; differ: *the two books diverge in setting and in style* **3** to deviate (from a prescribed course)
> **divergence** *n* > **divergent** *adj*

diverse *adj* **1** having variety; assorted **2** different in kind

> **diverse** *adj* **1** = various, mixed, varied, assorted, miscellaneous, several, sundry, motley **2** = different, unlike, varying, separate, distinct, disparate, discrete, dissimilar

diversify *vb* **-fies, -fying, -fied** **1** to create different forms of; vary **2** (of an enterprise) to vary (products or operations) in order to expand or reduce the risk of loss > **diversification** *n*

> **diversify** *vb* **1** = vary, change, expand, spread out, branch out

diversion *n* **1** *chiefly Brit* an official detour used by traffic when a main route is closed **2** something that distracts someone's attention or concentration **3** the act of diverting from a specified course **4** a pleasant or amusing pastime or activity > **diversionary** *adj*

> **diversion** *n* **1** = detour, roundabout way, indirect course **2** = distraction, deviation, digression **3** = deviation, departure, straying, divergence, digression **4** = pastime, game, sport, entertainment, hobby, relaxation, recreation, distraction

diversity *n* **1** the quality of being different or varied **2** a point of difference

> **diversity** *n* **1** = difference, multiplicity, heterogeneity, diverseness

divert *vb* **1** to change the course or direction of (traffic) **2** to distract the attention of **3** to entertain or amuse

> **divert** *vb* **1** = redirect, switch, avert, deflect, deviate, turn aside **2** = distract, sidetrack, lead astray, draw *or* lead away from **3** = entertain, delight, amuse, please, charm, gratify, beguile, regale

divest *vb* **1** to strip (of clothes) **2** to deprive of a role, function, or quality: *the CEO felt duty-bound to stay with the company after it was divested of all its aviation interests*

divide *vb* **-viding, -vided** **1** to separate into parts **2** to share or be shared out in parts **3** to disagree or cause to disagree: *experts are divided over the plan* **4** to keep apart or be a boundary between **5** to categorize or classify **6** to calculate how many times one number can be contained in another ▸ *n* **7** a division or split **8** *chiefly US & Canad* an area of high ground separating drainage basins

> **divide** *vb* **1** = separate, split, segregate, bisect; ≠ join **2** = share, distribute, allocate, dispense, allot, mete, deal out **3** = split, break up, come between, estrange, cause to disagree

dividend *n* **1** a portion of a company's profits paid to its shareholders **2** an extra benefit: *Saudi progressives saw a dividend to the crisis* **3** *maths* a number to be divided by another number

> **dividend** *n* **1** = bonus, share, cut (*informal*), gain, extra, plus, portion, divvy (*informal*)

divider *n* a screen placed so as to divide a room into separate areas

divination *n* the art of discovering future events as though by supernatural powers

divine *adj* **1** of God or a god **2** godlike **3** *informal* splendid or perfect ▸ *n* **4** a priest who is learned in theology ▸ *vb* **-vining, -vined** **5** to discover (something) by intuition or guessing > **divinely** *adv* > **diviner** *n*

> **divine** *adj* **1** = heavenly, spiritual, holy, immortal, supernatural, celestial, angelic, superhuman **3** = wonderful, perfect, beautiful, excellent, lovely, glorious, marvellous, splendid ▸ *vb* = guess, suppose, perceive, discern, infer, deduce, apprehend, surmise

divining rod *n* a forked twig said to move when held over ground in which water or metal is to be found

divinity *n, pl* **-ties** **1** the study of religion **2** a god or goddess **3** the state of being divine

divisible *adj* capable of being divided
> **divisibility** *n*

division *n* **1** the separation of something into two or more distinct parts **2** the act of dividing or sharing out **3** one of the parts into which something is divided **4** the mathematical operation of dividing **5** a difference of opinion **6** a part of an organization that has been made into a unit for administrative or other reasons **7** a formal vote in Parliament **8** one of the groups of teams that make up a football or other sports league **9** *army* a major formation containing the necessary arms to sustain independent combat **10** *biol* one of the major groups into which the plant kingdom is divided, corresponding to a phylum > **divisional** *adj*

division *n* **1** = separation, dividing, splitting up, partition, cutting up **2** = sharing, distribution, assignment, rationing, allocation, allotment, apportionment **3** = part, bit, piece, section, class, category, fraction **5** = disagreement, split, rift, rupture, abyss, chasm, variance, discord; ≠ unity **6** = department, group, branch

divisive (div-**vice**-iv) *adj* tending to cause disagreement: *she played an important role in defusing potentially divisive issues*

divisor *n* a number to be divided into another number

divorce *n* **1** the legal ending of a marriage **2** a separation, esp. one that is permanent ▸ *vb* **-vorcing, -vorced 3** to separate or be separated by divorce **4** to remove or separate

divorce *n* **1** = separation, split, break-up, parting, split-up, rift, dissolution, annulment ▸ *vb* **3** = split up, separate, part company, dissolve your marriage

divorcee *or masc* **divorcé** *n* a person who is divorced

divulge *vb* **-vulging, -vulged** to make known: *I am not permitted to divulge his name* > **divulgence** *n*

Dixie *n* the southern states of the US. Also called: **Dixieland**

DIY *or* **d.i.y.** *Brit, Austral & NZ* do-it-yourself

dizzy *adj* **-zier, -ziest 1** feeling giddy **2** unable to think clearly; confused **3** tending to cause giddiness or confusion ▸ *vb* **-zies, -zying, -zied 4** to cause to feel giddy or confused > **dizzily** *adv* > **dizziness** *n*

dizzy *adj* **1** = giddy, faint, light-headed, swimming, reeling, shaky, wobbly, off balance **2** = confused, dazzled, at sea, bewildered, muddled, bemused, dazed, disorientated

DJ *or* **dj 1** disc jockey **2** *Brit* dinner jacket

DM direct message

DNA deoxyribonucleic acid, the main constituent of the chromosomes of all organisms

do *vb* **does, doing, did, done 1** to perform or complete (a deed or action): *we do a fair amount of entertaining* **2** to be adequate: *it's not what I wanted but it will have to do* **3** to provide: *this hotel only does bed and breakfast* **4** to make tidy or elegant: *he watched her do her hair* **5** to improve: *that style does nothing for you* **6** to find an answer to (a problem or puzzle) **7** to conduct oneself: *do as you want* **8** to cause or produce: *herbal teas have active ingredients that can do good* **9** to give or grant: *do me a favour* **10** to work at as a course of study or a job **11** to mimic **12** to achieve a particular speed, amount, or rate: *this computer system can do 40 different cross checks; this car will do 120 mph* **13** **A** used to form questions: *do you like it?* **B** used to intensify positive statements and commands: *tensions do exist* **C** used to form negative

statements or commands: *do not talk while I'm talking!* **D** used to replace an earlier verb: *she exercises much more than I do* **14** *informal* to visit (a place) as a tourist: *we plan to do the States this year* **15** *slang* to serve (a period of time) as a prison sentence **16** *informal* to cheat or rob: *I was done out of ten pounds* **17** *slang* **A** to arrest **B** to convict of a crime: *he was done for burglary* **18** *slang, chiefly Brit* to assault **19** *slang* to take or use (drugs) **20** **make do** to manage with whatever is available ▸ *n, pl* **dos** *or* **do's 21** *informal, chiefly Brit & NZ* a party or other social event **22** **do's and don'ts** *informal* rules ▸ See also **do away with**

do *vb* **1, 3, 5** = perform, achieve, carry out, complete, accomplish, execute, pull off **2** = be adequate, be sufficient, satisfy, suffice, pass muster, cut the mustard, meet requirements **6** = solve, work out, resolve, figure out, decode, decipher, puzzle out ▸ *n* **21** = party, gathering, function, event, affair, occasion, celebration, reception

do away with *vb* to get rid of (someone or something)

do away with *vb* = get rid of, remove, eliminate, abolish, discard, put an end to, dispense with, discontinue

Doberman pinscher *or* **Doberman** *n* a large dog with a glossy black-and-tan coat

dob in *vb* **dobbing, dobbed** *Austral & NZ informal* **1** to inform against **2** to contribute to a fund

DOC (in New Zealand) Department of Conservation

docile *adj* (of a person or animal) easily controlled > **docilely** *adv* > **docility** *n*

dock¹ *n* **1** an enclosed area of water where ships are loaded, unloaded, or repaired **2** a wharf or pier ▸ *vb* **3** to moor or be moored at a dock **4** to link (two spacecraft) or (of two spacecraft) to be linked together in space

dock *n* = port, haven, harbour, pier, wharf, quay, waterfront, anchorage ▸ *vb* **3** = moor, land, anchor, put in, tie up, berth, drop anchor **4** = link up, unite, join, couple, rendezvous, hook up

dock² *vb* **1** to deduct (an amount) from (a person's wages) **2** to remove part of (an animal's tail) by cutting through the bone

dock *vb* **1** = deduct, subtract **2** = cut off, crop, clip, shorten, curtail, cut short

dock³ *n* an enclosed space in a court of law where the accused person sits or stands

dock⁴ *n* a weed with broad leaves

docker *n Brit* a person employed to load and unload ships

docket *chiefly Brit* ▸ *n* **1** a label on a package or other delivery, stating contents, delivery instructions, etc. ▸ *vb* **-eting, -eted 2** to fix a docket to (a package or other delivery)

dockyard *n* a place where ships are built or repaired

doctor *n* **1** a person licensed to practise medicine **2** a person who has been awarded a doctorate **3** *chiefly US & Canad* a person licensed to practise dentistry or veterinary medicine ▸ *vb* **4** to change in order to deceive: *she confessed to having doctored the figures* **5** to poison or drug (food or drink) **6** to castrate (an animal) ▹ **doctoral** *adj*

> **doctor** *n* **1** = physician, medic (*informal*), general practitioner, medical practitioner, G.P. ▸ *vb* **4** = change, alter, interfere with, disguise, pervert, tamper with, tinker with, misrepresent **5** = add to, spike, cut, mix something with something, dilute, water down, adulterate

doctorate *n* the highest academic degree in any field of knowledge

doctrinaire *adj* stubbornly insistent on the application of a theory without regard to practicality

doctrine (**dock-trin**) *n* **1** a body of teachings of a religious, political, or philosophical group **2** a principle or body of principles that is taught or advocated ▹ **doctrinal** *adj*

> **doctrine** *n* = teaching, principle, belief, opinion, conviction, creed, dogma, tenet, kaupapa (*NZ*)

document *n* **1** a piece of paper that provides an official record of something **2** an item of text or graphics that is stored as a file on a computer ▸ *vb* **3** to record or report (something) in detail **4** to support (a claim) with evidence

> **document** *n* **1** = paper, form, certificate, report, record, testimonial, authorization ▸ *vb* = support, certify, verify, detail, validate, substantiate, corroborate, authenticate

documentary *n*, *pl* **-ries 1** a film or television programme presenting the facts about a particular subject ▸ *adj* **2** of or based on documents: *vital documentary evidence has been found*

documentation *n* documents supplied as proof or evidence of something

docu-soap *n* a television documentary series presenting the lives of the people filmed as entertainment

dodder *vb* to move unsteadily ▹ **dodderer** *n* ▹ **doddery** *adj*

dodecagon (**doe-deck-a-gon**) *n* a polygon with twelve sides

dodecahedron (**doe-deck-a-heed-ron**) *n* a solid figure with twelve plane faces

dodge *vb* **dodging**, **dodged 1** to avoid being hit, caught, or seen by moving suddenly **2** to evade by cleverness or trickery: *the Government will not be able to dodge the issue* ▸ *n* **3** a cunning and deceitful trick

> **dodge** *vb* **1** = duck (*informal*), dart, swerve, sidestep, shoot, turn aside **2** = evade, avoid, escape, get away from, elude ▸ *n* = trick, scheme, ploy, trap, device, fraud, manoeuvre, deception, fastie (*Austral slang*)

Dodgem *n* trademark a small electric car driven and bumped against similar cars in a rink at a funfair

dodger *n* a person who evades a duty or obligation

dodgy *adj* **dodgier**, **dodgiest** *Brit*, *Austral & NZ informal* **1** dangerous, risky, or unreliable: *he's in a very dodgy political position* **2** untrustworthy: *they considered him a very dodgy character*

> **dodgy** *adj* **1** = risky, difficult, tricky, dangerous, delicate, uncertain, dicey (*informal, chiefly Brit*), chancy (*informal*), shonky (*Austral, NZ informal*)

dodo *n*, *pl* **dodos** *or* **dodoes 1** a large extinct bird that could not fly **2 as dead as a dodo** no longer existing

doe *n*, *pl* **does** *or* **doe** the female of the deer, hare, or rabbit

does *vb* third person singular of the present tense of **do**

doesn't does not

doff *vb* to take off or lift (one's hat) in salutation

dog *n* **1** a domesticated canine mammal occurring in many different breeds **2** any other member of the dog family, such as the dingo or coyote. Related adjective: **canine 3** the male of animals of the dog family **4** *informal* a person: *you lucky dog!* **5** *US & Canad informal* something unsatisfactory or inferior **6 a dog's life** a wretched existence **7 dog eat dog** ruthless competition **8 like a dog's dinner** dressed smartly and ostentatiously ▸ *vb* **dogging**, **dogged 9** to follow (someone) closely **10** to trouble: *dogged by ill health*

> **dog** *n* **1** = hound, canine, pooch (*slang*), cur, man's best friend, kuri *or* goorie (*NZ*), brak (*S African*) ▸ *vb* **9** = pursue, follow, track, chase, trail, hound, stalk **10** = plague, follow, trouble, haunt, hound, torment

dogcart *n* a light horse-drawn two-wheeled cart

dog collar *n* **1** a collar for a dog **2** *informal* a clerical collar

doge (**doje**) *n* (formerly) the chief magistrate of Venice or Genoa

dog-eared *adj* **1** (of a book) having pages folded down at the corner **2** shabby or worn

dogfight *n* **1** close-quarters combat between fighter aircraft **2** any rough fight

dogfish *n*, *pl* **-fish** *or* **-fishes** a small shark

dogged (**dog-gid**) *adj* obstinately determined ▹ **doggedly** *adv* ▹ **doggedness** *n*

> **dogged** *adj* = determined, persistent, stubborn, resolute, tenacious, steadfast, obstinate, indefatigable; ≠ irresolute

doggerel *n* poorly written, usually comic, verse

doggo *adv* **lie doggo** *informal* to hide and keep quiet

doggy *or* **doggie** *n, pl* **-gies** **1** a child's word for a **dog** ▸ *adj* **-gier, -giest** **2** of or like a dog **3** fond of dogs: *I suppose dogs are all right but doggy folk can be real bores*

doghouse *n* **1** *US & Canad* a kennel **2 in the doghouse** *informal* in disfavour

dogleg *n* a sharp bend

dogma *n* a doctrine or system of doctrines proclaimed by authority as true

dogmatic *adj* habitually stating one's opinions in a forceful or arrogant manner ▸ **dogmatically** *adv* ▸ **dogmatism** *n*

dogsbody *n, pl* **-bodies** *informal* a person who carries out boring or unimportant tasks for others

dog-tired *adj informal* exhausted

doh *or* **do** *n music* (in tonic sol-fa) the first note of any ascending major scale

doily *or* **doyley** *n, pl* **-lies** *or* **-leys** a decorative lacelike paper mat laid on a plate

do-it-yourself *n* the practice of constructing and repairing things oneself

doldrums *n* **the doldrums** **1 A** a feeling of depression **B** a state of inactivity **2** a belt of sea along the equator noted for absence of winds

dole *n* **1 the dole** *Brit, Austral & NZ informal* money received from the state while unemployed **2 on the dole** *Brit, Austral & NZ informal* receiving benefit while unemployed ▸ *vb* **doling, doled** **3 dole out** to distribute in small quantities

> **dole** *vb* **dole something out** = give out, distribute, assign, allocate, hand out, dispense, allot, apportion

doleful *adj* dreary or mournful ▸ **dolefully** *adv* ▸ **dolefulness** *n*

doll *n* **1** a small model of a human being, used as a toy **2** *slang* a pretty girl or young woman

dollar *n* the standard monetary unit of various countries

dollop *n informal* an amount of food served in a lump: *he shook the bottle and added a large dollop of ketchup*

dolly *n, pl* **-lies** **1** a child's word for a **doll** (sense 1) **2** *films & television* a wheeled support on which a camera may be mounted **3** Also called: **dolly bird** *old-fashioned slang, chiefly Brit* an attractive and fashionable girl

dolman sleeve *n* a sleeve that is very wide at the armhole and tapers to a tight wrist

dolmen *n* a prehistoric monument consisting of a horizontal stone supported by vertical stones, thought to be a tomb

dolomite *n* a mineral consisting of calcium magnesium carbonate

dolorous *adj* sad, mournful

dolphin *n* a sea mammal of the whale family, with a long pointed snout

dolt *n* a stupid person ▸ **doltish** *adj*

domain *n* **1** a particular area of activity or interest **2** land under one ruler or government **3** a group of computers that have the same suffix in their names on the internet, specifying the country, type of institution, etc. where they are located **4** *NZ* a public park

dome *n* **1** a rounded roof built on a circular base **2** something shaped like this

domed *adj* shaped like a dome

domestic *adj* **1** of one's own country or a specific country: *the domestic economy was generally better* **2** of the home or family **3** enjoying home or family life: *she was never a very domestic sort of person* **4** intended for use in the home: *the kitchen was equipped with all the latest domestic appliances* **5** (of an animal) bred or kept as a pet or for the supply of food ▸ *n* **6** a household servant ▸ **domestically** *adv*

> **domestic** *adj* **1** = home, internal, native, indigenous **2** = household, home, family, private **3** = home-loving, homely, stay-at-home, domesticated **5** = domesticated, trained, tame, pet, house-trained ▸ *n* = servant, help, maid, daily, char (*informal*), charwoman

domesticate *vb* **-cating, -cated** **1** to bring or keep (wild animals or plants) under control or cultivation **2** to accustom (someone) to home life ▸ **domestication** *n*

domesticity *n, pl* **-ties** **1** home life **2** devotion to home life

domestic science *n* the study of cooking, needlework, and other household skills

domicile (dom-miss-ile) *n* **1** *formal* a person's regular dwelling place **2** *law* the country in which a person has his or her permanent legal residence ▸ **domiciliary** *adj*

dominant *adj* **1** having control, authority, or influence: *a dominant leader* **2** main or chief: *coal is still, worldwide, the dominant fuel* **3** *genetics* (in a pair of genes) designating the gene that produces a particular character in an organism ▸ **dominance** *n*

> **dominant** *adj* **1** = controlling, ruling, commanding, supreme, governing, superior, authoritative **2** = main, chief, primary, principal, prominent, predominant, pre-eminent; ≠ minor

dominate *vb* **-nating, -nated** **1** to control or govern **2** to tower above (surroundings): *the building had been designed to dominate the city skyscape* **3** to predominate in ▸ **dominating** *adj* ▸ **domination** *n*

> **dominate** *vb* **1** = control, rule, direct, govern, monopolize, tyrannize, have the whip hand over **2** = tower above, overlook, survey, stand over, loom over, stand head and shoulders above

domineering *adj* acting arrogantly or tyrannically

Dominican *n* **1** a friar or nun of the Christian order founded by Saint Dominic ▸ *adj* **2** of the Dominican order

dominion *n* **1** control or authority **2** the land governed by one ruler or government **3** (formerly) a self-governing division of the British Empire

domino *n, pl* **-noes** a small rectangular block marked with dots, used in dominoes

dominoes *n* a game in which dominoes with matching halves are laid together

don¹ *vb* **donning, donned** to put on (clothing)

> **don** *vb* = put on, get into, dress in, pull on, change into, get dressed in, clothe yourself in, slip on *or* into

don² *n* **1** *Brit* a member of the teaching staff at a university or college **2** a Spanish gentleman or nobleman **3** (in the Mafia) the head of a family

donate *vb* **-nating, -nated** to give (something) to a charity or other organization

> **donate** *vb* = give, present, contribute, grant, subscribe, endow, entrust, impart

donation *n* **1** the act of donating **2** a contribution to a charity or other organization

> **donation** *n* **2** = contribution, gift, subscription, offering, present, grant, hand-out, koha (NZ)

done *vb* **1** the past participle of **do** ▸ *interj* **2** an expression of agreement: *£60 seems reasonable, done!* ▸ *adj* **3** (of a task) completed **4** (of food) cooked enough **5** used up: *the milk is done* **6** *Brit, Austral & NZ* socially acceptable: *the done thing* **7** *informal* cheated or tricked **8** **done in** *or* **up** *informal* exhausted

doner kebab *n* a dish of grilled minced lamb, served in a split slice of unleavened bread

dongle *n computers* a plug-in device that allows a computer user to access the internet via mobile broadband

donkey *n* **1** a long-eared member of the horse family **2** a person who is considered to be stupid or stubborn

donkey jacket *n Brit, Austral & NZ* a man's thick hip-length jacket with a waterproof panel across the shoulders

donkey's years *pl n informal* a long time

donkey-work *n* uninteresting groundwork

donnish *adj* resembling a university don; pedantic or fussy

donor *n* **1** *med* a person who gives blood or organs for use in the treatment of another person **2** a person who makes a donation

> **donor** *n* **2** = giver, contributor, benefactor, philanthropist, donator; ≠ recipient

don't do not

doodle *vb* **-dling, -dled 1** to scribble or draw aimlessly ▸ *n* **2** a shape or picture drawn aimlessly

doom *n* **1** death or a terrible fate ▸ *vb* **2** to destine or condemn to death or a terrible fate

> **doom** *n* = destruction, ruin, catastrophe, downfall ▸ *vb* = condemn, sentence, consign, destine

doomsday *or* **domesday** *n* **1** the day on which the Last Judgment will occur **2** any dreaded day

door *n* **1** a hinged or sliding panel for closing the entrance to a building, room, or cupboard **2** a doorway or entrance **3** a means of access or escape: *the door to happiness* **4** **lay something at someone's door** to blame someone for something **5** **out of doors** in the open air

> **door** *n* **2** = opening, entry, entrance, exit, doorway

doormat *n* **1** a mat, placed at an entrance, for wiping dirt from shoes **2** *informal* a person who offers little resistance to being treated badly

doorway *n* an opening into a building or room

dope *n* **1** *slang* an illegal drug, such as cannabis **2** a drug administered to a person or animal to affect performance in a race or other sporting competition **3** *informal* a slow-witted person **4** *informal* confidential information **5** a thick liquid, such as a lubricant ▸ *vb* **doping, doped 6** to administer a drug to

> **dope** *n* **1** = drugs, narcotics, opiates, dadah (*Austral slang*) **3** = idiot, fool, twit (*informal, chiefly Brit*), dunce, nitwit (*informal*), dumb-ass (*slang*), dorba *or* dorb (*Austral slang*), mampara (*S African informal*) ▸ *vb* = drug, knock out, sedate, stupefy, anaesthetize, narcotize

dopey *or* **dopy** *adj* **dopier, dopiest 1** *informal* half-asleep, as when under the influence of a drug **2** *slang* silly

dorba *n Austral informal* a stupid, inept, or clumsy person

dormant *adj* **1** temporarily quiet, inactive, or not being used **2** *biol* alive but in a resting condition > **dormancy** *n*

dormer *or* **dormer window** *n* a window that is built upright in a sloping roof

dormitory *n, pl* **-ries 1** a large room, esp. at a school, containing several beds **2** a building, esp. at a college, providing living accommodation ▸ *adj* **3** *Brit & Austral* denoting an area from which most of the residents commute to work: *the swelling suburban dormitory areas*

dormouse *n, pl* **-mice** a small rodent resembling a mouse with a furry tail

dorp *n S African* a small town or village

> **dorp** *n* = town, village, settlement, municipality, kainga *or* kaika (NZ)

dorsal *adj anatomy & zool* of or on the back

dory *n, pl* **-ries** a spiny-finned food fish. Also called: **John Dory**

dose *n* **1** a specific quantity of a medicine taken at one time **2** *informal* something unpleasant to experience: *a dose of the cold* **3** the total energy of radiation absorbed **4** *slang* a sexually transmitted infection ▸ *vb* **dosing, dosed 5** to administer a quantity of medicine to (someone) ▸ **dosage** *n*

> **dose** *n* **1** = measure, amount, allowance, portion, prescription, ration, draught, dosage

doss *slang* ▸ *vb* **1 doss down** to sleep on a makeshift bed **2** to pass time aimlessly: *I doss around a lot* ▸ *n* **3** a task requiring little effort

dosshouse *n slang* a cheap lodging house for homeless people

dossier (**doss**-ee-ay) *n* a collection of papers about a subject or person

dot *n* **1** a small round mark **2** the small round mark used to represent the short sound in Morse code **3 on the dot** at exactly the arranged time ▸ *vb* **dotting, dotted 4** to mark with a dot **5** to scatter or intersperse: *there are numerous churches dotted around Rome* **6 dot one's i's and cross one's t's** *informal* to pay meticulous attention to detail

> **dot** *n* **1** = spot, point, mark, fleck, jot, speck, speckle **3 on the dot** = on time, promptly, precisely, exactly (*informal*), to the minute, on the button (*informal*), punctually ▸ *vb* **5** = spot, stud, fleck, speckle

dotage *n* feebleness of mind as a result of old age

dotcom *or* **dot.com** *n* a company that conducts most of its business on the internet

dote *vb* **doting, doted** > **dote on** *or* **upon** to love (someone or something) to an excessive degree > **doting** *adj*

dotty *adj* **-tier, -tiest** *slang* slightly crazy > **dottiness** *n*

double *adj* **1** as much again in size, strength, number, etc.: *a double scotch* **2** composed of two equal or similar parts **3** designed for two users: *a double bed* **4** folded in half: *the blanket had been folded double* **5** stooping: *she was bent double over the flower bed* **6** ambiguous: *a double meaning* **7** false, deceitful, or hypocritical: *double standards* **8** *music* (of an instrument) sounding an octave lower: *a double bass* ▸ *adv* **9** twice over: *that's double the amount requested* ▸ *n* **10** twice the size, strength, number, etc. **11** a double measure of spirits **12** a person who closely resembles another person **13** a bet on two horses in different races in which any winnings from the first race are placed on the horse in the later race **14 at** *or* **on the double** quickly or immediately ▸ *vb* **-bling, -bled 15** to make or become twice as much **16** to bend or fold so that one part covers another **17** to play two parts or serve two roles **18** to turn sharply **19** *bridge* to make a call that will double certain scoring points if the preceding bid becomes the contract **20 double for** to act as substitute for > **doubler** *n*

double *adj* **2** = matching, coupled, paired, twin, duplicate, in pairs **6** = dual, enigmatic, twofold ▸ *n* **12** = twin, lookalike, spitting image, clone, replica, dead ringer (*slang*), Doppelgänger, duplicate **14 at or on the double** = at once, now, immediately, directly, quickly, promptly, straight away, right away ▸ *vb* **15** = multiply by two, duplicate, increase twofold, enlarge, magnify **16** = fold up *or* over

double agent *n* a spy employed by two enemy countries at the same time

double bass *n* a stringed instrument, the largest and lowest member of the violin family

double chin *n* a fold of fat under the chin

double cream *n Brit & Austral* thick cream with a high fat content

double-cross *vb* **1** to cheat or betray ▸ *n* **2** an instance of double-crossing

double-dealing *n* treacherous or deceitful behaviour

double-decker *n* **1** *chiefly Brit* a bus with two passenger decks one on top of the other ▸ *adj* **2** *informal* having two layers: *a double-decker sandwich*

double Dutch *n informal* speech or writing that is difficult to understand: *it was double Dutch to me*

double entendre (**doob-bl** on-**tond**-ra) *n* a word or phrase with two interpretations, esp. with one meaning that is rude

double glazing *n* a window consisting of two layers of glass separated by a space, fitted to reduce heat loss

doublet (**dub**-lit) *n history* a man's close-fitting jacket, with or without sleeves

double talk *n* deceptive or ambiguous talk

double whammy *n informal* a devastating setback made up of two elements

doubloon *n* a former Spanish gold coin

doubly *adv* **1** to or in a greater degree, quantity, or measure: *I have to be doubly careful* **2** in two ways: *the defence debate was doubly complicated*

doubt *n* **1** uncertainty about the truth, facts, or existence of something **2** an unresolved difficulty or point **3 give someone the benefit of the doubt** to accept that someone is speaking the truth **4 no doubt** almost certainly ▸ *vb* **5** to be inclined to disbelieve: *I doubt that we are late* **6** to distrust or be suspicious of: *he doubted their motives* > **doubter** *n*

> **doubt** *n* **1** = uncertainty, confusion, hesitation, suspense, indecision, hesitancy, lack of conviction, irresolution; ≠ certainty ▸ *vb* **6** = disbelieve, question, suspect, query, distrust, mistrust, lack confidence in; ≠ believe

doubtful *adj* **1** unlikely or improbable: *it's doubtful that I will marry again* **2** unsure or uncertain: *I was doubtful about some of his ideas* > **doubtfully** *adv* > **doubtfulness** *n*

doubtful *adj* **1** = unlikely, unclear, dubious, questionable, improbable, debatable, equivocal; ≠ certain **2** = unsure, uncertain, hesitant, suspicious, hesitating, sceptical, tentative, wavering; ≠ certain

doubtless *adv* probably or almost certainly: *somebody will know and doubtless somebody will ring us*

doubtless *adv* = probably, presumably, most likely

douche (doosh) *n* **1** a stream of water directed onto or into the body for cleansing or medical purposes **2** an instrument for applying a douche ▸ *vb* **douching**, **douched** **3** to cleanse or treat by means of a douche

dough *n* **1** a thick mixture of flour and water or milk, used for making bread, pastry, or biscuits **2** *slang* money

doughnut *n* a small cake of sweetened dough cooked in hot fat

doughty (dowt-ee) *adj* **-tier**, **-tiest** *old-fashioned* brave and determined

do up *vb* **1** to wrap and make into a bundle: *he did up the parcel* **2** to fasten: *to do up one's blouse* **3** to renovate or redecorate

dour (doo-er, dow-er) *adj* sullen and unfriendly ▹ **dourness** *n*

douse *or* **dowse** (rhymes with **mouse**) *vb* **dousing**, **doused** *or* **dowsing**, **dowsed** **1** to drench with water or other liquid **2** to put out (a light)

dove *n* **1** a bird with a heavy body, small head, and short legs **2** *politics* a person opposed to war

dovecote *or* **dovecot** *n* a box, shelter, or part of a house built for doves or pigeons to live in

dovetail *n* **1** Also called: **dovetail joint** a wedge-shaped joint used to fit two pieces of wood tightly together ▸ *vb* **2** to fit together closely or neatly: *her resignation dovetails well with the new structure*

dowager *n* a woman possessing property or a title obtained from her dead husband

dowdy *adj* **-dier**, **-diest** wearing dull and unfashionable clothes ▹ **dowdily** *adv* ▹ **dowdiness** *n*

dowel *n* a wooden or metal peg that fits into two corresponding holes to join larger pieces of wood or metal together

dower *n* **1** the life interest in a part of her husband's estate allotted to a widow by law **2** *archaic* a dowry

do with *vb* **1** **could do with** need or would benefit from: *I could do with some royal treatment* **2** **have to do with** to be associated with: *his illness has a lot to do with his failing the exam* **3** **to do with** concerning; related to: *this book has to do with the occult*

do without *vb* to manage without

do without *vb* **do without something or someone** = manage without, give up, dispense with, forgo, kick (*informal*), abstain from, get along without

down¹ *prep* **1** from a higher to a lower position in or on **2** at a lower or further level or position on, in, or along: *I wandered down the corridor* ▸ *adv* **3** at or to a lower level or position: *he bent down* **4** indicating lowering or destruction: *to bring down an aircraft* **5** indicating intensity or completion: *calm down and mind your manners* **6** immediately: *cash down* **7** on paper: *she copied it down* **8** away from a more important place: *she came down from head office* **9** reduced to a state of lack: *he was down to his last pound* **10** lacking a specified amount: *down several pounds* **11** lower in price **12** from an earlier to a later time: *the ring was handed down from my grandmother* **13** to a finer state: *to grind down* **14** *sport* being a specified number of points or goals behind an opponent **15** (of a person) being inactive, owing to illness: *down with the cold* ▸ *adj* **16** depressed or unhappy: *she seems very down today* ▸ *vb* **17** *informal* to eat or drink quickly **18** to fell (someone or something) ▸ *n* **19** **have a down on** *informal* to feel hostile towards: *you seem to have a down on the family tonight*

down *adj* = depressed, low, sad, unhappy, discouraged, miserable, fed up, dejected ▸ *vb* **17** = swallow, drink (down), drain, gulp (down), put away (*informal*), toss off

down² *n* soft fine feathers ▹ **downy** *adj*

down-and-out *n* **1** a person who is homeless and destitute ▸ *adj* **2** without any means of support; destitute

downbeat *adj informal* **1** depressed or gloomy: *she was in one of her downbeat moods* **2** casual and restrained: *the statement was decidedly downbeat* ▸ *n* **3** *music* the first beat of a bar

downcast *adj* **1** sad and dejected **2** (of the eyes) directed downwards

downfall *n* **1** a sudden loss of position or reputation **2** the cause of this

downfall *n* **1** = ruin, fall, destruction, collapse, disgrace, overthrow, undoing, comeuppance (*slang*)

downgrade *vb* **-grading**, **-graded** to reduce in importance or value

downgrade *vb* = demote, degrade, take down a peg (*informal*), lower *or* reduce in rank; ≠ promote

downhearted *adj* sad and discouraged

downhill *adj* **1** going or sloping down ▸ *adv* **2** towards the bottom of a hill **3** **go downhill** *informal* to deteriorate

download *vb* **1** to transfer (data) from the memory of one computer to that of another ▸ *n* **2** a file transferred in this way

downpour *n* a heavy continuous fall of rain

downright *adv* **1** extremely: *it's just downright cruel* ▸ *adj* **2** absolute; utter: *Crozier is a downright thief*

downright *adj* = complete, absolute, utter, total, plain, outright, unqualified, out-and-out

downs *pl n* an area of low grassy hills, esp. in S England

Down's syndrome *or esp US, Canad & Austral* **Down syndrome** *n pathol* a congenital condition characterized by learning difficulties and physical differences, such as shorter stature

downstairs *adv* **1** down the stairs; to or on a lower floor ▸ *n* **2** a lower or ground floor

down-to-earth *adj* sensible or practical

> **down-to-earth** *adj* = sensible, practical, realistic, matter-of-fact, sane, no-nonsense, unsentimental, plain-spoken, grounded

downtrodden *adj* oppressed and lacking the will to resist

down under *informal* ▸ *n* **1** Australia or New Zealand ▸ *adv* **2** in or to Australia or New Zealand

downward *adj* **1** descending from a higher to a lower level, condition, or position ▸ *adv* **2** same as **downwards** > **downwardly** *adv*

> **downward** *adj* = descending, declining, heading down, earthward

downwards *or* **downward** *adv* **1** from a higher to a lower level, condition, or position **2** from an earlier time or source to a later one

dowry *n, pl* **-ries** the property brought by a woman to her husband at marriage

dowse (rhymes with **cows**) *vb* **dowsing, dowsed** to search for underground water or minerals using a divining rod > **dowser** *n*

doxology *n, pl* **-gies** *Christianity* a hymn or verse of praise to God

doyen (doy-en) *or fem* **doyenne** (doy-en) *n* the senior member of a group, profession, or society

doze *vb* **dozing, dozed** **1** to sleep lightly or for a short period **2** **doze off** to fall into a light sleep ▸ *n* **3** a short sleep

dozen *adj, n* twelve > **dozenth** *adj*

dozy *adj* **dozier, doziest** **1** feeling sleepy **2** *Brit informal* stupid and slow-witted

DPB (in New Zealand) Domestic Purposes Benefit

DPP (in Britain) Director of Public Prosecutions

Dr **1** Doctor **2** Drive

drab *adj* **drabber, drabbest** **1** dull and dreary **2** light olive-brown > **drabness** *n*

drachm (dram) *n Brit* a unit of liquid measure equal to one eighth of a fluid ounce (3.55 ml)

drachma *n, pl* **-mas** *or* **-mae** a former monetary unit of Greece

draconian *adj* severe or harsh: *draconian measures were taken by the government*

draft *n* **1** a preliminary outline of a letter, book, or speech **2** a written order for payment of money by a bank **3** *US & Austral* selection for compulsory military service ▸ *vb* **4** to write a preliminary outline of a letter, book, or speech **5** to send (personnel) from one place to another to carry out a specific job **6** *chiefly US* to select for compulsory military service ▸ *n, vb* **7** *US* same as **draught**

draft *n* **1** = outline, plan, sketch, version, rough, abstract **2** = money order, bill (of exchange), cheque, postal order ▸ *vb* **4** = outline, write, plan, produce, create, design, draw, compose

drag *vb* **dragging, dragged** **1** to pull with force along the ground **2** to trail on the ground **3** to persuade (someone) to go somewhere: *he didn't want to come so I had to drag him along* **4** to move (oneself) slowly and with difficulty: *I had to drag myself out of bed this morning* **5** to linger behind: *she dragged along behind her mother* **6** to search (a river) with a dragnet or hook **7** to draw (on a cigarette) **8** *computers* to move (a graphics image) from one place to another on the screen by manipulating a mouse with its button held down **9** **drag away** *or* **from** to force (oneself) to come away from something interesting: *I was completely spellbound and couldn't drag myself away from the film* **10** **drag on** *or* **out** to last or be prolonged tediously: *winter dragged on* **11** **drag one's feet** *informal* to act with deliberate slowness ▸ *n* **12** a person or thing that slows up progress **13** *informal* a tedious or boring thing: *it was a drag having to walk two miles to the station every day* **14** *informal* a draw on a cigarette **15** an implement, such as a dragnet, used for dragging **16** *aeronautics* the resistance to the motion of a body passing through air **17** **in drag** (of a man) wearing women's clothes, usually as a form of entertainment

drag *vb* **1** = pull, draw, haul, trail, tow, tug, jerk, lug ▸ *n* **13** = nuisance, bore, bother, pest, hassle (*informal*), inconvenience, annoyance

dragnet *n* a net used to scour the bottom of a pond or river when searching for something

dragon *n* **1** a mythical monster that resembles a large fire-breathing lizard **2** *informal, derogatory* a fierce woman **3** **chase the dragon** *slang* to smoke opium or heroin

dragonfly *n, pl* **-flies** a brightly coloured insect with a long slender body and two pairs of wings

dragoon *n* **1** a heavily armed cavalryman ▸ *vb* **2** to coerce or force: *we were dragooned into participating*

drag race *n* a race in which specially built or modified cars or motorcycles are timed over a measured course > **drag racing** *n*

drain *n* **1** a pipe that carries off water or sewage **2** a cause of a continuous reduction in energy or resources: *the expansion will be a drain on resources* **3** a metal grid on a road or pavement through which rainwater flows **4** **down the drain** wasted ▸ *vb* **5** to draw off or remove (liquid) from **6** to flow (away) or filter (off) **7** to dry or be emptied as a result of liquid running off or flowing away **8** to drink the entire contents of (a glass or cup) **9** to make constant demands on (energy or resources); exhaust **10** (of a river) to carry off the surface water from (an area)

drain n 1 = sewer, channel, pipe, sink, ditch, trench, conduit, duct 2 = reduction, strain, drag, exhaustion, sapping, depletion ▸ vb 5 = remove, draw, empty, withdraw, tap, pump, bleed (informal) 6 = flow out, leak, trickle, ooze, seep, exude, well out, effuse 7 = empty 8 = drink up, swallow, finish, put away (informal), quaff, gulp down 9 = consume, exhaust, empty, use up, sap, dissipate

drainage n 1 a system of pipes, drains, or ditches used to drain water or other liquids 2 the process or a method of draining

drake n the male of a duck

dram n 1 a small amount of spirits, such as whisky 2 a unit of weight equal to one sixteenth of an ounce (avoirdupois)

drama n 1 a serious play for theatre, television, or radio 2 plays in general, as a form of literature 3 the art of writing, producing, or acting in a play 4 a situation that is exciting or highly emotional

drama n 1 = play, show, stage show, dramatization 2, 3 = theatre, acting, stagecraft, dramaturgy 4 = excitement, crisis, spectacle, turmoil, histrionics

dramatic adj 1 of or relating to drama 2 like a drama in suddenness or effectiveness: the government's plan has had a dramatic effect on employment in television 3 acting or performed in a flamboyant way: he spread his hands in a dramatic gesture of helplessness ▸ **dramatically** adv

dramatic adj 1 = theatrical, Thespian, dramaturgical 2 = exciting, thrilling, tense, sensational, breathtaking, electrifying, melodramatic, climactic; ≠ ordinary 3 = expressive

dramatist n a playwright: Austria's greatest living dramatist

dramatize or **-tise** vb -tizing, -tized or -tising, -tised 1 to rewrite (a book or story) in a form suitable for performing on stage 2 to express (something) in a dramatic or exaggerated way: he dramatizes his illness ▸ **dramatization** or **-tisation** n

drank vb the past tense of **drink**

drape vb draping, draped 1 to cover with material or fabric 2 to hang or arrange in folds 3 to place casually: he draped his arm across the back of the seat

drape vb 1 = cover, wrap, fold, swathe

draper n Brit a person who sells fabrics and sewing materials

drapery n, pl -peries 1 fabric or clothing arranged and draped 2 fabrics and cloth collectively

drastic adj strong and severe: the police are taking drastic measures against car thieves ▸ **drastically** adv

drastic adj = extreme, strong, radical, desperate, severe, harsh

draught or US **draft** n 1 a current of cold air, usually one coming into a room or vehicle 2 a portion of liquid to be drunk, esp. a dose of medicine 3 a gulp or swallow: she took a deep draught then a sip 4 one of the flat discs used in the game of draughts. US and Canad equivalent: **checker** 5 **feel the draught** to be short of money 6 **on draught** (of beer) drawn from a cask ▸ adj 7 (of an animal) used for pulling heavy loads: horses are specialized draught animals

draught or **draft** n 1 = breeze, current, movement, flow, puff, gust, current of air 3 = drink

draught beer n beer stored in a cask

draughtsman or US **draftsman** n, pl -men 1 a person employed to prepare detailed scale drawings of equipment, machinery, or buildings 2 a person skilled in drawing 3 Brit a flat disc used in the game of draughts. US and Canad equivalent: **checker** ▸ **draughtsmanship** n

draughty or US **drafty** adj draughtier, draughtiest or US draftier, draftiest exposed to draughts of air ▸ **draughtily** adv ▸ **draughtiness** n

draw vb drawing, drew, drawn 1 to sketch (a picture, pattern, or diagram) with a pen or pencil 2 to cause (a person or thing) to move closer or further away from a place by pulling 3 to bring, take, or pull (something) out of a container: he drew a gun and laid it on the table 4 to take (something) from a particular source: the inhabitants drew water from the well two miles away 5 to move in a specified direction: she drew alongside me 6 to attract: she drew enthusiastic audiences from all over the country 7 to formulate or decide: he drew similar conclusions 8 to cause to flow: the barman nodded and drew two pints 9 to choose or be given by lottery: Brazil have drawn Spain in the semi-final 10 (of two teams or contestants) to finish a game with an equal number of points 11 archery to bend (a bow) by pulling the string 12 to cause (pus) to discharge from an abscess or wound ▸ n 13 a raffle or lottery 14 informal a person, place, show, or event that attracts a large audience 15 a contest or game ending in a tie ▸ See also **drawback**

draw vb 1 = sketch, design, outline, trace, portray, paint, depict, mark out 2 = pull, drag, haul, tow, tug 4, 12 = extract, take, remove 6 = entice 7 = deduce, make, take, derive, infer ▸ n 14 = appeal, pull (informal), charm, attraction, lure, temptation, fascination, allure 15 = tie, deadlock, stalemate, impasse, dead heat

drawback n 1 a disadvantage or hindrance ▸ vb draw back 2 to move backwards: the girl drew back as though in pain 3 to turn aside from an undertaking: the prime minister drew back from his original intention

drawback n = disadvantage, difficulty, handicap, deficiency, flaw, hitch, snag, downside; ≠ advantage

drawbridge n a bridge that may be raised to prevent access or to enable vessels to pass

drawer n **1** a sliding box-shaped part of a piece of furniture used for storage **2** a person or thing that draws

drawing n **1** a picture or plan made by means of lines on a surface **2** the art of making drawings

drawing n **1** = picture, illustration, representation, cartoon, sketch, portrayal, depiction, study

drawing pin n Brit & NZ a short tack with a broad smooth head used for fastening papers to a drawing board or other surface

drawing room n a room where visitors are received and entertained

drawl vb **1** to speak slowly with long vowel sounds ▸ n **2** the way of speech of someone who drawls > **drawling** adj

drawn vb **1** the past participle of **draw** ▸ adj **2** haggard, tired, or tense in appearance

drawn adj = tense, worn, stressed, tired, pinched, haggard

draw out vb **1** (of a train) to leave a station **2** to encourage (someone) to talk freely: therapy groups will continue to draw her out **3** **draw out of** to find out (information) from

drawstring n a cord run through a hem around an opening, so that when it is pulled tighter, the opening closes

draw up vb **1** to prepare and write out: the signatories drew up a draft agreement **2** (of a vehicle) to come to a halt

dray n a low cart used for carrying heavy loads

dread vb **1** to anticipate with apprehension or terror ▸ n **2** great fear

dread vb = fear, shrink from, cringe at the thought of, quail from, shudder to think about, have cold feet about (informal), tremble to think about ▸ n = fear, alarm, horror, terror, dismay, fright, apprehension, trepidation (formal)

dreadful adj **1** extremely disagreeable or shocking **2** extreme: there were dreadful delays > **dreadfully** adv

dreadful adj **1** = terrible, shocking (informal), awful, appalling, horrible, fearful (informal), hideous, atrocious **2** = serious, terrible, awful, horrendous, monstrous, abysmal

dreadlocks pl n hair worn in the Rastafarian style of tightly curled strands

dream n **1** an imagined series of events experienced in the mind while asleep **2** a daydream: she escaped into dreams of the perfect job

3 a goal or aim: unity has been their constant dream **4** a wonderful person or thing: her house is a dream ▸ vb **dreaming**, **dreamed** or **dreamt 5** to experience (a dream) **6** to indulge in daydreams **7** to be unrealistic: you're dreaming if you think we can win **8** **dream of** to consider the possibility of: she would not dream of taking his advice **9** **dream of** or **about** to have an image of or fantasy about: they often dream about what life will be like for them on the outside ▸ adj **10** beautiful or pleasing: a dream kitchen > **dreamer** n

dream n **1** = vision, illusion, delusion, hallucination **2** = daydream **3** = ambition, wish, fantasy, desire, pipe dream **4** = delight, pleasure, joy, beauty, treasure, gem, marvel, pearler (Austral slang), beaut (Austral, NZ slang) ▸ vb **5** = have dreams, hallucinate **6** = daydream, stargaze, build castles in the air or in Spain **9 dream of something or someone** = daydream about, fantasize about

dreamy adj **dreamier**, **dreamiest 1** vague or impractical: she was wild-eyed and dreamy **2** relaxing or gentle: I felt this dreamy contentment **3** informal wonderful or impressive: he drives a dreamy Jaguar > **dreamily** adv > **dreaminess** n

dreary adj **drearier**, **dreariest** dull or uninteresting: there are long streets of dreary red houses spreading everywhere > **drearily** adv > **dreariness** n

dreary adj = dull, boring, tedious, drab, tiresome, monotonous, humdrum, uneventful; ≠ exciting

dredge¹ n **1** a machine used to scoop or suck up silt or mud from a river bed or harbour ▸ vb **dredging**, **dredged 2** to remove silt or mud from (a river bed or harbour) by means of a dredge > **dredger** n

dredge² vb **dredging**, **dredged** to sprinkle (food) with a substance, such as flour > **dredger** n

dregs pl n **1** solid particles that settle at the bottom of some liquids **2** **the dregs** the worst or most despised elements: the dregs of colonial society

drench vb **1** to make completely wet **2** to give medicine to (an animal) > **drenching** n, adj

drench vb **1** = soak, flood, wet, drown, steep, swamp, saturate, inundate

dress n **1** a one-piece garment consisting of a skirt and bodice and sometimes sleeves **2** complete style of clothing: contemporary dress ▸ adj **3** suitable for a formal occasion: he was wearing a dress shirt ▸ vb **4** to put clothes on **5** to put on formal clothes **6** to apply protective covering to (a wound) **7** to cover (a salad) with dressing **8** to prepare (meat, poultry, or fish) for selling or cooking by cleaning or gutting **9** to put a finish on (the surface of stone, metal, or other building material)

dress n **1** = frock, gown, robe **2** = clothing, clothes, costume, garments, apparel (old-fashioned), attire, garb, togs ▸ vb **4** = put on clothes, don clothes, slip on or into something; ≠ undress **6** = bandage, treat, plaster, bind up

dressage (dress-ahzh) n **A** the method of training horses to perform manoeuvres as a display of obedience **B** the manoeuvres performed

dress circle n the first gallery in a theatre

dresser[1] n **1** a piece of furniture with shelves and cupboards, used for storing or displaying dishes **2** US a chest of drawers

dresser[2] n **1** a person who dresses in a specified way: Lars was a meticulous, elegant dresser **2** theatre a person employed to assist performers with their costumes

dressing n **1** a sauce for food: salad dressing **2** US & Canad same as **stuffing** (sense 1) **3** a covering for a wound **4** manure or fertilizer spread on land **5** a gluey material used for stiffening paper, textiles, etc.

dressing-down n informal a severe reprimand

dressing gown n a loose-fitting garment worn over one's pyjamas or nightdress

dressing room n a room used for changing clothes and applying make-up, esp. a backstage room in a theatre

dressmaker n a person who makes clothes for women > **dressmaking** n

dress rehearsal n **1** the last rehearsal of a play, opera, or show using costumes, lighting, and other effects **2** any full-scale practice: astronauts are in the midst of a two-day dress rehearsal of their launch countdown

dressy adj **dressier**, **dressiest 1** (of clothes or occasions) elegant **2** (of people) dressing stylishly > **dressiness** n

drew vb the past tense of **draw**

drey or **dray** n Brit & Austral a squirrel's nest

dribble vb **-bling**, **-bled 1** to flow or allow to flow in a thin stream or drops **2** to allow saliva to trickle from the mouth **3** (in football, hockey, etc.) to propel (the ball) by kicking or tapping in quick succession ▸ n **4** a small quantity of liquid falling in drops or flowing in a thin stream **5** a small supply: there's only a dribble of milk left **6** an act or instance of dribbling > **dribbler** n

dribble vb **1** = run, drip, trickle, drop, leak, ooze, seep, fall in drops **2** = drool, drivel, slaver, slobber

dried vb the past of **dry**

drier[1] adj a comparative of **dry**

drier[2] n same as **dryer**

driest adj a superlative of **dry**

drift vb **1** to be carried along by currents of air or water **2** to move aimlessly from one place to another **3** to wander away from a fixed course or point **4** (of snow) to pile up in heaps ▸ n **5** something piled up by the wind or current, as a snowdrift **6** a general movement or development: there has been a drift away from family control **7** the main point of an argument or speech: I was beginning to get his drift **8** the extent to which a vessel or aircraft is driven off course by winds, etc. **9** a current of water created by the wind

drift vb **1** = float, go (aimlessly), bob, coast, slip, sail, slide, glide **2** = wander, stroll, stray, roam, meander, rove, range **3** = stray, wander, digress, get off the point **4** = pile up, gather, accumulate, amass, bank up ▸ n **5** = pile, bank, mass, heap, mound, accumulation **7** = meaning, point, gist, direction, import, intention, tendency, significance

drifter n **1** a person who moves aimlessly from place to place **2** a boat used for drift-net fishing

driftwood n wood floating on or washed ashore by the sea

drill[1] n **1** a machine or tool for boring holes **2** military training in procedures or movements, as for parades **3** strict and often repetitious training **4** informal correct procedure: he knows the drill as well as anybody ▸ vb **5** to bore a hole in (something) with or as if with a drill **6** to instruct or be instructed in military procedures or movements **7** to teach by rigorous exercises or training

drill n **1** = bit, borer, gimlet, boring tool **2, 3** = training, exercise, discipline, instruction, preparation, repetition **4** = practice ▸ vb **5** = bore, pierce, penetrate, sink in, puncture, perforate **6, 7** = train, coach, teach, exercise, discipline, practise, instruct, rehearse

drill[2] n **1** a machine for planting seeds in rows **2** a furrow in which seeds are sown **3** a row of seeds planted by means of a drill ▸ vb **4** to plant (seeds) by means of a drill

drill[3] n a hard-wearing cotton cloth, used for uniforms

drily or **dryly** adv in a dry manner

drink vb **drinking**, **drank**, **drunk 1** to swallow (a liquid) **2** to consume alcohol, esp. to excess **3** to bring (oneself) into a specified condition by consuming alcohol: he drank himself senseless every night **4 drink someone's health** to wish someone health or happiness with a toast **5 drink in** to pay close attention to: I drank in what the speaker said **6 drink to** to drink a toast to: I drank to their engagement ▸ n **7** liquid suitable for drinking **8** a portion of liquid for drinking **9** alcohol, or the habit of drinking too much of it > **drinkable** adj > **drinker** n

drink vb **1** = swallow, sip, suck, gulp, sup, guzzle, imbibe (formal), quaff **2** = booze (informal), tipple, tope, tope (literary), hit the bottle (informal) ▸ n **7** = beverage, refreshment, potion, liquid **8** = glass, cup, draught

9 = alcohol, booze (*informal*), liquor, spirits, the bottle (*informal*), hooch or hootch (*informal, chiefly US, Canad*)

drip *vb* **dripping**, **dripped 1** to fall or let fall in drops ▸ *n* **2** a drop of liquid **3** the falling of drops of liquid **4** the sound made by falling drops **5** *informal* a weak or foolish person **6** *med* a device that administers a liquid drop by drop into a vein

> **drip** *vb* = drop, splash, sprinkle, trickle, dribble, exude, plop ▸ *n* **2** = drop, bead, trickle, dribble, droplet, globule, pearl **5** = weakling, wet (*Brit informal*), weed (*informal*), softie (*informal*), mummy's boy (*informal*), namby-pamby

drip-dry *adj* **1** (of clothes or fabrics) designed to dry without creases if hung up when wet ▸ *vb* **-dries**, **-drying**, **-dried 2** to dry or become dry thus

dripping *n* the fat that comes from meat while it is being roasted

drive *vb* **driving**, **drove**, **driven 1** to guide the movement of (a vehicle) **2** to transport or be transported in a vehicle **3** to force into a specified state: *work drove him to despair* **4** to push or propel: *he drove the nail into the wall with a hammer* **5** *sport* to hit (a ball) very hard and straight **6** *golf* to strike (the ball) with a driver **7** to chase (game) from cover **8 drive home** to make (a point) clearly understood by emphasis ▸ *n* **9** a journey in a driven vehicle **10** a road for vehicles, esp. a private road leading to a house **11** a special effort made by a group of people for a particular purpose: *a charity drive* **12** energy, ambition, or initiative **13** *psychol* a motive or interest: *sex drive* **14** a sustained and powerful military offensive **15** the means by which power is transmitted in a machine **16** *sport* a hard straight shot or stroke

> **drive** *vb* **1** = operate, manage, direct, guide, handle, steer **2** = go (by car), ride (by car), motor, travel by car **3** = force, press, prompt, spur, prod, coerce, goad **4** = push, propel **7** = herd, urge, impel ▸ *n* **9** = run, ride, trip, journey, spin (*informal*), outing, excursion, jaunt **11** = campaign, push (*informal*), crusade, action, effort, appeal **12** = initiative, energy, enterprise, ambition, motivation, zip (*informal*), vigour, get-up-and-go (*informal*)

drive at *vb* to intend or mean: *he had no idea what she was driving at*

drive-in *n* **1** a cinema, restaurant, etc. offering a service where people remain in their cars while using the service provided ▸ *adj* **2** denoting a cinema, etc. of this kind

drivel *n* **1** foolish talk ▸ *vb* **-velling**, **-velled** or US **-veling**, **-veled 2** to speak foolishly **3** to allow (saliva) to flow from the mouth

driver *n* **1** a person who drives a vehicle **2** *golf* a long-shafted club with a large head and steep face, used for tee shots ▸ **driverless** *adj*

driveway *n* a path for vehicles connecting a building to a public road

drizzle *n* **1** very light rain ▸ *vb* **-zling**, **-zled 2** to rain lightly ▸ **drizzly** *adj*

droll *adj* quaintly amusing ▸ **drollery** *n* ▸ **drolly** *adv*

dromedary (drom-mid-er-ee) *n*, *pl* **-daries** a camel with a single hump

drone¹ *n* **1** a male honeybee **2** a person who lives off the work of others **3** a pilotless remote-controlled aircraft

drone² *vb* **droning**, **droned 1** to make a monotonous low dull sound **2 drone on** to talk in a monotonous tone without stopping ▸ *n* **3** a monotonous low dull sound **4** a single-reed pipe in a set of bagpipes

drongo *n*, *pl* **-gos** a tropical songbird with a glossy black plumage, a forked tail, and a stout bill

drool *vb* **1 drool over** to show excessive enthusiasm for or pleasure in **2** same as **drivel** (senses 2, 3)

droop *vb* **1** to sag, as from weakness or lack of support **2** to be overcome by weariness: *her eyelids drooped as if she were falling asleep* ▸ **drooping** *adj*

droopy *adj* **droopier**, **droopiest** hanging or sagging downwards: *a droopy moustache*

drop *vb* **dropping**, **dropped 1** to fall or allow (something) to fall vertically **2** to decrease in amount, strength, or value **3** to fall to the ground, as from exhaustion **4** to sink to a lower position, as on a scale **5** to mention casually: *she dropped a hint* **6** to set down (passengers or goods): *can you drop me at the hotel?* **7** *informal* to send: *drop me a letter* **8** to discontinue: *can we drop the subject?* **9** *informal* to be no longer friendly with: *I dropped him when I discovered his political views* **10** to leave out in speaking: *she has a tendency to drop her h's* **11** (of animals) to give birth to (offspring) **12** *sport* to omit (a player) from a team **13** to lose (a game or point) **14 drop back** to progress more slowly than other people going in the same direction **15 drop in** or **by** *informal* to pay someone a casual visit ▸ *n* **16** a small quantity of liquid forming a round shape **17** a small quantity of liquid **18** a small round sweet: *a lemon drop* **19** a decrease in amount, strength, or value **20** the vertical distance that anything may fall **21** the act of unloading troops or supplies by parachute ▸ See also **drop off**, **dropout**

> **drop** *vb* **1** = plunge, fall, tumble, descend, plummet **2** = fall, decline, diminish **3** = sink, fall, descend **4** = decline, fall, sink **8** = quit, give up, axe (*informal*), kick (*informal*), relinquish, discontinue ▸ *n* **16** = droplet, bead, globule, bubble, pearl, drip **17** = dash, shot (*informal*), spot, trace, sip, tot, trickle, mouthful **19** = decrease, fall, cut, lowering, decline, reduction, slump, fall-off **20** = fall, plunge, descent

d

droplet *n* a very small drop of liquid

drop off *vb* **1** to set down (passengers or goods) **2** to fall asleep **3** to decrease or decline: *sales dropped off during our period of transition*

> **drop off** *vb* **2** = fall asleep, nod (off), doze (off), snooze (*informal*), have forty winks (*informal*) **3** = decrease, lower, decline, shrink, diminish, dwindle, lessen, subside

dropout *n* **1** a person who rejects conventional society **2** a student who does not complete a course of study ▸ *vb* **drop out 3** to abandon or withdraw (from an institution or group)

> **dropout** *vb* **drop out** = leave, stop, give up, withdraw, quit, pull out, fall by the wayside

droppings *pl n* the dung of certain animals, such as rabbits or birds

dropsy *n* an illness in which watery fluid collects in the body > **dropsical** *adj*

dross *n* **1** the scum formed on the surfaces of molten metals **2** anything of inferior quality: *we can't publish this dross*

> **dross 2** = nonsense, garbage (*informal*), twaddle, rot, trash, hot air (*informal*), tripe (*informal*), claptrap (*informal*), bizzo (*Austral slang*), bull's wool (*Austral, NZ slang*)

drought (rhymes with **out**) *n* a prolonged period of time during which no rain falls

> **drought** *n* = water shortage, dryness, dry spell, aridity; ≠ flood

drove¹ *vb* the past tense of **drive**

drove² *n* **1** a herd of livestock being driven together **2** a moving crowd of people

> **drove** *n* = herd, company, crowds, collection, mob, flocks, swarm, horde

drover *n* a person who drives sheep or cattle

drown *vb* **1** to die or kill by immersion in liquid **2** to drench thoroughly **3** to make (a sound) impossible to hear by making a loud noise

> **drown** *vb* **1** = go down, go under **2** = drench, flood, soak, steep, swamp, saturate, engulf, submerge **3** = overwhelm, overcome, wipe out, overpower, obliterate, swallow up

drowse *vb* **drowsing, drowsed** to be sleepy, dull, or sluggish

drowsy *adj* **drowsier, drowsiest 1** feeling sleepy **2** peaceful and quiet: *row upon row of windows looked out over drowsy parkland* > **drowsily** *adv* > **drowsiness** *n*

drubbing *n* an utter defeat, as in a contest: *the Communists received a drubbing*

drudge *n* **1** a person who works hard at an uninteresting task ▸ *vb* **drudging, drudged 2** to work at such tasks

drudgery *n* uninteresting work that must be done

drug *n* **1** any substance used in the treatment, prevention, or diagnosis of disease **2** a chemical substance, such as a narcotic, taken for the effects it produces ▸ *vb* **drugging, drugged 3** to administer a drug to (a person or animal) in order to induce sleepiness or unconsciousness **4** to mix a drug with (food or drink): *who drugged my wine?*

> **drug** *n* **1** = medication, medicine, remedy, physic, medicament **2** = narcotic (*slang*), stimulant, opiate ▸ *vb* **3** = knock out, dope (*slang*), numb, deaden, stupefy, anaesthetize

drugstore *n US & Canad* a pharmacy where a wide variety of goods are available

Druid *n* a member of an ancient order of Celtic priests > **Druidic** *or* **Druidical** *adj*

drum *n* **1** a percussion instrument sounded by striking a skin stretched across the opening of a hollow cylinder **2** the sound produced by a drum **3** an object shaped like a drum: *an oil drum* **4** same as **eardrum** ▸ *vb* **drumming, drummed 5** to play (music) on a drum **6** to tap rhythmically or regularly: *he drummed his fingers on the desk* **7** to fix in someone's mind by constant repetition: *my father always drummed into us how privileged we were* ▸ See also **drum up** > **drummer** *n*

> **drum** *vb* **5, 6** = pound, beat, tap, rap, thrash, tattoo, throb, pulsate

drumstick *n* **1** a stick used for playing a drum **2** the lower joint of the leg of a cooked fowl

drum up *vb* to obtain (support or business) by making requests or canvassing

drunk *vb* **1** the past participle of **drink** ▸ *adj* **2** intoxicated with alcohol to the extent of losing control over normal functions **3** overwhelmed by strong influence or emotion: *they are drunk with joy at their unexpected victory* ▸ *n* **4** a person who is drunk or drinks habitually to excess

> **drunk** *adj* **2** = intoxicated, plastered (*slang*), drunken, merry (*Brit informal*), under the influence (*informal*), tipsy, legless (*informal*), inebriated, out to it (*Austral, NZ slang*), babalas (*S African*) ▸ *n* = drunkard, alcoholic, lush (*slang*), boozer (*informal*), wino (*informal*), inebriate

drunkard *n* a person who is frequently or habitually drunk

drunken *adj* **1** intoxicated with alcohol **2** habitually drunk **3** caused by or relating to alcoholic intoxication: *a drunken argument* > **drunkenly** *adv* > **drunkenness** *n*

dry *adj* **drier, driest** *or* **dryer, dryest 1** lacking moisture **2** having little or no rainfall **3** having the water drained away or evaporated: *a dry gully for the most part of the year* **4** not providing milk: *a dry cow* **5** (of the eyes) free from tears **6** *Brit, Austral & NZ informal* thirsty **7** eaten without butter or jam: *a dry cracker* **8** (of wine) not sweet **9** dull and uninteresting: *a dry subject* **10** (of humour) subtle and sarcastic **11** prohibiting the sale of alcoholic liquor: *a dry district* ▸ *vb* **dries, drying, dried** **12** to make or become dry **13** to preserve (food) by removing the moisture ▸ See also **dry out** ▹ **dryness** *n*

> **dry** *adj* **2** = dehydrated, dried-up, arid, parched, desiccated; ≠ wet **6** = thirsty, parched **9** = dull, boring, tedious, dreary, tiresome, monotonous, run-of-the-mill, humdrum; ≠ interesting **10** = sarcastic, cynical, low-key, sly, sardonic, deadpan, droll, ironical ▸ *vb* **12** = drain, make dry **13** = dehydrate, make dry, desiccate, sear, parch, dehumidify; ≠ wet

dryad *n*, *pl* **dryads** *or* **dryades** (dry-ad-deez) *Greek myth* a wood nymph
dry-clean *vb* to clean (clothes, etc.) with a solvent other than water ▹ **dry-cleaner** *n* ▹ **dry-cleaning** *n*
dryer *n* any device that removes moisture by heating or by hot air
dry out *vb* **1** Also: **dry up** to make or become dry **2** to undergo or cause to undergo treatment for alcoholism or drug addiction

> **dry out** *vb* **1 dry out or up** = become dry, harden, wither, shrivel up, wizen

dry rot *n* **1** crumbling and drying of timber, caused by certain fungi **2** a fungus causing this decay
dry run *n informal* a rehearsal
dry stock *n NZ* cattle raised for meat
dual *adj* having two parts, functions, or aspects: *dual controls*; *dual nationality* ▹ **duality** *n*

> **dual** *adj* = twofold, double, twin, matched, paired, duplicate, binary, duplex

dual carriageway *n Brit, Austral & NZ* a road with a central strip of grass or concrete to separate traffic travelling in opposite directions
dub¹ *vb* **dubbing, dubbed** to give (a person or place) a name or nickname: *he is dubbed a racist despite his strong denials*
dub² *vb* **dubbing, dubbed** **1** to provide (a film) with a new soundtrack in a different language **2** to provide (a film or tape) with a soundtrack ▸ *n* **3** *music* a style of reggae record production involving exaggeration of instrumental parts, echo, etc.
dubbin *n* a kind of thick grease applied to leather to soften it and make it waterproof
dubious (dew-bee-uss) *adj* **1** not entirely honest, safe, or reliable: *this allegation was at best dubious and at worst an outright fabrication* **2** unsure or undecided: *she felt dubious about the entire proposition* **3** of doubtful quality or worth: *she had the dubious honour of being taken for his mother* ▹ **dubiety** (dew-by-it-ee) *n* ▹ **dubiously** *adv*

> **dubious** *adj* **1, 3** = suspect, suspicious, crooked (*informal*), dodgy (*Brit, Austral, NZ informal*), questionable, unreliable, fishy (*informal*), disreputable; ≠ trustworthy **2** = unsure, uncertain, suspicious, hesitating, doubtful, sceptical, tentative, wavering; ≠ sure

ducal (duke-al) *adj* of a duke
ducat (duck-it) *n* a former European gold or silver coin
duchess *n* **1** a woman who holds the rank of duke **2** the wife or widow of a duke
duchy *n*, *pl* **duchies** the area of land owned or ruled by a duke or duchess
duck¹ *n*, *pl* **ducks** *or* **duck** **1** a water bird with short legs, webbed feet, and a broad blunt bill **2** the flesh of this bird used for food **3** the female of such a bird **4** *cricket* a score of nothing **5 like water off a duck's back** without effect: *I reprimanded him but it was like water off a duck's back*
duck² *vb* **1** to move (the head or body) quickly downwards, to escape being seen or avoid a blow **2** to plunge suddenly under water **3** *informal* to dodge (a duty or responsibility)

> **duck** *vb* **1** = bob, drop, lower, bend, bow, dodge, crouch, stoop **2** = dunk, wet, plunge, dip, submerge, immerse, douse, souse **3** = dodge, avoid, escape, evade, elude, sidestep, shirk

duck-billed platypus *n* See **platypus**
duckling *n* a young duck
duct *n* **1** a tube, pipe, or channel through which liquid or gas is sent **2** a tube in the body through which liquid such as tears or bile can pass
ductile *adj* (of a metal) able to be shaped into sheets or drawn out into threads ▹ **ductility** *n*
dud *informal* ▸ *n* **1** an ineffectual person or thing: *they had the foresight to pick on someone who was not a total dud* ▸ *adj* **2** bad or useless: *a dud cheque*
dude *n informal* **1** a man: *a fair-haired dude in his late twenties* **2** *chiefly US & Canad old-fashioned* a dandy **3** *Western US & Canad* a city dweller who spends his or her holiday on a ranch
dudgeon *n* **in high dudgeon** angry or resentful: *the scientist departed in high dudgeon*
due *adj* **1** expected to happen, be done, or arrive at a particular time: *he is due to return on Thursday* **2** immediately payable: *the balance is now due* **3** owed as a debt: *they finally agreed to pay her the money she was due* **4** fitting or proper: *he was found guilty of driving without due care and attention* **5 due to** happening or existing as a direct result of someone or something else: *the cause of death was chronic kidney failure due to diabetes* ▸ *n* **6** something that is owed or required **7 give someone his** or **her due** to acknowledge someone's good points: *I'll give him his due, he's resourceful* ▸ *adv* **8** directly or exactly: *due west*

due adj **1** = expected, scheduled **2, 3** = payable, outstanding, owed, owing, unpaid, in arrears **4** = fitting, deserved, appropriate, justified, suitable, merited, proper, rightful ▸ n **6** = right(s), privilege, deserts, merits, comeuppance (informal) ▸ adv = directly, dead, straight, exactly, undeviatingly

duel n **1** a formal fight between two people using guns, swords, or other weapons to settle a quarrel ▸ vb **duelling, duelled** or US **dueling, dueled 2** to fight in a duel > **duellist** or US **duelist** n

duel n = single combat, affair of honour ▸ vb = fight, struggle, clash, compete, contest, contend, vie with, lock horns

duet n a piece of music sung or played by two people > **duettist** n

duff adj **1** chiefly Brit informal broken or useless: my car had a duff clutch ▸ vb **2** golf informal to bungle (a shot) **3 duff up** Brit slang to beat (someone) severely

duff adj = bad, poor, useless, inferior, unsatisfactory, defective, imperfect, substandard, bodger or bodgie (Austral slang)

duffel or **duffle** n same as **duffel coat**
duffel bag n a cylinder-shaped canvas bag fastened with a drawstring
duffel coat n a wool coat usually with a hood and fastened with toggles
duffer n informal a dull or incompetent person
dug[1] vb the past of **dig**
dug[2] n a teat or udder of a female animal
dugite (doo-gyte) n a medium-sized Australian venomous snake
dugong n a whalelike mammal found in tropical waters
dugout n **1** a canoe made by hollowing out a log **2** Brit (at a sports ground) the covered bench where managers and substitutes sit **3** military a covered shelter dug in the ground to provide protection
duke n **1** a nobleman of the highest rank **2** the prince or ruler of a small principality or duchy > **dukedom** n
dulcet (dull-sit) adj (of a sound) soothing or pleasant: she smiled and, in dulcet tones, told me I would be next
dulcimer n a tuned percussion instrument consisting of a set of strings stretched over a sounding board and struck with hammers
dull adj **1** not interesting: the finished article would make dull reading **2** slow to learn or understand **3** (of an ache) not intense: I have a dull ache in the middle of my back **4** (of weather) not bright or clear **5** not lively or energetic: she appeared, looking dull and apathetic **6** (of colour) lacking brilliance **7** (of the blade of a knife) not sharp **8** (of a sound) not loud or clear: his head fell back to the carpet with a dull thud ▸ vb **9** to make or become dull > **dullness** n > **dully** adv

dull adj **1** = boring, tedious, dreary, flat, plain, monotonous, run-of-the-mill, humdrum; ≠ exciting **4** = cloudy, dim, gloomy, dismal, overcast, leaden; ≠ bright **5** = lifeless, indifferent, apathetic, listless, unresponsive, passionless; ≠ lively **7** = blunt, blunted, unsharpened; ≠ sharp

dullard n old-fashioned a dull or stupid person
duly adv **1** in a proper manner: my permit was duly stamped **2** at the proper time: the photographer duly arrived

duly adv **1** = properly, fittingly, correctly, appropriately, accordingly, suitably, deservedly, rightfully **2** = on time, promptly, punctually, at the proper time

dumb adj **1** offensive lacking the power to speak **2** lacking the power of human speech: the event was denounced as cruelty to dumb animals **3** temporarily unable to speak: I was struck dumb when I heard the news **4** done or performed without speech: I looked at her in dumb puzzlement **5** informal stupid or slow to understand ▸ See also **dumb down** > **dumbly** adv

dumb adj **1** = unable to speak, mute (old-fashioned, offensive); ≠ articulate **3, 4** = silent, mute, speechless, tongue-tied, wordless, voiceless, soundless, mum **5** = stupid, thick, dull, foolish, dense, unintelligent, asinine, dim-witted (informal); ≠ clever

dumbbell n **1** a short bar with a heavy ball or disc at either end, used for physical exercise **2** slang, chiefly US & Canad a stupid person
dumb down vb to make (something) less intellectually demanding or sophisticated: a move to dumb down its news coverage
dumbfounded adj speechless with amazement: she sat open-mouthed and dumbfounded
dumb show n meaningful gestures without speech
dumdum or **dumdum bullet** n a soft-nosed bullet that expands on impact and causes large and serious wounds
dummy n, pl **-mies 1** a large model that looks like a human being, used for displaying clothes in a shop, as a target, etc. **2** a copy of an object, often lacking some essential feature of the original **3** slang a stupid person **4** bridge **a** the hand exposed on the table by the declarer's partner and played by the declarer **b** the declarer's partner **5** a rubber teat for babies to suck ▸ adj **6** imitation or substitute: you can train them with dummy bombs and live ammunition

dummy n **1** = model, figure, mannequin, form, manikin **2** = imitation, copy, duplicate, sham, counterfeit, replica **3** = fool, idiot, dunce, nitwit (informal), blockhead, dumb-ass (slang), dorba or dorb (Austral slang), mampara (S African informal) ▸ adj = imitation, false, fake, artificial, mock, bogus, simulated, sham

dummy run *n* a practice or test carried out to test if any problems remain: *we'll do a dummy run on the file to see if the program works*

dump *vb* **1** to drop or let fall in a careless manner: *he dumped the books on the bed* **2** *informal* to abandon (someone or something) without proper care: *the unwanted babies were dumped in orphanages* **3** to dispose of (nuclear waste) **4** *commerce* to sell (goods) in bulk and at low prices, usually in another country, in order to keep prices high in the home market **5** *computers* to record (the contents of the memory) on a storage device at a series of points during a computer run ▸ *n* **6** a place where rubbish is left **7** *informal* a dirty, unattractive place: *you're hardly in this dump out of choice* **8** *military* a place where weapons or supplies are stored

> **dump** *vb* **1** = drop, deposit, throw down, let fall, fling down **2** = get rid of, tip, dispose of, unload, jettison, empty out, throw away *or* out ▸ *n* **6** = rubbish tip, tip (*Brit*), junkyard, rubbish heap, refuse heap **7** = pigsty, hole (*informal*), slum, hovel

dumpling *n* **1** a small ball of dough cooked and served with stew **2** a round pastry case filled with fruit: *an apple dumpling*

dumpy *adj* **dumpier**, **dumpiest** short and plump

dun *adj* brownish-grey

dunce *n Brit, Austral & NZ* a person who is stupid or slow to learn

dunderhead *n Brit, Austral & NZ* a slow-witted person

dune *n* a mound or ridge of drifted sand

dung *n* the faeces from large animals

dungarees *pl n* trousers with a bib attached

dungeon *n* a prison cell, often underground

dunk *vb* **1** to dip (a biscuit or piece of bread) in a drink or soup before eating it **2** to put (something) in liquid: *dunk the garment in the dye for 15 minutes* **3** *basketball* to drop (the ball) through the hoop after having leapt high enough to have the hands above the rim ▸ *n* **4** *basketball* a scoring shot in which one player drops the ball through the hoop after having leapt high enough to have the hands above the rim

dunny *n, pl* **-nies** *Austral & NZ informal* a toilet

> **dunny** *n* = toilet, lavatory, bathroom, loo (*Brit informal*), W.C., bog (*slang*), Gents *or* Ladies, can (*US, Canad slang*), bogger (*Austral slang*), brasco (*Austral slang*)

duo *n, pl* **duos 1** two singers or musicians who sing or play music together as a pair **2** *informal* two people who have something in common or do something together: *when they're together they make an impressive duo*

duodenum (dew-oh-**deen**-um) *n* the first part of the small intestine, just below the stomach > **duodenal** *adj*

dupe *vb* **duping**, **duped 1** to deceive or cheat: *you duped me into doing exactly what you wanted* ▸ *n* **2** a person who is easily deceived

duple *adj* **1** same as **double 2** *music* having two beats in a bar

duplex *n* **1** *US & Canad* **A** an apartment on two floors **B** *US & Austral* a semidetached house ▸ *adj* **2** having two parts

duplicate *adj* **1** copied exactly from an original: *he had a duplicate key to the front door* ▸ *n* **2** an exact copy **3** **in duplicate** in two exact copies: *submit the draft in duplicate, please* ▸ *vb* **-cating**, **-cated 4** to make an exact copy of **5** to do again (something that has already been done) > **duplication** *n* > **duplicator** *n*

> **duplicate** *adj* = identical, matched, matching, twin, corresponding, twofold ▸ *n* **2** = copy, facsimile ▸ *vb* **4** = copy **5** = repeat, reproduce, copy, clone, replicate

duplicity *n* deceitful behaviour: *he is a man of duplicity, who turns things to his advantage*

durable *adj* strong and long-lasting: *the car's body was made of a light but durable plastic* > **durability** *n*

> **durable** *adj* = hard-wearing, strong, tough, reliable, resistant, sturdy, long-lasting; ≠ fragile

durable goods *pl n* goods that do not require frequent replacement. Also called: **durables**

duration *n* the length of time that something lasts

> **duration** *n* = length, time, period, term, stretch, extent, spell, span, time frame, timeline

duress *n* physical or moral pressure used to force someone to do something: *confessions obtained under duress*

during *prep* throughout or within the limit of (a period of time)

dusk *n* the time just before nightfall when it is almost dark

> **dusk** *n* = twilight, evening, evo (*Austral slang*), nightfall, sunset, dark, sundown, eventide, gloaming (*Scot poetic*); ≠ dawn

dusky *adj* **duskier**, **duskiest 1** dark in colour: *her gold earrings gleamed against her dusky cheeks* **2** dim or shadowy: *the dusky room was crowded with absurd objects* > **duskily** *adv* > **duskiness** *n*

dust *n* **1** small dry particles of earth, sand, or dirt **2** **bite the dust** **A** to stop functioning: *my television has finally bitten the dust* **B** to fall down dead **3** **shake the dust off one's feet** to depart angrily **4** **throw dust in someone's eyes** to confuse or mislead someone ▸ *vb* **5** to remove dust from (furniture) by wiping **6** to sprinkle (something) with a powdery substance: *serve dusted with brown sugar and cinnamon*

> **dust** *n* **1** = grime, grit ▸ *vb* **6** = sprinkle, cover, powder, spread, spray, scatter, sift, dredge

dustbin *n* a large, usually cylindrical, container for household rubbish

dust bowl *n* a dry area in which the surface soil is exposed to wind erosion

duster *n* a cloth used for dusting

dust jacket *or* **dust cover** *n* a removable paper cover used to protect a book

dustman *n, pl* **-men** *Brit* a man whose job is to collect household rubbish

dustpan *n* a short-handled shovel into which dust is swept from floors

dusty *adj* **dustier**, **dustiest** **1** covered with dust **2** (of a colour) tinged with grey

> **dusty** *adj* **1** = dirty, grubby, unclean, unswept

Dutch *adj* **1** of the Netherlands ▸ *n* **2** the language of the Netherlands ▸ *pl n* **3** **the Dutch** the people of the Netherlands ▸ *adv* **4** **go Dutch** *informal* to share expenses equally, for example in a restaurant

Dutch courage *n* false courage gained from drinking alcohol

dutiable *adj* (of goods) requiring payment of duty

dutiful *adj* doing what is expected: *she is a responsible and dutiful mother* > **dutifully** *adv*

duty *n, pl* **-ties** **1** the work performed as part of one's job: *it is his duty to supervise the memorial services* **2** a obligation to fulfil one's responsibilities: *it's my duty as a doctor to keep it confidential* **3** a government tax on imports **4** **on** *or* **off duty** at (*or* not at) work

> **duty** *n* **1, 2** = responsibility, job, task, work, role, function, obligation, assignment **3** = tax, toll, levy, tariff, excise **4 on duty** = at work, busy, engaged, on active service

duvet (**doo**-vay) *n* a large quilt used as a bed cover in place of the top sheet and blankets

DVD Digital Versatile *or* Video Disk: a type of compact disc that can store large amounts of video and audio information

DVT deep-vein thrombosis

dwang *n NZ & S African* a short piece of wood inserted in a timber-framed wall

dwarf *vb* **1** to cause (someone or something) to seem small by being much larger ▸ *adj* **2** (of an animal or plant) much below the average size for the species: *a dwarf evergreen shrub* ▸ *n, pl* **dwarfs** *or* **dwarves** **3** a person who is smaller than average size as a result of a medical condition **4** (in folklore) a small ugly manlike creature, often possessing magical powers

> **dwarf** *vb* = tower above *or* over, dominate, overlook, stand over, loom over, stand head and shoulders above ▸ *adj* = miniature, small, baby, tiny, diminutive, bonsai, undersized ▸ *n* **4** = gnome, midget, Lilliputian, Tom Thumb, pygmy *or* pigmy

dwell *vb* **dwelling**, **dwelt** *or* **dwelled** *formal, literary* to live as a permanent resident > **dweller** *n*

> **dwell** *vb* = live, reside (*formal*), lodge, abide

dwelling *n formal, literary* a place of residence

> **dwelling** *n* = home, house, residence, abode, quarters, lodging, habitation, domicile, whare (NZ)

dwell on *or* **dwell upon** *vb* to think, speak, or write at length about (something)

dwindle *vb* **-dling**, **-dled** to grow less in size, strength, or number

> **dwindle** *vb* = lessen, decline, fade, shrink, diminish, decrease, wane, subside; ≠ increase

dye *n* **1** a colouring substance **2** the colour produced by dyeing ▸ *vb* **dyeing**, **dyed** **3** to colour (hair or fabric) by applying a dye > **dyer** *n*

> **dye** *n* **2** = colouring, colour, pigment, stain, tint, tinge, colorant ▸ *vb* = colour, stain, tint, tinge, pigment

dyed-in-the-wool *adj* having strong and unchanging attitudes or opinions: *he's a dyed-in-the-wool communist*

dying *vb* **1** the present participle of **die¹** ▸ *adj* **2** occurring at the moment of death: *in accordance with his dying wish* **3** (of a person or animal) very ill and likely to die soon **4** becoming less important or less current: *coal mining is a dying industry*

> **dying** *adj* **2** = final, last, parting, departing **3** = near death, moribund, in extremis (*Latin*), at death's door, not long for this world **4** = failing, declining, foundering, diminishing, decreasing, dwindling, subsiding

dyke¹ *or esp US* **dike** *n* **1** a wall built to prevent flooding **2** a ditch **3** *Scot* a dry-stone wall

dyke² *or* **dike** *n offensive slang* a lesbian

dynamic *adj* **1** (of a person) full of energy, ambition, or new ideas **2** relating to a force of society, history, or the mind that produces a change: *the government needs a more dynamic policy towards the environment* **3** *physics* relating to energy or forces that produce motion > **dynamically** *adv*

> **dynamic** *adj* **1, 2** = energetic, powerful, vital, go-ahead, lively, animated, high-powered, forceful; ≠ apathetic

dynamics *n* **1** the branch of mechanics concerned with the forces that change or produce the motions of bodies ▸ *pl n* **2** those forces that produce change in any field or system **3** *music* the various degrees of loudness called for in a performance

dynamism *n* great energy or enthusiasm

dynamite *n* **1** an explosive made of nitroglycerine **2** *informal* a dangerous or exciting person or thing: *she's still dynamite* ▸ *vb* **-miting**, **-mited** **3** to mine or blow (something) up with dynamite

dynamo *n, pl* **-mos** a device for converting mechanical energy into electricity

dynasty *n, pl* **-ties** 1 a series of rulers or influential people from the same family 2 a period of time during which a country is ruled by the same family > **dynastic** *adj*

> **dynasty** *n* = empire, house, rule, regime, sovereignty

dysentery *n* infection of the intestine which causes severe diarrhoea

dysfunction *n* 1 *med* any disturbance or abnormality in the function of an organ or part 2 (esp. of a family) failure to show the characteristics or fulfil the purposes accepted as normal or beneficial > **dysfunctional** *adj*

dyslexia *n* a developmental disorder that causes learning difficulty with reading, writing, and numeracy > **dyslexic** *adj, n*

dysmenorrhoea *or esp US* **dysmenorrhea** *n* painful or difficult menstruation

dyspepsia *n* indigestion > **dyspeptic** *adj, n*

dystrophy (diss-trof-fee) *n* See **muscular dystrophy**

Ee

E 1 *music* the third note of the scale of C major 2 East(ern) 3 English 4 *physics* **A** energy **B** electromotive force 5 *slang* the drug ecstasy or an ecstasy tablet

e- *prefix* electronic: *e-card; e-banking*

E- *prefix* used with a number following it to indicate that something, such as a food additive, conforms to an EU standard

each *adj* 1 every one of two or more people or things considered individually: *each year* ▸ *pron* 2 every one of two or more people or things: *each had been given one room to design* ▸ *adv* 3 for, to, or from each person or thing: *twenty pounds each* 4 **each other** (of two or more people) each one to or at the other or others; one another: *they stared at each other*

> **each** *adj* = every, every single ▸ *pron* = every one, all, each one, each and every one, one and all ▸ *adv* 3 = apiece, individually, for each, to each, respectively, per person, per head, per capita

eager *adj* very keen to have or do something > **eagerly** *adv* > **eagerness** *n*

> **eager** *adj* = anxious, keen, hungry, impatient, itching, thirsty; ≠ unenthusiastic

eagle *n* 1 a large bird of prey with broad wings and strong soaring flight 2 *golf* a score of two strokes under par for a hole

eaglet *n* a young eagle

ear¹ *n* 1 the part of the body with which a person or animal hears 2 the external visible part of the ear 3 the ability to hear musical and other sounds and interpret them accurately: *a good ear for languages* 4 willingness to listen: *they are always willing to lend an ear* 5 **be all ears** to be prepared to listen attentively to something 6 **fall on deaf ears** to be ignored: *his words fell on deaf ears* 7 **in one ear and out the other** heard but quickly forgotten or ignored 8 **out on one's ear** *informal* dismissed suddenly and unpleasantly 9 **play by ear** to play without written music 10 **play it by ear** *informal* to make up one's plan of action as one goes along 11 **turn a deaf ear to** to be deliberately unresponsive to: *many countries have turned a deaf ear to their cries for help* 12 **up to one's ears in** *informal* deeply involved in

> **ear** *n* 3 = sensitivity, taste, discrimination, appreciation

ear² *n* the part of a cereal plant, such as wheat or barley, that contains the seeds

earache *n* pain in the ear

earbash *vb Brit, Austral & NZ informal* to talk incessantly ▷ **earbashing** *n*

eardrum *n* the thin membrane separating the external ear from the middle ear

earl *n* (in Britain) a nobleman ranking below a marquess and above a viscount ▷ **earldom** *n*

early *adj* **-lier, -liest 1** before the correct or expected time **2** in the first part of a period of time: *early April* **3** near the beginning of the development or history of something: *early Britain was very primitive; early models of this car rust easily* ▶ *adv* **4** occurring or arriving before the correct or expected time **5** in the first part of a period of time **6** near the beginning of the development or history of something: *early in the war*

> **early** *adj* **1** = premature, forward, advanced, untimely, unseasonable; ≠ belated **2** = first, opening, initial, introductory **3** = primitive, first, earliest, young, original, undeveloped, primordial, primeval; ≠ developed ▶ *adv* **4** = in good time, beforehand, ahead of schedule, in advance, with time to spare; ≠ late

earmark *vb* **1** to set (something) aside for a specific purpose ▶ *n* **2** a feature that enables the nature of something to be identified: *it had all the earmarks of a disaster*

> **earmark** *vb* = set aside, reserve, label, flag, allocate, designate, mark out

earn *vb* **1** to gain or be paid (money) in return for work **2** to acquire or deserve through one's behaviour or action: *you've earned a good night's sleep* **3** to make (money) as interest or profit: *her savings earned 8% interest* ▷ **earner** *n*

> **earn** *vb* **1** = be paid, make, get, receive, gain, net, collect, bring in **2** = deserve, win, gain, attain, justify, merit, warrant, be entitled to

earnest *adj* **1** serious and sincere, often excessively so ▶ *n* **2** **in earnest** with serious or sincere intentions ▷ **earnestly** *adv* ▷ **earnestness** *n*

> **earnest** *adj* = serious, grave, intense, dedicated, sincere, thoughtful, solemn, ardent; ≠ frivolous

earnings *pl n* money earned

> **earnings** *pl n* = income, pay, wages, revenue, proceeds, salary, receipts, remuneration

earring *n* a piece of jewellery worn attached to the ear

earshot *n* the range within which a sound can be heard: *out of earshot*

earth *n* **1** (*sometimes cap*) the planet that we live on, the third planet from the sun, the only one on which life is known to exist. Related adjective: **terrestrial 2** the part of the surface of this planet that is not water **3** the soil in which plants grow **4** the hole in which a fox lives **5** a wire in a piece of electrical equipment through which electricity can escape into the ground if a fault develops **6 come down to earth** to return to reality from a daydream or fantasy **7 on earth** used for emphasis: *what on earth happened?* ▶ *vb* **8** to fit (a piece of electrical equipment) with an earth

> **earth** *n* **1** = world, planet, globe, sphere, orb, earthly sphere **2** = ground, land, dry land, terra firma **3** = soil, ground, land, dust, clay, dirt, turf, silt

earthen *adj* made of earth or baked clay: *an earthen floor*

earthenware *n* dishes and other objects made of baked clay: *an earthenware flowerpot*

earthly *adj* **-lier, -liest 1** of life on earth as opposed to any heavenly or spiritual state **2** *informal* conceivable or possible: *what earthly reason would they have for lying?*

> **earthly** *adj* **1** = worldly, material, secular, mortal, temporal, human; ≠ spiritual **2** = possible, likely, practical, feasible, conceivable, imaginable

earthquake *n* a series of vibrations at the earth's surface caused by movement of the earth's crust

earthwork *n* **1** excavation of earth, as in engineering construction **2** a fortification made of earth

earthworm *n* a common worm that burrows in the soil

earthy *adj* **earthier, earthiest 1** open and direct in the treatment of sex, excretion, etc. **2** of or like earth: *earthy colours* ▷ **earthiness** *n*

earwig *n* a thin brown insect with pincers at the tip of its abdomen

ease *n* **1** lack of difficulty **2** freedom from discomfort or worry **3** rest, leisure, or relaxation **4** freedom from poverty: *a life of leisure and ease* **5 at ease A** *military* (of a soldier) standing in a relaxed position with the feet apart **B** in a relaxed attitude or frame of mind ▶ *vb* **easing, eased 6** to make or become less difficult or severe: *the pain gradually eased* **7** to move into or out of a place or situation slowly and carefully **8 ease off** *or* **up** to lessen or cause to lessen in severity, pressure, tension, or strain: *the rain eased off*

> **ease** *n* **1** = straightforwardness, simplicity, readiness **2** = peace of mind, peace, content, quiet, comfort, happiness, serenity, tranquillity; ≠ agitation **3, 4** = comfort, luxury, leisure, relaxation, prosperity, affluence, rest, repose; ≠ hardship ▶ *vb* **6** = relieve, calm, soothe, lessen, alleviate, lighten, lower, relax; ≠ aggravate **7** = move carefully, edge, slip, inch, slide, creep, manoeuvre

easel *n* a frame on legs, used for supporting an artist's canvas or a display

easily *adv* **1** without difficulty **2** without doubt; by far: *easily the most senior Chinese leader to visit the West*

easily *adv* **1** = without difficulty, smoothly, readily, comfortably, effortlessly, with ease, straightforwardly

east *n* **1** one of the four cardinal points of the compass, at 90° clockwise from north **2** the direction along a line of latitude towards the sunrise **3 the east** any area lying in or towards the east ▸ *adj* **4** situated in, moving towards, or facing the east **5** (esp. of the wind) from the east ▸ *adv* **6** in, to, or towards the east

Easter *n* **1** *Christianity* a festival commemorating the Resurrection of Christ ▸ *adj* **2** taking place at the time of the year when this festival is celebrated: *the Easter weekend*

Easter egg *n* a chocolate egg given at Easter

easterly *adj* **1** of or in the east ▸ *adv, adj* **2** towards the east **3** from the east: *an easterly breeze*

eastern *adj* **1** situated in or towards the east **2** facing or moving towards the east **3** (*sometimes cap*) of or characteristic of the east or East > **easternmost** *adj*

eastward *adj, adv* also **eastwards 1** towards the east ▸ *n* **2** the eastward part or direction

easy *adj* **easier, easiest 1** not difficult; simple: *the house is easy to keep clean* **2** free from pain, care, or anxiety: *an easy life* **3** tolerant and undemanding; easy-going **4** defenceless or readily fooled: *easy prey* **5** moderate and not involving any great effort: *an easy ride* **6** *informal* ready to fall in with any suggestion made: *he wanted to do something and I was easy about it* **7** *informal* pleasant and not involving any great effort to enjoy: *easy on the eye* ▸ *adv* **8 go easy on A** to avoid using too much of: *he'd tried to go easy on the engines* **B** to treat less severely than is deserved: *go easy on him, he's just a kid* **9 take it easy** to relax and avoid stress or undue hurry > **easiness** *n*

easy *adj* **1** = simple, straightforward, no trouble, not difficult, effortless, painless, uncomplicated, child's play (*informal*); ≠ hard **2** = untroubled, relaxed, peaceful, serene, tranquil, quiet; ≠ difficult **3** = tolerant, soft, mild, laid-back (*informal*), indulgent, easy-going, lenient, permissive; ≠ strict

easy chair *n* a comfortable upholstered armchair

easy-going *adj* relaxed in manner or attitude; very tolerant

eat *vb* **eating, ate, eaten 1** to take (food) into the mouth and swallow it **2** to have a meal: *sometimes we eat out of doors* **3** *informal* to make anxious or worried: *what's eating you?* **4 eat away** or **into** or **up** to destroy or use up partly or wholly: *inflation ate into the firm's profits* > **eater** *n*

eat *vb* **1** = consume, swallow, chew, scoff (*slang*), devour, munch, tuck into (*informal*), put away **2** = have a meal, lunch, breakfast, dine, snack, feed, graze (*informal*), have lunch

eatable *adj* fit or suitable for eating

eau de Cologne (oh de kol-**lone**) *n* full form of **cologne**

eaves *pl n* the edge of a sloping roof that overhangs the walls

eavesdrop *vb* **-dropping, -dropped** to listen secretly to a private conversation > **eavesdropper** *n*

ebb *vb* **1** (of the sea or the tide) to flow back from its highest point **2** to fall away or decline: *her anger ebbed away* ▸ *n* **3** the flowing back of the tide from high to low water **4 at a low ebb** in a weak state: *her creativity was at a low ebb*

ebb *vb* **1** = flow back, go out, withdraw, retreat, wane, recede **2** = decline, flag, diminish, decrease, dwindle, lessen, subside, fall away ▸ *n* **3** = flowing back, going out, withdrawal, retreat, wane, low water, low tide, outgoing tide

Ebola virus *n* a virus that causes severe infectious disease

ebony *n* **1** a very hard dark-coloured wood used to make furniture, etc. ▸ *adj* **2** very deep black

e-book *n* **1** a book in electronic form ▸ *vb* **2** to book (tickets, appointments, etc.) through the internet

ebullient *adj* full of enthusiasm or excitement > **ebullience** *n*

EC 1 European Commission **2** European Community: a former name for the European Union

eccentric *adj* **1** unconventional or odd **2** (of circles) not having the same centre ▸ *n* **3** a person who behaves unconventionally or oddly > **eccentrically** *adv*

eccentric *adj* **1** = odd, strange, peculiar, irregular, quirky, unconventional, idiosyncratic, outlandish, daggy (*Austral, NZ informal*); ≠ normal ▸ *n* = crank (*informal*), character (*informal*), oddball (*informal*), nonconformist

eccentricity *n* **1** unconventional or odd behaviour **2** *pl* **-ties** an unconventional or odd habit or act

ecclesiastic *n* **1** a member of the Christian clergy ▸ *adj* **2** of or relating to the Christian Church or its clergy

ecclesiastical *adj* of or relating to the Christian Church or its clergy

ECG electrocardiogram

echelon (esh-a-lon) *n* **1** a level of power or responsibility: *the upper echelons of society* **2** *military* a formation in which units follow one another but are spaced out sideways to allow each a line of fire ahead

e

echidna (ik-**kid**-na) *n, pl* **-nas, -nae** (-nee) an Australian spiny egg-laying mammal. Also called: **spiny anteater**

echo *n, pl* **-oes** **1 A** the reflection of sound by a solid object **B** a sound reflected by a solid object **2** a repetition or imitation of someone else's opinions **3** something that brings back memories: *an echo of the past* **4** the signal reflected back to a radar transmitter by an object ► *vb* **-oing, -oed 5** (of a sound) to be reflected off an object in such a way that it can be heard again **6** (of a place) to be filled with a sound and its echoes: *the church echoed with singing* **7** (of people) to repeat or imitate (what someone else has said): *his conclusion echoed that of Jung* › **echoing** *adj*

echo *n* **1** = reverberation, ringing, repetition, answer, resonance, resounding **2** = copy, reflection, clone, reproduction, imitation, duplicate, double, reiteration ► *vb* **5, 6** = reverberate, repeat, resound, ring, resonate **7** = recall, reflect, copy, mirror, resemble, imitate, ape

echo sounder *n* a navigation device that determines depth by measuring the time taken for a pulse of sound to reach the sea bed and for the echo to return

e-cigarette *n* an electronic vaporizer that simulates the effect of smoking. Often shortened to: **e-cig**

éclair *n* a finger-shaped cake of choux pastry, filled with cream and coated with chocolate

eclectic *adj* **1** composed of elements selected from a wide range of styles, ideas, or sources: *the contenders for this year's Turner Prize are an eclectic bunch* **2** selecting elements from a wide range of styles, ideas, or sources: *an eclectic approach that takes the best from all schools of psychology* ► *n* **3** a person who takes an eclectic approach › **eclecticism** *n*

eclipse *n* **1** the obscuring of reflected light from a celestial body as it passes through the shadow of another; a **lunar eclipse** occurs when the moon passes through the shadow of the earth **2** a loss of importance, power, or fame: *communism eventually went into eclipse* ► *vb* **eclipsing, eclipsed 3** to overshadow or surpass **4** (of a star or planet) to hide (another planet or star) from view

eclipse *n* **1** = obscuring, covering, blocking, shading, dimming, extinction, darkening, blotting out ► *vb* **3** = surpass, exceed, overshadow, excel, transcend, outdo, outclass, outshine

ecliptic *n astron* the great circle on the celestial sphere representing the apparent annual path of the sun relative to the stars

ecological *adj* **1** of or relating to ecology **2** tending or intended to benefit or protect the environment: *an ecological approach to agriculture* › **ecologically** *adv*

ecology *n* the study of the relationships between people, animals, and plants, and their environment › **ecologist** *n*

e-commerce *or* **ecommerce** *n* business transactions conducted on the internet

economic *adj* **1** of or relating to an economy or economics **2** *Brit & Austral* capable of being produced or operated for profit **3** *informal* inexpensive or cheap

economic *adj* **1** = financial, industrial, commercial **2** = profitable, successful, commercial, rewarding, productive, lucrative, worthwhile, viable **3** = economical, cheap, reasonable, modest, low-priced, inexpensive

economical *adj* **1** not requiring a lot of money to use: *low fuel consumption makes this car very economical* **2** (of a person) spending money carefully and sensibly **3** using no more time, effort, or resources than is necessary **4 economical with the truth** *euphemistic* deliberately withholding information › **economically** *adv*

economical *adj* **2** = thrifty, sparing, careful, prudent, provident, frugal, parsimonious, scrimping; ≠ extravagant **3** = efficient, sparing, cost-effective, money-saving, time-saving; ≠ wasteful

economics *n* **1** the study of the production and consumption of goods and services and the commercial activities of a society ► *pl n* **2** financial aspects: *the economics of health care*

economist *n* a person who specializes in economics

economize *or* **-mise** *vb* **-mizing, -mized** *or* **-mising, -mised** to reduce expense or waste: *people are being advised to economize on fuel use*

economy *n, pl* **-mies 1** the system by which the production, distribution, and consumption of goods and services is organized in a country or community: *the rural economy* **2** the ability of a country to generate wealth through business and industry: *unless the economy improves, more jobs will be lost* **3** careful use of money or resources to save expense, time, or energy **4** an instance of this: *we can make economies by reusing envelopes* ► *adj* **5** denoting a class of air travel that is cheaper than first-class **6** offering a larger quantity for a lower price: *an economy pack*

economy *n* **2** = financial system, financial state **3** = thrift, restraint, prudence, husbandry, frugality, parsimony

ecosystem *n ecology* the system of relationships between animals and plants and their environment

ecru *adj* pale creamy-brown

ecstasy *n, pl* **-sies 1** a state of extreme delight or joy **2** *slang* a strong drug that acts as a stimulant and can cause hallucinations › **ecstatic** *adj* › **ecstatically** *adv*

ecstasy n 1 = rapture, delight, joy, bliss, euphoria, fervour, elation; ≠ agony

ectoplasm n (in spiritualism) the substance that supposedly is emitted from the body of a medium during a trance

ecumenical adj 1 of or relating to the Christian Church throughout the world 2 tending to promote unity among Christian churches

eczema (ek-sim-a, ig-zeem-a) n pathol a condition in which the skin becomes inflamed and itchy

Edam n a round yellow Dutch cheese with a red waxy covering

eddy n, pl **-dies** 1 a circular movement of air, water, or smoke ▸ vb **-dies, -dying, -died** 2 to move with a gentle circular motion; swirl gently

edelweiss (ade-el-vice) n a small white alpine flower

edema (id-deem-a) n, pl **-mata** same as **oedema**

Eden n 1 Also called: **Garden of Eden** Bible the garden in which Adam and Eve were placed at the Creation 2 a place of great delight or contentment

edge n 1 a border or line where something ends or begins: the edge of the city 2 a line along which two faces or surfaces of a solid meet 3 the sharp cutting side of a blade 4 keenness, sharpness, or urgency: there was a nervous edge to his voice 5 **have the edge on** to have a slight advantage over 6 **on edge** nervous and irritable 7 **set someone's teeth on edge** to make someone acutely irritated ▸ vb **edging, edged** 8 to make, form, or be an edge or border for: a pillow edged with lace 9 to move very gradually in a particular direction: I edged through to the front of the crowd

> **edge** n 1 = border, side, limit, outline, boundary, fringe, verge, brink 4 = sharpness, point, bitterness, keenness 6 **on edge** = tense, nervous, impatient, irritable, apprehensive, edgy, ill at ease, on tenterhooks, adrenalized ▸ vb 8 = border, fringe, hem, pipe 9 = inch, ease, creep, slink, steal, sidle, move slowly

edgeways or esp US & Canad **edgewise** adv 1 with the edge forwards or uppermost 2 **get a word in edgeways** to interrupt a conversation in which someone else is talking continuously

edging n anything placed along an edge for decoration

edgy adj **edgier, edgiest** nervous, irritable, or anxious > **edginess** n

edible adj fit to be eaten; eatable > **edibility** n

edict (ee-dikt) n a decree or order given by any authority

edifice (ed-if-iss) n 1 a large or impressive building 2 an elaborate system of beliefs and institutions: the entire crumbling edifice of a former superpower

edify (ed-if-fie) vb **-fies, -fying, -fied** to inform or instruct (someone) with a view to improving his or her morals or understanding > **edification** n > **edifying** adj

edit vb **editing, edited** 1 to prepare (text) for publication by checking and improving its accuracy or clarity 2 to be in charge of (a newspaper or magazine) 3 to prepare (a film, television or radio programme, etc.) by rearranging or selecting material 4 **edit out** to remove (a section) from a text, film, etc.

> **edit** vb 1 = revise, improve, correct, polish, adapt, rewrite, condense, redraft

edition n 1 a particular version of a book, newspaper, or magazine produced at one time: the revised paperback edition 2 a single television or radio programme which forms part of a series: the first edition goes on the air in 30 minutes

> **edition** n 1 = printing, publication 2 = programme (television, radio)

editor n 1 a person who edits 2 a person in overall charge of a newspaper or magazine 3 a person in charge of one section of a newspaper or magazine: the Political Editor 4 a person in overall control of a television or radio programme > **editorship** n

editorial n 1 an article in a newspaper expressing the opinion of the editor or publishers ▸ adj 2 of editing or editors: an editorial meeting 3 relating to the contents and opinions of a magazine or newspaper: the paper's editorial policy > **editorially** adv

educate vb **-cating, -cated** 1 to teach (someone) over a long period of time so that he or she acquires knowledge and understanding of a range of subjects 2 to send (someone) to a particular educational establishment: he was educated at a boarding school in Switzerland 3 to teach (someone) about a particular matter: a campaign to educate people to the dangers of smoking > **educative** adj

> **educate** vb 1 = teach, school, train, develop, improve, inform, discipline, tutor

education n 1 the process of acquiring knowledge and understanding 2 knowledge and understanding acquired through study and training: education is the key to a good job 3 the process of teaching, esp. at a school, college, or university 4 the theory of teaching and learning > **educational** adj > **educationally** adv > **educationalist** or **educationist** n

> **education** n 1, 2 = learning, schooling, cultivation, refinement 3 = teaching, schooling, training, development, discipline, instruction, nurture, tuition, e-learning or elearning

Edwardian adj of or in the reign of King Edward VII of Great Britain and Ireland (1901–10)

EEG electroencephalogram

eel n a slimy snakelike fish

e

eerie *adj* **eerier, eeriest** strange and frightening > **eerily** *adv*

> **eerie** *adj* = uncanny, strange, frightening, ghostly, weird, mysterious, scary (*informal*), sinister

efface *vb* **-facing, -faced 1** to obliterate or make dim: *nothing effaced the memory* **2** to rub out or erase **3 efface oneself** to make oneself inconspicuous > **effacement** *n*

effect *n* **1** a change or state of affairs caused by something or someone: *the gales have had a serious effect on the crops* **2** power to influence or produce a result: *antibiotics have no effect on viruses – they only work against bacteria* **3** the condition of being operative: *a new law has come into effect* **4** the overall impression: *the whole effect is one of luxury* **5** basic meaning or purpose: *words to that effect* **6** an impression, usually a contrived one: *he paused for effect* **7** a physical phenomenon: *the greenhouse effect* **8 in effect** for all practical purposes: *in effect he has no choice* **9 take effect** to begin to produce results ▸ *vb* **10** to cause (something) to take place: *a peace treaty was effected*

> **effect** *n* **1** = result, consequence, conclusion, outcome, event, end result, upshot **2** = impression, feeling, impact, influence **5** = purpose, impression, sense, intent, essence, thread, tenor ▸ *vb* = bring about, produce, complete, achieve, perform, fulfil, accomplish, execute

effective *adj* **1** producing a desired result: *polio's spread was checked by the creation of an effective vaccine in the 1950s* **2** officially coming into operation: *the new rates become effective at the end of May* **3** impressive: *a highly effective speech* **4** in reality, although not officially or in theory: *he is in effective control of the company* > **effectively** *adv* > **effectiveness** *n*

> **effective** *adj* **1** = efficient, successful, useful, active, capable, valuable, helpful, adequate; ≠ ineffective **2** = in operation, official, current, legal, active, in effect, valid, operative; ≠ inoperative **3** = powerful, strong, convincing, persuasive, telling, impressive, compelling, forceful; ≠ weak **4** = virtual, essential, practical, implied, implicit, tacit, unacknowledged

effectual *adj* **1** producing the intended result **2** (of a document, etc.) having legal force > **effectually** *adv*

effeminate *adj* (of a man) displaying characteristics regarded as typical of a woman > **effeminacy** *n*

effervescent *adj* **1** (of a liquid) giving off bubbles of gas **2** (of a person) lively and enthusiastic > **effervescence** *n*

effete (if-**feet**) *adj* weak, powerless, and decadent

efficacious *adj* producing the intended result > **efficacy** *n*

efficient *adj* working or producing effectively without wasting effort, energy, or money > **efficiency** *n* > **efficiently** *adv*

> **efficient** *adj* = effective, successful, structured, productive, systematic, streamlined, cost-effective, methodical; ≠ inefficient

effigy (ef-fij-ee) *n, pl* **-gies 1** a statue or carving of someone, often as a memorial: *a 14th-century wooden effigy of a knight* **2** a crude representation of someone, used as a focus for contempt: *an effigy of the president was set on fire*

efflorescence *n* **1** the blooming of flowers on a plant **2** a brief period of high-quality artistic activity

effluent *n* liquid discharged as waste, for instance from a factory or sewage works

effluvium *n, pl* **-via** an unpleasant smell, such as the smell of decaying matter

effort *n* **1** physical or mental energy needed to do something **2** a determined attempt to do something **3** an achievement or creation: *his earliest literary efforts* > **effortless** *adj* > **effortlessly** *adv*

> **effort** *n* **1** = exertion, work, trouble, energy, struggle, application, graft, toil **2** = attempt, try, endeavour, shot (*informal*), bid, essay (*formal*), go (*informal*), stab (*informal*)

effrontery *n* insolence or boldness

effusion *n* **1** an unrestrained verbal expression of emotions or ideas **2** a sudden pouring out: *small effusions of blood*

effusive *adj* enthusiastically showing pleasure, gratitude, or approval > **effusively** *adv* > **effusiveness** *n*

EFTA European Free Trade Association

eg *or* **e.g.** for example

egalitarian *adj* **1** expressing or supporting the idea that all people should be equal ▸ *n* **2** a person who believes that all people should be equal > **egalitarianism** *n*

egg *n* **1** the oval or round object laid by the females of birds, reptiles, and other creatures, containing a developing embryo **2** a hen's egg used for food **3** a type of cell produced in the body of a female animal which can develop into a baby if fertilized by a male reproductive cell **4 have egg on one's face** *informal* to have been made to look ridiculous **5 put all one's eggs in one basket** to rely entirely on one action or decision, with no alternative in case of failure

> **egg** *n* **3** = ovum, gamete, germ cell

egghead *n informal* an intelligent person

eggplant *n US, Canad, Austral & NZ* a dark purple tropical fruit, cooked and eaten as a vegetable

ego *n, pl* **egos 1** the part of a person's self that is able to recognize that person as being distinct from other people and things **2** a person's opinion of his or her own worth: *as well as the physical injuries, there were one or two bruised egos*

egocentric *adj* thinking only of one's own interests and feelings > **egocentricity** *n*

egotism *or* **egoism** *n* concern only for one's own interests and feelings > **egotist** *or* **egoist** *n* > **egotistical, egoistical, egotistic** *or* **egoistic** *adj*

egregious (ig-greej-uss) *adj* shockingly bad: *egregious government waste*

egress (ee-gress) *n formal* **1** the act of going out **2** a way out or exit

egret (ee-grit) *n* a wading bird like a heron, with long white feathery plumes

Egyptian *adj* **1** of Egypt **2** of the ancient Egyptians ▸ *n* **3** a person from Egypt **4** a member of an ancient people who established an advanced civilization in Egypt **5** the language of the ancient Egyptians

Egyptology *n* the study of the culture of ancient Egypt > **Egyptologist** *n*

eider *or* **eider duck** *n* a large sea duck of the N hemisphere

eiderdown *n* a thick warm cover for a bed, filled with soft feathers, originally the breast feathers of the female eider duck

eight *n* **1** the cardinal number that is the sum of one and seven **2** a numeral, 8 or VIII, representing this number **3** something representing or consisting of eight units **4** *rowing* a light narrow boat rowed by eight people **B** the crew of such a boat ▸ *adj* **5** amounting to eight: *eight apples* > **eighth** *adj, n*

eighteen *n* **1** the cardinal number that is the sum of ten and eight **2** a numeral, 18 or XVIII, representing this number **3** something representing or consisting of 18 units ▸ *adj* **4** amounting to eighteen: *eighteen months* > **eighteenth** *adj, n*

eighty *n, pl* **eighties 1** the cardinal number that is the product of ten and eight **2** a numeral, 80 or LXXX, representing this number **3** something representing or consisting of 80 units ▸ *adj* **4** amounting to eighty: *eighty miles* > **eightieth** *adj, n*

eisteddfod (ice-sted-fod) *n* a Welsh festival with competitions in music, poetry, drama, and art

either *adj, pron* **1** one or the other (of two): *we were offered either fish or beef* **2** both one and the other: *we sat at either end of a long sofa* ▸ *conj* **3** used preceding two or more possibilities joined by *or*: *it must be stored either in the fridge or in a cool place* ▸ *adv* **4** likewise: *I don't eat meat and my husband doesn't either* **5** used to qualify or modify a previous statement: *he wasn't exactly ugly, but he wasn't handsome either*

ejaculate *vb* **-lating, -lated 1** to discharge semen from the penis while having an orgasm **2** *literary* to say or shout suddenly > **ejaculation** *n* > **ejaculatory** *adj*

eject *vb* **1** to push or send out forcefully **2** to compel (someone) to leave a place or position

3 to leave an aircraft rapidly in mid-flight, using an ejector seat > **ejection** *n* > **ejector** *n*

> **eject** *vb* **2** = throw out, remove, turn out, expel, oust, banish, drive out, evict **3** = bail out, escape, get out

eke out *vb* **eking, eked 1** to make (a supply) last for a long time by using as little as possible **2** to manage to sustain (a living) despite having barely enough food or money

elaborate *adj* **1** very complex because of having many different parts: *elaborate equipment* **2** having a very complicated design: *elaborate embroidery* ▸ *vb* **-rating, -rated 3** elaborate on to describe in more detail: *he did not elaborate on his plans* **4** to develop (a plan or theory) in detail > **elaborately** *adv* > **elaboration** *n*

> **elaborate** *adj* **1** = complicated, detailed, studied, complex, precise, thorough, intricate, painstaking **2** = ornate, involved, complex, fancy, complicated, intricate, baroque, ornamented; ≠ plain ▸ *vb* **3** = expand upon, extend upon, enlarge on, amplify upon, embellish, flesh out, add detail to; ≠ simplify **4** = develop, flesh out

élan (ale-an) *n* style and liveliness

eland (eel-and) *n* a large spiral-horned antelope of southern Africa

elapse *vb* **elapsing, elapsed** (of time) to pass by

elastic *adj* **1** capable of returning to its original shape after stretching, compression, or other distortion **2** capable of being adapted to meet the demands of a particular situation: *an elastic interpretation of the law* **3** made of elastic ▸ *n* **4** tape, cord, or fabric containing flexible rubber > **elastically** *adv* > **elasticated** *adj* > **elasticity** *n*

> **elastic** *adj* **1** = flexible, supple, rubbery, pliable, plastic, springy, pliant, tensile; ≠ rigid **2** = adaptable, yielding, variable, flexible, accommodating, tolerant, adjustable, supple; ≠ inflexible

elated *adj* extremely happy and excited > **elatedly** *adv*

elation *n* a feeling of great happiness and excitement

elbow *n* **1** the joint between the upper arm and the forearm **2** the part of a garment that covers the elbow ▸ *vb* **3** to push with one's elbow or elbows: *she elbowed him aside; he elbowed his way to the bar*

elbow grease *n facetious* vigorous physical labour, esp. hard rubbing

elbow room *n* sufficient scope to move or to function

elder[1] *adj* **1** (of one of two people) born earlier ▸ *n* **2** an older person: *have some respect for your elders* **3** a senior member of a tribe, who has authority **4** (in certain Protestant Churches) a member of the church who has certain administrative, teaching, or preaching powers

elder *adj* = older, first, senior, first-born ▸ *n*
2 = older person, senior

elder² *n* a shrub or small tree with clusters of
small white flowers and dark purple berries
elderly *adj* **1** rather old ▸ *pl n* **2 the elderly** old
people
eldest *adj* (of a person, esp. a child) oldest
El Dorado (el dor-*rah*-doe) *n* **1** a fabled city in
South America, supposedly rich in treasure
2 Also: **eldorado** any place of great riches or
fabulous opportunity
eldritch *adj poetic Scot* unearthly or weird
elect *vb* **1** to choose (someone) to fill a position
by voting for him or her: *she was elected President in*
1990 **2** to choose or decide: *those who elected to stay*
▸ *adj* **3** voted into office but not yet having taken
over from the current office-bearer: *the President*
elect ▸ *pl n* **4 the elect** any group of people
specially chosen for some privilege
> **electable** *adj*

elect *vb* **1** = vote for, choose, pick, determine,
select, appoint, opt for, settle on **2** = choose,
decide, prefer, select, opt

election *n* **1** **A** a process whereby people vote for
a person or party to fill a position: *last month's*
presidential election **B** short for **general election**
2 the gaining of political power or taking up of a
position in an organization as a result of being
voted for: *he will be seeking election as the President of*
Romania

election *n* **1A** = vote, poll, ballot, referendum,
franchise, plebiscite, show of hands
2 = appointment, picking, choice, selection

electioneering *n* the act of taking an active
part in a political campaign, for example by
canvassing
elective *adj* **1** of or based on selection by vote:
an elective office **2** not compulsory or necessary:
an elective hysterectomy
elector *n* **1** someone who is eligible to vote in
an election **2** (in the Holy Roman Empire) any
of the German princes who were entitled to
elect a new emperor: *the Elector of Hanover*
electoral *adj* of or relating to elections: *the*
electoral system > **electorally** *adv*
electorate *n* **1** all the people in an area or
country who have the right to vote in an
election **2** the rank or territory of an elector of
the Holy Roman Empire
electric *adj* **1** produced by, transmitting, or
powered by electricity: *an electric fire* **2** very tense
or exciting: *the atmosphere was electric* ▸ *n*
3 electrics *Brit* an electric circuit or electric
appliances

electric *adj* **1** = electric-powered, powered,
cordless, battery-operated, electrically-
charged, mains-operated **2** = charged,
exciting, stirring, thrilling, stimulating,
dynamic, tense, rousing, adrenalized

electrical *adj* of or relating to electricity
> **electrically** *adv*
electric chair *n* (in the US) a chair for
executing criminals by passing a strong electric
current through them
electrician *n* a person trained to install and
repair electrical equipment
electricity *n* **1** a form of energy associated with
stationary or moving electrons, ions, or other
charged particles **2** the supply of electricity to
houses, factories, etc., for heating, lighting, etc.
electrify *vb* **-fies**, **-fying**, **-fied 1** to adapt or
equip (a system or device) to work by electricity:
the whole track has now been electrified **2** to provide
(an area) with electricity **3** to startle or excite
intensely > **electrification** *n*
electro- *combining form* electric or electrically:
electroconvulsive
electrocardiograph *n* an instrument for
making tracings (**electrocardiograms**) recording
the electrical activity of the heart
electrocute *vb* **-cuting**, **-cuted** to kill or injure
by an electric shock > **electrocution** *n*
electrode *n* a small piece of metal used to take
an electric current to or from a power source,
piece of equipment, or living body
electrodynamics *n* the branch of physics
concerned with the interactions between
electrical and mechanical forces
electroencephalograph (ill-lek-tro-en-*sef*-
a-loh-graf) *n* an instrument for making
tracings (**electroencephalograms**) recording the
electrical activity of the brain
electrolysis (ill-lek-*troll*-iss-iss) *n* **1** the process
of passing an electric current through a liquid
in order to produce a chemical reaction in the
liquid **2** the destruction of living tissue, such as
hair roots, by an electric current
electrolyte *n* a solution or molten substance
that conducts electricity > **electrolytic** *adj*
electromagnet *n* a magnet consisting of a coil
of wire wound round an iron core through
which a current is passed
electromagnetic *adj* **1** of or operated by an
electromagnet **2** of or relating to
electromagnetism > **electromagnetically** *adv*
electromagnetism *n* magnetism produced
by an electric current
electron *n* *physics* an elementary particle in all
atoms that has a negative electric charge
electronic *adj* **1** (of a device, circuit, or system)
containing transistors, silicon chips, etc. which
control the current passing through it
2 making use of electronic systems: *electronic*
surveillance devices > **electronically** *adv*
electronics *n* the technology concerned with
the development, behaviour, and applications of
devices and circuits
electron microscope *n* a powerful
microscope that uses electrons, rather than
light, to produce a magnified image
electronvolt *n* *physics* a unit of energy equal to

the work done on an electron accelerated through a potential difference of 1 volt

electroplate *vb* **-plating, -plated 1** to coat (an object) with metal by dipping it in a special liquid through which an electric current is passed ▸ *n* **2** electroplated articles collectively

elegant *adj* **1** attractive and graceful or stylish **2** cleverly simple and clear: *an elegant summary* > **elegance** *n* > **elegantly** *adv*

> **elegant** *adj* **1** = stylish, fine, sophisticated, delicate, handsome, refined, chic, exquisite, schmick (*Austral informal*); ≠ inelegant

elegiac *adj literary* sad, mournful, or plaintive

elegy (el-lij-ee) *n, pl* **-gies** a mournful poem or song, esp. a lament for the dead

element *n* **1** one of the fundamental components making up a whole **2** *chem* any of the known substances that cannot be separated into simpler substances by chemical means **3** a distinguishable section of a social group: *liberal elements in Polish society* **4** a degree: *an element of truth* **5** a metal part in an electrical device, such as a kettle, that changes the electric current into heat **6** one of the four substances (earth, air, water, and fire) formerly believed to make up the universe **7** *maths* any of the members of a set **8 in one's element** in a situation in which one is happy and at ease: *she was in her element behind the wheel* **9 elements A** the basic principles of something **B** weather conditions, esp. wind, rain, and cold: *only 200 braved the elements*

> **element** *n* **1** = component, part, unit, section, factor, principle, aspect, detail, foundation **3** = group, faction, clique, set, party, circle **4** = trace, suggestion, hint, dash, suspicion, tinge, smattering, soupçon **8 in one's element** = in a situation you enjoy, in your natural environment, in familiar surroundings **9B** = weather conditions, climate, the weather, wind and rain, atmospheric conditions, powers of nature

elemental *adj* of or like basic and powerful natural forces or passions

elementary *adj* **1** simple, basic, and straightforward: *elementary precautions* **2** involving only the most basic principles of a subject: *elementary mathematics*

> **elementary** *adj* **1** = simple, clear, easy, plain, straightforward, rudimentary, uncomplicated, undemanding; ≠ complicated

elephant *n* **1** a very large four-legged animal that has a very long flexible nose called a trunk, large ears, and two ivory tusks, and lives in Africa or India **2 elephant in the room** an obvious truth deliberately ignored by all parties in a situation

elephantiasis (el-lee-fan-**tie**-a-siss) *n pathol* a skin disease, caused by parasitic worms, in which the affected parts of the body become extremely enlarged

elephantine *adj* like an elephant, esp. in being huge, clumsy, or ponderous

elevate *vb* **-vating, -vated 1** to raise in rank or status: *he had elevated flirting to an art form* **2** to lift to a higher place: *this action elevates the upper back*

> **elevate** *vb* **1** = promote, raise, advance, upgrade, exalt, kick upstairs (*informal*), aggrandize, give advancement to **2** = raise, lift, heighten, uplift, hoist, lift up, raise up, hike up

elevation *n* **1** the act of elevating someone or something: *his elevation to the peerage* **2** height above sea level **3** a raised area **4** a scale drawing of one side of a building

elevator *n* **1** *Austral, US & Canad* a lift for carrying people **2** a mechanical hoist

eleven *n* **1** the cardinal number that is the sum of ten and one **2** a numeral, 11 or XI, representing this number **3** something representing or consisting of 11 units **4** a team of 11 players in football, cricket, etc. ▸ *adj* **5** amounting to eleven: *eleven years* > **eleventh** *adj, n*

elevenses *pl n Brit, Austral, S African & NZ informal* a mid-morning snack

elf *n, pl* **elves** (in folklore) a small mischievous fairy

elfin *adj* **1** small and delicate: *her elfin features* **2** of or relating to elves

elicit *vb* **1** to bring about (a response or reaction): *her remarks elicited a sharp retort* **2** to draw out (information) from someone: *a phone call elicited the fact that she had just awakened*

> **elicit** *vb* **1** = bring about, cause, derive, bring out, evoke, give rise to, draw out, bring forth **2** = obtain, extract, exact, evoke, wrest, draw out, extort

elide *vb* **eliding, elided** to omit (a syllable or vowel) from a spoken word

eligible *adj* **1** meeting the requirements or qualifications needed: *he may be eligible for free legal services* **2** *old-fashioned* desirable as a spouse > **eligibility** *n*

> **eligible** *adj* **1** = entitled, fit, qualified, suitable; ≠ ineligible **2** = available, free, single, unmarried, unattached

eliminate *vb* **-nating, -nated 1** to get rid of (something or someone unwanted, unnecessary, or not meeting the requirements needed): *he can be eliminated from the list of suspects* **2** to remove (a competitor or team) from a contest, esp. following a defeat: *they were eliminated in the third round* **3** *slang* to murder in cold blood: *Stalin had thousands of his former comrades eliminated* > **elimination** *n*

> **eliminate** *vb* **1** = remove, end, stop, withdraw, get rid of, abolish, cut out, dispose of

elision *n* omission of a syllable or vowel from a spoken word

elite (ill-**eet**) *n* the most powerful, rich, or gifted members of a group or community

> **elite** *n* = aristocracy, best, pick, cream, upper class, nobility, the crème de la crème, flower; ≠ rabble

elitism *n* **1** the belief that society should be governed by a small group of people who are superior to everyone else **2** pride in being part of an elite > **elitist** *n, adj*

elixir (ill-**ix**-er) *n* **1** an imaginary substance that is supposed to be capable of prolonging life and changing base metals into gold **2** a liquid medicine mixed with syrup

Elizabethan *adj* **1** of or in the reign of Queen Elizabeth I of England (1558–1603) ▸ *n* **2** a person who lived during the reign of Queen Elizabeth I

elk *n* a very large deer of N Europe and Asia with broad flat antlers

ellipse *n* an oval shape resembling a flattened circle

ellipsis (ill-**lip**-siss) *n, pl* **-ses** (-seez) **1** the omission of a word or words from a sentence **2** *printing* three dots (...) indicating an omission

elliptical *or* **elliptic** *adj* **1** oval-shaped **2** (of speech or writing) obscure or ambiguous

elm *n* **1** a tall tree with broad leaves **2** the hard heavy wood of this tree

elocution *n* the art of speaking clearly in public > **elocutionist** *n*

elongate (eel-**long**-gate) *vb* **-gating, -gated** to make or become longer > **elongation** *n*

elope *vb* **eloping, eloped** (of two people) to run away secretly to get married > **elopement** *n*

eloquence *n* the ability to speak or write in a skilful and convincing way

eloquent *adj* **1** (of speech or writing) fluent and persuasive **2** (of a person) able to speak in a fluent and persuasive manner **3** visibly or vividly expressive: *he raised an eloquent eyebrow* > **eloquently** *adv*

> **eloquent** *adj* **1, 2** = silver-tongued, moving, powerful, effective, stirring, articulate, persuasive, forceful; ≠ inarticulate **3** = expressive, telling, pointed, significant, vivid, meaningful, indicative, suggestive

else *adv* **1** in addition or more: *what else do you want to know?* **2** other or different: *it was unlike anything else that had happened* **3** **or else A** if not, then: *tell us soon or else we shall go mad* **B** *informal* or something terrible will result: used as a threat: *do it our way or else*

elsewhere *adv* in or to another place

> **elsewhere** *adv* = in *or* to another place, away, abroad, hence (*archaic*), somewhere else, not here, in other places, in *or* to a different place

elucidate *vb* **-dating, -dated** to make (something obscure or difficult) clear > **elucidation** *n*

elude *vb* **eluding, eluded 1** to avoid or escape from (someone or something) **2** to fail to be understood or remembered by: *the mysteries of commerce elude me*

> **elude** *vb* **1** = evade, escape, lose, avoid, flee, duck (*informal*), dodge, get away from **2** = escape, baffle, frustrate, puzzle, stump, be beyond (someone)

elusive *adj* **1** difficult to find or catch **2** difficult to remember or describe > **elusiveness** *n*

> **elusive** *adj* **1** = difficult to catch, tricky, slippery, difficult to find, evasive, shifty (*informal*) **2** = indefinable, fleeting, subtle, indefinite, transient, intangible, indescribable, transitory

elver *n* a young eel

elves *n* the plural of **elf**

emaciated (im-**mace**-ee-ate-id) *adj* extremely thin through illness or lack of food > **emaciation** *n*

email *or* **e-mail** (**ee**-mail) *n* **1** the transmission of messages from one computer terminal to another ▸ *vb* **2** to contact (a person) by email **3** to send (a message) by email

emanate (**em**-a-nate) *vb* **-nating, -nated** to come or seem to come from someone or something: *an aura of power emanated from him* > **emanation** *n*

> **emanate** *vb* = flow, emerge, spring, proceed, arise, stem, derive, originate

emancipate *vb* **-pating, -pated** to free from social, political, or legal restrictions > **emancipation** *n*

emasculate *vb* **-lating, -lated** to deprive of power or strength > **emasculation** *n*

embalm *vb* to preserve (a corpse) by the use of chemicals and oils

embankment *n* a man-made ridge of earth or stone that carries a road or railway or prevents a river or lake from overflowing

embargo *n, pl* **-goes 1** an order by a government or international body prohibiting trade with a country: *America lifted its trade embargo on China* ▸ *vb* **-going, -goed 2** to place an official prohibition on

> **embargo** *n* = ban, bar, restriction, boycott, restraint, prohibition, moratorium, stoppage, rahui (NZ) ▸ *vb* = block, stop, bar, ban, restrict, boycott, prohibit, blacklist

embark *vb* **1** to go on board a ship or aircraft **2 embark on** to begin (a new project or venture) > **embarkation** *n*

> **embark** *vb* **1** = go aboard, climb aboard, board ship, step aboard, go on board, take ship; ≠ get off **2 embark on something** = begin, start, launch, enter, take up, set out, set about, plunge into

embarrass *vb* **1** to make (someone) feel shy, ashamed, or guilty about something **2** to cause

political problems for (a government or party) **3** to cause to have financial difficulties
› **embarrassed** *adj* › **embarrassing** *adj*
› **embarrassingly** *adv* › **embarrassment** *n*

embarrass *vb* **1** = shame, distress, show up (*informal*), humiliate, disconcert, fluster, mortify, discomfit

embassy *n*, *pl* **-sies** **1** the residence or place of business of an ambassador **2** an ambassador and his or her assistants and staff

embattled *adj* **1** (of a country) involved in fighting a war, esp. when surrounded by enemies **2** facing many problems and difficulties: *the embattled Mayor*

embed *vb* **-bedding, -bedded** **1** to fix firmly in a surrounding solid mass: *the boy has shrapnel embedded in his spine* **2** to fix (an attitude or idea) in a society or in someone's mind: *corruption was deeply embedded in the ruling party*

embellish *vb* **1** to make (something) more attractive by adding decorations **2** to make (a story) more interesting by adding details which may not be true › **embellishment** *n*

ember *n* a smouldering piece of coal or wood remaining after a fire has died

embezzle *vb* **-zling, -zled** to steal (money that belongs to the company or organization that one works for) › **embezzlement** *n*
› **embezzler** *n*

embittered *adj* feeling anger and despair as a result of misfortune: *embittered by poverty*
› **embitterment** *n*

emblazon (im-blaze-on) *vb* **1** to decorate with a coat of arms, slogan, etc.: *a jacket emblazoned with his band's name* **2** to proclaim or publicize: *I am not sure he would want his name emblazoned in my column*

emblem *n* an object or design chosen to symbolize an organization or idea
› **emblematic** *adj*

embody *vb* **-bodies, -bodying, -bodied** **1** to be an example of or express (an idea or other abstract concept) **2** to include as part of a whole: *the proposal has been embodied in a draft resolution*
› **embodiment** *n*

embody *vb* **1** = personify, represent, stand for, manifest, exemplify, symbolize, typify, actualize **2** = incorporate, include, contain, combine, collect, take in, encompass

embolden *vb* to make bold

embolism *n pathol* the blocking of a blood vessel by a blood clot, air bubble, etc.

emboss *vb* to mould or carve a decoration on (a surface) so that it stands out from the surface

embrace *vb* **-bracing, -braced** **1** to clasp (someone) with one's arms as an expression of affection or a greeting **2** to accept eagerly: *he has embraced the Islamic faith* **3** to include or be made up of: *a church that embraces two cultures* ▸ *n* **4** an act of embracing

embrace *vb* **1** = hug, hold, cuddle, seize, squeeze, clasp, envelop, canoodle (*slang*) **2** = accept, support, welcome, adopt, take up, seize, espouse, take on board **3** = include, involve, cover, contain, take in, incorporate, comprise, encompass ▸ *n* = hug, hold, cuddle, squeeze, clinch (*slang*), clasp

embrasure *n* **1** an opening for a door or window which is wider on the inside of the wall than on the outside **2** an opening in a battlement or wall, for shooting through

embrocation *n* a lotion rubbed into the skin to ease sore muscles

embroider *vb* **1** to do decorative needlework on (a piece of cloth or a garment) **2** to add imaginary details to (a story) › **embroiderer** *n*

embroidery *n* **1** decorative needlework, usually on cloth or canvas **2** the act of adding imaginary details to a story

embroil *vb* to involve (oneself or another person) in problems or difficulties
› **embroilment** *n*

embroil *vb* = involve, mix up, implicate, entangle, mire, ensnare, enmesh

embryo (em-bree-oh) *n*, *pl* **-bryos** **1** an unborn animal or human being in the early stages of development, in humans up to approximately the end of the second month of pregnancy **2** something in an early stage of development: *the embryo of a serious comic novel*

embryo *n* **1** = fetus, unborn child, fertilized egg **2** = germ, beginning, source, root, seed, nucleus, rudiment

embryology *n* the scientific study of embryos

embryonic *adj* **1** of or relating to an embryo **2** in an early stage

emend *vb* to make corrections or improvements to (a text) › **emendation** *n*

emerald *n* **1** a green transparent variety of beryl highly valued as a gem ▸ *adj* **2** bright green

emerge *vb* **emerging, emerged** **1** to come into view out of something: *a man emerged from the shadows* **2** to come out of a particular state of mind or way of existence: *she emerged from the trance* **3** to come to the end of a particular event or situation: *no party emerged from the election with a clear majority* **4** to become apparent, esp. as the result of a discussion or investigation: *it emerged that he had made up much of his CV to get a job as a teacher* **5** to come into existence over a long period of time: *a new style of dance music emerged in the late 1980s* › **emergence** *n* › **emergent** *adj*

emerge *vb* **1** = come out, appear, surface, rise, arise, turn up, spring up, emanate; ≠ withdraw **4** = become apparent, come out, become known, come to light, crop up, transpire, become evident, come out in the wash

emergency *n, pl* **-cies 1** an unforeseen or sudden occurrence, esp. of danger demanding immediate action **2 state of emergency** a time of crisis, declared by a government, during which normal laws and civil rights can be suspended ▸ *adj* **3** for use in an emergency: *the emergency exit* **4** made necessary because of an emergency: *emergency surgery*

> **emergency** *n* **1** = crisis, danger, difficulty, accident, disaster, necessity, plight, scrape (*informal*) ▸ *adj* = urgent, crisis, immediate

emeritus (im-mer-rit-uss) *adj* retired, but retaining one's title on an honorary basis: *a professor emeritus*

emery *n* a hard greyish-black mineral used for smoothing and polishing

emery board *n* a strip of cardboard coated with crushed emery, for filing one's fingernails

emetic (im-met-ik) *n* **1** a substance that causes vomiting ▸ *adj* **2** causing vomiting

emigrate *vb* **-grating, -grated** to leave one's native country to settle in another country > **emigrant** *n, adj* > **emigration** *n*

> **emigrate** *vb* = move abroad, move, relocate, migrate, resettle, leave your country

émigré (em-mig-gray) *n* someone who has left his or her native country for political reasons

eminence *n* **1** the state of being well-known and well-respected **2** a piece of high ground

Eminence *n* **Your** *or* **His Eminence** a title used to address or refer to a cardinal

eminent *adj* well-known and well-respected

> **eminent** *adj* = prominent, noted, respected, famous, celebrated, distinguished, well-known, esteemed; ≠ unknown

eminently *adv* extremely: *eminently sensible*

emir (em-meer) *n* an independent ruler in the Islamic world > **emirate** *n*

emissary *n, pl* **-saries** an agent sent on a mission by a government or head of state

emission *n* **1** the act of giving out heat, light, a smell, etc. **2** energy or a substance given out by something: *exhaust emissions from motor vehicles*

> **emission** *n* **1** = giving off *or* out, release, shedding, leak, radiation, discharge, transmission, ejaculation

emit *vb* **emitting, emitted 1** to give or send forth (heat, light, a smell, etc.) **2** to produce (a sound)

> **emit** *vb* **1** = give off, release, leak, transmit, discharge, send out, radiate, eject; ≠ absorb **2** = utter, produce, voice, give out, let out

emoji (im-moh-jee) *n* a small image used in electronic messaging to express an idea or emotion

emollient *adj* **1** (of skin cream or lotion) having a softening effect **2** helping to avoid confrontation; calming: *his emollient political style* ▸ *n* **3** a cream or lotion that softens the skin

emolument *n* fees or wages from employment

emoticon (im-mote-ik-kon) *n* a series of symbols used in electronic messaging to express an idea or emotion

emotion *n* **1** any strong feeling, such as joy or fear **2** the part of a person's character based on feelings rather than thought: *the conflict between emotion and logic*

> **emotion** *n* **1** = feeling, spirit, soul, passion, excitement, sensation, sentiment, fervour **2** = instinct, sentiment, sensibility, intuition, tenderness, gut feeling, soft-heartedness

emotional *adj* **1** of or relating to the emotions: *emotional abuse* **2** influenced by feelings rather than rational thinking: *he was too emotional to be a good doctor* **3** appealing to the emotions: *emotional appeals for public support* **4** showing one's feelings openly, esp. when upset: *he became very emotional and burst into tears* > **emotionalism** *n* > **emotionally** *adv*

> **emotional** *adj* **1** = psychological, private, personal, hidden, spiritual, inner **2, 4** = passionate, sentimental, temperamental, excitable, demonstrative, hot-blooded **3** = moving, touching, affecting, stirring, sentimental, poignant, emotive, heart-rending

emotive *adj* tending or designed to arouse emotion

empathy *n* the ability to sense and understand someone else's feelings as if they were one's own > **empathic** *adj*

emperor *n* a man who rules an empire

emphasis *n, pl* **-ses 1** special importance or significance given to something, such as an object or idea **2** stress on a particular syllable, word, or phrase in speaking

> **emphasis** *n* **1** = importance, attention, weight, significance, stress, priority, prominence **2** = stress, accent, force, weight

emphasize *or* **-sise** *vb* **-sizing, -sized** *or* **-sising, -sised** to give emphasis or prominence to: *to emphasize her loyalty*

> **emphasize** *or* **-sise** *vb* = highlight, stress, underline, draw attention to, dwell on, play up, make a point of, give priority to; ≠ minimize

emphatic *adj* **1** expressed, spoken, or done forcefully: *an emphatic denial of the allegations* **2** forceful and positive: *he was emphatic about his desire for peace talks* > **emphatically** *adv*

> **emphatic** *adj* **1** = significant, pronounced, decisive, resounding, conclusive **2** = forceful, positive, definite, vigorous, unmistakable, insistent, unequivocal, vehement; ≠ hesitant

emphysema (em-fiss-see-ma) *n pathol* a condition in which the air sacs of the lungs are grossly enlarged, causing breathlessness

empire *n* **1** a group of countries under the rule of a single person or sovereign state **2** a large industrial organization that is controlled by one person: *the heiress to a jewellery empire*

> **empire** *n* **1** = kingdom, territory, province, federation, commonwealth, realm, domain **2** = organization, company, business, firm, concern, corporation, consortium, syndicate

empirical *adj* derived from experiment, experience, and observation rather than from theory or logic: *there is no empirical data to support this claim* > **empirically** *adv*

> **empirical** *adj* = first-hand, direct, observed, practical, actual, experimental, pragmatic, factual; ≠ hypothetical

empiricism *n philosophy* the doctrine that all knowledge derives from experience > **empiricist** *n*

emplacement *n* a prepared position for an artillery gun

employ *vb* **1** to hire (someone) to do work in return for money **2** to keep busy or occupy: *she was busily employed cutting the grass* **3** to use as a means: *you can employ various methods to cut your heating bills* ▸ *n* **4 in the employ of** doing regular paid work for: *he is in the employ of The Sunday Times* > **employable** *adj*

> **employ** *vb* **1** = hire, commission, appoint, take on, retain, engage, recruit, sign up **2** = spend, fill, occupy, involve, engage, take up, make use of, use up **3** = use, apply, exercise, exert, make use of, utilize, ply, bring to bear

employee *n* a person who is hired to work for someone in return for payment

> **employee** *n* = worker, labourer, workman *or* woman *or* person, staff member, member of staff, hand, wage-earner, white-collar worker

employer *n* a person or company that employs workers

> **employer** *n* = boss (*informal*), manager, head, leader, director, chief, owner, master, sherang (*Austral, NZ*)

employment *n* **1** the act of employing or state of being employed **2** a person's work or occupation **3** the availability of jobs for the population of a town, country, etc.: *the party's commitment to full employment*

> **employment** *n* **1** = taking on, commissioning, appointing, hire, hiring, retaining, engaging, appointment **2** = job, work, position, trade, post, situation, profession, occupation

emporium *n, pl* **-riums** *or* **-ria** *old-fashioned* a large retail shop with a wide variety of merchandise

empower *vb* to give (someone) the power or authority to do something

> **empower** *vb* = authorize, allow, commission, qualify, permit, sanction, entitle, delegate

empress *n* **1** a woman who rules an empire **2** the wife or widow of an emperor

empty *adj* **-tier, -tiest 1** containing nothing **2** without inhabitants; unoccupied **3** without purpose, substance, or value: *he contemplated yet another empty weekend* **4** insincere or trivial: *empty words* **5** informal drained of energy or emotion **6** *maths & logic* (of a set or class) containing no members ▸ *vb* **-ties, -tying, -tied 7** to make or become empty **8** to remove from something: *they emptied out the remains of the tin of paint* ▸ *n, pl* **-ties 9** an empty container, esp. a bottle > **emptiness** *n*

> **empty** *adj* **1, 2** = bare, clear, abandoned, deserted, vacant, free, void (*old-fashioned*), desolate; ≠ full **3** = worthless, meaningless, hollow, pointless, futile, senseless, fruitless, inane; ≠ meaningful **4** = meaningless, cheap, hollow, vain, idle, futile, insincere ▸ *vb* **7** = clear, drain, void, unload, pour out, unpack, remove the contents of; ≠ fill

emu *n* a large Australian long-legged bird that cannot fly

emulate *vb* **-lating, -lated** to imitate (someone) in an attempt to do as well as or better than him or her > **emulation** *n* > **emulator** *n*

> **emulate** *vb* = imitate, follow, copy, mirror, echo, mimic, model yourself on

emulsifier *n* a substance that helps to combine two liquids, esp. a water-based liquid and an oil

emulsify *vb* **-fies, -fying, -fied** to make or form into an emulsion

emulsion *n* **1** a mixture of two liquids in which particles of one are suspended evenly throughout the other **2** *photog* a light-sensitive coating for photographic film **3** a type of water-based paint

enable *vb* **-abling, -abled 1** to provide (someone) with the means or opportunity to do something **2** to make possible: *to enable the best possible chance of cure*

> **enable** *vb* = allow, permit, empower, give someone the opportunity, give someone the means; ≠ prevent

enact *vb* **1** to establish by law: *plans to enact a bill of rights* **2** to perform (a story or play) by acting > **enactment** *n*

> **enact** *vb* **1** = establish, order, command, approve, sanction, proclaim, decree, authorize **2** = perform, play, present, stage, represent, put on, portray, depict

enamel n 1 a coloured glassy coating on the surface of articles made of metal, glass, or pottery 2 an enamel-like paint or varnish 3 the hard white substance that covers teeth ▸ vb -elling, -elled or US -eling, -eled 4 to decorate or cover with enamel

enamoured or US **enamored** adj **enamoured of** A in love with B very fond of and impressed by: he is not enamoured of Hollywood

en bloc (on blok) adv as a whole; all together

encamp vb formal to set up a camp > **encampment** n

encapsulate vb -lating, -lated 1 to put in a concise form; summarize 2 to enclose in, or as if in, a capsule > **encapsulation** n

encephalitis (en-sef-a-lite-iss) n inflammation of the brain > **encephalitic** adj

encephalogram n an electroencephalogram

enchant vb 1 to delight and fascinate 2 to cast a spell on > **enchanted** adj > **enchantment** n > **enchanter** or fem **enchantress** n

enchant vb 1 = fascinate, delight, charm, entrance, dazzle, captivate, enthral, beguile

encircle vb -cling, -cled to form a circle round > **encirclement** n

enclave n a part of a country entirely surrounded by foreign territory: a Spanish enclave

enclose vb -closing, -closed 1 to surround completely: the house enclosed a courtyard 2 to include along with something else: he enclosed a letter with the parcel

enclose vb 1 = surround, circle, bound, fence, confine, close in, wall in, encircle 2 = send with, include, put in, insert

enclosure n 1 an area of land enclosed by a fence, wall, or hedge 2 something, such as a cheque, enclosed with a letter

encomium n a formal expression of praise

encompass vb 1 to enclose within a circle; surround 2 to include all of: the programme encompasses the visual arts, music, literature, and drama

encompass vb 1 = surround, circle, enclose, close in, envelop, encircle, fence in, ring 2 = include, hold, cover, admit, deal with, contain, take in, embrace

encore interj 1 again: used by an audience to demand a short extra performance ▸ n 2 an extra song or piece performed at a concert in response to enthusiastic demand from the audience

encounter vb 1 to meet (someone) unexpectedly 2 to be faced with: he had rarely encountered such suffering 3 to meet (an opponent or enemy) in a competition or battle ▸ n 4 a casual or unexpected meeting 5 a game or battle: a fierce encounter between the army and armed rebels

encounter vb 1 = meet, confront, come across, bump into (informal), run across, come upon, chance upon, meet by chance 2 = experience, meet, face, suffer, have, go through, sustain, endure ▸ n 4 = meeting, brush, confrontation, rendezvous, chance meeting 5 = battle, conflict, clash, contest, run-in (informal), confrontation, head-to-head

encourage vb -raging, -raged 1 to give (someone) the confidence to do something 2 to stimulate (something or someone) by approval or help > **encouragement** n > **encouraging** adj

encourage vb 1 = inspire, comfort, cheer, reassure, console, hearten, cheer up, embolden; ≠ discourage 2 = urge, persuade, prompt, spur, coax, egg on; ≠ dissuade

encroach vb to intrude gradually on someone's rights or on a piece of land > **encroachment** n

encrust vb to cover (a surface) with a layer of something, such as jewels or ice > **encrustation** n

encrypt vb to put (a message or data) into a coded form > **encryption** n

encumber vb 1 to hinder or impede: neither was greatly encumbered with social engagements 2 to burden with a load or with debts

encumbrance n something that impedes or is burdensome

encyclical (en-sik-lik-kl) n a letter sent by the pope to all Roman Catholic bishops

encyclopedia or **encyclopaedia** n a book or set of books, often in alphabetical order, containing facts about many different subjects or about one particular subject

encyclopedic or **encyclopaedic** adj (of knowledge or information) very full and thorough; comprehensive

end n 1 one of the two extreme points of something such as a road 2 the surface at one of the two extreme points of an object: a pencil with a rubber at one end 3 the extreme extent or limit of something: the end of the runway 4 the most distant place or time that can be imagined: the ends of the earth 5 the act or an instance of stopping doing something or stopping something from continuing: I want to put an end to all the gossip 6 the last part of something: at the end of the story 7 a remnant or fragment: cigarette ends 8 death or destruction 9 the purpose of an action: he will only use you to achieve his own ends 10 sport either of the two defended areas of a playing field 11 **in the end** finally 12 **make ends meet** to have just enough money to meet one's needs 13 **no end** used for emphasis: these moments give me no end of trouble 14 **on end** informal without pause or interruption: for months on end 15 **the end** slang the worst, esp. beyond the limits of endurance ▸ vb 16 to bring or come to a finish 17 **end it all** informal to die by suicide

end n **1, 3** = extremity, limit, edge, border, extent, extreme, margin, boundary **2** = tip, point, head, peak, extremity **5** = close, ending, finish, expiry, expiration; ≠ beginning **6** = conclusion, ending, climax, completion, finale, culmination, denouement, consummation; ≠ start **7** = remnant, butt, stub, scrap, fragment, stump, remainder, leftover **8** = death, dying, ruin, destruction, passing on, doom, demise (euphemistic), extinction **9** = purpose, point, reason, goal, target, aim, object, mission ▶ vb **16** = stop, finish, halt, cease, wind up, terminate, call off, discontinue; ≠ start

endanger vb to put in danger

endanger vb = put at risk, risk, threaten, compromise, jeopardize, imperil, put in danger, expose to danger; ≠ save

endear vb to cause to be liked: his wit endeared him to a great many people > **endearing** adj
endearment n an affectionate word or phrase
endeavour or US **endeavor** formal ▶ vb **1** to try (to do something) ▶ n **2** an effort to do something

endeavour or **endeavor** vb = try, labour, attempt, aim, struggle, venture, strive, aspire ▶ n = attempt, try, effort, trial, bid, venture, enterprise, undertaking

endemic adj present within a localized area or only found in a particular group of people: he found 100 species of plant endemic to that ridge
ending n **1** the last part or conclusion of something: the film has a happy ending **2** the tip or end of something: nerve endings

ending n **1** = finish, end, close, conclusion, summing up, completion, finale, culmination; ≠ start

endive n a plant with crisp curly leaves, used in salads
endless adj **1** having no end; eternal or infinite **2** continuing too long or continually recurring: an endless stream of visitors > **endlessly** adv

endless adj **1** = eternal, infinite, continual, unlimited, interminable, incessant, boundless, everlasting; ≠ temporary

endocrine adj of or denoting a gland that secretes hormones directly into the bloodstream, or a hormone secreted by such a gland
endogenous (en-**dodge**-in-uss) adj biol developing or originating from within
endorse vb -**dorsing**, -**dorsed** **1** to give approval or support to **2** to sign the back of (a cheque) to specify the payee **3** chiefly Brit to record a conviction on (a driving licence) > **endorsement** n

endorse vb **1** = approve, back, support, champion, promote, recommend, advocate, uphold **2** = sign, initial, countersign, sign on the back of

endow vb **1** to provide with a source of permanent income, esp. by leaving money in a will **2 endowed with** provided with or possessing (a quality or talent)

endow vb **1** = finance, fund, pay for, award, confer, bestow, bequeath, donate money to **2** = provided, favoured, graced, blessed, supplied, furnished

endowment n **1** the money given to an institution, such as a hospital **2** a natural talent or quality

endowment n **1** = provision, funding, award, grant, gift, contribution, subsidy, donation, koha (NZ)

endurance n the ability to withstand prolonged hardship

endurance n = staying power, strength, resolution, determination, patience, stamina, fortitude, persistence

endure vb -**during**, -**dured** **1** to bear (hardship) patiently **2** to tolerate or put up with: I cannot endure your disloyalty any longer **3** to last for a long time > **endurable** adj

endure vb **1** = experience, suffer, bear, meet, encounter, cope with, sustain, undergo **3** = last, continue, remain, stay, stand, go on, survive, live on

endways or esp US & Canad **endwise** adv having the end forwards or upwards
enema (en-im-a) n med a quantity of fluid inserted into the rectum to empty the bowels, for example before an operation
enemy n, pl -**mies** **1** a person who is hostile or opposed to a person, group, or idea **2** a hostile nation or people **3** something that harms or opposes something: oil is an enemy of the environment. ▶ Related adjective: **inimical** ▶ adj **4** of or belonging to an enemy: enemy troops

enemy n **1** = foe (formal, literary), rival, opponent, the opposition, competitor, the other side, adversary, antagonist; ≠ friend

energetic adj **1** having or showing energy and enthusiasm: an energetic campaigner for democracy **2** involving a lot of movement and physical effort: energetic exercise > **energetically** adv

energetic adj **1** = forceful, determined, active, aggressive, dynamic, vigorous, hard-hitting, strenuous; ≠ lethargic **2** = strenuous, hard, taxing, demanding, tough, exhausting, vigorous, arduous

e

energize or **-gise** vb **-gizing, -gized** or **-gising,
-gised** to stimulate or enliven
energy n, pl **-gies 1** capacity for intense activity;
vigour **2** intensity or vitality of action or
expression; forcefulness **3** physics the capacity to
do work and overcome resistance **4** a source of
power, such as electricity

> **energy** n **1** = strength, might, stamina,
> forcefulness **2** = liveliness, drive,
> determination, pep, vitality, vigour, verve,
> resilience **4** = power

energy drink n a soft drink designed to boost
the drinker's energy levels
enervate vb **-vating, -vated** to deprive of
strength or vitality > **enervating** adj
> **enervation** n
enfant terrible (on-fon ter-reeb-la) n, pl
enfants terribles a talented but unconventional
or indiscreet person
enfeeble vb **-bling, -bled** to make (someone or
something) weak
enfold vb **1** to cover (something) by, or as if by,
wrapping something round it: darkness enfolded
the city **2** to embrace or hug
enforce vb **-forcing, -forced 1** to ensure that
(a law or decision) is obeyed **2** to impose
(obedience) by, or as if by, force > **enforceable** adj
> **enforcement** n

> **enforce** vb **1** = carry out, apply, implement,
> fulfil, execute, administer, put into effect, put
> into action **2** = impose, force, insist on

enfranchise vb **-chising, -chised** to grant (a
person or group of people) the right to vote
> **enfranchisement** n
engage vb **-gaging, -gaged 1** Also: **be engaged**
(usually foll. by in) to take part or participate: he
engaged in criminal and illegal acts; they were engaged in
espionage **2** to involve (a person or his or her
attention) intensely: there's nothing to engage the
intellect in this film **3** to employ (someone) to do
something **4** to promise (to do something)
5 military to begin a battle with **6** to bring
(part of a machine or other mechanism) into
operation, esp. by causing components to
interlock **7 engage in conversation** to start a
conversation with

> **engage** vb **1** = participate in, join in, take
> part in, undertake, embark on, enter into,
> become involved in, set about **2** = captivate,
> catch, arrest, fix, capture **3** = employ, appoint,
> take on, hire, retain, recruit, enlist, enrol;
> ≠ dismiss **5** = begin battle with, attack, take
> on, encounter, fall on, battle with, meet, assail
> **6** = set going, apply, trigger, activate, switch
> on, energize, bring into operation

engaged adj **1** having made a promise to get
married **2** Brit (of a telephone line or a toilet)
already being used

engaged adj **1** = betrothed (old-fashioned),
promised, pledged, affianced (old-fashioned),
promised in marriage; ≠ unattached **2** = in
use, busy, tied up, unavailable; ≠ free

engagement n **1** a business or social
appointment **2** the period when a couple has
agreed to get married but the wedding has not
yet taken place **3** a limited period of employment,
esp. in the performing arts **4** a battle

> **engagement** n **1** = appointment, meeting,
> interview, date, commitment, arrangement,
> rendezvous **2** = betrothal (old-fashioned),
> marriage contract, troth (archaic), agreement
> to marry **4** = battle, fight, conflict, action,
> struggle, clash, encounter, combat

engaging adj pleasant and charming
> **engagingly** adv

> **engaging** adj = charming, interesting,
> pleasing, attractive, lovely, entertaining,
> winning, fetching (informal); ≠ unpleasant

engender vb to produce (a particular feeling,
atmosphere, or situation)
engine n **1** any machine designed to convert
energy into mechanical work, esp. one used to
power a vehicle **2** a railway locomotive

> **engine** n **1** = machine, motor, mechanism,
> generator, dynamo

engineer n **1** a person trained in any branch
of engineering **2** a person who repairs and
maintains mechanical or electrical devices **3** a
soldier trained in engineering and construction
work **4** an officer responsible for a ship's
engines **5** US & Canad a train driver ▶ vb **6** to
cause or plan (an event or situation) in a clever
or devious manner **7** to design or construct as a
professional engineer

> **engineer** n **1** = designer, producer, architect,
> developer, deviser, creator, planner, inventor
> **2** = worker, specialist, operator, practitioner,
> operative, driver, conductor, technician ▶ vb
> **6** = bring about, plan, effect, set up (informal),
> scheme, arrange, plot, mastermind **7** = design,
> plan, create, construct, devise

engineering n the profession of applying
scientific principles to the design and
construction of engines, cars, buildings,
bridges, roads, and electrical machines
English adj **1** of England or the English
language ▶ n **2** the principal language of
Britain, Ireland, Australia, New Zealand,
the US, Canada, and several other countries
▶ pl n **3 the English** the people of England
engrave vb **-graving, -graved 1** to carve or etch
a design or inscription into (a surface) **2** to print
(designs or characters) from a plate into which
they have been cut or etched **3** to fix deeply or
permanently in the mind > **engraver** n

engraving n 1 a printing surface that has been engraved 2 a print made from this

> **engraving** n = print, carving, etching, inscription, plate, woodcut, dry point

engross (en-**groce**) vb to occupy the attention of (someone) completely > **engrossing** adj

engulf vb 1 to immerse, plunge, or swallow up: *engulfed by flames* 2 to overwhelm: *a terrible fear engulfed her*

> **engulf** vb 1 = immerse, swamp, submerge, overrun, inundate, envelop, swallow up 2 = overwhelm, overcome, crush, swamp

enhance vb -**hancing**, -**hanced** to improve or increase in quality, value, or power: *grilling on the barbecue enhances the flavour* > **enhancement** n > **enhancer** n

> **enhance** vb = improve, better, increase, lift, boost, add to, strengthen, reinforce; ≠ reduce

enigma n something or someone that is mysterious or puzzling > **enigmatic** adj > **enigmatically** adv

enjoin vb 1 to order (someone) to do something 2 to impose (a particular kind of behaviour) on someone: *the sect enjoins poverty on its members* 3 law to prohibit (someone) from doing something by an injunction

enjoy vb 1 to receive pleasure from 2 to have or experience (something, esp. something good): *many older people enjoy excellent health* 3 **enjoy oneself** to have a good time > **enjoyable** adj > **enjoyably** adv > **enjoyment** n

> **enjoy** vb 1 = take pleasure in or from, like, love, appreciate, relish, delight in, be pleased with, be fond of; ≠ hate 2 = have, use, own, experience, possess, have the benefit of, reap the benefits of, be blessed or favoured with

enlarge vb -**larging**, -**larged** 1 to make or grow larger 2 **enlarge on** to speak or write about in greater detail > **enlargement** n > **enlarger** n

> **enlarge** vb 1 = expand, increase, extend, add to, build up, widen, intensify, broaden; ≠ reduce 2 **enlarge on something** = expand on, develop, add to, fill out, elaborate on, flesh out, expatiate on, give further details about

enlighten vb to give information or understanding to > **enlightening** adj

> **enlighten** vb = inform, tell, teach, advise, counsel, educate, instruct, illuminate

enlightenment n the act of enlightening or the state of being enlightened

> **enlightenment** n = understanding, learning, education, knowledge, instruction, awareness, wisdom, insight

enlist vb 1 to enter the armed forces 2 to obtain (someone's help or support) > **enlistment** n

> **enlist** vb 1 = join up, join, enter (into), register, volunteer, sign up, enrol 2 = obtain, get, gain, secure, engage, procure

enliven vb to make lively, cheerful, or bright > **enlivening** adj

en masse (on **mass**) adv all together; as a group

enmeshed adj deeply involved: *enmeshed in turmoil*

enmity n a feeling of hostility or ill will

ennoble vb -**bling**, -**bled** 1 to make (someone) a member of the nobility 2 to make (someone or his or her life) noble or dignified: *poverty does not ennoble people*

ennui (on-**nwee**) n literary boredom and dissatisfaction resulting from lack of activity or excitement

enormity n 1 extreme wickedness 2 pl -**ties** an act of great wickedness 3 the vastness or extent of a problem or difficulty

enormous adj unusually large in size, extent, or degree > **enormously** adv

> **enormous** adj = huge, massive, vast, extensive, tremendous, gross, immense, gigantic, supersize; ≠ tiny

enough adj 1 as much or as many as necessary 2 **that's enough!** used to stop someone behaving in a particular way ▸ pron 3 an adequate amount or number: *I don't know enough about the subject to be able to speak about it* ▸ adv 4 as much as necessary 5 fairly or quite: *that's a common enough experience* 6 very: used to give emphasis to the preceding word: *funnily enough, I wasn't alarmed* 7 just adequately: *he sang well enough*

> **enough** adj 1 = sufficient, adequate, ample, abundant, as much as you need, as much as is necessary ▸ pron = sufficiency, plenty, sufficient, abundance, adequacy, right amount, ample supply ▸ adv 4, 5 = sufficiently, amply, reasonably, adequately, satisfactorily, abundantly, tolerably

en passant (on pass-**on**) adv in passing: *references made en passant*

enquire vb -**quiring**, -**quired** same as **inquire** > **enquiry** n

enraptured adj filled with delight and fascination

enrich vb 1 to improve or increase the quality or value of: *his poetry has vastly enriched the English language* 2 to improve in nutritional value, colour, or flavour: *a sauce enriched with beer* 3 to make wealthy or wealthier > **enriched** adj > **enrichment** n

> **enrich** vb 1 = enhance, develop, improve, boost, supplement, refine, heighten, augment 3 = make rich, make wealthy, make affluent, make prosperous, make well-off

enrol or US **enroll** vb -**rolling**, -**rolled** to become or cause to become a member > **enrolment** or US **enrollment** n

enrol *or* **enroll** *vb* = enlist, register, be accepted, be admitted, join up, put your name down for, sign up *or* on

en route (on root) *adv* on or along the way

en route *adv* = on *or* along the way, travelling, on the road, in transit, on the journey

ensconce *vb* **-sconcing, -sconced** to settle firmly or comfortably

ensemble (on-som-bl) *n* **1** all the parts of something considered as a whole **2** the complete outfit of clothes a person is wearing **3** a group of musicians or actors performing together **4** *music* a passage in which all or most of the performers are playing or singing at once

ensemble *n* **1** = collection, set, body, whole, total, sum, combination, entity **2** = outfit, suit, get-up (*informal*), costume **3** = group, company, band, troupe, cast, orchestra, chorus

enshrine *vb* **-shrining, -shrined** to contain and protect (an idea or right) in a society, legal system, etc.: *the university's independence is enshrined in its charter*

ensign *n* **1** a flag flown by a ship to indicate its nationality **2** any flag or banner **3** (in the US Navy) a commissioned officer of the lowest rank **4** (formerly, in the British infantry) a commissioned officer of the lowest rank

enslave *vb* **-slaving, -slaved** to make a slave of (someone) > **enslavement** *n*

ensnare *vb* **-snaring, -snared** **1** to trap or gain power over (someone) by dishonest or underhand means **2** to catch (an animal) in a snare

ensue *vb* **-suing, -sued** **1** to happen next **2** to occur as a consequence: *if glaucoma is not treated, blindness can ensue* > **ensuing** *adj*

ensue *vb* = follow, result, develop, proceed, arise, stem, derive, issue; ≠ come first

en suite (on *sweet*) *adj, adv* (of a bathroom) connected to a bedroom and entered directly from it: *an en-suite bathroom; a room with a bathroom en suite*

ensure *or esp US* **insure** *vb* **-suring, -sured** **1** to make certain: *we must ensure that similar accidents do not happen again* **2** to make safe or protect: *to ensure against fraud, voters will have to bring a piece of identification*

ensure *or* **insure** *vb* **1** = make certain, guarantee, secure, make sure, confirm, warrant, certify **2** = protect, defend, secure, safeguard, guard, make safe

entail *vb* **1** to bring about or impose inevitably: *he wasn't ready for all that marriage entails* **2** *Brit, Austral & NZ property law* to restrict the ability to inherit (a piece of property) to designated heirs

entail *vb* **1** = involve, require, produce, demand, call for, occasion (*formal*), need, bring about

entangle *vb* **-gling, -gled** **1** to catch very firmly in something, such as a net or wire: *a fishing line had entangled his legs* **2** to involve in a complicated series of problems or difficulties: *he entangles himself in contradictions* **3** to involve in a troublesome relationship: *Harvey soon got entangled with a certain Miss Gilmour* > **entanglement** *n*

enter *vb* **1** to come or go into (a particular place): *he entered the room* **2** to join (a party or organization) **3** to become involved in or take part in: *1500 schools entered the competition* **4** to become suddenly present or noticeable in: *a note of anxiety entered his voice* **5** to record (an item) in a journal or list **6** *theatre* to come on stage: used as a stage direction: *enter Joseph* **7** to begin (a new process or period of time): *the occupation of the square has entered its eleventh day*

enter *vb* **1** = come *or* go in *or* into, arrive, set foot in somewhere, cross the threshold of somewhere, make an entrance; ≠ exit **2** = join, start work at, begin work at, enrol in, enlist in; ≠ leave **3** = participate in, join (in), be involved in, get involved in, play a part in, partake in, associate yourself with, start to be in **5** = record, note, register, log, list, write down, take down, inscribe **7** = begin, start, take up, move into, commence, set out on, embark upon

enteric (en-*ter*-ik) *adj* of the intestines

enteritis (en-ter-*rite*-iss) *n* inflammation of the small intestine

enterprise *n* **1** a business firm **2** a project or undertaking, esp. one that requires boldness or effort **3** boldness and energy

enterprise *n* **1** = firm, company, business, concern, operation, organization, establishment, commercial undertaking **2** = venture, operation, project, adventure, undertaking, programme, pursuit, endeavour **3** = initiative, energy, daring, enthusiasm, imagination, drive, ingenuity, originality

enterprising *adj* full of boldness and initiative > **enterprisingly** *adv*

enterprising *adj* = resourceful, original, spirited, daring, bold, enthusiastic, imaginative, energetic

entertain *vb* **1** to provide amusement for (a person or audience) **2** to show hospitality to (guests) **3** to consider (an idea or suggestion)

entertain *vb* **1** = amuse, interest, please, delight, charm, enthral, cheer, regale **2** = show hospitality to, receive, accommodate, treat, put up, lodge, be host to, have company of **3** = consider, imagine, think about, contemplate, conceive of, bear in mind, keep in mind, give thought to

entertainer *n* a person who entertains, esp. professionally

entertainment n 1 enjoyment and interest: *a match of top-quality entertainment and goals* 2 an act or show that entertains, or such acts and shows collectively

> **entertainment** n 1 = enjoyment, fun, pleasure, leisure, relaxation, recreation, amusement 2 = pastime, show, sport, performance, treat, presentation, leisure activity

enthral or US **enthrall** (en-thrawl) vb **-thralling, -thralled** to hold the attention or interest of > **enthralling** adj > **enthralment** or US **enthrallment** n

enthuse vb **-thusing, -thused** to feel or cause to feel enthusiasm

enthusiasm n ardent and lively interest or eagerness: *your enthusiasm for literature*

> **enthusiasm** n = keenness, interest, passion, motivation, relish, zeal, zest, fervour

enthusiast n a person who is very interested in and keen on something > **enthusiastic** adj > **enthusiastically** adv

> **enthusiast** n = fan, supporter, lover, follower, addict, buff (*informal*), fanatic, devotee

entice vb **-ticing, -ticed** to attract (someone) away from one place or activity to another > **enticement** n > **enticing** adj

> **entice** vb = lure, attract, invite, persuade, tempt, induce, seduce, lead on

entire adj made up of or involving all of something, including every detail, part, or aspect > **entirely** adv

> **entire** adj = whole, full, complete, total

entirety n, pl **-ties** 1 all of a person or thing: *you must follow this diet for the entirety of your life* 2 **in its entirety** as a whole

entitle vb **-tling, -tled** 1 to give (someone) the right to do or have something 2 to give a name or title to (a book or film) > **entitlement** n

> **entitle** vb 1 = give the right to, allow, enable, permit, sanction, license, authorize, empower 2 = call, name, title, term, label, dub, christen, give the title of

entity n, pl **-ties** something that exists in its own right and not merely as part of a bigger thing

> **entity** n = thing, being, individual, object, substance, creature, organism

entomology n the study of insects > **entomological** adj > **entomologist** n

entourage (on-toor-ahzh) n a group of people who assist or travel with an important or well-known person

entrails pl n 1 the internal organs of a person or animal; intestines 2 the innermost parts of anything

entrance[1] n 1 something, such as a door or gate, through which it is possible to enter a place 2 the act of coming into a place, esp. with reference to the way in which it is done: *she made a sudden startling entrance* 3 *theatre* the act of appearing on stage 4 the right to enter a place: *he refused her entrance because she was carrying her Scottie dog* 5 ability or permission to join or become involved with a group or organization: *entrance to the profession should be open to men and women alike* ▸ adj 6 necessary in order to enter something: *they have paid entrance fees for English-language courses*

> **entrance** n 1 = way in, opening, door, approach, access, entry, gate, passage; ≠ exit 2, 3 = appearance, coming in, entry, arrival, introduction; ≠ exit 4, 5 = admission, access, entry, entrée, admittance, permission to enter, right of entry

entrance[2] vb **-trancing, -tranced** to fill with delight > **entrancement** n > **entrancing** adj

> **entrance** vb = enchant, delight, charm, fascinate, dazzle, captivate, enthral, beguile; ≠ bore

entrant n a person who enters a university, competition, etc.

> **entrant** n = competitor, player, candidate, entry, participant, applicant, contender, contestant

entreat vb to ask (someone) earnestly to do something

entreaty n, pl **-treaties** an earnest request or plea

entrée (on-tray) n 1 the right to enter a place 2 a dish served before a main course 3 *chiefly US* the main course

entrench vb 1 to fix or establish firmly: *the habit had become entrenched* 2 *military* to fortify (a position) by digging trenches around it > **entrenchment** n

entrepreneur n the owner of a business who attempts to make money by risk and initiative > **entrepreneurial** adj

> **entrepreneur** n = businessperson, tycoon, executive, industrialist, speculator, magnate, impresario, business executive

entropy (en-trop-ee) n 1 *formal* lack of pattern or organization 2 *physics* a thermodynamic quantity that represents the amount of energy present in a system that cannot be converted into work because it is tied up in the atomic structure of the system

entrust vb 1 to give (someone) a duty or responsibility: *Miss Conway, who was entrusted with the child's education* 2 to put (something) into the care of someone: *he stole all the money we had entrusted to him*

> **entrust** vb 1 = give custody of, deliver, commit, delegate, hand over, turn over, confide (*formal*) 2 = assign

entry *n, pl* **-tries 1** something, such as a door or gate, through which it is possible to enter a place **2** the act of coming in to a place, esp. with reference to the way in which it is done **3** the right to enter a place: *he was often refused entry to Boston's bars because he looked so young* **4** the act of joining an organization or group: *Poland's entry into the EU* **5** a brief note, article, or group of figures in a diary, book, or computer file **6** a quiz form, painting, etc. submitted in an attempt to win a competition **7** a person, horse, car, etc. entering a competition ▸ *adj* **8** necessary in order to enter something: *entry fee*

> **entry** *n* **1** = way in, opening, door, approach, access, gate, passage, entrance **2** = coming in, entering, appearance, arrival, entrance; ≠ exit **3** = admission, access, entrance, admittance, entrée, permission to enter, right of entry **4** = introduction, presentation, initiation, inauguration, induction, debut, investiture **5** = record, listing, account, note, statement, item

entwine *vb* **-twining, -twined** to twist together or round something else

E number *n* any of a series of numbers with the prefix E- indicating a specific food additive recognized by the EU

enumerate *vb* **-ating, -ated 1** to name or list one by one **2** to count **3** *Canad* to include in the voting list for an area > **enumeration** *n* > **enumerator** *n*

enunciate *vb* **-ating, -ated 1** to pronounce (words) clearly **2** to state precisely or formally > **enunciation** *n*

envelop *vb* to cover, surround, or enclose > **envelopment** *n*

envelope *n* **1** a flat covering of paper, that can be sealed, used to enclose a letter, etc. **2** any covering, wrapper, or enclosing structure: *an envelope of filo pastry* **3** *geom* a curve that is tangential to each one of a group of curves

> **envelope** *n* **2** = wrapping, casing, case, covering, cover, jacket, sleeve, wrapper

enviable *adj* so desirable or fortunate that it is likely to cause envy > **enviably** *adv*

envious *adj* feeling, showing, or resulting from envy > **enviously** *adv*

environment (en-**vire**-on-ment) *n* **1** the surroundings in which a person, animal, or plant lives **2** *ecology* **the environment** the natural world of land, sea, air, plants, and animals: *nuclear waste must be prevented from leaking into the environment* > **environmental** *adj*

> **environment** *n* **1** = surroundings, setting, conditions, situation, medium, circumstances, background, atmosphere

environmentalist *n* a person concerned with the protection of the natural environment

environmentalist *n* = conservationist, ecologist, green

environs *pl n* a surrounding area, esp. the outskirts of a city

envisage *or US* **envision** *vb* **-aging, -aged** *or* **-ioning, -ioned** to believe to be possible or likely in the future: *the commission envisages a mix of government and private funding*

> **envisage** *or* **envision** *vb* = foresee, see, expect, predict, anticipate, envision

envoy *n* **1** a messenger or representative **2** a diplomat ranking next below an ambassador

> **envoy** *n* **1** = messenger, agent, representative, delegate, courier, intermediary, emissary **2** = ambassador, diplomat, emissary

envy *n, pl* **-vies 1** a feeling of discontent aroused by someone else's possessions, achievements, or qualities **2** something that causes envy: *their standards are the envy of the world* ▸ *vb* **-vies, -vying, -vied 3** to wish that one had the possessions, achievements, or qualities of (someone else) > **envyingly** *adv*

> **envy** *n* **1** = covetousness, resentment, jealousy, bitterness, resentfulness, enviousness (*informal*) ▸ *vb* = be jealous (of), resent, begrudge, be envious (of)

enzyme *n* any of a group of complex proteins that act as catalysts in specific biochemical reactions > **enzymatic** *adj*

Eolithic *adj* of the early period of the Stone Age, when crude stone tools were used

epaulette *n* a piece of ornamental material on the shoulder of a garment, esp. a military uniform

ephemeral *adj* lasting only for a short time

epic *n* **1** a long exciting book, poem, or film, usually telling of heroic deeds **2** a long narrative poem telling of the deeds of a legendary hero ▸ *adj* **3** very large or grand: *a professional feud of epic proportions*

epicentre *or US* **epicenter** *n* the point on the earth's surface immediately above the origin of an earthquake

epicure *n* a person who enjoys good food and drink > **epicurism** *n*

epicurean *adj* **1** devoted to sensual pleasures, esp. food and drink ▸ *n* **2** same as **epicure** > **epicureanism** *n*

epidemic *n* **1** a widespread occurrence of a disease **2** a rapid development or spread of something: *the epidemic of childhood obesity* ▸ *adj* **3** (esp. of a disease) affecting many people in an area: *stress has now reached epidemic proportions*

> **epidemic** *n* **1** = outbreak, plague, growth, spread, scourge, contagion **2** = spate, plague, outbreak, wave, rash, eruption, upsurge

epidermis *n* the thin protective outer layer of the skin > **epidermal** *adj*

epidural (ep-pid-dure-al) *adj* **1** on or over the outermost membrane covering the brain and spinal cord (**dura mater**) ▸ *n* **2** ▲ an injection of anaesthetic into the space outside the outermost membrane enveloping the spinal cord **B** anaesthesia produced by this method

epiglottis *n* a thin flap of cartilage at the back of the mouth that covers the entrance to the larynx during swallowing

epigram *n* **1** a witty remark **2** a short poem with a witty ending > **epigrammatic** *adj*

epigraph *n* **1** a quotation at the beginning of a book **2** an inscription on a monument or building

epilepsy *n* a disorder of the central nervous system which causes periodic loss of consciousness and sometimes convulsions

epileptic *adj* **1** of or having epilepsy ▸ *n* **2** *sometimes offensive* a person who has epilepsy

epilogue *n* a short concluding passage or speech at the end of a book or play

Epiphany *n*, *pl* **-nies** a Christian festival held on January 6 commemorating, in the Western church, the manifestation of Christ to the Magi and, in the Eastern church, the baptism of Christ

episcopal (ip-**piss**-kop-al) *adj Christianity* of or relating to bishops

episcopalian *adj also* **episcopal** *Christianity* **1** practising or advocating Church government by bishops ▸ *n* **2** an advocate of such Church government

episode *n* **1** an event or series of events **2** any of the sections into which a novel or a television or radio serial is divided

> **episode** *n* **1** = event, experience, happening, matter, affair, incident, adventure, occurrence **2** = instalment, part, act, scene, section, chapter, passage, webisode

episodic *adj* **1** resembling or relating to an episode **2** occurring at irregular and infrequent intervals

epistemology (ip-iss-stem-**ol**-a-jee) *n* the theory of knowledge, esp. the critical study of its validity, methods, and scope > **epistemological** *adj* > **epistemologist** *n*

epistle *n* **1** *formal or humorous* a letter **2** a literary work in letter form, esp. a poem

epistolary *adj* **1** of or relating to letters **2** (of a novel) presented in the form of a series of letters

epitaph *n* **1** a commemorative inscription on a tombstone **2** a commemorative speech or written passage

epithet *n* a word or short phrase used to describe someone or something: *these tracks truly deserve that overworked epithet 'classic'*

epitome (ip-**pit**-a-mee) *n* **1** a person or thing that is a typical example of a characteristic or class: *the epitome of rural tranquillity* **2** a summary, esp. of a written work

epitomize *or* **-mise** *vb* **-mizing, -mized** *or* **-mising, -mised** to be or make a perfect or typical example of

epoch (**ee**-pok) *n* **1** a long period of time marked by some predominant characteristic: *the cold-war epoch* **2** the beginning of a new or distinctive period: *the invention of nuclear weapons marked an epoch in the history of warfare* **3** *geol* a unit of time within a period during which a series of rocks is formed > **epochal** *adj*

epoch-making *adj* very important or significant

eponymous (ip-**pon**-im-uss) *adj* **1** (of a person) being the person after whom a literary work, film, etc. is named: *the eponymous heroine in the film of Jane Eyre* **2** (of a literary work, film, etc.) named after its central character or creator: *The Stooges' eponymous debut album*

equable (ek-**wab**-bl) *adj* **1** even-tempered and reasonable **2** (of a climate) not varying much throughout the year, and neither very hot nor very cold > **equably** *adv*

equal *adj* **1** identical in size, quantity, degree, or intensity **2** having identical privileges, rights, or status **3** applying in the same way to all people or in all circumstances: *equal rights* **4** **equal to** having the necessary strength, ability, or means for: *she was equal to any test the corporation put to her* ▸ *n* **5** a person or thing equal to another ▸ *vb* **equalling, equalled** *or US* **equaling, equaled** **6** to be equal to; match **7** to make or do something equal to: *he has equalled his world record in the men's 100 metres* > **equally** *adv*

> **equal** *adj* **1** = identical, the same, matching, equivalent, uniform, alike, corresponding; ≠ unequal **2, 3** = fair, just, impartial, egalitarian, unbiased, even-handed; ≠ unfair ▸ *n* = match, equivalent, twin, counterpart ▸ *vb* **6** = be equal to, match, reach **7** = be as good as, match, compare with, equate with, measure up to, be as great as

equality *n*, *pl* **-ties** the state of being equal

> **equality** *n* = fairness, equal opportunity, equal treatment, egalitarianism, fair treatment, justness; ≠ inequality

equalize *or* **-ise** *vb* **-izing, -ized** *or* **-ising, -ised** **1** to make equal or uniform **2** (in a sport) to reach the same score as one's opponent or opponents > **equalization** *or* **-isation** *n* > **equalizer** *or* **-iser** *n*

equal opportunity *n* the offering of employment or promotion equally to all, without discrimination as to sex, ethnicity, colour, etc.

equanimity *n* calmness of mind or temper; composure

equate *vb* **equating, equated** **1** to make or regard as equivalent **2** *maths* to form an equation from > **equatable** *adj*

equation | 276

equate *vb* **1** = identify, associate, connect, compare, relate, mention in the same breath, think of in connection with

equation *n* **1** a mathematical statement that two expressions are equal **2** a situation or problem in which a number of different factors need to be considered: *this plan leaves human nature out of the equation* **3** the act of equating **4** *chem* a representation of a chemical reaction using symbols of the elements

equation *n* **3** = equating, comparison, parallel, correspondence

equator *n* an imaginary circle around the earth at an equal distance from the North Pole and the South Pole

equatorial *adj* of, like, or existing at or near the equator

equestrian *adj* **1** of or relating to horses and riding **2** on horseback: *an equestrian statue of the Queen* > **equestrianism** *n*

equidistant *adj* equally distant

equilateral *adj* **1** having all sides of equal length ► *n* **2** a geometric figure having all sides of equal length

equilibrium *n*, *pl* **-ria** **1** a stable condition in which forces cancel one another **2** a state of mental and emotional balance; composure

equilibrium *n* **1** = stability, balance, symmetry, steadiness, evenness, equipoise

equine *adj* of or like a horse

equinoctial *adj* **1** relating to or occurring at an equinox ► *n* **2** a storm at or near an equinox

equinox *n* either of the two occasions when day and night are of equal length, around March 21 and September 23

equip *vb* **equipping**, **equipped** **1** to provide with supplies, components, etc.: *the car comes equipped with a catalytic converter* **2** to provide with abilities, understanding, etc.: *stress is something we are all equipped to cope with*

equip *vb* **1** = supply, provide, stock, arm, array, furnish, fit out, kit out **2** = prepare, qualify, educate, get ready

equipment *n* **1** a set of tools or devices used for a particular purpose: *communications equipment* **2** an act of equipping

equipment *n* **1** = apparatus, stock, supplies, stuff, tackle, gear, tools, provisions

equipoise *n* the state of being perfectly balanced; equilibrium

equitable *adj* fair and reasonable > **equitably** *adv*

equitable *adj* = even-handed, just, fair, reasonable, proper, honest, impartial, unbiased

equity *n*, *pl* **-ties** **1** the quality of being impartial; fairness **2** *law* a system of using

principles of natural justice and fair conduct to reach a judgment when common law is inadequate or inappropriate **3** the difference in value between a person's debts and the value of the property on which they are secured: *negative equity*

equivalent *n* **1** something that has the same use or function as something else: *Denmark's equivalent to Silicon Valley* ► *adj* **2** equal in value, quantity, significance, etc. **3** having the same or a similar effect or meaning > **equivalence** *n*

equivalent *n* = equal, counterpart, twin, parallel, match, opposite number ► *adj* = equal, same, comparable, parallel, identical, alike, corresponding, tantamount; ≠ different

equivocal *adj* **1** capable of varying interpretations; ambiguous **2** deliberately misleading or vague **3** of doubtful character or sincerity: *the party's commitment to genuine reform is equivocal* > **equivocally** *adv*

equivocate *vb* **-cating**, **-cated** to use vague or ambiguous language in order to deceive someone or to avoid telling the truth > **equivocation** *n* > **equivocator** *n*

ER Queen Elizabeth

era *n* **1** a period of time considered as distinctive; epoch **2** an extended period of time measured from a fixed point: *the Communist era* **3** *geol* a major division of time

era *n* **1, 2** = age, time, period, date, generation, epoch, day *or* days

eradicate *vb* **-cating**, **-cated** to destroy or get rid of completely: *measures to eradicate racism* > **eradicable** *adj* > **eradication** *n* > **eradicator** *n*

eradicate *vb* = wipe out, eliminate, remove, destroy, get rid of, erase, extinguish, obliterate

erase *vb* **erasing**, **erased** **1** to destroy all traces of: *he could not erase the memory of his earlier defeat* **2** to rub or wipe out (something written) **3** to remove sound or information from (a magnetic tape or disk) > **erasable** *adj*

erase *vb* **1** = delete, cancel out, wipe out, remove, eradicate, obliterate, blot out, expunge (*formal*) **2** = rub out, remove, wipe out, delete

eraser *n* an object, such as a piece of rubber, for erasing something written

erasure *n* **1** an erasing **2** the place or mark where something has been erased

ere *conj*, *prep poetic* before

e-reader *n* a portable device that allows users to download and read texts in electronic form

erect *vb* **1** to build **2** to raise to an upright position **3** to found or form: *the caricature of socialism erected by Lenin* ► *adj* **4** upright in posture or position **5** *physiol* (of the penis, clitoris, or nipples) firm or rigid after swelling with blood, esp. as a result of sexual excitement > **erection** *n*

erect *vb* **1, 2** = build, raise, set up, construct, put up, assemble, put together; ≠ demolish **3** = found, establish, form, create, set up, institute, organize, put up ▸ *adj* **4** = upright, straight, stiff, vertical, elevated, perpendicular; ≠ bent

erectile *adj physiol* (of an organ, such as the penis) capable of becoming erect

ergonomic *adj* **1** designed to minimize effort and discomfort **2** of or relating to ergonomics

ergonomics *n* the study of the relationship between workers and their environment

ergot *n* **1** a disease of a cereal, such as rye, caused by a fungus **2** the dried fungus used in medicine

ermine *n, pl* **-mines** *or* **-mine** **1** the stoat in northern regions, where it has a white winter coat **2** the fur of this animal, used to trim state robes of judges, nobles, etc.

erode *vb* **eroding, eroded** **1** to wear down or away **2** to deteriorate or cause to deteriorate

erode *vb* **1** = disintegrate, crumble, deteriorate, corrode, break up, grind down, waste away, wear down *or* away **2** = weaken, destroy, undermine, diminish, impair, lessen, wear away

erogenous (ir-roj-in-uss) *adj* sensitive to sexual stimulation: *an erogenous zone*

erosion *n* **1** the wearing away of rocks or soil by the action of water, ice, or wind **2** a gradual lessening or reduction: *an erosion of national sovereignty* › **erosive** *or* **erosional** *adj*

erosion *n* **1** = disintegration, deterioration, wearing down *or* away, grinding down **2** = deterioration, undermining, destruction, weakening, attrition, eating away, abrasion, grinding down

erotic *adj* of, concerning, or arousing sexual desire or giving sexual pleasure › **erotically** *adv*

erotic *adj* = sexual, sexy (*informal*), crude, explicit, sensual, seductive, vulgar

erotica *pl n* explicitly sexual literature or art

eroticism *n* **1** erotic quality or nature **2** the use of sexually arousing symbolism in literature or art **3** sexual excitement or desire

err *vb* **1** to make a mistake **2** to sin

errand *n* **1** a short trip to get or do something for someone **2** **run an errand** to make such a trip

errant *adj* **1** behaving in a way considered to be unacceptable: *an errant schoolboy* **2** old-fashioned or literary wandering in search of adventure: *a knight errant* › **errantry** *n*

erratic *adj* **1** irregular or unpredictable: *his increasingly erratic behaviour* ▸ *n* **2** *geol* a rock that has been transported by glacial action › **erratically** *adv*

erratic *adj* = unpredictable, variable, unstable, irregular, inconsistent, uneven, unreliable, wayward; ≠ regular

erratum *n, pl* **-ta** an error in writing or printing

erroneous *adj* based on or containing an error or errors; incorrect › **erroneously** *adv*

error *n* **1** a mistake, inaccuracy, or misjudgment **2** the act or state of being wrong or making a misjudgment: *the plane was shot down in error* **3** the amount by which the actual value of a quantity might differ from an estimate: *a 3% margin of error*

error *n* = mistake, slip, blunder, oversight, howler (*informal*), bloomer (*Brit informal*), miscalculation, solecism (*formal*), barry *or* Barry Crocker (*Austral slang*)

ersatz (air-zats) *adj* made in imitation of something more expensive: *ersatz coffee*

erstwhile *adj* **1** former ▸ *adv* **2** *archaic* formerly

erudite (air-rude-ite) *adj* having or showing great academic knowledge › **erudition** *n*

erupt *vb* **1** (of a volcano) to throw out molten lava, ash, and steam in a sudden and violent way **2** to burst forth suddenly and violently: *riots erupted across the country* **3** (of a group of people) to suddenly become angry and aggressive: *the meeting erupted in fury* **4** (of a blemish) to appear on the skin › **eruptive** *adj* › **eruption** *n*

erupt *vb* **1** = explode, blow up, emit lava **2** = gush, burst out, pour forth, belch forth, spew forth *or* out **4** = break out, appear, flare up

erysipelas (air-riss-sip-ill-ass) *n* an acute disease of the skin, with fever and raised purplish patches

escalate *vb* **-lating, -lated** to increase or be increased in size, seriousness, or intensity › **escalation** *n*

escalate *vb* = grow, increase, extend, intensify, expand, surge, mount, heighten; ≠ decrease

escalator *n* a moving staircase consisting of stair treads fixed to a conveyor belt

escalope (**ess**-kal-lop) *n* a thin slice of meat, usually veal

escapade *n* a mischievous act or adventure

escape *vb* **-caping, -caped** **1** to get away or break free from (confinement) **2** to manage to avoid (something dangerous, unpleasant, or difficult) **3** (of gases, liquids, etc.) to leak gradually **4** to elude; be forgotten by: *those little round cakes whose name escapes me* ▸ *n* **5** the act of escaping or state of having escaped **6** a way of avoiding something difficult, dangerous, or unpleasant: *his frequent illnesses provided an escape from intolerable stress* **7** a means of relaxation or relief: *he found temporary escape through the local cinema* **8** a leakage of gas or liquid

escape *vb* 1 = get away, flee, take off, fly, bolt, slip away, abscond, make a break for it, do a Skase (*Austral informal*) 2 = avoid, miss, evade, dodge, shun, elude, duck (*informal*), steer clear of 3 = leak out, flow out, gush out, emanate, seep out, exude, spill out, pour forth ▸ *n* 5 = getaway, break, flight, break-out 6 = avoidance, evasion, circumvention 7 = relaxation, recreation, distraction, diversion, pastime 8 = leak, emission, outpouring, seepage, issue, emanation

escapee *n* a person who has escaped, esp. from prison

escapism *n* an inclination to retreat from unpleasant reality, for example through fantasy > **escapist** *n, adj*

escapologist *n* an entertainer who specializes in freeing himself or herself from chains, ropes, etc. > **escapology** *n*

escarpment *n* the long continuous steep face of a ridge or mountain

eschew (iss-**chew**) *vb* to avoid doing or being involved in (something disliked or harmful) > **eschewal** *n*

escort *n* 1 people or vehicles accompanying another to protect or guard them 2 a person who accompanies someone on a social occasion ▸ *vb* 3 to act as an escort to

escort *n* 1 = guard, bodyguard, train, convoy, entourage, retinue, cortege 2 = companion, partner, attendant, guide, beau (*old-fashioned*), chaperon ▸ *vb* = accompany, lead, partner, conduct, guide, shepherd, usher, chaperon

escudo (ess-**kew**-doe) *n, pl* **-dos** a former monetary unit of Portugal

escutcheon *n* 1 a shield displaying a coat of arms 2 **blot on one's escutcheon** a stain on one's honour

Eskimo *sometimes offensive* ▸ *n* 1 *pl* **-mos** or **-mo** a member of a group of peoples who live in N Canada, Greenland, Alaska, and E Siberia 2 a language of these peoples ▸ *adj* 3 of these peoples

esoteric (ee-so-**ter**-rik) *adj* understood by only a small number of people, esp. because they have special knowledge > **esoterically** *adv*

ESP extrasensory perception

esp. especially

espadrille (ess-pad-**drill**) *n* a light canvas shoe with a braided cord sole

espalier (ess-**pal**-yer) *n* 1 a shrub or fruit tree trained to grow flat 2 the trellis on which such plants are grown

esparto or **esparto grass** *n, pl* **-tos** any of various grasses of S Europe and N Africa, used to make ropes, mats, etc.

especial *adj formal* same as **special**

especially *adv* 1 particularly: *people are dying, especially children and babies* 2 more than usually: *an especially virulent disease*

especially *adv* 1 = notably, mostly, strikingly, conspicuously, outstandingly 2 = very, specially, extremely, remarkably, unusually, exceptionally, markedly, uncommonly

Esperanto *n* an international artificial language > **Esperantist** *n, adj*

espionage (ess-**pyon**-ahzh) *n* 1 the use of spies to obtain secret information, esp. by governments 2 the act of spying

espionage *n* = spying, intelligence, surveillance, counter-intelligence, undercover work

esplanade *n* a long open level stretch of ground, esp. beside the seashore or in front of a fortified place

espousal *n* 1 adoption or support: *his espousal of the free market* 2 *old-fashioned* a marriage or engagement ceremony

espouse *vb* **-pousing, -poused** 1 to adopt or give support to (a cause, ideal, etc.) 2 *old-fashioned* (esp. of a man) to marry

espresso *n, pl* **-sos** coffee made by forcing steam or boiling water through ground coffee

esprit (ess-**pree**) *n* spirit, liveliness, or wit

esprit de corps (de **kore**) *n* consciousness of and pride in belonging to a particular group

espy *vb* **espies, espying, espied** to catch sight of

Esq. esquire

esquire *n* 1 *chiefly Brit* a title of respect placed after a man's name and usually shortened to *Esq.*: *I Davies, Esquire* 2 (in medieval times) the attendant of a knight

essay *n* 1 a short literary composition on a single subject 2 a short piece of writing on a subject done as an exercise by a student 3 an attempt ▸ *vb* 4 *formal* to attempt: *he essayed a faint smile*

essay *n* 1, 2 = composition, study, paper, article, piece, assignment, discourse, tract ▸ *vb* = attempt, try, undertake, endeavour

essayist *n* a person who writes essays

essence *n* 1 the most important and distinctive feature of something, which determines its identity 2 a concentrated liquid used to flavour food 3 **in essence** essentially 4 **of the essence** vitally important

essence *n* 1 = fundamental nature, nature, being, heart, spirit, soul, core, substance 2 = concentrate, spirits, extract, tincture, distillate

essential *adj* 1 vitally important; absolutely necessary: *it is essential to get this finished on time* 2 basic or fundamental: *she translated the essential points of the lecture into English* ▸ *n* 3 something fundamental or indispensable > **essentially** *adv*

essential adj 1 = vital, important, needed, necessary, critical, crucial (informal), key, indispensable; ≠ unimportant
2 = fundamental, main, basic, principal, cardinal, elementary, innate, intrinsic; ≠ secondary ▸ n = prerequisite, fundamental, necessity, must, basic, sine qua non (Latin), rudiment, must-have

establish vb 1 to create or set up (an organization, link, etc.): the regime wants to establish better relations with neighbouring countries 2 to become firmly associated with a particular activity or reputation: the play that established him as a major dramatist 3 to prove: a test to establish if your baby has any chromosomal disorder 4 to cause (a principle) to be accepted: our study establishes the case for further research

establish vb 1 = set up, found, create, institute, constitute, inaugurate 2 = secure, form, ground, settle 3 = prove, confirm, demonstrate, certify, verify, substantiate, corroborate, authenticate

establishment n 1 the act of establishing or state of being established 2 **A** a business organization or other institution **B** a place of business 3 the people employed by an organization

establishment n 1 = creation, founding, setting up, foundation, institution, organization, formation, installation
2**A** = organization, company, business, firm, concern, operation, institution, corporation

Establishment n **the Establishment** a group of people having authority within a society: usually seen as conservative

Establishment n **the Establishment** = the authorities, the system, the powers that be, the ruling class

estate n 1 a large piece of landed property, esp. in the country 2 Brit & Austral a large area of land with houses or factories built on it: an industrial estate 3 law property or possessions, esp. of a deceased person 4 history any of the orders or classes making up a society

estate n 1 = lands, property, area, grounds, domain, manor, holdings, homestead (US, Canad) 2 = area, centre, park, development, site, zone, plot 3 = property, capital, assets, fortune, goods, effects, wealth, possessions

estate agent n Brit & Austral a person whose job is to help people buy and sell houses and other property

estate car n Brit a car which has a long body with a door at the back end and luggage space behind the rear seats

esteem n 1 admiration and respect ▸ vb 2 to have great respect or high regard for (someone)

3 formal to judge or consider: I should esteem it a kindness > **esteemed** adj

esteem n = respect, regard, honour, admiration, reverence, estimation, veneration
▸ vb 2 = respect, admire, think highly of, love, value, prize, treasure, revere

ester n chem a compound produced by the reaction between an acid and an alcohol

estimable adj worthy of respect

estimate vb **-mating, -mated** 1 to form an approximate idea of (size, cost, etc.); calculate roughly 2 to form an opinion about; judge 3 to submit an approximate price for a job to a prospective client ▸ n 4 an approximate calculation 5 a statement of the likely charge for certain work 6 an opinion > **estimator** n

estimate vb 1 = calculate roughly, value, guess, judge, reckon, assess, evaluate, gauge 2 = think, believe, consider, rate, judge, hold, rank, reckon (informal) ▸ n 4 = approximate calculation, guess, assessment, judgment, valuation, guesstimate (informal), rough calculation, ballpark figure (informal) 6 = assessment, opinion, belief, appraisal, evaluation, judgment, estimation

estimation n 1 a considered opinion; judgment: overall, he went up in my estimation 2 the act of estimating

estranged adj 1 no longer living with one's husband or wife: his estranged wife 2 having quarrelled and lost touch with one's family or friends: I am estranged from my son
> **estrangement** n

estuary n, pl **-aries** the widening channel of a river where it nears the sea > **estuarine** adj

estuary n = inlet, mouth, creek, firth, fjord

ETA estimated time of arrival

et al. 1 and elsewhere 2 and others

etc. et cetera

et cetera or **etcetera** (et set-ra) adv 1 and the rest; and others; or the like 2 and so forth

etch vb 1 to wear away the surface of (a metal, glass, etc.) by the action of an acid 2 to cut (a design or pattern) into a printing plate with acid 3 to imprint vividly: the scene is etched on my mind > **etcher** n

etch vb 1 = corrode, eat into, burn into 2, 3 = engrave, cut, impress, stamp, carve, imprint, inscribe

etching n 1 the art or process of preparing or printing etched designs 2 a print made from an etched plate

etching n = print, carving, engraving, imprint, inscription

eternal adj 1 without beginning or end; lasting for ever 2 unchanged by time: eternal truths 3 seemingly unceasing: his eternal whingeing

4 of or like God or a god: *the Eternal Buddha*
> **eternally** *adv*

> **eternal** *adj* **1, 2** = everlasting, lasting,
> permanent, enduring, endless, perpetual,
> timeless, unending; ≠ transitory
> **3** = interminable, endless, infinite, continual,
> immortal, never-ending, everlasting;
> ≠ occasional

eternity *n, pl* **-ties 1** endless or infinite time
2 a seemingly endless period of time: *it seemed an
eternity before he could feel his heart beating again* **3** the
timeless existence after death **4** the state of
being eternal

> **eternity** *n* **1, 4** = perpetuity, immortality,
> infinity, timelessness, endlessness **2** = ages
> **3** = the afterlife, heaven (*informal*), paradise, the
> next world, the hereafter

eternity ring *n* a ring given as a token of
lasting affection, esp. one set all around with
stones to symbolize continuity
ether *n* **1** a colourless sweet-smelling liquid
used as a solvent and anaesthetic **2** the
substance formerly believed to fill all space and
to transmit electromagnetic waves **3** the upper
regions of the atmosphere; clear sky ▷ Also (for
senses 2 and 3): **aether**
ethereal (eth-eer-ee-al) *adj* **1** extremely
delicate or refined **2** heavenly or spiritual
> **ethereally** *adv*
ethic *n* a moral principle or set of moral values
held by an individual or group
ethical *adj* **1** of or based on a system of moral
beliefs about right and wrong **2** in accordance
with principles of professional conduct **3** of or
relating to ethics > **ethically** *adv*

> **ethical** *adj* **1, 2** = right, morally acceptable,
> good, just, fair, responsible, principled;
> ≠ unethical **3** = moral, behavioural

ethics *pl n* **1** a code of behaviour, esp. of a
particular group, profession, or individual:
business ethics **2** the moral fitness of a decision,
course of action, etc. ▸ *n* **3** the study of the
moral value of human conduct

> **ethics** *pl n* **1** = moral code, standards,
> principles, morals, conscience, morality,
> moral values, moral principles, tikanga (NZ)

ethnic *or* **ethnical** *adj* **1** of or relating to a
human group with racial, religious, and
linguistic characteristics in common
2 characteristic of another culture, esp. a
peasant one: *ethnic foodstuffs* > **ethnically** *adv*

> **ethnic** *or* **ethnical** *adj* = cultural, national,
> traditional, native, folk, racial, genetic,
> indigenous

ethnic cleansing *n* the practice, by the
dominant ethnic group in an area, of removing
other ethnic groups by expulsion or extermination

ethnology *n* the branch of anthropology that
deals with races and peoples and their relations
to one another > **ethnological** *adj* > **ethnologist** *n*
ethos (eeth-oss) *n* the distinctive spirit and
attitudes of a people, culture, etc.
ethyl (eth-ill) *adj* of, consisting of, or containing
the monovalent group $C_2H_5–$
ethylene *or* **ethene** *n* a colourless flammable
gaseous alkene used to make polythene and
other chemicals
etiolate (ee-tee-oh-late) *vb* **-lating, -lated**
1 *formal* to become or cause to become weak
2 *botany* to make a green plant paler through
lack of sunlight > **etiolation** *n*
etiology *n, pl* **-gies 1** the study of causation
2 the study of the cause of diseases > **etiological**
adj
etiquette *n* **1** the customs or rules of behaviour
regarded as correct in social life **2** a conventional
code of practice in certain professions
étude (ay-tewd) *n music* a short composition for
a solo instrument, esp. intended to be played as
an exercise or to demonstrate virtuosity
etymology *n, pl* **-gies 1** the study of the sources
and development of words **2** an account of the
source and development of a word
> **etymological** *adj* > **etymologist** *n*
EU European Union
eucalyptus *or* **eucalypt** *n, pl* **-lyptuses, -lyptus**
or **-lypts** any of a mostly Australian genus of
trees, widely cultivated for timber and gum, and
for the medicinal oil in their leaves (**eucalyptus
oil**)
Eucharist (yew-kar-ist) *n* **1** the Christian
sacrament commemorating Christ's Last
Supper by the consecration of bread and wine
2 the consecrated elements of bread and wine
> **Eucharistic** *adj*
eugenics (yew-jen-iks) *n* the study of methods
of improving the human race, esp. by selective
breeding > **eugenic** *adj* > **eugenically** *adv*
> **eugenicist** *n*
eulogize *or* **-gise** *vb* **-gizing, -gized** *or* **-gising,
-gised** to praise (a person or thing) highly in
speech or writing > **eulogistic** *adj*
eulogy *n, pl* **-gies 1** a speech or piece of writing
praising a person or thing, esp. a person who
has recently died **2** high praise
eunuch *n* a man who has been castrated, esp.
(formerly) a guard in a harem
euphemism *n* an inoffensive word or phrase
substituted for one considered offensive or
upsetting, such as *departed* for *dead*
> **euphemistic** *adj* > **euphemistically** *adv*
euphonious *adj* pleasing to the ear
euphonium *n* a brass musical instrument
with four valves, resembling a small tuba
euphony *n, pl* **-nies** a pleasing sound, esp. in
speech
euphoria *n* a feeling of great but often
unjustified or exaggerated happiness
> **euphoric** *adj*

euphoria *n* = elation, joy, ecstasy, rapture, exhilaration, jubilation; ≠ despondency

Eurasian *adj* **1** of Europe and Asia **2** of mixed European and Asian descent ▸ *n* **3** a person of mixed European and Asian descent

eureka (yew-reek-a) *interj* an exclamation of triumph on discovering or solving something

euro *n*, *pl* **euros** the unit of the European Union's single currency

European *adj* **1** of Europe ▸ *n* **2** a person from Europe **3** a person of European descent **4** an advocate of closer links between the countries of Europe, esp. those in the European Union ▸ **Europeanism** *n*

European Union *n* an economic organization of European states, which have some shared monetary, social, and political goals

Eustachian tube *n* a tube that connects the middle ear with the pharynx and equalizes the pressure between the two sides of the eardrum

euthanasia *n* the act of killing someone painlessly, esp. to relieve suffering from an incurable illness

euthanasia *n* = assisted suicide, mercy killing

euthanize *or* **-nise** *vb* **-nizing, -nized** *or* **-nising, -nised** to kill (a person or animal) painlessly, esp. to relieve suffering from an incurable illness. Also (Austral): **euthanaze**

evacuate *vb* **-ating, -ated** **1** to send away from a dangerous place to a safe place: *200 people were evacuated from their homes because of the floods* **2** to empty (a place) because it has become dangerous: *the entire street was evacuated until the fire was put out* **3** *physiol* to discharge waste from the body ▸ **evacuation** *n* ▸ **evacuee** *n*

evacuate *vb* **1** = remove, clear, withdraw, expel, move out, send to a safe place **2** = abandon, leave, clear, desert, quit, withdraw from, pull out of, move out of

evade *vb* **evading, evaded** **1** to get away from or avoid (imprisonment, captors, etc.) **2** to get around, shirk, or dodge (the law, a duty, etc.) **3** to avoid answering (a question)

evade *vb* **1, 2** = avoid, escape, dodge, get away from, elude, steer clear of, sidestep, duck (*informal*); ≠ face **3** = avoid answering, parry, fend off, fudge, hedge, equivocate

evaluate *vb* **-ating, -ated** to find or judge the quality or value of (something) ▸ **evaluation** *n*

evaluate *vb* = assess, rate, judge, estimate, reckon, weigh, calculate, gauge

evanescent *adj formal* quickly fading away; ephemeral or transitory ▸ **evanescence** *n*

evangelical *adj* **1** of or following from the Christian Gospels **2** of certain Protestant sects which emphasize salvation through faith alone and a belief in the absolute authority of the Bible **3** displaying missionary zeal in promoting something ▸ *n* **4** a member of an evangelical sect ▸ **evangelicalism** *n* ▸ **evangelically** *adv*

evangelism *n* the practice of spreading the Christian gospel

evangelist *n Christianity* a preacher, sometimes itinerant ▸ **evangelistic** *adj*

Evangelist *n Christianity* any of the writers of the Gospels: Matthew, Mark, Luke, or John

evangelize *or* **-lise** *vb* **-lizing, -lized** *or* **-lising, -lised** to preach the Christian gospel (to) ▸ **evangelization** *or* **-lisation** *n*

evaporate *vb* **-rating, -rated** **1** to change from a liquid or solid to a vapour **2** to become less and less and finally disappear: *faith in the government evaporated rapidly after the election* ▸ **evaporable** *adj* ▸ **evaporation** *n*

evaporate *vb* **1** = disappear, vaporize, dematerialize, vanish, dissolve, dry up, fade away, melt away **2** = fade away, disappear, vanish, dissolve, melt away

evaporated milk *n* thick unsweetened tinned milk from which some of the water has been removed

evasion *n* **1** the act of evading something, esp. a duty or responsibility, by cunning or illegal means: *tax evasion* **2** cunning or deception used to dodge a question, duty, etc.

evasive *adj* **1** seeking to evade; not straightforward: *an evasive answer* **2** avoiding or seeking to avoid trouble or difficulties: *evasive action* ▸ **evasively** *adv*

eve *n* **1** the evening or day before some special event **2** the period immediately before an event: *on the eve of the Second World War* **3** *poetic or old-fashioned* evening

eve *n* **1** = night before, day before, vigil **2** = brink, point, edge, verge, threshold

even *adj* **1** level and regular; flat **2** on the same level: *make sure the surfaces are even with one another* **3** regular and unvarying: *an even pace* **4** equally balanced between two sides **5** equal in number, quantity, etc. **6** (of a number) divisible by two **7** denoting alternatives, events, etc. that have an equal probability: *they have a more than even chance of winning the next election* **8** having scored the same number of points **9 even money** *or* **evens** a bet in which the winnings are exactly the same as the amount staked **10 get even with** *informal* to exact revenge on; settle accounts with ▸ *adv* **11** used to suggest that the content of a statement is unexpected or paradoxical: *it's chilly in Nova Scotia, even in August* **12** used to intensify a comparative adjective or adverb: *an even greater demand* **13** used to introduce a word that is stronger and more accurate than one already used: *a normal, even inevitable aspect of ageing* **14** used preceding a hypothesis to emphasize that whether or not the condition is fulfilled, the statement remains valid: *the remark didn't call for an answer even if he could have thought of one* **15 even so** in spite of any assertion to the contrary; nevertheless **16 even though** despite the fact that > **evenly** *adv* > **evenness** *n*

> **even** *adj* **1, 2** = level, straight, flat, smooth, true, steady, uniform, parallel; ≠ uneven **3** = regular, stable, constant, steady, smooth, uniform, unbroken, uninterrupted; ≠ variable **4, 8** = equally matched, level, tied, on a par, neck and neck, fifty-fifty (*informal*), all square; ≠ ill-matched **5** = equal, like, matching, similar, identical, comparable; ≠ unequal

evening *n* **1** the latter part of the day, esp. from late afternoon until nightfall ▸ *adj* **2** of or in the evening: *the evening meal*

> **evening** *n* = dusk (*archaic*), night, sunset, twilight, sundown, gloaming (*Scot poetic*), close of day, evo (*Austral slang*)

evensong *n* *Church of England* the daily evening service. Also called: **Evening Prayer**

event *n* **1** anything that takes place, esp. something important **2** a planned and organized occasion: *the wedding was one of the social events of the year* **3** any one contest in a sporting programme **4 in any event** *or* **at all events** whatever happens **5 in the event** when it came to the actual or final outcome: *in the event, neither of them turned up* **6 in the event of** if (such a thing) happens **7 in the event that** if it should happen that

> **event** *n* **1, 2** = incident, happening, experience, affair, occasion, proceeding, business, circumstance **3** = competition, game, tournament, contest, bout

eventful *adj* full of exciting or important incidents

eventing *n* *Brit, Austral & NZ* riding competitions (esp. **three-day events**), usually involving cross-country riding, jumping, and dressage

eventual *adj* happening or being achieved at the end of a situation or process: *the Fascists' eventual victory in the Spanish Civil War* > **eventually** *adv*

> **eventual** *adj* = final, overall, concluding, ultimate

eventuality *n, pl* **-ties** a possible occurrence or result: *I was utterly unprepared for such an eventuality*

ever *adv* **1** at any time: *it was the fourth fastest time ever* **2** always: *ever present* **3** used to give emphasis: *tell him to put to sea as soon as ever he can* **4 ever so** *or* **ever such** *informal, chiefly Brit* used to give emphasis: *I'm ever so sorry*

> **ever** *adv* **1** = at any time, at all, in any case, at any point, by any chance, on any occasion, at any period **2** = always, for ever, at all times, evermore

evergreen *adj* **1** (of certain trees and shrubs) bearing foliage throughout the year ▸ *n* **2** an evergreen tree or shrub

everlasting *adj* **1** never coming to an end; eternal **2** lasting so long or occurring so often as to become tedious > **everlastingly** *adv*

evermore *adv* all time to come

every *adj* **1** each without exception: *they were winning every battle* **2** the greatest or best possible: *there is every reason to believe in the sincerity of their commitment* **3** each: *every 20 years* **4 every bit as** informal just as: *she's every bit as clever as you* **5 every other** each alternate: *every other month*

> **every** *adj* **1** = each, each and every, every single

everybody *pron* every person; everyone

> **everybody** *pron* = everyone, each one, the whole world, each person, every person, all and sundry, one and all

everyday *adj* **1** commonplace or usual **2** happening each day **3** suitable for or used on ordinary days

> **everyday** *adj* **1, 3** = ordinary, common, usual, routine, stock, customary, mundane, run-of-the-mill; ≠ unusual

everyone *pron* every person; everybody

> **everyone** *pron* = everybody, each one, the whole world, each person, every person, all and sundry, one and all

everything *pron* **1** the whole; all things: *everything had been carefully packed* **2** the thing that is most important: *work was everything to her*

> **everything** *pron* **1** = all, the lot, the whole lot, each thing

everywhere *adv* to or in all parts or places

> **everywhere** *adv* = all over, all around, the world over, high and low, in every nook and cranny, far and wide *or* near, to *or* in every place

evict *vb* to expel (someone) legally from his or her home or land > **eviction** *n*

evidence *n* **1** something which provides ground for belief or disbelief: *there is no evidence that depression is inherited* **2** *law* matter produced before a court of law in an attempt to prove or disprove a point in issue **3 in evidence** on display; apparent ▸ *vb* **-dencing, -denced 4** to show clearly; demonstrate: *you evidenced no talent for music*

> **evidence** *n* **1** = proof, grounds, demonstration, confirmation, verification, corroboration, authentication, substantiation **2** = testimony, statement, submission, avowal ▸ *vb* = show, prove, reveal, display, indicate, witness, demonstrate, exhibit

evident *adj* easy to see or understand
> **evidently** *adv*

evident *adj* = obvious, clear, plain, apparent, visible, manifest, noticeable, unmistakable; ≠ hidden

evidential *adj* of, serving as, or based on evidence > **evidentially** *adv*

evil *n* **1** a force or power that brings about wickedness and harm: *the battle between good and evil* **2** a wicked or morally wrong act or thing: *the evil of racism* ▸ *adj* **3** (of a person) deliberately causing great harm and misery; wicked: *an evil dictator* **4** (of an act, idea, etc.) causing great harm and misery; morally wrong: *what you did was deeply evil* **5** very unpleasant: *it was fascinating to see people vanish as if we had some very evil smell*
> **evilly** *adv*

evil *n* **1** = wickedness, bad, vice, sin, wrongdoing, depravity, badness, villainy **2** = act of cruelty, crime, ill, horror, outrage, misfortune, mischief, affliction ▸ *adj* **3** = wicked, bad, malicious, immoral, sinful, malevolent, depraved, villainous **4** = harmful, disastrous, destructive, dire, catastrophic, pernicious (*formal*), ruinous **5** = offensive, nasty, foul, unpleasant, vile, noxious, disagreeable, pestilential

evildoer *n* a person who does evil > **evildoing** *n*
evince *vb* **evincing, evinced** *formal* to show or display (a quality or feeling) clearly: *a humility which he had never evinced in earlier days*
eviscerate *vb* **-ating, -ated** to remove the internal organs of; disembowel > **evisceration** *n*
evocation *n* the act of evoking > **evocative** *adj*
evoke *vb* **evoking, evoked** **1** to call or summon up (a memory or feeling) from the past **2** to provoke or bring about: *his sacking evoked a huge public protest*

evoke *vb* **2** = arouse, cause, induce, awaken, give rise to, stir up, rekindle, summon up; ≠ suppress

evolution *n* **1** *biol* a gradual change in the characteristics of a population of animals or plants over successive generations **2** a gradual development, esp. to a more complex form
> **evolutionary** *adj*

evolution *n* **1** = rise, development, adaptation, natural selection, Darwinism, survival of the fittest **2** = development, growth, advance, progress, working out, expansion, extension, unfolding

evolve *vb* **evolving, evolved** **1** to develop gradually **2** (of animal or plant species) to undergo evolution

evolve *vb* **1** = develop, metamorphose, adapt yourself **2** = grow, develop, advance, progress, mature

ewe *n* a female sheep
ewer *n* a large jug with a wide mouth
ex *n, pl* **exes** *informal* one's former wife, husband, or romantic partner
ex- *prefix* **1** out of, outside, or from: *exit* **2** former: *his famous ex-wife*
exacerbate (ig-zass-er-bate) *vb* **-bating, -bated** to make (pain, emotion, or a situation) worse > **exacerbation** *n*
exact *adj* **1** correct in every detail; strictly accurate **2** precise, as opposed to approximate **3** based on measurement and the formulation of laws: *forecasting floods is not an exact science* ▸ *vb* **4** to obtain or demand as a right, esp. through force or strength: *the rebels called for revenge to be exacted for the killings*

exact *adj* **1** = accurate, correct, true, right, specific, precise, definite, faultless; ≠ approximate ▸ *vb* = demand, claim, force, command, extract, compel, extort

exacting *adj* making rigorous or excessive demands

exacting *adj* = demanding, hard, taxing, difficult, tough; ≠ easy

exactly *adv* **1** with complete accuracy and precision: *I don't know exactly where they live* **2** in every respect: *he looks exactly like his father* ▸ *interj* **3** just so! precisely!

exactly *adv* **1** = accurately, correctly, precisely, faithfully, explicitly, scrupulously, truthfully, unerringly **2** = precisely, specifically, bang on (*informal*), to the letter

exaggerate *vb* **-rating, -rated** **1** to regard or represent as greater than is true **2** to make greater or more noticeable > **exaggerated** *adj*
> **exaggeratedly** *adv* > **exaggeration** *n*

exaggerate *vb* = overstate, enlarge, embroider, amplify, embellish, overestimate, overemphasize, pile it on about (*informal*)

exalt *vb* **1** to praise highly **2** to raise to a higher rank > **exalted** *adj* > **exaltation** *n*
exam *n* short for **examination**
examination *n* **1** the act of examining **2** *education* exercises, questions, or tasks set to test a person's knowledge and skill **3** *med* physical inspection of a patient **4** *law* the formal questioning of a person on oath

examination *n* **2** = exam, test, research, paper, investigation, practical, assessment, quiz **3** = checkup, analysis, going-over (*informal*), exploration, health check, check

examine *vb* **-mining, -mined** **1** to inspect carefully or in detail; investigate **2** *education* to test the knowledge of (a candidate) in (a subject) **3** *med* to investigate the state of health of (a patient) **4** *law* to formally question (someone) on oath > **examinee** *n* > **examiner** *n*

e

example | 284

examine *vb* **1** = inspect, study, survey, investigate, explore, analyse, scrutinize, peruse **2** = test, question, assess, quiz, evaluate, appraise **3** = check, analyse, check over **4** = question, quiz, interrogate, cross-examine, grill (*informal*), give the third degree to (*informal*)

example *n* **1** a specimen that is typical of its group; sample: *a fine example of Georgian architecture* **2** a particular event, object, or person that demonstrates a point or supports an argument, theory, etc.: *Germany is a good example of how federalism works in practice* **3** a person, action, or thing that is worthy of imitation **4** a punishment or the person punished regarded as a warning to others **5 for example** as an illustration

example *n* **1** = instance, specimen, case, sample, illustration, particular case, particular instance, typical case **2, 3** = illustration, model, ideal, standard, prototype, paradigm, archetype, paragon **4** = warning, lesson, caution, deterrent

exasperate *vb* **-rating, -rated** to cause great irritation to ▷ **exasperated** *adj* ▷ **exasperating** *adj* ▷ **exasperation** *n*

excavate *vb* **-vating, -vated** **1** to unearth (buried objects) methodically to discover information about the past **2** to make a hole in something by digging into it or hollowing it out: *one kind of shrimp excavates a hole for itself* ▷ **excavation** *n* ▷ **excavator** *n*

exceed *vb* **1** to be greater in degree or quantity **2** to go beyond the limit of (a restriction)

exceed *vb* **1** = surpass, better, pass, eclipse, beat, cap (*informal*), top, be over **2** = go over the limit of, go beyond, overstep

exceedingly *adv* very; extremely

excel *vb* **-celling, -celled** **1** to be better than; surpass **2 excel in** *or* **at** to be outstandingly good at

excel *vb* **1** = be superior, eclipse, beat, surpass, transcend, outdo, outshine **2 excel in or at something** = be good at, shine at, be proficient in, show talent in, be skilful at, be talented at

excellence *n* the quality of being exceptionally good

excellence *n* = high quality, merit, distinction, goodness, superiority, greatness, supremacy, eminence

Excellency *or* **Excellence** *n, pl* **-lencies** *or* **-lences** ▷ **Your** *or* **His** *or* **Her Excellency** a title used to address a high-ranking official, such as an ambassador

excellent *adj* exceptionally good; outstanding

excellent *adj* = outstanding, good, great (*informal*), fine, cool (*informal*), brilliant, very good, superb, booshit (*Austral slang*), exo (*Austral slang*), sik (*Austral slang*), rad (*informal*), phat (*slang*), schmick (*Austral informal*); ≠ terrible

except *prep* **1** Also: **except for** not including; apart from: *everyone except Jill laughed* **2 except that** but for the fact that ▷ *vb* **3** to leave out or exclude

except *prep* **1** = apart from, but for, saving, barring, excepting, other than, excluding, omitting ▷ *vb* = exclude, leave out, omit, disregard, pass over

excepting *prep* except

exception *n* **1** anything excluded from or not conforming to a general rule or classification **2 take exception to** to make objections to

exception *n* **1** = special case, freak, anomaly, inconsistency, deviation, oddity, peculiarity, irregularity

exceptional *adj* **1** forming an exception **2** having much more than average intelligence, ability, or skill ▷ **exceptionally** *adv*

exceptional *adj* **1** = unusual, special, odd, strange, extraordinary, unprecedented, peculiar, abnormal; ≠ ordinary **2** = remarkable, special, excellent, extraordinary, outstanding, superior, first-class, marvellous; ≠ average

excerpt *n* **1** a passage taken from a book, speech, etc.; extract ▷ *vb* **2** to take a passage from a book, speech, etc.

excerpt *n* = extract, part, piece, section, selection, passage, fragment, quotation

excess *n* **1** the state or act of going beyond normal or permitted limits **2** an immoderate or abnormal amount **3** the amount, number, etc. by which one thing exceeds another **4** behaviour regarded as too extreme or immoral to be acceptable: *a life of sex, drugs, and drunken excess* **5 excesses** acts or actions that are unacceptably cruel or immoral: *one of the bloodiest excesses of a dictatorial regime* **6 in excess of** more than **7 to excess** to an extreme or unhealthy extent: *he had started to drink to excess* ▷ *adj* **8** more than normal, necessary, or permitted: *excess fat* ▷ **excessive** *adj* ▷ **excessively** *adv*

excess *n* **2** = surfeit, surplus, overload, glut, superabundance, superfluity; ≠ shortage **4** = overindulgence, extravagance, profligacy, debauchery, dissipation, intemperance, indulgence, prodigality; ≠ moderation

exchange *vb* **-changing, -changed** **1** (of two or more people, governments, etc.) to give each other (something similar) at the same time: *they nervously exchanged smiles* **2** to replace (one thing) with another, esp. to replace unsatisfactory goods: *could I exchange this for a larger size, please?* ▷ *n* **3** the act of exchanging **4** anything given or received as an equivalent or substitute for something else **5** an argument **6** Also called: **telephone exchange** a centre in which

telephone lines are interconnected **7** a place where securities or commodities are traded, esp. by brokers or merchants **8** a transfer of sums of money of equivalent value, as between different currencies **9** the system by which commercial debts are settled, esp. by bills of exchange, without direct payment of money
> **exchangeable** *adj*

exchange *vb* = interchange, change, trade, switch, swap, barter, give to each other, give to one another ▸ *n* **3** = interchange, trade, switch, swap, trafficking, swapping, substitution, barter **5** = conversation, talk, word, discussion, chat, dialogue, natter, powwow

Exchequer *n government* (in Britain and certain other countries) the accounting department of the Treasury

excise[1] *n* **1** a tax on goods, such as alcoholic drinks, produced for the home market **2** *Brit* that section of the government service responsible for the collection of excise, now the Board of Customs and Excise

excise[2] *vb* **-cising, -cised 1** to delete a passage from a book **2** to remove an organ or part surgically > **excision** *n*

excitable *adj* nervous and easily excited
> **excitability** *n*

excite *vb* **-citing, -cited 1** to make (a person) feel so highly excited he or she is unable to relax because he or she is looking forward eagerly to something: *he was excited at the long-awaited arrival of a son* **2** to cause or arouse (an emotion, response, etc.): *the idea strongly excited his interest* **3** to arouse sexually **4** *physiol* to cause a response in (an organ, tissue, or part) **5** *physics* to raise (an atom, molecule, etc.) to a higher energy level
> **excited** *adj* > **excitedly** *adv*

excite *vb* **1** = thrill, inspire, stir, provoke, animate, rouse, exhilarate, inflame **2** = arouse, provoke, rouse, stir up **3** = titillate, thrill, stimulate, electrify

excitement *n* **1** the state of being excited **2** a person or thing that excites

excitement *n* **1** = exhilaration, action, activity, passion, thrill, animation, furore, agitation

exclaim *vb* to cry out or speak suddenly or excitedly, as from surprise, delight, horror, etc.

exclaim *vb* = cry out, declare, shout, proclaim, yell, utter, call out

exclamation *n* **1** an abrupt or excited cry or utterance **2** the act of exclaiming
> **exclamatory** *adj*

exclamation mark *or US* **exclamation point** *n* the punctuation mark (!) used after exclamations and forceful commands

exclude *vb* **-cluding, -cluded 1** to keep out; prevent from entering **2** to leave out of consideration > **exclusion** *n*

exclude *vb* **1** = keep out, bar, ban, refuse, forbid, boycott, prohibit, disallow; ≠ let in **2** = omit, reject, eliminate, rule out, miss out, leave out; ≠ include

exclusive *adj* **1** excluding or incompatible with anything else: *these two theories are mutually exclusive* **2** not shared: *exclusive rights* **3** used or lived in by a privileged minority, esp. a fashionable clique: *an exclusive skiing resort* **4** not including the numbers, dates, etc. mentioned **5** *exclusive of* except for; not taking account of **6 exclusive to** limited to; found only in ▸ *n* **7** a story reported in only one newspaper > **exclusively** *adv* > **exclusivity** *or* **exclusiveness** *n*

exclusive *adj* **2** = entire, full, whole, complete, total, absolute, undivided **3** = select, fashionable, stylish, restricted, posh (*informal, chiefly Brit*), chic, high-class, up-market; ≠ unrestricted

excommunicate *vb* **-cating, -cated** *Christianity* to expel (someone) from membership of a church and ban him or her from taking part in its services > **excommunication** *n*

excoriate *vb* **-ating, -ated 1** *literary* to censure severely **2** to strip skin from (a person or animal) > **excoriation** *n*

excrement *n* waste matter discharged from the body; faeces > **excremental** *adj*

excrescence *n* something that protrudes, esp. an outgrowth from a part of the body
> **excrescent** *adj*

excreta (ik-skree-ta) *pl n* urine and faeces discharged from the body

excrete *vb* **-creting, -creted** to discharge waste matter, such as urine, sweat, or faeces, from the body > **excretion** *n* > **excretory** *adj*

excruciating *adj* **1** unbearably painful; agonizing **2** hard to bear: *never had an afternoon passed with such excruciating slowness*
> **excruciatingly** *adv*

exculpate *vb* **-pating, -pated** to free from blame or guilt

excursion *n* a short outward and return journey, esp. for sightseeing, etc.; outing

excursion *n* = trip, tour, journey, outing, expedition, ramble, day trip, jaunt

excuse *n* **1** an explanation offered to justify an action which has been criticized or as a reason for not fulfilling an obligation, etc. ▸ *vb* **-cusing, -cused 2** to put forward a reason or justification for (an action, fault, or offending person) **3** to pardon (a person) or overlook (a fault) **4** to free (someone) from having to carry out a task, obligation, etc.: *a doctor's letter excusing him from games at school* **5** to allow to leave **6 be excused** *euphemistic* to go to the toilet **7 excuse me!** an expression used to catch someone's attention or to apologize for an interruption, disagreement, etc. > **excusable** *adj*

excuse *n* = justification, reason, explanation, defence, grounds, plea, apology, vindication; ≠ accusation ▸ *vb* **2** = justify, explain, defend, vindicate, mitigate, apologize for, make excuses for; ≠ blame **3** = forgive, pardon, overlook, tolerate, acquit, turn a blind eye to, exonerate, make allowances for **4** = free, relieve, exempt, release, spare, discharge, let off, absolve; ≠ convict

ex-directory *adj Brit & NZ* not listed in a telephone directory by request

execrable (eks-sik-rab-bl) *adj* of very poor quality > **execrably** *adv*

execute *vb* **-cuting, -cuted** **1** to put (a condemned person) to death **2** to carry out or accomplish **3** to produce or create (a work of art) **4** *law* to render (a deed) effective, for example by signing it **5** to carry out the terms of (a contract, will, etc.) > **executer** *n*

execute *vb* **1** = put to death, kill, shoot, hang, behead, decapitate, guillotine, electrocute **2** = perform, carry out, accomplish **3** = carry out, effect, implement, accomplish, discharge, administer, prosecute, enact

execution *n* **1** the act of executing **2** the carrying out or undergoing of a sentence of death **3** the manner in which something is performed; technique

execution *n* **1** = carrying out, performance, operation, administration, prosecution, enforcement, implementation, accomplishment **2** = killing, hanging, the death penalty, the rope, capital punishment, beheading, the electric chair, the guillotine

executioner *n* a person whose job is to kill people who have been sentenced to death

executive *n* **1** a person or group responsible for the administration of a project or business **2** the branch of government responsible for carrying out laws, decrees, etc. ▸ *adj* **3** having the function of carrying plans, orders, laws, etc. into effect: *the executive producer* **4** of or for executives: *the executive car park* **5** *informal* very expensive or exclusive: *executive cars*

executive *n* **1** = administrator, official, director, manager, managing director, controller, chief executive officer **2** = administration, government, directors, management, leadership, hierarchy, directorate ▸ *adj* **3** = administrative, controlling, directing, governing, regulating, decision-making, managerial

executor *or fem* **executrix** *n law* a person appointed by someone to ensure that the conditions set out in his or her will are carried out > **executorial** *adj*

exegesis (eks-sij-jee-siss) *n, pl* **-ses** (-seez) explanation of a text, esp. of the Bible

exemplar *n* **1** a person or thing to be copied; model **2** a typical specimen; example

exemplary *adj* **1** so good as to be an example worthy of imitation **2** (of a punishment) extremely harsh, so as to discourage others from committing a similar crime

exemplify *vb* **-fies, -fying, -fied** **1** to show by example **2** to serve as an example of > **exemplification** *n*

exemplify *vb* = show, represent, display, demonstrate, illustrate, exhibit, embody, serve as an example of

exempt *adj* **1** not subject to an obligation, tax, etc. ▸ *vb* **2** to release (someone) from an obligation, tax, etc. > **exemption** *n*

exempt *adj* = immune, free, excepted, excused, released, spared, not liable to; ≠ liable ▸ *vb* = grant immunity, free, excuse, release, spare, relieve, discharge, let off

exequies (eks-sik-weez) *pl n, sing* **-quy** funeral rites

exercise *n* **1** physical exertion, esp. for training or keeping fit **2** an activity planned to achieve a particular purpose: *the group's meeting was mainly an exercise in mutual reassurance* **3** a set of movements, tasks, etc. designed to improve or test one's ability or fitness **4** the use or practice of (a right, power, or authority) **5** *military* a manoeuvre or simulated combat operation ▸ *vb* **-cising, -cised** **6** to put into use; make use of: *we urge all governments involved to exercise restraint* **7** to take exercise or perform exercises **8** to practise using in order to develop or train: *to exercise one's voice* **9** to worry or vex: *the government has been exercised by the threat from international criminal groups* **10** *military* to carry out simulated combat, manoeuvres, etc. > **exerciser** *n*

exercise *n* **1** = exertion, training, activity, work, labour, effort, movement, toil **3** = task, problem, lesson, assignment, practice **4** = use, practice, application, operation, discharge, implementation, fulfilment, utilization **5** = manoeuvre, campaign, operation, movement, deployment ▸ *vb* **6** = put to use, use, apply, employ, exert, utilize, bring to bear, avail yourself of **7, 8** = train, work out, practise, keep fit, do exercises

exert *vb* **1** to use influence, authority, etc. forcefully or effectively **2 exert oneself** to make a special effort

exert *vb* **1** = apply, use, exercise, employ, wield, make use of, utilize, bring to bear **2 exert oneself** = make an effort, work, labour, struggle, strain, strive, endeavour, toil

exertion *n* **1** effort or exercise, esp. physical effort: *the sudden exertion of running for a bus* **2** the act or an instance of using one's influence, powers, or authority: *the exertion of parental authority*

exeunt (eks-see-unt) they go out: used as a stage direction

exfoliate *vb* **-ating, -ated 1** to peel off in scales or layers **2** to remove dead cells from the skin by washing with a granular cosmetic preparation > **exfoliation** *n*

ex-gratia (eks-gray-sha) *adj* given as a favour where no legal obligation exists: *an ex-gratia payment*

exhale *vb* **-haling, -haled 1** to expel breath or smoke from the lungs; breathe out **2** to give off or be given off as gas, fumes, etc.: *the crater exhaled smoke* > **exhalation** *n*

exhaust *vb* **1** to tire out **2** to use up totally **3** to discuss (a topic) so thoroughly that no more remains to be said ▸ *n* **4** gases ejected from an engine as waste products **5** the parts of an engine through which waste gases pass > **exhausted** *adj* > **exhaustible** *adj*

> **exhaust** *vb* **1** = tire out, fatigue, drain, weaken, weary, sap, wear out, debilitate **2** = use up, spend, consume, waste, go through, run through, deplete, squander

exhaustion *n* **1** extreme tiredness **2** the act of exhausting or state of being exhausted

> **exhaustion** *n* **1** = tiredness, fatigue, weariness, debilitation **2** = depletion, emptying, consumption, using up

exhaustive *adj* very thorough; comprehensive > **exhaustively** *adv*

exhibit *vb* **1** to display (a work of art) to the public **2** to show (a quality or feeling): *they exhibited extraordinary courage* ▸ *n* **3** an object exhibited to the public **4** *law* a document or object produced in court as evidence > **exhibitor** *n*

> **exhibit** *vb* **1** = display, show, set out, parade, unveil, put on view **2** = show, reveal, display, demonstrate, express, indicate, manifest

exhibition *n* **1** a public display of art, skills, etc. **2** the act of exhibiting or the state of being exhibited: *an exhibition of bad temper* **3 make an exhibition of oneself** to behave so foolishly that one attracts public attention

> **exhibition** *n* **1** = show, display, representation, presentation, spectacle, showcase, exposition, ex (*Canad informal*) **2** = display, show, performance, demonstration, revelation

exhibitionism *n* **1** a compulsive desire to attract attention to oneself **2** a compulsive desire to expose one's genitals publicly > **exhibitionist** *n*

exhilarate *vb* **-rating, -rated** to make (someone) feel lively and cheerful > **exhilaration** *n*

exhort *vb formal* to urge (someone) earnestly > **exhortation** *n*

exhume (ig-zyume) *vb* **-huming, -humed** *formal* to dig up something buried, esp. a corpse > **exhumation** *n*

exigency *n*, *pl* **-gencies** *formal* **1** an urgent demand or need **2** an emergency > **exigent** *adj*

exiguous *adj formal* scanty or meagre > **exiguity** *n*

exile *n* **1** a prolonged, usually enforced absence from one's country **2** a person banished or living away from his or her country ▸ *vb* **-iling, -iled 3** to expel (someone) from his or her country; banish

> **exile** *n* **1** = banishment, expulsion, deportation, eviction, expatriation **2** = expatriate, refugee, outcast, émigré, deportee ▸ *vb* = banish, expel, throw out, deport, drive out, eject, expatriate, cast out

exist *vb* **1** to have being or reality; be: *does God exist?* **2** to only just be able to keep oneself alive, esp. because of poverty or hunger **3** to be living; live **4** to be present under specified conditions or in a specified place > **existing** *adj*

> **exist** *vb* **2** = survive, stay alive, make ends meet, subsist, eke out a living, scrape by, scrimp and save, support yourself **3** = live, be present, survive, endure, be in existence, be, have breath **4** = occur, be present

existence *n* **1** the fact or state of being real, live, or actual **2** a way of life, esp. a poor or hungry one **3** everything that exists > **existent** *adj*

> **existence** *n* **1** = reality, being, life, subsistence, actuality **2** = life, situation, way of life, lifestyle

existential *adj* **1** of or relating to existence, esp. human existence **2** of or relating to existentialism

existentialism *n* a philosophical movement stressing personal experience and responsibility of the individual, who is seen as a free agent > **existentialist** *adj*, *n*

exit *n* **1** a way out **2** the act of going out **3** *theatre* the act of going offstage **4** *Brit & Austral* a point at which vehicles may leave a motorway ▸ *vb* **exiting, exited 5** to go away or out; depart **6** *theatre* he or she goes offstage: used as a stage direction: *exit bleeding from the room*

> **exit** *n* **1** = way out, door, gate, outlet, doorway, gateway, escape route; ≠ entry **2** = departure, withdrawal, retreat, farewell, going, goodbye, exodus, decamping ▸ *vb* **5** = depart, leave, go out, withdraw, retire, quit, retreat, go away; ≠ enter

exocrine *adj* of or denoting a gland, such as the sweat gland, that discharges its product through a duct

exodus (eks-so-duss) *n* the departure of a large number of people

> **exodus** *n* = departure, withdrawal, retreat, leaving, flight, exit, migration, evacuation

ex officio (eks off-fish-ee-oh) *adv*, *adj* by right of position or office

exonerate *vb* -ating, -ated to clear (someone) of blame or a criminal charge > **exoneration** *n*

exorbitant *adj* (of prices, demands, etc.) excessively great or high: *an exorbitant rent* > **exorbitantly** *adv*

exorcize *or* **-cise** *vb* -cizing, -cized *or* -cising, -cised to expel (evil spirits) by prayers and religious rites > **exorcism** *n* > **exorcist** *n*

exotic *adj* 1 having a strange allure or beauty 2 originating in a foreign country; not native ► *n* 3 a non-native plant > **exotically** *adv*

> **exotic** *adj* 1 = unusual, striking, strange, fascinating, mysterious, colourful, glamorous, unfamiliar; ≠ ordinary 2 = foreign, alien, tropical, external, naturalized

exotica *pl n* exotic objects, esp. as a collection

expand *vb* 1 to make or become greater in extent, size, or scope 2 to spread out; unfold 3 **expand on** to go into more detail about (a story or subject) 4 to become increasingly relaxed, friendly, and talkative 5 *maths* to express a function or expression as the sum or product of terms > **expandable** *adj*

> **expand** *vb* 1 = get bigger, increase, grow, extend, swell, widen, enlarge, become bigger; ≠ contract 2 = spread (out), stretch (out), unfold, unravel, diffuse, unfurl, unroll 3 **expand on something** = go into detail about, embellish, elaborate on, develop, flesh out, expound on, enlarge on, expatiate on

expanse *n* an uninterrupted wide area; stretch: *a large expanse of water*

expansion *n* 1 the act of expanding 2 an increase or development, esp. in the activities of a company

> **expansion** *n* 1 = enlargement, increase, growth, opening out 2 = increase, development, growth, spread, magnification, amplification

expansive *adj* 1 wide or extensive 2 friendly, open, and talkative > **expansiveness** *n*

expat *adj*, *n* short for **expatriate**

expatiate (iks-pay-shee-ate) *vb* -ating, -ated > **expatiate on** *formal* to speak or write at length on (a subject) > **expatiation** *n*

expatriate (eks-pat-ree-it) *adj* 1 living away from one's native country: *an expatriate American* 2 exiled ► *n* 3 a person living away from his or her native country 4 an exile > **expatriation** *n*

> **expatriate** *adj* = exiled, refugee, banished, emigrant, émigré, expat ► *n* = exile, refugee, emigrant, émigré

expect *vb* 1 to regard as likely 2 to look forward to or be waiting for 3 to require (something) as an obligation: *he expects an answer by January* 4 **be expecting** *informal* to be pregnant

> **expect** *vb* 1 = think, believe, suppose, assume, trust, imagine, reckon (*informal*), presume 2 = anticipate, look forward to, predict, envisage, await, hope for, contemplate 3 = require, demand, want, call for, ask for, hope for, insist on

expectancy *n* 1 something expected, esp. on the basis of a norm: *a life expectancy of 78* 2 anticipation or expectation

expectant *adj* 1 expecting or hopeful 2 **A** pregnant **B** being the partner of a woman who is pregnant: *an expectant father* > **expectantly** *adv*

expectation *n* 1 the state of expecting or of being expected 2 something looked forward to, whether feared or hoped for 3 belief that someone should behave in a particular way: *unrealistic expectations of yourself and others*

> **expectation** *n* 1 = projection, supposition, assumption, belief, forecast, likelihood, probability, presumption 2 = anticipation, hope, promise, excitement, expectancy, apprehension, suspense

expectorant *med* ► *adj* 1 helping to bring up phlegm from the respiratory passages ► *n* 2 an expectorant medicine

expectorate *vb* -rating, -rated *formal* to cough up and spit out (phlegm from the respiratory passages) > **expectoration** *n*

expediency *or* **expedience** *n*, *pl* -encies *or* -ences 1 the use of methods that are advantageous rather than fair or just 2 appropriateness or suitability

expedient (iks-pee-dee-ent) *n* 1 something that achieves a particular purpose: *income controls were used only as a short-term expedient* ► *adj* 2 useful or advantageous in a given situation: *they only talk about human rights when it is politically expedient*

expedite *vb* -diting, -dited *formal* 1 to hasten the progress of 2 to do quickly

expedition *n* 1 an organized journey or voyage, esp. for exploration 2 the people and equipment comprising an expedition 3 a pleasure trip or excursion: *an expedition to the seaside* > **expeditionary** *adj*

> **expedition** *n* 1 = journey, mission, voyage, tour, quest, trek

expeditious *adj* done quickly and efficiently

expel *vb* -pelling, -pelled 1 to drive out with force 2 to dismiss from a school, club, etc. permanently

expel *vb* **1** = drive out, discharge, force out, let out, eject, issue, spew, belch **2** = throw out, exclude, ban, dismiss, kick out (*informal*), ask to leave, turf out (*informal*), debar; ≠ let in

expend *vb formal* to spend or use up (time, energy, or money)

expendable *adj* **1** not worth preserving **2** able to be sacrificed to achieve an objective, esp. a military one

expenditure *n* **1** something expended, esp. money **2** the amount expended

expenditure *n* **1** = spending, payment, expense, outgoings, cost, outlay **2** = consumption, using, output

expense *n* **1** a particular payment of money; expenditure **2** the amount of money needed to buy or do something; cost **3 expenses** money spent in the performance of a job, etc. **4** something requiring money for its purchase or upkeep **5 at the expense of** to the detriment of

expense *n* **1, 2** = cost, charge, expenditure, payment, spending, outlay

expensive *adj* costing a great deal of money > **expensiveness** *n*

expensive *adj* = costly, high-priced, lavish, extravagant, dear, stiff, steep (*informal*), pricey; ≠ cheap

experience *n* **1** direct personal participation or observation of something: *his experience of prison life* **2** a particular incident, feeling, etc. that a person has undergone **3** accumulated knowledge, esp. of practical matters ▸ *vb* **-encing, -enced 4** to participate in or undergo **5** to be moved by; feel

experience *n* **1, 3** = knowledge, practice, skill, contact, expertise, involvement, exposure, participation **2** = event, affair, incident, happening, encounter, episode, adventure, occurrence ▸ *vb* = undergo, feel, face, taste, go through, sample, encounter, endure

experienced *adj* skilful or knowledgeable as a result of having done something many times before

experienced *adj* = knowledgeable, skilled, tried, tested, seasoned, expert, veteran, practised; ≠ inexperienced

experiment *n* **1** a test or investigation to provide evidence for or against a theory: *a scientific experiment* **2** the trying out of a new idea or method ▸ *vb* **3** to carry out an experiment or experiments > **experimentation** *n* > **experimenter** *n*

experiment *n* **1** = test, trial, investigation, examination, procedure, demonstration, observation, try-out **2** = research, investigation, analysis, observation, research and development, experimentation ▸ *vb* = test, investigate, trial, research, try, examine, pilot, sample

experimental *adj* **1** relating to, based on, or having the nature of an experiment **2** trying out new ideas or methods > **experimentally** *adv*

experimental *adj* **1** = test, trial, pilot, preliminary, provisional, tentative, speculative, exploratory **2** = innovative, new, original, radical, creative, ingenious, avant-garde, inventive

expert *n* **1** a person who has extensive skill or knowledge in a particular field ▸ *adj* **2** skilful or knowledgeable **3** of, involving, or done by an expert > **expertly** *adv*

expert *n* = specialist, authority, professional, master, genius, guru, pundit, maestro, fundi (*S African*), geek (*informal*); ≠ amateur ▸ *adj* **2** = skilful, experienced, professional, masterly, qualified, talented, outstanding, practised, leet (*computers slang*); ≠ unskilled

expertise (eks-per-**teez**) *n* special skill, knowledge, or judgment

expertise *n* = skill, knowledge, know-how (*informal*), facility, judgment, mastery, proficiency, adroitness

expiate *vb* **-ating, -ated** *formal* to make amends for (a sin or wrongdoing) > **expiation** *n*

expiration *n* **1** the finish of something; expiry **2** the act, process, or sound of breathing out > **expiratory** *adj*

expire *vb* **-piring, -pired 1** to finish or run out; come to an end **2** to breathe out air **3** to die

expire *vb* **1** = become invalid, end, finish, conclude, close, stop, run out, cease **3** = die, depart, perish, kick the bucket (*informal*), depart this life, meet your maker, cark it (*Austral, NZ slang*), pass away *or* on

expiry *n, pl* **-ries** a coming to an end, esp. of the period of a contract

explain *vb* **1** to make something easily understandable, esp. by giving a clear and detailed account of it **2 explain oneself** to justify or attempt to justify oneself by giving reasons for one's actions **3 explain away** to offer excuses or reasons for (mistakes)

explain *vb* **1** = make clear *or* plain, describe, teach, define, resolve, clarify, clear up, simplify **3 explain away** = account for, excuse, justify, give a reason for

explanation *n* **1** the reason or reasons why a particular event or situation happened: *there is no reasonable explanation for her behaviour* **2** a detailed account or description: *a 90-minute explanation of his love of jazz*

explanation n 1 = reason, answer, account, excuse, motive, justification, vindication 2 = description, report, definition, teaching, interpretation, illustration, clarification, simplification

explanatory adj serving or intended to serve as an explanation

expletive (iks-**plee**-tiv) n an exclamation or swearword expressing emotion rather than meaning

explicable adj capable of being explained

explicate vb -cating, -cated formal to make clear; explain ▸ **explication** n

explicit adj 1 precisely and clearly expressed, leaving nothing to implication: an explicit commitment to democracy 2 leaving little to the imagination; graphically detailed: the film contains some sexually explicit scenes 3 (of a person) expressing something in a precise and clear way, so as to leave no doubt about what is meant ▸ **explicitly** adv

explicit adj 1 = clear, obvious, specific, direct, precise, straightforward, definite, overt; ≠ vague 3 = frank, specific, graphic, unambiguous, unrestricted, unrestrained, uncensored; ≠ indirect

explode vb -ploding, -ploded 1 to burst with great violence; blow up 2 (of a gas) to undergo a sudden violent expansion as a result of a fast chemical or nuclear reaction 3 to react suddenly or violently with emotion 4 (esp. of a population) to increase rapidly 5 to show (a theory, etc.) to be baseless

explode vb 1 = blow up, erupt, burst, go off, shatter 3 = lose your temper, rage, erupt, become angry, hit the roof (informal), go crook (Austral, NZ slang) 4 = increase, grow, develop, extend, advance, shoot up, soar, boost 5 = disprove, discredit, refute, demolish, repudiate, put paid to, invalidate, debunk

exploit vb 1 to take advantage of (a person or situation) for one's own ends 2 to make the best use of ▸ n 3 a notable deed or feat ▸ **exploitation** n ▸ **exploiter** n

exploit vb 1 = take advantage of, abuse, use, manipulate, milk, misuse, ill-treat, play on or upon 2 = make the best use of, use, make use of, utilize, cash in on (informal), capitalize on, use to good advantage, profit by or from ▸ n = feat, act, achievement, enterprise, adventure, stunt, deed, accomplishment

explore vb -ploring, -plored 1 to examine or investigate, esp. systematically 2 to travel into an unfamiliar region, esp. for scientific purposes ▸ **exploration** n ▸ **exploratory** or **explorative** adj ▸ **explorer** n

explore vb 1 = investigate, consider, research, survey, search, examine, probe, look into

2 = travel around, tour, survey, scout, reconnoitre

explosion n 1 an exploding 2 a violent release of energy resulting from a rapid chemical or nuclear reaction 3 a sudden or violent outburst of activity, noise, emotion, etc. 4 a rapid increase

explosion n 1, 2 = blast, crack, burst, bang, discharge, report, blowing up, clap 3 = outburst, fit, storm, attack, surge, flare-up, eruption 4 = increase, rise, development, growth, boost, expansion, enlargement, escalation

explosive adj 1 able or likely to explode 2 potentially violent: an explosive situation ▸ n 3 a substance capable of exploding ▸ **explosiveness** n

explosive adj 1 = unstable, dangerous, volatile, hazardous, unsafe, perilous, combustible, inflammable 2 = fiery, violent, volatile, stormy, touchy, vehement ▸ n = bomb, mine, shell, missile, rocket, grenade, charge, torpedo

expo n, pl -**pos** short for **exposition** (sense 3)

exponent n 1 a person who advocates an idea, cause, etc.: an exponent of free speech 2 a person who is a skilful performer of some activity: one of the greatest modern exponents of the blues 3 maths a number placed as a superscript to another number indicating how many times the number is to be used as a factor

exponential adj 1 maths of or involving numbers raised to an exponent 2 informal very rapid ▸ **exponentially** adv

export n 1 the sale of goods and services to a foreign country: a ban on the export of arms 2 **exports** goods or services sold to a foreign country ▸ vb 3 to sell (goods or services) or transport (goods) to a foreign country ▸ **exporter** n

expose vb -posing, -posed 1 to uncover (something previously covered) 2 to reveal the truth about (someone or something), esp. when it is shocking or scandalous: an MP whose private life was recently exposed in the press 3 to leave (a person or thing) unprotected in a potentially harmful situation: workers were exposed to relatively low doses of radiation 4 **expose someone to** to give someone an introduction to or experience of (something new) 5 photog to subject (a film) to light when using a camera 6 **expose oneself** to display one's sexual organs in public

expose vb 1 = uncover, show, reveal, display, exhibit, present, unveil, lay bare; ≠ hide 3 = make vulnerable, subject, leave open, lay open

exposé (iks-**pose**-ay) n the bringing of a scandal, crime, etc. to public notice

exposition n **1** a systematic explanation of a subject **2** the act of expounding or setting out a viewpoint **3** a large public exhibition **4** *music* the first statement of the themes of a movement

expostulate vb **-lating, -lated** > **expostulate with** to reason or argue with, esp. in order to dissuade or as a protest > **expostulation** n > **expostulatory** adj

exposure n **1** the state of being exposed to, or lacking protection from, something: *the body cannot cope with sudden exposure to stress* **2** the revealing of the truth about someone or something, esp. when it is shocking or scandalous: *the exposure of a loophole in the tax laws* **3** the harmful effect on a person's body caused by lack of shelter from the weather, esp. the cold **4** appearance before the public, as on television **5** *photog* **A** the act of exposing a film to light **B** an area on a film that has been exposed **6** *photog* **A** the intensity of light falling on a film multiplied by the time for which it is exposed **B** a combination of lens aperture and shutter speed used in taking a photograph

> **exposure** n **3** = hypothermia, frostbite, extreme cold, intense cold

expound vb to explain (a theory, belief, etc.) in detail

express vb **1** to state (an idea or feeling) in words; utter: *two record labels have expressed an interest in signing the band* **2** to show (an idea or feeling): *his body and demeanour expressed distrust* **3** to indicate through a symbol or formula **4** to squeeze out (juice, etc.) **5 express oneself** to communicate one's thoughts or ideas ▸ adj **6** explicitly stated **7** deliberate and specific: *she came with the express purpose of causing a row* **8** of or for rapid transportation of people, mail, etc. ▸ n **9** a fast train stopping at only a few stations **10** *chiefly US & Canad* a system for sending mail rapidly ▸ adv **11** using a system for rapid transportation of people, mail, etc.: *please send this letter express: it's very urgent!* > **expressible** adj

> **express** vb **1** = state, communicate, convey, articulate, say, word, voice, declare **2** = show, indicate, exhibit, demonstrate, reveal, intimate, convey, signify ▸ adj **6** = explicit, clear, plain, distinct, definite, unambiguous, categorical **7** = specific, exclusive, particular, sole, special, singular, clear-cut, especial **8** = fast, direct, rapid, priority, prompt, swift, high-speed, speedy

expression n **1** the transforming of ideas into words **2** a showing of emotion without words **3** communication of emotion through music, painting, etc. **4** a look on the face that indicates mood or emotion **5** a particular phrase used conventionally to express something **6** *maths* a variable, function, or some combination of these > **expressionless** adj

> **expression** n **1** = statement, declaration, announcement, communication, utterance, articulation **2** = indication, demonstration, exhibition, display, showing, show, sign, symbol **4** = look, countenance (*literary*), face, air, appearance, aspect **5** = phrase, saying, word, term, remark, maxim, idiom, adage

expressionism n an early 20th-century artistic and literary movement which sought to express emotions rather than to represent the physical world > **expressionist** n, adj

expressive adj **1** of or full of expression **2 expressive of** showing or suggesting: *looks expressive of hatred and revenge*

> **expressive** adj **1** = vivid, striking, telling, moving, poignant, eloquent; ≠ impassive

expropriate vb **-ating, -ated** *formal* (of a government or other official body) to take (money or property) away from its owners > **expropriation** n > **expropriator** n

expulsion n the act of expelling or the fact of being expelled > **expulsive** adj

> **expulsion** n = ejection, exclusion, dismissal, removal, eviction, banishment

expunge (iks-**sponge**) vb **-punging, -punged** *formal* to remove all traces of: *he had tried to expunge his failure from his mind*

expurgate (**eks**-per-gate) vb **-gating, -gated** to amend (a piece of writing) by removing sections thought to be offensive > **expurgation** n > **expurgator** n

exquisite adj **1** extremely beautiful or attractive **2** showing unusual delicacy and craftsmanship **3** sensitive or discriminating: *exquisite manners* **4** intensely felt: *exquisite joy* > **exquisitely** adv

> **exquisite** adj **1** = beautiful, elegant, graceful, pleasing, attractive, lovely, charming, comely (*old-fashioned*); ≠ unattractive **2** = fine, beautiful, lovely, elegant, precious, delicate, dainty **4** = intense, acute, severe, sharp, keen, extreme

extant adj still in existence; surviving

extemporize or **-rise** vb **-rizing, -rized** or **-rising, -rised** to perform or speak without preparation > **extemporization** or **-risation** n > **extemporizer** or **-riser** n

extend vb **1** to make bigger or longer than before: *they extended the house by building a conservatory* **2** to reach to a certain distance or in a certain direction: *the suburbs extend for many miles* **3** to last for a certain time: *in Norway maternity leave extends to 52 weeks* **4** to broaden the meaning or scope of: *the law was extended to ban all guns* **5** to make something exist or be valid for longer than before: *her visa was extended for three months* **6** to present or offer: *a tradition of extending asylum to refugees* **7** to straighten or stretch out (part of

the body): *she extended a hand in welcome*
8 extend oneself to make use of all one's
ability or strength, often because forced to:
she'll have to really extend herself if she wants to win
> **extendable** *adj*

extend *vb* **1, 4** = widen, increase, expand, add
to, enhance, supplement, enlarge, broaden;
≠ reduce **2** = spread out, reach, stretch **3** = last,
continue, go on, stretch, carry on **6** = offer,
present, confer, stick out, impart, proffer;
≠ withdraw **7** = stretch, stretch out, spread
out, straighten out

extension *n* **1** a room or rooms added to an
existing building **2** a development that
includes or affects more people or things than
before: *an extension of democracy within the EU* **3** an
additional telephone connected to the same line
as another **4** an extra period of time in which
something continues to exist or be valid: *an
extension of the contract for another 2 years* ▸ *adj*
5 denoting something that can be extended or
that extends another object: *an extension ladder*
6 of or relating to the provision of teaching and
other facilities by a school or college to people
who cannot attend full-time courses

extension *n* **1** = annexe, addition,
supplement, appendix, appendage
2 = development, expansion, widening,
increase, broadening, enlargement,
diversification **4** = lengthening, extra time,
continuation, additional period of time

extensive *adj* **1** covering a large area: *extensive
moorland* **2** very great in effect: *the bomb caused
extensive damage* **3** containing many details,
ideas, or items on a particular subject: *an
extensive collection of modern art* > **extensively** *adv*

extensive *adj* **1** = large, considerable,
substantial, spacious, wide, broad, expansive;
≠ confined **2** = great, vast, widespread,
large-scale, far-reaching, far-flung,
voluminous; ≠ limited **3** = comprehensive,
complete, wide, pervasive; ≠ restricted

extensor *n* any muscle that stretches or
extends an arm, leg, or other part of the body
extent *n* **1** the length, area, or size of something
2 the scale or seriousness of a situation or
difficulty: *the extent of the damage* **3** the degree or
amount to which something applies: *to a certain
extent that's true*

extent *n* **1** = size, area, length, width,
breadth **2, 3** = magnitude, amount, scale, level,
stretch, expanse

extenuate *vb* **-ating, -ated** *formal* to make (an
offence or fault) less blameworthy, by giving
reasons that partly excuse it > **extenuating** *adj*
> **extenuation** *n*
exterior *n* **1** a part or surface that is on the
outside **2** the outward appearance of a person:

Amir's grumpy exterior concealed a warm heart **3** a film
scene shot outside ▸ *adj* **4** of, situated on, or
suitable for the outside **5** coming or acting from
outside or abroad

exterior *n* **1** = outside, face, surface, covering,
skin, shell, coating, facade ▸ *adj* **4** = outer,
outside, external, surface, outward,
outermost; ≠ inner

exterminate *vb* **-nating, -nated** to destroy
(a group or type of people, animals, or plants)
completely > **extermination** *n* > **exterminator** *n*
external *adj* **1** of, situated on, or suitable for the
outside: *there was damage to the house's external walls*
2 coming or acting from outside: *most ill health is
caused by external influences* **3** of or involving
foreign nations: *Hong Kong's external trade*
4 *anatomy* situated on or near the outside of the
body: *the external ear* **5** brought into an
organization to do a task which must be done
impartially, esp. one involving testing or
checking: *external examiners* **6** of or relating to
someone taking a university course, but not
attending a university: *an external degree* ▸ *n*
7 externals obvious circumstances or aspects,
esp. superficial ones: *despite the war, the externals of
life in the city remain normal* > **externality** *n*
> **externally** *adv*

external *adj* **1** = outer, outside, surface,
outward, exterior, outermost; ≠ internal
3 = foreign, international, alien, extrinsic;
≠ domestic **5, 6** = outside, visiting; ≠ inside

extinct *adj* **1** (of an animal or plant species)
having died out **2** no longer in existence, esp.
because of social changes: *shipbuilding is virtually
extinct in Scotland* **3** (of a volcano) no longer liable
to erupt

extinct *adj* **1** = dead, lost, gone, vanished,
defunct; ≠ living

extinction *n* **1** the dying out of a plant or
animal species **2** the end of a particular way of
life or type of activity

extinction *n* = dying out, destruction,
abolition, oblivion, extermination,
annihilation, eradication, obliteration

extinguish *vb* **1** to put out (a fire or light) **2** to
remove or destroy entirely > **extinguishable** *adj*
> **extinguisher** *n*
extirpate (eks-ter-pate) *vb* **-pating, -pated**
to remove or destroy completely: *the Romans
attempted to extirpate the Celtic religion*
> **extirpation** *n*
extol *or US* **extoll** *vb* **-tolling, -tolled** to praise
lavishly
extort *vb* to obtain (money or favours) by
intimidation, violence, or the misuse of
authority > **extortion** *n*
extortionate *adj* (of prices, profits, etc.) much
higher than is fair > **extortionately** *adv*

extra *adj* **1** more than is usual, expected, or needed; additional ▸ *n* **2** a person or thing that is additional **3** something for which an additional charge is made **4** *films* a person temporarily engaged, usually for crowd scenes **5** *cricket* a run not scored from the bat **6** an additional edition of a newspaper ▸ *adv* **7** unusually; exceptionally

extra *adj* = surplus, excess, spare, redundant, unused, leftover, superfluous; ≠ vital ▸ *n* **2** = addition, bonus, supplement, accessory; ≠ necessity ▸ *adv* = exceptionally, very, specially, especially, particularly, extremely, remarkably, unusually

extra- *prefix* outside or beyond an area or scope: *extracellular*; *extraterrestrial*

extract *vb* **1** to pull out or uproot by force **2** to remove from a container **3** to derive (pleasure, information, etc.) from some source **4** *informal* to obtain (money, information, etc.) from someone who is not willing to provide it: *a confession extracted by force* **5** to obtain (a substance) from a material or the ground by mining, distillation, digestion, etc.: *oil extracted from shale* **6** to copy out (an article, passage, etc.) from a publication ▸ *n* **7** something extracted, such as a passage from a book, etc. **8** a preparation containing the concentrated essence of a substance > **extractive** *adj* > **extractor** *n*

extract *vb* **1** = pull out, remove, take out, draw, uproot, pluck out **2** = take out, draw, pull, remove, withdraw, pull out, bring out **4** = elicit, obtain, force, draw, derive, glean, coerce ▸ *n* **7** = passage, selection, excerpt, cutting, clipping, quotation, citation **8** = essence, solution, concentrate, juice, distillation

extraction *n* **1** the act or an instance of extracting **2** the removal of a tooth by a dentist: *few patients need an extraction* **3** the origin or ancestry of a person: *he is of German extraction*

extradite *vb* **-diting, -dited** to hand over (an alleged offender) to the country where the crime took place for trial: *an agreement to extradite him to Hong Kong* > **extraditable** *adj* > **extradition** *n*

extramural *adj* connected with but outside the normal courses of a university or college

extraneous (iks-**train**-ee-uss) *adj* not essential or relevant to the situation or subject being considered

extraordinary *adj* **1** very unusual or surprising: *the award of a Victoria Cross for an act of extraordinary bravery under hostile fire* **2** having some special or extreme quality: *an extraordinary first novel* **3** (of a meeting, ambassador, etc.) specially called or appointed to deal with one particular topic > **extraordinarily** *adv*

extraordinary *adj* **1** = unusual, strange, remarkable, uncommon; ≠ ordinary **2** = remarkable, outstanding, amazing, fantastic (*informal*), astonishing, exceptional, phenomenal, extremely good; ≠ unremarkable

extraordinary rendition *n* the process by which a country seizes a terrorist suspect and then transports him or her for interrogation to a country where due process of law is unlikely to be respected

extrapolate (iks-**trap**-a-late) *vb* **-lating, -lated** **1** to infer (something not known) from the known facts, using logic and reason **2** *maths* to estimate (the value of a function or measurement) beyond the known values, by the extension of a curve > **extrapolation** *n*

extrasensory *adj* of or relating to extrasensory perception

extravagant *adj* **1** spending more than is reasonable or affordable **2** costing more than is reasonable or affordable: *an extravagant gift* **3** going beyond usual or reasonable limits: *extravagant expectations* **4** (of behaviour or gestures) extreme, esp. in order to make a particular impression: *an extravagant display of affection* **5** very elaborate and impressive: *extravagant costumes* > **extravagance** *n*

extravagant *adj* **1** = wasteful, lavish, prodigal, profligate, spendthrift; ≠ economical **3, 4** = excessive, outrageous, over the top (*slang*), unreasonable, preposterous; ≠ moderate

extravaganza *n* **1** an elaborate and lavish entertainment **2** any fanciful display, literary composition, etc.

extreme *adj* **1** of a high or the highest degree or intensity **2** exceptionally severe or unusual: *people can survive extreme conditions* **3** (of an opinion, political group, etc.) beyond the limits regarded as acceptable; fanatical **4** farthest or outermost ▸ *n* **5** either of the two limits of a scale or range **6** **go to extremes** to be unreasonable in speech or action **7** **in the extreme** to the highest or furthest degree: *the effect was dramatic in the extreme* > **extremely** *adv*

extreme *adj* **1** = great, highest, supreme, acute, severe, maximum, intense, ultimate; ≠ mild **2** = severe, radical, strict, harsh, rigid, drastic, uncompromising **3** = radical, excessive, fanatical, immoderate; ≠ moderate **4** = farthest, furthest, far, remotest, far-off, outermost, most distant; ≠ nearest ▸ *n* **5** = limit, end, edge, opposite, pole, boundary, antithesis, extremity

extreme sport *n* any of various sports with a high risk of injury or death

extremist *n* **1** a person who favours or uses extreme or violent methods, esp. to bring about

political change ▸ *adj* **2** holding extreme opinions or using extreme methods
> **extremism** *n*

extremist *n* = radical, activist, militant, fanatic, die-hard, bigot, zealot ▸ *adj* = extreme, wild, passionate, frenzied, obsessive, fanatical, fervent, zealous

extremity *n*, *pl* **-ties 1** the farthest point **2** an unacceptable or extreme nature or degree: *the extremity of his views alienated other nationalists* **3** an extreme condition, such as misfortune **4 extremities** hands and feet

extricate *vb* **-cating, -cated** to free from a difficult or complicated situation or place
> **extricable** *adj* > **extrication** *n*

extrovert *adj* **1** lively and outgoing **2** *psychol* concerned more with external reality than inner feelings ▸ *n* **3** a person who has these characteristics > **extroverted** *adj*

extrude *vb* **-truding, -truded 1** to squeeze or force out **2** to produce (moulded sections of plastic, metal, etc.) by forcing through a shaped die > **extruded** *adj* > **extrusion** *n*

exuberant *adj* **1** full of vigour and high spirits **2** (of vegetation) growing thickly; flourishing
> **exuberance** *n*

exude *vb* **-uding, -uded 1** (of a liquid or smell) to seep or flow out slowly and steadily **2** to seem to have (a quality or feeling) to a great degree: *the Chancellor exuded confidence* > **exudation** *n*

exult *vb* to be joyful or jubilant > **exultation** *n*
> **exultant** *adj*

eye *n* **1** the organ of sight in humans and animals **2** the external part of an eye, often including the area around it **3** (*often pl*) the ability to see or record what is happening: *the eyes of an entire nation were upon us* **4** a look, glance, or gaze **5** attention or observation: *his new shirt caught my eye* **6** the ability to judge or appreciate something: *his shrewd eye for talent* **7** (*often pl*) opinion, judgment, or authority: *in the eyes of the law* **8** a dark spot on a potato from which new shoots can grow **9** a small hole, such as the one at the blunt end of a sewing needle **10** a small area of calm in the centre of a storm, hurricane, or tornado **11 all eyes** *informal* acutely vigilant **12 an eye for an eye** justice consisting of an equivalent action to the original wrong or harm **13 have eyes for** to be interested in **14 in one's mind's eye** imagined or remembered vividly **15 in the public eye** exposed to public curiosity **16 keep an eye on** to take care of **17 keep an eye open** or **out for** to watch with special attention for **18 keep one's eyes peeled** or **skinned** to watch vigilantly **19 look someone in the eye** to look openly and without embarrassment at someone **20 make eyes at someone** to look at someone in an obviously attracted manner **21 more than meets the eye** hidden motives, meanings, or facts **22 my eye!** *old-fashioned, informal* nonsense! **23 see eye to eye with** to

agree with **24 set** or **lay** or **clap eyes on** to see: *I never laid eyes on him again* **25 turn a blind eye to** or **close one's eyes to** to pretend not to notice **26 up to one's eyes in** extremely busy with **27 with an eye to** with the intention of **28 with one's eyes open** in full knowledge of all the facts ▸ *vb* **eyeing** or **eying, eyed 29** to look at carefully or warily > **eyeless** *adj* > **eyelike** *adj*

eye *n* **1, 2** = eyeball, optic (*informal*), organ of vision, organ of sight **3** = eyesight, sight, vision, perception, ability to see, power of seeing **5** = observance, observation, surveillance, vigil, watch, lookout **6** = appreciation, taste, recognition, judgment, discrimination, perception, discernment **10** = centre, heart, middle, mid, core, nucleus ▸ *vb* = look at, view, study, watch, survey, observe, contemplate, check out (*informal*)

eyeball *n* **1** the entire ball-shaped part of the eye **2 eyeball to eyeball** in close confrontation ▸ *vb* **3** *slang* to stare at

eyebrow *n* **1** the bony ridge over each eye **2** the arch of hair on this ridge **3 raise an eyebrow** to show doubt or disapproval

eyeglass *n* a lens for aiding defective vision

eyelash *n* any of the short hairs that grow from the edge of the eyelids

eyelet *n* **1** a small hole for a lace or cord to be passed through **2** a small metal ring reinforcing such a hole

eyelid *n* either of the two folds of skin that cover an eye when it is closed

eyeliner *n* a cosmetic used to outline the eyes

eye-opener *n informal* something startling or revealing

eye shadow *n* a coloured cosmetic worn on the upper eyelids

eyesight *n* the ability to see: *poor eyesight*

eyesore *n* something very ugly

eyewitness *n* a person present at an event who can describe what happened

eyrie *n* **1** the nest of an eagle, built in a high inaccessible place **2** any high isolated place

Ff

F 1 *music* the fourth note of the scale of C major **2** Fahrenheit **3** farad(s) **4** *chem* fluorine **5** *physics* force **6** franc(s)

FA (in Britain) Football Association

fable *n* **1** a short story, often one with animals as characters, that illustrates a moral **2** an unlikely story which is usually untrue **3** a story about mythical characters or events

> **fable** *n* **1, 3** = legend, myth, parable, allegory, story, tale **2** = fiction, fantasy, myth, invention, yarn (*informal*), fabrication, urban myth, tall story (*informal*); ≠ fact

fabled *adj* well-known from anecdotes and stories rather than experience

fabric *n* **1** any cloth made from yarn or fibres by weaving or knitting **2** the structure that holds a system together: *the fabric of society* **3** the walls, floor, and roof of a building

> **fabric** *n* **1** = cloth, material, stuff, textile, web **2** = framework, structure, make-up, organization, frame, foundations, construction, constitution **3** = structure, foundations, construction, framework

fabricate *vb* **-cating, -cated 1** to invent (a story or lie): *fabricated reports about the opposition* **2** to make or build ▷ **fabrication** *n*

fabulous *adj* **1** *informal* extremely good **2** almost unbelievable: *a city of fabulous wealth* **3** told of in fables and legends: *a fabulous horned creature* ▷ **fabulously** *adv*

> **fabulous** *adj* **1** = wonderful, excellent, brilliant, superb, spectacular, fantastic (*informal*), marvellous, sensational (*informal*); ≠ ordinary **2** = astounding, amazing, extraordinary, remarkable, incredible (*informal*), astonishing, unbelievable, breathtaking **3** = legendary, imaginary, mythical, fictitious, made-up, fantastic, invented, unreal

facade (fass-**sahd**) *n* **1** the front of a building **2** a front or deceptive outer appearance

> **facade** *n* **1** = front, face, exterior **2** = show, front, appearance, mask, exterior, guise, pretence, semblance

face *n* **1** the front of the head from the forehead to the lower jaw **2A** one's expression: *as his eyes met hers his face sobered* **B** a distorted expression to show disgust or defiance: *she was pulling a face*

at him **3** the front or main side of an object, building, etc. **4** the surface of a clock or watch that has the numbers or hands on it **5** the functional side of an object, such as a tool or playing card **6** the exposed area of a mine from which coal or metal can be mined **7** *Brit slang* a well-known or important person **8 in the face of** in spite of: *a determined character in the face of adversity* **9 lose face** to lose one's credibility **10 on the face of it** to all appearances **11 put a good** *or* **brave face on something** to maintain a cheerful appearance despite misfortune **12 save face** to keep one's reputation **13 set one's face against** to oppose with determination **14 to someone's face** directly and openly ▷ *vb* **facing, faced 15** to look towards **16** to be opposite **17** to be confronted by: *they were faced with the prospect of high inflation* **18** to provide with a surface of a different material ▷ See also **face up to**

> **face** *n* **1** = countenance, features, profile, mug (*slang*), visage **2A** = expression, look, air, appearance, aspect, countenance (*literary*) **3** = side, front, outside, surface, exterior, elevation, vertical surface ▷ *vb* **16** = look onto, overlook, be opposite, look out on, front onto **17** = confront, meet, encounter, deal with, oppose, tackle, experience, brave

faceless *adj* without individual identity or character: *faceless government officials*

facelift *n* **1** cosmetic surgery for tightening sagging skin and smoothing wrinkles on the face **2** an outward improvement designed to give a more modern appearance: *the stadium was given a facelift*

face-saving *adj* preventing damage to one's reputation ▷ **face-saver** *n*

facet *n* **1** an aspect of something, such as a personality **2** any of the surfaces of a cut gemstone

facetious (fass-**see**-shuss) *adj* joking, or trying to be amusing, esp. at inappropriate times ▷ **facetiously** *adv*

face up to *vb* to accept (an unpleasant fact or reality)

> **face up to** *vb* = accept, deal with, tackle, acknowledge, cope with, confront, come to terms with, meet head-on

face value *n* apparent worth or meaning: *only a fool would take it at face value*

facia (**fay**-shee-a) *n, pl* **-ciae** (-shee-ee) same as **fascia**

facial *adj* **1** of the face ▷ *n* **2** a beauty treatment for the face ▷ **facially** *adv*

facile (**fass**-ile) *adj* **1** (of a remark, argument, etc.) overly simple and showing lack of real thought **2** easily performed or achieved: *a facile winner of his only race this year*

facilitate *vb* **-tating, -tated** to make easier the progress of: *the agreement helped facilitate trade between the countries* ▷ **facilitation** *n*

facilitate *vb* = further, help, forward, promote, speed up, pave the way for, make easy, expedite; ≠ hinder

facility *n*, *pl* **-ties 1 facilities** the means or equipment needed for an activity: *leisure and shopping facilities* **2** the ability to do things easily and well **3** skill or ease: *grown human beings can forget with remarkable facility*

facility *n* **1** = amenity, means, aid, opportunity, advantage, resource, equipment, provision **2** = ability, skill, efficiency, fluency, proficiency, dexterity, adroitness **3** = ease, fluency, effortlessness; ≠ difficulty

facing *n* **1** a piece of material used esp. to conceal the seam of a garment **2 facings** contrasting collar and cuffs on a jacket **3** an outer layer of material applied to the surface of a wall

facsimile (fak-**sim**-ill-ee) *n* an exact copy

fact *n* **1** an event or thing known to have happened or existed **2** a truth that can be proved from experience or observation **3** a piece of information **4 after** *or* **before the fact** *criminal law* after or before the commission of the offence **5 as a matter of fact** *or* **in fact** in reality or actuality **6 fact of life** an inescapable truth, esp. an unpleasant one

fact *n* **1** = event, happening, act, performance, incident, deed, occurrence, fait accompli (*French*) **2** = truth, reality, certainty, verity; ≠ fiction

faction *n* **1** a small group of people within a larger body, but differing from it in certain aims and ideas **2** strife within a group > **factional** *adj*

faction *n* **1** = group, set, party, gang, bloc, contingent, clique, coterie, public-interest group (*US, Canad*) **2** = dissension, division, conflict, rebellion, disagreement, variance, discord, infighting; ≠ agreement

factious *adj* inclined to quarrel and cause divisions: *a factious political party is unelectable*

factor *n* **1** an element that contributes to a result: *reliability was an important factor in the success of the car* **2** *maths* any whole number that will divide exactly into a given number, for example 2 and 3 are factors of 6 **3** a quantity by which an amount is multiplied or divided to become that number of times bigger or smaller: *production increased by a factor of 3* **4** *med* any of several substances that participate in the clotting of blood: *factor VIII* **5** a level on a scale of measurement: *sun cream with a protection factor of 30* **6** (in Scotland) the manager of an estate

factor *n* **1** = element, part, cause, influence, item, aspect, characteristic, consideration

factorial *maths* ► *n* **1** the product of all the whole numbers from one to a given whole number ► *adj* **2** of factorials or factors

factorize *or* **-rise** *vb* **-rizing, -rized** *or* **-rising, -rised** *maths* to resolve (a whole number) into factors > **factorization** *or* **-risation** *n*

factory *n*, *pl* **-ries** a building where goods are manufactured in large quantities

factory *n* = works, plant, mill, workshop, assembly line, shop floor

factual *adj* concerning facts rather than opinions or theories: *a factual report* > **factually** *adv*

factual *adj* = true, authentic, real, correct, genuine, exact, precise, dinkum (*Austral, NZ informal*), true-to-life; ≠ fictitious

faculty *n*, *pl* **-ties 1** one of the powers of the mind or body, such as memory, sight, or hearing **2** any ability or power, either inborn or acquired: *his faculties of reasoning were considerable* **3 A** a department within a university or college **B** its staff **C** *chiefly US & Canad* all the teaching staff of a university, school, or college

faculty *n* **1** = power, reason, sense, intelligence, mental ability, physical ability **2** = ability, power, skill, facility, capacity, propensity, aptitude; ≠ failing **3A** = department, school **3B, 3C** = teaching staff, staff, teachers, professors, lecturers

fad *n informal* **1** an intense but short-lived fashion: *the latest healthy-eating fad* **2** a personal whim > **faddish** *adj*

fad *n* **1** = craze, fashion, trend, rage, vogue, whim, mania

faddy *adj* **-dier, -diest** unreasonably fussy, particularly about food

fade *vb* **fading, faded 1** to lose brightness, colour, or strength **2 fade away** *or* **out** to vanish slowly

fade *vb* **1** = become pale, bleach, wash out, discolour, lose colour, decolour

faeces *or esp US* **feces** (**fee**-seez) *pl n* bodily waste matter discharged through the anus > **faecal** *or esp US* **fecal** (**fee**-kl) *adj*

fag¹ *n informal* a boring or tiring task: *weeding was a fag*

fag² *n slang* a cigarette

fag end *n* **1** the last and worst part: *another dull game at the fag end of the football season* **2** *Brit & NZ informal* the stub of a cigarette

faggot¹ *or esp US* **fagot** *n* **1** *Brit, Austral & NZ* a ball of chopped liver bound with herbs and bread **2** a bundle of sticks

faggot² *n offensive slang* a homosexual man

Fahrenheit (**far**-ren-hite) *adj* of or measured according to the scale of temperature in which 32° represents the melting point of ice and 212° the boiling point of water

faïence (**fie**-ence) *n* tin-glazed earthenware

fail *vb* **1** to be unsuccessful in an attempt

2 to stop operating **3** to judge or be judged as being below the officially accepted standard required in a course or examination **4** to prove disappointing or useless to (someone): *the government has failed the homeless* **5** to neglect or be unable (to do something): *he failed to repair the car* **6** to go bankrupt ▸ *n* **7** a failure to attain the required standard **8 without fail A** regularly or without exception: *use this shampoo once a week without fail* **B** definitely: *they agreed to enforce the embargo without fail*

fail *vb* **1** = be unsuccessful, founder, fall, break down, flop (*informal*), fizzle out (*informal*), come unstuck, miscarry; ≠ succeed **2** = stop working, stop, die, break down, stall, cut out, malfunction, conk out (*informal*), crash **4** = disappoint, abandon, desert, neglect, omit, let down, forsake, be disloyal to **6** = go bankrupt, collapse, fold (*informal*), close down, go under, go bust (*informal*), go out of business, be wound up ▸ *n* **8A without fail** = without exception, regularly, constantly, invariably, religiously, unfailingly, conscientiously, like clockwork

failing *n* **1** a weak point ▸ *prep* **2 failing that** alternatively: *your doctor will normally be able to advise you or, failing that, one of the self-help agencies*

failing *n* = shortcoming, fault, weakness, defect, deficiency, flaw, drawback, blemish; ≠ strength

failure *n* **1** the act or an instance of failing **2** someone or something that is unsuccessful: *he couldn't help but regard his own son as a failure* **3** the fact of something required or expected not being done or not happening: *his failure to appear at the meeting* **4** a halt in normal operation: *heart failure* **5** a decline or loss of something: *crop failure* **6** the fact of not reaching the required standard in an examination or test

failure *n* **1** = lack of success, defeat, collapse, breakdown, overthrow, miscarriage, fiasco, downfall; ≠ success **2** = loser, disappointment, flop (*informal*), write-off, no-hoper (*chiefly Austral*), dud (*informal*), black sheep, washout (*informal*), dead duck (*slang*)

faint *adj* **1** lacking clarity, brightness, or volume: *her voice was very faint* **2** feeling dizzy or weak **3** lacking conviction or force: *a faint attempt to smile* ▸ *vb* **4** to lose consciousness ▸ *n* **5** a sudden loss of consciousness › **faintly** *adv*

faint *adj* **1** = dim, low, soft, faded, distant, vague, unclear, muted; ≠ clear **2** = dizzy, giddy, light-headed, weak, exhausted, wobbly, muzzy, woozy (*informal*); ≠ energetic ▸ *vb* = pass out, black out, lose consciousness, keel over (*informal*), go out, collapse, swoon (*literary*), flake out (*informal*) ▸ *n* = blackout, collapse, coma, swoon (*literary*), unconsciousness

fair[1] *adj* **1** reasonable and just: *a move towards fair trade* **2** in agreement with rules **3** light in colour: *her fair skin* **4** old-fashioned young and beautiful: *a fair maiden* **5** quite good: *a fair attempt at making a soufflé* **6** quite large: *they made a fair amount of money* **7** (of the tide or wind) favourable to the passage of a ship or plane **8** fine or cloudless **9 fair and square** in a correct or just way ▸ *adv* **10** in a fair way **11** absolutely or squarely: *he was caught fair off his guard* › **fairness** *n*

fair *adj* **1, 2** = unbiased, impartial, even-handed, unprejudiced, just, reasonable, proper, legitimate; ≠ unfair **3** = light, golden, blonde, blond, yellowish, fair-haired, light-coloured, flaxen-haired **4** = beautiful, pretty, attractive, lovely, handsome, good-looking, bonny (*Scot, N English dialect*), comely (*old-fashioned*), fit (*Brit informal*); ≠ ugly **5, 6** = respectable, average, reasonable, decent, acceptable, moderate, adequate, satisfactory **8** = fine, clear, dry, bright, pleasant, sunny, cloudless, unclouded

fair[2] *n* **1** a travelling entertainment with sideshows, rides, and amusements **2** an exhibition of goods produced by a particular industry to promote business: *the Frankfurt book fair*

fair *n* **1** = carnival, fête, gala, bazaar **2** = exhibition, show, festival, mart

fairground *n* an open space used for a fair

Fair Isle *n* an intricate multicoloured knitted pattern

fairly *adv* **1** to a moderate degree or extent: *in the Philippines labour is fairly cheap* **2** to a great degree or extent: *the folder fairly bulged with documents* **3** as deserved: *the shares are fairly valued*

fairly *adv* **1** = moderately, rather, quite, somewhat, reasonably, adequately, pretty well, tolerably **2** = positively, really, simply, absolutely **3** = equitably, objectively, legitimately, honestly, justly, lawfully, without prejudice, dispassionately

fair trade *n* the practice of buying goods from producers in the developing world at a guaranteed price

fairway *n* **1** (on a golf course) the mown areas between tees and greens **2** *naut* a part of a river or sea on which ships may sail

fairy *n, pl* **fairies 1** an imaginary supernatural being with magical powers **2** *offensive slang* a homosexual man

fairy *n* **1** = sprite, elf, brownie, pixie, puck, imp, leprechaun, peri

fairy godmother *n* a generous friend who appears unexpectedly and offers help in time of trouble

fairyland *n* **1** an imaginary place where fairies live **2** an enchanted or wonderful place

fairy lights *pl n* small coloured electric bulbs used as decoration, esp. on a Christmas tree

fairy penguin *n* a small penguin with a bluish head and back, found on the Australian coast

fairy tale *or* **fairy story** *n* **1** a story about fairies or magical events **2** a highly improbable account: *his report was little more than a fairy tale* ▸ *adj* **fairy-tale 3** of or like a fairy tale: *a fairy-tale wedding* **4** highly improbable: *a fairy-tale account of his achievements*

> **fairy tale** *or* **fairy story** *n* **1** = folk tale, romance, traditional story **2** = lie, fiction, invention, fabrication, untruth, urban myth, tall story, urban legend

fait accompli (fate ak-kom-plee) *n* something already done and beyond alteration: *they had to accept the invasion as a fait accompli*

faith *n* **1** strong belief in something, esp. without proof **2** a specific system of religious beliefs **3** complete confidence or trust, such as in a person or remedy **4** allegiance to a person or cause **5 bad faith** dishonesty **6 good faith** honesty

> **faith** *n* **2** = religion, church, belief, persuasion, creed, communion, denomination, dogma; ≠ agnosticism **3** = confidence, trust, credit, conviction, assurance, dependence, reliance, credence; ≠ distrust

faithful *adj* **1** remaining true or loyal **2** maintaining sexual loyalty to one's lover or spouse **3** consistently reliable: *my old, but faithful, four-cylinder car* **4** accurate in detail: *a faithful translation of the book* ▸ *pl n* **the faithful 5 A** the believers in a religious faith **B** loyal followers
> **faithfully** *adv* > **faithfulness** *n*

> **faithful** *adj* **1, 3** = loyal, true, committed, constant, devoted, dedicated, reliable, staunch; ≠ disloyal **4** = accurate, close, true, strict, exact, precise

faithless *adj* treacherous or disloyal

faith school *n Brit* a school that provides a general education within a framework of a specific religious belief

fake *vb* **faking, faked 1** to cause (something not genuine) to appear real or more valuable by fraud **2** to pretend to have (an illness, emotion, etc.) ▸ *adj* **3** an object, person, or act that is not genuine ▸ *adj* **4** not genuine: *fake fur*

> **fake** *vb* **1** = forge, copy, reproduce, fabricate, counterfeit, falsify **2** = sham, put on, pretend, simulate, feign, go through the motions of ▸ *n* = forgery, copy, fraud (*informal*), reproduction, dummy, imitation, hoax, counterfeit ▸ *adj* = artificial, false, forged, counterfeit, put-on, pretend (*informal*), mock, imitation; ≠ genuine

falcon *n* a type of bird of prey that can be trained to hunt other birds and small animals

falconry *n* **1** the art of training falcons to hunt **2** the sport of hunting with falcons
> **falconer** *n*

fall *vb* **falling, fell, fallen 1** to descend by the force of gravity from a higher to a lower place **2** to drop suddenly from an upright position **3** to collapse to the ground **4** to become less or lower in number or quality: *inflation fell by one percentage point* **5** to slope downwards **6** to be badly wounded or killed **7** to give in to attack: *in 1939 Barcelona fell to the Nationalists* **8** to lose power or status **9** to pass into a specified condition: *I fell asleep* **10** to adopt a downhearted expression: *his face fell and he pouted like a child* **11** (of night or darkness) to begin **12** to occur at a specified time: *Christmas falls on a Sunday* **13** to give in to temptation or sin **14 fall apart A** to break owing to long use or poor construction: *the chassis is falling apart* **B** to become disorganized and ineffective: *since you resigned, the office has fallen apart* **15 fall short** to prove inadequate **16 fall short of** to fail to reach (a standard) ▸ *n* **17** an instance of falling **18** an amount of something, such as snow or soot, that has fallen **19** a decrease in value or number **20** a decline in status or importance: *the town's fall from prosperity* **21** a capture or overthrow: *the fall of Budapest in February 1945* **22** *wrestling* a scoring move, pinning both shoulders of one's opponent to the floor for a specified period **23** *chiefly US* autumn

> **fall** *vb* **1, 2, 3** = drop, plunge, tumble, plummet, collapse, sink, go down, come down; ≠ rise **4** = decrease, drop, decline, go down, slump, diminish, dwindle, lessen; ≠ increase **6** = be killed, die, perish, meet your end; ≠ survive **7** = be overthrown, surrender, succumb, submit, capitulate, be conquered, pass into enemy hands; ≠ triumph **12** = occur, happen, come about, chance, take place, befall, come to pass ▸ *n* **17** = drop, slip, plunge, dive, tumble, descent, plummet, nose dive **19** = decrease, drop, lowering, decline, reduction, slump, dip, lessening **21** = collapse, defeat, downfall, ruin, destruction, overthrow, submission, capitulation

fallacy *n, pl* **-cies 1** an incorrect or misleading notion based on inaccurate facts or faulty reasoning: *the fallacy underlying the government's industrial policy* **2** reasoning that is unsound
> **fallacious** *adj*

fall for *vb* **1** to become strongly attracted to (someone) **2** to be deceived by (a lie or trick)

fall guy *n informal* **1** the victim of a confidence trick **2** a person who is publicly blamed for something, though it may not be his or her fault

fallible *adj* **1** (of a person) liable to make mistakes **2** capable of error: *our all-too-fallible economic indicators* > **fallibility** *n*

Fallopian tube *n* either of a pair of slender tubes through which eggs pass from the ovaries to the uterus in female mammals

fallout *n* 1 radioactive material in the atmosphere following a nuclear explosion 2 unpleasant circumstances following an event: *the political fallout of the riots* ▸ *vb* **fall out** 3 *informal* to disagree and quarrel: *I hope we don't fall out over this issue* 4 to leave a military formation

fallow *adj* (of land) left unseeded after being ploughed to regain fertility for a future crop

false *adj* 1 not in accordance with the truth or facts: *false allegations* 2 not real or genuine but intended to seem so: *false teeth* 3 misleading or deceptive: *their false promises* 4 forced or insincere: *false cheer* 5 based on mistaken ideas > **falsely** *adv* > **falseness** *n*

> **false** *adj* 1 = incorrect, wrong, mistaken, misleading, faulty, inaccurate, invalid, erroneous; ≠ correct 2 = artificial, forged, fake, reproduction, replica, imitation, bogus, simulated; ≠ real 3 = untrue, fraudulent, trumped up, fallacious, untruthful; ≠ true

falsehood *n* 1 the quality of being untrue 2 a lie

falsetto *n, pl* **-tos** a voice pitch higher than one's normal range

falsify *vb* **-fies, -fying, -fied** to make (a report or evidence) false by alteration in order to deceive > **falsification** *n*

falsity *n, pl* **-ties** 1 the state of being false 2 a lie

falter *vb* 1 to be hesitant, weak, or unsure 2 (of a machine) to lose power or strength in an uneven way: *the engine began to falter and the plane lost height* 3 to speak nervously and without confidence 4 to stop moving smoothly and start moving unsteadily: *as he neared the house his steps faltered* > **faltering** *adj*

> **falter** *vb* 1 = hesitate, delay, waver, vacillate; ≠ persevere 3 = stutter, pause, stumble, hesitate, stammer

fame *n* the state of being widely known or recognized

> **fame** *n* = prominence, glory, celebrity, stardom, reputation, honour, prestige, stature; ≠ obscurity

famed *adj* extremely well-known: *a nation famed for its efficiency*

familial *adj formal* of or relating to the family

familiar *adj* 1 well-known 2 frequent or common: *it was a familiar argument* 3 **familiar with** well acquainted with 4 friendly and informal 5 more intimate than is acceptable ▸ *n* 6 an animal or bird believed to share with a witch her supernatural powers 7 a friend > **familiarly** *adv* > **familiarity** *n*

> **familiar** *adj* 1, 2 = well-known, recognized, common, ordinary, routine, frequent, accustomed, customary; ≠ unfamiliar 4 = friendly, close, dear, intimate, amicable; ≠ formal 5 = disrespectful, forward, bold, intrusive, presumptuous, impudent, overfamiliar

familiarize *or* **-rise** *vb* **-rizing, -rized** *or* **-rising, -rised** to make (oneself or someone else) fully aware of a particular subject > **familiarization** *or* **-risation** *n*

family *n, pl* **-lies** 1 a social group consisting of parents and their offspring. Related adjective: **familial** 2 one's wife or husband and one's children 3 one's children 4 a group descended from a common ancestor 5 all the people living together in one household 6 any group of related objects or beings: *a family of chemicals* 7 *biol* one of the groups into which an order is divided, containing one or more genera: *the cat family* ▸ *adj* 8 of or suitable for a family or any of its members: *films for a family audience* 9 **in the family way** *informal* pregnant

> **family** *n* 1, 2 = relations, relatives, household, folk (*informal*), kin, nuclear family, next of kin, kith and kin, ainga (NZ), cuzzies *or* cuzzie-bros (NZ), rellies (*Austral slang*) 3 = children, kids (*informal*), offspring, little ones, littlies (*Austral informal*) 4 = ancestors, house, race, tribe, clan, dynasty, line of descent 6 = species, group, class, system, order, network, genre, subdivision

family planning *n* the control of the number of children in a family by the use of contraceptives

famine *n* a severe shortage of food

> **famine** *n* = hunger, want, starvation, deprivation, scarcity, dearth

famish *vb* **be famished** *or* **famishing** to be very hungry

famous *adj* known to or recognized by many people

> **famous** *adj* = well-known, celebrated, acclaimed, noted, distinguished, prominent, legendary, renowned; ≠ unknown

famously *adv* 1 well-known: *her famously relaxed manner* 2 very well: *the two got on famously*

fan[1] *n* 1 any device for creating a current of air, esp. a rotating machine of blades attached to a central hub 2 a hand-held object, usually made of paper, which creates a draught of cool air when waved 3 something shaped like such a fan, such as the tail of certain birds ▸ *vb* **fanning, fanned** 4 to create a draught of air in the direction of (someone or something) 5 **fan out** to spread out in the shape of a fan: *the troops fanned out along the beach*

> **fan** *n* 1 = blower, ventilator, air conditioner ▸ *vb* 4 = blow, cool, refresh, air-condition, ventilate

fan[2] *n* a person who admires or is enthusiastic about a pop star, actor, sport, or hobby: *he was a big fan of American football*

> **fan** *n* = supporter, lover, follower, enthusiast, admirer, fanboy (*informal*), fangirl (*informal*)

fanatic n 1 a person whose enthusiasm for something, esp. a political or religious cause, is extreme 2 informal a person devoted to a particular hobby or pastime ▸ adj also **fanatical** 3 excessively enthusiastic ⊳**fanatically** adv ⊳**fanaticism** n

> **fanatic** n = extremist, activist, militant, bigot, zealot

fanbase n a body of admirers of a particular pop singer, sports team, etc.

fan belt n the belt that drives a cooling fan in a car engine

fanciful adj 1 not based on fact 2 made in a curious or imaginative way: fanciful architecture 3 guided by unrestrained imagination: fanciful tales of fairy folk ⊳**fancifully** adv

fancy adj **-cier, -ciest** 1 special, unusual, and elaborate 2 (often used ironically) superior in quality 3 (of a price) higher than expected ▸ n, pl **-cies** 4 a sudden imaginative idea 5 a sudden or irrational liking for a person or thing 6 old-fashioned or literary a person's imagination ▸ vb **-cies, -cying, -cied** 7 Brit informal to be physically attracted to (another person) 8 informal to have a wish for 9 to picture in the imagination 10 to think or suppose: I fancy I am redundant here 11 **fancy oneself** to have a high opinion of oneself ▸ interj 12 Also: **fancy that!** an exclamation of surprise ⊳**fancily** adv

> **fancy** adj 1 = elaborate, decorative, extravagant, intricate, baroque, ornamental, ornate, embellished; ≠ plain ▸ n 4, 5 = whim, thought, idea, desire, urge, notion, humour, impulse ▸ vb 7 = be attracted to, find attractive, lust after, like, take to, be captivated by, have a thing about (informal), have eyes for 8 = wish for, want, desire, hope for, long for, crave, yearn for, thirst for 10 = suppose, think, believe, imagine, reckon, conjecture, think likely

fancy dress n clothing worn for a party at which people dress up to look like a particular animal or character

fancy-free adj free from commitments, esp. marriage

fandango n, pl **-gos** 1 a lively Spanish dance 2 music for this dance

fanfare n a short rousing tune played on brass instruments

fang n 1 the long pointed tooth of a poisonous snake through which poison is injected 2 the canine tooth of a meat-eating mammal

fantail n 1 a breed of domestic pigeon with a large tail like a fan 2 a fly-catching bird of Australia, New Zealand, and SE Asia with a broad fan-shaped tail

fantasia n 1 any musical work not composed in a strict form 2 a mixture of popular tunes arranged as a continuous whole

fantasize or **-sise** vb **-sizing, -sized** or **-sising, -sised** to imagine pleasant but unlikely events

fantastic adj 1 informal excellent 2 informal very large in degree or amount: a fantastic amount of money 3 strange or exotic in appearance: fantastic costumes 4 difficult to believe or unlikely to happen ⊳**fantastically** adv

> **fantastic** adj 1 = wonderful, great (informal), excellent, very good, smashing (informal), superb, tremendous (informal), magnificent, booshit (Austral slang), exo (Austral slang), sik (Austral slang), rad (informal), phat (slang), schmick (Austral informal); ≠ ordinary 3 = strange, bizarre, grotesque, fanciful, outlandish 4 = implausible, unlikely, incredible, absurd, preposterous, cock-and-bull (informal)

fantasy n, pl **-sies** 1 a far-fetched idea 2 imagination unrestricted by reality 3 a daydream 4 fiction with a large fantasy content 5 music same as **fantasia**

> **fantasy** n 1, 3 = daydream, dream, wish, reverie, flight of fancy, pipe dream 2 = imagination, fancy (old-fashioned, literary), invention, creativity, originality

FAQ n computers frequently asked question or questions: a document containing basic information on a particular subject

far adv **farther, farthest** or **further, furthest** 1 at, to, or from a great distance 2 at or to a remote time: as far back as 1984 3 by a considerable degree: far greater 4 **as far as** A to the degree or extent that B to the distance or place of C informal with reference to 5 **by far** by a considerable margin 6 **far and away** by a very great margin: far and away the ugliest building in the city 7 **far and wide** in a great many places over a large area 8 **go far** A to be successful B to be sufficient or last long: her wages didn't go far 9 **go too far** to go beyond reasonable limits: the press have gone too far this time 10 **so far** A up to the present moment B up to a certain point, extent, or degree ▸ adj 11 distant in space or time: the far south 12 extending a great distance 13 more distant: over in the far corner 14 **far from** by no means: the battle is far from over

> **far** adv 1 = a long way, miles, deep, a good way, afar, a great distance 3 = much, greatly, very much, extremely, significantly, considerably, decidedly, markedly ▸ adj 11 = remote, distant, far-flung, faraway, out-of-the-way, outlying, off the beaten track; ≠ near

farad n physics the SI unit of electric capacitance

farce n 1 a humorous play involving characters in unlikely and ridiculous situations 2 the style of comedy of this kind 3 a ludicrous situation: the game degenerated into farce ⊳**farcical** adj ⊳**farcically** adv

> **farce** n 1, 2 = comedy, satire, slapstick, burlesque, buffoonery 3 = mockery, joke, nonsense, parody, shambles, sham, travesty

fare n 1 the amount charged or paid for a journey in a bus, train, or plane 2 a paying passenger 3 a range of food and drink: *marvellous picnic fare* ▸ vb **faring**, **fared** 4 to get on (in a specified way): *he fared well in the exam*

> **fare** n 1 = charge, price, ticket price, ticket money 3 = food, provisions, board, rations, kai (NZ informal), nourishment, sustenance, victuals, nutriment ▸ vb = get on, do, manage, make out, prosper, get along

farewell interj 1 old-fashioned goodbye ▸ n 2 the act of saying goodbye and leaving ▸ vb 3 NZ to say goodbye ▸ adj 4 parting or closing: *the President's farewell speech*

> **farewell** interj = goodbye, bye (informal), so long, see you, take care, good morning, bye-bye (informal), good day, haere ra (NZ) ▸ n = goodbye, parting, departure, leave-taking, adieu, valediction, sendoff (informal)

far-fetched adj unlikely to be true
farinaceous adj containing starch or having a starchy texture
farm n 1 a tract of land, usually with a house and buildings, cultivated as a unit or used to rear livestock 2 a unit of land or water devoted to the growing or rearing of some particular type of fruit, animal, or fish: *a salmon farm; an ostrich farm* ▸ vb 3 ᴀ to cultivate (land) ʙ to rear (animals or fish) on a farm 4 to do agricultural work as a way of life 5 to collect and keep the profits from (a tax district or business) ▸ See also **farm out**

> **farm** n = smallholding, ranch (chiefly US, Canad), farmstead, station (Austral, NZ), vineyard, plantation, croft (Scot), grange, homestead ▸ vb 3ᴀ = cultivate, work, plant, grow crops on

farmer n a person who owns or manages a farm
farmers' market n a market at which farm produce is sold directly to the public by the producer
farmhouse n a house attached to a farm
farm out vb 1 to send (work) to be done by another person or firm 2 (of the state) to put (a child) into the care of a private individual
farmstead n a farm and its main buildings
farmyard n the small area of land enclosed by or around the farm buildings
farrago (far-rah-go) n, pl **-gos** or **-goes** a hotchpotch or mixture, esp. a ridiculous or unbelievable one: *a farrago of patriotic nonsense*
farrier n chiefly Brit a person who shoes horses
farrow n 1 a litter of piglets ▸ vb 2 (of a sow) to give birth to a litter
fart vulgar ▸ n 1 an emission of intestinal gas from the anus ▸ vb 2 to break wind
farther adv 1 to or at a greater distance in space or time 2 in addition ▸ adj 3 more distant or remote in space or time

farthest adv 1 to or at the greatest distance in space or time ▸ adj 2 most distant or remote in space or time
farthing n a former British coin worth a quarter of an old penny
fascia or **facia** (fay-shee-a) n, pl **-ciae** (-shee-ee) 1 the flat surface above a shop window 2 archit a flat band or surface 3 Brit the outer panel which surrounds the instruments and dials of a motor vehicle 4 a detachable cover for a mobile phone
fascinate vb **-nating**, **-nated** to attract and delight by arousing interest > **fascinating** adj > **fascinatingly** adv > **fascination** n

> **fascinate** vb = entrance, absorb, intrigue, rivet, captivate, enthral, beguile, transfix; ≠ bore

Fascism (fash-iz-zum) n 1 the authoritarian and nationalistic political movement in Italy (1922–43) 2 any ideology or movement like this > **Fascist** n, adj
fashion n 1 style in clothes, hairstyles, behaviour, etc., that is popular at a particular time 2 the way that something happens or is done: *conversing in a very animated fashion* 3 **after a fashion** in some way, but not very well: *she apologized, after a fashion, for her haste* ▸ vb 4 to form, make, or shape: *he had fashioned a crude musical instrument*

> **fashion** n 1 = style, look, trend, rage, custom, mode, vogue, craze 2 = method, way, style, manner, mode ▸ vb = make, shape, cast, construct, form, create, manufacture, forge

fashionable adj 1 popular with a lot of people at a particular time 2 popular among well-off or famous people: *the fashionable Côte d'Azur* > **fashionably** adv

> **fashionable** adj = popular, in fashion, trendy (Brit informal), in (informal), modern, with it (old-fashioned, informal), stylish, chic, schmick (Austral informal), funky (old-fashioned); ≠ unfashionable

fast¹ adj 1 acting or moving quickly 2 accomplished in or lasting a short time 3 adapted to or allowing for rapid movement: *the fast lane* 4 (of a clock or watch) indicating a time in advance of the correct time 5 given to a life of expensive and exciting activities: *the desire for a fast life* 6 firmly fixed, fastened, or shut 7 (of colours and dyes) not likely to fade 8 photog (of film) very sensitive and able to be used in low-light conditions 9 **fast friends** devoted and loyal friends 10 **pull a fast one** informal to play an unscrupulous trick ▸ adv 11 quickly 12 **fast asleep** in a deep sleep 13 firmly and tightly: *stuck fast* 14 **play fast and loose** to behave in an insincere or unreliable manner

f

fast *adj* **1, 2** = quick, flying, rapid, fleet, swift, speedy, brisk, hasty; ≠ slow **5** = dissipated, wild, exciting, loose (*old-fashioned*), extravagant, reckless, self-indulgent, wanton **6** = fixed, firm, sound, stuck, secure, tight, jammed, fastened; ≠ unstable **9** = close, firm, devoted, faithful, steadfast ▸ *adv* **11** = quickly, rapidly, swiftly, hastily, hurriedly, speedily, in haste, at full speed; ≠ slowly **13** = securely, firmly, tightly, fixedly

fast² *vb* **1** to go without food for a period of time, esp. for religious reasons ▸ *n* **2** a period of fasting

fast *vb* = go hungry, abstain, go without food, deny yourself ▸ *n* = fasting, diet, abstinence

fasten *vb* **1** to make or become secure or joined **2** to close by fixing firmly in place or locking **3 fasten on A** to direct one's attention in a concentrated way towards: *the mind needs such imagery to fasten on to* **B** to take a firm hold on > **fastener** *n*

fasten *vb* **1** = tie, bind, tie up **2** = secure, close, do up

fast food *n* food, such as hamburgers, that is prepared and served very quickly

fastidious *adj* **1** paying great attention to neatness, detail, and order: *a fastidious dresser* **2** excessively concerned with cleanliness > **fastidiously** *adv* > **fastidiousness** *n*

fastness *n Brit & Austral literary* a stronghold or safe place that is hard to get to

fast-track *adj* **1** taking the quickest but most competitive route to success or personal advancement: *a fast-track marketer's dream* ▸ *vb* **2** to speed up the progress of (a project or person)

fat *adj* **fatter, fattest 1** having more flesh on the body than is thought necessary or desirable; overweight **2** (of meat) containing a lot of fat **3** thick or wide: *his obligatory fat cigar* **4** profitable or productive: *fat years for the farmers are few and far between* **5 a fat chance** *slang* not much likelihood at all **6 a fat lot of good** *slang* not at all good or useful ▸ *n* **7** extra or unwanted flesh on the body **8** a greasy or oily substance obtained from animals or plants and used in cooking **9 the fat is in the fire** an action has been taken from which disastrous consequences are expected **10 the fat of the land** the best that is obtainable > **fatless** *adj* > **fatness** *n*

fat *adj* **1** = overweight, large, heavy, plump, stout, obese, tubby, portly; ≠ thin **2** = fatty, greasy, adipose, oleaginous, oily; ≠ lean ▸ *n* **7** = fatness, flesh (*informal*), bulk, obesity, flab, blubber, paunch, fatty tissue

fatal *adj* **1** resulting in death: *a fatal accident* **2** resulting in unfortunate consequences: *the consortium's second fatal mistake* > **fatally** *adv*

fatal *adj* **1** = lethal, deadly, mortal, causing death, final, killing, terminal, malignant; ≠ harmless **2** = disastrous, devastating, crippling, catastrophic, ruinous, calamitous, baleful, baneful; ≠ minor

fatalism *n* the belief that all events are decided in advance by God or Fate so that human beings are powerless to alter their destiny > **fatalist** *n* > **fatalistic** *adj* > **fatalistically** *adv*

fatality *n, pl* **-ties** a death caused by an accident or disaster

fate *n* **1** the ultimate force that supposedly predetermines the course of events **2** the inevitable fortune that happens to a person or thing **3** death or downfall: *Custer met his fate at Little Bighorn*

fate *n* **1** = destiny, chance, fortune, luck, the stars, providence, nemesis, kismet **2** = fortune, destiny, lot, portion, cup, horoscope

fated *adj* **1** certain to be or do something: *he was always fated to be a musician* **2** doomed to death or destruction

fated *adj* **1** = destined, doomed, predestined, preordained, foreordained

fateful *adj* having important, and usually disastrous, consequences > **fatefully** *adv*

fathead *n informal* a stupid person > **fatheaded** *adj*

father *n* **1** a male parent **2** a person who founds a line or family; forefather **3** a man who starts, creates, or invents something: *the father of democracy in Costa Rica* **4** a leader of an association or council: *the city fathers* ▸ *vb* **5** (of a man) to be the biological cause of the conception and birth of (a child) > **fatherhood** *n*

father *n* **1** = daddy (*informal*), dad (*informal*), male parent, pop (*US informal*), old man (*Brit informal*), pa (*informal*), papa (*old-fashioned, informal*), pater (*old-fashioned*) **2** = forefather, predecessor, ancestor, forebear, progenitor, tupuna or tipuna (*NZ*) **3** = founder, author, maker, architect, creator, inventor, originator, prime mover ▸ *vb* = sire, parent, conceive, bring to life, beget, procreate (*formal*), bring into being, give life to

Father *n* **1** God **2** a title used for Christian priests **3** any of the early writers on Christian doctrine

Father *n* **2** = priest, minister, vicar, parson, pastor, cleric, churchman, padre (*informal*)

father-in-law *n, pl* **fathers-in-law** the father of one's wife or husband

fatherland *n* a person's native country

fatherly *adj* kind or protective, like a father

fatherly *adj* = paternal, kindly, protective, supportive, benign, affectionate, patriarchal, benevolent

fathom n 1 a unit of length, used in navigation, equal to six feet (1.83 metres) ▸ vb 2 to understand by thinking carefully about: *I couldn't fathom his intentions* > **fathomable** adj

fathomless adj too deep or difficult to fathom

fatigue (fat-**eeg**) n 1 extreme physical or mental tiredness 2 the weakening of a material caused by repeated stress or movement 3 the duties of a soldier that are not military 4 **fatigues** a soldier's clothing for nonmilitary or battlefield duties ▸ vb **-tiguing, -tigued** 5 to make or become weary or exhausted

> **fatigue** n 1 = tiredness, lethargy, weariness, heaviness, languor, listlessness; ≠ freshness ▸ vb = tire, exhaust, weaken, weary, drain, wear out, take it out of (*informal*), tire out; ≠ refresh

fatten vb to grow or cause to grow fat or fatter > **fattening** adj

fatty adj **-tier, -tiest** 1 containing or derived from fat 2 greasy or oily ▸ n, pl **-ties** 3 *informal* a fat person

> **fatty** adj = greasy, fat, creamy, oily, adipose, oleaginous, suety, rich

fatuity n, pl **-ties** 1 foolish thoughtlessness 2 a fatuous remark

fatuous adj foolish, inappropriate, and showing no thought > **fatuously** adv

faucet (**faw**-set) n 1 a tap fitted to a barrel 2 *US & Canad* a tap

> **faucet** n 1 = tap, spout, spigot, stopcock, valve

fault n 1 responsibility for something wrong 2 a defect or failing: *they shut the production line to remedy a fault* 3 a weakness in a person's character 4 *geol* a fracture in the earth's crust with displacement of the rocks on either side 5 *tennis & squash etc.* a serve that bounces outside the proper service court or fails to get over the net 6 (in showjumping) a penalty mark for failing to clear, or refusing, a fence 7 **at fault** to be to blame for something wrong 8 **find fault with** to seek out minor imperfections in 9 **to a fault** more than is usual or necessary: *generous to a fault* ▸ vb 10 to criticize or blame 11 *geol* to undergo or cause to undergo a fault > **faultless** adj > **faultlessly** adv

> **fault** n 1 = responsibility, liability, guilt, accountability, culpability 2, 3 = failing, weakness, defect, deficiency, flaw, shortcoming, blemish, imperfection; ≠ strength 8 **find fault with something or someone** = criticize, complain about, whinge about (*informal*), whine about (*informal*), quibble, carp at, take to task, pick holes in, nit-pick (*informal*) 9 **to a fault** = excessively, unduly, in the extreme, overmuch, immoderately ▸ vb 10 = criticize, blame, complain, condemn, moan about, censure, hold (someone) responsible, find fault with

faulty adj **faultier, faultiest** badly designed or not working properly: *a faulty toaster*

> **faulty** adj = defective, damaged, malfunctioning, broken, flawed, impaired, imperfect, out of order, buggy

faun n (in Roman legend) a creature with the head and torso of a man and the legs, ears, and horns of a goat

fauna n, pl **-nas** or **-nae** all the animal life of a given place or time: *the fauna of the Arctic*

faux pas (foe pah) n, pl **faux pas** (foe pahz) a socially embarrassing action or mistake

favour or US **favor** n 1 an approving attitude: *the company looked with favour on his plan* 2 an act done out of goodwill or generosity 3 bias at the expense of others: *his fellow customs officers, showing no favour, demanded to see his luggage* 4 **in** or **out of favour** regarded with approval or disapproval 5 **in favour of** A approving B to the benefit of ▸ vb 6 to prefer 7 to show bias towards (someone) at the expense of others: *parents sometimes favour the youngest child in the family* 8 to support or agree with (something): *he favours the abolition of capital punishment* > **favoured** or US **favored** adj

> **favour** or **favor** n 1 = approval, goodwill, commendation, approbation; ≠ disapproval 2 = good turn, service, benefit, courtesy, kindness, indulgence, boon (*archaic*), good deed; ≠ wrong 3 = favouritism, preferential treatment ▸ vb 6 = prefer, opt for, like better, incline towards, choose, pick, desire, go for; ≠ object to 7 = indulge, reward, side with, smile upon 8 = support, champion, encourage, approve, advocate, subscribe to, commend, stand up for; ≠ oppose

favourable or US **favorable** adj 1 advantageous, encouraging, or promising: *a favourable climate for business expansion* 2 giving consent or approval > **favourably** or US **favorably** adv

> **favourable** or **favorable** adj 1 = positive, encouraging, approving, praising, reassuring, enthusiastic, sympathetic, commending; ≠ disapproving 2 = affirmative, agreeing, confirming, positive, assenting, corroborative

favourite or US **favorite** adj 1 most liked ▸ n 2 a person or thing regarded with especial preference or liking 3 *sport* a competitor thought likely to win

> **favourite** or **favorite** adj = preferred, favoured, best-loved, most-liked, special, choice, dearest, pet ▸ n 2 = darling, pet, blue-eyed boy (*informal*), beloved, idol, fave (*informal*), teacher's pet, the apple of your eye

favouritism or US **favoritism** n the practice of giving special treatment to a person or group: *favouritism in the allocation of government posts*

fawn¹ *n* **1** a young deer aged under one year ▸ *adj* **2** pale greyish-brown

fawn² *vb* **fawn on** **1** to seek attention from (someone) by insincere flattery: *people in suits fawning over the boss* **2** (of a dog) to try to please (someone) by a show of extreme friendliness >**fawning** *adj*

fax *n* **1** an electronic system for transmitting an exact copy of a document **2** a document sent by this system **3** Also called: **fax machine, facsimile machine** a machine which transmits and receives exact copies of documents ▸ *vb* **4** to send (a document) by this system

FBI (in the US) Federal Bureau of Investigation

FC (in Britain) Football Club

Fe *chem* iron

fealty *n*, *pl* **-ties** (in feudal society) the loyalty sworn to a lord by his tenant or servant

fear *n* **1** a feeling of distress or alarm caused by danger or pain that is about to happen **2** something that causes fear **3** possibility or likelihood: *there is no fear of her agreeing to that* **4 no fear** *informal* certainly not ▸ *vb* **5** to be afraid of (someone or something) **6** *formal* to be sorry: *I fear the children were not very good yesterday* **7 fear for** to feel anxiety about >**fearless** *adj* >**fearlessly** *adv*

> **fear** *n* **1** = dread, horror, panic, terror, fright, alarm, trepidation (*formal*), fearfulness **2** = bugbear, bête noire, horror, nightmare, anxiety, terror, dread, spectre ▸ *vb* **5** = be afraid of, dread, shudder at, be fearful of, tremble at, be terrified by, take fright at, shake in your shoes about **6** = regret, feel, suspect, have a feeling, have a hunch, have a sneaking suspicion, have a funny feeling **7 fear for something or someone** = worry about, be anxious about, feel concern for

fearful *adj* **1** afraid and full of fear **2** frightening or causing fear: *the ship hit a fearful storm* **3** *informal* very bad: *they were making a fearful noise* >**fearfully** *adv*

> **fearful** *adj* **1** = scared, afraid, alarmed, frightened, nervous, terrified, petrified; ≠ unafraid **3** = frightful, terrible, awful, dreadful, horrific, dire, horrendous, gruesome

fearsome *adj* terrible or frightening

feasible *adj* able to be done: *a manned journey to Mars is now feasible* >**feasibility** *n* >**feasibly** *adv*

> **feasible** *adj* = practicable, possible, reasonable, viable, workable, achievable, attainable, likely; ≠ impracticable

feast *n* **1** a large and special meal for many people **2** something extremely pleasing: *a feast of colour* **3** an annual religious celebration ▸ *vb* **4** to take part in a feast **5** to give a feast to **6 feast on** to eat a large amount of: *down come hundreds of vultures to feast on the remains* **7 feast one's eyes on** to look at (someone or something) with a great deal of attention and pleasure

> **feast** *n* **1** = banquet, repast, spread (*informal*), dinner, treat, hakari (NZ) **3** = festival, holiday, fête, celebration, holy day, red-letter day, religious festival, saint's day ▸ *vb* **4** = eat your fill, wine and dine, overindulge, consume, indulge, gorge, devour, pig out (*slang*)

feat *n* a remarkable, skilful, or daring action: *an extraordinary feat of engineering*

> **feat** *n* = accomplishment, act, performance, achievement, enterprise, undertaking, exploit, deed

feather *n* **1** any of the flat light structures that form the plumage of birds, each consisting of a shaft with soft thin hairs on either side **2 feather in one's cap** a cause for pleasure at one's achievements ▸ *vb* **3** to fit, cover, or supply with feathers **4** *rowing* to turn an oar parallel to the water between strokes, in order to lessen wind resistance **5 feather one's nest** to collect possessions and money to make one's life comfortable, often dishonestly >**feathered** *adj* >**feathery** *adj*

> **feather** *n* **1** = plume

featherweight *n* **1** a professional or an amateur boxer weighing up to 126 pounds (57 kg) **2** something very light or of little importance

feature *n* **1 features** any one of the parts of the face, such as the nose, chin, or mouth **2** a prominent or distinctive part of something: *regular debates were a feature of our final year* **3** the main film in a cinema programme **4** an item appearing regularly in a newspaper or magazine **5** a prominent story in a newspaper ▸ *vb* **-turing, -tured** **6** to have as a feature or make a feature of: *this cooker features a fan-assisted oven* **7** to give special prominence to: *the film features James Mason as Rommel* >**featureless** *adj*

> **feature** *n* **1** = face, countenance (*literary*), physiognomy, lineaments **2** = aspect, quality, characteristic, property, factor, trait, hallmark, facet **4, 5** = article, report, story, piece, item, column ▸ *vb* **6** = spotlight, present, emphasize, play up, foreground, give prominence to

Feb. February

febrile (fee-brile) *adj* *formal* **1** very active and nervous: *increasingly febrile activity at the Stock Exchange* **2** of or relating to fever

February *n*, *pl* **-aries** the second month of the year

feckless *adj* irresponsible and lacking character and determination: *her feckless brother was always in debt*

fecund *adj* *literary* **1** fertile or capable of producing many offspring **2** intellectually productive or creative: *an extraordinarily fecund year even by Mozart's standards* >**fecundity** *n*

fed *vb* the past of **feed**

federal *adj* **1** of a form of government in which power is divided between one central and several regional governments **2** of the central government of a federation **3** *Austral* of a style of house built around the time of Federation ▷ **federalism** *n* ▷ **federalist** *n, adj*

federate *vb* **-rating, -rated** to unite in a federal union ▷ **federative** *adj*

federation *n* **1** the union of several provinces, states, etc. **2** any alliance or association of organizations which have freely joined together for a common purpose: *a federation of twenty regional unions*

> **federation** *n* = union, league, association, alliance, combination, coalition, partnership, consortium

fedora (fid-**or**-a) *n* a type of soft hat with a brim

fed up *adj informal* annoyed or bored

> **fed up** *adj* = cheesed off, depressed, bored, tired, discontented, dissatisfied, glum, sick and tired (*informal*), hoha (NZ)

fee *n* **1** a charge paid to be allowed to do something: *many people resent the licence fee* **2** a payment asked by professional people for their services **3** *property law* an interest in land that can be inherited. The interest can be with unrestricted rights (**fee simple**) or restricted (**fee tail**)

> **fee** *n* **1, 2** = charge, price, cost, bill, payment, wage, salary, toll

feeble *adj* **1** lacking in physical or mental strength **2** not effective or convincing: *feeble excuses for Scotland's latest defeat* ▷ **feebly** *adv*

> **feeble** *adj* **1** = weak, frail, debilitated, sickly, puny, weedy (*informal*), infirm, effete; ≠ strong **2** = inadequate, pathetic, insufficient, lame; ≠ effective

feeble-minded *adj* unable to think or understand effectively

feed *vb* **feeding, fed** **1** to give food to (a person or an animal) **2** to give (something) as food: *people feeding bread to their cattle* **3** to eat food: *red squirrel feed in the pines* **4** to supply or prepare food for **5** to provide what is needed for the continued existence, operation, or growth of: *illustrations which will feed an older child's imagination; pools fed by waterfalls* ▶ *n* **6** the act of feeding **7** food, esp. that given to animals or babies **8** *Brit, Austral & NZ informal* a meal

> **feed** *vb* **3** = graze, eat, browse, pasture **4** = cater for, provide for, nourish, provide with food, supply, sustain, cook for, wine and dine ▶ *n* **7** = food, fodder, provender, pasturage **8** = meal, spread (*informal*), dinner, lunch, tea, breakfast, feast, supper

feedback *n* **1** information in response to an inquiry or experiment: *considerable feedback from the customers* **2** the return of part of the output of an electronic circuit to its input **3** the return of part of the sound output of a loudspeaker to the microphone, so that a high-pitched whine is produced

feeder *n* **1** a device used to feed an animal, child, or sick person **2** an animal or a person who feeds: *these larvae are voracious feeders* **3** a road, rail, or air service that links outlying areas to the main network **4** a tributary or channel of a river

feel *vb* **feeling, felt** **1** to have a physical or emotional sensation of: *he felt a combination of shame and relief* **2** to become aware of or examine by touching **3** Also: **feel in one's bones** to sense by intuition **4** to believe or think: *I felt I got off pretty lightly* **5** **feel for** to show compassion towards **6** **feel like** to have an inclination for (something or doing something): *I feel like going to the cinema* **7** **feel up to** to be fit enough for (something or doing something) ▶ *n* **8** the act of feeling **9** an impression: *all this mixing and matching has a French feel to it* **10** the sense of touch **11** an instinctive ability: *a feel for art*

> **feel** *vb* **1** = experience, bear **2** = touch, handle, manipulate, finger, stroke, paw, caress, fondle **3** = sense, be aware, be convinced, have a feeling, intuit **4** = believe, consider, judge, deem, think, hold ▶ *n* **9** = impression, feeling, air, sense, quality, atmosphere, mood, aura

feeler *n* **1** an organ on an insect's head that is sensitive to touch **2** **put out feelers** to make informal suggestions or remarks designed to probe the reactions of others

feeling *n* **1** an emotional reaction: *a feeling of discontent* **2** **feelings** emotional sensitivity: *I don't want to hurt your feelings* **3** instinctive appreciation and understanding: *your feeling for language* **4** an intuitive understanding that cannot be explained: *I began to have a sinking feeling that I was not going to get rid of her* **5** opinion or view: *it was his feeling that the report was a misinterpretation of what had been said* **6** capacity for sympathy or affection: *moved by feeling for his fellow citizens* **7** ᴀ the ability to experience physical sensations: *he has no feeling in his left arm* ʙ the sensation so experienced **8** the impression or mood created by something: *a feeling of excitement in the air* **9** **bad feeling** resentment or anger between people, for example after an argument or an injustice: *his refusal may have triggered bad feeling between the two men* ▷ **feelingly** *adv*

> **feeling** *n* **1** = emotion, sentiment **4** = impression, idea, sense, notion, suspicion, hunch, inkling, presentiment **5** = opinion, view, attitude, belief, point of view, instinct, inclination **6** = ardour, love, care, warmth, tenderness, fervour **7ᴀ** = sense of touch, perception, sensation **7ʙ** = sensation, sense, impression, awareness **8** = atmosphere, mood, aura, ambience, feel, air, quality

f

feet n 1 the plural of **foot** 2 **be run** or **rushed off one's feet** to be very busy 3 **feet of clay** a weakness that is not widely known 4 **have** or **keep one's feet on the ground** to be practical and reliable 5 **put one's feet up** to take a rest 6 **stand on one's own feet** to be independent 7 **sweep off one's feet** to fill with enthusiasm

feign (fane) vb to pretend to experience (a particular feeling): *he didn't have to feign surprise* >**feigned** adj

feint¹ (faint) n 1 a misleading movement designed to distract an opponent, such as in boxing or fencing ▸ vb 2 to make a feint

feint² (faint) n *printing* paper that has pale lines across it for writing on

feldspar or **felspar** n a hard mineral that is the main constituent of igneous rocks >**feldspathic** or **felspathic** adj

felicitations pl n, interj expressions of pleasure at someone's success or good fortune; congratulations

felicitous adj appropriate and well-chosen: *a felicitous combination of architectural styles*

felicity n 1 great happiness and pleasure 2 the quality of being pleasant or desirable: *small moments of architectural felicity amidst acres of monotony* 3 pl **-ties** an appropriate and well-chosen remark: *Nietzsche's verbal felicities are not lost in translation*

feline adj 1 of or belonging to the cat family 2 like a cat, esp. in stealth or grace ▸ n 3 any member of the cat family >**felinity** n

fell¹ vb the past tense of **fall**

fell² vb 1 to cut down (a tree) 2 to knock down (a person), esp. in a fight

> **fell** vb 1 = cut down, cut, level, demolish, knock down, hew 2 = knock down

fell³ adj **in one fell swoop** in one single action or on one single occasion: *they arrested all the hooligans in one fell swoop*

fell⁴ n Scot & N English a mountain, hill, or moor

felloe or **felly** n, pl **-loes** or **-lies** a segment or the whole rim of a wooden wheel

fellow n 1 a man or boy 2 a comrade or associate 3 a person in the same group or condition: *he earned the respect of his fellows at Dunkirk* 4 a member of the governing body at any of various universities or colleges 5 (in Britain) a postgraduate research student ▸ adj 6 in the same group or condition: *a conversation with a fellow passenger*

> **fellow** n 1 = man, person, individual, character, guy (informal), bloke (Brit informal), chap (informal), boykie (S African informal) 2 = associate, colleague, peer, partner, companion, comrade, crony

fellowship n 1 the state of sharing mutual interests or activities 2 a society of people sharing mutual interests or activities 3 companionship or friendship 4 *education* a financed research post providing study facilities

> **fellowship** n 2 = society, club, league, association, organization, guild, fraternity (US, Canad), sorority (US, Canad), brotherhood 3 = camaraderie, brotherhood, sisterhood, companionship, sociability

felon n *criminal law* (formerly) a person who committed a serious crime

felony n, pl **-nies** *criminal law* (formerly) a serious crime, such as murder or arson >**felonious** adj

felspar n same as **feldspar**

felt¹ vb the past of **feel**

felt² n a matted fabric of wool, made by working the fibres together under pressure

felt-tip pen n a pen with a writing point made from pressed fibres

fem. 1 female 2 feminine

female adj 1 of the sex producing offspring 2 of or characteristic of a woman 3 (of reproductive organs such as the ovary and carpel) capable of producing reproductive cells (**gametes**) that are female 4 (of flowers) not having parts in which pollen is produced (**stamens**) 5 (of a mechanical component) having an opening into which a projecting male component can be fitted ▸ n 6 a female person, animal, or plant

feminine adj 1 possessing qualities considered typical of or appropriate to a woman 2 of women 3 *grammar* denoting a gender of nouns that includes some female animate things >**femininity** n

> **feminine** adj 1 = female, womanly, ladylike; ≠ masculine

feminism n a doctrine or movement that advocates equal rights for women >**feminist** n, adj

femme fatale (fam fat-tahl) n, pl **femmes fatales** (fam fat-tahlz) an alluring or seductive woman who leads men into dangerous or difficult situations by her charm

femur (fee-mer) n, pl **femurs** or **femora** (fee-mer-ra) the thighbone >**femoral** adj

fen n Brit low-lying flat marshy land

fence n 1 a barrier that encloses an area such as a garden or field, usually made of posts connected by wire rails or boards 2 an obstacle for a horse to jump in steeplechasing or showjumping 3 *slang* a dealer in stolen property 4 *machinery* a guard or guide, esp. in a circular saw or plane 5 (**sit**) **on the fence** (to be) unwilling to commit oneself ▸ vb **fencing, fenced** 6 to construct a fence on or around (a piece of land) 7 **fence in** or **off** to close in or separate off with or as if with a fence 8 to fight using swords or foils 9 to argue cleverly but evasively: *they fenced for a while, weighing each other up*

> **fence** n 1 = barrier, wall, defence, railings, hedge, barricade, hedgerow, rampart ▸ vb 6 = enclose, surround, bound, protect, pen, confine, encircle

fencing *n* **1** the sport of fighting with swords or foils **2** materials used for making fences

fend *vb* **1 fend for oneself** to look after oneself; be independent **2 fend off** to defend oneself against (verbal or physical attack)

fender *n* **1** a low metal barrier that stops coals from falling out of a fireplace **2** a soft but solid object, such as a coil of rope, hung over the side of a vessel to prevent damage when docking **3** *US & Canad* the wing of a car

feng shui (fung shway) *n* the Chinese art of deciding the best design or position of a grave, building, etc., in order to bring good luck

fennel *n* a fragrant plant whose seeds, leaves, and root are used in cookery

fenugreek *n* a Mediterranean plant grown for its heavily scented seeds

feral *adj* **1** (of animals and plants) existing in a wild state, esp. after being domestic or cultivated **2** savage

ferment *n* **1** excitement and unrest caused by change or uncertainty **2** any substance, such as yeast, that causes fermentation ▸ *vb* **3** to undergo or cause to undergo fermentation

fermentation *n* a chemical reaction in which an organic molecule splits into simpler substances, esp. the conversion of sugar to ethyl alcohol by yeast

fern *n* a flowerless plant with roots, stems, and long feathery leaves that reproduces by releasing spores ▸ **ferny** *adj*

ferocious *adj* savagely fierce or cruel ▸ **ferocity** *n*

ferocious *adj* = cruel, bitter, brutal, vicious, ruthless, bloodthirsty; ≠ gentle

ferret *n* **1** a small yellowish-white animal related to the weasel and bred for hunting rats and rabbits ▸ *vb* **-reting, -reted** **2** to hunt rabbits or rats with ferrets **3** to search around **4 ferret out** **A** to drive from hiding **B** to find by determined investigation: *she could ferret out little knowledge of his background*

ferric *adj* of or containing iron in the trivalent state

Ferris wheel *n* a large vertical fairground wheel with hanging seats for riding on

ferrous *adj* of or containing iron in the divalent state

ferry *n, pl* **-ries 1** a boat for transporting passengers and vehicles across a body of water, esp. as a regular service **2** such a service ▸ *vb* **-ries, -rying, -ried 3** to transport or go by ferry **4** to transport (passengers or goods) on a regular basis ▸ **ferryman** *n*

ferry *n* **1** = ferry boat, boat, ship, passenger boat, packet boat, packet ▸ *vb* = transport, bring, carry, ship, take, run, shuttle, convey

fertile *adj* **1** capable of producing offspring, crops, or vegetation **2** *biol* capable of growth and development: *fertile seeds* **3** highly productive: *a fertile imagination* **4** *physics* (of a substance) able to

be transformed into fissile or fissionable material ▸ **fertility** *n*

fertile *adj* **3** = productive, rich, lush, prolific, abundant, plentiful, fruitful, teeming; ≠ barren

fertilize *or* **-lise** *vb* **-lizing, -lized** *or* **-lising, -lised 1** to provide (an animal or plant) with sperm or pollen to bring about fertilization **2** to supply (soil) with nutrients ▸ **fertilization** *or* **-lisation** *n*

fertilizer *or* **-liser** *n* any substance, such as manure, added to soil to increase its productivity

fertilizer *or* **-liser** *n* = compost, muck, manure, dung, bone meal, dressing, toad juice (*Austral*)

fervent *or* **fervid** *adj* intensely sincere and passionate ▸ **fervently** *adv*

fervour *or US* **fervor** *n* great intensity of feeling or belief

fescue *n* a pasture and lawn grass with stiff narrow leaves

fester *vb* **1** to grow worse and increasingly hostile: *the bitterness which had been festering beneath the surface* **2** (of a wound) to form pus **3** to rot and decay: *rubbish festered in the heat*

festival *n* **1** an organized series of special events and performances: *the Edinburgh Festival* **2** a day or period set aside for celebration

festival *n* **1** = celebration, fair, carnival, gala, fête, entertainment, jubilee, fiesta **2** = holy day, holiday, feast, commemoration, feast day, red-letter day, saint's day, fiesta

festive *adj* of or like a celebration

festive *adj* = celebratory, happy, merry, jubilant, cheery, joyous, joyful, jovial; ≠ mournful

festivity *n, pl* **-ties 1** happy celebration: *a spirit of joy and festivity* **2 festivities** celebrations

festoon *vb* **1** to drape with decorations: *Christmas trees festooned with fairy lights* ▸ *n* **2** a decorative chain of flowers or ribbons suspended in loops

feta *n* a white Greek cheese made from sheep's or goat's milk

fetch *vb* **1** to go after and bring back **2** to be sold for (a certain price): *Impressionist pictures fetch very high prices* **3** *informal* to give someone (a blow or slap) **4 fetch and carry** to perform menial tasks

fetch *vb* **1** = bring, pick up, collect, go and get, get, carry, deliver, transport **2** = sell for, make, raise, earn, realize, go for, yield, bring in

fetching *adj informal* attractive: *a fetching dress*

fetching *adj* = attractive, charming, cute, enticing, captivating, alluring, winsome

fetch up *vb* **1** *US & NZ informal* to arrive or end up **2** *slang* to vomit food

fete (fate) n **1** an event, usually outdoors, with stalls, competitions, etc., held to raise money for charity ▸ vb **feting**, **feted 2** to honour and entertain (someone) publicly: *the President was feted with an evening of music and dancing*

fetid or **foetid** adj having a stale and unpleasant smell

fetish n **1** a a form of behaviour in which a person derives sexual satisfaction from handling an object **b** any object that is involved in such behaviour **2** any object, activity, etc., to which one is excessively devoted: *cleanliness is almost a fetish with her* **3** an object that is believed to have magical powers > **fetishism** n > **fetishist** n

fetlock n **1** the back part of a horse's leg, just behind the hoof **2** the tuft of hair growing from this part

fetter n **1 fetters** checks or restraints: *free from the fetters of religion* **2** a chain fixed around a prisoner's ankle ▸ vb **3** to prevent from behaving freely and naturally: *fettered by bureaucracy* **4** to tie up in fetters

fettle n **in fine fettle** in good spirits or health

fetus or **foetus** (fee-tuss) n, pl **-tuses** the embryo of a mammal in the later stages of development > **fetal** or **foetal** adj

feu n *Scots law* a right to the use of land in return for a fixed annual payment (**feu duty**)

feud n **1** long and bitter hostility between two families, clans, or individuals ▸ vb **2** to carry on a feud

> **feud** n = hostility, row, conflict, argument, disagreement, rivalry, quarrel, vendetta ▸ vb = quarrel, row, clash, dispute, fall out (*informal*), contend, war, squabble

feudal adj of or characteristic of feudalism

feudalism n the legal and social system in medieval Europe, in which people were given land and protection by a lord in return for which they worked and fought for him. Also called: **feudal system**

fever n **1** an abnormally high body temperature, accompanied by a fast pulse rate, shivering, and nausea. Related adjective: **febrile 2** any disease characterized by a high temperature **3** intense nervous excitement: *she waited in a fever of anxiety*

> **fever** n **3** = excitement, frenzy, ferment, agitation, fervour, restlessness, delirium

feverish or **fevered** adj **1** suffering from fever **2** in a state of nervous excitement: *a feverish scramble to buy shares* > **feverishly** adv

few adj **1** hardly any: *few homes had telephones in Paris in the 1930s* **2 a few** a small number of: *a few days ago* **3 a good few** *informal* several **4 few and far between** scarce **5 quite a few** *informal* several

> **few** adj **1** = not many, one or two, scarcely any, rare, meagre, negligible, sporadic, sparse

fey adj **1** vague and whimsically strange **2** having the ability to look into the future

fez n, pl **fezzes** a round red brimless hat with a flat top and a tassel hanging from it. Formerly worn by men in Turkey and some Arab countries

fiancé or *fem* **fiancée** (fee-on-say) n a person who is engaged to be married

fiasco n, pl **-cos** or **-coes** an action or attempt that fails completely in a ridiculous or disorganized way: *the invasion of Cuba ended in a fiasco*

> **fiasco** n = flop (*informal*), failure, disaster, mess (*informal*), catastrophe, debacle, cock-up (*Brit slang*), washout (*informal*)

fiat (fie-at) n **1** an official order issued without the consultation of those expected to obey it: *the junta ruled by fiat* **2** official permission

fib n **1** a trivial and harmless lie ▸ vb **fibbing**, **fibbed 2** to tell such a lie ▸ **fibber** n

fibre or *US* **fiber** n **1** a natural or synthetic thread that may be spun into yarn **2** a threadlike animal or plant tissue: *a simple network of nerve fibres* **3** a fibrous substance that helps the body digest food: *fruits, vegetables, grains, lentils, and beans are high in fibre* **4** strength of character: *moral fibre* **5** essential substance or nature: *my every fibre sang out in sudden relief* > **fibrous** adj

> **fibre** or **fiber** n = thread, strand, filament, tendril, pile, texture, wisp

fibreglass n **1** material consisting of matted fine glass fibres, used as insulation **2** a light strong material made by bonding fibreglass with a synthetic resin, used for boats and car bodies

fibre optics n the transmission of information by light along very thin flexible fibres of glass > **fibre optic** adj

fibrillation n uncontrollable twitching of muscle fibres, esp. those of the heart

fibro n *Austral* a mixture of cement and asbestos fibre, formerly used in building materials. Short for: **fibrocement**

fibroid (fibe-royd) adj **1** *anatomy* (of structures or tissues) containing or resembling fibres ▸ n **2** a harmless tumour composed of fibrous connective tissue

fibrositis (fibe-roh-site-iss) n inflammation of fibrous tissue, esp. of the back muscles, causing pain and stiffness

fibula (fib-yew-la) n, pl **-lae** (-lee) or **-las** the outer and thinner of the two bones between the knee and ankle of the human leg > **fibular** adj

fickle adj **1** changeable in purpose, affections, etc.: *notoriously fickle voters* **2** (of the weather) changing often and suddenly > **fickleness** n

fiction n **1** literary works invented by the imagination, such as novels **2** an invented story or explanation: *the fiction that cricket is more noble than other sports* **3** *law* something assumed to be true for the sake of convenience, though probably false > **fictional** adj

fiction *n* **1** = tale, story, novel, legend, myth, romance, narration, creative writing **2** = lie, invention, fabrication, falsehood, untruth, urban myth, tall story, urban legend

fictionalize *or* **-lise** *vb* **-lizing, -lized** *or* **-lising, -lised** to make into fiction

fictitious *adj* **1** not genuine: *rumours of false accounting and fictitious loans had surrounded the bank for years* **2** of or in fiction

fiddle *n* **1** *informal or derogatory* the violin **2** a violin played as a folk instrument **3** *Brit & NZ informal* a dishonest action or scheme **4 on the fiddle** *informal* engaged in an illegal or fraudulent undertaking **5 fit as a fiddle** *informal* in very good health **6 play second fiddle** *informal* to undertake a role that is less important or powerful than someone else's ▸ *vb* **-dling, -dled** **7** to play (a tune) on the fiddle **8** *informal* to do (something) by illegal or dishonest means **9** *informal* to falsify (accounts) **10 fiddle with** to move or touch (something) restlessly or nervously **11 fiddle about** *or* **around** *informal* to waste time

fiddle *n* **3** = fraud, racket, scam (*slang*), fix, swindle ▸ *vb* **8, 9** = cheat, cook (*informal*), fix, diddle (*informal*), wangle (*informal*)

fiddlesticks *interj* an expression of annoyance or disagreement

fiddling *adj* small or unimportant

fiddling *adj* = trivial, small, petty, trifling, insignificant, unimportant, pettifogging, futile

fiddly *adj* **-dlier, -dliest** small and awkward to do or handle

fidelity *n, pl* **-ties** **1** faithfulness to one's spouse or lover **2** loyalty to a person, belief, or cause **3** accuracy in reporting detail: *an account of the invasion written with objectivity and fidelity* **4** *electronics* the degree to which an amplifier or radio accurately reproduces the input signal

fidelity *n* **1, 2** = loyalty, devotion, allegiance, constancy, faithfulness, dependability, trustworthiness, staunchness; ≠ disloyalty **3** = accuracy, precision, correspondence, closeness, faithfulness, exactness, scrupulousness; ≠ inaccuracy

fidget *vb* **-dgeting, -dgeted** **1** to move about restlessly **2 fidget with** to make restless or uneasy movements with (something): *he broke off, fidgeting with the papers, unable to meet their gaze* ▸ *n* **3** a person who fidgets **4 the fidgets** a state of restlessness: *these youngsters are very highly strung and tend to get the fidgets* ▸ **fidgety** *adj*

fiduciary (fid-yewsh-ya-ree) *law* ▸ *n* **1** a person bound to act for someone else's benefit, as a trustee ▸ *adj* **2** of or relating to a trust or trustee

fief (feef) *n* (in feudal Europe) land granted by a lord in return for military service

field *n* **1** an area of uncultivated grassland; meadow **2** a piece of cleared land used for pasture or growing crops **3** a marked off area on which sports or athletic competitions are held **4** an area that is rich in minerals or other natural resources: *an oil field* **5 a** all the competitors in a competition **b** the competitors in a competition excluding the favourite **6** a battlefield **7** *cricket* the fielders collectively **8** a wide expanse of land covered by some substance such as snow or lava **9** an area of human activity or knowledge: *the most distinguished physicist in the field of quantum physics* **10** a place away from the laboratory or classroom where practical work is done **11** the surface or background of something, such as a flag **12** *physics* In full: **field of force** the region surrounding a body, such as a magnet, within which it can exert a force on another similar body not in contact with it **13 play the field** *informal* to have many romantic relationships ▸ *adj* **14** *military* of equipment or personnel for operations in the field: *field guns* ▸ *vb* **15** *sport* to catch or return (the ball) as a fielder **16** *sport* to send (a player or team) onto the field to play **17** *sport* (of a player or team) to act or take turn as a fielder or fielders **18** *informal* to deal successfully with (a question or remark)

field *n* **1, 2** = meadow, land, green, lea (*poetic*), pasture **5a** = competitors, competition, candidates, runners, applicants, entrants, contestants **9** = speciality, line, area, department (*informal*), territory, discipline, province, sphere ▸ *vb* **15** = retrieve, return, stop, catch, pick up **18** = deal with, answer, handle, respond to, reply to, deflect, turn aside

field day *n* **1** *informal* an opportunity or occasion for unrestrained action, esp. if previously denied or restricted: *the revelations gave the press a field day* **2** *military* a day devoted to manoeuvres or exercises

fielder *n* *sport* a member of the fielding side

fieldfare *n* a type of large thrush

field glasses *pl n* binoculars

field marshal *n* an officer holding the highest rank in certain armies

field sports *pl n* sports carried on in the countryside, such as hunting or fishing

fieldwork *n* *military* a temporary structure used in defending a place or position

field work *n* an investigation made in the field as opposed to the classroom or laboratory > **field worker** *n*

fiend (feend) *n* **1** an evil spirit **2** a cruel or wicked person **3** *informal* a person who is extremely interested in or fond of something: *a fitness fiend* > **fiendish** *adj* > **fiendishly** *adv*

fierce *adj* **1** very aggressive or angry: *a fierce dog* **2** intense or strong: *a fierce wind* > **fiercely** *adv*

fierce *adj* **1** = ferocious, wild, dangerous, cruel, savage, brutal, aggressive, menacing, aggers (*Austral slang*), biffo (*Austral slang*); ≠ gentle **2** = intense, strong, keen, relentless, cut-throat; ≠ tranquil

fiery (fire-ee) *adj* **fierier, fieriest 1** consisting of or like fire: *a fiery explosion* **2** displaying strong passion, esp. anger: *a fiery speech* **3** (of food) very spicy ⊳ **fierily** *adv* ⊳ **fieriness** *n*

fiery *adj* **1** = burning, flaming, blazing, on fire, ablaze, aflame, afire **2** = excitable, fierce, passionate, irritable, impetuous, irascible, hot-headed

fiesta *n* (esp. in Spain and Latin America) a religious festival or carnival

FIFA (fee-fa) International Association Football Federation

fifteen *n* **1** the cardinal number that is the sum of ten and five **2** a numeral, 15 or XV, representing this number **3** something representing or consisting of 15 units **4** a Rugby Union team ▸ *adj* **5** amounting to fifteen: *fifteen trees* ⊳ **fifteenth** *adj, n*

fifth *adj* **1** of or being number five in a series **2** denoting the fifth from lowest (usually the highest) forward gear in a motor vehicle ▸ *n* **3** one of five equal parts of something **4** *music* the interval between one note and the note three-and-a-half tones higher or lower than it **5** the fifth from lowest (usually the highest) forward gear in a motor vehicle

fifth column *n* any group that secretly helps the enemies of its own country or organization ⊳ **fifth columnist** *n*

fifty *n, pl* **-ties 1** the cardinal number that is the product of ten and five **2** a numeral, 50 or L, representing this number **3** something representing or consisting of 50 units ▸ *adj* **4** amounting to fifty: *fifty bodies* ⊳ **fiftieth** *adj, n*

fig *n* **1** a soft sweet fruit full of tiny seeds, which grows on a tree **2** not care *or* give a fig not to care at all: *he did not give a fig for his enemies*

fight *vb* **fighting, fought 1** to struggle against (an enemy) in battle or physical combat **2** to struggle to overcome or destroy: *to fight drug trafficking* **3** to carry on (a battle or contest) **4** to make (one's way) somewhere with difficulty: *they fought their way upstream* **5** fight for to uphold (a cause) by struggling: *fight for your rights* **6** fight it out to struggle or compete until a decisive result is obtained **7** fight shy of to avoid: *they fought shy of direct involvement in the conflict* ▸ *n* **8** a battle **9** a quarrel or contest **10** a boxing match **11** put up a fight to offer resistance ⊳ **fighting** *n*

fight *vb* **1** = oppose, campaign against, dispute, contest, resist, defy, contend, withstand **3** = engage in, conduct, wage, pursue, carry on ▸ *n* **8** = battle, campaign, movement, struggle **9** = row, argument, dispute, quarrel, squabble **10** = brawl, scrap (*informal*), confrontation, rumble (*US, NZ slang*), duel, skirmish, tussle, biffo (*Austral slang*), boilover (*Austral*)

fighter *n* **1** a professional boxer **2** a person who has determination **3** *military* an armed aircraft for destroying other aircraft

fighter *n* **1** = boxer, wrestler, pugilist, prize fighter

fight off *vb* **1** to drive away (an attacker) **2** to struggle to avoid: *to fight off infection*

figment *n* **a figment of one's imagination** something nonexistent and only imagined by someone

figurative *adj* **1** (of language) abstract, imaginative, or symbolic; not literal **2** (of art) involving realistic representation of people and things ⊳ **figuratively** *adv*

figure *n* **1** a written symbol for a number **2** an amount expressed in numbers **3 figures** calculations with numbers **4** visible shape or form; outline **5** a slim bodily shape: *it's not good for your figure* **6** a well-known person: *a public figure* **7** a representation in painting or sculpture, esp. of the human body **8** an illustration or diagram in a text **9** a decorative pattern **10** a fixed set of movements in dancing or skating **11** *geom* any combination of points, lines, curves, or planes **12** *music* a characteristic short pattern of notes **13 figure of fun** a person who is often laughed at by other people ▸ *vb* **-uring, -ured 14** to calculate (sums or amounts) **15** *US, Canad, Austral & NZ informal* to consider **16** to be included or play a part: *a house which figures in several of White's novels* **17** *informal* to be consistent with expectation: *he's a small-time crook, earns most of his cash as an informer. – That figures*

figure *n* **1** = digit, character, symbol, number, numeral **5** = shape, build, body, frame, proportions, physique **6** = personage, person, individual, character (*informal*), personality, celebrity, big name, dignitary **8** = diagram, drawing, picture, illustration, representation, sketch **9** = design, shape, pattern ▸ *vb* **14** = calculate, work out, compute, tot up, total, count, reckon, tally **16** = feature, act, appear, contribute to, play a part, be featured

figurehead *n* **1** a person who is formally the head of a movement or an organization, but has no real authority **2** a carved bust on the bow of some sailing vessels

figurehead *n* **1** = nominal head, titular head, frontman *or* woman *or* person, puppet, mouthpiece

figure of speech *n* an expression, such as a simile, in which words do not have their literal meaning

figure out *vb informal* to work out, solve, or understand: *I can't figure him out*

figure out *vb* **figure something or someone out** = understand, make out, fathom, see, solve, comprehend, make sense of, decipher

figurine *n* a small carved or moulded figure

filament *n* **1** the thin wire inside a light bulb that emits light **2** *electronics* a high-resistance wire forming the cathode in some valves **3** a single strand of fibre **4** *botany* the stalk of a stamen > **filamentary** *adj*

filbert *n* the brown edible nuts of the hazel

filch *vb* to steal in small amounts

file¹ *n* **1** a folder or box used to keep documents in order **2** the documents, etc., kept in this way **3** documents or information about a specific subject or person: *the doctor handed him his file* **4** a line of people in marching formation, one behind another **5** *computers* an organized collection of related records **6** **on file** recorded for reference, as in a file ▸ *vb* **filing, filed 7** to place (a document) in a file **8** to place (a legal document) on public or official record **9** to bring a lawsuit, esp. for divorce **10** to submit (a report or story) to a newspaper **11** to march or walk in a line

file *n* **1** = folder, case, portfolio, binder **2, 3** = dossier, record, information, data, documents, case history, report, case **4** = line, row, chain, column, queue, procession ▸ *vb* **7** = arrange, order, classify, put in place, categorize, pigeonhole, put in order **8** = register, record, enter, log, put on record **11** = march, troop, parade, walk in line, walk behind one another

file² *n* **1** a hand tool consisting of a steel blade with small cutting teeth on its faces, used for shaping or smoothing ▸ *vb* **filing, filed 2** to shape or smooth (a surface) with a file

file *vb* = smooth, shape, polish, rub, scrape, rasp, abrade

filial *adj* of or suitable to a son or daughter: *filial duty*

filibuster *n* **1** the process of obstructing legislation by means of long speeches so that time runs out and a vote cannot be taken **2** a legislator who engages in such obstruction ▸ *vb* **3** to obstruct (legislation) with such delaying tactics

filigree *n* **1** delicate ornamental work of gold or silver wire ▸ *adj* **2** made of filigree

filings *pl n* shavings or particles removed by a file: *iron filings*

Filipino (fill-lip-pee-no) *adj* **1** of the Philippines ▸ *n, pl* **-nos 2** Also (fem): **Filipina** a person from the Philippines

fill *vb* (often foll. by *up*) **1** to make or become full **2** to occupy the whole of: *their supporters filled the entire stand* **3** to plug (a gap or crevice) **4** to meet (a requirement or need) satisfactorily: *this book fills a major gap* **5** to cover (a page or blank space)

with writing or drawing **6** to hold and perform the duties of (an office or position) **7** to appoint or elect an occupant to (an office or position) ▸ *n* **8 one's fill** sufficient for one's needs or wants

fill *vb* **1** = top up, fill up, make full, become full, brim over **2** = pack, crowd, squeeze, cram, throng **3** = plug, close, stop, seal, cork, bung, block up, stop up **4** = fulfil, hold, perform, carry out, occupy, execute, discharge

filler *n* **1** a paste used for filling in cracks or holes in a surface before painting **2** *journalism* an item to fill space between more important articles

fillet *n* **1** a piece of boneless meat or fish **2** a thin strip of ribbon or lace worn in the hair or around the neck **3** *archit* a narrow flat moulding ▸ *vb* **-leting, -leted 4** to cut or prepare (meat or fish) as a fillet

filling *n* **1** a substance or thing used to fill something: *a sandwich filling* **2** *dentistry* a substance that fills a gap or cavity of a tooth ▸ *adj* **3** (of food or a meal) substantial and satisfying

filling *n* **1** = stuffing, padding, filler, wadding, inside, insides, contents ▸ *adj* = satisfying, heavy, square, substantial, ample

filling station *n chiefly Brit* a place where petrol and other supplies for motorists are sold

fillip *n* **1** something that adds stimulation or enjoyment **2** the action of holding a finger towards the palm with the thumb and suddenly releasing it with a snapping sound

filly *n, pl* **-lies** a young female horse

film *n* **1 A** a sequence of images projected onto a screen, creating the illusion of movement **B** a form of entertainment in such a sequence of images. ▸ Related adjective: **cinematic 2** a thin flexible strip of cellulose coated with a photographic emulsion, used to make negatives and slides **3** a thin coating, covering, or layer: *a fine film of dust covered the floor* **4** a thin sheet of any material, as of plastic for packaging ▸ *vb* **5 A** to photograph with a movie or video camera **B** to make a film of (a screenplay or event) **6 film over** to cover or become covered with a thin layer ▸ *adj* **7** of or relating to films or the cinema

film *n* **1A** = movie, picture, flick (*slang*), motion picture, MPEG, MP4 **1B** = cinema, the movies **3** = layer, covering, cover, skin, coating, dusting, tissue, membrane ▸ *vb* **5A** = photograph, record, shoot, video, videotape, take **5B** = adapt for the screen, make into a film

filmy *adj* **filmier, filmiest** very thin and almost transparent: *a shirt of filmy black chiffon* > **filmily** *adv* > **filminess** *n*

filter *n* **1** a substance, such as paper or sand, that allows fluid to pass but retains solid particles **2** any device containing such a substance, esp. a tip on the mouth end of a cigarette **3** any electronic or acoustic device that blocks signals of certain frequencies while allowing others to pass **4** a computer program that processes data in order to remove certain items: *a spam filter* **5** any transparent disc of gelatine or glass used to reduce the intensity of given frequencies from the light leaving a lamp or entering a camera **6** *Brit* a traffic signal which permits vehicles to turn either left or right when the main signals are red ▸ *vb* **7** Also: **filter out** to remove or separate (particles) from (a liquid or gas) by a filter **8** Also: **filter through** to pass through a filter or something like a filter

> **filter** *n* **1** = sieve, mesh, gauze, strainer, membrane, riddle, sifter ▸ *vb* **8** = purify, treat, strain, refine, riddle, sift, sieve, winnow

filth *n* **1** disgusting dirt and muck **2** offensive material or language > **filthiness** *n* > **filthy** *adj*
filtrate *n* **1** a liquid or gas that has been filtered ▸ *vb* **-trating, -trated 2** to filter > **filtration** *n*
fin *n* **1** any of the winglike projections from a fish's body enabling it to balance and swim **2** *Brit* a vertical surface to which the rudder is attached at the rear of an aeroplane **3** a swimmer's flipper > **finned** *adj*
finagle (fin-nay-gl) *vb* **-gling, -gled** *informal* to use or achieve by craftiness or trickery
final *adj* **1** of or occurring at the end; last **2** having no possibility of further discussion, action, or change: *a final decision* ▸ *n* **3** a deciding contest between the winners of previous rounds in a competition > **finality** *n* > **finally** *adv*

> **final** *adj* **1** = last, latest, closing, finishing, concluding, ultimate, terminal; ≠ first **2** = irrevocable, absolute, definitive, decided, settled, definite, conclusive, irrefutable

finale (fin-nah-lee) *n* the concluding part of a dramatic performance or musical composition

> **finale** *n* = climax, ending, close, conclusion, culmination, denouement, last part, epilogue; ≠ opening

finalist *n* a contestant who has reached the last stage of a competition
finalize *or* **-lise** *vb* **-lizing, -lized** *or* **-lising, -lised** to put into final form; settle: *plans have yet to be finalized* > **finalization** *or* **-lisation** *n*
finance *vb* **-nancing, -nanced 1** to provide or obtain funds for (a project or large purchase) ▸ *n* **2** the system of money, credit, and investment **3** management of money, loans, or credits: *the dangerous political arena of public-sector finance* **4** funds or the provision of funds **5 finances** money resources: *the company's crumbling finances*

> **finance** *vb* = fund, back, support, pay for, guarantee, invest in, underwrite, endow ▸ *n* **2** = economics, business, money, banking, accounts, investment, commerce **5** = resources, money, funds, capital, cash, affairs, budgeting, assets

financial *adj* **1** of or relating to finance, finances, or people who manage money **2** *Austral & NZ informal* having ready money > **financially** *adv*

> **financial** *adj* **1** = economic, business, commercial, monetary, fiscal, pecuniary, pocketbook

financial year *n* any annual accounting period
financier *n* a person who is engaged in large-scale financial operations
finch *n* a small songbird with a short strong beak
find *vb* **finding, found 1** to discover by chance **2** to discover by search or effort **3** to realize or become aware: *I have found that if you make the effort then people will be more willing to help you* **4** to consider (someone or something) to have a particular quality: *his business partner had found that odd* **5** to experience (a particular feeling): *she found comfort in his words* **6** *law* to pronounce (the defendant) guilty or not guilty **7** to reach (a target) **8** to provide, esp. with difficulty: *we'll find room for you too* **9 find one's feet** to become capable or confident ▸ *n* **10** a person or thing that is found, esp. a valuable discovery: *the archaeological find of the century*

> **find** *vb* **1** = discover, uncover, spot, locate, detect, come across, hit upon, put your finger on; ≠ lose **3** = observe, learn, note, discover, notice, realize, come up with, perceive ▸ *n* = discovery, catch, asset, bargain, acquisition, good buy

finder *n* **1** a small telescope fitted to a larger one **2** a person or thing that finds
finding *n* the conclusion reached after an inquiry or investigation
find out *vb* **1** to learn something that one did not already know **2 find someone out** to discover that someone has been dishonest or deceitful

> **find out** *vb* **1 find something out** = learn, discover, realize, observe, perceive, detect, become aware, come to know

fine¹ *adj* **1** very good **2** superior in skill: *a fine doctor* **3** (of weather) clear and dry **4** *informal* quite well: *I felt fine* **5** satisfactory: *as far as we can tell, everything is fine* **6** of delicate or careful workmanship: *fine porcelain* **7** subtle: *too fine a distinction* **8** very thin or slender: *fine soft hair* **9** very small: *fine print* **10** (of edges or blades) sharp **11** fancy, showy, or smart **12** good-looking **13** *humorous* disappointing or terrible: *a fine mess!* ▸ *adv* **14** *informal* very well: *that's what we've always done, and it suits us just fine* ▸ *vb* **fining, fined 15** to make (something) finer or thinner **16 fine down** to make (a theory or criticism) more precise or exact > **finely** *adv*

fine *adj* **1** = excellent, good, striking, masterly, very good, impressive, outstanding, magnificent; ≠ poor **2** = brilliant, quick, keen, alert, clever, penetrating, astute **3** = sunny, clear, fair, dry, bright, pleasant, clement, balmy; ≠ cloudy **5** = satisfactory, good, all right, suitable, acceptable, convenient, fair, O.K. *or* okay (*informal*) **6** = delicate, light, thin, sheer, flimsy, wispy, gossamer, diaphanous; ≠ coarse **8** = thin, light, narrow, wispy **11** = stylish, expensive, elegant, refined, tasteful, quality, schmick (*Austral informal*)

fine² *n* **1** a payment imposed as a penalty ▸ *vb* **fining, fined 2** to impose a fine on

fine *n* = penalty, damages, punishment, forfeit, financial penalty ▸ *vb* = penalize, charge, punish

fine art *n* **1** art produced chiefly to appeal to the sense of beauty **2** any of the fields in which such art is produced, such as painting, sculpture, and engraving

finery *n* elaborate or showy decoration, esp. clothing and jewellery: *the princess dressed up in her finery*

finesse (fin-**ness**) *n* **1** elegant and delicate skill **2** subtlety and tact in handling difficult situations: *a lack of diplomatic finesse* **3** *bridge & whist* an attempt to win a trick when opponents hold a high card in the suit led by playing a lower card ▸ *vb* -**nessing**, -**nessed 4** to bring about with finesse **5** *bridge & whist* to play (a card) as a finesse

fine-tune *vb* -**tuning**, -**tuned** to make fine adjustments to (something) so that it works really well

finger *n* **1** one of the four long jointed parts of the hand **2** the part of a glove made to cover a finger **3** something that resembles a finger in shape or function **4** a quantity of liquid in a glass as deep as a finger is wide **5 get** *or* **pull one's finger out** *Brit & NZ informal* to begin or speed up activity, esp. after initial delay **6 put one's finger on** to identify precisely **7 put the finger on** *informal* to inform on or identify, esp. for the police **8 twist around one's little finger** to have easy and complete influence over ▸ *vb* **9** to touch or manipulate with the fingers; handle **10** to use one's fingers in playing (a musical instrument) **11** *informal*, *chiefly US* to identify as a criminal or suspect > **fingerless** *adj*

finger *vb* **9** = touch, feel, handle, play with, manipulate, paw (*informal*), maul, toy with

fingerboard *n* the long strip of hard wood on a violin, guitar, etc., upon which the strings are stopped by the fingers

fingering *n* **1** the technique of using one's fingers in playing a musical instrument **2** the numerals in a musical part indicating this

fingerprint *n* **1** an impression of the pattern of ridges on the inner surface of the end of each finger and thumb ▸ *vb* **2** to take an inked impression of the fingerprints of (a person) **3** to take a sample of the DNA of (a person)

finicky *or* **finicking** *adj* **1** extremely fussy **2** overelaborate or ornate: *finicky designer patterns*

finish *vb* **1** to bring to an end; conclude or stop **2** to be at or come to the end; use up **3** to bring to a desired or complete condition **4** to put a particular surface texture on (wood, cloth, or metal) **5 finish off A** to complete by doing the last part of: *she finished off her dissertation last week* **B** to destroy or defeat completely: *the physical demands of two young children nearly finished me off* **6 finish with** to end a relationship with (someone) ▸ *n* **7** the final stage or part; end **8** death or absolute defeat **9** the surface texture of wood, cloth, or metal **10** a thing or event that completes

finish *vb* **1** = end, stop, conclude, wind up, terminate; ≠ start **2** = stop, close, complete, conclude, cease, wrap up (*informal*), terminate, round off; ≠ start **3** = get done, complete, conclude **4** = coat, polish, stain, texture, wax, varnish, gild, veneer ▸ *n* **7** = end, close, conclusion, run-in, completion, finale, culmination, cessation; ≠ beginning **9** = surface, polish, shine, texture, glaze, veneer, lacquer, lustre

finite (**fine**-ite) *adj* **1** having limits in size, space, or time: *finite supplies of fossil fuels* **2** *maths & logic* having a countable number of elements **3** *grammar* denoting any form of a verb inflected for person, number, and tense

Finn *n* a person from Finland

Finnish *adj* **1** of Finland ▸ *n* **2** the language of Finland

fiord (**fee**-ord) *n* same as **fjord**

fir *n* a pyramid-shaped tree with needle-like leaves and erect cones

fire *n* **1** the state of combustion producing heat, flames, and often smoke **2** burning coal or wood, esp. in a hearth to heat a room **3** a destructive uncontrolled burning that destroys buildings, crops, etc. **4** *Brit* an electric or gas device for heating a room **5** the act of shooting weapons **6** passion and enthusiasm: *her questions brought new fire to the debate* **7 catch fire** to start burning **8 on fire A** burning **B** ardent or eager **9 open fire** to start firing a gun, artillery, etc. **10 play with fire** to be involved in something risky **11 set fire to** *or* **set on fire A** to ignite **B** to arouse or excite **12 under fire** being attacked, such as by weapons or by harsh criticism ▸ *vb* **firing, fired 13** to discharge (a firearm) **14** to detonate (an explosive device) **15** *informal* to dismiss from employment **16** to ask (a lot of questions) quickly in succession **17** *ceramics* to bake in a kiln to harden the clay **18** to kindle or be kindled **19** (of an internal-combustion engine) to produce an electrical spark which causes the fuel to burn and the engine to start **20** to provide with fuel **21** to arouse to strong emotion: *he fired his team mates with enthusiasm*

> **fire** *n* **3** = flames, blaze, combustion, inferno, conflagration, holocaust **5** = bombardment, shooting, firing, shelling, hail, volley, barrage, gunfire **6** = passion, energy, spirit, enthusiasm, excitement, intensity, sparkle, vitality ▸ *vb* **13, 14** = shoot, explode, discharge, detonate, pull the trigger **15** = dismiss, sack (*informal*), get rid of, discharge, lay off, make redundant, cashier, give notice, kennet (*Austral slang*), jeff (*Austral slang*) **21** = inspire, excite, stir, stimulate, motivate, awaken, animate, rouse

firearm *n* a weapon, such as a pistol, that fires bullets

firebrand *n* a person who arouses passionate political feelings, often causing trouble

firebreak *n* a strip of open land in a forest to stop the advance of a fire

fire brigade *n Brit & Austral* an organized body of firefighters

firedamp *n Brit, Austral & NZ* an explosive mixture of hydrocarbons, chiefly methane, formed in coal mines

fire drill *n* a rehearsal of procedures for escape from a fire

fire engine *n* a vehicle that carries firefighters and firefighting equipment to a fire

fire escape *n* a metal staircase or ladder on the outside of a building for escape in the event of fire

firefighter *n* a person whose job is to put out fires and rescue people endangered by them
> **firefighting** *adj, n*

firefly *n, pl* **-flies** a beetle that glows in the dark

fireguard *n* a screen made of wire mesh put before an open fire to protect against sparks

fire irons *pl n* a shovel, poker, and tongs for tending a domestic fire

fireplace *n* an open recess at the base of a chimney for a fire; hearth

fire power *n military* the amount of fire that can be delivered by a unit or weapon

fire station *n* a building where firefighting vehicles and equipment are stationed

firewall *n* software that prevents unauthorized access to a computer network from the internet

firework *n* a device containing chemicals that is ignited to produce coloured sparks and sometimes bangs

firie *n Austral informal* a firefighter

firing squad *n* a group of soldiers appointed to shoot a condemned criminal dead

firm¹ *adj* **1** not soft or yielding to a touch or pressure **2** securely in position **3** definitely established: *a firm agreement* **4** having determination or strength: *if you are firm and consistent she will come to see things your way* ▸ *adv*

5 stand firm to refuse to give in ▸ *vb* **6** to make or become firm: *to firm up flabby thighs* > **firmly** *adv* > **firmness** *n*

> **firm** *adj* **1** = hard, solid, dense, set, stiff, compacted, rigid, inflexible; ≠ soft **2** = secure, fixed, rooted, stable, steady, fast, embedded, immovable; ≠ unstable **3** = definite, hard, clear, confirmed, settled, fixed, hard-and-fast, cut-and-dried (*informal*) **4** = determined, resolved, definite, set on, adamant, resolute, inflexible, unyielding; ≠ wavering

firm² *n* a business company

> **firm** *n* = company, business, concern, association, organization, corporation, venture, enterprise

firmament *n literary* the sky or the heavens

first *adj* **1** earliest in time or order **2** rated, graded, or ranked above all other levels: *the First Lord of the Admiralty* **3** denoting the lowest forward gear in a motor vehicle **4** *music* denoting the highest voice part in a chorus or one of the sections of an orchestra: *the first violin* ▸ *n* **5** the person or thing coming before all others **6** the beginning or outset **7** *education, chiefly Brit* an honours degree of the highest class **8** the lowest forward gear in a motor vehicle ▸ *adv* **9** before anything else: *I would advise you to try surgery first* **10** for the first time: *this story first came to public attention in January 1984*

> **first** *adj* **1** = earliest, initial, opening, introductory, original, maiden, primordial **2** = top, best, winning, premier ▸ *adv* **9** = to begin with, firstly, initially, at the beginning, in the first place, beforehand, to start with, at the outset

first aid *n* immediate medical assistance given in an emergency

first-hand *adj* **1** obtained directly from the original source ▸ *adv* **2** directly from the original source **3 at first hand** directly

firstly *adv* same as **first** (sense 9)

first mate *n* an officer second in command to the captain of a merchant ship

first person *n* the form of a pronoun or verb used by the speaker to refer to himself or herself, or a group including himself or herself

first-rate *adj* of the best quality; excellent

firth *n* a narrow inlet of the sea, esp. in Scotland

fiscal *adj* **1** of or relating to government finances, esp. tax revenues ▸ *n* **2** (in Scotland) same as **procurator fiscal**

fish *n, pl* **fish** *or* **fishes** **1** a cold-blooded animal with a backbone, gills, and usually fins and a skin covered in scales, that lives in water. Related adjective: **piscine** **2** the flesh of fish used as food **3 cold fish** a person who shows little emotion **4 drink like a fish** to drink alcohol to excess **5 have other fish to fry** to have other more important concerns **6 like a fish out of**

water ill at ease in an unfamiliar situation
▸ *vb* **7** to attempt to catch fish **8** to fish in (a particular area of water): *the first trawler to fish these waters* **9** to grope for and find with some difficulty: *he fished a cigarette from his pocket* **10 fish for** to seek (something) indirectly: *he was fishing for compliments*

fish *vb* **7** = angle, net, cast, trawl

fisherman *n, pl* **-men** a person who fishes as a profession or for sport

fishery *n, pl* **-eries 1 A** the industry of catching, processing, and selling fish **B** a place where this is carried on **2** a place where fish are reared

fishfinger *n* an oblong piece of fish coated in breadcrumbs

fishmeal *n* ground dried fish used as feed for farm animals or as a fertilizer

fishmonger *n chiefly Brit* a seller of fish

fishnet *n* an open mesh fabric resembling netting, sometimes used for tights or stockings

fishplate *n* a flat piece of metal joining one rail or beam to the next, esp. on railway tracks

fishwife *n, pl* **-wives** *derogatory* a coarse or bad-tempered woman with a loud voice

fishy *adj* **fishier, fishiest 1** of or suggestive of fish **2** *informal* suspicious or questionable: *something a bit fishy about his explanation* > **fishily** *adv*

fissile *adj* **1** capable of undergoing nuclear fission **2** tending to split

fission *n* **1** the act or process of splitting into parts **2** *biol* a form of asexual reproduction involving a division into two or more equal parts **3** the splitting of atomic nuclei with the release of a large amount of energy > **fissionable** *adj*

fissure (fish-er) *n* any long narrow cleft or crack, esp. in a rock

fist *n* a hand with the fingers clenched into the palm

fisticuffs *pl n* fighting with the fists

fit¹ *vb* **fitting, fitted 1** to be appropriate or suitable for **2** to be of the correct size or shape (for) **3** to adjust in order to make appropriate **4** to try clothes on (someone) and note any adjustments needed **5** to make competent or ready: *the experience helped to fit him for the task* **6** to correspond with the facts or circumstances: *this part doesn't fit in with the rest of his theory* ▸ *adj* **fitter, fittest 7** appropriate **8** in good health **9** worthy or suitable: *houses fit for human habitation* **10** *slang* (of a person) sexually attractive ▸ *n* **11** the manner in which something fits: *the suit was an excellent fit* ▸ See also **fit in, fit out** > **fitly** *adv* > **fitness** *n*

fit *vb* **1, 6** = suit, meet, match, belong to, conform to, correspond to, accord with, be appropriate to **3** = adapt, shape, arrange, alter, adjust, modify, tweak (*informal*), customize **5** = equip, provide, arm, prepare, fit out, kit out ▸ *adj* **7, 9** = appropriate, suitable, right, becoming, seemly, fitting, skilled, correct; ≠ inappropriate **8** = healthy, strong, robust, sturdy, well, trim, strapping, hale (*old-fashioned*); ≠ unfit

fit² *n* **1** a sudden attack or convulsion, such as an epileptic seizure **2** a sudden short burst or spell: *fits of laughter; a fit of pique* **3 in fits and starts** in spasmodic spells **4 have a fit** *informal* to become very angry

fit *n* **1** = seizure, attack, bout, spasm, convulsion, paroxysm **2** = bout, burst, outbreak, outburst, spell

fitful *adj* occurring in irregular spells > **fitfully** *adv*

fit in *vb* **1** to give a place or time to (someone or something) **2** to belong or conform, esp. after adjustment

fitment *n* **1** an accessory attached to a machine **2** *chiefly Brit* a detachable part of the furnishings of a room

fit out *vb* to equip: *he started to fit out a ship in secret*

fitter *n* **1** a person who is skilled in the installation and adjustment of machinery **2** a person who fits garments

fitting *adj* **1** appropriate or proper ▸ *n* **2** an accessory or part **3** the trying-on of clothes so that they can be adjusted to fit **4 fittings** furnishings or accessories in a building > **fittingly** *adv*

fitting *adj* = appropriate, suitable, proper, apt, right, becoming, seemly, correct; ≠ unsuitable ▸ *n* **2** = accessory, part, piece, unit, component, attachment

five *n* **1** the cardinal number that is the sum of one and four **2** a numeral, 5 or V, representing this number **3** something representing or consisting of five units ▸ *adj* **4** amounting to five: *five years* ▸ See also **fives**

fiver *n Brit, Austral & NZ informal* a five-pound or five-dollar note

fives *n* a ball game similar to squash but played with bats or the hands

fix *vb* **1** to make or become firm, stable, or secure **2** to repair **3** to attach or place permanently: *fix the mirror to the wall* **4** to settle definitely or decide upon: *the meeting is fixed for the 12th* **5** to direct (the eyes, etc.) steadily: *she fixed her eyes upon the jewels* **6** *informal* to unfairly influence the outcome of: *the fight was fixed by the promoter* **7** *informal* to put a stop to the activities of (someone): *the Party was determined to fix him* **8** *informal* to prepare: *let me fix you a drink* **9** *photog* to treat (a film, plate, or paper) with fixer to make the image permanent **10** to convert (atmospheric nitrogen) into nitrogen compounds **11** *slang* to inject a narcotic drug ▸ *n* **12** *informal* a difficult situation **13** the reckoning of a navigational position of a ship by radar, etc. **14** *slang* an injection of a narcotic ▸ See also **fix up**

fix *vb* **2** = repair, mend, service, correct, restore, see to, overhaul, patch up **3** = place, join, stick (*informal*), attach, set, position, plant, link **4** = decide, set, choose, establish, determine, settle, arrange, arrive at **5** = focus, direct at, fasten on **6** = rig, set up (*informal*), influence, manipulate, fiddle (*informal*) ▸ *n* **12** = mess, corner, difficulty, dilemma, embarrassment, plight, pickle (*informal*), uphill (*S African*)

fixation *n* **1** an obsessive interest in something **2** *psychol* a strong attachment of a person to another person or an object in early life **3** *chem* the conversion of nitrogen in the air into a compound, esp. a fertilizer > **fixated** *adj*

fixative *n* **1** a fluid sprayed over drawings to prevent smudging **2** a liquid used to hold objects, esp. dentures, in place **3** a substance added to a perfume to make it less volatile

fixed *adj* **1** attached or placed so as to be immovable **2** stable: *fixed rates* **3** unchanging and appearing artificial: *a fixed smile* **4** established as to relative position: *a fixed point* **5** always at the same time **6** (of ideas) firmly maintained **7** *informal* equipped or provided for, esp. with money or possessions **8** *informal* illegally arranged: *a fixed trial* > **fixedly** (fix-id-lee) *adv*

fixed *adj* **1** = immovable, set, established, secure, rooted, permanent, rigid; ≠ mobile **5** = agreed, set, planned, decided, established, settled, arranged, resolved **6** = inflexible, set, steady, resolute, unwavering; ≠ wavering

fixer *n* **1** a solution used in photographic development that fixes the image in place, preventing further chemical reactions **2** *slang* a person who makes arrangements, esp. illegally

fixture *n* **1** an object firmly fixed in place, esp. a household appliance **2** something or someone regarded as fixed in a particular place or position: *the regatta has become a fixture of the sporting calendar* **3** **A** a sports match **B** the date of it

fix up *vb* **1** to arrange **2 fix up with** to provide with: *can you fix me up with tickets?*

fix up *vb* **1 fix something up** = arrange, plan, settle, fix, organize, sort out, agree on, make arrangements for

fizz *vb* **1** to make a hissing or bubbling sound **2** (of a drink) to produce bubbles of carbon dioxide ▸ *n* **3** a hissing or bubbling sound **4** releasing of small bubbles of gas by a liquid **5** any effervescent drink > **fizzy** *adj* > **fizziness** *n*

fizz *vb* **1** = sputter, buzz, sparkle, hiss, crackle **2** = bubble, froth, fizzle, effervesce, produce bubbles

fizzle *vb* **-zling, -zled 1** to make a hissing or bubbling sound **2 fizzle out** *informal* to fail or die out, esp. after a promising start

fjord (fee-ord) *n* a long narrow inlet of the sea between high cliffs, esp. in Norway

Fl flerovium

flab *n* unsightly or unwanted fat on the body

flabbergasted *adj informal* completely astonished

flabby *adj* **-bier, -biest 1** having flabby flesh **2** loose or limp **3** weak and lacking purpose: *flabby hesitant leaders* > **flabbiness** *n*

flaccid (flass-id) *adj* soft and limp > **flaccidity** *n*

flag[1] *n* **1** a piece of cloth often attached to a pole, used as an emblem or for signalling ▸ *vb* **flagging, flagged 2** to mark with a tag or sticker **3 flag down** to signal (a vehicle) to stop **4 flag up** to bring (something) to someone's attention

flag *n* = banner, standard, colours, pennant, ensign, streamer, pennon ▸ *vb* **2** = mark, identify, indicate, label, pick out, note **3** = hail, stop, signal, wave down

flag[2] *n* same as **iris** (sense 2)

flag[3] *vb* **flagging, flagged** to lose enthusiasm or energy

flag *vb* = weaken, fade, weary, falter, wilt, wane, sag, languish

flag[4] *n* short for **flagstone**

flagellate *vb* (flaj-a-late) **-lating, -lated 1** to whip, esp. in religious penance or for sexual pleasure ▸ *adj* (flaj-a-lit) **2** possessing one or more flagella **3** like a whip > **flagellation** *n*

flageolet (flaj-a-let) *n* a high-pitched musical instrument of the recorder family

flagged *adj* paved with flagstones

flagon *n* **1** a large bottle of wine, cider, etc. **2** a narrow-necked jug for containing liquids

flagpole *or* **flagstaff** *n* a pole on which a flag is flown

flagrant (flayg-rant) *adj* openly outrageous: *flagrant violation of international law* > **flagrancy** *n*

flagship *n* **1** a ship aboard which the commander of a fleet is quartered **2** the most important ship belonging to a shipping company **3** the most modern or impressive product or asset of an organization: *the company has opened its own flagship store*

flagstone *n* a flat slab of hard stone for paving

flail *n* **1** a tool formerly used for threshing grain by hand ▸ *vb* **2** to wave about wildly: *arms flailing, they staggered about* **3** to beat with or as if with a flail

flair *n* **1** natural ability: *she has a flair for languages* **2** originality and stylishness: *to dress with flair*

flair *n* **1** = ability, feel, talent, gift, genius, faculty, mastery, knack **2** = style, taste, dash, chic, elegance, panache, discernment, stylishness

flak *n* **1** anti-aircraft fire **2** severe criticism: *most of the flak was directed at the umpire*

flake[1] *n* **1** a small thin piece chipped off an object or substance **2** a small piece: *flakes of snow*

3 slang an eccentric or unreliable person ▸ vb
flaking, flaked 4 to peel or cause to peel off in flakes **5** to break into small thin pieces: bake for 30 minutes, or until the fish is firm and flakes easily ▷**flaky** adj

flake n **1** = chip, scale, layer, peeling, shaving, wafer, sliver ▸ vb **4** = chip, scale, layer, peeling, shaving, wafer, sliver

flake² n (in Australia) the commercial name for the meat of the gummy shark

flake out vb informal to collapse or fall asleep from exhaustion

flambé (flahm-bay) vb **flambéing, flambéd** to cook or serve (food) in flaming brandy

flamboyant adj **1** behaving in a very noticeable, extravagant way: a flamboyant jazz pianist **2** very bright and showy ▷**flamboyance** n

flamboyant adj **1** = camp (informal), dashing, theatrical **2** = showy, elaborate, extravagant, ornate, ostentatious

flame n **1** a hot luminous body of burning gas coming in flickering streams from burning material **2 flames** the state of burning: half the building was in flames **3** intense passion: the flame of love ▸ vb **flaming, flamed 4** to burn brightly **5** to become red or fiery: colour flamed in Sally's cheeks **6** to become angry or excited

flame n **1** = fire, light, spark, glow, blaze, brightness, inferno ▸ vb **4** = burn, flash, shine, glow, blaze, flare, glare

flamenco n, pl **-cos 1** a rhythmic Spanish dance accompanied by a guitar and vocalist **2** music for this dance

flamingo n, pl **-gos** or **-goes** a large pink wading bird with a long neck and legs

flammable adj easily set on fire; inflammable ▷**flammability** n

flan n an open sweet or savoury tart

flange n a projecting collar or rim on an object for strengthening it or for attaching it to another object

flank n **1** the side of a man or animal between the ribs and the hip **2** a cut of beef from the flank **3** the side of a naval or military formation ▸ vb **4** to be positioned at the side of (a person or thing)

flank n **1** = side, hip, thigh, loin **3** = wing, side, sector, aspect

flannel n **1** Brit a small piece of towelling cloth used to wash the face **2** a soft light woollen fabric used for clothing **3 flannels** trousers made of flannel **4** Brit informal evasive talk that avoids giving any commitment or direct answer ▸ vb **-nelling, -nelled** or US **-neling, -neled 5** Brit informal to flatter or talk evasively

flannelette n a cotton imitation of flannel, used to make sheets and nightdresses

flap vb **flapping, flapped 1** to move backwards and forwards or up and down, like a bird's wings in flight ▸ n **2** the action of or noise made by flapping **3** a piece of material attached at one edge and usually used to cover an opening, such as on a pocket **4** a hinged section of an aircraft wing that is raised or lowered to control the aircraft's speed **5** informal a state of panic or agitation

flap vb = flutter, wave, flail ▸ n **2** = flutter, beating, waving, shaking, swinging, swish **5** = panic, state (informal), agitation, commotion, sweat (informal), dither (chiefly Brit), fluster, tizzy (informal)

flapjack n **1** Brit a chewy biscuit made with rolled oats **2** NZ a small thick pancake

flare vb **flaring, flared 1** to burn with an unsteady or sudden bright flame **2** (of temper, violence, or trouble) to break out suddenly **3** to spread outwards from a narrow to a wider shape ▸ n **4** an unsteady flame **5** a sudden burst of flame **6 A** a blaze of light used to illuminate, signal distress, alert, etc. **B** the device producing such a blaze **7 flares** trousers with legs that flare out at the bottom ▷**flared** adj

flare vb **1** = blaze, flame, glare, flicker, burn up **3** = widen, spread, broaden, spread out, dilate, splay ▸ n **4, 5** = flame, burst, flash, blaze, glare, flicker

flash n **1** a sudden short blaze of intense light or flame **2** a sudden occurrence of a particular emotion or experience: a flash of anger **3** a very brief time: in a flash he was inside and locked the door behind him **4** a short unscheduled news announcement **5** Brit & Austral an emblem on a uniform or vehicle to identify its military formation **6** photog short for **flashlight 7 flash in the pan** a project, person, etc., that enjoys only short-lived success ▸ adj **8** informal ostentatious or vulgar **9** brief and rapid: a flash fire ▸ vb **10** to burst or cause to burst suddenly into flame **11** to shine with a bright light suddenly or repeatedly **12** to move very fast **13** to come rapidly (into the mind or vision) **14 A** to signal very fast: a warning was flashed onto a screen in the cockpit **B** to signal by use of a light, such as car headlights **15** informal to display in a boastful and extravagant way: flashing banknotes around **16** informal to show briefly **17** Brit slang to expose oneself indecently ▷**flasher** n

flash n **1** = blaze, burst, spark, beam, streak, flare, dazzle, glare ▸ adj **8** = ostentatious, smart, trendy, showy, bling (slang) ▸ vb **10, 11** = blaze, shine, beam, sparkle, flare, glare, gleam, light up **12** = speed, race, shoot, fly, tear, dash, whistle, streak **14A, 15, 16** = show quickly, display, expose, exhibit, flourish, show off, flaunt

flashback n a scene in a book, play, or film that shows earlier events

flash drive n a portable storage device such as a memory card

flash flood n a sudden short-lived flood

flashing n a weatherproof material used to cover the joins in a roof

flashlight n **1** photog a brief bright light emitted by a camera when taking a photograph **2** chiefly US & Canad a torch

flash point n **1** a critical time beyond which a situation will inevitably erupt into violence **2** the lowest temperature at which the vapour above a liquid can be ignited

flashy adj **flashier, flashiest** showy in a vulgar way: a loud and flashy tie ▸ **flashily** adv ▸ **flashiness** n

flask n **1** same as **vacuum flask 2** a small flat container for alcoholic drink designed to be carried in a pocket **3** a bottle with a narrow neck, esp. used in a laboratory

flat¹ adj **flatter, flattest 1** horizontal or level: roofs are now flat instead of slanted **2** even or smooth: a flat surface **3** lying stretched out at full length **4** (of a tyre) deflated **5** (of shoes) having an unraised heel **6** without qualification; total: a flat rejection **7** fixed: a flat rate **8** unexciting: a picture curiously flat in tone **9** without variation or emotion: a flat voice **10** (of drinks) no longer fizzy **11** (of a battery) fully discharged **12** (of paint) without gloss **13** music **A** denoting a note that has been lowered in pitch by one chromatic semitone: B flat **B** (of an instrument, voice, etc.) out of tune by being too low in pitch ▸ adv **14** in or into a level or flat position: the boat was knocked almost flat **15** completely: flat broke **16** exactly: in three months flat **17** music **A** lower than a standard pitch **B** too low in pitch: singing flat **18** **fall flat (on one's face)** to fail to achieve a desired effect **19** **flat out** informal with maximum speed and effort ▸ n **20** a flat object or part **21** low-lying land, esp. a marsh **22** a mud bank exposed at low tide **23** music **A** an accidental that lowers the pitch of a note by one semitone. Symbol: ♭ **B** a note affected by this accidental **24** theatre a wooden frame covered with painted canvas, used to form part of a stage setting **25** a punctured car tyre **26** **the flat** chiefly Brit the season of flat racing ▸ **flatly** adv

> **flat** adj **1, 2** = even, level, levelled, smooth, horizontal; ≠ uneven **4** = punctured, collapsed, burst, blown out, deflated, empty **6** = absolute, firm, positive, explicit, definite, outright, downright, unequivocal **8** = dull, dead, empty, boring, depressing, tedious, lacklustre, tiresome; ≠ exciting **9** = monotonous, boring, dull, tedious, tiresome, unchanging **11** = used up, finished, empty, drained, expired ▸ adv **15** = completely, directly, absolutely, categorically, precisely, exactly, utterly, outright **19 flat out** = at full speed, all out, to the full, hell for leather (informal), as hard as possible, at full tilt, for all you are worth

flat² n **1** a set of rooms forming a home entirely on one floor of a building ▸ vb **flatting, flatted**

2 Austral & NZ to share a flat **3 go flatting** Austral & NZ to leave home to share a flat

> **flat** n = apartment (chiefly US), rooms, quarters, digs, suite, penthouse, living quarters, duplex (US, Canad), bachelor apartment (Canad)

flatfish n, pl **-fish** or **-fishes** a sea fish, such as the sole, which has a flat body with both eyes on the uppermost side

flatlet n Brit, Austral & S African a small flat

flatmate n a person with whom one shares a flat

flat-pack adj (of furniture, etc.) supplied in pieces in a flat box for assembly by the buyer

flat racing n the racing of horses on racecourses without jumps

flatscreen n a slimline television set or computer monitor with a flat screen

flatten vb **1** to make or become flat or flatter **2** informal **A** to knock down or injure **B** to crush or subdue

> **flatten** vb **1** = level, squash, compress, trample, iron out, even out, smooth off **2A** = destroy, level, ruin, demolish, knock down, pull down, raze, kennel (Austral slang), jeff (Austral slang)

flatter vb **1** to praise insincerely, esp. in order to win favour **2** to show to advantage: she wore a simple green cotton dress which she knew flattered her **3** to make (a person) appear more attractive than in reality: a portrait that flattered him **4** to cater to the vanity of (a person): I was flattered by her praise **5** **flatter oneself** to believe, perhaps mistakenly, something good about oneself ▸ **flatterer** n

> **flatter** vb **1** = praise, compliment, pander to, sweet-talk (informal), wheedle, soft-soap (informal), butter up **2** = suit, become, enhance, set off, embellish, do something for, show to advantage

flattery n, pl **-teries** excessive or insincere praise

flattie n NZ & S African informal a flat tyre

flatulent adj suffering from or caused by too much gas in the stomach or intestines ▸ **flatulence** n

flaunt vb to display (oneself or one's possessions) arrogantly: flaunting his new car

flautist (**flaw-tist**) n a flute player

flavour or US **flavor** n **1** taste perceived in food or liquid in the mouth **2** a distinctive quality or atmosphere: Rome has its own particular flavour ▸ vb **3** to give flavour to: salmon flavoured with dill ▸ **flavourless** or US **flavorless** adj

> **flavour** or **flavor** n **1** = taste, seasoning, flavouring, savour, relish, smack, aroma, zest; ≠ blandness **2** = quality, feeling, feel, style, character, tone, essence, tinge ▸ vb = season, spice, add flavour to, enrich, infuse, imbue, pep up, leaven

flavouring *or US* **flavoring** *n* a substance used to flavour food

flaw *n* 1 an imperfection or blemish 2 a mistake in something that makes it invalid: *a flaw in the system* ▸ **flawed** *adj* ▸ **flawless** *adj*

> **flaw** = weakness, failing, defect, weak spot, fault, blemish, imperfection, chink in your armour

flax *n* 1 a plant that has blue flowers and is cultivated for its seeds and the fibres of its stems 2 its fibres, made into linen fabrics 3 NZ a perennial plant producing a fibre that is used by Maoris for decorative work and weaving baskets

flaxen *adj* 1 of flax 2 (of hair) pale yellow

flay *vb* 1 to strip off the skin of, esp. by whipping 2 to criticize severely

flea *n* 1 a small wingless jumping insect feeding on the blood of mammals and birds 2 **flea in one's ear** *informal* a sharp rebuke

flea market *n* an open-air market selling cheap second-hand goods

fleapit *n informal* a shabby cinema or theatre

fleck *n* 1 a small marking or streak 2 a small or tiny piece of something: *a fleck of grit* ▸ *vb* 3 to speckle: *a grey suit flecked with white*

fled *vb* the past of **flee**

fledged *adj* 1 (of young birds) able to fly 2 qualified and competent: *a fully fledged doctor*

fledgling *or* **fledgeling** *n* 1 a young bird that has grown feathers ▸ *adj* 2 new or inexperienced: *her fledgling legal practice*

flee *vb* **fleeing, fled** 1 to run away from (a place, danger, etc.) 2 to run or move quickly

> **flee** *vb* = run away, escape, bolt, fly, take off (*informal*), depart, run off, take flight

fleece *n* 1 the coat of wool that covers a sheep 2 the wool removed from a sheep at one shearing 3 sheepskin or a fabric with soft pile, used as a lining for coats, etc. 4 *Brit* a jacket or top made of this fabric 5 a warm outdoor jacket or top made from a polyester fabric with a brushed nap ▸ *vb* **fleecing, fleeced** 6 to defraud or overcharge 7 same as **shear** (sense 1)

fleecy *adj* 1 of or resembling fleece ▸ *n, pl* **-ies** 2 NZ *informal* a person who collects fleeces after shearing and prepares them for baling

fleet¹ *n* 1 a number of warships organized as a tactical unit 2 all the ships of a nation or company: *the British merchant fleet* 3 a number of vehicles under the same ownership

> **fleet** *n* 1, 2 = navy, task force, flotilla, armada

fleet² *adj* rapid in movement

fleeting *adj* rapid and soon passing: *a fleeting moment* ▸ **fleetingly** *adv*

> **fleeting** *adj* = momentary, passing, brief, temporary, short-lived, transient, ephemeral, transitory; ≠ lasting

Flemish *adj* 1 of Flanders, in Belgium ▸ *n* 2 one of the two official languages of Belgium ▸ *pl n* 3 **the Flemish** people from Flanders or Flemish-speaking Belgium

flerovium *n chem* a synthetic element. Symbol: **Fl**

flesh *n* 1 the soft part of the body of an animal or human, esp. muscular tissue. Related adjective: **carnal** 2 *informal* excess weight; fat 3 the meat of animals as opposed to that of fish or, sometimes, fowl 4 the thick soft part of a fruit or vegetable 5 **the flesh** sexuality or sensuality: *pleasures of the flesh* 6 **flesh and blood** human beings or human nature: *it is almost more than flesh and blood can bear* 7 **in the flesh** in person; actually present 8 **one's own flesh and blood** one's own family 9 **press the flesh** *informal* to shake hands with large numbers of people, esp. in political campaigning

> **flesh** *n* 1 = fat, muscle, tissue, brawn 2 = fatness, fat, adipose tissue, corpulence, weight 3 = meat 8 **one's own flesh and blood** = family, blood, relations, relatives, kin, kith and kin, blood relations, kinsfolk, ainga (NZ), rellies (Austral slang)

flesh-coloured *adj* yellowish-pink

fleshly *adj* **-lier, -liest** 1 relating to sexuality or sensuality: *the fleshly implications of their love* 2 worldly as opposed to spiritual

flesh wound *n* a wound affecting superficial tissues

fleshy *adj* **fleshier, fleshiest** 1 plump 2 resembling flesh 3 *botany* (of some fruits) thick and pulpy ▸ **fleshiness** *n*

fleur-de-lys *or* **fleur-de-lis** (flur-de-lee) *n, pl* **fleurs-de-lys** *or* **fleurs-de-lis** (flur-de-leez) a representation of a lily with three distinct petals

flew *vb* the past tense of **fly¹**

flex *n* 1 *Brit & Austral* a flexible insulated electric cable: *a coiled kettle flex* ▸ *vb* 2 to bend 3 to bend and stretch (a muscle)

flexible *adj* 1 able to be bent easily without breaking 2 adaptable to changing circumstances: *flexible working arrangements* ▸ **flexibility** *n* ▸ **flexibly** *adv*

> **flexible** *adj* 1 = pliable, plastic, elastic, supple, lithe, springy, pliant, stretchy; ≠ rigid 2 = adaptable, open, variable, adjustable, discretionary; ≠ inflexible

flexitime *n* a system permitting flexibility of working hours at the beginning or end of the day, provided an agreed total is worked

flick *vb* 1 to touch or move with the finger or hand in a quick jerky movement 2 to move with a short sudden movement, often repeatedly: *the windscreen wipers flicked back and forth* 3 **flick through** to look at (a book or magazine) quickly or idly ▸ *n* 4 a tap or quick stroke 5 **give the flick** *informal, chiefly Austral* to dismiss or reject

flick *vb* **1** = strike, tap, remove quickly, hit, touch, stroke, flip, whisk **2** = jerk, pull, tug, lurch, jolt **3 flick through something** = browse, glance at, skim, leaf through, flip through, thumb through, skip through

flicker *vb* **1** to give out an unsteady or irregular light **2** to move quickly to and fro ▸ *n* **3** an unsteady or brief light **4** a brief or faint indication of emotion: *a flicker of fear in his voice*

flicker *vb* **1** = twinkle, flash, sparkle, flare, shimmer, gutter, glimmer **2** = flutter, waver, quiver, vibrate ▸ *n* **3** = glimmer, flash, spark, flare, gleam **4** = trace, breath, spark, glimmer, iota

flick knife *n* a knife with a retractable blade that springs out when a button is pressed
flier *n* same as **flyer**
flight¹ *n* **1** a journey by aircraft **2** the act or manner of flying **3** a group of flying birds or aircraft **4** an aircraft flying on a scheduled journey **5** a set of stairs between one landing and the next **6 flight of fancy** an idea that is imaginative but not practical **7** small plastic or feather fins at the rear of an arrow or dart which make it stable in flight

flight *n* **1** = journey, trip, voyage **2** = aviation, flying, aeronautics **3** = flock, group, unit, cloud, formation, squadron, swarm, flying group

flight² *n* **1** the act of running away, esp. from danger **2 put to flight** to cause to run away **3 take (to) flight** to run away

flight *n* **1** = escape, fleeing, departure, retreat, exit, running away, exodus, getaway

flight attendant *n* a person who attends to the needs of passengers on a commercial flight
flight deck *n* **1** the crew compartment in an airliner **2** the upper deck of an aircraft carrier from which aircraft take off
flightless *adj* (of certain birds and insects) unable to fly
flight recorder *n* an electronic device in an aircraft for storing information concerning its performance in flight. It is often used to determine the cause of a crash. Also called: **black box**
flighty *adj* **flightier**, **flightiest** frivolous and not very reliable or serious ⊳ **flightiness** *n*
flimsy *adj* **-sier**, **-siest 1** not strong or substantial **2** light and thin: *a flimsy gauze mask* **3** not very convincing: *flimsy evidence* ⊳ **flimsily** *adv* ⊳ **flimsiness** *n*
flinch *vb* **1** to draw back suddenly from pain or something unpleasant **2 flinch from** to avoid: *I wouldn't flinch from saying that to his face*
fling *vb* **flinging**, **flung 1** to throw with force **2** to move or go hurriedly or violently: *she flung her arms open wide* **3** to put or send without

warning: *they used to fling me in jail* **4** to put (something) somewhere hurriedly or carelessly **5 fling oneself into** to apply oneself with enthusiasm to ▸ *n* **6** a short spell of self-indulgent enjoyment **7** a brief romantic or sexual relationship **8** a vigorous Scottish country dance: *a Highland fling*

fling *vb* **1** = throw, toss, hurl, launch, cast, propel, sling (*informal*), catapult ▸ *n* **6** = binge (*informal*), good time, bash, party, spree, night on the town, rave-up (*Brit slang*)

flint *n* **1** a very hard stone that produces sparks when struck with steel **2** any piece of flint, esp. one used as a primitive tool **3** a small piece of an iron alloy, used in cigarette lighters ⊳ **flinty** *adj*
flip *vb* **flipping**, **flipped 1** to throw (something light or small) carelessly **2** to turn (something) over: *flip the fish on its back* **3** to turn (a device or machine) on or off by quickly pressing a switch **4** to throw (an object such as a coin) so that it turns in the air **5** to buy and sell an asset (often property) quickly for profit **6 flip through** to look at (a book or magazine) idly **7** Also: **flip one's lid** *slang* to fly into an emotional outburst ▸ *n* **8** a snap or tap, usually with the fingers ▸ *adj* **9** *informal* flippant or pert

flip *vb* **1** = toss, throw, flick, fling, sling (*informal*) **2** = spin, turn, overturn, turn over, roll over **3** = flick, switch, snap, click ▸ *n* = toss, throw, spin, snap, flick

flip-flop *n* **1** *Brit & S African* a rubber-soled sandal attached to the foot by a thong between the big toe and the next toe **2** *informal* a reversal of opinion, policy, etc. ▸ *vb* *informal* **3** to reverse one's opinion, policy, etc.
flippant *adj* treating serious matters with inappropriate light-heartedness or lack of respect ⊳ **flippancy** *n*
flipper *n* **1** the flat broad limb of seals, whales, and other aquatic animals specialized for swimming **2** either of a pair of rubber paddle-like devices worn on the feet as an aid in swimming
flirt *vb* **1** to behave as if sexually attracted to someone **2** (foll. by *with*) to consider lightly; toy with: *he had often flirted with the idea of emigrating* ▸ *n* **3** a person who flirts ⊳ **flirtation** *n* ⊳ **flirtatious** *adj*

flirt *vb* **1** = chat up, lead on (*informal*), make advances at, make eyes at, philander, make sheep's eyes at **2** = toy with, consider, entertain, play with, dabble in, trifle with, give a thought to, expose yourself to ▸ *n* = tease, philanderer, coquette, heart-breaker

flit *vb* **flitting**, **flitted 1** to fly or move along rapidly and lightly **2** to pass quickly: *a shadow flitted across his face* **3** *Scot & N English dialect* to move house **4** *Brit informal* to leave hurriedly and stealthily in order to avoid debts ▸ *n* **5** the act of flitting **6 do a flit** NZ *informal* to abandon rented accommodation

float *vb* **1** to rest on the surface of a fluid without sinking **2** to move lightly or freely across a surface or through air or water **3** to move about aimlessly, esp. in the mind: *a pleasant image floated into his mind* **4 A** to launch (a commercial enterprise, etc.) **B** to offer for sale on the stock market **5** *finance* to allow (a currency) to fluctuate against other currencies ▸ *n* **6** an inflatable object that helps people learning to swim stay afloat **7** *angling* an indicator attached to a baited line that moves when a fish bites **8** a long rigid boatlike structure, of which there are usually two, attached to an aircraft instead of wheels so that it can land on and take off from water **9** a decorated lorry that is part of a procession **10** a small delivery vehicle: *a milk float* **11** *Austral & NZ* a vehicle for transporting horses **12** a sum of money used to cover small expenses or provide change **13** the hollow floating ball of a ball cock

> **float** *vb* **1** = be buoyant, hang, hover; ≠ sink **2** = glide, sail, drift, move gently, bob, coast, slide, be carried **4** = launch, offer, sell, set up, promote, get going

floating *adj* **1** (of a population) moving about; not settled **2** (of an organ or part) displaced or abnormally movable: *a floating kidney* **3** (of a voter) not committed to one party **4** *finance* **A** (of capital) available for current use **B** (of a currency) free to fluctuate against other currencies

> **floating** *adj* **1** = free, wandering, variable, fluctuating, unattached, movable **3** = uncommitted, wavering, undecided, indecisive, vacillating, sitting on the fence (*informal*), unaffiliated, independent

flock¹ *n* **1** a group of animals of one kind, esp. sheep or birds **2** a large number of people **3** a congregation of Christians regarded as the responsibility of a member of the clergy ▸ *vb* **4** to gather together or move in large numbers

> **flock** *n* **1** = herd, group, flight, drove, colony, gaggle, skein **2** = crowd, company, group, host, collection, mass, gathering, herd ▸ *vb* = stream, crowd, mass, swarm, throng

flock² *n* **1** waste from fabrics such as cotton or wool, used for stuffing mattresses ▸ *adj* **2** (of wallpaper) having a velvety raised pattern

floe *n* a sheet of floating ice

flog *vb* **flogging**, **flogged 1** to beat harshly, esp. with a whip or stick **2** (sometimes foll. by *off*) *informal* to sell **3** *Austral & NZ informal* to steal **4 flog a dead horse** *chiefly Brit* to waste one's energy › **flogging** *n*

> **flog** *vb* **1** = beat, whip, lash, thrash, whack, scourge, hit hard, trounce

flood *n* **1** an overflowing of water on an area that is normally dry **2** a large amount of water **3** the rising of the tide from low to high water. Related adjective: **diluvial**, **diluvian 4** a large amount: *a flood of letters* **5** *theatre* short for **floodlight** ▸ *vb* **6** to cover or become covered with water **7** to fill to overflowing **8** to put a large number of goods on sale on (a market) at the same time, often at a cheap price: *the US was flooded with cheap televisions* **9** to flow or surge: *the memories flooded back* **10** to supply excess petrol to (a petrol engine) so that it cannot work properly **11** to bleed profusely from the womb › **flooding** *n*

> **flood** *n* **1** = deluge, downpour, inundation, tide, overflow, torrent, spate **2** = torrent, flow, rush, stream, tide, abundance, glut, profusion **4** = series, stream, avalanche, barrage, spate, torrent ▸ *vb* **6** = immerse, swamp, submerge, inundate, drown, cover with water **7** = pour over, swamp, run over, overflow, inundate **8** = saturate, fill, choke, swamp, glut, oversupply, overfill **9** = stream, flow, rush, pour, surge

floodgate *n* **1** a gate used to control the flow of water **2 floodgates** controls against an outpouring of emotion: *it had opened the floodgates of her anxiety*

floodlight *n* **1** a lamp that casts a broad intense light, used in the theatre or to illuminate sports grounds or the exterior of buildings ▸ *vb* **-lighting**, **-lit 2** to illuminate by floodlight

floor *n* **1** the lower surface of a room **2** a storey of a building **3** a flat bottom surface: *the ocean floor* **4** that part of a legislative hall in which debate is conducted **5** a minimum limit: *a wages floor for low-paid employees* **6 have the floor** to have the right to speak in a debate or discussion ▸ *vb* **7** to knock to the ground **8** *informal* to disconcert or defeat

> **floor** *n* **1** = ground **2** = storey, level, stage, tier ▸ *vb* **7** = knock down, fell, knock over, prostrate, deck (*slang*) **8** = disconcert, stump, baffle, confound, throw (*informal*), defeat, puzzle, bewilder

floored *adj* covered with a floor: *an attic floored with pine planks*

flooring *n* **1** the material used in making a floor: *pine flooring* **2** a floor

floor show *n* a series of entertainments, such as singing and dancing, in a nightclub

floozy, **floozie** *or* **floosie** *n*, *pl* **-zies** *or* **-sies** *old-fashioned*, *derogatory slang* a woman considered to be disreputable or immoral

flop *vb* **flopping**, **flopped 1** to bend, fall, or collapse loosely or carelessly **2** *informal* to fail: *his first big film flopped* **3** to fall or move with a sudden noise ▸ *n* **4** *informal* a complete failure **5** the act of flopping › **floppy** *adj*

flop *vb* **1** = hang down, hang, dangle, sag, droop **2** = fail, fold (*informal*), founder, fall flat, come unstuck, misfire, go belly-up (*slang*); ≠ succeed **3** = slump, fall, drop, collapse, sink ▸ *n* **4** = failure, disaster, fiasco, debacle, washout (*informal*), nonstarter; ≠ success

flora *n* all the plant life of a given place or time

floral *adj* decorated with or consisting of flowers or patterns of flowers

floral *adj* = flowery, flower-patterned

floret (**flaw**-ret) *n* a small flower forming part of a composite flower head

floribunda *n* a type of rose whose flowers grow in large clusters

florid *adj* **1** having a red or flushed complexion **2** very ornate and extravagant: *florid prose*

florin *n* a former British, Australian, and New Zealand coin, equivalent to ten pence or twenty cents

florist *n* a person or shop selling flowers

floss *n* **1** fine silky fibres, such as those obtained from silkworm cocoons **2** See **dental floss** ▸ *vb* **3** to clean (between the teeth) with dental floss >**flossy** *adj*

flotation *or* **floatation** *n* the launching or financing of a commercial enterprise by bond or share issues

flotilla *n* a small fleet or a fleet of small ships

flotsam *n* **1** floating wreckage from a ship **2 flotsam and jetsam** ᴀ odds and ends ʙ *Brit* homeless or vagrant people

flounce¹ *vb* **flouncing, flounced** **1** to move or go with emphatic movements ▸ *n* **2** the act of flouncing

flounce² *n* an ornamental frill on a garment or tablecloth

flounder¹ *vb* **1** to struggle to move or stay upright, esp. in water or mud **2** to behave or speak in an awkward, confused way

flounder *vb* **1** = struggle, toss, thrash, stumble, fumble, grope **2** = falter, struggle, stall, slow down, run into trouble, come unstuck (*informal*), be in difficulties, hit a bad patch

flounder² *n, pl* **-der** *or* **-ders** an edible flatfish

flour *n* **1** a powder prepared by grinding grain, esp. wheat ▸ *vb* **2** to sprinkle (food or utensils) with flour >**floury** *adj*

flourish *vb* **1** to be active, successful, or widespread; prosper **2** to be at the peak of development **3** to wave (something) dramatically ▸ *n* **4** a dramatic waving or sweeping movement: *she created a flourish with an imaginary wand* **5** an ornamental curly line in writing **6** a fancy or extravagant action or part of something: *he took his tie off with a flourish* >**flourishing** *adj*

flourish *vb* **1** = thrive, increase, advance, abound, progress, boom, bloom, blossom, prosper; ≠ fail **3** = wave, brandish, display, shake, wield, flaunt ▸ *n* **4** = wave, sweep, brandish, swish, swing, twirl **5** = curlicue, sweep, decoration, swirl, plume, embellishment, ornamentation **6** = show, display, parade, fanfare

flout (rhymes with **out**) *vb* to deliberately disobey (a rule, law, etc.)

flow *vb* **1** (of liquids) to move in a stream **2** (of blood, electricity, etc.) to circulate **3** to move steadily and smoothly: *a golf club with rich-looking cars flowing into it* **4** to be produced effortlessly: *words flowed from him in a steady stream* **5** to hang freely: *her hair loose and flowing down her back* **6** to be abundant: *at the buffet lunch, wine flowed like water* **7** (of tide water) to rise ▸ *n* **8** the act, rate, or manner of flowing: *the abundant flow of water through domestic sprinklers* **9** a continuous stream or discharge **10** the advancing of the tide

flow *vb* **1** = run, course, rush, sweep, move, pass, roll, flood **3** = pour, move, sweep, flood, stream **4** = issue, follow, result, emerge, spring, proceed, arise, derive ▸ *n* **8** = stream, current, movement, motion, course, flood, drift, tide

flow chart *or* **flow sheet** *n* a diagram showing a sequence of operations in an industrial process, computer program, etc.

flower *n* **1** the part of a plant that is, usually, brightly coloured, and quickly fades, producing seeds **2** a plant grown for its colourful flowers. Related adjective: **floral** **3** the best or finest part: *in the flower of her youth* **4 in flower** with flowers open ▸ *vb* **5** to produce flowers; bloom **6** to reach full growth or maturity: *liberty only flowers in times of peace*

flower *n* **1** = bloom, blossom, efflorescence **3** = elite, best, prime, finest, pick, choice, cream, the crème de la crème ▸ *vb* **5** = bloom, open, mature, flourish, unfold, blossom **6** = blossom, grow, develop, progress, mature, thrive, flourish, bloom

flowered *adj* decorated with flowers or a floral design

flowery *adj* **1** decorated with flowers or floral patterns **2** (of language or style) containing elaborate literary expressions >**floweriness** *n*

flown *vb* the past participle of **fly¹**

fl. oz. fluid ounce(s)

flu *n informal* short for **influenza**

fluctuate *vb* **-ating, -ated** to change frequently and erratically: *share prices fluctuated wildly throughout the day* >**fluctuation** *n*

fluctuate *vb* = change, swing, vary, alternate, waver, veer, seesaw

flue *n* a passage or pipe in a chimney, used to carry off smoke, gas, or hot air

fluent *adj* **1** able to speak or write with ease: *they spoke fluent English; fluent in French* **2** spoken or written with ease ▷ **fluency** *n* ▷ **fluently** *adv*

> **fluent** *adj* **2** = effortless, natural, articulate, well-versed, voluble

fluff *n* **1** soft light particles, such as the down of cotton or wool **2** *informal* a mistake, esp. in speaking or reading lines ▶ *vb* **3** to make or become soft and puffy **4** *informal* to make a mistake in performing ▷ **fluffy** *adj* ▷ **fluffiness** *n*

fluid *n* **1** a substance, such as a liquid or gas, that can flow and has no fixed shape ▶ *adj* **2** capable of flowing and easily changing shape **3** constantly changing or apt to change ▷ **fluidity** *n*

> **fluid** *n* = liquid, solution, juice, liquor, sap ▶ *adj* **2** = liquid, flowing, watery, molten, melted, runny, liquefied; ≠ solid

fluid ounce *n* **1** *Brit* a unit of liquid measure equal to one twentieth of an Imperial pint (28.4 ml) **2** *US* a unit of liquid measure equal to one sixteenth of a US pint (29.6 ml)

fluke¹ *n* an accidental stroke of luck ▷ **fluky** *adj*

fluke² *n* **1** the flat triangular point of an anchor **2** either of the two lobes of the tail of a whale

fluke³ *n* any parasitic flatworm, such as the liver fluke

flume *n* **1** a narrow sloping channel for water **2** an enclosed water slide at a swimming pool

flummox *vb* to puzzle or confuse

flung *vb* the past of **fling**

flunk *vb* *US, Canad, Austral, NZ & S African informal* to fail (an examination, course, etc.)

flunky *or* **flunkey** *n, pl* **flunkies** *or* **flunkeys** **1** a manservant who wears ceremonial dress **2** a person who performs small unimportant tasks for a powerful or important person in the hope of being rewarded

fluoresce *vb* **-rescing, -resced** to exhibit fluorescence

fluorescence *n* **1** *physics* the emission of light from atoms or molecules that are bombarded by particles, such as electrons, or by radiation from a separate source **2** the radiation emitted as a result of fluorescence ▷ **fluorescent** *adj*

fluoridate *vb* **-dating, -dated** to add fluoride to (water) as protection against tooth decay ▷ **fluoridation** *n*

fluoride *n* *chem* any compound containing fluorine and another element or radical

fluorine *n* *chem* a poisonous strong-smelling pale yellow gas that is the most reactive of all the elements. Symbol: **F**

flurry *n, pl* **-ries 1** a short rush of vigorous activity or movement **2** a light gust of wind or rain, or fall of snow ▶ *vb* **-ries, -rying, -ried** **3** to confuse or bewilder

flurry *n* **1** = commotion, stir, bustle, flutter, excitement, fuss, disturbance, ado **2** = gust, shower, gale, swirl, squall, storm

flush¹ *vb* **1** to blush or cause to blush **2** to send water quickly through (a pipe or a toilet) so as to clean it **3** to elate: *she was flushed with excitement* ▶ *n* **4** a rosy colour, esp. in the cheeks **5** a sudden flow, such as of water **6** a feeling of elation: *in the flush of victory* **7** freshness: *in the first flush of youth* ▷ **flushed** *adj*

> **flush** *vb* **1** = blush, colour, glow, redden, turn red, go red **2** = cleanse, wash out, rinse out, flood, swill, hose down ▶ *n* **4** = blush, colour, glow, reddening, redness, rosiness

flush² *adj* **1** level with another surface **2** *informal* having plenty of money ▶ *adv* **3** so as to be level

> **flush** *adj* **1** = level, even, true, flat, square **2** = wealthy, rich, well-off, in the money (*informal*), well-heeled (*informal*), replete, moneyed, minted (*Brit slang*)

flush³ *vb* to drive out of a hiding place

flush⁴ *n* (in poker and similar games) a hand containing only one suit

fluster *vb* **1** to make or become nervous or upset ▶ *n* **2** a nervous or upset state

flute *n* **1** a wind instrument consisting of a tube of wood or metal with holes in the side stopped either by the fingers or keys. The breath is directed across a mouth hole in the side **2** a tall narrow wineglass, used esp. for champagne ▶ *vb* **fluting, fluted 3** to utter in a high-pitched tone ▷ **fluty** *adj*

fluted *adj* having decorated grooves

flutter *vb* **1** to wave rapidly **2** (of birds or butterflies) to flap the wings **3** to move with an irregular motion **4** *pathol* (of the heart) to beat abnormally rapidly **5** to move about restlessly ▶ *n* **6** a quick flapping or vibrating motion **7** a state of nervous excitement or confusion **8** excited interest **9** *Brit informal* a modest bet **10** *pathol* an abnormally rapid beating of the heart **11** *electronics* a slow variation in pitch in a sound-reproducing system

> **flutter** *vb* **1** = beat, flap, tremble, ripple, waver, quiver, vibrate, palpitate **3, 5** = flit ▶ *n* **6** = tremor, tremble, shiver, shudder, palpitation **7** = agitation, state (*informal*), confusion, excitement, flap (*informal*), dither (*chiefly Brit*), commotion, fluster

fluvial (flew-vee-al) *adj* of or relating to a river

flux *n* **1** continuous change or instability **2** a flow or discharge **3** a substance mixed with a metal oxide to assist in fusion **4** *physics* **a** the rate of flow of particles, energy, or a fluid **b** the strength of a field in a given area: *magnetic flux*

fly¹ *vb* **flies, flying, flew, flown 1** to move through the air on wings or in an aircraft **2** to control the flight of (an aircraft) **3** to float, flutter, display, or be displayed in the air: *the Red Cross flag flew at each corner of the compound* **4** to transport or be transported through the air by aircraft, wind, etc. **5** to move very quickly or suddenly: *the front door flew open* **6** to pass quickly: *how time flies* **7** to escape from (an enemy or a place) **8 fly a kite** to release information or take a step in order to test public opinion **9 fly at** to attack (someone) **10 fly high** *informal* to have a high aim **11 let fly** *informal* to lose one's temper: *a young child letting fly at you in a sudden moment of temper* ▸ *n, pl* **flies 12** Also: **flies** a closure that conceals a zip, buttons, or other fastening, as on trousers **13** a flap forming the entrance to a tent **14 flies** *theatre* the space above the stage, used for storing scenery

> **fly** *vb* **1** = take wing, soar, glide, wing, sail, hover, flutter, flit **2** = pilot, control, operate, steer, manoeuvre, navigate **3** = display, show, flourish, brandish **4** = airlift, send by plane, take by plane, take in an aircraft **5** = rush, race, shoot, career, speed, tear, dash, hurry **6** = pass swiftly, pass, glide, slip away, roll on, flit, elapse, run its course **7** = leave, get away, escape, flee, run for it, skedaddle (*informal*), take to your heels

fly² *n, pl* **flies 1** a small insect with two pairs of wings **2** any of various similar but unrelated insects, such as the dragonfly **3** *angling* a lure made from a fish-hook attached with feathers to resemble a fly **4 fly in the ointment** *informal* a slight flaw that detracts from value or enjoyment **5 fly on the wall** a person who watches others, while not being noticed himself or herself **6 there are no flies on him** *or* **her** *informal* he or she is no fool

fly³ *adj slang, chiefly Brit* sharp and cunning
flycatcher *n* a small insect-eating songbird
flyer *or* **flier** *n* **1** a small advertising leaflet **2** a person or thing that flies or moves very fast **3** *old-fashioned* an aircraft pilot
fly-fishing *n angling* fishing using artificial flies as lures
flying *n* **1** the act of piloting, navigating, or travelling in an aircraft ▸ *adj* **2** hurried and brief: *a flying visit* **3** fast or built for speed: *Australia's flying fullback* **4** hanging, waving, or floating freely: *flags flying proudly*

> **flying** *adj* **2** = hurried, brief, rushed, fleeting, short-lived, hasty, transitory

flying boat *n* a seaplane in which the fuselage consists of a hull that provides buoyancy
flying colours *pl n* conspicuous success; triumph: *they passed with flying colours*
flying fish *n* a fish of warm and tropical seas, with winglike fins used for gliding above the water
flying fox *n* **1** a large fruit bat of tropical Africa and Asia **2** *Austral & NZ* a platform suspended from an overhead cable, used for transporting people or materials

flying saucer *n* an unidentified disc-shaped flying object alleged to come from outer space
flying squad *n* a small group of police or soldiers ready to move into action quickly
flying start *n* **1** any promising beginning: *a flying start to the new financial year* **2** a start to a race in which the competitor is already travelling at speed as he or she passes the starting line
flyleaf *n, pl* **-leaves** the inner leaf of the endpaper of a book
flyover *n* an intersection of two roads at which one is carried over the other by a bridge
flypaper *n* paper with a sticky and poisonous coating, hung up to trap flies
flyweight *n* a professional or an amateur boxer weighing up to 112 pounds (51 kg)
flywheel *n* a heavy wheel that regulates the speed of a machine
FM 1 frequency modulation **2** First Minister
foal *n* **1** the young of a horse or related animal ▸ *vb* **2** to give birth to a foal
foam *n* **1** a mass of small bubbles of gas formed on the surface of a liquid **2** frothy saliva **3** a light spongelike solid used for insulation, packing, etc. ▸ *vb* **4** to produce or cause to produce foam **5 foam at the mouth** to be very angry > **foamy** *adj*

> **foam** *n* **1** = froth, spray, bubbles, lather, suds, spume, head ▸ *vb* **4** = bubble, boil, fizz, froth, lather, effervesce

fob *n* **1** a chain by which a pocket watch is attached to a waistcoat **2** a small pocket in a man's waistcoat, for holding a watch
fob off *vb* **fobbing, fobbed 1** to pretend to satisfy (a person) with lies or excuses **2** to sell or pass off (inferior goods) as valuable
focal *adj* **1** of or relating to a focus **2** situated at or measured from the focus
focus (**foe-kuss**) *vb* **-cusing, -cused** *or* **-cussing, -cussed 1** to adjust one's eyes or an instrument on an object so that its image is clear **2** to concentrate ▸ *n, pl* **-cuses** *or* **-ci** (-sigh, -kye, -kee) **3** a point of convergence of light or sound waves, or a point from which they appear to diverge **4 in focus** (of an object or image being viewed) clear and sharp **5 out of focus** (of an object or image being viewed) blurred and fuzzy **6** *optics* the state of an optical image when it is distinct or the state of an instrument producing this image **7** a point upon which attention or activity is concentrated: *the focus was on health and education* **8** *geom* a fixed reference point on the concave side of a conic section, used when defining its eccentricity

> **focus** *vb* **1** = fix, train, direct, aim **2** = concentrate, centre, spotlight, direct, aim, pinpoint, zoom in ▸ *n* **3** = centre, focal point, central point

focus group *n* a group of people gathered by a market research company to discuss and assess a product or service

fodder *n* bulk feed for livestock, esp. hay or straw

foe *n formal or literary* an enemy

> **foe** *n* = enemy, rival, opponent, adversary, antagonist; ≠ friend

foetid *adj* same as **fetid**

foetus *n, pl* **-tuses** same as **fetus**

fog *n* **1** a mass of droplets of condensed water vapour suspended in the air, often greatly reducing visibility **2** *photog* a blurred area on a developed negative, print, or transparency ▸ *vb* **fogging, fogged 3** to envelop or become enveloped with or as if with fog › **foggy** *adj*

> **fog** *n* **1** = mist, gloom, haze, smog, murk, miasma, peasouper (*informal*)

fogey *or* **fogy** *n, pl* **-geys** *or* **-gies** an extremely old-fashioned person: *a stick-in-the-mud old fogey* › **fogeyish** *or* **fogyish** *adj*

foghorn *n* a large horn sounded at intervals as a warning to ships in fog

foible *n* a slight peculiarity or minor weakness: *he was intolerant of other people's foibles*

foil¹ *vb* to baffle or frustrate (a person or an attempt)

> **foil** *vb* = thwart, stop, defeat, disappoint, counter, frustrate, hamper, balk

foil² *n* **1** metal in the form of very thin sheets **2** a person or thing setting off another thing to advantage: *mint sauce is an excellent foil to lamb*

> **foil** *n* **2** = complement, relief, contrast, antithesis

foil³ *n* a light slender flexible sword tipped by a button, used in fencing

foist *vb* **foist on** to force (someone) to have or experience (something): *the tough economic policies which have been foisted on the developing world*

fold¹ *vb* **1** to bend double so that one part covers another **2** to bring together and intertwine (the arms or legs) **3 fold up** to enclose in a surrounding material **4** *literary* to clasp (a person) in one's arms **5** Also: **fold in** to mix (ingredients) by gently turning one over the other with a spoon **6** *informal* (of a business, organization, or project) to fail or go bankrupt ▸ *n* **7** a piece or section that has been folded **8** a mark, crease, or hollow made by folding **9** a bend in stratified rocks that results from movements within the earth's crust

> **fold** *vb* **1** = bend, crease, double over **6** = go bankrupt, fail, crash, collapse, founder, shut down, go under, go bust (*informal*) ▸ **7, 8** = crease, gather, bend, overlap, wrinkle, pleat, ruffle, furrow

fold² *n* **1** *Brit, Austral & S African* a small enclosure for sheep **2** a church or the members of it

folder *n* **1** a binder or file for holding loose papers **2** an area of a computer disk which contains one or more files or other folders

foliage *n* **1** the green leaves of a plant **2** leaves together with the stems, twigs, and branches they are attached to, esp. when used for decoration

foliation *n* **1** *botany* **A** the process of producing leaves **B** the state of being in leaf **2** a leaflike decoration

folio *n, pl* **-lios 1** a sheet of paper folded in half to make two leaves for a book **2** a book of the largest common size made up of such sheets **3 A** a leaf of paper numbered on the front side only **B** the page number of a book **4** *NZ* a collection of related material ▸ *adj* **5** of or made in the largest book size, common esp. in early centuries of European printing: *the entire series is being reissued, several in the original folio format*

folk *pl n* **1** people in general, esp. those of a particular group or class: *ordinary folk* **2** Also: **folks** *informal* members of one's family; relatives ▸ *n* **3** a people or tribe ▸ *adj* **4** originating from or traditional to the common people of a country: *folk art*

> **folk** *pl n* **1** = people, persons, individuals, men and women, humanity, inhabitants, humankind, mankind, mortals **2** = family, parents, relations, relatives, tribe, clan, kin, kindred, ainga (NZ), rellies (*Austral slang*)

folk dance *n* **1** a traditional country dance **2** music for such a dance

folklore *n* the traditional beliefs of a people as expressed in stories and songs

folk song *n* **1** a song handed down among ordinary people **2** a modern song like this › **folk singer** *n*

folksy *adj* **-sier, -siest** simple and unpretentious, sometimes in an artificial way

follicle *n* any small sac or cavity in the body, esp. one from which a hair grows › **follicular** *adj*

follow *vb* **1** to go or come after **2** to accompany: *he followed Isabel everywhere* **3** to be a logical or natural consequence of **4** to keep to the course or track of **5** to act in accordance with: *follow the rules below and it will help you a great deal* **6** to accept the ideas or beliefs of **7** to understand (an explanation) **8** to have a keen interest in: *he's followed the singer's career for more than 25 years* **9** to choose to receive messages or blogs posted online by (a particular person) ▸ See also **follow up**

> **follow** *vb* **1** = pursue, track, dog, hunt, chase, shadow, trail, hound; ≠ avoid **2** = accompany, attend, escort, go behind, tag along behind, come behind **3** = result, issue, develop, spring, flow, proceed, arise, ensue **5** = obey, observe, adhere to, stick to, heed, conform to, keep to, pay attention to; ≠ ignore **7** = understand, realize, appreciate, take in, grasp, catch on (*informal*), comprehend, fathom **8** = keep up with, support, be interested in, cultivate, be a fan of, keep abreast of

follower n **1** a person who accepts the teachings of another: *a follower of Nietzsche* **2** a supporter, such as of a sport or team

follower n = supporter, fan, disciple, devotee, apostle, pupil, adherent, groupie (*slang*); ≠ leader

following adj **1** about to be mentioned **2** next in time **3** (of winds or currents) moving in the same direction as a vessel ▸ prep **4** as a result of: *uncertainty following the collapse of communism* ▸ n **5** a group of supporters or enthusiasts

following adj **1** = coming, about to be mentioned **2** = next, subsequent, successive, ensuing, later, succeeding, consequent ▸ n = supporters, backing, train, fans, suite, clientele, entourage, coterie

follow up vb **1** to investigate (a person, evidence, etc.) closely **2** to continue (action) after a beginning, esp. to increase its effect ▸ n **follow-up 3** something done to reinforce an initial action: *a routine follow-up to his operation*

folly n, pl **-lies 1** the quality of being foolish **2** a foolish action, idea, etc. **3** an imitation castle, temple, etc., built as a decoration in a large garden or park

folly n **1, 2** = foolishness, nonsense, madness, stupidity, indiscretion, imprudence, rashness; ≠ wisdom

foment (foam-ent) vb to encourage or stir up (trouble) ▸ **fomentation** n

fond adj **1 fond of** having a liking for **2** loving and affectionate: *his fond parents* **3** (of hopes or wishes) cherished but unlikely to be realized ▸ **fondly** adv ▸ **fondness** n

fond adj **1 fond of** = attached to, in love with, keen on, attracted to, having a soft spot for, enamoured of **2** = loving, caring, warm, devoted, tender, adoring, affectionate, indulgent; ≠ indifferent **3** = unrealistic, empty, naive, vain, foolish, deluded, overoptimistic, delusive; ≠ sensible

fondant n (a sweet made from) a thick flavoured paste of sugar and water

fondle vb **-dling, -dled** to touch or stroke tenderly

fondue n a Swiss dish, consisting of melted cheese into which small pieces of bread are dipped

font¹ n a large bowl in a church for baptismal water

font² n *printing* a complete set of type of one style and size

fontanelle or esp US **fontanel** n *anatomy* a soft membranous gap between the bones of a baby's skull

food n any substance that can be taken into the body by a living organism and changed into energy and body tissue. Related adjective: **gastronomic**

food n = nourishment, fare, diet, tucker (*Austral, NZ informal*), rations, nutrition, cuisine, refreshment, nibbles, kai (*NZ informal*)

food group n any of the categories into which different foods may be placed according to the type of nourishment they supply

foodie n *informal* a person with a keen interest in food and cookery

foodstuff n any substance that can be used as food

fool¹ n **1** a person who lacks sense or judgment **2** a person who is made to appear ridiculous **3** (formerly) a professional jester living in a royal or noble household **4 play** or **act the fool** to deliberately act foolishly ▸ vb **5** to deceive (someone), esp. in order to make them look ridiculous **6 fool around** or **about with** *informal* to act or play with irresponsibly or aimlessly **7** to speak or act in a playful or jesting manner

fool n **1** = idiot, mug (*Brit slang*), dummy (*slang*), twit (*informal, chiefly Brit*), dunce, dorba or dorb (*Austral slang*), mampara (*S African informal*); ≠ genius **2** = dupe, mug (*Brit slang*), sucker (*slang*), stooge (*slang*), laughing stock, pushover (*informal*), fall guy (*informal*) **3** = jester, clown, harlequin, buffoon, court jester ▸ vb **5** = deceive, mislead, delude, trick, take in, con (*informal*), dupe, beguile, scam (*slang*)

fool² n *chiefly Brit* a dessert made from a puree of fruit with cream

foolery n foolish behaviour

foolhardy adj **-hardier, -hardiest** recklessly adventurous ▸ **foolhardily** adv ▸ **foolhardiness** n

foolish adj very silly, unwise, or absurd ▸ **foolishly** adv ▸ **foolishness** n

foolish adj = unwise, silly, absurd, rash, senseless, foolhardy, ill-judged, imprudent; ≠ sensible

foolproof adj *informal* **1** incapable of going wrong; infallible: *a foolproof identification system* **2** (of machines, etc.) guaranteed to function as intended despite human misuse or error

foosball n *US & Canad* a game in which opponents on either side of a purpose-built table attempt to strike a ball into the other side's goal by moving horizontal bars with miniatures of footballers attached

foot n, pl **feet 1** the part of the leg below the ankle joint that is in contact with the ground during standing and walking **2** the part of a garment covering a foot **3** a unit of length equal to 12 inches (0.3048 metre) **4** the bottom, base, or lower end of something: *at the foot of the hill; the foot of the page* **5** *old-fashioned* infantry **6** *prosody* a group of two or more syllables in which one syllable has the major stress, forming the basic unit of poetic rhythm **7 one foot in the grave** *informal* near to death **8 on foot** walking **9 put one's best foot forward** to try to do one's best

10 put one's foot down *informal* to act firmly **11 put one's foot in it** *informal* to make an embarrassing and tactless mistake **12 under foot** on the ground ▸ *vb* **13 foot it** *informal* to travel on foot **14 foot the bill** to pay the entire cost of something ▸ See also **feet** › **footless** *adj*

footage *n* **1** a length of film **2** the sequences of filmed material: *footage of refugees leaving the city*

foot-and-mouth disease *n* a highly infectious viral disease of cattle, pigs, sheep, and goats, in which blisters form in the mouth and on the feet

football *n* **1** any of various games played with a ball in which two teams compete to kick, head, or propel the ball into each other's goal **2** the ball used in any of these games › **footballer** *n*

footbridge *n* a narrow bridge for the use of pedestrians

footfall *n* the sound of a footstep

foothills *pl n* relatively low hills at the foot of a mountain

foothold *n* **1** a secure position from which further progress may be made: *a firm foothold in Europe's telecommunications market* **2** a ledge or other place where a foot can be securely positioned, as during climbing

footing *n* **1** basis or foundation: *on a sound financial footing* **2** the relationship between two people or groups: *on an equal footing* **3** a secure grip by or for the feet

> **footing** *n* **1** = basis, foundation, base position, groundwork **2** = relationship, position, basis, standing, rank, status, grade

footlights *pl n theatre* lights set in a row along the front of the stage floor

footloose *adj* free to go or do as one wishes

footman *n, pl* -**men** a male servant in uniform

footnote *n* a note printed at the bottom of a page

footpath *n* **1** a narrow path for walkers only **2** *Austral* a raised space alongside a road, for pedestrians

> **footpath** *n* **2** = pavement, sidewalk (*US, Canad*)

footplate *n chiefly Brit* a platform in the cab of a steam locomotive on which the crew stand to operate the controls

footprint *n* **1** an indentation or outline of the foot on a surface **2** the shape and size of the area something occupies: *enlarging the footprint of the building* **3** impact on the environment

footsie *n informal* flirtation involving the touching together of feet

footstep *n* **1** a step in walking **2** the sound made by walking **3** a footmark **4 follow in someone's footsteps** to continue the example of another

> **footstep** *n* **1** = step, tread, footfall

footstool *n* a low stool used for supporting the feet of a seated person

footwear *n* anything worn to cover the feet

footwork *n* the way in which the feet are used, for example in sports or dancing: *nimble footwork*

fop *n* a man who is excessively concerned with fashion › **foppery** *n* › **foppish** *adj*

for *prep* **1** directed or belonging to: *a bottle of beer for himself* **2** to the advantage of: *he spelt it out for her* **3** in the direction of: *he headed for the door* **4** over a span of (time or distance): *she considered him coolly for a moment* **5** in favour of: *support for the war* **6** in order to get: *for a bit of company* **7** designed to meet the needs of: *the instructions are for right-handed players* **8** at a cost of: *two dishes for one* **9** in place of: *she had to substitute for her mother because they woke late* **10** because of: *dancing for joy* **11** regarding the usual characteristics of: *unusually warm for the time of year* **12** concerning: *our idea for the last scene* **13** as being: *do you take me for an idiot?* **14** at (a specified time): *multiparty elections are planned for next year* **15** to do or take part in: *two guests for dinner* **16** in the duty or task of: *that's for you to decide* **17** in relation to; as it affects: *it's too hard for me* **18** in order to preserve or retain: *fighting for survival* **19** as a direct equivalent to: *word for word* **20** in order to become or enter: *training for the priesthood* **21** in exchange for: *the cash was used to pay for food, shelter, and medical supplies* **22 for all** See **all** (sense 12) **23 for it** *Brit & Austral informal* liable for punishment or blame: *you'll be for it if you get caught* ▸ *conj* **24** *formal* because or seeing that: *implausibility cries aloud, and this is a pity, for much of the narrative is entertaining*

forage (**for**-*ridge*) *vb* -**aging**, -**aged** **1** to search for food **2** to obtain (something) by searching about: *she foraged for her shoes* ▸ *n* **3** food for horses or cattle, esp. hay or straw **4** the act of searching for food or provisions

foray *n* **1** a short raid or incursion **2** a first attempt or new undertaking: *his first foray into films*

> **foray** *n* **1** = raid, sally, incursion, inroad, attack, assault, invasion, swoop

forbear *vb* -**bearing**, -**bore**, -**borne** to cease or refrain (from doing something) › **forbearance** *n*

forbid *vb* -**bidding**, -**bade** *or* -**bad**, -**bidden** *or* -**bid** to prohibit or refuse to allow

> **forbid** *vb* = prohibit, ban, disallow, exclude, rule out, veto, outlaw, preclude; ≠ permit

forbidding *adj* severe and threatening in appearance or manner: *a very large and forbidding building*

> **forbidding** *adj* = threatening, severe, frightening, hostile, menacing, sinister, daunting, ominous; ≠ inviting

force *n* **1** strength or power: *the force of the impact had thrown him into the fireplace* **2** exertion or the use of exertion against a person or thing that resists: *they used force and repression against those who opposed their policies* **3** *physics* an influence that changes a body from a state of rest to one of motion or changes its rate of motion. Symbol: F **4 ◣** intellectual or moral influence: *the Superintendent acknowledged the force of the Chief Constable's argument* **B** a person or thing with such influence: *the major force behind the group's success* **5** drive or intensity: *she reacted with frightening speed and force* **6** a group of people organized for particular duties or tasks: *a UN peacekeeping force* **7 in force ◣** (of a law) having legal validity **B** in great strength or numbers ▸ *vb* **forcing, forced 8** to compel (a person, group, etc.) to do something through effort, superior strength, etc.: *forced into an arranged marriage* **9** to acquire or produce through effort, superior strength, etc.: *I forced a smile* **10** to propel or drive despite resistance **11** to break down or open (a lock, door, etc.) **12** to impose or inflict: *a series of opposition strikes forced the appointment of a coalition government* **13** to cause (plants or farm animals) to grow at an increased rate

force *n* **1** = power, might, pressure, energy, strength, momentum, impulse, vigour; ≠ weakness **2** = compulsion, pressure, violence, constraint, oppression, coercion, duress, arm-twisting (*informal*) **5** = intensity, vigour, vehemence, fierceness, emphasis **6** = army, unit, company, host, troop, squad, patrol, regiment **7a in force** = valid, working, current, effective, binding, operative, operational, in operation **7b in force** = in great numbers, all together, in full strength ▸ *vb* **8** = compel, make, drive, press, oblige, constrain, coerce, impel **10** = push, thrust, propel **11** = break open, blast, wrench, prise, wrest

forced *adj* **1** done because of force: *forced labour* **2** false or unnatural: *forced jollity* **3** due to an emergency: *a forced landing*

forced *adj* **1** = compulsory, enforced, mandatory, obligatory, involuntary, conscripted; ≠ voluntary **2** = false, affected, strained, wooden, stiff, artificial, contrived, unnatural; ≠ natural

forceful *adj* **1** strong, emphatic, and confident: *a forceful speech* **2** effective > **forcefully** *adv*

forceful *adj* **1** = dynamic, powerful, assertive; ≠ weak **2** = powerful, strong, convincing, effective, compelling, persuasive, cogent

forceps *n, pl* **-ceps** a surgical instrument in the form of a pair of pincers

forcible *adj* **1** involving physical force **2** convincing or effective: *a strong shrewd mind and a steady forcible manner* > **forcibly** *adv*

ford *n* **1** a shallow area in a river that can be crossed by car, on horseback, etc. ▸ *vb* **2** to cross (a river) over a shallow area > **fordable** *adj*

fore *adj* **1** at, in, or towards the front: *the fore foot* ▸ *n* **2** the front part **3 fore and aft** located at

both ends of a vessel: *two double cabins fore and aft* **4 to the fore** to the front or prominent position ▸ *interj* **5** a golfer's shouted warning to a person in the path of a flying ball

fore- *prefix* **1** before in time or rank: *foregoing* **2** at or near the front: *foreground*

forearm[1] *n* the part of the arm from the elbow to the wrist

forearm[2] *vb* to prepare or arm beforehand

forebear *or* **forbear** *n* an ancestor

foreboding *n* a strong feeling that something bad is about to happen

forecast *vb* **-casting, -cast** *or* **-casted 1** to predict or calculate (weather, events, etc.), in advance ▸ *n* **2** a statement predicting the weather **3** a prediction > **forecaster** *n*

forecast *vb* = predict, anticipate, foresee, foretell, divine, prophesy, augur, forewarn ▸ *n* **3** = prediction, prognosis, guess, prophecy, conjecture, forewarning

forecastle, fo'c's'le *or* **fo'c'sle** (foke-sl) *n* the raised front part of a ship

foreclose *vb* **-closing, -closed** *law* to take possession of property bought with borrowed money because repayment has not been made: *the banks have been reluctant to foreclose on troubled borrowers* > **foreclosure** *n*

forecourt *n* a courtyard in front of a building, such as one in a filling station

forefather *n* an ancestor

forefinger *n* the finger next to the thumb. Also called: **index finger**

forefront *n* **1** the most active or prominent position: *at the forefront of medical research* **2** the very front

forefront *n* **1** = lead, centre, front, fore, spearhead, prominence, vanguard, foreground

foregather *or* **forgather** *vb* to gather together or assemble

forego *vb* **-goes, -going, -went, -gone** to precede in time, place, etc.

foregoing *adj* (esp. of writing or speech) going before; preceding

foregone conclusion *n* an inevitable result

foreground *n* **1** the part of a view, esp. in a picture, nearest the viewer **2** an important or prominent position

forehand *tennis & squash etc.* ▸ *adj* **1** (of a stroke) made so that the racket is held with the wrist facing the direction of play ▸ *n* **2** a forehand stroke

forehead *n* the part of the face between the natural hairline and the eyes

foreign *adj* **1** of, located in, or coming from another country, area, or people **2** dealing or concerned with another country, area, or people: *the Foreign Minister* **3** not familiar; strange **4** in an abnormal place or position: *a foreign body in the food*

foreign *adj* **1** = alien, exotic, unknown, strange, imported, remote, external, unfamiliar; ≠ native

foreigner *n* **1** a person from a foreign country **2** an outsider

foreigner *n* = alien, incomer, immigrant, non-native, stranger, settler

foreleg *n* either of the front legs of an animal
forelock *n* a lock of hair growing or falling over the forehead
foreman *n, pl* **-men 1** a person who supervises other workers **2** *law* the leader of a jury
foremast *n* the mast nearest the bow of a ship
foremost *adj* **1** first in time, place, or importance: *Germany's foremost conductor* ▸ *adv* **2** first in time, place, or importance

foremost *adj* = leading, best, highest, chief, prime, primary, supreme, most important

forename *n* first name
forenoon *n* the daylight hours before noon
forensic (for-ren-sik) *adj* used in or connected with a court of law ▸ **forensically** *adv*
forensic medicine *n* the application of medical knowledge for the purposes of the law, such as in determining the cause of death
foreplay *n* sexual stimulation before intercourse
forerunner *n* **1** a person or thing that existed or happened before another and is similar in some way: *a forerunner of the surrealist painters* **2** a person or thing that is a sign of what will happen in the future
foresail *n* the main sail on the foremast of a ship
foresee *vb* **-seeing, -saw, -seen** to see or know beforehand ▸ **foreseeable** *adj*

foresee *vb* = predict, forecast, anticipate, envisage, prophesy, foretell

foreshadow *vb* to show, indicate, or suggest in advance
foreshore *n* the part of the shore between high- and low-tide marks
foreshorten *vb* to see or draw (an object) from such an angle that it appears to be shorter than it really is
foresight *n* **1** the ability to anticipate and provide for future needs **2** the front sight on a firearm
foreskin *n anatomy* the fold of skin covering the tip of the penis
forest *n* **1** a large wooded area with a thick growth of trees and plants **2** a group of narrow or tall objects standing upright: *a forest of waving arms* **3** NZ an area planted with pines or other trees that are not native to the country ▸ **forested** *adj*
forestall *vb* to delay, stop, or guard against beforehand: *an action forestalling any further talks*

forester *n* a person skilled in forestry or in charge of a forest
forestry *n* the science or skill of growing and maintaining trees in a forest, esp. to obtain wood
foretaste *n* an early but limited experience of something to come
foretell *vb* **-telling, -told** *literary* to correctly predict (an event, a result, etc.) beforehand
forethought *n* thoughtful planning for future events: *a little forethought can avoid a lot of problems later*
for ever *or* **forever** *adv* **1** without end **2** at all times **3** *informal* for a long time: *I could go on for ever about similar incidents*

for ever *or* **forever** *adv* **1** = evermore, always, ever, for good, for keeps, for all time, in perpetuity, till the cows come home (*informal*) **2** = constantly, always, all the time, continually, endlessly, persistently, eternally, perpetually

forewarn *vb* to warn beforehand
foreword *n* an introductory statement to a book
forfeit (for-fit) *n* **1** something lost or given up as a penalty for a fault, mistake, etc. ▸ *vb* **2** to lose as a forfeit ▸ *adj* **3** lost as a forfeit ▸ **forfeiture** *n*

forfeit *n* = penalty, fine, damages, forfeiture, loss, mulct ▸ *vb* = relinquish, lose, give up, surrender, renounce, be deprived of, say goodbye to, be stripped of

forge[1] *n* **1** a place in which metal is worked by heating and hammering; smithy **2** a furnace used for heating metal ▸ *vb* **forging, forged 3** to shape (metal) by heating and hammering **4** to make a fraudulent imitation of (a signature, money, a painting, etc.) **5** to create (an alliance, relationship, etc.) ▸ **forger** *n*

forge *vb* **3** = create, make, work, found, form, model, fashion, shape **4** = fake, copy, reproduce, imitate, counterfeit, feign, falsify **5** = form, build, create, establish, set up, fashion, shape, frame

forge[2] *vb* **forging, forged 1** to move at a steady pace **2 forge ahead** to increase speed or progress; take the lead
forgery *n, pl* **-geries 1** an illegal copy of a painting, banknote, antique, etc. **2** the crime of making a fraudulent imitation
forget *vb* **-getting, -got, -gotten 1** to fail to remember (someone or something once known) **2** to neglect, either by mistake or on purpose **3** to leave behind by mistake **4 forget oneself** to act in an uncharacteristically unrestrained or unacceptable manner: *behave yourself or I might forget myself and slap your wrists* ▸ **forgettable** *adj*

forget *vb* **2** = neglect, overlook, omit, not remember, be remiss, fail to remember **3** = leave behind, lose, lose sight of, mislay

forgetful adj **1** tending to forget **2 forgetful of** inattentive to or neglectful of: *Fiona, forgetful of the time, was still in bed* > **forgetfully** adv > **forgetfulness** n

forget-me-not n a low-growing plant with clusters of small blue flowers

forgive vb **-giving, -gave, -given 1** to stop feeling anger and resentment towards (a person) or at (an action that has caused upset or harm) **2** to pardon (a mistake) **3** to free from (a debt)

> **forgive** vb **1** = excuse, pardon, not hold something against, understand, acquit, condone, let off (*informal*), turn a blind eye to; ≠ blame

forgiveness n the act of forgiving or the state of being forgiven

> **forgiveness** n = pardon, mercy, absolution, exoneration, amnesty, acquittal, remission

forgo or **forego** vb **-goes, -going, -went, -gone** to give up or do without

forgot vb **1** the past tense of **forget 2** oldfashioned or dialect a past participle of **forget**

forgotten vb a past participle of **forget**

fork n **1** a small tool with long thin prongs on the end of a handle, used for lifting food to the mouth **2** a larger similar-shaped gardening tool, used for lifting or digging **3 forks** the part of a bicycle that links the handlebars to the front wheel **4** **A** (of a road, river, etc.) a division into two or more branches **B** the point where the division begins **C** such a branch ▸ vb **5** to pick up, dig, etc., with a fork **6** to be divided into two or more branches **7** to take one or other branch at a fork in a road, etc.

> **fork** vb **6** = branch, part, separate, split, divide, diverge, subdivide, bifurcate

forked adj **1** having a fork or forklike parts **2** zigzag: *forked lightning*

> **forked** adj = branching, split, branched, divided, angled, pronged, zigzag, Y-shaped

fork-lift truck n a vehicle with two moveable arms at the front that can be raised and lowered for transporting and unloading goods

fork out vb slang to pay, esp. with reluctance

forlorn adj **1** lonely, unhappy, and uncared-for **2** (of a place) having a deserted appearance **3** desperate and without any expectation of success: *a final, apparently forlorn attempt to save the war-torn country* > **forlornly** adv

forlorn hope n **1** a hopeless enterprise **2** a faint hope

form n **1** the shape or appearance of something **2** a visible person or animal **3** the particular mode in which a thing or person appears: *wood in the form of paper* **4** a type or kind: *shells were used as a form of currency* **5** physical or mental condition **6** a printed document, esp. one with spaces in which to fill details or answers **7** the previous record of a horse, athlete, etc. **8** Brit slang a criminal record **9** education, chiefly Brit & NZ a group of children who are taught together **10** manners and etiquette: *it is considered bad form not to wear a tie* **11** the structure and arrangement of a work of art or piece of writing as distinguished from its content **12** a bench **13** a hare's nest **14** any of the various ways in which a word may be spelt or inflected ▸ vb **15** to give shape to or take shape, esp. a particular shape **16** to come or bring into existence: *glaciers dammed the valley bottoms with debris behind which lakes have formed* **17** to make or construct or be made or constructed **18** to train or mould by instruction or example **19** to acquire or develop: *they've formed this impression; we formed a bond* **20** to be an element of: *they had formed part of a special murder unit*

> **form** n **1** = shape, formation, configuration, structure, pattern, appearance **4** = type, sort, kind, variety, class, style **5** = condition, health, shape, nick (*informal*), fitness, trim, fettle **6** = document, paper, sheet, questionnaire, application **9** = class, year, set, rank, grade, stream **10** = procedure, etiquette, use, custom, convention, usage, protocol, wont, kawa (NZ), tikanga (NZ) ▸ vb **15** = arrange, combine, line up, organize, assemble, draw up **16** = establish, start, launch **17** = make, produce, fashion, build, create, shape, construct, forge **19** = develop, pick up, acquire, cultivate, contract **20** = constitute, make up, compose, comprise

formal adj **1** of or following established conventions: *formal talks; a formal announcement* **2** characterized by conventional forms of ceremony and behaviour: *a small formal dinner party* **3** suitable for occasions organized according to conventional ceremony: *formal cocktail frocks* **4** methodical and organized: *a formal approach* **5** (of education and training) given officially at a school, college, etc.: *he had no formal training in maths* **6** symmetrical in form: *a formal garden* **7** relating to the form or structure of something as distinguished from its substance or content: *they addressed the formal elements of the structure of police work* **8** philosophy logically deductive rather than based on facts and observation > **formally** adv

> **formal** adj **1** = official, authorized, endorsed, certified, solemn **2** = ceremonial, traditional, solemn, ritualistic, dressy

formaldehyde (for-**mal**-de-hide) n a colourless poisonous strong-smelling gas, used as formalin and in synthetic resins. Also: **methanal**

formalin n a solution of formaldehyde in water, used as a disinfectant and as a preservative for biological specimens

formality *n, pl* **-ties 1** something done as a requirement of custom or good manners: *he dealt with the formalities regarding the cremation* **2** a necessary procedure without real effect: *trials were often a mere formality with the verdict decided beforehand* **3** strict observance of ceremony

> **formality** *n* **1, 2** = convention, procedure, custom, ritual, rite **3** = correctness, seriousness, decorum, protocol, etiquette

formalize *or* **-ise** *vb* **-izing, -ized** *or* **-ising, -ised 1** to make official or valid **2** to give a definite form to ▷ **formalization** *or* **-isation** *n*

format *n* **1** the shape, size, and general appearance of a publication **2** style or arrangement, such as of a television programme: *a chat-show format* **3** *computers* the arrangement of data on disk or magnetic tape to comply with a computer's input device ▶ *vb* **-matting, -matted 4** to arrange in a specified format

> **format** *n* **1** = arrangement, form, style, make-up, look, plan, design, type

formation *n* **1** the act of having or taking form or existence **2** something that is formed **3** the manner in which something is arranged **4** an arrangement of people or things acting as a unit, such as a troop of soldiers **5** a series of rocks or clouds of a particular structure or shape

> **formation** *n* **1** = establishment, founding, forming, setting up, starting, production, generation, manufacture **3** = development, shaping, constitution, moulding, genesis **4, 5** = arrangement, grouping, design, structure, pattern, organization, array, configuration

formative *adj* **1** of or relating to formation, development, or growth: *formative years at school* **2** shaping or moulding: *the formative influence on his life*

former *adj* **1** belonging to or occurring in an earlier time: *a grotesque parody of a former greatness* **2** having been at a previous time: *the former prime minister* ▶ *n* **3 the former** the first or first mentioned of two

> **former** *adj* **2** = previous, one-time, erstwhile, earlier, prior, sometime, foregoing; ≠ current

formerly *adv* in the past

> **formerly** *adv* = previously, earlier, in the past, at one time, before, lately, once

Formica *n trademark* a hard laminated plastic used esp. for heat-resistant surfaces

formic acid *n* an acid derived from ants

formidable *adj* **1** frightening because very difficult to deal with or overcome: *the Finnish winter presents formidable problems to drivers* **2** extremely impressive: *a formidable Juventus squad* ▷ **formidably** *adv*

formidable *adj* **2** = impressive, great (*informal*), powerful, tremendous, mighty, terrific, awesome, invincible

formless *adj* without a definite shape or form

formula (**form-yew-la**) *n, pl* **-las** *or* **-lae** (-lee) **1** a group of letters, numbers, or other symbols which represents a mathematical or scientific rule **2** a plan or set of rules for doing or producing something: *a formula for peace in the Middle East* **3** an established form of words, as used in religious ceremonies, legal proceedings, etc. **4** a powder used to make a milky drink for babies **5** *motor racing* the category in which a car competes, judged according to various criteria including engine size ▷ **formulaic** *adj*

> **formula** *n* **2** = method, plan, policy, rule, principle, procedure, recipe, blueprint

formulate *vb* **-lating, -lated 1** to express in a formula **2** to plan or describe precisely and clearly: *formulate a regional energy strategy* ▷ **formulation** *n*

> **formulate** *vb* **1** = express, detail, frame, define, specify, articulate, set down, put into words **2** = devise, plan, develop, prepare, work out, invent, forge, draw up

fornicate *vb* **-cating, -cated** to have sexual intercourse without being married ▷ **fornicator** *n*

fornication *n* voluntary sexual intercourse outside marriage

forsake *vb* **-saking, -sook, -saken 1** to withdraw support or friendship from **2** to give up (something valued or enjoyed)

forsooth *adv old-fashioned* in truth or indeed

forswear *vb* **-swearing, -swore, -sworn 1** to reject or renounce with determination **2** to testify falsely in a court of law

forsythia (for-syth-ee-a) *n* a shrub with yellow flowers which appear in spring before the leaves

fort *n* **1** a fortified building or position **2 hold the fort** *informal* to keep things in operation during someone's absence

> **fort** *n* **1** = fortress, keep, camp, tower, castle, garrison, stronghold, citadel, fortified pa (NZ) **2 hold the fort** = take responsibility, cover, stand in, carry on, take over the reins, deputize, keep things on an even keel

forte[1] (for-tay) *n* something at which a person excels: *cooking is his forte*

> **forte** *n* = speciality, strength, talent, strong point, métier, long suit (*informal*), gift; ≠ weak point

forte[2] *adv music* loudly

forth *adv* **1** *formal or old-fashioned* forward, out, or away: *running back and forth across the street; Christopher Columbus set forth on his epic voyage of discovery* **2 and so forth** and so on

> **forth** *adv* **1** = out

forthcoming *adj* **1** about to appear or happen: *the forthcoming elections* **2** given or made available **3** (of a person) willing to give information

> **forthcoming** *adj* **1** = approaching, coming, expected, future, imminent, prospective, impending, upcoming **2** = available, ready, accessible, at hand, in evidence, obtainable, on tap (*informal*) **3** = communicative, open, free, informative, expansive, sociable, chatty, talkative

forthright *adj* direct and outspoken
forthwith *adv* at once
fortification *n* **1** the act of fortifying **2 fortifications** walls, mounds, etc., used to strengthen the defences of a place
fortify *vb* **-fies, -fying, -fied 1** to make (a place) defensible, such as by building walls **2** to strengthen physically, mentally, or morally: *the news fortified their resolve to succeed* **3** to increase the nutritious value of (a food), such as by adding vitamins

> **fortify** *vb* **1** = protect, defend, strengthen, reinforce, support, shore up, augment, buttress

fortissimo *adv music* very loudly
fortitude *n* calm and patient courage in trouble or pain

> **fortitude** *n* = courage, strength, resolution, grit, bravery, backbone, perseverance, valour

fortnight *n* a period of 14 consecutive days
fortnightly *chiefly Brit* ▸ *adj* **1** occurring or appearing once each fortnight ▸ *adv* **2** once a fortnight
fortress *n* a large fort or fortified town

> **fortress** *n* = castle, fort, stronghold, citadel, redoubt, fastness, fortified pa (NZ)

fortuitous (for-**tyew**-it-uss) *adj* happening by chance, esp. by a lucky chance ▸ **fortuitously** *adv*
fortunate *adj* **1** having good luck **2** occurring by good luck ▸ **fortunately** *adv*

> **fortunate** *adj* **1** = lucky, favoured, jammy (*Brit slang*), in luck; ≠ unfortunate **2** = providential, fortuitous, felicitous, timely, helpful, convenient, favourable, advantageous

fortune *n* **1** a very large sum of money **2** luck, esp. when favourable **3** (*often pl*) a person's destiny **4** a power regarded as being responsible for human affairs **5** wealth or material prosperity

> **fortune** *n* **2** = luck, fluke (*informal*), stroke of luck, serendipity, twist of fate, run of luck **3** = destiny, lot, experiences, history, condition, success, means, adventures **4** = chance, fate, destiny, providence, the stars, Lady Luck, kismet **5** = wealth, means, property, riches, resources, assets, possessions, treasure; ≠ poverty

fortune-teller *n* a person who claims to predict events in other people's lives
forty *n, pl* **-ties 1** the cardinal number that is the product of ten and four **2** a numeral, 40 or XL, representing this number **3** something representing or consisting of 40 units ▸ *adj* **4** amounting to forty: *forty pages* > **fortieth** *adj, n*
forum *n* **1** a meeting or medium for the open discussion of subjects of public interest **2** (in ancient Roman cities) an open space serving as a marketplace and centre of public business **3** (in South Africa) a pressure group of leaders and representatives
forward *adj* **1** directed or moving ahead **2** at, in, or near the front **3** overfamiliar or disrespectful **4** well developed or advanced **5** of or relating to the future or favouring change ▸ *n* **6** an attacking player in any of various sports, such as soccer ▸ *adv* **7** same as **forwards** ▸ *vb* **8** to send (a letter, etc.) on to an ultimate destination **9** to advance or promote: *the veneer of street credibility he had used to forward his career*

> **forward** *adj* **2** = leading, first, head, front, advance, foremost **3** = presumptuous, familiar, bold, cheeky, brash, pushy (*informal*), brazen, shameless; ≠ shy **4** = future, advanced, premature, prospective ▸ *vb* **8** = send on, send, post, pass on, dispatch, redirect **9** = further, advance, promote, assist, hurry, hasten, expedite

forwards *or* **forward** *adv* **1** towards or at a place ahead or in advance, esp. in space but also in time **2** towards the front

> **forwards** *or* **forward** *adv* **1** = forth (*formal, old-fashioned*), on, ahead, onwards; ≠ backward(s)

fossick *vb Austral & NZ* **1** to search for gold or precious stones in abandoned workings, rivers, etc. **2** to search for, through, or in something; to forage

> **fossick** *vb* **2** = search, hunt, explore, ferret, check, forage, rummage

fossil *n* **1** remains of a plant or animal that existed in a past geological age, occurring in the form of mineralized bones, shells, etc. ▸ *adj* **2** of, like, or being a fossil
fossilize *or* **-ise** *vb* **-izing, -ized** *or* **-ising, -ised 1** to convert or be converted into a fossil **2** to become out-of-date or inflexible: *fossilized political attitudes*
foster *adj* **1** of or involved in the bringing up of a child not one's own: *foster care* ▸ *vb* **2** to bring up (a child not one's own) **3** to promote the growth or development of: *Catherine fostered knowledge and patronized the arts* > **fostering** *n*

> **foster** *vb* **2** = bring up, raise, parent, nurse, look after, rear, care for, take care of **3** = develop, support, further, encourage, feed, promote, stimulate, uphold; ≠ suppress

fought *vb* the past of **fight**

foul *adj* 1 offensive or loathsome: *a foul deed* 2 stinking or dirty 3 full of dirt or offensive matter 4 (of language) obscene or vulgar 5 unfair: *by fair or foul means* 6 (of weather) unpleasant 7 very bad-tempered and irritable: *he was in a foul mood* 8 *informal* disgustingly bad ▸ *n* 9 *sport* a violation of the rules ▸ *vb* 10 to make dirty or polluted 11 to make or become entangled 12 to make or become clogged 13 *sport* to commit a foul against (an opponent) ▸ *adv* 14 **fall foul of** to come into conflict with

> **foul** *adj* 1 = offensive, bad, wrong, evil, corrupt, disgraceful, shameful, immoral; ≠ admirable 2, 3 = dirty, unpleasant, stinking, filthy, grubby, repellent, squalid, repulsive, festy (*Austral slang*), yucko (*Austral slang*); ≠ clean 4 = obscene, crude, indecent, blue, abusive, coarse, vulgar, lewd 5 = unfair, illegal, crooked (*informal*), shady (*informal*), fraudulent, dishonest, unscrupulous, underhand ▸ *vb* 10 = dirty, stain, contaminate, pollute, taint, sully, defile, besmirch; ≠ clean

foul-mouthed *adj* habitually using swearwords and bad language

foul play *n* 1 violent activity, esp. murder 2 a violation of the rules in a game

found¹ *vb* the past of **find**

found² *vb* 1 to bring into being or establish (something, such as an institution) 2 to lay the foundation of 3 **founded on** to have a basis in: *a political system founded on fear* > **founder** *n* > **founding** *adj*

> **found** *vb* 1, 2 = establish, start, set up, begin, create, institute, organize, constitute

found³ *vb* 1 to cast (metal or glass) by melting and pouring into a mould 2 to make (articles) in this way > **founder** *n*

foundation *n* 1 the basic experience, idea, or attitude on which a way of life or belief is based: *respect for the law is the foundation of commercial society* 2 a construction below the ground that distributes the load of a building, wall, etc. 3 the base on which something stands 4 the act of founding 5 an endowment for the support of an institution, such as a college 6 an institution supported by an endowment 7 a cosmetic used as a base for make-up

> **foundation** *n* 1 = basis 2, 3 = substructure, underpinning, groundwork, bedrock, base, footing, bottom 4 = setting up, institution, instituting, organization, settlement, establishment, initiating, originating

founder *vb* 1 to break down or fail: *his negotiations have foundered on economic grounds* 2 (of a ship) to sink 3 to sink into or become stuck in soft ground 4 (of a horse) to stumble or go lame

> **founder** *vb* 1 = fail, collapse, break down, fall through, be unsuccessful, come unstuck, miscarry, misfire 2 = sink, go down, be lost, submerge, capsize, go to the bottom

foundling *n chiefly Brit* an abandoned baby whose parents are not known

foundry *n, pl* **-ries** a place where metal is melted and cast

fount¹ *n* 1 *poetic* a spring or fountain 2 a source or supply: *a fount of knowledge*

fount² *n printing, chiefly Brit* same as **font²**

fountain *n* 1 an ornamental feature in a pool or lake consisting of a jet of water forced into the air by a pump 2 a jet or spray of water 3 a natural spring of water 4 a cascade of sparks, lava, etc.

> **fountain** *n* 1, 3 = font, spring, reservoir, spout, fount, water feature, well 2 = jet, stream, spray, gush

fountainhead *n* a principal or original source

fountain pen *n* a pen supplied with ink from a container inside it

four *n* 1 the cardinal number that is the sum of one and three 2 a numeral, 4 or IV, representing this number 3 something representing or consisting of four units 4 *cricket* a score of four runs, obtained by hitting the ball so that it crosses the boundary after hitting the ground 5 *rowing* **A** a rowing boat propelled by four oarsmen **B** the crew of such a rowing boat ▸ *adj* 6 amounting to four: *four zones*

four-letter word *n* any of several short English words referring to sex or excrement: regarded generally as offensive or obscene

four-poster *n* a bed with posts at each corner supporting a canopy and curtains

foursome *n* 1 a group of four people 2 *golf* a game between two pairs of players

fourteen *n* 1 the cardinal number that is the sum of ten and four 2 a numeral, 14 or XIV, representing this number 3 something representing or consisting of 14 units ▸ *adj* 4 amounting to fourteen: *fourteen points* > **fourteenth** *adj, n*

fourth *adj* 1 of or being number four in a series 2 denoting the fourth from lowest forward gear in a motor vehicle ▸ *n* 3 the fourth from lowest forward gear in a motor vehicle

fourth dimension *n* 1 the dimension of time, which in addition to three spatial dimensions specifies the position of a point or particle 2 the concept in science fiction of an extra dimension > **fourth-dimensional** *adj*

fourth estate *n* the press

fowl *n* 1 a domesticated bird such as a hen 2 any other bird that is used as food or hunted as game 3 the meat of fowl 4 *old-fashioned* a bird ▸ *vb* 5 to hunt or snare wild birds

> **fowl** *n* 2, 3 = poultry

f

fox *n, pl* **foxes** *or* **fox 1** a doglike wild animal with a pointed muzzle and a bushy tail **2** its reddish-brown or grey fur **3** a person who is cunning and sly ▸ *vb* **4** *informal* to confuse or puzzle

foxglove *n* a tall plant with purple or white flowers

foxhole *n military* a small pit dug to provide shelter against enemy fire

foxhound *n* a breed of short-haired terrier, originally kept for hunting foxes

foxtrot *n* **1** a ballroom dance with slow and quick steps **2** music for this ▸ *vb* **-trotting, -trotted 3** to perform this dance

foxy *adj* **foxier, foxiest 1** of or resembling a fox, esp. in craftiness **2** reddish-brown > **foxily** *adv* > **foxiness** *n*

foyer (foy-ay) *n* an entrance hall in a hotel, theatre, or cinema

> **foyer** *n* = entrance hall, lobby, reception area, vestibule, anteroom, antechamber

fracas (frak-ah) *n* a noisy quarrel or fight

fracking *n* a method of extracting oil or gas from rock by forcing liquid at high pressure into the rock

fraction *n* **1** *maths* a numerical quantity that is not a whole number **2** any part or subdivision **3** a very small proportion or amount of something **4** *chem* a component of a mixture separated by distillation > **fractional** *adj* > **fractionally** *adv*

> **fraction** *n* **2** = fragment, part, piece, section, sector, segment

fractious *adj* (esp. of children) easily upset and angered, often due to tiredness

fracture *n* **1** breaking, esp. the breaking or cracking of a bone ▸ *vb* **-turing, -tured 2** to break > **fractural** *adj*

> **fracture** *n* = break, split, crack ▸ *vb* = break, crack

fragile *adj* **1** able to be broken or damaged easily **2** in a weakened physical state: *you're looking a bit fragile this morning* > **fragility** *n*

> **fragile** *adj* **1** = unstable, weak, vulnerable, delicate, uncertain, insecure, precarious, flimsy; ≠ durable **2** = unwell, poorly (*informal*), weak, delicate, crook (*Austral, NZ informal*), shaky, frail, feeble, sickly

fragment *n* **1** a piece broken off **2** an incomplete piece: *fragments of information* ▸ *vb* **3** to break into small pieces or different parts > **fragmentation** *n*

> **fragment** *n* = piece, bit, scrap, particle, portion, shred, speck, sliver ▸ *vb* = break, shatter, crumble, disintegrate, splinter, come apart, break into pieces, come to pieces; ≠ fuse

fragmentary *adj* made up of small or unconnected pieces: *fragmentary evidence to support his theory*

fragrance *n* **1** a pleasant smell **2** a perfume or scent

> **fragrance** *n* **1** = scent, smell, perfume, bouquet, aroma, sweet smell, sweet odour, redolence; ≠ stink **2** = perfume, scent, cologne, eau de toilette, eau de Cologne, toilet water, Cologne water

fragrant *adj* having a pleasant smell

> **fragrant** *adj* = aromatic, perfumed, balmy, redolent, sweet-smelling, sweet-scented, odorous; ≠ stinking

frail *adj* **1** physically weak and delicate **2** easily damaged: *the frail aircraft* **3** easily tempted

> **frail** *adj* **1** = feeble, weak, puny, infirm; ≠ strong **2** = flimsy, weak, vulnerable, delicate, fragile, insubstantial

frailty *n* **1** physical or moral weakness **2** *pl* **-ties** an inadequacy or fault resulting from moral weakness

frame *n* **1** an open structure that gives shape and support to something, such as a building **2** an enclosing case or border into which something is fitted: *the window frame* **3** the system around which something is built up: *caught up in the frame of the revolution* **4** the structure of the human body **5** one of a series of exposures on film used in making motion pictures **6** a television picture scanned by electron beams at a particular frequency **7** *snooker* **A** a single game in a match **B** a wooden triangle used to arrange the red balls in formation before the start of a game **8** *slang* a frame-up **9 frame of mind** a state of mind: *in a complacent frame of mind* ▸ *vb* **framing, framed 10** to construct by fitting parts together **11** to create and develop (plans or a policy) **12** to construct (a statement) in a particular kind of language **13** to provide or enclose with a frame **14** *slang* to conspire to incriminate (someone) on a false charge

> **frame** *n* **2** = casing, framework, structure, shell, construction, skeleton, chassis **4** = physique, build, form, body, figure, anatomy, carcass **9 frame of mind** = mood, state, attitude, humour, temper, outlook, disposition, mind-set ▸ *vb* **11** = devise, draft, compose, sketch, put together, draw up, formulate, map out **13** = mount, case, enclose

frame-up *n slang* a conspiracy to incriminate someone on a false charge

framework *n* **1** a particular set of beliefs, ideas, or rules referred to in order to solve a problem: *a moral framework* **2** a structure supporting something

framework *n* **1** = system, plan, order, scheme, arrangement, the bare bones **2** = structure, body, frame, foundation, shell, skeleton

franc *n* the standard monetary unit of Switzerland, various African countries, and formerly of France and Belgium

franchise *n* **1** the right to vote, esp. for a member of parliament **2** any exemption, privilege, or right granted by a public authority **3** **A** *commerce* authorization granted by a manufacturing or entertainment enterprise to market its products **B** an organization that receives such an authorization **4** a series of films, video games, etc that has a strong identity and lends itself to merchandising ▸ *vb* **-chising, -chised 5** *commerce, chiefly US & Canad* to grant (a person, firm, etc.) a franchise

Franciscan *n* **1** a member of a Christian religious order of friars or nuns founded by Saint Francis of Assisi ▸ *adj* **2** of this order

francium *n chem* an unstable radioactive element of the alkali-metal group. Symbol: **Fr**

Franco- *combining form* indicating France or French: *the Franco-Prussian war*

frangipani (fran-jee-pah-nee) *n* **1** an Australian evergreen tree with large yellow fragrant flowers **2** a tropical shrub with fragrant white or pink flowers

frank *adj* **1** honest and straightforward in speech or attitude ▸ *vb* **2** to put a mark on (a letter), ensuring free carriage ▸ *n* **3** an official mark stamped to a letter ensuring free delivery ▹ **frankly** *adv* ▹ **frankness** *n*

> **frank** *adj* = candid, open, direct, straightforward, blunt, sincere, outspoken, honest; ≠ secretive

frankfurter *n* a smoked sausage of pork or beef

frankincense *n* an aromatic gum resin burnt as incense

frantic *adj* **1** distracted with fear, pain, joy, etc. **2** hurried and disorganized: *frantic activity* ▹ **frantically** *adv*

> **frantic** *adj* **1** = frenzied, wild, furious, distracted, distraught, berserk, at the end of your tether, beside yourself, berko (*Austral slang*); ≠ calm **2** = hectic, desperate, frenzied, fraught (*informal*), frenetic

fraternal *adj* **1** of a brother; brotherly **2** designating twins that developed from two separate fertilized ova ▹ **fraternally** *adv*

fraternity *n, pl* **-ties 1** a body of people united in interests, aims, etc. **2** friendship between groups of people **3** *US & Canad* a society of male students

> **fraternity** *n* **1** = brotherhood, club, union, society, league, association **2** = companionship, fellowship, brotherhood, kinship, camaraderie

fraternize *or* **-nise** *vb* **-nizing, -nized** *or* **-nising, -nised** to associate on friendly terms: *fraternizing with the customers is off-limits* ▹ **fraternization** *or* **-nisation** *n*

fratricide *n* **1** the act of killing one's brother **2** a person who kills his or her brother ▹ **fratricidal** *adj*

Frau (rhymes with **how**) *n, pl* **Frauen** *or* **Fraus** a German form of address equivalent to *Mrs* or *Ms*

fraud *n* **1** deliberate deception or cheating intended to gain an advantage **2** an act of such deception **3** *informal* a person who acts in a false or deceitful way

> **fraud** *n* **1** = deception, deceit, treachery, swindling, trickery, duplicity, double-dealing, chicanery; ≠ honesty **2** = scam, deception (*slang*) **3** = impostor, fake, hoaxer, pretender, charlatan, fraudster, swindler, phoney *or* phony (*informal*)

fraudulent *adj* **1** acting with intent to deceive **2** proceeding from fraud: *fraudulent income* ▹ **fraudulence** *n*

> **fraudulent** *adj* = deceitful, crooked (*informal*), untrue, sham, treacherous, dishonest, swindling, double-dealing; ≠ genuine

fraught (frawt) *adj* **1 fraught with** involving or filled with: *we expected the trip to be fraught with difficulties* **2** tense or anxious

Fräulein (froy-line) *n, pl* **-lein** *or* **-leins** a German form of address equivalent to *Miss*

fray[1] *n* **1** *Brit, Austral & NZ* a noisy quarrel or brawl **2 the fray** any challenging conflict: *at the last minute a rival bidder entered the fray*

fray[2] *vb* **1** to wear away into loose threads, esp. at an edge **2** to make or become strained or irritated

> **fray** *vb* **1** = wear thin, wear, rub, wear out, chafe

frazzle *n informal* the state of being exhausted: *worn to a frazzle*

freak *n* **1** a person, animal, or plant that is abnormal or deformed **2** an object, event, etc., that is abnormal: *a statistical freak* **3** *informal* a person whose appearance or behaviour is very unusual **4** *informal* a person who is very enthusiastic about something specified: *a health freak* ▸ *adj* **5** abnormal or unusual: *a freak accident* ▹ **freakish** *adj* ▹ **freaky** *adj*

> **freak** *n* **3** = eccentric, character (*informal*), oddball (*informal*), nonconformist **4** = enthusiast, fan, nut (*slang*), addict, buff (*informal*), fanatic, devotee, fiend (*informal*) ▸ *adj* = abnormal, chance, unusual, exceptional, unparalleled

freak out *vb informal* to be or cause to be in a heightened emotional state

freckle *n* **1** a small brownish spot on the skin ▸ *vb* **-ling, -led 2** to mark or become marked with freckles ▹ **freckled** *adj*

free *adj* **freer, freest 1** able to act at will; not under compulsion or restraint **2** not enslaved or confined **3** (of a country) independent **4** (of a translation) not exact or literal **5** provided without charge: *free school meals* **6** not occupied or in use; available: *is this seat free?* **7** (of a person) not busy **8** open or available to all **9** not fixed or joined; loose: *the free end* **10** without obstruction or blockage: *the free flow of capital* **11** *chem* chemically uncombined: *free nitrogen* **12** **free and easy** casual or tolerant **13** **free from** not subject to: *free from surveillance* **14** **free with** using or giving (something) a lot: *he was free with his tongue* **15** **make free with** to behave too familiarly towards ▸ *adv* **16** in a free manner **17** without charge or cost ▸ *vb* **freeing, freed 18** to release or liberate **19** to remove obstructions or impediments from **20** to make available or usable: *capital freed by the local authority* **21** **free of** or **from** to relieve or rid of (obstacles, pain, etc.) ▹ **freely** *adv*

> **free** *adj* **1** = allowed, permitted, unrestricted, unimpeded, clear, able **2** = at liberty, loose, liberated, at large, on the loose; ≠ confined **5** = complimentary, for free (*informal*), for nothing, unpaid, for love, free of charge, on the house, without charge, open *or* open source (*computers*) **6** = available, empty, spare, vacant, unused, unoccupied, untaken ▸ *vb* **18** = clear, disengage, cut loose, release, rescue, extricate; ≠ confine **19** = disentangle, extricate, disengage, loose, unravel, disconnect, untangle

-free *combining form* free from: *duty-free; gluten-free*
Freecycle *n trademark* **1** a network of citizens who promote recycling online by offering one another unwanted items free of charge ▸ *vb* **freecycle 2** to recycle (an unwanted item) by offering it free of charge
freedom *n* **1** the state of being free, esp. to enjoy political and civil liberties **2** exemption or immunity: *freedom from government control* **3** liberation, such as from slavery **4** the right or privilege of unrestricted access: *freedom of the skies* **5** self-government or independence **6** the power to order one's own actions **7** ease or frankness of manner

> **freedom** *n* **3** = liberty, release, discharge, emancipation, deliverance; ≠ captivity **5** = independence, democracy, sovereignty, self-determination, emancipation, autarchy, rangatiratanga (NZ) **6** = licence, latitude, free rein, opportunity, discretion, carte blanche, blank cheque; ≠ restriction

free fall *n* **1** the part of a parachute descent before the parachute opens **2** free descent of a body in which gravity is the only force acting on it
free-for-all *n informal* a disorganized brawl or argument involving all those present

free hand *n* **1** unrestricted freedom to act: *the president must be able to deal with foreign hostilities with a free hand* ▸ *adj, adv* **freehand 2** (done) by hand without the use of guiding instruments
freehold *property law* ▸ *n* **1** tenure of property for life without restrictions ▸ *adj* **2** of or held by freehold ▹ **freeholder** *n*
free house *n Brit* a public house not bound to sell only one brewer's products
freelance *n* **1** a self-employed person doing specific pieces of work for various employers ▸ *vb* **-lancing, -lanced 2** to work as a freelance ▸ *adj, adv* **3** of or as a freelance
freeloader *n slang* a person who habitually depends on others for food, accommodation, etc.
Freemason *n Also called* **Mason** a member of a widespread secret order whose members are pledged to help each other ▹ **Freemasonry** *n*
free-range *adj* kept or produced in natural conditions: *free-range eggs*
freesia *n* a plant with fragrant tubular flowers
Freeview *n trademark* (in Britain) a free service providing digital terrestrial television
freeway *n US & Austral* a motorway

> **freeway** *n* = motorway (*Brit*), autobahn (*German*), autoroute (*French*), autostrada (*Italian*)

freewheel *vb* **1** to travel downhill on a bicycle without pedalling ▸ *n* **2** a device in the rear hub of a bicycle wheel that permits it to rotate freely while the pedals are stationary
freeze *vb* **freezing, froze, frozen 1** to change from a liquid to a solid by the reduction of temperature, such as water to ice **2** to preserve (food) by subjection to extreme cold **3** to cover or become covered with ice **4** to fix fast or become fixed (to something) because of frost **5** to feel or cause to feel the effects of extreme cold **6** to die of extreme cold **7** to become motionless through fear, shock, etc. **8** to cause (moving film) to stop at a particular frame **9** to fix (prices, incomes, etc.) at a particular level **10** to forbid by law the exchange or collection of (loans, assets, etc.) ▸ *n* **11** the act of freezing or state of being frozen **12** *meteorol* a spell of temperatures below freezing point **13** the fixing of incomes, prices, etc. by legislation

> **freeze** *vb* **1** = ice over *or* up, harden, stiffen, solidify, become solid **5** = chill **9** = fix, hold, limit, hold up **10** = suspend, stop, shelve, curb, cut short, discontinue

freeze-dry *vb* **-dries, -drying, -dried** to preserve (food) by rapid freezing and drying in a vacuum
freezer *n* an insulated cabinet for cold-storage of perishable foods
freezing *adj informal* very cold

> **freezing** *adj* = icy, biting, bitter, raw, chill, arctic (*informal*), frosty, glacial

freight (frate) *n* **1 A** commercial transport of goods **B** the cargo transported **C** the cost of this

2 *chiefly Brit* a ship's cargo or part of it ▸ *vb* **3** to transport (goods) by freight **4** to load with goods for transport

freight *n* **1A** = transportation, traffic, delivery, carriage, shipment, haulage, conveyance, transport **2** = cargo, goods, load, delivery, burden, shipment, merchandise, consignment

freighter *n* a ship or aircraft designed for transporting cargo

French *adj* **1** of France ▸ *n* **2** the official language of France and an official language of Switzerland, Belgium, Canada, and certain other countries ▸ *pl n* **3 the French** the people of France

French *adj* = Gallic

French bread *n* white bread in a long thin crusty loaf

French dressing *n* a salad dressing made from oil and vinegar with seasonings

French fries *pl n chiefly US & Canad* potato chips

French horn *n music* a valved brass wind instrument with a coiled tube

French letter *n Brit & NZ slang* a condom

French polish *n* a shellac varnish for wood, giving a high gloss

frenetic (frin-net-ik) *adj* wild, excited, and uncontrolled > **frenetically** *adv*

frenzy *n, pl* **-zies 1** violent or wild and uncontrollable behaviour **2** excited or agitated activity: *a frenzy of speculation* > **frenzied** *adj*

frenzy *n* **1** = fury, passion, rage, seizure, hysteria, paroxysm; ≠ calm

frequency *n, pl* **-cies 1** the number of times that an event occurs within a given period **2** the state of being frequent **3** *physics* the number of times a wave repeats itself in a given time

frequent *adj* **1** happening often **2** habitual ▸ *vb* **3** to visit often: *a spa town frequented by the Prussian nobility* > **frequently** *adv*

frequent *adj* = common, repeated, usual, familiar, everyday, persistent, customary, recurrent; ≠ infrequent ▸ *vb* = visit, attend, haunt, be found at, patronize, hang out at (*informal*), visit often, go to regularly; ≠ keep away

fresco *n, pl* **-coes** *or* **-cos 1** a method of wall-painting with watercolours on wet plaster **2** a painting done in this way

fresh *adj* **1** newly made, acquired, etc. **2** not thought of before; novel: *fresh ideas* **3** most recent: *fresh allegations* **4** further or additional: *a fresh supply* **5** (of food) not canned or frozen **6** (of water) not salty **7** bright and clear: *a fresh morning* **8** (of a wind) cold and fairly strong **9** not tired; alert **10** not worn or faded: *the fresh colours of spring* **11** having a healthy or ruddy appearance **12** having recently come (from

somewhere): *cakes fresh from the oven* **13** youthful or inexperienced **14** *informal* overfamiliar or disrespectful ▸ *adv* **15** recently: *a delicious fresh-baked cake* > **freshly** *adv* > **freshness** *n*

fresh *adj* **2, 3** = new, original, novel, different, recent, modern, up-to-date, unorthodox; ≠ old **4** = additional, more, new, other, added, further, extra, supplementary **5** = natural, unprocessed, unpreserved; ≠ preserved **8** = cool, cold, refreshing, brisk, chilly, nippy **9** = lively, keen, alert, refreshed, vigorous, energetic, sprightly, spry; ≠ weary **14** = cheeky (*informal*), impertinent, forward, familiar, audacious, disrespectful, presumptuous, insolent; ≠ well-mannered

freshen *vb* **1** to make or become fresh or fresher **2** (of the wind) to become stronger **3 freshen up** to wash and tidy up one's appearance: *I'll go and freshen up*

fresher *or* **freshman** *n, pl* **-ers** *or* **-men** *Brit & US* a first-year student at college or university

fret¹ *vb* **fretting, fretted 1** to worry: *he would fret about the smallest of problems* **2** to rub or wear away **3** to feel or give annoyance ▸ *n* **4** a state of irritation or anxiety

fret *vb* **1** = worry, brood, agonize, obsess, lose sleep, upset yourself, distress yourself

fret² *n* a small metal bar set across the fingerboard of a musical instrument, such as a guitar, as a guide to fingering

fretful *adj* irritable or upset > **fretfully** *adv*

fret saw *n* a fine-toothed saw with a long thin narrow blade, used for cutting designs in thin wood or metal

fretwork *n* decorative geometrical carving in wood

Freudian (froy-dee-an) *adj* of or relating to Sigmund Freud (1856–1939), Austrian psychiatrist, or his ideas > **Freudianism** *n*

friable (fry-a-bl) *adj* easily broken up > **friability** *n*

friar *n* a member of a male Roman Catholic religious order

friary *n, pl* **-aries** a house of friars

fricassee *n* stewed meat, esp. chicken or veal, served in a thick white sauce

friction *n* **1** a resistance encountered when one body moves relative to another body with which it is in contact **2** the act of rubbing one object against another **3** disagreement or conflict > **frictional** *adj*

friction *n* **1** = resistance, rubbing, scraping, grating, rasping, chafing, abrasion **3** = conflict, hostility, resentment, disagreement, animosity, discord, bad blood, dissension

Friday *n* the sixth day of the week

fridge *n* a cabinet for keeping food and drink cool. In full: **refrigerator**

fried vb the past of **fry**¹

friend n 1 a person known well to another and regarded with liking, affection, and loyalty 2 an ally in a fight or cause 3 a patron or supporter: *our cause has many influential friends throughout Europe* 4 **make friends (with)** to become friendly (with) ▸ vb 5 to add (a person) as a contact on a social networking site > **friendless** adj > **friendship** n

> **friend** n 1 = companion, pal (*informal*), mate (*informal*), buddy (*informal*), best friend, close friend, comrade, chum (*informal*), blood (*Brit slang*), cobber (*Austral, NZ*), cuzzie or cuzzie-bro (*NZ*), E hoa (*NZ old-fashioned, informal*); ≠ foe 2, 3 = supporter, ally, associate, sponsor, patron, well-wisher

Friend n a member of the Society of Friends; Quaker

friendly adj **-lier, -liest** 1 showing or expressing liking, goodwill, or trust 2 on the same side; not hostile 3 tending to help or support ▸ n, pl **-lies** 4 sport a match played for its own sake and not as part of a competition > **friendliness** n

> **friendly** adj 1 = amiable, welcoming, warm, neighbourly, pally (*informal*), helpful, sympathetic, affectionate; ≠ unfriendly

-friendly combining form helpful, easy, or good for the person or thing specified: *a user-friendly computer system*; *the development of an environment-friendly weedkiller*

friendly society n Brit an association of people who pay regular dues in return for old-age pensions, sickness benefits, etc.

Friesian (free-zhan) n any of several breeds of black-and-white dairy cattle

frieze (freeze) n 1 a sculptured or decorated band on a wall 2 archit the horizontal band between the architrave and cornice of a classical temple

frigate (frig-it) n 1 a fast warship, smaller than a destroyer 2 a medium-sized warship of the 18th and 19th centuries

fright n 1 sudden fear or alarm 2 a sudden alarming shock 3 informal a very strange or unattractive person or thing

> **fright** n 1 = fear, shock, alarm, horror, panic, dread, consternation, trepidation (*formal*); ≠ courage 2 = scare, start, turn (*informal*), surprise, shock, jolt, the creeps (*informal*), the willies (*slang*)

frighten vb 1 to terrify or scare 2 to force (someone) to do something from fear > **frightening** adj

> **frighten** vb 1 = scare, shock, alarm, terrify, startle, intimidate, unnerve, petrify; ≠ reassure

frightful adj 1 very alarming or horrifying 2 annoying or disagreeable: *a frightful pair of socks* 3 informal extreme: *a frightful mess* > **frightfully** adv

frigid (frij-id) adj 1 (esp. of a woman) lacking sexual responsiveness 2 very cold: *the frigid air* 3 formal or stiff in behaviour or temperament > **frigidity** n

frill n 1 a long narrow strip of fabric with many folds in it, attached at one edge of something as a decoration 2 an unnecessary part of something added to make it more attractive or interesting: *no fuss, no frills, just a purity of sound and clarity of vision* > **frilly** or **frilled** adj

frilled lizard n a large tree-living Australian lizard with an erectile fold of skin around the neck

fringe n 1 chiefly Brit hair cut short and hanging over the forehead 2 an ornamental edge of hanging threads, tassels, etc. 3 an outer edge: *London's southern fringe* 4 the minor and less important parts of an activity or organization: *two agents on the fringes of espionage activity* 5 a small group of people within a larger body, but differing from it in certain aims and ideas: *the radical fringe of the Green Party* ▸ adj 6 (of theatre) unofficial or unconventional ▸ vb **fringing, fringed** 7 to form a border for: *sandy paths fringing the water's edge* 8 to decorate with a fringe: *tinsel fringed the desk*

> **fringe** n 2 = border, edging, edge, trimming, hem, frill, flounce 3 = edge, limits, border, margin, outskirts, perimeter, periphery, borderline ▸ adj = unofficial, alternative, radical, innovative, avant-garde, unconventional, unorthodox

fringe benefit n a benefit given in addition to a regular salary or wage

fringed adj 1 (of clothes, curtains, etc.) decorated with a fringe 2 **fringed with** or **by** bordered with or by: *a field fringed with trees*

frippery n, pl **-peries** 1 showy but useless ornamentation 2 unimportant or trivial matters

frisk vb 1 to leap, move about, or act in a playful manner 2 informal to search (someone) by feeling for concealed weapons, etc. ▸ n 3 a playful movement 4 informal an instance of frisking a person

frisky adj **friskier, friskiest** lively, high-spirited, or playful > **friskily** adv

frisson (freess-on) n a short sudden feeling of fear or excitement

fritter n a piece of food, such as apple, that is dipped in batter and fried in deep fat

fritter away vb to waste: *he did not fritter away his energy on trivialities*

frivolous adj 1 not serious or sensible in content, attitude, or behaviour 2 unworthy of serious or sensible treatment: *frivolous distractions* > **frivolity** n

frizz vb 1 (of hair) to form or cause (hair) to form tight curls ▸ n 2 hair that has been frizzed > **frizzy** adj

frock n old-fashioned 1 a dress 2 a loose garment, formerly worn by peasants

frock coat *n* a man's skirted coat, as worn in the 19th century

frog *n* **1** a smooth-skinned tailless amphibian with long back legs used for jumping **2 a frog in one's throat** phlegm on the vocal cords, hindering speech

frogman *n, pl* **-men** a swimmer equipped with a rubber suit, flippers, and breathing equipment for working underwater

frogspawn *n* a jelly-like substance containing a frog's eggs

frolic *vb* **-icking, -icked 1** to run and play in a lively way ▸ *n* **2** lively and merry behaviour **3** a light-hearted occasion

frolicsome *adj* merry and playful

from *prep* **1** indicating the original location, situation, etc.: *from America* **2** in a period of time starting at: *from 1950 to the current year* **3** indicating the distance between two things or places: *60 miles from the Iraqi border* **4** indicating a lower amount: *from 5 to 6* **5** showing the model of: *drawn from life* **6** used with a verbal noun to denote prohibition, etc.: *she was banned from smoking at meetings* **7** because of: *five hundred horses collapsed from exhaustion*

frond *n* **1** the compound leaf of a fern **2** the leaf of a palm

front *n* **1** that part or side that is forward, or most often seen or used **2** a position or place directly before or ahead **3** the beginning, opening, or first part **4** the position of leadership **5** a promenade at a seaside resort **6** *military* **A** the total area in which opposing armies face each other **B** the space in which a military unit is operating **7** *meteorol* the dividing line between two different air masses **8** an outward appearance: *he put on a bold front* **9** *informal* a business or other activity serving as a respectable cover for another, usually criminal, organization **10** Also called: **front man, front woman** a nominal leader of an organization **11** a particular field of activity: *on the economic front* **12** a group of people with a common goal: *the National Liberation Front* ▸ *adj* **13** of, at, or in the front ▸ *vb* **14** to face (onto) **15** to be a front of or for **16** to appear as a presenter in (a television show, etc.) **17** to be the leader of (a band) on stage

> **front** *n* **1** = foreground, fore, forefront, nearest part **2** = exterior, face, facade, frontage **3** = head, start, lead, forefront **6A** = front line, trenches, vanguard, firing line **9** = disguise, cover, blind, mask, cover-up, cloak, facade, pretext ▸ *adj* = foremost, at the front; ≠ back ▸ *vb* **14** = face onto, overlook, look out on, have a view of, look over *or* onto

frontage *n* **1** the facade of a building or the front of a plot of ground **2** the extent of the front of a shop, plot of land, etc.

frontal *adj* **1** of, at, or in the front **2** of or relating to the forehead

front bench *n* (in Britain) the leadership of either the Government or Opposition in the House of Commons or in various other legislative assemblies > **front-bencher** *n*

frontier *n* **1** the region of a country bordering on another, or a line marking such a boundary **2** the edge of the settled area of a country **3 frontiers** the limit of knowledge in a particular field: *at that time, laser spectroscopy was on the frontiers of chemical research*

> **frontier** *n* **1** = border, limit, edge, boundary, verge (*Brit*), perimeter, borderline, dividing line

frontispiece *n* an illustration facing the title page of a book

frontrunner *n informal* the leader or a favoured contestant in a race or election

frost *n* **1** a white deposit of ice particles **2** an atmospheric temperature of below freezing point, producing this deposit ▸ *vb* **3** to cover with frost **4** to kill or damage (plants) with frost

> **frost** *n* = hoarfrost, freeze, rime

frostbite *n* destruction of tissues, esp. of the fingers, ears, toes, and nose, by freezing > **frostbitten** *adj*

frosted *adj* (of glass) having the surface roughened so that it cannot be seen through clearly

frosting *n chiefly US & Canad* icing

frosty *adj* **frostier, frostiest 1** characterized by frost: *the frosty air* **2** covered by frost **3** unfriendly or disapproving: *a frosty reception from the bank manager* > **frostily** *adv* > **frostiness** *n*

froth *n* **1** a mass of small bubbles of air or a gas in a liquid **2** a mixture of saliva and air bubbles formed at the lips in certain diseases, such as rabies **3** trivial but superficially attractive ideas or entertainment ▸ *vb* **4** to produce or cause to produce froth > **frothy** *adj*

frown *vb* **1** to wrinkle one's brows in worry, anger, or concentration **2 frown on** to disapprove of: *unnecessary waste is frowned on* ▸ *n* **3** the act of frowning **4** a look of disapproval or displeasure

> **frown** *vb* **1** = scowl, glare, glower, make a face, look daggers, knit your brows, lour *or* lower ▸ *n* **4** = scowl, glare, glower, dirty look

frowsty *adj* **frowstier, frowstiest** *Brit* stale or musty

frowzy *or* **frowsy** *adj* **frowzier, frowziest** *or* **frowsier, frowsiest 1** slovenly or unkempt in appearance **2** musty and stale

froze *vb* the past tense of **freeze**

frozen *vb* **1** the past participle of **freeze** ▸ *adj* **2** turned into or covered with ice **3** killed or stiffened by extreme cold **4** (of food) preserved by a freezing process **5 A** (of prices or wages) officially fixed at a certain level **B** (of business assets) not convertible into cash **6** motionless: *she was frozen in horror*

frozen *adj* **2** = icy, hard, solid, frosted, arctic (*informal*), ice-covered, icebound **3** = ice-cold, freezing, numb, very cold, frigid, frozen stiff **4** = chilled, cold, iced, refrigerated, ice-cold

frugal (froo-gl) *adj* **1** economical in the use of money or resources; thrifty **2** meagre and inexpensive: *a frugal meal* ▷ **frugality** *n* ▷ **frugally** *adv*

fruit *n* **1** any fleshy part of a plant that supports the seeds and is edible, such as the strawberry **2** *botany* the ripened ovary of a flowering plant, containing one or more seeds **3** any plant product useful to man, including grain and vegetables **4 fruits** the results of an action or effort, esp. if pleasant: *they have enjoyed the fruits of a complete victory* ▶ *vb* **5** to bear fruit

fruit *n* **4** = result, reward, outcome, end result, return, effect, benefit, profit

fruiterer *n chiefly Brit & Austral* a person who sells fruit

fruit fly *n* **1** a small fly that feeds on and lays its eggs in plant tissues **2** a similar fly that feeds on plant sap, decaying fruit, etc., and is widely used in genetic experiments

fruitful *adj* **1** producing good and useful results: *a fruitful relationship* **2** bearing much fruit ▷ **fruitfully** *adv*

fruition (froo-ish-on) *n* **1** the fulfilment of something worked for or desired **2** the act or condition of bearing fruit

fruitless *adj* **1** producing nothing of value: *a fruitless debate* **2** without fruit ▷ **fruitlessly** *adv*

fruit machine *n Brit & NZ* a coin-operated gambling machine that pays out money when a particular combination of symbols, usually representing fruit, appears on a screen

fruity *adj* **fruitier, fruitiest 1** of or like fruit **2** (of a voice) mellow or rich **3** *informal, chiefly Brit* referring humorously to things relating to sex ▷ **fruitiness** *n*

frump *n derogatory* a woman whose appearance is considered dull or old-fashioned ▷ **frumpy** or **frumpish** *adj*

frustrate *vb* **-trating, -trated 1** to upset or anger (a person) by presenting difficulties that cannot be overcome: *his lack of ambition frustrated me* **2** to hinder or prevent (the efforts, plans, or desires of) ▷ **frustrating** *adj* ▷ **frustration** *n*

frustrate *vb* **2** = thwart, stop, check, block, defeat, disappoint, counter, spoil, crool or cruel (*Austral slang*); ≠ further

frustrated *adj* dissatisfied or unfulfilled

frustrated *adj* = disappointed, discouraged, infuriated, exasperated, resentful, embittered, disheartened

fry¹ *vb* **fries, frying, fried 1** to cook or be cooked in fat or oil, usually over direct heat ▶ *n, pl* **fries 2** *Also:* **fry-up** *informal* a dish of mixed fried food ▷ **fryer** or **frier** *n*

fry² *pl n* the young of various species of fish

ft. foot or feet

ftp file transfer protocol: a standard protocol for transferring files across a network, esp. the internet

fuchsia (fyew-sha) *n* an ornamental shrub with hanging purple, red, or white flowers

fuddle *vb* **-dling, -dled 1** to cause to be confused or intoxicated ▶ *n* **2** a confused state ▷ **fuddled** *adj*

fuddy-duddy *n, pl* **-dies** *informal* a person, esp. an elderly one, who is extremely conservative or dull

fudge¹ *n* a soft sweet made from sugar, butter, and milk

fudge² *vb* **fudging, fudged 1** to make (an issue or problem) less clear deliberately **2** to avoid making a firm statement or decision

fudge *vb* = misrepresent, hedge, stall, flannel (*Brit informal*), equivocate

fuel *n* **1** any substance burned for heat or power, such as coal or petrol **2** the material that produces energy by fission in a nuclear reactor **3 add fuel to** to make (a difficult situation) worse ▶ *vb* **fuelling, fuelled** or *US* **fueling, fueled 4** to supply with or receive fuel **5** to intensify or make worse (a feeling or situation): *the move is bound to fuel speculation*

fug *n chiefly Brit & NZ* a hot stale atmosphere ▷ **fuggy** *adj*

fugitive (fyew-jit-iv) *n* **1** a person who flees, esp. from arrest or pursuit ▶ *adj* **2** fleeing **3** not permanent; fleeting

fugitive *n* = runaway, refugee, deserter, outlaw, escapee

fugue (fyewg) *n* a musical form consisting of a theme repeated above or below the continuing first statement ▷ **fugal** *adj*

fulcrum *n, pl* **-crums** or **-cra** the pivot about which a lever turns

fulfil or *US* **fulfill** *vb* **-filling, -filled 1** to bring about the achievement of (a desire or promise) **2** to carry out (a request or order) **3** to satisfy (demands or conditions) **4 fulfil oneself** to achieve one's potential ▷ **fulfilment** or *US* **fulfillment** *n*

fulfil or **fulfill** *vb* **1** = achieve, realize, satisfy, attain, consummate, bring to fruition **2** = carry out, perform, complete, achieve, accomplish; ≠ neglect **3** = satisfy, please, content, cheer, refresh, gratify, make happy

full *adj* **1** holding as much or as many as possible **2** abundant in supply: *full of enthusiasm* **3** having consumed enough food or drink **4** (of the face or figure) rounded or plump **5** complete: *the full amount* **6** with all privileges or rights: *full membership* **7** *music* powerful or rich in volume and sound **8** (of a garment) containing a large amount of fabric **9 full of** engrossed with: *she* had been full of her own plans lately **10 full of oneself** full of pride or conceit **11 full up** filled to capacity ▸ adv **12** completely or entirely **13** directly or right: *she hit him full in the face* **14 full well** very or extremely well: *we knew full well that she was watching every move we made* ▸ n **15 in full** without omitting or shortening **16 to the full** thoroughly or fully ▸**fullness** or esp US **fulness** n

> **full** adj **1** = filled, stocked, brimming, replete, complete, loaded, saturated **3** = satiated, having had enough, replete **4** = plump, rounded, voluptuous, shapely, well-rounded, buxom, curvaceous (*informal*) **6** = comprehensive, complete, exhaustive, all-embracing **7** = rich, strong, deep, loud, distinct, resonant, sonorous, clear; ≠ thin **8** = voluminous, large, loose, baggy, billowing, puffy, capacious, loose-fitting; ≠ tight

full-blooded adj **1** vigorous or enthusiastic **2** (esp. of horses) having ancestors of a single race or breed
full-blown adj fully developed
full moon n the phase of the moon when it is visible as a fully illuminated disc
full-scale adj **1** (of a plan) of actual size **2** using all resources; all-out

> **full-scale** adj **2** = major, wide-ranging, all-out, sweeping, comprehensive, thorough, in-depth, exhaustive

full stop n the punctuation mark (.) used at the end of a sentence and after abbreviations. Also called (esp. US and Canad): **period**
fully adv **1** to the greatest degree or extent **2** amply or adequately **3** at least: *fully a hundred people*

> **fully** adv **1** = completely, totally, perfectly, entirely, altogether, thoroughly, wholly, utterly

fulmar n a heavily-built Arctic sea bird with a short tail
fulminate vb **-nating, -nated** ▸**fulminate against** to criticize or denounce angrily ▸**fulmination** n
fulsome adj **1** exaggerated and elaborate, and often sounding insincere: *fulsome praise* **2** *not standard* extremely complimentary
fumble vb **-bling, -bled 1** to use the hands clumsily or grope about blindly: *fumbling for a torch* **2** to say or do awkwardly ▸ n **3** the act of fumbling

> **fumble** vb **1** = grope, flounder, scrabble, feel around

fume vb **fuming, fumed 1** to be overcome with anger or fury **2** to give off (fumes) or (of fumes) to be given off, esp. during a chemical reaction **3** to treat with fumes ▸ n **4** (*often pl*) pungent or toxic vapour, gas, or smoke: *exhaust fumes*

fume vb **1** = rage, seethe, see red (*informal*), storm, rant, smoulder, get hot under the collar (*informal*) ▸ n = smoke, gas, exhaust, pollution, vapour, smog

fumigate (fyew-mig-gate) vb **-gating, -gated** to treat (something contaminated) with fumes ▸**fumigation** n
fun n **1** pleasant, enjoyable, and light-hearted activity or amusement **2 for** or **in fun** for amusement or as a joke **3 make fun of** or **poke fun at** to ridicule or tease ▸ adj **4** (of a person) amusing and likeable **5** (of a place or activity) amusing and enjoyable

> **fun** n **1** = amusement, sport, pleasure, entertainment, recreation, enjoyment, merriment, jollity; ≠ gloom **3 make fun of something or someone** = mock, tease, ridicule, poke fun at, laugh at, mimic, parody, send up (*Brit informal*) ▸ adj **5** = enjoyable, entertaining, pleasant, amusing, lively, diverting, witty, convivial

function n **1** the intended role or purpose of a person or thing **2** an official or formal social gathering **3** a factor, the precise nature of which depends upon another thing in some way: *muscle breakdown is a function of vitamin E deficiency* **4** *maths* a quantity, the value of which depends on the varying value of another quantity **5** a sequence of operations that a computer or calculator performs when a specified key is pressed ▸ vb **6** to operate or work **7 function as** to perform the action or role of (something or someone else)

> **function** n **1** = purpose, business, job, use, role, responsibility, task, duty **2** = reception, party, affair, gathering, bash (*informal*), social occasion, soiree, do (*informal*) ▸ vb **6** = work, run, operate, perform, act **7** = act, operate, perform, behave, do duty, have the role of

functional adj **1** of or performing a function **2** practical rather than decorative **3** in working order **4** *med* affecting a function of an organ without structural change ▸**functionally** adv

> **functional** adj **2** = practical, utilitarian, serviceable, hard-wearing, useful **3** = working, operative, operational, going, prepared, ready, viable, up and running

functionary n, pl **-aries** a person acting in an official capacity, such as for a government; official
fund n **1** a reserve of money set aside for a certain purpose **2** a supply or store of something ▸ vb **3** to provide money to **4** *finance* to convert (short-term debt) into long-term debt bearing fixed interest ▸**funder** n

> **fund** n **1** = reserve, stock, supply, store, collection, pool ▸ vb **3** = finance, back, support, pay for, subsidize, provide money for, put up the money for

fundamental *adj* **1** essential or primary: *fundamental mathematical concepts* **2** basic: *a fundamental error* ▸ *n* **3** **fundamentals** the most important and basic parts of a subject or activity **4** the lowest note of a harmonic series ▷ **fundamentally** *adv*

> **fundamental** *adj* **1** = central, key, basic, essential, primary, principal, cardinal; ≠ incidental **2** = basic, essential, underlying, profound, elementary, rudimentary

fundamentalism *n* **1** *Christianity* the view that the Bible is literally true **2** *Islam* a movement favouring strict observance of Islamic law ▷ **fundamentalist** *n, adj*

fundi (foon-dee) *n S African* an expert

> **fundi** *n* = expert

funding *n* **1** the provision of money for a project or organization **2** the amount of money provided

funeral *n* **1** a ceremony at which a dead person is buried or cremated **2** **it's your funeral** *informal* a mistake has been made and you alone will be responsible for its consequences ▸ *adj* **3** of or for a funeral ▷ **funerary** *adj*

> **funeral** *n* **1** = burial, committal, laying to rest, cremation, interment, obsequies, entombment

funereal (fyew-neer-ee-al) *adj* suggestive of a funeral; gloomy or sombre ▷ **funereally** *adv*

funfair *n Brit* an amusement park with machines to ride on and stalls

fungicide *n* a substance used to destroy fungi

fungus *n, pl* **fungi** *or* **funguses** a plant without leaves, flowers, or roots, that reproduces by spores, including moulds, yeasts, and mushrooms ▷ **fungal** *adj*

funicular (fyew-nik-yew-lar) *n* a railway up the side of a mountain, consisting of two cars at either end of a cable passing round a driving wheel at the summit. Also called: **funicular railway**

funk[1] *old-fashioned Brit* ▸ *n* **1** a state of nervousness, fear, or depression **2** a coward ▸ *vb* **3** to avoid doing (something) through fear

funk[2] *n* a type of dance music with a strong beat

funky *adj* **-kier, -kiest** (of jazz or pop) having a strong beat

funnel *n* **1** a tube with a wide mouth tapering to a small hole, used for pouring liquids into narrow openings **2** a chimney of a ship or steam train ▸ *vb* **-nelling, -nelled** *or US* **-neling, -neled** **3** to move or cause to move through, or as if through, a funnel

funnel-web *n Austral* a large poisonous black spider that builds funnel-shaped webs

funny *adj* **-nier, -niest** **1** causing amusement or laughter; humorous **2** peculiar or odd **3** *informal* faint or ill: *this smell is making me feel a bit funny* **4** **funny business** *informal* suspicious or dubious behaviour ▷ **funnily** *adv* ▷ **funniness** *n*

funny *adj* **1** = humorous, amusing, comical, entertaining, comic, witty, hilarious, riotous; ≠ unfunny **2** = peculiar, odd, strange, unusual, bizarre, curious, weird, mysterious **3** = ill, poorly (*informal*), sick, odd, crook (*Austral, NZ informal*), ailing, unhealthy, unwell, off-colour (*informal*)

funny bone *n* a sensitive area near the elbow where the nerve is close to the surface of the skin

fur *n* **1** the dense coat of fine silky hairs on many mammals **2** the skin of certain animals, with the hair left on **3** a garment made of fur **4** **make the fur fly** to cause a scene or disturbance **5** *informal* a whitish coating on the tongue, caused by illness **6** *Brit* a deposit on the insides of water pipes or kettles, caused by hard water ▸ *vb* **furring, furred 7** Also: **fur up** to cover or become covered with a furlike deposit

furbish *vb formal* to brighten up or renovate

furious *adj* **1** extremely angry or annoyed **2** violent or unrestrained, such as in speed or energy: *fast and furious dance routines* ▷ **furiously** *adv*

> **furious** *adj* **1** = angry, raging, fuming, infuriated, incensed, enraged, inflamed, very angry, tooshie (*Austral slang*); ≠ pleased **2** = violent, intense, fierce, savage, turbulent, vehement, unrestrained

furl *vb* to roll up (an umbrella, flag, or sail) neatly and securely

furlong *n* a unit of length equal to 220 yards (201.168 metres)

furlough (fur-loh) *n* leave of absence from military or other duty

furnace *n* **1** an enclosed chamber in which heat is produced to destroy refuse or smelt ores **2** *informal* a very hot place

furnish *vb* **1** to provide (a house or room) with furniture, etc. **2** to supply or provide ▷ **furnished** *adj*

> **furnish** *vb* **1** = decorate, fit out, stock, equip **2** = supply, give, offer, provide, present, grant, hand out

furnishings *pl n* furniture, carpets, and fittings with which a room or house is furnished

furniture *n* the large movable articles, such as chairs and tables, that equip a room or house

> **furniture** *n* = household goods, furnishings, fittings, house fittings, goods, things (*informal*), possessions, appliances

furore (fyew-ror-ee) *n* a very angry or excited reaction by people to something: *the latest furore over executive pay*

> **furore** *n* = commotion, to-do, stir, disturbance, outcry, uproar, hullabaloo

furrier *n* a person who makes or sells fur garments

furrow n 1 a long narrow trench made in the ground by a plough 2 any long deep groove, esp. a deep wrinkle on the forehead ▸ vb 3 to become wrinkled 4 to make furrows in (land)

furry adj **-rier, -riest** like or covered with fur or something furlike

further adv 1 in addition 2 to a greater degree or extent 3 to or at a more advanced point 4 to or at a greater distance in time or space ▸ adj 5 additional 6 more distant or remote in time or space ▸ vb 7 to assist the progress of (something) >**furtherance** n

> **further** adv 1 = in addition, moreover, besides, furthermore, also, to boot, additionally, into the bargain ▸ adj 5 = additional, more, new, other, extra, fresh, supplementary ▸ vb = promote, help, develop, forward, encourage, advance, work for, assist; ≠ hinder

further education n (in Britain, Australia, and South Africa) formal education beyond school other than at university

furthermore adv in addition

> **furthermore** adv = moreover, further, in addition, besides, too, as well, to boot, additionally

furthest adv 1 to the greatest degree or extent 2 to or at the greatest distance in time or space; farthest ▸ adj 3 most distant in time or space; farthest

> **furthest** adj = most distant, extreme, ultimate, remotest, furthermost, outmost

furtive adj sly, cautious, and secretive >**furtively** adv

fury n, pl **-ries** 1 violent anger 2 uncontrolled violence: the fury of the sea 3 an outburst of violent anger 4 a person with a violent temper 5 **like fury** old-fashioned with great energy, strength, or power

> **fury** n 1 = anger, passion, rage, madness (informal), frenzy, wrath, impetuosity; ≠ calmness 2 = violence, force, intensity, severity, ferocity, savagery, vehemence, fierceness; ≠ peace

furze n gorse >**furzy** adj

fuse[1] or US **fuze** n 1 a lead containing an explosive for detonating a bomb ▸ vb **fusing, fused** or US **fuzing, fuzed** 2 to equip with such a fuse

fuse[2] n 1 a protective device for safeguarding electric circuits, containing a wire that melts and breaks the circuit when the current exceeds a certain value ▸ vb **fusing, fused** 2 Brit to fail or cause to fail as a result of a fuse blowing 3 to equip (a plug or circuit) with a fuse 4 to join or become combined: the two ideas fused in his mind 5 to unite or become united by melting 6 to become or cause to become liquid, esp. by the action of heat

fuselage (**fyew**-zill-lahzh) n the main body of an aircraft

fusilier (fyew-zill-**leer**) n (formerly) an infantryman armed with a light musket: a term still used in the names of certain British regiments

fusillade (fyew-zill-**lade**) n 1 a rapid continual discharge of firearms 2 a sudden outburst of criticism, questions, etc.

fusion n 1 the act or process of melting together 2 something produced by fusing 3 a kind of popular music that is a blend of two or more styles, such as jazz and funk 4 something new created by a mixture of qualities, ideas, or things 5 See **nuclear fusion** ▸ adj 6 relating to a style of cooking that combines traditional Western techniques and ingredients with those used in Eastern cuisine

fuss n 1 needless activity and worry 2 complaint or objection: it was silly to make a fuss over seating arrangements 3 an exhibition of affection or admiration: when I arrived my nephews made a big fuss of me ▸ vb 4 to worry unnecessarily 5 to be excessively concerned over trivial matters 6 to bother (a person) 7 **fuss over** to show great or excessive concern or affection for

> **fuss** n 1 = commotion, to-do, bother, stir, excitement, ado, hue and cry, palaver 2 = complaint, row, protest, objection, trouble, argument, squabble, furore ▸ vb 4 = worry, flap (informal), fret, fidget, take pains, be agitated, get worked up

fussy adj **fussier, fussiest** 1 inclined to fuss 2 very particular about detail 3 overelaborate: a fussy, overdecorated palace >**fussily** adv

fusty adj **-tier, -tiest** 1 smelling of damp or mould 2 old-fashioned >**fustiness** n

futile (**fyew**-tile) adj 1 useless or having no chance of success 2 foolish and of no value: her futile remarks began to annoy me >**futility** n

> **futile** adj 1 = useless, vain, unsuccessful, pointless, worthless, fruitless, ineffectual, unprofitable; ≠ useful

futon (**foo**-tonn) n a Japanese padded quilt, laid on the floor as a bed

future n 1 the time yet to come 2 undetermined events that will occur in that time 3 the condition of a person or thing at a later date 4 prospects: he had faith in its future 5 grammar a tense of verbs used when the action specified has not yet taken place 6 **in future** from now on ▸ adj 7 that is yet to come or be 8 of or expressing time yet to come 9 destined to become 10 grammar in or denoting the future as a tense of verbs

> **future** n 1 = time to come, hereafter, what lies ahead 4 = prospect, expectation, outlook ▸ adj 7, 9 = forthcoming, coming, later, approaching, to come, succeeding, fated, subsequent; ≠ past

futuristic *adj* **1** of design or technology that appears to belong to some future time **2** of futurism

fuzz¹ *n* a mass or covering of fine or curly hairs, fibres, etc.

fuzz² *n Brit, Austral & NZ slang* the police or a police officer

fuzzy *adj* **fuzzier, fuzziest 1** of, like, or covered with fuzz **2** unclear, blurred, or distorted: *just a few fuzzy pictures of the creature exist* **3** (of hair) tightly curled ›**fuzzily** *adv* ›**fuzziness** *n*

> **fuzzy** *adj* **1** = frizzy, fluffy, woolly, downy **2** = indistinct, blurred, vague, distorted, unclear, bleary, out of focus, ill-defined; ≠ distinct

FYI for your information

g

Gg

g 1 gallon(s) **2** gram(s) **3** acceleration due to gravity

gab *informal* ▸ *vb* **gabbing, gabbed 1** to talk a lot, esp. about unimportant things ▸ *n* **2** idle talk **3 gift of the gab** the ability to talk easily and persuasively

gabardine *or* **gaberdine** *n* **1** a strong twill cloth used esp. for raincoats **2** a coat made of this cloth

gabble *vb* **-bling, -bled 1** to speak rapidly and indistinctly: *the interviewee started to gabble furiously* ▸ *n* **2** rapid and indistinct speech

gable *n* the triangular upper part of a wall between the sloping ends of a ridged roof ›**gabled** *adj*

gad *vb* **gadding, gadded** (foll. by *about* or *around*) to go about in search of pleasure

gadabout *n informal* a person who restlessly seeks amusement

gadfly *n, pl* **-flies 1** a large fly that bites livestock **2** a constantly irritating person

gadget *n* a small mechanical device or appliance ›**gadgetry** *n*

> **gadget** *n* = device, thing, appliance, machine, tool, implement, invention, instrument

Gael (**gayl**) *n* a Gaelic-speaker of Scotland, Ireland, or the Isle of Man ›**Gaeldom** *n*

Gaelic (**gal**-lik, **gay**-lik) *n* **1** any of the closely related Celtic languages of Scotland, Ireland, or the Isle of Man ▸ *adj* **2** of the Celtic people of Scotland, Ireland, or the Isle of Man, or their language

gaff¹ *n* **1** *angling* a pole with a hook attached for landing large fish **2** *naut* a spar hoisted to support a fore-and-aft sail

gaff² *n* **blow the gaff** *Brit slang* to give away a secret

gaffe *n* something said or done that is socially upsetting or incorrect

gaffer *n* **1** *informal, chiefly Brit* a boss or foreman **2** an old man: often used affectionately **3** *informal* the senior electrician on a television or film set

gag¹ *vb* **gagging, gagged 1** to choke as if about to vomit or as if struggling for breath **2** to stop up (a person's mouth), usually with a piece of cloth, to prevent them from speaking or crying out **3** to deprive of free speech ▸ *n* **4** something, usually a piece of cloth, stuffed into or tied across the mouth **5** any restraint on free speech **6** a device for keeping the jaws apart: *a dentist's gag*

gag vb 1 = retch, heave 3 = suppress, silence, muffle, curb, stifle, muzzle, quieten ▸ n 4 = muzzle, tie, restraint

gag² informal ▸ n 1 a joke, usually one told by a professional comedian ▸ vb **gagging, gagged** 2 to tell jokes

gag n = joke, crack (slang), funny (informal), quip, pun, jest, wisecrack (informal), witticism

gaga (gah-gah) adj informal 1 confused and having some memory loss, esp. as a result of old age 2 foolishly doting: she's gaga over him

gaggle n 1 informal a group of people gathered together 2 a flock of geese

gaiety n, pl **-ties** 1 a state of lively good spirits 2 festivity; merrymaking

gaily adv 1 in a lively manner; cheerfully 2 with bright colours

gain vb 1 to acquire (something desirable) 2 to increase, improve, or advance: wholesale prices gained 5.6 percent 3 to get to; reach: gaining the top of the hill 4 (of a watch or clock) to become or be too fast 5 **gain on** to get nearer to or catch up on ▸ n 6 something won or acquired; profit; advantage: a clear gain would result 7 an increase in size or amount 8 electronics the ratio of the output signal of an amplifier to the input signal, usually measured in decibels

gain vb 1 = acquire, get, receive, pick up, secure, collect, gather, obtain 5 **gain on something or someone** = get nearer to, close in on, approach, catch up with, narrow the gap on ▸ n 6 = profit, return, benefit, advantage, yield, dividend; ≠ loss

gainful adj useful or profitable > **gainfully** adv

gainsay vb **-saying, -said** archaic or literary to deny or contradict

gait n 1 manner of walking 2 (of horses and dogs) the pattern of footsteps at a particular speed, such as a trot

gaiters pl n cloth or leather coverings for the legs or ankles

gala (gah-la) n 1 a special social occasion, esp. a special performance 2 chiefly Brit a sporting occasion with competitions in several events: next week's sports gala

gala n 1 = festival, fête, celebration, carnival, festivity, pageant, jamboree

galactic adj of the Galaxy or other galaxies

galaxy n, pl **-axies** 1 a star system held together by gravitational attraction 2 a collection of brilliant people or things: a galaxy of legal talent

gale n 1 a strong wind, specifically one of force 8 on the Beaufort scale 2 **gales** a loud outburst: gales of laughter

gale n 1 = storm, hurricane, tornado, cyclone, blast, typhoon, tempest (literary), squall 2 = outburst, scream, roar, fit, storm, shout, burst, explosion

gall¹ (gawl) n 1 informal bold impudence: she was stunned I had the gall to ask 2 a feeling of great bitterness 3 physiol obsolete same as **bile**

gall² (gawl) vb 1 to annoy or irritate 2 to make the skin sore by rubbing ▸ n 3 something that causes annoyance 4 a sore on the skin caused by rubbing

gall vb 1 = annoy, provoke, irritate, trouble, disturb, madden, exasperate, vex

gall³ (gawl) n an abnormal outgrowth on a tree or plant caused by parasites

gallant adj 1 persistent and courageous in the face of overwhelming odds: a gallant fight 2 (of a man) making a show of polite attentiveness to women 3 having a reputation for bravery: Police Medal for gallant and meritorious services ▸ n 4 history a young man who tried to impress women with his fashionable clothes or daring acts > **gallantly** adv

gallantry n 1 showy, attentive treatment of women 2 great bravery in war or danger

gall bladder n a muscular sac, attached to the liver, that stores bile

galleon n a large three-masted sailing ship used from the 15th to the 18th centuries

gallery n, pl **-leries** 1 a room or building for displaying works of art 2 a balcony running along or around the inside wall of a church, hall, or other building 3 theatre **A** an upper floor that projects from the rear and contains the cheapest seats **B** the audience seated there 4 an underground passage in a mine or cave 5 a group of spectators, for instance at a golf match 6 **play to the gallery** to try to gain approval by appealing to popular taste

galley n 1 the kitchen of a ship, boat, or aircraft 2 a ship propelled by oars or sails, used in ancient or medieval times

galley slave n 1 a criminal or slave forced to row in a galley 2 informal a drudge

Gallic adj 1 French 2 of ancient Gaul or the Gauls

gallium n chem a silvery metallic element used in high-temperature thermometers and low-melting alloys. Symbol: **Ga**

gallivant vb to go about in search of pleasure

gallon n 1 Brit a unit of liquid measure equal to 4.55 litres 2 US a unit of liquid measure equal to 3.79 litres

gallop vb 1 (of a horse) to run fast with a two-beat stride in which all four legs are off the ground at once 2 to ride (a horse) at a gallop 3 to move or progress rapidly ▸ n 4 the fast two-beat gait of horses 5 an instance of galloping

gallop vb 1 = run, race, career, speed, bolt 3 = dash, run, race, career, speed, rush, sprint

gallows n, pl **-lowses** or **-lows** 1 a wooden structure consisting of two upright posts with a crossbeam, used for hanging criminals 2 **the gallows** execution by hanging

gallstone *n* a small hard mass formed in the gall bladder or its ducts

Gallup Poll *n* a sampling of the views of a representative cross section of the population, usually used to forecast voting

galore *adj* in abundance: *there were bargains galore*

galoshes *pl n Brit, Austral & NZ* a pair of waterproof overshoes

galumph *vb Brit, Austral & NZ informal* to leap or move about clumsily or joyfully

galvanic *adj* 1 of or producing an electric current by chemical means, such as in a battery 2 *informal* stimulating, startling, or energetic

galvanize *or* **-nise** *vb* **-nizing, -nized** *or* **-nising, -nised** 1 to stimulate into action 2 to cover (metal) with a protective zinc coating 3 to stimulate by an electric current › **galvanization** *or* **-nisation** *n*

gambit *n* 1 an opening remark or action intended to gain an advantage 2 *chess* an opening move in which a piece, usually a pawn, is sacrificed to gain an advantageous position

gamble *vb* **-bling, -bled** 1 to play games of chance to win money or prizes 2 to risk or bet (something) on the outcome of an event or sport 3 **gamble away** to lose by gambling 4 **gamble on** to act with the expectation of: *she has gambled on proving everyone wrong* ▸ *n* 5 a risky act or venture 6 a bet or wager › **gambler** *n* › **gambling** *n*

> **gamble** *vb* 1 = bet, play, game, speculate, punt (*chiefly Brit*), wager, have a flutter (*informal*) 2 = risk, chance, hazard, wager 4 = take a chance, speculate, stick your neck out (*informal*) ▸ *n* 5 = risk, chance, venture, lottery, speculation, uncertainty, leap in the dark; ≠ certainty 6 = bet, flutter (*informal*), punt (*chiefly Brit*), wager

gamboge (gam-**boje**) *n* a gum resin obtained from a tropical Asian tree, used as a yellow pigment and as a purgative

gambol *vb* **-bolling, -bolled** *or US* **-boling, -boled** 1 to jump about playfully; frolic ▸ *n* 2 a playful jumping about; frolicking

game¹ *n* 1 an amusement for children 2 a competitive activity with rules 3 a single period of play in such an activity 4 (in some sports) the score needed to win 5 a single contest in a series; match 6 style or ability in playing a game: *in the second set his overall game improved markedly* 7 an activity that seems to operate according to unwritten rules: *the political game of power* 8 an activity undertaken in a spirit of playfulness: *people who regard life as a game* 9 wild animals, birds, or fish, hunted for sport or food 10 the flesh of such animals, used as food 11 an object of pursuit: *fair game* 12 *informal* a trick or scheme: *what's his game?* 13 **games** an event consisting of various sporting contests, usually in athletics: *Commonwealth Games* 14 **give the game away** to reveal one's intentions or a secret

15 **on the game** *slang* working as a prostitute 16 **play the game** to behave fairly 17 **the game is up** the scheme or trick has been found out and so cannot succeed ▸ *adj* 18 *informal* full of fighting spirit; plucky 19 *informal* prepared or willing: *I'm always game for a new sensation* ▸ *vb* **gaming, gamed** 20 to play games of chance for money; gamble 21 to play computer games › **gamely** *adv* › **gameness** *n*

> **game** *n* 1, 8 = amusement, joke, entertainment, diversion 5 = match, meeting, event, competition, tournament, clash, contest, head-to-head 9 = wild animals or birds, prey, quarry 12 = scheme, plan, design, trick, plot, tactic, manoeuvre, ploy, fastie (*Austral slang*) ▸ *adj* 18 = brave, courageous, spirited, daring, persistent, gritty, feisty (*informal*), intrepid, plucky, (as) game as Ned Kelly (*Austral slang*); ≠ cowardly 19 = willing, prepared, ready, keen, eager, interested, desirous

game² *adj Brit, Austral & NZ* lame: *he had a game leg*

gamekeeper *n Brit* a person employed to take care of game on an estate

gamer *n* a person who plays computer games

games console *n* an electronic device, linked to a television set, used for playing video games

gamesmanship *n informal* the art of winning by cunning practices without actually cheating

gamete (gam-**eet**) *n* a cell that can fuse with another in reproduction › **gametic** *or* **gametal** *adj*

gamine (gam-**een**) *n* a slim and boyish girl or young woman

gaming *n* gambling

gamma *n* the third letter in the Greek alphabet (Γ, γ)

gammon *n* 1 cured or smoked ham 2 the hindquarter of a side of bacon

gammy *adj* **-mier, -miest** *Brit & NZ slang* (of the leg) lame

gamut *n* 1 entire range or scale: *a rich gamut of facial expressions* 2 *music* A a scale B the whole range of notes

gander *n* 1 a male goose 2 *informal* a quick look: *have a gander*

gang *n* 1 a group of people who go around together, often to commit crime 2 an organized group of manual workers ▸ *vb* 3 to become or act as a gang

> **gang** *n* 1 = group, crowd, pack, company, band, bunch, mob

gangland *n* the criminal underworld

gangling *or* **gangly** *adj* lanky and awkward in movement

ganglion *n, pl* **-glia** *or* **-glions** a collection of nerve cells outside the brain and spinal cord › **ganglionic** *adj*

gangplank *n naut* a portable bridge for boarding and leaving a ship

gangrene n decay of body tissue caused by the blood supply being interrupted by disease or injury > **gangrenous** adj

gangsta rap n a style of rap music, often with lyrics referring to crime or violence

gangster n a member of an organized gang of criminals > **gangsterism** n

> **gangster** n = hoodlum (chiefly US), crook (informal), bandit, hood (US slang), robber, mobster (US slang), racketeer, ruffian, tsotsi (S African)

gangway n 1 Brit an aisle between rows of seats 2 same as **gangplank** 3 an opening in a ship's side to take a gangplank

gannet n 1 a heavily built white sea bird 2 Brit slang a greedy person

gantry n, pl **-tries** a large metal framework used to support something, such as a travelling crane, or to position a rocket on its launch pad

gaol (jayl) n, vb Brit & Austral same as **jail** > **gaoler** n

gap n 1 a break or opening in something 2 an interruption or interval 3 a difference in ideas or viewpoint: the generation gap > **gappy** adj

> **gap** n 1 = opening, space, hole, break, crack, slot, aperture, cleft 2 = interval, pause, interruption, respite, lull, interlude, breathing space, hiatus 3 = difference, gulf, contrast, disagreement, discrepancy, inconsistency, disparity, divergence

gape vb **gaping, gaped 1** to stare in wonder with the mouth open 2 to open the mouth wide, as in yawning 3 to be or become wide open: a hole gaped in the roof > **gaping** adj

> **gape** vb 1 = stare, wonder, goggle, gawp (Brit slang), gawk 3 = open, split, crack, yawn

garage n 1 a building used to keep cars 2 a place where cars are repaired and petrol is sold ▸ vb **-aging, -aged 3** to put or keep a car in a garage

garb n 1 clothes, usually the distinctive dress of an occupation or group: modern military garb ▸ vb 2 to clothe

garbage n 1 US, Austral & NZ household waste 2 worthless rubbish or nonsense

garbled adj (of a story, message, etc.) jumbled and confused

garden n 1 an area of land usually next to a house, for growing flowers, fruit, or vegetables. Related adjective: **horticultural** 2 Also: **gardens** a cultivated area of land open to the public: Kensington Gardens 3 **lead someone up the garden path** informal to mislead or deceive someone ▸ vb 4 to work in or take care of a garden > **gardener** n > **gardening** n

garden centre n a place where plants and gardening tools and equipment are sold

gardenia (gar-deen-ya) n 1 a large fragrant waxy white flower 2 the evergreen shrub on which it grows

garfish n 1 a freshwater fish with a long body and very long toothed jaws 2 a sea fish with similar characteristics

gargantuan adj huge or enormous

gargle vb **-gling, -gled 1** to rinse the mouth and throat with (a liquid) by slowly breathing out through the liquid ▸ n 2 the liquid used for gargling 3 the act or sound of gargling

gargoyle n (on ancient buildings) a waterspout below the roof, carved in the form of a grotesque face or figure

garish adj crudely bright or colourful > **garishly** adv > **garishness** n

garland n 1 a wreath of flowers and leaves worn round the head or neck or hung up ▸ vb 2 to decorate with a garland or garlands

> **garland** n = wreath, band, bays, crown, honours, laurels, festoon, chaplet ▸ vb = adorn, crown, deck, festoon, wreathe

garlic n the bulb of a plant of the onion family, with a strong taste and smell, made up of small segments which are used in cooking > **garlicky** adj

garment n an article of clothing

> **garment** n = clothes, dress, clothing, gear (slang), uniform, outfit, costume, apparel

garner vb to collect or gather: the financial rewards garnered by his book

garnet n a red semiprecious gemstone

garnish vb 1 to decorate (food) with something to add to its appearance or flavour ▸ n 2 a decoration for food

> **garnish** vb = decorate, adorn, ornament, embellish, trim; ≠ strip ▸ n = decoration, embellishment, adornment, ornamentation, trimming

garret n an attic in a house

garrison n 1 soldiers who guard a base or fort 2 the place itself ▸ vb 3 to station (soldiers) in (a fort or base)

> **garrison** n 1 = troops, group, unit, section, command, armed force, detachment 2 = fort, fortress, camp, base, post, station, stronghold, fortification, fortified pa (NZ) ▸ vb = station, position, post, install, assign, put on duty

garrotte or **garotte** n 1 a Spanish method of execution by strangling 2 a cord, wire, or iron collar, used to strangle someone ▸ vb **-rotting, -rotted 3** to execute with a garrotte

garrulous adj constantly chattering; talkative > **garrulousness** n

garter n 1 a band, usually of elastic, worn round the leg to hold up a sock or stocking 2 US & Canad a suspender

gas n, pl **gases** or **gasses 1** an airlike substance that is neither liquid nor solid at room temperature and atmospheric pressure 2 a fossil fuel in the form of a gas, used as a source of heat **3** an anaesthetic in the form of a gas **4** *mining* firedamp or the explosive mixture of firedamp and air **5** *US, Canad, Austral & NZ* petrol **6** a poisonous gas used in war **7** *informal* idle talk or boasting **8** *slang* an entertaining person or thing: *Monterey was a gas for musicians and fans alike* **9** *US informal* gas generated in the alimentary canal ▸ *vb* **gases** or **gasses**, **gassing**, **gassed** **10** to subject to gas fumes so as to make unconscious or to suffocate **11** *informal* to talk a lot; chatter

> **gas** *n* **1** = fumes, vapour **5** = petrol, gasoline (*US, Canad, NZ*)

gasbag *n informal* a person who talks too much

gas chamber *n* an airtight room which is filled with poison gas to kill people

gaseous (**gass**-ee-uss, **gay**-see-uss) *adj* of or like a gas

gash *n* **1** a long deep cut ▸ *vb* **2** to make a long deep cut in

gasholder *n* a large tank for storing gas before distributing it to users

gasket *n* a piece of paper, rubber, or metal sandwiched between the faces of a metal joint to provide a seal

gas mask *n* a mask fitted with a chemical filter to protect the wearer from breathing in harmful gases

gasoline or **gasolene** *n US & Canad* petrol

gasp *vb* **1** to draw in the breath sharply or with difficulty **2** to utter breathlessly ▸ *n* **3** a short convulsive intake of breath

> **gasp** *vb* **1** = pant, blow, puff, choke, gulp, catch your breath ▸ *n* = pant, puff, gulp, sharp intake of breath

gassy *adj* **-sier, -siest** filled with, containing, or like gas > **gassiness** *n*

gastric *adj* of the stomach

gastritis *n* inflammation of the lining of the stomach, causing vomiting or gastric ulcers

gastroenteritis *n* inflammation of the stomach and intestine, causing vomiting and diarrhoea

gastronomy *n* the art of good eating > **gastronomic** *adj*

gastropod *n* a mollusc, such as a snail or whelk, that has a single flat muscular foot, eyes on stalks, and usually a spiral shell

gastropub *n* a pub that serves high-quality food

gate *n* **1** a movable barrier, usually hinged, for closing an opening in a wall or fence **2** **A** the number of people admitted to a sporting event or entertainment **B** the total entrance money received from them **3** an exit at an airport by which passengers get to an aircraft **4** *electronics* a circuit with one or more input terminals and one output terminal, the output being determined by the combination of input signals **5** a slotted metal frame that controls the positions of the gear lever in a motor vehicle

> **gate** *n* **1** = barrier, opening, door, entrance, exit, gateway, portal (*literary*)

gateau (**gat**-toe) *n, pl* **-teaux** (-toes) a large rich layered cake

gate-crash *vb informal* to gain entry to (a party) without invitation > **gate-crasher** *n*

gatehouse *n* a building at or above a gateway

gateway *n* **1** an entrance that may be closed by a gate **2** a means of entry or access: *his only gateway to the outside world* **3** *computers* hardware and software that connect incompatible computer networks, allowing them to communicate

gather *vb* **1** to come or bring together **2** to increase gradually in (pace, speed, or momentum) **3** to prepare oneself for a task or challenge by collecting one's thoughts, strength, or courage **4** to learn from information given; conclude: *this is pretty important, I gather* **5** to draw (fabric) into small folds or tucks **6** to pick or harvest (crops) ▸ *n* **7 gathers** small folds or tucks in fabric

> **gather** *vb* **1** = congregate, assemble, collect, meet, mass, come together, muster, converge; ≠ scatter **2** = build up, rise, increase, grow, expand, swell, intensify, heighten **4** = understand, believe, hear, learn, assume, conclude, presume, infer **5** = fold, tuck, pleat **6** = pick, harvest, pluck, reap, garner, glean

gathering *n* a group of people, usually meeting for some particular purpose: *the Braemar Highland Gathering*

> **gathering** *n* = assembly, group, crowd, meeting, conference, company, congress, mass, hui (*NZ*), runanga (*NZ*)

gatvol (**hhut**-fol) *adj S African vulgar slang* annoyed; fed up

gauche (**gohsh**) *adj* socially awkward

gaucho (**gow**-choh) *n, pl* **-chos** a cowboy of the South American pampas

gaudy *adj* **gaudier, gaudiest** vulgarly bright or colourful > **gaudily** *adv* > **gaudiness** *n*

gauge (**gayj**) *vb* **1** to estimate or judge (people's feelings or reactions) **2** to measure using a gauge ▸ *n* **3** an instrument for measuring quantities: *a petrol gauge* **4** a scale or standard of measurement **5** a standard for estimating people's feelings or reactions: *a gauge of public opinion* **6** the diameter of the barrel of a gun **7** the distance between the rails of a railway track

> **gauge** *vb* **1** = judge, estimate, guess, assess, evaluate, rate, appraise, reckon **2** = measure, calculate, evaluate, value, determine, count, weigh, compute ▸ *n* **3** = meter, dial, measuring instrument

gaunt *adj* **1** bony and emaciated in appearance **2** (of a place) bleak or desolate: *the gaunt disused flour mill* > **gauntness** *n*

gauntlet[1] *n* **1** a long heavy protective glove **2** a medieval armoured glove **3 take up the gauntlet** to accept a challenge **4 throw down the gauntlet** to offer a challenge

gauntlet[2] *n* **run the gauntlet** to be exposed to criticism or harsh treatment

gauze *n* a transparent, loosely woven cloth, often used for surgical dressings ▷ **gauzy** *adj*

gave *vb* the past tense of **give**

gavel (gav-vl) *n* a small hammer used by a judge, auctioneer, or chair of a meeting to call for order or attention

gavotte *n* **1** an old formal dance in quadruple time **2** music for this dance

gawk *vb* **1** to stare stupidly ▸ *n* **2** a clumsy stupid person

gawky *adj* **gawkier**, **gawkiest** clumsy and awkward

gawp *vb slang* to stare stupidly ▷ **gawper** *n*

gay *adj* **1** homosexual **2** *old-fashioned* carefree and merry: *with gay abandon* **3** *old-fashioned* bright and cheerful: *smartly dressed in gay colours* ▸ *n* **4** a homosexual person

> **gay** *adj* **1** = homosexual, lesbian **2** = cheerful, lively, sparkling, merry, upbeat (*informal*), buoyant, cheery, carefree; ≠ sad **3** = colourful, rich, bright, brilliant, vivid, flamboyant, flashy, showy; ≠ drab ▸ *n* = homosexual, lesbian; ≠ heterosexual

gayness *n* homosexuality

gaze *vb* **gazing**, **gazed 1** to look long and steadily at someone or something ▸ *n* **2** a long steady look

> **gaze** *vb* = stare, look, view, watch, regard, gape ▸ *n* = stare, look, fixed look

gazebo (gaz-zee-boh) *n, pl* **-bos** a summerhouse or pavilion with a good view

gazelle *n* a small graceful fawn-coloured antelope of Africa and Asia

gazette *n* an official newspaper that gives lists of announcements, for instance in legal or military affairs

> **gazette** *n* = newspaper, paper, journal, periodical, news-sheet

gazetteer *n* a book or section of a book that lists and describes places

gazump *vb Brit & Austral informal* to raise the price of a house after agreeing a price verbally with an intending buyer

GB 1 Great Britain **2** Also: **Gb** gigabyte

GBH (in Britain and South Africa) grievous bodily harm

GCE 1 (formerly in Britain) General Certificate of Education **2** *informal* a pass in a GCE examination

GCSE 1 (in Britain) General Certificate of Secondary Education; an examination in specified subjects which replaced the GCE O level and CSE **2** *informal* a pass in a GCSE examination

g'day *interj Austral & NZ* a variant of **gidday**

GDP gross domestic product

gear *n* **1** a set of toothed wheels that engages with another or with a rack in order to change the speed or direction of transmitted motion **2** a mechanism for transmitting motion by gears **3** the setting of a gear to suit engine speed or direction: *a higher gear; reverse gear* **4** clothing or personal belongings **5** equipment for a particular task: *police in riot gear* **6 in** or **out of gear** with the gear mechanism engaged or disengaged ▸ *vb* **7** to prepare or organize for something: *to gear for war* ▸ See also **gear up**

> **gear** *n* **1, 2** = mechanism, works, machinery, cogs, cogwheels, gearwheels **4** = clothing, wear, dress, clothes, outfit, costume, garments, togs **5** = equipment, supplies, tackle, tools, instruments, apparatus, paraphernalia, accoutrements ▸ *vb* = equip, fit, adjust, adapt

gearbox *n* the metal casing enclosing a set of gears in a motor vehicle

gear up *vb* to prepare for an activity: *to gear up for a massive relief operation*

gecko *n, pl* **geckos** a small tropical lizard

geebung (gee-bung) *n* **1** an Australian tree or shrub with an edible but tasteless fruit **2** the fruit of this tree

geek *n informal* **1** a person who is knowledgeable and enthusiastic about a specific subject **2** a boring and unattractive person ▷ **geeky** *adj*

geelbek (heel-bek) *n S African* an edible marine fish with yellow jaws

geese *n* the plural of **goose**

geezer *n Brit, Austral & NZ informal* a man

Geiger counter (guy-ger) or **Geiger-Müller counter** *n* an instrument for detecting and measuring radiation

geisha (gay-sha) *n* a professional female companion for men in Japan, trained in music, dancing, and conversation

gel (jell) *n* **1** a thick jelly-like substance, esp. one used to keep a hairstyle in shape ▸ *vb* **gelling**, **gelled 2** to become a gel **3** same as **jell 4** to apply gel to (one's hair)

gelatine (jell-a-teen) or **gelatin** *n* a clear water-soluble protein made by boiling animal hides and bones, used in cooking, in glue, and in photographic film processes

gelatinous (jill-at-in-uss) *adj* with a thick, semiliquid consistency

geld *vb* **gelding**, **gelded** or **gelt** to castrate (a horse or other animal)

gelding *n* a castrated male horse

gelignite *n* a type of dynamite used for blasting

gem *n* **1** a precious stone used for decoration. Related adjective: **lapidary 2** a person or thing regarded as precious or special: *a perfect gem of a hotel*

gem n 1 = precious stone, jewel, stone
2 = treasure, prize, jewel, pearl, masterpiece,
humdinger (*slang*), taonga (*NZ*)

gemfish n an Australian food fish with a
delicate flavour

gen n Brit, Austral & NZ informal information: *I want
to get as much gen as I can about the American market.*
See also **gen up on**

gender n 1 the state of being male or female
with reference to socially and culturally defined
characteristics of masculinity or femininity
2 the classification of nouns in certain
languages as masculine, feminine, or neuter

gender identity n a person's understanding
of having a particular gender, which may or
may not correspond with the gender assigned to
them at birth

gender-neutral adj 1 suitable for both female
and male genders: *gender-neutral toys* 2 not
referring to one gender only: *gender-neutral
language*

gene (jean) n a unit composed of DNA forming
part of a chromosome, by which inherited
characteristics are transmitted from parent to
offspring

genealogy (jean-ee-**al**-a-jee) n 1 the direct
descent of an individual or group from an
ancestor 2 pl **-gies** a chart showing the descent
of an individual or group > **genealogical** adj
> **genealogist** n

genera (**jen**-er-a) n a plural of **genus**

general adj 1 common or widespread: *general
goodwill* 2 of, affecting, or including all or most
of the members of a group 3 not specialized or
specializing: *a general hospital* 4 including various
or miscellaneous items: *general knowledge* 5 not
definite; vague: *the examples used will give a general
idea* 6 highest in authority or rank: *the club's
general manager* ▸ n 7 a very senior military officer
8 **in general** generally; mostly or usually

general adj 1, 4 = widespread, accepted,
popular, public, common, broad, extensive,
universal; ≠ individual 2 = universal, overall,
widespread, collective, across-the-board;
≠ exceptional 5 = vague, loose, blanket,
sweeping, unclear, approximate, woolly,
indefinite; ≠ specific

general election n an election in which
representatives are chosen in all constituencies
of a state

generality n 1 pl **-ties** a general principle or
observation: *speaking in generalities* 2 old-fashioned
the majority: *the generality of mankind*

generalization or **-lisation** n a principle or
statement based on specific instances but
applied generally: *the argument sinks to
generalizations and name-calling*

generalize or **-lise** vb **-lizing, -lized** or **-lising,
-lised** 1 to form general principles or
conclusions from specific instances 2 to speak

in generalities 3 to make widely used or known:
generalized violence

generally adv 1 usually; as a rule: *these protests
have generally been peaceful* 2 commonly or widely:
it's generally agreed he has performed well 3 not
specifically; broadly: *what are your thoughts generally
about the war?*

generally adv 1 = usually, commonly,
typically, normally, on the whole, by and large,
ordinarily, as a rule; ≠ occasionally
2 = commonly, widely, publicly, universally,
extensively, popularly, conventionally,
customarily; ≠ individually

general practitioner n a doctor who does not
specialize but has a general medical practice in
which he or she treats all illnesses

generate vb **-rating, -rated** to produce or
create

generate vb = produce, create, make, cause,
give rise to, engender; ≠ end

generation n 1 all the people of approximately
the same age: *the younger generation* 2 a successive
stage in descent of people or animals: *passed on
from generation to generation* 3 the average time
between two generations of a species, about 35
years for humans: *an alliance which has lasted a
generation* 4 a specified stage of development: *the
next generation of fighter aircraft* 5 production, esp.
of electricity or heat

generation n 1 = age group, peer group
2, 3 = age, period, era, time, lifetime, span,
epoch

generative adj capable of producing or
originating something

generator n a device for converting
mechanical energy into electrical energy

generic (jin-**ner**-ik) adj of a whole class, or
group, or genus > **generically** adv

generic adj = collective, general, common,
wide, comprehensive, universal, blanket,
inclusive; ≠ specific

generous adj 1 ready to give freely; unselfish
2 free from pettiness in character and mind
3 large or plentiful: *a generous donation*
> **generously** adv > **generosity** n

generous adj 1 = liberal, lavish, charitable,
hospitable, bountiful, open-handed,
unstinting, beneficent; ≠ mean
2 = magnanimous, kind, noble, good,
high-minded, unselfish, big-hearted
3 = plentiful, lavish, ample, abundant, full,
rich, liberal, copious; ≠ meagre

genesis (**jen**-iss-iss) n, pl **-ses** (-seez) the
beginning or origin of anything

genesis n = beginning, origin, start, birth,
creation, formation, inception; ≠ end

g

gene therapy n genetics the replacement or alteration of defective genes in order to prevent the occurrence of inherited diseases

genetic (jin-**net**-tik) adj of genetics, genes, or the origin of something > **genetically** adv

genetic engineering n alteration of the genetic structure of an organism in order to produce more desirable traits

genetic fingerprinting n the use of a person's unique pattern of DNA, which can be obtained from blood, saliva, or tissue, as a means of identification > **genetic fingerprint** n

genetics n the study of heredity and variation in organisms > **geneticist** n

genial (**jean**-ee-al) adj cheerful, easy-going, and friendly > **geniality** n > **genially** adv

genie (**jean**-ee) n (in fairy tales) a servant who appears by magic and fulfils a person's wishes

genital adj of the sexual organs or reproduction

genitals or **genitalia** (jen-it-**ail**-ya) pl n the external sexual organs

genitive n grammar a grammatical case in some languages used to indicate a relation of ownership or association

genius (**jean**-yuss) n, pl -**uses** **1** a person with exceptional ability in a particular subject or activity **2** such ability **3** a person considered as exerting influence of a certain sort: the evil genius behind the drug-smuggling empire

genius n **1** = master, expert, mastermind, maestro, virtuoso, whiz (informal), hotshot (informal), brainbox, fundi (S African) **2** = brilliance, ability, talent, capacity, gift, bent, excellence, flair

genocide (**jen**-no-side) n the deliberate killing of a people or nation > **genocidal** adj

genome n **1** the full complement of genetic material within an organism **2** all the genes comprising a haploid set of chromosomes

genre (**zhahn**-ra) n **1** a kind or type of literary, musical, or artistic work: the mystery and supernatural genres **2** a kind of painting depicting incidents from everyday life

genre n **1** = type, group, order, sort, kind, class, style, species

gent n Brit, Austral & NZ informal short for **gentleman**

genteel adj **1** overly concerned with being polite **2** respectable, polite, and well-bred > **genteelly** adv

gentian (**jen**-shun) n a mountain plant with blue or purple flowers

Gentile n **1** a person who is not a Jew ▶ adj **2** not Jewish

gentle adj **1** kind and calm in character **2** temperate or moderate: gentle autumn rain **3** soft; not sharp or harsh: gentle curves > **gentleness** n > **gently** adv

gentle adj **1, 3** = kind, kindly, tender, mild, humane, compassionate, meek, placid; ≠ unkind **2** = moderate, light, soft, slight, mild, soothing; ≠ violent

gentleman n, pl -**men** **1** a cultured, courteous, and well-bred man **2** a man who comes from a family of high social position **3** a polite name for a man > **gentlemanly** adj

gentrification n a process by which the character of a traditionally working-class area is made fashionable by middle-class people > **gentrify** vb

gentry n Brit old-fashioned people just below the nobility in social rank

gents n Brit & Austral informal a men's public toilet

genuflect vb to bend the knee as a sign of reverence or deference, esp. in church > **genuflection** n

genuine adj **1** real and exactly what it appears to be: a genuine antique **2** sincerely felt: genuine concern **3** (of a person) honest and without pretence > **genuinely** adv > **genuineness** n

genuine adj **1** = authentic, real, actual, true, valid, legitimate, veritable, bona fide, dinkum (Austral, NZ informal); ≠ counterfeit **2** = heartfelt, sincere, honest, earnest, real, true, frank, unaffected; ≠ affected **3** = sincere, honest, frank, candid, dinkum (Austral, NZ informal), guileless; ≠ hypocritical

gen up on vb genning, genned Brit & Austral informal to become, or make someone else, fully informed about

genus (**jean**-uss) n, pl genera or genuses **1** biol one of the groups into which a family is divided, containing one or more species **2** a class or group

geocentric adj **1** having the earth as a centre **2** measured as from the centre of the earth

geography n **1** the study of the earth's surface, including physical features, climate, and population **2** the physical features of a region > **geographer** n > **geographical** or **geographic** adj > **geographically** adv

geology n **1** the study of the origin, structure, and composition of the earth **2** the geological features of an area > **geological** adj > **geologically** adv > **geologist** n

geometric or **geometrical** adj **1** of geometry **2** consisting of shapes used in geometry, such as circles, triangles, and straight lines: geometric design > **geometrically** adv

geometry n the branch of mathematics concerned with points, lines, curves, and surfaces > **geometrician** n

Geordie Brit ▶ n **1** a person from Tyneside **2** the Tyneside dialect ▶ adj **3** of Tyneside: a Geordie accent

Georgian adj **1** of or in the reigns of any of the kings of Great Britain and Ireland called George **2** denoting a style of architecture or furniture prevalent in Britain in the 18th century: *an elegant Georgian terrace in Edinburgh*

geostationary *adj* (of a satellite) orbiting so as to remain over the same point on the earth's surface

geothermal *adj* of or using the heat in the earth's interior

geranium *n* a cultivated plant with scarlet, pink, or white flowers

gerbil (jur-bill) *n* a small rodent with long back legs, often kept as a pet

geriatric *adj* 1 of geriatrics or old people ▸ *n* 2 *old-fashioned, offensive* an older person

geriatrics *n* the branch of medicine concerned with illnesses affecting old people

germ *n* 1 a tiny living thing, esp. one that causes disease: *a diphtheria germ* 2 the beginning from which something may develop: *the germ of a book*

> **germ** *n* 1 = microbe, virus, bug (*informal*), bacterium, bacillus, microorganism 2 = beginning, root, seed, origin, spark, embryo, rudiment

German *adj* 1 of Germany ▸ *n* 2 a person from Germany 3 the official language of Germany, Austria, and parts of Switzerland

germane *adj* relevant: *the studies provided some evidence germane to these questions*

Germanic *n* 1 the ancient language from which English, German, and the Scandinavian languages developed ▸ *adj* 2 of this ancient language or the languages that developed from it 3 characteristic of German people or things: *Germanic-looking individuals*

germanium *n chem* a brittle grey metalloid element that is a semiconductor and is used in transistors. Symbol: **Ge**

German measles *n* same as **rubella**

German shepherd dog *n* same as **Alsatian**

germinal *adj* 1 of or in the earliest stage of development: *the germinal phases of the case* 2 of germ cells

germinate *vb* -nating, -nated to grow or cause to grow > **germination** *n*

gerrymandering *n* the practice of dividing the constituencies of a voting area so as to give one party an unfair advantage

gerund (jer-rund) *n* a noun formed from a verb, ending in *-ing*, denoting an action or state, for example *running*

Gestapo *n* the secret state police of Nazi Germany

gestation *n* 1 the process of carrying and developing babies in the womb during pregnancy, or the time during which this process takes place 2 the process of developing a plan or idea in the mind

gesticulate *vb* -lating, -lated to make expressive movements with the hands and arms, usually while talking > **gesticulation** *n*

gesture *n* 1 a movement of the hands, head, or body to express or emphasize an idea or emotion 2 something said or done to indicate intention, or as a formality: *a gesture of goodwill* ▸ *vb* -turing, -tured 3 to make expressive movements with the hands and arms

> **gesture** *n* 1 = sign, action, signal, motion, indication, gesticulation ▸ *vb* = signal, sign, wave, indicate, motion, beckon, gesticulate

get *vb* **getting, got** 1 to come into possession of 2 to bring or fetch 3 to catch (an illness) 4 to become: *they get frustrated and angry* 5 to cause to be done or to happen: *he got a wart removed; to get steamed up* 6 to hear or understand: *did you get that joke?* 7 to reach (a place or point): *we could not get to the airport in time* 8 to catch (a bus or train) 9 to persuade: *she was trying to get him to give secrets away* 10 *informal* to annoy: *you know what really gets me?* 11 *informal* to baffle: *now you've got me* 12 *informal* to hit: *a bit of grenade got me on the left hip* 13 *informal* to be revenged on 14 *informal* to start: *we got talking about it; it got me thinking* ▸ See also **get across** *etc.*

> **get** *vb* 1 = obtain, receive, gain, acquire, win, land (*informal*), net, pick up 2 = fetch, bring, collect 3 = catch, develop, contract, succumb to, fall victim to, go down with, come down with 4 = become, grow, turn, come to be 6 = understand, follow, catch, see, realize, take in, perceive, grasp 9 = persuade, convince, induce, influence, entice, incite, impel, prevail upon 10 = annoy, upset, anger, disturb, trouble, bug (*informal*), irritate, gall

get across *vb* to make (something) understood

> **get across** *vb* **get something across** = communicate, pass on, transmit, convey, impart, bring home, make known, put over

get at *vb* 1 to succeed in reaching or discovering: *the inquiry tried to get at the truth* 2 to imply or mean: *it is hard to see quite what he is getting at* 3 to annoy or criticize persistently: *people who know they're being got at*

> **get at** *vb* 1 **get at something** = reach, touch, grasp, get (a) hold of, stretch to 2 **get at something** = imply, mean, suggest, hint, intimate, lead up to, insinuate 3 **get at someone** = criticize, attack, blame, put down, knock (*informal*), nag, pick on, disparage

get away *vb* 1 to escape or leave 2 **get away with** to do (something wrong) without being caught or punished ▸ *interj* 3 an exclamation of disbelief ▸ *n* **getaway** 4 the act of escaping, usually by criminals ▸ *adj* **getaway** 5 used to escape: *the getaway car was abandoned*

get by *vb informal* to manage in spite of difficulties: *he saw for himself what people did to get by*

> **get by** *vb* = manage, survive, cope, fare, exist, get along, make do, muddle through

get off *vb* **1** to leave (a bus, train, etc.) **2** to escape the consequences of or punishment for an action: *the real culprits have got off scot-free* **3** **get off with** *Brit & Austral informal* to begin a romantic or sexual relationship with

get over *vb* **1** to recover from (an illness or unhappy experience) **2** to overcome (a problem) **3** **get over with** to bring (something necessary but unpleasant) to an end: *better to get it over with*

get through *vb* **1** to complete (a task or process) **2** to use up (money or supplies) **3** to succeed in (an examination or test) **4** **get through to** **A** to succeed in making (someone) understand **B** to contact (someone) by telephone

geyser (geez-er) *n* **1** a spring that discharges steam and hot water **2** *Brit & S African* a domestic gas water heater

GF *or* **gf** girlfriend

ghastly *adj* **-lier, -liest 1** *informal* very unpleasant **2** deathly pale **3** horrible: *a ghastly accident*

ghastly *adj* **1** = horrible, shocking (*informal*), terrible (*informal*), awful, dreadful, horrendous, hideous, frightful; ≠ lovely

ghat *n* (in India) **1** stairs leading down to a river **2** a place of cremation **3** a mountain pass

ghee (gee) *n* clarified butter, used in Indian cookery

gherkin *n* a small pickled cucumber

ghetto *n, pl* **-tos** *or* **-toes** an area that is inhabited by people of a particular race, religion, nationality, or class

ghillie *n* same as **gillie**

ghost *n* **1** the disembodied spirit of a dead person, supposed to haunt the living **2** a faint trace: *the ghost of a smile on his face* **3** a faint secondary image in an optical instrument or on a television screen

ghost *n* **1** = spirit, soul, phantom, spectre, spook (*informal*), apparition, wraith, atua (NZ), kehua (NZ), wairua (NZ) **2** = trace, shadow, suggestion, hint, suspicion, glimmer, semblance

ghost gum *n Austral* a eucalyptus with a white trunk and branches

ghostly *adj* **-lier, -liest** frightening in appearance or effect: *ghostly noises*

ghostly *adj* = unearthly, phantom, eerie, supernatural, spooky (*informal*), spectral

ghost town *n* a town that used to be busy but is now deserted

ghoul (gool) *n* **1** a person who is interested in morbid or disgusting things **2** a demon that eats corpses > **ghoulish** *adj* > **ghoulishly** *adv*

GI *n, pl* **GIs** *or* **GI's** *US informal* a soldier in the US Army

giant *n* **1** a mythical figure of superhuman size and strength **2** a person or thing of exceptional size, ability, or importance: *industrial giants* ▸ *adj* **3** remarkably large **4** (of an atom or ion or its structure) having large numbers of particles present in a crystal lattice, with each particle exerting a strong force of attraction on those near to it

giant *n* = ogre, monster, titan, colossus ▸ *adj* = huge, vast, enormous, tremendous, immense, titanic, gigantic, monumental (*informal*), supersize; ≠ tiny

gibber¹ (jib-ber) *vb* to talk in a fast and unintelligible manner

gibber² (gib-ber) *n Austral* **1** a boulder **2** barren land covered with stones

gibberish (jib-ber-rish) *n* rapid incomprehensible talk; nonsense

gibbet (jib-bit) *n* a gallows

gibbon (gib-bon) *n* a small agile ape of the forests of S Asia

gibbous (gib-bus) *adj* (of the moon) more than half but less than fully illuminated

gibe (jibe) *n, vb* **gibing, gibed** same as **jibe¹**

giblets (jib-lits) *pl n* the gizzard, liver, heart, and neck of a fowl

gidday *or* **g'day** *interj Austral & NZ* an expression of greeting used during the day

giddy *adj* **-dier, -diest 1** feeling weak and unsteady on one's feet, as if about to faint **2** happy and excited: *a state of giddy expectation* > **giddiness** *n*

gift *n* **1** something given to someone: *a birthday gift* **2** a special ability or power: *a gift for caricature*

gift *n* **1** = donation, offering, present, contribution, grant, legacy, hand-out, endowment, bonsela (*S African*), koha (NZ) **2** = talent, ability, capacity, genius, power, capability, flair, knack

gifted *adj* having natural talent or aptitude: *that era's most gifted director*

gifted *adj* = talented, able, skilled, expert, masterly, brilliant, capable, clever; ≠ talentless

gig¹ *n* **1** a single performance by jazz or pop musicians ▸ *vb* **gigging, gigged 2** to play gigs

gig² *n* a light open two-wheeled one-horse carriage

gig³ *n computers informal* short for **gigabyte**

gigabyte *n computers* one thousand and twenty-four megabytes

gigantic *adj* extremely large: *the most gigantic gold paperweight ever*

gigantic *adj* = huge, large, giant, massive, enormous, tremendous, immense, titanic, supersize; ≠ tiny

gig economy *n informal* an economy in which there are few permanent employees and most jobs are assigned to temporary or freelance workers

giggle *vb* **-gling, -gled 1** to laugh nervously or foolishly ▸ *n* **2** a nervous or foolish laugh

3 *informal* an amusing person or thing
> **giggly** *adj*

giggle *vb* = laugh, chuckle, snigger, chortle, titter, twitter ▸ *n* **2** = laugh, chuckle, snigger, chortle, titter, twitter

gigolo (jig-a-lo) *n, pl* **-los** a man who is paid by an older woman to be her escort or lover

gigot *n chiefly Brit* a leg of lamb or mutton

gild *vb* **gilding, gilded** *or* **gilt 1** to cover with a thin layer of gold **2** to make (something) appear golden: *the morning sun gilded the hills* **3 gild the lily A** to adorn unnecessarily something already beautiful **B** to praise someone excessively

gill (jill) *n* a unit of liquid measure equal to one quarter of a pint (0.14 litres)

gillie *or* **ghillie** *n Scot* an attendant or guide for hunting or fishing

gills (gillz) *pl n* the breathing organs of fish and other water creatures

gilt *vb* **1** a past of **gild** ▸ *adj* **2** covered with a thin layer of gold ▸ *n* **3** a thin layer of gold, used as decoration

gilt-edged *adj* denoting government securities on which interest payments and final repayments are guaranteed

gimcrack (jim-krak) *adj* showy but cheap; shoddy

gimlet (gim-let) *n* **1** a small hand tool with a pointed spiral tip, used for boring holes in wood ▸ *adj* **2** penetrating or piercing: *gimlet eyes*

gimmick *n informal* something designed to attract attention or publicity > **gimmickry** *n* > **gimmicky** *adj*

gin[1] *n* an alcoholic drink distilled from malted grain and flavoured with juniper berries

gin[2] *n* a noose of thin strong wire for catching small mammals

ginger *n* **1** the root of a tropical plant, chopped or powdered and used as a spice, or sugared and eaten as a sweet ▸ *adj* **2** light reddish-brown: *ginger hair* ▸ **gingery** *adj*

ginger ale *n* a nonalcoholic fizzy drink flavoured with ginger extract

gingerbread *n* a moist brown cake flavoured with ginger

ginger group *n Brit, Austral & NZ* a group within a larger group that agitates for a more active policy

gingerly *adv* carefully or cautiously: *she sat gingerly on the edge of the chair*

ginger nut *or* **ginger snap** *n* a hard biscuit flavoured with ginger

gingham *n* a cotton fabric with a checked or striped design

gingivitis (jin-jiv-vite-iss) *n* inflammation of the gums

ginseng (jin-seng) *n* the root of a plant of China and N America, believed to have tonic and energy-giving properties

Gipsy *n, pl* **-sies** same as **Gypsy**

giraffe *n* a cud-chewing African mammal with a very long neck and long legs and a spotted yellowy skin

gird *vb* **girding, girded** *or* **girt 1** to put a belt or girdle around **2 gird (up) one's loins** to prepare oneself for action

girder *n* a large steel or iron beam used in the construction of bridges and buildings

girdle *n* **1** an elastic corset that covers the stomach and hips **2** anything that surrounds something or someone: *encased in a girdle of concrete* **3** *anatomy* an encircling arrangement of bones: *the shoulder girdle* ▸ *vb* **-dling, -dled 4** to surround: *a ring of volcanic ash girdling the earth*

girl *n* **1** a female child **2** a young woman
> **girlhood** *n* > **girlish** *adj*

girl *n* **1** = female child, lass, lassie (*informal*), miss (*old-fashioned or derogatory*), maiden (*archaic*), maid (*archaic*)

girlfriend *n* **1** a female friend with whom a person is romantically or sexually involved **2** any female friend

girlfriend *n* **1** = sweetheart, love, girl, lover, beloved, valentine, truelove, steady (*informal*), GF *or* gf (*informal*), bae (*US informal*)

girlie *adj informal* **1** featuring naked or scantily dressed women: *girlie magazines* **2** suited to or designed to appeal to young women: *a real girlie night out*

giro (jire-oh) *n, pl* **-ros 1** (in some countries) a system of transferring money within a bank or post office, directly from one account into another **2** *Brit informal* an unemployment or income support payment by giro cheque

girt *vb* a past of **gird**

girth *n* **1** the measurement around something **2** a band fastened round a horse's middle to keep the saddle in position

gist (jist) *n* the main point or meaning of something: *the gist of the letter*

give *vb* **giving, gave, given 1** to present or hand (something) to someone **2** to pay (an amount of money) for a purchase **3** to grant or provide: *to give an answer* **4** to utter (a shout or cry) **5** to perform, make, or do: *the prime minister gave a speech* **6** to host (a party) **7** to sacrifice or devote: *comrades who gave their lives for their country* **8** to concede: *he was very efficient, I have to give him that* **9** to yield or break under pressure: *something has got to give* **10 give or take** plus or minus: *about one hundred metres, give or take five* ▸ *n* **11** a tendency to yield under pressure; elasticity ▸ See also **give away, give in** *etc.* > **giver** *n*

give *vb* **1** = present, contribute, donate, provide, supply, award, grant, deliver; ≠ take **4** = communicate, announce, transmit, pronounce, utter, issue **5** = perform, do, carry out, execute **7** = surrender, yield, devote, hand over, relinquish, part with **8** = concede, allow, grant

give away *vb* **1** to donate as a gift **2** to reveal (a secret) **3** to present (a bride) formally to her spouse in a marriage ceremony **4 give something away** NZ to give something up ▸ *n* **giveaway 5** something that reveals hidden feelings or intentions ▸ *adj* **giveaway 6** very cheap or free: *a giveaway rent*

> **give away** *vb* **2 give something away**
> = reveal, expose, leak, disclose, betray, uncover, let out, divulge

give in *vb* to admit defeat

> **give in** *vb* = admit defeat, yield, concede, collapse, quit, submit, surrender, succumb

give off *vb* to send out (heat, light, or a smell)

> **give off** *vb* **give something off or out** = emit, produce, release, discharge, send out, throw out, exude

give out *vb* **1** to hand out: *the bloke that was giving out those tickets* **2** to send out (heat, light, or a smell) **3** to make known: *the woman who gave out the news* **4** to fail: *the engine gave out*

give over *vb* **1** to set aside for a specific purpose: *the amount of space given over to advertisements* **2** *informal* to stop doing something annoying: *tell him to give over*

give up *vb* **1** to stop (doing something): *I did give up smoking* **2** to resign from (a job or position) **3** to admit defeat or failure **4** to abandon (hope) **5 give oneself up A** to surrender to the police or other authorities **B** to devote oneself completely: *she gave herself up to her work*

> **give up** *vb* **1 give something up** = abandon, stop, quit, cease, renounce, leave off, desist

gizzard *n* the part of a bird's stomach in which hard food is broken up

glacé (glass-say) *adj* preserved in a thick sugary syrup: *glacé cherries*

glacial *adj* **1** of glaciers or ice **2** extremely cold **3** cold and unfriendly: *a glacial stare*

glaciation *n* the process of covering part of the earth's surface with glaciers or masses of ice > **glaciated** *adj*

glacier *n* a slowly moving mass of ice formed by an accumulation of snow

glad *adj* **gladder, gladdest 1** happy and pleased **2** very willing: *he was only too glad to help* **3** *archaic* causing happiness: *glad tidings* > **gladly** *adv* > **gladness** *n* > **gladden** *vb*

> **glad** *adj* **1** = happy, pleased, delighted, contented, gratified, joyful, overjoyed; ≠ unhappy **3** = pleasing, happy, cheering, pleasant, cheerful, gratifying

glade *n* an open space in a forest: *a peaceful and sheltered glade*

gladiator *n* (in ancient Rome) a man trained to fight in arenas to provide entertainment > **gladiatorial** *adj*

gladiolus (glad-ee-oh-luss) *n, pl* **-li** (-lie) a garden plant with brightly coloured funnel-shaped flowers

glad rags *pl n informal* one's best clothes

gladwrap *Austral, NZ & S African* ▸ *n* **1** *trademark* thin polythene material for wrapping ▸ *vb* **2** to wrap in gladwrap

glamorous *adj* attractive or fascinating

> **glamorous** *adj* = attractive, elegant, dazzling; ≠ unglamorous

glamour *or US* **glamor** *n* exciting or alluring charm or beauty > **glamorize** *or* **-ise** *vb*

> **glamour** *or* **glamor** *n* = charm, appeal, beauty, attraction, fascination, allure, enchantment

glance *n* **1** a quick look ▸ *vb* **glancing, glanced 2** to look quickly at something **3** to be deflected off an object at an oblique angle: *the ball glanced off a spectator* > **glancing** *adj*

> **glance** *n* = peek, look, glimpse, peep, dekko (*slang, old-fashioned*); ≠ good look ▸ *vb* **2** = peek, look, view, glimpse, peep; ≠ scrutinize

gland *n* **1** an organ that synthesizes and secretes chemical substances for the body to use or eliminate **2** a similar organ in plants

glandular *adj* of or affecting a gland or glands

glare *vb* **glaring, glared 1** to stare angrily **2** (of light or colour) to be too bright ▸ *n* **3** an angry stare **4** a dazzling light or brilliance **5 in the glare of publicity** receiving a lot of attention from the media or the public

> **glare** *vb* **1** = scowl, frown, glower, look daggers, lour *or* lower **2** = dazzle, blaze, flare, flame ▸ *n* **3** = scowl, frown, glower, dirty look, black look, lour *or* lower **4** = dazzle, glow, blaze, flame, brilliance

glaring *adj* conspicuous or obvious: *glaring inconsistencies* > **glaringly** *adv*

> **glaring** *adj* = obvious, gross, outrageous, manifest, blatant, conspicuous, flagrant, unconcealed; ≠ inconspicuous

glass *n* **1** a hard brittle transparent solid, consisting of metal silicates or similar compounds **2** a drinking vessel made of glass **3** the amount contained in a drinking glass: *a glass of wine* **4** objects made of glass, such as drinking glasses and bowls

glasshouse *n Brit & NZ* same as **greenhouse**

glassy *adj* **glassier, glassiest 1** smooth, clear, and shiny, like glass: *the glassy sea* **2** expressionless: *that glassy look*

glaucoma *n* an eye disease in which increased pressure in the eyeball causes gradual loss of sight

glaze *vb* **glazing, glazed 1** to fit or cover with glass **2** to cover (a piece of pottery) with a protective shiny coating **3** to cover (food) with beaten egg or milk before cooking, in order to produce a shiny coating ▸ a protective shiny coating applied to a piece of pottery **5** a shiny coating of beaten egg or milk applied to food > **glazed** *adj* > **glazing** *n*

> **glaze** *vb* **2** = coat, polish, gloss, varnish, enamel, lacquer ▸ *n* **4** = coat, finish, polish, shine, gloss, varnish, enamel, lacquer

glazier *n* a person who fits windows or doors with glass

gleam *n* **1** a small beam or glow of light **2** a brief or dim indication: *a gleam of anticipation in his eye* ▸ *vb* **3** to shine > **gleaming** *adj*

> **gleam** *n* **1** = glimmer, flash, beam, glow, sparkle **2** = trace, suggestion, hint, flicker, glimmer, inkling ▸ *vb* = shine, flash, glow, sparkle, glitter, shimmer, glint, glimmer

glean *vb* **1** to gather (information) bit by bit **2** to gather the useful remnants of (a crop) after harvesting > **gleaner** *n*

glee *n* great merriment or joy, esp. caused by the misfortune of another person

gleeful *adj* merry or joyful, esp. over someone else's mistake or misfortune > **gleefully** *adv*

glen *n* a deep narrow mountain valley

glib *adj* **glibber, glibbest** fluent and easy, often in an insincere or deceptive way: *there were no glib or easy answers* > **glibly** *adv* > **glibness** *n*

glide *vb* **gliding, glided** **1** to move easily and smoothly **2** (of an aircraft) to land without engine power **3** to fly a glider **4** to float on currents of air

> **glide** *vb* **1** = slip, sail, slide

glider *n* **1** an aircraft that does not use an engine, but flies by floating on air currents **2** *Austral* a flying phalanger

gliding *n* the sport of flying in a glider

glimmer *vb* **1** (of a light) to glow faintly or flickeringly ▸ *n* **2** a faint indication: *a glimmer of hope* **3** a glow or twinkle

glimpse *n* **1** a brief view: *a glimpse of a rare snow leopard* **2** a vague indication: *glimpses of insecurity* ▸ *vb* **glimpsing, glimpsed** **3** to catch sight of momentarily

> **glimpse** *n* = look, sighting, sight, glance, peep, peek ▸ *vb* = catch sight of, spot, sight, view, spy, espy

glint *vb* **1** to gleam brightly ▸ *n* **2** a bright gleam

glissando *n, pl* **-dos** *music* a slide between two notes in which all intermediate notes are played

glisten *vb* (of a wet or glossy surface) to gleam by reflecting light: *sweat glistened above her eyes*

glitch *n* a small problem that stops something from working properly

glitter *vb* **1** (of a surface) to reflect light in bright flashes **2** (of light) to be reflected in bright flashes **3** to be brilliant in a showy way: *she glitters socially* ▸ *n* **4** a sparkling light **5** superficial glamour: *the trappings and glitter*

of the European aristocracy **6** tiny pieces of shiny decorative material **7** *Canad* ice formed from freezing rain > **glittering** *adj* > **glittery** *adj*

> **glitter** *vb* = shine, flash, sparkle, glare, gleam, shimmer, twinkle, glint ▸ *n* **4** = sparkle, flash, shine, glare, gleam, sheen, shimmer, brightness **5** = glamour, show, display, splendour, tinsel, pageantry, gaudiness, showiness

glitzy *adj* **glitzier, glitziest** *slang* showily attractive

gloaming *n Scot poetic* twilight; dusk

gloat *vb* to regard one's own good fortune or the misfortune of others with smug or malicious pleasure

glob *n informal* a rounded mass of thick fluid

global *adj* **1** of or applying to the whole earth: *global environmental problems* **2** of or applying to the whole of something: *a global total for local-authority revenue* > **globally** *adv*

> **global** *adj* **1** = worldwide, world, international, universal **2** = comprehensive, general, total, unlimited, exhaustive, all-inclusive; ≠ limited

globalize *or* **-lise** *vb* **-izing, -ized** *or* **-ising, -ised** **1** to do business in countries all around the world **2** to put (something) into effect worldwide > **globalization** *or* **-lisation** *n*

global warming *n* an increase in the overall temperature worldwide believed to be caused by the greenhouse effect

globe *n* **1** a sphere on which a map of the world is drawn **2** **the globe** the earth **3** a spherical object, such as a glass lamp shade or fishbowl **4** *S African* an electric light bulb

> **globe** *n* **1, 2** = planet, world, earth, sphere, orb

globetrotter *n* a habitual worldwide traveller > **globetrotting** *n, adj*

globular *adj* shaped like a globe or globule

globule *n* a small round drop of liquid

glockenspiel *n* a percussion instrument consisting of tuned metal plates played with a pair of small hammers

gloom *n* **1** depression or melancholy: *all doom and gloom* **2** partial or total darkness

> **gloom** *n* **1** = depression, sorrow, woe, melancholy, unhappiness, despondency, dejection, low spirits; ≠ happiness **2** = darkness, dark, shadow, shade, twilight, dusk (*poetic*), obscurity, blackness; ≠ light

gloomy *adj* **gloomier, gloomiest** **1** despairing or sad **2** causing depression or gloom: *gloomy economic forecasts* **3** dark or dismal > **gloomily** *adv*

> **gloomy** *adj* **1** = miserable, sad, pessimistic, melancholy, glum, dejected, dispirited, downcast; ≠ happy **2** = depressing, bad, dreary, sombre, dispiriting, disheartening, cheerless **3** = dark, dull, dim, dismal, black, grey, murky, dreary; ≠ light

g

glorify vb **-fies, -fying, -fied 1** to make (something) seem more important than it really is: *the discussion forum is just a glorified noticeboard* **2** to praise: *few countries have glorified success in business more than the United States* **3** to worship (God) > **glorification** n

glorious adj **1** brilliantly beautiful: *in glorious colour* **2** delightful or enjoyable: *the glorious summer weather* **3** having or full of glory: *glorious successes* > **gloriously** adv

> **glorious** adj **1** = splendid, beautiful, brilliant, shining, superb, gorgeous, dazzling; ≠ dull **2** = delightful, fine, wonderful, excellent, marvellous, gorgeous **3** = illustrious, famous, celebrated, distinguished, honoured, magnificent, renowned, eminent; ≠ ordinary

glory n, pl **-ries 1** fame, praise, or honour: *tales of glory* **2** beauty: *the glory of the tropical day* **3** something worthy of praise: *the Lady Chapel is the great glory of Lichfield* **4** adoration or worship: *the greater glory of God* ▸ vb **-ries, -rying, -ried 5 glory in** to take great pleasure in: *the workers were glorying in their new-found freedom*

> **glory** n **1** = honour, praise, fame, distinction, acclaim, prestige, eminence, renown; ≠ shame ▸ vb = triumph, boast, relish, revel, exult, take delight in, pride yourself on

glory hole n an untidy cupboard or storeroom
gloss[1] n **1** a bright shine on a surface **2** a superficially attractive appearance **3** a paint with a shiny finish **4** a cosmetic used to give a shiny appearance: *lip gloss* ▸ vb **5** to paint with gloss **6 gloss over** to conceal (an error, failing, or awkward moment) by minimizing it: *don't try to gloss over bad news*

> **gloss** n **1** = shine, gleam, sheen, polish, brightness, veneer, lustre, patina

gloss[2] n **1** an explanatory comment added to the text of a book ▸ vb **2** to add a gloss or glosses to

> **gloss** n = interpretation, comment, note, explanation, commentary, translation, footnote, elucidation ▸ vb = interpret, explain, comment, translate, annotate, elucidate

glossary n, pl **-ries** an alphabetical list of technical or specialist words in a book, with explanations
glossy adj **glossier, glossiest 1** smooth and shiny: *glossy black hair* **2** superficially attractive or sophisticated: *his glossy Manhattan flat* **3** (of a magazine) produced on expensive shiny paper

> **glossy** adj **1** = shiny, polished, shining, glazed, bright, silky, glassy, lustrous; ≠ dull

glottis n the opening at the top of the windpipe, between the vocal cords
glove n **1** a shaped covering for the hand with individual sheaths for each finger and the thumb **2** a protective hand covering worn in sports such as boxing

glove compartment n a small storage area in the dashboard of a car
gloved adj covered by a glove or gloves: *a gloved hand*
glow n **1** light produced as a result of great heat **2** a steady light without flames **3** brightness of complexion **4** a feeling of wellbeing or satisfaction ▸ vb **5** to produce a steady light without flames **6** to shine intensely **7** to experience a feeling of wellbeing or satisfaction: *she glowed with pleasure* **8** (of the complexion) to have a strong bright colour: *his pale face glowing at the recollection*

> **glow** n **1, 2** = light, gleam, splendour, glimmer, brilliance, brightness, radiance, luminosity; ≠ dullness ▸ vb **5, 6** = shine, burn, gleam, brighten, glimmer, smoulder

glower (rhymes with **power**) vb **1** to stare angrily ▸ n **2** an angry stare
glow-worm n a European beetle, the females and larvae of which have organs producing a soft greenish light
gloxinia n a plant with white, red, or purple bell-shaped flowers
glucose n a white crystalline sugar found in plant and animal tissues
glue n **1** a substance used for sticking things together ▸ vb **gluing** or **glueing, glued 2** to join or stick together with glue **3 glued to** paying full attention to: *she lay on the sofa, glued to her phone* > **gluey** adj

> **glue** n = adhesive, cement, gum, paste ▸ vb **2** = stick, fix, seal, cement, gum, paste, affix

glue-sniffing n the practice of inhaling glue fumes to produce intoxicating or hallucinatory effects > **glue-sniffer** n
glum adj **glummer, glummest** gloomy and quiet, usually because of a disappointment > **glumly** adv
glut n **1** an excessive supply ▸ vb **glutting, glutted 2** to supply (a market) with a commodity in excess of the demand for it **3 glut oneself** to eat or drink more than one really needs
gluten (gloo-ten) n a sticky protein found in cereal grains, such as wheat
glutinous (gloo-tin-uss) adj gluelike in texture
glutton n **1** someone who eats and drinks too much **2** a person who has a great capacity for something: *a glutton for work* > **gluttonous** adj
gluttony n the practice of eating too much
glycerine (gliss-ser-reen) or **glycerin** n a nontechnical name for **glycerol**
glycerol (gliss-ser-ol) n a colourless odourless syrupy liquid obtained from animal and vegetable fats, used as a solvent, antifreeze, and sweetener, and in explosives
gm gram
GM 1 genetically modified **2** Brit grant-maintained
GMO genetically modified organism

GMT Greenwich Mean Time

gnarled *adj* rough, twisted, and knobbly, usually through age

gnash *vb* to grind (the teeth) together in pain or anger

gnat *n* a small biting two-winged insect

gnaw *vb* 1 to bite or chew constantly so as to wear away bit by bit 2 **gnaw at** to cause constant distress or anxiety to: *uneasiness gnawed at his mind* ▸ **gnawing** *adj*

gneiss *n* a coarse-grained layered metamorphic rock

gnome *n* 1 an imaginary creature in fairy tales that looks like a little old man 2 a small statue of a gnome in a garden

gnomic (no-mik) *adj literary* of or containing short clever sayings: *gnomic pronouncements*

Gnosticism (noss-tiss-siz-zum) *n* a religious movement involving belief in intuitive spiritual knowledge ▸ **Gnostic** *n, adj*

gnu (noo) *n, pl* **gnus** *or* **gnu** a sturdy African antelope with an oxlike head

go *vb* **goes, going, went, gone** 1 to move or proceed to or from a place: *go forward* 2 to be in regular attendance at (work, church, or a place of learning) 3 to lead to a particular place: *the path that goes right along the bank* 4 to be kept in a particular place: *where does this go?* 5 to do or become as specified: *he went white; the gun went bang* 6 to be or continue to be in a specified state: *to go to sleep* 7 to operate or function: *the car wouldn't go* 8 to follow a specified course; fare: *I'd hate the meeting to go badly* 9 to be allotted to a particular purpose or recipient: *a third of the total budget goes on the army* 10 to be sold: *the portrait went for a fortune to a telephone bidder* 11 (of words or music) to be expressed or sung: *the song goes like this* 12 to fail or break down: *my eyesight is going; he was on lap 19 when the engine went* 13 to die: *she went quickly at the end* 14 to be spent or finished: *all tension and all hope had gone* 15 to proceed up to or beyond certain limits: *I think this is going too far* 16 to carry authority: *what Mummy says goes* 17 to endure or last out: *they go for eight or ten hours without resting* 18 *not standard* to say: *then she goes, 'shut up'* 19 **anything goes** anything is acceptable 20 **be going to** to intend or be about to: *he was afraid of what was going to happen next* 21 **let go** to relax one's hold on; release 22 **let oneself go** **A** to act in an uninhibited manner **B** to lose interest in one's appearance 23 **to go** remaining: *two days to go till the holidays* ▸ *n, pl* **goes** 24 an attempt: *he had a go at the furniture business* 25 a verbal or physical attack: *she couldn't resist having another go at me* 26 a turn to do something in a game: *'Your go now!' I shouted* 27 *informal* the quality of being active and energetic: *a grand old man, full of go and determination* 28 **from the word go** *informal* from the very beginning 29 **make a go of** *informal* to be successful in (a business venture or a relationship) 30 **on the go** *informal* active and energetic

go *vb* 1 = move, travel, advance, journey, proceed, pass, set off; ≠ **stay** 7 = function, work, run, move, operate, perform; ≠ **fail** 9 = be given, be spent, be awarded, be allotted ▸ *n* 24 = attempt, try, effort, bid, shot (*informal*), crack (*informal*) 26 = turn, shot (*informal*), stint 27 = energy, life, drive, spirit, vitality, vigour, verve, force

goad *vb* 1 to provoke (someone) to take some kind of action, usually in anger ▸ *n* 2 something that provokes someone to take some kind of action 3 a sharp pointed stick for driving cattle

goal *n* 1 *sport* the space into which players try to propel the ball or puck to score 2 *sport* **A** a successful attempt at scoring **B** the score so made 3 an aim or purpose: *the goal is to get homeless people on their feet* ▸ **goalless** *adj*

goal *n* 3 = aim, end, target, purpose, object, intention, objective, ambition

goalie *n informal* a goalkeeper

goalkeeper *n sport* a player whose duty is to prevent the ball or puck from entering the goal

goalpost *n* 1 either of two uprights supporting the crossbar of a goal 2 **move the goalposts** to change the aims of an activity to ensure the desired results

goanna *n* a large Australian lizard

goat *n* 1 an agile cud-chewing mammal with hollow horns 2 **act the goat** *informal* to behave in a silly manner 3 **get someone's goat** *slang* to annoy someone

goatee *n* a small pointed beard that does not cover the cheeks

gob¹ *n* a thick mass of a soft substance

gob² *n Brit, Austral & NZ slang* the mouth

go back on *vb* to fail to fulfil (a promise): *he went back on his promise not to raise taxes*

gobbet *n* a chunk or lump

gobble¹ *vb* **-bling, -bled** to eat quickly and greedily

gobble² *n* 1 the loud rapid gurgling sound made by a turkey ▸ *vb* **-bling, -bled** 2 to make this sound

gobbledegook *or* **gobbledygook** *n* pretentious or unintelligible language

go-between *n* a person who acts as a messenger between two people or groups

goblet *n* a drinking vessel with a base and stem but without handles

goblin *n* a small grotesque creature in fairy tales that causes trouble for people

goby *n, pl* **-by** *or* **-bies** a small spiny-finned fish

god *n* 1 a supernatural being, worshipped as the controller of the universe or some aspect of life, or as the personification of some force 2 an image of such a being 3 a person or thing to which excessive attention is given: *the All Blacks are gods in New Zealand* 4 **the gods** the top balcony in a theatre

god *n* 1 = deity, immortal, divinity, divine being, supreme being, atua (NZ)

God n **1** the sole Supreme Being, Creator and ruler of all, in religions such as Christianity, Judaism, and Islam ▸ interj **2** an oath or exclamation of surprise or annoyance

godchild n, pl **-children** a person who is sponsored by godparents at baptism

goddaughter n a female godchild

goddess n a female god

godetia n a garden plant with showy flowers

godfather n **1** a male godparent **2** the head of a Mafia family or other criminal ring

godforsaken adj desolate or dreary: some godforsaken village in the Himalayas

godly adj **-lier, -liest** deeply religious ▷ **godliness** n

> **godly** adj = devout, religious, holy, righteous, pious, good, saintly, god-fearing

godmother n a female godparent

godparent n a person who promises at a person's baptism to look after his or her religious upbringing

godsend n a person or thing that comes unexpectedly but is very welcome

godson n a male godchild

go for vb **1** to choose: any politician will go for the soft option **2** informal to like very much **3** to attack **4** to apply equally to: the same might go for the other woman

go-getter n informal an ambitious enterprising person ▷ **go-getting** adj

gogga (hohh-a) n S African informal an insect

> **gogga** n = insect, bug, creepy-crawly (Brit informal)

goggle vb **-gling, -gled** to stare with wide-open eyes. See also **goggles** ▷ **goggle-eyed** adj

goggles pl n close-fitting protective spectacles

going n **1** the condition of the ground with regard to walking or riding: the going for the cross-country is perfect **2** informal speed or progress: not bad going for a lad of 58 ▸ adj **3** thriving: the racecourse was a going concern **4** current or accepted: this is the going rate for graduates

going-over n, pl **goings-over** informal **1** a thorough examination or investigation **2** a physical beating

goings-on pl n informal mysterious or shady activities

goitre or US **goiter** (goy-ter) n pathol a swelling of the thyroid gland in the neck

go-kart n a small four-wheeled motor vehicle, used for racing

gold n **1** a bright yellow precious metal, used as a monetary standard and in jewellery and plating. Symbol: **Au** **2** jewellery or coins made of this metal **3** short for **gold medal** ▸ adj **4** deep yellow

goldcrest n a small bird with a bright yellow-and-black crown

gold-digger n informal someone who enters into a relationship with a more affluent person in order to get money or expensive things

golden adj **1** made of gold: golden bangles **2** of the colour of gold: golden corn **3** informal very successful or destined for success: the golden girl of British athletics **4** excellent or valuable: a golden opportunity for peace **5** (of an anniversary) the fiftieth: golden wedding; Golden Jubilee

> **golden** adj **2** = yellow, blonde, blond, flaxen; ≠ dark **3** = successful, glorious, prosperous, rich, flourishing, halcyon; ≠ worst **4** = promising, excellent, favourable, opportune (formal); ≠ unfavourable

golden eagle n a large mountain eagle of the N hemisphere with golden-brown feathers

golden handshake n informal money given to an employee either on retirement or to compensate for loss of employment

golden rule n an important principle: the golden rule is to start with the least difficult problems

golden wattle n an Australian plant with yellow flowers that yields a useful gum and bark

goldfinch n a European finch, the adult of which has yellow-and-black wings

goldfish n, pl **-fish** or **-fishes** a gold or orange-red freshwater fish, often kept as a pet

gold leaf n very thin gold sheet made by rolling or hammering gold and used for gilding

gold medal n a medal made of gold, awarded to the winner of a race or competition

golf n **1** a game in which a ball is struck with clubs into a series of eighteen holes in a grassy course ▸ vb **2** to play golf ▷ **golfer** n

gondola n **1** a long narrow flat-bottomed boat with a high ornamented stem, traditionally used on the canals of Venice **2** a moving cabin suspended from a cable, used as a ski lift

gondolier n a person who propels a gondola

gone vb **1** the past participle of **go** ▸ adj **2** no longer present or no longer in existence

> **gone** adj = past, over, ended, finished, elapsed

goner n slang a person who is about to die or who is beyond help

gong n **1** a flat circular metal disc that is hit with a hammer to give out a loud sound **2** Brit slang a medal

gonorrhoea or esp US **gonorrhea** (gon-or-ree-a) n a sexually transmitted disease that causes inflammation and a discharge from the genital organs

good adj **better, best** **1** having admirable, pleasing, or superior qualities: a good listener **2** morally excellent; virtuous: a good person **3** beneficial: exercise is good for the heart **4** kindly or generous: he is so good to us **5** competent or talented: she's good at physics **6** obedient or well-behaved: a good boy **7** reliable or recommended: a good make **8** complete or thorough: she went to have a good look round **9** appropriate or opportune: a good time to clear the air **10** satisfying or enjoyable: a good holiday **11** newest or of the best quality: keep the good dishes

g

for guests **12** fairly large, extensive, or long: *they contain a good amount of protein* **13 as good as** virtually or practically: *the war was as good as over* ▶ *n* **14** advantage or benefit: *what is the good of it all?* **15** positive moral qualities; virtue **16 for good** for ever; permanently: *his political career was over for good*

> **good** *adj* **1, 10** = excellent, great (*informal*), fine, pleasing, acceptable, first-class, splendid, satisfactory, booshit (*Austral slang*), exo (*Austral slang*), sik (*Austral slang*), rad (*informal*), phat (*slang*), schmick (*Austral informal*); ≠ bad **2** = honourable, moral, worthy, ethical, upright, admirable, honest, righteous; ≠ bad **3** = beneficial, useful, helpful, favourable, wholesome, advantageous; ≠ harmful **4** = kind, kindly, friendly, obliging, charitable, humane, benevolent, merciful; ≠ unkind **5** = proficient, able, skilled, expert, talented, clever, accomplished, first-class; ≠ bad **6** = well-behaved, polite, orderly, obedient, dutiful, well-mannered; ≠ naughty **7** = true, real, genuine, proper, dinkum (*Austral, NZ informal*) **8** = considerable, large, substantial, sufficient, adequate, ample **9** = convenient, timely, fitting, appropriate, suitable; ≠ inconvenient **12** = full, complete, extensive; ≠ scant ▶ *n* **14** = benefit, interest, gain, advantage, use, profit, welfare, usefulness; ≠ disadvantage **15** = virtue, goodness, righteousness, worth, merit, excellence, morality, rectitude; ≠ evil

goodbye *interj* **1** an expression used on parting ▶ *n* **2** the act of saying goodbye: *he said his goodbyes*

> **goodbye** *interj* = farewell, see you, see you later, ciao (*Italian*), cheerio, adieu, ta-ta, au revoir (*French*), haere ra (*NZ*) ▶ *n* = farewell, parting, leave-taking

good-for-nothing *n* **1** an irresponsible or worthless person ▶ *adj* **2** irresponsible or worthless

goodly *adj* **-lier, -liest** fairly large: *a goodly number of children*

goodness *n* **1** the quality of being good ▶ *interj* **2** an exclamation of surprise

> **goodness** *n* = kindness, charity, humanity, goodwill, mercy, compassion, generosity, friendliness; ≠ badness

Good Samaritan *n* a person who helps someone in difficulty or distress

goodwill *n* **1** kindly feelings towards other people **2** the popularity and good reputation of a well-established business, considered as a valuable asset

> **goodwill** *n* **1** = friendliness, friendship, benevolence, amity (*formal*), kindliness

goody *interj* **1** a child's exclamation of pleasure ▶ *n, pl* **goodies 2** *informal* the hero in a film or book

goody-goody *informal* ▶ *n, pl* **-goodies 1** a person who behaves well in order to please people in authority ▶ *adj* **2** behaving well in order to please people in authority

gooey *adj* **gooier, gooiest** *informal* **1** sticky, soft, and often sweet **2** sentimental: *one knows the whole gooey performance is an act*

goof *vb informal* **1** to bungle or botch **2 goof off** *US & Canad* to spend time in a lazy or foolish way: *he's goofing off on the Costa del Sol*

go off *vb* **1** to stop functioning: *the heating went off* **2** to make a sudden loud noise: *a bomb went off* **3** to occur as specified: *the actual launch went off perfectly* **4** *informal* (of food) to become stale or rotten **5** *Brit informal* to stop liking

> **go off** *vb* **2** = explode, fire, blow up, detonate **3** = take place, come about **4** = go bad, turn, spoil, rot, go stale

google *vb* **1** to search for (something) on the internet using a search engine **2** to check the credentials of (someone) by searching for websites containing his or her name

googly *n, pl* **-lies** *cricket* a ball bowled like a leg break but spinning from off to leg on pitching

goon *n* **1** a stupid person **2** *US informal* a hired thug

goose *n, pl* **geese 1** a fairly large web-footed long-necked migratory bird **2** the female of such a bird **3** the flesh of the goose used for food **4** *informal* a silly person

gooseberry *n, pl* **-ries 1** a small edible green berry with tiny hairs on the skin **2 play gooseberry** *Brit & NZ informal* to be an unwanted single person accompanying a couple

goose flesh *n* the bumpy condition of the skin due to cold or fear, in which the muscles at the base of the hair follicles contract, making the hair bristle. Also: **goose pimples**

go out *vb* **1** to go to entertainments or social functions **2** to be extinguished or cease to function: *the lights went out* **3** (of information) to be released publicly **4** (of a broadcast) to be transmitted **5 go out with** to have a romantic relationship with

> **go out** *vb* **2** = be extinguished, die out, fade out **5 go out with** = see someone, court, date (*informal*), woo, go steady with (*informal*), be romantically involved with, step out with (*informal*)

go over *vb* **1** to examine very carefully **2 go over to** to change to: *he went over to the Free Orthodox Church*

gopher (**go**-fer) *n* an American burrowing rodent with wide cheek pouches

gore[1] *n* blood shed from a wound

> **gore** *n* = blood, slaughter, bloodshed, carnage, butchery

gore[2] *vb* **goring, gored** (of an animal) to pierce or stab (a person or another animal) with a horn or tusk

g

gore *vb* = pierce, wound, transfix, impale

gorge *n* **1** a deep narrow steep-sided valley **2 one's gorge rises** one feels disgusted or nauseated ▸ *vb* **gorging, gorged 3** Also: **gorge oneself** to eat greedily

gorge *n* **1** = ravine, canyon, pass, chasm, cleft, fissure, defile, gulch (*US, Canad*) ▸ *vb* = stuff, feed, cram, glut

gorgeous *adj* **1** strikingly beautiful or attractive **2** *informal* warm, sunny, and very pleasant: *a gorgeous day* ▸ **gorgeously** *adv*

gorgeous *adj* **1** = beautiful, lovely, stunning (*informal*), elegant, handsome, exquisite, ravishing, hot (*informal*); ≠ shabby

Gorgon *n* **1** *Greek myth* one of three monstrous sisters who had live snakes for hair, and were so horrifying that anyone who looked at them was turned to stone **2** *derogatory* a terrifying or repulsive woman

Gorgonzola *n* a sharp-flavoured blue-veined Italian cheese

gorilla *n* a very large W African ape with coarse black hair

gormless *adj Brit & NZ informal* stupid or dull-witted

gorse *n* an evergreen shrub with small yellow flowers and prickles, which grows wild in the countryside

gory *adj* **gorier, goriest 1** horrific or bloodthirsty: *the gory details* **2** bloody: *gory remains*

goshawk *n* a large swift short-winged hawk

gosling *n* a young goose

go-slow *n Brit & NZ* a deliberate slowing of the rate of production by workers as a tactic in industrial conflict

gospel *n* **1** *Christianity* **A** the teachings of Jesus Christ **B** the story of Christ's life and teachings **2** a doctrine held to be of great importance: *the gospel of self-help* **3** Also called: **gospel truth** unquestionable truth: *gross inaccuracies which are sometimes taken as gospel* ▸ *adj* **4** denoting a kind of religious music originating in the churches of Black people in the Southern US

gospel *n* **1, 2** = doctrine, news, teachings, message, revelation, creed, credo, tidings **3** = truth, fact, certainty, the last word

Gospel *n* *Christianity* any of the first four books of the New Testament, namely Matthew, Mark, Luke, and John, which tell the story of Jesus Christ

gossamer *n* **1** a very fine fabric **2** a filmy cobweb often seen on foliage or floating in the air

gossip *n* **1** idle talk, usually about other people's private lives, esp. of a disapproving or malicious nature: *office gossip* **2** an informal conversation, esp. about other people's private lives: *to have a gossip and a giggle* **3** a person who habitually talks about other people, usually maliciously ▸ *vb*

4 to talk idly or maliciously, esp. about other people's private lives ▸ **gossipy** *adj*

gossip *n* **1** = idle talk, scandal, hearsay, tittle-tattle, goss (*informal*), small talk, chitchat, blether, chinwag (*Brit informal*) **3** = busybody, chatterbox (*informal*), chatterer, scandalmonger, gossipmonger, tattletale (*chiefly US, Canad*) ▸ *vb* = chat, chatter, jaw (*slang*), blether

got *vb* **1** the past of **get 2 have got** to possess **3 have got to** must: *you have got to be prepared to work hard*

Gothic *adj* **1** of a style of architecture used in W Europe from the 12th to the 16th centuries, characterized by pointed arches, ribbed vaults, and flying buttresses **2** of a literary style featuring stories of gloom, horror, and the supernatural, popular in the late 18th century **3** of or in a heavy ornate script typeface ▸ *n* **4** Gothic architecture or art

go through *vb* **1** to experience (a difficult time or process) **2** to name or describe: *the president went through a list of government ministers* **3** to qualify for the next stage of a competition: *Belgium, Spain and Uruguay all went through from Group E* **4** to be approved: *the bill went through parliament* **5 go through with** to bring to a successful conclusion, often by persistence

go through *vb* **1 go through something** = suffer, experience, bear, endure, brave, undergo, tolerate, withstand

gouache (goo-ahsh) *n* opaque watercolour paint bound with glue

Gouda *n* a round mild-flavoured Dutch cheese

gouge (gowj) *vb* **gouging, gouged 1** to scoop or force (something) out of its position **2** to cut (a hole or groove) in something with a pointed object ▸ *n* **3** a mark or groove made by gouging

goulash (goo-lash) *n* a rich stew seasoned with paprika, originating in Hungary

gourd (goord) *n* **1** a large hard-shelled fruit similar to a cucumber or marrow **2** a container made from a dried gourd shell

gourmand (goor-mand) *n* a person devoted to eating and drinking, usually to excess

gourmet (goor-may) *n* an expert on good food and drink

gourmet *n* = connoisseur, foodie (*informal*), bon vivant (*French*), epicure, gastronome

gout (gowt) *n* a disease that causes painful inflammation of certain joints, for example of the big toe ▸ **gouty** *adj*

govern *vb* **1** to direct and control the policy and affairs of (a country or an organization) **2** to control or determine: *the international organizations governing athletics and rugby* ▸ **governable** *adj*

govern *vb* **1** = rule, lead, control, command, manage, direct, guide, handle

governance n government, control, or authority

governess n a woman employed in a private household to teach the children

government n 1 the executive policy-making body of a country or state 2 the state and its administration: *the assembled heads of state and government* 3 the system by which a country or state is ruled: *the old hard-line government* > **governmental** adj

> **government** n 1, 2 = administration, executive, ministry, regime, powers-that-be, e-government or egovernment 3 = rule, authority, administration, sovereignty, governance, statecraft

governor n 1 the chief political administrator of a region, such as a US state or a colony. Related adjective: **gubernatorial** 2 *Brit* the senior administrator of a school, prison, or other institution 3 *Brit informal* one's employer or father > **governorship** n

> **governor** n 1 = leader, administrator, ruler, head, director, manager, chief, executive

governor general n, pl **governors general** or **governor generals** the chief representative of the British government in a Commonwealth country

gown n 1 a woman's long formal dress 2 a surgeon's overall 3 a loose wide official robe worn by judges, lawyers, and academics

> **gown** n 1 = dress, costume, garment, robe, frock, garb, habit

goy n, pl **goyim** or **goys** a Jewish word for a **Gentile**

GP general practitioner

GPS Global Positioning System: a satellite-based navigation system

grab vb **grabbing**, **grabbed** 1 to seize hold of 2 to take (food, drink, or rest) hurriedly 3 to take (an opportunity) eagerly 4 to seize illegally or unscrupulously: *land grabbing* 5 *informal* to interest or impress ▸ n 6 the act of grabbing

> **grab** vb 1 = snatch, catch, seize, capture, grip, grasp, clutch, snap up

grace n 1 elegance and beauty of movement, form, or expression 2 a pleasing or charming quality: *architecture with few redeeming graces* 3 courtesy or decency: *at least she had the grace to laugh* 4 a delay granted for the completion of a task or payment of a debt: *another year's grace* 5 *Christian theol* the free and unmerited favour of God shown towards humankind 6 a short prayer of thanks for a meal 7 **airs and graces** an affected manner 8 **with bad grace** unwillingly or grudgingly: *independence was granted with bad grace* 9 **with good grace** willingly or ungrudgingly: *to accept with good grace* ▸ vb **gracing**, **graced** 10 to honour or favour: *graced by the presence of the ambassador* 11 to decorate or make more attractive: *bedsit walls graced by Che Guevara and James Dean*

> **grace** n 1 = elegance, poise, ease, polish, refinement, fluency, suppleness, gracefulness; ≠ ungainliness 3 = manners, decency, etiquette, consideration, propriety, tact, decorum; ≠ bad manners 4 = indulgence, mercy, pardon, reprieve 5 = benevolence, favour, goodness, goodwill, generosity, kindness, kindliness; ≠ ill will 6 = prayer, thanks, blessing, thanksgiving, benediction ▸ vb 10 = honour, favour, dignify; ≠ insult 11 = adorn, enhance, decorate, enrich, set off, ornament, embellish

Grace n **Your** or **His** or **Her Grace** a title used to address or refer to a duke, duchess, or archbishop

graceful adj having beauty of movement, style, or form > **gracefully** adv > **gracefulness** n

> **graceful** adj = elegant, easy, pleasing, beautiful; ≠ inelegant

graceless adj 1 lacking elegance 2 lacking manners

grace note n *music* a note that ornaments a melody

gracious adj 1 showing kindness and courtesy 2 characterized by elegance, ease, and indulgence: *gracious living* ▸ interj 3 an expression of mild surprise or wonder > **graciously** adv > **graciousness** n

> **gracious** adj 1 = courteous, polite, civil, accommodating, kind, friendly, cordial, well-mannered; ≠ ungracious

gradation n 1 a series of systematic stages; gradual progression 2 a stage in such a series or progression > **gradate** vb

grade n 1 a place on a scale of quality, rank, or size 2 a mark or rating indicating a student's level of achievement 3 a rank or level of importance in a company or organization 4 *US, Canad, Austral & S African* a class or year in a school 5 **make the grade** *informal* to be successful by reaching a required standard ▸ vb **grading**, **graded** 6 to arrange according to quality or rank: *passes are graded from A down to E* 7 to give a grade to: *students are graded by teachers based entirely on their coursework*

> **grade** n 1 = class 2 = mark, degree (*archaic*) 3 = level, rank, group, class, stage, category, echelon ▸ vb 6 = classify, rate, order, class, group, sort, range, rank

gradient n 1 Also (esp. US): **grade** a sloping part of a railway, road, or path 2 Also (esp. US): **grade** a measure of the steepness of such a slope 3 a measure of the change in something, such as the angle of a curve, over a specified distance

gradual adj occurring, developing, or moving in small stages: *a gradual handover of power* > **gradually** adv

gradual *adj* = steady, slow, regular, gentle, progressive, piecemeal, unhurried; ≠ sudden

graduate *n* **1** a person who holds a university or college degree **2** *US & Canad* a student who has completed a course of studies at a high school and received a diploma **3** same as **postgraduate** ▸ *vb* **-ating, -ated 4** to receive a degree or diploma **5** to change by degrees: *the winds graduate from tropical storms to cyclones* **6** to mark (a measuring flask or instrument) with units of measurement

graduate *vb* **6** = mark off, grade, proportion, regulate, gauge, calibrate, measure out

graduation *n* **1** the act of graduating from university or college **2** *US & Canad* the act of graduating from high school **3** the ceremony at which degrees and diplomas are given to graduating students **4** a mark indicating measure on an instrument or container

graffiti (graf-**fee**-tee) *n* drawings or words scribbled or sprayed on walls or posters

graft¹ *n* **1** *surgery* a piece of tissue transplanted to an area of the body in need of the tissue **2** a small piece of tissue from one plant that is joined to another plant so that they grow together as one ▸ *vb* **3** to transplant (tissue) to an area of the body in need of the tissue **4** to join (part of one plant) onto another plant so that they grow together as one **5** to attach or incorporate: *to graft Japanese production methods onto the American talent for innovation*

graft *n* **2** = shoot, bud, implant, sprout, splice, scion ▸ *vb* **4** = join, insert, transplant, implant, splice, affix

graft² *n* **1** *Brit informal* hard work **2** the practice of obtaining money by taking advantage of one's position ▸ *vb* **3** *informal* to work hard

graft *n* **1** = labour, work, effort, struggle, sweat, toil, slog, exertion ▸ *vb* = work, labour, struggle, sweat (*informal*), slave, strive, toil

Grail *n* See **Holy Grail**

grain *n* **1** the small hard seedlike fruit of a cereal plant **2** a mass of such fruits gathered for food **3** cereal plants in general **4** a small hard particle: *a grain of salt* **5** a very small amount: *a grain of compassion* **6** ▴ the arrangement of the fibres, layers, or particles in wood, leather, or stone ▸ the pattern or texture resulting from this **7 go against the grain** to be contrary to one's natural inclinations ▸ **grainy** *adj*

grain *n* **1** = seed, kernel, grist **2,3** = cereal, corn **4,5** = bit, piece, trace, scrap, particle, fragment, speck, morsel **6** = texture, pattern, surface, fibre, weave, nap

gram *or* **gramme** *n* a metric unit of weight equal to one thousandth of a kilogram

grammar *n* **1** the rules of a language, that show how sentences are formed, or how words are inflected **2** the way in which grammar is used: *the teacher found errors of spelling and grammar* **3** a book on the rules of grammar

grammarian *n* a person who studies or writes about grammar for a living

grammar school *n* **1** *Brit* (esp. formerly) a secondary school for children of high academic ability **2** *Austral* a private school, usually one controlled by a church

grammatical *adj* **1** of grammar **2** (of a sentence) following the rules of grammar ▸ **grammatically** *adv*

gramme *n* same as **gram**

gramophone *n* an old-fashioned type of record player

grampus *n, pl* **-puses** a dolphin-like mammal with a blunt snout

gran *n Brit, Austral & NZ informal* a grandmother

granary *n, pl* **-ries 1** a building for storing threshed grain **2** a region that produces a large amount of grain

grand *adj* **1** large or impressive in size or appearance; magnificent: *the grand hall* **2** ambitious or important: *grand themes* **3** dignified or haughty **4** *informal* excellent or wonderful **5** comprehensive or complete: *the grand total* ▸ *n* **6** *pl* **grand** *slang* a thousand pounds or dollars **7** short for **grand piano** ▸ **grandly** *adv*

grand *adj* **1** = impressive, great, large, magnificent, imposing, splendid, regal, stately; ≠ unimposing **2** = ambitious, great, grandiose **3** = superior, great, dignified, stately **4** = excellent, great (*informal*), fine, wonderful, outstanding, smashing (*informal*), first-class, splendid; ≠ bad

grandchild *n, pl* **-children** a son or daughter of one's son or daughter

granddaughter *n* a daughter of one's son or daughter

grandee *n* **1** a high-ranking Spanish nobleman **2** a person who has a high rank or position: *the Party's grandees*

grandeur *n* **1** personal greatness, dignity, or nobility: *delusions of grandeur* **2** magnificence or splendour: *cathedral-like grandeur*

grandeur *n* **2** = splendour, glory, majesty, nobility, pomp, magnificence, sumptuousness, sublimity

grandfather *n* the father of one's father or mother

grandfather clock *n* an old-fashioned clock in a tall wooden case that stands on the floor

grandiloquent *adj* using pompous or unnecessarily complicated language ▸ **grandiloquence** *n*

grandiose *adj* impressive, or meant to impress: *grandiose plans for constructing a new stadium*

grandmother *n* the mother of one's father or mother

g

grandparent *n* the father or mother of one's father or mother

grand piano *n* a large piano in which the strings are arranged horizontally

grand slam *n* the achievement of winning all the games or major tournaments in a sport in one season

grandson *n* a son of one's son or daughter

grandstand *n* the main block of seats giving the best view at a sports ground

grange *n* *Brit* a farmhouse or country house with its farm buildings

granite (gran-nit) *n* a very hard rock consisting of quartz and feldspars that is widely used for building

granny *or* **grannie** *n*, *pl* **-nies** *informal* a grandmother

granny flat *n* a flat in or joined on to a house, suitable for an elderly relative to live in

grant *vb* **1** to give (a sum of money or a right) formally: *to grant a 38% pay rise; only the President can grant a pardon* **2** to consent to perform or fulfil: *granting the men's request for sanctuary* **3** to admit that (something) is true: *I grant that her claims must be true* **4** **take for granted** **A** to accept that something is true without requiring proof **B** to take advantage of (someone or something) without showing appreciation ▸ *n* **5** a sum of money provided by a government or public fund to a person or organization for a specific purpose: *student grants*

> **grant** *vb* **2** = give, allow, present, award, permit, assign, allocate, hand out **3** = accept, allow, admit, acknowledge, concede ▸ *n* = award, allowance, donation, endowment, gift, subsidy, hand-out

granular *adj* of, like, or containing granules: *granular materials such as powders*

granulated *adj* (of sugar) in the form of coarse grains

granule *n* a small grain of something: *gravy granules*

grape *n* a small round sweet juicy fruit with a purple or green skin, which can be eaten raw, dried to make raisins, currants, or sultanas, or used to make wine

grapefruit *n*, *pl* **-fruit** *or* **-fruits** a large round yellow juicy citrus fruit with a slightly bitter taste

grapevine *n* **1** a vine grown for its grapes **2** *informal* an unofficial means of passing on information from person to person: *he'd doubtless heard rumours on the grapevine*

graph *n* a diagram showing the relation between certain sets of numbers or quantities by means of a series of dots or lines plotted with reference to a set of axes

graphene *n* a very thin, strong material consisting of a single layer of carbon atoms arranged in a hexagonal pattern

graphic *adj* **1** vividly described: *a graphic account*

of her three days in captivity **2** of the graphic arts: *graphic design* **3** Also: **graphical** *maths* of or using a graph: *a graphic presentation* > **graphically** *adv*

> **graphic** *adj* **1** = vivid, clear, detailed, striking, explicit, expressive; ≠ vague **2, 3** = pictorial, visual, diagrammatic; ≠ impressionistic

graphics *n* **1** the art of drawing in accordance with mathematical rules ▸ *pl n* **2** the illustrations in a magazine or book, or in a television or film production **3** *computers* information displayed in the form of diagrams or graphs

graphite *n* a soft black form of carbon used in pencils, as a lubricant, and in some nuclear reactors

graphology *n* the study of handwriting, usually to analyse the writer's character > **graphologist** *n*

grapnel *n* a device with several hooks at one end, which is used to grasp or secure an object, esp. in sailing

grapple *vb* **-pling, -pled** > **grapple with** **A** to try to cope with: *a difficult concept to grapple with* **B** to come to grips with (someone) in hand-to-hand combat

> **grapple** *vb* **1A** = deal, tackle, struggle, take on, confront, get to grips, address yourself to **1B** = struggle, fight, combat, wrestle, battle, clash, tussle, scuffle

grappling iron *n* same as **grapnel**

grasp *vb* **1** to grip firmly **2** to understand: *his failure to grasp the gravity of the crisis* ▸ *n* **3** a very firm grip **4** understanding or comprehension: *a good grasp of detail* **5** **within someone's grasp** almost certain to be accomplished or won: *she now has that prize within her grasp*

> **grasp** *vb* **1** = grip, hold, catch, grab, seize, snatch, clutch, clinch **2** = understand, realize, take in, get, see, catch on (*informal*), comprehend, catch or get the drift of ▸ *n* **3** = grip, hold, possession, embrace, clutches, clasp **4** = understanding, knowledge, grip, awareness, mastery, comprehension

grasping *adj* greedy for money

> **grasping** *adj* = greedy, acquisitive, rapacious, avaricious, covetous, snoep (*S African informal*); ≠ generous

grass *n* **1** a very common green plant with jointed stems and long narrow leaves, eaten by animals such as sheep and cows, and used for lawns and sports fields **2** a particular kind of grass, such as bamboo **3** a lawn **4** *slang* marijuana **5** *Brit & Austral slang* a person who informs, usually on criminals ▸ *vb* **6** **grass on** or **up** *Brit slang* to inform on (someone) to the police or some other authority **7** **grass over** to cover with grass > **grassy** *adj*

grasshopper *n* an insect with long hind legs which it uses for leaping

grass roots *pl n* **1** ordinary members of a group or organization, as distinct from its leaders ▸ *adj* **grassroots 2** of the ordinary members of a group or organization: *the focus of a virulent grassroots campaign*

grass tree *n* an Australian plant with stiff grass-like leaves and small white flowers

grate¹ *vb* **grating, grated 1** to reduce to shreds by rubbing against a rough surface: *grated cheese* **2** to produce a harsh rasping sound by scraping against an object or surface: *the clutch plates grated* **3 grate on** to annoy: *his manner always grated on me*

> **grate** *vb* **1** = shred, mince, pulverize **2** = scrape, grind, rub, scratch, creak, rasp

grate² *n* **1** a framework of metal bars for holding coal or wood in a fireplace **2** same as **grating¹**

grateful *adj* feeling or showing thanks > **gratefully** *adv*

> **grateful** *adj* = thankful, obliged, in (someone's) debt, indebted, appreciative, beholden

grater *n* a tool with a sharp surface for grating food

gratify *vb* **-fies, -fying, -fied 1** to satisfy or please (someone) **2** to yield to (a desire or whim): *all his wishes were to be gratified* > **gratification** *n*

grating¹ *n* a framework of metal bars covering an opening in a wall or in the ground

> **grating** *n* = grille, grid, grate, lattice, trellis, gridiron

grating² *adj* **1** (of a sound) rough or unpleasant **2** annoying or irritating: *his cringing obsequiousness was grating*

> **grating** *adj* = irritating, harsh, annoying, jarring, unpleasant, raucous, strident, discordant; ≠ pleasing

gratis *adv, adj* without payment; free: *the gifts are gratis*

gratitude *n* a feeling of being grateful for gifts or favours

> **gratitude** *n* = thankfulness, thanks, recognition, obligation, appreciation, indebtedness, gratefulness; ≠ ingratitude

gratuitous (grat-tyoo-it-uss) *adj* **1** unjustified or unreasonable: *gratuitous violence* **2** given or received without charge or obligation: *his gratuitous voluntary services* > **gratuitously** *adv*

gratuity (grat-tyoo-it-ee) *n, pl* **-ties** money given for services rendered; tip

grave¹ *adj* (rhymes with **save**) **1** serious and worrying: *grave concern* **2** serious and solemn in appearance or behaviour: *the woman looked grave and respectful* **3** (rhymes with **halve**) denoting an accent (`) over a vowel in some languages, such as French, which indicates that the vowel is pronounced in a particular way ▸ *n* (rhymes with **halve**) **4** a grave accent > **gravely** *adv*

grave *adj* **1** = serious, important, critical, pressing, threatening, dangerous, acute, severe; ≠ trifling **2** = solemn, sober, sombre, dour, unsmiling; ≠ carefree

grave² (rhymes with **save**) *n* a place where a dead person is buried. Related adjective: **sepulchral**

> **grave** *n* = tomb, vault, crypt, mausoleum, sepulchre, pit, burying place

gravel *n* **1** a mixture of rock fragments and pebbles that is coarser than sand **2** *pathol* small rough stones in the kidneys or bladder ▸ *vb* **-elling, -elled** or US **-eling, -eled 3** to cover with gravel

gravelly *adj* **1** covered with gravel **2** (of a voice or sound) harsh and grating

gravestone *n* a stone marking a grave

graveyard *n* a place where dead people are buried, esp. one by a church

> **graveyard** *n* = cemetery, churchyard, burial ground, charnel house, necropolis

gravid (grav-id) *adj med* pregnant

gravitate *vb* **-tating, -tated 1 gravitate towards** to be attracted or influenced by: *the mathematically inclined often gravitate towards computers* **2** *physics* to move under the influence of gravity

gravitation *n physics* **1** the force of attraction that bodies exert on one another as a result of their mass **2** the process or result of this interaction > **gravitational** *adj*

gravity *n, pl* **-ties 1** *physics* **A** the force that attracts bodies towards the centre of the earth, a moon, or any planet **B** same as **gravitation 2** seriousness or importance: *the gravity of the situation* **3** seriousness or solemnity of appearance or behaviour: *his priestly gravity*

> **gravity** *n* **2** = seriousness, importance, significance, urgency, severity, acuteness, weightiness, momentousness; ≠ triviality **3** = solemnity, seriousness, gravitas; ≠ frivolity

gravy *n, pl* **-vies A** the juices that come from meat during cooking **B** the sauce made by thickening and flavouring these juices

gray *adj, n, vb chiefly US* grey

graze¹ *vb* **grazing, grazed A** (of an animal) to eat (grass or other growing plants) **B** to feed (animals) on grass or other growing plants

> **graze** *vb* **1A** = feed, crop, browse, pasture

graze² *vb* **grazing, grazed 1** to break the skin of (a part of the body) by scraping **2** to brush against someone gently in passing ▸ *n* **3** an injury on the skin caused by scraping

> **graze** *vb* **1** = scratch, skin, scrape, chafe, abrade **2** = touch, brush, rub, scrape, shave, skim, glance off ▸ *n* = scratch, scrape, abrasion

grease *n* **1** soft melted animal fat **2** a thick oily substance, such as the kind put on machine parts to make them work smoothly ▸ *vb* **greasing, greased 3** to apply grease to: *lightly grease a baking tin* **4 grease someone's palm** *slang* to bribe someone

greasepaint *n* theatrical make-up

greasy *adj* **greasier, greasiest 1** covered with or containing grease **2** excessively pleasant or flattering in an insincere manner ▸ **greasiness** *n*

> **greasy** *adj* **1** = fatty, slippery, oily, slimy (*Brit*), oleaginous

great *adj* **1** large in size **2** large in number or amount: *the great majority* **3** larger than others of its kind: *the great white whale* **4** extreme or more than usual: *great difficulty* **5** of importance or consequence: *a great discovery* **6** of exceptional talents or achievements: *a great artist* **7** skilful: *he's a great storyteller; they are great at problem solving* **8** *informal* excellent ▸ *n* **9 the greats** the most successful people in a particular field: *the all-time greats of golf* ▸ **greatly** *adv* ▸ **greatness** *n*

> **great** *adj* **1, 2** = large, big, huge, vast, enormous, immense, gigantic, prodigious, supersize; ≠ small **8** = excellent, fine, wonderful, superb, fantastic (*informal*), tremendous (*informal*), marvellous (*informal*), terrific (*informal*), booshit (*Austral slang*), exo (*Austral slang*), sik (*Austral slang*), rad (*informal*), phat (*slang*), schmick (*Austral informal*); ≠ poor

great- *prefix* (in expressing relationship) one generation older or younger than: *great-grandmother*

greatcoat *n* a heavy overcoat

Great Dane *n* a very large dog with short smooth hair

grebe *n* a diving water bird

Grecian (gree-shan) *adj* of ancient Greece

greed *n* excessive desire for something, such as food or money

> **greed** *n* = avarice, longing, desire, hunger, craving, selfishness, acquisitiveness, covetousness; ≠ generosity

greedy *adj* **greedier, greediest** having an excessive desire for something, such as food or money: *greedy for personal possessions* ▸ **greedily** *adv*

> **greedy** *adj* = avaricious, grasping, selfish, insatiable, acquisitive, rapacious, materialistic, desirous; ≠ generous

Greek *adj* **1** of Greece ▸ *n* **2** a person from Greece **3** the language of Greece

green *adj* **1** of a colour between yellow and blue; of the colour of grass **2** covered with grass, plants, or trees: *green fields* **3** of or concerned with conservation and improvement of the environment: used in a political context: *green issues* **4** (of fruit) fresh, raw, or unripe **5** pale and sick-looking **6** inexperienced or gullible **7 green with envy** very envious ▸ *n* **8** a colour

between yellow and blue **9** anything green, such as green clothing or green ink: *printed in green* **10** a small area of grassy land: *the village green* **11** an area of smooth turf kept for a special purpose: *putting greens* **12 greens** the leaves and stems of certain plants, eaten as a vegetable: *turnip greens* **13 Green** a person who supports environmentalist issues ▸ **greenish** *or* **greeny** *adj* ▸ **greenness** *n*

> **green** *adj* **2** = verdant (*literary*), leafy, grassy **3** = ecological, conservationist, environment-friendly, ozone-friendly, non-polluting, sustainable, recyclable, green-collar **6** = inexperienced, new, raw, naive, immature, gullible, untrained, wet behind the ears (*informal*) ▸ *n* **10, 11** = lawn, common, turf, sward

green belt *n* a protected zone of parkland or open country surrounding a town or city

greenery *n* green leaves or growing plants: *lush greenery*

greenfinch *n* a European finch, the male of which has olive-green feathers

green fingers *pl n* skill in growing plants

greenfly *n, pl* **-flies** a green aphid commonly occurring as a pest on plants

greengage *n* a green sweet variety of plum

greengrocer *n Brit & Austral* a shopkeeper who sells fruit and vegetables

greenhorn *n* an inexperienced person; novice

greenhouse *n* **1** a building with glass walls and roof where plants are grown under controlled conditions ▸ *adj* **2** relating to or contributing to the greenhouse effect: *greenhouse gases such as carbon dioxide*

greenhouse effect *n* the gradual rise in temperature in the earth's atmosphere due to heat being absorbed from the sun and being trapped by gases such as carbon dioxide in the air around the earth

greenhouse gas *n* any gas that contributes to the greenhouse effect

green light *n* **1** a signal to go **2** permission to proceed with a project ▸ *vb* **greenlight, -lighting, -lighted 3** to permit (a project) to proceed

greenstone *n NZ* a type of green jade used for Māori carvings and ornaments

greet *vb* **1** to address or meet with expressions of friendliness or welcome **2** to receive in a specified manner: *a direct request would be greeted coolly* **3** to be immediately noticeable to: *the scene of devastation which greeted him*

> **greet** *vb* **1** = welcome, meet, receive, karanga (NZ), mihi (NZ), haeremai (NZ) **2** = receive, take, respond to, react to

greeting *n* the act or words of welcoming on meeting

> **greeting** *n* = welcome, reception, salute, address, salutation (*formal*), hongi (NZ), kia ora (NZ)

gregarious *adj* **1** enjoying the company of others **2** (of animals) living together in herds or in flocks

gremlin *n* an imaginary imp jokingly blamed for malfunctions in machinery

grenade *n* a small bomb filled with explosive or gas, thrown by hand or fired from a rifle

grenadier *n military* **1** (in the British Army) a member of the senior regiment of infantry in the Household Brigade (the **Grenadier Guards**) **2** (formerly) a soldier trained to throw grenades

grenadine (gren-a-**deen**) *n* a syrup made from pomegranate juice, often used as an ingredient in cocktails

grevillea *n* any of various Australian evergreen trees and shrubs

grew *vb* the past tense of **grow**

grey *or US* **gray** *adj* **1** of a colour between black and white; of the colour of ashes **2** **A** (of hair) having partly turned white **B** (of a person) having grey hair **3** dismal, dark, or gloomy: *a grey and misty morning* **4** dull or boring: *in 1948 life generally was grey* ▸ *n* **5** a colour between black and white **6** anything grey, such as grey paint or grey clothing: *available in grey or brown* **7** a grey or whitish horse ➤ **greyness** *n* ➤ **greyish** *adj*

> **grey** *or* **gray** *adj* **1, 3** = dull, dark, dim, gloomy, drab **4** = boring, dull, anonymous, faceless, colourless, nondescript, characterless

greyed out *adj* (of a navigation button, menu item, etc. on a computer screen) not highlighted, indicating that the function is not available

greyhound *n* a tall slender dog that can run very fast and is used for racing

greying *adj* becoming grey: *greying hair*

grey matter *n informal* intellect or brains: *those who don't have lots of grey matter*

grid *n* **1** a network of crossing parallel lines on a map, plan, or graph paper for locating points **2 the grid** the national network of cables or pipes by which electricity, gas, or water is distributed **3** *electronics* an electrode that controls the flow of electrons between the cathode and anode of a valve

griddle *n* a thick round iron plate placed on top of a cooker and used to cook food

gridiron *n* **1** a utensil of parallel metal bars, used to grill food **2** the field of play in American football

gridlock *n* **1** obstruction of traffic caused by queues of vehicles forming across junctions and so causing queues in intersecting streets **2** a point in a dispute at which no agreement can be reached: *political gridlock* ▸ *vb* **3** (of traffic) to obstruct (an area)

grief *n* **1** deep or intense sorrow **2** *informal* trouble or annoyance: *people were giving me grief for leaving ten minutes early* **3 come to grief** to have an unfortunate or unsuccessful end or outcome

> **grief** *n* **1** = sadness, suffering, regret, distress, misery, sorrow, woe, anguish; ≠ joy

grievance *n* **1** a real or imaginary cause for complaint **2** a feeling of resentment at having been unfairly treated

> **grievance** *n* **1** = complaint, gripe (*informal*), axe to grind

grieve *vb* **grieving**, **grieved** to feel or cause to feel great sorrow or distress ➤ **grieved** *adj* ➤ **grieving** *adj*

> **grieve** *vb* = sadden, hurt, injure, distress, wound, pain, afflict, upset; ≠ gladden

grievous *adj* **1** very severe or painful: *grievous injuries* **2** very serious or worrying: *a grievous loss* ➤ **grievously** *adv*

griffin, griffon *or* **gryphon** *n* a mythical winged monster with an eagle's head and a lion's body

grill *vb* **1** to cook by direct heat under a grill or over a hot fire **2** *informal* to subject to relentless questioning: *the jury pool was grilled for signs of prejudice* ▸ *n* **3** a device on a cooker that radiates heat downwards for grilling food **4** a gridiron for cooking food **5** a dish of grilled food ➤ **grilled** *adj* ➤ **grilling** *n*

grille *or* **grill** *n* a metal or wooden grating, used as a screen or partition

grilse (grillss) *n, pl* **grilses** *or* **grilse** a salmon on its first return from the sea to fresh water

grim *adj* **grimmer**, **grimmest** **1** unfavourable and worrying: *grim figures on unemployment* **2** harsh and unpleasant: *grim conditions in the detention centres* **3** stern or resolute: *a grim determination to fight on* **4** *informal* unpleasant or disagreeable ➤ **grimly** *adv* ➤ **grimness** *n*

> **grim** *adj* **1** = terrible, severe, harsh, forbidding, formidable, sinister

grimace *n* **1** an ugly or distorted facial expression of disgust, pain, or displeasure ▸ *vb* **-macing**, **-maced** **2** to make a grimace

grime *n* **1** ingrained dirt **2** a type of British rap music ▸ *vb* **griming**, **grimed** **3** to make very dirty: *sweat-grimed faces* ➤ **grimy** *adj*

grin *vb* **grinning**, **grinned** **1** to smile broadly, showing one's teeth **2 grin and bear it** *informal* to suffer hardship without complaint ▸ *n* **3** a broad smile ➤ **grinning** *adj*

grind *vb* **grinding**, **ground** **1** to reduce to small particles by pounding or rubbing: *grinding coffee* **2** to smooth, sharpen, or polish by friction **3** (of two objects) to scrape together with a harsh rasping sound **4 an axe to grind** See **axe** (sense 2) **5 grind one's teeth** to rub one's upper and lower teeth against each other, as if chewing **6 grind to a halt** to come to an end or a standstill: *without enzymes life would grind to a halt* ▸ *n* **7** *informal* hard or tedious work: *the grind of everyday life*

grind vb 1 = crush, mill, powder, grate, pulverize, pound, abrade, granulate 2 = sharpen, polish, sand, smooth, whet 3 = grate, scrape, gnash ▸ n = hard work (*informal*), labour, sweat (*informal*), chore, toil, drudgery

grind out n to produce (a result) in a routine or uninspired manner

grindstone n 1 a revolving stone disc used for sharpening, grinding, or polishing things 2 **keep one's nose to the grindstone** to work hard and steadily

grip n 1 a very tight hold: *he felt a grip at his throat* 2 the style or manner of holding something, such as a golf club or tennis racket 3 power or control over a situation, person, or activity: *rebel forces tighten their grip around the capital* 4 a travelling bag or holdall 5 a small bent clasp used to fasten the hair 6 a handle 7 a person who manoeuvres the cameras in a film or television studio 8 **get** or **come to grips with** to face up to and deal with (a problem or subject) ▸ vb **gripping**, **gripped** 9 to take a tight hold of 10 to affect strongly: *sudden panic gripped her* 11 to hold the interest or attention of: *gripped by the intensity of the film; the story gripped him*

grip n 1 = clasp, hold, grasp 3 = control, rule, influence, command, power, possession, domination, mastery ▸ vb 9 = grasp, hold, catch, seize, clutch, clasp, take hold of 11 = engross, fascinate, absorb, entrance, hold, compel, rivet, enthral

gripe vb **griping**, **griped** 1 *informal* to complain persistently 2 to cause sudden intense pain in the bowels ▸ n 3 *informal* a complaint 4 **the gripes** a sudden intense pain in the bowels

gripping adj very interesting and exciting: *a gripping story*

gripping adj = fascinating, exciting, thrilling, entrancing, compelling, riveting, enthralling, engrossing

grisly adj **-lier**, **-liest** causing horror or dread: *grisly murders*

grist n 1 grain that is to be or that has been ground 2 **grist to the mill** anything that can be turned to profit or advantage

gristle n tough stringy animal tissue found in meat > **gristly** adj

grit n 1 small hard particles of sand, earth, or stone 2 courage and determination ▸ vb **gritting**, **gritted** 3 to cover (an icy road) with grit 4 **grit one's teeth** A to rub one's upper and lower teeth against each other, as if chewing B to decide to carry on in a difficult situation: *he urged the Cabinet to grit its teeth and continue cutting public spending*

grit n 1 = gravel, sand, dust, pebbles 2 = courage, spirit, resolution, determination, guts (*informal*), backbone, fortitude, tenacity

gritty adj **-tier**, **-tiest** 1 courageous and tough 2 covered with grit

gritty adj 1 = courageous, dogged, determined, spirited, brave, feisty (*informal*), resolute, tenacious, plucky, (as) game as Ned Kelly (*Austral slang*) 2 = rough, sandy, dusty, rasping, gravelly, granular

grizzle vb **-zling**, **-zled** Brit, Austral & NZ informal to whine or complain

grizzled adj 1 (of hair) streaked or mixed with grey 2 (of a person) having grey hair

grizzly n, pl **-zlies** a large fierce greyish-brown bear of N America. In full: **grizzly bear**

groan n 1 a long deep cry of pain, grief, or disapproval 2 *informal* a grumble or complaint ▸ vb 3 to give a long deep cry of pain, grief, or disapproval 4 *informal* to complain or grumble 5 **groan under** to be weighed down by: *chemists' shelves groan under the weight of slimming aids* > **groaning** adj, n

groan n 1 = moan, cry, sigh, whine 2 = complaint, protest, objection, grumble, grouse, gripe (*informal*) ▸ vb 3 = moan, cry, sigh 4 = complain, object, moan (*informal*), grumble, gripe (*informal*), carp, lament, whine

groat n a former British coin worth four old pennies

grocer n a shopkeeper who sells food and other household supplies

grocery n, pl **-ceries** the business or premises of a grocer

grog n 1 an alcoholic drink, usually rum, diluted with water 2 Brit, Austral & NZ informal any alcoholic drink

groggy adj **-gier**, **-giest** informal faint, weak, or dizzy

groin n 1 the part of the body where the abdomen joins the legs 2 archit a curved edge formed where two intersecting vaults meet

grommet n 1 a rubber, plastic, or metal ring or eyelet 2 med a small tube inserted into the eardrum to drain fluid from the middle ear

groom n 1 a person employed to clean and look after horses 2 short for **bridegroom** ▸ vb 3 to clean and smarten (a horse or other animal) 4 to keep (oneself or one's appearance) clean and tidy: *carefully groomed hair* 5 to train (someone) for a particular task or occupation: *groomed for future leadership* > **grooming** n

groom n 1 = stableman, stableboy, hostler or ostler (*archaic*) ▸ vb 3 = brush, clean, tend, rub down, curry 4 = smarten up, clean, tidy, preen, spruce up, primp 5 = train, prime, prepare, coach, ready, educate, drill, nurture

groove n 1 a long narrow furrow cut into a surface 2 *informal* a pleasing rhythm > **grooved** adj

groove n 1 = indentation, cut, hollow, channel, trench, flute, trough, furrow

grope *vb* **groping, groped** **1** to feel about uncertainly for something **2** to find (one's way) by groping **3** to search uncertainly for a solution or expression: *the new democracies are groping for stability* **4** *slang* to fondle (someone) in a rough sexual way ► *n* **5** an instance of groping

> **grope** *vb* **1, 3** = feel, search, fumble, flounder, fish, scrabble, cast about, fossick (*Austral, NZ*)

gross *adj* **1** outrageously wrong: *gross violations of human rights* **2** very coarse or vulgar: *gross bad taste* **3** *slang* disgusting or repulsive: *I think beards are gross* **4** repulsively fat **5** with no deductions for tax or the weight of the container; total: *gross income; a gross weight of 20 000 lbs* ► *n* **6** *pl* **gross** twelve dozen (144) **7** the entire amount or weight ► *vb* **8** to earn as total revenue, before deductions > **grossly** *adv*

> **gross** *adj* **1** = flagrant, blatant, rank, sheer, utter, grievous, heinous, unmitigated; ≠ qualified **2, 3** = vulgar, offensive, crude, obscene, coarse, indelicate; ≠ decent **4** = fat, obese, overweight, hulking, corpulent; ≠ slim **5** = total, whole, entire, aggregate, before tax, before deductions; ≠ net ► *vb* = earn, make, take, bring in, rake in (*informal*)

grotesque (groh-**tesk**) *adj* **1** strangely distorted or bizarre: *a grotesque and pervasive personality cult* **2** ugly or repulsive ► *n* **3** a grotesque person or thing **4** an artistic style in which parts of human, animal, and plant forms are distorted and mixed, or a work of art in this style > **grotesquely** *adv*

> **grotesque** *adj* **1** = absurd, preposterous; ≠ natural

grotto *n, pl* **-toes** *or* **-tos** a small picturesque cave
grotty *adj* **-tier, -tiest** *Brit & NZ slang* **1** nasty or unattractive **2** in bad condition
grouch *informal* ► *vb* **1** to complain or grumble ► *n* **2** a person who is always complaining **3** a persistent complaint
grouchy *adj* **grouchier, grouchiest** bad-tempered
ground[1] *n* **1** the land surface **2** earth or soil **3** an area used for a particular purpose: *a cricket ground* **4** a matter for consideration or discussion: *there is no need to cover the same ground* **5** an advantage in an argument or competition: *neither side seems willing to give ground in this trial of strength* **6** the background colour of a painting **7** *US & Canad* an electrical earth **8** **grounds** ʌ the land around a building ʙ reason or justification: *the hostages should be freed on humanitarian grounds* ᴄ sediment or dregs: *coffee grounds* **9 break new ground** to do something that has not been done before **10 common ground** an agreed basis for identifying issues in an argument **11 get something off the ground** to get something started: *to get the peace conference off the ground* **12 into the ground** to exhaustion or excess: *he was running himself into the ground* **13 suit someone**

down to the ground *Brit informal* to be totally suitable or appropriate for someone ► *adj* **14** on the ground: *ground troops* ► *vb* **15** to confine (an aircraft or pilot) to the ground **16** *naut* to move (a ship) onto the bottom of shallow water, so that it cannot move **17** to instruct in the basics of a subject: *the student who is not grounded in the elements cannot understand the advanced teaching* **18** to provide a basis for; establish: *a scientifically grounded documentation* **19** to go out and enjoy himself or herself as a punishment **20** *US & Canad* to connect (a circuit or electrical device) to an earth

> **ground** *n* **1** = earth, land, dry land, terra firma **3** = arena, pitch, stadium, park, field, enclosure **8ᴀ** = estate, land, fields, gardens, territory **8ʙ** = reason, cause, basis, occasion, foundation, excuse, motive, justification **8ᴄ** = dregs, lees, deposit, sediment ► *vb* **17** = instruct, train, teach, initiate, tutor, acquaint with, familiarize with **18** = base, found, establish, set, settle, fix

ground[2] *vb* **1** the past of **grind** ► *adj* **2** reduced to fine particles by grinding: *ground glass*
ground-breaking *adj* innovative
ground floor *n* the floor of a building that is level, or almost level, with the ground
grounding *n* a foundation, esp. the basic general knowledge of a subject
groundless *adj* without reason or justification: *the scare turned out to be groundless*
groundnut *n Brit* a peanut
groundsheet *n* a waterproof sheet placed on the ground in a tent to keep out damp
groundsman *n, pl* **-men** a person employed to maintain a sports ground or park
groundswell *n* a rapidly developing general feeling or opinion
groundwork *n* preliminary work as a foundation or basis
group *n* **1** a number of people or things considered as a unit **2** a small band of players or singers, esp. of popular music **3** an association of business firms that have the same owner **4** *chem* two or more atoms that are bound together in a molecule and behave as a single unit: *a methyl group* $-CH_3$ **5** *chem* a vertical column of elements in the periodic table that all have similar properties: *the halogen group* ► *vb* **6** to put into or form into a group

> **group** *n* **1** = crowd, party, band, pack, gang, bunch (*informal*) ► *vb* = arrange, order, sort, class, classify, marshal, bracket

grouse[1] *n, pl* **grouse** **1** a game bird with a stocky body and feathered legs and feet **2** the flesh of this bird used for food
grouse[2] *vb* **grousing, groused** **1** to complain or grumble ► *n* **2** a persistent complaint
grout *n* **1** a thin mortar for filling joints between tiles or masonry ► *vb* **2** to fill with grout

grove *n* a small wood or group of trees: *orange groves*

> **grove** *n* = wood, plantation, covert, thicket, copse, coppice, spinney

grovel (grov-el) *vb* **-elling, -elled** or US **-eling, -eled** 1 to behave excessively humbly towards someone, esp. a superior, in an attempt to win his or her favour 2 to crawl on the floor, often in search of something: *grovelling on the floor for missing cards* > **grovelling** or US **groveling** *adj, n*

grow *vb* **growing, grew, grown** 1 (of a person or animal) to increase in size and develop physically 2 (of a plant) to exist and increase in size: *an ancient meadow where wild flowers grow* 3 to produce (a plant) by planting seeds, bulbs, or cuttings, and looking after it: *many farmers have expressed a wish to grow more cotton* 4 to let (one's hair or nails) develop: *to grow a beard* 5 to increase in size or degree: *the gulf between rich and poor is growing* 6 to originate or develop: *Melbourne grew from a sheep-farming outstation and occasional port to a city* 7 to become increasingly as specified: *as the night wore on the audience grew more intolerant* > **growing** *adj* > **grower** *n*

> **grow** *vb* 1 = develop, get bigger; ≠ shrink 3 = cultivate, produce, raise, farm, breed, nurture, propagate 5 = get bigger, spread, swell, stretch, expand, enlarge, multiply 6 = originate, spring, arise, stem, issue 7 = become, get, turn, come to be

growl *vb* 1 (of a dog or other animal) to make a low rumbling sound, usually in anger 2 to say in a gruff or angry manner: *'You're late,' he growled* 3 to make a deep rumbling sound: *her stomach growled* ▸ *n* 4 the act or sound of growling

grown-up *adj* 1 having reached maturity; adult 2 of or suitable for an adult ▸ *n* 3 an adult

> **grown-up** *adj* = mature, adult, of age, fully-grown ▸ *n* = adult, man, woman

growth *n* 1 the process of growing 2 an increase in size, number, or significance: *the growth of drug trafficking* 3 something grown or growing: *a thick growth of ivy* 4 any abnormal tissue, such as a tumour ▸ *adj* 5 of or relating to growth: *growth hormone*

> **growth** *n* 1 = increase, development, expansion, proliferation, enlargement, multiplication; ≠ decline 2 = progress, success, improvement, expansion, advance, prosperity; ≠ failure 4 = tumour, cancer, swelling, lump, carcinoma (*pathol*), sarcoma (*med*)

grow up *vb* to reach maturity; become adult

groyne *n* a wall or breakwater built out from a shore to control erosion

grub *n* 1 *slang* food 2 the short legless larva of certain insects, such as beetles ▸ *vb* **grubbing, grubbed** 3 to search carefully for something by digging or by moving things about 4 **grub up** to dig (roots or plants) out of the ground

grubby *adj* **-bier, -biest** 1 rather dirty 2 unsavoury or morally unacceptable: *grubby activities* > **grubbiness** *n*

grudge *n* 1 a persistent feeling of resentment against a person who has caused harm or upset ▸ *vb* **grudging, grudged** 2 to give unwillingly: *the rich men who grudged pennies for poor people* 3 to resent or envy the success or possessions of: *none of their guests grudged them this celebration* ▸ *adj* 4 planned or carried out in order to settle a grudge: *a grudge match*

> **grudge** *n* = resentment, bitterness, grievance, dislike, animosity, antipathy, enmity, rancour; ≠ goodwill ▸ *vb* = resent, mind, envy, covet, begrudge; ≠ welcome

gruel *n* thin porridge made by boiling oatmeal in water or milk

gruelling or US **grueling** *adj* extremely severe or tiring: *a gruelling journey*

> **gruelling** or **grueling** *adj* = exhausting, demanding, tiring, taxing, severe, punishing, strenuous, arduous; ≠ easy

gruesome *adj* inspiring horror and disgust

> **gruesome** *adj* = horrific, shocking, terrible, horrible, grim, ghastly, grisly, macabre; ≠ pleasant

gruff *adj* 1 rough or surly in manner or speech 2 (of a voice) low and throaty > **gruffly** *adv* > **gruffness** *n*

grumble *vb* **-bling, -bled** 1 to complain in a nagging way: *his neighbour grumbled about the long wait* 2 to make low rumbling sounds: *the storm grumbled in the distance* ▸ *n* 3 a complaint 4 a low rumbling sound: *a distant grumble of artillery fire* > **grumbling** *adj, n*

> **grumble** *vb* 1 = complain, moan (*informal*), gripe (*informal*), whinge (*informal*), carp, whine, grouse, bleat 2 = rumble, growl, gurgle ▸ *n* 3 = complaint, protest, objection, moan (*informal*), grievance, grouse, gripe (*informal*), grouch (*informal*) 4 = rumble, growl, gurgle

grumpy *adj* **grumpier, grumpiest** sulky and bad-tempered > **grumpily** *adv*

grunge *n* 1 a style of rock music with a fuzzy guitar sound 2 a deliberately untidy and uncoordinated fashion style

grunt *vb* 1 to make a low short gruff noise, such as the sound made by a pig, or by a person to express annoyance 2 to express (something) gruffly: *he grunted his thanks* ▸ *n* 3 a low short gruff noise, such as the sound made by a pig, or by a person to express annoyance

Gruyère (grew-yair) *n* a hard flat pale yellow cheese with holes

gryphon *n* same as **griffin**

GST (in Australia, New Zealand, and Canada) Goods and Services Tax

G-string *n* a strip of cloth worn between the legs and attached to a waistband

GT gran turismo: a touring car, usually a fast sports car with a hard fixed roof

guano (**gwah**-no) *n* the dried manure of sea birds, used as a fertilizer

guarantee *n* **1** a formal assurance in writing that a product or service will meet certain standards or specifications **2** something that makes a specified condition or outcome certain: *there was no guarantee that there would not be another military coup* ▸ *vb* **-teeing, -teed 3** to promise or make certain: *to guarantee absolute loyalty* **4** (of a company) to provide a guarantee in writing for (a product or service) **5** to take responsibility for the debts or obligations of (another person)

> **guarantee** *n* **1** = warranty, contract, bond
> ▸ *vb* **3** = promise, pledge, undertake

guarantor *n* a person who gives or is bound by a guarantee or guaranty

guard *vb* **1** to watch over or shield from danger or harm; protect: *US marines who guard the American embassy* **2** to keep watch over (a prisoner) to prevent escape **3** to protect (a right or privilege) **4** to take precautions: *to guard against a possible coup attempt* ▸ *n* **5** a person or group of people who protect or watch over people or things **6** *Brit, Austral & NZ* the official in charge of a train **7** a device or part of a machine designed to protect the user against injury **8** anything that provides protection: *a guard against future shocks* **9** **off guard** having one's defences down; unprepared: *England were caught off guard as the Dutch struck two telling blows* **10** **on guard** on duty to protect or watch over people or things **11** **on one's guard** prepared to face danger or difficulties: *parents have been warned to be on their guard against kidnappers* **12** **stand guard** (of a sentry) to keep watch

> **guard** *vb* **1, 3, 4** = protect, defend, secure, mind, preserve, shield, safeguard, watch over
> ▸ *n* **8** = shield, security, defence, screen, protection, safeguard, buffer

guarded *adj* cautious and avoiding any commitment: *a guarded welcome* > **guardedly** *adv*

> **guarded** *adj* = cautious, reserved, careful, suspicious, wary, prudent, reticent, circumspect

guardian *n* **1** one who looks after, protects, or defends someone or something: *the nation's moral guardians* **2** someone legally appointed to manage the affairs of another person, such as a child or other vulnerable person > **guardianship** *n*

> **guardian** *n* **1** = keeper, champion, defender, guard, warden, curator, protector, custodian

guardsman *n, pl* **-men** *military* a member of a regiment responsible for ceremonial duties

guava (**gwah**-va) *n* a round tropical fruit with yellow skin and pink pulp

gudgeon *n* a small slender European freshwater fish, used as bait by anglers

Guernsey (**gurn**-zee) *n* a breed of dairy cattle that produces rich creamy milk, originating from Guernsey, in the Channel Islands

guerrilla *or* **guerilla** *n* a member of an irregular, politically motivated, armed force that fights regular forces

> **guerrilla** *or* **guerilla** *n* = freedom fighter, partisan, underground fighter

guess *vb* **1** to form an estimate or conclusion about (something), without proper knowledge: *a competition to guess the weight of the cake* **2** to arrive at a correct estimate of (something) by guessing: *I had a notion that he guessed my thoughts* **3** *informal* to think or suppose: *I guess he must have been a great athlete* ▸ *n* **4** an estimate or conclusion arrived at by guessing: *we can hazard a guess at the answer*

> **guess** *vb* **1, 2** = estimate, predict, work out, speculate, conjecture, postulate, hypothesize; ≠ know **3** = suppose, think, believe, suspect, judge, imagine, reckon (*informal*), fancy
> ▸ *n* = estimate, speculation, judgment, hypothesis, conjecture, shot in the dark; ≠ certainty

guesswork *n* the process of arriving at conclusions or estimates by guessing

guest *n* **1** a person who receives hospitality at someone else's home **2** a person who is taken out socially by someone else who pays all the expenses **3** a performer or speaker taking part in an event, show, or programme by special invitation **4** a person who is staying in a hotel ▸ *vb* **5** to be a guest in an event, show, or programme: *she guested in concert with Kylie Minogue*

> **guest** *n* **1** = visitor, company, caller, manu(w)hiri (NZ)

guesthouse *n* a private home or boarding house offering accommodation

guff *n Brit, Austral & NZ slang* ridiculous talk; nonsense

guffaw *vb* **1** to laugh loudly and raucously ▸ *n* **2** a loud raucous laugh

guidance *n* help, advice, or instruction, usually from someone more experienced or more qualified: *marriage guidance*

> **guidance** *n* = advice, direction, leadership, instruction, help, management, teaching, counselling

guide *n* **1** a person who conducts parties of tourists around places of interest, such as museums **2** a person who leads travellers to a place, usually in a dangerous area: *a mountain guide* **3** something that can be used to gauge something or to help in planning one's actions: *starting salary was not an accurate guide to future earnings* **4** a book that explains the basics of a subject or skill: *a guide to higher education* ▸ *vb* **guiding, guided 5** to lead the way for (tourists or travellers) **6** to control the movement or course of; steer **7** to direct the affairs of (a person, team, or country): *he will stay with the club he guided to promotion to the First Division* **8** to influence (a person) in his or her actions or opinions: *to be guided by the law* ▷ **guiding** *adj*

guide *n* **1, 2** = escort, leader, usher **3** = model, example, standard, ideal, inspiration, paradigm **4** = handbook, manual, guidebook, instructions, catalogue ▸ *vb* **5** = lead, direct, escort, conduct, accompany, shepherd, usher, show the way **6** = steer, control, manage, direct, handle, command, manoeuvre **7, 8** = supervise, train, teach, influence, advise, counsel, instruct, oversee

Guide *n* a member of an organization for girls that encourages discipline and practical skills

guided missile *n* a missile whose course is controlled electronically

guide dog *n* a dog that has been trained to lead a blind person

guideline *n* a principle put forward to set standards or determine a course of action: *guidelines for arms exporting*

guild *n* **1** an organization or club for people with shared interests **2** (in Medieval Europe) an association of men in the same trade or craft

guild *n* **1** = society, union, league, association, company, club, order, organization

guilder *n*, *pl* **-ders** *or* **-der** a former monetary unit of the Netherlands

guile (gile) *n* craftiness or deviousness ▷ **guileless** *adj*

guillemot (gil-lee-mot) *n* a northern oceanic black-and-white diving sea bird

guillotine *n* **1** a device formerly used, esp. in France, for beheading people, consisting of a weighted blade between two upright posts, which was dropped on the neck **2** a device with a blade for cutting paper ▸ *vb* **-tining, -tined 3** to behead with a guillotine

guilt *n* **1** the fact or state of having done wrong: *the court was unable to establish guilt* **2** remorse or self-reproach caused by feeling that one has done something wrong: *he feels no guilt about the planned cutbacks*

guilt *n* **1** = culpability, blame, responsibility, misconduct, wickedness, sinfulness, guiltiness; ≠ innocence **2** = shame, regret, remorse, contrition, guilty conscience, self-reproach; ≠ pride

guiltless *adj* free of all responsibility for wrongdoing or crime; innocent

guilty *adj* **guiltier, guiltiest 1** *law* judged to have committed a crime: *she has been found guilty of drug trafficking* **2** responsible for doing something wrong: *students who are guilty of cheating* **3** showing, feeling, or indicating guilt: *guilty conscience* ▷ **guiltily** *adv*

guilty *adj* **1, 2** = culpable, responsible, to blame, offending, erring, at fault, reprehensible, blameworthy; ≠ innocent **3** = ashamed, sorry, rueful, sheepish, contrite, remorseful, regretful, shamefaced; ≠ proud

guinea *n* a former British unit of currency worth £1.05 (21 shillings), sometimes still used in quoting professional fees

guinea fowl *n* a domestic bird with a heavy rounded body and speckled feathers

guinea pig *n* **1** a tailless S American rodent, commonly kept as a pet or used in scientific experiments **2** a person used in an experiment

guise (rhymes with **size**) *n* **1** a false appearance: *in the guise of a wood-cutter* **2** general appearance or form: *haricot beans are best known in Britain in their popular guise of baked beans*

guise *n* **1** = pretence, disguise, aspect, semblance **2** = form, appearance, shape, aspect, mode, semblance

guitar *n* a stringed instrument with a flat back and a long neck with a fretted fingerboard, which is played by plucking or strumming ▷ **guitarist** *n*

gulch *n* US & Canad a narrow ravine with a stream running through it

gulch *n* = ravine, canyon, defile, gorge, gully, pass

gulf *n* **1** a large deep bay **2** something that divides or separates people, such as a lack of understanding: *gradually the gulf between father and son has lessened*

gulf *n* **1** = bay, bight, sea inlet **2** = chasm, opening, split, gap, separation, void, rift, abyss

gull *n* a large sea bird with white feathers tipped with black or grey

gullet *n* the muscular tube through which food passes from the throat to the stomach

gullible *adj* easily tricked; too trusting ▷ **gullibility** *n*

gully *or* **gulley** *n*, *pl* **-lies** *or* **-leys 1** a channel or small valley originally worn away by running water **2** *cricket* a fielding position on the off side, between the slips and point

gulp *vb* **1** to swallow (a drink or food) rapidly in large mouthfuls **2** to gasp or breathe in violently, for example when nervous or when swimming **3 gulp back** to stifle or suppress: *he gulped back the tears as he said his goodbyes* ▸ *n* **4** the act of gulping **5** the quantity taken in a gulp

gum[1] *n* **1** a sticky substance obtained from certain plants, which hardens on exposure to air and dissolves in water **2** a substance used for sticking things together **3** short for **chewing gum 4** chiefly Brit a gumdrop ▸ vb **gumming, gummed 5** to stick with gum

> **gum** n **1, 2** = glue, adhesive, resin, cement, paste ▸ vb = stick, glue, affix, cement, paste

gum² n the fleshy tissue that covers the bases of the teeth

gumboots pl n Brit & NZ long rubber boots, worn in wet or muddy conditions

gumdrop n a small hard fruit-flavoured jelly-like sweet

gummy¹ adj **-mier, -miest** sticky or tacky

gummy² adj **-mier, -miest** toothless

gumption n Brit & NZ informal common sense or initiative

gun n **1** a weapon with a metallic tube or barrel from which a missile is fired, usually by force of an explosion **2** a device used to force out (a substance, such as grease or paint) under pressure: a spray gun **3 jump the gun** informal to act prematurely **4 stick to one's guns** informal to stand by one's opinions or intentions in spite of opposition ▸ vb **gunning, gunned 5** to press hard on the accelerator of (a vehicle's engine) **6 gun down** to shoot (someone) with a gun ▸ adj **7** NZ slang expert: a gun surfer ▸ See also **gun for**

> **gun** n **1** = firearm, shooter (slang), piece (slang), handgun

gunboat n a small ship carrying mounted guns

gun dog n **1** a dog trained to locate or retrieve birds or animals that have been shot in a hunt **2** a dog belonging to any breed traditionally used for these activities

gun for vb informal to search for (someone) in order to harm him or her in some way

gunge n informal a sticky or congealed substance > **gungy** adj

gunman n, pl **-men** a man who uses a gun to commit a crime

> **gunman** n = armed man or woman or person, gunslinger (US slang)

gunmetal n **1** a type of bronze containing copper, tin, and zinc ▸ adj **2** dark grey

gunnel (gun-nel) n same as **gunwale**

gunner n a member of the armed forces who works with, uses, or specializes in guns

gunnery n the art and science of the efficient design and use of large guns

gunny n chiefly US a coarse hard-wearing fabric, made from jute and used for sacks

gunpowder n an explosive mixture of potassium nitrate, charcoal, and sulphur, used to make fireworks

gunrunning n the practice of smuggling guns and ammunition into a country > **gunrunner** n

gunshot n **1** bullets fired from a gun **2** the sound of a gun being fired **3** the firing range of a gun: within gunshot

gunwale (gun-nel) n naut the top of the side of a ship

gunyah n Austral a hut or shelter in the bush

guppy n, pl **-pies** a small brightly coloured tropical fish, often kept in aquariums in people's homes

gurgle vb **-gling, -gled 1** (of water) to make low bubbling noises when flowing **2** to make low throaty bubbling noises: the baby gurgled in delight ▸ n **3** the sound of gurgling

Gurkha n **1** a member of a Hindu people living mainly in Nepal **2** a member of a Gurkha regiment in the Indian or British Army

guru n **1** a Hindu or Sikh religious teacher or leader **2** a leader or adviser of a person or group of people: inside a team of advertising gurus are at work

> **guru** n **1** = teacher, mentor, sage, master, tutor **2** = authority, expert, leader, master, pundit, Svengali, fundi (S African)

gush vb **1** to pour out suddenly and profusely **2** to speak or behave in an overenthusiastic manner: I'm not about to start gushing about raspberry coulis ▸ n **3** a sudden large flow of liquid **4** a sudden surge of strong feeling: she felt a gush of pure affection for her mother

> **gush** vb **1** = flow, run, rush, flood, pour, stream, cascade, spurt ▸ n **3** = stream, flow, rush, flood, jet, cascade, torrent, spurt

gusher n **1** a person who gushes **2** a spurting oil well

gusset n a piece of material sewn into a garment to strengthen it

gust n **1** a sudden blast of wind **2** a sudden surge of strong feeling: a gust of joviality ▸ vb **3** to blow in gusts > **gusty** adj

gusto n vigorous enjoyment: we all sang with great gusto

gut n **1** same as **intestine 2** slang the belly; paunch **3** short for **catgut 4** a silky fibrous substance extracted from silkworms and used in the manufacture of fishing tackle ▸ vb **gutting, gutted 5** to remove the internal organs from (a dead animal or fish) **6** (of a fire) to destroy the inside of (a building): a local pub was gutted ▸ adj **7** informal basic, essential, or natural: I have a gut feeling she's after something

> **gut** n **2** = paunch (informal), belly, spare tyre (Brit slang), potbelly, puku (NZ) ▸ vb **5** = disembowel, clean **6** = ravage, empty, clean out, despoil (formal) ▸ adj = instinctive, natural, basic, spontaneous, intuitive, involuntary, heartfelt, unthinking

gutsy adj **gutsier, gutsiest** slang **1** bold or courageous: the gutsy kid who lost a leg to cancer **2** robust or vigorous: a gutsy rendering of 'Bobby Shaftoe'

gutta-percha n a whitish rubber substance, obtained from a tropical Asian tree and used in electrical insulation and dentistry

gutted *adj Brit, Austral & NZ informal* disappointed and upset: *the supporters will be absolutely gutted if the manager leaves the club*

gutter *n* 1 a channel on the roof of a building or alongside a kerb, used to collect and carry away rainwater 2 *tenpin bowling* one of the channels on either side of an alley 3 **the gutter** a poverty-stricken, degraded, or criminal environment: *he dragged himself up from the gutter* ▸ *vb* 4 (of a candle) to flicker and be about to go out › **guttering** *n*

> **gutter** *n* 1 = drain, channel, ditch, trench, trough, conduit, sluice

gutter press *n informal* the section of the popular press that concentrates on the sensational aspects of the news

guttersnipe *n Brit* a child who spends most of his or her time in the streets, usually in a slum area

guttural (gut-ter-al) *adj* 1 *phonetics* pronounced at the back of the throat 2 harsh-sounding

guy¹ *n* 1 *informal* a man or boy 2 *informal* a person of either sex: *it's been very nice talking to you guys again* 3 *Brit* a crude model of Guy Fawkes, that is burnt on top of a bonfire on Guy Fawkes Day (November 5)

> **guy** *n* 1, 2 = man, person, fellow (*old-fashioned*), lad, bloke (*Brit informal*), chap

guy² *n* a rope or chain for steadying or securing something such as a tent. Also: **guyrope**

guzzle *vb* **-zling, -zled** to eat or drink quickly or greedily: *the guests guzzled their way through squid with mushrooms*

gybe *or* **jibe** (jibe) *naut* ▸ *vb* **gybing, gybed** *or* **jibing, jibed** 1 (of a fore-and-aft sail) to swing suddenly from one side of a ship to the other 2 to change the course of (a ship) by letting the sail gybe ▸ *n* 3 an instance of gybing

gym *n* short for **gymnasium** or **gymnastics**

gymkhana (jim-kah-na) *n Brit, Austral & NZ* an event in which horses and riders take part in various races and contests

gymnasium *n* a large room containing equipment such as bars, weights, and ropes, for physical exercise

gymnast *n* a person who is skilled or trained in gymnastics

gymnastics *n* 1 practice or training in exercises that develop physical strength and agility ▸ *pl n* 2 such exercises › **gymnastic** *adj*

gynaecology *or US* **gynecology** (guy-nee-kol-la-jee) *n* the branch of medicine concerned with diseases and conditions specific to women › **gynaecological** *or US* **gynecological** *adj* › **gynaecologist** *or US* **gynecologist** *n*

gypsophila *n* a garden plant with small white flowers

gypsum *n* a mineral used in making plaster of Paris

Gypsy *or* **Gipsy** *n, pl* **-sies** *sometimes offensive* a member of a travelling people, esp. a Roma or Irish traveller

gyrate (jire-rate) *vb* **-rating, -rated** to turn round and round in a circle › **gyration** *n*

gyrocompass *n* a nonmagnetic compass that uses a motor-driven gyroscope to indicate true north

gyroscope (jire-oh-skope) *n* a device containing a disc rotating on an axis that can turn freely in any direction, so that the disc maintains the same position regardless of the movement of the surrounding structure › **gyroscopic** *adj*

Hh

H 1 *chem* hydrogen **2** *physics* henry
habeas corpus (hay-bee-ass kor-puss) *n law* a writ ordering a person to be brought before a judge, so as to decide whether his or her detention is lawful
haberdasher *n Brit, Austral & NZ* a dealer in small articles used for sewing > **haberdashery** *n*
habit *n* **1** a tendency to act in a particular way **2** established custom or use: *the English habit of taking tea in the afternoon* **3** an addiction to a drug **4** mental disposition or attitude: *deference was a deeply ingrained habit of mind* **5** the costume of a nun or monk **6** a woman's riding costume

> **habit** *n* **1** = mannerism, custom, way, practice, characteristic, tendency, quirk, propensity **3** = addiction, dependence, compulsion

habitable *adj* fit to be lived in > **habitability** *n*
habitat *n* the natural home of an animal or plant
habitation *n* **1** occupation of a dwelling place: *unfit for human habitation* **2** *formal* a dwelling place
habitual *adj* **1** done regularly and repeatedly: *habitual behaviour patterns* **2** by habit: *a habitual criminal* > **habitually** *adv*
habituate *vb* **-ating, -ated** to accustom; get used to: *habituated to failure* > **habituation** *n*
habitué (hab-it-yew-ay) *n* a frequent visitor to a place
hacienda (hass-ee-end-a) *n* (in Spanish-speaking countries) a ranch or large estate with a house on it
hack¹ *vb* **1** to chop roughly or violently **2** to cut and clear (a way) through undergrowth **3** (in sport) to foul (an opposing player) by kicking his or her shins **4** *Brit & NZ informal* to tolerate **5** to manipulate a computer program skilfully, esp. to gain unauthorized access to another computer system ► *n* **6** a cut or gash **7** a tool, such as a pick **8** a chopping blow **9** a kick on the shins, such as in rugby > **hacker** *n* > **hacking** or **hackery** *n*

> **hack** *vb* **1, 2** = cut, chop, slash, mutilate, mangle, mangulate (*Austral slang*), hew, lacerate

hack² *n* **1** a writer or journalist who produces work fast and on a regular basis **2** a horse kept for riding, often one for hire **3** *Brit* a country ride on horseback ► *vb* **4** *Brit* to ride (a horse) cross-country for pleasure ► *adj* **5** unoriginal or of a low standard: *clumsily contrived hack verse*

hack *n* **1** = reporter, writer, correspondent, journalist, scribbler, contributor, literary hack
hackles *pl n* **1** the hairs or feathers on the back of the neck of certain animals or birds, which rise when they are angry **2** **raise someone's hackles** to make someone feel angry or hostile
hackney *n* **1** *Brit* a taxi **2** same as **hack²** (sense 2)
hackneyed (hak-need) *adj* (of a word or phrase) unoriginal and overused
hacksaw *n* a small saw for cutting metal
had *vb* the past of **have**
haddock *n, pl* **-dock** a North Atlantic food fish
Hades (hay-deez) *n Greek myth* **1** the underworld home of the souls of the dead **2** the god of the underworld
hadj *n* same as **hajj**
haematology or US **hematology** *n* the branch of medical science concerned with the blood > **haematologist** or US **hematologist** *n*
haemoglobin or US **hemoglobin** (hee-moh-globe-in) *n* a protein in red blood cells that carries oxygen from the lungs to the tissues
haemophilia or US **hemophilia** (hee-moh-fill-lee-a) *n* a hereditary disorder, usually affecting males, in which the blood does not clot properly > **haemophiliac** *n*
haemorrhage or US **hemorrhage** (hem-or-ij) *n* **1** heavy bleeding from ruptured blood vessels ► *vb* **-rhaging, -rhaged** **2** to bleed heavily

> **haemorrhage** or **hemorrhage** *n* = drain, outpouring, rapid loss ► *vb* = drain, bleed (*informal*), flow rapidly

haemorrhoids or US **hemorrhoids** (hem-or-oydz) *pl n pathol* swollen veins in the wall of the anus
hafnium *n chem* a metallic element found in zirconium ores. Symbol: **Hf**
haft *n* the handle of an axe, knife, or dagger
hag *n* **1** *derogatory* an unpleasant or ugly old woman **2** a witch > **haggish** *adj*
haggard *adj* looking tired and ill
haggis *n* a Scottish dish made from sheep's or calf's offal, oatmeal, suet, and seasonings boiled in a skin made from the animal's stomach
haggle *vb* **-gling, -gled** to bargain or wrangle (over a price)
hagiography *n, pl* **-phies** the writing of lives of the saints > **hagiographer** *n*
hag-ridden *adj* distressed or worried
hail¹ *n* **1** small pellets of ice falling from thunderclouds **2** words, ideas, missiles, etc., directed with force and in great quantity: *a hail of abuse* ► *vb* **3** to fall as hail: *it's hailing* **4** to fall like hail: *blows hailed down on him*

> **hail** *n* **1** = hailstones, sleet, hailstorm, frozen rain **2** = shower, rain, storm, battery, volley, barrage, bombardment, downpour ► *vb* **3** = rain, shower, pelt **4** = batter, rain, bombard, pelt, rain down on, beat down upon

h

hail² *vb* **1** to call out to; greet: *a voice from behind hailed him* **2** to praise, acclaim, or acknowledge: *his crew had been hailed as heroes* **3** to stop (a taxi) by shouting or gesturing **4 hail from** to come originally from: *she hails from Nova Scotia* **5 within hailing distance** within hearing range ▸ *interj* **6** *poetic* an exclamation of greeting

> **hail** *vb* **1** = salute, greet, address, welcome, say hello to, halloo; ≠ snub **2** = acclaim, honour, acknowledge, cheer, applaud; ≠ condemn **3** = flag down, summon, signal to, wave down **4 hail from somewhere** = come from, be born in, originate in, be a native of, have your roots in

hailstone *n* a pellet of hail

hair *n* **1** any of the threadlike outgrowths on the skin of mammals **2** a mass of such outgrowths, such as on a person's head or an animal's body **3** *botany* a threadlike growth from the outer layer of a plant **4** a very small distance or margin: *he missed death by a hair* **5 get in someone's hair** *informal* to annoy someone **6 hair of the dog** an alcoholic drink taken as a cure for a hangover **7 let one's hair down** to enjoy oneself without restraint **8 not turn a hair** to show no reaction **9 split hairs** to make petty and unnecessary distinctions > **hairless** *adj*

> **hair** *n* **2** = locks, mane, tresses, shock, mop, head of hair

hairclip *n* a small clip used to hold the hair in place

hairdo *n, pl* **-dos** *informal* the style of a person's hair

hairdresser *n* **1** a person who cuts and styles hair. Related adjective: **tonsorial 2** a hairdresser's premises > **hairdressing** *n*

> **hairdresser** *n* **1** = stylist, barber, coiffeur *or* coiffeuse

hairgrip *n chiefly Brit* a small bent clasp used to fasten the hair

hairline *n* **1** the edge of hair at the top of the forehead ▸ *adj* **2** very fine or narrow: *a hairline crack*

hairpin *n* a thin U-shaped pin used to fasten the hair

hairpin bend *n* a bend in the road that curves very sharply

hair-raising *adj* very frightening or exciting

hairstyle *n* the cut and arrangement of a person's hair > **hairstylist** *n*

hairy *adj* **hairier, hairiest 1** covered with hair **2** *slang* dangerous, exciting, and difficult > **hairiness** *n*

> **hairy** *adj* **1** = shaggy, woolly, furry, stubbly, bushy, unshaven, hirsute (*formal*) **2** = dangerous, risky, unpredictable, hazardous, perilous

hajj *or* **hadj** *n* the pilgrimage a Muslim makes to Mecca

haka *n NZ* **1** a Māori war chant accompanied by actions **2** a similar chant by a sports team

hake *n, pl* **hake** *or* **hakes 1** an edible fish of the cod family **2** *Austral* same as **barracuda**

hakea (hah-kee-a) *n* an Australian tree or shrub with hard woody fruit

halal *or* **hallal** *n* meat from animals that have been slaughtered according to Muslim law

halberd *n history* a tall spear that includes an axe blade and a pick

halcyon (hal-see-on) *adj* **1** peaceful, gentle, and calm **2 halcyon days** a time, usually in the past, of greatest happiness or success

hale *adj* healthy and robust: *hale and hearty*

> **hale** *adj* = healthy, well, strong, sound, fit, flourishing, robust, vigorous

half *n, pl* **halves 1** either of two equal or corresponding parts that together make up a whole **2** the fraction equal to one divided by two **3** half a pint, esp. of beer **4** *sport* one of two equal periods of play in a game **5** a half-price ticket **6 by half** to an excessive degree: *too clever by half* **7 by halves** without being thorough: *they rarely do things by halves* **8 go halves** to share expenses ▸ *adj* **9** denoting one of two equal parts: *a half chicken* ▸ *adv* **10** half in degree or quantity: *half as much* **11** partially; to an extent: *half hidden in the trees* **12 not half** *Brit informal* **A** very; indeed: *it isn't half hard to look at these charts* **B** yes, indeed

> **half** *n* **1, 2** = fifty per cent, equal part ▸ *adj* = partial, limited, moderate, halved ▸ *adv* **11** = partially, partly, in part

half-baked *adj informal* poorly planned: *half-baked policies*

half-brother *n* the son of either one's mother or father by another partner

half-caste *n offensive* a person of mixed race

half-hearted *adj* without enthusiasm or determination > **half-heartedly** *adv*

half-life *n* the time taken for radioactive material to lose half its radioactivity

half-nelson *n* a wrestling hold in which a wrestler places an arm under the opponent's arm from behind and exerts pressure with his or her palm on the back of the opponent's neck

halfpenny *or* **ha'penny** (hayp-nee) *n, pl* **-pennies** a former British coin worth half a penny

half-pie *adj NZ informal* badly planned; not properly thought out: *a half-pie scheme*

half-pipe *n* a structure with a U-shaped cross section, used in skateboarding, snowboarding, Rollerblading, etc.

half-timbered *adj* (of a building) having an exposed timber framework filled with brick or plaster

half-time *n sport* an interval between the two halves of a game

halftone *n* a photographic illustration in which the image is composed of a large number of black and white dots

halfway *adv* **1** at or to half the distance **2** at or towards the middle of a period of time or of an event or process **3** rather: *halfway decent* **4 meet someone halfway** to compromise with someone ▸ *adj* **5** at the same distance from two points: *the halfway line*

> **halfway** *adv* **1, 2** = midway, to or in the middle ▸ *adj* = midway, middle, mid, central, intermediate, equidistant

halfwit *n* a foolish or inane person > **halfwitted** *adj*

halibut *n* a large edible flatfish

halitosis *n* bad-smelling breath

hall *n* **1** an entry area to other rooms in a house **2** a building or room for public meetings, dances, etc. **3** a residential building in a college or university **4** *Brit* a great house of an estate; manor **5** a large dining room in a college or university **6** the large room of a castle or stately home

> **hall** *n* **1** = passage, lobby, corridor, hallway, foyer, entry, passageway, entrance hall **2** = meeting place, chamber, auditorium, concert hall, assembly room

hallelujah, halleluiah (hal-ee-**loo**-ya) or **alleluia** *interj* an exclamation of praise to God

hallmark *n* **1** a typical feature: *secrecy became the hallmark of government* **2** *Brit* an official seal stamped on gold, silver, or platinum articles to guarantee purity and date of manufacture **3** a mark of authenticity or excellence ▸ *vb* **4** to stamp with a hallmark

> **hallmark** *n* **1** = trademark, sure sign, telltale sign **2, 3** = mark, sign, device, stamp, seal, symbol

hallo *interj, n* same as **hello**

hallowed *adj* **1** regarded as holy: *hallowed ground* **2** respected and revered because of age, importance, or reputation: *the hallowed pitch at Lord's*

Halloween or **Hallowe'en** *n* October 31, celebrated by children by dressing up as ghosts, witches, etc.

hallucinate *vb* **-nating, -nated** to seem to see something that is not really there

hallucination *n* the experience of seeming to see something that is not really there > **hallucinatory** *adj*

hallucinogen *n* any drug that causes hallucinations > **hallucinogenic** *adj*

hallway *n* an entrance area

halo (**hay**-loh) *n, pl* **-loes** or **-los 1** a ring of light around the head of a sacred figure **2** a circle of refracted light around the sun or moon ▸ *vb* **-loes** or **-los, -loing, -loed 3** to surround with a halo

halogen (**hal**-oh-jen) *n chem* any of the nonmetallic chemical elements fluorine, chlorine, bromine, iodine, and astatine, which form salts when combined with metal

halt *vb* **1** to come to a stop or bring (someone or something) to a stop ▸ *n* **2** a temporary standstill **3** a military command to stop **4** *chiefly Brit* a minor railway station without a building: *Deeside Halt* **5 call a halt to** to put an end to

> **halt** *vb* = stop, break off, stand still, wait, rest; ≠ continue ▸ *n* **2** = stop, end, close, pause, standstill, stoppage; ≠ continuation

halter *n* **1** a strap around a horse's head with a rope to lead it with ▸ *vb* **2** to put a halter on (a horse)

halterneck *n* a woman's top or dress which fastens behind the neck, leaving the back and arms bare

halting *adj* hesitant or uncertain: *she spoke halting Italian*

> **halting** *adj* = faltering, stumbling, awkward, hesitant, laboured, stammering, stuttering

halve *vb* **halving, halved 1** to divide (something) into two equal parts **2** to reduce (the size or amount of something) by half **3** *golf* to draw with one's opponent on (a hole or round)

> **halve** *vb* **1** = split in two, cut in half, bisect, divide in two, share equally, divide equally **2** = cut in half, reduce by fifty per cent, decrease by fifty per cent, lessen by fifty per cent

halyard *n naut* a line for hoisting or lowering a ship's sail or flag

ham[1] *n* smoked or salted meat from a pig's thigh

ham[2] *n* **1** *informal* an amateur radio operator **2** *theatre informal* an actor who overacts and exaggerates the emotions and gestures of a part ▸ *adj* **3** (of actors or their performances) exaggerated and overstated ▸ *vb* **hamming, hammed 4 ham it up** *informal* to overact

hamburger *n* a flat round of minced beef, often served in a bread roll

ham-fisted or **ham-handed** *adj informal* very clumsy or awkward

hamlet *n* a small village

hammer *n* **1** a hand tool consisting of a heavy metal head on the end of a handle, used for driving in nails, beating metal, etc. **2** the part of a gun that causes the bullet to shoot when the trigger is pulled **3** *athletics* **A** a heavy metal ball attached to a flexible wire: thrown in competitions **B** the sport of throwing the hammer **4** an auctioneer's mallet **5** the part of a piano that hits a string when a key is pressed **6 come** or **go under the hammer** to be on sale at auction **7 hammer and tongs** with great effort or energy ▸ *vb* **8** to hit with or as if with a hammer **9** _Brit_ to criticize severely **10** _informal_ to defeat heavily **11** to feel or sound like hammering: _his heart was hammering_ **12 hammer in** to force (facts or ideas) into someone through repetition **13 hammer away at** to work at (something) constantly: _the paper hammered away at the same theme all the way through the campaign_

hammer _vb_ **8** = hit, drive, knock, beat, strike, tap, bang **10** = defeat, beat, thrash, trounce, run rings around (_informal_), wipe the floor with (_informal_), drub

hammerhead _n_ a shark with a wide flattened head

hammock _n_ a hanging bed made of canvas or net

hamper¹ _vb_ to make it difficult for (someone or something) to move or progress

hamper _vb_ = hinder, handicap, prevent, restrict, frustrate, hamstring, interfere with, obstruct; ≠ help

hamper² _n_ **1** a large basket with a lid **2** _Brit_ a selection of food and drink packed as a gift

hamster _n_ a small rodent with a stocky body, short tail, and cheek pouches

hamstring _n_ **1** one of the tendons at the back of the knee ▸ _vb_ **-stringing, -strung 2** to make it difficult for someone to take any action

hand _n_ **1** the part of the body at the end of the arm, consisting of a thumb, four fingers, and a palm. Related adjective: **manual 2** a person's style of writing: _scrolls written in her own hand_ **3** the influence a person or thing has over a particular situation: _the hand of the military in shaping policy was obvious_ **4** a part in some activity: _I remember with gratitude Fortune's hand in starting my collection_ **5** assistance: _give me a hand with the rice_ **6** a round of applause: _give a big hand to the most exciting duo in the game_ **7** consent to marry someone: _he asked for her hand in marriage_ **8** a manual worker **9** a member of a ship's crew **10** a pointer on a dial or gauge, esp. on a clock **11 A** the cards dealt in one round of a card game **B** one round of a card game **12** a position indicated by its location to the side of an object or the observer: _on the right hand_ **13** a contrasting aspect or condition: _on the other hand_ **14** source: _I had experienced at first hand many management styles_ **15** a person who creates something: _a good hand at baking_ **16** a unit of length equalling four inches, used for measuring the height of horses **17 by hand A** by manual rather than mechanical means **B** by messenger: _the letter was delivered by hand_ **18 from hand to mouth** with no food or money in reserve: _living from hand to mouth_ **19 hand in glove** in close association **20 hand over fist** steadily and quickly: _losing money hand over fist_ **21 in hand A** under control **B** receiving attention: _the business in hand_ **C** available in reserve: _Pakistan have a game in hand_ **22 keep one's hand in** to continue to practise something **23 (near) at hand** very close

24 on hand close by; available **25 out of hand A** beyond control **B** decisively, without possible reconsideration: _he dismissed the competition out of hand_ **26 show one's hand** to reveal one's plans **27 to hand** accessible ▸ _vb_ **28** to pass or give by the hand or hands **29 hand it to someone** to give credit to someone › **handless** _adj_

hand _n_ **1** = palm, fist, paw (_informal_), mitt (_slang_) **2** = writing, script, handwriting, calligraphy **6** = round of applause, clap, ovation, big hand **8** = worker, employee, labourer, workman, operative, craftsman _or_ woman _or_ person, artisan, hired hand ▸ _vb_ **28** = give, pass, hand over, present to, deliver

handbag _n_ a small bag carried to contain personal articles

handbill _n_ a small printed notice for distribution by hand

handbook _n_ a reference manual giving practical information on a subject

handbook _n_ = guidebook, guide, manual, instruction book

handcuff _n_ **1 handcuffs** a linked pair of locking metal rings used for securing prisoners ▸ _vb_ **2** to put handcuffs on (a person)

handcuff _n_ = shackles, cuffs (_informal_), fetters, manacles ▸ _vb_ = shackle, secure, restrain, fetter, manacle

handful _n_, _pl_ **-fuls 1** the amount that can be held in the hand **2** a small number: _a handful of parents_ **3** _informal_ a person or animal that is difficult to control: _as a child she was a real handful_

handful _n_ **2** = few, sprinkling, small amount, smattering, small number; ≠ a lot

hand-held _adj_ **1** held in position by the hand ▸ _n_ **2** a device, such as a computer, that can be held in the hand

handicap _n_ **1** _old-fashioned, offensive_ a physical or mental disability **2** something that makes progress difficult **3 A** a contest in which competitors are given advantages or disadvantages in an attempt to equalize their chances **B** the advantage or disadvantage given **4** _golf_ the number of strokes by which a player's averaged score exceeds par for the course ▸ _vb_ **-capping, -capped 5** to make it difficult for (someone) to do something

handicap _n_ **2** = disadvantage, barrier, restriction, obstacle, limitation, drawback, stumbling block, impediment; ≠ advantage **3B** = advantage, head start ▸ _vb_ = hinder, limit, restrict, burden, hamstring, hamper, hold back, impede; ≠ help

handicraft _n_ **1** a skill performed with the hands, such as weaving **2** the objects produced by people with such skills

handiwork *n* **1** the result of someone's work or activity **2** work produced by hand

handkerchief *n* a small square of fabric used to wipe the nose

handle *n* **1** the part of an object that is held or operated in order that it may be used **2** a small lever used to open and close a door or window **3** *slang* a person's name **4** a means of understanding or dealing with something: *trying to get a handle on why companies borrow money* **5** **fly off the handle** *informal* to become suddenly extremely angry ▸ *vb* **-dling, -dled** **6** to hold, move, operate, or touch with the hands **7** to have responsibility for: *she handles all their affairs personally* **8** to manage successfully: *I can handle this challenge* **9** to discuss (a subject) **10** to deal with in a specified way: *the affair was neatly handled* **11** to trade or deal in (specified merchandise): *we handle 1800 properties in Normandy* **12** to react or respond in a specified way to operation or control: *it's light and handles well* ▸ **handling** *n*

> **handle** *n* **1** = grip, hilt, haft, stock ▸ *vb* **6** = control, manage, direct, guide, manipulate, manoeuvre **8** = manage, deal with, tackle, cope with

handlebars *pl n* a metal tube with handles at each end, used for steering a bicycle or motorcycle

handler *n* **1** a person who trains and controls an animal **2** a person who handles something: *a baggage handler*

hand-out *n*, *pl* **hand-outs** **1** clothing, food, or money given to a needy person **2** a leaflet, free sample, etc., given out to publicize something **3** a piece of written information given out to the audience at a talk, lecture, etc. ▸ *vb* **hand out** **4** to distribute

hands-free *adj*, *n* (of) a device allowing the user to make and receive telephone calls without holding the handset

handsome *adj* **1** (esp. of a man) good-looking **2** (of a building, garden, etc.) large, well-made, and with an attractive appearance: *a handsome building* **3** (of an amount of money) generous or large: *a handsome dividend* ▸ **handsomely** *adv*

> **handsome** *adj* **1** = good-looking, attractive, gorgeous (*informal*), elegant, personable, dishy (*informal*, *chiefly Brit*), comely (*old-fashioned*), hot (*informal*), fit (*Brit informal*); ≠ ugly **3** = generous, large, princely, liberal, considerable, lavish, ample, abundant; ≠ mean

hands-on *adj* involving practical experience of equipment: *Navy personnel joined the 1986 expedition for hands-on operating experience*

handstand *n* the act of supporting the body on the hands in an upside-down position

handwriting *n* **1** writing by hand rather than by typing or printing **2** a person's characteristic writing style ▸ **handwritten** *adj*

handy *adj* **handier, handiest** **1** conveniently within reach **2** easy to handle or use **3** good at manual work ▸ **handily** *adv*

> **handy** *adj* **1** = convenient, close, available, nearby, accessible, on hand, at hand, within reach; ≠ inconvenient **2** = useful, practical, helpful, neat, convenient, easy to use, manageable, user-friendly; ≠ useless **3** = skilful, skilled, expert, adept, deft, proficient, adroit, dexterous; ≠ unskilled

handyman *n*, *pl* **-men** a man skilled at odd jobs

hang *vb* **hanging, hung** **1** to fasten or be fastened from above **2** to place (something) in position, for instance by a hinge, so as to allow free movement: *to hang a door* **3** to be suspended so as to allow movement from the place where it is attached: *her long hair hung over her face* **4** to decorate with something suspended, such as pictures **5** (of cloth or clothing) to fall or flow in a particular way: *the fine gauge knit hangs loosely with graceful femininity* **6** *past tense & past participle* **hanged** to suspend or be suspended by the neck until dead **7** to hover: *clouds hung over the mountains* **8** to fasten to a wall: *to hang wallpaper* **9** to exhibit or be exhibited in an art gallery **10** *past tense & past participle* **hanged** *slang* to damn: used in mild curses or interjections **11** **hang fire** to put off doing something **12** **hang over** to threaten or overshadow: *the threat of war hung over the Middle East* ▸ *n* **13** the way in which something hangs **14** **get the hang of something** *informal* to understand the technique of doing something ▸ See also **hang back**

> **hang** *vb* **1** = dangle, swing, suspend **2** = lower, suspend, dangle **6** = execute, lynch, string up (*informal*) ▸ *n* **14** **get the hang of something** = grasp, understand, learn, master, comprehend, catch on to, acquire the technique of

hangar *n* a large building for storing aircraft

hang back *vb* to be reluctant to do something

> **hang back** *vb* = be reluctant, hesitate, hold back, recoil, demur

hangdog *adj* dejected, ashamed, or guilty in appearance or manner

hanger *n* same as **coat hanger**

hang-glider *n* an unpowered aircraft consisting of a large cloth wing stretched over a light framework from which the pilot hangs in a harness ▸ **hang-gliding** *n*

hangi (hung-ee) *n* NZ **1** an open-air cooking pit **2** the food cooked in it **3** the social gathering at the resultant meal

hangman *n*, *pl* **-men** an official who carries out a sentence of hanging

hangover *n* a feeling of sickness and headache after drinking too much alcohol

hangover *n* = aftereffects, morning after (*informal*)

hank *n* a loop or coil, esp. of yarn

hank *n* = coil, roll, length, bunch, piece, loop, clump, skein

hanker *vb* (foll. by *for* or *after*) to have a great desire for ⟩ **hankering** *n*

hanky *or* **hankie** *n, pl* **hankies** *informal* short for **handkerchief**

hanky-panky *n informal* **1** casual sexual relations **2** mischievous behaviour

hansom *n* (formerly) a two-wheeled one-horse carriage with a fixed hood. Also called: **hansom cab**

haphazard *adj* not organized or planned ⟩ **haphazardly** *adv*

hapless *adj* unlucky: *the hapless victim of a misplaced murder attempt*

happen *vb* **1** to take place; occur **2** to chance (to be or do something): *I happen to know him* **3** to be the case, esp. by chance: *it happens that I know him* **4 happen to** (of some unforeseen event, such as death) to be the experience or fate of: *if anything happens to me you will know*

happen *vb* **1** = occur, take place, come about, result, develop, transpire (*informal*), come to pass **2** = chance, turn out (*informal*)

happening *n* an event that often occurs in a way that is unexpected or hard to explain: *some strange happenings in the village recently*

happening *n* = event, incident, experience, affair, proceeding, episode, occurrence

happy *adj* **-pier, -piest** **1** feeling or expressing joy **2** causing joy or gladness: *the happiest day of my life* **3** fortunate or lucky: *it was a happy coincidence* **4** satisfied or content: *he seems happy to let things go on as they are* **5** willing: *I'll be happy to arrange a loan for you* ⟩ **happily** *adv* ⟩ **happiness** *n*

happy *adj* **1** = pleased, delighted, content, thrilled, glad, cheerful, merry, ecstatic, stoked (*informal*); ≠ sad **2** = contented, joyful, blissful; ≠ unhappy **3** = fortunate, lucky, timely, favourable, auspicious, propitious, advantageous; ≠ unfortunate

happy-go-lucky *adj* carefree or easy-going

hara-kiri *n* (formerly, in Japan) ritual suicide by disembowelment when disgraced or under sentence of death

harangue *vb* **-ranguing, -rangued** **1** to address (a person or group) in an angry or forcefully persuasive way ▸ *n* **2** a forceful or angry speech

harass *vb* to trouble or annoy (someone) by repeated attacks, questions, or problems ⟩ **harassed** *adj* ⟩ **harassment** *n*

harass *vb* = annoy, trouble, bother, harry, plague, hound, hassle (*informal*), persecute

harbinger (har-binge-er) *n literary* a person or thing that announces or indicates the approach of something: *a harbinger of death*

harbour *or US* **harbor** *n* **1** a sheltered port **2** a place of refuge or safety ▸ *vb* **3** to maintain secretly in the mind: *he might be harbouring a death wish* **4** to give shelter or protection to: *the government accused her of harbouring criminals*

harbour *or* **harbor** *n* **1** = port, haven, dock, mooring, marina, pier, wharf, anchorage ▸ *vb* **3** = hold, bear, maintain, nurse, retain, foster, entertain, nurture **4** = shelter, protect, hide, shield, provide refuge, give asylum to

hard *adj* **1** firm, solid, or rigid **2** difficult to do or understand: *a hard sum* **3** showing or requiring a lot of effort or application: *hard work* **4** unkind or unfeeling: *she's very hard, no pity for anyone* **5** causing pain, sorrow, or hardship: *the hard life of a northern settler* **6** tough or violent: *a hard man* **7** forceful: *a hard knock* **8** cool or uncompromising: *we took a long hard look at our profit factor* **9** indisputable and proven to be true: *hard facts* **10** (of water) containing calcium salts which stop soap lathering freely **11** practical, shrewd, or calculating: *I am a hard businesswoman* **12** harsh: *hard light* **13** (of currency) high and stable in exchange value **14** (of alcoholic drink) being a spirit rather than a wine or beer **15** (of a drug) highly addictive **16** hard-core **17** *phonetics* denoting the consonants *c* and *g* when they are pronounced as in *cat* and *got* **18** politically extreme: *the hard left* **19 hard of hearing** slightly deaf **20 hard up** *informal* in need of money ▸ *adv* **21** with great energy or force: *they fought so hard and well in Spain* **22** with great intensity: *thinking hard about the conversation* **23 hard by** very close to: *Cleveland Place, hard by Bruntsfield Square* **24 hard put (to it)** scarcely having the capacity (to do something) ▸ *n* **25 have a hard on** *vulgar slang* to have an erection of the penis ⟩ **hardness** *n*

hard *adj* **1** = tough, strong, firm, solid, stiff, rigid, resistant, compressed; ≠ soft **2** = difficult, involved, complicated, puzzling, intricate, perplexing, impenetrable, thorny; ≠ easy **3** = exhausting, tough, exacting, rigorous, gruelling, strenuous, arduous, laborious; ≠ easy **4** = harsh, cold, cruel, stern, callous, unkind, unsympathetic, pitiless; ≠ kind **5** = grim, painful, distressing, harsh, unpleasant, intolerable, grievous, disagreeable ▸ *adv* **21** = forcefully, strongly, heavily, sharply, severely, fiercely, vigorously, intensely; ≠ softly **22** = intently, closely, carefully, sharply, keenly

hardback *n* **1** a book with stiff covers ▸ *adj* **2** of or denoting a hardback

hard-bitten *adj informal* tough and determined

hardboard *n* stiff board made in thin sheets of compressed sawdust and wood pulp

hard-boiled *adj* **1** (of an egg) boiled until solid **2** *informal* tough, realistic, and unemotional

hard copy *n* computer output printed on paper

hard disk *n* *computers* a rigid magnetic storage disk that is permanently mounted in a computer

hard drive *n* *computers* the mechanism that handles the reading, writing, and storage of data on the hard disk

harden *vb* **1** to make or become hard; freeze, stiffen, or set **2** to make or become tough or unfeeling: *life in the camp had hardened her considerably* **3** to make or become stronger or firmer: *they hardened defences* **4** to make or become more determined or resolute: *the government has hardened its attitude to the crisis* **5** *commerce* (of prices or a market) to cease to fluctuate

> **harden** *vb* **1** = solidify, set, freeze, cake, bake, clot, thicken, stiffen **2** = accustom, season, toughen, train, inure, habituate

hardfill *n NZ & S African* a stone waste material used for landscaping

hard-headed *adj* tough, realistic, or shrewd, esp. in business

hardhearted *adj* unsympathetic and uncaring

hardly *adv* **1** scarcely; barely: *he'd hardly sipped his whisky* **2** *humorous* not at all: *it was hardly in the Great Train Robbery league* **3** with difficulty: *their own families would hardly recognize them*

> **hardly** *adv* **1** = barely, only just, scarcely, just, with difficulty, with effort; ≠ completely

hard sell *n* an aggressive insistent technique of selling

hardship *n* **1** conditions of life that are difficult to endure **2** something that causes suffering

> **hardship** *n* = suffering, need, difficulty, misfortune, adversity, discomfort, tribulation, privation (*formal*); ≠ ease

hard shoulder *n Brit & NZ* a surfaced verge running along the edge of a motorway and other roads for emergency stops

hardware *n* **1** metal tools or implements, esp. cutlery or cooking utensils **2** the physical equipment used in a computer system **3** heavy military equipment, such as tanks and missiles

hardwood *n* the wood of a deciduous tree such as oak, beech, or ash

hardy *adj* **-dier, -diest 1** able to stand difficult conditions **2** (of plants) able to live out of doors throughout the winter > **hardiness** *n*

> **hardy** *adj* **1** = strong, tough, robust, sound, rugged (*US, Canad*), sturdy, stout; ≠ frail

hare *n, pl* **hares** *or* **hare 1** a mammal like a large rabbit, with longer ears and legs ▸ *vb* **haring, hared 2** (foll. by *off* or *after*) *Brit & Austral informal* to run fast or wildly

harebell *n* a blue bell-shaped flower

harebrained *adj* foolish or impractical: *harebrained schemes*

haricot bean *or* **haricot** (har-rik-oh) *n* a white edible bean, which can be dried

harissa *n* a hot paste or sauce made from chilli peppers, tomatoes, spices, and olive oil, used in North African cuisine

harlequin *n* **1** *theatre* a stock comic character, usually wearing a diamond-patterned multicoloured costume and a black mask ▸ *adj* **2** in varied colours

harlot *n literary* a prostitute > **harlotry** *n*

harm *vb* **1** to injure physically, morally, or mentally ▸ *n* **2** physical, moral, or mental injury

> **harm** *vb* = injure, hurt, wound, abuse, ill-treat, maltreat; ≠ heal ▸ *n* = injury, suffering, damage, ill, hurt, distress

harmful *adj* causing or tending to cause harm, esp. to a person's health

> **harmful** *adj* = damaging, dangerous, negative, destructive, hazardous, unhealthy, detrimental, hurtful, toxic; ≠ harmless

harmless *adj* **1** safe to use, touch, or be near **2** unlikely to annoy or worry people: *a harmless habit*

> **harmless** *adj* **1** = safe, benign, wholesome, innocuous, nontoxic; ≠ dangerous **2** = inoffensive, innocent, innocuous, gentle, tame, unobjectionable

harmonic *adj* **1** of, producing, or characterized by harmony; harmonious ▸ *n* **2** *music* an overtone of a musical note produced when that note is played, but not usually heard as a separate note ▸ See also **harmonics** > **harmonically** *adv*

harmonica *n* a small wind instrument in which reeds enclosed in a narrow oblong box are made to vibrate by blowing and sucking

harmonics *n* the science of musical sounds

harmonious *adj* **1** (esp. of colours or sounds) consisting of parts which blend together well **2** showing agreement, peacefulness, and friendship: *a harmonious relationship* **3** tuneful or melodious > **harmoniously** *adv*

harmonium *n* a musical keyboard instrument in which air from pedal-operated bellows causes the reeds to vibrate

harmonize *or* **-nise** *vb* **-nizing, -nized** *or* **-nising, -nised 1** to sing or play in harmony, such as with another singer or player **2** to make or become harmonious

harmony *n, pl* **-nies 1** a state of peaceful agreement and cooperation **2** *music* a pleasant combination of two or more notes sounded at the same time **3** the way parts combine well together or into a whole

h

harmony *n* **1** = accord, peace, agreement, friendship, sympathy, cooperation, rapport, compatibility; ≠ conflict **2** = tune, melody, unison, tunefulness, euphony; ≠ discord

harness *n* **1** an arrangement of straps for attaching a horse to a cart or plough **2** something resembling this, for attaching something to a person's body: *a parachute harness* **3 in harness** at one's routine work ▸ *vb* **4** to put a harness on (a horse or other animal) **5** to control something in order to make use of it: *learning to harness the power of your own mind*

> **harness** *n* **1, 2** = equipment, tackle, gear, tack ▸ *vb* **5** = exploit, control, channel, employ, utilize, mobilize

harp *n* **1** a large upright triangular stringed instrument played by plucking the strings with the fingers ▸ *vb* **2 harp on** to speak in a persistent and tedious manner (about a subject) > **harpist** *n*

harpoon *n* **1** a barbed spear attached to a long rope and thrown or fired when hunting whales, etc. ▸ *vb* **2** to spear with a harpoon

harpsichord *n* a keyboard instrument, resembling a small piano, with strings that are plucked mechanically > **harpsichordist** *n*

harridan *n* *derogatory* a scolding old woman; nag

harrier *n* a cross-country runner

harrow *n* **1** an implement used to break up clods of soil ▸ *vb* **2** to draw a harrow over (land)

harrowing *adj* very upsetting or disturbing

> **harrowing** *adj* = distressing, disturbing, painful, terrifying, traumatic, tormenting, agonizing, nerve-racking

harry *vb* **-ries, -rying, -ried** to keep asking (someone) to do something; pester

> **harry** *vb* = pester, bother, plague, harass, hassle (*informal*), badger, chivvy (*Brit*)

harsh *adj* **1** severe and difficult to cope with: *harsh winters* **2** unkind and showing no understanding: *the judge was very harsh on the demonstrators* **3** excessively hard, bright, or rough: *harsh sunlight* **4** (of sounds) unpleasant and grating > **harshly** *adv* > **harshness** *n*

> **harsh** *adj* **1** = severe, hard, tough, stark, austere, inhospitable, bare-bones **2** = cruel, savage, ruthless, barbarous, pitiless; ≠ kind **4** = raucous, rough, grating, strident, rasping, discordant, guttural, dissonant; ≠ soft

harvest *n* **1** the gathering of a ripened crop **2** the crop itself **3** the season for gathering crops **4** the product of an effort or action ▸ *vb* **5** to gather (a ripened crop) **6** *chiefly US* to remove (an organ) from the body for transplantation

> **harvest** *n* **1** = harvesting, picking, gathering, collecting, reaping, harvest-time **2** = crop, yield, year's growth, produce ▸ *vb* **5** = gather, pick, collect, bring in, pluck, reap

harvester *n* **1** a harvesting machine, esp. a combine harvester **2** a person who harvests

has *vb* third person singular of the present tense of **have**

has-been *n* *informal* a person who is no longer popular or successful

hash¹ *n* **1** a dish of diced cooked meat, vegetables, etc., reheated: *corned-beef hash* **2** a reworking of old material **3 make a hash of** *informal* to mess up or destroy

hash² *n* *slang* short for **hashish**

hash³ *or* **hashmark** *n* the character (#) used to precede a number

hashish (hash-eesh) *n* a drug made from the hemp plant, smoked for its intoxicating effects

hashtag *n* (on the Twitter website) a word or phrase preceded by a hash, indicating the topic being discussed

hasp *n* a clasp which fits over a staple and is secured by a pin, bolt, or padlock, used as a fastening

hassle *informal* ▸ *n* **1** a great deal of trouble **2** a prolonged argument ▸ *vb* **-sling, -sled** **3** to cause annoyance or trouble to (someone): *stop hassling me!*

> **hassle** *n* **1** = trouble, problem, difficulty, bother, grief (*informal*), uphill (*S African*), inconvenience ▸ *vb* = bother, bug (*informal*), annoy, hound, harass, badger, pester

hassock *n* a cushion for kneeling on in church

haste *n* **1** speed, esp. in an action **2** the act of hurrying in a careless manner **3 make haste** to hurry or rush ▸ *vb* **hasting, hasted** **4** *poetic* to hasten

hasten *vb* **1** to hurry or cause to hurry **2** to be anxious (to say something)

hasty *adj* **-tier, -tiest** **1** done or happening suddenly or quickly **2** done too quickly and without thought; rash > **hastily** *adv*

hat *n* **1** a head covering, often with a brim, usually worn to give protection from the weather **2** *informal* a role or capacity: *I'm wearing my honorary consul's hat* **3 keep something under one's hat** to keep something secret **4 pass the hat round** to collect money for a cause **5 take off one's hat to someone** to admire or congratulate someone

hatch¹ *vb* **1** to cause (the young of various animals, esp. birds) to emerge from the egg or (of young birds, etc.) to emerge from the egg **2** (of eggs) to break and release the young animal within **3** to devise (a plot or plan)

> **hatch** *vb* **1** = incubate, breed, sit on, brood, bring forth **3** = devise, design, invent, put together, conceive, brew, formulate, contrive

hatch² *n* **1** a hinged door covering an opening in a floor or wall **2 A** short for **hatchway** **B** a door in an aircraft or spacecraft **3** Also called: **serving hatch** an opening in a wall between a kitchen and a dining area **4** *informal* short for **hatchback**

hatchback *n* a car with a single lifting door in the rear

hatchet *n* **1** a short axe used for chopping wood, etc. **2 bury the hatchet** to make peace or resolve a disagreement ▸ *adj* **3** narrow and sharp: *a hatchet face*

hatchet job *n informal* a malicious verbal or written attack

hatchet man *n informal* a person who carries out unpleasant tasks on behalf of an employer

hatchway *n* an opening in the deck of a vessel to provide access below

hate *vb* **hating, hated** **1** to dislike (someone or something) intensely **2** to be unwilling (to do something): *I hate to trouble you* ▸ *n* **3** intense dislike **4** *informal* a person or thing that is hated: *my own pet hate is restaurants* ▷ **hater** *n*

> **hate** *vb* **1** = detest, loathe, despise, dislike, abhor, recoil from, not be able to bear; ≠ love **2** = be unwilling, regret, be reluctant, hesitate, be sorry, be loath, feel disinclined ▸ *n* **3** = dislike, hostility, hatred, loathing, animosity, aversion, antipathy, enmity; ≠ love

hateful *adj* causing or deserving hate

hatred *n* intense dislike

> **hatred** *n* = hate, dislike, animosity, aversion, revulsion, antipathy, enmity, repugnance; ≠ love

hat trick *n* **1** *cricket* the achievement of a bowler in taking three wickets with three successive balls **2** any achievement of three successive goals, victories, etc.

haughty *adj* **-tier, -tiest** having or showing excessive pride or arrogance ▷ **haughtily** *adv* ▷ **haughtiness** *n*

haul *vb* **1** to drag or pull (something) with effort **2** to transport, such as in a lorry **3** *naut* to alter the course of (a vessel) ▸ *n* **4** the act of dragging with effort **5** a quantity of something obtained: *a good haul of fish; a huge haul of stolen goods* **6 long haul** **A** a long journey **B** a long difficult process

> **haul** *vb* **1** = drag, draw, pull, heave ▸ *n* **5** = yield, gain, spoils, catch, harvest, loot, takings, booty

haulage *n* **1** the business of transporting goods **2** a charge for transporting goods

haulier *n Brit & Austral* a person or firm that transports goods by road

haunch *n* **1** the human hip or fleshy hindquarter of an animal **2** the leg and loin of an animal, used for food

haunt *vb* **1** to visit (a person or place) in the form of a ghost **2** to remain in the memory or thoughts of: *it was a belief which haunted her* **3** to visit (a place) frequently ▸ *n* **4** a place visited frequently

> **haunt** *vb* **2** = plague, trouble, obsess, torment, possess, stay with, recur, prey on ▸ *n* = meeting place, hangout (*informal*), rendezvous, stamping ground

haunted *adj* **1** (of a place) frequented or visited by ghosts **2** (of a person) obsessed or worried

> **haunted** *adj* **1** = possessed, ghostly, cursed, eerie, spooky (*informal*), jinxed **2** = preoccupied, worried, troubled, plagued, obsessed, tormented

haunting *adj* having a quality of great beauty or sadness so as to be memorable: *a haunting melody*

> **haunting** *adj* = evocative, poignant, unforgettable

haute couture (oat koo-ture) *n* high fashion

hauteur (oat-ur) *n* haughtiness

have *vb* **has, having, had** **1** to possess: *he has a collection of classic cars; I have an iron constitution* **2** to receive, take, or obtain: *I had a long letter* **3** to hold in the mind: *she always had a yearning to be a schoolteacher* **4** to possess a knowledge of: *I have no German* **5** to experience or be affected by: *a good way to have a change* **6** to suffer from: *to have a blood pressure problem* **7** to gain control of or advantage over: *you have me on that point* **8** *slang* to cheat or outwit: *I've been had* **9** to show: *have mercy on me* **10** to take part in; hold: *I had a telephone conversation* **11** to cause to be done: *have my shoes mended by Friday* **12** to eat or drink **13** *vulgar slang* to have sexual intercourse with **14** to tolerate or allow: *I won't have all this noise* **15** to receive as a guest: *we have visitors* **16** to be pregnant with or give birth to (offspring) **17** used to form past tenses: *I have gone; I had gone* **18 have had it** *informal* **A** to be exhausted or killed **B** to have lost one's last chance **19 have it off** *Brit vulgar slang* to have sexual intercourse **20 have to** used to express compulsion or necessity: *you'd have to wait six months* ▸ *n* **21 haves** *informal* people who have wealth, security, etc.: *the haves and the have-nots* ▸ See also **have on**

> **have** *vb* **1** = own, keep, possess, hold, retain, boast, be the owner of **2** = get, obtain, take, receive, accept, gain, secure, acquire **5** = experience, go through, undergo, meet with, come across, run into, be faced with **6** = suffer, experience, undergo, sustain, endure, be suffering from **16** = give birth to, bear, deliver, bring forth, beget **20 have to** = must, should, be forced, ought, be obliged, be bound, have got to, be compelled

haven *n* **1** a place of safety **2** a harbour for shipping

> **haven** *n* **1** = sanctuary, shelter, retreat, asylum, refuge, oasis, sanctum

have on vb **1** to wear: *he had a pair of long trousers on* **2** to have a commitment: *what do you have on this afternoon?* **3** *informal* to trick or tease: *he's having you on* **4** to have (information, esp. when incriminating) about (a person): *she has something on him*

> **have on** vb **1 have something on** = wear, be wearing, be dressed in, be clothed in, be attired in **3 have someone on** = tease, kid (*informal*), wind up (*Brit slang*), trick, deceive, take the mickey, pull someone's leg

haversack n a canvas bag carried on the back or shoulder

have up vb to bring to trial: *what, and get me had up for kidnapping?*

havoc n **1** *informal* chaos, disorder, and confusion **2 play havoc with** to cause a great deal of damage or confusion to

> **havoc** n **1** = disorder, confusion, chaos, disruption, mayhem, shambles

haw n the fruit of the hawthorn

hawk¹ n **1** a bird of prey with short rounded wings and a long tail **2** a supporter or advocate of warlike policies ▸ vb **3** to hunt with falcons or hawks ▸ **hawkish** adj ▸ **hawklike** adj

hawk² vb to offer (goods) for sale in the street or door-to-door

hawk³ vb **1** to clear the throat noisily **2** to force (phlegm) up from the throat

hawker n a person who travels from place to place selling goods

hawk-eyed adj having extremely keen eyesight

hawser n *naut* a large heavy rope

hawthorn n a thorny tree or shrub with white or pink flowers and reddish fruits

hay n **1** grass cut and dried as fodder **2 hit the hay** *slang* to go to bed **3 make hay while the sun shines** to take full advantage of an opportunity

hay fever n an allergic reaction to pollen, which causes sneezing, runny nose, and watery eyes

haystack *or* **hayrick** n a large pile of hay built in the open and covered with thatch

haywire adj **go haywire** *informal* to stop functioning properly

hazard n **1** a thing likely to cause injury, loss, etc. **2** risk or likelihood of injury, loss, etc.: *evaluate the level of hazard in a situation* **3** *golf* an obstacle such as a bunker **4 at hazard** at risk ▸ vb **5** to risk: *hazarding the health of his crew* **6 hazard a guess** to make a guess

> **hazard** n **1, 2** = danger, risk, threat, problem, menace, peril, jeopardy, pitfall ▸ vb **5** = jeopardize, risk, endanger, threaten, expose, imperil, put in jeopardy **6 hazard a guess** = guess, conjecture, presume, take a guess

hazardous adj involving great risk

hazardous adj = dangerous, risky, difficult, insecure, unsafe, precarious, perilous, dicey (*informal, chiefly Brit*); ≠ safe

haze n **1** *meteorol* reduced visibility as a result of condensed water vapour, dust, etc., in the air **2** confused or unclear understanding or feeling

> **haze** n **1** = mist, cloud, fog, obscurity, vapour

hazel n **1** a shrub with edible rounded nuts ▸ adj **2** greenish-brown: *hazel eyes*

hazelnut n the nut of a hazel shrub, which has a smooth shiny hard shell

hazy adj **-zier, -ziest 1** (of the sky or a view) unable to be seen clearly because of dust or heat **2** dim or vague: *my memory is a little hazy on this* ▸ **hazily** adv ▸ **haziness** n

H-bomb n short for **hydrogen bomb**

HD high definition

he pron **1** (refers to) a male person or animal ▸ n **2** (refers to) a male person or animal: *a he-goat*

head n **1** the upper or front part of the body that contains the brain, eyes, mouth, nose, and ears **2** a person's mind and mental abilities: *I haven't any head for figures* **3** the most forward part of a thing: *the head of a queue* **4** the highest part of a thing; upper end: *the head of the pass* **5** something resembling a head in form or function, such as the top of a tool **6** the position of leadership or command **7** the person commanding most authority within a group or an organization **8** *botany* the top part of a plant, where the leaves or flowers grow in a cluster **9** a culmination or crisis: *the matter came to a head in December 1928* **10** the froth on the top of a glass of beer **11** the pus-filled tip of a pimple or boil **12** part of a computer or tape recorder that can read, write, or erase information **13** the source of a river or stream **14** the side of a coin that usually bears a portrait of the head of a monarch, etc. **15** a headland or promontory: *Beachy Head* **16** pressure of water or steam in an enclosed space **17** *pl* **head** a person or animal considered as a unit: *the cost per head of Paris's refuse collection; six hundred head of cattle* **18** a headline or heading **19** *informal* short for **headache 20 give someone his** *or* **her head** to allow someone greater freedom or responsibility **21 go to one's head** **A** (of an alcoholic drink) to make one slightly drunk **B** to make one conceited: *success has gone to his head* **22 head over heels (in love)** very much (in love) **23 keep one's head** to remain calm **24 not make head nor tail of** not to understand (a problem, etc.) **25 off one's head** *slang* very foolish or mentally unstable **26 on one's own head** at one's own risk **27 over someone's head** **A** to a higher authority: *the taboo of going over the head of their immediate boss* **B** beyond a person's understanding **28 put our** *or* **your** *or* **their heads together** *informal* to consult together **29 turn someone's head** to make someone conceited ▸ vb **30** to be at the front or top of: *Barnes headed* *the list* **31** to be in charge of **32** (often foll. by *for*) to go or cause to go (towards): *to head for the Channel ports* **33** *soccer* to propel (the ball) by striking it with the head **34** to provide with a heading ▸ See also **heads**

head *n* **1** = skull, crown, pate, nut (*slang*), loaf (*slang*) **2** = mind, reasoning, understanding, thought, sense, brain, brains (*informal*), intelligence **4** = top, crown, summit, peak, crest, pinnacle **7** = leader, president, director, manager, chief, boss (*informal*), captain, master, sherang (*Austral, NZ*) **21ᴀ go to one's head** = intoxicate **21ʙ go to one's head** = make someone conceited, puff someone up, make someone full of themselves **22 head over heels** = completely, thoroughly, utterly, intensely, wholeheartedly, uncontrollably ▸ *vb* **30** = lead, precede, be the leader of, be *or* go first, be *or* go at the front of, lead the way **31** = be in charge of, run, manage, lead, control, direct, guide, command

headache *n* **1** a continuous pain in the head **2** *informal* any cause of worry, difficulty, or annoyance: *financial headaches*

headache *n* **1** = migraine, head (*informal*), neuralgia **2** = problem, worry, trouble, bother, nuisance, inconvenience, bane, vexation

headboard *n* a vertical board at the head of a bed
headdress *n* any decorative head covering
header *n* **1** *soccer* the action of striking a ball with the head **2** *informal* a headlong fall or dive
heading *n* **1** a title for a page, chapter, etc. **2** a main division, such as of a speech **3** *mining* a horizontal tunnel

heading *n* **1** = title, name, caption, headline, rubric

headland *n* a narrow area of land jutting out into a sea
headlight *or* **headlamp** *n* a powerful light on the front of a vehicle
headline *n* **1** a phrase in heavy large type at the top of a newspaper or magazine article indicating the subject **2 headlines** the main points of a television or radio news broadcast ▸ *vb* **-lining**, **-lined 3** to provide with a headline **4** to be the main performer in (a show) ▸ **headliner** *n*
headlong *adv* **1** with the head foremost; headfirst **2** with great haste and without much thought: *they rushed headlong into buying a house* ▸ *adj* **3** hasty or reckless
headphones *pl n* two small loudspeakers held against the ears, worn to listen to the radio or recorded music without other people hearing it
headquarters *pl n* any centre from which operations are directed
headroom *or* **headway** *n* the space below a roof or bridge which allows an object to pass or stay underneath it without touching it

heads *adv* with the side of a coin uppermost which has a portrait of a head on it
head start *n* an initial advantage in a competitive situation
headstone *n* a memorial stone at the head of a grave
headstrong *adj* determined to do something in one's own way and ignoring the advice of others
headway *n* **1** progress towards achieving something: *have the police made any headway?* **2** motion forward: *we felt our way out to the open sea, barely making headway* **3** same as **headroom**
headwind *n* a wind blowing directly against the course of an aircraft or ship
heady *adj* **headier**, **headiest 1** (of an experience or period of time) extremely exciting **2** (of alcoholic drink, atmosphere, etc.) strongly affecting the physical senses: *a powerful, heady scent of cologne* **3** rash and impetuous

heady *adj* **1** = exciting, thrilling, stimulating, exhilarating, intoxicating **2** = intoxicating, strong, potent, inebriating

heal *vb* **1** (of a wound) to repair by natural processes, such as by scar formation **2** to restore (someone) to health **3** to repair (a rift in a personal relationship or an emotional wound) ▸ **healer** *n* ▸ **healing** *n, adj*

heal *vb* **1** = mend, get better, get well, regenerate, show improvement **2** = cure, restore, mend, make better, remedy, make good, make well; ≠ injure

health *n* **1** the general condition of body and mind: *better health* **2** the state of being bodily and mentally vigorous and free from disease **3** the condition of an organization, society, etc.: *the economic health of the republics*

health *n* **1** = condition, state, shape, constitution, fettle **2** = wellbeing, strength, fitness, vigour, good condition, soundness, robustness, healthiness; ≠ illness **3** = state, condition, shape

health food *n* natural food, organically grown and free from additives
healthy *adj* **healthier**, **healthiest 1** having or showing good health **2** likely to produce good health: *healthy seaside air* **3** functioning well or being sound: *this is a very healthy business to be in* **4** *informal* considerable: *healthy profits* **5** sensible: *a healthy scepticism about his promises* ▸ **healthily** *adv* ▸ **healthiness** *n*

healthy *adj* **1** = well, fit, strong, active, robust, in good shape (*informal*), in the pink, in fine fettle; ≠ ill **2** = wholesome, beneficial, nourishing, nutritious, salutary, hygienic, salubrious; ≠ unwholesome

heap *n* **1** a pile of things lying one on top of another **2** (*often pl*) *informal* a large number or quantity ▸ *adv* **3 heaps** *informal* much: *he was*

h

heaps better ▸ *vb* **4** to collect into a pile **5** to give freely (to): *film roles were heaped on her*

> **heap** *n* **1** = pile, lot, collection, mass, stack, mound, accumulation, hoard **2** = a lot, lots, plenty, masses, load(s) (*informal*), great deal, tons (*informal*), stack(s) ▸ *vb* **4** = pile, collect, gather, stack, accumulate, amass, hoard

hear *vb* **hearing**, **heard** **1** to perceive (a sound) with the sense of hearing **2** to listen to: *I didn't want to hear what he had to say* **3** to be informed (of something); receive information (about something): *I hear you mean to join the crusade* **4** *law* to give a hearing to (a case) **5** **hear from** to receive a letter or telephone call from **6** **hear!** **hear!** an exclamation of approval **7** **hear of** to allow: *she wouldn't hear of it* ▸ **hearer** *n*

> **hear** *vb* **1** = overhear, catch, detect **2** = listen to **3** = learn, discover, find out, pick up, gather, ascertain, get wind of (*informal*) **4** = try, judge, examine, investigate

hearing *n* **1** the sense by which sound is perceived **2** an opportunity for someone to be listened to **3** the range within which sound can be heard; earshot **4** the investigation of a matter by a court of law

> **hearing** *n* **4** = inquiry, trial, investigation, industrial tribunal

hearsay *n* gossip or rumour

hearse *n* a large car used to carry a coffin at a funeral

heart *n* **1** a hollow muscular organ whose contractions pump the blood throughout the body **2** this organ considered as the centre of emotions, esp. love **3** tenderness or pity: *my heart went out to her* **4** courage or spirit **5** the most central part or important part: *at the heart of Italian motor racing* **6** (of vegetables such as cabbage) the inner compact part **7** the breast: *she held him to her heart* **8** a shape representing the heart, with two rounded lobes at the top meeting in a point at the bottom **9** **A** a red heart-shaped symbol on a playing card **B** a card with one or more of these symbols or (*when pl*) the suit of cards so marked **10** **break someone's heart** to cause someone to grieve very deeply, esp. by ending a love affair **11** **by heart** by memorizing **12** **have a change of heart** to experience a profound change of outlook or attitude **13** **have one's heart in one's mouth** to be full of apprehension, excitement, or fear **14** **have the heart** to have the necessary will or callousness (to do something): *I didn't have the heart to tell him* **15** **set one's heart on something** to have something as one's ambition **16** **take heart** to become encouraged **17** **take something to heart** to take something seriously or be upset about something **18** **wear one's heart on one's sleeve** to show one's feelings openly **19** **with all one's heart** deeply and sincerely

> **heart** *n* **2** = emotions, feelings, love, affection **4** = courage, will, spirit, purpose, bottle (*Brit informal*), resolution, resolve, stomach **5** = root, core, centre, nucleus, hub, gist, nitty-gritty (*informal*), nub **11** **by heart** = from or by memory, verbatim, word for word, pat, word-perfect, by rote, off by heart, off pat

heartache *n* very great sadness and emotional suffering

heart attack *n* a sudden severe malfunction of the heart

heartbeat *n* one complete pulsation of the heart

heartbreak *n* intense and overwhelming grief, esp. after the end of a love affair
> **heartbreaking** *adj* > **heartbroken** *adj*

heartburn *n* a burning sensation in the chest caused by indigestion

hearten *vb* to encourage or make cheerful
> **heartening** *adj*

heart failure *n* **1** a condition in which the heart is unable to pump an adequate amount of blood to the tissues **2** sudden stopping of the heartbeat, resulting in death

heartfelt *adj* sincerely and strongly felt: *heartfelt thanks*

hearth *n* **1** the floor of a fireplace **2** this as a symbol of the home

heartless *adj* unkind or cruel > **heartlessly** *adv*

heart-rending *adj* causing great sadness and pity: *a heart-rending story*

heart-throb *n* a man, esp. a film or pop star, who is attractive to a lot of people

hearty *adj* **heartier**, **heartiest** **1** warm, friendly, and enthusiastic **2** strongly felt: *a hearty dislike* **3** (of a meal) substantial and nourishing
> **heartily** *adv*

heat *vb* **1** to make or become hot or warm ▸ *n* **2** the state of being hot **3** the energy transferred as a result of a difference in temperature. Related adjectives: **thermal**, **calorific** **4** hot weather: *he loves the heat of Africa* **5** intensity of feeling: *the heat of their argument* **6** the most intense part: *in the heat of an election campaign* **7** pressure: *political heat on the government* **8** *sport* a preliminary eliminating contest in a competition **9** **on** or **in heat** (of some female mammals) ready for mating > **heating** *n*

> **heat** *vb* = warm (up), cook, boil, roast, reheat, make hot; ≠ chill ▸ *n* **2** = warmth, hotness, temperature; ≠ cold **4** = hot weather, warmth, closeness, high temperature, heatwave, warm weather, hot climate, mugginess **5** = passion, excitement, intensity, fury, fervour, vehemence; ≠ calmness

heated *adj* impassioned or highly emotional: *a heated debate* > **heatedly** *adv*

> **heated** *adj* = impassioned, intense, spirited, excited, angry, furious, fierce, lively; ≠ calm

heater *n* a device for supplying heat

heath *n* **1** *Brit* a large open area, usually with sandy soil, low shrubs, and heather **2** a low-growing evergreen shrub with small bell-shaped pink or purple flowers

heathen *old-fashioned* ▸ *n, pl* **-thens** *or* **-then 1** a person who does not believe in an established religion; pagan ▸ *adj* **2** of or relating to heathen peoples

heather *n* a shrub with small bell-shaped flowers growing on heaths and mountains

heave *vb* **heaving**, **heaved 1** to lift or move (something) with a great effort **2** to throw (something heavy) with effort **3** to utter (a sigh) noisily or unhappily **4** to rise and fall heavily **5** *past tense & past participle* **hove** *naut* **A** to move in a specified direction: *heave her bows around and head north* **B** (of a vessel) to pitch or roll **6** to vomit or retch ▸ *n* **7** the act of heaving

heaven *n* **1** (in some religions) the place where God is believed to live and where those leading good lives are believed to go when they die **2** a place or state of happiness **3 heavens** the sky **4** Also: **heavens** God or the gods, used in exclamatory phrases: *for heaven's sake!*

> **heaven** *n* **1** = paradise, next world, hereafter, nirvana (*Buddhism, Hinduism*), bliss, Zion (*Christianity*), life everlasting, Elysium *or* Elysian fields (*Greek myth*) **2** = happiness, paradise, ecstasy, bliss, utopia, rapture, seventh heaven **3 the heavens** = sky, ether, firmament

heavenly *adj* **1** *informal* wonderful or very enjoyable: *a heavenly meal* **2** of or occurring in space: *a heavenly body* **3** of or relating to heaven

> **heavenly** *adj* **1** = wonderful, lovely, delightful, beautiful, divine (*informal*), exquisite, sublime, blissful; ≠ awful **3** = celestial, holy, divine, blessed, immortal, angelic; ≠ earthly

heavy *adj* **heavier**, **heaviest 1** of comparatively great weight **2** with a relatively high density: *lead is a heavy metal* **3** great in degree or amount: *heavy traffic* **4** considerable: *heavy emphasis* **5** hard to fulfil: *an exceptionally heavy demand for this issue* **6** using or consuming a lot of something quickly: *a heavy drinker* **7** deep and loud: *heavy breathing* **8** clumsy and slow: *a heavy lumbering trot* **9** (of a movement or action) with great downward force or pressure: *a heavy blow with a club* **10** solid or fat: *mountain animals acquire a heavy layer of fat* **11** not easily digestible: *a heavy meal* **12** (of cakes or bread) insufficiently raised **13** (of soil) with a high clay content **14** sad or dejected: *you feel heavy or sad afterwards* **15** (of facial features) looking sad and tired **16** (of a situation) serious and causing anxiety or sadness **17** cloudy or overcast: *heavy clouds obscured the sun* **18** (of an industry) engaged in the large-scale manufacture of large objects or extraction of

raw materials **19** *military* (of guns, etc.) large and powerful **20** dull and uninteresting: *Helen finds his friends very heavy going* **21** (of music, literature, etc.) difficult to understand or not immediately appealing **22** *slang* (of rock music) loud and having a powerful beat **23** *slang* using, or prepared to use, violence or brutality ▸ *n, pl* **heavies 24** *slang* a large strong man hired to threaten violence or deter others by his presence **25 A** a villainous role **B** an actor who plays such a part **26 the heavies** *informal* serious newspapers ▸ *adv* **27** heavily: *time hung heavy* › **heavily** *adv* › **heaviness** *n*

> **heavy** *adj* **1** = weighty, large, massive, hefty, bulky, ponderous; ≠ light **3** = intensive, severe, serious, concentrated, fierce, excessive, relentless **4** = considerable, large, huge, substantial, abundant, copious, profuse; ≠ slight

heavy metal *n* a type of very loud rock music featuring guitar riffs

heavyweight *n* **1** a professional boxer weighing over 195 pounds (88.5 kg) or an amateur weighing over 91 kg **2** a person who is heavier than average **3** *informal* an important or highly influential person

Hebrew *n* **1** the ancient language of the Hebrews, revived as the official language of Israel **2** a member of an ancient Semitic people; an Israelite ▸ *adj* **3** of the Hebrews or their language

heckle *vb* **-ling**, **-led** to interrupt (a public speaker) with comments, questions, or taunts › **heckler** *n*

hectare *n* a unit of measure equal to one hundred ares (10 000 square metres or 2.471 acres)

hectic *adj* involving a lot of rushed activity

> **hectic** *adj* = frantic, chaotic, heated, animated, turbulent, frenetic, feverish; ≠ peaceful

hector *vb* **1** to bully or torment ▸ *n* **2** a blustering bully

hedge *n* **1** a row of shrubs or bushes forming a boundary **2** a barrier or protection against something, esp. against the risk of loss on an investment ▸ *vb* **hedging**, **hedged 3** to avoid making a decision by making noncommittal statements **4 hedge against** to guard against the risk of loss in (a bet or disagreement), by supporting the opposition as well

> **hedge** *vb* **3** = prevaricate, evade, sidestep, duck (*informal*), dodge, flannel (*Brit informal*), equivocate, temporize **4 hedge against something** = protect, insure, guard, safeguard, shield, cover

hedge fund *n* *finance* a speculative fund which offers substantial returns for high-risk investments

hedgehog *n* a small mammal with a protective covering of spines

hedgerow *n* a hedge of shrubs or low trees bordering a field

hedonism *n* the doctrine that the pursuit of pleasure is the most important thing in life > **hedonist** *n* > **hedonistic** *adj*

heed *formal* ▸ *n* **1** careful attention: *he must have taken heed of her warning* ▸ *vb* **2** to pay close attention to (a warning or piece of advice)

> **heed** *n* = thought, care, mind, attention, regard, respect, notice; ≠ disregard ▸ *vb* = pay attention to, listen to, take notice of, follow, consider, note, observe, obey; ≠ ignore

heedless *adj* taking no notice; careless or thoughtless > **heedlessly** *adv*

heel¹ *n* **1** the back part of the foot **2** the part of a stocking or sock designed to fit the heel **3** the part of a shoe supporting the heel **4** *slang* a contemptible person **5 at one's heels** following closely behind one **6 down at heel** untidy and in poor condition **7 kick** *or* **cool one's heels** to be kept waiting **8 take to one's heels** to run off **9 to heel** under control, such as a dog walking by a person's heel ▸ *vb* **10** to repair or replace the heel of (a shoe or boot)

> **heel** *n* **4** = swine, cad (*Brit informal*), bounder (*Brit old-fashioned slang*), rotter (*old-fashioned, chiefly Brit*), wrong 'un (*slang*)

heel² *vb* to lean to one side

heeler *n Austral & NZ* a dog that herds cattle by biting at their heels

hefty *adj* **heftier, heftiest** *informal* **1** large in size, weight, or amount **2** forceful and vigorous: *a hefty slap on the back* **3** involving a large amount of money: *a hefty fine*

> **hefty** *adj* **1** = big, strong, massive, strapping, robust, muscular, burly, hulking; ≠ small

hegemony (hig-em-on-ee) *n, pl* **-nies** domination of one state, country, or class within a group of others

Hegira *n* the flight of Mohammed from Mecca to Medina in 622 AD, regarded as being the starting point of the Muslim era

heifer (hef-fer) *n* a young cow

height *n* **1** the vertical distance from the bottom of something to the top **2** the vertical distance of a place above sea level **3** relatively great distance from bottom to top **4** the topmost point; summit **5** the period of greatest intensity: *the height of the shelling* **6** an extreme example: *the height of luxury* **7 heights** extremes: *dizzy heights of success*

> **height** *n* **1, 2** = altitude, measurement, highness, elevation, tallness; ≠ depth **3** = tallness, stature, highness, loftiness; ≠ shortness **4** = peak, top, crown, summit, crest, pinnacle, apex; ≠ valley **5** = culmination, climax, zenith, limit, maximum, ultimate; ≠ low point

heighten *vb* to make or become higher or more intense > **heightened** *adj*

> **heighten** *vb* = intensify, increase, add to, improve, strengthen, enhance, sharpen, magnify

heinous *adj* evil and shocking

heir *or fem* **heiress** *n* the person legally succeeding to the property of a deceased person

> **heir** *or* **heiress** *n* = successor, beneficiary, inheritor, heiress (*fem.*), next in line

heirloom *n* an object that has been in a family for generations

held *vb* the past of **hold¹**

helical *adj* of or like a helix

helicopter *n* an aircraft, powered by rotating overhead blades, that is capable of hovering, vertical flight, and horizontal flight in any direction

heliotrope *n* a plant with small fragrant purple flowers

heliport *n* an airport for helicopters

helium (heel-ee-um) *n chem* a very light colourless odourless inert gas. Symbol: **He**

helix (heel-iks) *n, pl* **helices** (hell-iss-seez) *or* **helixes** a spiral

hell *n* **1** (in Christianity and some other religions) the place or state of eternal punishment of the wicked after death **2** (in various religions and cultures) the abode of the spirits of the dead **3** *informal* a situation that causes suffering or extreme difficulty: *war is hell* **4 come hell or high water** *informal* whatever difficulties may arise **5 for the hell of it** *informal* for the fun of it **6 from hell** *informal* denoting a person or thing that is particularly bad or alarming: *the neighbour from hell* **7 give someone hell** *informal* **a** to give someone a severe reprimand or punishment **b** to be a torment to someone **8 hell for leather** at great speed **9 the hell** *informal* **a** used for emphasis: *what the hell* **b** an expression of strong disagreement: *the hell you do!* ▸ *interj* **10** *informal* an exclamation of anger or surprise

> **hell** *n* **1, 2** = the underworld, the abyss, Hades (*Greek myth*), hellfire, the inferno, fire and brimstone, the nether world, the bad fire (*informal*) **3** = torment, suffering, agony, nightmare, misery, ordeal, anguish, wretchedness

hellbent *adj informal* rashly intent: *hellbent on revenge*

Hellenic *adj* **1** of the Greeks or their language **2** of or relating to ancient Greece during the classical period (776–323 BC)

hellish *adj informal* very unpleasant

hello, hallo or **hullo** interj **1** an expression of greeting or surprise **2** a call used to attract attention ▸ n, pl **-los 3** the act of saying 'hello'

> **hello, hallo** or **hullo** interj **1** = hi (informal), greetings, how do you do?, good morning, good evening, good afternoon, welcome, kia ora (NZ), gidday or g'day (Austral, NZ)

helm n **1** naut the tiller or wheel for steering a ship **2 at the helm** in a position of leadership or control > **helmsman** n

> **helm** n **1** = tiller, wheel, rudder

helmet n a piece of protective headgear worn by motorcyclists, soldiers, police officers, divers, etc.

help vb **1** to assist (someone to do something) **2** to contribute to: to help Latin America's economies **3** to improve a situation: a felt or rubber underlay will help **4 A** to refrain from: I couldn't help feeling foolish **B** to be responsible for: you must not blame him, he simply can't help it **5** to serve (a customer) **6 help oneself** to take something, esp. food or drink, for oneself, without being served ▸ n **7** the act of helping **8** a person or thing that helps, esp. a farm worker or domestic servant **9** a remedy: there's no help for it ▸ interj **10** used to call for assistance > **helper** n

> **help** vb **1, 2** = aid, support, assist, cooperate with, abet, lend a hand, succour; ≠ hinder **3** = improve, ease, relieve, facilitate, alleviate, mitigate, ameliorate; ≠ make worse **4A** = resist, refrain from, avoid, prevent, keep from ▸ n **7** = assistance, aid, support, advice, guidance, cooperation, helping hand; ≠ hindrance

helpful adj giving help > **helpfully** adv > **helpfulness** n

> **helpful** adj = cooperative, accommodating, kind, friendly, neighbourly, sympathetic, supportive, considerate

helping n a single portion of food

> **helping** n = portion, serving, ration, piece, dollop (informal), plateful

helpless adj **1** unable to manage independently **2** made weak: it reduced her to helpless laughter > **helplessly** adv > **helplessness** n

> **helpless** adj **2** = powerless, weak, incapable, paralysed, impotent, infirm; ≠ powerful

helpline n a telephone line set aside for callers to contact an organization for help with a problem

helpmate or **helpmeet** n a companion and helper, esp. a husband or wife

helter-skelter adj **1** hurried or disorganized ▸ adv **2** in a hurried or disorganized manner ▸ n **3** Brit a high spiral slide at a fairground

hem n **1** the bottom edge of a garment, folded under and stitched down ▸ vb **hemming, hemmed 2** to provide (a garment) with a hem ▸ See also **hem in**

> **hem** n = edge, border, margin, trimming, fringe

hem in vb to surround and prevent from moving

> **hem in** vb **hem something or someone in** = surround, confine, enclose, shut in

hemisphere n one half of a sphere, esp. of the earth (**northern** and **southern hemisphere**) or of the brain > **hemispherical** adj

hemline n the level to which the hem of a skirt or dress hangs: a mid-calf hemline

hemlock n a poisonous drug derived from a plant with spotted stems and small white flowers

hemp n **1** an Asian plant with tough fibres **2** the fibre of this plant, used to make canvas and rope **3** a narcotic drug obtained from this plant > **hempen** adj

hen n the female of any bird, esp. the domestic fowl

hence adv **1** for this reason; therefore **2** from this time: two weeks hence **3** archaic from here

> **hence** adv **1** = therefore, thus, consequently, for this reason, in consequence, ergo, on that account

henceforth or **henceforward** adv from now on

henchman or fem **henchwoman** n, pl **-men** or **-women** a person employed by someone powerful to carry out orders

henna n **1** a reddish dye, obtained from a shrub or tree of Asia and N Africa which is used to colour hair ▸ vb **2** to dye (the hair) with henna

hen night or **hen party** n informal a party for women only, esp. held for a woman shortly before she is married

henpecked adj (of a man) harassed by the persistent nagging of his wife

henry n, pl **-ry**, **-ries** or **-rys** the SI unit of electric inductance

hepatitis n inflammation of the liver, causing fever, jaundice, and weakness

heptagon n geom a figure with seven sides > **heptagonal** adj

heptathlon n an athletic contest for women in which athletes compete in seven different events

her pron **1** (refers to) a female person or animal: he loves her **2** (refers to) things personified as feminine, such as ships and nations ▸ adj **3** of, belonging to, or associated with her: her hair

Hera or **Here** n Greek myth the queen of the gods

herald n **1** a person who announces important news **2** often literary a forerunner ▸ vb **3** to announce or signal the approach of: his arrival was heralded by excited barking > **heraldic** adj

h

herald *n* **1** = messenger, courier, proclaimer, announcer, crier, town crier **2** = forerunner, sign, signal, indication, token, omen, precursor, harbinger (*literary*) ▸ *vb* = indicate, promise, usher in, presage, portend, foretoken

heraldry *n*, *pl* **-ries** the study of coats of arms and family trees

herb *n* **1** an aromatic plant that is used for flavouring in cookery, and in medicine **2** *botany* a seed-bearing plant whose parts above ground die back at the end of the growing season > **herbal** *adj* > **herby** *adj*

herbaceous *adj* designating plants that are soft-stemmed rather than woody

herbalist *n* a person who grows or specializes in the use of medicinal herbs

herbicide *n* a substance used to destroy plants, esp. weeds

herbivore (her-biv-vore) *n* **1** an animal that feeds only on plants **2** *informal* a liberal or idealistic person > **herbivorous** (her-biv-or-uss) *adj*

herculean (her-kew-lee-an) *adj* **1** (of a task) requiring tremendous effort or strength **2** (*sometimes cap*) resembling Hercules, hero of classical myth, in strength or courage

herd *n* **1** a large group of mammals, esp. cattle, living and feeding together ▸ *vb* **2** *often derogatory* a large group of people ▸ *vb* **3** to collect or be collected into, or as if into, a herd

herd *n* = flock, crowd, collection, mass, drove, mob, swarm, horde

herdsman *n*, *pl* **-men** *chiefly Brit* a man who looks after a herd of animals

here *adv* **1** in, at, or to this place, point, case, or respect: *I am pleased to be back here* **2 here and there** at several places in or throughout an area **3 here's to** a convention used in proposing a toast **4 neither here nor there** of no relevance ▸ *n* **5** this place: *they leave here tonight*

hereabouts or **hereabout** *adv* in this region

hereafter *adv* **1** *formal or law* in a subsequent part of this document, matter, or case **2** at some time in the future ▸ *n* **3 the hereafter** **A** life after death **B** the future

hereby *adv* (used in official statements and documents) by means of or as a result of this

hereditary *adj* **1** passed on genetically from one generation to another **2** *law* passed on to succeeding generations by inheritance

hereditary *adj* **1** = genetic, inborn, inbred, transmissible, inheritable **2** = inherited, passed down, traditional, ancestral

heredity (hir-red-it-ee) *n*, *pl* **-ties** the passing on from one generation to another of genetic factors that determine individual characteristics

herein *adv formal or law* in this place, matter, or document

heresy (herr-iss-ee) *n*, *pl* **-sies** **1** an opinion contrary to the principles of a religion **2** any belief thought to be contrary to official or established theory

heretic (herr-it-ik) *n* **1** *chiefly RC Church* a person who maintains beliefs contrary to the established teachings of the Church **2** a person who holds unorthodox opinions in any field > **heretical** (hir-ret-ik-kl) *adj*

herewith *adv formal* together with this: *a schedule of the event is appended herewith*

heritage *n* **1** something inherited at birth **2** anything that has been carried over from the past or handed down by tradition **3** the evidence of the past, such as historical sites, considered as the inheritance of present-day society

heritage *n* **1** = inheritance, legacy, birthright, tradition, endowment, bequest

hermaphrodite (her-maf-roe-dite) *n* an animal, flower, or person that has both male and female reproductive organs > **hermaphroditic** *adj*

hermetic *adj* sealed so as to be airtight > **hermetically** *adv*

hermit *n* a person living in solitude, esp. for religious reasons

hermitage *n* **1** the home of a hermit **2** any retreat

hernia *n* protrusion of an organ or part through the lining of the body cavity in which it is normally situated

hero *n*, *pl* **-roes** **1** the principal male character in a novel, play, etc. **2** a man of exceptional courage, nobility, etc. **3** a man who is idealized for having superior qualities in any field

hero *n* **1** = protagonist, leading man **2** = star, champion, victor, superstar, conqueror **3** = idol, favourite, pin-up (*slang*), fave (*informal*)

heroic *adj* **1** brave and courageous: *heroic work by the army engineers* **2** of, like, or befitting a hero > **heroically** *adv*

heroic *adj* **1** = courageous, brave, daring, fearless, gallant, intrepid, valiant, lion-hearted; ≠ cowardly

heroics *pl n* behaviour or language considered too melodramatic or extravagant for the particular situation in which they are used

heroin *n* a highly addictive drug derived from morphine

heroine *n* **1** the principal female character in a novel, play, etc. **2** a woman of exceptional courage, nobility, etc. **3** a woman who is idealized for having superior qualities in any field

heroine *n* **1** = protagonist, leading lady, diva, prima donna **3** = idol, favourite, pin-up (*slang*), fave (*informal*)

heroism (herr-oh-izz-um) *n* great courage and bravery

heron *n* a wading bird with a long neck, long legs, and grey or white feathers

herpes (her-peez) *n* any of several inflammatory skin diseases, including shingles and cold sores

Herr (hair) *n, pl* **Herren** a German form of address equivalent to *Mr*

herring *n, pl* **-rings** *or* **-ring** a food fish of northern seas, with a long silver-coloured body

herringbone *n* a zigzag pattern consisting of short lines of V shapes

herself *pron* **1 A** the reflexive form of *she* or *her*: *she busied herself with work* **B** used for emphasis: *none other than The Great Mother herself* **2** her normal self: *she hasn't been herself all week*

hertz *n, pl* **hertz** the SI unit of frequency, equal to one cycle per second

hesitant *adj* doubtful and unsure in speech or action > **hesitancy** *n* > **hesitantly** *adv*

hesitate *vb* **-tating, -tated 1** to be slow and uncertain in acting **2** to be reluctant (to do something): *I hesitate to use the word 'squandered'* **3** to pause during speech because of uncertainty > **hesitation** *n*

> **hesitate** *vb* **1** = waver, delay, pause, wait, doubt, falter, dither (*chiefly Brit*), vacillate; ≠ be decisive **2** = be reluctant, be unwilling, shrink from, think twice, scruple, demur, hang back, be disinclined; ≠ be determined

hessian *n* a coarse jute fabric similar to sacking

heterodox *adj* different from established or accepted doctrines or beliefs > **heterodoxy** *n*

heterogeneous (het-er-oh-jean-ee-uss) *adj* varied in content; composed of different parts: *a heterogeneous collection of art* > **heterogeneity** *n*

heterosexual *n* **1** a person who is sexually attracted to members of the opposite sex ▸ *adj* **2** (of a person) sexually attracted to members of the opposite sex **3** (of a sexual relationship) between a man and a woman > **heterosexuality** *n*

heuristic (hew-rist-ik) *adj* (of a method of teaching) allowing students to learn things for themselves by trial and error

hew *vb* **hewing, hewed, hewed** *or* **hewn 1** to chop or cut with an axe **2** to carve (something) from a substance: *a tunnel hewn out of the living rock*

hexagon *n geom* a figure with six sides > **hexagonal** *adj*

hey *interj* **1** an expression of surprise or for catching attention **2 hey presto!** an exclamation used by conjurors at the climax of a trick

heyday *n* the time of most power, popularity, or success: *the heyday of classical composition*

hiatus (hie-ay-tuss) *n, pl* **-tuses** *or* **-tus** a pause or an interruption in continuity: *diplomatic relations restored after a four-year hiatus*

hibernate *vb* **-nating, -nated** (of some animals) to pass the winter in a resting state in which heartbeat, temperature, and breathing rate are very low > **hibernation** *n*

hibiscus *n, pl* **-cuses** a tropical plant with large brightly coloured flowers

hiccup *n* **1** a spasm of the breathing organs with a sharp coughlike sound **2 hiccups** the state of having such spasms **3** *informal* a minor difficulty ▸ *vb* **-cuping, -cuped** *or* **-cupping, -cupped 4** to make a hiccup or hiccups. Also: **hiccough**

hick *n* US, *Austral & NZ informal* an unsophisticated country person

hickory *n, pl* **-ries 1** a North American tree with edible nuts **2** the hard wood of this tree

hide¹ *vb* **hiding, hid, hidden** *or* **hid 1** to conceal (oneself or an object) from view or discovery: *in an attempt to hide from his wife* **2** to keep (information or one's feelings) secret **3** to obscure or cover (something) from view: *the collar hid his face* ▸ *n* **4** *Brit* a place of concealment, disguised to appear as part of its surroundings, used by hunters, bird-watchers, etc.

> **hide** *vb* **1** = conceal, stash (*informal*), secrete, put out of sight; ≠ display **2** = keep secret, suppress, withhold, keep quiet about, hush up, draw a veil over, keep dark, keep under your hat; ≠ disclose **3** = obscure, cover, mask, disguise, conceal, veil, cloak, shroud; ≠ reveal

hide² *n* the skin of an animal, either tanned or raw

> **hide** *n* = skin, leather, pelt

hidebound *adj* restricted by petty rules and unwilling to accept new ideas

hideous (hid-ee-uss) *adj* extremely ugly or unpleasant > **hideously** *adv*

> **hideous** *adj* = ugly, revolting, ghastly, monstrous, grotesque, gruesome, grisly, unsightly; ≠ beautiful

hide-out *n* a hiding place

hiding¹ *n* a state of concealment: *in hiding*

hiding² *n informal* a severe beating

> **hiding** *n* = beating, whipping, thrashing, licking (*informal*), spanking, walloping (*informal*), drubbing

hierarchy (hire-ark-ee) *n, pl* **-chies 1** a system of people or things arranged in a graded order **2 the hierarchy** the people in power in any organization > **hierarchical** *adj*

> **hierarchy** *n* **1** = grading, ranking, social order, pecking order, class system, social stratum

hieroglyphic (hire-oh-gliff-ik) *adj* **1** of or relating to a form of writing using picture symbols, as used in ancient Egypt ▸ *n also* **hieroglyph 2** a symbol that is difficult to decipher **3** a picture or symbol representing an object, idea, or sound

hi-fi *n informal* **1** a set of high-quality sound-reproducing equipment ▸ *adj* **2** producing high-quality sound: *a hi-fi amplifier*

higgledy-piggledy *informal* ▸ *adj, adv* in a muddle

high *adj* **1** being a relatively great distance from top to bottom: *a high stone wall* **2** being at a relatively great distance above sea level: *a high village* **3** being a specified distance from top to bottom: *three feet high* **4** coming up to a specified level: *waist-high* **5** being at its peak: *high summer* **6** of greater than average height: *a high ceiling* **7** greater than usual in intensity or amount: *high blood pressure*; *high fees* **8** (of a sound) acute in pitch **9** (of food) slightly decomposed, regarded as enhancing the flavour of game **10** towards the top of a scale of importance or quality: *high fashion* **11** intensely emotional: *high drama* **12** very cheerful: *high spirits* **13** *informal* under the influence of alcohol or drugs **14** luxurious or extravagant: *high life* **15** advanced in complexity: *high finance* **16** *formal* and elaborate: *High Mass* **17 high and dry** abandoned in a difficult situation **18 high and mighty** *informal* too confident and full of self-importance **19 high opinion** a favourable opinion ▸ *adv* **20** at or to a height: *flying high* ▸ *n* **21** a high level **22** same as **anticyclone 23 on a high** *informal* **A** in a state of intoxication by alcohol or drugs **B** in a state of great excitement and happiness

> **high** *adj* **1, 6** = tall, towering, soaring, steep, elevated, lofty; ≠ short **7** = extreme, great, acute, severe, extraordinary, excessive; ≠ low **8** = high-pitched, piercing, shrill, penetrating, strident, sharp, acute, piping; ≠ deep **10** = important, chief, powerful, superior, eminent, exalted, skookum (*Canad*); ≠ lowly **13** = intoxicated, stoned (*slang*), tripping (*informal*) ▸ *adv* = way up, aloft, far up, to a great height

highbrow *often derogatory* ▸ *adj* **1** concerned with serious, intellectual subjects ▸ *n* **2** a person with such tastes

high definition *n* a digital technology that produces a television picture with superior definition to the standard

higher education *n* education at universities and colleges

high-flown *adj* extravagant or pretentious: *high-flown language*

> **high-flown** *adj* = extravagant, elaborate, pretentious, exaggerated, inflated, lofty, grandiose, overblown; ≠ straightforward

high-handed *adj* using authority in an unnecessarily forceful way ▸ **high-handedness** *n*

Highland *adj* of or denoting the Highlands, a mountainous region of NW Scotland ▸ **Highlander** *n*

highlands *pl n* relatively high ground

highlight *n* **1** Also called: **high spot** the most exciting or memorable part of something **2** an area of the lightest tone in a painting or photograph **3** a lightened streak in the hair produced by bleaching ▸ *vb* **4** to give emphasis to: *the prime minister repeatedly highlighted the need for lower pay*

> **highlight** *n* **1** = high point, peak, climax, feature, focus, focal point, high spot; ≠ low point ▸ *vb* = emphasize, stress, accent, show up, underline, spotlight, accentuate, flag, call attention to; ≠ play down

highly *adv* **1** extremely: *highly desirable* **2** towards the top of a scale of importance, admiration, or respect: *highly paid doctors*

> **highly** *adv* = extremely, very, greatly, vastly, exceptionally, immensely, tremendously

highly strung or *US & Canad* **high-strung** *adj* tense and easily upset

high-maintenance *adj* **1** (of a piece of equipment, motor vehicle, etc.) requiring regular maintenance to keep it in working order **2** *informal* (of a person) requiring a high level of care and attention; demanding

Highness *n* (preceded by *Your, His* or *Her*) a title used to address or refer to a royal person

high-rise *adj* **1** of or relating to a building that has many storeys: *a high-rise estate* ▸ *n* **2** a building that has many storeys

high street *n* the main street of a town, usually containing the most important shops

high tea *n Brit* an early evening meal consisting of a cooked dish, bread, cakes, and tea

high time *adv informal* the latest possible time, which is almost too late: *it's high time we mended that shelf*

highway *n* **1** a public road that everyone may use **2** *US, Canad, Austral & NZ* a main road, esp. one that connects towns

Highway Code *n* (in Britain) a booklet of regulations and recommendations for all road users

highwayman *n, pl* **-men** (formerly) a robber, usually on horseback, who held up travellers on public roads

hijab or **hejab** *n* a covering for the head and face, worn by some Muslim women

hijack *vb* **1** to seize control of or divert (a vehicle or aircraft) while travelling ▸ *n* **2** an instance of hijacking ▸ **hijacker** *n*

> **hijack** *vb* = seize, take over, commandeer, expropriate (*formal*)

hike *vb* **hiking, hiked 1** to walk a long way in the country, usually for pleasure **2** to raise (prices) **3** to pull up with a quick movement: *he hiked up his trouser legs* ▸ *n* **4** a long walk **5** a rise in price ▸ **hiker** *n*

hike *vb* **1** = walk, march, trek, ramble, tramp, back-pack ▸ *n* **4** = walk, march, trek, ramble, tramp, traipse

hilarious *adj* very funny ▷ **hilariously** *adv* ▷ **hilarity** *n*

hilarious *adj* = funny, entertaining, amusing, hysterical (*informal*), humorous, comical, side-splitting

hill *n* **1** a natural elevation of the earth's surface, less high than a mountain **2** a heap or mound **3** an incline or slope ▷ **hilly** *adj*

hill *n* **1** = mount, fell, height, mound, hilltop, tor, knoll, hillock, kopje *or* koppie (*S African*)

hillbilly *n, pl* **-lies 1** *usually derogatory* an unsophisticated person from the mountainous areas in the southeastern US **2** same as **country and western**

hillock *n* a small hill or mound

hilt *n* **1** the handle or shaft of a sword, dagger, or knife **2 to the hilt** to the full: *he plays the role to the hilt*

him *pron* refers to a male person or animal: *I greeted him at the hotel; I must send him a note of congratulation*

himself *pron* **1 A** the reflexive form of *he* or *him*: *he secretly asked himself* **B** used for emphasis: *approved of by the Creator himself* **2** his normal self: *he was almost himself again*

hind¹ *adj* **hinder, hindmost** situated at the back: *a hind leg*

hind² *n, pl* **hinds** *or* **hind** the female of the deer, esp. the red deer

hinder (hin-der) *vb* to get in the way of (someone or something)

hinder *vb* = obstruct, stop, check, block, delay, frustrate, handicap, interrupt; ≠ help

Hindi *n* **1** a language or group of dialects of N central India **2** a formal literary dialect of this language, the official language of India

hindrance *n* **1** an obstruction or snag **2** the act of hindering

Hindu *n, pl* **-dus 1** a person who practises Hinduism ▸ *adj* **2** of Hinduism

Hinduism *n* the dominant religion of India, which involves the worship of many gods and belief in reincarnation

hinge *n* **1** a device for holding together two parts, such as a door and its frame, so that one can swing freely ▸ *vb* **hinging, hinged 2** to join or open (something) by means of a hinge **3 hinge on** to depend on: *billions of dollars of western aid hinged on the outcome of the talks* ▷ **hinged** *adj*

hint *n* **1** a suggestion given in an indirect or subtle manner **2** a helpful piece of advice **3** a small amount: *a hint of irony* ▸ *vb* **4** (sometimes foll. by *at*) to suggest indirectly: *a solution has been hinted at by a few politicians*

hint *n* **1** = clue, suggestion, implication, indication, pointer, allusion, innuendo, intimation **2** = advice, help, tip(s), suggestion(s), pointer(s) **3** = trace, touch, suggestion, dash, suspicion, tinge, undertone ▸ *vb* = suggest, indicate, imply, intimate, insinuate

hinterland *n* **1** land lying behind a coast or the shore of a river **2** an area near and dependent on a large city, esp. a port

hip¹ *n* either side of the body below the waist and above the thigh

hip² *n* the berry-like brightly coloured fruit of a rose bush. Also called: **rosehip**

hip³ *adj* **hipper, hippest** *slang* aware of or following the latest trends

hip-hop *n* a US pop-culture movement originating in the 1980s, comprising rap music, graffiti, and break dancing

hippie *n* same as **hippy**

hippo *n, pl* **-pos** *informal* short for **hippopotamus**

hippodrome *n* **1** a music hall, variety theatre, or circus **2** (in ancient Greece or Rome) an open-air course for horse and chariot races

hippopotamus *n, pl* **-muses** *or* **-mi** a very large mammal with thick wrinkled skin and short legs, which lives around the rivers of tropical Africa

hippy *or* **hippie** *n, pl* **-pies** (esp. during the 1960s) a person whose behaviour and dress imply a rejection of conventional values

hipster *n* *informal* a person who believes he or she is following trends that are outside the mainstream

hire *vb* **hiring, hired 1** to acquire the temporary use of (a thing) or the services of (a person) in exchange for payment **2** to employ (a person) for wages **3** to provide (something) or the services of (oneself or others) for payment **4 hire out** *chiefly Brit* to pay independent contractors for (work to be done) ▸ *n* **5** the act of hiring **6 for hire** available to be hired

hire *vb* **1, 2** = employ, commission, take on, engage, appoint, sign up, enlist **3** = rent, charter, lease, let, engage ▸ *n* **5** = rental, hiring, rent, lease

hireling *n* *derogatory* a person who works only for money

hire-purchase *n* a system in which a buyer takes possession of merchandise on payment of a deposit and completes the purchase by paying a series of instalments while the seller retains ownership until the final instalment is paid

hirsute (her-suit) *adj* hairy

his *adj* **1** of, belonging to, or associated with him: *his birthday* ▸ *pron* **2** something belonging to him: *his is on the left; that book is his* **3 of his** belonging to him

Hispanic *adj* **1** of or derived from Spain or the Spanish ▸ *n* **2** *US* a US citizen of Spanish or Latin-American descent

hiss *n* **1** a sound like that of a prolonged *s* **2** such a sound as an expression of dislike or disapproval ▸ *vb* **3** to utter a hiss **4** to express with a hiss: *she hissed the name* **5** to show dislike or disapproval towards (a speaker or performer) by hissing

> **hiss** *n* **1** = fizz, buzz, hissing, fizzing, sibilation ▸ *vb* **3, 4** = whistle, wheeze, whiz, whirr, sibilate **5** = jeer, mock, deride

histamine (hiss-ta-meen) *n* a chemical compound released by the body tissues in allergic reactions

histogram *n* a statistical graph that represents the frequency of values of a quantity by vertical bars of varying heights and widths

histology *n* the study of the tissues of an animal or plant

historian *n* a person who writes or studies history

historic *adj* important in history, or likely to be seen as important in the future

> **historic** *adj* = significant, notable, momentous, famous, extraordinary, outstanding, remarkable, ground-breaking; ≠ unimportant

historical *adj* **1** occurring in the past **2** describing or representing situations or people that existed in the past: *a historical novel* **3** belonging to or typical of the study of history: *historical perspective* > **historically** *adv*

> **historical** *adj* **1** = factual, real, documented, actual, authentic, attested; ≠ contemporary

history *n, pl* **-ries 1** a record or account of past events and developments **2** all that is preserved of the past, esp. in written form **3** the study of interpreting past events **4** the past events or previous experiences of a place, thing, or person: *he knew the whole history of the place* **5** a play that depicts historical events

> **history** *n* **1** = chronicle, record, story, account, narrative, recital, annals **2** = the past, antiquity, yesterday, yesteryear, olden days

histrionic *adj* **1** very dramatic and full of exaggerated emotion: *histrionic bursts of invective* ▸ *n* **2 histrionics** behaviour of this kind > **histrionically** *adv*

hit *vb* **hitting, hit 1** to strike or touch (a person or thing) **2** to come into violent contact with: *a helicopter hit a Volvo* **3** to propel (a ball) by striking **4** *cricket* to score (runs) **5** to affect (a person, place, or thing) badly: *the airline says that its revenue will be hit* **6** to reach (a point or place): *the city's crime level hit new heights* **7 hit the bottle** *slang* to start drinking excessive amounts of alcohol **8 hit the road** *informal* to set out on a journey ▸ *n* **9** an impact or collision **10** a shot or blow that reaches its target **11** *informal* a person or thing that gains wide appeal: *those early*

collections made her a hit with the club set **12** a single visit to a website: *over 500,000 hits a day to its site* ▸ See also **hit on**

> **hit** *vb* **1** = strike, beat, knock, bang, slap, smack, thump, clout (*informal*) **2** = collide with, run into, bump into, clash with, smash into, crash against, bang into **5** = affect, damage, harm, ruin, devastate, overwhelm, touch, impact on **6** = reach, gain, achieve, arrive at, accomplish, attain ▸ *n* **9** = shot, blow **10** = blow, knock, stroke, belt (*informal*), slap, smack, clout (*informal*) **11** = success, winner, triumph, smash (*informal*), sensation

hit-and-miss *adj informal* happening in an unplanned way: *farming can be very much a hit-and-miss affair*

hitch *n* **1** a temporary or minor problem or difficulty **2** a knot that can be undone by pulling against the direction of the strain that holds it ▸ *vb* **3** *informal* **A** to obtain (a ride) by hitchhiking **B** to hitchhike **4** to fasten with a knot or tie **5 get hitched** *slang* to get married **6 hitch up** to pull up (one's trousers, etc.) with a quick jerk

> **hitch** *n* **1** = problem, catch (*informal*), difficulty, hold-up, obstacle, drawback, snag, uphill (*S African*), impediment ▸ *vb* **3B** = hitchhike, thumb a lift **4** = fasten, join, attach, couple, tie, connect, harness, tether **6 hitch something up** = pull up, tug, jerk, yank

hitchhike *vb* **-hiking, -hiked** to travel by getting free lifts in motor vehicles > **hitchhiker** *n*

hi-tech *adj* using sophisticated, esp. electronic, technology

hither *adv old-fashioned* to or towards this place: *come hither*

hitherto *adv formal* until this time: *fundamental questions which have hitherto been ignored*

> **hitherto** *adv* = previously, so far, until now, thus far, heretofore

hit man *n* a person hired by terrorists or gangsters to murder someone

hit on *or* **hit upon** *vb* to think of (an idea or a solution)

> **hit on** *or* **hit upon** *vb* **hit on something** = think up, discover, arrive at, invent, stumble on, light upon, strike upon

HIV human immunodeficiency virus, the cause of AIDS

hive *n* **1** a structure in which bees live **2 hive of activity** a busy place with many people working hard

hive off *vb* **hiving, hived** to transfer (part of a business, esp. the profitable part of a nationalized industry) to new ownership

hives *n pathol* an allergic reaction in which itchy red or whitish raised patches develop on the skin

HM (in Britain) Her (or His) Majesty

H.M.S. or **HMS** (in Britain) Her (or His) Majesty's Ship

HNC (in Britain) Higher National Certificate; a qualification recognized by many national technical and professional institutions

HND (in Britain) Higher National Diploma; a qualification in a technical subject equivalent to an ordinary degree

hoard n **1** a store of money, food, etc., hidden away for future use ▸ vb **2** to save or store (money, food, etc.) > **hoarder** n

hoarding n a large board at the side of a road, used for displaying advertising posters

hoarfrost n a white layer of ice crystals formed on the ground by condensation at temperatures below freezing point

hoarse adj **1** (of a voice) rough and unclear through illness or too much shouting **2** having a rough and unclear voice > **hoarsely** adv > **hoarseness** n

hoary adj **hoarier, hoariest 1** having grey or white hair **2** very old: a hoary old problem

hoax n **1** a deception, esp. a practical joke ▸ vb **2** to deceive or play a joke on (someone) > **hoaxer** n

hob n Brit the flat top part of a cooker, or a separate flat surface, containing hotplates or burners

hobble vb **-bling, -bled 1** to walk with a lame awkward movement **2** to tie the legs of (a horse) together in order to restrict its movement

hobby n, pl **-bies** an activity pursued in one's spare time for pleasure or relaxation

hobby n = pastime, relaxation, leisure pursuit, diversion, avocation (formal), (leisure) activity

hobbyhorse n **1** a favourite topic about which a person likes to talk at every opportunity: public transport is his hobbyhorse **2** a toy consisting of a stick with a figure of a horse's head at one end **3** a figure of a horse attached to a performer's waist in a morris dance

hobgoblin n a small, mischievous creature in fairy stories

hobnail boots pl n old-fashioned heavy boots with short nails in the soles to lessen wear and tear

hobnob vb **-nobbing, -nobbed** to socialize or talk informally: hobnobbing with the rich

hobo n, pl **-bos** or **-boes** US, Canad, Austral & NZ a tramp or vagrant

hock¹ n the joint in the leg of a horse or similar animal that corresponds to the human ankle

hock² n a white wine from the German Rhine

hock³ informal ▸ vb **1** to pawn or pledge ▸ n **2 in hock ᴀ** in debt **ʙ** in pawn

hockey n **1** a game played on a field by two teams of 11 players who try to hit a ball into their opponents' goal using long sticks curved at the end **2** US & Canad ice hockey

hocus-pocus n informal something said or done in order to confuse or trick someone

hod n an open metal or plastic box attached to a pole, for carrying bricks or mortar

hodgepodge n chiefly US & Canad same as **hotchpotch**

hoe n **1** a long-handled implement used to loosen the soil or to weed ▸ vb **hoeing, hoed 2** to scrape or weed with a hoe

hog n **1** a castrated male pig **2** US & Canad any mammal of the pig family **3** informal a greedy person **4 go the whole hog** slang to do something in the most complete way possible ▸ vb **hogging, hogged 5** slang to take more than one's share of (something)

Hogmanay n New Year's Eve in Scotland

hogshead n a large cask for storing alcoholic drinks

hogwash n informal nonsense

hoick vb **1** to raise abruptly and sharply **2** NZ to clear the throat and spit

hoi polloi pl n the ordinary people when compared to the rich or well-educated

hoisin n a sweet spicy sauce of soya beans, sugar, garlic, and vinegar, used in Chinese cookery

hoist vb **1** to raise or lift up, esp. by mechanical means ▸ n **2** any apparatus or device for lifting things

hoist vb = raise, lift, erect, elevate, heave ▸ n = lift, crane, elevator, winch

hoity-toity adj informal arrogant or haughty

hokey-pokey n NZ a brittle toffee sold in lumps

hold¹ vb **holding, held 1** to keep (an object or a person) with or within the hands or arms **2** to support: a rope made from 1000 hairs would hold a large adult **3** to maintain in a specified state or position: his reputation continued to hold secure **4** to have the capacity for: trains designed to hold more than 400 **5** to set aside or reserve: they will hold our tickets until tomorrow **6** to restrain or keep back: designed to hold dangerous criminals **7** to remain unbroken: if the elastic holds **8** (of the weather) to remain dry and bright **9** to keep (the attention of): a writer holds a reader by his temperament **10** to arrange and cause to take place: we must hold an inquiry **11** to have the ownership or possession of: she holds a degree in Egyptology **12** to have responsibility for: she cannot hold an elective office **13** to be able to control the outward effects of drinking (alcohol): he can't hold his drink **14** to (cause to) remain committed to (a promise, etc.) **15** to claim or believe: some Sufis hold that all religious leaders were prophets **16** to remain valid or true: the categories are not the same and equivalency does not hold **17** to consider in a specified manner: philosophies which we hold so dear **18** to defend successfully: the Russians were holding the Volga front **19** music to sustain the sound of (a note) ▸ n **20** a way of holding something or the act of holding it **21** something to hold onto for support **22** controlling influence: *drugs will take a hold* **23 with no holds barred** with all limitations removed ▸ **holder** *n*

hold *vb* **1** = embrace, grasp, clutch, hug, squeeze, cradle, clasp, enfold **4** = accommodate, take, contain, seat, have a capacity for **6** = restrain; ≠ release **10** = conduct, convene, call, run, preside over; ≠ cancel **12** = occupy, have, fill, maintain, retain, possess, hold down (*informal*) **15** = consider, think, believe, judge, regard, assume, reckon, deem; ≠ deny ▸ *n* **20** = grip, grasp, clasp **22** = control, influence, mastery, mana (*NZ*)

hold² *n* the space in a ship or aircraft for storing cargo or luggage

holdall *n Brit* a large strong travelling bag

holding *n* **1** land held under a lease **2** property to which the holder has legal title, such as land, stocks, or shares

hold-up *n* **1** an armed robbery **2** a delay: *a traffic hold-up* ▸ *vb* **3** to delay **4** to support (an object) **5** to stop and rob (someone), using a weapon **6** to exhibit or present (something) as an example: *he was held up as a model professional*

hold-up *n* **1** = robbery, theft, mugging (*informal*), stick-up (*slang, chiefly US*) **2** = delay, wait, hitch, setback, snag, traffic jam, stoppage, bottleneck

hole *n* **1** an area hollowed out in a solid **2** an opening in or through something **3** an animal's burrow **4** *informal* a fault or error: *this points to a very big hole in parliamentary security* **5** *informal* an unattractive town or other place **6** (on a golf course) any one of the divisions of a course (usually 18) represented by the distance between the tee and the sunken cup on the green into which the ball is to be played **7 in a hole** *slang* in a difficult and embarrassing situation **8 make a hole in** *informal* to use a great amount of (one's money or food supply) **9 pick holes in** to point out faults in ▸ *vb* **holing, holed 10** to make a hole or holes in (something) **11** to hit (a golf ball) into a hole ▸ **holey** *adj*

hole *n* **1** = cavity, pit, hollow, chamber, cave, cavern **2** = opening, crack, tear, gap, breach, vent, puncture, aperture **3** = burrow, den, earth, shelter, lair **5** = hovel, dump (*informal*), dive (*slang*), slum

holiday *n* **1** a period of time spent away from home for enjoyment and relaxation **2** (*often pl*) *chiefly Brit & NZ* a period in which a break is taken from work or studies for rest or recreation **3** a day on which work is suspended by law or custom, such as a bank holiday ▸ *vb* **4** *chiefly Brit* to spend a holiday

holiday *n* **1** = vacation, leave, break, time off, recess, schoolie (*Austral*), accumulated day off or ADO (*Austral*), staycation or stacation (*informal*) **3** = festival, fête, celebration, feast, gala

holier-than-thou *adj* offensively self-righteous

Holiness *n* (preceded by *His* or *Your*) a title reserved for the pope

holism *n* **1** the view that a whole is greater than the sum of its parts **2** (in medicine) consideration of the complete person in the treatment of disease ▸ **holistic** *adj*

hollow *adj* **1** having a hole or space within; not solid: *a hollow tree* **2** curving inwards: *hollow cheeks* **3** (of sounds) as if echoing in a hollow place **4** without any real value or worth: *a hollow enterprise, lacking purpose, and lacking soul* ▸ *adv* **5 beat someone hollow** *Brit & NZ informal* to defeat someone thoroughly ▸ *n* **6** a cavity or space in something **7** a dip in the land ▸ *vb* **8** (often foll. by *out*) to form a hole or cavity in ▸ **hollowly** *adv*

hollow *adj* **1** = empty, vacant, void, unfilled; ≠ solid **3** = dull, low, deep, muted, toneless, reverberant; ≠ vibrant **4** = worthless, useless, vain, meaningless, pointless, futile, fruitless; ≠ meaningful ▸ *n* **6** = cavity, hole, bowl, depression, pit, basin, crater, trough; ≠ mound **7** = valley, dale, glen, dell, dingle; ≠ hill ▸ *vb* = scoop out, dig out, excavate, gouge out

holly *n* an evergreen tree with prickly leaves and bright red berries, used for Christmas decorations

hollyhock *n* a tall garden plant with spikes of colourful flowers

holocaust *n* **1** destruction or loss of life on a massive scale **2 the Holocaust** mass murder of the Jews in Europe by the Nazis (1940–45)

holocaust *n* **1** = devastation, destruction, genocide, annihilation, conflagration

hologram *n* a three-dimensional photographic image produced by means of a split laser beam

holograph *n* a book or document handwritten by its author

holster *n* a sheathlike leather case for a pistol, worn attached to a belt

holy *adj* **-lier, -liest 1** of or associated with God or a deity **2** (of a person) religious and leading a virtuous life ▸ **holiness** *n*

holy *adj* **1** = sacred, blessed, hallowed, venerable, consecrated, sacrosanct, sanctified; ≠ unsanctified **2** = devout, godly, religious, pure, righteous, pious, virtuous, saintly; ≠ sinful

Holy Communion *n Christianity* a church service in which people take bread and wine in remembrance of Christ's Last Supper and His atonement for the sins of the world

Holy Grail *n* **1 the Holy Grail** (in medieval legend) the bowl used by Jesus at the Last Supper **2** *informal* any ambition or goal

Holy Spirit *n* **the Holy Spirit** *Christianity* one of the three aspects of God

Holy Week *n* *Christianity* the week before Easter Sunday

homage *n* a public show of respect or honour towards someone or something: *the master's jazzy-classical homage to Gershwin*

> **homage** *n* = respect, honour, worship, devotion, reverence, deference, adulation, adoration; ≠ contempt

home *n* **1** the place where one lives **2** the country or area of one's birth **3** a building or organization set up to care for people in a certain category, such as orphans or elderly people **4** the place where something is invented or started: *the home of the first aircraft* **5** *sport* a team's own ground: *the match is at home* **6** *baseball & rounders etc.* the objective towards which a player runs after striking the ball **7 at home A** in one's own home or country **B** at ease: *he felt more at home with the Russians* **c** receiving visitors ▸ *adj* **8** of one's home, birthplace, or native country **9** (of an activity) done in one's house: *home movies* **10** *sport* played on one's own ground: *a home game* **11 home and dry** *Brit slang* definitely safe or successful ▸ *adv* **12** to or at home: *I came home* **13** to or on the point: *the message struck home* **14** to the fullest extent: *they drove their spears home* **15 bring something home to someone** to make something clear to someone ▸ *vb* **homing, homed 16** (of birds) to return home accurately from a distance **17 home in on** to be directed towards (a goal or target)

> **home** *n* **1** = dwelling (*formal, literary*), house, residence, abode, habitation (*formal*), pad (*slang, old-fashioned*), domicile **2** = birthplace, homeland, home town, native land, Godzone (*Austral informal*) **7A at home** = in, present, available **7B at home** = at ease, relaxed, comfortable, content, at peace ▸ *adj* **8** = domestic, local, internal, native ▸ *adv* **15 bring something home to someone** = make clear, emphasize, drive home, press home, impress upon

home-brew *n* beer or other alcoholic drink brewed at home

homeland *n* **1** the country from which the ancestors of a person or group came: *defending their homeland* **2** *S African* (formerly) an area reserved for occupation by a Black African people

> **homeland** *n* **1** = native land, birthplace, motherland, fatherland, country of origin, mother country, Godzone (*Austral informal*)

homeless *adj* **1** having nowhere to live ▸ *pl n* **2 the homeless** people who have nowhere to live: *night shelters for the homeless* > **homelessness** *n*

> **homeless** *adj* = destitute, displaced, dispossessed, down-and-out

homely *adj* **-lier, -liest 1** simple, ordinary, and comfortable **2 A** *Brit* (of a person) warm and friendly **B** *chiefly US & Canad* (of a person) plain or unattractive > **homeliness** *n*

> **homely** *adj* **1** = comfortable, welcoming, friendly, cosy, homespun; ≠ elaborate

home-made *adj* (esp. of foods) made at home or on the premises

homeopathy *or* **homoeopathy** (home-ee-op-ath-ee) *n* a method of treating disease by the use of small amounts of a drug that produces symptoms of the disease in healthy people > **homeopath** *or* **homoeopath** (home-ee-oh-path) *n* > **homeopathic** *or* **homoeopathic** *adj*

home page *n* *internet* the introductory information about a website with links to the information or services provided

homesick *adj* depressed by being away from home and family > **homesickness** *n*

homestead *n* **1** a farmhouse and the adjoining land **2** (in the western US & Canada) a house and adjoining tract of land (originally often 160 acres) that was granted by the government for development as a farm

home truths *pl n* unpleasant facts told to a person about himself or herself

homeward *adj* **1** going home ▸ *adv also* **homewards 2** towards home

homework *n* **1** school work done at home **2** research or preparation

homicide *n* **1** the act of killing someone **2** a person who kills someone > **homicidal** *adj*

> **homicide** *n* **1** = murder, killing, manslaughter, slaying, bloodshed

homily *n, pl* **-lies** a moralizing talk or piece of writing > **homiletic** *adj*

hominid *n* **1** any member of the family of primates that includes modern humans and the extinct forerunners of humans ▸ *adj* **2** of or belonging to this family

homo- *combining form* same or like: *homologous*

homogeneous (home-oh-**jean**-ee-uss) *adj* having parts or members which are all the same or which consist of only one substance: *the Arabs are not a single, homogeneous nation* > **homogeneity** *n*

homogenize *or* **-nise** *vb* **-nizing, -nized** *or* **-nising, -nised 1** to break up the fat globules in (milk or cream) so that they are evenly distributed **2** to make different elements the same or similar: *homogenized products for a mass market*

homograph *n* a word spelt the same as another, but having a different meaning, such as *bear* (to carry) and *bear* (the animal)

h

homologous (hom-ol-log-uss) *adj* **1** having a related or similar position or structure **2** *biol* (of organs and parts) having the same origin but different functions: *the wing of a bat and the arm of a monkey are homologous*

homonym *n* a word pronounced and spelt the same as another, but having a different meaning, such as *novel* (a book) and *novel* (new)

homophobia *n* intense hatred or fear of homosexuals > **homophobic** *adj*

homophone *n* a word pronounced the same as another, but having a different meaning or spelling or both, such as *bear* and *bare*

Homo sapiens (home-oh sap-ee-enz) *n* the name for modern humans as a species

homosexual *n* **1** a person who is sexually attracted to members of the same sex ▸ *adj* **2** (of a person) sexually attracted to members of the same sex **3** (of a sexual relationship) between members of the same sex > **homosexuality** *n*

Hon. Honourable (title)

hone *vb* **honing, honed** **1** to develop and improve (a quality or ability): *a workshop to hone interview techniques* **2** to sharpen (a tool) ▸ *n* **3** a fine whetstone used for sharpening edged tools and knives

> **hone** *vb* **1** = improve, better, enhance, upgrade, refine, sharpen, help **2** = sharpen, point, grind, edge, file, polish, whet

honest *adj* **1** truthful and moral in behaviour; trustworthy **2** open and sincere in relationships and attitudes; without pretensions **3** gained or earned fairly: *an honest income*

> **honest** *adj* **1** = trustworthy, upright, ethical, honourable, reputable, truthful, virtuous, law-abiding; ≠ dishonest **2** = open, direct, frank, plain, sincere, candid, forthright, upfront (*informal*); ≠ secretive

honestly *adv* **1** in an honest manner **2** truly: *honestly, that's all I can recall*

> **honestly** *adv* **1** = ethically, legally, lawfully, honourably, by fair means

honesty *n, pl* **-ties** **1** the quality of being truthful and trustworthy **2** a plant with flattened silvery pods which are used for indoor decoration

> **honesty** *n* **1** = integrity, honour, virtue, morality, probity (*formal*), rectitude, truthfulness, trustworthiness

honey *n* **1** a sweet edible sticky substance made by bees from nectar **2** *chiefly US & Canad* a term of affection **3** *informal, chiefly US & Canad* something very good of its kind: *a honey of a picture about American family life*

honeycomb *n* a waxy structure, constructed by bees in a hive, that consists of many six-sided cells in which honey is stored

honeydew melon *n* a melon with yellow skin and sweet pale flesh

honeymoon *n* **1** a holiday taken by a newly married couple **2** the early period of an undertaking or activity, such as the start of a new government's term of office, when an attitude of goodwill prevails ▸ *vb* **3** to take a honeymoon > **honeymooner** *n*

honeysuckle *n* a climbing shrub with sweet-smelling white, yellow, or pink flowers

hongi (hong-jee) *n NZ* a Māori greeting in which people touch noses

honk *n* **1** the sound made by a motor horn **2** the sound made by a goose ▸ *vb* **3** to make or cause (something) to make a honking sound

honorary *adj* **A** held or given as a mark of respect, without the usual qualifications, payment, or work: *an honorary degree* **B** (of a secretary, treasurer, etc.) unpaid

> **honorary** *adj* **1A** = nominal, unofficial, titular, in name or title only

honorific *adj* showing respect: *an honorific title*

honour *or US* **honor** *n* **1** allegiance to moral principles **2** a person's good reputation and the respect they are given by other people **3 A** fame or glory **B** a person who wins fame or glory for his or her country, school, etc.: *he was an honour to his nation* **4** great respect or esteem, or an outward sign of this **5** a privilege or pleasure: *it was an honour to meet him* **6** *old-fashioned* a woman's virginity **7** *bridge & whist* any of the top four or five cards in a suit **8** *golf* the right to tee off first **9 in honour of** out of respect for **10 on one's honour** under a moral obligation ▸ *vb* **11** to hold someone in respect **12** to give (someone) special praise, attention, or an award **13** to accept and then pay (a cheque or bill) **14** to keep (one's promise); fulfil (a previous agreement)

> **honour** *or* **honor** *n* **1** = integrity, morality, honesty, goodness, fairness, decency, probity (*formal*), rectitude; ≠ dishonour **2** = reputation, standing, prestige, image, status, stature, good name, cachet **3A** = prestige, credit, reputation, glory, fame, distinction, dignity, renown **4** = acclaim, praise, recognition, compliments, homage, accolades, commendation; ≠ contempt **5** = privilege, credit, pleasure, compliment ▸ *vb* **11** = respect, value, esteem, prize, appreciate, adore; ≠ scorn **12** = acclaim, praise, decorate, commemorate, commend **13** = pay, take, accept, pass, acknowledge; ≠ refuse **14** = fulfil, keep, carry out, observe, discharge, live up to, be true to

honourable *or US* **honorable** *adj* **1** principled **2** worthy of respect or esteem > **honourably** *adv*

> **honourable** *or* **honorable** *adj* **1** = principled, moral, ethical, fair, upright, honest, virtuous, trustworthy **2** = proper, respectable, virtuous, creditable

hood[1] *n* **1** a loose head covering either attached to a coat or made as a separate garment **2** *US, Canad & Austral* the bonnet of a car **3** the folding roof of a convertible car or a pram ▸ *vb* **4** to cover with or as if with a hood ▸ **hoodlike** *adj*

hood[2] *n slang* short for **hoodlum**

hooded *adj* **1** (of a garment) having a hood **2** (of eyes) having heavy eyelids that appear to be half-closed

hoodie *n informal* **1** a hooded sweatshirt **2** a young person who wears a hooded sweatshirt, regarded by some as a potential hooligan

hoodlum *n* a violent criminal, esp. one who is a member of a gang

hoodoo *n, pl* **-doos 1** *informal* bad luck **2** *informal* a person or thing that brings bad luck **3** *chiefly US* same as **voodoo**

hoodwink *vb* to trick or deceive

hoof *n, pl* **hooves** or **hoofs 1** the horny covering of the end of the foot in the horse, deer, and certain other mammals **2 on the hoof** **A** (of livestock) alive **B** in an impromptu way: *thinking on the hoof* ▸ *vb* **3 hoof it** *slang* to walk ▸ **hoofed** *adj*

hoo-ha *n informal* a noisy commotion or fuss

hook *n* **1** a curved piece of metal or plastic used to hang, hold, or pull something **2** something resembling a hook, such as a sharp bend in a river or a sharply curved strip of land **3** *boxing* a short swinging blow with the elbow bent **4** *cricket & golf* a shot that causes the ball to go to the player's left **5 by hook or by crook** by any means: *get into the charts by hook or by crook* **6 hook, line, and sinker** *informal* completely: *we fell for it hook, line, and sinker* **7 let someone off the hook** *slang* to free someone from an obligation or a difficult situation **8 sling one's hook** *Brit & Austral slang* to leave ▸ *vb* **9** to fasten with, or as if with, a hook **10** to catch (a fish) on a hook **11** *cricket & golf* to play (a ball) with a hook **12** *rugby* to obtain and pass (the ball) backwards from a scrum, using the feet

> **hook** *n* **1** = fastener, catch, link, peg, clasp ▸ *vb* **9** = fasten, fix, secure, clasp **10** = catch, land, trap, entrap

hookah *n* (esp. in Arab countries) a pipe for smoking marijuana or tobacco, with a long flexible stem connected to a container of water through which smoke is drawn and cooled

hooked *adj* **1** bent like a hook **2** (often foll. by *on*) **A** *slang* addicted (to): *hooked on drugs* **B** obsessed (with): *hooked on football*

> **hooked** *adj* **1** = bent, curved, aquiline, hook-shaped **2A** = addicted, dependent, using (*informal*), having a habit **2B** = obsessed, addicted, taken, devoted, turned on (*slang*), enamoured

hooker *n* **1** *slang* a prostitute **2** *rugby* a player who uses his feet to get the ball in a scrum

hook-up *n* the linking of broadcasting equipment or stations to transmit a special programme

hookworm *n* a blood-sucking worm with hooked mouthparts

hooligan *n slang* a young person who behaves in a noisy and violent way in public ▸ **hooliganism** *n*

> **hooligan** *n* = delinquent, vandal, hoon (*Austral, NZ informal*), ruffian, lager lout, yob or yobbo (*Brit slang*), cougan (*Austral slang*), scozza (*Austral slang*), bogan (*Austral slang*), hoodie (*informal*)

hoon *Austral & NZ informal* ▸ *n* **1** a loutish youth who drives irresponsibly ▸ *vb* **2** to drive irresponsibly

hoop *n* **1** a rigid circular band of metal, plastic, or wood **2** a child's toy shaped like a hoop and rolled on the ground or whirled around the body **3** *croquet* any of the iron arches through which the ball is driven **4** a large ring through which performers or animals jump **5 go** or **be put through the hoops** to go through an ordeal or test ▸ *vb* **6** to surround (something) with a hoop ▸ **hooped** *adj*

> **hoop** *n* **1** = ring, band, loop, wheel, round, girdle, circlet

hoopla *n Brit & Austral* a fairground game in which hoops are thrown over objects in an attempt to win them

hoop pine *n* an Australian tree or shrub with flowers in dense spikes

hooray *interj, n* same as **hurrah**

hoot *n* **1** the sound of a car horn **2** the cry of an owl **3** a high-pitched noise showing disapproval **4** *informal* an amusing person or thing ▸ *vb* **5** *Brit* to blow (a car horn) **6** to make a hoot **7** to jeer or yell contemptuously at someone **8** to drive (speakers or performers on stage) off by hooting

hooter *n chiefly Brit* **1** a device that hoots, such as a car horn **2** *slang* a nose

Hoover *n* **1** *trademark* a vacuum cleaner ▸ *vb* **hoover** **2** to vacuum-clean (a carpet) **3** (often foll. by *up*) to devour (something) quickly and completely

hooves *n* a plural of **hoof**

hop[1] *vb* **hopping, hopped 1** to jump forwards or upwards on one foot **2** (of frogs, birds, etc.) to move forwards in short jumps **3** to jump over something **4** *informal* to move quickly (in, on, out of, etc.): *hop into bed* **5 hop it** *Brit & Austral slang* to go away ▸ *n* **6** an instance of hopping **7** *informal* an informal dance **8** *informal* a short journey, usually in an aircraft **9 on the hop** *informal* **A** active or busy: *he keeps me on the hop* **B** unawares or unprepared: *you caught me on the hop*

> **hop** *vb* **3** = jump, spring, bound, leap, skip, vault, caper ▸ *n* **6** = jump, step, spring, bound, leap, bounce, skip, vault

h

hop² *n* a climbing plant with green conelike flowers

hope *vb* **hoping, hoped 1** to desire (something), usually with some possibility of fulfilment: *you would hope for their cooperation* **2** to trust or believe: *I hope I've arranged that* ▸ *n* **3** a feeling of desire for something, usually with confidence in the possibility of its fulfilment: *the news was greeted by some as hope for further interest rate cuts* **4** a reasonable ground for this feeling: *there is hope for you yet* **5** the person, thing, situation, or event that gives cause for hope or is desired: *the young are a symbol of hope for the future*

> **hope** *vb* **2** = believe, look forward to, cross your fingers ▸ *n* **3** = belief, confidence, expectation, longing, dream, desire, ambition, assumption; ≠ despair

hopeful *adj* **1** having, inspiring, or expressing hope ▸ *n* **2** a person considered to be on the brink of success: *a young hopeful*

> **hopeful** *adj* = optimistic, confident, looking forward to, buoyant, sanguine, expectant; ≠ despairing

hopefully *adv* **1** in a hopeful manner **2** *informal* it is hoped: *hopefully I've got a long career ahead of me*

> **hopefully** *adv* **1** = optimistically, confidently, expectantly, with anticipation

hopeless *adj* **1** having or offering no hope **2** impossible to solve **3** *informal* without skill or ability: *I'm hopeless at maths* > **hopelessly** *adv* > **hopelessness** *n*

> **hopeless** *adj* **1** = impossible, pointless, futile, useless, vain, no-win, unattainable

hopper *n* a funnel-shaped device from which solid materials can be discharged into a receptacle below

hopscotch *n* a children's game in which a player throws a stone to land in one of a pattern of squares marked on the ground and then hops over to it to pick it up

horde *n* a very large crowd, often frightening or unpleasant

> **horde** *n* = crowd, mob, swarm, host, band, pack, drove, gang

horizon *n* **1** the apparent line that divides the earth and the sky **2 horizons** the limits of a person's interests and activities: *seeking to broaden his horizons at college* **3 on the horizon** almost certainly going to happen or be done in the future: *a new type of computer is on the horizon*

> **horizon** *n* **1** = skyline, view, vista

horizontal *adj* **1** flat and level with the ground or with a line considered as a base **2** affecting or happening at one level in a system or organization: *a horizontal division of labour* ▸ *n* **3** a horizontal plane, position, or line > **horizontally** *adv*

> **horizontal** *adj* **1** = level, flat, parallel

hormone *n* **1** a chemical substance produced in an endocrine gland and transported in the blood to a certain tissue, on which it has a specific effect **2** a similar substance produced by a plant that is essential for growth **3** a synthetic substance having the same effects > **hormonal** *adj*

horn *n* **1** either of a pair of permanent bony outgrowths on the heads of animals such as cattle and antelopes **2** any hornlike projection, such as the eyestalk of a snail **3** the antler of a deer **4** the hard substance of which horns are made **5** a musical wind instrument made from horn **6** any musical instrument consisting of a pipe or tube of brass fitted with a mouthpiece **7** a device, such as on a vehicle, for producing a warning or signalling noise > **horned** *adj*

hornbeam *n* a tree with smooth grey bark

hornbill *n* a tropical bird with a bony growth on its large beak

hornblende *n* a green-to-black mineral containing aluminium, calcium, sodium, magnesium, and iron

hornet *n* **1** a large wasp that can inflict a severe sting **2 hornet's nest** a very unpleasant situation that is difficult to deal with: *you'll stir up a hornet's nest*

hornpipe *n* **1** a solo dance, traditionally performed by sailors **2** music for this dance

horny *adj* **hornier, horniest 1** of, like, or hard as horn **2** *slang* **A** sexually aroused **B** provoking sexual arousal **C** sexually eager

horoscope *n* **1** the prediction of a person's future based on the positions of the planets, sun, and moon at the time of birth **2** a diagram showing the positions of the planets, sun, and moon at a particular time and place

horrendous *adj* very unpleasant or shocking

horrible *adj* **1** disagreeable and unpleasant: *a horrible hotel room* **2** causing fear, shock, or disgust: *he died a horrible death* > **horribly** *adv*

> **horrible** *adj* **2** = dreadful, terrible, awful, nasty, cruel, mean, unpleasant, horrid (*informal*); ≠ wonderful

horrid *adj* **1** disagreeable or unpleasant: *it had been a horrid day at school* **2** *informal* (of a person) unkind and nasty: *her horrid parents*

horrific *adj* provoking horror: *horrific injuries* > **horrifically** *adv*

> **horrific** *adj* = horrifying, shocking (*informal*), appalling, awful, terrifying, dreadful, horrendous, ghastly

horrify *vb* **-fies, -fying, -fied** to cause feelings of horror in (someone); shock (someone) greatly

> **horrify** *vb* = terrify, alarm, frighten, scare, intimidate, petrify, make your hair stand on end; ≠ comfort

horror *n* **1** extreme fear or terror **2** intense hatred: *she had a horror of violence* **3** a thing or person causing fear, loathing, or distaste ▸ *adj* **4** having a frightening subject, usually concerned with the supernatural: *a horror film*

> **horror** *n* **1** = terror, fear, alarm, panic, dread, fright, consternation, trepidation (*formal*) **2** = hatred, disgust, loathing, aversion, revulsion, repugnance, odium (*formal*), detestation; ≠ love

hors d'oeuvre (or **durv**) *n*, *pl* **hors d'oeuvre** or **hors d'oeuvres** (or **durv**) an appetizer, usually served before the main meal

horse *n* **1** a four-footed mammal with hooves, a mane, and a tail, used for riding and pulling carts, etc. Related adjectives: **equestrian**, **equine 2** the adult male of this species; stallion **3** *gymnastics* a padded apparatus on legs, used for vaulting **4 be** or **get on one's high horse** *informal* to act in a haughty manner **5 the horses** *informal* horse races on which bets may be placed: *an occasional flutter on the horses* **6 the horse's mouth** the most reliable source: *I'll tell you straight from the horse's mouth* ▸ See also **horse around**

> **horse** *n* **1** = nag, mount, mare, colt, filly, stallion, steed (*archaic, literary*), moke (*Austral slang*), yarraman or yarramin (*Austral*), gee-gee (*slang*)

horse around or **horse about** *vb informal* to play roughly or boisterously

horse chestnut *n* **1** a tree with broad leaves and brown shiny inedible nuts enclosed in a spiky case **2** the nut of this tree

horsefly *n*, *pl* **-flies** a large fly which sucks the blood of horses, cattle, and people

horsehair *n* hair from the tail or mane of a horse, used in upholstery

horse laugh *n* a loud and coarse laugh

horseman or *fem* **horsewoman** *n*, *pl* **-men** or **-women 1** a person who is skilled in riding **2** a person riding a horse > **horsemanship** *n*

horseplay *n* rough or rowdy play

horsepower *n* a unit of power (equivalent to 745.7 watts), used to measure the power of an engine

horseradish *n* a plant with a white strong-tasting root, which is used to make a sauce

horseshoe *n* **1** a piece of iron shaped like a U, nailed to the bottom of a horse's hoof to protect the foot **2** an object of similar shape: often regarded as a symbol of good luck

horsey or **horsy** *adj* **horsier**, **horsiest 1** of or relating to horses: *a horsey smell* **2** devoted to horses: *the horsey set* **3** like a horse: *a horsey face*

horticulture *n* the art or science of growing gardens > **horticultural** *adj* > **horticulturalist** or **horticulturist** *n*

hosanna *interj* an exclamation of praise to God

hose¹ *n* **1** a flexible pipe, for conveying a liquid or gas ▸ *vb* **hosing**, **hosed 2** to wash or water (a person or thing) with a hose

hose² *n* **1** *old-fashioned* stockings, socks, and tights collectively **2** *history* a man's garment covering the legs and reaching up to the waist

hosiery *n* stockings, socks, and knitted underclothing collectively

hospice (**hoss-piss**) *n* **1** a nursing home that specializes in caring for the terminally ill **2** *archaic* a place of shelter for travellers, esp. one kept by a religious order

hospitable *adj* generous, friendly, and welcoming to guests or strangers: *charming and hospitable lodgings* > **hospitably** *adv*

hospital *n* an institution for the medical or psychiatric care and treatment of patients

hospitality *n*, *pl* **-ties** kindness in welcoming strangers or guests

> **hospitality** *n* = welcome, warmth, kindness, friendliness, sociability, conviviality, neighbourliness, cordiality

hospitalize or **-lise** *vb* **-lizing**, **-lized** or **-lising**, **-lised** to admit or send (a person) into a hospital > **hospitalization** or **-lisation** *n*

host¹ *n* **1** a person who receives or entertains guests, esp. in his or her own home **2** the organization or country providing the facilities for a function or event: *Rio de Janeiro, host of the 2016 Olympic Games* **3** the compere of a radio or television programme **4** *biol* an animal or plant in or on which a parasite lives **5** a computer connected to a network and providing facilities to other computers and their users **6** *old-fashioned* the owner or manager of an inn ▸ *vb* **7** to be the host of (a party, programme, or event): *he's hosting a radio show*

> **host** *n* **3** = presenter, compere (*Brit*), anchorman or anchorwoman ▸ *vb* = present, introduce, compere (*Brit*), front (*informal*)

host² *n* a great number; multitude

> **host** *n* = multitude, lot, load (*informal*), wealth, array, myriad, great quantity, large number

Host *n* *Christianity* the bread used in Holy Communion

hostage *n* a person who is illegally held prisoner until certain demands are met by other people

> **hostage** *n* = captive, prisoner, pawn

hostel *n* **1** a building providing overnight accommodation at a low cost for particular groups of people, such as the homeless **2** same as **youth hostel 3** *Brit & NZ* a supervised lodging house for nurses, students, etc. > **hosteller** or *US* **hosteler** *n*

hostelry *n*, *pl* **-ries** *archaic or facetious* an inn

hostess *n* **1** a woman who receives and entertains guests, esp. in her own house **2** a woman who receives and entertains patrons of a club, restaurant, or dance hall

hostile adj **1** unfriendly and aggressive
2 opposed (to): hostile to the referendum **3** relating
to or involving the enemies of a country

> **hostile** adj **1** = unfriendly, belligerent,
> antagonistic, rancorous, ill-disposed;
> ≠ friendly **2** = antagonistic, opposed, contrary,
> ill-disposed

hostility n, pl **-ties 1** unfriendly and aggressive
feelings or behaviour **2 hostilities** acts of
warfare

> **hostility** n **1** = unfriendliness, hatred,
> animosity, spite, bitterness, malice, venom,
> enmity; ≠ friendliness **2** = warfare, war,
> fighting, conflict, combat, armed conflict;
> ≠ peace

hot adj **hotter**, **hottest 1** having a relatively
high temperature **2** having a temperature
higher than desirable **3** spicy or causing a
burning sensation on the tongue: hot chillies
4 (of a temper) quick to flare up **5** (of a contest
or conflict) intense **6** recent or new: hot from the
press **7** much favoured: a hot favourite **8** informal
having a dangerously high level of radioactivity
9 slang stolen or otherwise illegally obtained
10 (of a colour) intense; striking: hot pink
11 following closely: this album appeared hot on the
heels of the debut smash **12** informal dangerous or
unpleasant: they're making it hot for me here **13** (in
various games) very near the answer **14 hot on**
informal **A** strict about: they are extremely hot on
sloppy language **B** particularly knowledgeable
about **15 hot under the collar** informal aroused
with anger, annoyance, or resentment **16 in hot
water** informal in trouble > **hotly** adv

> **hot** adj **1** = heated, boiling, steaming,
> roasting, searing, scorching, scalding
> **2** = warm, close, stifling, humid, torrid, sultry,
> sweltering, balmy; ≠ cold **3** = spicy, pungent,
> peppery, piquant, biting, sharp; ≠ mild
> **4** = fiery, violent, raging, passionate, stormy;
> ≠ calm **5** = fierce, intense, strong, keen,
> competitive, cut-throat **6** = new, latest, fresh,
> recent, up to date, just out, up to the minute,
> bang up to date (informal); ≠ old

hot air n informal empty and usually boastful
talk

hotbed n a place offering ideal conditions for
the growth of an idea or activity: a hotbed of
resistance

hot-blooded adj passionate or excitable

hotchpotch or esp US & Canad **hodgepodge** n
a jumbled mixture

hot dog n a long roll split lengthways with a
hot sausage inside

hotel n a commercially run establishment
providing lodging and meals for guests

hotelier n an owner or manager of a hotel

hotfoot adv with all possible speed: hotfoot
to the accident

hot-headed adj impetuous, rash, or hot-
tempered > **hot-headedness** n

hothouse n a greenhouse in which the
temperature is maintained at a fixed level

hotline n a direct telephone link between heads
of government for emergency use

hotplate n **1** a heated metal surface on an
electric cooker **2** a portable device on which
food can be kept warm

hot pool n NZ a geothermally heated pool

hound n **1** a dog used for hunting: to ride with the
hounds ▶ vb **2** to pursue, disturb, or criticize
relentlessly: hounded by the press

> **hound** vb = harass, harry, bother, provoke,
> annoy, torment, hassle (informal), badger

hour n **1** a period of time equal to 60 minutes;
$1/_{24}$ of a day **2** any of the points on the face of a
clock or watch that indicate intervals of 60
minutes: in my hurry I mistook the hour **3** the time of
day **4** the time allowed for, or used for,
something: a three-and-a-half-hour test **5** the
distance covered in an hour: an hour from the heart
of Tokyo **6** a special moment: the decisive hour

hourglass n a device consisting of two
transparent sections linked by a narrow
channel, containing a quantity of sand that
takes an hour to trickle from one section to the
other

houri n, pl **-ris** (in Muslim belief) any of the
nymphs of Paradise

hourly adj **1** of, occurring, or done once every
hour **2** measured by the hour: hourly charges
3 frequent ▶ adv **4** once every hour **5** by the
hour: hourly paid **6** frequently **7** at any moment:
the arrival of the men was hourly expected

house n **1** a building used as a home; dwelling
2 the people in a house **3** a building for some
specific purpose: beach house **4** a family or
dynasty: the House of Windsor **5** a commercial
company: auction house **6** a law-making body or
the hall where it meets **7** a division of a large
school: he was captain of the house rugby team **8** the
audience in a theatre or cinema **9** astrol any of
the 12 divisions of the zodiac **10** informal a
brothel **11 get on like a house on fire** informal (of
people) to get on very well together **12 on the
house** (usually of drinks) paid for by the
management **13 put one's house in order** to
settle or organize one's affairs ▶ adj **14** (of wine)
sold unnamed by a restaurant, at a lower price
than wines specified on the wine list: house red
▶ vb **housing**, **housed 15** to give accommodation
to **16** to contain or cover (something)

> **house** n **1** = home, residence, dwelling (formal,
> literary), pad (slang, old-fashioned), homestead,
> abode, habitation (formal), domicile, whare
> (NZ) **2** = household, family **4** = dynasty, tribe,
> clan **5** = firm, company, business,
> organization, outfit (informal) **6** = assembly,
> parliament, Commons, legislative body

h

12 on the house = free, for free (*informal*), for nothing, free of charge, gratis ▸ *vb* **15** = accommodate, quarter, take in, put up, lodge, harbour, billet **16** = contain, keep, hold, cover, store, protect, shelter

house arrest *n* confinement to one's own home rather than in prison

houseboat *n* a stationary boat used as a home

housecoat *n* a woman's loose robelike garment for indoor wear

household *n* **1** all the people living together in one house ▸ *adj* **2** relating to the running of a household: *household budget*

household *n* = family, home, house, family circle, ainga (NZ)

householder *n* a person who owns or rents a house

housekeeper *n* a person employed to run someone else's household

housekeeping *n* **1** the running of a household **2** money allotted for this

housemaid *n* (esp. formerly) a female servant employed to do housework

House music *or* **House** *n* a type of dance music of the late 1980s, based on funk, with fragments of other recordings edited in electronically

house officer *n* a junior doctor in a hospital

house-train *vb* to train (a pet) to urinate and defecate outside

house-warming *n* a party given after moving into a new home

housewife *n*, *pl* **-wives** a woman who runs her own household and does not have a paid job > **housewifely** *adj*

housework *n* the work of running a home, such as cleaning, cooking, and shopping

housing *n* **1** houses collectively **2** the job of providing people with accommodation **3** a part designed to contain and support a component or mechanism: *the inspection panel set within the concrete housing*

housing *n* **1** = accommodation, homes, houses, dwellings, domiciles **3** = case, casing, covering, cover, shell, jacket, holder, container

hovea *n* an Australian plant with purple flowers

hovel *n* a small house or hut that is dirty or badly in need of repair

hover *vb* **1** (of a bird, insect, or helicopter) to remain suspended in one place in the air **2** to linger uncertainly in a place **3** to be in an unsettled or uncertain situation or frame of mind: *hovering between two options*

hover *vb* **1** = float, fly, hang, drift, flutter **2** = linger, loiter, hang about *or* around (*informal*) **3** = waver, fluctuate, dither (*chiefly Brit*), oscillate, vacillate

hovercraft *n* a vehicle that is able to travel across both land and water on a cushion of air

how *adv* **1** in what way, by what means: *how did you spend the evening?*; observing how elderly people coped **2** to what extent: *they don't know how tough I am* **3** how good, how well, what ... like: *how good are the copies?*; *so that's how things are* **4 how about?** used to suggest something: *how about some tea?* **5 how are you?** what is your state of health? **6 how's that?** A what is your opinion?: *we'll go out for a late-night supper – how's that?* B *cricket* Also written: **howzat** (an appeal to the umpire) is the batsman out?

howdah *n* a seat for riding on an elephant's back

however *adv* **1** still; nevertheless: *the book does, however, almost get funny* **2** by whatever means: *get there however you can* **3** (with an adjective or adverb) no matter how: *however low we plunge, there is always hope*

however *adv* **1** = but, nevertheless, still, though, yet, nonetheless, notwithstanding, anyhow

howitzer *n* a large gun that fires shells at a steep angle

howl *n* **1** the long, loud wailing noise made by a wolf or dog **2** a similar cry of pain or sorrow **3** a loud burst of laughter ▸ *vb* **4** to express (something) in a howl or utter such cries **5** (of the wind, etc.) to make a wailing noise

howl *n* **1** = baying, cry, bay, bark, barking, yelping **2** = cry, scream, roar, bay, wail, shriek, clamour, bawl ▸ *vb* **4** = bay, cry

howler *n informal* a glaring mistake

hoyden *n old-fashioned* a wild boisterous girl; tomboy > **hoydenish** *adj*

HP *or* **h.p. 1** *Brit* hire-purchase **2** horsepower

HQ *or* **h.q.** headquarters

HRH Her (*or* His) Royal Highness

HRT 1 hormone replacement therapy **2** *Austral & NZ* high rising terminal

HTML *n computers* hypertext markup language: a text description language that is used on the internet

hub *n* **1** the central portion of a wheel, through which the axle passes **2** the central, most important, or active part of a place or organization **3** an airport, railway station, etc. from which many services operate and connecting journeys can be made **4** a device for connecting computers in a network

hub *n* **2** = centre, heart, focus, core, middle, focal point, nerve centre

hubbub *n* **1** a confused noise of many voices **2** great confusion or excitement

hubby *n*, *pl* **-bies** *informal* a husband

hubris (hew-briss) *n formal* pride or arrogance > **hubristic** *adj*

huckster n 1 a person who uses aggressive methods of selling 2 *rare* a person who sells small articles or fruit in the street

huddle n 1 a small group of people or things standing or lying close together 2 **go into a huddle** *informal* to have a private conference ▸ vb **-dling, -dled** 3 (of a group of people) to crowd or nestle closely together 4 to curl up one's arms and legs close to one's body through cold or fear

> **huddle** vb 1 = crowd, press, gather, collect, squeeze, cluster, flock, herd 4 = curl up, crouch, hunch up

hue n 1 the feature of colour that enables an observer to classify it as red, blue, etc. 2 a shade of a colour

> **hue** n = colour, tone, shade, dye, tint, tinge

huff n 1 a passing mood of anger or resentment: *in a huff* ▸ vb 2 to blow or puff heavily 3 *draughts* to remove (an opponent's draught) from the board for failure to make a capture 4 **huffing and puffing** empty threats or objections > **huffy** adj > **huffily** adv

hug vb **hugging, hugged** 1 to clasp (someone or something) tightly, usually with affection 2 to keep close to (a shore or the kerb) ▸ n 3 a tight or fond embrace

> **hug** vb 1 = embrace, cuddle, squeeze, clasp, enfold, hold close, take in your arms ▸ n = embrace, squeeze, bear hug, clinch (*slang*), clasp

huge adj extremely large > **hugely** adv

> **huge** adj = enormous, large, massive, vast, tremendous, immense, gigantic, monumental (*informal*); ≠ tiny

huh interj an exclamation of derision, bewilderment, or inquiry

hui (hoo-ee) n, pl **huis** NZ 1 a Māori social gathering 2 a meeting to discuss Māori matters 3 any party

> **hui** n 1, 2 = meeting, gathering, assembly, conference, congress, rally, convention, get-together (*informal*)

hula n a Hawaiian dance performed by a woman

Hula Hoop n *trademark* a plastic hoop swung round the body by wiggling the hips

hulk n 1 the body of an abandoned ship 2 *derogatory* a large ungainly person or thing

hulking adj big and ungainly

hull n 1 the main body of a boat 2 the outer covering of a fruit or seed such as a pea or bean 3 the leaves round the stem of a strawberry, raspberry, or similar fruit ▸ vb 4 to remove the hulls from (fruit or seeds)

> **hull** n 1 = framework, casing, body, covering, frame

hullabaloo n, pl **-loos** a loud confused noise or commotion

hullo interj, n same as **hello**

hum vb **humming, hummed** 1 to make a low continuous vibrating sound 2 (of a person) to sing with the lips closed 3 to utter an indistinct sound when hesitating 4 *informal* to be in a state of feverish activity: *the town is humming* 5 *slang* to smell unpleasant ▸ n 6 a low continuous murmuring sound 7 an unpleasant smell ▸ interj, n 8 an indistinct sound of hesitation

> **hum** vb 1 = drone, buzz, murmur, throb, vibrate, purr, thrum, whir 4 = be busy, buzz, bustle, stir, pulse, pulsate

human adj 1 of or relating to people: *human occupants* 2 having the qualities of people as opposed to animals, divine beings, or machines: *human nature* 3 kind or considerate ▸ n 4 a human being

> **human** adj 1 = mortal, manlike; ≠ nonhuman ▸ n = human being, person, individual, creature, mortal, man or woman; ≠ nonhuman

human being n a man, woman, or child

humane adj 1 showing kindness and sympathy 2 inflicting as little pain as possible: *a humane method of reducing animal numbers* 3 considered to have a civilizing effect on people: *the humane tradition of a literary education* > **humanely** adv

> **humane** adj 1 = kind, compassionate, understanding, forgiving, tender, sympathetic, benign, merciful; ≠ cruel

humanism n the rejection of religion in favour of a belief in the advancement of humanity by its own efforts > **humanist** n, adj > **humanistic** adj

humanitarian adj 1 having the interests of mankind at heart ▸ n 2 a person who has the interests of mankind at heart > **humanitarianism** n

> **humanitarian** adj = charitable, philanthropic, public-spirited ▸ n = philanthropist, benefactor, Good Samaritan, altruist

humanity n, pl **-ties** 1 the human race 2 the quality of being human 3 kindness or mercy 4 **humanities** the study of literature, philosophy, and the arts

> **humanity** n 1 = the human race, humankind, mankind, man, men and women, people, mortals, Homo sapiens 2 = human nature, mortality 3 = kindness, charity, compassion, sympathy, mercy, philanthropy, fellow feeling, kind-heartedness

humanize or **-ise** vb **-izing, -ized** or **-ising, -ised** to make human or humane > **humanization** or **-isation** n

humankind *n* the human race; humanity

humanly *adv* by human powers or means: *as fast as is humanly possible*

humble *adj* **1** conscious of one's failings **2** modest and unpretentious: *humble domestic objects* **3** ordinary or not very important: *humble beginnings* ▸ *vb* **-bling, -bled** **4** to cause to become humble; humiliate ▹ **humbly** *adv*

> **humble** *adj* **1** = modest, meek, unassuming, unpretentious, self-effacing, unostentatious; ≠ proud **2** = lowly, poor, mean, simple, ordinary, modest, obscure, undistinguished; ≠ distinguished ▸ *vb* = humiliate, disgrace, crush, subdue, chasten, put (someone) in their place, take down a peg (*informal*); ≠ exalt

humbug *n* **1** *Brit* a hard peppermint sweet with a striped pattern **2** a speech or piece of writing that is obviously untrue, dishonest, or nonsense **3** a dishonest person

humdinger *n slang* **1** something unusually large **2** an excellent person or thing

humdrum *adj* ordinary, dull, and uninteresting

humerus (hew-mer-uss) *n, pl* **-meri** (-mer-rye) the bone from the shoulder to the elbow ▹ **humeral** *adj*

humid *adj* (of the weather) damp and warm

humidify *vb* **-fies, -fying, -fied** to make the air in (a room) more humid or damp ▹ **humidifier** *n*

humidity *n* **1** dampness **2** a measure of the amount of moisture in the air

> **humidity** *n* **1** = damp, moisture, dampness, wetness, moistness, dankness, clamminess, mugginess

humiliate *vb* **-ating, -ated** to hurt the dignity or pride of: *the English cricket team was humiliated by Australia* ▹ **humiliating** *adj* ▹ **humiliation** *n*

> **humiliate** *vb* = embarrass, shame, humble, crush, put down, degrade, chasten, mortify; ≠ honour

humility *n* the quality of being humble and modest

hummingbird *n* a very small brightly-coloured American bird with a long slender bill, and powerful wings that hum as they vibrate

hummock *n* a very small hill or a mound

humorist *n* a person who speaks or writes in a humorous way

humorous *adj* amusing, esp. in a witty or clever way ▹ **humorously** *adv*

> **humorous** *adj* = funny, comic, amusing, entertaining, witty, comical, droll, jocular; ≠ serious

humour *or US* **humor** *n* **1** the quality of being funny **2** the ability to appreciate or express things that are humorous: *a sense of humour* **3** situations, speech, or writings that are humorous **4** a state of mind; mood: *in astoundingly good humour* **5** *archaic* any of various fluids in the body: *aqueous humour* ▸ *vb* **6** to be kind and indulgent to: *he decided the patient needed to be humoured* ▹ **humourless** *adj*

> **humour** *or* **humor** *n* **1** = comedy, funniness, fun, amusement, funny side, jocularity, facetiousness, ludicrousness; ≠ seriousness **3** = joking, comedy, wit, farce, jesting, wisecracks (*informal*), witticisms **4** = mood, spirits, temper, disposition, frame of mind ▸ *vb* = indulge, accommodate, go along with, flatter, gratify, pander to, mollify; ≠ oppose

hump *n* **1** a rounded lump on the ground **2** a rounded deformity of the back **3** a rounded lump on the back of a camel or related animal **4** **the hump** *Brit informal* a fit of sulking: *you've got the hump today* ▸ *vb* **5** *slang* to carry or heave: *who would be responsible if they were injured humping heavy gear around?*

humus (hew-muss) *n* a dark brown or black mass of partially decomposed plant and animal matter in the soil

hunch *n* **1** a feeling or suspicion not based on facts: *she said that she had had a hunch that the coup would not succeed* **2** same as **hump** ▸ *vb* **3** to draw (oneself or one's shoulders) up or together

> **hunch** *n* **1** = feeling, idea, impression, suspicion, intuition, premonition, inkling, presentiment ▸ *vb* = crouch, bend, curve, arch, draw in

hunchback *n old-fashioned, offensive* a person who has an abnormal curvature of the spine ▹ **hunchbacked** *adj*

hundred *n, pl* **-dreds** *or* **-dred** **1** the cardinal number that is the product of ten and ten **2** a numeral, 100 or C, representing this number **3** (*often pl*) a large but unspecified number ▸ *adj* **4** amounting to a hundred: *a hundred yards* ▹ **hundredth** *adj, n*

hundredweight *n, pl* **-weights** *or* **-weight** **1** *Brit* a unit of weight equal to 112 pounds or 50.802kg **2** *US & Canad* a unit of weight equal to 100 pounds or 45.359kg **3** a metric unit of weight equal to 50 kilograms

hung *vb* **1** the past of **hang** ▸ *adj* **2** (of a parliament or jury) with no side having a clear majority **3** **hung over** *informal* suffering the effects of a hangover

Hungarian *adj* **1** of Hungary ▸ *n* **2** a person from Hungary **3** the language of Hungary

hunger *n* **1** a feeling of emptiness or weakness caused by lack of food **2** a lack of food that causes suffering or death: *refugees dying of hunger and disease* **3** desire or craving: *Europe's hunger for bullion* ▸ *vb* **4** **hunger for** *or* **after** to have a great desire for

> **hunger** *n* **1** = appetite, emptiness, hungriness, ravenousness **2** = starvation, famine, malnutrition, undernourishment

h

3 = desire, appetite, craving, ache, lust, yearning, itch, thirst ▸ *vb* **hunger for or after something** = want, desire, crave, long for, wish for, yearn for, hanker after, ache for

hunger strike *n* a refusal of all food, usually by a prisoner, as a means of protest

hungry *adj* **-grier, -griest 1** desiring food **2** (foll. by *for*) having a craving, desire, or need for: *hungry for revenge* **3** expressing greed, craving, or desire: *the media's hungry search for impact* ▸ **hungrily** *adv*

hungry *adj* **1** = starving, ravenous, famished, starved, empty (*informal*), voracious, peckish (*informal, chiefly Brit*) **2, 3** = eager, keen, craving, yearning, greedy, avid, desirous, covetous

hunk *n* **1** a large piece: *a hunk of bread* **2** *slang* a well-built, sexually attractive man

hunk *n* **1** = lump, piece, chunk, block, mass, wedge, slab, nugget

hunt *vb* **1** to seek out and kill (animals) for food or sport **2 hunt down** to track in an attempt to capture (someone): *hunting down villains* **3 hunt for** to search for: *Western companies are hunting for opportunities to invest* ▸ *n* **4** the act or an instance of hunting **5** a party organized for the pursuit of wild animals for sport **6** the members of such a party ▸ **hunting** *n*

hunt *vb* **1** = stalk, track, chase, pursue, trail, hound **3 hunt for something or someone** = search for, look for, seek for, forage for, scour for, fossick for (*Austral, NZ*), ferret about for ▸ *n* **4** = search, hunting, investigation, chase, pursuit, quest

huntaway *n NZ* a sheepdog trained to drive sheep by barking

hunter *n* **1** a person or animal that seeks out and kills or captures game **2** a person who looks carefully for something: *a house hunter* **3** a horse or dog bred for hunting **4** a watch with a hinged metal lid or case to protect the glass

huntsman *n, pl* **-men 1** a person who hunts **2** a person who trains hounds and manages them during a hunt

hurdle *n* **1** *athletics* one of a number of light barriers over which runners leap in certain events **2** a difficulty or problem: *the main technical hurdle is the environment* **3 hurdles** a race involving hurdles ▸ *vb* **-dling, -dled 4** to jump over (a hurdle or other obstacle) ▸ **hurdler** *n*

hurdle *n* **1** = fence, barrier, barricade **2** = obstacle, difficulty, barrier, handicap, hazard, uphill (*S African*), obstruction, stumbling block

hurdy-gurdy *n, pl* **hurdy-gurdies** a mechanical musical instrument, such as a barrel organ

hurl *vb* **1** to throw (something) with great force **2** to utter (something) with force; yell: *onlookers hurled abuse at them*

hurl *vb* **1** = throw, fling, launch, cast, pitch, toss, propel, sling (*informal*)

hurling or **hurley** *n* a traditional Irish game resembling hockey

hurly-burly *n* great noise and activity; commotion

hurrah or **hooray** *interj, n* a cheer of joy or victory

hurricane *n* a severe, often destructive storm, esp. a tropical cyclone

hurricane *n* = storm, gale, tornado, cyclone, typhoon, tempest (*literary*), twister (*US informal*), willy-willy (*Austral*)

hurricane lamp *n* a paraffin lamp with a glass covering

hurry *vb* **-ries, -rying, -ried 1** to move or act, or cause to move or act, in great haste: *the umpires hurried the players off the ground* **2** to speed up the completion or progress of: *eat a small snack rather than hurry a main meal* ▸ *n* **3** haste **4** urgency or eagerness **5 in a hurry** *informal* **a** easily: *a striking old guy, not the sort you'd forget in a hurry* **b** willingly: *he would not ease interest rates again in a hurry*

hurry *vb* **1** = rush, fly, dash, scurry, scoot; ≠ dawdle ▸ *n* **3, 4** = rush, haste, speed, urgency, flurry, quickness; ≠ slowness

hurt *vb* **hurting, hurt 1** to cause physical or mental injury to: *is she badly hurt?* **2** to cause someone to feel pain: *my head hurt* **3** *informal* to feel pain: *she was hurting* ▸ *n* **4** physical or mental pain or suffering ▸ *adj* **5** injured or pained: *his hurt head; a hurt expression* ▸ **hurtful** *adj*

hurt *vb* **1** = injure, damage, wound, cut, bruise, scrape, impair; ≠ heal **2** = ache, be sore, be painful, burn, smart, sting, throb, be tender ▸ *n* = distress, suffering, pain, grief, misery, sorrow, heartache, wretchedness; ≠ happiness ▸ *adj* = injured, wounded, damaged, harmed, cut, bruised, scarred; ≠ healed

hurtle *vb* **-ling, -led** to move very quickly or violently

hurtle *vb* = rush, charge, race, shoot, fly, speed, tear, crash

husband *n* **1** the man to whom a person is married ▸ *vb* **2** to use (resources, finances, etc.) economically

husband *n* = partner, spouse, mate, better half (*humorous*) ▸ *vb* = conserve, budget, save, store, hoard, economize on, use economically; ≠ squander

husbandry *n* **1** the art or skill of farming **2** management of resources

hush *vb* **1** to make or be silent ▸ *n* **2** stillness or silence ▸ *interj* **3** a plea or demand for silence ▸ See also **hush up** ▸ **hushed** *adj*

hush *vb* = quieten, silence, mute, muzzle, shush ▸ *n* = quiet, silence, calm, peace, tranquillity, stillness

hush-hush *adj informal* (esp. of official work) secret and confidential

hush up *vb* to suppress information or rumours about (something)

husk *n* 1 the outer covering of certain fruits and seeds ▸ *vb* 2 to remove the husk from

husky¹ *adj* **huskier, huskiest** 1 (of a voice) slightly hoarse 2 *informal* (of a man) big and strong ▸ **huskily** *adv*

husky² *n, pl* **huskies** an Arctic sledge dog with thick hair and a curled tail

hussar (hoo-**zar**) *n history* a member of a light cavalry regiment

hussy *n, pl* **-sies** *old-fashioned, derogatory* a woman considered to be sexually immoral

hustings *pl n* the campaigns and speeches at a parliamentary election

hustle *vb* **-tling, -tled** 1 to make (someone) move by pushing or jostling them: *he hustled her away* 2 to deal with (something) hurriedly: *they did not heedlessly hustle the tempo* 3 *US & Canad slang* (of a prostitute) to solicit clients ▸ *n* 4 lively activity and excitement

hut *n* a small house or shelter

hut *n* = cabin, shack, shanty, hovel, whare (NZ)

hutch *n* a cage for small animals

hyacinth *n* a plant with bell-shaped sweet-smelling flowers

hyaena *n* same as **hyena**

hybrid *n* 1 an animal or plant resulting from a cross between two different types of animal or plant 2 a vehicle that is powered by an internal-combustion engine and another source of power 3 anything that is a mixture of two different things ▸ *adj* 4 of mixed origin 5 (of a vehicle) powered by an internal-combustion engine and another source of power

hybrid *n* 1 = crossbreed, cross, mixture, compound, composite, amalgam, mongrel, half-breed 3 = mixture, compound, composite, amalgam

hydra *n* 1 a mythical many-headed serpent 2 a persistent problem: *killing the hydra of drug production is impossible* 3 a microscopic freshwater creature with a slender tubular body and tentacles around the mouth

hydrangea *n* an ornamental shrub with large clusters of white, pink, or blue flowers

hydrant *n* an outlet from a water main, from which water can be tapped for fighting fires

hydrate *chem* ▸ *n* 1 a compound containing water chemically combined with a substance: *chloral hydrate* ▸ *vb* **-drating, -drated** 2 to treat or impregnate (a substance) with water ▸ **hydration** *n*

hydraulic *adj* operated by pressure transmitted through a pipe by a liquid, such as water or oil ▸ **hydraulically** *adv*

hydraulics *n* the study of the mechanical properties of fluids as they apply to practical engineering

hydro¹ *n, pl* **-dros** *Brit* a hotel offering facilities for hydropathic treatment

hydro² *adj* 1 short for **hydroelectric** ▸ *n* 2 *Canad* electricity as supplied to a residence, business, etc.

hydro- *or before a vowel* **hydr-** *combining form* 1 indicating water or fluid: *hydrodynamics* 2 *chem* indicating hydrogen in a chemical compound: *hydrochloric acid*

hydrocarbon *n chem* a compound containing only carbon and hydrogen

hydrochloric acid *n chem* a solution of hydrogen chloride in water: a strong acid used in many industrial and laboratory processes

hydroelectric *adj* 1 generated by the pressure of falling water: *hydroelectric power* 2 of the generation of electricity by water pressure: *a hydroelectric scheme* ▸ **hydroelectricity** *n*

hydrofoil *n* 1 a fast light vessel the hull of which is raised out of the water on one or more pairs of fins 2 any of these fins

hydrogen *n chem* a colourless gas that burns easily and is the lightest element in the universe. It occurs in water and in most organic compounds. Symbol: **H** ▸ **hydrogenous** *adj*

hydrogen bomb *n* an extremely powerful bomb in which energy is released by fusion of hydrogen nuclei to give helium nuclei

hydrogen peroxide *n* a colourless oily unstable liquid chemical used as a hair bleach and as an antiseptic

hydrolysis (hide-**rol**-iss-iss) *n chem* a process of decomposition in which a compound reacts with water to produce other compounds

hydrometer (hide-**rom**-it-er) *n* an instrument for measuring the density of a liquid

hydropathy *n* a method of treating disease by the use of large quantities of water both internally and externally ▸ **hydropathic** *adj*

hydrophobia *n* 1 same as **rabies** 2 (esp. of a person with rabies) a fear of drinking fluids ▸ **hydrophobic** *adj*

hydroplane *n* 1 a motorboat that raises its hull out of the water at high speeds 2 a fin on the hull of a submarine for controlling its vertical motion

hydroponics *n* a method of growing plants in gravel, etc., through which water containing the necessary nutrients is pumped

hydrotherapy *n med* the treatment of certain diseases by exercise in water

hyena *or* **hyaena** *n* a meat-eating doglike mammal of Africa and S Asia

hygiene *n* 1 the principles and practices of health and cleanliness: *personal hygiene* 2 Also called: **hygienics** the science concerned with the maintenance of health > **hygienic** *adj* > **hygienically** *adv* > **hygienist** *n*

hygiene *n* **1** = cleanliness, sanitation, disinfection, sterility

hymen *n anatomy* a membrane that partly covers the entrance to the vagina and is usually ruptured when sexual intercourse takes place for the first time

hymn *n* a Christian song of praise sung to God or a saint

hymn *n* = religious song, song of praise, carol, chant, anthem, psalm, paean

hymnal *n* a book of hymns. Also: **hymn book**

hype *slang* ▸ *n* **1** intensive or exaggerated publicity or sales promotion ▸ *vb* **hyping, hyped 2** to market or promote (a commodity) using intensive or exaggerated publicity

hype *n* = publicity, promotion, plugging (*informal*), razzmatazz (*slang*), brouhaha, ballyhoo (*informal*)

hyper *adj informal* overactive or overexcited

hyper- *prefix* above, over, or in excess: *hypercritical*

hyperbola (hie-per-bol-a) *n geom* a curve produced when a cone is cut by a plane at a steeper angle to its base than its side

hyperbole (hie-per-bol-ee) *n* a deliberate exaggeration of speech or writing used for effect, such as *he embraced her a thousand times*

hyperbolic *or* **hyperbolical** *adj* **1** exaggerated **2** of a hyperbola or a hyperbole

hyperlink *computers* ▸ *n* **1** a word, picture, etc., in a computer document on which a user may click to move to another part of the document or to another document ▸ *vb* **2** to link (files) in this way

hypermarket *n* a huge self-service store

hypersensitive *adj* **1** unduly emotionally vulnerable **2** abnormally sensitive to an allergen, a drug, or high or low temperatures

hypersonic *adj* having a speed of at least five times the speed of sound

hypertension *n pathol* abnormally high blood pressure

hypertext *n* computer software and hardware that allows users to store and view text and move between related items easily

hyphen *n* the punctuation mark (-), used to separate parts of compound words and between syllables of a word split between two consecutive lines

hyphenated *adj* having two words or syllables connected by a hyphen

hypnosis *n* an artificially induced state of relaxation in which the mind is more than usually receptive to suggestion

hypnotic *adj* **1** of or producing hypnosis or sleep **2** having an effect resembling hypnosis:

the film makes for hypnotic viewing ▸ *n* **3** a drug that induces sleep > **hypnotically** *adv*

hypnotism *n* the practice of or process of inducing hypnosis > **hypnotist** *n*

hypnotize *or* **-tise** *vb* **-tizing, -tized** *or* **-tising, -tised 1** to induce hypnosis in (a person) **2** to hold the attention of (someone) completely; fascinate; mesmerize: *hypnotized by her beauty*

hypo- *or before a vowel* **hyp-** *prefix* beneath; less than: *hypodermic*

hypoallergenic *adj* not likely to cause an allergic reaction

hypochondria *n* abnormal anxiety concerning one's health

hypochondriac *n* a person abnormally concerned about his or her health

hypocrisy (hip-ok-rass-ee) *n, pl* **-sies 1** the practice of claiming to have standards or beliefs that are contrary to one's real character or actual behaviour **2** an act or instance of this

hypocrisy *n* **1** = insincerity, pretence, deception, cant, duplicity, deceitfulness; ≠ sincerity

hypocrite (hip-oh-krit) *n* a person who pretends to be what he or she is not > **hypocritical** *adj*

hypodermic *adj* **1** used for injecting ▸ *n* **2** a hypodermic syringe or needle

hypotension *n pathol* abnormally low blood pressure

hypotenuse (hie-pot-a-news) *n* the side in a right-angled triangle that is opposite the right angle

hypothalamus *n, pl* **-mi** an area at the base of the brain, which controls hunger, thirst, and other functions

hypothermia *n pathol* an abnormally low body temperature, as a result of exposure to cold weather

hypothesis (hie-poth-iss-iss) *n, pl* **-ses** (-seez) a suggested explanation for a group of facts, accepted either as a basis for further verification or as likely to be true > **hypothesize** *or* **-ise** *vb*

hypothesis *n* = theory, premise, proposition, assumption, thesis, postulate, supposition

hypothetical *adj* based on assumption rather than fact or reality > **hypothetically** *adv*

hyrax (hire-ax) *n, pl* **hyraxes** *or* **hyraces** (hire-a-seez) a genus of hoofed rodent-like animals

hysterectomy *n, pl* **-mies** surgical removal of the womb

hysteria *n* **1** a psychological disorder marked by emotional outbursts and, often, symptoms such as paralysis **2** any uncontrolled emotional state, such as of panic, anger, or excitement

hysteria *n* **2** = frenzy, panic, madness, agitation, delirium, hysterics

hysterical *adj* **1** in a state of uncontrolled panic, anger, or excitement **2** *informal* wildly funny > **hysterically** *adv*

> **hysterical** *adj* **1** = frenzied, frantic, raving, distracted, distraught, crazed, overwrought; ≠ calm **2** = hilarious, uproarious, side-splitting, comical; ≠ serious

hysterics *n* **1** an attack of hysteria **2** *informal* wild uncontrollable bursts of laughter
Hz hertz

I *pron* used by a speaker or writer to refer to himself or herself as the subject of a verb
Iberian *adj* **1** of Iberia, the peninsula made up of Spain and Portugal ▸ *n* **2** a person from Iberia
ibex (ibe-eks) *n, pl* **ibexes** *or* **ibex** a wild mountain goat with large backward-curving horns
ibid. in the same place: used to refer to a book, page, or passage previously cited
ibis (ibe-iss) *n, pl* **ibises** *or* **ibis** a large wading bird with a long thin curved bill
ice *n* **1** water that has frozen and become solid **2** *chiefly Brit* a portion of ice cream **3 break the ice** to relax the atmosphere, esp. between strangers **4 on ice** in readiness or reserve **5 on thin ice** in a dangerous situation: *he knew he was on thin ice* **6 the Ice** NZ *informal* Antarctica ▸ *vb* **icing, iced 7** (foll. by *up* or *over*) to become covered with ice **8** to cover with icing **9** to cool or chill with ice
iceberg *n* **1** a large mass of ice floating in the sea **2 tip of the iceberg** the small visible part of a problem that is much larger
icebox *n* **1** *US & Canad* a refrigerator **2** a compartment in a refrigerator for making or storing ice **3** a container packed with ice for keeping food and drink cold
icecap *n* a thick mass of glacial ice that permanently covers an area
ice cream *n* a sweet frozen food, made from cream, milk, or a custard base, flavoured in various ways
iced *adj* **1** served very cold **2** covered with icing
ice floe *n* a sheet of ice floating in the sea
ice hockey *n* a game like hockey played on ice by two teams wearing skates
Icelander *n* a person from Iceland
Icelandic *adj* **1** of Iceland ▸ *n* **2** the official language of Iceland
ice lolly *n Brit informal* a water ice or an ice cream on a stick
ice skate *n* **1** a boot with a steel blade fitted to the sole, which enables the wearer to glide over ice ▸ *vb* **ice-skate, -skating, -skated 2** to glide over ice on ice skates > **ice-skater** *n*
icicle *n* a tapering spike of ice hanging where water has dripped
icing *n* **1** Also (esp. US and Canad.): **frosting** a mixture of sugar and water or egg whites used to cover and decorate cakes **2** the formation of ice on a ship or aircraft **3 icing on the cake** any unexpected extra or bonus

icing sugar *n* a very finely ground sugar used for making icing or sweets

icon *or* **ikon** *n* **1** a picture of Christ, the Virgin Mary, or a saint, venerated in the Orthodox Church **2** a picture on a computer screen representing a computer function that can be activated by moving the cursor over it **3** a person or thing regarded as a symbol of a belief or cultural movement: *a feminist icon*

> **icon** *or* **ikon** *n* **1** = representation, image, likeness, avatar, favicon (*computers*) **3** = idol, hero, superstar

iconoclast *n* **1** a person who attacks established or traditional ideas or principles **2** a destroyer of religious images or objects > **iconoclastic** *adj* > **iconoclasm** *n*

ICT Information and Communications Technology

icy *adj* **icier, iciest 1** freezing or very cold **2** covered with ice: *an icy runway* **3** cold or reserved in manner > **icily** *adv* > **iciness** *n*

> **icy** *adj* **1** = cold, freezing, bitter, biting, raw, chill, chilly, frosty; ≠ hot **2** = slippery, glassy, slippy (*informal, dialect*), like a sheet of glass **3** = unfriendly, cold, distant, aloof, frosty, frigid, unwelcoming; ≠ friendly

id *n psychoanalysis* the primitive instincts and energies in the unconscious mind that underlie all psychological impulses

ID 1 Idaho **2** identification

idea *n* **1** any product of mental activity; thought **2** a scheme, intention, or plan **3** the thought of something: *the idea excites me* **4** a belief or opinion **5** a vague notion; inkling: *they had no idea of the severity of my injuries* **6** a person's conception of something: *his idea of integrity is not the same as mine* **7** aim or purpose: *the idea is to economize on transport* **8** *philosophy* (in Plato) a universal model of which all things in the same class are only imperfect imitations

> **idea** *n* **1, 4** = notion, thought, view, teaching, opinion, belief, conclusion, hypothesis **6** = understanding, thought, view, opinion, concept, impression, perception **7** = intention, aim, purpose, object, plan, objective

ideal *n* **1** (*often pl*) a principle or model of ethical behaviour **2** a conception of something that is perfect **3** a person or thing considered to represent perfection **4** something existing only as an idea ▸ *adj* **5** most suitable: *the ideal person to head the delegation* **6** of, involving, or existing only as an idea; imaginary: *an ideal world* > **ideally** *adv*

> **ideal** *n* **2** = model, prototype, paradigm **3** = epitome, standard, dream, pattern, perfection, last word, paragon ▸ *adj* **5** = perfect, best, model, classic, supreme, ultimate, archetypal, exemplary; ≠ imperfect

idealism *n* **1** belief in or striving towards ideals **2** the tendency to represent things in their ideal forms, rather than as they are **3** *philosophy* the doctrine that material objects and the external world do not exist in reality, but are creations of the mind > **idealist** *n* > **idealistic** *adj*

idealize *or* **-lise** *vb* **-lizing, -lized** *or* **-lising, -lised** to consider or represent (something) as ideal or more nearly perfect than is true > **idealization** *or* **-lisation** *n*

idem *pron, adj* the same: used to refer to an article, chapter, or book already quoted

identical *adj* **1** that is the same: *they got the identical motel room as last year* **2** exactly alike or equal **3** (of twins) developed from a single fertilized ovum that has split into two, and thus of the same sex and very much alike > **identically** *adv*

> **identical** *adj* **1, 2** = alike, matching, twin, duplicate, indistinguishable, interchangeable; ≠ different

identify *vb* **-fies, -fying, -fied 1** to prove or recognize as being a certain person or thing; determine the identity of **2** (often foll. by *with*) to understand and sympathize with a person or group because one regards oneself as being similar or similarly situated **3** to consider or treat as the same **4** to connect or associate closely: *he was closely identified with the community charge* > **identifiable** *adj* > **identification** *n*

> **identify** *vb* **1** = recognize, place, name, remember, spot, diagnose, make out, pinpoint **2 identify with someone** = relate to, respond to, feel for, empathize with **4** = equate with, associate with

Identikit *n* **1** *trademark* a composite picture, assembled from descriptions given, of a person wanted by the police ▸ *adj* **2** artificially created; formulaic: *an identikit pop group* **3** stereotypical: *the identikit tenacious lawyer*

identity *n, pl* **-ties 1** the state of being a specified person or thing: *the identity of his murderers was not immediately established* **2** the individual characteristics by which a person or thing is recognized **3** the state of being the same **4** *maths* Also called: **identity element** a member of a set that when combined with any other member of the set, leaves it unchanged: *the identity for multiplication of numbers is 1*

> **identity** *n* **2** = individuality, self, character, personality, existence, originality, separateness

identity card *n* a card with a person's name, photograph, and other personal information on it

identity theft *n* the fraudulent use of another person's name and personal details to open a bank account, obtain credit, etc.

ideology *n, pl* **-gies** the body of ideas and beliefs of a person, group, or nation ▷ **ideological** *adj* ▷ **ideologically** *adv* ▷ **ideologist** *n*

idiocy *n, pl* **-cies** 1 utter stupidity 2 a foolish act or remark

idiom *n* 1 a group of words which, when used together, have a different meaning from the one suggested by the individual words, eg *it was raining cats and dogs* 2 linguistic usage that is grammatical and natural to native speakers 3 the characteristic vocabulary or usage of a person or group 4 the characteristic artistic style of an individual or school ▷ **idiomatic** *adj*

idiosyncrasy *n, pl* **-sies** a personal peculiarity of mind, habit, or behaviour; quirk ▷ **idiosyncratic** *adj*

idiot *n* 1 a foolish or senseless person 2 *old-fashioned, offensive* a person with severe learning difficulties ▷ **idiotic** *adj* ▷ **idiotically** *adv*

> **idiot** *n* 1 = fool, twit (*informal, chiefly Brit*), chump, halfwit, galah (*Austral, NZ informal*), dorba or dorb (*Austral slang*), dill (*Austral, NZ informal*), mampara (*S African informal*)

idle *adj* 1 not doing anything 2 not operating or being used 3 not wanting to work; lazy 4 ineffective or useless: *it would be idle to look for a solution at this stage* 5 frivolous or trivial: *idle pleasures* 6 without basis; unfounded: *idle rumours* ▶ *vb* **idling, idled** 7 (often foll. by *away*) to waste or pass (time) in idleness 8 (of an engine) to run at low speed without transmitting any power ▷ **idleness** *n* ▷ **idler** *n* ▷ **idly** *adv*

> **idle** *adj* 1 = unoccupied, unemployed, redundant, inactive; ≠ occupied 2 = unused, inactive, out of order, out of service 3 = lazy, slow, slack, sluggish, lax, negligent, inactive, inert; ≠ busy 4 = useless, vain, pointless, unsuccessful, ineffective, worthless, futile, fruitless; ≠ useful ▶ *vb* 7 = fritter, lounge, potter, loaf, dally, loiter, dawdle, laze

idol (eye-dl) *n* 1 an object of excessive devotion or admiration 2 an image of a god used as an object of worship

> **idol** *n* 1 = hero, pin-up, favourite, pet, darling, beloved (*slang*), fave (*informal*) 2 = graven image, god, deity

idolatry (ide-ol-a-tree) *n* 1 the worship of idols 2 excessive devotion or reverence ▷ **idolater** *n* ▷ **idolatrous** *adj*

idolize *or* **-lise** *vb* **-lizing, -lized** *or* **-lising, -lised** 1 to love or admire excessively 2 to worship as an idol ▷ **idolization** *or* **-lisation** *n*

idyll *or US sometimes* **idyl** (id-ill) *n* 1 a scene or time of peace and happiness 2 a poem or prose work describing a charming rural scene or episode ▷ **idyllic** *adj*

i.e. that is to say

IED improvised explosive device

if *conj* 1 in the event that, or on condition that: *if you work hard you'll succeed* 2 used to introduce an indirect question to which the answer is either yes or no; whether: *it doesn't matter if the play is any good or not* 3 even though: *a splendid if slightly decaying house* 4 used to introduce an unfulfilled wish, with only: *if only you had told her* ▶ 5 a condition or stipulation: *there are no hidden ifs or buts*

> **if** *conj* 1 = provided, assuming, given that, providing, supposing, presuming, on condition that, as long as

iffy *adj* **iffier, iffiest** *informal* full of uncertainty

igloo *n, pl* **-loos** a dome-shaped Inuit dwelling, built of blocks of solid snow

igneous (ig-nee-uss) *adj* 1 (of rocks) formed as molten rock cools and hardens 2 of or like fire

ignite *vb* **-niting, -nited** 1 to catch fire 2 to set fire to ▷ **ignitable** *adj*

> **ignite** *vb* 1 = catch fire, burn, burst into flames, inflame, flare up, take fire 2 = set fire to, light, set alight, torch, kindle

ignition *n* 1 the system used to ignite the fuel in an internal-combustion engine 2 an igniting or the process of igniting

ignoble *adj* 1 dishonourable 2 of humble origin or social status ▷ **ignobly** *adv*

ignominy (ig-nom-in-ee) *n, pl* **-minies** disgrace or public shame: *the ignominy of being replaced* ▷ **ignominious** *adj*

ignoramus *n, pl* **-muses** an ignorant person

ignorance *n* lack of knowledge or education

> **ignorance** *n* = lack of education, stupidity, foolishness; ≠ knowledge

ignorant *adj* 1 lacking in knowledge or education 2 rude through lack of knowledge of good manners: *an ignorant remark* 3 **ignorant of** lacking in awareness or knowledge of: *ignorant of Asian culture*

> **ignorant** *adj* 1 = uneducated, illiterate; ≠ educated 2 = insensitive, rude, crass 3 = uninformed of, unaware of, oblivious to, innocent of, unconscious of, inexperienced of, uninitiated about, unenlightened about; ≠ informed

ignore *vb* **-noring, -nored** to refuse to notice; disregard deliberately

> **ignore** *vb* = pay no attention to, neglect, disregard, slight, overlook, scorn, spurn, rebuff; ≠ pay attention to

iguana *n* a large tropical tree lizard of the W Indies and S America with a spiny back

ill *adj* **worse, worst** 1 not in good health 2 bad, harmful, or hostile: *ill effects* 3 promising an unfavourable outcome: *ill omen* 4 **ill at ease** unable to relax ▶ *n* 5 evil or harm ▶ *adv* 6 badly, wrongly: *the title ill befits him* 7 with difficulty; hardly: *we can ill afford another scandal*

ill *adj* 1 = unwell, sick, poorly (*informal*), diseased, weak, crook (*Austral, NZ slang*), ailing, frail; ≠ healthy 2 = harmful, bad, damaging, evil, foul, unfortunate, destructive, detrimental; ≠ favourable ▸ *n* = problem, trouble, suffering, worry, injury, hurt, strain, harm ▸ *adv* 7 = hardly, barely, scarcely, just, only just, by no means, at a push; ≠ well

ill-advised *adj* 1 (of a plan or action) badly thought out 2 (of a person) acting without reasonable care or thought
ill-disposed *adj* unfriendly or unsympathetic
illegal *adj* against the law > **illegally** *adv* > **illegality** *n*

illegal *adj* = unlawful, banned, forbidden, prohibited, criminal, outlawed, illicit, unlicensed; ≠ legal

illegible *adj* unable to be read or deciphered > **illegibility** *n*
illegitimate *adj* 1 born of parents who were not married to each other at the time 2 illegal; unlawful > **illegitimacy** *n*
ill-fated *adj* doomed or unlucky
ill-gotten *adj* obtained dishonestly or illegally: *ill-gotten gains*
ill-health *n* the condition of being unwell
illicit *adj* 1 same as **illegal** 2 forbidden or disapproved of by society: *an illicit kiss*

illicit *adj* 1 = illegal, criminal, prohibited, unlawful, illegitimate, unlicensed, unauthorized, felonious; ≠ legal 2 = forbidden, improper, immoral, guilty, clandestine, furtive

illiterate *adj* 1 unable to read and write 2 uneducated or ignorant: *linguistically illiterate* ▸ *n* 3 an illiterate person > **illiteracy** *n*
ill-mannered *adj* having bad manners
illness *n* 1 a disease or indisposition 2 a state of ill health

illness *n* = sickness, disease, infection, disorder, bug (*informal*), ailment, affliction, malady

illogical *adj* 1 senseless or unreasonable 2 not following logical principles > **illogicality** *n* > **illogically** *adv*
ill-treat *vb* to treat cruelly or harshly > **ill-treatment** *n*
illuminate *vb* **-nating, -nated** 1 to light up 2 to make easily understood; explain: *the report obscures rather than illuminates the most relevant facts* 3 to decorate with lights 4 to decorate (an initial letter or manuscript) with designs of gold, silver, or bright colours > **illuminating** *adj* > **illuminative** *adj*

illuminate *vb* 1 = light up, brighten; ≠ darken 2 = explain, interpret, make clear, clarify, clear up, enlighten, shed light on, elucidate; ≠ obscure

illumination *n* 1 an illuminating or being illuminated 2 a source of light 3 **illuminations** *chiefly Brit* lights used as decorations in streets or towns 4 the decoration in colours, gold, or silver used on some manuscripts
illusion *n* 1 a false appearance or deceptive impression of reality: *her upswept hair gave the illusion of above average height* 2 a false or misleading idea or belief: *we may suffer from the illusion that we are special*

illusion *n* 1 = false impression, appearance, impression, deception, fallacy; ≠ reality 2 = delusion, misconception, misapprehension, fancy, fallacy, false impression, false belief

illusionist *n* a conjuror
illusory *or* **illusive** *adj* seeming to be true, but actually false: *the economic benefits of such reforms were largely illusory*
illustrate *vb* **-trating, -trated** 1 to clarify or explain by use of examples or comparisons 2 to provide (a book or text) with pictures 3 to be an example of > **illustrative** *adj* > **illustrator** *n*

illustrate *vb* 1 = explain, sum up, summarize, bring home, point up, elucidate 3 = demonstrate, emphasize

illustration *n* 1 a picture or diagram used to explain or decorate a text 2 an example: *an illustration of the brutality of the regime* 3 the art of illustrating

illustration *n* 1 = picture, drawing, painting, image, print, plate, figure, portrait 2 = example, case, instance, sample, specimen, exemplar

illustrious *adj* famous and distinguished
ill will *n* unkind feeling; hostility
IM instant messaging
image *n* 1 a mental picture of someone or something produced by the imagination or memory 2 the appearance or impression given to the public by a person or organization 3 a simile or metaphor 4 a representation of a person or thing in a work of art or literature 5 an optical reproduction of an object, formed by the lens of an eye or camera, or by a mirror 6 a person or thing that resembles another closely 7 a personification of a specified quality; epitome: *the image of good breeding* ▸ *vb* **imaging, imaged** 8 to picture in the mind 9 to mirror or reflect an image of 10 to portray or describe

image *n* 1 = thought, idea, vision, concept, impression, perception, mental picture, conceptualization 3 = figure of speech 4 = figure, idol, icon, fetish, talisman, avatar 5 = reflection, likeness, mirror image 6 = replica, copy, reproduction, counterpart, clone, facsimile, spitting image (*informal*), Doppelgänger

imagery *n*, *pl* **-ries** **1** figurative or descriptive language in a literary work **2** mental images **3** images collectively, esp. statues or carvings

imaginary *adj* **1** existing only in the imagination **2** *maths* relating to the square root of a negative number

> **imaginary** *adj* **1** = fictional, made-up, invented, imagined, unreal, hypothetical, fictitious, illusory; ≠ real

imagination *n* **1** the faculty or action of producing mental images of what is not present or in one's experience **2** creative mental ability

> **imagination** *n* **1** = mind's eye, fancy (*old-fashioned*, *literary*) **2** = creativity, vision, invention, ingenuity, enterprise, originality, inventiveness, resourcefulness

imaginative *adj* **1** produced by or showing a creative imagination **2** having a vivid imagination > **imaginatively** *adv*

> **imaginative** *adj* **1** = creative, original, inspired, enterprising, clever, ingenious, inventive; ≠ unimaginative

imagine *vb* **-ining**, **-ined** **1** to form a mental image of **2** to think, believe, or guess: *I would imagine they'll be here soon* > **imaginable** *adj*

> **imagine** *vb* **1** = envisage, see, picture, plan, think of, conjure up, envision, visualize **2** = believe, think, suppose, assume, suspect, guess (*informal*), take it, reckon (*informal*)

imago (im-**may**-go) *n*, *pl* **imagoes** *or* **imagines** (im-**maj**-in-eez) a sexually mature adult insect

imam *n* *Islam* **1** a leader of congregational prayer in a mosque **2** the title of some Muslim leaders

IMAX (**eye**-max) *n* a film projection process that produces an image ten times larger than standard

imbalance *n* a lack of balance, for instance in emphasis or proportion: *a chemical imbalance in the brain*

imbecile (im-**biss**-eel) *n* **1** *informal* an extremely stupid person **2** *psychol obsolete* a person of abnormally low intelligence ▸ *adj* **3** stupid or senseless: *imbecile fanaticism* > **imbecility** *n*

imbibe *vb* **-bibing**, **-bibed** *formal* **1** to drink (alcoholic drinks) **2** to take in or assimilate (ideas): *values she had imbibed as a child*

imbroglio (im-**role**-ee-oh) *n*, *pl* **-glios** a confusing and complicated situation

imbue *vb* **-buing**, **-bued** to fill or inspire (with ideals or principles)

IMF International Monetary Fund

imitate *vb* **-tating**, **-tated** **1** to copy the manner or style of, or take as a model: *he remains rock's most imitated guitarist* **2** to mimic or impersonate, esp. for amusement **3** to make a copy or reproduction of; duplicate > **imitable** *adj* > **imitator** *n*

imitate *vb* **1** = copy, follow, repeat, echo, emulate, ape, simulate, mirror **2** = do an impression of, mimic, copy

imitation *n* **1** a copy of an original or genuine article **2** an instance of imitating someone: *her Coward imitations were not the best thing she did* **3** behaviour modelled on the behaviour of someone else: *to learn by imitation* ▸ *adj* **4** made to resemble something which is usually superior or more expensive: *imitation leather*

> **imitation** *n* **1** = replica, fake, reproduction, sham, forgery, counterfeiting, likeness, duplication **2** = impression, impersonation **3** = copying, resemblance, mimicry ▸ *adj* = artificial, mock, reproduction, dummy, synthetic, man-made, simulated, sham; ≠ real

imitative *adj* **1** imitating or tending to copy **2** copying or reproducing an original, esp. in an inferior manner: *imitative painting* **3** onomatopoeic

immaculate *adj* **1** completely clean or tidy: *an immaculate pinstripe suit* **2** completely flawless: *his equestrian pedigree is immaculate* > **immaculately** *adv*

> **immaculate** *adj* **1** = clean, spotless, neat, spruce, squeaky-clean, spick-and-span; ≠ dirty **2** = perfect, flawless, impeccable, faultless, unblemished, untarnished, unexceptionable; ≠ tainted

immanent *adj* **1** present within and throughout something **2** (of God) present throughout the universe > **immanence** *n*

immaterial *adj* **1** of no real importance or relevance **2** not formed of matter

immature *adj* **1** not fully grown or developed **2** lacking wisdom, insight, or stability because of youth > **immaturity** *n*

immediate *adj* **1** taking place without delay: *an immediate cut in interest rates* **2** next or nearest in space, time, or relationship: *our immediate neighbour* **3** present; current: *they had no immediate plans to close it* > **immediacy** *n* > **immediately** *adv*

> **immediate** *adj* **1** = instant, prompt, instantaneous, quick, on-the-spot, split-second; ≠ later **2** = nearest, next, direct, close, near; ≠ far

immemorial *adj* having existed or happened for longer than anyone can remember: *this has been the custom since time immemorial*

immense *adj* **1** huge or vast **2** *informal* very great > **immensely** *adv* > **immensity** *n*

> **immense** *adj* **1** = huge, great, massive, vast, enormous, extensive, tremendous, very big, supersize; ≠ tiny

immerse *vb* **-mersing**, **-mersed** **1** to plunge or dip into liquid **2** to involve deeply: *he immersed himself in the history of Rome* **3** to baptize by dipping the whole body into water > **immersion** *n*

i

immerse *vb* **1** = plunge, dip, submerge, sink, duck, bathe, douse, dunk **2** = engross, involve, absorb, busy, occupy, engage

immersion heater *n* an electrical device in a domestic hot-water tank for heating water

immersive *adj* making one feel completely surrounded by and involved in something

immigrant *n* a person who comes to a foreign country in order to settle there

immigrant *n* = settler, incomer, alien, stranger, outsider, newcomer, migrant, emigrant

immigration *n* the act of coming to a foreign country in order to settle there > **immigrate** *vb*

imminent *adj* likely to happen soon > **imminence** *n* > **imminently** *adv*

imminent *adj* = near, coming, close, approaching, gathering, forthcoming, looming, impending; ≠ remote

immobile *adj* **1** not moving **2** not able to move or be moved > **immobility** *n*

immobilize *or* **-lise** *vb* **-lizing, -lized** *or* **-lising, -lised** to make unable to move or work: *a device for immobilizing steering wheels* > **immobilization** *or* **-lisation** *n*

immoderate *adj* excessive or unreasonable: *immoderate consumption of alcohol* > **immoderately** *adv*

immolate *vb* **-lating, -lated** *literary* to kill or offer as a sacrifice, esp. by fire > **immolation** *n*

immoral *adj* morally wrong; corrupt > **immorality** *n*

immoral *adj* = wicked, bad, wrong, corrupt, indecent, sinful, unethical, depraved; ≠ moral

immortal *adj* **1** not subject to death or decay **2** famous for all time **3** everlasting ▸ *n* **4** a person whose fame will last for all time **5** an immortal being > **immortality** *n*

immortal *adj* **1** = undying, eternal, imperishable, deathless; ≠ mortal **3** = timeless, eternal, everlasting, lasting, traditional, classic, enduring, perennial; ≠ ephemeral ▸ *n* **4** = hero, genius, great **5** = god, goddess, deity, divine being, immortal being, atua (NZ)

immortalize *or* **-ise** *vb* **-izing, -ized** *or* **-ising, -ised** **1** to give everlasting fame to: *a name immortalized by countless writers* **2** to give immortality to

immune *adj* **1** protected against a specific disease by inoculation or as the result of natural resistance **2** exempt from obligation or penalty **3** **immune to** secure against: *football is not immune to economic recession*

immune *adj* **1** **immune to** = resistant to, free from, protected from, safe from, not open to, spared from, secure against, invulnerable to **3** **immune to** = unaffected by, invulnerable to

immunity *n, pl* **-ties 1** the ability of an organism to resist disease **2** freedom from prosecution, tax, etc.

immunity *n* **1** = resistance, protection, resilience, inoculation, immunization; ≠ susceptibility **2** = exemption, amnesty, indemnity, release, freedom, invulnerability

immunize *or* **-nise** *vb* **-nizing, -nized** *or* **-nising, -nised** to make (someone) immune to a disease, esp. by inoculation > **immunization** *or* **-nisation** *n*

immunodeficiency *n* a deficiency in or breakdown of a person's ability to fight diseases

immunology *n* the branch of medicine concerned with the study of immunity > **immunological** *adj* > **immunologist** *n*

immutable (im-mute-a-bl) *adj* unchangeable or unchanging: *the immutable sequence of night and day* > **immutability** *n*

imp *n* **1** a small demon **2** a mischievous child

impact *n* **1** the effect or impression made by something **2** the act of one object striking another; collision **3** the force of a collision ▸ *vb* **4** to press firmly against or into **5** **impact on** to have an effect on > **impaction** *n*

impact *n* **1** = effect, influence, consequences, impression, repercussions, ramifications **2** = collision, contact, crash, knock, stroke, smash, bump, thump ▸ *vb* **4** = hit, strike, crash, clash, crush, ram, smack, collide

impair *vb* to damage or weaken in strength or quality > **impairment** *n*

impair *vb* = worsen, reduce, damage, injure, harm, undermine, weaken, diminish; ≠ improve

impala (imp-ah-la) *n, pl* **-las** *or* **-la** an African antelope with lyre-shaped horns

impale *vb* **-paling, -paled** to pierce through or fix with a sharp object: *they impaled his severed head on a spear* > **impalement** *n*

impalpable *adj formal* **1** not able to be felt by touching: *impalpable shadows* **2** difficult to understand > **impalpability** *n*

impart *vb* **1** to communicate (information or knowledge) **2** to give (a specified quality): *flavouring to impart a sweet taste*

impartial *adj* not favouring one side or the other > **impartiality** *n* > **impartially** *adv*

impassable *adj* (of terrain or roads) not able to be travelled through or over > **impassability** *n*

impasse (am-pass) *n* a situation in which progress or escape is impossible

impasse *n* = deadlock, stalemate, standstill, dead end, standoff

impassioned *adj* full of emotion: *an impassioned plea to the United Nations*

impassive *adj* not showing or feeling emotion > **impassively** *adv* > **impassivity** *n*

impatient *adj* **1** irritable at any delay or difficulty **2** restless to have or do something > **impatience** *n* > **impatiently** *adv*

> **impatient** *adj* **1** = cross, annoyed, irritated, prickly, touchy, bad-tempered, intolerant, ill-tempered **2** = eager, longing, keen, anxious, hungry, enthusiastic, restless, avid; ≠ calm

impeach *vb* **1** *chiefly US* to charge (a public official) with an offence committed in office **2** *Brit & Austral criminal law* to accuse of treason or serious crime **3** to challenge or question (a person's honesty or honour) > **impeachable** *adj* > **impeachment** *n*

impeccable *adj* without flaw or error: *impeccable manners* > **impeccably** *adv*

> **impeccable** *adj* = faultless, perfect, immaculate, flawless, squeaky-clean, unblemished, unimpeachable, irreproachable; ≠ flawed

impecunious *adj formal* without money; penniless

impedance (imp-eed-anss) *n electronics* the total effective resistance in an electric circuit to the flow of an alternating current

impede *vb* **-peding, -peded** to block or make progress or action difficult

impediment *n* **1** a hindrance or obstruction **2** a physical disability that makes speech or walking difficult

impel *vb* **-pelling, -pelled** **1** to urge or force (a person) to do something **2** to push, drive, or force into motion

impending *adj* (esp. of something bad) about to happen

> **impending** *adj* = looming, coming, approaching, near, forthcoming, imminent, upcoming, in the pipeline

impenetrable *adj* **1** impossible to get through: *an impenetrable barrier* **2** impossible to understand **3** not receptive to ideas or influence: *impenetrable ignorance* > **impenetrability** *n* > **impenetrably** *adv*

imperative *adj* **1** extremely urgent; essential **2** commanding or authoritative: *an imperative tone of voice* **3** *grammar* denoting a mood of verbs used in commands ▸ *n* **4** *grammar* the imperative mood

> **imperative** *adj* **1** = urgent, essential, pressing, vital, crucial (*informal*); ≠ unnecessary

imperceptible *adj* too slight, subtle, or gradual to be noticed > **imperceptibly** *adv*

imperfect *adj* **1** having faults or errors **2** not complete **3** *grammar* denoting a tense of verbs describing continuous, incomplete, or repeated past actions ▸ *n* **4** *grammar* the imperfect tense > **imperfectly** *adv*

imperfection *n* **1** the state of being imperfect **2** a fault or defect

imperial *adj* **1** of an empire, emperor, or empress **2** majestic; commanding **3** exercising supreme authority; imperious **4** (of weights or measures) conforming to the standards of a system formerly official in Great Britain ▸ *n* **5** a wine bottle holding the equivalent of eight normal bottles

> **imperial** *adj* **1** = royal, regal, kingly, queenly, princely, sovereign, majestic, monarchial

imperialism *n* **1** the policy or practice of extending a country's influence over other territories by conquest, colonization, or economic domination **2** an imperial system, authority, or government > **imperialist** *adj*, *n* > **imperialistic** *adj*

imperil *vb* **-rilling, -rilled** *or US* **-riling, -riled** *formal* to put in danger

imperious *adj* used to being obeyed; domineering > **imperiously** *adv*

impersonal *adj* **1** without reference to any individual person; objective: *Buddhism began as a very impersonal doctrine* **2** without human warmth or sympathy: *an impersonal manner* **3** *grammar* **A** (of a verb) having no subject, as in *it is raining* **B** (of a pronoun) not referring to a person > **impersonality** *n* > **impersonally** *adv*

impersonate *vb* **-ating, -ated** **1** to pretend to be (another person) **2** to imitate the character or mannerisms of (another person) for entertainment > **impersonation** *n* > **impersonator** *n*

impertinent *adj* disrespectful or rude > **impertinence** *n*

imperturbable *adj* not easily upset; calm > **imperturbability** *n* > **imperturbably** *adv*

impervious *adj* **1** not letting water, etc. through **2** not influenced by a feeling, argument, etc.

impetigo (imp-it-tie-go) *n* a contagious skin disease causing spots or pimples

impetuous *adj* **1** acting without consideration **2** done rashly or hastily > **impetuosity** *n*

impetus (imp-it-uss) *n*, *pl* **-tuses** **1** an incentive or impulse **2** *physics* the force that starts a body moving or that tends to resist changes in its speed or direction once it is moving

> **impetus** *n* **1** = incentive, push, spur, motivation, impulse, stimulus, catalyst, goad **2** = force, power, energy, momentum

impinge *vb* **-pinging, -pinged** (often foll. by *on*) to encroach (on), affect or restrict: *international economic forces impinging on the local economy* > **impingement** *n*

impious (imp-e-uss) *adj* showing a lack of respect or religious reverence

impish *adj* mischievous > **impishness** *n*

implacable *adj* **1** incapable of being appeased or pacified **2** unyielding > **implacability** *n* > **implacably** *adv*

implant *vb* **1** to fix firmly in the mind: *to implant sound moral principles* **2** to plant or embed **3** *surgery* to graft or insert (a tissue or hormone) into the body ▸ *n* **4** anything implanted in the body, such as a tissue graft > **implantation** *n*

> **implant** *vb* **1** = instil, infuse, inculcate **2** = insert, fix, graft

implement *vb* **1** to carry out (instructions, etc.): *she refused to implement the agreed plan* ▸ *n* **2** a tool or other piece of equipment > **implementation** *n*

> **implement** *vb* = carry out, effect, carry through, complete, apply, perform, realize, fulfil; ≠ hinder ▸ *n* = tool, machine, device, instrument, appliance, apparatus, gadget, utensil

implicate *vb* **-cating, -cated** **1** to show (someone) to be involved, esp. in a crime **2** to imply

> **implicate** *vb* **1** = incriminate, involve, embroil, entangle, inculpate (*formal*); ≠ dissociate

implication *n* **1** something that is suggested or implied **2** an act or instance of suggesting, implying, or being implied **3** a probable consequence (of something)

> **implication** *n* **1, 2** = suggestion, hint, inference, meaning, significance, presumption, overtone, innuendo **3** = consequence, result, development, upshot

implicit *adj* **1** expressed indirectly: *an implicit agreement* **2** absolute and unquestioning: *implicit trust* **3** contained in, although not stated openly: *this view of the mind was implicit in all his work* > **implicitly** *adv*

> **implicit** *adj* **1** = implied, understood, suggested, hinted at, taken for granted, unspoken, inferred, tacit; ≠ explicit **2** = absolute, full, complete, firm, fixed, constant, utter, outright **3** = inherent, underlying, intrinsic, latent, ingrained, inbuilt

implode *vb* **-ploding, -ploded** to collapse inwards

implore *vb* **-ploring, -plored** to beg desperately

imply *vb* **-plies, -plying, -plied** **1** to express or indicate by a hint; suggest **2** to suggest or involve as a necessary consequence: *a spending commitment implies a corresponding tax imposition*

> **imply** *vb* **1** = suggest, hint, insinuate, indicate, intimate, signify **2** = involve, mean, entail, require, indicate, point to, signify, presuppose

impolitic *adj* ill-advised; unwise

imponderable *adj* **1** unable to be weighed or assessed ▸ *n* **2** something difficult or impossible to assess

import *vb* **1** to bring in (goods) from another country **2** *formal* to signify; mean: *to import doom* ▸ *n* **3** something imported **4** *formal* importance: *his new work is of great import* **5** meaning **6** *informal* a sportsperson who is not native to the area where they play > **importer** *n* > **importation** *n*

> **import** *vb* = bring in, buy in, ship in, introduce ▸ *n* **4** = significance, concern, value, weight, consequence, substance, moment, magnitude **5** = meaning, implication, significance, sense, intention, substance, drift, thrust

important *adj* **1** of great significance, value, or consequence **2** of social significance: *the second most important person in the government* **3** of great concern: *it was important to me to know* > **importance** *n* > **importantly** *adv*

> **important** *adj* **1** = significant, critical, substantial, urgent, serious, far-reaching, momentous, seminal; ≠ unimportant **2** = powerful, prominent, commanding, dominant, influential, eminent, high-ranking, authoritative, skookum (*Canad*)

importunate *adj formal* persistent or demanding

importune *vb* **-tuning, -tuned** *formal* to harass with persistent requests > **importunity** *n*

impose *vb* **-posing, -posed** **1** to establish (a rule, condition, etc.) as something to be obeyed or complied with **2** to force (oneself) on others **3** *printing* to arrange (pages) in the correct order for printing **4** to pass off (something) deceptively on someone **5** **impose on** to take advantage of (a person or quality): *she imposed on his kindness*

> **impose** *vb* **1** **impose something on someone** = levy, introduce, charge, establish, fix, institute, decree, ordain (*formal*)

imposing *adj* grand or impressive: *an imposing building*

> **imposing** *adj* = impressive, striking, grand, powerful, commanding, awesome, majestic, dignified; ≠ unimposing

imposition *n* **1** the act of imposing **2** something imposed, esp. unfairly on someone **3** the arrangement of pages for printing **4** *old-fashioned* a task set as a school punishment

> **imposition** *n* **1** = application, introduction, levying **2** = intrusion, liberty, presumption

impossibility *n, pl* **-ties** **1** the state or quality of being impossible **2** something that is impossible

impossible *adj* **1** not able to be done or to happen **2** absurd or unreasonable **3** *informal* intolerable or outrageous: *those children are impossible* > **impossibly** *adv*

impossible *adj* **1** = not possible, out of the question, impracticable, unfeasible; ≠ possible **2** = absurd, crazy (*informal*), ridiculous, outrageous, ludicrous, unreasonable, preposterous, farcical

impostor *or* **imposter** *n* a person who cheats or swindles by pretending to be someone else

impotent (imp-a-tent) *adj* **1** not having the power to influence people or events **2** (of a man) incapable of sexual intercourse > **impotence** *n*

impound *vb* **1** to take legal possession of; confiscate **2** to confine (an animal) in a pound

impoverish *vb* **1** to make (someone) poor **2** weaken the quality of something > **impoverished** *adj* > **impoverishment** *n*

impoverish *vb* **1** = bankrupt, ruin, beggar, break **2** = deplete, drain, exhaust, diminish, use up, sap, wear out, reduce

impracticable *adj* **1** not able to be put into practice **2** unsuitable for a desired use > **impracticability** *n*

impractical *adj* **1** not sensible or workable: *the use of force was viewed as impractical* **2** not having practical skills > **impracticality** *n*

imprecation *n formal* a curse > **imprecate** *vb*

impregnable *adj* **1** unable to be broken into or taken by force: *an impregnable fortress* **2** unable to be affected or overcome: *a confident, impregnable person* > **impregnability** *n*

impregnate *vb* **-nating, -nated** **1** to saturate, soak, or fill throughout **2** to make pregnant **3** to imbue or permeate: *the party has been impregnated with an enthusiasm for reform* > **impregnation** *n*

impresario *n*, *pl* **-sarios** a person who runs theatre performances, concerts, etc.

impress *vb* **1** to make a strong, lasting, or favourable impression on: *he was impressed by the standard of play* **2** to stress or emphasize **3** to imprint or stamp by pressure: *a pattern impressed in paint on the rock* ▶ *n* **4** an impressing **5** a mark produced by impressing > **impressible** *adj*

impress *vb* **1** = excite, move, strike, touch, affect, inspire, amaze, overcome

impression *n* **1** an effect produced in the mind by a person or thing: *she was keen to create a relaxed impression* **2** a vague idea or belief: *he only had a vague impression of how it worked* **3** a strong, favourable, or remarkable effect **4** an impersonation for entertainment **5** an imprint or mark produced by pressing **6** *printing* the number of copies of a publication printed at one time

impression *n* **1** = effect, influence, impact **2** = idea, feeling, thought, sense, view, assessment, judgment, reaction **4** = imitation, parody, impersonation, send-up (*Brit informal*), takeoff (*informal*) **5** = mark, imprint, stamp, outline, hollow, dent, indentation

impressionable *adj* easily impressed or influenced: *the promotion of smoking to the impressionable young* > **impressionability** *n*

Impressionism *n* a style of painting developed in 19th-century France, with the aim of reproducing the immediate impression or mood of things, esp. the effects of light and atmosphere, rather than form or structure

impressive *adj* capable of impressing, esp. by size, magnificence, or importance > **impressively** *adv*

impressive *adj* = grand, striking, splendid, good, great (*informal*), fine, powerful, exciting; ≠ unimpressive

imprimatur (imp-rim-ah-ter) *n* official approval for something to be printed, usually given by the Roman Catholic Church

imprint *n* **1** a mark or impression produced by pressing, printing, or stamping **2** the publisher's name and address, often with the date of publication, printed on the title page of a book ▶ *vb* **3** to produce (a mark) by pressing, printing, or stamping: *T-shirts imprinted with slogans* **4** to establish firmly; impress: *he couldn't dislodge the images imprinted on his brain*

imprint *n* **1** = mark, impression, stamp, indentation ▶ *vb* **3** = engrave, print, stamp, impress, etch, emboss

imprison *vb* to confine in or as if in prison > **imprisonment** *n*

imprison *vb* = jail, confine, detain, lock up, put away, intern, incarcerate, send down (*informal*); ≠ free

improbable *adj* not likely or probable > **improbability** *n* > **improbably** *adv*

improbable *adj* = doubtful, unlikely, dubious, questionable, fanciful, far-fetched, implausible; ≠ probable

impromptu *adj* **1** without planning or preparation; improvised ▶ *adv* **2** in a spontaneous or improvised way: *he spoke impromptu* ▶ *n* **3** a short piece of instrumental music resembling improvisation **4** something that is impromptu

improper *adj* **1** indecent **2** irregular or incorrect > **improperly** *adv*

improper *adj* **1** = indecent, vulgar, suggestive, unseemly, untoward, risqué, smutty, unbecoming; ≠ decent

improper fraction *n* a fraction in which the numerator is greater than the denominator, as $7/6$

impropriety (imp-roe-pry-a-tee) *n*, *pl* **-ties** *formal* unsuitable or slightly improper behaviour

improve *vb* **-proving, -proved** **1** to make or become better in quality **2** **improve on**

to achieve a better standard or quality in comparison with: *both had improved on their previous performance* > **improvable** *adj*

improve *vb* **1** = enhance, better, add to, upgrade, touch up, ameliorate; ≠ worsen

improvement *n* **1** the act of improving or the state of being improved **2** a change that makes something better or adds to its value: *home improvements* **3** *Austral & NZ* a building on a piece of land, adding to its value

improvement *n* **1** = enhancement, advancement, betterment **2** = advance, development, progress, recovery, upswing

improvident *adj* **1** not providing for the future **2** incautious or rash > **improvidence** *n*

improvise *vb* **-vising, -vised** **1** to do or make quickly from whatever is available, without previous planning **2** to make up (a piece of music, speech, etc.) as one goes along > **improvisation** *n*

improvise *vb* **1** = devise, contrive, concoct, throw together **2** = ad-lib, invent, busk, wing it (*informal*), play it by ear (*informal*), extemporize, speak off the cuff (*informal*)

impudent *adj* impertinent or insolent > **impudence** *n* > **impudently** *adv*

impugn (imp-**yoon**) *vb formal* to challenge or attack as false > **impugnment** *n*

impulse *n* **1** a sudden desire or whim **2** an instinctive drive; urge: *the mothering impulse* **3** *physics* **A** the product of a force acting on a body and the time for which it acts **B** the change in the momentum of a body as a result of a force acting upon it **4** *physiol* a stimulus transmitted in a nerve or muscle

impulse *n* **1, 2** = urge, longing, wish, notion, yearning, inclination, itch, whim

impulsive *adj* **1** tending to act without thinking first: *an impulsive man* **2** done without thinking first **3** forceful or impelling

impunity (imp-**yoon**-it-ee) *n* **with impunity** without punishment or unpleasant consequences

impure *adj* **1** having unwanted substances mixed in **2** immoral or obscene: *impure thoughts* **3** dirty or unclean

impurity *n, pl* **-ties** **1** an impure element or thing: *impurities in the water* **2** the quality of being impure

impute *vb* **-puting, -puted** **1** to attribute (blame or a crime) to a person **2** to attribute to a source or cause: *I impute your success to nepotism* > **imputation** *n*

in *prep* **1** inside; within: *in the room* **2** at a place where there is: *in the shade* **3** indicating a state, situation, or condition: *in silence* **4** when (a period of time) has elapsed: *come back in one year* **5** using: *written in code* **6** wearing: *the man in the blue suit* **7** with regard to (a specified activity or occupation): *in journalism* **8** while performing the action of: *in crossing the street he was run over* **9** having as purpose: *in honour of the president* **10** (of certain animals) pregnant with: *in calf* **11** into: *he fell in the water* **12** **have it in one** to have the ability (to do something) **13** **in that** or **in so far as** because or to the extent that: *it was of great help in that it gave me more confidence* ▸ *adv* **14** in or into a particular place; indoors: *come in* **15** at one's home or place of work: *he's not in at the moment* **16** in office or power: *the Conservatives got in at the last election* **17** so as to enclose: *block in* **18** (in certain games) so as to take one's turn of the play: *you have to get the other side out before you go in* **19** *Brit* (of a fire) alight **20** (*in combination*) indicating prolonged activity, esp. by a large number: *teach-in; sit-in* **21** **have got it in for** *informal* to wish or intend harm towards **22** **in for** about to experience (something, esp. something unpleasant): *they're in for a shock* **23** **in on** acquainted with or sharing in: *I was in on all his plans* **24** **in with** friendly with ▸ *adj* **25** fashionable; modish: *the in thing to do* ▸ *n* **26** **ins and outs** the detailed points or facts (of a situation)

inability *n* the fact of not being able to do something

inaccessible *adj* **1** impossible or very difficult to reach **2** unable to be used or seen: *his works are inaccessible to English-speaking readers* **3** difficult to understand or appreciate: *Webern's music is still considered inaccessible* > **inaccessibility** *n*

inaccuracy *n, pl* **-cies** **1** lack of accuracy; imprecision **2** an error or mistake > **inaccurate** *adj*

inadequacy *n, pl* **-cies** **1** lack or shortage **2** the state of being or feeling inferior **3** a weakness or failing: *their own failures or inadequacies*

inadequacy *n* **1** = shortage, poverty, dearth, paucity (*formal*), insufficiency, meagreness, scantiness **2** = incompetence, inability, deficiency, incapacity, ineffectiveness **3** = shortcoming, failing, weakness, defect, imperfection

inadequate *adj* **1** not enough; insufficient **2** not good enough > **inadequately** *adv*

inadequate *adj* **1** = insufficient, meagre, poor, lacking, scant, sparse, sketchy; ≠ adequate **2** = incapable, incompetent, faulty, deficient, unqualified, not up to scratch (*informal*); ≠ capable

inadvertent *adj* done unintentionally > **inadvertence** *n* > **inadvertently** *adv*

inalienable *adj* not able to be taken away or transferred to another: *the inalienable rights of the citizen*

inane *adj* senseless or silly: *inane remarks* > **inanity** *n*

inanimate *adj* lacking the qualities of living beings: *inanimate objects*

inappropriate *adj* not suitable or proper
> **inappropriately** *adv*

inarticulate *adj* unable to express oneself
clearly or well

inasmuch as *conj* **1** since; because **2** in so far as

inaugural *adj* **1** of or for an inauguration ▸ *n*
2 US a speech made at an inauguration

> **inaugural** *adj* = first, opening, initial,
> maiden, introductory

inaugurate *vb* **-rating, -rated 1** to open or
celebrate the first public use of ceremonially:
the newest electrified line was inaugurated today **2** to
formally establish (a new leader) in office **3** to
begin officially or formally > **inauguration** *n*
> **inaugurator** *n*

inauspicious *adj* unlucky; suggesting an
unfavourable outcome

inauthentic *adj* not genuine or real

inboard *adj* **1** (of a boat's motor or engine)
situated within the hull **2** situated close to the
fuselage of an aircraft ▸ *adv* **3** within the sides
of, or towards the centre of, a vessel or aircraft

inborn *adj* existing from birth: *an inborn sense of
optimism*

inbox *n* a folder in a computer mailbox in which
incoming messages are stored

inbred *adj* **1** produced as a result of inbreeding
2 inborn or ingrained: *inbred good manners*

inbreeding *n* breeding from closely related
individuals

inbuilt *adj* (of a quality or feeling) present from
the beginning: *an inbuilt prejudice*

Inc. US & Austral (of a company) incorporated

incalculable *adj* impossible to estimate or
predict > **incalculability** *n*

in camera *adv* in private session: *the proceedings
were held in camera*

incandescent *adj* **1** glowing with heat
2 (of artificial light) produced by a glowing
filament > **incandescence** *n*

incantation *n* **1** ritual chanting of
magic words or sounds **2** a magic spell
> **incantatory** *adj*

incapable *adj* **1** helpless: *drunk and incapable*
2 **incapable of** lacking the ability to

incapacitate *vb* **-tating, -tated** to deprive (a
person) of strength, power, or ability; disable

incapacity *n, pl* **-ties 1** lack of power, strength,
or ability **2** *law* legal disqualification or
ineligibility

incarcerate *vb* **-rating, -rated** *formal* to confine
or imprison > **incarceration** *n*

incarnate *adj* **1** possessing human form: *a devil
incarnate* **2** personified or typified: *stupidity
incarnate* ▸ *vb* **-nating, -nated 3** to give a bodily
or concrete form to **4** to be representative or
typical of

incarnation *n* **1** the act of embodying or state
of being embodied in human form **2** a person or
thing that typifies some quality or idea

incarnation *n* **2** = embodiment,
manifestation, epitome, type, personification,
avatar

Incarnation *n* *Christian theol* God's coming to
earth in human form as Jesus Christ

incendiary (in-send-ya-ree) *adj* **1** (of bombs,
etc.) designed to cause fires **2** tending to create
strife or violence **3** relating to the illegal
burning of property or goods ▸ *n, pl* **-aries 4** a
bomb that is designed to start fires **5** a person
who illegally sets fire to property or goods
> **incendiarism** *n*

incense¹ *n* an aromatic substance burnt for its
fragrant odour, esp. in religious ceremonies

incense² *vb* **-censing, -censed** to make very
angry > **incensed** *adj*

> **incense** *vb* = anger, infuriate, enrage, irritate,
> madden, inflame, rile (*informal*), make your
> blood boil (*informal*)

incentive *n* **1** something that encourages effort
or action **2** an additional payment made to
employees to increase production ▸ *adj*
3 encouraging greater effort: *an incentive scheme for
workers*

> **incentive** *n* **1** = inducement,
> encouragement, spur, lure, bait, motivation,
> carrot (*informal*), stimulus; ≠ disincentive

inception *n* the beginning of a project

incessant *adj* never stopping > **incessantly** *adv*

incest *n* sexual intercourse between two people
who are too closely related to marry
> **incestuous** *adj*

inch *n* **1** a unit of length equal to one twelfth of
a foot (2.54cm) **2** *meteorol* the amount of rain or
snow that would cover a surface to a depth of
one inch **3** a very small distance, degree, or
amount: *neither side was prepared to give an inch*
4 **every inch** in every way: *she arrived looking every
inch a star* **5** **inch by inch** gradually **6** **within an
inch of one's life** almost to death ▸ *vb* **7** to move
very slowly or gradually: *I inched my way to the bar*

incidence *n* **1** extent or frequency of
occurrence: *the rising incidence of car fires* **2** *physics*
the arrival of a beam of light or particles at a
surface **3** *geom* the partial overlapping of two
figures or a figure and a line

incident *n* **1** an occurrence or event, esp. a
minor one **2** a relatively insignificant event
that might have serious consequences **3** a
public disturbance ▸ *adj* **4** *physics* (of a beam of
light or particles) arriving at or striking a
surface **5** **incident to** *formal* likely to occur in
connection with: *the dangers are incident to a police
officer's job*

> **incident** *n* **1** = happening, event, affair,
> business, fact, matter, occasion, episode
> **3** = disturbance, scene, clash, disorder,
> confrontation, brawl, fracas, commotion

incidental *adj* **1** happening in connection with or resulting from something more important **2** secondary or minor: *incidental expenses* > **incidentally** *adv*

incidental music *n* background music for a film or play

incinerate *vb* **-ating, -ated** to burn up completely > **incineration** *n*

incinerator *n* a furnace for burning rubbish

incipient *adj formal* just starting to be or happen

incise *vb* **-cising, -cised** to cut into with a sharp tool

incision *n* a cut, esp. one made during a surgical operation

incisive *adj* direct and forceful: *witty and incisive comments*

incisor *n* a sharp cutting tooth at the front of the mouth

incite *vb* **-citing, -cited** to stir up or provoke to action > **incitement** *n*

incivility *n, pl* **-ties 1** rudeness **2** an impolite act or remark

inclement *adj formal* (of weather) stormy or severe > **inclemency** *n*

inclination *n* **1** a liking, tendency, or preference: *he showed no inclination to change his routine* **2** the degree of slope from a horizontal or vertical plane **3** a slope or slant **4** *surveying* the angular distance of the horizon below the plane of observation

> **inclination** *n* **1** = desire, longing, aspiration, craving, hankering; ≠ aversion

incline *vb* **-clining, -clined 1** to veer from a vertical or horizontal plane; slope or slant **2** to have or cause to have a certain tendency or disposition: *that does not incline me to think that you are right* **3** to bend or lower (part of the body, esp. the head) **4 incline one's ear** to listen favourably ▸ *n* **5** an inclined surface or slope > **inclined** *adj*

> **incline** *vb* **2** = predispose, influence, persuade, prejudice, sway, dispose ▸ *n* = slope, rise, dip, grade, descent, ascent, gradient

include *vb* **-cluding, -cluded 1** to have as part of the whole **2** to put in as part of a set, group, or category

> **include** *vb* **1** = contain, involve, incorporate, cover, consist of, take in, embrace, comprise; ≠ exclude **2** = add, enter, put in, insert

inclusion *n* **1** an including or being included **2** something included

> **inclusion** *n* **1** = addition, incorporation, introduction, insertion; ≠ exclusion

inclusive *adj* **1** including everything: *capital inclusive of profit* **2** including the limits specified: *Monday to Friday inclusive* **3** comprehensive

> **inclusive** *adj* **1, 3** = comprehensive, general, global, sweeping, blanket, umbrella, across-the-board, all-embracing; ≠ limited

incognito (in-kog-nee-toe) *adv, adj* **1** under an assumed name or appearance ▸ *n, pl* **-tos 2** a false identity **3** a person who is incognito

incoherent *adj* **1** unable to express oneself clearly **2** not logically connected or ordered: *an incoherent argument* > **incoherence** *n*

income *n* the total amount of money earned from work or obtained from other sources over a given period of time

> **income** *n* = revenue, earnings, pay, returns, profits, wages, yield, proceeds

income support *n chiefly Brit* an allowance paid to people with a very low income

income tax *n* a personal tax levied on annual income

incoming *adj* **1** about to arrive **2** about to come into office

> **incoming** *adj* **1** = arriving, landing, approaching, entering, returning, homeward; ≠ departing **2** = new

incommode *vb* **-moding, -moded** *formal* to bother, disturb, or inconvenience

incommunicado *adv, adj* not allowed to communicate with other people, for instance while in solitary confinement

incomparable *adj* so excellent as to be beyond or above comparison > **incomparably** *adv*

incompatible *adj* not able to exist together in harmony; conflicting or inconsistent > **incompatibility** *n*

> **incompatible** *adj* = inconsistent, conflicting, contradictory, incongruous, unsuited, mismatched; ≠ compatible

incompetent *adj* **1** not having the necessary ability or skill to do something **2** *law* not legally qualified: *an incompetent witness* ▸ *n* **3** an incompetent person > **incompetence** *n*

> **incompetent** *adj* **1** = inept, useless (*informal*), incapable, floundering, bungling, unfit, ineffectual, inexpert; ≠ competent

inconceivable *adj* so unlikely to be true as to be unthinkable > **inconceivability** *n*

inconclusive *adj* not giving a final decision or result

incongruous *adj* out of place; inappropriate: *an incongruous figure among the tourists* > **incongruously** *adv* > **incongruity** *n*

inconsequential *or* **inconsequent** *adj* **1** unimportant or insignificant **2** not following logically as a consequence > **inconsequentially** *adv*

inconsiderable *adj* **1** not worth considering; insignificant **2 not inconsiderable** fairly large: *he gets not inconsiderable royalties from his musicals* > **inconsiderably** *adv*

inconstant *adj* **1** liable to change one's loyalties or opinions **2** variable: *their household income is inconstant* > **inconstancy** *n*

incontinent *adj* **1** unable to control the bladder and bowels **2** lacking self-restraint
> **incontinence** *n*

incontrovertible *adj* absolutely certain; undeniable > **incontrovertibly** *adv*

inconvenience *n* **1** a state or instance of trouble or difficulty ▶ *vb* **-iencing, -ienced** **2** to cause trouble or difficulty to (someone)
> **inconvenient** *adj*

> **inconvenience** *n* = trouble, difficulty, bother, fuss, disadvantage, disturbance, disruption, nuisance, uphill (*S African*) ▶ *vb* = trouble, bother, disturb, upset, disrupt, put out, discommode

incorporate *vb* **-rating, -rated** **1** to include or be included as part of a larger unit **2** to form a united whole or mass **3** to form into a corporation ▶ *adj* **4** incorporated > **incorporated** *adj* > **incorporation** *n*

> **incorporate** *vb* **1** = include, contain, take in, embrace, integrate, encompass, assimilate, comprise of **2** = blend, combine, compound, mingle

incorporeal (in-kore-**pore**-ee-al) *adj* without material form, substance, or existence

incorrigible *adj* (of a person or behaviour) beyond correction or reform; incurably bad
> **incorrigibility** *n* > **incorrigibly** *adv*

incorruptible *adj* **1** too honest to be bribed or corrupted **2** not prone to decay or disintegration
> **incorruptibility** *n*

increase *vb* **-creasing, -creased** **1** to make or become greater in size, degree, or frequency ▶ *n* **2** a rise in size, degree, or frequency **3** the amount by which something increases **4 on the increase** becoming more common
> **increasingly** *adv*

> **increase** *vb* = raise, extend, boost, expand, develop, advance, strengthen, widen; ≠ decrease ▶ *n* **2, 3** = growth, rise, development, gain, expansion, extension, proliferation, enlargement

incredible *adj* **1** unbelievable **2** *informal* marvellous; amazing > **incredibility** *n*
> **incredibly** *adv*

> **incredible** *adj* **1** = unbelievable, unthinkable, improbable, inconceivable, preposterous, unconvincing, unimaginable, far-fetched **2** = amazing, wonderful, stunning (*informal*), extraordinary, overwhelming, astonishing, staggering, sensational (*informal*)

incredulity *n* unwillingness to believe

incredulous *adj* not prepared or willing to believe something

increment *n* **1** the amount by which something increases **2** a regular salary increase **3** *maths* a small positive or negative change in a variable or function > **incremental** *adj*

incriminate *vb* **-nating, -nated** **1** to make (someone) seem guilty of a crime **2** to charge (someone) with a crime > **incrimination** *n*
> **incriminatory** *adj*

incubate (in-cube-ate) *vb* **-bating, -bated** **1** (of birds) to hatch (eggs) by sitting on them **2** to cause (bacteria) to develop, esp. in an incubator or culture medium **3** (of disease germs) to remain inactive in an animal or human before causing disease **4** to develop gradually
> **incubation** *n*

incubator *n* **1** *med* a heated enclosed apparatus for rearing premature babies **2** an apparatus for hatching birds' eggs or growing bacterial cultures

incubus (in-cube-uss) *n, pl* **-bi** *or* **-buses** **1** a demon believed in folklore to have sexual intercourse with sleeping women **2** a nightmarish burden or worry

inculcate *vb* **-cating, -cated** to fix in someone's mind by constant repetition > **inculcation** *n*

incumbency *n, pl* **-cies** the office, duty, or tenure of an incumbent

incumbent *formal* ▶ *n* **1** a person who holds a particular office or position ▶ *adj* **2** morally binding as a duty: *it is incumbent on cricketers to respect the umpire's impartiality*

> **incumbent** *n* = holder, keeper, bearer ▶ *adj* = obligatory, required, necessary, essential, binding, compulsory, mandatory, imperative

incur *vb* **-curring, -curred** to bring (something undesirable) upon oneself

> **incur** *vb* = sustain, experience, suffer, gain, earn, collect, meet with, provoke

incurable *adj* **1** not able to be cured: *an incurable tumour* **2** not able to be changed: *he is an incurable romantic* ▶ *n* **3** a person with an incurable disease > **incurability** *n* > **incurably** *adv*

incurious *adj* showing no curiosity or interest
> **incuriously** *adv*

incursion *n* **1** a sudden or brief invasion **2** an inroad or encroachment: *a successful incursion into the American book-shop market* > **incursive** *adj*

indebted *adj* **1** owing gratitude for help or favours **2** owing money > **indebtedness** *n*

indecent *adj* **1** morally or sexually offensive **2** unseemly or improper: *indecent haste*
> **indecency** *n* > **indecently** *adv*

> **indecent** *adj* **1** = obscene, lewd, dirty, inappropriate, rude, crude, filthy, improper; ≠ decent **2** = unbecoming, unsuitable, vulgar, unseemly, undignified, indecorous; ≠ proper

indecent assault *n* a sexual attack which does not include rape

indecent exposure *n* the crime of showing of one's genitals in public

indecipherable *adj* impossible to read

indeed *adv* **1** certainly; actually: *indeed, the sea featured heavily in his poems* **2** truly, very: *it has* *become a dangerous place indeed* **3** in fact; what is more: *it is necessary, indeed indispensable* ▸ *interj* **4** an expression of doubt or surprise

indeed *adv* **1** = certainly, yes, definitely, surely, truly, undoubtedly, without doubt, indisputably **3** = really, actually, in fact, certainly, genuinely, in truth, in actuality

indefatigable *adj* never getting tired or giving up: *an indefatigable organizer* ▸ **indefatigably** *adv*
indefensible *adj* **1** (of behaviour or statements) unable to be justified or supported **2** (of places or buildings) impossible to defend against attack ▸ **indefensibility** *n*
indefinite *adj* **1** without exact limits: *an indefinite number* **2** vague or unclear ▸ **indefinitely** *adv*
indefinite article *n grammar* either of the words 'a' or 'an'
indelible *adj* **1** impossible to erase or remove **2** making indelible marks: *indelible ink* ▸ **indelibly** *adv*
indelicate *adj* **1** offensive, embarrassing, or tasteless **2** coarse, crude, or rough ▸ **indelicacy** *n*
indemnify *vb* **-fies, -fying, -fied 1** to secure against loss, damage, or liability **2** to compensate for loss or damage ▸ **indemnification** *n*
indemnity *n, pl* **-ties 1** insurance against loss or damage **2** compensation for loss or damage **3** legal exemption from penalties incurred
indent *vb* **1** to start (a line of text) or position (a block of text) further from the margin than the main part of the text **2** to order (goods) using a special order form **3** to notch (an edge or border) **4** to write out (a document) in duplicate **5** to bind (an apprentice) by indenture ▸ *n* **6** *chiefly Brit* an official order for goods, esp. foreign merchandise
indentation *n* **1** a hollow, notch, or cut, as on an edge or on a coastline **2** an indenting or being indented **3** Also: **indention** the leaving of space or the amount of space left between a margin and the start of an indented line
indenture *n* **1** a contract, esp. one binding an apprentice to his or her employer ▸ *vb* **-turing, -tured 2** to bind (an apprentice) by indenture **3** to enter into an agreement by indenture
independent *adj* **1** free from the influence or control of others **2** not dependent on anything else for function or validity **3** not relying on the support, esp. financial support, of others **4** capable of acting for oneself or on one's own **5** of or having a private income large enough to enable one to live without working: *independent means* **6** *maths* (of a variable) not dependent on another variable ▸ *n* **7** an independent person or thing **8** a politician who does not represent any political party ▸ **independence** *n* ▸ **independently** *adv*

independent *adj* **1** = separate, unattached, uncontrolled, unconstrained; ≠ controlled **3** = self-sufficient, free, liberated, self-contained, self-reliant, self-supporting **4** = self-governing, free, autonomous, liberated, sovereign, self-determining, nonaligned; ≠ subject

in-depth *adj* detailed or thorough: *an in-depth analysis*
indescribable *adj* too intense or extreme for words ▸ **indescribably** *adv*
indeterminate *adj* **1** uncertain in extent, amount, or nature **2** left doubtful; inconclusive: *an indeterminate reply* **3** *maths* **A** having no numerical meaning, as $^0/_0$ **B** (of an equation) having more than one variable and an unlimited number of solutions ▸ **indeterminable** *adj* ▸ **indeterminacy** *n*
index *n, pl* **-dexes** or **-dices 1** an alphabetical list of names or subjects dealt with in a book, indicating where they are referred to **2** a file or catalogue in a library which enables a book or reference to be found **3** a number indicating the level of wages or prices as compared with some standard value **4** an indication or sign: *national birth rate was once an index of military power* **5** *maths* **A** same as **exponent B** a superscript number placed to the left of a radical sign indicating the root to be extracted: *the index of $^3\sqrt{8}$ is 3* **6** a number or ratio indicating a specific characteristic or property: *refractive index* ▸ *vb* **7** to put an index in (a book) **8** to enter (a word or item) in an index **9** to make index-linked
index finger *n* the finger next to the thumb. Also called: **forefinger**
index-linked *adj* (of pensions, wages, or interest rates) rising and falling in line with the cost of living
Indian *adj* **1** of India **2** of the original inhabitants of the American continent ▸ *n* **3** a person from India **4** a person descended from the original inhabitants of the American continent
Indian summer *n* **1** a period of warm sunny weather in autumn **2** a period of tranquillity or of renewed productivity towards the end of a person's life or career
indicate *vb* **-cating, -cated 1** to be or give a sign or symptom of: *to concede 18 goals in 7 games indicates a serious malaise* **2** to point out or show **3** to state briefly **4** to switch on the indicators in a motor vehicle to show that one is changing direction **5** (of measuring instruments) to show a reading of **6** (*usually passive*) to recommend or require: *surgery seems to be indicated for this patient* ▸ **indication** *n*

indicate *vb* **1** = show, suggest, reveal, display, demonstrate, point to, imply, manifest, flag up **2** = point to, point out, specify, gesture towards, designate **5** = register, show, record, read, express, display, demonstrate

indicative (in-dik-a-tiv) *adj* **1 indicative of** suggesting: *the symptoms aren't indicative of anything serious* **2** *grammar* denoting a mood of verbs used to make a statement ▸ *n* **3** *grammar* the indicative mood

indicator *n* **1** something that acts as a sign or indication: *an indicator of the moral decline of our society* **2** a device for indicating that a motor vehicle is about to turn left or right, esp. two pairs of lights that flash **3** an instrument, such as a gauge, that registers or measures something **4** *chem* a substance used to indicate the completion of a chemical reaction, usually by a change of colour

> **indicator** *n* **1** = sign, mark, measure, guide, signal, symbol, meter, gauge

indict (in-dite) *vb criminal law* to charge (a person) formally with a crime, esp. in writing
> **indictable** *adj*

> **indict** *vb* = charge, accuse, prosecute, summon, impeach, arraign

indictment *n* **1** *criminal law* a formal charge of crime, esp. in writing: *the indictment contained three similar charges against each of the defendants* **2** a serious criticism: *a scathing indictment of faith healing*

> **indictment** *n* **1** = charge, allegation, prosecution, accusation, impeachment, summons, arraignment

indie *n informal* an independent record or film company

indifference *n* **1** lack of concern or interest: *elite indifference to mass opinion* **2** lack of importance: *a matter of indifference to me*

> **indifference** *n* **1** = disregard, apathy, negligence, detachment, coolness, coldness, nonchalance, aloofness; ≠ concern

indifferent *adj* **1** showing no concern or interest: *he was indifferent to politics* **2** of only average standard or quality **3** not at all good: *she had starred in several very indifferent movies* **4** unimportant **5** showing or having no preferences

> **indifferent** *adj* **1** = unconcerned, detached, cold, cool, callous, aloof, unmoved, unsympathetic; ≠ concerned **2** = mediocre, ordinary, moderate, so-so (*informal*), passable, undistinguished, no great shakes (*informal*), half-pie (NZ *informal*); ≠ excellent

indigenous (in-dij-in-uss) *adj* originating or occurring naturally in a country or area: *the indigenous population is under threat*

indigent *adj formal* so poor as to lack even necessities: *the indigent widow of a fellow writer*
> **indigence** *n*

indigestible *adj* difficult or impossible to digest > **indigestibility** *n*

indigestion *n* difficulty in digesting food, accompanied by stomach pain, heartburn, and belching

indignant *adj* feeling or showing indignation
> **indignantly** *adv*

indignation *n* anger aroused by something felt to be unfair or wrong

> **indignation** *n* = resentment, anger, rage, exasperation, pique, umbrage

indignity *n, pl* **-ties** embarrassing or humiliating treatment

indigo *adj* **1** deep violet-blue ▸ *n, pl* **-gos** *or* **-goes** **2** a dye of this colour originally obtained from plants

indirect *adj* **1** done or caused by someone or something else: *indirect benefits* **2** not going in a direct course or line: *he took the indirect route home* **3** not coming straight to the point: *an indirect question* > **indirectly** *adv*

> **indirect** *adj* **1** = related, secondary, subsidiary, incidental, unintended **2** = circuitous, roundabout, curving, wandering, rambling, deviant (*old-fashioned*), meandering, tortuous; ≠ direct

indirect object *n grammar* the person or thing indirectly affected by the action of a verb and its direct object, as *John* in the sentence *I bought John a newspaper*

indirect tax *n* a tax levied on goods or services which is paid indirectly by being added to the price

indiscreet *adj* incautious or tactless in revealing secrets

indiscretion *n* **1** lack of discretion **2** an indiscreet act or remark

indiscriminate *adj* lacking discrimination or careful choice: *an indiscriminate bombing campaign* > **indiscriminately** *adv* > **indiscrimination** *n*

indispensable *adj* absolutely necessary: *an indispensable guide for any traveller* > **indispensability** *n*

> **indispensable** *adj* = essential, necessary, needed, key, vital, crucial (*informal*), imperative, requisite; ≠ dispensable

indisposed *adj* **1** sick or ill **2** unwilling
> **indisposition** *n*

indisputable *adj* beyond doubt
> **indisputably** *adv*

indissoluble *adj* permanent: *joining a political party is not an indissoluble marriage*

indium *n chem* a rare soft silvery metallic element. Symbol: **In**

individual *adj* **1** of, relating to, or meant for a single person or thing: *small sums from individual donors* **2** separate or distinct from others of its kind: *please mark the individual pages* **3** characterized by unusual and striking qualities ▸ *n* **4** a single person, esp. when regarded as distinct from others: *respect for the individual* **5** *informal* a person: *a most annoying* *individual* **6** *biol* a single animal or plant, esp. as distinct from a species > **individually** *adv*

individual *adj* **1** = separate, independent, isolated, lone, solitary; ≠ collective **3** = unique, special, fresh, novel, exclusive, singular, idiosyncratic, unorthodox; ≠ conventional ▶ *n* **4** = person, being, human, unit, character (*informal*), soul, creature

individualism *n* **1** the principle of leading one's life in one's own way **2** same as **laissez faire 3** egotism > **individualist** *n* > **individualistic** *adj*

individuality *n, pl* **-ties 1** distinctive or unique character or personality: *a house of great individuality* **2** the qualities that distinguish one person or thing from another **3** a separate existence

indoctrinate *vb* **-nating, -nated** to teach (someone) systematically to accept a doctrine or opinion uncritically > **indoctrination** *n*

Indo-European *adj* **1** of a family of languages spoken in most of Europe and much of Asia, including English, Russian, and Hindi ▶ *n* **2** the Indo-European family of languages

indolent *adj* lazy; idle > **indolence** *n*

indomitable *adj* too strong to be defeated or discouraged: *an indomitable work ethic*

indoor *adj* situated, happening, or used inside a building: *an indoor pool*

indoors *adv, adj* inside or into a building

indubitable (in-**dew**-bit-a-bl) *adj* beyond doubt; definite > **indubitably** *adv*

induce *vb* **-ducing, -duced 1** to persuade or use influence on **2** to cause or bring about **3** *med* to cause (labour) to begin by the use of drugs or other means **4** *logic obsolete* to draw (a general conclusion) from particular instances **5** to produce (an electromotive force or electrical current) by induction **6** to transmit (magnetism) by induction > **inducible** *adj*

induce *vb* **1** = persuade, encourage, influence, convince, urge, prompt, sway, entice; ≠ dissuade **2** = cause, produce, create, effect, lead to, occasion (*formal*), generate, bring about; ≠ prevent

inducement *n* **1** something that encourages someone to do something **2** the act of inducing

induct *vb* **1** to bring in formally or install in a job, rank, or position **2** to initiate in knowledge of (a group or profession): *boys are inducted into the world of men*

inductance *n* the property of an electric circuit as a result of which an electromotive force is created by a change of current in the same or in a neighbouring circuit

induction *n* **1** *logic* a process of reasoning by which a general conclusion is drawn from particular instances **2** *med* the process of inducing labour **3** the process by which electrical or magnetic properties are transferred, without physical contact, from one circuit or body to another **4** a formal introduction or entry into an office or position **5** (in an internal-combustion engine) the drawing in of mixed air and fuel from the carburettor to the cylinder > **inductional** *adj*

induction coil *n* a transformer for producing a high voltage from a low voltage. It consists of a soft-iron core, a primary coil of few turns, and a concentric secondary coil of many turns

induction course *n* a training course to help familiarize someone with a new job

inductive *adj* **1** *logic* of or using induction: *inductive reasoning* **2** of or operated by electrical or magnetic induction

indulge *vb* **-dulging, -dulged 1** (often foll. by *in*) to yield to or gratify (a whim or desire for): *to indulge in new clothes* **2** to allow (someone) to have or do everything he or she wants: *he had given her too much, indulged her in everything* **3** to allow (oneself) the pleasure of something: *he indulged himself* **4** *informal* to take alcoholic drink

indulge *vb* **1** = gratify, satisfy, feed, give way to, yield to, pander to, gladden **2** = spoil, pamper, cosset, humour, give in to, coddle, mollycoddle, overindulge **3 indulge yourself** = treat yourself, splash out, spoil yourself, luxuriate in something, overindulge yourself

indulgence *n* **1** something that is allowed because it gives pleasure; extravagance **2** the act of indulging oneself or someone else **3** liberal or tolerant treatment **4** something granted as a favour or privilege **5** *RC Church* a remission of the temporal punishment for sin after its guilt has been forgiven

indulgence *n* **1, 4** = luxury, treat, extravagance, favour, privilege

indulgent *adj* kind or lenient, often to excess > **indulgently** *adv*

industrial *adj* **1** of, used in, or employed in industry **2** with an economy relying heavily on industry: *northern industrial cities*

industrial action *n* action, such as a strike or work-to-rule, by which workers complain about their conditions

industrial estate *n Brit, Austral, NZ & S African* an area of land set aside for factories and warehouses

industrialize *or* **-lise** *vb* **-lizing, -lized** *or* **-lising, -lised** to develop industry on a large scale in (a country or region) > **industrialization** *or* **-lisation** *n*

industrial relations *pl n* the relations between management and workers

industrious *adj* hard-working

industry *n, pl* **-tries 1** the work and process involved in manufacture: *Japanese industry increased output considerably last year* **2** a branch of commercial enterprise concerned with the manufacture of a specified product: *the steel industry* **3** the quality of working hard

industry n 1 = business, production, manufacturing, trade, commerce 2 = trade, world, business, service, line, field, profession, occupation 3 = diligence, effort, labour, hard work, trouble, activity, application, endeavour

inebriate n 1 a person who is habitually drunk
▸ adj 2 drunk, esp. habitually ▸ **inebriation** n

inebriated adj drunk

inedible adj not fit to be eaten

ineffable adj too great or intense to be expressed in words ▸ **ineffably** adv

ineffectual adj having no effect or an inadequate effect: the raids were costly and ineffectual

ineligible adj not qualified for or entitled to something

ineluctable adj formal impossible to avoid: the ineluctable collapse of the coalition

inept adj 1 awkward, clumsy, or incompetent 2 not suitable or fitting; out of place ▸ **ineptitude** n

inequitable adj unjust or unfair

ineradicable adj impossible to remove or root out: an ineradicable sense of guilt

inert adj 1 without the power to move or to resist motion 2 inactive or lifeless 3 having only a limited ability to react chemically

inertia n 1 a feeling of unwillingness to do anything 2 physics the tendency of a body to remain still or continue moving unless a force is applied to it ▸ **inertial** adj

inescapable adj not able to be avoided

inestimable adj too great to be calculated

inevitable adj 1 unavoidable; sure to happen 2 informal so regular as to be predictable: the inevitable guitar solo ▸ n 3 (often preceded by the) something that is unavoidable ▸ **inevitability** n ▸ **inevitably** adv

inevitable adj 1 = unavoidable, inescapable, inexorable, sure, certain, fixed, assured, fated; ≠ avoidable

inexorable adj unable to be prevented from continuing or progressing: an inexorable trend ▸ **inexorably** adv

inexpert adj lacking skill

inexplicable adj impossible to explain ▸ **inexplicably** adv

in extremis adv 1 in dire straits 2 at the point of death

inextricable adj 1 impossible to escape from: an inextricable dilemma 2 impossible to disentangle or separate: an inextricable mass of twisted metal ▸ **inextricably** adv

infallible adj 1 incapable of error 2 always successful: an infallible cure 3 (of the Pope, in Roman Catholic belief) incapable of error in setting forth matters of doctrine on faith and morals ▸ **infallibility** n ▸ **infallibly** adv

infamous (in-fam-uss) adj well-known for something bad

infamous adj = notorious, ignominious, disreputable, ill-famed; ≠ esteemed

infamy n, pl -mies 1 the state of being infamous 2 an infamous act or event

infancy n, pl -cies 1 the state or period of being an infant 2 an early stage of growth or development: the technology is still in its infancy 3 law the state or period of being a minor

infancy n 2 = beginnings, start, birth, roots, seeds, origins, dawn (literary), outset; ≠ end

infant n 1 a very young child; baby 2 law same as **minor** (sense 4) 3 Brit a young schoolchild ▸ adj 4 of, relating to, or designed for young children: infant school 5 in an early stage of development: an infant democracy

infant n 1 = baby, child, babe, toddler, tot, bairn (Scot, N English), littlie (Austral informal), ankle-biter (Austral slang), tacker (Austral slang)

infanticide n 1 the act of killing an infant 2 a person who kills an infant

infantile adj 1 childishly immature 2 of infants or infancy

infantry n, pl -tries soldiers who fight on foot

infatuated adj (often foll. by with) carried away by an intense and unreasoning passion for someone

infect vb 1 to contaminate (a person or thing) with a germ or virus or its consequent disease 2 to taint or contaminate 3 to affect with an opinion or feeling as if by contagion: even she was infected by the excitement

infect vb 1 = contaminate 2 = pollute, poison, corrupt, contaminate, taint, defile 3 = affect, move, upset, overcome, stir, disturb

infection n 1 an infectious disease 2 contamination of a person or thing by a germ or virus or its consequent disease

infection n 1 = disease, condition, complaint, illness, virus, disorder, corruption, poison

infectious adj 1 (of a disease) capable of being transmitted without actual contact 2 causing or transmitting infection 3 spreading from one person to another: infectious laughter

infectious adj = catching, spreading, contagious, communicable, virulent, transmittable

infer vb -ferring, -ferred 1 to conclude by reasoning from evidence; deduce 2 not standard to imply or suggest

inference n 1 the act or process of reaching a conclusion by reasoning from evidence 2 an inferred conclusion or deduction

inferior adj 1 lower in quality, quantity, or usefulness 2 lower in rank, position, or status 3 of poor quality 4 lower in position 5 printing (of a character) printed at the foot of an ordinary character ▸ *n* **6** a person inferior to another, esp. in rank > **inferiority** *n*

> **inferior** *adj* **1, 2** = lower, minor, secondary, subsidiary, lesser, humble, subordinate, lowly; ≠ superior ▸ *n* = underling (*derogatory*), junior, subordinate, lesser, menial, minion

infernal *adj* **1** of or relating to hell **2** *informal* irritating: *stop that infernal noise*

inferno *n, pl* **-nos 1** an intense raging fire **2** a place or situation resembling hell, because it is crowded and noisy **3 the inferno** hell

infertile *adj* **1** not capable of producing offspring **2** (of soil) not productive; barren > **infertility** *n*

infest *vb* to inhabit or overrun (a place, plant, etc.) in unpleasantly large numbers: *the area was infested with moles* > **infestation** *n*

infidel *n* **1** a person who has no religious belief **2** a person who rejects a specific religion, esp. Christianity or Islam ▸ *adj* **3** of unbelievers or unbelief

infidelity *n, pl* **-ties 1** sexual unfaithfulness to one's husband, wife, or lover **2** an act or instance of unfaithfulness

infighting *n* **1** rivalry or quarrelling between members of the same group or organization **2** *boxing* combat at close quarters

infiltrate *vb* **-trating, -trated 1** to enter (an organization, area, etc.) gradually and in secret, so as to gain influence or control: *they infiltrated the party structure* **2** to pass (a liquid or gas) through (a substance) by filtering or (of a liquid or gas) to pass through (a substance) by filtering > **infiltration** *n* > **infiltrator** *n*

> **infiltrate** *vb* **1** = penetrate, pervade, permeate, percolate, filter through to, make inroads into, sneak into (*informal*), insinuate yourself

infinite (in-fin-it) *adj* **1** having no limits or boundaries in time, space, extent, or size **2** extremely or immeasurably great or numerous: *infinite wealth* **3** *maths* having an unlimited or uncountable number of digits, factors, or terms > **infinitely** *adv*

> **infinite** *adj* **1** = limitless, endless, unlimited, eternal, never-ending, boundless, everlasting, inexhaustible; ≠ finite **2** = vast, enormous, immense, countless, measureless

infinitesimal *adj* **1** extremely small: *an infinitesimal risk* **2** *maths* of or involving a small change in the value of a variable that approaches zero as a limit ▸ *n* **3** *maths* an infinitesimal quantity

infinitive (in-fin-it-iv) *n* *grammar* a form of the verb which in most languages is not inflected for tense or person and is used without a particular subject: in English, the infinitive usually consists of the word *to* followed by the verb

infinity *n, pl* **-ties 1** an infinitely great number or amount **2** endless time, space, or quantity **3** *maths* the concept of a value greater than any finite numerical value

infirm *adj* physically or mentally weak, esp. from old age

infirmary *n, pl* **-ries** a place for the treatment of sick or injured people; hospital

infirmity *n, pl* **-ties 1** the state of being infirm **2** physical weakness or frailty

inflame *vb* **-flaming, -flamed 1** to make angry or excited **2** to increase or intensify; aggravate **3** to produce inflammation in or become inflamed **4** to set or be set on fire

> **inflame** *vb* **1** = enrage, stimulate, provoke, excite, anger, arouse, rouse, infuriate; ≠ calm

inflamed *adj* (of part of the body) red, swollen, and painful because of infection

inflammable *adj* **1** liable to catch fire **2** easily aroused to anger or passion > **inflammability** *n*

inflammation *n* **1** the reaction of living tissue to injury or infection, characterized by heat, redness, swelling, and pain **2** an inflaming or being inflamed

inflammatory *adj* **1** likely to provoke anger **2** characterized by or caused by inflammation

inflatable *adj* **1** capable of being inflated ▸ *n* **2** a plastic or rubber object which can be inflated

inflate *vb* **-flating, -flated 1** to expand or cause to expand by filling with gas or air **2** to give an impression of greater importance than is justified: *something to inflate their self-esteem* **3** to cause or undergo economic inflation

> **inflate** *vb* **1** = blow up, pump up, swell, dilate, distend, bloat, puff up or out; ≠ deflate **2** = increase, expand, enlarge; ≠ diminish

inflation *n* **1** an inflating or being inflated **2** *econ* a progressive increase in the general level of prices brought about by an increase in the amount of money in circulation or by increases in costs **3** *informal* the rate of increase of prices > **inflationary** *adj*

> **inflation** *n* **1** = increase, expansion, extension, swelling, escalation, enlargement

inflection *or* **inflexion** *n* **1** change in the pitch of the voice **2** *grammar* a change in the form of a word, signalling change in such grammatical functions as tense or number **3** an angle or bend **4** an inflecting or being inflected **5** *maths* a change in curvature from concave to convex or vice versa > **inflectional** *or* **inflexional** *adj*

inflexible *adj* **1** unwilling to be persuaded; obstinate **2** (of a rule, etc.) firmly fixed: *inflexible schedules* **3** incapable of being bent: *inflexible joints* > **inflexibility** *n*

inflict *vb* **1** to impose (something unpleasant) on **2** to deliver (a blow or wound) > **infliction** *n* > **inflictor** *n*

inflict vb **1** = impose, administer, visit, apply, deliver, levy, wreak, mete or deal out

inflorescence n botany **1** the part of a plant that consists of the flower-bearing stalks **2** the arrangement of the flowers on the stalks **3** the process of flowering; blossoming

influence n **1** an effect of one person or thing on another **2** the power of a person or thing to have such an effect **3** power resulting from ability, wealth, or position **4** a person or thing with influence **5 under the influence** informal drunk ▸ vb **-encing, -enced 6** to have an effect upon (actions or events) **7** to persuade or induce > **influencer** n

influence n **2** = power, authority, pull (informal), importance, prestige, clout (informal), leverage **3** = control, power, authority, direction, command, domination, supremacy, mastery, mana (NZ) ▸ vb **6** = affect, have an effect on, have an impact on, control, concern, direct, guide, bear upon **7** = persuade, prompt, urge, induce, entice, coax, incite, instigate

influential adj having or exerting influence

influential adj = important, powerful, telling, leading, inspiring, potent, authoritative, weighty; ≠ unimportant

influenza n a highly contagious viral disease characterized by fever, muscular pains, and catarrh

influx n **1** the arrival or entry of many people or things **2** the act of flowing in

influx n **1** = arrival, rush, invasion, incursion, inundation, inrush

info n informal short for **information**

inform vb **1** to give information to; tell: he informed me that he would be free after lunch **2** to make knowledgeable (about) or familiar (with): he'll be informed of his rights **3** to give incriminating information to the police **4** to impart some essential or formative characteristic to **5** to animate or inspire > **informed** adj

inform vb **1, 2** = tell, advise, notify, instruct, enlighten, communicate to, tip someone off

informal adj **1** relaxed and friendly: an informal interview **2** appropriate to everyday life or use rather than formal occasions: informal clothes **3** (of speech or writing) appropriate to ordinary conversation rather than to formal written language > **informality** n > **informally** adv

informal adj **1** = natural, relaxed, casual, familiar, unofficial, laid-back, easy-going, colloquial; ≠ formal **2** = casual, comfortable, leisure, everyday, simple

informant n a person who gives information

information n **1** knowledge acquired in any manner; facts **2** computers **A** the meaning given to data by the way it is interpreted **B** same as **data** (sense 2)

information n **1** = facts, news, report, message, notice, knowledge, data, intelligence, drum (Austral informal), heads up

information technology n the production, storage, and communication of information using computers and electronic technology

informative adj giving useful information

informative adj = instructive, revealing, educational, forthcoming, illuminating, enlightening, chatty, communicative

informer n a person who informs to the police

infra dig adj informal beneath one's dignity

infrared adj **1** of or using rays with a wavelength just beyond the red end of the visible spectrum ▸ n **2** the infrared part of the spectrum

infrastructure n **1** the basic structure of an organization or system **2** the stock of facilities, services, and equipment in a country, including factories, roads, and schools, that are needed for it to function properly

infringe vb **-fringing, -fringed 1** to violate or break (a law or agreement) **2 infringe on** or **upon** to encroach or trespass on: the press infringed on their privacy > **infringement** n

infuriate vb **-ating, -ated** to make very angry > **infuriating** adj > **infuriatingly** adv

infuriate vb = enrage, anger, provoke, irritate, incense, madden, exasperate, rile; ≠ soothe

infuse vb **-fusing, -fused 1** to fill with (an emotion or quality) **2** to soak or be soaked in order to extract flavour

infusion n **1** the act of infusing **2** a liquid obtained by infusing

ingenious (in-jean-ee-uss) adj showing cleverness and originality: a truly ingenious invention

ingenious adj = creative, original, brilliant, clever, bright, shrewd, inventive, crafty; ≠ unimaginative

ingenue (an-jay-new) n an innocent or inexperienced young woman, esp. as a role played by an actress

ingenuity (in-jen-new-it-ee) n cleverness at inventing things

ingenuous (in-jen-new-uss) adj **1** unsophisticated and trusting **2** frank and straightforward

ingest vb to take (food or liquid) into the body > **ingestion** n

inglorious adj dishonourable or shameful

ingot n a piece of metal cast in a form suitable for storage, usually a bar

ingrained or **engrained** adj **1** (of a habit, feeling, or belief) deeply impressed or instilled

2 (of dirt) worked into or through the fibre or pores

ingratiate vb **-ating, -ated** to act in order to bring (oneself) into favour (with someone) > **ingratiating** adj

ingredient n a component of a mixture or compound, esp. in cooking

> **ingredient** n = component, part, element, feature, piece, unit, item, aspect

ingress n formal **1** the act of going or coming in **2** the right or permission to enter

ingrowing adj (esp. of a toenail) growing abnormally into the flesh > **ingrown** adj

inhabit vb to live or dwell in > **inhabitable** adj

> **inhabit** vb = live in, occupy, populate, reside in, dwell in, abide in

inhabitant n a person or animal that is a permanent resident of a particular place or region

> **inhabitant** n = occupant, resident, citizen, local, native, tenant, inmate, dweller

inhalant (in-hale-ant) n a medicinal preparation inhaled to help breathing problems

inhale vb **-haling, -haled** to breathe in (air, smoke, or vapour) > **inhalation** n

> **inhale** vb = breathe in, gasp, draw in, suck in, respire; ≠ exhale

inhaler n a container used to administer an inhalant

inherent adj existing as an inseparable part > **inherently** adv

> **inherent** adj = intrinsic, natural, essential, native, fundamental, hereditary, instinctive, innate; ≠ extraneous

inherit vb **1** to receive money, property, or a title from someone who has died **2** to receive (a characteristic) from an earlier generation by heredity **3** to receive (a position or situation) from a predecessor: he inherited a mess > **inheritor** n

> **inherit** vb **1** = be left, come into, be willed, succeed to, fall heir to

inheritance n **1** law **A** hereditary succession to an estate or title **B** the right of an heir to succeed on the death of an ancestor **2** something inherited or to be inherited **3** the act of inheriting **4** the fact of receiving characteristics from an earlier generation by heredity

> **inheritance** n **2** = legacy, heritage, bequest, birthright, patrimony

inheritance tax n (in Britain) a tax consisting of a percentage levied on the part of an inheritance that exceeds a specified allowance

inhibit vb **1** to restrain or hinder (an impulse or desire) **2** to prohibit or prevent: an attempt to inhibit nuclear proliferation **3** chem to stop, prevent, or decrease the rate of (a chemical reaction) > **inhibited** adj > **inhibitor** n

> **inhibit** vb **1** = hinder, check, frustrate, curb, restrain, constrain, obstruct, impede; ≠ further **2** = prevent, stop, frustrate; ≠ allow

inhibition n **1** psychol a feeling of fear or embarrassment that stops one from behaving naturally **2** an inhibiting or being inhibited **3** the process of stopping or retarding a chemical reaction

inhospitable adj **1** not welcoming; unfriendly **2** (of a place or climate) not easy to live in; harsh

inhuman adj **1** cruel or brutal **2** not human

inhumane adj extremely cruel or brutal

inhumanity n, pl **-ties 1** lack of kindness or compassion **2** an inhumane act

inimical adj **1** adverse or unfavourable: inimical to change **2** unfriendly or hostile

inimitable adj impossible to imitate > **inimitably** adv

iniquity n, pl **-ties 1** injustice or wickedness **2** a wicked act > **iniquitous** adj

initial adj **1** of or at the beginning ▸ n **2** the first letter of a word, esp. a person's name **3** printing a large letter set at the beginning of a chapter or work ▸ vb **-tialling, -tialled** or US **-tialing, -tialed 4** to sign with one's initials, esp. to indicate approval > **initially** adv

> **initial** adj = opening, first, earliest, beginning, primary, maiden, introductory, embryonic; ≠ final

initiate vb **-ating, -ated 1** to begin or set going: they wanted to initiate a discussion **2** to accept (new members) into a group, often through secret ceremonies **3** to teach the fundamentals of a skill or knowledge to (someone) ▸ n **4** a person who has been initiated, esp. recently **5** a beginner > **initiation** n > **initiator** n

> **initiate** vb **1** = begin, start, open, launch, kick off (informal), embark on, originate, set about **2** = introduce, admit, enlist, enrol, launch, establish, invest, recruit ▸ n **4** = novice, member, pupil, convert, amateur, newcomer, beginner, trainee

initiative n **1** a first step; a commencing move: a peace initiative **2** the right or power to initiate something: it forced local people to take the initiative **3** enterprise: the drive and initiative to create new products **4 on one's own initiative** without being prompted

> **initiative** n **2** = advantage, start, lead, upper hand **3** = enterprise, drive, energy, leadership, ambition, daring, enthusiasm, dynamism

inject vb **1** med to put (a fluid) into the body with a syringe **2** to introduce (a new element): to inject a dose of realism into the assessment > **injection** n

inject vb 1 = vaccinate, administer, inoculate 2 = introduce, bring in, insert, instil, infuse, breathe

injudicious adj showing poor judgment; unwise

injunction n 1 law a court order not to do something 2 an authoritative command > **injunctive** adj

injunction n 2 = order, ruling, command, instruction, mandate, precept, exhortation (formal)

injure vb -juring, -jured 1 to hurt physically or mentally 2 to do wrong to (a person), esp. by an injustice: the injured party 3 to damage: an opportunity to injure your reputation > **injured** adj

injure vb 1 = hurt, wound, harm, damage, smash, crush, mar, shatter, mangulate (Austral slang) 2 = undermine, damage 3 = damage, harm, ruin, wreck, spoil, impair, crool or cruel (Austral slang)

injurious adj 1 causing harm 2 abusive, slanderous, or libellous

injury n, pl -ries 1 physical hurt 2 a specific instance of this: a leg injury 3 harm done to the feelings 4 damage: inflict no injury on the wealth of the nation

injury n 1 = harm, suffering, damage, ill, hurt, misfortune, affliction 2 = wound, cut, damage, trauma (pathol), gash, lesion, laceration 3 = wrong, offence, insult, detriment, disservice

injury time n sport playing time added at the end of a match to compensate for time spent treating injured players. Also called: **stoppage time**

injustice n 1 unfairness 2 an unfair action

injustice n 1 = unfairness, discrimination, prejudice, bias, inequality, oppression, intolerance, bigotry; ≠ justice 2 = wrong, injury, crime, error, offence, sin, misdeed, transgression

ink n 1 a black or coloured liquid used for printing, writing, and drawing 2 a dark brown fluid squirted for self-concealment by an octopus or cuttlefish 3 informal a tattoo or a series of tattoos ▸ vb 4 to mark or cover with ink 5 **ink in** to arrange or confirm definitely

inkling n a vague idea or suspicion

inky adj inkier, inkiest 1 dark or black, like ink 2 stained with ink > **inkiness** n

inlaid adj 1 set in another material so that the surface is smooth, such as a design in wood 2 made in this way: an inlaid table-top

inland adj 1 of or in the interior of a country or region, away from a sea or border 2 chiefly Brit operating within a country or region; domestic: inland trade ▸ n 3 the interior of a country or region ▸ adv 4 towards or into the interior of a country or region

inland adj 1 = interior, internal, upcountry

Inland Revenue n (in New Zealand and formerly in Britain) a government department that collects major direct taxes, such as income tax

in-law n 1 a relative by marriage ▸ adj 2 (in combination) related by marriage: his brother-in-law

inlay vb -laying, -laid 1 to decorate (an article, esp. of furniture) by inserting pieces of wood, ivory, or metal so that the surfaces are smooth and flat ▸ n 2 decoration made by inlaying 3 an inlaid article 4 dentistry a filling shaped to fit a cavity

inlet n 1 a narrow strip of water extending from the sea into the land 2 a passage or valve through which a liquid or gas enters a machine

in loco parentis (par-rent-iss) in place of a parent: said of a person acting for a parent

inmate n a person who is confined to an institution such as a prison or hospital

inmost adj same as **innermost**

inn n a pub or small hotel providing food and accommodation

innards pl n informal 1 the internal organs of the body, esp. the entrails 2 the working parts of a machine

innate adj existing from birth, rather than acquired; inborn: his innate decency > **innately** adv

inner adj 1 happening or located inside or further inside: the door to the inner office 2 of the mind or spirit: her inner self 3 exclusive or private: the inner sanctum of the party secretariat 4 more profound; less apparent: the inner meaning ▸ n 5 archery A the red innermost ring on a target B a shot which hits this ring

inner adj 1 = inside, internal, interior, inward; ≠ outer 4 = hidden, deep, secret, underlying, obscure, repressed, unrevealed; ≠ obvious

inner city n the parts of a city in or near its centre, where there are often social and economic problems

innermost adj 1 most intimate or private: innermost secrets 2 furthest within

innings n 1 cricket A the batting turn of a player or team B the runs scored during such a turn 2 a period of opportunity or action

innkeeper n an owner or manager of an inn

innocence n the quality or state of being innocent

innocence n = naiveté, simplicity, inexperience, credulity, gullibility, ingenuousness, artlessness, unworldliness; ≠ worldliness

innocent adj 1 not guilty of a particular crime 2 without experience of evil 3 harmless or innocuous 4 **innocent of** without or lacking:

innocent of prejudice ▸ *n* **5** an innocent person, esp. a young child or a naive adult > **innocently** *adv*

> **innocent** *adj* **1** = not guilty, in the clear, blameless, clean, honest, uninvolved, irreproachable, guiltless; ≠ guilty **3** = harmless, innocuous, inoffensive, well-meant, unobjectionable, well-intentioned

innocuous *adj* having no adverse or harmful effect

innovate *vb* **-vating, -vated** to introduce new ideas or methods > **innovative** *or* **innovatory** *adj* > **innovator** *n*

innovation *n* **1** something newly introduced, such as a new method or device **2** the act of innovating

> **innovation** *n* = change, revolution, departure, introduction, variation, transformation, upheaval, alteration

innuendo *n, pl* **-dos** *or* **-does** an indirect or subtle reference to something rude or unpleasant

innumerable *adj* too many to be counted > **innumerably** *adv*

innumerate *adj* having no understanding of mathematics or science > **innumeracy** *n*

inoculate *vb* **-lating, -lated 1** to protect against disease by injecting with a vaccine **2** to introduce (microorganisms, esp. bacteria) into (a culture medium) > **inoculation** *n*

inoperable *adj surgery* unable to be safely operated on: *an inoperable tumour*

inopportune *adj* badly timed or inappropriate

inordinate *adj* **1** excessive: *an inordinate amount of time spent arguing* **2** unrestrained, as in behaviour or emotion: *inordinate anger* > **inordinately** *adv*

inorganic *adj* **1** not having the structure or characteristics of living organisms **2** *chem* of or denoting chemical compounds that do not contain carbon **3** not resulting from or produced by growth; artificial: *inorganic fertilizers*

inpatient *n* a patient who stays in a hospital for treatment

input *n* **1** resources, such as money, labour, or power, put into a project **2** *computers* the data fed into a computer ▸ *vb* **-putting, -put 3** to enter (data) in a computer

inquest *n* **1** an official inquiry into an unexplained, sudden, or violent death, held by a coroner **2** *informal* an investigation or discussion

> **inquest** *n* **1** = inquiry, investigation, probe, inquisition

inquire *or* **enquire** *vb* **-quiring, -quired 1** to seek information (about) **2 inquire after** to ask about the health or progress of (a person) **3 inquire into** to make an investigation **4 inquire of** to ask (a person) for information: *I'll inquire of my aunt when she is coming* > **inquirer** *or* **enquirer** *n*

inquire *or* **enquire** *vb* **1** = ask, question, query, quiz **3 inquire into** = investigate, study, examine, research, explore, look into, probe into, make inquiries into

inquiry *or* **enquiry** *n, pl* **-ries 1** a question **2** an investigation

> **inquiry** *or* **enquiry** *n* **1** = question, query, investigation **2** = investigation, study, review, survey, examination, probe, inspection, exploration

inquisition *n* **1** a thorough investigation **2** *archaic* a judicial or official inquiry > **inquisitional** *adj*

Inquisition *n history* an organization within the Catholic Church (1232–1820) for suppressing heresy

inquisitive *adj* **1** excessively curious about other people's business **2** eager to learn > **inquisitively** *adv* > **inquisitiveness** *n*

inquisitor *n* **1** a person who inquires, esp. deeply or ruthlessly **2 Inquisitor** an officer of the Inquisition

inquisitorial *adj* **1** of or like an inquisition or an inquisitor **2** offensively curious > **inquisitorially** *adv*

inquorate *adj* without enough people present to make a quorum

inroads *pl n* **make inroads into** to start affecting or reducing: *my gambling has made great inroads into my savings*

insane *adj* **1** of unsound mind **2** stupidly irresponsible: *acting on an insane impulse* > **insanely** *adv*

> **insane** *adj* **2** = stupid, foolish, daft (*informal*), irresponsible, irrational, senseless, preposterous, impractical; ≠ reasonable

insanitary *adj* dirty or unhealthy

insanity *n, pl* **-ties 1** the state of being insane **2** stupidity

insatiable (in-**saysh**-a-bl) *adj* impossible to satisfy > **insatiability** *n* > **insatiably** *adv*

inscribe *vb* **-scribing, -scribed 1** to mark or engrave with (words, symbols, or letters) **2** to write one's name, and sometimes a brief dedication, on (a book) before giving to someone **3** to enter (a name) on a list **4** *geom* to draw (a geometric construction) inside another construction so that the two are in contact at as many points as possible but do not intersect

inscription *n* **1** something inscribed, esp. words carved or engraved on a coin, tomb, or ring **2** a signature or brief dedication in a book or on a work of art

inscrutable *adj* mysterious or enigmatic > **inscrutability** *n*

insect *n* **1** a small animal that has six legs and usually has wings, such as an ant, fly, or butterfly **2** (loosely) any similar invertebrate, such as a spider, tick, or centipede

insect n **2** = bug, creepy-crawly (Brit informal), gogga (S African informal)

insecticide n a substance used to destroy insects

insecure adj **1** anxious or uncertain **2** not adequately protected: low-paid or insecure employment **3** unstable or shaky > **insecurity** n

insecure adj **1** = unconfident, worried, anxious, afraid, shy, uncertain, unsure, timid; ≠ confident **2** = unsafe, exposed, vulnerable, wide-open, unprotected, defenceless, unguarded; ≠ safe

inseminate vb **-nating, -nated** to impregnate (a female) with semen > **insemination** n

insensate adj **1** lacking sensation or consciousness **2** insensitive or unfeeling **3** foolish

insensible adj **1** unconscious **2** without feeling **3** imperceptible **4** **insensible of** or **to** unaware of or indifferent to: insensible to suffering > **insensibility** n

insensitive adj unaware of or ignoring other people's feelings > **insensitivity** n

inseparable adj **1** constantly together because of mutual liking: they became inseparable companions **2** too closely connected to be separated > **inseparably** adv

insert vb **1** to place or fit (something) inside something else **2** to introduce (a clause or comment) into text or a speech ▸ n **3** something inserted, esp. an advertisement in between the pages of a magazine

insert vb **1** = put, place, position, slip, slide, slot, thrust, stick in

insertion n **1** the act of inserting **2** something inserted, such as an advertisement in a newspaper

inset vb **-setting, -set 1** to place in or within; insert ▸ n **2** something inserted **3** printing a small map or diagram set within the borders of a larger one ▸ adj **4** decorated with something inserted

inshore adj **1** in or on the water, but close to the shore: inshore fishermen ▸ adv, adj **2** towards the shore from the water: the boat was forced inshore; a strong wind blowing inshore

inside prep **1** in or to the interior of: a bomb had gone off inside the parliament building **2** in a period of time less than: they took the lead inside seven minutes ▸ adj **3** on or of the inside: an article on the paper's inside pages **4** by or from someone within an organization, esp. illicitly: inside information **5** of or being the lane in a road which is nearer the side than other lanes going in the same direction: all the lorries were in the inside lane ▸ adv **6** on, in, or to the inside; indoors: when the rain started we took our drinks inside **7** Brit, Austral & NZ slang in or into prison ▸ n **8** the inner side, surface, or part of something **9** **inside out** with

the inside facing outwards **10** **know inside out** to know thoroughly

inside adj **3** = inner, internal, interior, inward; ≠ outside **4** = confidential, private, secret, internal, exclusive, restricted, privileged, classified ▸ adv **6** = indoors, in, within, under cover ▸ n **8** = interior, contents, core, nucleus

insider n a member of a group or organization who therefore has exclusive information about it

insidious adj working in a subtle or apparently harmless way, but nevertheless dangerous or deadly: an insidious virus > **insidiously** adv > **insidiousness** n

insight n **1** a penetrating understanding, as of a complex situation or problem **2** the ability to perceive clearly or deeply the inner nature of things

insight n **1** = perception, understanding, sense, knowledge, vision, judgment, awareness, grasp

insignia (in-sig-nee-a) n, pl **-nias** or **-nia** a badge or emblem of membership, office, or honour

insignificant adj having little or no importance > **insignificance** n

insignificant adj = unimportant, minor, irrelevant, petty, trivial, meaningless, trifling, paltry; ≠ important

insincere adj pretending what one does not feel > **insincerely** adv > **insincerity** n

insinuate vb **-ating, -ated 1** to suggest indirectly by allusion, hints, or innuendo **2** to get (someone, esp. oneself) into a position by gradual manoeuvres: she insinuated herself into the conversation

insinuation n **1** an indirect or devious hint or suggestion **2** an act or the practice of insinuating

insipid adj **1** dull and boring **2** lacking flavour > **insipidity** n

insist vb (often foll. by on or upon) **1** to make a determined demand (for): he insisted on his rights **2** to express a convinced belief (in) or assertion (of): she insisted that she had been given permission

insist vb **1** = demand, order, require, command, dictate, entreat **2** = assert, state, maintain, claim, declare, repeat, vow, swear

insistent adj **1** making continual and persistent demands **2** demanding attention: the chirruping of an insistent bird > **insistence** n > **insistently** adv

in situ adv, adj in the original position

in so far as or **insofar as** prep to the degree or extent that

insole n **1** the inner sole of a shoe or boot **2** a loose inner sole used to give extra warmth or to make a shoe fit

insolent *adj* rude and disrespectful › **insolence** *n* › **insolently** *adv*

insoluble *adj* **1** impossible to solve **2** not able to be dissolved › **insolubility** *n*

insolvent *adj* **1** unable to pay one's debts ▸ *n* **2** a person who is insolvent › **insolvency** *n*

insomnia *n* inability to sleep › **insomniac** *n, adj*

insouciant *adj* carefree or unconcerned › **insouciance** *n*

inspect *vb* **1** to examine closely, esp. for faults or errors **2** to examine officially › **inspection** *n*

> **inspect** *vb* **1** = examine, check, look at, view, survey, look over, scrutinize, go over *or* through **2** = check, examine, investigate, look at, survey, vet, look over, go over *or* through

inspector *n* **1** an official who checks that things or places meet certain regulations and standards **2** a police officer ranking below a superintendent and above a sergeant

> **inspector** *n* **1** = examiner, investigator, supervisor, monitor, superintendent, auditor, censor, surveyor

inspiration *n* **1** stimulation of the mind or feelings to activity or creativity **2** a person or thing that causes this state **3** an inspired idea or action › **inspirational** *adj*

> **inspiration** *n* **1** = imagination, creativity, ingenuity, insight, originality, inventiveness, cleverness **2** = influence, spur, stimulus, muse; ≠ deterrent

inspire *vb* **-spiring, -spired** **1** to stimulate (a person) to activity or creativity **2** to arouse (an emotion or a reaction): *he inspires confidence*

> **inspire** *vb* **1** = motivate, stimulate, encourage, influence, spur, animate, enliven, galvanize; ≠ discourage

instability *n* lack of steadiness or reliability

> **instability** *n* = uncertainty, insecurity, vulnerability, volatility, unpredictability, fluctuation, impermanence, unsteadiness; ≠ stability

install *vb* **1** to put in and prepare (equipment) for use **2** to place (a person) formally in a position or rank **3** to settle (a person, esp. oneself) in a position or state: *Tony installed himself in an armchair*

> **install** *vb* **1** = set up, put in, place, position, station, establish, lay, fix **2** = institute, establish, introduce, invest, ordain, inaugurate, induct **3** = settle, position, plant, establish, lodge, ensconce

installation *n* **1** installing **2** equipment that has been installed **3** a place containing equipment for a particular purpose: *radar installation*

> **installation** *n* **1** = setting up, fitting, instalment, placing, positioning, establishment

instalment *or US* **installment** *n* **1** one of the portions into which a debt is divided for payment at regular intervals **2** a portion of something that is issued, broadcast, or published in parts

> **instalment** *or* **installment** *n* **1** = payment, repayment, part payment **2** = part, section, chapter, episode, portion, division

instance *n* **1** a case or particular example **2** urgent request or order: *at the instance of* **3 for instance** as an example **4 in the first instance** in the first place; initially ▸ *vb* **-stancing, -stanced** **5** to mention as an example

> **instance** *n* **1** = example, case, occurrence, occasion, sample, illustration

instant *n* **1** a very brief time; moment **2** a particular moment: *at the same instant* ▸ *adj* **3** immediate **4** (of foods) able to be prepared very quickly and easily: *instant coffee* **5** urgent or pressing **6** of the present month: *a letter of the 7th instant*

> **instant** *n* **1** = moment, second, flash, split second, jiffy (*informal*), trice, twinkling of an eye (*informal*) **2** = time, point, hour, moment, stage, occasion, phase, juncture ▸ *adj* **3** = immediate, prompt, instantaneous, direct, quick, on-the-spot, split-second **4** = ready-made, fast, convenience, ready-mixed, ready-cooked, precooked

instantaneous *adj* happening at once: *the applause was instantaneous* › **instantaneously** *adv*

instantly *adv* immediately

> **instantly** *adv* = immediately, at once, straight away, now, directly, right away, instantaneously, this minute

instead *adv* **1** as a replacement or substitute for the person or thing mentioned **2 instead of** in place of or as an alternative to

> **instead** *adv* **1** = rather, alternatively, preferably, in preference, in lieu, on second thoughts **2 instead of** = in place of, rather than, in preference to, in lieu of, in contrast with

instep *n* **1** the middle part of the foot forming the arch between the ankle and toes **2** the part of a shoe or stocking covering this

instigate *vb* **-gating, -gated** **1** to cause to happen: *to instigate rebellion* **2** to urge on to some action › **instigation** *n* › **instigator** *n*

instil *or US* **instill** *vb* **-stilling, -stilled** **1** to introduce (an idea or feeling) gradually in someone's mind **2** *rare* to pour in or inject drop by drop › **instillation** *n* › **instiller** *n*

instinct *n* **1** the inborn tendency to behave in a particular way without the need for thought: *maternal instinct* **2** natural reaction: *my first instinct was to get out of the car* **3** intuition: *Mr Barr's mother said she knew by instinct that her son was safe*

> **instinct** *n* **1** = natural inclination, talent, tendency, faculty, inclination, knack, predisposition, proclivity (*formal*) **3** = intuition, impulse

instinctive *or* **instinctual** *adj* done or happening without any logical thought: *an instinctive understanding of people* > **instinctively** *or* **instinctually** *adv*

> **instinctive** *or* **instinctual** *adj* = natural, inborn, automatic, unconscious, inherent, spontaneous, reflex, innate; ≠ acquired

institute *n* **1** an organization set up for a specific purpose, esp. research or teaching **2** the building where such an organization is situated **3** a rule, custom, or precedent ▸ *vb* **-tuting, -tuted** **4** to start or establish **5** to install in a position or office

> **institute** *n* **1** = establishment, body, centre, school, university, society, association, college ▸ *vb* **4** = establish, start, found, launch, set up, introduce, fix, organize; ≠ end

institution *n* **1** a large important organization such as a university or bank **2** an organization providing residential care for people with special needs **3** an established custom, law, or principle: *the institution of marriage* **4** *informal* a well-established person or feature: *the programme has became an institution* **5** an instituting or being instituted

> **institution** *n* **1** = establishment, body, centre, school, university, society, association, college **3** = custom, practice, tradition, law, rule, procedure, convention, ritual

institutional *adj* **1** of or relating to an institution: *institutional care* **2** dull, routine, and uniform: *institutional meals* > **institutionalism** *n*

> **institutional** *adj* **1** = conventional, accepted, established, formal, routine, orthodox, procedural

institutionalize *or* **-lise** *vb* **-lizing, -lized** *or* **-lising, -lised** **1** (*often passive*) to subject (a person) to institutional life, often causing apathy and dependence on routine **2** to make or become an institution: *institutionalized religion* **3** to place in an institution

instruct *vb* **1** to order to do something **2** to teach (someone) how to do something **3** to brief (a solicitor or barrister)

> **instruct** *vb* **1** = order, tell, direct, charge (*formal*), bid, command, mandate, enjoin **2** = teach, school, train, coach, educate, drill, tutor

instruction *n* **1** a direction or order **2** the process or act of teaching > **instructional** *adj*

> **instruction** *n* **1** = order, ruling, command, rule, demand, regulation, dictate, decree **2** = teaching, schooling, training, grounding, education, coaching, lesson(s), guidance

instructive *adj* informative or helpful

instructor *n* **1** a person who teaches something **2** *US & Canad* a college teacher ranking below assistant professor

> **instructor** *n* **1** = teacher, coach, guide, adviser, trainer, demonstrator, tutor, mentor

instrument *n* **1** a tool or implement, esp. one used for precision work **2** *music* any of various devices that can be played to produce musical sounds **3** a measuring device to show height, speed, etc.: *the pilot's eyes never left his instruments* **4** *informal*: a person used by another to gain an end **5** an important factor in something: *her evidence was an instrument in his arrest* **6** a formal legal document

> **instrument** *n* **1** = tool, device, implement, mechanism, appliance, apparatus, gadget, contraption (*informal*) **5** = agent, means, medium, agency (*old-fashioned*), vehicle, mechanism, organ

instrumental *adj* **1** helping to cause **2** played by or composed for musical instruments **3** of or done with an instrument: *instrumental error*

> **instrumental** *adj* **1** = active, involved, influential, useful, helpful, contributory

instrumentalist *n* a person who plays a musical instrument

instrumentation *n* **1** a set of instruments in a car, etc. **2** the arrangement of music for instruments **3** the list of instruments needed for a piece of music

insubordinate *adj* not submissive to authority > **insubordination** *n*

insufferable *adj* unbearable > **insufferably** *adv*

insular *adj* **1** not open to change or new ideas: *theatre tradition become rather insular* **2** of or like an island > **insularity** *n*

insulate *vb* **-lating, -lated** **1** to prevent or reduce the transfer of electricity, heat, or sound by surrounding or lining with a nonconducting material **2** to isolate or set apart > **insulator** *n*

> **insulate** *vb* **2** = isolate, protect, screen, defend, shelter, shield, cut off, cushion

insulation *n* **1** material used to insulate something **2** the act of insulating

insulin (in-syoo-lin) *n* a hormone produced in the pancreas which controls the amount of sugar in the blood

insult *vb* **1** to treat or speak to rudely: *they insulted us and even threatened to kill us* ▸ *n* **2** an offensive remark or action **3** a person or thing producing the effect of an insult: *their explanation is an insult to our intelligence*

> **insult** *vb* = offend, abuse, wound, slight, put down, snub, malign, affront; ≠ praise ▸ *n* **2** = jibe, slight, put-down, abuse, snub, barb, affront, abusive remark **3** = offence, slight, snub, slur, affront, slap in the face (*informal*), kick in the teeth (*informal*), insolence

insuperable *adj* impossible to overcome; insurmountable > **insuperability** *n*

insupportable *adj* **1** impossible to tolerate **2** incapable of being upheld or justified: *an insupportable accusation*

insurance *n* **1** the agreement by which one makes regular payments to a company who pay an agreed sum if damage, loss, or death occurs **2** the money paid for insurance or by an insurance company **3** a means of protection: *sensible insurance against heart attacks*

> **insurance** *n* **1** = assurance, cover, security, protection, safeguard, indemnity **3** = protection, security, guarantee, shelter, safeguard, warranty

insurance policy *n* a contract of insurance

insure *vb* **-suring, -sured 1** to guarantee or protect (against risk or loss) **2** (often foll. by *against*) to issue (a person) with an insurance policy or take out an insurance policy (on): *the players were insured against accidents* **3** *chiefly US* same as **ensure** > **insurable** *adj* > **insurability** *n*

> **insure** *vb* **1** = assure, cover, protect, guarantee, warrant, underwrite, indemnify **2** = protect, cover, safeguard

insurgent *adj* **1** rebellious or in revolt against an established authority ▸ *n* **2** a person who takes part in a rebellion > **insurgency** *n*

insurmountable *adj* impossible to overcome: *insurmountable problems*

insurrection *n* the act of rebelling against an established authority > **insurrectionist** *n*, *adj*

intact *adj* not changed or damaged in any way

> **intact** *adj* = undamaged, whole, complete, sound, perfect, entire, unscathed, unbroken; ≠ damaged

intaglio (in-tah-lee-oh) *n, pl* **-lios** *or* **-li 1** a seal or gem decorated with an engraved design **2** an engraved design > **intagliated** *adj*

intake *n* **1** a thing or a quantity taken in: *an intake of students* **2** the act of taking in **3** the opening through which fluid or gas enters a pipe or engine

intangible *adj* **1** difficult for the mind to grasp: *intangible ideas* **2** incapable of being felt by touch > **intangibility** *n*

integer *n* any positive or negative whole number or zero, as opposed to a number with fractions or decimals

integral *adj* **1** being an essential part of a whole **2** whole or complete **3** *maths* ▲ of or involving an integral ▪ involving or being an integer ▸ *n* **4** *maths* the sum of a large number of minute quantities, summed either between stated limits (**definite integral**) or in the absence of limits (**indefinite integral**)

> **integral** *adj* **1** = essential, basic, fundamental, necessary, component, constituent, indispensable, intrinsic; ≠ inessential

integrate *vb* **-grating, -grated 1** to make or be made into a whole **2** to amalgamate (an ethnic or a religious group) with an existing community **3** to designate (an institution) for use by all ethnicities or groups **4** *maths* to determine the integral of a function or variable > **integration** *n*

> **integrate** *vb* **1** = join, unite, combine, blend, incorporate, merge, fuse, assimilate; ≠ separate

integrated circuit *n* a tiny electronic circuit

integrity *n* **1** honesty **2** the quality of being whole or united: *respect for a state's territorial integrity* **3** the quality of being unharmed or sound: *the integrity of the cell membrane*

> **integrity** *n* **1** = honesty, principle, honour, virtue, goodness, morality, purity, probity (*formal*); ≠ dishonesty **2** = unity, unification, cohesion, coherence, wholeness, soundness, completeness

intel *n informal* information collected by the military about the plans and movements of an enemy

intellect *n* **1** the ability to understand, think, and reason **2** a particular person's mind or intelligence, esp. a brilliant one: *his intellect is wasted on that job* **3** *informal* a person who has a brilliant mind

> **intellect** *n* **1** = intelligence, mind, reason, understanding, sense, brains (*informal*), judgment

intellectual *adj* **1** of, involving, or appealing to the intellect: *intellectual literature* **2** clever or intelligent ▸ *n* **3** a person who has a highly developed intellect > **intellectuality** *n* > **intellectually** *adv*

> **intellectual** *adj* **2** = scholarly, learned, academic, lettered, intelligent, cerebral, erudite, scholastic; ≠ stupid ▸ *n* = academic, expert, genius, thinker, master, mastermind, maestro, highbrow, fundi (*S African*), acca (*Austral slang*)

intelligence *n* **1** the ability to understand, learn, and think things out quickly **2** the collection of secret information, esp. for military purposes **3** a group or department collecting military information **4** *old-fashioned* news or information

intelligence *n* **1** = intellect, understanding, brains (*informal*), sense, knowledge, judgment, wit, perception; ≠ stupidity **4** = information, news, facts, report, findings, knowledge, data, notification, heads up; ≠ misinformation

intelligent *adj* **1** having or showing intelligence: *an intelligent child; an intelligent guess* **2** (of a computerized device) able to initiate or modify action in the light of ongoing events > **intelligently** *adv*

intelligent *adj* **1** = clever, bright, smart, sharp, enlightened, knowledgeable, well-informed, brainy (*informal*); ≠ stupid

intelligent design *n* a theory that rejects the theory of natural selection, arguing for an intelligent cause in the form of a creator
intelligentsia *n* **the intelligentsia** the educated or intellectual people in a society
intelligible *adj* able to be understood > **intelligibility** *n*
intemperate *adj* **1** unrestrained or uncontrolled: *intemperate remarks* **2** drinking alcohol too much or too often **3** extreme or severe: *an intemperate climate* > **intemperance** *n*
intend *vb* **1** to propose or plan (something or to do something) **2** to have as one's purpose **3** to mean to express or indicate: *no criticism was intended* **4** (often foll. by *for*) to design or destine (for a certain purpose or person): *the plane was never intended for combat*

intend *vb* **1, 2** = plan, mean, aim, propose, purpose, have in mind *or* view

intense *adj* **1** of very great force, strength, degree, or amount: *intense heat* **2** characterized by deep or forceful feelings: *an intense person* > **intensely** *adv* > **intenseness** *n*

intense *adj* **1** = extreme, great, severe, fierce, deep, powerful, supreme, acute; ≠ mild **2** = passionate, emotional, fierce, heightened, ardent, fanatical, fervent, heartfelt; ≠ indifferent

intensify *vb* **-fies, -fying, -fied** to make or become intense or more intense > **intensification** *n*

intensify *vb* = increase, raise, add to, strengthen, reinforce, widen, heighten, sharpen; ≠ decrease

intensity *n, pl* **-ties 1** the state or quality of being intense **2** extreme force, degree, or amount **3** *physics* the amount or degree of strength of electricity, heat, light, or sound per unit area of volume

intensity *n* **1** = passion, emotion, fervour, force, strength, fanaticism, ardour, vehemence **2** = force, strength, fierceness

intensive *adj* **1** of or needing concentrated effort or resources: *intensive training* **2** using one specified factor more than others: *labour-intensive* **3** *agriculture* designed to increase production from a particular area: *intensive farming* **4** *grammar* (of a word) giving emphasis, for example, *very* in *the very same* > **intensively** *adv* > **intensiveness** *n*

intensive *adj* **1** = concentrated, thorough, exhaustive, full, demanding, detailed, complete, serious

intent *n* **1** something that is intended **2** *law* the will or purpose to commit a crime: *loitering with intent* **3 to all intents and purposes** in almost every respect; virtually ▸ *adj* **4** having one's attention firmly fixed: *an intent look* **5 intent on** *or* **upon** strongly resolved on: *intent on winning the election* > **intently** *adv* > **intentness** *n*

intent *n* **1** = intention, aim, purpose, meaning, end, plan, goal, design; ≠ chance ▸ *adj* **4** = absorbed, intense, fascinated, preoccupied, enthralled, attentive, watchful, engrossed; ≠ indifferent

intention *n* something intended; a plan, idea, or purpose: *he had no intention of resigning*

intention *n* = aim, plan, idea, goal, end, design, target, wish

intentional *adj* done on purpose > **intentionally** *adv*
inter (in-ter) *vb* **-terring, -terred** to bury (a corpse)

inter *vb* = bury, lay to rest, entomb, consign to the grave

inter- *prefix* **1** between or among: *international* **2** together, mutually, or reciprocally: *interdependent*
interact *vb* to act on or in close relation with each other > **interaction** *n* > **interactive** *adj*
interbreed *vb* **-breeding, -bred 1** to breed within a related group so as to produce particular characteristics in the offspring **2** same as **crossbreed** (sense 1)
intercede *vb* **-ceding, -ceded 1** to plead in favour of **2** to act as a mediator in order to end a disagreement: *a police officer was watching the beatings without interceding*
intercept *vb* **1** to stop or seize on the way from one place to another **2** *maths* to mark off or include (part of a line, curve, plane, or surface) between two points or lines ▸ *n* **3** *maths* **A** a point at which two figures intersect **B** the distance from the origin to the point at which a line, curve, or surface cuts a coordinate axis > **interception** *n* > **interceptor** *n*

intercept *vb* **1** = catch, stop, block, seize, cut off, interrupt, head off, obstruct

intercession *n* **1** the act of interceding **2** a prayer offered to God on behalf of others > **intercessor** *n*

interchange *vb* **-changing, -changed 1** to change places or cause to change places ▸ *n* **2** the act of interchanging **3** a motorway junction of interconnecting roads and bridges designed to prevent streams of traffic crossing one another › **interchangeable** *adj* › **interchangeably** *adv*

intercom *n* an internal communication system with loudspeakers

intercontinental *adj* travelling between or linking continents

intercourse *n* **1** the act of having sex **2** communication or dealings between individuals or groups

> **intercourse** *n* **1** = sexual intercourse, sex (*informal*), copulation (*formal*) **2** = contact, communication, commerce (*literary*), dealings

interdict *n* **1** *law* an official prohibition or restraint **2** *RC Church* the exclusion of a person or place from certain sacraments, although not from communion ▸ *vb* **3** to prohibit or forbid › **interdiction** *n* › **interdictory** *adj*

interdisciplinary *adj* involving more than one branch of learning

interest *n* **1** curiosity or concern about something or someone **2** the power of causing this: *to have great interest* **3** something in which one is interested; a hobby or pursuit **4** (*often pl*) advantage: *in one's own interests* **5** money paid for the use of credit or borrowed money: *she borrowed money at 25 per cent interest* **6** (*often pl*) a right, share, or claim, esp. in a business or property **7** (*often pl*) a group of people with common aims: *foreign interests* ▸ *vb* **8** to arouse the curiosity or concern of **9** to cause to become interested or involved in something

> **interest** *n* **3** = hobby, activity, pursuit, entertainment, recreation, amusement, preoccupation, diversion **4** = advantage, good, benefit, profit **6** = stake, investment ▸ *vb* = arouse your curiosity, fascinate, attract, grip, entertain, intrigue, divert, captivate; ≠ bore

interested *adj* **1** showing or having interest **2** involved in or affected by: *a consultation paper sent to interested parties*

> **interested** *adj* **1** = curious, attracted, excited, drawn, keen, gripped, fascinated, captivated; ≠ uninterested **2** = involved, concerned, affected, implicated

interesting *adj* causing interest › **interestingly** *adv*

> **interesting** *adj* = intriguing, absorbing, appealing, attractive, engaging, gripping, entrancing, stimulating; ≠ uninteresting

interface *n* **1** an area where two things interact or link: *the interface between Islamic culture and Western modernity* **2** an electrical circuit linking one device, esp. a computer, with another **3** the way that a piece of computer software appears to users, esp. in terms of being easy or difficult to operate **4** *physics & chem* a surface that forms the boundary between two liquids or chemical phases that cannot be mixed ▸ *vb* **-facing, -faced 5** to connect or be connected with by interface › **interfacial** *adj*

> **interface** *n* **1** = connection, link, boundary, border, frontier

interfaith *adj* relating to, between, or involving different religions

interfere *vb* **-fering, -fered 1** to try to influence other people's affairs where one is not involved or wanted **2** *physics* to produce or cause to produce interference **3 interfere with A** to clash with or hinder: *I try not to let personal feelings interfere with my work* **B** *Brit, Austral & NZ euphemistic* to abuse sexually › **interfering** *adj*

> **interfere** *vb* **1** = meddle, intervene, intrude, butt in, tamper, pry, encroach, stick your oar in (*informal*) **3A interfere with something or someone** = conflict with, check, clash, handicap, hamper, disrupt, inhibit, thwart

interference *n* **1** the act of interfering **2** any undesired signal that interferes with the reception of radio waves **3** *physics* the meeting of two waves which reinforce or neutralize each other depending on whether they are in or out of phase

> **interference** *n* **1** = intrusion, intervention, meddling, opposition, conflict, obstruction, prying

interferon *n* *biochem* a protein made by cells that stops the development of an invading virus

interim *adj* **1** temporary or provisional: *an interim government* ▸ *n* **2 in the interim** during the intervening time

> **interim** *adj* = temporary, provisional, makeshift, acting, caretaker, improvised, stopgap

interior *n* **1** a part or region that is on the inside: *the interior of the earth* **2** the inside of a building or room, with respect to design and decoration **3** the central area of a country or continent, furthest from the sea **4** a picture of the inside of a room or building ▸ *adj* **5** of, situated on, or suitable for the inside **6** mental or spiritual: *interior development* **7** coming or acting from within **8** of a nation's domestic affairs

> **interior** *n* **1** = inside, centre, heart, middle, depths, core, nucleus ▸ *adj* **5,7** = inside, internal, inner; ≠ exterior **6** = mental, emotional, psychological, private, personal, secret, hidden, spiritual

interject *vb* to make (a remark) suddenly or as an interruption

interjection *n* a word or phrase which is used on its own and which expresses sudden emotion

interlace *vb* **-lacing, -laced** to join by lacing or weaving together: *interlaced fingers*

interlink *vb* to connect together

interlock *vb* **1** to join or be joined firmly together ▶ *n* **2** a device used to prevent a mechanism from operating independently or unsafely

interlocutor (in-ter-**lock**-yew-ter) *n formal* a person who takes part in a conversation

interloper (in-ter-**lope**-er) *n* a person in a place or situation where he or she has no right to be

interlude *n* **1** a period of time or different activity between longer periods or events **2 A** a pause between the acts of a play **B** a brief piece of music or other entertainment performed during this pause

intermarry *vb* **-ries, -rying, -ried 1** (of different ethnicities, religions, or social groups) to become connected by marriage **2** to marry within one's own family or tribe
› **intermarriage** *n*

intermediary *n, pl* **-aries 1** a person who tries to bring about agreement between others **2** a messenger ▶ *adj* **3** acting as an intermediary **4** intermediate

> **intermediary** *n* **1** = mediator, agent, middleman, broker, go-between

intermediate *adj* **1** occurring between two points or extremes **2** (of a class, course, etc.) suitable for learners with some level of skill or competence ▶ *n* **3** something intermediate **4** *chem* a substance formed between the first and final stages of a chemical process
› **intermediation** *n*

> **intermediate** *adj* **1** = middle, mid, halfway, in-between (*informal*), midway, intervening, transitional, median

interment *n* a burial

intermezzo (in-ter-**met**-so) *n, pl* **-zos** *or* **-zi 1** a short piece of instrumental music performed between the acts of a play or opera **2 A** a short composition between two longer movements in an extended musical work **B** a similar composition intended for independent performance

interminable *adj* seemingly endless because boring: *an interminable rambling anecdote*
› **interminably** *adv*

intermingle *vb* **-gling, -gled** to mix together

intermission *n* an interval between parts of a play, film, etc.

intermittent *adj* occurring at intervals
› **intermittently** *adv*

intern *vb* **1** to imprison, esp. during wartime ▶ *n* **2** a student or recent graduate receiving practical training in a working environment **3** *chiefly US* a trainee doctor in a hospital
› **internment** *n*

internal *adj* **1** of, situated on, or suitable for the inside **2** *anatomy* affecting or relating to the inside of the body: *internal bleeding* **3** of a nation's domestic affairs: *internal politics* **4** coming or acting from within an organization: *an internal reorganization* **5** spiritual or mental: *internal conflict*
› **internally** *adv*

> **internal** *adj* **1** = inner, inside, interior;
> ≠ external **3** = domestic, home, national, local, civic, in-house, intramural

internal-combustion engine *n* an engine in which power is produced by the explosion of a fuel-and-air mixture within the cylinders

international *adj* **1** of or involving two or more nations **2** controlling or legislating for several nations: *an international court* **3** available for use by all nations: *international waters* ▶ *n* **4** *sport* **A** a game or match between the national teams of different countries **B** a member of a national team › **internationally** *adv*

> **international** *adj* **1** = global, world, worldwide, universal, cosmopolitan, intercontinental

International Style *or* **Modernism** *n* a 20th-century architectural style characterized by undecorated straight forms and the use of glass, steel, and reinforced concrete

internecine *adj formal* destructive to both sides: *internecine war*

internee *n* a person who is interned

internet *n* (*sometimes cap*) a large public access computer network linked to others worldwide

> **internet** *n* **the internet** = the information superhighway, the net (*informal*), the web (*informal*), the World Wide Web, cyberspace, the cloud, blogosphere, the interweb (*facetious*), blogostream, extranet, podosphere

interplanetary *adj* of or linking planets

interplay *n* the action and reaction of things upon each other

interpolate (in-ter-**pole**-ate) *vb* **-lating, -lated 1** to insert (a comment or passage) into (a conversation or text) **2** *maths* to estimate (a value of a function) between the values already known › **interpolation** *n*

interpose *vb* **-posing, -posed 1** to place (something) between or among other things **2** to interrupt (with comments or questions) **3** to put forward so as to interrupt: *he ended the discussion by interposing a veto* › **interposition** *n*

interpret *vb* **1** to explain the meaning of **2** to work out the significance of: *his remarks were widely interpreted as a promise not to raise taxes* **3** to convey the meaning of (a poem, song, etc.) in performance **4** to act as an interpreter
› **interpretive** *adj*

interpret *vb* **1** = explain, make sense of, decode, decipher, elucidate **2** = take, understand, explain, construe **3** = portray, present, perform, render, depict, enact, act out **4** = translate, transliterate

interpretation *n* **1** the act or result of interpreting or explaining **2** the particular way in which a performer expresses his or her view of a composition: *an interpretation of Mahler's fourth symphony* **3** explanation, as of a historical site, provided by the use of original objects, visual display material, etc.

interpretation *n* **1** = explanation, analysis, exposition, elucidation **2** = performance, portrayal, presentation, reading, rendition

interpreter *n* **1** a person who translates orally from one language into another **2** *computers* a program that translates a statement in a source program to machine language and executes it before translating and executing the next statement

interpreter *n* **1** = translator

interregnum *n, pl* **-nums** *or* **-na** a period between the end of one ruler's reign and the beginning of the next > **interregnal** *adj*

interrogate *vb* **-gating, -gated** to question (someone) closely > **interrogation** *n* > **interrogator** *n*

interrogative (in-ter-rog-a-tiv) *adj* **1** used in asking a question: *an interrogative pronoun* **2** of or like a question: *an interrogative look* ▶ *n* **3** an interrogative word, phrase, sentence, or construction

interrupt *vb* **1** to break into (a conversation or discussion) by questions or comment **2** to stop (a process or activity) temporarily > **interrupted** *adj* > **interruptive** *adj*

interrupt *vb* **1** = intrude, disturb, intervene, interfere (with), break in, heckle, butt in, barge in (*informal*) **2** = suspend, stop, end, delay, cease, postpone, shelve, put off

interruption *n* **1** something that interrupts, such as a comment or question **2** an interval or intermission **3** the act of interrupting or the state of being interrupted

interruption *n* **2** = disruption, break, disturbance, hitch, intrusion **3** = stoppage, pause, suspension

intersect *vb* **1** (of roads or lines) to cross (each other) **2** to divide or mark off (a place, area, or surface) by passing through or across

intersection *n* **1** a point at which things intersect, esp. a road junction **2** the act of intersecting or the state of being intersected **3** *maths* **A** a point or set of points common to two or more geometric figures **B** the set of elements that are common to two sets > **intersectional** *adj*

intersex *n* **1** the condition of having both male and female characteristics **2** an individual exhibiting such characteristics

intersperse *vb* **-spersing, -spersed** **1** to scatter among, between, or on **2** to mix (something) with other things scattered here and there > **interspersion** *n*

interstellar *adj* between or among stars

interstice (in-ter-stiss) *n* (*usually pl*) **1** a small gap or crack between things **2** *physics* the space between adjacent atoms in a crystal lattice

intertwine *vb* **-twining, -twined** to twist together

interval *n* **1** the period of time between two events **2** *Brit & Austral* a short period between parts of a play, concert, etc. **3** *music* the difference of pitch between two notes **4** **at intervals** **A** now and then: *add water to the mix at intervals* **B** with a certain amount of space between: *the poles were placed at intervals of twenty metres*

interval *n* **1** = period, spell, space, stretch, pause, span **2** = break, interlude, intermission, rest, gap, pause, respite, lull

intervene *vb* **-vening, -vened** **1** (often foll. by *in*) to involve oneself in a situation, esp. to prevent conflict **2** to interrupt a conversation **3** to happen so as to stop something: *he hoped to play but a serious injury intervened* **4** to come or be among or between: *ten years had intervened since he had seen Joe*

intervene *vb* **1** = step in (*informal*), interfere, mediate, intrude, intercede, arbitrate, take a hand (*informal*) **2** = interrupt, involve yourself **3** = happen, occur, take place, follow, arise, ensue, befall, materialize

intervention *n* the act of intervening, esp. to influence or alter a situation in some way > **interventionist** *n, adj*

intervention *n* = mediation, interference, intrusion, arbitration, conciliation, agency (*old-fashioned*)

interview *n* **1** a formal discussion, esp. one in which an employer assesses a job applicant **2** a conversation in which a well-known person is asked about his or her views, career, etc., by a reporter ▶ *vb* **3** to question (someone) > **interviewee** *n* > **interviewer** *n*

interview *n* **1** = meeting **2** = audience, talk, conference, exchange, dialogue, consultation, press conference ▶ *vb* = question, interrogate, examine, investigate, pump, grill (*informal*), quiz, cross-examine

interweave *vb* **-weaving, -wove** *or* **-weaved**, **-woven** *or* **-weaved** to weave together

intestate *adj* **1** (of a person) not having made a will ▶ *n* **2** a person who dies without having made a will > **intestacy** *n*

intestine *n* the part of the alimentary canal between the stomach and the anus
>**intestinal** *adj*

intimacy *n, pl* **-cies 1** close or warm friendship **2** (*often pl*) intimate words or acts within a close relationship

> **intimacy** *n* **1** = familiarity, closeness, confidentiality; ≠ aloofness

intimate¹ *adj* **1** characterized by a close or warm personal relationship: *an intimate friend* **2** deeply personal, private, or secret **3** (of knowledge) extensive and detailed **4** *euphemistic* having sexual relations **5** having a friendly quiet atmosphere: *an intimate nightclub* ▸ *n* **6** a close friend >**intimately** *adv*

> **intimate** *adj* **1** = close, dear, loving, near, familiar, thick (*informal*), devoted, confidential; ≠ distant **2** = private, personal, confidential, special, individual, secret, exclusive; ≠ public **3** = detailed, minute, full, deep, particular, immediate, comprehensive, profound **5** = cosy, relaxed, friendly, informal, harmonious, snug, comfy (*informal*), warm ▸ *n* = friend, close friend, crony, cobber (*Austral, NZ old-fashioned, informal*), confidant *or* confidante, (constant) companion, E hoa (NZ); ≠ stranger

intimate² *vb* **-mating, -mated** *formal* **1** to make (something) known in an indirect way: *he has intimated his intention to retire* **2** to announce
>**intimation** *n*

> **intimate** *vb* **1** = suggest, indicate, hint, imply, insinuate **2** = announce, state, declare, communicate, make known

intimidate *vb* **-dating, -dated** to subdue or influence (someone) through fear
>**intimidating** *adj* >**intimidation** *n*

> **intimidate** *vb* = frighten, pressure, threaten, scare, bully, plague, hound, daunt

into *prep* **1** to the inner part of: *they went into the house* **2** to the middle of so as to be surrounded by: *into the bushes* **3** against; up against: *he drove into a wall* **4** used to indicate the result of a change: *they turned the theatre into a garage* **5** *maths* used to indicate division: *three into six is two* **6** *informal* interested in: *I'm really into healthy food*

intolerable *adj* more than can be endured
>**intolerably** *adv*

intolerant *adj* refusing to accept practices and beliefs that differ from one's own
>**intolerance** *n*

intonation *n* **1** the sound pattern produced by variations in the voice **2** the act of intoning **3** *music* the ability to play or sing in tune
>**intonational** *adj*

intone *vb* **-toning, -toned 1** to speak or recite in a monotonous tone **2** to speak with a particular tone

intoxicant *n* **1** something, such as an alcoholic drink, that causes intoxication ▸ *adj* **2** causing intoxication

intoxicate *vb* **-cating, -cated 1** (of an alcoholic drink) to make (a person) drunk **2** to stimulate or excite to a point beyond self-control
>**intoxicated** *adj* >**intoxicating** *adj*

intoxication *n* **1** the state of being drunk **2** great excitement and exhilaration

intractable *adj* **1** (of a person) difficult to influence or direct **2** (of a problem or illness) difficult to solve or cure >**intractability** *n*
>**intractably** *adv*

intranet *n* *computers* an internal network that makes use of internet technology

intransigent *adj* **1** refusing to change one's attitude ▸ *n* **2** an intransigent person, esp. in politics >**intransigence** *n*

intransitive *adj* (of a verb) not taking a direct object: *'to faint' is an intransitive verb*
>**intransitively** *adv*

intrauterine *adj* situated within the womb

intravenous (in-tra-vee-nuss) *adj anatomy* into a vein: *intravenous drug users*
>**intravenously** *adv*

intrepid *adj* fearless or bold >**intrepidity** *n*
>**intrepidly** *adv*

intricate *adj* **1** difficult to sort out: *an intricate problem* **2** full of complicated detail: *intricate Arab mosaics* >**intricacy** *n* >**intricately** *adv*

> **intricate** *adj* = complicated, involved, complex, fancy, elaborate, tangled, tortuous, convoluted; ≠ simple

intrigue *vb* **-triguing, -trigued 1** to make interested or curious: *a question which has intrigued him for years* **2** to plot secretly or dishonestly ▸ *n* **3** secret plotting **4** a secret love affair
>**intriguing** *adj* >**intriguingly** *adv*

> **intrigue** *vb* **1** = interest, fascinate, attract, rivet, titillate **2** = plot, scheme, manoeuvre, conspire, connive, machinate ▸ *n* **3** = plot, scheme, conspiracy, manoeuvre, collusion, stratagem, chicanery, wile **4** = affair, romance, intimacy, liaison, amour

intrinsic *adj* **1** essential to the real nature of a thing: *hedgerows are an intrinsic part of the countryside* **2** *anatomy* situated within or peculiar to a part: *intrinsic muscles* >**intrinsically** *adv*

introduce *vb* **-ducing, -duced 1** to present (someone) by name (to another person) **2** to present (a radio or television programme) **3** to present for consideration or approval: *he introduced the bill to Parliament in 1967* **4** to bring into use: *they introduced a new system into our political life* **5** to insert **6 introduce to** to cause to experience for the first time: *his father introduced him to golf* **7 introduce with** to start: *he introduced his talk with some music* >**introducible** *adj*

introduce vb 1 = present, acquaint, make known, familiarize 3 = suggest, air, advance, submit, bring up, put forward, broach, moot 4 = bring in, establish, set up, start, found, launch, institute, pioneer 5 = add, insert, inject, throw in (informal), infuse

introduction n 1 the act of introducing something or someone 2 a preliminary part, as of a book or musical composition 3 a book that explains the basic facts about a particular subject to a beginner 4 a presentation of one person to another or others

introduction n 1 = launch, institution, pioneering, inauguration; ≠ elimination 2 = opening, prelude, preface, lead-in, preamble, foreword, prologue, intro (informal); ≠ conclusion

introductory adj serving as an introduction

introductory adj = preliminary, first, initial, inaugural, preparatory; ≠ concluding

introspection n the examining of one's own thoughts, impressions, and feelings > **introspective** adj

introversion n psychol the directing of interest inwards towards one's own thoughts and feelings rather than towards the external world or making social contacts

introvert adj 1 shy and quiet 2 psychol concerned more with inner feelings than with external reality ▸ n 3 such a person > **introverted** adj

intrude vb -truding, -truded to come in or join in without being invited

intruder n a person who enters a place without permission

intruder n = trespasser, invader, prowler, interloper, infiltrator, gate-crasher (informal)

intrusion n 1 the act of intruding; an unwelcome visit, etc.: an intrusion into her private life 2 geol A the forcing of molten rock into spaces in the overlying strata B molten rock formed in this way > **intrusive** adj

intrusion n 1 = interruption, interference, infringement, trespass, encroachment

intuition n instinctive knowledge of or belief about something without conscious reasoning: intuition told her something was wrong > **intuitional** adj

intuition n = instinct, perception, insight, sixth sense

intuitive adj of, possessing, or resulting from intuition: an intuitive understanding > **intuitively** adv

Inuit n, pl -it or -its an indigenous inhabitant of North America or Greenland

inundate vb -dating, -dated 1 to cover completely with water 2 to overwhelm, as if with a flood: the police were inundated with calls > **inundation** n

inured adj able to tolerate something unpleasant because one has become accustomed to it: he became inured to the casual brutality of his captors > **inurement** n

invade vb -vading, -vaded 1 to enter (a country or territory) by military force 2 to enter in large numbers: the town was invaded by rugby supporters 3 to disturb (privacy, etc.) > **invader** n

invade vb 1 = attack, storm, assault, capture, occupy, seize, raid, overwhelm 2 = infest, swarm, overrun, ravage, beset, pervade, permeate

invalid¹ n 1 a person who is weak or disabled by illness or injury ▸ adj 2 weak or disabled by illness or injury ▸ vb 3 chiefly Brit to dismiss (a soldier, etc.) from active service because of illness > **invalidity** n

invalid n = patient, sufferer, convalescent, valetudinarian ▸ adj = disabled, challenged, ill, sick, ailing, frail, infirm, bedridden

invalid² adj 1 having no legal force: an invalid cheque 2 (of an argument, result, etc.) not valid because it has been based on a mistake > **invalidity** n

invalid adj 1 = null and void, void, worthless, inoperative; ≠ valid 2 = unfounded, false, illogical, irrational, unsound, fallacious, untenable; ≠ sound

invalidate vb -dating, -dated 1 to make or show (an argument) to be invalid 2 to take away the legal force of (a contract) > **invalidation** n

invaluable adj having great value that is impossible to calculate

invaluable adj = precious, valuable, priceless, inestimable, worth your or its weight in gold; ≠ worthless

invasion n 1 the act of invading with armed forces 2 any intrusion: an invasion of privacy > **invasive** adj

invasion n 1 = attack, assault, capture, takeover, raid, offensive, occupation, conquering 2 = intrusion, breach, violation, disturbance, disruption, infringement, encroachment, infraction

invective n abusive speech or writing

inveigh (in-vay) vb **inveigh against** formal to make harsh criticisms against

inveigle vb -gling, -gled to coax or manipulate (someone) into an action or situation > **inveiglement** n

invent vb 1 to think up or create (something new) 2 to make up (a story, excuse, etc.) > **inventor** n

invent vb 1 = create, make, produce, design, discover, manufacture, devise, conceive 2 = make up, devise, concoct, forge, fake, fabricate, feign, falsify

invention *n* **1** something that is invented **2** the act of inventing **3** creative power; inventive skill **4** *euphemistic* a lie: *his story is a malicious invention*

invention *n* **1** = creation, machine, device, design, instrument, discovery, innovation, gadget **2** = development, design, production, setting up, foundation, construction, creation, discovery **3** = creativity, imagination, initiative, enterprise, genius, ingenuity, originality, inventiveness **4** = fiction, fantasy, lie, yarn (*informal*), fabrication, falsehood, untruth

inventive *adj* creative and resourceful: *her inventive use of colour* > **inventiveness** *n*

inventive *adj* = creative, original, innovative, imaginative, inspired, fertile, ingenious, resourceful; ≠ uninspired

inventory (in-ven-tree) *n*, *pl* **-tories** **1** a detailed list of the objects in a particular place ▸ *vb* **-tories, -torying, -toried** **2** to make a list of

inventory *n* = list, record, catalogue, listing, account, roll, file, register

inverse *adj* **1** opposite in effect, sequence, direction, etc. **2** *maths* linking two variables in such a way that one increases as the other decreases ▸ *n* **3** the exact opposite: *the inverse of this image* **4** *maths* an inverse element

inversion *n* **1** the act of inverting or state of being inverted **2** something inverted, esp. a reversal of order, functions, etc.: *an inversion of their previous relationship* > **inversive** *adj*

invert *vb* **1** to turn upside down or inside out **2** to reverse in effect, sequence, or direction > **invertible** *adj*

invertebrate *n* **1** any animal without a backbone, such as an insect, worm, or octopus ▸ *adj* **2** of or designating invertebrates

inverted commas *pl n* same as **quotation marks**

invest *vb* **1** (often foll. by *in*) to put (money) into an enterprise with the expectation of profit **2** (often foll. by *in*) to devote (time or effort to a project) **3** to give power or authority to: *invested with the powers of government* **4** (often foll. by *in*) to install someone (in an official position) **5** (foll. by *with* or *in*) to credit or provide (a person with qualities): *he was invested with great common sense* **6 invest in** to buy: *she invested in some barbecue equipment* **7 invest with** *usually poetic* to cover, as if with a coat: *when spring invests the trees with leaves* > **investor** *n*

invest *vb* **1, 2** = spend, expend, advance, venture, put in, devote, lay out, sink in **3** = empower, provide, charge, sanction, license, authorize, vest **6 invest in something** = buy, get, purchase, pay for, obtain, acquire, procure

investigate *vb* **-gating, -gated** to inquire into

(a situation or problem) thoroughly in order to discover the truth: *the police are currently investigating the case* > **investigative** *adj* > **investigator** *n*

investigate *vb* = examine, study, research, go into, explore, look into, inspect, probe into

investigation *n* a careful search or examination in order to discover facts

investigation *n* = examination, study, inquiry, review, search, survey, probe, inspection

investiture *n* the formal installation of a person in an office or rank

investment *n* **1** the act of investing **2** money invested **3** something in which money is invested

investment *n* **1** = investing, backing, funding, financing, contribution, speculation, transaction, expenditure **2** = stake, interest, share, concern, portion, ante (*informal*) **3** = buy, asset, acquisition, venture, risk, gamble

inveterate *adj* **1** deep-rooted or ingrained: *an inveterate enemy of Marxism* **2** confirmed in a habit or practice: *an inveterate gambler* > **inveteracy** *n*

invidious *adj* likely to cause resentment or unpopularity

invigilate (in-vij-il-late) *vb* **-lating, -lated** *Brit* to supervise people who are sitting an examination > **invigilation** *n* > **invigilator** *n*

invigorate *vb* **-rating, -rated** to give energy to or refresh > **invigorating** *adj*

invincible *adj* incapable of being defeated: *an army of invincible strength* > **invincibility** *n* > **invincibly** *adv*

inviolable *adj* that must not be broken or violated: *an inviolable oath* > **inviolability** *n*

inviolate *adj* free from harm or injury > **inviolacy** *n*

invisible *adj* **1** not able to be seen by the eye: *invisible radiation* **2** concealed from sight **3** *econ* relating to services, such as insurance and freight, rather than goods: *invisible earnings* > **invisibility** *n* > **invisibly** *adv*

invisible *adj* **1** = unseen, imperceptible, indiscernible, unseeable; ≠ visible

invitation *n* **1** a request to attend a dance, meal, etc. **2** the card or paper on which an invitation is written

invitation *n* **1** = request, call, invite (*informal*), summons

invite *vb* **-viting, -vited** **1** to ask (a person) in a friendly or polite way (to do something, attend an event, etc.) **2** to make a request for, esp. publicly or formally: *we invite applications for six scholarships* **3** to bring on or provoke: *his theory invites disaster* **4** to tempt ▸ *n* **5** *informal* an invitation

invite vb 1 = ask 2 = request, look for, bid for, appeal for 3 = encourage, attract, cause, court, ask for (informal), generate, foster, tempt

inviting adj tempting or attractive

inviting adj = tempting, appealing, attractive, welcoming, enticing, seductive, alluring, mouthwatering; ≠ uninviting

in vitro adv, adj (of biological processes or reactions) happening outside the body of the organism in an artificial environment

invocation n 1 the act of invoking 2 a prayer to God or another deity asking for help, forgiveness, etc. > **invocatory** adj

invoice n 1 a bill for goods and services supplied ▸ vb -voicing, -voiced 2 to present (a customer) with an invoice

invoke vb -voking, -voked 1 to put (a law or penalty) into use: chapter 8 of the UN charter was invoked 2 to bring about: the hills invoked a feeling of serenity 3 to call on (God or another deity) for help, inspiration, etc. 4 to summon (a spirit) by uttering magic words

invoke vb 1 = apply, use, implement, initiate, resort to, put into effect 3, 4 = call upon, appeal to, pray to, petition, beseech, entreat, supplicate

involuntary adj 1 carried out without one's conscious wishes; unintentional 2 physiol (esp. of a movement or muscle) performed or acting without conscious control > **involuntarily** adv

involve vb -volving, -volved 1 to include as a necessary part 2 to have an effect on: around fifty riders were involved and some were hurt 3 to implicate: several people were involved in the crime 4 to make complicated: the situation was further involved by her disappearance > **involvement** n

involve vb 1 = entail, mean, require, occasion (formal), imply, give rise to, necessitate

involved adj 1 complicated 2 **involved in** concerned in

involved adj 1 = complicated, complex, intricate, hard, confused, confusing, elaborate, tangled; ≠ straightforward

invulnerable adj not able to be wounded or damaged > **invulnerability** n

inward adj 1 directed towards the middle of something 2 situated within 3 of the mind or spirit: inward meditation 4 of one's own country or a specific country: inward investment ▸ adv 5 same as **inwards**

inward adj 1 = incoming, entering, inbound, ingoing 3 = internal, inner, private, personal, inside, secret, hidden, interior; ≠ outward

inwardly adv 1 within the private thoughts or feelings: inwardly troubled, he kept smiling 2 not aloud: to laugh inwardly 3 in or on the inside

inwards or **inward** adv towards the inside or middle of something

iodine n chem a bluish-black element found in seaweed and used in medicine and in the manufacture of dyes. Symbol: **I**

iodize or **-dise** vb -dizing, -dized or -dising, -dised to treat with iodine > **iodization** or **-disation** n

ion n an electrically charged atom or group of atoms formed by the loss or gain of one or more electrons

ionic adj of or in the form of ions

ionize or **-ise** vb -izing, -ized or -ising, -ised to change or become changed into ions > **ionization** or **-isation** n

ionosphere n a region of ionized layers of air in the earth's upper atmosphere, which reflects radio waves > **ionospheric** adj

iota (eye-oh-ta) n 1 the ninth letter in the Greek alphabet (I, ι) 2 a very small amount: I don't feel one iota of guilt

IOU n a written promise or reminder to pay a debt

IP address computers internet protocol address: a unique code that identifies each computer connected to the internet

iPod n trademark a small portable digital audio player capable of storing thousands of tracks in a variety of formats including MP3

IQ intelligence quotient

Iranian adj 1 of Iran ▸ n 2 a person from Iran 3 a branch of the Indo-European family of languages, including Persian

Iraqi adj 1 of Iraq ▸ n 2 a person from Iraq

irascible adj easily angered > **irascibility** n > **irascibly** adv

irate adj very angry

ire n literary anger

iridescent (ir-rid-ess-ent) adj having shimmering changing colours like a rainbow > **iridescence** n

iridium n chem a hard yellowish-white chemical element that occurs in platinum ores and is used as an alloy with platinum. Symbol: **Ir**

iris n 1 the coloured muscular membrane in the eye that surrounds and controls the size of the pupil 2 a tall plant with long pointed leaves and large flowers

Irish adj 1 of Ireland ▸ n 2 the dialect of English spoken in Ireland ▸ pl n 3 **the Irish** the people of Ireland

irk vb to irritate or vex

irksome adj annoying or tiresome

iron n 1 a strong silvery-white metallic element, widely used for structural and engineering purposes. Symbol: **Fe** 2 a tool made of iron 3 a small electrically heated device with a weighted flat bottom for pressing clothes 4 golf a club with an angled metal head 5 a splintlike support for a malformed leg 6 great strength or resolve: a will of iron 7 **strike while the iron is hot** to act at a suitable moment ▸ adj 8 made of iron 9 very hard or merciless: iron determination

10 very strong: *an iron constitution* ▶ *vb* **11** to smooth (clothes or fabric) by removing (creases) with an iron ▶ See also **iron out**

iron *adj* **8** = ferrous, ferric **9, 10** = inflexible, hard, strong, tough, rigid, adamant, unconditional, steely; ≠ weak

Iron Age *n* a phase of human culture that began in the Middle East about 1100 BC, during which iron tools and weapons were used

ironbark *n* an Australian eucalyptus with hard rough bark

ironic *or* **ironical** *adj* of, characterized by, or using irony ▷ **ironically** *adv*

ironic *or* **ironical** *adj* = sarcastic, dry, acid, bitter, mocking, wry, satirical, tongue-in-cheek

ironing *n* clothes to be ironed

ironing board *n* a narrow cloth-covered board, usually with folding legs, on which to iron clothes

iron out *vb* to settle (a problem or difficulty) through negotiation or discussion

iron out *vb* **iron something out** = settle, resolve, sort out, get rid of, reconcile, clear up, put right, straighten out

irony *n, pl* **-nies** **1** the mildly sarcastic use of words to imply the opposite of what they normally mean **2** a situation or result that is the direct opposite of what was expected or intended

irony *n* **1** = sarcasm, mockery, ridicule, satire, cynicism, derision **2** = paradox, incongruity

irrational *adj* **1** not based on logical reasoning **2** incapable of reasoning **3** *maths* (of an equation or expression) involving radicals or fractional exponents ▷ **irrationality** *n* ▷ **irrationally** *adv*

irrational *adj* **1** = illogical, crazy (*informal*), absurd, unreasonable, preposterous, nonsensical; ≠ rational

irrefutable *adj* impossible to deny or disprove

irregular *adj* **1** uneven in shape, position, arrangement, etc. **2** not conforming to accepted practice or routine **3** (of a word) not following the usual pattern of formation in a language **4** not occurring at expected or equal intervals: *an irregular pulse* **5** (of troops) not belonging to regular forces ▶ *n* **6** a soldier not in a regular army ▷ **irregularity** *n* ▷ **irregularly** *adv*

irregular *adj* **1** = uneven, rough, ragged, crooked, jagged, bumpy, contorted, lopsided; ≠ even **2** = inappropriate, unconventional, unethical, unusual, extraordinary, exceptional, peculiar, unofficial **4** = variable, erratic, occasional, random, casual, shaky, sporadic, haphazard; ≠ steady **5** = unofficial, underground, guerrilla, resistance, partisan, rogue, paramilitary, mercenary

irrelevant *adj* not connected with the matter in hand ▷ **irrelevance** *or* **irrelevancy** *n*

irrelevant *adj* = unconnected, unrelated, unimportant, inappropriate, peripheral, immaterial, extraneous, beside the point; ≠ relevant

irreparable *adj* not able to be repaired or put right: *irreparable damage to his reputation* ▷ **irreparably** *adv*

irreplaceable *adj* impossible to replace: *acres of irreplaceable moorland were devastated*

irrepressible *adj* not capable of being repressed, controlled, or restrained ▷ **irrepressibility** *n* ▷ **irrepressibly** *adv*

irreproachable *adj* blameless or faultless ▷ **irreproachability** *n*

irresistible *adj* **1** not able to be resisted or refused: *irresistible pressure from the financial markets* **2** extremely attractive: *an irresistible woman* ▷ **irresistibility** *n* ▷ **irresistibly** *adv*

irresistible *adj* **1** = overwhelming, compelling, overpowering, urgent, compulsive

irresponsible *adj* **1** not showing or done with due care for the consequences of one's actions or attitudes; reckless **2** not capable of accepting responsibility ▷ **irresponsibility** *n* ▷ **irresponsibly** *adv*

irresponsible *adj* **1** = thoughtless, reckless, careless, unreliable, untrustworthy, shiftless, scatterbrained; ≠ responsible

irreverence *n* **1** lack of due respect **2** a disrespectful remark or act ▷ **irreverent** *adj*

irreversible *adj* not able to be reversed or put right again: *irreversible loss of memory* ▷ **irreversibly** *adv*

irrevocable *adj* not possible to change or undo ▷ **irrevocably** *adv*

irrigate *vb* **-gating, -gated** **1** to supply (land) with water through ditches or pipes in order to encourage the growth of crops **2** *med* to bathe (a wound or part of the body) ▷ **irrigation** *n* ▷ **irrigator** *n*

irritable *adj* **1** easily annoyed or angered **2** *pathol* abnormally sensitive **3** *biol* (of all living organisms) capable of responding to such stimuli as heat, light, and touch ▷ **irritability** *n*

irritant *n* **1** something that annoys or irritates **2** a substance that causes a part of the body to become tender or inflamed ▶ *adj* **3** causing irritation

irritate *vb* **-tating, -tated** **1** to annoy or anger (someone) **2** *pathol* to cause (an organ or part of the body) to become inflamed or tender **3** *biol* to stimulate (an organ) to respond in a characteristic manner ▷ **irritation** *n*

irritate *vb* **1** = annoy, anger, bother, needle (*informal*), infuriate, exasperate, nettle, irk; ≠ placate **2** = inflame, pain, rub, scratch, scrape, chafe

is *vb* third person singular of the present tense of **be**

ISA (**eye**-sa) *n* (in Britain) individual savings account

isinglass (**ize**-ing-glass) *n* **1** a gelatine made from the air bladders of freshwater fish **2** same as **mica**

Islam *n* **1** the Muslim religion teaching that there is only one God and that Mohammed is his prophet **2** Muslim countries and civilization > **Islamic** *adj* > **Islamist** *adj, n*

island *n* **1** a piece of land that is completely surrounded by water **2** something isolated, detached, or surrounded **3** See **traffic island**. ▶ Related adjective: **insular**

> **island** *n* **1** = isle, atoll, islet, ait *or* eyot (*dialect*), cay *or* key

islander *n* **1** a person who lives on an island **2 Islander** NZ a Pacific Islander

isle *n* (except when part of a place name) a poetic name for an island

islet *n* a small island

isobar (**ice**-oh-bar) *n* **1** a line on a map connecting places of equal atmospheric pressure **2** *physics* any of two or more atoms that have the same mass number but different atomic numbers > **isobaric** *adj* > **isobarism** *n*

isolate *vb* **-lating, -lated 1** to place apart or alone **2** *chem* to obtain (a substance) in an uncombined form **3** *med* to quarantine (a person or animal) with a contagious disease > **isolation** *n*

> **isolate** *vb* **1** = separate, break up, cut off, detach, split up, insulate, segregate, disconnect **3** = quarantine

isolationism *n* policy of not participating in international affairs > **isolationist** *adv*

isomer (**ice**-oh-mer) *n* *chem* a substance whose molecules contain the same atoms as another but in a different arrangement > **isomeric** *adj*

isometric *adj* **1** having equal dimensions or measurements **2** *physiol* relating to muscular contraction that does not produce shortening of the muscle **3** (of a three-dimensional drawing) having the three axes equally inclined and all lines drawn to scale > **isometrically** *adv*

isometrics *n* a system of isometric exercises

isosceles triangle (**ice**-soss-ill-eez) *n* a triangle with two sides of equal length

isotherm (**ice**-oh-therm) *n* a line on a map linking places of equal temperature

isotope (**ice**-oh-tope) *n* one of two or more atoms with the same number of protons in the nucleus but a different number of neutrons > **isotopic** *adj* > **isotopy** *n*

ISP internet service provider: a business providing its customers with connection to the internet

Israeli *adj* **1** of Israel ▶ *n, pl* **-lis** *or* **-li 2** a person from Israel

issue *n* **1** a topic of interest or discussion **2** an important subject requiring a decision **3** a particular edition of a magazine or newspaper **4** a consequence or result **5** *law* the descendants of a person **6** the act of sending or giving out something **7** the act of emerging; outflow **8** something flowing out, such as a river **9 at issue A** under discussion **B** in disagreement **10 force the issue** to compel decision on some matter **11 join issue** to join in controversy **12 take issue (with)** to disagree (with) ▶ *vb* **-suing, -sued 13** to make (a statement, etc.) publicly **14** to supply officially (with) **15** to send out or distribute **16** to publish **17** to come forth or emerge > **issuable** *adj*

> **issue** *n* **1** = topic, point, matter, problem, question, subject, theme **2** = point, question, bone of contention **3** = edition, printing, copy, publication, number, version **5** = children, offspring, babies, kids (*informal*), heirs, descendants, progeny; ≠ parent **12 take issue with something or someone** = disagree with, question, challenge, oppose, dispute, object to, argue with, take exception to ▶ *vb* **13, 15, 16** = give out, release, publish, announce, deliver, spread, broadcast, distribute

isthmus (**iss**-muss) *n* a narrow strip of land connecting two relatively large land areas

it *pron* **1** refers to a nonhuman, animal, plant, or inanimate thing, or sometimes to a small baby **2** refers to something unspecified or implied or to a previous or understood clause, phrase, or word: *I knew it* **3** used to represent human life or experience in respect of the present situation: *how's it going?* **4** used as the subject of impersonal verbs: *it is snowing; it's Friday* **5** *informal* the crucial or ultimate point: *the steering failed and I thought that was it* ▶ *n* **6** *informal* **A** sexual intercourse **B** sex appeal **7** a desirable quality or ability

IT information technology

Italian *adj* **1** of Italy ▶ *n* **2** a person from Italy **3** the official language of Italy and one of the official languages of Switzerland

italic *adj* **1** of a style of printing type in which the characters slant to the right ▶ *pl n* **2 italics** italic type or print, used for emphasis

italicize *or* **-cise** *vb* **-cizing, -cized** *or* **-cising, -cised** to print (text) in italic type > **italicization** *or* **-cisation** *n*

itch *n* **1** a skin irritation causing a desire to scratch **2** a restless desire **3** any skin disorder, such as scabies, characterized by intense itching ▶ *vb* **4** to feel an irritating or tickling sensation **5** to have a restless desire (to do something): *they were itching to join the fight*

> **itch** *n* **1** = irritation, tingling, prickling, itchiness **2** = desire, longing, craving, passion, yen (*informal*), hunger, lust, yearning ▶ *vb* **4** = prickle, tickle, tingle **5** = long, ache, crave, pine, hunger, lust, yearn, hanker

itchy *adj* **itchier, itchiest 1** having an itch **2 have itchy feet** to have a desire to travel ▷ **itchiness** *n*

itém *n* **1** a single thing in a list or collection **2** a piece of information: *a news item* **3** *accounting* an entry in an account **4** *informal* a couple

> **item** *n* **1** = article, thing, object, piece, unit, component **2** = report, story, piece, account, note, feature, notice, article

itemize or **-ise** *vb* **-izing, -ized** or **-ising, -ised** to put on a list or make a list of ▷ **itemization** or **-isation** *n*

iterate *vb* **-ating, -ated** to say or do again ▷ **iteration** *n* ▷ **iterative** *adj*

itinerant *adj* **1** working for a short time in various places ▶ *n* **2** an itinerant worker or other person

itinerary *n, pl* **-aries 1** a detailed plan of a journey **2** a record of a journey **3** a guidebook for travellers

> **itinerary** *n* **1** = schedule, programme, route, timetable

its *adj* **1** of or belonging to it: *its left rear wheel; I can see its logical consequence* ▶ *pron* **2** something belonging to it: *its is over there*

it's it is *or* it has

itself *pron* **1 A** the reflexive form of it: *the cat scratched itself* **B** used for emphasis: *even the money itself won't convince me* **2** its normal or usual self: *my parrot doesn't seem itself these days*

ITV (in Britain) Independent Television

IUD intrauterine device: a coil-shaped contraceptive fitted into the womb

IVF in vitro fertilization

ivory *n, pl* **-ries 1** a hard smooth creamy white type of bone that makes up a major part of the tusks of elephants ▶ *adj* **2** yellowish-white ▷ **ivory-like** *adj*

ivory tower *n* remoteness from the realities of everyday life ▷ **ivory-towered** *adj*

ivy *n, pl* **ivies 1** a woody climbing or trailing plant with evergreen leaves and black berry-like fruits **2** any of various other climbing or creeping plants, such as the poison ivy

iwi (ee-wee) *n* NZ a Māori tribe

jab *vb* **jabbing, jabbed 1** to poke sharply ▶ *n* **2** a quick short punch **3** *informal* an injection: *a flu jab* **4** a sharp poke

> **jab** *vb* **=** poke, dig, punch, thrust, tap, stab, nudge, prod ▶ *n* **4** = poke, dig, punch, thrust, tap, stab, nudge, prod

jabber *vb* **1** to speak very quickly and excitedly; chatter ▶ *n* **2** quick excited chatter

jabiru *n* a large white-and-black Australian stork

jacaranda *n* a tropical American tree with sweet-smelling wood and pale purple flowers

jack *n* **1** a mechanical device used to raise a motor vehicle or other heavy object **2** a playing card with a picture of a pageboy on it **3** *bowls* a small white bowl at which the players aim their bowls **4** *electrical engineering* a socket into which a plug can be inserted **5** a flag flown at the bow of a ship, showing nationality **6** one of the pieces used in the game of jacks **7 every man jack** everyone without exception ▶ See also **jack up**

jackal *n* a doglike wild animal of Africa and Asia, which feeds on the decaying flesh of dead animals

jackaroo or **jackeroo** *n, pl* **-roos** *Austral* a trainee on a sheep station

jackass *n* **1** a fool **2** a male donkey **3 laughing jackass** same as **kookaburra**

jackboot *n* **1** a leather military boot reaching up to the knee **2** brutal and authoritarian rule

jackdaw *n* a large black-and-grey crowlike bird of Europe and Asia

jacket *n* **1** a short coat with a front opening and long sleeves **2** the skin of a potato **3** same as **dust jacket**

jackknife *vb* **-knifing, -knifed 1** (of an articulated lorry) to go out of control in such a way that the trailer swings round at a sharp angle to the cab ▶ *n, pl* **-knives 2** a knife with a blade that can be folded into the handle **3** a dive in which the diver bends at the waist in midair

jackpot *n* **1** the most valuable prize that can be won in a gambling game **2 hit the jackpot** *informal* to be very fortunate or very successful

> **jackpot** *n* **1** = prize, winnings, award, reward, bonanza

jack up *vb* **1** to raise (a motor vehicle) with a jack **2** to increase (prices or salaries) **3** NZ *informal* to organize something through unorthodox channels ▶ *n* **jack-up 4** NZ *informal* something achieved dishonestly

Jacobean (jak-a-**bee**-an) *adj* of or in the reign of James I of England and Ireland (1603–25)

Jacobite *n history* a supporter of James II and his descendants

Jacquard (jak-ard) *n* a fabric with an intricate design incorporated into the weave

Jacuzzi (jak-oo-zee) *n trademark* a large circular bath with a mechanism that swirls the water

jade *n* 1 an ornamental semiprecious stone, usually green in colour ▸ *adj* 2 bluish-green

jaded *adj* tired or bored from overindulgence or overwork

jagged (jag-gid) *adj* having an uneven edge with sharp points

jaguar *n* a large wild cat of south and central America, with a spotted coat

jail *or* **gaol** *n* 1 a prison ▸ *vb* 2 to confine in prison

> **jail** *or* **gaol** *n* = prison, penitentiary (*US*), confinement, dungeon, nick (*Brit slang*), slammer (*slang*), reformatory, boob (*Austral slang*) ▸ *vb* = imprison, confine, detain, lock up, put away, intern, incarcerate, send down

jailbird *n informal* a person who is or has often been in jail

jailer *or* **gaoler** *n* a person in charge of a jail

jalopy (jal-**lop**-ee) *n*, *pl* -**lopies** *informal* a dilapidated old car

jam¹ *vb* **jamming, jammed** 1 to wedge (an object) into a tight space or against another object: *the table was jammed against the wall* 2 to fill (a place) with people or vehicles: *the surrounding roads were jammed for miles* 3 to make or become stuck or locked: *the window was jammed open* 4 *radio* to prevent the clear reception of (radio communications) by transmitting other signals on the same wavelength 5 *slang* to play in a jam session 6 **jam on the brakes** to apply the brakes of a vehicle very suddenly ▸ *n* 7 a situation where a large number of people or vehicles are crowded into a place: *a traffic jam* 8 *informal* a difficult situation: *you are in a bit of a jam* 9 same as **jam session**

> **jam** *vb* 1 = pack, force, press, stuff, squeeze, ram, wedge, cram 2 = congest, block, clog, stick, stall, obstruct ▸ *n* 8 = predicament, tight spot, situation, trouble, hole (*slang*), fix (*informal*), mess, pinch

jam² *n* a food made from fruit boiled with sugar until the mixture sets, used for spreading on bread

jamb *n* a side post of a doorframe or window frame

jamboree *n* a large gathering or celebration

jam-packed *adj* filled to capacity

jam session *n slang* an improvised performance by jazz or rock musicians

Jan. January

Jandal *n trademark NZ* a rubber-soled sandal attached to the foot by a thong between the big toe and the next toe

jangle *vb* -**gling, -gled** 1 to make a harsh unpleasant ringing noise 2 to produce an irritating or unpleasant effect on: *the caffeine in coffee can jangle the nerves*

janitor *n chiefly Scot, US & Canad* the caretaker of a school or other building

January *n* the first month of the year

japan *n* 1 a glossy black lacquer, originally from E Asia, which is used on wood or metal ▸ *vb* -**panning, -panned** 2 to varnish with japan

Japanese *adj* 1 of Japan ▸ *n* 2 *pl* -**nese** a person from Japan 3 the language of Japan

jape *n old-fashioned* a joke or prank

japonica *n* 1 a Japanese shrub with red flowers and yellowish fruit 2 same as **camellia**

jar¹ *n* 1 a wide-mouthed cylindrical glass container, used for storing food 2 *Brit informal* a glass of beer

> **jar** *n* 1 = pot, container, drum, vase, jug, pitcher, urn, crock

jar² *vb* **jarring, jarred** 1 to have an irritating or unpleasant effect: *sometimes a light remark jarred on her father* 2 to be in disagreement or conflict: *their very different temperaments jarred* 3 to jolt or bump ▸ *n* 4 a jolt or shock ˃ **jarring** *adj*

> **jar** *vb* 1 = irritate, annoy, offend, nettle, irk, grate on, get on your nerves (*informal*) 3 = jolt, rock, shake, bump, rattle, vibrate, convulse

jargon *n* 1 specialized language relating to a particular subject, profession, or group 2 pretentious or unintelligible language

> **jargon** *n* 1 = parlance, idiom, usage, argot, leetspeak, l33tspeak *or* 1337speak (*computers*), netspeak (*computers*)

jarrah *n* an Australian eucalypt yielding valuable timber

jasmine *n* a shrub or climbing plant with sweet-smelling flowers

jasper *n* a kind of quartz, usually red in colour, which is used as a gemstone and for ornamental decoration

jaundice *n* yellowing of the skin and the whites of the eyes, caused by an excess of bile pigments in the blood

jaundiced *adj* 1 bitter or cynical: *the financial markets are taking a jaundiced view of the Government's motives* 2 having jaundice

jaunt *n* 1 a pleasure trip or outing ▸ *vb* 2 to go on a jaunt

jaunty *adj* -**tier, -tiest** 1 cheerful and energetic: *he managed to keep up a jaunty air* 2 smart and attractive: *a jaunty little hat* ˃ **jauntily** *adv*

javelin *n* a light spear thrown in a sports competition

jaw *n* 1 either of the bones that hold the teeth and frame the mouth 2 the lower part of the face below the mouth 3 *slang* a long chat ▸ *vb* 4 *slang* to have a long chat

jaw vb = talk, chat, gossip, chatter, spout (*informal*), natter

jay n **1** a bird of Europe and Asia with a pinkish-brown body and blue-and-black wings **2** a N American bird with bright blue feathers

jaywalking n crossing the road in a dangerous or careless manner >**jaywalker** n

jazz n **1** a kind of popular music of African-American origin that has an exciting rhythm and often involves improvisation **2 and all that jazz** slang and other related things

jazz up vb informal **1** to play (a piece of music) in a jazzy style **2** to make (something) appear more interesting or lively: *never seek to jazz up a plain story*

jazzy adj **-zier, -ziest 1** colourful and modern: *jazzy shop fronts* **2** of or like jazz

JCB n trademark Brit a large machine used in building, that has a shovel on the front and a digger arm on the back

jealous adj **1** suspicious or fearful of being displaced by a rival **2** envious: *I was jealous of the girls who had boyfriends* **3** resulting from jealousy: *my jealous tears* >**jealously** adv

jealous adj **1** = suspicious, protective, wary, doubtful, sceptical, vigilant, watchful, possessive; ≠ trusting **2** = envious, grudging, resentful, green, green with envy, desirous, covetous; ≠ satisfied

jealousy n, pl **-ousies** the state of or an instance of feeling jealous

jealousy n = suspicion, mistrust, possessiveness, doubt, spite, resentment, wariness, dubiety

jeans pl n casual denim trousers

Jeep n trademark a small road vehicle with four-wheel drive

jeer vb **1** to be derisive towards (someone) ▸ n **2** a cry of derision >**jeering** adj, n

jeer vb = mock, deride, heckle, barrack, ridicule, taunt, scoff, gibe; ≠ cheer ▸ n = mockery, abuse, ridicule, taunt, boo, derision, gibe, catcall; ≠ applause

Jehovah n God

jejune adj **1** simple and unsophisticated **2** dull and uninteresting

jell vb **1** to take on a definite form: *the changes have had little time to jell* **2** same as **gel** (sense 2)

jellied adj prepared in a jelly: *jellied eels*

jelly n, pl **-lies 1** a fruit-flavoured dessert set with gelatine **2** a food made from fruit juice boiled with sugar until the mixture sets, used for spreading on bread **3** a savoury food preparation set with gelatine >**jelly-like** adj

jellyfish n, pl **-fish** a small sea creature with a jelly-like umbrella-shaped body and trailing tentacles

jemmy or US **jimmy** n, pl **-mies** a short steel crowbar, used by burglars to prise open doors and windows

jenny n, pl **-nies** a female donkey, ass, or wren

jeopardize or **-dise** vb **-dizing, -dized** or **-dising, -dised** to put (something) at risk: *the escalating violence that is jeopardizing current peace moves*

jeopardy n danger of harm, loss, or death: *the survival of public hospitals is in jeopardy*

jeopardy n = danger, risk, peril, vulnerability, insecurity

jerboa n a small rodent of Asia and N Africa with long hind legs used for jumping

jerk vb **1** to move with an irregular or spasmodic motion **2** to pull or push (something) abruptly or spasmodically ▸ n **3** an abrupt or spasmodic movement **4** an irregular jolting motion: *the irritating jerk that heralded a gear change* **5** slang, chiefly US & Canad a stupid or ignorant person

jerk vb = jolt, bang, bump, lurch ▸ n **3, 4** = lurch, movement, thrust, twitch, jolt

jerkin n a short jacket

jerky adj **jerkier, jerkiest** having an irregular jolting motion: *avoid any sudden or jerky movements* >**jerkily** adv >**jerkiness** n

jerry-built adj (of houses) built badly with cheap materials

jerry can n a flat-sided can used for carrying petrol or water

jersey n **1** a knitted garment covering the upper part of the body **2** a soft, slightly stretchy, machine-knitted fabric

Jersey n a breed of reddish-brown dairy cattle that produces milk with a high butterfat content

Jerusalem artichoke n a small yellowish-white vegetable that grows underground

jest n **1** something done or said to amuse people **2 in jest** as a joke: *many a true word is spoken in jest* ▸ vb **3** to do or say something to amuse people

jester n a professional clown employed by a king or nobleman during the Middle Ages

Jesuit (jezz-yew-it) n a member of the Society of Jesus, a Roman Catholic religious order >**Jesuitical** adj

jet¹ n **1** an aircraft driven by jet propulsion **2** a thin stream of liquid or gas forced out of a small hole **3** an outlet or nozzle through which a stream of liquid or gas is forced ▸ vb **jetting, jetted 4** to travel by jet aircraft

jet n **2** = stream, current, spring, flow, rush, flood, burst, spray ▸ vb = fly, wing, cruise, soar, zoom

jet² n a hard black mineral that is polished and used in jewellery

jet-black adj deep black

jetboat n a motorboat propelled by a jet of water

j

jet lag *n* a feeling of fatigue and disorientation often experienced by air passengers who have crossed several time zones in a short space of time

jet-propelled *adj* driven by jet propulsion

jet propulsion *n* a method of propulsion by which an aircraft is moved forward by the force of the exhaust gases ejected from the rear

jetsam *n* **1** goods thrown overboard to lighten a ship during a storm **2 flotsam and jetsam** See **flotsam** (sense 2)

jet set *n* rich and fashionable people who travel widely for pleasure >**jet-setter** *n* >**jet-setting** *adj*

jettison *vb* **1** to abandon or give up: *jettisoning democracy in favour of fascism* **2** to throw overboard

jetty *n, pl* **-ties 1** a landing pier or dock **2** a structure built from a shore out into the water to protect a harbour

Jew *n* **1** a person whose religion is Judaism **2** a descendant of the ancient Hebrews

jewel *n* **1** a precious or semiprecious stone **2** a person or thing regarded as precious or special: *a fantastic little car, a real little jewel* **3** a gemstone used as part of the machinery of a watch

> **jewel** *n* **1** = gemstone, gem, ornament, sparkler (*informal*), rock (*slang*) **2** = treasure, wonder, darling, pearl, gem, paragon, pride and joy, taonga (*NZ*)

jeweller *or US* **jeweler** *n* a person who buys, sells, and repairs jewellery

jewellery *or US* **jewelry** *n* objects such as rings, necklaces, and bracelets, worn for decoration

> **jewellery** *or* **jewelry** *n* = jewels, treasure, gems, trinkets, ornaments, finery, regalia, bling (*slang*)

jewfish *n Austral* a freshwater catfish

Jewish *adj* of Jews or Judaism

Jewry *n* Jews collectively

jew's-harp *n* a small musical instrument held between the teeth and played by plucking a metal strip with the finger

jib¹ *n* **1** *naut* a triangular sail set in front of the foremast **2 the cut of someone's jib** a person's manner or style

jib² *vb* **jibbing, jibbed** *chiefly Brit* **1** (of an animal) to stop short and refuse to go forwards: *my animal jibbed three times* **2 jib at** to object to: *he jibs at any suggestion that his side are the underdogs*

jib³ *n* the projecting arm of a crane

jibe¹ *n* **1** an insulting or taunting remark ▸ *vb* **jibing, jibed 2** to make insulting or taunting remarks

jibe² *vb* **jibing, jibed** *informal* to be in accord or be consistent: *their apparent devotion hardly jibed with what he had heard about them*

jiffy *n, pl* **jiffies** *informal* a very short time: *won't be a jiffy!*

jig *n* **1** a lively folk dance **2** music for this dance **3** a mechanical device that holds and locates a

part during machining ▸ *vb* **jigging, jigged 4** to dance a jig **5** to move with quick jerky movements

jiggery-pokery *n informal, chiefly Brit* dishonest behaviour; cheating

jiggle *vb* **-gling, -gled** to move with quick jerky movements

jigsaw *n* **1** Also called: **jigsaw puzzle** a puzzle in which the player has to put together a picture that has been cut into irregularly shaped interlocking pieces **2** a mechanical saw with a fine steel blade for cutting along curved or irregular lines in sheets of material

jihad *n* an Islamic holy war against unbelievers

jilt *vb* to leave or reject (a lover) abruptly or callously

jingle *n* **1** a short catchy song used to advertise a product **2** a light ringing sound ▸ *vb* **-gling, -gled 3** to make a light ringing sound

jingoism *n* excessive and aggressive patriotism >**jingoistic** *or* **jingoist** *adj*

jinks *pl n* **high jinks** boisterous or mischievous behaviour

jinni *or* **djinni** *n, pl* **jinn** *or* **djinn** (in Islamic belief) a being or spirit that can take on human or animal form

jinx *n* **1** someone or something believed to bring bad luck ▸ *vb* **2** to bring bad luck to

jitters *pl n* **the jitters** *informal* a feeling of extreme nervousness experienced before an important event: *I had a case of the jitters before my first two speeches*

jittery *adj* nervous

jive *n* **1** a lively jerky dance that was popular in the 1940s and 1950s ▸ *vb* **jiving, jived 2** to dance the jive >**jiver** *n*

job *n* **1** a person's occupation or paid employment **2** a piece of work; task **3** the performance of a task: *he made a good job of the repair* **4** *informal* a difficult task: *they are having a job to fill his shoes* **5** *Brit, Austral & NZ informal* a crime, esp. a robbery **6 just the job** *informal* exactly what is required **7 make the best of a bad job** to cope as well as possible in unsatisfactory circumstances

> **job** *n* **1** = position, work, calling, business, field, career, employment, profession **2** = task, duty, work, venture, enterprise, undertaking, assignment, chore

jobbing *adj* doing individual jobs for payment: *a jobbing gardener*

jobless *adj* **1** unemployed ▸ *pl n* **2** people who are unemployed: *the young jobless*

> **jobless** *adj* = unemployed, redundant, out of work, inactive, unoccupied, idle

job lot *n* a miscellaneous collection of articles sold together

job sharing *n* an arrangement by which a job is shared by two part-time workers

jockey *n* **1** a person who rides horses in races as a profession ▸ *vb* **2 jockey for position** to try to obtain an advantage by skilful manoeuvring

jockstrap *n* an elasticated belt with a pouch to support the genitals, worn by male athletes. Also called: **athletic support**

jocose (joke-**kohss**) *adj old-fashioned* playful or humorous ▹**jocosely** *adv*

jocular *adj* **1** (of a person) often joking; good-humoured **2** (of a remark) meant lightly or humorously ▹**jocularity** *n* ▹**jocularly** *adv*

jocund (**jok**-kund) *adj literary* cheerful or merry

jodhpurs *pl n* trousers worn for riding, which are loose-fitting around the thighs and tight-fitting below the knees

joey *n Austral* a young kangaroo

jog *vb* **jogging, jogged 1** to run at a gentle pace for exercise **2** to nudge slightly **3 jog along** to continue in a plodding way: *many people jog along in second gear for the whole of their lives* **4 jog someone's memory** to remind someone of something ▸ *n* **5** a slow run as a form of exercise ▹**jogger** *n* ▹**jogging** *n*

> **jog** *vb* **1** = run, trot, canter, lope **2** = nudge, push, shake, prod

joggle *vb* **-gling, -gled** to shake or move with a slightly jolting motion

joie de vivre (zhwah de **veev**-ra) *n* enjoyment of life

join *vb* **1** to become a member of (a club or organization) **2** to become part of (a queue or list) **3** to meet (someone) as a companion: *join me for a cup of coffee* **4** to take part in (an activity): *join the relief effort* **5** (of two roads or rivers) to meet and come together **6** to bring into contact: *join hands* **7 join forces** to combine efforts with someone ▸ *n* **8** a place where two things are joined together ▸ See also **join up**

> **join** *vb* **1** = enrol in, enter, sign up for, enlist in **6** = connect, unite, couple, link, combine, attach, fasten, add; ≠ detach

joined-up *adj* integrated by an overall strategy: *joined-up government*

joiner *n* a person whose job is making finished woodwork, such as window frames and stairs

joinery *n* the skill or work of a joiner

joint *adj* **1** shared by or belonging to two or more parties: *the two countries have issued a joint statement* ▸ *n* **2** *anatomy* the junction between two or more bones: *a hip joint* **3** a junction of two or more parts or objects: *a mortar joint* **4** a piece of meat suitable for roasting **5** *slang* a building or place of entertainment: *fast-food joints* **6** *slang* a cannabis cigarette **7 out of joint** **A** *informal* out of order or out of keeping: *they find their routine lives out of joint with their training* **B** (of a bone) knocked out of its normal position **8 put someone's nose out of joint** See **nose** (sense 10) ▸ *vb* **9** to provide a joint or joints **10** to cut or divide (meat) into joints ▹**jointed** *adj* ▹**jointly** *adv*

joint *adj* = shared, mutual, collective, communal, united, joined, allied, combined ▸ *n* **3** = junction, connection, brace, bracket, hinge, intersection, node, nexus

join up *vb* to become a member of a military organization

joist *n* a beam made of timber, steel, or concrete, used as a support in the construction of floors and roofs

jojoba (hoe-**hoe**-ba) *n* a shrub whose seeds contain an oil used in cosmetics

joke *n* **1** something that is said or done to amuse people **2** someone or something that is ridiculous: *the country's inexperienced leaders are regarded as something of a joke* **3 no joke** *informal* a serious or difficult matter: *getting over mountain passes at ten thousand feet is no joke* ▸ *vb* **joking, joked 4** to say or do something to amuse people ▹**jokey** *adj* ▹**jokingly** *adv*

> **joke** *n* **1** = jest, gag (*informal*), wisecrack (*informal*), witticism, crack (*informal*), quip, pun, one-liner (*informal*) **2** = laughing stock, clown, buffoon ▸ *vb* = jest, kid (*informal*), mock, tease, taunt, quip, banter, play the fool

joker *n* **1** a person who jokes a lot **2** *slang* a person regarded without respect: *waiting for the next jokers to sign up* **3** an extra playing card in a pack, which can replace any other card in some games **4** *Austral & NZ informal* a chap

> **joker** *n* = comedian, comic, wit, clown, wag, jester, prankster, buffoon

jollification *n* a merry festivity

jollity *n* the condition of being jolly

jolly *adj* **-lier, -liest 1** full of good humour **2** involving a lot of fun: *big jolly birthday parties* ▸ *adv* **3** *Brit informal* very: *I'm going to have a jolly good try* ▸ *vb* **-lies, -lying, -lied 4 jolly along** *informal* to try to keep (someone) cheerful by flattery or cheerful chat

> **jolly** *adj* = happy, cheerful, merry, upbeat, playful, cheery, genial, chirpy (*informal*); ≠ miserable

jolt *n* **1** a severe shock **2** a sudden violent movement ▸ *vb* **3** to surprise or shock: *he was momentarily jolted by the news* **4** to bump against (someone or something) with a sudden violent movement **5** to move in a jerking manner

> **jolt** *n* **1** = surprise, blow, shock, setback, bombshell, bolt from the blue **2** = jerk, start, jump, shake, bump, jar, jog, lurch ▸ *vb* **3** = surprise, stun, disturb, stagger, startle, perturb, discompose **4** = jerk, push, shake, knock, jar, shove, jog, jostle

jonquil *n* a narcissus with sweet-smelling yellow or white flowers

josh *vb slang* to joke or tease

joss stick *n* a stick of incense, giving off a sweet smell when burnt

jostle *vb* **-tling, -tled 1** to bump or push roughly: *television crews filming the scene were jostled by police* **2** to compete with someone: *jostling for power*

jot *vb* **jotting, jotted 1 jot down** to write a brief note of: *quickly jot down the answers to these questions* ▸ *n* **2** the least bit: *it makes not one jot of difference*

jotter *n* a small notebook

jottings *pl n* notes jotted down

joule (jool) *n physics* the SI unit of work or energy

journal *n* **1** a newspaper or magazine **2** a daily record of events

> **journal** *n* **1** = newspaper, paper, daily, weekly, monthly **2** = diary, record, history, log, notebook, chronicle, annals, yearbook, blog (*informal*)

journalese *n* a superficial style of writing regarded as typical of newspapers and magazines

journalism *n* the profession of collecting, writing, and publishing news through newspapers and magazines or by radio, television, and other media

journalist *n* a person who writes or edits news items for a newspaper or magazine or for radio, television, or other media ▸ **journalistic** *adj*

> **journalist** *n* = reporter, writer, correspondent, newsman *or* newswoman, commentator, broadcaster, hack (*derogatory*), columnist

journey *n* **1** the process of travelling from one place to another **2** the time taken or distance travelled on a journey ▸ *vb* **3** to make a journey

> **journey** *n* **1** = trip, drive, tour, flight, excursion, trek, expedition, voyage ▸ *vb* = travel, go, move, tour, progress, proceed, wander, trek, go walkabout (*Austral*)

journeyman *n, pl* **-men** a qualified craftsman who works for an employer

joust *history* ▸ *n* **1** a combat with lances between two mounted knights ▸ *vb* **2** to take part in such a tournament

jovial *adj* happy and cheerful ▸ **joviality** *n* ▸ **jovially** *adv*

jowl¹ *n* **1** the lower jaw **2 cheek by jowl** See **cheek** (sense 4) **3 jowls** cheeks ▸ **jowled** *adj*

jowl² *n* fatty flesh hanging from the lower jaw

joy *n* **1** deep happiness and contentment **2** something that brings deep happiness: *a thing of beauty is a joy for ever* **3** *informal* success or satisfaction: *we checked ports and airports without any joy*

> **joy** *n* **1** = delight, pleasure, satisfaction, ecstasy, enjoyment, bliss, glee, rapture; ≠ sorrow

joyful *adj* feeling or bringing great joy: *joyful crowds; a joyful event* ▸ **joyfully** *adv*

joyless *adj* feeling or bringing no joy

joyous *adj* extremely happy and enthusiastic ▸ **joyously** *adv*

joyride *n* a drive in a car one has stolen ▸ **joyriding** *n* ▸ **joyrider** *n*

joystick *n* the control lever of an aircraft or a computer

JP (in Britain) Justice of the Peace

JPEG (jay-peg) *n computers* **A** a standard compressed file format used for pictures **B** a picture held in this file format

Jr Junior

JSA jobseeker's allowance: in Britain, a payment made to unemployed people

jubilant *adj* feeling great joy ▸ **jubilantly** *adv*

jubilation *n* a feeling of great joy and celebration

jubilee *n* a special anniversary, esp. a 25th (**silver jubilee**) or 50th one (**golden jubilee**)

> **jubilee** *n* = celebration, holiday, festival, festivity

Judaic *adj* of Jews or Judaism

Judaism *n* the religion of the Jews, based on the Old Testament and the Talmud

judder *vb informal, chiefly Brit* to shake or vibrate violently: *the van juddered before it moved away*

judder bar *n NZ* a raised strip across a road designed to slow down vehicles

judge *n* **1** a public official with authority to hear cases and pass sentences in a court of law **2** a person appointed to determine the result of a competition **3** a person whose opinion on a particular subject is usually reliable: *a fine judge of character* ▸ *vb* **judging, judged 4** to determine the result of (a competition) **5** to appraise critically: *she hopes people judge her on her work rather than her appearance* **6** to decide (something) after inquiry: *we use a means test to judge the most needy cases* **7** to believe or consider: *doctors judged that the benefits of such treatment outweighed the risk*

> **judge** *n* **1** = magistrate, justice, beak (*Brit slang*), His, Her *or* Your Honour **2** = referee, expert, specialist, umpire, umpie (*Austral slang*), mediator, examiner, connoisseur, assessor **3** = critic, assessor, arbiter ▸ *vb* **4** = adjudicate, referee, umpire, mediate, officiate, arbitrate **5** = evaluate, rate, consider, view, value, esteem (*formal*) **6** = estimate, guess, assess, calculate, evaluate, gauge

judgment *or* **judgement** *n* **1** a decision formed after careful consideration: *the editorials reserve their judgment about the new political plan* **2** the verdict pronounced by a court of law **3** the ability to make critical distinctions and achieve a balanced viewpoint: *their judgment was unsound on foreign and defence issues* **4** the formal decision of the judge of a competition **5 against one's better judgment** contrary to what one thinks is sensible: *against my better judgment, I applied to study law* **6 pass judgment** to give one's opinion, usually a critical one, on a matter

judgment or **judgement** n 1 = opinion, view, estimate, belief, assessment, diagnosis, valuation, appraisal 2 = verdict, finding, ruling, decision, sentence, decree, arbitration, adjudication 3 = sense, good sense, understanding, discrimination, perception, wisdom, wit, prudence

judgmental or **judgemental** adj making judgments, esp. critical ones, about other people's conduct

judicial adj 1 of judges or the administration of justice 2 showing or using good judgment: *judicial self-restraint* > **judicially** adv

> **judicial** adj 1 = legal, official

judiciary n the branch of the central authority in a country that administers justice

judicious adj having or showing good judgment: *the judicious use of herbal remedies* > **judiciously** adv

judo n a sport derived from jujitsu, in which the two opponents try to throw or force each other on to the ground

jug n a container with a handle and a small spout, used for holding and pouring liquids

> **jug** n = container, pitcher, urn, carafe, creamer (US, Canad), vessel, jar, crock

jugged hare n hare stewed in an earthenware pot

juggernaut n 1 Brit a very large heavy lorry 2 any terrible force that demands complete self-sacrifice

juggle vb **-gling, -gled** 1 to throw and catch several objects continuously so that most are in the air at the same time 2 to keep (several activities) in progress at the same time: *people who are adept at juggling priorities* 3 to manipulate (facts or figures) to suit one's purpose > **juggler** n

> **juggle** vb 3 = manipulate, change, alter, modify, manoeuvre

jugular n a large vein in the neck that carries blood to the heart from the head. Also called: **jugular vein**

juice n 1 a drink made from the liquid part of a fruit or vegetable: *grapefruit juice* 2 informal **A** petrol **B** electricity 3 juices **A** the fluids in a person's or animal's body: *digestive juices* **B** the liquid that comes out of meat when it is cooked

> **juice** n 1 = liquid, extract, fluid, liquor, sap, nectar 3**A** = secretion

juicy adj **juicier, juiciest** 1 full of juice 2 informal interesting and exciting: *juicy details*

> **juicy** adj 1 = moist, lush, succulent 2 = interesting, colourful, sensational, vivid, provocative, spicy (*informal*), suggestive, racy

jujitsu n the traditional Japanese system of unarmed self-defence

juju n 1 a magic charm or fetish used by some tribes in W Africa 2 the power associated with a juju

jukebox n a machine that plays music when a payment is made

Jul. July

julep n a sweet alcoholic drink, usually garnished with sprigs of mint

July n, pl **-lies** the seventh month of the year

jumble n 1 a disordered mass or state 2 articles donated for a jumble sale ▶ vb **-bling, -bled** 3 to mix up

> **jumble** n 2 = muddle, mixture, mess, disorder, confusion, clutter, disarray, mishmash ▶ vb = mix, mistake, confuse, disorder, shuffle, muddle, disorganize

jumble sale n a sale, usually of second-hand articles, often in aid of charity

jumbo adj Brit, Austral & NZ informal very large: *jumbo prawns*

> **jumbo** adj = giant, large, huge, immense, gigantic, oversized, supersize; ≠ tiny

jumbuck n Austral old-fashioned slang sheep

jump vb 1 to move suddenly up into the air by using the muscles in the legs and feet 2 to move quickly: *he jumps on a No. 6 bus* 3 to jerk with astonishment or shock: *he jumped when he heard a loud noise* 4 (of prices) to rise suddenly or abruptly 5 to change quickly from one subject to another: *any other comments before I jump on to the next section?* 6 informal to attack without warning: *the officer was jumped by three prisoners who broke his jaw* 7 **jump down someone's throat** informal to speak sharply to someone 8 **jump the gun** See **gun** (sense 3) 9 **jump the queue** **A** to take a place in a queue ahead of people who are already queuing **B** to have an unfair advantage over other people: *squatters should not be able to jump the queue for housing* 10 **jump to it** informal to begin doing something immediately ▶ n 11 the act or an instance of jumping 12 sport any of several contests that involve jumping: *the long jump* 13 a sudden rise: *a 78% jump in taxable profits* 14 a sudden change from one subject to another: *stunning jumps from thought to thought* 15 a step or degree: *one jump ahead of the competition* 16 **take a running jump** informal a contemptuous expression of dismissal ▶ See also **jump at, jump on**

> **jump** vb 1 = leap, spring, bound, bounce, hop, skip 3 = recoil, start, jolt, flinch, shake, jerk, quake, shudder 4 = increase, rise, climb, escalate, advance, soar, surge, spiral ▶ n 11 = leap, spring, skip, bound, hop, vault 13 = rise, increase, upswing, advance, upsurge, upturn, increment

jump at vb to accept eagerly: *I jumped at the chance to return to English county cricket*

jumped-up adj informal having suddenly risen in significance and appearing arrogant: *a jumped-up bunch of ex-student-leaders*

jumped-up adj = conceited, arrogant, pompous, overbearing, presumptuous, insolent

jumper n 1 Brit & Austral a knitted garment covering the upper part of the body 2 US & Canad a pinafore dress

jumper n 1 = sweater, top, jersey, cardigan, woolly, pullover

jump jet n informal a fixed-wing jet aircraft that can land and take off vertically

jump leads pl n two heavy cables used to start a motor vehicle with a flat battery by connecting the flat battery to the battery of another vehicle

jump on vb informal to make a sudden physical or verbal attack on: the press really jumped on him

jump suit n a one-piece garment combining trousers and top

jumpy adj **jumpier**, **jumpiest** nervous or apprehensive

Jun. 1 June 2 Junior

junction n a place where roads or railway lines meet, link, or cross each other

juncture n a point in time, esp. a critical one: trade has been halted at a crucial juncture

June n the sixth month of the year

jungle n 1 a forest area in a hot country with luxuriant vegetation 2 a confused or confusing situation: the administrative jungle 3 a situation where there is an intense struggle for survival: the economic jungle

junior adj 1 lower in rank or position: junior officers 2 younger: world junior champion 3 (in England and Wales) of schoolchildren between the ages of 7 and 11 approximately 4 US of the third year of a four-year course at college or high school ▸ n 5 a person holding a low rank or position 6 a person who is younger than another person: the man she is to marry is 20 years her junior 7 (in England and Wales) a junior schoolchild 8 US a junior student

junior adj 1 = minor, lower, secondary, lesser, subordinate, inferior 2 = younger; ≠ senior

juniper n an evergreen shrub with purple berries which are used to make gin

junk¹ n 1 old or unwanted objects 2 informal rubbish: the sheer junk written about astrology 3 slang narcotic drugs, esp. heroin

junk n 1 = rubbish, refuse, waste, scrap, litter, debris, garbage (chiefly US), trash (chiefly US, Canad)

junk² n a Chinese sailing boat with a flat bottom and square sails

junket n 1 an excursion made by a public official and paid for out of public funds 2 a sweet dessert made of flavoured milk set with rennet 3 a feast > **junketing** n

junk food n food with a low nutritional value

junkie n informal a drug addict

junk mail n unsolicited mail advertising goods or services

junta n a group of military officers holding the power in a country after a revolution

Jupiter n 1 the king of the Roman gods 2 the largest planet

juridical adj of law or the administration of justice

jurisdiction n 1 the right or power to administer justice and to apply laws 2 the exercise or extent of such a right or power 3 authority in general: under the jurisdiction of the referee

jurisdiction n = authority, power, control, rule, influence, command, mana (NZ)

jurisprudence n the science or philosophy of law

jurist n a person who is an expert on law

juror n a member of a jury

jury n, pl **-ries** 1 a group of, usually, twelve people, sworn to deliver a true verdict according to the evidence upon a case presented in a court of law 2 a group of people appointed to judge a competition

just adv 1 very recently: the results have just been published 2 at this very instant or in the very near future: news is just coming in of a nuclear explosion 3 no more than; only: nothing fancy, just simple, honest fare 4 exactly: just the opposite 5 barely: the swimmers arrived just in time for the opening ceremony 6 **just about** practically or virtually: just about everyone 7 **just about to** very soon going to: it was just about to explode 8 **just a moment** or **second** or **minute** an expression requesting someone to wait for a short time 9 **just now** A a short time ago: as you said just now B at the present time: he needs all the support he can get just now C S African informal in a little while 10 **just so** arranged with precision: a cottage with the gardens and rooms all just so ▸ adj 11 fair and right: a just war > **justly** adv > **justness** n

just adv 1, 2 = recently, lately, only now 3 = merely, only, simply, solely 4 = exactly, really, quite, completely, totally, perfectly, entirely, truly 5 = barely, hardly, by a whisker, by the skin of your teeth ▸ adj = fair, good, legitimate, upright, honest, equitable, conscientious, virtuous; ≠ unfair

justice n 1 the quality of being just 2 the administration of law according to prescribed and accepted principles 3 a judge 4 **bring to justice** to capture, try, and punish (a criminal) 5 **do justice to** to show to full advantage: the choir was not able to do justice to Handel's music

justice n 1 = fairness, equity, integrity, honesty, decency, rightfulness, right; ≠ injustice 3 = judge, magistrate, beak (Brit slang), His, Her or Your Honour

justifiable adj having a good cause or reason: I reacted with justifiable indignation > **justifiably** adv

justify *vb* **-fies**, **-fying**, **-fied** **1** to prove (something) to be just or valid: *the idea of the end justifying the means* **2** to defend (an action) as being warranted: *an essay justifying his conversion to Catholicism* **3** to arrange (text) when typing or printing so that both margins are straight ▷ **justification** *n*

> **justify** *vb* **1, 2** = explain, support, warrant, defend, excuse, uphold, vindicate, exonerate

jute *n* a fibre that comes from the bark of an Asian plant, used in making rope, sacks, and mats

jut out *vb* **jutting**, **jutted** to stick out

juvenile *adj* **1** young; not fully adult: *juvenile offenders* **2** of or for young people: *juvenile court* **3** immature in behaviour ▶ *n* **4** a young person

> **juvenile** *adj* **1** = young, junior, adolescent, youthful, immature; ≠ adult **2** = merely, only, simply, solely **3** = immature, childish, infantile, puerile, young, youthful, inexperienced, callow ▶ *n* = child, youth, minor, girl, boy, teenager, infant, adolescent; ≠ adult

juvenile delinquent *n* a young person who is guilty of a crime ▷ **juvenile delinquency** *n*

juvenilia *pl n* works produced in an artist's youth

juxtapose *vb* **-posing**, **-posed** to place (two objects or ideas) close together or side by side ▷ **juxtaposition** *n*

Kk

K **1** kelvin(s) **2** *chess* king **3** *chem* potassium **4** one thousand **5** *computers* a unit of 1024 words, bits, or bytes

Kaffir (kaf-fer) *n S African taboo* a Black African

kaftan *or* **caftan** *n* **1** a long loose garment worn by men in eastern countries **2** a dress resembling this

kai *n NZ informal* food

> **kai** *n* = food, grub (*slang*), provisions, fare, tucker (*Austral, NZ informal*), refreshment, foodstuffs

kaiser (kize-er) *n history* a German or Austro-Hungarian emperor

kak (kuck) *n S African vulgar slang* **1** faeces **2** rubbish

> **kak** *n* **1** = faeces, excrement, manure, dung, droppings, waste matter **2** = rubbish, nonsense, garbage (*informal*), rot, drivel, tripe (*informal*), bizzo (*Austral slang*), bull's wool (*Austral, NZ slang*)

Kalashnikov *n* a Russian-made automatic rifle

kale *n* a type of cabbage with crinkled leaves

kaleidoscope *n* **1** a tube-shaped toy lined with angled mirrors and containing loose pieces of coloured paper that form intricate patterns when viewed through a hole in the end **2** any complicated or rapidly changing set of colours, circumstances, etc.: *a kaleidoscope of shifting political groups and alliances* ▷ **kaleidoscopic** *adj*

kamikaze (kam-mee-kah-zee) *n* **1** (in World War II) a Japanese pilot who performed a suicidal mission ▶ *adj* **2** (of an action) undertaken in the knowledge that it will result in the death or injury of the person performing it: *a kamikaze attack*

kangaroo *n, pl* **-roos** a large Australian marsupial with powerful hind legs used for leaping

kangaroo court *n* an unofficial court set up by a group to discipline its members

kangaroo paw *n* an Australian plant with green-and-red flowers

kaolin *n* a fine white clay used in making porcelain and in some medicines

kapok *n* a fluffy fibre from a tropical tree, used for stuffing pillows and padding sleeping bags

kaput (kap-poot) *adj informal* ruined or broken: *the chronometer, incidentally, is kaput*

karaoke *n* a form of entertainment in which members of the public sing well-known songs over a prerecorded backing tape

k

karate n a Japanese system of unarmed combat, in which punches, chops, and kicks are made with the hands, feet, elbows, and legs

karma n *Hinduism & Buddhism* a person's actions affecting his or her fate in the next incarnation

karoo or **karroo** n, pl **-roos** *S African* an arid semidesert plateau of Southern Africa

karri n, pl **-ris 1** an Australian eucalypt **2** its wood, used for building

katipo n, pl **-pos** a small venomous New Zealand spider, commonly black with a red or orange stripe on the abdomen

kauri n a large New Zealand conifer grown for its valuable wood and resin

kayak n **1** an Inuit canoe-like boat consisting of a frame covered with animal skins **2** a fibreglass or canvas-covered canoe of similar design

kbps *computers* kilobits per second

kbyte *computers* kilobyte

kebab n a dish consisting of small pieces of meat and vegetables, usually threaded onto skewers and grilled

kedgeree n *chiefly Brit* a dish consisting of rice, fish, and eggs

keel n **1** one of the main lengthways steel or timber pieces along the base of a ship, to which the frames are fastened **2 on an even keel** working or progressing smoothly without any sudden changes

keel over vb **1** (of an object) to turn upside down **2** *informal* (of a person) to collapse suddenly

keen¹ adj **1** eager or enthusiastic: *a keen gardener* **2** intense or strong: *a keen interest in environmental issues* **3** intelligent, quick, and perceptive: *a keen sense of humour* **4** (of sight, smell, or hearing) capable of recognizing fine distinctions **5** (of a knife or blade) having a sharp cutting edge **6** very strong and cold: *a keen wind* **7** very competitive: *keen prices* **8 keen on** fond of; devoted to: *he is very keen on sport* > **keenly** adv > **keenness** n

> **keen** adj **1, 8** = eager, intense, enthusiastic, passionate, ardent, avid, fervent, impassioned; ≠ unenthusiastic **2** = earnest, fierce, intense, vehement, passionate, heightened, ardent, fanatical **3** = perceptive, quick, sharp, acute, smart, wise, clever, shrewd; ≠ obtuse **5** = sharp, incisive, cutting, edged, razor-like; ≠ dull **7** = intense, strong, fierce, relentless, cut-throat

keen² vb **1** to lament the dead ▸ n **2** a lament for the dead

keep vb **keeping, kept 1** to have or retain possession of (something) **2** to have temporary charge of: *he'd kept my broken beads in his pocket for me all evening* **3** to store in a customary place: *I keep it at the back of the drawer with my journal* **4** to remain or cause (someone or something) to remain in a specified state or condition: *keep still* **5** to continue or cause (someone) to continue: *keep*

going straight on **6** to stay (in, on, or at a place or position): *keep to the paths* **7** to have as part of normal stock: *they keep a small stock of first-class German wines* **8** to support (someone) financially **9** to detain (someone) **10** to be faithful to (something): *to keep a promise* **11** (of food) to stay in good condition for a certain time: *fish doesn't keep very well* **12** to observe (a religious festival) with rites or ceremonies **13** to maintain by writing regular records in: *I keep a nature diary in my spare time* **14** to look after or maintain for use, pleasure, or profit: *an old man who kept goats and cows* **15** to associate with: *she has started keeping bad company* **16 how are you keeping?** are you well? **17 keep in with** to stay friendly with a person as they may be useful to one ▸ n **18** the cost of food and other everyday expenses: *I have to earn my keep* **19** the main tower within the walls of a medieval castle or fortress **20 for keeps** *informal* permanently

> **keep** vb **1** = hold on to, maintain, retain, save, preserve, nurture, cherish, conserve; ≠ lose **2, 3** = store, put, place, house, hold, deposit, stack, stow **7** = carry, stock, sell, supply, handle **8** = support, maintain, sustain, provide for, mind, fund, finance, feed **9** = delay, detain, hinder, impede, obstruct, set back; ≠ release **14** = raise, own, maintain, tend, farm, breed, look after, rear ▸ n **18** = board, food, maintenance, living, kai (*NZ informal*) **19** = tower, castle

keeper n **1** a person in charge of animals in a zoo **2** a person in charge of a museum, collection, or section of a museum **3** a person who supervises a person or thing: *the self-appointed keeper of the village conscience* **4** short for **gamekeeper** or **goalkeeper**

> **keeper** n **2** = curator, guardian, steward, attendant, caretaker, preserver

keep fit n exercises designed to promote physical fitness if performed regularly

keeping n **1 in keeping with** suitable or appropriate to or for **2 out of keeping with** unsuitable or inappropriate to or for

> **keeping** n **1** = care, charge, protection, possession, custody, guardianship, safekeeping

keepsake n a gift kept in memory of the giver

keep up vb **1** to maintain at the present level **2** to maintain in good condition **3 keep up with** **A** to maintain a pace set by (someone) **B** to remain informed about: *he liked to think he kept up with current musical trends* **C** to remain in contact with (someone) **4 keep up with the Joneses** *informal* to compete with one's friends or neighbours in material possessions

> **keep up** vb **1 keep something up** = maintain, sustain, perpetuate, retain, preserve, prolong

keg *n* a small barrel in which beer is transported and stored

kelp *n* a large brown seaweed rich in iodine and potash

kelpie *n* **1** (in Scottish folklore) a water spirit in the form of a horse **2** an Australian sheepdog with a smooth coat and upright ears

kelvin *n physics* the basic SI unit of thermodynamic temperature

Kelvin scale *n physics* a thermodynamic temperature scale starting at absolute zero

ken *n* **1 beyond one's ken** beyond one's range of knowledge ▸ *vb* **kenning, kenned** or **kent 2** *Scot & N English dialect* to know

kendo *n* the Japanese sport of fencing using wooden staves

kennel *n* **1** a hutlike shelter for a dog **2 kennels** a place where dogs are bred, trained, or boarded ▸ *vb* **-nelling, -nelled** or US **-neling, -neled 3** to keep (a dog) in a kennel

kept *vb* **1** the past of **keep 2 kept woman** or **man** a person who is financially supported by a sexual partner

keratin *n* a fibrous protein found in the hair and nails

kerb or US & Canad **curb** *n* a line of stone or concrete forming an edge between a pavement and a roadway

kerb crawling *n Brit* the act of driving slowly beside a kerb to pick up a prostitute
> **kerb crawler** *n*

kerchief *n* a piece of cloth worn over the head or round the neck

kerfuffle *n informal* a noisy and disorderly incident

kernel *n* **1** the edible seed of a nut or fruit within the shell or stone **2** the grain of a cereal, such as wheat, consisting of the seed in a hard husk **3** the central or essential part of something: *there is a kernel of truth in these remarks*

kerosene *n US, Canad, Austral & NZ* same as **paraffin** (sense 1)

kestrel *n* a small falcon that feeds on small animals such as mice

ketchup *n* a thick cold sauce, usually made of tomatoes

kettle *n* **1** a metal container with a handle and spout, for boiling water **2** any of various metal containers for heating liquid, cooking, etc. **3 a different kettle of fish** a different matter entirely **4 a fine kettle of fish** a difficult or awkward situation ▸ *vb* **-tling, -tled 5** (of police) to force (demonstrators) into an enclosed space

kettledrum *n* a large bowl-shaped metal drum that can be tuned to play specific notes

key *n* **1** a specially shaped metal instrument for moving the bolt of a lock so as to lock or unlock a door, suitcase, etc. **2** an instrument that is turned to operate a valve, clock winding mechanism, etc. **3** any of a set of levers pressed to operate a computer, typewriter, or musical keyboard instrument **4** a scale of musical notes that starts at one specific note **5** something that is crucial in providing an explanation or interpretation **6** a means of achieving a desired end: *education is the key to success in most walks of life today* **7** a list of explanations of symbols, codes, or abbreviations **8** pitch: *he spoke in a low key* ▸ *adj* **9** of great importance: *key prosecution witnesses have been giving evidence* ▸ *vb* **10** to harmonize with: *training and educational programmes uniquely keyed for local needs* **11** to adjust or fasten (something) with a key or some similar device **12** to enter (information or instructions) into a computer by means of a keyboard ▸ See also **key in**

> **key** *n* **1** = opener, door key, latchkey
> **6** = answer ▸ *adj* = essential, leading, major, main, important, necessary, vital, crucial; ≠ minor

keyboard *n* **1** a set of keys on a computer, typewriter, or piano **2** a musical instrument played using a keyboard

keyhole *n* an opening for inserting a key into a lock

key in *vb* to enter (information or instructions) into a computer by means of a keyboard

keynote *n* **1** a central or dominant idea in a speech or literary work **2** the note on which a scale or key is based ▸ *adj* **3** central or dominating: *his keynote speech to the party conference*

keypad *n* a small panel with a set of buttons for operating an electronic device

keystone *n* **1** the most important part of a process, organization, etc.: *the keystone of the government's economic policy* **2** the central stone at the top of an arch

key worker *n chiefly Brit* **1** a social worker, mental health worker, or nursery nurse assigned to an individual case, patient, or child **2** (in Britain) a worker in a public sector profession considered by the government to be essential to society

kg kilogram

khaki *adj* **1** dull yellowish-brown ▸ *n* **2** a hard-wearing fabric of this colour, used for military uniforms

kHz kilohertz

kia ora *interj NZ* a Māori greeting

> **kia ora** *interj* = hello, hi (*informal*), greetings, gidday or g'day (*Austral, NZ*), how do you do?, good morning, good evening, good afternoon

kibbutz *n, pl* **kibbutzim** a farm, factory, or other workplace in Israel, owned and run communally by its members

kick *vb* **1** to drive, push, or hit with the foot or feet **2** to strike out with the feet, as in swimming **3** to raise a leg high, as in dancing **4** *rugby* to score (a conversion, drop kick, or penalty) with a kick: *he kicked his third penalty* **5** (of a firearm) to recoil when fired **6** *informal* to object or resist: *school uniforms give children something to kick against* **7** *informal* to free oneself of (an addiction): *smokers who want to kick the habit* **8 alive and kicking** *informal* active and in good health **9 kick someone upstairs** to promote someone to a higher but effectively powerless position ▸ *n* **10** a thrust or blow with the foot **11** any of certain rhythmic leg movements used in swimming **12** the recoil of a firearm **13** *informal* an exciting effect: *I always get a kick out of decorating the Christmas cake* **14** *informal* the intoxicating effect of an alcoholic drink: *a cocktail with a kick in it* **15 kick in the teeth** *slang* a humiliating rebuff

> **kick** *vb* **1** = boot, knock, punt **7** = give up, break, stop, abandon, quit, cease, eschew, leave off ▸ *n* **13** = thrill, buzz (*slang*), tingle, high (*informal*)

kickback *n* **1** part of an income paid to a person in return for an opportunity to make a profit, esp. in an illegal arrangement **2** a strong reaction

kick off *vb* **1** to start play in a game of football by kicking the ball from the centre of the field **2** *informal* to commence (a discussion, event, etc.) ▸ *n* **kick-off 3 A** the kick that officially starts a game of football **B** the time when the first kick is due to take place **4** *informal* the time when an event is due to begin

> **kick off** *vb* **2 kick something off** = begin, start, open, commence, initiate, get on the road

kick out *vb informal* to dismiss (someone) or throw (someone) out forcefully

> **kick out** *vb* **kick someone out** = dismiss, remove, get rid of, expel, eject, evict, sack (*informal*), kennet (*Austral slang*), jeff (*Austral slang*)

kick-start *n* **1** Also: **kick-starter** a pedal on a motorcycle that is kicked downwards to start the engine **2** an action or event that reactivates something ▸ *vb* **3** to start (a motorcycle) with a kick-start **4** to do something bold or drastic in order to begin or improve the performance of something: *to kick-start the economy*

kick up *vb informal* to cause (trouble)

kid¹ *n* **1** *informal* a young person; child **2** a young goat **3** soft smooth leather made from the hide of a kid ▸ *adj* **4** younger: *my kid sister* ▸ *vb* **kidding, kidded 5** (of a goat) to give birth to (young)

> **kid** *n* **1** = child, baby, teenager, youngster, infant, adolescent, juvenile, toddler, littlie (*Austral informal*), ankle-biter (*Austral slang*), tacker (*Austral slang*)

kid² *vb* **kidding, kidded** *informal* **1** to tease or deceive (someone) for fun **2** to fool (oneself) into believing something: *don't kid yourself that no-one else knows* ▸ **kidder** *n*

> **kid** *vb* **1** = tease, joke, trick, fool, pretend, wind up (*Brit slang*), hoax, delude

kiddie *n informal* a child

kidnap *vb* **-napping, -napped** *or US* **-naping, -naped** to capture and hold (a person), usually for ransom ▸ **kidnapper** *or US* **-naper** *n* ▸ **kidnapping** *or US* **-naping** *n*

> **kidnap** *vb* = abduct, capture, seize, snatch (*slang*), hijack, hold to ransom

kidney *n* **1** either of two bean-shaped organs at the back of the abdominal cavity. They filter waste products from the blood, which are excreted as urine **2** the kidneys of certain animals used as food

kidney bean *n* a reddish-brown kidney-shaped bean, edible when cooked

kill *vb* **1** to cause the death of (a person or animal) **2** *informal* to cause (someone) pain or discomfort: *my feet are killing me* **3** to put an end to: *his obsession with work has killed his marriage* **4** *informal* to quash or veto: *the main opposition party tried to kill the bill* **5** *informal* to overwhelm (someone) completely with laughter, attraction, or surprise: *her jokes really kill me* **6 kill oneself** *informal* to overexert oneself **7 kill time** to spend time on something unimportant or trivial while waiting for something: *I'm just killing time until I can talk to the other witnesses* **8 kill two birds with one stone** to achieve two results with one action ▸ *n* **9** the act of causing death at the end of a hunt or bullfight **10** the animal or animals killed during a hunt **11 in at the kill** present when something comes to a dramatic end with unpleasant results for someone else ▸ **killer** *n*

> **kill** *vb* **1** = slay, murder, execute, slaughter, destroy, massacre, butcher, cut down **3, 4** = destroy, crush, scotch, stop, halt, wreck, shatter, suppress

killer whale *n* a black-and-white toothed whale, most common in cold seas

killing *adj* **1** *informal* very tiring: *a killing pace* **2** *informal* extremely funny **3** causing death; fatal ▸ *n* **4** the act of causing death; slaying **5 make a killing** *informal* to have a sudden financial success

> **killing** *adj* **1** = tiring, taxing, exhausting, punishing, fatiguing, gruelling, sapping, debilitating ▸ *n* **4** = murder, massacre, slaughter, dispatch, manslaughter, elimination, slaying, homicide **5 make a killing** = profit, gain, clean up (*informal*), be lucky, be successful, make a fortune, strike it rich (*informal*), make a bomb (*slang*)

killjoy *n* a person who spoils other people's pleasure

kiln *n* a large oven for burning, drying, or processing pottery, bricks, etc.

kilo *n*, *pl* **kilos** short for **kilogram** or **kilometre**

kilo- *combining form* **1** denoting one thousand (10^3): *kilometre* **2** (in computers) denoting 2^{10} (1024): *kilobyte*. In computer usage, *kilo-* is restricted to sizes of storage (eg *kilobit*) when it means 1024: in other computer contexts it retains its usual meaning of 1000

kilobyte *n computers* 1024 bytes

kilogram *or* **kilogramme** *n* **1** one thousand grams **2** the basic SI unit of mass

kilohertz *n, pl* **kilohertz** one thousand hertz; one thousand cycles per second

kilometre *or US* **kilometer** *n* a unit of length equal to one thousand metres

kilowatt *n* one thousand watts

kilt *n* **1** a knee-length pleated tartan skirt-like garment, worn by men in Highland dress and by women and girls ▸ *vb* **2** to put pleats in (cloth) ▸ **kilted** *adj*

kimono (kim-moan-no) *n, pl* **-nos** **1** a loose wide-sleeved Japanese robe, fastened with a sash **2** a European dressing gown resembling this

kin *n* a person's relatives collectively

kind¹ *adj* **1** considerate, friendly, and helpful: *a good, kind man; a few kind words* **2** cordial; courteous: *reprinted by kind permission*

> **kind** *adj* **1** = considerate, kindly, concerned, friendly, generous, obliging, charitable, benign; ≠ unkind

kind² *n* **1** a class or group having characteristics in common: *what kind of music do you like?* **2** essential nature or character: *differences of degree rather than of kind* **3** **in kind** **A** (of payment) in goods or services rather than in money **B** with something of the same sort: *the government threatened to retaliate in kind to any act of hostility* **4** **kind of** to a certain extent; loosely: *kind of hard; a kind of socialist* **5** **of a kind** of a poorer quality or standard than is wanted or expected: *a few farmers wrest subsistence of a kind from the thin topsoil*

> **kind** *n* **1** = class, sort, type, variety, brand, category, genre

kindergarten *n* a class or school for children under six years old

kind-hearted *adj* considerate and sympathetic

kindle *vb* **-dling, -dled** **1** to set (a fire) alight or (of a fire) to start to burn **2** to arouse or be aroused: *his passions were kindled as quickly as her own*

kindling *n* material for starting a fire, such as dry wood or straw

kindly *adj* **-lier, -liest** **1** having a warm-hearted and caring nature **2** pleasant or agreeable: *a kindly climate* ▸ *adv* **3** in a considerate or humane way **4** please: *will you kindly stop prattling on about it!* **5** **not take kindly to** to react unfavourably towards ▸ **kindliness** *n*

> **kindly** *adj* **1** = benevolent, kind, caring, warm, helpful, pleasant, sympathetic, benign; ≠ cruel ▸ *adv* **3** = benevolently, politely, generously, thoughtfully, tenderly, lovingly, cordially, affectionately; ≠ unkindly

kindness *n* **1** the quality of being kind **2** a kind or helpful act

> **kindness** *n* **1** = goodwill, understanding, charity, humanity, compassion, generosity, philanthropy, benevolence; ≠ malice

kindred *adj* **1** having similar qualities: *cholera, and other kindred diseases* **2** related by blood or marriage **3** **kindred spirit** a person with whom one has something in common ▸ *n* **4** relationship by blood or marriage **5** similarity in character **6** a person's relatives collectively

kindy *or* **kindie** *n, pl* **-dies** *Austral & NZ informal* a kindergarten

kinetic (kin-net-ik) *adj* relating to or caused by motion ▸ **kinetically** *adv*

king *n* **1** a male ruler of a country who has inherited the throne from his parents **2** a ruler or chief: *the king of the fairies* **3** a person, animal, or thing considered as the best or most important of its kind: *the king of rock and roll* **4** a playing card with a picture of a king on it **5** a chess piece, able to move one square in any direction: *the object of the game is to checkmate one's opponent's king* **6** *draughts* a piece which has moved entirely across the board and been crowned and which may therefore move backwards as well as forwards ▸ **kingship** *n*

> **king** *n* **1, 2** = ruler, monarch, sovereign, leader, lord, Crown, emperor, head of state

kingdom *n* **1** a territory or state ruled by a king or queen **2** any of the three groups into which natural objects may be divided: the animal, plant, and mineral kingdoms **3** a place or area considered to be under the total power and control of a person, organization, or thing: *the kingdom of God*

> **kingdom** *n* **1** = country, state, nation, territory, realm

kingfisher *n* a fish-eating bird with a greenish-blue and orange plumage

king prawn *n* a large prawn, fished commercially in Australian waters

king-size *or* **king-sized** *adj* larger than a standard size

kink *n* **1** a twist or bend in something such as a rope or hair **2** *informal* a flaw or quirk in someone's personality ▸ *vb* **3** to form or cause to form a kink

kinky *adj* **kinkier, kinkiest** **1** *slang* given to unusual sexual practices **2** tightly looped or curled

kinsfolk *pl n* one's family or relatives

kinship *n* **1** blood relationship **2** the state of having common characteristics

kiosk *n* a small booth from which cigarettes, newspapers, and sweets are sold

kip *Brit slang* ▸ *n* **1** sleep: *a couple of hours' kip* **2** a bed ▸ *vb* **kipping, kipped** **3** to sleep or take a nap **4** **kip down** to sleep in a makeshift bed

kipper *n* **1** a herring that has been cleaned, salted, and smoked ▸ *vb* **2** to cure (a herring) by salting and smoking it

k

kirk n Scot a church

Kirsch or **Kirschwasser** n a brandy distilled from black cherries

kismet n fate or destiny

kiss vb **1** to touch with the lips as an expression of love, greeting, or respect **2** to join lips with another person as an act of love or desire **3** literary to touch lightly: a long high free kick that kissed the top of the crossbar ▸ n **4** a caress with the lips **5** a light touch ▸ **kissable** adj

> **kiss** vb **1, 2** = peck (informal), osculate, neck (informal) **3** = brush, touch, shave, scrape, graze, glance off, stroke ▸ n **4** = peck (informal), snog (Brit slang), smacker (slang), French kiss, osculation

kissagram n Brit, Austral & NZ a greetings service in which a person is employed to present greetings by kissing the person celebrating

kisser n slang the mouth or face

kissing crust n NZ the soft end of a loaf of bread where two loaves have been separated

kist n Scot & S African a large wooden chest

kit n **1** a set of tools or supplies for use together or for a purpose: a first-aid kit **2** the container for such a set **3** a set of parts sold ready to be assembled: a model aircraft kit **4** a basket or box for holding fish **5** clothing and other personal effects, such as those of a soldier: a complete set of school team kit ▸ See also **kit out**

> **kit** n **1** = equipment, materials, tackle, tools, apparatus, paraphernalia **5** = gear, things, stuff, equipment, uniform

kitbag n a canvas or other bag for a soldier's or sailor's kit

kitchen n a room equipped for preparing and cooking food

kitchenette n a small kitchen or part of a room equipped for use as a kitchen

kitchen garden n a garden for growing vegetables, herbs, etc.

kite n **1** a light frame covered with a thin material flown in the wind at the end of a length of string **2** a bird of prey with a long forked tail and large wings **3** a four-sided geometrical shape in which each side is equal in length to one of the sides joining it

Kite mark n Brit the official mark in the form of a kite on articles approved by the British Standards Institution

kith n kith and kin old-fashioned one's friends and relations

kit out or **kit up** vb **kitting, kitted** chiefly Brit to provide with clothes or equipment needed for a particular activity

> **kit out** or **kit up** vb kit something or someone out or up = equip, fit, supply, provide with, arm, stock, costume, furnish

kitsch n tawdry or sentimental art or literature ▸ **kitschy** adj

kitten n **1** a young cat **2** have kittens informal to react with disapproval or anxiety: she had kittens when she discovered the price

kittenish adj lively and flirtatious

kittiwake n a type of seagull with pale grey black-tipped wings and a square-cut tail

kitty¹ n, pl **-ties** a diminutive or affectionate name for a **kitten** or **cat**

kitty² n, pl **-ties** any shared fund of money

kiwi n, pl **kiwis 1** a flightless bird of New Zealand with a long beak, stout legs, and no tail **2** informal a New Zealander

kiwi fruit n an edible fruit with a fuzzy brown skin and green flesh

klaxon n a type of loud horn used on fire engines and ambulances as a warning signal

kleptomania n psychol a strong impulse to steal ▸ **kleptomaniac** n

kloof n S African a mountain pass or gorge

km kilometre(s)

knack n **1** a skilful way of doing something **2** an ability to do something difficult with apparent ease

> **knack** n = skill, art, ability, facility, talent, gift, capacity, trick; ≠ ineptitude

knacker n Brit a person who buys up old horses for slaughter

knackered adj slang **1** extremely tired: they'd been marching for three hours and were absolutely knackered **2** broken or no longer functioning: a knackered TV set

knapsack n a canvas or leather bag carried strapped on the back or shoulder

knave n **1** cards the jack **2** archaic a dishonest man ▸ **knavish** adj

knead vb **1** to work and press (a soft substance, such as dough) into a smooth mixture with the hands **2** to squeeze or press with the hands ▸ **kneader** n

knee n **1** the joint of the leg between the thigh and the lower leg **2** the area around this joint **3** the upper surface of a sitting person's thigh: a little girl being cuddled on her father's knee **4** the part of a garment that covers the knee **5** bring someone to his or her knees to force someone into submission ▸ vb **kneeing, kneed 6** to strike, nudge, or push with the knee

kneecap n **1** anatomy a small flat triangular bone in front of and protecting the knee ▸ vb **-capping, -capped 2** (of terrorists) to shoot (a person) in the kneecap

knee-jerk n **1** physiol a sudden involuntary kick of the lower leg caused by a sharp tap on the tendon just below the kneecap ▸ adj **kneejerk 2** made or occurring as a predictable and automatic response: a kneejerk reaction

kneel vb **kneeling, knelt** or **kneeled 1** to rest, fall, or support oneself on one's knees ▸ n **2** the act or position of kneeling

> **kneel** vb = genuflect, stoop

knees-up n Brit informal a party

knell n **1** the sound of a bell rung to announce a death or a funeral **2** something that indicates death or destruction ▸ vb **3** to ring a knell **4** to proclaim by a tolling bell

knew vb the past tense of **know**

knickerbockers pl n loose-fitting short trousers gathered in at the knee or calf

knickers pl n a woman's or girl's undergarment covering the lower trunk and having separate legs or leg-holes

> **knickers** pl n = underwear, smalls, briefs, drawers, panties, bloomers

knick-knack n a small ornament or trinket

knife n, pl **knives** **1** a cutting instrument or weapon consisting of a sharp-edged blade of metal fitted into a handle ▸ vb **knifing, knifed** **2** to stab or kill with a knife > **knifelike** adj

> **knife** n = blade, carver, cutter ▸ vb = cut, wound, stab, slash, thrust, pierce, spear, jab

knight n **1** a man who has been given a knighthood in recognition of his achievements **2** **A** (in medieval Europe) a person who served his lord as a mounted and heavily armed soldier **B** (in medieval Europe) a devoted male admirer of a noblewoman, esp. her champion in a jousting tournament **3** a chess piece shaped like a horse's head, able to move either two squares horizontally and one square vertically or two squares vertically and one square horizontally ▸ vb **4** to make (a man) a knight

knighthood n an honorary title given to a man by the British sovereign in recognition of his achievements

knightly adj of, resembling, or appropriate for a knight > **knightliness** n

knit vb **knitting, knitted** or **knit** **1** to make (a garment) by looping (wool) using long eyeless needles or a knitting machine **2** to join together closely **3** to draw (one's eyebrows) together ▸ n **4** a fabric made by knitting > **knitter** n

> **knit** vb **2** = join, unite, link, tie, bond, combine, bind, weave **3** = furrow, tighten, knot, wrinkle, crease, screw up, pucker, scrunch up

knitting n knitted work or the process of producing it

knitwear n knitted clothes, such as sweaters

knob n **1** a rounded projection from a surface, such as a rotating switch on a radio **2** a rounded handle of a door or drawer **3** a small amount of butter or margarine > **knoblike** adj

> **knob** n **1** = ball, stud, knot, lump, bump, projection, hump, protrusion

knobbly adj having or covered with small bumps: a curious knobbly root vegetable

knobkerrie n S African a club or a stick with a rounded end

knock vb **1** to give a blow or push to **2** to rap sharply with the knuckles: he knocked on the door of the guest room **3** to make by striking: he knocked a hole in the wall **4** to collide (with) **5** to bring into a certain condition by striking: he was knocked unconscious in a collision **6** informal to criticize adversely **7** to emit a regular banging sound as a result of a fault: the engine was knocking badly **8** **knock on the head** to prevent the further development of (a plan) ▸ n **9** **A** a blow, push, or rap: he gave the table a knock **B** the sound so caused **10** the sound of knocking in an engine or bearing **11** informal a misfortune, rejection, or setback **12** informal criticism ▸ See also **knock about, knock back** etc.

> **knock** vb **1** = hit, strike, punch, belt (informal), smack, thump, cuff **2** = bang, strike, tap, rap, thump, pummel **6** = criticize, condemn, put down, run down, abuse, slate (informal), censure, denigrate, nit-pick (informal) ▸ n **9A** = blow, hit, punch, crack (informal), clip, slap, bash, smack **11** = setback, check, defeat, blow, reverse, disappointment, hold-up, hitch

knock about or **knock around** vb **1** to wander or travel about: I have knocked about the world through three continents **2** (foll. by with) to associate **3** to treat brutally: they used to knock me about a bit and try and make me cry **4** to consider or discuss informally ▸ adj **knockabout 5** (of comedy) lively, boisterous, and physical

> **knock about** or **knock around** vb **1** **knock about or around** = wander, travel, roam, rove, range, drift, stray, ramble, go walkabout (Austral) **2** **knock about or around with someone** = mix with, associate with, mingle with, consort with, hobnob with, socialize with, accompany **3** **knock someone about or around** = hit, attack, beat, strike, abuse, injure, assault, batter

knock back vb informal **1** to drink quickly: he fell over after knocking back eight pints of lager **2** to cost: lunch for two here will knock you back a small fortune **3** to reject or refuse: I don't know anyone who'd knock back an offer like that ▸ n **knockback 4** slang a refusal or rejection

knock down vb **1** to strike to the ground with a blow, such as in boxing **2** (in auctions) to declare an article sold **3** to demolish **4** informal to reduce (a price) ▸ adj **knockdown 5** powerful: a knockdown argument **6** chiefly Brit (of a price) very cheap **7** easily dismantled: knockdown furniture

> **knock down** vb **1** **knock someone down** = run over, hit, run down, knock over, mow down **3** **knock something down** = demolish, destroy, flatten, tear down, level, fell, dismantle, bulldoze, kennet (Austral slang), jeff (Austral slang)

k

knocker *n* **1** a metal object attached to a door by a hinge and used for knocking **2 knockers** *vulgar slang* a woman's breasts

knock-knees *pl n* legs that are bent inwards at the knees ▸ **knock-kneed** *adj*

knock off *vb* **1** *informal* to finish work: *around ten, the day shift knocked off* **2** *informal* to make or do hastily or easily: *she knocked off 600 books in all during her long life* **3** *informal* to take (an amount) off the price of (an article): *I'll knock off 10% if you pay cash* **4** *Brit, Austral & NZ informal* to steal **5** *slang* to kill **6** *slang* to stop doing something; used as a command: *knock it off!*

> **knock off** *vb* = stop work, get out, call it a day (*informal*), finish work, clock off, clock out **4 knock something off** = steal, take, nick (*slang, chiefly Brit*), thieve, rob, pinch (*Brit informal*)

knockout *n* **1** the act of rendering someone unconscious **2** *boxing* a blow that renders an opponent unable to continue after the referee has counted to ten **3** a competition in which competitors are eliminated progressively **4** *informal* a person or thing that is very impressive or attractive: *at my youngest sister's wedding she was a knockout in navy and scarlet* ▸ *vb* **knock out 5** to render (someone) unconscious **6** *boxing* to defeat (an opponent) by a knockout **7** to destroy: *communications in many areas were knocked out by the earthquake* **8** to eliminate from a knockout competition **9** *informal* to amaze: *the fantastic audience reaction knocked me out*

> **knockout** *n* = killer blow, coup de grâce (*French*), KO or K.O. (*slang*) **4** = success, hit, winner, triumph, smash (*informal*), sensation, smash hit; ≠ failure

knock up *vb* **1** Also: **knock together** *informal* to make or assemble quickly: *my boyfriend can knock up a wonderful lasagne* **2** *Brit informal* to waken: *to knock someone up early* **3** *slang* to make pregnant **4** to practise before a game of tennis, squash, or badminton ▸ *n* **knock-up 5** a practice session at tennis, squash, or badminton

knoll *n* a small rounded hill

knot *n* **1** a fastening formed by looping and tying pieces of rope, cord, or string **2** a tangle, such as in hair **3** a decorative bow, such as of ribbon **4** a small cluster or huddled group: *a knot of passengers gathered on the platform* **5** a bond: *to tie the knot of friendship* **6 A** a hard mass of wood where a branch joins the trunk of a tree **B** a cross section of this, visible in timber **7** a feeling of tightness, caused by tension or nervousness: *a dull knot of anxiety that sat in the pit of her stomach* **8** a unit of speed used by ships and aircraft, equal to one nautical mile per hour **9 at a rate of knots** very fast **10 tie someone in knots** to confuse someone completely ▸ *vb* **knotting, knotted 11** to tie or fasten in a knot **12** to form into a knot **13** to entangle or become entangled > **knotted** *adj* > **knotless** *adj*

> **knot** *n* **1, 3** = connection, tie, bond, joint, loop, ligature ▸ *vb* **11** = tie, secure, bind, loop, tether

knotty *adj* **-tier, -tiest 1** full of knots **2** extremely difficult or puzzling: *a knotty problem*

know *vb* **knowing, knew, known 1** to be or feel certain of the truth or accuracy of (a fact, answer, or piece of information) **2** to be acquainted with: *I'd known him for many years, since I was seventeen* **3** to have a grasp of or understand (a skill or language) **4** to understand or be aware of (something, or how to do or be something): *she knew how to get on with people* **5** to experience: *you had to have known poverty before you could give money its true value, he claimed* **6** to be intelligent, informed, or sensible enough (to do something): *how did he know to send the letter in the first place?* **7** to be able to distinguish: *I don't know one flower from another* **8 know what's what** to know how one thing or things in general work **9 you never know** things are uncertain ▸ *n* **10 in the know** *informal* aware or informed > **knowable** *adj*

> **know** *vb* **1** = have knowledge of, see, understand, recognize, perceive, be aware of, be conscious of **2** = be acquainted with, recognize, be familiar with, be friends with, be friendly with, have knowledge of, have dealings with, socialize with; ≠ be unfamiliar with **3, 4, 5** = be familiar with, understand, comprehend, have knowledge of, be acquainted with, feel certain of, have dealings in, be versed in; ≠ be ignorant of

know-all *n informal, derogatory* a person who pretends or appears to know a lot more than other people

know-how *n informal* the ability to do something that is difficult or technical

> **know-how** *n* = expertise, ability, skill, knowledge, facility, talent, command, capability

knowing *adj* **1** suggesting secret knowledge: *Paul saw the knowing look that passed between them* **2** cunning or shrewd **3** deliberate > **knowingly** *adv* > **knowingness** *n*

> **knowing** *adj* **1** = meaningful, significant, expressive, enigmatic, suggestive

knowledge *n* **1** the facts or experiences known by a person or group of people **2** the state of knowing **3** specific information about a subject **4 to my knowledge** as I understand it

> **knowledge** *n* **1** = learning, education, intelligence, instruction, wisdom, scholarship, enlightenment, erudition; ≠ ignorance **2** = understanding, sense, judgment, perception, awareness, insight, grasp, appreciation; ≠ unfamiliarity

knowledgeable or **knowledgable** adj intelligent or well-informed ▸ **knowledgeably** or **knowledgably** adv

> **knowledgeable** or **knowledgable** adj = intelligent, learned, educated, scholarly, erudite

knuckle n **1** a joint of a finger **2** the knee joint of a calf or pig **3 near the knuckle** informal likely to offend people because of frankness or rudeness ▸ See also **knuckle under**

knuckle-duster n a metal appliance worn over the knuckles to add force to a blow

knuckle under vb **-ling, -led** to give way under pressure or authority

KO or **k.o.** vb **KO'ing, KO'd** or **k.o.'ing, k.o.'d 1** to knock out ▸ n, pl **KO's** or **k.o.'s 2** a knockout

koala or **koala bear** n a tree-dwelling Australian marsupial with dense grey fur

kohanga reo or **kohanga** n NZ an infant class where children are taught in Māori

kohl n a cosmetic powder used to darken the area around the eyes

kookaburra n a large Australian kingfisher with a cackling cry

koori n, pl **-ris** Austral a member of an Aboriginal people

kopje or **koppie** (kop-ee) n S African a small isolated hill

> **kopje** or **koppie** n = hill, down (archaic), fell, mount, hilltop, knoll, hillock, brae (Scot)

Koran n the sacred book of Islam, believed by Muslims to be the infallible word of God dictated to Mohammed ▸ **Koranic** adj

kosher (koh-sher) adj **1** Judaism **a** conforming to religious law **b** (of food) prepared in accordance with the dietary laws **2** informal legitimate, genuine, or proper ▸ n **3** kosher food

kowhai (koh-wye, koh-fye) n a small tree of New Zealand and Chile with clusters of yellow flowers

kowtow vb **1** to be humble and very respectful (towards): the senior editors accused each other of kowtowing to his demands **2** to touch the forehead to the ground in deference ▸ n **3** the act of kowtowing

kph kilometres per hour

kraal n **1** a Southern African hut village surrounded by a strong fence **2** S African an enclosure for livestock

Kremlin n the central government of Russia and, formerly, the Soviet Union

krill n, pl **krill** a small shrimplike crustacean

krypton n chem an inert gaseous element occurring in trace amounts in air and used in fluorescent lights and lasers. Symbol: **Kr**

kudos (kew-doss) n personal fame or glory

kugel (koog-el) n S African a rich, fashion-conscious, materialistic young Jewish woman

kumera or **kumara** (koo-ma-ra) n NZ a tropical root vegetable with yellow flesh

kumquat (kumm-kwott) n a citrus fruit resembling a tiny orange

kung fu n any of various Chinese systems of martial art, esp. unarmed combat in which punches, chops, and kicks are made with the hands and feet; certain styles involve the use of weapons

kura kaupapa Māori n NZ a primary school where the teaching is done in Māori

kurrajong n an Australian tree or shrub with tough fibrous bark

kW kilowatt

kWh kilowatt-hour

k

Ll

l litre(s)

L 1 large **2** Latin **3** learner driver **4** usually written: **£** pound **5** the Roman numeral for 50

lab *n informal* short for **laboratory**

label *n* **1** a piece of card or other material attached to an object to show its contents, ownership, use, or destination **2** a brief descriptive term given to a person, group, or school of thought: *we would need a handy label to explain the new company* ▸ *vb* **-belling, -belled** *or US* **-beling, -beled 3** to attach a label to **4** to describe or classify in a word or phrase

> **label** *n* **1** = tag, ticket, tab, marker, sticker ▸ *vb* **3** = tag, mark, stamp, ticket, tab

labial (lay-bee-al) *adj* **1** of or near the lips **2** *phonetics* relating to a speech sound made using the lips ▸ *n* **3** *phonetics* a speech sound such as English *p* or *m*, that involves the lips

labium (lay-bee-um) *n, pl* **-bia** (-bee-a) **1** a lip or liplike structure **2** any one of the four lip-shaped folds of the vulva

labor *n US, Austral & sometimes Canad* same as **labour**

laboratory *n, pl* **-ries** a building or room equipped for conducting scientific research or for teaching practical science

Labor Day *n* **1** (in the US and Canada) a public holiday in honour of labour, held on the first Monday in September **2** (in Australia) a public holiday observed on different days in different states

laborious *adj* involving great exertion or prolonged effort > **laboriously** *adv*

Labor Party *n* the main left-wing political party in Australia

labour *or US, Austral & sometimes Canad* **labor** *n* **1** productive work, esp. physical work done for wages **2** the people involved in this, as opposed to management **3** the final stage of pregnancy, leading to childbirth **4** difficult work or a difficult job ▸ *vb* **5** to do physical work: *the girls were labouring madly on it* **6** to work hard (for something) **7** to make one's way with difficulty: *she was now labouring down the return length* **8** to emphasize too persistently: *I have laboured the point* **9** (usually foll. by *under*) to be at a disadvantage because of a mistake or false belief: *she laboured under the illusion that I understood her*

> **labour** *or* **labor** *n* **1** = work, effort, employment, toil, industry **2** = workers, employees, workforce, labourers, hands

3 = childbirth, birth, delivery, parturition ▸ *vb* **5** = work, toil, strive, work hard, sweat (*informal*), slave, endeavour, slog away (*informal*), ≠ rest **6** = struggle, work, strain, work hard, strive, grapple, toil, make an effort **8** = overemphasize, stress, elaborate, exaggerate, strain, dwell on, overdo, go on about **9** = be disadvantaged by, suffer from, be a victim of, be burdened by

Labour Day *n* **1** a public holiday in honour of work, held in Britain on May 1 **2** (in New Zealand) a public holiday commemorating the introduction of the eight-hour day, held on the fourth Monday in October

laboured *or US, Austral & sometimes Canad* **labored** *adj* undertaken with difficulty: *laboured breathing*

> **laboured** *or* **labored** *adj* = difficult, forced, strained, heavy, awkward

labourer *or US, Austral & sometimes Canad* **laborer** *n* a person engaged in physical work

> **labourer** *or* **laborer** *n* = worker, manual worker, hand, blue-collar worker, drudge, navvy (*Brit informal*)

Labour Party *n* the main left-wing political party in a number of countries including Britain and New Zealand

Labrador *or* **Labrador retriever** *n* a powerfully built dog with short dense black, brown, or golden hair

laburnum *n* a small ornamental tree that has clusters of yellow drooping flowers. It is highly poisonous

labyrinth (lab-er-inth) *n* **1** a mazelike network of tunnels or paths, either natural or man-made **2** any complex or confusing system **3** the interconnecting cavities of the internal ear > **labyrinthine** *adj*

lace *n* **1** a delicate decorative fabric made from threads woven in an open web of patterns **2** a cord or string drawn through eyelets to fasten a shoe or garment ▸ *vb* **lacing, laced 3** to fasten (shoes) with a lace **4** to draw (a cord or thread) through holes as when tying shoes **5** to add a small amount of alcohol, a drug, or poison to (food or drink) **6** to intertwine; interlace

> **lace** *n* **1** = netting, net, filigree, meshwork, openwork **2** = cord, tie, string, lacing, shoelace, bootlace ▸ *vb* **3** = fasten, tie, tie up, do up, secure, bind, thread **5** = mix, drug, doctor, add to, spike, contaminate, fortify, adulterate **6** = intertwine, interweave, entwine, twine, interlink

lacerate (lass-er-rate) *vb* **-ating, -ated 1** to tear (the flesh) jaggedly **2** to hurt (the feelings): *it would only lacerate an overburdened conscience* > **laceration** *n*

lachrymose *adj* **1** given to weeping; tearful **2** mournful; sad

lack *n* **1** shortage or absence of something required or desired: *a lack of confidence* ▶ *vb* **2** (often foll. by *in*) to be short (of) or have need (of): *lacking in sparkle*

> **lack** *n* = shortage, want, absence, deficiency, need, inadequacy, scarcity, dearth; ≠ abundance
> ▶ *vb* = miss, want, need, require, not have, be without, be short of, be in need of; ≠ have

lackadaisical *adj* **1** lacking vitality and purpose **2** lazy and careless in a dreamy way

lackey *n* **1** a servile follower; hanger-on **2** a liveried male servant or valet

lacklustre *or US* **lackluster** *adj* lacking brilliance, force, or vitality

laconic *adj* (of a person's speech) using few words > **laconically** *adv*

lacquer *n* **1** a hard glossy coating made by dissolving natural or synthetic resins in a solvent that evaporates quickly **2** a black resin, obtained from certain trees, used to give a hard glossy finish to wooden furniture **3** a clear sticky substance for spraying onto the hair to hold a style in place

lacrimal *or* **lachrymal** (lack-rim-al) *adj* of tears or the glands that secrete tears

lacrosse *n* a sport in which two teams try to propel a ball into each other's goal using long-handled sticks with a pouched net at the end

lactation *n* **1** the secretion of milk from the mammary glands **2** the period during which milk is secreted

lactic *adj* relating to or derived from milk

lactose *n* a white crystalline sugar occurring in milk

lacuna (lak-kew-na) *n, pl* **-nae** (-nee) a gap or space in a book or manuscript

lacy *adj* **lacier**, **laciest** of or like lace

lad *n* **1** a boy or young man **2** *informal* any male **3 the lads** *informal* a group of males

> **lad** *n* **1** = boy, kid (*informal*), guy (*informal*), youth, fellow (*old-fashioned*), youngster, juvenile, nipper (*informal*)

ladder *n* **1** a portable frame consisting of two long parallel supports connected by steps, for climbing up or down **2** any system thought of as having a series of ascending stages: *the career ladder* **3** *chiefly Brit* a line of connected stitches that have come undone in tights or stockings ▶ *vb* **4** *chiefly Brit* to have or cause to have a line of undone stitches

laden *adj* **1** loaded **2** burdened

> **laden** *adj* = loaded, burdened, full, charged, weighed down, encumbered

la-di-da *or* **lah-di-dah** *adj informal* affected or pretentious in speech or manners

ladle *n* **1** a long-handled spoon with a deep bowl for serving soup, stew, etc. ▶ *vb* **-dling, -dled** **2** to serve out as with a ladle

lady *n, pl* **-dies 1** a woman regarded as having the characteristics of a good family, such as dignified manners **2** a polite name for a woman ▶ *adj* **3** *old-fashioned* female: *a lady chef*

> **lady** *n* **1** = gentlewoman, duchess, noble, dame, baroness, countess, aristocrat, viscountess **2** = woman, female, girl, damsel (*archaic, poetic*), charlie (*Austral old-fashioned slang*), chook (*Austral slang, sometimes derogatory*), wahine (NZ)

Lady *n, pl* **-dies 1** (in Britain) a title borne by various classes of women of the peerage **2 Our Lady** a title of the Virgin Mary

ladybird *n* a small red beetle with black spots

lady-in-waiting *n, pl* **ladies-in-waiting** a woman who attends a queen or princess

lady-killer *n informal* a man who is, or believes he is, irresistible to women

ladylike *adj* (of a woman) refined and fastidious

lag¹ *vb* **lagging, lagged 1** (often foll. by *behind*) to hang (back) or fall (behind) in movement, progress, or development **2** to fall away in strength or intensity ▶ *n* **3** a slowing down or falling behind **4** the interval of time between two events, esp. between an action and its effect: *the time lag between mobilization and combat*

> **lag** *vb* **1** = hang back, delay, trail, linger, loiter, straggle, dawdle, tarry

lag² *vb* **lagging, lagged 1** to wrap (a pipe, cylinder, or boiler) with insulating material to prevent heat loss ▶ *n* **2** the insulating casing of a steam cylinder or boiler

lag³ *n* **old lag** *Brit, Austral & NZ slang* a convict or ex-convict

lager *n* a light-bodied effervescent beer, fermented in a closed vessel using yeasts that sink to the bottom of the brew

laggard *n* a person who lags behind

lagging *n* insulating material wrapped around pipes, boilers, or tanks to prevent loss of heat

lagoon *n* a body of water cut off from the open sea by coral reefs or sand bars

laid *vb* the past of **lay¹**

laid-back *adj* relaxed in style or character

> **laid-back** *adj* = relaxed, calm, casual, easy-going, unflappable (*informal*), unhurried, free and easy, chilled (*informal*); ≠ tense

lain *vb* the past participle of **lie²**

lair *n* **1** the resting place of a wild animal **2** *informal* a place of seclusion or hiding

laird *n Scot* a landowner, esp. of a large estate

laissez faire *or* **laisser faire** (less-ay fair) *n* the policy of nonintervention, esp. by a government in commerce

laity (lay-it-ee) *n* **1** people who are not members of the clergy **2** all the people who do not belong to a specific profession

lake¹ *n* an expanse of water entirely surrounded by land

lake *n* = pond, pool, reservoir, loch (*Scot*), lagoon, mere, lough (*Irish*), tarn

lake² *n* **1** a bright pigment produced by combining organic colouring matter with an inorganic compound **2** a red dye obtained by combining a metallic compound with cochineal

lama *n* a Buddhist priest or monk in Mongolia or Tibet

lamb *n* **1** the young of a sheep **2** the meat of a young sheep eaten as food **3** someone who is innocent, gentle, and good ▸ *vb* **4** (of a ewe) to give birth

lambast *or* **lambaste** *vb* **1** to beat severely **2** to reprimand severely

lambent *adj* **1** (of a flame or light) flickering softly over a surface **2** (of wit or humour) light or brilliant › **lambency** *n*

lamb's fry *n Austral & NZ* lamb's liver for cooking

lambskin *n* the skin of a lamb, usually with the wool still on, used to make coats, slippers, etc.

lame *adj* **1** unable to walk properly because of an injury or illness affecting the legs or feet **2** weak; unconvincing: *lame arguments* ▸ *vb* **laming, lamed 3** to make lame › **lamely** *adv* › **lameness** *n*

lame *adj* **1** = crippled, limping, hobbling, game **2** = unconvincing, poor, pathetic, inadequate, thin, weak, feeble, unsatisfactory

lamé (lah-may) *n* a fabric interwoven with gold or silver threads

lame duck *n* a person who is unable to cope without the help of other people

lament *vb* **1** to feel or express sorrow or regret (for or over) ▸ *n* **2** an expression of sorrow **3** a poem or song in which a death is lamented › **lamentation** *n*

lament *vb* = bemoan, grieve, mourn, weep over, complain about, regret, wail about, deplore ▸ *n* **2** = complaint, moan, wailing, lamentation **3** = dirge, requiem, elegy, threnody (*formal*)

lamentable *adj* very unfortunate or disappointing › **lamentably** *adv*

lamented *adj* grieved for: usually said of someone dead

laminate *vb* **-nating, -nated 1** to make (material in sheet form) by sticking together thin sheets **2** to cover with a thin sheet of material **3** to split or be split into thin sheets ▸ *n* **4** a material made by sticking sheets together ▸ *adj* **5** composed of lamina; laminated › **lamination** *n*

laminated *adj* **1** composed of many layers stuck together **2** covered with a thin protective layer of plastic

lamington *n Austral & NZ* a sponge cake covered with a sweet coating

lamp *n* **1** a device that produces light: *an electric lamp; a gas lamp; an oil lamp* **2** a device that produces radiation, esp. for therapeutic purposes: *an ultraviolet lamp*

lampoon *n* **1** a piece of writing ridiculing a person ▸ *vb* **2** to ridicule and criticize (someone) in a lampoon › **lampooner** *or* **lampoonist** *n*

lamppost *n* a metal or concrete pole supporting a lamp in a street

lamprey *n* an eel-like fish with a round sucking mouth

LAN *computers* local area network

lance *n* **1** a long weapon with a pointed head used by horsemen ▸ *vb* **lancing, lanced 2** to pierce (an abscess or boil) with a lancet **3** to pierce with or as with a lance

lance corporal *n* a noncommissioned officer of the lowest rank

lancer *n* (formerly) a cavalryman armed with a lance

lancet *n* a pointed surgical knife with two sharp edges

land *n* **1** the solid part of the surface of the earth as distinct from seas and lakes. Related adjective: **terrestrial 2** ground, esp. with reference to its use or quality: *agricultural land* **3** rural or agricultural areas: *he couldn't leave the land* **4** *law* ground owned as property **5** a country, region, or area: *to bring peace and riches to your land* ▸ *vb* **6** to come down or bring (something) down to earth after a flight or jump **7** to transfer (something) or go from a ship to the shore: *sacks of malt were landed from barges* **8** to come to or touch shore **9** *informal* to obtain: *he landed a handsomely paid job in a bank* **10** *angling* to retrieve (a hooked fish) from the water **11** *informal* to deliver (a blow or punch) ▸ See also **land up** › **landless** *adj*

land *n* **1** = ground, earth, dry land, terra firma **2** = soil, ground, earth, clay, dirt, sod, loam **3** = countryside, farmland **4** = property, grounds, estate, real estate, realty, acreage, homestead (*US, Canad*) **5** = country, nation, region, state, district, territory, province, kingdom ▸ *vb* **8** = arrive, dock, put down, moor, alight, touch down, disembark, come to rest **9** = gain, get, win, secure, acquire

landau (lan-daw) *n* a four-wheeled horse-drawn carriage with two folding hoods

landed *adj* **1** owning land: *landed gentry* **2** consisting of land: *landed property*

landfall *n* the act of sighting or nearing land, esp. from the sea

landing *n* **1** the floor area at the top of a flight of stairs **2** the act of coming to land, esp. after a flight or sea voyage **3** a place of disembarkation

landlady *n, pl* **-dies 1** a woman who owns and leases property **2** a woman who owns or runs a lodging house or pub

land line *n* a telecommunications wire or cable laid over land

landlocked *adj* (of a country) completely surrounded by land

landlord *n* **1** a man who owns and leases property **2** a man who owns or runs a lodging house or pub

> **landlord** *n* **1** = owner, landowner, proprietor, freeholder, lessor, landholder **2** = innkeeper, host, hotelier

landlubber *n naut* any person without experience at sea

landmark *n* **1** a prominent object in or feature of a particular landscape **2** an important or unique event or development: *a landmark in scientific progress*

> **landmark** *n* **1** = feature, spectacle, monument **2** = milestone, turning point, watershed, critical point, tipping point

landscape *n* **1** an extensive area of land regarded as being visually distinct **2** a painting, drawing, or photograph depicting natural scenery ▸ *vb* **-scaping, -scaped 3** to improve the natural features of (an area of land) ▸ *adj* **4** (of a page or screen) having greater width than height

> **landscape** *n* **1** = scenery, country, view, land, scene, prospect, countryside, outlook

landslide *n* **1** Also called: **landslip** **A** the sliding of a large mass of rocks and soil down the side of a mountain or cliff **B** the material dislodged in this way **2** an overwhelming electoral victory

> **landslide** *n* **1A** = landslip, avalanche, mudslide, rockfall

land up *vb* to arrive at a final point or condition

> **land up** *vb* = end up, turn up, wind up, finish up, fetch up (*informal*)

landward *adj* **1** lying, facing, or moving towards land **2** in the direction of the land ▸ *adv also* **landwards 3** towards land

lane *n* **1** a narrow road, esp. in the country **2** one of the parallel strips into which the carriageway of a major road or motorway is divided **3** any well-defined route or course, such as for ships or aircraft **4** one of the parallel strips into which a running track or swimming pool is divided for races

> **lane** *n* **1** = road, street, track, path, way, passage, trail, pathway

language *n* **1** a system of spoken sounds or conventional symbols for communicating thought **2** the language of a particular nation or people **3** the ability to use words to communicate **4** any other means of communicating: *body language* **5** the specialized vocabulary used by a particular group: *legal language* **6** a particular style of verbal expression: *rough language* **7** *computers* See **programming language**

> **language** *n* **1, 2** = tongue, dialect, vernacular, patois **3** = speech, communication, expression, speaking, talk, talking, discourse, parlance

languid *adj* lacking energy; dreamy and inactive > **languidly** *adv*

languish *vb literary* **1** to suffer deprivation, hardship, or neglect: *she won't languish in jail for it* **2** to lose or diminish in strength or energy: *the design languished into oblivion* **3** (often foll. by *for*) to be listless with desire; pine > **languishing** *adj*

> **languish** *vb* **1** = decline, fade away, wither away, flag, weaken, wilt; ≠ flourish **2** = waste away, suffer, rot, be abandoned, be neglected; ≠ thrive **3** = pine, long, desire, hunger, yearn, hanker

languor (lang-ger) *n literary* a pleasant state of dreamy relaxation > **languorous** *adj*

lank *adj* **1** (of hair) straight and limp **2** thin or gaunt: *a tall, lank, lean man*

lanky *adj* **lankier, lankiest** ungracefully tall and thin > **lankiness** *n*

lanolin *n* a yellowish sticky substance extracted from wool: used in some ointments

lantana (lan-**tay**-na) *n* a shrub with orange or yellow flowers, considered a weed in Australia

lantern *n* **1** a light with a transparent protective case **2** a raised part on top of a dome or roof which lets in light or air **3** the upper part of a lighthouse that houses the light

lantern jaw *n* a long hollow jaw that gives the face a drawn appearance > **lantern-jawed** *adj*

lanthanide series *n chem* a class of 15 chemically related elements (**lanthanides**) with atomic numbers from 57 (lanthanum) to 71 (lutetium)

lanthanum *n chem* a silvery-white metallic element of the lanthanide series: used in electronic devices and glass manufacture. Symbol: **La**

lanyard *n* **1** a cord worn round the neck to hold a whistle, identity card, etc. **2** *naut* a line for extending or tightening rigging

lap¹ *n* **1** the area formed by the upper surface of the thighs of a seated person **2** a protected place or environment: *in the lap of luxury* **3** the part of a person's clothing that covers the lap **4 drop in someone's lap** to give someone the responsibility of

lap² *n* **1** one circuit of a racecourse or track **2** a stage or part of a journey **3** **A** an overlapping part **B** the extent of overlap ▸ *vb* **lapping, lapped 4** to overtake (an opponent) in a race so as to be one or more circuits ahead **5** to enfold or wrap around **6** to place or lie partly or completely over, or project beyond: *deep-pile carpet that lapped against his ankles* **7** to envelop or surround with comfort, love, or peace: *she was lapped by the luxury of Seymour House*

> **lap** *n* **1** = circuit, tour, leg, stretch, circle, orbit, loop

lap³ *vb* **lapping, lapped 1** (of small waves) to wash against (the shore or a boat) with light splashing sounds **2** (often foll. by *up*) (esp. of animals) to scoop (a liquid) into the mouth with the tongue ▸ *n* **3** the act or sound of lapping ▸ See also **lap up**

> **lap** *vb* **1** = ripple, wash, splash, swish, gurgle, slosh, purl, plash **2** = drink, sip, lick, swallow, gulp, sup

lapel (lap-**pel**) *n* the part on the front of a jacket or coat that folds back towards the shoulders

lapidary *n, pl* **-daries 1** a person who cuts, polishes, sets, or deals in gemstones ▸ *adj* **2** of or relating to gemstones or the work of a lapidary

lapis lazuli (lap-iss **lazz**-yew-lie) *n* a brilliant blue mineral used as a gemstone

lapse *n* **1** a temporary drop in standard as a result of forgetfulness or lack of concentration **2** a moment or instance of bad behaviour, esp. by someone who is usually well-behaved **3** a period of time sufficient for a change to take place: *we returned after a lapse of two years* **4** a gradual decline to a lower degree, condition, or state: *its lapse from the tradition of Disraeli* **5** *law* the loss of some right by neglecting to exercise or renew it ▸ *vb* **lapsing, lapsed 6** to drop in standard or fail to maintain a standard **7** to decline gradually in status, condition, or degree **8** to allow to end or become no longer valid, esp. through negligence: *a bid that lapsed last July* **9** (usually foll. by *into*) to drift (into a condition): *she appeared to lapse into a brief reverie* **10** (often foll. by *from*) to turn away (from beliefs or standards) **11** (of time) to slip away › **lapsed** *adj*

> **lapse** *n* **1** = mistake, failing, fault, failure, error, slip, negligence, omission **2, 4** = decline, fall, drop, deterioration **3** = interval, break, gap, pause, interruption, lull, breathing space, intermission ▸ *vb* **6, 7** = slip, fall, decline, sink, drop, slide, deteriorate, degenerate **8** = end, stop, run out, expire, terminate

laptop *adj* **1** (of a computer) small and light enough to be held on the user's lap ▸ *n* **2** a personal computer that is small and light enough to be held on the user's lap

lap up *vb* **1** to eat or drink **2** to accept (information or attention) eagerly: *the public are lapping up the scandal*

> **lap up** *vb* **2 lap something up** = relish, like, enjoy, delight in, savour, revel in, wallow in, accept eagerly

lapwing *n* a bird of the plover family with a crested head. Also called: **peewit**

larboard *n naut* an old word for **port²** (sense 1)

larceny *n, pl* **-nies** *law* theft › **larcenist** *n*

larch *n* **1** a coniferous tree with deciduous needle-like leaves and egg-shaped cones **2** the wood of this tree

lard *n* **1** the soft white fat obtained from pigs and prepared for use in cooking ▸ *vb* **2** to prepare (lean meat or poultry) by inserting small strips of bacon or fat before cooking **3** to add unnecessary material to (speech or writing)

larder *n* a room or cupboard used for storing food

large *adj* **1** having a relatively great size, quantity, or extent; big **2** of wide or broad scope, capacity, or range; comprehensive: *a large effect* ▸ *n* **3 at large A** as a whole; in general: *both the Navy and the country at large* **B** (of a dangerous criminal or wild animal) out of captivity; free **c** in full detail ▸ *vb* **larging, larged 4 large it** *Brit slang* to enjoy oneself or celebrate in an extravagant way › **largeness** *n*

> **large** *adj* **1** = big, great, huge, heavy, massive, vast, enormous, tall, supersize; ≠ small ▸ *n* **3A at large** = in general, generally, chiefly, mainly, as a whole, in the main **3B at large** = free, on the run, fugitive, at liberty, on the loose, unchained, unconfined

largely *adv* principally; to a great extent

> **largely** *adv* = mainly, generally, chiefly, mostly, principally, primarily, predominantly, by and large

large-scale *adj* **1** wide-ranging or extensive **2** (of maps and models) constructed or drawn to a big scale

> **large-scale** *adj* **1** = wide-ranging, global, sweeping, broad, wide, vast, extensive, wholesale

largesse *or* **largess** (lar-**jess**) *n* the generous giving of gifts, favours, or money

largish *adj* fairly large

largo *music* ▸ *adv* **1** in a slow and stately manner ▸ *n, pl* **-gos 2** a piece or passage to be performed in a slow and stately manner

lariat *n US & Canad* **1** a lasso **2** a rope for tethering animals

lark¹ *n* a small brown songbird, esp. the skylark

lark² *informal* ▸ *n* **1** a carefree adventure or frolic **2** a harmless piece of mischief **3** an activity or job viewed with disrespect ▸ *vb* **4 lark about** to have a good time frolicking or playing pranks › **larky** *adj*

larkspur *n* a plant with blue, pink, or white flowers with slender spikes at the base

larrikin *n Austral & NZ old-fashioned slang* a mischievous or unruly person

larva *n, pl* **-vae** the immature form of many insects before it develops into its adult form › **larval** *adj*

laryngeal *adj* of or relating to the larynx

laryngitis *n* inflammation of the larynx, causing huskiness or loss of voice

larynx (lar-**rinks**) *n, pl* **larynges** (lar-**rin**-jeez) *or* **larynxes** a hollow organ forming part of the air passage to the lungs: it contains the vocal cords

lasagne *or* **lasagna** (laz-zan-ya) *n* **1** a form of pasta in wide flat sheets **2** a dish made from layers of lasagne, meat, and cheese

lascivious (lass-iv-ee-uss) *adj* showing or producing sexual desire; lustful › **lasciviously** *adv*

laser (lay-zer) *n* **1** a device that produces a very narrow intense beam of light, which is used for cutting very hard materials and in surgery, etc. ▸ *vb* **2** to use a laser on (something), esp. as part of medical treatment **3** Also: **laser off** to remove (a tattoo, fat, etc.) with laser treatment

lash¹ *n* **1** an eyelash **2** a sharp cutting blow from a whip **3** the flexible end of a whip ▸ *vb* **4** to hit (a person or thing) sharply with a whip, esp. formerly as punishment **5** (of rain or waves) to beat forcefully against **6** to attack (someone) with words of ridicule or scolding **7** to flick or wave sharply to and fro: *his tail lashing in irritation* **8** to urge as with a whip: *to lash the audience into a violent mood* ▸ See also **lash out**

> **lash** *n* **2** = blow, hit, strike, stroke, stripe, swipe (*informal*) ▸ *vb* **4** = whip, beat, thrash, birch, flog, scourge **5** = pound, beat, strike, hammer, drum, smack (*dialect*) **6** = censure, attack, blast, put down, criticize, slate (*informal, chiefly Brit*), scold, tear into (*informal*)

lash² *vb* to bind or secure with rope, string, or cord

> **lash** *vb* = fasten, tie, secure, bind, strap, make fast

lashings *pl n old-fashioned, informal* large amounts; lots: *lashings of cream*

lash out *vb* **1** to make a sudden verbal or physical attack **2** *informal* to spend extravagantly

lass *n* a girl or young woman

lassie *n Scot & N English informal* a little lass; girl

lassitude *n* physical or mental weariness

lasso (lass-oo) *n*, *pl* **-sos** *or* **-soes** **1** a long rope with a noose at one end used for catching horses and cattle ▸ *vb* **-soing**, **-soed** **2** to catch as with a lasso › **lassoer** *n*

last¹ *adj* **1** being, happening, or coming at the end or after all others **2** most recent: *last April* **3** only remaining: *that's the last one* **4** most extreme; utmost **5** least suitable or likely: *it's the last place on earth I would have expected to be recognized* ▸ *adv* **6** after all others **7** most recently: *we last saw him on Thursday night* **8** as the last or latest item ▸ *n* **9** **the last A** a person or thing that is last **B** the final moment; end **10** the final appearance, mention, or occurrence: *the last of this season's visitors* **11** **at last** in the end; finally **12** **at long last** finally, after difficulty or delay

> **last** *adj* **1** = hindmost, final, at the end, remotest, furthest behind, most distant, rearmost; ≠ foremost **2** = most recent, latest, previous **3, 4** = final, closing, concluding, ultimate; ≠ first ▸ *adv* **6, 8** = in *or* at the end, after, in the rear, bringing up the rear

last² *vb* **1** to continue to exist for a length of time: *the soccer war lasted 100 hours* **2** to be sufficient for the needs of (a person) for a length of time: *I shall make a couple of bottles to last me until next summer* **3** to remain fresh, uninjured, or unaltered for a certain time: *the flowers haven't lasted well*

> **last** *vb* **1, 3** = continue, remain, survive, carry on, endure, persist, keep on, abide; ≠ end

last³ *n* the wooden or metal form on which a shoe or boot is made or repaired

last-ditch *adj* done as a final resort: *a last-ditch attempt*

lasting *adj* existing or remaining effective for a long time

> **lasting** *adj* = continuing, long-term, permanent, enduring, remaining, abiding, long-standing, perennial; ≠ passing

lastly *adv* **1** at the end or at the last point **2** finally

last post *n military* **1** a bugle call used to signal the time to retire at night **2** a similar call sounded at military funerals

last straw *n* a small incident, irritation, or setback that coming after others is too much to cope with

last word *n* **1** the final comment in an argument **2** **the last word in** the most recent or best example of something: *the last word in luxury*

latch *n* **1** a fastening for a gate or door that consists of a bar that may be slid or lowered into a groove, hole, or notch **2** a spring-loaded door lock that can only be opened by a key from outside ▸ *vb* **3** to fasten, fit, or be fitted with a latch

> **latch** *n* **1** = fastening, catch, bar, lock, hook, bolt, hasp ▸ *vb* = fasten, bar, secure, bolt, make fast

late *adj* **1** occurring or arriving after the correct or expected time: *the plane will be late* **2** towards or near the end: *the late afternoon* **3** occurring or being at a relatively advanced time: *a late starter, his first novel was effectively his last* **4** at an advanced time in the evening or at night: *it's late, I have to get back* **5** having died recently: *her late father* **6** recent: *recollect the late defeats which your enemies have experienced* **7** former: *the late manager of the team* **8** **of late** recently ▸ *adv* **9** after the correct or expected time: *Leela arrived late* **10** at a relatively advanced age: *coming late to motherhood* **11** recently: *as late as in 1983, only 9 per cent of that labour force was unionized* **12** **late in the day A** at a late or advanced stage **B** too late › **lateness** *n*

> **late** *adj* **1** = overdue, delayed, last-minute, belated, tardy, behind time, behindhand; ≠ early **5** = dead, deceased, departed (*euphemistic*), passed on, former, defunct; ≠ alive **6** = recent, new, advanced, fresh; ≠ old ▸ *adv* **9** = behind time, belatedly, tardily, behindhand, dilatorily; ≠ early

lately *adv* in recent times; of late

> **lately** *adv* = recently, of late, just now, in recent times, not long ago, latterly

latent *adj* lying hidden and not yet developed within a person or thing > **latency** *n*

lateral (lat-ter-al) *adj* of or relating to the side or sides > **laterally** *adv*

latex *n* a milky fluid produced by many plants: latex from the rubber plant is used in the manufacture of rubber

lath *n* one of several thin narrow strips of wood used as a supporting framework for plaster or tiles

lathe *n* a machine for shaping metal or wood by turning it against a fixed tool

lather *n* **1** foam formed by soap or detergent in water **2** foamy sweat, as produced by a horse **3** *informal* a state of agitation ▸ *vb* **4** to coat or become coated with lather **5** to form a lather **6** *informal* to beat; flog > **lathery** *adj*

Latin *n* **1** the language of ancient Rome and the Roman Empire **2** a member of any of those peoples whose languages are derived from Latin ▸ *adj* **3** of the Latin language **4** of those peoples whose languages are derived from Latin **5** of the Roman Catholic Church

Latin America *n* those areas of South and Central America whose official languages are Spanish and Portuguese > **Latin American** *adj, n*

latitude *n* **1** **A** an angular distance measured in degrees north or south of the equator **B** (*often pl*) a region considered with regard to its distance from the equator **2** scope for freedom of action and thought > **latitudinal** *adj*

> **latitude** *n* **2** = scope, liberty, freedom, play, space, licence, leeway, laxity

latrine *n* a toilet in a barracks or camp

latte (lat-tay) *n* a drink of strong coffee mixed with hot milk

latter *n* **1** **the latter** the second or second mentioned of two ▸ *adj* **2** near or nearer the end: *the latter half of the season* **3** more advanced in time or sequence; later

> **latter** *n* = second, last, last-mentioned, second-mentioned ▸ *adj* = last, ending, closing, final, concluding; ≠ earlier

latter-day *adj* present-day; modern

latterly *adv* recently; lately

lattice (lat-iss) *n* **1** Also called: **latticework** a framework of strips of wood or metal interlaced in a diagonal pattern **2** a gate, screen, or fence formed of such a framework **3** an array of atoms, ions, or molecules in a crystal, or an array of points indicating their positions in space ▸ *vb* **-ticing, -ticed** **4** to make, adorn, or supply with a lattice > **latticed** *adj*

laud *literary* ▸ *vb* **1** to praise or glorify ▸ *n* **2** praise or glorification

laudable *adj* deserving praise; commendable > **laudability** *n* > **laudably** *adv*

laudanum (lawd-a-num) *n* a sedative extracted from opium

laudatory *adj* (of speech or writing) expressing praise

laugh *vb* **1** to express amusement or happiness by producing a series of inarticulate sounds **2** to utter or express with laughter: *he laughed his derision at the play* **3** to bring or force (oneself) into a certain condition by laughter: *laughing herself silly* **4** **laugh at** to make fun of; jeer at **5** **laugh up one's sleeve** to laugh secretly ▸ *n* **6** the act or an instance of laughing **7** *informal* a person or thing that causes laughter: *he's a laugh, that one* **8** **the last laugh** final success after previous defeat ▸ See also **laugh off** > **laughingly** *adv*

> **laugh** *vb* **1** = chuckle, giggle, snigger, cackle, chortle, guffaw, titter, be in stitches ▸ *n* **6** = chortle, giggle, chuckle, snigger, guffaw, titter **7** = clown, character (*informal*), scream (*informal*), entertainer, card (*informal*), joker, hoot (*informal*)

laughable *adj* ridiculous because so obviously inadequate or unsuccessful

laughing gas *n* nitrous oxide used as an anaesthetic: it may cause laughter and exhilaration when inhaled

laughing stock *n* a person or thing that is treated with ridicule

laugh off *vb* to treat (something serious or difficult) lightly

> **laugh off** *vb* **laugh something off** = disregard, ignore, dismiss, overlook, shrug off, minimize, brush aside, make light of

laughter *n* the action or noise of laughing

> **laughter** *n* = amusement, entertainment, humour, glee, fun, mirth, hilarity, merriment

launch[1] *vb* **1** to move (a vessel) into the water, esp. for the first time **2** **A** to start off or set in motion: *to launch an appeal* **B** to put (a new product) on the market **3** to set (a rocket, missile, or spacecraft) into motion **4** to involve (oneself) totally and enthusiastically: *Francis launched himself into the transfer market with gusto* **5** **launch into** to start talking or writing (about) **6** (usually foll. by *out*) to start (out) on a new enterprise ▸ *n* **7** an act or instance of launching > **launcher** *n*

> **launch** *vb* **2A** = begin, start, open, initiate, introduce, found, set up, originate **3** = propel, fire, dispatch, discharge, project, send off, set in motion, send into orbit **5** **launch into something** = start enthusiastically, begin, initiate, embark on, instigate, inaugurate, embark upon

launch[2] *n* an open motorboat

launder *vb* **1** to wash and iron (clothes and linen) **2** to make (money illegally obtained) appear to be legally gained by passing it through foreign banks or legitimate enterprises

Launderette *n Brit, Austral & NZ trademark* an establishment where clothes can be washed and dried, using coin-operated machines. Also called (US, Canad, Austral, NZ): **Laundromat**

laundry *n, pl* **-dries 1** the clothes or linen to be laundered or that have been laundered **2** a place where clothes and linen are washed and ironed

laureate (lor-ee-at) *adj* **1** *literary* crowned with laurel leaves as a sign of honour ▸ *n* **2** short for **poet laureate** ▷ **laureateship** *n*

laurel *n* **1** a small Mediterranean evergreen tree with glossy leaves **2 laurels** a wreath of laurel, worn on the head as an emblem of victory or honour in classical times **3 laurels** honour, distinction, or fame **4 look to one's laurels** to be on guard against one's rivals **5 rest on one's laurels** to be satisfied with what one has already achieved and stop striving for further success

> **laurel** *n* **5 rest on one's laurels** = sit back, relax, take it easy, relax your efforts

lava *n* **1** molten rock discharged by volcanoes **2** any rock formed by the solidification of lava

lavatory *n, pl* **-ries** same as **toilet**

lavender *n* **1** a plant grown for its bluish-purple flowers and as the source of a sweet-smelling oil **2** its dried flowers, used to perfume clothes ▸ *adj* **3** pale bluish-purple

lavender water *n* a light perfume made from lavender

lavish *adj* **1** great in quantity or richness: *lavish banquets* **2** very generous in giving **3** extravagant; wasteful: *lavish spending habits* ▸ *vb* **4** to give or spend very generously or in great quantities ▷ **lavishly** *adv*

> **lavish** *adj* **1** = grand, magnificent, splendid, abundant, copious, profuse; ≠ stingy
> **2** = generous, free, liberal, bountiful, open-handed, unstinting, munificent; ≠ stingy **3** = extravagant, wild, excessive, exaggerated, wasteful, prodigal, unrestrained, immoderate; ≠ thrifty ▸ *vb* = shower, pour, heap, deluge, dissipate; ≠ stint

law *n* **1** a rule or set of rules regulating what may or may not be done by members of a society or community **2** a rule or body of rules made by the legislature or other authority. Related adjectives: **legal**, **judicial**, **juridical 3** the control enforced by such rules: *scant respect for the rule of law* **4 the law A** the legal or judicial system **B** the profession or practice of law **C** *informal* the police or a police officer **5 law and order** the policy of strict enforcement of the law, esp. against crime and violence **6** a rule of behaviour: *an unwritten law that teacher knows best* **7** Also called: **law of nature** a generalization based on a recurring fact or event **8** the science or knowledge of law; jurisprudence **9** a general principle, formula, or rule in mathematics,

science, or philosophy: *the law of gravity* **10 the Law** the laws contained in the first five books of the Old Testament **11 go to law** to resort to legal proceedings on some matter **12 lay down the law** to speak in an authoritative manner

> **law** *n* **1** = statute, act, bill, rule, order, command, regulation, resolution
> **2, 8** = constitution, code, legislation, charter **4B** = the legal profession, the bar, barristers **6, 9** = principle, code, canon, precept, axiom, kaupapa (NZ)

law-abiding *adj* obeying the laws: *a law-abiding citizen*

lawful *adj* allowed, recognized, or sanctioned by law; legal ▷ **lawfully** *adv*

lawless *adj* **1** breaking the law, esp. in a wild or violent way: *lawless butchery* **2** not having laws ▷ **lawlessness** *n*

lawn¹ *n* an area of cultivated and mown grass

lawn² *n* a fine linen or cotton fabric

lawn mower *n* a hand-operated or power-operated machine for cutting grass

lawn tennis *n* **1** tennis played on a grass court **2** same as **tennis**

lawsuit *n* a case in a court of law brought by one person or group against another

> **lawsuit** *n* = case, action, trial, suit, proceedings, dispute, prosecution, legal action

lawyer *n* a member of the legal profession who can advise clients about the law and represent them in court

> **lawyer** *n* = legal adviser, attorney, solicitor, counsel, advocate, barrister, counsellor, legal representative

lax *adj* lacking firmness; not strict ▷ **laxity** *n*

laxative *n* **1** a medicine that induces the emptying of the bowels ▸ *adj* **2** easing the emptying of the bowels

lay¹ *vb* **lays**, **laying**, **laid 1** to put in a low or horizontal position; cause to lie: *Mary laid a clean square of white towelling carefully on the grass* **2** to establish as a basis: *ready to lay your new fashion foundations?* **3** to place in a particular state or position: *he laid a finger in his lips* **4** to regard as the responsibility of: *ridiculous attempts to lay the loss at the door of the Admiralty* **5** to put forward: *ruses by which we lay claim on one another* **6** to arrange or prepare: *she would lay her plans* **7** to place in position: *he laid a wreath* **8** (of birds, esp. the domestic hen) to produce (eggs) **9** to make (a bet) with (someone): *I'll lay money he's already gone home* **10** to arrange (a table) for a meal **11** to prepare (a fire) by arranging fuel in the grate **12** *vulgar slang* to have sexual intercourse with **13 lay bare** to reveal or explain: *a century of neurophysiology has now laid bare the structures of the brain* **14 lay hold of** to seize or grasp **15 lay oneself open** to make oneself vulnerable (to criticism or attack) **16 lay open** to reveal or

disclose **17 lay waste** to destroy completely ▸ *n*
18 the manner or position in which something
lies or is placed **19** *vulgar slang* **A** an act of sexual
intercourse **B** a sexual partner

> **lay** *vb* **1, 3, 7** = place, put, set, spread, plant,
> leave, deposit, put down **4** = attribute, assign,
> allocate, allot, ascribe, impute **5** = put forward,
> offer, present, advance, lodge, submit, bring
> forward **6** = arrange, prepare, make, organize,
> position, set out, devise, put together
> **8** = produce, bear, deposit **9** = bet, stake,
> venture, gamble, chance, risk, hazard, wager

lay² *vb* the past tense of **lie²**
lay³ *adj* **1** of or involving people who are not
members of the clergy **2** nonprofessional or
nonspecialist

> **lay** *adj* **1** = nonclerical, secular, non-ordained
> **2** = nonspecialist, amateur, unqualified,
> untrained, inexpert, nonprofessional

lay⁴ *n* a short narrative poem intended to be
sung
layabout *n* a lazy person
lay-by *n* **1** *Brit* a place where drivers can stop by
the side of a main road **2** *Austral & NZ* a system of
payment whereby a buyer pays a deposit on an
article, which is reserved for him or her until he
or she has paid the full price
layer *n* **1** a single thickness of something, such
as a cover or a coating on a surface **2** a laying
hen **3** *horticulture* a shoot that forms its own root
while still attached to the parent plant ▸ *vb* **4** to
form or make a layer or layers
layette *n* a complete set of clothing, bedclothes,
and other accessories for a newborn baby
layman *or fem* **laywoman** *n, pl* **-men** *or* **-women**
1 a person who is not a member of the clergy
2 a person who does not have specialized
knowledge of a subject: *the layman's guide to nuclear
power*
lay off *vb* **1** to suspend (staff) during a slack
period at work **2** *informal* to leave (a person,
thing, or activity) alone: *'Lay off the defence counsel
bit!' he snapped* ▸ *n* **lay-off 3** a period of imposed
unemployment

> **lay off** *vb* **1 lay someone off** = dismiss, fire
> (*informal*), release, sack (*informal*), pay off,
> discharge, let go, make redundant, kennet
> (*Austral slang*), jeff (*Austral slang*)

lay on *vb* **1** to provide or supply: *they laid on a
treat for the entourage* **2 lay it on thick** *slang* to
exaggerate, esp. when flattering
lay out *vb* **1** to arrange or spread out **2** to plan or
design: *the main streets were laid out on a grid system*
3 to prepare (a corpse) for burial or cremation
4 *informal* to spend (money), esp. lavishly
5 *informal* to knock (someone) unconscious
▸ *n* **layout 6** the arrangement or plan of
something, such as a building **7** the
arrangement of printed material

lay out *vb* **1 lay something out** = arrange,
order, design, display, exhibit, put out, spread
out **4 lay something out** = spend, pay, invest,
fork out (*slang*), expend, shell out (*informal*),
disburse **5 lay someone out** = knock out, fell,
floor, knock unconscious, knock for six ▸ *n*
6 layout = arrangement, design, outline,
format, plan, formation

laze *vb* **lazing, lazed 1** to be idle or lazy **2** (often
foll. by *away*) to spend (time) in idleness ▸ *n*
3 time spent lazing
lazy *adj* **lazier, laziest 1** not inclined to work or
exert oneself **2** done in a relaxed manner with
little effort **3** moving in a sluggish manner: *the
lazy drift of the bubbles* > **lazily** *adv* > **laziness** *n*

> **lazy** *adj* **1** = idle, inactive, indolent, slack,
> negligent, inert, workshy, slothful (*formal*);
> ≠ industrious **2, 3** = lethargic, languorous,
> slow-moving, languid, sleepy, sluggish,
> drowsy, somnolent; ≠ quick

lb 1 pound (weight) **2** *cricket* leg bye
lbw *cricket* leg before wicket
lea *n* **1** *poetic* a meadow or field **2** grassland
leach *vb* **1** to remove or be removed from a
substance by a liquid passing through it **2** to
lose soluble substances by the action of a liquid
passing through

> **leach** *vb* **1** = extract, strain, drain, filter, seep,
> percolate

lead¹ (rhymes with *seed*) *vb* **leading, led 1** to
show the way to (an individual or a group) by
going with or ahead: *he led her into the house* **2** to
guide, control, or direct: *he dismounted and led his
horse back* **3** to influence someone to act, think,
or behave in a certain way: *researching our family
history has led her to correspond with relatives abroad*
4 to have the principal part in (something):
planners led the development of policy **5** to go at the
head of or have the top position in (something):
the pair led the field by almost two minutes **6** (of a road
or way) to be the means of reaching a place: *the
footbridge leads on to a fine promenade* **7** to pass or
spend: *I've led a happy life* **8** to guide or be guided
by physical means: *she took him firmly by the arm and
led him home* **9** to direct the course of (water, a
rope, or wire) along, or as if along, a channel
10 (foll. by *with*) to have as the most important
item: *the Review leads with a critique of A Place of
Greater Safety* **11** *Brit music* to play first violin in (an
orchestra) **12** to begin a round of cards by putting
down the first card ▸ *n* **13** the first or most
prominent place **14** example or leadership: *some
of his children followed his lead* **15** an advantage over
others: *Essex have a lead of 24 points* **16** an indication;
clue: *we've got a lead on how the body got into the water*
17 a length of leather, nylon, or chain used to
walk or control a dog **18** the principal role in a
play, film, or other production, or the person
playing such a role **19** the most important news

story in a newspaper: *the shooting makes the lead in The Times* **20** the act of playing the first card in a round of cards or the card so played **21** a wire, cable, or other conductor for making an electrical connection ▸ *adj* **22** acting as a leader or lead: *lead singer*

lead *vb* **1** = go in front (of), head, be in front, be at the head (of), walk in front (of) **2, 8** = guide, conduct, steer, escort, precede, usher, pilot, show the way **3** = cause, prompt, persuade, move, draw, influence, motivate, prevail **4** = command, rule, govern, preside over, head, control, manage, direct **5** = be ahead (of), be first, exceed, be winning, excel, surpass, come first, transcend **6** = connect to, link, open onto **7** = live, have, spend, experience, pass, undergo ▸ *n* **13** = first place, winning position, primary position, vanguard **14** = example, direction, leadership, guidance, model, pattern **15** = advantage, start, edge, margin, winning margin **16** = clue, suggestion, hint, indication, pointer, tip-off **17** = leash, line, cord, rein, tether **18** = leading role, principal, protagonist, title role, principal part ▸ *adj* = main, prime, top, leading, first, head, chief, premier

lead² (rhymes with *bed*) *n* **1** a heavy toxic bluish-white metallic element: used in alloys, cable sheaths, paints, and as a radiation shield. Symbol: **Pb 2 A** graphite used for drawing **B** a thin stick of this as the core of a pencil **3** a lead weight suspended on a line, used to take soundings of the depth of water **4** lead weights or shot, as used in cartridges or fishing lines **5** a thin strip of lead for holding small panes of glass or pieces of stained glass **6 leads A** thin sheets or strips of lead used as a roof covering **B** a roof covered with such sheets **7** Also called: **leading** *printing* a thin strip of metal, formerly used for spacing between lines of type ▸ *adj* **8** of, relating to, or containing lead ▸ *vb* **9** to surround, cover, or secure with lead or leads

leaded *adj* **1** (of petrol) containing tetraethyl lead in order to improve combustion **2** (of windows) made from many small panes of glass held together by lead strips

leaden *adj* **1** heavy or sluggish: *my limbs felt leaden* **2** of a dull greyish colour: *leaden November sky* **3** made of lead **4** gloomy, spiritless, or lifeless: *hollow characters and leaden dialogue*

leader *n* **1** a person who rules, guides, or inspires others; head **2** Also: **leading article** *Brit & Austral* the leading editorial in a newspaper **3** *music* the principal first violinist of an orchestra who acts as the conductor's deputy **4** the person or animal who is leading in a race **5** the best or the most successful of its kind: *the company is a world leader in its field* **6** the leading horse or dog in a team **7** *botany* any of the long slender shoots that grow from the stem or branch of a tree ▸ **leadership** *n*

leader *n* **1** = principal, president, head, chief, boss (*informal*), director, manager, chairperson, sherang (*Austral, NZ*); ≠ follower

lead-in *n* an introduction to a subject

leading *adj* **1** principal or primary: *the leading designers* **2** in the first position: *the leading driver*

leading *adj* **1** = principal, top, major, main, first, highest, greatest, chief; ≠ minor

leading question *n* a question worded to suggest the desired answer, such as *What do you think of the horrible effects of pollution?*

leaf *n, pl* **leaves 1** one of the flat usually green blades attached to the stem of a plant **2** the foliage of a tree or plant: *shrubs have been planted for their leaf interest* **3 in leaf** (of shrubs or trees) with all its leaves fully opened **4** a very thin sheet of metal **5** one of the sheets of paper in a book **6** a hinged, sliding, or detachable part, such as an extension to a table **7 take a leaf out of someone's book** to imitate someone in a particular course of action **8 turn over a new leaf** to begin a new and improved course of behaviour ▸ *vb* **9** (usually foll. by *through*) to turn pages casually or hurriedly without reading them **10** (of plants) to produce leaves ▸ **leafless** *adj*

leaf *n* **1** = frond, blade, cotyledon **5** = page, sheet, folio ▸ *vb* **9 leaf through something** = skim, glance, scan, browse, look through, dip into, flick through, flip through

leaflet *n* **1** a sheet of printed matter distributed, usually free, for advertising or information **2** any small leaf **3** one of the divisions of a compound leaf ▸ *vb* **-leting, -leted 4** to distribute leaflets (to)

leaflet *n* **1** = booklet, notice, brochure, circular, flyer, tract, pamphlet, handout

leaf mould *n* a rich soil consisting of decayed leaves

leafy *adj* **leafier, leafiest 1** covered with leaves **2** having many trees or shrubs: *a leafy suburb*

leafy *adj* = green, shaded, shady, verdant (*literary*)

league¹ *n* **1** an association of people or nations formed to promote the interests of its members **2** an association of sporting clubs that organizes matches between member teams **3** *informal* a class or level: *the guy is not even in the same league* **4 in league (with)** working or planning together with ▸ *vb* **leaguing, leagued 5** to form or be formed into a league

league *n* **1** = association, union, alliance, coalition, group, corporation, partnership, federation **3** = class, group, level, category

league² *n* an obsolete unit of distance of varying length: commonly equal to 3 miles (4.8 km)

leak *n* **1 A** a crack or hole that allows the accidental escape or entrance of liquid, gas, radiation, etc. **B** such escaping or entering liquid, etc. **2** a disclosure of secret information **3** the loss of current from an electrical conductor because of faulty insulation **4** the act or an instance of leaking **5** *slang* urination ▸ *vb* **6** to enter or escape, or allow to enter or escape, through a crack or hole **7** to make (secret information) public, esp. deliberately
> **leaky** *adj*

leak *n* **1A** = hole, opening, crack, puncture, aperture, chink, crevice, fissure **1B, 4** = leakage, discharge, drip, seepage, percolation **2** = disclosure, exposé, exposure, admission, revelation, uncovering, betrayal, unearthing ▸ *vb* **6** = escape, pass, spill, release, drip, trickle, ooze, seep **7** = disclose, tell, reveal, pass on, give away, make public, divulge, let slip

leakage *n* the act, an instance, or the result of leaking: *the leakage of 60 tonnes of oil*

lean¹ *vb* **leaning, leaned** *or* **leant 1** (foll. by *against, on* or *upon*) to rest or put (something) so that it rests against a support **2** to bend or make (something) bend from an upright position **3** (foll. by *to* or *towards*) to have or express a tendency or preference ▸ *n* **4** the condition of bending from an upright position ▸ See also **lean on**

lean *vb* **1** = rest, prop, be supported, recline, repose **2** = bend, tip, slope, incline, tilt, heel, slant **3** = tend, prefer, favour, incline, be prone to, be disposed to

lean² *adj* **1** (esp. of a person) having a trim body with no surplus flesh **2** (of meat) having little or no fat **3** (of a period) sparse, difficult, or causing hardship: *we've been through some lean times in recent years* ▸ *n* **4** the part of meat that contains little or no fat > **leanness** *n*

lean *adj* **1** = thin, slim, slender, skinny, angular, trim, spare, gaunt; ≠ fat

leaning *n* a tendency or inclination

leaning *n* = tendency, bias, inclination, bent, disposition, penchant, propensity, predilection

lean on *vb* **1** *informal* to try to influence (someone) by using threats **2** to depend on (someone) for help and advice

lean on *vb* **2 lean on someone** = depend on, trust, rely on, cling to, count on, have faith in

lean-to *n, pl* **-tos** a building with a sloping roof attached to another building or a wall

leap *vb* **leaping, leapt** *or* **leaped 1** to jump suddenly from one place to another **2** (often foll. by *at*) to move or react quickly **3** to jump over ▸ *n* **4** the act of jumping **5** an abrupt or important change or increase: *it's been a huge leap to the Premiership from where I started with Wigan* **6 a leap in the dark** an action performed without knowledge of the consequences **7 by leaps and bounds** with unexpectedly rapid progress

leap *vb* **1** = jump, spring, bound, bounce, hop, skip ▸ *n* **4** = jump, spring, bound, vault **5** = rise, change, increase, soaring, surge, escalation, upsurge, upswing

leapfrog *n* **1** a children's game in which each player in turn leaps over the others' bent backs ▸ *vb* **-frogging, -frogged 2 A** to play leapfrog **B** to leap over (something) **3** to advance by jumps or stages

leap year *n* a calendar year of 366 days, February 29 (**leap day**) being the additional day, that occurs every four years

learn *vb* **learning, learned** *or* **learnt 1** to gain knowledge (of something) or acquire skill in (some art or practice) **2** to memorize (something) **3** to gain by experience, example, or practice: *I learned everything the hard way* **4** (often foll. by *of* or *about*) to become informed; find out: *Captain Nelson learned of the disaster from his wireless*
> **learnable** *adj* > **learner** *n*

learn *vb* **1, 3** = master, grasp, pick up, take in, familiarize yourself with **2** = memorize, commit to memory, learn by heart, learn by rote, learn parrot-fashion, get off pat **4** = discover, hear, understand, find out about, become aware, discern, ascertain, come to know

learned (lurn-id) *adj* **1** having great knowledge **2** involving or characterized by scholarship: *your learned paper on the subject*

learned *adj* = scholarly, academic, intellectual, versed, well-informed, erudite, highbrow, well-read; ≠ uneducated

learning *n* knowledge gained by studying

learning *n* = knowledge, study, education, scholarship, enlightenment, e-learning *or* elearning

lease *n* **1** a contract by which an owner rents buildings or land to another person for a specified period **2 a new lease of life** a prospect of renewed energy, health, or happiness ▸ *vb* **leasing, leased 3** to let or rent (land or buildings) by lease

lease *vb* = hire, rent, let, loan, charter, rent out, hire out

leasehold *n* **1** land or property held under a lease **2** the holding of such property under lease
> **leaseholder** *n*

leash *n* **1** a dog's lead **2 straining at the leash** eagerly impatient to begin something ▸ *vb* **3** to put a leash on

least *adj, adv* **1 the least** the superlative of **little**: *without encountering the least sign of civilization;*

the least talented player on the team ▸ adj 2 of very little importance 3 smallest ▸ adv 4 **at least** if nothing else: at least I wrote 5 **at the least** at the minimum: at the very least you should have some self-respect 6 **not in the least** not at all: you're not detaining me, not in the least

> **least** adj 3 = smallest, meanest, fewest, lowest, tiniest, minimum, slightest, minimal

leather n 1 the skin of an animal made smooth and flexible by tanning and removing the hair 2 **leathers** leather clothes, esp. as worn by motorcyclists ▸ adj 3 made of leather ▸ vb 4 to whip as if with a leather strap 5 to dress in leather

leathery adj looking or feeling like leather, esp. in toughness

leave¹ vb **leaving, left 1** to go away (from a person or place) 2 to cause to remain behind, often by mistake, in a place: I left the paper under the table 3 to cause to be or remain in a specified state: the poll leaves the parties neck-and-neck 4 to stop attending or belonging to a particular organization or institution: at seventeen she left the convent 5 to not eat something or not deal with something: he left a half-eaten lunch 6 to result in; cause: I have been terribly hurt by past partners, it leaves indelible marks 7 to allow (someone) to do something without interfering: the governor left them to it for a further few hours 8 to be survived by (members of one's family): he leaves a widow and one daughter 9 to bequeath: her adored son left his millions to an unknown half-sister 10 to have as a remainder: 37 - 14 leaves 23 11 **leave (someone) alone** A to stop annoying (someone) B to permit to stay or be alone ▸ See also **leave out**

> **leave** vb 1 = depart from, withdraw from, go from, escape from, quit, flee, exit, pull out of; ≠ arrive 2 = forget, leave behind, mislay 4 = quit, give up, get out of, resign from, drop out of 6 = cause, produce, result in, generate, deposit 7 = entrust, commit, delegate, refer, hand over, assign, consign, allot 9 = bequeath, will, transfer, endow, confer, hand down

leave² n 1 permission to be absent, for instance from work: so I asked for leave 2 the length of such absence: weekend leave 3 permission to do something: they were refused leave to appeal 4 **on leave** officially excused from work or duty 5 **take (one's) leave of** to say farewell to

> **leave** n 1, 2 = holiday, break, vacation, time off, sabbatical, leave of absence, furlough, schoolie (Austral), accumulated day off or ADO (Austral) 3 = permission, freedom, sanction, liberty, concession, consent, allowance, warrant; ≠ refusal

leaven (lev-ven) n also **leavening 1** any substance, such as yeast, that produces fermentation in dough and makes it rise 2 an influence that produces a gradual change

▸ vb 3 to cause fermentation in (dough) 4 to spread through, causing a gradual change

leave out vb to omit or exclude: leave out everything not necessary to living

> **leave out** vb **leave something or someone out** = omit, exclude, miss out, forget, reject, ignore, overlook, neglect

lecherous (letch-er-uss) adj having or showing strong and uncontrolled sexual desire ▸ **lecher** n ▸ **lechery** n

lectern n a sloping reading desk, esp. in a church

lecture n 1 a talk on a particular subject delivered to an audience 2 a lengthy scolding ▸ vb **-turing, -tured 3** to deliver a lecture (to an audience or class) 4 to scold (someone) at length ▸ **lecturer** n ▸ **lectureship** n

> **lecture** n 1 = talk, address, speech, lesson, instruction, presentation, discourse, sermon, webinar 2 = telling-off (informal), rebuke, reprimand, talking-to (informal), scolding, dressing-down (informal), reproof ▸ vb 3 = talk, speak, teach, address, discourse, spout (informal), expound, hold forth 4 = tell off (informal), berate, scold, reprimand, censure, castigate, admonish, reprove

LED electronics light-emitting diode: a semiconductor that gives out light when an electric current is applied to it

ledge n 1 a narrow horizontal surface that projects from a wall or window 2 a narrow shelflike projection on a cliff or mountain

ledger n accounting the principal book in which the commercial transactions of a company are recorded

lee n 1 a sheltered part or side; the side away from the direction from which the wind is blowing ▸ adj 2 naut on, at, or towards the side away from the wind: her lee rail was awash

leech n 1 a worm which has a sucker at each end of the body and feeds on the blood or tissues of other animals 2 a person who lives off another person; parasite

leek n a vegetable of the onion family with a slender white bulb and broad flat green overlapping leaves: the national emblem of Wales

leer vb 1 to give a sneering or suggestive look or grin ▸ n 2 such a look

leery adj **leerier, leeriest 1** slang (foll. by of) suspicious or wary 2 chiefly dialect knowing or sly

lees pl n the sediment from an alcoholic drink

> **lees** pl n = sediment, grounds, deposit, dregs

leeward chiefly naut ▸ adj 1 of, in, or moving in the direction towards which the wind blows ▸ n 2 the side towards the lee ▸ adv 3 towards the lee

leeway n 1 flexibility of action or expenditure: he gave me a lot of leeway in the work I did 2 sideways drift of a boat or aircraft

left¹ *adj* **1** denoting the side of something or someone that faces west when the front is turned towards the north **2** on the left side of the body: *I grabbed it with my left hand* **3** liberal, radical, or socialist ▸ *adv* **4** on or in the direction of the left ▸ *n* **5** a left side, direction, position, area, or part **6 the left** the people in a political party or society who have more socialist or liberal views: *the biggest party of the French Left* **7** *boxing* **A** a blow with the left hand **B** the left hand

> **left** *adj* **1, 2** = left-hand, port, larboard (*naut*) **3** = socialist, radical, left-wing, leftist

left² *vb* the past of **leave¹**

left-handed *adj* **1** better at using the left hand than the right **2** done with the left hand **3** designed for use by the left hand **4** awkward or clumsy **5** ambiguous or insincere: *a left-handed compliment* **6** turning from right to left; anticlockwise ▸ *adv* **7** with the left hand: *I write left-handed* > **left-hander** *n*

leftist *adj* **1** of or relating to the political left or its principles ▸ *n* **2** a person who supports the political left ▸ **leftism** *n*

leftover *n* **1** (*often pl*) an unused portion, esp. of cooked food ▸ *adj* **2** left as an unused portion

left-wing *adj* **1** socialist or radical: *the party ditched many of its more left-wing policies* **2** belonging to the more radical part of a political party: *a group of left-wing Conservatives* ▸ *n* **left wing 3** the more radical or progressive section, esp. of a political party: *the left wing of the Labour Party* **4** *sport* **A** the left-hand side of the field of play **B** a player positioned in this area in certain games > **left-winger** *n*

> **left-wing** *adj* **1** = socialist, communist, red (*informal*), radical, revolutionary, militant, Bolshevik, Leninist

leg *n* **1** either of the two lower limbs in humans, or any similar structure in animals, that is used for movement or support **2** the part of a garment that covers the leg **3** a lower limb of an animal, esp. the thigh, used for food: *leg of lamb* **4** something similar to a leg in appearance or function, such as one of the supports of a chair **5** a section of a journey **6** a single stage, lap, or length in a relay race **7** one of a series of games, matches, or parts of games **8** *cricket* the side of the field to the left of a right-handed batsman as he faces the bowler **9 not have a leg to stand on** *informal* to have no reasonable basis for an opinion or argument **10 on one's last legs** worn out or exhausted **11 pull someone's leg** *informal* to tease or make fun of someone **12 shake a leg** *informal* to hurry up **13 stretch one's legs** to stand up or walk around, esp. after sitting for some time ▸ *vb* **legging, legged 14 leg it** *informal* to walk, run, or hurry

leg *n* **1** = limb, member, shank, lower limb, pin (*informal*), stump (*informal*) **4** = support, prop, brace, upright **5, 6** = stage, part, section, stretch, lap, segment, portion **11 pull someone's leg** = tease, trick, fool, kid (*informal*), wind up (*Brit slang*), hoax, make fun of, lead up the garden path

legacy *n, pl* **-cies 1** money or personal property left to someone by a will **2** something handed down to a successor

> **legacy** *n* **1** = bequest, inheritance, gift, estate, heirloom

legal *adj* **1** established by or permitted by law; lawful **2** of or relating to law **3** relating to or characteristic of lawyers > **legally** *adv*

> **legal** *adj* **1** = lawful, allowed, sanctioned, constitutional, valid, legitimate, authorized, permissible **2, 3** = judicial, judiciary, forensic, juridical, jurisdictive

legality *n, pl* **-ties** the state or quality of being legal or lawful

legalize *or* **-lise** *vb* **-lizing, -lized** *or* **-lising, -lised** to make lawful or legal > **legalization** *or* **-lisation** *n*

legate *n* a messenger, esp. one representing the Pope

legatee *n* the recipient of a legacy

legation *n* **1** a diplomatic mission headed by a minister **2** the official residence and office of a diplomatic minister

legato (leg-ah-toe) *music* ▸ *adv* **1** smoothly and evenly ▸ *n, pl* **-tos 2** a style of playing with no gaps between notes

legend *n* **1** a popular story handed down from earlier times which may or may not be true **2** such stories collectively **3** a person whose fame makes him or her seem exceptional: *he is a living legend* **4** modern stories about a famous person which may or may not be true: *no Garland fan could complain about sordid revelations tarnishing the legend* **5** words written on something to explain it: *a pub mirror spelling out the legend 'Saloon Bar'* **6** an explanation on a table, map, or chart, of the symbols used

> **legend** *n* **1** = myth, story, tale, fiction, saga, fable, folk tale, folk story **3** = celebrity, star, phenomenon, genius, prodigy, luminary, megastar (*informal*) **5** = inscription, title, caption, device, motto, rubric

legendary *adj* **1** very famous: *the legendary beauty of the Alps* **2** of or relating to legend **3** described in legend: *the legendary birthplace of Aphrodite*

> **legendary** *adj* **1** = famous, celebrated, well-known, acclaimed, renowned, famed, immortal, illustrious; ≠ unknown **2, 3** = mythical, fabled, traditional, romantic, fabulous, fictitious, storybook, apocryphal; ≠ factual

legerdemain (lej-er-de-main) *n* **1** same as **sleight of hand** **2** cunning deception

leggings *pl n* **1** an extra outer covering for the lower legs **2** very close-fitting trousers

leggy *adj* **1** having unusually long legs **2** (of a plant) having a long weak stem

legible *adj* (of handwriting) able to be read > **legibility** *n* > **legibly** *adv*

legion *n* **1** any large military force: *the French Foreign Legion* **2** (*often pl*) any very large number **3** an infantry unit in the ancient Roman army of three to six thousand men **4** an association of veterans > **legionary** *adj, n*

> **legion** *n* **1** = army, company, force, division, troop, brigade **2** = multitude, host, mass, drove, number, horde, myriad, throng

legionnaire *n* (*often cap*) a member of a legion

legislate *vb* **-lating, -lated 1** to make or pass laws **2** to bring into effect by legislation > **legislator** *n*

legislation *n* **1** the act or process of making laws **2** the laws so made

> **legislation** *n* **1** = lawmaking, regulation, prescription, enactment **2** = law, act, ruling, rule, bill, measure, regulation, charter

legislative *adj* **1** of or relating to the process of making laws **2** having the power or function of making laws: *the House of Lords is one of the largest legislative assemblies in the world*

> **legislative** *adj* **2** = law-making, judicial, law-giving

legislature *n* a body of people authorized to make, amend, and repeal laws

> **legislature** *n* = parliament, congress, senate, assembly, chamber

legit *adj informal* short for **legitimate**

legitimate *adj* **1** authorized by or in accordance with law: *legitimate accounting practices* **2** based on correct or acceptable principles of reasoning: *a legitimate argument* **3** (of a child) born of parents legally married to each other **4** of, relating to, or ruling by hereditary right: *under their legitimate ruling house* **5** of or relating to serious drama as distinct from films, television, or vaudeville ▸ *vb* **-mating, -mated 6** to make, pronounce, or show to be legitimate > **legitimacy** *n* > **legitimately** *adv*

> **legitimate** *adj* **1** = lawful, legal, genuine, authentic, authorized, rightful, kosher (*informal*), dinkum (*Austral, NZ informal*), licit; ≠ unlawful **2** = reasonable, correct, sensible, valid, warranted, logical, justifiable, well-founded; ≠ unreasonable ▸ *vb* = legitimize, allow, permit, sanction, authorize, legalize, pronounce lawful

legitimize *or* **-mise** *vb* **-mizing, -mized** *or* **-mising, -mised** to make legitimate; legalize > **legitimization** *or* **-misation** *n*

legless *adj* **1** without legs **2** *slang* very drunk

Lego *n trademark* a construction toy consisting of plastic bricks and other components that fit together

leguaan *n* a large amphibious S African lizard

legume *n* **1** the pod of a plant of the pea or bean family **2** the seed from such pods, esp. beans or peas

leguminous *adj* of or relating to any family of flowering plants having pods (or legumes) as fruits

lei *n* (in Hawaii) a garland of flowers, worn around the neck

leisure *n* **1** time or opportunity for relaxation or hobbies **2 at leisure** **A** having free time **B** not occupied **3 at one's leisure** when one has free time > **leisured** *adj*

> **leisure** *n* **1** = spare time, free time, rest, ease, relaxation, recreation; ≠ work

leisure centre *n* a building providing facilities, such as a swimming pool, gym, and café, for a range of leisure pursuits

leisurely *adj* **1** unhurried; relaxed ▸ *adv* **2** in a relaxed way > **leisureliness** *n*

leitmotif *or* **leitmotiv** (lite-mote-eef) *n* **1** *music* a recurring melodic phrase used to suggest a character, thing, or idea **2** an often repeated image in a literary work

lekker *adj S African slang* pleasing, enjoyable, or tasty

> **lekker** *adj* = delicious, tasty, luscious, palatable, delectable, mouthwatering, scrumptious (*informal*), appetizing, yummo (*Austral slang*)

lemming *n* **1** a small rodent of northern and arctic regions, reputed to rush into the sea in large groups and drown **2** a member of any group following an unthinking course towards destruction

lemon *n* **1** a yellow oval edible fruit with juicy acidic flesh that grows on an evergreen tree in warm and tropical regions **2** *slang* a person or thing considered to be useless or defective ▸ *adj* **3** light yellow > **lemony** *adj*

lemonade *n* a drink made from lemon juice, sugar, and water, or from carbonated water, citric acid, and sweetener

lemon sole *n* an edible European flatfish

lemur *n* a nocturnal animal, related to the monkey, with a foxy face and long tail, found on Madagascar

lend *vb* **lending, lent 1** to permit the temporary use of **2** to provide (money) temporarily, often at interest **3** to contribute (some abstract quality): *a painted trellis lends a classical air to any garden* **4 lend an ear** to listen **5 lend itself to** to be appropriate for: *the building lends itself to loft conversion* > **lender** *n*

> **lend** *vb* **1, 2** = loan, advance, sub (*Brit informal*) **3** = give, provide, add, supply, grant, confer, bestow, impart **5 lend itself to something** = be appropriate for, suit, be suitable for, be appropriate to, be serviceable for

length *n* **1** the extent or measurement of something from end to end **2** a specified distance, esp. between two positions: *the length of a cricket pitch* **3** a period of time, as between specified limits or moments **4** the quality, state, or fact of being long rather than short **5** a piece of something, usually longer than it is wide: *a length of twine* **6** (*usually pl*) the amount of trouble taken in doing something: *to go to great lengths* **7** *prosody & phonetics* the duration of a vowel or syllable **8 at length A** after a long interval or period of time **B** in great detail

> **length** *n* **1** = distance, reach, measure, extent, span, longitude **3** = duration, term, period, space, stretch, span, expanse **5** = piece, measure, section, segment, portion **8A at length** = at last, finally, eventually, in time, in the end, at long last **8B at length** = for a long time, completely, fully, thoroughly, for hours, in detail, for ages, in depth

lengthen *vb* to make or become longer

> **lengthen** *vb* = protract, extend, prolong, draw out, spin out, make longer; ≠ cut down

lengthways *or* **lengthwise** *adv, adj* in, according to, or along the direction of length

lengthy *adj* **lengthier**, **lengthiest** very long or tiresome > **lengthily** *adv* > **lengthiness** *n*

> **lengthy** *adj* = very long, rambling, interminable, long-winded, wordy, discursive, extended; ≠ brief

lenient (lee-nee-ent) *adj* tolerant, not strict or severe > **leniency** *n* > **leniently** *adv*

lens *n* **1** a piece of glass or other transparent material with a curved surface or surfaces, used to bring together or spread rays of light passing through it: used in cameras, telescopes, and spectacles **2** *anatomy* a transparent structure in the eye, behind the iris, that focuses images on the retina

lent *vb* the past of **lend**

Lent *n Christianity* the period from Ash Wednesday to Easter Saturday, during which some Christians give up doing something they enjoy > **Lenten** *adj*

lentil *n* any of the small edible seeds of a leguminous Asian plant

lento *music* ▸ *adv* **1** slowly ▸ *n, pl* **-tos 2** a movement or passage performed slowly

leonine *adj* of or like a lion

leopard *or fem* **leopardess** *n* a large African and Asian mammal of the cat family, which has a tawny yellow coat with black spots. Also called: **panther**

leotard *n* a tight-fitting garment covering the body from the shoulders to the thighs and worn by acrobats, ballet dancers, and people doing exercises

leper *n* **1** *offensive* a person who has leprosy **2** a person who is avoided

lepidopterist *n* a person who studies or collects moths and butterflies

leprechaun *n* (in Irish folklore) a mischievous elf

leprosy *n pathol* a chronic infectious disease, characterized by painful inflamed lumps beneath the skin and disfigurement and wasting away of affected parts > **leprous** *adj*

lesbian *n* **1** a female homosexual ▸ *adj* **2** of or characteristic of lesbians > **lesbianism** *n*

> **lesbian** *adj* = homosexual, gay, sapphic

lese-majesty (lezz-maj-ist-ee) *n* **1** an offence against the sovereign power in a state; treason **2** an act of disrespect towards authority

lesion *n* **1** any structural change in an organ or tissue resulting from injury or disease **2** an injury or wound

less *adj* **1** the comparative of **little**: *less fibre* **2** *not standard* fewer ▸ *adv* **3** the comparative of **little**: *eat less* **4 less of** to a smaller extent or degree: *it would become less of a problem* **5 no less** *sometimes humorous* used to indicate admiration or surprise: *sculpted by a famous Frenchman, Rodin no less* ▸ *prep* **6** minus: *a two pounds-a-week rise (less tax)*

> **less** *adj* **1** = smaller, shorter, not so much

lessee *n* a person to whom a lease is granted

lessen *vb* to make or become less

> **lessen** *vb* = grow less, diminish, decrease, contract, ease, shrink; ≠ increase

lesser *adj* not as great in quantity, size, or worth

> **lesser** *adj* = lower, secondary, subsidiary, inferior, less important; ≠ greater

lesson *n* **1 A** a single period of instruction in a subject **B** the content of such a period **2** material assigned for individual study **3** something from which useful knowledge or principles can be learned: *one could still learn an important lesson from these masters* **4** an experience that serves as a warning or example: *the experience will prove a sobering lesson for the military* **5** a passage of Scripture read during a church service

> **lesson** *n* **1** = class, schooling, period, teaching, coaching, session, instruction, lecture **3, 4** = example, warning, message, moral, deterrent **5** = Bible reading, reading, text, Bible passage, Scripture passage

lest *conj* **1** so as to prevent any possibility that: *one grabbed it lest a neighbour got there first* **2** for fear that: *his anxiety lest anything mar the family event*

let¹ *vb* **letting**, **let 1** to allow: *a child lets a friend play with his favourite toy* **2 A** an auxiliary expressing a request, proposal, or command, or conveying a warning or threat: *well, let's try it; just let me catch you here again!* **B** an auxiliary expressing an assumption or hypothesis: *let 'a' equal 'b'* **C** an auxiliary used to convey resigned acceptance of the inevitable: *let the worst happen* **3** to allow someone to rent (property or accommodation) **4** to cause the movement of (something) in a specified direction: *he let the air out of the tire* **5 let alone** not to mention: *I could hardly think, let alone find words to say* **6 let alone** *or* **be** stop annoying or interfering with: *let the poor cat alone* **7 let go** to relax one's hold (on) **8 let loose A** to allow (a person or animal) to leave or escape **B** *informal* to make (a sound) suddenly: *he let loose a laugh* **C** *informal* to fire (ammunition) from a gun ▸ *n* **9** *Brit & Austral* the act of letting property or accommodation ▸ See also **let down**, **let off** *etc.*

> **let** *vb* **1** = allow, permit, authorize, give the go-ahead, give permission **3** = lease, hire, rent, rent out, hire out, sublease

let² *n* **1** *tennis & squash* a minor infringement or obstruction of the ball, requiring a point to be replayed **2 without let or hindrance** without obstruction

let down *vb* **1** to fail to satisfy the expectations of (someone); disappoint **2** to lower **3** to lengthen a garment by decreasing the hem **4** to deflate: *to let down a tyre* ▸ *n* **letdown 5** a disappointment

> **let down** *vb* **1 let someone down** = disappoint, fail, abandon, desert, disillusion, fall short, leave stranded, leave in the lurch **4 let something down** = deflate, empty, exhaust, flatten, puncture

lethal *adj* capable of causing death ▸ **lethally** *adv*

> **lethal** *adj* = deadly, terminal, fatal, dangerous, devastating, destructive, mortal, murderous; ≠ harmless

lethargy *n, pl* **-gies 1** sluggishness or dullness **2** an abnormal lack of energy ▸ **lethargic** *adj* ▸ **lethargically** *adv*

let off *vb* **1** to excuse from (work or duties): *I'll let you off homework for a week* **2** to spare (someone) the expected punishment: *lots were let off because they couldn't be bothered to prosecute anybody* **3** to explode or fire (a bomb, gun, or firework) **4** to release (liquid, air, or steam)

> **let off** *vb* **1, 2 let someone off** = excuse, release, discharge, pardon, spare, forgive, exempt, exonerate **3 let something off** = fire, explode, set off, discharge, detonate **4 let something off** = emit, release, leak, exude, give off

let on *vb informal* **1** to reveal (a secret) **2** to pretend: *he let on that he was a pilgrim*

> **let on** *vb* **1** = reveal, disclose, say, tell, admit, give away, divulge, let slip

let out *vb* **1** to emit: *he let out a scream* **2** to allow to leave; release **3** to make (property) available for people to rent **4** to make (a garment) wider by reducing the seams **5** to reveal (a secret) ▸ *n* **let-out 6** a chance to escape

> **let out** *vb* **1 let something out** = emit, make, produce, give vent to

letter *n* **1** a written or printed message, usually enclosed in an envelope and sent by post **2** any of a set of conventional symbols used in writing or printing a language: character of the alphabet **3** the strict meaning of an agreement or document; exact wording: *the letter of the law* **4 to the letter** precisely: *you have to follow treatment to the letter for it to be effective* ▸ *vb* **5** to write or mark letters on (a sign) ▸ **lettering** *n*

> **letter** *n* **1** = message, line, note, communication, dispatch, missive, epistle, email *or* e-mail **2** = character, mark, sign, symbol, glyph (*computers*)

letter bomb *n* an explosive device in an envelope or parcel that explodes when the envelope or parcel is opened

letter box *n chiefly Brit* **1** a slot in a door through which letters are delivered **2** Also called: **pillar box, postbox** a public box into which letters and postcards are put for collection

lettered *adj* **1** well educated **2** printed or marked with letters

letterhead *n* a printed heading on stationery giving the name and address of the sender

lettuce *n* a plant cultivated for its large edible leaves, which are used in salads

let up *vb* **1** to diminish or stop **2** (foll. by *on*) *informal* to be less harsh (towards someone) ▸ *n* **let-up 3** *informal* a lessening: *there has been no let-up in the war*

> **let up** *vb* **1** = stop, diminish, decrease, subside, relax, ease (up), moderate, lessen

leucocyte (loo-koh-site) *n* any of the various large white cells in the blood of vertebrates

leukaemia *or esp US* **leukemia** (loo-kee-mee-a) *n* an acute or chronic disease characterized by extreme overproduction of white blood cells

levee *n US* **1** a natural or artificial river embankment **2** a quay

level *adj* **1** on a horizontal plane **2** having an even surface **3** being of the same height as something else: *the floor of the lean-to was level with the patio* **4** equal to or even with (something or someone else): *Johnson was level with the overnight leader* **5** not exceeding the upper edge of (a spoon, etc.) **6** consistent or regular: *a level pulse* **7 one's level best** the best one can do ▸ *vb* **-velling, -velled** *or US* **-veling, -veled 8** (sometimes foll. by *off*) to make horizontal or even **9** to make equal in position or status **10** to direct (an accusation or criticism) emphatically at someone **11** to focus (a look) directly at someone **12** to aim (a weapon) horizontally **13** to demolish completely ▸ *n* **14** a horizontal line or plane **15** a device, such as a spirit level, for determining whether a surface is horizontal **16** position or status in a scale of values: *a high-level* delegation **17** stage or degree of progress: *primary-school level* **18** a specified vertical position: *floor level* **19** the topmost horizontal line or plane from which the height of something is calculated: *sea level* **20** a flat even surface or area of land **21** a degree or intensity reached on a measurable or notional scale: *noise level* **22 on the level** *informal* sincere or genuine

> **level** *adj* **1, 2** = horizontal, even, flat, smooth, uniform; ≠ slanted **3** = equal, balanced, at the same height **4** = even, tied, equal, drawn, neck and neck, all square, level pegging ▸ *vb* **8** = flatten, plane, smooth, even off *or* out **9** = equalize, balance, even up **10, 11, 12** = direct, point, turn, train, aim, focus **13** = destroy, devastate, demolish, flatten, knock down, pull down, tear down, bulldoze, kennet (*Austral slang*), jeff (*Austral slang*); ≠ build ▸ *n* **16, 17** = position, standard, degree (*archaic*), grade, standing, stage, rank, status **22 on the level** = honest, genuine, straight, fair, square, dinkum (*Austral, NZ informal*), above board

level crossing *n* *Brit, Austral & NZ* a point at which a railway line and a road cross

level-headed *adj* calm and sensible

lever *n* **1** a handle used to operate machinery **2** a bar used to move a heavy object or to prise something open **3** a rigid bar that turns on a fixed support (fulcrum) to transfer effort and motion, for instance to move a load **4** a means of exerting pressure in order to achieve an aim: *using the hostages as a lever to gain concessions from the government* ▸ *vb* **5** to open or move with a lever

> **lever** *n* **1, 2, 3** = handle, bar ▸ *vb* = prise, force

leverage *n* **1** the mechanical advantage gained by using a lever **2** the ability to influence people or events: *information gives leverage*

> **leverage** *n* **1** = force, hold, pull, strength, grip, grasp **2** = influence, authority, pull (*informal*), weight, clout (*informal*)

leveret (lev-ver-it) *n* a young hare

leviathan (lev-vie-ath-an) *n* any huge or powerful thing

Levis *pl n trademark* denim jeans

levitate *vb* **-tating, -tated** to rise or cause to rise, suspended, in the air › **levitation** *n*

levity *n, pl* **-ties** a frivolous or too light-hearted attitude to serious matters

levy (lev-vee) *vb* **levies, levying, levied** **1** to impose and collect (a tax, tariff, or fine) **2** to conscript troops for service ▸ *n, pl* **levies** **3** ᴀ the imposition and collection of taxes, tariffs, or fines ʙ the money so raised **4** troops conscripted for service

> **levy** *vb* **1** = impose, charge, collect, demand, exact ▸ *n* **3** = tax, fee, toll, tariff, duty, excise, exaction

lewd *adj* indecently vulgar; obscene › **lewdly** *adv* › **lewdness** *n*

lexical *adj* **1** relating to the vocabulary of a language **2** relating to a lexicon › **lexically** *adv*

lexicography *n* the process or profession of compiling dictionaries › **lexicographer** *n*

lexicon *n* **1** a dictionary, esp. one of an ancient language such as Greek **2** the vocabulary of a language or of an individual

LGBT lesbian, gay, bisexual, and transgender

LGBTQ lesbian, gay, bisexual, transgender, and queer (or questioning)

liability *n, pl* **-ties** **1** someone or something that is a problem or embarrassment **2** the state of being legally responsible **3** (*often pl*) sums of money owed by an organization

> **liability** *n* **1** = disadvantage, burden, drawback, inconvenience, handicap, nuisance, hindrance, millstone **2** = responsibility, accountability, culpability, answerability

liable *adj* **1** probable or likely: *weak and liable to give way* **2** commonly suffering a condition: *he's liable to colds in the chest* **3** legally obliged or responsible; answerable

> **liable** *adj* **1** = likely, tending, inclined, disposed, prone, apt **2** = vulnerable, subject, exposed, prone, susceptible, open, at risk of **3** = responsible, accountable, answerable, obligated

liaise *vb* **-aising, -aised** (usually foll. by *with*) to communicate and maintain contact with

liaison *n* **1** communication and cooperative contact between groups **2** a secretive or adulterous sexual relationship

> **liaison** *n* **1** = contact, communication, connection, interchange **2** = affair, romance, intrigue, fling, love affair, amour, entanglement

liana *n* a woody climbing and twining plant of tropical forests

liar *n* a person who tells lies

> **liar** *n* = falsifier, perjurer, fibber, fabricator

lib *n informal* liberation: used in the name of certain movements: *women's lib*

libel *n* **1** *law* the publication of something false which damages a person's reputation **2** any damaging or unflattering representation or statement ▸ *vb* **-belling, -belled** *or US* **-beling, -beled 3** *law* to make or publish a false damaging statement or representation about (a person) › **libellous** *or US* **libelous** *adj*

> **libel** *n* = defamation, misrepresentation, denigration, smear, calumny, aspersion ▸ *vb* = defame, smear, slur, blacken, malign, denigrate, revile, vilify

liberal *adj* 1 having social and political views that favour progress and reform 2 generous in temperament or behaviour 3 tolerant of other people 4 using or existing in large quantities; lavish: *the world's finest gadgetry, in liberal quantities* 5 not rigid; free: *a more liberal interpretation* 6 (of an education) designed to develop general cultural interests and intellectual ability 7 **Liberal** of or relating to a Liberal Party ▸ *n* 8 a person who has liberal ideas or opinions > **liberalism** *n* > **liberally** *adv*

> **liberal** *adj* 1 = progressive, radical, reformist, libertarian, forward-looking, free-thinking; ≠ conservative 2 = generous, kind, charitable, extravagant, open-hearted, bountiful, magnanimous, open-handed; ≠ stingy 4 = abundant, generous, handsome, lavish, ample, rich, plentiful, copious; ≠ limited

Liberal Democrat *n* a member or supporter of the Liberal Democrats, a British centrist political party that advocates proportional representation

liberality *n, pl* **-ties** 1 generosity 2 the quality of being broad-minded

liberalize *or* **-lise** *vb* **-lizing, -lized** *or* **-lising, -ised** to make (a law) less strict > **liberalization** *or* **-lisation** *n*

Liberal Party *n* 1 *history* a British non-Socialist political party which advocated progress and reform 2 any similar party in various other countries 3 the main right-wing political party in Australia

liberate *vb* **-rating, -rated** 1 to free (someone) from social prejudices or injustices 2 to give liberty to; make free 3 to release (a country) from enemy occupation > **liberation** *n* > **liberator** *n*

> **liberate** *vb* 2, 3 = free, release, rescue, save, deliver, let out, set free, let loose; ≠ imprison

libertarian *n* 1 a person who believes in freedom of thought and action ▸ *adj* 2 believing in freedom of thought and action

libertine (lib-er-teen) *n* 1 a person who is promiscuous and unscrupulous ▸ *adj* 2 promiscuous and unscrupulous

liberty *n, pl* **-ties** 1 the freedom to choose, think, and act for oneself 2 the right of unrestricted movement and access; freedom 3 (*often pl*) a social action regarded as being forward or improper 4 **at liberty** free or unconfined 5 **at liberty (to)** unrestricted or authorized: *I am not at liberty to divulge his name* 6 **take liberties** *or* **a liberty (with)** to be overfamiliar (towards someone)

> **liberty** *n* 1 = independence, sovereignty, liberation, autonomy, immunity, self-determination, emancipation, self-government 4 **at liberty** = free, escaped, unlimited, at large, not confined, untied,

on the loose, unchained 5 **at liberty** = able, free, allowed, permitted, entitled, authorized 6 **take liberties** *or* **a liberty** = not show enough respect, show disrespect, act presumptuously, behave too familiarly, behave impertinently

libidinous *adj* characterized by excessive sexual desire > **libidinously** *adv*

libido (lib-ee-doe) *n, pl* **-dos** 1 *psychoanalysis* psychic energy from the id 2 sexual urge or desire > **libidinal** *adj*

librarian *n* a person in charge of or assisting in a library > **librarianship** *n*

library *n, pl* **-braries** 1 a room or building where books and other literary materials are kept 2 a collection of literary materials, films, CDs, toys, etc., kept for borrowing or reference 3 the building or institution that houses such a collection 4 a set of books published as a series, often in a similar format 5 *computers* a collection of standard programs, usually stored on disk

libretto *n, pl* **-tos** *or* **-ti** a text written for an opera > **librettist** *n*

lice *n* the plural of **louse**

licence *or US* **license** *n* 1 a document giving official permission to do, use, or own something 2 formal permission or exemption 3 intentional disregard of conventional rules to achieve a certain effect: *poetic licence* 4 excessive freedom

> **licence** *or* **license** *n* 1 = certificate, document, permit, charter, warrant 2 = permission, the right, authority, leave, sanction, liberty, immunity, entitlement; ≠ denial 3 = freedom, creativity, latitude, independence, liberty, deviation, leeway, free rein; ≠ restraint 4 = laxity, excess, indulgence, irresponsibility, licentiousness, immoderation; ≠ moderation

license *vb* **-censing, -censed** 1 to grant a licence to or for 2 to give permission to or for > **licensable** *adj*

> **license** *vb* = permit, sanction, allow, warrant, authorize, empower, certify, accredit; ≠ forbid

licensee *n* a person who holds a licence, esp. one to sell alcoholic drink

licentiate *n* a person who holds a certificate of competence to practise a certain profession

licentious *adj* sexually unrestrained or promiscuous > **licentiousness** *n*

lichen *n* any of various small mossy plants that grow in patches on tree trunks, bare ground, rocks, and stone walls

licit *adj formal* lawful; permitted

lick *vb* 1 to pass the tongue over in order to taste, wet, or clean 2 to flicker over or round (something): *flames licked the gutters* 3 *informal* **A** to defeat **B** to thrash 4 **lick into shape** to put into a satisfactory condition 5 **lick one's wounds** to retire after a defeat ▸ *n* 6 an instance of passing the tongue over something **7** a small amount: *a lick of paint* **8** *informal* a blow **9** *informal* a fast pace: *a pulsating rhythm taken at a lick* **10 a lick and a promise** something hastily done, esp. a hurried wash

> **lick** *vb* **1** = taste, lap, tongue **2** = flicker, touch, flick, dart, ripple, play over **3A** = beat, defeat, overcome, rout, outstrip, outdo, trounce, vanquish ► *n* **7** = dab, touch, stroke **9** = pace, rate, speed, clip (*informal*)

licorice *n US & Canad* same as **liquorice**

lid *n* **1** a removable or hinged cover: *a saucepan lid* **2** short for **eyelid 3 put the (tin) lid on** *informal* to put an end to ► **lidded** *adj*

lido (lee-doe) *n, pl* **-dos** *Brit* an open-air swimming pool or a part of a beach used by the public for swimming and sunbathing

lie¹ *vb* **lying, lied 1** to speak untruthfully with the intention of deceiving **2** to convey a false impression: *the camera cannot lie* ► *n* **3** an untrue statement deliberately used to mislead **4** something that is deliberately intended to deceive **5 give the lie to A** to disprove **B** to accuse of lying

> **lie** *vb* = fib, fabricate, falsify, prevaricate, not tell the truth, equivocate, dissimulate, tell untruths ► *n* **3, 4** = falsehood, deceit, fabrication, fib, fiction, invention, deception, untruth **5A give the lie to something** = disprove, expose, discredit, contradict, refute, negate, invalidate, rebut

lie² *vb* **lying, lay, lain 1** (often foll. by *down*) to place oneself or be in a horizontal position **2** to be situated: *I left the money lying on the table; Nepal became the only country lying between China and India* **3** to be and remain (in a particular state or condition): *others of their species lie asleep* **4** to stretch or extend: *an enormous task lies ahead* **5** (usually foll. by *in*) to exist or comprise: *her charm lies in her inner beauty* **6** (foll. by *with*) to rest (with): *the fault lies with them* ► *n* **7** the manner, place, or style in which something is situated **8** an animal's lair **9 lie of the land** the way in which a situation is developing ► See also **lie in**

> **lie** *vb* **1** = recline, rest, lounge, sprawl, stretch out, loll, repose **2** = be placed, be, rest, exist, be situated

lied (leed) *n, pl* **lieder** *music* a musical setting for solo voice and piano of a romantic or lyrical poem

liege (leej) *adj* **1** (of a lord) owed feudal allegiance: *their liege lord* **2** (of a vassal or subject) owing feudal allegiance: *a liege subject* **3** faithful; loyal ► *n* **4** a liege lord **5** a subject

lie in *vb* **1** to remain in bed late into the morning ► *n* **lie-in 2** a long stay in bed in the morning

lien *n law* a right to retain possession of someone else's property until a debt is paid

lieu (lyew) *n* **in lieu of** instead of

lieutenant (lef-**ten**-ant, loo-**ten**-ant) *n* **1** a junior officer in the army, navy, or the US police force **2** a person who acts as principal assistant ► **lieutenancy** *n*

life *n, pl* **lives 1** the state or quality that identifies living beings, characterized chiefly by growth, reproduction, and response to stimuli **2** the period between birth and death or between birth and the present time **3** a living person or being: *riots which claimed 22 lives* **4** the remainder or extent of one's life: *in that house for the rest of her life* **5** the process of living: *rituals gave his life stability* **6** *informal* a sentence of life imprisonment, usually approximating to fifteen years **7** a characteristic state or mode of existence: *country life is best* **8** the length of time that something is active or functioning: *the life of a battery* **9** a present condition or mode of existence: *they are leading a joyous life* **10** a biography **11** the sum or course of human events and activities **12** liveliness or high spirits: *full of life* **13** a source of strength, animation, or vitality: *he was the life of the show* **14** all living things collectively: *there is no life on Mars; marine life* **15 a matter of life and death** a matter of extreme urgency **16 as large as life** *informal* real and living **17 not on your life** *informal* certainly not **18 to the life** (of a copy of a painting or drawing) resembling the original exactly **19 true to life** faithful to reality

> **life** *n* **1** = being, existence, vitality, sentience **2, 4** = existence, being, lifetime, time, days, span **5, 7, 9** = way of life, situation, conduct, behaviour, lifestyle **10** = biography, story, history, profile, confessions, autobiography, memoirs, life story **12** = liveliness, energy, spirit, vitality, animation, vigour, verve, zest

life belt *n* an inflatable ring used to keep a person afloat when in danger of drowning

lifeboat *n* a boat used for rescuing people at sea

life cycle *n* the series of changes occurring in each generation of an animal or plant

lifeless *adj* **1** inanimate; dead **2** lacking liveliness or animation **3** unconscious

lifelike *adj* closely resembling or representing life

lifeline *n* **1** a single means of contact or support on which a person or an area relies **2** a rope used for life-saving

lifelong *adj* lasting for a lifetime

> **lifelong** *adj* = long-lasting, enduring, lasting, persistent, long-standing, perennial

life science *n* any of the sciences concerned with the structure and behaviour of living organisms, such as biology, botany, or zoology

lifespan *n* **1** the period of time for which a creature normally lives **2** the period of time for which a product normally functions

lifestyle *n* a set of attitudes, habits, and possessions regarded as typical of a particular group or an individual

life-support *adj* (of equipment or treatment) necessary to sustain life

lifetime *n* **1** the length of time a person is alive **2** **of a lifetime** (of an opportunity or experience) the most important or memorable

> **lifetime** *n* **1** = existence, time, day(s), span

lift *vb* **1** to rise or raise upwards to a higher place: *the breakdown truck was lifting the lorry* **2** to move upwards: *he slowly lifted his hand* **3** to raise in status or estimation: *lifted from poverty* **4** to revoke or cancel: *the government lifted its restrictions on imported beef* **5** to remove (plants or underground crops) from the ground for harvesting **6** to disappear or disperse: *the tension lifted* **7** *informal* to plagiarize (music or writing) ▸ *n* **8** a compartment raised or lowered in a vertical shaft to transport people or goods to another floor in a building **9** a ride in a car or other vehicle as a passenger **10** a rise in morale or feeling of cheerfulness **11** the act of lifting **12** the force that lifts airborne objects

> **lift** *vb* **1, 2** = raise, pick up, hoist, draw up, elevate, uplift, heave up, upraise; ≠ lower **4** = revoke, end, remove, withdraw, stop, cancel, terminate, rescind; ≠ impose **6** = disappear, clear, vanish, disperse, dissipate, rise, be dispelled ▸ *n* **8** = elevator (*chiefly US*), hoist, paternoster **9** = ride, run, drive, hitch (*informal*) **10** = boost, encouragement, stimulus, pick-me-up, fillip, shot in the arm (*informal*), gee-up; ≠ blow

liftoff *n* the initial movement of a rocket as it leaves its launch pad

ligament *n anatomy* a band of tough tissue that connects various bones or cartilage

ligature *n* **1** a link, bond, or tie **2** *printing* a character of two or more joined letters **3** *music* a slur or the group of notes connected by it ▸ *vb* **-turing, -tured 4** to bind with a ligature

light¹ *n* **1** the natural medium, electromagnetic radiation, that makes sight possible **2** anything that illuminates, such as a lamp or candle **3** a particular type of light: *dim yellow light* **4 A** daylight **B** daybreak; dawn **5** anything that lets in light, such as a window **6** an aspect or view: *we have seen the light in a new light* **7** mental understanding or spiritual insight: *suddenly he saw the light* **8** an outstanding person: *a leading light of the movement* **9** brightness of countenance, esp. a sparkle in the eyes **10 A** something that ignites, such as a spark or flame **B** something used for igniting, such as a match **11** See **lighthouse 12 come to light** to become known or visible **13 in (the) light of** taking into account **14 see the light** to understand **15 see the light (of day) A** to come into being **B** to come to public notice ▸ *adj* **16** full of light **17** (of a colour) pale: *light blue* ▸ *vb* **lighting, lighted** or **lit 18** to ignite **19** (often foll. by *up*) to illuminate or cause to illuminate **20** to guide by light > **lightish** *adj*

> **light** *n* **1, 14** = brightness, illumination, luminosity, shining, glow, glare, gleam, brilliance; ≠ dark **2** = lamp, torch, candle, flare, beacon, lantern, taper **6** = aspect, context, angle, point of view, interpretation, viewpoint, slant, standpoint **10** = match, spark, flame, lighter ▸ *adj* **16** = bright, brilliant, shining, illuminated, luminous, well-lit, lustrous, well-illuminated; ≠ dark **17** = pale, fair, faded, blonde, blond, bleached, pastel, light-coloured; ≠ dark ▸ *vb* **18** = ignite, inflame, kindle, touch off, set alight; ≠ put out **19** = illuminate, light up, brighten; ≠ darken

light² *adj* **1** not heavy; weighing relatively little **2** relatively low in density, strength, amount, degree, etc.: *light oil; light alloy* **3** lacking sufficient weight **4** not bulky or clumsy: *light bedclothes* **5** not serious or difficult to understand; entertaining: *light music* **6** graceful or agile: *light movements* **7** without strong emphasis or serious meaning: *he gazed about with a light inattentive smile* **8** easily digested: *a light lunch* **9** relatively low in alcohol: *a light wine* **10** without burdens, difficulties, or problems: *a light heart lives longest* **11** dizzy or unclear: *a light head* **12** (of bread or cake) spongy or well risen **13 A** (of transport) designed to carry light loads **B** (of a vessel, aircraft, or other transport) not loaded **14** carrying light arms or equipment: *light infantry* **15** (of an industry) producing small consumer goods using light machinery **16 make light of** to treat as insignificant or unimportant ▸ *adv* **17** with little equipment or luggage: *travelling light* ▸ *vb* **lighting, lighted** or **lit 18** (esp. of birds) to settle or land after flight **19** (foll. by *on* or *upon*) to discover by chance ▸ See also **lights** > **lightish** *adj* > **lightly** *adv* > **lightness** *n*

> **light** *adj* **1, 4** = insubstantial, thin, slight, portable, buoyant, airy, flimsy, underweight; ≠ heavy **2** = weak, soft, gentle, moderate, slight, mild, faint, indistinct; ≠ strong **5** = light-hearted, funny, entertaining, amusing, witty, humorous, frivolous, unserious; ≠ serious **6** = nimble, graceful, deft, agile, sprightly, lithe, limber, lissom(e); ≠ clumsy **8** = digestible, modest, frugal; ≠ substantial ▸ *vb* **19 light on something** = come across, find, discover, encounter, stumble on, hit upon, happen upon

light bulb *n* a hollow rounded glass fitting containing a gas and a thin metal filament that gives out light when an electric current is passed through it

lighten¹ *vb* to make less dark

> **lighten** *vb* = brighten, illuminate, light up, irradiate, become light

lighten² *vb* **1** to make or become less heavy **2** to make or become more cheerful or lively

lighten *vb* 2 = ease, relieve, alleviate, allay, reduce, lessen, mitigate, assuage; ≠ intensify

lighter¹ *n* a small device for lighting cigarettes, etc.

lighter² *n* a flat-bottomed barge used in loading or unloading a ship

light-fingered *adj* skilful at thieving, esp. by picking pockets

light-headed *adj* giddy; feeling faint

light-hearted *adj* cheerful or carefree in mood or disposition > **light-heartedly** *adv*

lighthouse *n* a tower with a light to guide ships and warn of obstructions

lighting *n* 1 the apparatus for and design of artificial light effects to a stage, film, or television set 2 the act or quality of illumination

lightning *n* 1 a flash of light in the sky caused by a discharge of electricity ▸ *adj* 2 fast and sudden: *a lightning attack*

lights *pl n* the lungs of sheep, bullocks, and pigs, used for feeding pets

lightweight *adj* 1 not serious 2 of relatively light weight ▸ *n* 3 *informal* a person of little importance or influence 4 a person or animal of relatively light weight 5 a professional boxer weighing up to 135 pounds (61 kg) or an amateur weighing up to 60 kg

lightweight *adj* 1 = unimportant, shallow, trivial, insignificant, slight, petty, worthless, trifling; ≠ significant 2 = thin, fine, delicate, sheer, flimsy, gossamer, diaphanous, filmy

light year *n astron* the distance travelled by light in one mean solar year, i.e. 9.4607×10^{15} metres

ligneous *adj* of or like wood

lignite (**lig**-nite) *n* a brown sedimentary rock with a woody texture: used as a fuel

like¹ *adj* 1 resembling ▸ *prep* 2 in the manner of; similar to: *she was like a child; it looks like a traffic cone* 3 such as: *a modern material, like carbon fibre* 4 characteristic of ▸ *adv* 5 in the manner of: *cheering like mad* ▸ *conj* 6 *not standard* as though; as if: *I don't want to make it seem like I had this bad childhood* 7 in the same way that: *she doesn't dance like you do* ▸ *n* 8 the equal or counterpart of a person or thing

like *adj* = similar to, same as, equivalent to, parallel to, identical to, alike, corresponding to, comparable to; ≠ different

like² *vb* **liking, liked** 1 to find enjoyable 2 to be fond of 3 to prefer or choose: *I'd like to go home* 4 to feel disposed or inclined; choose; wish: *do as you like* 5 to indicate approval of (an item posted on a social media site) ▸ *n* 6 (*usually pl*) a favourable feeling, desire, or preference: *tell me your likes and dislikes* 7 an indication of approval for an item posted on a social media site > **likeable** *or* **likable** *adj*

like *vb* 1, 2 = enjoy, love, delight in, go for, relish, savour, revel in, be fond of; ≠ dislike 3, 4 = wish, want, choose, prefer, desire, fancy (*Brit informal*), care, feel inclined

likelihood *n* chance; probability

likelihood *n* = probability, chance, possibility, prospect

likely *adj* 1 tending or inclined: *likely to win* 2 probable: *the likely effects of the tunnel* 3 appropriate for a purpose or activity: *a likely candidate* ▸ *adv* 4 probably or presumably 5 **not likely** *informal* definitely not

likely *adj* 1 = inclined, disposed, prone, liable, tending, apt 2 = probable, expected, anticipated, odds-on, on the cards, to be expected

liken *vb* to compare

liken *vb* = compare, match, relate, parallel, equate, set beside

likeness *n* 1 resemblance 2 portrait 3 an imitative appearance; semblance: *in the likeness of a dragon*

likewise *adv* 1 in addition; also 2 similarly

likewise *adv* 2 = similarly, the same, in the same way, in similar fashion, in like manner

liking *n* 1 fondness 2 what one likes or prefers: *if it's not to your liking, do let me know*

liking *n* = fondness, love, taste, weakness, preference, affection, inclination, penchant; ≠ dislike

lilac *n* 1 a small tree with large sprays of purple or white sweet-smelling flowers ▸ *adj* 2 pale purple

Lilliputian (lil-lip-**pew**-shun) *n* 1 a tiny person or being ▸ *adj* 2 tiny; very small

Lilo *n, pl* **-los** *trademark* a type of inflatable plastic mattress

lilt *n* 1 a pleasing musical quality in a speaking voice 2 (in music) a jaunty rhythm 3 a graceful rhythmic motion ▸ *vb* 4 (of a voice, tune, or song) to rise and fall in a pleasant way 5 to move gracefully and rhythmically > **lilting** *adj*

lily *n, pl* **lilies** 1 a perennial plant, such as the tiger lily, with scaly bulbs and showy white or coloured flowers 2 a water lily

limb *n* 1 an arm, leg, or wing 2 any of the main branches of a tree 3 **out on a limb** **A** in a precarious or questionable position **B** *Brit & NZ* isolated, esp. because of unpopular opinions > **limbless** *adj*

limb *n* 1 = part, member, arm, leg, wing, extremity, appendage 2 = branch, spur, projection, offshoot, bough

limber *adj* 1 pliant; supple 2 able to move or bend the body freely; agile

limbo[1] *n, pl* **-bos 1** (*often cap*) *RC Church* (formerly) the supposed region intermediate between heaven and hell for the unbaptized **2 in limbo** not knowing the result or next stage of something and powerless to influence it

limbo[2] *n, pl* **-bos** a West Indian dance in which dancers lean backwards and pass under a horizontal bar which is gradually lowered

lime[1] *n agriculture* **1** calcium hydroxide spread as a dressing on acidic land ▸ *vb* **liming, limed 2** to spread a calcium compound upon (land)

lime[2] *n* the green oval fruit of a small Asian citrus tree with acid fleshy pulp rich in vitamin C

lime[3] *n* a European linden tree planted for ornament

lime-green *adj* light yellowish-green

limelight *n* **1 the limelight** glare of publicity: *this issue will remain in the limelight* **2** ᴀ a type of lamp, formerly used in stage lighting, in which lime is heated to white heat ʙ brilliant white light produced in this way

> **limelight** *n* **1** = publicity, recognition, fame, the spotlight, attention, prominence, stardom, public eye

limerick (lim-mer-ik) *n* a form of comic verse consisting of five lines

limestone *n* rock consisting mainly of calcium carbonate: used as a building stone and in making cement

limey *n US, Canad & Austral slang* **1** a British person **2** a British sailor or ship

limit *n* **1** (*sometimes pl*) the ultimate extent or amount of something: *each soloist was stretched to his or her limit by the demands of the vocal writing* **2** (*often pl*) the boundary of a specific area: *beyond the city limits* **3** the largest quantity or amount allowed **4 the limit** *informal* a person or thing that is intolerably exasperating ▸ *vb* **-iting, -ited 5** to restrict > **limitable** *adj* > **limitless** *adj*

> **limit** *n* **1** = end, ultimate, deadline, breaking point, extremity **2** = boundary, edge, border, frontier, perimeter ▸ *vb* = restrict, control, check, bound, confine, curb, restrain, ration

limitation *n* **1** a restriction or controlling of quantity, quality, or achievement **2 limitations** the limit or extent of an ability to achieve something: *learn your own limitations*

> **limitation** *n* **1** = restriction, control, check, curb, restraint, constraint

limousine *n* any large luxurious car

limp[1] *vb* **1** to walk with an uneven step, esp. with a weak or injured leg **2** to advance in a labouring or faltering manner ▸ *n* **3** an uneven walk or progress > **limping** *adj, n*

> **limp** *vb* **1** = hobble, stagger, stumble, shuffle, hop, falter, shamble, totter ▸ *n* = lameness, hobble

limp[2] *adj* **1** lacking firmness or stiffness **2** not energetic or vital **3** (of the binding of a book) paperback > **limply** *adv*

> **limp** *adj* **1** = floppy, soft, slack, drooping, flabby, pliable, flaccid; ≠ stiff

limpet *n* **1** a conical shellfish that clings tightly to rocks with its muscular foot ▸ *adj* **2** denoting certain weapons that are magnetically attached to their targets and resist removal: *limpet mines*

limpid *adj* **1** clear or transparent **2** (of speech or writing) clear and easy to understand > **limpidity** *n*

linchpin *or* **lynchpin** *n* **1** a pin inserted through an axle to keep a wheel in position **2** an essential person or thing: *she was the linchpin of the experiment*

linctus *n, pl* **-tuses** a soothing syrupy cough mixture

linden *n* a large tree with heart-shaped leaves and fragrant yellowish flowers. See also **lime**[3]

line[1] *n* **1** a narrow continuous mark, such as one made by a pencil or brush **2** a thin indented mark or wrinkle on skin **3** a continuous length without breadth **4** a boundary: *the United Nations established a provisional demarcation line* **5** *sport* ᴀ a white band indicating a division on a field or track ʙ a mark or imaginary mark at which a race begins or ends **6** a boundary or limit: *there's a thin dividing line between confidence and arrogance* **7** the edge or contour of a shape: *the shoulder line* **8** a wire or string with a particular function: *a long washing line* **9** a telephone connection: *it was a very bad line* **10** a conducting wire, cable, or circuit for electric-power transmission or telecommunications **11** a system of travel or transportation: *a shipping line* **12** a route between two points on a railway **13** a railway track **14** a course or direction of movement: *the birds' line of flight* **15** a course of action or behaviour: *to adopt a more aggressive line* **16** a policy or prescribed way of thinking: *city commentators supported the CBI line* **17** a field of interest or activity: *computer gaming – that's their line* **18** straight or orderly alignment: *stand in line* **19** one kind of product or article: *a line of smart suits* **20** a row of people or things **21** a row of printed or written words **22** a unit of verse consisting of words in a single row **23** one of a number of narrow horizontal bands forming a television picture **24** *music* any of the five horizontal marks that make up the stave **25** the most forward defensive position: *the front line* **26** a formation of ships or soldiers abreast of each other **27** the combatant forces of certain armies and navies **28** *US & Canad* a queue **29 all along the line** at every stage in a series **30 draw the line (at)** to object (to) or set a limit (on): *I'm not a killer, I draw the line at that* **31 drop someone a line** to send someone a short note **32 get a line on** *informal* to obtain information about **33 in line for** likely to receive: *high achievers are in line for cash bonuses* **34 in line with** conforming to **35 lay** or **put on the line A** to speak frankly and directly **B** to risk (one's career or reputation) on something ▸ vb **lining, lined 36** to mark with a line or lines **37** to be or form a border: *the square was lined with stalls selling snacks* **38** to place in or form a row, series, or alignment ▸ See also **line-up** ▸ **lined** adj

line n 1, 3 = stroke, mark, score, band, scratch, slash, streak, stripe 2 = wrinkle, mark, crease, furrow, crow's foot 4, 6 = boundary, limit, edge, border, frontier, partition, borderline 8 = string, cable, wire (*old-fashioned*), rope, thread, cord 14 = trajectory, way, course, track, channel, direction, route, path 17 = occupation, work, calling, business, job, area, trade, field 20 = row, queue, rank, file, column, convoy, procession 33 in line for = due for, shortlisted for, in the running for ▸ vb 36 = mark, crease, furrow, rule, score 37 = border, edge, bound, fringe

line² vb **lining, lined 1** to attach an inside layer to **2** to cover the inside of: *the works of Shakespeare lined his walls* **3 line one's pockets** to make a lot of money, esp. dishonestly

lineage (lin-ee-ij) n direct descent from an ancestor

lineament n (*often pl*) a facial outline or feature

linear (lin-ee-er) adj **1** of or in lines **2** of or relating to length **3** represented by a line or lines ▸ **linearity** n

line dancing n a form of dancing performed by rows of people to country and western music

linen n **1** a hard-wearing fabric woven from the spun fibres of flax **2** articles, such as sheets or tablecloths, made from linen cloth or from cotton

liner¹ n **1** a passenger ship or aircraft, esp. one that is part of a commercial fleet **2** Also called: **eyeliner** a cosmetic used to outline the eyes

liner² n something used as a lining: *a plastic bin liner*

linesman n, pl **-men 1** an official who helps the referee or umpire in various sports, by indicating when the ball has gone out of play **2** a person who maintains railway, electricity, or telephone lines

line-up n **1** people or things assembled for a particular purpose: *Christmas TV line-up* **2** the members of such an assembly ▸ vb **line up 3** to form or organize a line-up

line-up n = arrangement, team, row, selection, array ▸ vb = arrangement, team, row, selection, array

ling¹ n, pl **ling** or **lings** a fish with a long slender body

ling² n heather

linger vb **1** to delay or prolong departure **2** to survive in a weakened condition for some time before death **3** to spend a long time doing or considering something ▸ **lingering** adj

linger vb **1** = stay, remain, stop, wait, delay, hang around, idle, dally

lingerie (lan-zher-ee) n women's underwear and nightwear

lingo n, pl **-goes** informal any foreign or unfamiliar language or jargon

lingua franca n, pl **lingua francas** or **linguae francae 1** a language used for communication among people of different mother tongues **2** any system of communication providing mutual understanding

lingual adj **1** anatomy of the tongue **2** articulated with the tongue **3** rare of language or languages ▸ **lingually** adv

linguist n **1** a person who is skilled in foreign languages **2** a person who studies linguistics

linguistic adj **1** of language **2** of linguistics ▸ **linguistically** adv

linguistics n the scientific study of language

liniment n a medicated oily liquid applied to the skin to relieve pain or stiffness

lining n **1** material used to line a garment or curtain **2** any interior covering: *the lining of the womb*

link n **1** any of the separate rings that form a chain **2** an emotional or logical relationship between people or things; association **3** a connecting part or episode **4** a type of communications connection: *a rail link; radio link* **5** short for **hyperlink** (sense 1) ▸ vb **6** (*often foll. by up*) to connect with or as if with links **7** to connect by association

link n 2 = relationship, association, bond, connection, attachment, affinity 3 = component, part, piece, element, constituent ▸ vb 6 = connect, join, unite, couple, tie, bind, attach, fasten; ≠ separate 7 = associate, relate, identify, connect, bracket

linkage n **1** the act of linking or the state of being linked **2** a system of links

links pl n a golf course beside the sea·

link-up n a joining together of two systems or groups

linnet n a brownish finch: the male has a red breast and forehead

lino n short for **linoleum**

linoleum n a floor covering made of hessian or jute with a smooth decorative coating of powdered cork

linseed n the seed of the flax plant

lint n **1** an absorbent material with raised fibres on one side, used to dress wounds **2** tiny shreds of yarn or cloth; fluff

lintel n a horizontal beam over a door or window

lion or fem **lioness** n **1** a large animal of the cat family found in Africa and India, with a tawny yellow coat and, in the male, a shaggy mane **2** a courageous and strong person **3 the lion's share** the largest portion

lion-hearted *adj* very brave; courageous

lip *n* **1** *anatomy* either of the two fleshy folds surrounding the mouth **2** any structure resembling a lip, such as the rim of a jug **3** *slang* impudent talk or backchat **4 bite one's lip** to avoid showing feelings of anger or distress **5 keep a stiff upper lip** to maintain one's composure during a time of trouble **6 lick** or **smack one's lips** to anticipate or recall something with glee or relish

> **lip** *n* **2** = edge, rim, brim, margin, brink **3** = impudence, insolence, impertinence, cheek (*informal*), effrontery, backchat (*informal*), brass neck (*informal*)

lipo *n informal* short for **liposuction**

liposuction *n* a cosmetic surgical operation in which fat is removed from the body by suction

lip-reading *n* a method used by deaf people to understand spoken words by interpreting movements of the speaker's lips > **lip-reader** *n*

lip service *n* **pay lip service to** to appear to support or obey something publicly while actually disregarding it

lipstick *n* a cosmetic in the form of a stick, for colouring the lips

liquefy *vb* **-fies, -fying, -fied** (esp. of a gas) to make or become liquid > **liquefaction** *n*

liqueur (lik-**cure**) *n* a highly flavoured sweetened alcoholic spirit, intended to be drunk after a meal

liquid *n* **1** a substance in a physical state which can change shape but not size ▸ *adj* **2** of or being a liquid: *liquid medicines* **3** shining and clear: *liquid sunlight days* **4** flowing, fluent, or smooth **5** (of assets) in the form of money or easily convertible into money

> **liquid** *n* = fluid, solution, juice, sap ▸ *adj* **2** = fluid, running, flowing, melted, watery, molten, runny, aqueous **5** = convertible, disposable, negotiable, realizable

liquidate *vb* **-dating, -dated 1** to settle or pay off (a debt or claim) **2** to dissolve (a company) and divide its assets among creditors **3** to convert (assets) into cash **4** to eliminate or kill

liquidation *n* **1 A** the dissolving of a company by selling its assets to pay off its debts **B go into liquidation** (of a business firm) to have its affairs so terminated **2** destruction; elimination

liquidator *n* an official appointed to liquidate a business

liquidity *n* the state of being able to meet financial obligations

liquidize *or* **-dise** *vb* **-dizing, -dized** *or* **-dising, -dised 1** to make or become liquid; liquefy **2** to process (food) in a liquidizer to make it liquid

liquidizer *or* **-diser** *n* a kitchen appliance with blades for liquidizing food

liquor *n* **1** spirits or other alcoholic drinks **2** any liquid in which food has been cooked

liquor *n* **1** = alcohol, drink, spirits, booze (*informal*), hard stuff (*informal*), strong drink **2** = juice, stock, liquid, extract, broth

liquorice *or US & Canad* **licorice** (lik-ker-**iss**) *n* **1** a chewy black sweet with a strong flavour **2** the dried black root of a Mediterranean plant, used as a laxative and in confectionery

lira *n, pl* **lire** *or* **liras 1** a former monetary unit of Italy **2** the standard monetary unit of Turkey

lisle (rhymes with **mile**) *n* a strong fine cotton thread or fabric, formerly used to make stockings

lisp *n* **1** a speech defect in which *s* and *z* are pronounced like the *th* sounds in English *thin* and *then* respectively ▸ *vb* **2** to speak with a lisp

lissom *or* **lissome** *adj* slim and graceful and agile in movement

list¹ *n* **1** an item-by-item record of names or things, usually written one below the other ▸ *vb* **2** to make a list of **3** to include in a list

> **list** *n* = inventory, record, series, roll, index, register, catalogue, directory ▸ *vb* = itemize, record, enter, register, catalogue, enumerate, note down, tabulate

list² *vb* **1** (esp. of ships) to lean to one side ▸ *n* **2** a leaning to one side: *developed a list to starboard*

> **list** *vb* = lean, tip, incline, tilt, heel over, careen ▸ *n* = tilt, leaning, slant, cant

listen *vb* **1** to concentrate on hearing something **2** to take heed or pay attention: *listen, let me explain* > **listener** *n*

> **listen** *vb* **1** = hear, attend, pay attention, lend an ear, prick up your ears **2** = pay attention, observe, obey, mind, heed, take notice, take note of, take heed of

listen in *vb* (often foll. by *on* or *to*) to listen secretly to; eavesdrop

listeriosis *n* a serious form of food poisoning, caused by bacteria of the genus *Listeria*

listless *adj* lacking interest or energy > **listlessly** *adv*

lit *vb* a past of **light¹** or **light²**

lit. **1** literal(ly) **2** literary **3** literature

litany *n, pl* **-nies 1** *Christianity* a prayer consisting of a series of invocations, each followed by the same response **2** any tedious recital: *a litany of complaints*

liter *n US* same as **litre**

literacy *n* **1** the ability to read and write **2** the ability to use language effectively

> **literacy** *n* = education, learning, knowledge

literal *adj* **1** in exact accordance with the explicit meaning of a word or text **2** word for word: *a literal translation* **3** dull or unimaginative: *she's very, very literal and flat in how she interprets what she sees* **4** true; actual ▸ *n* **5** a misprint or misspelling in a text > **literally** *adv*

literal *adj* **1, 2** = exact, close, strict, accurate, faithful, verbatim, word for word **4** = actual, real, true, simple, plain, genuine, bona fide, unvarnished

literary *adj* **1** of or characteristic of literature: *literary criticism* **2** knowledgeable about literature **3** (of a word) used chiefly in written work; not colloquial › **literariness** *n*

literary *adj* **1, 2** = well-read, learned, formal, intellectual, scholarly, erudite, bookish

literate *adj* **1** able to read and write **2** educated ▸ *n* **3** a literate person

literate *adj* = educated, informed, knowledgeable

literati *pl n* literary or scholarly people

literature *n* **1** written material such as poetry, novels, or essays **2** the body of written work of a particular culture, people, or era: *Elizabethan literature* **3** written or printed matter of a particular type or genre: *medical literature* **4** the art or profession of a writer **5** *informal* printed matter on any subject

literature *n* **1, 2** = writings, letters, compositions, lore, creative writing

lithe *adj* attractively graceful and supple in movement

lithium *n* *chem* a soft silvery element of the alkali metal series: the lightest known metal. Symbol: **Li**

litho *n*, *pl* **-thos**, *adj*, *adv* short for **lithography** or **lithograph**

lithograph *n* **1** a print made by lithography ▸ *vb* **2** to reproduce (pictures or text) by lithography › **lithographic** *adj* › **lithographically** *adv*

lithography (lith-**og**-ra-fee) *n* a method of printing from a metal or stone surface on which the printing areas are made ink-receptive › **lithographer** *n*

litigant *n* a person involved in a lawsuit

litigate *vb* **-gating, -gated 1** to bring or contest a lawsuit **2** to engage in legal proceedings › **litigator** *n*

litigation *n* the process of bringing or contesting a lawsuit

litigation *n* = lawsuit, case, action, prosecution

litigious (lit-ij-uss) *adj* frequently going to law

litmus *n* a soluble powder obtained from lichens, which is turned red by acids and blue by alkalis. Paper treated with it (**litmus paper**) is used as an indicator in chemistry

litmus test *n* something which is regarded as a simple and accurate test of a particular thing, such as a person's attitude to an issue

litotes *n*, *pl* **-tes** understatement used for effect, for example 'She was not a little upset' meaning 'She was extremely upset'

litre *or US* **liter** *n* a measure of volume equivalent to 1 cubic decimetre

litter *n* **1** small items of rubbish carelessly dropped in public places **2** a disordered or untidy collection of objects **3** a group of animals produced at one birth **4** straw or hay used as bedding for animals **5** dry material used to line a receptacle in which a domestic cat can urinate and defecate **6** (esp. formerly) a bed or seat held between parallel poles and used for carrying people ▸ *vb* **7** to strew with litter **8** to scatter or be scattered in an untidy fashion **9** (of animals) to give birth to offspring **10** to provide (an animal) with straw or hay for bedding

litter *n* **1** = rubbish, refuse, waste, junk, debris, garbage (*chiefly US*), trash (*chiefly US, Canad*), muck **3** = brood, young, offspring, progeny ▸ *vb* **7** = clutter, mess up, clutter up, be scattered about, disorder, disarrange, derange, muss (*US, Canad*) **8** = scatter, spread, shower, strew

little *adj* **1** of small or less than average size **2** young: *a little boy* **3** endearingly familiar: *he was a sweet little man* **4** contemptible, mean, or disagreeable: *he was an arrogant little squirt* **5** of small quantity, extent, or duration: *there was little money circulating; I could see little evidence of it* ▸ *adv* **6** (usually preceded by *a*) to a small extent or degree; not a lot: *to sleep a little* **7** not at all, or hardly: *army life varied little as the years passed* **8** not much or often: *we go there very little now* **9 little by little** by small degrees ▸ *n* **10 make little of** to treat as insignificant: *one episode in their history is made little of in the guide books* **11 think little of** to have a low opinion of ▸ See also **less**, **lesser**, **least**

little *adj* **1** = small, minute, short, tiny, wee, compact, miniature, diminutive; ≠ big **2** = young, small, junior, infant, immature, undeveloped, babyish ▸ *adv* **6 a little** = to a small extent, slightly, to some extent, to a certain extent, to a small degree **7** = hardly, barely, scarcely; ≠ much **8** = rarely, seldom, scarcely, not often, infrequently, hardly ever; ≠ always

littoral *adj* **1** of or by the shore ▸ *n* **2** a coastal region

liturgy *n*, *pl* **-gies** the forms of public services officially prescribed by a Church › **liturgical** *adj*

live¹ (rhymes with **give**) *vb* **living, lived 1** to show the characteristics of life; be alive **2** to remain alive or in existence **3** to exist in a specified way: *to live at ease* **4** to have one's home: *he went to live in Switzerland* **5** to continue or last: *his childhood had always lived inside him* **6** (foll. by *on*, *upon* or *by*) to support one's style of life: *forest dwellers who live by extracting rubber* **7** (foll. by *with*) to endure the effects (of a crime or mistake); tolerate **8** to pass or spend (one's life) **9** to enjoy life to the full: *he likes to live every day to the full*

10 to put into practice in one's daily life: *the freedom to live his own life as he chooses* **11 live and let live** to be tolerant ▸ See also **live down**

> **live** *vb* **1, 2** = exist, last, prevail, be, have being, breathe, persist, be alive **4** = dwell (*formal, literary*), board, settle, lodge, occupy, abide, inhabit, reside **6** = survive, get along, make a living, make ends meet, subsist, eke out a living, support yourself, maintain yourself **9** = thrive, flourish, prosper, have fun, enjoy yourself, live life to the full

live² (rhymes with *hive*) *adj* **1** alive; living **2** *radio & television* transmitted at the time of performance, rather than being prerecorded: *a live broadcast* **3** actual: *I was able to speak to a real live Hurricane pilot* **4** (of a recording) recorded during a performance **5** connected to a source of electric power: *a live cable* **6** of current interest; controversial: *the document has become a live political issue* **7** loaded or capable of exploding: *a live firing exercise with a 4.5in gun* **8** (of a coal or ember) glowing or burning ▸ *adv* **9** during, at, or in the form of a live performance

> **live** *adj* **1** = living, alive, breathing, animate **5, 7** = active, unexploded **6** = topical, important, pressing, current, hot, burning, controversial, prevalent

live down *vb* to withstand people's reactions to a crime or mistake until they forget it
livelihood *n* one's job or other source of income

> **livelihood** *n* = occupation, work, employment, living, job, bread and butter (*informal*)

lively *adj* **-lier, -liest 1** full of life or vigour **2** vivacious or animated **3** vivid ▸ **liveliness** *n*

> **lively** *adj* **1, 2** = animated, spirited, quick, keen, active, alert, dynamic, vigorous; ≠ dull **3** = vivid, strong, striking, bright, exciting, stimulating, bold, colourful; ≠ dull

liver *n* **1** a large glandular organ which secretes bile, balances nutrients, and removes certain poisons from the body **2** the liver of certain animals used as food
liveried *adj* wearing livery
liverish *adj* **1** *informal* having a disorder of the liver **2** feeling disagreeable and slightly irritable
livermorium *n chem* a synthetic element. Symbol: **Lv**
livery *n, pl* **-eries 1** the identifying uniform of a servant **2** distinctive dress or outward appearance **3** the stabling, keeping, or hiring out of horses for money
livestock *n* animals kept on a farm
live together *vb* (of an unmarried couple) to live in the same house; cohabit
live up to *vb* to fulfil (an expectation, obligation, or principle)

live with *vb* to tolerate: *I don't like it, but I have to live with it*
livid *adj* **1** *informal* extremely angry **2** of a dark grey or purple colour: *livid bruises*
living *adj* **1** possessing life; not dead or inanimate **2** currently in use or valid: *a living alliance* **3** seeming to be real: *a living doll* **4** (of people or animals) existing in the present age **5** very: *the living image* **6** of or like everyday life: *living costs* **7** of or involving those now alive: *one of our greatest living actors* ▸ *n* **8** the condition of being alive **9** the manner of one's life: *high living* **10** one's financial means **11** *Church of England* a benefice

> **living** *adj* **1, 4, 7** = alive, existing, moving, active, breathing, animate; ≠ dead **2** = current, present, active, contemporary, in use, extant; ≠ obsolete ▸ *n* **8** = alive, existing, moving, active, breathing, animate; ≠ dead **9** = lifestyle, ways, situation, conduct, behaviour, customs, way of life

living room *n* a room in a private house or flat used for relaxation and entertainment
lizard *n* a reptile with an elongated body, four limbs, and a long tail
llama *n* a South American mammal of the camel family, that is used as a beast of burden and is valued for its woolly fleece
LLB Bachelor of Laws
loach *n* a freshwater fish with a long narrow body and barbels around the mouth
load *n* **1** something to be borne or conveyed; weight **2** the amount borne or conveyed **3** something that weighs down or burdens: *I have enough of a load to carry right now* **4** *electronics* the power delivered by a machine, generator, or circuit **5** an external force applied to a component or mechanism **6 a load of** *informal* a quantity of: *a load of half-truths* **7 get a load of** *informal* to pay attention to ▸ *vb* **8** to place cargo or goods upon (a ship or vehicle) **9** to burden or oppress **10** to supply in abundance: *other treats are loaded with fat* **11** to cause to be biased: *the dice are loaded* **12** to put ammunition into (a firearm) **13** *photog* to insert film in (a camera) **14** to weight or bias (a roulette wheel or dice) **15** *computers* to transfer (a program) to a memory ▸ **loader** *n*

> **load** *n* **1, 2** = cargo, delivery, haul, shipment, batch, freight, consignment **3** = oppression, charge, worry, trouble, weight, responsibility, burden, onus ▸ *vb* **8** = fill, stuff, pack, pile, stack, heap, cram, freight **12** = make ready, charge, prime

loaded *adj* **1** carrying a load **2** charged with ammunition **3** (of a question or statement) containing a hidden trap or implication **4** (of dice or a roulette wheel) weighted or otherwise biased **5** *slang* wealthy **6** *slang, chiefly US & Canad* drunk

loaded *adj* **3** = tricky, charged, sensitive, delicate, manipulative, emotive, insidious, artful **5** = rich, wealthy, affluent, well off, flush (*informal*), well-heeled (*informal*), well-to-do, moneyed, minted (*Brit slang*)

loaf¹ *n*, *pl* **loaves 1** a shaped mass of baked bread **2** any shaped or moulded mass of food, such as cooked meat **3** *slang* the head; common sense: *use your loaf!*

loaf *n* **1, 2** = lump, block, cake, cube, slab **3** = head, mind, sense, common sense, nous (*Brit slang*), gumption (*Brit informal*)

loaf² *vb* to loiter or lounge around in an idle way

loaf *vb* = idle, hang around, take it easy, lie around, loiter, laze, lounge around

loafer *n* **1** a person who avoids work; idler **2** a moccasin-like shoe
loam *n* fertile soil consisting of sand, clay, and decaying organic material > **loamy** *adj*
loan *n* **1** money lent at interest for a fixed period of time **2** the act of lending: *I am grateful to her for the loan of her book* **3** property lent **4 on loan** lent out; borrowed ▸ *vb* **5** to lend (something, esp. money)

loan *n* **1** = advance, credit, overdraft ▸ *vb* = lend, advance, let out

loan shark *n* a person who lends money at an extremely high interest rate, esp. illegally
loath *or* **loth** (rhymes with **both**) *adj* (usually foll. by *to*) reluctant or unwilling
loathe *vb* **loathing**, **loathed** to feel strong disgust for

loathe *vb* = hate, dislike, despise, detest, abhor, abominate

loathing *n* strong disgust

loathing *n* = hatred, hate, disgust, aversion, revulsion, antipathy, repulsion, abhorrence

loathsome *adj* causing loathing
lob *sport* ▸ *n* **1** a ball struck or bowled in a high arc ▸ *vb* **lobbing**, **lobbed 2** to hit or kick (a ball) in a high arc **3** *informal* to throw
lobby *n*, *pl* **-bies 1** a room or corridor used as an entrance hall or vestibule **2** a group which attempts to influence legislators on behalf of a particular interest **3** *chiefly Brit* a hall in a legislative building used for meetings between legislators and members of the public **4** *chiefly Brit* one of two corridors in a legislative building in which members vote ▸ *vb* **-bies**, **-bying**, **-bied 5** to attempt to influence (legislators) in the formulation of policy

lobby *n* **1** = corridor, passage, entrance, porch, hallway, foyer, entrance hall, vestibule **2** = pressure group, group, camp, faction, lobbyists, interest group, special-interest

group, ginger group, public-interest group (*US, Canad*) ▸ *vb* = campaign, press, pressure, push, influence, promote, urge, persuade

lobbyist *n* a person who lobbies on behalf of a particular interest
lobe *n* **1** any rounded projection **2** the fleshy lower part of the external ear **3** any subdivision of a bodily organ
lobelia *n* a plant with blue, red, white, or yellow five-lobed flowers
lobola *n S African* (in southern Africa) an African custom by which a bridegroom's family makes a payment in cattle or cash to the bride's family shortly before the marriage

lobola *n* = dowry, portion, marriage settlement, dot (*archaic*)

lobotomy *n*, *pl* **-mies** the surgical cutting of nerves in the frontal lobe of the brain, formerly performed to treat severe mental illness
lobster *n*, *pl* **-sters** *or* **-ster 1** a large edible crustacean with large pincers and a long tail, which turns red when boiled **2** its edible flesh **3** *Austral informal* a $20 note
local *adj* **1** of or concerning a particular area **2** restricted to a particular place **3** *med* of, affecting, or confined to a limited area or part: *a local anaesthetic* **4** (of a train or bus) stopping at all stations or stops ▸ *n* **5** an inhabitant of a specified locality: *we swim, sunbathe, meet the locals, unwind* **6** *Brit informal* a pub close to one's home > **locally** *adv*

local *adj* **1** = community, regional **2, 3** = confined, limited, restricted ▸ *n* **5** = resident, native, inhabitant

local anaesthetic *n med* See **anaesthesia**
local authority *n* the governing body of a county, district, or region
locale (loh-**kahl**) *n* the place where something happens or has happened
local government *n* the government of the affairs of counties, towns, and districts by locally elected political bodies
locality *n*, *pl* **-ties 1** a neighbourhood or area **2** the site or scene of an event
localize *or* **-lise** *vb* **-lizing**, **-lized** *or* **-lising**, **-lised** to restrict (something) to a particular place
locate *vb* **-cating**, **-cated 1** to discover the whereabouts of; find **2** to situate or build: *located around the corner from the church* **3** to become established or settled

locate *vb* **1** = find, discover, detect, come across, track down, pinpoint, unearth, pin down **2** = place, put, set, position, seat, site, establish, settle

location *n* **1** a site or position; situation **2** the act of locating or the state of being located: *make their location and rescue a top priority* **3** a place outside a studio where filming is done: *shot on* *location* **4** (in South Africa) a Black African or Coloured township

> **location** *n* **1** = place, point, setting, position, situation, spot, venue, locale

loch *n Scot* **1** a lake **2** a long narrow arm of the sea

lock¹ *n* **1** a device for fastening a door, drawer, lid, etc., and preventing unauthorized access **2** a section of a canal or river closed off by gates between which the water level can be altered to aid boats moving from one level to the next **3** *Brit & NZ* the extent to which a vehicle's front wheels will turn: *they adopted more steering lock* **4** the interlocking of parts **5** a mechanism that fires a gun **6 lock, stock, and barrel** completely; entirely **7** a wrestling hold **8** Also called: **lock forward** *rugby* a player in the second row of the scrum ▸ *vb* **9** to fasten or become fastened to prevent entry or exit **10** to secure (a building) by locking all doors and windows **11** to fix or become fixed together securely **12** to become or cause to become immovable: *just before your knees lock* **13** to clasp or entangle in a struggle or embrace ▸ See also **lock out, lock up**

> **lock** *n* **1** = fastening, catch, bolt, clasp, padlock ▸ *vb* **9, 10** = fasten, close, secure, shut, bar, seal, bolt **11** = unite, join, link, engage, clench, entangle, interlock, entwine **13** = embrace, press, grasp, clutch, hug, enclose, clasp, encircle

lock² *n* **1** a strand or curl of hair **2 locks** *chiefly literary* hair

> **lock** *n* **1** = strand, curl, tuft, tress, ringlet

locker *n* a small compartment with a lock, used for temporarily storing clothes, valuables, or luggage

locket *n* a small hinged ornamental pendant that holds a picture or keepsake

lockjaw *n pathol* a nontechnical name for **tetanus**

lock out *vb* **1** to prevent from entering by locking a door **2** to prevent (employees) from working during an industrial dispute, by shutting them out of the premises ▸ *n* **lockout** **3** the closing of a place of employment by an employer, in order to force employees to accept terms

locksmith *n* a person who makes or repairs locks

lock up *vb* **1** to imprison **2** to secure a building by locking all the doors and windows ▸ *n* **lockup** **3** a jail **4** *Brit* a garage or store separate from the main premises **5** *Brit* a small shop with no attached quarters for the owner ▸ *adj* **lock-up** **6** *Brit & NZ* (of premises) without living quarters: *a lock-up garage*

> **lock up** *vb* **1 lock someone up** = imprison, jail, confine, cage, detain, shut up, incarcerate, send down (*informal*)

locomotion *n* the act or power of moving

locomotive *n* **1** a self-propelled engine for pulling trains ▸ *adj* **2** of locomotion

locum *n* a person who stands in temporarily for a doctor or a member of the clergy

locus (loh-kuss) *n, pl* **loci** **1** an area or place where something happens **2** *maths* a set of points or lines whose location satisfies, or is determined by, one or more specified conditions: *the locus of points equidistant from a given point is a circle*

locust *n* **1** an African insect, related to the grasshopper, which travels in vast swarms, stripping large areas of vegetation **2** a North American leguminous tree with prickly branches; the carob tree

lode *n* a vein of metallic ore

lodestar *n* **1** a star, esp. the North Star, used in navigation or astronomy as a point of reference **2** something that serves as a guide

lodestone *n* **1 A** magnetic iron ore **B** a piece of this, used as a magnet **2** a person or thing regarded as a focus of attraction

lodge *n* **1** *chiefly Brit* the gatekeeper's house at the entrance to the grounds of a country mansion **2** a house or cabin used occasionally by hunters, skiers, etc.: *a hunting lodge* **3** *chiefly Brit* a room used by porters in a university or college **4** a local branch of certain societies **5** a beaver's home ▸ *vb* **lodging, lodged** **6** to provide or be provided with rented accommodation **7** to live temporarily in rented accommodation **8** to embed or be embedded: *the bullet lodged in his brain* **9** to leave for safety or storage: *he lodged his wages in the bank* **10** to bring (a charge or accusation) against someone: *the Brazilians lodged a complaint* **11** (often foll. by *in* or *with*) to place (authority or power) in the control (of someone)

> **lodge** *n* **2** = cabin, shelter, cottage, hut, chalet, gatehouse **4** = society, group, club, section, wing, chapter, branch ▸ *vb* **6, 7** = stay, room, board, reside (*formal*) **8** = stick, remain, implant, come to rest, imbed **10** = register, enter, file, submit, put on record

lodger *n* a person who pays rent in return for accommodation in someone else's home

lodging *n* **1** a temporary residence: *where might I find a night's lodging?* **2 lodgings** a rented room or rooms in another person's home

> **lodging** *n* = accommodation, rooms, apartments, quarters, digs (*Brit informal*), shelter, residence, abode, bachelor apartment (*Canad*)

loft *n* **1** the space inside a roof **2** a gallery in a church **3** a room over a stable used to store hay **4** a raised house or coop in which pigeons are kept **5** *golf* **A** the angle of the face of the club used to elevate a ball **B** the height reached by a struck ball ▸ *vb* **6** *sport* to strike or kick (a ball) high in the air

lofty *adj* **loftier, loftiest 1** of majestic or imposing height **2** morally admirable: *lofty ideals* **3** unpleasantly superior: *a lofty contempt* ▸ **loftily** *adv* ▸ **loftiness** *n*

> **lofty** *adj* **1** = high, raised, towering, soaring, elevated; ≠ low **2** = noble, grand, distinguished, renowned, elevated, dignified, illustrious, exalted; ≠ humble **3** = haughty, proud, arrogant, patronizing, condescending, disdainful, supercilious; ≠ modest

log¹ *n* **1** a section of a felled tree stripped of branches **2 A** a detailed record of a voyage of a ship or aircraft **B** a record of the hours flown by pilots and aircrews **C** a book in which these records are made; logbook **3** a device consisting of a float with an attached line, formerly used to measure the speed of a ship **4 sleep like a log** to sleep without stirring ▸ *vb* **logging, logged 5** to saw logs from (trees) **6** to enter (a distance or event) in a logbook or log ▸ See also **log in**

> **log** *n* **1** = stump, block, branch, chunk, trunk **2** = record, account, register, journal, diary, logbook, blog (*informal*) ▸ *vb* **6** = record, enter, note, register, chart, put down, set down

log² *n* short for **logarithm**

loganberry *n, pl* **-ries** a purplish-red fruit, similar to a raspberry, that grows on a trailing prickly plant

logarithm *n* the exponent indicating the power to which a fixed number, the base, must be raised to obtain a given number or variable ▸ **logarithmic** *adj*

logbook *n* **1** a book containing the official record of trips made by a ship or aircraft **2** *Brit informal* the registration document of a car

loggerhead *n* **1** a large-headed turtle occurring in most seas **2 at loggerheads** engaged in dispute or confrontation

loggia (loj-ya) *n* a covered gallery on the side of a building

logging *n* the work of felling, trimming, and transporting timber ▸ **logger** *n*

logic *n* **1** the branch of philosophy that analyses the patterns of reasoning **2** a particular system of reasoning **3** reasoned thought or argument, as distinguished from irrationality **4** the interdependence of a series of events or facts **5** *electronics & computers* the principles underlying the units in a computer system that produce results from data

> **logic** *n* **3** = reason, reasoning, sense, good sense

logical *adj* **1** relating to or characteristic of logic **2** using or deduced from the principles of logic: *a logical conclusion* **3** capable of or using clear and valid reasoning **4** reasonable because of facts or events: *the logical choice* ▸ **logically** *adv*

> **logical** *adj* **1, 2, 3** = rational, clear, reasoned, sound, consistent, valid, coherent, well-organized; ≠ illogical **4** = reasonable, sensible, natural, wise, plausible; ≠ unlikely

logician *n* a person who specializes in or is skilled at logic

log in *or* **log on** *vb* to gain entrance to a computer system by keying in a special command

logistics *n* the detailed planning and organization of a large complex operation, such as a military campaign ▸ **logistical** *or* **logistic** *adj* ▸ **logistically** *adv*

logo (loh-go) *n, pl* **-os** a special design that identifies a company or an organization and appears on all its products, printed material, etc.

loin *n* **1** the part of the body between the pelvis and the ribs **2** a cut of meat from this part of an animal

loincloth *n* a piece of cloth covering only the loins

loiter *vb* to stand or wait aimlessly or idly

loll *vb* **1** to lounge in a lazy manner **2** to hang loosely: *a wet lolling tongue; his head lolled back and forth*

lollipop *n* **1** a boiled sweet stuck on a small wooden stick **2** *Brit* an ice lolly

lollipop man *or* **lollipop lady** *n Brit informal* a person holding a circular sign on a pole who stops traffic to enable children to cross the road safely

lolly *n, pl* **-lies 1** *informal* a lollipop **2** *Brit* short for **ice lolly 3** *Brit, Austral & NZ slang* money **4** *Austral & NZ informal* a sweet

lone *adj* **1** solitary: *a lone figure* **2** isolated: *a lone isle guarded by the great Atlantic swell* **3** *Brit* having no partner: *a lone parent*

> **lone** *adj* **1** = solitary, single, one, only, sole, unaccompanied

lonely *adj* **-lier, -liest 1** unhappy as a result of solitude **2** resulting from the state of being alone: *command can be a lonely business* **3** isolated and not much visited by people: *a lonely beach* ▸ **loneliness** *n*

> **lonely** *adj* **1** = solitary, alone, isolated, abandoned, lone, withdrawn, single, forsaken, lonesome (*chiefly US, Canad*); ≠ accompanied **3** = desolate, deserted, remote, isolated, out-of-the-way, secluded, uninhabited, godforsaken; ≠ crowded

loner *n informal* a person who prefers to be alone

lonesome *adj* **1** *chiefly US & Canad* lonely **2** causing feelings of loneliness: *it was lonesome up here on the mountain*

> **lonesome** *adj* = lonely, gloomy, dreary, desolate, forlorn, friendless, companionless

long¹ *adj* **1** having relatively great length in space or time **2** having greater than the average or expected range, extent, or duration: *a long session of talks* **3** seeming to occupy a greater time than is really so: *she was quiet a long moment* **4** of a specified extent or duration: *trimmed to about two cms long* **5** consisting of a large number of parts: *a long list* **6** *phonetics & prosody* (of a vowel) of relatively considerable duration **7** from end to end; lengthwise **8** *finance* having large holdings of securities or commodities in anticipation of rising prices **9 in the long run** ultimately; after or over a period of time **10 long on** *informal* plentifully supplied or endowed with: *long on showbiz gossip* ▸ *adv* **11** for a certain time or period: *how long have we got?* **12** for or during an extensive period of time: *to talk long into the night* **13** a considerable amount of time: *long after I met you*; *long ago* **14** **as** or **so long as A** for or during the same length of time that **B** provided that; if ▸ *n* **15** anything that is long **16 before long** soon **17 for long** for a long time **18 the long and the short of it** the essential points or facts › **longish** *adj*

> **long** *adj* **1** = elongated, extended, stretched, expanded, extensive, lengthy, far-reaching, spread out; ≠ short **2, 3** = prolonged, sustained, lengthy, lingering, protracted, interminable, spun out, long-drawn-out; ≠ brief

long² *vb* to have a strong desire for something or to do something: *I longed for a baby*; *the more I think of him the more I long to see him*

> **long** *vb* = desire, want, wish, burn, pine, lust, crave, yearn

long-distance *adj* **1** covering relatively long distances: *a long-distance race* **2** (of a telephone call) connecting points relatively far apart
longevity (lon-jev-it-ee) *n* long life
long face *n* a glum expression
longhand *n* ordinary handwriting, as opposed to typing or shorthand
longing *n* **1** a strong feeling of wanting something one is unlikely ever to have ▸ *adj* **2** having or showing desire: *longing glances* › **longingly** *adv*

> **longing** *n* = desire, hope, wish, burning, urge, ambition, hunger, yen (*informal*); ≠ indifference

longitude *n* distance in degrees east or west of the prime meridian at o°
longitudinal *adj* **1** of longitude or length **2** placed or extended lengthways
long johns *pl n informal* long underpants
long-life *adj* (of milk, batteries, etc.) lasting longer than the regular kind
long-lived *adj* living or lasting for a long time
long-range *adj* **1** of or extending into the future: *a long-range economic forecast* **2** (of vehicles, aircraft, or weapons) capable of covering great distances

longshoreman *n, pl* **-men** *US & Canad* a docker
long shot *n* **1** an undertaking, guess, or possibility with little chance of success **2** a bet against heavy odds **3 not by a long shot** not by any means: *she wasn't beaten, not by a long shot*
long-sighted *adj* **1** able to see only distant objects in focus **2** far-sighted
long-standing *adj* existing for a long time

> **long-standing** *adj* = established, fixed, enduring, abiding, long-lasting, long-established, time-honoured

long-suffering *adj* enduring trouble or unhappiness without complaint
long-term *adj* **1** lasting or extending over a long time: *a long-term commitment* ▸ *n* **long term** **2 in the long term** over a long period of time: *in the long term the cost of energy will have to go up*
long wave *n* a radio wave with a wavelength greater than 1000 metres
long-winded *adj* tiresomely long › **long-windedness** *n*
loo *n, pl* **loos** *Brit & NZ informal* a toilet
loofah *n* a long rough-textured bath sponge made from the dried pod of a gourd
look *vb* **1** (often foll. by *at*) to direct the eyes (towards): *he turned to look at her* **2** (often foll. by *at*) to consider: *let's look at the issues involved* **3** to give the impression of being; seem: *Luxembourg's timetable looks a winner* **4** to face in a particular direction: *Morgan's Rock looks south* **5** (foll. by *for*) to search or seek: *the department looks for reputable firms* **6** (foll. by *into*) to carry out an investigation **7** to direct a look at (someone) in a specified way: *she looks at Teresina suspiciously* **8** to match in appearance with (something): *looking your best* **9** to expect or hope (to do something): *we would look to derive a procedure that would account for most cases* **10 look alive** or **lively** or **sharp** or **smart** to hurry up; get busy **11 look here** an expression used to attract someone's attention or add emphasis to a statement ▸ *n* **12** an instance of looking: *a look of icy contempt* **13** a view or sight (of something): *take a look at my view* **14** (often *pl*) appearance to the eye or mind; aspect: *I'm not happy with the look of things here*; *better than you by the looks of it* **15** style or fashion: *the look made famous by the great Russian* ▸ *conj* **16** an expression demanding attention or showing annoyance: *look, I won't be coming back* ▸ See also **look after** › **looker** *n*

> **look** *vb* **1, 7** = see, view, consider, watch, eye, study, survey, examine **2** = consider, contemplate **3** = seem, appear, look like, strike you as **4** = face, overlook **5** = search, seek, hunt, forage, fossick (*Austral, NZ*) **9** = hope, expect, await, anticipate, reckon on ▸ *n* **12, 13** = glimpse, view, glance, observation, sight, examination, gaze, inspection **14, 15** = appearance, bearing, air, style, aspect, manner, expression, impression

look after *vb* to take care of

> **look after** *vb* **look after something or someone** = take care of, mind, protect, tend, guard, nurse, care for, supervise

lookalike *n* a person or thing that is the double of another, often well-known, person or thing
look forward to *vb* to anticipate with pleasure

> **look forward to** *vb* **look forward to something** = anticipate, expect, look for, wait for, await, hope for, long for

look on *vb* **1** to be a spectator **2** to consider or regard: *I just looked on her as a friend* > **looker-on** *n*
lookout *n* **1** the act of watching for danger or for an opportunity: *on the lookout for attack* **2** a person or people keeping such a watch **3** a viewpoint from which a watch is kept **4** *informal* worry or concern: *that is my lookout rather than theirs* **5** *chiefly Brit* chances or prospect: *it's a bad lookout for Europe* ▸ *vb* **6** to be careful **7** to watch out for: *look out particularly for oils that have been flavoured* **8** to find and take out: *little time to look out clothes that she might need* **9** (foll. by *on* or *over*) to face in a particular direction: *looking out over the courtyard*

> **lookout** *n* **1** = watch, guard, vigil **2** = watchman, guard, sentry, sentinel **3** = watchtower, post, observatory, observation post **4** = concern, business, worry ▸ *vb* **7 look out for something** = be careful of, beware, watch out for, pay attention to, be wary of, keep an eye out for

look up *vb* **1** to discover or confirm by checking in a reference book **2** to improve: *things were looking up* **3 look up to** to have respect for: *she looked up to him as a kind of father* **4** to visit (a person): *I'll look you up when I'm in town*

> **look up** *vb* **1 look something up** = research, find, search for, hunt for, track down, seek out **2** = improve, develop, advance, pick up, progress, get better, shape up (*informal*), perk up **3 look up to someone** = respect, honour, admire, esteem, revere, defer to, think highly of **4 look someone up** = visit, call on, drop in on (*informal*), look in on

loom¹ *n* a machine for weaving yarn into cloth
loom² *vb* **1** to appear indistinctly, esp. as a tall and threatening shape **2** (of an event) to seem ominously close

> **loom** *vb* **1** = appear, emerge, hover, take shape, threaten, bulk, menace, come into view

loony *slang* ▸ *adj* **loonier, looniest 1** *offensive* insane **2** foolish or ridiculous ▸ *n, pl* **loonies 3** *offensive* an insane person **4** a foolish person
loop *n* **1** the rounded shape formed by a curved line that crosses itself: *a loop of the highway* **2** any round or oval-shaped thing that is closed or nearly closed **3** *electronics* a closed circuit

through which a signal can circulate **4** a flight manoeuvre in which an aircraft flies vertically in a complete circle **5** a continuous strip of film or tape **6** *computers* a series of instructions in a program, performed repeatedly until some specified condition is satisfied ▸ *vb* **7** to make into a loop **8** to fasten or encircle with a loop **9** Also: **loop the loop** to fly or be flown vertically in a complete circle

> **loop** *n* **1, 2** = curve, ring, circle, twist, curl, spiral, coil, twirl ▸ *vb* **7** = twist, turn, roll, knot, curl, spiral, coil, wind round

loophole *n* an ambiguity or omission in the law, which enables one to evade it

> **loophole** *n* = let-out, escape, excuse

loose *adj* **1** (of clothing) not close-fitting: *the jacket loose and unbuttoned* **2** free or released from confinement or restraint **3** not tight, fastened, fixed, or tense **4** not bundled, fastened, or put in a container: *loose tobacco* **5** inexact or imprecise: *a loose translation* **6** (of cash) accessible: *a lot of the loose money is floating around the city* **7** *old-fashioned* sexually promiscuous **8** lacking a sense of propriety: *loose talk* **9 at a loose end** bored because one has nothing to do ▸ *n* **10 on the loose** free from confinement or restraint **11 the loose** *rugby* the part of play when the forwards close round the ball in a ruck or loose scrum ▸ *adv* **12** in a loose manner; loosely ▸ *vb* **loosing, loosed 13** to free or release from restraint or obligation: *he loosed the dogs* **14** to unfasten or untie: *the guards loosed his arms* **15** to make or become less strict, tight, firmly attached, or compact **16** to let fly (a bullet, arrow, or other missile) > **loosely** *adv* > **looseness** *n*

> **loose** *adj* **1** = slack, easy, relaxed, sloppy, loose-fitting; ≠ tight **3** = free, detached, insecure, unfettered, unrestricted, untied, unattached, unfastened **5** = vague, random, inaccurate, rambling, imprecise, ill-defined, indistinct, inexact; ≠ precise **7** = promiscuous, fast, abandoned, immoral, dissipated, profligate, debauched, dissolute; ≠ chaste ▸ *vb* **13, 14** = free, release, liberate, detach, unleash, disconnect, set free, untie; ≠ fasten

loose-leaf *adj* (of a binder) allowing the removal and addition of pages
loosen *vb* **1** to make or become less tight: *loosen and relax the ankle* (often foll. by *up*) **2** to make or become less firm, compact, or rigid: *massage is used first to loosen up the muscles* **3** to untie **4** (often foll. by *up*) to make or become less strict: *the churches loosen up on sexual teachings*

> **loosen** *vb* **3** = untie, undo, release, separate, detach, unloose **4 loosen up** = relax, chill (*slang*), soften, unwind, go easy (*informal*), hang loose (*slang*), outspan (*S African*), ease up *or* off

loot n **1** goods stolen in wartime or during riots; plunder **2** informal money ▸ vb **3** to plunder (a city) during war or riots **4** to steal (money or goods) during war or riots ⊳ **looter** n

> **loot** n = plunder, goods, prize, haul, spoils, booty, swag (slang) ▸ vb = plunder, rob, raid, sack, rifle, ravage, ransack, pillage

lop vb **lopping**, **lopped** (usually foll. by off) **1** to cut (parts) off a tree or body **2** to cut out or eliminate any unnecessary parts: some parts of the legislature were lopped off

lope vb **loping**, **loped 1** to move or run with a long easy stride ▸ n **2** a long steady gait or stride

lop-eared adj (of animals) having ears that droop

lopsided adj greater in weight, height, or size on one side

loquacious adj talkative ⊳ **loquacity** n

lord n **1** a person with power or authority over others, such as a monarch or master **2** a male member of the nobility **3** (in medieval Europe) a feudal superior **4 my lord** a respectful form of address used to a judge, bishop, or nobleman ▸ vb **5 lord it over someone** to act in a superior manner towards someone

> **lord** n = ruler, leader, chief, master, governor, commander, superior, liege **2** = peer, nobleman, count, duke, gentleman, earl, noble, baron ▸ vb **lord it over someone** = boss around or about (informal), order around, threaten, bully, menace, intimidate, hector, bluster

Lord n **1** Christianity a title given to God or Jesus Christ **2** Brit a title given to certain male peers **3** Brit a title given to certain high officials and judges ▸ interj **4** an exclamation of dismay or surprise: Good Lord!

> **Lord** n **1 the Lord or Our Lord** = Jesus Christ, God, Christ, Messiah, Jehovah, the Almighty

lordly adj **-lier**, **-liest 1** haughty or arrogant **2** of or suitable to a lord ⊳ **lordliness** n

Lordship n (preceded by Your or His) Brit a title used to address or refer to a bishop, a judge of the high court, or any peer except a duke

lore n collective knowledge or wisdom on a particular subject

lorgnette (lor-**nyet**) n a pair of spectacles or opera glasses mounted on a long handle

lorikeet n a small brightly coloured Australian parrot

lorry n, pl **-ries** Brit & S African a large motor vehicle for transporting heavy loads

lose vb **losing**, **lost 1** to come to be without, through carelessness or by accident or theft **2** to fail to keep or maintain: to lose control **3** to suffer the loss of: he will lose his redundancy money **4** to get rid of: I've lost a stone this summer **5** to fail to get or make use of: Lysenko never lost a chance to show his erudition **6** to be defeated in a fight or competition **7** to fail to see, hear, or understand: she lost sight of him **8** to waste: so I'd lost a fortune **9** to go astray from: psychologists lose the trail **10** to allow to go astray or out of sight: he lost, at the Gare de Lyon, a case with most of his early manuscripts **11** to cause the loss of: I came in to have the gear attended to, which lost me a lap **12** to absorb or engross: lost in thought **13** to die or cause the death of: two lost as yacht sinks in storm **14** to outdistance or escape from: there's some satisfaction in knowing that they've lost us **15** (of a timepiece) to run slow (by a specified amount)

> **lose** vb **1, 10** = mislay, drop, forget, be deprived of, lose track of, misplace **3** = forfeit, miss, yield, be deprived of, pass up (informal) **6** = be defeated, be beaten, lose out, come to grief

loser n **1** a person or thing that loses **2** informal a person or thing that seems destined to fail: he's a bit of a loser

> **loser** n = failure, flop (informal), also-ran, no-hoper (Austral slang), dud (informal), non-achiever, luser (computers slang)

loss n **1** the act or an instance of losing **2** the person, thing, or amount lost: the only loss was a sleeping bag **3** the disadvantage or deprivation resulting from losing: a loss of sovereignty **4 at a loss A** uncertain what to do; bewildered **B** with income less than outlay: they cannot afford to run branches at a loss

> **loss** n **1** = losing, waste, squandering, forfeiture; ≠ gain **2** = deficit, debt, deficiency, debit, depletion; ≠ gain **3** = damage, cost, injury, hurt, harm; ≠ advantage **4a at a loss** = confused, puzzled, baffled, bewildered, helpless, stumped, perplexed, mystified

loss leader n an article offered at a low price to attract customers

lost vb **1** the past of **lose** ▸ adj **2** unable to find one's way **3** unable to be found or recovered **4** confused or bewildered: she seemed a bit lost **5** (sometimes foll. by on) not used, noticed, or understood by: not that the propaganda value of the game was lost on the authorities **6** no longer possessed or existing: lost credit **7** (foll. by in) engrossed (in): he remained lost in his own thoughts **8** morally ruined: in a lost condition **9** damned: a lost soul

> **lost** adj **3** = missing, disappeared, vanished, wayward, misplaced, mislaid

lot pron **1 a lot** a great number or quantity: not that there was a lot to tell; a lot of people ▸ n **2** a collection of things or people: your lot have wasted enough time **3** destiny or fortune: helping the less well-off to improve their lot **4** any object, such as a straw or slip of paper, drawn from others at random to make a selection or choice: they could only be split by the drawing of lots; the casting by lots **5** the use of lots in making a choice: chosen by lot

6 an item or set of items for sale in an auction **7** US, Canad, Austral & NZ an area of land: *to the parking lot* **8 a bad lot** an unpleasant or disreputable person **9 cast** or **throw in one's lot with someone** to join with voluntarily and share the fortunes of someone **10 the lot** the entire amount or number ▸ *adv* **11** (preceded by *a*) *informal* to a considerable extent, degree, or amount: *steroids are used a lot in weightlifting*

> **lot** *pron* **a lot** or **lots** = plenty, scores, masses (*informal*), load(s) (*informal*), wealth, piles (*informal*), a great deal, stack(s) ▸ *n* **2** = bunch (*informal*), group, crowd, crew (*informal*), set, band, quantity, assortment **3** = destiny, situation, circumstances, fortune, chance, accident, fate, doom ▸ *adv* **a lot** or **lots** = often, regularly, a great deal, frequently, a good deal

loth (rhymes with *both*) *adj* same as **loath**
lotion *n* a liquid preparation having a soothing, cleansing, or antiseptic action, applied to the skin

> **lotion** *n* = cream, solution, balm, salve, liniment, embrocation

lottery *n*, *pl* **-teries 1** a method of raising money by selling tickets by which a winner is selected at random **2** a venture whose outcome is a matter of luck: *hospital treatment is a lottery*

> **lottery** *n* **1** = raffle, draw, lotto (*Brit, NZ, S African*), sweepstake **2** = gamble, chance, risk, hazard, toss-up (*informal*)

lotto *n* **1** a game of chance similar to bingo **2 Lotto** (in certain countries) the national lottery
lotus *n* **1** (in Greek mythology) a fruit that induces dreamy forgetfulness in those who eat it **2** any of several water lilies of tropical Africa and Asia, regarded as sacred **3** a symbolic representation of such a plant
loud *adj* **1** (of sound) relatively great in volume: *loud applause* **2** making or able to make sounds of relatively great volume: *a loud voice* **3** insistent and emphatic: *loud appeals* **4** (of colours or patterns) harsh to look at **5** noisy, vulgar, and offensive ▸ *adv* **6** in a loud manner **7 out loud** audibly > **loudly** *adv* > **loudness** *n*

> **loud** *adj* **1, 2, 3** = noisy, booming, roaring, thundering, forte (*music*), resounding, deafening, thunderous; ≠ quiet **4** = garish, bold, glaring, flamboyant, brash, flashy, lurid, gaudy; ≠ sombre

loudspeaker *n* a device for converting electrical signals into sounds
lough *n Irish* **1** a lake **2** a long narrow arm of the sea
lounge *n* **1** a living room in a private house **2** same as **lounge bar 3** a communal room in a hotel, ship, or airport, used for waiting or relaxing in **4** the act of lounging ▸ *vb* **lounging,**

lounged 5 (often foll. by *about* or *around*) to sit or lie in a relaxed manner **6** to pass time lazily or idly

> **lounge** *n* **1** = sitting room (*Brit*), living room, parlour (*old-fashioned*), drawing room, front room, reception room, television room ▸ *vb* = relax, loaf, sprawl, lie about, take it easy, loiter, loll, laze, outspan (*S African*)

lounge bar *n* a more expensive and comfortable bar in a pub or hotel
lounge suit *n* a man's suit for daytime wear
lour *vb* same as **lower²**
louse *n* **1** *pl* **lice** a wingless blood-sucking insect which feeds off humans and some animals **2** *pl* **louses** *slang* an unpleasant or dishonourable person
lousy *adj* **lousier, lousiest 1** *slang* very mean or unpleasant **2** *slang* inferior or bad **3** *slang* ill or unwell **4** infested with lice
lout *n* a crude or oafish person; boor > **loutish** *adj*
louvre or US **louver** (loo-ver) *n* **A** any of a set of horizontal slats in a door or window, slanted to admit air but not rain **B** the slats and frame supporting them > **louvred** or US **louvered** *adj*
love *vb* **loving, loved 1** to have a great affection for a person or thing **2** to have passionate desire for someone **3** to like (to do something) very much ▸ *n* **4** an intense emotion of affection towards a person or thing **5** a deep feeling of sexual attraction **6** wholehearted liking for or pleasure in something **7** a beloved person: often used as an endearment **8** *Brit informal* a commonplace term of address, not necessarily restricted to people one knows or has regard for **9** (in tennis, squash, etc.) a score of zero **10 fall in love** to become in love **11 for love or money** in any circumstances **12 in love** feeling a strong emotional and sexual attraction **13 make love to A** to have sexual intercourse with **B** *archaic* to court > **lovable** or **loveable** *adj*

> **love** *vb* **1, 2** = adore, care for, treasure, cherish, prize, worship, be devoted to, dote on; ≠ hate **3** = enjoy, like, appreciate, relish, delight in, savour, take pleasure in, have a soft spot for; ≠ dislike ▸ *n* **4, 5** = passion, affection, warmth, attachment, intimacy, devotion, tenderness, adoration, aroha (NZ); ≠ hatred **6** = liking, taste, bent for, weakness for, relish for, enjoyment, devotion to, penchant for **7** = beloved, dear, dearest, lover, darling, honey, sweetheart, truelove; ≠ enemy

love affair *n* a romantic or sexual relationship between two people who are not married to each other

> **love affair** *n* = romance, relationship, affair, intrigue, liaison, amour

lovebird *n* any of several small African parrots often kept as cage birds

love child *n euphemistic* a child whose parents have not been married to each other

loveless *adj* without love: *a loveless marriage*

love life *n* a person's romantic or sexual relationships

lovelorn *adj* miserable because of unreturned love or unhappiness in love

lovely *adj* **-lier, -liest** 1 very attractive or beautiful 2 highly pleasing or enjoyable: *thanks for a lovely evening* ▶ *n, pl* **-lies** 3 *slang* an attractive woman: *suntanned lovelies* > **loveliness** *n*

> **lovely** 1 = beautiful, appealing, attractive, charming, pretty, handsome, good-looking, exquisite, fit (Brit *informal*); ≠ ugly
> 2 = wonderful, pleasing, nice, pleasant, engaging, marvellous, delightful, enjoyable; ≠ horrible

lovemaking *n* 1 sexual play and activity between lovers, including sexual intercourse 2 *archaic* courtship

lover *n* 1 a person having a sexual relationship with another person outside marriage 2 (*often pl*) either of the people involved in a love affair 3 someone who loves a specified person or thing: *an animal-lover*

> **lover** 1,2 = sweetheart, beloved, loved one, flame (*informal*), mistress, admirer, suitor

loving *adj* feeling or showing love and affection > **lovingly** *adv*

> **loving** = tender, kind, caring, warm, gentle, sympathetic, considerate; ≠ cruel

low¹ *adj* 1 having a relatively small distance from base to top: *a low wall* 2 of less than usual amount, degree, quality, or cost: *low score; low inflation* 3 situated at a relatively short distance above the ground, sea level, or the horizon: *heavy weather with low driving cloud* 4 (of numbers) small 5 involving or containing a relatively small amount of something: *low-fat cheese and crackers* 6 having little value or quality: *it sounds as if your self-confidence is low* 7 coarse or vulgar: *low comedy* 8 unworthy or contemptible: *that's a low trick, Justin* 9 inferior in culture or status 10 in a weakened physical or mental state 11 with a hushed tone: *in a low, scared voice* 12 low-necked: *a low evening gown* 13 *music* of or having a relatively low pitch 14 (of latitudes) situated not far north or south of the equator 15 having little or no money 16 unfavourable: *he has a low opinion of Ford* 17 deep: *a low bow* 18 (of a gear) providing a relatively low speed ▶ *adv* 19 in a low position, level, or degree: *the pilot flew low over the area* 20 at a low pitch; deeply: *he's singing very low* 21 cheaply: *the bank is having to buy high and sell low* 22 **lay low** A to make (someone) fall by a blow B to overcome or destroy 23 **lie low** to keep or be concealed or quiet ▶ *n* 24 a low position, level, or degree: *shares hit new low* 25 an area of low atmospheric pressure; depression > **lowness** *n*

> **low** *adj* 1 = small, little, short, stunted, squat; ≠ tall 7 = coarse, common, rough, crude, rude, vulgar, undignified, disreputable 10 = ill, weak, frail, stricken, debilitated; ≠ strong 11 = quiet, soft, gentle, whispered, muted, subdued, hushed, muffled; ≠ loud

low² *n* 1 Also: **lowing** the sound uttered by cattle; moo ▶ *vb* 2 to make a mooing sound

lowbrow *derogatory* ▶ *n* 1 a person with uncultivated or nonintellectual tastes ▶ *adj* 2 of or for such a person

Low Church *n* a section of the Church of England which stresses evangelical beliefs and practices > **Low-Church** *adj*

low-down *informal* ▶ *adj* 1 mean, underhand, and dishonest ▶ *n* **lowdown** 2 **the lowdown** information

lower¹ (rhymes with **goer**) *adj* 1 being below one or more other things: *the lower branches* 2 reduced in amount or value: *lower rates* 3 **Lower** *geol* denoting the early part of a period or formation ▶ *vb* 4 to cause or allow to move down: *she lowered her head* 5 to behave in a way that damages one's respect: *she'd never lowered herself enough to make a call* 6 to lessen or become less: *the cholesterol was lowered by medication* 7 to make quieter or reduce the pitch of

> **lower** *adj* 1 = subordinate, under, smaller, junior, minor, secondary, lesser, inferior
> 2 = reduced, cut, diminished, decreased, lessened, curtailed; ≠ increased ▶ *vb* 4 = drop, sink, depress, let down, submerge, take down, let fall; ≠ raise 6 = lessen, cut, reduce, diminish, slash, decrease, prune, minimize; ≠ increase

lower² *or* **lour** (rhymes with **sour**) *vb* (of the sky or weather) to be overcast and menacing > **lowering** *or* **louring** *adj*

lower case *n* (in printing) small letters, as opposed to capital letters > **lower-case** *adj*

low-key *or* **low-keyed** *adj* 1 restrained or subdued 2 having a low intensity or tone

> **low-key** *or* **low-keyed** *adj* = subdued, quiet, restrained, muted, understated, toned down

lowland *n* 1 relatively low ground 2 (*often pl*) a low generally flat region ▶ *adj* 3 of a lowland or lowlands > **lowlander** *n*

Lowland *adj* of the Lowlands or the dialects of English spoken there > **Lowlander** *n*

lowly *adj* **-lier, -liest** 1 humble in position or status 2 simple and unpretentious > **lowliness** *n*

low profile *n* a deliberate shunning of publicity: *he kept a low profile* > **low-profile** *adj*

low-spirited *adj* depressed or dejected

loyal *adj* 1 faithful to one's friends, country, or government 2 of or expressing loyalty: *the loyal toast* > **loyally** *adv*

loyal *adj* **1** = faithful, true, devoted, dependable, constant, staunch, trustworthy, trusty; ≠ disloyal

loyalist *n* a patriotic supporter of the sovereign or government › **loyalism** *n*

loyalty *n, pl* **-ties 1** the quality of being loyal **2** a feeling of friendship or duty towards someone or something

loyalty *n* = faithfulness, commitment, devotion, allegiance, fidelity, homage, obedience, constancy

loyalty card *n* a swipe card issued by a supermarket or chain store to a customer, used to record credit points awarded for money spent in the store

lozenge *n* **1** *med* a medicated tablet held in the mouth until it has dissolved **2** *geom* a rhombus

L-plate *n Brit & Austral* a letter 'L' on a square piece of plastic attached to a motor vehicle to indicate that the driver is a learner

LSD *n* lysergic acid diethylamide; an illegal hallucinogenic drug

Lt Lieutenant

Ltd *Brit* Limited (Liability)

lubricant *n* a lubricating substance, such as oil

lubricate (loo-brik-ate) *vb* **-cating, -cated 1** to cover with an oily substance to lessen friction **2** to make greasy, slippery, or smooth › **lubrication** *n*

lubricious (loo-brish-uss) *adj formal or literary* lewd

lucerne *n Brit & Austral* same as **alfalfa**

lucid *adj* **1** clear and easily understood **2** capable of clear thought, particularly between periods of mental illness or confusion **3** shining or glowing › **lucidity** *n* › **lucidly** *adv*

Lucifer *n* Satan

luck *n* **1** events that are subject to chance; fortune, good or bad **2** success or good fortune **3 down on one's luck** lacking good fortune to the extent of suffering hardship **4 no such luck** *informal* unfortunately not **5 try one's luck** to attempt something that is uncertain

luck *n* **1** = fortune, lot, stars, chance, accident, fate, destiny, twist of fate **2** = good fortune, success, advantage, prosperity, blessing, windfall, godsend, serendipity

luckless *adj* unfortunate or unlucky

lucky *adj* **luckier, luckiest 1** having or bringing good fortune **2** happening by chance, esp. as desired › **luckily** *adv*

lucky *adj* **1** = fortunate, successful, favoured, charmed, blessed, jammy (*Brit slang*), serendipitous; ≠ unlucky

lucky dip *n Brit, Austral & NZ* a box filled with sawdust containing small prizes for which children search

lucrative *adj* profitable

lucrative *adj* = profitable, rewarding, productive, fruitful, well-paid, advantageous, remunerative

lucre (loo-ker) *n usually facetious* money or wealth: *filthy lucre*

Luddite *Brit history* ▸ *n* **1** any of the textile workers opposed to mechanization, who organized machine-breaking between 1811 and 1816 **2** any opponent of industrial change or innovation ▸ *adj* **3** of the Luddites

luderick *n* an Australian fish, usually black or dark brown in colour

ludicrous *adj* absurd or ridiculous › **ludicrously** *adv*

ludicrous *adj* = ridiculous, crazy (*informal*), absurd, preposterous, silly, laughable, farcical, outlandish; ≠ sensible

ludo *n Brit & Austral* a simple board game in which players move counters forward by throwing dice

lug[1] *vb* **lugging, lugged** to carry or drag with great effort

lug[2] *n* **1** a projecting piece by which something is connected, supported, or lifted **2** *informal Scot* an ear

luggage *n* suitcases, trunks, and bags

luggage *n* = baggage, things, cases, bags, gear, suitcases, paraphernalia, impedimenta

lugubrious (lug-goo-bree-uss) *adj* mournful or gloomy

lugworm *n* a large worm which lives in burrows on sandy shores and is often used as bait by fishermen

lukewarm *adj* **1** (of a liquid) moderately warm; tepid **2** lacking enthusiasm or conviction

lull *vb* **1** to soothe (a person or animal) by soft sounds or motions **2** to calm (fears or suspicions) by deception ▸ *n* **3** a short period of calm

lull *vb* = calm, soothe, subdue, quell, allay, pacify, tranquillize ▸ *n* = respite, pause, quiet, silence, calm, hush, let-up (*informal*)

lullaby *n, pl* **-bies** a quiet song to lull a child to sleep

lumbago (lum-bay-go) *n* pain in the lower back; low backache

lumbar *adj* relating to the lower back

lumber[1] *n* **1** *Brit* unwanted disused household articles **2** *chiefly US & Canad* logs; sawn timber ▸ *vb* **3** *informal* to burden with something unpleasant: *somebody gets lumbered with the extra costs* **4** to fill up with useless household articles **5** *chiefly US & Canad* to convert trees into marketable timber

lumber *n* **1** = junk, refuse, rubbish, trash (*chiefly US, Canad*), clutter, jumble ▸ *vb* **3** = burden, land, load, saddle, encumber

lumber² *vb* to move awkwardly and heavily ⊳**lumbering** *adj*

lumber *vb* = plod, shuffle, shamble, trudge, stump, waddle, trundle

lumberjack *n* (esp. in North America) a person who fells trees and prepares the timber for transport

luminary *n, pl* -naries 1 A a famous person B an expert in a particular subject 2 *literary* something, such as the sun or moon, that gives off light

luminescence *n physics* the emission of light at low temperatures by any process other than burning ⊳**luminescent** *adj*

luminous *adj* 1 reflecting or giving off light: *luminous colours* 2 *not in technical use* luminescent: *luminous sparklers* 3 enlightening or wise ⊳**luminosity** *n*

lump¹ *n* 1 a small solid mass without definite shape 2 *pathol* any small swelling or tumour 3 *informal* an awkward, heavy, or stupid person 4 **a lump in one's throat** a tight dry feeling in one's throat, usually caused by great emotion 5 **the lump** *Brit* self-employed workers in the building trade considered collectively ▸ *adj* 6 in the form of a lump or lumps: *lump sugar* ▸ *vb* 7 (often foll. by *together*) to consider as a single group, often without justification 8 to grow into lumps or become lumpy

lump *n* 1 = piece, ball, block, mass, chunk, hunk, nugget 2 = swelling, growth, bump, tumour, bulge, hump, protrusion ▸ *vb* 7 = group, throw, mass, combine, collect, pool, consolidate, conglomerate

lump² *vb* **lump it** *informal* to accept something irrespective of personal preference: *if you don't like it, you can lump it*

lump sum *n* a relatively large sum of money, paid at one time

lumpy *adj* lumpier, lumpiest full of or having lumps ⊳**lumpiness** *n*

lunacy *n, pl* -cies 1 foolishness 2 (formerly) any severe mental illness

lunar *adj* relating to the moon: *lunar eclipse*

lunatic *adj* 1 foolish; eccentric 2 *archaic* having severe mental illness ▸ *n* 3 a foolish or annoying person 4 *archaic* a person with severe mental illness

lunch *n* 1 a meal eaten during the middle of the day ▸ *vb* 2 to eat lunch

luncheon *n* a lunch, often a formal one

luncheon meat *n* a ground mixture of meat (often pork) and cereal, usually tinned

luncheon voucher *n Brit* a voucher for a specified amount issued to employees and accepted by some restaurants as payment for food

lung *n* the part of the body that allows an animal or bird to breathe air. Humans have two lungs, contained within the chest cavity

lunge *n* 1 a sudden forward motion 2 *fencing* a thrust made by advancing the front foot and straightening the back leg ▸ *vb* **lunging, lunged** 3 to move with a lunge 4 *fencing* to make a lunge

lunge *n* 1 = thrust, charge, pounce, spring, swing, jab ▸ *vb* 3 = pounce, charge, dive, leap, plunge, thrust

lungfish *n, pl* -fish *or* -fishes a freshwater fish with an air-breathing lung

lupin *n* a garden plant with large spikes of brightly coloured flowers and flattened pods

lupine *adj* of or like a wolf

lurch¹ *vb* 1 to lean or tilt suddenly to one side 2 to stagger ▸ *n* 3 a lurching movement

lurch *vb* 1 = tilt, roll, pitch, list, rock, lean, heel 2 = stagger, reel, stumble, weave, sway, totter

lurch² *n* **leave someone in the lurch** to abandon someone in trouble

lure *vb* **luring, lured** 1 (sometimes foll. by *away* or *into*) to tempt or attract by the promise of reward ▸ *n* 2 a person or thing that lures 3 *angling* a brightly coloured artificial spinning bait 4 *falconry* a feathered decoy to which small pieces of meat can be attached

lure *vb* = tempt, draw, attract, invite, trick, seduce, entice, allure ▸ *n* 2 = temptation, attraction, incentive, bait, carrot (*informal*), inducement, enticement, allurement

lurid *adj* 1 vivid in shocking detail; sensational: *magazines whose lurid covers sickened him* 2 glaring in colour: *a lurid red tartan* 3 horrible in savagery or violence: *reporting lurid crimes* ⊳**luridly** *adv*

lurk *vb* 1 to move stealthily or be concealed, esp. for evil purposes 2 to be present in an unobtrusive way; be latent

lurk *vb* = hide, sneak, prowl, lie in wait, slink, skulk, conceal yourself

luscious (lush-uss) *adj* 1 extremely pleasurable to taste or smell 2 very attractive

lush¹ *adj* 1 (of vegetation) growing thickly and healthily 2 luxurious, elaborate, or opulent 3 *slang* very attractive or pleasing

lush *adj* 1 = abundant, green, flourishing, dense, rank, verdant (*literary*) 2 = luxurious, grand, elaborate, lavish, extravagant, sumptuous, plush (*informal*), ornate

lush² *n slang* an alcoholic

lust *n* 1 a strong sexual desire 2 a strong desire or drive: *a lust for power* ▸ *vb* 3 (often foll. by *after* or *for*) to have a passionate desire (for) ⊳**lustful** *adj* ⊳**lustfully** *adv*

lust *n* 1 = lechery, sensuality, lewdness, lasciviousness 2 = desire, longing, passion, appetite, craving, greed, thirst ▸ *vb* **lust for or after someone or something** = desire, want, crave, yearn for, covet, hunger for *or* after

lustre *or US* **luster** *n* **1** soft shining light reflected from a surface; sheen **2** great splendour or glory **3** a shiny metallic surface on some pottery and porcelain > **lustrous** *adj*

lusty *adj* **lustier, lustiest** **1** healthy and full of strength and energy **2** strong or invigorating > **lustily** *adv* > **lustiness** *n*

lute *n* an ancient plucked stringed instrument with a long fingerboard and a body shaped like a half pear

Lutheran *n* **1** a follower of Martin Luther (1483–1546), German leader of the Reformation, or a member of a Lutheran Church ▸ *adj* **2** of or relating to Luther, his doctrines, or any of the Churches that follow these doctrines > **Lutheranism** *n*

luxuriant *adj* **1** rich and abundant; lush: *luxuriant foliage* **2** very elaborate or ornate > **luxuriance** *n* > **luxuriantly** *adv*

luxuriate *vb* **-ating, -ated** **1** **luxuriate in** to take self-indulgent pleasure in; revel in **2** to flourish profusely

luxurious *adj* **1** characterized by luxury **2** enjoying or devoted to luxury > **luxuriously** *adv*

> **luxurious** *adj* **1** = sumptuous, expensive, comfortable, magnificent, splendid, lavish, plush (*informal*), opulent

luxury *n, pl* **-ries** **1** indulgence in rich and sumptuous living **2** something considered an indulgence rather than a necessity ▸ *adj* **3** relating to, indicating, or supplying luxury: *a luxury hotel*

> **luxury** *n* **1** = opulence, splendour, richness, extravagance, affluence, hedonism, a bed of roses, the life of Riley; ≠ poverty **2** = extravagance, treat, extra, indulgence, frill; ≠ necessity

Lv livermorium

lychee (lie-**chee**) *n* a Chinese fruit with a whitish juicy pulp

lych gate *or* **lich gate** *n* a roofed gate to a churchyard, formerly used as a temporary shelter for a coffin

Lycra *n trademark* a synthetic elastic fabric used for tight-fitting garments, such as swimsuits

lye *n* **1** a caustic solution obtained from wood ash **2** a concentrated solution of sodium hydroxide or potassium hydroxide

lying *vb* the present participle of **lie¹** or **lie²**

lymph *n* the almost colourless body fluid containing chiefly white blood cells > **lymphatic** *adj*

lymphocyte *n* a type of white blood cell

lynch *vb* (of a mob) to kill (a person) for some supposed offence without a trial > **lynching** *n*

lynchpin *n* same as **linchpin**

lynx *n, pl* **lynxes** *or* **lynx** a mammal of the cat family, with grey-brown mottled fur, tufted ears, and a short tail

lyre *n* an ancient Greek U-shaped stringed instrument, similar to a harp but plucked with a plectrum

lyric *adj* **1** **A** (of poetry) expressing the writer's personal feelings **B** (of poetry) having the form and manner of a song **2** of or relating to such poetry **3** (of a singing voice) light and melodic ▸ *n* **4** a short poem of songlike quality **5 lyrics** the words of a popular song: *Cole invests all her lyrics with a touch of drama*

lyrical *adj* **1** same as **lyric** (senses 1, 2) **2** enthusiastic or effusive > **lyrically** *adv*

> **lyrical** *adj* **2** = enthusiastic, inspired, poetic, impassioned, effusive, rhapsodic

lyricist *n* a person who writes the words for a song, opera, or musical

Mm

m 1 metre(s) 2 mile(s) 3 milli- 4 million 5 minute(s)

M 1 mach 2 medium 3 mega- 4 (in Britain) motorway 5 the Roman numeral for 1000

m. 1 male 2 married 3 masculine 4 meridian 5 month

ma *n* an informal word for mother

MA 1 Massachusetts 2 Master of Arts

ma'am *n* short for **madam** (sense 1)

mac *or* **mack** *n* Brit informal a mackintosh

macabre (mak-**kahb**-ra) *adj* strange and horrible; gruesome

macadam *n* a road surface made of compressed layers of small broken stones, esp. one bound together with tar or asphalt

macadamia (mak-a-**day**-mee-a) *n* an Australian tree with edible nuts

macaroni *n, pl* **-nis** *or* **-nies** 1 pasta tubes made from wheat flour 2 (in 18th-century Britain) a man who was excessively concerned with his clothes and appearance

macaroon *n* a sweet biscuit made of ground almonds

macaw *n* a large tropical American parrot with a long tail and brightly coloured feathers

mace¹ *n* 1 a ceremonial staff carried by certain officials 2 a club with a spiked metal head used in the Middle Ages

mace² *n* a spice made from the dried outer casing of the nutmeg

macerate (**mass**-er-ate) *vb* **-ating, -ated** to soften or be softened by soaking > **macerated** *adj* > **maceration** *n*

machete (mash-**ett**-ee) *n* a broad heavy knife used for cutting or as a weapon

Machiavellian (mak-ee-a-**vel**-yan) *adj* cleverly deceitful and unscrupulous > **Machiavellianism** *n*

machinations (mak-in-**nay**-shuns) *pl n* cunning schemes or plots to gain power or harm an opponent: *the machinations of a power-hungry institution*

machine *n* 1 an assembly of components arranged so as to perform a particular task and usually powered by electricity 2 a vehicle, such as a car or aircraft 3 a system within an organization that controls activities and policies: *the party machine* ▸ *vb* **-chining, -chined** 4 to shape, cut, or make something using a machine > **machinable** *adj*

> **machine** *n* 1 = appliance, device, apparatus, engine (*obsolete*), tool, instrument, mechanism, gadget 3 = system, structure, organization, machinery, setup (*informal*)

machine gun *n* 1 a rapid-firing automatic gun, using small-arms ammunition ▸ *vb* **machine-gun, -gunning, -gunned** 2 to shoot or fire at with a machine gun

machine-readable *adj* in a form suitable for processing by a computer

machinery *n, pl* **-eries** 1 machines, machine parts, or machine systems collectively 2 the mechanism of a machine 3 the organization and procedures by which a system functions: *the machinery of international politics*

> **machinery** *n* 1, 2 = equipment, gear, instruments, apparatus, technology, tackle, tools, gadgetry

machinist *n* 1 a person who operates machines to cut or process materials 2 a maker or repairer of machines

machismo (mak-**izz**-moh) *n* strong or exaggerated masculinity

Mach number (mak) *n* the ratio of the speed of a body in a particular medium to the speed of sound in that medium

macho (**match**-oh) *adj* 1 strongly or exaggeratedly masculine ▸ *n* 2 strong or exaggerated masculinity

> **macho** *adj* = manly, masculine, chauvinist, virile

mackerel *n, pl* **-rel** *or* **-rels** an edible sea fish

mackintosh *or* **macintosh** *n* Brit 1 a raincoat made of rubberized cloth 2 any raincoat

macramé (mak-**rah**-mee) *n* 1 the art of knotting and weaving coarse thread into patterns 2 ornaments made in this way

macrobiotics *n* a dietary system which advocates whole grains and vegetables grown without chemical additives > **macrobiotic** *adj*

macrocosm *n* a complex structure, such as the universe or society, regarded as a whole

mad *adj* **madder, maddest** 1 *informal* of unsound mind 2 extremely foolish; senseless: *that was a mad thing to do!* 3 *informal* angry or annoyed: *he's mad at her for the unjust accusation* 4 wildly excited or confused: *a mad rush* 5 **A** (of animals) unusually ferocious: *a mad bear* **B** (of animals) afflicted with rabies 6 **like mad** *informal* with great energy, enthusiasm, or haste 7 **mad about** *or* **on** *or* **over** wildly enthusiastic about or fond of > **madness** *n*

> **mad** *adj* 2 = foolish, absurd, wild, stupid, daft (*informal*), irrational, senseless, preposterous; ≠ sensible 3 = angry, furious, incensed, enraged, livid (*informal*), berserk, berko (*Austral slang*), toshie (*Austral slang*), off the air (*Austral slang*); ≠ calm 4 = frenzied, wild, excited, frenetic, uncontrolled, unrestrained 7 = enthusiastic, wild, crazy (*informal*), ardent, fanatical, avid, impassioned, infatuated; ≠ nonchalant

m

madam *n, pl* **madams 1** *pl* **mesdames** a polite term of address for a woman **2** a woman who runs a brothel **3** *Brit & Austral informal* a spoilt or pert girl: *a precocious little madam*

madame (mad-**dam**) *n, pl* **mesdames** (may-**dam**) a French form of address equivalent to *Mrs*

madcap *adj* **1** impulsive, reckless, or unlikely to succeed: *a madcap expansion of council bureaucracy* ▸ *n* **2** an impulsive or reckless person

madden *vb* to make or become mad or angry > **maddening** *adj*

> **madden** *vb* = infuriate, irritate, incense, enrage, upset, annoy, inflame, drive you crazy; ≠ calm

madder *n* **1** a plant with small yellow flowers and a red fleshy root **2** a dark reddish-purple dye formerly obtained from its root **3** an artificial pigment of this colour

made *vb* **1** the past of **make** ▸ *adj* **2** (*in combination*) produced or shaped as specified: *handmade* **3 get** or **have it made** *informal* to be assured of success

Madeira (mad-**deer**-a) *n* a fortified white wine from Madeira, an island in the N Atlantic

Madeira cake *n* a type of rich sponge cake

mademoiselle (mad-mwah-**zel**) *n, pl* **mesdemoiselles** (maid-mwah-**zel**) **1** a French form of address equivalent to *Miss* **2** a French teacher or governess

madly *adv* **1** in an crazy or foolish manner: *I yelled and waved madly* **2** with great speed and energy **3** *informal* extremely or excessively: *she was madly in love with him*

> **madly** *adv* **1** = insanely, frantically, hysterically, crazily, deliriously, distractedly, frenziedly **2** = energetically, wildly, furiously, excitedly, recklessly, speedily, like mad (*informal*) **3** = passionately, wildly, desperately, intensely, to distraction, devotedly

madman *or fem* **madwoman** *n, pl* **-men** *or* **-women 1** a person who behaves recklessly **2** *offensive* a person who is insane

Madonna *n* **1** *chiefly RC Church* the Virgin Mary **2** a picture or statue of the Virgin Mary

madrigal *n* a type of 16th- or 17th-century part song for unaccompanied voices > **madrigalist** *n*

maelstrom (**male**-strom) *n* **1** a large powerful whirlpool **2** any confused, violent, and destructive turmoil: *a maelstrom of adulterous passion*

maestro (**my**-stroh) *n, pl* **-tri** *or* **-tros 1** a distinguished musician or conductor **2** any master of an art: *Milan's maestro of minimalism*

Mafia *n* **the Mafia** a secret criminal organization founded in Sicily, and carried to the US by Italian immigrants

mafioso (maf-fee-**oh**-so) *n, pl* **-sos** *or* **-si** (-see) a member of the Mafia

magazine *n* **1** a periodic publication containing written pieces and illustrations, usually on a particular subject **2** a television or radio programme made up of short nonfictional items **3** a metal case holding several cartridges used in some firearms **4** a rack for automatically feeding slides through a projector **5** a place for storing weapons, explosives, or military equipment

> **magazine** *n* **1** = journal, publication, supplement, rag (*informal*), issue, glossy (*informal*), pamphlet, periodical, ezine *or* e-zine

magenta (maj-**jen**-ta) *adj* deep purplish-red

maggot *n* the limbless larva of various insects, esp. the housefly and blowfly > **maggoty** *adj*

magi (**maje**-eye) *pl n, sing* **magus** (**may**-guss) **the three Magi** *Christianity* the wise men from the East who came to worship the infant Jesus (Matthew 2:1–12)

magic *n* **1** the supposed power to make things happen by using supernatural means **2** tricks done to entertain; conjuring **3** any mysterious or extraordinary quality or power: *the magic of Placido Domingo* **4 like magic** very quickly ▸ *adj also* **magical 5** of magic **6** possessing or considered to possess mysterious powers **7** unaccountably enchanting **8** *informal* wonderful or marvellous ▸ *vb* **-gicking, -gicked 9** to transform or produce as if by magic: *he had magicked up a gourmet meal at a moment's notice* > **magically** *adv*

> **magic** *n* **1** = sorcery, wizardry, witchcraft, enchantment, black art, necromancy **2** = conjuring, illusion, trickery, sleight of hand, legerdemain, prestidigitation **3** = charm, power, glamour, fascination, magnetism, enchantment, allurement, mojo (*slang*) ▸ *adj* **7** *also* **magical** = miraculous, entrancing, charming, fascinating, marvellous, magical, enchanting, bewitching

magician *n* **1** a conjuror **2** a person with magic powers

> **magician** *n* **1** = conjuror, illusionist, prestidigitator **2** = sorcerer, witch, wizard, illusionist, warlock, necromancer, enchanter *or* enchantress

magisterial *adj* **1** commanding and authoritative **2** of a magistrate > **magisterially** *adv*

magistrate *n* **1** a public officer concerned with the administration of law **2** *Austral & NZ* a former name for **district court judge**

> **magistrate** *n* **1** = judge, justice, justice of the peace, J.P.

magma *n, pl* **-mas** *or* **-mata** hot molten rock within the earth's crust which sometimes finds its way to the surface where it solidifies to form igneous rock

magnanimous *adj* generous and forgiving, esp. towards a defeated enemy > **magnanimity** *n* > **magnanimously** *adv*

magnate *n* an influential or wealthy person, esp. in industry

magnesia *n* a white tasteless substance used as an antacid and laxative; magnesium oxide

magnesium *n* *chem* a light silvery-white metallic element that burns with a very bright white flame. Symbol: **Mg**

magnet *n* **1** a piece of iron, steel, or lodestone that has the property of attracting iron to it **2** a person or thing that exerts a great attraction: *these woods are a magnet for bird watchers*

magnetic *adj* **1** of, producing, or operated by means of magnetism **2** of or like a magnet **3** capable of being made into a magnet **4** exerting a powerful attraction: *political leaders of magnetic appeal* > **magnetically** *adv*

> **magnetic** *adj* **4** = attractive, irresistible, seductive, captivating, charming, fascinating, charismatic, hypnotic; ≠ repulsive

magnetic tape *n* a long plastic strip coated with a magnetic substance, used to record sound or video signals or to store information in computers

magnetism *n* **1** the property of attraction displayed by magnets **2** powerful personal charm **3** the branch of physics concerned with magnetic phenomena

magnetize *or* **-tise** *vb* **-tizing, -tized** *or* **-tising, -tised 1** to make a substance or object magnetic **2** to attract strongly: *he was magnetized by her smile* > **magnetizable** *or* **-tisable** *adj* > **magnetization** *or* **-tisation** *n*

magneto (mag-nee-toe) *n, pl* **-tos** a small electric generator in which the magnetic field is produced by a permanent magnet, esp. one used to provide the spark in an internal-combustion engine

magnification *n* **1** the act of magnifying or the state of being magnified **2** the degree to which something is magnified **3** a magnified copy of something

magnificent *adj* **1** splendid or impressive in appearance **2** superb or very fine: *a magnificent performance* > **magnificence** *n* > **magnificently** *adv*

> **magnificent** *adj* **1** = splendid, impressive, imposing, glorious, gorgeous, majestic, regal, sublime; ≠ ordinary **2** = brilliant, fine, excellent, outstanding, superb, splendid

magnify *vb* **-fies, -fying, -fied 1** to make something look bigger than it really is, for instance by using a lens or microscope **2** to make something seem more important than it really is; exaggerate: *you are magnifying the problem out of all proportion* **3** to make something sound louder than it really is: *the stethoscope magnifies internal body sounds* **4** *archaic* to glorify or praise > **magnified** *adj*

magnify *vb* **1** = enlarge, increase, boost, expand, intensify, blow up (*informal*), heighten, amplify; ≠ reduce **2** = make worse, exaggerate, intensify, worsen, exacerbate, increase, inflame; ≠ understate

magnitude *n* **1** relative importance: *an evil of the first magnitude* **2** relative size or extent **3** *astron* the apparent brightness of a celestial body expressed on a numerical scale on which bright stars have a low value

> **magnitude** *n* **1** = importance, consequence, significance, moment, note, weight, greatness; ≠ unimportance **2** = immensity, size, extent, enormity (*informal*), volume, vastness; ≠ smallness

magnolia *n* an Asian and North American tree or shrub with white, pink, purple, or yellow showy flowers

magnum *n, pl* **-nums** a wine bottle of twice the normal size, holding 1.5 litres

magpie *n* **1** a bird of the crow family with black-and-white plumage, a long tail, and a chattering call **2** any of various similar Australian birds, eg the butcherbird **3** *Brit* a person who hoards small objects

maharaja *or* **maharajah** *n* the head of one of the royal families which formerly ruled parts of India

maharani *or* **maharanee** *n* the wife of a maharaja

mah jong *or* **mah-jongg** *n* a game of Chinese origin, played using tiles bearing various designs, in which the players try to obtain a winning combination of tiles

mahogany *n, pl* **-nies 1** the hard reddish-brown wood of any of several tropical trees ▸ *adj* **2** reddish-brown: *wonderful mahogany tones*

mahout (ma-**howt**) *n* (in India) an elephant driver or keeper

maid *n* **1** a female servant **2** *archaic or literary* a young unmarried girl; maiden

> **maid** *n* **1** = servant, chambermaid, housemaid, menial, maidservant, female servant, domestic (*archaic*), parlourmaid **2** = girl, maiden (*archaic, literary*), lass, damsel, lassie (*informal*)

maiden *n* **1** *archaic or literary* a young unmarried girl, esp. a virgin **2** *horse racing* a horse that has never won a race ▸ *adj* **3** unmarried: *a maiden aunt* **4** first or earliest: *maiden voyage* > **maidenhood** *n* > **maidenly** *adj*

> **maiden** *n* **1** = girl, maid (*archaic, literary*), lass, damsel (*archaic, poetic*), virgin, lassie (*informal*) ▸ *adj* **3** = unmarried, unwed, single **4** = first, initial, inaugural, introductory

maidenhead *n* **1** the hymen **2** virginity or maidenhood

maiden name *n* a woman's surname before marriage

maiden over n cricket an over in which no runs are scored

maidservant n a female servant

mail¹ n 1 letters and packages transported and delivered by the post office 2 the postal system 3 a single collection or delivery of mail 4 a train, ship, or aircraft that carries mail 5 short for **email** ▸ vb 6 chiefly US & Canad to send by mail 7 to contact or send by email

> **mail** n 1 = letters, post, correspondence ▸ vb 6 = post, send, forward, dispatch 7 = email or e-mail, send, forward

mail² n flexible armour made of riveted metal rings or links > **mailed** adj

mailbox n 1 US, Canad & Austral a box outside a house into which the postman puts letters for the occupiers of the house 2 (on a computer) the directory in which email messages are stored

mail order n a system of buying and selling goods by post

mailshot n a posting of circulars, leaflets, or other advertising to a selected large number of people at once

maim vb to injure badly or cruelly, with some permanent damage resulting

main adj 1 chief or principal ▸ n 2 a principal pipe or line in a system used to distribute water, electricity, or gas 3 **mains** the main distribution network for water, gas, or electricity 4 great strength or force: with might and main 5 literary the open ocean 6 **in the main** on the whole

> **main** adj = chief, leading, head, central, essential, primary, principal, foremost; ≠ minor ▸ n 2 = pipeline, channel, pipe, conduit, duct 3 = cable, line, electricity supply, mains supply 6 **in the main** = on the whole, generally, mainly, mostly, in general, for the most part

mainframe n a high-speed, general-purpose computer, with a large storage capacity

mainland n the main part of a land mass as opposed to an island

mainly adv for the most part; principally

> **mainly** adv = chiefly, mostly, largely, principally, primarily, on the whole, predominantly, in the main

mainmast n naut the chief mast of a sailing vessel with two or more masts

mainsail n naut the largest and lowermost sail on the mainmast

mainspring n 1 the chief cause or motive of something: the mainspring of a dynamic economy 2 the chief spring of a watch or clock

mainstay n 1 a chief support 2 naut a rope securing a mainmast

mainstream n 1 the people or things representing the most common or generally accepted ideas and styles in a society, art form,

etc.: the mainstream of academic life 2 the main current of a river ▸ adj 3 belonging to the social or cultural mainstream: mainstream American movies

> **mainstream** adj = conventional, general, established, received, accepted, current, prevailing, orthodox, lamestream (informal); ≠ unconventional

maintain vb 1 to continue or keep in existence: we must maintain good relations with them 2 to keep in proper or good condition: an expensive car to maintain 3 to sustain or keep up a particular level or speed: he set off at a high speed, but couldn't maintain it all the way 4 to enable a person to have the money, food and other things he or she needs to live: the money maintained us for a month 5 to assert: he had always maintained that he never wanted children 6 to defend against contradiction: he maintained his innocence

> **maintain** vb 1, 3 = continue, retain, preserve, sustain, carry on, keep up, prolong, perpetuate; ≠ end 2 = look after, care for, take care of, conserve, keep in good condition 5 = assert, state, claim, insist, declare, contend, profess, avow; ≠ disavow

maintenance n 1 the act of maintaining or the state of being maintained 2 the process of keeping a car, building, etc. in good condition 3 law financial provision ordered to be made by way of periodical payments or a lump sum, usually for a separated or divorced spouse

> **maintenance** n 1 = continuation, carrying-on, perpetuation, prolongation 2 = upkeep, keeping, care, repairs, conservation, nurture, preservation 3 = allowance, support, keep, alimony

maisonette n Brit & S African a flat with more than one floor

maitre d'hotel (met-ra dote-tell) n, pl **maitres d'hotel** a head waiter

maize n a type of corn grown for its large yellow edible grains, which are used for food and as a source of oil. See also **sweet corn**

majestic adj beautiful, dignified, and impressive > **majestically** adv

> **majestic** adj = grand, magnificent, impressive, superb, splendid, regal, stately, monumental; ≠ modest

majesty n 1 great dignity and grandeur 2 supreme power or authority

> **majesty** n 1 = grandeur, glory, splendour, magnificence, nobility; ≠ triviality

major adj 1 greater in size, frequency, or importance than others of the same kind: the major political parties 2 very serious or significant: a major investigation 3 main or principal: a major road 4 music **A** (of a scale) having notes separated by a whole tone, except for the third and fourth notes, and seventh and eighth notes, which are separated by a semitone **B** of or based on the major scale: *the key of D major* ▸ *n* **5** a middle-ranking military officer **6** *music* a major key, chord, mode, or scale **7** a person who has reached the age of legal majority **8** *US, Canad, S African, Austral & NZ* the principal field of study of a student ▸ *vb* **9** *US, Canad, S African, Austral & NZ* to study as one's principal subject: *he majored in economics*

major *adj* **1, 3** = main, higher, greater, bigger, leading, chief, senior, supreme; ≠ minor **2** = important, critical, significant, great, serious, crucial (*informal*), outstanding, notable

major-domo *n, pl* **-mos** the chief steward or butler of a great household

majority *n, pl* **-ties 1** the greater number or part of something **2** (in an election) the number of votes or seats by which the strongest party or candidate beats the combined opposition or the runner-up **3** the largest party or group that votes together in a meeting, council or parliament **4** the age at which a person legally becomes an adult **5 in the majority** forming or part of the group of people or things made up of more than half of a larger group

majority *n* **1** = most, mass, bulk, best part, better part, lion's share, preponderance, greater number **4** = adulthood, maturity, age of consent, seniority, manhood *or* womanhood

make *vb* **making, made 1** to create, construct, establish, or draw up; bring into being: *houses made of stone; he will have to make a will* **2** to cause to do or be; compel or induce: *please make her go away* **3** to bring about or produce: *don't make a noise* **4** to carry out or perform: *he made his first trip to China in 1987; she made an obscene gesture* **5** to appoint: *they made him caretaker manager* **6** to come into a specified state or condition: *to make merry* **7** to become: *she will make a good diplomat* **8** to cause or ensure the success of: *that news has made my day* **9** to amount to: *5 and 5 make 10* **10** to earn or be paid: *they must be making a fortune* **11** to have the qualities of or be suitable for: *what makes this book such a good read?* **12** to prepare for use: *she forgot to make her bed* **13** to be the essential element in: *confidence makes a good salesperson* **14** to use for a specified purpose: *they will make this town their base* **15** to deliver: *he made a very good speech* **16** to consider to be: *what time do you make it?* **17** to cause to seem or represent as being: *her girlish pigtails made her look younger than she was; she made the experience sound most unpleasant* **18** to acquire: *she doesn't make friends easily* **19** to engage in: *they made war on the Turks* **20** to travel a certain distance or to a certain place: *we can make at least three miles before it gets dark* **21** to arrive in time for: *he didn't make the first act of the play* **22** to win or score: *he made a break of 125* **23** *informal* to gain a place or position on or in: *to make the headlines* **24 make a day** *or* **night of it** to cause an activity to last a day or night **25 make eyes at** *old-fashioned* to flirt with or ogle **26 make it** *informal* **A** to be able to attend: *I'm afraid I can't make it to your party* **B** to be successful **27 make like** *slang, chiefly US & Canad* **A** to imitate **B** to pretend **28 make to** *or* **as if to** *or* **as though to** to act with the intention or with a show of doing something: *she made as if to hit him* ▸ *n* **29** manufacturer; brand: *what make of car is that?* **30** the way in which something is made **31 on the make** *slang* out for profit or conquest ▸ See also **make for** *etc*. > **maker** *n*

make *vb* **1, 3** = produce, cause, create, effect, lead to, generate, bring about, give rise to **2** = force, cause, compel, drive, require, oblige, induce, constrain **4** = perform, do, effect, carry out, execute **9** = amount to, total, constitute, add up to, count as, tot up to (*informal*) **10** = earn, get, gain, net, win, clear, obtain, bring in **26B make it** = succeed, prosper, arrive (*informal*), get on, crack it (*informal*) ▸ *n* **29** = brand, sort, style, model, kind, type, variety, marque

make for *vb* **1** to head towards **2** to prepare to attack **3** to help bring about: *this will make for a spectacular race*

make for *vb* **1 make for something** = head for, aim for, head towards, be bound for

makeshift *adj* serving as a temporary substitute

makeshift *adj* = temporary, provisional, substitute, expedient, stopgap

make-up *n* **1** cosmetics, such as powder or lipstick **2** the cosmetics used by an actor to adapt his or her appearance **3** the arrangement of the parts of something **4** mental or physical constitution ▸ *vb* **make up 5** to form or constitute: *these arguments make up the case for the defence* **6** to devise or compose, sometimes with the intent to deceive: *she was well known for making up stories about herself* **7** to supply what is lacking in; complete: *I'll make up the difference* **8** Also: **make it up** to settle differences amicably **9 make up for** to compensate for: *one good year can make up for several bad ones* **10** to apply cosmetics to the face **11 make up to** *informal* **A** to make friendly overtures to **B** to flirt with

make-up *n* **1, 2** = cosmetics, paint (*informal*), powder, face (*informal*), greasepaint (*theatre*) **3** = structure, organization, arrangement, construction, assembly, constitution, format, composition **4** = nature, character, constitution, temperament, disposition ▸ *vb* **5 make up something** = form, account for, constitute, compose, comprise **6 make something up** = invent, create, construct, compose, frame, coin, devise, originate

7 make up something = complete, supply, fill, round off **8 make up** = settle your differences, bury the hatchet, call it quits, declare a truce, be friends again **9 make up for something** = compensate for, make amends for, atone for, balance out, offset, make recompense for

makeweight n an unimportant person or thing added to make up a lack

making n **1** the act or process of producing something **2 be the making of** to cause the success of **3 in the making** in the process of becoming or being made

making n **1** = creation, production, manufacture, construction, assembly, composition, fabrication

mal- combining form bad or badly; wrong or wrongly: maladjusted; malfunction

malachite (mal-a-kite) n a green mineral used as a source of copper, and for making ornaments

maladjustment n psychol a failure to meet the demands of society, such as coping with problems and social relationships > **maladjusted** adj

maladroit (mal-a-droyt) adj clumsy, awkward, or tactless > **maladroitly** adv > **maladroitness** n

malady (mal-a-dee) n, pl **-dies** old-fashioned any disease or illness

malaise (mal-laze) n **1** a vague feeling of unease, illness, or depression **2** a complex of problems affecting a country, economy, etc.: decades of economic malaise

malapropism n the comic misuse of a word by confusion with one which sounds similar, for example under the affluence of alcohol

malaria n a disease with recurring attacks of fever, caused by the bite of some types of mosquito > **malarial** adj

Malay n **1** a member of a people living chiefly in Malaysia and Indonesia **2** the language of this people ▸ adj **3** of the Malays or their language

Malayan adj **1** of Malaya ▸ n **2** a person from Malaya

malcontent n a person who is discontented with the existing situation

male adj **1** of the sex that can fertilize female reproductive cells **2** of or characteristic of a man **3** for or composed of men or boys: a male choir **4** (of flowers) bearing stamens but lacking a pistil **5** electronics & engineering having a projecting part or parts that fit into a hollow counterpart: a male plug ▸ n **6** a male person, animal, or plant > **maleness** n

male adj **2** = masculine, manly, macho, virile; ≠ female

malediction (mal-lid-dik-shun) n the utterance of a curse against someone or something > **maledictory** adj

malefactor (mal-if-act-or) n a criminal or wrongdoer > **malefaction** n

malevolent (mal-lev-a-lent) adj wishing evil to others; malicious > **malevolence** n > **malevolently** adv

malfeasance (mal-fee-zanss) n law wrongful or illegal behaviour, esp. by a public official

malformation n **1** the condition of being faulty or abnormal in form or shape **2** pathol a deformity, esp. when congenital > **malformed** adj

malfunction vb **1** to fail to function properly or fail to function at all ▸ n **2** failure to function properly or failure to function at all

malfunction vb = break down, fail, go wrong, stop working, be defective, conk out (informal), crash ▸ n = fault, failure, breakdown, defect, flaw, glitch

malice (mal-iss) n the desire to do harm or cause mischief to others > **malicious** adj > **maliciously** adv

malign (mal-line) vb **1** to say unpleasant and untrue things about someone; slander ▸ adj **2** evil in influence or effect

malignant (mal-lig-nant) adj **1** seeking to harm others **2** tending to cause great harm; injurious **3** pathol (of a tumour) uncontrollable or resistant to therapy > **malignancy** n

malignity (mal-lig-nit-ee) n the condition of being malign or deadly

malinger (mal-ling-ger) vb to pretend to be ill, or exaggerate how ill one is, to avoid work > **malingerer** n

mall (mawl) n a shaded avenue, esp. one open to the public

mallard n, pl **-lard** or **-lards** a common N hemisphere duck, the male of which has a dark green head

malleable (mal-lee-a-bl) adj **1** (esp. of metal) capable of being hammered or pressed into shape without breaking **2** able to be influenced > **malleability** n > **malleably** adv

mallee n a low-growing eucalypt found in dry regions of Australia

mallet n **1** a hammer with a large wooden head **2** a long stick with a head like a hammer used to strike the ball in croquet or polo

mallow n any of a group of plants, with purple, pink, or white flowers

malnutrition n physical weakness resulting from insufficient food or an unbalanced diet

malodorous (mal-lode-or-uss) adj having an unpleasant smell: the malodorous sludge of Boston harbour

malpractice n illegal, unethical, or negligent professional conduct

malt n **1** grain, such as barley, that is kiln-dried after it has been germinated by soaking in water ▸ vb **2** to make into or become malt **3** to make from malt or to add malt to > **malted** adj > **malty** adj

maltreat vb to treat badly, cruelly, or violently > **maltreatment** n

malware *n* a computer program designed specifically to damage or disrupt a system, such as a virus

mama *or esp US* **mamma** (mam-**mah**) *n* *old-fashioned*, *informal* same as **mother**

mamba *n* a very poisonous tree snake found in tropical and Southern Africa

mammal *n* a warm-blooded animal, such as a human being, dog or whale, the female of which produces milk to feed her babies
> **mammalian** *adj*, *n*

mammary *adj* of the breasts or milk-producing glands

mammon *n* wealth regarded as a source of evil and corruption, personified in the New Testament as a false god (**Mammon**)

mammoth *n* **1** a large extinct elephant with a hairy coat and long curved tusks ▸ *adj* **2** gigantic

> **mammoth** *adj* = colossal, huge, giant, massive, enormous, immense, gigantic, monumental (*informal*), supersize; ≠ tiny

mampara *n* *S African derogatory*, *informal* a foolish or stupid person

man *n*, *pl* **men 1** an adult male human being **2** a human being of either sex; person: *all men are born equal* **3** human beings collectively; mankind. Related adjective: **anthropoid 4** a human being regarded as representative of a particular period or category: *Neanderthal man* **5** an adult male human being with qualities associated with the male, such as courage or virility: *take it like a man* **6** an employee, servant, or representative **7** a member of the armed forces who is not an officer **8** a member of a group or team **9** a husband, boyfriend, or male lover **10** a movable piece in various games, such as draughts **11** *S African slang* any person: used as a term of address **12** **as one man** with unanimous action or response **13** **he's your man** he's the person needed **14** **man and boy** from childhood **15** **sort out the men from the boys** to discover who can cope with difficult or dangerous situations and who cannot **16** **to a man** without exception ▸ *vb* **manning**, **manned 17** to provide with sufficient people for operation or defence **18** to take one's place at or near in readiness for action > **manhood** *n*

> **man** *n* **1** = male, guy (*informal*), fellow (*old-fashioned*), gentleman, bloke (*Brit informal*), chap (*Brit informal*), dude (*US informal*), geezer (*informal*) **2** = human, human being, person, individual, soul **3** = humankind, humanity, mankind, people, human race, Homo sapiens ▸ *vb* **17** = staff, people, crew, occupy, garrison

mana *n NZ* authority, influence and prestige

> **mana** *n* = authority, influence, power, might, standing, status, importance, eminence

manacle (man-a-kl) *n* **1** a metal ring or chain put round the wrists or ankles, used to restrict the movements of a prisoner or convict ▸ *vb* **-cling, -cled 2** to put manacles on

manage *vb* **-naging, -naged 1** to succeed in doing something: *we finally managed to sell our old house* **2** to be in charge of; administer: *the company is badly managed* **3** to have room or time for: *can you manage lunch tomorrow?* **4** to keep under control: *she disapproved of taking drugs to manage stress* **5** to struggle on despite difficulties, esp. financial ones: *most people cannot manage on a cleaner's salary* > **manageable** *adj*

> **manage** *vb* **2** = be in charge of, run, handle, direct, conduct, command, administer, supervise **4** = control, handle, manipulate **5** = cope, survive, succeed, carry on, make do, get by (*informal*), muddle through

management *n* **1** the people responsible for running an organization or business **2** managers or employers collectively **3** the technique or practice of managing or controlling

> **management** *n* **1, 2** = directors, board, executive(s), administration, employers **3** = administration, control, running, operation, handling, direction, command, supervision

manager *n* **1** a person who manages an organization or business **2** a person in charge of a sports team **3** a person who controls the business affairs of an actor or entertainer
> **manageress** *fem n*

> **manager** *n* **1** = supervisor, head, director, executive, boss (*informal*), governor, administrator, organizer, sherang (*Austral*, *NZ*)

managerial *adj* of a manager or management

manatee *n* a large plant-eating mammal occurring in tropical coastal waters of the Atlantic

mandarin *n* **1** (in the Chinese Empire) a member of a senior grade of the bureaucracy **2** a high-ranking official with extensive powers **3** a person of standing and influence, esp. in literary or intellectual circles **4** a small citrus fruit resembling the tangerine

Mandarin Chinese *or* **Mandarin** *n* the official language of China since 1917

mandate *n* **1** an official or authoritative command to carry out a particular task: *the UN force's mandate does not allow it to intervene* **2** *politics* the political authority given to a government or an elected representative through an electoral victory **3** Also: **mandated territory** (formerly) a territory administered by one country on behalf of an international body ▸ *vb* **-dating, -dated 4** to delegate authority to **5** to assign territory to a nation under a mandate

> **mandate** *n* **1** = command, order, commission, instruction, decree, directive, edict

m

mandatory *adj* **1** obligatory; compulsory
2 having the nature or powers of a mandate
> **mandatorily** *adv*

> **mandatory** *adj* **1** = compulsory, required,
> binding, obligatory, requisite; ≠ optional

mandible *n* **1** the lower jawbone of a vertebrate
2 either of the jawlike mouthparts of an insect
3 either part of the bill of a bird, esp. the lower
part

mandolin *n* a musical instrument with four
pairs of strings stretched over a small light body,
usually played with a plectrum

mandrel *or* **mandril** *n* **1** a spindle on which the
object being worked on is supported in a lathe
2 a shaft on which a machining tool is mounted

mane *n* **1** the long hair that grows from the
neck in such mammals as the lion and horse
2 long thick human hair > **maned** *adj*

maneuver *n, vb US* same as **manoeuvre**

manful *adj* determined and brave
> **manfully** *adv*

manganese *n chem* a brittle greyish-white
metallic element used in making steel.
Symbol: **Mn**

mange *n* a skin disease of domestic animals,
characterized by itching and loss of hair

mangelwurzel *n* a variety of beet with a large
yellowish root

manger *n* a trough in a stable or barn from
which horses or cattle feed

mangetout (mawnzh-too) *n* a variety of
garden pea with an edible pod

mangle¹ *vb* **-gling, -gled** **1** to destroy or
damage by crushing and twisting **2** to spoil
> **mangled** *adj*

mangle² *n* **1** a machine for pressing or
squeezing water out of washed clothes,
consisting of two heavy rollers between
which the clothes are passed ▸ *vb* **-gling, -gled**
2 to put through a mangle

mango *n, pl* **-goes** *or* **-gos** the egg-shaped edible
fruit of a tropical Asian tree, with a smooth rind
and sweet juicy flesh

mangrove *n* a tropical evergreen tree or shrub
with intertwining aerial roots that forms dense
thickets along coasts

mangy *adj* **-gier, -giest** **1** having mange
2 scruffy or shabby > **mangily** *adv*
> **manginess** *n*

manhandle *vb* **-handling, -handled** **1** to handle
or push someone about roughly **2** to move
something by manpower rather than by
machinery

manhole *n* a hole with a detachable cover,
through which a person can enter a sewer or
pipe to inspect or repair it

man-hour *n* a unit of work in industry, equal to
the work done by one person in one hour

mania *n* **1** an obsessional enthusiasm or liking
2 a mental illness characterized by great or
violent excitement

maniac *n* **1** a wild disorderly person **2** a person
who has a great craving or enthusiasm for
something > **maniacal** (man-**eye**-ak-kl) *adj*

manic *adj* **1** extremely excited or energetic;
frenzied: *manic, cavorting dancers* **2** of, involving,
or affected by mania: *deep depression broken by
periods of manic excitement*

manic-depressive *old-fashioned* ▸ *adj* **1** relating
to or having bipolar disorder ▸ *n* **2** a person with
bipolar disorder

manicure *n* **1** cosmetic care of the hands and
fingernails ▸ *vb* **-curing, -cured** **2** to care for the
fingernails and hands > **manicurist** *n*

manifest *adj* **1** easily noticed, obvious ▸ *vb*
2 to reveal or display: *an additional symptom now
manifested itself* **3** to show by the way one
behaves: *he manifested great personal bravery*
4 (of a disembodied spirit) to appear in visible
form ▸ *n* **5** a customs document containing
particulars of a ship and its cargo **6** a list of
the cargo and passengers on an aeroplane
> **manifestation** *n*

> **manifest** *adj* = obvious, apparent, patent,
> evident, clear, glaring, noticeable, blatant;
> ≠ concealed ▸ *vb* **2, 3** = display, show, reveal,
> express, demonstrate, expose, exhibit;
> ≠ conceal

manifesto *n, pl* **-tos** *or* **-toes** a public
declaration of intent or policy issued by a
group of people, for instance by a political
party

manifold *adj formal* **1** numerous and varied:
her talents are manifold ▸ *n* **2** a pipe with a number
of inlets or outlets, esp. one in a car engine

manikin *n* **1** a little man; dwarf or child
2 a model of the human body

manila *or* **manilla** *n* a strong usually brown
paper used to make envelopes

manipulate *vb* **-lating, -lated** **1** to handle or
use skilfully **2** to control something or someone
cleverly or deviously > **manipulation** *n*
> **manipulator** *n* > **manipulative** *adj*

> **manipulate** *vb* **1** = work, use, operate,
> handle **2** = influence, control, direct,
> negotiate, exploit, manoeuvre

mankind *n* **1** human beings collectively **2** men
collectively

> **mankind** *n* **1** = people, man, humanity,
> human race, humankind, Homo sapiens

manly *adj* **-lier, -liest** **1** possessing qualities,
such as vigour or courage, traditionally
regarded as appropriate to a man; masculine
2 characteristic of a man > **manliness** *n*

> **manly** *adj* **1** = virile, masculine; ≠ effeminate

man-made *adj* made by humans; artificial

> **man-made** *adj* = artificial, manufactured,
> mock, synthetic, ersatz

manna n 1 Bible the miraculous food which sustained the Israelites in the wilderness (Exodus 16:14–36) 2 a windfall: manna from heaven

mannequin n 1 a woman who wears the clothes displayed at a fashion show; model 2 a life-size dummy of the human body used to fit or display clothes

manner n 1 the way a thing happens or is done 2 a person's bearing and behaviour 3 the style or customary way of doing something: sculpture in the Greek manner 4 type or kind 5 **in a manner of speaking** in a way; so to speak 6 **to the manner born** naturally fitted to a specified role or activity

> **manner** n 1, 3 = style, way, fashion, method, custom, mode 2 = behaviour, air, bearing, conduct, aspect, demeanour 4 = type, form, sort, kind, variety, brand, category

mannered adj 1 (of speech or behaviour) unnaturally formal and put on to impress others 2 having manners as specified: ill-mannered

> **mannered** adj 1 = affected, artificial, pretentious, stilted, arty-farty (informal); ≠ natural

mannerism n 1 a distinctive and individual gesture or way of speaking 2 excessive use of a distinctive or affected manner, esp. in art or literature

mannish adj (of a woman) displaying an appearance or qualities regarded as typical of a man

manoeuvre or US **maneuver** (man-**noo**-ver) vb **-vring, -vred** or **-vering, -vered** 1 to move or do something with dexterity and skill: she manoeuvred the car easily into the parking space 2 to manipulate a situation in order to gain some advantage 3 to perform a manoeuvre or manoeuvres ▸ n 4 a movement or action requiring dexterity and skill 5 a contrived, complicated, and possibly deceptive plan or action 6 **manoeuvres** military or naval exercises, usually on a large scale 7 a change in course of a ship or aircraft, esp. a complicated one 8 **room for manoeuvre** the possibility of changing one's plans or behaviour if it becomes necessary or desirable > **manoeuvrable** or US **maneuverable** adj > **manoeuvrability** or US **maneuverability** n

> **manoeuvre** or **maneuver** vb 2 = scheme, wangle (informal), machinate ▸ n 5 = stratagem, scheme, trick, tactic, intrigue, dodge, ploy, ruse 6 = movement, operation, exercise, war game

manor n 1 (in medieval Europe) the lands and property controlled by a lord 2 Brit a large country house and its lands 3 Brit slang an area of operation, esp. of a local police force > **manorial** adj

manpower n the number of people needed or available for a job

manqué (**mong**-kay) adj unfulfilled; would-be: an actor manqué

manse n the house provided for a minister of some Christian denominations

manservant n, pl **menservants** a male servant, esp. a valet

mansion n 1 a large and imposing house 2 **Mansions** Brit a name given to some blocks of flats as part of their address: 18 Wilton Mansions

> **mansion** n 1 = residence, manor, hall, villa, seat

manslaughter n law the unlawful but not deliberately planned killing of one human being by another

mantel n a wooden, stone, or iron frame around a fireplace

mantelpiece n a shelf above a fireplace often forming part of the mantel. Also: **mantel shelf, chimneypiece**

mantilla n a woman's lace or silk scarf covering the shoulders and head, worn esp. in Spain

mantis n, pl **-tises** or **-tes** a carnivorous insect resembling a grasshopper, that rests with the first pair of legs raised as if in prayer. Also: **praying mantis**

mantle n 1 old-fashioned a loose wrap or cloak 2 anything that covers completely or envelops: a mantle of snow covered the ground 3 the responsibilities and duties which go with a particular job or position: he refuses to accept the mantle of leader 4 a small mesh dome used to increase illumination in a gas or oil lamp by becoming incandescent 5 geol the part of the earth between the crust and the core ▸ vb **-tling, -tled** 6 to spread over or become spread over: mountains mantled in lush vegetation

> **mantle** n 1 = cloak, wrap, cape, hood, shawl 2 = covering, screen, curtain, blanket, veil, shroud, canopy, pall

mantra n 1 Hinduism & Buddhism any sacred word or syllable used as an object of concentration 2 Hinduism a Vedic psalm of praise 3 any phrase that is consciously repeated because it is believed to contain an important truth

manual adj 1 of a hand or hands: manual dexterity 2 physical as opposed to mental: manual labour 3 operated or done by human labour rather than automatic or computer-aided means: a manual gearbox ▸ n 4 a book of instructions or information 5 music one of the keyboards on an organ > **manually** adv

> **manual** adj 2 = physical, human 3 = hand-operated, hand, non-automatic ▸ n 4 = handbook, guide, instructions, bible

manufacture vb **-turing, -tured** 1 to process or make goods on a large scale, esp. using machinery 2 to invent or concoct evidence, an excuse, etc. ▸ *n* **3** the production of goods, esp. by industrial processes > **manufacturer** *n* > **manufacturing** *n*, *adj*

manufacture *vb* **1** = make, build, produce, construct, create, turn out, assemble, put together **2** = concoct, make up, invent, devise, fabricate, think up, cook up (*informal*), trump up ▸ *n* = making, production, construction, assembly, creation

manure *n* **1** animal excrement used as a fertilizer ▸ *vb* **-nuring, -nured 2** to spread manure upon fields or soil

manuscript *n* **1** a book or other document written by hand **2** the original handwritten or typed version of a book or article submitted by an author for publication

Manx *adj* **1** of the Isle of Man ▸ *n* **2** an almost extinct Celtic language of the Isle of Man ▸ *pl n* **3 the Manx** the people of the Isle of Man > **Manxman** *or fem* **Manxwoman** *n*

Manx cat *n* a short-haired breed of cat without a tail

many *adj* **1** a large number of; numerous: *many times; many people think the government is incompetent* ▸ *pron* **2** a number of people or things, esp. a large one: *many are seated already; have as many as you want* **3 many a** each of a considerable number of: *many a man* ▸ *n* **4 the many** the majority of mankind, esp. ordinary people

many *adj* = numerous, various, countless, abundant, myriad, innumerable, manifold (*formal*), umpteen (*informal*) ▸ *pron* **2** = a lot, lots (*informal*), plenty, scores, heaps (*informal*)

Maoism *n* Communism as interpreted in the theories and policies of Mao Zedong (1893–1976), Chinese statesman > **Maoist** *n*, *adj*

Māori *n pl* **-ri** *or* **-ris** a member of the Polynesian people living in New Zealand since before the arrival of European settlers **2** the language of this people ▸ *adj* **3** of this people or their language

map *n* **1** a diagrammatic representation of the earth's surface or part of it, showing the geographical distributions or positions of features such as roads, towns, relief, and rainfall **2** a diagrammatic representation of the stars or of the surface of a celestial body **3** *maths* same as **function 4 put on the map** to make (a town or company) well-known: *William Morris put Kelmscott on the map* ▸ *vb* **mapping, mapped 5** to make a map of **6** *maths* to represent or transform (a function, figure, or set) ▸ See also **map out**

maple *n* **1** any of various trees or shrubs with five-pointed leaves and winged seeds borne in pairs **2** the hard wood of any of these trees

map out *vb* to plan or design

mapping *n* *maths* same as **function**

mar *vb* **marring, marred** to spoil or be the one bad feature of: *the coastline is marred by high-rise hotels*

mar *vb* = harm, damage, hurt, spoil, stain, taint, tarnish; ≠ improve

Mar. March

marabou *n* **1** a large black-and-white African stork **2** the soft white down of this bird, used to trim hats, etc.

maraca (mar-**rak**-a) *n* a shaken percussion instrument, usually one of a pair, consisting of a gourd or plastic shell filled with dried seeds or pebbles

marae (mar-**rye**) *n* NZ **1** an enclosed space in front of a Māori meeting house **2** a Māori meeting house and its buildings

maraschino cherry *n* a cherry preserved in maraschino

marathon *n* **1** a race on foot of 26 miles 385 yards (42.195 kilometres) **2** any long or arduous task or event ▸ *adj* **3** of or relating to a race on foot of 26 miles 385 yards (42.195 kilometres): *marathon runners* **4** long and arduous: *a marathon nine hour meeting*

marble *n* **1** a hard limestone rock, which usually has a mottled appearance and can be given a high polish **2** a block of marble or work of art made of marble **3** a small round glass ball used in playing marbles ▸ *vb* **-bling, -bled 4** to mottle with variegated streaks in imitation of marble > **marbled** *adj*

march¹ *vb* **1** to walk with very regular steps, like a soldier **2** to walk in a quick and determined manner, esp. when angry: *he marched into the kitchen without knocking* **3** to make a person or group proceed: *he was marched back to his cell* **4** (of an army, procession, etc.) to walk as an organized group: *the demonstrators marched down the main street* **5** to advance or progress steadily: *time marches on* ▸ *n* **6** a regular stride **7** a long or exhausting walk **8** the steady development or progress of something: *the continuous march of industrial development* **9** a distance covered by marching **10** an organized protest in which a large group of people walk somewhere together: *a march against racial violence* **11** a piece of music suitable for marching **12 steal a march on** to gain an advantage over, esp. by a trick > **marcher** *n* > **marching** *adj*

march *vb* **1, 4** = parade, walk, file, pace, stride, swagger **2** = walk, strut, storm, sweep, stride, flounce ▸ *n* **7** = walk, trek, slog, yomp (*Brit informal*), routemarch **8** = progress, development, advance, evolution, progression

march² *n* **1** a border or boundary **2** the land lying along a border or boundary, often of disputed ownership

March *n* the third month of the year

marching girl *n Austral & NZ* a girl who does team formation marching as a sport

marchioness (marsh-on-**ness**) *n* **1** a woman who holds the rank of marquis or marquess **2** the wife or widow of a marquis or marquess

Mardi Gras (mar-dee grah) *n* the festival of Shrove Tuesday, celebrated in some cities with great revelry

mare *n* the adult female of a horse or zebra

margarine *n* a butter substitute made from vegetable and animal fats

marge *n Brit & Austral informal* margarine

margin *n* **1** an edge, rim, or border: *we came to the margin of the wood; people on the margin of society* **2** the blank space surrounding the text on a page **3** an additional amount or one beyond the minimum necessary: *the margin of victory was seven lengths; a small margin of error* **4** *chiefly Austral* a payment made in addition to a basic wage, esp. for special skill or responsibility **5** a limit beyond which something can no longer exist or function: *the margin of physical survival* **6** *econ* the minimum return below which an enterprise becomes unprofitable

> **margin** *n* **1** = edge, side, border, boundary, verge (*Brit*), brink, rim, perimeter

marginal *adj* **1** of, in, on, or forming a margin **2** not important; insignificant: *he remained a rather marginal political figure* **3** close to a limit, esp. a lower limit: *marginal legal ability* **4** *econ* relating to goods or services produced and sold at the margin of profitability: *marginal cost* **5** *politics* of or designating a constituency in which elections tend to be won by small margins: *a marginal seat* **6** designating agricultural land on the edge of fertile areas ▸ *n* **7** *politics, chiefly Brit & NZ* a marginal constituency > **marginally** *adv*

> **marginal** *adj* **2** = insignificant, small, minor, slight, minimal, negligible **3** = borderline, bordering, on the edge, peripheral

marguerite *n* a garden plant with flowers resembling large daisies

marigold *n* any of various plants cultivated for their yellow or orange flowers

marijuana *or* **marihuana** (mar-ree-wah-na) *n* the dried leaves and flowers of the hemp plant, used as a drug, esp. in cigarettes

> **marijuana** *or* **marihuana** *n* = cannabis, pot (*slang*), dope (*slang*), grass (*slang*), hemp, dagga (*S African*)

marina *n* a harbour for yachts and other pleasure boats

marinade *n* **1** a mixture of oil, wine, vinegar, etc., in which meat or fish is soaked before cooking ▸ *vb* **-nading, -naded** **2** same as **marinate**

marinate *vb* **-nating, -nated** to soak in marinade > **marinated** *adj*

marine *adj* **1** of, found in, or relating to the sea **2** of shipping or navigation **3** used or adapted for use at sea ▸ *n* **4** (esp. in Britain and the US) a soldier trained for land and sea combat **5** a country's shipping or navy collectively: *the merchant marine*

> **marine** *adj* **1, 2** = nautical, maritime, naval, seafaring, seagoing

mariner (mar-in-er) *n* a sailor

> **mariner** *n* = sailor, seaman *or* woman, sea dog, seafarer, salt

marionette *n* a puppet whose limbs are moved by strings

marital *adj* of or relating to marriage > **maritally** *adv*

> **marital** *adj* = matrimonial, nuptial, conjugal, connubial (*formal*)

maritime *adj* **1** of or relating to shipping **2** of, near, or living near the sea

> **maritime** *adj* **1** = nautical, marine, naval, oceanic, seafaring **2** = coastal, seaside, littoral

marjoram *n* a plant with sweet-scented leaves, used for seasoning food and in salads

mark[1] *n* **1** a visible impression on a surface, such as a spot or scratch **2** a sign, symbol, or other indication that distinguishes something **3** a written or printed symbol, as used for punctuation **4** a letter, number, or percentage used to grade academic work **5** a thing that indicates position; marker **6** an indication of some quality: *a mark of respect* **7** a target or goal **8** impression or influence: *this book displays the mark of its author's admiration of Kafka* **9** (in trade names) a particular model or type of a vehicle, machine, etc.: *a Spitfire Mark XI* **10** one of the temperature settings at which a gas oven can work: *bake at gas mark 5 for thirty minutes* **11** **make one's mark** to achieve recognition **12** **on your mark** *or* **marks** a command given to runners in a race to prepare themselves at the starting line **13** **up to the mark** meeting the desired standard ▸ *vb* **14** to make a visible impression, trace, or stain on **15** to have a tendency to become dirty, scratched, or damaged: *this material marks easily* **16** to characterize or distinguish: *the gritty determination that has marked his career* **17** to designate someone as a particular type of person: *she would now be marked as a troublemaker* **18** to label, esp. to indicate price **19** to celebrate or commemorate an occasion or its anniversary: *events marking the anniversary of Shakespeare's birth* **20** to pay attention to: *mark my words* **21** to observe or notice **22** to grade or evaluate academic work **23** *sport* to stay close to an opponent to hamper his or her play **24** **mark off** *or* **out** to set boundaries or limits on **25** **mark time** **A** to move the feet alternately as in marching but without advancing **B** to wait for something more interesting to happen

> **mark** *n* **1** = spot, stain, streak, smudge, line, scratch, scar, blot **2** = characteristic, feature, standard, quality, measure, stamp, attribute, criterion **6** = indication, sign, symbol, token **7** = target, goal, aim, purpose, object, objective

▶ *vb* **14** = scar, scratch, stain, streak, blot, smudge, blemish **16** = distinguish, show, illustrate, exemplify, denote **17** = label, identify, brand, flag, stamp, characterize **20, 21** = observe, mind, note, notice, attend to, pay attention to, pay heed to **22** = grade, correct, assess, evaluate, appraise

mark² *n* See **Deutschmark**

marked *adj* **1** obvious or noticeable: *a marked improvement* **2** singled out, esp. as the target of attack: *a marked man* ▷ **markedly** (mark-id-lee) *adv*

marked *adj* **1** = noticeable, clear, decided, striking, obvious, prominent, patent, distinct; ≠ imperceptible

marker *n* **1** an object used to show the position of something **2** Also called: **marker pen** a thick felt-tipped pen used for drawing and colouring

market *n* **1** an occasion at which people meet to buy and sell merchandise **2** a place at which a market is held **3** the buying and selling of goods and services, esp. when unrestrained by political or social considerations: *the market has been brought into health care* **4** the trading opportunities provided by a particular group of people: *the youth market* **5** demand for a particular product **6 be in the market for** to wish to buy **7 on the market** available for purchase **8 seller's** or **buyer's market** a market characterized by excess demand (or supply) and thus favourable to sellers (or buyers) ▶ *adj* **9** of, relating to, or controlled by the buying and selling of goods and services, esp. when unrestrained by political or social considerations: *a market economy* ▶ *vb* **-keting, -keted 10** to offer or produce for sale ▷ **marketable** *adj*

market *n* **1, 2** = fair, mart, bazaar, souk (*Arabic*) ▶ *vb* = sell, promote, retail, peddle, vend

market garden *n chiefly Brit & NZ* a place where fruit and vegetables are grown for sale ▷ **market gardener** *n*

marketing *n* the part of a business which controls the way that goods or services are sold

market maker *n* a dealer in securities on the London Stock Exchange who can also deal with the public as a broker

marketplace *n* **1** a place where a public market is held **2** the commercial world of buying and selling

market research *n* the study of customers' wants and purchases, and of the forces influencing them

marksman *n, pl* **-men** a person skilled in shooting ▷ **marksmanship** *n*

marl *n* a fine-grained rock consisting of clay, limestone, and silt used as a fertilizer ▷ **marly** *adj*

marlin *n, pl* **-lin** or **-lins** a large fish with a long spear-like upper jaw, found in warm and tropical seas

marlinspike or **marlinespike** (mar-lin-spike) *n naut* a pointed metal tool used in separating strands of rope

marmalade *n* a jam made from citrus fruits, esp. oranges

marmoreal (mar-**more**-ee-al) *adj* of or like marble

marmoset *n* a small South American monkey with a long bushy tail

marmot *n* any of various burrowing rodents of Europe, Asia, and North America. They are heavily built and have coarse fur

maroon¹ *vb* **1** to abandon someone in a deserted area, esp. on an island **2** to isolate in a helpless situation: *we're marooned here until the snow stops* ▷ **marooned** *adj*

maroon *vb* = abandon, leave, desert, strand, leave high and dry (*informal*)

maroon² *adj* dark purplish-red

marquee *n* a large tent used for a party, exhibition, etc.

marquess (mar-kwiss) *n* **1** (in the British Isles) a nobleman ranking between a duke and an earl **2** See **marquis**

marquetry *n, pl* **-quetries** a pattern of inlaid veneers of wood or metal used chiefly as ornamentation in furniture

marquis *n, pl* **-quises** or **-quis** (in various countries) a nobleman ranking above a count, corresponding to a British marquess

marram grass *n* a grass that grows on sandy shores: often planted to stabilize sand dunes

marriage *n* **1** the state or relationship of being married: *the institution of marriage* **2** the contract made by two people to live together in a partnership. Related adjectives: **connubial, nuptial 3** the ceremony formalizing this union; wedding **4** a close union or relationship: *the marriage of scientific knowledge and industry*

marriage *n* **1, 3** = wedding, match, nuptials, wedlock, matrimony

marriageable *adj* suitable for marriage, usually with reference to age

marrow *n* the fatty tissue that fills the cavities of bones

marry *vb* **-ries, -rying, -ried 1** to take (someone) as one's partner in marriage **2** to join or give in marriage **3** Also: **marry up** to fit together or unite; join: *their playing marries Irish traditional music and rock*

marry *vb* **2** = tie the knot (*informal*), wed, get hitched (*slang*) **3** = unite, join, link, bond, ally, merge, knit, unify

Mars *n* **1** the Roman god of war **2** the fourth planet from the sun

marsh *n* low poorly drained land that is wet, muddy, and sometimes flooded > **marshy** *adj*

> **marsh** *n* = swamp, bog, slough, fen, quagmire, morass, muskeg (*Canad*)

marshal *n* **1** (in some armies and air forces) an officer of the highest rank: *Field Marshall* **2** an officer who organizes or controls ceremonies or public events **3** *US* the chief police or fire officer in some states **4** (formerly in England) an officer of the royal family or court ▸ *vb* **-shalling, -shalled** *or US* **-shaling, -shaled 5** to arrange in order: *she marshalled her facts and came to a conclusion* **6** to assemble and organize people or vehicles in readiness for onward movement **7** to guide or lead, esp. in a ceremonious way: *she marshalled them towards the lecture theatre* > **marshalcy** *n*

> **marshal** *vb* **5, 6** = arrange, group, order, line up, organize, deploy, array, draw up **7** = conduct, take, lead, guide, steer, escort, shepherd, usher

marshalling yard *n railways* a place where railway wagons are shunted and made up into trains

marshmallow *n* a spongy pink or white sweet

marsh mallow *n* a plant that grows in salt marshes and has pale pink flowers. It was formerly used to make marshmallows

marsupial (mar-**soop**-ee-al) *n* **1** a mammal, such as a kangaroo or an opossum, the female of which carries her babies in a pouch at the front of her body until they reach a mature state ▸ *adj* **2** of or like a marsupial

mart *n* a market or trading centre

Martello tower *n* a round tower used for coastal defence, formerly much used in Europe

marten *n, pl* **-tens** *or* **-ten 1** any of several agile weasel-like mammals with bushy tails and golden-brown to blackish fur **2** the fur of these animals

martial *adj* of or characteristic of war, soldiers, or the military life: *martial music*

> **martial** *adj* = military, belligerent, warlike, bellicose

martial art *n* any of various philosophies and techniques of self-defence originating in China, Japan, and Korea, such as judo or karate

martial law *n* rule of law maintained by military forces in the absence of civil law

Martian (**marsh**-an) *adj* **1** of the planet Mars ▸ *n* **2** an inhabitant of Mars, in science fiction

martin *n* a bird of the swallow family with a square or slightly forked tail

martinet *n* a person who maintains strict discipline

martini *n* **1** (*often cap*) *trademark* an Italian vermouth **2** a cocktail of gin and vermouth

martyr *n* **1** a person who chooses to die rather than renounce his or her religious beliefs **2** a person who suffers greatly or dies for a cause

or belief **3 a martyr to** suffering constantly from: *a martyr to arthritis* ▸ *vb* **4** to make a martyr of > **martyrdom** *n*

marvel *vb* **-velling, -velled** *or US* **-veling, -veled 1** to be filled with surprise or wonder ▸ *n* **2** something that causes wonder

> **marvel** *vb* = be amazed, wonder, gape, be awed ▸ *n* = wonder, phenomenon, miracle, portent

marvellous *or US* **marvelous** *adj* **1** excellent or splendid: *a marvellous idea* **2** causing great wonder or surprise; extraordinary: *electricity is a marvellous thing* > **marvellously** *or US* **marvelously** *adv*

> **marvellous** *or* **marvelous** *adj* **1** = excellent, great, wonderful, brilliant, amazing, extraordinary, superb, spectacular, booshit (*Austral slang*), exo (*Austral slang*), sik (*Austral slang*), rad (*informal*), phat (*slang*), schmick (*Austral informal*); ≠ terrible

Marxism *n* the economic and political theories of Karl Marx (1818–83), German political philosopher, which argue that class struggle is the basic agency of historical change, and that capitalism will be superseded by communism > **Marxist** *n*, *adj*

marzipan *n* a mixture made from ground almonds, sugar, and egg whites that is put on top of cakes or used to make sweets

masala *n Indian cookery* a mixture of spices ground into a paste

masc. masculine

mascara *n* a cosmetic for darkening the eyelashes

mascot *n* a person, animal, or thing considered to bring good luck

masculine *adj* **1** possessing qualities or characteristics considered typical of or appropriate to a man **2** of men **3** *grammar* denoting a gender of nouns that includes some male animate things **4** *prosody* denoting a rhyme between pairs of single final stressed syllables > **masculinity** *n*

> **masculine** *adj* **1, 2** = male, manly, mannish, boyish, manlike, virile

mash *n* **1** a soft pulpy mass **2** *agriculture* bran, meal, or malt mixed with warm water and used as food for horses, cattle, or poultry **3** *Brit informal* mashed potatoes ▸ *vb* **4** to beat or crush into a mash > **mashed** *adj*

mask *n* **1** any covering for the whole or a part of the face worn for amusement, protection, or disguise **2** behaviour that hides one's true feelings: *his mask of detachment* **3** *surgery* a sterile gauze covering for the nose and mouth worn to minimize the spread of germs **4** a device placed over the nose and mouth to facilitate or prevent inhalation of a gas **5** a moulded likeness of a face or head, such as a death mask **6** the face or

m

head of an animal such as a fox ▸ *vb* **7** to cover with or put on a mask **8** to hide or disguise: *a high brick wall that masked the front of the building* **9** to cover so as to protect > **masked** *adj*

> **mask** *n* **2** = facade, disguise, front (*informal*), cover, screen, veil, guise, camouflage ▸ *vb* **8** = disguise, hide, conceal, obscure, cover (up), screen, blanket, veil

masochism (mass-oh-kiz-zum) *n* **1** *psychiatry* a condition in which pleasure, esp. sexual pleasure, is obtained from feeling pain or from being humiliated **2** a tendency to take pleasure from one's own suffering > **masochist** *n, adj* > **masochistic** *adj*

mason *n* a person skilled in building with stone

Mason *n* a Freemason

Masonic *adj* of Freemasons or Freemasonry

masonry *n* **1** stonework or brickwork **2** the craft of a mason

Masonry *n* Freemasonry

masque (mask) *n* a dramatic entertainment of the 16th to 17th centuries, consisting of dancing, dialogue, and song > **masquer** *n*

masquerade (mask-er-aid) *vb* **-ading, -aded** **1** to pretend to be someone or something else ▸ *n* **2** an attempt to keep secret the real identity or nature of something: *he was unable to keep up his masquerade as the war's victor* **3** a party at which the guests wear masks and costumes

mass *n* **1** a large body of something without a definite shape **2** a collection of the component parts of something: *a mass of fibres* **3** a large amount or number, as of people **4** the main part or majority **5** the size of a body; bulk **6** *physics* a physical quantity expressing the amount of matter in a body **7** (in painting or drawing) an area of unified colour, shade, or intensity ▸ *adj* **8** done or occurring on a large scale: *mass hysteria* **9** consisting of a mass or large number, esp. of people: *a mass meeting* ▸ *vb* **10** to join together into a mass > **massed** *adj*

> **mass** *n* **1** = piece, block, lump, chunk, hunk **2** = lot, collection, load (*informal*), pile, quantity, bunch, stack, heap **5** = size, matter, weight, extent, bulk, magnitude, greatness ▸ *adj* **8** = large-scale, general, widespread, extensive, universal, wholesale, indiscriminate ▸ *vb* = gather, assemble, accumulate, collect, rally, swarm, throng, congregate

Mass *n* **1** (in the Roman Catholic Church and certain other Christian churches) a service in which bread and wine are consecrated to represent the body and blood of Christ **2** a musical setting of parts of this service

massacre (mass-a-ker) *n* **1** the wanton or savage killing of large numbers of people **2** *informal* an overwhelming defeat ▸ *vb* **-cring, -cred 3** to kill people indiscriminately in large numbers **4** *informal* to defeat overwhelmingly

> **massacre** *n* **1** = slaughter, murder, holocaust, carnage, extermination, annihilation, butchery, blood bath ▸ *vb* **3** = slaughter, kill, murder, butcher, wipe out, exterminate, mow down, cut to pieces

massage (mass-ahzh) *n* **1** the kneading or rubbing of parts of the body to reduce pain or stiffness or help relaxation ▸ *vb* **-saging, -saged 2** to give a massage to **3** to manipulate statistics or evidence to produce a desired result

> **massage** *n* = rub-down, manipulation ▸ *vb* **2** = rub down, manipulate, knead **3** = manipulate, alter, distort, doctor, cook (*informal*), fix (*informal*), rig, fiddle (*informal*)

masseur (mass-ur) *or fem* **masseuse** (mass-**uhz**) *n* a person who gives massages

massif (mass-seef) *n* a series of connected masses of rock forming a mountain range

massive *adj* **1** (of objects) large, bulky, heavy, and usually solid **2** impressive or imposing **3** intensive or considerable: *a massive overdose* > **massively** *adv*

> **massive** *adj* **1** = huge, big, enormous, immense, hefty, gigantic, monumental (*informal*), mammoth, supersize; ≠ tiny

mass-market *adj* of, for, or appealing to a large number of people; popular: *mass-market newspapers*

mass media *pl n* the means of communication that reach large numbers of people, such as television, newspapers, and radio

mass-produce *vb* **-producing, -produced** to manufacture standardized goods on a large scale by extensive use of machinery > **mass-produced** *adj* > **mass-production** *n*

mast[1] *n* **1** *naut* a vertical pole for supporting sails, radar equipment, etc., above the deck of a ship **2** a tall upright pole used as an aerial for radio or television broadcasting: *a television mast* **3** **before the mast** *naut* as an apprentice seaman

mast[2] *n* the fruit of forest trees, such as beech or oak, used as food for pigs

mastectomy (mass-tek-tom-ee) *n, pl* **-mies** surgical removal of a breast

master *n* **1** the man who has authority over others, such as the head of a household, the employer of servants, or the owner of animals or, formerly, slaves **2** a person with exceptional skill at a certain thing: *a master of her craft* **3** a person who has complete control of a situation: *the master of his portfolio* **4** an original copy or tape from which duplicates are made **5** a craftsman fully qualified to practise his trade and to train others **6** a player of a game, esp. chess or bridge, who has won a specified number of tournament games **7** a highly regarded teacher or leader **8** a graduate holding a master's degree **9** the chief officer aboard a merchant ship **10** *chiefly Brit* a male teacher **11** the superior person or side in a contest **12** the heir apparent of a Scottish viscount or baron: *the Master of Ballantrae* ▸ *adj* **13** (of a craftsman) fully qualified to practise and to train others **14** overall or controlling: *master plan* **15** designating a mechanism that controls others: *master switch* **16** main or principal: *master bedroom* ▸ *vb* **17** to become thoroughly proficient in **18** to overcome or defeat

master *n* **1** = lord, ruler, commander, chief, director, manager, boss (*informal*), head; ≠ servant **2** = expert, maestro, ace (*informal*), genius, wizard, virtuoso, doyen, past master, fundi (*S African*); ≠ amateur **10** = teacher, tutor, instructor; ≠ student ▸ *adj* **16** = main, principal, chief, prime, foremost, predominant; ≠ lesser ▸ *vb* **17** = learn, understand, pick up, grasp, get the hang of (*informal*), know inside out, know backwards **18** = overcome, defeat, conquer, tame, triumph over, vanquish (*literary*); ≠ give in to

masterful *adj* **1** showing great skill **2** domineering or authoritarian > **masterfully** *adv*

master key *n* a key that opens all the locks of a set; passkey

masterly *adj* showing great skill; expert

masterly *adj* = skilful, expert, crack (*informal*), supreme, world-class, consummate, first-rate, masterful

mastermind *vb* **1** to plan and direct a complex task or project ▸ *n* **2** a person who plans and directs a complex task or project

mastermind *vb* = plan, manage, direct, organize, devise, conceive ▸ *n* = organizer, director, manager, engineer, brain(s) (*informal*), architect, planner

masterpiece *or* **masterwork** *n* **1** an outstanding work or performance **2** the most outstanding piece of work of an artist or craftsman

masterpiece *or* **masterwork** *n* = classic, tour de force (*French*), pièce de résistance (*French*), magnum opus, jewel

mastery *n, pl* -**teries 1** outstanding skill or expertise **2** complete power or control: *he had complete mastery over the country*

mastery *n* **1** = understanding, skill, know-how (*informal*), expertise, prowess, finesse, proficiency, virtuosity **2** = control, command, domination, superiority, supremacy, upper hand, ascendancy, mana (*NZ*), whip hand

mastic *n* **1** an aromatic resin obtained from a Mediterranean tree and used to make varnishes and lacquers **2** any of several putty-like substances used as a filler, adhesive, or seal

masticate *vb* -**cating**, -**cated** to chew food > **mastication** *n*

mastiff *n* a large powerful short-haired dog, usually fawn or brown with dark streaks

mastitis *n* inflammation of the breast

mastodon *n* an extinct elephant-like mammal

mastoid *adj* **1** shaped like a nipple or breast ▸ *n* **2** a nipple-like projection of bone behind the ear **3** *informal* mastoiditis

masturbate *vb* -**bating**, -**bated** to fondle one's own genitals, or those of someone else, to cause sexual pleasure > **masturbation** *n*

mat *n* **1** a thick flat piece of fabric used as a floor covering, a place to wipe one's shoes, etc. **2** a small pad of material used to protect a surface from heat or scratches from an object placed upon it **3** a large piece of thick padded material put on the floor as a surface for wrestling, gymnastics, etc. ▸ *vb* **matting**, **matted 4** to tangle or become tangled into a dense mass

matador *n* the bullfighter armed with a sword, who attempts to kill the bull

match¹ *n* **1** a formal game or sports event in which people or teams compete **2** a person or thing able to provide competition for another: *he has met his match* **3** a person or thing that resembles, harmonizes with, or is equivalent to another: *the colours aren't a perfect match, but they're close enough; white wine is not a good match for steak* **4** a person or thing that is an exact copy or equal of another **5** a partnership between two people, as in marriage **6** a person regarded as a possible partner in marriage: *for any number of men she would have been a good match* ▸ *vb* **7** to fit parts together **8** to resemble, harmonize with, or equal one another or something else: *our bedroom curtains match the bedspread; she walked at a speed that he could barely match* **9** to find a match for **10 match with** *or* **against A** to compare in order to determine which is the superior **B** to arrange a competition between > **matching** *adj*

match *n* **1** = game, test, competition, trial, tie, contest, fixture, bout **2** = equal, rival, peer, counterpart **5** = marriage, pairing, alliance, partnership ▸ *vb* **8** = correspond with, go with, fit with, harmonize with

match² *n* **1** a thin strip of wood or cardboard tipped with a chemical that ignites when scraped against a rough or specially treated surface **2** a fuse used to fire cannons' explosives

matchbox *n* a small box for holding matches

matchless *adj* unequalled

matchmaker *n* a person who introduces people in the hope that they will form a couple > **matchmaking** *n, adj*

matchstick *n* **1** the wooden part of a match ▸ *adj* **2** (esp. of drawn figures) thin and straight: *little matchstick men*

matchwood *n* **1** wood suitable for making matches **2** splinters

mate¹ *n* **1 A** *informal, chiefly Brit, Austral & NZ* a friend: often used as a term of address between males: *I spotted my mate Jimmy McCrae at the other end of the bar; that's all right, mate* **B** an associate or colleague: *a classmate; the governor's running mate* **2** the sexual partner of an animal **3** a marriage partner **4** *naut* any officer below the master on a commercial ship **5** (in some trades) an assistant: *a plumber's mate* **6** one of a pair of matching items ▸ *vb* **mating, mated 7** to pair (a male and female animal) or (of animals) to pair for breeding **8** to marry **9** to join as a pair

> **mate** *n* **1A** = friend, pal (*informal*), companion, buddy (*informal*), comrade, chum (*informal*), mucker (*Brit informal, old-fashioned*), crony, cobber (*Austral, NZ old-fashioned, informal*), E hoa (*NZ*) **1B** = colleague, associate, companion **3** = partner, lover, companion, spouse, consort, helpmeet, husband *or* wife **5** = assistant, subordinate, apprentice, helper, accomplice, sidekick (*informal*) ▸ *vb* **7** = pair, couple, breed

mate² *n, vb* **mating, mated** *chess* same as **checkmate**

material *n* **1** the substance of which a thing is made **2** cloth **3** ideas or notes that a finished work may be based on: *the material of the story resembles an incident in his own life* ▸ *adj* **4** concerned with or composed of physical matter or substance; not relating to spiritual or abstract things: *the material universe* **5** of or affecting economic or physical wellbeing: *material prosperity* **6** relevant or pertinent: *material evidence*

> **material** *n* **1** = substance, matter, stuff **2** = cloth, fabric, textile **3** = information, details, facts, notes, evidence, particulars, data, info (*informal*) ▸ *adj* **4** = physical, solid, substantial (*formal*), concrete, bodily, tangible, palpable, corporeal **6** = relevant, important, significant, essential, vital, serious, meaningful, applicable

materialism *n* **1** excessive interest in and desire for money or possessions **2** the belief that only the material world exists > **materialist** *n, adj* > **materialistic** *adj*

materialize *or* **-lise** *vb* **-lizing, -lized** *or* **-lising, -lised 1** to become fact; actually happen: *the promised pay rise never materialized* **2** to appear after being invisible: *trees materialized out of the gloom* **3** to take shape: *after hours of talks, a plan began to materialize* > **materialization** *or* **-lisation** *n*

materially *adv* to a significant extent: *we were not materially affected*

> **materially** *adv* = significantly, much, greatly, essentially, seriously, gravely, substantially; ≠ insignificantly

maternal *adj* **1** of or characteristic of a mother **2** related through the mother's side of the family: *his maternal uncle* > **maternally** *adv*

> **maternal** *adj* **1** = motherly, protective, nurturing, maternalistic

maternity *n* **1** motherhood **2** motherliness ▸ *adj* **3** relating to women during pregnancy or childbirth: *maternity leave*

> **maternity** *n* = motherhood, parenthood, motherliness

matey *adj Brit informal* friendly or intimate

math *n US & Canad informal* short for **mathematics**

mathematical *adj* **1** using, used in, or relating to mathematics **2** having the precision of mathematics > **mathematically** *adv*

mathematician *n* an expert or specialist in mathematics

mathematics *n* **1** a group of related sciences, including algebra, geometry, and calculus, which use a specialized notation to study number, quantity, shape, and space **2** numerical calculations involved in the solution of a problem

maths *n Brit & Austral informal* short for **mathematics**

matinee (mat-in-nay) *n* an afternoon performance of a play or film

matins *n* an early morning service in various Christian Churches

matriarch (mate-ree-ark) *n* the female head of a tribe or family > **matriarchal** *adj*

matriarchy *n, pl* **-chies** a form of social organization in which a female is head of the family or society, and descent and kinship are traced through the female line

matricide *n* **1** the act of killing one's mother **2** a person who kills his or her mother > **matricidal** *adj*

matriculate *vb* **-lating, -lated** to enrol or be enrolled in a college or university > **matriculation** *n*

matrimony *n* the state of being married > **matrimonial** *adj*

matrix (may-trix) *n, pl* **-trices** *or* **matrixes 1** the context or framework in which something is formed or develops: *a highly complex matrix of overlapping interests* **2** the rock in which fossils or pebbles are embedded **3** a mould, esp. one used in printing **4** *maths* a rectangular array of elements set out in rows and columns

matron *n* **1** a staid or dignified married woman **2** a woman in charge of the domestic or medical arrangements in an institution **3** *Brit* (formerly) the administrative head of the nursing staff in a hospital > **matronly** *adj*

matt *or* **matte** *adj* having a dull surface rather than a shiny one

matter *n* **1** the substance of which something, esp. a physical object, is made; material **2** substance that occupies space and has mass, as distinguished from substance that is mental or spiritual **3** substance of a specified type: *vegetable matter* **4** an event, situation, or subject: *a matter of taste; the break-in is a matter for the police* **5** a quantity or amount: *a matter of a few pounds*

6 the content of written or verbal material as distinct from its style or form **7** written material in general: *advertising matter* **8** a secretion or discharge, such as pus **9 for that matter** as regards that **10 no matter** regardless of; irrespective of: *you have to leave, no matter what she thinks* **11 the matter** wrong; the trouble: *there's nothing the matter* ▸ *vb* **12** to be of importance ▸ *interj* **no matter** **13** it is unimportant

> **matter** *n* **1** = substance, material, body, stuff **4** = situation, concern, business, question, event, subject, affair, incident ▸ *vb* = be important, make a difference, count, be relevant, make any difference, carry weight, cut any ice (*informal*), be of account

mattock *n* a type of large pick that has one flat, horizontal end to its blade, used for loosening soil

mattress *n* a large flat cushion with a strong cover, filled with cotton, foam rubber, etc., and often including coiled springs, used as a bed

maturation *n* the process of becoming mature

mature *adj* **1** fully developed physically or mentally; grown-up **2** (of plans or theories) fully considered and thought-out **3** sensible and balanced in personality and emotional behaviour **4** due or payable: *a mature insurance policy* **5** (of fruit, wine, or cheese) ripe or fully aged ▸ *vb* **-turing, -tured** **6** to make or become mature **7** (of bills or bonds) to become due for payment or repayment > **maturity** *n*

> **mature** *adj* **1** = grown-up, adult, of age, fully fledged, full-grown; ≠ immature **5** = matured, seasoned, ripe, mellow ▸ *vb* **6** = develop, grow up, bloom, blossom, come of age, age

maudlin *adj* foolishly or tearfully sentimental, esp. as a result of drinking

maul *vb* **1** to tear with the claws: *she was badly mauled by a lion* **2** to criticize a play, performance, etc., severely: *the film was mauled by the critics* **3** to handle roughly or clumsily ▸ *n* **4** *rugby* a loose scrum

> **maul** *vb* **1** = mangle, claw, lacerate, tear, mangulate (*Austral slang*) **3** = ill-treat, abuse, batter, molest, manhandle

maunder *vb* to move, talk, or act aimlessly or idly

mausoleum (maw-so-lee-um) *n* a large stately tomb

mauve *adj* light purple

maverick *n* **1** a person of independent or unorthodox views **2** (in the US and Canada) an unbranded stray calf ▸ *adj* **3** (of a person or his or her views) independent and unorthodox

> **maverick** *n* **1** = rebel, radical, dissenter, individualist, protester, eccentric, heretic, nonconformist; ≠ traditionalist ▸ *adj* = rebel, radical, dissenting, individualistic, eccentric, heretical, iconoclastic, nonconformist

maw *n* the mouth, throat, or stomach of an animal

mawkish *adj* foolishly or embarrassingly sentimental > **mawkishness** *n*

maxim *n* a brief expression of a general truth, principle, or rule of conduct

maximal *adj* of or being a maximum; the greatest possible

maximize or **-mise** *vb* **-mizing, -mized** or **-mising, -mised** to make as high or great as possible; increase to a maximum > **maximization** or **-misation** *n*

maximum *n, pl* **-mums** or **-ma** **1** the greatest possible amount or degree: *he gave the police the maximum of cooperation* **2** the greatest amount recorded, allowed, or reached: *keep to a maximum of two drinks a day* ▸ *adj* **3** of, being, or showing a maximum or maximums: *maximum speed*

> **maximum** *n* **2** = top, peak, ceiling, utmost, upper limit; ≠ minimum ▸ *adj* = greatest, highest, supreme, paramount, utmost, most, topmost; ≠ minimal

may *vb, past tense* **might** **1** used as an auxiliary to indicate that permission is requested by or granted to someone: *she may leave* **2** used as an auxiliary to indicate the possibility that something could happen: *problems which may well have tragic consequences* **3** used as an auxiliary to indicate ability or capacity, esp. in questions: *may I help you?* **4** used as an auxiliary to indicate a strong wish: *long may she reign*

May *n* the fifth month of the year

maybe *adv* perhaps

> **maybe** *adv* = perhaps, possibly, perchance (*archaic*)

Mayday *n* the international radio distress signal

mayfly *n, pl* **-flies** a short-lived insect with large transparent wings

mayhem *n* **1** any violent destruction or confusion: *a driver caused motorway mayhem* **2** *law* the maiming of a person

> **mayhem** *n* **1** = chaos, trouble, violence, disorder, destruction, confusion, havoc (*informal*), fracas

mayo *n informal* short for **mayonnaise**

mayonnaise *n* a thick creamy sauce made from egg yolks, oil, and vinegar

mayor *n* the civic head of a municipal council in many countries > **mayoral** *adj*

mayoralty *n, pl* **-ties** the office or term of office of a mayor

mayoress *n* **1** *chiefly Brit* the wife of a mayor **2** a female mayor

maypole *n* a tall pole around which people dance during May-Day celebrations

maze *n* **1** a complex network of paths or passages designed to puzzle people who try and find their way through or out of it **2** a puzzle in

m

which the player must trace a path through a complex network of lines without touching or crossing any of them **3** any confusing network or system: *a maze of regulations*

maze *n* **3** = web, confusion, tangle, labyrinth, imbroglio, complex network

mazurka *n* **1** a lively Polish dance in triple time **2** music for this dance
MB 1 Bachelor of Medicine **2** Manitoba
MBE (in Britain) Member of the Order of the British Empire
Mc moscovium
MC 1 Master of Ceremonies **2** (in the US) Member of Congress **3** (in Britain) Military Cross
MD 1 Doctor of Medicine **2** Managing Director **3** Maryland
me *pron* (objective) **1** refers to the speaker or writer: *that hurts me* ▸ *n* **2** *informal* the personality of the speaker or writer or something that expresses it: *the real me*
ME 1 Maine **2** Middle English
mead *n* a wine-like alcoholic drink made from honey, often with spices added
meadow *n* **1** a grassy field used for hay or for grazing animals **2** a low-lying piece of grassland, often near a river

meadow *n* = field, pasture, grassland, lea (*poetic*)

meadowsweet *n* a plant with dense heads of small fragrant cream-coloured flowers
meagre *or US* **meager** *adj* **1** not enough in amount or extent: *meagre wages* **2** thin or emaciated
meal¹ *n* **1** any of the regular occasions, such as breakfast or dinner, when food is served and eaten **2** the food served and eaten **3 make a meal of** *informal* to perform a task with unnecessarily great effort
meal² *n* **1** the edible part of a grain or bean pulse (excluding wheat) ground to a coarse powder **2** *Scot* oatmeal **3** *chiefly US* maize flour ▸ **mealy** *adj*
mealie *or* **mielie** *n* (*often pl*) *S African* same as **maize**
mealy-mouthed *adj* unwilling or afraid to speak plainly
mean¹ *vb* **meaning, meant 1** to intend to convey or express: *what do you mean by that?* **2** to denote, represent, or signify: *a red light means 'stop!'; 'gravid' is a technical term meaning 'pregnant'* **3** to intend: *I meant to phone you earlier, but didn't have time* **4** to say or do in all seriousness: *the boss means what she says* **5** to have the importance specified: *music means everything to him* **6** to destine or design for a certain person or purpose: *those sweets weren't meant for you* **7** to produce, cause, or result in: *major road works will mean long traffic delays* **8** to foretell: *those black clouds mean rain* **9 mean well** to have good intentions

mean *vb* **1** = imply, suggest, intend, hint at, insinuate **2** = signify, indicate, represent, express, stand for, convey, spell out, symbolize **3** = intend, want, plan, expect, design, aim, wish, think

mean² *adj* **1** not willing to give or use much of something, esp. money: *she was noticeably mean; don't be mean with the butter* **2** unkind or spiteful: *a mean trick* **3** *informal* ashamed: *she felt mean about not letting the children stay out late* **4** *informal, chiefly US, Canad & Austral* bad-tempered or vicious **5** shabby and poor: *a mean little room* **6** *slang* excellent or skilful: *he plays a mean trumpet* **7 no mean A** of high quality: *no mean player* **B** difficult: *no mean feat* > **meanly** *adv* > **meanness** *n*

mean *adj* **1** = miserly, stingy, parsimonious, niggardly, mercenary, penny-pinching, ungenerous, tight-fisted, snoep (*S African informal*); ≠ generous

mean³ *n* **1** the middle point, state, or course between limits or extremes **2** *maths* **A** the mid-point between the highest and lowest number in a set **B** the average ▸ *adj* **3** intermediate in size or quantity **4** occurring halfway between extremes or limits; average

mean *n* **1, 2** = average, middle, balance, norm, midpoint ▸ *adj* = average, middle, standard

meander (mee-and-er) *vb* **1** (of a river, road, etc.) to follow a winding course **2** to wander without definite aim or direction ▸ *n* **3** a curve or bend, as in a river **4** a winding course or movement
meaning *n* **1** the sense or significance of a word, sentence, or symbol **2** the inner, symbolic, or true interpretation or message: *the meaning of the New Testament*

meaning *n* **1** = significance, message, substance, drift, connotation, gist

meaningful *adj* **1** serious and important: *a meaningful relationship* **2** intended to express a feeling or opinion: *a meaningful pause*

meaningful *adj* **1** = significant, important, material, useful, relevant, valid, worthwhile, purposeful; ≠ trivial

meaningless *adj* having no meaning or purpose; futile

meaningless *adj* = nonsensical, senseless, inconsequential, inane; ≠ worthwhile

means test *n* the checking of a person's income to determine whether he or she qualifies for financial aid > **means-tested** *adj*
meantime *n* **1** the intervening period: *in the meantime* ▸ *adv* **2** same as **meanwhile**

meantime *adv* = at the same time, simultaneously, concurrently

meanwhile *adv* **1** during the intervening period **2** at the same time, esp. in another place

meanwhile *adv* **1** = for now, in the interim

measles *n* a highly contagious viral disease common in children, characterized by fever and a rash of small red spots. See also **German measles**

measly *adj* **-slier, -sliest** **1** *informal* too small in quantity or value **2** having or relating to measles

measure *n* **1** the size, quantity, or degree of something, as discovered by measurement or calculation **2** a device for measuring distance, volume, etc., such as a graduated scale or container **3** a system or unit of measurement: *the joule is a measure of energy* **4** an amount of alcoholic drink, esp. that served as standard in a bar **5** degree or extent: *a measure of success* **6** a particular action intended to achieve an effect: *radical measures are needed to cut unemployment* **7** a legislative bill, act, or resolution **8** *music* same as **bar¹** (sense 9) **9** *prosody* poetic rhythm or metre **10** *prosody* a metrical foot **11** *old-fashioned* a dance **12 for good measure** as an extra precaution or beyond requirements ▸ *vb* **-suring, -sured** **13** to determine the size, amount, etc., of by measurement: *he measured the room for a new carpet* **14** to indicate or record the size, speed, force, etc., of: *this dial measures the pressure in the pipe* **15** to have the size, quantity, etc., specified: *the room measures six feet* **16** to estimate or assess: *you cannot measure intelligence purely by exam results* **17** to function as a measurement of: *the ohm measures electrical resistance* **18** to bring into competition or conflict with: *he measured his strength against that of his opponent* > **measurable** *adj*

measure *n* **1** = quantity, share, amount, allowance, portion, quota, ration, allotment **2** = gauge, rule, scale, metre, ruler, yardstick **6** = action, act, step, procedure, means, control, initiative, manoeuvre **7** = law, act, bill, legislation, resolution, statute ▸ *vb* **13, 14, 16** = quantify, determine, assess, weigh, calculate, evaluate, compute, gauge

measured *adj* **1** slow or stately **2** carefully considered; deliberate

measured *adj* **1** = steady, even, slow, regular, dignified, stately, solemn, leisurely **2** = considered, reasoned, studied, calculated, deliberate, sober, well-thought-out

measurement *n* **1** the act or process of measuring **2** an amount, extent, or size determined by measuring **3** a system or unit used for measuring: *the kilometre is the standard measurement of distance in most countries* **4 measurements** the size of a person's waist, chest, hips, etc., used when buying clothes

measurement *n* **1** = calculation, assessment, evaluation, valuation, computation, calibration, mensuration

meat *n* **1** the flesh of animals used as food **2** the essence or gist: *get to the meat of your lecture as quickly as possible* > **meatless** *adj*

meaty *adj* **meatier, meatiest** **1** of, like, or full of meat **2** heavily built; fleshy or brawny **3** full of import or interest: *a meaty historical drama*

Mecca *n* **1** the holy city of Islam **2** a place that attracts many visitors

mechanic *n* a person skilled in maintaining or operating machinery or motors

mechanical *adj* **1** made, performed, or operated by machinery **2** able to understand how machines work and how to repair or maintain them **3** **A** (of an action) done without thought or feeling **B** (of a task) not requiring any thought; routine or repetitive **4** of or involving the science of mechanics > **mechanically** *adv*

mechanical *adj* **1** = automatic, automated, mechanized, power-driven, motor-driven; ≠ manual **3** = unthinking, routine, automatic, instinctive, involuntary, impersonal, cursory, perfunctory

mechanics *n* **1** the scientific study of motion and force **2** the science of designing, constructing, and operating machines ▸ *pl n* **3** the technical aspects of something

mechanism *n* **1** a system of moving parts that performs some function, esp. in a machine **2** any mechanical device or part of such a device **3** a process or technique: *the body's defence mechanisms* > **mechanistic** *adj*

mechanism *n* **1** = machine, device, tool, instrument, appliance, apparatus, contrivance **3** = process, way, means, system, operation, agency (*old-fashioned*), method, technique

mechanize *or* **-nise** *vb* **-nizing, -nized** *or* **-nising, -nised** **1** to equip a factory or industry with machinery **2** to make mechanical or automatic **3** *military* to equip an army with armoured vehicles > **mechanization** *or* **-nisation** *n*

med. **1** medical **2** medicine **3** medieval **4** medium

medal *n* a small flat piece of metal bearing an inscription or image, given as an award or in commemoration of some outstanding event

medallion *n* **1** a disc-shaped ornament worn on a chain round the neck **2** a large medal **3** a circular decorative device used in architecture

medallist *or* US **medalist** *n* *chiefly sport* a winner of a medal or medals

meddle *vb* **-dling, -dled** to interfere annoyingly > **meddler** *n* > **meddlesome** *adj*

media *n* **1** a plural of **medium** **2 the media** the mass media collectively ▸ *adj* **3** of or relating to the mass media: *media hype*

mediaeval (med-ee-**eve**-al) *adj* same as **medieval**

m

m

medial (mee-dee-al) *adj* of or situated in the middle > **medially** *adv*

median *n* **1** a middle point, plane, or part **2** *geom* a straight line joining one corner of a triangle to the midpoint of the opposite side **3** *statistics* the middle value in a frequency distribution, below and above which lie values with equal total frequencies

mediate (mee-dee-ate) *vb* **-ating, -ated 1** to intervene between people or in a dispute in order to bring about agreement **2** to resolve differences by mediation **3** to be changed slightly by (an experience or event): *clients' attitudes to social workers have often been mediated by their past experiences* > **mediation** *n* > **mediator** *n*

> **mediate** *vb* **1** = intervene, step in (*informal*), intercede, referee, umpire, reconcile, arbitrate, conciliate

medic *n informal* a doctor, medical orderly, or medical student

medical *adj* **1** of or relating to the science of medicine or to the treatment of patients without surgery ▸ *n* **2** *informal* a medical examination > **medically** *adv*

medicate *vb* **-cating, -cated 1** to treat a patient with a medicine **2** to add a medication to a bandage, shampoo, etc. > **medicative** *adj*

medication *n* **1** treatment with drugs or remedies **2** a drug or remedy

medicinal (mid-**diss**-in-al) *adj* relating to or having therapeutic properties > **medicinally** *adv*

medicine *n* **1** any substance used in treating or alleviating the symptoms of disease **2** the science of preventing, diagnosing, or curing disease **3** any nonsurgical branch of medical science **4 take one's medicine** to accept a deserved punishment

> **medicine** *n* **1** = remedy, drug, cure, prescription, medication, nostrum, medicament

medicine man *n* (among certain peoples) a person believed to have supernatural powers of healing

medieval *or* **mediaeval** (med-ee-**eve**-al) *adj* **1** of, relating to, or in the style of the Middle Ages **2** *informal* old-fashioned or primitive > **medievalist** *or* **mediaevalist** *n*

mediocre (mee-dee-**oak**-er) *adj* not very high quality; average or second rate > **mediocrity** (mee-dee-**ok**-rit-ee) *n*

> **mediocre** *adj* = second-rate, average, ordinary, indifferent, middling, pedestrian, inferior, so-so (*informal*), half-pie (NZ *informal*); ≠ excellent

meditate *vb* **-tating, -tated 1** to think about something deeply: *he meditated on the problem* **2** to reflect deeply on spiritual matters **3** to plan, consider, or think of doing something > **meditative** *adj* > **meditator** *n*

meditation *n* **1** the act of meditating; reflection **2** contemplation of spiritual matters, esp. as a religious practice

> **meditation** *n* **1** = reflection, thought, study, musing, pondering, contemplation, rumination, cogitation

medium *adj* **1** midway between extremes of size, amount, or degree: *fry over a medium heat; a man of medium height* ▸ *n, pl* **-dia** *or* **-diums 2** a middle state, degree, or condition: *the happy medium* **3** a substance which has a particular effect or can be used for a particular purpose: *linseed oil is used as a thinning medium for oil paint* **4** a means for communicating information or news to the public **5** a person who can supposedly communicate with the dead **6** the substance or surroundings in which an organism naturally lives or grows **7** *art* the category of a work of art, as determined by its materials: *his works in the photographic medium*

> **medium** *adj* = average, mean, middle, middling, fair, intermediate, midway, mediocre; ≠ extraordinary ▸ *n* **2** = middle, mean, centre, average, compromise, midpoint **5** = spiritualist, seer, clairvoyant, fortune teller, channeller

medium wave *n* a radio wave with a wavelength between 100 and 1000 metres

medlar *n* the apple-like fruit of a small Eurasian tree, which is not edible until it has begun to decay

medley *n* **1** a mixture of various elements **2** a musical composition consisting of various tunes arranged as a continuous whole **3** *swimming* a race in which a different stroke is used for each length

medulla (mid-**dull**-la) *n, pl* **-las** *or* **-lae** (-lee) **1** *anatomy* the innermost part of an organ or structure **2** *anatomy* the lower stalklike section of the brain **3** *botany* the central pith of a plant stem > **medullary** *adj*

meek *adj* quiet, and ready to do what other people say > **meekly** *adv*

meerkat *n* a South African mongoose

meerschaum (meer-shum) *n* **1** a white, heat-resistant, claylike mineral **2** a tobacco pipe with a bowl made of this mineral

meet¹ *vb* **meeting, met 1** to be in or come to the same place at the same time as, either by arrangement or by accident: *I met him in town* **2** to come into contact with something or each other: *his head met the ground with a crack; the town where the Rhine and the Moselle meet* **3** to come to or be at the place of arrival of: *he met his train at noon* **4** to make the acquaintance of, or be introduced to, someone or each other **5** (of people) to gather together for a purpose: *the board meets once a week* **6** to compete, play, or fight against **7** to cope with effectively; satisfy: *they were unable to meet his demands* **8** to pay for (something): *it is difficult to* meet the cost of medical insurance **9** Also: **meet with** to experience or suffer: *he met his death at the Somme* **10 there is more to this than meets the eye** there is more involved in this than appears ▶ *n* **11** a sports meeting **12** *chiefly Brit* the assembly of hounds and huntsmen prior to a hunt

> **meet** *vb* **1** = encounter, come across, run into, happen on, find, contact, confront, bump into (*informal*); ≠ avoid **2** = converge, join, cross, touch, connect, come together, link up, intersect; ≠ diverge **5** = gather, collect, assemble, get together, come together, muster, convene, congregate; ≠ disperse **7** = fulfil, match (up to), answer, satisfy, discharge, comply with, come up to, conform to; ≠ fall short of **9** = experience, face, suffer, bear, go through, encounter, endure, undergo

meet² *adj archaic* proper, fitting, or correct: *meet and proper*

meeting *n* **1** an act of coming together: *a meeting was fixed for the following day* **2** an assembly or gathering of people: *the meeting voted in favour* **3** a sporting competition, as of athletes, or of horse racing

> **meeting** *n* **1** = encounter, introduction, confrontation, engagement, rendezvous, tryst, assignation **2** = conference, gathering, assembly, congress, session, convention, get-together (*informal*), reunion, hui (NZ)

meg *n computers informal* short for **megabyte**
mega- *combining form* **1** denoting 10⁶: *megawatt* **2** (in computer technology) denoting 2²⁰ (1 048 576): *megabyte* **3** large or great: *megalith* **4** *informal* very great: *megastar*
megabyte *n computers* 2²⁰ or 1 048 576 bytes
megahertz *n, pl* **megahertz** one million hertz; one million cycles per second
megalith *n* a very large stone, esp. one forming part of a prehistoric monument > **megalithic** *adj*
megalomania *n* **1** an obsessional delusion of power and importance **2** *informal* a craving for power > **megalomaniac** *adj, n*
megaphone *n* a funnel-shaped instrument used to make someone's voice sound louder, esp. out of doors
megapixel *n* one million pixels: used to describe the resolution of digital images
megapode *n* any of various ground-living birds of Australia, New Guinea, and adjacent islands. Their eggs incubate in mounds of sand or rotting vegetation
megaton *n* **1** one million tons **2** an explosive power, esp. of a nuclear weapon, equal to the power of one million tons of TNT
meh *interj* expression of indifference or boredom
melaleuca (mel-a-loo-ka) *n* an Australian shrub or tree with a white trunk and black branches

melancholia (mel-an-kole-lee-a) *n* an old name for **depression** (sense 1)
melancholy (mel-an-kol-lee) *n, pl* **-cholies** **1** a tendency to gloominess or depression **2** a sad, thoughtful state of mind ▶ *adj* **3** characterized by, causing, or expressing sadness > **melancholic** *adj, n*

> **melancholy** *n* = sadness, depression, misery, gloom, sorrow, unhappiness, despondency, dejection; ≠ happiness ▶ *adj* = sad, depressed, miserable, gloomy, glum, mournful, despondent, dispirited; ≠ happy

melange (may-lahnzh) *n* a mixture or assortment: *a melange of historical facts and legends*
melanin *n* a black pigment present in the hair, skin, and eyes of humans and animals
melee (mel-lay) *n* a noisy riotous fight or crowd
mellifluous (mel-lif-flew-uss) *adj* (of sound) smooth and sweet
mellow *adj* **1** (esp. of colours, light, or sounds) soft or rich: *the mellow stillness of a sunny Sunday morning* **2** kind-hearted, esp. through maturity or old age **3** genial and relaxed, for instance through the effects of alcohol or good food **4** (esp. of fruits) sweet, ripe, and full-flavoured **5** (esp. of wine or cheese) having developed a full smooth flavour as a result of maturing **6** (of soil) soft and loamy ▶ *vb* **7** to make or become mellow **8** (foll. by *out*) to make or become calm and relaxed

> **mellow** *adj* **4, 5** = full-flavoured, rich, sweet, delicate; ≠ unripe ▶ *vb* **7** = season, develop, improve, ripen **8** = relax, improve, settle, calm, mature, soften, sweeten

melodic (mel-lod-ik) *adj* **1** of or relating to melody **2** tuneful and pleasant to the ear; melodious > **melodically** *adv*
melodious (mel-lode-ee-uss) *adj* **1** pleasant to the ear: *he gave a melodious chuckle* **2** tuneful and melodic > **melodiousness** *n*
melodrama *n* **1** a play or film full of extravagant action and emotion **2** overdramatic emotion or behaviour > **melodramatic** *adj* > **melodramatics** *pl n*
melody *n, pl* **-dies** **1** *music* a succession of notes forming a distinctive sequence; tune **2** sounds that are pleasant because of their tone or arrangement, esp. words of poetry

> **melody** *n* **1** = tune, song, theme, air, music, strain **2** = tunefulness, harmony, musicality, euphony, melodiousness

melon *n* any of various large edible fruits which have a hard rind and juicy flesh
melt *vb* **1** to change from a solid into a liquid as a result of the action of heat **2** to dissolve: *these sweets melt in the mouth* **3** Also: **melt away** to diminish and finally disappear; fade away: *he felt his inner doubts melt away* **4** to blend so that it is impossible to tell where one thing ends and

m

another begins: *they melted into the trees until the gamekeeper had passed* **5** to make or become emotional or sentimental; soften: *she melted into tears* ▶ *n* **6** a quantity of a melted substance **7** *US & Canad* a sandwich containing and melted cheese: *a tuna melt* > **meltingly** *adv*

melt *vb* **1, 2** = dissolve, run, soften, fuse, thaw, defrost, liquefy, unfreeze **5** = soften, relax, disarm, mollify

meltdown *n* **1** (in a nuclear reactor) the melting of the fuel rods, with the possible escape of radioactivity **2** *informal* a sudden disastrous failure **3** *informal* a process of irreversible decline

member *n* **1** a person who belongs to a group or organization such as a club or political party **2** any part of a plant or animal, such as a limb or petal **3** a Member of Parliament: *the member for Glasgow Central* ▶ *adj* **4** (of a country or group) belonging to an organization or alliance: *a summit of the member countries' heads of state is due*

member *n* **1** = representative, associate, supporter, fellow, subscriber, comrade, disciple

Member of Parliament *n* a person who has been elected to the House of Commons or the equivalent assembly in another country

membership *n* **1** the members of an organization collectively **2** the number of members **3** the state of being a member

membership *n* **1** = members, body, associates, fellows **3** = participation, belonging, fellowship, enrolment

membrane *n* a thin flexible tissue that covers, lines, or connects plant and animal organs or cells > **membranous** *adj*

meme *n* a video, photo, or story that is spread widely on the internet, often altered by users for humorous effect

memento *n*, *pl* **-tos** *or* **-toes** something that reminds one of past events; a souvenir

memo *n*, *pl* **memos** short for **memorandum**

memoir (mem-wahr) *n* a biography or historical account based on personal knowledge

memoir *n* = account, life, record, journal, essay, biography, narrative, monograph

memorable *adj* worth remembering or easily remembered because it is very special or important > **memorably** *adv*

memorable *adj* = noteworthy, celebrated, historic, striking, famous, significant, remarkable, notable; ≠ forgettable

memorandum *n*, *pl* **-dums** *or* **-da** **1** a note sent by one person or department to another within a business organization **2** a note of things to be remembered **3** *law* a short written summary of the terms of a transaction

memorandum *n* **1, 2** = note, minute, message, communication, reminder, memo, jotting, email *or* e-mail

memorial *n* **1** something, such as a statue, built or displayed to preserve the memory of someone or something: *a war memorial* ▶ *adj* **2** in memory of someone or something: *a memorial service*

memorial *n* = monument, shrine, plaque, cenotaph ▶ *adj* = commemorative, remembrance, monumental

memorize *or* **-rise** *vb* **-rizing, -rized** *or* **-rising, -rised** to commit to memory; learn by heart

memory *n*, *pl* **-ries** **1** the ability of the mind to store and recall past sensations, thoughts, and knowledge: *she can do it from memory* **2** the sum of everything retained by the mind **3** a particular recollection of an event or person: *he started awake with a sudden memory* **4** the length of time one can remember: *my memory doesn't go that far back* **5** commemoration: *in memory of our leader* **6** a person's reputation after death: *a conductor of fond memory* **7** a part of a computer in which information is stored

memory *n* **1** = recall, mind, retention, ability to remember, powers of recall, powers of retention **3** = recollection, reminder, reminiscence, impression, echo, remembrance **5** = commemoration, respect, honour, recognition, tribute, remembrance, observance

memory card *n* a small removable data storage device, used in mobile phones, digital cameras, etc.

Memory Stick *n computers* **1** a standard format for memory cards **2 memory stick** also: **USB memory stick** same as **USB drive**

men *n* the plural of **man**

menace *vb* **-acing, -aced** **1** to threaten with violence or danger ▶ *n* **2** a threat; a source of danger **3** *informal* an annoying person or thing; nuisance > **menacing** *adj*

menace *vb* = bully, threaten, intimidate, terrorize, frighten, scare ▶ *n* **2** = threat, warning, intimidation, ill-omen, ominousness **3** = nuisance, plague (*informal*), pest, annoyance, troublemaker

ménage (may-nahzh) *n* a household

menagerie (min-naj-er-ee) *n* a collection of wild animals kept for exhibition

mend *vb* **1** to repair something broken or not working **2** to heal or recover: *a wound like that will take a while to mend* **3** (esp. of behaviour) to improve; make or become better: *if you don't mend your ways you'll be in serious trouble* ▶ *n* **4** a mended area, esp. on a garment **5 on the mend** regaining one's health

mend *vb* **1** = repair, fix, restore, renew, patch up, renovate, refit, retouch **2** = heal, improve, recover, get better, be all right, be cured, recuperate, pull through **3** = improve, reform, correct, revise, amend, rectify, ameliorate, emend ▸ *n* **5 on the mend** = convalescent, improving, recovering, getting better, recuperating

mendacity *n* the tendency to be untruthful › **mendacious** *adj*

mendicant *adj* **1** begging **2** (of a monk, nun, etc.) dependent on charity for food ▸ *n* **3** a mendicant friar **4** a beggar

menhir (men-hear) *n* a single standing stone, dating from prehistoric times

menial (mean-nee-al) *adj* **1** involving or doing boring work of low status ▸ *n* **2** a domestic servant

meningitis (men-in-jite-iss) *n* inflammation of the meninges, caused by infection and causing severe headache, fever, and rigidity of the neck muscles

meniscus *n, pl* **-nisci** *or* **-niscuses 1** the curved upper surface of a liquid standing in a tube, produced by the surface tension **2** a crescent-shaped lens

menopause *n* the period during which a woman's menstrual cycle ceases, normally at an age of 45 to 50 › **menopausal** *adj*

menstrual *adj* of or relating to menstruation: *the menstrual cycle*

menstruate *vb* **-ating, -ated** to undergo menstruation

menstruation *n* the approximately monthly discharge of blood from the womb in women of childbearing age who are not pregnant

mensuration *n* **1** the study of the measurement of geometric magnitudes such as length **2** the act or process of measuring

mental *adj* **1** of, done by, or involving the mind: *mental alertness* **2** done in the mind without using speech or writing: *mental arithmetic* **3** concerned with the care of people with mental health problems: *a mental hospital* **4** *slang* extremely foolish or eccentric › **mentally** *adv*

mental *adj* **1** = intellectual, rational, theoretical, cognitive, brain, conceptual, cerebral

mentality *n, pl* **-ties** a particular attitude or way of thinking: *the traditional civil service mentality*

mentality *n* = attitude, character, personality, psychology (*informal*), make-up, outlook, disposition, cast of mind

menthol *n* an organic compound found in peppermint oil and used as an antiseptic, decongestant, and painkiller › **mentholated** *adj*

mention *vb* **1** to refer to or speak about briefly or incidentally **2** to include in a report, list, etc., because of high standards or an outstanding achievement: *the hotel is mentioned in all the guidebooks; he was twice mentioned in dispatches during the war* **3 not to mention (something)** to say nothing of (something too obvious to mention) ▸ *n* **4** a slight reference or allusion **5** a recognition or acknowledgment of high quality or an outstanding achievement

mention *vb* **1** = refer to, point out, bring up, state, reveal, declare, disclose, intimate ▸ *n* **4** = reference, observation, indication, remark, allusion **5** = acknowledgment, recognition, tribute, citation, honourable mention

mentor *n* an adviser or guide

mentor *n* = guide, teacher, coach, adviser, tutor, instructor, counsellor, guru

menu *n* **1** a list of dishes served at a meal or that can be ordered in a restaurant **2** a list of options displayed on a visual display unit from which the operator can choose

menu *n* **1** = bill of fare, tariff (*chiefly Brit*), set menu, table d'hôte, carte du jour (*French*)

meow *or* **miaow** (mee-ow) *n* **1** the characteristic high-pitched cry of a cat; mew ▸ *vb* **2** to make such a sound

MEP Member of the European Parliament

mercantile *adj* of trade or traders; commercial

mercenary *n, pl* **-naries 1** a soldier who fights for a foreign army for money ▸ *adj* **2** motivated by greed or the desire for gain: *calculating and mercenary businesspeople* **3** of or relating to a mercenary or mercenaries

merchandise *n* **1** goods for buying, selling, or trading with; commodities ▸ *vb* **-dising, -dised 2** to engage in the commercial purchase and sale of goods or services; trade

merchandise *n* = goods, produce, stock, products, commodities, wares

merchant *n* **1** a person who buys and sells goods in large quantities and usually of one type: *a wine merchant* **2** *chiefly Scot, US & Canad* a person engaged in retail trade; shopkeeper **3** *slang* a person dealing in something undesirable: *a gossip merchant* ▸ *adj* **4** of ships involved in commercial trade or their crews: *a merchant sailor; the British merchant fleet*

merchant *n* **1, 2** = tradesperson, dealer, trader, broker, retailer, supplier, seller, salesman *or* woman *or* person

merchant bank *n* a financial institution that deals primarily with foreign trade and business finance › **merchant banker** *n*

merchantman *n, pl* **-men** a merchant ship

merchant navy *n* the ships or crew engaged in a nation's commercial shipping

merciful *adj* **1** (of an act or event) giving relief from pain or suffering: *after months of illness, death*

m

came as a merciful release **2** showing or giving mercy; compassionate > **mercifully** adv

merciless adj without mercy; pitiless, cruel, or heartless > **mercilessly** adv

mercurial (mer-**cure**-ee-al) adj **1** lively and unpredictable: a mercurial and temperamental chess player **2** of or containing mercury

mercury n, pl **-ries** chem a silvery toxic metal, the only element liquid at normal temperatures, used in thermometers, barometers, lamps, and dental amalgams. Symbol: **Hg**

Mercury n **1** Roman myth the messenger of the gods **2** the second smallest planet and the one nearest the sun

mercy n, pl **-cies 1** compassionate treatment of, or attitude towards, an offender or enemy who is in one's power **2** they threw themselves on the King's mercy **3** a relieving or welcome occurrence or act: it was a mercy you turned up when you did **4 at the mercy of** in the power of ▸ adj **5** done or undertaken in an attempt to relieve suffering or bring help: a mercy mission

> **mercy** n **1, 2** = compassion, pity, forgiveness, grace, kindness, clemency, leniency, forbearance; ≠ cruelty **3** = blessing, boon, godsend

mere[1] adj nothing more than: the election in Slovenia seems a mere formality > **merely** adv

> **mere** adj = simple, nothing more than, common, plain, pure

mere[2] n Brit dialect or archaic a lake

meretricious adj superficially or garishly attractive but of no real value

merganser (mer-**gan**-ser) n, pl **-sers** or **-ser** a large crested marine diving duck

merge vb **merging, merged 1** to combine, esp. so as to become part of a larger whole: the two airlines merged in 1983 **2** to blend gradually, without any sudden change being apparent: late afternoon merged imperceptibly into early evening

> **merge** vb **1** = combine, blend, fuse, amalgamate, unite, join, mix, mingle; ≠ separate **2** = melt, blend, mingle

merger n the act of merging, esp. the combination of two or more companies

> **merger** n = union, fusion, consolidation, amalgamation, combination, coalition, incorporation

meridian n **1** one of the imaginary lines joining the north and south poles at right angles to the equator, designated by degrees of longitude from 0° at Greenwich to 180° **2** (in acupuncture, etc.) any of various channels through which vital energy is believed to circulate round the body

meringue (mer-**rang**) n **1** stiffly beaten egg whites mixed with sugar and baked **2** a small cake made from this mixture

merino n, pl **-nos 1** a sheep with long fine wool, originally reared in Spain **2** the yarn made from this wool

merit n **1** worth or superior quality; excellence: the film had two sequels, neither of much merit **2** an admirable or advantageous quality: the relative merits of film and video as a medium of communication **3** have the merit of to have a positive feature or advantage that the alternatives do not have: the first version has the merit of being short **4 on its merits** on its intrinsic qualities or virtues ▸ vb **-riting, -rited 5** to be worthy of; deserve: the issue merits much fuller discussion

> **merit** n **2** = advantage, value, quality, worth, strength, asset, virtue, strong point ▸ vb = deserve, warrant, be entitled to, earn, have a right to, be worthy of

meritocracy (mer-it-**tok**-rass-ee) n, pl **-cies** a social system in which power is held by the most talented or intelligent people > **meritocrat** n > **meritocratic** adj

meritorious adj deserving praise for being good or worthwhile

merlin n a small falcon with dark plumage

mermaid n an imaginary sea creature with a woman's head and upper body and a fish's tail > **merman** masc n

merry adj **-rier, -riest 1** cheerful and jolly **2** Brit & Austral informal slightly drunk **3 make merry** to take part in noisy cheerful celebrations or fun > **merrily** adv > **merriment** n

> **merry** adj **1** = cheerful, happy, carefree, jolly, festive, joyous, convivial, blithe (archaic); ≠ gloomy **2** = tipsy, happy, mellow, tiddly (rare, chiefly Brit), squiffy (Brit informal, old-fashioned)

merry-go-round n **1** a fairground roundabout **2** a whirl of activity

merrymaking n noisy cheerful celebrations or fun > **merrymaker** n

mesdames (may-**dam**) n the plural of **madame, madam** (sense 1)

mesdemoiselles (maid-mwah-**zel**) n the plural of **mademoiselle**

mesh n **1** a material resembling a net made from intersecting strands with a space between each strand **2** an open space between the strands of a net or network: the minimum permitted size of fishing net mesh **3** (often pl) the strands surrounding these spaces **4** anything that ensnares or holds like a net ▸ adj **5** made from mesh: a wire mesh fence ▸ vb **6** to entangle or become entangled **7** (of gear teeth) to engage or interlock **8** to fit together closely or work in harmony: she schedules her holidays to mesh with theirs

> **mesh** n **1** = net, netting, network, web, tracery ▸ vb **8** = engage, combine, connect, knit, coordinate, interlock, dovetail, harmonize

mesmerize or **-ise** vb **-izing**, **-ized** or **-ising**, **-ised**
1 to fascinate and hold spellbound: *his voice had the entire audience mesmerized* **2** archaic to hypnotize > **mesmerism** n > **mesmerizing** adj

meson (mee-zon) n physics any of a group of elementary particles that has a mass between those of an electron and a proton

mess n **1** a state of untidiness or confusion, esp. a dirty or unpleasant one: *the house was in a mess* **2** a confused and difficult situation; muddle: *the firm is in a terrible financial mess* **3** informal a dirty or untidy person or thing: *there was a nasty burnt mess in the saucepan* **4** a building providing catering, and sometimes recreation, facilities for service personnel **5** a group of service personnel who regularly eat together **6** old-fashioned a portion of soft or runny food: *a mess of pottage* ▸ vb **7** (of service personnel) to eat in a group

> **mess** n **1** = untidiness, disorder, confusion, chaos, litter, clutter, disarray, jumble **2** = difficulty, dilemma, plight, hole (informal), fix (informal), jam (informal), muddle, pickle (informal), uphill (S African)

message n **1** a communication from one person or group to another **2** an implicit meaning or moral, as in a work of art **3** a religious or political belief that someone attempts to communicate to others: *paintings with a fierce feminist message* **4 get the message** informal to understand

> **message** n **1** = communication, note, bulletin, word, letter, dispatch, memorandum, communiqué, email or e-mail, text or text message, SMS, IMS, tweet, mention or @ mention **2** = point, meaning, idea, moral, theme, import, purport

message board n an internet discussion forum

messaging n the sending of a message by any form of electronic communication: *text messaging*

messenger n a person who takes messages from one person or group to another

> **messenger** n = courier, runner, carrier, herald, envoy, go-between, emissary, delivery boy

Messiah n **1** Judaism the awaited king of the Jews, who will be sent by God to free them **2** Christianity Jesus Christ, when regarded in this role **3** a liberator of a country or people

Messianic adj **1** of or relating to a Messiah, or the arrival on Earth of a Messiah **2 messianic** of or relating to the belief that someone or something will bring about a complete transformation of the existing social order: *a messianic zeal for the free market*

messieurs (may-**syuh**) n the plural of **monsieur**

Messrs (mess-erz) n the plural of **Mr**

messy adj **messier**, **messiest 1** untidy **2** dirty **3** unpleasantly confused or complicated: *the messy, uncontrollable world of real life* > **messily** adv > **messiness** n

> **messy** adj **1** = disorganized, sloppy (informal), untidy; ≠ tidy **2** = dirty **3** = confusing, difficult, complex, confused, tangled, chaotic, tortuous

met vb the past of **meet**[1]

metabolism (met-**tab**-ol-liz-zum) n the chemical processes that occur in living organisms, resulting in growth, production of energy, and elimination of waste > **metabolic** adj

metabolize or **-lise** vb **-lizing**, **-lized** or **-lising**, **-lised** to produce or be produced by metabolism

metal n **1** ᴀ chem a chemical element, such as iron or copper, that reflects light and can be shaped, forms positive ions, and is a good conductor of heat and electricity ʙ an alloy, such as brass or steel, containing one or more of these elements **2** informal short for **heavy metal** **3 metals** the rails of a railway ▸ adj **4** made of metal

metallic adj **1** of or consisting of metal **2** sounding like two pieces of metal hitting each other: *a metallic click* **3** (of a voice) harsh, unpleasant, and unemotional **4** shining like metal: *metallic paint* **5** (of a taste) unpleasantly harsh and bitter

metallurgy n the scientific study of the structure, properties, extraction, and refining of metals > **metallurgical** adj > **metallurgist** n

metal road n NZ an unsealed road covered in gravel

metamorphic adj **1** (of rocks) altered considerably from the original structure and composition by pressure and heat **2** of metamorphosis or metamorphism

metamorphose vb **-phosing**, **-phosed** to change from one state or thing into something different: *hysterical laughter which gradually metamorphosed into convulsive sobs*

metamorphosis (met-a-**mor**-foss-is) n, pl **-ses** (-seez) **1** a complete change of physical form or substance **2** a complete change of character or appearance **3** zool the change of form that accompanies transformation into an adult in certain animals, for example the butterfly or frog

metaphor n a figure of speech in which a word or phrase is applied to an object or action that it does not literally apply to in order to imply a resemblance, for example *he is a lion in battle* > **metaphorical** adj > **metaphorically** adv

> **metaphor** n = figure of speech, image, symbol, analogy, conceit (literary), allegory, trope, figurative expression

metaphysical adj **1** of metaphysics **2** abstract, abstruse, or unduly theoretical

metaphysics n **1** the philosophical study of the nature of reality **2** abstract or subtle discussion or reasoning

m

meteor n 1 a small piece of rock or metal that has entered the earth's atmosphere from space 2 Also: **shooting star** the bright streak of light appearing in the sky due to a piece of rock or metal burning up because of friction as it falls through the atmosphere

meteoric (meet-ee-or-rik) adj 1 of or relating to meteors 2 brilliant and very rapid: *his meteoric rise to power* ▷ **meteorically** adv

meteorite n the rocklike remains of a meteoroid that has collided with the earth

meteorol. or **meteor.** 1 meteorological 2 meteorology

meteorology n the study of the earth's atmosphere and weather-forming processes, esp. for weather forecasting ▷ **meteorological** adj ▷ **meteorologist** n

mete out vb **meting, meted** to impose or deal out something, usually something unpleasant: *the sentence meted out to him has proved controversial*

meter n 1 any device that measures and records the quantity or number of units of something that was used during a specified period or is being used at that moment: *a gas meter* ▶ vb 2 to measure the amount of something used, or a rate of flow, with a meter

methane n a colourless odourless flammable gas, the main constituent of natural gas

methanol n a colourless poisonous liquid used as a solvent and fuel. Also: **methyl alcohol**

methinks vb, *past tense* **methought** archaic it seems to me that

method n 1 a way of doing something, esp. a systematic or regular one 2 orderliness of thought or action 3 the techniques of a particular field or subject

> **method** n 1 = manner, process, approach, technique, way, system, style, procedure 2 = orderliness, planning, order, system, purpose, pattern, organization, regularity

methodical adj careful, well-organized, and systematic ▷ **methodically** adv

Methodist n 1 a member of any of the Christian Nonconformist denominations that derive from the beliefs and practices of John Wesley and his followers ▶ adj 2 of or relating to Methodists or their Church ▷ **Methodism** n

methodology n, *pl* **-gies** 1 the system of methods and principles used in a particular discipline 2 the philosophical study of method ▷ **methodological** adj

meths n Brit, Austral & NZ informal methylated spirits

methyl adj of or containing the monovalent saturated hydrocarbon group of atoms CH_3: *methyl mercury*

methyl alcohol n same as **methanol**

methylated spirits n alcohol that has been rendered undrinkable by the addition of methanol and a violet dye, used as a solvent or as a fuel for small lamps or heaters. Also: **methylated spirit**

meticulous adj very precise about details; careful and thorough ▷ **meticulously** adv ▷ **meticulousness** n

métier (met-ee-ay) n 1 a profession or trade 2 a person's strong point or speciality

metonymy (mit-on-im-ee) n, *pl* **-mies** a figure of speech in which one thing is replaced by another associated with it, for instance the use of *Downing Street* to mean *the British government*

metre or US **meter** n the basic SI unit of length, equal to 100 centimetres (39.37 inches): *the majority of people are between one and a half and two metres tall*

metric adj of or relating to the metre or metric system: *use either all metric or all imperial measurements*

metrical or **metric** adj 1 of or relating to measurement 2 of or in poetic metre ▷ **metrically** adv

metro n, *pl* **-ros** an urban, usually underground, railway system in certain cities, such as Paris

metronome n a device which indicates the speed music should be played at by producing a clicking sound from a pendulum with an adjustable period of swing

metropolis (mit-trop-oh-liss) n the main city of a country or region

metropolitan adj 1 of or characteristic of a metropolis 2 of or consisting of a city and its suburbs: *the Tokyo metropolitan region* 3 of or belonging to the home territories of a country, as opposed to overseas territories: *metropolitan France* ▶ n 4 Christianity the senior member of the clergy, esp. an archbishop, in charge of an ecclesiastical province 5 an inhabitant of a large city

metrosexual n informal a heterosexual man who spends a lot of time and money on his appearance

mettle n 1 courage or spirit: *it's the first real test of the team's mettle this season* 2 character or abilities: *the mettle saints are made of* 3 **on one's mettle** roused to making one's best efforts

mew n 1 the characteristic high-pitched cry of a cat; meow ▶ vb 2 to make such a sound

mews n chiefly Brit 1 a yard or street lined by buildings originally used as stables but now often converted into dwellings ▶ adj 2 (of a flat or house) located in a mews: *a mews cottage*

Mexican adj 1 of Mexico ▶ n 2 a person from Mexico

mezzanine (mez-zan-een) n an intermediate storey, esp. one between the ground and first floor

mezzotint (met-so-tint) n 1 a method of engraving done by scraping and burnishing the roughened surface of a copper plate 2 a print made from a plate so treated

mg milligram

MHz megahertz

miasma (mee-azz-ma) *n, pl* **-mata** *or* **-mas** an unwholesome or foreboding atmosphere

mica (my-ka) *n* any of a group of minerals consisting of flakelike crystals of aluminium or potassium silicates. They have a high resistance to electricity and heat

mice *n* the plural of **mouse**

Michaelmas (mik-kl-mass) *n* Sept 29, the feast of St Michael the archangel: one of the four quarter days in England, Ireland, and Wales

Michaelmas daisy *n Brit* a garden plant with small daisy-shaped purple, pink, or white flowers in autumn

mickey *n* **take the mickey (out of)** *informal* to tease (someone)

micro *n, pl* **micros** short for **microcomputer** or **microprocessor**

microbe *n* any microscopic organism, esp. a disease-causing bacterium > **microbial** *or* **microbic** *adj*

microblog *n* a blog in which there is a limitation on the length of individual postings > **microblogger** *n* > **microblogging** *n*

microchip *n* a tiny wafer of semiconductor material, such as silicon, containing an integrated circuit. Often shortened to: **chip**

microcomputer *n* a compact computer built around a central processing unit on a single microchip

microcosm *n* **1** a miniature representation of something: *this area is a microcosm of France as a whole* **2 in microcosm** on a small scale > **microcosmic** *adj*

microfiche (my-kroh-feesh) *n* a small sheet of film on which writing or other information is stored, greatly reduced in size

microfilm *n* **1** a strip of film on which books or documents can be recorded in miniaturized form ▸ *vb* **2** to photograph a page or document on microfilm

microlight *or* **microlite** *n* a very small, light aircraft

micrometer (my-krom-it-er) *n* an instrument for the accurate measurement of small distances or angles

micron (my-kron) *n* a unit of length equal to one millionth of a metre

microorganism *n* any organism of microscopic size, such as a virus or bacterium

microphone *n* a device for converting sound into electrical energy

microprocessor *n computers* a single integrated circuit which acts as the central processing unit in a small computer

microscope *n* **1** an optical instrument that uses a lens or combination of lenses to produce a greatly magnified image of a small close object **2** any instrument, such as the electron microscope, for producing a greatly magnified visual image of a small object

microscopic *adj* **1** too small to be seen except with a microscope **2** very small; minute **3** of or

using a microscope > **microscopically** *adv*

microscopy *n* the use of microscopes

microsurgery *n* intricate surgery performed using a special microscope and miniature precision instruments

microwave *n* **1** an electromagnetic wave with a wavelength of between 0.3 and 0.001 metres: used in radar and cooking **2** short for **microwave oven** ▸ *vb* **-waving, -waved** **3** to cook in a microwave oven

microwave oven *n* a type of cooker which uses microwaves to cook food quickly

mid *adj* middle

midday *n* **1** twelve o'clock in the day; noon **2** the middle part of the day, from late morning to early afternoon: *the midday sun*

midday *n* **1** = noon, twelve o'clock, noonday

midden *n Brit & Austral* a dunghill or pile of refuse

middle *n* **1** an area or point equal in distance from the ends or edges of a place: *a hotel in the middle of town* **2** the time between the first part and last part of an event or period of time: *the middle of June; the film got a bit boring in the middle* **3** the part of the body around the stomach; waist **4 in the middle of** busy doing something: *I'm in the middle of washing the dishes* ▸ *adj* **5** equally distant from the ends or outer edges of something; central: *the middle finger* **6** having an equal number of elder and younger brothers and sisters: *he was the middle child of three* **7** intermediate in status or situation: *middle management* **8** avoiding extremes; moderate: *we must find a middle course between authoritarianism and anarchy*

middle *n* **1** = centre, heart, midst, halfway point, midpoint, midsection ▸ *adj* **5** = central, medium, mid, intervening, halfway, intermediate, median **7** = intermediate, intervening

middle age *n* the period of life between youth and old age, usually considered to occur between the ages of 40 and 60 > **middle-aged** *adj*

middle class *n* **1** the social class between the working and upper classes. It consists of business and professional people ▸ *adj* **middle-class 2** of or characteristic of the middle class

middle class *adj* **middle-class** = bourgeois, traditional, conventional

Middle East *n* the area around the E Mediterranean, esp. Israel and the Arab countries from Turkey to North Africa and eastwards to Iran > **Middle Eastern** *adj*

middleman *n, pl* **-men** **1** a trader who buys from the producer and sells to the consumer **2** an intermediary or go-between

middle-of-the-road *adj* **1** not extreme, esp. in political views; moderate **2** of or denoting popular music of wide general appeal

m

middleweight n a professional boxer weighing up to 160 pounds (72.5 kg) or an amateur weighing up to 75 kg

middling adj **1** neither very good nor very bad **2** moderate in size **3 fair to middling** neither good nor bad, esp. in health ▸ adv **4** informal moderately: middling well

> **middling** adj **1** = mediocre, all right, indifferent, so-so (informal), unremarkable, tolerable (informal), run-of-the-mill, passable, half-pie (NZ informal) **2** = moderate, medium, average, fair, ordinary, modest, adequate

midge n a small mosquito-like biting insect occurring in swarms, esp. near water

midget n old-fashioned, offensive **1** a dwarf whose skeleton and features are of normal proportions ▸ adj **2** much smaller than normal: a midget submarine

midland n the central or inland part of a country

midnight n **1** the middle of the night; 12 o'clock at night ▸ adj **2** happening or apparent at midnight or in the middle of the night: midnight Mass **3 burn the midnight oil** to work or study late into the night

> **midnight** n = twelve o'clock, middle of the night, dead of night, the witching hour

midriff n **1** the middle part of the human body between waist and chest **2** anatomy same as **diaphragm** (sense 1)

midshipman n, pl **-men** a naval officer of the lowest commissioned rank

midst n **1 in our midst** among us **2 in the midst of A** surrounded by **B** at a point during

> **midst** n **2A in the midst of** = among, in the middle of, surrounded by, amidst, in the thick of **2B in the midst of** = during, in the middle of, amidst

midsummer n the middle or height of summer

Midsummer's Day or **Midsummer Day** n June 24, the feast of St John the Baptist: one of the four quarter days in England, Ireland, and Wales

midway adj **1** in or at the middle of the distance; halfway: the midway point ▸ adv **2** to the middle of the distance

> **midway** adv = halfway, in the middle of, part-way, equidistant, at the midpoint, betwixt and between

midwife n, pl **-wives** a person qualified to deliver babies and to care for women before, during, and after childbirth ▸ **midwifery** (mid-**wiff**-fer-ree) n

midwinter n the middle or depth of winter

mien (mean) n literary a person's manner, bearing, or appearance

miffed adj informal offended or upset

might¹ vb **1** the past tense or subjunctive mood of **may**: he might have come **2** (used as an auxiliary) expressing possibility: he might well have gone already. See **may** (sense 2)

might² n **1** great power, strength, or vigour **2 with all one's might** using all one's strength and energy **3 (with) might and main** See **main**

> **might** n **1** = power, force, energy, strength, vigour

mighty adj **mightier, mightiest 1** powerful or strong **2** very great in extent or importance ▸ adv **3** informal, chiefly US, Canad & Austral very: mighty hungry ▸ **mightily** adv ▸ **mightiness** n

> **mighty** adj **1** = powerful, strong, strapping, robust, vigorous, sturdy, forceful, lusty; ≠ weak

migraine (mee-grain, mye-grain) n a throbbing headache usually affecting only one side of the head and commonly accompanied by nausea and visual disturbances

migrant n **1** a person or animal that moves from one place to another ▸ adj **2** moving from one place to another: migrant farm labourers

> **migrant** n = wanderer, immigrant, traveller, rover, nomad, emigrant, itinerant, drifter ▸ adj = itinerant, wandering, drifting, roving, travelling, shifting, immigrant, transient

migrate vb **-grating, -grated 1** to go from one place to settle in another, esp. in a foreign country **2** (of living creatures, esp. birds) to journey between different habitats at specific times of the year ▸ **migration** n ▸ **migratory** adj

> **migrate** vb **1** = move, travel, journey, wander, trek, voyage, roam, emigrate

mike n informal a microphone

milch (miltch) adj chiefly Brit (esp. of cattle) kept for milk

mild adj **1** (of a taste or sensation) not strong; bland **2** gentle or temperate in character, climate, or behaviour **3** not extreme; moderate: mild criticism of senior officers **4** feeble; unassertive: a mild protest ▸ n **5** Brit a dark beer flavoured with fewer hops than bitter ▸ **mildly** adv

> **mild** adj **1** = bland, thin, smooth, tasteless, insipid, flavourless **2** = temperate, warm, calm, moderate, tranquil, balmy; ≠ cold

mildew n **1** a disease of plants caused by a parasitic fungus **2** same as **mould²** ▸ vb **3** to affect or become affected with mildew ▸ **mildewy** adj

mile n **1** Also: **statute mile** a unit of length used in the UK, the US and certain other countries, equal to 1760 yards. 1 mile is equivalent to 1.60934 kilometres **2** See **nautical mile 3** Also: **miles** informal a great distance; great deal: he missed by miles **4** a race extending over a mile ▸ adv **5 miles** very much: it's miles better than their first album

m

mileage *n* **1** a distance expressed in miles **2** the total number of miles that a motor vehicle has travelled **3** the number of miles a motor vehicle will travel on one gallon of fuel **4** *informal* the usefulness or benefit of something: *the opposition is trying to make political mileage out of the issue*

mileometer *or* **milometer** (mile-om-it-er) *n* Brit a device that records the number of miles that a vehicle has travelled

milestone *n* **1** a stone pillar that shows the distance in miles to or from a place **2** a significant event in a life or history: *a milestone in Turkish-Bulgarian relations*

milieu (meal-yuh) *n*, *pl* **milieux** *or* **milieus** (meal-yuhz) the social and cultural environment in which a person or thing exists: *the film takes for its milieu an apparently wholesome small town*

militant *adj* **1** very active or aggressive in the support of a cause **2** *formal* warring; engaged in warfare ▸ *n* **3** a militant person > **militancy** *n* > **militantly** *adv*

> **militant** *adj* = aggressive, active, vigorous, assertive, combative; ≠ peaceful

militarism *n* the pursuit of policies intended to create and maintain aggressive and influential armed forces > **militarist** *n*, *adj* > **militaristic** *adj*

militarized *or* **-rised** *adj* occupied by armed forces: *one of the most heavily militarized borders in the world* > **militarization** *or* **-risation** *n*

military *adj* **1** of or relating to the armed forces or war **2** of or characteristic of soldiers ▸ *n* **3 the military** the armed services, esp. the army > **militarily** *adv*

> **military** *adj* = warlike, armed, soldierly, martial ▸ *n* **the military** = the armed forces, the forces, the services, the army

militate *vb* **-tating, -tated** (of facts or events) to have a strong influence or effect: *our position militated against counter-attacks*

militia (mill-ish-a) *n* a military force of trained civilians enlisted for use in emergency only > **militiaman** *n*

milk *n* **1** ᴀ a whitish fluid secreted by the mammary glands of mature female mammals and used for feeding their young ʙ the milk of cows, goats, etc., used by humans as a food and to make cheese, butter, and yogurt **2** any similar fluid, such as the juice of a coconut ▸ *vb* **3** to draw milk from the udder of a cow or other animal **4** to extract as much money, help, or value as possible from: *he was accused of milking the situation for his own ends* > **milker** *n* > **milkiness** *n* > **milky** *adj*

> **milk** *vb* **4** = exploit, pump, take advantage of

milk float *n* Brit a small electrically powered vehicle used to deliver milk to houses

milkmaid *n* a girl or woman who milks cows

milkman *n*, *pl* **-men** Brit, Austral & NZ a man who delivers milk to people's houses

milk shake *n* a cold frothy drink made of milk, flavouring, and sometimes ice cream, whisked or beaten together

milksop *n* a feeble or ineffectual man or youth

Milky Way *n* **1** the diffuse band of light stretching across the night sky that consists of millions of distant stars in our galaxy **2** the galaxy in which the Earth is situated

mill *n* **1** a building where grain is crushed and ground to make flour **2** a factory, esp. one which processes raw materials: *a steel mill* **3** any of various processing or manufacturing machines, esp. one that grinds, presses, or rolls **4** a small device for grinding solids: *a pepper mill* **5 go** *or* **be put through the mill** to have an unpleasant experience or ordeal ▸ *vb* **6** to grind, press, or process in or as if in a mill **7** to groove or flute the edge of a coin **8** (often foll. by *about* or *around*) to move about in a confused manner: *the corridor was full of people milling about*

> **mill** *n* **2** = factory, works, plant, workshop, foundry **4** = grinder, crusher, quern ▸ *vb* **6** = grind, pound, crush, powder, grate **8 mill about** *or* **around** = swarm, crowd, stream, surge, throng

millennial (mill-en-nee-al) *adj* **1** of or relating to a millennium ▸ *n* **2** a member of the generation who became adults in the early 21st century

millennium (mill-en-nee-um) *n*, *pl* **-nia** (-nee-a) *or* **-niums** **1** a period of one thousand years **2 the Millennium** Christianity the period of a thousand years of Christ's awaited reign upon earth **3** a future period of peace and happiness

miller *n* history a person who owns or operates a mill, esp. a corn mill

millet *n* a cereal grass cultivated for its edible grain and as animal fodder

milli- *combining form* denoting 10^{-3}: *millimetre*

millibar *n* a unit of atmospheric pressure equal to 100 newtons per square metre

millimetre *or* US **millimeter** *n* a unit of length equal to one thousandth of a metre

milliner *n* a person who makes or sells women's hats > **millinery** *n*

million *n*, *pl* **-lions** *or* **-lion** **1** the number equal to one thousand thousands: 1 000 000 or 10^6 **2** (often *pl*) *informal* an extremely large but unspecified number: *I've got a million things to do today* > **millionth** *n*, *adj*

millionaire *n* a person who has money or property worth at least a million pounds, dollars, etc. > **millionairess** *fem n*

millipede *or* **millepede** *n* a small crawling animal with a cylindrical many-segmented body, each segment of which bears two pairs of legs

millstone *n* **1** one of a pair of heavy flat stones that are rotated one against the other to grind grain **2** a heavy burden of responsibility or obligation: *the debt had become a millstone round his neck*

m

millwheel *n* a water wheel that drives a mill

milometer (mile-om-it-er) *n* same as
 mileometer

milt *n* the male reproductive gland, sperm, or
 semen of a fish

mime *n* **1** a style of acting using only gesture
 and bodily movement and not words **2** a
 performer specializing in this **3** a performance
 in this style ▸ *vb* **miming, mimed 4** to express
 or describe something in actions or gestures
 without using speech **5** (of musicians) to
 pretend to be singing or playing music that is
 actually prerecorded ▹ **mimer** *n*

mimic *vb* **-icking, -icked 1** to imitate a person or
 a way of acting or speaking, esp. to entertain or
 make fun of **2** to take on the appearance of:
 certain flies mimic wasps **3** to copy closely or in a
 servile manner: *social climbers in the colonies began to
 mimic their conquerors* ▸ *n* **4** a person or an animal,
 such as a parrot, that is clever at mimicking

> **mimic** *vb* **1** = imitate, do (*informal*), take off
> (*informal*), ape, parody, caricature, impersonate
> ▸ *n* = imitator, impressionist, copycat (*informal*),
> impersonator, caricaturist

mimicry *n, pl* **-ries 1** the act or art of copying or
 imitating closely **2** *biol* the resemblance shown
 by one animal species to another dangerous or
 inedible one, which protects it from predators

min. 1 minimum **2** minute *or* minutes

minaret *n* a slender tower of a mosque with
 one or more balconies

mince *vb* **mincing, minced 1** to chop, grind, or
 cut into very small pieces **2** to walk or speak in
 an affected dainty manner **3 not mince one's
 words** to be direct and to the point rather than
 making an effort to avoid upsetting people ▸ *n*
 4 *chiefly Brit & NZ* minced meat ▹ **minced** *adj*
 ▹ **mincer** *n*

> **mince** *vb* **1** = cut, grind, crumble, dice, hash,
> chop up

mincemeat *n* **1** a mixture of dried fruit and
 spices used for filling pies **2 make mincemeat
 of** *informal* to defeat completely

mince pie *n* a small round pastry tart filled
 with mincemeat

mincing *adj* (of a person or their style of
 walking or speaking) affectedly elegant

> **mincing** *adj* = affected, precious, pretentious,
> dainty, foppish

mind *n* **1** the part of a person responsible for
 thought, feelings, and intention. Related
 adjective: **mental 2** intelligence as opposed to
 feelings or wishes **3** memory or recollection: *his
 name didn't spring to mind immediately* **4** a person
 considered as an intellectual being: *one of Europe's
 greatest minds* **5** the condition or state of a
 person's feelings or thoughts: *a confused state of
 mind* **6** an intention or desire: *I have a mind to go*
 7 attention or thoughts: *keep your mind on the job*

8 a sound mental state; sanity: *he's out of his mind*
 9 change one's mind to alter one's decision or
 opinion **10 give someone a piece of one's mind**
 to scold someone severely **11 in two minds**
 undecided or wavering **12 make up one's mind**
 to reach a decision **13 on one's mind** in one's
 thoughts **14 to my mind** in my opinion ▸ *vb*
 15 to take offence at: *do you mind if I open a window?*
 16 to pay attention to: *to mind one's own business*
 17 to make certain; ensure: *mind you tell him*
 18 to take care of: *mind the shop* **19** to be cautious
 or careful about: *mind how you go* **20** *dialect* to
 remember

> **mind** *n* **2** = intelligence, reason, reasoning,
> understanding, sense, brain(s) (*informal*),
> wits, intellect **3** = memory, recollection,
> remembrance, powers of recollection
> **6** = intention, wish, desire, urge, fancy,
> leaning, notion, inclination **8** = sanity, reason,
> senses, judgment, wits, marbles (*informal*),
> rationality, mental balance ▸ *vb* **15** = take
> offence at, dislike, care about, object to, resent,
> disapprove of, be bothered by, be affronted by
> **16** = pay attention to, mark, note, listen to,
> observe, obey, heed, take heed of **18** = look
> after, watch, protect, tend, guard, take care of,
> attend to, keep an eye on **19** = be careful, watch,
> take care, be wary, be cautious, be on your guard

minded *adj* having a mind or inclination as
 specified: *commercially minded*

minder *n* *slang* an aide or assistant, esp. one
 employed as a bodyguard or public relations
 officer for someone

mindful *adj* **mindful of** being aware of and
 taking into account: *the company is ever mindful of
 the need to find new markets*

mindless *adj* **1** stupid or careless **2** requiring
 little or no intellectual effort **3** heedless: *mindless
 of the risks involved* ▹ **mindlessly** *adv*
 ▹ **mindlessness** *n*

mine[1] *pron* **1** something or someone belonging
 to or associated with me: *it's a great favourite of mine*
 2 of mine belonging to or associated with me
 ▸ *adj* **3** *archaic* same as **my**: *mine eyes; mine host*

mine[2] *n* **1** a place where minerals, esp. coal,
 ores, or precious stones, are dug from the
 ground **2** a type of bomb placed in water or
 under the ground, and designed to destroy
 ships, vehicles, or people passing over or near
 it **3** a profitable source or abundant supply: *a
 mine of information* ▸ *vb* **mining, mined 4** to dig
 minerals from the ground: *lead has been mined here
 for over three centuries* **5** to dig a hole or tunnel, esp.
 in order to obtain minerals **6** to place explosive
 mines in or on: *the retreating troops had mined the
 bridge*

> **mine** *n* **1** = pit, deposit, shaft, colliery,
> excavation **3** = source, store, fund, stock, supply,
> reserve, treasury, wealth ▸ *vb* **4** = dig up,
> extract, quarry, unearth, excavate, hew, dig for

minefield n **1** an area of ground or water containing explosive mines **2** a subject or situation full of hidden problems

miner n a person who works in a mine, esp. a coal mine

> **miner** n = coalminer, pitman (Brit), collier (Brit)

mineral n **1** a naturally occurring solid inorganic substance with a characteristic chemical composition and structure **2** any inorganic matter **3** any substance obtained by mining, esp. a metal ore **4** Brit a soft drink containing carbonated water and flavourings ▸ adj **5** of, containing, or resembling minerals

mineralogy (min-er-al-a-jee) n the scientific study of minerals > **mineralogical** adj > **mineralogist** n

mineral water n water containing dissolved mineral salts or gases

minestrone (min-ness-strone-ee) n a soup made from a variety of vegetables and pasta

minesweeper n a naval vessel equipped to clear mines

minger n Brit informal an unattractive person

minging n Brit informal unattractive or unpleasant

mingle vb **-gling, -gled 1** to mix or blend **2** to associate or mix with a group of people: the performers mingled with the audience after the show

> **mingle** vb **1** = mix, combine, blend, merge, unite, join, interweave, intermingle; ≠ separate **2** = associate, consort, socialize, rub shoulders (informal), hobnob, fraternize, hang about or around; ≠ dissociate

mingy adj **-gier, -giest** Brit & NZ informal mean or miserly

mini adj **1** small; miniature **2** (of a skirt or dress) very short ▸ n, pl **minis 3** something very small of its kind, esp. a miniskirt

miniature n **1** a model or representation on a very small scale **2** a very small painting, esp. a portrait **3** a very small bottle of whisky or other spirits, which can hold 50 millilitres **4 in miniature** on a small scale ▸ adj **5** much smaller than usual; small-scale > **miniaturist** n

> **miniature** adj = small, little, minute, tiny, toy, scaled-down, diminutive, minuscule; ≠ giant

miniaturize or **-rise** vb **-rizing, -rized** or **-rising, -rised** to make a very small version of something, esp. electronic components > **miniaturization** or **-risation** n

minibar n a selection of drinks and confectionery provided in a hotel room

minibus n a small bus

minicab n Brit an ordinary car used as a taxi

minicomputer n a small computer which is more powerful than a microcomputer

minidisc n a small recordable compact disc

minim n **1** a unit of fluid measure equal to one sixtieth of a drachm **2** music a note with the time value of half a semibreve

minimal adj of the least possible quantity or degree

> **minimal** adj = minimum, smallest, least, slightest, token, nominal, negligible, least possible

minimize or **-mise** vb **-mizing, -mized** or **-mising, -mised 1** to reduce to the lowest possible degree or amount: these measures should help minimize our costs **2** to regard or treat as less important than it really is; belittle: I don't want to minimize the importance of her contribution

> **minimize** or **-mise** vb **1** = reduce, decrease, shrink, diminish, prune, curtail, miniaturize; ≠ increase **2** = play down, discount, belittle, disparage, decry, underrate, deprecate, make light or little of; ≠ praise

minimum n, pl **-mums** or **-ma 1** the least possible amount, degree, or quantity: fry the burgers in the minimum of oil **2** the least amount recorded, allowed, or reached: soak the beans for a minimum of eight hours ▸ adj **3** of, being, or showing a minimum or minimums: the minimum age

> **minimum** n **1** = lowest, least, lowest level, nadir ▸ adj = lowest, smallest, least, slightest, minimal, least possible; ≠ maximum

minion n a servile assistant

miniseries n, pl **-series** a television programme in several parts that is shown on consecutive days over a short period

minister n **1** (esp. in Presbyterian and some Nonconformist Churches) a member of the clergy **2** a head of a government department **3** a diplomat with a lower rank than an ambassador ▸ vb **4 minister to** to attend to the needs of > **ministerial** adj

> **minister** n **1** = clergyman or woman, priest, vicar, parson, preacher, pastor, cleric, rector ▸ vb **minister to** = attend to, serve, tend to, take care of, cater to, pander to, administer to

ministry n, pl **-tries 1** the profession or duties of a minister of religion **2** ministers considered as a group **3 A** a government department headed by a minister **B** the buildings of such a department

> **ministry** n **1** = the priesthood, the church, the cloth, holy orders **2** = administration, council **3A** = department, office, bureau, government department

mink n, pl **mink** or **minks 1** a mammal of Europe, Asia, and North America, resembling a large stoat **2** its highly valued fur **3** a garment made of this, esp. a coat or stole

minnow n, pl **-nows** or **-now** a small slender European freshwater fish

minor *adj* **1** lesser or secondary in size, frequency, or importance than others of the same kind: *a minor poet* **2** not very serious or significant: *minor injuries* **3** *music* **A** (of a scale) having a semitone between the second and third and fifth and sixth notes (**natural minor**) **B** of or based on the minor scale: *his quintet in C minor; a minor third* ▸ *n* **4** a person below the age of legal majority **5** *US, Canad & Austral education* a subsidiary subject **6** *music* a minor key, chord, mode, or scale ▸ *vb* **7 minor in** *US & Canad education* to study as a subsidiary subject: *to minor in politics*

> **minor** *adj* **2** = small, lesser, slight, petty, trivial, insignificant, unimportant, inconsequential; ≠ major

minority *n, pl* **-ties 1** the smaller of two parts, factions, or groups **2** a group that is different, esp. racially or politically, from a larger group of which it is a part **3 in the minority** forming or part of the group of people or things making up or less than half of a larger group ▸ *adj* **4** relating to or being a minority: *a minority sport*

minster *n Brit* any of certain cathedrals and large churches, usually originally connected to a monastery

minstrel *n* **1** a medieval singer and musician **2** a performer in a minstrel show

mint[1] *n* **1** any of various plants with aromatic leaves used for seasoning and flavouring **2** a sweet flavoured with mint ▸ **minty** *adj*

mint[2] *n* **1** a factory where the official coins of a country are made **2** a very large amount of money ▸ *adj* **3 in mint condition** in perfect condition; as if new ▸ *vb* **4** to make coins by stamping metal **5** to invent or create: *no-one knows who first minted the term 'yuppie'*

> **mint** *vb* **4** = make, produce, strike, cast, stamp, punch, coin

minuet (min-new-et) *n* **1** a stately court dance of the 17th and 18th centuries in triple time **2** music for this dance

minus *prep* **1** reduced by the subtraction of: *six minus two equals four* **2** *informal* without or lacking: *he returned minus his jacket* ▸ *adj* **3** indicating or involving subtraction: *a minus sign* **4** Also: **negative** less than zero: *it's minus eight degrees in Montreal today* **5** *education* slightly below the standard of a particular grade: *a C minus for maths* ▸ *n* **6** a negative quantity **7** *informal* something detrimental or negative

minuscule (min-niss-skyool) *adj* very small

minute[1] *n* **1** 60 seconds; one sixtieth of an hour **2** any very short period of time; moment: *I'll be with you in a minute* **3** the distance that can be travelled in a minute: *it's about ten minutes away* **4** a measure of angle equal to one sixtieth of a degree **5 up to the minute** the very latest or newest ▸ *vb* **-nuting, -nuted 6** to record in minutes: *the decision was minuted in 1990*

minute *n* **2** = moment, second, bit, flash, instant, tick (*Brit informal*), sec (*informal*), short time

minute[2] *adj* **1** very small; tiny **2** precise or detailed: *a minute examination* ▸ **minutely** *adv*

> **minute** *adj* **1** = small, little, tiny, miniature, microscopic, diminutive, minuscule, infinitesimal; ≠ huge **2** = precise, close, detailed, critical, exact, meticulous, exhaustive, painstaking; ≠ imprecise

minutiae (my-new-shee-eye) *pl n, sing* **-tia** trifling or precise details

minx *n* a bold or flirtatious girl

miracle *n* **1** an event contrary to the laws of nature and attributed to a supernatural cause **2** any amazing and fortunate event: *it's a miracle that no-one was killed in the accident* **3** a marvellous example of something: *a miracle of organization*

> **miracle** *n* **3** = wonder, phenomenon, sensation, marvel, amazing achievement, astonishing feat

miracle play *n* a medieval play based on a biblical story or the life of a saint

miraculous *adj* **1** like a miracle **2** surprising or remarkable ▸ **miraculously** *adv*

> **miraculous** *adj* **2** = wonderful, amazing, extraordinary, incredible (*informal*), astonishing, unbelievable, phenomenal, astounding; ≠ ordinary

mirage (mir-rahzh) *n* **1** an image of a distant object or sheet of water, often inverted or distorted, caused by atmospheric refraction by hot air **2** something illusory: *the mirage of economic recovery*

mire *n* **1** a boggy or marshy area **2** mud, muck, or dirt **3** an unpleasant or difficult situation that is difficult to get out of: *the country sank deeper into the economic mire* ▸ *vb* **miring, mired 4** to sink or be stuck in a mire: *the company has been mired in financial scandal*

mirror *n* **1** a sheet of glass with a metal coating on its back, that reflects an image of an object placed in front of it **2** a thing that reflects or depicts something else ▸ *vb* **3** to reflect or represent faithfully: *the book inevitably mirrors my own interests*

> **mirror** *n* **1** = looking-glass, glass (*Brit*), reflector ▸ *vb* = reflect, follow, copy, echo, emulate

mirth *n* laughter, gaiety, or merriment ▸ **mirthful** *adj* ▸ **mirthless** *adj*

mis- *prefix* **1** wrong or bad; wrongly or badly: *misunderstanding; mislead* **2** lack of; not: *mistrust*

misadventure *n* **1** an unlucky event; misfortune **2** *law* accidental death not due to crime or negligence

misanthrope (miz-zan-thrope) or **misanthropist** (miz-**zan**-throp-ist) n a person who dislikes or distrusts people in general > **misanthropic** (miz-zan-**throp**-ik) adj > **misanthropy** (miz-**zan**-throp-ee) n

misapprehend vb to misunderstand > **misapprehension** n

misappropriate vb -ating, -ated to take and use money dishonestly > **misappropriation** n

miscarriage n 1 spontaneous premature expulsion of a fetus from the womb, esp. before the 20th week of pregnancy 2 an act of mismanagement or failure: a miscarriage of justice

miscarriage n 2 = failure, error, breakdown, mishap, perversion

miscarry vb -ries, -rying, -ried 1 to expel a fetus prematurely from the womb 2 to fail

miscast vb -casting, -cast to cast a role or an actor in a play or film inappropriately: the role of the avaricious boss was miscast; she was miscast as Cassandra

miscegenation (miss-ij-in-**nay**-shun) n old-fashioned interbreeding of races, esp. where differences of colour are involved

miscellaneous (miss-sel-**lane**-ee-uss) adj composed of or containing a variety of things; mixed or assorted

miscellany (miss-**sell**-a-nee) n, pl -nies a mixed assortment of items

mischance n 1 bad luck 2 an unlucky event or accident

mischief n 1 annoying but not malicious behaviour that causes trouble or irritation 2 an inclination to tease 3 injury or harm caused by a person or thing

mischievous (miss-**chiv**-uss) adj 1 full of mischief 2 teasing; slightly malicious 3 intended to cause harm: a purveyor of mischievous disinformation > **mischievously** adv

miscible (miss-**sib**-bl) adj able to be mixed: miscible with water > **miscibility** n

misconception n a false or mistaken view, idea, or belief

misconduct n behaviour, such as adultery or professional negligence, that is regarded as immoral or unethical

misconduct n = immorality, wrongdoing, mismanagement, malpractice, impropriety

miscreant (miss-**kree**-ant) n a wrongdoer or villain

misdeed n an evil or illegal action

misdemeanour or US **misdemeanor** n 1 a minor wrongdoing 2 criminal law (formerly) an offence less serious than a felony

miser n a person who hoards money and hates spending it: I'm married to a miser > **miserly** adj

miserable adj 1 unhappy or depressed; wretched 2 causing misery or discomfort: a miserable existence 3 sordid or squalid: miserable living conditions 4 mean or ungenerous: a miserable pension > **miserableness** n > **miserably** adv

miserable adj 1 = sad, depressed, gloomy, forlorn, dejected, despondent, sorrowful, wretched; ≠ happy 4 = pathetic, sorry, shameful, despicable, deplorable, lamentable; ≠ respectable

misery n, pl -eries 1 intense unhappiness or suffering 2 something which causes such unhappiness 3 squalid or poverty-stricken conditions 4 Brit informal a person who is habitually depressed: he is such a misery

misery n 1 = unhappiness, distress, despair, grief, suffering, depression, gloom, torment; ≠ happiness 4 = moaner, pessimist, killjoy, spoilsport (informal), prophet of doom, wet blanket (informal), sourpuss (informal), wowser (Austral, NZ slang)

misfire vb -firing, -fired 1 (of a firearm) to fail to fire as expected 2 (of a motor engine or vehicle) to fail to fire at the appropriate time 3 to fail to have the intended result; go wrong: he was injured when a practical joke misfired ▸ n 4 the act or an instance of misfiring

misfit n a person who is not suited to the role, social group, etc., he or she finds himself or herself in

misfortune n 1 bad luck 2 an unfortunate event

misfortune n 1 = bad luck, adversity, hard luck, ill luck, infelicity, bad trot (Austral slang) 2 = mishap, trouble, disaster, reverse, tragedy, setback, calamity, affliction; ≠ good luck

misgivings pl n feelings of uncertainty, fear, or doubt

misguided adj mistaken or unwise

misguided adj = unwise, mistaken, misplaced, deluded, ill-advised, imprudent, injudicious

mishandle vb -dling, -dled to handle or treat badly or inefficiently

mishap n a minor accident

misinform vb to give incorrect information to > **misinformation** n

misjudge vb -judging, -judged to judge wrongly or unfairly > **misjudgment** or **misjudgement** n

mislay vb -lays, -laying, -laid to lose something temporarily, esp. by forgetting where it is

mislead vb -leading, -led to give false or confusing information to

mislead vb = deceive, fool, delude, take someone in (informal), misdirect, misinform, hoodwink, misguide

misleading adj giving a false or confusing impression: misleading use of statistical data

misleading adj = confusing, false, ambiguous, deceptive, evasive, disingenuous; ≠ straightforward

m

mismanage *vb* **-naging, -naged** to organize or run something badly ▷ **mismanagement** *n*

misnomer (miss-no-mer) *n* **1** an incorrect or unsuitable name for a person or thing **2** the use of the wrong name

misogyny (miss-oj-in-ee) *n* hatred of women ▷ **misogynist** *n* ▷ **misogynous** *adj*

misplace *vb* **-placing, -placed** **1** to lose something temporarily by forgetting where it was placed **2** to put something in the wrong place

misprint *n* **1** an error in printing ▶ *vb* **2** to print a letter incorrectly

misrepresent *vb* to represent wrongly or inaccurately ▷ **misrepresentation** *n*

miss *vb* **1** to fail to notice, see, or hear: *it's right at the top of the hill, so you can't miss it; I missed what he said because I was talking at the time* **2** to fail to hit something aimed at: *he threw the ball at the stumps but missed* **3** to fail to achieve or reach: *they narrowly missed promotion last season* **4** to fail to take advantage of: *he never missed a chance to make money* **5** to fail or be unable to be present: *he had missed the last three meetings* **6** to be too late for: *we missed the bus and had to walk* **7** to discover or regret the loss or absence of: *the boys miss their father when he's away on business* **8** to escape or avoid narrowly: *it missed the helicopter's rotors by inches* ▶ *n* **9** a failure to hit, reach, etc.: *an easy miss in the second frame gave his opponent the advantage* **10** **give something a miss** to decide not to do, go to, or take part in something: *I'll give the pub a miss and have a quiet night in*

> **miss** *vb* **1** = fail to notice, overlook, pass over **5** = not go to, skip (*informal*), cut, omit, be absent from, fail to attend, skive off (*informal*), play truant from, bludge (*Austral, NZ informal*) **7** = long for, yearn for, pine for, long to see, ache for, feel the loss of, regret the absence of **8** = avoid, beat, escape, skirt, duck (*informal*), cheat, bypass, dodge ▶ *n* **9** = mistake, failure, error, blunder, omission, oversight

Miss *n* a title of a girl or unmarried woman, usually used before the surname: *Miss Brown to you*

missal *n* *RC Church* a book containing the prayers and rites of the Masses for a complete year

misshapen *adj* badly shaped; deformed

missile *n* **1** a rocket with an exploding warhead, used as a weapon **2** an object or weapon that is thrown, launched, or fired at a target

> **missile** *n* = projectile, weapon, shell, rocket

missing *adj* **1** not in its proper or usual place and unable to be found **2** not able to be traced and not known to be dead: *seven men were reported missing after the raid* **3** not included in something although it perhaps should have been: *two things are missing from the report*

> **missing** *adj* **1** = lost, misplaced, not present, astray, unaccounted for, mislaid

mission *n* **1** a specific task or duty assigned to a person or group of people **2** a task or duty that a person believes he or she must achieve; vocation: *he felt it was his mission to pass on his knowledge to other people* **3** a group of people representing or working for a particular country or organization in a foreign country: *the UN peacekeeping mission* **4** a group of people sent by a church to a foreign country to do religious and social work **5** the place in which a church or government mission is based **6** the dispatch of aircraft or spacecraft to achieve a particular task **7** a charitable centre that offers shelter or aid to poor or needy people **8** *S African* a long and difficult process

> **mission** *n* **2** = task, job, commission, duty, undertaking, quest, assignment, vocation

missionary *n*, *pl* **-naries** **1** a person sent abroad by a church to do religious and social work ▶ *adj* **2** of or relating to missionaries: *missionary work* **3** resulting from a desire to convert people to one's own beliefs: *missionary zeal*

> **missionary** *n* = evangelist, preacher, apostle

missive *n* a formal or official letter

missus *or* **missis** *n* **1** *Brit, Austral & NZ informal* one's wife or the wife of the person addressed or referred to: *the missus is a teacher* **2** an informal term of address for a woman

mist *n* **1** a thin fog **2** a fine spray of liquid, such as that produced by an aerosol container **3** condensed water vapour on a surface **4** something that causes haziness or lack of clarity, such as a film of tears ▶ *vb* **5** to cover or be covered with mist: *the windscreen has misted up again; his eyes misted over and he shook with rage* ▷ **misty** *adj* ▷ **mistiness** *n*

> **mist** *n* **1, 2** = fog, cloud, steam, spray, film, haze, vapour, smog

mistake *n* **1** an error or blunder **2** a misconception or misunderstanding ▶ *vb* **-taking, -took, -taken** **3** to misunderstand or misinterpret: *the chaplain quite mistook her meaning* **4** (foll. by *for*) to confuse a person or thing with another: *they saw the HMS Sheffield and mistook her for the Bismarck* **5** to choose badly or incorrectly: *he mistook his path*

> **mistake** *n* **1** = error, blunder, oversight, slip, gaffe (*informal*), miscalculation, faux pas, barry or Barry Crocker (*Austral slang*) **2** = oversight, error, slip, fault, howler (*informal*), erratum, barry or Barry Crocker (*Austral slang*) ▶ *vb* **3** = misunderstand, misinterpret, misjudge, misread, misconstrue, misapprehend **4 mistake something or someone for something or someone** = confuse with, take for, mix up with

Mister *n* the full form of **Mr**

mistletoe *n* a Eurasian evergreen shrub with waxy white berries, which grows as a parasite on various trees

mistral *n* a strong cold dry northerly wind of S France

mistress *n* **1** a woman who has a continuing sexual relationship with a man who is usually married to somebody else **2** a woman in a position of authority, ownership, or control **3** a woman having control over something specified: *she is a mistress of disguise* **4** *chiefly Brit* a female teacher

> **mistress** *n* **1** = lover, girlfriend, concubine (*old-fashioned*), kept woman, paramour (*old-fashioned*)

mistrial *n law* a trial which is invalid because of some error

mistrust *vb* **1** to have doubts or suspicions about ▸ *n* **2** lack of trust > **mistrustful** *adj* > **mistrustfully** *adv*

misunderstand *vb* **-standing, -stood** to fail to understand properly

> **misunderstand** *vb* = misinterpret, misread, mistake, misjudge, misconstrue, misapprehend, be at cross-purposes with

misunderstanding *n* **1** a failure to understand properly **2** a disagreement

> **misunderstanding** *n* **1** = mistake, error, mix-up, misconception, misinterpretation, misjudgment

misuse *n* **1** incorrect, improper, or careless use: *misuse of drugs* **2** cruel or inhumane treatment ▸ *vb* **-using, -used** **3** to use wrongly **4** to treat badly or harshly

> **misuse** *n* **1** = waste, squandering ▸ *vb* **3** = abuse, misapply, prostitute (*old-fashioned, derogatory*)

mite[1] *n* any of numerous very small creatures of the spider family, some of which live as parasites

mite[2] *n* **1** a very small creature or thing **2 a mite** *informal* somewhat: *the main course was a mite bland*

mitigate *vb* **-gating, -gated** to make less severe or harsh > **mitigating** *adj* > **mitigation** *n*

mitre *or US* **miter** (my-ter) *n* **1** *Christianity* the headdress of a bishop or abbot, consisting of a tall pointed cleft cap **2** Also: **mitre joint** a corner joint formed by cutting bevels of equal angles at the ends of each piece of material ▸ *vb* **-tring, -tred** *or* **-tering, -tered** **3** to join with a mitre joint

mitt *n* **1** a glovelike hand covering that does not cover the fingers **2** short for **mitten 3** *slang* a hand **4** a baseball glove

mitten *n* a glove with one section for the thumb and a single section for the fingers

mix *vb* **1** to combine or blend into one mass or substance: *mix the water, yeast, and flour into a smooth dough* **2** to be able to combine into one substance: *oil and water do not mix* **3** to form by combining different substances: *to mix cement* **4** to do at the same time: *to mix business and pleasure* **5** to be outgoing in social situations: *he mixed well* **6** *music* to balance and adjust individual performers' parts to make an overall sound by electronic means ▸ *n* **7** something produced by mixing; mixture **8** a mixture of ingredients, esp. one commercially prepared for making a cake **9** *music* the sound produced by mixing ▸ See also **mix-up** > **mixed** *adj*

> **mix** *vb* **1** = combine, blend, merge, join, cross, fuse, mingle, jumble **4** = combine, marry, blend, integrate, amalgamate, coalesce, meld **5** = socialize, associate, hang out (*informal*), mingle, circulate, consort, hobnob, fraternize ▸ *n* **7** = mixture, combination, blend, fusion, compound, assortment, alloy, medley

mixer *n* **1** a kitchen appliance, usually electrical, used for mixing foods **2** any of various other devices or machines used for mixing things: *a cement mixer* **3** a nonalcoholic drink such as tonic water or ginger ale that is mixed with an alcoholic drink **4** *informal* a person considered in relation to his or her ability to mix socially: *he's not a good mixer*

mixture *n* **1** something produced by blending or combining other things: *top with the cheese and breadcrumb mixture* **2** a combination of different things, such as feelings: *he speaks of her with a mixture of loyalty and regret* **3** *chem* a substance consisting of two or more substances mixed together without any chemical bonding between them

> **mixture** *n* **1** = composite, compound **2** = blend, mix, variety, fusion, assortment, brew, jumble, medley

mix-up *n* **1** a confused condition or situation ▸ *vb* **mix up 2** to make into a mixture **3** to confuse: *he mixes Ryan up with Lee* **4 mixed up in** involved in (an activity or group, esp. one that is illegal): *she's mixed up in a drugs racket*

> **mix-up** *n* = confusion, mistake, misunderstanding, mess, tangle, muddle ▸ *vb* **2 mix something up** = blend, beat, mix, stir, fold

mizzenmast *n naut* (on a vessel with three or more masts) the third mast from the bow

mm millimetre(s)

mnemonic (nim-on-ik) *n* **1** something, for instance a verse, intended to help the memory ▸ *adj* **2** aiding or meant to aid one's memory > **mnemonically** *adv*

mo *n informal, chiefly Brit* short for **moment** (sense 1)

MO 1 Medical Officer **2** Missouri

moa *n* a recently extinct large flightless bird of New Zealand that resembled the ostrich

moan *n* **1** a low prolonged cry of pain or suffering **2** any similar sound, esp. that made by the wind **3** *informal* a grumble or complaint ▶ *vb* **4** to make a low cry of, or talk in a way suggesting, pain or suffering: *he moaned in pain* **5** to make a sound like a moan: *the wind moaned through the trees* **6** *informal* to grumble or complain > **moaner** *n*

> **moan** *n* **1** = groan, sigh, sob, lament, wail, grunt, whine **3** = complaint, protest, grumble, whine, grouse, gripe (*informal*), grouch (*informal*) ▶ *vb* **4** = groan, sigh, sob, whine, lament **6** = grumble, complain, groan (*informal*), whine, carp, grouse, whinge (*informal*), bleat

moat *n* a wide ditch, originally filled with water, surrounding a fortified place such as a castle

mob *n* **1** a riotous or disorderly crowd of people **2** *informal* any group of people **3** the masses **4** *slang* a gang of criminals ▶ *vb* **mobbing, mobbed** **5** to attack in a group resembling a mob **6** to surround in a crowd to acclaim or attack: *she was mobbed by her fans when she left the theatre*

> **mob** *n* **1** = crowd, pack, mass, host, drove, flock, swarm, horde **2** = gang, group, set, lot, crew (*informal*) ▶ *vb* **6** = surround, besiege, jostle, fall on, set upon, crowd around, swarm around

mobile *adj* **1** able to move or be moved: *mobile toilets* **2** changing quickly in expression: *a mobile face* **3** *sociol* (of individuals or social groups) moving within and between classes, occupations, and localities ▶ *n* **4** a light structure suspended in midair with delicately balanced parts that are set in motion by air currents **5** short for **mobile phone** > **mobility** *n*

> **mobile** *adj* **1** = movable, moving, travelling, wandering, portable, itinerant, peripatetic

mobile phone *n* a portable telephone powered by batteries

mobilize *or* **-lise** *vb* **-lizing, -lized** *or* **-lising, -lised** **1** to prepare for war or another emergency by organizing resources and the armed services **2** to organize for a purpose: *we must mobilize local residents behind our campaign* > **mobilization** *or* **-lisation** *n*

> **mobilize** *or* **-lise** *vb* **1** = deploy, prepare, ready, rally, assemble, call up, marshal, muster **2** = rally, organize, stimulate, excite, prompt, marshal, activate, awaken

moccasin *n* **1** a type of soft leather shoe traditionally worn by some Native American peoples **2** a soft leather shoe with a raised seam at the front above the toe

mocha (**mock-a**) *n* **1** a dark brown coffee originally imported from the port of Mocha in Arabia **2** a flavouring made from coffee and chocolate

mock *vb* **1** to behave with scorn or contempt towards a person or thing: *her husband mocked her attempts to educate herself* **2** to imitate or mimic, esp. in fun **3** to defy or frustrate: *the team mocked the visitors' attempts to score* ▶ *n* **4 mocks** *informal* (in England and Wales) school examinations taken as practice before public exams ▶ *adj* **5** sham or imitation: *mock Georgian windows* **6** serving as an imitation or substitute, esp. for practice purposes: *a mock battle* ▶ See also **mock-up** > **mocking** *n, adj*

> **mock** *vb* **1** = laugh at, tease, ridicule, taunt, scorn, sneer, scoff, deride; ≠ respect ▶ *adj* = imitation, pretended, artificial, fake, false, dummy, sham, feigned; ≠ genuine

mockers *pl n* **put the mockers on** *Brit, Austral & NZ informal* to ruin the chances of success of

mockery *n, pl* **-eries** **1** ridicule, contempt, or derision **2** a person, thing, or action that is so worthless that it seems like a parody: *the interview was a mockery from start to finish* **3 make a mockery of something** to make something appear worthless or foolish: *the judge's decision makes a mockery of the law*

mockingbird *n* an American songbird which can mimic the song of other birds

mock orange *n* a shrub with white fragrant flowers like those of the orange

mock-up *n* a working full-scale model of a machine or apparatus for test or research purposes

mod *n* an annual Highland Gaelic meeting with musical and literary competitions

MOD (in Britain) Ministry of Defence

mod. **1** moderate **2** modern

mode *n* **1** a manner or way of doing, acting, or existing **2** a particular fashion or style **3** *music* any of the various scales of notes within one octave **4** *maths* the most frequently occurring of a range of values

> **mode** *n* **1** = method, way, system, form, process, style, technique, manner **2** = fashion, style, trend, rage, vogue, look, craze

model *n* **1** a three-dimensional representation, usually on a smaller scale, of a device or structure: *an architect's model of the proposed new housing estate* **2** an example or pattern that people might want to follow: *her success makes her an excellent role model for other women* **3** an outstanding example of its kind: *the report is a model of clarity* **4** a person who poses for a sculptor, painter, or photographer **5** a person who wears clothes to display them to prospective buyers; mannequin **6** a design or style of a particular product: *the cheapest model of this car has a 1300cc engine* **7** a theoretical description of the way a system or process works: *a working model of the human immune system*

▸ *adj* **8** excellent or perfect: *a model husband* **9** being a small-scale representation of: *a model aeroplane* ▸ *vb* **-elling, -elled** or *US* **-eling, -eled** **10** to make a model of: *he modelled a plane out of balsa wood* **11** to plan or create according to a model or models: *it had a constitution modelled on that of the United States* **12** to display (clothing and accessories) as a mannequin **13** to pose for a sculptor, painter, or photographer

model *n* **1** = representation, image, copy, miniature, dummy, replica, imitation, duplicate **2** = pattern, example, standard, original, ideal, prototype, paradigm, archetype **4** = sitter, subject, poser ▸ *vb* **10** = shape, form, design, fashion, carve, mould, sculpt **12** = show off (*informal*), wear, display, sport (*informal*)

modem (mode-em) *n* *computers* a device for transmitting information between two computers by a telephone line, consisting of a modulator that converts computer signals into audio signals and a corresponding demodulator

moderate *adj* **1** not extreme or excessive: *a man of moderate views*; *moderate consumption of alcohol* **2** (of a size, rate, intensity, etc.) towards the middle of the range of possible values: *a moderate-sized garden*; *a moderate breeze* **3** of average quality or extent: *moderate success* ▸ *n* **4** a person who holds moderate views, esp. in politics ▸ *vb* **-rating, -rated** **5** to make or become less extreme or violent: *he has moderated his opinions since then* **6** to preside over a meeting, discussion, etc. > **moderately** *adv*

moderate *adj* **1** = mild, reasonable, controlled, limited, steady, modest, restrained, middle-of-the-road; ≠ extreme **2, 3** = average, middling, fair, ordinary, indifferent, mediocre, so-so (*informal*), passable, half-pie (*NZ informal*) ▸ *vb* **5** = soften, control, temper, regulate, curb, restrain, subdue, lessen; ≠ intensify

moderation *n* **1** the quality of being moderate **2** the act of moderating **3 in moderation** within moderate or reasonable limits

moderator *n* **1** *Presbyterian Church* a minister appointed to preside over a Church court, synod, or general assembly **2** a person who presides over a public or legislative assembly **3** a material, such as heavy water, used for slowing down neutrons in nuclear reactors

modern *adj* **1** of the present or a recent time; contemporary: *there have been very few outbreaks of the disease in modern times* **2** using the latest techniques, equipment, etc.; up-to-date: *modern and efficient railways* **3** of contemporary styles or schools of art, literature, and music, esp. those of an experimental kind ▸ *n* **4** a contemporary person > **modernity** *n*

modern *adj* **1** = current, contemporary, recent, present-day, latter-day **2** = up-to-date, fresh, new, novel, newfangled; ≠ old-fashioned

modernism *n* an early- and mid-twentieth century movement in art, literature, and music that rejected traditional styles and techniques > **modernist** *n, adj*

modernize or **-nise** *vb* **-nizing, -nized** or **-nising, -nised** **1** to make modern in style, methods, or equipment: *a commitment to modernizing industry* **2** to adopt modern ways or ideas > **modernization** or **-nisation** *n*

modest *adj* **1** having a humble opinion of oneself or one's accomplishments **2** not extreme or excessive: *a modest increase in inflation* **3** not ostentatious or pretentious: *a modest flat in the suburbs* **4** shy or easily embarrassed **5** *old-fashioned* (esp. of clothes) not revealing much of the body: *a modest dress* > **modestly** *adv* > **modesty** *n*

modest *adj* **2** = moderate, small, limited, fair, ordinary, middling, meagre, frugal **3, 4** = unpretentious, reserved, retiring, shy, coy, reticent, self-effacing, demure

modicum *n* a small amount

modifier *n* *grammar* a word or phrase that makes the sense of another word more specific: for example, the noun *garage* is a modifier of *door* in *garage door*

modify *vb* **-fies, -fying, -fied** **1** to change or alter slightly **2** to make less extreme or uncompromising **3** *grammar* (of a word or phrase) to act as a modifier to another word or phrase > **modification** *n*

modify *vb* **1** = change, reform, convert, alter, adjust, adapt, revise, remodel **2** = tone down, lower, qualify, ease, moderate, temper, soften, restrain

modish (mode-ish) *adj* in the current fashion or style > **modishly** *adv*

modulate *vb* **-lating, -lated** **1** to change the tone, pitch, or volume of (one's voice) **2** to adjust or regulate the degree of: *the hormone which modulates the development of the sexual organs* **3** *music* to change from one key to another **4** *physics & electronics* to superimpose the amplitude, frequency, or phase of a wave or signal onto another wave or signal > **modulation** *n* > **modulator** *n*

module *n* **1** a standard self-contained unit, such as an assembly of electronic components or a standardized piece of furniture, that can be used in combination with other units **2** *astronautics* a self-contained separable unit making up a spacecraft **3** *education* a short course of study that together with other such courses counts towards a qualification > **modular** *adj*

m

modus operandi (mode-uss op-er-an-die) *n, pl* **modi operandi** (mode-eye) method of operating

mogul (moh-gl) *n* an important or powerful person

> **mogul** *n* = tycoon, baron (*old-fashioned*), magnate, big shot (*informal*), big noise (*informal*), big hitter (*informal*), heavy hitter (*informal*), V.I.P.

mohair *n* **1** the long soft silky hair of the Angora goat **2** a fabric made from yarn of this hair and cotton or wool

mohican *n* a punk hairstyle in which the head is shaved at the sides and the remaining strip of hair is worn stiffly erect and often brightly coloured

moiety (moy-it-ee) *n, pl* **-ties** *archaic* **1** a half **2** one of two parts or divisions of something

moist *adj* slightly damp or wet

> **moist** *adj* = damp, wet, soggy, humid, clammy, dewy

moisten *vb* to make or become moist

moisture *n* water diffused as vapour or condensed on or in objects

> **moisture** *n* = damp, water, liquid, dew, wetness

moisturize *or* **-rise** *vb* **-rizing, -rized** *or* **-rising, -rised** to add moisture to the air or the skin > **moisturizer** *or* **-riser** *n*

mojo *n, pl* **mojos** *or* **mojoes** *US slang* **1** a charm or magic spell **2** the art of casting magic spells **3** uncanny personal power or influence, esp. the power to attract sexually

moke *n* **1** *Brit slang* a donkey **2** *Austral & NZ* a horse of inferior quality

molar *n* **1** a large back tooth specialized for crushing and chewing food ▸ *adj* **2** of any of these teeth

molasses *n* **1** the thick brown bitter syrup obtained from sugar during refining **2** *US & Canad* same as **treacle**

mold *n, vb US* same as **mould¹**

mole¹ *n* a small dark raised spot on the skin

mole² *n* **1** a small burrowing mammal with velvety dark fur and forelimbs specialized for digging **2** *informal* a spy who has infiltrated an organization and become a trusted member of it

mole³ *n chem* the basic SI unit of amount of substance: the amount that contains as many elementary entities as there are atoms in 0.012 kilogram of carbon-12

mole⁴ *n* **1** a breakwater **2** a harbour protected by a breakwater

molecular (mol-lek-yew-lar) *adj* of or relating to molecules

molecule (mol-lik-kyool) *n* **1** the simplest unit of a chemical compound that can exist, consisting of two or more atoms held together by chemical bonds **2** a very small particle

> **molecule** *n* **2** = particle, jot, speck

molest *vb* **1** to accost or attack someone with the intention of assaulting her or him sexually **2** to disturb or injure, esp. by using or threatening violence: *killing, capturing, or molesting the local wildlife was strictly forbidden* > **molestation** *n* > **molester** *n*

moll *n slang* a gangster's female accomplice or girlfriend

mollify *vb* **-fies, -fying, -fied** to make someone less angry or upset; soothe: *he sought to mollify his critics* > **mollification** *n*

mollusc *or US* **mollusk** *n* an invertebrate with a soft unsegmented body and often a shell, such as a snail, mussel, or octopus

mollycoddle *vb* **-coddling, -coddled** to give an excessive amount of care and protection to

Molotov cocktail *n* a simple bomb made from a bottle filled with petrol and a cloth wick; petrol bomb

molt *vb, n US* same as **moult**

molten *adj* so hot that it has melted and formed a liquid: *molten metal*

molybdenum (mol-lib-din-um) *n chem* a very hard silvery-white metallic element used in alloys, esp. to harden and strengthen steels. Symbol: **Mo**

moment *n* **1** a short period of time **2** a specific instant or point in time: *at that moment the phone rang* **3 the moment** the present point of time: *for the moment he is out of prison* **4** importance, significance, or value: *a matter of greatest moment* **5** *physics* **A** a tendency to produce motion, esp. rotation about a point or axis **B** the product of a physical quantity, such as force or mass, and its distance from a fixed reference point

> **moment** *n* **1** = instant, second, flash, twinkling, split second, jiffy (*informal*), trice **2** = time, point, stage, juncture

momentary *adj* lasting for only a moment; temporary > **momentarily** *adv*

momentous (moh-men-tuss) *adj* of great significance > **momentousness** *n*

> **momentous** *adj* = significant, important, vital, critical, crucial (*informal*), historic, pivotal, fateful; ≠ unimportant

momentum (moh-men-tum) *n* **1** the impetus to go forward, develop, or get stronger: *the campaign steadily gathered support and momentum* **2** the impetus of a moving body: *the sledge gathered momentum as it slid ever faster down the slope* **3** *physics* the product of a body's mass and its velocity

> **momentum** *n* **1** = impetus, force, power, drive, push (*informal*), energy, strength, thrust

monarch *n* a sovereign head of state, esp. a king, queen, or emperor, who rules by hereditary right > **monarchical** *or* **monarchic** *adj*

monarch *n* = ruler, king *or* queen, sovereign, tsar, potentate, emperor *or* empress, prince *or* princess

monarchy *n, pl* **-chies 1** a form of government in which supreme authority is held by a single hereditary ruler, such as a king **2** a country reigned over by a monarch

monarchy *n* **1** = sovereignty, autocracy, kingship, queenship, royalism, monocracy **2** = kingdom, empire, realm, principality

monastery *n, pl* **-teries** the building or group of buildings where a community of monks lives

monastery *n* = abbey, convent, priory, cloister, nunnery, friary

monastic *adj* **1** of or relating to monasteries, monks, or nuns **2** (of a way of life) simple and austere; ascetic › **monasticism** *n*

Monday *n* the second day of the week, and the first day of the working week

monetarism *n* **1** the theory that inflation is caused by an excess quantity of money in an economy **2** an economic policy based on this theory and a belief in the efficiency of free market forces › **monetarist** *n, adj*

monetary *adj* of money or currency

monetary *adj* = financial, money, economic, capital, cash, fiscal, budgetary, pecuniary

money *n* **1** a means of payment and measure of value: *some cultures used to use shells as money* **2** the official currency, in the form of banknotes or coins, issued by a government **3 moneys** *or* **monies** *law old-fashioned* a financial sum or income **4** an unspecified amount of wealth: *money to lend* **5** *informal* a rich person or rich people: *he married money* **6 for my money** in my opinion **7 one's money's worth** full value for the money one has paid for something **8 put money on** to place a bet on. ‣ Related adjective: **pecuniary**

money *n* **1, 2** = cash, capital, currency, hard cash, readies (*informal*), riches, silver, coin, kembla (*Austral slang*)

moneyed *or* **monied** *adj* having a great deal of money; rich

mongol *n offensive* (not in technical use) a person affected by Down's syndrome › **mongoloid** *n, adj*

Mongolian *adj* **1** of Mongolia ‣ *n* **2** a person from Mongolia **3** the language of Mongolia

mongolism *n offensive* a former name (not in technical use) for **Down's syndrome**

mongoose *n, pl* **-gooses** a small long-tailed predatory mammal of Asia and Africa that kills snakes

mongrel *n* **1** a dog of mixed breeding **2** something made up of things from a variety of sources: *despite using components from three other cars, this new model is no mongrel* ‣ *adj* **3** of mixed breeding or origin

monitor *n* **1** a person or device that warns, checks, controls, or keeps a continuous record of something **2** *Brit, Austral & NZ* a pupil assisting a teacher with various duties **3** a screen used to display certain kinds of information, for example in airports or television studios **4** a large predatory lizard inhabiting warm regions of Africa, Asia, and Australia ‣ *vb* **5** to act as a monitor of **6** to observe or record the condition or performance of a person or thing **7** to check a broadcast for acceptable quality or content › **monitorial** *adj*

monitor *n* **1** = guide, observer, supervisor, invigilator **2** = prefect (*Brit*), head girl, head boy, senior boy, senior girl ‣ *vb* **5, 6** = check, follow, watch, survey, observe, keep an eye on, keep track of, keep tabs on

monk *n* a male member of a religious community bound by vows of poverty, chastity, and obedience. Related adjective: **monastic** › **monkish** *adj*

monk *n* = friar, brother

monkey *n* **1** any long-tailed primate that is not a lemur or tarsier **2** (loosely) any primate that is not a human **3** a naughty or mischievous child **4** *slang* £500 or $500 **5 give a monkey's** *Brit slang* to care about or regard as important: *who gives a monkey's what he thinks?* ‣ *vb* **6 monkey around** *or* **about with** to meddle or tinker with

monkey *n* **1, 2** = simian, ape, primate **3** = rascal, horror (*informal*), devil, rogue, imp, tyke, scallywag, scamp, nointer (*Austral slang*)

monkey nut *n Brit* a peanut

monkey puzzle *n* a South American coniferous tree with branches shaped like a candelabrum and stiff sharp leaves

monkey wrench *n chiefly Brit* a wrench with adjustable jaws

mono- *or before a vowel* **mon-** *combining form* **1** one; single: *monorail*; *monolingual* **2** *chem* indicating that a chemical compound contains a single specified atom or group: *monoxide*

monochrome *adj* **1** *photog & television* black-and-white ‣ *n* **2** a painting or drawing done in a range of tones of a single colour

monocle (mon-a-kl) *n* (formerly) a lens worn for correcting defective sight in one eye only, held in position by the facial muscles › **monocled** *adj*

monogamy *n* the state or practice of having only one husband or wife at a time › **monogamous** *adj*

monogram *n* a design of one or more letters, esp. initials, on clothing, stationery, etc.

monograph *n* a paper, book, or other work concerned with a single subject or aspect of a subject

m

monolith *n* **1** a large block of stone **2** a statue, obelisk, or column cut from one block of stone **3** something which can be regarded as forming one large, single, whole: *the Christian religion should not be thought of as a monolith* > **monolithic** *adj*

monologue *n* **1** a long speech made by one actor in a play or film; soliloquy **2** a dramatic piece for a single performer **3** any long speech by one person, esp. one which prevents other people talking or expressing their views

monomania *n* an obsession with one thing or idea > **monomaniac** *n, adj*

monoplane *n* an aeroplane with only one pair of wings

monopolize *or* **-lise** *vb* **-lizing, -lized** *or* **-lising, -lised** **1** to have full control or use of, to the exclusion of others **2** to hold exclusive control of a market or supply

monopoly *n, pl* **-lies** **1** exclusive control of the market supply of a product or service **2** **A** an enterprise exercising this control **B** the product or service so controlled **3** *law* the exclusive right granted to a person or company by the state to trade in a specified commodity or area **4** exclusive control, possession, or use of something > **monopolist** *n* > **monopolistic** *adj*

Monopoly *n trademark* a board game for two to six players who deal in 'property' as they move tokens around the board

monorail *n* a single-rail railway

monotheism *n* the belief or doctrine that there is only one God > **monotheist** *n, adj* > **monotheistic** *adj*

monotone *n* **1** a single unvaried pitch level in speech or sound **2** a way of speaking which lacks variety of pitch or expression: *he rambled on in a dull monotone* **3** lack of variety in style or expression ▸ *adj* **4** unvarying

monotonous *adj* tedious because of lack of variety > **monotonously** *adv*

monotony *n, pl* **-nies** **1** wearisome routine; dullness **2** lack of variety in pitch or tone

Monseigneur (mon-sen-**nyur**) *n, pl* **Messeigneurs** (may-sen-**nyur**) a title given to French prelates and princes

monsieur (muss-**syuh**) *n, pl* **messieurs** (may-**syuh**) a French form of address equivalent to *sir* or *Mr*

Monsignor *n, pl* **Monsignors** *or* **Monsignori** *RC Church* a title given to certain senior clergymen

monsoon *n* **1** a seasonal wind of S Asia which blows from the southwest in summer and from the northeast in winter **2** the rainy season when the SW monsoon blows, from about April to October

monster *n* **1** an imaginary beast, usually frightening in appearance **2** a very large person, animal, or thing **3** an exceptionally cruel or wicked person **4** a person, animal, or plant with a marked deformity

monster *n* **2** = giant, mammoth, titan, colossus, monstrosity **3** = brute, devil, beast, demon, villain, fiend

monstrance *n RC Church* a vessel in which the consecrated Host is exposed for adoration

monstrosity *n, pl* **-ties** **1** an outrageous or ugly person or thing **2** the state or quality of being monstrous

monstrous *adj* **1** hideous or unnatural in size or character **2** atrocious, unjust, or shocking: *the President described the invasion as monstrous* **3** huge **4** of or like a monster **5** (of plants and animals) abnormal in structure > **monstrously** *adv*

monstrous *adj* **1** = unnatural, horrible, hideous, grotesque, gruesome, frightful, freakish, fiendish; ≠ normal **2** = outrageous, shocking, foul, intolerable, disgraceful, scandalous, inhuman, diabolical; ≠ decent **3** = huge, massive, enormous, tremendous, immense, mammoth, colossal, prodigious; ≠ tiny

montage (mon-**tahzh**) *n* **1** a picture made by combining material from various sources, such as other pictures or photographs **2** the technique of producing pictures in this way **3** a method of film editing by juxtaposition or partial superimposition of several shots to form a single image **4** a film sequence of this kind

month *n* **1** one of the twelve divisions (**calendar months**) of the calendar year **2** a period of time extending from one date to a corresponding date in the next calendar month **3** a period of four weeks or of 30 days

monthly *adj* **1** happening or payable once every month: *a monthly magazine* **2** lasting or valid for a month: *a monthly travel pass* ▸ *adv* **3** once a month ▸ *n, pl* **-lies** **4** a magazine published once a month

monument *n* **1** something, such as a statue or building, erected in commemoration of a person or event **2** an ancient building which is regarded as an important part of a country's history **3** an exceptional example of the results of something: *the whole town is a monument to bad sixties' architecture*

monument *n* **1** = memorial, cairn, marker, shrine, tombstone, mausoleum, commemoration, headstone

monumental *adj* **1** large, impressive, or likely to last or be remembered for a long time: *a monumental three-volume biography* **2** of or being a monument **3** *informal* extreme: *a monumental gamble*

monumental *adj* **1** = important, significant, enormous, historic, memorable, awesome, majestic, unforgettable; ≠ unimportant **3** = immense, great, massive, staggering, colossal; ≠ tiny

moo n 1 the characteristic deep long sound made by a cow ▸ vb 2 to make this sound; low

mooch vb slang 1 to loiter or walk aimlessly 2 to cadge or scrounge

mood¹ n 1 a temporary state of mind or temper: a happy mood 2 a sullen or gloomy state of mind, esp. when temporary: she's in a mood 3 a prevailing atmosphere or feeling: the current mood of disenchantment with politics 4 **in the mood** inclined to do or have (something)

> **mood** n 1 = state of mind, spirit, humour, temper, disposition, frame of mind

mood² n grammar a form of a verb indicating whether the verb expresses a fact (indicative mood), a wish or supposition (subjunctive mood), or a command (imperative mood)

moody adj **moodier, moodiest** 1 sullen, sulky, or gloomy 2 temperamental or changeable > **moodily** adv > **moodiness** n

> **moody** adj 1 = gloomy, sad, sullen, glum, morose; ≠ cheerful 2 = changeable, volatile, unpredictable, erratic, fickle, temperamental, impulsive, mercurial; ≠ stable

moon n 1 the natural satellite of the earth. Related adjective: **lunar** 2 this satellite as it is seen during its revolution around the earth, esp. at one of its phases: new moon; full moon 3 any natural satellite of a planet 4 a month 5 **over the moon** informal extremely happy; ecstatic 6 **moon about** or **around** to be idle in a listless or dreamy way > **moonless** adj

> **moon** n 3 = satellite ▸ vb = idle, drift, loaf, languish, waste time, daydream, mope

moonlight n 1 light from the sun received on earth after reflection by the moon ▸ adj 2 illuminated by the moon: a moonlight walk ▸ vb **-lighting, -lighted** 3 informal to work at a secondary job, esp. illegally > **moonlighter** n

moonshine n 1 US & Canad illegally distilled or smuggled whisky 2 foolish or nonsensical talk or thought

moonstone n a white translucent form of feldspar, used as a gem

moonstruck adj slightly mad or odd, as if affected by the moon

moor¹ n Brit an expanse of open uncultivated ground covered with heather, coarse grass, and bracken

> **moor** n = moorland, fell (Brit), heath

moor² vb to secure a ship or boat with cables, ropes, or anchors so that it remains in one place > **moorage** n

> **moor** vb = tie up, secure, anchor, dock, lash, berth, make fast

Moor n a member of a Muslim people of North Africa who ruled much of Spain and Portugal between the 8th and 15th centuries

moorhen n a waterfowl with black plumage and a red bill

mooring n a place where a ship or boat can be tied up or anchored

Moorish adj 1 of or relating to the Moors 2 of a style of architecture used in Spain from the 8th to the 15th centuries, characterized by the horseshoe arch

moose n, pl **moose** a large North American deer with large flattened antlers; the American elk

moot adj 1 subject or open to debate: a moot point ▸ vb 2 to suggest or bring up for debate: a compromise proposal, involving building fewer flats, was mooted ▸ n 3 (in Anglo-Saxon England) a local administrative assembly

mop n 1 a tool with a head made of twists of cotton or sponge and a long handle used for washing or polishing floors 2 a similar tool, except smaller and without a long handle, used to wash dishes 3 a thick untidy mass of hair ▸ vb **mopping, mopped** 4 to clean or soak up with or as if with a mop: she mopped her brow with a handkerchief

> **mop** n 1, 2 = squeegee, sponge, swab 3 = mane, shock, mass, tangle, mat, thatch ▸ vb = clean, wash, wipe, sponge, swab

mope vb **moping, moped** 1 to be gloomy or apathetic 2 to walk around in a gloomy and aimless manner

moped n a light motorcycle not over 50cc

mopoke n 1 a small spotted owl of Australia and New Zealand 2 Austral slang a slow or lugubrious person

moraine n a ridge or mound formed from debris deposited by a glacier

moral adj 1 concerned with or relating to the distinction between good and bad or right and wrong behaviour: moral sense 2 based on a sense of right and wrong according to conscience: moral duty 3 displaying a sense of right and wrong; (of support or a victory) psychological rather than practical ▸ n 4 a lesson about right or wrong behaviour that is shown in a fable or event 5 **morals** principles of behaviour in accordance with standards of right and wrong > **morally** adv

> **moral** adj 3 = good, just, right, principled, decent, noble, ethical, honourable; ≠ immoral ▸ n 4 = lesson, meaning, point, message, teaching, import, significance, precept 5 = morality, standards, conduct, principles, behaviour, manners, habits, ethics

morale (mor-**rahl**) n the degree of confidence or optimism of a person or group

> **morale** = confidence, heart, spirit, self-esteem, team spirit, esprit de corps

moralist n 1 a person who has a strong sense of right and wrong 2 someone who criticizes other

people for doing what he or she thinks is
morally correct > **moralistic** adj

morality n, pl **-ties 1** good moral conduct
2 the degree to which something is morally
acceptable: *we discussed the morality of fox-hunting*
3 a system of moral principles

> **morality** n **1** = virtue, justice, morals,
> honour, integrity, goodness, honesty, decency
> **2** = rights and wrongs, ethics **3** = ethics,
> conduct, principles, morals, manners,
> philosophy, mores

morality play n a medieval type of drama
concerned with the conflict between
personified virtues and vices

moralize or **-lise** vb **-lizing, -lized** or **-lising,
-lised 1** to discuss or consider something in the
light of one's own moral beliefs, esp. with
disapproval **2** to interpret or explain in a moral
sense **3** to improve the morals of

morass n **1** a tract of swampy low-lying land
2 a disordered, confusing, or muddled state of
affairs

moratorium n, pl **-ria** or **-riums 1** a legally
authorized postponement of the payment
of a debt **2** an agreed suspension of activity

> **moratorium** n = postponement, freeze, halt,
> suspension, standstill

moray n a large marine eel marked with
brilliant colours

morbid adj **1** having an unusual interest in
death or unpleasant events **2** med relating to or
characterized by disease > **morbidity** n
> **morbidly** adv

mordant adj **1** sarcastic or caustic: *mordant wit*
> n **2** a substance used in dyeing to fix colours
3 an acid or other corrosive fluid used to etch
lines on a printing plate

more adj **1** the comparative of **much** or **many**:
more joy than you know; even more are leaving the country
2 additional or further: *no more apples* **3** **more of**
to a greater extent or degree: *more of a nuisance*
> adv **4** used to form the comparative of some
adjectives and adverbs: *more quickly* **5** the
comparative of **much**: *people listen to the radio more
now* **6** **more or less** **A** as an estimate;
approximately **B** to an unspecified extent or
degree: *the film was a disaster, more or less*

> **more** adj **2** = extra, additional, new, other,
> added, further, new-found, supplementary

moreover adv in addition to what has already
been said

> **moreover** adv = furthermore, also, further,
> in addition, too, as well, besides, additionally

mores (**more**-rayz) pl n the customs and
conventions embodying the fundamental
values of a community

Moreton Bay bug n an Australian flattish
edible shellfish

morgue n **1** a mortuary **2** informal a store of
clippings and back numbers used for reference
in a newspaper

moribund adj **1** near death **2** no longer
performing effectively or usefully: *a moribund
economy*

Mormon n **1** a member of the Church of Jesus
Christ of Latter-day Saints, founded in 1830 in
New York by Joseph Smith ▸ adj **2** of the Church
of Jesus Christ of Latter-day Saints, its members,
or their beliefs > **Mormonism** n

morn n poetic or Austral morning

morning n **1** the first part of the day, ending at
noon **2** daybreak; dawn **3** **the morning after**
informal the aftereffects of excess, esp. a
hangover ▸ adj **4** of or in the morning: *morning
coffee*

> **morning** n **1** = before noon, forenoon, morn
> (*poetic*), a.m. **2** = dawn, sunrise, first light,
> daybreak, break of day

morning-glory n, pl **-ries** a tropical climbing
plant with trumpet-shaped blue, pink, or white
flowers, which close in late afternoon

Moroccan adj **1** of Morocco ▸ n **2** a person from
Morocco

morocco n a fine soft leather made from
goatskins

moron n **1** informal, derogatory a foolish or stupid
person **2** not in technical use, offensive a person
having an intelligence quotient of between 50
and 70 > **moronic** adj

morose (mor-**rohss**) adj ill-tempered, sullen,
and unwilling to talk very much > **morosely** adv

morphine or **morphia** n a drug extracted from
opium: used in medicine as an anaesthetic and
sedative

morphology n the science of forms and
structures of organisms or words
> **morphological** adj

morris dance n an old English folk dance
performed by men (**morris men**) who wear a
traditional costume decorated with bells

morrow n the morrow old-fashioned or poetic
1 the next day **2** the morning

Morse code n a code formerly used
internationally for transmitting messages, in
which letters and numbers are represented by
groups of dots and dashes, or by shorter and
longer sounds

morsel n a small piece of something, esp. of food

mortal adj **1** (of living beings, esp. humans)
destined to die sometime rather than living
forever **2** causing death; fatal: *a mortal wound*
3 deadly or unrelenting: *he is my mortal enemy*
4 of or resulting from the fear of death: *mortal
terror* **5** of or involving life or the world: *the
hangman's noose ended his mortal existence* **6** great
or very intense: *mortal pain* **7** informal conceivable
or possible: *there was no mortal reason to leave*
8 slang long and tedious: *for three mortal hours* ▸ n
9 a human being > **mortally** adv

mortal *adj* **1, 5** = human, worldly, passing, fleshly, temporal, transient, ephemeral, perishable **2** = fatal, killing, terminal, deadly, destructive, lethal, murderous, death-dealing ▸ *n* = human being, being, man, woman, person, human, individual, earthling

mortality *n*, *pl* **-ties 1** the condition of being mortal **2** great loss of life, as in war or disaster **3** the number of deaths in a given period

mortality *n* **1** = humanity, transience, impermanence, corporeality, impermanency **2, 3** = death, dying, fatality

mortal sin *n* *Christianity* a sin that will lead to damnation unless repented of

mortar *n* **1** a small cannon that fires shells in high arcs **2** a mixture of cement or lime or both with sand and water, used to hold bricks or stones together **3** a vessel, usually bowl-shaped, in which substances are crushed with a pestle ▸ *vb* **4** to fire on with mortars **5** to join bricks or stones with mortar

mortarboard *n* **1** a black tasselled academic cap with a flat square top **2** a small square board with a handle on the underside for carrying mortar

mortgage *n* **1** an agreement under which a person borrows money to buy property, esp. a house, and the lender can take possession of the property if the borrower fails to repay the money **2** a loan obtained under such an agreement: *a mortgage of three times one's income* **3** a regular repayment of money borrowed under such an agreement: *the monthly mortgage on the building* ▸ *vb* **-gaging, -gaged 4** to pledge a house or other property as security for the repayment of a loan ▸ *adj* **5** of or relating to a mortgage: *a mortgage payment*

mortgagee *n* the person or organization who lends money in a mortgage agreement

mortgagor *or* **-ger** *n* the person who borrows money in a mortgage agreement

mortice *or* **mortise** (mor-tiss) *n* **1** a slot or recess cut into a piece of wood or stone to receive a matching projection (tenon) on another piece, or a mortice lock ▸ *vb* **-ticing, -ticed** *or* **-tising, -tised 2** to cut a slot or recess in a piece of wood or stone **3** to join two pieces of wood or stone by means of a mortice and tenon

mortice lock *n* a lock set into the edge of a door so that the mechanism of the lock is enclosed by the door

mortify *vb* **-fies, -fying, -fied 1** to make someone feel ashamed or embarrassed **2** *Christianity* to subdue one's emotions, the body, etc., by self-denial **3** (of flesh) to become gangrenous > **mortification** *n* > **mortifying** *adj*

mortuary *n*, *pl* **-aries** a building or room where dead bodies are kept before cremation or burial

mosaic (moh-**zay**-ik) *n* a design or decoration made up of small pieces of coloured glass or stone

Mosaic *adj* of or relating to Moses or the laws and traditions ascribed to him

moscovium *n* *chem* a synthetic radioactive element produced in small quantities. Symbol: **Mc**

moselle *n* a German white wine from the valley of the river Moselle

Moslem *n*, *pl* **-lems** *or* **-lem**, *adj* same as **Muslim**

mosque *n* a Muslim place of worship

mosquito *n*, *pl* **-toes** *or* **-tos** a two-winged insect, the females of which pierce the skin of humans and animals to suck their blood

moss *n* **1** a very small flowerless plant typically growing in dense mats on trees, rocks, or moist ground **2** *Scot & N English* a peat bog or marsh > **mossy** *adj*

most *n* **1** the greatest number or degree: *the most I can ever remember being paid* **2** the majority: *most of his records are dreadful* **3 at (the) most** at the maximum: *she is fifteen at the most* **4 make the most of** to use to the best advantage: *they made the most of their chances* ▸ *adj* **5** of or being the majority of a group of things or people or the largest part of something: *most people don't share your views* **6 the most** the superlative of **many** or **much**: *he has the most talent* ▸ *adv* **7 the most** used to form the superlative of some adjectives and adverbs: *the most beautiful places in the world* **8** the superlative of **much**: *what do you like most about your job?* **9** very; exceedingly: *a most unfortunate accident*

mostly *adv* **1** almost entirely; generally: *the men at the party were mostly young* **2** on many or most occasions; usually: *rattlesnakes mostly hunt at night*

mostly *adv* **1** = mainly, largely, chiefly, principally, primarily, on the whole, predominantly **2** = generally, usually, on the whole, as a rule

MOT 1 *Brit* short for **MOT test 2** *Brit* the certificate showing that a vehicle has passed its MOT test **3** *NZ* Ministry of Transport

motel *n* a roadside hotel for motorists

motet (moh-**tet**) *n* a religious song for a choir in which several voices, usually unaccompanied, sing contrasting parts simultaneously

moth *n* any of numerous chiefly nocturnal insects resembling butterflies, that typically have stout bodies and do not have club-shaped antennae

mothball *n* **1** a small ball of camphor or naphthalene placed in stored clothing to repel clothes moths **2 put in mothballs** to postpone work on ▸ *vb* **3** to take something out of operation but maintain it for future use **4** to postpone work on

moth-eaten *adj* **1** decayed or scruffy **2** eaten away by or as if by moths: *a moth-eaten suit*

mother *n* **1** a female who has given birth to offspring **2** a person's own mother **3** a title given to certain members of female religious orders **4** motherly qualities, such as maternal

m

affection: *it appealed to the mother in her* **5 the mother of** a female or thing that creates, founds, or protects something: *the mother of modern feminism; necessity is the mother of invention* **6 the mother of all** *informal* the greatest example of its kind: *the mother of all parties* ▸ *adj* **7** of or relating to a female or thing that creates, founds, or protects something: *our mother company is in New York* **8** native or innate: *mother wit* ▸ *vb* **9** to give birth to or produce **10** to nurture or protect > **motherless** *adj* > **motherly** *adj*

mother *n* **1, 2** = female parent, mum (*Brit informal*), mummy (*Brit informal*), ma (*informal*), mater, dam, foster mother, biological mother ▸ *adj* **8** = native, natural, innate, inborn ▸ *vb* **10** = nurture, raise, protect, tend, nurse, rear, care for, cherish

motherboard *n electronics* a printed circuit board through which signals between all other boards are routed

motherhood *n* the state of being a mother

mother-in-law *n, pl* **mothers-in-law** the mother of one's wife or husband

mother tongue *n* the language first learned by a child

motif (moh-**teef**) *n* **1** a distinctive idea, esp. a theme elaborated on in a piece of music or literature **2** a recurring shape in a design **3** a single decoration, such as a symbol or name on a piece of clothing

motif *n* **1** = theme, idea, subject, concept, leitmotif, trope **2, 3** = design, shape, decoration, ornament

motion *n* **1** the process of continual change in the position of an object; movement: *the motion of the earth round the sun.* Related adjective: **kinetic 2** a movement or gesture: *he made stabbing motions with the spear* **3** a way or style of moving: *massage the back with steady circular motions* **4** a formal proposal to be discussed and voted on in a debate or meeting **5** *Brit* **A** the evacuation of the bowels **B** excrement **6 go through the motions** to do something mechanically or without sincerity **7 set in motion** to make operational or start functioning ▸ *vb* **8** to signal or direct a person by a movement or gesture: *she motioned to me to sit down* > **motionless** *adj*

motion *n* **1** = movement, mobility, travel, progress, flow, locomotion **4** = proposal, suggestion, recommendation, proposition, submission ▸ *vb* = gesture, direct, wave, signal, nod, beckon, gesticulate

motion picture *n US & Canad* a film; movie

motivate *vb* **-vating, -vated 1** to give a reason or inspiration for a course of action to someone: *he was motivated purely by greed* **2** to inspire and encourage someone to do something: *a good teacher must motivate her pupils* > **motivation** *n*

motivate *vb* **1** = inspire, drive, stimulate, move, cause, prompt, stir, induce **2** = stimulate, drive, inspire, stir, arouse, galvanize, incentivize

motive *n* **1** the reason, whether conscious or unconscious, for a certain course of action **2** same as **motif** (sense 2) ▸ *adj* **3** of or causing motion: *a motive force*

motive *n* **1** = reason, ground(s), purpose, object, incentive, inspiration, stimulus, rationale

motley *adj* **1** made up of people or things of different types: *a motley assortment of mules, donkeys, and camels* **2** multicoloured ▸ *n* **3** *history* the costume of a jester

motocross *n* the sport of motorcycle racing across rough ground

motor *n* **1** the engine, esp. an internal-combustion engine, of a vehicle **2** a machine that converts energy, esp. electrical energy, into mechanical energy **3** *chiefly Brit informal* a car ▸ *adj* **4** *chiefly Brit* of or relating to cars and other vehicles powered by petrol or diesel engines: *the motor industry* **5** powered by or relating to a motor: *a new synthetic motor oil* **6** *physiol* producing or causing motion ▸ *vb* **7** to travel by car **8** *informal* to move fast > **motorized** *or* **-ised** *adj*

motorbike *n informal* a motorcycle

motorboat *n* any boat powered by a motor

motorcar *n* a more formal word for **car**

motorcycle *n* a two-wheeled vehicle driven by an engine > **motorcyclist** *n*

motorhome *n* a large motor vehicle designed for living in while travelling

motorist *n* a driver of a car

motor scooter *n* a light motorcycle with small wheels and an enclosed engine

motorway *n Brit, Austral & NZ* a dual carriageway for fast-moving traffic, with no stopping permitted and no crossroads

MOT test *n* (in Britain) a compulsory annual test of the roadworthiness of motor vehicles over 3 years old

mottled *adj* coloured with streaks or blotches of different shades > **mottling** *n*

motto *n, pl* **-toes** *or* **-tos 1** a short saying expressing the guiding maxim or ideal of a family or organization, esp. when part of a coat of arms **2** a verse or maxim contained in a paper cracker **3** a quotation prefacing a book or chapter of a book

motto *n* **1** = saying, slogan, maxim, rule, adage, proverb, dictum, precept

mould¹ *or US* **mold** *n* **1** a shaped hollow container into which a liquid material is poured so that it can set in a particular shape: *pour the mixture into a buttered mould, cover, and steam for two hours* **2** a shape, nature, or type: *an orthodox Communist in the Stalinist mould* **3** a framework around which something is constructed or shaped: *the heated glass is shaped round a mould inside a kiln* **4** something, esp. a food, made in or on a mould: *salmon mould* ▸ *vb* **5** to make in a mould **6** to shape or form: *a figure moulded out of clay* **7** to influence or direct: *cultural factors moulding our everyday life*

> **mould** *or* **mold** *n* **1** = cast, shape, pattern **2** = nature, character, sort, kind, quality, type, stamp, calibre ▸ *vb* **6** = shape, make, work, form, create, model, fashion, construct **7** = influence, make, form, control, direct, affect, shape

mould² *or US* **mold** *n* a coating or discoloration caused by various fungi that develop in a damp atmosphere on food, fabrics, and walls

> **mould** *or* **mold** *n* = fungus, blight, mildew

mould³ *or US* **mold** *n* loose soil, esp. when rich in organic matter: *leaf mould*

moulder *or US* **molder** *vb* to crumble or cause to crumble, as through decay: *John Brown's body lies mouldering in the grave*

moulding *or US* **molding** *n* a shaped ornamental edging

mouldy *or US* **moldy** *adj* **-dier, -diest 1** covered with mould **2** stale or musty, esp. from age or lack of use **3** *slang* dull or boring

moult *or US* **molt** *vb* **1** (of birds and animals) to shed feathers, hair, or skin so that they can be replaced by a new growth ▸ *n* **2** the periodic process of moulting

mound *n* **1** a heap of earth, debris, etc. **2** any heap or pile **3** a small natural hill

> **mound** *n* **1, 2** = heap, pile, drift, stack, rick **3** = hill, bank, rise, dune, embankment, knoll, hillock, kopje *or* koppie (*S African*)

mount¹ *vb* **1** to climb or ascend: *he mounted the stairs to his flat* **2** to get up on a horse, a platform, etc. **3** Also: **mount up** to increase or accumulate: *costs do mount up; the tension mounted* **4** to fix onto a backing, setting, or support: *sensors mounted on motorway bridges* **5** to organize and stage a campaign, play, etc.: *the Allies mounted a counter attack on the eastern front* ▸ *n* **6** a backing, setting, or support onto which something is fixed: *a diamond set in a gold mount* **7** a horse for riding: *none of his mounts at yesterday's race meeting finished better than third*

> **mount** *vb* **1** = ascend, scale, climb (up), go up, clamber up; ≠ descend **2** = get (up) on, jump on, straddle, climb onto, hop on to, bestride, get on the back of; ≠ get off **3** = accumulate, increase, collect, gather, build up, pile up, amass; ≠ decrease **5** = display, present, prepare, put on, organize, put on display ▸ *n* **6** = backing, setting, support, stand, base, frame **7** = horse, steed (*literary*)

mount² *n* a mountain or hill: used in literature and (when cap.) in proper names: *Mount Etna*

mountain *n* **1** a very large, high, and steep hill: *the highest mountain in the Alps* **2** a huge heap or mass: *a mountain of papers* **3** a surplus of a commodity, esp. in the European Union: *a butter mountain* ▸ *adj* **4** of, found on, or for use on a mountain or mountains: *a mountain village*

> **mountain** *n* **1** = peak, mount, horn, ridge, fell (*Brit*), berg (*S African*), alp, pinnacle **2** = heap, mass, masses, pile, a great deal, ton, stack, abundance

mountain bike *n* a type of bicycle with straight handlebars and heavy-duty tyres, originally designed for use over rough hilly ground

mountaineer *n* **1** a person who climbs mountains ▸ *vb* **2** to climb mountains › **mountaineering** *n*

mountainous *adj* **1** having many mountains: *a mountainous region* **2** like a mountain or mountains, esp. in size: *mountainous waves*

mountain oyster *n NZ informal* a sheep's testicle eaten as food

mountebank *n* **1** (formerly) a person who sold quack medicines in public places **2** a charlatan or fake

Mountie *or* **Mounty** *n, pl* **Mounties** *informal* a member of the Royal Canadian Mounted Police

mourn *vb* to feel or express sadness for the death or loss of someone or something › **mourner** *n*

> **mourn** *vb* = grieve for, lament, weep for, wail for

mournful *adj* **1** feeling or expressing grief and sadness: *he stood by, a mournful expression on his face* **2** (of a sound) suggestive or reminiscent of grief or sadness: *the locomotive gave a mournful bellow* › **mournfully** *adv*

mourning *n* **1** sorrow or grief, esp. over a death **2** the conventional symbols of grief for a death, such as the wearing of black **3** the period of time during which a death is officially mourned ▸ *adj* **4** of or relating to mourning

> **mourning** *n* **1** = grieving, grief, bereavement, weeping, woe, lamentation **2** = black, sackcloth and ashes, widow's weeds

mouse *n, pl* **mice 1** a small long-tailed rodent similar to but smaller than a rat **2** a quiet, timid, or cowardly person **3** a hand-held device used to control cursor movements and computing functions without using a keyboard ▸ *vb* **mousing, moused 4** *rare* to stalk and catch mice

mouser *n* a cat or other animal that is used to catch mice

mousse *n* **1** a light creamy dessert made with eggs, cream, and fruit set with gelatine **2** a similar dish made from fish or meat

moustache *or US* **mustache** *n* unshaved hair growing on the upper lip

mousy *or* **mousey** *adj* **mousier, mousiest**
1 (of hair) dull light brown in colour **2** shy or ineffectual **> mousiness** *n*

mouth *n, pl* **mouths 1** the opening through which many animals take in food and issue sounds **2** the visible part of the mouth; lips **3** a person regarded as a consumer of food: *three mouths to feed* **4** a particular manner of speaking: *a foul mouth* **5** *informal* boastful, rude, or excessive talk: *she is all mouth* **6** the point where a river issues into a sea or lake **7** an opening, such as that of a bottle, tunnel, or gun **8 down in the mouth** in low spirits **> vb 9** to form words with movements of the lips but without speaking **10** to speak or say something insincerely, esp. in public: *ministers mouthing platitudes*

> **mouth** *n* **1, 2** = lips, jaws, gob (*slang, esp Brit*), maw, cakehole (*Brit slang*) **6** = inlet, outlet, estuary, firth, outfall, debouchment **7** = entrance, opening, gateway, door, aperture, orifice

mouthful *n, pl* **-fuls 1** the amount of food or drink put into the mouth at any one time when eating or drinking **2** a long word, phrase, or name that is difficult to say **3** *Brit informal* an abusive response: *I asked him to move and he just gave me a mouthful*

mouth organ *n* same as **harmonica**

mouthpiece *n* **1** the part of a wind instrument into which the player blows **2** the part of a telephone receiver into which a person speaks **3** a person or publication expressing the views of an organization

movable *or* **moveable** *adj* **1** able to be moved; not fixed **2** (of a festival, esp. Easter) varying in date from year to year **> n 3 movables** movable articles, esp. furniture

move *vb* **moving, moved 1** to go or take from one place to another; change in position: *I moved your books off the table* **2** to start to live or work in a different place: *I moved to Brighton from Bristol last year* **3** to be or cause to be in motion: *the trees were moving in the wind; the car moved slowly down the road* **4** to act or begin to act: *the government plans to move to reduce crime* **5** to cause or prompt to do something: *public opinion moved the President to act* **6** to change the time when something is scheduled to happen: *can I move the appointment to Friday afternoon, please?* **7** to arouse affection, pity, or compassion in; touch: *her story moved me to tears* **8** to change, progress, or develop in a specified way: *the conversation moved to more personal matters* **9** to suggest a proposal formally, as in a debate: *to move a motion* **10** to spend most of one's time with a specified social group: *they both move in theatrical, arty circles* **11** (in board games) to change the position of a piece **12** (of machines) to work or operate **13 A** (of the bowels) to excrete waste **B** to cause the bowels to excrete waste **14** (of merchandise) to be disposed of by being bought **15** to travel quickly: *this car can really move*

16 move heaven and earth to do everything possible to achieve a result **> n 17** the act of moving; movement **18** one of a sequence of actions, usually part of a plan: *the first real move towards disarmament* **19** the act of moving one's home or place of business **20 A** (in a boardgame) a player's turn to move his piece **B** (in a boardgame) a manoeuvre of a piece **21 get a move on** *informal* to hurry up **22 make a move** *informal* **A** to prepare or begin to leave a place to go somewhere else: *we'd better make a move if we want to be home before dark* **B** to do something which will produce a response: *neither of us wanted to make the first move* **23 on the move** travelling from place to place

> **move** *vb* **1, 6** = transfer, change, switch, shift, transpose **2** = relocate, leave, remove, quit, migrate, emigrate, decamp, up sticks (*Brit informal*) **5** = drive, cause, influence, persuade, shift, inspire, prompt, induce; ≠ discourage **7** = touch, affect, excite, impress, stir, disquiet **9** = propose, suggest, urge, recommend, request, advocate, submit, put forward **> n 17** = action, step, manoeuvre **18** = ploy, action, measure, step, initiative, stroke, tactic, manoeuvre **19** = transfer, posting, shift, removal, relocation **20** = turn, go, play, chance, shot (*informal*), opportunity

movement *n* **1** the act, process, or an instance of moving **2** the manner of moving: *their movement is jerky* **3 A** a group of people with a common ideology **B** the organized action and campaigning of such a group: *a successful movement to abolish child labour* **4** a trend or tendency: *a movement towards shorter working hours* **5** *finance* a change in the price or value of shares, a currency, etc.: *adverse currency movements* **6** *music* a principal self-contained section of a large-scale work, such as a symphony **7 movements** a person's location and activities during a specific time: *police were trying to piece together the recent movements of the two men* **8 A** the evacuation of the bowels **B** the matter evacuated **9** the mechanism which drives and regulates a watch or clock

> **movement** *n* **1, 2** = move, action, motion, manoeuvre **3A** = group, party, organization, grouping, front, faction **3B** = campaign, drive, push (*informal*), crusade **5** = development, change, variation, fluctuation **6** = section, part, division, passage

movie *n* **1** *informal* a cinema film **2 the movies** the cinema: *I want to go to the movies tonight*

> **movie** *n* **1** = film, picture, feature, flick (*slang, old-fashioned*), MP4, MPEG

mow *vb* **mowing, mowed, mowed** *or* **mown 1** to cut down grass or crops: *a tractor chugged along, mowing hay* **2** to cut the growing vegetation of a field or lawn: *to mow a meadow* **> mower** *n*

mow *vb* = cut, crop, trim, shear, scythe

mow down *vb* to kill in large numbers, esp. by gunfire

> **mow down** *vb* **mow something or someone down** = massacre, butcher, slaughter, cut down, shoot down, cut to pieces

mozzarella (mot-sa-rel-la) *n* a moist white curd cheese originally made in Italy from buffalo milk

MP 1 Member of Parliament **2** Military Police **3** Mounted Police

MP3 *n* a format for processing a digital audio file so as to remove unneeded data and produce a smaller file for transmission on the internet, for use in portable players, etc.

MP3 player *n* a small portable digital audio player capable of storing and playing files downloaded from the internet or transferred from a CD

MPEG (em-peg) *n computers* **A** a standard compressed file format used for audio and video files **B** a file in this format

mpg miles per gallon

mph miles per hour

Mr *n, pl* **Messrs** a title used before a man's name or before some office that he holds: *Mr Pickwick; Mr President*

Mrs *n, pl* **Mrs** *or* **Mesdames** a title used before the name of a married woman

Ms (mizz) *n* a title used before the name of a woman to avoid indicating whether she is married or not

MS 1 Mississippi **2** multiple sclerosis

MS. *or* **ms.** *pl* **MSS.** *or* **mss.** manuscript

MSc Master of Science

MSP (in Britain) Member of the Scottish Parliament

Mt Mount: *Mt Everest*

much *adj* **more, most 1** a large amount or degree of: *there isn't much wine left* ▶ *n* **2** a large amount or degree **3 a bit much** *informal* rather excessive **4 make much of A** to make sense of: *he couldn't make much of her letter* **B** to give importance to: *the press made much of the story* **5 not much of** not to any appreciable degree or extent: *he's not much of a cook* **6 not up to much** *informal* of a low standard: *this beer is not up to much* ▶ *adv* **7** considerably: *I'm much better now* **8** practically or nearly: *it's much the same* **9** often or a great deal: *that doesn't happen much these days* **10 (as) much as** even though; although: *much as I'd like to, I can't come* ▶ See also **more, most**

> **much** *adj* = great, a lot of, plenty of, considerable, substantial, piles of (*informal*), ample, abundant, shedful (*slang*); ≠ little ▶ *n* **2** = a lot, plenty, a great deal, lots (*informal*), masses (*informal*), loads (*informal*), tons (*informal*), heaps (*informal*); ≠ little ▶ *adv* **7** = greatly, a lot, considerably, decidedly, exceedingly, appreciably; ≠ hardly

9 = often, a lot, routinely, a great deal, many times, habitually, on many occasions, customarily

muck *n* **1** dirt or filth **2** farmyard dung or decaying vegetable matter **3** *slang, chiefly Brit & NZ* something of poor quality; rubbish: *I don't want to eat this muck* **4 make a muck of** *slang, chiefly Brit & NZ* to ruin or spoil ▶ *vb* **5** to spread manure upon

> **muck** *n* **1** = dirt, mud, filth, ooze, sludge, mire, slime, gunge (*informal*), kak (*S African vulgar slang*) **2** = manure, dung, ordure

mucky *adj* **1** dirty or muddy: *don't come in here with your mucky boots on!* **2** sexually explicit; obscene: *a mucky book*

mucous membrane *n* a mucus-secreting tissue that lines body cavities or passages

mucus (mew-kuss) *n* the slimy protective secretion of the mucous membranes > **mucosity** *n* > **mucous** *adj*

mud *n* **1** soft wet earth, as found on the ground after rain or at the bottom of ponds **2 (someone's) name is mud** *informal* (someone) is disgraced **3 throw mud at** *informal* to slander or vilify ▶ *adj* **4** made from mud or dried mud: *a mud hut*

> **mud** *n* **1** = dirt, clay, ooze, silt, sludge, mire, slime

muddle *n* **1** a state of untidiness or confusion: *the files are in a terrible muddle* **2** a state of mental confusion or uncertainty: *the government are in a muddle over the economy* ▶ *vb* **-dling, -dled** *Also:* **muddle up** to mix up or confuse (objects or items): *you've got your books all muddled up with mine* **4** to make (someone) confused: *don't muddle her with too many suggestions* > **muddled** *adj*

> **muddle** *n* = confusion, mess, disorder, chaos, tangle, mix-up, disarray, predicament ▶ *vb* **3** = jumble, disorder, scramble, tangle, mix up **4** = confuse, bewilder, daze, confound, perplex, disorient, stupefy, befuddle

muddy *adj* **-dier, -diest 1** covered or filled with mud **2** not clear or bright: *muddy colours* **3** cloudy: *a muddy liquid* **4** (esp. of thoughts) confused or vague ▶ *vb* **-dies, -dying, -died 5** to make muddy **6** to make a situation or issue less clear: *the allegations of sexual misconduct only serve to muddy the issue* > **muddily** *adv*

> **muddy** *adj* **1** = boggy, swampy, marshy, quaggy

mudguard *n* a curved part of a bicycle or other vehicle attached above the wheels to reduce the amount of water or mud thrown up by them

muesli (mewz-lee) *n* a mixture of rolled oats, nuts, and dried fruit, usually eaten with milk

muezzin (moo-ezz-in) *n Islam* the official of a mosque who calls the faithful to prayer from the minaret

muff[1] *n* a tube of fur or cloth into which the hands are placed for warmth

muff[2] *vb* **1** to do (something) badly: *I muffed my chance to make a good impression* **2** to bungle (a shot or catch)

muffin *n* **1** a small cup-shaped sweet bread roll, usually eaten hot with butter **2** a thick round baked yeast roll, usually toasted and served with butter

muffle *vb* **-fling, -fled 1** to deaden (a sound or noise), esp. by wrapping the source of it in something: *the sound was muffled by the double glazing* **2** to wrap up in a scarf or coat for warmth **3** to censor or restrict: *an attempt to muffle criticism* > **muffled** *adj*

muffler *n* **1** *Brit* a thick scarf worn for warmth **2** *US & Canad* a device to deaden sound, esp. one on a car exhaust; silencer

mug[1] *n* **1** a large drinking cup with a handle **2** the quantity held by a mug or its contents: *a mug of coffee*

> **mug** *n* = cup, pot (*informal*), beaker, tankard

mug[2] *n* **1** *slang* a person's face or mouth: *keep your ugly mug out of this* **2** *slang* a gullible person, esp. one who is swindled easily **3** **a mug's game** a worthless activity

> **mug** *n* **1** = face, features, countenance (*literary*), visage (*formal*) **2** = fool, sucker (*slang*), chump (*informal*), simpleton, easy *or* soft touch (*slang*), dorba *or* dorb (*Austral slang*), bogan (*Austral slang*)

mug[3] *vb* **mugging, mugged** to attack someone in order to rob them > **mugger** *n* > **mugging** *n*

> **mug** *vb* = attack, assault, beat up, rob, set about *or* upon

muggins *n slang* **A** a stupid or gullible person **B** a title used humorously to refer to oneself

muggy *adj* **-gier, -giest** (of weather or air) unpleasantly warm and humid > **mugginess** *n*

mulatto (mew-lat-toe) *n, pl* **-tos** *or* **-toes** *old-fashioned, offensive* a person with one Black and one White parent

mulberry *n, pl* **-ries 1** a tree with edible blackberry-like fruit, the leaves of which are used to feed silkworms **2** the fruit of any of these trees ▸ *adj* **3** dark purple

mulch *n* **1** a mixture of half-rotten vegetable matter and peat used to protect the roots of plants or enrich the soil ▸ *vb* **2** to cover soil with mulch

mule[1] *n* **1** the sterile offspring of a male donkey and a female horse **2** a machine that spins cotton into yarn

mule[2] *n* a backless shoe or slipper

mulga *n* **1** an Australian acacia shrub growing in desert regions **2** *Austral* the outback

mulish *adj* stubborn; obstinate

mull *n Scot* a promontory or headland: *the Mull of Galloway*

mullah *n* (formerly) a Muslim scholar, teacher, or religious leader

mulled *adj* (of wine or ale) flavoured with sugar and spices and served hot

mullet *n, pl* **mullets** *or* **mullet** any of various marine food fishes

mulligatawny *n* a curry-flavoured soup of Anglo-Indian origin

mullion *n* a slender vertical bar between the casements or panes of a window > **mullioned** *adj*

mulloway *n* a large Australian sea fish, valued for sport and food

multi- *combining form* **1** many or much: *multimillion* **2** more than one: *multistorey*

multifarious (mull-tee-fare-ee-uss) *adj* many and varied: *multifarious religious movements and political divisions sprang up around this time*

multilateral *adj* of or involving more than two nations or parties: *multilateral trade negotiations*

multiple *adj* **1** having or involving more than one part, individual, or element ▸ *n* **2** a number or polynomial which can be divided by another specified one an exact number of times: *6 is a multiple of 2* > **multiply** *adv*

> **multiple** *adj* = many, several, various, numerous, sundry, manifold (*formal*), multitudinous

multiplex *n, pl* **-plexes 1** a purpose-built complex containing several cinemas and usually restaurants and bars ▸ *adj* **2** having many elements; complex

multiplicand *n* a number to be multiplied by another number (the **multiplier**)

multiplication *n* **1** a mathematical operation, equivalent to adding a number to itself a specified number of times. For instance, 4 multiplied by 3 equals 12 (i.e. 4+4+4) **2** the act of multiplying or state of being multiplied

multiplicity *n, pl* **-ties 1** a large number or great variety **2** the state of being multiple

multiply *vb* **-plies, -plying, -plied 1** to increase or cause to increase in number, quantity, or degree **2** to combine numbers or quantities by multiplication **3** to increase in number by reproduction

> **multiply** *vb* **1** = increase, extend, expand, spread, build up, proliferate; ≠ decrease **3** = reproduce, breed, propagate

multipurpose *adj* having many uses: *a giant multipurpose enterprise*

multipurpose vehicle *n* a large car, similar to a van, designed to carry up to eight passengers

multitude *n* **1** a large number of people or things: *a multitude of different pressure groups* **2** **the multitude** ordinary people collectively > **multitudinous**

> **multitude** *n* **1** = great number, host, army, mass, horde, myriad

mum[1] *n chiefly Brit informal* same as **mother**

mum[2] *adj* **1 keep mum** remain silent **2 mum's the word** keep quiet (about something)

mumble *vb* **-bling, -bled 1** to speak or say something indistinctly, with the mouth partly closed: *I could hear him mumbling under his breath* ▸ *n* **2** an indistinct or low utterance or sound

mumbo jumbo *n* **1** meaningless language; nonsense or gibberish **2** foolish religious ritual or incantation

mummer *n* one of a group of masked performers in a folk play or mime

mummified *adj* (of a body) preserved as a mummy > **mummification** *n*

mummy[1] *n, pl* **-mies** *chiefly Brit* an embalmed body as prepared for burial in ancient Egypt

mummy[2] *n, pl* **-mies** a child's word for **mother**

mumps *n* an infectious viral disease in which the glands below the ear become swollen and painful

munch *vb* to chew noisily and steadily

mundane *adj* **1** everyday, ordinary, and therefore not very interesting **2** relating to the world or worldly matters

> **mundane** *adj* **1** = ordinary, routine, commonplace, banal, everyday, day-to-day, prosaic, humdrum; ≠ extraordinary **2** = earthly, worldly, secular, mortal, terrestrial, temporal; ≠ spiritual

municipal *adj* of or relating to a town or city or its local government

> **municipal** *adj* = civic, public, local, council, district, urban, metropolitan

municipality *n, pl* **-ties 1** a city, town, or district enjoying local self-government **2** the governing body of such a unit

munificent (mew-niff-fiss-sent) *adj* very generous > **munificence** *n*

muniments (mew-nim-ments) *pl n law* the title deeds and other documentary evidence relating to the title to land

munitions (mew-nish-unz) *pl n* military equipment and stores, esp. ammunition

munted *adj NZ slang* **1** destroyed or ruined **2** abnormal or peculiar

mural (myoor-al) *n* **1** a large painting on a wall ▸ *adj* **2** of or relating to a wall > **muralist** *n*

murder *n* **1** the unlawful intentional killing of one human being by another **2** *informal* something dangerous, difficult, or unpleasant: *shopping on Christmas Eve is murder* **3 cry blue murder** *informal* to make an outcry **4 get away with murder** *informal* to do as one pleases without ever being punished ▸ *vb* **5** to kill someone intentionally and unlawfully **6** *informal* to ruin a piece of music or drama by performing it very badly: *he absolutely murdered that song* **7** *informal* to beat decisively > **murderer** *or fem* **murderess** *n* > **murderous** *adj*

> **murder** *n* **1** = killing, homicide, massacre, assassination, slaying, bloodshed, carnage, butchery ▸ *vb* **5** = kill, massacre, slaughter, assassinate, eliminate (*slang*), butcher, slay, bump off (*slang*)

murk *n* thick gloomy darkness

murky *adj* **murkier, murkiest 1** gloomy or dark **2** cloudy or hard to see through: *a murky stagnant pond* **3** obscure and suspicious; shady: *murky goings-on; his murky past* > **murkily** *adv* > **murkiness** *n*

> **murky** *adj* **1** = dark, gloomy, grey, dull, dim, cloudy, misty, overcast; ≠ bright **2** = dark, cloudy

murmur *vb* **1** to speak or say in a quiet indistinct way **2** to complain ▸ *n* **3** a continuous low indistinct sound, such as that of a distant conversation **4** an indistinct utterance: *a murmur of protest* **5** a complaint or grumble: *he left without a murmur* **6** *med* any abnormal soft blowing sound heard usually over the chest: *a heart murmur* > **murmuring** *n, adj* > **murmurous** *adj*

> **murmur** *vb* **1** = mumble, whisper, mutter ▸ *n* **4** = whisper, drone, purr

muscle *n* **1** a tissue in the body composed of bundles of elongated cells which produce movement in an organ or part by contracting or relaxing **2** an organ composed of muscle tissue: *the heart is essentially just another muscle* **3** strength or force: *we do not have the political muscle to force through these reforms* ▸ *vb* **-cling, -cled 4 muscle in** to force one's way into a situation; intrude: *I don't like the way he's trying to muscle in here*

> **muscle** *n* **1** = tendon, sinew **3** = strength, might, power, weight, stamina, brawn ▸ *vb* **muscle in** = impose yourself, encroach, butt in, force your way in

muscular *adj* **1** having well-developed muscles; brawny **2** of or consisting of muscle: *great muscular effort is needed* **3** forceful or powerful: *a muscular account of Schumann's Fourth Symphony* > **muscularity** *n*

> **muscular** *adj* **1, 3** = strong, powerful, athletic, strapping, robust, vigorous, sturdy, sinewy

muscular dystrophy *n* a hereditary disease in which the muscles gradually weaken and waste away

muse[1] *vb* **musing, mused** to think deeply and at length about: *she mused unhappily on how right her sister had been*

> **muse** *vb* = ponder, consider, reflect, contemplate, deliberate, brood, meditate, mull over

muse[2] *n* a force or person that inspires a creative artist

museum *n* a building where objects of historical, artistic, or scientific interest are exhibited and preserved

mush *n* 1 a soft pulpy mass 2 *informal* cloying sentimentality

mushroom *n* 1 an edible fungus consisting of a cap at the end of a stem 2 something resembling a mushroom in shape or rapid growth ▸ *vb* 3 to grow rapidly: *the deficit has mushroomed*

mushy *adj* **mushier, mushiest** 1 soft and pulpy 2 *informal* excessively sentimental

music *n* 1 an art form consisting of sequences of sounds organized melodically, harmonically, and rhythmically 2 such sounds, esp. when produced by singing or musical instruments 3 any written or printed representation of musical sounds: *I can't read music* 4 any sequence of sounds perceived as pleasing or harmonious 5 **face the music** *informal* to confront the consequences of one's actions 6 **music to one's ears** something, such as a piece of news, that one is pleased to hear

musical *adj* 1 of or used in music 2 talented in or fond of music 3 pleasant-sounding; harmonious: *musical laughter* 4 involving or set to music: *a musical biography of Judy Garland* ▸ *n* 5 a play or film that has dialogue interspersed with songs and dances ▸ **musicality** *n* ▸ **musically** *adv*

> **musical** *adj* 3 = melodious, lyrical, harmonious, melodic, tuneful, dulcet, sweet-sounding, euphonious; ≠ discordant

music hall *n chiefly Brit* 1 (formerly) a variety entertainment consisting of songs and comic turns 2 a theatre at which such entertainments were staged

musician *n* a person who plays or composes music, esp. as a profession

musicology *n* the scholarly study of music ▸ **musicologist** *n*

musk *n* 1 a strong-smelling glandular secretion of the male musk deer, used in perfumery 2 any similar substance produced by animals or plants, or manufactured synthetically

musket *n* a long-barrelled muzzle-loading gun fired from the shoulder, a forerunner of the rifle ▸ **musketeer** *n*

muskrat *n, pl* **-rats** *or* **-rat** 1 a North American beaver-like amphibious rodent 2 the brown fur of this animal

musky *adj* **muskier, muskiest** having a heady sweet smell ▸ **muskiness** *n*

Muslim *or* **Moslem** *n, pl* **-lims** *or* **-lim** 1 a follower of the religion of Islam ▸ *adj* 2 of or relating to Islam

muslin *n* a very fine plain-weave cotton fabric

mussel *n* an edible shellfish, with a dark slightly elongated hinged shell, which lives attached to rocks

must[1] *vb* 1 used as an auxiliary to express or indicate the need or necessity to do something: *I must go to the shops* 2 used as an auxiliary to express or indicate obligation or requirement: *you must not smoke in here* 3 used as an auxiliary to express or indicate the probable correctness of a statement: *he must be finished by now* 4 used as an auxiliary to express or indicate inevitability: *all good things must come to an end* 5 used as an auxiliary to express or indicate determination: *I must try and finish this* 6 used as an auxiliary to express or indicate conviction or certainty on the part of the speaker: *you must be kidding!* ▸ *n* 7 an essential or necessary thing: *strong boots are a must for hill walking*

> **must** *n* = necessity, essential, requirement, fundamental, imperative, requisite, prerequisite, sine qua non (*Latin*)

must[2] *n* the pressed juice of grapes or other fruit ready for fermentation

mustache *n US* same as **moustache**

mustang *n* a small breed of horse, often wild or half wild, found in the southwestern US

mustard *n* 1 a hot, spicy paste made from the powdered seeds of any of a family of plants 2 any of these plants, which have yellow flowers and slender pods ▸ *adj* 3 brownish-yellow

mustard gas *n* an oily liquid with poisonous vapour used in chemical warfare, esp. in World War I, which can cause blindness, burns, and sometimes death

muster *vb* 1 to summon or gather: *I put as much disbelief in my expression as I could muster* 2 to call or be called together for duty or inspection: *the battalion mustered on the bank of the river* ▸ *n* 3 an assembly of military personnel for duty or inspection 4 a collection, assembly, or gathering 5 **pass muster** to be acceptable

> **muster** *vb* 1 = summon up, marshal 2 = rally, gather, assemble, marshal, mobilize, call together ▸ *n* 4 = assembly, meeting, collection, gathering, rally, convention, congregation, roundup, hui (NZ), runanga (NZ)

musty *adj* **-tier, -tiest** 1 smelling or tasting old, stale, or mouldy 2 old-fashioned, dull, or hackneyed: *musty ideas* ▸ **mustily** *adv* ▸ **mustiness** *n*

mutable (mew-tab-bl) *adj* able to or tending to change ▸ **mutability** *n*

mutant (mew-tant) *n* 1 an animal, organism, or gene that has undergone mutation ▸ *adj* 2 of or resulting from mutation

mutate (mew-tate) *vb* **-tating, -tated** to undergo or cause to undergo mutation

mutation (mew-tay-shun) *n* 1 a change or alteration 2 a change in the chromosomes or genes of a cell which may affect the structure and development of the resultant offspring 3 a physical characteristic in an organism resulting from this type of chromosomal change

mutation *n* 1, 2 = change, variation, evolution, transformation, modification, alteration, metamorphosis, transfiguration 3 = anomaly, variation, deviant (*old-fashioned*), freak of nature

mute *adj* 1 not giving out sound or speech; silent 2 *old-fashioned, offensive* unable to speak 3 unspoken or unexpressed: *she shot him a look of mute entreaty* 4 (of a letter in a word) silent: *the 'k' in 'know' is mute* ▸ *n* 5 *old-fashioned, offensive* a person who is unable to speak 6 any of various devices used to soften the tone of stringed or brass instruments ▸ *vb* **muting, muted** 7 to reduce the volume or soften the tone of a musical instrument by means of a mute or soft pedal 8 to reduce the volume of a sound: *the double glazing muted the noise* > **mutely** *adv* > **muteness** *n*

mute *adj* 1 = close-mouthed, silent 2 = dumb (*old-fashioned, offensive*), speechless, voiceless 3 = silent, dumb, unspoken, tacit, wordless, voiceless, unvoiced

muted *adj* 1 (of a sound or colour) softened: *a muted pink shirt* 2 (of an emotion or action) subdued or restrained: *his response was muted* 3 (of a musical instrument) being played while fitted with a mute: *muted trumpet*

muti (moo-tee) *n S African* medicine, esp. herbal

mutilate (mew-till-ate) *vb* **-lating, -lated** 1 to injure by tearing or cutting off a limb or essential part; maim 2 to damage a book or text so as to render it unintelligible 3 to spoil or damage severely > **mutilated** *adj* > **mutilation** *n* > **mutilator** *n*

mutineer *n* a person who mutinies

mutinous *adj* 1 openly rebellious 2 characteristic or indicative of mutiny

mutiny (mew-tin-ee) *n, pl* **-nies** 1 open rebellion against authority, esp. by sailors or soldiers against their officers ▸ *vb* **-nies, -nying, -nied** 2 to engage in mutiny: *soldiers who had mutinied and taken control*

mutt *n slang* 1 a foolish or stupid person 2 a mongrel dog

mutter *vb* 1 to say something or speak in a low and indistinct tone: *he muttered an excuse* 2 to grumble ▸ *n* 3 a muttered sound or complaint > **muttering** *n, adj*

mutter *vb* = grumble, complain, murmur, rumble, whine, mumble, grouse, bleat

mutton *n* 1 the flesh of mature sheep, used as food 2 **mutton dressed as lamb** *derogatory* an older woman dressed up to look young

mutton bird *n* 1 *Austral* a migratory sea bird with dark plumage 2 *NZ* any of a number of migratory sea birds, the young of which are a Māori delicacy

mutual (mew-chew-al) *adj* 1 experienced or expressed by each of two or more people about the other; reciprocal: *mutual respect* 2 common to or shared by two or more people: *a mutual friend* 3 denoting an organization, such as an insurance company, in which the policyholders or investors share the profits and expenses and there are no shareholders > **mutuality** *n* > **mutually** *adv*

mutual *adj* 1, 2 = shared, common, joint, returned, reciprocal, interchangeable, requited

Muzak *n trademark* recorded light music played in places such as restaurants and shops

muzzle *n* 1 the projecting part of an animal's face, usually the jaws and nose 2 a guard, made of plastic or strap of strong material, fitted over an animal's nose and jaws to prevent it biting or eating 3 the front end of a gun barrel ▸ *vb* **-zling, -zled** 4 to prevent from being heard or noticed: *an attempt to muzzle the press* 5 to put a muzzle on an animal

muzzy *adj* **-zier, -ziest** 1 confused and groggy: *he felt muzzy and hung over* 2 blurred or hazy: *the picture was muzzy and out of focus* > **muzzily** *adv* > **muzziness** *n*

MW 1 megawatt 2 *radio* medium wave

my *adj* 1 of, belonging to, or associated with the speaker or writer (me): *my own way of doing things* 2 used in various forms of address: *my lord* ▸ *interj* 3 an exclamation of surprise or awe: *my, how you've grown!*

myall *n* an Australian acacia with hard scented wood

mycology *n* the study of fungi

mynah *or* **myna** *n* a tropical Asian starling which can mimic human speech

myopia (my-oh-pee-a) *n* inability to see distant objects clearly because the images are focused in front of the retina; short-sightedness > **myopic** (my-op-ik) *adj*

myriad (mir-ree-ad) *adj* 1 innumerable: *the myriad demands of the modern world* ▸ *n* 2 a large indefinite number: *myriads of tiny yellow flowers*

myriad *adj* = innumerable, countless, untold, incalculable, immeasurable, multitudinous ▸ *n* = multitude, host, army, swarm, horde

myrrh (mur) *n* the aromatic resin of an African or Asian shrub or tree, used in perfume, incense, and medicine

myrtle (mur-tl) *n* an evergreen shrub with pink or white flowers and aromatic blue-black berries

myself *pron* 1 the reflexive form of *I* or *me*: *I really enjoyed myself at the party* 2 I or me in person, as distinct from anyone else: *I myself know of no answer* 3 my usual self: *I'm not myself today*

mysterious *adj* 1 of unknown cause or nature: *a mysterious illness* 2 creating a feeling of strangeness, curiosity, or wonder: *a fascinating and mysterious place* > **mysteriously** *adv*

m

mysterious *adj* 1 = strange, puzzling, secret, weird, perplexing, uncanny, mystifying, arcane; ≠ clear 2 = secretive, enigmatic, evasive, discreet, covert, reticent, furtive, inscrutable

mystery *n, pl* **-teries** 1 an unexplained or inexplicable event or phenomenon 2 a person or thing that arouses curiosity or suspense because of an unknown, obscure, or enigmatic quality 3 a story or film which arouses suspense and curiosity because of facts concealed 4 a religious rite, such as the Eucharist in Christianity

mystery *n* 1, 2 = puzzle, problem, question, secret, riddle, enigma, conundrum, teaser

mystic *n* 1 a person who achieves mystical experience ▸ *adj* 2 same as **mystical**

mystical *adj* 1 relating to or characteristic of mysticism 2 *Christianity* having a sacred significance that is beyond human understanding 3 having occult or metaphysical significance > **mystically** *adv*

mystical *adj* 1, 3 = supernatural, mysterious, transcendental, occult, metaphysical, paranormal, inscrutable, otherworldly

mysticism *n* 1 belief in or experience of a reality beyond normal human understanding or experience 2 the use of prayer and meditation in an attempt to achieve direct intuitive experience of the divine

mystify *vb* **-fies**, **-fying**, **-fied** 1 to confuse, bewilder, or puzzle: *his success mystifies many in the fashion industry* 2 to make obscure: *it is important for us not to mystify the function of the scientist* > **mystification** *n* > **mystifying** *adj*

mystique (miss-**steek**) *n* an aura of mystery, power, and awe that surrounds a person or thing

myth *n* 1 **A** a story about superhuman beings of an earlier age, usually of how natural phenomena or social customs came into existence **B** same as **mythology** (senses 1, 2) 2 **A** an idea or explanation which is widely held but untrue or unproven: *the myth that the USA is a classless society* **B** a person or thing whose existence is fictional or unproven: *the Loch Ness Monster is a myth*

myth *n* 1**A** = legend, story, fiction, saga, fable, allegory, fairy story, folk tale 2 = illusion, story, fancy, fantasy, imagination, invention, delusion, superstition

myth. 1 mythological 2 mythology

mythical *or* **mythic** *adj* 1 of or relating to myth 2 imaginary or fictitious > **mythically** *adv*

mythology *n, pl* **-gies** 1 myths collectively, esp. those associated with a particular culture or person 2 a body of stories about a person, institution, etc. 3 the study of myths > **mythological** *adj*

mythology *n* 1, 2 = legend, folklore, tradition, lore

myxomatosis (mix-a-mat-**oh**-siss) *n* an infectious and usually fatal viral disease of rabbits causing swellings and tumours

m

Nn

n *n* **1** *maths* a number whose value is not stated: *two to the power n* ▸ *adj* **2** an indefinite number of: *there are n objects in the box* > **nth** *adj*

N 1 *chess* knight **2** *chem* nitrogen **3** *physics* newton(s) **4** North(ern) **5** nuclear: *N plant*

n. 1 neuter **2** noun **3** number

Na *chem* sodium

Naafi *n* **1** Brit Navy, Army, and Air Force Institutes **2** a canteen or shop run by this organization, esp. for military personnel

naan *n* same as **nan bread**

naartjie (nahr-chee) *n S African* a tangerine

nab *vb* **nabbing, nabbed** *informal* **1** to arrest (someone) **2** to catch (someone) doing something wrong

> **nab** *vb* **1** = catch, arrest, apprehend, seize, grab, capture, collar (*informal*), snatch

nadir *n* **1** the point in the sky directly below an observer and opposite the zenith **2** the lowest or worst point of anything: *I had touched the very nadir of despair*

naevus *or US* **nevus** (nee-vuss) *n, pl* -**vi** a birthmark or mole

naff *adj Brit slang* in poor taste: *naff frocks and trouser suits* > **naffness** *n*

nag¹ *vb* **nagging, nagged 1** to scold or find fault constantly **2 nag at** to be a constant source of discomfort or worry to ▸ *n* **3** a person who nags > **nagging** *adj, n*

> **nag** *vb* **1** = scold, harass, badger, pester, worry, plague, hassle (*informal*), upbraid ▸ *n* = complainer, grumbler, moaner

nag² *n* **1** often derogatory an old horse **2** a small riding horse

> **nag** *n* = horse, hack

naiad (nye-ad) *n, pl* **naiads** *or* **naiades** (nye-ad-deez) *Greek myth* a water nymph

nail *n* **1** a piece of metal with a point at one end and a head at the other, hit with a hammer to join two objects together **2** the hard covering of the upper tips of the fingers and toes **3 hit the nail on the head** to say something exactly correct or accurate **4 on the nail** at once: *he paid always in cash, always on the nail* ▸ *vb* **5** to attach (something) with nails **6** *informal* to arrest or catch (someone) **7** *informal* to execute (an act or performance) to the highest level: *you nailed that song!*

> **nail** *n* **1** = tack, spike, rivet, hobnail, brad (*technical*) **2** = fingernail, toenail, talon, thumbnail, claw ▸ *vb* **5** = fasten, fix, secure, attach, pin, hammer (*informal*), tack **6** = catch, arrest, capture, apprehend, trap, snare, ensnare, entrap

nail varnish *or* **nail polish** *n* a thick liquid applied to the nails as a cosmetic

naive *or* **naïve** (nye-eev) *adj* **1** innocent and gullible **2** simple and lacking sophistication: *naive art* > **naively** *adv*

> **naive** *or* **naïve** *adj* **1** = gullible, trusting, credulous, unsuspicious, green, simple, innocent, callow; ≠ worldly

naivety (nye-eev-tee) *or* **naïveté** *n* the state or quality of being naive

naked *adj* **1** without clothes **2** not concealed: *naked aggression* **3** without any covering: *it was dimly lit by naked bulbs* **4 the naked eye** the eye unassisted by any optical instrument: *difficult to spot with the naked eye* > **nakedly** *adv* > **nakedness** *n*

> **naked** *adj* **1** = nude, stripped, exposed, bare, undressed, starkers (*informal*), stark-naked, unclothed; ≠ dressed

namby-pamby *adj Brit, Austral & NZ* excessively sentimental or prim

name *n* **1** a word or term by which a person or thing is known. Related adjective: **nominal** **2** reputation, esp. a good one: *he was making a name for himself* **3** a famous person: *she's a big name now* **4 call someone names** *or* **a name** to insult someone by using rude words to describe him or her **5 in name only** not possessing the powers or status implied by one's title: *a leadership in name only* **6 in the name of A** for the sake of: *in the name of decency* **B** by the authority of: *in the name of the law* **7 name of the game** the most significant or important aspect of something: *survival is the name of the game in wartime* **8 to one's name** in one's possession: *she hasn't a penny to her name* ▸ *vb* **naming, named 9** to give a name to **10** to refer to by name: *he refused to name his source* **11** to fix or specify: *he named a time for the meeting* **12** to appoint: *she was named Journalist of the Year* **13** to ban (an MP) from the House of Commons by mentioning him or her formally by name as being guilty of disorderly conduct **14 name names** to cite people in order to blame or accuse them

> **name** *n* **1** = title, nickname, designation, term, handle (*slang*), epithet, sobriquet, moniker *or* monicker (*slang*) ▸ *vb* **9** = call, christen, baptize, dub, term, style, label, entitle **11, 12** = nominate, choose, select, appoint, specify, designate

nameless *adj* **1** without a name **2** unspecified: *the individual concerned had better remain nameless* **3** too horrible to speak about: *the nameless dread*

namely *adv* that is to say

> **namely** *adv* = specifically, to wit, viz.

namesake *n* a person or thing with the same name as another

nan bread *or* **naan** *n* a slightly leavened Indian bread in a large flat leaf shape

nanny *n, pl* **-nies 1** a person, usually a woman, whose job is looking after young children ▸ *vb* **nannies, nannying, nannied 2** to nurse or look after someone else's children **3** to be too protective towards (someone)

nanny goat *n* a female goat

nano- *combining form* denoting one thousand millionth (10^{-9}): *nanosecond*

nap¹ *n* **1** a short sleep ▸ *vb* **napping, napped 2** to have a short sleep **3 catch someone napping** to catch someone unprepared: *they don't want to be caught napping when the army moves again*

> **nap** *n* = sleep, rest, kip (*Brit slang*), siesta, catnap, forty winks (*informal*) ▸ *vb* **2** = sleep, rest, drop off (*informal*), doze, kip (*Brit slang*), snooze (*informal*), nod off (*informal*), catnap

nap² *n* the raised fibres of velvet or similar cloth

> **nap** *n* = pile, down, fibre, weave, grain

nap³ *n* **1** a card game similar to whist **2** *horse racing* a tipster's choice for a certain winner ▸ *vb* **napping, napped 3** *horse racing* to name (a horse) as a likely winner

napalm *n* **1** a highly inflammable jellied petrol, used in firebombs and flame-throwers ▸ *vb* **2** to attack (people or places) with napalm

nape *n* the back of the neck

naphtha *n* *chem* a liquid mixture distilled from coal tar or petroleum, used as a solvent and in petrol

naphthalene *n* *chem* a white crystalline substance distilled from coal tar or petroleum, used in mothballs, dyes, and explosives

napkin *n* a piece of cloth or paper for wiping the mouth or protecting the clothes while eating

> **napkin** *n* = serviette, cloth

nappy *n, pl* **-pies** *Brit & NZ* a piece of soft absorbent material, usually disposable, wrapped around the waist and between the legs of a baby to absorb its urine and excrement

narcissism *n* an exceptional interest in or admiration for oneself › **narcissistic** *adj*

narcissus (nahr-**siss**-uss) *n, pl* **-cissi** (-**siss**-eye) a yellow, orange, or white flower related to the daffodil

narcosis *n* unconsciousness caused by a narcotic or general anaesthetic

narcotic *n* **1** a drug, such as opium or morphine, that produces numbness and drowsiness, used medicinally but addictive ▸ *adj* **2** of narcotics or narcosis

narcotic *n* = drug, anaesthetic, painkiller, sedative, opiate, tranquillizer, anodyne, analgesic ▸ *adj* = sedative, calming, hypnotic, analgesic, soporific, painkilling

nark *slang* ▸ *vb* **1** to annoy ▸ *n* **2** an informer or spy: *copper's nark* **3** *Brit* someone who complains in an irritating or whining manner

narky *adj* **narkier, narkiest** *slang* irritable, complaining, or sarcastic

narrate *vb* **-rating, -rated 1** to tell (a story); relate **2** to speak the words accompanying and telling what is happening in a film or TV programme › **narrator** *n*

narration *n* **1** a narrating **2** a narrated account or story

narrative *n* **1** an account of events **2** the part of a literary work that relates events ▸ *adj* **3** telling a story: *a narrative account of the main events* **4** of narration: *narrative clarity*

> **narrative** *n* **1** = story, report, history, account, statement, tale, chronicle

narrow *adj* **1** small in breadth in comparison to length **2** limited in range, extent, or outlook: *a narrow circle of academics* **3** with little margin: *a narrow advantage* ▸ *vb* **4** to make or become narrow **5 narrow down** to restrict or limit: *the search can be narrowed down to a single room* ▸ See also **narrows** › **narrowly** *adv* › **narrowness** *n*

> **narrow** *adj* **1** = thin, fine, slim, slender, tapering, attenuated; ≠ broad **2** = limited, restricted, confined, tight, close, meagre, constricted; ≠ wide ▸ *vb* **4** = get narrower, taper, shrink, tighten, constrict **5** = restrict, limit, reduce, constrict

narrow boat *n* *Brit* a long bargelike canal boat

narrow-minded *adj* bigoted, intolerant, or prejudiced › **narrow-mindedness** *n*

narrows *pl n* a narrow part of a strait, river, or current

narwhal *n* an arctic whale with a long spiral tusk

NASA (in the US) National Aeronautics and Space Administration

nasal *adj* **1** of the nose **2** (of a sound) pronounced with air passing through the nose **3** (of a voice) characterized by nasal sounds › **nasally** *adv*

nascent *adj formal* starting to grow or develop

NASDAQ (in the US) National Association of Securities Dealers Automated Quotations (System)

nasturtium *n* a plant with yellow, red, or orange trumpet-shaped flowers

nasty *adj* **-tier, -tiest 1** unpleasant: *a nasty odour* **2** dangerous or painful: *a nasty burn* **3** (of a person) spiteful or ill-natured ▸ *n, pl* **-ties 4** something unpleasant: *free from chemical nasties* › **nastily** *adv* › **nastiness** *n*

nasty *adj* **1** = unpleasant, ugly, disagreeable; ≠ pleasant **2** = serious, bad, dangerous, critical, severe, painful (*informal*) **3** = spiteful, mean (*informal*), offensive, vicious, unpleasant, vile, malicious, despicable; ≠ pleasant

natal (**nay**-tl) *adj* of or relating to birth
nation *n* a large body of people of one or more cultures or ethnicities, organized into a single state: *a major industrialized nation*

nation *n* = country, state, realm, micronation

national *adj* **1** of or serving a nation as a whole **2** characteristic of a particular nation: *the national character* ▸ *n* **3** a citizen of a particular country: *Belgian nationals* **4** a national newspaper > **nationally** *adv*

national *adj* **1** = nationwide, public, widespread, countrywide ▸ *n* **3** = citizen, subject, resident, native, inhabitant

National Curriculum *n* (in England and Wales) the curriculum of subjects taught in state schools since 1989
National Health Service *n* (in Britain) the system of national medical services financed mainly by taxation
national insurance *n* (in Britain) state insurance based on contributions from employees and employers, providing payments to unemployed, sick, and retired people
nationalism *n* **1** a policy of national independence **2** patriotism, sometimes to an excessive degree > **nationalist** *n, adj* > **nationalistic** *adj*

nationalism *n* **2** = patriotism, loyalty to your country, chauvinism, jingoism, allegiance

nationality *n, pl* **-ties 1** the fact of being a citizen of a particular nation **2** a group of people of the same ethnicity: *young men of all nationalities*

nationality *n* **1** = citizenship, birth **2** = race, nation

nationalize *or* **-lise** *vb* **-lizing, -lized** *or* **-lising, -lised** to put (an industry or a company) under state control > **nationalization** *or* **-lisation** *n*
national park *n* an area of countryside protected by a national government for its scenic or environmental importance and visited by the public
national service *n chiefly Brit* compulsory military service
native *adj* **1** relating to a place where a person was born: *native land* **2** born in a specified place: *a native New Yorker* **3** **native to** originating in: *a plant native to alpine regions* **4** natural or inborn: *native genius* **5** relating to the original inhabitants of a country: *archaeology may uncover magnificent native artefacts* **6** **go native** (of a settler) to adopt the lifestyle of the local population ▸ *n* **7** a person born in a specified place: *a native of*

Palermo **8** an indigenous animal or plant: *the saffron crocus is a native of Asia Minor* **9** a member of the original race of a country, as opposed to colonial immigrants

native *n* **7, 9** = inhabitant, national, resident, citizen, countryman, aborigine, dweller

Native American *n* **1** a member of any of the original peoples of North America ▸ *adj* **2** of any of these peoples
native bear *n Austral* same as **koala**
native companion *n Austral* same as **brolga**
native dog *n Austral* same as **dingo**
Nativity *n Christianity* **1** the birth of Jesus Christ **2** the feast of Christmas celebrating this
NATO *or* **Nato** North Atlantic Treaty Organization: an international organization established for purposes of collective security
natter *Brit & NZ informal* ▸ *vb* **1** to talk idly and at length ▸ *n* **2** a long idle chat
natty *adj* **-tier, -tiest** *informal* smart and spruce > **nattily** *adv*
natural *adj* **1** as is normal or to be expected: *the natural consequence* **2** genuine or spontaneous: *talking in a relaxed, natural manner* **3** of, according to, existing in, or produced by nature: *natural disasters* **4** not acquired; inborn: *their natural enthusiasm* **5** not created by human beings **6** not synthetic: *natural fibres such as wool* **7** (of a parent) not adoptive **8** *music* not sharp or flat: *F natural* ▸ *n* **9** *informal* a person with an inborn talent or skill: *she's a natural at bridge* **10** *music* a note that is neither sharp nor flat > **naturalness** *n*

natural *adj* **1** = logical, valid, legitimate; ≠ abnormal **2** = unaffected, open, genuine, spontaneous, unpretentious, unsophisticated, dinkum (*Austral, NZ informal*), ingenuous, real; ≠ affected **4** = innate, native, characteristic, inherent, instinctive, intuitive, inborn, essential **6** = pure, plain, organic, whole, unrefined; ≠ processed

natural gas *n* a gaseous mixture, consisting mainly of methane, found below ground; used widely as a fuel
natural history *n* the study of animals and plants in the wild
naturalism *n* a movement in art and literature advocating detailed realism > **naturalistic** *adj*
naturalist *n* **1** a student of natural history **2** a person who advocates or practises naturalism
naturalize *or* **-lise** *vb* **-lizing, -lized** *or* **-lising, -lised 1** to give citizenship to (a person born in another country) **2** to introduce (a plant or animal) into another region **3** to cause (a foreign word or custom) to be adopted > **naturalization** *or* **-lisation** *n*
naturally *adv* **1** of course; surely **2** in a natural or normal way **3** instinctively

naturally *adv* **1** = of course, certainly **2** = typically, simply, normally, spontaneously

natural selection *n* a process by which only those creatures and plants well adapted to their environment survive

nature *n* 1 the whole system of the existence, forces, and events of the physical world that are not controlled by human beings 2 fundamental or essential qualities: *the theory and nature of science* 3 kind or sort: *problems of a financial nature* 4 temperament or personality: *an amiable and pleasant nature* 5 **by nature** essentially: *he was by nature a cautious man* 6 **in the nature of** essentially; by way of: *it was in the nature of a debate rather than an argument*

> **nature** *n* 1 = creation, world, earth, environment, universe, cosmos, natural world 2 = quality, character, make-up, constitution, essence, complexion 3 = kind, sort, style, type, variety, species, category, description 4 = temperament, character, personality, disposition, outlook, mood, humour, temper

naturism *n* the practice of not wearing clothes; nudism > **naturist** *n, adj*

naught *n* 1 *archaic or literary* nothing 2 *chiefly US* the figure o ▸ *adv* 3 *archaic or literary* not at all: *I care naught*

naughty *adj* **-tier, -tiest** 1 (of children) mischievous or disobedient 2 mildly indecent: *naughty lingerie* > **naughtily** *adv* > **naughtiness** *n*

> **naughty** *adj* 1 = disobedient, bad, mischievous, badly behaved, wayward, wicked, impish, refractory; ≠ good 2 = obscene, vulgar, improper, lewd, risqué, smutty, ribald; ≠ clean

nausea (naw-zee-a) *n* 1 the feeling of being about to vomit 2 disgust

> **nausea** *n* 1 = sickness, vomiting, retching, squeamishness, queasiness, biliousness

nauseate *vb* **-ating, -ated** 1 to cause (someone) to feel sick 2 to arouse feelings of disgust in (someone) > **nauseating** *adj*

nauseous *adj* 1 as if about to be sick: *he felt nauseous* 2 sickening

nautical *adj* of the sea, ships, or navigation

nautical mile *n* a unit of length, used in navigation, standardized as 6080 feet

nautilus *n, pl* **-luses** *or* **-li** a sea creature with a shell and tentacles

naval *adj* of or relating to a navy or ships

> **naval** *adj* = nautical, marine, maritime

nave *n* the long central part of a church

navel *n* the slight hollow in the centre of the abdomen, where the umbilical cord was attached

navigable *adj* 1 wide, deep, or safe enough to be sailed through: *the navigable portion of the Nile* 2 able to be steered: *the boat has to be watertight and navigable*

navigate *vb* **-gating, -gated** 1 to direct or plot the course or position of a ship or aircraft 2 to travel over or through safely: *your cousin, who's just navigated the Amazon* 3 *informal* to direct (oneself) carefully or safely: *he navigated his unsteady way to the bar* 4 (of a passenger in a vehicle) to read the map and give directions to the driver
> **navigation** *n* > **navigational** *adj* > **navigator** *n*

navvy *n, pl* **-vies** *Brit & Austral informal* a labourer on a building site or road

navy *n, pl* **-vies** 1 the branch of a country's armed services comprising warships with their crews, and all their supporting services 2 the warships of a nation ▸ *adj* 3 short for **navy-blue**

> **navy** *n* 2 = fleet, flotilla, armada

navy-blue *adj* very dark blue

nay *interj* 1 *old-fashioned* no ▸ *n* 2 a person who votes against a motion ▸ *adv* 3 used for emphasis: *I want, nay, need to know*

Nazi *n, pl* **-zis** 1 a member of the fascist National Socialist German Workers' Party, which came to power in Germany in 1933 under Adolf Hitler ▸ *adj* 2 of or relating to the Nazis > **Nazism** *n*

NB 1 New Brunswick 2 note well

NCO noncommissioned officer

NE 1 Nebraska 2 northeast(ern)

Neanderthal (nee-ann-der-tahl) *adj* 1 of a type of primitive human that lived in Europe before 12 000 BC 2 *informal* having or characterized by excessively conservative views: *his notoriously Neanderthal attitude to women*

neap tide *n* a tide that occurs at the first and last quarter of the moon when there is the smallest rise and fall in tidal level

near *prep* 1 at or to a place or time not far away from ▸ *adv* 2 at or to a place or time not far away 3 short for **nearly**: *the pain damn near crippled him* ▸ *adj* 4 at or in a place or time not far away: *in the near future* 5 closely connected or intimate: *a near relation* 6 almost being the thing specified: *a mood of near rebellion* ▸ *vb* 7 to draw close (to): *the participants are nearing agreement* > **nearness** *n*

> **near** *adj* 4 = close, neighbouring, nearby, adjacent, adjoining; ≠ far

nearby *adj* 1 not far away: *a nearby village* ▸ *adv* 2 close at hand: *I live nearby*

> **nearby** *adj* = neighbouring, adjacent, adjoining

nearly *adv* 1 almost 2 **not nearly** nowhere near: *it's not nearly as easy as it looks*

> **nearly** *adv* 1 = practically, almost, virtually, just about, as good as, well-nigh

nearside *n* 1 *chiefly Brit* the side of a vehicle that is nearer the kerb 2 the left side of an animal

neat *adj* 1 clean and tidy 2 smoothly or competently done: *a neat answer* 3 (of alcoholic drinks) undiluted 4 *slang, chiefly US & Canad* admirable; excellent > **neatly** *adv* > **neatness** *n*

neat *adj* **1** = tidy, trim, orderly, spruce, shipshape, spick-and-span; ≠ untidy **2** = graceful, elegant, adept, nimble, adroit, efficient; ≠ clumsy **3** = undiluted, straight, pure, unmixed **4** = cool, great (*informal*), excellent, brilliant, superb, fantastic (*informal*), tremendous, fabulous (*informal*), booshit (*Austral slang*), exo (*Austral slang*), sik (*Austral slang*), rad (*informal*), phat (*slang*), schmick (*Austral informal*); ≠ terrible

nebula (neb-yew-la) *n, pl* **-lae** (-lee) *astron* a hazy cloud of particles and gases > **nebular** *adj*

nebulous *adj* vague and unclear: *a nebulous concept*

necessarily *adv* **1** as a certainty: *the factors were not necessarily connected with one another* **2** inevitably: *tourism is an industry that has a necessarily close connection with governments*

necessarily *adv* **1** = automatically, naturally, definitely, undoubtedly, certainly **2** = inevitably, of necessity, unavoidably, incontrovertibly, nolens volens (*Latin*)

necessary *adj* **1** needed in order to obtain the desired result: *the necessary skills* **2** certain or unavoidable: *the necessary consequences* ▸ *n* **3** do the necessary *informal* to do something that is necessary in a particular situation **4** the necessary *informal* the money required for a particular purpose

necessary *adj* **1** = needed, required, essential, vital, compulsory, mandatory, imperative, indispensable; ≠ unnecessary **2** = inevitable, certain, unavoidable, inescapable; ≠ avoidable

necessitate *vb* **-tating, -tated** to compel or require

necessity *n, pl* **-ties** **1** a set of circumstances that inevitably requires a certain result: *the necessity to maintain safety standards* **2** something needed: *the daily necessities* **3** great poverty **4** of necessity inevitably

necessity *n* **2** = essential, need, requirement, fundamental, requisite, prerequisite, sine qua non (*Latin*), desideratum, must-have

neck *n* **1** the part of the body connecting the head with the rest of the body **2** the part of a garment around the neck **3** the long narrow part of a bottle or violin **4** the length of a horse's head and neck taken as the distance by which one horse beats another in a race: *to win by a neck* **5** *informal* impudence **6** by a neck by a very small margin: *beaten only by a neck* **7** get it in the neck *informal* to be reprimanded or punished severely **8** neck and neck absolutely level in a race or competition **9** neck of the woods *informal* a particular area: *how did they get to this neck of the woods?* **10** stick one's neck out *informal* to risk criticism or ridicule by speaking one's mind

11 up to one's neck in *informal* to be deeply involved in: *he was up to his neck in the scandal* ▸ *vb* **12** *slang* to swallow quickly **13** *informal* (of two people) to kiss each other passionately

neckerchief *n* a piece of cloth worn tied round the neck

necklace *n* a decorative piece of jewellery worn round the neck

necromancy (neck-rome-man-see) *n* **1** communication with the dead **2** sorcery > **necromancer** *n*

necropolis (neck-rop-pol-liss) *n* a cemetery

nectar *n* **1** a sugary fluid produced by flowers and collected by bees **2** *classical myth* the drink of the gods **3** any delicious drink

nectarine *n* a smooth-skinned variety of peach

ned *n Scot slang* a hooligan

née *prep* indicating the maiden name of a married woman: *Jane Gray (née Blandish)*

need *vb* **1** to require or be in want of: *they desperately need success* **2** to be obliged: *the government may need to impose a statutory levy* **3** used to express necessity or obligation and does not add -s when used with singular nouns or pronouns: *need he go?* ▸ *n* **4** the condition of lacking something: *he has need of a new coat* **5** a requirement: *the need for closer economic co-operation* **6** necessity: *there was no need for an explanation* **7** poverty or destitution: *the money will go to those areas where need is greatest* **8** distress: *help has been given to those in need* ▸ See also **needs**

need *vb* **1** = require, want, demand, call for, entail, necessitate **2** = have to, be obliged to ▸ *n* **5** = requirement, demand, essential, necessity, requisite, desideratum, must-have **6** = necessity, call, demand, obligation **7** = poverty, deprivation, destitution, penury **8** = emergency, want, necessity, urgency, exigency

needful *adj* **1** necessary or required ▸ *n* **2** the needful *informal* what is necessary, usually money

needle *n* **1** a pointed slender piece of metal with a hole in it through which thread is passed for sewing **2** a long pointed rod used in knitting **3** same as **stylus** **4** *med* the long hollow pointed part of a hypodermic syringe, which is inserted into the body **5** a pointer on the scale of a measuring instrument **6** a long narrow stiff leaf: *pine needles* **7** *Brit informal* intense rivalry or ill-feeling in a sports match **8** have *or* get the needle *Brit informal* to be or become annoyed ▸ *vb* **-dling, -dled** **9** *informal* to goad or provoke

needle *vb* = irritate, provoke, annoy, harass, taunt, nag, goad, rile

needless *adj* not required; unnecessary > **needlessly** *adv*

needless *adj* = unnecessary, pointless, gratuitous, useless, unwanted, redundant, superfluous, groundless; ≠ essential

n

needlework *n* sewing and embroidery

needs *adv* **1** necessarily: *they must needs be admired* ▸ *pl n* **2** what is required: *he provides them with their needs*

needy *adj* **needier**, **neediest** in need of financial support

> **needy** *adj* = poor, deprived, disadvantaged, impoverished, penniless, destitute, poverty-stricken, underprivileged; ≠ wealthy

ne'er *adv poetic* never

ne'er-do-well *n* **1** an irresponsible or lazy person ▸ *adj* **2** useless; worthless: *his ne'er-do-well brother*

nefarious (nif-fair-ee-uss) *adj literary* evil; wicked

negate *vb* **-gating, -gated 1** to cause to have no value or effect: *his prejudices largely negate his accomplishments* **2** to deny the existence of

negation *n* **1** the opposite or absence of something **2** a negative thing or condition **3** the act of negating

negative *adj* **1** expressing a refusal or denial: *a negative response* **2** lacking positive qualities, such as enthusiasm or optimism **3** *med* indicating absence of the condition for which a test was made **4** *physics* **A** (of an electric charge) having the same electrical charge as an electron **B** (of a body or system) having a negative electric charge; having an excess of electrons **5** same as **minus** (sense 4) **6** measured in a direction opposite to that regarded as positive **7** of a photographic negative ▸ *n* **8** a statement or act of denial or refusal **9** *photog* a piece of photographic film, exposed and developed, bearing an image with a reversal of tones or colours, from which positive prints are made **10** a word or expression with a negative meaning, such as *not* **11** a quantity less than zero **12 in the negative** indicating denial or refusal > **negatively** *adv*

> **negative** *adj* **1** = dissenting, contradictory, refusing, denying, rejecting, opposing, resisting, contrary; ≠ assenting **2** = pessimistic, cynical, unwilling, gloomy, jaundiced, uncooperative; ≠ optimistic ▸ *n* **8** = denial, no, refusal, rejection, contradiction

neglect *vb* **1** to fail to give due care or attention to: *she had neglected her child* **2** to fail (to do something) through carelessness: *he neglected to greet his guests* **3** to disregard: *he neglected his duty* ▸ *n* **4** lack of due care or attention: *the city had a look of shabbiness and neglect* **5** the state of being neglected

> **neglect** *vb* **1** = disregard, ignore, fail to look after; ≠ look after **2** = shirk, forget, overlook, omit, evade, pass over, skimp, be remiss in *or* about ▸ *n* **4** = negligence, inattention; ≠ care

neglectful *adj* not paying enough care or attention: *abusive and neglectful parents*

negligee (neg-lee-zhay) *n* a woman's light, usually lace-trimmed dressing gown

negligence *n* neglect or carelessness > **negligent** *adj* > **negligently** *adv*

> **negligence** *n* = carelessness, neglect, disregard, dereliction, slackness, inattention, laxity, thoughtlessness

negligible *adj* so small or unimportant as to not worth considering

negotiable *adj* **1** able to be changed or agreed by discussion: *the prices were negotiable* **2** (of a bill of exchange or promissory note) legally transferable

negotiate *vb* **-ating, -ated 1** to talk with others in order to reach (an agreement) **2** to succeed in passing round or over (a place or a problem) > **negotiation** *n* > **negotiator** *n*

> **negotiate** *vb* **1** = bargain, deal, discuss, debate, mediate, hold talks, cut a deal, conciliate **2** = arrange, work out, bring about, transact

Negro *old-fashioned, offensive* ▸ *n, pl* **-groes 1** a member of any of the dark-skinned peoples originating in Africa ▸ *adj* **2** of Black people

Negroid *adj old-fashioned, offensive* of or relating to the dark-skinned peoples originating in Africa

neigh *n* **1** the high-pitched sound made by a horse ▸ *vb* **2** to make this sound

neighbour *or US* **neighbor** *n* **1** a person who lives near or next to another **2** a person, thing, or country near or next to another

neighbourhood *or US* **neighborhood** *n* **1** a district where people live **2** the immediate environment; surroundings **3** the people in a district **4 in the neighbourhood of** approximately ▸ *adj* **5** in and for a district: *our neighbourhood cinema*

> **neighbourhood** *or US* **neighborhood** *n* **1** = district, community, quarter, region, locality, locale **2** = vicinity, environs

neighbouring *or US* **neighboring** *adj* situated nearby: *the neighbouring island*

> **neighbouring** *or US* **neighboring** *adj* = nearby, next, near, bordering, surrounding, connecting, adjacent, adjoining; ≠ remote

neighbourly *or US* **neighborly** *adj* kind, friendly, and helpful

> **neighbourly** *or US* **neighborly** *adj* = helpful, kind, friendly, obliging, harmonious, considerate, sociable, hospitable

neither *adj* **1** not one nor the other (of two): *neither enterprise went well* ▸ *pron* **2** not one nor the other (of two): *neither completed the full term* ▸ *conj* **3 A** used preceding alternatives joined by *nor*; not: *sparing neither strength nor courage* **B** same as **nor** (sense 2) ▸ *adv* **4** *not standard* same as **either** (sense 4)

nemesis (nem-miss-iss) *n, pl* **-ses** (-seez) a means of retribution or vengeance

neo- *combining form* new, recent, or a modern form of: *neoclassicism; neo-Nazi*

neocon *n, adj chiefly US* short for **neoconservative**

neoconservative *adj* **1** favouring a return to a set of established (esp. political) conservative values which have been updated to suit current conditions ▸ *n* **2** a person subscribing to neoconservative philosophy

Neolithic *adj* of the period that lasted in Europe from about 4000 to 2400 BC, characterized by primitive farming and the use of polished stone and flint tools and weapons

neologism (nee-ol-a-jiz-zum) *n* a newly coined word, or an established word used in a new sense

neon *n* **1** *chem* a colourless odourless rare gas, used in illuminated signs and lights. Symbol: **Ne** ▸ *adj* **2** of or illuminated by neon: *a flashing neon sign*

neonatal *adj* relating to the first few weeks of a baby's life ▸ **neonate** *n*

neophyte *n formal* **1** a beginner **2** a person newly converted to a religious faith **3** a novice in a religious order

nephew *n* a son of one's sister or brother

nephritis (nif-frite-tiss) *n* inflammation of the kidney

nepotism (nep-a-tiz-zum) *n* favouritism shown to relatives and friends by those with power

Neptune *n* **1** the Roman god of the sea **2** the eighth planet from the sun

nerd *or* **nurd** *n slang* **1** a boring or unpopular person, esp. one who is obsessed with a particular subject: *a computer nerd* **2** a stupid and feeble person ▸ **nerdish, nurdish, nerdy** *or* **nurdy** *adj*

> **nerd** *or* **nurd** *n* **1** = bore, obsessive, anorak (*informal*), geek (*informal*), trainspotter (*informal*), dork (*slang*), wonk (*informal*), techie (*informal*), alpha geek

nerve *n* **1** a cordlike bundle of fibres that conducts impulses between the brain and other parts of the body **2** bravery and determination **3** *informal* impudence: *you've got a nerve!* **4 lose one's nerve** to lose self-confidence and become afraid about what one is doing **5 strain every nerve** to make every effort (to do something) ▸ *vb* **nerving, nerved 6 nerve oneself** to prepare oneself (to do something difficult or unpleasant)

> **nerve** *n* **2** = bravery, courage, bottle (*Brit slang*), resolution, daring, guts (*informal*), pluck, grit **3** = impudence, cheek (*informal*), audacity, boldness, temerity, insolence, impertinence, brazenness ▸ *vb* **nerve oneself** = brace yourself, prepare yourself, steel yourself, fortify yourself, gear yourself up, gee yourself up

nerve centre *n* **1** a place from which a system or organization is controlled: *an underground nerve centre of intelligence* **2** a group of nerve cells associated with a specific function

nerveless *adj* **1** (of fingers or hands) without feeling; numb **2** (of a person) fearless

nerve-racking *or* **nerve-wracking** *adj* very distressing or harrowing

nervous *adj* **1** apprehensive or worried **2** excitable; highly strung **3** of or relating to the nerves: *the nervous system* > **nervously** *adv* > **nervousness** *n*

> **nervous** *adj* **1** = apprehensive, anxious, uneasy, edgy, worried, tense, fearful, uptight (*informal*), toey (*Austral slang*), adrenalized; ≠ calm

nervous breakdown *n* a mental illness in which a person ceases to function properly, and experiences symptoms including tiredness, anxiety, and severe depression

nervy *adj* **nervier, nerviest** *Brit & Austral informal* excitable or nervous

nest *n* **1** a place or structure in which birds or other animals lay eggs or give birth to young **2** a cosy or secluded place **3** a set of things of graduated sizes designed to fit together: *a nest of tables* ▸ *vb* **4** to make or inhabit a nest **5** (of a set of objects) to fit one inside another **6** *computers* to position (data) within other data at different ranks or levels

> **nest** *n* **2** = refuge, retreat, haunt, den, hideaway

nest egg *n* a fund of money kept in reserve

nestle *vb* **-tling, -tled 1** to snuggle or cuddle closely **2** to be in a sheltered position: *honey-coloured stone villages nestling in wooded valleys*

> **nestle** *vb* **1** = snuggle, cuddle, huddle, curl up, nuzzle

nestling *n* a young bird not yet able to fly

> **nestling** *n* = chick, fledgling, baby bird

net¹ *n* **1** a very fine fabric made from intersecting strands of material with a space between each strand **2** a piece of net, used to protect or hold things or to trap animals **3** (in certain sports) a strip of net over which the ball or shuttlecock must be hit **4** the goal in soccer or hockey **5** a strategy intended to trap people: *innocent fans were caught in the police net* **6** *informal* short for **internet** ▸ *vb* **netting, netted 7** to catch (a fish or other animal) in a net

> **net** *n* **1, 2** = mesh, netting, network, web, lattice, openwork ▸ *vb* = catch, bag, capture, trap, entangle, ensnare, enmesh

net² *or* **nett** *adj* **1** remaining after all deductions, as for taxes and expenses: *net income* **2** (of weight) excluding the weight of wrapping or container **3** final or conclusive: *the net effect*

n

▸ *vb* **netting, netted 4** to yield or earn as a clear profit

net *or* **nett** *adj* **1** = after taxes, final, clear, take-home ▸ *vb* = earn, make, clear, gain, realize, bring in, accumulate, reap

netball *n* a team game, usually played by women, in which a ball has to be thrown through a net hanging from a ring at the top of a pole

nether *adj old-fashioned* lower or under: *nether regions*

nett *adj, vb* same as **net²**

netting *n* a fabric or structure made of net

nettle *n* **1** a plant with stinging hairs on the leaves **2 grasp the nettle** to attempt something unpleasant with boldness and courage

nettled *adj* irritated or annoyed

network *n* **1** a system of intersecting lines, roads, veins, etc. **2** an interconnecting group or system: *a network of sympathizers and safe-houses* **3** *radio & television* a group of broadcasting stations that all transmit the same programme at the same time **4** *electronics & computers* a system of interconnected components or circuits ▸ *vb* **5** *radio & television* to broadcast (a programme) over a network **6** to form business contacts through informal social meetings

network *n* **1** = web, system, arrangement, grid, lattice

neural *adj* of a nerve or the nervous system

neuralgia *n* severe pain along a nerve ▸ **neuralgic** *adj*

neuritis (nyoor-**rite**-tiss) *n* inflammation of a nerve or nerves, often causing pain and loss of function in the affected part

neurology *n med* the scientific study of the nervous system ▸ **neurological** *adj* ▸ **neurologist** *n*

neurosis (nyoor-**oh**-siss) *n, pl* **-ses** (-seez) a mental health condition characterized by anxiety, depression, or obsessive behaviour

neurotic *adj* **1** tending to be emotionally unstable **2** affected by neurosis ▸ *n* **3** a person with a neurosis or tending to be emotionally unstable

neuter *adj* **1** *grammar* denoting a gender of nouns which are neither male nor female **2** (of animals and plants) sexually underdeveloped ▸ *n* **3** *grammar* **a** the neuter gender **b** a neuter noun **4** a sexually underdeveloped female insect, such as a worker bee **5** a castrated animal ▸ *vb* **6** to castrate (an animal)

neutral *adj* **1** not taking any side in a war or dispute **2** of or belonging to a neutral party or country **3** not displaying any emotions or opinions **4** (of a colour) not definite or striking **5** *chem* neither acidic nor alkaline **6** *physics* having zero charge or potential ▸ *n* **7** a neutral person or nation **8** the position of the controls of a gearbox that leaves the gears unconnected to the engine ▸ **neutrality** *n*

neutral *adj* **1, 2** = unbiased, impartial, disinterested, even-handed, uninvolved, nonpartisan, unprejudiced, nonaligned; ≠ biased **3** = expressionless, dull **4** = colourless

neutralize *or* **-lise** *vb* **-lizing, -lized** *or* **-lising, -lised 1** to make electrically or chemically neutral **2** to make ineffective by counteracting **3** to make (a country) neutral by international agreement: *the great powers neutralized Belgium in the 19th century* ▸ **neutralization** *or* **-lisation** *n*

neutrino (new-**tree**-no) *n, pl* **-nos** *physics* an elementary particle with no mass or electrical charge

neutron *n physics* a neutral elementary particle of about the same mass as a proton

neutron bomb *n* a nuclear weapon designed to kill people and animals while leaving buildings virtually undamaged

never *adv* **1** at no time; not ever **2** certainly not; not at all **3** Also: **well I never!** surely not!

never *adv* **1** = at no time, not once, not ever; ≠ always **2** = under no circumstances, not at all, on no account, not ever

never-never *n* **the never-never** *informal* hire-purchase: *they are buying it on the never-never*

nevertheless *adv* in spite of that

nevertheless *adv* = even so, still, however, yet, regardless, nonetheless, notwithstanding, in spite of that

new *adj* **1** recently made, brought into being, or acquired: *a new car* **2** of a kind never before existing; novel: *a new approach to monetary policy* **3** recently discovered: *testing new drugs* **4** recently introduced to or inexperienced in a place or situation: *new to this game* **5** fresh; additional: *you can acquire new skills* **6** unknown: *this is new to me* **7** (of a cycle) beginning again: *a new era* **8** (of crops) harvested early: *new potatoes* **9** changed for the better: *she returned a new woman* ▸ *adv* **10** recently, newly: *new-laid eggs* ▸ See also **news** ▸ **newish** *adj* ▸ **newness** *n*

new *adj* **1** = brand new **3** = modern, recent, contemporary, up-to-date, latest, current, original, fresh; ≠ old-fashioned **4, 6** = unfamiliar, strange **5** = extra, more, added, new-found, supplementary **9** = renewed, changed, improved, restored, altered, revitalized

New Age *n* **1** a philosophy, originating in the late 1980s, characterized by a belief in alternative medicine, astrology, and spiritualism ▸ *adj* **2** of the New Age: *New Age therapies* ▸ **New Ager** *n*

newbie *n informal* a person new to a job, club, etc.

newborn *adj* recently or just born

newcomer *n* a recent arrival or participant

newcomer *n* = new arrival, stranger

newel *n* **1** Also called: **newel post** the post at the top or bottom of a flight of stairs that supports the handrail **2** the central pillar of a winding staircase

newfangled *adj* objectionably or unnecessarily modern

newlyweds *pl n* a recently married couple

new moon *n* the moon when it appears as a narrow crescent at the beginning of its cycle

news *n* **1** important or interesting new happenings **2** information about such events, reported in the mass media **3 the news** a television or radio programme presenting such information **4** interesting or important new information: *it's news to me* **5** a person or thing widely reported in the mass media: *reggae is suddenly big news again*

> **news** *n* **1, 2** = information, latest (*informal*), report, story, exposé, intelligence, rumour, revelation, goss (*informal*)

newsagent *n Brit* a shopkeeper who sells newspapers and magazines

newsflash *n* a brief item of important news, which interrupts a radio or television programme

newsletter *n* a periodical bulletin issued to members of a group

newspaper *n* a weekly or daily publication consisting of folded sheets and containing news, features, and advertisements

newsprint *n* an inexpensive wood-pulp paper used for newspapers

newsreader *n* a news announcer on radio or television

newsreel *n* a short film with a commentary which presents current events

newsroom *n* a room in a newspaper office or radio or television station where news is received and prepared for publication or broadcasting: *a journalist who was in the newsroom at the time*

newsworthy *adj* sufficiently interesting to be reported as news

newsy *adj* **newsier, newsiest** (of a letter) full of news

newt *n* a small amphibious creature with a long slender body and tail and short legs

newton *n* the SI unit of force that gives an acceleration of 1 metre per second per second to a mass of 1 kilogram

next *adj* **1** immediately following: *the next generation* **2** immediately adjoining: *in the next room* **3** closest to in degree: *the next-best thing* ▸ *adv* **4** at a time immediately to follow: *the patient to be examined next* **5 next to A** adjacent to: *the house next to ours* **B** following in degree: *next to my wife, I love you most* **C** almost: *the evidence is next to totally useless*

> **next** *adj* **1** = following, later, succeeding, subsequent **2** = adjacent, closest, nearest, neighbouring, adjoining ▸ *adv* **4** = afterwards, then, later, following, subsequently, thereafter

nexus *n, pl* **nexus 1** a connection or link **2** a connected group or series

Nh nihonium

NHS (in Britain) National Health Service

nib *n* the writing point of a pen

nibble *vb* **-bling, -bled 1** to take little bites (of) **2** to bite gently: *she nibbled at her lower lip* ▸ *n* **3** a little bite **4** a light hurried meal

nibs *n* **his** *or* **her nibs** *slang* a mock title used of an important or self-important person

nice *adj* **1** pleasant **2** kind: *it's really nice of you to worry about me* **3** good or satisfactory: *a nice clean operation* **4** subtle: *a nice distinction* > **nicely** *adv* > **niceness** *n*

> **nice** *adj* **1** = pleasant, delightful, agreeable, good, attractive, charming, pleasurable, enjoyable; ≠ unpleasant **2** = kind, helpful, obliging, considerate; ≠ unkind **4** = precise, fine, careful, strict, subtle, delicate, meticulous, fastidious; ≠ vague

nicety *n, pl* **-ties 1** a subtle point: *the niceties of our arguments* **2** a refinement or delicacy: *social niceties* **3 to a nicety** precisely

niche (neesh) *n* **1** a recess in a wall for a statue or ornament **2** a position exactly suitable for the person occupying it: *perhaps I will find my niche in a desk job* ▸ *adj* **3** of or aimed at a specialist group or market: *niche retailing ventures*

> **niche** *n* **1** = recess, opening, corner, hollow, nook, alcove **2** = position, calling, place, slot (*informal*), vocation, pigeonhole (*informal*)

nick *vb* **1** to make a small cut in **2** *chiefly Brit slang* to steal **3** *chiefly Brit slang* to arrest ▸ *n* **4** a small notch or cut **5** *slang* a prison or police station **6** *informal* condition: *in good nick* **7 in the nick of time** just in time

> **nick** *vb* **1** = cut, mark, score, chip, scratch, scar, notch, dent **2** = steal, pinch (*informal*), swipe (*slang*), pilfer ▸ *n* **4** = cut, mark, scratch, chip, scar, notch, dent

nickel *n* **1** *chem* a silvery-white metallic element that is often used in alloys. Symbol: **Ni 2** a US or Canadian coin worth five cents

nickelodeon *n US* an early type of jukebox

nickname *n* **1** a familiar, pet, or derisory name given to a person or place ▸ *vb* **-naming, -named 2** to call (a person or place) by a nickname: *Gaius Caesar Augustus Germanicus, nicknamed Caligula*

> **nickname** *n* = pet name, label, diminutive, epithet, sobriquet, moniker *or* monicker (*slang*)

nicotine *n* a poisonous alkaloid found in tobacco > **nicotinic** *adj*

niece *n* a daughter of one's sister or brother

nifty *adj* **-tier, -tiest** *informal* neat or smart

niggard *n* a stingy person

niggardly *adj* not generous: *it pays its staff on a niggardly scale* > **niggardliness** *n*

niggle vb **-gling**, **-gled** 1 to worry slightly 2 to find fault continually ▸ n 3 a small worry or doubt 4 a trivial objection or complaint ▸ **niggling** adj

nigh archaic, poetic ▸ adv 1 nearly ▸ adj 2 near ▸ prep 3 close to

night n 1 the period of darkness that occurs each 24 hours, between sunset and sunrise. Related adjective: **nocturnal** 2 the period between sunset and bedtime; evening 3 the time between bedtime and morning 4 nightfall or dusk 5 an evening designated for a specific activity: *opening night* 6 **make a night of it** to celebrate the whole evening ▸ adj 7 of, occurring, or working at night: *the night sky*

> **night** n 1 = darkness, dark, night-time

nightcap n 1 a drink taken just before bedtime 2 a soft cap formerly worn in bed

nightclub n a place of entertainment open until late at night, that offers drink and dancing

nightdress n a loose dress worn in bed by women or girls

nightfall n the approach of darkness; dusk

nightie n informal short for **nightdress**

nightingale n a small bird with a musical song, usually heard at night

nightjar n a nocturnal bird with a harsh cry

nightlife n the entertainment and social activities available at night in a town or city: *New York nightlife*

nightly adj 1 happening each night ▸ adv 2 each night

> **nightly** adj = nocturnal, night-time ▸ adv = every night, nights (informal), each night, night after night

nightmare n 1 a terrifying or deeply distressing dream 2 a terrifying or unpleasant experience 3 a thing that is feared: *wheels and loose straps are a baggage handler's nightmare* ▸ **nightmarish** adj

> **nightmare** n 1 = bad dream, hallucination 2 = ordeal, trial, hell (informal), horror, torture, torment, tribulation, purgatory

night school n an educational institution that holds classes in the evening

nightshade n a plant which produces poisonous berries with bell-shaped flowers

nightshirt n a long loose shirtlike garment worn in bed

night-time n the time from sunset to sunrise

nihilism (nye-ill-liz-zum) n a total rejection of all established authority and institutions ▸ **nihilist** n, adj ▸ **nihilistic** adj

nihonium n chem a synthetic radioactive element produced in small quantities. Symbol: **Nh**

nil n nothing: esp. as a score in games

> **nil** n = nothing, love, zero

nimble adj 1 agile and quick in movement 2 mentally alert or acute ▸ **nimbly** adv

nimbus n, pl **-bi** or **-buses** 1 a dark grey rain cloud 2 a halo

nincompoop n informal a stupid person

nine n 1 the cardinal number that is the sum of one and eight 2 a numeral, 9 or IX, representing this number 3 something representing or consisting of nine units 4 **dressed up to the nines** informal elaborately dressed 5 **999** (in Britain) the telephone number of the emergency services ▸ adj 6 amounting to nine: *nine men* ▸ **ninth** adj, n

ninepins n the game of skittles

nineteen n 1 the cardinal number that is the sum of ten and nine 2 a numeral, 19 or XIX, representing this number 3 something representing or consisting of nineteen units 4 **talk nineteen to the dozen** to talk very fast ▸ adj 5 amounting to nineteen: *nineteen years* ▸ **nineteenth** adj, n

ninety n, pl **-ties** 1 the cardinal number that is the product of ten and nine 2 a numeral, 90 or XC, representing this number 3 something representing or consisting of ninety units ▸ adj 4 amounting to ninety: *ninety degrees* ▸ **ninetieth** adj, n

niobium n chem a white superconductive metallic element. Symbol: **Nb**

nip[1] vb **nipping**, **nipped** 1 informal to hurry 2 to pinch or squeeze 3 to bite lightly 4 (of the cold) to affect (someone) with a stinging sensation 5 to check the growth of (something): *a trite script nips all hope in the bud* ▸ n 6 a pinch or light bite 7 sharp coldness: *a nip in the air*

> **nip** vb 1 = pop, go, run, rush, dash 2 = pinch, squeeze, tweak 3 = bite ▸ n 6 = pinch, squeeze, tweak

nip[2] n a small drink of spirits

> **nip** n = dram, shot (informal), drop, sip, draught, mouthful, snifter (informal)

nipper n Brit, Austral & NZ informal a small child

nipple n 1 the small projection in the centre of each breast, which in females contains the outlet of the milk ducts 2 a small projection through which oil or grease can be put into a machine or component

nippy adj **-pier**, **-piest** 1 (of weather) frosty or chilly 2 informal quick or nimble 3 (of a motor vehicle) small and relatively powerful

niqab n a veil of lightweight opaque fabric, covering all the face except the eyes, worn by some Muslim women

nirvana (near-vah-na) n Buddhism & Hinduism the ultimate state of spiritual enlightenment and bliss attained by extinction of all desires and individual existence

> **nirvana** n = paradise, peace, joy, bliss, serenity, tranquillity

n

nit[1] *n* the egg or larva of a louse

nit[2] *n informal* short for **nitwit**

nit-picking *informal* ▸ *n* **1** a concern with insignificant details, usually with the intention of finding fault ▸ *adj* **2** showing such concern

nitrate *chem* ▸ *n* **1** a salt or ester of nitric acid **2** a fertilizer containing nitrate salts ▸ *vb* **-trating**, **-trated 3** to treat with nitric acid or a nitrate **4** to convert or be converted into a nitrate > **nitration** *n*

nitric *adj chem* of or containing nitrogen

nitrogen (nite-roj-jen) *n chem* a colourless odourless gas that forms four-fifths of the air and is an essential part of all animal and plant life. Symbol: **N** > **nitrogenous** *adj*

nitroglycerine *or* **nitroglycerin** *n chem* a thick pale yellow explosive liquid made from glycerol and nitric and sulphuric acids

nitty-gritty *n* **the nitty-gritty** *informal* the basic facts of a matter or situation

nitwit *n informal* a stupid person

no[1] *interj* **1** used to express denial, disagreement, or refusal ▸ *n*, *pl* **noes** *or* **nos 2** an answer or vote of no **3** a person who answers or votes no

> **no** *interj* = not at all, certainly not, of course not, absolutely not, never, no way, nay; ≠ yes ▸ *n* **2** = refusal, rejection, denial, negation; ≠ consent

no[2] *adj* **1** not any, not a, or not one: *I have no money*; *no comment* **2** not at all: *he's no exception*

No *chem* nobelium

No. *or* **no.** *pl* **Nos.** *or* **nos.** number

nob *n chiefly Brit old-fashioned slang* a person of wealth or social distinction

nobble *vb* **-bling**, **-bled** *chiefly Brit, Austral & NZ slang* **1** to bribe or threaten **2** to disable (a racehorse) to stop it from winning **3** to steal

nobelium *n chem* a radioactive element produced artificially from curium. Symbol: **No**

Nobel prize (no-**bell**) *n* a prize for outstanding contributions to chemistry, physics, physiology and medicine, literature, economics, and peace that may be awarded annually

nobility *n* **1** the quality of being noble; dignity **2** the class of people who hold titles and high social rank

noble *adj* **1** having or showing high moral qualities: *a noble cause* **2** belonging to a class of people who hold titles and high social rank **3** impressive and magnificent: *a noble beast* **4** *chem* (of certain metals) resisting oxidation ▸ *n* **5** a person who holds a title and high social rank > **nobly** *adv*

> **noble** *adj* **1** = worthy, generous, upright, honourable, virtuous, magnanimous; ≠ despicable **2** = aristocratic, lordly, titled, patrician, blue-blooded, highborn (*old-fashioned*); ≠ humble **3** = dignified, great, imposing, impressive, distinguished, splendid, stately; ≠ lowly ▸ *n* = lord *or* lady, peer, aristocrat, nobleman *or* woman; ≠ commoner

nobleman *or fem* **noblewoman** *n*, *pl* **-men** *or* **-women** a person of noble rank

nobody *pron* **1** no person; no-one ▸ *n*, *pl* **-bodies 2** a person of no importance

> **nobody** *pron* = no-one ▸ *n* = nonentity, lightweight (*informal*), zero, no-mark (*Brit slang*, *old-fashioned*), cipher; ≠ celebrity

no-brainer *n slang* something, esp. a decision that requires little or no thought

nocturnal *adj* **1** of the night **2** (of animals) active at night

nocturne *n* a short dreamy piece of music

nod *vb* **nodding**, **nodded 1** to lower and raise (one's head) briefly, to express agreement or greeting **2** to express by nodding: *he nodded his approval* **3** to sway or bend forwards and back **4** to let one's head fall forward with sleep **5** **nodding acquaintance** a slight knowledge (of a subject or person) ▸ *n* **6** a quick down-and-up movement of the head, in agreement **7** **land of Nod** an imaginary land of sleep

> **nod** *vb* **2** = signal, indicate, motion, gesture **3** = incline, bow ▸ *n* **6** = signal, sign, motion, gesture, indication

noddle *n chiefly Brit informal* the head or brains

node *n* **1** *botany* the point on a plant stem from which the leaves grow **2** *maths* a point at which a curve crosses itself **3** a knot or knob **4** *physics* a point in a vibrating body at which there is practically no vibration **5** *anatomy* any natural bulge or swelling: *lymph node* **6** *astron* either of the two points at which the orbit of a body intersects the path of the sun or the orbit of another body > **nodal** *adj*

nod off *vb informal* to fall asleep

nodule *n* **1** a small rounded lump, knot, or node **2** a rounded mineral growth on the root of a plant such as clover > **nodular** *adj*

Noel *or* **Noël** *n* same as **Christmas**

noggin *n* **1** *informal* the head **2** a small quantity of spirits

no-go area *n* a district that is barricaded off so that the police or army can enter only by force

noise *n* **1** a sound, usually a loud or disturbing one **2** loud shouting; din **3** an undesired electrical disturbance in a signal **4** unwanted or irrelevant elements in a visual image: *removing noise from pictures* **5** **noises** conventional utterances conveying a reaction: *he made the appropriate noises* ▸ *vb* **noising**, **noised 6** **be noised abroad** (of news or gossip) to be spread

> **noise** *n*, **1, 2** = sound, row, racket, clamour, din, uproar, commotion, hubbub; ≠ silence

noiseless *adj* making little or no sound > **noiselessly** *adv*

noisome *adj formal* **1** (of smells) offensive **2** extremely unpleasant

noisy *adj* **noisier**, **noisiest 1** making a lot of noise **2** (of a place) full of noise > **noisily** *adv*

n

noisy adj 1 = rowdy, strident, boisterous, vociferous, uproarious, clamorous; ≠ quiet

nomad n 1 a member of a tribe who move from place to place to find pasture and food 2 a wanderer > **nomadic** adj

no-man's-land n land between boundaries, esp. an unoccupied zone between opposing forces

nom de plume n, pl **noms de plume** same as **pen name**

nomenclature (no-men-klatch-er) n formal the system of names used in a particular subject

nominal adj 1 in name only: nominal independence 2 very small in comparison with real worth: a nominal amount of aid > **nominally** adv

nominal adj 1 = titular, formal, purported, in name only, supposed, so-called, theoretical, professed 2 = token, small, symbolic, minimal, trivial, trifling, insignificant, inconsiderable

nominate vb -nating, -nated 1 to propose (someone) as a candidate 2 to appoint (someone) to an office or position > **nomination** n

nominate vb 1 = propose, suggest, recommend, put forward 2 = appoint, name, choose, select, elect, assign, designate

nominative n grammar a grammatical case in some languages that identifies the subject of a verb

nominee n a person who is nominated to an office or as a candidate

nominee n = candidate, applicant, entrant, contestant, aspirant, runner

non- prefix 1 indicating negation: nonexistent 2 indicating refusal or failure: noncooperation 3 indicating exclusion from a specified class: nonfiction 4 indicating lack or absence: nonevent

nonagenarian n a person who is from 90 to 99 years old

nonaggression n the policy of not attacking other countries

nonagon n geom a figure with nine sides > **nonagonal** adj

nonalcoholic adj containing no alcohol

nonaligned adj (of a country) not part of a major alliance or power bloc > **nonalignment** n

nonbinary adj relating to a gender identity that does not belong to the categories of male or female

nonce n **for the nonce** for the present

nonchalant (non-shall-ant) adj casually unconcerned or indifferent > **nonchalance** n > **nonchalantly** adv

noncombatant n a member of the armed forces whose duties do not include fighting, such as a chaplain or surgeon

noncommissioned officer n (in the armed forces) a person who is appointed as a subordinate officer, from the lower ranks, rather than by a commission

noncommittal adj not committing oneself to any particular opinion

non compos mentis adj of unsound mind

nonconductor n a substance that is a poor conductor of heat, electricity, or sound

nonconformist n 1 a person who does not conform to generally accepted patterns of behaviour or thought ▸ adj 2 (of behaviour or ideas) not conforming to accepted patterns: people who pride themselves on their nonconformist past > **nonconformity** n

Nonconformist n 1 a member of a Protestant group separated from the Church of England ▸ adj 2 of or relating to Nonconformists

noncontributory adj Brit denoting a pension scheme for employees, the premiums of which are paid entirely by the employer

nondescript adj lacking outstanding features

none pron 1 not any: none of the men was represented by a lawyer; none of it meant anything to him 2 no-one; nobody: none could deny it 3 **none the** in no degree: her parents were none the wiser

none pron 1 = not any, nothing, zero, not one, nil 2 = no-one, nobody, not one

nonentity (non-enn-tit-tee) n, pl -ties an insignificant person or thing

nonetheless adv despite that; however

nonetheless adv = nevertheless, however, yet, even so, despite that, in spite of that

nonevent n a disappointing or insignificant occurrence which was expected to be important

nonflammable adj not easily set on fire

nonintervention n refusal to intervene in the affairs of others

nonpareil (non-par-rail) n a person or thing that is unsurpassed

non-payment n failure to pay money owed

nonplussed or US **nonplused** adj perplexed

nonsense n 1 something that has or makes no sense 2 unintelligible language 3 foolish behaviour: she'll stand no nonsense > **nonsensical** adj

nonsense n 1 = rubbish, hot air (informal), twaddle, drivel, tripe (informal), gibberish, claptrap (old-fashioned), double Dutch (Brit informal), bizzo (Austral slang), bull's wool (Austral, NZ slang); ≠ sense 3 = idiocy, stupidity

non sequitur (sek-wit-tur) n a statement having little or no relation to what preceded it

nonstandard adj denoting words, expressions, or pronunciations that are not regarded as correct by educated native speakers of a language

nonstarter n a person or an idea that has little chance of success

nonstick *adj* (of cooking utensils) coated with a substance that food will not stick to when cooked

nonstop *adj* **1** without a stop: *two weeks of nonstop rain* ▸ *adv* **2** without a stop: *most days his phone rings nonstop*

> **nonstop** *adj* = continuous, constant, relentless, uninterrupted, endless, unbroken, interminable, incessant; ≠ occasional
> ▸ *adv* = continuously, constantly, endlessly, relentlessly, perpetually, incessantly, ceaselessly, interminably

nontoxic *adj* not poisonous

noodles *pl n* ribbon-like strips of pasta

nook *n* **1** a corner or recess **2** a secluded or sheltered place

noon *n* the middle of the day; 12 o'clock

> **noon** *n* = midday, high noon, noonday, twelve noon, noontide

noonday *adj* happening or appearing at noon

no-one *or* **no one** *pron* no person; nobody

noose *n* a loop in the end of a rope, tied with a slipknot, such as one used to hang people

nor *conj* **1** used to join alternatives, the first of which is preceded by *neither*; and not: *neither willing nor able* **2** and not … either: *he had not arrived yet, nor had any of the models*

Nordic *adj* of Scandinavia or its typically tall, blond, and blue-eyed people

norm *n* a standard that is required or regarded as normal

> **norm** *n* = standard, rule, pattern, average, par, criterion, benchmark, yardstick

normal *adj* **1** usual, regular, or typical: *the study of normal behaviour* **2** free from serious mental or physical health problems **3** *geom* same as **perpendicular** (sense 1) ▸ *n* **4** the usual, regular, or typical state, degree, or form **5** *geom* a perpendicular line or plane › **normality** *or esp US* **normalcy** *n*

> **normal** *adj* **1** = usual, common, standard, average, natural, regular, ordinary, typical; ≠ unusual **2** = sane, reasonable, rational, well-adjusted, compos mentis (*Latin*), in your right mind, mentally sound

normalize *or* **-lise** *vb* **-lizing, -lized** *or* **-lising, -lised 1** to make or become normal **2** to bring into conformity with a standard › **normalization** *or* **-lisation** *n*

normally *adv* **1** as a rule; usually **2** in a normal manner

> **normally** *adv* **1** = usually, generally, commonly, regularly, typically, ordinarily, as a rule, habitually **2** = as usual, naturally, properly, conventionally, in the usual way

Norse *adj* **1** of ancient and medieval Scandinavia **2** of Norway ▸ *n* **3** **A** the N group of Germanic languages spoken in Scandinavia **B** any one of these languages, esp. in their ancient or medieval forms

north *n* **1** one of the four cardinal points of the compass, at 0° or 360° **2** the direction along a meridian towards the North Pole **3** the direction in which a compass needle points; magnetic north **4** **the north** any area lying in or towards the north ▸ *adj* **5** in or towards the north **6** (esp. of the wind) from the north ▸ *adv* **7** in, to, or towards the north

> **north** *adj* = northern, polar, arctic, boreal, northerly ▸ *adv* = northward(s), in a northerly direction

North *n* **1** **the North A** the northern part of England, generally regarded as reaching the southern boundaries of Yorkshire, Derbyshire, and Cheshire **B** (in the US) the states north of the Mason-Dixon Line that were known as the Free States during the Civil War **C** the economically and technically advanced countries of the world ▸ *adj* **2** of or denoting the northern part of a country or area

northerly *adj* **1** of or in the north ▸ *adv, adj* **2** towards the north **3** from the north: *a cold northerly wind*

northern *adj* **1** situated in or towards the north **2** facing or moving towards the north **3** (*sometimes cap*) of or characteristic of the north or North › **northernmost** *adj*

Northerner *n* a person from the north of a country or area, esp. England

North Pole *n* the northernmost point on the earth's axis, at a latitude of 90°N, which has very low temperatures

northward *adj, adv also* **northwards 1** towards the north ▸ *n* **2** the northward part or direction

Nos. *or* **nos.** numbers

nose *n* **1** the organ situated above the mouth, used for smelling and breathing **2** the sense of smell **3** the front part of a vehicle **4** the distinctive smell of a wine or perfume **5** instinctive skill in detecting something: *he had a nose for media events* **6** **get up someone's nose** *informal* to annoy someone **7** **keep one's nose clean** to stay out of trouble **8** **look down one's nose at** *informal* to be haughty towards **9** **pay through the nose** *informal* to pay a high price **10** **put someone's nose out of joint** *informal* to make someone envious by doing what he or she would have liked to do or had expected to do **11** **rub someone's nose in it** *informal* to remind someone unkindly of a failing or error **12** **turn up one's nose at** *informal* to show contempt for **13** **win by a nose** to win by a narrow margin ▸ *vb* **nosing, nosed 14** to move forward slowly and carefully: *a motorboat nosed out of the mist* **15** to pry or snoop **16** **nose out** to discover by searching or prying

nose n 1 = snout, bill, beak (slang), hooter (slang), proboscis ▸ vb 14 = ease forward, push, edge, shove, nudge

nose dive n 1 (of an aircraft) a sudden plunge with the nose pointing downwards 2 informal a sudden drop: when we fail our self-confidence takes a nose dive ▸ vb **nose-dive, -diving, -dived** 3 to take a nose dive

nosegay n a small bunch of flowers

nosey or **nosy** adj **nosier, nosiest** informal prying or inquisitive > **nosiness** n

nosh Brit, Austral & NZ slang ▸ n 1 food ▸ vb 2 to eat

nostalgia n 1 a sentimental yearning for the past 2 homesickness > **nostalgic** adj > **nostalgically** adv

nostalgia n 1 = reminiscence, longing, pining, yearning, remembrance, homesickness, wistfulness

nostril n either of the two openings at the end of the nose

nostrum n 1 a quack medicine 2 a favourite remedy

not adv 1 used to negate the sentence, phrase, or word that it modifies: I will not stand for it 2 **not that** which is not to say that: not that I've ever heard him complain

notable (note-a-bl) adj 1 worthy of being noted; remarkable ▸ n 2 a person of distinction > **notability** n > **notably** adv

notable adj = remarkable, striking, unusual, extraordinary, outstanding, memorable, uncommon, conspicuous; ≠ imperceptible ▸ n = celebrity, big name, dignitary, luminary, personage, V.I.P.

notary or **notary public** (note-a-ree) n, pl **notaries** or **notaries public** a public official, usually a solicitor, who is legally authorized to attest and certify documents

notation (no-tay-shun) n 1 representation of numbers or quantities in a system by a series of symbols 2 a set of such symbols

notch n 1 a V-shaped cut 2 informal a step or level: the economy moved up another notch ▸ vb 3 to cut a notch in 4 **notch up** informal to score or achieve: he notched up a hat trick of wins

notch n 1 = cut, nick, incision, indentation, mark, score, cleft 2 = level, step, degree, grade ▸ vb 3 = cut, mark, score, nick, scratch, indent

note n 1 a brief informal letter 2 a brief record in writing for future reference 3 a critical comment or explanation in a book 4 an official written communication, as from a government or from a doctor 5 short for **banknote** 6 Brit & NZ a musical sound of a particular pitch 7 a written symbol representing the pitch and duration of a musical sound 8 chiefly Brit a key on a piano, organ, or other keyboard instrument 9 a particular feeling or atmosphere: an optimistic note 10 a distinctive vocal sound, as of a type of animal 11 a sound used as a signal or warning: the note to retreat was sounded 12 **of note** a distinguished or famous B important: nothing of note 13 **strike the right note** to behave appropriately 14 **take note of** to pay attention to ▸ vb **noting, noted** 15 to notice; pay attention to: such criticism should be noted 16 to make a written note of: he noted it in his diary 17 to remark upon: I note that you do not wear shoes

note n 1 = message, letter, communication, memo, memorandum, epistle, email or e-mail, text 2 = record, reminder, memo, memorandum, jotting, minute 3 = annotation, comment, remark 4 = document, form, record, certificate 7 = symbol, mark, sign, indication, token 9 = tone, touch, trace, hint, sound ▸ vb 15 = notice, see, observe, perceive 16 = write down, record, scribble, set down, jot down 17 = mention, record, mark, indicate, register, remark

notebook n a book for writing in

notebook n = notepad, exercise book, journal, diary

noted adj well-known: a noted scholar

noted adj = famous, celebrated, distinguished, well-known, prominent, acclaimed, notable, renowned; ≠ unknown

noteworthy adj worth noting; remarkable

nothing pron 1 not anything: I felt nothing 2 a matter of no importance: don't worry, it's nothing 3 absence of meaning, value, or worth: the industry shrank to almost nothing 4 the figure o 5 **have** or **be nothing to do with** to have no connection with 6 **nothing but** not something other than; only 7 **nothing doing** informal an expression of dismissal or refusal 8 **nothing less than** downright: nothing less than complete withdrawal 9 **think nothing of something** to regard something as easy or natural ▸ adv 10 not at all: he looked nothing like his brother ▸ n 11 informal a person or thing of no importance or significance

nothing pron 1, 4 = nought, zero, nil, not a thing, zilch (slang) 2 = a trifle 3 = void, emptiness, nothingness, nullity ▸ n = nobody, cipher, nonentity

nothingness n 1 nonexistence 2 total insignificance

notice n 1 observation or attention: to attract notice 2 a displayed placard or announcement giving information 3 advance notification of something such as intention to end a contract of employment: she handed in her notice 4 a theatrical or literary review: the film reaped ecstatic notices 5 **at short notice** with very little notification 6 **take no notice of** to ignore or

disregard **7 take notice** to pay attention ▸ vb
-ticing, -ticed 8 to become aware (of) **9** to point
out or remark upon

> **notice** n **1** = attention, interest, note, regard,
> consideration, observation, scrutiny, heed;
> ≠ oversight **3** = notification, warning,
> advice, intimation, news, communication,
> announcement, instruction, heads up (US,
> Canad) ▸ vb = observe, see, note, spot,
> distinguish, perceive, detect, discern;
> ≠ overlook

noticeable adj easily seen or detected
> **noticeably** adv

> **noticeable** adj = obvious, clear, striking,
> plain, evident, manifest, conspicuous,
> perceptible

notifiable adj having to be reported to the
authorities: a notifiable disease
notification n **1** the act of notifying someone
of something **2** a formal announcement
notify vb **-fies, -fying, -fied** to inform: notify gas
and electricity companies of your moving date

> **notify** vb = inform, tell, advise, alert to,
> announce, warn

notion n **1** an idea or opinion **2** a whim

> **notion** n **1** = idea, view, opinion, belief,
> concept, impression, sentiment, inkling
> **2** = whim, wish, desire, fancy, impulse,
> inclination, caprice

notional adj hypothetical, imaginary, or
unreal: a notional dividend payment
notorious adj well known for some bad reason
> **notoriety** n > **notoriously** adv

> **notorious** adj = infamous, disreputable,
> opprobrious

notwithstanding prep **1** in spite of ▸ adv
2 nevertheless

> **notwithstanding** prep = despite, in spite of,
> regardless of

nougat n a hard chewy pink or white sweet
containing chopped nuts
nought n **1** the figure o ▸ n, adv **2** same as
naught

> **nought** n = zero, nil, aught or ought

noughties pl n informal the decade from 2000 to
2009
noun n a word that refers to a person, place, or
thing
nourish vb **1** to provide with the food necessary
for life and growth **2** to encourage or foster (an
idea or feeling) > **nourishing** adj

> **nourish** vb **1** = feed, supply, sustain, nurture
> **2** = encourage, support, maintain, promote,
> sustain, foster

nourishment n the food needed to nourish
the body
nouvelle cuisine (noo-vell kwee-**zeen**) n a
style of preparing and presenting food with
light sauces and unusual combinations of
flavours
Nov. November
nova n, pl **-vae** or **-vas** a star that undergoes an
explosion and fast increase of brightness, then
gradually decreases to its original brightness
novel[1] n a long fictional story in book form

> **novel** n = story, tale, fiction, romance,
> narrative

novel[2] adj fresh, new, or original: a novel
approach

> **novel** adj = new, different, original, fresh,
> unusual, innovative, uncommon; ≠ ordinary

novelist n a writer of novels
novella n, pl **-las** a short narrative tale or short
novel
novelty n, pl **-ties 1** the quality of being new
and interesting **2** a new or unusual experience
or thing **3** a small cheap toy or trinket

> **novelty** n **1** = newness, originality,
> freshness, innovation, surprise, uniqueness,
> strangeness, unfamiliarity **2** = curiosity,
> rarity, oddity, wonder **3** = trinket, souvenir,
> memento, bauble, trifle, knick-knack

November n the eleventh month of the year
novena (no-**vee**-na) n, pl **-nas** or **-nae** (-nee)
RC Church a set of prayers or services on nine
consecutive days
novice (**nov**-viss) n **1** a beginner **2** a person
who has entered a religious order but has not
yet taken vows

> **novice** n **1** = beginner, pupil, amateur,
> newcomer, trainee, apprentice, learner,
> probationer; ≠ expert

now adv **1** at or for the present time
2 immediately: bring it now **3** in these times;
nowadays **4** given the present circumstances:
now do you understand why? **5 A** used as a hesitation
word: now, I can't really say **B** used for emphasis:
now listen to this **C** used at the end of a command:
run along now **6 just now A** very recently: he left
just now **B** very soon: I'm going just now **7 now and
again** or **then** occasionally **8 now now!** an
exclamation used to tell someone off or to calm
someone ▸ conj **9** Also: **now that** seeing that:
now you're here, you can help me ▸ n **10** the present
time: now is the time to go

> **now** adv **2** = immediately, promptly,
> instantly, at once, straight away **3** = nowadays,
> at the moment **7 now and then** or **again**
> = occasionally, sometimes, from time to time,
> on and off, intermittently, infrequently,
> sporadically

n

nowadays *adv* in these times: *nowadays his work is regarded as out-of-date*

> **nowadays** *adv* = now, today, at the moment, in this day and age

nowhere *adv* 1 in, at, or to no place 2 **getting nowhere** *informal* making no progress 3 **nowhere near** far from: *the stadium is nowhere near completion* ▸ *n* 4 **in the middle of nowhere** (of a place) completely isolated

noxious *adj* 1 poisonous or harmful 2 extremely unpleasant

nozzle *n* a projecting spout from which fluid is discharged

NSPCC (in Britain) National Society for the Prevention of Cruelty to Children

NSW New South Wales

NT 1 (in Britain) National Trust 2 New Testament 3 Northern Territory 4 Nunavut

nuance (new-ahnss) *n* a subtle difference, as in colour, meaning, or tone

nub *n* the point or gist: *this is the nub of his theory*

nubile (new-bile) *adj* 1 (of a young woman) sexually attractive 2 (of a young woman) old enough or mature enough for marriage

nuclear *adj* 1 of nuclear weapons or energy 2 of an atomic nucleus: *nuclear fission*

nuclear energy *n* energy released during a nuclear reaction as a result of fission or fusion

nuclear fission *n physics* the splitting of an atomic nucleus, either spontaneously or by bombardment by a neutron: used in atomic bombs and nuclear power plants

nuclear fusion *n physics* the combination of two nuclei to form a heavier nucleus with the release of energy: used in hydrogen bombs

nuclear power *n* power produced by a nuclear reactor

nuclear reaction *n physics* a process in which the structure and energy content of an atomic nucleus is changed by interaction with another nucleus or particle

nuclear reactor *n* a device in which a nuclear reaction is maintained and controlled to produce nuclear energy

nuclear winter *n* a theoretical period of low temperatures and little light that has been suggested would occur after a nuclear war

nucleic acid *n biochem* a complex compound, such as DNA or RNA, found in all living cells

nucleus *n, pl* **-clei** 1 *physics* the positively charged centre of an atom, made of protons and neutrons, about which electrons orbit 2 a central thing around which others are grouped 3 a centre of growth or development: *the nucleus of a new relationship* 4 *biol* the part of a cell that contains the chromosomes and associated molecules that control the characteristics and growth of the cell 5 *chem* a fundamental group of atoms in a molecule serving as the base structure for related compounds

> **nucleus** *n* 2, 3 = centre, heart, focus, basis, core, pivot, kernel, nub

nude *adj* 1 completely undressed ▸ *n* 2 a naked figure in painting, sculpture, or photography 3 **in the nude** naked > **nudity** *n*

> **nude** *adj* = naked, stripped, bare, undressed, stark-naked, disrobed, unclothed, unclad; ≠ dressed

nudge *vb* **nudging**, **nudged** 1 to push (someone) gently with the elbow to get attention 2 to push (something or someone) lightly: *the dog nudged the stick with its nose* 3 to persuade (someone) gently ▸ *n* 4 a gentle poke or push

> **nudge** *vb* 1, 2 = push, touch, dig, jog, prod, elbow, shove, poke 3 = prompt, influence, persuade, spur, prod, coax ▸ *n* = push, touch, dig, elbow, bump, shove, poke, jog

nudism *n* the practice of not wearing clothes, esp. on beaches or in camps set aside for this purpose > **nudist** *n, adj*

nugatory (new-gat-tree) *adj formal* 1 of little value 2 not valid: *their rejection rendered the treaty nugatory*

nugget *n* 1 a small lump of gold in its natural state 2 something small but valuable: *a nugget of useful knowledge* ▸ *vb* **-geting**, **-geted** 3 NZ to polish footwear

nuisance *n* 1 a person or thing that causes annoyance or bother ▸ *adj* 2 causing annoyance or bother: *nuisance calls*

> **nuisance** *n* = trouble, problem, trial, drag (*informal*), bother, pest, irritation, hassle (*informal*); ≠ benefit

nuke *slang* ▸ *vb* **nuking**, **nuked** 1 to attack with nuclear weapons ▸ *n* 2 a nuclear bomb

null *adj* 1 **null and void** not legally valid 2 **null set** *maths* a set with no members > **nullity** *n*

nulla-nulla *n* a wooden stick used by Australian Aboriginal people for hunting, digging, fighting, and for ceremonial purposes

nullify *vb* **-fies**, **-fying**, **-fied** 1 to make (something) ineffective 2 to make (something) legally void > **nullification** *n*

numb *adj* 1 deprived of feeling through cold, shock, or fear 2 unable to move; paralysed ▸ *vb* 3 to make numb > **numbly** *adv* > **numbness** *n*

> **numb** *adj* 1 = unfeeling, dead, frozen, paralysed, insensitive, deadened, immobilized, torpid; ≠ sensitive ▸ *vb* = stun, knock out, paralyse, daze

numbat *n* a small Australian marsupial with a long snout and tongue

number *n* 1 a concept of quantity that is or can be derived from a single unit, a sum of units, or zero 2 the word or symbol used to represent a number 3 a numeral or string of numerals used to identify a person or thing: *an account number*

4 the person or thing so identified: *he was seeded number two* **5** sum or quantity: *a very large number of people have telephoned* **6** one of a series, as of a magazine **7** a self-contained piece of pop or jazz music **8** a group of people: *one of their number might be willing* **9** *informal* an admired article: *that little number is by Dior* **10** *grammar* classification of words depending on how many people or things are referred to **11 any number of** many **12 beyond** *or* **without number** innumerable **13 have someone's number** *informal* to have discovered someone's true character or intentions **14 one's number is up** *Brit & Austral informal* one is about to die ▸ *vb* **15** to count **16** to assign a number to: *numbered seats* **17** to add up to: *the illustrations numbered well over fifty* **18** to include in a group: *he numbered several Americans among his friends* **19 one's days are numbered** something unpleasant, such as death, is likely to happen to one soon

> **number** *n* **2** = numeral, figure, character, digit, integer **5** = amount, quantity, collection, aggregate; ≠ shortage **6** = issue, copy, edition, imprint, printing **8** = group, set, band, crowd, gang ▸ *vb* **15** = calculate, account, reckon, compute, enumerate; ≠ guess **17** = amount to, come to, total, add up to **18** = include, count

number crunching *n informal* the large-scale processing of numerical data
> **number cruncher** *n*

numberless *adj* too many to be counted

number one *n* **1** *informal* oneself: *he looks after number one* **2** *informal* the bestselling pop record in any one week ▸ *adj* **3** first in importance, urgency, or quality: *he's their number one suspect*

numberplate *n* a plate on a motor vehicle showing the registration number

numbskull *or* **numskull** *n informal, derogatory* a stupid person

numeral *n* a word or symbol used to express a sum or quantity

numerate *adj* able to do basic arithmetic
> **numeracy** *n*

numeration *n* **1** the act or process of numbering or counting **2** a system of numbering

numerator *n maths* the number above the line in a fraction

numerical *or* **numeric** *adj* measured or expressed in numbers: *record the severity of your symptoms in numerical form* ▸ **numerically** *adv*

numerous *adj* **1** many: *they carried out numerous bombings* **2** consisting of a large number of people or things: *the cast is not as numerous as one might suppose*

> **numerous** *adj* = many, several, countless, lots, abundant, plentiful, innumerable, copious; ≠ few

numskull *n* same as **numbskull**

nun *n* a female member of a religious order

nuncio *n*, *pl* **-cios** *RC Church* a papal ambassador

nunnery *n*, *pl* **-neries** a convent

nuptial *adj* relating to marriage: *a nuptial blessing*

nuptials *pl n* a wedding

nurd *n slang* same as **nerd**

nurse *n* **1** a person trained to look after sick people, usually in a hospital **2** short for **nursemaid** ▸ *vb* **nursing, nursed 3** to look after (a sick person) **4** to breast-feed (a baby) **5** (of a baby) to feed at its mother's breast **6** to try to cure (an ailment) **7** to harbour or foster (a feeling) **8** to clasp fondly: *she nursed her drink* ▸ **nursing** *n, adj*

> **nurse** *vb* **3** = look after, treat, tend, care for, take care of, minister to **4** = breast-feed, feed, nurture, nourish, suckle, wet-nurse **7** = harbour, have, maintain, preserve, entertain, cherish

nursemaid *or* **nurserymaid** *n* a woman employed to look after children

nursery *n*, *pl* **-ries** **1** a room in a house where children sleep or play **2** a place providing care for children during the working day **3** a place where plants and young trees are grown for sale

> **nursery** *n* **2** = crèche, kindergarten, playgroup, play-centre (NZ)

nurseryman *n*, *pl* **-men** a person who raises plants and trees for sale

nursery nurse *n* a person trained to look after children of pre-school age

nursery school *n* a school for young children from three to five years old

nursery slopes *pl n* gentle slopes used by beginners in skiing

nursing home *n* a private hospital or home for people who are old or ill

nursing officer *n* (in Britain) the administrative head of the nursing staff of a hospital

nurture *n* **1** the act or process of promoting the development of a child or young plant ▸ *vb* **-turing, -tured 2** to promote or encourage the development of

> **nurture** *n* = upbringing, training, education, instruction, rearing, development ▸ *vb* = bring up, raise, look after, rear, care for, develop; ≠ neglect

nut *n* **1** a dry one-seeded fruit that grows inside a hard shell **2** the edible inner part of such a fruit **3** a small piece of metal with a hole in it, that screws on to a bolt **4** *slang* a foolish or eccentric person **5** *offensive* a person with a mental illness **6** *slang* an enthusiast: *a health nut* **7** *slang* the head **8** *Brit* a small piece of coal **9 a hard** *or* **tough nut to crack** a person or thing that presents difficulties **10 do one's nut** *Brit & Austral slang* to be very angry

> **nut** *n* **7** = head, skull

nutcase *n slang* **1** a foolish or eccentric person **2** *offensive* a person with a mental illness

nutcracker *n* a device for cracking the shells of nuts. Also: **nutcrackers**

nuthatch *n* a songbird that feeds on insects, seeds, and nuts

nutmeg *n* a spice made from the seed of a tropical tree

nutria (**new-tree-a**) *n* the fur of the coypu

nutrient (**new-tree-ent**) *n* **1** a substance that provides nourishment: *their only source of nutrient* ▶ *adj* **2** providing nourishment

nutriment (**new-tree-ment**) *n* the food or nourishment required by all living things to grow and stay healthy

nutrition (**new-trish-un**) *n* **1** the process of taking in and absorbing nutrients **2** the process of being nourished **3** the study of nutrition › **nutritional** *adj* › **nutritionist** *n*

> **nutrition** *n* **1** = food, nourishment, sustenance, nutriment

nutritious *adj* providing nourishment

nutter *n Brit & NZ slang* **1** a foolish or eccentric person **2** *offensive* a person with a mental illness

nutty *adj* **-tier, -tiest 1** containing or resembling nuts **2** *slang* foolish or eccentric › **nuttiness** *n*

nuzzle *vb* **-zling, -zled** to push or rub gently with the nose or snout

NW northwest(ern)

nylon *n* a synthetic material used for clothing and many other products

nymph *n* **1** *myth* a spirit of nature, represented as a beautiful young woman **2** the larva of certain insects, resembling the adult form **3** *chiefly poetic* a beautiful young woman

nymphet *n* a girl who is attractive and sexually precocious

nymphomaniac *n* a woman with an abnormally intense sexual desire › **nymphomania** *n*

NZ *or* **N.Z.** New Zealand

NZE New Zealand English

NZRFU New Zealand Rugby Football Union

O 1 *chem* oxygen **2** Old **3** same as **nought**

oaf *n* a stupid or clumsy person › **oafish** *adj*

oak *n* **1** a large forest tree with hard wood, acorns as fruits, and leaves with rounded projections **2** the wood of this tree, used as building timber and for making furniture › **oaken** *adj*

oak apple *or* **oak gall** *n* a brownish round lump or ball produced on oak trees by certain wasps

oakum *n* loose fibre obtained by unravelling old rope, used for filling cracks in wooden ships

OAP (in Britain) old age pensioner

oar *n* **1** a long pole with a broad blade, used for rowing a boat **2** **put** *or* **stick one's oar in** to interfere or interrupt

oasis *n, pl* **-ses 1** a fertile patch in a desert **2** a place or situation offering relief in the midst of difficulty

oast *n chiefly Brit* an oven for drying hops

oat *n* **1** a hard cereal grown as food **2** **oats** the edible grain of this cereal **3** **sow one's wild oats** to have casual sexual relationships while young › **oaten** *adj*

oath *n, pl* **oaths 1** a solemn promise, esp. to tell the truth in a court of law **2** an offensive or blasphemous expression; a swearword **3** **on** *or* **under oath** having made a solemn promise to tell the truth, esp. in a court of law

> **oath** *n* **1** = promise, bond, pledge, vow, word, affirmation, avowal **2** = swear word, curse, obscenity, blasphemy, expletive, four-letter word, profanity

oatmeal *n* **1** a coarse flour made by grinding oats ▶ *adj* **2** greyish-yellow

obbligato (**ob-lig-gah-toe**) *music* ▶ *adj* **1** not to be omitted in performance ▶ *n, pl* **-tos 2** an essential part or accompaniment: *an aria with bassoon obbligato*

obdurate *adj* not to be persuaded; hardhearted or obstinate › **obduracy** *n*

OBE (in Britain) Officer of the Order of the British Empire

obedient *adj* obeying or willing to obey › **obedience** *n* › **obediently** *adv*

obeisance (**oh-bay-sanss**) *n formal* **1** an attitude of respect or humble obedience **2** a bow or curtsy showing this attitude › **obeisant** *adj*

obelisk (**ob-bill-isk**) *n* **1** a four-sided stone pillar that tapers to a pyramid at the top **2** *printing* same as **dagger** (sense 2)

obese (oh-**beess**) *adj* very fat ▷ **obesity** *n*

obey *vb* **1** to carry out instructions or orders; be obedient **2** to act in accordance with one's feelings, an impulse, etc.: *I had obeyed the impulse to open the gate and had walked up the drive*

> **obey** *vb* **1** = carry out, follow, implement, act upon, carry through; ≠ disregard **2** = abide by, keep, follow, comply with, observe, heed, conform to, keep to

obfuscate *vb* **-cating, -cated** *formal* to make something unnecessarily difficult to understand ▷ **obfuscation** *n* ▷ **obfuscatory** *adj*

obituary *n, pl* **-aries** a published announcement of a death, usually with a short biography of the dead person ▷ **obituarist** *n*

object[1] *n* **1** a thing that can be touched or seen **2** a person or thing seen as a focus for feelings, actions, or thought: *she had become for him an object of compassion* **3** an aim or purpose: *the main object of the exercise* **4** *philosophy* that which can be perceived by the mind, as contrasted with the thinking subject **5** *grammar* a noun, pronoun, or noun phrase that receives the action of a verb or is governed by a preposition, such as *the bottle* in *she threw the bottle* **6** **no object** not a hindrance or obstacle: *money's no object*

> **object** *n* **1** = thing, article, body, item, entity **2** = target, victim, focus, recipient **3** = purpose, aim, end, point, plan, idea, goal, design

object[2] *vb* **1** to express disapproval or opposition: *my colleagues objected strongly to further delays* **2** to state as one's reason for opposing: *he objected that his small staff would be unable to handle the added work* ▷ **objector** *n*

> **object** *vb* **1** = protest against, oppose, argue against, draw the line at, take exception to, cry out against, complain against, expostulate against; ≠ accept

objection *n* **1** an expression or feeling of opposition or disapproval **2** a reason for opposing something: *the planning officer had raised no objection to the proposals*

> **objection** *n* = protest, opposition, complaint, doubt, dissent, outcry, protestation, scruple; ≠ agreement

objectionable *adj* offensive or unacceptable

objective *n* **1** an aim or purpose: *the objective is to highlight the environmental threat to the planet* **2** *grammar* a grammatical case in some languages that identifies the direct object of a verb or preposition **3** *optics* the lens nearest to the object observed in an optical instrument ▶ *adj* **4** not distorted by personal feelings or bias: *I have tried to be as objective as possible in my presentation* **5** of or relating to actual facts as opposed to thoughts or feelings: *stand back and try to take a more objective view of your life as a whole* **6** existing independently of the mind; real ▷ **objectival** *adj* ▷ **objectively** *adv* ▷ **objectivity** *n*

> **objective** *n* **1** = purpose, aim, goal, end, plan, hope, idea, target ▶ *adj* **4, 5** = unbiased, detached, fair, open-minded, impartial, impersonal, disinterested, even-handed; ≠ subjective **6** = factual, real

objet d'art (ob-zhay **dahr**) *n, pl* **objets d'art** (ob-zhay **dahr**) a small object considered to be of artistic worth

oblation *n* **1** *Christianity* the offering of bread and wine to God at Communion **2** any offering made for religious purposes ▷ **oblational** *adj*

obligated *adj* being morally or legally bound to do something: *they are obligated to provide temporary accommodation* ▷ **obligative** *adj*

obligation *n* **1** a moral or legal duty **2** the binding power of such a duty: *I feel under some obligation to help you with your education* **3** a sense of being in debt because of a service or favour: *I don't want him marrying me out of obligation*

> **obligation** *n* **1** = duty, compulsion **2** = responsibility, duty, liability, accountability, answerability

obligatory *adj* required or compulsory because of custom or law

oblige *vb* **obliging, obliged** **1** to compel someone by legal, moral, or physical means to do something **2** to make (someone) indebted or grateful for a favour: *I am obliged to you for your help* **3** to do a favour to someone: *she obliged the guests with a song*

> **oblige** *vb* **1** = compel, make, force, require, bind, constrain, necessitate, impel **3** = help, assist, benefit, please, humour, accommodate, indulge, gratify; ≠ bother

obliging *adj* willing to be helpful ▷ **obligingly** *adv*

> **obliging** *adj* = accommodating, kind, helpful, willing, polite, cooperative, agreeable, considerate; ≠ unhelpful

oblique (oh-**bleak**) *adj* **1** at an angle; slanting **2** *geom* (of lines or planes) neither perpendicular nor parallel to one another **3** indirect or evasive: *only oblique references have been made to the anti-government unrest* ▷ **obliquely** *adv* ▷ **obliqueness** *n*

oblique angle *n* an angle that is not a right angle or any multiple of a right angle

obliterate *vb* **-rating, -rated** to destroy every trace of; wipe out completely ▷ **obliteration** *n*

oblivion *n* **1** the condition of being forgotten or disregarded: *the Marxist-Leninist wing of the party looks set to sink into oblivion* **2** the state of being unaware or unconscious: *guests seemed to feel a social obligation to drink themselves into oblivion*

oblivious *adj* unaware or unconscious: *oblivious of her soaking clothes; I was oblivious to the beauty* ▷ **obliviousness** *n*

oblong *adj* **1** having an elongated, rectangular shape ▶ *n* **2** a figure or object having this shape ▷ **obliviousness** *n*

obloquy (ob-lock-wee) *n, pl* **-quies** *formal*
1 abusive statements or blame: *the British press was held up to moral obloquy* **2** disgrace brought about by this: *the punishment of lifelong public obloquy and private embarrassment*

obnoxious *adj* extremely unpleasant
> **obnoxiousness** *n*

oboe *n* a double-reeded woodwind instrument with a penetrating nasal tone > **oboist** *n*

obscene *adj* **1** offensive to accepted standards of decency or modesty **2** *law* tending to deprave or corrupt: *an obscene publication* **3** disgusting: *a great dark obscene pool of blood* > **obscenity** *n*

> **obscene** *adj* **1** = indecent, dirty, offensive, filthy, improper, immoral, pornographic, lewd; ≠ decent **3** = offensive, shocking, evil, disgusting, outrageous, revolting, sickening, vile

obscure *adj* **1** not well-known: *the concerts feature several obscure artists* **2** not easily understood: *the contracts are written in obscure language* **3** unclear or indistinct ▸ *vb* **-scuring, -scured 4** to make unclear or vague; hide: *no amount of bluster could obscure the fact that the prime minister had run out of excuses* **5** to cover or cloud over > **obscuration** *n*
> **obscurity** *n*

> **obscure** *adj* **1** = unknown, little-known, humble, unfamiliar, out-of-the-way, lowly, unheard-of, undistinguished; ≠ famous **2** = abstruse, complex, confusing, mysterious, vague, unclear, ambiguous, enigmatic; ≠ straightforward **3** = unclear, uncertain, confused, mysterious, doubtful, indeterminate; ≠ well-known ▸ *vb* **4** = hide, screen, mask, disguise, conceal, veil, cloak, camouflage; ≠ expose **5** = obstruct, hinder

obsequies (ob-sick-weez) *pl n, sing* **-quy** *formal* funeral rites

obsequious (ob-seek-wee-uss) *adj* being overattentive in order to gain favour
> **obsequiousness** *n*

observance *n* **1** the observing of a law or custom **2** a ritual, ceremony, or practice, esp. of a religion

observant *adj* quick to notice details around one; sharp-eyed

observation *n* **1** the act of watching or the state of being watched **2** a comment or remark **3** detailed examination of something before analysis, diagnosis, or interpretation: *you may be admitted to hospital for observation and rest* **4** the facts learned from observing **5** the ability to notice things: *she has good powers of observation*
> **observational** *adj*

> **observation** *n* **1, 3** = watching, study, survey, review, investigation, monitoring, examination, inspection **2** = comment, thought, note, statement, opinion, remark, explanation, reflection

observatory *n, pl* **-ries** a building specially designed and equipped for studying the weather and the stars

observe *vb* **-serving, -served 1** to see or notice: *after some hours I observed a change in the animal's behaviour* **2** to watch (something) carefully **3** to make scientific examinations of **4** to remark: *the speaker observed that times had changed* **5** to keep (a law or custom) > **observable** *adj* > **observer** *n*

> **observe** *vb* **1** = notice, see, note, discover, spot, regard, witness, distinguish **2** = watch, study, view, look at, check, survey, monitor, keep an eye on (*informal*) **4** = remark, say, comment, state, note, reflect, mention, opine (*formal*) **5** = comply with, keep, follow, respect, carry out, honour, discharge, obey; ≠ disregard

obsess *vb* **1** to be constantly in the thoughts of (someone): *maps obsess Tim* **2** (foll. by *about* or *over*) to be constantly worried: *I tend to obsess about my work* > **obsessive** *adj, n*

obsessed *adj* thinking about someone or something all the time: *he had become obsessed with her*

> **obsessed** *adj* = absorbed, dominated, gripped, haunted, distracted, hung up (*slang*), preoccupied; ≠ indifferent

obsession *n* **1** something that preoccupies a person to the exclusion of other things: *his principal obsession was with trying to economize* **2** *psychiatry* a persistent idea or impulse, often associated with anxiety and mental illness
> **obsessional** *adj*

> **obsession** *n* = preoccupation, thing (*informal*), complex, hang-up (*informal*), mania, phobia, fetish, fixation

obsidian *n* a dark glassy volcanic rock

obsolescent *adj* becoming obsolete or out of date > **obsolescence** *n*

obsolete *adj* no longer used; out of date

> **obsolete** *adj* = outdated, old, passé, old-fashioned, discarded, extinct, out of date, archaic; ≠ up-to-date

obstacle *n* **1** a situation or event that prevents something being done: *there are obstacles which could slow the development of a vaccine* **2** a person or thing that hinders movement

> **obstacle** *n* **1** = hindrance, bar, difficulty, barrier, handicap, hurdle, hitch, drawback, uphill (*S African*); ≠ help **2** = obstruction, block, barrier, hurdle, snag, impediment, blockage, hindrance

obstetrician *n* a doctor who specializes in obstetrics

obstetrics *n* the branch of medicine concerned with pregnancy and childbirth > **obstetric** *adj*

obstinate *adj* **1** keeping stubbornly to a particular opinion or course of action **2** difficult

to treat or deal with: *obstinate weeds* ▸ **obstinacy** *n*
▸ **obstinately** *adv*

obstreperous *adj* noisy and difficult to
control: *her obstreperous teenage son*

obstruct *vb* **1** to block a way with an obstacle
2 to make progress or activity difficult: *this
government will never obstruct the course of justice*
3 to block a clear view of

> **obstruct** *vb* **1** = block, close, bar, plug,
> barricade, stop up, bung up (*informal*) **2** = hold
> up, stop, check, block, restrict, slow down,
> hamper, hinder; ≠ help **3** = obscure, screen,
> cover

obstruction *n* **1** a person or thing that
obstructs **2** the act of obstructing or being
obstructed **3** *sport* the act of unfairly impeding
an opposing player

obstructive *adj* deliberately causing
difficulties or delays ▸ **obstructively** *adv*
▸ **obstructiveness** *n*

obtain *vb* **1** to gain possession of; get **2** *formal* to
be customary or accepted: *silence obtains from eight
in the evening* ▸ **obtainable** *adj*

> **obtain** *vb* **1** = get, gain, acquire, land (*informal*),
> net, pick up, secure, procure; ≠ lose **2** = prevail,
> hold, exist, be the case, abound, predominate,
> be in force, be current

obtrude *vb* **-truding, -truded 1** to push oneself
or one's opinions on others in an unwelcome
way **2** to be or make unpleasantly noticeable
▸ **obtrusion** *n*

obtrusive *adj* unpleasantly noticeable: *the music
should fit your mood, it shouldn't be too obtrusive*
▸ **obtrusiveness** *n*

obtuse *adj* **1** slow to understand or emotionally
insensitive **2** *maths* (of an angle) between 90°
and 180° **3** not sharp or pointed; blunt
▸ **obtuseness** *n*

obverse *n* **1** a counterpart or opposite:
his true personality being the obverse of his outer image
2 the side of a coin that bears the main design
3 the front, top, or main surface of anything

obviate *vb* **-ating, -ated** *formal* to avoid or
prevent (a need or difficulty): *a mediator will
obviate the need for independent legal advice*

obvious *adj* **1** easy to see or understand
▸ *n* **2 state the obvious** to say something
that is unnecessary or already known:
he is prone to stating the obvious ▸ **obviously** *adv*
▸ **obviousness** *n*

> **obvious** *adj* = clear, plain, apparent, evident,
> distinct, manifest, noticeable, conspicuous;
> ≠ unclear

ocarina *n* a small egg-shaped wind instrument
with a mouthpiece and finger holes

occasion *n* **1** a particular event or the time at
which it happens **2** a need or reason to do or be
something: *we barely knew him and never had occasion
to speak of him* **3** a suitable time or opportunity to

do something **4** a special event, time, or
celebration: *a wedding day is a truly special occasion*
5 on occasion every so often **6 rise to the
occasion** to meet the special demands of a
situation ▸ *vb* **7** *formal* to cause, esp. incidentally

> **occasion** *n* **1** = time, moment, point, stage,
> instance, juncture **2** = reason, cause, call,
> ground(s), excuse, incentive, motive,
> justification **3** = opportunity, chance, time,
> opening, window **4** = function, event, affair,
> do (*informal*), happening, experience,
> gathering, celebration ▸ *vb* = cause, produce,
> lead to, inspire, result in, generate, prompt,
> provoke

occasional *adj* happening from time to time;
not frequent or regular ▸ **occasionally** *adv*

> **occasional** *adj* = infrequent, odd, rare,
> irregular, sporadic, intermittent, few and far
> between, periodic; ≠ constant

Occident *n* the western hemisphere, esp.
Europe and America ▸ **Occidental** *adj*

occiput (ox-sip-putt) *n* *anatomy* the back of the
head or skull ▸ **occipital** *adj*

occlude *vb* **-cluding, -cluded** *formal* **1** to block or
stop up (a passage or opening): *the arteries are
occluded by deposits of plaque* **2** to shut in or out:
slowly occluding him from Nash's vision **3** *chem* (of a
solid) to absorb and retain (a gas or other
substance) ▸ **occlusion** *n*

occluded front *n* *meteorol* the front formed
when the cold front of a depression overtakes a
warm front, raising the warm air from ground
level

occult *adj* **1** involving mystical or supernatural
phenomena or powers **2** beyond ordinary
human understanding **3** secret or mysterious
▸ *n* **4 the occult** the knowledge and study of
occult phenomena and powers

> **occult** *adj* **1** = supernatural, magical,
> mysterious, psychic, mystical, unearthly,
> esoteric, uncanny ▸ *n* **the occult** = magic,
> witchcraft, sorcery, wizardry, enchantment,
> black art, necromancy

occupancy *n, pl* **-cies 1** the act of occupying a
property **2** the period of time during which one
is an occupant of a property

occupant *n* a person occupying a property,
position, or place

> **occupant** *n* = occupier, resident, tenant,
> inmate, inhabitant, incumbent, dweller,
> lessee

occupation *n* **1** a person's job or profession
2 any activity on which someone's time is
spent: *a pleasant and rewarding occupation* **3** the
control of a country by a foreign military
power **4** the act of occupying or the state of
being occupied: *the occupation of Kuwait*
▸ **occupational** *adj*

O

occupation n 1 = job, calling, business, line (of work), trade, career, employment, profession 2 = hobby, pastime, diversion, relaxation, leisure pursuit, (leisure) activity 3, 4 = invasion, seizure, conquest, incursion, subjugation

occupational therapy n treatment of people with physical, emotional, or social problems using purposeful activity to help them overcome or learn to accept their problems

occupier n Brit the person who lives in a particular house, whether as owner or tenant

occupy vb **-pies**, **-pying**, **-pied** 1 to live, stay, or work in (a house, flat, or office) 2 to keep (someone or someone's mind) busy 3 to take up (time or space) 4 to move in and take control of (a country or other place): *soldiers have occupied the country's television station* 5 to fill or hold (a position or office)

occupy vb 1 = inhabit, own, live in, dwell in, reside in, abide in; ≠ vacate 2 = engage, involve, employ, divert, preoccupy, engross 3 = take up, consume, tie up, use up, monopolize 4 = invade, take over, capture, seize, conquer, overrun, annex, colonize, cybersquat (*computers*); ≠ withdraw 5 = hold, control, dominate, possess

occur vb **-curring**, **-curred** 1 to happen 2 to be found or be present; exist 3 **occur to** to come into the mind of

occur vb 1 = happen, take place, come about, turn up (*informal*), crop up (*informal*), transpire (*informal*), befall 2 = exist, appear, be found, develop, turn up, be present, manifest itself, present itself 3 **occur to someone** = come to mind, strike someone, dawn on someone, spring to mind, cross someone's mind, enter someone's head, suggest itself to someone

occurrence n 1 something that happens 2 the fact of occurring: *the likelihood of its occurrence increases with age*

occurrence n 1 = incident, happening, event, fact, matter, affair, circumstance, episode 2 = existence, instance, appearance, manifestation, materialization

OCD n obsessive-compulsive disorder: a condition that causes people to feel anxiety and repeat certain acts over and over again

ocean n 1 the vast area of salt water covering about 70 per cent of the earth's surface 2 one of the five principal divisions of this: the Atlantic, Pacific, Indian, Arctic, and Antarctic 3 *informal* a huge quantity or expanse: *oceans of replies* 4 *literary* the sea > **oceanic** adj

ocean-going adj (of a ship or boat) suited for travel on the open ocean

oceanography n the study of oceans and their environment > **oceanographer** n > **oceanographic** adj

ocelot (oss-ill-lot) n a large cat of Central and South America with a dark-spotted yellow-grey coat

oche (ok-kee) n darts a mark on the floor behind which a player must stand when throwing a dart

ochre or US **ocher** (oak-er) n 1 a yellow or reddish-brown earth used in paints or dyes ▸ adj 2 moderate yellow-orange to orange

o'clock adv used after a number between one and twelve to specify an hour: *five o'clock in the morning*

Oct. October

octagon n a geometric figure with eight sides > **octagonal** adj

octahedron (ok-ta-heed-ron) n, pl **-drons** or **-dra** a solid figure with eight plane faces

octane n a liquid hydrocarbon found in petroleum

octane number or **octane rating** n a number indicating the quality of a petrol

octave n 1 **A** the musical interval between the first note and the eighth note of a major or minor scale **B** the higher of these two notes **C** the series of notes filling this interval 2 *prosody* a rhythmic group of eight lines of verse

octet n 1 a group of eight instrumentalists or singers 2 a piece of music for eight performers

October n the tenth month of the year

octogenarian n 1 a person between 80 and 89 years old ▸ adj 2 between 80 and 89 years old

octopus n, pl **-puses** a sea creature with a soft oval body and eight long tentacles with suckers

ocular adj of or relating to the eyes or sight

OD *informal* ▸ n 1 an overdose of a drug ▸ vb **OD'ing**, **OD'd** 2 to take an overdose of a drug

odd adj 1 unusual or peculiar: *his increasingly odd behaviour* 2 occasional or incidental: *the odd letter from a friend abroad, the occasional postcard from a chum* 3 leftover or additional: *we use up odd pieces of fabric to make up jerseys in wild designs* 4 (of a number) not divisible by two 5 being part of a pair or set when the other or others are missing: *the drawer was full of odd socks* 6 somewhat more than the round number specified: *I had known him for the past twenty-odd years* 7 **odd man** or **one out** a person or thing excluded from others forming a group or unit ▸ See also **odds** > **oddly** adv > **oddness** n

odd adj 1 = peculiar, strange, unusual, extraordinary, bizarre, offbeat, freakish, daggy (*Austral, NZ informal*); ≠ normal 2 = occasional, various, random, casual, irregular, periodic, sundry, incidental; ≠ regular 3 = spare, remaining, extra, surplus, solitary, leftover, unmatched, unpaired; ≠ matched

oddity n, pl **-ties** 1 an odd person or thing 2 a peculiar characteristic 3 the quality of being or appearing unusual or strange

oddments pl n odd pieces or things; leftovers: *oddments of wool*

odds *pl n* **1** the probability, expressed as a ratio, that something will or will not happen: *the odds against an acquittal had stabilized at six to four* **2** the difference, expressed as a ratio, between the money placed on a bet and the amount that would be received as winning payment: *the current odds are ten to one* **3** the likelihood that a certain state of affairs will be so: *the odds are that you are going to fail* **4** the advantage that one contender is judged to have over another: *the odds are in his favour* **5 at odds A** on bad terms **B** at variance **6 it makes no odds** *Brit & Austral* it does not matter **7 over the odds** more than is expected or necessary

> **odds** *pl n* **3** = probability, chances, likelihood **5A at odds** = in conflict, arguing, quarrelling, at loggerheads, at daggers drawn **5B at odds** = at variance, conflicting, contrary to, at odds, out of line, out of step, at sixes and sevens (*informal*)

odds and ends *pl n* small, usually unimportant, objects, jobs to be done, etc.: *I have brought a few odds and ends with me*

> **odds and ends** *pl n* = scraps, bits, remains, fragments, debris, remnants, bits and pieces, bric-a-brac

ode *n* a lyric poem, usually addressed to a particular subject, with lines of varying lengths and metres

odious *adj* offensive or hateful: *I steeled myself for the odious task* > **odiousness** *n*

odium (oh-dee-um) *n formal* widespread dislike or disapproval of a person or action

odour *or US* **odor** *n* a particular and distinctive scent or smell > **odorous** *adj* > **odourless** *adj*

> **odour** *or* **odor** *n* = smell, scent, perfume, fragrance, stink, bouquet, aroma, stench

odyssey (odd-iss-ee) *n* a long eventful journey

> **odyssey** *n* = journey, tour, trip, quest, trek, expedition, voyage, crusade

OE *NZ informal* overseas experience: *he's away on his OE*

OECD Organization for Economic Cooperation and Development

oedema *or* **edema** (id-deem-a) *n, pl* **-mata** *pathol* an abnormal accumulation of fluid in the tissues of the body, causing swelling

oesophagus *or US* **esophagus** (ee-soff-a-guss) *n, pl* **-gi** (-guy) the tube through which food travels from the throat to the stomach; gullet > **oesophageal** *or US* **esophageal** *adj*

oestrogen *or US* **estrogen** (ee-stra-jen) *n* a female sex hormone that controls the reproductive cycle, and prepares the body for pregnancy

of *prep* **1** belonging to; situated in or coming from; because of: *the inhabitants of former East Germany; I saw five people die of chronic hepatitis*

2 used after words or phrases expressing quantities: *a pint of milk* **3** specifying an amount or value: *we had to release the bombs at a height of 400 metres* **4** made up of, containing, or characterized by: *a length of rope; she was a woman of strong character* **5** used to link a verbal noun with a following noun or noun phrase that is either the subject or the object of the verb: *the sudden slipping of the plates of the Earth's crust; the bombing of civilian targets* **6** at a given distance or space of time from: *you can still find wood within a mile of the village; he had been within hours of leaving for Romania* **7** used to specify or give more information about: *the city of Glasgow; a meeting on the subject of regional security* **8** about or concerning: *speaking of boycotts* **9** *US* before the hour of: *about quarter of eight in the evening*

off *prep* **1** so as to be no longer in contact with: *take the wok off the heat* **2** so as to be no longer attached to or associated with: *to take the tax off children's clothes* **3** away from: *he was driven off the road* **4** situated near to or leading away from: *they were laying out a bombing range off the coast* **5** no longer having a liking for: *she's gone off you lately* **6** no longer using: *he was off heroin for a year* ▸ *adv* **7** so as to deactivate or disengage: *turn off the gas supply* **8 A** so as to get rid of: *he was flying at midnight so he had to sleep off his hangover* **B** as a reduction in price: *she took 20% off* **9** spent away from work or other duties: *it was the assistant manager's day off* **10** away; at a distance: *the men dashed back to their car and sped off* **11** away in the future: *the date was six weeks off* **12** so as to be no longer taking place: *the investigation was hastily called off* **13** removed from contact with something: *he took the jacket off* **14 off and on** occasionally; not regularly or continuously: *we lived together off and on* ▸ *adj* **15** not on; no longer operating: *her bedroom light was off* **16** cancelled or postponed: *the deal is off and your deposit will be returned in full* **17** in a specified condition, esp. regarding money or provisions: *I'd be better off without this job; how are you off for money?* **18** not up to the usual standard: *an off year for good wine* **19** no longer on the menu: *haddock is off* **20** (of food or drink) having gone bad or sour: *this milk is off* ▸ *n* **21** *cricket* the side of the field to the right of a right-handed batsman when he is facing the bowler

> **off** *adv* **9** = absent, gone, unavailable **10** = away, out, apart, elsewhere, aside, hence, from here ▸ *adj* **16** = cancelled, abandoned, postponed, shelved **20** = bad, rotten, rancid, mouldy, turned, spoiled, sour, decayed

offal *n* the edible internal parts of an animal, such as the heart or liver

offal pit *or* **offal hole** *n NZ* a place on a farm for the disposal of animal offal

off colour *adj* **1** slightly ill; unwell **2** slightly indecent: *an off-colour joke*

offcut *n* a piece of paper, wood, or fabric remaining after the main pieces have been cut; remnant

offence or US **offense** n **1** a breaking of a law or rule; crime **2** annoyance or anger **3** a cause of annoyance or anger **4 give offence** to cause to feel upset or angry **5 take offence** to feel hurt or offended

> **offence** or **offense** n **1** = crime, sin, fault, violation, wrongdoing, trespass, felony, misdemeanour **2** = outrage, shock, anger, trouble, bother, resentment, irritation, hassle (informal) **3** = insult, slight, hurt, outrage, injustice, snub, affront, indignity

offend vb **1** to hurt the feelings of (a person); insult **2** to be disagreeable to; disgust: she was offended by what she saw **3** to commit a crime > **offender** n > **offending** adj

> **offend** vb **1** = distress, upset, outrage, wound, slight, insult, annoy, snub; ≠ please **3** = break the law, sin, err, do wrong, fall, go astray

offensive adj **1** unpleasant or disgusting to the senses: there was an offensive smell of beer **2** causing annoyance or anger; insulting **3** for the purpose of attack rather than defence ▸ n **4** an attitude or position of aggression: to go on the offensive **5** an attack or hostile action: troops had launched a major offensive against the rebel forces > **offensively** adv

> **offensive** adj **1** = disgusting, gross, foul, unpleasant, revolting, vile, repellent, obnoxious, festy (Austral slang), yucko (Austral slang); ≠ pleasant **2** = insulting, rude, abusive, degrading, contemptuous, disparaging, objectionable, disrespectful; ≠ respectful **3** = attacking, threatening, aggressive, striking, hostile, invading, combative; ≠ defensive ▸ n **5** = attack, charge, campaign, strike, push (informal), assault, raid, drive

offer vb **1** to present for acceptance or rejection: I offered her a lift **2** to provide: this department offers a wide range of courses **3** to present itself: if an opportunity should offer **4** to be willing (to do something): his father offered to pay his tuition **5** to put forward (a proposal, information, or opinion) for consideration: may I offer a different view? **6** to present for sale **7** to propose as payment; bid **8** to present (a prayer or sacrifice) as an act of worship **9** to show readiness for: to offer resistance ▸ n **10** something that is offered **11** the act of offering

> **offer** vb **2** = provide, present, furnish, afford; ≠ withhold **4** = volunteer, come forward, offer your services **5** = propose, suggest, advance, submit **6** = put up for sale, sell **7** = bid, submit, propose, tender, proffer **9** = give, show, bring, provide, render, impart ▸ n **10** = proposal, suggestion, proposition, submission

offering n **1** something that is offered **2** a contribution to the funds of a religious organization **3** a sacrifice to a god

> **offering** n **2** = contribution, gift, donation, present, subscription, hand-out **3** = sacrifice, tribute, libation, burnt offering

offertory n, pl -tories Christianity **1** the part of a church service when the bread and wine for communion are offered for consecration **2** the collection of money at this service **3** the prayers said or sung while the worshippers' offerings are being brought to the altar

offhand adj also **offhanded** **1** curt or casual in manner: I felt calm enough to adopt a casual offhand manner ▸ adv **2** without preparation: I don't know offhand why that should be so > **offhandedly** adv > **offhandedness** n

office n **1** a room, set of rooms, or building in which business, professional duties, or clerical work are carried out **2** a department of an organization dealing with particular business: Zoe worked in the store's cash office for 18 months **3** the group of people working in an office: she assured him that the office was running smoothly **4** a government department or agency: Serious Fraud Office **5** a position of trust or authority, as in a government: he would not seek a second term of office **6** a place where tickets, information, or some service can be obtained: why don't you give the ticket office a ring? **7** Christianity a religious ceremony or service **8 good offices** the help given by someone to someone else: Syria's good offices finally led to the release of two Western hostages **9 in** or **out of office** (of a government) in or out of power

> **office** n **1** = place of work, workplace, base, workroom, place of business **2** = branch, department, division, section, wing, subdivision, subsection **5** = post, place, role, situation, responsibility, function, occupation

officer n **1** a person in the armed services, or on a non-naval ship, who holds a position of authority **2** a member of a police force, esp. a constable **3** a person holding a position of authority in a government or organization

> **officer** n **2** = police officer, detective, PC, police constable, policeman, policewoman **3** = official, executive, agent, representative, appointee, functionary, office-holder, office bearer

official adj **1** of an office or position of authority: I'm not here in any official capacity **2** approved by or derived from authority: there has been no official announcement **3** formal or ceremonial: he was speaking at an official dinner in Warsaw ▸ n **4** a person holding a position of authority > **officially** adv

> **official** adj **1, 2** = authorized, formal, sanctioned, licensed, proper, legitimate, authentic, certified; ≠ unofficial **3** = formal, bureaucratic, ceremonial, solemn, ritualistic ▸ n = officer, executive, agent, representative, bureaucrat, appointee, functionary, office-holder

officialdom *n* officials or bureaucrats collectively

Official Receiver *n Brit* an officer appointed by the government to deal with the affairs of a bankrupt person or company

officiate *vb* **-ating, -ated 1** to perform the duties of an office; act in an official capacity: *the referee will officiate at the match* **2** to conduct a religious or other ceremony: *the priest officiated at the wedding* > **officiation** *n* > **officiator** *n*

officious *adj* offering unwanted advice or services; interfering > **officiousness** *n*

offing *n* **1** the part of the sea that can be seen from the shore **2 in the offing** *Brit, Austral & NZ* not far off; likely to occur soon

off-licence *n Brit* a shop or a counter in a shop where alcoholic drink is sold for drinking elsewhere

offline *adj* **1** disconnected from a computer or the internet ▸ *adv* **2** while not connected to a computer or the internet

off-road *adj* (of a motor vehicle) designed for use away from public roads

offset *vb* **-setting, -set 1** to cancel out or compensate for **2** to print (something) using the offset process ▸ *n* **3** a printing method in which the impression is made onto a surface, such as a rubber roller, which transfers it to the paper **4** *botany* a short runner in certain plants that produces roots and shoots at the tip

> **offset** *vb* **1** = cancel out, balance, set off, make up for, compensate for, counteract, neutralize, counterbalance

offshoot *n* **1** a shoot growing from the main stem of a plant **2** something that has developed from something else

offside *adj, adv* **1** *sport* (of a player) in a position illegally ahead of the ball when it is played ▸ *n* **2** *chiefly Brit* the side of a vehicle nearest the centre of the road

offspring *n* **1** the immediate descendant or descendants of a person or animal **2** a product, outcome, or result: *the women's liberation movement was the offspring of the 1960s*

> **offspring** *n* **1** = child, baby, kid (*informal*), youngster, infant, successor, babe, toddler, littlie (*Austral informal*), ankle-biter (*Austral slang*), tacker (*Austral slang*); ≠ parent

oft *adv* old-fashioned or poetic short for **often**

often *adv* **1** frequently; much of the time **2 as often as not** quite frequently **3 every so often** occasionally **4 more often than not** in more than half the instances

> **often** *adv* **1** = frequently, generally, commonly, repeatedly, time and again, habitually, not infrequently; ≠ never

Og oganesson

oganesson *n chem* a synthetic radioactive element produced in small quantities. Symbol: **Og**

ogle *vb* **ogling, ogled** to stare at (someone) lustfully

ogre *n* **1** (in folklore) a giant that eats human flesh **2** any monstrous or cruel person > **ogreish** *adj* > **ogress** *fem n*

oh *interj* an exclamation of surprise, pain, pleasure, fear, or annoyance

ohm *n* the SI unit of electrical resistance

OHMS (in Britain and the Commonwealth) On Her (*or* His) Majesty's Service

oil *n* **1** any of a number of viscous liquids with a smooth sticky feel, which are usually flammable, insoluble in water, and are obtained from plants, animals, or mineral deposits by synthesis **2** same as **petroleum 3** a substance derived from petroleum and used for lubrication **4** *Brit* paraffin as a domestic fuel **5** oil colour or paint **6** an oil painting ▸ *vb* **7** to lubricate with oil or apply oil to **8 oil the wheels** to make things run smoothly

> **oil** *n* **3** = lubricant, grease, lubrication, fuel oil ▸ *vb* **7** = lubricate, grease

oilfield *n* an area containing reserves of oil

oil rig *n* a structure used as a base when drilling an oil well

oilskin *n* **1** a thick cotton fabric treated with oil to make it waterproof **2** a protective outer garment made of this fabric

oily *adj* **oilier, oiliest 1** soaked or covered with oil **2** of, containing, or like oil **3** attempting to gain favour by insincere behaviour and flattery > **oiliness** *n*

> **oily** *adj* **1, 2** = greasy, slimy (*Brit*), fatty, slippery, oleaginous

ointment *n* a smooth greasy substance applied to the skin to heal or protect, or as a cosmetic: *home-made creams and ointments*

O.K. *informal* ▸ *interj* **1** an expression of approval or agreement ▸ *adj* **2** in good or satisfactory condition ▸ *adv* **3** reasonably well or in a satisfactory manner ▸ *vb* **O.K.ing, O.K.ed** **4** to approve or endorse ▸ *n, pl* **O.K.s 5** approval or agreement

> **O.K.** *interj* = all right, right, yes, agreed, very good, roger, very well, ya (*S African*), righto (*Brit informal*), yebo (*S African informal*) ▸ *adj* = all right, fine, fitting, in order, permitted, suitable, acceptable, allowable; ≠ unacceptable ▸ *vb* = approve, allow, agree to, permit, sanction, endorse, authorize, rubber-stamp (*informal*) ▸ *n* = authorization, agreement, sanction, approval, go-ahead (*informal*), blessing, permission, consent

okapi (oh-kah-pee) *n, pl* **-pis** *or* **-pi** an African mammal related to the giraffe, but with a shorter neck, a reddish coat, and white stripes on the legs

okay *interj, adj, adv, vb, n* same as **O.K.**

okra *n* a tall plant with long green pods that are used as food

old *adj* **1** having lived or existed for a long time: *the old woman; burning witches is one old custom I've no desire to see revived* **2** of or relating to advanced years or a long life: *I twisted my knee as I tried to squat and cursed old age* **3** worn with age or use: *the old bathroom fittings* **4** having lived or existed for a specified period: *he is 60 years old* **5** the earlier or earliest of two or more things with the same name: *the old edition; the Old Testament* **6** designating the form of a language in which the earliest known records are written: *Old English* **7** familiar through long acquaintance or repetition: *an old acquaintance; the legalization argument is an old and familiar one* **8** dear: used as a term of affection or familiarity: *always rely on old Tom to turn out* **9** out of date; unfashionable **10** former or previous: *my old housekeeper lent me some money* **11** of long standing: *he's an old and respected member of staff* **12 good old days** an earlier period of time regarded as better than the present ▸ *n* **13** an earlier or past time: *in days of old* ⊳ **oldish** *adj*

> **old** *adj* **1** = aged, elderly, ancient, mature, venerable, antiquated; ≠ young **5, 10** = former, earlier, past, previous, prior, one-time, erstwhile

olden *adj archaic or poetic* old: *the steam trains of olden times*

old-fashioned *adj* **1** in the style of a previous period; outdated: *she wore her hair in a strangely old-fashioned tight hairdo* **2** favouring or denoting the styles or ideas of a former time: *old-fashioned values*

> **old-fashioned** *adj* **1** = out of date, dated, outdated, unfashionable, outmoded, passé, old hat, behind the times; ≠ up-to-date **2** = oldfangled, square (*informal*), outdated, unfashionable, obsolescent

old guard *n* a group of people in an organization who have traditional values: *the company's old guard is making way for a new, more youthful team*

old hat *adj* old-fashioned or dull

oldie *n informal* an old song, film, or person

old maid *n sometimes offensive* a woman regarded as unlikely ever to marry

old master *n* **1** one of the great European painters of the period 1500 to 1800 **2** a painting by one of these

Old Nick *n informal* Satan

old school tie *n* the system of mutual help supposed to operate among the former pupils of independent schools

Old Testament *n* the first part of the Christian Bible, containing the sacred Scriptures of the Hebrews

Old World *n* that part of the world that was known to Europeans before the discovery of the Americas; the eastern hemisphere

oleaginous (oh-lee-**aj**-in-uss) *adj* like or producing oil; oily

oleander (oh-lee-**ann**-der) *n* an evergreen Mediterranean shrub with fragrant white, pink, or purple flowers

olfactory *adj* of the sense of smell

oligarch (**ol**-lee-gark) *n* a member of a small group of powerful people

oligarchy (**ol**-lee-gark-ee) *n, pl* **-chies** **1** government by a small group of people **2** a state governed this way **3** a small group of people governing such a state ⊳ **oligarchic** or **oligarchical** *adj*

olive *n* **1** an evergreen Mediterranean tree **2** the small green or black fruit of this tree

olive branch *n* a peace offering: *I should offer some kind of olive branch and get in touch with them*

olive-green *adj* deep yellowish-green

Olympian *adj* **1** of Mount Olympus or the classical Greek gods **2** majestic or godlike ▸ *n* **3** *trademark* a competitor in the Olympic Games **4** a god of Mount Olympus

Olympic Games *n* **1** an ancient Greek festival, held every fourth year in honour of Zeus, consisting of games and festivities **2** Also called: **the Olympics** *trademark* the modern revival of these games, consisting of international athletic and sporting contests held every four years in a selected country

ombudsman *n, pl* **-men** an official who investigates citizens' complaints against the government or its servants

omelette *or esp US* **omelet** *n* a dish of beaten eggs cooked in a flat pan and often folded round a savoury filling

omen *n* **1** a thing or occurrence regarded as a sign of future happiness or disaster **2** prophetic significance: *birds of ill omen*

ominous *adj* warning of evil ⊳ **ominously** *adv*

> **ominous** *adj* = threatening, sinister, grim, fateful, foreboding, unpromising, portentous, inauspicious; ≠ promising

omission *n* **1** something that has been left out or passed over **2** an act of missing out or failing to do something: *we regret the omission of these and the names of the other fine artists*

> **omission** *n* **1** = gap, space, exclusion, lacuna **2** = exclusion, removal, elimination, deletion, excision; ≠ inclusion

omit *vb* **omitting, omitted 1** to fail to include; leave out **2** to fail (to do something)

> **omit** *vb* **1** = leave out, drop, exclude, eliminate, skip; ≠ include **2** = forget, overlook, neglect, pass over, lose sight of

omnibus *n, pl* **-buses 1** a collection of works by one author or several works on a similar topic, reprinted in one volume **2** Also called: **omnibus edition** a television or radio programme consisting of two or more episodes of a serial broadcast earlier in the week **3** *old-fashioned* a bus ▸ *adj* **4** consisting of or dealing with several different things at once: *this year's version of an omnibus crime bill*

omnipotent (om-nip-a-tent) *adj* having very great or unlimited power › **omnipotence** *n*

omnipresent *adj* (esp. of a god) present in all places at the same time › **omnipresence** *n*

omniscient (om-niss-ee-ent) *adj* knowing or seeming to know everything › **omniscience** *n*

omnivore (om-niv-vore) *n* an animal that eats any type of food

omnivorous (om-niv-or-uss) *adj* 1 eating any type of food 2 taking in everything indiscriminately: *he was an omnivorous reader*

on *prep* 1 in contact with or at the surface of: *let the cakes stand in the tins on a wire rack; she had dirt on her dress* 2 attached to: *a piece of paper on a clipboard* 3 carried with: *the message found on her* 4 near to or along the side of: *the hotel is on the coast* 5 within the time limits of (a day or date): *they returned to Moscow on 22nd September* 6 being performed upon or relayed through the medium of: *a construction of refined sounds played on special musical instruments; what's on television?* 7 at the occasion of: *she had received numerous letters congratulating her on her election* 8 immediately after or at the same time as: *check with the tourist office on arrival* 9 through the use of: *an extraordinarily vigorous man who thrives on physical activity; the program runs on the Unix operating system* 10 regularly taking (a drug): *she's on the pill* 11 by means of (a mode of transport): *his only way up the hill had to be on foot; they get around on bicycles* 12 in the process or course of: *he is away on a climbing expedition; the miners went on strike* 13 concerned with or relating to: *an emotional documentary on homelessness among war veterans* 14 (of a statement or action) having as basis or grounds: *I have it on good authority* 15 charged to: *all drinks are on the house for the rest of the evening* 16 staked as a bet: *I'll have a bet on the favourite* ▸ *adv* 17 in operation; functioning: *the lights had been left on all night* 18 attached to, surrounding, or placed in contact with something: *they escaped with nothing on except sleeveless shirts and shorts* 19 taking place: *what do you have on tonight?* 20 continuously or persistently: *the crisis must not be allowed to drag on indefinitely* 21 forwards or further: *they trudged on* 22 **on and off** occasionally; not regularly or continuously 23 **on and on** without ceasing; continually ▸ *adj* 24 *informal* performing: *who's on next?* 25 *informal* definitely tolerable taking place: *is the party still on?* 26 *informal* tolerable, practicable, or acceptable: *that's just not on* 27 **on at** *informal* nagging: *he was always on at her to stop smoking* ▸ *n* 28 *cricket* the side of the field to the left of a right-handed batsman when he is facing the bowler

once *adv* 1 one time; on one occasion only 2 at some past time, but no longer: *I was in love once* 3 by one degree (of relationship): *he was Deirdre's cousin once removed* 4 **once and for all** conclusively; for the last time 5 **once in a while** occasionally; now and then 6 **once or twice** a few times 7 **once upon a time** used to begin fairy tales and children's stories ▸ *conj* 8 as soon as: *once you have learned good grammar you can leave it to nature and forget it* ▸ *n* 9 one occasion or case: *once is enough* 10 **all at once** ʌ suddenly ʙ simultaneously 11 **at once** ʌ immediately ʙ simultaneously 12 **for once** this time, even if at no other time

> **once** *adv* 1 = on one occasion, one time, one single time 2 = at one time, previously, formerly, long ago, once upon a time ▸ *conj* = as soon as, when, after, the moment, immediately, the instant ▸ *n* 10ʙ **all at once** = simultaneously, together, at the same time, concurrently 11ʌ **at once** = immediately, now, straight away, directly, promptly, instantly, right away, forthwith

once-over *n informal* a quick examination or appraisal

oncogene (ong-koh-jean) *n* a gene present in all cells, that when abnormally activated can cause cancer

oncology *n* the branch of medicine concerned with cancerous tumours › **oncologist** *n*

oncoming *adj* coming nearer in space or time; approaching: *oncoming traffic*

one *adj, n* 1 single or lone (person or thing); not two or more: *one civilian has died and thirty-three have been injured* 2 only or unique (person or thing): *he is the one to make correct judgments and influence the public; she was unique, inimitable, one of a kind* 3 a specified (person or thing) as distinct from another or others of its kind: *place one hand under the knee and the other under the ankle; which one is correct?* 4 **one or two** a few ▸ *adj* 5 a certain, indefinite, or unspecified (time): *one day he would learn the truth about her* 6 *informal, emphatic* a: *we're on to one hell of a story* ▸ *pron* 7 an indefinite person regarded as typical of every person: *one can always hope that there won't be an accident* 8 any indefinite person: *one can catch fine trout in this stream* 9 I or me: *one only wonders what he has against the dogs* ▸ *n* 10 the smallest natural number and first cardinal number 11 a numeral, 1 or I, representing this number 12 something representing or consisting of one unit 13 *informal* a joke or story: *have you heard the one about the actress and the bishop?* 14 **(all) in one** combined or united 15 **all one** of no consequence: *leave if you want to, it's all one to me* 16 **at one with** in agreement or harmony with 17 **one and all** everyone, without exception 18 **one by one** one at a time; individually

one-armed bandit *n informal* a fruit machine operated by pulling down a lever at one side

one-liner *n informal* a short joke or witty remark

oneness *n* 1 agreement 2 uniqueness 3 sameness

one-night stand *n* 1 *informal* a sexual encounter lasting only one evening or night 2 a performance given only once at any one place

O

onerous (own-er-uss) *adj* (of a task) difficult to carry out › **onerousness** *n*

oneself *pron* **1** the reflexive form of *one* **2** one's normal or usual self: *one doesn't feel oneself after such an experience*

one-sided *adj* **1** considering or favouring only one side of a matter: *a one-sided version of events* **2** having all the advantage on one side: *it was a one-sided match with Brazil missing a succession of chances*

> **one-sided** *adj* **1** = biased, prejudiced, weighted, unfair, partial, distorted, partisan, slanted; ≠ unbiased **2** = unequal, unfair, uneven, unjust, unbalanced, lopsided, ill-matched; ≠ equal

one-way *adj* **1** moving or allowing travel in one direction only: *the town centre has a baffling one-way system* **2** involving no reciprocal obligation or action: *he does not get anything back out of the one-way relationship*

ongoing *adj* in progress; continuing: *there are still ongoing discussions about the future role of NATO*

> **ongoing** *adj* = in progress, developing, progressing, evolving, unfolding, unfinished

onion *n* **1** a vegetable with an edible bulb with a strong smell and taste **2 know one's onions** *Brit & NZ slang* to be fully acquainted with a subject › **oniony** *adj*

online *adj* **1** connected to a computer or the internet ▸ *adv* **2** while connected to a computer or the internet

onlooker *n* a person who observes without taking part › **onlooking** *adj*

> **onlooker** *n* = spectator, witness, observer, viewer, looker-on, watcher, eyewitness, bystander

only *adj* **1** alone of its or their kind: *I will be talking to the only journalist to have been inside the prison* **2** (of a child) having no brothers or sisters **3** unique by virtue of superiority; best: *first class is the only way to travel* **4 one and only** incomparable: *the one and only Usain Bolt* ▸ *adv* **5** without anyone or anything else being included; alone: *only you can decide if you can abide by this compromise* **6** merely or just: *it's only Henry* **7** no more or no greater than: *I was talking to a priest only a minute ago* **8** merely: *they had only to turn up to win the competition* **9** not earlier than; not until: *I've only found out today why you wouldn't come* **10 if only** or **if … only** used to introduce a wish or hope **11 only too** extremely: *they were only too willing to do anything to help* ▸ *conj* **12** but or however: *those countries are going through the same cycle, only a little later than us*

> **only** *adj* **1** = sole, one, single, individual, exclusive, unique, lone, solitary ▸ *adv* **6, 8** = just, simply, purely, merely **7** = hardly, just, barely, only just, scarcely, at a push

onomatopoeia (on-a-mat-a-pee-a) *n* use of a word which imitates the sound it represents, such as *hiss* › **onomatopoeic** or **onomatopoetic** *adj*

onset *n* a start; beginning

> **onset** *n* = beginning, start, birth, outbreak, inception, commencement; ≠ end

onside *adj, adv* **1** *sport* (of a player) in a legal position, for example, behind the ball or with a required number of opponents between oneself and the opposing team's goal line **2** in a position of support or sympathy: *phoning shareholders in an attempt to bring them onside*

onslaught *n* a violent attack

> **onslaught** *n* = attack, charge, campaign, strike, assault, raid, invasion, offensive; ≠ retreat

onto or **on to** *prep* **1** to a position that is on: *step onto the train* **2** having discovered or become aware of: *the police are onto us* **3** into contact with: *get onto the factory*

ontology *n* *philosophy* the study of the nature of being › **ontological** *adj*

onus (own-uss) *n, pl* **onuses** a responsibility, task, or burden: *the courts put the onus on parents*

onward *adj* **1** directed or moving forward ▸ *adv also* **onwards** **2** continuing; progressing

> **onward** *adv also* **onwards** = forward, on, forwards, ahead, beyond, in front, forth (*formal, old-fashioned*)

onyx *n* a kind of quartz with alternating coloured layers, used as a gemstone

oodles *pl n informal* great quantities: *he has shown he can raise oodles of cash*

ooze[1] *vb* **oozing, oozed** **1** to flow or leak out slowly; seep **2** (of a substance) to discharge moisture **3** to overflow with (a feeling or quality): *he oozes confidence* ▸ *n* **4** a slow flowing or leaking › **oozy** *adj*

> **ooze** *vb* **1** = seep, well, escape, leak, drain, filter, drip, trickle **2** = emit, release, leak, drip, dribble, give off, pour forth **3** = exude, emit

ooze[2] *n* a soft thin mud, such as that found at the bottom of a lake, river, or sea

> **ooze** *n* = mud, clay, dirt, silt, sludge, mire, slime, alluvium

opacity (ohp-ass-it-tee) *n, pl* **-ties** **1** the state or quality of being opaque **2** the quality of being difficult to understand; unintelligibility

opal *n* a precious stone, usually milky or bluish in colour, with shimmering changing reflections

opalescent *adj* having shimmering changing reflections, like opal › **opalescence** *n*

opaque *adj* **1** not able to be seen through; not transparent or translucent **2** hard to understand; unintelligible

op. cit. (op sit) (in textual annotations) in the work cited

OPEC Organization of Petroleum-Exporting Countries

open *adj* **1** not closed, fastened, or blocked up: *the doctor's office was open* **2** not enclosed, covered, or wrapped: *the parcel was open* **3** extended, expanded, or unfolded: *an open flower* **4** ready for business: *some of the crafts rooms and photography shops are open all night* **5** (of a job) available: *all the positions on the council should be open to everyone* **6** unobstructed by buildings or trees: *we lived in a small market town surrounded by open countryside* **7** free to all to join in, enter, or use: *there was an open competition and I was appointed* **8** (of a season or period) not restricted for purposes of hunting game of various kinds **9** not decided or finalized: *the legality of these sales is still an open question* **10** ready to consider new ideas: *I was able to approach their problem with an open mind* **11** honest and frank **12** generous: *she has given me love and the open hand* **13** exposed to view; blatant: *there has never been such sustained and open criticism of the President* **14** unprotected; susceptible: *a change of policy which would leave vulnerable youths open to exploitation* **15** having spaces or gaps: *open ranks; an open texture* **16** *computers* designed to an internationally agreed standard to allow communication between computers irrespective of size or manufacturer **17** *music* **A** (of a string) not stopped with the finger **B** (of a note) played on such a string **18** *sport* (of a goal or court) unguarded or relatively unprotected **19** (of a wound) exposed to the air ▸ *vb* **20** to make or become open: *it was easy to open the back door and to slip noiselessly outside; she knelt and tried to open the drawer* **21** to set or be set in action; start: *the US will have to open talks on Palestinian rights; I want to open a dress shop* **22** to arrange for (a bank account), usually by making an initial deposit **23** to declare open ceremonially or officially ▸ *n* **24** *sport* a competition which anyone may enter **25** **the open** any wide or unobstructed area ⊳ **opener** *n* ⊳ **openly** *adv* ⊳ **openness** *n*

> **open** *adj* **1** = unclosed, unlocked, ajar, unfastened, yawning; ≠ closed **2** = unsealed, unstoppered; ≠ unopened **3** = extended, unfolded, stretched out, unfurled, straightened out, unrolled; ≠ shut **5** = vacant, free, available, empty, unoccupied, unfilled **6** = clear, passable, unhindered, unimpeded, navigable, unobstructed; ≠ obstructed **7** = general, public, free, universal, blanket, across-the-board, unrestricted, overarching; ≠ restricted **9** = unresolved, unsettled, undecided, debatable, moot, arguable **10** = receptive, sympathetic, responsive, amenable **11** = frank, direct, straightforward, sincere, transparent, honest, candid, truthful; ≠ sly ▸ *vb* **20** = unfasten, unlock, unzip; ≠ close **21** = begin, start, commence; ≠ end

opencast mining *n* mining by excavating from the surface

open day *n* a special occasion on which a school, university, or other institution is open for the public to visit

open-handed *adj* generous

open-hearted *adj* **1** kind or generous **2** willing to speak one's mind; candid

open-heart surgery *n* surgical repair of the heart during which the heart is exposed and the blood circulation is maintained mechanically

open house *n* a situation in which people allow friends or visitors to come to their house whenever they want

opening *n* **1** the beginning or first part of something **2** the first performance of a theatrical production **3** a chance or opportunity: *an opening into show business* **4** a hole or gap

> **opening** *n* **1** = beginning, start, launch, dawn (*literary*), outset, initiation, inception, commencement; ≠ ending **3** = opportunity, chance, time, moment, occasion, look-in (*informal*) **4** = hole, space, tear, crack, gap, slot, puncture, aperture; ≠ blockage

open letter *n* a letter, esp. one of protest, addressed to an individual but published in a newspaper or magazine for all to read

open-minded *adj* willing to consider new ideas; unprejudiced

> **open-minded** *adj* = unprejudiced, liberal, balanced, objective, reasonable, tolerant, impartial, receptive; ≠ narrow-minded

open-plan *adj* having no or few dividing walls between areas: *the house includes an open-plan living room and dining area*

open prison *n* a prison in which the prisoners are not locked up, thus extending the range of work they can do

open source *n* **1** intellectual property, esp. computer source code, made freely available to the public by its creators ▸ *adj* **open-source** **2** relating to this code: *open-source software*

open verdict *n* a finding by a coroner's jury of death, without stating the cause

opera[1] *n* **1** a dramatic work in which most or all of the text is sung to orchestral accompaniment **2** the branch of music or drama relating to operas **3** a group that produces or performs operas **4** a theatre where opera is performed

opera[2] *n* a plural of **opus**

operate *vb* **-ating, -ated 1** to work **2** to control the working of (a machine) **3** to manage, direct, or run (a business or system) **4** to perform a surgical operation (upon a person or animal) **5** to conduct military or naval operations

> **operate** *vb* **1** = function, work, act; ≠ break down **2** = run, work, use, control, manoeuvre **3** = manage, run, direct, handle, supervise, be in charge of

operatic adj 1 of or relating to opera
2 overdramatic or exaggerated: *he was about to go out with his operatic strut*

operation n 1 the act or method of operating
2 the condition of being in action: *there are 20 teleworking centres in operation around the country*
3 an action or series of actions done to produce a particular result: *a large-scale police operation has been in place to manage the heavy traffic* 4 surgery a surgical procedure carried out to remove, replace, or repair a diseased or damaged part of the body 5 a military or naval manoeuvre
6 *maths* any procedure, such as addition, in which a number is derived from another number or numbers by applying specific rules

> **operation** n 1 = performance, action, movement, motion

operational adj 1 in working order and ready for use 2 of or relating to an action done to produce a particular result

> **operational** adj 1 = working, going, running, ready, functioning, operative, viable, functional; ≠ inoperative

operative (op-rat-tiv) adj 1 in force, effect, or operation: *these pension provisions became operative from 1978* 2 (of a word) particularly relevant or significant: *'if' is the operative word* 3 of or relating to a surgical operation ▸ n 4 a worker with a special skill

> **operative** adj 1 = in force, effective, functioning, active, in effect, operational, in operation; ≠ inoperative ▸ n = worker, employee, labourer, workman or woman or person, artisan

operator n 1 a person who operates a machine or instrument, esp. a telephone switchboard 2 a person who runs a business: *your tour operator will arrange a visa for you* 3 *informal* a person who manipulates affairs and other people: *she considered him a shrewd operator who only liked to appear to be simple* 4 *maths* any symbol, term, or letter used to indicate or express a specific operation or process

> **operator** n 1 = worker, driver, mechanic, operative, conductor, technician, handler

operetta n a type of comic or light-hearted opera
ophthalmic adj of or relating to the eye
ophthalmic optician n See optician (sense 1)
ophthalmology n the branch of medicine concerned with the eye and its diseases
> **ophthalmologist** n

opiate (oh-pee-it) n 1 a narcotic or sedative drug containing opium 2 something that causes mental dullness or inactivity
opine vb **opining**, **opined** *formal* to hold or express an opinion: *he opined that the navy would have to start again from the beginning*

opinion n 1 belief not founded on certainty or proof but on what seems probable 2 evaluation or estimation of a person or thing: *they seemed to share my high opinion of her* 3 a judgment given by an expert: *medical opinion* 4 **a matter of opinion** a point open to question

> **opinion** n 1 = belief, feeling, view, idea, theory, conviction, point of view, sentiment 2, 3 = estimation, view, impression, assessment, judgment, appraisal, considered opinion

opinionated adj holding very strong opinions which one is convinced are right
opinion poll n same as poll (sense 1)
opium (oh-pee-um) n an addictive narcotic drug made from the seed capsules of the opium poppy and used in medicine as a painkiller and sedative
opossum n, pl **-sums** or **-sum** 1 a thick-furred American marsupial, with a long snout and a hairless prehensile tail 2 *Austral & NZ* a similar Australian animal, such as a phalanger
opponent n a person who opposes another in a contest, battle, or argument

> **opponent** n = adversary, rival, enemy, competitor, challenger, foe (*formal*, *literary*), contestant, antagonist; ≠ ally

opportune adj *formal* 1 happening at a time that is suitable or advantageous: *there was an opportune knock at the door* 2 (of time) suitable for a particular purpose: *I have arrived at a very opportune moment*
opportunist n 1 a person who adapts his or her actions to take advantage of opportunities and circumstances without regard for principles ▸ adj 2 taking advantage of opportunities and circumstances in this way > **opportunism** n > **opportunistic** adj
opportunity n, pl **-ties** 1 a favourable combination of circumstances 2 a good chance or prospect

> **opportunity** n 2 = chance, opening, time, turn, moment, possibility, occasion, slot (*informal*)

opportunity shop n *Austral & NZ* a shop selling second-hand clothes, sometimes for charity. Sometimes shortened to: **op-shop**
oppose vb **-posing**, **-posed** 1 Also: **be opposed to** to be against (something or someone) in speech or action 2 **as opposed to** in strong contrast with: *I'm a realist as opposed to a theorist* > **opposing** adj

> **oppose** vb 1 = be against, fight (against), block, take on, counter, contest, resist, combat; ≠ support

opposite adj 1 situated on the other or further side 2 facing or going in contrary directions: *he saw another small craft heading the opposite way* 3 completely different: *I have a different, in fact,* *opposite view on this subject* **4** *maths* (of a side in a triangle) facing a specified angle ▸ *n* **5** a person or thing that is opposite; antithesis ▸ *prep* **6** facing; across from ▸ *adv* **7** in an opposite position: *fragments smashed through the windows of the house opposite*

opposite *adj* **1, 2** = facing, other, opposing **3** = different, conflicting, contrasted, contrasting, unlike, contrary, dissimilar, divergent; ≠ alike ▸ *n* = reverse, contrary, converse, antithesis, contradiction, inverse, obverse ▸ *prep* = facing, face to face with, across from, eyeball to eyeball with (*informal*)

opposition *n* **1** the act of opposing or being opposed **2** hostility, resistance, or disagreement **3** a person or group antagonistic or opposed to another **4** a political party or group opposed to the ruling party or government **5** *astrol* a diametrically opposite position of two heavenly bodies

opposition *n* **2** = hostility, resistance, resentment, disapproval, obstruction, animosity, antagonism, antipathy; ≠ support **3** = opponent(s), competition, rival(s), enemy, competitor(s), other side, challenger(s), foe

oppress *vb* **1** to put down or control by cruelty or force **2** to make anxious or uncomfortable > **oppression** *n* > **oppressor** *n*

oppress *vb* **1** = subjugate, abuse, suppress, wrong, master, overcome, subdue, persecute; ≠ liberate **2** = depress, burden, discourage, torment, harass, afflict, sadden, vex

oppressive *adj* **1** cruel, harsh, or tyrannical **2** uncomfortable or depressing: *a small flat can become rather oppressive* **3** (of weather) hot and humid > **oppressiveness** *n*

oppressive *adj* **1** = tyrannical, severe, harsh, cruel, brutal, authoritarian, unjust, repressive; ≠ merciful **3** = stifling, close, sticky, stuffy, humid, sultry, airless, muggy

opprobrium (op-*probe*-ree-um) *n formal* **1** the state of being abused or scornfully criticized **2** a cause of disgrace or shame > **opprobrious** *adj*
op-shop *n Austral & NZ* short for **opportunity shop**
opt *vb* to show preference (for) or choose (to do something)

opt *vb* = choose, decide, prefer, select, elect; ≠ reject

optic *adj* of the eye or vision
optical *adj* **1** of or involving light or optics **2** of the eye or the sense of sight; optic **3** (of a lens) helping vision
optical fibre *n* a thin flexible glass fibre used in fibre optics to transmit information
optician *n* **1** Also called: **ophthalmic optician** a person who is qualified to examine the eyes and

prescribe and supply spectacles and contact lenses **2** Also called: **dispensing optician** a person who supplies and fits spectacle frames and lenses, but is not qualified to prescribe lenses
optics *n* the science dealing with light and vision
optimal *adj* best or most favourable
optimism *n* **1** the tendency to take the most hopeful view in all matters **2** *philosophy* the doctrine of the ultimate triumph of good over evil > **optimist** *n* > **optimistic** *adj* > **optimistically** *adv*
optimize *or* **-mise** *vb* **-mizing, -mized** *or* **-mising, -mised** to make the most of
optimum *n, pl* **-ma** *or* **-mums 1** the most favourable conditions or best compromise possible ▸ *adj* **2** most favourable or advantageous; best: *balance is a critical part of an optimum diet*

optimum *adj* = ideal, best, highest, finest, perfect, supreme, peak, outstanding; ≠ worst

option *n* **1** the power or liberty to choose: *we have no option other than to fully comply* **2** something that is or may be chosen: *the menu includes a vegetarian option* **3** an exclusive right, usually for a limited period, to buy or sell something at a future date: *a producer could extend his option on the material for another six months* **4 keep** *or* **leave one's options open** not to commit oneself **5 soft option** an easy alternative ▸ *vb* **6** to obtain or grant an option on: *the film rights are optioned by an international film director*

option *n* **1** = choice, alternative, selection, preference, freedom of choice, power to choose

optional *adj* possible but not compulsory; open to choice

optional *adj* = voluntary, open, discretionary, possible, extra, elective; ≠ compulsory

optometrist (op-tom-met-trist) *n* a person qualified to examine the eyes and prescribe and supply spectacles and contact lenses > **optometry** *n*
opt out *vb* **1** (often foll. by *of*) to choose not to be involved (in) or part (of), used esp. of schools and hospitals that leave the public sector ▸ *n* **opt-out 2** the act of opting out, esp. of a local authority administration
opulent (op-*pew*-lent) *adj* **1** having or indicating wealth **2** abundant or plentiful > **opulence** *n*
opus (oh-puss) *n, pl* **opuses** *or* **opera** an artistic creation, esp. a musical work by a particular composer, numbered in order of publication: *Beethoven's opus 61*

opus *n* = work, piece, production, creation, composition, work of art, brainchild, oeuvre (*French*)

or *conj* **1** used to join alternatives: *do you want to go out or stay at home?* **2** used to join rephrasings of the same thing: *twelve, or a dozen*

oracle *n* **1** a shrine in ancient Greece or Rome at which gods were consulted through the medium of a priest or priestess for advice or prophecy **2** a prophecy or statement made by an oracle **3** any person believed to indicate future action with infallible authority

oracular *adj* **1** of or like an oracle **2** wise and prophetic **3** mysterious or ambiguous

oral *adj* **1** spoken or verbal; using spoken words **2** of or for use in the mouth: *an oral thermometer* **3** (of a drug) to be taken by mouth: *an oral contraceptive* ▸ *n* **4** an examination in which the questions and answers are spoken rather than written > **orally** *adv*

> **oral** *adj* **1** = spoken, vocal, verbal, unwritten

orange *n* **1** a round reddish-yellow juicy citrus fruit **2** the evergreen tree on which it grows **3** a colour between red and yellow; the colour of an orange ▸ *adj* **4** of a colour between red and yellow

orangeade *n Brit* a usually fizzy orange-flavoured drink

orangery *n, pl* **-eries** a conservatory or greenhouse in which orange trees are grown in cooler climates

orang-utan *or* **orang-utang** *n* a large ape of the forests of Sumatra and Borneo, with shaggy reddish-brown hair and long arms

oration *n* a formal or ceremonial public speech

orator (or-rat-tor) *n* a person who gives an oration, esp. one skilled in persuasive public speaking

oratorio (or-rat-tor-ee-oh) *n, pl* **-rios** a musical composition for soloists, chorus, and orchestra, based on a religious theme

oratory[1] (or-rat-tree) *n* the art or skill of public speaking

oratory[2] *n, pl* **-ries** a small room or building set apart for private prayer

orb *n* **1** an ornamental sphere with a cross on top, carried by a king or queen in important ceremonies **2** a sphere; globe **3** *poetic* the eye **4** *obsolete or poetic* a heavenly body, such as the sun

orbit *n* **1** the curved path followed by something, such as a heavenly body or spacecraft, in its motion around another body **2** a range or sphere of action or influence **3** *anatomy* the eye socket ▸ *vb* **-biting, -bited 4** to move around (a heavenly body) in an orbit **5** to send (a satellite or spacecraft) into orbit > **orbital** *adj*

> **orbit** *n* **1** = path, course, cycle, circle, revolution, rotation, trajectory, sweep **2** = sphere of influence, reach, range, influence, province, scope, domain, compass ▸ *vb* **4** = circle, ring, go round, revolve around, encircle, circumscribe, circumnavigate

orca *n* same as **killer whale**

orchard *n* an area of land on which fruit trees are grown

orchestra *n* **1** a large group of musicians whose members play a variety of different instruments **2** Also called: **orchestra pit** the space, in front of or under the stage, reserved for musicians in a theatre > **orchestral** *adj*

orchestrate *vb* **-trating, -trated 1** to score or arrange (a piece of music) for orchestra **2** to arrange (something) in order to produce a particular result: *he had orchestrated today's meeting* > **orchestration** *n*

> **orchestrate** *vb* **1** = score, set, arrange, adapt **2** = organize, plan, run, set up, arrange, put together, marshal, coordinate

orchid *n* a plant having flowers of unusual shapes and beautiful colours, usually with one lip-shaped petal which is larger than the other two

ordain *vb* **1** to make (someone) a member of the clergy **2** *formal* to decree or order with authority > **ordainment** *n*

> **ordain** *vb* **1** = appoint, name, commission, select, invest, nominate, anoint, consecrate **2** = order, will, rule, demand, require, direct, command, dictate

ordeal *n* **1** a severe or trying experience **2** *history* a method of trial in which the accused person was subjected to physical danger

> **ordeal** *n* **1** = hardship, trial, difficulty, test, suffering, nightmare, torture, agony; ≠ pleasure

order *n* **1** an instruction that must be obeyed; command **2** a state in which everything is arranged logically, comprehensibly, or naturally: *she strove to keep more order in the house* **3** an arrangement of things in succession; sequence: *group them by letter and then put them in numerical order* **4** an established or customary system of society: *there is an opportunity here for a new world order* **5** a peaceful or harmonious condition of society: *riot police were called in to restore order* **6** **A** an instruction to supply something in return for payment: *the waitress came to take their order* **B** the thing or things supplied **7** a written instruction to pay money: *post the coupon below with a cheque or postal order* **8** a social class: *the result will be harmful to society as a whole and to the lower orders in particular* **9** *biol* one of the groups into which a class is divided, containing one or more families **10** kind or sort: *the orchestra played superbly and the singing was of the highest order* **11** Also called: **religious order** a religious community of monks or nuns **12** a group of people who have been awarded a particular honour: *the Order of the Garter* **13** the office or rank of a Christian minister: *he studied for the priesthood as a young man, but never took Holy Orders* **14** the procedure and rules followed by an assembly or meeting: *a point of order* **15** one of the five major classical styles of architecture, classified by the type of columns used **16 a tall order** something difficult or demanding **17 in order A** in sequence **B** properly arranged: *everything is in order for your trip* **C** appropriate or fitting **18 in order that** so that **19 in order to** so that it is possible to: *a healthy diet is necessary in order to keep fit* **20 in** *or* **of the order of** amounting approximately to: *summer temperatures are usually in the order of 35°* **21 keep order** to ensure that people obey the law or behave in an acceptable manner **22 on order** having been ordered but not yet delivered **23 out of order A** not in sequence **B** not working: *the lift was out of order, so we had to use the stairs* **C** not following the rules or customary procedure: *the chairperson ruled the motion out of order* **24 to order** according to a buyer's specifications ▸ *vb* **25** to command or instruct (to do something): *she ordered her son to wash the dishes; the police ordered her into the house* **26** to request (something) to be supplied in return for payment: *I ordered a new car three weeks ago, but it hasn't been delivered yet* **27** to arrange (things) methodically or in their proper places ▸ *interj* **28** an exclamation demanding that orderly behaviour be restored

order *n* **1** = instruction, ruling, demand, direction, command, dictate, decree, mandate **2** = organization, system, method, pattern, symmetry, regularity, neatness, tidiness; ≠ chaos **3** = sequence, grouping, series, structure, chain, arrangement, line-up, array **5** = peace, control, law, quiet, calm, discipline, law and order, tranquillity **6A** = request, booking, demand, commission, application, reservation, requisition **8** = class, set, rank, grade, caste **9** = kind, group, class, family, sort, type, variety, category **12** = society, company, group, club, community, association, institute, organization ▸ *vb* **25** = command, instruct, direct, charge (*formal*), demand, require, bid, compel; ≠ forbid **26** = request, ask (for), book, seek, reserve, apply for, solicit, send away for **27** = arrange, group, sort, position, line up, organize, catalogue, sort out; ≠ disarrange

orderly *adj* **1** tidy or well-organized: *they evacuated the building in an orderly manner* **2** well-behaved; law-abiding ▸ *n, pl* **-lies 3** *med* a male hospital attendant **4** *military* a soldier whose duty is to carry out orders or perform minor tasks for a more senior officer ▸ **orderliness** *n*

orderly *adj* **1** = well-organized, regular, in order, organized, precise, neat, tidy, systematic; ≠ disorganized **2** = well-behaved, controlled, disciplined, quiet, restrained, law-abiding, peaceable; ≠ disorderly

ordinal number *n* a number indicating position in a sequence, such as *first, second, third*
ordinance *n* an official rule or order

ordinarily *adv* in ordinary or usual practice; usually; normally
ordinary *adj* **1** usual or normal: *it was an ordinary working day for them* **2** not special or different in any way: *her campaign speech dwells on the problems faced by ordinary Americans* **3** dull or unexciting: *the restaurant charged very high prices for very ordinary cooking* ▸ *n, pl* **-naries 4** *RC Church* the parts of the Mass that do not vary from day to day **5 out of the ordinary** unusual

ordinary *adj* **1** = usual, standard, normal, common, regular, typical, conventional, routine **2** = commonplace, plain, modest, humble, mundane, banal, unremarkable, run-of-the-mill

ordination *n* the act or ceremony of making someone a member of the clergy
ordnance *n* **1** weapons and other military supplies **2 the ordnance** a government department dealing with military supplies
Ordnance Survey *n* the British government organization that produces detailed maps of Britain and Ireland
ordure *n* excrement; dung
ore *n* rock or mineral from which valuable substances such as metals can be extracted
oregano (or-rig-**gah**-no) *n* a sweet-smelling herb used as seasoning
organ *n* **1** a part in animals and plants that is adapted to perform a particular function, for example the heart or lungs **2 A** a musical keyboard instrument which produces sound by forcing air through pipes of a variety of lengths **B** Also called: **electric organ** a keyboard instrument which produces similar sounds electronically **3** a means of communication, such as a newspaper issued by a specialist group or party **4** *euphemistic* a penis

organ *n* **1** = body part, part of the body, element, biological structure **3** = newspaper, medium, voice, vehicle, gazette, mouthpiece

organdie *n* a fine, slightly stiff cotton fabric
organic *adj* **1** of, produced by, or found in plants or animals: *the rocks were carefully searched for organic remains* **2** not using, or grown without, artificial fertilizers or pesticides: *organic vegetables; an organic farm* **3** *chem* of or belonging to the class of chemical compounds that are formed from carbon **4** (of change or development) gradual and natural rather than sudden or forced **5** made up of many different parts which contribute to the way in which the whole society or structure works: *an organic whole* ▸ **organically** *adv*

organic *adj* **1** = natural, biological, living, live, animate **5** = systematic, ordered, structured, organized, integrated, orderly, methodical

organism _n_ **1** an animal or plant **2** anything resembling a living creature in structure, behaviour, or complexity: _cities are more complicated organisms than farming villages_

> **organism** _n_ **1** = creature, being, thing, body (_informal_), animal, structure, beast, entity

organist _n_ a person who plays the organ

organization _or_ **-nisation** _n_ **1** an organized group of people, such as a club, society, union, or business **2** the act of organizing: _setting up the European tour took a lot of organization_ **3** the structure and arrangement of the different parts of something: _the report recommended radical changes in the organization of the social services department_ **4** the state of being organized: _the material in this essay lacks any sort of organization_ > **organizational** _or_ **-isational** _adj_

> **organization** _or_ **-nisation** _n_ **1** = group, company, party, body, association, band, institution, corporation **2** = management, running, planning, control, operation, handling, structuring, administration **3, 4** = structure, form, pattern, make-up, arrangement, construction, format, formation

organize _or_ **-nise** _vb_ **-nizing, -nized** _or_ **-nising, -nised** **1** to plan and arrange (something): _we organized a protest meeting in the village hall_ **2** to arrange systematically: _the files are organized in alphabetical order and by date_ **3** to form, join, or recruit (people) into a trade union: _the seasonal nature of tourism makes it difficult for hotel workers to organize_ > **organizer** _or_ **-niser** _n_

> **organize** _or_ **-nise** _vb_ **1** = arrange, run, plan, prepare, set up, devise, put together, take care of, jack up (NZ _informal_); ≠ disrupt **2** = put in order, arrange, group, list, file, index, classify, inventory; ≠ muddle

orgasm _n_ the most intense point of pleasure and excitement during sexual activity > **orgasmic** _adj_

orgy _n, pl_ **-gies** **1** a wild party involving promiscuous sexual activity and excessive drinking **2** an act of immoderate or frenzied indulgence: _the rioters were engaged in an orgy of destruction_ > **orgiastic** _adj_

oriel window _or_ **oriel** _n_ a window built out from the wall of a house at an upper level

orient _vb_ **1** to position or set (for example, a map or chart) with relation to the points of the compass or other specific directions **2 orient oneself** to adjust or align oneself or one's ideas according to new surroundings or circumstances: _new employees can take some time to orient themselves to the company's procedures_ **3 be oriented to** _or_ **towards** to work or act with a particular aim, idea, or person in mind: _training programmes oriented towards older people_ ▸ _n_ **4** _poetic_ the east

> **orient** _vb_ **2** = adjust, adapt, alter, accustom, align, familiarize, acclimatize

Orient _n_ **the Orient** East Asia

Oriental _adj_ **1** of East Asia ▸ _n_ **2** _offensive_ a person from East Asia

orientate _vb_ **-tating, -tated** same as **orient**

orientation _n_ **1** the activities and aims that a person or organization is interested in: _the course has a practical rather than theoretical orientation_ **2** the position of an object with relation to the points of the compass or other specific directions: _the room's southerly orientation means that it receives a lot of light_ ▸ _adj_ **3** of or providing information or training needed to understand a new situation or environment: _nearly every college has an orientation programme_

> **orientation** _n_ **1** = inclination, tendency, disposition, predisposition, predilection, proclivity (_formal_), partiality **2** = position, situation, location, bearings, direction, arrangement, whereabouts

orienteering _n_ a sport in which contestants race on foot over a cross-country course consisting of checkpoints found with the aid of a map and compass

orifice (or-rif-fiss) _n_ an opening or hole through which something can pass, esp. one in the body such as the mouth or anus

origami (or-rig-**gah**-mee) _n_ the art, originally Japanese, of folding paper intricately into decorative shapes

origin _n_ **1** the point, source, or event from which something develops: _the origin of the term 'jazz' is obscure; the war had its origin in the clash between rival nationalists_ **2** the country, race, or social class of a person's parents or ancestors: _an Australian of Greek origin; he was proud of his working-class origins_ **3** _maths_ the point at which the horizontal and vertical axes intersect

> **origin** _n_ **1** = beginning, start, birth, launch, foundation, creation, emergence, onset; ≠ end

original _adj_ **1** first or earliest: _the dining room also has attractive original beams_ **2** fresh and unusual; not copied from or based on something else: _the composer's work has created some original and attractive choreography_ **3** able to think of or carry out new ideas or concepts: _he is an excitingly original writer_ **4** being the first and genuine form of something, from which a copy or translation is made: _all French recipes were translated from the original abridged versions_ ▸ _n_ **5** the first and genuine form of something, from which others are copied or translated: _the original is in the British Museum_ **6** a person or thing used as a model in art or literature: _she claimed to be the original on whom Lawrence based Lady Chatterley_ > **originality** _n_ > **originally** _adv_

original adj **1** = first, earliest, initial; ≠ final **2** = new, fresh, novel, unusual, unprecedented, innovative, unfamiliar, seminal; ≠ unoriginal **3** = creative, inspired, imaginative, artistic, fertile, ingenious, visionary, inventive ▶ n **5** = prototype, master, pattern; ≠ copy

original sin n a state of sin believed by some Christians to be inborn in all human beings as a result of Adam's disobedience

originate vb **-nating, -nated** to come or bring (something) into existence: *humans probably originated in East Africa* > **origination** n > **originator** n

originate vb = begin, start, emerge, come, happen, rise, appear, spring; ≠ end

oriole n a songbird with a long pointed bill and a mostly yellow-and-black plumage

ormolu n a gold-coloured alloy of copper, tin, or zinc, used to decorate furniture and other articles

ornament n **1** anything that adorns someone or something; decoration: *the room's only ornament was a dim, oily picture of the Holy Family* **2** decorations collectively: *he had no watch, nor ornament of any kind* **3** a small decorative object: *I hit a garden ornament while parking* **4** a person whose character or talent makes them an asset to society or the group to which they belong: *an ornament of the firm* **5** *music* a note or group of notes which embellishes the melody but is not an integral part of it, for instance a trill ▶ vb **6** to decorate or adorn: *the hall had a high ceiling, ornamented with plaster fruits and flowers* > **ornamental** adj > **ornamentation** n > **ornamented** adj

ornament n **1** = decoration, trimming, accessory, festoon, trinket, bauble, knick-knack **2** = embellishment, decoration, embroidery, elaboration, adornment, ornamentation ▶ vb = decorate, adorn, array, do up (*informal*), embellish, festoon, beautify, prettify

ornate adj **1** heavily or elaborately decorated: *an ornate ceiling painted with allegorical figures* **2** (of style in writing) overelaborate; using many literary expressions > **ornately** adv

ornithology n the study of birds > **ornithological** adj > **ornithologist** n

orphan n **1** a child whose parents are dead ▶ vb **2** to cause (someone) to become an orphan: *she was orphaned at 16 when her parents died in a car crash*

orphanage n a children's home for orphans and abandoned children

orphaned adj having no living parents

orrery n, pl **-ries** a mechanical model of the solar system in which the planets can be moved around the sun

orris n **1** a kind of iris that has fragrant roots **2** Also: **orrisroot** the root of this plant prepared and used as perfume

orthodontics n the branch of dentistry concerned with correcting irregularities of the teeth > **orthodontic** adj > **orthodontist** n

orthodox adj conforming to traditional or established standards in religion, behaviour, or attitudes: *orthodox medicine; the concerto has a more orthodox structure than is usual for this composer* > **orthodoxy** n

orthodox adj = established, official, accepted, received, common, traditional, normal, usual; ≠ unorthodox

Orthodox adj **1** of the Orthodox Church of Eastern Europe **2** of or being the form of Judaism characterized by traditional interpretation of and strict adherence to Mosaic Law: *an Orthodox Jew*

Orthodox Church n the Christian Church dominant in Greece, Russia, and some Eastern European countries, which has the Greek Patriarch of Constantinople as its head

orthography n **1** spelling considered to be correct: *British and American orthography is different in many cases* **2** the study of spelling > **orthographic** adj

orthopaedics or US **orthopedics** n the branch of surgery concerned with disorders of the bones and joints > **orthopaedic** or US **orthopedic** adj > **orthopaedist** or US **orthopedist** n

oryx n any of various large straight-horned African antelopes

Oscar n an award in the form of a small gold statuette awarded annually in the US for outstanding achievements in various aspects of the film industry: *he won an Oscar for Best Supporting Actor in 1974*

oscillate (oss-ill-late) vb **-lating, -lated** **1** to swing repeatedly back and forth: *its wings oscillate up and down many times a second* **2** to waver between two extremes of opinion, attitude, or behaviour: *the government oscillates between a desire for reform and a desire to keep its powers intact* **3** *physics* (of an electric current) to vary between minimum and maximum values > **oscillation** n > **oscillator** n

oscilloscope (oss-sill-oh-scope) n an instrument that produces a visual representation of an oscillating electric current on the screen of a cathode-ray tube

osier (oh-zee-er) n **1** a willow tree whose flexible branches or twigs are used for making baskets and furniture **2** a twig or branch from this tree

osmium n *chem* a very hard brittle bluish-white metal, the heaviest known element. Symbol: **Os**

osmosis n **1** the diffusion of liquids through a membrane until they are mixed **2** the process by which people or ideas influence each other gradually and subtly > **osmotic** adj

osprey n a large fish-eating bird of prey, with a dark back and whitish head and underparts

ossify vb **-fies, -fying, -fied** **1** to change into bone; harden **2** to become rigid, inflexible, or unprogressive: *ossified traditions* > **ossification** n

ostensible *adj* apparent or seeming; alleged: *our ostensible common interest is boats* **> ostensibly** *adv*

ostentation *n* pretentious, showy, or vulgar display: *she felt the gold taps in the bathroom were tasteless ostentation* **> ostentatious** *adj* **> ostentatiously** *adv*

osteopathy *n* a system of healing based on the manipulation of bones or muscle **> osteopath** *n*

osteoporosis (ost-ee-oh-pore-**oh**-siss) *n* brittleness of the bones, caused by lack of calcium

ostracize *or* **-cise** *vb* **-cizing, -cized** *or* **-cising, -cised** to exclude or banish (a person) from a particular group or from society: *he was ostracized from his family when his affair became known* **> ostracism** *n*

ostrich *n* **1** a large African bird which runs fast but cannot fly, and has a long neck, long legs, and soft dark feathers **2** a person who refuses to recognize an unpleasant truth: *he accused the Minister of being 'an ostrich with its head stuck in the sand, while all around him unemployment soars'*

other *adj* **1** remaining (one or ones) in a group of which one or some have been specified: *she wasn't getting on with the other children* **2** being a different one or ones from the one or ones already specified or understood: *other people might not be so tolerant of your behaviour; are you sure it's not in your other pocket?* **3** refers to a place or time which is not the one the speaker or writer is in: *results in other countries have been most encouraging* **4** additional; further: *there is one other thing for the government to do* **5 every other** every alternate: *the doctor sees me every other week* **6 other than A** apart from: *he knew little of the country other than it was Muslim* **B** different from: *treatment other than a hearing aid will be possible for those with inner ear deafness* **7 or other** used to add vagueness to the preceding word or phrase: *she could take some evening course or other which could lead to an extra qualification; he was called away from the house on some pretext or other* **8 the other day** a few days ago ▸ *n* **9** an additional person or thing: *show me one other* **10 others** people apart from the person who is being spoken or written about: *she devoted her entire life to helping others* **11 the others** the people or things remaining in a group of which one or some have been specified: *I can't speak for the others* ▸ *adv* **12** otherwise; differently: *they couldn't behave other than they do* **> otherness** *n*

other *adj* **2, 3** = different, alternative, contrasting, distinct, diverse, dissimilar, separate, alternative **4** = additional, more, further, new, added, extra, fresh, spare

otherwise *conj* **1** or else; if not, then: *you need to leave by ten o'clock, otherwise you'll be late* ▸ *adv* **2** differently: *it was fruitless to pretend or to hope otherwise* **3** in other respects: *shrewd psychological twists perk up an otherwise predictable storyline* ▸ *adj* **4** different: *circumstances beyond our control dictated that it should be otherwise* ▸ *pron* **5 or otherwise**

or not; or the opposite: *he didn't want company, talkative or otherwise*

otherwise *conj* = or else, or, if not, or then ▸ *adv* **2** = differently, any other way, contrarily **3** = apart from that, in other ways, in (all) other respects

otherworldly *adj* **1** concerned with spiritual rather than practical matters: *his otherworldly manner concealed a ruthless business mind* **2** mystical or supernatural: *this part of Italy has an otherworldly beauty*

otiose (**oh**-tee-oze) *adj* serving no useful purpose: *such a strike is almost otiose*

otter *n* a small freshwater fish-eating animal with smooth brown fur, a streamlined body, and webbed feet

ottoman *n, pl* **-mans** a storage chest with a padded lid for use as a seat

Ottoman *adj* **1** *history* of the Ottomans or the Ottoman Empire, the Turkish empire which lasted from the late 13th century until the end of World War I, and at its height included the Balkans and much of N Africa ▸ *n, pl* **-mans** **2** a member of a Turkish people who formed the basis of this empire

ouch *interj* an exclamation of sharp sudden pain

ought *vb* **1** used to express duty or obligation: *she ought to tell this to the police* **2** used to express advisability: *we ought to get the roof repaired before the attics get any damper* **3** used to express probability or expectation: *a good lawyer ought to be able to fix it for you* **4** used to express a desire on the part of the speaker: *you ought to have a good breakfast before you hit the road*

Ouija board *or* **Ouija** (**weej**-a) *n trademark* a board on which are marked the letters of the alphabet. Answers to questions are spelt out by a pointer, which is supposedly guided by spirits

ounce *n* **1** a unit of weight equal to one sixteenth of a pound or 28.4 grams **2** short for **fluid ounce 3** a small amount: *you haven't got one ounce of control over her*

ounce *n* **3** = shred, bit, drop, trace, scrap, grain, fragment, atom

our *adj* **1** of, belonging to, or associated with us: *our daughter* **2** a formal word for *my* used by monarchs

ours *pron* **1** something belonging to us: *our son has blue eyes while ours are brown; the money is ours* **2 of ours** belonging to or associated with us: *my wife and a friend of ours had both deserted me*

ourselves *pron* **1 A** the reflexive form of *we* or *us*: *we humiliated ourselves* **B** used for emphasis: *we ourselves will finish it* **2** our usual selves: *we've not been feeling quite ourselves since the accident* **3** *not standard* used instead of *we* or *us* in compound noun phrases: *other people and ourselves*

ousel *n* same as **ouzel**

oust *vb* to force (someone) out of a position; expel: *the coup which ousted the President*

oust *vb* = expel, turn out, dismiss, exclude, exile, throw out, displace, topple

out *adv, adj* **1** away from the inside of a place: *she took her purse out; inspection of the eggs should be done when the hen is out of the nest* **2** away from one's home or place of work for a short time: *I called earlier but you were out; a search party is out looking for survivors* **3** no longer burning, shining, or functioning: *he switched the light out; the living-room fire went out while we were next door eating* **4** used up; not having any more of: *their supplies ran out after two weeks; we're out of milk* **5** public; revealed: *our dirty little secret is out* **6** available to the public: *her biography will be out in December* **7** (of the sun, stars, or moon) visible **8** in bloom: *the roses are out early this year* **9** not in fashion or current usage: *'skinny' is out* **10** excluded from consideration: *pricey ski holidays are out* **11** not allowed: *smoking on duty is out* **12 out for** *or* **to** wanting or intent on (something or doing something): *the young soldiers were out for revenge; they're out to get me* **13** *sport* (of a player in a sport like cricket or baseball) no longer batting because he or she has been dismissed by being caught, bowled, etc. **14** on strike **15** in or into a state of unconsciousness: *he went outside and passed out in an alley* **16** used to indicate a burst of activity as indicated by a verb: *war broke out in the Gulf* **17** out of existence: *the mistakes were scored out* **18** to the fullest extent: *spread out* **19** loudly; clearly: *he cried out in shock and pain* **20** to a conclusion; completely: *she'd worked it out for herself* **21** existing: *the friendliest dog out* **22** inaccurate or incorrect: *the estimate was out by £60* **23** not in office or authority: *she was finally voted out as party leader* **24** (of a period of time) completed: *before the year is out* **25** having made it known that one is not heterosexual: *I came out as a lesbian when I was still in my teens* **26** *old-fashioned* (of a young woman) in or into upper-class society life: *Lucinda had a large party when she came out* **27 out of** **A** at or to a point outside: *the train pulled out of the station* **B** away from; not in: *they're out of touch with reality; out of focus* **c** because of; motivated by: *out of jealousy* **D** from (a material or source): *made out of plastic* **E** no longer in a specified state or condition: *out of work; out of practice* ▸ *adj* **28** *informal* not concealing one's homosexuality ▸ *prep* **29** *US or not standard* out of; out through: *he ran out the door* ▸ *interj* **30** **A** an exclamation of dismissal **B** (in signalling and radio) an expression used to signal that the speaker is signing off: *over and out!* ▸ *vb informal* **31** to name (a person, esp. a public figure) as being not heterosexual, often against their will **32** to reveal something embarrassing or unknown about (a person): *he was outed as a talented goal scorer*

> **out** *adv, adj* **2** = not in, away, elsewhere, outside, gone, abroad, from home, absent **3** = extinguished, ended, finished, dead, exhausted, expired, used up, at an end; ≠ alight **5** = revealed, exposed, common knowledge, public knowledge, (out) in the open; ≠ kept secret **6** = available, on sale, in the shops, to be had, purchasable **8** = in bloom, opening, open, flowering, blooming, in flower, in full bloom ▸ *vb* **31** = expose

out- *prefix* **1** excelling or surpassing in a particular action: *outlast; outlive* **2** at or from a point away, outside: *outpost; outpatient* **3** going away, outward: *outcrop; outgrowth*

outback *n* the remote bush country of Australia

outbid *vb* **-bidding, -bidded** *or* **-bid** to offer a higher price than (another person)

outboard motor *n* a portable petrol engine that can be attached externally to the stern of a boat to propel it

outbox *n* a folder in a computer mailbox in which outgoing messages are stored

outbreak *n* a sudden occurrence of disease or war

> **outbreak** *n* = eruption, burst, explosion, epidemic, rash, outburst, flare-up, upsurge

outburst *n* **1** a sudden strong expression of emotion, esp. of anger: *such emotional outbursts do nothing to help calm discussion of the matter* **2** a sudden period of violent activity: *this sudden outburst of violence has come as a shock*

> **outburst** *n* **1** = explosion, surge, outbreak, eruption, flare-up **2** = fit, flare-up, eruption, spasm, outpouring

outcast *n* a person who is rejected or excluded from a particular group or from society

outclass *vb* to surpass (someone) in performance or quality

outcome *n* the result or consequence of something

> **outcome** *n* = result, end, consequence, conclusion, payoff (*informal*), upshot

outcrop *n* part of a rock formation that sticks out of the earth

outcry *n, pl* **-cries** a widespread or vehement protest: *there was great popular outcry against the plan for a dual carriageway*

> **outcry** *n* = protest, complaint, objection, dissent, outburst, clamour, uproar, commotion

outdated *adj* old-fashioned or obsolete

> **outdated** *adj* = old-fashioned, dated, obsolete, out of date, passé, archaic, unfashionable, antiquated; ≠ modern

outdo *vb* **-does, -doing, -did, -done** to be more successful or better than (someone or something) in performance: *this car easily outdoes its rivals when it comes to comfort*

outdoor *adj* **1** taking place, existing, or intended for use in the open air: *have a swim at the* *beach or outdoor pool; she was just taking off her outdoor clothing* **2** fond of the outdoors: *Paul was a butch outdoor type*

> **outdoor** *adj* **1** = open-air, outside, out-of-door(s), alfresco; ≠ indoor

outdoors *adv* **1** in the open air; outside: *he hardly ever went outdoors* ▸ *n* **2** the world outside or far away from buildings; the open air: *he'd forgotten his fear of the outdoors*

outer *adj* **1** on the outside; external: *the building's outer walls were painted pale pink* **2** further from the middle: *the outer suburbs* ▸ *n* **3** *archery* **A** the white outermost ring on a target **B** a shot that hits this ring

> **outer** *adj* **1** = external, outside, outward, exterior, exposed, outermost; ≠ inner
> **2** = outlying, distant, provincial, out-of-the-way, peripheral, far-flung; ≠ central

outermost *adj* furthest from the centre or middle

outer space *n* space beyond the atmosphere of the earth

outface *vb* **-facing, -faced** to subdue or disconcert (someone) by staring

outfield *n* **1** *cricket* the area of the field far from the pitch **2** *baseball* the area of the playing field beyond the lines connecting first, second, and third bases > **outfielder** *n*

outfit *n* **1** a set of clothes worn together **2** *informal* a group of people working together as a unit **3** a set of equipment for a particular task; kit: *a complete anti-snakebite outfit*

> **outfit** *n* **1** = costume, dress, clothes, clothing, suit, get-up (*informal*), kit, ensemble **2** = group, company, team, party, unit, crowd, squad, organization

outfitter *n old-fashioned* a shop or person that sells men's clothes

outflank *vb* **1** to go around and beyond the side of (an enemy army) **2** to get the better of (someone)

outgoing *adj* **1** leaving: *some members of the outgoing government continued to attend the peace talks* **2** friendly and sociable

> **outgoing** *adj* **1** = leaving, former, previous, retiring, withdrawing, prior, departing, erstwhile; ≠ incoming **2** = sociable, open, social, warm, friendly, expansive, affable, extrovert; ≠ reserved

outgoings *pl n* expenses

> **outgoings** *pl n* = expenses, costs, payments, expenditure, overheads, outlay

outgrow *vb* **-growing, -grew, -grown 1** to grow too large for (clothes or shoes): *it's amazing how quickly children outgrow their clothes* **2** to lose (a way of behaving or thinking) in the course of becoming more mature: *most teenagers outgrow*

their moodiness as they near adulthood **3** to grow larger or faster than (someone or something): *the weeds threatened to outgrow and choke the rice plants*

outgrowth *n* **1** a natural development or consequence: *he argued that religion was an outgrowth of magic* **2** a thing growing out of a main body; offshoot

outhouse *n* a building near to, but separate from, a main building

outing *n* **1** a trip or excursion **2** *informal* the naming of people as being not heterosexual, often against their will

> **outing** *n* **1** = journey, run, trip, tour, expedition, excursion, spin (*informal*), jaunt

outlandish *adj* extremely unconventional; bizarre

outlaw *n* **1** *history* a criminal who has been deprived of legal protection and rights ▸ *vb* **2** to make (something) illegal: *racial discrimination was formally outlawed* **3** *history* to make (someone) an outlaw > **outlawed** *adj*

> **outlaw** *n* = bandit, criminal, thief, robber, fugitive, outcast, felon, highwayman *or* woman ▸ *vb* **2** = ban, bar, veto, forbid, exclude, prohibit, disallow, proscribe; ≠ legalize **3** = banish, put a price on (someone's) head

outlay *n* the money, effort, or time spent on something

outlet *n* **1** a means of expressing one's feelings: *the shock would give her an outlet for her own grief* **2** **A** a market for a product: *there is a huge sales outlet for personal computers* **B** a shop or organization selling the goods of a particular producer or wholesaler or manufacturer: *her own brand is now sold to outlets throughout the world* **3** an opening permitting escape or release: *make sure the exhaust outlet is not blocked*

> **outlet** *n* **1** = channel, release, medium, avenue, vent, conduit **2B** = shop, store, supermarket, market, boutique, emporium (*old-fashioned*), hypermarket **3** = pipe, opening, channel, exit, duct

outline *n* **1** a general explanation or description of something, which does not give all the details: *the course gave a brief outline of twentieth-century music* **2** **outlines** the important features of something: *the outlines of his theory are correct, we just need to fill in the details* **3** the general shape of something, esp. when only the profile and not the details are visible: *it was still light enough to see the outline of the distant mountains* **4** a drawing showing only the external lines of an object ▸ *vb* **-lining, -lined 5** to give the main features or general idea of (something): *I outlined what we had done and what we had still to do* **6** to show the general shape of an object but not its details, as light does coming from behind an object: *we could see the towers of the city outlined against the night sky*

outline n **1** = summary, review, résumé, rundown, synopsis, précis, thumbnail sketch, recapitulation **3** = shape, lines, form, figure, profile, silhouette, configuration, contour(s) ▸ vb **5** = summarize, draft, plan, trace, sketch (in), sum up, encapsulate, delineate **6** = silhouette, etch

outlook n **1** a general attitude to life: *my whole outlook on life had changed* **2** the probable condition or outcome of something: *the economic outlook is not good* **3** the weather forecast for the next few days: *the outlook for the weekend* **4** the view from a place: *a dreary outlook of chimneys and smoke*

outlook n **1** = attitude, opinion, position, approach, mood, perspective, point of view, stance **2** = prospect(s), future, expectations, forecast, prediction, probability, prognosis

outlying adj far away from the main area

outmanoeuvre or US **outmaneuver** vb **-vring, -vred** or **-vering, -vered** to gain an advantage over (someone) by skilful dealing: *the management outmanoeuvred us into accepting redundancies*

outmoded adj no longer fashionable or accepted

outnumber vb to exceed in number: *they were outnumbered by fifty to one*

out-of-date adj, adv old-fashioned; outmoded

outpatient n a patient who visits a hospital for treatment but does not stay there overnight

outpost n a small settlement in a distant part of the country or in a foreign country, which is used for military or trading purposes

outpouring n **1** a great amount of something that is produced very rapidly: *a prolific outpouring of ideas and energy* **2** a passionate outburst: *the hysterical outpourings of fanatics*

output n **1** the amount of something that is made or produced: *our weekly output has increased by 240 tonnes* **2** *electronics* the power, voltage, or current delivered by a circuit or component **3** *computers* the information produced by a computer ▸ vb **-putting, -putted** or **-put** **4** *computers* to produce (data) at the end of a process

output n **1** = production, manufacture, manufacturing, yield, productivity

outrage n **1** deep indignation, anger, or resentment: *she felt a sense of outrage that he should abandon her like that* **2** an extremely vicious or cruel act; gross violation of decency, morality, or honour: *there have been reports of another bombing outrage in the capital* ▸ vb **-raging, -raged** **3** to cause deep indignation, anger, or resentment in (someone): *they were outraged by the news of the assassination*

outrage n **1** = indignation, shock, anger, rage, fury, hurt, resentment, scorn ▸ vb = offend, shock, upset, wound, insult, infuriate, incense, madden

outrageous adj **1** unusual and shocking: *his sense of humour made him say and do the most outrageous things* **2** shocking and socially or morally unacceptable: *I will fight these outrageous accusations of corruption in the courts if necessary* ▸ **outrageously** adv

outrageous adj **1** = atrocious, shocking, terrible, offensive, appalling, cruel, savage, horrifying; ≠ mild **2** = unreasonable, unfair, steep (*informal*), shocking, extravagant, scandalous, preposterous, unwarranted; ≠ reasonable

outré (oo-tray) adj eccentric and rather shocking

outrider n a person who rides a motorcycle or horse in front of or beside an official vehicle as an attendant or guard

outrigger n **1** a stabilizing framework projecting from the side of a boat or canoe **2** a boat or canoe equipped with such a framework

outright adj **1** complete; total: *he is close to an outright victory* **2** straightforward and direct: *outright hostility* ▸ adv **3** completely: *the film was banned outright* **4** instantly: *my driver was killed outright* **5** openly: *ask her outright why she treated you as she did*

outright adj **1** = absolute, complete, total, perfect, sheer, thorough, unconditional, unqualified **2** = definite, clear, certain, flat, absolute, black-and-white, straightforward, unequivocal ▸ adv **3** = absolutely, completely, totally, fully, entirely, thoroughly, wholly, utterly **5** = openly, frankly, plainly, overtly, candidly, unreservedly, unhesitatingly, forthrightly

outrun vb **-running, -ran, -run** **1** to run faster or further than (someone) **2** to develop faster than (something): *the population of the city is in danger of outrunning the supply of houses*

outset n a start; beginning: *we never really hit it off from the outset*

outset n = beginning, start, opening, onset, inauguration, inception, commencement, kickoff (*informal*); ≠ finish

outshine vb **-shining, -shone** to be better than (someone) at something: *by university she had begun to outshine me in sports*

outside prep **1** on or to the exterior of: *a crowd gathered outside the court* **2** beyond the limits of: *it was outside my experience and beyond my ability* **3** apart from; other than: *no-one knows outside us* ▸ adj **4** on or of the outside: *an outside light is also a good idea* **5** remote; unlikely: *I still had an outside chance of the title* **6** coming from outside a particular group or organization: *the patient had been subjected to outside influences* **7** of or being the lane in a road which is further from the side than other lanes going in the same direction: *he was doing 120 in the outside lane* ▸ adv **8** outside a thing or place; out of doors: *we went outside to get some fresh air* **9** *slang* not in prison ▸ *n* **10** the external side or surface of something **11 at the outside** *informal* at the very most: *I'll be away four days at the outside*

> **outside** *adj* **4** = external, outer, exterior, outward, extraneous; ≠ inner **5** = remote, small, unlikely, slight, slim, distant, faint, marginal ▸ *adv* **8** = outdoors, out of the house, out-of-doors ▸ *n* **10** = exterior, face, front, covering, skin, surface, shell, coating

outsider *n* **1** a person excluded from a group **2** a contestant thought unlikely to win

> **outsider** *n* **1** = stranger, incomer, visitor, newcomer, intruder, interloper, odd one out

outsize *adj* **1** Also: **outsized** very large or larger than normal ▸ *n* **2** an outsize garment

outskirts *pl n* the parts of a town or city that are furthest from the centre: *an office in the northernmost outskirts of Glasgow*

> **outskirts** *pl n* = edge, boundary, suburbs, fringe, perimeter, periphery, suburbia, environs

outsmart *vb* same as **outwit**

outspan *S African* ▸ *n* **1** an area on a farm kept available for travellers to rest and refresh their animals ▸ *vb* **-spanning, -spanned 2** to unharness or unyoke (animals) **3** to relax

> **outspan** *vb* **3** = relax, chill out (*slang*), take it easy, loosen up, put your feet up

outspoken *adj* **1** saying exactly what one thinks: *an outspoken critic of human rights abuses* **2** spoken candidly: *she is known for her outspoken views* > **outspokenness** *n*

> **outspoken** *adj* = forthright, open, frank, straightforward, blunt, explicit, upfront (*informal*), unequivocal; ≠ reserved

outstanding *adj* **1** very good; excellent: *an outstanding performance* **2** still to be dealt with or paid: *outstanding bills; a few outstanding problems have to be put right* **3** very obvious or important: *there are significant exceptions, of which oil is the outstanding example* > **outstandingly** *adv*

> **outstanding** *adj* **1** = excellent, good, great (*informal*), important, special, fine, brilliant, impressive, booshit (*Austral slang*), exo (*Austral slang*), sik (*Austral slang*), rad (*informal*), phat (*slang*), schmick (*Austral informal*); ≠ mediocre **2** = unpaid, remaining, due, pending, payable, unsettled, uncollected

outstrip *vb* **-stripping, -stripped 1** to surpass (someone) in a particular activity: *his newspapers outstrip all others in vulgarity* **2** to go faster than (someone)

outtake *n* an unreleased take from a recording session, film, or television programme

outward *adj* **1** apparent or superficial: *to outward appearances the house is largely unchanged today* **2** of or relating to the outside: *outward shape* **3** (of a journey) away from a place to which one intends to return ▸ *adv also* **outwards 4** in an outward direction; towards the outside > **outwardly** *adv*

> **outward** *adj* **1** = apparent, seeming, surface, ostensible; ≠ inward

outweigh *vb* **1** to be more important, significant, or influential than: *these niggles are outweighed by the excellent cooking and service* **2** to be heavier than

> **outweigh** *vb* **1** = override, cancel (out), eclipse, offset, compensate for, supersede, neutralize, counterbalance

outwit *vb* **-witting, -witted** to gain an advantage over (someone) by cunning or ingenuity

ouzel *or* **ousel** (ooze-el) *n* same as **dipper** (sense 2)

ova *n* the plural of **ovum**

oval *adj* **1** egg-shaped ▸ *n* **2** anything that is oval in shape, such as a sports ground

> **oval** *adj* = elliptical, egg-shaped, ovoid

ovary *n, pl* **-ries 1** a reproductive organ in women and female animals in which eggs are produced **2** *botany* the lower part of a pistil, containing the ovules > **ovarian** *adj*

ovation *n* an enthusiastic round of applause

> **ovation** *n* = applause, hand, cheers, praise, tribute, acclaim, clapping, accolade; ≠ derision

oven *n* **1** an enclosed heated compartment or container for baking or roasting food, or for drying or firing ceramics ▸ *vb* **2** to cook in an oven

over *prep* **1** directly above; across the top or upper surface of: *set the frying pan over a low heat* **2** on or to the other side of: *the pilot flew over the Channel* **3** during or throughout (a period of time): *over the next few months it became clear what was happening* **4** throughout the whole extent of: *the effects are being felt all over the country now* **5** by means of (an instrument of telecommunication): *there was an announcement over the Tannoy system* **6** more than: *she had met him over a year ago* **7** concerning; about: *there has been much argument over these figures* **8** while occupied in: *I'll tell you over dinner tonight* **9** having recovered from the effects of: *he appeared to be over his niggling injury problems* **10 all over someone** *informal* extremely affectionate or attentive towards someone **11 over and above** added to; in addition to ▸ *adv* **12** in a state, condition, or position over something: *to climb over* **13** onto its side: *the jug toppled over* **14** at or to a point across an intervening space: *she carried him over to the other side of the river* **15** covering the whole area: *there's poverty the world over* **16** from beginning to end: *to read a document over* **17 all over** ᴀ finished

B over one's entire body **C** typically: *that's him all over* **18 over again** once more **19 over and over (again)** repeatedly ▸ *interj* **20** (in signalling and radio) it is now your turn to speak ▸ *adj* **21** finished; no longer in progress: *the second round of voting is over* ▸ *adj, adv* **22** remaining: *there wasn't any money left over* ▸ *n* **23** *cricket* **A** a series of six balls bowled by a bowler from the same end of the pitch **B** the play during this

> **over** *prep* **1** = above, on top of **2** = across, (looking) onto **6** = more than, above, exceeding, in excess of, upwards of **7** = about, regarding, relating to, concerning, apropos of ▸ *adj* = finished, done (with), through, ended, closed, past, completed, complete ▸ *adj, adv* = extra, more, further, beyond, additional, in addition, surplus, in excess

over- *prefix* **1** excessive or excessively: *overcharge*; *overdue* **2** superior in rank: *overlord* **3** indicating location or movement above: *overhang* **4** indicating movement downwards: *overthrow*

overall *adj* **1** from one end to the other: *the overall length* **2** including everything; total: *the overall cost* ▸ *adv* **3** in general; on the whole: *overall, I think this is the better car* ▸ *n* **4** *Brit & NZ* a coat-shaped work garment worn over ordinary clothes as a protection against dirt **5 overalls** work trousers with a bib and braces or jacket attached, worn over ordinary clothes as a protection against dirt and wear

> **overall** *adj* **2** = total, full, whole, general, complete, entire, global, comprehensive ▸ *adv* = in general, generally, mostly, all things considered, on average, on the whole, predominantly, in the main

overarm *sport* ▸ *adj* **1** bowled, thrown, or performed with the arm raised above the shoulder ▸ *adv* **2** with the arm raised above the shoulder

overawe *vb* **-awing, -awed** to affect (someone) with an overpowering sense of awe: *he was overawed by the prospect of meeting the Prime Minister*

overbalance *vb* **-lancing, -lanced** to lose one's balance

overbearing *adj* **1** imposing one's views in an unpleasant or forceful manner **2** of particular or overriding importance: *an overbearing need*

overblown *adj* inflated or excessive: *humiliation comes from having overblown expectations for yourself*

overboard *adv* **1** from a boat or ship into the water: *many passengers drowned when they jumped overboard to escape the flames* **2 go overboard** *informal* **A** to be extremely enthusiastic **B** to go to extremes **3 throw overboard** to reject or abandon (an idea or a plan)

overcast *adj* (of the sky or weather) cloudy

overcoat *n* a warm heavy coat worn in cold weather

overcome *vb* **-coming, -came, -come 1** to deal successfully with or control (a problem or feeling): *once I'd overcome my initial nerves I discovered hang-gliding was great fun* **2** (of an emotion or a feeling) to affect (someone) strongly or make (someone) powerless: *he was overcome by a sudden surge of jealousy* **3** to defeat (someone) in a conflict

> **overcome** *vb* **1** = conquer, beat, master, subdue, triumph over, vanquish (*literary*) **3** = defeat, beat, conquer, master, overwhelm, subdue, rout, overpower

overcrowded *adj* containing more people or things than is desirable: *overcrowded commuter trains*

overdo *vb* **-does, -doing, -did, -done 1** to do (something) to excess **2** to exaggerate (something) **3** to cook (something) too long **4 overdo it** *or* **things** to do something to a greater degree than is advisable or healthy

overdose *n* **1** a larger dose of a drug than is safe: *she tried to kill herself with an overdose of alcohol and drugs* ▸ *vb* **-dosing, -dosed 2** to take more of a drug than is safe, either accidentally or deliberately: *this drug is rarely prescribed because it is easy to overdose fatally on it*

overdraft *n* **1** the withdrawal of more money from a bank account than there is in it **2** the amount of money withdrawn thus

overdraw *vb* **-drawing, -drew, -drawn** to withdraw more money from a bank account than is in it

overdrawn *adj* **1** having overdrawn one's bank account **2** (of an account) in debit

overdrive *n* **1** a very high gear in a motor vehicle, used at high speeds to reduce wear **2** a state of great activity or excitement: *the government propaganda machine went into overdrive to try to play down the Minister's comments*

overdue *adj* **1** not having arrived or happened by the time expected or desired: *a reassessment of policy on this issue is long overdue* **2** (of money) not having been paid by the required date: *by this time his rent was three weeks overdue* **3** (of a library book) not having been returned to the library by the required date

> **overdue** *adj* **1** = delayed, belated, late, behind schedule, tardy, unpunctual, behindhand; ≠ early **2** = unpaid, owing

overgrown *adj* covered over with plants or weeds: *they headed up the overgrown and winding trail*

overhaul *vb* **1** to examine (a system or an idea) carefully for faults **2** to make repairs or adjustments to (a vehicle or machine) **3** to overtake (a vehicle or person) ▸ *n* **4** a thorough examination and repair

> **overhaul** *vb* **1, 2** = check, service, maintain, examine, restore, tune (up), repair, go over **3** = overtake, pass, leave behind, catch up with, get past, outstrip, get ahead of, outdistance ▸ *n* = check, service, examination, going-over (*informal*), inspection, once-over (*informal*), checkup, reconditioning

overhead adj **1** situated or operating above head height: *overhead compartments* ▶ adv **2** over or above head height: *the missile streaked overhead*

> **overhead** adj = raised, suspended, elevated, aerial, overhanging ▶ adv = above, in the sky, on high, aloft, up above; ≠ underneath

overheads pl n the general costs of running a business, such as rent, electricity, and stationery

> **overheads** pl n = running costs, expenses, outgoings, operating costs

overhear vb **-hearing, -heard** to hear (a speaker or remark) unintentionally or without the knowledge of the speaker

overjoyed adj extremely pleased

overkill n any treatment that is greater than that required: *the overkill in negative propaganda resulted in this upsurge*

overland adj, adv by land

overlap vb **-lapping, -lapped 1** (of two things) to share part of the same space as or lie partly over (each other): *slice the meat and lay it in overlapping slices in a serving dish* **2** to coincide partly in time or subject: *their careers have overlapped for the last ten years* ▶ n **3** a part that overlaps **4** the amount or length of something overlapping

overleaf adv on the other side of the page

overlook vb **1** to fail to notice (something) **2** to disregard or ignore (misbehaviour or a fault): *I'm prepared to overlook your failure, but don't do it again* **3** to give a view of (something) from above: *a cliff overlooking the Atlantic*

> **overlook** vb **1** = miss, forget, neglect, omit, disregard, pass over; ≠ notice **2** = ignore, excuse, forgive, pardon, disregard, condone, turn a blind eye to, wink at **3** = look over or out on, have a view of

overly adv too; excessively

overnight adv **1** during the night **2** in or as if in the course of one night; suddenly: *we are not saying that a change like this would happen overnight* ▶ adj **3** done in, occurring in, or lasting the night: *the army has ordered an overnight curfew* **4** staying for one night: *overnight guests* **5** for use during a single night: *should I pack an overnight case?* **6** happening very quickly; sudden: *he doesn't expect the programme to be an overnight success*

overpower vb **1** to conquer or subdue (someone) by superior force **2** to have such a strong effect on (someone) as to make him or her helpless or ineffective: *I was so appalled, so overpowered by my guilt and my shame that I was unable to speak* > **overpowering** adj

> **overpower** vb **1** = overcome, master, overwhelm, overthrow, subdue, quell, subjugate, prevail over **2** = overwhelm, overcome, bowl over (*informal*), stagger

overreach vb **overreach oneself** to fail by trying to be too clever or achieve too much:

he built up a successful media empire before he overreached himself and lost much of his fortune

override vb **-riding, -rode, -ridden 1** to set aside or disregard (a person or a person's decisions) by having superior authority or power: *the managing director can override any decision he doesn't like* **2** to be more important than or replace (something): *unsurprisingly the day-to-day struggle for survival overrode all moral considerations* > **overriding** adj

> **override** vb **1** = overrule, cancel, overturn, repeal, rescind, annul, nullify, countermand **2** = outweigh, eclipse, supersede, take precedence over, prevail over

overrule vb **-ruling, -ruled 1** to reverse the decision of (a person or organization with less power): *the President overruled the hardliners in the party who wanted to use force* **2** to rule or decide against (an argument or decision): *the initial judgment was overruled by the Supreme Court*

overrun vb **-running, -ran, -run 1** to conquer (territory) rapidly by force of numbers **2** to spread over (a place) rapidly: *dirty tenements, overrun by lice, rats, and roaches* **3** to extend or run beyond a set limit: *Tuesday's lunch overran by three-quarters of an hour*

> **overrun** vb **1** = overwhelm, attack, assault, occupy, raid, invade, penetrate, rout **2** = spread over, overwhelm, choke, swamp, infest, inundate, permeate, swarm over **3** = exceed, go beyond, surpass, overshoot, run over or on

overseas adv **1** across the sea; abroad ▶ adj **2** of, to, from, or in a distant country or countries ▶ n **3** *informal* a foreign country or foreign countries collectively

oversee vb **-seeing, -saw, -seen** to watch over and direct (someone or something); supervise > **overseer** n

overshadow vb **1** to make (someone or something) seem insignificant or less important by comparison **2** to sadden the atmosphere of: *news of their team-mate's injury overshadowed the victory celebrations*

> **overshadow** vb **1** = outshine, eclipse, surpass, dwarf, tower above, leave or put in the shade **2** = spoil, ruin, mar, wreck, blight, crool or cruel (*Austral slang*), mess up, put a damper on

oversight n a mistake caused by not noticing something

overspill n *Brit* the rehousing of people from crowded cities in smaller towns

overstay vb **overstay one's welcome** to stay as a guest longer than one's host or hostess would like

overstayer n a person who remains in a country after his or her permit has expired

overt adj done or shown in an open and obvious way: *jurors were now looking at the defendant with overt hostility* > **overtly** adv

overt *adj* = open, obvious, plain, public, manifest, blatant, observable, undisguised; ≠ hidden

overtake *vb* **-taking, -took, -taken 1** *chiefly Brit* to move past (another vehicle or person) travelling in the same direction **2** to do better than (someone) after catching up with him or her **3** to come upon (someone) suddenly or unexpectedly: *a mortal tiredness overtook him*

overtake *vb* **1** = pass, leave behind, overhaul, catch up with, get past, outdistance, go by *or* past **2** = outdo, top, exceed, eclipse, surpass, outstrip, get the better of, outclass **3** = befall (*archaic, literary*), hit, happen to, catch off guard, catch unawares

overthink *vb* **-thinking, -thought** to think about (something) for longer than is necessary or productive

overthrow *vb* **-throwing, -threw, -thrown 1** to defeat and replace (a ruler or government) by force **2** to replace (standards or values) ▸ *n* **3** downfall or destruction: *the overthrow of the US-backed dictatorship*

overthrow *vb* **1** = defeat, overcome, conquer, bring down, oust, topple, rout, overpower; ≠ uphold ▸ *n* = downfall, fall, defeat, collapse, destruction, ousting, undoing, unseating; ≠ preservation

overtime *n* **1** work at a regular job done in addition to regular working hours **2** pay for such work ▸ *adv* **3** in addition to one's regular working hours: *she had been working overtime and she fell asleep at the wheel*

overtone *n* **1** an additional meaning or hint: *I don't want to deny that from time to time there are political overtones* **2** *music & acoustics* any of the tones, with the exception of the principal or lowest one, that make up a musical sound

overture *n* **1** *music* **A** a piece of orchestral music played at the beginning of an opera, oratorio, ballet, musical comedy, or film, often containing the main musical themes of the work **B** a one-movement orchestral piece, usually having a descriptive or evocative title: *the 1812 Overture* **2 overtures** opening moves towards a new relationship or agreement: *the German government made a variety of friendly overtures towards the French*

overturn *vb* **1** to turn over or upside down **2** to overrule or reverse (a legal decision) **3** to overthrow or destroy (a government)

overturn *vb* **1** = tip over, topple, upturn, capsize, upend, keel over, overbalance **2** = reverse, change, cancel, abolish, overthrow, set aside, repeal, quash **3** = overthrow, defeat, destroy, overcome, bring down, oust, topple, depose

overweight *adj* **1** (of a person) weighing more than is healthy **2** weighing more than is usual or permitted

overweight *adj* **1** = fat, heavy, stout, hefty, plump, bulky, chunky, chubby; ≠ underweight

overwhelm *vb* **1** to overpower the thoughts, emotions, or senses of (someone): *we were overwhelmed with grief* **2** to overcome (people) with irresistible force: *gang violence has overwhelmed an ailing police force* ▸ **overwhelming** *adj* ▸ **overwhelmingly** *adv*

overwhelm *vb* **1** = overcome, devastate (*informal*), stagger, bowl over (*informal*), knock (someone) for six (*informal*), sweep (someone) off their feet, take (someone's) breath away **2** = destroy, defeat, overcome, crush, massacre, conquer, wipe out, overthrow

overwrought *adj* tense, nervous, and agitated

ovoid (oh-void) *adj* egg-shaped

ovulate (ov-yew-late) *vb* **-lating, -lated** *biol* to produce or release eggs from an ovary ▸ **ovulation** *n*

ovum (oh-vum) *n, pl* **ova** an unfertilized female egg cell

owe *vb* **owing, owed 1** to be under an obligation to pay an amount of money to (someone): *he owes me a lot of money* **2** to feel an obligation to do or give: *I think I owe you an apology* **3 owe something to** to have something as a result of: *many serving officers owe their present position to the former president*

owe *vb* **1** = be in debt (to), be in arrears (to), be overdrawn (by), be obligated *or* indebted (to)

owl *n* a bird of prey which has a flat face, large eyes, and a small hooked beak, and which is active at night ▸ **owlish** *adj*

own *adj* (*preceded by a possessive*) **1** used to emphasize that something belongs to a particular person: *rely on your own instincts* ▸ *pron* (*preceded by a possessive*) **2** the one or ones belonging to a particular person: *I had one of my own* **3** the people that owes loyalty to, esp. relations: *we all look after our own around here* **4 come into one's own** to fulfil one's potential **5 hold one's own** to have the necessary ability to deal successfully with a situation: *he chose a partner who could hold her own with the best* **6 on one's own A** without help: *you'll never manage to lift that on your own* **B** by oneself; alone: *he lives on his own in a flat in town* ▸ *vb* **7** to have (something) as one's possession: *he owns homes in four countries* **8** Also: **own up to** to confess or admit: *I own I could not bear to think of it; I thought she was going to own up to an affair* ▸ **owner** *n* ▸ **ownership** *n*

own *adj* = personal, special, private, individual, particular, exclusive ▸ *vb* **7** = possess, have, keep, hold, enjoy, retain, be in possession of, have to your name

OX *n, pl* **oxen** a castrated bull used for pulling heavy loads and for meat

Oxbridge *n Brit* the universities of Oxford and Cambridge considered together

Oxfam Oxford Committee for Famine Relief

oxide *n chem* a compound of oxygen with another element

oxidize *or* **-dise** *vb* **-dizing, -dized** *or* **-dising, -dised** to react chemically with oxygen, as in burning or rusting ▷ **oxidization** *or* **-disation** *n*

oxygen *n chem* a colourless, odourless gaseous element essential to life processes and to combustion. Symbol: **O**

oxygenate *vb* **-nating, -nated** to add oxygen to: *to oxygenate blood*

oxymoron (ox-see-**more**-on) *n* a figure of speech that combines two apparently contradictory terms, for example *cruel kindness*

oyez *or* **oyes** *interj* a cry usually uttered three times by a public crier or court official calling for silence and attention

oyster *n* **1** an edible shellfish, some types of which produce pearls **2 the world is your oyster** you are in a position where there is every possible chance of personal advancement and satisfaction ▶ *adj* **3** greyish-white

oystercatcher *n* a wading bird with black-and-white plumage and a long stout red bill

oz *or* **oz.** ounce

Oz *n slang* Australia

ozone *n* **1** a form of oxygen with a strong odour, formed by an electric discharge in the atmosphere **2** *informal* clean bracing air, as found at the seaside

ozone layer *n* a layer of ozone in the upper atmosphere that absorbs harmful ultraviolet rays from the sun

Pp

p *or* **P** *n, pl* **p's, P's** *or* **Ps 1** the 16th letter of the English alphabet **2 mind one's p's and q's** to be careful to behave correctly and use polite language

p 1 *Brit, Austral & NZ* penny **2** *Brit* pence

P 1 *chem* phosphorus **2** (on road signs) parking **3** *chess* pawn

p. 1 *pl* **pp.** page **2** per

pa¹ *n informal* father

pa² *n NZ* (formerly) a fortified Māori settlement

PA 1 Pennsylvania **2** personal assistant **3** public-address system

p.a. yearly

pace *n* **1 A** a single step in walking **B** the length of a step **2** speed of walking or running **3** speed of doing some other activity: *efforts to accelerate the pace of change are unlikely to succeed* **4** manner of walking **5 keep pace with** to advance at the same speed as **6 put someone through his** *or* **her paces** to test someone's ability **7 set the pace** to determine the speed at which a group advances ▶ *vb* **pacing, paced 8** to walk with regular steps, often in anxiety or impatience: *he paced up and down the foyer impatiently* **9** to set the speed for (the competitors) in a race **10 pace out** to measure by paces

> **pace** *n* **1A** = footstep, step, stride **3** = speed, rate, tempo, velocity **4** = step, walk, stride, tread, gait ▶ *vb* **8** = stride, walk, pound, patrol, march up and down

pacemaker *n* **1** an electronic device positioned in the body, next to the heart, to regulate the heartbeat **2** a competitor who, by leading a race, causes it to be run at a particular speed

pachyderm (pak-ee-durm) *n* a large thick-skinned mammal, such as an elephant or rhinoceros

pacifist *n* a person who is totally opposed to violence and refuses to take part in war ▷ **pacifism** *n*

pacify *vb* **-fies, -fying, -fied** to soothe or calm ▷ **pacification** *n*

pack *n* **1** a bundle or load carried on the back **2** *Brit & NZ* a complete set of playing cards **3** a group of animals that hunt together: *a pack of hounds* **4** any collection of people or things: *a pack of lies* **5** *chiefly US & Canad* same as **packet** (sense 1) ▶ *vb* **6** to put (articles) in a case or container for moving **7** to roll (articles) up into a bundle **8** to press tightly together; cram: *thousands of people packed into the city's main square* **9** (foll. by *off*) to send away hastily: *their young son came in to say good night and was packed off to bed* ▶ See also **pack in**

pack *n* **1** = bundle, parcel, load, burden, rucksack, knapsack, back pack, kitbag **4** = group, crowd, company, band, troop, gang, bunch (*informal*), mob **5** = packet, box, package, carton ▶ *vb* **6** = package, load, store, bundle, stow **8** = cram, crowd, press, fill, stuff, jam, ram, compress **9 pack someone off** = send away, dismiss, send packing (*informal*)

package *n* **1** a small parcel **2** Also: **package deal** a deal in which separate items are presented together as a unit **3** *US & Canad* same as **packet** (sense 1) ▶ *vb* **-aging, -aged 4** to put (something) into a package ▷ **packaging** *n*

package *n* **1** = parcel, box, container, packet, carton **2** = collection, lot, unit, combination, compilation ▶ *vb* = pack, box, parcel (up)

package holiday *n* a holiday in which everything is arranged by one company for a fixed price

packet *n* **1** a container, together with its contents: *a packet of crisps* **2** a small parcel **3** Also: **packet boat** a boat that transports mail, passengers, or goods on a fixed short route **4** *slang* a large sum of money: *she was paid a packet* **5** *computers* a unit into which a larger piece of data is broken down for more efficient transmission

packet *n* **1** = container, box, package, carton **2** = package, parcel **4** = a fortune, a bomb (*Brit slang*), a pile (*informal*), a small fortune, a tidy sum (*informal*), a king's ransom (*informal*), top whack (*informal*)

packhorse *n* a horse used to carry goods

pack ice *n* a large area of floating ice, consisting of pieces that have become massed together

pack in *vb informal* to stop doing (something): *I'm going to pack it in and resign*

pack in *vb* **pack something in** = stop, give up, kick (*informal*), cease, chuck (*informal*)

pact *n* a formal agreement between two or more parties

pact *n* = agreement, alliance, treaty, deal (*informal*), understanding, bargain, covenant

pad[1] *n* **1** a thick piece of soft material used for comfort, shape, protection, or absorption **2** a number of sheets of paper fastened together along one edge **3** the fleshy cushioned underpart of an animal's paw **4** a level area or flat-topped structure, from which rockets are launched or helicopters take off **5** *informal* a person's residence ▶ *vb* **padding, padded 6** to fill (something) out with soft material for comfort, shape, or protection **7 pad out** to lengthen (a speech or piece of writing) with unnecessary words or pieces of information

pad *n* **1** = wad, dressing, pack, padding, compress, wadding **2** = notepad, block, notebook, jotter, writing pad **3** = paw, foot, sole **5** = home, flat, apartment (*chiefly US*), place, bachelor apartment (*Canad*) ▶ *vb* **6** = pack, fill, protect, stuff, cushion

pad[2] *vb* **padding, padded** to walk with a soft or muffled step

pad *vb* = sneak, creep, steal, go barefoot

padding *n* **1** any soft material used to pad something **2** unnecessary information put into a speech or written work to make it longer

padding *n* **1** = filling, stuffing, packing, wadding **2** = waffle (*informal, chiefly Brit*), hot air (*informal*), verbiage, wordiness, verbosity

paddle[1] *n* **1** a short light oar with a flat blade at one or both ends **2** a paddle wheel used to move a boat **3** a blade of a water wheel or paddle wheel ▶ *vb* **-dling, -dled 4** to move (a boat) with a paddle **5** to swim with short rapid strokes, like a dog **6** *US & Canad informal* to spank

paddle *n* **1** = oar, scull ▶ *vb* **4** = row, pull, scull

paddle[2] *vb* **-dling, -dled 1** to walk barefoot in shallow water **2** to dabble (one's fingers, hands, or feet) in water ▶ *n* **3** the act of paddling in water

paddle *vb* **1** = wade, splash (about), slop

paddle steamer *n* a ship propelled by paddle wheels turned by a steam engine

paddle wheel *n* a large wheel fitted with paddles, turned by an engine to propel a ship

paddock *n* **1** a small enclosed field for horses **2** (in horse racing) the enclosure in which horses are paraded and mounted before a race **3** *Austral & NZ* any area of fenced land

paddy[1] *n, pl* **-dies 1** Also: **paddy field** a field planted with rice **2** rice as a growing crop or when harvested but not yet milled

paddy[2] *n, pl* **-dies** *Brit & NZ informal* a fit of temper

pademelon or **paddymelon** (pad-ee-mel-an) *n* a small Australian wallaby

padlock *n* **1** a detachable lock with a hinged hoop fastened through a ring on the object to be secured ▶ *vb* **2** to fasten (something) with a padlock

padre (pah-dray) *n informal* a chaplain to the armed forces

paean (pee-an) *n literary* an expression of praise or joy

paediatrician or US **pediatrician** *n* a doctor who specializes in children's diseases

paediatrics or US **pediatrics** *n* the branch of medicine concerned with children and their diseases ▷ **paediatric** or US **pediatric** *adj*

paedophile or US **pedophile** *n* a person who is sexually attracted to children

paedophilia or US **pedophilia** *n* the condition of being sexually attracted to children

paella (pie-ell-a) *n* a Spanish dish made from rice, shellfish, chicken, and vegetables

pagan *adj* 1 having, being, or relating to religious beliefs, esp. ancient ones, which are not part of any of the world's major religions: *this was the site of a pagan temple to the sun* 2 irreligious ▸ *n* 3 a person who does not belong to any of the world's major religions 4 a person without any religion ▹ **paganism** *n*

> **pagan** *adj* = heathen, infidel, polytheistic, idolatrous ▸ *n* = heathen (*old-fashioned*), infidel, polytheist, idolater

page¹ *n* 1 one side of one of the leaves of a book, newspaper, or magazine 2 one of the leaves of a book, newspaper, or magazine 3 *literary* a period or event: *a new page in the country's political history* 4 a screenful of information from a website or teletext service

> **page** *n* 1, 2 = folio, side, leaf, sheet

page² *n* 1 a small boy who attends a bride at a wedding 2 a youth employed to run errands for the guests in a hotel or club 3 *medieval history* a boy in training for knighthood ▸ *vb* **paging**, **paged** 4 to summon (a person), by bleeper or loudspeaker, in order to pass on a message

> **page** *n* 1 = servant, attendant, squire, pageboy 2 = attendant, pageboy ▸ *vb* = call, summon, send for

pageant *n* 1 an outdoor show portraying scenes from history 2 any magnificent display or procession

pageantry *n* spectacular display or ceremony

pageboy *n* 1 a hairstyle in which the hair is smooth and the same medium length with the ends curled under 2 same as **page²** (senses 1, 2)

pagination *n* the numbering in sequence of the pages of a book or manuscript ▹ **paginate** *vb*

pagoda *n* a pyramid-shaped Asian temple or tower

paid *vb* 1 past of **pay** 2 **put paid to** to end or destroy: *a knee injury put paid to his promising sporting career*

pail *n* 1 a bucket 2 Also called: **pailful** the amount contained in a pail: *a pail of water*

pain *n* 1 physical hurt or discomfort caused by injury or illness 2 emotional suffering 3 Also called: **pain in the neck** *informal* a person or thing that is annoying or irritating 4 **on pain of** subject to the penalty of: *orders which their soldiers were bound to follow on pain of death* ▸ *vb* 5 to cause (a person) physical or mental suffering 6 *informal* to annoy; irritate ▹ **painless** *adj*

> **pain** *n* 1 = suffering, discomfort, hurt, irritation, tenderness, soreness 2 = sorrow, suffering, torture, distress, despair, misery, agony, sadness ▸ *vb* 5 = distress, hurt, torture, grieve, torment, sadden, agonize, cut to the quick

painful *adj* 1 causing pain or distress: *painful inflammation of the joints; he began the painful task of making funeral arrangements* 2 affected with pain: *the symptoms include fever and painful joints* 3 tedious or difficult: *the hours passed with painful slowness* 4 *informal* extremely bad: *a painful so-called comedy* ▹ **painfully** *adv*

> **painful** *adj* 1 = distressing, unpleasant, grievous, distasteful, agonizing, disagreeable; ≠ pleasant 2 = sore, smarting, aching, tender; ≠ painless 3 = difficult, arduous, trying, hard, troublesome, laborious; ≠ easy

painkiller *n* a drug that relieves pain

painstaking *adj* extremely careful and thorough ▹ **painstakingly** *adv*

paint *n* 1 a coloured substance, spread on a surface with a brush or a roller, that forms a hard coating 2 a dry film of paint on a surface 3 *informal* face make-up ▸ *vb* 4 to apply paint to paper or canvas to make a picture of 5 to coat (a surface) with paint 6 to describe vividly in words: *the survey paints a dismal picture of growing hunger and disease* 7 to apply make-up to (the face) 8 to apply (liquid) to (a surface): *paint the varnish on and leave it to dry for at least four hours* 9 **paint the town red** *informal* to celebrate in a lively way

> **paint** *n* 1 = colouring, colour, stain, dye, tint, pigment, emulsion ▸ *vb* 4 = depict, draw, portray, picture, represent, sketch 5 = colour, cover, coat, stain, whitewash, daub, distemper, apply paint to

painter *n* 1 an artist who paints pictures 2 a person who paints surfaces of buildings as a trade

painting *n* 1 a picture produced by using paint 2 the art of producing pictures by applying paints to paper or canvas 3 the act of applying paint to a surface

pair *n* 1 two identical or similar things matched for use together: *a pair of shoes* 2 two people, animals, or things used or grouped together: *a pair of tickets* 3 an object consisting of two identical or similar parts joined together: *a pair of jeans* 4 a male and a female animal of the same species kept for breeding purposes 5 *parliament* two opposed members who both agree not to vote on a specified motion 6 two playing cards of the same denomination 7 one member of a matching pair: *I can't find the pair to this glove* ▸ *vb* 8 to group (people or things) in twos 9 **pair off** to separate into groups of two

> **pair** *n* 1 = set 2 = couple, brace, duo ▸ *vb* 8 = team, match (up), join, couple, twin, bracket

paisley pattern *or* **paisley** *n* a detailed pattern of small curving shapes, used in fabric

pajamas *pl n* US pyjamas

pakeha (pah-kee-hah) *n*, *pl* **pakeha** *or* **pakehas** NZ a person of European descent, as distinct from a Māori

Pakistani *adj* 1 of Pakistan ▶ *n* 2 a person from Pakistan

pal *informal* ▶ *n* 1 a close friend ▶ *vb* **palling**, **palled** 2 **pal up with** to become friends with

> **pal** *n* = friend, companion, mate (*informal*), buddy (*informal*), comrade, chum (*informal*), crony, cobber (*Austral*, *NZ old-fashioned*, *informal*), E hoa (*NZ*)

palace *n* 1 the official residence of a king, queen, president, or archbishop 2 a large and richly furnished building

palaeography *or US* **paleography** (pal-ee-**og**-ra-fee) *n* the study of ancient handwriting

Palaeolithic *or US* **Paleolithic** (pal-ee-oh-**lith**-ik) *adj* of the period from about 2.5 to 3 million years ago until about 12,000 BC, during which primitive humans emerged and unpolished chipped stone tools were made

palaeontology *or US* **paleontology** (pal-ee-on-**tol**-a-jee) *n* the study of past geological periods and fossils > **palaeontologist** *or US* **paleontologist** *n*

Palagi (pa-**lang**-gee) *n*, *pl* **-gis** *NZ* the Samoan name for a Pakeha

palatable *adj* 1 (of food or drink) pleasant to taste 2 (of an experience or idea) acceptable or satisfactory

palate *n* 1 the roof of the mouth 2 the sense of taste: *a range of dishes to tempt every palate*

palatial *adj* like a palace; magnificent: *his palatial home*

palaver (pal-**lah**-ver) *n* time-consuming fuss: *all the palaver involved in obtaining a visa*

pale¹ *adj* 1 (of a colour) whitish and not very strong: *pale yellow* 2 (of a complexion) having a whitish appearance, usually because of illness, shock, or fear 3 lacking brightness or colour: *the pale, chill light of an October afternoon* ▶ *vb* **paling**, **paled** 4 to become pale or paler: *the girl paled at the news* > **paleness** *n*

> **pale** *adj* 1 = light, soft, faded, subtle, muted, bleached, pastel, light-coloured 2 = white, pasty, bleached, wan, colourless, pallid, ashen; ≠ rosy-cheeked 3 = dim, weak, faint, feeble, thin, wan, watery ▶ *vb* = become pale, blanch, whiten, go white, lose colour

pale² *n* 1 a wooden post used in fences 2 **A** a fence made of pales **B** a boundary 3 **beyond the pale** outside the limits of social convention: *the destruction of forests is beyond the pale*

palette *n* 1 a flat board used by artists to mix paints 2 the range of colours characteristic of a particular artist or school of painting: *he uses a cool palette with no strong red* 3 the range of colours or patterns that can be displayed on the visual display unit of a computer

palindrome *n* a word or phrase that reads the same backwards or forwards, such as *able was I ere I saw Elba*

paling *n* 1 a fence made of pales 2 pales collectively 3 a single pale

palisade *n* 1 a fence made of stakes driven into the ground 2 one of the stakes used in such a fence

pall¹ *n* 1 a cloth spread over a coffin 2 a coffin at a funeral ceremony 3 a dark heavy covering: *a pall of smoke and dust hung in the air* 4 a depressing atmosphere: *a pall hung on them all after his death*

pall² *vb* to become boring or uninteresting, esp. by continuing for too long: *any pleasure had palled long before the two-hour programme was over*

palladium *n chem* a rare silvery-white element of the platinum metal group, used in jewellery. Symbol: **Pd**

pallbearer *n* a person who helps to carry or who escorts the coffin at a funeral

pallet¹ *n* a straw-filled mattress or bed

pallet² *n* 1 a tool with a flat, sometimes flexible, blade used for shaping pottery 2 a portable platform for storing and moving goods

palliate *vb* **-ating**, **-ated** 1 to lessen the severity of (pain or disease) without curing it 2 to cause (an offence) to seem less serious

palliative *adj* 1 relieving without curing ▶ *n* 2 something that palliates, such as a sedative drug 3 something that alleviates or lessens a problem: *a scheme offered as a palliative for economic pain*

pallid *adj* 1 lacking colour, brightness, or vigour: *a pallid autumn sun* 2 lacking energy or vitality; insipid: *many militants find the party's socialism too pallid*

pallor *n* paleness of complexion, usually because of illness, shock, or fear

pally *adj* **-lier**, **-liest** *informal* on friendly terms

palm¹ *n* 1 the inner surface of the hand from the wrist to the base of the fingers 2 the part of a glove that covers the palm 3 **in the palm of one's hand** at one's mercy or command: *he had the jury in the palm of his hand* ▶ *vb* 4 to hide (something) in the hand: *he palmed the key* ▶ See also **palm off**

palm² *or* **palm tree** *n* a tropical or subtropical tree with a straight unbranched trunk crowned with long pointed leaves

palmistry *n* fortune-telling by examining the lines and bumps of the hand > **palmist** *n*

palm off *vb* 1 to get rid of (someone or something) by passing it on to another: *the risk has to be shared with subcontractors, not simply palmed off on them* 2 to divert (someone) by a lie or excuse: *Mark was palmed off with a series of excuses*

Palm Sunday *n Christianity* the Sunday before Easter

palmtop *adj* 1 (of a computer) small enough to be held in the hand ▶ *n* 2 a personal computer that is small enough to be held in the hand

palomino *n*, *pl* **-nos** a golden or cream horse with a white mane and tail

palpable *adj* 1 obvious: *palpable nonsense* 2 (of a feeling or an atmosphere) so intense that it seems capable of being touched: *an air of palpable gloom hung over him* ▷ **palpably** *adv*

palpate *vb* **-pating, -pated** *med* to examine (an area of the body) by touching ▷ **palpation** *n*

palpitate *vb* **-tating, -tated 1** (of the heart) to beat rapidly **2** to flutter or tremble ▷ **palpitation** *n*

palsy (pawl-zee) *n pathol* paralysis of a specified type: *cerebral palsy* ▷ **palsied** *adj*

paltry *adj* **-trier, -triest** insignificant

pampas *n* the extensive grassy plains of South America

pampas grass *n* a South American grass with large feathery silver-coloured flower branches

pamper *vb* to treat (someone) with excessive indulgence or care; spoil

> **pamper** *vb* = spoil, indulge, pet, cosset, coddle, mollycoddle

pamphlet *n* a thin paper-covered booklet, often on a subject of current interest

> **pamphlet** *n* = booklet, leaflet, brochure, circular, tract

pamphleteer *n* a person who writes or issues pamphlets

pan¹ *n* **1** a wide long-handled metal container used in cooking **2** any of various similar containers used in industry, etc. **3** either of the two dishes on a set of scales **4** *Brit* the bowl of a lavatory **5** a natural or artificial hollow in the ground: *a saltpan* ▷ *vb* **panning, panned 6** to sift gold from (a river) in a shallow pan **7** *informal* to criticize harshly: *his first film was panned by the critics* ▷ See also **pan out**

> **pan** *n* **1** = pot, container, saucepan ▷ *vb* **6** = sift out, look for, search for **7** = criticize, knock (*informal*), slam (*slang*), censure, tear into (*informal*)

pan² *vb* **panning, panned 1** to move (a film camera) or (of a film camera) to be moved to follow a moving object or to take in a whole scene ▷ *n* **2** the act of panning

> **pan** *vb* = move along *or* across, follow, track, sweep

pan- *combining form* including or relating to all parts or members: *Pan-American*

panacea (pan-a-see-a) *n* a remedy for all diseases or problems

panache (pan-ash) *n* a confident and stylish manner: *the orchestra played with great panache*

panama hat *or* **panama** *n* a straw hat with a rounded crown and a wide brim

panatella *n* a long slender cigar

pancake *n* **1** a thin flat circle of fried batter **2** Also called: **pancake landing** an aircraft landing made by levelling out a few feet from the ground and then dropping onto it

panchromatic *adj photog* (of an emulsion or film) sensitive to light of all colours

pancreas (pang-kree-ass) *n* a large gland behind the stomach, that produces insulin and aids digestion ▷ **pancreatic** *adj*

panda *n* **1** Also called: **giant panda** a large black-and-white bearlike animal from the high mountain bamboo forests of China **2** Also called: **lesser panda, red panda** a raccoon-like animal of the mountain forests of S Asia, with a reddish-brown coat and ringed tail

panda car *n Brit* a police patrol car

pandemic *n, adj* (a disease) occurring over a wide geographical area

pandemonium *n* wild confusion; uproar

pander *vb* **1** (foll. by *to*) to indulge (a person or his or her desires): *he pandered to popular fears* ▷ *n* **2** *chiefly archaic* a person who procures a sexual partner for someone

p & p *Brit* postage and packing

pane *n* a sheet of glass in a window or door

panegyric (pan-ee-jirr-rik) *n* a formal speech or piece of writing that praises a person or event

panel *n* **1** a distinct section of a larger surface area, such as that in a door **2** any distinct section of something formed from a sheet of material, such as part of a car body **3** a piece of material inserted in a garment **4** a group of people acting as a team, such as in a quiz or a discussion before an audience **5** *law* **A** a list of jurors **B** the people on a jury ▷ *adj* **6** of a group acting as a panel: *a panel game* ▷ *vb* **-elling, -elled** *or US* **-eling, -eled 7** to cover or decorate with panels

panel beater *n* a person who repairs damage to car bodies

panelling *or US* **paneling** *n* panels collectively, such as on a wall or ceiling

panellist *or US* **panelist** *n* a member of a panel, usually on radio or television

pang *n* a sudden sharp feeling of pain or sadness

pangolin *n* an animal of tropical countries with a scaly body and a long snout for feeding on ants and termites. Also called: **scaly anteater**

panic *n* **1** a sudden overwhelming feeling of terror or anxiety, sometimes affecting a whole group of people ▷ *adj* **2** of or resulting from such terror: *panic measures* ▷ *vb* **-nicking, -nicked 3** to feel or cause to feel panic ▷ **panicky** *adj*

> **panic** *n* = fear, alarm, terror, anxiety, hysteria, fright, trepidation (*formal*), a flap (*informal*) ▷ *vb* = go to pieces, become hysterical, lose your nerve

panic-stricken *adj* affected by panic

panini *n, pl* **-ni** *or* **-nis** a type of Italian bread usually served grilled with a variety of fillings

pannier *n* **1** one of a pair of bags fixed on either side of the back wheel of a bicycle or motorcycle **2** one of a pair of large baskets slung over a beast of burden

p

panoply (pan-a-plee) *n* a magnificent array: *ambassadors equipped with the full panoply of diplomatic bags, codes and ciphers*

panorama *n* **1** a wide unbroken view in all directions: *the beautiful panorama of the Cornish coast* **2** a wide or comprehensive survey of a subject: *the panorama of American life* **3** a picture of a scene unrolled before spectators a part at a time so as to appear continuous ▷ **panoramic** *adj*

> **panorama** *n* **1** = view, prospect, vista
> **2** = survey, perspective, overview, overall picture

pan out *vb* **1** *informal* to work out; result: *Parker's research did not pan out too well* **2** (of gravel) to yield gold by panning

pansy *n, pl* **-sies** **1** a garden plant whose flowers have rounded white, yellow, or purple velvety petals **2** *offensive slang* an effeminate or homosexual man or boy

pant *vb* **1** to breathe with noisy gasps after exertion **2** to say (something) while breathing in this way **3** (foll. by *for*) to have a frantic desire for ▸ *n* **4** the act of panting

> **pant** *vb* **1** = puff, blow, breathe, gasp, wheeze, heave

pantaloons *pl n* baggy trousers gathered at the ankles

pantechnicon *n Brit* a large van used for furniture removals

pantheism *n* **1** the belief that God is present in everything **2** readiness to worship all gods ▷ **pantheist** *n* ▷ **pantheistic** *adj*

pantheon *n* **1** (in ancient Greece or Rome) a temple built to honour all the gods **2** all the gods of a particular creed: *the Celtic pantheon of horse gods* **3** a group of very important people: *he deserves a place in the pantheon of social reformers*

panther *n* a leopard, usually a black one

panties *pl n* women's or children's underpants

pantile *n* a roofing tile, with an S-shaped cross section

pantomime *n* **1** (in Britain) a play based on a fairy tale and performed at Christmas time **2** a theatrical entertainment in which words are replaced by gestures and bodily actions **3** *informal, chiefly Brit* a confused or farcical situation

pantry *n, pl* **-tries** a small room or large cupboard in which food is kept

pants *pl n* **1** *Brit* an undergarment with two leg holes, covering the body from the waist or hips to the thighs **2** *US, Canad, Austral & NZ* trousers or shorts **3** **bore** or **scare the pants off someone** *informal* to bore or scare someone very much

> **pants** *pl n* **1** = underpants, briefs, drawers, knickers, panties, boxer shorts, broekies (*S African*), underdaks (*Austral slang*)
> **2** = trousers, slacks

pap *n* **1** a soft food for babies or invalids **2** worthless or oversimplified entertainment or information **3** *S African* maize porridge

papacy (pay-pa-see) *n, pl* **-cies** **1** the office or term of office of a Pope **2** the system of government in the Roman Catholic Church that has the Pope as its head

papal *adj* of the Pope or the papacy

paparazzo (pap-a-rat-so) *n, pl* **-razzi** (-rat-see) a freelance photographer who specializes in taking shots of famous people without their knowledge or consent

papaya (pap-pie-a) *n* a large green fruit with sweet yellow flesh, that grows in the West Indies

paper *n* **1** a flexible material made in sheets from wood pulp or other fibres and used for writing on, decorating walls, or wrapping parcels **2** short for **newspaper** or **wallpaper** **3** **papers** documents, such as a passport, which can identify the bearer **4** a set of examination questions **5** **papers** the collected diaries or letters of someone's private or public life **6** a lecture or an essay on a specific subject **7** **on paper** in theory, as opposed to fact: *countless ideas which look good on paper just don't work in practice* ▸ *adj* **8** made of paper: *paper towels; a paper bag* **9** recorded on paper but not yet existing in practice: *a paper profit of more than $50 million* ▸ *vb* **10** to cover (walls) with wallpaper ▷ **papery** *adj*

> **paper** *n* **2** = newspaper, daily, journal, gazette **3** = documents, records, certificates, identification, deeds, identity papers, I.D. (*informal*) **4** = examination, test, exam **5** = letters, records, documents, file, diaries, archive, paperwork, dossier **6** = essay, article, treatise, dissertation ▸ *vb* = wallpaper, hang

paperback *n* **1** a book with covers made of flexible card ▸ *adj* **2** of a paperback or publication of paperbacks: *a paperback novel*

paperweight *n* a small heavy object placed on top of loose papers to prevent them from scattering

paperwork *n* clerical work, such as the writing of reports or letters

papier-mâché (pap-yay mash-ay) *n* **1** a hard substance made of layers of paper mixed with paste and moulded when moist ▸ *adj* **2** made of papier-mâché

papist *n, adj offensive* (a) Roman Catholic

papoose *n* a Native American baby

paprika *n* a mild powdered seasoning made from red peppers

papyrus (pap-ire-uss) *n, pl* **-ri** (-rye) or **-ruses** **1** a tall water plant of Africa **2** a kind of paper made from the stem of this plant, used by the ancient Egyptians, Greeks, and Romans **3** an ancient document written on this paper

par *n* **1** the usual or average condition: *I feel slightly below par most of the time* **2** *golf* a standard score for a hole or course that a good player should make: *four under par with two holes to play*

3 *finance* the established value of the unit of one national currency in terms of the unit of another **4 on a par with** equal or equivalent to: *an environmental disaster on a par with Chernobyl* **5 par for the course** to be expected: *random acts of violence were par for the course in the capital*

parable *n* a short story that uses familiar situations to illustrate a religious or moral point

parabola (par-ab-bol-a) *n geom* an open plane curve formed by the intersection of a cone by a plane parallel to its side ▸ **parabolic** *adj*

paracetamol *n* a mild pain-relieving drug

parachute *n* **1** a large fabric canopy connected by a harness, that slows the descent of a person or package from an aircraft ▸ *vb* **-chuting, -chuted 2** to land or to drop (supplies or troops) by parachute from an aircraft ▸ **parachutist** *n*

parade *n* **1** an ordered march or procession **2** a public promenade or street of shops **3** a blatant but sometimes insincere display: *a man who made a parade of liking his own company best* ▸ *vb* **-rading, -raded 4** to exhibit or flaunt: *he neither paraded nor disguised his devout faith* **5** to walk or march, esp. in a procession

> **parade** *n* **1** = procession, march, pageant, cavalcade ▸ *vb* **4** = flaunt, display, exhibit, show off (*informal*) **5** = march, process, promenade

paradigm (par-a-dime) *n* a model or example: *his experience is a paradigm for the young artist*

> **paradigm** *n* = model, example, pattern, ideal

paradise *n* **1** heaven; where the good go after death **2** the Garden of Eden **3** any place or condition that fulfils a person's desires

> **paradise** *n* **1** = heaven, Promised Land, Elysian fields **3** = bliss, delight, heaven (*informal*), felicity, utopia

paradox *n* **1** a statement that seems self-contradictory but may be true: *it's a strange paradox that a musician must practise improvising to become a good improviser* **2** a self-contradictory proposition, such as *I always tell lies* **3** a person or thing that is made up of contradictory elements ▸ **paradoxical** *adj* ▸ **paradoxically** *adv*

> **paradox** *n* = contradiction, puzzle, anomaly, enigma, oddity

paraffin *n Brit* a liquid mixture distilled from petroleum or shale and used as a fuel or solvent

paragon *n* a model of perfection: *a paragon of integrity and determination*

paragraph *n* **1** a section of a piece of writing, usually devoted to one idea, which begins on a new line and is often indented **2** *printing* the character ¶, used to indicate the beginning of a new paragraph ▸ *vb* **3** to put (a piece of writing) into paragraphs

> **paragraph** *n* **1** = section, part, item, passage, clause, subdivision

parakeet *n* a small colourful parrot with a long tail

parallax *n* an apparent change in an object's position due to a change in the observer's position

parallel *adj* **1** separated by an equal distance at every point: *parallel lines; a path parallel to the main road* **2** precisely corresponding: *we decide our salaries by comparison with parallel jobs in other charities* **3** *computers* operating on several items of information or instructions at the same time ▸ *n* **4** *maths* one of a set of parallel lines or planes **5** something with similar features to another **6** a comparison; similarity between two things: *she attempted to excuse herself by drawing a parallel between her behaviour and ours* **7** Also called: **parallel of latitude** any of the imaginary lines around the earth parallel to the equator, marking degrees of latitude **8** *printing* the character ‖, used as a reference mark ▸ *vb* **9** to correspond to: *the increase in smoking is paralleled by an increase in lung cancer*

> **parallel** *adj* **1** = equidistant, alongside, side by side; ≠ divergent **2** = matching, corresponding, like, similar, resembling, analogous; ≠ different ▸ *n* **5** = equivalent, counterpart, match, equal, twin, analogue; ≠ opposite **6** = similarity, comparison, analogy, resemblance, likeness; ≠ difference

parallelogram *n geom* a plane figure whose opposite sides are parallel and equal in length

paralyse *or US* **-lyze** *vb* **-lysing, -lysed** *or* **-lyzing, -lyzed 1** *pathol* to affect with paralysis **2** to make immobile: *he was paralysed by fear*

> **paralyse** *or* **-lyze** *vb* **1** = disable, cripple, lame, incapacitate **2** = freeze, stun, numb, petrify, halt, immobilize

paralysis *n* **1** *pathol* inability to move all or part of the body due to damage to the nervous system **2** a state of inactivity: *the economic chaos and political paralysis into which the country has sunk*

> **paralysis** *n* **1** = immobility, palsy **2** = standstill, breakdown, stoppage, halt

paralytic *adj* **1** of or relating to paralysis **2** *Brit informal* very drunk ▸ *n* **3** a person who is paralysed

paramedic *n* a person, such as a member of an ambulance crew, whose work supplements that of the medical profession ▸ **paramedical** *adj*

parameter (par-am-it-er) *n* **1** *maths* an arbitrary constant that determines the specific form of a mathematical expression, such as a and b in $y = ax^2 + b$ **2** *informal* any limiting factor: *exchange rates are allowed to fluctuate only within designated parameters*

> **parameter** *n* **2** = limit, restriction, framework, limitation, specification

paramilitary *adj* denoting a group of people organized on military lines

paramount *adj* of the greatest importance

> **paramount** *adj* = principal, prime, first, chief, main, primary, supreme, cardinal; ≠ secondary

paramour *n old-fashioned* someone's lover

paranoia *n* **1** a mental health condition which causes delusions of grandeur or of persecution **2** *informal* intense fear or suspicion, usually unfounded > **paranoid** or **paranoiac** *adj, n*

paranormal *adj* **1** beyond normal scientific explanation ▸ *n* **2 the paranormal** paranormal happenings or matters generally

parapet *n* **1** a low wall or railing along the edge of a balcony or roof **2** *military* a mound of sandbags in front of a trench to conceal and protect troops from fire

paraphernalia *n* various articles or bits of equipment

paraphrase *n* **1** an expression of a statement or text in other words ▸ *vb* **-phrasing, -phrased** **2** to put (a statement or text) into other words

paraplegia (par-a-**pleej**-ya) *n pathol* paralysis of the lower half of the body > **paraplegic** *adj, n*

parapsychology *n* the study of mental phenomena such as telepathy

Paraquat *n trademark* an extremely poisonous weedkiller

parasite *n* **1** an animal or plant that lives in or on another from which it obtains nourishment **2** a person who habitually lives at the expense of others; sponger > **parasitic** *adj*

> **parasite** *n* **2** = sponger (*informal*), leech, hanger-on, scrounger (*informal*), bloodsucker (*informal*), quandong (*Austral slang*)

parasol *n* an umbrella-like sunshade

paratrooper *n* a member of the paratroops

paratroops *pl n* troops trained to be dropped by parachute into a battle area

parboil *vb* to boil (food) until partially cooked

parcel *n* **1** something wrapped up; a package **2** a group of people or things sharing something in common: *a parcel of fools* **3** a distinct portion of land: *he was the recipient of a substantial parcel of land* ▸ *vb* **-celling, -celled** or US **-celing, -celed 4** (often foll. by *up*) to wrap (something) up into a parcel **5** (foll. by *out*) to divide (something) into portions: *the children were parcelled out to relatives*

> **parcel** *n* **1** = package, case, box, pack, bundle ▸ *vb* **4** = wrap, pack, package, tie up, do up, gift-wrap, box up, fasten together

parch *vb* **1** to deprive (something) of water; dry up: *the summer sun parched the hills* **2** to make (someone) very thirsty: *I'm parched. Have we got any lemonade?*

parchment *n* **1** a thick smooth material made from animal skin and used for writing on **2** a manuscript made of this material **3** a stiff yellowish paper resembling parchment

pardon *vb* **1** to forgive or excuse (a person) for (an offence, mistake, etc.): *I hope you'll pardon the wait* ▸ *n* **2** forgiveness **3** official release from punishment for a crime ▸ *interj* **4** Also: **pardon me, I beg your pardon** *A* sorry; excuse me **B** what did you say? > **pardonable** *adj*

> **pardon** *vb* = acquit, let off (*informal*), exonerate, absolve; ≠ punish ▸ *n* **2** = forgiveness, absolution; ≠ condemnation **3** = acquittal, amnesty, exoneration; ≠ punishment ▸ *interj* **4A pardon me** = forgive me, excuse me

pare *vb* **paring, pared 1** to peel (the outer layer) from (something): *thinly pare the rind from the grapefruit* **2** to trim or cut the edge of **3** to decrease bit by bit: *the government is prepared to pare down the armed forces*

parent *n* **1** a father or mother **2** a person acting as a father or mother; guardian **3** a plant or animal that has produced one or more plants or animals > **parental** *adj* > **parenthood** *n*

> **parent** *n* **1** = father or mother, sire, progenitor, procreator, old (*Austral, NZ informal*), oldie (*Austral informal*), patriarch

parentage *n* ancestry or family

parenthesis (par-en-**thiss**-iss) *n, pl* **-ses** (-seez) **1** a word or phrase inserted into a passage, and marked off by brackets or dashes **2** Also called: **bracket** either of a pair of characters ( ), used to enclose such a phrase > **parenthetical** *adj* > **parenthetically** *adv*

parenting *n* the activity of bringing up children

pariah (par-**rye**-a) *n* a social outcast: *the man they regard as a pariah*

parietal (par-**rye**-it-al) *adj anatomy & biol* of or forming the walls of a body cavity: *the parietal bones of the skull*

paring *n* something that has been cut off something

parish *n* **1** an area that has its own church and a priest or pastor. Related adjective: **parochial 2** the people who live in a parish **3** (in England and, formerly, Wales) the smallest unit of local government

> **parish** *n* **2** = community, flock, church, congregation **3** = district, community

parishioner *n* a person who lives in a particular parish

parity *n* **1** equality, for example of rank or pay **2** close or exact equivalence: *the company maintained parity with the competition* **3** *finance* equivalence between the units of currency of two countries

park *n* **1** a large area of open land for recreational use by the public **2** a piece of open land for public recreation in a town **3** *Brit* a large area of private land surrounding a country house **4** an area designed to accommodate a

number of related enterprises: *a science park*
5 *US & Canad* a playing field or sports stadium
6 the park *Brit informal* the pitch in soccer ▸ *vb*
7 to stop and leave (a vehicle) temporarily:
*I parked between the two cars already outside; police vans
were parked on every street corner* **8** *informal* to leave
or put (someone or something) somewhere: *she
parked herself on the sofa and stayed there all evening*
▸ **parking** *n*

park *n* **1** = recreation ground, garden,
playground, pleasure garden, playpark,
domain (NZ), forest park (NZ) **2, 3** = parkland,
grounds, estate (Brit), lawns, woodland,
grassland **5** = field, pitch, playing field

parka *n* a long jacket with a quilted lining and
a fur-trimmed hood
Parkinson's disease *or* **Parkinsonism** *n*
a progressive disorder of the central nervous
system which causes tremor, rigidity, and
impaired muscular coordination
parky *adj* **parkier**, **parkiest** *Brit informal* (of the
weather) chilly
parlance *n* the manner of speaking associated
with a particular group or subject: *he had, in
Marxist parlance, a 'petit bourgeois' mentality*
parley *old-fashioned* ▸ *n* **1** a discussion between
members of opposing sides to decide terms of
agreement ▸ *vb* **2** to have a parley
parliament *n* a law-making assembly of a
country

parliament *n* = assembly, council, congress,
senate, convention, legislature

parliamentary *adj* **1** of or from a parliament:
parliamentary elections **2** conforming to the
procedures of a parliament: *parliamentary
language*

parliamentary *adj* **1** = governmental,
legislative, law-making

parlour *or US* **parlor** *n* **1** *old-fashioned* a living
room for receiving visitors **2** a room or shop
equipped as a place of business: *an ice-cream
parlour*

parlour *or* **parlor** *n* **1** = sitting room (Brit),
lounge, living room, drawing room, front
room **2** = establishment, shop, store, salon

parlous *adj archaic or humorous* dangerously bad;
dire: *the parlous state of the economy*
Parmesan (par-miz-zan) *n* a hard strong-
flavoured cheese used grated on pasta dishes
and soups
parochial *adj* **1** narrow in outlook; provincial
2 of or relating to a parish ▸ **parochialism** *n*
parody *n, pl* **-dies 1** a piece of music or literature
that mimics the style of another composer or
author in a humorous way **2** something done so
badly that it seems like an intentional mockery
▸ *vb* **-dies, -dying, -died 3** to make a parody of
▸ **parodist** *n*

parody *n* **1** = takeoff (*informal*), satire,
caricature, send-up (Brit *informal*), spoof
(*informal*), skit, burlesque, piss-take (*informal*)
▸ *vb* = take off (*informal*), caricature, send up
(Brit *informal*), burlesque, satirize, do a takeoff
of (*informal*)

parole *n* **1** the freeing of a prisoner before his or
her sentence has run out, on condition that he
or she behaves well **2** a promise given by a
prisoner to behave well if granted liberty or
partial liberty **3 on parole** conditionally
released from prison ▸ *vb* **-roling, -roled**
4 to place (a person) on parole
paroxysm *n* **1** an uncontrollable outburst of
emotion: *a paroxysm of grief* **2** *pathol* **A** a sudden
attack or recurrence of a disease **B** a fit or
convulsion ▸ **paroxysmal** *adj*
parquet (par-kay) *n* **1** a floor covering made of
blocks of wood ▸ *vb* **2** to cover (a floor) with
parquetry
parquetry (par-kit-tree) *n* pieces of wood
arranged in a geometric pattern, used to cover
floors
parricide *n* **1** a person who kills one of his or
her parents **2** the act of killing either of one's
parents ▸ **parricidal** *adj*
parrot *n* **1** a tropical bird with a short hooked
beak, bright plumage, and an ability to mimic
human speech **2** a person who repeats or
imitates someone else's words **3 sick as a parrot**
usually facetious extremely disappointed ▸ *vb*
-roting, -roted 4 to repeat or imitate (someone
else's words) without understanding them

parrot *vb* = repeat, echo, imitate, copy,
mimic

parry *vb* **-ries, -rying, -ried 1** to ward off (an
attack) **2** to avoid answering (questions) in a
clever way ▸ *n, pl* **-ries 3** an instance of parrying
4 a skilful evasion of a question

parry *vb* **1** = ward off, block, deflect, repel,
rebuff, repulse **2** = evade, avoid, dodge,
sidestep

parse (parz) *vb* **parsing, parsed** to analyse
(a sentence or the words in a sentence)
grammatically
parsimony *n formal* extreme caution in
spending ▸ **parsimonious** *adj*
parsley *n* a herb with curled pleasant-smelling
leaves, used for seasoning and garnishing food
parsnip *n* a long tapering cream-coloured root
vegetable
parson *n* **1** a parish priest in the Church of
England **2** any member of the clergy **3** NZ a
nonconformist minister

parson *n* **2** = clergyman, minister, priest,
vicar, preacher, pastor, cleric, churchman

parsonage *n* the residence of a parson,
provided by the parish

part n 1 a piece or portion 2 one of several equal divisions: *a salad dressing made with two parts oil to one part vinegar* 3 an actor's role in a play 4 a person's duty: *his ancestors had done their part nobly and well at Bannockburn* 5 an involvement in or contribution to something: *he was jailed for his part in the fraud* 6 a region or area: *he's well known in these parts; the weather in this part of the country is extreme* 7 *anatomy* an area of the body 8 a component that can be replaced in a vehicle or machine 9 *US, Canad & Austral* same as **parting** (sense 2) 10 *music* a melodic line assigned to one or more instrumentalists or singers 11 **for my part** as far as I am concerned 12 **for the most part** generally 13 **in part** to some degree; partly 14 **on the part of** on behalf of 15 **part and parcel of** an essential ingredient of 16 **play a part** A to pretend to be what one is not B (foll. by in) to have something to do with: *examinations play a large part in education and in schools* 17 **take part in** to participate in 18 **take someone's part** to support someone, for example in an argument 19 **take something in good part** to respond to (teasing or criticism) with good humour ▸ vb 20 to divide or separate from one another: *her lips parted in laughter; the cord parted with a pop* 21 to go away from one another: *we parted with handshakes all round* 22 to split: *the path parts here* 23 to arrange (the hair) in such a way that a line of scalp is left showing 24 **part from** to cause (someone) to give up: *I was astonished at the way Henry parted his audience from their money* 25 **part with** to give up: *check carefully before you part with your cash* ▸ adv 26 to some extent; partly: *this book is part history, part travelogue*

> **part** n 1 = piece, share, proportion, percentage, bit, section, scrap, portion; ≠ entirety 2, 8 = component, bit, unit, constituent 3 = role, representation, persona, portrayal, depiction, character part 6 = region, area, district, neighbourhood, quarter, vicinity 7 = organ, member, limb ▸ vb 20 = divide, separate, break, tear, split, rend (*literary*), detach, sever; ≠ join 21 = part company, separate, split up; ≠ meet

partake vb **-taking, -took, -taken** 1 **partake in** to take part in 2 **partake of** to take (food or drink)

partial adj 1 relating to only a part; not complete: *partial deafness* 2 biased: *religious programmes can be as partial as they like* 3 **be partial to** to have a particular liking for > **partiality** n > **partially** adv

> **partial** adj 1 = incomplete, unfinished, imperfect, uncompleted; ≠ complete 2 = biased, prejudiced, discriminatory, partisan, unfair, one-sided, unjust; ≠ unbiased

participate vb **-pating, -pated** > **participate in** to become actively involved in > **participant** n > **participation** n > **participatory** adj

participle n *grammar* a form of a verb that is used in compound tenses or as an adjective > **participial** adj

particle n 1 an extremely small piece or amount: *clean thoroughly to remove all particles of dirt* 2 *grammar* an uninflected part of speech, such as an interjection or preposition 3 *physics* a minute piece of matter, such as an electron or proton

> **particle** n 1 = bit, piece, scrap, grain, shred, mite, jot, speck

particular adj 1 of, belonging to, or being one person or thing; specific: *the particular type of tuition on offer* 2 exceptional or special: *the report voices particular concern over the state of the country's manufacturing industry* 3 providing specific details or circumstances: *a particular account* 4 difficult to please; fussy ▸ n 5 a separate distinct item as opposed to a generalization: *moving from the general to the particular* 6 an item of information; detail: *she refused to go into particulars* 7 **in particular** especially or exactly: *three painters in particular were responsible for these developments* > **particularly** adv

> **particular** adj 1 = specific, special, exact, precise, distinct, peculiar; ≠ general 2 = special, exceptional, notable, uncommon, marked, unusual, remarkable, singular 4 = fussy, demanding, fastidious, choosy (*informal*), picky (*informal*), finicky, pernickety (*informal*), nit-picky (*informal*); ≠ indiscriminate ▸ n 6 = detail, fact, feature, item, circumstance, specification

particularize or **-rise** vb **-rizing, -rized** or **-rising, -rised** to give details about (something) > **particularization** or **-risation** n

parting n 1 a departure or leave-taking 2 *Brit & NZ* the line of scalp showing when sections of hair are combed in opposite directions 3 the act of dividing (something): *the parting of the Red Sea*

> **parting** n 1 = farewell, goodbye 3 = division, breaking, split, separation, rift, rupture

partisan n 1 a person who supports a particular cause or party 2 a member of an armed resistance group within occupied territory ▸ adj 3 prejudiced or one-sided > **partisanship** n

> **partisan** n 1 = supporter, devotee, adherent, upholder; ≠ opponent 2 = underground fighter, guerrilla, freedom fighter, resistance fighter ▸ adj = prejudiced, one-sided, biased, partial, sectarian; ≠ unbiased

partition n 1 a large screen or thin wall that divides a room 2 the division of a country into two or more independent countries ▸ vb 3 to separate (a room) into sections: *the shower is partitioned off from the rest of the bathroom* 4 to divide (a country) into separate self-governing parts: *the subcontinent was partitioned into India and Pakistan*

partition *n* **1** = screen, wall, barrier **2** = division, separation, segregation ▸ *vb* **3** = separate, screen, divide

partly *adv* not completely

partly *adv* = partially, somewhat, slightly; ≠ completely

partner *n* **1** either member of a couple in a relationship **2** a member of a business partnership **3** one of a pair of dancers or of players on the same side in a game: *her bridge partner* **4** an ally or companion: *the country's main European trading partner* ▸ *vb* **5** to be the partner of (someone)

partner *n* **1** = spouse, consort, significant other (*informal, chiefly US*), mate, husband *or* wife, plus-one (*informal*) **2** = associate, colleague, collaborator **4** = companion, ally, colleague, associate, mate, comrade

partnership *n* **1** a relationship in which two or more people or organizations work together in a business venture **2** the condition of being a partner

partnership *n* **1** = cooperation, alliance, sharing, union, connection, participation, copartnership

part of speech *n grammar* a class of words, such as a noun, verb, or adjective, sharing important syntactic or semantic features

partridge *n, pl* **-tridges** *or* **-tridge** a game bird with an orange-brown head, greyish neck, and a short rust-coloured tail

part-time *adj* **1** for less than the normal full working time: *a part-time job* ▸ *adv* **part time 2** on a part-time basis: *he works part time* ▸ **part-timer** *n*

parturition *n formal* the process of giving birth

party *n, pl* **-ties 1** a social gathering for pleasure **2** a group of people involved in the same activity: *a search party* **3** a group of people sharing a common political aim **4** the person or people who take part in or are involved in something, esp. a legal action or dispute: *a judge will decide who the guilty party is* **5** *informal, humorous* a person: *he's an odd old party* ▸ *vb* **-ties, -tying, -tied 6** *informal* to celebrate; have a good time

party *n* **1** = get-together (*informal*), celebration, do (*informal*), gathering, function, reception, festivity, social gathering **2** = group, team, band, company, unit, squad, crew, gang **3** = faction, set, side, league, camp, clique, coterie

party line *n* **1** the policies of a political party **2** a telephone line shared by two or more subscribers

party wall *n property law* a common wall separating two properties

parvenu *or fem* **parvenue** (par-ven-new) *n* a person newly risen to a position of power or wealth who is considered to lack culture or education

pascal *n* the SI unit of pressure; the pressure exerted on an area of 1 square metre by a force of 1 newton

pash *Austral & NZ slang* ▸ *vb* **1** to kiss or embrace passionately ▸ *n* **2** a passionate kiss or embrace

pashmina (pash-mee-na) *n* a type of cashmere scarf or shawl made from the underfur of Tibetan goats

paspalum (pass-pale-um) *n Austral & NZ* a type of grass with wide leaves

pass *vb* **1** to go by or past (a person or thing) **2** to continue or extend in a particular direction: *the road to Camerino passes through some fine scenery* **3** to go through or cause (something) to go through (an obstacle or barrier): *the bullet passed through his head* **4** to be successful in (a test or examination) **5** to spend (time) or (of time) go by: *the time passed surprisingly quickly* **6** to hand over or be handed over: *she passed me her glass* **7** to be inherited by: *his mother's small estate had passed to him after her death* **8** *sport* to hit, kick, or throw (the ball) to another player **9** (of a law-making body) to agree to (a law or proposal): *the bill was passed by parliament last week* **10** to pronounce (judgment): *the court is expected to pass sentence later today* **11** to move onwards or over: *a flicker of amusement passed over his face* **12** to exceed: *Australia's population has just passed the 25 million mark* **13** to go without comment: *the insult passed unnoticed* **14** to choose not to answer a question or not to make a bid or a play in card games **15** to discharge (urine, etc.) from the body **16** to come to an end or disappear: *today's jitters will soon pass* **17** (foll. by *for* or *as*) to be likely to be mistaken for (someone or something else): *the few sunny days that pass for summer in this country* **18** *old-fashioned* to take place: *what passed at the meeting?* **19 pass away** *or* **on** *euphemistic* to die ▸ *n* **20** a successful result in an examination or test **21** *sport* the transfer of a ball from one player to another **22** a route through a range of mountains where there is a gap between peaks **23** a permit or licence **24** *military* a document authorizing leave of absence **25** *bridge etc.* an instance of choosing not to answer a question or not to make a bid or a play in card games **26 a pretty pass** a bad state of affairs **27 make a pass at** *informal* to try to persuade (someone) to have sex ▸ See also **pass out** *etc.*

pass *vb* **1** = go by *or* past, overtake, drive past, lap, leave behind, pull ahead of; ≠ stop **3, 11** = go, move, travel, progress, flow, proceed **4** = be successful in, qualify (in), succeed (in), graduate (in), get through, do, gain a pass (in); ≠ fail **5** = elapse, progress, go by, lapse, wear on, go past, tick by **6** = give, hand, send, transfer, deliver, convey **7** = be left, come, be bequeathed, be inherited by **8** = kick, hit, loft, head, lob **9** = approve, accept, decree, enact, ratify, ordain (*formal*), legislate (for); ≠ ban **12** = exceed, beat, overtake, go beyond, surpass, outstrip, outdo **16** = end, go, cease, blow over **19 pass away or on** = die, pass on, expire, pass over, snuff it (*informal*), kick the bucket (*slang*), shuffle off this mortal coil, cark it (*Austral, NZ informal*) ▸ *n* **22** = gap, route, canyon, gorge, ravine **23** = licence, ticket, permit, passport, warrant, authorization

passable *adj* **1** adequate or acceptable: *passable if hardly faultless German* **2** (of a road, path, etc.) capable of being travelled along: *most main roads are passable with care despite the snow* > **passably** *adv*

passage *n* **1** a channel or opening providing a way through **2** a hall or corridor **3** a section of a written work, speech, or piece of music **4** a journey by ship **5** the act of passing from one place or condition to another: *Ireland faced a tough passage to qualify for the World Cup finals* **6** the right or freedom to pass: *the aid convoys were guaranteed safe passage through rebel-held areas* **7** the establishing of a law by a law-making body

passage *n* **1** = alley, way, close (*Brit*), course, road, channel, route, path **2** = corridor, hall, lobby, vestibule **3** = extract, reading, piece, section, text, excerpt, quotation **4** = journey, crossing, trip, trek, voyage **6** = safe-conduct, right to travel, freedom to travel, permission to travel

passageway *n* a corridor or passage

passbook *n* **1** a book issued by a bank or building society for recording deposits and withdrawals **2** *S African* (formerly) an official identity document

passé (pas-say) *adj* out-of-date: *smoking is a bit passé these days*

passenger *n* **1** a person travelling in a vehicle driven by someone else **2** *Brit & NZ* a member of a team who does not take an equal share of the work: *you'll have to pull your weight – we can't afford passengers*

passenger *n* **1** = traveller, rider, fare, commuter, fare payer

passer-by *n, pl* **passers-by** a person who is walking past someone or something

passer-by *n* = bystander, witness, observer, viewer, spectator, looker-on, watcher, onlooker

passim *adv* throughout: used to indicate that what is referred to occurs frequently in a particular piece of writing

passing *adj* **1** momentary or short-lived: *a passing fad* **2** casual or superficial: *a passing resemblance* ▸ *n* **3** *euphemistic* death **4** the ending of something: *the passing of the old order in Eastern Europe* **5 in passing** briefly and without going into detail; incidentally: *this fact is only noted in passing*

passing *adj* **1** = momentary, fleeting, short-lived, transient, ephemeral, brief, temporary, transitory **2** = superficial, short, quick, glancing, casual, summary, cursory, perfunctory

passion *n* **1** intense sexual love **2** any strongly felt emotion **3** a strong enthusiasm for something: *a passion for football* **4** the object of an intense desire or enthusiasm: *flying is his abiding passion* > **passionless** *adj*

passion *n* **1** = love, desire, lust, infatuation, ardour **2** = emotion, feeling, fire, heat, excitement, intensity, warmth, zeal; ≠ indifference **3, 4** = mania, enthusiasm, obsession, bug (*informal*), craving, fascination, craze

Passion *n* *Christianity* the sufferings of Christ from the Last Supper to his death on the cross

passionate *adj* **1** showing intense sexual desire **2** capable of or revealing intense emotion: *a passionate speech* > **passionately** *adv*

passionate *adj* **1** = loving, ardent, amorous, lustful; ≠ cold **2** = emotional, eager, strong, intense, fierce, ardent, fervent, heartfelt; ≠ unemotional

passionflower *n* a tropical plant with brightly coloured showy flowers

passion fruit *n* the edible egg-shaped fruit of the passionflower

Passion play *n* a play about the Passion of Christ

passive *adj* **1** not taking an active part **2** submissive and receptive to outside forces **3** *grammar* denoting a form of verbs used to indicate that the subject is the recipient of the action, as *was broken* in *The glass was broken by that boy over there* **4** *chem* (of a substance) chemically unreactive ▸ *n* **5** *grammar* the passive form of a verb > **passively** *adv* > **passivity** *n*

passive *adj* **1** = inactive, uninvolved; ≠ active **2** = submissive, compliant, receptive, docile, quiescent; ≠ spirited

passive-aggressive *adj* *psychol* of or relating to a personality that harbours aggressive emotions while behaving in a calm or detached manner

passive resistance *n* resistance to a government or the law by nonviolent acts such as fasting, peaceful demonstrations, or refusing to cooperate

passive smoking *n* the unwilling inhalation of smoke from other people's cigarettes by a nonsmoker

pass out *vb* **1** *informal* to become unconscious; faint **2** *Brit* (of an officer cadet) to qualify for a military commission

pass out *vb* **1** = faint, black out (*informal*), lose consciousness, become unconscious

P

Passover *n* an eight-day Jewish festival commemorating the sparing of the Israelites in Egypt

passport *n* **1** an official document issued by a government, which identifies the holder and grants him or her permission to travel abroad **2** an asset that gains a person admission or acceptance: *good qualifications are no automatic passport to a job*

pass up *vb informal* to let (something) go by; disregard: *am I passing up my one chance to be really happy?*

> **pass up** *vb* **pass something up** = miss, let slip, decline, neglect, forgo, abstain from, give (something) a miss (*informal*)

password *n* a secret word or phrase that ensures admission by proving identity or membership

past *adj* **1** of the time before the present: *the past history of the world* **2** no longer in existence: *past happiness* **3** immediately previous: *the past year* **4** former: *a past president* **5** *grammar* indicating a tense of verbs used to describe actions that have been begun or completed at the time of speaking ▸ *n* **6** **the past** the period of time before the present: *a familiar face from the past* **7** the history of a person or nation **8** an earlier disreputable period of someone's life: *a man with a bit of a past* **9** *grammar* **A** the past tense **B** a verb in the past tense ▸ *adv* **10** on or onwards: *I called but he just walked past* **11** at a time before the present; ago: *three years past* ▸ *prep* **12** beyond in time: *it's past midnight* **13** beyond in place: *a procession of mourners filed past the coffin* **14** beyond the limit of: *riches past his wildest dreams* **15** **not put it past someone** to consider someone capable of (a particular action): *I wouldn't put it past him to double-cross us* **16** **past it** *informal* unable to do the things one could do when younger

> **past** *adj* **1** = former, early, previous, ancient, bygone, olden; ≠ future **2** = over, done, ended, finished, gone **3** = last, previous **4** = previous, former, one-time, ex- ▸ *n* **6** = former times, long ago, days gone by, the olden days; ≠ future **7** = background, life, history, past life, life story, career to date ▸ *adv* **10** = on, by, along ▸ *prep* **12** = after, beyond, later than **13** = by, across, in front of

pasta *n* a type of food, such as spaghetti, that is made from a dough of flour and water and formed into different shapes

paste *n* **1** a soft moist mixture, such as toothpaste **2** an adhesive made from water and flour or starch, for use with paper **3** a smooth creamy preparation of fish, meat, or vegetables for spreading on bread: *sausage paste* **4** *Brit & NZ* dough for making pastry **5** a hard shiny glass used to make imitation gems ▸ *vb* **pasting**, **pasted 6** to attach by paste: *she bought a scrapbook and carefully pasted in it all her clippings* **7** *slang* to beat or defeat (someone)

paste *n* **2** = adhesive, glue, cement, gum **3** = purée, pâté, spread ▸ *vb* **6** = stick, glue, cement, gum

pasteboard *n* a stiff board made by pasting layers of paper together

pastel *n* **1 A** a crayon made of ground pigment bound with gum **B** a picture drawn with such crayons **2** a pale delicate colour ▸ *adj* **3** (of a colour) pale and delicate: *pastel pink*

> **pastel** *adj* = pale, light, soft, delicate, muted; ≠ bright

pasteurize *or* **-rise** *vb* **-rizing, -rized** *or* **-rising, -rised** to destroy bacteria (in beverages or solid foods) by a special heating process
> **pasteurization** *or* **-risation** *n*

pastiche (past-*eesh*) *n* a work of art that mixes styles or copies the style of another artist

pastille *n* a small fruit-flavoured and sometimes medicated sweet

pastime *n* an activity which makes time pass pleasantly

> **pastime** *n* = activity, game, entertainment, hobby, recreation, amusement, diversion

pasting *n* **1** *slang* a thrashing or heavy defeat **2** *informal* strong criticism

past master *n* a person with a talent for or experience in a particular activity: *a past master at manipulating the media*

pastor *n* a member of the Christian clergy in charge of a congregation

> **pastor** *n* = clergyman *or* woman, minister, priest, vicar, parson, rector, curate, churchman *or* woman

pastoral *adj* **1** of or depicting country life or scenery **2** (of land) used for pasture **3** of or relating to a member of the Christian clergy or his or her duties **4** of or relating to shepherds or their work ▸ *n* **5** a literary work, picture, or piece of music portraying country life **6** *Christianity* a letter from a bishop to the clergy or people of his diocese

> **pastoral** *adj* **1** = rustic, country, rural, bucolic **3** = ecclesiastical, priestly, ministerial, clerical

pastrami *n* highly seasoned smoked beef

pastry *n* **1** a dough of flour, water, and fat **2** *pl* **-tries** an individual cake or pie **3** baked foods, such as tarts, made with this dough

pasture *n* **1** land covered with grass, suitable for grazing by farm animals **2** the grass growing on this land

> **pasture** *n* **1** = grassland, grass, meadow, grazing

pasty¹ (pay-*stee*) *adj* **pastier, pastiest** (of the complexion) pale and unhealthy-looking

pasty² (past-*ee*) *n, pl* **pasties** a round of pastry folded over a filling of meat and vegetables

pat¹ *vb* **patting, patted** 1 to tap (someone or something) lightly with the hand ▸ *n* 2 a gentle tap or stroke 3 a small shaped lump of something soft, such as butter

> **pat** *vb* = stroke, touch, tap, pet, caress, fondle ▸ *n* 2 = tap, stroke, clap

pat² *adv* 1 Also: **off pat** thoroughly learned: *he had all his answers off pat* ▸ *adj* 2 quick, ready, or glib: *a pat generalization*

patch *n* 1 a piece of material used to cover a hole in a garment 2 a small contrasting section: *there was a bald patch on the top of his head* 3 a small plot of land 4 *med* a protective covering for an injured eye 5 a scrap or remnant 6 the area under someone's supervision, such as a police officer or social worker 7 **a bad patch** a difficult time 8 **not a patch on** not nearly as good as ▸ *vb* 9 to mend (a garment) with a patch 10 **patch together** to produce (something) by piecing parts together hurriedly or carelessly 11 **patch up A** to mend (something) hurriedly or carelessly **B** to make up (a quarrel)

> **patch** *n* 1 = reinforcement, piece of fabric, piece of cloth, piece of material, piece sewn on 2, 5 = spot (Brit), bit, scrap, shred, small piece 3 = plot, area, ground, land, tract ▸ *vb* 9 = sew (up), mend, repair, reinforce, stitch (up) 11A = mend, cover, reinforce

patchwork *n* 1 needlework done by sewing together pieces of different materials 2 something made up of various parts

patchy *adj* **patchier, patchiest** 1 of uneven quality or intensity: *since then her career has been patchy* 2 having or forming patches

pate *n* *old-fashioned or humorous* the head or the crown of the head

pâté (pat-ay) *n* a spread of finely minced meat, fish, or vegetables often served as a starter

patella (pat-tell-a) *n, pl* **-lae** (-lee) *anatomy* kneecap > **patellar** *adj*

patent *n* 1 **A** an official document granting the exclusive right to make, use, and sell an invention for a limited period **B** the right granted by such a document 2 an invention protected by a patent ▸ *adj* 3 open or available for inspection: *letters patent* 4 obvious: *their scorn was patent to everyone* 5 concerning protection of or appointment by a patent 6 (of food, drugs, etc.) made or held under a patent ▸ *vb* 7 to obtain a patent for (an invention)

> **patent** *n* 1 = copyright, licence, franchise, registered trademark ▸ *adj* 4 = obvious, apparent, evident, clear, glaring, manifest

patent leather *n* leather processed with lacquer to give a hard glossy surface

patently *adv* clearly and obviously: *an outdated and patently absurd promise*

paternal *adj* 1 fatherly: *paternal authority* 2 related through one's father: *his paternal grandmother* > **paternally** *adv*

paternalism *n* authority exercised in a way that limits individual responsibility > **paternalistic** *adj*

paternity *n* 1 the fact or state of being a father 2 descent or derivation from a father

path *n, pl* **paths** 1 a road or way, often a narrow trodden track 2 a surfaced walk, such as through a garden 3 the course or direction in which something moves: *his car skidded into the path of an oncoming lorry* 4 a course of conduct: *the path of reconciliation and forgiveness*

> **path** *n* 1, 2 = way, road, walk, track, trail, avenue, footpath, berm (NZ) 3 = route, way, course, direction 4 = course, way, road, route

pathetic *adj* 1 arousing pity or sympathy 2 distressingly inadequate: *his pathetic attempt to maintain a stiff upper lip failed* > **pathetically** *adv*

> **pathetic** *adj* 1 = sad, moving, touching, affecting, distressing, tender, poignant, plaintive; ≠ funny

pathname *n* *computers* the name of a file or directory together with its position in relation to other directories

pathogen *n* any agent, such as a bacterium, that can cause disease > **pathogenic** *adj*

pathological *adj* 1 of or relating to pathology 2 *informal* compulsively motivated: *pathological jealousy*

pathology *n* the branch of medicine that studies diseases > **pathologist** *n*

pathos *n* the power, for example in literature, of arousing feelings of pity or sorrow

patience *n* 1 the capacity for calmly enduring difficult situations: *the endless patience of the nurses* 2 the ability to wait calmly for something to happen without complaining or giving up: *he urged the international community to have patience to allow sanctions to work* 3 Brit & NZ a card game for one player only

> **patience** *n* 1 = forbearance, tolerance, serenity, restraint, calmness, sufferance; ≠ impatience 2 = endurance, resignation, submission, fortitude, long-suffering, perseverance, stoicism, constancy

patient *adj* 1 enduring difficult situations with an even temper 2 persevering or diligent: *his years of patient work may finally pay off* ▸ *n* 3 a person who is receiving medical care > **patiently** *adv*

> **patient** *adj* 1 = forbearing, understanding, forgiving, mild, tolerant, indulgent, lenient, even-tempered; ≠ impatient 2 = long-suffering, resigned, calm, enduring, philosophical, persevering, stoical, submissive ▸ *n* = sick person, case, sufferer, invalid

patina *n* 1 a film formed on the surface of a metal 2 the sheen on the surface of an old object, caused by age and much handling

p

patio *n, pl* **-tios 1** a paved area adjoining a house: *a barbecue on the patio* **2** an open inner courtyard in a Spanish or Spanish-American house

patois (pat-wah) *n, pl* **patois** (pat-wahz) **1** a regional dialect of a language **2** the jargon of a particular group

patriarch *n* **1** the male head of a tribe or family **2** *Bible* any of the men regarded as the fathers of the human race or of the Hebrew people **3 A** *RC Church* the pope **B** *Eastern Orthodox Church* a highest-ranking bishop **4** an old man who is respected ▷ **patriarchal** *adj*

patriarchy *n* **1** a form of social organization in which males hold most of the power **2** *pl* **-chies** a society governed by such a system

patrician *n* **1** a member of the nobility of ancient Rome **2** an aristocrat **3** a person of refined conduct and tastes ▷ *adj* **4** (in ancient Rome) of or relating to patricians **5** aristocratic

patricide *n* **1** the act of killing one's father **2** a person who kills his or her father ▷ **patricidal** *adj*

patrimony *n, pl* **-nies** an inheritance from one's father or other ancestor

patriot *n* a person who loves his or her country and passionately supports its interests ▷ **patriotic** *adj* ▷ **patriotically** *adv* ▷ **patriotism** *n*

> **patriot** *n* = nationalist, loyalist, chauvinist

patrol *n* **1** the action of going round an area or building at regular intervals for purposes of security or observation **2** a person or group that carries out such an action **3** a group of soldiers or ships involved in patrolling a particular area **4** a division of a troop of Scouts or Guides ▷ *vb* **-trolling, -trolled 5** to engage in a patrol of (a place): *peacekeepers patrolled several areas of the city*

> **patrol** *n* **2** = guard, watch, watchman, sentinel, patrolman ▷ *vb* = police, guard, keep watch (on), inspect, safeguard, keep guard (on)

patron *n* **1** a person who financially supports artists, writers, musicians, or charities **2** a regular customer of a shop, hotel, etc.

> **patron** *n* **1** = supporter, friend, champion, sponsor, backer, helper, benefactor, philanthropist **2** = customer, client, buyer, frequenter, shopper, habitué

patronage *n* **1** the support or custom given by a patron **2** (in politics) the ability or power to appoint people to jobs **3** a condescending manner

> **patronage** *n* **1** = support, promotion, sponsorship, backing, help, aid, assistance

patronize *or* **-nise** *vb* **-nizing, -nized** *or* **-nising, -nised 1** to treat (someone) in a condescending way **2** to be a patron of ▷ **patronizing** *or* **-nising** *adj* ▷ **patronizingly** *or* **-nisingly** *adv*

patron saint *n* a saint regarded as the particular guardian of a country or a group of people

patronymic *n* a name derived from one's father's or a male ancestor's

patter[1] *vb* **1** to make repeated light tapping sounds **2** to walk with quick soft steps ▷ *n* **3** a quick succession of light tapping sounds, such as by feet: *the steady patter of rain against the window*

patter[2] *n* **1** the glib rapid speech of comedians or salespeople **2** chatter **3** the jargon of a particular group ▷ *vb* **4** to speak glibly and rapidly

pattern *n* **1** an arrangement of repeated parts or decorative designs **2** a regular recognizable way that something is done: *I followed a normal eating pattern* **3** a plan or diagram used as a guide to making something: *a knitting pattern* **4** a model worthy of imitation: *a pattern of kindness* **5** a representative sample ▷ *vb* **6** (foll. by *after* or *on*) to model: *an orchestra patterned after Count Basie's*

> **pattern** *n* **1** = design, arrangement, motif, figure, device, decoration **2** = order, plan, system, method, sequence **3** = plan, design, original, guide, diagram, stencil, template

patterned *adj* having a decorative pattern on it: *a selection of plain and patterned fabrics*

patty *n, pl* **-ties 1** a small flattened cake of minced food **2** a small round pie filled with meat or vegetables

paucity *n formal* **1** scarcity **2** smallness of amount or number

paunch *n* a protruding belly or abdomen ▷ **paunchy** *adj*

pauper *n* **1** a person who is extremely poor **2** (formerly) a person supported by public charity

pause *vb* **pausing, paused 1** to stop doing (something) for a short time **2** to hesitate: *she answered him without pausing* ▷ *n* **3** a temporary stop or rest in speech or action **4** *music* a continuation of a note or rest beyond its normal length **5 give someone pause** to cause someone to hesitate: *it gave him pause for reflection*

> **pause** *vb* = stop briefly, delay, break, wait, rest, halt, cease, interrupt; ≠ continue ▷ *n* **3** = stop, break, interval, rest, gap, halt, respite, lull; ≠ continuance

pave *vb* **paving, paved 1** to cover (a road or area of ground) with a firm surface to make it suitable for walking or travelling on **2 pave the way for** to prepare or make easier: *the arrests paved the way for the biggest-ever Mafia trial*

> **pave** *vb* **1** = cover, floor, surface, concrete, tile

pavement *n* **1** a hard-surfaced path for pedestrians, alongside and a little higher than a road **2** the material used in paving **3** *US* the surface of a road

pavilion *n* **1** a building at a sports ground, esp. a cricket pitch, in which players can wash and change **2** an open building or temporary structure used for exhibitions **3** a summerhouse or other decorative shelter **4** a large ornate tent

paw *n* **1** a four-legged mammal's foot with claws and pads **2** *informal* a hand ▸ *vb* **3** to scrape or hit with the paws **4** *informal* to touch or caress (someone) in a rough or overfamiliar manner

> **paw** *vb* **4** = manhandle, grab, maul, molest, handle roughly

pawn¹ *vb* **1** to deposit (an article) as security for money borrowed **2** to stake or risk: *I will pawn my honour on this matter* ▸ *n* **3** an article deposited as security **4** the condition of being so deposited: *in pawn*

pawn² *n* **1** a chessman of the lowest value, usually able to move only one square forward at a time **2** a person or thing manipulated by someone else: *our city is just a pawn in their power games*

pawnbroker *n* a person licensed to lend money on goods deposited > **pawnbroking** *n*

pay *vb* **pays, paying, paid** **1** to give (money) in return for goods or services: *Willie paid for the drinks; nurses are not very well paid* **2** to settle (a debt or obligation) by giving or doing something: *he has paid his debt to society* **3** to suffer: *she paid dearly for her mistake* **4** to give (a compliment, regards, attention, etc.) **5** to profit or benefit (someone): *it doesn't always pay to be honest* **6** to make (a visit or call) **7** to yield a return of: *the account pays 5% interest* **8 pay one's way** **A** to contribute one's share of expenses **B** to remain solvent without outside help ▸ *n* **9** money given in return for work or services; a salary or wage **10 in the pay of** employed by ▸ See also **pay off, pay out**

> **pay** *vb* **1** = reward, compensate, reimburse, recompense, requite, remunerate (*formal*), front up **2** = settle **4** = give, extend, present with, grant, hand out, bestow **5** = be profitable, make money, make a return **7** = bring in, earn, return, net, yield ▸ *n* **9** = wages, income, payment, earnings, fee, reward, salary, allowance

payable *adj* **1** (often foll. by *on*) due to be paid: *the instalments are payable on the third of each month* **2** that is capable of being paid: *pensions are payable to those disabled during the wars*

> **payable** *adj* **1** = due, outstanding, owed, owing

payday *n* the day on which wages or salaries are paid

PAYE (in Britain, Australia, and New Zealand) pay as you earn; a system by which income tax is deducted by employers and paid directly to the government

payee *n* the person to whom a cheque or money order is made out

paying guest *n euphemistic* a lodger

payload *n* **1** the amount of passengers, cargo, or bombs which an aircraft can carry **2** the part of a cargo which earns revenue **3** the explosive power of a warhead or bomb carried by a missile or aircraft

payment *n* **1** the act of paying **2** a sum of money paid **3** something given in return; punishment or reward

> **payment** *n* **1** = settlement, paying, discharge, remittance **2** = remittance, advance, deposit, premium, instalment, e-payment **3** = wages, fee, reward, hire, remuneration

pay off *vb* **1** to pay the complete amount of (a debt) **2** to pay (someone) all that is due in wages and dismiss him or her from employment **3** to turn out successfully: *her persistence finally paid off* **4** *informal* to give a bribe to ▸ *n* **payoff** **5** *informal* the climax or outcome of events **6** *informal* a bribe **7** the final payment of a debt **8** the final settlement, esp. in retribution: *the payoff came when the gang besieged the squealer's house*

> **pay off** *vb* **1 pay something off** = settle, clear, square, discharge, pay in full **3** = succeed, work, be effective

payola *n informal* a bribe to secure special treatment, esp. to promote a commercial product

pay out *vb* **1** to spend (money) on a particular thing **2** to release (a rope) gradually, bit by bit ▸ *n* **payout** **3** a sum of money paid out

payroll *n* a list of employees, giving the salary or wage of each

paywall *n* a system preventing a user from accessing certain information on a website unless a fee is paid

pc 1 per cent **2** postcard

PC 1 personal computer **2** (in Britain) Police Constable **3** politically correct **4** (in Britain) Privy Council *or* Counsellor **5** (in Canada) Progressive Conservative

PDA personal digital assistant

PDF portable document format: a format in which electronic documents may be viewed

PE 1 physical education **2** Prince Edward Island

pea *n* **1** an annual climbing plant with green pods containing green seeds **2** the seed of this plant, eaten as a vegetable

peace *n* **1** stillness or silence **2** absence of mental anxiety: *peace of mind* **3** absence of war **4** harmony between people or groups **5** a treaty marking the end of a war **6** law and order within a state: *a breach of the peace* **7 at peace** **A** dead: *the woman is at peace now* **B** in a state of harmony or serenity **8 hold** *or* **keep one's peace** to keep silent **9 keep the peace** to maintain law and order

peace n 1 = stillness, rest, quiet, silence, calm, hush, tranquillity, seclusion 2 = serenity, calm, composure, contentment, repose, equanimity, peacefulness, harmoniousness 4 = harmony, accord, agreement, concord 5 = truce, ceasefire, treaty, armistice; ≠ war

peaceable adj 1 inclined towards peace 2 tranquil or calm

peaceful adj 1 not in a state of war or disagreement 2 calm or tranquil
> **peacefully** adv

peaceful adj 1 = friendly, at peace, harmonious, amicable, nonviolent; ≠ hostile 2 = calm, still, quiet, tranquil, restful, chilled (*informal*); ≠ agitated

peach n 1 a soft juicy fruit with a downy skin, yellowish-orange sweet flesh, and a single stone 2 *informal* a person or thing that is especially pleasing: *a peach of a goal* ▸ adj 3 pale pinkish-orange

peacock n, pl **-cocks** or **-cock** 1 a large male bird of the pheasant family with a crested head and a very large fanlike tail with blue and green eyelike spots 2 a vain strutting person
> **peahen** fem n

peak n 1 a pointed tip or projection: *the peak of the roof* 2 **A** the pointed summit of a mountain **B** a mountain with a pointed summit 3 the point of greatest success or achievement: *the peak of his career* 4 a projecting piece on the front of some caps ▸ vb 5 to form or reach a peak ▸ adj 6 of or relating to a period of greatest demand: *hotels are generally dearer in peak season*

peak n 1, 2A = point, top, tip, summit, brow, crest, pinnacle, apex 3 = high point, crown, climax, culmination, zenith, acme ▸ vb = culminate, climax, come to a head

peaked adj having a peak

peaky adj **peakier, peakiest** pale and sickly

peal n 1 a long loud echoing sound, such as of bells or thunder ▸ vb 2 to sound with a peal or peals

peanut n a plant with edible nutlike seeds which ripen underground

pear n 1 a sweet juicy fruit with a narrow top and a rounded base 2 **go pear-shaped** *informal* to go wrong: *the plan started to go pear-shaped*

pearl n 1 a hard smooth greyish-white rounded object found inside the shell of a clam or oyster and much valued as a gem 2 a person or thing that is like a pearl in beauty or value ▸ adj 3 of, made of, or set with pearl or mother-of-pearl ▸ vb 4 to set with or as if with pearls 5 to shape into or assume a pearl-like form or colour 6 to dive for pearls

pearly adj **pearlier, pearliest** 1 resembling a pearl, esp. in lustre 2 decorated with pearls or mother-of-pearl

peasant n 1 a member of a low social class employed in agricultural labour 2 *informal* an uncouth or uncultured person

peasant n 1 = rustic, countryman

peasantry n peasants as a class

peat n decaying vegetable matter found in uplands and bogs and used as a fuel (when dried) and as a fertilizer

pebble n 1 a small smooth rounded stone, esp. one worn by the action of water ▸ vb **-bling, -bled** 2 to cover with pebbles > **pebbly** adj

pebble dash n Brit & Austral a finish for external walls consisting of small stones set in plaster

pecan (pee-kan) n a smooth oval nut with a sweet oily kernel that grows on hickory trees in the Southern US

peccadillo n, pl **-loes** or **-los** a trivial misdeed

peck vb 1 to strike or pick up with the beak 2 *informal* to kiss (a person) quickly and lightly 3 **peck at** to eat slowly and reluctantly: *pecking away at your lunch* ▸ n 4 a quick light blow from a bird's beak 5 a mark made by such a blow 6 *informal* a quick light kiss

peck vb 1 = pick, hit, strike, tap, poke, jab, prick 2 = kiss, plant a kiss, give someone a smacker, give someone a peck or kiss ▸ n 6 = kiss, smacker, osculation (*rare*)

peckish adj *informal* feeling slightly hungry

pectin n *biochem* a water-soluble carbohydrate that occurs in ripe fruit: used in the manufacture of jams because of its ability to gel

pectoral adj 1 of or relating to the chest, breast, or thorax: *pectoral fins* 2 worn on the breast or chest: *a pectoral cross* ▸ n 3 a pectoral organ or part, esp. a muscle or fin

peculiar adj 1 strange or odd: *a peculiar idea* 2 distinct or special 3 (foll. by to) belonging exclusively (to): *a fish peculiar to these waters*

peculiar adj 1 = odd, strange, unusual, bizarre, funny, extraordinary, curious, weird; ≠ ordinary 2 = special, particular, unique, characteristic; ≠ common

peculiarity n, pl **-ties** 1 a strange or unusual habit; eccentricity 2 a distinguishing trait 3 the state or quality of being peculiar

pecuniary adj 1 of or relating to money 2 *law* (of an offence) involving a monetary penalty

pedagogue or sometimes US **pedagog** n a teacher, esp. a pedantic one > **pedagogic** adj

pedal n 1 a foot-operated lever used to control a vehicle or machine, or to modify the tone of a musical instrument ▸ vb **-dalling, -dalled** or US **-daling, -daled** 2 to propel (a bicycle) by operating the pedals 3 to operate the pedals of an organ or piano

pedant n a person who is concerned chiefly with insignificant detail or who relies too much on academic learning > **pedantic** adj
> **pedantically** adv

pedantry *n, pl* **-ries** the practice of being a pedant, esp. in the minute observance of petty rules or details

peddle *vb* **-dling, -dled** 1 to sell (goods) from place to place 2 to sell (illegal drugs) 3 to advocate (an idea or information) persistently: *the version of events being peddled by his opponents*

> **peddle** *vb* 1 = sell, trade, push (*informal*), market, hawk, flog (*slang*)

pederast *or* **paederast** *n* a man who has homosexual relations with boys › **pederasty** *or* **paederasty** *n*

pedestal *n* 1 a base that supports something, such as a statue 2 **put someone on a pedestal** to admire someone very much

pedestrian *n* 1 a person who travels on foot ▸ *adj* 2 dull or commonplace: *a pedestrian performance*

> **pedestrian** *n* = walker, foot-traveller; ≠ driver ▸ *adj* = dull, ordinary, boring, commonplace, mundane, mediocre, banal, prosaic, half-pie (NZ *informal*); ≠ exciting

pedestrian crossing *n* Brit & Austral a path across a road marked as a crossing for pedestrians

pedestrian precinct *n* Brit an area of a town for pedestrians only, esp. an area of shops

pedicure *n* medical or cosmetic treatment of the feet

pedigree *n* 1 the line of descent of a purebred animal 2 a document recording this 3 a genealogical table, esp. one indicating pure ancestry

> **pedigree** *n* 1 = lineage, family, line, race, stock, blood, breed, descent

pediment *n* a triangular part over a door, as used in classical architecture

pedlar *or esp US* **peddler** *n* a person who peddles

pee *informal* ▸ *vb* **peeing, peed** 1 to urinate ▸ *n* 2 urine 3 the act of urinating

peek *vb* 1 to glance quickly or secretly ▸ *n* 2 such a glance

peel *vb* 1 to remove the skin or rind of (a fruit or vegetable) 2 to come off in flakes 3 (of a person or part of the body) to shed skin in flakes as a result of sunburn ▸ *n* 4 the skin or rind of a fruit, etc.

> **peel** *vb* 1 = skin, scale, strip, pare, shuck, flake off, take the skin *or* rind off ▸ *n* = rind, skin, peeling

peelings *pl n* strips of skin or rind that have been peeled off: *potato peelings*

peep¹ *vb* 1 to peep slyly or quickly, such as through a small opening or from a hidden place 2 to appear partially or briefly: *the sun peeped through the clouds* ▸ *n* 3 a quick or sly look 4 the first appearance: *the peep of dawn*

peep *vb* 1 = peek, look, eyeball (*slang*), sneak a look, steal a look ▸ *n* 3 = look, glimpse, peek, look-see (*slang*)

peep² *vb* 1 (esp. of young birds) to make small shrill noises ▸ *n* 2 a peeping sound

Peeping Tom *n* a man who furtively observes people undressing

peer¹ *n* 1 a member of a nobility 2 a person who holds any of the five grades of the British nobility: duke, marquess, earl, viscount, and baron 3 a person of equal social standing, rank, age, etc.: *he is greatly respected by his peers in the arts world*

> **peer** *n* 1,2 = noble, lord, aristocrat, nobleman *or* woman 3 = equal, like, fellow (*old-fashioned*), contemporary, compeer

peer² *vb* 1 to look intently or as if with difficulty: *Amir peered anxiously at his father's face* 2 to appear dimly: *the sun peered through the fog*

> **peer** *vb* 1 = squint, look, spy, gaze, scan, inspect, peep, peek

peerage *Brit* ▸ *n* 1 the whole body of peers; aristocracy 2 the position, rank, or title of a peer

peeress *n* 1 (in Britain) a woman holding the rank of a peer 2 the wife or widow of a peer

peer group *n* a social group composed of people of similar age and status

peerless *adj* having no equals; unsurpassed

peer pressure *n* influence from one's peer group

peevish *adj* fretful or irritable › **peevishly** *adv*

peewee *n* a black-and-white Australian bird

peewit *or* **pewit** *n* same as **lapwing**

peg *n* 1 a small pin or bolt used to join two parts together, to fasten, or to mark 2 a hook or knob for hanging things on 3 *music* a pin on a stringed instrument which can be turned to tune the string wound around it 4 Also called: **clothes peg** a split or hinged pin for fastening wet clothes to a line to dry 5 Brit a small drink of spirits 6 an opportunity or pretext for doing something: *the play's subject matter provides a perfect peg for a discussion of issues like morality and faith* 7 **bring** *or* **take (someone) down a peg** to lower the pride of (someone) 8 **off the peg** Brit & NZ (of clothes) ready-to-wear, as opposed to tailor-made ▸ *vb* **pegging, pegged** 9 to insert a peg into 10 to secure with pegs: *the balloon was pegged down to stop it drifting away* 11 to mark (a score) with pegs, as in some card games 12 *chiefly Brit* to work steadily: *he pegged away at his job for years* 13 to fix or maintain something, such as prices, at a particular level or value: *a fixed-rate mortgage, pegged at 4.6 per cent*

> **peg** *n* 1 = pin, spike, rivet, skewer, dowel, spigot ▸ *vb* 10 = fasten, join, fix, secure, attach

peggy square *n* NZ a small hand-knitted square

peignoir (pay-nwahr) *n* a woman's light dressing gown

pejorative (pij-jor-a-tiv) *adj* **1** (of a word or expression) having an insulting or critical sense ▸ *n* **2** a pejorative word or expression

Pekingese *or* **Pekinese** *n* **1** *pl* **-ese** a small dog with a long straight coat, curled plumed tail, and short wrinkled muzzle **2** the dialect of Mandarin Chinese spoken in Beijing

pelargonium *n* a plant with circular leaves and red, pink, or white flowers: includes many cultivated geraniums

pelican *n* a large water bird with a pouch beneath its long bill for holding fish

pelican crossing *n* (in Britain) a type of road crossing with a pedestrian-operated traffic-light system

pellagra *n pathol* a disease caused by a diet lacking in vitamin B, which results in scaling of the skin, diarrhoea, and mental disorder

pellet *n* **1** a small round ball, esp. of compressed matter **2 A** an imitation bullet used in toy guns **B** a piece of small shot **3** a small pill

pell-mell *adv* **1** in a confused headlong rush: *the hounds ran pell-mell into the yard* **2** in a disorderly manner: *the things were piled pell-mell in the room*

pellucid *adj literary* **1** transparent or translucent **2** extremely clear in style and meaning

pelmet *n* a board or piece of fabric used to conceal the curtain rail

pelt[1] *vb* **1** to throw (missiles) at **2** (foll. by *along* etc.) to hurry **3** to rain heavily ▸ *n* **4** a blow **5 at full pelt** very quickly: *she ran down the street at full pelt*

pelt[2] *n* the skin or fur of an animal, esp. as material for clothing or rugs: *the lucrative international trade in beaver pelts*

pelvis *n, pl* **-vises** *or* **-ves 1** the framework of bones at the base of the spine, to which the hips are attached **2** the bones that form this structure ▸ **pelvic** *adj*

pen[1] *n* **1** an instrument for writing or drawing using ink. See also **ballpoint**, **fountain pen 2 the pen** writing as an occupation ▸ *vb* **penning, penned 3** to write or compose

pen *vb* = write (down), draft, compose, pencil, draw up, scribble, take down, inscribe

pen[2] *n* **1** an enclosure in which domestic animals are kept **2** any place of confinement ▸ *vb* **penning, penned** *or* **pent 3** to enclose (animals) in a pen **4 penned in** being or feeling trapped or confined: *she stood penned in by bodies at the front of the crowd*

pen *n* **1** = enclosure, pound, fold, cage, coop, hutch, sty ▸ *vb* **3** = enclose, confine, cage, fence in, coop up, hedge in, shut up *or* in

pen[3] *n US & Canad informal* short for **penitentiary** (sense 1)

pen[4] *n* a female swan

penal (pee-nal) *adj* **1** of or relating to punishment **2** used as a place of punishment: *a penal colony* ▸ **penally** *adv*

penalize *or* **-ise** *vb* **-izing, -ized** *or* **-ising, -ised 1** to impose a penalty on (someone) for breaking a law or rule **2** to inflict a disadvantage on: *use of the car is penalized by increasing parking charges* ▸ **penalization** *or* **-isation** *n*

penalty *n, pl* **-ties 1** a legal punishment for a crime or offence **2** loss or suffering as a result of one's own action: *we are now paying the penalty for neglecting to keep our equipment up to date* **3** *sport & games etc.* a handicap awarded against a player or team for illegal play, such as a free shot at goal by the opposing team

penalty *n* **1** = punishment, price, fine, handicap, forfeit

penance *n* **1** voluntary self-punishment to make amends for a sin **2** *RC Church* a sacrament in which repentant sinners are forgiven provided they confess their sins to a priest and perform a penance

pence *n* a plural of **penny**

penchant (pon-shon) *n* strong inclination or liking: *a stylish woman with a penchant for dark glasses*

pencil *n* **1** a rod of graphite encased in wood which is used for writing or drawing ▸ *vb* **-cilling, -cilled** *or US* **-ciling, -ciled 2** to draw, colour, write, or mark with a pencil **3 pencil in** to note, arrange, or include provisionally or tentatively

pendant *n* **A** an ornament worn on a chain round the neck: *a beautiful pearl pendant* **B** an ornament that hangs from a piece of jewellery

pendent *adj literary* **1** dangling **2** jutting

pending *prep* **1** while waiting for ▸ *adj* **2** not yet decided or settled **3** imminent: *these developments have been pending for some time*

pending *prep* = awaiting, until, waiting for, till ▸ *adj* **2** = undecided, unsettled, in the balance, undetermined **3** = forthcoming, imminent, prospective, impending, in the wind

pendulous *adj literary* hanging downwards and swinging freely

pendulum *n* **1** a weight suspended so it swings freely under the influence of gravity **2** such a device used to regulate a clock mechanism **3** a movement from one attitude or belief towards its opposite: *the pendulum has swung back to more punitive measures*

penetrate *vb* **-trating, -trated 1** to find or force a way into or through **2** to diffuse through; permeate: *the smell of cooking penetrated through to the sitting room* **3** to see through: *the sunlight did not penetrate the thick canopy of leaves* **4** (of a man) to insert the penis into the vagina or anus of (a person) **5** to grasp the meaning of (a principle, etc.) ▸ **penetrable** *adj* ▸ **penetrative** *adj*

penetrate *vb* **1** = pierce, enter, go through, bore, stab, prick **5** = grasp, work out, figure out (*informal*), comprehend, fathom, decipher, suss (out) (*slang*), get to the bottom of

penetrating *adj* tending to or able to penetrate: *a penetrating mind; a penetrating voice*

> **penetrating** *adj* = sharp, harsh, piercing, carrying, piping, loud, strident, shrill; ≠ sweet

penetration *n* **1** the act or an instance of penetrating **2** the ability or power to penetrate **3** keen insight or perception

> **penetration** *n* **1** = piercing, entry, entrance, puncturing, incision

pen friend *n* a person with whom one exchanges letters, often a person in another country whom one has not met

penguin *n* a flightless black-and-white sea bird with webbed feet and wings modified as flippers for swimming

penicillin *n* an antibiotic used to treat diseases caused by bacteria

peninsula *n* a narrow strip of land projecting from the mainland into a sea or lake > **peninsular** *adj*

penis *n, pl* **-nises** *or* **-nes** the organ of copulation in higher vertebrates, also used for urinating in many mammals > **penile** *adj*

penitent *adj* **1** feeling regret for one's sins; repentant ▸ *n* **2** a person who is penitent > **penitence** *n*

penitential *adj* of, showing, or as a penance

penitentiary *n, pl* **-ries 1** (in the US and Canada) a state or federal prison ▸ *adj* **2** of or for penance **3** used for punishment and reformation: *the penitentiary system*

penknife *n, pl* **-knives** a small knife with one or more blades that fold into the handle

pen name *n* a name used by a writer instead of his or her real name; nom de plume

pennant *n* **1** a long narrow flag, esp. one used by ships as identification or for signalling **2** *chiefly US, Canad & Austral* a flag indicating the winning of a championship in certain sports

penniless *adj* very poor

penny *n, pl* **pennies** *or* **pence 1** a British bronze coin worth one hundredth of a pound **2** a former British and Australian coin worth one twelfth of a shilling **3** *pl* **pennies** *US & Canad* a cent **4** *informal, chiefly Brit* the least amount of money: *I don't have a penny* **5 a pretty penny** *informal* a considerable sum of money **6 spend a penny** *Brit & NZ informal* to urinate **7 the penny dropped** *informal* the explanation of something was finally understood

pension¹ *n* **1** a regular payment made by the state or a former employer to a person who has retired or to a widowed or disabled person ▸ *vb* **2** to grant a pension to ▸ See also **pension off** > **pensionable** *adj* > **pensioner** *n*

> **pension** *n* = allowance, benefit, welfare, annuity, superannuation

pension² (pon-syon) *n* (in France and some other countries) a relatively cheap boarding house

pension off *vb* to cause (someone) to retire from a job and pay him or her a pension

pensive *adj* deeply thoughtful, often with a tinge of sadness > **pensively** *adv*

pentagon *n* *geom* a figure with five sides > **pentagonal** *adj*

Pentagon *n* a five-sided building in Washington DC that houses the headquarters of the US Department of Defense

pentameter (pen-tam-it-er) *n* a line of poetry consisting of five metrical feet

Pentateuch (pent-a-tyuke) *n* the first five books of the Old Testament > **Pentateuchal** *adj*

Pentecost *n* a Christian festival occurring on Whit Sunday celebrating the descent of the Holy Ghost to the apostles

penthouse *n* a luxurious flat built on the top floor or roof of a building

pent-up *adj* not released; repressed: *full of pent-up emotional violence*

penultimate *adj* second last

penumbra *n, pl* **-brae** *or* **-bras 1** the partially shadowed region which surrounds the full shadow in an eclipse **2** *literary* a partial shadow > **penumbral** *adj*

penurious *adj formal* **1** niggardly with money **2** lacking money or means

penury *n formal* **1** extreme poverty **2** extreme scarcity

peony *n, pl* **-nies** a garden plant with showy pink, red, white, or yellow flowers

people *pl n* **1** persons collectively or in general **2** a group of persons considered together: *young people* **3** *pl* **-ples** the persons living in a particular country: *the American people* **4** one's family or ancestors: *her people originally came from Skye* **5 the people A** the mass of ordinary persons without rank or privileges **B** the body of persons in a country who are entitled to vote ▸ *vb* **-pling, -pled 6** to provide with inhabitants: *the centre of the continent is sparsely peopled*

> **people** *pl n* **1** = humankind, persons, individuals, folk (*informal*), men and women, humanity, mankind, mortals, the human race **3** = nation, public, community, subjects, population, residents, citizens, folk **4** = family, parents, relations, relatives, folk, folks (*informal*), clan, kin, rellies (*Austral slang*) ▸ *vb* = inhabit, occupy, settle, populate, colonize

people mover *n* *Brit, Austral & NZ* same as **multipurpose vehicle**

pep *n* **1** high spirits, energy, or vitality ▸ *vb* **pepping, pepped 2 pep up** to make more lively or interesting: *the company has spent thousands trying to pep up its image*

pepper *n* **1** a sharp hot condiment obtained from the fruit of an Asian climbing plant **2** Also called: **capsicum** a colourful tropical fruit used as a vegetable and a condiment ▸ *vb* **3** to season with pepper **4** to sprinkle liberally: *his speech is heavily peppered with Americanisms* **5** to pelt with small missiles

pepper *n* **1** = seasoning, flavour, spice
▶ *vb* **4** = sprinkle, spot, scatter, dot, fleck, intersperse, speck, spatter **5** = pelt, hit, shower, blitz, rake, bombard, assail, strafe

peppercorn *n* the small dried berry of the pepper plant

peppercorn rent *n Brit* a rent that is very low or nominal

peppermint *n* **1** a mint plant which produces a pungent oil, used as a flavouring **2** a sweet flavoured with peppermint

pepper spray *n* a defence spray agent derived from hot cayenne peppers, which causes temporary blindness and breathing difficulty

peppery *adj* **1** tasting of pepper **2** irritable

pep talk *n informal* a talk designed to increase confidence and enthusiasm

peptic *adj* **1** of or relating to digestion **2** of or caused by pepsin or the action of the digestive juices: *a peptic ulcer*

per *prep* **1** for every: *three pence per pound; 30 pounds per week* **2** by; through **3 as per** according to: *proceed as per the instructions* **4 as per usual** or **as per normal** *informal* as usual

perambulate *vb* **-lating, -lated** *formal* to walk about (a place) > **perambulation** *n*

perambulator *n formal* same as **pram**

per annum *adv* in each year

per capita *adj, adv* of or for each person: *the average per capita wage has increased*

perceive *vb* **-ceiving, -ceived** **1** to become aware of (something) through the senses **2** to understand or grasp > **perceivable** *adj*

perceive *vb* **1** = see, notice, note, identify, discover, spot, observe, recognize **2** = understand, gather, see, learn, realize, grasp, comprehend, suss (out) (*slang*)

per cent *adv* **1** in each hundred. Symbol: **%**
▶ *n also* **percent 2** a percentage or proportion

percentage *n* **1** proportion or rate per hundred parts **2** any proportion in relation to the whole: *a small percentage of the population* **3** *informal* profit or advantage

perceptible *adj* able to be perceived; recognizable > **perceptibly** *adv*

perception *n* **1** the act of perceiving **2** insight or intuition: *his acute perception of other people's emotions* **3** the ability to perceive **4** way of viewing: *advertising affects the customer's perception of a product* > **perceptual** *adj*

perception *n* **2** = understanding, intelligence, observation, discrimination, insight, sharpness, cleverness, keenness **4** = awareness, understanding, sense, impression, feeling, idea, notion, consciousness

perceptive *adj* **1** observant **2** able to perceive > **perceptively** *adv* > **perceptiveness** *n*

perch¹ *n* **1** a branch or other resting place above

ground for a bird **2** any raised resting place: *from his perch on the bar stool* ▶ *vb* **3** (of birds) to alight or rest on a perch: *it fluttered to the branch and perched there for a moment* **4** to place or position precariously: *he was perched uneasily on the edge of his chair*

perch *n* **1** = resting place, post, branch, pole
▶ *vb* **3** = sit, rest, balance, settle **4** = place, put, rest, balance

perch² *n, pl* **perch** or **perches** **1** a spiny-finned edible freshwater fish of Europe and North America **2** any of various similar or related fishes

perchance *adv archaic or poetic* **1** perhaps **2** by chance

percipient *adj formal* quick at perceiving; observant > **percipience** *n*

percolate *vb* **-lating, -lated** **1** to pass or filter through very small holes: *the light percolating through the stained-glass windows cast coloured patterns on the floor* **2** to spread gradually: *his theories percolated through the academic community* **3** to make (coffee) or (of coffee) to be made in a percolator > **percolation** *n*

percolator *n* a coffee pot in which boiling water is forced up through a tube and filters down through the coffee grounds into a container

percussion *n* **1** the striking of one thing against another **2** *music* percussion instruments collectively > **percussive** *adj*

percussion instrument *n* a musical instrument, such as the drums, that produces a sound when struck directly

perdition *n* **1** *Christianity* final and unalterable spiritual ruin; damnation **2** same as **hell**

peregrine falcon *n* a European falcon with dark plumage on the back and wings and lighter underparts

peremptory *adj* **1** urgent or commanding: *a peremptory knock on the door* **2** expecting immediate obedience without any discussion: *he gave peremptory instructions to his son* **3** dogmatic > **peremptorily** *adv*

perennial *adj* **1** lasting throughout the year or through many years ▶ *n* **2** a plant that continues its growth for at least three years > **perennially** *adv*

perennial *adj* = continual, lasting, constant, enduring, persistent, abiding, recurrent, incessant

perfect *adj* **1** having all essential elements **2** faultless: *a perfect circle* **3** correct or precise: *perfect timing* **4** utter or absolute: *a perfect stranger* **5** excellent in all respects: *a perfect day* **6** *maths* exactly divisible into equal integral or polynomial roots: *36 is a perfect square* **7** *grammar* denoting a tense of verbs used to describe a completed action ▶ *n* **8** *grammar* the perfect tense ▶ *vb* **9** to improve to one's satisfaction:

he is in Paris to perfect his French **10** to make fully accomplished: *he perfected the system*
> **perfectly** *adv*

> **perfect** *adj* **1, 2** = faultless, correct, pure, impeccable, exemplary, flawless, foolproof; ≠ deficient **3** = exact, true, accurate, precise, correct, faithful, unerring **4** = complete, absolute, sheer, utter, consummate, unmitigated; ≠ partial **5** = excellent, ideal, supreme, superb, splendid, sublime, superlative ▸ *vb* **9** = improve, develop, polish, refine; ≠ mar

perfection *n* the state or quality of being perfect

> **perfection** *n* = excellence, integrity, superiority, purity, wholeness, sublimity, exquisiteness, faultlessness

perfectionism *n* the demand for the highest standard of excellence > **perfectionist** *n, adj*
perfidious *adj literary* treacherous or deceitful
> **perfidy** *n*
perforate *vb* **-rating, -rated 1** to make a hole or holes in **2** to punch rows of holes between (stamps) for ease of separation > **perforable** *adj*
> **perforator** *n*
perforation *n* **1** a hole or holes made in something **2** a series of punched holes, such as that between individual stamps
perforce *adv formal* of necessity
perform *vb* **1** to carry out (an action): *the hospital performs more than a hundred such operations each year* **2** to present (a play or concert): *he performed a couple of songs from his new album* **3** to fulfil: *you have performed the first of two conditions* > **performable** *adj*
> **performer** *n*

> **perform** *vb* **1** = do, achieve, carry out, complete, fulfil, accomplish, execute, pull off **2** = present, act (out), stage, play, produce, represent, put on, enact **3** = fulfil, carry out, execute, discharge

performance *n* **1** the act or process of performing **2** an artistic or dramatic production: *the concert includes the first performance of a new trumpet concerto* **3** manner or quality of functioning: *the car's overall performance is excellent* **4** *informal* conduct or behaviour, esp. when distasteful: *what did you mean by that performance at the restaurant?*

> **performance** *n* **1** = presentation, playing, acting (out), staging, production, exhibition, rendering, portrayal **2** = show, appearance, concert, gig (*informal*), recital

perfume *n* **1** a liquid cosmetic worn for its pleasant smell **2** a fragrant smell ▸ *vb* **-fuming, -fumed 3** to impart a perfume to > **perfumed** *adj*

> **perfume** *n* **1** = fragrance, scent **2** = scent, smell, fragrance, bouquet, aroma, odour

perfunctory *adj formal* done only as a matter of routine: *he gave his wife a perfunctory kiss*
> **perfunctorily** *adv* > **perfunctoriness** *n*
pergola *n* an arched trellis or framework that supports climbing plants
perhaps *adv* **1** possibly; maybe **2** approximately; roughly: *it would have taken perhaps three or four minutes*

> **perhaps** *adv* **1** = maybe, possibly, it may be, it is possible (that), conceivably, perchance (*archaic*), feasibly, happen (*N English dialect*)

pericardium *n, pl* **-dia** the membranous sac enclosing the heart > **pericardial** *adj*
perihelion *n, pl* **-lia** *astron* the point in its orbit around the sun when a planet or comet is nearest the sun
peril *n* great danger or jeopardy > **perilous** *adj*
> **perilously** *adv*

> **peril** *n* = danger, risk, threat, hazard, menace, jeopardy, perilousness

perimeter (per-rim-it-er) *n* **1** *maths* **A** the curve or line enclosing a plane area **B** the length of this curve or line **2** any boundary around something

> **perimeter** *n* **2** = boundary, edge, border, bounds, limit, margin, confines, periphery; ≠ centre

perinatal *adj* of or occurring in the period from about three months before to one month after birth
period *n* **1** a portion of time: *six inches of rain fell in a 24-hour period* **2** a portion of time specified in some way: *the President's first period of office* **3** an occurrence of menstruation **4** *geol* a unit of geological time during which a system of rocks is formed: *the Jurassic period* **5** a division of time at school, college, or university when a particular subject is taught **6** *physics & maths* the time taken to complete one cycle of a regularly recurring phenomenon **7** *chem* one of the horizontal rows of elements in the periodic table **8** *chiefly US & Canad* same as **full stop** ▸ *adj* **9** dating from or in the style of an earlier time: *a performance on period instruments*

> **period** *n* **1** = time, term, season, space, run, stretch, spell, phase

periodic *adj* recurring at intervals > **periodically** *adv* > **periodicity** *n*

> **periodic** *adj* = recurrent, regular, repeated, occasional, cyclical, sporadic, intermittent

periodical *n* **1** a publication issued at regular intervals, usually monthly or weekly ▸ *adj* **2** of or relating to such publications **3** periodic or occasional
periodic table *n chem* a table of the elements, arranged in order of increasing atomic number, based on the periodic law

peripatetic (per-rip-a-**tet**-ik) adj **1** travelling from place to place **2** Brit employed in two or more educational establishments and travelling from one to another: a peripatetic violin teacher ▸ n **3** a peripatetic person

peripheral (per-if-er-al) adj **1** not relating to the most important part of something; incidental **2** of or relating to a periphery ▸ n **3** computers any device, such as a printer, that can be connected to a computer

> **peripheral** adj **1** = secondary, minor, marginal, irrelevant, unimportant, incidental, inessential **2** = outermost, outside, external, outer, exterior

periphery (per-if-er-ee) n, pl **-eries 1** the boundary or edge of an area or group: slums sprouted up on the periphery of the city **2** fringes of a field of activity: less developed countries on the periphery of the capitalist system

periscope n an optical instrument used, esp. in submarines, to give a view of objects on a different level

perish vb **1** to be destroyed or die **2** to cause to suffer: we were perished with cold **3** to rot or cause to rot: to prevent your swimsuit from perishing, rinse it in clean water before it dries

> **perish** vb **1** = be destroyed, fall, decline, collapse, disappear, vanish **3** = rot, waste away, decay, disintegrate, decompose, moulder

perishable adj **1** liable to rot ▸ n **2** (often pl) a perishable article, esp. food

perishing adj **1** informal (of weather) extremely cold **2** slang confounded or blasted: get rid of the perishing lot!

peritoneum (per-rit-toe-**nee**-um) n, pl **-nea** (-**nee**-a) or **-neums** a serous sac that lines the walls of the abdominal cavity and covers the abdominal organs > **peritoneal** adj

peritonitis (per-rit-tone-ite-iss) n inflammation of the peritoneum, causing severe abdominal pain

periwinkle[1] n same as **winkle** (sense 1)

periwinkle[2] n a Eurasian evergreen plant with trailing stems and blue flowers

perjury (per-jer-ee) n, pl **-juries** criminal law the act of deliberately giving false evidence while under oath

perk n informal an incidental benefit gained from a job, such as a company car

> **perk** n = bonus, benefit, extra, plus (informal), fringe benefit, perquisite (formal)

perk up vb **1** to make or become more cheerful **2** to rise or cause to rise briskly: the dog's ears perked up suddenly

perky adj **perkier**, **perkiest 1** jaunty or lively **2** confident or spirited

perlemoen (per-la-moon) n S African same as **abalone**

perm n **1** a hairstyle with long-lasting waves or curls produced by treating the hair with chemicals ▸ vb **2** to give a perm to (hair)

permafrost n ground that is permanently frozen

permanent adj **1** existing or intended to exist forever: a permanent solution **2** not expected to change: a permanent condition > **permanence** n > **permanently** adv

> **permanent** adj **1** = lasting, constant, enduring, persistent, eternal, abiding, perpetual, everlasting; ≠ temporary **2** = long-term, established, secure, stable, steady; ≠ temporary

permeable adj capable of being permeated, esp. by liquids > **permeability** n

permeate vb **-ating**, **-ated 1** to penetrate or spread throughout (something): his mystical philosophy permeates everything he creates **2** to pass through or cause to pass through by osmosis or diffusion: the rain permeated her anorak > **permeation** n

permissible adj permitted or allowable > **permissibility** n

permission n authorization to do something

> **permission** n = authorization, sanction, licence, approval, leave, go-ahead (informal), liberty, consent; ≠ prohibition

permissive adj tolerant or lenient, esp. in sexual matters: the so-called permissive society > **permissiveness** n

permit vb **-mitting**, **-mitted 1** to allow (something) to be done or to happen: smoking is not permitted in the office **2** to allow (someone) to do something: her father does not permit her to eat sweets **3** to allow the possibility (of): they saw each other as often as time and circumstances permitted ▸ n **4** an official document granting permission to do something

> **permit** vb **1, 2** = allow, grant, sanction, let, entitle, license, authorize, consent to; ≠ forbid **3** = enable, let, allow, cause ▸ n = licence, pass, document, certificate, passport, visa, warrant, authorization; ≠ prohibition

permutation n **1** maths an ordered arrangement of the numbers or terms of a set into specified groups: the permutations of a, b, and c, taken two at a time, are ab, ba, ac, ca, bc, cb **2** a combination of items made by reordering **3** a transformation **4** a fixed combination for selections of results on football pools

pernicious adj formal **1** wicked or malicious: pernicious lies **2** causing grave harm; deadly

pernickety adj informal **1** excessively fussy about details **2** (of a task) requiring close attention

peroration n formal the concluding part of a speech which sums up the points made previously

peroxide *n* **1** hydrogen peroxide used as a hair bleach **2** any of a class of metallic oxides, such as sodium peroxide, Na_2O_2 ▸ *adj* **3** bleached with or resembling peroxide: *a peroxide blonde* ▸ *vb* **-iding, -ided** **4** to bleach (the hair) with peroxide

perp *n* *US & Canad informal* a person who has committed a crime

perpendicular *adj* **1** at right angles to a given line or surface **2** upright; vertical **3** denoting a style of English Gothic architecture characterized by vertical lines ▸ *n* **4** *geom* a line or plane perpendicular to another › **perpendicularity** *n*

perpetrate *vb* **-trating, -trated** to perform or be responsible for (a deception or crime) › **perpetration** *n* › **perpetrator** *n*

perpetual *adj* **1** never ending or never changing: *Mexico's colourful scenery and nearly perpetual sunshine* **2** continually repeated: *his mother's perpetual worries about his health* › **perpetually** *adv*

> **perpetual** *adj* **1** = everlasting, permanent, endless, eternal, lasting, perennial, infinite, never-ending; ≠ temporary **2** = continual, repeated, constant, endless, continuous, persistent, recurrent, never-ending; ≠ brief

perpetuate *vb* **-ating, -ated** to cause to continue: *we must not perpetuate the divisions of the past* › **perpetuation** *n*

> **perpetuate** *vb* = maintain, preserve, keep going, immortalize; ≠ end

perpetuity *n, pl* **-ties** **1** eternity **2** the state of being perpetual **3** something perpetual, such as a pension that is payable indefinitely **4** **in perpetuity** forever

perplex *vb* **1** to puzzle or bewilder **2** to complicate: *this merely perplexes the issue* › **perplexing** *adj*

perplexity *n, pl* **-ties** **1** the state of being perplexed **2** something that perplexes

perquisite *n formal* same as **perk**

perry *n, pl* **-ries** an alcoholic drink made from fermented pear juice

per se (per **say**) *adv* in itself

persecute *vb* **-cuting, -cuted** **1** to oppress or maltreat (someone), because of ethnicity or religion **2** to harass (someone) persistently › **persecution** *n* › **persecutor** *n*

> **persecute** *vb* **1** = victimize, torture, torment, oppress, pick on, ill-treat, maltreat; ≠ mollycoddle **2** = harass, bother, annoy, tease, hassle (*informal*), badger, pester; ≠ leave alone

perseverance *n* continued steady belief or efforts; persistence

persevere *vb* **-severing, -severed** (often foll. by *with* or *in*) to continue to make an effort despite difficulties

Persian *adj* **1** of ancient Persia or modern Iran ▸ *n* **2** a person from Persia (now Iran) **3** the language of Iran or of Persia

Persian carpet *n* a hand-made carpet or rug with flowing or geometric designs in rich colours

Persian cat *n* a long-haired variety of domestic cat

persimmon *n* a sweet red tropical fruit

persist *vb* **1** to continue without interruption: *if the symptoms persist, see your doctor* **2** (often foll. by *in* or *with*) to continue obstinately despite opposition: *she persisted in using these controversial methods*

> **persist** *vb* **1** = continue, last, remain, carry on, keep up, linger **2** = persevere, continue, go on, carry on, keep on, keep going, press on, not give up, crack on (*informal*)

persistent *adj* **1** unrelenting: *persistent rain* **2** showing persistence: *a persistent critic of the government* › **persistence** *n* › **persistently** *adv*

> **persistent** *adj* **1** = continuous, constant, repeated, endless, perpetual, continual, never-ending, incessant; ≠ occasional **2** = determined, dogged, steady, stubborn, persevering, tireless, tenacious, steadfast; ≠ irresolute

person *n, pl* **people** *or* **persons** **1** an individual human being **2** the body of a human being: *he was found to have a knife concealed about his person* **3** *grammar* a category into which pronouns and forms of verbs are subdivided to show whether they refer to the speaker, the person addressed, or some other individual or thing **4** **in person** actually doing something or being somewhere oneself: *I had the chance to hear her speak in person*

> **person** *n* **1** = individual, being, body (*informal*), human, soul, creature, mortal, man *or* woman **4** **in person** = personally, yourself

persona (per-**soh**-na) *n, pl* **-nae** (-nee) the personality that a person adopts and presents to other people

personable *adj* pleasant in appearance and personality

personage *n* **1** an important or distinguished person **2** any person

personal *adj* **1** of the private aspects of a person's life: *redundancy can put an enormous strain on personal relationships* **2** of a person's body: *personal hygiene* **3** belonging to, or for the sole use of, a particular individual: *he disappeared, leaving his passport, diary and other personal belongings in his flat* **4** undertaken by an individual: *the sponsorship deal requires him to make a number of personal appearances for publicity purposes* **5** offensive in respect of an individual's personality or intimate affairs: *he has suffered a lifetime of personal remarks about his weight* **6** having the attributes of an individual conscious being: *a personal God* **7** *grammar* of person **8** *law* of movable property, such as money

P

personal *adj* 1 = private 3 = own, special, private, individual, particular, peculiar 5 = offensive, nasty, insulting, disparaging, derogatory

personal computer *n* a computer that is used by one person at a time in a business or school or at home

personality *n, pl* **-ties** 1 *psychol* the distinctive characteristics which make an individual unique 2 the distinctive character of a person which makes him or her socially attractive: *some people find him lacking in personality and a bit colourless* 3 a well-known person in a certain field; celebrity 4 a remarkable person: *she is a personality to be reckoned with* 5 (*often pl*) an offensive personal remark: *the argument never degenerated into personalities*

personality *n* 1 = nature, character, make-up, identity, temperament, disposition, individuality 2 = character, charm, attraction, charisma, magnetism 3 = celebrity, star, notable, household name, famous name, personage, megastar (*informal*)

personally *adv* 1 without the help of others: *she had seen to it personally that permission was granted* 2 in one's own opinion: *personally, I think it's overrated* 3 as if referring to oneself: *yes, he was rather rude but it's not worth taking it personally* 4 as a person: *I don't like him personally, but he's fine to work with*

personally *adv* 1 = by yourself, alone, independently, solely, on your own 2 = in your opinion, in your book, for your part, from your own viewpoint, in your own view

personal pronoun *n* a pronoun such as I, you, he, she, it, we, and they that represents a definite person or thing

personal stereo *n chiefly Brit* a small portable cassette or CD player used with lightweight headphones

personify *vb* **-fies, -fying, -fied** 1 to give human characteristics to (a thing or abstraction) 2 to represent (an abstract quality) in human or animal form 3 (of a person or thing) to represent (an abstract quality), as in art 4 to be the embodiment of: *she can be charm personified* > **personification** *n*

personnel *n* 1 the people employed in an organization or for a service 2 the department in an organization that appoints or keeps records of employees 3 (in the armed forces) people, as opposed to machinery or equipment

personnel *n* 1 = employees, people, staff, workers, workforce, human resources, helpers

perspective *n* 1 a way of regarding situations or facts and judging their relative importance: *recent events have given her a new perspective on life* 2 objectivity: *Kiara's problems helped me put my minor worries into perspective* 3 a method of drawing that gives the effect of solidity and relative distances and sizes 4 the appearance of objects or buildings relative to each other, determined by their distance from the viewer

perspective *n* 1 = outlook, attitude, context, angle, frame of reference 2 = objectivity, proportion, relation, relativity, relative importance

Perspex *n trademark* a clear acrylic resin used as a substitute for glass

perspicacious *adj formal* acutely perceptive or discerning > **perspicacity** *n*

perspiration *n* 1 the salty fluid secreted by the sweat glands of the skin; sweat 2 the act of sweating

perspire *vb* **-spiring, -spired** to sweat

persuade *vb* **-suading, -suaded** 1 to make (someone) do something by reason or charm: *we tried to persuade him not to come up the mountain with us* 2 to cause to believe; convince: *persuading people of the need for enforced environmental protection may be difficult* > **persuadable** *adj*

persuade *vb* 1 = talk (someone) into, urge, influence, win (someone) over, induce, sway, entice, coax; ≠ dissuade 2 = convince, satisfy, assure, cause to believe

persuasion *n* 1 the act of persuading 2 the power to persuade 3 a set of beliefs; creed: *the Roman Catholic persuasion; literary intellectuals of the modernist persuasion*

persuasion *n* 1 = urging, inducement, wheedling, enticement, cajolery 3 = belief, views, opinion, party, school, side, camp, faith

persuasive *adj* able to persuade: *a persuasive argument* > **persuasively** *adv*

persuasive *adj* = convincing, telling, effective, sound, compelling, influential, valid, credible; ≠ unconvincing

pert *adj* 1 saucy or impudent 2 attractive in a neat way: *pert buttocks*

pertain *vb* (*often foll. by to*) 1 to have reference or relevance: *the notes pertaining to the case* 2 to be appropriate: *the product pertains to real user needs* 3 to belong (to) or be a part (of)

pertinacious *adj* 1 doggedly resolute in purpose or belief 2 stubbornly persistent > **pertinacity** *n*

pertinent *adj* relating to the matter at hand; relevant > **pertinence** *n*

perturb *vb* 1 to disturb the composure of 2 to throw into disorder

perturbation *n literary* anxiety or worry

peruse *vb* **-rusing, -rused** 1 to read or examine with care 2 to browse or read in a leisurely way > **perusal** *n*

pervade *vb* **-vading, -vaded** to spread through or throughout (something) > **pervasion** *n* > **pervasive** *adj*

perverse *adj* **1** deliberately acting in a way different from what is regarded as normal or proper **2** wayward or contrary; obstinate ▷ **perversely** *adv* ▷ **perversity** *n*

perverse *adj* **1** = abnormal, unhealthy, improper, deviant (*old-fashioned*) **2** = stubborn, contrary, dogged, troublesome, rebellious, wayward, intractable, wilful; ≠ cooperative

perversion *n* **1** any means of obtaining sexual satisfaction that is considered abnormal or unacceptable **2** the act of perverting

pervert *vb* **1** to use wrongly or badly **2** to interpret wrongly or badly; distort **3** to lead (someone) into abnormal behaviour, esp. sexually; corrupt **4** to debase ▶ *n* **5** a person who practises sexual perversion ▷ **perverted** *adj*

pervert *vb* **1, 2** = distort, abuse, twist, misuse, warp, misrepresent, falsify **3, 4** = corrupt, degrade, deprave, debase (*formal*), debauch, lead astray ▶ *n* = deviant (*old-fashioned*), degenerate, sicko (*informal*), weirdo or weirdie (*informal*)

pervious *adj* **1** able to be penetrated; permeable: *the thin walls were pervious to the slightest sound* **2** receptive to new ideas; open-minded

peseta (pess-**say**-ta) *n* a former monetary unit of Spain

pessary *n, pl* **-ries** *med* **1** a device worn in the vagina, either as a support for the uterus or as a contraceptive **2** a vaginal suppository

pessimism *n* **1** the tendency to expect the worst in all things **2** the doctrine of the ultimate triumph of evil over good ▷ **pessimist** *n* ▷ **pessimistic** *adj* ▷ **pessimistically** *adv*

pest *n* **1** an annoying person or thing; nuisance **2** any organism that damages crops, or injures or irritates livestock or humans

pest *n* **1** = nuisance, trial, pain (*informal*), drag (*informal*), bother, irritation, annoyance, bane **2** = infection, bug, insect, plague, epidemic, blight, scourge, pestilence, gogga (*S African informal*)

pester *vb* to annoy or nag continually

pesticide *n* a chemical used to destroy pests, esp. insects

pestilence *n literary* any deadly epidemic disease, such as the plague

pestilent *adj* **1** annoying or irritating **2** highly destructive morally or physically **3** likely to cause infectious disease ▷ **pestilential** *adj*

pestle *n* a club-shaped instrument for grinding or pounding substances in a mortar

pet *n* **1** a tame animal kept for companionship or pleasure **2** a person who is favoured or indulged: *teacher's pet* ▶ *adj* **3** kept as a pet: *a pet hamster* **4** of or for pet animals: *pet food* **5** strongly felt or particularly cherished: *my pet hate; he would not stand by and let his pet project be abandoned* ▶ *vb* **petting**, **petted 6** to treat as a

pet; pamper **7** to pat or stroke affectionately **8** *informal* (of two people) to caress each other in an erotic manner

pet *n* **2** = favourite, treasure, darling, jewel, idol ▶ *adj* **5** = favourite, favoured, dearest, cherished, fave (*informal*), dear to your heart ▶ *vb* **6** = pamper, spoil, indulge, cosset, baby, dote on, coddle, mollycoddle **7** = fondle, pat, stroke, caress **8** = cuddle, kiss, snog (*Brit slang*), smooch (*informal*), neck (*informal*), canoodle (*slang*)

petal *n* any of the brightly coloured leaflike parts which form the head of a flower ▷ **petalled** *adj*

petard *n* **1** (formerly) a device containing explosives used to break through a wall or door **2 hoist with one's own petard** being the victim of one's own schemes

peter out *vb* to come gradually to an end: *the road petered out into a rutted track*

petite (pit-**eat**) *adj* (of a woman) small and dainty

petition *n* **1** a written document signed by a large number of people demanding some form of action from a government or other authority **2** any formal request to a higher authority **3** *law* a formal application in writing made to a court asking for some specific judicial action: *she filed a petition for divorce* ▶ *vb* **4** to address or present a petition to (a government or to someone in authority): *he petitioned the Crown for mercy* **5** (foll. by *for*) to seek by petition: *the firm's creditors petitioned for liquidation* ▷ **petitioner** *n*

petition *n* **1** = appeal, round robin, list of signatures **2, 3** = entreaty, appeal, suit, application, request, prayer, plea, solicitation ▶ *vb* **4** = appeal, plead, ask, pray, beg, solicit, beseech, entreat

petrel *n* a sea bird with a hooked bill and tubular nostrils, such as the albatross, storm petrel, or shearwater

petrify *vb* **-fies, -fying, -fied 1** to stun or daze with fear: *he was petrified of going to jail* **2** (of organic material) to turn to stone **3** to make or become unable to change or develop: *a society petrified by outmoded conventions* ▷ **petrification** *n*

petrochemical *n* a substance, such as acetone, obtained from petroleum ▷ **petrochemistry** *n*

petrol *n* a volatile flammable liquid obtained from petroleum and used as a fuel for internal-combustion engines

petrol bomb *n* a simple grenade consisting of a bottle filled with petrol. A piece of cloth is put in the neck of the bottle and set alight just before the bomb is thrown

petroleum *n* a dark-coloured thick flammable crude oil occurring in sedimentary rocks, consisting mainly of hydrocarbons: the source of petrol and paraffin

petticoat *n* a woman's underskirt

pettifogging adj old-fashioned excessively concerned with unimportant detail > **pettifogger** n

petty adj **-tier, -tiest 1** trivial or unimportant: petty details **2** small-minded: petty spite **3** low in importance: petty criminals > **pettily** adv > **pettiness** n

> **petty** adj **1** = trivial, insignificant, little, small, slight, trifling, negligible, unimportant; ≠ important **2** = small-minded, mean, shabby, spiteful, ungenerous, mean-minded; ≠ broad-minded

petty cash n a small cash fund for minor incidental expenses

petty officer n a noncommissioned officer in the navy

petulant adj unreasonably irritable or peevish > **petulance** n > **petulantly** adv

petunia n a tropical American plant with pink, white, or purple funnel-shaped flowers

pew n **1 A** (in a church) a long benchlike seat with a back, used by the congregation **B** (in a church) an enclosed compartment reserved for the use of a family or group **2 take a pew** informal take a seat

pewter n **1** an alloy containing tin, lead, and sometimes copper and antimony **2** dishes or kitchen utensils made from pewter

pH n potential of hydrogen; a measure of the acidity or alkalinity of a solution

phalanger n an Australian marsupial with dense fur and a long tail

phalanx (fal-lanks) n, pl **phalanxes** or **phalanges** (fal-lan-jeez) **1** any closely grouped mass of people: a solid phalanx of reporters and photographers **2** a number of people united for a common purpose **3** an ancient Greek battle formation of infantry in close ranks

phallic adj of or resembling a phallus: a phallic symbol

phallus (fal-luss) n, pl **-luses** or **-li** (-lie) **1** same as **penis 2** an image of the penis as a symbol of reproductive power

phantasm n **1** a phantom **2** an unreal vision; illusion > **phantasmal** adj

phantasmagoria n psychol a shifting medley of dreamlike figures > **phantasmagoric** adj

phantom n **1** an apparition or spectre **2** the visible representation of something abstract, such as in a dream or hallucination: the phantom of liberty ▸ adj **3** deceptive or unreal: she regularly took days off for what her bosses considered phantom illnesses

> **phantom** n **1** = spectre, ghost, spirit, shade (literary), spook (informal), apparition, wraith, phantasm

Pharaoh (fare-oh) n the title of the ancient Egyptian kings

pharmaceutical adj of or relating to drugs or pharmacy

pharmacist n a person qualified to prepare and dispense drugs

pharmacology n the science or study of drugs > **pharmacological** adj > **pharmacologist** n

pharmacopoeia (far-ma-koh-pee-a) n an authoritative book containing a list of medicinal drugs along with their uses, preparation, and dosages

pharmacy n **1** the preparation and dispensing of drugs **2** pl **-cies** a dispensary

pharyngitis (far-rin-jite-iss) n inflammation of the pharynx, causing a sore throat

pharynx (far-rinks) n, pl **pharynges** (far-rin-jeez) or **pharynxes** the part of the alimentary canal between the mouth and the oesophagus > **pharyngeal** adj

phase n **1** any distinct or characteristic stage in a sequence of events: two distinct phases in the singer's career **2** astron one of the recurring shapes of the portion of the moon, Mercury, or Venus illuminated by the sun **3** physics a particular stage in a periodic process or phenomenon **4** physics **in** or **out of phase** (of two waves or signals) reaching or not reaching corresponding phases at the same time ▸ vb **phasing, phased 5** to do or introduce gradually: the redundancies will be phased over two years ▸ See also **phase in**

> **phase** n **1** = stage, time, point, position, step, development, period, chapter

phase in vb to introduce in a gradual or cautious manner: the scheme was phased in over seven years

> **phase in** vb **phase something in** = introduce, incorporate, ease in, start

PhD Doctor of Philosophy

pheasant n a long-tailed bird with a brightly coloured plumage in the male: native to Asia but introduced elsewhere

phenobarbitone or **phenobarbital** n a sedative used to treat insomnia and epilepsy

phenol n a white crystalline derivative of benzene, used as an antiseptic and disinfectant and in the manufacture of resins, explosives, and pharmaceutical substances

phenomenal adj **1** extraordinary or outstanding: a phenomenal success **2** of or relating to a phenomenon > **phenomenally** adv

> **phenomenal** adj **1** = extraordinary, outstanding, remarkable, fantastic (informal), unusual, marvellous, exceptional, miraculous; ≠ unremarkable

phenomenon n, pl **-ena** or **-enons 1** anything that can be perceived as an occurrence or fact **2** any remarkable occurrence or person

> **phenomenon** n **1** = occurrence, happening, fact, event, incident, circumstance, episode **2** = wonder, sensation, exception, miracle, marvel, prodigy, rarity

phial *n* a small bottle for liquid medicine

philadelphus *n* a shrub grown for its strongly scented showy flowers

philanthropy *n, pl* **-pies** **1** the practice of helping people well-off than oneself **2** love of mankind in general › **philanthropic** *adj* › **philanthropist** *n*

philately (fill-**lat**-a-lee) *n* the collection and study of postage stamps › **philatelist** *n*

philharmonic *adj* **1** fond of music ▸ *n* **2** a specific choir, orchestra, or musical society: *the Vienna Philharmonic*

philistine *n* **1** a person who is hostile towards culture and the arts ▸ *adj* **2** boorishly uncultured › **philistinism** *n*

philology *n* the science of the structure and development of languages › **philological** *adj* › **philologist** *n*

philosopher *n* **1** a person who studies philosophy **2** a person who remains calm and stoical in the face of difficulties or disappointments

> **philosopher** *n* **1** = thinker, theorist, sage, wise man, logician, metaphysician

philosophical *or* **philosophic** *adj* **1** of or relating to philosophy or philosophers **2** calm and stoical in the face of difficulties or disappointments › **philosophically** *adv*

> **philosophical** *or* **philosophic** *adj*
> **1** = theoretical, abstract, wise, rational, logical, thoughtful, sagacious; ≠ **practical 2** = stoical, calm, composed, cool, collected, serene, tranquil, unruffled; ≠ **emotional**

philosophize *or* **-phise** *vb* **-phizing, -phized** *or* **-phising, -phised** to discuss in a philosophical manner › **philosophizer** *or* **-phiser** *n*

philosophy *n, pl* **-phies** **1** the academic study of knowledge, thought, and the meaning of life **2** the particular doctrines of a specific individual or school relating to these issues: *the philosophy of John Locke* **3** any system of beliefs or values **4** a personal outlook or viewpoint

> **philosophy** *n* **1, 2** = thought, knowledge, thinking, reasoning, wisdom, logic, metaphysics **3, 4** = outlook, values, principles, convictions, thinking, beliefs, doctrine, ideology

philtre *or US* **philter** *n* a drink supposed to arouse desire

phishing *n* the practice of using fraudulent emails and copies of legitimate websites to extract financial data from computer users for criminal purposes

phlebitis (fleb-**bite**-iss) *n* inflammation of a vein, usually in the legs › **phlebitic** *adj*

phlegm (flem) *n* **1** the thick yellowish substance secreted by the walls of the respiratory tract **2** apathy or stolidity **3** calmness › **phlegmy** *adj*

phlegm *n* **1** = mucus, catarrh, sputum, mucous secretion

phlegmatic (fleg-**mat**-ik) *adj* having an unemotional disposition

phlox *n, pl* **phlox** *or* **phloxes** a plant with clusters of white, red, or purple flowers

phobia *n psychiatry* an intense and irrational fear of a given situation or thing › **phobic** *adj, n*

phoenix *n* a legendary Arabian bird said to set fire to itself and rise anew from the ashes every 500 years

phone *n, vb* **phoning, phoned** short for **telephone**

phone-in *n* a radio or television programme in which telephone questions or comments from the public are broadcast live as part of a discussion

phonetic *adj* **1** of phonetics **2** denoting any perceptible distinction between one speech sound and another **3** conforming to pronunciation: *phonetic spelling* › **phonetically** *adv*

phonetics *n* the study of speech processes, including the production, perception, and analysis of speech sounds

phoney *or esp US* **phony** *informal* ▸ *adj* **-nier, -niest** **1** not genuine: *a phoney two-pound coin* **2** (of a person) insincere or pretentious ▸ *n, pl* **-neys** *or esp US* **-nies** **3** an insincere or pretentious person **4** something that is not genuine

phonograph *n* **1** an early form of record player capable of recording and reproducing sound on wax cylinders **2** *US & Canad* a record player

phosphate *n* **1** any salt or ester of any phosphoric acid **2** (*often pl*) chemical fertilizer containing phosphorous compounds › **phosphatic** *adj*

phosphorescence *n* **1** *physics* a fluorescence that persists after the bombarding radiation producing it has stopped **2** the light emitted in phosphorescence › **phosphorescent** *adj*

phosphorus *n chem* a toxic flammable nonmetallic element which appears luminous in the dark. It exists in two forms, white and red. Symbol: P

photo *n, pl* **-tos** short for **photograph**

photocopier *n* a machine using light-sensitive photographic materials to reproduce written, printed, or graphic work

photocopy *n, pl* **-copies** **1** a photographic reproduction of written, printed, or graphic work ▸ *vb* **-copies, -copying, -copied** **2** to reproduce on photographic material

photoelectric *adj* of or concerned with electric or electronic effects caused by light or other electromagnetic radiation › **photoelectricity** *n*

photo finish *n* a finish of a race in which contestants are so close that a photograph is needed to decide the result

photogenic *adj* **1** (esp. of a person) always looking attractive in photographs **2** *biol* producing or emitting light

photograph *n* **1** a picture made using a camera, either by the chemical action of light on sensitive film or by the creation of a digital image ▶ *vb* **2** to take a photograph of

> **photograph** *n* = picture, photo (*informal*), shot, print, snap (*informal*), snapshot, selfie (*informal*), transparency, JPEG, thumbnail, avatar ▶ *vb* = take a picture of, record, film, shoot, snap (*informal*), take (someone's) picture

photographic *adj* **1** of or like photography or a photograph **2** (of a person's memory) able to retain facts or appearances in precise detail
> **photographically** *adv*

> **photographic** *adj* **1** = pictorial, visual, graphic, cinematic, filmic **2** = accurate, exact, precise, faithful, retentive

photography *n* **1** the process of recording images either on sensitized material by the action of light or by equipment which enables images to be stored digitally and viewed on a screen **2** the practice of taking photographs
> **photographer** *n*

Photoshop *n* **1** *trademark* a software application for managing and editing digital images ▶ *vb* **-shopping, -shopped** **2** *informal* to alter (a digital image) using Photoshop or a similar application

photostat *n* **1** a type of photocopying machine or process **2** any copy made by such a machine ▶ *vb* **-statting, -statted** *or* **-stating, -stated** **3** to make a photostat copy (of)

photosynthesis *n* (in plants) the process by which a green plant uses sunlight to build up carbohydrate reserves > **photosynthesize** *or* **-sise** *vb* > **photosynthetic** *adj*

phrasal verb *n* a phrase that consists of a verb plus an adverb or preposition, esp. one whose meaning cannot be deduced from its parts, such as *take in* meaning *deceive*

phrase *n* **1** a group of words forming a unit of meaning in a sentence **2** an idiomatic or original expression **3** *music* a small group of notes forming a coherent unit of melody ▶ *vb* **phrasing, phrased** **4** to express orally or in a phrase: *I could have phrased that better* **5** *music* to divide (a melodic line or part) into musical phrases, esp. in performance > **phrasal** *adj*

> **phrase** *n* **1, 2** = expression, saying, remark, construction, quotation, maxim, idiom, adage ▶ *vb* **4** = express, say, word, put, voice, communicate, convey, put into words

phraseology (fray-zee-**ol**-a-jee) *n, pl* **-gies** the manner in which words or phrases are used

physical *adj* **1** of the body, as distinguished from the mind or spirit **2** of material things or nature: *the physical world* **3** of or concerned with matter and energy **4** of or relating to physics
> **physically** *adv*

physical *adj* **1** = corporal, fleshly, bodily, corporeal **2** = earthly, fleshly, mortal, incarnate **3** = material, real, substantial (*formal*), natural, solid, tangible, palpable

physical education *n* training and practice in sports and gymnastics

physician *n* **1** a medical doctor **2** *archaic* a healer

> **physician** *n* **1** = doctor, doc (*informal*), medic (*informal*), general practitioner, medical practitioner, doctor of medicine, G.P., M.D.

physicist *n* a person versed in or studying physics

physics *n* **1** the branch of science concerned with the properties of matter and energy and the relationships between them **2** physical properties of behaviour: *the physics of the electron*

physiognomy (fiz-ee-**on**-om-ee) *n formal* **1** a person's face considered as an indication of personality **2** the outward appearance of something: *the changed physiognomy of the forests*

physiology *n* **1** the branch of science concerned with the functioning of organisms **2** the processes and functions of all or part of an organism > **physiologist** *n* > **physiological** *adj*

physiotherapy *n* the treatment of disease or injury by physical means, such as massage or exercises, rather than by drugs
> **physiotherapist** *n*

physique *n* a person's bodily build and muscular development

pi *n, pl* **pis** **1** the 16th letter in the Greek alphabet (Π, π) **2** *maths* a number that is the ratio of the circumference of a circle to its diameter; approximate value: 3.141592.... Symbol: π

pianissimo *adj, adv music* to be performed very quietly

piano *n, pl* **-anos** a musical instrument played by depressing keys that cause hammers to strike strings and produce audible vibrations

Pianola (pee-an-**oh**-la) *n trademark* a type of mechanical piano, the music for which is encoded in perforations in a paper roll

piazza *n* **1** a large open square in an Italian town **2** *chiefly Brit* a covered passageway or gallery

pic *n, pl* **pics** *or* **pix** *informal* a photograph or illustration

picador *n bullfighting* a horseman who wounds the bull with a lance to weaken it

picaresque *adj literary* of or relating to a type of fiction in which the hero, a rogue, goes through a series of episodic adventures

piccalilli *n* a pickle of mixed vegetables in a mustard sauce

piccolo *n, pl* **-los** a woodwind instrument an octave higher than the flute

pick[1] *vb* **1** to choose or select **2** to gather (fruit, berries, or crops) from (a tree, bush, or field) **3** to remove loose particles from: *she picked some bits of* *fluff off her sleeve* **4** (foll. by *at*) to nibble (at) without appetite **5** to provoke (an argument or fight) deliberately **6** to separate (strands or fibres), as in weaving **7** to steal from (someone's pocket) **8** to open (a lock) with an instrument other than a key **9** to make (one's) way) carefully on foot: *they picked their way through the rubble* **10 pick and choose** to select fastidiously or fussily ▸ *n* **11** choice: *take your pick* **12** the best: *the pick of the country's young cricketers* ▸ See also **pick on** etc.

> **pick** *vb* **1** = select, choose, identify, elect, nominate, specify, opt for, single out, flag up; ≠ reject **2** = gather, pull, collect, take in, harvest, pluck, garner **5** = provoke, start, cause, stir up, incite, instigate **8** = open, force, crack (*informal*), break into, break open ▸ *n* **11** = choice, decision, option, selection, preference **12** = best, prime, finest, elect, elite, cream, jewel in the crown, the crème de la crème

pick² *n* **1** a tool with a handle and a long curved steel head, used for loosening soil or breaking rocks **2** any tool used for picking, such as an ice pick or toothpick **3** a plectrum ▸ *vb* **4** to pierce or break up (a hard surface) with a pick

pickaxe *or US* **pickax** *n* a large pick

picket *n* **1** a person or group standing outside a workplace to dissuade strikebreakers from entering **2** a small unit of troops posted to give early warning of attack **3** a pointed stake that is driven into the ground to support a fence ▸ *vb* **-eting, -eted 4** to act as pickets outside (a workplace)

> **picket** *n* **1** = protester, demonstrator, picketer **2** = lookout, watch, guard, patrol, sentry, sentinel **3** = stake, post, pale, paling, upright, stanchion ▸ *vb* = blockade, boycott, demonstrate outside

picket line *n* a line of people acting as pickets

pickings *pl n* money or profits acquired easily

pickle *n* **1** (*often pl*) food, esp. vegetables preserved in vinegar or brine **2** a liquid or marinade, such as spiced vinegar, for preserving vegetables, meat, or fish **3** *informal* an awkward or difficult situation: *to be in a pickle; they are in a pickle over what to do with toxic waste* ▸ *vb* **-ling, -led 4** to preserve or treat in a pickling liquid

> **pickle** *n* **1** = chutney, relish, piccalilli **3** = predicament, fix (*informal*), difficulty, bind (*informal*), jam (*informal*), dilemma, scrape (*informal*), hot water (*informal*), uphill (*S African*) ▸ *vb* = preserve, marinade, steep

pickled *adj* **1** (of food) preserved in a pickling liquid **2** *informal* drunk

pick-me-up *n informal* a tonic, esp. a special drink taken as a stimulant

pick on *vb* to continually treat someone unfairly

pick on *vb* **pick on someone** = torment, bully, bait, tease, get at (*informal*), badger, persecute, hector

pick out *vb* **1** to select for use or special consideration: *she picked out a wide gold wedding ring* **2** to distinguish (an object from its surroundings), such as in painting: *the wall panels are light brown, with their edges picked out in gold* **3** to recognize (a person or thing): *she picked the man out in a police identity parade* **4** to play (a tune) tentatively, as by ear

> **pick out** *vb* **3 pick something or someone out** = identify, recognize, distinguish, perceive, discriminate, make someone *or* something out, tell someone *or* something apart

pickpocket *n* a person who steals from the pockets of others in public places

pick up *vb* **1** to lift or raise: *he picked up his glass* **2** to obtain or purchase: *a couple of pictures she has picked up in a flea market in Paris* **3** to improve in health or condition: *business had picked up after a difficult first quarter* **4** to learn as one goes along: *she had a good ear and picked up languages quickly* **5** to raise (oneself) after a fall or setback: *she picked herself up and got on with her life* **6** to resume; return to **7** to accept the responsibility for paying (a bill) **8** to collect or give a lift to (passengers or goods) **9** *informal* to become acquainted with for a sexual purpose **10** *informal* to arrest **11** to receive (sounds or signals)

> **pick up** *vb* **1 pick something or someone up** = lift, raise, gather, take up, grasp, uplift **2 pick something up** = obtain, get, find, buy, discover, purchase, acquire, locate **3** = improve, recover, rally, get better, bounce back, make progress, perk up, turn the corner **4 pick something up** = learn, master, acquire, get the hang of (*informal*), become proficient in **8 pick something or someone up** = collect, get, call for

pick-up *n* **1** a small truck with an open body used for light deliveries **2** *informal* a casual acquaintance made for a sexual purpose **3** *informal* **A** a stop to collect passengers or goods **B** the people or things collected **4** a device which converts vibrations into electrical signals, such as that to which a record player stylus is attached

picnic *n* **1** an excursion on which people bring food to be eaten in the open air **2** an informal meal eaten out-of-doors **3 no picnic** *informal* a hard or disagreeable task ▸ *vb* **-nicking, -nicked 4** to eat or take part in a picnic ▸ **picnicker** *n*

> **picnic** *n* **1, 2** = excursion, barbecue, barbie (*informal*), cookout (*US, Canad*), alfresco meal, clambake (*US, Canad*), outdoor meal, outing

Pict *n* a member of any of the peoples who lived in N Britain in the first to the fourth centuries AD ▸ **Pictish** *adj*

pictorial *adj* **1** relating to or expressed by pictures ▸ *n* **2** a periodical containing many pictures

picture *n* **1** a visual representation produced on a surface, such as in a photograph or painting **2** a mental image: *neither had any clear picture of whom they were looking for* **3** a description or account of a situation considered as an observable scene: *the reports do not provide an accurate picture of the spread of the disease* **4** a person or thing resembling another: *he is the picture of a perfect host* **5** a person or scene typifying a particular state: *his face was a picture of dejection* **6** the image on a television screen **7** a cinema film **8 in the picture** informed about a situation **9 the pictures** a cinema or film show ▸ *vb* **-turing, -tured 10** to visualize or imagine **11** to describe or depict vividly: *a documentary that had pictured them as good-natured dolts* **12** to put in a picture or make a picture of: *the people pictured above are all the same age*

> **picture** *n* **1** = representation, drawing, painting, portrait, image, print, illustration, sketch, avatar **2** = idea, vision, concept, impression, notion, visualization, mental picture, mental image **3** = description, impression, explanation, report, account, image, sketch, depiction **5** = personification, embodiment, essence, epitome, avatar **7** = film, movie (US informal), flick (slang), feature film, motion picture ▸ *vb* **10** = imagine, see, envision, visualize, conceive of, fantasize about, conjure up an image of **11** = represent, show, draw, paint, illustrate, sketch, depict **12** = show, photograph, capture on film

picturesque *adj* **1** visually pleasing, as in being striking or quaint: *a small picturesque harbour* **2** (of language) graphic or vivid

> **picturesque** *adj* **1** = interesting, pretty, beautiful, attractive, charming, scenic, quaint; ≠ unattractive **2** = vivid, striking, graphic, colourful, memorable; ≠ dull

picture window *n* a large window with a single pane of glass, usually facing a view

piddle *vb* **-dling, -dled** *informal* **1** to urinate **2 piddle about** or **around** or **away** to spend (one's time) aimlessly: *we have been piddling around for seven months*

pidgin *n* a language made up of elements of two or more languages and used between the speakers of the languages involved

pie *n* **1** a sweet or savoury filling baked in pastry **2 pie in the sky** illusory hope or promise of some future good

piebald *adj* **1** marked in two colours, esp. black and white ▸ *n* **2** a black-and-white horse

piece *n* **1** a separate bit or part **2** an instance or occurrence: *a piece of luck* **3** an example or specimen of a style or type: *each piece of furniture is crafted from native red pine by traditional methods*

4 a literary, musical, or artistic composition **5** a coin: *a fifty-pence piece* **6** a firearm or cannon **7** a small object used in playing various games: *a chess piece* **8 go to pieces** (of a person) to lose control of oneself; have a breakdown ▸ *vb* **piecing, pieced 9** (often foll. by *together*) to fit or assemble bit by bit **10** (often foll. by *up*) to patch or make up (a garment) by adding pieces

> **piece** *n* **1** = bit, slice, part, block, quantity, segment, portion, fragment **4** = composition, work, production, opus

pièce de résistance (pyess de ray-**zeest**-onss) *n* the most outstanding item in a series

piecemeal *adv* **1** bit by bit; gradually ▸ *adj* **2** fragmentary or unsystematic: *a piecemeal approach*

piecework *n* work paid for according to the quantity produced

pie chart *n* a circular graph divided into sectors proportional to the sizes of the quantities represented

pied *adj* having markings of two or more colours

pied-à-terre (pyay-da-**tair**) *n, pl* **pieds-à-terre** (pyay-da-**tair**) a flat or other lodging for occasional use

pier *n* **1** a structure with a deck that is built out over water and used as a landing place or promenade **2** a pillar or support that bears heavy loads **3** the part of a wall between two adjacent openings

> **pier** *n* **1** = jetty, wharf, quay, promenade, landing place **2** = pillar, support, post, column, pile, upright, buttress

pierce *vb* **piercing, pierced 1** to make a hole in (something) with a sharp point **2** to force (a way) through (something) **3** (of light) to shine through (darkness) **4** (of sounds or cries) to sound sharply through (the silence) **5** to penetrate: *the cold pierced the air*

> **pierce** *vb* **1** = penetrate, stab, spike, enter, bore, drill, puncture, prick

piercing *adj* **1** (of a sound) unpleasantly loud and sharp: *a piercing scream* **2** very intense: *a piercing stare* ▸ *n* **3** a hole made in the body so that an item of jewellery can be inserted into it: *a nose piercing*

Pierrot (pier-roe) *n* a male character from French pantomime with a whitened face, white costume, and pointed hat

piety *n, pl* **-ties 1** dutiful devotion to God and observance of religious principles **2** the quality of being pious **3** a pious action or saying

piffle *n informal* nonsense

pig *n* **1** a mammal with a long head, a snout, and bristle-covered skin, which is kept and killed for pork, ham, and bacon. Related adjective: **porcine 2** *informal* a dirty, greedy, or bad-mannered person **3** *offensive slang* a police officer **4** a mass of metal cast into a simple shape **5** *Brit informal* something that is difficult or unpleasant: *the coast is a pig for little boats* **6 a pig in a poke** something bought or received without previous sight or knowledge **7 make a pig of oneself** *informal* to overeat ▸ *vb* **pigging, pigged 8** (of a sow) to give birth **9** (often foll. by *out*) *slang* to eat greedily or to excess: *she had pigged out on pizza before the show*

> **pig** *n* **1** = hog (US), sow, boar, swine, porker **2** = slob, glutton

pigeon¹ *n* **1** a bird which has a heavy body, small head, and short legs, and is usually grey in colour **2** *slang* a victim or dupe

pigeon² *n informal* concern or responsibility: *this is our pigeon – there's nothing to keep you*

pigeonhole *n* **1** a small compartment, such as in a bureau, for filing papers ▸ *vb* **-holing, -holed 2** to classify or categorize **3** to put aside

pigeon-toed *adj* with the toes or feet turned inwards

piggery *n, pl* **-geries** a place where pigs are kept

piggish *adj* **1** like a pig in appetite or manners **2** stubborn > **piggishness** *n*

piggyback or **pickaback** *n* **1** a ride on the back and shoulders of another person ▸ *adv, adj* **2** on the back and shoulders of another person

pig-headed *adj* stupidly stubborn

pig iron *n* crude iron produced in a blast furnace and poured into moulds

pigment *n* **1** any substance which gives colour to paint or dye **2** a substance which occurs in plant or animal tissue and produces a characteristic colour > **pigmentary** *adj*

> **pigment** *n* **1** = colour, colouring, paint, stain, dye, tint, tincture

pigmentation *n* colouring in plants, animals, or humans, caused by the presence of pigments

Pigmy *n, pl* **-mies** same as **Pygmy**

pigsty or US & Canad **pigpen** *n, pl* **-sties 1** a pen for pigs **2** an untidy place

pigtail *n* a plait of hair or one of two plaits on either side of the face

pike¹ *n, pl* **pike** or **pikes** a large predatory freshwater fish with a broad flat snout, strong teeth, and a long body covered with small scales

pike² *n* a medieval weapon consisting of a metal spearhead on a long pole > **pikeman** *n*

pikelet *n* a small thick pancake

piker *n Austral & NZ slang* a shirker

pikey *n Brit slang, derogatory* **1** a traveller or vagrant **2** a member of the underclass

pilaster *n* a shallow rectangular column attached to the face of a wall > **pilastered** *adj*

Pilates (pil-**lah**-teez) *n* a system of gentle exercises that stretch and lengthen the muscles, designed to improve posture and flexibility

pilau or **pilaf** *n* a Middle Eastern dish, consisting of rice flavoured with spices and cooked in stock, to which meat, poultry, or fish may be added

pilchard *n* a small edible sea fish of the herring family, with a rounded body covered with large scales

pile¹ *n* **1** a collection of objects laid on top of one another **2** *informal* a large amount: *boxing has made him a pile of money; I've got piles of work to do* **3** same as **pyre 4** a large building or group of buildings **5** *physics* a nuclear reactor ▸ *vb* **piling, piled 6** (often foll. by *up*) to collect or be collected into a pile: *snow piled up in the drive* **7** (foll. by *in, into, off* or *out* etc.) to move in a group, often in a hurried manner: *the crew piled into the van* **8 pile it on** *informal* to exaggerate

> **pile** *n* **1** = heap, collection, mountain, mass, stack, mound, accumulation, hoard **2** = lot(s), mountain(s), load(s) (*informal*), oceans, wealth, great deal, stack(s), abundance **4** = mansion, building, residence, manor, country house, seat, big house, stately home ▸ *vb* **6** = load, stuff, pack, stack, charge, heap, cram, lade **7** = crowd, pack, rush, climb, flood, stream, crush, squeeze

pile² *n* a long heavy beam driven into the ground as a foundation for a structure

> **pile** *n* = foundation, support, post, column, beam, upright, pillar

pile³ *n* the fibres in a fabric that stand up or out from the weave, such as in carpeting or velvet

> **pile** *n* = nap, fibre, down, hair, fur, plush

piles *pl n* swollen veins in the rectum; haemorrhoids

pilfer *vb* to steal (minor items) in small quantities

pilgrim *n* **1** a person who journeys to a holy place **2** any wayfarer

> **pilgrim** *n* = traveller, wanderer, devotee, wayfarer

pilgrimage *n* **1** a journey to a shrine or other holy place **2** a journey or long search made for sentimental reasons: *a pilgrimage to the poet's birthplace*

> **pilgrimage** *n* **2** = journey, tour, trip, mission, excursion

pill *n* **1** a small mass of medicine intended to be swallowed whole **2 the pill** *informal* an oral contraceptive taken by a woman **3** something unpleasant that must be endured: *her reinstatement was a bitter pill to swallow; the pill was sweetened by a reduction in interest*

> **pill** *n* **1** = tablet, capsule, pellet

pillage *vb* **-laging, -laged 1** to steal property violently, often in war ▸ *n* **2** the act of pillaging **3** something obtained by pillaging; booty

pillar *n* **1** an upright support of stone, brick, or metal; column **2** something resembling this: *a pillar of smoke* **3** a prominent supporter or member: *a pillar of society* **4 from pillar to post** from one place to another

P

pillar n **1** = support, post, column, prop, shaft, upright, pier, stanchion **3** = supporter, leader, mainstay, leading light (informal), upholder

pillar box n (in Britain) a red pillar-shaped public letter box situated in the street

pillion n **1** a seat for a passenger behind the rider of a motorcycle or horse ▸ adv **2** on a pillion: *the motorbike on which he was riding pillion*

pillory n, pl **-ries 1** (formerly) a wooden frame in which offenders were locked by the neck and wrists and exposed to public abuse and ridicule ▸ vb **-ries, -rying, -ried 2** to expose to public ridicule **3** (formerly) to punish by putting in a pillory

pillow n **1** a cloth bag stuffed with feathers, polyester fibre, or pieces of foam rubber used to support the head in bed ▸ vb **2** to rest (one's head) on or as if on a pillow: *he pillowed his head in her lap*

pillowcase or **pillowslip** n a removable washable cover for a pillow

pilot n **1** a person who is qualified to fly an aircraft or spacecraft **2** a person employed to steer a ship into or out of a port **3** a person who acts as a guide ▸ adj **4** serving as a test or trial: *a pilot scheme* **5** serving as a guide: *a pilot beacon* ▸ vb **-loting, -loted 6** to act as pilot of **7** to guide or lead (a project or people): *the legislation was piloted through its committee stage*

pilot n **1** = airman, flyer (old-fashioned), aviator, aeronaut **2, 3** = helmsman, navigator, steersman or woman or person ▸ adj **4** = trial, test, model, sample, experimental ▸ vb **6** = fly, operate, be at the controls of **7** = direct, conduct, steer

pilot light n a small flame that lights the main burner of a gas appliance

pimento n, pl **-tos** same as **allspice**

pimp n **1** a man who obtains customers for a prostitute, in return for a share of his or her earnings ▸ vb **2** to act as a pimp **3** informal (often foll. by up or out) to make (someone or something, esp. a car) more extravagantly decorated, as with flashy accessories, etc.

pimpernel n a plant, such as the scarlet pimpernel, typically having small star-shaped flowers

pimple n a small swollen infected spot on the skin > **pimpled** adj > **pimply** adj

pin n **1** a short stiff straight piece of wire with a pointed end and a rounded head: used mainly for fastening **2** a wooden or metal peg **3** a pin-shaped brooch **4** (in various bowling games) a club-shaped wooden object set up in groups as a target **5** a clip that prevents a hand grenade from exploding until it is removed or released **6** golf the flagpole marking the hole on a green **7** informal a leg ▸ vb **pinning, pinned 8** to fasten with a pin or pins **9** to seize and hold fast: *they pinned his arms behind his back* **10 pin something on someone** informal to place the blame for something on someone: *corruption*

charges are the easiest to pin on former dictators ▸ See also **pin down**

pin n **1** = tack, nail, needle, safety pin **2** = peg, rod, brace, bolt ▸ vb **8** = fasten, stick, attach, join, fix, secure, nail, clip **9** = hold fast, hold down, constrain, immobilize, pinion

PIN Personal Identification Number: a secret number used to gain access an automated system, for example to authorize a financial transaction

pinafore n **1** chiefly Brit an apron with a bib **2** a dress with a sleeveless bodice or bib top, worn over a jumper or blouse

pinball n an electrically operated table game in which the player shoots a small ball through several hazards

pince-nez (panss-nay) n, pl **pince-nez** glasses that are held in place only by means of a clip over the bridge of the nose

pincers pl n **1** a gripping tool consisting of two hinged arms and curved jaws **2** the jointed grasping arms of crabs and lobsters

pinch vb **1** to squeeze (something, esp. flesh) between a finger and thumb **2** to squeeze by being too tight: *shoes that pinch* **3** to cause stinging pain to: *the cold pinched his face* **4** to make thin or drawn-looking, such as from grief or cold **5** informal to steal **6** informal to arrest **7** (usually foll. by out or back) to remove the tips of (a plant shoot) to correct or encourage growth ▸ n **8** a squeeze or sustained nip **9** the quantity that can be taken up between a thumb and finger: *a pinch of ground ginger* **10** extreme stress or need: *most companies are feeling the pinch of recession* **11 at a pinch** if absolutely necessary **12 feel the pinch** to be forced to economize

pinch vb **1** = nip, press, squeeze, grasp, compress **2** = hurt, crush, squeeze, pain, cramp **5** = steal, lift (informal), nick (slang, chiefly Brit), swipe (slang), knock off (slang), pilfer, purloin, filch ▸ n **8** = nip, squeeze **9** = dash, bit, mite, jot, speck, soupçon (French) **10** = emergency, crisis, difficulty, plight, scrape (informal), strait, uphill (S African), predicament

pinchbeck n **1** an alloy of copper and zinc, used as imitation gold ▸ adj **2** sham or cheap

pin down vb **1** to force (someone) to make a decision or carry out a promise **2** to define clearly: *the courts have found it difficult to pin down what exactly obscenity is*

pin down vb **1 pin someone down** = force, pressure, compel, put pressure on, pressurize, nail someone down, make someone commit themselves **2 pin something down** = determine, identify, locate, name, specify, pinpoint

pine¹ n **1** an evergreen tree with long needle-shaped leaves and brown cones **2** the light-coloured wood of this tree

pine² *vb* **pining, pined 1** (often foll. by *for*) to feel great longing (for) **2** (often foll. by *away*) to become ill or thin through grief or longing

> **pine** *vb* **1 pine for something or someone** = long, ache, crave, yearn, eat your heart out over **2** = waste, decline, sicken, fade, languish

pineal gland *or* **pineal body** (pin-ee-al) *n* a small cone-shaped gland at the base of the brain

pineapple *n* a large tropical fruit with juicy flesh and a thick hard skin

pine cone *n* the woody seed case of a pine tree

pine marten *n* a mammal of N European and Asian coniferous woods, with dark brown fur and a creamy-yellow patch on the throat

ping *n* **1** a short high-pitched sound, such as of a bullet striking metal ▸ *vb* **2** to make such a noise

ping-pong *n* same as **table tennis**

pinion¹ *n* **1** *chiefly poetic* a bird's wing **2** the outer part of a bird's wing including the flight feathers ▸ *vb* **3** to immobilize (someone) by holding or tying his or her arms **4** to confine

pinion² *n* a cogwheel that engages with a larger wheel or rack

pink *n* **1** a colour between red and white **2** anything pink, such as pink paint or pink clothing: *packaged in pink* **3** a garden plant with pink, red, or white fragrant flowers **4 in the pink** in good health ▸ *adj* **5** of a colour between red and white **6** *informal* having mild left-wing sympathies **7** *informal* relating to homosexuals or homosexuality: *the pink vote* ▸ *vb* **8** same as **knock** (sense 7) > **pinkish** *or* **pinky** *adj*

> **pink** *adj* **5** = rosy, rose, salmon, flushed, reddish, roseate

pinking shears *pl n* scissors with a serrated edge that give a wavy edge to material cut and so prevent fraying

pin money *n* a small amount of extra money earned to buy small luxuries

pinnacle *n* **1** the highest point of fame or success **2** a towering peak of a mountain **3** a slender spire

> **pinnacle** *n* **1** = height, top, crown, crest, zenith, apex, vertex **2** = summit, top, height, peak

pinotage (pin-oh-tazh) *n* a red wine blended from the Pinot Noir and Hermitage grapes that is unique to South Africa

pinpoint *vb* **1** to locate or identify exactly: *we've pinpointed the fault* ▸ *adj* **2** exact: *pinpoint accuracy*

> **pinpoint** *vb* = locate, find, identify, zero in on

pinstripe *n* (in textiles) a very narrow stripe in fabric or the fabric itself

pint *n* **1** *Brit* a unit of liquid measure equal to one eighth of an imperial gallon (0.568 litre) **2** *US* a unit of liquid measure equal to one eighth of a US gallon (0.473 litre) **3** *Brit informal* a pint of beer

pin-up *n* **1** *informal* a picture of a sexually attractive person, often partially or totally undressed **2** *slang* a person who has appeared in such a picture: *your favourite pin-up* **3** a photograph of a famous personality

pioneer *n* **1** an explorer or settler of a new land or region **2** an originator or developer of something new ▸ *vb* **3** to be a pioneer (in or of) **4** to initiate or develop: *the new technique was pioneered in France*

> **pioneer** *n* **1** = settler, explorer, colonist **2** = founder, leader, developer, innovator, trailblazer ▸ *vb* **4** = develop, create, establish, start, discover, institute, invent, initiate

pious *adj* **1** religious or devout **2** insincerely reverent; sanctimonious > **piousness** *n*

pip¹ *n* the seed of a fleshy fruit, such as an apple or pear

pip² *n* **1** a short high-pitched sound used as a time signal on radio **2** any of the spots on a playing card, dice, or domino **3** *informal* the emblem worn on the shoulder by junior officers in the British Army, indicating their rank

pip³ *n* **1** a contagious disease of poultry **2** *facetious slang* a minor human ailment **3 get** *or* **have the pip** *NZ slang* to sulk **4 give someone the pip** *Brit, NZ & S African slang* to annoy someone: *it really gives me the pip*

pipe *n* **1** a long tube for conveying water, oil, or gas **2** a tube with a small bowl at the end for smoking tobacco **B** the amount of tobacco that fills the bowl of a pipe **3** *zool & botany* any of various hollow organs, such as the respiratory passage of certain animals **A** a tubular instrument in which air vibrates and produces a musical sound **B** any of the tubular devices on an organ **5** a boatswain's whistle **6 put that in your pipe and smoke it** *informal* accept that fact if you can **7 the pipes** See **bagpipes** ▸ *vb* **piping, piped 8** to play (music) on a pipe or on bagpipes **9** to summon or lead by a pipe: *to pipe in the haggis* **10 A** to signal orders to (the crew) by a boatswain's pipe **B** to signal the arrival or departure of: *he piped his entire ship's company on deck* **11** to utter in a shrill tone **12** to convey (water, oil, or gas) by pipe **13** to force (cream or icing) through a shaped nozzle to decorate food ▸ See also **pipe down, pipe up**

> **pipe** *n* **1** = tube, drain, canal, pipeline, line, main, passage, cylinder ▸ *vb* **12** = convey, channel, conduct

piped music *n* light music played as background music in public places

pipe down *vb informal* to stop talking or making noise

> **pipe down** *vb* = be quiet, shut up (*informal*), hush, stop talking, quieten down, shush, shut your mouth, hold your tongue

P

pipe dream *n* a fanciful or impossible plan or hope

pipeline *n* **1** a long pipe for transporting oil, water, or gas **2** a means of communication **3 in the pipeline** in preparation

> **pipeline** *n* **1** = tube, passage, pipe, conduit, duct

piper *n* a person who plays a pipe or bagpipes

pipette *n* a slender glass tube for transferring or measuring out liquids

pipe up *vb* to speak up unexpectedly

pipi *n*, *pl* **pipi** or **pipis** *Austral & NZ* an edible mollusc of Australia and New Zealand

piping *n* **1** a system of pipes **2** a string of icing or cream to decorate cakes and desserts **3** a thin strip of covered cord or material, used to edge hems or cushions **4** the sound of a pipe or bagpipes **5** a shrill voice or whistling sound: *a dove's cool piping* ▸ *adj* **6** making a shrill sound ▸ *adv* **7 piping hot** extremely hot

pipit *n* a small songbird with a brownish speckled plumage and a long tail

pippin *n* a type of eating apple

piquant (pee-kant) *adj* **1** having a spicy taste **2** stimulating to the mind: *love was a forbidden piquant secret* > **piquancy** *n*

pique (peek) *n* **1** a feeling of resentment or irritation, such as from hurt pride ▸ *vb* **piquing, piqued 2** to hurt (someone's) pride **3** to excite (curiosity or interest)

piqué (pee-kay) *n* a stiff ribbed fabric of cotton, silk, or spun rayon

piquet (pik-ket) *n* a card game for two people played with a reduced pack

piracy *n*, *pl* **-cies 1** robbery on the seas **2** a crime, such as hijacking, committed aboard a ship or aircraft **3** the unauthorized use of patented or copyrighted material

piranha *n* a small fierce freshwater fish of tropical America, with strong jaws and sharp teeth

pirate *n* **1** a person who commits piracy **2** a vessel used by pirates **3** a person who illegally sells or publishes someone else's literary or artistic work **4** a person or group of people who broadcast illegally ▸ *vb* **-rating, -rated 5** to sell or reproduce (artistic work, ideas, etc.) illegally > **piratical** *adj*

> **pirate** *n* **1** = buccaneer, raider, marauder, corsair, freebooter ▸ *vb* = copy, steal, reproduce, bootleg, appropriate, poach, crib (*informal*), plagiarize

pirouette *n* **1** a body spin performed on the toes or the ball of the foot ▸ *vb* **-etting, -etted 2** to perform a pirouette

piss *vulgar* ▸ *vb* **1** to urinate **2** to discharge as or in one's urine: *to piss blood* ▸ *n* **3** an act of urinating **4** urine **5 take the piss** to make fun of or mock someone

pistachio *n*, *pl* **-chios** a Mediterranean nut with a hard shell and an edible green kernel

piste (peest) *n* a slope or course for skiing

pistil *n* the seed-bearing part of a flower

pistol *n* a short-barrelled handgun

piston *n* a cylindrical part that slides to and fro in a hollow cylinder: in an engine it is attached by a rod to other parts, thus its movement causes the other parts to move

pit *n* **1** a large deep opening in the ground **2** a coal mine **3** *anatomy* **A** a small natural depression on the surface of a body or organ **B** the floor of any natural bodily cavity: *the pit of the stomach* **4** *pathol* a pockmark **5** a concealed danger or difficulty **6** an area at the side of a motor-racing track for servicing or refuelling vehicles **7** the area occupied by the orchestra in a theatre **8** *Brit history* an enclosure for fighting animals or birds **9** the back of the ground floor of a theatre **10** same as **pitfall** (sense 2) **11 the pit** hell ▸ *vb* **pitting, pitted 12** (often foll. by *against*) to match in opposition, esp. as antagonists: *sister pitted against sister* **13** to mark with small dents or scars **14** to place or bury in a pit **15 pit one's wits against** to compete against in a test or contest

> **pit** *n* **1** = hole, depression, hollow, crater, trough, cavity, abyss, chasm **2** = coal mine, mine, shaft, colliery, mine shaft ▸ *vb* **13** = scar, mark, dent, indent, pockmark

pit bull terrier *n* a strong muscular terrier with a short coat

pitch[1] *vb* **1** to hurl or throw **2** to set up (a tent or camp) **3** to slope or fall forwards or downwards: *she pitched forwards like a diver* **4** (of a ship or plane) to dip and raise its back and front alternately **5** to set the level or tone of: *his ambitions were pitched too high* **6** to aim to sell (a product) to a specified market or on a specified basis **7** *music* to sing or play (a note or interval) accurately ▸ *n* **8** *chiefly Brit* (in many sports) the field of play **9** a level of emotion: *children can wind their parents up to a pitch of anger and guilt* **10** the degree or angle of slope **11** the distance between corresponding points or adjacent threads on a screw thread **12** the pitching motion of a ship or plane **13** *music* the highness or lowness of a note in relation to other notes: *low pitch* **14** the act or manner of pitching a ball **15** *chiefly Brit* the place where a street or market trader regularly sells **16** *slang* a persuasive sales talk, esp. one routinely repeated ▸ See also **pitch in, pitch into**

> **pitch** *vb* **1** = throw, cast, toss, hurl, fling, chuck (*informal*), sling, lob (*informal*) **2** = set up, raise, settle, put up, erect **3** = fall, drop, plunge, dive, tumble, topple, plummet, fall headlong **4** = toss (about), roll, plunge, lurch ▸ *n* **8** = sports field, ground, stadium, arena, park, field of play **9** = level, point, degree, summit, extent, height, intensity, high point **13** = tone, sound, key, frequency, timbre, modulation **16** = talk, patter, spiel (*informal*)

pitch² *n* **1** a thick sticky substance formed from coal tar and used for paving or waterproofing **2** any similar substance, such as asphalt, occurring as a natural deposit ▸ *vb* **3** to apply pitch to

pitch-black *adj* extremely dark; unlit: *it was a wild night, pitch-black, with howling gales*

pitchblende *n* a blackish mineral which is the principal source of uranium and radium

pitcher *n* a large jug, usually rounded with a narrow neck

pitchfork *n* **1** a long-handled fork with two or three long curved prongs for tossing hay ▸ *vb* **2** to use a pitchfork on (something)

pitch in *vb* to cooperate or contribute

> **pitch in** *vb* = help, contribute, participate, join in, cooperate, chip in (*informal*), get stuck in (*Brit informal*), lend a hand

pitch into *vb informal* to attack (someone) physically or verbally

piteous *adj* arousing or deserving pity: *the piteous mewing of an injured kitten* > **piteousness** *n*

pitfall *n* **1** an unsuspected difficulty or danger **2** a trap in the form of a concealed pit, designed to catch people or wild animals

> **pitfall** *n* **1** = danger, difficulty, peril, catch (*informal*), trap, hazard, drawback, snag, uphill (*S African*)

pith *n* **1** the soft white lining inside the rind of fruits such as the orange **2** the essential part: *policy, though, isn't the pith of what happened yesterday* **3** the soft spongy tissue in the centre of the stem of certain plants

pithy *adj* **pithier, pithiest 1** terse and full of meaning **2** of, resembling, or full of pith > **pithiness** *n*

pitiful *adj* arousing or deserving great pity or contempt > **pitifully** *adv* > **pitifulness** *n*

pitiless *adj* feeling no pity or mercy > **pitilessly** *adv*

piton (**peet-on**) *n mountaineering* a metal spike that may be driven into a crack and used to secure a rope

pittance *n* a very small amount of money

pituitary *or* **pituitary gland** *n* the gland at the base of the brain which secretes hormones that affect skeletal growth, development of the sex glands, and other functions of the body

pity *n, pl* **pities 1** sorrow felt for the sufferings of others **2** a cause of regret: *it's a great pity he did not live longer* **3** **have** *or* **take pity on** to have sympathy or show mercy for ▸ *vb* **pities, pitying, pitied 4** to feel pity for > **pitying** *adj*

> **pity** *n* **1** = compassion, charity, sympathy, kindness, fellow feeling; ≠ mercilessness **2** = shame, sin (*informal*), misfortune, bummer (*slang*), crying shame ▸ *vb* = feel sorry for, feel for, sympathize with, grieve for, weep for, bleed for, have compassion for

pivot *n* **1** a central shaft around which something turns **2** the central person or thing necessary for progress or success ▸ *vb* **-oting, -oted 3** to turn on or provide with a pivot

pivotal *adj* **1** of crucial importance **2** of or acting as a pivot

> **pivotal** *adj* **1** = crucial, central, vital, critical, decisive

pix *n informal* a plural of **pic**

pixel *n* the smallest constituent unit of an image, as on a computer screen

pixelate *or* **pixellate** *vb* **-lating, -lated** to blur (a video image) by overlaying it with a grid of squares, often to disguise the identity of a person > **pixelation** *or* **pixellation** *n*

pixie *or* **pixy** *n, pl* **pixies** (in folklore) a fairy or elf

pizza *n* a dish of Italian origin consisting of a baked disc of dough covered with a wide variety of savoury toppings

pizzazz *or* **pizazz** *n informal* an attractive combination of energy and style

pizzicato (pit-see-kah-toe) *adj, adv music* (in music for the violin family) to be plucked with the finger

placard *n* **1** a notice that is paraded in public ▸ *vb* **2** to attach placards to

placate *vb* **-cating, -cated** to calm (someone) to stop him or her feeling angry or upset > **placatory** *adj*

place *n* **1** a particular part of a space or of a surface **2** a geographical point, such as a town or city **3** a position or rank in a sequence or order **4** an open square lined with houses in a city or town **5** space or room **6** a house or living quarters: *he's buying his own place* **7** any building or area set aside for a specific purpose **8** the point reached in reading or speaking: *her finger was pressed to the page as if marking her place* **9** right or duty: *it's not my place to do their job for them* **10** appointment, position, or job: *she won a place at university* **11** position, condition, or state: *if I were in your place, I'd change things* **12** a space or seat, as at a dining table **13** *maths* the relative position of a digit in a number **14 all over the place** in disorder or disarray **15 go places** *informal* to become successful **16 in** *or* **out of place** in or out of the proper or customary position **17 in place of** **A** instead of: *leeks can be used in place of the broccoli* **B** in exchange for: *he gave her it in place of her ring* **18 know one's place** to be aware of one's inferior position **19 put someone in his** *or* **her place** to humble someone who is arrogant, conceited, etc. **20 take place** to happen or occur **21 take the place of** to be a substitute for ▸ *vb* **placing, placed 22** to put in a particular or appropriate place **23** to find or indicate the place of: *I bet you the media couldn't have placed Neath on the map before the by-election* **24** to identify or classify by linking with an appropriate context: *I felt I should know him, but could not quite place him* **25** to make (an order or bet) **26** to find a home or job for (someone) **27** (often foll. by *with*) to put under the care (of) **28** (of a racehorse, greyhound, athlete, etc.) to arrive in first, second, third, or sometimes fourth place

> **place** n **1, 7** = spot, point, position, site, area, location, venue, whereabouts **2** = region, quarter, district, neighbourhood, vicinity, locality, locale, dorp (*S African*) **3** = position, point, spot, location **6** = home, house, room, property, accommodation, pad (*slang, old-fashioned*), residence, dwelling (*formal, literary*), bachelor apartment (*Canad*) **9** = duty, right, job, charge, concern, role, affair, responsibility **11** = situation, position, circumstances, shoes (*informal*) **12** = space, position, seat, chair **18 know one's place** = know one's rank, know one's standing, know one's position, know one's footing, know one's station, know one's status, know one's grade, know one's niche **20 take place** = happen, occur, go on, go down (*US, Canad*), arise, come about, crop up, transpire (*informal*) ▸ vb **22** = lay (down), put (down), set (down), stand, position, rest, station, stick (*informal*) **24** = identify, remember, recognize, pin someone down, put your finger on, put a name to **26, 27** = entrust to, give to, assign to, appoint to, allocate to, find a home for

placebo (plas-see-bo) *n*, *pl* **-bos** *or* **-boes** *med* an inactive substance given to a patient usually to compare its effects with those of a real drug but sometimes for the psychological benefit gained by the patient through believing that he or she is receiving treatment

placenta (plass-ent-a) *n*, *pl* **-tas** *or* **-tae** the organ formed in the womb of most mammals during pregnancy, providing oxygen and nutrients for the fetus ▹ **placental** *adj*

placid *adj* having a calm appearance or nature: *placid waters; a placid temperament* ▹ **placidity** *or* **placidness** *n* ▹ **placidly** *adv*

plagiarize *or* **-rise** (play-jer-ize) *vb* **-rizing, -rized** *or* **-rising, -rised** to steal ideas or passages from (another's work) and present them as one's own ▹ **plagiarism** *n* ▹ **plagiarizer** *or* **-riser** *n*

plague *n* **1** any widespread and usually highly contagious disease with a high fatality rate **2** an infectious disease of rodents transmitted to humans by the bite of the rat flea; bubonic plague **3** something that afflicts or harasses: *a plague of locusts* **4** *informal* a nuisance ▸ vb **plaguing, plagued** **5** to afflict or harass: *a playing career plagued by injury* **6** *informal* to annoy or pester

> **plague** n **1** = disease, infection, epidemic, pestilence **3** = infestation, invasion, epidemic, influx, host, swarm, multitude ▸ vb **5** = torment, trouble, torture **6** = pester, trouble, bother, annoy, tease, harry, harass, hassle

plaice *n*, *pl* **plaice** *or* **plaices** an edible European flatfish with a brown body marked with red or orange spots

plaid *n* **1** a long piece of tartan cloth worn over the shoulder as part of Highland costume **2** a crisscross weave or cloth

plain *adj* **1** flat or smooth **2** easily understood: *he made it plain what he wanted from me* **3** honest or blunt: *the plain fact is that my mother has no time for me* **4** without adornment: *a plain brown envelope* **5** not good-looking **6** (of fabric) without pattern or of simple weave **7** lowly, esp. in social rank or education: *the plain people of the nation* **8** *knitting* of or done in plain stitch ▸ **9** a level stretch of country **10** a simple stitch in knitting made by passing the wool round the front of the needle ▸ *adv* **11** clearly or simply: *that's just plain stupid!* ▹ **plainly** *adv* ▹ **plainness** *n*

> **plain** adj **2** = clear, obvious, patent, evident, visible, distinct, understandable, manifest; ≠ hidden **3** = straightforward, open, direct, frank, blunt, outspoken, honest, downright; ≠ roundabout **4** = unadorned, simple, basic, severe, bare, stark, austere, spartan, bare-bones; ≠ ornate **5** = ugly, unattractive, homely (*US, Canad*), unlovely, unprepossessing, not beautiful, no oil painting (*informal*), ill-favoured; ≠ attractive **7** = ordinary, common, simple, everyday, commonplace, unaffected, unpretentious; ≠ sophisticated ▸ n **9** = flatland, plateau, prairie, grassland, steppe, veld

plain clothes *pl n* ordinary clothes, as opposed to uniform, worn by a detective on duty

plain sailing *n* **1** *informal* smooth or easy progress **2** *naut* sailing in a body of water that is unobstructed; clear sailing

plainsong *n* the style of unaccompanied choral music used in the medieval Church, esp. in Gregorian chant

plain speaking *n* saying exactly what one thinks ▹ **plain-spoken** *adj*

plaintiff *n* a person who sues in a court of law

plaintive *adj* sad and mournful ▹ **plaintively** *adv*

plait (platt) *n* **1** a length of hair that has been plaited ▸ vb **2** to intertwine (strands or strips) in a pattern

plan *n* **1** a method thought out for doing or achieving something **2** a detailed drawing to scale of a horizontal section through a building **3** an outline or sketch ▸ vb **planning, planned** **4** to form a plan (for) **5** to make a plan of (a building) **6** to intend

> **plan** n **1** = scheme, system, design, programme, proposal, strategy, method, suggestion **2, 3** = diagram, map, drawing, chart, representation, sketch, blueprint, layout ▸ vb **4** = devise, arrange, scheme, plot, draft, organize, outline, formulate **5** = design, outline, draw up a plan of **6** = intend, aim, mean, propose, purpose

plane¹ n 1 an aeroplane 2 maths a flat surface in which a straight line joining any two of its points lies entirely on that surface 3 a level surface: *an inclined plane* 4 a level of existence or attainment: *her ambition was set on a higher plane than pulling pints in a pub* ▸ adj 5 level or flat 6 maths lying entirely in one plane ▸ vb **planing, planed** 7 to glide or skim: *they planed over the ice*

> **plane** n 1 = aeroplane, aircraft, jet, airliner, jumbo jet 3 = flat surface, the flat, horizontal, level surface 4 = level, position, stage, condition, standard, degree (*archaic*), rung, echelon ▸ adj 5 = level, even, flat, regular, smooth, horizontal ▸ vb = skim, sail, skate, glide

plane² n 1 a tool with a steel blade for smoothing timber ▸ vb **planing, planed** 2 to smooth (timber) using a plane 3 (often foll. by *away* or *off*) to remove using a plane

planet n any of the eight celestial bodies, Mercury, Venus, Earth, Mars, Jupiter, Saturn, Uranus, or Neptune, that revolve around the sun in oval-shaped orbits ▷ **planetary** adj

planetarium n, pl **-riums** or **-ria** 1 an instrument for projecting images of the sun, moon, stars, and planets onto a domed ceiling 2 a building in which such an instrument is housed

plane tree or **plane** n a tree with rounded heads of fruit and leaves with pointed lobes

plangent (plan-jent) adj (of sounds) mournful and resounding

plank n 1 a long flat piece of sawn timber 2 one of the policies in a political party's programme 3 **walk the plank** to be forced by sailors to walk to one's death off the end of a plank jutting out from the side of a ship

plankton n the small drifting plants and animals on the surface layer of a sea or lake

planner n 1 a person who makes plans, esp. for the development of a town, building, etc. 2 a chart for recording future appointments, etc.

plant n 1 a living organism that grows in the ground and lacks the power of movement 2 the land, building, and equipment used in an industry or business 3 a factory or workshop 4 mobile mechanical equipment for construction or road-making 5 *informal* a thing positioned secretly for discovery by someone else, often in order to incriminate an innocent person ▸ vb 6 to set (seeds or crops) into the ground to grow: *it's the wrong time of year for planting roses* 7 to place firmly in position: *I planted my chair beside hers* 8 to introduce into someone's mind: *once Wendy had planted the idea in the minds of the owners, they quite fancied selling* 9 *slang* to deliver (a blow or kiss) 10 *informal* to position or hide (someone) in order to deceive or observe 11 *informal* to hide or secrete (something), usually for some illegal purpose or in order to incriminate someone

> **plant** n 1 = flower, bush, vegetable, herb, weed, shrub 3 = factory, works, shop, yard, mill, foundry 4 = machinery, equipment, gear, apparatus ▸ vb 6 = sow, scatter, transplant, implant, put in the ground 7 = place, put, set, fix 8 = place, put, establish, found, fix, insert 10, 11 = hide, put, place, conceal

plantain¹ n a plant with a rosette of broad leaves and a slender spike of small greenish flowers

plantain² n 1 a large tropical fruit like a green-skinned banana 2 the tree on which this fruit grows

plantation n 1 an estate, esp. in tropical countries, where cash crops such as rubber or coffee are grown on a large scale 2 a group of cultivated trees or plants 3 (formerly) a colony of settlers

plant-based adj using foods and materials derived from plants rather than animals: *a plant-based diet*

planter n 1 the owner or manager of a plantation 2 a decorative pot for house plants

plaque n 1 a commemorative inscribed stone or metal plate 2 Also called: **dental plaque** a filmy deposit on teeth consisting of mucus, bacteria, and food, that causes decay

plasma n 1 the clear yellowish fluid portion of blood which contains the corpuscles and cells 2 a sterilized preparation of such fluid, taken from the blood, for use in transfusions 3 a former name for **protoplasm** 4 physics a hot ionized gas containing positive ions and free electrons

plasma screen n a type of flat television or computer screen that produces high-quality images

plaster n 1 a mixture of lime, sand, and water that is applied to a wall or ceiling as a soft paste and dries as a hard coating 2 Brit, Austral & NZ an adhesive strip of material for dressing a cut or wound ▸ vb 3 to coat (a wall or ceiling) with plaster 4 to apply like plaster: *he plastered his face with shaving cream* 5 to cause to lie flat or to adhere: *his hair was plastered to his forehead* ▷ **plasterer** n

> **plaster** n 1 = mortar, stucco, gypsum, plaster of Paris 2 = bandage, dressing, sticking plaster, Elastoplast (*trademark*), adhesive plaster ▸ vb 4 = cover, spread, coat, smear, overlay, daub

plastered adj slang drunk

plaster of Paris n a white powder that sets to a hard solid when mixed with water, used for making sculptures and casts for setting broken limbs

plastic n 1 any of a large number of synthetic materials that can be moulded when soft and then set 2 *informal* Also called: **plastic money** credit cards, etc. as opposed to cash ▸ adj 3 made

P

of plastic **4** easily influenced **5** capable of being moulded or formed **6** of moulding or modelling: *the plastic arts* **7** *slang* superficially attractive yet artificial or false: *glamorous models with plastic smiles* > **plasticity** *n*

> **plastic** *adj* **5** = pliant, soft, flexible, supple, pliable, ductile, mouldable; ≠ rigid

plastic bullet *n* a solid PVC cylinder fired by the police in riot control

Plasticine *n trademark* a soft coloured material used, esp. by children, for modelling

plastic surgery *n* the branch of surgery concerned with the repair or reconstruction of missing, injured, or malformed tissues or parts > **plastic surgeon** *n*

plate *n* **1** a shallow dish made of porcelain, earthenware, glass, etc., on which food is served **2** Also called: **plateful** the contents of a plate **3** a shallow dish for receiving a collection in church **4** flat metal of even thickness obtained by rolling **5** a thin coating of metal usually on another metal **6** dishes or cutlery made of gold or silver **7** a sheet of metal, plastic, or rubber having a printing surface produced by a process such as stereotyping **8** a print taken from such a sheet or from a woodcut **9** a thin flat sheet of a substance, such as glass **10** a small piece of metal or plastic with an inscription, fixed to another surface: *a brass name plate* **11** *photog* a sheet of glass coated with photographic emulsion on which an image can be formed by exposure to light **12** *informal* same as **denture** **13** *anatomy* any flat platelike structure **14** a cup awarded to the winner of a sporting contest, esp. a horse race **15** any of the rigid layers of the earth's crust **16 have a lot on one's plate** to have many pressing things to deal with **17 on a plate** acquired without trouble: *he got the job handed to him on a plate* ▶ *vb* **plating, plated 18** to coat (a metal surface) with a thin layer of another metal **19** to cover with metal plates, usually for protection **20** to form (metal) into plate, usually by rolling

> **plate** *n* **1** = platter, dish, dinner plate, salver, trencher (*archaic*) **2** = helping, course, serving, dish, portion, platter, plateful **5** = layer, panel, sheet, slab **8** = illustration, picture, photograph, print, engraving, lithograph ▶ *vb* **18** = coat, gild, laminate, cover, overlay

plateau (plat-oh) *n, pl* **-teaus** *or* **-teaux** (-ohs) **1** a wide level area of high land **2** a relatively long period of stability: *the body temperature rises to a plateau that it keeps until shortly before bedtime* ▶ *vb* **3** to remain stable for a long period

> **plateau** *n* **1** = upland, table, highland, tableland **2** = levelling off, level, stage, stability

plate glass *n* glass produced in thin sheets, used for windows and mirrors

platen *n* **1** the roller on a typewriter, against which the keys strike **2** a flat plate in a printing press that presses the paper against the type

platform *n* **1** a raised floor **2** a raised area at a railway station where passengers get on or off the trains **3** the declared aims of a political party **4** the thick raised sole of some shoes **5** a type of computer hardware or operating system

> **platform** *n* **1** = stage, stand, podium, rostrum, dais, pulpit, soapbox **3** = policy, programme, principle, objective(s), manifesto, party line

platinum *n* a silvery-white metallic element, very resistant to heat and chemicals: used in jewellery, laboratory apparatus, electrical contacts, dentistry, electroplating, and as a catalyst. Symbol: **Pt**

platinum blonde *n* a girl or woman with silvery-blonde hair

platitude *n* a trite or unoriginal remark: *it's a platitude, but people need people* > **platitudinous** *adj*

platonic *adj* friendly or affectionate but without physical desire: *platonic love*

platoon *n military* a subunit of a company, usually comprising three sections of ten to twelve men

platteland *n* **the platteland** (in South Africa) the country districts or rural areas

platter *n* a large shallow, usually oval, dish

platypus *or* **duck-billed platypus** *n, pl* **-puses** an Australian egg-laying amphibious mammal, with dense fur, webbed feet, and a ducklike bill

plaudit *n* (*usually pl*) an expression of enthusiastic approval

plausible *adj* **1** apparently reasonable or true: *a plausible excuse* **2** apparently trustworthy or believable: *he is an extraordinarily plausible liar* > **plausibility** *n* > **plausibly** *adv*

> **plausible** *adj* **1** = believable, possible, likely, reasonable, credible, probable, persuasive, conceivable; ≠ unbelievable **2** = glib, smooth, specious, smooth-talking, smooth-tongued

play *vb* **1** to occupy oneself in (a sport or recreation) **2** to compete against (someone) in a sport or game: *I saw Brazil play Argentina recently* **3** to fulfil (a particular role) in a team game: *he usually plays in midfield* **4** (often foll. by *about* or *around*) to behave carelessly: *he's only playing with your affections, you know* **5** to act the part (of) in a dramatic piece: *he has played Hamlet to packed Broadway houses* **6** to perform (a dramatic piece) **7 A** to perform (music) on a musical instrument **B** to be able to perform on (a musical instrument): *she plays the bassoon* **8** to send out (water) or cause to send out (water): *they played a hose across the wrecked building* **9** to cause (a radio, etc.) to emit sound **10** to move freely or quickly: *the light played across the water* **11** *Stock Exchange* to speculate for gain in (a market) **12** *angling* to tire (a hooked fish) by alternately letting out and reeling in the line **13** to put (a card) into play **14** to gamble **15 play fair** *or* **false with** to act fairly *or* unfairly with **16 play for time** to gain time to one's advantage by the use of delaying tactics **17 play into the hands of** to act unwittingly to the advantage of (an opponent) **18 play politics A** to negotiate politically **B** to exploit an important issue merely for political gain **C** to make something into a political issue ▸ *n* **19 A** a dramatic piece written for performance by actors **B** the performance of such a piece **20** games or other activity undertaken for pleasure **21** the playing of a game or the time during which a game is in progress: *rain stopped play* **22** conduct: *fair play* **23** gambling **24** activity or operation: *radio allows full play to your imagination* **25** scope for freedom of movement: *there was a lot of play in the rope* **26** free or rapidly shifting motion: *the play of light on the water* **27** fun or jest: *I used to throw cushions at her in play* **28 in** *or* **out of play** (of a ball in a game) in *or* not in a position of continuing play according to the rules **29 make a play for** *informal* to make an obvious attempt to gain (something) ▸ **playable** *adj*

> **play** *vb* **1** = amuse yourself, have fun, sport, fool, romp, revel, trifle, entertain yourself **2** = compete against, challenge, take on, oppose, contend against **5** = act, portray, represent, perform, act the part of **7A** = perform on, strum, make music on ▸ *n* **19** = drama, show, piece, comedy, tragedy, farce, soapie *or* soapy (*Austral slang*), pantomime **20** = amusement, pleasure, leisure, games, sport, fun, entertainment, relaxation, me-time

playboy *n* a rich man who devotes himself to such pleasures as nightclubs and female company

> **playboy** *n* = womanizer, philanderer, rake, roué, ladies' man

playcentre *n NZ* a centre for preschool children run by parents

playdate *n* an arrangement for children from different families to meet and play

play down *vb* to minimize the importance of: *she played down the problems of the company*

> **play down** *vb* **play something down** = minimize, make light of, gloss over, talk down, underrate, underplay, pooh-pooh (*informal*), soft-pedal (*informal*)

player *n* **1** a person who takes part in a game or sport **2** a person who plays a musical instrument **3** *informal* a leading participant in a particular field or activity: *one of the key players in Chinese politics* **4** an actor

> **player** *n* **1** = sportsman *or* sportswoman, competitor, participant, contestant **2** = musician, artist, performer, virtuoso, instrumentalist **4** = performer, entertainer, Thespian, trouper, actor *or* actress

playful *adj* **1** good-natured and humorous: *a playful remark* **2** full of high spirits and fun: *a playful child* ▸ **playfully** *adv*

playgroup *n* a regular meeting of infants for supervised creative play

playhouse *n* a theatre

playing field *n* (*sometimes pl*) *Brit & NZ* a field or open space used for sport

play-lunch *n Austral & NZ* a child's mid-morning snack at school

play off *vb* **1** to set (two people) against each other for one's own ends: *she delighted in playing one parent off against the other* **2** to take part in a play-off ▸ *n* **play-off 3** *sport* an extra contest to decide the winner when there is a tie **4** *chiefly US & Canad* a contest or series of games to determine a championship

play on *vb* to exploit (the feelings or weakness of another): *he played on my sympathy*

> **play on** *vb* **play on something** = take advantage of, abuse, exploit, impose on, trade on, capitalize on

playschool *n* a nursery group for preschool children

PlayStation *n trademark* a type of games console

plaything *n* **1** a toy **2** a person regarded or treated as a toy

play up *vb* **1** to highlight: *the temptation is to play up the sensational aspects of the story* **2** *Brit & Austral informal* to behave in an unruly way **3** to give (one) trouble or not be working properly: *my back's playing me up again*; *the photocopier's started to play up* **4 play up to** to try to please by flattery

> **play up** *vb* **1 play something up** = emphasize, highlight, underline, stress, accentuate **2** = be awkward, misbehave, give trouble, be disobedient, be stroppy (*Brit slang*) **3** = hurt, be painful, bother you, trouble you, be sore, pain you

playwright *n* a person who writes plays

plaza *n* **1** an open public square, usually in Spain **2** *chiefly US & Canad* a modern shopping complex

PLC *or* **plc** (in Britain) Public Limited Company

plea *n* **1** an emotional appeal **2** *law* a statement by or on behalf of a defendant **3** an excuse: *his plea of poverty rings a little hollow*

> **plea** *n* **1** = appeal, request, suit, prayer, petition, entreaty, intercession, supplication (*formal*) **3** = excuse, defence, explanation, justification

plead *vb* **pleading, pleaded, plead** *or esp Scot & US* **pled 1** (sometimes foll. by *with*) to ask with deep feeling **2** to give as an excuse: *whenever she invites him to dinner, he pleads a prior engagement* **3** *law* to declare oneself to be (guilty or not guilty) of the charge made against one **4** *law* to present (a case) in a court of law

> **plead** *vb* **1** = appeal, ask, request, beg, petition, implore, beseech, entreat

pleasant *adj* **1** pleasing or enjoyable: *what a pleasant surprise* **2** having pleasing manners or appearance: *he was a pleasant boy* ▸ **pleasantly** *adv*

> **pleasant** *adj* **1** = pleasing, nice, fine, lovely, amusing, delightful, enjoyable, agreeable, lekker (*S African slang*); ≠ horrible **2** = friendly, nice, agreeable, likable *or* likeable, engaging, charming, amiable, genial; ≠ disagreeable

pleasantry *n, pl* **-ries** (*often pl*) a polite or jocular remark: *we exchanged pleasantries about the weather* **2** agreeable jocularity

please *vb* **pleasing, pleased** **1** to give pleasure or satisfaction to (a person) **2** to regard as suitable or satisfying: *he can get almost anyone he pleases to work with him* **3** **if you please** if you wish, sometimes used in ironic exclamation **4** **pleased with** happy because of **5** **please oneself** to do as one likes ▸ *adv* **6** used in making polite requests or pleading: *please sit down* **7** **yes please** a polite phrase used to accept an offer or invitation ▸ **pleased** *adj*

> **please** *vb* **1** = delight, entertain, humour, amuse, suit, satisfy, indulge, gratify; ≠ annoy

pleasing *adj* giving pleasure

> **pleasing** *adj* = enjoyable, satisfying, charming, delightful, gratifying, agreeable, pleasurable; ≠ unpleasant

pleasurable *adj* enjoyable or agreeable ▸ **pleasurably** *adv*

pleasure *n* **1** a feeling of happiness and contentment: *the pleasure of hearing good music* **2** something that gives enjoyment: *his garden was his only pleasure* **3** the activity of enjoying oneself: *business before pleasure* **4** *euphemistic* sexual gratification: *he took his pleasure of her* **5** a person's preference

> **pleasure** *n* **1** = happiness, delight, satisfaction, enjoyment, bliss, gratification, gladness, delectation (*formal*); ≠ displeasure **2** = amusement, joy; ≠ duty

pleat *n* **1** a fold formed by doubling back fabric and pressing or stitching into place ▸ *vb* **2** to arrange (material) in pleats

pleb *n Brit informal, often offensive* a common vulgar person

plebeian (pleb-ee-an) *adj* **1** of the lower social classes **2** unrefined: *plebeian tastes* ▸ *n* **3** one of the common people, usually of ancient Rome **4** a coarse or unrefined person

plebiscite (pleb-iss-ite) *n* a direct vote by all the electorate on an issue of national importance

plectrum *n, pl* **-trums** *or* **-tra** an implement for plucking the strings of a guitar or similar instrument

pledge *n* **1** a solemn promise **2** ʌ something valuable given as a guarantee that a promise will be kept or a debt paid **b** the condition of being used as security: *in pledge* **3** a token: *a pledge of good faith* **4** an assurance of support or goodwill, given by drinking a toast: *we drank a pledge to their success* **5** **take** *or* **sign the pledge** to vow not to drink alcohol ▸ *vb* **pledging, pledged** **6** to promise solemnly **7** to promise to give (money to charity, etc.) **8** to bind by or as if by a pledge: *I was pledged to secrecy* **9** to give (one's word or property) as a guarantee **10** to drink a toast to (a person or cause)

> **pledge** *n* **1** = promise, vow, assurance, word, undertaking, warrant, oath, covenant **2** = guarantee, security, deposit, bail, collateral, pawn, surety ▸ *vb* **6** = promise, vow, swear, contract, engage, give your word, give your oath

plenary *adj* **1** (of an assembly) attended by all the members **2** full or complete: *plenary powers*

plenipotentiary *adj* **1** (usually of a diplomat) invested with full authority ▸ *n, pl* **-aries** **2** a diplomat or representative who has full authority to transact business

plenitude *n literary* **1** abundance **2** fullness or completeness

plenteous *adj literary* **1** abundant: *a plenteous supply* **2** producing abundantly: *a plenteous harvest*

plentiful *adj* existing in large amounts or numbers ▸ **plentifully** *adv*

> **plentiful** *adj* = abundant, liberal, generous, lavish, ample, overflowing, copious, bountiful; ≠ scarce

plenty *n, pl* **-ties** **1** (often foll. by *of*) a great number or amount: *plenty of time* **2** abundance: *an age of plenty* ▸ *adj* **3** very many: *there's plenty more fish in the sea* ▸ *adv* **4** *informal* more than adequately: *that's plenty fast enough for me*

> **plenty** *n* **1** = lots of (*informal*), enough, a great deal of, masses of, piles of (*informal*), stacks of, heaps of (*informal*), an abundance of **2** = abundance, wealth, prosperity, fertility, profusion, affluence, plenitude, fruitfulness

pleonasm *n rhetoric* **1** the use of more words than necessary, such as *a tiny little child* **2** an unnecessary word or phrase ▸ **pleonastic** *adj*

plethora *n* an excess

pleurisy *n* inflammation of the pleura, making breathing painful ▸ **pleuritic** *adj, n*

pliable *adj* **1** easily bent: *pliable branches* **2** easily influenced: *his easy and pliable nature* ▸ **pliability** *n*

p

pliant *adj* **1** easily bent; supple: *pliant young willow and hazel twigs* **2** easily influenced: *he was a far more pliant subordinate than his predecessor* > **pliancy** *n*

pliers *pl n* a gripping tool consisting of two hinged arms usually with serrated jaws

plight¹ *n* a dangerous or difficult situation: *the plight of the British hostages*

> **plight** *n* = difficulty, condition, state, situation, trouble, predicament

plight² *vb* **plight one's troth** *old-fashioned* to make a promise to marry

Plimsoll line *n* a line on the hull of a ship showing the level that the water should reach if the ship is properly loaded

plimsolls *pl n Brit* light rubber-soled canvas sports shoes

plinth *n* **1** a base on which a statue stands **2** the slab that forms the base of a column or pedestal

PLO Palestine Liberation Organization

plod *vb* **plodding, plodded 1** to walk with heavy slow steps **2** to work slowly and steadily ▸ *n* **3** the act of plodding **4** *Brit slang* a police officer > **plodder** *n*

plonk¹ *vb* **1** to put down heavily and carelessly: *he plonked himself down on the sofa* ▸ *n* **2** the act or sound of plonking

plonk² *n informal* cheap inferior wine

plop *n* **1** the sound made by an object dropping into water without a splash ▸ *vb* **plopping, plopped 2** to drop with such a sound: *a tear rolled down his cheek and plopped into his soup* **3** to fall or be placed heavily or carelessly: *we plopped down on the bed and went straight to sleep*

plot¹ *n* **1** a secret plan for an illegal purpose **2** the story of a play, novel, or film ▸ *vb* **plotting, plotted 3** to plan secretly; conspire **4** to mark (a course) on a map **5** to make a plan or map of **6** **A** to locate (points) on a graph by means of coordinates **B** to draw (a curve) through these points **7** to construct the plot of (a play, novel, or film) > **plotter** *n*

> **plot** *n* **1** = plan, scheme, intrigue, conspiracy, cabal, stratagem, machination **2** = story, action, subject, theme, outline, scenario, narrative, story line ▸ *vb* **3** = plan, scheme, conspire, intrigue, manoeuvre, contrive, collude, machinate **4** = chart, mark, map, locate, calculate, outline **7** = devise, design, lay, conceive, hatch, contrive, concoct, cook up (*informal*)

plot² *n* a small piece of land: *there was a small vegetable plot in the garden*

> **plot** *n* = patch, lot, area, ground, parcel, tract, allotment

plough *or US* **plow** *n* **1** an agricultural tool for cutting or turning over the earth **2** a similar tool used for clearing snow ▸ *vb* **3** to turn over (the soil) with a plough **4** to make (furrows or grooves) in (something) with or as if with a plough **5** (sometimes foll. by *through*) to move (through something) in the manner of a plough: *the ship ploughed through the water* **6** (foll. by *through*) to work at slowly or perseveringly **7** to invest (money): *he ploughed the profits back into the business* **8 plough into** (of a vehicle, plane, etc.) to go out of control and crash into (something): *the aircraft ploughed into a motorway embankment*

> **plough** *or* **plow** *vb* **3, 4** = turn over, dig, till, cultivate **5 plough through something** = forge, cut, drive, press, push, plunge, wade

ploughman *or US* **plowman** *n, pl* **-men** a man who ploughs

ploughshare *or US* **plowshare** *n* the cutting blade of a plough

plover *n* a shore bird with a round head, straight bill, and long pointed wings

plow *n, vb US* same as **plough**

ploy *n* a manoeuvre designed to gain an advantage in a situation: *a cheap political ploy*

> **ploy** *n* = tactic, move, trick, device, scheme, manoeuvre, dodge, ruse

pluck *vb* **1** to pull or pick off **2** to pull out the feathers of (a bird for cooking) **3** (foll. by *off* or *away* etc.) to pull (something) forcibly or violently (from something or someone) **4** to sound the strings of (a musical instrument) with the fingers or a plectrum ▸ *n* **5** courage **6** a pull or tug ▸ See also **pluck up**

> **pluck** *vb* **1, 4** = tug, catch, snatch, clutch, jerk, yank, tweak, pull at **2** = pull out *or* off, pick, draw, collect, gather, harvest ▸ *n* **5** = courage, nerve, bottle (*Brit slang*), guts (*informal*), grit, bravery, backbone, boldness

pluck up *vb* to summon up (courage)

plucky *adj* **pluckier, pluckiest** courageous > **pluckily** *adv* > **pluckiness** *n*

plug *n* **1** an object used to block up holes or waste pipes **2** a device with one or more pins which connects an appliance to an electricity supply **3** *informal* a favourable mention of a product, etc., for example on television, to encourage people to buy it **4** See **spark plug 5** a piece of tobacco for chewing ▸ *vb* **plugging, plugged 6** to block or seal (a hole or gap) with a plug **7** *informal* to make frequent favourable mentions of (a product, etc.), for example on television **8** *slang* to shoot **9** *slang* to punch **10** (foll. by *along* or *away* etc.) *informal* to work steadily ▸ See also **plug in**

> **plug** *n* **1** = stopper, cork, bung, spigot **3** = mention, advertisement, advert (*Brit*), push, publicity, hype ▸ *vb* **6** = seal, close, stop, fill, block, stuff, pack, cork **7** = mention, push, promote, publicize, advertise, build up, hype **10 plug away** = slog away, labour, toil away, grind away (*informal*), peg away, plod away

P

plug in *vb* to connect (an electrical appliance) to a power source by pushing a plug into a socket

plum *n* **1** an oval dark red or yellow fruit with a stone in the middle, that grows on a small tree **2** a raisin, as used in a cake or pudding **3** *informal* something of a superior or desirable kind ▸ *adj* **4** made from plums: *plum cake* **5** dark reddish-purple **6** very desirable: *plum targets for attack*

> **plum** *adj* **6** = choice, prize, first-class

plumage *n* the feathers of a bird

plumb *vb* **1** to understand (something obscure): *to plumb a mystery* **2** to test the alignment of or make vertical with a plumb line **3** (foll. by *in* or *into*) to connect (an appliance or fixture) to a water pipe or drainage system: *the shower should be plumbed in professionally* **4** **plumb the depths** (usually foll. by *of*) to experience the worst extremes (of something): *to plumb the depths of despair* ▸ *n* **5** a lead weight hanging at the end of a string and used to test the depth of water or to test whether something is vertical **6** **out of plumb** not vertical ▸ *adv* **7** vertical or perpendicular **8** *informal, chiefly US* utterly: *plumb stupid* **9** *informal* exactly: *plumb in the centre*

> **plumb** *adv* **7, 9** = exactly, precisely, bang, slap, spot-on (*Brit informal*)

plumber *n* a person who fits and repairs pipes and fixtures for water, drainage, or gas systems

plumbing *n* **1** the pipes and fixtures used in a water, drainage, or gas system **2** the trade or work of a plumber

plumb line *n* a string with a metal weight at one end, used to test the depth of water or to test whether something is vertical

plume *n* **1** a large ornamental feather **2** a group of feathers worn as a badge or ornament on a hat **3** something like a plume: *a plume of smoke* ▸ *vb* **pluming, plumed 4** to adorn with plumes **5** (of a bird) to preen (its feathers) **6** **plume oneself** (foll. by *on* or *upon*) to be proud of oneself or one's achievements, esp. unjustifiably: *she was pluming herself on her figure*

plummet *vb* **-meting, -meted 1** to drop down; plunge ▸ *n* **2** the weight on a plumb line or fishing line

> **plummet** *vb* = drop, fall, crash, nosedive, descend rapidly

plump¹ *adj* **1** full or rounded: *until puberty I was really quite plump* ▸ *vb* **2** (often foll. by *up* or *out*) to make (something) fuller or rounded: *she plumped up the cushions on the couch* > **plumpness** *n*

> **plump** *adj* = chubby, fat, stout, round, tubby, dumpy, roly-poly, rotund; ≠ scrawny

plump² *vb* **1** (often foll. by *down* or *into* etc.) to drop or sit suddenly and heavily: *he plumped down on the seat* **2** **plump for** to choose (one) from a selection ▸ *n* **3** a heavy abrupt fall or the sound

of this ▸ *adv* **4** suddenly or heavily **5** directly: *the plane landed plump in the middle of the field*

plunder *vb* **1** to seize (valuables or goods) from (a place) by force, usually in wartime; loot ▸ *n* **2** anything plundered; booty **3** the act of plundering; pillage

> **plunder** *vb* = steal, rob, take, nick (*informal*), pinch (*informal*), embezzle, pilfer, thieve ▸ *n* **2** = loot, spoils, booty, swag (*slang*), ill-gotten gains **3** = pillage

plunge *vb* **plunging, plunged 1** (usually foll. by *into*) to thrust or throw (something or oneself) forcibly or suddenly: *they plunged into the sea*; *he plunged the knife in to the hilt* **2** to throw or be thrown into a certain condition: *the room was plunged into darkness* **3** (usually foll. by *into*) to involve or become involved deeply (in) **4** to move swiftly or impetuously **5** to descend very suddenly or steeply: *temperatures were plunging* ▸ *n* **6** a leap or dive **7** *informal* a swim **8** a pitching motion **9** **take the plunge** *informal* to make a risky decision which cannot be reversed later

> **plunge** *vb* **1** = submerge, dip **4** = hurtle, charge, career, jump, tear, rush, dive, dash **5** = descend, fall, drop, crash, pitch, sink, dive, tumble ▸ *n* **6** = dive, jump, duck, descent **8** = fall, crash (*informal*), slump, drop, tumble

plunger *n* **1** a rubber suction cup used to clear blocked drains **2** a device with a plunging motion; piston

Plunket baby *n* *NZ* a baby brought up according to the principles of the Plunket Society

pluperfect *grammar* ▸ *adj* **1** denoting a tense of verbs used to describe an action completed before a past time. In English this is a compound tense formed with *had* plus the past participle ▸ *n* **2** the pluperfect tense

plural *adj* **1** of or consisting of more than one **2** *grammar* denoting a word indicating more than one ▸ *n* **3** *grammar* **A** the plural number **B** a plural form

pluralism *n* **1** the existence and toleration in a society of a variety of groups of different ethnic origins, cultures, or religions **2** the holding of more than one office by a person > **pluralist** *n*, *adj* > **pluralistic** *adj*

plus *prep* **1** increased by the addition of: *four plus two* **2** with the addition of: *a good salary, plus a company car* ▸ *adj* **3** indicating addition: *a plus sign* **4** *maths* same as **positive** (sense 7) **5** on the positive part of a scale **6** indicating the positive side of an electrical circuit **7** involving advantage: *a plus factor* **8** *informal* having a value above the value stated: *it must be worth a thousand pounds plus* **9** slightly above a specified standard: *he received a B plus for his essay* ▸ *n* **10** a plus sign (+), indicating addition **11** a positive quantity **12** *informal* something positive or an advantage **13** a gain, surplus, or advantage

plus *prep* **2** = and, with, added to, coupled with ▸ *adj* **7** = additional, added, extra, supplementary, add-on ▸ *n* **12, 13** = advantage, benefit, asset, gain, extra, bonus, good point

plus fours *pl n* men's baggy knickerbockers gathered in at the knee, now only worn for hunting or golf

plush *n* **1** a velvety fabric with a long soft pile, used for furniture coverings ▸ *adj* **2** Also: **plushy** *informal* luxurious

plush *adj* = luxurious, luxury, lavish, rich, sumptuous, opulent, de luxe

plus-one *n informal* someone who accompanies an invited person to a social function

Pluto *n* **1** *classical myth* the god of the underworld **2** a dwarf planet in the solar system, classified as a planet until 2006

plutocrat *n* a person who is powerful because of being very rich

plutonium *n chem* a toxic radioactive metallic element, used in nuclear reactors and weapons. Symbol: **Pu**

ply[1] *vb* **plies, plying, plied 1** to work at (a job or trade) **2** to use (a tool) **3** (usually foll. by *with*) to provide (with) or subject (to) persistently: *he plied us with drink; he plied me with questions* **4** to work steadily **5** (of a ship) to travel regularly along (a route): *to ply the trade routes*

ply *vb* **1** = work at, follow, exercise, pursue, carry on, practise

ply[2] *n, pl* **plies 1** a layer or thickness, such as of fabric or wood **2** one of the strands twisted together to make rope or yarn

plywood *n* a board made of thin layers of wood glued together under pressure, with the grain of one layer at right angles to the grain of the next

PM 1 Prime Minister **2** Postmaster **3** Paymaster **4** project manager

p.m. 1 after noon **2** postmortem (examination)

PMS premenstrual syndrome

PMT premenstrual tension

pneumatic *adj* **1** operated by compressed air: *pneumatic drill* **2** containing compressed air: *a pneumatic tyre* **3** of or concerned with air, gases, or wind

pneumonia *n* inflammation of one or both lungs

PO 1 Also: **p.o.** *Brit* postal order **2** Post Office **3** petty officer **4** Pilot Officer

poach[1] *vb* **1** to catch (game or fish) illegally on someone else's land **2** A to encroach on (someone's rights or duties) B to steal (an idea, employee, or player) ▸ **poacher** *n*

poach[2] *vb* to simmer (food) very gently in liquid

pocket *n* **1** a small pouch sewn into clothing for carrying small articles **2** any pouchlike container, esp. for catching balls at the edge of a snooker table **3** a small isolated area or group: *a pocket of resistance* **4** a cavity in the earth, such as one containing ore **5 in one's pocket** under one's control **6 out of pocket** having made a loss ▸ *vb* **-eting, -eted 7** to put into one's pocket **8** to take secretly or dishonestly **9** *billiards etc.* to drive (a ball) into a pocket **10** to conceal or suppress: *he pocketed his pride and asked for help* ▸ *adj* **11** small: *a pocket edition*

pocket *n* **2** = pouch, bag, sack, compartment, receptacle ▸ *vb* **8** = steal, take, lift (*informal*), appropriate, pilfer, purloin (*formal*), filch ▸ *adj* = small, compact, miniature, portable, little

pocket money *n* **1** a small weekly sum of money given to children by parents **2** money for small personal expenses

pockmarked *adj* **1** (of the skin) marked with pitted scars after the healing of smallpox **2** (of a surface) covered in many small hollows: *the building is pockmarked with bullet holes* ▸ **pockmark** *n*

pod *n* **1** A a long narrow seedcase containing peas, beans, etc. B the seedcase as distinct from the seeds ▸ *vb* **podding, podded 2** to remove the pod from

pod *n* **1B** = shell, case, hull, husk, shuck

podcast *n* **1** an audio file similar to a radio broadcast, which can be downloaded and listened to on a computer, mobile electronic device, etc. ▸ *vb* **-casts, -casting, -cast** *or* **-casted 2** to create such files and make them available for downloading **3** to make (music, interviews, etc.) available using this format ▸ **podcaster** *n* ▸ **podcasting** *n*

podgy *adj* **podgier, podgiest** short and fat ▸ **podginess** *n*

podiatry (pod-eye-a-tree) *n* another word for **chiropody** ▸ **podiatrist** *n*

podium *n, pl* **-diums** *or* **-dia 1** a small raised platform used by conductors or speakers **2** a plinth that supports a colonnade or wall

podium *n* **1** = platform, stand, stage, rostrum, dais

poem *n* **1** a literary work, often in verse, usually dealing with emotional or descriptive themes in a rhythmic form **2** a literary work that is not in verse but deals with emotional or descriptive themes in a rhythmic form: *a prose poem* **3** anything like a poem in beauty or effect: *his painting is a poem on creation*

poem *n* **1** = verse, song, lyric, rhyme, sonnet, ode, verse composition

poep (poop) *n S African vulgar* **1** an emission of intestinal gas from the anus **2** a mean or despicable person

poesy *n archaic* poetry

poet *n* **1** a writer of poetry **2** a person with great imagination and creativity

poet *n* **1** = bard (*archaic, literary*), rhymer, lyricist, lyric poet, versifier, elegist

p

poetic *or* **poetical** *adj* **1** like poetry, by being expressive or imaginative **2** of poetry or poets **3** recounted in verse

> **poetic** *or* **poetical** *adj* **1** = figurative, creative, lyric, symbolic, lyrical, lyric, elegiac, metrical

poetic justice *n* an appropriate punishment or reward for previous actions

poet laureate *n*, *pl* **poets laureate** *Brit* the poet selected by the British sovereign to write poems on important occasions

poetry *n* **1** poems in general **2** the art or craft of writing poems **3** a poetic quality that prompts an emotional response: *her acting was full of poetry*

> **poetry** *n* **1, 2** = verse, poems, rhyme, rhyming, verse composition

pogrom *n* an organized persecution and massacre

poignant *adj* **1** sharply painful to the feelings: *a poignant reminder* **2** cutting: *poignant wit* **3** pertinent in mental appeal: *a poignant subject* > **poignancy** *n*

> **poignant** *adj* **1** = moving, touching, sad, bitter, intense, painful, distressing, pathetic

poinsettia *n* a shrub of Mexico and Central America, widely grown for its showy scarlet bracts, which resemble petals

point *n* **1** the essential idea in an argument or discussion: *I agreed with the point he made* **2** a reason or aim: *what is the point of this exercise?* **3** a detail or item **4** a characteristic: *he has his good points* **5** a location or position **6** a dot or tiny mark **7** a dot used as a decimal point or a full stop **8** the sharp tip of anything: *the point of the spear* **9** a headland: *the soaring cliffs at Dwerja Point in the southwest of the island* **10** *maths* a geometric element having a position located by coordinates, but no magnitude **11** a specific condition or degree: *freezing point* **12** a moment: *at that point he left* **13** (*often pl*) any of the extremities, such as the tail, ears, or feet, of a domestic animal **14** (*often pl*) *ballet* the tip of the toes **15** a single unit for measuring something such as value, or of scoring in a game **16** *printing* a unit of measurement equal to one twelfth of a pica **17** *naut* one of the 32 direction marks on the compass **18** *cricket* a fielding position at right angles to the batsman on the off side **19** either of the two electrical contacts that make or break the circuit in the distributor of a motor vehicle **20** *Brit, Austral & NZ* (*often pl*) a movable section of railway track used to direct a train from one line to another **21** *Brit* short for **power point** **22** *boxing* a mark awarded for a scoring blow or knockdown **23** **beside the point** irrelevant **24** **make a point of** **A** to make a habit of (something) **B** to do (something) because one thinks it important **25** **on** *or* **at the point of** about to; on the verge of: *on the point of leaving* **26** **to the point** relevant **27** **up to a point** not completely ▸ *vb* **28** (usually foll. by *at* or *to*) to show the position or direction of something by extending a finger or other pointed object towards it **29** (usually foll. by *at* or *to*) to single out one person or thing from among several: *all the symptoms pointed to epilepsy* **30** to direct or face in a specific direction: *point me in the right direction* **31** to finish or repair the joints in brickwork with mortar or cement **32** (of a gun dog) to show where game is lying by standing rigidly with the muzzle turned towards it

> **point** *n* **1** = essence, meaning, subject, question, heart, import, drift, thrust **2** = purpose, aim, object, end, reason, goal, intention, objective **3, 4** = aspect, detail, feature, quality, particular, respect, item, characteristic **5** = place, area, position, site, spot, location, locality, locale **6** = pinpoint, mark, spot, dot, fleck **8** = end, tip, sharp end, top, spur, spike, apex, prong **11** = stage, level, position, condition, degree, pitch, circumstance, extent **12** = moment, time, stage, period, phase, instant, juncture, moment in time **15** = score, tally, mark ▸ *vb* **28 point at or to something or someone** = indicate, show, signal, point to, point out, specify, designate, gesture towards **30** = aim, level, train, direct

point-blank *adj* **1** fired at a very close target **2** plain or blunt: *a point-blank refusal to discuss the matter* ▸ *adv* **3** directly or bluntly: *the Minister was asked point-blank if he intended to resign*

point duty *n* the control of traffic by a police officer at a road junction

pointed *adj* **1** having a sharp tip **2** cutting or incisive: *pointed wit* **3** obviously directed at a particular person: *a pointed remark* **4** emphasized or obvious: *pointed ignorance* > **pointedly** *adv*

> **pointed** *adj* **1** = sharp, edged, acute, barbed **2** = cutting, telling, biting, sharp, keen, acute, penetrating, pertinent

pointer *n* **1** something that is a helpful indicator of how a situation has arisen or may turn out: *a significant pointer to the likely resumption of talks* **2** an indicator on a measuring instrument **3** a long stick used by teachers, to point out particular features on a map, chart, etc. **4** a large smooth-coated gun dog

> **pointer** *n* **1** = hint, tip, suggestion, recommendation, caution, piece of information, piece of advice **2** = indicator, hand, guide, needle, arrow

pointless *adj* without meaning or purpose

> **pointless** *adj* = senseless, meaningless, futile, fruitless, stupid, silly, useless, absurd; ≠ worthwhile

point of view *n*, *pl* **points of view** **1** a mental viewpoint or attitude: *she refuses to see the other* *person's point of view* **2** a way of considering something: *a scientific point of view*

point-to-point *n Brit* a steeplechase organized by a hunt

poise *n* **1** dignified manner **2** physical balance: *the poise of a natural model* **3** mental balance: *he recovered his poise* ▸ *vb* **poising**, **poised 4** to be balanced or suspended **5** to hold in readiness: *to poise a lance*

poised *adj* **1** absolutely ready **2** behaving with or showing poise

> **poised** *adj* **1** = ready, waiting, prepared, standing by, all set **2** = composed, calm, together (*informal*), collected, dignified, self-confident, self-possessed; ≠ agitated

poison *n* **1** a substance that causes death or injury when swallowed or absorbed **2** something that destroys or corrupts: *the poison of Nazism* ▸ *vb* **3** to give poison to someone **4** to add poison to (something) **5** to have a harmful or evil effect on **6** (foll. by *against*) to turn (a person's mind) against: *he poisoned her mind against me* > **poisoner** *n*

> **poison** *n* **1** = toxin, venom, bane (*archaic*) ▸ *vb* **3** = give someone poison, murder, kill, administer poison to **5** = contaminate, foul, infect, spoil, pollute, blight, taint, befoul **6** = corrupt, colour, undermine, bias, sour, pervert, warp, taint

poisonous *adj* **1** of or like a poison **2** malicious

> **poisonous** *adj* **1** = toxic, fatal, deadly, lethal, mortal, virulent, noxious, venomous **2** = evil, malicious, corrupting, pernicious (*formal*), baleful

poison-pen letter *n* a malicious anonymous letter

poke *vb* **poking**, **poked 1** to jab or prod with an elbow, finger, etc. **2** to make a hole by poking **3** (sometimes foll. by *at*) to thrust (at): *she poked at the food with her fork* **4** (usually foll. by *in* or *through* etc.) to thrust forward or out: *yellow hair poked from beneath his cap* **5** to stir (a fire) by poking **6** (often foll. by *about* or *around*) to search or pry **7 poke one's nose into** to meddle in ▸ *n* **8** a jab or prod

> **poke** *vb* **1** = jab, push, stick, dig, stab, thrust, shove, nudge **4** = protrude, stick, thrust, jut ▸ *n* = jab, dig, thrust, nudge, prod

poker[1] *n* a metal rod with a handle for stirring a fire

poker[2] *n* a card game of bluff and skill in which players bet on the hands dealt

poky *adj* **pokier**, **pokiest** (of a room) small and cramped > **pokiness** *n*

polar *adj* **1** of or near either of the earth's poles or the area inside the Arctic or Antarctic Circles **2** of or having a pole or polarity **3** directly opposite in tendency or nature: *polar opposites*

polar bear *n* a white bear of coastal regions of the North Pole

polarization *or* **-risation** *n* **1** the condition of having or giving polarity **2** *physics* the condition in which waves of light or other radiation are restricted to certain directions of vibration

polarize *or* **-rise** *vb* **-rizing, -rized** *or* **-rising, -rised 1** to cause people to adopt directly opposite opinions: *political opinion had polarized since the restoration of democracy* **2** to have or give polarity or polarization

Polaroid *n trademark* **1** a type of plastic that polarizes light: used in sunglasses to eliminate glare **2 Polaroid camera** a camera that produces a finished print by developing and processing it inside the camera within a few seconds **3 Polaroids** sunglasses with Polaroid plastic lenses

polder *n* a stretch of land reclaimed from the sea

pole[1] *n* **1** a long slender rounded piece of wood, metal, or other material **2 up the pole** *Brit*, *Austral & NZ informal* **A** slightly mad **B** in a predicament

> **pole** *n* **1** = rod, post, support, staff, bar, stick, stake, paling

pole[2] *n* **1** either end of the earth's axis of rotation. See also **North Pole**, **South Pole 2** *physics* **A** either of the opposite forces of a magnet **B** either of two points at which there are opposite electric charges **3** either of two directly opposite tendencies or opinions **4 poles apart** having widely divergent opinions or tastes

poleaxe *or US* **poleax** *vb* **-axing, -axed 1** to hit or stun with a heavy blow ▸ *n* **2** an axe formerly used in battle or used by a butcher

polecat *n, pl* **-cats** *or* **-cat 1** a dark brown mammal like a weasel that gives off a foul smell **2** *US* a skunk

pole dancing *n* a form of entertainment in which a scantily dressed woman dances erotically, turning on and posing against a vertically fixed pole on stage > **pole dancer** *n*

polemic (pol-em-ik) *n* **1** a fierce attack on or defence of a particular opinion, belief, etc.: *anti-capitalist polemic* ▸ *adj also* **polemical 2** of or involving dispute or controversy > **polemicist** *n*

Pole Star *n* **the Pole Star** the star closest to the northern celestial pole

police *n* **1** (often preceded by *the*) the organized civil force in a state which keeps law and order **2** the men and women who are members of such a force **3** an organized body with a similar function: *security police* ▸ *vb* **-licing, -liced 4** to maintain order or control by means of a police force or similar body

> **police** *n* **1, 2** = the law (*informal*), police force, constabulary, the fuzz (*slang*), boys in blue (*informal, archaic*), the Old Bill (*slang*), the rozzers (*slang*) ▸ *vb* = control, patrol, guard, watch, protect, regulate

P

policeman *or fem* **policewoman** *n, pl* **-men** *or* **-women** a member of a police force; police officer

policy[1] *n, pl* **-cies** 1 a plan of action adopted by a person, group, or government 2 *archaic* wisdom or prudence

> **policy** *n* 1 = procedure, plan, action, practice, scheme, code, custom

policy[2] *n, pl* **-cies** a document containing an insurance contract > **policyholder** *n*

polio *n* short for **poliomyelitis**

poliomyelitis (pole-ee-oh-my-el-lite-iss) *n* a viral disease which affects the brain and spinal cord, often causing paralysis

polish *vb* 1 to make smooth and shiny by rubbing 2 to perfect or complete: *media experts he had hired to polish his image* 3 to make or become elegant or refined: *not having polished his accent didn't help his career* ▸ *n* 4 a substance used for polishing 5 a shine or gloss 6 elegance or refinement ▸ See also **polish off**

> **polish** *vb* 1 = shine, wax, smooth, rub, buff, brighten, burnish 2, 3 = perfect, improve, enhance, refine, finish, brush up, touch up ▸ *n* 4 = varnish, wax, glaze, lacquer, japan 5 = sheen, finish, glaze, gloss, brightness, lustre 6 = style, class (*informal*), finish, breeding, grace, elegance, refinement, finesse

Polish *adj* 1 of Poland ▸ *n* 2 the language of Poland

polished *adj* 1 accomplished: *a polished actor* 2 done or performed well or professionally: *a polished performance*

> **polished** *adj* = accomplished, professional, masterly, fine, expert, skilful, adept, superlative; ≠ amateurish

polish off *vb informal* 1 to finish completely 2 to dispose of or kill

polite *adj* 1 having good manners; courteous 2 cultivated or refined: *polite society* 3 socially correct but insincere: *he smiled a polite response and stifled an urge to scream* > **politely** *adv* > **politeness** *n*

> **polite** *adj* 1 = mannerly, civil, courteous, gracious, respectful, well-behaved, complaisant, well-mannered; ≠ rude 2 = refined, cultured, civilized, polished, sophisticated, elegant, genteel, well-bred; ≠ uncultured

politic *adj* 1 wise or possibly advantageous: *I didn't feel it was politic to mention it* 2 artful or shrewd: *a politic manager* 3 crafty; cunning: *a politic old scoundrel* 4 *archaic* political

> **politic** *adj* 1 = wise, diplomatic, sensible, prudent, advisable, expedient, judicious

political *adj* 1 of the state, government, or public administration 2 relating to or interested in politics: *she was always a very political*

person 3 of the parties and the partisan aspects of politics: *the government blames political opponents for fanning the unrest* > **politically** *adv*

> **political** *adj* = governmental, government, state, parliamentary, constitutional, administrative, legislative, ministerial

politically correct *adj* displaying progressive attitudes, esp. in using vocabulary which is intended to avoid any implied prejudice > **political correctness** *n*

political prisoner *n* a person imprisoned for holding particular political beliefs

politician *n* a person actively engaged in politics, esp. a member of parliament

> **politician** *n* = statesman *or* woman *or* person, representative, senator (*US*), Member of Parliament (*Brit*), congressman *or* woman *or* person (*US*), legislator, public servant

politics *n* 1 (*functioning as sing*) the art and science of government 2 (*functioning as pl*) political opinions or sympathies: *his conservative politics* 3 (*functioning as pl*) political activities or affairs: *party politics* 4 (*functioning as sing*) the business or profession of politics 5 (*functioning as sing or pl*) any activity concerned with the acquisition of power: *company politics are often vicious*

> **politics** *n* 1 = affairs of state, government, public affairs, civics 2 = political beliefs, party politics, political allegiances, political leanings, political sympathies

polka *n* 1 a lively 19th-century dance 2 music for this dance ▸ *vb* **-kaing, -kaed** 3 to dance a polka

polka dots *pl n* a regular pattern of small bold spots on a fabric

poll *n* 1 Also called: **opinion poll** the questioning of a random sample of people to find out the general opinion 2 the casting, recording, or counting of votes in an election 3 the result of such a voting: *a marginal poll* 4 the head ▸ *vb* 5 to receive (a certain number of votes) 6 to record the votes of: *he polled the whole town* 7 to question (a person, etc.) as part of an opinion poll 8 to vote in an election 9 to clip or shear 10 to remove or cut short the horns of (cattle)

> **poll** *n* 1 = survey, figures, count, sampling, returns, ballot, tally, census 2 = election, vote, voting, referendum, ballot, plebiscite ▸ *vb* 5 = gain, return, record, register, tally 7 = question, interview, survey, sample, ballot, canvass

pollen *n* a fine powder produced by flowers to fertilize other flowers of the same species

pollen count *n* a measure of the amount of pollen in the air over a 24-hour period, often published as a warning to people with hay fever

pollinate *vb* **-nating, -nated** to fertilize by the transfer of pollen > **pollination** *n*

polling station n a building where voters go during an election to cast their votes

pollster n a person who conducts opinion polls

pollutant n a substance that pollutes, usually the chemical waste of an industrial process

pollute vb **-luting, -luted 1** to contaminate with poisonous or harmful substances **2** to corrupt morally > **pollution** n

> **pollute** vb **1** = contaminate, dirty, poison, soil, foul, infect, spoil, stain; ≠ decontaminate **2** = defile, corrupt, sully, deprave, debase, profane, desecrate, dishonour; ≠ honour

polo n **1** a game like hockey played on horseback with long-handled mallets and a wooden ball **2** short for **water polo**

polonaise n **1** a stately Polish dance **2** music for this dance

polo neck n a sweater with a high tight turned-over collar

polonium n chem a rare radioactive element found in trace amounts in uranium ores. Symbol: **Po**

poltergeist n a spirit believed to be responsible for noises and acts of mischief, such as throwing objects about

poltroon n obsolete a complete coward

poly- combining form many or much: polyhedron; polysyllabic

polyandry n the practice of having more than one husband at the same time > **polyandrous** adj

polyanthus n, pl **-thuses** a hybrid garden primrose with brightly coloured flowers

polychromatic adj **1** having many colours **2** (of radiation) containing more than one wavelength

polyester n a synthetic material used to make plastics and textile fibres

polygamy (pol-ig-a-mee) n the practice of having more than one wife or husband at the same time > **polygamist** n > **polygamous** adj

polyglot adj **1** able to speak many languages **2** written in or using many languages ▸ n **3** a person who can speak many languages

polygon n a geometrical figure with three or more sides and angles > **polygonal** adj

polyhedron n, pl **-drons** or **-dra** a solid figure with four or more sides > **polyhedral** adj

polymer n a natural or synthetic compound with large molecules made up of simple molecules of the same kind

polymerization or **-isation** n the process of forming a polymer > **polymerize** or **-ise** vb

polyp n **1** zool a small sea creature that has a hollow cylindrical body with a ring of tentacles around the mouth **2** pathol a small growth on the surface of a mucous membrane

polyphonic adj music consisting of several melodies played together

polystyrene n a synthetic material used esp. as white rigid foam for insulating and packing

polytechnic n **1** (in New Zealand and formerly in Britain) a college offering courses in many subjects at and below degree level ▸ adj **2** of or relating to technical instruction

polytheism n belief in more than one god > **polytheistic** adj > **polytheist** n

polythene n a light plastic material made from ethylene, usually made into thin sheets or bags

polyunsaturated adj of a group of fats that are less likely to contribute to the build-up of cholesterol in the body

polyurethane n a synthetic material used esp. in paints

pom n Austral & NZ slang same as **pommy**

pomander n **1** a mixture of sweet-smelling substances in a container, used to perfume drawers or cupboards **2** a container for such a mixture

pomegranate n a round tropical fruit with a tough reddish rind containing many seeds in a juicy red pulp

Pomeranian n a toy dog with a long straight silky coat

pommel n **1** the raised part on the front of a saddle **2** a knob at the top of a sword handle ▸ vb **-melling, -melled** or US **-meling, -meled 3** same as **pummel**

pommy n, pl **-mies** (sometimes cap) slang a word used by Australians and New Zealanders for a British person. Sometimes shortened to: **pom**

pomp n **1** stately display or ceremony **2** ostentatious display

pompom n **1** a decorative ball of tufted silk or wool **2** the small round flower head of some dahlias and chrysanthemums

pompous adj **1** foolishly dignified or self-important **2** foolishly grand in style: a pompous speech > **pomposity** n > **pompously** adv

ponce offensive slang, chiefly Brit ▸ n **1** an effeminate man **2** same as **pimp** ▸ vb **poncing, ponced 3** (often foll. by around or about) Brit & Austral to act stupidly or waste time

poncho n, pl **-chos** a type of cloak made of a piece of cloth with a hole in the middle for the head

pond n a pool of still water

> **pond** n = pool, tarn, small lake, fish pond, duck pond, millpond

ponder vb (sometimes foll. by on or over) to consider thoroughly or deeply > **ponderable** adj

> **ponder** vb = think about, consider, reflect on, contemplate, deliberate about, muse on, brood on, meditate on

ponderous adj **1** serious and dull: much of the film is ponderous and pretentious **2** heavy or huge **3** (of movement) slow and clumsy

pong Brit & Austral informal ▸ n **1** a strong unpleasant smell ▸ vb **2** to give off a strong unpleasant smell > **pongy** adj

pontiff n the Pope

P

pontificate *vb* **-cating, -cated 1** to speak in a dogmatic manner **2** to officiate as a pontiff ▸ *n* **3** the term of office of a Pope

pontoon¹ *n* a floating platform used to support a bridge

pontoon² *n* a card game in which players try to obtain sets of cards worth 21 points

pony *n, pl* **-nies** a breed of small horse

ponytail *n* a hairstyle in which the hair is tied in a bunch at the back of the head and hangs down like a tail

poodle *n* a dog with curly hair, which is sometimes clipped

poof *n Brit, Austral & NZ offensive slang* a homosexual man > **poofy** *adj*

pool¹ *n* **1** a small body of still water **2** a small body of spilt liquid: *a pool of blood* **3** See **swimming pool 4** a deep part of a stream or river

> **pool** *n* **1** = pond, lake, mere, tarn **2** = puddle, drop, patch

pool² *n* **1** a shared fund of resources or workers: *a typing pool* **2** a billiard game in which all the balls are potted with the cue ball **3** the combined stakes of those betting in many gambling games **4** *commerce* a group of producers who agree to maintain output levels and high prices ▸ *vb* **5** to put into a common fund

> **pool** *n* **1** = supply, reserve, fall-back **3** = kitty, bank, fund, stock, store, pot, jackpot, stockpile ▸ *vb* = combine, share, merge, put together, amalgamate, lump together, join forces on

poop *n naut* a raised part at the back of a sailing ship

poor *adj* **1** having little money and few possessions **2** less than is necessary or expected: *it was a poor reward for all his effort* **3** (sometimes foll. by *in*) lacking in (something): *a food which is rich in energy but poor in vitamins* **4** inferior: *poor quality* **5** disappointing or disagreeable: *a poor play* **6** pitiable; unlucky: *poor John is ill* **7 poor man's (something)** a cheaper substitute for (something): *pewter, sometimes known as poor man's silver*

> **poor** *adj* **1** = impoverished, broke (*informal*), hard up (*informal*), short, needy, penniless, destitute, poverty-stricken; ≠ rich **2, 3** = meagre, inadequate, insufficient, lacking, incomplete, scant, deficient, skimpy; ≠ ample **4, 5** = inferior, unsatisfactory, mediocre, second-rate, rotten (*informal*), low-grade, below par, substandard, half-pie (*NZ informal*), bodger *or* bodgie (*Austral slang*); ≠ excellent **6** = unfortunate, unlucky, hapless, pitiful, luckless, wretched, ill-starred, pitiable; ≠ fortunate

poorly *adv* **1** badly ▸ *adj* **2** *informal* rather ill

> **poorly** *adv* = badly, incompetently, inadequately, unsuccessfully, insufficiently, unsatisfactorily, inexpertly; ≠ well ▸ *adj* = ill, sick, unwell, crook (*Austral, NZ informal*), seedy (*informal*), below par, off colour, under the weather (*informal*), feeling rotten (*informal*); ≠ healthy

pop¹ *vb* **popping, popped 1** to make or cause to make a small explosive sound **2** (often foll. by *in* or *out* etc.) *informal* to enter or leave briefly or suddenly: *his mother popped out to buy him an ice cream* **3** to place suddenly or unexpectedly: *Benny popped a sweet into his mouth* **4** to burst with a small explosive sound **5** (of the eyes) to protrude **6** *informal* to pawn **7 pop the question** *informal* to propose marriage ▸ *n* **8** a light sharp explosive sound **9** *Brit informal* a nonalcoholic fizzy drink ▸ *adv* **10** with a pop

> **pop** *vb* **1, 4** = burst, crack, snap, bang, explode, go off (with a bang) **3** = put, insert, push, stick, slip, thrust, tuck, shove ▸ *n* **8** = bang, report, crack, noise, burst, explosion

pop² *n* **1** music of general appeal, esp. to young people, that usually has a strong rhythm and uses electrical amplification ▸ *adj* **2** relating to pop music: *a pop concert* **3** *informal* short for **popular**

pop³ *n informal* **1** father **2** an old man

popcorn *n* grains of maize heated until they puff up and burst

Pope *n* the bishop of Rome as head of the Roman Catholic Church

> **Pope** *n* = Holy Father, pontiff, His Holiness, Bishop of Rome, Vicar of Christ

popish (**pope-ish**) *adj offensive* relating to Roman Catholicism

poplar *n* a tall slender tree with light soft wood, triangular leaves, and catkins

poplin *n* a strong plain-woven fabric, usually of cotton, with fine ribbing

poppadom *or* **poppadum** *n* a thin round crisp fried Indian bread

poppy *n, pl* **-pies 1** a plant with showy red, orange, or white flowers **2** a drug, such as opium, obtained from these plants **3** an artificial red poppy worn to mark Remembrance Sunday and in New Zealand to mark Anzac Day ▸ *adj* **4** reddish-orange

populace *n* the ordinary people of an area; masses

popular *adj* **1** widely liked or admired **2** (often foll. by *with*) liked by a particular person or group: *the bay is popular with windsurfers and water-skiers* **3** common among the general public: *the groundswell of popular feeling* **4** designed to appeal to a mass audience: *an attack on him in the popular press* > **popularity** *n* > **popularly** *adv*

popular *adj* **1, 2** = well-liked, liked, in, accepted, favourite, approved, in favour, fashionable, trending; ≠ unpopular **3** = common, general, prevailing, current, conventional, universal, prevalent; ≠ rare

popularize *or* **-rise** *vb* **-rizing, -rized** *or* **-rising, -rised 1** to make popular **2** to make easily understandable > **popularization** *or* **-risation** *n*

populate *vb* **-lating, -lated 1** (*often passive*) to live in: *a mountainous region populated mainly by Armenians* **2** to provide with inhabitants > **populated** *adj*

populate *vb* **1** = inhabit, people, live in, occupy, reside in, dwell in (*formal*) **2** = settle, occupy, pioneer, colonize

population *n* **1** all the inhabitants of a place **2** the number of such inhabitants **3** all the people of a particular class in a place: *the bulk of the rural population lives in poverty* **4** *ecology* a group of individuals of the same species inhabiting a given area: *a population of grey seals*

population *n* **1** = inhabitants, people, community, society, residents, natives, folk, occupants

populism *n* a political strategy based on a calculated appeal to the interests or prejudices of ordinary people: *they preach a heady message of populism and religion* > **populist** *adj, n*

populous *adj* containing many inhabitants

pop-up *adj* **1** (of an appliance) characterized by or having a mechanism that pops up **2** (of a book) having pages that rise when opened, to simulate a three-dimensional form **3** *computers* (of a menu on a computer screen, etc.) suddenly appearing when an option is selected **4** (of a shop, restaurant, etc.) intentionally trading for a short time only: *a pop-up boutique* ▸ *n* **5** *computers* something that appears over or above the open window on a computer screen

porbeagle *n* a large shark of the N Atlantic and Mediterranean

porcelain *n* **1** a delicate type of china **2** an object or objects made of this

porch *n* a covered approach to the entrance of a building

porcine *adj* of or like a pig

porcupine *n* a large rodent covered with long pointed quills

pore[1] *vb* **poring, pored** > **pore over** to examine or study intently: *I pored over account books and ledgers all day*

pore[2] *n* a small opening in the skin or surface of an animal or plant

pore *n* = opening, hole, outlet, orifice

pork *n* the flesh of pigs used as food

porker *n* a pig fattened for food

porn *or* **porno** *n, adj informal* short for **pornography** *or* **pornographic**

pornography *n* writings, pictures, or films

designed to be sexually exciting > **pornographer** *n* > **pornographic** *adj*

pornography *n* = obscenity, porn (*informal*), dirt, filth, indecency, smut

porous *adj* **1** allowing air and liquids to be absorbed **2** *biol & geol* having pores > **porosity** *n*

porphyry (por-fir-ee) *n, pl* **-ries** a reddish-purple rock with large crystals of feldspar in it > **porphyritic** *adj*

porpoise *n, pl* **-poises** *or* **-poise** a small mammal of the whale family with a blunt snout

porridge *n* **1** a dish made of oatmeal or other cereal, cooked in water or milk **2** *chiefly Brit slang* a term of imprisonment

port[1] *n* a town with a harbour where ships can load and unload

port *n* = harbour, haven, anchorage, seaport

port[2] *n* **1** the left side of an aircraft or ship when facing the front of it ▸ *vb* **2** to turn or be turned towards the port

port[3] *n* a strong sweet fortified wine, usually dark red

port[4] *n naut* **A** an opening with a watertight door in the side of a ship, used for loading, etc. **B** See **porthole 2** a location on a computer where peripherals and other components can be plugged in

portable *adj* **1** easily carried ▸ *n* **2** an article designed to be easily carried, such as a television or a games console > **portability** *n*

portable *adj* = light, compact, convenient, handy, manageable, movable, easily carried

portal *n* **1** *literary* a large and impressive gateway or doorway **2** *computers* an internet site providing links to other sites

portcullis *n* an iron grating suspended in a castle gateway, that can be lowered to bar the entrance

portend *vb* to be an omen of: *the 0.5% increase certainly portends higher inflation ahead*

portent *n* **1** a sign of a future event **2** great or ominous significance: *matters of great portent* **3** a marvel

portentous *adj* **1** of great or ominous significance **2** self-important or pompous: *there was nothing portentous or solemn about him*

porter[1] *n* **1** a person employed to carry luggage at a railway station or hotel **2** a hospital worker who transfers patients from one part of the hospital to another > **porterage** *n*

porter *n* **1** = baggage attendant, carrier, bearer, baggage-carrier

porter[2] *n chiefly Brit* a doorman or gatekeeper of a building

porter *n* = doorman, caretaker, janitor, concierge, gatekeeper

portfolio *n, pl* **-os 1** a flat case for carrying maps, drawings, or papers **2** selected examples,

P

such as drawings or photographs, that show an artist's recent work **3** the area of responsibility of the head of a government department: *the defence portfolio* **4** a list of investments held by an investor **5 Minister without portfolio** a cabinet minister without responsibility for a government department

porthole *n* a small round window in a ship or aircraft

portico *n, pl* **-coes** *or* **-cos** a porch or covered walkway with columns supporting the roof

portion *n* **1** a part of a whole **2** a part belonging to a person or group **3** a helping of food served to one person **4** *law* a dowry **5** *literary* someone's fate or destiny: *utter disaster was my portion* ▸ *vb* **6** to divide (something) into shares

> **portion** *n* **1** = part, bit, piece, section, scrap, segment, fragment, chunk **2** = share, allowance, lot, measure, quantity, quota, ration, allocation **3** = helping, serving, piece, plateful

portly *adj* **-lier, -liest** stout or rather fat

portmanteau *n, pl* **-teaus** *or* **-teaux** *old-fashioned* a large suitcase made of stiff leather that opens out into two compartments

portrait *n* **1** a painting, drawing, or photograph of a person, often only of the face **2** a description ▸ *adj* **3** (of a page or screen) having greater height than width › **portraitist** *n*

> **portrait** *n* **1** = picture, painting, image, photograph, representation, likeness **2** = description, profile, portrayal, depiction, characterization, thumbnail sketch

portray *vb* to describe or represent (someone) by artistic means, such as in writing or on film › **portrayal** *n*

> **portray** *vb* = play, take the role of, act the part of, represent, personate (*rare*)

Portuguese *adj* **1** of Portugal ▸ *n* **2** *pl* **-guese** a person from Portugal **3** the language of Portugal and Brazil

Portuguese man-of-war *n* a large sea creature like a jellyfish, with long stinging tentacles

pose *vb* **posing, posed 1** to take up a particular position to be photographed or drawn **2** to behave in an affected way in order to impress others **3** (often foll. by *as*) to pretend to be (someone one is not) **4** to create or be (a problem, threat, etc.): *dressing complicated wounds has always posed a problem for doctors* **5** to put forward or ask: *the question you posed earlier* ▸ *n* **6** a position taken up for an artist or photographer **7** behaviour adopted for effect

> **pose** *vb* **1** = position yourself, sit, model, arrange yourself **2** = put on airs, posture, show off (*informal*) **3 pose as something or someone** = impersonate, pretend to be, profess to be,

masquerade as, pass yourself off as ▸ *n* **6** = posture, position, bearing, attitude, stance **7** = act, facade, air, front, posturing, pretence, mannerism, affectation

poser¹ *n Brit, Austral & NZ informal* a person who likes to be seen in trendsetting clothes in fashionable bars, clubs, etc.

poser² *n* a baffling question

poseur *n* a person who behaves in an affected way in order to impress others

posh *adj informal, chiefly Brit* **1** smart or elegant **2** upper-class

> **posh** *adj* **1** = smart, grand, stylish, luxurious, classy (*slang*), swish (*informal, chiefly Brit*), up-market, swanky (*informal*), schmick (*Austral informal*) **2** = upper-class, high-class

posit (pozz-it) *vb* **-iting, -ited** to lay down as a basis for argument: *the archetypes posited by modern psychology*

position *n* **1** place or location: *the hotel is in an elevated position above the River Wye* **2** the proper or usual place **3** the way in which a person or thing is placed or arranged: *an upright position* **4** point of view; attitude: *the Catholic Church's position on contraception* **5** social status, esp. high social standing **6** a job; appointment **7** *sport* a player's allotted role or place in the playing area **8** *military* a place occupied for tactical reasons **9 in a position to** able to: *you were not in a position to repay the money* ▸ *vb* **10** to put in the proper or usual place; locate › **positional** *adj*

> **position** *n* **1** = location, place, point, area, post, situation, station, spot **3** = posture, attitude, arrangement, pose, stance **4** = attitude, view, perspective, point of view, opinion, belief, stance, outlook **5** = status, place, standing, footing, station, rank, reputation, importance **6** = job, place, post, opening, office, role, situation, duty ▸ *vb* = place, put, set, stand, arrange, locate, lay out

positive *adj* **1** expressing certainty: *a positive answer* **2** definite or certain: *are you absolutely positive about the date?* **3** tending to emphasize what is good; constructive: *positive thinking* **4** tending towards progress or improvement: *investment that could have a positive impact on the company's fortunes* **5** *philosophy* constructive rather than sceptical **6** *informal* complete; downright: *a positive delight* **7** *maths* having a value greater than zero: *a positive number* **8** *grammar* denoting the unmodified form of an adjective as opposed to its comparative or superlative form **9** *physics* (of an electric charge) having an opposite charge to that of an electron **10** *med* (of the result of an examination or test) indicating the presence of a suspected condition or organism ▸ *n* **11** something positive **12** *maths* a quantity greater than zero **13** *photog* a print showing an image whose colours and tones correspond to those of the original subject **14** *grammar* the positive degree of an adjective or adverb **15** a positive object, such as a terminal in a voltaic cell ▸ **positively** *adv* ▸ **positiveness** *or* **positivity** *n*

> **positive** *adj* **1** = definite, real, clear, firm, certain, express, absolute, decisive, nailed-on (*slang*); ≠ inconclusive **2** = certain, sure, convinced, confident, satisfied, assured, free from doubt; ≠ uncertain **4** = beneficial, useful, practical, helpful, progressive, productive, worthwhile, constructive; ≠ harmful **6** = absolute, complete, perfect, right (*Brit informal*), real, total, sheer, utter

positive discrimination *n* the provision of special opportunities for a disadvantaged group

positron *n physics* the antiparticle of the electron, having the same mass but an equal and opposite charge

posse (poss-ee) *n* **1** *US* a selected group of men on whom the sheriff may call for assistance **2** *informal* a group of friends or associates: *a posse of reporters* **3** (in W Canada) a troop of horses and riders who perform at rodeos

possess *vb* **1** to have as one's property; own **2** to have as a quality or attribute: *he possessed an innate elegance, authority, and wit on screen* **3** to gain control over or dominate: *absolute terror possessed her* ▸ **possessor** *n*

> **possess** *vb* **1** = own, have, hold, be in possession of, be the owner of, have in your possession **2** = be endowed with, have, enjoy, benefit from, be possessed of, be gifted with **3** = seize, hold, control, dominate, occupy, take someone over, have power over, have mastery over

possession *n* **1** the state of possessing; ownership: *how had this compromising picture come into the possession of the press?* **2** anything that is possessed **3 possessions** wealth or property **4** the state of being controlled by or as if by evil spirits **5** the occupancy of land or property: *troops had taken possession of the airport* **6** a territory subject to a foreign state **7** the criminal offence of having something illegal on one's person: *arrested for drug dealing and possession* **8** *sport* control of the ball by a team or player: *City had most of the possession, but couldn't score*

> **possession** *n* **1** = ownership, control, custody, hold, hands, tenure **3** = property, things, effects, estate, assets, belongings, chattels

possessive *adj* **1** of possession **2** desiring excessively to possess, control, or dominate: *a possessive partner* **3** *grammar* denoting a form of a noun or pronoun used to convey possession, as *my* or *Harry's*: *a possessive pronoun* ▸ *n* **4** *grammar* **A** the possessive case **B** a word in the possessive case ▸ **possessiveness** *n*

possibility *n, pl* **-ties 1** the state of being possible **2** anything that is possible **3** a competitor or candidate with a chance of success **4** a future prospect or potential: *all sorts of possibilities began to open up*

> **possibility** *n* **1** = feasibility, likelihood, potentiality, practicability, workableness **4** = potential, promise, prospects, talent, capabilities, potentiality

possible *adj* **1** capable of existing, happening, or proving true: *the earliest possible moment* **2** capable of being done: *I am grateful to the library staff for making this work possible* **3** having potential: *a possible buyer* **4** feasible but less than probable: *it's possible that's what he meant, but I doubt it* ▸ *n* **5** same as **possibility** (sense 3)

> **possible** *adj* **1, 2** = feasible, viable, workable, achievable, practicable, attainable, doable, realizable; ≠ unfeasible **3** = aspiring, would-be, promising, hopeful, prospective, wannabe (*informal*) **4** = conceivable, likely, credible, plausible, hypothetical, imaginable, believable, thinkable; ≠ inconceivable

possibly *adv* **1** perhaps or maybe **2** by any means; at all: *he can't possibly come*

> **possibly** *adv* **1** = perhaps, maybe, perchance (*archaic*)

possum *n* **1** *informal* an opossum **2** *Austral & NZ* a phalanger **3 play possum** to pretend to be dead, ignorant, or asleep in order to deceive an opponent

post[1] *n* **1** an official system of mail delivery **2** letters or packages that are transported and delivered by the Post Office; mail **3** a single collection or delivery of mail **4** a postbox or post office: *take this to the post* **5** *computers* a blog or message made publicly available ▸ *vb* **6** to send by post **7** *computers* to make (a blog or message) publicly available **8** *accounting* **A** to enter (an item) in a ledger **B** (often foll. by *up*) to enter all paper items in (a ledger) **9 keep someone posted** to inform someone regularly of the latest news

> **post** *n* **1, 3** = mail, collection, delivery, postal service, snail mail (*informal*) **2** = correspondence, letters, cards, mail ▸ *vb* **6** = send (off), forward, mail, get off, transmit, dispatch, consign **9 keep someone posted** = notify, brief, advise, inform, report to, keep someone informed, keep someone up to date, apprise

post[2] *n* **1** a length of wood, metal, or concrete fixed upright to support or mark something **2** *horse racing* **A** either of two upright poles marking the beginning and end of a racecourse **B** the finish of a horse race ▸ *vb* **3** (sometimes foll. by *up*) to put up (a notice) in a public place **4** to publish (a name) on a list

p

post *n* **1** = support, stake, pole, column, shaft, upright, pillar, picket ▸ *vb* **3** = put up, display, affix, pin something up

post³ *n* **1** a position to which a person is appointed; job **2** a position to which a soldier or guard is assigned for duty **3** a permanent military establishment **4** *Brit* either of two military bugle calls (**first post** and **last post**) giving notice of the time to retire for the night ▸ *vb* **5** *Brit & Austral* to send (someone) to a new place to work **6** to assign to or station at a particular place or position: *guards were posted at the doors*

post *n* **1** = job, place, office, position, situation, employment, appointment, assignment **2** = position, place, base, beat, station ▸ *vb* = station, assign, put, place, position, situate, put on duty

post- *prefix* **1** after in time: *postgraduate* **2** behind: *postorbital*

postage *n* the charge for sending a piece of mail by post

postage stamp *n* same as **stamp** (sense 1)

postal *adj* of a post office or the mail-delivery service

postal order *n* a written money order sent by post and cashed at a post office by the person who receives it

postbag *n* **1** *chiefly Brit* a mailbag **2** the mail received by a magazine, radio programme, or public figure

postcard *n* a card, often with a picture on one side, for sending a message by post without an envelope

postcode *n* a system of letters and numbers used to aid the sorting of mail

postdate *vb* **-dating, -dated 1** to write a future date on (a cheque or document) **2** to occur at a later date than **3** to assign a date to (an event or period) that is later than its previously assigned date

poster *n* **1** a large notice displayed in a public place as an advertisement **2** a large printed picture

poster *n* **1** = notice, bill, announcement, advertisement, sticker, placard, public notice

posterior *n* **1** *formal or humorous* the buttocks ▸ *adj* **2** at the back of or behind something: *posterior leg muscles* **3** coming after in a series or time

posterity *n* **1** future generations **2** all of one's descendants

postern *n* a small back door or gate

postgraduate *n* **1** a person who is studying for a more advanced qualification after obtaining a degree ▸ *adj* **2** of or for postgraduates

posthaste *adv* with great speed

posthumous (poss-tume-uss) *adj* **1** happening after one's death **2** born after the death of one's

father **3** (of a book) published after the author's death > **posthumously** *adv*

postie *n Scot, Austral & NZ informal* a postman

postilion *or* **postillion** *n* (esp. formerly) a person who rides one of a pair of horses drawing a coach

postman *or fem* **postwoman** *n, pl* **-men** *or fem* **-women** a person who collects and delivers mail as a profession

postmark *n* **1** an official mark stamped on mail, showing the place and date of posting ▸ *vb* **2** to put such a mark on (mail)

postmaster *n* **1** Also (fem): **postmistress** an official in charge of a post office **2** a person who is responsible for managing the email system in an organization

postmortem *n* **1** In full: **postmortem examination** medical examination of a dead body to discover the cause of death **2** analysis of a recent event: *a postmortem on the party's recent appalling by-election results* ▸ *adj* **3** occurring after death

postnatal *adj* occurring after childbirth: *postnatal depression*

post office *n* a building where stamps are sold and postal business is conducted

postpone *vb* **-poning, -poned** to put off until a future time > **postponement** *n*

postpone *vb* = put off, delay, suspend, adjourn, shelve, defer, put back, put on the back burner (*informal*); ≠ go ahead with

postscript *n* a message added at the end of a letter, after the signature

postulant *n* an applicant for admission to a religious order

postulate *formal* ▸ *vb* **-lating, -lated 1** to assume to be true as the basis of an argument or theory **2** to ask, demand, or claim ▸ *n* **3** something postulated > **postulation** *n*

posture *n* **1** a position or way in which a person stands, walks, etc.: *good posture* **2** a mental attitude: *a cooperative posture* **3** an affected attitude: *an intellectual posture* ▸ *vb* **-turing, -tured 4** to behave in an exaggerated way to attract attention **5** to assume an affected attitude > **postural** *adj*

posture *n* **1** = bearing, set, attitude, stance, carriage, disposition ▸ *vb* **4** = show off (*informal*), pose, affect, put on airs

posy *n, pl* **-sies** a small bunch of flowers

pot¹ *n* **1** a round deep container, often with a handle and lid, used for cooking **2** the amount that a pot will hold **3** short for **teapot 4** a handmade piece of pottery **5** *billiards etc.* a shot by which a ball is pocketed **6** a chamber pot **7** the money in the pool in gambling games **8** (*often pl*) *informal* a large sum of money **9** *informal* a cup or other trophy **10 go to pot** *informal* to go to ruin ▸ *vb* **potting, potted 11** to put (a plant) in soil in a flowerpot **12** *billiards etc.*

to pocket (a ball) **13** to preserve (food) in a pot **14** to shoot (game) for food rather than for sport **15** to shoot casually or without careful aim **16** *informal* to capture or win

pot *n* **1, 4** = container, bowl, pan, vessel, basin, cauldron, skillet

pot² *n slang* cannabis

potable (pote-a-bl) *adj formal* drinkable

potash *n* **1** potassium carbonate, used as fertilizer **2** a compound containing potassium: *permanganate of potash*

potassium *n chem* a light silvery element of the alkali metal group. Symbol: **K**

potato *n, pl* **-toes 1** a starchy vegetable that grows underground **2** the plant from which this vegetable is obtained

poteen *or* **poitín** *n* (in Ireland) illegally made alcoholic drink

potent *adj* **1** having great power or influence **2** (of arguments) persuasive or forceful **3** highly effective: *a potent poison* **4** (of a male) capable of having sexual intercourse ▷ **potency** *n*

potent *adj* **1** = powerful, commanding, dynamic, dominant, influential, authoritative **3** = strong, powerful, mighty, vigorous, forceful; ≠ weak

potentate *n* a ruler or monarch

potential *adj* **1 A** possible but not yet actual: *potential buyers* **B** capable of being or becoming; latent: *potential danger* ▷ *n* **2** ability or talent not yet in full use: *she has great potential as a painter* **3** In full: **electric potential** the work required to transfer a unit positive electric charge from an infinite distance to a given point ▷ **potentially** *adv*

potential *adj* **1** = possible, future, likely, promising, probable ▷ *n* **2** = ability, possibilities, capacity, capability, aptitude, wherewithal, potentiality

potentiality *n, pl* **-ties** latent capacity for becoming or developing

pothole *n* **1** a hole in the surface of a road **2** a deep hole in a limestone area

potholing *n* the sport of exploring underground caves ▷ **potholer** *n*

potion *n* a drink of medicine, poison, or some supposedly magic liquid

pot luck *n* **take pot luck** *informal* to accept whatever happens to be available: *we'll take pot luck at whatever restaurant might still be open*

potoroo *n, pl* **-roos** an Australian leaping rodent

potpourri (po-poor-ee) *n, pl* **-ris 1** a fragrant mixture of dried flower petals **2** an assortment or medley

pot shot *n* **1** a shot taken without careful aim **2** a shot fired at an animal within easy range

pottage *n* a thick soup or stew

potted *adj* **1** grown in a pot: *potted plant* **2** cooked or preserved in a pot: *potted shrimps* **3** *informal* shortened or abridged: *a potted history*

potter¹ *n* a person who makes pottery

potter² *or esp US & Canad* **putter** *vb* **1** to move with little energy or direction: *I saw him pottering off to see his canaries* **2 potter about** *or* **around** *or* **away** to be busy in a pleasant but aimless way: *he potters away doing God knows what all day*

potter *or* **putter** *vb* **2** = mess about, tinker, dabble, footle (*informal*)

pottery *n, pl* **-teries 1** articles made from baked clay **2** a place where such articles are made **3** the craft of making such articles

pottery *n* **1** = ceramics, terracotta, crockery, earthenware, stoneware

potting shed *n* a garden hut in which plants are put in flowerpots and potting materials are stored

potty¹ *adj* **-tier, -tiest** *informal* **1** foolish or slightly crazy **2** trivial or insignificant **3** (foll. by *about*) very keen (on) ▷ **pottiness** *n*

potty² *n, pl* **-ties** a bowl used as a toilet by a small child

pouch *n* **1** a small bag **2** a baglike pocket in various animals, such as the cheek fold in hamsters ▷ *vb* **3** to place in or as if in a pouch **4** to make or be made into a pouch

pouf *or* **pouffe** (poof) *n* a large solid cushion used as a seat

poulterer *n Brit* a person who sells poultry

poultice (pole-tiss) *n med* a moist dressing, often heated, applied to painful and swollen parts of the body

poultry *n* domestic fowls

pounce *vb* **pouncing, pounced 1** (often foll. by *on* or *upon*) to spring upon suddenly to attack or capture ▷ *n* **2** the act of pouncing; a spring or swoop

pounce *vb* = attack, strike, jump, leap, swoop

pound¹ *n* **1** the standard monetary unit of the United Kingdom and some other countries, made up of 100 pence. Official name: **pound sterling 2** the standard monetary unit of various other countries, such as Cyprus and Malta **3** a unit of weight made up of 16 ounces and equal to 0.454 kilograms

pound² *vb* **1** (sometimes foll. by *on* or *at*) to hit heavily and repeatedly **2** to crush to pieces or to powder **3** (foll. by *out*) to produce, by typing heavily **4** (of the heart) to throb heavily **5** to run with heavy steps

pound *vb* **1** = beat, strike, hammer (*informal*), batter, thrash, thump, clobber (*slang*), pummel **2** = crush, powder, pulverize **4** = pulsate, beat, pulse, throb, palpitate **5** = stomp, tramp, march, thunder (*informal*)

pound³ *n* an enclosure for stray dogs or officially removed vehicles

P

pound n = enclosure, yard, pen, compound, kennels

pour vb **1** to flow or cause to flow out in a stream **2** to rain heavily **3** to be given or obtained in large amounts: *suggestions are pouring in* **4** to move together in large numbers: *the fans poured onto the pitch*

pour vb **1** = let flow, spill, splash, dribble, drizzle, slop (*informal*), slosh (*informal*), decant **2** = rain, pelt (down), teem, bucket down (*informal*) **4** = stream, crowd, flood, swarm, gush, throng, teem

pout vb **1** to thrust out (the lips) sullenly or provocatively ▸ n **2** a pouting

pout vb = sulk, glower, look petulant, pull a long face ▸ n = sullen look, glower, long face

poverty n **1** the state of lacking adequate food or money **2** lack or scarcity: *a poverty of information* **3** inferior quality or inadequacy: *the poverty of political debate in this country*

poverty n **1** = pennilessness, want, need, hardship, insolvency, privation (*formal*), penury, destitution; ≠ wealth **2** = scarcity, lack, absence, want, deficit, shortage, deficiency, inadequacy; ≠ abundance

POW prisoner of war

powder n **1** a substance in the form of tiny loose particles **2** a medicine or cosmetic in this form ▸ vb **3** to cover or sprinkle with powder ▸ **powdery** adj

powder n **1** = dust, talc, fine grains, loose particles ▸ vb = dust, cover, scatter, sprinkle, strew, dredge

powdered adj **1** sold in the form of a powder, esp. one which has been formed by grinding or drying the original material: *powdered milk* **2** covered or made up with a cosmetic in the form of a powder: *liveried footmen in powdered wigs*

powder room n euphemistic a women's cloakroom or toilet

power n **1** ability to do something **2** (often pl) a specific ability or faculty **3** political, financial, or social force or authority: *the strong have power over the weak; economic power is the bedrock of political power* **4** a position of control, esp. over the running of a country: *he seized power in a coup in 1966* **5** a state with political, industrial, or military strength **6** a person or group having authority **7** a prerogative or privilege: *the power of veto* **8** official or legal authority **9** maths the value of a number or quantity raised to some exponent **10** physics & engineering a measure of the rate of doing work expressed as the work done per unit of time **11** the rate at which electrical energy is fed into or taken from a device or system, measured in watts **12** mechanical energy as opposed to manual labour

13 a particular form of energy: *nuclear power* **14** the magnifying capacity of a lens or optical system **15** informal a great deal: *a power of good* **16 the powers that be** established authority ▸ vb **17** to supply with power ▸ adj **18** producing or using electrical energy: *a large selection of power tools*

power n **1** = ability, capacity, faculty, property, potential, capability, competence, competency; ≠ inability **3** = strength, might, energy, muscle, vigour, potency, brawn, hard power; ≠ weakness **4** = control, authority, influence, command, dominance, domination, mastery, dominion, mana (NZ) **7** = authority, right, licence, privilege, warrant, prerogative, authorization

power cut n a temporary interruption in the supply of electricity

powerful adj **1** having great power or influence **2** having great physical strength **3** extremely effective: *a powerful drug* ▸ **powerfully** adv ▸ **powerfulness** n

powerful adj **1** = influential, dominant, controlling, commanding, prevailing, authoritative, skookum (*Canad*); ≠ powerless **2** = strong, strapping, mighty, vigorous, potent, energetic, sturdy; ≠ weak

powerless adj without power or authority; unable to act ▸ **powerlessly** adv ▸ **powerlessness** n

powerless adj = defenceless, vulnerable, dependent, subject, tied, ineffective, unarmed

power point n an electrical socket fitted into a wall for plugging in electrical appliances

power station n an installation for generating and distributing electricity

powwow n **1** a talk or meeting **2** a meeting of Native Americans ▸ vb **3** to hold a powwow

pox n **1** a disease in which pus-filled blisters or pimples form on the skin **2 the pox** informal syphilis

pp 1 past participle **2** (in signing documents on behalf of someone else) by delegation to

pp. pages

PPTA (in New Zealand) Post Primary Teachers' Association

PR 1 proportional representation **2** public relations

practicable adj **1** capable of being done **2** usable ▸ **practicability** n

practical adj **1** involving experience or actual use rather than theory **2** concerned with everyday matters: *the kind of practical and emotional upheaval that divorce can bring* **3** sensible, useful, and effective rather than fashionable or attractive: *it's a marvellous design, because it's comfortable, it's practical, and it actually looks good* **4** involving the simple basics: *practical skills* **5** being very close to (a state); virtual: *it's a practical certainty* ▸ n **6** an examination or lesson in which something has to be made or done ▸ **practicality** n ▸ **practically** adv

practical *adj* 1 = empirical, real, applied, actual, hands-on, in the field, experimental, factual; ≠ theoretical 2 = sensible, ordinary, realistic, down-to-earth, matter-of-fact, businesslike, hard-headed, grounded; ≠ impractical 3 = functional, realistic, pragmatic; ≠ impractical 4 = useful, ordinary, appropriate, sensible, everyday, functional, utilitarian, serviceable

practical joke *n* a trick intended to make someone look foolish > **practical joker** *n*

practice *n* 1 something done regularly or repeatedly 2 repetition of an activity in order to gain skill: *regular practice is essential if you want to play an instrument well* 3 the business or surgery of a doctor or lawyer 4 the act of doing something: *I'm not sure how effective these methods will be when put into practice* 5 **in practice** A what actually happens as distinct from what is supposed to happen: *many ideas which look good on paper just don't work in practice* B skilled in something through having had a lot of regular recent experience at it: *I still go shooting, just to keep in practice* 6 **out of practice** not having had much regular recent experience at an activity: *although out of practice, I still love playing my violin*

practice *n* 1 = custom, way, system, rule, method, tradition, habit, routine, tikanga (NZ) 2 = training, study, exercise, preparation (*old-fashioned*), drill, rehearsal, repetition 3 = profession, work, business, career, occupation, pursuit, vocation 4 = use, experience, action, operation, application, enactment

practise *or US* **practice** *vb* **-tising, -tised** *or* **-ticing, -ticed** 1 to do repeatedly in order to gain skill 2 to take part in or follow (a religion, etc.): *none of them practise Islam* 3 to work at (a profession): *he originally intended to practise medicine* 4 to do regularly: *they practise meditation*

practise *or* **practice** *vb* 1 = rehearse, study, prepare, perfect, repeat, go through, go over, refine 2 = carry out, follow, apply, perform, observe, engage in 3 = work at, pursue, carry on 4 = do, train, exercise, drill

practitioner *n* a person who practises a profession

pragmatic *adj* 1 concerned with practical consequences rather than theory 2 *philosophy of* pragmatism > **pragmatically** *adv*

pragmatic *adj* 1 = practical, sensible, realistic, down-to-earth, utilitarian, businesslike, hard-headed; ≠ idealistic

pragmatism *n* 1 policy dictated by practical consequences rather than by theory 2 *philosophy* the doctrine that the content of a concept consists only in its practical applicability > **pragmatist** *n, adj*

prairie *n* (*often pl*) a large treeless area of grassland of North America

prairie dog *n* a rodent that lives in burrows in the N American prairies

praise *vb* **praising, praised** 1 to express admiration or approval for 2 to express thanks and worship to (one's God) ▸ *n* 3 the expression of admiration or approval 4 **sing someone's praises** to praise someone highly

praise *vb* 1 = acclaim, approve of, honour, cheer, admire, applaud, compliment, congratulate; ≠ criticize 2 = give thanks to, bless, worship, adore, glorify, exalt ▸ *n* 3 = approval, acclaim, tribute, compliment, congratulations, eulogy, commendation, approbation; ≠ criticism

praiseworthy *adj* deserving praise; commendable

praline (prah-leen) *n* a sweet made of nuts with caramelized sugar

pram *n* a four-wheeled carriage for a baby, pushed by a person on foot

prance *vb* **prancing, pranced** 1 to walk with exaggerated movements 2 (of an animal) to move with high springing steps ▸ *n* 3 the act of prancing

prang *Brit & Austral slang* ▸ *n* 1 a crash in an aircraft or car ▸ *vb* 2 to crash or damage (an aircraft or car)

prank *n* a mischievous trick > **prankster** *n*

prat *n Brit, Austral & NZ slang* an incompetent or ineffectual person

prattle *vb* **-tling, -tled** 1 to chatter in a foolish or childish way ▸ *n* 2 foolish or childish talk

prawn *n* a small edible shellfish

praxis *n* 1 practice as opposed to the theory 2 accepted practice or custom

pray *vb* 1 to say prayers (to one's God) 2 to ask earnestly; beg ▸ *adv* 3 *archaic* I beg you; please: *pray, leave us alone*

pray *vb* 1 = say your prayers, offer a prayer, recite the rosary 2 = beg, ask, plead, petition, request, solicit, implore, beseech

prayer *n* 1 a thanksgiving or an appeal spoken to one's God 2 a set form of words used in praying: *the Lord's Prayer* 3 an earnest request 4 the practice of praying: *call the faithful to prayer* 5 (*often pl*) a form of devotion spent mainly praying: *morning prayers* 6 something prayed for

prayer *n* 1 = orison, litany, invocation, intercession 3 = plea, appeal, request, petition, entreaty, supplication (*formal*) 5 = supplication, devotion

pre- *prefix* before in time or position: *predate*; *pre-eminent*

preach *vb* 1 to talk on a religious theme as part of a church service 2 to speak in support of (something) in a moralizing way

p

preach vb 1 = deliver a sermon, address, evangelize, preach a sermon 2 = urge, teach, champion, recommend, advise, counsel, advocate, exhort

preacher n a person who preaches

preacher n = clergyman or woman, minister, parson, missionary, evangelist

preamble n an introduction that comes before something spoken or written

prearranged adj arranged beforehand
> **prearrangement** n

prebendary n, pl **-daries** a member of the clergy who is a member of the chapter of a cathedral

precarious adj (of a position or situation) dangerous or insecure > **precariously** adv

precarious adj = dangerous, shaky, insecure, unsafe, unreliable; ≠ stable

precaution n an action taken in advance to prevent an undesirable event > **precautionary** adj

precaution n = safeguard, insurance, protection, provision, safety measure

precede vb **-ceding, -ceded** to go or be before (someone or something) in time, place, or rank

precede vb = go before, antedate

precedence (press-i-denss) n formal order of rank or position

precedent n 1 a previous occurrence used to justify taking the same action in later similar situations 2 law a judicial decision that serves as an authority for deciding a later case ▸ adj 3 preceding

precedent n 1 = instance, example, standard, model, pattern, prototype, paradigm, antecedent

precentor n a person who leads the singing in church services

precept n 1 a rule of conduct 2 a rule for morals 3 law a writ or warrant > **preceptive** adj

precinct n 1 Brit, Austral & S African an area in a town closed to traffic: a shopping precinct 2 Brit, Austral & S African an enclosed area around a building 3 US an administrative area of a city

precinct n 3 = area, quarter, section, sector, district, zone

precious adj 1 very costly or valuable: precious jewellery 2 loved and treasured 3 very affected in speech, manners, or behaviour ▸ adv 4 informal very: there's precious little to do in this town

precious adj 1 = valuable, expensive, fine, prized, dear, costly, invaluable, priceless; ≠ worthless 2 = loved, prized, dear, treasured, darling, beloved, adored, cherished 3 = affected, artificial, twee (Brit informal), overrefined, overnice

precious metal n gold, silver, or platinum

precious stone n a rare mineral, such as diamond, ruby, or opal, that is highly valued as a gem

precipice n the very steep face of a cliff

precipitate vb **-tating, -tated** 1 to cause to happen earlier than expected: the scandal could bring the government down, precipitating a general election 2 to condense or cause to condense and fall as snow or rain 3 chem to cause to be deposited in solid form from a solution 4 to throw from a height: the encircled soldiers chose to precipitate themselves into the ocean ▸ adj 5 done rashly or hastily 6 rushing ahead ▸ n 7 chem a precipitated solid

precipitate vb 1 = quicken, trigger, accelerate, advance, hurry, speed up, bring on, hasten 4 = throw, launch, cast, hurl, fling, let fly ▸ adj 5 = hasty, rash, reckless, impulsive, precipitous, impetuous, heedless 6 = sudden, quick, brief, rushing, rapid, unexpected, swift, abrupt

precipitation n 1 the formation of a chemical precipitate 2 meteorol A rain, hail, snow, or sleet formed by condensation of water vapour in the atmosphere B the falling of these 3 rash haste: they decamped with the utmost precipitation

precipitous adj 1 very steep: precipitous cliffs 2 very quick and severe: a precipitous decline 3 rapid and unplanned; hasty: European governments urged the Americans not to make a precipitous decision

précis (pray-see) n, pl **précis** 1 a short summary of a longer text ▸ vb 2 to make a précis of

precise adj 1 particular or exact: this precise moment 2 strictly correct in amount or value: precise measurements 3 working with total accuracy: precise instruments 4 strict in observing rules or standards > **precisely** adv

precise adj 1 = exact, specific, particular, express, correct, absolute, accurate, explicit; ≠ vague 4 = strict, particular, exact, formal, careful, stiff, rigid, meticulous; ≠ inexact

precision n 1 the quality of being precise ▸ adj 2 accurate: precision engineering

precision n = exactness, care, accuracy, particularity, meticulousness, preciseness

preclude vb **-cluding, -cluded** formal to make impossible to happen

precocious adj having developed or matured early or too soon > **precocity** n

precognition n psychol the alleged ability to foresee future events

preconceived adj (of ideas, etc.) formed without real experience or reliable information > **preconception** n

precondition n something that is necessary before something else can come about

precursor n 1 something that comes before and signals something to follow; a forerunner 2 a predecessor

predate vb **-dating, -dated 1** to occur at an earlier date than **2** to write a date on (a document) that is earlier than the actual date

predator n an animal that kills and eats other animals

predatory (pred-a-tree) adj **1** (of animals) habitually hunting and killing other animals for food **2** eager to gain at the expense of others

predecease vb **-ceasing, -ceased** to die before (someone else)

predecessor n **1** a person who precedes another in an office or position **2** an ancestor **3** something that precedes something else: *the library will be more extravagant than its predecessors*

> **predecessor** n **1** = previous job holder, precursor, forerunner, antecedent **2** = ancestor, forebear, antecedent, forefather, tupuna or tipuna (NZ)

predestination n *Christian theol* the belief that future events have already been decided by God

predestined adj *Christian theol* determined in advance by God

predicament n an embarrassing or difficult situation

> **predicament** n = fix (*informal*), situation, spot (*informal*), hole (*slang*), mess, jam (*informal*), dilemma, pinch

predicate n **1** *grammar* the part of a sentence in which something is said about the subject **2** *logic* something that is asserted about the subject of a proposition ▸ vb **-cating, -cated 3** to base or found: *the process of unification is predicated on the hope of economic growth* **4** to declare or assert: *it has been predicated that the consequence of the budget will be immediate recession* **5** *logic* to assert (something) about the subject of a proposition > **predication** n > **predicative** adj

predict vb to tell about in advance; prophesy > **predictable** adj > **predictably** adv > **predictor** n

> **predict** vb = foretell, forecast, divine, prophesy, augur, portend

prediction n **1** the act of forecasting in advance **2** something that is forecast in advance

> **prediction** n = prophecy, forecast, prognosis, divination, prognostication, augury

predictive adj **1** relating to or able to make predictions **2** (of mobile phone technology) enabling mobile phones to predict the word being entered in a text message from the first few letters: *predictive text*

predilection n *formal* a preference or liking

predispose vb **-posing, -posed** (often foll. by *to*) **1** to influence (someone) in favour of something: *some scientists' social class background predisposes them to view the natural world in a certain way* **2** to make (someone) susceptible to something: *a high-fat diet appears to predispose men towards heart disease* > **predisposition** n

predominant adj being more important or noticeable than others: *improved living conditions probably played the predominant role in reducing disease in the nineteenth century* > **predominance** n > **predominantly** adv

predominate vb **-nating, -nated 1** to be the most important or controlling aspect or part: *the image of brutal repression that has tended to predominate since the protests were crushed* **2** to form the greatest part or be most common: *women predominate in this gathering*

pre-eminent adj outstanding > **pre-eminence** n

pre-empt vb to prevent an action by doing something which makes it pointless or impossible: *he pre-empted his expulsion from the party by resigning*

pre-emption n *law* the purchase of or right to buy property in advance of others

pre-emptive adj *military* designed to damage or destroy an enemy's attacking strength before it can be used: *a pre-emptive strike*

preen vb **1** (of birds) to clean or trim (feathers) with the beak **2** to smarten (oneself) carefully **3 preen oneself** (often foll. by *on*) to be self-satisfied

prefab n a prefabricated house

prefabricated adj (of a building) made in shaped sections for quick assembly

preface (pref-iss) n **1** an introduction to a book, usually explaining its intention or content **2** anything introductory ▸ vb **-facing, -faced 3** to say or do something before proceeding to the main part **4** to act as a preface to

prefatory adj concerning a preface

prefect n **1** *Brit, Austral & NZ* a senior pupil in a school with limited power over the behaviour of other pupils **2** (in some countries) the chief administrative officer in a department

prefecture n the office or area of authority of a prefect

prefer vb **-ferring, -ferred 1** to like better: *most people prefer television to reading books* **2** *law* to put (charges) before a court for judgment **3** (*often passive*) to promote over another or others

> **prefer** vb **1** = like better, favour, go for, pick, fancy (*Brit informal*), opt for, incline towards, be partial to

preferable adj more desirable or suitable > **preferably** adv

> **preferable** adj = better, best, chosen, preferred, recommended, favoured, superior, more suitable; ≠ undesirable

preference n **1** a liking for one thing above the rest **2** a person or thing preferred

> **preference** n **1** = liking, wish, taste, desire, leaning, bent, bias, inclination **2** = first choice, choice, favourite, pick, option, selection

P

preferential *adj* **1** showing preference: *preferential treatment* **2** indicating a special favourable status in business affairs: *the President is to renew China's preferential trading status* **3** indicating a voting system which allows voters to rank candidates in order of preference: *a multi-option referendum with preferential voting*

preferment *n* promotion to a higher position

prefigure *vb* **-guring, -gured** **1** to represent or suggest in advance **2** to imagine beforehand

prefix *n* **1** *grammar* a letter or group of letters put at the beginning of a word to make a new word, such as *un-* in *unhappy* **2** a title put before a name, such as *Mr* ▸ *vb* **3** *grammar* to add (a letter or group of letters) as a prefix to the beginning of a word **4** to put before

pregnant *adj* **1** carrying a fetus or fetuses within the womb **2** full of meaning or significance: *a pregnant pause* › **pregnancy** *n*

> **pregnant** *adj* **1** = expectant, expecting, with child (*archaic*), in the club (*Brit slang*), up the duff (*Brit slang, rare*), big *or* heavy with child (*archaic*) **2** = meaningful, pointed, charged, significant, telling, loaded, expressive, eloquent

prehensile *adj* capable of curling round objects and grasping them: *a prehensile tail*

prehistoric *adj* of human development before the appearance of the written word › **prehistory** *n*

prejudice *n* **1** an unreasonable or unfair dislike or preference **2** intolerance of or dislike for people because they belong to a specific race, religion, or group: *class prejudice* **3** the act or condition of holding such opinions **4** harm or detriment: *conduct to the prejudice of good order and military discipline* **5 without prejudice** *law* without harm to an existing right or claim ▸ *vb* **-dicing, -diced** **6** to cause (someone) to have a prejudice **7** to harm: *the incident prejudiced his campaign*

> **prejudice** *n* **1** = bias, preconception, partiality, preconceived notion, prejudgment **2, 3** = discrimination, injustice, intolerance, bigotry, unfairness, chauvinism, narrow-mindedness, faith hate ▸ *vb* **6** = bias, influence, colour, poison, distort, slant, predispose **7** = harm, damage, hurt, injure, mar, undermine, spoil, impair, crool *or* cruel (*Austral slang*)

prejudicial *adj* harmful; damaging

prelate (prel-it) *n* a high-ranking member of the clergy, such as a bishop

preliminary *adj* **1** occurring before or in preparation; introductory ▸ *n, pl* **-naries** **2** an action or event occurring before or in preparation for an activity: *the discussions are a preliminary to the main negotiations* **3** a qualifying contest held before a main competition

preliminary *adj* = first, opening, trial, initial, test, pilot, prior, introductory ▸ *n* **2** = introduction, opening, beginning, start, prelude, preface, overture, preamble

prelude (prel-yewd) *n* **1 A** an introductory movement in music **B** a short piece of music for piano or organ **2** an event introducing or preceding the main event ▸ *vb* **-luding, -luded** **3** to act as a prelude to (something) **4** to introduce by a prelude

> **prelude** *n* **1A** = overture, opening, introduction, introductory movement **2** = introduction, beginning, start

premarital *adj* occurring before marriage: *premarital sex*

premature *adj* **1** happening or done before the normal or expected time: *premature ageing* **2** impulsive or hasty: *a premature judgment* **3** (of a baby) born weeks before the date when it was due to be born › **prematurely** *adv*

> **premature** *adj* **1** = early, untimely, before time, unseasonable **2** = hasty, rash, too soon, untimely, ill-timed, overhasty

premeditated *adj* planned in advance › **premeditation** *n*

premenstrual *adj* occurring or experienced before a menstrual period

premier *n* **1** a prime minister **2** a head of government of a Canadian province or Australian state ▸ *adj* **3** first in importance or rank: *Torbay, Devon's premier resort* **4** first in occurrence › **premiership** *n*

> **premier** *n* **1** = head of government, prime minister, chancellor, chief minister, P.M. ▸ *adj* **3** = chief, leading, first, highest, head, main, prime, primary

premiere *n* **1** the first public performance of a film, play, or opera ▸ *vb* **-ering, -ered** **2** to give, or (of a film, play, or opera) be, a premiere: *the play was premiered last year in Johannesburg; the movie premieres tomorrow*

> **premiere** *n* = first night, opening, debut

premise *or* **premiss** *n* *logic* a statement that is assumed to be true and is used as a basis for an argument

> **premise** *or* **premiss** *n* = assumption, proposition, argument, hypothesis, assertion, supposition, presupposition, postulation

premises *pl n* **1** a piece of land together with its buildings **2** *law* (in a deed) the matters referred to previously

> **premises** *pl n* **1** = building(s), place, office, property, site, establishment

premium *n* **1** an extra sum of money added to a standard rate, price, or wage: *the superior taste* persuades me to pay the premium for bottled water **2** the (regular) amount paid for an insurance policy **3** the amount above the usual value at which something sells: *some even pay a premium of up to 15% for the privilege* **4** great value or regard: *we do put a very high premium on common sense* **5 at a premium** **A** in great demand, usually because of scarcity **B** at a higher price than usual

> **premium** *n* **1** = surcharge, extra charge, additional fee *or* charge **2** = fee, charge, payment, instalment **3** = bonus, reward, prize, perk (*Brit informal*), bounty, perquisite (*formal*) **5A at a premium** = in great demand, rare, scarce, in short supply, hard to come by

premonition *n* a feeling that something unpleasant is going to happen; foreboding > **premonitory** *adj*

prenatal *adj* before birth; during pregnancy

preoccupy *vb* **-pies, -pying, -pied** to fill the thoughts or mind of (someone) to the exclusion of other things > **preoccupation** *n*

preordained *adj* decreed or determined in advance

prep. **1** preparation **2** preparatory **3** preposition

prepacked *adj* (of goods) sold already wrapped

prepaid *adj* paid for in advance

preparation *n* **1** the act of preparing or being prepared **2** (*often pl*) something done in order to prepare for something else: *to make preparations for a wedding* **3** something that is prepared, such as a medicine **4** *Brit old-fashioned* **A** homework **B** the period reserved for this

> **preparation** *n* **1** = groundwork, preparing, getting ready **2** = arrangement, plan, measure, provision **3** = mixture, medicine, compound, concoction

preparatory (prip-par-a-tree) *adj* **1** preparing for: *a preparatory meeting to organize the negotiations* **2** introductory **3** **preparatory to** before: *Imran cleared his throat preparatory to speaking*

preparatory school *n* **1** *Brit & S African* a private school for children between the ages of 6 and 13, generally preparing pupils for public school **2** (in the US) a private secondary school preparing pupils for college

prepare *vb* **-paring, -pared** **1** to make or get ready: *the army prepared for battle* **2** to put together using parts or ingredients: *he had spent most of the afternoon preparing the meal* **3** to equip or outfit, as for an expedition **4** **be prepared to** to be willing and able to: *I'm not prepared to say*

> **prepare** *vb* **1** = make *or* get ready, arrange, jack up (*NZ informal*) **2** = make, cook, put together, get, produce, assemble, muster, concoct

preponderant *adj* greater in amount, force, or influence > **preponderance** *n*

preposition *n* a word used before a noun or pronoun to relate it to the other words, for example *in* in *he is in the car* > **prepositional** *adj*

prepossessing *adj* making a favourable impression; attractive

preposterous *adj* utterly absurd

prep school *n informal* See **preparatory school**

prepuce (pree-pyewss) *n* **1** the retractable fold of skin covering the tip of the penis; foreskin **2** the retractable fold of skin covering the tip of the clitoris

prequel *n* a film, novel, or play that portrays events that occurred before the events of an existing work

prerequisite *n* **1** something that is required before something else is possible ▸ *adj* **2** required before something else is possible

prerogative *n* a special privilege or right

presage (press-ij) *vb* **-aging, -aged** **1** to be a warning or sign of something about to happen: *the windless air presaged disaster* ▸ *n* **2** an omen **3** a misgiving

Presbyterian *adj* **1** of any of the Protestant Churches governed by lay elders ▸ *n* **2** a member of a Presbyterian Church > **Presbyterianism** *n*

presbytery *n, pl* **-teries** **1** *Presbyterian Church* a local Church court **2** *RC Church* the residence of a parish priest **3** elders collectively **4** the part of a church east of the choir; a sanctuary

prescience (press-ee-enss) *n formal* knowledge of events before they happen > **prescient** *adj*

prescribe *vb* **-scribing, -scribed** **1** *med* to recommend the use of (a medicine or other remedy) **2** to lay down as a rule

> **prescribe** *vb* **1** = specify, order, direct, stipulate, write a prescription for **2** = ordain (*formal*), set, order, rule, recommend, dictate, lay down, decree

prescription *n* **1** **A** written instructions from a doctor for the preparation and use of a medicine **B** the medicine prescribed **2** written instructions from an optician specifying the lenses needed to correct bad eyesight **3** a prescribing

> **prescription** *n* **1A** = instruction, direction, formula, script (*informal*), recipe **1B** = medicine, drug, treatment, preparation, cure, mixture, dose, remedy

prescriptive *adj* **1** laying down rules **2** based on tradition

presence *n* **1** the fact of being in a specified place: *the test detects the presence of sugar in the urine* **2** impressive personal appearance or bearing: *a person of dignified and commanding presence* **3** the company or nearness of a person: *she seemed completely unaware of my presence* **4** *military* a force stationed in another country: *the American-led military presence in the Gulf* **5** an invisible spirit felt to be nearby: *I felt a presence in the room*

> **presence** *n* **1** = being, existence, residence, attendance, showing up, occupancy, inhabitance **2** = personality, bearing, appearance, aspect, air, carriage, aura, poise

presence of mind *n* the ability to stay calm and act sensibly in a crisis

> **presence of mind** *n* = level-headedness, assurance, composure, poise, cool (*slang*), wits, countenance, coolness

present[1] *adj* **1** being in a specified place: *he had been present at the birth of his son* **2** existing or happening now **3** current: *the present exchange rate* **4** *grammar* of a verb tense used when the action described is happening now ▸ *n* **5** *grammar* the present tense **6 at present** now **7 for the present** for now; temporarily **8 the present** the time being; now

> **present** *adj* **1** = here, there, near, ready, nearby, at hand; ≠ absent **2, 3** = current, existing, immediate, contemporary, present-day, existent ▸ *n* **8 the present** = now, today, the time being, here and now, the present moment

present[2] *n* (prez-int) **1** a gift ▸ *vb* (pri-zent) **2** to introduce (a person) formally to another **3** to introduce to the public: *the Museum of Modern Art is presenting a retrospective of his work* **4** to introduce and compere (a radio or television show) **5** to show or exhibit: *they took advantage of every tax dodge that presented itself* **6** to bring about: *the case presented a large number of legal difficulties* **7** to put forward or submit: *they presented a petition to the Prime Minister* **8** to give or offer formally: *he was presented with a watch to celebrate his twenty-five years with the company* **9** to hand over for action or payment: *to present a bill* **10** to portray in a particular way: *his lawyer presented him as a naive young man who had got into bad company* **11** to aim (a weapon) **12 present arms** to salute with one's weapon

> **present** *n* = gift, offering, grant, donation, hand-out, endowment, boon (*archaic*), gratuity, bonsela (*S African*), koha (*NZ*) ▸ *vb* **2** = introduce, make known, acquaint someone with **3** = put on, stage, perform, give, show, render **8** = give, award, hand over, grant, hand out, confer, bestow

presentable *adj* **1** fit to be seen by or introduced to other people **2** acceptable: *the team reached a presentable total* > **presentability** *n*

presentation *n* **1** the act of presenting or being presented **2** the manner of presenting **3** a talk or lecture; the manner of presenting **4** a formal ceremony in which an award is made **5** a public performance, such as a play or a ballet

> **presentation** *n* **1** = giving, award, offering, donation, bestowal, conferral **3** = appearance, look, display, packaging, arrangement, layout **5** = performance, production, show

presenter *n* a person who introduces a radio or television show and links the items in it

presentiment (priz-zen-tim-ent) *n* a sense that something unpleasant is about to happen; premonition

presently *adv* **1** soon: *you will understand presently* **2** *chiefly Scot, US & Canad* at the moment: *these methods are presently being developed*

> **presently** *adv* **1** = soon, shortly, directly, before long, momentarily (*US, Canad*), by and by, in a jiffy (*informal*) **2** = at present, currently, now, today, these days, nowadays, at the present time, in this day and age

preservative *n* **1** a chemical added to foods to prevent decay ▸ *adj* **2** preventing decay

preserve *vb* **-serving, -served 1** to keep safe from change or extinction; protect: *we are interested in preserving world peace* **2** to protect from decay or damage: *the carefully preserved village of Cregneish* **3** to treat (food) in order to prevent it from decaying **4** to maintain; keep up: *the 1.2% increase in earnings needed to preserve living standards* ▸ *n* **5** an area of interest restricted to a particular person or group: *tattoos were once the preserve of sailors* **6** (*usually pl*) fruit preserved by cooking in sugar **7** an area where game is kept for private hunting or fishing > **preservation** *n*

> **preserve** *vb* **1** = protect, keep, save, maintain, defend, shelter, shield, care for; ≠ attack **4** = maintain, keep, continue, sustain, keep up, prolong, uphold, conserve; ≠ end ▸ *n* **5** = area, department (*informal*), field, territory, province, arena, sphere

preshrunk *adj* (of fabric or a garment) having been shrunk during manufacture so that further shrinkage will not occur when washed

preside *vb* **-siding, -sided 1** to chair a meeting **2** to exercise authority: *he presided over the burning of the books*

> **preside** *vb* **1** = officiate, chair, moderate, be chairperson

presidency *n, pl* **-cies** the office or term of a president

president *n* **1** the head of state of a republic, such as the US **2** the head of a company, society, or institution **3** a person who presides over a meeting **4** the head of certain establishments of higher education > **presidential** *adj*

press[1] *vb* **1** to apply weight or force to: *he pressed the button on the camera* **2** to squeeze: *she pressed his hand* **3** to compress to alter in shape **4** to smooth out creases by applying pressure or heat **5** to make (objects) from soft material by pressing with a mould **6** to crush to force out (juice) **7** to urge (someone) insistently: *they pressed for an answer* **8** to force or compel: *I was pressed into playing rugby at school* **9** to plead or put forward strongly: *they intend to press their claim for damages in the courts* **10** to be urgent: *time presses* **11** (sometimes foll. by *on* or *forward*) to continue in a determined way: *they pressed on with their* journey **12** to crowd; push: *shoppers press along the pavements* **13 pressed for** short of: *pressed for time* ▶ *n* **14** any machine that exerts pressure to form or cut materials or to extract liquids or compress solids **15** the art or process of printing **16** the opinions and reviews in the newspapers: *the government is not receiving a good press at the moment* **17** the act of pressing or state of being pressed: *at the press of a button* **18** a crowd: *a press of people at the exit* **19** a cupboard for storing clothes or linen **20 go to press** to go to be printed: *when is this book going to press?* **21 the press A** news media collectively, esp. newspapers **B** journalists collectively

> **press** *vb* **1** = push (down), depress, lean on, press down, force down **2** = hug, squeeze, embrace, clasp, crush, hold close, fold in your arms **3** = compress, grind, reduce, mill, crush, pound, squeeze, tread **4** = iron, steam, smooth, flatten **8** = urge, beg, petition, exhort (*formal*), implore, pressurize, entreat **9** = plead, present, lodge, submit, tender, advance insistently **12** = crowd, push, gather, surge, flock, herd, swarm, seethe

press² *vb* **1** to recruit (men) forcibly for military service **2** to use for a purpose other than intended: *press into service*

press box *n* a room at a sports ground reserved for reporters

press conference *n* an interview for reporters given by a prominent person

press gang *n* **1** (formerly) a group of men used to capture men and boys and force them to join the navy ▶ *vb* **press-gang 2** to force (a person) to join the navy by a press gang **3** to persuade (someone) to do something that he or she does not want to do: *he was press-ganged into joining the family business*

pressie *or* **prezzie** *n informal* a present

pressing *adj* demanding immediate attention

> **pressing** *adj* = urgent, serious, vital, crucial (*informal*), imperative, important, high-priority, importunate (*formal*); ≠ unimportant

pressure *n* **1** the state of pressing or being pressed **2** the application of force by one body on the surface of another **3** urgent claims or demands: *to work under pressure* **4** a condition that is hard to bear: *the pressure of grief* **5** *physics* the force applied to a unit area of a surface **6 bring pressure to bear on** to use influence or authority to persuade ▶ *vb* **-suring, -sured 7** to persuade forcefully: *he was pressured into resignation*

> **pressure** *n* **1, 2** = force, crushing, squeezing, compressing, weight, compression **3** = stress, demands, strain, heat, load, burden, urgency, hassle (*informal*), uphill (*S African*) **4** = power, influence, force, constraint, sway, compulsion, coercion

pressure cooker *n* an airtight pot which cooks food quickly by steam under pressure > **pressure-cook** *vb*

pressure group *n* a group that tries to influence policies or public opinion

prestidigitation *n formal* same as **sleight of hand** > **prestidigitator** *n*

prestige *n* **1** high status or respect resulting from success or achievements: *a symbol of French power and prestige* **2** the power to impress: *a humdrum family car with no prestige* > **prestigious** *adj*

> **prestige** *n* **1** = status, standing, credit, reputation, honour, importance, fame, distinction, mana (NZ)

presto *music* ▶ *adv, adj* **1** very fast ▶ *n, pl* **-tos 2** a passage to be played very quickly

presumably *adv* one supposes or guesses; probably: *he emerged from what was presumably the kitchen carrying a tray*

> **presumably** *adv* = it would seem, probably, apparently, seemingly, on the face of it, in all probability, in all likelihood

presume *vb* **-suming, -sumed 1** to take (something) for granted: *I presume he's dead* **2** to dare (to): *I would not presume to lecture you on medical matters, Dr Jacobs* **3** (foll. by on or upon) to rely or depend: *don't presume on his agreement* **4** (foll. by on or upon) to take advantage (of): *I'm afraid I presumed on Aunt Ginny's generosity* > **presumedly** *adv* > **presuming** *adj*

> **presume** *vb* **1** = believe, think, suppose, assume, guess (*informal*), take for granted, infer, conjecture **2** = dare, venture, go so far as, take the liberty, make so bold as

presumption *n* **1** the act of presuming **2** a basis on which an assumption is made **3** bold insolent behaviour **4** a belief or assumption based on reasonable evidence > **presumptive** *adj*

presumptuous *adj* bold and insolent

presuppose *vb* **-posing, -posed 1** to require as a previous condition in order to be true: *the idea of integration presupposes a disintegrated state* **2** to take for granted > **presupposition** *n*

pretence *or US* **pretense** *n* **1** an action or claim that could mislead people into believing something which is not true: *the pretence that many unemployed people are on 'training schemes'* **2** a false display; affectation: *she abandoned all pretence of work and watched me* **3** a claim, esp. a false one, to a right, title, or distinction **4** make-believe **5** a pretext: *they were placed in a ghetto on the pretence that they would be safe there*

pretend *vb* **1** to claim or give the appearance of (something untrue): *he pretended to be asleep* **2** to make believe: *the children pretended to be pop stars* **3** (foll. by to) to present a claim, esp. a doubtful one: *to pretend to the throne*

p

pretend *vb* 1 = feign, affect, assume, allege, fake, simulate, profess, sham 2 = make believe, suppose, imagine, act, make up

pretender *n* a person who makes a false or disputed claim to a throne or title

pretension *n* 1 (*often pl*) a false claim to merit or importance 2 the quality of being pretentious

pretentious *adj* 1 making (unjustified) claims to special merit or importance: *many critics thought her work and ideas pretentious and empty* 2 vulgarly showy; ostentatious: *a family restaurant with no pretentious furnishing*

preternatural *adj* beyond what is natural; supernatural

pretext *n* a false reason given to hide the real one: *delivering the book had been a good pretext for seeing her again*

pretty *adj* **-tier, -tiest** 1 attractive in a delicate or graceful way 2 pleasant to look at 3 *informal, often humorous* excellent or fine: *well, this is a pretty state of affairs to have got into* ▸ *adv* 4 *informal* fairly: *I think he and Nicholas got on pretty well* 5 **sitting pretty** *informal* in a favourable state ▹ **prettily** *adv* ▹ **prettiness** *n*

pretty *adj* 1 = attractive, beautiful, lovely, charming, fair, good-looking, bonny (*Scot, N English dialect*), comely (*old-fashioned*), fit (*Brit informal*); ≠ plain ▸ *adv* 4 = fairly, rather, quite, kind of (*informal*), somewhat, moderately, reasonably

pretzel *n* a brittle salted biscuit in the shape of a knot

prevail *vb* 1 (*often foll. by* over *or* against) to prove superior; gain mastery: *moderate nationalists have until now prevailed over the radicals* 2 to be the most important feature: *a casual good-natured mood prevailed* 3 to be generally established: *this attitude has prevailed for many years* 4 **prevail on** *or* **upon** to succeed in persuading: *he had easily been prevailed upon to accept a lift*

prevail *vb* 1 = win, succeed, triumph, overcome, overrule, be victorious 3 = be widespread, abound, predominate, be current, be prevalent, exist generally

prevailing *adj* 1 widespread: *the prevailing mood* 2 most usual: *the prevailing wind is from the west*

prevailing *adj* 1 = widespread, general, established, popular, common, current, usual, ordinary 2 = predominating, ruling, main, existing, principal

prevalent *adj* widespread or common ▹ **prevalence** *n*

prevalent *adj* = common, established, popular, general, current, usual, widespread, universal; ≠ rare

prevaricate *vb* **-cating, -cated** to avoid giving a direct or truthful answer ▹ **prevarication** *n* ▹ **prevaricator** *n*

prevent *vb* 1 to keep from happening: *vitamin C prevented scurvy* 2 (*often foll. by* from) to keep (someone from doing something): *circumstances prevented her from coming* ▹ **preventable** *adj* ▹ **prevention** *n*

prevent *vb* = stop, avoid, frustrate, hamper, foil, inhibit, avert, thwart; ≠ help

preventive *adj* 1 intended to prevent or hinder 2 *med* tending to prevent disease ▸ *n* 3 something that serves to prevent 4 *med* any drug or agent that tends to prevent disease. Also: **preventative**

preview *n* 1 an opportunity to see a film, exhibition, or play before it is shown to the public ▸ *vb* 2 to view in advance

preview *n* = sample, sneak preview, trailer, taster, foretaste, advance showing

previous *adj* 1 coming or happening before 2 *informal* happening too soon; premature: *such criticism is a bit previous because no definite decision has yet been taken* 3 **previous to** before ▹ **previously** *adv*

previous *adj* 1 = earlier, former, past, prior, preceding, erstwhile; ≠ later

prey *n* 1 an animal hunted and killed for food by another animal 2 the victim of a hostile person, influence, emotion, or illness: *children are falling prey to the disease* 3 **bird** *or* **beast of prey** a bird or animal that kills and eats other birds or animals ▸ *vb* (*often foll. by* on *or* upon) 4 to hunt and kill for food 5 to worry or obsess: *it preyed on his conscience* 6 to make a victim (of others), by profiting at their expense

prey *n* 1 = quarry, game, kill 2 = victim, target, mug (*Brit slang*), dupe, fall guy (*informal*)

price *n* 1 the amount of money for which a thing is bought or sold 2 the cost at which something is obtained: *the price of making the wrong decision* 3 *gambling* odds 4 **at any price** whatever the price or cost 5 **at a price** at a high price 6 **what price (something)?** what are the chances of (something) happening now? ▸ *vb* **pricing, priced** 7 to fix the price of 8 to discover the price of

price *n* 1 = cost, value, rate, charge, figure, worth, damage (*informal*), amount 2 = consequences, penalty, cost, result, toll, forfeit ▸ *vb* 7 = evaluate, value, estimate, rate, cost, assess

priceless *adj* 1 extremely valuable 2 *informal* extremely amusing

priceless *adj* 1 = valuable, expensive, precious, invaluable, dear, costly; ≠ worthless

pricey *adj* **pricier, priciest** *informal* expensive

prick *vb* 1 to pierce lightly with a sharp point 2 to cause a piercing sensation (in): *a needle* pricked her finger **3** to cause a sharp emotional pain (in): *the film pricked our consciences about the plight of the Afghan refugees* **4 prick up one's ears** A (of a dog) to make the ears stand erect B (of a person) to listen attentively ▸ *n* **5** a sudden sharp pain caused by pricking **6** a mark made by a sharp point **7** a sharp emotional pain: *a prick of conscience* **8** *vulgar slang* a penis **9** *vulgar derogatory slang* a man who provokes contempt

> **prick** *vb* **1** = pierce, stab, puncture, punch, lance, jab, perforate ▸ *n* **6** = puncture, hole, wound, perforation, pinhole

prickle *n* **1** *botany* a thorn or spike on a plant **2** a pricking or stinging sensation ▸ *vb* **-ling, -led 3** to feel a stinging sensation
prickly *adj* **-lier, -liest 1** having prickles **2** tingling or stinging: *he had a prickly feeling down his back* **3** touchy or irritable: *you know how prickly they can be about the issue*

> **prickly** *adj* **1** = spiny, barbed, thorny, bristly **2** = itchy, sharp, smarting, stinging, crawling, tingling, scratchy

prickly heat *n* an itchy rash that occurs in very hot moist weather
pride *n* **1** satisfaction in one's own or another's success or achievements: *his obvious pride in his son's achievements* **2** an excessively high opinion of oneself **3** a sense of dignity and self-respect: *he must swallow his pride and ally himself with his political enemies* **4** one of the better or most admirable parts of something: *the pride of the main courses is the Japanese fish and vegetable tempura* **5** a group of lions **6 pride and joy** the main source of pride: *the car was his pride and joy* **7 pride of place** the most important position ▸ *vb* **priding, prided 8** (foll. by *on* or *upon*) to take pride in (oneself) for

> **pride** *n* **1** = satisfaction, achievement, fulfilment, delight, content, pleasure, joy, gratification **2** = conceit, vanity, arrogance, pretension, hubris, self-importance, egotism, self-love; ≠ humility **3** = self-respect, honour, ego, dignity, self-esteem, self-image, self-worth

priest *or fem* **priestess** *n* **1** (in the Christian Church) a person ordained to administer the sacraments and preach **2** a minister of any religion **3** an official who performs religious ceremonies > **priesthood** *n* > **priestly** *adj*

> **priest** *or* **priestess** *n* **1, 2** = clergyman *or* woman, minister, father, divine, vicar, pastor, cleric, curate

prig *n* a person who is smugly self-righteous and narrow-minded > **priggish** *adj* > **priggishness** *n*
prim *adj* **primmer, primmest** affectedly proper, or formal, and rather prudish > **primly** *adv*
prima ballerina *n* a leading female ballet dancer

primacy *n*, *pl* **-cies 1** the state of being first in rank, grade, or order **2** *Christianity* the office of an archbishop
prima donna *n*, *pl* **prima donnas 1** a leading female opera singer **2** *informal* a temperamental person
primaeval *adj* same as **primeval**
prima facie (prime-a fay-shee) *adj, adv* as it seems at first
primal *adj* **1** of basic causes or origins **2** chief or most important
primarily *adv* **1** chiefly or mainly **2** originally

> **primarily** *adv* **1** = chiefly, largely, generally, mainly, essentially, mostly, principally, fundamentally **2** = at first, originally, initially, in the first place, in the beginning, first and foremost, at *or* from the start

primary *adj* **1** first in importance **2** first in position or time, as in a series: *he argued that the country was only in the primary stage of socialism* **3** fundamental or basic: *the new policy will put the emphasis on primary health care rather than hospital care* **4** being the first stage; elementary: *all new recruits participated in the same primary training courses* **5** relating to the education of children up to the age of 11 or 12 **6** (of an industry) involving the obtaining of raw materials **7** (of the flight feathers of a bird's wing) outer and longest **8** being the part of an electric circuit in which a changing current causes a current in a neighbouring circuit: *a primary coil* ▸ *n*, *pl* **-ries 9** a person or thing that is first in position, time, or importance **10** (in the US) an election in which the voters of a state choose a candidate for office. Full name: **primary election 11** a primary school **12** a primary colour **13** any of the outer and longest flight feathers of a bird's wing **14** a primary part of an electric circuit

> **primary** *adj* **1** = chief, main, first, highest, greatest, prime, principal, cardinal; ≠ subordinate

primary colours *pl n* **1** *physics* the colours red, green, and blue from which all other colours can be obtained by mixing **2** *art* the colours red, yellow, and blue from which all other colours can be obtained by mixing
primary school *n* **1** (in England and Wales) a school for children between the ages of 5 and 11 **2** (in Scotland, Australia and New Zealand) a school for children between the ages of 5 and 12 **3** (in the US and Canada) a school equivalent to the first three or four grades of elementary school
primate¹ *n* a mammal with flexible hands and feet and a highly developed brain, such as a monkey, an ape, or a human being
primate² *n* an archbishop
prime *adj* **1** first in importance: *the prime aim* **2** of the highest quality: *prime beef* **3** typical: *a prime example* ▸ *n* **4** the time when a thing is at its best

5 a period of power, vigour, and activity: *he was in the prime of life* **6** *maths* short for **prime number** ▸ *vb* **priming, primed 7** to give (someone) information in advance to prepare him or her **8** to prepare (a surface) for painting **9** to prepare (a gun or mine) before detonating or firing **10** to fill (a pump) with its working fluid, to expel air from it before starting **11** to prepare (something)

prime *adj* **1** = main, leading, chief, central, major, key, primary, supreme **2** = best, top, select, highest, quality, choice, excellent, first-class ▸ *n* **4, 5** = peak, flower, bloom, height, heyday, zenith ▸ *vb* **7** = inform, tell, train, coach, brief, fill in (*informal*), notify, clue in (*informal*) **9, 11** = prepare, set up, load, equip, get ready, make ready

Prime Minister *n* the leader of a government
prime number *n* an integer that cannot be divided into other integers but is only divisible by itself or 1, such as 2, 3, 5, 7, and 11
primer¹ *n* **1** a substance applied to a surface as a base coat or sealer **2** a device for detonating the main charge in a gun or mine
primer² *n* an introductory text, such as a school textbook
primeval (prime-ee-val) *adj* of the earliest age of the world
primitive *adj* **1** of or belonging to the beginning **2** *biol* of an early stage in development: *primitive amphibians* **3** characteristic of an early simple state, esp. in being crude or basic: *a primitive dwelling* ▸ *n* **4** a primitive person or thing **5** a painter of any era whose work appears childlike or untrained **6** a work by such an artist

primitive *adj* **1** = early, first, earliest, original, primary, elementary, primordial, primeval; ≠ modern **3** = crude, simple, rough, rudimentary, unrefined

primogeniture *n* **1** *formal* the state of being the first-born child **2** *law* the right of an eldest son to inherit all the property of his parents
primordial *adj formal* existing at or from the beginning
primrose *n* **1** a wild plant which has pale yellow flowers in spring ▸ *adj* **2** Also: **primrose yellow** pale yellow **3** of primroses
primula *n* a type of primrose with brightly coloured funnel-shaped flowers
Primus *n trademark* a portable paraffin cooking stove, used esp. by campers
prince *n* **1** a male member of a royal family, esp. the son of the king or queen **2** the male ruler of a small country **3** an outstanding member of a specified group: *Dryden, that prince of poets*

prince *n* **2** = ruler, lord, monarch, sovereign, crown prince, liege, prince regent, crowned head

prince consort *n* the husband of a queen, who is himself a prince

princely *adj* **-lier, -liest 1** of or characteristic of a prince **2** generous or lavish

princely *adj* **1** = regal, royal, imperial, noble, sovereign, majestic **2** = substantial, considerable, large, huge, massive, enormous, sizable *or* sizeable

Prince of Wales *n* the eldest son of the British sovereign
princess *n* **1** a female member of a royal family, esp. the daughter of the king or queen **2** the wife of a prince

princess *n* **2** = ruler, lady, monarch, sovereign, liege, crowned head, crowned princess, dynast

Princess Royal *n* a title sometimes given to the eldest daughter of the British sovereign
principal *adj* **1** first in importance, rank, or value: *salt is the principal source of sodium in our diets; the Republic's two principal parties* ▸ *n* **2** the head of a school or other educational institution **3** a person who holds one of the most important positions in an organization: *she became a principal in the home finance department* **4** the leading actor in a play **5** *law* **A** a person who engages another to act as his or her agent **B** a person who takes an active part in a crime **C** the person held responsible for fulfilling an obligation **6** *finance* **A** capital or property, as contrasted with income **B** the original amount of a debt on which interest is calculated › **principally** *adv*

principal *adj* = main, leading, chief, prime, first, key, essential, primary; ≠ minor ▸ *n* **2** = headmaster *or* headmistress, head (*informal*), dean, head teacher, rector, master *or* mistress **4** = star, lead, leader, prima ballerina, leading man *or* lady, coryphée **6A** = capital, money, assets, working capital

principal boy *n Brit* the leading male role in a pantomime, traditionally played by a woman
principality *n, pl* **-ties** a territory ruled by a prince
principle *n* **1** a moral rule guiding personal conduct: *he'd stoop to anything – he has no principles* **2** a set of such moral rules: *a man of principle* **3** a basic or general truth: *the principle of freedom of expression* **4** a basic law or rule underlying a particular theory or philosophy: *the government has been deceitful and has violated basic principles of democracy* **5** a general law in science: *the principle of the conservation of mass* **6** *chem* a constituent of a substance that determines its characteristics **7 in principle** in theory though not always in practice **8 on principle** because of one's beliefs

principle *n* **2** = morals, standards, ideals, honour, virtue, ethics, integrity, conscience, kaupapa (NZ) **3, 4, 5** = rule, law, truth, precept **7 in principle** = in theory, ideally, on paper, theoretically, in an ideal world, en principe (*French*)

print *vb* **1** to reproduce (a newspaper, book, etc.) in large quantities by mechanical or electronic means **2** to reproduce (text or pictures) by applying ink to paper **3** to write in letters that are not joined up **4** to stamp (fabric) with a design **5** to produce (a photograph) from a negative **6** to fix in the mind or memory ▸ *n* **7** printed content, such as newsprint **8** a printed publication, such as a book **9** a picture printed from an engraved plate or wood block **10** printed text, with regard to the typeface: *italic print* **11** a photograph produced from a negative **12** a fabric with a printed design **13** a mark made by pressing something onto a surface **14** See **fingerprint 15 in print A** in printed or published form **B** (of a book) available from a publisher **16 out of print** no longer available from a publisher

print *vb* **1** = publish, release, circulate, issue, disseminate **2** = run off, publish, copy, reproduce, issue, engrave **4** = mark, impress, stamp, imprint ▸ *n* **9** = picture, plate, etching, engraving, lithograph, woodcut, linocut **11** = photograph, photo, snap

printed circuit *n* an electronic circuit in which the wiring is a metallic coating printed on a thin insulating board

printer *n* **1** a person or business engaged in printing **2** a machine that prints **3** a machine connected to a computer that makes copies on paper of documents or other information held by the computer

printing *n* **1** the process of producing printed matter **2** printed text **3** all the copies of a book printed at one time **4** a form of writing in which the letters are not joined together

prior[1] *adj* **1** previous: *prior knowledge* **2 prior to** before

prior *adj* **1** = earlier, previous, former, preceding, foregoing, pre-existing, pre-existent **2 prior to** = before, preceding, earlier than, in advance of, previous to

prior[2] *n* **1** the head monk in a priory **2** the abbot's deputy in a monastery ▸ **prioress** *fem n*

priority *n, pl* **-ties 1** the most important thing that must be dealt with first **2** the right to be or go before others

priority *n* **1** = prime concern **2** = precedence, preference, primacy, predominance

priory *n, pl* **-ories** a religious house where certain orders of monks or nuns live

prise *or* **prize** *vb* **prising, prised** *or* **prizing, prized** to force open or out by levering

prism *n* **1** a transparent block, often with triangular ends and rectangular sides, used to disperse light into a spectrum or refract it in optical instruments **2** *maths* a polyhedron with parallel bases and sides that are parallelograms

prismatic *adj* **1** of or shaped like a prism **2** exhibiting bright spectral colours; rainbow-like: *prismatic light*

prison *n* **1** a public building used to hold convicted criminals and accused people awaiting trial **2** any place of confinement

prison *n* **1** = jail, confinement, nick (*Brit slang*), cooler (*slang, old-fashioned*), jug (*slang, old-fashioned*), dungeon, clink (*slang*), gaol, boob (*Austral slang*)

prisoner *n* **1** a person kept in prison as a punishment for a crime, or while awaiting trial **2** a person confined by any restraints: *he's a prisoner of his own past* **3 take (someone) prisoner** to capture and hold (someone) as a prisoner

prisoner *n* **1** = convict, con (*slang*), lag (*slang*), jailbird

prisoner of war *n* a member of the armed forces captured by an enemy in wartime

prissy *adj* **-sier, -siest** prim and prudish ▸ **prissily** *adv*

pristine *adj* **1** completely new, clean, and pure: *pristine white plates* **2** of or involving the original, unchanged, and unspoilt period or state: *the viewing of wild game in its pristine natural state*

privacy *n* **1** the condition of being private **2** secrecy

privacy *n* **1** = seclusion, isolation, solitude, retirement, retreat

private *adj* **1** not for general or public use: *a private bathroom* **2** confidential or secret: *a private conversation* **3** involving someone's domestic and personal life rather than his or her work or business: *what I do in my private life is none of your business* **4** owned or paid for by individuals rather than by the government: *private enterprise* **5** not publicly known: *they had private reasons for the decision* **6** having no public office, rank, or position: *the Red Cross received donations from private citizens* **7** (of a place) quiet and secluded: *the garden is completely private* **8** (of a person) quiet and retiring: *she was private – her life was her own* ▸ *n* **9** a soldier of the lowest rank in the army **10 in private** in secret ▸ **privately** *adv*

private *adj* **1** = exclusive, individual, privately owned, own, special, reserved; ≠ public **2** = secret, confidential, covert, unofficial, clandestine, off the record, hush-hush (*informal*); ≠ public **5** = personal, individual, secret, intimate, undisclosed, unspoken, innermost, unvoiced **7** = secluded, secret, separate, isolated, sequestered; ≠ busy **8** = solitary, reserved, retiring, withdrawn, discreet, secretive, self-contained, reclusive; ≠ sociable

privateer *n* **1** a privately owned armed vessel authorized by the government to take part in a war **2** a captain of such a ship

privation n formal loss or lack of the necessities of life

privatize or **-tise** vb **-tizing, -tized** or **-tising, -tised** to sell (a state-owned company) to individuals or a private company › **privatization** or **-tisation** n

privet n a bushy evergreen shrub used for hedges

privilege n 1 a benefit or advantage granted only to certain people: a privilege of rank 2 the opportunity to do something which gives you great satisfaction and which most people never have the chance to do: I had the privilege of meeting the Queen when she visited our school 3 the power and advantages that come with great wealth or high social class: the use of violence to protect class privilege and thwart popular democracy

> **privilege** n 1 = right, due, advantage, claim, freedom, liberty, concession, entitlement

privileged adj enjoying a special right or immunity

> **privileged** adj = special, advantaged, favoured, honoured, entitled, elite

privy adj **privier, priviest** 1 archaic secret 2 **privy to** sharing in the knowledge of something secret ▸ n, pl **privies** 3 obsolete a toilet, esp. an outside one

Privy Council n 1 the private council of the British king or queen 2 (in Canada) a formal body of advisers of the governor general › **Privy Counsellor** n

prize[1] n 1 something of value, such as a trophy, given to the winner of a contest or game 2 something given to the winner of any game of chance, lottery, etc. 3 something striven for ▸ adj 4 winning or likely to win a prize: a prize bull

> **prize** n 1 = reward, cup, award, honour, medal, trophy, accolade 2 = winnings, haul, jackpot, stakes, purse ▸ adj = champion, best, winning, top, outstanding, award-winning, first-rate

prize[2] vb **prizing, prized** to value highly

> **prize** vb = value, treasure, esteem, cherish, hold dear

pro[1] adv 1 in favour of a motion, etc. ▸ prep 2 in favour of ▸ See also **pros and cons**

pro[2] informal ▸ adj 1 short for **professional** (senses 2, 4) ▸ n, pl **pros** 2 short for **professional** (sense 5) 3 a prostitute

pro- prefix 1 in favour of; supporting: pro-Chinese 2 acting as a substitute for: pronoun

probability n, pl **-ties** 1 the condition of being probable 2 an event or other thing that is likely to happen or be true 3 statistics a measure of the likelihood of an event happening

> **probability** n 1 = likelihood, prospect, chance, odds, expectation, liability, likeliness 3 = chance, odds, possibility, likelihood

probable adj 1 likely to happen or be true 2 most likely: the probable cause of the accident ▸ n 3 a person who is likely to be chosen for a team, event, etc.

> **probable** adj = likely, possible, apparent, reasonable to think, credible, plausible, feasible, presumable; ≠ unlikely

probably adv in all likelihood or probability: the wedding's probably going to be in late August

> **probably** adv = likely, perhaps, maybe, possibly, presumably, most likely, doubtless, perchance (archaic)

probate n 1 the process of officially proving the validity of a will 2 the official certificate stating that a will is genuine

probation n 1 a system of dealing with offenders, esp. juvenile ones, by placing them under supervision 2 **on probation A** under the supervision of a probation officer **B** undergoing a test or trial period, such as at the start of a new job › **probationary** adj

probationer n 1 a person on a trial period in a job 2 a person under the supervision of a probation officer

probe vb **probing, probed** 1 to investigate, or look into, closely 2 to poke or examine (something) with or as if with a probe: he probed carefully with his fingertips ▸ n 3 surgery a slender instrument for exploring a wound, etc. 4 a thorough inquiry, such as one into corrupt practices

> **probe** vb 1 = examine, go into, investigate, explore, search, look into, analyze, dissect 2 = explore, examine, poke, prod, feel around ▸ n 4 = investigation, study, inquiry, analysis, examination, exploration, scrutiny, scrutinization

probiotic n 1 a bacterium that protects the body from harmful bacteria ▸ adj 2 of or relating to probiotics: probiotic yogurts

probity n formal honesty; integrity

problem n 1 something or someone that is difficult to deal with 2 a puzzle or question set for solving 3 maths a statement requiring a solution usually by means of several operations ▸ adj 4 of a literary work that deals with difficult moral questions: a problem play 5 difficult to deal with or creating difficulties for others: a problem child

> **problem** n 1 = difficulty, trouble, dispute, plight, obstacle, dilemma, headache (informal), complication 2 = puzzle, question, riddle, enigma, conundrum, poser

problematic or **problematical** adj difficult to solve or deal with

> **problematic** or **problematical** adj = tricky, puzzling, doubtful, dubious, debatable, problematical; ≠ clear

proboscis (pro-**boss**-iss) n 1 a long flexible trunk or snout, such as an elephant's 2 the elongated mouthpart of certain insects

procedure n 1 a way of doing something, esp. an established method 2 the established form of conducting the business of a legislature > **procedural** adj

> **procedure** n 1 = method, policy, process, course, system, action, practice, strategy

proceed vb 1 to advance or carry on, esp. after stopping 2 (often foll. by with) to start or continue doing: he proceeded to pour himself a cup of tea 3 formal to walk or go 4 (often foll. by against) to start a legal action 5 formal to arise (from): their mutual dislike proceeded from differences of political opinion

> **proceed** vb 1 = continue, go on, progress, carry on, go ahead, press on, crack on (informal); ≠ discontinue 2 = begin, go ahead 3 = go on, continue, progress, carry on, go ahead, move on, move forward, press on, crack on (informal); ≠ stop 5 = arise, come, issue, result, spring, flow, stem, derive

proceeds pl n the amount of money obtained from an event or activity

> **proceeds** pl n = income, profit, revenue, returns, products, gain, earnings, yield

process n 1 a series of actions or changes: a process of genuine national reconciliation 2 a series of natural developments which result in an overall change: the ageing process 3 a method of doing or producing something: the various production processes use up huge amounts of water 4 a a summons to appear in court b an action at law 5 a natural outgrowth or projection of a part or organism 6 **in the process of** during or in the course of ▸ vb 7 to handle or prepare by a special method of manufacture 8 computers to perform operations on (data) in order to obtain the required information

> **process** n 1 = procedure, means, course, system, action, performance, operation, measure 2 = development, growth, progress, movement, advance, evolution, progression 3 = method, system, practice, technique, procedure

processed adj (of food) treated by adding colouring, preservatives, etc., to improve its appearance or the period it will stay edible: processed cheese

procession n 1 a line of people or vehicles moving forwards in an orderly or ceremonial manner 2 the act of proceeding in a regular formation

> **procession** n 1 = parade, train, march, file, cavalcade, cortege

processor n a person or thing that carries out a process

proclaim vb 1 to announce publicly; declare: Greece was proclaimed an independent kingdom in 1832 2 to indicate plainly: the sharp hard glint in the eye proclaimed her determination > **proclamation** n

> **proclaim** vb 1 = pronounce, announce, declare 2 = announce, declare, advertise, publish, indicate, herald, circulate, profess; ≠ keep secret

proclivity n, pl -ties formal a tendency or inclination

procrastinate vb -nating, -nated to put off (an action) until later; delay > **procrastination** n > **procrastinator** n

procreate vb -ating, -ated formal to produce (offspring) > **procreative** adj > **procreation** n

procurator fiscal n (in Scotland) a legal officer who acts as public prosecutor and coroner

procure vb -curing, -cured 1 to get or provide: it remained very difficult to procure food and fuel 2 to obtain (people) to act as prostitutes > **procurement** n

procurer n a person who obtains people to act as prostitutes

prod vb prodding, prodded 1 to poke with a pointed object 2 to rouse (someone) to action ▸ n 3 the act of prodding 4 a reminder

> **prod** vb 1 = poke, push, dig, shove, nudge, jab 2 = prompt, move, urge, motivate, spur, stimulate, rouse, incite ▸ n 3 = poke, push, dig, shove, nudge, jab 4 = prompt, signal, cue, reminder, stimulus

prodigal adj 1 recklessly wasteful or extravagant 2 **prodigal of** lavish with: you are prodigal of both your toil and your talent ▸ n 3 a person who squanders money > **prodigality** n

prodigious adj 1 very large or immense 2 wonderful or amazing

prodigy n, pl -gies 1 a person, esp. a child, with marvellous talent 2 anything that is a cause of wonder

> **prodigy** n 1 = genius, talent, wizard, mastermind, whizz (informal), up-and-comer (informal)

produce vb -ducing, -duced 1 to bring (something) into existence 2 to present to view: he produced his passport 3 to make: this area produces much of Spain's best wine 4 to give birth to 5 to present on stage, film, or television: the girls and boys write and produce their own plays 6 to act as producer of ▸ n 7 food grown for sale: farm produce 8 something produced > **producible** adj

> **produce** vb 1 = cause, effect, generate, bring about, give rise to 2 = display, show, present, proffer 3 = make, create, develop, manufacture, construct, invent, fabricate 4 = bring forth, bear, deliver, breed, give birth to, beget (old-fashioned), bring into the world

p

5 = present, stage, direct, put on, do, show, mount, exhibit ▸ *n* = fruit and vegetables, goods, food, products, crops, yield, harvest, greengrocery (*Brit*)

producer *n* **1** a person with the financial and administrative responsibility for a film or television programme **2** a person responsible for the artistic direction of a play **3** a person who supervises the arrangement, performance, and mixing of a recording **4** a person or thing that produces

> **producer** *n* **1, 2** = director, promoter, impresario **4** = maker, manufacturer, builder, creator, fabricator

product *n* **1** something produced **2** a consequence: *their skill was the product of hours of training* **3** *maths* the result achieved by multiplication

> **product** *n* **1** = goods, produce, creation, commodity, invention, merchandise, artefact **2** = result, consequence, effect, outcome, upshot

production *n* **1** the act of producing **2** anything that is produced **3** the amount produced or the rate at which it is produced **4** *econ* the creation or manufacture of goods and services **5** any work created as a result of literary or artistic effort **6** the presentation of a play, opera, etc. **7** the artistic direction of a play **8** the overall sound of a recording

> **production** *n* **1** = producing, making, manufacture, manufacturing, construction, formation, fabrication **6** = presentation, staging, mounting **7** = management, administration, direction

productive *adj* **1** producing or having the power to produce **2** yielding favourable results **3** *econ* producing goods and services that have exchange value: *the country's productive capacity* **4** (foll. by *of*) resulting in: *a period highly productive of books and ideas* > **productivity** *n*

> **productive** *adj* **1** = creative, inventive **2** = useful, rewarding, valuable, profitable, effective, worthwhile, beneficial, constructive; ≠ useless **4** = fertile, rich, prolific, plentiful, fruitful, fecund; ≠ barren

profane *adj* **1** showing disrespect for religion or something sacred **2** secular **3** coarse or blasphemous: *profane language* ▸ *vb* **-faning, -faned 4** to treat (something sacred) with irreverence **5** to put to an unworthy use > **profanation** *n*

profanity *n, pl* **-ties 1** the quality of being profane **2** coarse or blasphemous action or speech

profess *vb* **1** to claim (something as true), often falsely: *he professes not to want the job of Prime Minister* **2** to acknowledge openly: *he professed great relief at*

getting some rest **3** to have as one's belief or religion: *most Indonesians profess the Islamic faith* > **professed** *adj*

> **profess** *vb* **1** = claim, allege, pretend, fake, make out, purport, feign **2** = state, admit, announce, declare, confess, assert, proclaim, affirm

profession *n* **1** a type of work that requires special training, such as in law or medicine **2** the people employed in such an occupation **3** a declaration of a belief or feeling: *a profession of faith*

> **profession** *n* **1** = occupation, calling, business, career, employment, office, position, sphere

professional *adj* **1** of a profession **2** taking part in an activity, such as sport or music, as a means of livelihood **3** displaying a high level of competence or skill: *a professional and polished performance* **4** undertaken or performed by people who are paid: *professional golf* ▸ *n* **5** a professional person > **professionalism** *n* > **professionally** *adv*

> **professional** *adj* **1** = qualified, trained, skilled, white-collar **3** = expert, experienced, skilled, masterly, efficient, competent, adept, proficient; ≠ amateurish ▸ *n* = expert, master, pro (*informal*), specialist, guru, adept, maestro, virtuoso, fundi (*S African*)

professor *n* **1** the highest rank of teacher in a university **2** *chiefly US & Canad* any teacher in a university or college **3** *rare* a person who professes his or her opinions or beliefs > **professorial** *adj* > **professorship** *n*

> **professor** *n* **1** = don (*Brit*), fellow (*Brit*), prof (*informal*)

proffer *vb formal* to offer for acceptance

proficient *adj* skilled; expert > **proficiency** *n*

profile *n* **1** an outline, esp. of the human face, as seen from the side **2** a short biographical sketch **3** an area of a social media site containing a person's name, picture, and personal information

> **profile** *n* **1** = outline, lines, form, figure, silhouette, contour, side view **2** = biography, sketch, vignette, characterization, thumbnail sketch

profiling *n* the practice of categorizing people and predicting their behaviour according to particular characteristics such as race or age

profit *n* **1** (*often pl*) money gained in business or trade **2** a benefit or advantage ▸ *vb* **-iting, -ited 3** to gain a profit or advantage: *we do not want to profit from someone else's problems*

> **profit** *n* **1** = earnings, return, revenue, gain, yield, proceeds, receipts, takings; ≠ loss **2** = benefit, good, use, value, gain, advantage, advancement; ≠ disadvantage ▸ *vb* = benefit, help, serve, gain, promote, be of advantage to

profitable adj making money or gaining an advantage or benefit > **profitability** n > **profitably** adv

> **profitable** adj = money-making, lucrative, paying, commercial, worthwhile, cost-effective, fruitful, remunerative; ≠ useless

profiteer n 1 a person who makes excessive profits at the expense of the public ▸ vb 2 to make excessive profits > **profiteering** n

profligate adj 1 recklessly extravagant 2 shamelessly immoral ▸ n 3 a profligate person > **profligacy** n

pro forma adj 1 laying down a set form ▸ adv 2 performed in a set manner

profound adj 1 showing or needing great knowledge: *a profound knowledge of Greek literature* 2 strongly felt; intense: *profound relief* 3 extensive: *profound changes* 4 situated at or having a great depth > **profoundly** adv > **profundity** n

> **profound** adj 1 = wise, learned, deep, penetrating, philosophical, sage, abstruse, sagacious (*formal*); ≠ uninformed 2 = sincere, acute, intense, great, keen, extreme, heartfelt, deeply felt; ≠ insincere

profuse adj 1 plentiful or abundant: *he broke out in a profuse sweat* 2 (often foll. by *in*) generous in the giving (of): *he was profuse in his apologies* > **profusely** adv > **profusion** n

progenitor (pro-jen-it-er) n 1 a direct ancestor 2 an originator or founder

progeny (proj-in-ee) n, pl **-nies** 1 offspring; descendants 2 an outcome

progesterone n a hormone, produced in the ovary, that prepares the womb for pregnancy and prevents further ovulation

prognosis n, pl **-noses** 1 med a forecast about the course or outcome of an illness 2 any forecast

program n 1 a sequence of coded instructions which enables a computer to perform various tasks ▸ vb **-gramming, -grammed** 2 to arrange (data) so that it can be processed by a computer 3 to feed a program into (a computer) > **programmer** n

programmable or **programable** adj capable of being programmed for computer processing

programme or US **program** n 1 a planned series of events 2 a broadcast on radio or television 3 a printed list of items or performers in an entertainment ▸ vb **-gramming, -grammed** or US **-graming, -gramed** 4 to schedule (something) as a programme > **programmatic** adj

> **programme** or **program** n 1 = schedule, plan, agenda, timetable, listing, list, line-up, calendar 2 = show, performance, production, broadcast, episode, presentation, transmission, telecast, podcast

programming language n a language system by which instructions to a computer are coded, that is understood by both user and computer

progress n 1 improvement or development 2 movement forward or advance 3 **in progress** taking place ▸ vb 4 to become more advanced or skilful 5 to move forwards

> **progress** n 1 = development, growth, advance, gain, improvement, breakthrough, headway; ≠ regression 2 = movement forward, passage, advancement, course, advance, headway; ≠ movement backward 3 **in progress** = going on, happening, continuing, being done, occurring, taking place, proceeding, under way ▸ vb 4 = develop, improve, advance, grow, gain; ≠ get behind 5 = move on, continue, travel, advance, proceed, go forward, make headway, crack on (*informal*); ≠ move back

progression n 1 the act of progressing; advancement 2 the act or an instance of moving from one thing in a sequence to the next 3 maths a sequence of numbers in which each term differs from the succeeding term by a fixed ratio

> **progression** n 1 = progress, advance, advancement, gain, headway, furtherance, movement forward 3 = sequence, course, series, chain, cycle, string, succession

progressive adj 1 favouring political or social reform 2 happening gradually: *a progressive illness* 3 (of a dance, card game, etc.) involving a regular change of partners ▸ n 4 a person who favours political or social reform > **progressively** adv

> **progressive** adj 1 = enlightened, liberal, modern, advanced, radical, revolutionary, avant-garde, reformist 2 = growing, continuing, increasing, developing, advancing, ongoing

prohibit vb **-biting, -bited** 1 to forbid by law or other authority 2 to hinder or prevent: *the paucity of information prohibits us from drawing reliable conclusions* > **prohibitor** n

> **prohibit** vb 1 = forbid, ban, veto, outlaw, disallow, proscribe, debar; ≠ permit 2 = prevent, restrict, stop, hamper, hinder, impede; ≠ allow

prohibition n 1 the act of forbidding 2 a legal ban on the sale or drinking of alcohol 3 an order or decree that forbids > **prohibitionist** n

> **prohibition** n 3 = ban, boycott, embargo, bar, veto, prevention, exclusion, injunction, restraining order (US *law*)

prohibitive adj 1 (esp. of prices) too high to be affordable 2 prohibiting or tending to prohibit: *a prohibitive distance* > **prohibitively** adv

p

project n 1 a proposal or plan 2 a detailed study of a particular subject ▸ vb 3 to make a prediction based on known data and observations 4 to cause (an image) to appear on a surface 5 to communicate (an impression): *he wants to project an image of a deep-thinking articulate gentleman* 6 to jut out 7 to cause (one's voice) to be heard clearly at a distance 8 to transport in the imagination: *it's hard to project oneself into his situation*

> **project** n 1 = scheme, plan, job, idea, campaign, operation, activity, venture 2 = assignment, task, homework, piece of research ▸ vb 3 = forecast, expect, estimate, predict, reckon, calculate, gauge, extrapolate 6 = stick out, extend, stand out, bulge, protrude, overhang, jut

projectile n 1 an object thrown as a weapon or fired from a gun ▸ adj 2 designed to be thrown forwards 3 projecting forwards

projection n 1 a part that juts out 2 a forecast based on known data 3 the process of showing film on a screen 4 the representation on a flat surface of a three-dimensional figure or curved line

> **projection** n 1 = forecast, estimate, reckoning, calculation, estimation, computation, extrapolation

projectionist n a person who operates a film projector

projector n an apparatus for projecting photographic images, film, or slides onto a screen

prolapse pathol ▸ n 1 Also: **prolapsus** the slipping down of an internal organ of the body from its normal position ▸ vb -**lapsing**, -**lapsed** 2 (of an internal organ) to slip from its normal position

prole n chiefly Brit offensive slang a proletarian

proletarian (pro-lit-air-ee-an) adj 1 of the proletariat ▸ n 2 a member of the proletariat

proletariat (pro-lit-**air**-ee-at) n the working class

proliferate vb -**rating**, -**rated** 1 to increase rapidly in numbers 2 to grow or reproduce (new parts, such as cells) rapidly > **proliferation** n

prolific adj 1 producing a constant creative output: *a prolific author* 2 producing fruit or offspring in abundance 3 (often foll. by *in* or *of*) rich or fruitful > **prolifically** adv

> **prolific** adj 1 = productive, creative, fertile, inventive, copious 3 = fruitful, fertile, abundant, luxuriant, profuse, fecund; ≠ unproductive

prolix adj (of a speech or piece of writing) overlong and boring > **prolixity** n

prologue or often US **prolog** n 1 an introduction to a play or book 2 an event that comes before another: *this success was a happy prologue to their transatlantic tour*

prolong vb to make (something) last longer > **prolongation** n

> **prolong** vb = lengthen, continue, perpetuate, draw out, extend, delay, stretch out, spin out; ≠ shorten

prom n 1 Brit short for **promenade** (sense 1) or **promenade concert** 2 informal a formal dance held at a high school or college

promenade n 1 chiefly Brit a paved walkway along the seafront at a holiday resort 2 old-fashioned a leisurely walk for pleasure or display ▸ vb -**nading**, -**naded** 3 old-fashioned to take a leisurely walk

promenade concert n a concert at which some of the audience stand rather than sit

prominent adj 1 standing out from the surroundings; noticeable 2 widely known; famous 3 jutting or projecting outwards: *prominent eyes* > **prominence** n > **prominently** adv

> **prominent** adj 1 = noticeable, obvious, outstanding, pronounced, conspicuous, eye-catching, obtrusive; ≠ inconspicuous 2 = famous, leading, top, important, main, distinguished, well-known, notable; ≠ unknown

promiscuous adj 1 taking part in many casual sexual relationships 2 formal consisting of different elements mingled indiscriminately > **promiscuity** n

promise vb -**mising**, -**mised** 1 to say that one will definitely do or not do something: *I promise I'll have it finished by the end of the week* 2 to undertake to give (something to someone): *he promised me a car for my birthday* 3 to show signs of; seem likely: *she promises to be a fine singer* 4 to assure (someone) of the certainty of something: *everything's fine, I promise you* ▸ n 5 an undertaking to do or not do something 6 indication of future success: *a young player who shows great promise*

> **promise** vb 1, 2 = guarantee, pledge, vow, swear, contract, assure, undertake, warrant 3 = seem likely, look like, show signs of, augur, betoken ▸ n 5 = guarantee, word, bond, vow, commitment, pledge, undertaking, assurance 6 = potential, ability, talent, capacity, capability, aptitude

promising adj likely to succeed or turn out well

> **promising** adj = encouraging, likely, bright, reassuring, hopeful, favourable, rosy, auspicious; ≠ unpromising

promo n, pl -**mos** informal an item produced to promote a product, esp. a video used to promote a pop record

promontory n, pl -**ries** a point of high land that juts out into the sea

promote vb -**moting**, -**moted** 1 to encourage the progress or success of: *all attempts to promote a lasting ceasefire have failed* 2 to raise to a higher rank or position **3** to encourage the sale of (a product) by advertising **4** to work for: *he actively promoted reform* › **promotion** *n* › **promotional** *adj*

> **promote** *vb* **1, 4** = help, back, support, aid, forward, encourage, advance, boost; ≠ impede **2** = raise, upgrade, elevate, exalt; ≠ demote **3** = advertise, sell, hype, publicize, push, plug (*informal*)

promoter *n* **1** a person who helps to organize and finance an event, esp. a sports one **2** a person or thing that encourages the progress or success of: *a promoter of peace*

prompt *vb* **1** to cause (an action); bring about: *the killings prompted an anti-Mafia crackdown* **2** to motivate or cause someone to do something: *I still don't know what prompted me to go* **3** to remind (an actor) of lines forgotten during a performance **4** to refresh the memory of ▸ *adj* **5** done without delay **6** quick to act ▸ *adv* **7** *informal* punctually: *at 8 o'clock prompt* ▸ *n* **8** anything that serves to remind › **promptly** *adv* › **promptness** *n*

> **prompt** *vb* **1, 2** = cause, occasion (*formal*), provoke, give rise to, elicit **3, 4** = remind, assist, cue, help out ▸ *adj* **5** = immediate, quick, rapid, instant, timely, early, swift, speedy; ≠ slow ▸ *adv* = exactly, sharp, promptly, on the dot, punctually

prompter *n* **A** a person offstage who reminds the actors of forgotten lines **B** a device which performs a similar function for public speakers, TV presenters, etc.

promulgate *vb* **-gating, -gated 1** to put (a law or decree) into effect by announcing it officially **2** to make widely known › **promulgation** *n* › **promulgator** *n*

prone *adj* **1** having a tendency to be affected by or do something: *I am prone to indigestion* **2** lying face downwards; prostrate

> **prone** *adj* **1** = liable, given, subject, inclined, tending, bent, disposed, susceptible; ≠ disinclined **2** = face down, flat, horizontal, prostrate, recumbent; ≠ face up

prong *n* a long pointed projection from an instrument or tool such as a fork

pronoun *n* a word, such as *she* or *it*, that replaces a noun or noun phrase that has already been or is about to be mentioned

pronounce *vb* **-nouncing, -nounced 1** to speak (a sound or sounds), esp. clearly or in a certain way **2** to announce or declare officially: *a specialist pronounced her fully fit* **3** to declare as one's judgment: *he pronounced the wine drinkable* › **pronounceable** *adj*

> **pronounce** *vb* **1** = say, speak, sound, articulate, enunciate **2, 3** = declare, announce, deliver, proclaim, decree, affirm

pronounced *adj* very noticeable: *he speaks with a pronounced lisp*

> **pronounced** *adj* = noticeable, decided, marked, striking, obvious, evident, distinct, definite; ≠ imperceptible

pronouncement *n* a formal announcement
pronto *adv informal* at once
pronunciation *n* **1** the recognized way to pronounce sounds in a given language **2** the way in which someone pronounces words

proof *n* **1** any evidence that confirms that something is true or exists **2** *law* the total evidence upon which a court bases its verdict **3** *maths & logic* a sequence of steps or statements that establishes the truth of a proposition **4** the act of testing the truth of something **5** an early copy of printed matter for checking before final production **6** *photog* a trial print from a negative **7** (esp. formerly) a defined level of alcoholic content used as a standard measure for comparing the alcoholic strength of other liquids: *Moldavian ruby port, 17° proof* ▸ *adj* **8** (foll. by *against*) able to withstand: *proof against tears* **9** (esp. formerly) having a level of alcoholic content used as a standard measure for comparing the alcoholic strength of other liquids ▸ *vb* **10** to take a proof from (type matter) **11** to render (something) proof, esp. to waterproof

> **proof** *n* **1** = evidence, demonstration, testimony, confirmation, verification, corroboration, authentication, substantiation ▸ *adj* **8** = impervious, strong, resistant, impenetrable, repellent

proofread *vb* **-reading, -read** to read and correct (printers' proofs) › **proofreader** *n*
prop¹ *vb* **propping, propped** (often foll. by *up*) **1** to support (something or someone) in an upright position: *she was propped up by pillows* **2** to sustain or support: *the type of measures necessary to prop up the sagging economy* **3** (often foll. by *against*) to place or lean ▸ *n* **4** something that gives rigid support, such as a pole **5** a person or thing giving moral support

> **prop** *vb* **1, 2** = support, sustain, hold up, brace, uphold, bolster, buttress **3** = lean, place, set, stand, position, rest, lay, balance ▸ *n* **4** = support, stay, brace, mainstay, buttress, stanchion **5** = mainstay, support, sustainer, anchor, backbone, cornerstone, upholder

prop² *n* a movable object used on the set of a film or play
prop³ *n informal* a propeller
propaganda *n* **1** the organized promotion of information to assist or damage the cause of a government or movement **2** such information › **propagandist** *n, adj*

> **propaganda** *n* = information, advertising, promotion, publicity, hype, disinformation

p

propagate *vb* **-gating, -gated 1** to spread (information or ideas) **2** *biol* to reproduce or breed **3** *horticulture* to produce (plants) **4** *physics* to transmit, esp. in the form of a wave: *the electrical signal is propagated through a specialized group of conducting fibres* ▷ **propagation** *n* ▷ **propagator** *n*

propane *n* a flammable gas found in petroleum and used as a fuel

propel *vb* **-pelling, -pelled** to cause to move forwards ▷ **propellant** *n, adj*

> **propel** *vb* = drive, launch, force, send, shoot, push, thrust, shove; ≠ stop

propeller *n* a revolving shaft with blades to drive a ship or aircraft

propensity *n, pl* **-ties** *formal* a natural tendency: *his problem had always been a propensity to live beyond his means*

proper *adj* **1** real or genuine: *a proper home* **2** appropriate or usual: *good wine must have the proper balance of sugar and acid* **3** suited to a particular purpose: *they set out without any proper climbing gear* **4** correct in behaviour: *they denied that they doctored reports or did anything that was not proper* **5** excessively moral: *she was very strait-laced and proper* **6** being or forming the main or central part of something: *a suburb some miles west of the city proper* **7** *Brit, Austral & NZ informal* complete: *you made him look a proper fool* ▷ **properly** *adv*

> **proper** *adj* **1** = real, actual, genuine, true, bona fide, dinkum (*Austral, NZ informal*) **2,3** = correct, accepted, established, appropriate, right, formal, conventional, precise; ≠ improper **4** = polite, right, becoming, seemly, fitting, fit, mannerly, suitable; ≠ unseemly

property *n, pl* **-ties 1** something owned **2** *law* the right to possess, use, and dispose of anything **3** possessions collectively **4** land or buildings owned by someone **5** a quality or attribute: *the oils have healing properties* **6** same as **prop²**

> **property** *n* **3** = possessions, goods, effects, holdings, capital, riches, estate, assets **4** = land, holding, estate, real estate, freehold **5** = quality, feature, characteristic, attribute, trait, hallmark

prophecy *n, pl* **-cies 1** a prediction **2** ᴀ a message revealing God's will ᴮ the act of uttering such a message **3** the function or activity of a prophet

> **prophecy** *n* **1** = prediction, forecast, prognostication, augury **3** = second sight, divination, augury, telling the future, soothsaying

prophesy *vb* **-sies, -sying, -sied** to foretell

prophet *n* **1** a person supposedly chosen by God to pass on His message **2** a person who predicts the future: *a prophet of doom* **3** a spokesman for, or advocate of, some cause: *a prophet of revolution* ▷ **prophetess** *fem n*

> **prophet** *n* **2** = soothsayer, forecaster, diviner, oracle, seer, sibyl, prophesier

prophetic *adj* **1** foretelling what will happen **2** of the nature of a prophecy ▷ **prophetically** *adv*

prophylactic *adj* **1** preventing disease ▶ *n* **2** a drug or device that prevents disease **3** *chiefly US* a condom

propitiate *vb* **-ating, -ated** to appease (someone, esp. a god or spirit); make well disposed ▷ **propitiable** *adj* ▷ **propitiation** *n* ▷ **propitiator** *n* ▷ **propitiatory** *adj*

propitious *adj* **1** favourable or auspicious: *a propitious moment* **2** likely to prove favourable; advantageous: *his origins were not propitious for a literary career*

proponent *n* a person who argues in favour of something

proportion *n* **1** relative size or extent: *a large proportion of our revenue comes from advertisements* **2** correct relationship between parts **3** a part considered with respect to the whole: *the proportion of women in the total workforce* **4** **proportions** dimensions or size: *a building of vast proportions* **5** *maths* a relationship between four numbers in which the ratio of the first pair equals the ratio of the second pair **6 in proportion** ᴀ comparable in size, rate of increase, etc. ᴮ without exaggerating ▶ *vb* **7** to adjust in relative amount or size: *the size of the crops are very rarely proportioned to the wants of the inhabitants* **8** to cause to be harmonious in relationship of parts

> **proportion** *n* **1** = part, share, amount, division, percentage, segment, quota, fraction **2** = balance, harmony, correspondence, symmetry, concord, congruity **3** = relative amount, relationship, ratio **4** = dimensions, size, volume, capacity, extent, expanse

proportional *adj* **1** being in proportion ▶ *n* **2** *maths* an unknown term in a proportion, for example in $a/b = c/x$, x is the fourth proportional ▷ **proportionally** *adv*

> **proportional** *adj* = correspondent, corresponding, even, balanced, consistent, compatible, equitable, in proportion; ≠ disproportionate

proposal *n* **1** the act of proposing **2** a suggestion put forward for consideration **3** an offer of marriage

> **proposal** *n* **2** = suggestion, plan, programme, scheme, offer, project, bid, recommendation

propose *vb* **-posing, -posed 1** to put forward (a plan) for consideration **2** to nominate (someone) for a position **3** to intend (to do something): *I don't propose to waste any more time* discussing it **4** to ask people to drink (a toast) **5** (often foll. by *to*) to make an offer of marriage

propose *vb* **1** = put forward, present, suggest, advance, submit **2** = nominate, name, present, recommend **3** = intend, mean, plan, aim, design, scheme, have in mind **5** = offer marriage, pop the question (*informal*), ask for someone's hand (in marriage)

proposition *n* **1** a proposal or offer **2** *logic* a statement that affirms or denies something and is capable of being true or false **3** *maths* a statement or theorem, usually containing its proof **4** *informal* a person or matter to be dealt with: *even among experienced climbers the mountain is considered a tough proposition* **5** *informal* an invitation to engage in sexual intercourse ► *vb* **6** *informal* to invite (someone) to engage in sexual intercourse

proposition *n* **1** = proposal, plan, suggestion, scheme, bid, recommendation **2** = theory, idea, argument, concept, thesis, hypothesis, theorem, premise **4** = task, problem, activity, job, affair, venture, undertaking **5** = advance, pass (*informal*), proposal, overture, improper suggestion, come-on (*informal*) ► *vb* = make a pass at, solicit, accost, make an improper suggestion to

propound *vb* to put forward for consideration
proprietary *adj* **1** denoting a product manufactured and distributed under a trade name **2** possessive: *she watched them with a proprietary eye* **3** privately owned and controlled
proprietor *n* an owner of a business establishment > **proprietress** *fem n* > **proprietorial** *adj*

proprietor *n* = owner, titleholder, landlord *or* landlady

propriety *n, pl* **-ties 1** the quality or state of being appropriate or fitting **2** correct conduct **3 the proprieties** the standards of behaviour considered correct by polite society
propulsion *n* **1** a force that moves (something) forward **2** the act of propelling or the state of being propelled > **propulsive** *adj*
pro rata *adv, adj* in proportion
prorogue *vb* **-roguing, -rogued** to suspend (Parliament) without dissolving it > **prorogation** *n*
prosaic (pro-*zay*-ik) *adj* **1** lacking imagination; dull **2** having the characteristics of prose > **prosaically** *adv*
pros and cons *pl n* the advantages and disadvantages of a situation
proscenium (proh-*see*-nee-um) *n, pl* **-nia** *or* **-niums** the arch in a theatre separating the stage from the auditorium
proscribe *vb* **-scribing, -scribed 1** to prohibit (something) **2** to condemn (something); outlaw or banish > **proscription** *n* > **proscriptive** *adj*

prose *n* **1** ordinary spoken or written language in contrast to poetry **2** a passage set for translation into a foreign language **3** commonplace or dull talk
prosecute *vb* **-cuting, -cuted 1** to bring a criminal charge against (someone) **2** to continue to do (something): *the business of prosecuting a cold war through propaganda* **3 A** to seek redress by legal proceedings **B** to institute or conduct a prosecution > **prosecutor** *n*

prosecute *vb* **1** = take someone to court, try, sue, indict, arraign, put someone on trial, litigate, bring someone to trial

prosecution *n* **1** the act of bringing criminal charges against someone **2** the institution and conduct of legal proceedings against a person **3** the lawyers acting for the Crown to put the case against a person **4** the carrying out of something begun
proselyte (*pross*-ill-ite) *n* a recent convert > **proselytism** *n*
proselytize *or* **-tise** (*pross*-ill-it-ize) *vb* **-tizing, -tized** *or* **-tising, -tised** to attempt to convert (someone)
prospect *n* **1** (*pl*) chances or opportunities for future success: *a job with impossible workloads and poor career prospects* **2** expectation, or something anticipated: *she was terrified at the prospect of bringing up two babies on her own* **3** old-fashioned a view or scene: *a prospect of spires, domes, and towers* ► *vb* **4** (sometimes foll. by *for*) to search for gold or other valuable minerals

prospect *n* **1** = possibilities, chances, future, potential, expectations, outlook, scope **2** = idea, outlook **3** = view, landscape, scene, sight, outlook, spectacle, vista ► *vb* = look, search, seek, dowse

prospective *adj* **1** future: *prospective customers* **2** expected or likely: *the prospective loss* > **prospectively** *adv*

prospective *adj* **1** = potential, possible **2** = expected, coming, future, likely, intended, anticipated, forthcoming, imminent

prospector *n* a person who searches for gold or other valuable minerals
prospectus *n, pl* **-tuses** a booklet produced by a university, company, etc., giving details about it and its activities

prospectus *n* = catalogue, list, programme, outline, syllabus, synopsis

prosper *vb* to be successful

prosper *vb* = succeed, advance, progress, thrive, get on, do well, flourish

prosperity *n* success and wealth

prosperity *n* = success, riches, plenty, fortune, wealth, luxury, good fortune, affluence; ≠ poverty

prosperous *adj* wealthy and successful

> **prosperous** *adj* = wealthy, rich, affluent, well-off, well-heeled (*informal*), well-to-do, moneyed, minted (*Brit slang*); ≠ poor

prostate *n* a gland in male mammals that surrounds the neck of the bladder. Also called: **prostate gland**

prosthesis (pross-theess-iss) *n*, *pl* **-ses** (-seez) *surgery* **A** the replacement of a missing body part with an artificial substitute **B** an artificial body part such as a limb, eye, or tooth > **prosthetic** *adj*

prostitute *n* **1** a person who offers sexual intercourse in return for payment ▸ *vb* **-tuting**, **-tuted 2** to offer (oneself or another) in sexual intercourse for money **3** to offer (oneself or one's talent) for unworthy purposes > **prostitution** *n*

> **prostitute** *n* = sex worker, call girl, hooker (*US slang*, *derogatory*), pro (*slang*) ▸ *vb* **3** = cheapen, sell out, pervert, degrade, devalue, squander, demean, debase

prostrate *adj* **1** lying face downwards **2** physically or emotionally exhausted ▸ *vb* **-trating, -trated 3 prostrate oneself** to cast (oneself) face downwards, as in submission **4** to exhaust physically or emotionally > **prostration** *n*

protagonist *n* **1** a supporter of a cause: *a great protagonist of the ideas and principles of mutuality* **2** the leading character in a play or story

> **protagonist** *n* **1** = supporter, champion, advocate, exponent **2** = leading character, principal, central character, hero *or* heroine

protea (pro-tee-a) *n* an African shrub with showy heads of flowers

protean (pro-tee-an) *adj* capable of constantly changing shape or form: *he is a protean stylist who can move from blues to ballads with consummate ease*

protect *vb* **1** to defend from trouble, harm, or loss **2** *econ* to assist (domestic industries) by taxing imports

> **protect** *vb* **1** = keep someone safe, defend, support, save, guard, preserve, look after, shelter; ≠ endanger

protection *n* **1** the act of protecting or the condition of being protected **2** something that keeps one safe **3 A** the charging of taxes on imports, to protect domestic industries **B** Also called: **protectionism** the policy of such taxation **4** *informal* Also called: **protection money** money paid to gangsters to avoid attack or damage > **protectionism** *n* > **protectionist** *n*, *adj*

> **protection** *n* **1** = safety, care, defence, protecting, security, custody, safeguard, aegis **2** = safeguard, cover, guard, shelter, screen, barrier, shield, buffer

protective *adj* **1** giving protection: *protective clothing* **2** tending or wishing to protect someone > **protectively** *adv* > **protectiveness** *n*

> **protective** *adj* **1** = protecting **2** = caring, defensive, motherly, fatherly, maternal, vigilant, watchful, paternal

protector *n* **1** a person or thing that protects **2** *history* a person who acts for the king or queen during his or her childhood, absence, or incapacity > **protectress** *fem n*

> **protector** *n* **1** = defender, champion, guard, guardian, patron, bodyguard

protectorate *n* **1** a territory largely controlled by a stronger state **2** the office or term of office of a protector

protégé *or fem* **protégée** (pro-tizh-ay) *n* a person who is protected and helped by another

protein *n* any of a large group of nitrogenous compounds that are essential for life

pro tempore *adv*, *adj* for the time being. Often shortened to: **pro tem**

protest *n* **1** public, often organized, demonstration of objection **2** a strong objection **3** a formal statement declaring that a debtor has dishonoured a bill **4** the act of protesting ▸ *vb* **5** to take part in a public demonstration to express one's support for or disapproval of an action, proposal, etc.: *the workers marched through the city to protest against the closure of their factory* **6** to disagree or object: *'I'm OK,' she protested* **7** to assert in a formal or solemn manner: *all three repeatedly protested their innocence* **8** *US & NZ* to object forcefully to: *students and teachers have protested the budget reductions* > **protestant** *adj*, *n* > **protester** *n*

> **protest** *n* **1** = demonstration, march, rally, sit-in, demo (*informal*), hikoi (*NZ*) **2** = objection, complaint, dissent, outcry, protestation, remonstrance ▸ *vb* **5** = object, demonstrate, oppose, complain, disagree, cry out, disapprove, demur **7** = assert, insist, maintain, declare, affirm, profess, attest, avow

Protestant *n* **1** a follower of any of the Christian Churches that separated from the Roman Catholic Church in the 16th century ▸ *adj* **2** of or relating to any of these Churches or their followers > **Protestantism** *n*

protestation *n* *formal* a strong declaration

proto- *or sometimes before a vowel* **prot-** *combining form* **1** first: *protomartyr* **2** original: *prototype*

protocol *n* **1** the rules of behaviour for formal occasions **2** a record of an agreement in international negotiations **3** *computers* a standardized format for exchanging data, esp. between different computer systems

> **protocol** *n* **1** = code of behaviour, manners, conventions, customs, etiquette, propriety, decorum

p

proton (pro-ton) n a positively charged elementary particle, found in the nucleus of an atom

protoplasm n biol a complex colourless substance forming the living contents of a cell > **protoplasmic** adj

prototype n 1 an early model of a product, which is tested so that the design can be changed if necessary 2 a person or thing that serves as an example of a type

> **prototype** n = original, model, first, example, standard

protozoan (pro-toe-zoe-an) n, pl -**zoa** a very tiny single-celled invertebrate, such as an amoeba. Also: **protozoon**

protractor n an instrument for measuring angles, usually a flat semicircular piece of plastic

protrude vb -**truding**, -**truded** to stick out or project > **protrusion** n > **protrusive** adj

protuberant adj swelling out; bulging > **protuberance** n

proud adj 1 feeling pleasure or satisfaction: she was proud of her daughter's success 2 feeling honoured 3 haughty or arrogant 4 causing pride: the city's proud history 5 dignified: too proud to accept charity 6 (of a surface or edge) projecting or protruding ▸ adv 7 **do someone proud** to entertain someone on a grand scale: Mum did us all proud last Christmas > **proudly** adv

> **proud** adj 1 = satisfied, pleased, content, thrilled, glad, gratified, joyful, well-pleased; ≠ dissatisfied 3 = conceited, arrogant, lordly, imperious, overbearing, haughty, snobbish, self-satisfied; ≠ humble

prove vb **proving**, **proved**, **proved** or **proven** 1 to establish the truth or validity of: such a claim is difficult to prove scientifically 2 law to establish the genuineness of (a will) 3 to show (oneself) to be: he proved equal to the task 4 to be found to be: it proved to be a trap 5 (of dough) to rise in a warm place before baking > **provable** adj

> **prove** vb 1 = verify, establish, determine, show, confirm, demonstrate, justify, substantiate; ≠ disprove 4 = turn out, come out, end up

proven vb 1 a past participle of **prove** ▸ adj 2 known from experience to work: a proven ability to make money

> **proven** adj = established, proved, confirmed, tested, reliable, definite, verified, attested

provenance (prov-in-anss) n a place of origin

provender n old-fashioned fodder for livestock

proverb n a short memorable saying that expresses a truth or gives a warning, for example half a loaf is better than no bread

proverbial adj 1 well-known because commonly or traditionally referred to 2 of a proverb > **proverbially** adv

provide vb -**viding**, -**vided** 1 to make available 2 to afford; yield: social activities providing the opportunity to meet new people 3 (often foll. by for or against) to take careful precautions: we provide for the possibility of illness in the examination regulations 4 (foll. by for) to support financially: both parents should be expected to provide for their children 5 **provide for** formal (of a law, treaty, etc.) to make possible: a bill providing for stiffer penalties for racial discrimination > **provider** n

> **provide** vb 1 = supply, give, distribute, outfit, equip, donate, furnish, dispense; ≠ withhold 2 = give, bring, add, produce, present, serve, afford, yield 4 **provide for someone** = support, care for, keep, maintain, sustain, take care of, fend for

providence n 1 God or nature seen as a protective force that oversees people's lives 2 the foresight shown by a person in the management of his or her affairs

provident adj 1 thrifty 2 showing foresight

providential adj fortunate, as if through divine involvement

province n 1 a territory governed as a unit of a country or empire 2 an area of learning, activity, etc. 3 **the provinces** those parts of a country lying outside the capital

> **province** n 1 = region, section, district, zone, patch, colony, domain

provincial adj 1 of a province 2 unsophisticated or narrow-minded 3 NZ denoting a football team representing a province ▸ n 4 an unsophisticated person 5 a person from a province or the provinces > **provincialism** n

> **provincial** adj 1 = regional, state, local, county, district, territorial, parochial 2 = parochial, insular, narrow-minded, unsophisticated, limited, narrow, small-town (chiefly US), inward-looking; ≠ cosmopolitan

provision n 1 the act of supplying something 2 something supplied 3 **provisions** food and other necessities 4 a condition incorporated in a document 5 **make provision for** to make arrangements for beforehand: the company has made provision for future losses ▸ vb 6 to supply with provisions

> **provision** n 1 = supplying, giving, providing, supply, delivery, distribution, catering, presentation 3 = food, supplies, stores, fare, rations, foodstuff, kai (NZ informal), victuals (old-fashioned), edibles 4 = condition, term, requirement, demand, rider, restriction, qualification, clause

provisional adj temporary or conditional: a provisional diagnosis > **provisionally** adv

> **provisional** adj = conditional, limited, qualified, contingent, tentative; ≠ definite

P

proviso (pro-**vize**-oh) *n, pl* **-sos** *or* **-soes** a condition or stipulation ➤ **provisory** *adj*

provocation *n* **1** the act of provoking or inciting **2** something that causes indignation or anger

> **provocation** *n* **1** = cause, reason, grounds, motivation, stimulus, incitement **2** = offence, challenge, insult, taunt, injury, dare, grievance, annoyance

provocative *adj* provoking or inciting, esp. to anger or sexual desire: *a provocative remark* ➤ **provocatively** *adv*

> **provocative** *adj* = offensive, provoking, insulting, stimulating, annoying, galling, goading

provoke *vb* **-voking, -voked** **1** to deliberately act in a way intended to anger someone: *waving a red cape, Delgado provoked the animal into charging* **2** to incite or stimulate: *the army seems to have provoked this latest confrontation* **3** (often foll. by *into*) to cause a person to react in a particular, often angry, way: *keeping your true motives hidden may provoke others into being just as two-faced with you* **4** to bring about: *the case has provoked furious public debate* ➤ **provoking** *adj*

> **provoke** *vb* **1** = anger, annoy, irritate, infuriate, hassle (*informal*), aggravate (*informal*), incense, enrage; ≠ pacify **4** = rouse, cause, produce, promote, occasion (*formal*), prompt, stir, induce; ≠ curb

provost *n* **1** the head of certain university colleges or schools **2** the chief councillor of a Scottish town

prow *n* the bow of a vessel

prowess *n* **1** superior skill or ability **2** bravery or fearlessness

> **prowess** *n* **1** = skill, ability, talent, expertise, genius, excellence, accomplishment, mastery; ≠ inability **2** = bravery, daring, courage, heroism, mettle, valour, fearlessness, valiance; ≠ cowardice

prowl *vb* **1** (sometimes foll. by *around* or *about*) to move stealthily around (a place) as if in search of prey or plunder ▶ *n* **2** the act of prowling **3** **on the prowl** moving around stealthily ➤ **prowler** *n*

proximate *adj* **1** next or nearest in space or time **2** very near **3** immediately coming before or following in a series **4** approximate

proximity *n* **1** nearness in space or time **2** nearness or closeness in a series

> **proximity** *n* = nearness, closeness

proxy *n, pl* **proxies** **1** a person authorized to act on behalf of someone else: *the firm's creditors can vote either in person or by proxy* **2** the authority to act on behalf of someone else

> **proxy** *n* **1** = representative, agent, deputy, substitute, factor (*Scot*), delegate

prude *n* a person who is excessively modest or prim, esp. regarding sex ➤ **prudery** *n* ➤ **prudish** *adj*

prudent *adj* **1** sensible and careful **2** discreet or cautious **3** exercising good judgment ➤ **prudence** *n* ➤ **prudently** *adv*

> **prudent** *adj* **1, 2** = cautious, careful, wary, discreet, vigilant; ≠ careless **3** = wise, politic, sensible, shrewd, discerning, judicious; ≠ unwise

prudential *adj* old-fashioned showing prudence: *prudential reasons* ➤ **prudentially** *adv*

prune[1] *n* a purplish-black partially dried plum

prune[2] *vb* **pruning, pruned** **1** to cut off dead or surplus branches of (a tree or shrub) **2** to shorten or reduce

> **prune** *vb* **1** = cut, trim, clip, dock, shape, shorten, snip **2** = reduce, cut, cut back, trim, cut down, pare down, make reductions in

prurient *adj* **1** excessively interested in sexual matters **2** exciting lustfulness ➤ **prurience** *n*

pry *vb* **pries, prying, pried** (often foll. by *into*) to make an impertinent or uninvited inquiry (about a private matter)

PS **1** *Also:* **ps** postscript **2** private secretary

PSA (in New Zealand) Public Service Association

psalm *n* (*often cap*) any of the sacred songs that make up a book (Psalms) of the Old Testament

psalmist *n* a writer of psalms

Psalter *n* **1** the Book of Psalms **2** a book containing a version of Psalms

psaltery *n, pl* **-teries** an ancient musical instrument played by plucking strings

PSBR (in Britain) public sector borrowing requirement: the money needed by the public sector of the economy for items not paid for by income

psephology (sef-**fol**-a-jee) *n* the statistical and sociological study of elections ➤ **psephologist** *n*

pseud *n informal* a pretentious person

pseudo- *or sometimes before a vowel* **pseud-** *combining form* false, pretending, or unauthentic: *pseudo-intellectual*

pseudonym *n* a fictitious name adopted, esp. by an author ➤ **pseudonymity** *n* ➤ **pseudonymous** *adj*

psittacosis *n* a viral disease of parrots that can be passed on to humans

psoriasis (so-**rye**-a-siss) *n* a skin disease with reddish spots and patches covered with silvery scales

psyche *n* the human mind or soul

> **psyche** *n* = soul, mind, self, spirit, personality, individuality, anima, wairua (NZ)

psychedelic *adj* **1** denoting a drug that causes hallucinations **2** *informal* having vivid colours and complex patterns similar to those experienced during hallucinations

psychiatry *n* the branch of medicine concerned with the study and treatment of mental health conditions > **psychiatric** *adj* > **psychiatrist** *n*

psychic *adj* **1** relating to or having powers (esp. mental powers) which cannot be explained by natural laws **2** relating to the mind ▸ *n* **3** a person who has psychic powers > **psychical** *adj*

> **psychic** *adj* **1** = supernatural, mystic, occult **2** = psychological, emotional, mental, spiritual, inner, psychiatric, cognitive ▸ *n* = clairvoyant, fortune teller

psycho *informal* ▸ *n*, *pl* **-chos 1** same as **psychopath** ▸ *adj* **2** same as **psychopathic**

psychoanalyse *or US* **-lyze** *vb* **-lysing, -lysed** *or* **-lyzing, -lyzed** to examine or treat (a person) by psychoanalysis

psychoanalysis *n* a method of treating mental and emotional conditions by discussion and analysis of the patient's thoughts and feelings > **psychoanalyst** *n* > **psychoanalytical** *or* **psychoanalytic** *adj*

psychological *adj* **1** relating to the mind or mental activity **2** relating to psychology **3** having its origin in the mind: *his backaches are purely psychological* > **psychologically** *adv*

> **psychological** *adj* **1** = mental, emotional, intellectual, inner, cognitive, cerebral **3** = imaginary, psychosomatic, irrational, unreal, all in the mind

psychology *n*, *pl* **-gies 1** the scientific study of all forms of human and animal behaviour **2** *informal* the mental make-up of a person > **psychologist** *n*

> **psychology** *n* **1** = behaviourism, study of personality, science of mind **2** = way of thinking, attitude, behaviour, temperament, mentality, thought processes, mental processes, what makes you tick

psychopath *n* a person with a personality disorder which can cause him or her to commit antisocial and sometimes violent acts > **psychopathic** *adj*

psychosis (sike-oh-siss) *n*, *pl* **-ses** (-seez) a severe mental disorder in which the individual's contact with reality becomes highly distorted: *a classic case of psychosis* > **psychotic** *adj*

psychosomatic *adj* (of a physical disorder) thought to have psychological causes, such as stress

psychotherapy *n* the treatment of nervous disorders by psychological methods > **psychotherapeutic** *adj* > **psychotherapist** *n*

psych up *vb* to prepare (oneself or another) mentally for a contest or task

pt 1 part **2** past tense **3** point **4** port **5** pro tempore

PT *old-fashioned* physical training

pt. pint

PTA Parent Teacher Association

ptarmigan (**tar**-mig-an) *n* a bird of the grouse family that turns white in winter

pterodactyl (terr-roe-**dak**-til) *n* an extinct flying reptile with batlike wings

PTO *or* **pto** please turn over

ptomaine *or* **ptomain** (**toe**-main) *n* any of a group of poisonous alkaloids found in decaying matter

Pty *Austral & S African* Proprietary

pub *n* **1** *chiefly Brit* a building with a licensed bar where alcoholic drinks may be bought and drunk **2** *Austral & NZ* a hotel

> **pub** *n* **1** = tavern, bar, inn, saloon, beer parlour (*Canad*), beverage room (*Canad*)

puberty (**pew**-ber-tee) *n* the beginning of sexual maturity > **pubertal** *adj*

pubescent *adj* **1** arriving or arrived at puberty **2** covered with down, as some plants and animals > **pubescence** *n*

pubic (**pew**-bik) *adj* of or relating to the pubes or pubis: *pubic hair*

public *adj* **1** relating to the people as a whole **2** provided by the government: *public service* **3** open to all: *public gardens* **4** well-known: *a public figure* **5** performed or made openly: *a public proclamation* **6** maintained by and for the community: *a public library* **7** open, acknowledged, or notorious: *a public scandal* **8 go public A** (of a private company) to offer shares for sale to the public: *few German firms have gone public in recent years* **B** to make information, plans, etc., known: *the group would not have gone public with its suspicions unless it was fully convinced of them* ▸ *n* **9** the community or people in general **10** a particular section of the community: *the racing public* > **publicly** *adv*

> **public** *adj* **1** = general, popular, national, shared, common, widespread, universal, collective **2** = civic, government, state, national, local, official, community, social **3** = open, accessible, communal, unrestricted; ≠ private **4** = well-known, leading, important, respected, famous, celebrated, recognized, distinguished **7** = known, open, obvious, acknowledged, plain, patent, overt; ≠ secret ▸ *n* **9** = people, society, community, nation, everyone, citizens, electorate, populace

publican *n* *Brit*, *Austral & NZ* a person who owns or runs a pub

publication *n* **1** the publishing of a printed work **2** any printed work offered for sale **3** the act of making information known to the public

> **publication** *n* **2** = pamphlet, newspaper, magazine, issue, title, leaflet, brochure, periodical, blog (*informal*) **3** = publishing, announcement, broadcasting, reporting, declaration, disclosure, proclamation, notification

P

public house n 1 Brit a pub 2 US & Canad an inn or small hotel

publicist n a person, such as a press agent or journalist, who publicizes something

publicity n 1 the process or information used to arouse public attention 2 the public interest so aroused

> **publicity** n 1 = advertising, press, promotion, hype, boost, plug (informal) 2 = attention, exposure, fame, celebrity, fuss, public interest, limelight, notoriety

publicize or **-cise** vb **-cizing, -cized** or **-cising, -cised** to bring to public attention

public relations n the practice of gaining the public's goodwill and approval for an organization

public school n 1 (in England and Wales) a private independent fee-paying secondary school 2 (in certain Canadian provinces) a public elementary school as distinguished from a separate school 3 (in the US) any school that is part of a free local educational system

public-spirited adj having or showing an active interest in the good of the community

publish vb 1 to produce and issue (printed matter) for sale 2 to have one's written work issued for publication 3 to announce formally or in public > **publishing** n

> **publish** vb 1 = put out, issue, produce, print 3 = announce, reveal, spread, advertise, broadcast, disclose, proclaim, circulate

publisher n 1 a company or person that publishes books, periodicals, music, etc. 2 US & Canad the proprietor of a newspaper

puce adj dark brownish-purple: his face suddenly turned puce with futile rage

puck¹ n a small disc of hard rubber used in ice hockey

puck² n a mischievous or evil spirit > **puckish** adj

pucker vb 1 to gather into wrinkles ▸ n 2 a wrinkle or crease

pudding n 1 a dessert, esp. a cooked one served hot 2 a savoury dish with pastry or batter: steak-and-kidney pudding 3 a sausage-like mass of meat: black pudding

> **pudding** n 1 = dessert, afters (Brit informal), sweet, pud (informal)

puddle n 1 a small pool of water, esp. of rain 2 a worked mixture of wet clay and sand that is impervious to water ▸ vb **-dling, -dled** 3 to make (clay, etc.) into puddle > **puddly** adj

puerile adj silly and childish > **puerility** n

puerperal (pew-er-per-al) adj concerning the period following childbirth

puff n 1 a short quick blast of breath, wind, or smoke 2 the amount of wind or smoke released in a puff 3 the sound made by a puff 4 an act of inhaling and expelling cigarette smoke

5 a light pastry usually filled with cream and jam 6 **out of puff** out of breath: by the third flight of stairs she was out of puff ▸ vb 7 to blow or breathe in short quick blasts 8 (often foll. by out) to cause to be out of breath 9 to take draws at (a cigarette) 10 to move with or by the emission of puffs: the steam train puffed up the incline 11 (often foll. by up or out) to swell > **puffy** adj

> **puff** n 1, 2 = blast, breath, whiff, draught, gust 4 = drag, pull (slang), smoke ▸ vb 7 = breathe heavily, pant, exhale, blow, gasp, gulp, wheeze, fight for breath 9 = smoke, draw, drag (slang), suck, inhale, pull at or on

puffball n a ball-shaped fungus that sends out a cloud of brown spores when mature

puffin n a black-and-white sea bird with a brightly coloured beak

puff pastry or US **puff paste** n a light flaky pastry

pug n a small dog with a smooth coat, lightly curled tail, and a short wrinkled nose

pugilist (pew-jil-ist) n a boxer > **pugilism** n > **pugilistic** adj

pugnacious adj formal ready and eager to fight > **pugnacity** n

pug nose n a short stubby upturned nose > **pug-nosed** adj

puissance n a showjumping competition that tests a horse's ability to jump large obstacles

puke slang ▸ vb **puking, puked** 1 to vomit ▸ n 2 the act of vomiting 3 the matter vomited

pulchritude n formal or literary physical beauty > **pulchritudinous** adj

pull vb 1 to exert force on (an object) to draw it towards the source of the force 2 to strain or stretch 3 to remove or extract: he pulled a crumpled handkerchief from his pocket 4 informal to draw out (a weapon) for use: he pulled a knife on his attacker 5 informal to attract: the game is expected to pull a large crowd 6 Brit slang to attract a sexual partner 7 (usually foll. by on or at) to drink or inhale deeply: he pulled on his pipe 8 to possess or exercise the power to move: this car doesn't pull well on hills 9 to withdraw or remove: the board pulled their support 10 printing to take (a proof) from type 11 golf & baseball etc. to hit (the ball) in the direction of one's follow-through 12 cricket to hit (a ball) to the leg side 13 to row (a boat) or take a stroke of (an oar) in rowing 14 **pull a face** to make a grimace 15 **pull a fast one** slang (often foll. by on) to play a sly trick 16 **pull apart** or **to pieces** to criticize harshly 17 **pull (one's) punches** to limit the force of one's criticisms or blows ▸ n 18 the act of pulling 19 the force used in pulling: the pull of the moon affects the tides 20 the act of taking in drink or smoke 21 printing a proof taken from type 22 something used for pulling, such as a handle 23 informal power or influence: his uncle is chairman of the company, so he has quite a lot of pull 24 informal the power to attract attention or support 25 a single stroke of an oar in rowing

26 the act of pulling the ball in golf, cricket, etc. ▸ See also **pull in** etc.

> **pull** *vb* **1** = draw, haul, drag, trail, tow, tug, jerk, yank; ≠ push **2** = strain, tear, stretch, rip, wrench, dislocate, sprain **3** = extract, pick, remove, gather, take out, pluck, uproot, draw out; ≠ insert **5, 6** = attract, draw, bring in, tempt, lure, interest, entice, pull in; ≠ repel ▸ *n* **18** = tug, jerk, yank, twitch, heave; ≠ shove **20** = puff, drag (*slang*), inhalation **23** = influence, power, weight, muscle, clout (*informal*), kai (*NZ informal*)

pullet *n* a hen less than one year old

pulley *n* a wheel with a grooved rim in which a belt, chain, or piece of rope runs in order to lift weights by a downward pull

pull in *vb* **1** Also: **pull over** (of a motor vehicle) to draw in to the side of the road **2** (often foll. by *to*) to reach a destination: *the train pulled in to the station* **3** to attract: *his appearance will pull in the crowds* **4** *Brit, Austral & NZ slang* to arrest **5** to earn (money): *he pulls in at least thirty thousand a year*

Pullman *n, pl* **-mans** *chiefly Brit* a luxurious railway coach

pull off *vb informal* to succeed in accomplishing (something difficult): *superheroes who pull off the impossible*

> **pull off** *vb* **pull something off** = succeed in, manage, carry out, accomplish

pull out *vb* **1 A** (of a motor vehicle) to draw away from the side of the road **B** (of a motor vehicle) to move out from behind another vehicle to overtake **2** to depart: *the train pulled out of the station* **3** to withdraw: *several companies have pulled out of the student market* **4** to remove by pulling **5** to abandon a situation

> **pull out** *vb* **3 pull out (of)** = withdraw, quit **4 pull something out** = produce, draw, bring out, draw out **5 pull out (of)** = leave, abandon, get out, quit, retreat from, depart (*US*), evacuate

pullover *n* a sweater that is pulled on over the head

pull up *vb* **1** (of a motor vehicle) to stop **2** to remove by the roots **3** to rebuke

> **pull up** *vb* **1** = stop, halt, brake **3 pull someone up** = reprimand, rebuke, admonish, read the riot act to, tell someone off (*informal*), reprove, bawl someone out (*informal*), tear someone off a strip (*Brit informal*)

pulmonary *adj* **1** of or affecting the lungs **2** having lungs or lunglike organs

pulp *n* **1** a soft wet substance made from matter which has been crushed or beaten: *mash the strawberries to a pulp* **2** the soft fleshy part of a fruit or vegetable: *halve the tomatoes then scoop the seeds and pulp into a bowl* **3** printed or recorded material with little depth or designed to shock: *a music player churned out disco pulp* ▸ *vb* **4** to reduce (a material) to pulp: *he began to pulp the orange in his fingers* ▸ **pulpy** *adj*

> **pulp** *n* **1** = paste, mash, mush **2** = flesh, meat, soft part ▸ *vb* = crush, squash, mash, pulverize

pulpit *n* **1** a raised platform in churches used for preaching **2** (usually preceded by *the*) preaching or the clergy

pulsar *n* a very small star which emits regular pulses of radio waves

pulsate *vb* **-sating, -sated 1** to expand and contract rhythmically, like a heartbeat **2** to quiver or vibrate: *the images pulsate with energy and light* **3** *physics* to vary in intensity or magnitude ▸ **pulsation** *n*

pulse [1] *n* **1** *physiol* **A** the regular beating of blood through the arteries at each heartbeat **B** a single such beat **2** *physics & electronics* a sudden change in a quantity, such as a voltage, that is normally constant in a system **3** a regular beat or vibration **4** bustle or excitement: *the lively pulse of a city* **5** the feelings or thoughts of a group as they can be measured: *the political pulse of the capital* ▸ *vb* **pulsing, pulsed 6** to beat, throb, or vibrate

> **pulse** *n* **3** = beat, rhythm, vibration, beating, throb, throbbing, pulsation ▸ *vb* = beat, throb, vibrate, pulsate

pulse [2] *n* the edible seeds of pod-bearing plants, such as peas, beans, and lentils

pulverize *or* **-rise** *vb* **-rizing, -rized** *or* **-rising, -rised 1** to reduce to fine particles by crushing or grinding **2** to destroy completely ▸ **pulverization** *or* **-risation** *n*

puma *n* a large American wild cat with a plain greyish-brown coat and a long tail

pumice (pumm-iss) *n* a light porous stone used for scouring and for removing hard skin. Also called: **pumice stone**

pummel *vb* **-melling, -melled** *or US* **-meling, -meled** to strike repeatedly with the fists

pump [1] *n* **1** a device to force a gas or liquid to move in a particular direction ▸ *vb* **2** (sometimes foll. by *from* or *out* etc.) to raise or drive (air, liquid, etc.) with a pump, esp. into or from something **3** (usually foll. by *in* or *into*) to supply in large amounts: *pumping money into the economy* **4** to operate (a handle, etc.) in the manner of a pump: *he was warmly applauded, and his hand was pumped by well-wishers* **5** to obtain information from (someone) by persistent questioning **6 pump iron** *slang* to exercise with weights; do body-building exercises

> **pump** *vb* **3** = supply, send, pour, inject **5** = interrogate, probe, quiz, cross-examine

pump [2] *n* **1** *chiefly Brit* a shoe with a rubber sole, used in games such as tennis; plimsoll **2** a woman's flat-heeled shoe that does not cover the top part of the foot

P

pumpkin *n* **1** a large round fruit with a thick orange rind, pulpy flesh, and many seeds **2** the creeping plant that bears this fruit

pun *n* **1** the use of words to exploit double meanings for humorous effect, for example *my dog's a champion boxer* ▸ *vb* **punning, punned 2** to make puns

punch¹ *vb* **1** to strike at with a clenched fist ▸ *n* **2** a blow with the fist **3** *informal* point or vigour: *the jokes are mildly amusing but lack any real punch*

> **punch** *vb* = hit, strike, box, smash, belt (*informal*), sock (*slang, old-fashioned*), swipe (*informal*), bop (*informal*) ▸ *n* **2** = blow, hit, sock (*slang*), jab, swipe (*informal*), bop (*informal*), wallop (*informal*) **3** = effectiveness, bite, impact, drive, vigour, verve, forcefulness

punch² *n* **1** a tool or machine for shaping, piercing, or engraving ▸ *vb* **2** to pierce, cut, stamp, shape, or drive with a punch

> **punch** *vb* = pierce, cut, bore, drill, stamp, puncture, prick, perforate

punch³ *n* a mixed drink containing fruit juice and, usually, wine or spirits, generally hot and spiced

punch-drunk *adj* dazed and confused through suffering repeated blows to the head

punchy *adj* **punchier, punchiest** *informal* effective or forceful: *learn to compose short concise punchy letters*

punctilious *adj formal* **1** paying careful attention to correct social behaviour **2** attentive to detail > **punctiliously** *adv*

punctual *adj* **1** arriving or taking place at an arranged time **2** (of a person) always keeping exactly to arranged times > **punctuality** *n* > **punctually** *adv*

punctuate *vb* **-ating, -ated 1** to insert punctuation marks into (a written text) **2** to interrupt at frequent intervals: *the meeting was punctuated by heckling* **3** to emphasize: *he punctuated the question by pressing the muzzle into the pilot's neck*

> **punctuate** *vb* **2** = interrupt, break, pepper, sprinkle, intersperse

punctuation *n* **1** the use of symbols, such as commas, to indicate speech patterns and meaning not otherwise shown by the written language **2** the symbols used for this purpose

puncture *n* **1** a small hole made by a sharp object **2** a tear and loss of pressure in a tyre **3** the act of puncturing or perforating ▸ *vb* **-turing, -tured 4** to pierce a hole in (something) with a sharp object **5** to cause (a tyre, etc.) to lose pressure by piercing

> **puncture** *n* **1** = hole, opening, break, cut, nick, leak, slit **2** = flat tyre, flat, flattie (NZ) ▸ *vb* **4** = pierce, cut, nick, penetrate, prick, rupture, perforate, bore a hole (in)

pundit *n* **1** an expert on a subject who often speaks or writes about it for a non-specialist audience: *Spain's leading sports pundit, who hosts two TV programmes* **2** a Hindu scholar learned in Sanskrit, religion, philosophy, or law

pungent *adj* **1** having a strong sharp bitter smell or taste **2** (of speech or writing) biting; critical > **pungency** *n*

punish *vb* **1** to force (someone) to undergo a penalty for some crime or misbehaviour **2** to inflict punishment for (some crime or misbehaviour) **3** to treat harshly, esp. by overexertion: *he continued to punish himself in the gym* > **punishable** *adj* > **punishing** *adj*

> **punish** *vb* **1** = discipline, correct, castigate, chastise, sentence, chasten, penalize

punishment *n* **1** a penalty for a crime or offence **2** the act of punishing or state of being punished **3** *informal* rough physical treatment: *the boxer's face could not withstand further punishment*

> **punishment** *n* **1** = penalty, penance **2** = penalizing, discipline, correction, retribution, chastening, chastisement

punitive (pew-nit-tiv) *adj* relating to punishment: *punitive measures*

> **punitive** *adj* = retaliatory, in reprisal, retaliative

punk *n* **1** *US informal* a worthless person **2** a youth movement of the late 1970s, characterized by anti-Establishment slogans, short spiky hair, and the wearing of worthless articles such as safety pins for decoration **3** a follower of the punk movement or of punk rock ▸ *adj* **4** relating to the punk youth movement of the late 1970s: *a punk band* **5** *US informal* worthless or insignificant

punnet *n* a small basket for fruit

punt¹ *n* **1** an open flat-bottomed boat, propelled by a pole ▸ *vb* **2** to propel (a punt) by pushing with a pole on the bottom of a river

punt² *n* **1** a kick in certain sports, such as rugby, in which the ball is dropped and kicked before it hits the ground ▸ *vb* **2** to kick (a ball) using a punt

punt³ *chiefly Brit* ▸ *vb* **1** to gamble or bet ▸ *n* **2** a gamble or bet, esp. against the bank, such as in roulette

> **punt** *vb* = bet, back, stake, gamble, lay, wager ▸ *n* = bet, stake, gamble, wager

punter *n* **1** a person who places a bet **2** *Brit, Austral & NZ informal* any member of the public, esp. when a customer: *the punters are flocking into the sales*

> **punter** *n* **1** = gambler, better, backer

puny *adj* **-nier, -niest** small and weakly

pup *n* **1** **A** a young dog; puppy **B** the young of various other animals, such as the seal ▸ *vb* **pupping, pupped 2** (of dogs, seals, etc.) to give birth to pups

pupa (pew-pa) *n*, *pl* **-pae** (-pee) *or* **-pas** an insect at the stage of development between larva and adult > **pupal** *adj*

pupil[1] *n* a student who is taught by a teacher

> **pupil** *n* = student, schoolboy *or* schoolgirl, schoolchild; ≠ teacher

pupil[2] *n* the dark circular opening at the centre of the iris of the eye

puppet *n* **1** a small doll or figure moved by strings attached to its limbs or by the hand inserted in its cloth body **2** a person or state that appears independent but is controlled by another: *the former cabinet ministers have denied that they are puppets of a foreign government*

> **puppet** *n* **1** = marionette, doll, glove puppet, sock puppet, finger puppet **2** = pawn, tool, instrument (*informal*), mouthpiece, stooge (*slang*), cat's-paw

puppeteer *n* a person who operates puppets

puppy *n*, *pl* **-pies 1** a young dog **2** *informal*, *derogatory* a brash or conceited young man > **puppyish** *adj*

purchase *vb* **-chasing, -chased 1** to obtain (goods) by payment **2** to obtain by effort or sacrifice: *he had purchased his freedom at the expense of his principles* ▶ *n* **3** something that is bought **4** the act of buying **5** the mechanical advantage achieved by a lever **6** a firm leverage or grip > **purchaser** *n*

> **purchase** *vb* **1** = buy, pay for, obtain, get, score (*slang*), gain, pick up, acquire; ≠ sell ▶ *n* **3** = acquisition, buy, investment, property, gain, asset, possession **6** = grip, hold, support, leverage, foothold

purdah *n* the custom in some Muslim and Hindu communities of keeping women in seclusion, with clothing that conceals them completely when they go out

pure *adj* **1** not mixed with any other materials or elements: *pure wool* **2** free from tainting or polluting matter: *pure water* **3** innocent: *pure love* **4** complete: *Pamela's presence on that particular flight was pure chance* **5** (of a subject) studied in its theoretical aspects rather than for its practical applications: *pure mathematics* **6** of unmixed descent: *a pure Dalmatian* > **purely** *adv* > **pureness** *n*

> **pure** *adj* **1** = unmixed, real, simple, natural, straight, genuine, neat, authentic; ≠ adulterated **2** = clean, wholesome, sanitary, spotless, sterilized, squeaky-clean, untainted, uncontaminated; ≠ contaminated **3** = innocent, modest, good, moral, impeccable, righteous, virtuous, squeaky-clean; ≠ corrupt **4** = complete, total, perfect, absolute, sheer, patent, utter, outright; ≠ qualified

puree (pure-ray) *n* **1** a smooth thick pulp of sieved fruit, vegetables, meat, or fish ▶ *vb* **-reeing, -reed 2** to make (foods) into a puree

purgative *med* ▶ *n* **1** a medicine for emptying the bowels ▶ *adj* **2** causing emptying of the bowels

purgatory *n* **1** *chiefly RC Church* a place in which the souls of those who have died undergo limited suffering for their sins on earth before they go to heaven **2** a situation of temporary suffering or torment: *it was purgatory living in the same house as him* > **purgatorial** *adj*

purge *vb* **purging, purged 1** to rid (something) of undesirable qualities **2** to rid (an organization, etc.) of undesirable people: *the party was purged* **3 A** to empty (the bowels) **B** to cause (a person) to empty his or her bowels **4 A** *law* to clear (a person) of a charge **B** to free (oneself) of guilt by showing repentance **5** to be purified ▶ *n* **6** the act or process of purging **7** the removal of undesirables from a state, organization, or political party **8** a medicine that empties the bowels

> **purge** *vb* **1** = rid, clear, cleanse, strip, empty, void ▶ *n* **7** = removal, elimination, expulsion, eradication, ejection

purify *vb* **-fies, -fying, -fied 1** to free (something) of harmful or inferior matter **2** to free (a person) from sin or guilt **3** to make clean, for example in a religious ceremony > **purification** *n*

puritan *n* **1** a person who follows strict moral or religious principles ▶ *adj* **2** of or like a puritan: *he maintained a streak of puritan self-denial* > **puritanism** *n*

Puritan *history* ▶ *n* **1** a member of the extreme English Protestants who wished to strip the Church of England of most of its rituals ▶ *adj* **2** of or relating to the Puritans > **Puritanism** *n*

puritanical *adj* **1** *usually derogatory* strict in moral or religious outlook **2** (*sometimes cap*) of or relating to a puritan or the Puritans > **puritanically** *adv*

purity *n* the state or quality of being pure

> **purity** *n* = cleanness, cleanliness, wholesomeness, pureness, faultlessness, immaculateness; ≠ impurity

purl *n* **1** a knitting stitch made by doing a plain stitch backwards **2** a decorative border, such as of lace ▶ *vb* **3** to knit in purl stitch

purloin *vb* *formal* to steal

purple *n* **1** a colour between red and blue **2** cloth of this colour, often used to symbolize royalty or nobility **3** the official robe of a cardinal **4** anything purple, such as purple paint or purple clothing: *dressed in purple* ▶ *adj* **5** of a colour between red and blue **6** (of writing) excessively elaborate: *purple prose* > **purplish** *adj*

purport *vb* **1** to claim to be or do something, esp. falsely: *painkillers may actually cause the headaches they purport to cure* **2** (of speech or writing) to signify or imply ▶ *n* **3** meaning or significance

> **purport** *vb* **1** = claim, allege, assert, profess

p

purpose *n* **1** the reason for which anything is done, created, or exists **2** a fixed design or idea that is the object of an action **3** determination: *his easy manner only lightly conceals a clear sense of purpose* **4** practical advantage or use: *we debated senseless points of dogma for hours to no fruitful purpose* **5 on purpose** intentionally ▶ *vb* **-posing, -posed** **6** to intend or determine to do (something)

> **purpose** *n* **1** = reason, point, idea, aim, object, intention **2** = aim, end, plan, hope, goal, wish, desire, object **3** = determination, resolve, will, resolution, ambition, persistence, tenacity, firmness **5 on purpose** = deliberately, purposely, intentionally, knowingly, designedly

purposely *adv* on purpose

> **purposely** *adv* = deliberately, expressly, consciously, intentionally, knowingly, with intent, on purpose; ≠ accidentally

purr *vb* **1** (esp. of cats) to make a low vibrant sound, usually considered as expressing pleasure **2** to express (pleasure) by this sound or by a sound suggestive of purring ▶ *n* **3** a purring sound

purse *n* **1** a small pouch for carrying money **2** *US, Canad, Austral & NZ* a woman's handbag **3** wealth or resources: *the public purse appeared bottomless* **4** a sum of money that is offered as a prize ▶ *vb* **pursing, pursed 5** to pull (the lips) into a small rounded shape

> **purse** *n* **1** = pouch, wallet, money-bag, e-wallet *or* eWallet **2** = handbag, bag, shoulder bag, pocket book, clutch bag **3** = funds, means, money, resources, treasury, wealth, exchequer ▶ *vb* = pucker, contract, tighten, pout, press together

purser *n* an officer aboard a ship who keeps the accounts

pursue *vb* **-suing, -sued 1** to follow (a person, vehicle, or animal) in order to capture or overtake **2** to try hard to achieve (some desire or aim) **3** to follow the guidelines of (a plan or policy) **4** to apply oneself to (studies or interests) **5** to follow persistently or seek to become acquainted with **6** to continue to discuss or argue (a point or subject) > **pursuer** *n*

> **pursue** *vb* **1** = follow, track, hunt, chase, dog, shadow, tail (*informal*), hound; ≠ flee **2** = try for, seek, desire, search for, aim for, work towards, strive for **3** = engage in, perform, conduct, carry on, practise **6** = continue, maintain, carry on, keep on, persist in, proceed in, persevere in

pursuit *n* **1** the act of pursuing **2** an occupation or pastime

> **pursuit** *n* **1** = quest, seeking, search, aim, aspiration, striving towards **2** = occupation, activity, interest, line, pleasure, hobby, pastime

purulent (pure-yew-lent) *adj* of, relating to, or containing pus > **purulence** *n*

purvey *vb* **1** to sell or provide (foodstuffs) **2** to provide or make available: *the foreign ministry used him to purvey sensitive items of diplomatic news* > **purveyor** *n*

purview *n* **1** scope of operation: *each designation falls under the purview of a different ministry* **2** breadth or range of outlook: *he hopes that the purview of science will be widened*

pus *n* the yellowish fluid that comes from inflamed or infected tissue

push *vb* **1** (sometimes foll. by *off* or *away* etc.) to apply steady force to in order to move **2** to thrust (one's way) through something, such as a crowd **3** (sometimes foll. by *for*) to be an advocate or promoter (of): *there are many groups you can join to push for change* **4** to spur or drive (oneself or another person) in order to achieve more effort or better results: *you must be careful not to push your children too hard* **5** *informal* to sell (narcotic drugs) illegally ▶ *n* **6** the act of pushing; thrust **7** *informal* drive or determination: *everything depends on him having the push to obtain the money* **8** *informal* a special effort to achieve something: *when this push spent itself it was obvious the bid had failed* **9 the push** *Brit & NZ informal* dismissal from employment

> **push** *vb* **1** = shove, force, press, thrust, drive, knock, sweep, plunge; ≠ pull **2** = make *or* force your way, move, shoulder, inch, squeeze, thrust, elbow, shove **4** = urge, encourage, persuade, spur, press, incite, impel; ≠ discourage ▶ *n* **6** = shove, thrust, butt, elbow, nudge; ≠ pull **7** = drive, go (*informal*), energy, initiative, enterprise, ambition, vitality, vigour **9 the push** = dismissal, the sack (*informal*), discharge, the boot (*slang*), your cards (*informal*)

pushchair *n Brit* a small folding chair on wheels in which a small child can be wheeled around: *escalators are difficult with pushchairs*

pusher *n informal* a person who sells illegal drugs

pushy *adj* **pushier, pushiest** *informal* offensively assertive or ambitious

pusillanimous *adj formal* timid and cowardly: *pusillanimous behaviour* > **pusillanimity** *n*

puss *n* **1** *informal* a cat **2** *slang* a girl or woman

pussy[1] *n, pl* **pussies 1** Also called: **pussycat** *informal* a cat **2** *vulgar slang* the female genitals

pussy[2] *adj* **-sier, -siest** containing or full of pus

pussyfoot *vb informal* **1** to move about stealthily **2** to avoid committing oneself: *don't let's pussyfoot about naming the hit man*

pustule *n* a small inflamed raised area of skin containing pus > **pustular** *adj*

put *vb* **putting, put 1** to cause to be (in a position or place): *he put the book on the table* **2** to cause to be (in a state or condition): *what can be done to put things right?* **3** to lay (blame, emphasis, etc.) on a person or thing: *don't try to put the blame on someone* *else!* **4** to set or commit (to an action, task, or duty), esp. by force: *she put him to work weeding the garden* **5** to estimate or judge: *I wouldn't put him in the same class as Verdi as a composer* **6** (foll. by *to*) to utilize: *he put his culinary skills to good use when he opened a restaurant* **7** to express: *he didn't put it quite as crudely as that* **8** to make (an end or limit): *opponents claim the scheme will put an end to much of the sailing and boating in the area* **9** to present for consideration; propose: *he put the question to the committee* **10** to invest (money) in or expend (time or energy) on: *they put a lot of money into the sport* **11** to throw or cast: *put the shot* ▸ *n* **12** a throw, esp. in putting the shot ▸ See also **put across** *etc.*

put *vb* **1** = place, leave, set, position, rest, park (*informal*), plant, lay **7** = express, state, word, phrase, utter

put across *vb* to communicate successfully: *he's not very good at putting his ideas across*. Also: **put over**

put across *vb* put something across or over = communicate, explain, convey, make clear, get across, make yourself understood

putative (pew-tat-iv) *adj formal* **1** commonly regarded as being: *the desire of the putative father to establish his possible paternity* **2** considered to exist or have existed; inferred: *a putative earlier form*

put off *vb* **1** to postpone: *ministers have put off making a decision until next month* **2** to evade (a person) by delay: *they tried to put him off, but he came anyway* **3** to cause dislike in: *he was put off by her appearance* **4** to cause to lose interest in: *the accident put him off sailing* **5** to distract: *a swerving cyclist may have put off the driver*

put off *vb* **1** put something off = postpone, delay, defer, adjourn, hold over, put on the back burner (*informal*), take a rain check on (*US, Canad informal*) **4** put someone off = discourage, intimidate, deter, daunt, dissuade, demoralize, scare off, dishearten **5** put someone off = disconcert, confuse, unsettle, throw (*informal*), dismay, perturb, faze, discomfit

putrefy *vb* **-fies**, **-fying**, **-fied** *formal* (of organic matter) to rot and produce an offensive smell > **putrefaction** *n*

putrescent *adj formal* becoming putrid; rotting: *putrescent toadstools* > **putrescence** *n*

putrid *adj* **1** (of organic matter) rotting: *putrid meat* **2** sickening or foul: *a putrid stench* **3** *informal* deficient in quality or value: *a penchant for putrid puns* **4** morally corrupt > **putridity** *n*

putsch *n* a violent and sudden political revolt: *an attempted putsch against the general*

putt *golf* ▸ *n* **1** a stroke on the green with a putter to roll the ball into or near the hole ▸ *vb* **2** to strike (the ball) in this way

putter *n golf* a club, usually with a short shaft, for putting

putty *n, pl* **-ties** **1** a stiff paste used to fix glass into frames and fill cracks in woodwork ▸ *vb* **-ties**, **-tying**, **-tied** **2** to fix or fill with putty

put up *vb* **1** to build or erect: *I want to put up a fence round the garden* **2** to display (a poster, sign, etc.) **3** to accommodate or be accommodated at: *can you put me up for tonight?* **4** to increase (prices) **5** to submit (a plan, case, etc.) **6** to offer: *the factory is being put up for sale* **7** to give: *they put up a good fight* **8** to provide (money) for: *they put up 35% of the film's budget* **9** to nominate or be nominated as a candidate: *the party have yet to decide whether to put up a candidate* **10** **put up to** to incite to: *I wonder who put them up to it?* **11** **put up with** *informal* to endure or tolerate ▸ *adj* **put-up** **12** *informal* dishonestly or craftily prearranged: *a put-up job*

put up *vb* **1** put something up = build, raise, set up, construct, erect, fabricate **3** put someone up = accommodate, house, board, lodge, quarter, take someone in, billet **5** put something up = offer, present, mount, put forward **9** put someone up = nominate, put forward, offer, present, propose, recommend, submit

puzzle *vb* **-zling**, **-zled** **1** to baffle or bewilder **2** **puzzle out** to solve (a problem) by mental effort **3** **puzzle over** to think deeply about in an attempt to understand: *he puzzled over the squiggles and curves on the paper* ▸ *n* **4** a problem that cannot be easily solved **5** a toy, game, or question presenting a problem that requires skill or ingenuity for its solution > **puzzlement** *n* > **puzzled** *adj* > **puzzler** *n* > **puzzling** *adj*

puzzle *vb* **1** = perplex, confuse, baffle, stump, bewilder, confound, mystify, faze ▸ *n* **4** = mystery, problem, paradox, enigma, conundrum **5** = problem, riddle, question, conundrum, poser

PVC polyvinyl chloride

pygmy *n, pl* **-mies** **1** something that is a very small example of its type **2** an abnormally undersized person **3** a person of little importance or significance ▸ *adj* **4** very small: *the pygmy anteater*

Pygmy *n, pl* **-mies** a member of one of the very short peoples of Equatorial Africa

pyjamas *or US* **pajamas** *pl n* a loose-fitting jacket or top and trousers worn to sleep in

pylon *n* **1** *chiefly Brit* a large vertical steel tower-like structure supporting high-tension electrical cables **2** *US & Canad* a plastic cone used to demarcate areas, esp. on public roads

pyramid *n* **1** a huge stone building with a square base and four sloping triangular sides meeting in a point, such as the royal tombs built by the ancient Egyptians **2** *maths* a solid figure with a polygonal base and triangular sides that meet in a common vertex > **pyramidal** *adj*

pyre *n* a pile of wood for cremating a corpse

Pyrex *n trademark* a variety of heat-resistant glassware used in cookery and chemical apparatus

pyromania *n psychiatry* the uncontrollable impulse and practice of setting things on fire > **pyromaniac** *n, adj*

pyrotechnics *n* **1** the art of making fireworks **2** a firework display **3** a brilliant display of skill: *all those courtroom pyrotechnics* > **pyrotechnic** *adj*

Pyrrhic victory (pir-ik) *n* a victory in which the victor's losses are as great as those of the defeated

python *n* a large nonpoisonous snake of Australia, Africa, and S Asia which kills its prey by crushing it with its body

Qq

QC 1 Queen's Counsel **2** Quebec

QED which was to be shown or proved

QLD *or* **Qld** Queensland

QM Quartermaster

qr. *pl* **qrs 1** quarter **2** quire

QR code *n* a type of bar code that can be read both horizontally and vertically

qt *pl* **qt** *or* **qts** quart

qua (kwah) *prep* in the capacity of; by virtue of being

quack¹ *vb* **1** (of a duck) to utter a harsh guttural sound **2** to make a noise like a duck ▶ *n* **3** the sound made by a duck

quack² *n* **1** an unqualified person who claims medical knowledge **2** *Brit, Austral & NZ informal* a doctor > **quackery** *n*

quad¹ *n* short for **quadrangle** (sense 1)

quad² *n informal* a quadruplet

quad bike *or* **quad** *n* a vehicle like a small motorcycle, with four large wheels, designed for agricultural and sporting uses

quadrangle *n* **1** a rectangular courtyard with buildings on all four sides **2** *geom* a figure consisting of four points connected by four lines > **quadrangular** *adj*

quadrant *n* **1** *geom* **A** a quarter of the circumference of a circle **B** the area enclosed by two perpendicular radii of a circle **2** a piece of a mechanism in the form of a quarter circle **3** an instrument formerly used in astronomy and navigation for measuring the altitudes of stars

quadraphonic *adj* using four independent channels to reproduce or record sound > **quadraphonics** *n*

quadratic *maths* ▶ *n* **1** Also called: **quadratic equation** an equation in which the variable is raised to the power of two, but nowhere raised to a higher power: *solve the quadratic equation* $2x^2-3x-6=3$ ▶ *adj* **2** of or relating to the second power

quadrennial *adj* **1** occurring every four years **2** lasting four years

quadri- *or before a vowel* **quadr-** *combining form* four: *quadrilateral*

quadrilateral *adj* **1** having four sides ▶ *n* **2** a polygon with four sides

quadrille *n* **1** a square dance for four couples **2** music for this dance

quadriplegia (kwod-rip-**pleej**-ya) *n* paralysis of all four limbs > **quadriplegic** *adj, n*

quadruped (**kwod**-roo-ped) *n* an animal, esp. a mammal, that has four legs

quadruple vb **-pling, -pled 1** to multiply by four ▸ adj **2** four times as much or as many **3** consisting of four parts **4** music having four beats in each bar ▸ n **5** a quantity or number four times as great as another

quadruplet n one of four children born at one birth

quaff (kwoff) vb old-fashioned to drink heartily or in one draught

quagmire (kwog-mire) n a soft wet area of land that gives way under the feet; bog

quail[1] n, pl **quails** or **quail** a small game bird of the partridge family

quail[2] vb to shrink back with fear; cower

quaint adj attractively unusual, esp. in an old-fashioned style

quake vb **quaking, quaked 1** to shake or tremble with or as if with fear **2** to shudder because of instability ▸ n **3** informal an earthquake

> **quake** vb = shake, tremble, quiver, move, rock, shiver, shudder, vibrate

Quaker n a member of a Christian sect, the Religious Society of Friends > **Quakerism** n

qualification n **1** an official record of achievement awarded on the successful completion of a course of training or passing of an examination **2** an ability, quality, or attribute, esp. one that fits a person to perform a particular job or task **3** a condition that modifies or limits; restriction **4** the act of qualifying or being qualified

> **qualification** n **2** = eligibility, quality, ability, skill, fitness, attribute, capability, aptitude **3** = condition, proviso, requirement, rider, reservation, limitation, modification, caveat

qualified adj **1** having successfully completed a training course or passed the exams necessary in order to be entitled to work in a particular profession: a qualified lawyer **2** having the abilities, qualities, or attributes necessary to perform a particular job or task **3** having completed a training or degree course and gained the relevant certificates **4** limited or restricted; not wholehearted: the mission was only a qualified success

> **qualified** adj **1, 2, 3** = capable, trained, experienced, seasoned, able, fit, expert, chartered; ≠ untrained **4** = restricted, limited, provisional, conditional, reserved, bounded, adjusted, moderated; ≠ unconditional

qualify vb **-fies, -fying, -fied 1** to have the abilities or attributes required in order to do or have something, such as a job: he qualified as a teacher; she did not qualify for a State pension at that time **2** to moderate or restrict (a statement one has made) **3** to describe or be described as having a particular quality: it was neither witty nor subtle

enough to qualify as a spoof **4** to be successful in one stage of a competition and as a result progress to the next stage: Lewis failed to qualify for the semi-final **5** grammar to modify the sense of (a word) > **qualifier** n

> **qualify** vb **2** = restrict, limit, reduce, ease, moderate, regulate, diminish, temper

qualitative adj involving or relating to distinctions based on quality

quality n, pl **-ties 1** degree or standard of excellence **2** a distinguishing characteristic or attribute **3** the basic character or nature of something **4** a feature of personality **5** (formerly) high social status ▸ adj **6** excellent or superior: a quality product

> **quality** n **1** = excellence, status, merit, position, value, worth, distinction, virtue **2, 4** = characteristic, feature, attribute, point, side, mark, property, aspect **3** = nature, character, make, sort, kind

quality assurance n commerce the process of verifying that a product conforms to required standards, often performed by an independent assessor

qualm (kwahm) n **1** a pang of conscience; scruple **2** a sudden sensation of misgiving **3** a sudden feeling of sickness or nausea

quandary n, pl **-ries** a situation in which it is difficult to decide what to do; predicament; dilemma

quandong (kwon-dong) n **1** a small Australian tree with edible fruit and nuts used in preserves **2** an Australian tree with pale timber

quango n, pl **-gos** a semipublic government-financed administrative body whose members are appointed by the government

quantify vb **-fies, -fying, -fied** to discover or express the quantity of > **quantifiable** adj > **quantification** n

quantitative adj **1** involving considerations of amount or size **2** capable of being measured

quantitative easing or **quantitive easing** n the practice of increasing the supply of money in order to stimulate economic activity

quantity n, pl **-ties 1** a specified or definite amount or number **2** the aspect of anything that can be measured, weighed, or counted **3** a large amount **4** maths an entity having a magnitude that may be denoted by a numerical expression

> **quantity** n **1** = amount, lot, total, sum, part, number **2** = size, measure, mass, volume, length, capacity, extent, bulk

quantity surveyor n a person who estimates the cost of the materials and labour necessary for a construction job

quantum n, pl **-ta 1** an amount or quantity, esp. a specific amount **2** physics the smallest quantity of some physical property that a system can possess ▸ *adj* **3** of or designating a major breakthrough or sudden advance: *a quantum leap in business computing*

quantum theory *n* a theory concerning the behaviour of physical systems based on the idea that they can only possess certain properties, such as energy and angular momentum, in discrete amounts (quanta)

quarantine *n* **1** a period of isolation, esp. of people or animals arriving from abroad, to prevent the spread of disease ▸ *vb* **-tining, -tined** **2** to isolate in or as if in quarantine

quark *n physics* the hypothetical elementary particle supposed to be a fundamental unit of all baryons and mesons

quarrel *n* **1** an angry disagreement; argument **2** a cause of dispute; grievance ▸ *vb* **-relling, -relled** *or US* **-reling, -reled** (often foll. by *with*) **3** to engage in a disagreement or dispute; argue **4** to find fault; complain

> **quarrel** *n* **1** = disagreement, fight, row, argument, dispute, controversy, breach, contention, biffo (*Austral slang*); ≠ accord ▸ *vb* **3** = disagree, fight, argue, row, clash, dispute, differ, fall out (*informal*); ≠ get on *or* along (with)

quarrelsome *adj* inclined to quarrel or disagree

quarry¹ *n, pl* **-ries 1** a place where stone is dug from the surface of the earth ▸ *vb* **-ries, -rying, -ried 2** to extract (stone) from a quarry

quarry² *n, pl* **-ries 1** an animal that is being hunted; prey **2** anything pursued

> **quarry** *n* = prey, victim, game, goal, aim, prize, objective

quart *n* a unit of liquid measure equal to one quarter of a gallon or two pints (1.136 litres)

quarter *n* **1** one of four equal parts of something such as an object or quantity **2** the fraction equal to one divided by four ($\frac{1}{4}$) **3** a fourth part of a year; three months **4** *Brit informal* a unit of weight equal to four ounces (113.4 grams) **5** a region or district of a town or city: *the French quarter of New Orleans* **6** a region, direction, or point of the compass **7** *US & Canad* a coin worth 25 cents **8** *astron* **A** one fourth of the moon's period of revolution around the earth **B** either of two phases of the moon when half of the lighted surface is visible **9** (*sometimes pl*) an unspecified person or group of people: *it met stiff opposition in some quarters* **10** mercy or pity shown to a defeated opponent: *no quarter was asked or given* **11** any of the four limbs of a quadruped ▸ *vb* **12** to divide into four equal parts **13** (*formerly*) to dismember (a human body) **14** to billet or be billeted in lodgings **15** *heraldry* to divide (a shield) into four separate bearings ▸ *adj* **16** being or consisting of one of four equal parts

> **quarter** *n* **5** = district, region, neighbourhood, place, part, side, area, zone **10** = mercy, pity, compassion, charity, sympathy, tolerance, kindness, forgiveness ▸ *vb* **14** = accommodate, house, lodge, place, board, post, station, billet

quarter day *n Brit* any of four days in the year when certain payments become due

quarterdeck *n naut* the rear part of the upper deck of a ship, traditionally for official or ceremonial use

quarter-final *n* the round before the semi-final in a competition

quarterly *adj* **1** occurring, done, due, or issued at intervals of three months ▸ *n, pl* **-lies 2** a periodical issued every three months ▸ *adv* **3** once every three months

quartermaster *n* **1** a military officer responsible for accommodation, food, and equipment **2** a naval officer responsible for navigation

quartet *n* **1** a group of four singers or instrumentalists **2** a piece of music for four performers **3** any group of four

quarto *n, pl* **-tos** a book size resulting from folding a sheet of paper into four leaves or eight pages

quartz *n* a hard glossy mineral consisting of crystalline silicon dioxide

quasar (kway-zar) *n* any of a class of extremely distant starlike objects that are powerful sources of radio waves and other forms of energy

quash *vb* **1** to officially reject (something, such as a judgment or decision) as invalid **2** to defeat or suppress forcefully and completely

> **quash** *vb* **1** = annul, overturn, reverse, cancel, overthrow, revoke, overrule, rescind **2** = suppress, crush, put down, beat, overthrow, squash, subdue, repress

quasi- (kway-zie) *combining form* **1** almost but not really; seemingly: *a quasi-religious cult* **2** resembling but not actually being; so-called: *a quasi-scholar*

quatrain *n* a stanza or poem of four lines

quaver *vb* **1** (esp. of the voice) to quiver or tremble **2** to say or sing (something) with a trembling voice ▸ *n* **3** *music* a note having the time value of an eighth of a semibreve **4** a tremulous sound or note ⟩ **quavering** *adj*

quay (kee) *n* a wharf built parallel to the shoreline

queasy *adj* **-sier, -siest 1** having the feeling that one is about to vomit; nauseous **2** feeling or causing uneasiness ⟩ **queasily** *adv* ⟩ **queasiness** *n*

queen *n* **1** a female sovereign who is the official ruler or head of state **2** the wife of a king **3** a woman, thing, or place considered the best or most important of her or its kind: *the rose is considered the queen of garden flowers* **4** *offensive slang* an effeminate homosexual man **5** the only fertile female in a colony of bees, wasps, or ants **6** a playing card with a picture of a queen on it **7** a chess piece, able to move in a straight line in any direction ▸ *vb* **8** *chess* to promote (a pawn) to a queen when it reaches the eighth rank **9 queen it** *informal* to behave in an overbearing manner: *she is more beautiful than ever and still queening it over everybody* ▷ **queenly** *adj*

> **queen** *n* **1, 2** = sovereign, ruler, monarch, leader, Crown, princess, majesty, head of state **3** = leading light, star, favourite, celebrity, darling, mistress, big name

Queen's Counsel *n* **1** (in Britain, Australia, and New Zealand) a barrister or advocate appointed Counsel to the Crown **2** (in Canada and New Zealand) an honorary title bestowed on a lawyer with long experience

queer *adj* **1** not normal or usual; odd or strange **2** dubious; shady **3** *Brit* faint, giddy, or queasy **4** *informal, sometimes offensive* not heterosexual **5** *informal* eccentric or slightly mad ▸ *n* **6** *informal, sometimes offensive* a person who is not heterosexual ▸ *vb* **7 queer someone's pitch** *informal* to spoil or thwart someone's chances of something

> **queer** *adj* **1, 2** = strange, odd, funny, unusual, extraordinary, curious, weird, peculiar; ≠ normal **3** = faint, dizzy, giddy, queasy, light-headed

quell *vb* **1** to suppress (rebellion or unrest); subdue **2** to overcome or allay

quench *vb* **1** to satisfy (one's thirst) **2** to put out; extinguish **3** to suppress or subdue **4** *metallurgy* to cool (hot metal) by plunging it into cold water

quern *n* a stone hand mill for grinding corn

querulous (kwer-yew-luss) *adj* complaining; whining or peevish ▷ **querulously** *adv*

query *n, pl* **-ries 1** a question, esp. one expressing doubt **2** a question mark ▸ *vb* **-ries, -rying, -ried 3** to express uncertainty, doubt, or an objection concerning (something) **4** to express as a query; ask

> **query** *n* **1** = question, inquiry, enquiry, problem ▸ *vb* **3** = question, challenge, doubt, suspect, dispute, object to, distrust, mistrust **4** = ask, inquire *or* enquire, question

quest *n* **1** a looking for or seeking; search **2** the object of a search; a goal or target ▸ *vb* **3 quest for** to go in search of **4** (of dogs) to search for game

> **quest** *n* **1** = search, hunt, mission, enterprise, crusade

question *n* **1** a form of words addressed to a person in order to obtain an answer; interrogative sentence **2** a point at issue: *they were silent on the question of social justice* **3** a difficulty or uncertainty **4 A** an act of asking **B** an

investigation into some problem **5** a motion presented for debate **6 beyond (all) question** beyond (any) doubt **7 call something into question A** to make something the subject of disagreement **B** to cast doubt upon the validity or truth of something **8 in question** under discussion: *the area in question was not contaminated* **9 out of the question** beyond consideration; impossible ▸ *vb* **10** to put a question or questions to (a person); interrogate **11** to make (something) the subject of dispute **12** to express uncertainty; doubt

> **question** *n* **1** = inquiry, enquiry, query, investigation, examination, interrogation; ≠ answer **2** = issue, point, matter, subject, problem, debate, proposal, theme **3** = difficulty, problem, doubt, argument, dispute, controversy, query, contention **9 out of the question** = impossible, unthinkable, inconceivable, not on (*informal*), hopeless, unimaginable, unworkable, unattainable ▸ *vb* **10** = interrogate, cross-examine, interview, examine, probe, quiz, ask questions **11, 12** = dispute, challenge, doubt, suspect, oppose, query, mistrust, disbelieve; ≠ accept

questionable *adj* **1** (esp. of a person's morality or honesty) doubtful **2** of disputable value or authority ▷ **questionably** *adv*

> **questionable** *adj* = dubious, suspect, doubtful, controversial, suspicious, dodgy (*Brit, Austral, NZ informal*), debatable, moot, shonky (*Austral, NZ informal*); ≠ indisputable

question mark *n* **1** the punctuation mark (?), used at the end of questions **2** a doubt or uncertainty: *a question mark still hangs over their success*

questionnaire *n* a set of questions on a form, used to collect statistical information or opinions from people

> **questionnaire** *n* = set of questions, form, survey form, question sheet

queue *n* **1** a line of people or vehicles waiting for something ▸ *vb* **queuing** *or* **queueing, queued 2** (often foll. by *up*) to form or remain in a line while waiting

> **queue** *n* = line, row, file, train, series, chain, string, column

quibble *vb* **-bling, -bled 1** to make trivial objections ▸ *n* **2** a trivial objection or equivocation, esp. one used to avoid an issue **3** *archaic* a pun

quiche (keesh) *n* a savoury flan with an egg custard filling to which cheese, bacon, or vegetables are added

quick *adj* **1** characterized by rapidity of movement or action; fast **2** lasting or taking a short time **3** immediate or prompt: *her quick*

q

action minimized the damage **4** eager or ready to perform (an action): *quick to condemn* **5** responsive to stimulation; alert; lively: *they were impressed by his quick mind* **6** easily excited or aroused: *he is impulsive and has a quick temper* **7** nimble in one's movements or actions; deft: *she has quick hands* ▸ *n* **8** any area of sensitive flesh, esp. that under a nail **9 cut someone to the quick** to hurt someone's feelings deeply **10 the quick** *archaic* living people ▸ *adv* **11** in a rapid manner; swiftly > **quickly** *adv* > **quickness** *n*

quick *adj* **1** = fast, swift, speedy, express, cracking (*Brit informal*), smart, rapid, fleet; ≠ slow **2** = brief, passing, hurried, flying, fleeting, summary, lightning, short-lived; ≠ long **3** = immediate, instant, prompt, sudden, abrupt, instantaneous **4, 6** = excitable, passionate, irritable, touchy, irascible, testy; ≠ calm **5** = intelligent, bright, alert, sharp, acute, smart, clever, shrewd; ≠ stupid

quicken *vb* **1** to make or become faster; accelerate **2** to impart to or receive vigour or enthusiasm: *science quickens the imagination* **3 A** (of a fetus) to begin to show signs of life **B** (of a pregnant woman) to reach the stage of pregnancy at which movements of the fetus can be felt

quicken *vb* **1** = speed up, hurry, accelerate, hasten, gee up (*informal*) **2** = stimulate, inspire, arouse, excite, revive, incite, energize, invigorate

quicklime *n* a white caustic solid, mainly composed of calcium oxide, used in the manufacture of glass and steel

quicksand *n* a deep mass of loose wet sand that submerges anything on top of it

quicksilver *n* the metal mercury

quickstep *n* **1** a modern ballroom dance in rapid quadruple time **2** music for this dance

quid *n*, *pl* **quid** *Brit slang* **1** a pound (sterling) **2 be quids in** to be in a very favourable or advantageous position

quid pro quo *n*, *pl* **quid pro quos** one thing, esp. an advantage or object, given in exchange for another

quiescent (kwee-ess-ent) *adj formal* quiet, inactive, or dormant > **quiescence** *n*

quiet *adj* **1** characterized by an absence of noise **2** calm or tranquil: *the sea is quiet today* **3** untroubled: *a quiet life* **4** not busy: *business is quiet this morning* **5** private or secret: *I had a quiet word with her* **6** free from anger, impatience, or other extreme emotion **7** not showy: *quiet colours; a quiet wedding* **8** modest or reserved: *quiet humour* ▸ *n* **9** the state of being silent, peaceful, or untroubled **10 on the quiet** without other people knowing ▸ *vb* **11** to make or become calm or silent > **quietly** *adv* > **quietness** *n*

quiet *adj* **1** = soft, low, muted, lowered, whispered, faint, suppressed, stifled; ≠ loud **2, 6** = calm, peaceful, tranquil, mild, serene, placid, restful, chilled (*informal*); ≠ exciting **3** = still, calm, peaceful, tranquil; ≠ troubled **8** = reserved, retiring, shy, gentle, mild, sedate, meek; ≠ excitable ▸ *n* **9** = peace, rest, tranquillity, ease, silence, solitude, serenity, stillness; ≠ noise

quieten *vb* *Brit & NZ* **1** (often foll. by *down*) to make or become calm or silent **2** to allay (fear or doubts)

quietism *n* *formal* passivity and calmness of mind towards external events > **quietist** *n*, *adj*

quietude *n* *formal* quietness, peace, or tranquillity

quiff *n* *Brit* a tuft of hair brushed up above the forehead

quill *n* **1** Also called: **quill pen** a feather made into a pen **A** any of the large stiff feathers of the wing or tail of a bird **B** the hollow stem of a feather **3** any of the stiff hollow spines of a porcupine or hedgehog

quilt *n* **1** a cover for a bed, consisting of a soft filling sewn between two layers of material, usually with crisscross seams **2** a continental quilt; duvet ▸ *vb* **3** to stitch together two layers of (fabric) with padding between them > **quilted** *adj*

quilt *n* = bedspread, duvet, coverlet, eiderdown, counterpane, doona (*Austral*), continental quilt

quin *n* a quintuplet

quince *n* the acid-tasting pear-shaped fruit of an Asian tree, used in preserves

quinine *n* a bitter drug extracted from cinchona bark, used as a tonic and formerly in malaria therapy

quinquennial *adj* occurring once every five years or over a period of five years

quinsy *n* inflammation of the tonsils and throat, with abscesses

quintessence *n* **1** the perfect representation of a quality or state **2** an extract of a substance containing its central nature in its most concentrated form > **quintessential** *adj*

quintet *n* **1** a group of five singers or instrumentalists **2** a piece of music for five performers **3** any group of five

quintuplet *n* one of five children born at one birth

quip *n* **1** a witty saying ▸ *vb* **quipping**, **quipped** **2** to make a quip

quip *n* = joke, sally, jest, riposte, wisecrack (*informal*), retort, pleasantry, gibe

quire *n* a set of 24 or 25 sheets of paper

quirk *n* **1** a peculiarity of character; mannerism or foible **2** an unexpected twist or turn: *a strange quirk of fate* > **quirky** *adj*

quisling *n* a traitor who aids an occupying enemy force; collaborator

quit *vb* **quitting, quit 1** to stop (doing something) **2** to resign (from): *the Prime Minister's decision to quit*; *he quit his job as an editor* **3** to leave (a place) > **quitter** *n*

> **quit** *vb* **1** = stop, give up, cease, end, drop, abandon, halt, discontinue; ≠ continue **2** = resign (from), leave, retire (from), pull out (of), step down (from) (*informal*), abdicate **3** = leave, depart from, go out of, go away from, pull out from

quite *adv* **1** (*not used with a negative*) to a greater than average extent; somewhat: *he found her quite attractive* **2** absolutely: *you're quite right* **3** in actuality; truly **4 quite a** *or* **an** of an exceptional kind: *she is quite a girl* **5 quite something** a remarkable thing or person ▸ *interj* **6** an expression used to indicate agreement

> **quite** *adv* **1** = somewhat, rather, fairly, reasonably, relatively, moderately **2** = absolutely, perfectly, completely, totally, fully, entirely, wholly

quits *adj informal* **1** on an equal footing **2 call it quits** to end a dispute or contest, agreeing that honours are even

quiver¹ *vb* **1** to shake with a tremulous movement; tremble ▸ *n* **2** a shaking or trembling > **quivering** *adj*

quiver² *n* a case for holding or carrying arrows

quixotic (kwik-**sot**-ik) *adj* unrealistically optimistic or chivalrous > **quixotically** *adv*

quiz *n, pl* **quizzes 1** an entertainment in which the knowledge of the players is tested by a series of questions **2** any set of quick questions designed to test knowledge **3** an investigation by close questioning ▸ *vb* **quizzing, quizzed 4** to investigate by close questioning; interrogate

> **quiz** *n* **3** = examination, questioning, interrogation, interview, investigation, grilling (*informal*), cross-examination, cross-questioning ▸ *vb* = question, ask, interrogate, examine, investigate

quizzical *adj* questioning and mocking or supercilious: *the question elicits a quizzical expression* > **quizzically** *adv*

quoit *n* a large ring used in the game of quoits

quokka *n* a small Australian wallaby

quorum *n* the minimum number of members required to be present in a meeting or assembly before any business can be transacted

quota *n* **1** the share that is due from, due to, or allocated to a person or group **2** the prescribed number or quantity allowed, required, or admitted

> **quota** *n* = share, allowance, ration, part, limit, slice, quantity, portion

quotation *n* **1** a written or spoken passage repeated exactly in a later work, speech, or conversation, usually with an acknowledgment of its source **2** the act of quoting **3** an estimate of costs submitted by a contractor to a prospective client

> **quotation** *n* **1, 2** = passage, quote (*informal*), excerpt, reference, extract, citation **3** = estimate, price, tender, rate, cost, charge, figure, quote (*informal*)

quotation marks *pl n* the punctuation marks used to begin and end a quotation, either " and " or ' and '

quote *vb* **quoting, quoted 1** to repeat (words) exactly from (an earlier work, speech, or conversation), usually with an acknowledgment of their source **2** to state a price for goods or a job of work **3** to put quotation marks round (words) ▸ *n* **4** *informal* a quotation **5 quotes** *informal* quotation marks ▸ *interj* **6** an expression used to indicate that the words that follow are a quotation > **quotable** *adj*

> **quote** *vb* **1** = repeat, recite, recall

quoth *vb archaic* (foll. by *I, he* or *she*) said

quotidian *adj* **1** daily **2** *literary* commonplace **3** (esp. of fever) recurring daily

quotient *n* the result of the division of one number or quantity by another

q.v. (denoting a cross-reference) which (word, item, etc.) see

q

Rr

r 1 radius **2** ratio **3** right **4** *cricket* run(s)
R 1 *chem* radical **2** Regina **3** Registered
Trademark **4** *physics & electronics* resistance **5** Rex
6 River **7** *chess* rook
RA 1 rear admiral **2** (in Britain) Royal Academy
3 (in Britain) Royal Artillery
RAAF Royal Australian Air Force
rabbi (rab-bye) *n, pl* **-bis 1** the spiritual leader of
a Jewish congregation **2** an expert in or teacher
of Jewish Law ▸ **rabbinical** *adj*
rabbit *n, pl* **-bits** *or* **-bit 1** a common burrowing
mammal with long ears and a short fluffy tail
▸ *vb* **-biting, -bited 2** *informal* to talk too much: *he
keeps rabbiting on about interrogation*
rabble *n* **1** a disorderly crowd of noisy people
2 the rabble *derogatory* ordinary people
collectively
rabid *adj* **1** fanatical: *a rabid separatist* **2** having
rabies ▸ **rabidity** *n*
rabies (ray-beez) *n pathol* a fatal infectious viral
disease of the nervous system transmitted by
dogs and certain other animals
RAC (in Britain) Royal Automobile Club
raccoon *or* **racoon** *n, pl* **-coons** *or* **-coon** a small
American mammal with a long striped tail
race¹ *n* **1** a contest of speed **2** any competition
or rivalry: *the arms race* **3** a rapid current of water
4 a channel of a stream: *a mill race* **5** *Austral & NZ* a
narrow passage through which sheep pass
individually, as to a sheep dip ▸ *vb* **racing, raced
6** to take part in a contest of speed with
(someone) **7** to enter (an animal or vehicle) in a
race: *to race greyhounds* **8** to travel as fast as
possible **9** (of an engine) to run faster than
normal **10** (of the heart) to beat faster than
normal ▸ **racer** *n* ▸ **racing** *adj, n*

> **race** *n* **1** = competition, contest, chase, dash,
> pursuit **2** = contest, competition, rivalry ▸ *vb*
> **6** = compete, run, contend, take part in a race
> **8** = run, fly, career, speed, tear, dash, hurry,
> dart

race² *n* **1** a group of people of common ancestry
with distinguishing physical features, such as
skin colour or build **2 the human race** human
beings collectively **3** a group of animals or
plants having common characteristics that
distinguish them from other members of the
same species

> **race** *n* **1** = people, nation, blood, stock, type,
> folk, tribe

racecourse *n* a long broad track on which
horses are raced
racehorse *n* a horse specially bred for racing
raceme (rass-eem) *n botany* a cluster of flowers
along a central stem, as in the foxglove
racetrack *n* **1** a circuit used for races between
cars, bicycles, or runners **2** *US & Canad* a
racecourse
racial *adj* **1** relating to the division of the
human species into races **2** typically associated
with any such group ▸ **racially** *adv*

> **racial** *adj* **1** = ethnic, ethnological, national,
> folk, genetic, tribal, genealogical

racism *or* **racialism** *n* **1** hostile or oppressive
behaviour towards people because they belong
to a different race **2** the belief that some races
are innately superior to others because of
hereditary characteristics ▸ **racist** *or*
racialist *n, adj*
rack¹ *n* **1** a framework for holding particular
articles, such as coats or luggage **2** a straight
bar with teeth on its edge, to work with a
cogwheel **3 the rack** *history* an instrument of
torture that stretched the body of the victim ▸ *vb*
4 to cause great suffering to: *Italy was racked by
internal disputes* **5 rack one's brains** to try very
hard to think of something

> **rack** *n* **1** = frame, stand, structure, framework
> ▸ *vb* **4** = torture, torment, afflict, oppress,
> harrow, crucify, agonize, pain

rack² *n* **go to rack and ruin** to be destroyed
through neglect
racket¹ *n* **1** a noisy disturbance **2** an illegal
activity done to make money **3** *slang* a business
or occupation: *I've been in the racket since I was sixteen*
▸ *vb* **-eting, -eted 4** to make a commotion
▸ **rackety** *adj*

> **racket** *n* **1** = noise, row, fuss, disturbance,
> outcry, clamour, din, pandemonium **2** = fraud,
> scheme

racket² *or* **racquet** *n* a bat consisting of an oval
frame surrounding a mesh of strings, with a
handle, used in tennis, badminton, and squash.
See also **rackets**
racketeer *n* a person who makes money from
illegal activities ▸ **racketeering** *n*
rackets *n* a game similar to squash, played by
two or four people
raconteur (rak-on-tur) *n* a person skilled in
telling stories
racquet *n* same as **racket²**
racy *adj* **racier, raciest 1** slightly shocking:
a racy comedy **2** spirited or lively: *a racy literary style*
▸ **racily** *adv* ▸ **raciness** *n*
radar *n* **1** a method of detecting the
position and velocity of a distant object by
bouncing a narrow beam of extremely
high-frequency radio pulses off it **2** the
equipment used in this

radial *adj* **1** spreading out from a common central point **2** of a radius or ray **3** short for **radial-ply** ▸ *n* **4** a radial-ply tyre > **radially** *adv*

radial-ply *adj* (of a tyre) having the fabric cords in the outer casing running radially to enable the sidewalls to be flexible

radiant *adj* **1** characterized by health and happiness: *radiant good looks* **2** shining **3** emitted as radiation: *radiant heat* **4** sending out heat by radiation: *radiant heaters* > **radiance** *n*

radiate *vb* **-ating, -ated** **1** to spread out from a central point **2** to show (an emotion or quality) to a great degree: *she radiated competence and composure* **3** to emit or be emitted as radiation ▸ *adj* **4** having rays or a radial structure

> **radiate** *vb* **1** = spread out, diverge, branch out **2** = show, display, demonstrate, exhibit, emanate, give off *or* out **3** = shine, be diffused

radiation *n* **1** *physics* **A** the emission of energy as particles, electromagnetic waves or sound **B** the particles or waves emitted by radiating **2** the process of radiating

radiator *n* **1** *Brit* a device for heating a room or building, consisting of a series of pipes containing hot water **2** a device for cooling an internal-combustion engine, consisting of thin-walled tubes containing water **3** *Austral & NZ* an electric fire

radical *adj* **1** favouring fundamental change in political or social conditions: *a radical student movement* **2** of the essential nature of a person or thing; fundamental: *a radical fault* **3** searching or thorough: *a radical interpretation* **4** *maths* of or containing roots of numbers or quantities ▸ *n* **5** a person who favours fundamental change in existing institutions or in political, social, or economic conditions **6** *maths* a root of a number or quantity, such as $^3\sqrt{5}$, $\sqrt{x}$ **7** *chem* an atom or group of atoms that acts as a unit during chemical reactions > **radicalism** *n* > **radically** *adv*

> **radical** *adj* **1** = revolutionary, extremist, fanatical **2, 3** = fundamental, natural, basic, profound, innate, deep-seated; ≠ superficial ▸ *n* **5** = extremist, revolutionary, militant, fanatic; ≠ conservative

radicle *n* *botany* **A** the part of the embryo of seed-bearing plants that develops into the main root **B** a very small root or rootlike part

radii *n* a plural of **radius**

radio *n, pl* **-dios** **1** the use of electromagnetic waves for broadcasting or two-way communication without the use of linking wires **2** an electronic device for converting radio signals into sounds **3** a communications device for sending and receiving messages using radio waves **4** sound broadcasting ▸ *vb* **5** to transmit (a message) by radio ▸ *adj* **6** of, relating to, or using radio broadcasting or radio signals: *a radio interview* **7** using or producing electromagnetic

waves in the range used for radio signals: *radio astronomy*

radio- *combining form* **1** (denoting) radio: *radio-controlled* **2** (denoting) radioactivity or radiation: *radiocarbon*

radioactive *adj* showing or using radioactivity

radioactivity *n* the spontaneous emission of radiation from atomic nuclei. The radiation can consist of alpha or beta particles, or gamma rays

radiography (ray-dee-**og**-ra-fee) *n* the production of radiographs for use in medicine or industry > **radiographer** *n*

radiology (ray-dee-**ol**-a-jee) *n* the use of X-rays and radioactive substances in the diagnosis and treatment of disease > **radiologist** *n*

radiotherapy *n* the treatment of disease, esp. cancer, by radiation

radish *n* a small hot-flavoured red root vegetable eaten raw in salads

radium *n* *chem* a highly radioactive luminescent metallic element, found in pitchblende. Symbol: **Ra**

radius (ray-dee-**uss**) *n, pl* **-dii** (-dee-eye) *or* **-diuses** **1** a straight line joining the centre of a circle to any point on the circumference **2** the length of this line **3** *anatomy* the outer, slightly shorter of the two bones of the forearm **4** a circular area of a specified size round a central point: *within a seven-mile radius of the club*

radon (ray-don) *n* *chem* a colourless radioactive element of the noble gas group. Symbol: **Rn**

RAF (in Britain) Royal Air Force

raffia *n* a fibre obtained from the leaves of a palm tree, used for weaving

raffish *adj* unconventional or slightly disreputable

raffle *n* **1** a lottery, often to raise money for charity, in which the prizes are goods rather than money ▸ *vb* **-fling, -fled** **2** to offer as a prize in a raffle

raft *n* a floating platform of logs or planks tied together

rafter *n* any of the parallel sloping beams that form the framework of a roof

rag[1] *n* **1** a small piece of cloth **2** *Brit, Austral & NZ informal* a newspaper **3 rags** old tattered clothing **4 from rags to riches** from being extremely poor to being extremely wealthy

rag[2] *Brit* ▸ *vb* **ragging, ragged** **1** to tease **2** to play rough practical jokes on ▸ *n* **3** a boisterous practical joke ▸ *adj* **4** (in British universities and colleges) of various events organized to raise money for charity: *a rag week*

ragamuffin *n* a ragged dirty child

rage *n* **1** intense anger or passion **2** a fashion or craze: *the dance was the rage of Europe* **3** aggressive behaviour associated with a specified activity or environment: *road rage; school rage* **4 all the rage** *informal* very popular **5** *Austral & NZ informal* a dance or party ▸ *vb* **raging, raged** **6** to feel or show intense anger **7** to proceed violently and without restraint: *the argument was still raging*

r

rage n **1** = anger, passion, madness, wrath, ire; ≠ calmness **2** = craze, fashion, enthusiasm, vogue, fad (*informal*), latest thing ▶ vb **6** = be furious, blow up (*informal*), fume, lose it (*informal*), seethe, lose the plot (*informal*), go ballistic (*slang*), lose your temper; ≠ stay calm

ragged (rag-gid) *adj* **1** dressed in shabby or torn clothes **2** (of clothes) tattered and torn **3** having a rough or uneven surface or edge **4** neglected or untidy: *the ragged stone-built village*

ragged *adj* **1**, **2** = tatty (*Brit*), worn, torn, rundown, shabby, seedy, scruffy, in tatters; ≠ smart **3** = rough, rugged, unfinished, uneven, jagged, serrated

raglan *adj* **1** (of a sleeve) joined to the garment by diagonal seams from the collar to the underarm **2** (of a garment) with this style of sleeve

ragout (rag-goo) *n* a richly seasoned stew of meat and vegetables

ragtime *n* a style of jazz piano music with a syncopated melody

raid *n* **1** a sudden surprise attack: *a bombing raid* **2** a surprise visit by police searching for people or goods: *a drugs raid* ▶ vb **3** to make a raid on **4** to sneak into (a place) in order to steal ⊳ **raider** *n*

raid *n* **1** = attack, invasion, foray, sortie, incursion, sally, inroad **2** = bust (*informal*), swoop ▶ vb **3** = attack, invade, assault **4** = steal from, plunder, pillage, sack

rail[1] *n* **1** a horizontal bar supported by vertical posts, used as a fence or barrier **2** a horizontal bar on which to hang things: *a curtain rail* **3** one of a pair of parallel bars that serve as a running surface for the wheels of a train **4** railway: *by car or by rail* **5** **go off the rails** to start behaving improperly or eccentrically ▶ vb **6** to fence (an area) with rails

rail[2] *vb* **rail against** *or* **at** to complain bitterly or loudly about

rail[3] *n* a small wading marsh bird

railing *n* a fence made of rails supported by posts

railing *n* = fence, rails, barrier, paling, balustrade

raillery *n, pl* **-leries** good-natured teasing

railway *n* **1** a track composed of a line of parallel metal rails fixed to sleepers, on which trains run **2** any track on which the wheels of a vehicle may run: *a cable railway* **3** the rolling stock, buildings, and tracks used in such a transport system **4** the organization responsible for operating a railway network

raiment *n archaic or poetic* clothing

rain *n* **1** **A** water falling from the sky in drops formed by the condensation of water vapour in the atmosphere **B** a fall of rain. ▶ Related adjective: **pluvial 2** a large quantity of anything

falling rapidly: *a rain of stones descended on the police* **3** **(come) rain or shine** regardless of circumstances **4** **right as rain** *informal* perfectly all right ▶ vb **5** to fall as rain: *it's raining back home* **6** to fall rapidly and in large quantities: *steel rungs and sawdust raining down* **7** **rained off** cancelled or postponed because of rain. US and Canad term: **rained out** ⊳ **rainy** *adj*

rain *n* **1A** = rainfall, fall, showers, deluge, drizzle, downpour, raindrops, cloudburst ▶ vb **5** = pour, pelt (down), teem, bucket down (*informal*), drizzle, come down in buckets (*informal*) **6** = fall, shower, be dropped, sprinkle, be deposited

rainbow *n* an arched display in the sky of the colours of the spectrum, caused by the refraction and reflection of the sun's rays through rain

rainbow nation *n* the South African nation

raincoat *n* a coat made of a waterproof material

rainfall *n* the amount of rain, hail, or snow in a specified place and time

rainforest *n* dense forest found in tropical areas of heavy rainfall

raise *vb* **raising, raised 1** to lift to a higher position or level **2** to place in an upright position **3** to increase in amount, quality, or intensity: *to raise interest rates* **4** to collect or gather together: *to raise additional capital; to raise an army* **5** to cause to be expressed: *to raise a smile* **6** to stir up **7** to bring up: *to raise a family* **8** to grow: *to raise a crop* **9** to put forward for consideration: *they raised controversial issues* **10** to arouse from sleep or death **11** to build: *to raise a barn* **12** to bring to an end: *to raise a siege* **13** to establish radio communications with: *we raised Moscow last night* **14** to advance in rank; promote **15** *maths* to multiply (a number) by itself a specified number of times: *8 is 2 raised to the power 3* **16** to cause (dough) to rise, as by the addition of yeast **17** *cards* to bet more than (the previous player) **18** **raise Cain A** to create a disturbance **B** to protest vehemently ▶ *n* **19** *US, Canad & NZ* an increase in pay

raise *vb* **1** = lift, elevate, uplift, heave **2** = set upright, lift, elevate **3** = increase, intensify, heighten, advance, boost, strengthen, enhance, enlarge; ≠ reduce **4** = collect, gather, obtain **5** = cause, start, produce, create, occasion (*formal*), provoke, originate, engender **7** = bring up, develop, rear, nurture **9** = put forward, suggest, introduce, advance, broach, moot **11** = build, construct, put up, erect; ≠ demolish

raisin *n* a dried grape

raison d'être (ray-zon det-ra) *n, pl* **raisons d'être** (ray-zon **det**-ra) reason or justification for existence

Raj *n* **the Raj** the British government in India before 1947

raja or **rajah** n history an Indian prince or ruler

rake¹ n **1** a farm or garden tool consisting of a row of teeth set in a headpiece attached to a long shaft and used for gathering leaves or straw, or for smoothing loose earth **2** any of various implements similar in shape or function ▸ vb **raking**, **raked 3** to scrape or gather with a rake **4** to smooth (a surface) with a rake **5** Also: **rake out** to clear (ashes) from (a fire) **6 rake together** or **up** to gather (items or people) with difficulty, as from a limited supply **7** to search or examine carefully: raking over the past is not always popular **8** to direct (gunfire) along the length of (a target): the machine guns raked up and down their line **9** to scrape or graze: he raked the tip of his shoe across the pavement ▸ See also **rake-off** etc.

rake vb **3** = gather, collect, remove **7** = search, comb, scour, scrutinize, fossick (Austral, NZ)

rake² n an immoral man

rake n = libertine, playboy, swinger (slang), lecher, roué, debauchee; ≠ puritan

rake-off n slang a share of profits, esp. an illegal one

rake up vb to bring back memories of (a forgotten unpleasant event): she doesn't want to rake up the past

rakish (ray-kish) adj dashing or jaunty: a hat which he wore at a rakish angle

rally n, pl **-lies 1** a large gathering of people for a meeting **2** a marked recovery of strength, as during illness **3** Stock Exchange a sharp increase in price or trading activity after a decline **4** tennis & squash etc. an exchange of several shots before one player wins the point **5** a car-driving competition on public roads ▸ vb **-lies**, **-lying**, **-lied 6** to bring or come together after being dispersed **7** to bring or come together for a common cause **8** to summon up (one's strength or spirits) **9** to recover (sometimes only temporarily) from an illness **10** Stock Exchange to increase sharply after a decline

rally n **1** = gathering, convention, meeting, congress, assembly, hui (NZ) **2** = recovery, improvement, revival, recuperation; ≠ relapse ▸ vb **6,7** = gather together, unite, regroup, reorganize, reassemble **9** = recover, improve, revive, get better, recuperate; ≠ get worse

ram n **1** an uncastrated adult male sheep **2** a hydraulically or pneumatically driven piston **3** the falling weight of a pile driver **4** short for **battering ram** ▸ vb **ramming**, **rammed 5** to strike against with force **6** to force or drive: he rammed his sword into the man's belly **7** to stuff or cram **8 ram something home** to make something clear or obvious: to ram home the message **9 ram something down someone's throat** to put forward or emphasize an argument or idea with excessive force

ram vb **5** = hit, force, drive into, crash, impact, smash, dash, butt **6,7** = cram, force, stuff, jam, thrust

RAM computers random access memory: a temporary storage space which loses its contents when the computer is switched off

Ramadan n **1** the ninth month of the Muslim year, 29 or 30 days long, during which strict fasting is observed from dawn to sunset **2** the fast itself

ramble vb **-bling**, **-bled 1** to walk for relaxation, sometimes with no particular direction **2** to speak or write in a confused style **3** to grow or develop in a random fashion ▸ n **4** a walk, esp. in the countryside

ramble vb **1** = walk, range, wander, stroll, stray, roam, rove, saunter, go walkabout (Austral) **2** = babble, rabbit (on) (Brit informal), waffle (informal, chiefly Brit), witter on (informal) ▸ n = walk, tour, stroll, hike, roaming, roving, saunter

rambler n **1** a person who takes country walks **2** a climbing rose

ramekin (ram-ik-in) n a small container for baking and serving one portion of food

ramp n **1** a slope that joins two surfaces at different levels **2** a place where the level of a road surface changes because of roadworks **3** a movable stairway by which passengers enter and leave an aircraft **4** Brit a small hump on a road to make traffic slow down

ramp n **1** = slope, incline, gradient, rise

rampage vb **-paging**, **-paged 1** to rush about violently ▸ n **2 on the rampage** behaving violently or destructively

rampage vb = go berserk, storm, rage, run riot, run amok ▸ n **on the rampage** = berserk, wild, violent, raging, out of control, amok, riotous, berko (Austral slang)

rampant adj **1** growing or spreading uncontrollably **2** heraldry (of a beast) standing on the hind legs, the right foreleg raised above the left: a lion rampant

rampant adj **1** = widespread, prevalent, rife, uncontrolled, unchecked, unrestrained, profuse, spreading like wildfire **2** = upright, standing, rearing, erect

rampart n a mound of earth or a wall built to protect a fort or city

ramshackle adj badly made or cared for: a curious ramshackle building

ran vb the past tense of **run**

ranch n **1** a large cattle farm in the American West **2** chiefly US & Canad a large farm for the rearing of a particular kind of livestock or crop: they owned a sheep ranch in Montana ▸ vb **3** to run a ranch ▸ **rancher** n

r

rancid *adj* (of fatty foods) stale and having an offensive smell > **rancidity** *n*

rancour *or US* **rancor** *n* deep bitter hate > **rancorous** *adj*

rand *n* the standard monetary unit of the Republic of South Africa

R & D research and development

random *adj* **1** lacking any definite plan or prearranged order: *a random sample* **2** *informal* unknown or unspecified: *some random guy* ▸ *n* **3** *informal* an unknown or unspecified person **4 at random** not following any prearranged order > **randomly** *adv* > **randomness** *n*

> **random** *adj* 1 = casual; ≠ planned ▸ *n* 4 **at random** = haphazardly, randomly, arbitrarily, by chance, willy-nilly, unsystematically

randy *adj* **randier**, **randiest** *informal* sexually aroused > **randily** *adv* > **randiness** *n*

> **randy** *adj* = lustful, hot, turned-on (*slang*), aroused, horny (*slang*), amorous, lascivious

rang *vb* the past tense of **ring¹**

range *n* **1** the limits within which a person or thing can function effectively: *academic ability range* **2** ʌ the maximum effective distance of a projectile fired from a weapon ʙ the distance between a target and a weapon **3** the total distance which a ship, aircraft, or vehicle can travel without taking on fresh fuel **4** the difference in pitch between the highest and lowest note of a voice or musical instrument **5** a whole set of related things: *a range of treatments was available* **6** the total products of a manufacturer, designer, or stockist: *the latest skin-care range* **7** the limits within which something can lie: *a range of prices* **8** *US & Canad* an extensive tract of open land on which livestock can graze **9** a chain of mountains **10** an area set aside for shooting practice or rocket testing **11** a large cooking stove with one or more ovens **12** *maths* the set of values that a function or variable can take ▸ *vb* **ranging**, **ranged 13** to vary between one point and another **14** to cover a specified period or specified things: *attitudes ranged from sympathy to indifference* **15** to roam (over) **16** to establish or be situated in a line or series **17** to put into a specific category: *they ranged themselves with the opposition*

> **range** *n* 1,7 = limits, reach 5 = series, variety, selection, assortment, lot, collection, gamut ▸ *vb* 13 = vary, run, reach (*informal*), extend, stretch 15 = roam, wander, rove, ramble, traverse

rangefinder *n* an instrument for finding how far away an object is

ranger *n* **1** an official in charge of a park or nature reserve **2** *US* an armed trooper employed to police a State or district: *a Texas ranger*

Ranger *or* **Ranger Guide** *n Brit & Austral* a member of the senior branch of the Guides

rangy (rain-jee) *adj* **rangier**, **rangiest** having long slender limbs

rank¹ *n* **1** a position within a social organization: *the rank of superintendent* **2** high social or other standing: *accusations were made against people of high rank* **3** a person's social class: *it was too grand for someone of his lowly rank* **4** the position of an item in any ordering or sequence **5** a line or row of people or things **6** a place where taxis wait to be hired **7** a line of people, esp. soldiers, positioned one beside the other **8** any of the eight horizontal rows of squares on a chessboard **9 close ranks** to maintain solidarity **10 pull rank** to get one's own way by virtue of one's superior position **11 rank and file** the ordinary people or members of a group **12 the ranks** the ordinary soldiers in an armed force ▸ *vb* **13** to give or hold a specific position in an organization or group **14** to arrange in rows or lines **15** to arrange in sequence: *to rank students according to their grades* **16** to be important: *the legendary coronation stone ranks high in the hearts of patriots*

> **rank** *n* 1 = status, level, position, grade, order, sort, type, division 3 = class, caste 5,7 = row, line, file, column, group, range, series, tier ▸ *vb* 13 = order, dispose 14,15 = arrange, sort, line up, array, align

rank² *adj* **1** complete or absolute: *rank incompetence* **2** smelling offensively strong **3** growing too quickly: *rank weeds*

> **rank** *adj* 2 = foul, bad, offensive, disgusting, revolting, stinking, noxious, rancid, festy (*Austral slang*) 3 = abundant, lush, luxuriant, dense, profuse

rankle *vb* **-kling**, **-kled** to continue to cause resentment or bitterness

ransack *vb* **1** to search through every part of (a place or thing) **2** to plunder or pillage

ransom *n* **1** the money demanded in return for the release of someone who has been kidnapped **2 hold to ransom** ʌ to keep (a prisoner) in confinement until payment is received ʙ to attempt to force (a person) to do something ▸ *vb* **3** to pay money to obtain the release of (a prisoner) **4** to set free (a prisoner) in return for money > **ransomer** *n*

> **ransom** *n* 1 = payment, money, price, payoff

ransomware *n* illegal software that disables a computer or blocks access to data until a payment is received

rant *vb* **1** to talk in a loud and excited way ▸ *n* **2** loud excited speech > **ranting** *adj*, *n*

> **rant** *vb* = shout, roar, yell, rave, cry, declaim

rap *vb* **rapping**, **rapped 1** to hit with a sharp quick blow **2** to knock loudly and sharply **3 rap out** to utter in sharp rapid speech: *he rapped out his address* **4** to perform a rhythmic monologue with musical backing **5** *slang* to talk in a relaxed and friendly way **6** to rebuke or criticize sharply **7 rap over the knuckles** to reprimand ▸ *n* **8** a sharp quick blow or the sound produced by it **9** a fast rhythmic monologue over a musical backing **10** a sharp rebuke or criticism **11** *slang* a legal charge: *a murder rap* **12 take the rap** *slang* to suffer the punishment for a crime, whether guilty or not > **rapper** *n*

> **rap** *vb* **1, 2** = hit, strike, knock, crack (*informal*), tap ▸ *n* **8** = blow, knock, crack (*informal*), tap, clout (*informal*) **10** = rebuke, blame, responsibility, punishment

rapacious *adj* **1** greedy or grasping **2** (of animals or birds) living by catching prey > **rapacity** *n*

rape¹ *vb* **raping, raped 1** to commit the offence of rape upon (a person) ▸ *n* **2** the offence of forcing a person to submit to sexual intercourse against that person's will **3** any violation or abuse: *the rape of the country's natural resources* > **rapist** *n*

> **rape** *vb* = sexually assault, violate, abuse ▸ *n* **2** = sexual assault, violation

rape² *n* a yellow-flowered plant cultivated for its seeds, **rapeseed**, which yield a useful oil, **rape oil**, and as a fodder plant

rapid *adj* **1** (of an action) taking or lasting a short time **2** acting or moving quickly: *a rapid advance* > **rapidly** *adv* > **rapidity** *n*

> **rapid** *adj* **1** = sudden, prompt, speedy, express, swift; ≠ gradual **2** = quick, fast, hurried, swift, brisk, hasty; ≠ slow

rapids *pl n* part of a river where the water is very fast and turbulent

rapier (ray-pyer) *n* a long narrow two-edged sword

rapport (rap-pore) *n* a sympathetic relationship or understanding

rapprochement (rap-prosh-mong) *n* a re-establishment of friendly relations: *diplomatic rapprochement with North Korea*

rapt *adj* **1** totally engrossed: *rapt attention* **2** arising from or showing rapture: *with a rapt look on his face*

rapture *n* **1** extreme happiness or delight **2 raptures** ecstatic joy: *they will be in raptures over the rugged scenery* > **rapturous** *adj*

rare¹ *adj* **1** uncommon or unusual: *a rare plant* **2** not happening or done very often: *a rare appearance in London* **3** of uncommonly high quality: *a rare beauty* **4** (of air at high altitudes) having low density; thin

> **rare** *adj* **1, 2** = uncommon, unusual, few, strange, scarce, singular, sparse, infrequent; ≠ common **3** = superb, great (*informal*), fine, excellent, superlative, choice, peerless

rare² *adj* (of meat) very lightly cooked

rarebit *n* short for **Welsh rarebit**

rarefied (rare-if-ide) *adj* **1** highly specialized: *the rarefied world of classical ballet* **2** (of air) thin **3** exalted in character: *the rarefied heights of academic excellence*

rarely *adv* **1** hardly ever **2** to an unusual degree; exceptionally

> **rarely** *adv* **1** = seldom, hardly, hardly ever, infrequently; ≠ often

raring *adj* **raring to do something** keen and willing to do something

> **raring** *adj* **raring to** = eager to, impatient to, longing to, ready to, keen to, desperate to, enthusiastic to

rarity *n*, *pl* **-ties 1** something that is valuable because it is unusual **2** the state of being rare

> **rarity** *n* **1** = curio, find, treasure, gem, collector's item **2** = uncommonness, scarcity, infrequency, unusualness, shortage, strangeness, sparseness

rascal *n* **1** a scoundrel or rogue **2** a mischievous child > **rascally** *adj*

rash¹ *adj* acting or done without proper thought or consideration; hasty: *rash actions* > **rashly** *adv* > **rashness** *n*

> **rash** *adj* = reckless, hasty, impulsive, imprudent, careless, ill-advised, foolhardy, impetuous; ≠ cautious

rash² *n* **1** an outbreak of spots or patches on the skin, caused by illness or allergy **2** an outbreak of occurrences: *a rash of censorship trials*

> **rash** *n* **1** = outbreak of spots, (skin) eruption **2** = spate, series, wave, flood, plague, outbreak

rasher *n* a thin slice of bacon

rasp *n* **1** a harsh grating noise **2** a coarse file with rows of raised teeth ▸ *vb* **3** to say or speak in a grating voice **4** to make a harsh grating noise **5** to scrape or rub (something) roughly **6** to irritate (one's nerves)

raspberry *n*, *pl* **-ries 1** the red fruit of a prickly shrub of Europe and North America **2** *informal* a spluttering noise made with the tongue and lips to express contempt: *she blew a loud raspberry*

Rastafarian or **Rasta** *n* **1** a believer in a religion of Jamaican origin that regards Ras Tafari, the former emperor of Ethiopia, Haile Selassie, as God ▸ *adj* **2** of Rastafarians

rat *n* **1** a long-tailed rodent, similar to but larger than a mouse **2** *informal* someone who is disloyal or treacherous **3 smell a rat** to detect something suspicious ▸ *vb* **ratting, ratted 4 rat on A** to betray (someone): *good friends don't rat on each other* **B** to go back on (an agreement): *his ex-wife claims he ratted on their divorce settlement* **5** to hunt and kill rats

ratafia (rat-a-fee-a) *n* **1** a liqueur made from fruit **2** an almond-flavoured biscuit

r

ratatouille (rat-a-**twee**) *n* a vegetable casserole made of stewed tomatoes, aubergines, etc.

ratchet *n* **1** a device in which a toothed rack or wheel is engaged by a pivoted lever which permits motion in one direction only **2** the toothed rack or wheel in such a device **3** to operate using a ratchet **4** (usually foll. by *up* or *down*) to increase or decrease, esp. irreversibly: *the director ratchets up the tension once again*

rate *n* **1** a quantity or amount considered in relation to or measured against another quantity or amount: *he was publishing at the rate of about 10 books a year* **2** a price or charge with reference to a standard or scale: *an exchange rate* **3** the speed of progress or change: *crime is increasing at an alarming rate* **4** a charge made per unit for a commodity or service **5** relative quality: *a third-rate power* **6 at any rate** in any case ► *vb* **rating, rated 7** to assign a position on a scale of relative values: *he is rated as one of the top caterers in the country* **8** to estimate the value of: *we rate your services highly* **9** to consider or regard: *it could hardly be rated a success* **10** to be worthy of: *it barely rates a mention* **11** *informal* to have a high opinion of: *the cognoscenti have always rated his political skills*

> **rate** *n* **1** = degree, standard, scale, proportion, ratio **2, 4** = charge, price, cost, fee, figure **3** = speed, pace, tempo, velocity, frequency **6 at any rate** = in any case, anyway, anyhow, at all events ► *vb* **7, 8, 9** = evaluate, consider, rank, reckon, value, measure, estimate, count **10** = deserve, merit, be entitled to, be worthy of

rateable *adj* **1** able to be rated or evaluated **2** liable to payment of rates

ratepayer *n* a person who pays local rates on a building

rather *adv* **1** fairly: *that was a rather narrow escape* **2** to a limited extent: *I rather thought that was the case* **3** more truly or appropriately: *they tend to be cat rather than dog people* **4** more willingly: *I would rather go straight home* ► *interj* **5** an expression of strong affirmation: *Is it worth seeing? — Rather!*

> **rather** *adv* **1, 2** = to some extent, quite, a little, fairly, relatively, somewhat, moderately, to some degree **4** = preferably, sooner, more readily, more willingly

ratify *vb* **-fies, -fying, -fied** to give formal approval to: *they ratified the treaty* > **ratification** *n*

> **ratify** *vb* = approve, establish, confirm, sanction, endorse, uphold, authorize, affirm; ≠ annul

rating *n* **1** a valuation or assessment **2** a classification according to order or grade **3** a noncommissioned sailor **4 ratings** the size of the audience for a TV or radio programme

> **rating** *n* **2** = position, placing, rate, order, class, degree (*archaic*), rank, status

ratio *n*, *pl* **-tios 1** the relationship between two numbers or amounts expressed as a proportion: *a ratio of one instructor to every five pupils* **2** *maths* a quotient of two numbers or quantities

> **ratio** *n* **1** = proportion, rate, relation, percentage, fraction

ration *n* **1** a fixed allowance of something that is scarce, such as food or petrol in wartime **2 rations** a fixed daily allowance of food, such as that given to a soldier ► *vb* **3** to restrict the distribution of (something): *the government has rationed petrol* **4** to distribute a fixed amount of (something) to each person in a group > **rationing** *n*

> **ration** *n* **1** = allowance, quota, allotment, helping, part, share, measure, portion ► *vb* **3** = limit, control, restrict, budget

rational *adj* **1** reasonable or sensible **2** using reason or logic in thinking out a problem **3** capable of reasoning: *man is a rational being* **4** sane: *rational behaviour* **5** *maths* able to be expressed as a ratio of two integers: *a rational number* > **rationality** *n* > **rationally** *adv*

> **rational** *adj* **1** = sensible, sound, wise, reasonable, intelligent, realistic, logical, sane, grounded

rationale (rash-a-**nahl**) *n* the reason for an action or belief

> **rationale** *n* = reason, grounds, theory, principle, philosophy, logic, motivation, raison d'être (*French*)

rationalism *n* the philosophy that regards reason as the only basis for beliefs or actions > **rationalist** *n* > **rationalistic** *adj*

rationalize *or* **-ise** *vb* **-izing, -ized** *or* **-ising, -ised 1** to find reasons to justify or explain (one's actions) **2** to apply logic or reason to (something) **3** to get rid of unnecessary equipment or staff to make (a business) more efficient > **rationalization** *or* **-isation** *n*

rat race *n* a continual routine of hectic competitive activity: *get out of the rat race for a while*

rattan *n* a climbing palm with tough stems used for wickerwork and canes

rattle *vb* **-tling, -tled 1** to make a rapid succession of short sharp sounds, such as when loose pellets are shaken in a container **2** to send, move, or drive with such a sound: *rain rattled against the window* **3** to shake briskly causing sharp sounds **4** *informal* to frighten or confuse **5 rattle off** *or* **out** to recite perfunctorily or rapidly **6 rattle on** *or* **away** to talk quickly and at length about something unimportant **7 rattle through** to do (something) very quickly: *she rattled through a translation* ► *n* **8** a rapid succession of short sharp sounds **9** a baby's toy filled with small pellets that rattle when shaken > **rattly** *adj*

rattle vb **1, 2** = clatter, bang, jangle **3** = shake, jolt, vibrate, bounce, jar **4** = fluster, shake, upset, disturb, disconcert, perturb, faze

rattlesnake n a poisonous snake with loose horny segments on the tail that make a rattling sound

ratty adj **-tier, -tiest** informal **1** cross and irritable **2** (of the hair) straggly and greasy › **rattily** adv › **rattiness** n

raucous adj loud and harsh

raunchy adj **-chier, -chiest** slang sexy or earthy

ravage vb **-vaging, -vaged 1** to cause extensive damage to ▸ n **2 ravages** the damaging effects: the ravages of weather and pollution

ravage vb = destroy, ruin, devastate, spoil, demolish, ransack, lay waste, despoil (formal) ▸ n = damage, destruction, devastation, ruin, havoc, ruination, spoliation

rave vb **raving, raved 1** to talk in a wild or incoherent manner **2** informal to write or speak (about) with great enthusiasm ▸ n **3** informal an enthusiastically favourable review **4** slang a professionally organized large-scale party with electronic dance music **5** a name given to various types of dance music, such as techno, that feature a fast electronic rhythm

rave vb **1** = rant, rage, roar, go mad (informal), babble, be delirious **2** = enthuse, praise, gush, be mad about (informal), be wild about (informal)

ravel vb **-velling, -velled** or US **-veling, -veled 1** to tangle or become entangled **2** (of a fabric) to fray out in loose ends; unravel

raven n **1** a large bird of the crow family with shiny black feathers ▸ adj **2** (of hair) shiny black

ravenous adj very hungry › **ravenously** adv

ravine (rav-veen) n a deep narrow steep-sided valley worn by a stream

raving adj **1** delirious **2** informal great or exceptional: a raving beauty ▸ adv **3** to an excessive degree: raving mad ▸ n **4 ravings** frenzied or wildly extravagant talk

raving adj **1** = mad, wild, crazy, hysterical, irrational, crazed, delirious

ravioli pl n small squares of pasta with a savoury filling, such as meat or cheese

ravish vb **1** to enrapture or delight: tourists ravished by our brilliant costumes **2** literary to rape › **ravishment** n

ravishing adj lovely or delightful › **ravishingly** adv

raw adj **1** (of food) not cooked **2** in an unfinished or unrefined state: raw sewage **3** not selected or modified: raw data **4** (of the skin or a wound) painful, with the surface scraped away **5** untrained or inexperienced: a raw recruit **6** (of the weather) harshly cold and damp **7** frank or realistic: a raw reality **8 raw deal** informal unfair or dishonest treatment ▸ n **9 in the raw A** informal naked **B** in a natural and uncivilized state: to see life in the raw

raw adj **1** = uncooked, natural, fresh; ≠ cooked **2** = unrefined, natural, crude, unprocessed, basic, rough, coarse, unfinished; ≠ refined **5** = inexperienced, new, green, immature, callow; ≠ experienced **6** = chilly, biting, cold, freezing, bitter, piercing, parky (Brit informal)

rawhide n **1** untanned hide **2** a whip or rope made of strips of this

ray¹ n **1** a narrow beam of light **2** any of a set of lines spreading from a central point **3** a slight indication: a ray of hope **4** maths a straight line extending from a point **5** a thin beam of electromagnetic radiation or particles **6** any of the spines that support the fin of a fish

ray n **1** = beam, bar, flash, shaft, gleam

ray² n a sea fish related to the sharks, with a flattened body and a long whiplike tail

rayon n a textile fibre or fabric made from cellulose

raze or **rase** vb **razing, razed** or **rasing, rased** to destroy (buildings or a town) completely

razor n an implement with a sharp blade, used for shaving

razorbill n a black-and-white sea bird with a stout sideways flattened bill

razzle-dazzle or **razzmatazz** n slang **1** noisy or showy fuss or activity **2** a spree or frolic

RC 1 Red Cross **2** Roman Catholic

Rd road

re prep with reference to

re prep = concerning, about, regarding, with regard to, with reference to, apropos

RE (in Britain) **1** Religious Education **2** Royal Engineers

re- prefix **1** (used with many main words to mean) repetition of an action: remarry **2** (used with many main words to mean) return to a previous condition: renew

reach vb **1** to arrive at or get to (a place) **2** to make a movement (towards), as if to grasp or touch: she reached for her bag **3** to succeed in touching: I can't reach that shelf unless I stand on a chair **4** to make contact or communication with: to reach a wider audience **5** to extend as far as (a point or place): to reach the ceiling **6** to come to (a certain condition or situation): to reach a compromise **7** to arrive at or amount to (an amount or value): temperatures in Greece reached 35° yesterday **8** informal to give (something to a person) with the outstretched hand ▸ n **9** the extent or distance of reaching: within easy reach **10** the range of influence or power: it symbolized America's global reach **11 reaches** a section of river, land, or sky: the quieter reaches of the upper Thames › **reachable** adj

r

reach *vb* 1 = arrive at, get to, make, attain
2, 3 = touch, grasp, extend to, stretch to,
contact 4 = contact, get in touch with, get
through to, communicate with, get hold of
7 = attain, get to ▸ *n* 9 = grasp, range, distance,
stretch, capacity, extent, extension, scope
10 = jurisdiction, power, influence

reach out *vb* (often foll. by *to*) to attempt to
establish friendly or sympathetic relations
(with someone)

react *vb* 1 (of a person or thing) to act in
response to another person, a stimulus, or a
situation 2 **react against** to act in an opposing
or contrary manner 3 *chem* to undergo a
chemical reaction 4 *physics* to exert an equal
force in the opposite direction to an acting force

react *vb* 1 = respond, act, proceed, behave

reactance *n* *electronics* the resistance to the flow
of an alternating current caused by the
inductance or capacitance of the circuit

reaction *n* 1 a physical or emotional response
to a stimulus 2 any action resisting another
3 opposition to change 4 *med* any effect
produced by a drug or by a substance (allergen)
to which a person is allergic 5 *chem* a process
that involves changes in the structure and
energy content of atoms, molecules, or ions
6 the equal and opposite force that acts on a
body whenever it exerts a force on another body
7 **reactions** someone's ability to act in response
to something that happens

reaction *n* 1 = response, answer, reply
2 = counteraction, backlash, recoil
3 = conservatism, the right

reactionary *adj* 1 opposed to political or social
change ▸ *n*, *pl* **-aries** 2 a person opposed to
radical change

reactionary *adj* = conservative, right-wing;
≠ radical ▸ *n* = conservative, die-hard,
right-winger; ≠ radical

reactive *adj* 1 readily taking part in chemical
reactions: *ozone is a highly reactive form of oxygen gas*
2 of or having a reactance 3 responsive to
stimulus > **reactively** *adv* ▸ **reactivity** *n*

reactor *n* short for **nuclear reactor**

read *vb* **reading**, **read** 1 to look at and
understand or take in (written or printed
matter) 2 to look at and say aloud 3 to have a
certain wording: *the memorandum read as follows*
4 to interpret in a specified way: *it can be read as
satire* 5 to interpret the significance or meaning
of: *an astrologer who reads Tarot* 6 to register or
show: *the meter reads 100* 7 to make out the true
nature or mood of: *she had read his thoughts* 8 to
interpret (signs, characters, etc.) other than by
visual means: *to read Braille* 9 to have sufficient
knowledge of (a language) to understand the
written word 10 to undertake a course of study

in (a subject): *to read economics* 11 to gain
knowledge by reading: *he read about the war*
12 to hear and understand, esp. when using a
two-way radio: *we are reading you loud and clear*
13 *computers* to obtain (data) from a storage
device, such as magnetic tape ▸ *n* 14 matter
suitable for reading: *this book is a very good read*
15 a spell of reading

read *vb* 1, 9 = understand, interpret,
comprehend, construe, decipher, see, discover
6 = register, show, record, display, indicate

readable *adj* 1 enjoyable to read 2 (of
handwriting or print) legible

reader *n* 1 a person who reads 2 a person who
reads aloud in public 3 a person who reads and
judges manuscripts sent to a publisher 4 a book
of texts for those learning a foreign language
5 *Brit* a member of staff below a professor but
above a senior lecturer at a university
6 a proofreader

readership *n* all the readers collectively of a
publication or author: *a new format would alienate
its readership*

reading *n* 1 the act of reading 2 ability to read:
disputes over methods of teaching reading 3 material
for reading 4 a public recital of a literary work
5 a measurement indicated by a gauge or dial
6 one of the three stages in the passage of a bill
through a legislative assembly 7 the form of a
particular word or passage in a given text 8 an
interpretation of a situation or something said
▸ *adj* 9 of or for reading: *reading glasses*

reading *n* 1 = perusal, study, examination,
inspection, scrutiny 4 = recital, performance,
lesson, sermon 8 = interpretation, version,
impression, grasp

readjust *vb* to adapt to a new situation
> **readjustment** *n*

ready *adj* **readier**, **readiest** 1 prepared for use or
action 2 prompt or eager: *the ready use of corporal
punishment* 3 quick or intelligent: *a ready wit*
4 **ready to** on the point of or liable to: *ready to
pounce* 5 easily available: *his ready tears* ▸ *n*
6 **at the ready** poised for use: *with pen at the ready*
▸ *vb* **readies**, **readying**, **readied** 7 to make ready;
prepare > **readily** *adv* ▸ **readiness** *n*

ready *adj* 1 = prepared, set, primed,
organized; ≠ unprepared 2 = willing, happy,
glad, disposed, keen, eager, inclined, prone;
≠ reluctant 3 = prompt, smart, quick, bright,
sharp, keen, alert, clever; ≠ slow 5 = available,
handy, present, near, accessible, convenient;
≠ unavailable

ready-made *adj* 1 for immediate use by any
customer 2 extremely convenient or ideally
suited: *a ready-made audience*

reagent (ree-**age**-ent) *n* a chemical substance
that reacts with another, used to detect the
presence of the other

real *adj* **1** existing or occurring in the physical world **2** actual: *the real agenda* **3** important or serious: *the real challenge* **4** rightly so called: *a real friend* **5** genuine: *the council has no real authority* **6** (of food or drink) made in a traditional way to ensure the best flavour **7** relating to immovable property such as land or buildings: *real estate* **8** *econ* (of prices or incomes) considered in terms of purchasing power rather than nominal currency value **9 the real thing** the genuine article, not a substitute or imitation

real *adj* **1** = true, genuine, sincere, factual, dinkum (*Austral, NZ informal*), unfeigned **2, 5** = actual, true; ≠ fake **4** = proper, true, valid

real ale *n chiefly Brit* beer that has fermented in the barrel

real estate *n* immovable property, esp. land and houses

realism *n* **1** awareness or acceptance of things as they are, as opposed to the abstract or ideal **2** a style in art or literature that attempts to show the world as it really is **3** *philosophy* the theory that physical objects continue to exist whether they are perceived or not › **realist** *n* › **realistic** *adj* › **realistically** *adv*

reality *n, pl* **-ties 1** the state of things as they are or appear to be, rather than as one might wish them to be **2** something that is real **3** the state of being real **4 in reality** in fact

reality *n* **1, 3** = fact, truth, realism, validity, verity, actuality **2** = truth, fact, actuality

reality TV *n* television programmes focusing on members of the public living in conditions created especially by the programme makers

realize *or* **-lise** *vb* **-lizing, -lized** *or* **-lising, -lised 1** to be aware of or grasp the significance of **2** to achieve (a plan or ambition) **3** to convert (property or goods) into cash **4** (of goods or property) to sell for (a certain sum): *this table realized a large sum at auction* **5** to produce (a complete work of art) from an idea or draft › **realizable** *or* **-lisable** *adj* › **realization** *or* **-lisation** *n*

realize *or* **-lise** *vb* **1** = become aware of, understand, take in, grasp, comprehend, get the message **2** = fulfil, achieve, accomplish, make real **5** = achieve, do, effect, complete, perform, fulfil, accomplish, carry out *or* through

really *adv* **1** truly: *really boring* **2** in reality: *it's really quite harmless* ▸ *interj* **3** an exclamation of dismay, doubt, or surprise

really *adv* **2** = truly, actually, in fact, indeed, in actuality

realm *n* **1** a kingdom **2** a field of interest or study: *the realm of science*

realm *n* **1** = kingdom, country, empire, land, domain, dominion **2** = field, world, area, province, sphere, department (*informal*), branch, territory

ream *n* **1** a number of sheets of paper, now equal to 500 or 516 sheets (20 quires) **2 reams** *informal* a large quantity (of written material): *reams of verse*

reap *vb* **1** to cut and gather (a harvest) **2** to receive as the result of a previous activity: *reap the benefits of our efforts*

reap *vb* **1** = collect, gather, bring in, harvest, garner, cut **2** = get, gain, obtain, acquire, derive

reaper *n* **1** a person who reaps or a machine for reaping **2 the grim reaper** death

reappear *vb* to come back into view › **reappearance** *n*

rear¹ *n* **1** the back part **2** the area or position that lies at the back **3** *informal* the buttocks **4 bring up the rear** to come last ▸ *adj* **5** of or in the rear: *the rear carriage*

rear *n* **1** = back part, back; ≠ front **2** = back, end, tail, rearguard, tail end ▸ *adj* = back, hind, last, following; ≠ front

rear² *vb* **1** to care for and educate (children) until maturity **2** to breed (animals) or grow (plants) **3** (of a horse) to lift the front legs in the air and stand nearly upright **4** to place or lift (something) upright

rear *vb* **1** = bring up, raise, educate, train, foster, nurture **2** = breed, keep

rear admiral *n* a high-ranking naval officer

rearguard *n* **1** the troops who protect the rear of a military formation ▸ *adj* **2 rearguard action** an effort to prevent or postpone something that is unavoidable

rearmost *adj* nearest the back

rearrange *vb* **-ranging, -ranged** to organize differently › **rearrangement** *n*

reason *n* **1** a cause or motive for a belief or action: *he had two reasons for his dark mood* **2** the ability to think or argue rationally **3** an argument in favour of or a justification for something: *there is every reason to encourage people to keep fit* **4** soundness of mind **5 by reason of** because of **6 within reason** within moderate or justifiable bounds **7 it stands to reason** it is logical or obvious ▸ *vb* **8** to think logically in forming conclusions **9 reason with** to persuade by logical arguments into doing something **10 reason out** to work out (a problem) by reasoning

reason *n* **1** = cause, grounds, purpose, motive, goal, aim, object, intention **2** = sense, mind, understanding, judgment, logic, intellect, sanity, rationality; ≠ emotion ▸ *vb* **8** = deduce, conclude, work out, make out, infer, think **9 reason with someone** = persuade, bring round, urge, win over, prevail upon (*formal*), talk into *or* out of

reasonable *adj* **1** sensible **2** not making unfair demands **3** logical: *a reasonable explanation* **4** moderate in price **5** average: *a reasonable amount of luck* › **reasonably** *adv* › **reasonableness** *n*

r

reasonable adj **1, 3** = sensible, sound, practical, wise, logical, sober, plausible, sane, grounded; ≠ irrational **2** = fair, just, right, moderate, equitable, tenable; ≠ unfair **4** = low, cheap, competitive, moderate, modest, inexpensive **5** = average, fair, moderate, modest, O.K. or okay (informal)

reassess vb to reconsider the value or importance of › **reassessment** n

reassure vb **-assuring, -assured** to relieve (someone) of anxieties › **reassurance** n › **reassuring** adj

reassure vb = encourage, comfort, hearten, gee up, restore confidence to, put or set your mind at rest

rebate n a refund or discount

rebate n = refund, discount, reduction, bonus, allowance, deduction

rebel vb **-belling, -belled 1** to fight against the ruling power **2** to reject accepted conventions of behaviour ► n **3** a person who rebels **4** a person who rejects accepted conventions of behaviour ► adj **5** rebelling: rebel councillors

rebel vb **1** = revolt, resist, rise up, mutiny **2** = defy, dissent, disobey ► n **3** = revolutionary, insurgent, secessionist, revolutionist **4** = nonconformist, dissenter, heretic, apostate, schismatic ► adj = rebellious, revolutionary, insurgent, insurrectionary

rebellion n **1** organized opposition to a government or other authority involving the use of violence **2** nonviolent opposition to a government or other authority: a Tory backbenchers' rebellion **3** rejection of accepted conventions of behaviour

rebellion n **1** = resistance, rising, revolution, revolt, uprising, mutiny **2, 3** = nonconformity, defiance, heresy, schism

rebellious adj rebelling or showing a tendency towards rebellion › **rebelliously** adv

rebellious adj = revolutionary, rebel, disorderly, unruly, insurgent, disloyal, seditious, mutinous; ≠ obedient

rebirth n a revival or renaissance: the rebirth of their nation

reboot vb **1** to shut down and then restart (a computer system) ► n **2** an instance of shutting down and restarting a computer system **3** informal a new version of something

rebore or **reboring** n the boring of a cylinder to restore its true shape

reborn adj active again after a period of inactivity

rebound vb **1** to spring back from a sudden impact **2** (of a plan or action) to misfire so as to hurt the person responsible ► n **3** the act of

rebounding **4 on the rebound** informal while recovering from rejection: she married him on the rebound

rebound vb **1** = bounce, ricochet, recoil **2** = misfire, backfire, recoil, boomerang

rebuff vb **1** to snub and reject an offer or suggestion ► n **2** a blunt refusal; snub

rebuff vb = reject, refuse, turn down, cut (informal), slight, snub, spurn, knock back (slang); ≠ encourage ► n = rejection, snub, knock-back, slight, refusal, repulse, cold shoulder, slap in the face (informal); ≠ encouragement

rebuke vb **-buking, -buked 1** to scold sternly ► n **2** a stern scolding

rebuke vb = scold, censure, reprimand, castigate, chide, dress down (informal), admonish, tell off (informal); ≠ praise ► n = scolding, censure, reprimand, row, dressing-down (informal), telling-off (informal), admonition; ≠ praise

rebus (ree-buss) n, pl -buses a puzzle consisting of pictures and symbols representing syllables and words

rebut vb **-butting, -butted** to prove that (a claim) is untrue › **rebuttal** n

recalcitrant adj wilfully disobedient › **recalcitrance** n

recall vb **1** to bring back to mind **2** to order to return **3** to annul or cancel ► n **4** the ability to remember things **5** an order to return

recall vb **1** = recollect, remember, evoke, call to mind **2** = call back **3** = annul, withdraw, cancel, repeal, revoke, retract, countermand ► n **4** = recollection, memory, remembrance

recant vb to take back (a former belief or statement) publicly › **recantation** n

recap informal ► vb **-capping, -capped 1** to recapitulate ► n **2** a recapitulation

recapitulate vb **-lating, -lated** to restate the main points of (an argument or speech)

recapitulation n **1** the act of recapitulating **2** music the repeating of earlier themes, esp. in the final section of a movement

recapture vb **-turing, -tured 1** to relive vividly (a former experience or sensation): recaptured some of those first feelings **2** to capture again ► n **3** the act of recapturing

recce chiefly Brit slang ► vb **-ceing, -ced** or **-ceed 1** to reconnoitre ► n **2** reconnaissance

recede vb **-ceding, -ceded 1** to withdraw from a point or limit: the tide had receded **2** to become more distant: the threat of intervention had receded **3** (of a man's hair) to stop growing at the temples and above the forehead **4** to slope backwards: a receding chin

recede vb **1** = fall back, withdraw, retreat, return, retire, regress

receipt *n* **1** a written acknowledgment that money or goods have been received **2** the act of receiving **3 receipts** money taken in over a particular period by a shop or business

> **receipt** *n* **1** = sales slip, proof of purchase, counterfoil **2** = receiving, delivery, reception, acceptance

receive *vb* **-ceiving, -ceived 1** to get (something offered or sent to one) **2** to experience: *he received a knife wound* **3** to greet (guests) **4** to have (an honour) bestowed: *he received the Order of the Garter* **5** to admit (a person) to a society or condition: *he was received into the Church* **6** to convert (incoming radio or television signals) into sounds or pictures **7** to be informed of (news) **8** to react to: *the article was well received* **9** to support or sustain (the weight of something) **10** *tennis etc.* to play at the other end from the server **11** *Brit, Austral & NZ* to buy and sell stolen goods

> **receive** *vb* **1, 4** = get, accept, be given, pick up, collect, obtain, acquire, take **2** = experience, suffer, bear, encounter, sustain, undergo **3** = greet, meet, admit, welcome, entertain, accommodate

received *adj* generally accepted or believed: *contrary to received wisdom*

receiver *n* **1** the part of a telephone that is held to the ear **2** the equipment in a telephone, radio, or television that converts the incoming signals into sound or pictures **3** a person appointed by a court to manage property of a bankrupt **4** a person who receives stolen goods knowing they have been stolen

receivership *n law* the state of being administered by a receiver: *the company went into receivership*

recent *adj* **1** having happened lately **2** new > **recently** *adv*

> **recent** *adj* **2** = new, modern, up-to-date, late, current, fresh, novel, present-day; ≠ old

receptacle *n* **1** an object used to contain something **2** *botany* the enlarged or modified tip of the flower stalk that bears the flower

reception *n* **1** an area in an office, hotel, etc., where visitors are received or reservations dealt with **2** a formal party for guests, esp. after a wedding **3** the manner in which something is received: *an enthusiastic reception* **4** the act of formally welcoming **5** *radio & television* the quality of a received broadcast: *the reception was poor*

> **reception** *n* **2** = party, gathering, get-together, social gathering, function, celebration, festivity, soirée **3** = response, reaction, acknowledgment, treatment, welcome, greeting

receptionist *n* a person employed to receive guests or clients and deal with reservations and appointments

receptive *adj* willing to consider and accept new ideas or suggestions > **receptivity** *or* **receptiveness** *n*

recess *n* **1** a space, such as an alcove, set back in a wall **2** a holiday between sessions of work **3 recesses** secret hidden places: *the recesses of her brain* **4** *US & Canad* a break between classes at a school

> **recess** *n* **1** = alcove, corner, bay, hollow, niche, nook **2** = break, rest, holiday, interval, vacation, respite, intermission, schoolie (*Austral*)

recessed *adj* hidden or placed in a recess

recession *n* **1** a period of economic difficulty when little is being bought or sold **2** the act of receding

> **recession** *n* **1** = depression, drop, decline, credit crunch, slump; ≠ boom

recessive *adj* **1** tending to recede **2** *genetics* (in a pair of genes) designating a gene that has a characteristic which will only be passed on if the other gene has the same characteristic

recherché (rish-**air**-shay) *adj* **1** studiedly refined or elegant **2** known only to connoisseurs

recidivism *n* habitual relapse into crime > **recidivist** *n, adj*

recipe *n* **1** a list of ingredients and directions for making a particular dish **2** a method for achieving something: *a recipe for industrial chaos*

> **recipe** *n* **1** = directions, instructions, ingredients

recipient *n* a person who receives something

reciprocal (ris-**sip**-prə-kl) *adj* **1** done or felt by each of two people or groups to or about the other: *a reciprocal agreement* **2** given or done in return: *a reciprocal invitation* **3** *grammar* (of a pronoun) indicating that action is given and received by each subject, for example, *each other* in *they started to shout at each other* ► *n* **4** Also called: **inverse** *maths* a number or quantity that when multiplied by a given number or quantity gives a product of one: *the reciprocal of 2 is 0.5* > **reciprocally** *adv*

reciprocate *vb* **-cating, -cated 1** to give or feel in return: *not everyone reciprocated his enthusiasm* **2** (of a machine part) to move backwards and forwards > **reciprocation** *n*

reciprocity *n* **1** reciprocal action or relation **2** a mutual exchange of commercial or other privileges

recital (ris-**site**-al) *n* **1** a musical performance by a soloist or soloists **2** the act of reciting something learned or prepared **3** a narration or description: *she plagued her with the recital of constant ailments and illnesses*

> **recital** *n* **1** = performance, rendering, rehearsal, reading **2** = recitation **3** = account, telling, statement, relation, narrative

r

recitation n **1** the act of reciting poetry or prose from memory **2** something recited

recitative (ress-it-a-**teev**) n a narrative passage in an opera or oratorio, reflecting the natural rhythms of speech

recite vb **-citing, -cited 1** to repeat (a poem or passage) aloud from memory before an audience **2** to give a detailed account of

> **recite** vb **1** = perform, deliver, repeat, declaim

reckless adj having no regard for danger or consequences: reckless driving > **recklessly** adv
> **recklessness** n

> **reckless** adj = careless, wild, rash, precipitate, hasty, mindless, headlong, thoughtless; ≠ cautious

reckon vb **1** informal to be of the opinion: she reckoned she could find them **2** to consider: he reckoned himself a failure **3** to calculate or compute **4** to expect **5 reckon with** to take into account: there are a few problems to reckon with **6 reckon without** to fail to take into account **7 reckon on** or **upon** to rely on or expect: they can't reckon on your automatic support

> **reckon** vb **1** = think, believe, suppose, imagine, assume, guess (informal) **2** = consider, rate, account, judge, regard, count, esteem (formal), deem **3** = count, figure, total, calculate, compute, add up, tally, number

reckoning n **1** counting or calculating: by his reckoning, he owed him money **2** retribution for one's actions: the moment of reckoning came **3** settlement of an account or bill

> **reckoning** n **1** = count, estimate, calculation, addition

reclaim vb **1** to get back possession of: the club is now trying to reclaim the money from the blockaders **2** to convert (unusable or submerged land) into land suitable for farming or building on **3** to recover (useful substances) from waste products
> **reclamation** n

> **reclaim** vb **1** = retrieve, regain **2** = regain, salvage, recapture

recline vb **-clining, -clined** to rest in a leaning position

reclining adj (of a seat) with a back that can be adjusted to slope at various angles

recluse n a person who lives alone and avoids people > **reclusive** adj

recognition n **1** the act of recognizing **2** acceptance or acknowledgment **3** formal acknowledgment of a government or of the independence of a country **4 in recognition of** as a token of thanks for

> **recognition** n **1** = identification, recollection, discovery, remembrance **2** = acceptance, admission, allowance, confession

recognizance or **recognisance** (rik-og-nizz-anss) n law **A** an undertaking made before a court or magistrate to do something specified, such as to appear in court on a stated day **B** a sum of money promised as a guarantee of this undertaking

recognize or **-nise** vb **-nizing, -nized** or **-nising, -nised 1** to identify (a person or thing) as someone or something already known **2** to accept or be aware of (a fact or problem): to recognize change **3** to acknowledge formally the status or legality of (something or someone): an organization recognized by the UN **4** to show approval or appreciation of (something) **5** to make formal acknowledgment of (a claim or duty): I must ask for her to be recognized as a hostile witness
> **recognizable** or **-nisable** adj

> **recognize** or **-nise** vb **1** = identify, know, place, remember, spot, notice, recall, recollect **2** = acknowledge, allow, accept, admit, grant, concede; ≠ ignore **4** = appreciate, respect, notice

recoil vb **1** to jerk or spring back **2** to draw back in fear or horror **3** (of an action) to go wrong so as to hurt the person responsible ▸ n **4** the backward movement of a gun when fired **5** the act of recoiling

recollect vb to remember > **recollection** n

recommend vb **1** to advise as the best course or choice **2** to praise or commend: I would wholeheartedly recommend his books **3** to make attractive or advisable: she has everything to recommend her > **recommendation** n

> **recommend** vb **1** = advocate, suggest, propose, approve, endorse, commend; ≠ disapprove of

recompense vb **-pensing, -pensed 1** to pay or reward for work or help **2** to compensate or make up for loss or injury ▸ n **3** compensation for loss or injury **4** reward or repayment

reconcile vb **-ciling, -ciled 1** to make (two apparently conflicting things) compatible or consistent with each other: in many cases science and religion are reconciled **2** to re-establish friendly relations with (a person or people) or between (people) **3** to accept or cause to accept an unpleasant situation: we reconciled ourselves to a change

> **reconcile** vb **1** = resolve, settle, square, adjust, compose, rectify, put to rights **2** = reunite, bring back together, conciliate

reconciliation n **1** the state of being reconciled **2** the act of reconciling people or groups **3** S African a political term emphasizing the need to acknowledge the wrongs of the past

> **reconciliation** n **1** = reunion, conciliation, pacification, reconcilement; ≠ separation

r

recondite *adj formal* **1** requiring special knowledge **2** dealing with abstruse or profound subjects

recondition *vb* to restore to good condition or working order ▸ **reconditioned** *adj*

reconfigure *vb* **-guring, -gured** *computers* to rearrange the elements or settings of (a system, device, etc.)

reconnaissance (rik-kon-iss-anss) *n* **1** the process of obtaining information about the position and movements of an enemy **2** a preliminary inspection

reconnoitre *or US* **reconnoiter** (rek-a-noy-ter) *vb* to make a reconnaissance of

reconsider *vb* to think about again, with a view to changing one's policy or course of action ▸ **reconsideration** *n*

> **reconsider** *vb* = rethink, review, revise, think again, reassess

reconstitute *vb* **-tuting, -tuted** **1** to reorganize in a slightly different form **2** to restore (dried food) to its former state by adding water ▸ **reconstitution** *n*

reconstruct *vb* **1** to build again **2** to reorganize: *three works proved useful in reconstructing the training routine* **3** to form a picture of (a past event, esp. a crime) by piecing together evidence ▸ **reconstruction** *n*

> **reconstruct** *vb* **1** = rebuild, restore, re-create, remake, renovate, remodel, regenerate **3** = build up a picture of, build up, piece together, deduce

record *n* (rek-ord) **1** a document or other thing that preserves information **2 records** information or data on a subject collected over a long period: *dental records* **3** a thin disc of a plastic material upon which sound has been recorded in a continuous spiral groove on each side **4** the best recorded achievement in some field: *her score set a Games record* **5** the known facts about a person's achievements **6** a list of crimes of which an accused person has previously been convicted **7** anything serving as evidence or as a memorial: *the First World War is a record of human folly* **8** *computers* a group of data or piece of information preserved as a unit in machine-readable form **9 for the record** for the sake of strict factual accuracy **10 go on record** to state one's views publicly **11 have a record** to have previous criminal convictions **12 off the record** not for publication **13 on record A** stated in a public document **B** publicly known ▸ *adj* **14** being the highest or lowest, or best or worst ever achieved: *record losses* ▸ *vb* (rik-**kord**) **15** to put in writing to preserve the true facts: *to record the minutes of a meeting* **16** to preserve (sound, TV programmes, etc.) on plastic disc, magnetic tape, etc., for reproduction on a playback device **17** to show or register

> **record** *n* **1, 2** = document, file, register, log, report, account, entry, journal, blog (*informal*) **3** = disc (*old-fashioned*), single, album, LP, vinyl **5, 6** = background, history, performance, career **7** = evidence, trace, documentation, testimony, witness
> ▸ *vb* **15** = set down, minute, note, enter, document, register, log, chronicle **16** = make a recording of, video, tape, video-tape, tape-record **17** = register, show, indicate, give evidence of

recorder *n* **1** a person who keeps records **2** a device for recording sound, data, or pictures **3** *music* a wind instrument, blown through the end, with finger-holes and a reedlike tone **4** (in England and Wales) a barrister or solicitor appointed to sit as a part-time judge in the crown court

> **recorder** *n* **1** = chronicler, archivist, historian, clerk, scribe, diarist

recording *n* **1** something that has been recorded **2** the process of storing sounds or visual signals for later use

> **recording** *n* **1** = record, video, tape, disc (*old-fashioned*)

record player *n* a device for reproducing the sounds stored on a record

recount *vb* to tell the story or details of

> **recount** *vb* = tell, report, describe, relate, repeat, depict, recite, narrate

re-count *vb* **1** to count again ▸ *n* **2** a second or further count, esp. of votes in an election

recoup (rik-**koop**) *vb* **1** to regain or make good (a loss) **2** to reimburse or compensate (someone) for a loss ▸ **recoupment** *n*

recourse *n* **1 have recourse to** to turn to a source of help or course of action **2** a source of help or course of action that is turned to when in difficulty

recover *vb* **1** (of a person) to regain health, spirits, or composure **2** to regain a former and better condition: *real wages have recovered from the recession* **3** to find again or obtain the return of (something lost) **4** to get back or make good (expense or loss) **5** to obtain (useful substances) from waste **6** *law* to gain (something) by the judgment of a court: *it should be possible to recover damages* ▸ **recoverable** *adj*

> **recover** *vb* **1** = get better, improve, get well, recuperate, heal, revive, mend, convalesce; ≠ relapse **2** = rally **3, 6** = recoup, restore, get back, regain, retrieve, reclaim, redeem, recapture; ≠ lose **4** = save, rescue, retrieve, salvage, reclaim; ≠ abandon

recovery *n, pl* **-veries** **1** the act of recovering from sickness, a shock, or a setback **2** restoration to a former and better condition

r

3 the regaining of something lost 4 the extraction of useful substances from waste

> **recovery** n 1 = improvement, healing, revival, mending, recuperation, convalescence 3 = retrieval, repossession, reclamation, restoration

re-create vb **-creating, -created** to make happen or exist again > **re-creation** n

recreation n an activity done for pleasure or relaxation > **recreational** adj

> **recreation** n = leisure, play, sport, fun, entertainment, relaxation, enjoyment, amusement, me-time

recrimination n accusations made by two people or groups about each other: bitter recrimination > **recriminatory** adj

recruit vb 1 to enlist (people) for military service 2 to enrol or obtain (members or support) ▸ n 3 a newly joined member of a military service 4 a new member or supporter > **recruitment** n

> **recruit** vb 1 = enlist, draft, enrol; ≠ dismiss 2 = assemble, raise, levy, muster, mobilize ▸ n 4 = beginner, trainee, apprentice, novice, convert, initiate, helper, learner

rectangle n an oblong shape with four straight sides and four right angles > **rectangular** adj

rectify vb **-fies, -fying, -fied** 1 to put right; correct 2 chem to separate (a substance) from a mixture by distillation 3 electronics to convert (alternating current) into direct current > **rectification** n > **rectifier** n

rectilinear (rek-tee-lin-ee-er) adj formal 1 in a straight line 2 bounded by or formed of straight lines

rectitude n moral or religious correctness: a model of rectitude

recto n, pl **-tos** 1 the right-hand page of a book 2 the front of a sheet of printed paper

rector n 1 Church of England a member of the clergy in charge of a parish 2 RC Church a cleric in charge of a college or congregation 3 chiefly Brit the head of certain academic institutions 4 (in Scotland) a high-ranking official in a university, elected by the students > **rectorship** n

rectory n, pl **-ries** the house of a rector

rectum n, pl **-tums** or **-ta** the lower part of the alimentary canal, ending in the anus

recumbent adj lying down

recuperate vb **-rating, -rated** to recover from illness or exhaustion > **recuperation** n > **recuperative** adj

recur vb **-curring, -curred** 1 to happen or occur again 2 (of a thought or feeling) to come back to the mind > **recurrence** n > **recurrent** adj > **recurring** adj

> **recur** vb 1 = happen again, return, repeat, persist, revert, reappear, come again

recycle vb **-cling, -cled** 1 to reprocess (something already used) for further use: public demand for recycled paper 2 to pass (a substance) through a system again for further use > **recyclable** adj

> **recycle** vb 1 = reprocess, reuse, salvage, reclaim, save

red adj **redder, reddest** 1 of a colour varying from crimson to orange; of the colour of blood 2 reddish in colour or having parts or marks that are reddish: red deer 3 flushed in the face from anger or shame 4 (of the eyes) bloodshot 5 (of wine) made from black grapes and coloured by their skins ▸ n 6 the colour red; the colour of blood 7 anything red, such as red clothing or red paint: she had dressed in red 8 **in the red** informal in debt 9 **see red** informal to become very angry > **redness** n > **reddish** adj

> **red** adj 1 = crimson, scarlet, ruby, vermilion, cherry, coral, carmine 2 = chestnut, reddish, flame-coloured, sandy, Titian, carroty, ginger 3 = flushed, embarrassed, blushing, florid, shamefaced ▸ n 6 = crimson, scarlet, ruby, vermilion, cherry, coral, carmine 8 **in the red** = in debt, insolvent, in arrears, overdrawn 9 **see red** = lose your temper, lose it (informal), go mad (informal), crack up (informal), lose the plot (informal), go ballistic (slang), fly off the handle (informal), blow your top

Red informal ▸ n 1 a Communist or socialist ▸ adj 2 Communist or socialist

redback spider n a small venomous Australian spider with a red stripe on the back of the abdomen

red-blooded adj informal vigorous or virile

redbrick adj (of a British university) founded in the late 19th or early 20th century

red card soccer ▸ n 1 a piece of red pasteboard raised by a referee to indicate that a player has been sent off ▸ vb **red-card** 2 to send off (a player)

red carpet n very special treatment given to an important guest

redcoat n 1 history a British soldier 2 Canad informal a Mountie

Red Cross n an international organization (**Red Cross Society**) which helps victims of war or natural disaster

redcurrant n a very small red edible fruit that grows in bunches on a bush

redden vb 1 to make or become red or redder 2 to blush

redeem vb 1 to make up for 2 to reinstate (oneself) in someone's good opinion: he missed a penalty but redeemed himself by setting up the winning goal 3 Christianity (of Christ as Saviour) to free (humanity) from sin by death on the Cross 4 to buy back: she didn't have the money to redeem it 5 to pay off (a loan or debt) 6 to convert (bonds or shares) into cash 7 to exchange (coupons) for goods **8** to fulfil (a promise): *I vowed to abide by the bill and have redeemed my pledge* > **redeemable** *adj* > **redeemer** *n*

> **redeem** *vb* **1** = make up for, compensate for, atone for, make amends for **2** = reinstate, absolve, restore to favour **4** = buy back, recover, regain, retrieve, reclaim, repurchase

redemption *n* **1** the act of redeeming **2** the state of being redeemed **3** *Christianity* deliverance from sin through the incarnation and death of Christ > **redemptive** *adj*

> **redemption** *n* **1** = compensation, amends, reparation, atonement **2** = salvation, release, rescue, liberation, emancipation, deliverance

redeploy *vb* to assign (people) to new positions or tasks > **redeployment** *n*
redevelop *vb* to rebuild or renovate (an area or building) > **redeveloper** *n* > **redevelopment** *n*
red-handed *adj* **catch someone red-handed** to catch someone in the act of doing something wrong or illegal
red herring *n* something which diverts attention from the main issue
red-hot *adj* **1** (of metal) glowing hot **2** extremely hot **3** very keen or excited **4** furious: *one of those red-hot blazes of temper* **5** very recent or topical: *red-hot information*
red light *n* **1** a traffic signal to stop **2** a danger signal
red meat *n* meat, such as beef or lamb, that is dark brown when cooked
redolent *adj* **redolent of** *or* **with 1** reminiscent or suggestive of: *a castle redolent of historical novels* **2** smelling of: *the warm heavy air was redolent of sea and flowers* > **redolence** *n*
redouble *vb* **-bling, -bled 1** to make or become much greater: *the party will have to redouble its efforts* **2** *bridge* to double (an opponent's double)
redoubt *n* **1** a small fort defending a hill top or pass **2** a stronghold
redoubtable *adj* to be feared and respected: *the redoubtable Mr Brooks* > **redoubtably** *adv*
redound *vb* **1 redound to** to have an advantageous or disadvantageous effect on: *individual rights redound to the common good* **2 redound on** *or* **upon** to recoil or rebound on
redox *n* a chemical reaction between two substances, in which one is oxidized and the other reduced
redress *vb* **1** to make amends for **2** to adjust in order to make fair or equal: *to redress the balance* ▸ *n* **3** compensation or reparation **4** the setting right of a wrong

> **redress** *vb* **1** = make amends for, make up for, compensate for **2** = put right, balance, correct, adjust, regulate, rectify, even up ▸ *n* **3** = amends, payment, compensation, reparation, atonement, recompense

red tape *n* time-consuming official rules or procedure
reduce *vb* **-ducing, -duced 1** to bring down or lower: *monitoring could reduce the number of perinatal deaths* **2** to weaken or lessen: *vegetarian diets reduce cancer risk* **3** to bring by force or necessity to some state or action: *it reduced her to helpless laughter* **4** to slim **5** to set out systematically as an aid to understanding: *reducing the problem to three main issues* **6** *cookery* to thicken (a sauce) by boiling away some of its liquid **7** to impoverish: *to be in reduced circumstances* **8** *chem* **A** to undergo a chemical reaction with hydrogen **B** to lose oxygen atoms **C** to increase the number of electrons **9** *maths* to simplify the form of (an expression or equation), esp. by substitution of one term by another > **reducible** *adj*

> **reduce** *vb* **1, 2** = lessen, cut, lower, moderate, dial down, weaken, diminish, decrease, cut down, kennet (*Austral slang*), jeff (*Austral slang*); ≠ increase

reduction *n* **1** the act of reducing **2** the amount by which something is reduced **3** a reduced form of an original, such as a copy of a document on a smaller scale > **reductive** *adj*
redundant *adj* **1** deprived of one's job because it is no longer necessary or sufficiently profitable **2** surplus to requirements > **redundancy** *n*

> **redundant** *adj* **2** = superfluous, extra, surplus, unnecessary, unwanted, inessential, supernumerary; ≠ essential

reed *n* **1** a tall grass that grows in swamps and shallow water **2** a straight hollow stem of this plant **3** *music* **A** a thin piece of cane or metal in certain wind instruments, which vibrates producing a musical note when the instrument is blown **B** a wind instrument or organ pipe that sounds by means of a reed
reedy *adj* **reedier, reediest 1** harsh or thin in tone: *his reedy, hesitant voice* **2** (of a place) full of reeds > **reedily** *adv* > **reediness** *n*
reef[1] *n* **1** a ridge of rock, sand, or coral, lying just beneath the surface of the sea: *a coral reef* **2** a vein of ore
reef[2] *naut* ▸ *n* **1** the part of a sail which can be rolled up to reduce its area ▸ *vb* **2** to reduce the area of (sail) by taking in a reef
reefer *n* **1** Also called: **reefer jacket** a man's short heavy double-breasted woollen jacket **2** *old-fashioned slang* a hand-rolled cigarette containing cannabis
reef knot *n* a knot consisting of two overhand knots turned opposite ways
reek *vb* **1** to give off a strong unpleasant smell **2 reek of** to give a strong suggestion of: *the scene had reeked of insincerity* **3** *dialect* to give off smoke or fumes ▸ *n* **4** a strong unpleasant smell **5** *dialect* smoke or steam
reel[1] *n* **1** a cylindrical object or frame that turns on an axis and onto which film, tape, wire, or

r

thread is wound **2** a winding device attached to a fishing rod, used for casting and winding in the line **3** a roll of film for projection ▸ *vb* **4 reel in** to wind or draw in on a reel

reel² *vb* **1** to move unsteadily or spin round, as if about to fall **2** to be in a state of confusion or stress: *my mind was still reeling*

> **reel** *vb* **1** = whirl, spin, revolve, swirl

reel³ *n* **1** a lively Scottish dance **2** music for this dance

reel off *vb* to recite or write fluently or quickly

ref *n informal* the referee in a sport

refectory *n, pl* **-ries** a dining hall in a religious or academic institution

refer *vb* **-ferring, -ferred** > **refer to 1** to mention or allude to **2** to be relevant or relate (to): *the word cancer refers to many quite specific different diseases* **3** to seek information (from): *he referred to his notes* **4** to direct the attention of (someone) for information: *the reader is referred to the introduction* **5** to direct (a patient or client) to another doctor or agency: *her GP referred her to a specialist* **6** to hand over for consideration or decision: *to refer a complaint to another department* > **referable** or **referrable** *adj* > **referral** *n*

> **refer** *vb* **1 refer to something or someone** = allude to, mention, cite, speak of, bring up **2 refer to something or someone** = relate to, concern, apply to, pertain to, be relevant to **3 refer to something or someone** = consult, go, apply, turn to, look up **4** = direct, point, send, guide

referee *n* **1** the umpire in various sports, such as football and boxing **2** a person who is willing to provide a reference for someone for a job **3** a person referred to for a decision or opinion in a dispute ▸ *vb* **-reeing, -reed 4** to act as a referee

> **referee** *n* **1** = umpire, umpie (*Austral slang*), judge, ref (*informal*), arbiter, arbitrator, adjudicator ▸ *vb* = umpire, judge, mediate, adjudicate, arbitrate

reference *n* **1** the act of referring **2** a mention: *this book contains several references to the Civil War* **3** direction to a passage elsewhere in a book or to another book **4** a book or passage referred to **5** a written testimonial regarding one's character or capabilities **6** a person referred to for such a testimonial **7** relation or restriction, esp. to or by membership of a specific group: *without reference to sex or age* **8 with reference to** concerning ▸ *adj* **9** containing information or facts: *reference books* > **referential** *adj*

> **reference** *n* **2** = allusion, note, mention, quotation **4** = citation **5** = testimonial, recommendation, credentials, endorsement, character reference

referendum *n, pl* **-dums** or **-da** a direct vote of the electorate on a question of importance

referendum *n* = public vote, popular vote, plebiscite

refill *vb* **1** to fill (something) again ▸ *n* **2** a second or subsequent filling: *I held out my glass for a refill* **3** a replacement supply of something in a permanent container > **refillable** *adj*

refine *vb* **-fining, -fined 1** to make free from impurities; purify **2** to improve: *surgical techniques are constantly being refined* **3** to separate (a mixture) into pure constituents: *molasses is a residual syrup obtained during sugar refining*

> **refine** *vb* **1** = purify, process, filter, cleanse, clarify, distil **2** = improve, perfect, polish, hone

refined *adj* **1** cultured or polite **2** freed from impurities **3** highly developed and effective: *refined intelligence tests*

> **refined** *adj* **1** = cultured, polished, elegant, polite, cultivated, civilized, well-bred; ≠ coarse **2** = purified, processed, pure, filtered, clean, clarified, distilled; ≠ unrefined **3** = discerning, fine, sensitive, delicate, precise, discriminating, fastidious

refinement *n* **1** an improvement to something, such as a piece of equipment **2** fineness of taste or manners **3** a subtle point or distinction **4** the act of refining

refinery *n, pl* **-neries** a factory for purifying a raw material, such as sugar or oil

reflation *n* an increase in the supply of money and credit designed to encourage economic activity > **reflate** *vb* > **reflationary** *adj*

reflect *vb* **1** (of a surface or object) to throw back (light, heat, or sound) **2** (of a mirror) to form an image of (something) by reflection **3** to show: *many of her books reflect her obsession with fine art* **4** to consider carefully **5 reflect on** or **upon** to cause to be regarded in a specified way: *the incident reflects very badly on me* **6** to bring as a consequence: *the programme reflected great credit on the technicians*

> **reflect** *vb* **1, 2** = throw back, return, mirror, echo, reproduce **3** = show, reveal, display, indicate, demonstrate, manifest **4** = consider, think, muse, ponder, meditate, ruminate, cogitate, wonder

reflection *n* **1** the act of reflecting **2** the return of rays of light, heat, or sound **3** an image of an object given back in a mirror **4** careful or long consideration **5 on reflection** after careful consideration or reconsideration **6** discredit or blame: *it's a sad reflection on modern morality* **7** *maths* a transformation of a shape in which right and left, or top and bottom, are reversed

> **reflection** *n* **3** = image, echo, mirror image **4** = consideration, thinking, thought, idea, opinion, observation, musing, meditation

reflective *adj* **1** characterized by quiet thought or contemplation **2** capable of reflecting: *a reflective coating*

> **reflective** *adj* **1** = thoughtful, contemplative, meditative, pensive

reflector *n* **1** a polished surface for reflecting light **2** a reflecting telescope

reflex *n* **1** an immediate involuntary response to a given stimulus **2** a mechanical response to a particular situation, involving no conscious decision **3** an image produced by reflection ▸ *adj* **4** of or caused by a reflex: *a reflex action* **5** reflected **6** *maths* (of an angle) between 180° and 360°

reflexive *adj* **1** *grammar* denoting a pronoun that refers back to the subject of a sentence or clause. Thus, in *that man thinks a great deal of himself*, the pronoun *himself* is reflexive **2** *grammar* denoting a verb used with a reflexive pronoun as its direct object, as in *to dress oneself* **3** *physiol* of or relating to a reflex ▸ *n* **4** a reflexive pronoun or verb

reflexology *n* foot massage as a therapy in alternative medicine > **reflexologist** *n*

reform *n* **1** correction of abuses or malpractices: *a programme of economic reforms* **2** improvement of morals or behaviour ▸ *vb* **3** to improve (a law or institution) by correcting abuses **4** to give up or cause to give up a bad habit or way of life > **reformative** *adj* > **reformer** *n*

> **reform** *n* **1** = improvement, amendment, rehabilitation, betterment ▸ *vb* **3** = improve, correct, restore, amend, mend, rectify **4** = mend your ways, go straight (*informal*), shape up (*informal*), turn over a new leaf, clean up your act (*informal*), pull your socks up (*Brit informal*)

reformation (ref-fer-**may**-shun) *n* **1** a reforming **2 the Reformation** a religious movement in 16th-century Europe that began as an attempt to reform the Roman Catholic Church and resulted in the establishment of the Protestant Churches

reformatory *n, pl* **-ries** (formerly) a place where young offenders were sent to be reformed

refract *vb* to cause light, heat, or sound to undergo refraction > **refractive** *adj* > **refractor** *n*

refraction *n physics* **1** the change in direction of a wave, such as light or sound, in passing from one medium to another in which it has a different velocity **2** the amount by which a wave is refracted

refractory *adj* **1** *formal* stubborn or rebellious **2** *med* not responding to treatment **3** (of a material) able to withstand high temperatures without fusion or decomposition

refrain¹ *vb* **refrain from** to keep oneself from doing

> **refrain** *vb* = stop, avoid, cease, renounce, abstain, leave off, desist, forbear

refrain² *n* **1** a frequently repeated part of a song **2** a much repeated saying or idea

> **refrain** *n* **1** = chorus, tune, melody

refresh *vb* **1** to revive or reinvigorate, for example through rest, drink, or food **2** to stimulate (the memory) > **refresher** *n*

> **refresh** *vb* **1** = revive, freshen, revitalize, stimulate, brace, enliven, invigorate **2** = stimulate, prompt, renew, jog

refreshing *adj* **1** having a reviving effect **2** pleasantly different or new: *refreshing candour*

> **refreshing** *adj* **1** = stimulating, fresh, bracing, invigorating; ≠ tiring **2** = new, original, novel

refreshment *n* **1** the act of refreshing **2 refreshments** snacks and drinks served as a light meal

> **refreshment** *n* **2** = food and drink, drinks, snacks, titbits, kai (*NZ informal*)

refrigerate *vb* **-rating, -rated** to chill or freeze in order to preserve > **refrigeration** *n*

refrigerator *n* the full name for **fridge**

refuge *n* **1** shelter or protection from danger or hardship **2** a place, person, or thing that offers protection or help

> **refuge** *n* **1** = protection, shelter, asylum **2** = haven, retreat, sanctuary, hide-out

refugee *n* a person who has fled from some danger, such as war or political persecution

> **refugee** *n* = exile, émigré, displaced person, escapee

refulgent *adj literary* shining brightly > **refulgence** *n*

refund *vb* **1** to give back (money) **2** to pay back (a person) ▸ *n* **3** return of money to a purchaser or the amount returned > **refundable** *adj*

> **refund** *vb* **1** = repay, return, restore, pay back, reimburse ▸ *n* = repayment, reimbursement, return

refurbish *vb* to renovate and brighten up > **refurbishment** *n*

> **refurbish** *vb* = renovate, restore, repair, clean up, overhaul, revamp, mend, do up (*informal*)

refusal *n* **1** the act of refusing **2** the opportunity to reject or accept: *he was given first refusal on all three scripts*

> **refusal** *n* **1** = rejection, denial, rebuff, knock-back (*slang*)

refuse¹ (rif-**yooz**) *vb* **-fusing, -fused 1** to be determined not (to do something): *he refuses to consider it* **2** to decline to give or allow (something) to (someone): *if the judge refuses bail, he'll appeal* **3** to decline to accept (something offered):

r

he *refused the captaincy* **4** (of a horse) to be unwilling to jump a fence

> **refuse** vb **1, 3** = decline, reject, turn down, say no to **2** = deny, decline, withhold; ≠ allow

refuse² (**ref**-yoos) n anything thrown away; rubbish

> **refuse** n = rubbish, waste, junk (*informal*), litter, garbage (*chiefly US*), trash (*chiefly US, Canad*)

refute vb **-futing, -futed** to prove (a statement or theory) to be false or incorrect > **refutation** n
regain vb **1** to get back or recover **2** to reach again: *to regain the shore*

> **regain** vb **1** = recover, get back, retrieve, recapture, win back, take back, recoup **2** = get back to, return to, reach again

regal adj **1** of or fit for a king or queen **2** splendid and dignified; magnificent: *a luxury cruise liner on her serene and regal way around the better ports* > **regality** n > **regally** adv

> **regal** adj = royal, majestic, kingly *or* queenly, noble, princely, magnificent

regale vb **-galing, -galed 1** to give delight or amusement to: *she would regale her friends with stories* **2** to provide with abundant food or drink
regalia n the ceremonial emblems or robes of royalty or high office
regard vb **1** to look upon or think of in a specified way: *angina can therefore be regarded as heart cramp* **2** to look closely or attentively at (something or someone) **3** to take notice of: *he has never regarded the conventions* **4 as regards** on the subject of ▶ n **5** respect or affection: *you haven't a high regard for her opinion* **6** attention: *he eats what he wants with no regard to health* **7** a gaze or look **8** reference or connection: *with regard to my complaint* **9 regards** an expression of goodwill: *give her my regards*

> **regard** vb **1** = consider, see, rate, view, judge, think of, esteem (*formal*), deem **2** = look at, view, eye, watch, observe, clock (*Brit slang*), check out (*informal*), gaze at **4 as regards** = concerning, regarding, relating to, pertaining to ▶ n **5** = respect, esteem, thought, concern, care, consideration **7** = look, gaze, scrutiny, stare, glance **9** = good wishes, respects, greetings, compliments, best wishes

regardless adj **1 regardless of** taking no notice of: *the illness can affect anyone regardless of their social class* ▶ adv **2** in spite of everything: *I carried on regardless*

> **regardless** adj = irrespective of, heedless of, unmindful of ▶ adv = in spite of everything, anyway, nevertheless, in any case

regatta n a series of races of boats or yachts

regency n, pl **-cies 1** government by a regent **2** the status of a regent **3** a period when a regent is in power
regenerate vb (ri-**jen**-er-ate) **-rating, -rated 1** to undergo or cause to undergo physical, economic, or spiritual renewal **2** to come or bring into existence once again **3** to replace (lost or damaged tissues or organs) by new growth ▶ adj (ri-**jen**-er-it) **4** physically, economically, or spiritually renewed > **regeneration** n > **regenerative** adj
regent n **1** the ruler of a country during the childhood, absence, or illness of its monarch **2** US & Canad a member of the governing board of certain schools and colleges ▶ adj **3** acting as a regent: *the Prince Regent*
reggae n a type of popular music of Jamaican origin with a strong beat
regicide n **1** the killing of a king **2** a person who kills a king
regime (ray-**zheem**) n **1** a system of government **2** a particular administration: *the corrupt regime* **3** med a regimen

> **regime** n **1, 2** = government, rule, management, leadership, reign **3** = plan, course, system, policy, programme, scheme, regimen

regimen n a prescribed system of diet and exercise
regiment n **1** an organized body of troops as a unit in the army **2** a large number or group > **regimental** adj
regimented adj very strictly controlled: *the regimented confines of the school* > **regimentation** n
region n **1** an administrative division of a country **2** an area considered as a unit for geographical or social reasons **3** a sphere of activity or interest **4** a part of the body: *the lumbar region* **5 in the region of** approximately: *in the region of 100 000 troops* **6 the regions** the parts of a country away from the capital: *discord between Moscow and the regions* > **regional** adj

> **region** n **1, 2** = area, place, part, quarter, section, sector, district, territory

register n **1** an official list recording names, events, or transactions **2** the book in which such a list is written **3** a device that records data, totals sums of money, etc.: *a cash register* **4** a style of speaking or writing, such as slang, used in particular circumstances or social situations **5** music **A** the timbre characteristic of a certain manner of voice production **B** any of the stops on an organ in respect of its tonal quality: *the flute register* ▶ vb **6** to enter (an event, person's name, ownership, etc.) in a register **7** to show on a scale or other measuring instrument **8** to show in a person's face or bearing: *his face registered surprise* **9** informal to have an effect or make an impression: *the news did not register at first* > **registration** n

register *n* **1, 2** = list, record, roll, file, diary, catalogue, log, archives ▸ *vb* **6** = enrol, enlist, list, note, enter **7** = indicate, show **8** = show, mark, indicate, manifest

register office *n Brit* a government office where civil marriages are performed and births, marriages, and deaths are recorded

registrar *n* **1** a person who keeps official records **2** an official responsible for student records and enrolment in a college **3** *Brit, Austral & S African* a hospital doctor senior to a house officer but junior to a consultant **4** an organization that administers the reservation of internet domain names

registration number *n Brit* a sequence of letters and numbers given to a motor vehicle when it is registered, displayed on numberplates at the front and rear

Regius professor (reej-yuss) *n Brit* a person appointed by the Crown to a university chair founded by a royal patron

regress *vb* **1** to return to a former and worse condition ▸ *n* **2** a return to a former and worse condition ▸ **regressive** *adj*

regression *n* **1** the act of regressing **2** *psychol* the use by an adult of behaviour more appropriate to a child

regret *vb* **-gretting, -gretted 1** to feel sorry or upset about **2** to express apology or distress about: *we regret any misunderstanding caused* ▸ *n* **3** a feeling of repentance, guilt, or sorrow **4 regrets** a polite expression of refusal: *she had sent her regrets* ▸ **regretful** *adj* ▸ **regretfully** *adv* ▸ **regrettable** *adj* ▸ **regrettably** *adv*

regret *vb* **1** = mourn, miss, grieve for *or* over; ≠ be satisfied with ▸ *n* **3** = sorrow; ≠ satisfaction

regular *adj* **1** normal, customary, or usual **2** symmetrical or even: *regular features* **3** according to a uniform principle, arrangement, or order **4** occurring at fixed or prearranged intervals: *we run regular advertisements in the press* **5** following a set rule or normal practice **6** *grammar* following the usual pattern of formation in a language: *regular verbs* **7** of or serving in the permanent military services: *the regular armed forces* **8** *maths* (of a polygon) having all its sides and angles the same **9** officially qualified or recognized: *he's not a regular doctor* **10** *informal* not constipated: *eating fresh vegetables helps keep you regular* **11** *US & Canad informal* likeable: *a regular guy* **12** complete or utter: *a regular fool* **13** subject to the rule of an established religious community: *canons regular* ▸ *n* **14** a professional long-term serviceman or servicewoman in a military unit **15** *informal* a frequent customer or visitor ▸ **regularity** *n* ▸ **regularize** *or* **-rise** *vb* ▸ **regularly** *adv*

regular *adj* **1, 5** = normal, common, usual, ordinary, typical, routine, customary, habitual; ≠ infrequent **2** = even, level, balanced, straight, flat, fixed, smooth, uniform; ≠ uneven **4** = frequent

regulate *vb* **-lating, -lated 1** to control by means of rules: *a code of practice to regulate advertising by schools* **2** to adjust slightly: *he had to take drugs to regulate his heartbeat* ▸ **regulatory** *adj*

regulate *vb* **1** = control, run, rule, manage, direct, guide, handle, govern **2** = moderate, control, modulate, fit, tune, adjust

regulation *n* **1** a rule that governs procedure or behaviour **2** the act of regulating ▸ *adj* **3** in accordance with rules or conventions: *dressed in the orchestra's regulation black tie*

regulation *n* **1** = rule, order, law, dictate, decree, statute, edict, precept **2** = control, government, management, direction, supervision

regulator *n* **1** a mechanism that automatically controls pressure, temperature, etc. **2** the mechanism by which the speed of a clock is regulated

regurgitate *vb* **-tating, -tated 1** to vomit **2** (of some birds and animals) to bring back (partly digested food) to the mouth to feed the young **3** to reproduce (ideas or facts) without understanding them ▸ **regurgitation** *n*

rehabilitate *vb* **-tating, -tated 1** to help (a person) to readapt to society after illness or imprisonment **2** to restore to a former position or rank **3** to restore the good reputation of ▸ **rehabilitation** *n*

rehash *vb* **1** to use (old or already used ideas) in a slightly different form without real improvement ▸ *n* **2** old ideas presented in a new form

rehearse *vb* **-hearsing, -hearsed 1** to practise (a play, concert, etc.) for public performance **2** to repeat aloud: *he rehearsed his familiar views on the press* **3** to train (a person) for public performance ▸ **rehearsal** *n* ▸ **rehearser** *n*

rehearse *vb* **1** = practise, prepare, run through, go over, train, repeat, drill, recite

rehouse *vb* **-housing, -housed** to provide with a new and better home

reign *n* **1** the period during which a monarch is the official ruler of a country **2** a period during which a person or thing is dominant: *a reign of terror* ▸ *vb* **3** to rule (a country) **4** to be supreme: *a sense of confusion reigns in the capital*

reign *n* **1** = rule, power, control, command, monarchy, dominion ▸ *vb* **3** = rule, govern, be in power, influence, command **4** = be supreme, prevail, predominate, hold sway

reimburse *vb* **-bursing, -bursed** to repay (someone) for (expenses or losses) ▸ **reimbursement** *n*

rein *n* **1 reins a** long narrow straps attached to a bit to control a horse **b** narrow straps attached to a harness to control a young child **c** means of control: *to take up the reins of government* **2 give (a) free rein** to allow a considerable amount of

r

freedom **3 keep a tight rein on** to control carefully: *we have to keep a tight rein on expenditure* ▸ *vb* **4** to restrain or halt with reins **5** to control or limit: *reining her thoughts, she tried to be objective*

> **rein** *n* **1A, 1B** = control, harness, bridle, hold, check, brake, curb, restraint

reincarnate *vb* **-nating, -nated** (*often passive*) to be born again in a different body: *souls may be reincarnated in human forms*

reincarnation *n* **1** the belief that after death the soul is reborn in another body **2** an instance of rebirth in another body **3** reappearance in a new form of a principle or idea: *he was the reincarnation of the old Republican Party isolationist*

> **reincarnation** *n* **1** = rebirth

reindeer *n, pl* **-deer** *or* **-deers** a deer with large branched antlers that lives in the arctic regions

reinforce *vb* **-inforcing, -inforced 1** to give added emphasis to (an idea or feeling): *his tired face reinforced his own weariness* **2** to make physically stronger or harder: *the plastic panels were reinforced with carbon fibre* **3** to give added support to (a military force) by providing more men or equipment: *the army garrison had been reinforced with helicopters* > **reinforcement** *n*

> **reinforce** *vb* **2** = support, strengthen, fortify, toughen, stress, prop, supplement, emphasize **3** = increase, extend, add to, strengthen, supplement

reinforced concrete *n* concrete with steel bars or mesh embedded in it to strengthen it

reinstate *vb* **-stating, -stated 1** to restore to a former rank or status **2** to cause to exist or be important again: *reinstate some semblance of order* > **reinstatement** *n*

> **reinstate** *vb* **1** = restore, recall, re-establish, return

reiterate *vb* **-rating, -rated** *formal* to repeat again and again > **reiteration** *n*

> **reiterate** *vb* = repeat, restate, say again, do again

reject *vb* **1** to refuse to accept, use, or believe **2** to deny to (a person) the feelings hoped for: *the boy had been rejected by his mother* **3** to pass over or throw out as useless **4** (of an organism) to fail to accept (a tissue graft or organ transplant) ▸ *n* **5** a person or thing rejected as not up to standard > **rejection** *n*

> **reject** *vb* **1** = deny, exclude, veto, relinquish, renounce, disallow, forsake, disown; ≠ approve **2** = rebuff, jilt, turn down, spurn, refuse, say no to, repulse, unfollow, unfriend; ≠ accept **3** = discard, decline, eliminate, scrap, jettison, throw away *or* out; ≠ accept ▸ *n* = failure, loser, flop (*informal*); ≠ treasure

rejig *vb* **-jigging, -jigged 1** to re-equip (a factory or plant) **2** *informal* to rearrange or manipulate,

sometimes in an unscrupulous way: *the promoter hastily rejigged the running order*

rejoice *vb* **-joicing, -joiced** to feel or express great happiness > **rejoicing** *n*

> **rejoice** *vb* = be glad, celebrate, be happy, glory, be overjoyed, exult; ≠ lament

rejoin¹ *vb* to come together with (someone or something) again

rejoin² *vb* to reply in a sharp or witty way

> **rejoin** *vb* = reply, answer, respond, retort, riposte

rejoinder *n* a sharp or witty reply

rejuvenate *vb* **-nating, -nated** to give back youth or vitality to > **rejuvenation** *n*

relapse *vb* **-lapsing, -lapsed 1** to fall back into bad habits or illness ▸ *n* **2** the act of relapsing **3** the return of ill health after an apparent or partial recovery

relate *vb* **-lating, -lated 1** to establish a relation between **2** to have reference or relation to **3** to have an understanding (of people or ideas): *the inability to relate to others* **4** to tell (a story) or describe (an event)

> **relate** *vb* **1 relate to something or someone** = connect with, associate with, link with, couple with, join with, correlate to **2 relate to something or someone** = concern, refer to, apply to, have to do with, pertain to, be relevant to **4** = tell, recount, report, detail, describe, recite, narrate

related *adj* **1** linked by kinship or marriage **2** connected or associated: *salts and related compounds*

> **related** *adj* **1** = akin, kindred; ≠ unrelated **2** = associated, linked, joint, connected, affiliated, akin, interconnected; ≠ unconnected

relation *n* **1** the connection between things or people **2** a person who is connected by blood or marriage **3** connection by blood or marriage **4** an account or narrative **5 in** *or* **with relation to** with reference to: *an inquiry into export controls in relation to Iraq*

> **relation** *n* **1** = similarity, link, bearing, bond, comparison, correlation, connection **2** = relative, kin, kinsman *or* woman *or* person, rellie (*Austral slang*)

relationship *n* **1** the dealings and feelings that exist between people or groups **2** an emotional or sexual affair **3** the connection between two things: *the relationship between exercise and mental health* **4** association by blood or marriage

> **relationship** *n* **1** = association, bond, connection, affinity, rapport, kinship **2** = affair, romance, liaison, amour, intrigue **3** = connection, link, parallel, similarity, tie-up, correlation, read-across

r

relative *adj* **1** true to a certain degree or extent: *a zone of relative affluence* **2** having significance only in relation to something else: *time is relative* **3** **relative to** in proportion to: *it will benefit from high growth in earnings relative to prices* **4** respective: *the relative qualities of speed and accuracy* **5** relevant: *the facts relative to the enquiry* **6** *grammar* of a clause (**relative clause**) that modifies a noun or pronoun occurring earlier in the sentence **7** *grammar* of or belonging to a class of words, such as *who*, *which*, or *that*, which function as conjunctions introducing relative clauses ▸ *n* **8** a person who is related by blood or marriage > **relatively** *adv*

> **relative** *adj* **1** = comparative **3** = in proportion to, proportionate to **4** = corresponding ▸ *n* = relation, kinsman *or* woman *or* person, member of your *or* the family, cuzzie *or* cuzzie-bro (*NZ*), rellie (*Austral slang*)

relativity *n* **1** either of two theories developed by Albert Einstein, the **special theory of relativity**, which requires that the laws of physics shall be the same as seen by any two different observers in uniform relative motion, and the **general theory of relativity**, which considers observers with relative acceleration and leads to a theory of gravitation **2** the state of being relative

relax *vb* **1** to make or become less tense, looser, or less rigid **2** to ease up from effort or attention **3** to make (rules or discipline) less strict **4** to become more friendly **5** to lessen the intensity of: *he relaxed his vigilance in the lulls between attacks* > **relaxed** *adj* > **relaxing** *adj*

> **relax** *vb* **1** = make less tense, rest; ≠ be alarmed **2** = calm down, calm, unwind **3** = moderate, ease, relieve, weaken, slacken; ≠ tighten up **4** = be *or* feel at ease, chill out (*slang*), take it easy, lighten up (*slang*), outspan (*S African*); ≠ be alarmed **5** = lessen, reduce, ease, relieve, weaken, loosen, let up, slacken; ≠ tighten

relaxation *n* **1** rest after work or effort **2** a form of recreation: *his favoured form of relaxation was walking on the local moors* **3** the act of relaxing

> **relaxation** *n* **1, 2** = leisure, rest, fun, pleasure, recreation, enjoyment, me-time

relay *n* **1** a fresh set of people or animals relieving others **2** short for **relay race 3** an automatic device that controls a valve or switch, esp. one in which a small change in current or voltage controls the switching on or off of circuits **4** *radio* a combination of a receiver and transmitter designed to receive radio signals and retransmit them ▸ *vb* **5** to pass on (a message) **6** to retransmit (a signal) by means of a relay **7** *Brit* to broadcast (a performance or event) as it happens

> **relay** *vb* **6, 7** = broadcast, carry, spread, communicate, transmit, send out, stream

relay race *n* a race between teams in which each contestant covers a specified portion of the distance

release *vb* **-leasing, -leased 1** to free (a person or animal) from captivity or imprisonment **2** to free (someone) from obligation or duty **3** to free (something) from (one's grip) **4** to allow (news or information) to be made public or available **5** to allow (something) to move freely: *she released the handbrake* **6** to issue (a music recording, film, or book) for sale or public showing: *When was the film originally released?* **7** to give out (heat, energy, radiation, etc.): *the explosion released a cloud of toxic gas* ▸ *n* **8** the act of freeing or state of being freed **9** a statement to the press **10** the act of issuing for sale or publication **11** something issued for sale or public showing

> **release** *vb* **1** = set free, free, discharge, liberate, drop, loose, undo, extricate; ≠ imprison **2** = acquit, let go, let off, exonerate, absolve **4** = issue, publish, make public, make known, launch, distribute, put out, circulate; ≠ withhold ▸ *n* **8** = liberation, freedom, liberty, discharge, emancipation, deliverance; ≠ imprisonment **9** = issue, publication, proclamation

relegate *vb* **-gating, -gated 1** to put in a less important position **2** to demote (a sports team) to a lower division: *four clubs were relegated from the first division* > **relegation** *n*

> **relegate** *vb* = demote, degrade, downgrade

relent *vb* **1** to change one's mind about some decision **2** to become milder or less severe: *the weather relented*

relentless *adj* **1** never stopping or reducing in severity: *relentless deterioration in standards* **2** (of a person) determined and pitiless

> **relentless** *adj* **1** = unremitting, persistent, unrelenting, incessant, nonstop, unrelieved **2** = merciless, fierce, cruel, ruthless, unrelenting, implacable, remorseless, pitiless; ≠ merciful

relevant *adj* to do with the matter in hand > **relevance** *n*

> **relevant** *adj* = significant, appropriate, related, fitting, to the point, apt, pertinent, apposite; ≠ irrelevant

reliable *adj* able to be trusted > **reliability** *n* > **reliably** *adv*

> **reliable** *adj* = dependable, trustworthy, sure, sound, true, faithful, staunch; ≠ unreliable

reliance *n* the state of relying on or trusting (a person or thing) > **reliant** *adj*

> **reliance** *n* = trust, confidence, belief, faith

r

relic *n* **1** an object or custom that has survived from the past **2** something valued for its past associations **3 relics** remaining parts or traces **4** *RC Church & Eastern churches* a body part or possession of a saint, venerated as holy

> **relic** *n* **1, 2** = remnant, vestige, memento, trace, fragment, souvenir, keepsake

relict *n* **1** a group of animals or plants that exists as a remnant of a formerly widely distributed group in an environment different from that in which it originated **2** *archaic* anything that is left behind from an earlier time

relief *n* **1** a feeling of cheerfulness that follows the removal of anxiety, pain, or distress **2** a temporary pause in anxiety, pain, or distress **3** money, food, or clothing given to people in special need: *disaster relief* **4** the act of freeing a besieged town or fortress: *the relief of Mafeking* **5** a person who replaces another at some task or duty **6** a bus, plane, etc., that carries additional passengers when a scheduled service is full **7** Also called: **relievo** *sculpture & archit* the projection of a carved design from the surface **8** any vivid effect resulting from contrast: *a welcome relief* **9** the difference between the highest and lowest level: *study the map of relief and the rainfall map* **10 on relief** *US & Canad* (of people) in receipt of government aid because of personal need

> **relief** *n* **1, 8** = ease, release, comfort, cure, remedy, solace, deliverance, mitigation **2** = rest, respite, relaxation, break, breather (*informal*) **3** = aid, help, support, assistance, succour

relief map *n* a map showing the shape and height of the land surface by contours and shading

relieve *vb* **-lieving, -lieved 1** to lessen (pain, distress, boredom, etc.) **2** to bring assistance to (someone in need): *a plan to relieve those facing hunger* **3** to free (someone) from an obligation: *a further attempt to relieve the taxpayers of their burdens* **4** to take over the duties of (someone): *the night nurse came in to relieve her* **5** to free (a besieged town or fort) **6 relieve oneself** to urinate or defecate **7** to set off by contrast: *painted walls are marginally relieved by some abstract prints* **8** *informal* to take from: *the prince had relieved him of his duties* > **relieved** *adj*

> **relieve** *vb* **1** = ease, soothe, alleviate, relax, comfort, calm, cure, soften; ≠ intensify **2** = help, support, aid, sustain, assist, succour

religion *n* **1** belief in or worship of a supernatural power or powers considered to be divine or to have control of human destiny **2** any formal expression of such belief: *the Christian religion* **3** *chiefly RC Church* the way of life entered upon by monks and nuns: *to enter religion*

> **religion** *n* **1, 2** = belief, faith, theology, creed

religious *adj* **1** of religion **2** pious or devout **3** scrupulous or conscientious: *religious attention to detail* **4** *Christianity* relating to the way of life of monks and nuns ► *n* **5** *Christianity* a monk or nun > **religiously** *adv*

> **religious** *adj* **1** = spiritual, holy, sacred, devotional **3** = conscientious, faithful, rigid, meticulous, scrupulous, punctilious (*formal*)

relinquish *vb formal* **1** to give up: *that hope has to be relinquished* **2** to renounce (a claim or right) **3** to release one's hold on > **relinquishment** *n*

> **relinquish** *vb* **1, 2** = give up, leave, drop, abandon, surrender, let go, renounce, forsake

reliquary (rel-lik-wer-ee) *n, pl* **-quaries** a container for relics of saints

relish *vb* **1** to savour or enjoy (an experience) to the full **2** to anticipate eagerly ► *n* **3** liking or enjoyment: *he has an enormous relish for life* **4** pleasurable anticipation: *his early relish for a new challenge* **5** an appetizing or spicy food, such as a pickle, added to a main dish to improve its flavour **6** a zestful quality: *he tells stories with great relish*

> **relish** *vb* **1** = enjoy, like, savour, revel in; ≠ dislike **2** = look forward to, fancy (*informal*), delight in ► *n* **3** = enjoyment, liking, love, taste, fancy, penchant, fondness, gusto; ≠ distaste **5** = condiment, seasoning, sauce

relocate *vb* **-cating, -cated** to move or be moved to a new place of work > **relocation** *n*

reluctance *n* **1** unwillingness to do something **2** *physics* a measure of the resistance of a closed magnetic circuit to a magnetic flux

> **reluctance** *n* **1** = unwillingness, dislike, loathing, distaste, aversion, disinclination, repugnance

reluctant *adj* unwilling or disinclined > **reluctantly** *adv*

> **reluctant** *adj* = unwilling, hesitant, loath, disinclined, unenthusiastic; ≠ willing

rely *vb* **-lies, -lying, -lied** > **rely on** *or* **upon** **A** to be dependent on: *the organization relies on voluntary contributions* **B** to have trust or confidence in: *you can rely on his judgment*

> **rely** *vb* **1A** = depend on, lean on **1B** = be confident of, bank on, trust, count on, bet on

remain *vb* **1** to continue to be: *the situation remains alarming* **2** to stay behind or in the same place: *to remain at home* **3** to be left after use or the passage of time **4** to be left to be done, said, etc.: *whether this will be a long-term trend remains to be seen*

> **remain** *vb* **1** = stay, continue, go on, stand, dwell (*formal, literary*) **2** = stay behind, wait, delay; ≠ go

remainder *n* **1** a part or portion that is left after use or the passage of time: *we ate some biscuits and the remainder of the jam* **2** *maths* **A** the amount left over when one quantity cannot be exactly divided by another: *for 10 ÷ 3, the remainder is 1* **B** the amount left over when one quantity is subtracted from another **3** a number of copies of a book sold cheaply because it has been impossible to sell them at full price ▸ *vb* **4** to sell (copies of a book) as a remainder

remainder *n* **1** = rest, remains, balance, excess, surplus, remnant, residue, leavings

remains *pl n* **1** parts left over from something after use or the passage of time: *the remains of the old Roman fortress* **2** a corpse

remains *pl n* **1** = remnants, leftovers, rest, debris, residue, dregs, leavings **2** = corpse, body, carcass, cadaver

remand *vb* **1** *law* to send (a prisoner or accused person) back into custody or put on bail before trial ▸ *n* **2** the sending of a person back into custody or putting on bail before trial **3 on remand** in custody or on bail awaiting trial

remand centre *n* a place where accused people are detained while awaiting trial

remark *vb* **1** to pass a casual comment (about) **2** to say **3** to observe or notice ▸ *n* **4** a brief casually expressed thought or opinion

remark *vb* **1, 2** = comment, say, state, reflect, mention, declare, observe, pass comment **3** = notice, note, observe, perceive, see, mark, make out, espy ▸ *n* = comment, observation, reflection, statement, utterance

remarkable *adj* **1** worthy of note or attention: *a remarkable career* **2** striking or extraordinary: *a thing of remarkable beauty* > **remarkably** *adv*

remarkable *adj* = extraordinary, striking, outstanding, wonderful, rare, unusual, surprising, notable, ≠ ordinary

remedial *adj* **1** providing or intended as a remedy **2** of special teaching for slow learners: *remedial classes* > **remedially** *adv*

remedy *n, pl* **-edies 1** a drug or treatment for curing pain or disease **2** a way of solving a problem: *every statesman promised a remedy for unemployment* ▸ *vb* **-edies, -edying, -edied 3** to put right or improve > **remediable** *adj*

remedy *n* **1** = cure, treatment, medicine, nostrum ▸ *vb* = put right, rectify, fix, correct, set to rights

remember *vb* **1** to become aware of (something forgotten) again **2** to keep (an idea, intention, etc.) in one's mind: *remember to write* **3** to give money to (someone), as in a will or in tipping **4 remember to** to mention (a person's name) to another person, by way of greeting: *remember me to her* **5** to commemorate: *we are here to remember the dead*

remember *vb* **1** = recall, think back to, recollect, reminisce about, call to mind; ≠ forget **2** = bear in mind, keep in mind **5** = look back (on), commemorate

remembrance *n* **1** a memory **2** a memento or keepsake **3** the act of honouring some past event or person

remembrance *n* **1** = memory, recollection, thought, recall, reminiscence **2** = souvenir, token, reminder, monument, memento, keepsake **3** = commemoration, memorial

remind *vb* **1** to cause to remember: *remind her that she was on duty* **2** to put in mind (of someone or something): *you remind me of Alice in Wonderland*

remind *vb* **1** = jog your memory, prompt, make you remember

reminder *n* **1** something that recalls the past **2** a note to remind a person of something not done

reminisce *vb* **-niscing, -nisced** to talk or write about old times or past experiences

reminiscence *n* **1** the act of recalling or narrating past experiences **2** something remembered from the past **3 reminiscences** stories about a person's life, often presented in a book

reminiscent *adj* **1 reminiscent of** reminding or suggestive of **2** characterized by reminiscence

reminiscent *adj* **1** = suggestive, evocative, similar

remiss *adj formal* careless in attention to duty or responsibility

remission *n* **1** a reduction in the length of a prison term **2** forgiveness for sin **3** easing of intensity of the symptoms of a disease **4** a release from an obligation

remit *vb* (rim-mitt) **-mitting, -mitted 1** to send (money) for goods or services **2** to cancel (a punishment or debt) **3** *law* to send back (a case) to a lower court for further consideration **4** to slacken or ease off **5** *archaic* to forgive (crime or sins) ▸ *n* (ree-mitt) **6** area of authority: *within the review body's remit*

remittance *n* money sent as payment

remnant *n* **1** a part left over **2** a piece of material from the end of a roll **3** a surviving trace or vestige: *the authorities drafted in the military to crush any remnant of protest*

remnant *n* **1, 3** = remainder, remains, trace, fragment, end, rest, residue, leftovers

remonstrance *n formal* a strong protest about something

remonstrate *vb* **-strating, -strated** *formal* to argue in protest or objection: *the player remonstrated loudly with the official* > **remonstration** *n*

remorse *n* a sense of deep regret and guilt for something one did > **remorseful** *adj*

remorse *n* = regret, shame, guilt, grief, sorrow, anguish, repentance, contrition

r

remorseless adj 1 constantly unkind and lacking pity: *remorseless fate* 2 continually intense: *the superintendent's remorseless gaze*

remote adj 1 far away 2 far from civilization 3 distant in time 4 not relevant: *the issues seem remote from the general population* 5 (of a person's manner) aloof or abstracted 6 slight or faint: *a remote possibility* 7 operated from a distance; remote-controlled: *a remote manipulator arm* > **remotely** adv

> **remote** adj 1, 2 = distant, far, isolated, out-of-the-way, secluded, inaccessible, in the middle of nowhere; ≠ nearby 3 = far, distant 5 = aloof, cold, reserved, withdrawn, distant, abstracted, detached, uncommunicative; ≠ outgoing 6 = slight, small, outside, unlikely, slim, faint, doubtful, dubious; ≠ strong

remote control n control of an apparatus from a distance by radio or electrical signals > **remote-controlled** adj

remould vb 1 to change completely: *to remould the country* 2 Brit to bond a new tread onto the casing of (a worn pneumatic tyre) ▸ n 3 Brit a tyre made by this process

removable adj capable of being removed from a place or released from another object: *a farmer's truck with removable wooden sides*

removal n 1 the act of removing or state of being removed 2 the process of moving one's possessions from a previous address to a new one

> **removal** n 1 = dismissal, expulsion, elimination, ejection 2 = move, transfer, departure, relocation, flitting (*Scot, N English dialect*)

remove vb -moving, -moved 1 to take away and place elsewhere 2 to take (clothing) off 3 to get rid of 4 to dismiss (someone) from office 5 formal to change the location of one's home or place of business ▸ n 6 the degree of difference: *one remove away from complete rebuttal* 7 Brit (in certain schools) a class or form designed to prepare pupils for senior classes

> **remove** vb 1 = take away, detach, displace; ≠ put back 2 = take off; ≠ put on 3 = erase, eliminate, take out 4 = dismiss, eliminate, get rid of, discharge, abolish, expel, throw out, oust; ≠ appoint 5 = move, depart, relocate, flit (*Scot, N English dialect*)

remunerate vb -rating, -rated formal to reward or pay for work or service > **remuneration** n > **remunerative** adj

renaissance n a renewal of interest or creativity in an area: *a complete renaissance in maze building*

> **renaissance** n = rebirth, revival, restoration, renewal, resurgence, reappearance, reawakening

Renaissance n 1 **the Renaissance** the great revival of art, literature, and learning in Europe in the 14th, 15th, and 16th centuries ▸ adj 2 of or from the Renaissance

renal (ree-nal) adj of the kidneys

renascent adj literary becoming active or vigorous again: *renascent nationalism* > **renascence** n

rend vb **rending, rent** literary 1 to tear violently 2 (of a sound) to break (the silence) with a shrill or piercing tone

> **rend** vb = tear, rip, separate, wrench, rupture

render vb 1 to cause to become: *he was rendered unconscious by his wound* 2 to give or provide (aid, a service, etc.) 3 formal to present or submit (a bill) 4 to translate 5 to represent in painting, music, or acting 6 to yield or give: *he rendered up his soul to God* 7 to cover with plaster 8 to melt down (fat) > **rendering** n

> **render** vb 1 = make, cause to become, leave 2 = provide, give, pay, present, supply, submit, tender, hand out 5 = represent, portray, depict, do, give, play, act, perform

rendezvous (ron-day-voo) n, pl **-vous** (-vooz) 1 an appointment to meet at a specified time and place 2 a place where people meet ▸ vb 3 to meet at a specified time or place

rendition n formal 1 a performance of a piece of music or a dramatic role 2 a translation

renegade n a person who deserts a cause for another

renege (rin-nayg) vb **-neging, -neged** to go back (on an agreement or promise): *the politicians reneged on every promise*

renew vb 1 to begin again 2 to take up again after a break: *they wanted to renew diplomatic ties* 3 to make valid again: *we didn't renew the lease* 4 to grow again 5 to restore to a new or fresh condition 6 to replace (an old or worn-out part or piece) 7 to restate or reaffirm (a promise) > **renewal** n

> **renew** vb 1, 2 = recommence, continue, extend, repeat, resume, reopen, re-create, reaffirm 5 = restore, repair, overhaul, mend, refurbish, renovate, refit, modernize 6 = replace, refresh, replenish, restock

renewable adj 1 able to be renewed 2 (of energy or an energy source) inexhaustible or capable of being perpetually replenished ▸ pl n **renewables** 3 renewable energy sources, such as wind and wave power

rennet n a substance prepared from the stomachs of calves and used for curdling milk to make cheese

renounce vb **-nouncing, -nounced** 1 to give up (a belief or habit) voluntarily 2 to give up formally (a claim or right): *he would renounce his rights to the throne*

renounce vb **1** = disown, quit, forsake, recant, forswear, abjure **2** = disclaim, deny, give up, relinquish, waive, abjure; ≠ assert

renovate vb **-vating, -vated** to restore to good condition ⊳ **renovation** n ⊳ **renovator** n

renovate vb = restore, repair, refurbish, do up (informal), renew, overhaul, refit, modernize

renown n widespread good reputation
renowned adj famous

renowned adj = famous, noted, celebrated, well-known, distinguished, esteemed, notable, eminent; ≠ unknown

rent¹ vb **1** to give or have use of (land, a building, a machine, etc.) in return for periodic payments ▸ n **2** a payment made periodically for the use of land, a building, a machine, etc.

rent vb = let, lease ▸ n = hire, rental, lease, fee, payment

rent² n **1** a slit made by tearing ▸ vb **2** the past of **rend**

rent n = tear, split, rip, slash, slit, gash, hole

rental n **1** the amount paid or received as rent ▸ adj **2** of or relating to rent
renunciation n **1** the act or an instance of renouncing **2** a formal declaration renouncing something
reoffend vb to commit another offence
reorganize or **-nise** vb **-nizing, -nized** or **-nising, -nised** to organize in a new and more efficient way ⊳ **reorganization** or **-nisation** n
rep¹ n theatre short for **repertory company**
rep² n **1** a sales representative **2** someone elected to represent a group of people: the union rep **3** NZ informal a rugby player selected to represent his district
repair¹ vb **1** to restore (something damaged or broken) to good condition or working order **2** to make up for (a mistake or injury) **3** to heal (a breach or division) in (something): he is attempting to repair his country's relations with America ▸ n **4** the act, task, or process of repairing **5** a part that has been repaired **6** state or condition: many museums may have to close because they are in such bad repair ⊳ **repairable** adj

repair vb **1** = mend, fix, restore, heal, patch, renovate, patch up; ≠ damage **2** = put right, make up for, compensate for, rectify, redress ▸ n **4** = mending, restoration, overhaul **5** = darn, mend, patch **6** = condition, state, form, shape (informal)

repair² vb **repair to** formal to go to (a place)
reparation n **1** the act of making up for loss or injury **2 reparations** compensation paid by a defeated nation after a war for the damage and injuries it caused

repartee n **1** conversation consisting of witty remarks **2** a sharp witty remark made as a reply
repast n literary a meal
repatriate vb **-ating, -ated 1** to send back (a person) to the country of his or her birth or citizenship ▸ n **2** a person who has been repatriated: Algerian repatriates ⊳ **repatriation** n
repay vb **-paying, -paid 1** to refund or reimburse **2** to make a return for (something): to repay hospitality ⊳ **repayable** adj ⊳ **repayment** n

repay vb **1** = pay back, refund, settle up, return, square, compensate, reimburse, recompense

repeal vb **1** to cancel (a law) officially ▸ n **2** the act of repealing: the repeal of repressive legislation ⊳ **repealable** adj

repeal vb = abolish, reverse, revoke, annul, recall, cancel, invalidate, nullify; ≠ pass ▸ n = abolition, cancellation, annulment, invalidation, rescindment; ≠ passing

repeat vb **1** to say, write, or do again **2** to tell to another person (the secrets told to one by someone else) **3** to recite (a poem, etc.) from memory **4** to occur more than once: this pattern repeats itself many times **5** (of food) to be tasted again after eating as the result of belching **6** to say (the words or sounds) uttered by someone else; echo ▸ n **7** the act or an instance of repeating **8** a word, action, pattern, etc., that is repeated **9** radio & television a broadcast of a programme which has been broadcast before **10** music a passage that is an exact restatement of the passage preceding it ⊳ **repeated** adj ⊳ **repeatedly** adv ⊳ **repeatable** adj

repeat vb **1** = reiterate (formal), restate **2** = retell, echo, replay, reproduce, rerun, reshow ▸ n **7** = repetition, echo, reiteration **9** = rerun, replay, reshowing

repeater n **1** a gun capable of firing several shots without reloading **2** a clock or watch which strikes the hour or quarter-hour just past, when a spring is pressed
repel vb **-pelling, -pelled 1** to cause (someone) to feel disgusted **2** to force or drive back (someone or something) **3** to be effective in keeping away or controlling: these buzzers are claimed to repel female mosquitoes **4** to fail to mix with or absorb: water and oil repel each other **5** to reject or spurn: she repelled his advances

repel vb **1** = disgust, offend, revolt, sicken, nauseate, gross you out (US slang); ≠ delight **2, 3** = drive off, fight, resist, parry, hold off, rebuff, ward off, repulse; ≠ submit to

repellent adj **1** disgusting or distasteful **2** resisting water, etc. ▸ n **3** a chemical used to keep insects or other creatures away
repent vb to feel regret for (something bad one has done) ⊳ **repentance** n ⊳ **repentant** adj

r

repertoire n 1 all the works that a company or performer can perform 2 the entire stock of skills or techniques that someone or something, such as a computer, is capable of: *a superb repertoire of shots*

> **repertoire** n 2 = range, list, stock, supply, store, collection, repertory

repertory n, pl **-ries** 1 same as **repertoire** (sense 2) 2 short for **repertory company**
repertory company n a permanent theatre company producing a succession of plays
repetition n 1 the act of repeating 2 a thing that is repeated 3 a replica or copy > **repetitious** adj > **repetitive** adj

> **repetition** n 1 = recurrence, repeating, echo 2 = repeating, replication, restatement, reiteration, tautology

rephrase vb **-phrasing, -phrased** to express in different words > **rephrasing** n
repine vb **-pining, -pined** literary to be worried or discontented
replace vb **-placing, -placed** 1 to take the place of 2 to substitute a person or thing for (another): *we need to replace that chair* 3 to put (something) back in its rightful place

> **replace** vb 1 = take the place of, follow, succeed, oust, take over from, supersede, supplant 2 = substitute, change, exchange, switch, swap 3 = put back, restore

replacement n 1 the act or process of replacing 2 a person or thing that replaces another

> **replacement** n 1 = replacing 2 = successor, double, substitute, stand-in, proxy, surrogate, understudy

replay n 1 a showing again of a sequence of action immediately after it happens 2 a second sports match played because an earlier game was drawn ▸ vb 3 to play (a recording, match, etc.) again
replenish vb to make full or complete again by supplying what has been used up > **replenishment** n
replete adj 1 pleasantly full of food and drink 2 well supplied: *a world replete with true horror* > **repletion** n
replica n an exact copy

> **replica** n = duplicate, copy, carbon copy; ≠ original

replicate vb **-cating, -cated** to make or be an exact copy of; reproduce > **replication** n

> **replicate** vb = copy, reproduce, re-create, mimic, duplicate, reduplicate

reply vb **-plies, -plying, -plied** 1 to make answer (to) in words or writing or by an action 2 to say (something) in answer: *she replied that she did not believe him* ▸ n, pl **-plies** 3 an answer or response

> **reply** vb = answer, respond, retort, counter, rejoin, retaliate, reciprocate ▸ n = answer, response, reaction, counter, retort, retaliation, counterattack, rejoinder

report vb 1 to give an account (of) 2 to give an account of the results of an investigation (into): *the commission is to report on global warming* 3 to make a formal report on (a subject) 4 to make a formal complaint about 5 to present (oneself) at an appointed place or for a specific purpose: *report to the manager's office* 6 **report to** to be responsible to and under the authority of 7 to act as a reporter ▸ n 8 an account prepared after investigation and published or broadcast 9 an account of the discussions of a committee or other group of people: *I have the report of the mining union* 10 a story for which there is no absolute proof: *according to report, he is not dead* 11 a statement on the progress of a schoolchild 12 a loud bang made by a gun or explosion 13 comment on a person's character or actions: *he is of good report here* > **reportedly** adv

> **report** vb 1 = inform of, communicate, recount 2, 3 = communicate, tell, state, detail, describe, relate, broadcast, post, tweet, pass on 5 = present yourself, come, appear, arrive, turn up ▸ n 8 = article, story, piece, write-up 9 = account, record, statement, communication, description, narrative 10 = rumour, talk, buzz, gossip, goss (informal), hearsay 12 = bang, sound, crack, noise, blast, boom, explosion, discharge

reporter n a person who gathers news for a newspaper or broadcasting organization

> **reporter** n = journalist, writer, correspondent, hack (derogatory), pressman or presswoman, journo (slang)

repose n 1 a state of quiet restfulness 2 calmness or composure 3 sleep ▸ vb **-posing, -posed** 4 to lie or lay down at rest 5 to lie when dead
repository n, pl **-ries** 1 a place or container in which things can be stored for safety: *a repository for national treasures* 2 a person to whom a secret is entrusted
repossess vb (of a lender) to take back (property) from a customer who is behind with payments, for example mortgage repayments > **repossession** n
reprehensible adj deserving criticism: *Willie's reprehensible behaviour*
represent vb 1 to act as the authorized delegate for (a person, country, etc.): *she represented her country at the Olympic Games* 2 to act as a substitute (for) 3 to stand as an equivalent of 4 to be a means of expressing: *the lights are relit to represent resurrection* 5 to display the characteristics of: *romanticism in music is represented by Liszt* 6 to describe as having a specified character or quality: *the magical bird was often represented as having*

two heads **7** to state or explain **8** to present an image of through a picture or sculpture **9** to bring clearly before the mind

represent vb **1** = act for, speak for **2** = stand for, serve as **3** = express, correspond to, symbolize, mean **4, 8** = depict, show, describe, picture, illustrate, outline, portray, denote **5** = exemplify, embody, symbolize, typify, personify, epitomize

representation n **1** the state of being represented **2** anything that represents, such as a pictorial portrait **3 representations** formal statements made to an official body by a person making a complaint > **representational** adj

representation n **2** = portrayal, depiction, account, description

representative n **1** a person chosen to act for or represent a group **2** a person who tries to sell the products or services of a firm **3** a typical example ▸ adj **4** typical of a class or kind **5** representing **6** including examples of all the interests or types in a group **7** acting as deputy for another **8** of a political system in which people choose a person to make decisions on their behalf

representative n **1** = delegate, member, agent, deputy, proxy, spokesman or woman or person **2** = agent, salesperson, rep, commercial traveller ▸ adj **4, 6** = typical, characteristic, archetypal, exemplary; ≠ uncharacteristic **5** = symbolic

repress vb **1** to keep (feelings) under control **2** to restrict the freedom of: he continued to repress his people **3** psychol to banish (unpleasant thoughts) from one's conscious mind > **repression** n > **repressive** adj

repress vb **1** = control, suppress, hold back, bottle up, check, curb, restrain, inhibit; ≠ release **2** = subdue, abuse, wrong, persecute, quell, subjugate, maltreat; ≠ liberate

reprieve vb **-prieving, -prieved 1** to postpone the execution of (a condemned person) **2** to give temporary relief to ▸ n **3** a postponement or cancellation of a punishment **4** a warrant granting a postponement or cancellation **5** a temporary relief from pain or harm

reprieve vb **1** = grant a stay of execution to, pardon, let off the hook (slang) ▸ n **3** = stay of execution, amnesty, pardon, remission, deferment, postponement of punishment

reprimand vb **1** to blame (someone) officially for a fault ▸ n **2** an instance of blaming someone officially

reprint vb **1** to print further copies of (a book) ▸ n **2** a reprinted copy

reprisal n an act of taking revenge: many residents say they are living in fear of reprisals by the army

reproach n **1** blame or rebuke **2** a scolding **3 beyond reproach** beyond criticism ▸ vb **4** to express disapproval of (someone's actions) > **reproachful** adj

reprobate (rep-roh-bate) n **1** an unprincipled bad person ▸ adj **2** morally unprincipled

reproduce vb **-ducing, -duced 1** to make a copy or representation of **2** biol to produce offspring **3** to re-create > **reproducible** adj

reproduce vb **1** = print, copy **2** = breed, procreate (formal), multiply, spawn, propagate

reproduction n **1** biol a process by which an animal or plant produces one or more individuals similar to itself **2** a copy of a work of art **3** the quality of sound from an audio system **4** the act or process of reproducing ▸ adj **5** made in imitation of an earlier style: reproduction furniture > **reproductive** adj

reproduction n **1** = breeding, increase, generation, multiplication **2** = copy, picture, print, replica, imitation, duplicate, facsimile; ≠ original

reproof n a severe blaming of someone for a fault

reprove vb **-proving, -proved** to speak severely to (someone) about a fault > **reprovingly** adv

reptile n **1** a cold-blooded animal, such as a tortoise, snake, or crocodile, that has an outer covering of horny scales or plates and lays eggs **2** a contemptible grovelling person > **reptilian** adj

republic n **1** a form of government in which the people or their elected representatives possess the supreme power **2** a country in which the head of state is an elected or nominated president

Republican adj **1** belonging to the Republican Party, the more conservative of the two main political parties in the US **2** advocating a united Ireland ▸ n **3** a member or supporter of the Republican Party in the US **4** an advocate of a united Ireland > **Republicanism** n

repudiate (rip-pew-dee-ate) vb **-ating, -ated 1** to reject the authority or validity of **2** to disown (a person) **3** to refuse to acknowledge or pay (a debt) > **repudiation** n

repugnant adj offensive or disgusting > **repugnance** n

repulse vb **-pulsing, -pulsed 1** to be disgusting to: this act of feminist rage repulsed as many as it delighted **2** to drive (an army) back **3** to reject with coldness or discourtesy: she repulsed his advances ▸ n **4** a driving back **5** a cold discourteous rejection or refusal

repulsion n **1** a feeling of disgust or aversion **2** physics a force separating two objects, such as the force between two like electric charges

repulsive adj **1** disgusting or distasteful **2** physics of repulsion > **repulsively** adv

reputable (rep-pew-tab-bl) adj trustworthy or respectable > **reputably** adv

reputation n **1** the opinion generally held of a person or thing **2** a high opinion generally held about a person or thing **3** notoriety or fame, esp. for some specified characteristic

> **reputation** n **1** = name, standing, character, esteem, stature, renown, repute

repute n good reputation: *a sculptor of international repute*

reputed adj supposed or rumoured: *the island was reputed to have held a Roman temple; the reputed murderess* > **reputedly** adv

request vb **1** to ask for or politely demand: *we requested a formal meeting with the committee* ▶ n **2** the act or an instance of asking for something: *a polite request* **3** something asked for **4** **on request** if asked for: *most companies will send samples on request*

> **request** vb = seek, ask (for), solicit ▶ n **2** = asking, plea

Requiem (rek-wee-em) n **1** RC Church a Mass celebrated for the dead **2** a musical setting of this Mass

require vb **-quiring, -quired 1** to need **2** to impose as a necessary condition: *the decision requires a logical common-sense approach* **3** to insist upon **4** to order or command: *family doctors are required to produce annual reports*

> **require** vb **1** = need, crave, want, miss, lack, wish, desire **3** = order, demand, command, compel, exact, oblige, call upon, insist upon **4** = ask

requirement n **1** something demanded or imposed as an obligation **2** a specific need or want

> **requirement** n = necessity, demand, stipulation, want, need, must, essential, prerequisite

requisite (rek-wizz-it) adj **1** absolutely essential ▶ n **2** something essential

requisition vb **1** to demand and take for use, esp. for military or public use ▶ n **2** a formal request or demand for the use of something **3** the act of taking something over, esp. for military or public use **4** a formal written demand

requite vb **-quiting, -quited** to return to someone (the same treatment or feeling as received): *an Australian who requites her love* > **requital** n

reredos (rear-doss) n a screen or wall decoration at the back of an altar

rescind vb to annul or repeal > **rescission** n

rescue vb **-cuing, -cued 1** to bring (someone or something) out of danger or trouble ▶ n **2** the act or an instance of rescuing > **rescuer** n

> **rescue** vb = salvage, deliver, redeem; ≠ desert ▶ n = saving, salvage, deliverance, release, recovery, liberation, salvation, redemption

research n **1** systematic investigation to establish facts or collect information on a subject ▶ vb **2** to carry out investigations into (a subject) > **researcher** n

> **research** n = investigation, study, analysis, examination, probe, exploration ▶ vb = investigate, study, examine, explore, probe, analyse

resemble vb **-bling, -bled** to be or look like > **resemblance** n

> **resemble** vb = be like, look like, mirror, parallel, be similar to, bear a resemblance to

resent vb to feel bitter or indignant about > **resentful** adj > **resentment** n

> **resent** vb = be bitter about, object to, grudge, begrudge, take exception to, take offence at; ≠ be content with

reservation n **1** a doubt: *his only reservation was, did he have the stamina?* **2** an exception or limitation that prevents one's wholehearted acceptance: *work I admire without reservation* **3** a seat, room, etc. that has been reserved **4** (esp. in the US) an area of land set aside for Native American peoples: *the Cherokee reservation* **5** Brit short for **central reservation**

> **reservation** n **1** = doubt, scruples, hesitancy **4** = reserve, territory, preserve, sanctuary

reserve vb **-serving, -served 1** to keep back or set aside for future use **2** to obtain by arranging beforehand: *I phoned to reserve two tickets* **3** to keep for oneself: *the association reserves the right to charge a fee* **4** to delay announcing (a legal judgment) ▶ n **5** something kept back or set aside for future use **6** the state or condition of being reserved: *we're keeping these two in reserve* **7** sport a substitute **8** a protected area for wildlife: *an elephant reserve* **9** the hiding of one's feelings and personality **10** the part of a nation's armed services not in active service **11** **reserves** finance money or assets held by a bank or business to meet future expenses **12** Canad a reservation for an indigenous people

> **reserve** vb **1, 3** = keep, hold, save, store, retain, set aside, stockpile, hoard **2** = book, prearrange, engage ▶ n **5** = store, fund, savings, stock, supply, reservoir, hoard, cache **7** = substitute, extra, spare, fall-back, auxiliary **8** = park, reservation, preserve, sanctuary, tract, forest park (NZ) **9** = shyness, silence, restraint, constraint, reticence, secretiveness, taciturnity

reserved adj **1** not showing one's feelings **2** set aside for use by a particular person

> **reserved** adj **1** = uncommunicative, retiring, silent, shy, restrained, secretive, reticent, taciturn; ≠ uninhibited **2** = set aside, taken, kept, held, booked, retained, engaged, restricted

reservist *n* a member of a nation's military reserve

reservoir *n* 1 a natural or artificial lake for storing water for community use 2 a large supply of something: *a vast reservoir of youthful enthusiasm*

> **reservoir** *n* 1 = lake, pond, basin 2 = store, stock, source, supply, reserves, pool

reshuffle *n* 1 a reorganization of jobs in a government or company ▸ *vb* **-fling, -fled** 2 to reorganize jobs or duties in a government or company

reside *vb* **-siding, -sided** *formal* 1 to live permanently (in a place): *my daughter resides in Europe* 2 to be present (in): *desire resides in the unconscious*

> **reside** *vb* 1 = live, lodge, dwell (*formal*, *literary*), stay, abide; ≠ visit

residence *n* 1 a person's home or house 2 a large imposing house 3 the fact of residing in a place 4 a period of residing in a place 5 **in residence** **A** living in a particular place: *the Monarch was not in residence* **B** (of an artist) working for a set period at a college, gallery, etc.: *composer in residence*

> **residence** *n* 1 = home, house, dwelling (*formal*, *literary*), place, flat, lodging, abode, habitation (*formal*)

resident *n* 1 a person who lives in a place 2 a bird or animal that does not migrate ▸ *adj* 3 living in a place 4 living at a place in order to carry out a job: *a resident custodian* 5 employed for one's specialized abilities: *the Museum's resident expert on seventeenth-century Dutch art* 6 (of birds and animals) not in the habit of migrating

> **resident** *n* 1 = tenant, occupant, lodger; ≠ nonresident

residential *adj* 1 (of a part of a town) consisting mainly of houses 2 providing living accommodation: *residential clubs for homeless boys*

residual *adj* 1 of or being a remainder ▸ *n* 2 something left over as a residue

residue *n* 1 what is left over after something has been removed 2 *law* what is left of an estate after the discharge of debts and distribution of specific gifts

> **residue** *n* 1 = remainder, remains, remnant, leftovers, rest, extra, excess, surplus

resign *vb* 1 to give up office or a job 2 to accept (an unpleasant fact): *he resigned himself to the inevitable* 3 to give up (a right or claim)

> **resign** *vb* 1 = quit, leave, step down (*informal*), vacate, abdicate, give *or* hand in your notice 2 **resign yourself to something** = accept, succumb to, submit to, give in to, yield to, acquiesce to 3 = give up, abandon, yield, surrender, relinquish, renounce, forsake, forgo

resignation *n* 1 the act of resigning 2 a formal document stating one's intention to resign 3 passive endurance of difficulties: *full of quiet resignation*

> **resignation** *n* 1 = leaving, departure, abandonment, abdication 3 = acceptance, patience, submission, compliance, endurance, passivity, acquiescence, sufferance; ≠ resistance

resigned *adj* content to endure something unpleasant > **resignedly** *adv*

> **resigned** *adj* = stoical, patient, subdued, long-suffering, compliant, unresisting

resilient *adj* 1 (of a person) recovering easily and quickly from misfortune or illness 2 (of an object) capable of regaining its original shape or position after bending or stretching > **resilience** *n*

resin (rezz-in) *n* 1 a solid or semisolid substance obtained from certain plants: *cannabis resin* 2 a similar substance produced synthetically > **resinous** *adj*

resist *vb* 1 to stand firm against or oppose: *the party's old guard continue to resist economic reform* 2 to refrain from in spite of temptation: *I couldn't resist a huge portion of almond cake* 3 to refuse to comply with: *to resist arrest* 4 to be proof against: *airport design should be strengthened to help resist explosion* > **resistible** *adj*

> **resist** *vb* 1 = oppose, battle against, combat, defy, stand up to, hinder; ≠ accept 2 = refrain from, avoid, keep from, forgo, abstain from, forbear; ≠ indulge in 4 = withstand, be proof against

resistance *n* 1 the act of resisting 2 the capacity to withstand something, esp. the body's natural capacity to withstand disease 3 *electronics* the opposition to a flow of electric current through a circuit, component, or substance 4 any force that slows or hampers movement: *wind resistance* 5 **line of least resistance** the easiest, but not necessarily the best, course of action > **resistant** *adj, n*

> **resistance** *n* 1 = fighting, fight, battle, struggle, defiance, obstruction, impediment, hindrance

resistor *n* an electrical component designed to introduce a known value of resistance into a circuit

resit *vb* **-sitting, -sat** 1 to sit (an examination) again ▸ *n* 2 an examination which one must sit again

resolute *adj* firm in purpose or belief > **resolutely** *adv*

resolution *n* 1 firmness or determination 2 a decision to do something 3 a formal expression of opinion by a meeting 4 the act of resolving 5 *music* the process in harmony whereby a dissonant note or chord is followed by a consonant one **6** the ability of a television, camera, etc. to reproduce fine detail **7** *physics* Also called: **resolving power** the ability of a telescope or microscope to produce separate images of closely placed objects

> **resolution** *n* **1** = determination, purpose, resolve, tenacity, perseverance, willpower, firmness, steadfastness **2** = decision, resolve, intention, aim, purpose, determination, intent **3** = declaration

resolve *vb* **-solving, -solved 1** to decide or determine firmly **2** to express (an opinion) formally by a vote **3** to separate or cause to separate into (constituent parts) **4** to find the answer or solution to **5** to explain away or dispel: *to resolve the controversy* **6** *music* to follow (a dissonant note or chord) by one producing a consonance **7** *physics* to distinguish between (separate parts) of (an image) as in a microscope, telescope, or other optical instrument ▸ *n* **8** absolute determination: *he spoke of his resolve to deal with the problem of terrorism*

> **resolve** *vb* **1** = decide, determine, agree, purpose, intend, fix, conclude **4** = work out, answer, clear up, crack, fathom ▸ *n* = determination, resolution, willpower, firmness, steadfastness, resoluteness; ≠ indecision

resolved *adj* determined
resonance *n* **1** the condition or quality of being resonant **2** sound produced by a body vibrating in sympathy with a neighbouring source of sound
resonant *adj* **1** resounding or re-echoing **2** producing resonance: *the resonant cavities of the mouth* **3** full of resonance: *his voice is a resonant baritone*
resonate *vb* **-nating, -nated** to resound or cause to resound > **resonator** *n*
resort *vb* **1 resort to** to have recourse to for help, use, etc.: *some people have resorted to begging for food* **2** to go, esp. often or habitually: *to resort to the beach* ▸ *n* **3** a place to which many people go for holidays **4** the use of something as a means or aid **5 last resort** the last possible course of action open to a person

> **resort** *n* **3** = holiday centre, spot, retreat, haunt, tourist centre

resound (riz-**zownd**) *vb* **1** to ring or echo with sound **2** (of sounds) to echo or ring **3** to be widely known: *his fame resounded throughout India*

> **resound** *vb* **1, 2** = ring

resounding *adj* **1** echoing **2** clear and emphatic: *he won a resounding victory* > **resoundingly** *adv*

> **resounding** *adj* **1** = echoing, full, ringing, powerful, booming, reverberating, resonant, sonorous

resource *n* **1 resources** sources of economic wealth, esp. of a country or business enterprise: *mineral resources* **2 resources** money available for use **3** something resorted to for aid or support: *he saw the university as a resource for the community* **4** the ability to deal with problems: *a man of resource* **5** a means of doing something: *resistance was their only resource*

> **resource** *n* **1** = reserves, supplies, stocks **2** = funds, holdings, money, capital, riches, assets, wealth **3** = facility **5** = means, course, resort, device, expedient

resourceful *adj* capable and full of initiative > **resourcefulness** *n*
respect *n* **1** consideration: *respect for my feelings* **2** an attitude of deference or esteem **3** the state of being honoured or esteemed **4** a detail or characteristic: *in virtually all respects boys develop more slowly than girls* **5 in respect of** or **with respect to** in reference or relation to **6 respects** polite greetings: *he paid his respects to her and left* ▸ *vb* **7** to have an attitude of esteem towards: *she is the person I most respect and wish to emulate* **8** to pay proper attention or consideration to: *he called on rebel groups to respect a cease-fire* > **respecter** *n*

> **respect** *n* **1** = consideration, kindness, deference, tact, thoughtfulness, considerateness **2** = regard, honour, recognition, esteem, admiration, estimation; ≠ contempt **4** = particular, way, point, matter, sense, detail, feature, aspect ▸ *vb* **7** = think highly of, value, honour, admire, esteem, look up to, defer to, have a good *or* high opinion of **8** = abide by, follow, observe, comply with, obey, heed, keep to, adhere to; ≠ disregard

respectable *adj* **1** worthy of respect **2** having good social standing or reputation **3** relatively or fairly good: *they obtained respectable results* **4** fit to be seen by other people > **respectability** *n* > **respectably** *adv*

> **respectable** *adj* **1, 2** = honourable, good, decent, worthy, upright, honest, reputable, estimable; ≠ disreputable **3** = reasonable, considerable, substantial, fair, ample, appreciable, sizable *or* sizeable; ≠ small **4** = decent, neat, spruce

respectful *adj* full of or showing respect > **respectfully** *adv*
respecting *prep* on the subject of
respective *adj* relating separately to each of several people or things: *the culprits will be repatriated to their respective countries*

> **respective** *adj* = specific, own, individual, particular, relevant

respectively *adv* (in listing things that refer to another list) separately in the order given: *Diotema and Mantinea were tutors to Pythagoras and Socrates respectively*

respiration (ress-per-ray-shun) *n* **1** breathing **2** the process in living organisms of taking in oxygen and giving out carbon dioxide **3** the breakdown of complex organic substances that takes place in the cells of animals and plants, producing energy and carbon dioxide > **respiratory** *adj*

respirator *n* **1** a device worn over the mouth and nose to prevent the breathing in of poisonous fumes **2** an apparatus for providing artificial respiration

respire *vb* **-spiring, -spired** **1** to breathe **2** to undergo respiration

respite *n* **1** an interval of rest: *I allowed myself a six month respite to enjoy my family* **2** a temporary delay

> **respite** *n* **1** = pause, break, rest, relief, halt, interval, recess, lull

resplendent *adj* **1** brilliant or splendid in appearance **2** shining > **resplendence** *n*

respond *vb* **1** to state or utter (something) in reply **2** to act in reply: *the government must respond accordingly to our recommendations* **3** to react favourably: *most headaches will respond to the use of relaxants*

> **respond** *vb* **1** = answer, return, reply, counter, retort, rejoin; ≠ remain silent **2** = react, retaliate, reciprocate

respondent *n law* a person against whom a petition is brought

response *n* **1** the act of responding **2** a reply or reaction **3** a reaction to stimulation of the nervous system **4 responses** *Christianity* the words recited or sung in reply to the priest at a church service

> **response** *n* **1, 2** = answer, return, reply, reaction, feedback, retort, counterattack, rejoinder

responsibility *n, pl* **-ties** **1** the state of being responsible **2** a person or thing for which one is responsible

> **responsibility** *n* **1** = fault, blame, liability, guilt, culpability **2** = job, task, function, role

responsible *adj* **1 responsible for** having control or authority over **2** being the agent or cause (of some action): *only a small number of students were responsible for the disturbances* **3 responsible to** being accountable for one's actions and decisions to: *management should be made more responsible to shareholders* **4** rational and accountable for one's own actions **5** (of a position or duty) involving decision and accountability > **responsibly** *adv*

> **responsible** *adj* **1** = in charge, in control, in authority **2** = to blame, guilty, at fault, culpable **3** = accountable, liable, answerable; ≠ unaccountable **4** = sensible, reliable, rational, dependable, trustworthy, level-headed; ≠ unreliable

responsive *adj* reacting quickly or favourably to something > **responsiveness** *n*

> **responsive** *adj* = sensitive, open, alive, susceptible, receptive, reactive, impressionable; ≠ unresponsive

rest¹ *n* **1** relaxation from exertion or labour **2** a period of inactivity **3** relief or refreshment **4** calm **5** death regarded as repose: *now he has gone to his eternal rest* **6 at rest A** not moving **B** calm **C** dead **D** asleep **7** a pause or interval **8** a mark in a musical score indicating a pause lasting a specific time **9** a thing or place on which to put something for support or to steady it **10 lay to rest** to bury (a dead person) ▸ *vb* **11** to become or make refreshed **12** to position (oneself, etc.) for rest or relaxation **13** to place for support or steadying: *he slumped forward to rest his head on his forearms* **14** to depend or rely: *his presidency rested on the outcome of the crisis* **15** to direct (one's eyes) or (of one's eyes) to be directed: *she rested her gaze on the face of the statue* **16** to be at ease **17** to cease or cause to cease from motion or exertion **18** to remain without further attention or action: *she refused to let the matter rest* **19** *law* to finish the introduction of evidence in (a case) **20** to put (pastry) in a cool place to allow the gluten to contract

> **rest** *n* **1** = relaxation, repose, leisure, me-time; ≠ work **3** = refreshment, release, relief, ease, comfort, cure, remedy, solace **4, 9** = calm, tranquillity, stillness **7** = pause, break, stop, halt, interval, respite, lull, interlude ▸ *vb* **11, 16** = relax, take it easy, sit down, be at ease, put your feet up, outspan (*S African*); ≠ work **13** = place, repose, sit, lean, prop **17** = stop, have a break, break off, take a breather (*informal*), halt, cease; ≠ keep going

rest² *n* **1 the rest A** something left; remainder **B** the others: *the rest of the world* ▸ *vb* **2** to continue to be (as specified): *your conscience can rest easy*

> **rest** *n* **1A** = remainder, remains, excess, remnants, others, balance, surplus, residue

restaurant *n* a place where meals are prepared and served to customers

> **restaurant** *n* = café, diner (*chiefly US, Canad*), bistro, cafeteria, tearoom, eatery *or* eaterie

restaurateur (rest-er-a-tur) *n* a person who owns or runs a restaurant

restful *adj* relaxing or soothing

restitution *n* **1** the act of giving back something that has been lost or stolen **2** *law* compensation for loss or injury

restive *adj* **1** restless or uneasy **2** impatient of control or authority

restless *adj* **1** bored or dissatisfied **2** unable to stay still or quiet **3** not restful: *a restless sleep* > **restlessly** *adv* > **restlessness** *n*

r

restless *adj* **2** = unsettled, nervous, edgy, fidgeting, on edge, restive, jumpy, fidgety; ≠ relaxed

restoration *n* **1** the act of restoring to a former or original condition, place, etc. **2** the giving back of something lost or stolen **3** something restored, replaced, or reconstructed **4** a model or representation of a ruin or extinct animal **5 the Restoration** *Brit* the re-establishment of the monarchy in 1660 or the reign of Charles II (1660–85)

restoration *n* **1** = repair, reconstruction, renewal, renovation, revitalization; ≠ demolition

restorative (rist-or-a-tiv) *adj* **1** giving back health or good spirits ► *n* **2** a food or medicine that gives back health or good spirits

restore *vb* **-storing, -stored 1** to return (something) to its original or former condition **2** to bring back to health or good spirits **3** to return (something lost or stolen) to its owner **4** to re-enforce or re-establish: *he must restore confidence in himself and his government; they worked to restore the monarchy* **5** to reconstruct (a ruin, extinct animal, etc.) > **restorer** *n*

restore *vb* **1, 5** = repair, refurbish, renovate, reconstruct, fix (up), renew, rebuild, mend; ≠ demolish **2** = revive, build up, strengthen, refresh, revitalize; ≠ make worse **3** = return, replace, recover, bring back, send back, hand back **4** = reinstate, re-establish, reintroduce; ≠ abolish

restrain *vb* **1** to hold (someone) back from some action **2** to limit or restrict: *restrain any tendency to impulse-buy* **3** to deprive (someone) of liberty

restrain *vb* **1** = hold back, control, check, contain, restrict, curb, hamper, hinder; ≠ encourage **2** = control, inhibit

restrained *adj* not displaying emotion

restrained *adj* = controlled, moderate, self-controlled, calm, mild, undemonstrative; ≠ hot-headed

restraint *n* **1** something that restrains **2** the ability to control one's impulses or passions **3** a restraining or being restrained

restraint *n* **1** = limitation, limit, check, ban, embargo, curb, rein, interdict, restraining order (*US law*); ≠ freedom **2** = self-control, self-discipline, self-restraint, self-possession; ≠ self-indulgence **3** = constraint, limitation, inhibition, control, restriction

restrict *vb* to confine or keep within certain limits > **restrictive** *adj*

restrict *vb* = limit, regulate, curb, ration; ≠ widen

restriction *n* a rule or situation that limits or controls something or someone: *operating under severe financial restrictions*

restriction *n* = control, rule, regulation, curb, restraint, confinement

restructure *vb* **-turing, -tured** to organize in a different way: *to restructure the world economy*

result *n* **1** the outcome or consequence of an action, policy, etc. **2** the final score of a sporting contest **3** a number or value obtained by solving a mathematical problem **4** a favourable result, esp. a victory or success: *the best chance of a result is at Cheltenham* **5 results** the marks or grades obtained in an examination ► *vb* **6 result from** to be the outcome or consequence of: *poverty resulting from high unemployment* **7 result in** to end in (a specified way): *negotiations which resulted in the Treaty of Paris*

result *n* **1** = outcome, end; ≠ cause ► *vb* **6** = arise, follow, issue, happen, appear, develop, spring, derive

resultant *adj* **1** arising as a result: *the resultant publicity* ► *n* **2** *maths & physics* a single vector that is the vector sum of two or more other vectors, such as a force which results from two other forces acting on a single point

resume *vb* **-suming, -sumed 1** to begin again or go on with (something interrupted) **2** to occupy again or recover: *he will resume his party post today*

resume *vb* **1** = begin again, continue, go on with, proceed with, carry on, reopen, restart; ≠ discontinue

résumé (rezz-yew-may) *n* **1** a short descriptive summary **2** *US, Canad & Austral* a curriculum vitae

résumé *n* **1** = summary, synopsis, précis, rundown, recapitulation

resumption *n* the act of resuming or beginning again

resumption *n* = continuation, carrying on, reopening, renewal, restart, resurgence, re-establishment

resurgence *n* a rising again to vigour: *worldwide religious resurgence* > **resurgent** *adj*

resurgence *n* = revival, return, renaissance, resurrection, resumption, rebirth, re-emergence

resurrect *vb* **1** to bring or be brought back to life from death **2** to bring back into use or activity

resurrect *vb* **1** = restore to life, raise from the dead **2** = revive, renew, bring back, reintroduce

resurrection *n* **1** a return to life by a dead person **2** revival or renewal **3 the Resurrection** *Christian theol* **a** the rising again of Christ from the tomb three days after his death **b** the rising again from the dead of all people at the Last Judgment

resurrection n 1, 3 = raising or rising from the dead, return from the dead 2 = revival, restoration, renewal, resurgence, return, renaissance, rebirth, reappearance; ≠ killing off

resuscitate (ris-suss-it-tate) vb **-tating, -tated** to restore to consciousness > **resuscitation** n

retail n 1 the sale of goods individually or in small quantities to the public ▸ adj 2 of or engaged in such selling: auctioneers have been successful in cornering the retail market ▸ adv 3 in small amounts or at a retail price ▸ vb 4 to sell or be sold in small quantities to the public 5 to relate (gossip or scandal) in detail: he gleefully retailed the story > **retailer** n

retain vb 1 to keep in one's possession 2 to be able to hold or contain: with this method the salmon retains its flavour and texture 3 law to engage the services of (a barrister) by payment of a preliminary fee 4 (of a person) to be able to remember (something) without difficulty 5 to hold in position

retain vb 1 = keep, save; ≠ let go

retainer n 1 a fee paid in advance to engage someone's services 2 Brit, Austral & NZ a reduced rent paid for a room or flat to reserve it for future use 3 a servant who has been with a family for a long time

retaliate vb **-ating, -ated** 1 to repay some injury or wrong in kind 2 to cast (accusations) back upon a person > **retaliation** n > **retaliatory** adj

retaliate vb 1 = pay someone back, hit back, strike back, reciprocate, take revenge, get even with (informal), get your own back (informal); ≠ turn the other cheek

retard vb to delay or slow down (the progress or development) of (something) > **retardant** n, adj > **retardation** n

retard vb = slow down, check, arrest, delay, handicap, hinder, impede, set back; ≠ speed up

retarded adj old-fashioned, offensive having learning difficulties

retch vb 1 to undergo spasms of the stomach as if one is vomiting ▸ n 2 an involuntary spasm of the stomach

retention n 1 the act of retaining or state of being retained 2 the capacity to remember 3 pathol the abnormal holding of something within the body, esp. fluid > **retentive** adj

rethink vb **-thinking, -thought** 1 to think about (something) again with a view to changing one's tactics ▸ n 2 the act or an instance of thinking again

reticent adj not willing to say or tell much > **reticence** n

retina n, pl **-nas** or **-nae** the light-sensitive inner lining of the back of the eyeball > **retinal** adj

retinue n a band of attendants accompanying an important person

retire vb **-tiring, -tired** 1 to give up or to cause (a person) to give up work, esp. on reaching pensionable age 2 to go away into seclusion 3 to go to bed 4 to withdraw from a sporting contest, esp. because of injury 5 to pull back (troops) from battle or (of troops) to fall back > **retired** adj > **retirement** n

retire vb 1 = stop working, give up work 2 = withdraw, leave, exit, go away, depart 3 = go to bed, turn in (informal), hit the sack (slang), hit the hay (slang)

retiring adj very shy

retiring adj = shy, reserved, quiet, timid, unassuming, self-effacing, bashful, unassertive; ≠ outgoing

retort[1] vb 1 to reply quickly, wittily, or angrily 2 to use (an argument) against its originator ▸ n 3 a sharp, angry, or witty reply 4 an argument used against its originator

retort vb = reply, return, answer, respond, counter, come back with, riposte ▸ n 3 = reply, answer, response, comeback, riposte, rejoinder

retort[2] n 1 a glass vessel with a long tapering neck that is bent down, used for distillation 2 a vessel used for heating ores in the production of metals or heating coal to produce gas

retouch vb to restore or improve (a painting or photograph) with new touches

retrace vb **-tracing, -traced** 1 to go back over (one's steps or a route) 2 to go over (a story) from the beginning

retract vb 1 to withdraw (a statement, charge, etc.) as invalid or unjustified 2 to go back on (a promise or agreement) 3 to draw in (a part or appendage): the rear wheels are retracted for tight spaces > **retractable** adj > **retraction** n

retread vb **-treading, -treaded** 1 to bond a new tread onto (a worn tyre) ▸ n 2 a remoulded tyre

retreat vb 1 military to withdraw or retire in the face of or from action with an enemy 2 to retire or withdraw to seclusion or shelter 3 to alter one's opinion about something ▸ n 4 the act of retreating or withdrawing 5 military A a withdrawal or retirement in the face of the enemy B a bugle call signifying withdrawal or retirement 6 a place to which one may retire, esp. for religious contemplation 7 a period of seclusion, esp. for religious contemplation 8 the act of altering one's opinion about something

retreat vb 1 = withdraw, back off, draw back, leave, go back, depart, fall back, pull back; ≠ advance ▸ n 4, 5A = flight, retirement, departure, withdrawal, evacuation 6 = refuge, haven, shelter, sanctuary, hideaway, seclusion

r

retrench *vb* to reduce expenditure
> **retrenchment** *n*

retrial *n* a second trial of a defendant in a court of law

retribution *n* punishment or vengeance for evil deeds > **retributive** *adj*

retrieve *vb* **-trieving, -trieved** 1 to get or fetch back again 2 to bring back to a more satisfactory state: *his attempt to retrieve the situation* 3 to rescue or save 4 to recover (stored information) from a computer system 5 (of dogs) to find and fetch (shot birds and animals) 6 to remember ▸ *n* 7 the chance of being retrieved: *beyond retrieve* > **retrievable** *adj* > **retrieval** *n*

> **retrieve** *vb* 1 = get back, regain, recover, restore, recapture 2, 3 = redeem, save, win back, recoup

retriever *n* a dog trained to retrieve shot birds and animals

retro *adj* associated with or revived from the past: *swap sandals for heeled mules to complete the retro look*

retroactive *adj* effective from a date in the past: *justice through retroactive legislation is never justice*

retrograde *adj* 1 tending towards an earlier worse condition 2 moving or bending backwards 3 (esp. of order) reverse or inverse ▸ *vb* **-grading, -graded** 4 to go backwards or deteriorate

retrorocket *n* a small rocket on a larger rocket or a spacecraft, that produces thrust in the opposite direction to the direction of flight in order to slow down

retrospect *n* **in retrospect** when looking back on the past

> **retrospect** *n* = hindsight, review, re-examination; ≠ foresight

retrospective *adj* 1 looking back in time 2 applying from a date in the past: *retrospective legislation* ▸ *n* 3 an exhibition of an artist's life's work

retroussé (rit-**troo**-say) *adj* (of a nose) turned upwards

retsina *n* a Greek wine flavoured with resin

return *vb* 1 to come back to a former place or state 2 to give, put, or send back 3 to repay with something of equivalent value: *she returned the compliment* 4 to hit, throw, or play (a ball) back 5 to recur or reappear: *as he relaxed his appetite returned* 6 to come back or revert in thought or speech: *let's return to what he said* 7 to earn or yield (profit or interest) 8 to answer or reply 9 to vote into office 10 *law* (of a jury) to deliver (a verdict) ▸ *n* 11 the act or an instance of coming back 12 the act of being returned 13 replacement or restoration: *the return of law and order* 14 something that is given or sent back 15 *sport* the act of playing or throwing a ball back 16 a recurrence or reappearance: *the return of tuberculosis* 17 the

yield or profit from an investment or venture 18 a statement of one's taxable income (a **tax return**) 19 an answer or reply 20 *Brit, Austral & NZ* short for **return ticket** 21 **in return** in exchange 22 **returns** statement of the votes counted at an election 23 **by return (of post)** *Brit* by the next post back to the sender 24 **many happy returns (of the day)** a conventional birthday greeting ▸ *adj* 25 of or being a return: *the team is keen on a return match* > **returnable** *adj*

> **return** *vb* 1, 4, 6 = come back, go back, retreat, turn back, revert, reappear; ≠ depart 2 = put back, replace, restore, reinstate; ≠ keep 5 = recur, repeat, persist, revert, happen again, reappear, come again 9 = elect, choose, vote in ▸ *n* 11 = reappearance; ≠ departure 12, 13 = restoration, reinstatement, re-establishment; ≠ removal 16 = recurrence, repetition, reappearance, reversion, persistence 17 = profit, interest, gain, income, revenue, yield, proceeds, takings 18 = statement, report, form, list, account, summary

returning officer *n* an official in charge of conducting an election in a constituency

return ticket *n* a ticket allowing a passenger to travel to a place and back

reunion *n* 1 a gathering of people who have been apart 2 the act of coming together again

reunite *vb* **-niting, -nited** to bring or come together again after a separation

reuse *n* 1 the act of using something again ▸ *vb* **-using, -used** 2 to use again > **reusable** *adj*

rev *informal* ▸ *n* 1 revolution per minute (of an engine) ▸ *vb* **revving, revved** 2 to increase the speed of revolution of (an engine)

Rev. Reverend

revalue *vb* **-valuing, -valued** to adjust the exchange value of (a currency) upwards > **revaluation** *n*

revamp *vb* to patch up or renovate

> **revamp** *vb* = renovate, restore, overhaul, refurbish, do up (*informal*), recondition

Revd. Reverend

reveal *vb* 1 to disclose or divulge (a secret) 2 to expose to view or show (something concealed) 3 (of God) to disclose (divine truths)

> **reveal** *vb* 1 = make known, disclose, give away, make public, tell, announce, proclaim, let out; ≠ keep secret 2 = show, display, exhibit, unveil, uncover, manifest, unearth, unmask; ≠ hide

reveille (riv-**val**-ee) *n* a signal given by a bugle or drum to awaken soldiers or sailors in the morning

revel *vb* **-velling, -velled** *or US* **-veling, -veled** 1 **revel in** to take pleasure or wallow in: *he would revel in his victory* 2 to take part in noisy festivities ▸ *n* 3 **revels** noisy merrymaking > **reveller** *n*

revel *vb* **2** = celebrate, carouse, live it up (*informal*), make merry ▸ *n* = merrymaking, party, celebration, spree (*old-fashioned*), festivity, carousal

revelation *n* **1** the act of making known a truth which was previously secret **2** a fact newly made known **3** a person or experience that proves to be different from expectations: *New York State could prove a revelation to first-time visitors* **4** *Christianity* God's disclosure of his own nature and his purpose for mankind

revelation *n* **1** = exhibition, publication, exposure, unveiling, uncovering, unearthing, proclamation

revelry *n, pl* **-ries** noisy or unrestrained merrymaking

revenge *n* **1** vengeance for wrongs or injury received **2** something done as a means of vengeance ▸ *vb* **-venging, -venged 3** to inflict equivalent injury or damage for (injury received) **4** to take vengeance for (oneself or another) > **revengeful** *adj*

revenge *n* **1** = retaliation, vengeance, reprisal, retribution, an eye for an eye ▸ *vb* **3** = avenge, repay, take revenge for, get your own back for (*informal*)

revenue *n* **1** income, esp. that obtained by a government from taxation **2** a government department responsible for collecting taxes

revenue *n* **1** = income, returns, profits, gain, yield, proceeds, receipts, takings; ≠ expenditure

reverberate *vb* **-rating, -rated 1** to resound or re-echo **2** to reflect or be reflected many times > **reverberation** *n*

revere *vb* **-vering, -vered** to be in awe of and respect deeply

revere *vb* = be in awe of, respect, honour, worship, reverence, exalt, look up to, venerate; ≠ despise

reverence *n* profound respect > **reverential** *adj*
Reverend *adj* a title of respect for a member of the clergy
reverent *adj* feeling or expressing reverence
reverie *n* an absent-minded daydream
revers (riv-veer) *n, pl* **-vers** the turned-back lining of part of a garment, such as the lapel or cuff
reverse *vb* **-versing, -versed 1** to turn or set in an opposite direction, order, or position **2** to change into something different or contrary: *the cabinet intends to reverse the trend of recent polls* **3** to move backwards or in an opposite direction: *as he started to reverse the car, the bomb exploded* **4** to run (machinery) in the opposite direction to normal **5** to turn inside out

6 *law* to revoke or set aside (a judgment or decree) **7 reverse the charges** *Brit* to make a telephone call at the recipient's expense ▸ *n* **8** the opposite or contrary of something **9** the back or rear side of something **10** a change to an opposite position, state, or direction **11** a change for the worse **12** the gear by which a motor vehicle can be made to go backwards **13** the side of a coin bearing a secondary design **14 in reverse** in an opposite or backward direction **15 the reverse of** not at all: *the result was the reverse of his expectations* ▸ *adj* **16** opposite or contrary in direction, position, etc. **17** denoting the gear by which a motor vehicle can be made to go backwards > **reversal** *n*

reverse *vb* **1** = turn round, turn over, turn upside down, upend **2** = transpose, change, move, exchange, transfer, switch, shift, alter **3** = go backwards, retreat, back up, turn back, move backwards, back; ≠ go forward **6** = change, cancel, overturn, overthrow, undo, repeal, quash, revoke; ≠ implement ▸ *n* **8** = opposite, contrary, converse, inverse **9, 13** = back, rear, other side, wrong side, underside; ≠ front **11** = misfortune, blow, failure, disappointment, setback, hardship, reversal, adversity

reversible *adj* **1** capable of being reversed: *the effect of the operation may not be reversible* **2** (of a garment) made so that either side may be used as the outer side
reversion *n* **1** a return to an earlier condition, practice, or belief **2** *biol* the return of individuals or organs to a more primitive condition or type **3** the rightful passing of property to the owner or designated heir
revert *vb* **1** to go back to a former state **2** *biol* (of individuals or organs) to return to a more primitive, earlier, or simpler condition or type **3** to come back to a subject **4** *property law* (of an estate) to return to its former owner

revert *vb* **1** = go back, return, come back, resume **4** = return

review *n* **1** a critical assessment of a book, film, etc. **2** a publication containing such articles **3** a general survey or report: *the new curriculum is to be set up a year after the conclusions of the review are due* **4** a formal or official inspection **5** the act or an instance of reviewing **6** a second consideration; re-examination **7** a retrospective survey **8** *law* a re-examination of a case ▸ *vb* **9** to hold or write a review of **10** to examine again: *the committee will review the ban in the summer* **11** to look back upon (a period of time or sequence of events): *he reviewed his achievements with pride* **12** to inspect formally or officially: *when he reviewed the troops they cheered him* **13** *law* to re-examine (a decision) judicially

r

review n 1 = critique, commentary, evaluation, notice, criticism, judgment 2 = magazine, journal, periodical, zine (informal) 3 = survey, study, analysis, examination, scrutiny 4 = inspection, parade, march past ▸ vb 9 = assess, study, judge, evaluate, criticize 10 = reconsider, revise, rethink, reassess, re-examine, re-evaluate, think over 11 = look back on, remember, recall, reflect on, recollect 12 = inspect, check, survey, examine, vet

reviewer n a person who writes reviews of books, films, etc.

reviewer n = critic, judge, commentator

revile vb **-viling, -viled** to be abusively scornful of: his works were reviled and admired in equal measure

revise vb **-vising, -vised 1** to change or alter: he grudgingly revised his opinion **2** to prepare a new edition of (a previously printed work) **3** to read (something) several times in order to learn it in preparation for an examination

revise vb 1 = change, review 2 = edit, correct, alter, update, amend, rework, redo, emend 3 = study, go over, run through, cram (informal), swot up on (Brit informal)

revision n **1** the act or process of revising **2** a corrected or new version of a book, article, etc.

revision n 1 = studying, cramming (informal), swotting (Brit informal), homework

revival n **1** a reviving or being revived **2** a reawakening of religious faith **3** a new production of a play that has not been recently performed **4** a renewed use or interest in: there has been an Art Deco revival

revival n 1, 4 = reawakening, renaissance, renewal, resurrection, rebirth, revitalization

revivalism n a movement that seeks to revive religious faith > **revivalist** n, adj

revive vb **-viving, -vived 1** to make or become lively or active again **2** to bring or be brought back to life, consciousness, or strength: revived by a drop of whisky **3** theatre to put on a new production of (an old play)

revive vb 1 = refresh; ≠ exhaust 2 = come round, recover

revoke vb **-voking, -voked 1** to take back or cancel (an agreement, will, etc.) **2** cards to break a rule by failing to follow suit when able to do so ▸ n 3 cards the act of revoking > **revocation** n

revolt n **1** a rebellion or uprising against authority **2 in revolt** in the state of rebelling ▸ vb **3** to rise up in rebellion against authority **4** to cause to feel disgust

revolt n 1 = uprising, rising, revolution, rebellion, mutiny, insurrection, insurgency ▸ vb 3 = rebel, rise up, resist, mutiny

4 = disgust, sicken, repel, repulse, nauseate, gross out (slang), turn your stomach, make your flesh creep

revolting adj horrible and disgusting

revolting adj = disgusting, foul, horrible, sickening, horrid (informal), repellent, repulsive, nauseating, yucko (Austral slang); ≠ delightful

revolution n **1** the overthrow of a regime or political system by the governed **2** (in Marxist theory) the transition from one system of production in a society to the next **3** a far-reaching and drastic change **4 A** movement in or as if in a circle **B** one complete turn in a circle: 33 revolutions per minute

revolution n 1 = revolt, rising, coup, rebellion, uprising, mutiny, insurgency 3 = transformation, shift, innovation, upheaval, reformation, sea change 4 = rotation, turn, cycle, circle, spin, lap, circuit, orbit

revolutionary adj **1** of or like a revolution **2** advocating or engaged in revolution **3** radically new or different: they have designed revolutionary new materials to build power stations ▸ n, pl **-aries 4** a person who advocates or engages in revolution

revolutionary adj 1, 2 = rebel, radical, extremist, subversive, insurgent; ≠ reactionary 3 = innovative, new, different, novel, radical, progressive, drastic, ground-breaking; ≠ conventional ▸ n = rebel, insurgent, revolutionist; ≠ reactionary

revolutionize or **-nise** vb **-nizing, -nized** or **-nising, -nised** to bring about a radical change in

revolve vb **-volving, -volved 1** to move or cause to move around a centre **2 revolve around** to be centred or focused upon: the campaign revolves around one man **3** to occur periodically or in cycles **4** to consider or be considered > **revolvable** adj

revolve vb 1 = rotate, turn, wheel, spin, twist, whirl

revolver n a pistol with a revolving cylinder that allows several shots to be fired without reloading

revue n a theatrical entertainment with topical sketches and songs

revulsion n a violent feeling of disgust

reward n **1** something given in return for a service **2** a sum of money offered for finding a criminal or missing property **3** something received in return for good or evil: sacrifice provided its own reward ▸ vb **4** to give something to (someone) for a service rendered

reward n 2 = payment, return, prize, wages, compensation, bonus, premium, repayment; ≠ penalty 3 = punishment, retribution, comeuppance (slang), just deserts ▸ vb = compensate, pay, repay, recompense, remunerate (formal); ≠ penalize

rewarding *adj* giving personal satisfaction: *my most professionally rewarding experience*

> **rewarding** *adj* = satisfying, fulfilling, valuable, profitable, productive, worthwhile, beneficial, enriching; ≠ unrewarding

rewind *vb* **-winding, -wound** to run (a tape or film) back to an earlier point in order to replay

rewire *vb* **-wiring, -wired** to provide (a house, engine, etc.) with new wiring

rewrite *vb* **-writing, -wrote, -written 1** to write again in a different way ▸ *n* **2** something rewritten

rhapsodize *or* **-dise** *vb* **-dizing, -dized** *or* **-dising, -dised** to speak or write with extravagant enthusiasm

rhapsody *n, pl* **-dies 1** *music* a freely structured and emotional piece of music **2** an expression of ecstatic enthusiasm > **rhapsodic** *adj*

rhea (ree-a) *n* a large fast-running flightless bird of South America, similar to the ostrich

rhenium (ree-nee-um) *n* *chem* a silvery-white metallic element with a high melting point. Symbol: **Re**

rheostat *n* a variable resistor in an electrical circuit, such as one used to dim lights > **rheostatic** *adj*

rhesus factor (ree-suss) *n* See **Rh factor**

rhesus monkey *n* a small long-tailed monkey of S Asia

rhetoric (ret-a-rik) *n* **1** the art of using speech or writing to persuade or influence **2** artificial or exaggerated language: *there's been no shortage of soaring rhetoric at this summit* > **rhetorical** (rit-**tor**-ik-kl) *adj*

> **rhetoric** *n* **1** = oratory, eloquence, public speaking, speech-making, elocution, declamation, grandiloquence, whaikorero (NZ) **2** = hyperbole, bombast, wordiness, verbosity, grandiloquence, magniloquence

rheumatic *adj* **1** caused by or affected by rheumatism ▸ *n* **2** a person with rheumatism > **rheumatically** *adv*

rheumatism *n* any painful disorder of joints, muscles, or connective tissue

rheumatoid *adj* (of symptoms) resembling rheumatism

Rh factor *n* an antigen commonly found in human blood: the terms **Rh positive** and **Rh negative** are used to indicate its presence or absence

rhinestone *n* an imitation diamond made of glass

rhino *n, pl* **-nos** *or* **-no** a rhinoceros

rhinoceros *n, pl* **-roses** *or* **-ros** a large plant-eating mammal of SE Asia and Africa with one or two horns on the nose and a very thick skin

rhizome *n* a thick horizontal underground stem whose buds develop into new plants

rhodium *n* *chem* a hard silvery-white metallic element, used to harden platinum and palladium. Symbol: **Rh**

rhododendron *n* an evergreen shrub with clusters of showy flowers

rhomboid *n* **1** a parallelogram with adjacent sides of unequal length. It resembles a rectangle but does not have 90° angles ▸ *adj* also **rhomboidal 2** having such a shape

rhombus (rom-buss) *n, pl* **-buses** *or* **-bi** (-bye) a parallelogram with sides of equal length but no right angles > **rhombic** *adj*

rhubarb *n* **1** a large-leaved plant with long green and red stalks which can be cooked and eaten **2** a related plant of central Asia, whose root can be dried and used as a laxative or astringent ▸ *interj, n* **3** the noise made by actors to simulate conversation, esp. by repeating the word *rhubarb*

rhyme *n* **1** sameness of the final sounds in lines of verse or in words **2** a word that is identical to another in its final sound: *'while' is a rhyme for 'mile'* **3** a piece of poetry with corresponding sounds at the ends of the lines **4 rhyme or reason** sense or meaning ▸ *vb* **rhyming, rhymed 5** (of a word) to form a rhyme with another word **6** to compose (verse) in a metrical structure

> **rhyme** *n* **3** = poem, song, verse, ode

rhythm *n* **1** any regular movement or beat: *the side-effects can cause changes in the rhythm of the heart beat* **2** any regular pattern that occurs over a period of time: *the seasonal rhythm of the agricultural year* **3 A** the arrangement of the durations of and stress on the notes of a piece of music, usually laid out in regular groups (**bars**) of beats **B** any specific arrangement of such groupings: *waltz rhythm* **4** (in poetry) the arrangement of words to form a regular pattern of stresses > **rhythmic** *or* **rhythmical** *adj* > **rhythmically** *adv*

> **rhythm** *n* **1, 3A** = beat, swing, accent, pulse, tempo, cadence, lilt **4** = metre, time

rhythm and blues *n* a kind of popular music derived from and influenced by the blues

rib¹ *n* **1** one of the curved bones forming the framework of the upper part of the body and attached to the spinal column **2** a cut of meat including one or more ribs **3** a curved supporting part, such as in the hull of a boat **4** one of a series of raised rows in knitted fabric ▸ *vb* **ribbing, ribbed 5** to provide or support with ribs **6** to knit to form a rib pattern > **ribbed** *adj*

rib² *vb* **ribbing, ribbed** *informal* to tease or ridicule > **ribbing** *n*

ribald *adj* coarse or obscene in a humorous or mocking way > **ribaldry** *n*

riband *or* **ribband** *n* a ribbon awarded for some achievement

ribbing *n* **1** a pattern of ribs in knitted material **2** a framework or structure of ribs

ribbon *n* **1** a narrow strip of fine material used for trimming, tying, etc. **2** a long narrow strip of inked cloth or plastic used to produce print in a typewriter **3** a small strip of coloured cloth

r

worn as a badge or as a symbol of an award
4 a long thin strip: *a ribbon of white water*
5 ribbons ragged strips or shreds: *his clothes were torn to ribbons*; *his credibility was shot to ribbons*

ribcage *n* the bony structure formed by the ribs that encloses the lungs

riboflavin (rye-boe-**flay**-vin) *n* a vitamin of the B complex that occurs in green vegetables, milk, fish, eggs, liver, and kidney: used as a yellow or orange food colouring (**E101**). Also called: **vitamin B₂**

rice *n* **1** the edible grain of an erect grass that grows on wet ground in warm climates ▸ *vb* **ricing, riced 2** *US & Canad* to sieve (potatoes or other vegetables) to a coarse mashed consistency

rich *adj* **1** owning a lot of money or property **2** well supplied (with a desirable substance or quality): *a country rich with cultural interest* **3** having an abundance of natural resources, minerals, etc.: *a land rich in unexploited minerals* **4** producing abundantly: *the island is a blend of hilly moorland and rich farmland* **5** luxuriant or prolific: *the meadows rich with corn* **6** (of food) containing much fat or sugar **7** having a full-bodied flavour: *a gloriously rich Cabernet-dominated wine* **8** (of colour) intense or vivid: *her hair had a rich auburn tint* **9** (of sound or a voice) full or resonant **10** very amusing or ridiculous: *a rich joke* **11** (of a fuel-air mixture) containing a relatively high proportion of fuel ▷ **richness** *n*

rich *adj* **1** = wealthy, affluent, well-off, loaded (*slang*), prosperous, well-heeled (*informal*), well-to-do, moneyed, minted (*Brit slang*); ≠ poor **2** = well-stocked, full, productive, ample, abundant, plentiful, copious, well-supplied; ≠ scarce **4** = fruitful, productive, fertile, prolific; ≠ barren **5** = abounding, luxurious, lush, abundant **6,7** = full-bodied, sweet, fatty, tasty, creamy, luscious, succulent; ≠ bland

riches *pl n* valuable possessions or desirable substances: *the unexpected riches of Georgian culture*

riches *pl n* = wealth, assets, plenty, fortune, substance, treasure, affluence, top whack (*informal*); ≠ poverty

richly *adv* **1** in a rich or elaborate manner: *the rooms are richly decorated with a variety of classical motifs* **2** fully and appropriately: *he left the field to a richly deserved standing ovation*

richly *adv* **1** = elaborately, lavishly, elegantly, splendidly, exquisitely, expensively, luxuriously, gorgeously **2** = fully, well, thoroughly, amply, appropriately, properly, suitably

Richter scale *n* a scale for expressing the intensity of an earthquake, ranging from 0 to over 8

rick¹ *n* a large stack of hay or straw

rick² *vb* **1** to wrench or sprain (a joint) ▸ *n* **2** a wrench or sprain of a joint

rickets *n* a disease of children, caused by a deficiency of vitamin D and characterized by softening of developing bone, and hence bow legs

rickety *adj* **1** likely to collapse or break: *a rickety wooden table* **2** resembling or having rickets ▷ **ricketiness** *n*

rickshaw *or* **ricksha** *n* **1** a small two-wheeled passenger vehicle pulled by one or two people, used in parts of Asia **2** a similar vehicle with three wheels, propelled by a person pedalling

ricochet (rik-osh-ay) *vb* **-cheting, -cheted** *or* **-chetting, -chetted 1** (of a bullet) to rebound from a surface ▸ *n* **2** the motion or sound of a rebounding bullet

rid *vb* **ridding, rid** *or* **ridded 1 rid of** to relieve (oneself) or make a place free of (something undesirable) **2 get rid of** to relieve or free oneself of (something undesirable)

rid *vb* **1** = free, clear, deliver, relieve, purge, unburden, make free, disencumber **2 get rid of something or someone** = dispose of, throw away *or* out, dump, remove, eliminate, expel, eject

ridden *vb* **1** the past participle of **ride** ▸ *adj* **2** afflicted or affected by the thing specified: *the police found three bullet-ridden bodies*

riddle¹ *n* **1** a question, puzzle, or verse phrased so that ingenuity is required to find the answer or meaning **2** a puzzling person or thing ▸ *vb* **-dling, -dled 3** to speak in riddles

riddle *n* **1** = puzzle, problem, conundrum, poser **2** = enigma, question, secret, mystery, puzzle, conundrum, teaser, problem

riddle² *vb* **-dling, -dled 1** to pierce with many holes **2** to put through a sieve ▸ *n* **3** a coarse sieve

riddle *vb* **1** = pierce, pepper, puncture, perforate, honeycomb

ride *vb* **riding, rode, ridden 1** to sit on and control the movements of (a horse or other animal) **2** to sit on and propel (a bicycle or motorcycle) **3** to travel on or in a vehicle: *he rides around in a chauffeur-driven Rolls-Royce* **4** to travel over: *they rode the countryside in search of shelter* **5** to travel through or be carried across (sea, sky, etc.): *the moon was riding high* **6** *US & Canad* to cause to be carried: *to ride someone out of town* **7** (of a vessel) to lie at anchor **8** to tyrannize over or dominate: *she was ridden by fear* **9 be riding on** to be dependent on (something) for success: *a lot is riding on the profits of the film* **10** *informal* to continue undisturbed: *let it ride* **11 riding high** popular and successful ▸ *n* **12** a journey on a bicycle, on horseback, or in a vehicle **13** transport in a vehicle: *most of us have been told not to accept rides from strangers* **14** the type of movement experienced in a vehicle: *a bumpy* *ride* **15** a path for riding on horseback **16 take for a ride** *informal* to cheat or deceive

> **ride** *vb* **1** = control, handle, manage **3** = travel, be carried, go, move ▸ **12, 13** = journey, drive, trip, lift, outing, jaunt

rider *n* **1** a person who rides **2** an extra clause or condition added to a document

ride up *vb* (of a garment) to move up from the proper position

ridge *n* **1** a long narrow raised land formation with sloping sides **2** a long narrow raised strip on a flat surface **3** the top of a roof where the two sloping sides meet **4** *meteorol* an elongated area of high pressure ▹ **ridged** *adj* ▹ **ridgy** *adj*

ridicule *n* **1** language or behaviour intended to humiliate or mock ▸ *vb* **-culing, -culed 2** to make fun of or mock

> **ridicule** *n* = mockery, scorn, derision, laughter, jeer, chaff, gibe, raillery ▸ *vb* = laugh at, mock, make fun of, sneer at, jeer at, deride, poke fun at, chaff

ridiculous *adj* worthy of or causing ridicule

> **ridiculous** *adj* = laughable, stupid, silly, absurd, ludicrous, farcical, comical, risible (*formal*); ≠ sensible

riding[1] *n* the art or practice of horsemanship

riding[2] *n* **1 Riding** any of the three former administrative divisions of Yorkshire: North Riding, East Riding, and West Riding **2** *Canad* an electoral constituency

riesling *n* a medium-dry white wine

rife *adj* **1** widespread or common **2 rife with** full of: *the media is rife with speculation*

> **rife** *adj* **1** = widespread, rampant, general, common, universal, frequent, prevalent, ubiquitous

riff *n* *jazz & rock* a short series of chords

riffle *vb* **-fling, -fled 1** to flick through (papers or pages) quickly: *I riffled through the rest of the memos* ▸ *n* **2** *US & Canad* **a** a rapid in a stream **b** a rocky shoal causing a rapid **c** a ripple on water **3** a riffling

riffraff *n* worthless or disreputable people

rifle[1] *n* **1** a firearm having a long barrel with a spirally grooved interior, which gives the bullet a spinning motion and thus greater accuracy over a longer range **2 Rifles** a unit of soldiers equipped with rifles: *the Burma Rifles* ▸ *vb* **-fling, -fled 3** to cut spiral grooves inside the barrel of (a gun) ▹ **rifled** *adj*

rifle[2] *vb* **-fling, -fled 1** to search (a house or safe) and steal from it **2** to steal and carry off: *he rifled whatever valuables he could lay his hands on*

> **rifle** *vb* **2** = ransack, rob, burgle, loot, strip, sack, plunder, pillage

rift *n* **1** a break in friendly relations between people or groups of people **2** a gap or space made by splitting

rift *n* **1** = breach, division, split, separation, falling out (*informal*), disagreement, quarrel **2** = split, opening, crack, gap, break, fault, flaw, cleft

rift valley *n* a long narrow valley resulting from the subsidence of land between two faults

rig *vb* **rigging, rigged 1** to arrange in a dishonest way, for profit or advantage: *he claimed that the poll was rigged* **2** to set up or prepare (something) hastily ready for use **3** *naut* to equip (a vessel or mast) with (sails or rigging) ▸ *n* **4** an apparatus for drilling for oil and gas **5** *naut* the arrangement of the sails and masts of a vessel **6** apparatus or equipment **7** *informal* an outfit of clothes **8** *US, Canad & Austral* an articulated lorry ▸ See also **rig up**

> **rig** *vb* **1** = fix (*informal*), engineer (*informal*), arrange, manipulate, tamper with, gerrymander **3** = equip, fit out, kit out, outfit, supply, furnish

rigging *n* the ropes and cables supporting a ship's masts and sails

right *adj* **1** morally or legally acceptable or correct: *his conduct seemed reasonable, even right* **2** correct or true: *the customer is always right* **3** appropriate, suitable, or proper: *there were problems involved in finding the right candidate* **4** most favourable or convenient: *she waited until the right moment to broach the subject* **5** in a satisfactory condition: *things are right again now* **6** accurate: *is that clock right?* **7** correct in opinion or judgment **8** sound in mind or body **9** of or on the side of something or someone that faces east when the front is turned towards the north **10** conservative or reactionary: *it was alleged he was an agent of the right wing* **11** *geom* formed by or containing a line or plane perpendicular to another line or plane: *a right angle* **12** of or on the side of cloth worn or facing outwards **13 in one's right mind** sane **14 she'll be right** *Austral & NZ informal* that's all right; not to worry **15 the right side of A** in favour with: *you'd better stay on the right side of him* **B** younger than: *he's still on the right side of fifty* **16 too right** *informal* an exclamation of agreement ▸ *adv* **17** correctly: *if we change the structure of local government we must do it right* **18** in the appropriate manner: *do it right next time!* **19** straight or directly: *let's go right to bed* **20** in the direction of the east from the point of view of a person or thing facing north **21** all the way: *he drove right up to the gate* **22** without delay: *I'll be right over* **23** exactly or precisely: *right here* **24** fittingly: *it serves him right* **25** to good or favourable advantage: *it all came out right in the end* ▸ *n* **26** a freedom or power that is morally or legally due to a person: *the defendant had an absolute right to a fair trial* **27** anything that accords with the principles of legal or moral justice **28 in the right** the state of being in accordance with reason or truth **29** the right side, direction, or part: *the right of the army* **30 the Right** the supporters or advocates of conservatism or reaction: *the rise of the far Right* **31** *boxing* a punch with the right hand **32 rights** *finance* the privilege of a company's shareholders to subscribe for new issues of the company's shares on advantageous terms **33 by right** or **rights** properly: *by rights he should have won* **34 in one's own right** having a claim or title oneself rather than through marriage or other connection **35 to rights** consistent with justice or orderly arrangement: *he put the matter to rights* ▸ *vb* **36** to bring or come back to a normal or correct state **37** to bring or come back to a vertical position: *he slipped and righted himself at once* **38** to compensate for or redress: *there is a wrong to be righted* **39** to make (something) accord with truth or facts ▸ *interj* **40** an expression of agreement or compliance

> **right** *adj* **1** = just, good, fair, moral, proper, ethical, honest, equitable; ≠ unfair **2, 7** = correct, true, genuine, accurate, exact, precise, valid, factual, dinkum (*Austral, NZ informal*); ≠ wrong **3** = proper, done, becoming, seemly, fitting, fit, appropriate, suitable; ≠ inappropriate ▸ *adv* **17** = correctly, truly, precisely, exactly, genuinely, accurately; ≠ wrongly **18** = suitably, fittingly, appropriately, properly, aptly; ≠ improperly **19, 22** = straight, directly, quickly, promptly, straight away; ≠ indirectly **23** = exactly, squarely, precisely ▸ *n* **26** = prerogative, business, power, claim, authority, due, freedom, licence **27** = justice, truth, fairness, legality, righteousness, lawfulness; ≠ injustice ▸ *vb* **38** = rectify, settle, fix, correct, sort out, straighten, redress, put right

right angle *n* **1** an angle of 90° or π/2 radians **2 at right angles** perpendicular or perpendicularly > **right-angled** *adj*
right away *adv* without delay

> **right away** *adv* = immediately, now, directly, instantly, at once, straight away, forthwith, pronto (*informal*)

righteous (rye-chuss) *adj* **1** moral, just, or virtuous: *the lieutenant was a righteous cop* **2** morally justifiable or right: *her eyes were blazing with righteous indignation* > **righteousness** *n*

> **righteous** *adj* **1** = virtuous, good, just, fair, moral, pure, ethical, upright; ≠ wicked

rightful *adj* **1** in accordance with what is right **2** having a legally or morally just claim: *he is the rightful heir to her fortune* **3** held by virtue of a legal or just claim: *these moves will restore them to their rightful homes* > **rightfully** *adv* > **rightfulness** *n*
right-handed *adj* **1** more adept with the right hand than with the left **2** made for or by the right hand **3** turning from left to right

rightist *adj* **1** of the political right or its principles ▸ *n* **2** a supporter of the political right > **rightism** *n*
rightly *adv* **1** in accordance with the true facts or justice **2** with good reason: *he was rightly praised for his constancy*
right of way *n, pl* **rights of way 1** the right of one vehicle or ship to go before another **2 ᴀ** the legal right of someone to pass over someone else's land **ʙ** the path used by this right
right-wing *adj* **1** conservative or reactionary: *there's a very fast-growing right-wing feeling in our country* **2** belonging to the more conservative part of a political party: *a group of right-wing Labour MPs* ▸ *n* **right wing 3** the more conservative or reactionary section, esp. of a political party: *the right wing of the Conservative Party* **4** *sport* **ᴀ** the right-hand side of the field of play **ʙ** a player positioned in this area in certain games > **right-winger** *n*
rigid *adj* **1** inflexible or strict: *the talks will be general, without a rigid agenda* **2** physically unyielding or stiff: *use only rigid plastic containers* > **rigidity** *n* > **rigidly** *adv*

> **rigid** *adj* **1** = inflexible, uncompromising, unbending; ≠ flexible **2** = stiff, inflexible, inelastic; ≠ pliable

rigmarole *n* **1** a long complicated procedure **2** a set of incoherent or pointless statements
rigor mortis *n* the stiffness of joints and muscles of a dead body
rigorous *adj* **1** harsh, strict, or severe: *rigorous enforcement of the libel laws* **2** severely accurate: *rigorous scientific testing*

> **rigorous** *adj* **1** = strict, hard, demanding, tough, severe, exacting, harsh, stern; ≠ soft

rigour or US **rigor** *n* **1** a severe or cruel circumstance: *the rigours of forced labour* **2** strictness in judgment or conduct **3** harsh but just treatment
rig up *vb* to set up or build temporarily: *they rigged up a loudspeaker system*

> **rig up** *vb* **rig something up** = set up, build, construct, put up, arrange, assemble, put together, erect

rile *vb* **riling, riled 1** to annoy or anger **2** *US & Canad* to stir up (a liquid)
rill *n* a small stream
rim *n* **1** the raised edge of an object **2** the outer part of a wheel to which the tyre is attached > **rimless** *adj*

> **rim** *n* **1** = edge, lip, brim

rime *literary* ▸ *n* **1** frost formed by the freezing of water droplets in fog onto solid objects ▸ *vb* **riming, rimed 2** to cover with rime or something resembling it > **rimy** *adj*
rind *n* a hard outer layer on fruits, bacon, or cheese

ring¹ *vb* **ringing, rang, rung 1** to give out a clear resonant sound, like that of a bell **2** to cause (a bell) to give out a ringing sound or (of a bell) to give out such a sound **3** *chiefly Brit & NZ* to call (a person) by telephone **4 ring for** to call by means of a bell: *ring for the maid* **5** (of a building or place) to be filled with sound: *the church rang with singing* **6** (of the ears) to have the sensation of humming or ringing **7** *slang* to change the identity of (a stolen vehicle) by using the licence plate or serial number of another, usually disused, vehicle **8 ring a bell** to bring something to the mind or memory: *the name doesn't ring a bell* **9 ring down the curtain** **a** to lower the curtain at the end of a theatrical performance **b ring down the curtain on** to put an end to **10 ring true** *or* **false** to give the impression of being true or false ▸ *n* **11** the act of or a sound made by ringing **12** a sound produced by or sounding like a bell **13** *informal, chiefly Brit & NZ* a telephone call **14** an inherent quality: *it has the ring of possibility to it* ▸ See also **ring off** *etc.*

> **ring** *vb* **1, 2** = chime, sound, toll, reverberate, clang, peal **3** = phone, call, telephone, buzz (*informal, chiefly Brit*) **5** = reverberate ▸ *n* **11, 12** = chime, knell, peal **13** = call, phone call, buzz (*informal, chiefly Brit*)

ring² *n* **1** a circular band of a precious metal worn on the finger **2** any object or mark that is circular in shape **3** a group of people or things standing or arranged in a circle: *a ring of standing stones* **4** a circular path or course: *crowds of people walking round in a ring* **5** a circular enclosure where circus acts perform or livestock is sold at a market **6** a square raised platform, marked off by ropes, in which contestants box or wrestle **7** a group of people, usually illegal, who control a specified market: *a drugs ring* **8** *chem* a closed loop of atoms in a molecule **9** one of the systems of circular bands orbiting the planets Saturn, Uranus, and Jupiter **10 the ring** the sport of boxing **11 throw one's hat in the ring** to announce one's intention to be a candidate or contestant **12 run rings around** *informal* to outclass completely ▸ *vb* **ringing, ringed 13** to put a ring round **14** to mark (a bird) with a ring or clip for subsequent identification **15** to kill (a tree) by cutting the bark round the trunk **16** to fit a ring in the nose of (a bull, etc.) so that it can be led easily › **ringed** *adj*

> **ring** *n* **2, 3** = circle, round, band, circuit, loop, hoop, halo **5, 6** = arena, enclosure, circus, rink **7** = gang, group, association, band, circle, mob, syndicate, cartel ▸ *vb* **13** = encircle, surround, enclose, girdle, gird

ringer *n informal* **1** Also called: **dead ringer** a person or thing that is almost identical to another **2** a person or thing that is presented under a false identity

ringleader *n* a person who leads others in illegal or mischievous actions

ringlet *n* a lock of hair hanging down in a spiral curl › **ringleted** *adj*

ring off *vb chiefly Brit & NZ* to end a telephone conversation by replacing the receiver

ring road *n chiefly Brit* a main road that bypasses a town or town centre

ringside *n* **1** the row of seats nearest a boxing or wrestling ring ▸ *adj* **2** providing a close uninterrupted view: *a ringside seat for the election*

ringtail *n Austral* a possum with a curling tail used to grip branches while climbing

ringtone *n* a tune or sound played by a mobile phone when it receives a call

ring up *vb* **1** *chiefly Brit* to make a telephone call to **2** to record on a cash register **3 ring up the curtain** **a** to begin a theatrical performance **b ring up the curtain on** to make a start on

ringworm *n* a fungal infection of the skin producing itchy patches

rink *n* **1** a sheet of ice for skating on, usually indoors **2** an area for roller-skating on **3** a building for ice-skating or roller-skating **4** **a** a strip of grass or ice on which a game of bowls or curling is played **b** the players on one side in a game of bowls or curling

rinkhals (rink-hals) *n, pl* **-hals** *or* **-halses** a highly venomous snake of Southern Africa capable of spitting its venom accurately at its victim's eyes

rinse *vb* **rinsing, rinsed 1** to remove soap or shampoo from (clothes, dishes, or hair) by washing it out with clean water **2** to wash lightly, esp. without using soap **3** to cleanse (the mouth) by swirling water or mouthwash in it and then spitting the liquid out **4** to give a light tint to (hair) ▸ *n* **5** the act or an instance of rinsing **6** *hairdressing* a liquid to tint hair: *a blue rinse*

> **rinse** *vb* **1, 2** = wash, clean, dip, splash, cleanse, bathe ▸ *n* **5** = wash, dip, splash, bath

riot *n* **1** a disturbance made by an unruly mob **2** *Brit, Austral & NZ* an occasion of lively enjoyment **3** a dazzling display: *the pansies provided the essential riot of colour* **4** *slang* a very amusing person or thing **5 read the riot act** to reprimand severely **6 run riot** **a** to behave without restraint **b** (of plants) to grow profusely ▸ *vb* **7** to take part in a riot › **rioter** *n* › **rioting** *n*

> **riot** *n* **1** = disturbance, disorder, confusion, turmoil, upheaval, strife, turbulence, lawlessness **3** = display, show, splash, extravaganza, profusion **4** = laugh (*informal*), joke, scream (*informal*), hoot (*informal*), lark **6a run riot** = rampage, go wild, be out of control **6b run riot** = grow profusely, spread like wildfire ▸ *vb* = rampage, run riot, go on the rampage

riotous *adj* **1** unrestrained and excessive: *riotous decadence* **2** unruly or rebellious **3** characterized by unrestrained merriment: *riotous celebration*

r

rip *vb* **ripping, ripped 1** to tear or be torn violently or roughly **2** to remove hastily or roughly **3** *informal* to move violently or hurriedly **4 let rip** to act or speak without restraint ▸ *n* **5** a tear or split ▸ See also **rip off**

> **rip** *vb* **1** = be torn, tear, split, burst **2** = tear, cut, split, burst, rend (*literary*), slash, claw, slit ▸ *n* = tear, cut, hole, split, rent, slash, slit, gash

RIP may he, she, *or* they rest in peace

riparian (rip-pair-ee-an) *adj formal* of or on the bank of a river

ripcord *n* a cord pulled to open a parachute from its pack

ripe *adj* **1** mature enough to be eaten or used: *a round ripe apple* **2** fully developed in mind or body **3** suitable: *wait until the time is ripe* **4 ripe for** ready or eager to (undertake or undergo an action): *China was ripe for revolution* **5 ripe old age** an elderly but healthy age

> **ripe** *adj* **1** = ripened, seasoned, ready, mature, mellow; ≠ unripe **3** = right, suitable

ripen *vb* **1** to make or become ripe **2** to mature

rip off *slang* ▸ *vb* **1** to cheat by overcharging **2** to steal (something) ▸ *n* **rip-off 3** a grossly overpriced article **4** the act of stealing or cheating

> **rip off** *vb* **1 rip someone off** = cheat, rob, con (*informal*), skin (*slang*), fleece, defraud, swindle, scam (*slang*) ▸ *n* **4 rip-off** = cheat, con (*informal*), scam (*slang*), con trick (*informal*), fraud, theft, swindle

riposte (rip-posst) *n* **1** a swift clever reply **2** *fencing* a counterattack made immediately after a successful parry ▸ *vb* **-posting, -posted 3** to make a riposte

ripple *n* **1** a slight wave on the surface of water **2** a slight ruffling of a surface **3** a sound like water flowing gently in ripples: *a ripple of applause* **4** vanilla ice cream with stripes of another ice cream through it: *raspberry ripple* ▸ *vb* **-pling, -pled 5** to form ripples or flow with a waving motion **6** (of sounds) to rise and fall gently > **rippling** *adj*

rip-roaring *adj informal* boisterous and exciting

rise *vb* **rising, rose, risen 1** to get up from a lying, sitting, or kneeling position **2** to get out of bed, esp. to begin one's day: *she rises at 5 am every day to look after her horse* **3** to move from a lower to a higher position or place **4** to appear above the horizon: *as the sun rises higher the mist disappears* **5** to slope upwards: *the road crossed the valley then rose to a low ridge* **6** to increase in height or level: *the tide rose* **7** to swell up: *dough rises* **8** to increase in strength or degree: *frustration is rising amongst sections of the population* **9** to increase in amount or value: *living costs are rising at an annual rate of nine per cent* **10** *informal* to respond (to a challenge or remark) **11** to revolt: *the people rose against their oppressors* **12** (of a court or parliament) to adjourn

13 to be resurrected **14** to become erect or rigid: *the hairs on his neck rose in fear* **15** to originate: *that river rises in the mountains* **16** *angling* (of fish) to come to the surface of the water ▸ *n* **17** the act or an instance of rising **18** a piece of rising ground **19** an increase in wages **20** an increase in amount, cost, or quantity **21** an increase in height **22** an increase in status or position **23** an increase in degree or intensity **24** the vertical height of a step or of a flight of stairs **25 get** *or* **take a rise out of** *slang* to provoke an angry reaction from **26 give rise to** to cause the development of

> **rise** *vb* **1** = get up, stand up, get to your feet **2** = arise (*old-fashioned*) **3** = go up, climb, ascend; ≠ descend **5** = get steeper, ascend, go uphill, slope upwards; ≠ drop **6, 9** = increase, mount; ≠ decrease **8** = grow, go up, intensify **11** = rebel, revolt, mutiny ▸ *n* **18** = upward slope, incline, elevation, ascent, kopje *or* koppie (*S African*) **19** = pay increase, raise (*US*), increment **20** = increase, upturn, upswing, upsurge, bounce; ≠ decrease **22** = advancement, progress, climb, promotion **26 give rise to something** = cause, produce, effect, result in, bring about

riser *n* **1** a person who rises from bed: *an early riser* **2** the vertical part of a step

risible (riz-zib-bl) *adj formal* ridiculous

rising *n* **1** a rebellion ▸ *adj* **2** increasing in rank or maturity

risk *n* **1** the possibility of bringing about misfortune or loss **2** a person or thing considered as a potential hazard: *in parts of the world transfusions carry the risk of infection* **3 at risk** in a dangerous situation **4 take** *or* **run a risk** to act without regard to the danger involved ▸ *vb* **5** to act in spite of the possibility of (injury or loss): *if they clamp down they risk a revolution* **6** to expose to danger or loss > **risky** *adj*

> **risk** *n* **1** = danger, chance, possibility, hazard **2** = gamble, chance, speculation, leap in the dark ▸ *vb* **5** = stand a chance of **6** = dare, endanger, jeopardize, imperil, venture, gamble, hazard

risotto *n, pl* **-tos** a dish of rice cooked in stock with vegetables, meat, etc.

risqué (risk-ay) *adj* making slightly rude references to sex: *risqué humour*

rissole *n* a mixture of minced cooked meat coated in egg and breadcrumbs and fried

rite *n* **1** a formal act which forms part of a religious ceremony: *the rite of burial* **2** a custom that is carried out within a particular group: *the barbaric rites of public execution* **3** a particular body of such acts, esp. of a particular Christian Church: *the traditional Anglican rite*

> **rite** *n* **1, 2** = ceremony, custom, ritual, practice, procedure, observance

ritual *n* **1** a religious or other ceremony involving a series of fixed actions performed in a certain order **2** these ceremonies collectively: *people need ritual* **3** a regular repeated action or behaviour **4** stereotyped activity or behaviour ▸ *adj* **5** of or like rituals › **ritually** *adv*

> **ritual** *n* **1, 2, 3** = ceremony, rite, observance ▸ *adj* = ceremonial, conventional, routine, customary, habitual

ritzy *adj* **ritzier, ritziest** *slang* luxurious or elegant

rival *n* **1** a person or group that competes with another for the same object or in the same field **2** a person or thing that is considered the equal of another: *she is without rival in the field of physics* ▸ *adj* **3** in the position of a rival ▸ *vb* **-valling, -valled** *or US* **-valing, -valed** **4** to be the equal or near equal of: *his inarticulateness was rivalled only by that of his brother* **5** to try to equal or surpass

> **rival** *n* **1** = opponent, competitor, contender, contestant, adversary; ≠ supporter ▸ *adj* = competing, conflicting, opposing ▸ *vb* = compete with, match, equal, compare with, come up to, be a match for

rivalry *n, pl* **-ries** active competition between people or groups

> **rivalry** *n* = competition, opposition, conflict, contest, contention

riven *adj old-fashioned* **1** split apart: *the party is riven by factions* **2** torn to shreds

river *n* **1** a large natural stream of fresh water flowing along a definite course into the sea, a lake, or a larger river. Related adjective: **fluvial** **2** an abundant stream or flow: *rivers of blood*

> **river** *n* **1** = stream, brook, creek (*US, Canad, Austral, NZ*), waterway, tributary, burn (*Scot*) **2** = flow, rush, flood, spate, torrent

rivet (**riv-vit**) *n* **1** a short metal pin for fastening metal plates, with a head at one end, the other end being hammered flat after being put through holes in the plates ▸ *vb* **-veting, -veted** **2** to join by riveting **3** to cause a person's attention to be fixed in fascination or horror: *he was riveted by the story* › **riveter** *n*

riveting *adj* very interesting or exciting

> **riveting** *adj* = enthralling, gripping, fascinating, absorbing, captivating, hypnotic, engrossing, spellbinding

rivulet *n* a small stream

RN 1 (in Canada and New Zealand) Registered Nurse **2** (in Britain) Royal Navy

RNA *n biochem* ribonucleic acid: any of a group of nucleic acids, present in all living cells, that play an essential role in the synthesis of proteins

RNZ Radio New Zealand

RNZAF Royal New Zealand Air Force

RNZN Royal New Zealand Navy

roach *n, pl* **roaches** *or* **roach** a European freshwater food fish

road *n* **1** a route, usually surfaced, used by travellers and vehicles to get from one place to another **2** a street **3** a way or course: *on the road to recovery* **4** **one for the road** *informal* a last alcoholic drink before leaving **5** **on the road** travelling about

> **road** *n* **1, 2** = roadway, highway, motorway, track, route, path, lane, pathway **3** = way, path

roadblock *n* a barrier set up across a road by the police or military, in order to stop and check vehicles

road hog *n informal* a selfish or aggressive driver

roadhouse *n* a pub or restaurant at the side of a road

roadie *n informal* a person who transports and sets up equipment for a band

road map *n* **1** a map for drivers **2** a plan or guide for future actions

roadside *n* **1** the edge of a road ▸ *adj* **2** by the edge or side of a road: *a roadside café*

road test *n* **1** a test of something, such as a vehicle in actual use ▸ *vb* **road-test** **2** to test (a vehicle, etc.) in actual use

roadway *n* the part of a road that is used by vehicles

roadworks *pl n* repairs to a road or cable under a road, esp. when they block part of the road

roadworthy *adj* (of a motor vehicle) mechanically sound › **roadworthiness** *n*

roam *vb* to walk about with no fixed purpose or direction

> **roam** *vb* = wander, walk, range, travel, stray, ramble, prowl, rove

roaming *n* the act of using a mobile phone in a foreign country

roan *adj* **1** (of a horse) having a brown or black coat sprinkled with white hairs ▸ *n* **2** a horse with such a coat

roar *vb* **1** (of lions and other animals) to make loud growling cries **2** to shout (something) with a loud deep cry: *'Don't do that!' he roared at me* **3** to make a very loud noise: *the engine roared* **4** to laugh in a loud hearty manner **5** (of a fire) to burn fiercely with a roaring sound ▸ *n* **6** a roaring noise: *there was a roar as the train came in* **7** a loud deep cry, uttered by a person or crowd, esp. in anger or triumph: *a roar of approval came from the crowd*

> **roar** *vb* **2, 4** = cry, shout, yell, howl, bellow, bawl, bay ▸ *n* **7** = cry, shout, yell, howl, outcry, bellow

roast *vb* **1** to cook (food) by dry heat in an oven or over a fire **2** to brown or dry (coffee or nuts) by exposure to heat **3** to make or be extremely hot **4** *informal* to criticize severely ▸ *n* **5** a roasted joint of meat ▸ *adj* **6** cooked by roasting: *roast beef* › **roaster** *n*

r

roasting *informal* ▸ *adj* **1** extremely hot ▸ *n*
2 severe criticism or scolding

rob *vb* **robbing, robbed 1** to take something
from (a person or place) illegally **2** to deprive,
esp. of something deserved: *I can't forgive him for
robbing me of an Olympic gold* > **robber** *n*

> **rob** *vb* **1** = steal from, hold up, mug (*informal*)
> **2** = deprive, do out of (*informal*)

robbery *n, pl* **-beries 1** *criminal law* the stealing of
property from a person by using or threatening
to use force **2** the act or an instance of robbing

> **robbery** *n* **1** = burglary, raid, hold-up, rip-off
> (*slang*), stick-up (*slang, chiefly US*), home
> invasion (*Austral, NZ*) **2** = theft, stealing,
> mugging (*informal*), plunder, swindle, pillage,
> larceny

robe *n* **1** a long loose flowing garment **2** a
dressing gown or bathrobe ▸ *vb* **robing, robed**
3 to put a robe on

> **robe** *n* **1** = gown, costume, habit

robin *n* **1** Also called: **robin redbreast** a small
Old World songbird with a brown back and an
orange-red breast and face **2** a North American
thrush similar to but larger than the Old World
robin

robot *n* **1** a machine programmed to perform
specific tasks in a human manner, esp. one with
a human shape **2** a person of machine-like
efficiency **3** *S African* a set of traffic lights
> **robotic** *adj*

> **robot** *n* **1** = machine, automaton, android,
> mechanical man *or* woman

robotics *n* the science of designing, building,
and using robots

robust *adj* **1** very strong and healthy **2** sturdily
built: *the new generation of robust lasers* **3** requiring
or displaying physical strength: *robust tackles*
> **robustly** *adv*

> **robust** *adj* **1, 2** = strong, tough, powerful, fit,
> healthy, strapping, hardy, vigorous; ≠ weak

roc *n* (in Arabian legend) a bird of enormous size
and power

rock¹ *n* **1** *geol* the mass of mineral matter that
makes up part of the earth's crust; stone **2** a
large rugged mass of stone **3** *chiefly US, Canad &
Austral* a stone **4** a hard peppermint-flavoured
sweet, usually in the shape of a long stick
5 a person or thing on which one can always
depend: *your loyalty is a rock* **6** *slang* a precious
jewel **7 on the rocks A** (of a marriage) about to
end **B** (of an alcoholic drink) served with ice

> **rock** *n* **2** = stone, boulder

rock² *vb* **1** to move from side to side or backwards
and forwards **2** to shake or move (something)
violently **3** to feel or cause to feel shock: *key
events have rocked both countries* **4** to dance to or

play rock music **5** *slang* to be very good ▸ *n*
6 Also called: **rock music** a style of pop music
with a heavy beat **7** a rocking motion ▸ *adj*
8 of or relating to rock music

> **rock** *vb* **3** = shock, surprise, shake, stun,
> astonish, stagger, astound

rock and roll *or* **rock'n'roll** *n* a type of pop
music originating in the 1950s as a blend of
rhythm and blues and country and western

rock bottom *n* the lowest possible level

rock cake *n* a small fruit cake with a rough
surface

rocker *n* **1** a rocking chair **2** either of two
curved supports on which a rocking chair stands
3 a rock music performer or fan **4 off one's
rocker** *slang* crazy

rockery *n, pl* **-eries** a garden built of rocks and
soil, for growing rock plants

rocket *n* **1** a self-propelling device, usually
cylindrical, which produces thrust by expelling
through a nozzle the gases produced by burning
fuel, such as one used as a firework or distress
signal **2** any vehicle propelled by a rocket
engine, as a weapon or carrying a spacecraft
3 *informal* a severe reprimand: *my sister gave me a
rocket for writing such dangerous nonsense* ▸ *vb* **-eting,
-eted 4** to increase rapidly: *within six years their
turnover had rocketed* **5** to attack with rockets

rocking chair *n* a chair set on curving supports
so that the sitter may rock backwards and
forwards

rock melon *n US, Austral & NZ* same as
cantaloupe

rocky¹ *adj* **rockier, rockiest** covered with rocks:
rocky and sandy shores > **rockiness** *n*

> **rocky** *adj* = rough, rugged, stony, craggy

rocky² *adj* **rockier, rockiest** shaky or unstable:
a rocky relationship > **rockiness** *n*

> **rocky** *adj* = unstable, shaky, wobbly, rickety,
> unsteady

rococo (rok-koh-koh) *adj* **1** relating to an
18th-century style of architecture, decoration,
and music characterized by elaborate
ornamentation **2** excessively elaborate in style

rod *n* **1** a thin straight pole made of wood or
metal **2** a cane used to beat people as a
punishment **3** a type of cell in the retina,
sensitive to dim light > **rodlike** *adj*

> **rod** *n* **1** = stick, bar, pole, shaft, cane **2** = staff,
> baton, wand

rode *vb* the past tense of **ride**

rodent *n* a small mammal with teeth
specialized for gnawing, such as a rat, mouse,
or squirrel > **rodent-like** *adj*

rodeo *n, pl* **-deos** a display of the skills of
cowboys, including bareback riding

roe¹ *n* the ovary and eggs of a female fish,
sometimes eaten as food

roe² or **roe deer** n a small graceful deer with short antlers

roentgen (ront-gan) n a unit measuring a radiation dose

rogue n 1 a dishonest or unprincipled person 2 a mischievous person 3 a crop plant which is inferior, diseased, or of a different variety 4 an inferior or defective specimen ▸ adj 5 (of a wild animal) having a savage temper and living apart from the herd: *a rogue elephant* 6 inferior or defective: *rogue heroin* ▸ **roguish** adj

rogue n 1 = scoundrel (*old-fashioned*), crook (*informal*), villain, fraud (*informal*), blackguard, skelm (*S African*), rorter (*Austral slang*), wrong 'un (*slang*) 2 = scamp, rascal, scally (*Northwest England dialect*), nointer (*Austral slang*)

roister vb old-fashioned to enjoy oneself noisily and boisterously ▸ **roisterer** n

role n 1 a task or function: *their role in international relations* 2 an actor's part in a production

role n 1 = job, part, position, post, task, duty, function, capacity 2 = part, character, representation, portrayal

roll vb 1 to move along by turning over and over 2 to move along on wheels or rollers 3 to curl or make by curling into a ball or tube 4 to move along in an undulating movement 5 to rotate wholly or partially: *he would snort in derision, roll his eyes, and heave a deep sigh* 6 to spread out flat or smooth with a roller or rolling pin: *roll the pastry out thinly* 7 (of a ship or aircraft) to turn from side to side around the longitudinal axis 8 to operate or begin to operate: *the cameras continued to roll as she pulled up to the nightclub* 9 to make a continuous deep reverberating sound: *the thunder rolled* 10 to walk in a swaying manner: *the drunks came rolling home* 11 to appear like a series of waves: *mountain ranges rolling away in every direction* 12 to pass or elapse: *watching the time roll away* 13 (of animals) to turn onto the back and kick 14 to trill or cause to be trilled: *she rolled her r's* 15 to throw (dice) ▸ n 16 the act or an instance of rolling 17 anything rolled up into a tube: *a roll of paper towels* 18 a small cake of bread for one person 19 a flat pastry or cake rolled up with a meat, jam, or other filling 20 an official list or register of names: *the electoral roll; the voters' roll* 21 a complete rotation about its longitudinal axis by an aircraft 22 a continuous deep reverberating sound: *the roll of musketry* 23 a swaying or unsteady movement or gait 24 a rounded mass: *rolls of fat* 25 a very rapid beating of the sticks on a drum 26 **on a roll** *slang* experiencing continued good luck or success 27 **strike off the roll** to expel from membership of a professional association ▸ See also **roll up**

roll vb 1 = turn, wheel, spin, go round, revolve, rotate, whirl, swivel 2 = trundle, go, move 4 = flow, run, course 6 = level, even, press,

smooth, flatten 7 = toss, rock, lurch, reel, tumble, sway ▸ n 20 = register, record, list, index, census 21 = turn, spin, rotation, cycle, wheel, revolution, reel, whirl 22 = rumble, boom, roar, thunder, reverberation

roll call n the reading aloud of an official list of names, to check who is present

rolled gold n a metal, such as brass, coated with a thin layer of gold

roller n 1 a rotating cylinder used for smoothing, supporting a thing to be moved, spreading paint, etc. 2 a small tube around which hair may be wound in order to make it curly 3 a long heavy wave of the sea 4 a cylinder fitted on pivots, used to enable heavy objects to be easily moved

Rollerblade n trademark a type of roller skate in which the wheels are set in a single straight line under the boot

roller coaster n (at a funfair) a narrow railway with open carriages, sharp curves and steep slopes

roller skate n 1 a shoe with four small wheels that enable the wearer to glide swiftly over a floor ▸ vb **roller-skate, -skating, -skated** 2 to move on roller skates ▸ **roller skater** n

rollicking adj boisterously carefree: *a rollicking read*

rolling pin n a cylinder with handles at both ends used for rolling pastry

rolling stock n the locomotives and coaches of a railway

rolling stone n a restless or wandering person

roll-on/roll-off adj denoting a ship designed so that vehicles can be driven straight on and straight off

roll-top adj (of a desk) having a slatted wooden panel that can be pulled down over the writing surface when not in use

roll up vb 1 to form into a cylindrical shape: *roll up a length of black material* 2 informal to arrive ▸ n **roll-up** 3 Brit informal a cigarette made by the smoker from loose tobacco and cigarette papers

roly-poly adj 1 plump or chubby ▸ n, pl **-lies** 2 Brit a strip of suet pastry spread with jam, rolled up, and baked or steamed

ROM n computers read only memory: a storage device that holds data permanently and cannot be altered by the programmer

Roma n pl **Roma** or **Romas** a member of a people scattered throughout Europe and N America, who have a nomadic way of life in industrialized societies

roman adj 1 in or relating to the vertical style of printing type used for most printed matter ▸ n 2 roman type

Roman adj 1 of Rome, a city in Italy, or its inhabitants in ancient or modern times 2 of Roman Catholicism or the Roman Catholic Church ▸ n 3 a person from ancient or modern Rome

r

Roman Catholic *adj* **1** of the Roman Catholic Church ▸ *n* **2** a member of this Church › **Roman Catholicism** *n*

Roman Catholic Church *n* the Christian Church over which the pope presides

romance *n* **1** a love affair: *a failed romance* **2** love, esp. romantic love idealized for its purity or beauty **3** a spirit of or inclination for adventure or mystery **4** a mysterious or sentimental quality **5** a story or film dealing with love, usually in an idealized way **6** a story or film dealing with events and characters remote from ordinary life **7** an extravagant, absurd, or fantastic account **8** a medieval narrative dealing with adventures of chivalrous heroes ▸ *vb* **-mancing, -manced** **9** to tell extravagant or improbable lies

> **romance** *n* **1** = love affair, relationship, affair, attachment, liaison, amour **3** = excitement, colour, charm, mystery, glamour, fascination **5, 6** = story, tale, fantasy, legend, fairy tale, love story, melodrama

Romance *adj* of the languages derived from Latin, such as French, Spanish, and Italian

Roman numerals *pl n* the letters used as numerals by the Romans, used occasionally today: I (= 1), V (= 5), X (= 10), L (= 50), C (= 100), D (= 500), and M (= 1000). VI = 6 (V + I) but IV = 4 (V – I)

romantic *adj* **1** of or dealing with love **2** idealistic but impractical: *a romantic notion* **3** evoking or given to thoughts and feelings of love: *romantic images* **4** **Romantic** relating to a movement in European art, music, and literature in the late 18th and early 19th centuries, characterized by an emphasis on feeling and content rather than order and form ▸ *n* **5** a person who is idealistic or amorous **6** a person who likes or produces artistic works in the style of Romanticism › **romantically** *adv*

> **romantic** *adj* **1, 3** = loving, tender, passionate, fond, sentimental, amorous, icky (*informal*); ≠ unromantic **2** = idealistic, unrealistic, impractical, dreamy, starry-eyed; ≠ realistic ▸ *n* **5** = idealist, dreamer, sentimentalist

romanticism *n* **1** idealistic but unrealistic thoughts and feelings **2** **Romanticism** the spirit and style of the Romantic art, music, and literature of the late 18th and early 19th centuries › **romanticist** *n*

romanticize *or* **-cise** *vb* **-cizing, -cized** *or* **-cising, -cised** to describe or regard (something or someone) in an unrealistic and idealized way: *the Victorian legacy of romanticizing family life*

Romany *n* **1** *pl* **-nies** a Roma **2** the language of the Roma

romp *vb* **1** to play or run about wildly or joyfully **2** **romp home** *or* **in** to win a race or other competition easily **3** **romp through** to do (something) quickly and easily ▸ *n* **4** a noisy or boisterous game or prank

romp *vb* **1** = frolic, sport, have fun, caper, cavort, frisk, gambol ▸ *n* = frolic, lark (*informal*), caper

rompers *pl n* a one-piece baby garment combining trousers and a top. Also called: **romper suit**

rondavel *n S African* a small circular building with a cone-shaped roof

rondo *n, pl* **-dos** a piece of music with a leading theme continually returned to: often forms the last movement of a sonata or concerto

roo *n, pl* **roos** *Austral informal* a kangaroo

rood *n* **1** *Christianity* the Cross **2** a crucifix

rood screen *n* (in a church) a screen separating the nave from the choir

roof *n, pl* **roofs** **1** a structure that covers or forms the top of a building **2** the top covering of a vehicle, oven, or other structure **3** the highest part of the mouth or a cave **4** **hit** *or* **go through the roof** *informal* to get extremely angry **5** **raise the roof** *informal* to be very noisy ▸ *vb* **6** to put a roof on

rooibos (roy-boss) *n S African* a kind of tea made from the leaves of a South African wild shrub. Also called: **rooibos tea, bush tea**

rook¹ *n* **1** a large European black bird of the crow family ▸ *vb* **2** *old-fashioned slang* to cheat or swindle

rook² *n* a chess piece that may move any number of unoccupied squares in a straight line, horizontally or vertically; castle

rookery *n, pl* **-eries** **1** a group of nesting rooks **2** a colony of penguins or seals

rookie *n informal* a newcomer without much experience

room *n* **1** an area within a building enclosed by a floor, a ceiling, and walls **2** the people present in a room: *the whole room was laughing* **3** unoccupied or unobstructed space: *there wasn't enough room* **4** **room for** opportunity or scope for: *there was no room for acts of heroism* **5** **rooms** lodgings ▸ *vb* **6** *US* to occupy or share a rented room: *I roomed with him for five years*

> **room** *n* **1** = chamber, office **3** = space, area, capacity, extent, expanse

roomy *adj* **roomier, roomiest** with plenty of space inside: *a roomy entrance hall* › **roominess** *n*

roost *n* **1** a place where birds rest or sleep ▸ *vb* **2** to rest or sleep on a roost **3** **come home to roost** to have unfavourable repercussions **4** **rule the roost** to have authority over people in a particular place

rooster *n* the male of the domestic fowl; a cock

root¹ *n* **1** the part of a plant that anchors the rest of the plant in the ground and absorbs water and mineral salts from the soil **2** a plant with an edible root, such as a carrot **3** *anatomy* the part of a tooth, hair, or nail that is below the skin **4** **roots** a person's sense of belonging in a place, esp. the one in which he or she was brought up **5** source or origin **6** the essential part or nature of something: *the root of a problem* **7** *linguistics* the form of a word from which other words and forms are derived **8** *maths* a quantity that when multiplied by itself a certain number of times equals a given quantity: *what is the cube root of a thousand?* **9** Also called: **solution** *maths* a number that when substituted for the variable satisfies a given equation **10** *Austral & NZ slang* sexual intercourse **11** **root and branch** entirely or utterly. ▸ Related adjective: **radical** ▸ *vb* **12** Also: **take root** to establish a root and begin to grow **13** Also: **take root** to become established or embedded **14** *Austral & NZ slang* to have sexual intercourse (with) ▸ See also **root out**

> **root** *n* **1** = stem, tuber, rhizome **4** = sense of belonging, origins, heritage, birthplace, home, family, cradle **5, 6** = source, cause, heart, bottom, base, seat, seed, foundation

root² *vb* **1** *Brit* to dig up the earth in search of food, using the snout: *dogs were rooting in the rushes for bones* **2** *informal* to search vigorously but unsystematically: *she was rooting around in her large untidy purse*

> **root** *vb* **2** = dig, burrow, ferret

root for *vb informal* to give support to (a team or contestant)

rootle *vb* **-ling, -led** *Brit* same as **root²**

rootless *adj* having no sense of belonging: *a rootless city dweller*

root out *vb* to get rid of completely: *a major drive to root out corruption*

> **root out** *vb* root something or someone out = get rid of, remove, eliminate, abolish, eradicate, do away with, weed out, exterminate

rope *n* **1** a fairly thick cord made of intertwined fibres or wire **2** a row of objects fastened to form a line: *a twenty-inch rope of pearls* **3** **know the ropes** to have a thorough understanding of a particular activity **4** **the rope A** a rope noose used for hanging someone **B** death by hanging ▸ *vb* **roping, roped 5** to tie with a rope **6** **rope off** to enclose or divide with a rope

> **rope** *n* **1** = cord, line, cable, strand, hawser **3 know the ropes** = be experienced, be knowledgeable, be an old hand

rope in *vb* to persuade to take part in some activity

> **rope in** *vb* rope someone in or into something = persuade, involve, engage, enlist, talk into, inveigle

ropey *or* **ropy** *adj* **ropier, ropiest** *Brit informal* **1** poor or unsatisfactory in quality: *a ropey performance* **2** slightly unwell > **ropiness** *n*

rorqual *n* a whalebone whale with a fin on the back

rort *Austral informal* ▸ *n* **1** a dishonest scheme ▸ *vb* **2** to take unfair advantage of something

rosary *n, pl* **-saries** *RC Church* **1** a series of prayers counted on a string of beads **2** a string of beads used to count these prayers as they are recited

rose¹ *n* **1** a shrub or climbing plant with prickly stems and fragrant flowers **2** the flower of any of these plants **3** a plant similar to this, such as the Christmas rose **4** a perforated cap fitted to a watering can or hose, causing the water to come out in a spray **5** **bed of roses** a situation of comfort or ease ▸ *adj* **6** reddish-pink

rose² *vb* the past tense of **rise**

rosé (roe-zay) *n* a pink wine

roseate (roe-zee-ate) *adj* **1** of the colour rose or pink **2** excessively optimistic

rosehip *n* the berry-like fruit of a rose plant

rosella *n* a type of Australian parrot

rosemary *n, pl* **-maries** an aromatic European shrub widely cultivated for its grey-green evergreen leaves, which are used in cookery and perfumes

rosette *n* a rose-shaped decoration, esp. a circular bunch of ribbons

rose window *n* a circular window with spokes branching out from the centre to form a symmetrical roselike pattern

rosewood *n* a fragrant dark wood used to make furniture

rosin (rozz-in) *n* **1** a translucent brittle substance produced from turpentine and used for treating the bows of stringed instruments ▸ *vb* **2** to apply rosin to

roster *n* **1** a list showing the order in which people are to perform a duty ▸ *vb* **2** to place on a roster

rostrum *n, pl* **-trums** *or* **-tra** a platform or stage

rosy *adj* **rosier, rosiest 1** of the colour rose or pink: *rosy cheeks* **2** hopeful or promising: *the analysis revealed a far from rosy picture* > **rosiness** *n*

> **rosy** *adj* **1** = glowing, blooming, radiant, ruddy, healthy-looking; ≠ pale **2** = promising, encouraging, bright, optimistic, hopeful, cheerful, favourable, auspicious; ≠ gloomy

rot *vb* **rotting, rotted 1** to decay or cause to decay **2** to deteriorate slowly, mentally and physically: *I thought he was either dead or rotting in a jail* ▸ *n* **3** the process of rotting or the state of being rotten **4** something decomposed **5** short for **dry rot 6** a plant or animal disease which causes decay of the tissues **7** nonsense

> **rot** *vb* **1** = decay, spoil, deteriorate, perish, decompose, moulder, go bad, putrefy (*formal*) **2** = deteriorate, decline, waste away ▸ *n* **3** = decay, decomposition, corruption, mould, blight, canker, putrefaction **7** = nonsense, rubbish, drivel, twaddle, garbage (*informal*), trash, tripe (*informal*), claptrap (*informal*), bizzo (*Austral slang*), bull's wool (*Austral, NZ slang*)

rota *n* a list of people who take it in turn to do a particular task

r

rotary *adj* **1** revolving **2** operating by rotation ▸ *n, pl* **-ries** **3** *US & Canad* a traffic roundabout

rotate *vb* **-tating, -tated** **1** to turn around a centre or pivot **2** to follow or cause to follow a set sequence **3** to regularly change the type of crop grown on a piece of land in order to preserve the fertility of the soil ▸ **rotation** *n* ▸ **rotational** *adj*

> **rotate** *vb* **1** = revolve, turn, wheel, spin, reel, go round, swivel, pivot **2** = follow in sequence, switch, alternate, take turns

rote *adj* **1** done by routine repetition: *rote learning* ▸ *n* **2** by repetition: *we learned by rote*

rotisserie *n* a rotating spit on which meat and poultry can be cooked

rotor *n* **1** the rotating part of a machine or device, such as the revolving arm of the distributor of an internal-combustion engine **2** a rotating device with blades projecting from a hub which produces thrust to lift a helicopter

rotten *adj* **1** decomposing or decaying: *rotten vegetables* **2** breaking up through age or hard use: *the window frames are rotten* **3** *informal* very bad: *what rotten luck!* **4** morally corrupt: *this country's politics are rotten and out of date* **5** *informal* miserably unwell: *I had glandular fever and spent that year feeling rotten* **6** *informal* distressed and embarrassed: *I'm feeling rotten as a matter of fact, rotten and guilty* ▸ *adv* **7** *informal* extremely; very much: *men fancy her rotten*

> **rotten** *adj* **1** = decaying, bad, rank, corrupt, sour, stinking, perished, festering, festy (*Austral slang*); ≠ fresh **2** = crumbling, perished **4** = corrupt, immoral, crooked (*informal*), dishonest, dishonourable, perfidious (*literary*); ≠ honourable

rotter *n chiefly Brit old-fashioned slang* a despicable person

Rottweiler (rot-vile-er) *n* a large sturdy dog with a smooth black-and-tan coat and a docked tail

rotund (roe-tund) *adj* **1** round and plump **2** (of speech) pompous or grand ▸ **rotundity** *n* ▸ **rotundly** *adv*

rotunda *n* a circular building or room, esp. with a dome

rouble *or* **ruble** (roo-bl) *n* the standard monetary unit of Russia, Belarus, and Transnistria

roué (roo-ay) *n* a man who leads a sensual and immoral life

rouge *n* **1** a red cosmetic for adding colour to the cheeks ▸ *vb* **rouging, rouged** **2** to apply rouge to

rough *adj* **1** not smooth; uneven or irregular **2** not using enough care or gentleness **3** difficult or unpleasant: *tomorrow will be a rough day* **4** approximate: *a rough guess* **5** violent or stormy **6** troubled by violence or crime: *he lived in a rough area* **7** incomplete or basic: *a rough draft* **8** lacking refinement: *a rough shelter*

9 (of ground) covered with scrub or rubble **10** harsh or grating to the ear **11** harsh or sharp: *the rough interrogation of my father* **12** unfair: *rough luck* **13** *informal* ill: *if you're feeling rough, you won't want to eat* **14** shaggy or hairy: *the rough wool of her sweater* **15** (of work, etc.) requiring physical rather than mental effort: *wear gloves for any rough work* ▸ *vb* **16** to make rough **17 rough it** *informal* to live without the usual comforts of life ▸ *n* **18** rough ground **19** a sketch or preliminary piece of artwork **20** *informal* a violent person **21 in rough** in an unfinished or crude state **22 the rough** *golf* the part of the course beside the fairways where the grass is untrimmed **23** the unpleasant side of something: *you have to take the rough with the smooth* ▸ *adv* **24** roughly **25 sleep rough** to spend the night in the open without shelter ▸ See also **rough out** ▸ **roughly** *adv*

> **rough** *adj* **1, 9** = uneven, broken, rocky, irregular, jagged, bumpy, stony, craggy; ≠ even **2** = ungracious, blunt, rude, coarse, brusque, uncouth, impolite, uncivil; ≠ refined **3** = unpleasant, hard, difficult, tough, uncomfortable; ≠ easy **4** = approximate, estimated; ≠ exact **5** = stormy, wild, turbulent, choppy, squally; ≠ calm **7** = basic, crude, unfinished, incomplete, imperfect, rudimentary, sketchy, unrefined; ≠ complete **11** = harsh, tough, nasty, cruel, unfeeling; ≠ gentle **15** = boisterous, hard, tough, arduous ▸ *n* **19** = outline, draft, mock-up, preliminary sketch

roughage *n* the coarse indigestible constituents of food, which help digestion

rough-and-ready *adj* **1** hastily prepared but adequate for the purpose **2** (of a person) without formality or refinement in manner or appearance

> **rough-and-ready** *adj* **1** = makeshift, crude, provisional, improvised, sketchy, stopgap **2** = unrefined, shabby, untidy, unkempt, unpolished, ill-groomed, daggy (*Austral, NZ informal*)

rough-and-tumble *n* **1** a playful fight **2** a disorderly situation

roughcast *n* **1** a mixture of plaster and small stones for outside walls ▸ *vb* **-casting, -cast** **2** to put roughcast on (a wall)

roughen *vb* to make or become rough

rough-hewn *adj* roughly shaped or cut without being properly finished

roughhouse *n slang* rough or noisy behaviour

rough out *vb* to prepare (a sketch or report) in preliminary form: *he offered to rough out some designs for the sets*

> **rough out** *vb* **rough something out** = outline, plan, draft, sketch

roughshod *adv* **ride roughshod over** to act with complete disregard for

roulette *n* a gambling game in which a ball is dropped onto a revolving wheel with numbered coloured slots

round *adj* **1** having a flat circular shape, like a hoop **2** having the shape of a ball **3** curved; not angular **4** involving or using circular motion **5** complete **6** *maths* **A** forming or expressed by a whole number, with no fraction **B** expressed to the nearest ten, hundred, or thousand: *in round figures* ▸ *adv* **7** on all or most sides **8** on or outside the circumference or perimeter: *ponds which are steeply sided all round* **9** in rotation or revolution: *she swung round on me* **10** by a circuitous route: *the road to the farm goes round by the pond* **11** to all members of a group: *handing chocolates round* **12** to a specific place: *the boys invited him round* **13** **all year round** throughout the year ▸ *prep* **14** surrounding or encircling: *wrap your sash round the wound* **15** on all or most sides of: *the man turned in a circle, looking all round him* **16** on or outside the circumference or perimeter of **17** from place to place in: *a trip round the island in an ancient bus* **18** reached by making a partial circuit about: *just round the corner* **19** revolving about: *if you have two bodies in orbit, they orbit round their common centre of gravity* ▸ *vb* **20** to move round: *as he rounded the last corner, he raised a fist* ▸ *n* **21** a round shape or object **22** a session: *a round of talks* **23** a series: *the petty round of domestic matters* **24** a series of calls: *a paper round* **25** **the daily round** the usual activities of a person's day **26** a playing of all the holes on a golf course **27** a stage of a competition: *the first round of the Portuguese Open* **28** one of a number of periods in a boxing or wrestling match **29** a single turn of play by each player in a card game **30** a number of drinks bought at one time for a group of people **31** a bullet or shell for a gun **32** a single discharge by a gun **33** *music* a part song in which the voices follow each other at equal intervals **34** circular movement **35** **A** a single slice of bread **B** a serving of sandwiches made from two complete slices of bread **36** a general outburst: *a round of applause* **37** **in the round A** in full detail **B** *theatre* with the audience all round the stage **38** **go the rounds** (of information or infection) to be passed around from person to person

> **round** *adj* **2, 3** = spherical, rounded, curved, circular, cylindrical, rotund, globular ▸ *vb* = go round, circle, skirt, flank, bypass, encircle, turn ▸ *n* **21** = sphere, ball, band, ring, circle, disc, globe, orb **22, 23** = series, session, cycle, sequence, succession **24** = course, tour, circuit, beat, series, schedule, routine **27** = stage, turn, level, period, division, session, lap

roundabout *n Brit* **1** a road junction in which traffic moves in one direction around a central island **2** a revolving circular platform, often with seats, on which people ride for amusement ▸ *adj* **3** not straightforward: *the roundabout sea route; she thought of asking about it in a roundabout way*

> ▸ *adv, prep* **round about 4** approximately: *round about 1900*

> **roundabout** *adj* = indirect, devious, tortuous, circuitous, evasive, discursive; ≠ direct

roundel *n* **1** a circular identifying mark on military aircraft **2** a small circular object

roundelay *n* a song in which a line or phrase is repeated as a refrain

rounders *n Brit & NZ* a bat and ball game in which players run between posts after hitting the ball

Roundhead *n English history* a supporter of Parliament against Charles I during the Civil War

roundly *adv* bluntly or thoroughly: *the Church roundly criticized the bill*

round robin *n* **1** a petition with the signatures in a circle to disguise the order of signing **2** a tournament in which each player plays against every other player

round-the-clock *adj* throughout the day and night

round trip *n* a journey to a place and back again

round up *vb* **1** to gather together: *the police had rounded up a circle of drug users* **2** to raise (a number) to the nearest whole number or ten, hundred, or thousand above it ▸ *n* **roundup 3** a summary or discussion of news and information **4** the act of gathering together livestock or people

> **round up** *vb* **1** **round something or someone up** = gather, muster, group, drive, collect, rally, herd, marshal

rouse¹ *vb* **rousing, roused 1** to wake up **2** to provoke or excite: *his temper was roused and he had a gun* **3** **rouse oneself** to become energetic

> **rouse** *vb* **1** = wake up, call, wake, awaken **2** = excite, move, stir, provoke, anger, animate, agitate, inflame

rouse² (rhymes with **mouse**) *vb* (foll. by *on*) *Austral* to scold or rebuke

rouseabout *n Austral & NZ* a labourer in a shearing shed

rousing *adj* lively or vigorous: *a rousing speech*

> **rousing** *adj* = lively, moving, spirited, exciting, inspiring, stirring, stimulating; ≠ dull

roustabout *n* an unskilled labourer on an oil rig

rout *n* **1** an overwhelming defeat **2** a disorderly retreat **3** a noisy rabble ▸ *vb* **4** to defeat and put to flight

> **rout** *n* **1, 2** = defeat, beating, overthrow, thrashing, pasting (*slang*), debacle, drubbing ▸ *vb* = defeat, beat, overthrow, thrash, destroy, crush, conquer, wipe the floor with (*informal*)

r

route *n* **1** the choice of roads taken to get to a place **2** a fixed path followed by buses, trains, etc. between two places **3** a chosen way or method: *the route to prosperity* ▸ *vb* **routeing, routed 4** to send by a particular route

> **route** *n* **1, 3** = way, course, road, direction, path, journey, itinerary **2** = beat, circuit

routine *n* **1** a usual or regular method of procedure **2** the boring repetition of tasks: *mindless routine* **3** a set sequence of dance steps **4** *computers* a program or part of a program performing a specific function: *an input routine* ▸ *adj* **5** relating to or characteristic of routine

> **routine** *n* **1** = procedure, programme, order, practice, method, pattern, custom ▸ *adj* = usual, standard, normal, customary, ordinary, typical, everyday, habitual; ≠ unusual

roux (roo) *n* a cooked mixture of fat and flour used as a basis for sauces

rove *vb* **roving, roved 1** to wander about (a place) **2** (of the eyes) to look around ▸ **rover** *n*

row¹ (rhymes with **know**) *n* **1** an arrangement of people or things in a line: *a row of shops* **2** a line of seats in a cinema or theatre **3** *Brit* a street lined with identical houses **4** *maths* a horizontal line of numbers **5** **in a row** in succession: *five championships in a row*

> **row** *n* **1** = line, bank, range, series, file, string, column **5** **in a row** = consecutively, running, in turn, one after the other, successively, in sequence

row² (rhymes with **know**) *vb* **1** to propel (a boat) by using oars **2** to carry (people or goods) in a rowing boat **3** to take part in the racing of rowing boats as a sport ▸ *n* **4** an act or spell of rowing **5** an excursion in a rowing boat ▸ **rowing** *n*

row³ (rhymes with **cow**) *informal* ▸ *n* **1** a noisy quarrel **2** a controversy or dispute: *the row over Europe* **3** a noisy disturbance: *go to the insurance offices and kick up a row about your money* **4** a reprimand ▸ *vb* **5** to quarrel noisily

> **row** *n* **1, 2** = quarrel, dispute, argument, squabble, tiff, trouble, brawl **3** = disturbance, noise, racket, uproar, commotion, rumpus, tumult ▸ *vb* = quarrel, fight, argue, dispute, squabble, wrangle

rowan *n* a European tree with white flowers and red berries; mountain ash

rowdy *adj* **-dier, -diest 1** rough, noisy, or disorderly ▸ *n, pl* **-dies 2** a person like this ▸ **rowdily** *adv*

rowel (rhymes with **towel**) *n* a small spiked wheel at the end of a spur

rowing boat *n* a small pleasure boat propelled by oars. Usual US and Canad word: **rowboat**

rowlock (rol-luk) *n* a swivelling device attached to the top of the side of a boat that holds an oar in place

royal *adj* **1** of or relating to a king or queen or a member of his or her family: *the royal yacht* **2 Royal** supported by or in the service of royalty: *the Royal Society of Medicine* **3** very grand: *royal treatment* ▸ *n* **4** *informal* a king or queen or a member of his or her family > **royally** *adv*

> **royal** *adj* **1** = regal, kingly *or* queenly, princely, imperial, sovereign **3** = splendid, grand, impressive, magnificent, majestic, stately

royalist *n* **1** a supporter of a monarch or monarchy ▸ *adj* **2** of or relating to royalists > **royalism** *n*

royalty *n, pl* **-ties 1** royal people **2** the rank or power of a king or queen **3** a percentage of the revenue from the sale of a book, performance of a work, use of a patented invention or of land, paid to the author, inventor, or owner

RPI (in Britain) retail price index: a measure of the changes in the average level of retail prices of selected goods

rpm revolutions per minute

RSA 1 Republic of South Africa **2** (in New Zealand) Returned Services Association **3** Royal Scottish Academy **4** Royal Society of Arts

RSI repetitive strain injury: pain in the arm caused by repeated awkward movements, such as in using a keyboard

RSPCA (in Britain) Royal Society for the Prevention of Cruelty to Animals

RSS Rich Site Summary *or* Really Simple Syndication: a way of allowing web users to receive updated information from selected websites on their browser

RSVP please reply

rub *vb* **rubbing, rubbed 1** to apply pressure and friction to (something) with a circular or backwards-and-forwards movement **2** to move (something) with pressure along or against (a surface) **3** to clean, polish, or dry by rubbing **4** to spread with pressure, esp. so that it can be absorbed: *rub beeswax into all polishable surfaces* **5** to chafe or fray through rubbing **6** to mix (fat) into flour with the fingertips, as in making pastry **7 rub it in** to emphasize an unpleasant fact **8 rub up the wrong way** to annoy ▸ *n* **9** the act of rubbing **10 the rub** the obstacle or difficulty: *there's the rub*

> **rub** *vb* **1** = stroke, massage, caress **3** = polish, clean, shine, wipe, scour **5** = chafe, scrape, grate, abrade ▸ *n* **9** = polish, stroke, shine, wipe

rubato *music* ▸ *n, pl* **-tos 1** flexibility of tempo in performance: *his playing brought much beautifully felt but never sentimental rubato to the music* ▸ *adj, adv* **2** to be played with a flexible tempo

rubber¹ *n* **1** an elastic material obtained from the latex of certain plants, such as the rubber tree **2** a similar substance produced synthetically **3** a piece of rubber used for erasing something written **4** *US slang* a condom **5 rubbers** US rubber-coated waterproof overshoes ▸ *adj* **6** made of or producing rubber ▸**rubbery** *adj*

rubber² *n* **1** *bridge & whist* a match of three games **2** a series of matches or games in various sports

rubberneck *slang* ▸ *vb* **1** to stare in a naive or foolish manner ▸ *n* **2** a person who stares inquisitively **3** a sightseer or tourist

rubber stamp *n* **1** a device used for imprinting dates or signatures on forms or invoices **2** automatic authorization of something **3** a person or body that gives official approval to decisions taken elsewhere but has no real power ▸ *vb* **rubber-stamp 4** *informal* to approve automatically

rubbish *n* **1** discarded or waste matter **2** anything worthless or of poor quality: *the rubbish on television* **3** foolish words or speech ▸ *vb* **4** *informal* to criticize ▸**rubbishy** *adj*

> **rubbish** *n* **1, 2** = waste, refuse, scrap, junk (*informal*), litter, garbage (*chiefly US*), trash (*chiefly US, Canad*), lumber (*Brit*) **3** = nonsense, garbage (*informal*), twaddle, rot, trash, hot air (*informal*), tripe (*informal*), claptrap (*informal*), bizzo (*Austral slang*), bull's wool (*Austral, NZ slang*)

rubble *n* **1** debris from ruined buildings **2** pieces of broken stones or bricks

rubella (roo-**bell**-a) *n* a mild contagious viral disease characterized by cough, sore throat, and skin rash. Also called: **German measles**

rubidium (roo-**bid**-ee-um) *n chem* a soft highly reactive radioactive metallic element used in electronic valves, photocells, and special glass. Symbol: **Rb**

rub out *vb* **1** to remove or be removed with a rubber **2** *US slang* to murder

rubric (roo-**brik**) *n* **1** a set of rules of conduct or procedure, esp. one for the conduct of Christian church services **2** a title or heading in a book

ruby *n, pl* **-bies 1** a deep red transparent precious gemstone ▸ *adj* **2** deep red **3** denoting a fortieth anniversary: *a ruby wedding*

ruck¹ *n* **1 the ruck** ordinary people, often in a crowd **2** *rugby* a loose scrum that forms over the ball when it is on the ground

ruck² *n* **1** a wrinkle or crease ▸ *vb* **2** to wrinkle or crease: *the toe of his shoe had rucked up one corner of the pale rug*

rucksack *n Brit, Austral & S African* a large bag, with two straps, carried on the back

rudder *n* **1** *naut* a vertical hinged piece that projects into the water at the stern, used to steer a boat **2** a vertical control surface attached to the rear of the fin used to steer an aircraft ▸**rudderless** *adj*

ruddy *adj* **-dier, -diest 1** (of the complexion) having a healthy reddish colour **2** red or pink: *a ruddy glow* ▸ *adv, adj* **3** *informal* bloody: *too ruddy slow; I just went through the ruddy ceiling*

rude *adj* **1** insulting or impolite **2** vulgar or obscene: *rude words* **3** unexpected and unpleasant: *we received a rude awakening* **4** roughly or crudely made: *the rude hovels* **5** robust or sturdy: *the very picture of rude health* **6** lacking refinement ▸**rudely** *adv* ▸**rudeness** *n*

> **rude** *adj* **1** = impolite, insulting, cheeky, abusive, disrespectful, impertinent, insolent, impudent; ≠ polite **2** = vulgar; ≠ refined **3** = unpleasant, sharp, sudden, harsh, startling, abrupt **4** = roughly-made, simple, rough, raw, crude, primitive, makeshift, artless; ≠ well-made **6** = uncivilized, rough, coarse, brutish, boorish, uncouth, loutish, graceless

rue¹ *vb* **ruing, rued** *literary* to feel regret for

> **rue** *vb* = regret, mourn, lament, repent, be sorry for, kick yourself for

rue² *n* an aromatic shrub with bitter evergreen leaves formerly used in medicine

rueful *adj* feeling or expressing sorrow or regret: *a rueful smile* ▸**ruefully** *adv*

ruff *n* **1** a circular pleated or fluted cloth collar **2** a natural growth of long or coloured hair or feathers around the necks of certain animals or birds **3** a bird of the sandpiper family

ruffian *n* a violent lawless person

ruffle *vb* **-fling, -fled 1** to disturb the smoothness of: *the wind was ruffling Dad's hair* **2** to annoy or irritate **3** (of a bird) to erect its feathers in anger or display **4** to flick cards or pages rapidly ▸ *n* **5** a strip of pleated material used as a trim

> **ruffle** *vb* **1** = disarrange, disorder, mess up, rumple, tousle, dishevel, muss (*US, Canad*) **2** = annoy, upset, irritate, agitate, nettle, fluster, peeve (*informal*); ≠ calm

rug *n* **1** a small carpet **2** a thick woollen blanket **3** *slang* a wig **4 pull the rug out from under** to betray or leave defenceless

rugby *or* **rugby football** *n* a form of football played with an oval ball in which the handling and carrying of the ball is permitted

rugged (rug-gid) *adj* **1** rocky or steep: *the rugged mountains of Sicily's interior* **2** with an uneven or jagged surface **3** (of the face) strong-featured **4** rough, sturdy, or determined in character **5** (of equipment or machines) designed to withstand rough treatment or use in rough conditions

> **rugged** *adj* **1, 2** = rocky, broken, rough, craggy, difficult, ragged, irregular, uneven; ≠ even **3** = strong-featured, rough-hewn, weather-beaten; ≠ delicate **4** = tough, strong, robust, muscular, sturdy, burly, husky (*informal*), brawny; ≠ delicate **5** = well-built, strong, tough, robust, sturdy

rugger *n chiefly Brit informal* rugby

r

ruin vb 1 to destroy or spoil completely: *the suit was ruined* 2 to cause (someone) to lose money: *the first war ruined him* ▸ n 3 the state of being destroyed or decayed 4 loss of wealth or position 5 a destroyed or decayed building or town 6 something that is severely damaged: *my heart was an aching ruin*

> **ruin** vb 1 = spoil, damage, mess up, blow (slang), screw up (informal), botch, make a mess of, crool or cruel (Austral slang); ≠ improve 2 = bankrupt, break, impoverish, beggar, pauperize ▸ n 3 = destruction, fall, breakdown, defeat, collapse, wreck, undoing, downfall; ≠ preservation 4 = bankruptcy, insolvency, destitution

ruination n 1 the act of ruining or the state of being ruined 2 something that causes ruin

ruinous adj 1 causing ruin or destruction 2 more expensive than can reasonably be afforded: *ruinous rates of exchange* > **ruinously** adv

rule n 1 a statement of what is allowed, for example in a game or procedure 2 a customary form or procedure: *he has his own rule: be firm, be clear, but never be rude* 3 **the rule** the common order of things: *humanitarian gestures were more the exception than the rule* 4 the exercise of governmental authority or control: *under the rule of the dictator* 5 the period of time in which a monarch or government has power: *four decades of Communist rule* 6 a device with a straight edge for guiding or measuring: *a slide rule* 7 printing a long thin line or dash 8 Christianity a systematic body of laws and customs followed by members of a religious order 9 law an order by a court or judge 10 **as a rule** usually ▸ vb **ruling, ruled** 11 to govern (people or a political unit) 12 to be pre-eminent or superior 13 to be customary or prevalent: *chaos ruled as the scene turned into one of total confusion* 14 to decide authoritatively: *the judges ruled that men could be prosecuted for rape offences against their wives* 15 to mark with straight parallel lines or one straight line 16 to restrain or control

> **rule** n 1 = regulation, law, direction, guideline, decree 4, 5 = government, power, control, authority, command, regime, reign, jurisdiction, mana (NZ) 10 **as a rule** = usually, generally, mainly, normally, on the whole, ordinarily ▸ vb 11 = govern, control, direct, have power over, command over, have charge of 12, 13 = be prevalent, prevail, predominate, be customary, preponderate 14 = decree, decide, judge, settle, pronounce

rule of thumb n a rough and practical approach, based on experience, rather than theory

rule out vb 1 to dismiss from consideration 2 to make impossible

rule out vb 1 **rule someone out** = exclude, eliminate, disqualify, ban, reject, dismiss, prohibit, leave out 2 **rule something out** = reject, exclude, eliminate

ruler n 1 a person who rules or commands 2 a strip of wood, metal, or plastic, with straight edges, used for measuring and drawing straight lines

> **ruler** n 1 = governor, leader, lord, commander, controller, monarch, sovereign, head of state 2 = measure, rule, yardstick

ruling adj 1 controlling or exercising authority 2 predominant ▸ n 3 a decision of someone in authority

> **ruling** adj 1 = governing, reigning, controlling, commanding 2 = predominant, dominant, prevailing, preponderant, chief, main, principal, pre-eminent; ≠ minor ▸ n = decision, verdict, judgment, decree, adjudication, pronouncement

rum[1] n an alcoholic drink made from sugar cane

rum[2] adj **rummer, rummest** Brit slang strange or unusual

rumba n 1 a rhythmic and syncopated dance of Cuban origin 2 music for this dance

rumble vb **-bling, -bled** 1 to make or cause to make a deep echoing sound: *thunder rumbled overhead* 2 to move with such a sound: *a slow freight train rumbled past* 3 Brit slang to find out about (someone or something): *his real identity was rumbled* ▸ n 4 a deep resonant sound 5 slang a gang fight > **rumbling** adj, n

rumbustious adj boisterous or unruly

ruminant n 1 a mammal that chews the cud, such as cattle, sheep, deer, goats, and camels ▸ adj 2 of ruminants 3 meditating or contemplating in a slow quiet way

ruminate vb **-nating, -nated** 1 (of ruminants) to chew (the cud) 2 to meditate or ponder > **rumination** n > **ruminative** adj

rummage vb **-maging, -maged** 1 to search untidily ▸ n 2 an untidy search through a collection of things

rummy n a card game based on collecting sets and sequences

rumour or US **rumor** n 1 information, often a mixture of truth and untruth, told by one person to another 2 gossip or common talk ▸ vb 3 **be rumoured** to be circulated as a rumour: *he is rumoured to have at least 53 yachts*

> **rumour** or **rumor** n = story, news, report, talk, word, whisper (informal), buzz, gossip, goss (informal)

rump n 1 a person's buttocks 2 the rear part of an animal's or bird's body 3 Also called: **rump steak** a cut of beef from the rump 4 a small core of members within a group who remain loyal to it: *the rump of the once-influential communist party*

rumple *vb* **-pling, -pled** to make or become crumpled or dishevelled

rumpus *n, pl* **-puses** a noisy or confused commotion

run *vb* **running, ran, run 1** to move on foot at a rapid pace **2** to pass over (a distance or route) in running: *being a man isn't about running the fastest mile* **3** to take part in (a race): *I ran a decent race* **4** to carry out as if by running: *he is running errands for his big brother* **5** to flee **6** to travel somewhere in a vehicle **7** to give a lift to (someone) in a vehicle: *one wet day I ran her down to the service* **8** to drive or maintain and operate (a vehicle) **9** to travel regularly between places on a route: *trains running through the night* **10** to move or pass quickly: *he ran his hand across his forehead* **11** to function or cause to function: *run the video tape backwards* **12** to manage: *she ran a small hotel* **13** to continue in a particular direction or for a particular time or distance: *a road running alongside the Nile; a performing arts festival running in the city for six weeks* **14** *law* to have legal force or effect: *the lease runs for two more years* **15** to be subjected to or affected by: *she ran a high risk of losing her hair* **16** to tend or incline: *he was of medium height and running to fat* **17** to recur persistently or be inherent: *the capacity for infidelity ran in the genes* **18** to flow or cause (liquids) to flow: *sweat ran down her face* **19** to dissolve and spread: *the soles of the shoes peeled off and the colours ran* **20** (of stitches) to unravel **21** to spread or circulate: *rumours ran around quickly* **22** to publish or be published in a newspaper or magazine: *our local newspaper ran a story on the appeal* **23** *chiefly US & Canad* to stand as a candidate for political or other office: *due to announce she is running for president* **24** to get past or through: *the oil tanker was hit as it tried to run the blockade* **25** to smuggle (goods, esp. arms) **26** (of fish) to migrate upstream from the sea, esp. in order to spawn **27** *cricket* to score (a run or number of runs) by hitting the ball and running between the wickets ▸ *n* **28** the act or an instance of running: *he broke into a run* **29** a distance covered by running or a period of running: *it's a short run of about 20 kilometres* **30** a trip in a vehicle, esp. for pleasure: *our only treat is a run in the car to Dartmoor* **31** free and unrestricted access: *he had the run of the house* **32 A** a period of time during which a machine or computer operates **B** the amount of work performed in such a period **33** a continuous or sustained period: *a run of seven defeats* **34** a continuous sequence of performances: *the play had a long run* **35** *cards* a sequence of winning cards in one suit: *a run of spades* **36** type, class, or category: *he had nothing in common with the usual run of terrorists* **37** a continuous and urgent demand: *a run on the pound* **38** a series of unravelled stitches, esp. in tights **39** a steeply inclined course, esp. a snow-covered one used for skiing **40** an enclosure for domestic fowls or other animals: *the chicken run* **41** (esp. in Australia and New Zealand) a tract of land for grazing livestock **42** the migration of fish upstream in order to spawn **43** *music* a rapid scalelike passage of notes **44** *cricket* a score of one, normally achieved by both batsmen running from one end of the wicket to the other after one of them has hit the ball **45** *baseball* an instance of a batter touching all four bases safely, thereby scoring **46 a run for one's money** *informal* **A** a close competition **B** pleasure or success from an activity **47 in the long run** as an eventual outcome **48 on the run** escaping from arrest **49 the runs** *slang* diarrhoea

> **run** *vb* **1** = race, rush, dash, hurry, sprint, bolt, gallop, hare (*Brit informal*); ≠ dawdle **3** = take part, compete **5** = flee, escape, take off (*informal*), bolt, beat it (*slang*), leg it (*informal*), take flight (*old-fashioned*), do a runner (*slang*); ≠ stay **10** = pass, go, move, roll, glide, skim **11** = go, work, operate, perform, function **12** = manage, lead, direct, be in charge of, head, control, operate, handle **13** = continue, go, stretch, reach, extend, proceed; ≠ stop **18** = flow, pour, stream, go, leak, spill, discharge, gush **19** = melt, dissolve, liquefy, go soft **22** = publish, feature, display, print **23** = compete, stand, contend, be a candidate, put yourself up for, take part **25** = smuggle, traffic in, bootleg ▸ *n* **28** = race, rush, dash, sprint, gallop, jog, spurt **30** = ride, drive, trip, spin (*informal*), outing, excursion, jaunt **33, 34** = sequence, period, stretch, spell, course, season, series, string **40** = enclosure, pen, coop

run away *vb* **1** to go away **2** to escape **3** (of a horse) to gallop away uncontrollably: *the horse ran away with him* **4 run away with A** to abscond or elope with: *I ran away with David* **B** to escape from the control of: *he let his imagination run away with him* **C** to win easily or be certain of victory in (a competition): *the Spaniards at one stage seemed to be running away with the match* ▸ *n* **runaway 5** a person or animal that runs away ▸ *adj* **runaway 6** no longer under control: *a runaway train* **7** (of a race or victory) easily won

> **run away** *vb* **1, 2, 3** = flee, escape, bolt, abscond, do a runner (*slang*), make a run for it, scram (*informal*), fly the coop (*US, Canad informal*), do a Skase (*Austral informal*)

run down *vb* **1** to be rude about: *he is busy running us down and insulting other Europeans* **2** to reduce in number or size: *it should be possible to run down the existing hospitals almost entirely* **3** (of a device such as a clock or battery) to lose power gradually and cease to function **4** to hit and knock to the ground with a moving vehicle **5** to pursue and find or capture: *while I was there, Moscow ran me down, convinced I was ready to defect* ▸ *adj* **rundown 6** tired or ill **7** shabby or dilapidated ▸ *n* **rundown 8** a reduction in number or size **9** a brief review or summary

run down *vb* **1 run something or someone down** = criticize, denigrate, belittle, knock (*informal*), rubbish (*informal*), slag (off) (*slang*), disparage, decry **2 run something or someone down** = downsize, cut, reduce, trim, decrease, cut back, curtail, kennet (*Austral slang*), jeff (*Austral slang*) **4 run something or someone down** = knock down, hit, run into, run over, knock over ▶ *adj* **6 rundown** = exhausted, weak, drained, weary, unhealthy, worn-out, debilitated, below par; ≠ fit **7 rundown** = dilapidated, broken-down, shabby, worn-out, seedy, ramshackle, decrepit

rune *n* **1** any of the characters of the earliest Germanic alphabet **2** an obscure piece of writing using mysterious symbols ▷ **runic** *adj*

rung¹ *n* **1** one of the bars forming the steps of a ladder **2** a crosspiece between the legs of a chair

rung² *vb* the past participle of **ring¹**

run into *vb* **1** to be beset by: *the mission has run into difficulty* **2** to meet unexpectedly **3** to extend to: *executives denied losses running into the thousands* **4** to collide with

run into *vb* **1 run into something** = be beset by, encounter, come across *or* upon, face, experience **2 run into someone** = meet, encounter, bump into, run across, come across *or* upon **4 run into something** = collide with, hit, strike

runnel *n literary* a small stream

runner *n* **1** a competitor in a race **2** a messenger for a firm **3** a person involved in smuggling **4 A** either of the strips of metal or wood on which a sledge runs **B** the blade of an ice skate **5** *botany* a slender horizontal stem of a plant, such as the strawberry, that grows along the surface of the soil and produces new roots and shoots **6** a long strip of cloth used to decorate a table or as a rug **7** a roller or guide for a sliding component **8 do a runner** *slang* to run away to escape trouble or to avoid paying for something

runner *n* **1** = athlete, sprinter, jogger **2** = messenger, courier, errand boy (*old-fashioned*), dispatch bearer

runner-up *n, pl* **runners-up** a person who comes second in a competition

running *adj* **1** maintained continuously: *a running battle* **2** without interruption: *for the third day running* **3 A** flowing: *rinse them under cold running water* **B** supplied through a tap: *there is no electricity, no running water, and no telephone* **4** operating: *running costs* **5** discharging pus: *a running sore* **6** accomplished at a run: *a running jump* **7** moving or slipping easily, as a rope or a knot ▶ *n* **8** the act of moving or flowing quickly **9** management or organization: *the running of the farm* **10** the operation or maintenance of a machine **11 in** *or* **out of the running** having *or* not having a good chance in a competition

12 make the running to set the pace in a competition or race

running *adj* **1** = continuous, constant, perpetual, uninterrupted, incessant **2** = in succession, unbroken **3A** = flowing, moving, streaming, coursing ▶ *n* **9** = management, control, administration, direction, leadership, organization, supervision **10** = working, performance, operation, functioning, maintenance

runny *adj* **-nier, -niest 1** tending to flow: *a runny egg* **2** producing moisture: *a runny nose*

run-of-the-mill *adj* ordinary or average

run out *vb* **1** to use up or (of a supply) to be used up: *we soon ran out of gas* **2** to become invalid: *my passport has run out* **3 run out on** *informal* to desert or abandon **4** *cricket* to dismiss (a running batsman) by breaking the wicket with the ball while he or she is running between the wickets ▶ *n* **run-out 5** *cricket* dismissal of a batsman by running him or her out

run out *vb* **1** = be used up, dry up, give out, fail, finish, be exhausted **2** = expire, end, terminate

run over *vb* **1** to knock down (a person) with a moving vehicle **2** to overflow **3** to examine hastily

run over *vb* **1 run over something or someone** = knock down, hit, run down, knock over **3 run over something** = review, check, go through, go over, run through, rehearse

runt *n* **1** the smallest and weakest young animal in a litter **2** *derogatory* an undersized or inferior person

run up *vb* **1** to amass: *running up massive debts* **2** to make by sewing together quickly **3 run up against** to experience (difficulties) ▶ *n* **run-up 4** the time just before an event: *the run-up to the elections*

runway *n* a hard level roadway where aircraft take off and land

rupee *n* the standard monetary unit of a number of countries including India and Pakistan

rupture *n* **1** the act of breaking or the state of being broken **2** a breach of peaceful or friendly relations **3** *pathol* a hernia ▶ *vb* **-turing, -tured 4** to break or burst **5** to cause a breach in relations or friendship **6** to affect or be affected with a hernia

rupture *n* **1** = break, tear, split, crack, rent, burst, breach, fissure ▶ *vb* **4** = break, separate, tear, split, crack, burst, sever

rural *adj* in or of the countryside

rural *adj* = agricultural, country

ruse (rooz) *n* an action or plan intended to mislead someone

rush[1] *vb* **1** to move or do very quickly **2** to force (someone) to act hastily **3** to make a sudden attack upon (a person or place): *scores of pubescent girls rushed the stage* **4** to proceed or approach in a reckless manner **5** to come or flow quickly or suddenly: *the water rushed in, and the next instant the boat was swamped* ▸ *n* **6** a sudden quick or violent movement **7** a sudden demand or need **8** a sudden surge towards someone or something: *the gold rush* **9** a sudden surge of sensation **10** a sudden flow of air or liquid **11** **rushes** (in film-making) the initial prints of a scene before editing ▸ *adj* **12** done with speed or urgency: *a rush job*

rush *vb* **1** = hurry, run, race, shoot, fly, career, speed, tear; ≠ dawdle **3** = attack, storm, charge at ▸ *n* **6** = dash, charge, race, scramble, stampede **9** = surge, flow, gush ▸ *adj* = hasty, fast, quick, hurried, rapid, urgent, swift; ≠ leisurely

rush[2] *n* a plant which grows in wet places and has a slender pithy stem > **rushy** *adj*

rush hour *n* a period at the beginning and end of the working day when large numbers of people are travelling to or from work

rusk *n* a hard brown crisp biscuit, often used for feeding babies

russet *adj* **1** *literary* reddish-brown: *a disarray of russet curls* ▸ *n* **2** an apple with a rough reddish-brown skin

Russian *adj* **1** of Russia ▸ *n* **2** a person from Russia **3** the official language of Russia and, formerly, of the Soviet Union

Russian roulette *n* an act of bravado in which a person spins the cylinder of a revolver loaded with only one cartridge and presses the trigger with the barrel against his or her own head

rust *n* **1** a reddish-brown oxide coating formed on iron or steel by the action of oxygen and moisture **2** a fungal disease of plants which produces a reddish-brown discoloration ▸ *adj* **3** reddish-brown ▸ *vb* **4** to become coated with a layer of rust **5** to deteriorate through lack of use: *my brain had rusted up*

rust *n* **1** = corrosion, oxidation **2** = mildew, must, mould, rot, blight ▸ *vb* **4** = corrode, oxidize

rustic *adj* **1** of or resembling country people **2** of or living in the country **3** crude, awkward, or uncouth **4** made of untrimmed branches: *rustic furniture* ▸ *n* **5** a person from the country > **rusticity** *n*

rustle[1] *vb* **-tling, -tled** **1** to make a low crisp whispering sound: *the leaves rustled in the breeze* ▸ *n* **2** this sound

rustle[2] *vb* **-tling, -tled** *chiefly US & Canad* to steal (livestock) > **rustler** *n*

rustle up *vb informal* to prepare or find at short notice: *Bob rustled up a meal*

rusty *adj* **rustier, rustiest** **1** affected by rust: *a rusty old freighter* **2** reddish-brown **3** out of practice in a skill or subject: *your skills may be a little rusty, but your past experience will more than make up for that* > **rustily** *adv* > **rustiness** *n*

rusty *adj* **1** = corroded, rusted, oxidized, rust-covered **2** = reddish-brown, chestnut, reddish, russet, coppery, rust-coloured **3** = out of practice, weak, stale, unpractised

rut[1] *n* **1** a groove or furrow in a soft road, caused by wheels **2** dull settled habits or way of living: *his career was in a rut*

rut[2] *n* **1** a recurrent period of sexual excitement in certain male ruminants ▸ *vb* **rutting, rutted** **2** (of male ruminants) to be in a period of sexual excitement

ruthenium *n chem* a rare hard brittle white metallic element. Symbol: **Ru**

ruthless *adj* **1** feeling or showing no mercy **2** thorough and forceful, regardless of effect: *the ruthless pursuit of cost-effectiveness* > **ruthlessly** *adv* > **ruthlessness** *n*

ruthless *adj* = merciless, harsh, cruel, brutal, relentless, callous, heartless, remorseless; ≠ merciful

rye *n* **1** a tall grasslike cereal grown for its light brown grain **2** the grain of this plant **3** Also called: **rye whiskey** whiskey distilled from rye

rye-grass *n* any of several grasses grown for fodder

r

Ss

s second (of time)

S 1 South(ern) **2** *chem* sulphur **3** *physics* siemens

SA 1 Salvation Army **2** South Africa **3** South America **4** South Australia

SAA South African Airways

Sabbath *n* **1** Saturday, observed by Jews as the day of worship and rest **2** Sunday, observed by Christians as the day of worship and rest

sabbatical *adj* **1** denoting a period of leave granted at intervals to university teachers for rest, study, or travel: *a sabbatical year* ▸ *n* **2** a sabbatical period

SABC South African Broadcasting Corporation

sable *n, pl* **-bles** *or* **-ble 1** a marten of N Asia, N Europe, and America, with dark brown luxuriant fur **2** the highly valued fur of this animal, used to make coats and hats ▸ *adj* **3** dark brown-to-black

sabot (**sab**-oh) *n* a heavy wooden or wooden-soled shoe; clog

sabotage *n* **1** the deliberate destruction or damage of equipment, for example by enemy agents or dissatisfied employees **2** deliberate obstruction of or damage to a cause or effort ▸ *vb* **-taging, -taged 3** to destroy or disrupt by sabotage

> **sabotage** *n* **1** = damage, destruction, wrecking ▸ *vb* = damage, destroy, wreck, disable, disrupt, subvert, incapacitate, vandalize

saboteur *n* a person who commits sabotage

sabre *or US* **saber** *n* **1** a heavy single-edged cavalry sword with a curved blade **2** a light sword used in fencing, with a narrow V-shaped blade

sac *n* a pouch or pouchlike part in an animal or plant

saccharin *n* an artificial sweetener

saccharine *adj* **1** excessively sweet or sentimental: *saccharine ballads* **2** like or containing sugar or saccharin

sacerdotal *adj formal* of priests or the priesthood

sachet *n* **1** a small sealed usually plastic envelope containing a small portion of a substance such as shampoo **2** a small soft bag of perfumed powder, placed in drawers to scent clothing

sack¹ *n* **1** a large bag made of coarse cloth or thick paper and used for carrying or storing goods **2** the amount contained in a sack

3 the sack *informal* dismissal from employment **4** *slang* bed **5 hit the sack** *slang* to go to bed ▸ *vb* **6** *informal* to dismiss from employment › **sacklike** *adj*

> **sack** *n* **1** = bag, pocket, sac, pouch, receptacle **3 the sack** = dismissal, discharge, the boot (*slang*), the axe (*informal*), the push (*slang*) ▸ *vb* = dismiss, fire (*informal*), axe (*informal*), discharge, kiss off (*slang, chiefly US, Canad*), give (someone) the push (*informal*), kennet (*Austral slang*), jeff (*Austral slang*)

sack² *n* **1** the plundering of a captured town or city by an army or mob ▸ *vb* **2** to plunder and partially destroy (a town or city)

> **sack** *n* = plundering, looting, pillage ▸ *vb* = plunder, loot, pillage, strip, rob, raid, ruin

sackcloth *n* **1** garments made of such cloth, worn formerly to indicate mourning **2 sackcloth and ashes** an exaggerated attempt to apologize or compensate for a mistake or wrongdoing

sacrament *n* **1** a symbolic religious ceremony in the Christian Church, such as baptism or communion **2** Holy Communion **3** something regarded as sacred › **sacramental** *adj*

sacred *adj* **1** exclusively devoted to a god or gods; holy **2** connected with religion or intended for religious use: *sacred music* **3** regarded as too important to be changed or interfered with: *sacred principles of free speech* **4 sacred to** dedicated to: *the site is sacred to Vishnu*

> **sacred** *adj* **1** = holy, hallowed, blessed, divine, revered, sanctified; ≠ secular **2** = religious, holy, ecclesiastical, hallowed; ≠ unconsecrated **3** = inviolable, protected, sacrosanct, hallowed, inalienable, unalterable

sacrifice *n* **1** a surrender of something of value in order to gain something more desirable or prevent some evil **2** a ritual killing of a person or animal as an offering to a god **3** a symbolic offering of something to a god **4** the person or animal killed or offered ▸ *vb* **-ficing, -ficed 5** to make a sacrifice (of) **6** *chess* to permit or force one's opponent to capture (a piece) as a tactical move › **sacrificial** *adj*

> **sacrifice** *n* **1** = surrender, loss, giving up, rejection, abdication, renunciation, repudiation, forswearing **2** = offering, oblation ▸ *vb* **5** = offer, offer up, immolate (*literary*)

sacrilege *n* **1** the misuse of or disrespect shown to something sacred **2** disrespect for a person who is widely admired or a belief that is widely accepted: *it is a sacrilege to offend democracy* › **sacrilegious** *adj*

sacristan *n* a person in charge of the contents of a church; sexton

sacristy *n, pl* **-ties** a room attached to a church or chapel where the sacred objects are kept

sacrosanct *adj* regarded as too important to be criticized or changed: *weekend rest days were considered sacrosanct by staff* > **sacrosanctity** *n*

sacrum (**say**-krum) *n, pl* **-cra** *anatomy* the large wedge-shaped bone in the lower part of the back

sad *adj* **sadder**, **saddest 1** feeling sorrow; unhappy **2** causing, suggesting, or expressing sorrow: *a sad story* **3** deplorably bad: *the garden was in a sad state* **4** regrettable: *it's rather sad he can't be with us* **5** *Brit informal* ridiculously pathetic: *a sad, boring little wimp* ▸ *n* **6 pack a sad** *NZ slang* to strongly express sadness or displeasure > **sadly** *adv* > **sadness** *n*

> **sad** *adj* **1** = unhappy, down, low, blue, depressed, melancholy, mournful, dejected; ≠ happy **2** = tragic, moving, upsetting, depressing, dismal, pathetic, poignant, harrowing **3** = deplorable, bad, sorry, terrible, unfortunate, regrettable, lamentable, wretched; ≠ good

sadden *vb* to make (someone) sad

> **sadden** *vb* = upset, depress, distress, grieve, make sad, deject

saddle *n* **1** a seat for a rider, usually made of leather, placed on a horse's back and secured under its belly **2** a similar seat on a bicycle, motorcycle, or tractor **3** a cut of meat, esp. mutton, consisting of both loins **4 in the saddle** in a position of control ▸ *vb* **-dling**, **-dled 5** to put a saddle on (a horse): *we saddled up at dawn* **6 saddle with** to burden with (a responsibility): *he was also saddled with debt*

> **saddle** *vb* **6** = burden, load, lumber (*Brit informal*), encumber

saddler *n* a person who makes, deals in, or repairs saddles and other leather equipment for horses

saddo *n Brit informal* a person perceived as socially inadequate

sadism (**say**-diz-zum) *n* the gaining of pleasure, esp. sexual pleasure, from infliction of suffering on another person > **sadist** *n* > **sadistic** *adj* > **sadistically** *adv*

sadomasochism *n* **1** the combination of sadistic and masochistic elements in one person, characterized by both submissive and aggressive periods in relationships with others **2** a sexual practice in which one partner adopts a masochistic role and the other a sadistic one > **sadomasochist** *n* > **sadomasochistic** *adj*

s.a.e. *Brit, Austral & NZ* stamped addressed envelope

safari *n, pl* **-ris** an overland expedition for hunting or observing animals, esp. in Africa

safari park *n* an enclosed park in which wild animals are kept uncaged in the open and can be viewed by the public from cars or buses

safe *adj* **1** giving security or protection from harm: *a safe environment* **2** free from danger: *she doesn't feel safe* **3** taking or involving no risks: *a safe bet* **4** not dangerous: *the beef is safe to eat* **5 on the safe side** as a precaution ▸ *n* **6** a strong metal container with a secure lock, for storing money or valuables > **safely** *adv*

> **safe** *adj* **1** = protected, secure, impregnable, out of danger, safe and sound, in safe hands, out of harm's way; ≠ endangered **2** = all right, intact, unscathed, unhurt, unharmed, undamaged, O.K. or okay (*informal*) **3** = risk-free, sound, secure, certain, impregnable ▸ *n* = strongbox, vault, coffer, repository, deposit box, safe-deposit box

safe-conduct *n* **1** a document giving official permission to travel through a dangerous region, esp. in time of war **2** the protection given by such a document

safeguard *vb* **1** to protect (someone or something) from being harmed or destroyed ▸ *n* **2** a person or thing that ensures protection against danger or harm: *safeguards to prevent air collisions*

> **safeguard** *vb* = protect, guard, defend, save, preserve, look after, keep safe ▸ *n* = protection, security, defence, guard

safekeeping *n* protection from theft or damage: *I put my money in a bank for safekeeping*

safety *n, pl* **-ties 1** the quality or state of being free from danger **2** shelter: *they swam to safety*

> **safety** *n* **1** = security, protection, safeguards, precautions, safety measures, impregnability; ≠ risk **2** = shelter, haven, protection, cover, retreat, asylum, refuge, sanctuary

safety net *n* **1** a large net under a trapeze or high wire to catch performers if they fall **2** something that can be relied on for help in the event of difficulties: *the social security safety net*

safety pin *n* a pin bent back on itself so that it forms a spring, with the point shielded by a guard when closed

safety valve *n* **1** a valve in a boiler or machine that allows fluid or gases to escape at excess pressure **2** an outlet that allows one to express strong feelings without harming or offending other people: *sport acted as a safety valve for his pent-up frustrations*

saffron *n* **1** a type of crocus with purple or white flowers with orange stigmas **2** the dried orange-coloured stigmas of this plant, used for colouring or flavouring ▸ *adj* **3** orange-yellow

sag *vb* **sagging**, **sagged 1** to sink in the middle, under weight or pressure: *the bed sagged nearly to the floor* **2** (of courage or spirits) to weaken or tire **3** (of clothes) to hang loosely or unevenly **4** to fall in value: *the stock market sagged* ▸ *n* **5** the act or state of sagging > **saggy** *adj*

S

sag *vb* **1** = drop, sink, slump, flop, droop, loll **2** = decline, tire, flag, weaken, wilt, wane, droop **3** = sink, bag, droop, fall, slump, dip, give way, hang loosely

saga (sah-ga) *n* **1** a medieval Scandinavian legend telling the adventures of a hero or a family **2** *informal* a long story or series of events: *the long-running saga of the hostage issue*

saga *n* **1** = epic, story, tale, narrative, yarn (*informal*) **2** = carry-on (*informal*), performance (*informal*), pantomime (*informal*)

sagacious *adj formal* wise or sensible > **sagaciously** *adv* > **sagacity** *n*

sage¹ *n* **1** a person, esp. an old man, regarded as being very wise ▸ *adj* **2** very wise or knowledgeable, esp. as the result of age or experience

sage *n* = wise man, philosopher, guru, master, elder, tohunga (NZ) ▸ *adj* = wise, sensible, judicious, sagacious (*formal*), sapient (*ironic*)

sage² *n* a Mediterranean plant with grey-green leaves which are used in cooking for flavouring

sago *n* an edible starch from the powdered pith of the sago palm tree, used for puddings and as a thickening agent

said *adj* **1** named or mentioned already: *she had heard that the said woman was also a medium* ▸ *vb* **2** the past of **say**

sail *n* **1** a sheet of canvas or other fabric, spread on rigging to catch the wind and move a ship over water **2** a voyage on such a ship: *a relaxing sail across the lake* **3** a ship or ships with sails: *to travel by sail* **4** one of the revolving arms of a windmill **5 set sail** to begin a voyage by water **6 under sail A** under way **B** with sail hoisted ▸ *vb* **7** to travel in a boat or ship: *to sail around the world* **8** to begin a voyage: *he hoped to sail at eleven* **9** (of a ship) to move over the water **10** to navigate (a ship): *she sailed the schooner up the channel* **11** to sail over: *he had already sailed the Pacific* **12** to move along smoothly **13 sail into** *informal* to make a violent attack on **14 sail through** to progress quickly or effortlessly: *the top seed sailed through to the second round*

sail *n* **1** = sheet, canvas ▸ *vb* **7** = go by water, cruise, voyage, ride the waves, go by sea **8** = set sail, embark, get under way, put to sea, put off, leave port, hoist sail, cast *or* weigh anchor **10** = pilot, steer **12** = glide, sweep, float, fly, wing, soar, drift, skim

sailboard *n* a board with a mast and a single sail, used for windsurfing

sailor *n* **1** any member of a ship's crew, esp. one below the rank of officer **2** a person considered as liable or not liable to seasickness: *a good sailor*

sailor *n* **1** = mariner, marine, seaman *or* woman, sea dog, seafarer

saint *n* **1** a person who after death is formally recognized by a Christian Church as deserving special honour because of having lived a very holy life **2** an exceptionally good person > **sainthood** *n* > **saintlike** *adj*

saintly *adj* behaving in a very good, patient, or holy way > **saintliness** *n*

sake¹ *n* **1 for someone's** *or* **one's own sake** for the benefit or in the interests of someone or oneself **2 for the sake of something** for the purpose of obtaining or achieving something **3 for its own sake** for the enjoyment obtained by doing something **4** used in various exclamations of annoyance, impatience, or urgency: *for God's sake*

sake *n* **1 for someone's sake** = in someone's interests, to someone's advantage, on someone's account, for the benefit of, for the good of, for the welfare of, out of respect for, out of consideration for

sake² *or* **saki** (sah-kee) *n* a Japanese alcoholic drink made from fermented rice

salaam (sal-ahm) *n* **1** a Muslim greeting consisting of a deep bow with the right palm on the forehead **2** a greeting signifying peace ▸ *vb* **3** to make a salaam (to)

salacious *adj* **1** having an excessive interest in sex **2** (of books, films, or jokes) concerned with sex in an unnecessarily detailed way > **salaciousness** *n*

salad *n* a dish of raw vegetables, often served with a dressing, eaten as a separate course or as part of a main course

salamander *n* **1** a tailed amphibian which looks like a lizard **2** a mythical creature supposed to live in fire

salami *n* a highly spiced sausage, usually flavoured with garlic

salaried *adj* earning or providing a salary: *a salaried employee; a salaried position*

salary *n, pl* **-ries** a fixed regular payment made by an employer, usually monthly, for professional or office work

salary *n* = pay, income, wage, fee, payment, wages, earnings, allowance

sale *n* **1** the exchange of goods or property for an agreed sum of money **2** the amount sold **3** an event at which goods are sold at reduced prices **4** an auction **5 sales** the department dealing with selling its company's products

sale *n* **1** = selling, marketing, dealing, transaction, disposal **4** = auction, fair, mart, bazaar

saleable *or US* **salable** *adj* fit for selling or capable of being sold > **saleability** *or US* **salability** *n*

salesman *n, pl* **-men** a man who sells goods in a shop or within an assigned area

salesmanship *n* the technique of or skill in selling

salesperson *n, pl* **-people** *or* **-persons** a person who sells goods in a shop or within an assigned area

saleswoman *n, pl* **-women** a woman who sells goods in a shop or within an assigned area

salient (**say**-lee-ent) *adj* **1** (of points or facts) most important: *the salient points of his speech* ▸ *n* **2** *military* a projection of the forward line of an army into enemy-held territory

saline (**say**-line) *adj* **1** of or containing salt: *a saline flavour* **2** *med* of or relating to a saline: *a saline drip* ▸ *n* **3** *med* a solution of sodium chloride and water › **salinity** *n*

saliva (sal-**lie**-va) *n* the watery fluid secreted by glands in the mouth, which aids digestion › **salivary** *adj*

salivate *vb* **-vating, -vated** to produce saliva, esp. an excessive amount › **salivation** *n*

sallee *n Austral* **1** a SE Australian eucalyptus with a pale grey bark **2** an acacia tree

sallow *adj* (of human skin) of an unhealthy pale or yellowish colour › **sallowness** *n*

sally *n, pl* **-lies** **1** a witty remark **2** a sudden brief attack by troops **3** an excursion ▸ *vb* **-lies, -lying, -lied** **4** **sally forth A** to set out on a journey **B** to set out in an energetic manner

salmon *n, pl* **-mons** *or* **-mon** a large pink-fleshed fish which is highly valued for food and sport: *salmon live in the sea but return to fresh water to spawn*

salmonella (sal-mon-**ell**-a) *n* a kind of bacteria that can cause food poisoning

salon *n* **1** a commercial establishment in which hairdressers or fashion designers carry on their business **2** an elegant room in a large house in which guests are received **3** an informal gathering, esp. in the 18th, 19th, and early 20th centuries, of major literary, artistic, and political figures in a fashionable household **4** an art exhibition

saloon *n* **1** a two-door or four-door car with a fixed roof **2** a comfortable but more expensive bar in a pub or hotel **3** a large public room on a passenger ship **4** *chiefly US & Canad* a place where alcoholic drink is sold and consumed

salt *n* **1** sodium chloride, a white crystalline substance, used for seasoning and preserving food **2** *chem* a crystalline solid compound formed from an acid by replacing its hydrogen with a metal **3** lively wit: *his humour added salt to the discussion* **4** **old salt** an experienced sailor **5** **rub salt into someone's wounds** to make an unpleasant situation even worse for someone **6** **salt of the earth** a person or people regarded as the finest of their kind **7** **take something with a pinch of salt** to refuse to believe something is completely true or accurate **8** **worth one's salt** worthy of one's pay; efficient ▸ *vb* **9** to season or preserve with salt **10** to scatter salt over (an iced road or path) to melt the ice ▸ *adj* **11** preserved in or tasting of salt: *salt beef* › **salted** *adj*

salt *n* **1** = seasoning ▸ *adj* = salty, saline, brackish, briny

saltbush *n* a shrub that grows in alkaline desert regions

saltire *n* **1** *heraldry* a diagonal cross on a shield **2** the national flag of Scotland, a white diagonal cross on a blue background

salty *adj* **saltier, saltiest** **1** of, tasting of, or containing salt **2** (esp. of humour) sharp and witty › **saltiness** *n*

salubrious *adj* favourable to health › **salubrity** *n*

Saluki *n* a tall hound with a smooth coat and long fringes on the ears and tail

salutary *adj* **1** (of an experience) producing a beneficial result despite being unpleasant: *a salutary reminder* **2** promoting health

salutation *n formal* a greeting by words or actions

salute *vb* **-luting, -luted** **1** to greet with friendly words or gestures of respect, such as bowing **2** to acknowledge with praise: *the statement salutes the changes of the past year* **3** *military* to pay formal respect to (someone) by raising the right hand to the forehead ▸ *n* **4** the act of saluting as a formal military gesture of respect **5** the act of firing guns as a military greeting of honour

salute *vb* **1** = greet, welcome, acknowledge, address, hail, mihi (NZ) **2** = honour, acknowledge, recognize, pay tribute *or* homage to

salvage *n* **1** the rescue of a ship or its cargo from loss at sea **2** the saving of any goods or property from destruction or waste **3** the goods or property so saved **4** compensation paid for the salvage of a ship or its cargo ▸ *vb* **-vaging, -vaged** **5** to save (goods or property) from shipwreck, destruction, or waste **6** to gain (something beneficial) from a failure: *it's too late to salvage anything from the whole dismal display* › **salvageable** *adj*

salvage *vb* **5** = save, recover, rescue, get back, retrieve, redeem

salvation *n* **1** the act of preserving someone or something from harm **2** a person or thing that preserves from harm **3** *Christianity* the fact or state of being saved from the influence or consequences of sin

salvation *n* **1** = saving, rescue, recovery, salvage, redemption, deliverance; ≠ ruin

salve *n* **1** an ointment for wounds **2** anything that heals or soothes ▸ *vb* **salving, salved** **3** **salve one's conscience** to do something in order to feel less guilty

salver *n* a tray, usually a silver one, on which something is presented

salvia *n* any small plant or shrub of the sage genus

S

salvo *n*, *pl* **-vos** *or* **-voes** **1** a simultaneous discharge of guns in battle or on a ceremonial occasion **2** an outburst of applause or questions

sal volatile (**sal** vol-**at**-ill-ee) *n* a solution of ammonium carbonate, used as smelling salts

SAM surface-to-air missile

Samaritan *n* **1** short for **Good Samaritan** **2** a member of a voluntary organization (**the Samaritans**) which offers counselling to people in despair, esp. by telephone

samba *n*, *pl* **-bas** **1** a lively Brazilian dance **2** music for this dance

same *adj* (usually preceded by *the*) **1** being the very one: *she is wearing the same hat* **2** being the one previously referred to: *it causes problems for the same reason* **3** alike in kind or quantity: *the same age* **4** unchanged in character or nature: *his attitude is the same as ever* **5** **all the same** *or* **just the same** nevertheless; even so **6** **be all the same** to be a matter of indifference: *it was all the same to me* ▸ *adv* **7** in the same way; similarly: *I felt much the same* ▸ *n* **8** **the same** something that is like something else in kind or quantity: *this is basically much more of the same* > **sameness** *n*

> **same** *adj* **1** = the very same, one and the same, selfsame **2** = aforementioned, aforesaid **3** = identical, similar, alike, equal, twin, corresponding, duplicate; ≠ different **4** = unchanged, consistent, constant, unaltered, invariable, unvarying, changeless; ≠ altered

samovar *n* a Russian metal tea urn in which the water is heated by an inner container

Samoyed *n* a dog with a thick white coat and a tightly curled tail

sampan *n* a small flat-bottomed boat with oars, used esp. in China

samphire *n* a European plant found on rocks by the seashore, with aromatic leaves sometimes eaten as a vegetable

sample *n* **1** a small part of anything, taken as being representative of a whole ▸ *vb* **-pling**, **-pled** **2** to take a sample or samples of **3** *music* **a** to take a short extract from (one record) and mix it into a different backing track **b** to record (a sound) and feed it into a computerized synthesizer so that it can be reproduced at any pitch > **sampling** *n*

> **sample** *n* = specimen, example, model, pattern, instance ▸ *vb* **2** = test, try, experience, taste, inspect

sampler *n* **1** a piece of embroidery done to show the embroiderer's skill in using many different stitches **2** *music* a piece of electronic equipment used for sampling

samurai *n*, *pl* **-rai** a member of the aristocratic warrior caste of feudal Japan

sanatorium *or US* **sanitarium** *n*, *pl* **-riums** *or* **-ria** **1** an institution providing medical treatment and rest for invalids or convalescents **2** *Brit* a room in a boarding school where sick pupils may be treated

sanctify *vb* **-fies**, **-fying**, **-fied** **1** to make holy **2** to free from sin **3** to approve (an action or practice) as religiously binding: *she is trying to make amends for her marriage not being sanctified* > **sanctification** *n*

sanctimonious *adj* pretending to be very religious and virtuous

sanction *n* **1** permission granted by authority: *official sanction* **2** support or approval: *they could not exist without his sanction* **3** something that gives binding force to a law, such as a penalty for breaking it or a reward for obeying it **4** **sanctions** coercive measures, such as boycotts and trade embargoes, taken by one or more states against another guilty of violating international law ▸ *vb* **5** to officially approve of or allow: *they do not want to sanction direct payments* **6** to confirm or ratify

> **sanction** *n* **1, 2** = permission, backing, authority, approval, authorization, O.K. *or* okay (*informal*), stamp *or* seal of approval; ≠ ban **4** = ban, boycott, embargo, exclusion, penalty, coercive measures; ≠ permission ▸ *vb* **5** = permit, allow, approve, endorse, authorize; ≠ forbid

sanctity *n* the quality of something considered so holy or important it must be respected totally: *the sanctity of the Sabbath*; *the sanctity of marriage*

sanctuary *n*, *pl* **-aries** **1** a holy place, such as a consecrated building or shrine **2** the part of a church nearest the main altar **3** a place of refuge or protection for someone who is being chased or hunted **4** refuge or safety: *the sanctuary of your own home* **5** a place, protected by law, where animals can live and breed without interference

> **sanctuary** *n* **3, 4** = protection, shelter, refuge, haven, retreat, asylum **5** = reserve, park, preserve, reservation, national park, tract, nature reserve, conservation area

sanctum *n*, *pl* **-tums** *or* **-ta** **1** a sacred or holy place **2** a room or place of total privacy

sand *n* **1** a powdery substance consisting of very small rock or mineral grains, found on the seashore and in deserts **2** **sands** a large sandy area, esp. on the seashore or in a desert ▸ *vb* **3** to smooth or polish the surface of (something) with sandpaper or a sander **4** to fill with sand: *the channel sanded up*

sandal *n* a light shoe consisting of a sole held on the foot by thongs or straps > **sandalled** *or US* **sandaled** *adj*

sandalwood *n* **1** the hard light-coloured wood of a S Asian or Australian tree, which is used for carving and for incense, and which yields an aromatic oil used in perfumes **2** a tree yielding this wood

sandbag n 1 a sack filled with sand used to make a temporary defence against gunfire or flood water ▸ vb -**bagging**, -**bagged** 2 to protect or strengthen with sandbags

sandblast n 1 a jet of sand blown from a nozzle under air or steam pressure ▸ vb 2 to clean or decorate (a surface) with a sandblast > **sandblaster** n

sander n a power-driven tool for smoothing surfaces, removing layers of paint from walls, etc.

S & M informal sadomasochism

sandpaper n 1 a strong paper coated with sand or other abrasive material for smoothing or polishing a surface ▸ vb 2 to smooth or polish (a surface) with sandpaper

sandpiper n a wading shore bird with a long bill and slender legs

sandstone n a sedimentary rock consisting mainly of sand grains, much used in building

sandstorm n a strong wind that whips up clouds of sand, esp. in a desert

sandwich n 1 two or more slices of bread, usually buttered, with a layer of food between them ▸ vb 2 to place between two other things: shops sandwiched between flats

sandwich board n one of two connected boards that are hung over the shoulders in front of and behind a person to display advertisements

sandy adj **sandier**, **sandiest** 1 resembling, containing, or covered with sand 2 (of hair) reddish-yellow > **sandiness** n

sane adj 1 having a healthy mind 2 sensible or well-judged: sane advice

> **sane** adj 1 = rational, of sound mind, compos mentis (Latin), in your right mind, mentally sound; ≠ insane 2 = sensible, sound, reasonable, balanced, judicious, level-headed, grounded; ≠ foolish

sang vb the past tense of **sing**

sang-froid (sahng-frwah) n composure and calmness in a difficult situation

sangoma (sang-go-ma) n S African a witch doctor

sanguinary adj formal 1 (of a battle or fight) involving much violence and bloodshed 2 (of a person) eager to see violence and bloodshed 3 of or stained with blood

sanguine adj 1 cheerful and confident 2 (of the complexion) ruddy

sanitary adj 1 promoting health by getting rid of dirt and germs 2 free from dirt or germs; hygienic

sanitation n 1 the use of sanitary measures to maintain public health 2 the drainage and disposal of sewage

sanity n 1 the state of having a healthy mind 2 good sense or soundness of judgment

sank vb the past tense of **sink**

Sanskrit n the classical literary language of India, used since ancient times for religious purposes > **Sanskritic** adj

sap[1] n 1 a thin liquid that circulates in a plant, carrying food and water 2 slang a gullible person ▸ vb **sapping**, **sapped** 3 to drain of sap

> **sap** n 1 = juice, essence, vital fluid, lifeblood 2 = fool, idiot, wally (slang), twit (informal), ninny, dorba or dorb (Austral slang)

sap[2] vb **sapping**, **sapped** 1 to weaken or exhaust the strength or confidence of 2 to undermine (an enemy position) by digging saps ▸ n 3 a deep and narrow trench used to approach or undermine an enemy position

> **sap** vb 1 = weaken, drain, undermine, exhaust, deplete

sapient (say-pee-ent) adj often humorous having great wisdom or sound judgment > **sapience** n

sapling n a young tree

sapper n a soldier who digs trenches 2 (in the British Army) a private of the Royal Engineers

sapphire n 1 a transparent blue precious stone ▸ adj 2 deep blue

sarabande or **saraband** n 1 a stately slow Spanish dance 2 music for this dance

Saracen n 1 an Arab or Muslim who opposed the Crusades ▸ adj 2 of the Saracens

sarcasm n 1 mocking or ironic language intended to insult someone 2 the use or tone of such language

sarcastic adj 1 full of or showing sarcasm 2 tending to use sarcasm: a sarcastic critic > **sarcastically** adv

sarcophagus (sahr-koff-a-guss) n, pl -**gi** (-guy) or -**guses** a stone or marble coffin or tomb, esp. one bearing sculpture or inscriptions

sardine n, pl -**dines** or -**dine** 1 a small fish of the herring family, often preserved in tightly packed tins 2 **like sardines** very closely crowded together

sardonic adj (of behaviour) mocking or scornful > **sardonically** adv

sargassum n a floating brown seaweed with long stringy fronds containing air sacs

sari or **saree** n, pl -**ris** or -**rees** the traditional dress of Hindu women, consisting of a very long piece of cloth swathed around the body with one end over the shoulder

sarmie n S African children's slang a sandwich

sarong n a garment worn by Malaysian men and women, consisting of a long piece of cloth tucked around the waist or under the armpits

sarsaparilla n a nonalcoholic drink prepared from the roots of a tropical American climbing plant

sartorial adj formal of men's clothes or tailoring: sartorial elegance

SAS (in Britain) Special Air Service

sash[1] n a long piece of cloth worn around the waist or over one shoulder, usually as a symbol of rank

sash² *n* **1** a frame that contains the panes of a window or door **2** a complete frame together with panes of glass

sash window *n* a window consisting of two sashes placed one above the other so that the window can be opened by sliding one frame over the front of the other

sassafras *n* a tree of North America, with aromatic bark used medicinally and as a flavouring

Sassenach *n* Scot & sometimes Irish an English person

sat *vb* the past of **sit**

Satan *n* the Devil

satanic *adj* **1** of Satan **2** supremely evil or wicked

> **satanic** *adj* **2** = evil, demonic, hellish, black, wicked, devilish, infernal (*informal*), fiendish; ≠ godly

Satanism *n* the worship of Satan > **Satanist** *n, adj*

satay (**sat-ay**) *n* an Indonesian and Malaysian dish consisting of pieces of chicken, pork, etc., grilled on skewers and served with peanut sauce

satchel *n* a small bag, usually with a shoulder strap

sate *vb* **sating, sated** to satisfy (a desire or appetite) fully

satellite *n* **1** a man-made device orbiting the earth or another planet, used in communications or to collect scientific information **2** a heavenly body orbiting a planet or star: *the earth is a satellite of the sun* **3** a country controlled by or dependent on a more powerful one ▸ *adj* **4** of, used in, or relating to the transmission of television signals from a satellite to the home: *satellite TV; a satellite dish*

satiate (**say-she-ate**) *vb* **-ating, -ated** to provide with more than enough, so as to disgust or weary: *enough cakes to satiate several children* > **satiable** *adj* > **satiation** *n*

satiety (**sat-tie-a-tee**) *n formal* the feeling of having had too much

satin *n* **1** a fabric, usually made from silk or rayon, closely woven to give a smooth glossy surface on one side ▸ *adj* **2** like satin in texture: *satin polyurethane varnish* > **satiny** *adj*

satinwood *n* **1** a hard wood with a satiny texture, used in fine furniture **2** the Asian tree yielding this wood

satire *n* **1** the use of ridicule to expose incompetence, evil, or corruption **2** a play, novel, or poem containing satire > **satirical** *adj*

> **satire** *n* **1** = mockery, irony, ridicule **2** = parody, mockery, caricature, lampoon, burlesque

satirist *n* **1** a writer of satire **2** a person who uses satire

satirize *or* **-rise** *vb* **-rizing, -rized** *or* **-rising, -rised** to ridicule (a person or thing) by means of satire > **satirization** *or* **-risation** *n*

satisfaction *n* **1** the pleasure obtained from the fulfilment of a desire **2** something that brings fulfilment: *craft workers get satisfaction from their work* **3** compensation or an apology for a wrong done: *consumers unable to get satisfaction from their gas supplier*

> **satisfaction** *n* **1** = fulfilment, pleasure, achievement, relish, gratification, pride; ≠ dissatisfaction **2** = contentment, content, comfort, pleasure, happiness, enjoyment, satiety, repletion; ≠ discontent

satisfactory *adj* **1** adequate or acceptable **2** giving satisfaction > **satisfactorily** *adv*

> **satisfactory** *adj* **1** = adequate, acceptable, good enough, average, fair, all right, sufficient, passable; ≠ unsatisfactory

satisfy *vb* **-fies, -fying, -fied 1** to fulfil the desires or needs of (a person): *his answer didn't satisfy me* **2** to provide sufficiently for (a need or desire): *to satisfy public demand* **3** to convince: *that trip did seem to satisfy her that he was dead* **4** to fulfil the requirements of: *unable to satisfy the conditions set by the commission* > **satisfiable** *adj* > **satisfying** *adj*

> **satisfy** *vb* **1** = content, please, indulge, gratify, pander to, assuage, pacify, quench; ≠ dissatisfy **2** = comply with, meet, fulfil, answer, serve, fill, observe, obey; ≠ fail to meet **3** = convince, persuade, assure, reassure; ≠ dissuade

satnav *n motoring informal* satellite navigation

satsuma *n* a small loose-skinned variety of orange with easily separable segments

saturate *vb* **-rating, -rated 1** to soak completely **2** to fill so completely that no more can be added: *saturating the area with their men* **3** *chem* to combine (a substance) or (of a substance) to be combined with the greatest possible amount of another substance

> **saturate** *vb* **1** = soak, steep, drench, imbue, suffuse, wet through, waterlog, souse **2** = flood, overwhelm, swamp, overrun

saturation *n* **1** the process or state that occurs when one substance is filled so full of another substance that no more can be added **2** *military* the use of very heavy force, esp. bombing, against an area

Saturday *n* the seventh day of the week

Saturn *n* **1** the Roman god of agriculture and vegetation **2** the sixth planet from the sun, second largest in the solar system, around which revolve concentric rings

Saturnalia *n, pl* **-lia** *or* **-lias 1** the ancient Roman festival of Saturn, renowned for its unrestrained revelry **2 saturnalia** a wild party or orgy

saturnine *adj* having a gloomy temperament or appearance

satyr *n* **1** *Greek myth* a woodland god represented as having a man's body with the ears, horns, tail, and legs of a goat **2** a man who has strong sexual desires

sauce n **1** a liquid added to food to enhance its flavour **2** anything that adds interest or zest **3** chiefly Brit informal impudent language or behaviour

> **sauce** n **1** = dressing, dip, relish, condiment

saucepan n a metal pan with a long handle and often a lid, used for cooking food

saucer n **1** a small round dish on which a cup is set **2** something shaped like a saucer
> **saucerful** n

saucy adj **saucier, sauciest 1** cheeky or slightly rude in an amusing and light-hearted way **2** jaunty and boldly smart: a saucy hat
> **sauciness** n

sauerkraut n a German dish of finely shredded pickled cabbage

sauna n **1** a Finnish-style hot steam bath, usually followed by a cold plunge **2** the place in which such a bath is taken

saunter vb **1** to walk in a leisurely manner; stroll ▸ n **2** a leisurely pace or stroll

sausage n **1** finely minced meat mixed with fat, cereal, and seasonings, in a tube-shaped casing **2** an object shaped like a sausage **3 not a sausage** informal nothing at all

> **sausage** n **1** = banger

sausage roll n a roll of sausage meat in pastry

sauté (so-tay) vb **-téing, -téed 1** to fry (food) quickly in a little fat ▸ n **2** a dish of sautéed food ▸ adj **3** sautéed until lightly brown: sauté potatoes

savage adj **1** wild and untamed: savage tigers **2** fierce and cruel: savage cries **3** (of peoples) uncivilized or primitive: savage tribes **4** rude, crude, and violent: savage behaviour on the terraces **5** (of terrain) wild and uncultivated ▸ n **6** a member of an uncivilized or primitive society **7** a fierce or vicious person ▸ vb **-vaging, -vaged 8** to attack ferociously and wound: savaged by a wild dog **9** to criticize extremely severely: savaged by the press for incompetence > **savagely** adv

> **savage** adj **1** = wild, fierce, ferocious, unbroken, feral, untamed, undomesticated; ≠ tame **2, 4** = cruel, brutal, vicious, fierce, harsh, ruthless, ferocious, sadistic; ≠ gentle **3** = primitive, undeveloped, uncultivated, uncivilized **5** = uncultivated, rugged, unspoilt, uninhabited, rough, uncivilized; ≠ cultivated ▸ n **7** = lout, yob (Brit slang), barbarian, yahoo, hoon (Austral, NZ informal), boor, cougan (Austral slang), scozza (Austral slang), bogan (Austral slang) ▸ vb **8** = maul, tear, claw, attack, mangle, lacerate, mangulate (Austral slang)

savagery n, pl **-ries** viciousness and cruelty

savannah or **savanna** n open grasslands, usually with scattered bushes or trees, in Africa

savant or fem **savante** n a very wise and knowledgeable person

save vb **saving, saved 1** to rescue or preserve (a person or thing) from danger or harm **2** to avoid the spending, waste, or loss of (something): an appeal on television for the public to save energy **3** to set aside or reserve (money or goods) for future use: I'm saving for a vintage Mercedes **4** to treat with care so as to preserve **5** to give a computer an instruction to store (newly entered data) **6** to prevent the necessity for: a chance saved him from having to make up his mind **7** sport to prevent (a goal) by stopping (a ball or puck) **8** Christianity to free (someone) from the influence or consequences of sin ▸ n **9** sport the act of saving a goal **10** computers the act or process of saving data to a storage location > **savable** or **saveable** adj > **saver** n

> **save** vb **1** = rescue, free, release, deliver, recover, get out, liberate, salvage; ≠ endanger **2** = keep, reserve, set aside, store, collect, gather, hold, hoard; ≠ spend **3** = put aside, keep, reserve, collect, retain, set aside, put by **4** = protect, keep, guard, preserve, look after, safeguard, salvage, conserve

saveloy n Brit, Austral & NZ a highly seasoned smoked sausage made from salted pork

saving n **1** preservation from destruction or danger **2** a reduction in the amount of time or money used **3 savings** money saved for future use ▸ adj **4** tending to rescue or preserve ▸ prep **5** with the exception of

> **saving** n **2** = economy, discount, reduction, bargain **3** = nest egg, fund, store, reserves, resources

saviour or US **savior** n a person who rescues another person or a thing from danger or harm

> **saviour** or **savior** n = rescuer, deliverer, defender, protector, liberator, redeemer, preserver

Saviour or US **Savior** n Christianity Jesus Christ, regarded as the saviour of people from sin

> **Saviour** or **Savior** n = Christ, Jesus, the Messiah, the Redeemer

savoir-faire (sav-wahr-**fair**) n the ability to say and do the right thing in any situation

savory n, pl **-vories** an aromatic plant whose leaves are used in cooking

savour or US **savor** vb **1** to enjoy and appreciate (food or drink) slowly **2** to enjoy (a pleasure) for as long as possible: an experience to be savoured **3 savour of** ⊿ to have a suggestion of: that could savour of ostentation ʙ to possess the taste or smell of: the vegetables savoured of coriander ▸ n **4** the taste or smell of something **5** a slight but distinctive quality or trace

> **savour** or **savor** vb **1** = enjoy, appreciate, relish, delight in, revel in, luxuriate in **2** = relish, delight in, revel in, luxuriate in ▸ n **4** = flavour, taste, smell, relish, smack, tang, piquancy

S

savoury *or US* **savory** *adj* **1** salty or spicy: *savoury foods* **2** attractive to the sense of taste or smell **3** pleasant or acceptable: *one of the book's less savoury characters* ▸ *n*, *pl* **-ries 4** *chiefly Brit* a savoury dish served before or after a meal › **savouriness** *or US* **savoriness** *n*

savoy *n* a cabbage with a compact head and wrinkled leaves

savvy *slang* ▸ *vb* **-vies, -vying, -vied 1** to understand ▸ *n* **2** understanding or common sense ▸ *adj* **3** shrewd

saw¹ *n* **1** a cutting tool with a toothed metal blade or edge, either operated by hand or powered by electricity ▸ *vb* **sawing, sawed, sawed** *or* **sawn 2** to cut with or as if with a saw **3** to form by sawing **4** to move (an object) from side to side as if moving a saw

saw² *vb* the past tense of **see¹**

saw³ *n old-fashioned* a wise saying or proverb

sawdust *n* particles of wood formed by sawing

sawfish *n*, *pl* **-fish** *or* **-fishes** a sharklike ray with a long toothed snout resembling a saw

sawmill *n* a factory where timber is sawn into planks

sawyer *n* a person who saws timber for a living

sax *n informal* short for **saxophone**

saxifrage *n* an alpine rock plant with small white, yellow, purple, or pink flowers

Saxon *n* **1** a member of a West Germanic people who raided and settled parts of Britain in the fifth and sixth centuries AD **2** any of the West Germanic dialects spoken by the ancient Saxons ▸ *adj* **3** of the ancient Saxons or their language

saxophone *n* a brass wind instrument with keys and a curved metal body › **saxophonist** *n*

say *vb* **saying, said 1** to speak or utter **2** to express (an idea) in words: *I can't say what I feel* **3** to state (an opinion or fact) positively: *I say you are wrong* **4** to indicate or show: *the clock says ten to nine* **5** to recite: *to say grace* **6** to report or allege: *they say we shall have rain today* **7** to suppose as an example or possibility: *let us say that he is lying* **8** to convey by means of artistic expression: *what does the artist have to say in this picture?* **9** to make a case for: *there is much to be said for it* **10 go without saying** to be so obvious as to need no explanation **11 to say the least** at the very least ▸ *adv* **12** approximately: *there were, say, 20 people present* **13** for example: *choose a number, say, four* ▸ *n* **14** the right or chance to speak: *the opposition has hardly had a say in these affairs* **15** authority, esp. to influence a decision: *he has a lot of say*

say *vb* **1** = speak, utter, voice, express, pronounce **2** = state, declare, remark, announce, maintain, mention, assert, affirm **7** = suppose, imagine, assume, presume **8** = suggest, express, imply, communicate, disclose, give away, convey, divulge ▸ *n* **14** = chance to speak, vote, voice **15** = influence, power, control, authority, weight, clout (*informal*), mana (*NZ*)

saying *n* a well-known phrase or sentence expressing a belief or a truth

saying *n* = proverb, maxim, adage, dictum, axiom, aphorism

scab *n* **1** the dried crusty surface of a healing skin wound or sore **2** *derogatory* a person who refuses to support a trade union's actions, and continues to work during a strike **3** a contagious disease of sheep, caused by a mite **4** a fungal disease of plants ▸ *vb* **scabbing, scabbed 5** to become covered with a scab **6** *derogatory* to work as a scab

scabbard *n* a holder for a sword or dagger

scabby *adj* **-bier, -biest 1** *pathol* covered with scabs **2** *informal* mean or despicable › **scabbiness** *n*

scabies (skay-beez) *n* a contagious skin infection caused by a mite, characterized by intense itching

scabrous (skay-bruss) *adj* **1** rough and scaly **2** indecent or crude: *scabrous stand-up comedy*

scaffold *n* **1** a temporary framework used to support workers and materials during the construction or repair of a building **2** a raised wooden platform on which criminals are hanged; gallows

scaffolding *n* **1** a scaffold or scaffolds **2** the building materials used to make scaffolds

scalar *maths* ▸ *n* **1** a quantity, such as time or temperature, that has magnitude but not direction ▸ *adj* **2** having magnitude but not direction

scald *vb* **1** to burn with hot liquid or steam **2** to sterilize with boiling water **3** to heat (a liquid) almost to boiling point ▸ *n* **4** a burn caused by scalding

scale¹ *n* **1** one of the thin flat overlapping plates covering the bodies of fishes and reptiles **2** a thin flat piece or flake **3** a coating which sometimes forms in kettles and hot-water pipes in areas where the water is hard **4** tartar formed on the teeth ▸ *vb* **scaling, scaled 5** to remove the scales or coating from **6** to peel off in flakes or scales **7** to cover or become covered with scales › **scaly** *adj*

scale *n* **1, 2** = flake, plate, layer, lamina

scale² *n* **1** (*often pl*) a machine or device for weighing **2** one of the pans of a balance **3 tip the scales** to have a decisive influence **4 tip the scales at** to amount in weight to

scale³ *n* **1** a sequence of marks at regular intervals, used as a reference in making measurements **2** a measuring instrument with such a scale **3** the ratio between the size of something real and that of a representation of it: *the map has a scale of 1:10 000* **4** a series of degrees or graded system of things: *the Western wage scale for the same work* **5** a relative degree or extent: *growing flowers on a very small scale* **6** *music* a sequence of notes taken in ascending or

descending order, esp. within one octave
7 *maths* the notation of a given number system: *the decimal scale* ▸ *vb* **scaling, scaled 8** to climb to the top of (an object or height): *the men scaled a wall* **9 scale up** *or* **down** to increase *or* reduce proportionately in size: *the design can easily be scaled up; after five days the search was scaled down*

scale *n* **1** = system of measurement, measuring system **3** = ratio, proportion **4** = ranking, ladder, hierarchy, series, sequence, progression **5** = degree, size, range, extent, dimensions, scope, magnitude, breadth ▸ *vb* **8** = climb up, mount, ascend, surmount, clamber up, escalade

scalene *adj maths* (of a triangle) having all sides of unequal length

scallop *n* **1** an edible marine mollusc with two fluted fan-shaped shells **2** a single shell of this mollusc **3** one of a series of small curves along an edge › **scalloping** *n*

scalloped *adj* decorated with small curves along the edge

scallywag *n informal* a badly behaved but likeable person; rascal

scalp *n* **1** *anatomy* the skin and hair covering the top of the head **2** (formerly among Native Americans of N America) a part of this removed as a trophy from a slain enemy ▸ *vb* **3** to cut the scalp from **4** *informal, chiefly US* to buy and resell so as to make a high or quick profit

scalpel *n* a small surgical knife with a very sharp thin blade

scam *n slang* a stratagem for gain; a swindle

scamp *n* a mischievous person, esp. a child

scamper *vb* **1** to run about hurriedly or quickly ▸ *n* **2** the act of scampering

scampi *n* large prawns, usually eaten fried in breadcrumbs

scan *vb* **scanning, scanned 1** to scrutinize carefully **2** to glance over quickly **3** *prosody* to analyse (verse) by examining its rhythmic structure **4** *prosody* (of a line or verse) to be metrically correct **5** to examine or search (an area) by systematically moving a beam of light or electrons, or a radar or sonar beam over it **6** *med* to obtain an image of (a part of the body) by means of ultrasound or a scanner ▸ *n* **7** an instance of scanning **8** *med* **A** the examination of part of the body by means of a scanner **B** the image produced by a scanner

scan *vb* **1** = survey, search, investigate, sweep, scour, scrutinize **2** = glance over, skim, look over, eye, check, examine, check out (*informal*), run over, surf (*computers*)

scandal *n* **1** a disgraceful action or event: *the manager resigned after a loans scandal* **2** shame or outrage arising from a disgraceful action or event: *the figures were a national scandal* **3** malicious gossip › **scandalous** *adj* › **scandalously** *adv*

scandal *n* **1** = disgrace, crime, offence, sin, embarrassment, wrongdoing, dishonourable behaviour, discreditable behaviour **2** = outrage, shame, insult, disgrace, injustice, crying shame **3** = gossip, goss (*informal*), talk, rumours, dirt (*informal*), slander, tattle, aspersion

scandalize *or* **-ise** *vb* **-izing, -ized** *or* **-ising, -ised** to shock (someone) or be shocked by improper behaviour

Scandinavian *adj* **1** of Scandinavia (Norway, Sweden, Denmark, and often Finland, Iceland, and the Faeroe Islands) ▸ *n* **2** a person from Scandinavia **3** the northern group of Germanic languages, consisting of Swedish, Danish, Norwegian, Icelandic, and Faeroese

scandium *n chem* a rare silvery-white metallic element. Symbol: **Sc**

scanner *n* **1** an aerial or similar device designed to transmit or receive signals, esp. radar signals **2** a device used in medical diagnosis to obtain an image of an internal organ or part

scansion *n* the metrical scanning of verse

scant *adj* scarcely sufficient: *some issues will get scant attention*

scant *adj* = inadequate, meagre, sparse, little, minimal, barely sufficient; ≠ adequate

scanty *adj* **scantier, scantiest** barely sufficient or not sufficient › **scantily** *adv* › **scantiness** *n*

scapegoat *n* **1** a person made to bear the blame for others ▸ *vb* **2** to make a scapegoat of

scapegoat *n* = fall guy, whipping boy

scapula (skap-pew-la) *n, pl* **-lae** (-lee) the technical name for **shoulder blade**

scapular *adj* **1** *anatomy* of the scapula ▸ *n* **2** a loose sleeveless garment worn by monks over their habits

scar *n* **1** a mark left on the skin following the healing of a wound **2** a permanent effect on a person's character resulting from emotional distress **3** a mark on a plant where a leaf was formerly attached **4** a mark of damage ▸ *vb* **scarring, scarred 5** to mark or become marked with a scar **6** to permanently effect or be permanently affected by mental trauma: *the disaster will scar the victims for life*

scar *n* **1** = mark, injury, wound, blemish **2** = trauma, suffering, pain, torture, anguish ▸ *vb* **5** = mark, disfigure, damage, mar, mutilate, blemish, deface

scarab *n* **1** the black dung-beetle, regarded by the ancient Egyptians as divine **2** an image or carving of this beetle

scarce *adj* **1** insufficient to meet the demand: *scarce water resources* **2** not common; rarely found **3 make oneself scarce** *informal* to go away ▸ *adv* **4** *archaic, literary* scarcely

S

scarce *adj* 1 = in short supply, insufficient; ≠ plentiful 2 = rare, few, uncommon, few and far between, infrequent; ≠ common

scarcely *adv* 1 hardly at all 2 *often humorous* probably or definitely not: *that is scarcely justification for your actions*

scarcely *adv* 1 = hardly, barely 2 = by no means, hardly, definitely not

scarcity *n, pl* **-ties** an inadequate supply

scare *vb* **scaring, scared** 1 to frighten or be frightened 2 **scare away** or **off** to drive away by frightening ▸ *n* 3 a sudden attack of fear or alarm: *you gave me a scare* 4 a period of general fear or alarm: *the bird flu scare*

scare *vb* 1 = frighten, alarm, terrify, panic, shock, startle, intimidate, dismay ▸ *n* 3 = fright, shock, start 4 = panic, hysteria

scarecrow *n* 1 an object, usually in the shape of a man, made out of sticks and old clothes, to scare birds away from crops 2 *informal* a raggedly dressed person

scaremonger *n* a person who starts or spreads rumours of disaster to frighten people > **scaremongering** *n*

scarf¹ *n, pl* **scarves** or **scarfs** a piece of material worn around the head, neck, or shoulders

scarf² *n, pl* **scarfs** 1 a joint between two pieces of timber made by notching the ends and strapping or gluing the two pieces together ▸ *vb* 2 to join (two pieces of timber) by means of a scarf

scarify *vb* **-fies, -fying, -fied** 1 *surgery* to make slight incisions in (the skin) 2 *agriculture* to break up and loosen (topsoil) 3 to criticize without mercy > **scarification** *n*

scarlatina *n* the technical name for **scarlet fever**

scarlet *adj* bright red

scarlet fever *n* an acute contagious disease characterized by fever, a sore throat, and a red rash on the body

scarp *n* 1 a steep slope or ridge of rock 2 *fortifications* the side of a ditch cut nearest to a rampart

scarper *vb chiefly Brit slang* to run away or escape

scary *adj* **scarier, scariest** *informal* quite frightening

scary *adj* = frightening, alarming, terrifying, chilling, horrifying, spooky (*informal*), creepy (*informal*), spine-chilling

scat¹ *vb* **scatting, scatted** *informal* to go away in haste

scat² *n* 1 a type of jazz singing using improvised vocal sounds instead of words ▸ *vb* **scatting, scatted** 2 to sing jazz in this way

scathing *adj* harshly critical: *there was a scathing review of the play in the paper* > **scathingly** *adv*

scatology *n* preoccupation with obscenity, esp. with references to excrement > **scatological** *adj*

scatter *vb* 1 to throw about in various directions: *scatter some oatmeal on top of the cake* 2 to separate and move in various directions; disperse: *the infantry were scattering* ▸ *n* 3 the act of scattering 4 a number of objects scattered about

scatter *vb* 1 = throw about, spread, sprinkle, strew, shower, fling, diffuse, disseminate; ≠ gather 2 = disperse, dispel, disband, dissipate; ≠ assemble

scatterbrain *n* a person who is incapable of serious thought or concentration > **scatterbrained** *adj*

scatty *adj* **-tier, -tiest** *informal* rather absent-minded > **scattiness** *n*

scavenge *vb* **-enging, -enged** to search for (anything usable) among discarded material

scavenger *n* 1 a person who collects things discarded by others 2 any animal that feeds on discarded or decaying matter

scenario *n, pl* **-narios** 1 a summary of the plot and characters of a play or film 2 an imagined sequence of future events: *the likeliest scenario is another general election*

scenario *n* 1 = story line, résumé, outline, summary, synopsis 2 = situation

scene *n* 1 the place where an action or event, real or imaginary, occurs 2 an incident or situation, real or imaginary, esp. as described or represented 3 a division of an act of a play, in which the setting is fixed and the action is continuous 4 *films* a shot or series of shots that constitutes a unit of the action 5 the backcloths or screens used to represent a location in a play or film set 6 the view of a place or landscape 7 a display of emotion or loss of temper in public: *you do not want to cause a scene* 8 *informal* a particular activity or aspect of life, and all the things associated with it: *the club scene* 9 **behind the scenes** A backstage B in secret or in private

scene *n* 1, 5 = setting, set, background, location, backdrop 3 = act, part, division, episode 6 = view, prospect, panorama, vista, landscape, outlook 7 = fuss, to-do, row, performance (*informal*), exhibition, carry-on (*informal, chiefly Brit*), tantrum, commotion, hissy fit (*informal*) 8 = world, business, environment, arena

scenery *n, pl* **-eries** 1 the natural features of a landscape 2 *theatre* the painted backcloths or screens used to represent a location in a theatre or studio

scenery *n* 1 = landscape, view, surroundings, terrain, vista 2 = set, setting, backdrop, flats, stage set

scenic *adj* 1 of or having beautiful natural scenery: *untouched scenic areas* 2 of the stage or stage scenery: *scenic artists*

scenic *adj* **1** = picturesque, beautiful, spectacular, striking, panoramic

scent *n* **1** a distinctive smell, esp. a pleasant one **2** a smell left in passing, by which a person or animal may be traced **3** a trail or series of clues by which something is followed: *he must have got on to the scent of the story through you* **4** perfume ▸ *vb* **5** to become aware of by smelling **6** to suspect: *he scented the beginnings of irritation in the car* **7** to fill with odour or fragrance > **scented** *adj*

scent *n* **1** = fragrance, smell, perfume, bouquet, aroma, odour **2** = trail, track, spoor ▸ *vb* **5** = smell, sense, detect, sniff, discern, nose out

sceptic *or US* **skeptic** (skep-tik) *n* **1** a person who habitually doubts generally accepted beliefs **2** a person who doubts the truth of a religion > **sceptical** *or US* **skeptical** *adj* > **sceptically** *or US* **skeptically** *adv* > **scepticism** *or US* **skepticism** *n*

sceptic *or* **skeptic** *n* **1** = doubter, cynic, disbeliever **2** = agnostic, doubter, unbeliever, doubting Thomas

sceptre *or US* **scepter** *n* an ornamental rod symbolizing royal power > **sceptred** *or US* **sceptered** *adj*

schedule *n* **1** a timed plan of procedure for a project **2** a list of details or items: *the schedule of priorities* **3** a timetable ▸ *vb* **-uling, -uled** **4** to plan and arrange (something) to happen at a certain time **5** to make a schedule or include in a schedule

schedule *n* **1, 3** = plan, programme, agenda, calendar, timetable ▸ *vb* **4** = plan, set up, book, programme, arrange, organize

schema *n, pl* **-mata** an outline of a plan or theory
schematic *adj* presented as a diagram or plan > **schematically** *adv*
scheme *n* **1** a systematic plan for a course of action **2** a systematic arrangement of parts or features: *colour scheme* **3** a secret plot **4** a chart, diagram, or outline **5** a plan formally adopted by a government or organization: *a pension scheme* ▸ *vb* **scheming, schemed** **6** to plan in an underhand manner > **schemer** *n* > **scheming** *adj, n*

scheme *n* **1** = plan, programme, strategy, system, project, proposal, tactics **3** = plot, ploy, ruse, intrigue, conspiracy, manoeuvre, subterfuge, stratagem ▸ *vb* = plot, plan, intrigue, manoeuvre, conspire, contrive, collude, machinate

scherzo (skairt-so) *n, pl* **-zos** a quick lively piece of music, often the second or third movement in a sonata or symphony
schism (skizz-um) *n* the division of a group, esp. a religious group, into opposing factions, due to differences in doctrine > **schismatic** *adj*

schist (shist) *n* a crystalline rock which splits into thin layers
schizoid *adj* **1** *psychol* having a personality disorder characterized by extreme shyness and extreme sensitivity **2** *informal* characterized by conflicting or contradictory ideas or attitudes ▸ *n* **3** *offensive* a person who has a schizoid personality
schizophrenia *n* **1** a psychotic disorder characterized by withdrawal from reality, hallucinations, or emotional instability **2** *informal* behaviour that seems to be motivated by contradictory or conflicting principles > **schizophrenic** *adj, n*
schmaltz *n* excessive sentimentality, esp. in music > **schmaltzy** *adj*
schnapps *n* a strong dry alcoholic drink distilled from potatoes
schnitzel *n* a thin slice of meat, esp. veal
scholar *n* **1** a person who studies an academic subject **2** a student who has a scholarship **3** a pupil > **scholarly** *adj*

scholar *n* **1** = intellectual, academic, savant, acca (*Austral slang*) **3** = student, pupil, learner, schoolboy *or* schoolgirl

scholarship *n* **1** academic achievement; learning gained by serious study **2** financial aid provided for a scholar because of academic merit

scholarship *n* **1** = learning, education, knowledge, erudition, book-learning **2** = grant, award, payment, endowment, fellowship, bursary

scholastic *adj* **1** of schools, scholars, or education **2** of or relating to scholasticism ▸ *n* **3** a scholarly person **4** a disciple or adherent of scholasticism
school¹ *n* **1** a place where children are educated **2** the staff and pupils of a school **3** a regular session of instruction in a school: *we stayed behind after school* **4** a faculty or department specializing in a particular subject: *the dental school* **5** a place or sphere of activity that instructs: *the school of hard knocks* **6** a group of artists, writers, or thinkers, linked by the same style, teachers, or methods **7** *informal* a group assembled for a common purpose, such as gambling: *a card school* ▸ *vb* **8** to educate or train: *she schooled herself to be as ambitious as her sister*

school *n* **1** = academy, college, institution, institute, seminary **6, 7** = group, set, circle, faction, followers, disciples, devotees, denomination ▸ *vb* = train, coach, discipline, educate, drill, tutor, instruct

school² *n* a group of sea-living animals that swim together, such as fish, whales, or dolphins
schoolchild *n* a child attending school
schoolie *n Austral informal* a schoolteacher or a high-school student

S

schoolies week *n Austral informal* a week of post-exam celebrations for students who have just completed their final year of high school

school run *n Brit* a journey to take children to school or to bring them home from school

schooner *n* **1** a sailing ship with at least two masts, one at the back and one at the front **2** a large glass for sherry **3** *US, Canad, Austral & NZ* a large glass for beer

sciatic *adj* **1** *anatomy* of the hip or the hipbone **2** of or having sciatica: *a sciatic injury*

sciatica *n* severe pain in the large nerve in the back of the leg

science *n* **1** the study of the nature and behaviour of the physical universe, based on observation, experiment, and measurement **2** the knowledge obtained by these methods **3** any particular branch of this knowledge: *medical science* **4** any body of knowledge organized in a way resembling that of the physical sciences but concerned with other subjects: *political science*

> **science** *n* **4** = discipline, body of knowledge, branch of knowledge

science fiction *n* stories and films that make imaginative use of scientific knowledge or theories

science park *n* an area where scientific research and commercial development are carried on in cooperation

scientific *adj* **1** relating to science or a particular science: *scientific discovery* **2** done in a systematic way, using experiments or tests > **scientifically** *adv*

> **scientific** *adj* **2** = systematic, accurate, exact, precise, controlled, mathematical

scientist *n* a person who studies or practises a science

> **scientist** *n* = researcher, inventor, boffin (*informal*), technophile

sci-fi *n* short for **science fiction**

scimitar *n* a curved Asian sword

scintillate *vb* **-lating, -lated** to give off (sparks); sparkle > **scintillation** *n*

scintillating *adj* (of conversation or humour) very lively and amusing

scion (**sy**-on) *n* **1** a descendant or young member of a family **2** a shoot of a plant for grafting onto another plant

scissors *pl n* a cutting instrument held in one hand, with two crossed blades pivoted so that they close together on what is to be cut

sclerosis (skleer-oh-siss) *n, pl* **-ses** (-seez) *pathol* an abnormal hardening or thickening of body tissues, esp. of the nervous system or the inner wall of arteries

scoff¹ *vb* **1** (often foll. by *at*) to speak in a scornful and mocking way about (something) ► *n* **2** a mocking expression; jeer > **scoffing** *adj, n*

> **scoff** *vb* = scorn, mock, laugh at, ridicule, knock (*informal*), despise, sneer, jeer

scoff² *vb informal* to eat (food) fast and greedily

> **scoff** *vb* = gobble (up), wolf, devour, bolt, guzzle, gulp down, gorge yourself on

scold *vb* **1** to find fault with or rebuke (a person) harshly **2** *old-fashioned* to use harsh or abusive language ► *n old-fashioned* **3** a person, esp. a woman, who constantly scolds > **scolding** *n*

sconce *n* a bracket fixed to a wall for holding candles or lights

scone (**skonn, skone**) *n* a small plain cake baked in an oven or on a griddle

scoop *n* **1** a spoonlike tool with a deep bowl, used for handling loose or soft materials such as flour or ice cream **2** the deep shovel of a mechanical digger **3** the amount taken up by a scoop **4** the act of scooping or dredging **5** a news story reported in one newspaper before all the others ► *vb* **6** (often foll. by *up*) to take up and remove (something) with or as if with a scoop **7 scoop out** to hollow out with or as if with a scoop **8** to beat (rival newspapers) in reporting a news item **9** to win (a prize, a large sum of money, etc.)

> **scoop** *n* **1** = ladle, spoon, dipper **5** = exclusive, exposé, revelation, sensation ► *vb* **6 scoop something or someone up** = gather up, lift, pick up, take up, sweep up *or* away **7 scoop something out** = dig, shovel, excavate, gouge, hollow out **9** = win, get, land (*informal*), gain, achieve, earn, secure, obtain

scoot *vb* to leave or move quickly

scooter *n* **1** a child's small cycle which is ridden by pushing the ground with one foot **2** a light motorcycle with a small engine

scope *n* **1** opportunity for using abilities: *ample scope for creative work* **2** range of view or grasp: *that is outside my scope* **3** the area covered by an activity or topic: *the scope of his essay was vast*

> **scope** *n* **1** = opportunity, room, freedom, space, liberty, latitude **2, 3** = range, capacity, reach, area, outlook, orbit, span, sphere

scorch *vb* **1** to burn or become burnt slightly on the surface **2** to parch or shrivel from heat **3** *informal* to criticize harshly ► *n* **4** a slight burn **5** a mark caused by the application of excessive heat > **scorching** *adj*

> **scorch** *vb* **1** = burn, sear, roast, wither, shrivel, parch, singe

scorcher *n informal* a very hot day

score *n* **1** the total number of points made by a side or individual in a game **2** the act of scoring a point or points: *there was no score and three minutes remained* **3 the score** *informal* the actual situation: *what's the score on this business?* **4** *old-fashioned* a group or set of twenty: *three score years and ten* **5 scores of** lots of: *we received scores of letters*

6 *music* a written version of a piece of music showing parts for each musician **7** ▲ the incidental music for a film or play **8** the songs and music for a stage or film musical **8** a mark or scratch **9** a record of money due: *what's the score for the drinks?* **10** an amount recorded as due **11** a reason: *some objections were made on the score of sentiment* **12** a grievance: *a score to settle* **13 over the score** *informal* excessive or unfair ▶ *vb* **scoring, scored 14** to gain (a point or points) in a game or contest **15** to make a total score of **16** to keep a record of the score (of) **17** to be worth (a certain number of points) in a game: *red aces score twenty* **18** to make cuts or lines in or on **19** *slang* to purchase an illegal drug **20** *slang* to succeed in finding a sexual partner **21** to arrange (a piece of music) for specific instruments or voices **22** to write the music for (a film or play) **23** to achieve (success or an advantage): *your idea scored with the boss*

> **score** *n* **1** = points, result, total, outcome **5** = lots, loads, many, millions, hundreds, masses, swarms, multitudes **6,7A** = composition, soundtrack, arrangement, orchestration **12** = grievance, wrong, injury, injustice, grudge ▶ *vb* **14, 15** = gain, win, achieve, make, get, attain, notch up (*informal*), chalk up (*informal*) **18** = cut, scratch, mark, slash, scrape, graze, gouge, deface **21, 22** = arrange, set, orchestrate, adapt

scorn *n* **1** open contempt for a person or thing ▶ *vb* **2** to treat with contempt: *she attacked the government for scorning her profession* **3** to refuse to have or do (something) because it is felt to be undesirable or wrong: *youths who scorn traditional morals* > **scornful** *adj* > **scornfully** *adv*

> **scorn** *n* = contempt, disdain, mockery, derision, sarcasm, disparagement; ≠ respect ▶ *vb* = despise, reject, disdain, slight, be above, spurn, deride, flout; ≠ respect

scorpion *n* a small lobster-shaped animal with a sting at the end of a jointed tail

Scot *n* a person from Scotland

scotch *vb* **1** to put an end to: *she had scotched the idea of bingo in the church* **2** to wound without killing

Scotch *n* whisky distilled in Scotland from fermented malted barley

Scotch broth *n Brit* a thick soup made from mutton or beef stock, vegetables, and pearl barley

scot-free *adv, adj* without harm or punishment: *the real crooks got off scot-free*

Scots *adj* **1** of Scotland ▶ *n* **2** any of the English dialects spoken or written in Scotland

Scotsman *or fem* **Scotswoman** *n, pl* **-men** *or* **-women** a person from Scotland

Scottish *adj* of Scotland

scoundrel *n old-fashioned* a person who cheats and deceives

scour¹ *vb* **1** to clean or polish (a surface) by rubbing with something rough **2** to clear (a channel) by the force of water ▶ *n* **3** the act of scouring > **scourer** *n*

> **scour** *vb* **1** = scrub, clean, polish, rub, buff, abrade

scour² *vb* **1** to search thoroughly and energetically: *he had scoured auction salerooms* **2** to move quickly over (land) in search or pursuit

> **scour** *vb* **1** = search, hunt, comb, ransack

scourge *n* **1** a person who or thing that causes affliction or suffering **2** a whip formerly used for punishing people ▶ *vb* **scourging, scourged 3** to cause severe suffering to **4** to whip

scout *n* **1** *military* a person sent to find out the position of the enemy **2** the act or an instance of scouting ▶ *vb* **3** to examine or observe (something) in order to obtain information **4 scout about** *or* **around** to go in search of something

> **scout** *n* **1** = vanguard, lookout, precursor, outrider, reconnoitrer, advance guard ▶ *vb* **3** = reconnoitre, investigate, watch, survey, observe, spy, probe, recce (*slang*)

Scout *or* **scout** *n* a member of the Scout Association, an organization for young people which aims to develop character and promote outdoor activities > **Scouting** *n*

scowl *vb* **1** to have an angry or bad-tempered facial expression ▶ *n* **2** an angry or bad-tempered facial expression

scrabble *vb* **-bling, -bled 1** to scrape at or grope for something with hands, feet, or claws: *scrabbling with his feet to find a foothold* **2** to move one's hands about in order to find something one cannot see: *scrabbling in her handbag for a comb*

scrag *n* **1** the thin end of a neck of veal or mutton **2** a thin or scrawny person or animal

scraggy *adj* **-gier, -giest** unpleasantly thin and bony > **scragginess** *n*

scram *vb* **scramming, scrammed** *informal* to leave very quickly

scramble *vb* **-bling, -bled 1** to climb or crawl hurriedly by using the hands to aid movement **2** to go hurriedly or in a disorderly manner **3** to compete with others in a rough and undignified way: *spectators scrambled for the best seats* **4** to jumble together in a haphazard manner **5** to cook (eggs that have been whisked up with milk) in a pan **6** *military* (of a crew or aircraft) to take off quickly in an emergency **7** to make (transmitted speech) unintelligible by the use of an electronic scrambler ▶ *n* **8** the act of scrambling **9** a climb or trek over difficult ground **10** a rough and undignified struggle to gain possession of something **11** *military* an immediate takeoff of crew or aircraft in an emergency **12** *Brit* a motorcycle race across rough open ground

S

scramble *vb* **1** = struggle, climb, crawl, swarm, scrabble **3** = strive, rush, contend, vie, run, push, jostle **4** = jumble, mix up, muddle, shuffle ▶ *n* **8, 9** = clamber, ascent **10** = race, competition, struggle, rush, confusion, commotion, melee *or* mêlée

scrambler *n* an electronic device that makes broadcast or telephone messages unintelligible without a special receiver

scrap[1] *n* **1** a small piece of something larger; fragment **2** waste material or used articles, often collected and reprocessed **3 scraps** pieces of leftover food ▶ *vb* **scrapping, scrapped** **4** to discard as useless

scrap *n* **1** = piece, fragment, bit, grain, particle, portion, part, crumb **2** = waste, junk, offcuts **3** = leftovers, remains, bits, leavings ▶ *vb* = get rid of, drop, abandon, ditch (*slang*), discard, write off, jettison, throw away *or* out; ≠ bring back

scrap[2] *informal* ▶ *n* **1** a fight or quarrel ▶ *vb* **scrapping, scrapped** **2** to quarrel or fight

scrap *n* = fight, battle, row, argument, dispute, disagreement, quarrel, squabble, biffo (*Austral slang*) ▶ *vb* = fight, argue, row, squabble, wrangle

scrapbook *n* a book of blank pages in which newspaper cuttings or pictures are stuck

scrape *vb* **scraping, scraped** **1** to move (a rough or sharp object) across (a surface) **2** (often foll. by *away* or *off*) to remove (a layer) by rubbing **3** to produce a grating sound by rubbing against (something else) **4** to injure or damage by scraping: *he had scraped his knees* **5 scrimp and scrape** See **scrimp** (sense 2) ▶ *n* **6** the act or sound of scraping **7** a scraped place: *a scrape on the car door* **8** *informal* an awkward or embarrassing situation **9** *informal* a conflict or struggle > **scraper** *n*

scrape *vb* **1** = rake, sweep, drag, brush **2** = clean, remove, scour **3** = grate, grind, scratch, squeak, rasp **4** = graze, skin, scratch, bark, scuff, rub ▶ *n* **8** = predicament, difficulty, fix (*informal*), mess, dilemma, plight, tight spot, awkward situation

scrape through *vb* to succeed in or survive with difficulty: *both teams had scraped through their semi-finals*

scrappy *adj* **-pier, -piest** badly organized or done: *a scrappy draft of a chapter of my thesis*

scratch *vb* **1** to mark or cut (the surface of something) with a rough or sharp instrument **2** (often foll. by *at* or *out* etc.) to tear or dig with the nails or claws **3** to scrape (the surface of the skin) with the nails to relieve itching **4** to rub against (the skin) causing a slight cut **5** to make or cause to make a grating sound **6** (sometimes foll. by *out*) to erase or cross out **7** to withdraw

from a race or (in the US) an election ▶ *n* **8** the act of scratching **9** a slight cut on a person's or an animal's body **10** a mark made by scratching **11** a slight grating sound **12 from scratch** *informal* from the very beginning **13 not up to scratch** *informal* not up to standard ▶ *adj* **14** put together at short notice: *a scratch team* **15** *sport* with no handicap allowed: *a scratch golfer* > **scratchy** *adj*

scratch *vb* **1** = mark, cut, score, damage, grate, graze, etch, lacerate **2** = rub, scrape, claw at ▶ *n* **10** = mark, scrape, graze, blemish, gash, laceration, claw mark **13 not up to scratch** = inadequate, unacceptable, unsatisfactory, insufficient, not up to standard

scratchcard *n* a ticket that reveals whether or not the holder is eligible for a prize when the surface is removed by scratching

scrawl *vb* **1** to write carelessly or hastily ▶ *n* **2** careless or scribbled writing > **scrawly** *adj*

scrawny *adj* **scrawnier, scrawniest** very thin and bony > **scrawniness** *n*

scream *vb* **1** to make a sharp piercing cry or sound because of fear or pain **2** (of a machine) to make a high-pitched noise **3** to laugh wildly **4** to utter with a scream: *he screamed abuse up into the sky* **5** to be unpleasantly conspicuous: *bad news screaming out from the headlines* ▶ *n* **6** a sharp piercing cry or sound, esp. of fear or pain **7** *informal* a very funny person or thing

scream *vb* **1** = cry, yell, shriek, screech, bawl, howl ▶ *n* **6** = cry, yell, howl, shriek, screech, yelp

scree *n* a pile of rock fragments at the foot of a cliff or hill, often forming a sloping heap

screech *n* **1** a shrill or high-pitched sound or cry ▶ *vb* **2** to utter a shrill cry > **screechy** *adj*

screed *n* a long tiresome speech or piece of writing

screen *n* **1** the blank surface of a television set, computer, or mobile phone, on which a visible image is formed **2** the white surface on which films or slides are projected **3 the screen** the film industry or films collectively **4** a light movable frame, panel, or partition used to shelter, divide, or conceal **5** anything that shelters, protects, or conceals: *a screen of leaves blocking out the sun* **6** a frame containing a mesh that is used to keep out insects ▶ *vb* **7** (sometimes foll. by *off*) to shelter, protect, or conceal with or as if with a screen **8** to test or check (an individual or group) so as to assess suitability for a task or to detect the presence of a disease or weapons: *women screened for breast cancer* **9** to show (a film) in the cinema or show (a programme) on television

screen *n* **4** = cover, guard, shade, shelter, shield, partition, cloak, canopy ▶ *vb* **7** = cover, hide, conceal, shade, mask, veil, cloak

8 = investigate, test, check, examine, scan
9 = broadcast, show, put on, present, air, cable, beam, transmit, stream

screen saver n software that produces changing images on a computer screen when the machine is operating but idle
screenshot n an image created by copying part or all of the display on a computer screen at a particular moment
screw n 1 a metal pin with a spiral ridge along its length, twisted into materials to fasten them together 2 a threaded cylindrical rod that engages with a similarly threaded cylindrical hole 3 a thread in a cylindrical hole corresponding with the one on the screw with which it is designed to engage 4 anything resembling a screw in shape 5 slang a prison guard 6 vulgar slang an act of or partner in sexual intercourse 7 **have a screw loose** informal **A** to be eccentric **B** offensive to be insane 8 **put the screws on** slang to use force on or threatening behaviour against ▸ vb 9 to rotate (a screw or bolt) so as to drive it into or draw it out of a material 10 to twist or turn: she screwed up the sheet of paper 11 to attach or fasten with or as if with a screw or screws 12 informal to take advantage of, esp. illegally: screwed by big business 13 informal to distort or contort: his face was screwed up in pain 14 (often foll. by out of) informal to force out of; extort 15 vulgar slang to have sexual intercourse (with) 16 **have one's head screwed on the right way** informal to be sensible ▸ See also **screw up**

> **screw** n 1 = nail, pin, tack, rivet, fastener, spike ▸ vb 10 = turn, twist, tighten 11 = fasten, fix, attach, bolt, clamp, rivet 12 = cheat, do (slang), rip (someone) off (slang), skin (slang), trick, con, sting (informal), fleece 14 = squeeze, wring, extract, wrest

screwdriver n 1 a tool used for turning screws, consisting of a long thin metal rod with a flattened tip that fits into a slot in the head of the screw 2 a drink consisting of orange juice and vodka
screw up vb 1 informal to mishandle or spoil (something): that screws up all my arrangements 2 to twist out of shape or distort 3 **screw up one's courage** to force oneself to be brave > **screwed-up** adj

> **screw up** vb 1 **screw something up** = bungle, botch, mess up, spoil, mishandle, make a mess of (slang), make a hash of (informal), crool or cruel (Austral slang) 2 **screw something up** = contort, wrinkle, distort, pucker

screwy adj screwier, screwiest informal crazy or eccentric
scribble vb -bling, -bled 1 to write or draw quickly and roughly 2 to make meaningless or illegible marks (on) ▸ n 3 something written or drawn quickly or roughly 4 meaningless or illegible marks > **scribbler** n > **scribbly** adj

> **scribble** vb 1 = scrawl, write, jot, dash off

scribe n 1 a person who made handwritten copies of manuscripts or documents before the invention of printing 2 Bible a recognized scholar and teacher of the Jewish Law
scrimmage n 1 a rough or disorderly struggle ▸ vb -maging, -maged 2 to take part in a scrimmage
scrimp vb 1 to be very sparing in the use of something: they were scrimping by on the last of the potatoes 2 **scrimp and save** or **scrape** to spend as little money as possible
scrip n finance a certificate representing a claim to shares or stocks
script n 1 the text of a play, TV programme, or film for the use of performers 2 an alphabet or system of writing: Cyrillic script 3 a candidate's answer paper in an examination 4 handwriting 5 a typeface which looks like handwriting ▸ vb 6 to write a script for

> **script** n 1 = text, lines, words, book, copy, dialogue, libretto 4 = handwriting, writing, calligraphy, penmanship (formal) ▸ vb = write, draft

scripture n the sacred writings of a religion > **scriptural** adj
scrofula n not in technical use tuberculosis of the lymphatic glands > **scrofulous** adj
scroggin n NZ a mixture of nuts and dried fruits
scroll n 1 a roll of parchment or paper, usually inscribed with writing 2 an ancient book in the form of a roll of parchment, papyrus, or paper 3 a decorative carving or moulding resembling a scroll ▸ vb 4 to move (text) on a computer or phone screen in order to view a section that cannot be fitted into a single display
scrotum n the pouch of skin containing the testicles in most male mammals
scrounge vb scrounging, scrounged informal to get (something) by asking for it rather than buying it or working for it > **scrounger** n
scrub¹ vb scrubbing, scrubbed 1 to rub (something) hard in order to clean it 2 to remove (dirt) by rubbing with a brush and water 3 **scrub up** (of a surgeon) to wash the hands and arms thoroughly before operating 4 informal to delete or cancel (an idea or plan) ▸ n 5 the act of scrubbing

> **scrub** vb 1 = scour, clean, polish, rub, wash, cleanse, buff, exfoliate 4 = cancel, drop, give up, abolish, forget about, call off, delete

scrub² n 1 vegetation consisting of stunted trees or bushes growing in a dry area 2 an area of dry land covered with such vegetation ▸ adj 3 stunted or inferior: scrub pines

S

scrubby *adj* **-bier, -biest 1** (of land) rough, dry, and covered with scrub **2** (of plants) stunted **3** *Brit informal* shabby or untidy

scruff¹ *n* the nape of the neck: *the sergeant had him by the scruff of the neck*

scruff² *n informal* a very untidy person

scruffy *adj* **scruffier, scruffiest** dirty and untidy in appearance

scrum *n* **1** *rugby* a formation in which players from each side form a tight pack and push against each other in an attempt to get the ball, which is thrown on the ground between them **2** *informal* a disorderly struggle ▸ *vb* **scrumming, scrummed 3** (usually foll. by *down*) *rugby* to form a scrum

scrummage *n*, *vb* **-maging, -maged 1** *rugby* same as **scrum 2** same as **scrimmage**

scrumptious *adj informal* delicious or very attractive

scrunch *vb* **1** to press or crush noisily or be pressed or crushed noisily ▸ *n* **2** the act or sound of scrunching: *the scrunch of tyres on gravel*

scruple *n* **1** a doubt or hesitation as to what is morally right in a certain situation: *he had no scruples about the drug trade* ▸ *vb* **-pling, -pled 2** to have doubts (about), esp. on moral grounds

scrupulous *adj* **1** taking great care to do what is fair, honest, or morally right **2** very careful or precise: *scrupulous attention to detail* ▸ **scrupulously** *adv*

scrutinize *or* **-nise** *vb* **-nizing, -nized** *or* **-nising, -nised** to examine carefully or in minute detail

scrutiny *n*, *pl* **-nies 1** very careful study or observation **2** a searching look

> **scrutiny** *n* **1** = examination, study, investigation, search, analysis, inspection, exploration, perusal

scuba (skew-ba) *n* an apparatus used in skin diving, consisting of cylinders containing compressed air attached to a breathing apparatus

scud *vb* **scudding, scudded 1** (esp. of clouds) to move along quickly **2** *naut* to run before a gale ▸ *n* **3** the act of scudding **4** spray, rain, or clouds driven by the wind

scuff *vb* **1** to drag (the feet) while walking **2** to scrape (one's shoes) by doing so ▸ *n* **3** a mark caused by scuffing **4** the act or sound of scuffing

scuffle *vb* **-fling, -fled 1** to fight in a disorderly manner ▸ *n* **2** a short disorganized fight **3** a scuffling sound

scull *n* **1** a single oar moved from side to side over the back of a boat **2** one of a pair of small oars, both of which are pulled by one oarsman **3** a racing boat rowed by one oarsman pulling two oars ▸ *vb* **4** to row (a boat) with a scull ▸ **sculler** *n*

scullery *n*, *pl* **-leries** *chiefly Brit* a small room where washing-up and other kitchen work is done

sculpt *vb* same as **sculpture**

sculptor *or fem* **sculptress** *n* a person who makes sculptures

sculpture *n* **1** the art of making figures or designs in wood, plaster, stone, or metal **2** works or a work made in this way ▸ *vb* **-turing, -tured 3** to carve (a material) into figures or designs **4** to represent (a person or thing) in sculpture **5** to form or be formed in the manner of sculpture: *limestone sculptured by fast-flowing streams* ▸ **sculptural** *adj*

> **sculpture** *n* **2** = statue, figure, model, bust, effigy, figurine, statuette ▸ *vb* **3, 5** = carve, form, model, fashion, shape, mould, sculpt, chisel

scum *n* **1** a layer of impure or waste matter that forms on the surface of a liquid: *the build-up of soap scum* **2** a person or people regarded as worthless or criminal ▸ *vb* **scumming, scummed 3** to remove scum from **4** *rare* to form a layer of or become covered with scum ▸ **scummy** *adj*

scungy (skun-jee) *adj* **scungier, scungiest** *Austral & NZ slang* miserable, sordid, or dirty

scupper *vb* **1** *Brit & NZ slang* to defeat or ruin: *a deliberate attempt to scupper the peace talks* **2** to sink (one's ship) deliberately

scurf *n* **1** same as **dandruff 2** any flaky or scaly matter sticking to or peeling off a surface ▸ **scurfy** *adj*

scurrilous *adj* untrue or unfair, insulting, and designed to damage a person's reputation: *scurrilous allegations* ▸ **scurrility** *n*

scurry *vb* **-ries, -rying, -ried 1** to run quickly with short steps ▸ *n*, *pl* **-ries 2** a quick hurrying movement or the sound of this movement **3** a short shower of rain or snow

scurvy *n* **1** a disease caused by a lack of vitamin C, resulting in weakness, spongy gums, and bleeding beneath the skin ▸ *adj* **-vier, -viest 2** *old-fashioned* deserving contempt ▸ **scurviness** *n*

scut *n* the short tail of animals such as the deer and rabbit

scuttle¹ *vb* **-tling, -tled 1** to run with short quick steps ▸ *n* **2** a hurried pace or run

scuttle² *vb* **-tling, -tled 1** *naut* to cause (a ship) to sink by making holes in the sides or bottom **2** to ruin (hopes or plans) or have them ruined: *a new policy scuttled by popular resistance* ▸ *n* **3** *naut* a small hatch in a ship's deck or side

scythe *n* **1** a long-handled tool for cutting grass or grain, with a curved sharpened blade that is swung parallel to the ground ▸ *vb* **scything, scythed 2** to cut (grass or grain) with a scythe

SE southeast(ern)

sea *n* **1 the sea** the mass of salt water that covers three-quarters of the earth's surface **2** **A** one of the smaller areas of this: *the Irish Sea* **B** a large inland area of water: *the Caspian Sea* **3** the area on or close to the edge of the sea, esp. as a place where holidays are taken: *a day by the sea* **4** strong and uneven swirling movement of waves: *rough seas* **5** anything resembling the sea in size or movement: *a sea of red and yellow flags* **6 at sea A** on the ocean **B** in a state of confusion or uncertainty **7 go to sea** to become a sailor **8 put out to sea** to start a sea voyage

> **sea** *n* **1** = ocean, the deep, the waves, main **5** = mass, army, host, crowd, mob, abundance, swarm, horde **6B at sea** = bewildered, lost, confused, puzzled, baffled, perplexed, mystified, flummoxed

sea anemone *n* a marine animal with a round body and rings of tentacles which trap food from the water

seaboard *n* land bordering on the sea

sea dog *n* an experienced or old sailor

seafaring *adj* **1** travelling by sea **2** working as a sailor ► *n* **3** the act of travelling by sea **4** the work of a sailor

seafood *n* edible saltwater fish or shellfish

seagull *n* same as **gull**

sea horse *n* a small marine fish with a horselike head, which swims upright

seal¹ *n* **1** a special design impressed on a piece of wax, lead, or paper, fixed to a letter or document as a mark of authentication **2** a stamp or signet ring engraved with a design to form such an impression **3** a substance placed over an envelope or container, so that it cannot be opened without the seal being broken **4** something that serves as an official confirmation of approval: *seal of approval* **5** any substance or device used to close an opening tightly **6 set the seal on** to confirm: *the experience set the seal on their friendship* ► *vb* **7** to close or secure with or as if with a seal: *once the manuscripts were sealed up, they were forgotten about* **8 seal off** to enclose or isolate (a place) completely **9** to close tightly so as to make airtight or watertight **10** to inject a compound around the edges of (something) to make it airtight or watertight **11** to attach a seal to or stamp with a seal **12** to finalize or authorize **13 seal one's fate** to make sure one dies or fails **14 seal one's lips** to promise not to reveal a secret > **sealable** *adj*

> **seal** *n* **4** = authentication, stamp, confirmation, ratification, insignia, imprimatur **5** = sealant, sealer, adhesive ► *vb* **12** = settle, clinch, conclude, consummate, finalize

seal² *n* **1** a fish-eating mammal with four flippers, which lives in the sea but comes ashore to breed **2** sealskin ► *vb* **3** to hunt seals

sealant *n* any substance, such as wax, used for sealing, esp. to make airtight or watertight

sea level *n* the average level of the sea's surface in relation to the land

sea lion *n* a type of large seal found in the Pacific Ocean

sealskin *n* the skin or prepared fur of a seal, used to make coats

seam *n* **1** the line along which pieces of fabric are joined by stitching **2** a ridge or line made by joining two edges: *the seam between the old and the new buildings* **3** a long narrow layer of coal, marble, or ore formed between layers of other rocks **4** a mark or line like a seam, such as a wrinkle or scar ► *adj* **5** *cricket* of a style of bowling in which the bowler uses the stitched seam round the ball in order to make it swing in flight and after touching the ground: *a seam bowler* ► *vb* **6** to join together by or as if by a seam **7** to mark with furrows or wrinkles

> **seam** *n* **2** = joint, closure **3** = layer, vein, stratum, lode

seaman *n*, *pl* **-men 1** a man ranking below an officer in a navy **2** a sailor

seamless *adj* **1** (of a garment) without seams **2** continuous or flowing: *a seamless performance* > **seamlessly** *adv* > **seamlessness** *n*

seamstress *n* a woman who sews, esp. professionally

seamy *adj* **seamier**, **seamiest** involving the sordid and unpleasant aspects of life, such as crime, prostitution, poverty, and violence > **seaminess** *n*

seance *or* **séance** (say-onss) *n* a meeting at which a spiritualist attempts to communicate with the spirits of the dead

seaplane *n* an aircraft with skis or floats, designed to land on and take off from water

sear *vb* **1** to scorch or burn the surface of **2** to cause to wither

> **sear** *vb* **2** = wither, burn, scorch, sizzle

search *vb* **1** to look through (a place) thoroughly in order to find someone or something **2** to examine (a person) for hidden objects **3** to look at or examine (something) closely: *I searched my heart for one good thing she had done* **4 search out** to find by searching **5** to make a search **6 search me** *informal* I don't know ► *n* **7** an attempt to find something by looking somewhere

> **search** *vb* **1** = examine, investigate, explore, inspect, comb, scour, ransack, scrutinize, fossick (*Austral, NZ*) ► *n* = hunt, look, investigation, examination, pursuit, quest, inspection, exploration, Google (*computers*), googlewhack (*computers informal*)

search engine *n* a service that enables users to search the internet for items of interest

searching *adj* keen or thorough: *a searching analysis* > **searchingly** *adv*

> **searching** *adj* = keen, sharp, probing, close, intent, piercing, penetrating, quizzical; ≠ superficial

searchlight *n* **1** a light with a powerful beam that can be shone in any direction **2** the beam of light produced by this device

searing adj **1** (of pain) very sharp **2** highly critical: *a searing satire of foreign policy*

seasick adj suffering from nausea and dizziness caused by the movement of a ship at sea ▷ **seasickness** n

seaside n an area, esp. a holiday resort, bordering on the sea

season n **1** one of the four divisions of the year (spring, summer, autumn, and winter), each of which has characteristic weather conditions **2** a period of the year characterized by particular conditions or activities: *the typhoon season*; *the football season* **3** the period during which any particular species of animal, bird, or fish is legally permitted to be caught or killed: *the deer season* **4** any definite or indefinite period: *the busy season* **5** any period during which a show or play is performed at one venue: *the show ran for three seasons* **6** **in season** **A** (of game) permitted to be killed **B** (of fresh food) readily available **C** (of animals) ready to mate ▶ vb **7** to add herbs, salt, pepper, or spice to (food) in order to enhance the flavour **8** (in the preparation of timber) to dry and harden **9** to make experienced: *old men seasoned by living* ▷ **seasoned** adj

> **season** n **2, 4** = period, time, term, spell ▶ vb **7** = flavour, salt, spice, enliven, pep up

seasonable adj **1** suitable for the season: *a seasonable Christmas snow scene* **2** coming or happening just at the right time: *seasonable advice*

seasonal adj of or depending on a certain season or seasons of the year: *seasonal employment* ▷ **seasonally** adv

seasoning n something that is added to food to enhance the flavour

> **seasoning** n = flavouring, spice, salt and pepper, condiment

season ticket n a ticket for a series of events or number of journeys, usually bought at a reduced rate

seat n **1** a piece of furniture designed for sitting on, such as a chair **2** the part of a chair or other piece of furniture on which one sits **3** a place to sit in a theatre, esp. one that requires a ticket: *there were two empty front-row seats at the pageant* **4** the part of a garment covering the buttocks **5** the part or surface on which an object rests **7** the place or centre in which something is based: *the seat of government* **8** Brit a country mansion **9** a membership or the right to membership of a legislative or administrative body: *a seat on the council* **10** chiefly Brit a parliamentary constituency **11** the manner in which a rider sits on a horse ▶ vb **12** to bring to or place on a seat **13** to provide seats for: *the dining hall seats 150 people* **14** to set firmly in place

> **seat** n **1** = chair, bench, stall, stool, pew, settle **7** = centre, place, site, heart, capital, situation, source, hub **8** = mansion, house, residence,

abode, ancestral hall **9** = membership, place, constituency, chair, incumbency ▶ vb **12** = sit, place, settle, set, fix, locate, install **13** = hold, take, accommodate, sit, contain, cater for

seat belt n a strap attached to a car or aircraft seat, worn across the body to prevent a person being thrown forward in the event of a collision

sea urchin n a small sea animal with a round body enclosed in a spiny shell

seaweed n any plant growing in the sea or on the seashore

seaworthy adj (of a ship) in a fit condition for a sea voyage ▷ **seaworthiness** n

sebaceous adj of, like, or secreting fat

secateurs pl n a small pair of gardening shears for pruning

secede vb **-ceding, -ceded** to make a formal withdrawal of membership from a political alliance, federation, or group: *it will secede from the federation within six months*

secession n the act of seceding ▷ **secessionism** n ▷ **secessionist** n, adj

seclude vb **-cluding, -cluded 1** to remove from contact with others **2** to shut off or screen from view

secluded adj **1** kept apart from the company of others: *a secluded private life* **2** private and sheltered: *a secluded cottage*

seclusion n the state of being secluded; privacy: *the seclusion of his winter retreat*

second¹ adj **1** coming directly after the first in order **2** rated, graded, or ranked between the first and third levels **3** alternate: *every second Saturday* **4** another of the same kind; additional: *a second chance* **5** resembling or comparable to a person or event from the past: *a second Virgin Mary* **6** of lesser importance or position; inferior **7** denoting the second lowest forward gear in a motor vehicle **8** *music* denoting a musical part, voice, or instrument subordinate to or lower in pitch than another (the first): *the second tenors* **9** **at second hand** by hearsay ▶ n **10** a person or thing that is second **11** Brit *education* an honours degree of the second class **12** the second lowest forward gear in a motor vehicle **13** (in boxing or duelling) an attendant who looks after a boxer or duellist **14** **seconds** **A** *informal* a second helping of food or the second course of a meal **B** goods that are sold cheaply because they are slightly faulty ▶ vb **15** to give aid or backing to **16** (in boxing or duelling) to act as second to (a boxer or duellist) **17** to express formal support for (a motion proposed in a meeting) ▶ adv **18** Also: **secondly** in the second place

> **second** adj **1** = next, following, succeeding, subsequent, sophomore (US, Canad) **4** = additional, other, further, extra, alternative **6** = inferior, secondary, subordinate, lower, lesser ▶ n **13** = supporter, assistant, aide, colleague, backer, helper, right-hand man *or* woman *or* person ▶ vb

15 = support, back, endorse, approve, go along with ► *adv* = next, second, moreover, furthermore, also, in the second place

second² *n* **1** the basic SI unit of time, equal to $\frac{1}{60}$ of a minute **2** $\frac{1}{60}$ of a minute of angle **3** a very short period of time

> **second** *n* **3** = moment, minute, instant, flash, sec (*informal*), jiffy (*informal*), trice

second³ (sik-kond) *vb Brit & NZ* to transfer (a person) temporarily to another job
> **secondment** *n*

secondary *adj* **1** below the first in rank or importance: *a secondary consideration* **2** coming next after the first: *secondary cancers* **3** derived from or depending on what is primary or first: *a secondary source* **4** of or relating to the education of people between the ages of 11 and 18 or, in New Zealand, between 13 and 18: *secondary education* **5** (of an industry) involving the manufacture of goods from raw materials ► *n, pl* **-aries** **6** a person or thing that is secondary

> **secondary** *adj* **1** = subordinate, minor, lesser, lower, inferior, unimportant; ≠ main **2** = resultant, contingent, derived, indirect; ≠ original

second-hand *adj* **1** previously owned or used **2** not from an original source or one's own experience: *second-hand opinions* **3** dealing in or selling goods that are not new: *second-hand furniture shops* ► *adv* **4** from a source of previously owned or used goods: *they preferred to buy second-hand* **5** not directly or from one's own experience: *his knowledge had been gleaned second-hand*

> **second-hand** *adj* **1** = used, old, hand-me-down (*informal*), nearly new, preloved (*informal*)

secondly *adv* same as **second¹** (sense 18)
second nature *n* a habit or characteristic practised for so long that it seems to be part of one's character
second sight *n* the supposed ability to foresee the future or see actions taking place elsewhere
second thoughts *pl n* a revised opinion or idea on a matter already considered
second wind *n* **1** the return of comfortable breathing following difficult or strenuous exercise **2** renewed ability to continue in an effort
secrecy *n, pl* **-cies** **1** the state of being secret **2** the ability or tendency to keep things secret

> **secrecy** *n* **1** = confidentiality, privacy **2** = mystery, stealth, concealment, furtiveness, secretiveness, clandestineness, covertness

secret *adj* **1** kept hidden or separate from the knowledge of all or all but a few others **2** secretive: *she had become a secret drinker* **3** operating without the knowledge of outsiders:

secret organizations ► *n* **4** something kept or to be kept hidden **5** something unrevealed; a mystery: *the secrets of nature* **6** an underlying explanation or reason: *the secret of great-looking hair* **7 in secret** without the knowledge of others
> **secretly** *adv*

> **secret** *adj* **1** = undisclosed, unknown, confidential, underground, undercover, unrevealed; ≠ unconcealed **2** = secretive, reserved, close; ≠ frank **3** = undercover, furtive; ≠ open ► *n* **4** = private affair **7 in secret** = secretly, surreptitiously, slyly

secretariat *n* **1 A** an office responsible for the secretarial, clerical, and administrative affairs of a legislative body or international organization **B** the staff of such an office or department **2** the premises of a secretariat
secretary *n, pl* **-taries** **1** a person who handles correspondence, keeps records, and does general clerical work for an individual or organization **2** the official manager of the day-to-day business of a society, club, or committee **3** (in Britain) a senior civil servant who assists a government minister **4** (in the US) the head of a government administrative department
> **secretarial** *adj*
secrete¹ *vb* **-creting, -creted** (of a cell, organ, or gland) to produce and release (a substance)
> **secretory** (sik-reet-or-ee) *adj*
secrete² *vb* **-creting, -creted** to put in a hiding place
secretion *n* **1** a substance that is released from a cell, organ, or gland **2** the process involved in producing and releasing such a substance
secretive *adj* hiding feelings and intentions
> **secretively** *adv*

> **secretive** *adj* = reticent, reserved, close, deep, uncommunicative, tight-lipped; ≠ open

sect *n* **1** a subdivision of a larger religious or political group, esp. one regarded as extreme in its beliefs or practices **2** a group of people with a common interest or philosophy

> **sect** *n* = group, division, faction, party, camp, denomination, schism

sectarian *adj* **1** of or belonging to a sect **2** narrow-minded as a result of supporting a particular sect ► *n* **3** a member of a sect
> **sectarianism** *n*
section *n* **1** a part cut off or separated from the main body of something: *a non-smoking section* **2** a part or subdivision of a piece of writing or a book: *the business section* **3** a distinct part of a country or community: *the Arabic section* **4** *surgery* the act or process of cutting or separating by cutting **5** *geom* a plane surface formed by cutting through a solid **6** short for **Caesarean section** **7** *NZ* a plot of land for building on **8** *Austral & NZ* a fare stage on a bus ► *vb* **9** to cut or divide into sections **10** to commit (a person)

S

to a psychiatric hospital under an appropriate section of mental health legislation

section n 1 = part, piece, portion, division, slice, passage, segment, fraction 3 = district, area, region, sector, zone

sectional adj 1 concerned with a particular area or group within a country or community, esp. to the exclusion of others: *narrow sectional interests* 2 made of sections 3 of a section

sector n 1 a part or subdivision, esp. of a society or an economy: *the public sector* 2 *geom* either portion of a circle bounded by two radii and the arc cut off by them 3 a portion into which an area is divided for military operations

sector n 1 = part, division 3 = area, part, region, district, zone, quarter

secular adj 1 relating to worldly as opposed to sacred things 2 not connected with religion or the church 3 (of clerics) not bound by religious vows to a monastic or other order

secular adj 1, 2 = worldly, lay, earthly, civil, temporal, nonspiritual; ≠ religious

secure adj 1 free from danger or damage 2 free from fear, doubt, or care 3 tightly locked or well protected 4 fixed or tied firmly in position 5 able to be relied on: *secure profits* ▸ vb **-curing**, **-cured** 6 to obtain: *to secure a change in German policy* 7 to make or become free from danger or fear 8 to make safe from loss, theft, or attack 9 to attach; make fast or firm 10 to guarantee (payment of a loan) by giving something as security > **securely** adv

secure adj 1 = safe, protected, immune, unassailable; ≠ unprotected 2 = confident, sure, easy, certain, assured, reassured; ≠ uneasy 4 = fast, firm, fixed, stable, steady, fastened, immovable; ≠ insecure ▸ vb 6 = obtain, get, acquire, score (*slang*), gain, procure; ≠ lose 9 = attach, stick, fix, bind, fasten; ≠ detach

security n, pl **-ties** 1 precautions taken to ensure against theft, espionage, or other danger 2 the state of being free from danger, damage, or worry 3 assured freedom from poverty: *the security of a weekly pay cheque* 4 a certificate of ownership, such as a share, stock, or bond 5 something given or pledged to guarantee payment of a loan

security n 1 = precautions, defence, safeguards, protection, safety measures 2 = assurance, confidence, conviction, certainty, reliance, sureness, positiveness; ≠ insecurity 5 = pledge, insurance, guarantee, hostage, collateral, pawn, gage, surety

sedan n US, Canad, Austral & NZ a saloon car
sedan chair n an enclosed chair for one passenger, carried on poles by two bearers,

commonly used in the 17th and 18th centuries
sedate[1] adj 1 quiet, calm, and dignified 2 slow or unhurried: *a sedate walk to the beach* > **sedately** adv
sedate[2] vb **-dating**, **-dated** to calm down or make sleepy by giving a sedative drug to
sedation n 1 a state of calm, esp. when brought about by sedatives 2 the administration of a sedative
sedative adj 1 having a soothing or calming effect ▸ n 2 *med* a sedative drug or agent that makes people sleep or calm down
sedentary (sed-en-tree) adj 1 done sitting down and involving very little exercise: *a sedentary job* 2 tending to sit about without taking much exercise
sedge n a coarse grasslike plant growing on wet ground > **sedgy** adj
sediment n 1 matter that settles to the bottom of a liquid 2 material that has been deposited by water, ice, or wind > **sedimentary** adj

sediment n 1 = dregs, grounds, residue, lees, deposit

sedition n speech, writing, or behaviour intended to encourage rebellion or resistance against the government > **seditionary** n, adj > **seditious** adj
seduce vb **-ducing**, **-duced** 1 to persuade to have sexual intercourse 2 to tempt into wrongdoing > **seduction** n

seduce vb 1 = corrupt, deprave, dishonour, debauch, deflower 2 = tempt, lure, entice, mislead, deceive, beguile, lead astray, inveigle

seductive adj 1 (of a person) sexually attractive 2 very attractive or tempting: *a seductive argument* > **seductively** adv > **seductiveness** n

seductive adj 1 = tempting, inviting, attractive, enticing, provocative, alluring, bewitching, hot (*informal*)

sedulous adj formal diligent or painstaking: *a sedulous concern with the achievements of western thought* > **sedulously** adv
see[1] vb **seeing, saw, seen** 1 to look at or recognize with the eyes 2 to understand: *I explained the problem but he could not see it* 3 to perceive or be aware of: *she had never seen him so angry* 4 to view, watch, or attend: *we had barely seen a dozen movies in our lives* 5 to foresee: *they could see what their fate was to be* 6 to find out (a fact): *I was ringing to see whether you'd got it* 7 to make sure (of something) or take care (of something): *see that he is never in a position to do these things again; you must see to it* 8 to consider or decide: *see if you can come next week* 9 to have experience of: *he had seen active service in the revolution* 10 to meet or pay a visit to: *I see my specialist every three months* 11 to receive: *the Prime Minister will see the deputation now* 12 to frequent the company of: *we've been seeing each other since then* 13 to accompany: *she saw him to the door*

14 to refer to or look up: see page 35 **15** (in gambling, esp. in poker) to match (another player's bet) or match the bet of (another player) by staking an equal sum **16 see fit** to consider it proper (to do something): *I did not see fit to send them home* **17 see you** or **see you later** or **be seeing you** an expression of farewell

> **see** *vb* **1** = perceive, spot, notice, sight, witness, observe, distinguish, glimpse **2** = understand, get, follow, realize, appreciate, grasp, comprehend, fathom **6** = find out, learn, discover, determine, verify, ascertain **7** = make sure, ensure, guarantee, make certain, see to it **8** = consider, decide, reflect, deliberate, think over **10** = meet, come across, happen on, bump into, run across, chance on **11** = speak to, receive, interview, consult, confer with **12** = go out with, court (*old-fashioned*), date (*informal*), go steady with (*informal, old-fashioned*), step out with (*old-fashioned*) **13** = accompany, show, escort, lead, walk, usher

see² *n* the diocese of a bishop or the place within it where his or her cathedral is situated

seed *n* **1** *botany* the mature fertilized grain of a plant, containing an embryo ready for germination. Related adjective: **seminal 2** such seeds used for sowing **3** the source, beginning, or origin of anything: *the seeds of dissent* **4** *chiefly Bible* descendants; offspring: *the seed of David* **5** *sport* a player ranked according to his or her ability **6 go** or **run to seed A** (of plants) to produce and shed seeds after flowering **B** to lose strength or usefulness ▸ *vb* **7** to plant (seeds) in (soil) **8** (of plants) to produce or shed seeds **9** to remove the seeds from (fruit or plants) **10** to scatter silver iodide in (clouds) in order to cause rain **11** to arrange (the draw of a tournament) so that outstanding teams or players will not meet in the early rounds ▸ **seedless** *adj*

> **seed** *n* **1** = grain, pip, germ, kernel, egg, embryo, spore, ovum **3** = beginning, start, germ **4** = offspring, children, descendants, issue, progeny (*old-fashioned*) **6B go** or **run to seed** = decline, deteriorate, degenerate, decay, go downhill (*informal*), let yourself go, go to pot

seedling *n* a plant produced from a seed, esp. a very young plant

seedy *adj* **seedier, seediest 1** shabby in appearance: *a seedy cinema* **2** *informal* physically unwell **3** (of a plant) at the stage of producing seeds ▸ **seediness** *n*

seeing *n* **1** the sense or faculty of sight ▸ *conj* **2** (often foll. by *that* or *as*) in light of the fact (that)

> **seeing** *conj* **seeing as** = since, as, in view of the fact that, inasmuch as

seek *vb* **seeking, sought 1** to try to find by searching: *to seek employment* **2** to try to obtain: *to seek a diplomatic solution* **3** to try (to do something): *we seek to establish a stable relationship*

> **seek** *vb* **1** = look for, pursue, search for, be after, hunt **3** = try, attempt, aim, strive, endeavour, essay (*formal*), aspire to

seem *vb* **1** to appear to the mind or eye; give the impression of: *the car seems to be running well* **2** to appear to be: *there seems no need for all this nonsense* **3** to have the impression: *I seem to remember you were there too*

> **seem** *vb* **1, 2** = appear, give the impression of being, look

seeming *adj* apparent but not real: *his seeming willingness to participate* ▸ **seemingly** *adv*

seemly *adj* **-lier, -liest** *formal* proper or fitting

seen *vb* the past participle of **see¹**

seep *vb* to leak through slowly; ooze ▸ **seepage** *n*

> **seep** *vb* = ooze, well, leak, soak, trickle, exude, permeate

seer *n* a person who can supposedly see into the future

seersucker *n* a light cotton fabric with a slightly crinkled surface

seesaw *n* **1** a plank balanced in the middle so that two people seated on the ends can ride up and down by pushing on the ground with their feet **2** an up-and-down or back-and-forth movement ▸ *vb* **3** to move up and down or back and forth alternately

seethe *vb* **seething, seethed 1** to be in a state of extreme anger or indignation without publicly showing these feelings **2** (of a liquid) to boil or foam ▸ **seething** *adj*

> **seethe** *vb* **1** = be furious, rage, fume, simmer, see red (*informal*), be livid, go ballistic (*slang*) **2** = boil, bubble, foam, fizz, froth

segment *n* **1** one of several parts or sections into which an object is divided **2** *maths* **A** a part of a circle cut off by an intersecting line **B** a part of a sphere cut off by an intersecting plane or planes ▸ *vb* **3** to cut or divide into segments ▸ **segmental** *adj* ▸ **segmentation** *n*

> **segment** *n* **1** = section, part, piece, division, slice, portion, wedge

segregate *vb* **-gating, -gated 1** to set apart from others or from the main group **2** to impose segregation on (a racial or minority group)

> **segregate** *vb* = set apart, divide, separate, isolate, discriminate against, dissociate; ≠ unite

segregation *n* **1** the practice or policy of creating separate facilities within the same society for the use of a racial or minority group **2** the act of segregating ▸ **segregational** *adj* ▸ **segregationist** *n*

> **segregation** *n* = separation, discrimination, apartheid, isolation

S

seine (sane) *n* **1** a large fishing net that hangs vertically in the water by means of floats at the top and weights at the bottom ▸ *vb* **seining**, **seined 2** to catch (fish) using this net

seismic *adj* relating to or caused by earthquakes

seismograph *n* an instrument that records the intensity and duration of earthquakes ›**seismographer** *n* ›**seismography** *n*

seismology *n* the branch of geology concerned with the study of earthquakes ›**seismologist** *n*

seize *vb* **seizing, seized 1** to take hold of forcibly or quickly; grab **2** to take immediate advantage of: *real journalists would have seized the opportunity* **3** to take legal possession of **4** (sometimes foll. by *on* or *upon*) to understand quickly: *she immediately seized his idea* **5** to affect or fill the mind of suddenly: *a wild frenzy seized her* **6** to take by force or capture: *the rebels seized a tank factory* **7** (often foll. by *up*) (of mechanical parts) to become jammed through overheating

> **seize** *vb* **1** = grab, grip, grasp, take, snatch, clutch, snap up, pluck; ≠ let go **6** = take by storm, take over, acquire, occupy, conquer; ≠ release

seizure *n* **1** *pathol* a sudden violent attack of an illness, such as an epileptic convulsion **2** the act of seizing: *a seizure of drug traffickers' assets*

> **seizure** *n* **1** = attack, fit, spasm, convulsion, paroxysm **2** = taking, grabbing, annexation, confiscation, commandeering

seldom *adv* rarely; not often

> **seldom** *adv* = rarely, not often, infrequently, hardly ever; ≠ often

select *vb* **1** to choose (someone or something) in preference to another or others ▸ *adj* **2** chosen in preference to others **3** restricted to a particular group; exclusive: *a select audience* ›**selector** *n*

> **select** *vb* = choose, take, pick, opt for, decide on, adopt, settle upon; ≠ reject ▸ *adj* **2** = choice, special, excellent, superior, first-class, hand-picked, top-notch (*informal*); ≠ ordinary **3** = exclusive, elite, privileged, cliquish; ≠ indiscriminate

selection *n* **1** a selecting or being selected **2** a thing or number of things that have been selected **3** a range from which something may be selected: *a good selection of reasonably priced wines* **4** *biol* the process by which certain organisms or individuals are reproduced and survive in preference to others

> **selection** *n* **1** = choice, choosing, pick, option, preference **2** = anthology, collection, medley, choice

selective *adj* **1** tending to choose carefully or characterized by careful choice: *they were selective in their reading* **2** of or characterized by selection ›**selectively** *adv* ›**selectivity** *n*

> **selective** *adj* **1** = particular, discriminating, careful, discerning, tasteful, fastidious; ≠ indiscriminate

selenium *n* *chem* a nonmetallic element used in photocells, solar cells, and in xerography. Symbol: **Se**

self *n, pl* **selves 1** the distinct individuality or identity of a person or thing **2** a person's typical bodily make-up or personal characteristics: *back to my old self after the scare* **3** one's own welfare or interests: *he only thinks of self* **4** an individual's consciousness of his or her own identity or being ▸ *pron* **5** *not standard* myself, yourself, himself, or herself: *setting goals for self and others*

self- *combining form* **1** (used with many main words to mean) of oneself or itself: *self-defence* **2** (used with many main words to mean) by, to, in, due to, for, or from the self: *self-employed*; *self-respect* **3** (used with many main words to mean) automatic or automatically: *self-propelled*

self-catering *adj* (of accommodation) for tenants providing and preparing their own food

self-coloured *or US* **self-colored** *adj* **1** having only a single and uniform colour: *a self-coloured tie* **2** (of cloth or wool) having the natural or original colour

self-conscious *adj* embarrassed or ill at ease through being unduly aware of oneself as the object of the attention of others ›**self-consciously** *adv* ›**self-consciousness** *n*

self-contained *adj* **1** containing within itself all parts necessary for completeness **2** (of a flat) having its own kitchen, bathroom, and toilet not shared by others

self-determination *n* **1** the ability to make a decision for oneself without influence from outside **2** the right of a nation or people to determine its own form of government ›**self-determined** *adj*

self-evident *adj* so obvious that no proof or explanation is needed ›**self-evidently** *adv*

self-harm *n* the practice of deliberately wounding oneself

self-help *n* **1** the use of one's own abilities and resources to help oneself without relying on the assistance of others **2** the practice of solving one's problems within a group of people with similar problems

selfie *n* *informal* a photograph taken by pointing the camera at oneself

selfie stick *n* *informal* a rod on which a camera or mobile phone may be mounted in order to take a photograph of oneself

self-interest *n* **1** one's personal interest or advantage **2** the pursuit of one's own interest ›**self-interested** *adj*

selfish *adj* **1** caring too much about oneself and not enough about others **2** (of behaviour or attitude) motivated by self-interest ›**selfishly** *adv* ›**selfishness** *n*

selfish *adj* = self-centred, self-interested, greedy, ungenerous, egoistic *or* egoistical, egotistic *or* egotistical; ≠ unselfish

selfless *adj* putting other people's interests before one's own > **selflessly** *adv* > **selflessness** *n*

self-made *adj* having achieved wealth or status by one's own efforts

self-possessed *adj* having control of one's emotions or behaviour, esp. in difficult situations > **self-possession** *n*

self-raising *adj* (of flour) having a raising agent, such as baking powder, already added

self-righteous *adj* thinking oneself more virtuous than others > **self-righteousness** *n*

selfsame *adj* the very same: *this was the selfsame woman I'd met on the train*

self-seeking *n* 1 the act or an instance of seeking one's own profit or interests ▸ *adj* 2 inclined to promote only one's own profit or interests: *self-seeking politicians* > **self-seeker** *n*

self-service *adj* 1 of or denoting a shop or restaurant where the customers serve themselves and then pay a cashier ▸ *n* 2 the practice of serving oneself and then paying a cashier

self-styled *adj* using a title or name that one has given oneself, esp. without right or justification; so-called: *the self-styled leader of the rebellion*

self-sufficient *adj* able to provide for or support oneself without the help of others > **self-sufficiency** *n*

self-willed *adj* stubbornly determined to have one's own way, esp. at the expense of others

sell *vb* **selling, sold** 1 to exchange (something) for money 2 to deal in (objects or property): *he sells used cars* 3 to give up or surrender for a price or reward: *to sell one's honour* 4 **sell for** to have a specified price: *they sell for 10 pence each* 5 to promote the sale of (objects or property): *sporting success sells newspapers* 6 to gain acceptance of: *he'll sell an idea to a producer* 7 to be in demand on the market: *his books did not sell well enough* 8 **sell down the river** *informal* to betray 9 **sell oneself** **A** to convince someone else of one's potential or worth **B** to give up one's moral standards for a price or reward 10 **sell someone short** *informal* to undervalue someone ▸ *n* 11 the act or an instance of selling: *the hard sell* ▸ See also **sell out** > **seller** *n*

sell *vb* 1 = trade, exchange, barter; ≠ buy 2 = deal in, market, trade in, stock, handle, retail, peddle, traffic in; ≠ buy

sell-by date *n* 1 *Brit* the date printed on packaged food specifying the date after which the food should not be sold 2 **past one's sell-by date** beyond one's prime

Sellotape *n* 1 *trademark* a type of transparent adhesive tape ▸ *vb* **-taping, -taped** 2 to seal or stick using adhesive tape

sell out *vb* 1 **A** to dispose of (something) completely by selling **B** (of items for sale) to be bought up completely: *these tickets will sell out in minutes* 2 *informal* to abandon one's principles, standards, etc. 3 *informal* to betray in order to gain an advantage or benefit ▸ *n* **sellout** 4 *informal* a performance of a show, etc. for which all tickets are sold 5 a commercial success 6 *informal* a betrayal

sell out *vb* 1**A** **sell out of something** = run out of, be out of stock of

selvage *or* **selvedge** *n* a specially woven edge on a length of fabric to prevent it from unravelling > **selvaged** *adj*

selves *n* the plural of **self**

semantic *adj* 1 of or relating to the meanings of words 2 of or relating to semantics

semantics *n* the branch of linguistics that deals with the study of meaning

semaphore *n* 1 a system of signalling by holding two flags in different positions to represent letters of the alphabet ▸ *vb* **-phoring, -phored** 2 to signal (information) by semaphore

semblance *n* outward or superficial appearance: *some semblance of order had been established*

semen *n* the thick whitish fluid containing spermatozoa that is produced by the male reproductive organs and ejaculated from the penis

semester *n* either of two divisions of the academic year

semi *n Brit, Austral & S African informal* short for **semidetached** (sense 2)

semi- *prefix* 1 half: *semicircle* 2 partly or almost: *semiprofessional* 3 occurring twice in a specified period: *semiweekly*

semibreve *n music* a note, now the longest in common use, with a time value that may be divided by any power of 2 to give all other notes

semicolon *n* the punctuation mark (;) used to separate clauses or items in a list, or to indicate a pause longer than that of a comma and shorter than that of a full stop

semiconductor *n physics* a substance, such as silicon, which has an electrical conductivity that increases with temperature

semidetached *adj* 1 (of a house) joined to another house on one side by a common wall ▸ *n* 2 *Brit* a semidetached house: *the mock Georgian semidetached*

semi-final *n* the round before the final in a competition > **semi-finalist** *n*

seminal *adj* 1 highly original and influential: *seminal thinkers* 2 potentially capable of development 3 of semen: *seminal fluid* 4 *biol* of seed

seminar *n* 1 a small group of students meeting regularly under the guidance of a tutor for study and discussion 2 one such meeting

seminary *n, pl* **-naries** a college for the training of priests > **seminarian** *n*

S

semiprecious *adj* (of certain stones) having less value than a precious stone

semiquaver *n music* a note having the time value of one-sixteenth of a semibreve

Semite *n* a member of the group of peoples who speak a Semitic language, such as the Jews and Arabs

Semitic *n* 1 a group of languages that includes Arabic, Hebrew, and Aramaic ▸ *adj* 2 of this group of languages 3 of any of the peoples speaking a Semitic language, esp. the Jews or the Arabs 4 same as **Jewish**

semitone *n* the smallest interval between two notes in Western music represented on a piano by the difference in pitch between any two adjacent keys > **semitonic** *adj*

semitrailer *n Austral* a large truck in two separate sections joined by a pivoted bar. Also called: **semi**

semolina *n* the large hard grains of wheat left after flour has been milled, used for making puddings and pasta

senate *n* the main governing body at some universities

Senate *n* the upper chamber of the legislatures of Australia, the US, Canada, and many other countries

senator *n* a member of a Senate > **senatorial** *adj*

send *vb* **sending, sent** 1 to cause (a person or thing) to go or be taken or transmitted to another place: *send a message* 2 **send for** to dispatch a request or command for (someone or something): *she had sent for me* 3 to cause to go to a place or point: *the bullet sent him flying into the air* 4 to bring to a state or condition: *his schemes to send her mad* 5 to cause to happen or come: *the thunderstorm sent by the gods* 6 *old-fashioned slang* to move to excitement or rapture: *this music really sends me* > **sender** *n*

send *vb* 1 = dispatch, forward, direct, convey, remit 3 = propel, hurl, fling, shoot, fire, cast, let fly

sendoff *n* 1 *informal* a show of good wishes to a person about to set off on a journey or start a new career ▸ *vb* **send off** 2 to dispatch (something, such as a letter) 3 *sport* (of a referee) to dismiss (a player) from the field of play for some offence

sendoff *n* = farewell, departure, leave-taking, valediction

send up *informal* ▸ *vb* 1 to make fun of by doing an imitation or parody ▸ *n* **send-up** 2 a parody or imitation

send up *vb* **send something or someone up** = mock, mimic, parody, spoof (*informal*), imitate, take off (*informal*), make fun of, lampoon

senile *adj* mentally or physically weak or infirm on account of old age > **senility** *n*

senior *adj* 1 higher in rank or length of service 2 older in years: *senior citizens* 3 *education* of or designating more advanced or older pupils or students ▸ *n* 4 a senior person

senior *adj* 1 = higher-ranking, superior; ≠ subordinate

seniority *n, pl* **-ties** 1 the state of being senior 2 degree of power or importance in an organization from length of continuous service

senna *n* 1 a tropical plant with yellow flowers and long pods 2 the dried leaves and pods of this plant, used as a laxative

señor (sen-nyor) *n* a Spanish form of address equivalent to *sir* or *Mr*

señora (sen-nyor-a) *n* a Spanish form of address equivalent to *madam* or *Mrs*

señorita (sen-nyor-ee-ta) *n* a Spanish form of address equivalent to *madam* or *Miss*

sensation *n* 1 the power of feeling things physically: *I lose all sensation in my hands* 2 a physical feeling: *a burning sensation in the throat* 3 a general feeling or awareness: *a sensation of vague resentment* 4 a state of excitement: *imagine the sensation in Washington!* 5 an exciting person or thing: *you'll be a sensation*

sensation *n* 1, 3 = feeling, sense, impression, perception, awareness, consciousness 4 = excitement, thrill, stir, furore, commotion

sensational *adj* 1 causing intense feelings of shock, anger, or excitement: *sensational allegations* 2 *informal* extremely good: *the views are sensational* 3 of the senses or sensation > **sensationally** *adv*

sensational *adj* 1 = amazing, dramatic, thrilling, astounding; ≠ dull 2 = excellent, superb (*old-fashioned*), mean (*slang*), impressive, smashing (*old-fashioned*), fabulous (*informal*), marvellous, out of this world (*informal*), booshit (*Austral slang*), exo (*Austral slang*), sik (*Austral slang*), rad (*informal*), phat (*slang*), schmick (*Austral informal*), funky; ≠ ordinary

sensationalism *n* the deliberate use of sensational language or subject matter to arouse feelings of shock, anger, or excitement > **sensationalist** *adj, n*

sense *n* 1 any of the faculties (sight, hearing, touch, taste, and smell) by which the mind receives information about the external world or the state of the body 2 the ability to perceive 3 a feeling perceived through one of the senses: *a sense of warmth* 4 a mental perception or awareness: *a sense of security* 5 ability to make moral judgments: *a sense of honour* 6 (*usually pl*) sound practical judgment or intelligence: *you must have lost your senses when you bought that* 7 reason or purpose: *no sense in continuing* 8 general meaning: *he couldn't understand every word but he got the sense of what they were saying* 9 specific meaning; definition: *the three senses of the word* 10 **make sense** to be understandable or practical

▸ *vb* **sensing, sensed** 11 to perceive without the evidence of the senses: *he sensed that she was impressed* 12 to perceive through the senses

sense *n* 1 = faculty 3, 4 = feeling, impression, perception, awareness, consciousness, atmosphere, aura 6 = intelligence, reason, understanding, brains (*informal*), judgment, wisdom, wit(s), common sense; ≠ foolishness 8, 9 = meaning, significance, import, implication, drift, gist ▸ *vb* = perceive, feel, understand, pick up, realize, be aware of, discern, get the impression; ≠ be unaware of

senseless *adj* 1 having no meaning or purpose: *a senseless act of violence* 2 unconscious ▸ **senselessly** *adv* ▸ **senselessness** *n*

sensibility *n, pl* **-ties** 1 (*often pl*) the ability to experience deep feelings 2 (*usually pl*) the tendency to be influenced or offended: *its sheer callousness offended her sensibilities* 3 the ability to perceive or feel

sensibility *n* 2 = feelings, emotions, sentiments, susceptibilities, moral sense

sensible *adj* 1 having or showing good sense or judgment 2 (of clothing and footwear) practical and hard-wearing 3 capable of receiving sensation 4 capable of being perceived by the senses 5 perceptible to the mind 6 *literary* aware: *sensible of your kindness* ▸ **sensibly** *adv*

sensible *adj* 1 = wise, practical, prudent, shrewd, judicious; ≠ foolish

sensitive *adj* 1 easily hurt; tender 2 responsive to feelings and moods 3 responsive to external stimuli or impressions 4 easily offended or shocked 5 (of a subject or issue) liable to arouse controversy or strong feelings 6 (of an instrument) capable of registering small differences or changes in amounts 7 (of photographic materials) responding readily to the action of light: *a sensitive emulsion* 8 *chiefly US* connected with matters affecting national security ▸ **sensitively** *adv* ▸ **sensitivity** *n*

sensitive *adj* 1 = delicate, tender 2 = thoughtful, kindly, concerned, patient, attentive, tactful, unselfish 3 = susceptible, responsive, easily affected 4 = touchy, oversensitive, easily upset, easily offended, easily hurt; ≠ insensitive 6 = precise, fine, acute, keen, responsive; ≠ imprecise

sensitize *or* **-tise** *vb* **-tizing, -tized** *or* **-tising, -tised** to make sensitive ▸ **sensitization** *or* **-tisation** *n*

sensor *n* a device that detects or measures a physical property, such as radiation

sensory *adj* relating to the physical senses

sensual *adj* 1 giving pleasure to the body and senses rather than the mind: *soft sensual music* 2 having a strong liking for physical, esp. sexual, pleasures 3 of the body and senses rather than the mind or soul ▸ **sensualist** *n*

sensual *adj* 2 = sexual, erotic, raunchy (*informal*), lewd, lascivious, lustful, lecherous 3 = physical, bodily, voluptuous, animal, luxurious, fleshly, carnal

sensuality *n* 1 the quality or state of being sensual 2 enjoyment of physical, esp. sexual, pleasures

sensuous *adj* 1 pleasing to the senses of the mind or body: *the sensuous rhythms of the drums* 2 (of a person) appreciating qualities perceived by the senses ▸ **sensuously** *adv*

sent *vb* the past of **send**

sentence *n* 1 a sequence of words constituting a statement, question, or a command that begins with a capital letter and ends with a full stop when written down 2 **A** the decision of a law court as to what punishment is passed on a convicted person **B** the punishment passed on a convicted person ▸ *vb* **-tencing, -tenced** 3 to pronounce sentence on (a convicted person) in a law court ▸ **sentential** *adj*

sentence *n* 2A = verdict, order, ruling, decision, judgment, decree 2B = punishment, condemnation ▸ *vb* = condemn, doom

sententious *adj formal* 1 trying to sound wise 2 making pompous remarks about morality ▸ **sententiously** *adv*

sentient (sen-tee-ent, sen-shent) *adj* capable of perception and feeling ▸ **sentience** *n*

sentiment *n* 1 a mental attitude based on a mixture of thoughts and feelings: *anti-American sentiment* 2 (*often pl*) a thought, opinion, or attitude expressed in words: *his sentiments were echoed by subsequent speakers* 3 feelings such as tenderness, romance, and sadness, esp. when exaggerated: *someone without the softness of sentiment*

sentiment *n* 2 = feeling, idea, view, opinion, attitude, belief, judgment 3 = sentimentality, emotion, tenderness, romanticism, sensibility, emotionalism, mawkishness

sentimental *adj* 1 feeling or expressing tenderness, romance, or sadness to an exaggerated extent 2 appealing to the emotions, esp. to romantic feelings: *she kept the ring for sentimental reasons* ▸ **sentimentalism** *n* ▸ **sentimentalist** *n* ▸ **sentimentality** *n* ▸ **sentimentally** *adv*

sentimental *adj* = romantic, touching, emotional, nostalgic, maudlin, weepy (*informal*), slushy (*informal*), schmaltzy (*slang*); ≠ unsentimental

sentimentalize *or* **-lise** *vb* **-lizing, -lized** *or* **-lising, -lised** to make sentimental or behave sentimentally

sentinel *n old-fashioned* a sentry

sentry *n, pl* **-tries** a soldier who keeps watch and guards a camp or building

S

sepal *n botany* a leaflike division of the calyx of a flower

separable *adj* able to be separated

separate *vb* **-rating, -rated 1** to act as a barrier between: *the narrow stretch of water which separates Europe from Asia* **2** to part or be parted from a mass or group **3** to distinguish: *it's what separates the good players from the poor ones* **4** to divide or be divided into component parts **5** to sever or be severed **6** (of a couple) to stop living together ▶ *adj* **7** existing or considered independently: *a separate issue* **8** set apart from the main body or mass **9** distinct or individual > **separately** *adv* > **separateness** *n* > **separator** *n*

> **separate** *vb* **1** = divide, detach, disconnect, disjoin; ≠ combine **2** = come apart, split, come away; ≠ connect **3** = distinguish, mark, single out, set apart; ≠ link **5** = sever, break apart, split in two, divide in two; ≠ join **6** = split up, part, divorce, break up, part company, get divorced, be estranged ▶ *adj* **7** = unconnected, individual, particular, divided, divorced, isolated, detached, disconnected; ≠ connected **8, 9** = individual, independent, apart, distinct; ≠ joined

separation *n* **1** the act of separating: *the separation of child from mother* **2** *family law* the living apart of a married couple without divorce **3** a mark, line, or object that separates one thing from another

> **separation** *n* **1** = division, break, dissociation, disconnection, disunion **2** = split-up, parting, split, divorce, break-up, rift

separatist *n* a person who advocates the separation of his or her own group from an organization or country > **separatism** *n*

sepia *adj* dark reddish-brown, like the colour of very old photographs

sepoy *n* (formerly) an Indian soldier in the service of the British

sepsis *n* poisoning caused by the presence of pus-forming bacteria in the body

Sept. September

September *n* the ninth month of the year

septet *n* **1** a group of seven performers **2** a piece of music for seven performers

septic *adj* of or caused by harmful bacteria > **septicity** *n*

septicaemia *or* **septicemia** (sep-tis-see-mee-a) *n* an infection of the blood which develops in a wound

septic tank *n* a tank in which sewage is decomposed by the action of bacteria

septuagenarian *n* **1** a person who is between 70 and 79 years old ▶ *adj* **2** between 70 and 79 years old

sepulchral (sip-pulk-ral) *adj* **1** gloomy and solemn, like a tomb or grave **2** of a sepulchre

sepulchre *or* US **sepulcher** (sep-pulk-er) *n* **1** a burial vault, tomb, or grave ▶ *vb* **-chring, -chred**

or US **-chering, -chered 2** to bury in a sepulchre

sequel *n* **1** a film, novel, or play that continues the story of an earlier one **2** anything that happens after or as a result of something else: *there was an amusing sequel to this incident*

> **sequel** *n* **1** = follow-up, continuation, development **2** = consequence, result, outcome, conclusion, end, upshot

sequence *n* **1** an arrangement of two or more things in a successive order **2** the successive order of two or more things: *chronological sequence* **3** an action or event that follows another or others **4** *maths* an ordered set of numbers or other quantities in one-to-one correspondence with the integers 1 to *n* **5** a section of a film forming a single uninterrupted episode ▶ *vb* **6** to arrange in a sequence

> **sequence** *n* **1** = succession, course, series, order, chain, cycle, arrangement, progression

sequential *adj* happening in a fixed order or sequence

sequester *vb* **1** to seclude: *he could sequester himself in his own home* **2** *law* same as **sequestrate**

sequestrate *vb* **-trating, -trated** *law* to confiscate (property) temporarily until creditors are satisfied or a court order is complied with > **sequestration** *n* > **sequestrator** *n*

sequin *n* a small piece of shiny metal foil used to decorate clothes > **sequined** *adj*

sequoia *n* a giant Californian coniferous tree

seraglio (sir-ah-lee-oh) *n, pl* **-raglios 1** the part of a Muslim house or palace where the owner's wives live **2** a Turkish sultan's palace

seraph *n, pl* **-raphim** *theol* a member of the highest order of angels > **seraphic** *adj*

Serb *adj, n* same as **Serbian**

Serbian *adj* **1** of Serbia ▶ *n* **2** a person from Serbia **3** the dialect of Serbo-Croat spoken in Serbia

Serbo-Croat *or* **Serbo-Croatian** *n* **1** the chief official language of Serbia and Croatia ▶ *adj* **2** of this language

serenade *n* **1** a piece of music played or sung to a person by a lover **2** a piece of music suitable for this **3** an orchestral suite for a small ensemble ▶ *vb* **-nading, -naded 4** to sing or play a serenade to (someone)

serendipity *n* the gift of making fortunate discoveries by accident

serene *adj* **1** peaceful or calm **2** (of the sky) clear or bright > **serenely** *adv* > **serenity** *n*

serf *n* (esp. in medieval Europe) a labourer who could not leave the land on which he worked > **serfdom** *n*

serge *n* a strong fabric made of wool, cotton, silk, or rayon, used for clothing

sergeant *n* **1** a noncommissioned officer in the armed forces **2** (in Britain, S Africa, Australia, and NZ) a police officer ranking between constable and inspector

sergeant at arms *n* a parliamentary or court officer responsible for keeping order

sergeant major *n* a noncommissioned officer of the highest rank in the army

serial *n* 1 a story published or broadcast in instalments at regular intervals 2 a publication that is regularly issued and consecutively numbered ▸ *adj* 3 of, in, or forming a series: *serial pregnancies* 4 published or presented as a serial ▹ **serially** *adv*

serialize *or* **-ise** *vb* **-izing, -ized** *or* **-ising, -ised** to publish or present in the form of a serial ▹ **serialization** *or* **-isation** *n*

serial killer *n* a person who commits a number of murders

series *n, pl* **-ries** 1 a group or succession of related things 2 a set of radio or television programmes dealing with the same subject, esp. one having the same characters but different stories 3 *maths* the sum of a finite or infinite sequence of numbers or quantities 4 *electronics* an arrangement of two or more components connected in a circuit so that the same current flows in turn through each of them: *a number of resistors in series* 5 *geol* a set of layers that represent the rocks formed during an epoch

> **series** *n* 1 = sequence, course, chain, succession, run, set, order, train 2 = drama, serial, soap (*informal*), sitcom (*informal*), soap opera, soapie *or* soapy (*Austral slang*), situation comedy

serious *adj* 1 giving cause for concern: *the situation is serious* 2 concerned with important matters: *there are some serious questions that need to be answered* 3 not cheerful; grave: *I am a serious person* 4 in earnest; sincere: *he believes we are serious* 5 requiring concentration: *a serious book* 6 *informal* impressive because of its substantial quantity or quality: *serious money* ▹ **seriously** *adv* ▹ **seriousness** *n*

> **serious** *adj* 1 = grave, bad, critical, dangerous, acute, severe 2 = important, crucial (*informal*), urgent, pressing, worrying, significant, grim, momentous; ≠ unimportant 3 = solemn, earnest, grave, sober, staid, humourless, unsmiling; ≠ light-hearted 4 = sincere, earnest, genuine, honest, in earnest; ≠ insincere 5 = thoughtful, detailed, careful, deep, profound, in-depth

sermon *n* 1 a speech on a religious or moral subject given by a member of the clergy as part of a church service 2 *derogatory* a serious talk on behaviour, morals, or duty, esp. a long and tedious one

> **sermon** *n* 1 = homily, address

serotonin (ser-roe-tone-in) *n biochem* a compound that occurs in the brain, intestines, and blood platelets and acts as a neurotransmitter

serpent *n* 1 *literary* a snake 2 a devious person

serpentine *adj* twisting like a snake

serrated *adj* having a notched or sawlike edge ▹ **serration** *n*

serum (seer-um) *n* 1 the yellowish watery fluid left after blood has clotted 2 this fluid from the blood of immunized animals used for inoculation or vaccination 3 *physiol & zool* any clear watery animal fluid

servant *n* 1 a person employed to do household work for another person 2 a person or thing that is useful or provides a service: *a distinguished servant of this country*

> **servant** *n* 1 = attendant, domestic, slave, maid, help, retainer, skivvy (*chiefly Brit*)

serve *vb* **serving, served** 1 to be of service to (a person, community, or cause); help 2 to perform an official duty or duties: *he served on several university committees* 3 to attend to (customers) in a shop 4 to provide (guests) with food or drink: *he served dinner guests German wine* 5 to provide (food or drink) for customers: *breakfast is served from 7 am* 6 to provide with something needed by the public: *the community served by the school* 7 to work as a servant for (a person) 8 to go through (a period of police or military service, apprenticeship, or imprisonment) 9 to meet the needs of: *they serve a purpose* 10 to perform a function: *the attacks only served to strengthen their resolve* 11 (of a male animal) to mate with (a female animal) 12 *tennis & squash etc.* to put (the ball) into play 13 to deliver (a legal document) to (a person) 14 **serve someone right** *informal* to be what someone deserves, esp. for doing something stupid or wrong ▸ *n* 15 *tennis & squash etc.* short for **service** (sense 12)

> **serve** *vb* 1 = work for, help, aid, assist, be in the service of 4, 5 = present, provide, supply, deliver, set out, dish up 8 = perform, do, complete, fulfil, discharge 9 = be adequate, do, suffice, suit, satisfy, be acceptable, answer the purpose

server *n* 1 a computer or program that supplies data to other machines on a network 2 a person who serves

service *n* 1 an act of help or assistance 2 an organization or system that provides something needed by the public: *a consumer information service* 3 a department of public employment and its employees: *the diplomatic service* 4 the installation or maintenance of goods provided by a dealer after a sale 5 availability for use by the public: *the new plane could be in service within fifteen years* 6 a regular check made on a machine or vehicle in which parts are tested, cleaned, or replaced if worn 7 the serving of guests or customers: *service is included on the wine list* 8 one of the branches of the armed forces 9 the serving of food: *silver service* 10 a set of dishes, cups, and plates for use at table 11 a formal religious ceremony 12 *tennis & squash etc.* ʌ the act, manner, or right of serving the ball **B** the game in which a particular player serves: *she dropped only one point on her service* ▸ *adj* **13** of or for the use of servants or employees: *a service elevator* **14** serving the public rather than producing goods: *service industries* ▸ *vb* **-vicing, -viced** **15** to provide service or services to **16** to check and repair (a vehicle or machine) **17** (of a male animal) to mate with (a female animal)

> **service** *n* **2** = facility, system, resource, utility, amenity **6** = check, maintenance check **11** = ceremony, worship, rite, observance ▸ *vb* **16** = overhaul, check, maintain, tune (up), go over, fine-tune

serviceable *adj* **1** performing effectively: *serviceable boots* **2** able or ready to be used: *five remaining serviceable aircraft* > **serviceability** *n*

service area *n* a place on a motorway with a garage, restaurants, and toilets

serviceman *or fem* **servicewoman** *n, pl* **-men** *or* **-women** **1** a person in the armed services **2** a person employed to service and maintain equipment

service road *n Brit & Austral* a narrow road running parallel to a main road that provides access to houses and shops situated along its length

service station *n* **1** a place that sells fuel, oil, and spare parts for motor vehicles **2** same as **service area**

serviette *n Brit & Canad* a table napkin

servile *adj* **1** too eager to obey people; fawning **2** of or suitable for a slave > **servility** *n*

servitude *n formal* **1** slavery or bondage **2** the state or condition of being completely dominated

sesame (sess-am-ee) *n* an Asian plant, grown for its seeds and oil, which are used in cooking

sesh *n slang* a session

session *n* **1** any period devoted to a particular activity **2** a meeting of a court, parliament, or council **3** a series or period of such meetings **4** a school or university term or year > **sessional** *adj*

> **session** *n* **2, 3** = meeting, hearing, sitting, period, conference, congress, discussion, assembly

set¹ *vb* **setting, set** **1** to put in a specified position or state: *I set him free* **2 set to** *or* **on** to bring (something) into contact with (something else): *three prisoners set fire to their cells* **3** to put into order or make ready: *set the table* **4** to make or become firm or rigid: *before the eggs begin to set* **5** to put (a broken bone) or (of a broken bone) to be put into a normal position for healing **6** to adjust (a clock or other instrument) to a particular position **7** to arrange or establish: *to set a date for diplomatic talks*; *it set the standards of performance* **8** to prescribe or assign (a task or material for study): *the examiners have set 'Paradise Lost'* **9** to arrange (hair) while wet, so that it

dries in position **10** to place a jewel in (a setting): *a ring set with diamonds* **11** to provide music for (a poem or other text to be sung) **12** *printing* **A** to arrange (type) for printing **B** to put (text) into type **13** to arrange (a stage or television studio) with scenery and props **14 set to** *or* **on** to value (something) at a specified price or worth: *he set a high price on his services* **15** (of the sun or moon) to disappear beneath the horizon **16** (of plants) to produce (fruits or seeds) or (of fruits or seeds) to develop **17** to place (a hen) on (eggs) to incubate them **18** (of a gun dog) to turn in the direction of game birds ▸ *n* **19** the act of setting **20** a condition of firmness or hardness **21** manner of standing; posture: *the set of his shoulders* **22** the scenery and other props used in a play or film **23** same as **sett** ▸ *adj* **24** fixed or established by authority or agreement: *set hours of work* **25** rigid or inflexible: *she is set in her ways* **26** unmoving; fixed: *a set expression on his face* **27** conventional or stereotyped: *she made her apology in set phrases* **28 set in** (of a scene or story) represented as happening at a certain time or place: *a European film set in Africa* **29 set on** *or* **upon** determined to (do or achieve something): *why are you so set upon avoiding me?* **30** ready: *all set to go* **31** (of material for study) prescribed for students' preparation for an examination ▸ See also **set back**, **set up**

> **set** *vb* **1** = put, place, lay, position, rest, plant, station, stick (*informal*) **3** = prepare, lay, spread, arrange, make ready **4** = harden, stiffen, solidify, cake, thicken, crystallize, congeal **7** = arrange, decide (upon), settle, establish, determine, fix, schedule, appoint **8** = assign, give, allot, prescribe **15** = go down, sink, dip, decline, disappear, vanish, subside ▸ *n* **21** = position, bearing, attitude, carriage, posture **22** = scenery, setting, scene, stage set ▸ *adj* **24** = established, planned, decided, agreed, arranged, rigid, definite, inflexible **25** = strict, rigid, stubborn, inflexible; ≠ flexible **27** = conventional, traditional, stereotyped, unspontaneous

set² *n* **1** a number of objects or people grouped or belonging together: *a set of slides* **2** a group of people who associate with each other or have similar interests: *the tennis set* **3** *maths* a collection of numbers or objects that satisfy a given condition or share a property **4** a television or piece of radio equipment **5** the scenery and other props used in a dramatic production, film, etc. **6** *sport* a group of games or points in a match, of which the winner must win a certain number **7** a series of songs or tunes performed by a musician or group on a given occasion

> **set** *n* **1** = series, collection, assortment, batch, compendium, ensemble **2** = group, company, crowd, circle, band, gang, faction, clique

set back *vb* **1** to delay or hinder **2** *informal* to cost (a person) a specified amount ▸ *n* **setback** **3** anything that delays progress

> **set back** *n* **setback** = hold-up, check, defeat, blow, reverse, disappointment, hitch, misfortune

set square *n* a thin flat piece of plastic or metal in the shape of a right-angled triangle, used in technical drawing

sett *or* **set** *n* **1** a badger's burrow **2** a small rectangular paving block made of stone

settee *n* a seat, for two or more people, with a back and usually with arms; couch

setter *n* a large long-haired dog originally bred for hunting

setting *n* **1** the surroundings in which something is set **2** the scenery, properties, or background used to create the location for a stage play or film **3** a piece of music written for the words of a text **4** the decorative metalwork in which a gem is set **5** the plates and cutlery for a single place at a table **6** one of the positions or levels to which the controls of a machine can be adjusted

> **setting** *n* **1, 2** = surroundings, site, location, set, scene, background, context, backdrop

settle¹ *vb* **-tling, -tled** **1** to put in order: *he settled his affairs before he died* **2** to arrange or be arranged firmly or comfortably: *he settled into his own chair by the fire* **3** to come down to rest: *a bird settled on top of the hedge* **4** to establish or become established as a resident: *they eventually settled in Glasgow* **5** to establish or become established in a way of life or a job **6** to migrate to (a country) and form a community; colonize **7** to make or become quiet, calm, or stable **8** to cause (sediment) to sink to the bottom in a liquid or (of sediment) to sink thus **9** to subside: *the dust settled* **10** (sometimes foll. by *up*) to pay off (a bill or debt) **11** to decide or dispose of: *to settle an argument* **12** (often foll. by *on* or *upon*) to agree or fix: *they settled on an elementary code* **13** (usually foll. by *on* or *upon*) to give (a title or property) to a person by gift or legal deed: *he settled his property on his wife* **14** to decide (a legal dispute) by agreement without court action: *they settled out of court*

> **settle** *vb* **1** = resolve, work out, put an end to, straighten out **3** = land, alight, descend, light, come to rest **4** = move to, take up residence in, live in, dwell in, inhabit, reside in, set up home in, put down roots in **6** = colonize, populate, people, pioneer **7** = calm, quiet, relax, relieve, reassure, soothe, lull, quell; ≠ disturb **10** = pay, clear, square (up), discharge

settle² *n* a long wooden bench with a high back and arms, sometimes having a storage space under the seat

settlement *n* **1** an act of settling **2** a place newly settled; colony **3** subsidence of all or part of a building **4** an official agreement ending a dispute **5** *law* ᴀ an arrangement by which property is transferred to a person's possession ʙ the deed transferring such property

> **settlement** *n* **2** = colony, community, outpost, encampment, kainga *or* kaika (NZ) **4** = agreement, arrangement, working out, conclusion, establishment, confirmation

settler *n* a person who settles in a new country or a colony

> **settler** *n* = colonist, immigrant, pioneer, frontiersman *or* frontierswoman

set-top box *n* a device which converts the signals from a digital television broadcast into a form which can be viewed on an analogue television, or that enables satellite, cable, or streaming services to be viewed

set up *vb* **1** to build or construct: *the soldiers had actually set up a munitions factory* **2** to put into a position of power or wealth **3** to begin or enable (someone) to begin (a new venture): *he set up a small shop* **4** to begin or produce: *to set up a nuclear chain reaction* **5** to establish: *Broad set up a world record* **6** *informal* to cause (a person) to be blamed or accused **7** to restore the health of: *a pub lunch set me up nicely* ▸ *n* **setup** **8** *informal* the way in which anything is organized or arranged **9** *slang* an event the result of which is prearranged

> **set up** *vb* **1 set something up** = build, raise, construct, put up, assemble, put together, erect **3 set something up** = establish, begin, found, institute, initiate ▸ *n* **8 setup** = arrangement, system, structure, organization, conditions, regime

seven *n* **1** the cardinal number that is the sum of one and six **2** a numeral, 7 or VII, representing this number **3** something representing or consisting of seven units ▸ *adj* **4** amounting to seven: *seven weeks* > **seventh** *adj, n*

seventeen *n* **1** the cardinal number that is the sum of ten and seven **2** a numeral, 17 or XVII, representing this number **3** something representing or consisting of seventeen units ▸ *adj* **4** amounting to seventeen: *seventeen children* > **seventeenth** *adj, n*

seventy *n, pl* **-ties** **1** the cardinal number that is the product of ten and seven **2** a numeral, 70 or LXX, representing this number **3** something representing or consisting of seventy units ▸ *adj* **4** amounting to seventy: *seventy countries* > **seventieth** *adj, n*

sever *vb* **1** to cut right through or cut off (something): *it accidentally severed the electrical cable* **2** to break off (a tie or relationship) > **severable** *adj* > **severance** *n*

> **sever** *vb* **1** = cut, separate, split, part, divide, detach, disconnect, cut in two; ≠ join **2** = discontinue, terminate, break off, put an end to, dissociate; ≠ continue

S

several *adj* **1** more than a few: *I spoke to several doctors* **2** *formal* various or separate: *the members with their several occupations* **3** *formal* distinct or different: *misfortune visited her three several times*

> **several** *adj* **2** = various, different, diverse, sundry

severally *adv formal* individually or separately: *the Western nations severally rather than jointly decided that they would have to act without Russia*

severance pay *n* compensation paid by a firm to an employee who has to leave because the job he or she was appointed to do no longer exists

severe *adj* **1** strict or harsh in the treatment of others: *a severe parent* **2** serious in appearance or manner: *a severe look*; *a severe hairdo* **3** very intense or unpleasant: *severe chest pains*; *the punishments are severe* **4** causing discomfort by its harshness: *severe frost* **5** hard to perform or accomplish: *a severe challenge* > **severely** *adv* > **severity** *n*

> **severe** *adj* **1** = strict, hard, harsh, cruel, rigid, drastic, oppressive, austere; ≠ lenient **2** = grim, serious, grave, forbidding, stern, unsmiling, tight-lipped; ≠ genial **3** = serious, critical, terrible, desperate, extreme, awful, drastic, catastrophic **4** = acute, intense, violent, piercing, harrowing, unbearable, agonizing, insufferable

sew *vb* **sewing**, **sewed**, **sewn** *or* **sewed** **1** to join with thread repeatedly passed through with a needle **2** to attach, fasten, or close by sewing

> **sew** *vb* **2** = stitch, tack (*Brit*), seam, hem

sewage *n* waste matter or excrement carried away in sewers or drains

sewer *n* a drain or pipe, usually underground, used to carry away surface water or sewage

sewerage *n* **1** a system of sewers **2** the removal of surface water or sewage by means of sewers

sewn *vb* a past participle of **sew**

sex *n* **1** the state of being male or female with reference to reproductive function **2** either of the two categories, male or female, into which organisms are divided **3** sexual intercourse **4** feelings or behaviour connected with having sex or the desire to have sex **5** sexual matters in general ▸ *adj* **6** of sexual matters: *sex education* **7** based on or resulting from the difference between the sexes: *sex discrimination* ▸ *vb* **8** to find out the sex of (an animal)

> **sex** *n* **1, 2** = gender **3** = lovemaking, sexual relations, copulation, fornication, coitus, cybersex

sexagenarian *n* **1** a person who is between 60 and 69 years old ▸ *adj* **2** between 60 and 69 years old

sexism *n* discrimination against the members of one sex, usually women > **sexist** *n, adj*

sextant *n* an instrument used in navigation for measuring angular distance, for example between the sun and the horizon, to calculate the position of a ship or aircraft

sextet *n* **1** a group of six performers **2** a piece of music for six performers **3** a group of six people or things

sexton *n* a person employed to look after a church and its churchyard

sexual *adj* **1** of or characterized by sex **2** (of reproduction) characterized by the union of male and female reproductive cells **3** of or relating to the differences between males and females > **sexuality** *n* > **sexually** *adv*

> **sexual** *adj* **1** = carnal, erotic, intimate

sexual intercourse *n* the sexual act in which, typically, the male's erect penis is inserted into the female's vagina

sex up *vb informal* to make (something) more exciting

sexy *adj* **sexier**, **sexiest** *informal* **1** sexually exciting or attractive: *a sexy voice* **2** interesting, exciting, or trendy: *a sexy project*; *a sexy new car* > **sexiness** *n*

> **sexy** *adj* **1** = erotic, sensual, seductive, arousing, naughty, provocative, sensuous, suggestive, hot (*informal*)

SF *or* **sf** science fiction

Sgt. Sergeant

shabby *adj* **-bier**, **-biest** **1** old and worn in appearance **2** wearing worn and dirty clothes **3** behaving in a mean or unfair way: *shabby manoeuvres* > **shabbily** *adv* > **shabbiness** *n*

> **shabby** *adj* **1, 2** = tatty (*Brit*), worn, ragged, scruffy, tattered, threadbare; ≠ smart **3** = mean, low, rotten (*informal*), cheap, dirty, despicable, contemptible, scurvy (*old-fashioned*); ≠ fair

shack *n* **1** a roughly built hut ▸ *vb* **2** **shack up with** *slang* to live with (a lover)

> **shack** *n* = hut, cabin, shanty, whare (NZ)

shackle *n* **1** one of a pair of metal rings joined by a chain for securing someone's wrists or ankles **2** **shackles** anything that confines or restricts freedom: *free from the shackles of its feudal past* **3** a metal loop or link closed by a bolt, used for securing ropes or chains ▸ *vb* **-ling**, **-led** **4** to fasten with shackles **5** to restrict or hamper: *an economy shackled by central control*

shad *n, pl* **shad** *or* **shads** a herring-like food fish

shade *n* **1** relative darkness produced by blocking out sunlight **2** a place sheltered from the sun by trees, buildings, etc. **3** something used to provide a shield or protection from a direct source of light, such as a lamp shade **4** a shaded area in a painting or drawing **5** any of the different hues of a colour: *a much darker shade of grey* **6** a slight amount: *a shade of reluctance* **7** **put someone** *or* **something in the shade** to be so impressive as to make another person or

thing seem unimportant by comparison
8 *literary* a ghost ▸ *vb* **shading, shaded 9** to
screen or protect from heat or light **10** to make
darker or dimmer **11** to represent (a darker area)
in (a painting or drawing), by graded areas of
tone, lines, or dots **12** to change slightly or by
degrees

> **shade** *n* **1, 2** = shadow **3** = screen, covering,
> cover, blind, curtain, shield, veil, canopy
> **5** = hue, tone, colour, tint **6** = dash, trace, hint,
> suggestion **8** = ghost, spirit, phantom, spectre,
> apparition, kehua (NZ) ▸ *vb* **9** = cover, protect,
> screen, hide, shield, conceal, obscure, veil
> **10** = darken, shadow, cloud, dim

shadow *n* **1** a dark image or shape cast on a
surface when something stands between a light
and the surface **2** a patch of shade **3** the dark
portions of a picture **4** a hint or faint trace:
a shadow of a doubt **5** a person less powerful or
vigorous than his or her former self **6** a
threatening influence: *news of the murder cast a
shadow over the village* **7** a person who always
accompanies another **8** a person who trails
another in secret, such as a detective ▸ *adj* **9** *Brit
& Austral* designating a member or members of
the main opposition party in Parliament who
would hold ministerial office if their party were
in power: *the shadow chancellor* ▸ *vb* **10** to cast a
shade or shadow over **11** to make dark or gloomy
12 to follow or trail secretly

> **shadow** *n* **1** = silhouette, shape, outline,
> profile **2** = shade, dimness, darkness, gloom,
> cover, dusk (*poetic*) ▸ *vb* **10, 11** = shade, screen,
> shield, darken, overhang **12** = follow, tail
> (*informal*), trail, stalk

shadowy *adj* **1** (of a place) full of shadows;
shady **2** faint or dark like a shadow: *a shadowy
figure* **3** mysterious or not well known: *the
shadowy world of espionage*
shady *adj* **shadier, shadiest 1** full of shade;
shaded **2** giving or casting shade **3** *informal* of
doubtful honesty or legality: *shady business dealings*
› **shadiness** *n*

> **shady** *adj* **1, 2** = shaded, cool, dim; ≠ sunny
> **3** = crooked (*informal*), dodgy (*Brit, Austral, NZ
> informal*), unethical, suspect, suspicious,
> dubious, questionable, shifty, shonky (*Austral,
> NZ informal*); ≠ honest

shaft *n* **1** ᴀ a spear or arrow ʙ its long narrow
stem **2 shaft of wit** *or* **humour** a clever or
amusing remark **3** a ray or streak of light
4 the long straight narrow handle of a tool or
golf club **5** a revolving rod in a machine that
transmits motion or power **6** one of the bars
between which an animal is harnessed to a
vehicle **7** *archit* the middle part of a column
or pier, between the base and the capital
8 a vertical passageway through a building
for a lift **9** a vertical passageway into a mine

> **shaft** *n* **3** = ray, beam, gleam **4** = handle, staff,
> pole, rod, stem, baton, shank **9** = tunnel, hole,
> passage, burrow, passageway, channel

shag¹ *n* **1** coarse shredded tobacco **2** a matted
tangle of hair or wool ▸ *adj* **3** (of a carpet) having
long thick woollen threads
shag² *n* a kind of cormorant
shag³ *vb* **shagging, shagged** *Brit, Austral & NZ
slang* to have sexual intercourse with (a person)
shaggy *adj* **-gier, -giest 1** having or covered
with rough unkempt fur, hair, or wool: *shaggy
cattle* **2** rough and untidy › **shagginess** *n*
shagreen *n* **1** the skin of a shark, used as an
abrasive **2** a rough grainy leather made from
certain animal hides
shah *n* the title of the former monarch of Iran
shake *vb* **shaking, shook, shaken 1** to move up
and down or back and forth with short quick
movements **2** to be or make unsteady
3 (of a voice) to tremble because of anger or
nervousness **4** to clasp or grasp (the hand)
of (a person) in greeting or agreement: *they
shook hands* **5 shake on it** *informal* to shake
hands in agreement or reconciliation **6** to wave
vigorously and angrily: *he shook his fist* **7** (often
foll. by *up*) to frighten or unsettle **8** to shock,
disturb, or upset: *he was badly shaken but unharmed*
9 to undermine or weaken: *a team whose morale
had been badly shaken* **10** *US & Canad informal* to get
rid of **11** *music* to perform a trill on (a note)
12 shake one's head to indicate disagreement
or disapproval by moving the head from side to
side ▸ *n* **13** the act or an instance of shaking **14** a
tremor or vibration **15 the shakes** *informal* a
state of uncontrollable trembling **16** *informal* a very
short period of time: *in half a shake* **17** *music* same
as **trill** (sense 1) **18** short for **milk shake**

> **shake** *vb* **1** = jiggle, agitate **2** = rock, totter
> **3** = tremble, shiver, quake, quiver **6** = wave,
> wield, flourish, brandish **8** = upset, shock,
> frighten, disturb, distress, rattle (*informal*),
> unnerve, traumatize ▸ *n* **14** = vibration,
> trembling, quaking, jerk, shiver, shudder, jolt,
> tremor

shaky *adj* **shakier, shakiest 1** weak and
unsteady, esp. due to illness or shock
2 uncertain or doubtful: *their prospects are shaky*
3 tending to shake or tremble › **shakily** *adv*

> **shaky** *adj* **1** = unstable, weak, precarious,
> rickety; ≠ stable **2** = uncertain, suspect,
> dubious, questionable, iffy (*informal*); ≠ reliable
> **3** = unsteady, faint, trembling, faltering,
> quivery

shale *n* a flaky sedimentary rock formed by
compression of successive layers of clay
shall *vb, past tense* **should 1** (with 'I' or 'we' as subject)
used as an auxiliary to make the future tense: *we
shall see you tomorrow* **2** (with 'you', 'he', 'she', 'it', 'they',
or a noun as subject*) ᴀ used as an auxiliary to indicate

S

determination on the part of the speaker: *you shall pay for this!* **B** used as an auxiliary to indicate compulsion or obligation, now esp. in official documents **3** (*with 'I' or 'we' as subject*) used as an auxiliary in questions asking for advice or agreement: *what shall we do now?; shall I shut the door?*

shallot (shal-lot) *n* a small, onion-like plant used in cooking for flavouring

shallow *adj* **1** having little depth **2** not involving sincere feelings or serious thought **3** (*of breathing*) consisting of short breaths ▸ *n* **4** (*often pl*) a shallow place in a body of water ▷ **shallowness** *n*

> **shallow** *adj* **2** = superficial, surface, empty, slight, foolish, trivial, meaningless, frivolous; ≠ deep

sham *n* **1** anything that is not genuine or is not what it appears to be **2** a person who pretends to be something other than he or she is ▸ *adj* **3** not real or genuine ▸ *vb* **shamming, shammed** **4** to fake or feign (something); pretend: *he made a point of shamming nervousness*

> **sham** *n* **1** = fraud (*informal*), imitation, hoax, pretence, forgery, counterfeit, humbug, impostor; ≠ the real thing ▸ *adj* = false, artificial, bogus, pretended, mock, imitation, simulated, counterfeit; ≠ real

shamble *vb* **-bling, -bled** **1** to walk or move along in an awkward shuffling way ▸ *n* **2** an awkward or shuffling walk ▷ **shambling** *adj, n*

shambles *n* **1** a disorderly or badly organized event or place: *the bathroom was a shambles* **2** *chiefly Brit* a butcher's slaughterhouse **3** *old-fashioned* any scene of great slaughter

> **shambles** *n* **1** = chaos, mess, disorder, confusion, muddle, havoc (*informal*), disarray, madhouse (*informal*)

shame *n* **1** a painful emotion resulting from an awareness of having done something wrong or foolish **2** capacity to feel such an emotion: *have they no shame?* **3** loss of respect; disgrace **4** a person or thing that causes this **5** a cause for regret or disappointment: *it's a shame to rush back* **6** **put to shame** to show up as being inferior by comparison: *his essay put mine to shame* ▸ *interj* **7** *S African informal* **A** an expression of sympathy **B** an expression of pleasure or endearment ▸ *vb* **shaming, shamed** **8** to cause to feel shame **9** to bring shame on **10** (*often foll. by into*) to force someone to do something by making him or her feel ashamed not to: *he was finally shamed into paying the bill*

> **shame** *n* **1** = embarrassment, humiliation, ignominy, mortification, abashment; ≠ shamelessness **3** = disgrace, scandal, discredit, smear, disrepute, reproach, dishonour, infamy; ≠ honour ▸ *vb* **8** = embarrass,

disgrace, humiliate, humble, mortify, abash; ≠ make proud **9** = dishonour, degrade, stain, smear, blot, debase, defile; ≠ honour

shamefaced *adj* embarrassed or guilty ▷ **shamefacedly** *adv*

shameful *adj* causing or deserving shame: *a shameful lack of concern* ▷ **shamefully** *adv*

> **shameful** *adj* = disgraceful, outrageous, scandalous, mean, low, base, wicked, dishonourable; ≠ admirable

shameless *adj* **1** having no sense of shame: *a shameless manipulator* **2** without decency or modesty: *a shameless attempt to stifle democracy* ▷ **shamelessly** *adv*

shammy *n, pl* **-mies** *informal* a piece of chamois leather

shampoo *n* **1** a soapy liquid used to wash the hair **2** a similar liquid for washing carpets or upholstery **3** the process of shampooing ▸ *vb* **-pooing, -pooed** **4** to wash (the hair, carpets, or upholstery) with shampoo

shamrock *n* a small clover-like plant with three round leaves on each stem: the national emblem of Ireland

shandy *n, pl* **-dies** a drink made of beer and lemonade

shanghai *slang* ▸ *vb* **-haiing, -haied** **1** to force or trick (someone) into doing something **2** *history* to kidnap (a man) and force him to serve at sea **3** *Austral & NZ* to shoot with a catapult ▸ *n* **4** *Austral & NZ* a catapult

shank *n* **1** the part of the leg between the knee and the ankle **2** a cut of meat from the top part of an animal's shank **3** the long narrow part of a tool, key, spoon, etc.

shan't shall not

shantung *n* a heavy Chinese silk with a knobbly surface

shanty[1] *n, pl* **-ties** a small rough hut; crude dwelling

shanty[2] *or* **chanty** *n, pl* **-ties** a rhythmic song originally sung by sailors when working

shantytown *n* a town of poor people living in shanties

shape *n* **1** the outward form of an object, produced by its outline **2** the figure or outline of the body of a person **3** organized or definite form: *to preserve the union in its present shape* **4** the specific form that anything takes on: *a gold locket in the shape of a heart* **5** a pattern or mould **6** condition or state of efficiency: *in poor shape* **7** **take shape** to assume a definite form ▸ *vb* **shaping, shaped** **8** (*often foll. by up or into*) to receive or cause to receive shape or form: *spinach shaped into a ball* **9** to mould into a particular pattern or form **10** to devise or develop: *to shape a system of free trade*

> **shape** *n* **1, 2** = form, profile, outline, lines, build, figure, silhouette, configuration **3** = appearance, form, aspect, guise, likeness,

semblance **5** = pattern, model, frame, mould **6** = condition, state, health, trim, fettle ▸ vb **8, 9** = mould, form, make, fashion, model, frame **10** = form, make, produce, create, model, fashion, mould

shapeless adj **1** (of a person or object) lacking a pleasing shape: *a shapeless dress* **2** having no definite shape or form: *a shapeless mound* ▸**shapelessness** n

shapely adj **-lier, -liest** (esp. of a woman's body or legs) pleasing or attractive in shape ▸**shapeliness** n

shard n a broken piece or fragment of pottery, glass, or metal

share[1] n **1** a part or portion of something that belongs to or is contributed by a person or group **2** (*often pl*) any of the equal parts into which the capital stock of a company is divided **3** (on a social networking site) an instance of transmitting another person's post to one's contacts ▸ vb **sharing, shared 4** (often foll. by *out*) to divide and distribute **5** to receive or contribute a portion of: *we shared a bottle of mineral water* **6** to join with another or others in the use of (something): *a programme about four women sharing a house* **7** to go through (a similar experience) as others: *we have all shared the nightmare of toothache* **8** to tell others about (something) **9** to have the same (beliefs or opinions) as others: *universal values shared by both east and west*

> **share** n **1** = part, portion, quota, ration, lot, due, contribution, allowance ▸ vb **4** = divide, split, distribute, assign **5** = go halves on, go fifty-fifty on (*informal*)

share[2] n short for **ploughshare**

shareholder n the owner of one or more shares in a company

sharemilker n NZ a person who works on a dairy farm belonging to someone else and gets a share of the proceeds from the sale of the milk

shark n **1** a large, usually predatory fish with a long body, two dorsal fins, and rows of sharp teeth **2** *derogatory* a person who swindles or extorts money from other people

sharkskin n a smooth glossy fabric used for sportswear

sharp adj **1** having a keen cutting edge **2** tapering to an edge or point **3** involving a sudden change in direction: *a sharp bend on a road*; *a sharp rise in prices* **4** moving, acting, or reacting quickly: *sharp reflexes* **5** clearly defined: *a sharp contrast* **6** quick to notice or understand things; keen-witted **7** clever in an underhand way: *sharp practices* **8** bitter or harsh: *a sharp response* **9** shrill or penetrating: *a sharp cry of horror* **10** having a bitter or sour taste **11** (of pain or cold) acute or biting: *a sharp gust of wind* **12** *music* **A** (of a note) raised in pitch by one semitone: *F sharp* **B** (of an instrument or voice) out of tune by being too

high in pitch **13** *informal* neat and stylish: *a sharp dresser* ▸ adv **14** promptly **15** exactly: *at ten o'clock sharp* **16** *music* **A** higher than a standard pitch **B** out of tune by being too high in pitch: *she sings sharp* ▸ n **17** *music* **A** an accidental that raises the pitch of a note by one semitone. Symbol: ♯ **B** a note affected by this accidental **18** *informal* a cheat; a cardsharp > **sharpish** adj > **sharply** adv > **sharpness** n

> **sharp** adj **1** = keen, jagged, serrated; ≠ blunt **3** = sudden, marked, abrupt, extreme, distinct; ≠ gradual **5** = clear, distinct, well-defined, crisp; ≠ indistinct **6** = quick-witted, clever, astute, knowing, quick, bright, alert, penetrating; ≠ slow **8** = cutting, biting, bitter, harsh, barbed, hurtful, caustic; ≠ gentle **10** = sour, tart, pungent, hot, acid, acrid, piquant; ≠ bland **11** = acute, severe, intense, painful, shooting, stabbing, piercing, gut-wrenching ▸ adv **14, 15** = promptly, precisely, exactly, on time, on the dot, punctually; ≠ approximately

sharpen vb to make or become sharp or sharper > **sharpener** n

> **sharpen** vb = make sharp, hone, whet, grind, edge

sharpshooter n a person who can fire a gun very accurately

shatter vb **1** to break suddenly into many small pieces **2** to damage badly or destroy: *to shatter American confidence* **3** to upset (someone) greatly: *the whole experience shattered me* > **shattering** adj

> **shatter** vb **1** = smash, break, burst, crack, crush, pulverize **2** = destroy, ruin, wreck, demolish, torpedo

shattered adj *informal* **1** completely exhausted **2** badly upset: *he was shattered by the separation*

> **shattered** adj **1** = exhausted, drained, worn out, done in (*informal*), all in (*slang*), knackered (*slang*), tired out, ready to drop **2** = devastated, crushed, gutted (*slang*)

shave vb **shaving, shaved, shaved** or **shaven 1** to remove (the beard or hair) from (the face, head, or body) by using a razor or shaver **2** to remove thin slices from (wood or other material) with a sharp cutting tool **3** to touch (someone or something) lightly in passing ▸ n **4** the act or an instance of shaving **5** the removal of hair from the face or body by a razor **6** a tool for cutting off thin slices **7 close shave** *informal* a narrow escape

> **shave** vb **1** = trim, crop **2** = scrape, trim, shear, pare

shaver n **1** an electrically powered razor **2** *old-fashioned* a young boy

shawarma n (in Arabic-speaking countries) a doner kebab

S

shawl *n* a piece of woollen cloth worn over the head or shoulders or wrapped around a baby

she *pron* **1** (refers to) the female person or animal previously mentioned or in question: *she is my sister* **2** (refers to) something regarded as female, such as a car, ship, or nation ▸ *n* **3** (refers to) a female person or animal

sheaf *n, pl* **sheaves 1** a bundle of papers tied together **2** a bundle of reaped corn tied together ▸ *vb* **3** to bind or tie into a sheaf

shear *vb* **shearing, sheared** *or Austral & NZ sometimes* **shore, sheared** *or* **shorn 1** to remove (the fleece) of (a sheep) by cutting or clipping **2** to cut or cut through (something) with shears or a sharp instrument **3** *engineering* to cause (a part) to break or (of a part) to break through strain or twisting ▸ *n* **4** breakage caused through strain or twisting ▸ See also **shears** > **shearer** *n*

shearing shed *n Austral & NZ* a farm building with equipment for shearing sheep

shears *pl n* **A** large scissors, used for sheep shearing **B** a large scissor-like cutting tool with flat blades, used for cutting hedges

sheath *n, pl* **sheaths 1** a case or covering for the blade of a knife or sword **2** *biol* a structure that encloses or protects **3** *Brit, Austral & NZ* same as **condom 4** a close-fitting dress

sheathe *vb* **sheathing, sheathed 1** to insert (a knife or sword) into a sheath **2** to cover with a sheath or sheathing

shebeen *or* **shebean** *n Scot, Irish & S African* a place where alcoholic drink is sold illegally

shed¹ *n* **1** a small, roughly made building used for storing garden tools etc. **2** a large barnlike building used for various purposes at factories, train stations, etc.: *a locomotive shed*

> **shed** *n* **1** = hut, shack, outhouse, whare (NZ)

shed² *vb* **shedding, shed 1** to get rid of: *250 workers shed by the company* **2 shed tears** to cry **3 shed light on** to make (a problem or situation) easier to understand **4** to cast off (skin, hair, or leaves): *the trees were already beginning to shed their leaves* **5** to cause to flow off: *this coat sheds water* **6** to separate or divide (a group of sheep)

> **shed** *vb* **4** = cast off, discard, moult, slough off **5** = drop, spill, scatter

sheen *n* a glistening brightness on the surface of something: *grass with a sheen of dew on it*

> **sheen** *n* = shine, gleam, gloss, polish, brightness, lustre

sheep *n, pl* **sheep 1** a cud-chewing mammal with a thick woolly coat, kept for its wool or meat. Related adjective: **ovine 2** a timid person **3 like sheep** (of a group of people) allowing a single person to dictate their actions or beliefs **4 separate the sheep from the goats** to pick out the members of a group who are superior in some respects > **sheeplike** *adj*

sheep-dip *n* **1** a liquid disinfectant and insecticide in which sheep are immersed **2** a deep trough containing such a liquid

sheepdog *n* **1** a dog used for herding sheep **2** a breed of dog reared originally for herding sheep

sheepish *adj* embarrassed because of feeling foolish > **sheepishly** *adv*

sheepskin *n* the skin of a sheep with the wool still attached, used to make clothing and rugs

sheer¹ *adj* **1** absolute; complete: *sheer amazement* **2** perpendicular; very steep: *the sheer rock face* **3** (of textiles) light, delicate, and see-through ▸ *adv* **4** steeply: *the cliff drops sheer to the sea*

> **sheer** *adj* **1** = total, complete, absolute, utter, pure, downright (*derogatory*), out-and-out, unmitigated; ≠ moderate **2** = steep, abrupt, precipitous; ≠ gradual **3** = fine, thin, transparent, see-through, gossamer, diaphanous, gauzy; ≠ thick

sheer² *vb* **sheer off** *or* **away (from) A** to change course suddenly **B** to avoid (an unpleasant person, thing, or topic)

sheet¹ *n* **1** a large rectangular piece of cloth used as an inner bed cover **2** a thin piece of material such as paper or glass, usually rectangular **3** a broad continuous surface or layer: *a sheet of ice* **4** a newspaper ▸ *vb* **5** to provide with, cover, or wrap in a sheet **6** (often foll. by *down*) to rain very heavily

> **sheet** *n* **2** = page, leaf, folio, piece of paper **3** = coat, film, layer, surface, stratum, veneer, overlay, lamina

sheet² *n naut* a line or rope for controlling the position of a sail

sheet anchor *n* **1** *naut* a large strong anchor for use in an emergency **2** a person or thing that can always be relied on

sheikh *or* **sheik** (shake) *n* **A** the head of an Arab tribe, village, or family **B** (in Muslim communities) a religious leader > **sheikhdom** *or* **sheikdom** *n*

sheila *n Austral & NZ old-fashioned, informal* a girl or woman

shelf *n, pl* **shelves 1** a board fixed horizontally against a wall or in a cupboard, for holding things **2** a projecting layer of ice or rock on land or in the sea **3 off the shelf** (of products in shops) sold as standard **4 on the shelf** put aside or abandoned; used esp. of unmarried women considered to be past the age of marriage

shelf life *n* the length of time a packaged product will remain fresh or usable

shell *n* **1** the protective outer layer of an egg, fruit, or nut **2** the hard outer covering of an animal such as a crab or tortoise **3** any hard outer case **4** the external structure of a building, car, or ship, esp. one that is unfinished or gutted by fire **5** an explosive artillery projectile that can be fired from a large gun **6** a small-arms cartridge **7** *rowing* a very light

s

narrow racing boat **8 come** or **bring out of one's shell** to become or help to become less shy and reserved ▸ *vb* **9** to remove the shell or husk from **10** to attack with artillery shells ▸ See also **shell out** › **shell-like** *adj*

> **shell** *n* **1** = husk, case, pod **2** = carapace **4** = frame, structure, hull, framework, chassis ▸ *vb* **10** = bomb, bombard, attack, blitz, strafe

shellac *n* **1** a yellowish resin used in varnishes and polishes **2** a varnish made by dissolving shellac in alcohol ▸ *vb* **-lacking, -lacked 3** to coat with shellac

shellfish *n*, *pl* **-fish** or **-fishes** a sea-living animal, esp. one that can be eaten, having a shell

shell out *vb informal* to pay out or hand over (money)

> **shell out** *vb* **shell something out** = pay out, fork out (*slang*), give, hand over

shell shock *n* a nervous disorder characterized by anxiety and depression that occurs as a result of lengthy exposure to battle conditions › **shell-shocked** *adj*

shell suit *n Brit* a lightweight tracksuit made of a waterproof nylon layer over a cotton layer

shelter *n* **1** something that provides cover or protection from weather or danger **2** the protection given by such a cover ▸ *vb* **3** to take cover from bad weather **4** to provide with a place to live or a hiding place: *to shelter refugees*

> **shelter** *n* **1** = cover, screen **2** = protection, safety, refuge, cover ▸ *vb* **3** = take shelter, hide, seek refuge, take cover **4** = protect, shield, harbour, safeguard, cover, hide, guard, defend; ≠ endanger

shelve¹ *vb* **shelving, shelved 1** to put aside or postpone: *to shelve a project* **2** to place (something, such as a book) on a shelf **3** to provide with shelves: *to shelve a cupboard* **4** to dismiss (someone) from active service

> **shelve** *vb* **1** = postpone, defer, freeze, suspend, put aside, put on ice, put on the back burner (*informal*), take a rain check on (*US, Canad informal*)

shelve² *vb* **shelving, shelved** to slope away gradually

shelving *n* **1** material for shelves **2** shelves collectively

shenanigans *pl n informal* **1** mischief or nonsense **2** trickery or deception

shepherd *n* **1** a person employed to tend sheep **2** *Christianity* a member of the clergy when considered as the moral and spiritual guide of the people in the parish ▸ *vb* **3** to guide or watch over (people) › **shepherdess** *fem n*

> **shepherd** *n* **1** = drover, stockman, herdsman or woman (*Brit*), herder, grazier ▸ *vb* = guide, conduct, steer, herd, usher

shepherd's pie *n* a baked dish of minced meat covered with mashed potato

sherbet *n* **1** *Brit, Austral & NZ* a fruit-flavoured slightly fizzy powder, eaten as a sweet or used to make a drink **2** *US, Canad & S African* same as **sorbet**

sheriff *n* **1** (in the US) the chief elected law-enforcement officer in a county **2** (in Canada) a municipal officer who enforces court orders and escorts convicted criminals to prison **3** (in England and Wales) the chief executive officer of the Crown in a county, having chiefly ceremonial duties **4** (in Scotland) a judge in a sheriff court **5** (in Australia) an officer of the Supreme Court

Sherpa *n*, *pl* **-pas** or **-pa** a member of a Tibetan people living on the southern slopes of the Himalayas

sherry *n*, *pl* **-ries** a pale or dark brown fortified wine, originally from southern Spain

shibboleth *n* **1** a slogan or catch phrase, usually considered outworn, that characterizes a particular party or sect: *the shibboleth of Western strategy* **2** a custom, phrase, or use of language that reliably distinguishes a member of one group or class from another

shield *n* **1** a piece of defensive armour carried in the hand or on the arm to protect the body from blows or missiles **2** any person or thing that protects, hides, or defends: *a wind shield* **3** *heraldry* a representation of a shield used for displaying a coat of arms **4** anything that resembles a shield in shape, such as a trophy in a sports competition ▸ *vb* **5** to protect, hide, or defend (someone or something) from danger or harm: *an industry shielded from competition*

> **shield** *n* **2** = protection, cover, defence, screen, guard, shelter, safeguard ▸ *vb* = protect, cover, screen, guard, defend, shelter, safeguard

shift *vb* **1** to move from one place or position to another **2** to pass (blame or responsibility) onto someone else: *he was trying to shift the blame to me* **3** to change (gear) in a motor vehicle **4** to remove or be removed: *no detergent can shift these stains* **5** *US* to change for another or others **6** *slang* to move quickly ▸ *n* **7** the act or an instance of shifting **8** **a** a group of workers who work during a specific period **b** the period of time worked by such a group **9** a method or scheme **10** a loose-fitting straight underskirt or dress

> **shift** *vb* **1** = move, move around, budge ▸ *n* **7** = change, shifting, displacement

shiftless *adj* lacking in ambition or initiative

shifty *adj* **shiftier, shiftiest** looking deceitful and not to be trusted › **shiftiness** *n*

shillelagh (shil-**lay**-lee) *n* (in Ireland) a heavy club

shilling *n* **1** a former British coin worth one twentieth of a pound, replaced by the 5p piece in

S

1970 **2** a former Australian coin, worth one twentieth of a pound **3** the standard monetary unit in several E African countries

shillyshally *vb* **-shallies, -shallying, -shallied** *informal* to be indecisive

shimmer *vb* **1** to shine with a faint unsteady light ▸ *n* **2** a faint unsteady light ▸ **shimmering** *or* **shimmery** *adj*

> **shimmer** *vb* = gleam, twinkle, glisten, scintillate ▸ *n* = gleam, iridescence

shin *n* **1** the front part of the lower leg **2** a cut of beef including the lower foreleg ▸ *vb* **shinning, shinned 3 shin up** to climb (something, such as a rope or pole) by gripping with the hands or arms and the legs and hauling oneself up

shinbone *n* the nontechnical name for **tibia**

shindig *or* **shindy** *n, pl* **-digs** *or* **-dies** *slang* **1** a noisy party or dance **2** a quarrel or brawl

shine *vb* **shining, shone 1** to give off or reflect light **2** to direct the light of (a lamp or torch): *I shone a torch at the ceiling* **3** *past tense & past participle* **shined** to make clean and bright by polishing: *they earned money by shining shoes* **4** to be very good at something: *she shone in most subjects; she shone at school* **5** to appear very bright and clear: *her hair shone like gold* ▸ *n* **6** brightness or lustre **7 take a shine to someone** *informal* to take a liking to someone

> **shine** *vb* **1** = gleam, flash, beam, glow, sparkle, glitter, glare, radiate **3** = polish, buff, burnish, brush **4** = be outstanding, stand out, excel, be conspicuous ▸ *n* **6** = polish, gloss, sheen, lustre

shiner *n informal* a black eye

shingle¹ *n* **1** a thin rectangular tile laid with others in overlapping rows to cover a roof or a wall **2** a woman's short-cropped hairstyle ▸ *vb* **-gling, -gled 3** to cover (a roof or a wall) with shingles **4** to cut (the hair) in a short-cropped style

shingle² *n* coarse gravel found on beaches

shingles *n* a disease causing a rash of small blisters along a nerve

shingle slide *n* NZ the loose stones on a steep slope

Shinto *n* a Japanese religion in which ancestors and nature spirits are worshipped ▸ **Shintoism** *n* ▸ **Shintoist** *n, adj*

shinty *n* **1** a game (of Scottish origin) like hockey but with taller goals **2** *pl* **-ties** the stick used in this game

shiny *adj* **shinier, shiniest 1** bright and polished **2** (of clothes or material) worn to a smooth and glossy state by continual wear or rubbing

> **shiny** *adj* **1** = bright, gleaming, glossy, glistening, polished, lustrous

ship *n* **1** a large seagoing vessel with engines or sails **2 when one's ship comes in** when one has become successful ▸ *vb* **shipping, shipped 3** to send or transport by any carrier, esp. a ship **4** *naut* to take in (water) over the side **5** to bring or go aboard a vessel: *to ship oars* **6** (often foll. by *off*) *informal* to send away: *they were shipped off to foreign countries* **7** to be hired to serve aboard a ship: *I shipped aboard a Liverpool liner*

> **ship** *n* **1** = vessel, boat, craft

shipment *n* **1** goods shipped together as part of the same lot: *a shipment of arms* **2** the act of shipping cargo

shipping *n* **1** the business of transporting freight, esp. by ship **2** ships collectively: *all shipping should stay clear of the harbour*

shipshape *adj* **1** neat or orderly ▸ *adv* **2** in a neat and orderly manner

shipwreck *n* **1** the destruction of a ship at sea **2** the remains of a wrecked ship **3** ruin or destruction: *the shipwreck of the old science* ▸ *vb* **4** to wreck or destroy (a ship) **5** to bring to ruin or destruction

shipyard *n* a place where ships are built and repaired

shire *n* **1** *Brit* a county **2** *Austral* a rural area with an elected council **3 the Shires** the Midland counties of England

shire horse *n* a large powerful breed of working horse

shirk *vb* to avoid doing (work or a duty); to be negligent: *no-one shirks when he's around* ▸ **shirker** *n*

shirt *n* **1** an item of clothing worn on the upper part of the body, usually with a collar and sleeves and buttoning up the front **2 keep your shirt on** *informal* keep your temper **3 put one's shirt on something** *informal* to bet all one has on something

shirty *adj* **shirtier, shirtiest** *slang* bad-tempered or annoyed

shish kebab *n* a dish of small pieces of meat and vegetables grilled on a skewer

shiver¹ *vb* **1** to tremble from cold or fear ▸ *n* **2** a tremble caused by cold or fear **3 the shivers** a fit of shivering through fear or illness ▸ **shivering** *n, adj* ▸ **shivery** *adj*

> **shiver** *vb* = shudder, shake, tremble, quake, quiver ▸ *n* **2** = tremble, shudder, quiver, trembling, flutter, tremor

shiver² *vb* **1** to break into fragments ▸ *n* **2** a splintered piece

shoal¹ *n* **1** a large group of fish swimming together **2** a large group of people or things

shoal² *n* **1** a stretch of shallow water **2** a sandbank or rocky area, esp. one that can be seen at low water ▸ *vb* **3** to make or become shallow

shock¹ *vb* **1** to cause (someone) to experience extreme horror, disgust, or astonishment: *the similarity shocked me* **2** to cause a state of shock in (a person) ▸ *n* **3** a sudden and violent blow or impact **4 a** a sudden and violent emotional disturbance **b** something causing this **5** *pathol* a condition in which a person's blood cannot flow properly because of severe injury, burns, or fright **6** pain and muscular spasm caused by an electric current passing through a person's body ▸ **shocker** *n*

> **shock** *vb* **1** = shake, stun, stagger, jolt, stupefy ▸ *n* **3** = impact, blow, clash, collision **4** = upset, blow, trauma, bombshell, turn (*informal*), distress, disturbance

shock² *n* **1** a number of grain sheaves set on end in a field to dry ▸ *vb* **2** to set up (sheaves) in shocks

shocking *adj* **1** *informal* very bad or terrible: *a shocking match at Leicester* **2** causing dismay or disgust: *a shocking lack of concern* **3 shocking pink** (of) a very bright shade of pink

> **shocking** *adj* **1** = terrible, appalling, dreadful, bad, horrendous, ghastly, deplorable, abysmal **2** = appalling, outrageous, disgraceful, disgusting, dreadful, horrifying, revolting, sickening; ≠ wonderful

shod *vb* the past of **shoe**

shoddy *adj* **-dier, -diest 1** made or done badly or carelessly: *shoddy goods* **2** of poor quality; shabby > **shoddily** *adv* > **shoddiness** *n*

shoe *n* **1** one of a matching pair of coverings shaped to fit the foot, made of leather or other strong material and ending below the ankle **2** anything resembling a shoe in shape, function, or position **3** short for **horseshoe 4 be in a person's shoes** *informal* to be in another person's situation ▸ *vb* **shoeing, shod 5** to fit (a horse) with horseshoes

shoehorn *n* a smooth curved piece of metal or plastic inserted at the heel of a shoe to ease the foot into it

shoestring *n* *informal* a very small amount of money: *the theatre will be run on a shoestring*

shone *vb* a past of **shine**

shonky *adj* **-kier, -kiest** *Austral & NZ informal* unreliable or unsound

shoo *interj* **1** go away!: used to drive away unwanted or annoying animals or people ▸ *vb* **shooing, shooed 2** to drive away by crying 'shoo'

shook *vb* the past tense of **shake**

shoot *vb* **shooting, shot 1** to hit, wound, or kill with a missile fired from a weapon **2** to fire (a missile or missiles) from a weapon **3** to fire (a weapon) **4** to hunt game with a gun for sport **5** to send out or be sent out quickly and aggressively: *he shot questions at her* **6** to move very rapidly: *the car shot forward* **7** to go or pass quickly over or through: *he was trying to shoot the white water* **8** to slide or push into or out of a fastening: *she shot the bolt quickly* **9** (of a plant) to sprout (a new growth) **10** to photograph or film (a subject, sequence, etc.) **11** *sport* to hit or kick the ball at goal ▸ *n* **12** the act of shooting **13** a new growth or sprout of a plant **14** *chiefly Brit* a meeting or party organized for hunting game with guns **15** an area where game can be hunted with guns **16** *informal* a photographic assignment: *a fashion shoot in New York*

> **shoot** *vb* **1** = open fire on, blast (*slang*), hit, kill, plug (*slang*), bring down **2** = fire, launch, discharge, project, hurl, fling, propel, emit **6** = speed, race, rush, charge, fly, tear, dash, barrel (along) (*informal, chiefly US, Canad*) ▸ *n* **13** = sprout, branch, bud, sprig, offshoot

shooting star *n* *informal* a meteor

shooting stick *n* a walking stick with a spike at one end and a folding seat at the other

shop *n* **1** a place for the sale of goods and services **2** a place where a specified type of work is done; workshop: *a repair shop* **3 all over the shop** *informal* scattered everywhere: *his papers were all over the shop* **4 shut up shop** to close business at the end of the day or permanently **5 talk shop** *informal* to discuss one's business or work on a social occasion ▸ *vb* **shopping, shopped 6** (often foll. by *for*) to visit a shop or shops in order to buy (goods) **7** *Brit, Austral & NZ slang* to inform on (someone), esp. to the police > **shopper** *n*

> **shop** *n* **1** = store, supermarket, boutique, emporium (*old-fashioned*), hypermarket, dairy (NZ)

shop around *vb* *informal* **1** to visit a number of shops or stores to compare goods and prices **2** to consider a number of possibilities before making a choice

shop floor *n* **1** the production area of a factory **2** workers, esp. factory workers, as opposed to management

shoplifter *n* a customer who steals goods from a shop > **shoplifting** *n*

shop steward *n* a trade-union official elected by his or her fellow workers to be their representative in dealing with their employer

shore¹ *n* the land along the edge of a sea, lake, or wide river. Related adjective: **littoral**

> **shore** *n* = beach, coast, sands, strand (*poetic*), seashore

shore² *vb* **shoring, shored shore up A** to prop up (an unsteady building or wall) with a strong support **B** to strengthen or support (something weak): *lower interest rates to shore up the economy*

shorn *vb* a past participle of **shear**

short *adj* **1** of little length; not long **2** of little height; not tall **3** not lasting long **4** not enough: *the number of places laid at the table was short by four* **5 short of** or **on** lacking in: *short of cash; short on detail* **6** concise: *a short book* **7** (of drinks) consisting chiefly of a spirit, such as whisky **8** (of someone's memory) lacking the ability to retain a lot of facts **9** (of a person's manner) abrupt and rather rude: *Kemp was short with her* **10** (of betting odds) almost even **11** *finance* **A** not possessing at the time of sale the stocks or commodities one sells **s** relating to such sales, which depend on falling prices for profit **12** *phonetics* (of a vowel) of relatively brief duration **13** (of pastry) crumbly in texture **14 in short supply** scarce **15 short and sweet** brief and to the point **16 short for** a shortened form of ▸ *adv* **17** abruptly: *to stop short* **18 be caught short** to have a sudden need to go to the toilet **19 go short** not to have enough **20 short of** except: *they want nothing short of his removal from power* ▸ *n* **21** a drink of spirits **22** a short film shown before the main feature in a cinema **23** same as **short circuit 24 for short** *informal* as a shortened form: *cystic fibrosis, CF for short* **25 in short** briefly ▸ *vb* **26** to short-circuit ▸ **shortness** *n*

> **short** *adj* **1, 2** = small, little, squat, diminutive, petite, dumpy; ≠ tall **3** = brief, fleeting, momentary; ≠ long **4, 14** = scarce, wanting, low, limited, lacking, scant, deficient; ≠ plentiful **6** = concise, brief, succinct, summary, compressed, terse, laconic, pithy; ≠ lengthy **9** = abrupt, sharp, terse, curt, brusque, impolite, discourteous, uncivil; ≠ polite ▸ *adv* **17** = abruptly, suddenly, without warning; ≠ gradually

shortage *n* not enough of something needed

> **shortage** *n* = deficiency, want, lack, scarcity, dearth, paucity (*formal*), insufficiency; ≠ abundance

shortbread *n* a rich crumbly biscuit made with butter

short-change *vb* **-changing, -changed 1** to give (someone) less than the correct change **2** *slang* to treat (someone), unfairly, esp. by giving less than is expected

short circuit *n* **1** a faulty or accidental connection in an electric circuit, which deflects current through a path of low resistance, usually causing the failure of the circuit ▸ *vb* **short-circuit 2** to develop a short circuit **3** to bypass (a procedure): *she wrote to them direct and short-circuited the job agency* **4** to hinder or frustrate (a plan)

shortcoming *n* a fault or weakness

> **shortcoming** *n* = failing, fault, weakness, defect, flaw, imperfection

short cut *n* **1** a route that is shorter than the usual one **2** a way of saving time or effort

shorten *vb* to make or become short or shorter

> **shorten** *vb* = cut, reduce, decrease, diminish, lessen, curtail, abbreviate, abridge; ≠ increase

shortfall *n* **1** failure to meet a requirement **2** the amount of such a failure; deficit

shorthand *n* a system of rapid writing using simple strokes and other symbols to represent words or phrases

short-handed *adj* (of a company or organization) lacking enough staff to do the required work

short list *n* **1** Also called (Scot): **short leet** a list of suitable candidates for a job or prize, from which the successful candidate will be selected ▸ *vb* **short-list 2** to put (someone) on a short list

shortly *adv* **1** in a short time; soon **2** spoken in a cross and impatient manner

> **shortly** *adv* = soon, presently, before long, in a little while

short shrift *n* brief and unsympathetic treatment

short-sighted *adj* **1** unable to see faraway things clearly **2** not taking likely future developments into account: *a short-sighted approach to the problem* ▸ **short-sightedness** *n*

short wave *n* a radio wave with a wavelength in the range 10–100 metres

shot[1] *n* **1** the act or an instance of firing a gun or rifle **2** *sport* the act or an instance of hitting, kicking, or throwing the ball **3** small round lead pellets used in shotguns **4** a person with specified skill in shooting: *my father was quite a good shot* **5** *informal* an attempt: *a second shot at writing a better treaty* **6** *informal* a guess **7 a** a single photograph **s** an uninterrupted sequence of film taken by a single camera **8** *informal* an injection of a vaccine or narcotic drug **9** *informal* a drink of spirits **10** the launching of a rocket or spacecraft to a specified destination: *a moon shot* **11** *sport* a heavy metal ball used in the shot put **12 like a shot** without hesitating **13 shot in the arm** *informal* something that brings back energy or confidence **14 shot in the dark** a wild guess

> **shot** *n* **1** = discharge, gunfire, crack, blast, explosion, bang **2** = strike, throw, lob **3** = ammunition, bullet, slug, pellet, projectile, lead, ball **4** = marksman *or* woman, shooter **5** = attempt, go (*informal*), try, turn, effort, stab (*informal*), endeavour

shot[2] *vb* **1** the past of **shoot** ▸ *adj* **2** (of textiles) woven to give a changing colour effect **3** streaked with colour: *dark hair shot with streaks of grey*

shotgun *n* a gun for firing a charge of shot at short range

shot put *n* an athletic event in which contestants hurl a heavy metal ball called a shot as far as possible ▸ **shot-putter** *n*

should *vb* the past tense of **shall**: used to indicate that an action is considered by the speaker to be obligatory (*you should go*) or to form the subjunctive mood (*I should like to see you; if I should die; should I be late, start without me*)

shoulder *n* **1** the part of the body where the arm, wing, or foreleg joins the trunk **2** a cut of meat including the upper part of the foreleg **3** the part of an item of clothing that covers the shoulder **4** the strip of unpaved land that borders a road **5 a shoulder to cry on** a person one turns to for sympathy with one's troubles **6 put one's shoulder to the wheel** *informal* to work very hard **7 rub shoulders with someone** *informal* to mix with someone socially **8 shoulder to shoulder** A side by side B working together ▸ *vb* **9** to accept (blame or responsibility) **10** to push with one's shoulder: *he shouldered his way through the crowd* **11** to lift or carry on one's shoulders **12 shoulder arms** *military* to bring one's rifle vertically close to one's right side

> **shoulder** *vb* **9** = bear, carry, take on, accept, assume, be responsible for **10** = push, elbow, shove, jostle, press

shoulder blade *n* either of two large flat triangular bones, one on each side of the back part of the shoulder

shouldn't should not

shout *n* **1** a loud call or cry **2** *informal* one's turn to buy a round of drinks ▸ *vb* **3** to cry out loudly **4** *Austral & NZ informal* to treat (someone) to (something, such as a drink)

> **shout** *n* **1** = cry, call, yell, scream, roar, bellow ▸ *vb* **3** = cry (out), call (out), yell, scream, roar, bellow, bawl, holler (*informal*)

shout down *vb* to silence (someone) by talking loudly

> **shout down** *vb* **shout someone down** = drown out, overwhelm, drown, silence

shove *vb* **shoving, shoved 1** to give a violent push to **2** to push (one's way) roughly **3** *informal* to put (something) somewhere quickly and carelessly: *shove it into the boot* ▸ *n* **4** a rough push

> **shove** *vb* **1, 2** = push, thrust, elbow, drive, press, propel, jostle, impel ▸ *n* = push, knock, thrust, elbow, bump, nudge, jostle

shovel *n* **1** a tool for lifting or moving loose material, consisting of a broad blade attached to a large handle **2** a machine or part of a machine resembling a shovel in function ▸ *vb* **-velling, -velled** *or US* **-veling, -veled 3** to lift or move (loose material) with a shovel **4** to put away large quantities of (something) quickly: *shovelling food into their mouths*

> **shovel** *vb* **3** = move, scoop, dredge, load, heap **4** = stuff, ladle

shove off *vb informal* to go away; depart

> **shove off** *vb* = go away, leave, clear off (*informal*), depart, push off (*informal*), scram (*informal*), rack off (*Austral, NZ slang*)

show *vb* **showing, showed, shown** *or* **showed 1** to make, be, or become visible or noticeable: *to show an interest; excitement showed on everyone's face* **2** to present for inspection: *someone showed me the plans* **3** to demonstrate or prove: *evidence showed that this was the most economical way* **4** to instruct by demonstration: *she showed me how to feed the pullets*

5 to indicate: *the device shows changes in the pressure* **6** to behave towards (someone) in a particular way: *to show mercy* **7** to exhibit or display works of art, goods, etc.: *three artists are showing at the gallery* **8** to present (a film or play) or (of a film or play) to be presented **9** to guide or escort: *he offered to show me around* **10** *informal* to arrive ▸ *n* **11** a theatrical or other entertainment: *a magic show* **12** a display or exhibition: *a show of paintings* **13** something done to create an impression: *a show of indignation* **14** vain and conspicuous display: *it was nothing but mere show* **15** *slang, chiefly Brit* a thing or affair: *jolly good show* ▸ See also **show off, show up**

> **show** *vb* **1, 3** = indicate, demonstrate, prove, reveal, display, point out, manifest, testify to, flag up; ≠ disprove **2, 7** = display, exhibit **4** = demonstrate, describe, explain, teach, illustrate, instruct **5** = express, display, reveal, indicate, register, demonstrate, manifest; ≠ hide **8** = broadcast, transmit, air, beam, relay, televise, put on the air, podcast **9** = guide, lead, conduct, accompany, direct, escort **10** = turn up, appear, attend ▸ *n* **11** = entertainment, production, presentation **12** = display, sight, spectacle, array **13** = appearance, display, pose, parade

show business *n* the entertainment industry. Also (*informal*): **show biz**

showcase *n* **1** a setting in which something is displayed to best advantage: *a showcase for young opera singers* **2** a glass case used to display objects in a museum or shop ▸ *vb* **-casing, -cased 3** to display something to its best advantage: *an exhibition showcasing new manufacturing technology*

showdown *n informal* a major confrontation that settles a dispute

> **showdown** *n* = confrontation, clash, face-off (*slang*)

shower *n* **1** A a kind of bathing in which a person stands upright and is sprayed with water from a nozzle B a device, room, or booth for such bathing **2** a brief period of rain, hail, sleet, or snow **3** a sudden fall of many small light objects: *a shower of loose gravel* **4** *Brit slang* a worthless or contemptible group of people **5** *US, Canad, Austral & NZ* a party held to honour and present gifts to a prospective bride or prospective mother ▸ *vb* **6** to take a shower **7** to sprinkle with or as if with a shower: *the walkers were showered by volcanic ash* **8** to present (someone) with things liberally: *he showered her with presents* > **showery** *adj*

> **shower** *n* **2** = deluge ▸ *vb* **7** = cover, dust, spray, sprinkle **8** = inundate, heap, lavish, pour, deluge

showjumping *n* the sport of riding horses in competitions to demonstrate skill in jumping > **showjumper** *n*

S

showman *n, pl* **-men 1** a person skilled at presenting anything in an effective manner **2** a person who presents or produces a show > **showmanship** *n*

shown *vb* a past participle of **show**

show off *vb* **1** to exhibit or display (something) so as to invite admiration: *he was eager to show off his new car* **2** *informal* to flaunt skills, knowledge, or looks in order to attract attention or impress people ▸ *n* **show-off** *informal* a person who flaunts his or her skills, knowledge, or looks in order to attract attention or impress people

show off *vb* **1 show something off** = exhibit, display, parade, demonstrate, flaunt **2** = boast, brag, blow your own trumpet, swagger ▸ *n* **show-off** = exhibitionist, boaster, poseur, braggart, figjam (*Austral slang*)

showpiece *n* **1** anything displayed or exhibited **2** something admired as a fine example of its type: *an orchestral showpiece*

showroom *n* a room in which goods for sale, esp. cars or electrical or gas appliances, are on display

show up *vb* **1** to reveal or be revealed clearly **2** to expose the faults or defects of (someone or something) by comparison **3** *informal* to put (someone) to shame; embarrass **4** *informal* to arrive

show up *vb* **1 show something up** = reveal, expose, highlight, lay bare **3 show someone up** = embarrass, let down, mortify, put to shame

showy *adj* **showier, showiest 1** colourful, bright in appearance, and very noticeable, and perhaps rather vulgar: *showy jewellery* **2** making an imposing display > **showily** *adv* > **showiness** *n*

shrank *vb* a past tense of **shrink**

shrapnel *n* **1** an artillery shell containing a number of small pellets or bullets which it is designed to scatter on explosion **2** fragments from this type of shell

shred *n* **1** a long narrow piece torn off something **2** a very small amount: *not a shred of truth* ▸ *vb* **shredding, shredded** *or* **shred 3** to tear into shreds > **shredder** *n*

shred *n* **1** = strip, bit, piece, scrap, fragment, sliver, tatter **2** = particle, trace, scrap, grain, atom, jot, iota

shrew *n* **1** a small mouselike animal with a long snout **2** *derogatory* a woman considered to be bad-tempered or nagging > **shrewish** *adj*

shrewd *adj* intelligent and making good judgments > **shrewdly** *adv* > **shrewdness** *n*

shrewd *adj* = astute, clever, sharp, keen, smart, calculating, intelligent, cunning; ≠ naive

shriek *n* **1** a high-pitched scream ▸ *vb* **2** to utter (words or sounds) in a high-pitched tone

shriek *n* = scream, cry, yell, screech, squeal ▸ *vb* = scream, cry, yell, screech, squeal

shrike *n* a bird with a heavy hooked bill, which kills small animals by dashing them on thorns

shrill *adj* **1** (of a sound) sharp and high-pitched ▸ *vb* **2** to utter (words or sounds) in a shrill tone > **shrillness** *n* > **shrilly** *adv*

shrimp *n* **1** a small edible shellfish with a long tail and a pair of pincers **2** *informal* a small person ▸ *vb* **3** to fish for shrimps

shrine *n* **1** a place of worship associated with a sacred person or object **2** a container for sacred relics **3** the tomb of a saint or other holy person **4** a place that is visited and honoured because of its association with a famous person or event: *he'd come to worship at the shrine of Mozart*

shrink *vb* **shrinking, shrank** *or* **shrunk, shrunk** *or* **shrunken 1** to become or cause to become smaller, sometimes because of wetness, heat, or cold **2 shrink from A** to withdraw or move away through fear: *they didn't shrink from danger* **B** to feel great reluctance (to perform a task or duty) ▸ *n* **3** *slang* a psychiatrist

shrink *vb* **1** = decrease, dwindle, lessen, grow or get smaller, contract, narrow, diminish, shorten; ≠ grow

shrinkage *n* **1** the fact of shrinking **2** the amount by which anything decreases in size, value, or weight

shrivel *vb* **-velling, -velled** *or US* **-veling, -veled** to become dry and withered

shroud *n* **1** a piece of cloth used to wrap a dead body **2** anything that hides things: *a shroud of smoke* ▸ *vb* **3** to hide or obscure (something): *shrouded in uncertainty; shrouded by smog*

shroud *n* **1** = winding sheet, grave clothes **2** = covering, veil, mantle, screen, pall ▸ *vb* = conceal, cover, screen, hide, blanket, veil, cloak, envelop

Shrove Tuesday *n* the day before Ash Wednesday

shrub *n* a woody plant, smaller than a tree, with several stems instead of a trunk > **shrubby** *adj*

shrubbery *n, pl* **-beries 1** an area planted with shrubs **2** shrubs collectively

shrug *vb* **shrugging, shrugged 1** to draw up and drop (the shoulders) as a sign of indifference or doubt ▸ *n* **2** the action of shrugging

shrug off *vb* **1** to treat (a matter) as unimportant **2** to get rid of (someone)

shrunk *vb* a past tense and past participle of **shrink**

shrunken *vb* **1** a past participle of **shrink** ▸ *adj* **2** reduced in size

shudder *vb* **1** to shake or tremble suddenly and violently from horror or fear **2** (of a machine) to shake violently ▸ *n* **3** a shiver of fear or horror

shudder *vb* **1** = shiver, shake, tremble, quake, quiver, convulse ▸ *n* = shiver, tremor, quiver, spasm

S

shuffle *vb* **-fling, -fled 1** to walk or move (the feet) with a slow dragging motion **2** to mix together in a jumbled mass: *the newsreader shuffled his papers* **3** to mix up (playing cards) so as to change their order ▸ *n* **4** an instance of shuffling **5** a rearrangement: *a shuffle of top management* **6** a dance with short dragging movements of the feet

> **shuffle** *vb* **1** = shamble, stagger, stumble, dodder **2** = rearrange, jumble, mix, disorder, disarrange

shun *vb* **shunning, shunned** to avoid deliberately

> **shun** *vb* = avoid, steer clear of, keep away from

shunt *vb* **1** to move (objects or people) to a different position **2** *railways* to transfer (engines or carriages) from track to track ▸ *n* **3** the act of shunting **4** a railway point **5** *electronics* a conductor connected in parallel across a part of a circuit to divert a known fraction of the current **6** *informal* a collision where one vehicle runs into the back of another

shush *interj* **1** be quiet! hush! ▸ *vb* **2** to quiet (someone) by saying 'shush'

shut *vb* **shutting, shut 1** to move (something) so as to cover an opening: *shut the door* **2** to close (something) by bringing together the parts: *Ridley shut the folder* **3 shut up** to close or lock the doors of: *let's shut up the shop* **4 shut in** to confine or enclose **5 shut out** to prevent from entering **6** (of a shop or other establishment) to stop operating for the day: *the late-night rush after the pubs shut* ▸ *adj* **7** closed or fastened ▸ See also **shutdown**

> **shut** *vb* **1** = close, secure, fasten, seal, slam; ≠ open ▸ *adj* = closed, fastened, sealed, locked; ≠ open

shutdown *n* **1** the closing of a factory, shop, or other business ▸ *vb* **shut down 2** to discontinue operations permanently

> **shutdown** *vb* **shut down** = stop work, halt work, close down

shutter *n* **1** a hinged doorlike cover, usually one of a pair, for closing off a window **2 put up the shutters** to close business at the end of the day or permanently **3** *photog* a device in a camera that opens to allow light through the lens so as to expose the film when a photograph is taken ▸ *vb* **4** to close or equip with a shutter or shutters

shuttle *n* **1** a bus, train, or aircraft that makes frequent journeys between two places which are fairly near to each other **2** a bobbin-like device used in weaving to pass the weft thread between the warp threads **3** a small bobbin-like device used to hold the thread in a sewing machine ▸ *vb* **-tling, -tled 4** to travel back and forth

> **shuttle** *vb* = go back and forth, commute, go to and fro, alternate

shuttlecock *n* a rounded piece of cork or plastic with feathers stuck in one end, struck to and fro in badminton

shy¹ *adj* **1** not at ease in the company of others **2** easily frightened; timid **3 shy of** cautious or wary of **4** reluctant or unwilling: *camera-shy*; *workshy* ▸ *vb* **shies, shying, shied 5** to move back or aside suddenly from fear: *with a terrified whinny the horse shied* **6 shy away from** to draw back from (doing something), through lack of confidence ▸ *n, pl* **shies 7** a sudden movement back or aside from fear > **shyly** *adv* > **shyness** *n*

> **shy** *adj* **1** = timid, self-conscious, bashful, retiring, shrinking, coy, self-effacing, diffident; ≠ confident **2** = cautious, wary, hesitant, suspicious, distrustful, chary; ≠ reckless ▸ *vb* **5** = recoil, flinch, draw back, start, balk

shy² *vb* **shies, shying, shied 1** to throw (something) ▸ *n, pl* **shies 2** a quick throw

Siamese *n, pl* **-mese 1** same as **Siamese cat** ▸ *adj, n, pl* **-mese 2** (formerly) same as **Thai**

Siamese cat *n* a breed of cat with cream fur, dark ears and face, and blue eyes

Siamese twins *pl n* a former name for **conjoined twins**

sibilant *adj* **1** having a hissing sound ▸ *n* **2** *phonetics* a consonant, such as *s* or *z*, that is pronounced with a hissing sound

sibling *n* a brother or sister

sibyl *n* (in ancient Greece and Rome) a prophetess > **sibylline** *adj*

sic *adv* thus: inserted in brackets in a text to indicate that an odd spelling or reading is in fact what was written, even though it is or appears to be wrong

sick *adj* **1** vomiting or likely to vomit **2** physically or mentally unwell **3** of or for ill people: *sick pay* **4** deeply affected with mental or spiritual distress: *sick at heart* **5** mentally disturbed **6** *informal* making fun of death, illness, or misfortune: *a sick joke* **7 sick of** or **sick and tired of** *informal* disgusted by or weary of: *I'm sick of this town* ▸ *n, vb* **8** *informal* same as **vomit**

> **sick** *adj* **1** = nauseous, ill, queasy, nauseated **2** = unwell, ill, poorly (*informal*), diseased, crook (*Austral, NZ informal*), ailing, under the weather (*informal*), indisposed; ≠ well **6** = morbid, sadistic, black, macabre, ghoulish **7** = tired, bored, fed up, weary, jaded

sicken *vb* **1** to make (someone) feel nauseated or disgusted **2 sicken for** to show symptoms of (an illness)

> **sicken** *vb* **1** = disgust, revolt, nauseate, repel, gross out (*slang*), turn your stomach

sickle *n* a tool for cutting grass and grain crops, with a curved blade and a short handle

sickly *adj* **-lier, -liest 1** weak and unhealthy **2** (of a person) looking pale and unwell: *sickly*

S

pallor **3** unpleasant to smell, taste, or look at **4** showing excessive emotion in a weak and rather pathetic way: *a sickly tune* ▸ *adv* **5** suggesting sickness: *sickly pale* > **sickliness** *n*

sickness *n* **1** a particular illness or disease: *sleeping sickness* **2** the state of being ill or unhealthy: *absent from work due to sickness* **3** a feeling of queasiness in the stomach followed by vomiting

> **sickness** *n* **1** = illness, disorder, ailment, disease, complaint, bug (*informal*), affliction, malady **3** = nausea, queasiness

side *n* **1** a line or surface that borders anything **2** *geom* a line forming part of the perimeter of a plane figure: *a square has four sides* **3** either of two parts into which an object, surface, or area can be divided: *the right side and the left side* **4** either of the two surfaces of a flat object: *write on both sides of the page* **5** the sloping part of a hill or bank **6** either the left or the right half of the body, esp. the area around the waist: *he took a nine millimetre bullet in the side* **7** the area immediately next to a person or thing: *at the side of my bed* **8** a place within an area identified by reference to a central point: *the south side of the island* **9** the area at the edge of something, as opposed to the centre: *the far side of the square* **10** aspect or part: *there is a positive side to things* **11** one of two or more contesting groups or teams: *the two sides will meet in the final* **12** a position held in opposition to another in a dispute **13** a line of descent through one parent: *a relative on his father's side* **14** *Brit slang* conceit or cheek: *to put on side* **15 on one side** apart from the rest **16 on the side** in addition to a person's main work: *she did a little public speaking on the side* **17 side by side** close together **18 side by side with** beside or near to **19 take sides** to support one party in a dispute against another ▸ *adj* **20** situated at the side: *the side entrance* **21** less important: *a side issue* ▸ *vb* **siding**, **sided 22 side with** to support (one party in a dispute)

> **side** *n* **1, 7, 9** = border, margin, boundary, verge (*Brit*), flank, rim, perimeter, edge; ≠ middle **4** = face, surface, facet **10** = aspect, feature, angle, facet **11** = party, camp, faction, cause **12** = point of view, viewpoint, position, opinion, angle, slant, standpoint ▸ *adj* **21** = subordinate, minor, secondary, subsidiary, lesser, marginal, incidental, ancillary; ≠ main
> ▸ *vb* **side with someone** = support, agree with, stand up for, favour, go along with, take the part of, ally yourself with

sidebar *n* (in a newspaper or website) a short article placed next to the main one and containing additional material

sideboard *n* a piece of furniture for a dining room, with drawers, cupboards, and shelves to hold tableware

sideboards *or esp US & Canad* **sideburns** *pl n* a man's whiskers grown down either side of the face in front of the ears

sidekick *n informal* a close friend or associate

sidelight *n* **1** *Brit* either of two small lights at the front of a motor vehicle **2** either of the two navigational lights used by ships at night

sideline *n* **1** an extra job in addition to one's main job ▸ *vb* **-lining**, **-lined 2** to prevent (a person) from pursuing a particular activity

sidelong *adj* **1** directed to the side; oblique ▸ *adv* **2** from the side; obliquely

sidereal (side-eer-ee-al) *adj* of or determined with reference to the stars: *the sidereal time*

side-saddle *n* **1** a riding saddle originally designed for women in skirts, allowing the rider to sit with both legs on the same side of the horse ▸ *adv* **2** on a side-saddle

sidestep *vb* **-stepping**, **-stepped 1** to step out of the way of (something) **2** to dodge (an issue) ▸ *n* **side step 3** a movement to one side, such as in dancing or boxing

sidetrack *vb* to distract (someone) from a main subject

sidewalk *n US & Canad* a raised space alongside a road, for pedestrians

> **sidewalk** *n* = pavement, footpath (*Austral, NZ*)

sideways *adv* **1** moving, facing, or inclining towards one side **2** from one side; obliquely **3** with one side forward ▸ *adj* **4** moving or directed to or from one side

> **sideways** *adv* **1** = to the side, laterally **2** = indirectly, obliquely ▸ *adj* = sidelong, oblique

siding *n* a short stretch of railway track connected to a main line, used for loading and unloading freight and storing engines and carriages

sidle *vb* **-dling**, **-dled** to walk slowly and carefully, not wanting to be noticed

SIDS sudden infant death syndrome; cot death

siege *n* **1** a military operation carried out to capture a place by surrounding and blockading it **2** a similar operation carried out by police, for example to force people out of a place **3 lay siege to** to subject (a place) to a siege

> **siege** *n* **1, 2** = blockade, encirclement, besiegement

sienna *n* **1** a natural earth used as a reddish-brown or yellowish-brown pigment ▸ *adj* **2 burnt sienna** reddish-brown **3 raw sienna** yellowish-brown

sierra *n* a range of mountains with jagged peaks in Spain or America

siesta *n* an afternoon nap, taken in hot countries

sieve (siv) *n* **1** a utensil with a mesh through which a substance is sifted or strained ▸ *vb* **sieving**, **sieved 2** to sift or strain through a sieve

sift *vb* **1** to sieve (a powdery substance) in order to remove the coarser particles **2** to examine (information or evidence) carefully to select what is important

> **sift** *vb* **1** = sieve, filter, strain, separate, part **2** = examine, investigate, go through, research, analyse, work over, scrutinize

sigh *vb* **1** to draw in and audibly let out a deep breath as an expression of sadness, tiredness, longing, or relief **2** to make a sound resembling this **3 sigh for** to long for **4** to say (something) with a sigh ▸ *n* **5** the act or sound of sighing

sight *n* **1** the ability to see; vision. Related adjective: **visual 2** an instance of seeing **3** the range of vision: *the cemetery was out of sight* **4** anything that is seen **5** point of view; judgment: *nothing has changed in my sight* **6** *informal* anything unpleasant to see: *she looked a sight in the streetlamps* **7** a device for guiding the eye in aiming a gun or making an observation with an optical instrument **8** an aim or observation made with such a device **9 sights** anything worth seeing: *the great sights of Barcelona* **10 a sight** *informal* a great deal: *it's a sight warmer than in the hall* **11 a sight for sore eyes** a welcome sight **12 catch sight of** to glimpse **13 know someone by sight** to be able to recognize someone without having ever been introduced **14 lose sight of A** to be unable to see (something) any longer **B** to forget: *we lose sight of priorities* **15 on sight** as soon as someone or something is seen **16 set one's sights on** to have (a specified goal) in mind **17 sight unseen** without having seen the object concerned: *he would have taken it sight unseen* ▸ *vb* **18** to see (someone or something) briefly or suddenly: *the two suspicious vessels were sighted* **19** to aim (a firearm) using the sight

> **sight** *n* **1** = vision, eyes, eyesight, seeing, eye **3** = view, range of vision, visibility **4** = spectacle, show, scene, display, exhibition, vista, pageant **6** = eyesore, mess, monstrosity ▸ *vb* **18** = spot, see, observe, distinguish, perceive, make out, discern, behold (*archaic, literary*)

sightless *adj* blind

sight-read *vb* **-reading, -read** to sing or play (music in a printed form) without previous preparation > **sight-reading** *n*

sightseeing *n informal* visiting famous or interesting sights in a place > **sightseer** *n*

sign *n* **1** something that indicates a fact or condition that is not immediately or outwardly observable: *a sign of tension* **2** a gesture, mark, or symbol intended to convey an idea or information **3** a board or placard displayed in public and intended to advertise, inform, or warn **4** a conventional mark or symbol that has a specific meaning, for example £ for pounds **5** *maths* **A** any symbol used to indicate an operation: *a minus sign* **B** a symbol used to indicate whether a number or expression is

positive or negative **6** a visible indication: *no sign of the enemy* **7** an omen **8** *med* any evidence of the presence of a disease or disorder ▸ *vb* **9** to write (one's name) on (a document or letter) to show its authenticity or one's agreement **10** to communicate using sign language **11** to make a sign to someone so as to convey an idea or information **12** to engage or be engaged by signing a contract: *he signed for another team*

> **sign** *n* **1, 6** = indication, evidence, mark, signal, symptom, hint, proof, gesture **2, 4** = symbol, mark, device, logo, badge, emblem **3** = notice, board, warning, placard **7** = omen, warning, portent, foreboding, augury, auspice ▸ *vb* **9** = autograph, initial, inscribe **11** = gesture, indicate, signal, beckon, gesticulate

signal *n* **1** any sign, gesture, sound, or action used to communicate information **2** anything that causes immediate action: *this is the signal for a detailed examination of the risk* **3 A** a variable voltage, current, or electromagnetic wave, by which information is conveyed through an electronic circuit **B** the information so conveyed ▸ *adj* **4** *formal* very important: *a signal triumph for the government* ▸ *vb* **-nalling, -nalled** or *US* **-naling, -naled 5** to communicate (information) by signal > **signally** *adv*

> **signal** *n* **1** = sign, gesture, indication, mark, note, expression, token **2** = cue, sign, prompting, reminder

signal box *n* a building from which railway signals are operated

signalman *n, pl* **-men** a railwayman in charge of the signals and points within a section

signatory (sig-na-tree) *n, pl* **-ries 1** a person, organization, or state that has signed a document such as a treaty ▸ *adj* **2** having signed a document or treaty

signature *n* **1** a person's name written by himself or herself, used in signing something **2** a distinctive characteristic that identifies a person or animal **3** *music* a sign at the beginning of a piece to show key or time **4** *printing* a sheet of paper printed with several pages, which when folded becomes a section of a book

signature tune *n* a piece of music used to introduce a particular television or radio programme

signet *n* a small seal used to make documents official

signet ring *n* a finger ring engraved with an initial or other emblem

significance *n* **1** the effect something is likely to have on other things: *an event of important significance in British history* **2** meaning: *the occult significance of the symbol*

> **significance** *n* **1** = importance, consequence, moment, weight

significant adj 1 very important 2 having or expressing a meaning ▸ **significantly** adv

> **significant** adj 1 = important, serious, material, vital, critical, momentous, weighty, noteworthy; ≠ insignificant 2 = meaningful, expressive, eloquent, indicative, suggestive; ≠ meaningless

signify vb -fies, -fying, -fied 1 to indicate or suggest 2 to stand as a symbol or sign for: *a blue line on the map signified a river* 3 to be important

> **signify** vb 1 = indicate, mean, suggest, imply, intimate, be a sign of, denote, connote, flag up

signing n a system of communication using hand and arm movements, such as one used by deaf people. Also called: **sign language**

sign on vb 1 Brit & Austral to register and report regularly at an unemployment-benefit office 2 to commit oneself to a job or activity by signing a form or contract

signor (see-nyor) n an Italian form of address equivalent to sir or Mr

signora (see-nyor-a) n an Italian form of address equivalent to madam or Mrs

signorina (see-nyor-ee-na) n an Italian form of address equivalent to madam or Miss

signpost n 1 a road sign displaying information, such as the distance to the next town 2 an indication as to how an event is likely to develop or advice on what course of action should be taken ▸ vb 3 to mark (the way) with signposts

Sikh (seek) n 1 a member of an Indian religion that teaches that there is only one God ▸ adj 2 of the Sikhs or their religious beliefs or customs ▸ **Sikhism** n

silage (sile-ij) n a fodder crop harvested while green and partially fermented in a silo

silence n 1 the state or quality of being silent 2 the absence of sound 3 refusal or failure to speak or communicate when expected: *he's broken his silence on the issue* ▸ vb -lencing, -lenced 4 to cause (someone or something) to become silent 5 to put a stop to: *a way of silencing criticism*

> **silence** n 1, 2 = quiet, peace, calm, hush, lull, stillness; ≠ noise 3 = reticence, dumbness, taciturnity, muteness; ≠ speech ▸ vb 4 = quieten, still, quiet, cut off, stifle, cut short, muffle, deaden; ≠ make louder

silencer n any device designed to reduce noise, for example one fitted to the exhaust system of a motor vehicle or one fitted to the muzzle of a gun

silent adj 1 tending to speak very little 2 failing to speak or communicate when expected: *they remained silent as minutes passed* 3 producing no noise: *the silent room* 4 not spoken: *silent reproach* 5 (of a letter) used in the spelling of a word but not pronounced, such as the k in *know* 6 (of a film) having no soundtrack ▸ **silently** adv

> **silent** adj 1 = uncommunicative, quiet, taciturn 2 = mute, dumb, speechless, wordless, voiceless; ≠ noisy 3 = quiet, still, hushed, soundless, noiseless, muted; ≠ loud

silhouette n 1 the outline of a dark shape seen against a light background 2 an outline drawing, often a profile portrait, filled in with black ▸ vb -etting, -etted 3 to show (something) in silhouette

> **silhouette** n 1 = outline, form, shape, profile ▸ vb = outline, etch

silica n a hard glossy mineral, silicon dioxide, which occurs naturally as quartz and is used in the manufacture of glass

silicon n 1 chem a brittle non-metallic element: used in transistors, solar cells, and alloys. Symbol: **Si** ▸ adj 2 denoting an area of a country that contains much high-technology industry: *the Silicon Glen*

silicon chip n same as **chip** (sense 3)

silicone n chem a tough synthetic material made from silicon and used in lubricants, paints, and resins

silicosis n pathol a lung disease caused by breathing in silica dust

silk n 1 the fine soft fibre produced by a silkworm 2 thread or fabric made from this fibre 3 **silks** clothing made of this 4 Brit **a** the gown worn by a Queen's (or King's) Counsel **b** informal a Queen's (or King's) Counsel **c take silk** to become a Queen's (or King's) Counsel

silky adj silkier, silkiest 1 soft, smooth, and shiny 2 (of a voice or manner) smooth and elegant ▸ **silkiness** n

sill n 1 a shelf at the bottom of a window, either inside or outside a room 2 the lower horizontal part of a window or door frame

silly adj -lier, -liest 1 behaving in a foolish or childish way 2 old-fashioned unable to think sensibly, as if from a blow 3 cricket (of a fielding position) near the batsman's wicket: *silly mid-off* ▸ n, pl -lies 4 informal a foolish person ▸ **silliness** n

> **silly** adj 1 = stupid, ridiculous, absurd, daft, inane, senseless, idiotic, fatuous; ≠ clever

silo n, pl -los 1 an airtight pit or tower in which silage or grain is made and stored 2 an underground structure in which missile systems are sited for protection

silt n 1 a fine sediment of mud or clay deposited by moving water ▸ vb 2 **silt up** to fill or choke up with silt: *the channels have been silted up*

silvan adj same as **sylvan**

silver n 1 a precious greyish-white metallic element: used in jewellery, tableware, and coins. Symbol: **Ag** 2 a coin or coins made of silver 3 any household articles made of silver ▸ adj 4 greyish-white: *silver hair* 5 (of anniversaries) the 25th in a series: *Silver Jubilee; silver wedding* ▸ vb 6 to coat with silver or a silvery substance:

a company that silvers their own mirrors **7** to cause (something) to become silvery in colour: *the sun silvered the tarmac*

silverbeet *n Austral & NZ* a beet of Australia and New Zealand with edible spinach-like leaves

silver birch *n* a tree with silvery-white peeling bark

silverfish *n, pl* **-fish** *or* **-fishes 1** a small wingless silver-coloured insect **2** a silver-coloured fish

silverside *n* a cut of beef from below the rump and above the leg

sim *n* a computer game that simulates an activity such as flying or playing a sport

SIM card *n* a small card used in a mobile phone to store data about the network, telephone number, etc.

simian *adj* **1** of or resembling a monkey or ape ▸ *n* **2** a monkey or ape

similar *adj* **1** alike but not identical **2** *geom* (of two or more figures) different in size or position, but with exactly the same shape > **similarity** *n* > **similarly** *adv*

> **similar** *adj* **1** = alike, resembling, comparable; ≠ different

simile (sim-ill-ee) *n* a figure of speech that likens one thing to another of a different category, introduced by *as* or *like*

similitude *n formal* likeness; similarity

simmer *vb* **1** to cook (food) gently at just below boiling point **2** (of violence or conflict) to threaten to break out: *revolt simmering among rural MPs* ▸ *n* **3** the state of simmering

> **simmer** *vb* **1** = bubble, boil gently, seethe **2** = fume, seethe, smoulder, rage, be angry

simmer down *vb informal* to calm down after being angry

> **simmer down** *vb* = calm down, control yourself, cool off *or* down

simnel cake *n Brit* a fruit cake with marzipan, traditionally eaten during Lent or at Easter

simper *vb* **1** to smile in a silly and mannered way **2** to say (something) with a simper ▸ *n* **3** a simpering smile > **simpering** *adj*

simple *adj* **1** easy to understand or do: *in simple English*; *simple exercises* **2** plain and not elaborate: *a simple red skirt*; *a simple answer* **3** not combined or complex: *simple diagnostic equipment* **4** leading an uncomplicated life: *I am a simple man myself* **5** sincere or frank: *a simple apology* **6** of humble background: *the simple country girl* **7** *informal* lacking in intelligence **8** straightforward: *a simple matter of choice* **9** *music* denoting a time where the number of beats per bar may be two, three, or four > **simplicity** *n*

> **simple** *adj* **1** = uncomplicated, clear, plain, understandable, lucid, recognizable, comprehensible, intelligible; ≠ complicated **2** = plain, natural, classic, unfussy,

unembellished, bare-bones; ≠ elaborate **3** = pure, mere, sheer, unalloyed **4** = artless, innocent, naive, natural, sincere, unaffected, childlike, unsophisticated; ≠ sophisticated **6** = unpretentious, modest, humble, homely, unfussy, unembellished; ≠ fancy

simple fraction *n maths* a fraction in which the numerator and denominator are both whole numbers

simpleton *n* a foolish or stupid person

simplify *vb* **-fies, -fying, -fied 1** to make (something) less complicated **2** *maths* to reduce (an equation or fraction) to its simplest form > **simplification** *n*

> **simplify** *vb* **1** = make simpler, streamline, disentangle, dumb down, reduce to essentials, declutter

simplistic *adj* (of an opinion or interpretation) too simple or naive

simply *adv* **1** in a simple manner: *an interesting book, simply written* **2** merely; just: *he's simply too slow* **3** absolutely: *a simply enormous success*

> **simply** *adv* **1** = clearly, straightforwardly, directly, plainly, intelligibly **2** = just, only, merely, purely, solely **3** = totally, really, completely, absolutely, wholly, utterly

simulate *vb* **-lating, -lated 1** to pretend to feel or perform (an emotion or action); imitate: *I tried to simulate anger* **2** to imitate the conditions of (a situation), as in carrying out an experiment: *we can then simulate global warming* **3** to have the appearance of: *the wood had been painted to simulate stone* > **simulated** *adj* > **simulation** *n*

> **simulate** *vb* **1** = pretend, act, feign, affect, put on, sham

simulator *n* a device that simulates specific conditions for the purposes of research or training: *a flight simulator*

simultaneous *adj* occurring or existing at the same time > **simultaneously** *adv* > **simultaneity** *n*

> **simultaneous** *adj* = coinciding, concurrent, contemporaneous, coincident, synchronous, happening at the same time

sin¹ *n* **1** the breaking of a religious or moral law **2** any offence against a principle or standard **3 live in sin** *old-fashioned, informal* (of an unmarried couple) to live together ▸ *vb* **sinning, sinned 4** to commit a sin > **sinner** *n*

> **sin** *n* **1** = wickedness, evil, crime, error, transgression, iniquity **2** = crime, offence, error, wrongdoing, misdeed, transgression, act of evil, guilt ▸ *vb* = transgress, offend, lapse, err, go astray, do wrong

sin² *maths* sine

since *prep* **1** during the period of time after: *one of their worst winters since 1945* ▸ *conj* **2** continuously from the time given: *they've been standing in line ever since she arrived* **3** for the reason that; because ▸ *adv* **4** from that time: *I have often been asked since*

sincere *adj* genuine and honest: *sincere concern* > **sincerely** *adv* > **sincerity** *n*

> **sincere** *adj* = honest, genuine, real, true, serious, earnest, frank, candid, dinkum (*Austral, NZ informal*); ≠ false

sine *n* (in trigonometry) the ratio of the length of the opposite side to that of the hypotenuse in a right-angled triangle

sinecure (sin-ee-cure) *n* a paid job that involves very little work or responsibility

sine die (sin-ay dee-ay) *adv* without fixing a day for future action or meeting

sine qua non (sin-ay kwah non) *n* an essential requirement

sinew *n* **1** *anatomy* a tough fibrous cord connecting muscle to bone **2** *literary* physical strength

sinewy *adj* lean and muscular

sinful *adj* **1** having committed or tending to commit sin: *I am a sinful man* **2** being a sin; wicked: *sinful acts*

sing *vb* **singing, sang, sung 1** to produce musical sounds with the voice **2** to perform (a song) **3** (of certain birds and insects) to make musical calls **4 sing of** to tell a story in song about: *the minstrels sang of courtly love* **5** to make a humming, ringing, or whistling sound: *the arrow sang past his ear* **6** (of one's ears) to be filled with a continuous ringing sound **7** to bring (someone) to a given state by singing: *I sang him to sleep* **8** *slang, chiefly US* to act as an informer > **singer** *n* > **singing** *adj, n*

> **sing** *vb* **1, 2** = croon, carol, chant, warble, yodel, pipe **3** = trill, chirp, warble

singe *vb* **singeing, singed 1** to burn slightly without setting alight; scorch: *it singed his sheepskin* ▸ *n* **2** a slight burn

singing telegram *n* **1** a service by which a person is employed to present greetings to someone on a special occasion by singing **2** the greetings presented in this way **3** the person who presents the greetings

single *adj* **1** existing alone; solitary: *the cottage's single chimney* **2** distinct from others of the same kind: *every single housing society* **3** designed for one user: *a single room* **4** unmarried **5** even one: *there was not a single bathroom* **6** (of a flower) having only one circle of petals **7 single combat** a duel or fight involving two individuals ▸ *n* **8** a hotel bedroom for one person **9** a song or recording that is marketed in its own right rather than as part of an album **10** *cricket* a hit from which one run is scored **11** *US & Canad* a dollar bill **12** a ticket valid for a one-way journey only ▸ *vb* **-gling, -gled 13 single out** to select from a group of people or things: *the judge had singled him out for praise*

single *adj* **1** = one, sole, lone, solitary, only, only one **2** = individual, separate, distinct **3** = separate, individual, exclusive, undivided, unshared **4** = unmarried, free, unattached, unwed ▸ *vb* **single something or someone out** = pick, choose, select, separate, distinguish, fix on, set apart, pick on *or* out, flag up

single file *n* a line of people, one behind the other

single-handed *adj* **1** alone; unaided: *a single-handed raid on the enemy camp* ▸ *adv* **2** unaided or working alone: *she had to take on the world single-handed* > **single-handedly** *adv*

single-minded *adj* having one purpose or aim only; dedicated > **single-mindedly** *adv* > **single-mindedness** *n*

singlet *n* *Brit & NZ* a man's sleeveless vest

singly *adv* one at a time; one by one

> **singly** *adv* = one by one, individually, one at a time, separately

sing-song *n* **1** an informal group singing session ▸ *adj* **2** (of a voice) having a repetitive rise and fall in tone

singular *adj* **1** *grammar* (of a word or form) denoting only one person or thing: *a singular noun* **2** remarkable; extraordinary: *one of the singular achievements* **3** unusual; odd: *a lovable but very singular old woman* ▸ *n* **4** *grammar* the singular form of a word > **singularity** *n* > **singularly** *adv*

> **singular** *adj* **1** = single, individual **2** = remarkable, outstanding, exceptional, notable, eminent, noteworthy; ≠ ordinary **3** = unusual, odd, strange, extraordinary, curious, peculiar, eccentric, queer (*old-fashioned*), daggy (*Austral, NZ informal*); ≠ conventional

sinister *adj* **1** threatening or suggesting evil or harm: *a sinister conspiracy* **2** *heraldry* of, on, or starting from the bearer's left side

> **sinister** *adj* **1** = threatening, evil, menacing, dire, ominous, malign, disquieting; ≠ reassuring

sink *vb* **sinking, sank, sunk 1** to submerge (in liquid) **2** to cause (a ship) to submerge by attacking it with bombs, torpedoes, etc. **3** to appear to descend towards or below the horizon **4** to make or become lower in amount or value: *the US dollar sank to a low against the euro* **5** to move or fall into a lower position, esp. due to tiredness or weakness: *she sank back in her chair* **6 sink into** to pass into a lower state or condition, esp. an unpleasant one: *to sink into debt* **7** (of a voice) to become quieter **8** to become weaker in health **9** to dig (something sharp) into a solid object: *she sank her teeth into the steak* **10** *informal* to drink (a number of alcoholic drinks) **11** to dig, drill, or excavate (a hole or shaft) **12** to drive (a stake) into the ground **13 sink in** *or* **into** to invest

S

(money) in (a venture) **14** *golf & snooker* to hit (the ball) into the hole or pocket: *she sank the putt* ▸ *n* **15** a fixed basin in a kitchen or bathroom, with a water supply and drainpipe ▸ *adj* **16** *informal* (of a housing estate or school) deprived or having low standards of achievement

> **sink** *vb* **1** = go down, founder, go under, submerge, capsize **4** = fall, drop, slip, plunge, subside, abate **5** = slump, drop **7** = drop, fall **8** = decline, fade, fail, flag, weaken, diminish, decrease, deteriorate; ≠ improve **11** = dig, bore, drill, drive, excavate

sinker *n* a weight attached to a fishing line or net to cause it to sink in water

sink in *vb* (of a fact) to become fully understood: *the euphoria started to wear off as the implications of it all sank in*

sinking fund *n* a fund set aside to repay a long-term debt

Sino- *combining form* Chinese: *Sino-European*; *Sinology*

sinuous *adj literary* **1** full of curves **2** having smooth twisting movements: *sinuous dances* > **sinuosity** *n*

sinus (sine-uss) *n anatomy* a hollow space in bone, such as one in the skull opening into a nasal cavity

sip *vb* **sipping, sipped** **1** to drink (a liquid) in small mouthfuls ▸ *n* **2** an amount sipped **3** an instance of sipping

> **sip** *vb* = drink, taste, sample, sup ▸ *n* **2** = swallow, drop, taste, thimbleful

siphon *or* **syphon** *n* **1** a tube which uses air pressure to draw liquid from a container ▸ *vb* **2 siphon off** **A** to draw (liquid) off through a siphon **B** to redirect (resources or money), esp. dishonestly, into other projects or bank accounts

sir *n* a polite term of address for a man

Sir *n* a title placed before the name of a knight or baronet: *Sir David Attenborough*

sire *n* **1** a male parent of a horse or other domestic animal **2** *archaic* a respectful form of address used to a king ▸ *vb* **siring, sired** **3** to father

siren *n* **1** a device that gives out a loud wailing sound as a warning or signal **2 Siren** *Greek myth* a sea nymph whose singing lured sailors to destruction on the rocks **3** a woman considered attractive but dangerous to men

sirloin *n* a prime cut of beef from the upper part of the loin

sirocco *n, pl* **-cos** a hot stifling wind blowing from N Africa into S Europe

sis¹ *n informal* short for **sister**

sis² *or* **sies** (siss) *interj S African informal* an exclamation of disgust

sisal (size-al) *n* a stiff fibre obtained from a Mexican plant and used for making rope

siskin *n* a yellow-and-black finch

sissy *or* **cissy** *n, pl* **-sies** *derogatory* **1** an effeminate or cowardly boy or man ▸ *adj* **2** effeminate or cowardly

sister *n* **1** a woman or girl having the same parents as another person **2** a female fellow member of a group, trade union, profession, etc. **3** a female nurse in charge of a ward **4** *chiefly RC Church* a nun ▸ *adj* **5** of the same class, origin, or design, as another: *its sister paper*

sisterhood *n* **1** the state of being sisters or like sisters **2** a religious group of women **3** a group of women united by a common interest or belief

sister-in-law *n, pl* **sisters-in-law** **1** the sister of one's husband or wife **2** the wife of one's sibling

sisterly *adj* of or like a sister; affectionate

sit *vb* **sitting, sat** **1** to rest one's body upright on the buttocks: *she had to sit on the ground* **2** to cause (someone) to rest in such a position: *they sat their grandfather in the shade* **3** (of an animal) to rest with the rear part of its body lowered to the ground **4** (of a bird) to perch or roost **5 sit on** (of a bird) to cover its eggs so as to hatch them **6** to be located: *the bank sits in the middle of the village* **7** to pose for a painting or photograph **8** to occupy a seat in some official capacity: *no police representatives will sit on the committee* **9** (of a parliament or court) to be in session **10** to remain unused: *his car sat in the garage* **11** (of clothes) to fit or hang in a certain way: *that dress sits well on you* **12** to take (an examination): *he's sitting his finals* **13** (in combination) to look after a specified person or thing for someone else: *is someone going to dog-sit for you?* **14 sit for** *chiefly Brit* to be a candidate for (a qualification): *he sat for a degree in medicine* **15 sit tight** *informal* **A** to wait patiently **B** to maintain one's position firmly

> **sit** *vb* **1** = take a seat, perch, settle down **2** = place, set, put, position, rest, lay, settle, deposit **8** = be a member of, serve on, have a seat on, preside on **9** = convene, meet, assemble, officiate

sitar *n* an Indian stringed musical instrument with a long neck and a rounded body

sitcom *n informal* (on television or radio) a comedy series involving the same characters in various everyday situations: *yet another unfunny sitcom set in Liverpool*

site *n* **1** the piece of ground where something was, is, or is intended to be located: *a building site; a car park is to be built on the site of a Roman fort* **2** same as **website** ▸ *vb* **siting, sited** **3** to locate (something) on a specific site

> **site** *n* **1** = area, plot ▸ *vb* = locate, put, place, set, position, establish, install, situate

sit-in *n* **1** a protest in which the demonstrators sit in a public place and refuse to move ▸ *vb* **sit in** **2 sit in for** to stand in as a substitute for (someone) **3 sit in on** to be present at (a meeting) as an observer

S

sitting room n a room in a house or flat where people sit and relax

situate vb -ating, -ated formal to place

situation n 1 A state of affairs B a complex or critical state of affairs 2 location and surroundings 3 social or financial circumstances 4 a position of employment

> **situation** n 1A = position, state, case, condition, circumstances, equation, plight, state of affairs 2 = location, place, setting, position, site, spot

situation comedy n same as **sitcom**

six n 1 the cardinal number that is the sum of one and five 2 a numeral, 6 or VI, representing this number 3 something representing or consisting of six units 4 cricket a score of six runs, obtained by hitting the ball so that it crosses the boundary without bouncing 5 **at sixes and sevens** in a state of confusion 6 **knock someone for six** informal to upset or overwhelm someone completely 7 **six of one and half a dozen of the other** a situation in which there is no real difference between the alternatives ▶ adj 8 amounting to six: six days > **sixth** adj, n

sixteen n 1 the cardinal number that is the sum of ten and six 2 a numeral, 16 or XVI, representing this number 3 something representing or consisting of sixteen units ▶ adj 4 amounting to sixteen: sixteen years > **sixteenth** adj, n

sixty n, pl -ties 1 the cardinal number that is the product of ten and six 2 a numeral, 60 or LX, representing this number 3 something representing or consisting of sixty units ▶ adj 4 amounting to sixty: sixty seconds > **sixtieth** adj, n

sizable or **sizeable** adj quite large

> **sizable** or **sizeable** adj = large, considerable, substantial, goodly, decent, respectable, largish

size[1] n 1 the dimensions, amount, or extent of something 2 large dimensions, amount, or extent: I was overwhelmed by the sheer size of the city 3 one of a series of standard measurements for goods: he takes size 11 shoes 4 informal state of affairs as summarized: that's about the size of it ▶ vb **sizing, sized** 5 to sort (things) according to size

> **size** n 1 = dimensions, extent, range, amount, mass, volume, proportions, bulk

size[2] n 1 a thin gluey substance that is used as a sealer ▶ vb **sizing, sized** 2 to treat (a surface) with size

size up vb informal to make an assessment of (a person or situation)

> **size up** vb **size something or someone up** = assess, evaluate, appraise, take stock of

sizzle vb -zling, -zled 1 to make a hissing sound like the sound of frying fat 2 informal to be very hot: the city was sizzling in a hot summer spell 3 informal to be very angry ▶ n 4 a hissing sound > **sizzling** adj

> **sizzle** vb 1 = hiss, spit, crackle, fry, frizzle

skanky adj skankier, skankiest slang 1 dirty or unattractive 2 promiscuous

skate[1] n 1 same as **ice skate** or **roller skate** 2 **get one's skates on** informal to hurry ▶ vb **skating, skated** 3 to glide on or as if on skates 4 **skate on thin ice** to place oneself in a dangerous situation > **skater** n > **skating** n

skate[2] n, pl **skate** or **skates** a large edible marine fish with a broad flat body

skateboard n 1 a narrow board mounted on roller-skate wheels, usually ridden while standing up ▶ vb 2 to ride on a skateboard > **skateboarding** n

skate round or **over** vb to avoid discussing or dealing with (a matter) fully: friends and admirers skated round the question

skedaddle vb -dling, -dled informal to run off hastily

skein n 1 a length of yarn or thread wound in a loose coil 2 a flock of geese in flight

skeleton n 1 the hard framework of bones that supports and protects the organs and muscles of the body 2 the essential framework of any structure: a metal skeleton supporting the roof and floors 3 informal an extremely thin person or animal 4 an outline consisting of bare essentials: the mere skeleton of a script 5 a small steel-frame sledge for racing down an ice-covered run 6 the sport of racing small steel-frame sledges down an ice-covered run 7 **skeleton in the cupboard** or **closet** an embarrassing or scandalous fact from the past that is kept secret ▶ adj 8 reduced to a minimum: a skeleton staff > **skeletal** adj

> **skeleton** n 1 = bones, bare bones

skeleton key n a key designed so that it can open many different locks

skeptic n US or archaic same as **sceptic**

sketch n 1 a quick rough drawing 2 a brief descriptive piece of writing 3 a short funny piece of acting forming part of a show 4 any brief outline ▶ vb 5 to make a quick rough drawing (of) 6 **sketch out** to make a brief description of: they sketched out plans for the invasion

> **sketch** n 1 = drawing, design, draft, delineation ▶ vb 5 = draw, outline, represent, draft, depict, delineate, rough out

sketchy adj sketchier, sketchiest giving only a rough or incomplete description > **sketchily** adv

skew adj 1 having a slanting position ▶ n 2 a slanting position ▶ vb 3 to take or cause to take a slanting position: our boat skewed off course 4 to distort or misrepresent: the takeover bid has skewed last month's figures

skewer n 1 a long pin for holding meat together during cooking ▶ vb 2 to fasten or pierce with or as if with a skewer

ski *n, pl* **skis** *or* **ski** **1** one of a pair of long runners that are used, fastened to boots, for gliding over snow ▸ *vb* **skiing, skied** *or* **ski'd 2** to travel on skis ▸ **skier** *n* ▸ **skiing** *n*

skid *vb* **skidding, skidded 1** (of a vehicle or person) to slide sideways while in motion ▸ *n* **2** an instance of skidding

skiff *n* a small narrow boat for one person

skilful *or US* **skillful** *adj* having or showing skill ▸ **skilfully** *or US* **skillfully** *adv*

> **skilful** *or* **skillful** *adj* = expert, deft, skilled, masterly, able, professional, clever, practised, competent; ≠ clumsy

skill *n* **1** special ability or expertise enabling one to perform an activity very well **2** something, such as a trade, requiring special training or expertise ▸ **skilled** *adj*

> **skill** *n* **1** = expertise, ability, proficiency, art, technique, facility, talent, craft; ≠ clumsiness

skillet *n* **1** a small frying pan **2** *chiefly Brit* a long-handled cooking pot

skim *vb* **skimming, skimmed 1** to remove (floating material) from the surface of (a liquid): *skim any impurities off the surface* **2** to glide smoothly over (a surface) **3** to throw (a flat stone) across a surface, so that it bounces: *two men skimmed stones on the surface of the sea* **4** (often foll. by *through*) to read (a piece of writing) quickly and without taking in the details

> **skim** *vb* **1** = remove, separate, cream **2** = glide, fly, coast, sail, float **4** = scan, glance, run your eye over

skimp *vb* **1** to be extremely sparing or supply (someone) sparingly **2** to do (something) carelessly or with inadequate materials

skimpy *adj* **skimpier, skimpiest** inadequate in amount or size; scant

skin *n* **1** the tissue forming the outer covering of the body **2** a person's complexion: *sallow skin* **3** any outer layer or covering: *potato skin* **4** a thin solid layer on the surface of a liquid: *custard with a thick skin on it* **5** the outer covering of a furry animal, removed and prepared for use **6** a container for liquids, made from animal skin **7 by the skin of one's teeth** by a narrow margin **8 get under one's skin** *informal* to annoy one **9 no skin off one's nose** *informal* not a matter that concerns one **10 save one's skin** to save one from death or harm **11 skin and bone** extremely thin **12 thick** *or* **thin skin** an insensitive *or* sensitive nature ▸ *vb* **skinning, skinned 13** to remove the outer covering from (fruit, vegetables, dead animals, etc.) **14** to injure (a part of the body) by scraping some of the skin off: *I had skinned my knuckles* **15** *slang* to swindle ▸ **skinless** *adj*

> **skin** *n* **3** = peel, rind, husk, casing, outside, crust **4** = film, coating **5** = hide, pelt, fell ▸ *vb* **13** = peel **14** = scrape, flay

skin-deep *adj* not of real importance; superficial: *beauty is only skin-deep*

skin diving *n* underwater swimming using only light breathing apparatus and without a special diving suit ▸ **skin-diver** *n*

skinflint *n* a very mean person

skinhead *n* **1** a member of a group of White youths, noted for their closely cropped hair, aggressive behaviour, and overt racism **2** a closely cropped hairstyle

skinny *adj* **-nier, -niest** extremely thin

> **skinny** *adj* = thin, lean, scrawny, emaciated, undernourished; ≠ fat

skip[1] *vb* **skipping, skipped 1** to move lightly by hopping from one foot to the other **2** to jump over a skipping-rope **3** to cause (a stone) to skim over a surface or (of a stone) to move in this way **4** to pass over or miss out; omit: *I skipped a few paragraphs* **5 skip through** *informal* to read or deal with (something) quickly or without great effort or concentration **6 skip it!** *informal* it doesn't matter! **7** *informal* to miss deliberately: *she skipped the class* **8** *informal, chiefly US, Canad & Austral* to leave (a place) in a hurry: *he skipped town three years later* ▸ *n* **9** a skipping movement or action

> **skip** *vb* **1** = hop, dance, bob, trip, bounce, caper, prance, frisk **4** = miss out, omit, leave out, overlook, pass over, eschew, give (something) a miss

skip[2] *n* **1** *Brit* a large open container for transporting building materials or rubbish **2** a cage used as a lift in mines

skipper *n* **1** the captain of a ship or aircraft **2** the captain of a sporting team ▸ *vb* **3** to be the captain of

skirmish *n* **1** a brief or minor fight or argument ▸ *vb* **2** to take part in a skirmish

skirt *n* **1** a woman's or girl's garment hanging from the waist **2** the part of a dress or coat below the waist **3** a circular hanging flap, for example round the base of a hovercraft **4** *Brit & NZ* a cut of beef from the flank **5 bit of skirt** *offensive slang* a girl or woman ▸ *vb* **6** to lie along or form the edge of (something): *a track skirting the foot of the mountain* **7** to go around the outer edge of (something): *we skirted the township* **8** to avoid dealing with (an issue): *I was skirting around the real issues*

> **skirt** *vb* **6** = border, edge, flank **7** = go round, circumvent **8** = avoid, evade, steer clear of, circumvent (*formal*)

skirting board *n* a narrow board round the bottom of an interior wall where it joins the floor

skit *n* a short funny or satirical sketch

skite *Austral & NZ* ▸ *vb* **1** to boast ▸ *n* **2** a boast

skittish *adj* **1** playful or lively **2** (of a horse) excitable and easily frightened

skittle *n* **1** a bottle-shaped object used as a target in a game of skittles **2 skittles** a bowling

S

game in which players knock over as many skittles as possible by rolling a wooden ball at them

skive *vb* **skiving, skived** (often foll. by *off*) *Brit informal* to avoid work or responsibility > **skiver** *n*

skivvy *chiefly Brit, often derogatory* ▸ *n, pl* **-vies 1** a servant who does menial work; drudge **2** *Austral & NZ* a garment resembling a sweater with long sleeves and a polo neck ▸ *vb* **-vies, -vying, -vied 3** to work as a skivvy

skulduggery *or US* **skullduggery** *n informal* underhand dealing to achieve an aim

skulk *vb* **1** to move stealthily, so as to avoid notice **2** to lie in hiding; lurk

skull *n* **1** the bony framework of the head **2** *informal* the head or mind: *that would have penetrated even your thick skull*

skullcap *n* a closely fitting brimless cap

skunk *n, pl* **skunks** *or* **skunk 1** a mammal with a black-and-white coat and bushy tail, which gives out a foul-smelling fluid when attacked **2** *informal* an unpleasant or unfair person

sky *n, pl* **skies 1** the upper atmosphere as seen from earth **2 praise to the skies** praise rather excessively ▸ *vb* **skies, skying, skied 3** *informal* to hit (a ball) high in the air: *the blond-haired forward skied the ball high over the bar*

> **sky** *n* **1** = heavens, firmament, rangi (NZ)

skydiving *n* the sport of jumping from an aircraft and falling freely or performing manoeuvres before opening the parachute > **skydiver** *n*

skylark *n* **1** a lark that sings while soaring at a great height ▸ *vb* **2** *old-fashioned* to play or frolic

skylight *n* a window placed in a roof or ceiling to let in daylight

Skype *n trademark* **1** a software application by which users can make voice and video calls over the internet ▸ *vb* **Skyping, Skyped 2** to make a call by Skype or call (someone) by Skype

skyscraper *n* a very tall building

slab *n* **1** a broad flat thick piece of wood, stone, or other material **2** *informal* a package containing 24 cans of beer

> **slab** *n* **1** = piece, slice, lump, chunk, wedge, portion

slack *adj* **1** not tight, tense, or taut: *the slack jaw hung open* **2** careless in one's work **3** (esp. of water) moving slowly **4** (of trade) not busy ▸ *n* **5** a part that is slack or hangs loose: *take up the slack* **6** a period of less busy activity ▸ *vb* **7** to neglect one's duty or work in a lazy manner: *stop slacking, you pair!* **8** (often foll. by *off*) to loosen or slacken > **slackness** *n*

> **slack** *adj* **1** = limp, relaxed, loose, lax; ≠ taut **2** = negligent, lazy, lax, idle, inactive, slapdash, neglectful, slipshod; ≠ strict **3, 4** = slow, quiet, inactive, dull, sluggish, slow-moving; ≠ busy ▸ *vb* **7** = shirk, idle, dodge, skive (Brit slang), bludge (Austral, NZ informal)

slacken *vb* (often foll. by *off*) **1** to make or become looser **2** to make or become slower or less intense: *to slacken the pace of reform*

slacker *n* a person who evades work or duty; shirker

slag *n* **1** the waste material left after metal has been smelted **2** *Brit & NZ derogatory slang* a woman considered sexually immoral ▸ *vb* **slagging, slagged 3** *Brit, Austral & NZ slang* (often foll. by *off*) to criticize in an unpleasant way: *I don't think anyone can slag it off* > **slagging** *n* > **slaggy** *adj*

slain *vb* the past participle of **slay**

slake *vb* **slaking, slaked 1** *literary* to satisfy (thirst or desire) **2** to add water to (lime) to produce calcium hydroxide

slalom *n skiing & rowing* a race over a winding course marked by artificial obstacles

slam *vb* **slamming, slammed 1** to close violently and noisily **2** to throw (something or someone) down violently **3** *slang* to criticize harshly: *his new proposals were slammed by the opposition* **4** to strike with violent force: *he slammed the ball into the back of the net* ▸ *n* **5** the act or noise of slamming

> **slam** *vb* **1** = bang, crash, smash **2** = throw, dash, hurl, fling

slander *n* **1** *law* a false and damaging statement about a person **2** the crime of making such a statement ▸ *vb* **3** to utter slander (about) > **slanderous** *adj*

slang *n* **1** informal language not used in formal speech or writing and often restricted to a particular social group or profession ▸ *vb* **2** to use insulting language to (someone) > **slangy** *adj*

slanging match *n* an angry quarrel in which people trade insults

slant *vb* **1** to lean at an angle; slope **2** to write or present (information) in a biased way ▸ *n* **3** a sloping line or position **4** a point of view, esp. a biased one: *a right-wing slant on the story* **5 on a** *or* **the slant** sloping ▸ *adj* **6** oblique; sloping > **slanting** *adj* > **slantwise** *adv*

> **slant** *vb* **1** = slope, incline, tilt, list, bend, lean, heel, cant **2** = bias, colour, twist, angle, distort ▸ *n* **3** = slope, incline, tilt, gradient, camber **4** = bias, emphasis, prejudice, angle, point of view, one-sidedness

slap *n* **1** a sharp blow or smack with something flat, such as the open hand **2** the sound made by or as if by such a blow **3 slap and tickle** *Brit old-fashioned, informal* sexual play **4 a slap in the face** an unexpected rejection or insult **5 a slap on the back** congratulations ▸ *vb* **slapping, slapped 6** to strike sharply with something flat, such as the open hand **7** to bring (something) down forcefully: *he slapped down a fiver* **8** (usually foll. by *against*) to strike (something) with a slapping sound **9** *informal* to cover with quickly or carelessly: *she slapped on some make-up*

10 slap on the back to congratulate ▸ *adv informal*
11 exactly: *slap in the middle* **12 slap into** forcibly or abruptly into: *he ran slap into the guard*

> **slap** *n* **1** = smack, blow, cuff, swipe (*informal*), spank ▸ *vb* **6** = smack, beat, clap, cuff, swipe (*informal*), spank, clobber (*slang*), wallop (*informal*)

slapdash *adv* **1** carelessly or hastily ▸ *adj* **2** careless or hasty
slap-happy *adj* **-pier, -piest** *informal* cheerfully careless
slapstick *n* rough and high-spirited comedy in which the characters behave childishly
slap-up *adj Brit informal* (esp. of meals) large and expensive
slash *vb* **1** to cut (a person or thing) with sharp sweeping strokes **2** to make large gashes in: *I slashed the tyres of his van* **3** to reduce drastically: *to slash costs* **4** to criticize harshly ▸ *n* **5** a sharp sweeping stroke **6** a cut made by such a stroke **7** *Brit & Austral slang* the act of urinating

> **slash** *vb* **1, 2** = cut, slit, gash, lacerate, score, rend (*literary*), rip, hack **3** = reduce, cut, decrease, drop, lower, moderate, diminish, cut down ▸ *n* **6** = cut, slit, gash, rent, rip, incision, laceration

slat *n* a narrow thin strip of wood or metal, such as used in a Venetian blind
slate[1] *n* **1** a dark grey rock that can be easily split into thin layers and is used as a roofing material **2** a roofing tile of slate **3** (formerly) a writing tablet of slate **4** *chiefly US & Canad* a list of candidates in an election **5 wipe the slate clean** forget about past mistakes or failures and start afresh **6 on the slate** *Brit & Austral informal* on credit ▸ *vb* **slating, slated 7** to cover (a roof) with slates **8** *chiefly US* to plan or schedule: *another exercise is slated for tomorrow* > **slaty** *adj*
slate[2] *vb* **slating, slated** *informal, chiefly Brit & Austral* to criticize harshly: *the new series was slated by the critics* > **slating** *n*

> **slate** *vb* = criticize, censure, rebuke, scold, tear into (*informal*)

slattern *n old-fashioned, derogatory* a dirty and untidy woman > **slatternliness** *n* > **slatternly** *adj*
slaughter *n* **1** the indiscriminate or brutal killing of large numbers of people **2** the savage killing of a person **3** the killing of animals for food ▸ *vb* **4** to kill indiscriminately or in large numbers **5** to kill brutally **6** to kill (animals) for food **7** *informal* (in sport) to defeat easily

> **slaughter** *n* **1, 2** = slaying, killing, murder, massacre, bloodshed, carnage, butchery ▸ *vb* **4** = butcher, kill, slay (*archaic, literary*), massacre **5** = kill (*informal*), murder, massacre, destroy, execute, assassinate

slaughterhouse *n* a place where animals are killed for food

Slav *n* a member of any of the peoples of Eastern and Central Europe who speak a Slavonic language
slave *n* **1** a person legally owned by another for whom he or she has to work without freedom, pay, or rights **2** a person under the domination of another or of some habit or influence: *a slave to party doctrine* **3** *informal* a badly-paid person doing menial tasks ▸ *vb* **slaving, slaved 4** (often foll. by *away* or *over*) to work very hard for little or no money

> **slave** *n* **1** = servant, serf, vassal **3** = drudge, skivvy (*chiefly Brit*) ▸ *vb* = toil, drudge, slog

slave-driver *n* **1** a person who makes people work very hard **2** (esp. formerly) a person forcing slaves to work
slaver[1] (slay-ver) *n* (esp. formerly) a dealer in slaves
slaver[2] (slav-ver) *vb* to dribble saliva
slavery *n* **1** the state or condition of being a slave **2** the practice of owning slaves **3** hard work with little reward

> **slavery** *n* **1** = enslavement, servitude, subjugation, captivity, bondage; ≠ freedom

slavish *adj* **1** of or like a slave **2** imitating or copying exactly without any originality: *a slavish adherence to the conventions of Italian opera* > **slavishly** *adv*
Slavonic *or esp US* **Slavic** *n* **1** a group of languages including Bulgarian, Russian, Polish, and Czech ▸ *adj* **2** of this group of languages **3** of the people who speak these languages
slay *vb* **slaying, slew, slain** *archaic, literary* to kill, esp. violently > **slayer** *n*

> **slay** *vb* = kill (*informal*), slaughter, massacre, butcher

sleaze *n informal* behaviour in public life considered immoral, dishonest, or disreputable: *political sleaze*

> **sleaze** *n* = corruption, fraud, dishonesty, bribery, extortion, venality, unscrupulousness

sleazy *adj* **-zier, -ziest** dirty, rundown, and not respectable: *a sleazy hotel* > **sleaziness** *n*
sledge[1] *or esp US & Canad* **sled** *n* **1** a vehicle mounted on runners, drawn by horses or dogs, for transporting people or goods over snow **2** a light wooden frame used, esp. by children, for sliding over snow ▸ *vb* **sledging, sledged 3** to travel by sledge
sledge[2] *n* short for **sledgehammer**
sledgehammer *n* **1** a large heavy hammer with a long handle, used for breaking rocks and concrete ▸ *adj* **2** crushingly powerful: *the sledgehammer approach*
sleek *adj* **1** smooth, shiny, and glossy: *sleek blond hair* **2** (of a person) elegantly dressed

> **sleek** *adj* **1** = glossy, shiny, lustrous, smooth; ≠ shaggy

S

sleep n 1 a state of rest during which the eyes are closed, the muscles and nerves are relaxed, and the mind is unconscious 2 a period spent sleeping 3 the substance sometimes found in the corner of the eyes after sleep 4 a state of inactivity, like sleep 5 poetic death ▸ vb **sleeping**, **slept** 6 to be in or as in the state of sleep 7 to be inactive or unaware: their defence slept as we scored another try 8 to have sleeping accommodation for (a certain number): the villa sleeps ten 9 poetic to be dead 10 **sleep on it** to delay making a decision about (something) until the next day, in order to think about it

sleep n 1 = slumber(s), nap, doze, snooze (informal), hibernation, siesta, forty winks (informal), zizz (Brit informal) ▸ vb 6 = slumber, doze, snooze (informal), hibernate, take a nap, catnap, drowse

sleeper n 1 a railway sleeping car or compartment 2 one of the blocks supporting the rails on a railway track 3 a small plain gold ring worn in a pierced ear lobe to prevent the hole from closing up 4 informal a person or thing that achieves success after an initial period of obscurity

sleeping bag n a large well-padded bag for sleeping in, esp. outdoors

sleeping sickness n an infectious, usually fatal, African disease transmitted by the bite of the tsetse fly, causing fever and sluggishness

sleepless adj 1 (of a night) during which one does not sleep 2 unable to sleep 3 chiefly poetic always active > **sleeplessness** n

sleepout n NZ a small building for sleeping in

sleepover n an occasion when a person stays overnight at a friend's house

sleep with vb to have sexual intercourse and, usually, spend the night with

sleepy adj **sleepier**, **sleepiest** 1 tired and ready for sleep 2 (of a place) without activity or excitement: a sleepy little town > **sleepily** adv

sleepy adj 1 = drowsy, sluggish, lethargic, heavy, dull, inactive; ≠ wide-awake

sleet n 1 partly melted falling snow or hail or (esp. US) partly frozen rain ▸ vb 2 to fall as sleet

sleeve n 1 the part of a garment covering the arm 2 a tubelike part which fits over or completely encloses another part 3 **up one's sleeve** secretly ready: he has a few more surprises up his sleeve > **sleeveless** adj

sleigh n 1 same as **sledge**¹ (sense 1) ▸ vb 2 to travel by sleigh

sleight of hand n 1 the skilful use of the hands when performing magic tricks 2 the performance of such tricks

slender adj 1 (esp. of a person's figure) slim and graceful 2 of small width relative to length or height 3 small or inadequate in amount or size: a slender advantage

slender adj 1 = slim, narrow, slight, lean, willowy; ≠ chubby 3 = meagre, little, small, scant, scanty; ≠ large

slept vb the past of **sleep**

sleuth (rhymes with **tooth**) n informal a detective

slew¹ vb the past tense of **slay**

slew² or esp US **slue** vb 1 to slide or skid sideways: the bus slewed across the road ▸ n 2 the act of slewing

slice n 1 a thin flat piece or wedge cut from something: a slice of tomato 2 a share or portion: the biggest slice of their income 3 a kitchen tool having a broad flat blade: a fish slice 4 sport a shot that causes the ball to go in the opposite direction from one's follow-through ▸ vb **slicing**, **sliced** 5 to cut (something) into slices 6 (usually foll. by through) to cut through cleanly and effortlessly, with or as if with a knife 7 (usually foll. by off, from or away) to cut or be cut from a larger piece 8 sport to play (a ball) with a slice

slice n 1 = piece, segment, portion, wedge, sliver, helping, share, cut (informal) ▸ vb 5 = cut, divide, carve, sever, dissect, bisect

slick adj 1 (esp. of speech) easy and persuasive: a slick answer 2 skilfully devised or executed: a slick marketing effort 3 informal, chiefly US & Canad shrewd; sly 4 informal well-made and attractive, but superficial: a slick publication 5 chiefly US & Canad slippery ▸ n 6 a slippery area, esp. a patch of oil floating on water ▸ vb 7 to make smooth or shiny: long hair slicked back with gel

slick adj 1, 4 = glib, smooth, plausible, polished, specious 2 = skilful, deft, adroit, dexterous, professional, polished; ≠ clumsy ▸ vb = smooth, sleek, plaster down

slide vb **sliding**, **slid** 1 to move smoothly along a surface in continual contact with it: doors that slide open 2 to slip: he slid on his back 3 (usually foll. by into, out of or away from) to pass or move smoothly and quietly: she slid out of her seat 4 (usually foll. by into) to go (into a specified condition) gradually: the republic will slide into political anarchy 5 (of a currency) to lose value gradually 6 **let slide** to allow to change to a worse state by neglect: past managers have undoubtedly let things slide ▸ n 7 the act or an instance of sliding 8 a small glass plate on which specimens are placed for study under a microscope 9 a piece of photographic film on a transparent base, mounted in a frame, that can be viewed by means of a projector 10 a smooth surface, such as ice, for sliding on 11 a structure with a steep smooth slope for sliding down in playgrounds 12 chiefly Brit an ornamental clip to hold hair in place 13 the sliding curved tube of a trombone that is moved in and out to allow different notes to be played

slide vb 1 = slip, slither, glide, skim, coast

slide rule *n* a device formerly used to make mathematical calculations consisting of two strips, one sliding along a central groove in the other, each strip graduated in two or more logarithmic scales of numbers

sliding scale *n* a variable scale according to which things such as wages or prices alter in response to changes in other factors

slight *adj* 1 small in quantity or extent: *a slight improvement* 2 not very important or lacking in substance: *her political career was honourable but relatively slight* 3 slim and delicate ▸ *vb* 4 to insult (someone) by behaving rudely; snub ▸ *n* 5 an act of snubbing (someone) › **slightly** *adv*

> **slight** *adj* 1, 2 = small, minor, insignificant, trivial, feeble, trifling, meagre, unimportant; ≠ large 3 = slim, small, delicate, spare, fragile, lightly-built; ≠ sturdy ▸ *vb* = snub, insult, ignore, affront, scorn, disdain; ≠ compliment ▸ *n* = insult, snub, affront, rebuff, slap in the face (*informal*), (the) cold shoulder; ≠ compliment

slim *adj* **slimmer**, **slimmest** 1 (of a person) attractively thin 2 small in width relative to height or length: *a slim book* 3 poor; meagre: *a slim chance of progress* ▸ *vb* **slimming**, **slimmed** 4 to make or become slim by diet and exercise 5 to reduce in size: *that would slim the overheads* › **slimmer** *n* › **slimming** *n*

> **slim** *adj* 1, 2 = slender, slight, trim, thin, narrow, lean, svelte, willowy; ≠ chubby 3 = slight, remote, faint, slender; ≠ strong ▸ *vb* 4 = lose weight, diet; ≠ put on weight

slime *n* 1 soft runny mud or any sticky substance, esp. when disgusting or unpleasant 2 a thick, sticky substance produced by some fish, slugs, and fungi

slimy *adj* **slimier**, **slimiest** 1 of, like, or covered with slime 2 pleasant and friendly in an insincere way

sling¹ *n* 1 *med* a wide piece of cloth suspended from the neck for supporting an injured hand or arm 2 a rope or strap by which something may be lifted 3 a simple weapon consisting of a strap tied to cords, in which a stone is whirled and then released ▸ *vb* **slinging**, **slung** 4 *informal* to throw 5 to carry or hang loosely from or as if from a sling: *her shoulder bag was slung across her chest* 6 to hurl with or as if with a sling

> **sling** *vb* 4 = throw, cast, toss, hurl, fling, chuck (*informal*), lob (*informal*), heave 5 = hang, suspend

sling² *n* a sweetened mixed drink with a spirit base: *gin sling*

slink *vb* **slinking**, **slunk** to move or act in a quiet and secretive way from fear or guilt

slinky *adj* **slinkier**, **slinkiest** *informal* 1 (of clothes) figure-hugging 2 moving in an alluring way

slip¹ *vb* **slipping**, **slipped** 1 to lose balance and slide unexpectedly: *he slipped on some leaves* 2 to let loose or be let loose: *the rope slipped from his fingers* 3 to move smoothly and easily: *small enough to slip into a pocket* 4 to place quickly or stealthily: *he slipped the pistol back into his holster* 5 to put on or take off easily or quickly: *we had slipped off our sandals* 6 to pass out of (the mind or memory) 7 to move or pass quickly and without being noticed: *we slipped out of the ballroom* 8 to make a mistake 9 to decline in health or mental ability 10 to become worse or lower: *sales had slipped below the level for June of last year* 11 to dislocate (a disc in the spine) 12 to pass (a stitch) from one needle to another without knitting it 13 **let slip** A to allow to escape B to say unintentionally ▸ *n* 14 a slipping 15 a mistake or oversight: *one slip in concentration that cost us the game* 16 a woman's sleeveless undergarment, worn under a dress 17 same as **slipway** 18 *cricket* a fielding position a little behind and to the offside of the wicketkeeper 19 **give someone the slip** to escape from someone ▸ See also **slip up**

> **slip** *vb* 1 = fall, skid 2 = slide, slither 7 = sneak, creep, steal ▸ *n* 15 = mistake, failure, error, blunder, lapse, omission, oversight, barry or Barry Crocker (*Austral slang*) 19 **give someone the slip** = escape from, get away from, evade, elude, lose (someone), flee, dodge

slip² *n* 1 a small piece of paper: *the registration slip* 2 a cutting taken from a plant 3 a young slim person: *a slip of a girl*

slip³ *n* clay mixed with water to a thin paste, used for decorating or patching a ceramic piece

slipknot *n* a nooselike knot tied so that it will slip along the rope round which it is made

slipped disc *n* *pathol* a painful condition in which one of the discs which connects the bones of the spine becomes displaced and presses on a nerve

slipper *n* a light soft shoe for indoor wear › **slippered** *adj*

slippery *adj* 1 liable or tending to cause objects to slip: *the road was slippery* 2 liable to slip from one's grasp: *a bar of slippery soap* 3 not to be trusted: *slippery politicians* › **slipperiness** *n*

> **slippery** *adj* 1 = smooth, icy, greasy, glassy, slippy (*informal*, *dialect*), unsafe 3 = untrustworthy, tricky, cunning, dishonest, devious, crafty, evasive, shifty (*informal*)

slippy *adj* **-pier**, **-piest** *informal*, *dialect* same as **slippery** (senses 1, 2) › **slippiness** *n*

slip road *n Brit* a short road connecting a motorway to another road

slipshod *adj* 1 (of an action) done in a careless way without attention to detail: *a slipshod piece of research* 2 (of a person's appearance) untidy and slovenly

slipstream *n* the stream of air forced backwards by an aircraft or car

slip up *informal* ▸ *vb* **1** to make a mistake ▸ *n* **slip-up 2** a mistake

> **slip up** *vb* = make a mistake, blunder, err, miscalculate

slipway *n* a large ramp that slopes down from the shore into the water, on which a ship is built or repaired and from which it is launched

slit *n* **1** a long narrow cut or opening ▸ *vb* **slitting, slit 2** to make a straight long cut in (something)

> **slit** *n* = opening, split ▸ *vb* = cut (open), rip, slash, knife, pierce, lance, gash

slither *vb* **1** to move or slide unsteadily, such as on a slippery surface **2** to move along the ground in a twisting way: *a snake slithered towards the tree* ▸ *n* **3** a slithering movement > **slithery** *adj*

sliver (sliv-ver) *n* **1** a small thin piece that is cut or broken off lengthwise ▸ *vb* **2** to cut into slivers

slob *n informal* a lazy and untidy person > **slobbish** *adj*

slobber *vb* **1** to dribble (liquid or saliva) from the mouth **2 slobber over** to behave in an excessively sentimental way towards (someone) ▸ *n* **3** liquid or saliva spilt from the mouth > **slobbery** *adj*

sloe *n* the small sour blue-black fruit of the blackthorn

slog *vb* **slogging, slogged 1** to work hard and steadily **2** to make one's way with difficulty: *we slogged our way through the snow* **3** to hit hard ▸ *n* **4** long exhausting work **5** a long and difficult walk: *a slog through heather and bracken* **6** a heavy blow

slogan *n* a catchword or phrase used in politics or advertising

> **slogan** *n* = catch phrase, motto, tag-line, catchword, catchcry (*Austral*)

sloop *n* a small sailing ship with a single mast

slop *vb* **slopping, slopped 1** (often foll. by *about*) to splash or spill (liquid) **2 slop over** *informal, chiefly US & Canad* to be excessively sentimental ▸ *n* **3** a puddle of spilt liquid **4 slops** liquid refuse and waste food used to feed animals, esp. pigs **5** (*often pl*) *informal* liquid food

slope *n* **1** a stretch of ground where one end is higher than the other **2 slopes** hills or foothills **3** any slanting surface **4** the angle of such a slant ▸ *vb* **5** to slant or cause to slant **6** (esp. of natural features) to have one end or part higher than another: *the bank sloped sharply down to the river* **7 slope off** or **away** *informal* to go quietly and quickly in order to avoid something or someone **8 slope arms** *military* (formerly) to hold a rifle in a sloping position against the shoulder

slope *n* **4** = inclination, rise, incline, tilt, slant, ramp, gradient, camber ▸ *vb* **5, 6** = slant, incline, drop away, fall, rise, lean, tilt **7 slope off** = slink away, slip away, creep away

sloppy *adj* **-pier, -piest 1** *informal* careless or untidy: *sloppy workmanship* **2** *informal* excessively sentimental and romantic **3** wet; slushy > **sloppily** *adv* > **sloppiness** *n*

> **sloppy** *adj* **1** = careless, slovenly, slipshod, messy, untidy **2** = sentimental, soppy (*Brit informal*), slushy (*informal*), gushing, mawkish, icky (*informal*)

slosh *vb* **1** *informal* to throw or pour (liquid) carelessly **2** (often foll. by *about* or *around*) *informal* **A** to shake or stir (something) in a liquid **B** (of a person) to splash (around) in water or mud **3** (usually foll. by *about* or *around*) *informal* to shake (a container of liquid) or (of liquid in a container) to be shaken **4** *Brit slang* to deal a heavy blow to ▸ *n* **5** the sound of splashing liquid **6** slush **7** *Brit slang* a heavy blow > **sloshy** *adj*

sloshed *adj slang, chiefly Brit & Austral* drunk

slot *n* **1** a narrow opening or groove, such as one in a vending machine for inserting a coin **2** *informal* a place in a series or scheme: *the late-night slot when people stop watching TV* ▸ *vb* **slotting, slotted 3** to make a slot or slots in **4** (usually foll. by *in* or *into*) to fit or be fitted into a slot: *I slotted my card into the machine*

> **slot** *n* **1** = opening, hole, groove, vent, slit, aperture **2** = place, time, space, opening, position, vacancy ▸ *vb* **4** = fit, insert

sloth (rhymes with **both**) *n* **1** a slow-moving shaggy-coated animal of Central and South America, which hangs upside down in trees by its long arms and feeds on vegetation **2** *formal* laziness, esp. regarding work

slothful *adj* lazy and unwilling to work

slot machine *n* a machine, esp. for vending food and cigarettes or featuring an electronic game on which to gamble, worked by placing a coin in a slot

slouch *vb* **1** to sit, stand, or move with a drooping posture ▸ *n* **2** a drooping posture **3 be no slouch** *informal* be very good or talented: *he was no slouch himself as a negotiator*

slough¹ (rhymes with **now**) *n* a swamp or marshy area

slough² (sluff) *vb* **slough off 1** to shed (an outer covering) or (of an outer covering) to be shed: *the dead cells would slough off* **2** to get rid of (something unwanted or unnecessary): *she tried hard to slough off her old personality*

sloven *n* a person who is always untidy or careless in appearance or behaviour

Slovene *adj* **1** Also: **Slovenian** of Slovenia ▸ *n* **2** a person from Slovenia **3** the language of Slovenia

slovenly *adj* **1** always unclean or untidy **2** negligent and careless: *to write in such a slovenly style* ▸ *adv* **3** in a slovenly manner ▸ **slovenliness** *n*

slow *adj* **1** taking a longer time than is usual or expected **2** lacking speed: *slow movements* **3** adapted to or producing slow movement: *the slow lane* **4** (of a clock or watch) showing a time earlier than the correct time **5** not quick to understand: *slow on the uptake* **6** dull or uninteresting: *the play was very slow* **7** not easily aroused: *he is slow to anger* **8** (of business) not busy; slack **9** (of a fire or oven) giving off low heat **10** (of photographic film) requiring a relatively long exposure time: *a slow film* ▸ *adv* **11** in a slow manner ▸ *vb* **12** (often foll. by *up* or *down*) to decrease or cause to decrease in speed or activity ▸ **slowly** *adv* ▸ **slowness** *n*

slow *adj* **1** = prolonged, protracted, long-drawn-out, lingering, gradual **2** = unhurried, sluggish, leisurely, lazy, ponderous, dawdling, laggard, lackadaisical; ≠ quick **5** = stupid, dim (*informal*), dense, thick, dozy (*Brit informal*), obtuse, braindead (*informal*); ≠ bright ▸ *vb* = decelerate, brake; ≠ speed up

slowcoach *n informal* a person who moves or works slowly

slowworm *n* a legless lizard with a brownish-grey snakelike body

sludge *n* **1** soft mud or snow **2** any muddy or slushy sediment **3** sewage ▸ **sludgy** *adj*

slug¹ *n* a mollusc like a snail but without a shell

slug² *n* **1** a bullet **2** *informal* a mouthful of alcoholic drink, esp. spirits: *he poured out a large slug of Scotch*

slug³ *vb* **slugging, slugged 1** to hit very hard ▸ *n* **2** a heavy blow

sluggard *n old-fashioned* a very lazy person

sluggish *adj* **1** lacking energy **2** moving or working at slower than the normal rate: *the sluggish waters of the canal*

sluggish *adj* **1** = inactive, slow, lethargic, heavy, dull, inert, indolent, torpid; ≠ energetic

sluice *n* **1** a channel that carries a rapid current of water, with a sluicegate to control the flow **2** the water controlled by a sluicegate **3** *mining* a sloping trough for washing ore ▸ *vb* **sluicing, sluiced 4** to draw off or drain with a sluice **5** to wash with a stream of water **6** (often foll. by *away* or *out*) (of water) to run or flow from or as if from a sluice

slum *n* **1** an overcrowded and badly maintained house **2** (*often pl*) a poor rundown overpopulated section of a city ▸ *vb* **slumming, slummed 3** to visit slums, esp. for curiosity **4 slum it** to temporarily and deliberately experience poorer places or conditions ▸ **slummy** *adj*

slum *n* **1** = hovel, ghetto, shanty

slumber *literary* ▸ *vb* **1** to sleep ▸ *n* **2** sleep ▸ **slumbering** *adj*

slump *vb* **1** (of commercial activity or prices) to decline suddenly **2** to sink or fall heavily and suddenly: *she slumped back with exhaustion* ▸ *n* **3** a severe decline in commercial activity or prices; depression **4** a sudden or marked decline or failure: *a slump in demand for oil*

slump *vb* **1** = fall, sink, plunge, crash, collapse, slip; ≠ increase **2** = sag, hunch, droop, slouch, loll ▸ *n* **3** = recession, depression, stagnation, inactivity, hard *or* bad times **4** = fall, drop, decline, crash, collapse, reverse, downturn, trough; ≠ increase

slung *vb* the past of **sling¹**

slunk *vb* the past of **slink**

slur *vb* **slurring, slurred 1** to pronounce or say (words) unclearly **2** to make insulting remarks about **3** *music* to sing or play (successive notes) smoothly by moving from one to the other without a break **4** (often foll. by *over*) to treat hastily or carelessly ▸ *n* **5** an insulting remark intended to damage someone's reputation **6** a slurring of words **7** *music* **A** a slurring of successive notes **B** the curved line (⌒ or ⌄) indicating this

slur *n* **5** = insult, stain, smear, affront, innuendo, calumny, insinuation, aspersion

slurp *informal* ▸ *vb* **1** to eat or drink (something) noisily ▸ *n* **2** a slurping sound

slurry *n, pl* **-ries** a thin watery mixture of something such as cement or mud

slush *n* **1** any watery muddy substance, esp. melting snow **2** *informal* sloppily sentimental language or writing ▸ **slushy** *adj*

slush fund *n* a fund for financing political or commercial corruption

slut *n derogatory* a woman who is considered promiscuous ▸ **sluttish** *adj*

sly *adj* **slyer, slyest** *or* **slier, sliest 1** (of a person's remarks or gestures) indicating that he or she knows something of which other people may be unaware: *she had the feeling they were poking sly fun at her* **2** secretive and skilled at deception: *a sly trickster* **3** roguish: *sly comedy* ▸ *n* **4 on the sly** secretively: *they were smoking on the sly behind the shed* ▸ **slyly** *adv*

sly *adj* **2** = cunning, scheming, devious, secret, clever, subtle, wily, crafty; ≠ open **3** = roguish, knowing, arch, mischievous, impish ▸ *n* **on the sly** = secretly, privately, covertly, surreptitiously, on the quiet

smack¹ *vb* **1** to slap sharply **2** to strike loudly or to be struck loudly **3** to open and close (the lips) loudly to show pleasure or anticipation ▸ *n* **4** a sharp loud slap, or the sound of such a slap **5** a loud kiss **6** a sharp sound made by the lips in enjoyment **7 smack in the eye** *informal* a snub or rejection ▸ *adv informal* **8** directly; squarely: *smack in the middle* **9** sharply and unexpectedly: *he ran smack into one of the men*

smack *vb* **1** = slap, hit, strike, clap, cuff, swipe (*informal*), spank **2** = drive, hit, strike ▸ *n* **4** = slap, blow, cuff, swipe (*informal*), spank ▸ *adv* **8** = directly, right, straight, squarely, precisely, exactly, slap (*informal*)

smack² *n* **1** a slight flavour or suggestion (of something): *the smack of loss of self-control* ▸ *vb* **2 smack of ʌ** to have a slight smell or flavour of (something) **ʙ** to have a suggestion of (something): *it smacks of discrimination*

smack³ *n* a slang word for **heroin**

smacker *n slang* **1** a loud kiss **2** a pound note or dollar bill

small *adj* **1** not large in size or amount **2** of little importance or on a minor scale: *a small detail* **3** mean, ungenerous, or petty: *a small mind* **4** modest or humble: *small beginnings* **5 feel small** to be humiliated **6** (of a child or animal) young; not mature **7** unimportant or trivial: *a small matter* **8** (of a letter) written or printed in lower case rather than as a capital ▸ *adv* **9** into small pieces: *cut it small* ▸ *n* **10** the small narrow part of the back **11 smalls** *informal, chiefly Brit* underwear > **smallish** *adj* > **smallness** *n*

small *adj* **1** = little, minute, tiny, mini, miniature, minuscule, diminutive, petite; ≠ big **2,7** = unimportant, minor, trivial, insignificant, little, petty, trifling, negligible; ≠ important **4** = modest, humble, unpretentious; ≠ grand **6** = young, little, junior, wee, juvenile, youthful, immature

smallholding *n* a piece of agricultural land smaller than a farm > **smallholder** *n*

small hours *pl n* the early hours of the morning, after midnight and before dawn

small-minded *adj* having narrow selfish attitudes; petty

smallpox *n* a contagious disease causing fever, a rash, and blisters which usually leave permanent scars

small talk *n* light conversation for social occasions

small-time *adj informal* operating on a limited scale; minor: *a small-time smuggler*

smarmy *adj* **smarmier**, **smarmiest** unpleasantly flattering or polite

smart *adj* **1** clean and neatly dressed **2** intelligent and shrewd **3** quick and witty in speech: *a smart talker* **4** (of places or events) fashionable; chic: *smart restaurants* **5** vigorous or brisk: *a smart pace* **6** causing a sharp stinging pain **7** (of a weapon) containing an electronic device which enables it to be guided to its target: *a smart bomb* ▸ *vb* **8** to feel or cause a sharp stinging physical or mental pain: *I was still smarting from the insult* ▸ *n* **9** a stinging pain or feeling ▸ *adv* **10** in a smart manner > **smartly** *adv* > **smartness** *n*

smart *adj* **1** = chic, trim, neat, stylish, elegant, spruce, snappy, natty (*informal*),

schmick (*Austral informal*); ≠ scruffy **2** = clever, bright, intelligent, quick, sharp, keen, acute, shrewd; ≠ stupid **5** = brisk, quick, lively, vigorous ▸ *vb* = sting, burn, hurt

smarten *vb* (usually foll. by *up*) to make or become smart

smartphone *n* a mobile phone that performs many of the functions of a computer, having internet access, a touchscreen interface, and the ability to run various apps

smart speaker *n* a wireless electronic device that is able to give information, play music, and perform certain tasks in response to spoken commands

smash *vb* **1** to break into pieces violently and noisily **2** (often foll. by *against*, *through* or *into*) to throw or crash (against) violently, causing shattering: *his head smashed against a window* **3** to hit or collide forcefully and suddenly **4** *sport* to hit (the ball) fast and powerfully with an overhead stroke **5** to defeat or destroy: *the police had smashed a major drug ring* ▸ *n* **6** an act or sound of smashing **7** a violent collision of vehicles **8** *sport* a fast and powerful overhead stroke **9** *informal* a show, record or film which is very popular with the public ▸ *adv* **10** with a smash

smash *vb* **1** = break, crush, shatter, crack, demolish, pulverize **3** = collide, crash, meet head-on, clash, come into collision **5** = destroy, ruin, wreck, trash (*slang*), lay waste ▸ *n* **7** = collision, crash, accident

smasher *n informal, chiefly Brit* a person or thing that is very attractive or outstanding

smashing *adj informal, chiefly Brit* excellent or first-rate

smashing *adj* = excellent, mean (*slang*), great (*informal*), wonderful, brilliant (*informal*), cracking (*Brit informal*), superb (*old-fashioned*), fantastic (*informal*), booshit (*Austral slang*), exo (*Austral slang*), sik (*Austral slang*), rad (*informal*), phat (*slang*), schmick (*Austral informal*); ≠ awful

smattering *n* a slight or superficial knowledge: *I knew a smattering of Russian*

smear *vb* **1** to spread with a greasy or sticky substance **2** to apply (a greasy or sticky substance) thickly **3** to rub so as to produce a smudge **4** to spread false and damaging rumours (about) ▸ *n* **5** a dirty mark or smudge **6** a false but damaging rumour spread by a rival or enemy **7** *med* a small amount of a substance smeared onto a glass slide for examination under a microscope > **smeary** *adj*

smear *vb* **1, 2** = spread over, daub, rub on, cover, coat, bedaub **3** = smudge, soil, dirty, stain, sully **4** = slander, malign, blacken, besmirch ▸ *n* **5** = smudge, daub, streak, blot, blotch, splotch **6** = slander, libel, defamation, calumny

smell vb **smelling, smelt** or **smelled 1** to perceive the scent of (a substance) with the nose **2** to have a specified kind of smell: *it smells fruity; your supper smells good* **3** (often foll. by *of*) to emit an odour (of): *the place smells of milk and babies* **4** to give off an unpleasant odour **5** (often foll. by *out*) to detect through instinct: *I smell trouble* **6** to use the sense of smell; sniff **7 smell of** to indicate or suggest: *anything that smells of devaluation* ▸ n **8** the sense by which scents or odours are perceived. Related adjective: **olfactory 9** an odour or scent **10** the act of smelling

> **smell** vb **1** = sniff, scent **4** = stink, reek, pong (*Brit informal*) ▸ n **9** = odour, scent, fragrance, perfume, bouquet, aroma

smelling salts pl n a preparation containing crystals of ammonium carbonate, used to revive a person feeling faint

smelly adj **smellier, smelliest** having a nasty smell > **smelliness** n

smelt[1] vb to extract (a metal) from (an ore) by heating

smelt[2] n, pl **smelt** or **smelts** a small silvery food fish

smelt[3] vb a past tense and past participle of **smell**

smelter n an industrial plant in which smelting is carried out

smile n **1** a facial expression in which the corners of the mouth are turned up, showing amusement or friendliness ▸ vb **smiling, smiled 2** to give a smile **3 smile at A** to look at with a kindly expression **B** to look with amusement at **4 smile on** or **upon** to regard favourably: *fortune smiled on us today* **5** to express by a smile: *he smiled a comrade's greeting*

> **smile** n = grin, beam, smirk ▸ vb **2** = grin, beam, smirk, twinkle, grin from ear to ear

smiley adj **1** cheerful **2** depicting a smile

smirch vb **1** to disgrace **2** to dirty or soil ▸ n **3** a disgrace **4** a smear or stain

smirk n **1** a smug smile ▸ vb **2** to give such a smile

smite vb **smiting, smote, smitten** or **smit** archaic **1** to strike with a heavy blow **2** to affect severely: *hunger smites him again* **3** to burden with an affliction in order to punish: *God smote the enemies of the righteous* **4 smite on** to strike abruptly and with force: *the sun smote down on him*

smith n **1** a person who works in metal: *goldsmith* **2** See **blacksmith**

smithereens pl n shattered fragments

smithy n, pl **smithies** the workshop of a blacksmith; forge

smitten vb **1** a past participle of **smite** ▸ adj **2** deeply affected by love (for)

smock n **1** a loose overall worn to protect the clothes **2** a loose blouselike garment **3** a loose protective overgarment decorated with smocking, worn formerly by farm workers ▸ vb **4** to gather (material) by sewing in a honeycomb pattern

smocking n ornamental needlework used to gather material

smog n a mixture of smoke and fog that occurs in some industrial areas > **smoggy** adj

smoke n **1** the cloudy mass that rises from something burning **2** the act of smoking tobacco **3** informal a cigarette or cigar **4 go up in smoke A** to come to nothing **B** to burn up vigorously ▸ vb **smoking, smoked 5** to give off smoke: *a smoking fireplace* **6 A** to draw the smoke of (burning tobacco) into the mouth and exhale it again **B** to do this habitually **7** to cure (meat, cheese, or fish) by treating with smoke

> **smoke** vb **5** = smoulder, fume **6A** = puff on, draw on, inhale, vape

smokeless adj having or producing little or no smoke: *smokeless fuel*

smoker n **1** a person who habitually smokes tobacco **2** a train compartment where smoking is permitted

smoke screen n **1** something said or done to hide the truth **2** military a cloud of smoke used to provide cover for manoeuvres

smoky adj **smokier, smokiest 1** filled with or giving off smoke, sometimes excessively: *smoky coal or wood fires* **2** having the colour of smoke **3** having the taste or smell of smoke **4** made dirty or hazy by smoke > **smokiness** n

smooch slang ▸ vb **1** (of two people) to kiss and cuddle **2** Brit to dance very slowly with one's arms around another person or (of two people) to dance together in such a way ▸ n **3** the act of smooching

smooth adj **1** having an even surface with no roughness, bumps, or holes **2** without obstructions or difficulties: *smooth progress towards an agreement* **3** without lumps: *a smooth paste* **4** free from jolts and bumps: *a smooth landing* **5** not harsh in taste; mellow: *an excellent smooth wine* **6** charming or persuasive but possibly insincere ▸ adv **7** in a smooth manner ▸ vb **8** (often foll. by *down*) to make or become even or without roughness **9** (often foll. by *out* or *away*) to remove in order to make smooth: *smoothing out the creases* **10** to make calm; soothe **11** to make easier: *Moscow smoothed the path to democracy* ▸ n **12** the smooth part of something **13** the act of smoothing > **smoothly** adv

> **smooth** adj **1** = even, level, flat, plane, flush, horizontal; ≠ uneven **2** = easy, effortless, well-ordered **4** = flowing, steady, regular, uniform, rhythmic **5** = mellow, pleasant, mild, agreeable **6** = suave, slick, persuasive, urbane, glib, facile, unctuous, smarmy (*Brit informal*) ▸ vb **8, 9** = flatten, level, press, plane, iron **11** = ease, facilitate; ≠ hinder

smoothie n **1** a smooth thick drink made from fresh fruit and yoghurt, ice cream, or milk

S

2 *slang* a man who is so confident, well-dressed, and charming that one is suspicious of his motives and doubts his honesty

smorgasbord *n* a variety of savoury dishes served as hors d'oeuvres or as a buffet meal

smote *vb* the past tense of **smite**

smother *vb* **1** to extinguish (a fire) by covering so as to cut it off from the air **2** to suffocate **3** to surround or overwhelm (with): *she smothered him with her idea of affection* **4** to suppress or stifle: *he smothered an ironic chuckle* **5** to cover over thickly: *ice cream smothered with sauce*

> **smother** *vb* **1** = extinguish, put out, stifle, snuff **2** = suffocate, choke, strangle, stifle **4** = suppress, stifle, repress, hide, conceal, muffle

smoulder *or US* **smolder** *vb* **1** to burn slowly without flames, usually giving off smoke **2** (of emotions) to exist in a suppressed state without being released

SMS short message system: used for sending data to mobile phones

smudge *vb* **smudging, smudged 1** to make or become smeared or soiled ▸ *n* **2** a smear or dirty mark **3** a blurred form or area: *the dull smudge of a ship* > **smudgy** *adj*

smug *adj* **smugger, smuggest** very pleased with oneself; self-satisfied > **smugly** *adv* > **smugness** *n*

> **smug** *adj* = self-satisfied, superior, complacent, conceited

smuggle *vb* **-gling, -gled 1** to import or export (goods that are prohibited or subject to taxation) secretly **2** (often foll. by *into* or *out of*) to bring or take secretly: *he was smuggled out of the country unnoticed* > **smuggler** *n* > **smuggling** *n*

smut *n* **1** stories, pictures, or jokes relating to sex or nudity **2** a speck of soot or a dark mark left by soot **3** a disease of cereals, in which black sooty masses cover the affected parts > **smutty** *adj*

snack *n* **1** a light quick meal eaten between or in place of main meals ▸ *vb* **2** to eat a snack

> **snack** *n* = light meal, bite, refreshment(s)

snack bar *n* a place where light meals or snacks are sold

snaffle *n* **1** a mouthpiece for controlling a horse ▸ *vb* **-fling, -fled 2** *Brit, Austral & NZ informal* to steal or take **3** to fit or control (a horse) with a snaffle

snag *n* **1** a small problem or difficulty: *one possible snag in his plans* **2** a sharp projecting point that may catch on things **3** a small hole in a fabric caused by a sharp object **4** a tree stump in a river bed that is a danger to navigation **5** *Austral slang* a sausage ▸ *vb* **snagging, snagged 6** to tear or catch on a snag

> **snag** *n* **1** = difficulty, hitch, problem, obstacle, catch (*informal*), disadvantage, complication, drawback ▸ *vb* = catch, tear, rip

snail *n* a slow-moving mollusc with a spiral shell

snail mail *informal* ▸ *n* **1** conventional post, as opposed to email or text messages **2** the conventional postal system ▸ *vb* **snail-mail 3** to send by the conventional postal system, rather than by email or text message

snail's pace *n* a very slow speed

snake *n* **1** a long scaly limbless reptile **2** *Also:* **snake in the grass** a person, esp. a colleague or friend, who secretly acts against one ▸ *vb* **snaking, snaked 3** to glide or move in a winding course, like a snake

> **snake** *n* **1** = serpent

snaky *adj* **snakier, snakiest 1** twisting or winding **2** treacherous

snap *vb* **snapping, snapped 1** to break suddenly, esp. with a sharp sound **2** to make or cause to make a sudden sharp cracking sound: *he snapped his fingers* **3** to move or close with a sudden sharp sound: *I snapped the lid shut* **4** to move in a sudden or abrupt way **5** to give way or collapse suddenly under strain: *one day someone's temper will snap* **6** to panic when a situation becomes too difficult to cope with: *he could snap at any moment* **7** (often foll. by *at* or *up*) to seize suddenly or quickly **8** (often foll. by *at*) (of animals) to bite at suddenly **9** to speak (words) sharply and angrily **10** to take a photograph of **11 snap one's fingers at** *informal* to defy or dismiss contemptuously **12 snap out of it** *informal* to recover quickly, esp. from depression or anger ▸ *n* **13** the act of breaking suddenly or the sound of a sudden breakage **14** a sudden sharp sound **15** a clasp or fastener that closes with a snapping sound **16** a sudden grab or bite **17** a thin crisp biscuit: *brandy snaps* **18** *informal* an informal photograph taken with a simple camera **19** *Brit & NZ* a card game in which the word *snap* is called when two similar cards are turned up ▸ *adj* **20** done on the spur of the moment: *snap judgments* ▸ *adv* **21** with a snap ▸ *interj* **22 a** *cards* the word called while playing snap **b** a cry used to draw attention to the similarity of two things ▸ *See also* **snap up**

> **snap** *vb* **1** = break, crack, separate **2, 3** = pop, click, crackle **8** = bite at, bite, nip **9** = speak sharply, bark, lash out at, jump down (someone's) throat (*informal*) ▸ *adj* = instant, immediate, sudden, spur-of-the-moment

snapdragon *n* a plant with spikes of colourful flowers that can open and shut like a mouth; antirrhinum

snapper *n* a food fish of Australia and New Zealand with a pinkish body covered with blue spots

snappy *adj* **-pier, -piest 1** smart and fashionable: *snappy designs* **2** *Also:* **snappish** (of someone's behaviour) irritable, unfriendly, and cross **3** brisk or lively: *short snappy movements* **4 make it snappy** *slang* hurry up! > **snappiness** *n*

snapshot *n* same as **snap** (sense 18)

snap up *vb* to take advantage of eagerly and quickly: *the tickets have been snapped up*

> **snap up** *vb* **snap something up** = grab, seize, take advantage of, pounce upon

snare *n* **1** a trap for birds or small animals, usually a flexible loop that is drawn tight around the prey **2** anything that traps someone or something unawares ▸ *vb* **snaring, snared 3** to catch in or as if in a snare

> **snare** *n* **1** = trap, net, wire, gin, noose ▸ *vb* = trap, catch, net, wire, seize, entrap

snarl¹ *vb* **1** (of an animal) to growl fiercely with bared teeth **2** to speak or say (something) fiercely: *he snarled out a command to a subordinate* ▸ *n* **3** a fierce growl or facial expression **4** the act of snarling

snarl² *n* **1** a complicated or confused state **2** a tangled mass ▸ *vb* **3 snarl up** to become, be, or make tangled, confused, or complicated: *the line became snarled up on the propeller; the postal service was snarled up at Christmas*

snarl-up *n informal* a confused, disorganized situation such as a traffic jam

snatch *vb* **1** to seize or grasp (something) suddenly: *she snatched the paper* **2** (usually foll. by *at*) to attempt to seize suddenly **3** to take hurriedly: *these players had snatched a few hours sleep* **4** to remove suddenly: *she snatched her hand away* ▸ *n* **5** an act of snatching **6** a small piece or incomplete part: *snatches of song* **7** a brief spell: *snatches of sleep* **8** *slang, chiefly US* an act of kidnapping **9** *Brit slang* a robbery: *a wages snatch*

> **snatch** *vb* **1** = grab, grip, grasp, clutch ▸ *n* **6** = bit, part, fragment, piece, snippet

snazzy *adj* **-zier, -ziest** *informal* (esp. of clothes) stylish and flashy

sneak *vb* **1** to move quietly, trying not to be noticed **2** to behave in a cowardly or underhand manner **3** to bring, take, or put secretly: *he sneaked him over the border* **4** *informal, chiefly Brit & NZ* (esp. in schools) to tell tales ▸ *n* **5** a person who acts in an underhand or cowardly manner ▸ *adj* **6** without warning: *a sneak attack* > **sneaky** *adj*

> **sneak** *vb* **1** = slink, slip, steal, pad, skulk **3** = slip, smuggle, spirit ▸ *n* = informer, betrayer, telltale, Judas, accuser, stool pigeon, nark (*Brit, Austral, NZ slang*), fizgig (*Austral slang*)

sneakers *pl n US, Canad, Austral & NZ* canvas shoes with rubber soles

sneaking *adj* **1** slight but nagging: *a sneaking suspicion* **2** secret: *a sneaking admiration* **3** acting in a cowardly and furtive way

> **sneaking** *adj* **1** = nagging, worrying, persistent, uncomfortable **2** = secret, private, hidden, unexpressed, unvoiced, undivulged

sneer *n* **1** a facial expression showing distaste or contempt, typically with a curled upper lip **2** a remark showing distaste or contempt ▸ *vb* **3** to make a facial expression of scorn or contempt **4** to say (something) in a scornful manner > **sneering** *adj, n*

> **sneer** *vb* **4** = say contemptuously, snigger

sneeze *vb* **sneezing, sneezed 1** to expel air from the nose suddenly and without control, esp. as the result of irritation in the nostrils ▸ *n* **2** the act or sound of sneezing

snib *n Scot & NZ* the catch of a door or window

snicker *n, vb chiefly US & Canad* same as **snigger**

snide *or* **snidey** *adj* (of comments) critical in an unfair and nasty way

sniff *vb* **1** to inhale through the nose in short audible breaths **2** (often foll. by *at*) to smell by sniffing ▸ *n* **3** the act or sound of sniffing > **sniffer** *n*

> **sniff** *vb* **1** = breathe in, inhale **2** = smell, scent

sniff at *vb* to express contempt or dislike for

sniffer dog *n* a police dog trained to locate drugs or explosives by smell

sniffle *vb* **-fling, -fled 1** to sniff repeatedly when the nasal passages are blocked up ▸ *n* **2** the act or sound of sniffling

snifter *n* **1** *informal* a small quantity of alcoholic drink **2** a pear-shaped brandy glass

snigger *n* **1** a quiet and disrespectful laugh kept to oneself ▸ *vb* **2** to utter such a laugh

snip *vb* **snipping, snipped 1** to cut with small quick strokes with scissors or shears ▸ *n* **2** *informal, chiefly Brit* a bargain **3** the act or sound of snipping **4** a small piece snipped off **5** a small cut made by snipping

snipe *n, pl* **snipe** *or* **snipes 1** a wading bird with a long straight bill ▸ *vb* **sniping, sniped** (often foll. by *at*) **2** to shoot (someone) from a place of hiding **3** (often foll. by *at*) to make critical remarks about > **sniper** *n*

snippet *n* a small scrap or fragment: *the odd snippet of knowledge*

snitch *slang* ▸ *vb* **1** to act as an informer **2** to steal small amounts ▸ *n* **3** an informer

snivel *vb* **-velling, -velled** *or US* **-veling, -veled 1** to cry and sniff in a self-pitying way **2** to say (something) tearfully; whine **3** to have a runny nose ▸ *n* **4** the act of snivelling

snob *n* **1** a person who tries to associate with those of higher social status and who hates those of lower social status **2** a person who feels smugly superior with regard to his or her tastes or interests: *a cultural snob* > **snobbery** *n* > **snobbish** *adj*

snoek (**snook**) *n* a South African edible marine fish

snog *Brit, NZ & S African slang* ▸ *vb* **snogging, snogged 1** to kiss and cuddle ▸ *n* **2** the act of kissing and cuddling

snood *n* a pouchlike hat loosely holding the hair at the back

snook *n* **cock a snook at** *Brit* **A** to make a rude gesture at (someone) by putting one thumb to the nose with the fingers of the hand outstretched **B** to show contempt for (someone in authority) without fear of punishment

snooker *n* **1** a game played on a billiard table with 15 red balls, six balls of other colours, and a white cue ball **2** a shot in which the cue ball is left in a position such that another ball blocks the target ball ▸ *vb* **3** to leave (an opponent) in an unfavourable position by playing a snooker **4** to put someone in a position where he or she can do nothing

snoop *informal* ▸ *vb* **1** (often foll. by *about* or *around*) to pry into the private business of others ▸ *n* **2** the act of snooping **3** a person who snoops > **snooper** *n* > **snoopy** *adj*

snooty *adj* **snootier, snootiest** *informal* behaving as if superior to other people; snobbish

snooze *informal* ▸ *vb* **snoozing, snoozed 1** to take a brief light sleep ▸ *n* **2** a nap

snore *vb* **snoring, snored 1** to breathe with snorting sounds while asleep ▸ *n* **2** the act or sound of snoring

snorkel *n* **1** a tube allowing a swimmer to breathe while face down on the surface of the water **2** a device supplying air to a submarine when under water ▸ *vb* **-kelling, -kelled** or *US* **-keling, -keled 3** to swim with a snorkel

snort *vb* **1** to exhale air noisily through the nostrils **2** to express contempt or annoyance by snorting **3** to say with a snort **4** *slang* to inhale (a powdered drug) through the nostrils ▸ *n* **5** a loud exhalation of air through the nostrils to express contempt or annoyance: *Clare gave a snort of disgust*

snot *n* **1** *informal* mucus from the nose **2** *slang* an annoying or disgusting person

snout *n* **1** the projecting nose and jaws of an animal **2** anything projecting like a snout: *the snout of a gun* **3** *slang* a person's nose

snow *n* **1** frozen vapour falling from the sky in flakes **2** a layer of snow on the ground **3** a falling of snow **4** *slang* cocaine ▸ *vb* **5** (with *'it'* as subject) to be the case that snow is falling: *it's snowing today* **6** to fall as or like snow **7 be snowed in** or **up** or **over** to be covered by or confined with a heavy fall of snow **8 be snowed under** to be overwhelmed, esp. with paperwork > **snowy** *adj*

snowball *n* **1** snow pressed into a ball for throwing ▸ *vb* **2** to increase rapidly in size or importance: *production snowballed between 1950 and 1970* **3** to throw snowballs at

snowboard *n* a shaped board, like a skateboard without wheels, on which a person stands to slide across the snow > **snowboarding** *n*

snowdrift *n* a bank of deep snow driven together by the wind

snowdrop *n* a plant with small drooping white bell-shaped flowers

snowflake *n* a single crystal of snow

snow line *n* (on a mountain) the altitude above which there is permanent snow

snowman *n, pl* **-men** a figure like a person, made of packed snow

snowplough or *esp US* **snowplow** *n* a vehicle for clearing away snow

snub *vb* **snubbing, snubbed 1** to insult (someone) deliberately ▸ *n* **2** a deliberately insulting act or remark ▸ *adj* **3** (of a nose) short and turned up

> **snub** *vb* = insult, slight, put down, humiliate, cut (*informal*), rebuff, cold-shoulder ▸ *n* = insult, put-down, affront, slap in the face (*informal*)

snub-nosed *adj* having a short turned-up nose

snuff¹ *n* finely powdered tobacco for sniffing up the nostrils

snuff² *vb* **1** (often foll. by *out*) to put out (a candle) **2 snuff it** *Brit & Austral informal* to die

snuffle *vb* **-fling, -fled 1** to breathe noisily or with difficulty **2** to say or speak through the nose **3** to cry and sniff in a self-pitying way ▸ *n* **4** an act or the sound of snuffling > **snuffly** *adj*

snug *adj* **snugger, snuggest 1** comfortably warm and well protected; cosy: *safe and snug in their homes* **2** small but comfortable: *a snug office* **3** fitting closely and comfortably ▸ *n* **4** (in Britain and Ireland) a small room in a pub > **snugly** *adv*

snuggle *vb* **-gling, -gled** to nestle into (a person or thing) for warmth or from affection

so *adv* **1** to such an extent: *the river is so dirty that it smells* **2** to the same extent as: *she is not so old as you* **3** extremely: *it's so lovely* **4** also: *I can speak Spanish and so can you* **5** thereupon: *and so we ended up in France* **6** in the state or manner expressed or implied: *they're happy and will remain so* **7 and so on** or **forth** and continuing similarly **8 or so** approximately: *fifty or so people came to see me* **9 so be it** an expression of agreement or resignation **10 so much A** a certain degree or amount (of) **B** a lot (of): *it's just so much nonsense* **11 so much for A** no more need be said about **B** used to express contempt for something that has failed: *so much for all our plans* ▸ *conj* (often foll. by *that*) **12** in order (that): *to die so that you might live* **13** with the consequence (that): *he was late home, so that there was trouble* **14 so as** in order (to): *to diet so as to lose weight* **15** *not standard* in consequence: *she wasn't needed, so she left* **16 so what!** *informal* that is unimportant ▸ *pron* **17** used to substitute for a clause or sentence, which may be understood: *you'll stop because I said so* ▸ *adj* **18** true: *it can't be so* ▸ *interj* **19** an exclamation of surprise or triumph

> **so** *conj* **15** = therefore, thus, hence, consequently, then, as a result, accordingly, thence

soak vb 1 to put or lie in a liquid so as to become thoroughly wet 2 (usually foll. by in or into) (of a liquid) to penetrate or permeate 3 (usually foll. by in or up) to take in; absorb: white clay soaks up excess oil ▸ n 4 a soaking or being soaked 5 slang a person who drinks very heavily ▸ **soaking** n, adj

> **soak** vb 1 = steep 2 = penetrate, permeate, seep 3 **soak something up** = absorb, suck up, assimilate

so-and-so n, pl **so-and-sos** informal 1 a person whose name is not specified 2 euphemistic a person regarded as unpleasant; a name used in place of a swear word: you're a dirty so-and-so

soap n 1 a compound of alkali and fat, used with water as a cleaning agent 2 informal short for **soap opera** ▸ vb 3 to apply soap to

soap opera n an on-going television or radio serial about the daily lives of a group of people

soapy adj **soapier**, **soapiest** 1 containing or covered with soap: a soapy liquid 2 like soap in texture, smell, or taste: the cheese had a soapy taste 3 slang flattering or persuasive ▸ **soapiness** n

soar vb 1 to rise or fly upwards into the air 2 (of a bird or aircraft) to glide while maintaining altitude 3 to rise or increase suddenly above the usual level: television ratings soared

> **soar** vb 1 = fly, wing, climb, ascend; ≠ plunge 3 = rise, increase, grow, mount, climb, go up, rocket, escalate

sob vb **sobbing**, **sobbed** 1 to cry noisily, breathing in short gasps 2 to speak with sobs ▸ n 3 the act or sound of sobbing

> **sob** vb = cry, weep, howl, shed tears ▸ n = cry, whimper, howl

sober adj 1 not drunk 2 tending to drink only moderate quantities of alcohol 3 serious and thoughtful: a sober and serious fellow 4 (of colours) plain and dull 5 free from exaggeration: a fairly sober version of what happened ▸ vb 6 (usually foll. by up) to make or become less drunk ▸ **sobering** adj

> **sober** adj 2 = abstinent, temperate, abstemious, moderate; ≠ drunk 3 = serious, cool, grave, reasonable, steady, composed, rational, solemn, grounded; ≠ frivolous 4 = plain, dark, sombre, quiet, subdued, drab; ≠ bright

sobriety n the state of being sober

sobriquet or **soubriquet** (so-brik-ay) n a nickname

sob story n a tale of personal misfortune or bad luck intended to arouse sympathy

so-called adj called (in the speaker's opinion, wrongly) by that name: so-called military experts

> **so-called** adj = alleged, supposed, professed, pretended, self-styled

soccer n a game in which two teams of eleven players try to kick or head a ball into their opponents' goal, only the goalkeeper on either side being allowed to touch the ball with his hands

sociable adj 1 friendly and enjoying other people's company 2 (of an occasion) providing the opportunity for relaxed and friendly companionship ▸ **sociability** n ▸ **sociably** adv

social adj 1 living or preferring to live in a community rather than alone 2 of or relating to human society or organization 3 of the way people live and work together in groups: social organization 4 of or for companionship or communal activities: social clubs 5 of or engaged in social services: a social worker 6 relating to a certain class of society: social misfits 7 (of certain species of insects) living together in organized colonies: social bees ▸ n 8 an informal gathering ▸ **socially** adv

> **social** adj 1 = communal, community, collective, group, public, general, common 3 = organized, gregarious ▸ n = get-together (informal), party, gathering, function, reception, social gathering

socialism n a political and economic theory or system in which the means of production, distribution, and exchange are owned by the community collectively, usually through the state ▸ **socialist** n, adj

socialite n a person who goes to many events attended by the rich, famous, and fashionable

socialize or **-lise** vb **-lizing**, **-lized** or **-lising**, **-lised** 1 to meet others socially 2 to prepare for life in society 3 chiefly US to organize along socialist principles ▸ **socialization** or **-lisation** n

social media n websites and applications that allow users to interact with each other

social security n state provision for the welfare of elderly, unemployed, or sick people, through pensions and other financial aid

social services pl n welfare services provided by local authorities or a state agency for people with particular social needs

social work n social services that give help and advice to elderly people, people with disabilities, and families with problems ▸ **social worker** n

society n, pl **-ties** 1 human beings considered as a group 2 a group of people forming a single community with its own distinctive culture and institutions 3 the structure, culture, and institutions of such a group 4 an organized group of people sharing a common aim or interest: a dramatic society 5 the rich and fashionable class of society collectively 6 old-fashioned companionship: I enjoy her society

> **society** n 1 = the community, people, the public, humanity, civilization, humankind, mankind 2 = culture, community, population 4 = organization, group, club, union, league, association, institute, circle 5 = upper classes, gentry, elite, high society, beau monde 6 = companionship, company, fellowship, friendship

S

sociology n the study of the development, organization, functioning, and classification of human societies ▸ **sociological** adj ▸ **sociologist** n

sociopath n another name for **psychopath**

sock¹ n 1 a cloth covering for the foot, reaching to between the ankle and knee and worn inside a shoe 2 **pull one's socks up** informal to make a determined effort to improve 3 **put a sock in it** slang be quiet!

sock² slang ▸ vb 1 to hit hard ▸ n 2 a hard blow

socket n 1 a device into which an electric plug can be inserted in order to make a connection in a circuit 2 anatomy a bony hollow into which a part or structure fits: the hip socket

sod¹ n 1 a piece of grass-covered surface soil; turf 2 poetic the ground

sod² slang, chiefly Brit ▸ n 1 an unpleasant person 2 humorous a person, esp. an unlucky one: the poor sod hasn't been out for weeks 3 **sod all** slang nothing ▸ interj 4 **sod it** an exclamation of annoyance ▸ **sodding** adj

soda n 1 a simple compound of sodium, such as sodium carbonate or sodium bicarbonate 2 same as **soda water** 3 US & Canad a sweet fizzy drink

soda water n a fizzy drink made by charging water with carbon dioxide under pressure

sodden adj 1 soaking wet 2 (of someone's senses) dulled, esp. by excessive drinking

sodium n chem a very reactive soft silvery-white metallic element. Symbol: **Na**

sodium bicarbonate n a white soluble crystalline compound used in fizzy drinks, baking powder, and in medicine as an antacid

sodium chloride n common table salt; a soluble colourless crystalline compound widely used as a seasoning and preservative for food and in the manufacture of chemicals, glass, and soap

sodium hydroxide n a white strongly alkaline solid used in the manufacture of rayon, paper, aluminium, and soap

sodomite n old-fashioned a person who practises sodomy

sodomy n anal intercourse

sofa n a long comfortable seat with back and arms for two or more people

> **sofa** n 1 = couch, settee, divan, chaise longue

soft adj 1 easy to dent, shape, or cut: soft material 2 not hard; giving way easily under pressure: a soft bed 3 fine, smooth, or fluffy to the touch: soft fur 4 (of music or sounds) quiet and pleasing 5 (of light or colour) not excessively bright or harsh 6 (of a breeze or climate) temperate, mild, or pleasant 7 with smooth curves rather than sharp edges: soft focus 8 kind or lenient, often to excess 9 easy to influence or make demands on 10 informal feeble or silly; simple: soft in the head 11 not strong or able to endure hardship 12 (of a drug) nonaddictive 13 informal requiring little effort; easy: a soft job 14 chem (of water) relatively

free of mineral salts and therefore easily able to make soap lather 15 loving and tender: soft words 16 phonetics denoting the consonants c and g when they are pronounced sibilantly, as in cent and germ 17 **soft on** A lenient towards: he was accused of being soft on criminals B experiencing romantic love for ▸ adv 18 in a soft manner: to speak soft ▸ interj 19 archaic quiet! ▸ **softly** adv

> **soft** adj 1 = pliable, flexible, supple, malleable, plastic, elastic, bendable, mouldable 2 = yielding, elastic; ≠ hard 3 = velvety, smooth, silky, feathery, downy, fleecy; ≠ rough 4 = quiet, gentle, murmured, muted, dulcet, soft-toned; ≠ loud 5 = pale, light, subdued, pastel, bland, mellow; ≠ bright 6 = mild, temperate, balmy 8 = lenient, easy-going, lax, indulgent, permissive, spineless, overindulgent; ≠ harsh 13 = easy, comfortable, undemanding, cushy (informal) 15 = kind, tender, sentimental, compassionate, sensitive, gentle, tenderhearted, touchy-feely (informal)

soft drink n a nonalcoholic drink

soften vb 1 to make or become soft or softer 2 to make or become more sympathetic and less critical: the farmers softened their opposition to the legislation 3 to lessen the severity or difficulty of: foreign relief softened the hardship of a terrible winter ▸ **softener** n

> **soften** vb 1 = melt, tenderize 2 = lessen, moderate, temper, ease, cushion, subdue, allay, mitigate

soft furnishings pl n curtains, hangings, rugs, and covers

soft option n the easiest of a number of choices

soft-pedal vb -dalling, -dalled or US -daling, -daled 1 to deliberately avoid emphasizing (something): he was soft-pedalling the question of tax increases ▸ n **soft pedal** 2 a pedal on a piano that softens the tone

soft-soap vb informal to flatter (a person)

software n the programs used by a computer

softwood n the wood of coniferous trees

soggy adj -gier, -giest 1 soaked with liquid: a soggy running track 2 moist and heavy: a soggy sandwich ▸ **sogginess** n

soigné or fem **soignée** (swah-nyay) adj neat, elegant, and well-dressed: the soignée deputy editor of Vogue

soil¹ n 1 the top layer of the land surface of the earth 2 a specific type of this material: sandy soil 3 land, country, or region: the first US side to lose on home soil

> **soil** n 1 = earth, ground, clay, dust, dirt 3 = territory, country, land

soil² vb 1 to make or become dirty or stained 2 to bring disgrace upon: he's soiled our reputation ▸ n 3 a soiled spot 4 refuse, manure, or excrement

soil *vb* **1** = dirty, foul, stain, pollute, tarnish, sully, defile, besmirch; ≠ clean

soiree (swah-ray) *n* an evening social gathering

sojourn (soj-urn) *literary* ▸ *n* **1** a short stay in a place ▸ *vb* **2** to stay temporarily: *he sojourned in Basle during a short illness*

solace (sol-iss) *n* **1** comfort in misery or disappointment: *it drove him to seek increasing solace in alcohol* **2** something that gives comfort or consolation: *his music was a solace to me during my illness* ▸ *vb* **-lacing, -laced 3** to give comfort or cheer to (a person) in time of sorrow or distress

solar *adj* **1** of the sun: *a solar eclipse* **2** operating by or using the energy of the sun: *solar cell*

solarium (sol-air-ee-um) *n, pl* **-lariums** *or* **-laria** a place with beds equipped with ultraviolet lights used for giving people an artificial suntan

solar plexus *n* **1** *anatomy* a network of nerves behind the stomach **2** *not in technical use* the vulnerable part of the stomach beneath the diaphragm

solar system *n* the system containing the sun and the planets, comets, and asteroids that go round it

sold *vb* **1** the past of **sell** ▸ *adj* **2 sold on** *slang* enthusiastic and uncritical about

solder *n* **1** an alloy used for joining two metal surfaces by melting the alloy so that it forms a thin layer between the surfaces ▸ *vb* **2** to join or mend or be joined or mended with solder

soldering iron *n* a hand tool with a copper tip that is heated and used to melt and apply solder

soldier *n* **1** ᴀ a person who serves or has served in an army ʙ a person who is not an officer in an army ▸ *vb* **2** to serve as a soldier ▸ **soldierly** *adj*

> **soldier** *n* **1**ᴀ = fighter, serviceman *or* servicewoman, trooper, warrior, man-at-arms, squaddie *or* squaddy (*Brit slang*)

soldier on *vb* to continue one's efforts despite difficulties or pressure

sole¹ *adj* **1** being the only one; only **2** not shared; exclusive: *sole ownership*

> **sole** *adj* = only, one, single, individual, alone, exclusive, solitary

sole² *n* **1** the underside of the foot **2** the underside of a shoe **3** the lower surface of an object ▸ *vb* **soling, soled 4** to provide (a shoe) with a sole

sole³ *n, pl* **sole** *or* **soles** an edible marine flatfish

sole charge school *n* NZ a country school with only one teacher

solecism (sol-iss-iz-zum) *n* *formal* **1** a minor grammatical mistake in speech or writing **2** an action considered not to be good manners ▸ **solecistic** *adj*

solely *adv* **1** only; completely: *an action intended solely to line his own pockets* **2** without others

> **solely** *adv* = only, completely, entirely, exclusively, alone, merely

solemn *adj* **1** very serious; deeply sincere: *my solemn promise* **2** marked by ceremony or formality: *a solemn ritual* **3** serious or glum: *a solemn look on her face* ▸ **solemnly** *adv*

> **solemn** *adj* **1,3** = serious, earnest, grave, sober, sedate, staid; ≠ cheerful **2** = formal, grand, grave, dignified, ceremonial, stately, momentous; ≠ informal

solemnity *n, pl* **-ties 1** the state or quality of being solemn **2** a solemn ceremony or ritual

solenoid (sole-in-oid) *n* a coil of wire, usually cylindrical, in which a magnetic field is set up by passing a current through it ▸ **solenoidal** *adj*

sol-fa *n*

solicit *vb* **1** *formal* to seek or request, esp. formally: *she was brushed aside when soliciting his support for the vote* **2** to approach a person with an offer of sex in return for money ▸ **solicitation** *n*

solicitor *n* *Brit, Austral & NZ* a lawyer who advises clients on matters of law, draws up legal documents, and prepares cases for barristers

solicitous *adj* *formal* **1** anxious about someone's welfare **2** eager ▸ **solicitousness** *n*

solicitude *n* *formal* anxiety or concern for someone's welfare

solid *adj* **1** (of a substance) in a physical state in which it resists changes in size and shape; not liquid or gaseous **2** consisting of matter all through; not hollow **3** of the same substance all through: *solid gold* **4** firm, strong, or substantial: *the solid door of a farmhouse* **5** proved or provable: *solid evidence* **6** law-abiding and respectable: *solid family men* **7** (of a meal or food) substantial **8** without interruption; continuous or unbroken: *solid bombardment* **9** financially sound: *a solid institution* **10** strongly united or established: *a solid marriage* **11** *geom* having or relating to three dimensions **12** adequate; sound, but not brilliant: *a solid career* **13** of a single uniform colour or tone ▸ *n* **14** *geom* a three-dimensional shape **15** a solid substance ▸ **solidity** *n* ▸ **solidly** *adv*

> **solid** *adj* **2** = firm, hard, compact, dense, concrete; ≠ unsubstantial **4** = strong, stable, sturdy, substantial, unshakable; ≠ unstable **5** = sound, real, reliable, good, genuine, dinkum (*Austral, NZ informal*); ≠ unsound **6** = reliable, dependable, upstanding, worthy, upright, trusty; ≠ unreliable

solidarity *n, pl* **-ties** agreement in interests or aims among members of a group; total unity

> **solidarity** *n* = unity, unification, accord, cohesion, team spirit, unanimity, concordance, like-mindedness, kotahitanga (NZ)

solidify *vb* **-fies, -fying, -fied 1** to make or become solid or hard **2** to make or become strong or unlikely to change: *a move that solidified the allegiance of our followers* ▸ **solidification** *n*

S

soliloquy *n, pl* **-quies** a speech made by a person while alone, esp. in a play

solipsism *n* *philosophy* the doctrine that the self is the only thing known to exist ▷ **solipsist** *n*

solitaire *n* **1** a game played by one person, involving moving and taking pegs in a pegboard with the object of being left with only one **2** a gem, esp. a diamond, set alone in a ring **3** *chiefly US* patience (the card game)

solitary *adj* **1** experienced or performed alone: *a solitary dinner* **2** living a life of solitude: *a solitary child* **3** single; alone: *the solitary cigarette in the ashtray* **4** having few friends; lonely **5** (of a place) without people; empty ▶ *n, pl* **-taries** **6** a person who lives on his or her own; hermit ▷ **solitariness** *n*

> **solitary** *adj* **1** = lone, alone **2, 4** = unsociable, reclusive, unsocial, isolated, lonely, cloistered, lonesome (*US, Canad*), friendless; ≠ sociable **5** = isolated, remote, out-of-the-way, hidden, unfrequented; ≠ busy

solitude *n* the state of being alone

solo *n, pl* **-los 1** a piece of music or section of a piece of music for one performer: *a trumpet solo* **2** any performance by an individual without assistance **3** Also: **solo whist** a card game in which each person plays on his or her own ▶ *adj* **4** performed by an individual without assistance: *a solo dance* ▶ *adv* **5** by oneself; alone: *to fly solo across the Atlantic* ▷ **soloist** *n*

so long *interj* **1** *informal* farewell; goodbye ▶ *adv* **2** *S African slang* for the time being; meanwhile

solo parent *n NZ* a parent bringing up a child or children alone

solstice *n* either the shortest day of the year (**winter solstice**) or the longest day of the year (**summer solstice**)

soluble *adj* **1** (of a substance) capable of being dissolved **2** (of a mystery or problem) capable of being solved ▷ **solubility** *n*

solution *n* **1** a specific answer to or way of answering a problem **2** the act or process of solving a problem **3** *chem* a mixture of two or more substances in which the molecules or atoms of the substances are completely dispersed **4** the act or process of forming a solution **5** the state of being dissolved: *the sugar is held in solution*

> **solution** *n* **1, 2** = answer, key, result, explanation **3** = mixture, mix, compound, blend, solvent

solve *vb* **solving, solved** to find the explanation for or solution to (a mystery or problem) ▷ **solvable** *adj*

> **solve** *vb* = answer, work out, resolve, crack, clear up, unravel, decipher, suss (out) (*slang*)

solvent *adj* **1** having enough money to pay off one's debts **2** (of a liquid) capable of dissolving other substances ▶ *n* **3** a liquid capable of dissolving other substances ▷ **solvency** *n*

solvent abuse *n* the deliberate inhaling of intoxicating fumes from certain solvents

sombre *or US* **somber** *adj* **1** serious, sad, or gloomy: *a sombre message* **2** (of a place) dim or gloomy **3** (of colour or clothes) dull or dark ▷ **sombrely** *or US* **somberly** *adv*

> **sombre** *or* **somber** *adj* **1** = gloomy, sad, sober, grave, dismal, mournful, lugubrious, joyless; ≠ cheerful **2, 3** = dark, dull, gloomy, sober, drab; ≠ bright

sombrero *n, pl* **-ros** a wide-brimmed Mexican hat

some *adj* **1** unknown or unspecified: *some man called for you* **2** an unknown or unspecified quantity or number of: *I've got some money* **3** **a** a considerable number or amount of: *he lived some years afterwards* **b** a little: *show some respect* **4** *informal* an impressive or remarkable: *that was some game!* ▶ *pron* **5** certain unknown or unspecified people or things: *some can teach and others can't* **6** an unknown or unspecified quantity of something or number of people or things: *he will sell some in his pub* ▶ *adv* **7** approximately: *some thirty pounds*

somebody *pron* **1** some person; someone ▶ *n, pl* **-bodies 2** a person of great importance: *he was a somebody*

> **somebody** *n* = celebrity, name, star, notable, household name, dignitary, luminary, personage; ≠ nobody

somehow *adv* **1** in some unspecified way **2** for some unknown reason: *somehow I can't do it*

> **somehow** *adv* **1** = one way or another, come what may, come hell or high water (*informal*), by fair means or foul, by hook or (by) crook, by some means or other

someone *pron* some person; somebody

somersault *n* **1** a leap or roll in which the head is placed on the ground and the trunk and legs are turned over it ▶ *vb* **2** to perform a somersault

something *pron* **1** an unspecified or unknown thing; some thing: *there was something wrong* **2** an unspecified or unknown amount: *something less than a hundred* **3** an impressive or important person, thing, or event: *isn't that something?* **4** **something else** *slang, chiefly US* a remarkable person or thing ▶ *adv* **5** to some degree; somewhat: *he looks something like me*

sometime *adv* **1** at some unspecified point of time ▶ *adj* **2** former: *a sometime actor*

sometimes *adv* now and then; from time to time

> **sometimes** *adv* = occasionally, at times, now and then; ≠ always

somewhat *adv* rather; a bit: *somewhat surprising*

somewhere *adv* **1** in, to, or at some unknown or unspecified place, point, or amount: *somewhere* down south; somewhere between 35 and 45 per cent **2 getting somewhere** *informal* making progress

somnambulism *n formal* the condition of walking in one's sleep > **somnambulist** *n*

somnolent *adj formal* drowsy; sleepy > **somnolence** *n*

son *n* **1** a male offspring **2** a form of address for a man or boy who is younger than the speaker **3** a male who comes from a certain place or one closely connected with a certain thing: *a good son of the church.* ▸ Related adjective: **filial**

sonar *n* a device that locates objects by the reflection of sound waves: used in underwater navigation and target detection

sonata *n* a piece of classical music, usually in three or more movements, for piano or for another instrument with or without piano

son et lumière (sonn ay **loom**-yair) *n* an entertainment staged at night at a famous building or historical site, at which its history is described by a speaker accompanied by lighting effects and music

song *n* **1** a piece of music with words, composed for the voice **2** the tuneful call made by certain birds or insects **3** the act or process of singing: *he broke into song* **4 for a song** at a bargain price **5 make a song and dance** *informal* to make an unnecessary fuss

> **song** *n* **1** = ballad, air, tune, carol, chant, chorus, anthem, number, waiata (NZ)

songbird *n* any bird that has a musical call

sonic *adj* of, involving, or producing sound

sonic boom *n* a loud explosive sound caused by the shock wave of an aircraft travelling at supersonic speed

son-in-law *n, pl* **sons-in-law** the husband of one's son or daughter

sonnet *n prosody* a verse form consisting of 14 lines with a fixed rhyme scheme and rhythm pattern

sonorous *adj* **1** (of a sound) deep or rich **2** (of speech) using language that is unnecessarily complicated and difficult to understand; pompous > **sonority** *n*

soon *adv* **1** in or after a short time; before long **2 as soon as** at the very moment that: *as soon as he had closed the door* **3 as soon ... as** used to indicate that the first alternative is slightly preferable to the second: *they'd just as soon die for him as live*

> **soon** *adv* **1** = before long, shortly, in the near future

sooner *adv* **1** the comparative of **soon**: *I only wish I'd been back sooner* **2** rather; in preference: *he would sooner leave the party than break with me* **3 no sooner ...than** immediately after or when: *no sooner had he spoken than the stench drifted up* **4 sooner or later** eventually

soot *n* a black powder formed by the incomplete burning of organic substances such as coal > **sooty** *adj*

soothe *vb* **soothing, soothed 1** to make (a worried or angry person) calm and relaxed **2** (of an ointment or cream) to relieve (pain) > **soothing** *adj*

> **soothe** *vb* **1** = calm, still, quiet, hush, appease, lull, pacify, mollify; ≠ upset **2** = relieve, ease, alleviate, assuage; ≠ irritate

soothsayer *n* a person who makes predictions about the future; prophet

sop *n* **1** a small bribe or concession given or made to someone to keep them from causing trouble: *a sop to her conscience* **2** *informal* a stupid or weak person **3 sops** food soaked in a liquid before being eaten ▸ *vb* **sopping, sopped 4 sop up** to soak up or absorb (liquid)

sophism *n* an argument that seems reasonable but is actually false and misleading

sophist *n* a person who uses clever but false arguments > **sophistic** *adj*

sophisticate *vb* **-cating, -cated 1** to make (someone) less natural or innocent, such as by education **2** to make (a machine or method) more complex or refined ▸ *n* **3** a sophisticated person > **sophistication** *n*

sophisticated *adj* **1** having or appealing to fashionable and refined tastes and habits: *a sophisticated restaurant* **2** intelligent, knowledgeable, or able to appreciate culture and the arts: *a sophisticated concert audience* **3** (of machines or methods) complex and using advanced technology

> **sophisticated** *adj* **2** = cultured, refined, cultivated, worldly, cosmopolitan, urbane; ≠ unsophisticated **3** = complex, advanced, complicated, subtle, delicate, elaborate, refined, intricate; ≠ simple

sophistry *n* **1** the practice of using arguments which seem clever but are actually false and misleading **2** *pl* **-ries** an instance of this

sophomore *n chiefly US & Canad* a second-year student at a secondary (high) school or college

soporific *adj* **1** causing sleep ▸ *n* **2** a drug that causes sleep

sopping *adj* completely soaked; wet through. Also: **sopping wet**

soppy *adj* **-pier, -piest** *informal* foolishly sentimental: *a soppy love song* > **soppily** *adv*

soprano *n, pl* **-pranos 1** the highest adult female voice **2** the voice of a young boy before puberty **3** a singer with such a voice **4** the highest or second highest instrument in a family of instruments ▸ *adj* **5** denoting a musical instrument that is the highest or second highest pitched in its family: *the soprano saxophone* **6** of or relating to the highest female voice, or the voice of a young boy: *the part is quite possibly the most demanding soprano role Wagner ever wrote*

sorbet (saw-bay) *n* a flavoured water ice

sorcerer *or fem* **sorceress** *n* a person who uses magic powers; a wizard

S

sorcery *n, pl* **-ceries** witchcraft or magic

sordid *adj* **1** dirty, depressing, and squalid: *a sordid backstreet in a slum area* **2** relating to sex in a crude or unpleasant way: *the sordid details of his affair* **3** involving immoral and selfish behaviour: *the sordid history of the slave trade*

sore *adj* **1** (of a wound, injury, etc.) painfully sensitive; tender **2** causing annoyance and resentment: **3** upset and angered: *she's still sore about last night* **4** *literary* urgent; pressing: *in sore need of firm government* ▸ *n* **5** a painful or sensitive wound or injury ▸ *adv* **6** **sore afraid** *archaic* greatly frightened ▸ **soreness** *n*

> **sore** *adj* = painful, smarting, raw, tender, burning, angry, sensitive, irritated **2** = annoying, troublesome **3** = annoyed, cross, angry, pained, hurt, upset, stung, irritated, tooshie (*Austral slang*), hoha (*NZ*) **4** = urgent, desperate, extreme, dire, pressing, critical, acute

sorely *adv* greatly: *sorely disappointed*

sorghum *n* a grass grown for grain and as a source of syrup

sorrel *n* a plant with bitter-tasting leaves which are used in salads and sauces

sorrow *n* **1** deep sadness or regret, associated with death or sympathy for another's misfortune **2** a particular cause of this ▸ *vb* **3** *literary* to feel deep sadness (about death or another's misfortunes); mourn ▸ **sorrowful** *adj* ▸ **sorrowfully** *adv*

> **sorrow** *n* **1** = grief, sadness, woe, regret, distress, misery, mourning, anguish; ≠ joy **2** = hardship, trial, tribulation, affliction, trouble, woe, misfortune; ≠ good fortune ▸ *vb* = grieve, mourn, lament, be sad, bemoan, agonize, bewail; ≠ rejoice

sorry *adj* **-rier, -riest 1** (often foll. by *for* or *about*) feeling or expressing pity, sympathy, grief, or regret: *I'm sorry about this* **2** in bad mental or physical condition: poor: *a sorry state* **3** poor: *a sorry performance* ▸ *interj* **4** an exclamation expressing apology or asking someone to repeat what he or she has said

> **sorry** *adj* **1** = regretful, apologetic, contrite, repentant, remorseful, penitent, shamefaced, conscience-stricken; ≠ unapologetic **3** = wretched, miserable, pathetic, mean, poor, sad, pitiful, deplorable

sort *n* **1** a class, group, or kind sharing certain characteristics or qualities **2** *informal* a type of character: *she was a good sort* **3** a more or less adequate example: *a sort of dream machine* **4 of sorts** or **of a sort** **A** of a poorer quality: *she was wearing a uniform of sorts* **B** of a kind not quite as intended or desired: *it was a reward, of sorts, for my efforts* **5 out of sorts** not in normal good health or temper **6 sort of** as it were; rather: *I sort of quit; sort of insensitive* ▸ *vb* **7** to arrange (things or

people) according to class or type **8** to put (something) into working order; fix **9** to arrange (information on a computer) in an order the user finds convenient

> **sort** *n* **1** = kind, type, class, make, order, style, quality, nature ▸ *vb* **7** = arrange, group, order, rank, divide, grade, classify, categorize

sortie *n* **1** a short or relatively short return trip **2** (of troops) a raid into enemy territory **3** an operational flight made by a military aircraft ▸ *vb* **-tieing, -tied 4** to make a sortie

SOS *n* **1** an international code signal of distress in which the letters SOS are repeatedly spelt out in Morse code **2** *informal* any call for help

so-so *informal* ▸ *adj* **1** neither good nor bad ▸ *adv* **2** in an average or indifferent way

sot *n* a person who is frequently drunk ▸ **sottish** *adj*

sotto voce (**sot**-toe **voe**-chay) *adv* with a soft voice

soubriquet *n* same as **sobriquet**

soufflé (**soo**-flay) *n* a light fluffy dish made with beaten egg whites and other ingredients such as cheese or chocolate

sough (rhymes with **now**) *vb literary* (of the wind) to make a sighing sound

sought (**sawt**) *vb* the past of **seek**

souk (**sook**) *n* an open-air marketplace in Muslim countries

soul *n* **1** the spiritual part of a person, regarded as the centre of personality, intellect, will, and emotions: believed by many to survive the body after death **2** the essential part or fundamental nature of anything: *the soul of contemporary America* **3** deep and sincere feelings: *you've got no soul* **4** Also called: **soul music** a type of music of Black American origin using blues and elements of jazz, gospel, and pop **5** a person regarded as a good example of some quality: *the soul of prudence* **6** a person: *there was hardly a soul there* **7 the life and soul** *informal* a person who is lively, entertaining, and fun to be with: *the life and soul of the campus*

> **soul** *n* **1** = spirit, essence, life, vital force, wairua (*NZ*) **2, 5** = embodiment, essence, epitome, personification, quintessence, type **6** = person, being, individual, body, creature, man *or* woman

soulful *adj* expressing deep feelings: *a soulful performance of one of Tchaikovsky's songs*

soulless *adj* **1** lacking human qualities; mechanical: *soulless materialism* **2** (of a person) lacking in sensitivity or emotion

sound¹ *n* **1** anything that can be heard; noise **2** *physics* mechanical vibrations that travel in waves through the air, water, etc. **3** the sensation produced by such vibrations in the organs of hearing **4** the impression one has of something: *I didn't really like the sound of it* **5 sounds** *slang* music, esp. rock, jazz, or pop

▸ *vb* **6** to make or cause (an instrument, etc.) to make a sound **7** to announce (something) by a sound: *guns sound the end of the two minutes silence* **8** to make a noise with a certain quality: *her voice sounded shrill* **9** to suggest (a particular idea or quality): *his argument sounded false* **10** to pronounce (something) clearly: *to sound one's r's*

> **sound** *n* **1** = noise, din, report, tone, reverberation **4** = idea, impression, drift
> ▸ *vb* **6** = toll, set off **9** = seem, seem to be, appear to be

sound² *adj* **1** free from damage, injury, or decay; in good condition **2** firm or substantial: *sound documentary evidence* **3** financially safe or stable: *a sound investment* **4** showing good judgment or reasoning; wise: *sound advice* **5** morally correct; honest **6** (of sleep) deep and uninterrupted **7** thorough: *a sound defeat* ▸ *adv* **8 sound asleep** in a deep sleep › **soundly** *adv*

> **sound** *adj* **1** = fit, healthy, perfect, intact, unhurt, uninjured, unimpaired; ≠ frail **2** = sturdy, strong, solid, stable **4** = sensible, wise, reasonable, right, correct, proper, valid, rational, grounded; ≠ irresponsible **6** = deep, unbroken, undisturbed, untroubled; ≠ troubled

sound³ *vb* **1** to measure the depth of (a well, the sea, etc.) **2** *med* to examine (a part of the body) by tapping or with a stethoscope

sound⁴ *n* a channel between two larger areas of sea or between an island and the mainland

sound barrier *n* a sudden increase in the force of air against an aircraft flying at or above the speed of sound

sound bite *n* a short pithy sentence or phrase extracted from a longer speech for use on television or radio: *complicated political messages cannot be properly reduced to fifteen-second sound bites*

sounding board *n* a person or group used to test a new idea or policy

soundings *pl n* **1** measurements of the depth of a river, lake, or sea **2** questions asked of someone in order to find out his or her opinion: *soundings among colleagues had revealed enthusiasm for the plan*

soundproof *adj* **1** (of a room) built so that no sound can get in or out ▸ *vb* **2** to make (a room) soundproof

soundtrack *n* the recorded sound accompaniment to a film

soup *n* **1** a food made by cooking meat, fish, or vegetables in a stock **2 in the soup** *slang* in trouble or difficulties › **soupy** *adj*

soupçon (soop-sonn) *n* a slight amount; dash

souped-up *adj slang* (of a car, motorbike, or engine) adjusted so as to be faster or more powerful than normal

soup kitchen *n* a place where food and drink are served to needy people

sour *adj* **1** having a sharp biting taste like the taste of lemon juice or vinegar **2** made acid or bad, such as when milk ferments **3** (of a person's mood) bad-tempered and unfriendly **4 go** *or* **turn sour** to become less enjoyable or happy: *the dream has turned sour* ▸ *vb* **5** to make or become less enjoyable or friendly: *relations soured shortly after the war* › **sourly** *adv*

> **sour** *adj* **1** = sharp, acid, tart, bitter, pungent, acetic; ≠ sweet **2** = rancid, turned, gone off, curdled, gone bad, off; ≠ fresh **3** = bitter, tart, acrimonious, embittered, disagreeable, ill-tempered, waspish, ungenerous; ≠ good-natured

source *n* **1** the origin or starting point: *the source of discontent among fishermen* **2** any person, book, or organization that provides information for a news report or for research **3** the area or spring where a river or stream begins ▸ *vb* **4** to establish a supplier of (a product, etc) **5** (foll. by *from*) to originate from

> **source** *n* **1** = cause, origin, derivation, beginning, author **2** = informant, authority **3** = origin, fount

souse *vb* **sousing, soused 1** to plunge (something) into water or other liquid **2** to drench **3** to steep or cook (food) in a marinade ▸ *n* **4** the liquid used in pickling **5** the act or process of sousing

soutane (soo-**tan**) *n RC Church* a priest's robe

south *n* **1** one of the four cardinal points of the compass, at 180° from north **2** the direction along a line of latitude towards the South Pole **3 the south** any area lying in or towards the south ▸ *adj* **4** situated in, moving towards, or facing the south **5** (esp. of the wind) from the south ▸ *adv* **6** in, to, or towards the south

South *n* **1 the South A** the southern part of England **B** (in the US) the Southern states that formed the Confederacy during the Civil War **C** the countries of the world that are not technically and economically advanced ▸ *adj* **2** of or denoting the southern part of a country, area, etc.

southerly *adj* **1** of or in the south ▸ *adv, adj* **2** towards the south **3** from the south: *light southerly winds*

southern *adj* **1** situated in or towards the south **2** facing or moving towards the south **3** (*sometimes cap*) of or characteristic of the south or South › **southernmost** *adj*

Southerner *n* a person from the south of a country or area, esp. England or the US

southpaw *informal* ▸ *n* **1** any left-handed person, esp. a boxer ▸ *adj* **2** left-handed

South Pole *n* the southernmost point on the earth's axis, at a latitude of 90°S, which has very low temperatures

southward *adj, adv also* **southwards 1** towards the south ▸ *n* **2** the southward part or direction

souvenir *n* an object that reminds one of a certain place, occasion, or person; memento

> **souvenir** *n* = keepsake, reminder, memento

S

sou'wester *n* a seaman's hat with a broad brim that covers the back of the neck

sovereign *n* **1** the Royal ruler of a country **2** a former British gold coin worth one pound sterling ▸ *adj* **3** independent of outside authority; not governed by another country: *a sovereign nation* **4** supreme in rank or authority: *a sovereign queen* **5** *old-fashioned* excellent or outstanding: *a sovereign remedy for epilepsy*

> **sovereign** *n* **1** = monarch, ruler, king *or* queen, chief, potentate, emperor *or* empress, prince *or* princess ▸ *adj* **4** = supreme, ruling, absolute, royal, principal, imperial, kingly *or* queenly **5** = excellent, efficient, effectual

sovereignty *n, pl* **-ties 1** the political power a nation has to govern itself **2** the position or authority of a sovereign

> **sovereignty** *n* **2** = supreme power, domination, supremacy, primacy, kingship, queenship, rangatiratanga (NZ)

soviet *n* (in the former Soviet Union) an elected government council at the local, regional, and national levels

Soviet *adj* **1** of the former Soviet Union ▸ *n* **2** a person from the former Soviet Union

sow¹ *vb* **sowing, sowed, sown** *or* **sowed 1** to scatter or plant (seed) in or on (the ground) so that it may grow: *sow sweet peas in pots; farmers sow their fields with fewer varieties* **2** to implant or introduce: *to sow confusion among the other members*

> **sow** *vb* **1** = scatter, plant, seed, implant

sow² *n* a female adult pig

soya bean *or US & Canad* **soybean** *n* a plant whose bean is used for food and as a source of oil

soy sauce *n* a salty dark brown sauce made from fermented soya beans, used in Chinese cookery

sozzled *adj Brit, Austral & NZ informal* drunk

spa *n* a mineral-water spring or a resort where such a spring is found

space *n* **1** the unlimited three-dimensional expanse in which all objects exist **2** an interval of distance or time between two points, objects, or events **3** a blank portion or area **4** unoccupied area or room: *barely enough space to walk around* **5** the region beyond the earth's atmosphere containing other planets, stars, and galaxies; the universe ▸ *vb* **spacing, spaced 6** (often foll. by *out*) to place or arrange (things) at intervals or with spaces between them

> **space** *n* **2** = period, interval, time, while, span, duration, time frame, timeline **3** = blank, gap, interval **4** = room, capacity, extent, margin, scope, play, expanse, leeway **5** = outer space, the universe, the galaxy, the solar system, the cosmos

spacecraft *n* a vehicle that can be used for travel in space

space shuttle *n* a manned reusable spacecraft designed for making regular flights

spacesuit *n* a sealed protective suit worn by astronauts

spacious *adj* having or providing a lot of space; roomy > **spaciousness** *n*

> **spacious** *adj* = roomy, large, huge, broad, extensive, ample, expansive, capacious; ≠ cramped

spade¹ *n* **1** a tool for digging, with a flat steel blade and a long wooden handle **2 call a spade a spade** to speak plainly and frankly

spade² *n* **1 ᴀ spades** the suit of playing cards marked with a black leaf-shaped symbol **ʙ** a card with one or more of these symbols on it **2 in spades** *informal* in plenty: *all you need is talent in spades*

spadework *n* dull or routine work done as preparation for a project or activity

spaghetti *n* pasta in the form of long strings

spam *vb* **spamming, spammed 1** to send unsolicited messages simultaneously to a typically large number of email addresses ▸ *n* **2** unsolicited messages sent in this way

span *n* **1** the interval or distance between two points, such as the ends of a bridge **2** the complete extent: *that span of time* **3** a unit of length based on the width of a stretched hand, usually taken as nine inches (23 centimetres) ▸ *vb* **spanning, spanned 4** to stretch or extend across, over, or around: *her career spanned fifty years; to span the Danube*

> **span** *n* **1, 2** = period, term, duration, spell ▸ *vb* = extend across, cross, bridge, cover, link, traverse

spangle *n* **1** a small piece of shiny material used as a decoration on clothes or hair; sequin ▸ *vb* **-gling, -gled 2** to cover or decorate (something) with spangles

Spaniard *n* a person from Spain

spaniel *n* a dog with long drooping ears and a silky coat

Spanish *adj* **1** of Spain ▸ *n* **2** the official language of Spain, Mexico, and most countries of South and Central America ▸ *pl n* **3 the Spanish** the people of Spain

spank *vb* **1** to slap (someone) with the open hand, on the buttocks or legs ▸ *n* **2** such a slap

spanking¹ *n* a series of spanks, usually as a punishment for children

spanking² *adj* **1** *informal* outstandingly fine or smart: *spanking new uniforms* **2** very fast: *a spanking pace*

spanner *n* **1** a tool for gripping and turning a nut or bolt **2 throw a spanner in the works** *informal* to cause a problem that prevents things from running smoothly

spar¹ *n* a pole used as a ship's mast, boom, or yard

spar² vb **sparring, sparred** 1 boxing & martial arts to fight using light blows for practice 2 to argue with someone ▸ n 3 an argument

> **spar** vb 2 = argue, row, squabble, scrap (informal), wrangle, bicker

spare adj 1 extra to what is needed: there are some spare chairs at the back 2 able to be used when needed: a spare parking space 3 (of a person) tall and thin 4 (of a style) plain and without unnecessary decoration or details; austere: a spare but beautiful novel 5 Brit slang frantic with anger or worry: the boss went spare ▸ n 6 an extra thing kept in case it is needed ▸ vb **sparing, spared** 7 to stop from killing, punishing, or injuring (someone) 8 to protect (someone) from (something) unpleasant: spare me the sermon 9 to be able to afford or give: can you spare me a moment to talk? 10 **not spare oneself** to try one's hardest 11 **to spare** more than is required: a few hours to spare

> **spare** adj 1 = back-up, reserve, second, extra, additional, auxiliary; ≠ necessary 3 = thin, lean, meagre, gaunt, wiry; ≠ plump ▸ vb 7 = have mercy on, pardon, leave, let off (informal), go easy on (informal), save (from harm); ≠ show no mercy to 9 = afford, give, grant, do without, part with, manage without, let someone have

sparing adj (sometimes foll. by of) economical (with): she was mercifully sparing in her use of jargon > **sparingly** adv

> **sparing** adj = economical, frugal, thrifty, saving, careful, prudent; ≠ lavish

spark n 1 a fiery particle thrown out from a fire or caused by friction 2 a short flash of light followed by a sharp crackling noise, produced by a sudden electrical discharge through the air 3 a trace or hint: a spark of goodwill 4 liveliness, enthusiasm, or humour: that spark in her eye ▸ vb 5 to give off sparks 6 to cause to start; trigger: the incident sparked off an angry exchange

> **spark** n 1 = flicker, flash, gleam, glint, flare 3 = trace, hint, scrap, atom, jot, vestige ▸ vb 6 = start, stimulate, provoke, inspire, trigger (off), set off, precipitate

sparkie n Brit, Austral & NZ informal electrician
sparkle vb **-kling, -kled** 1 to glitter with many bright points of light 2 (of wine or mineral water) to be slightly fizzy 3 to be lively, witty, and intelligent ▸ n 4 a small bright point of light 5 liveliness and wit > **sparkling** adj

> **sparkle** vb 1 = glitter, flash, shine, gleam, shimmer, twinkle, dance, glint ▸ n 4 = glitter, flash, gleam, flicker, brilliance, twinkle, glint 5 = vivacity, life, spirit, dash, vitality, élan, liveliness

sparkler n 1 a type of hand-held firework that throws out sparks 2 informal a sparkling gem; esp. a diamond

spark plug n a device in an internal-combustion engine that ignites the fuel by producing an electric spark
sparrow n a very common small brown or grey bird which feeds on seeds and insects
sparrowhawk n a small hawk which preys on smaller birds
sparse adj small in amount and spread out widely: a sparse population > **sparsely** adv
Spartan adj 1 of or relating to the ancient Greek city of Sparta 2 (of a way of life) strict or simple and with no luxuries: Spartan accommodation ▸ n 3 a citizen of Sparta 4 a person who leads a strict or simple life without luxuries
spasm n 1 a sudden tightening of the muscles, over which one has no control 2 a sudden burst of activity or feeling: a spasm of applause; sudden spasms of anger
spasmodic adj taking place in sudden short spells: spasmodic bouts of illness > **spasmodically** adv
spastic adj 1 old-fashioned, offensive a person who has cerebral palsy, and therefore has difficulty controlling his or her muscles ▸ adj 2 affected by involuntary muscle contractions: a spastic colon 3 old-fashioned, offensive having cerebral palsy
spat¹ n a slight quarrel
spat² vb a past of **spit¹**
spate n 1 a large number of things happening within a period of time: a spate of bombings 2 a fast flow or outpouring: an incomprehensible spate of words 3 **in spate** chiefly Brit (of a river) flooded

> **spate** n 1 = series, sequence, course, chain, succession, run, train 2 = flood, flow, torrent, rush, deluge, outpouring

spatial adj of or relating to size, area, or position: spatial dimensions > **spatially** adv
spats pl n cloth or leather coverings formerly worn by men over the ankle and instep
spatter vb 1 to scatter or splash (a substance, esp. a liquid) in scattered drops: spattering mud in all directions 2 to sprinkle (an object or a surface) with a liquid ▸ n 3 the sound of spattering 4 something spattered, such as a spot or splash
spatula n a utensil with a broad flat blade, used in cooking and by doctors
spawn n 1 the jelly-like mass of eggs laid by fish, amphibians, or molluscs ▸ vb 2 (of fish, amphibians, or molluscs) to lay eggs 3 to cause (something) to be created: the depressed economy spawned the riots
spay vb to remove the ovaries from (a female animal)
spaza shop n S African slang a small informal shop in a township, often run from a private house
speak vb **speaking, spoke, spoken** 1 to say words; talk 2 to communicate or express (something) in words 3 to give a speech or lecture 4 to know how to talk in (a specified language): I don't speak French 5 **on speaking**

S

terms on good terms; friendly **6 so to speak** as it were **7 speak one's mind** to express one's opinions honestly and plainly **8 to speak of** of a significant nature: *no licensing laws to speak of*

> **speak** *vb* **1** = talk, say something **2** = articulate, say, pronounce, utter, tell, state, talk, express **3** = lecture, address an audience

speaker *n* **1** a person who speaks, esp. someone making a speech **2** a person who speaks a particular language: *a fluent Tibetan and English speaker* **3** same as **loudspeaker**

> **speaker** *n* **1** = orator, public speaker, lecturer, spokesman *or* woman *or* person

Speaker *n* the official chair of a law-making body

speakerphone *n* a telephone that has an external microphone and loudspeaker, allowing several people to participate in a call at the same time

spear¹ *n* **1** a weapon consisting of a long pole with a sharp point ▸ *vb* **2** to pierce (someone or something) with a spear or other pointed object: *she took her fork and speared an oyster from its shell*

spear² *n* **1** a slender shoot, such as of grass **2** a single stalk of broccoli or asparagus

spearhead *vb* **1** to lead (an attack or a campaign) ▸ *n* **2** the leading force in an attack or campaign

> **spearhead** *vb* = lead, head, pioneer, launch, set off, initiate, set in motion

spearmint *n* a minty flavouring used for sweets and toothpaste, which comes from a purple-flowered plant

spec *n* **on spec** *informal* as a risk or gamble: *I still tend to buy on spec*

special *adj* **1** distinguished from or better than others of its kind: *a special occasion* **2** designed or reserved for a specific purpose: *special equipment* **3** not usual; different from normal: *a special case* **4** particular or primary: *a special interest in gifted children* **5** relating to the education of children with disabilities: *a special school* ▸ *n* **6** a product, TV programme, etc., which is only available or shown at a certain time: *a two-hour Christmas special live from Hollywood* **7** a meal, usually at a low price, in a bar or restaurant > **specially** *adv*

> **special** *adj* **1, 3** = exceptional, important, significant, particular, unique, unusual, extraordinary, memorable; ≠ ordinary **2** = specific, particular, distinctive, individual, appropriate, precise; ≠ general

specialist *n* **1** a person who is an expert in a particular activity or subject **2** a doctor who concentrates on treating one particular category of diseases or the diseases of one particular part of the body: *an eye specialist* ▸ *adj* **3** particular to or concentrating on one subject or activity: *a specialist comic shop*

> **specialist** *n* **1** = expert, authority, professional, master, consultant, guru, buff (*informal*), connoisseur, fundi (*S African*)

speciality *or esp US & Canad* **specialty** *n, pl* **-ties 1** a special interest or skill **2** a service, product, or type of food specialized in

> **speciality** *or* **specialty** *n* **1** = forte, métier, strength, strong point, bag (*slang*), pièce de résistance (*French*)

specialize *or* **-lise** *vb* **-lizing, -lized** *or* **-lising, -lised 1** (often foll. by *in*) to concentrate all one's efforts on studying a particular subject, occupation, or activity: *an expert who specializes in transport* **2** to modify (something) for a special use or purpose: *plants have evolved and specialized in every type of habitat* > **specialization** *or* **-lisation** *n*

specie *n* coins as distinct from paper money

species *n, pl* **-cies** *biol* one of the groups into which a genus is divided, the members of which are able to interbreed

> **species** *n* = kind, sort, type, group, class, variety, breed, category

specific *adj* **1** particular or definite: *a specific area of economic policy* **2** precise and exact: *try and be more specific* ▸ *n* **3** **specifics** particular qualities or aspects of something: *the specifics of the situation* **4** *med* any drug used to treat a particular disease > **specifically** *adv* > **specificity** *n*

> **specific** *adj* **1** = particular, special, characteristic, distinguishing; ≠ general **2** = precise, exact, explicit, definite, express, clear-cut, unequivocal; ≠ vague

specification *n* **1** a detailed description of features in the design of something: *engines built to racing specification* **2** a requirement or detail which is clearly stated: *the main specification was that a good degree was required* **3** the specifying of something

> **specification** *n* **2** = requirement, detail, particular, stipulation, condition, qualification

specific gravity *n* *physics* the ratio of the density of a substance to the density of water

specify *vb* **-fies, -fying, -fied 1** to state or describe (something) clearly **2** to state (something) as a condition: *the rules specify the number of prisoners to be kept in each cell*

> **specify** *vb* = state, designate, stipulate, name, detail, mention, indicate, define

specimen *n* **1** an individual or part regarded as typical of its group or class **2** *med* a sample of tissue, blood, or urine taken for analysis **3** *informal* a person: *I'm quite a healthy specimen*

> **specimen** *n* **1** = sample, example, model, type, pattern, instance, representative, exemplification

S

specious (spee-shuss) *adj* apparently correct or true, but actually wrong or false

speck *n* 1 a very small mark or spot 2 a small or tiny piece of something: *a speck of fluff*

speckle *vb* **-ling, -led** 1 to mark (something) with speckles ▸ *n* 2 a small mark or spot, such as on the skin or on an egg ▸ **speckled** *adj*

specs *pl n informal*

spectacle *n* 1 a strange, interesting, or ridiculous scene 2 an impressive public show: *the opening ceremony of the Olympics was an impressive spectacle* 3 **make a spectacle of oneself** to draw attention to oneself by behaving foolishly

> **spectacle** *n* 1 = sight, wonder, scene, phenomenon, curiosity, marvel 2 = show, display, exhibition, event, performance, extravaganza, pageant

spectacular *adj* 1 impressive, grand, or dramatic ▸ *n* 2 a spectacular show
▸ **spectacularly** *adv*

> **spectacular** *adj* = impressive, striking, dramatic, stunning (*informal*), grand, magnificent, splendid, dazzling; ≠ unimpressive ▸ *n* = show, display, spectacle

spectate *vb* **-tating, -tated** to be a spectator; watch

spectator *n* a person viewing anything; onlooker

> **spectator** *n* = onlooker, observer, viewer, looker-on, watcher, bystander; ≠ participant

spectre *or US* **specter** *n* 1 a ghost 2 an unpleasant or menacing vision in one's imagination: *the spectre of famine* ▸ **spectral** *adj*

> **spectre** *or US* **specter** *n* 1 = ghost, spirit, phantom, vision, apparition, wraith, kehua (NZ)

spectroscope *n physics* an instrument for forming or recording a spectrum by passing a light ray through a prism or grating

spectrum *n, pl* **-tra** 1 *physics* the distribution of colours produced when white light is dispersed by a prism or grating: *violet, indigo, blue, green, yellow, orange, and red* 2 *physics* the whole range of electromagnetic radiation with respect to its wavelength or frequency 3 a range or scale of anything such as opinions or emotions

speculate *vb* **-lating, -lated** 1 to form opinions about something, esp. its future consequences, based on the information available; conjecture: *it is too early to speculate about Jackie getting married* 2 to buy securities or property in the hope of selling them at a profit ▸ **speculation** *n*
▸ **speculative** *adj* ▸ **speculator** *n*

> **speculate** *vb* 1 = conjecture, consider, wonder, guess, surmise, theorize, hypothesize 2 = gamble, risk, venture, hazard

sped *vb* a past of **speed**

speech *n* 1 the ability to speak: *the loss of speech* 2 spoken language: *Doran's lack of coherent speech* 3 a talk given to an audience: *a speech to parliament* 4 a person's manner of speaking: *her speech was extremely slow* 5 a national or regional language or dialect: *Canadian speech*

> **speech** *n* 1, 2 = communication, talk, conversation, discussion, dialogue 3 = talk, address, lecture, discourse, homily, oration, spiel (*informal*), whaikorero (NZ) 4 = diction, pronunciation, articulation, delivery, fluency, inflection, intonation, elocution 5 = language, tongue, jargon, dialect, idiom, parlance, articulation, diction

speechless *adj* 1 unable to speak for a short time because of great emotion or shock 2 unable to be expressed in words: *speechless disbelief*

speed *n* 1 the quality of acting or moving fast; swiftness 2 the rate at which something moves or happens 3 a gear ratio in a motor vehicle or bicycle: *five-speed gearbox* 4 *photog* a measure of the sensitivity to light of a particular type of film 5 *slang* amphetamine 6 **at speed** quickly 7 **up to speed** A operating at an acceptable level B in possession of all the necessary information ▸ *vb* **speeding, sped** *or* **speeded** 8 to move or go somewhere quickly 9 to drive a motor vehicle faster than the legal limit ▸ See also **speed up**

> **speed** *n* 1 = swiftness, rush, hurry, haste, rapidity, quickness; ≠ slowness 2 = rate, pace ▸ *vb* 8 = race, rush, hurry, zoom, career, tear, barrel (along) (*informal, chiefly US, Canad*), gallop; ≠ crawl

speedboat *n* a high-speed motorboat

speed camera *n* a camera for photographing vehicles breaking the speed limit

speedometer *n* a dial in a vehicle which shows the speed of travel

speed up *vb* to accelerate or cause to accelerate

speedway *n* 1 the sport of racing on light powerful motorcycles round cinder tracks 2 *US, Canad & NZ* the track or stadium where such races are held

speedwell *n* a small blue or pinkish-white flower

speedy *adj* **speedier, speediest** 1 done without delay 2 (of a vehicle) able to travel fast
▸ **speedily** *adv*

> **speedy** *adj* = quick, fast, rapid, swift, express, immediate, prompt, hurried; ≠ slow

speleology *n* the scientific study of caves

spell[1] *vb* **spelling, spelt** *or* **spelled** 1 to write or name in correct order the letters that make up (a word): *how do you spell that name?* 2 (of letters) to make up (a word): *c-a-t spells cat* 3 to indicate (a particular result): *share price slump spells disaster* ▸ See also **spell out**

> **spell** *vb* 3 = indicate, mean, signify, point to, imply, augur, portend

spell² n **1** a sequence of words used to perform magic **2** the effect of a spell: *the wizard's spell was broken* **3 under someone's spell** fascinated by someone

> **spell** n **1** = incantation, charm, makutu (NZ) **2** = enchantment, magic, fascination, glamour, allure, bewitchment

spell³ n **1** a period of time of weather or activity: *the dry spell; a short spell in prison* **2** a period of duty after which one person or group relieves another **3** *Scot, Austral & NZ* a period of rest

> **spell** n **1** = period, time, term, stretch, course, season, interval, bout

spellbound adj completely fascinated; as if in a trance

spellchecker n *computers* a program that highlights any word in a word-processed document that is not recognized as being correctly spelt

spelling n **1** the way a word is spelt: *the British spelling of 'theatre'* **2** a person's ability to spell: *my spelling used to be excellent*

spell out vb **1** to make (something) as easy to understand as possible: *to spell out the implications* **2** to read with difficulty, working out each word letter by letter

spelt vb a past of **spell¹**

spend vb **spending, spent 1** to pay out (money) **2** to pass (time) in a specific way or place: *I spent a year in Budapest* **3** to concentrate (effort) on an activity: *a lot of energy was spent organizing the holiday* **4** to use up completely: *the hurricane spent its force* > **spending** n

> **spend** vb **1** = pay out, fork out (*slang*), expend, disburse; ≠ save **2** = pass, fill, occupy, while away **4** = use up, waste, squander, empty, drain, exhaust, consume, run through; ≠ save

spendthrift n **1** a person who spends money wastefully ▸ adj **2** of or like a spendthrift: *a spendthrift policy*

sperm n **1** pl **sperms** or **sperm** one of the male reproductive cells released in the semen during ejaculation **2** same as **semen**

spermaceti (sper-ma-**set**-ee) n a white waxy substance obtained from the sperm whale

spermatozoon (sper-ma-toe-**zoe**-on) n, pl **-zoa** same as **sperm** (sense 1)

spermicide n a substance, esp. a cream or jelly, that kills sperm, used as a means of contraception > **spermicidal** adj

sperm whale n a large whale which is hunted for spermaceti and ambergris

spew vb **1** to vomit **2** to send or be sent out in a stream: *the hydrant spewed a tidal wave of water*

sphagnum n a moss which is found in bogs and which decays to form peat

sphere n **1** *geom* a round solid figure in which every point on the surface is equally distant from the centre **2** an object having this shape,

such as a planet **3** a particular field of activity **4** people of the same rank or with shared interests: *a humbler social sphere*

> **sphere** n **2** = ball, globe, orb, globule, circle **3** = field, department (*informal*), function, territory, capacity, province, patch, scope

spherical adj shaped like a sphere

sphincter n *anatomy* a ring of muscle surrounding the opening of a hollow organ and contracting to close it

Sphinx n **1** the huge statue of a sphinx near the pyramids at El Gîza in Egypt **2** *Greek myth* a monster with a woman's head and a lion's body, who set a riddle for travellers, killing them when they failed to answer it. Oedipus answered the riddle and the Sphinx then killed herself

spice n **1 A** an aromatic substance, such as ginger or cinnamon, used as flavouring **B** such substances collectively **2** something that makes life or an activity more exciting ▸ vb **spicing, spiced 3** to flavour (food) with spices **4** (often foll. by *up*) to add excitement or interest to (something): *they spiced their letters with pointed demands*

> **spice** n **1A** = seasoning **2** = excitement, zest, colour, pep, zing (*informal*), piquancy

spick-and-span adj very neat and clean

spicy adj **spicier, spiciest 1** strongly flavoured with spices **2** *informal* slightly scandalous: *spicy new story lines*

> **spicy** adj **1** = hot, seasoned, aromatic, savoury, piquant **2** = risqué, racy, ribald, hot (*informal*), suggestive, titillating, indelicate

spider n a small eight-legged creature, many species of which weave webs in which to trap insects for food > **spidery** adj

spiel n a prepared speech made to persuade someone to buy or do something

spigot n **1** a stopper for the vent hole of a cask **2** a wooden tap fitted to a cask

spike n **1** a sharp-pointed metal object: *a high fence with iron spikes* **2** anything long and pointed: *a hedgehog bristling with spikes* **3** a long metal nail **4 spikes** sports shoes with metal spikes on the soles for greater grip ▸ vb **spiking, spiked 5** to secure or supply (something) with spikes: *spiked shoes* **6** to drive a spike or spikes into **7** to add alcohol to (a drink) > **spiky** adj

> **spike** n **1, 3** = point, stake, spine, barb, prong ▸ vb **6** = impale, spit, spear, stick

spill¹ vb **spilling, spilt** or **spilled 1** to pour from or as from a container by accident **2** (of large numbers of people) to come out of a place: *rival groups spilled out from the station* **3** to shed (blood) **4 spill the beans** *informal* to give away a secret ▸ n **5** *informal* a fall from a motorbike, bike, or horse, esp. in a competition **6** an amount of liquid spilt > **spillage** n

> **spill** vb **1** = shed, discharge, disgorge

spill² *n* a splinter of wood or strip of paper for lighting pipes or fires

spin *vb* **spinning, spun 1** to revolve or cause to revolve quickly **2** to draw out and twist (fibres, such as silk or cotton) into thread **3** (of a spider or silkworm) to form (a web or cocoon) from a silky fibre that comes out of the body **4 spin a yarn** to tell an unlikely story **5** *sport* to throw, hit, or kick (a ball) so that it spins and changes direction or changes speed on bouncing **6** same as **spin-dry 7** to grow dizzy: *her head was spinning* **8** *informal* to present information in a way that creates a favourable impression ▸ *n* **9** a fast rotating motion **10** a flight manoeuvre in which an aircraft flies in a downward spiral **11** *sport* a spinning motion given to a ball **12** *informal* a short car drive taken for pleasure **13** *informal* the presenting of information in a way that creates a favourable impression ▸ See also **spin out** › **spinning** *n*

> **spin** *vb* **1** = revolve, turn, rotate, reel, whirl, twirl, gyrate, pirouette **7** = reel, swim, whirl ▸ *n* **9** = revolution, roll, whirl, gyration **12** = drive, ride, joyride (*informal*)

spina bifida *n* a condition in which part of the spinal cord protrudes through a gap in the backbone, sometimes causing paralysis

spinach *n* a dark green leafy vegetable

spindle *n* **1** a rotating rod that acts as an axle **2** a rod with a notch in the top for drawing out, twisting and winding the thread in spinning

spindly *adj* **-dlier, -dliest** tall, thin, and frail

spin doctor *n informal* a person who provides a favourable slant to a news item or policy on behalf of a political personality or party

spindrift *n* spray blown up from the sea

spin-dry *vb* **-dries, -drying, -dried** to dry (clothes) in a spin-dryer

spin-dryer *n* a device that removes water from washed clothes by spinning them in a perforated drum

spine *n* **1** the row of bony segments that surround and protect the spinal cord **2** the back of a book, record sleeve, or video-tape box **3** a sharp point on the body of an animal or on a plant › **spinal** *adj*

> **spine** *n* **1** = backbone, vertebrae, spinal column, vertebral column **3** = barb, spur, needle, spike, ray, quill

spineless *adj* **1** behaving in a cowardly way **2** (of an animal) having no spine

spinet *n* a small harpsichord

spinifex *n* a coarse spiny Australian grass

spinnaker *n* a large triangular sail on a racing yacht

spinner *n* **1** *cricket* **A** a bowler who specializes in spinning the ball with his or her fingers to make it change direction when it bounces or strikes the batsman's bat **B** a ball that is bowled with a spinning motion **2** a small round object used in angling to attract fish to the bait by spinning in the water **3** a person who makes thread by spinning

spinney *n chiefly Brit* a small wood: *the hollow tree in the spinney*

spin-off *n* **1** a product or development that unexpectedly results from activities designed to achieve something else: *new energy sources could occur as a spin-off from the space effort* **2** a television series involving some of the characters from an earlier successful series

spin out *vb* **1** to take longer than necessary to do (something) **2** to make (money) last as long as possible

> **spin out** *vb* **1 spin something out** = prolong, extend, lengthen, draw out, drag out, delay, amplify

spinster *n old-fashioned* an unmarried woman › **spinsterish** *adj*

spiny *adj* **spinier, spiniest** (of animals or plants) covered with spines

spiral *n* **1** *geom* a plane curve formed by a point winding about a fixed point at an ever-increasing distance from it **2** something that follows a winding course or that has a twisting form **3** *econ* a continuous upward or downward movement in economic activity or prices ▸ *adj* **4** having the shape of a spiral: *a spiral staircase* ▸ *vb* **-ralling, -ralled** *or US* **-raling, -raled 5** to follow a spiral course or be in the shape of a spiral **6** to increase or decrease with steady acceleration: *oil prices continue to spiral* › **spirally** *adv*

> **spiral** *n* **1, 2** = coil, helix, corkscrew, whorl ▸ *adj* = coiled, winding, whorled, helical

spire *n* the tall cone-shaped structure on the top of a church

spirit¹ *n* **1** the nonphysical aspect of a person concerned with profound thoughts and emotions **2** the nonphysical part of a person believed to live on after death **3** a shared feeling: *a spirit of fun and adventure* **4** mood or attitude: *fighting spirit* **5** a person's character or temperament: *the indomitable spirit of the Polish people* **6** liveliness shown in what a person does: *it has been undertaken with spirit* **7** the feelings that motivate someone to survive in difficult times or live according to his or her beliefs: *someone had broken his spirit* **8 spirits** an emotional state: *in good spirits* **9** the way in which something, such as a law or an agreement, was intended to be interpreted: *they acted against the spirit of the treaty* **10** a supernatural being, such as a ghost ▸ *vb* **-riting, -rited 11 spirit away** *or* **off** to carry (someone or something) off mysteriously or secretly

spirit n 1 = soul, life 2 = life force, vital spark, mauri (NZ) 3 = feeling, atmosphere, character, tone, mood, tenor, ambience 4 = mood, feelings, morale, temper, disposition, state of mind, frame of mind 5 = attitude, character, temper, outlook, temperament, disposition 6 = liveliness, energy, vigour, life, force, fire, enthusiasm, animation 9 = intention, meaning, purpose, purport, gist 10 = ghost, phantom, spectre, apparition, atua (NZ), kehua (NZ)

spirit² n 1 (usually pl) distilled alcoholic liquor, such as whisky or gin 2 chem A a solution of ethanol obtained by distillation B the essence of a substance, extracted as a liquid by distillation 3 pharmacol a solution of a volatile oil in alcohol

spirited adj 1 showing liveliness or courage: a spirited rendition of Schubert's ninth symphony; a spirited defence of the government's policy 2 characterized by the mood as specified: high-spirited; mean-spirited

spirited adj 1 = lively, energetic, animated, active, feisty (informal), vivacious, mettlesome, (as) game as Ned Kelly (Austral slang); ≠ lifeless

spirit level n a device for checking whether a surface is level, consisting of a block of wood or metal containing a tube partially filled with liquid set so that the air bubble in it rests between two marks on the tube when the block is level

spiritual adj 1 relating to a person's beliefs as opposed to his or her physical or material needs 2 relating to religious beliefs 3 one's spiritual home the place where one feels one belongs ▸ n 4 Also called: **Negro spiritual** a type of religious folk song originally sung by African slaves in the American South > **spirituality** n > **spiritually** adv

spiritual adj 1 = nonmaterial, immaterial, incorporeal; ≠ material 2 = sacred, religious, holy, divine, devotional

spiritualism n the belief that the spirits of the dead can communicate with the living > **spiritualist** n

spit¹ vb spitting, spat or spit 1 to force saliva out of one's mouth 2 to force (something) out of one's mouth: he spat tobacco into an old coffee can 3 (of a fire or hot fat) to throw out sparks or particles violently and explosively 4 to rain very lightly 5 (often foll. by out) to say (words) in a violent angry way 6 to show contempt or hatred by spitting 7 **spit it out!** informal a command given to someone to say what is on his or her mind ▸ n 8 same as **spittle** 9 informal, chiefly Brit same as **spitting image**

spit vb 1, 2 = expectorate

spit² n 1 a pointed rod for skewering and roasting meat over a fire or in an oven 2 a long narrow strip of land jutting out into the sea

spite n 1 deliberate nastiness 2 **in spite of** regardless of: he loved them in spite of their shortcomings ▸ vb **spiting, spited** 3 to annoy (someone) deliberately, out of spite: it was to spite his father > **spiteful** adj > **spitefully** adv

spite n 1 = malice, malevolence, ill will, hatred, animosity, venom, spleen, spitefulness; ≠ kindness 2 **in spite of** = despite, regardless of, notwithstanding, (even) though ▸ vb = annoy, hurt, injure, harm, vex; ≠ benefit

spitfire n someone who is easily angered

spitting image n informal a person who looks very like someone else

spittle n the fluid that is produced in the mouth; saliva

spittoon n a bowl for people to spit into

spiv n Brit, Austral & NZ slang a smartly dressed man who makes a living by underhand dealings; black marketeer

splash vb 1 to scatter (liquid) on (something) 2 to cause (liquid) to fall or (of liquid) to be scattered in drops 3 to display (a photograph or story) prominently in a newspaper ▸ n 4 a splashing sound 5 an amount splashed 6 a patch (of colour or light) 7 **make a splash** informal to attract a lot of attention 8 a small amount of liquid added to a drink

splash vb 1, 2 = scatter, shower, spray, sprinkle, wet, spatter, slop ▸ n 5 = dash, touch, spattering 6 = spot (Brit), burst, patch, spurt

splash out vb to spend a lot of money on a treat or luxury: she planned to splash out on a good holiday

splatter vb 1 to splash (something or someone) with small blobs ▸ n 2 a splash of liquid

splay vb to spread out, with ends spreading out in different directions: her hair splayed over the pillow

spleen n 1 a spongy organ near the stomach, which filters bacteria from the blood 2 spitefulness or bad temper: we vent our spleen on drug barons

splendid adj 1 very good: a splendid match 2 beautiful or impressive: a splendid palace > **splendidly** adv

splendid adj 1 = excellent, wonderful, marvellous, great, cracking (Brit informal), fantastic, first-class, glorious, booshit (Austral slang), exo (Austral slang), sik (Austral slang), rad (informal), phat (slang), schmick (Austral informal); ≠ poor 2 = magnificent, grand, impressive, rich, superb, costly, gorgeous, lavish; ≠ squalid

splendour or US **splendor** n 1 beauty or impressiveness 2 **splendours** the impressive or beautiful features of something: the splendours of the Emperor's Palace

splendour or **splendor** n 1 = magnificence, grandeur, show, display, spectacle, richness, nobility, pomp; ≠ squalor

S

splenetic *adj literary* irritable or bad-tempered

splice *vb* **splicing, spliced 1** to join up the trimmed ends of (two pieces of wire, film, or tape) with an adhesive material **2** to join (two ropes) by interweaving the ends **3 get spliced** *informal* to get married

splint *n* a piece of wood used to support a broken bone

splinter *n* **1** a small thin sharp piece broken off, esp. from wood ▶ *vb* **2** to break or be broken into small sharp fragments

> **splinter** *n* = sliver, fragment, chip, flake
> ▶ *vb* = shatter, split, fracture, disintegrate

splinter group *n* a number of members of an organization, who split from the main body and form an independent group of their own

split *vb* **splitting, split 1** to break or cause (something) to break into separate pieces **2** to separate (a piece) or (of a piece) to be separated from (something) **3** (of a group) to separate into smaller groups, through disagreement: *the council is split over rent increases* **4** (often foll. by *up*) to divide (something) among two or more people **5** *slang* to leave a place **6 split on** *slang* to betray; inform on: *he didn't tell tales or split on him* **7 split one's sides** to laugh a great deal ▶ *n* **8** a gap or rift caused by splitting **9** a division in a group or the smaller group resulting from such a division **10** a dessert of sliced fruit and ice cream, covered with whipped cream and nuts: *banana split* ▶ *adj* **11** divided (esp. in opinion, etc.) **12** having a split or splits: *split ends*

> **split** *vb* **1** = break, crack, burst, open, give way, come apart, come undone **2** = cut, break, crack, snap, chop **3** = divide, separate, disunite, disband, cleave **4** = share out, divide, distribute, halve, allocate, partition, allot, apportion ▶ *n* **8** = crack, tear, rip, gap, rent, breach, slit, fissure **9** = division, breach, rift, rupture, discord, schism, estrangement, dissension ▶ *adj* **11** = divided **12** = broken, cracked, fractured, ruptured, cleft

split second *n* **1** an extremely short period of time; instant ▶ *adj* **split-second 2** made in an extremely short time: *split-second timing*

splodge *or US* **splotch** *n* **1** a large uneven spot or stain ▶ *vb* **splodging, splodged 2** to mark (something) with a splodge or splodges

splurge *n* **1** a bout of spending money extravagantly ▶ *vb* **splurging, splurged 2** (foll. by *on*) to spend (money) extravagantly: *they rushed out to splurge their pocket money on chocolate*

splutter *vb* **1** to spit out (something) from the mouth when choking or laughing **2** to say (words) with spitting sounds when choking or in a rage **3** to throw out or to be thrown out explosively: *sparks spluttered from the fire* ▶ *n* **4** the act or noise of spluttering

spoil *vb* **spoiling, spoilt** *or* **spoiled 1** to make (something) less valuable, beautiful, or useful **2** to weaken the character of (a child) by giving it all it wants **3** (of oneself) to indulge one's desires: *go ahead and spoil yourself* **4** (of food) to become unfit for consumption **5 be spoiling for** to have an aggressive urge for: *he is spoiling for a fight* ▶ See also **spoils**

> **spoil** *vb* **1** = ruin, destroy, wreck, damage, injure, harm, mar, trash (*slang*), crool *or* cruel (*Austral slang*); ≠ improve **2** = overindulge, indulge, pamper, cosset, coddle, mollycoddle; ≠ deprive **3** = indulge, pamper, satisfy, gratify, pander to **4** = go bad, turn, go off (*Brit informal*), rot, decay, decompose, curdle, addle

spoils *pl n* **1** valuables seized during war **2** the rewards and benefits of having political power

> **spoils** *pl n* **1** = booty, loot, plunder, prey, swag (*slang*)

spoilsport *n informal* a person who spoils the enjoyment of other people

spoke[1] *vb* the past tense of **speak**

spoke[2] *n* **1** a bar joining the centre of a wheel to the rim **2 put a spoke in someone's wheel** *Brit & NZ* to create a difficulty for someone

spoken *vb* **1** the past participle of **speak** ▶ *adj* **2** said in speech: *spoken commands* **3** having speech as specified: *quiet-spoken* **4 spoken for** engaged or reserved

> **spoken** *adj* **2** = verbal, voiced, expressed, uttered, oral, said, told, unwritten

spokesman, spokesperson *or* **spokeswoman** *n, pl* **-men, -people** *or* **-women** a person chosen to speak on behalf of another person or group

> **spokesman, spokesperson** *or* **spokeswoman** *n* = speaker, official, voice, spin doctor (*informal*), mouthpiece

spoliation *n* the act or an instance of plundering: *the spoliation of the countryside*

sponge *n* **1** a sea animal with a porous absorbent elastic skeleton **2** the skeleton of a sponge, or a piece of artificial sponge, used for bathing or cleaning **3** a soft absorbent material like a sponge **4** Also called: **sponge cake** a light cake made of eggs, sugar, and flour **5** Also called: **sponge pudding** *Brit & Austral* a light steamed or baked spongy pudding **6** a rub with a wet sponge ▶ *vb* **sponging, sponged 7** (often foll. by *down*) to clean (something) by rubbing it with a wet sponge **8** to remove (marks) by rubbing them with a wet sponge **9** (usually foll. by *off or on*) to get (something) from someone by taking advantage of his or her generosity: *stop sponging off the rest of us!* > **spongy** *adj*

sponger *n informal, derogatory* a person who lives off other people by continually taking advantage of their generosity

sponsor *n* **1** a person or group that promotes another person or group in an activity or the activity itself, either for profit or for charity **2** *chiefly US & Canad* a person or firm that pays the costs of a radio or television programme in return for advertising time **3** a person who presents and supports a proposal or suggestion **4** a person who makes certain promises on behalf of a person being baptized and takes responsibility for his or her Christian upbringing ▸ *vb* **5** to act as a sponsor for (someone or something) ▸ **sponsored** *adj* ▸ **sponsorship** *n*

> **sponsor** *n* **1** = backer, patron, promoter ▸ *vb* = back, fund, finance, promote, subsidize, patronize

spontaneous *adj* **1** not planned or arranged; impulsive: *a spontaneous celebration* **2** occurring through natural processes without outside influence: *a spontaneous explosion* ▸ **spontaneously** *adv* ▸ **spontaneity** *n*

> **spontaneous** *adj* **1** = unplanned, impromptu, unprompted, willing, natural, voluntary, instinctive, impulsive; ≠ planned

spoof *informal* ▸ *n* **1** an imitation of a film, TV programme, etc., that exaggerates in an amusing way the most memorable features of the original **2** a good-humoured trick or deception ▸ *vb* **3** to fool (a person) with a trick or deception

spook *informal* ▸ *n* **1** a ghost **2** a strange and frightening person ▸ *vb* **3** to frighten: *it was the wind that spooked her* ▸ **spooky** *adj*

spool *n* a cylinder around which film, thread, or tape can be wound

spoon *n* **1** a small shallow bowl attached to a handle, used for eating, stirring, or serving food **2** **be born with a silver spoon in one's mouth** to be born into a very rich and respected family ▸ *vb* **3** to scoop up (food or liquid) with a spoon **4** *old-fashioned slang* to kiss and cuddle

spoonbill *n* a wading bird with a long flat bill

spoonerism *n* the accidental changing over of the first sounds of a pair of words, often with an amusing result, such as *hush my brat* for *brush my hat*

spoon-feed *vb* **-feeding, -fed 1** to feed (someone, usually a baby) using a spoon **2** to give (someone) too much help

spoor *n* the trail of an animal

sporadic *adj* happening at irregular intervals; intermittent: *sporadic bursts of gunfire* ▸ **sporadically** *adv*

spore *n* a reproductive body, produced by nonflowering plants and bacteria, that develops into a new individual

sporran *n* a large pouch worn hanging from a belt in front of the kilt in Scottish Highland dress

sport *n* **1** an activity for exercise, pleasure, or competition: *your favourite sport* **2** such activities collectively: *the minister for sport* **3** the enjoyment

gained from a pastime: *just for the sport of it* **4** playful or good-humoured joking: *I only did it in sport* **5** *informal* a person who accepts defeat or teasing cheerfully **6** **make sport of someone** to make fun of someone **7** an animal or plant that is very different from others of the same species, usually because of a mutation **8** *Austral & NZ informal* a term of address between males ▸ *vb* **9** *informal* to wear proudly: *sporting a pair of bright yellow shorts*

> **sport** *n* **1, 2** = game, exercise, recreation, play, amusement, diversion, pastime **4** = fun, joking, teasing, banter, jest, badinage ▸ *vb* = wear, display, flaunt, exhibit, flourish, show off, vaunt

sporting *adj* **1** of sport **2** behaving in a fair and decent way **3** **a sporting chance** reasonable likelihood of happening: *a sporting chance of winning*

> **sporting** *adj* **2** = fair, sportsmanlike, game (*informal*); ≠ unfair

sportive *adj* playful or high-spirited

sports car *n* a fast car with a low body and usually seating only two people

sports jacket *n* a man's jacket, resembling a suit jacket. Also called (US, Austral & NZ): **sports coat**

sportsman *n, pl* **-men 1** a man who plays sports **2** a person who plays by the rules, is fair, and accepts defeat with good humour ▸ **sportsman-like** *adj* ▸ **sportsmanship** *n*

sporty *adj* **sportier, sportiest 1** (of a person) interested in sport **2** (of clothes) suitable for sport **3** (of a car) small and fast ▸ **sportily** *adv* ▸ **sportiness** *n*

> **sporty** *adj* **1** = athletic, outdoor, energetic

spot *n* **1** a small mark on a surface, which has a different colour or texture from its surroundings **2** a location: *a spot where they could sit* **3** a small mark or pimple on the skin **4** a feature of something that has the attribute mentioned: *the one bright spot in his whole day; the high spot of our trip* **5** *informal* a small amount: *a spot of bother* **6** *informal* an awkward situation: *I'm sometimes in a tight spot* **7** a part of a show, TV programme, etc., reserved for a specific performer or type of entertainment **8** short for **spotlight** (sense 1) **9** **in a tight spot** in a difficult situation **10** **knock spots off someone** to be much better than someone **11** **on the spot A** immediately: *he decided on the spot to fly down* **B** at the place in question: *the expert weapons man on the spot* **C** in an awkward situation: *the British government will be put on the spot* **12** **soft spot** a special affection for someone: *a soft spot for older men* ▸ *vb* **spotting, spotted 13** to see (something or someone) suddenly **14** to put stains or spots on (something) **15** (of some fabrics) to be prone to marking by liquids: *silk spots easily* **16** to take note of (the numbers of trains or planes observed) **17** (of scouts, agents, etc.) to look out for (talented but unknown actors, sportspersons, etc.) **18** *Brit* to rain lightly

spot *n* **1** = mark, stain, speck, scar, blot, smudge, blemish, speckle **2** = place, site, point, position, scene, location **3** = pimple, pustule, zit (*slang*) **6** = predicament, trouble, difficulty, mess, plight, hot water (*informal*), quandary, tight spot ► *vb* **13** = see, observe, catch sight of, sight, recognize, detect, make out, discern **14** = mark, stain, soil, dirty, fleck, spatter, speckle, splodge

spot check *n* a quick unplanned inspection

spotless *adj* **1** perfectly clean **2** free from moral flaws: *a spotless reputation* > **spotlessly** *adv*

spotlight *n* **1** a powerful light focused so as to light up a small area **2 the spotlight** the centre of attention: *the spotlight moved to the president* ► *vb* **-lighting, -lit** *or* **-lighted 3** to direct a spotlight on (something) **4** to focus attention on (something)

spotlight *n* **2** = attention, limelight, public eye, fame ► *vb* **4** = highlight, draw attention to, accentuate

spot-on *adj informal* absolutely correct; very accurate: *they're spot-on in terms of style*

spotty *adj* **-tier, -tiest 1** covered with spots or pimples **2** not consistent; irregular in quality: *a rather spotty performance* > **spottiness** *n*

spouse *n* a person's partner in marriage

spouse *n* = partner, mate, husband *or* wife, consort, significant other (*informal, chiefly US*)

spout *vb* **1** (of a liquid or flames) to pour out in a stream or jet **2** *informal* to talk about (something) in a boring way or without much thought ► *n* **3** a projecting tube or lip for pouring liquids **4** a stream or jet of liquid: *a spout of steaming water* **5 up the spout** *slang* **A** ruined or lost: *the motor industry is up the spout* **B** pregnant

sprain *vb* **1** to injure (a joint) by a sudden twist ► *n* **2** this injury, which causes swelling and temporary disability

sprang *vb* a past tense of **spring**

sprat *n* a small edible fish like a herring

sprawl *vb* **1** to sit or lie with one's arms and legs spread out **2** to spread out untidily over a large area: *the pulp mill sprawled over the narrow flats* ► *n* **3** the part of a city or town that has not been planned and spreads out untidily over a large area: *the huge Los Angeles sprawl* > **sprawling** *adj*

sprawl *vb* **1** = loll, slump, lounge, flop, slouch

spray¹ *n* **1** fine drops of a liquid **2 A** a liquid under pressure designed to be discharged in fine drops from an aerosol or atomizer: *hair spray* **B** the aerosol or atomizer itself **3** a number of small objects flying through the air: *a spray of bullets* ► *vb* **4** to scatter in fine drops **5** to squirt

(a liquid) from an aerosol or atomizer **6** to cover with a spray: *spray the crops* > **sprayer** *n*

spray *n* **1** = droplets, fine mist, drizzle **2B** = aerosol, sprinkler, atomizer ► *vb* **4** = scatter, shower, sprinkle, diffuse

spray² *n* **1** a sprig or branch with buds, leaves, flowers, or berries **2** an ornament or design like this

spray *n* **1** = sprig, floral arrangement, branch, corsage

spray gun *n* a device for spraying fine drops of paint, etc.

spread *vb* **spreading, spread 1** to open out or unfold to the fullest width: *spread the material out* **2** to extend over a larger expanse: *the subsequent unrest spread countrywide* **3** to apply as a coating: *spread the paste evenly over your skin* **4** to be displayed to its fullest extent: *the shining bay spread out below* **5** to send or be sent out in all directions or to many people: *the news spread quickly; the sandflies that spread the disease* **6** to distribute or be distributed evenly: *we were advised to spread the workload over the whole year* **7 spread out** (of people) to increase the distance between one another (to widen the scope of a search, for example) ► *n* **8** a spreading; distribution, dispersion, or expansion: *the spread of higher education* **9** *informal* a large meal **10** *informal* the wingspan of an aircraft or bird **11** *informal, chiefly US & Canad* a ranch or other large area of land **12** a soft food which can be spread: *cheese spread* **13** two facing pages in a book or magazine **14** a widening of the hips and waist: *middle-age spread*

spread *vb* **1** = open (out), extend, stretch, unfold, sprawl, unroll **2** = grow, increase, expand, widen, escalate, proliferate, multiply, broaden **4** = extend, open, stretch **5** = circulate, broadcast, propagate, disseminate, make known; ≠ suppress ► *n* **8** = increase, development, advance, expansion, proliferation, dissemination, dispersal **10** = extent, span, stretch, sweep

spread-eagled *adj* with arms and legs outstretched

spreadsheet *n* a computer program for manipulating figures, used mainly for financial planning

spree *n* a session of overindulgence, usually in drinking or spending money

sprig *n* **1** a shoot, twig, or sprout **2** an ornamental device like this **3** *NZ* a stud on the sole of a soccer or rugby boot > **sprigged** *adj*

sprightly *adj* **-lier, -liest** lively and active > **sprightliness** *n*

spring *vb* **springing, sprang** *or* **sprung, sprung 1** to jump suddenly upwards or forwards **2** to return or be returned into natural shape from a forced position by elasticity: *the coil sprang back* **3** to cause (something) to happen unexpectedly:

S

the national coach sprang a surprise **4** (usually foll. by *from*) to originate; be descended: *this motivation springs from their inborn curiosity; Truman sprang from ordinary people* **5** (often foll. by *up*) to come into being or appear suddenly: *new courses will spring up* **6** to provide (something, such as a mattress) with springs **7** *informal* to arrange the escape of (someone) from prison ▸ *n* **8** the season between winter and summer **9** a leap or jump **10** a coil which can be compressed, stretched, or bent and then return to its original shape when released **11** a natural pool forming the source of a stream **12** elasticity ▸ **springlike** *adj*

> **spring** *vb* **1, 2** = jump, bound, leap, bounce, vault **4** = originate, come, derive, start, issue, proceed, arise, stem ▸ *n* **12** = flexibility, bounce, resilience, elasticity, buoyancy

springboard *n* **1** a flexible board used to gain height or momentum in diving or gymnastics **2** anything that makes it possible for an activity to begin: *the meeting acted as a springboard for future negotiations*

springbok *n, pl* **-bok** *or* **-boks 1** a S African antelope which moves in leaps **2** a person who has represented S Africa in a national sports team

spring-clean *vb* **1** to clean (a house) thoroughly, traditionally at the end of winter ▸ *n* **2** an instance of this ▸ **spring-cleaning** *n*

spring tide *n* either of the two tides at or just after new moon and full moon: the greatest rise and fall in tidal level

springy *adj* **springier, springiest** (of an object) having the quality of returning to its original shape after being pressed or pulled ▸ **springiness** *n*

sprinkle *vb* **-kling, -kled 1** to scatter (liquid or powder) in tiny drops over (something) **2** to distribute over (something): *a dozen mud huts sprinkled around it* ▸ **sprinkler** *n*

> **sprinkle** *vb* **1** = scatter, dust, strew, pepper, shower, spray, powder, dredge

sprinkling *n* a small quantity or amount: *a sprinkling of diamonds*

> **sprinkling** *n* = scattering, dusting, few, dash, handful, sprinkle

sprint *n* **1** *athletics* **A** a short race run at top speed **B** a fast run at the end of a longer race **2** any quick run ▸ *vb* **3** to run or cycle a short distance at top speed ▸ **sprinter** *n*

> **sprint** *vb* = run, race, shoot, tear, dash, dart, hare (*Brit informal*)

sprite *n* **1** (in folklore) a fairy or elf **2** an icon in a computer game which can be manoeuvred around the screen

sprocket *n* **1** Also called: **sprocket wheel** a wheel with teeth on the rim, that drives or is driven by a chain **2** a cylindrical wheel with

teeth on one or both rims for pulling film through an analogue camera or projector

sprout *vb* **1** (of a plant or seed) to produce (new leaves or shoots) **2** (often foll. by *up*) to begin to grow or develop ▸ *n* **3** a new shoot or bud **4** same as **Brussels sprout**

> **sprout** *vb* **1** = germinate, bud, shoot, spring **2** = grow, develop, ripen

spruce¹ *n* **1** an evergreen pyramid-shaped tree with needle-like leaves **2** the light-coloured wood of this tree

spruce² *adj* neat and smart

spruce up *vb* **sprucing, spruced** to make neat and smart

sprung *vb* a past tense and the past participle of **spring**

spry *adj* **spryer, spryest** *or* **sprier, spriest** active and lively; nimble

spud *n informal* a potato

spume *n literary* **1** foam or froth on the sea ▸ *vb* **spuming, spumed 2** (of the sea) to foam or froth

spun *vb* **1** the past of **spin** ▸ *adj* **2** made by spinning: *spun sugar; spun silk*

spunk *n* **1** *old-fashioned, informal* courage or spirit **2** *chiefly Brit vulgar slang* semen **3** *Austral & NZ informal* a sexually attractive person, esp. a male ▸ **spunky** *adj*

spur *n* **1** an incentive to get something done **2** a sharp spiked wheel on the heel of a rider's boot used to urge the horse on **3** a sharp horny part sticking out from a cock's leg **4** a ridge sticking out from a mountain side **5 on the spur of the moment** suddenly and without planning; on impulse **6 win one's spurs** to prove one's ability ▸ *vb* **spurring, spurred 7** (often foll. by *on*) to encourage (someone)

> **spur** *n* **1** = stimulus, incentive, impetus, motive, impulse, inducement, incitement **5 on the spur of the moment** = on impulse, impulsively, on the spot, impromptu, without planning ▸ *vb* = incite, drive, prompt, urge, stimulate, animate, prod, prick

spurge *n* a plant with milky sap and small flowers

spurious *adj* not genuine or real

spurn *vb* to reject (a person or thing) with contempt

> **spurn** *vb* = reject, slight, scorn, rebuff, snub, despise, disdain, repulse; ≠ accept

spurt *vb* **1** to gush or cause (something) to gush out in a sudden powerful stream or jet **2** to make a sudden effort ▸ *n* **3** a short burst of activity, speed, or energy **4** a sudden powerful stream or jet

sputnik *n* a Russian artificial satellite

sputter *vb, n* same as **splutter**

sputum *n, pl* **-ta** saliva, usually mixed with mucus

S

spy n, pl **spies** 1 a person employed to find out secret information about other countries or organizations 2 a person who secretly keeps watch on others ▸ vb **spies**, **spying**, **spied** 3 (foll. by on) to keep a secret watch on someone 4 to work as a spy 5 to catch sight of (someone or something); notice

> **spy** n 1 = undercover agent, mole, nark (Brit, Austral, NZ slang) ▸ vb 5 = catch sight of, spot, notice, observe, glimpse, espy

spyware n software surreptitiously installed in a computer via the internet to gather and transmit information about the user

sq. square

squabble vb **-bling**, **-bled** 1 to quarrel over a small matter ▸ n 2 a petty quarrel

> **squabble** vb = quarrel, fight, argue, row, dispute, wrangle, bicker ▸ n = quarrel, fight, row, argument, dispute, disagreement, tiff

squad n 1 the smallest military formation, usually a dozen soldiers 2 any small group of people working together: the fraud squad 3 sport a number of players from which a team is to be selected

> **squad** n 2 = team, group, band, company, force, troop, crew, gang

squadron n the basic unit of an air force

squalid adj 1 dirty, untidy, and in bad condition 2 unpleasant, selfish, and often dishonest: this squalid affair

squall¹ n a sudden strong wind or short violent storm

squall² vb 1 to cry noisily; yell ▸ n 2 a noisy cry or yell

squalor n 1 dirty, poor, and untidy physical conditions 2 the condition of being squalid

squander vb to waste (money or resources)

> **squander** vb = waste, spend, fritter away, blow (slang), misuse, expend, misspend; ≠ save

square n 1 a geometric figure with four equal sides and four right angles 2 anything of this shape 3 an open area in a town bordered by buildings or streets 4 maths the number produced when a number is multiplied by itself: 9 is the square of 3, written 3² 5 informal a person who is dull or unfashionable 6 **go back to square one** to return to the start because of failure or lack of progress ▸ adj 7 being a square in shape 8 **A** having the same area as that of a square with sides of a specified length: 2,500 square metres of hillside **B** denoting a square having a specified length on each side: a cell of only four square metres 9 straight or level: I don't think that painting is square 10 fair and honest: a square deal 11 informal dull or unfashionable 12 having all debts or accounts settled: if I give you a pound, then we'll be square 13 **all square** on equal terms; even in score 14 **square peg in a round hole** informal a misfit

▸ vb **squaring**, **squared** 15 maths to multiply (a number or quantity) by itself 16 to position so as to be straight or level: bravely he squared his shoulders 17 to settle (a debt or account) 18 to level the score in (a game) 19 to be or cause to be consistent: it would not have squared with her image ▸ adv 20 informal same as **squarely**

> **square** adj 10 = fair, straight, genuine, ethical, honest, on the level (informal), kosher (informal), dinkum (Austral, NZ informal), above board ▸ vb 19 = agree, match, fit, correspond, tally, reconcile

square dance n a country dance in which the couples are arranged in squares

squarely adv 1 directly; straight: he looked her squarely in the eye 2 in an honest and frank way: you should face squarely anything that worries you

square meal n a meal which is large enough to leave the eater feeling full: we gave him his first square meal in days

square root n a number that when multiplied by itself gives a given number: the square roots of 4 are 2 and -2

squash¹ vb 1 to press or squeeze (something) so as to flatten it 2 to overcome (a difficult situation), often with force 3 **squash in** or **into** to push or force (oneself or a thing) into a confined space 4 to humiliate (someone) with a sarcastic reply ▸ n 5 Brit & Austral a drink made from fruit juice or fruit syrup diluted with water 6 a crowd of people in a confined space 7 Also called: **squash rackets** a game for two players played in an enclosed court with a small rubber ball and long-handled rackets

> **squash** vb 1 = crush, press, flatten, mash, smash, distort, pulp, compress 2 = suppress, quell, silence, crush, annihilate 4 = embarrass, put down, shame, degrade, mortify

squash² n, pl **squashes** or **squash** chiefly US & Canad a marrow-like vegetable

squashy adj **squashier**, **squashiest** soft and easily squashed

squat vb **squatting**, **squatted** 1 to crouch with the knees bent and the weight on the feet 2 law to occupy an unused building to which one has no legal right ▸ adj 3 short and thick ▸ n 4 a building occupied by squatters

squatter n an illegal occupier of an unused building

squaw n offensive a Native American woman of N America

squawk n 1 a loud harsh cry, esp. one made by a bird 2 informal a loud complaint ▸ vb 3 to make a squawk

squeak n 1 a short high-pitched cry or sound 2 **a narrow squeak** informal a narrow escape or success ▸ vb 3 to make a squeak 4 **squeak through** or **by** to pass (an examination), but only just > **squeaky** adj > **squeakiness** n

S

squeal *n* **1** a long high-pitched yelp ▸ *vb* **2** to make a squeal **3** *slang* to inform on someone to the police **4** *informal, chiefly Brit* to complain loudly › **squealer** *n*

squeamish *adj* easily shocked or upset by unpleasant sights or events

squeegee *n* a tool with a rubber blade used for wiping away excess water from a surface

squeeze *vb* **squeezing**, **squeezed** **1** to grip or press (something) firmly **2** to crush or press (something) so as to extract (a liquid): *squeeze the tomato and strain the juice; freshly squeezed lemon juice* **3** to push (oneself or a thing) into a confined space **4** to hug (someone) closely **5** to obtain (something) by great effort or force: *to squeeze the last dollar out of every deal* ▸ *n* **6** a squeezing **7** a hug **8** a crush of people in a confined space **9** *chiefly Brit & NZ* a restriction on borrowing made by a government to control price inflation **10** an amount extracted by squeezing: *a squeeze of lime* **11** **put the squeeze on someone** *informal* to put pressure on someone in order to obtain something

> **squeeze** *vb* **1** = press, crush, squash, pinch **3** = cram, press, crowd, force, stuff, pack, jam, ram **4** = hug, embrace, cuddle, clasp, enfold ▸ *n* **6** = press, grip, clasp, crush, pinch, squash, wring **7** = hug, embrace, clasp **8** = crush, jam, squash, press, crowd, congestion

squelch *vb* **1** to make a wet sucking noise, such as by walking through mud **2** *informal* to silence (someone) with a sarcastic or wounding reply ▸ *n* **3** a squelching sound › **squelchy** *adj*

squib *n* **1** a firework that burns with a hissing noise before exploding **2** **damp squib** something expected to be exciting or successful but turning out to be a disappointment

squid *n, pl* **squid** *or* **squids** a sea creature with ten tentacles and a long soft body

squiggle *n* a wavy line › **squiggly** *adj*

squint *vb* **1** to have eyes which face in different directions **2** to glance sideways ▸ *n* **3** an eye disorder in which one or both eyes turn inwards or outwards from the nose **4** *informal* a quick look; glance: *take a squint at the map* ▸ *adj* **5** *informal* not straight; crooked

squire *n* **1** a country gentleman in England, usually the main landowner in a country community **2** *informal, chiefly Brit* a term of address used by one man to another **3** *history* a knight's young attendant ▸ *vb* **squiring, squired** **4** *old-fashioned* (of a man) to escort (a woman)

squirm *vb* **1** to wriggle **2** to feel embarrassed or guilty ▸ *n* **3** a wriggling movement

squirrel *n* a small bushy-tailed animal that lives in trees

squirt *vb* **1** to force (a liquid) or (of a liquid) to be forced out of a narrow opening **2** to cover or spatter (a person or thing) with liquid in this way ▸ *n* **3** a jet of liquid **4** a squirting **5** *informal* a small or insignificant person

squish *vb* **1** to crush (something) with a soft squelching sound **2** to make a squelching sound ▸ *n* **3** a soft squelching sound › **squishy** *adj*

Sr **1** (after a name) senior **2** Señor **3** *chem* strontium

SS **1** an organization in the Nazi Party that provided Hitler's bodyguard, security forces, and concentration-camp guards **2** steamship

SSL *computers* secure sockets layer: a protocol for encrypting and transmitting sensitive data securely over the internet

St **1** Saint **2** Street

st. stone

stab *vb* **stabbing, stabbed** **1** to pierce with a sharp pointed instrument **2** (often foll. by *at*) to make a thrust (at); jab **3** **stab someone in the back** to do harm to someone by betraying him or her ▸ *n* **4** a stabbing **5** a sudden, usually unpleasant, sensation: *a stab of jealousy* **6** *informal* an attempt: *you've got to have a stab at it* **7** **stab in the back** an act of betrayal that harms a person › **stabbing** *n*

> **stab** *vb* **1** = pierce, stick, wound, knife, thrust, spear, jab, transfix ▸ *n* **5** = twinge, prick, pang, ache **6** = attempt, go (*informal*), try, endeavour

stability *n* the quality of being stable: *the security and stability of married life*

> **stability** *n* = firmness, strength, soundness, solidity, steadiness; ≠ instability

stabilize *or* **-lise** *vb* **-lizing, -lized** *or* **-lising, -lised** to make or become stable or more stable › **stabilization** *or* **-lisation** *n*

stabilizer *or* **-liser** *n* **1** a device for stabilizing a child's bicycle, an aircraft, or a ship **2** a substance added to food to preserve its texture

stable¹ *n* **1** a building where horses are kept **2** an organization that breeds and trains racehorses **3** an organization that manages or trains several entertainers or athletes ▸ *vb* **-bling, -bled** **4** to put or keep (a horse) in a stable

stable² *adj* **1** steady in position or balance; firm **2** lasting and not likely to experience any sudden changes: *a stable environment* **3** having a calm personality; not prone to changes in mood **4** *physics* (of an elementary particle) not subject to decay **5** *chem* (of a chemical compound) not easily decomposed

> **stable** *adj* **1** = solid, firm, fixed, substantial, durable, well-made, well-built, immovable; ≠ unstable **2** = secure, lasting, strong, sound, fast, sure, established, permanent; ≠ insecure **3** = well-balanced, balanced, sensible, reasonable, rational

staccato (stak-ah-toe) *adj* **1** *music* (of notes) short and separate **2** consisting of short abrupt sounds: *the staccato sound of high heels on the stairs* ▸ *adv* **3** in a staccato manner

stack *n* **1** a pile of things, one on top of the other **2** a large neat pile of hay or straw

3 stacks a large amount: *there's still stacks for us to do* **4** an area in a computer memory for temporary storage ▸ *vb* **5** to place (things) in a stack **6** to load or fill (something) up with piles of objects: *Henry was watching her stack the dishwasher* **7** to control (a number of aircraft) waiting to land at an airport so that each flies at a different altitude

> **stack** *n* **1** = pile, heap, mountain, mass, load (*informal*), mound ▸ *vb* **5** = pile, heap up, load, assemble, accumulate, amass

stadium *n, pl* **-diums** *or* **-dia** a large sports arena with tiered rows of seats for spectators

staff *n, pl* **staffs**, (for senses 3 and 4) **staffs** *or* **staves 1** the people employed in a company, school, or organization **2** *military* the officers appointed to assist a commander **3** a stick with some special use, such as a walking stick or an emblem of authority **4** *music* a set of five horizontal lines on which music is written and which, along with a clef, indicates pitch ▸ *vb* **5** to provide (a company, school, or organization) with a staff

> **staff** *n* **1** = workers, employees, personnel, workforce, team **3** = stick, pole, rod, crook, cane, stave, wand, sceptre

stag *n* the adult male of a deer

stag beetle *n* a beetle with large branched jaws

stage *n* **1** a step or period of development, growth, or progress **2** the platform in a theatre where actors perform **3 the stage** the theatre as a profession **4** the scene of an event or action **5** a part of a journey: *the last stage of his tour around France* **6** short for **stagecoach 7** *Brit & Austral* a division of a bus route for which there is a fixed fare ▸ *vb* **staging, staged 8** to present (a dramatic production) on stage: *to stage 'Hamlet'* **9** to organize and carry out (an event)

> **stage** *n* **1** = step, leg, phase, point, level, period, division, lap

stagecoach *n* a large four-wheeled horse-drawn vehicle formerly used to carry passengers and mail on a regular route

stage fright *n* feelings of fear and nervousness felt by a person about to appear in front of an audience

stage whisper *n* **1** a loud whisper from an actor, intended to be heard by the audience **2** any loud whisper that is intended to be overheard

stagger *vb* **1** to walk unsteadily **2** to amaze or shock (someone): *it staggered her that there was any liaison between them* **3** to arrange (events) so as not to happen at the same time: *staggered elections* ▸ *n* **4** a staggering > **staggering** *adj* > **staggeringly** *adv*

> **stagger** *vb* **1** = totter, reel, sway, lurch, wobble **2** = astound, amaze, stun, shock, shake, overwhelm, astonish, confound

stagnant *adj* **1** (of water) stale from not moving **2** unsuccessful or dull from lack of change or development

stagnate *vb* **-nating, -nated** to become inactive or unchanging: *people in old age only stagnate when they have no interests* > **stagnation** *n*

stag night *or* **stag party** *n informal* a party for men only, held for a man who is about to get married

stagy *or US* **stagey** *adj* **stagier, stagiest** too theatrical or dramatic

staid *adj* serious, rather dull, and old-fashioned in behaviour or appearance

stain *vb* **1** to discolour (something) with marks that are not easily removed **2** to dye (something) with a lasting pigment ▸ *n* **3** a mark or discoloration that is not easily removed **4** an incident in someone's life that has damaged his or her reputation: *a stain on his character* **5** a liquid used to penetrate the surface of a material, such as wood, and colour it without covering up the surface or grain

> **stain** *vb* **1** = mark, soil, discolour, dirty, tinge, spot, blot, blemish **2** = dye, colour, tint ▸ *n* **3** = mark, spot, blot, blemish, discoloration, smirch **4** = stigma, shame, disgrace, slur, dishonour **5** = dye, colour, tint

stainless steel *n* a type of steel that does not rust, as it contains large amounts of chromium

staircase *n* a flight of stairs, usually with a handrail or banisters

stairs *pl n* a flight of steps going from one level to another, usually indoors

stake¹ *n* **1** a stick or metal bar driven into the ground as part of a fence or as a support or marker **2 be burned at the stake** to be executed by being tied to a stake in the centre of a pile of wood that is then set on fire ▸ *vb* **staking, staked 3** to lay (a claim) to land or rights **4** to support (something, such as a plant) with a stake

> **stake** *n* **1** = pole, post, stick, pale, paling, picket, palisade

stake² *n* **1** the money that a player must risk in order to take part in a gambling game or make a bet **2** an interest, usually financial, held in something: *a 50% stake in a new consortium* **3 at stake** at risk **4 stakes a** the money that a player has available for gambling **b** a prize in a race or contest **c** a horse race in which all owners of competing horses contribute to the prize ▸ *vb* **staking, staked 5** to risk (something, such as money) on a result **6** to give financial support to (a business)

> **stake** *n* **1** = bet, ante, wager **2** = interest, share, involvement, concern, investment ▸ *vb* **5** = bet, gamble, wager, chance, risk, venture, hazard

S

stakeholder *n* **1** a person or group not owning shares in an enterprise but having an interest in its operations, such as the employees, customers, or local community ▸ *adj* **2** relating to policies intended to allow people to participate in decisions made by enterprises in which they have a stake: *stakeholder economy*

stalactite *n* an icicle-shaped mass of calcium carbonate hanging from the roof of a cave: formed by continually dripping water

stalagmite *n* a large pointed mass of calcium carbonate sticking up from the floor of a cave: formed by continually dripping water from a stalactite

stale *adj* **1** (esp. of food) no longer fresh, having being kept too long **2** (of air) stagnant and having an unpleasant smell **3** lacking in enthusiasm or ideas through overwork or lack of variety **4** uninteresting from having been done or seen too many times: *such achievements now seem stale today* **5** no longer new: *her war had become stale news* > **staleness** *n*

> **stale** *adj* **1** = old, hard, dry, decayed; ≠ fresh **2** = musty, fusty **4** = unoriginal, banal, trite, stereotyped, worn-out, threadbare, hackneyed, overused; ≠ original

stalemate *n* **1** a chess position in which any of a player's moves would place his king in check: in this position the game ends in a draw **2** a situation in which further action by two opposing forces is impossible or will not achieve anything; deadlock

stalk¹ *n* **1** the main stem of a plant **2** a stem that joins a leaf or flower to the main stem of a plant

stalk² *vb* **1** to follow (an animal or person) quietly and secretly in order to catch or kill them **2** to pursue persistently and, sometimes, attack (a person with whom one is obsessed) **3** to spread over (a place) in a menacing way: *danger stalked the streets* **4** to walk in an angry, arrogant, or stiff way > **stalker** *n*

> **stalk** *vb* **1** = pursue, follow, track, hunt, shadow, haunt

stalking-horse *n* something or someone used to hide a true purpose; pretext

stall¹ *n* **1** a small stand for the display and sale of goods **2** a compartment in a stable or shed for a single animal **3** any small room or compartment: *a shower stall* ▸ *vb* **4** to stop (a motor vehicle or its engine) or (of a motor vehicle or its engine) to stop, by incorrect use of the clutch or incorrect adjustment of the fuel mixture

> **stall** *n* **1** = stand, table, counter, booth, kiosk ▸ *vb* = stop dead, jam, seize up, catch, stick, stop short

stall² *vb* to employ delaying tactics towards (someone); be evasive

stall *vb* = play for time, delay, hedge, temporize

stallion *n* an uncastrated male horse, usually used for breeding

stalwart (**stawl**-wart) *adj* **1** strong and sturdy **2** loyal and reliable ▸ *n* **3** a hard-working and loyal supporter: *local party stalwarts*

> **stalwart** *adj* **1** = strong, strapping, sturdy, stout; ≠ puny **2** = loyal, faithful, firm, true, dependable, steadfast

stamen *n* the part of a flower that produces pollen

stamina *n* energy and strength sustained while performing an activity over a long time

> **stamina** *n* = staying power, endurance, resilience, force, power, energy, strength

stammer *vb* **1** to speak or say (something) with involuntary pauses or repetition, as a result of a speech disorder or through fear or nervousness ▸ *n* **2** a speech disorder characterized by involuntary repetitions and pauses

> **stammer** *vb* = stutter, falter, pause, hesitate, stumble over your words

stamp *n* **1** a printed paper label attached to a piece of mail to show that the required postage has been paid **2** a token issued by a shop or business after a purchase that can be saved and exchanged for other goods sold by that shop or business **3** the action or an act of stamping **4** an instrument for stamping a design or words **5** a design, device, or mark that has been stamped **6** a characteristic feature: *the stamp of inevitability* **7** type or class: *men of his stamp* ▸ *vb* **8** (often foll. by *on*) to bring (one's foot) down heavily **9** to walk with heavy or noisy footsteps **10** to characterize: *a performance that stamped him as a star* **11 stamp on** to subdue or restrain: *all of which have stamped on dissent* **12** to impress or mark (a pattern or sign) on **13** to mark (something) with an official seal or device **14** to have a strong effect on: *a picture vividly stamped on memory* **15** to stick a stamp on (an envelope or parcel)

> **stamp** *n* **5** = imprint, mark, brand, signature, earmark, hallmark ▸ *vb* **8** = trample, step, tread, crush **10** = identify, mark, brand, label, reveal, show to be, categorize **12** = print, mark, impress

stampede *n* **1** a sudden rush of frightened animals or of a crowd ▸ *vb* **-peding, -peded** **2** to run away in a stampede

stamping ground *n* a favourite meeting place

stamp out *vb* **1** to put an end to (something) by force; suppress: *an attempt to stamp out democracy* **2** to put out by stamping: *I stamped out my cigarette*

> **stamp out** *vb* **1 stamp something out** = eliminate, destroy, eradicate, crush, suppress, put down, scotch, quell

stance n **1** an attitude towards a particular matter: *a tough stance in the trade talks* **2** the manner and position in which a person stands **3** *sport* the position taken when about to play the ball

> **stance** n **1** = attitude, stand, position, viewpoint, standpoint **2** = posture, carriage, bearing, deportment

stanch (stahnch) vb same as **staunch²**
stanchion n a vertical pole or bar used as a support
stand vb **standing, stood 1** to be upright **2** to rise to an upright position **3** to place (something) upright **4** to be situated: *the property stands in a prime position* **5** to have a specified height when standing: *the structure stands sixty feet above the river* **6** to be in a specified position: *Turkey stands to gain handsomely* **7** to be in a specified state or condition: *how he stands in comparison to others* **8** to remain unchanged or valid: *the Conservatives were forced to let much of the legislation stand* **9 stand at** (of a score or an account) to be in the specified position: *now the total stands at nine* **10** to tolerate or bear: *Christopher can't stand him* **11** to survive: *stand the test of time* **12** (often foll. by for) to be a candidate: *to stand for president* **13** *informal* to buy: *to stand someone a drink* **14 stand a chance** to have a chance of succeeding **15 stand one's ground** to maintain a position in the face of opposition **16 stand to reason** to be obvious or logical: *it stands to reason you will play better* **17 stand trial** to be tried in a law court ▸ n **18** a stall or counter selling goods: *the hot dog stand* **19** a structure at a sports ground where people can sit or stand **20** the act or an instance of standing **21** a firmly held opinion: *its firm stand on sanctions* **22** *US & Austral* a place in a law court where a witness stands **23** a rack on which coats and hats may be hung **24** a base, support, or piece of furniture in or on which articles may be held or stored: *a guitar stand* **25** an effort to defend oneself or one's beliefs against attack or criticism: *a last stand against superior forces* **26** *cricket* a long period at the wicket by two batsmen **27** See **one-night stand**

> **stand** vb **1** = be upright, be erect, be vertical **2** = get to your feet, rise, stand up, straighten up **3** = put, place, position, set, mount **4** = be located, be, sit, be positioned, be situated or located **8** = be valid, continue, exist, prevail, remain valid **10** = tolerate, bear, abide, stomach, endure, brook **11** = resist, endure, tolerate, stand up to ▸ n **18** = stall, booth, kiosk, table **21** = position, attitude, stance, opinion, determination

standard n **1** a level of quality: *cuisine of a high standard* **2** an accepted example of something against which others are judged or measured: *the work was good by any standard* **3** a moral principle of behaviour **4** a flag of a nation or cause **5** an upright pole or beam used as a support: *a lamp standard* **6** a song that has remained popular for many years ▸ adj **7** of a usual, medium, or accepted kind: *a standard cost* **8** of recognized authority: *a standard reference book* **9** denoting pronunciations or grammar regarded as correct and acceptable by educated native speakers

> **standard** n **1** = level, grade **2** = criterion, measure, guideline, example, model, average, norm, gauge **3** = principles, ideals, morals, ethics **4** = flag, banner, ensign **7** = usual, normal, customary, average, basic, regular, typical, orthodox; ≠ unusual **8** = accepted, official, established, approved, recognized, definitive, authoritative; ≠ unofficial

standardize or **-dise** vb **-dizing, -dized** or **-dising, -dised** to make (things) standard: *to standardize the preparation process* > **standardization** or **-disation** n
standard lamp n a tall electric lamp that has a shade and stands on a base
stand for vb **1** to represent: *AIDS stands for Acquired Immune Deficiency Syndrome* **2** to support and represent (an idea or a belief): *to stand for liberty and truth* **3** *informal* to tolerate or bear: *I won't stand for this!*

> **stand for** vb **1 stand for something** = represent, mean, signify, denote, indicate, symbolize, betoken **3 stand for something** = tolerate, bear, endure, put up with, brook

stand in vb **1** to act as a substitute: *she stood in for her father* ▸ n **stand-in 2** a person who acts as a substitute for another

> **stand in** n **stand-in** = substitute, deputy, replacement, reserve, surrogate, understudy, locum, stopgap

standing adj **1** permanent, fixed, or lasting: *it was a standing joke* **2** used to stand in or on: *standing room only* **3** *athletics* (of a jump or the start of a race) begun from a standing position ▸ n **4** social or financial status or reputation: *her international standing* **5** duration: *a friendship of at least ten years' standing*

> **standing** adj **1** = permanent, lasting, fixed, regular ▸ n **4** = status, position, footing, rank, reputation, eminence, repute **5** = duration, existence, continuance

standoffish adj behaving in a formal and unfriendly way
standpipe n *chiefly Brit* a temporary vertical pipe installed in a street and supplying water when household water supplies are cut off
standpoint n a point of view from which a matter is considered
standstill n a complete stoppage or halt: *all traffic came to a standstill*
stank vb a past tense of **stink**
stanza n *prosody* a verse of a poem

staple¹ n **1** a short length of wire bent into a square U-shape, used to fasten papers or secure things ▸ vb **-pling, -pled 2** to secure (things) with staples

staple² adj **1** of prime importance; principal: *the staple diet of a country* ▸ n **2** something that forms a main part of the product, consumption, or trade of a region **3** a main constituent of anything: *the personal reflections which make up the staple of the book*

> **staple** adj = principal, chief, main, key, basic, fundamental, predominant

stapler n a device used to fasten things together with a staple

star n **1** a planet or meteor visible in the clear night sky as a point of light **2** a hot gaseous mass, such as the sun, that radiates energy as heat and light, or in some cases as radio waves and X-rays. Related adjectives: **astral, sidereal, stellar 3 stars** same as **horoscope** (sense 1) **4** an emblem with five or more radiating points, often used as a symbol of rank or an award: *the RAC awarded the hotel three stars* **5** same as **asterisk 6** a famous person from the sports, acting, or music professions **7 see stars** to see flashes of light after a blow on the head ▸ vb **starring, starred 8** to feature (an actor) or (of an actor) to be featured as a star: *he's starred in dozens of films* **9** to mark (something) with a star or stars

> **star** n **1, 2** = heavenly body, celestial body **6** = celebrity, big name, megastar (*informal*), name, luminary, leading man *or* lady, hero *or* heroine, principal, main attraction ▸ vb **8** = play the lead, appear, feature, perform

starboard n **1** the right side of an aeroplane or ship when facing forwards ▸ adj **2** of or on the starboard

starch n **1** a carbohydrate forming the main food element in bread, potatoes, and rice: in solution with water it is used to stiffen fabric **2** food containing a large amount of starch ▸ vb **3** to stiffen (cloth) with starch

starchy adj **starchier, starchiest 1** of or containing starch **2** (of a person's behaviour) very formal and humourless

stardom n the status of a star in the entertainment or sport world

stare vb **staring, stared 1** (often foll. by *at*) to look at for a long time **2 stare one in the face** to be glaringly obvious ▸ n **3** a long fixed look

> **stare** vb **1** = gaze, look, goggle, watch, gape, eyeball (*slang*), gawp (*Brit slang*), gawk

starfish n, pl **-fish** *or* **-fishes** a star-shaped sea creature with a flat body and five limbs

stark adj **1** harsh, unpleasant, and plain: *a stark choice* **2** grim, desolate, and lacking any beautiful features: *the stark landscapes* **3** utter; absolute: *in stark contrast* ▸ adv **4** completely: *stark staring bonkers* > **starkly** adv > **starkness** n

stark adj **1** = plain, harsh, basic, grim, straightforward, blunt **2** = austere, severe, plain, bare, harsh, bare-bones **3** = absolute, pure, sheer, utter, downright, out-and-out, unmitigated ▸ adv = absolutely, quite, completely, entirely, altogether, wholly, utterly

starling n a common songbird with shiny blackish feathers and a short tail

starry adj **-rier, -riest 1** (of a sky or night) full of or lit by stars **2** of or like a star or stars: *a starry cast*

starry-eyed adj full of unrealistic hopes and dreams; naive

start vb **1** to begin (something or to do something); come or cause to come into being: *to start a war; this conflict started years ago* **2** to set or be set in motion: *he started the van* **3** to make a sudden involuntary movement from fright or surprise; jump **4** to establish; set up: *to start a state lottery* **5** to support (someone) in the first part of a career or activity **6** *Brit informal* to begin quarrelling or causing a disturbance: *don't start with me* **7 to start with** in the first place ▸ n **8** the first part of something **9** the place or time at which something begins **10** a signal to begin, such as in a race **11** a lead or advantage, either in time or distance, in a competitive activity: *he had an hour's start on me* **12** a slight involuntary movement from fright or surprise: *I awoke with a start* **13** an opportunity to enter a career or begin a project **14 for a start** in the first place

> **start** vb **1** = set about, begin, proceed, embark upon, take the first step, make a beginning; ≠ stop **2** = start up, activate, get something going; ≠ turn off **3** = jump, shy, jerk, flinch, recoil **4** = establish, begin, found, create, launch, set up, institute, pioneer; ≠ terminate ▸ n **8, 9** = beginning, outset, opening, birth, foundation, dawn (*literary*), onset, initiation; ≠ end **12** = jump, spasm, convulsion

starter n **1** *chiefly Brit* the first course of a meal **2 for starters** *slang* in the first place **3** a device for starting an internal-combustion engine **4** a person who signals the start of a race **5** a competitor in a race or contest **6 under starter's orders** (of competitors in a race) waiting for the signal to start

startle vb **-tling, -tled** to slightly surprise or frighten (someone) > **startling** adj

> **startle** vb = surprise, shock, frighten, scare, make (someone) jump

starve vb **starving, starved 1** to die from lack of food **2** to deliberately prevent (a person or animal) from having any food **3** *informal* to be very hungry: *we're both starving* **4 starve of** to deprive (someone) of something needed: *the heart is starved of oxygen* **5 starve into** to force someone into a specified state by starving: *an attempt to starve him into submission* > **starvation** n

s

stash *informal* ▸ *vb* **1** (often foll. by *away*) *informal* to store (money or valuables) in a secret place for safekeeping ▸ *n* **2** a secret store, usually of illegal drugs, or the place where this is hidden

state *n* **1** the condition or circumstances of a person or thing **2** a sovereign political power or community **3** the territory of such a community **4** the sphere of power in such a community: *matters of state* **5** (*often cap*) one of a number of areas or communities having their own governments and forming a federation under a sovereign government, such as in the US or Australia **6** (*often cap*) the government, civil service, and armed forces **7 in a state** *informal* in an emotional or very worried condition **8 lie in state** (of a body) to be placed on public view before burial **9 state of affairs** circumstances or condition: *this wonderful state of affairs* **10** grand and luxurious lifestyle, as enjoyed by royalty, aristocrats, or the wealthy: *living in state* ▸ *adj* **11** controlled or financed by a state: *state ownership* **12** of or concerning the State: *state secrets* **13** involving ceremony: *a state visit* ▸ *vb* **stating, stated 14** to express (something) in words

> **state** *n* **1** = condition, shape **2, 3** = country, nation, land, republic, territory, federation, commonwealth, kingdom **6** = government, ministry, administration, executive, regime, powers-that-be **10** = ceremony, glory, grandeur, splendour, majesty, pomp ▸ *vb* = say, declare, present, voice, express, assert, utter

statehouse *n* NZ a rented house built by the government

stately *adj* **-lier, -liest** having a dignified, impressive, and graceful appearance or manner: *the Rolls-Royce approached him at a stately speed* > **stateliness** *n*

> **stately** *adj* = grand, majestic, dignified, royal, august, noble, regal, lofty; ≠ lowly

statement *n* **1** something stated, usually a formal prepared announcement or reply **2** *law* a declaration of matters of fact **3** an account prepared by a bank at regular intervals for a client to show all credits and debits and the balance at the end of the period **4** an account containing a summary of bills or invoices and showing the total amount due **5** the act of stating

> **statement** *n* **1** = announcement, declaration, communication, communiqué, proclamation **2** = account, report

stateroom *n* **1** a private room on a ship **2** *chiefly Brit* a large room in a palace, etc., used on ceremonial occasions

statesman *n, pl* **-men** an experienced and respected political leader > **statesmanship** *n*

static *adj* **1** not active, changing, or moving; stationary **2** *physics* (of a weight, force, or pressure) acting but causing no movement **3** *physics* of forces that do not produce movement ▸ *n* **4** hissing or crackling or a speckled picture caused by interference in the reception of radio or television transmissions **5** electric sparks or crackling produced by friction

static electricity *n* same as **static** (sense 5)

statin *n* *med* any of several drugs that inhibit the production of cholesterol

station *n* **1** a place along a route or line at which a bus or train stops to pick up passengers or goods **2** the headquarters of an organization such as the police or fire service **3** a building with special equipment for some particular purpose: *power station; a filling station* **4** a television or radio channel **5** *military* a place of duty **6** position in society: *he had ideas above his station* **7** *Austral & NZ* a large sheep or cattle farm **8** the place or position where a person is assigned to stand: *every man stood at his station* ▸ *vb* **9** to assign (someone) to a station

> **station** *n* **1** = railway station, stop, stage, halt, terminal, train station, terminus **2** = headquarters, base, depot (*US, Canad*) **6** = position, rank, status, standing, post, situation **8** = post, place, location, position, situation ▸ *vb* = assign, post, locate, set, establish, install

stationary *adj* not moving: *a line of stationary traffic*

stationer *n* a person or shop selling stationery

stationery *n* writing materials, such as paper, envelopes, and pens

station wagon *n* US, Austral & NZ an estate car

statistic *n* a numerical fact collected and classified systematically > **statistical** *adj* > **statistically** *adv* > **statistician** *n*

statistics *n* **1** the science dealing with the collection, classification, and interpretation of numerical information ▸ *pl n* **2** numerical information which has been collected, classified, and interpreted

statuary *n* statues collectively

statue *n* a sculpture of a human or animal figure, usually life-size or larger

statuesque (stat-yoo-**esk**) *adj* (of a woman) tall and well-proportioned; like a classical statue

statuette *n* a small statue

stature *n* **1** the height and size of a person **2** the reputation of a person or their achievements: *a batsman of international stature* **3** moral or intellectual distinction

> **stature** *n* **1** = height, build, size **2** = importance, standing, prestige, rank, prominence, eminence

status *n* **1** a person's position in society **2** the esteem in which people hold a person: *priests feel they have lost some of their status in society* **3** the legal or official standing or classification of a person or country: *the status of refugees; Ireland's non-aligned status* **4** degree of importance

S

status n 1 = position, rank, grade
2 = prestige, standing, authority, influence,
weight, honour, importance, fame, mana (NZ)
3 = state of play, development, progress,
condition, evolution

status quo n the existing state of affairs
statute n 1 a law made by a government and
expressed in a formal document 2 a permanent
rule made by a company or other institution
statutory adj 1 required or authorized by law
2 (of an action) declared by law to be punishable
staunch¹ adj strong and loyal: a staunch supporter
> **staunchly** adv

staunch adj = loyal, faithful, stalwart, firm,
sound, true, trusty, steadfast

staunch² or **stanch** vb to stop the flow of
(blood) from someone's body
stave n 1 one of the long strips of wood joined
together to form a barrel or bucket 2 a stick
carried as a symbol of office 3 a verse of a poem
4 music same as **staff** ▸ vb **staving, stove 5 stave
in** to burst a hole in (something)
stave off vb **staving, staved** to delay
(something) for a short time: to stave off political
rebellion
stay¹ vb 1 to continue or remain in a place,
position, or condition: to stay away; to stay inside
2 to lodge as a guest or visitor temporarily:
we stay with friends 3 Scot & S African to reside
permanently; live 4 to endure (something
testing or difficult): you have stayed the course this
long ▸ n 5 the period spent in one place 6 the
postponement of an order of a court of law:
a stay of execution

stay vb 1 = remain, continue to be, linger,
stop, wait, halt, pause, abide; ≠ go 2 = lodge,
visit, sojourn (literary), put up at, be
accommodated at 4 = continue, remain, go on,
survive, endure ▸ n 5 = visit, stop, holiday,
stopover, sojourn (literary) 6 = postponement,
delay, suspension, stopping, halt, deferment

stay² n something that supports or steadies
something, such as a prop or buttress
stay³ n a rope or chain supporting a ship's mast
or funnel
staying power n endurance to complete
something undertaken; stamina
STD sexually transmitted disease
stead n 1 **stand someone in good stead** to be
useful to someone in the future 2 rare the
function or position that should be taken by
another: I cannot let you rule in my stead
steadfast adj dedicated and unwavering
> **steadfastly** adv > **steadfastness** n
steady adj **steadier, steadiest 1** firm and not
shaking 2 without much change or variation:
we're on a steady course 3 continuous: a steady decline
4 not easily excited; sober 5 regular; habitual:
the steady drinking of alcohol ▸ vb **steadies,**

steadying, steadied 6 to make or become
steady ▸ adv 7 in a steady manner 8 **go steady**
old-fashioned, informal to date one person regularly
▸ n, pl **steadies 9** informal one's regular boyfriend
or girlfriend ▸ interj **10** a warning to keep calm
or be careful > **steadily** adv > **steadiness** n

steady adj 1 = stable, fixed, secure, firm, safe;
≠ unstable 2 = regular, established
3, 5 = continuous, regular, constant,
consistent, persistent, unbroken,
uninterrupted, incessant; ≠ irregular
4 = dependable, sensible, reliable, secure,
calm, supportive, sober, level-headed;
≠ undependable

steak n 1 a lean piece of beef for grilling or
frying 2 a cut of beef for braising or stewing
3 a thick slice of pork, veal, or fish
steal vb **stealing, stole, stolen 1** to take
(something) from someone without permission
or unlawfully 2 to use (someone else's ideas or
work) without acknowledgment 3 to move
quietly and carefully, not wanting to be noticed:
my father stole up behind her 4 **steal the show** (of a
performer) to draw the audience's attention to
oneself and away from the other performers
5 to obtain or do (something) stealthily: I stole a
glance behind ▸ n 6 informal something acquired
easily or at little cost

steal vb 1 = take, nick (slang, chiefly Brit), pinch
(informal), lift (informal), embezzle, pilfer,
misappropriate, purloin 2 = copy, take,
appropriate, pinch (informal), rip (computers)
3 = sneak, slip, creep, tiptoe, slink

stealth n 1 moving carefully and quietly, so as
to avoid being seen 2 cunning or underhand
behaviour ▸ adj 3 (of technology) able to render
an aircraft almost invisible to radar 4 disguised
or hidden > **stealthy** adj > **stealthily** adv

stealth n = secrecy, furtiveness, slyness,
sneakiness, unobtrusiveness, stealthiness,
surreptitiousness

steam n 1 the vapour into which water changes
when boiled 2 the mist formed when such
vapour condenses in the atmosphere 3 informal
power, energy, or speed 4 **let off steam** informal
to release pent-up energy or feelings 5 **pick up
steam** informal to gather momentum ▸ adj
6 operated, heated, or powered by steam: a steam
train ▸ vb 7 to give off steam 8 (of a vehicle) to
move by steam power 9 informal to proceed
quickly and often forcefully 10 to cook (food) in
steam 11 to treat (something) with steam, such
as in cleaning or pressing clothes 12 **steam
open** or **off** to use steam in order to open or
remove (something): let me steam open this letter
steam engine n an engine worked by steam
steamer n 1 a boat or ship driven by steam
engines 2 a container with holes in the bottom,
used to cook food by steam

S

steamroller *n* **1** a steam-powered vehicle with heavy rollers used for flattening road surfaces during road-making ▸ *vb* **2** to make (someone) do what one wants by overpowering force

steed *n archaic, literary* a horse

steel *n* **1** an alloy of iron and carbon, often with small quantities of other elements **2** a steel rod used for sharpening knives **3** courage and mental toughness ▸ *vb* **4** to prepare (oneself) for coping with something unpleasant: *he had steeled himself to accept the fact* ⟩ **steely** *adj*

steep[1] *adj* **1** having a sharp slope **2** *informal* (of a fee, price, or demand) unreasonably high; excessive ⟩ **steeply** *adv* ⟩ **steepness** *n*

> **steep** *adj* **1** = sheer, precipitous, abrupt, vertical; ≠ gradual **2** = high, exorbitant, extreme, unreasonable, overpriced, extortionate; ≠ reasonable

steep[2] *vb* **1** to soak or be soaked in a liquid in order to soften or cleanse **2 steeped in** filled with: *an industry steeped in tradition*

> **steep** *vb* **1** = soak, immerse, marinate (*cookery*), submerge, drench, moisten, souse

steeple *n* a tall ornamental tower on a church roof

steeplechase *n* **1** a horse race over a course with fences to be jumped **2** a track race in which the runners have to leap hurdles and a water jump ▸ *vb* **-chasing, -chased** **3** to race in a steeplechase

steeplejack *n* a person who repairs steeples and chimneys

steer[1] *vb* **1** to direct the course of (a vehicle or vessel) with a steering wheel or rudder **2** to direct the movements or course of (a person, conversation, or activity) **3** to follow (a specified course): *the Dutch government steered a middle course* **4 steer clear of** to avoid

> **steer** *vb* **1** = drive, control, direct, handle, pilot **2** = direct, lead, guide, conduct, escort

steer[2] *n* a castrated male ox or bull

steerage *n* **1** the cheapest accommodation on a passenger ship **2** steering

steering wheel *n* a wheel turned by the driver of a vehicle in order to change direction

stein (**stine**) *n* an earthenware beer mug

stellar *adj* **1** relating to the stars **2** *informal* outstanding or immense: *stellar profits*

stem[1] *n* **1** the long thin central part of a plant **2** a stalk that bears a flower, fruit, or leaf **3** the long slender part of anything, such as a wineglass **4** *linguistics* the form of a word that remains after removal of all inflectional endings ▸ *vb* **stemming, stemmed** **5 stem from** originate from: *this tradition stems from pre-Christian times*

> **stem** *n* **1, 2** = stalk, branch, trunk, shoot, axis ▸ *vb* **stem from something** = originate from, be caused by, derive from, arise from

stem[2] *vb* **stemming, stemmed** to stop or hinder the spread of (something): *to stem the flow of firearms*

> **stem** *vb* = stop, hold back, staunch, check, dam, curb

stench *n* a strong and very unpleasant smell

stencil *n* **1** a thin sheet with a cut-out pattern through which ink or paint passes to form the pattern on the surface below **2** a design or letters made in this way ▸ *vb* **-cilling, -cilled** or US **-ciling, -ciled** **3** to make (a design or letters) with a stencil

stenographer *n US & Canad* a shorthand typist

stent *n* a surgical implant used to keep an artery open

stentorian *adj* (of the voice) very loud: *a stentorian tone*

step *n* **1** the act of moving and setting down one's foot, such as when walking **2** the distance covered by such a movement **3** the sound made by such a movement **4** one of a sequence of foot movements that make up a dance **5** one of a sequence of actions taken in order to achieve a goal **6** a degree or rank in a series or scale **7** a flat surface for placing the foot on when going up or down **8** manner of walking: *he moved with a purposeful step* **9 steps** **A** a flight of stairs, usually out of doors **B** same as **stepladder 10** a short easily travelled distance: *Mexico and Brazil were only a step away* **11 break step** to stop marching in step **12 in step A** marching or dancing in time or at the same pace as other people **B** *informal* in agreement: *in step with public opinion* **13 out of step A** not marching or dancing in time or at the same pace as other people **B** *informal* not in agreement: *out of step with the political mood* **14 step by step** gradually **15 take steps** to do what is necessary (to achieve something) **16 watch one's step A** *informal* to behave with caution **B** to walk carefully ▸ *vb* **stepping, stepped 17** (often foll. by *on*) to move by taking a step, such as in walking **18** to place or press the foot; tread **19** to walk a short distance: *please step this way* **20 step into** to enter (a situation) apparently without difficulty: *she stepped into a life of luxury* ▸ See also **step in** *etc.*

> **step** *n* **2** = pace, stride, footstep **3** = footfall **5** = move, measure, action, means, act, deed, expedient **6** = level, rank, degree ▸ *vb* **17** = walk, pace, tread, move

step- *prefix* denoting a relationship created by the remarriage of a parent: *stepmother*

step in *vb informal* to intervene (in a quarrel or difficult situation)

> **step in** *vb* = intervene, take action, become involved

stepladder *n* a small folding portable ladder with a supporting frame

steppes *pl n* wide grassy plains without trees, in Siberia or SE Europe

S

stepping stone n 1 one of a series of stones acting as footrests for crossing a stream 2 a stage in a person's progress towards a goal: *it was a big stepping stone in his career*

step up vb 1 *informal* to increase (something) by stages; accelerate 2 **step up to the plate** A *baseball* to move into batting position B to come forward and take responsibility for something

> **step up** vb 1 **step something up** = increase, intensify, raise

stereo adj 1 (of a sound system) using two or more separate microphones to feed two or more loudspeakers through separate channels ▸ n, pl **stereos** 2 a music system in which sound is directed through two speakers 3 sound broadcast or played in stereo

stereophonic adj same as **stereo** (sense 1)

stereotype n 1 a set of characteristics or a fixed idea considered to represent a particular kind of person 2 an idea or convention that has grown stale through fixed usage ▸ vb **-typing, -typed** 3 to form a standard image or idea of (a type of person)

> **stereotype** n = formula, pattern ▸ vb = categorize, typecast, pigeonhole, standardize

sterile adj 1 free from germs 2 unable to produce offspring 3 (of plants) not producing or bearing seeds 4 lacking inspiration or energy; unproductive > **sterility** n

> **sterile** adj 1 = germ-free, sterilized, disinfected, aseptic; ≠ unhygienic 2, 3 = barren (*archaic*), infertile, unproductive; ≠ fertile

sterilize or **-lise** vb **-lizing, -lized** or **-lising, -lised** to make sterile > **sterilization** or **-lisation** n

sterling n 1 British money: *sterling fell against the dollar* ▸ adj 2 genuine and reliable; first-class: *he has a reputation for sterling honesty*

> **sterling** adj = excellent, sound, fine, superlative

stern¹ adj 1 strict and serious: *he's a very stern taskmaster* 2 difficult and often unpleasant: *the stern demands of the day* 3 (of a facial expression) severe and disapproving > **sternly** adv

> **stern** adj 1, 2 = strict, harsh, hard, grim, rigid, austere, inflexible; ≠ lenient 3 = severe, serious, forbidding; ≠ friendly

stern² n the rear part of a boat or ship

sternum n, pl **-na** or **-nums** a long flat bone in the front of the body, to which the collarbone and most of the ribs are attached

steroid n *biochem* an organic compound containing a carbon ring system, such as sterols and many hormones

stethoscope n *med* an instrument for listening to the sounds made inside the body, consisting of a hollow disc that transmits the sound through hollow tubes to earpieces

Stetson n *trademark* a felt hat with a broad brim and high crown, worn mainly by cowboys

stevedore n *chiefly US* a person employed to load or unload ships

stew n 1 a dish of meat, fish, or other food, cooked slowly in a closed pot 2 **in a stew** *informal* in a troubled or worried state ▸ vb 3 to cook by long slow simmering in a closed pot 4 *informal* (of a person) to be too hot 5 to cause (tea) to become bitter or (of tea) to become bitter through infusing for too long 6 **stew in one's own juice** to suffer the results of one's actions

steward n 1 a person who looks after passengers and serves meals on a ship or aircraft 2 an official who helps to supervise a public event, such as a race 3 a person who administers someone else's property 4 a person who manages the eating arrangements, staff, or service at a club or hotel 5 See **shop steward** ▸ vb 6 to act as a steward (of)

stewardess n a female steward on an aircraft or ship

stick¹ n 1 a small thin branch of a tree 2 A a long thin piece of wood B such a piece of wood shaped for a special purpose: *a walking stick; a hockey stick* 3 a piece of something shaped like a stick: *a stick of cinnamon* 4 *slang* verbal abuse, criticism: *they gave me a lot of stick* 5 **the sticks** a country area considered backward or unsophisticated: *places out in the sticks* 6 **sticks** pieces of furniture: *these few sticks are all I have* 7 *informal* a person: *not a bad old stick* 8 **get hold of the wrong end of the stick** to misunderstand a situation or an explanation completely

> **stick** n 1 = twig, branch 2 = cane, staff, pole, rod, crook, baton 4 = abuse, criticism, flak (*informal*), fault-finding

stick² vb **sticking, stuck** 1 to push (a pointed object) or (of a pointed object) to be pushed into another object 2 to fasten (something) in position by pins, nails, or glue: *she just stuck the label on* 3 to extend beyond something else; protrude: *he stuck his head out of the door* 4 *informal* to place (something) in a specified position: *stick it in the oven* 5 to fasten or be fastened by or as if by an adhesive 6 to come or be brought to a standstill: *stuck in a rut; two army lorries stuck behind us* 7 to remain for a long time: *the room that sticks in my mind the most* 8 *slang, chiefly Brit* to tolerate; abide: *you couldn't stick it for more than two days* 9 **be stuck** *informal* to be at a loss for; to be baffled or puzzled: *I'm stuck; stuck for words* ▸ See also **stick up for**

> **stick** vb 1 = poke, dig, stab, thrust, pierce, penetrate, spear, prod 2, 5 = fasten, fix, bind, hold, bond, attach, glue, paste 4 = put, place, set, lay, deposit 7 = stay, remain, linger, persist 8 = tolerate, take, stand, stomach, abide

sticker n a small piece of paper with a picture or writing on it that can be stuck to a surface

stick-in-the-mud n informal a person who is unwilling to try anything new or do anything exciting

stickleback n a small fish with sharp spines along its back

stickler n a person who insists on something: a stickler for punctuality

stick-up n slang, chiefly US a robbery at gunpoint; hold-up

stick up for vb informal to support or defend (oneself, another person, or a principle)

> **stick up for** vb **stick up for someone**
> = defend, support, champion, stand up for

sticky adj **stickier, stickiest** 1 covered with a substance that sticks to other things: sticky little fingers 2 intended to stick to a surface: sticky labels 3 informal difficult or painful: a sticky meeting 4 (of weather) unpleasantly warm and humid > **stickiness** n

> **sticky** adj 1 = gooey, tacky (informal), viscous, glutinous, gummy, icky (informal), gluey, clinging 2 = adhesive, gummed, adherent, grippy 3 = difficult, awkward, tricky, embarrassing, nasty, delicate, unpleasant, barro (Austral slang) 4 = humid, close, sultry, oppressive, sweltering, clammy, muggy

stiff adj 1 firm and not easily bent 2 moving with pain or difficulty: stiff and aching joints 3 not moving easily: the door is stiff 4 difficult or severe: a stiff challenge; stiff penalties 5 formal and not relaxed 6 fairly firm in consistency; thick 7 powerful: a stiff breeze 8 (of a drink) containing a lot of alcohol ▸ n 9 slang a corpse ▸ adv 10 completely or utterly: I was bored stiff > **stiffly** adv > **stiffness** n

> **stiff** adj 1 = inflexible, rigid, unyielding, hard, firm, tight, solid, tense; ≠ flexible 4 = difficult, hard, tough, exacting, arduous 5 = formal, constrained, forced, unnatural, stilted, unrelaxed; ≠ informal

stiffen vb to make or become stiff or stiffer

stiff-necked adj proud and stubborn

stifle vb **-fling, -fled** 1 to stop oneself from expressing (a yawn or cry) 2 to stop (something) from continuing: the new leadership stifled all internal debate 3 to feel discomfort and difficulty in breathing 4 to kill (someone) by preventing him or her from breathing

> **stifle** vb 1 = restrain, suppress, repress, smother 2 = suppress, repress, stop, check, silence, restrain, hush, smother

stigma n, pl **stigmas** or **stigmata** 1 a mark of social disgrace: a stigma attached to being redundant 2 botany the part of a flower that receives pollen 3 **stigmata** Christianity marks resembling the wounds of the crucified Christ, believed to appear on the bodies of certain people

> **stigma** n 1 = disgrace, shame, dishonour, stain, slur, smirch

stigmatize or **-tise** vb **-tizing, -tized** or **-tising, -tised** to regard as being shameful

stile n a set of steps in a wall or fence to allow people, but not animals, to pass over

stiletto n, pl **-tos** 1 Also called: **spike heel, stiletto heel** a high narrow heel on a woman's shoe or a shoe with such a heel 2 a small dagger with a slender tapered blade

still[1] adv 1 continuing now or in the future as in the past: she still loved the theatre 2 up to this or that time; yet 3 even or yet: still more pressure on the government 4 even then; nevertheless: the baby has been fed and still cries 5 quietly or without movement: keep still ▸ adj 6 motionless; stationary 7 undisturbed; silent and calm 8 (of a soft drink) not fizzy ▸ n 9 poetic silence or tranquillity: the still of night 10 a still photograph from a film ▸ vb 11 to make or become quiet or calm 12 to relieve or end: Fowler stilled his conscience > **stillness** n

> **still** adv 4 = however, but, yet, nevertheless, notwithstanding ▸ adj 6 = motionless, stationary, calm, peaceful, serene, tranquil, undisturbed, restful; ≠ moving 7 = silent, quiet, hushed; ≠ noisy ▸ vb 11 = quieten, calm, settle, quiet, silence, soothe, hush, lull; ≠ get louder

still[2] n an apparatus for distilling spirits

stillborn adj 1 (of a baby) dead at birth 2 (of an idea or plan) completely unsuccessful > **stillbirth** n

still life n, pl **still lifes** 1 a painting or drawing of objects such as fruit or flowers 2 this kind of painting or drawing

stilt n 1 either of a pair of long poles with footrests for walking raised from the ground 2 a long post or column used with others to support a building above ground level

stilted adj (of speech, writing, or behaviour) formal or pompous; not flowing continuously or naturally

stimulant n 1 a drug, food, or drink that makes the body work faster, increases heart rate, and makes sleeping difficult 2 any stimulating thing ▸ adj 3 stimulating

stimulate vb **-lating, -lated** 1 to encourage to start or progress further: a cut in interest rates should help stimulate economic recovery 2 to fill (a person) with ideas or enthusiasm: books satisfy a part of the intellect that needs to be stimulated 3 physiol to excite (a nerve or organ) with a stimulus > **stimulation** n

> **stimulate** vb 1 = encourage, inspire, prompt, fire, spur, provoke, arouse, rouse

stimulus (stim-myew-luss) n, pl **-li** (-lie) 1 something that acts as an incentive to (someone) 2 something, such as a drug or electrical impulse, that is capable of causing a response in a person or an animal

> **stimulus** n 1 = incentive, spur, encouragement, impetus, inducement, goad, incitement, fillip

S

sting *vb* **stinging, stung 1** (of certain animals and plants) to inflict a wound on (someone) by the injection of poison **2** to cause (someone) to feel a sharp physical pain: *her hand was stinging* **3** to offend or upset (someone) with a critical remark: *I was stung by what he said* **4** to provoke (a response) by angering: *the consulate would be stung into convulsive action* **5** *informal* to cheat (someone) by overcharging ▸ *n* **6** a skin wound caused by stinging **7** pain caused by or as if by a sting **8** a mental pain: *the sting of memory* **9** the sharp pointed organ of certain animals or plants used to inject poison **10** *slang* a deceptive trick **11** *slang* a trap set up by the police to entice a person to commit a crime, thereby producing evidence > **stinging** *adj*

> **sting** *vb* **1** = hurt, burn, wound **2** = smart, burn, pain, hurt, tingle

stingy *adj* **-gier, -giest** very mean > **stinginess** *n*

stink *n* **1** a strong unpleasant smell **2 make** or **create** or **kick up a stink** *slang* to make a fuss ▸ *vb* **stinking, stank** or **stunk, stunk 3** to give off a strong unpleasant smell **4** *slang* to be thoroughly bad or unpleasant: *the script stinks, the casting stinks* > **stinky** *adj*

> **stink** *n* **1** = stench, pong (*Brit informal*), foul smell, fetor ▸ *vb* **3** = reek, pong (*Brit informal*)

stint *vb* **1** to be miserly with (something): *don't stint on paper napkins* ▸ *n* **2** a given amount of work

> **stint** *vb* = be mean, hold back, be sparing, skimp on, be frugal ▸ *n* = term, time, turn, period, share, shift, stretch, spell

stipend (**sty**-pend) *n* a regular salary or allowance, esp. that paid to a member of the clergy > **stipendiary** *adj*

stipple *vb* **-pling, -pled** to draw, engrave, or paint (something) using dots or flecks

stipulate *vb* **-lating, -lated** to specify (something) as a condition of an agreement > **stipulation** *n*

> **stipulate** *vb* = specify, agree, require, contract, settle, covenant, insist upon

stir *vb* **stirring, stirred 1** to mix up (a liquid) by moving a spoon or stick around in it **2** to move slightly **3 stir from** to depart from (one's usual or preferred place) **4** to get up after sleeping **5** to excite or move (someone) emotionally **6** to move (oneself) quickly or vigorously; exert (oneself) **7** to wake up: *to stir someone from sleep* ▸ *n* **8** a stirring **9** a strong reaction, usually of excitement: *she created a stir wherever she went*

> **stir** *vb* **1** = mix, beat, agitate **5** = stimulate, move, excite, spur, provoke, arouse, awaken, rouse; ≠ inhibit ▸ *n* **9** = commotion, excitement, activity, disorder, fuss, disturbance, bustle, flurry

stir-fry *vb* **-fries, -frying, -fried 1** to cook (food) quickly by stirring it in a wok or frying pan over a high heat ▸ *n, pl* **-fries 2** a dish cooked in this way

stirrup *n* a metal loop attached to a saddle for supporting a rider's foot

stitch *n* **1** a link made by drawing a thread through material with a needle **2** a loop of yarn formed around a needle or hook in knitting or crocheting **3** a particular kind of stitch **4** *informal* a link of thread joining the edges of a wound together **5** a sharp pain in the side caused by running or exercising **6 in stitches** *informal* laughing uncontrollably **7 not a stitch** *informal* no clothes at all ▸ *vb* **8** to sew or fasten (something) with stitches > **stitching** *n*

stoat *n* a small brown N European mammal related to the weasel: in winter it has a white coat and is then known as an ermine

stock *n* **1** the total amount of goods kept on the premises of a shop or business **2** a supply of something stored for future use **3** *finance* **A** the money raised by a company through selling shares entitling their holders to dividends, partial ownership, and usually voting rights **B** the proportion of this money held by an individual shareholder **C** the shares of a specified company or industry **4** farm animals bred and kept for their meat, skins, etc. **5** the original type from which a particular race, family, or group is descended **6** the handle of a rifle, held by the firer against the shoulder **7** a liquid produced by simmering meat, fish, bones, or vegetables, and used to make soups and sauces **8** a kind of plant grown for its brightly coloured flowers **9** *old-fashioned* the degree of status a person has **10** See **laughing stock 11 in stock** stored on the premises or available for sale or use **12 out of stock** not immediately available for sale or use **13 take stock** to think carefully about a situation before making a decision ▸ *adj* **14** staple; standard: *stock sizes in clothes* **15** being a cliché; hackneyed: *the stock answer* ▸ *vb* **16** to keep (goods) for sale **17** to obtain a store of (something) for future use or sale: *to stock up on food* **18** to supply (a farm) with animals or (a lake or stream) with fish

> **stock** *n* **1** = goods, merchandise, wares, range, choice, variety, selection, commodities **2** = supply, store, reserve, fund, stockpile, hoard **3A** = property, capital, assets, funds **3B, 3C** = shares, holdings, securities, investments, bonds, equities **4** = livestock, cattle, beasts, domestic animals ▸ *adj* **14** = regular, usual, ordinary, conventional, customary **15** = hackneyed, routine, banal, trite, overused ▸ *vb* **16** = sell, supply, handle, keep, trade in, deal in **18** = fill, supply, provide with, equip, furnish, fit out

stockade *n* an enclosure or barrier of large wooden posts

stockbroker *n* a person who buys and sells stocks and shares for customers and receives a percentage of their profits > **stockbroking** *n*

stock car *n* a car that has been strengthened and modified for a form of racing in which the cars often collide

stock exchange *n* **1 A** a highly organized market for the purchase and sale of stocks and shares, operated by professional stockbrokers and market makers according to fixed rules **B** a place where stocks and shares are traded **2** the prices or trading activity of a stock exchange: *the stock exchange has been rising*

stocking *n* a long piece of close-fitting nylon or knitted yarn covering the foot and part or all of the leg

stockist *n Brit* a dealer who stocks a particular product

stockpile *vb* **-piling, -piled 1** to store a large quantity of (something) for future use ▶ *n* **2** a large store gathered for future use

stock-still *adv* absolutely still; motionlessly

stocktaking *n* **1** the counting and valuing of goods in a shop or business **2** a reassessment of a person's current situation and prospects

stocky *adj* **stockier, stockiest** (of a person) short but well-built > **stockily** *adv* > **stockiness** *n*

stodge *n Brit, Austral & NZ informal* heavy and filling starchy food

stodgy *adj* **stodgier, stodgiest 1** (of food) full of starch and very filling **2** (of a person) dull, serious, or excessively formal > **stodginess** *n*

stoep (stoop) *n* (in South Africa) a verandah

stoic (stow-ik) *n* **1** a person who suffers great difficulties without showing his or her emotions ▶ *adj* **2** same as **stoical**

stoical *adj* suffering great difficulties without showing one's feelings > **stoically** *adv* > **stoicism** (stow-iss-iz-zum) *n*

stoke *vb* **stoking, stoked 1** to feed and tend (a fire or furnace) **2** to excite or encourage (a strong emotion) in oneself or someone else

stoker *n* a person employed to tend a furnace on a ship or train powered by steam

stole¹ *vb* the past tense of **steal**

stole² *n* a long scarf or shawl

stolen *vb* the past participle of **steal**

stolid *adj* showing little or no emotion or interest in anything > **stolidity** *n* > **stolidly** *adv*

stomach *n* **1** an organ inside the body in which food is stored until it has been partially digested **2** the front of the body around the waist **3** desire or appetite: *he still has the stomach for a fight* ▶ *vb* **4** to put up with: *liberals could not stomach the rest of the package*

> **stomach** *n* **1** = belly, gut (*informal*), abdomen, tummy (*informal*), puku (NZ) **2** = tummy (*informal*), pot, spare tyre (*informal*) **3** = inclination, taste, desire, appetite, relish ▶ *vb* = bear, take, tolerate, endure, swallow, abide

stomp *vb* to tread or stamp heavily

stone *n* **1** the hard nonmetallic material of which rocks are made **2** a small lump of rock **3** Also called: **gemstone** a precious or semiprecious stone that has been cut and polished **4** a piece of rock used for some particular purpose: *gravestone; millstone* **5** the hard central part of fruits such as the peach or date **6** *pl* **stone** *Brit* a unit of weight equal to 14 pounds or 6.350 kilograms **7** *pathol* a hard deposit formed in the kidney or bladder **8 heart of stone** a hard or unemotional personality **9 leave no stone unturned** to do everything possible to achieve something ▶ *adj* **10** made of stoneware: *the polished stone planter* ▶ *vb* **stoning, stoned 11** to throw stones at (someone), for example as a punishment **12** to remove the stones from (a fruit)

> **stone** *n* **1** = masonry, rock **2** = rock, pebble **5** = pip, seed, pit, kernel

Stone Age *n* a phase of human culture identified by the use of tools made of stone

stone-cold *adj* **1** completely cold ▶ *adv* **2 stone-cold sober** completely sober

stoned *adj slang* under the influence of drugs or alcohol

stone-deaf *adj* completely deaf

stonewall *vb* **1** to deliberately prolong a discussion by being long-winded or evasive **2** *cricket* (of a batsman) to play defensively

stoneware *n* a hard type of pottery, fired at a very high temperature

stony *or* **stoney** *adj* **stonier, stoniest 1** (of ground) rough and covered with stones: *the stony path* **2** (of a face, voice, or attitude) unfriendly and unsympathetic > **stonily** *adv*

stony-broke *adj slang* completely without money

stood *vb* the past of **stand**

stooge *n* **1** an actor who feeds lines to a comedian or acts as the butt of his jokes **2** *slang* someone who is taken advantage of by someone in a superior position

stool *n* **1** a seat with legs but no back **2** waste matter from the bowels

stoop *vb* **1** to bend (the body) forward and downward **2** to stand or walk with head and shoulders habitually bent forward **3 stoop to** to lower one's normal standards of behaviour; degrade oneself: *no real journalist would stoop to faking* ▶ *n* **4** the act, position, or habit of stooping > **stooping** *adj*

> **stoop** *vb* **1** = bend, lean, bow, duck, crouch **2** = hunch ▶ *n* = slouch, bad posture, round-shoulderedness

stop *vb* **stopping, stopped 1** to cease from doing (something); discontinue **2** to cause (something moving) to halt or (of something moving) to come to a halt **3** to prevent the continuance or completion of (something) **4** (often foll. by *from*) to prevent or restrain: *I stopped her from going on any further* **5** to keep back: *no agreement to stop arms supplies* **6 stop up** to block or plug: *to stop up a pipe* **7** to stay or rest: *we stopped at a campsite for a change* **8** to instruct a bank not to honour (a cheque) **9** to deduct (money) from pay **10** *informal* to receive (a blow or hit) **11** *music* to alter the vibrating length of (a string on a violin, guitar, etc.) by pressing down on it at some point with the finger **12 stop at nothing** to be prepared to do anything; be ruthless ▸ *n* **13** prevention of movement or progress: *you can put a stop to it quite easily* **14** the act of stopping or the state of being stopped: *the car lurched to a stop* **15** a place where something halts or pauses: *a bus stop* **16** the act or an instance of blocking or obstructing **17** a device that prevents, limits, or ends the motion of a mechanism or moving part **18** *Brit* a full stop **19** *music* a knob on an organ that is operated to allow sets of pipes to sound **20 pull out all the stops** to make a great effort

stop *vb* **1** = quit, cease, refrain, put an end to, discontinue, desist; ≠ start **2** = halt, pause; ≠ keep going **3** = prevent, cut short, arrest, restrain, hold back, hinder, repress, impede; ≠ facilitate **7** = stay, rest, lodge ▸ *n* **14** = halt, standstill **15** = station, stage, depot (*US, Canad*), terminus

stopcock *n* a valve used to control or stop the flow of a fluid in a pipe

stopgap *n* a thing that serves as a substitute for a short time until replaced by something more suitable

stopover *n* **1** a break in a journey ▸ *vb* **stop over 2** to make a stopover

stoppage *n* **1** the act of stopping something or the state of being stopped: *a heart stoppage* **2** a deduction of money, such as taxation, from pay **3** an organized stopping of work during industrial action

stoppage time *n chiefly Brit* same as **injury time**

stopper *n* a plug for closing a bottle, pipe, etc.

stop press *n* news items inserted into a newspaper after the printing has been started

stopwatch *n* a watch which can be stopped instantly for exact timing of a sporting event

storage *n* **1** the act of storing or the state of being stored **2** space for storing **3** *computers* the process of storing information in a computer

storage heater *n* an electric device that accumulates and radiates heat generated by cheap off-peak electricity

store *vb* **storing, stored 1** to keep, set aside, or gather (things) for future use **2** to place (furniture or other possessions) in a warehouse for safekeeping **3** to supply or stock (certain goods) **4** *computers* to enter or keep (information) in a storage device ▸ *n* **5** a shop (in Britain usually a large one) **6** a large supply or stock kept for future use **7** short for **department store**

8 a storage place, such as a warehouse **9** *computers, chiefly Brit* same as **memory** (sense 7) **10 in store** about to happen; forthcoming: *you've got a treat in store* **11 set great store by something** to value something as important

store *vb* **1** = put by, save, hoard, keep, reserve, deposit, garner, stockpile **2** = put away, put in storage, put in store ▸ *n* **5** = shop, outlet, market, mart **6** = supply, stock, reserve, fund, quantity, accumulation, stockpile, hoard **8** = repository, warehouse, depository, storeroom

storey *or esp US* **story** *n, pl* **-reys** *or* **-ries** a floor or level of a building

stork *n* a large wading bird with very long legs, a long bill, and white-and-black feathers

storm *n* **1** a violent weather condition of strong winds, rain, hail, thunder, lightning, etc. **2** a violent disturbance or quarrel: *a storm of protest from the opposition* **3** (usually foll. by *of*) a heavy discharge of bullets or missiles **4 take a place by storm A** to capture or overrun a place by a violent attack **B** to surprise people, but receive their praise, by being extremely successful at something ▸ *vb* **5** to attack or capture (a place) suddenly and violently **6** to shout angrily **7** to move or rush violently or angrily: *she stormed into the study*

storm *n* **1** = tempest (*literary*), hurricane, gale, blizzard, squall **2** = outburst, row, outcry, furore, outbreak, turmoil, disturbance, strife ▸ *vb* **5** = attack, charge, rush, assault, assail **6** = rage, rant, thunder, rave, bluster **7** = rush, stamp, flounce, fly

stormy *adj* **stormier, stormiest 1** (of weather) violent with dark skies, heavy rain or snow, and strong winds **2** involving violent emotions: *a stormy affair*

stormy *adj* **1** = wild, rough, raging, turbulent, windy, blustery, inclement, squally **2** = angry, heated, fierce, passionate, fiery, impassioned

story *n, pl* **-ries 1** a description of a chain of events told or written in prose or verse **2** Also called: **short story** a piece of fiction, shorter and usually less detailed than a novel **3** Also called: **story line** the plot of a book or film **4** a news report **5** the event or material for such a report **6** *informal* a lie

story *n* **1** = anecdote, account, tale, report **2** = tale, romance, narrative, history, legend, yarn (*informal*) **4** = report, news, article, feature, scoop, news item

stoup *or* **stoop** (stoop) *n* a small basin in a church for holy water

stout *adj* **1** solidly built or fat **2** strong and sturdy: *stout footwear* **3** brave or determined: *we met unexpectedly stout resistance* ▸ *n* **4** a kind of strong, black beer > **stoutly** *adv*

stout *adj* 1 = fat, big, heavy, overweight, plump, bulky, burly, fleshy; ≠ slim 2 = strong, strapping, muscular, robust, sturdy, stalwart, brawny, able-bodied; ≠ puny 3 = brave, bold, courageous, fearless, resolute, gallant, intrepid, valiant; ≠ timid

stove[1] *n* 1 same as **cooker** (sense 1) 2 any apparatus for heating, such as a kiln

stove[2] *vb* a past tense and past participle of **stave**

stow *vb* (often foll. by *away*) to pack or store (something)

stowaway *n* 1 a person who hides aboard a ship or aircraft in order to travel free ▸ *vb* **stow away** 2 to travel in such a way: *he stowed away on a ferry*

straddle *vb* **-dling, -dled** 1 to have one leg or part on each side of (something) 2 *US & Canad informal* to be in favour of both sides of (an issue or argument)

strafe *vb* **strafing, strafed** to machine-gun (an enemy) from the air

straggle *vb* **-gling, -gled** 1 to spread out in an untidy and rambling way: *the town straggled off to the east* 2 to linger behind or wander from a main line or part ▹ **straggler** *n* ▹ **straggly** *adj*

straight *adj* 1 continuing in the same direction without bending; not curved or crooked 2 even, level, or upright 3 in keeping with the facts; accurate 4 outright or candid: *a straight rejection* 5 in continuous succession 6 (of an alcoholic drink) undiluted 7 not wavy or curly: *straight hair* 8 in good order 9 (of a play or acting style) straightforward or serious 10 honest, respectable, or reliable 11 heterosexual 12 *slang* conventional in views, customs, or appearance 13 *informal* no longer owing or being owed something: *if you buy the next round we'll be straight* ▸ *adv* 14 in a straight line or direct course 15 immediately; at once: *get straight back here* 16 in a level or upright position: *he sat up straight* 17 continuously; uninterruptedly: *we waited for three hours straight* 18 (often foll. by *out*) frankly; candidly: *she asked me straight out* 19 **go straight** *informal* to reform after having been a criminal 20 **straight away** or **straightaway** at once ▸ *n* 21 a straight line, form, part, or position 22 *Brit* a straight part of a racetrack 23 a heterosexual person

straight *adj* 1 = direct, unswerving; ≠ indirect 2 = level, even, right, square, true, smooth, aligned, horizontal; ≠ crooked 4 = frank, plain, straightforward, blunt, outright, honest, candid, forthright; ≠ evasive 5 = successive, consecutive, continuous, running, solid, nonstop; ≠ discontinuous 6 = undiluted, pure, neat, unadulterated, unmixed 8 = in order, organized, arranged, neat, tidy, orderly, shipshape; ≠ untidy 10 = honest, just, fair, reliable, respectable, upright, honourable, law-abiding; ≠ dishonest 12 = conventional, conservative,

bourgeois; ≠ fashionable ▸ *adv* 14 = directly, precisely, exactly, unswervingly, by the shortest route, in a beeline 15 = immediately, directly, promptly, instantly, at once, straight away, without delay, forthwith

straighten *vb* (sometimes foll. by *up* or *out*) 1 to make or become straight 2 to make (something) neat or tidy

straighten *vb* 2 = neaten, arrange, tidy (up), order, put in order

straight face *n* a serious facial expression which hides a desire to laugh ▹ **straight-faced** *adj*

straightforward *adj* 1 (of a person) honest, frank, and open 2 (of a task) easy to do

straightforward *adj* 1 = honest, open, direct, genuine, sincere, candid, truthful, forthright, dinkum (*Austral, NZ informal*); ≠ devious 2 = simple, easy, uncomplicated, routine, elementary, easy-peasy (*slang*); ≠ complicated

strain[1] *n* 1 tension or tiredness resulting from overwork or worry 2 tension between people or organizations: *there are signs of strain between the economic superpowers* 3 an intense physical or mental effort 4 the damage resulting from excessive physical exertion 5 a great demand on the emotions, strength, or resources 6 **strains** *music* a theme, melody, or tune ▸ *vb* 7 to subject (someone) to mental tension or stress 8 to make an intense effort: *the rest were straining to follow the conversation* 9 to use (resources) to, or beyond, their limits 10 to injure or damage (oneself or a part of one's body) by overexertion: *he appeared to have strained a muscle* 11 to pour (a substance) through a sieve or filter

strain *n* 1 = stress, anxiety 3 = worry, effort, struggle; ≠ ease 4 = injury, wrench, sprain, pull 5 = pressure, stress, demands, burden ▸ *vb* 8 = strive, struggle, endeavour, labour, go for it (*informal*), bend over backwards (*informal*), give it your best shot (*informal*), knock yourself out (*informal*); ≠ relax 9 = stretch, tax, overtax 11 = sieve, filter, sift, purify

strain[2] *n* 1 a group of animals or plants within a species or variety, distinguished by one or more minor characteristics 2 a trace or streak: *a strain of ruthlessness in their play*

strain *n* 1 = breed, family, race, blood, descent, extraction, ancestry, lineage 2 = trace, suggestion, tendency, streak

strained *adj* 1 (of an action, expression, etc.) not natural or spontaneous 2 (of an atmosphere, relationship, etc.) not relaxed; tense

strained *adj* 1 = forced, put on, false, artificial, unnatural; ≠ natural 2 = tense, difficult, awkward, embarrassed, stiff, uneasy; ≠ relaxed

S

strainer *n* a sieve used for straining sauces, vegetables, or tea

strait *n* **1** (*often pl*) a narrow channel of the sea linking two larger areas of sea **2 straits** a position of extreme difficulty: *in desperate straits*

> **strait** *n* **1** = channel, sound, narrows **2** = difficulty, dilemma, plight, hardship, uphill (*S African*), predicament, extremity

straitened *adj* **in straitened circumstances** not having much money

straitjacket *n* **1** a strong canvas jacket with long sleeves used to bind the arms of a violent person **2** anything which holds back or restricts development or freedom: *exporters are wrapped in a straitjacket of regulations*

strait-laced *or* **straight-laced** *adj* having a strict code of moral standards; puritanical

strand¹ *vb* **1** to leave or drive (ships or fish) ashore **2** to leave (someone) helpless, for example without transport or money ▸ *n* **3** *chiefly poetic* a shore or beach

strand² *n* **1** one of the individual fibres of string or wire that form a rope, cord, or cable **2** a single length of string, hair, wool, or wire **3** a string of pearls or beads **4** a part of something; element: *the many disparate strands of the Anglican Church*

> **strand** *n* **1** = filament, fibre, thread, string

strange *adj* **1** odd or unexpected **2** not known, seen, or experienced before; unfamiliar **3 strange to** inexperienced in or unaccustomed to: *they are in some degree strange to it* > **strangely** *adv* > **strangeness** *n*

> **strange** *adj* **1** = odd, curious, weird, wonderful, extraordinary, bizarre, peculiar, abnormal, daggy (*Austral, NZ informal*); ≠ ordinary **2** = unfamiliar, new, unknown, foreign, novel, alien, exotic, untried; ≠ familiar

stranger *n* **1** any person whom one does not know **2** a person who is new to a particular place **3 stranger to** a person who is unfamiliar with or new to something: *Paul is no stranger to lavish spending*

> **stranger** *n* **1** = unknown person **2** = newcomer, incomer, foreigner, guest, visitor, alien, outlander

strangle *vb* **-gling, -gled 1** to kill (someone) by pressing his or her windpipe; throttle **2** to prevent the growth or development of: *another attempt at strangling national identity* **3** to stifle (a voice, cry, or laugh) by swallowing suddenly: *the words were strangled by sobs* > **strangler** *n*

> **strangle** *vb* **1** = throttle, choke, asphyxiate, strangulate **2** = suppress, inhibit, subdue, stifle, repress, overpower, quash, quell

stranglehold *n* **1** a wrestling hold in which a wrestler's arms are pressed against his opponent's windpipe **2** complete power or control over a person or situation

strap *n* **1** a strip of strong flexible material used for carrying, lifting, fastening, or holding things in place **2** a loop of leather or rubber, hanging from the roof in a bus or train for standing passengers to hold on to **3 the strap** a beating with a strap as a punishment ▸ *vb* **strapping, strapped 4** to tie or bind (something) with a strap

> **strap** *n* **1** = tie, thong, belt ▸ *vb* = tie, thong, belt

strapped *adj* **strapped for** *slang* badly in need of: *strapped for cash*

strapping *adj* tall, strong, and healthy-looking: *a strapping young lad*

> **strapping** *adj* = well-built, big, powerful, robust, sturdy, husky (*informal*), brawny

strata *n* the plural of **stratum**

stratagem *n* a clever plan to deceive an enemy

strategic (strat-ee-jik) *adj* **1** planned to achieve an advantage; tactical **2** (of weapons, esp. missiles) directed against an enemy's homeland rather than used on a battlefield > **strategically** *adv*

> **strategic** *adj* **1** = tactical, calculated, deliberate, planned, politic, diplomatic

strategy *n, pl* **-gies 1** a long-term plan for success, such as in politics or business **2** the art of the planning and conduct of a war > **strategist** *n*

> **strategy** *n* **1** = plan, approach, scheme

strathspey *n* **1** a Scottish dance with gliding steps, slower than a reel **2** music for this dance

stratified *adj* **1** (of rocks) formed in horizontal layers of different materials **2** *sociol* (of a society) divided into different classes or groups > **stratification** *n*

stratosphere *n* the atmospheric layer between about 15 and 50 km above the earth

stratum (strah-tum) *n, pl* **-ta** (-ta) **1** any of the distinct layers into which certain rocks are divided **2** a layer of ocean or atmosphere marked off naturally or decided arbitrarily **3** a social class

straw *n* **1** dried stalks of threshed grain, such as wheat or barley **2** a single stalk of straw **3** a long thin hollow paper or plastic tube, used for sucking up liquids into the mouth **4 clutch at straws** to turn in desperation to something with little chance of success **5 draw the short straw** to be the person chosen to perform an unpleasant task ▸ *adj* **6** made of straw: *straw baskets*

strawberry *n, pl* **-ries** a sweet fleshy red fruit with small seeds on the outside

strawberry mark *n* a red birthmark

straw poll *or* **straw vote** *n* an unofficial poll

S

or vote taken to find out the opinion of a group or the public on some issue

stray *vb* **1** to wander away from the correct path or from a given area **2** to move away from the point or lose concentration **3** to fail to live up to certain moral standards: *her partner had strayed* ▶ *n* **4** a domestic animal that has wandered away from its home **5** *old-fashioned* a lost or homeless child ▶ *adj* **6** (of a domestic animal) having wandered away from its home **7** random or separated from the main group of things of their kind: *stray bombs and rockets*

> **stray** *vb* **1** = wander, go astray, drift **2** = digress, diverge, deviate, get off the point ▶ *adj* **6** = lost, abandoned, homeless, roaming, vagrant **7** = random, chance, accidental

streak *n* **1** a long thin stripe or trace of some contrasting colour **2** (of lightning) a sudden flash **3** a quality or characteristic: *a nasty streak* **4** a short stretch of good or bad luck: *a losing streak* **5** *informal* an instance of running naked through a public place ▶ *vb* **6** to mark (something) with a streak or streaks: *sweat streaking the grime of his face* **7** to move quickly in a straight line **8** *informal* to run naked through a public place > **streaked** *or* **streaky** *adj* > **streaker** *n*

> **streak** *n* **1, 3** = trace, touch, element, strain, dash, vein ▶ *vb* **7** = speed, fly, tear, flash, sprint, dart, zoom, whizz (*informal*)

stream *n* **1** a small river **2** any steady flow of water or other liquid **3** something that resembles a stream in moving continuously in a line or particular direction: *the stream of traffic* **4** a fast and continuous flow of speech: *the constant stream of jargon* **5** *Brit, Austral & NZ* a class of schoolchildren grouped together because of similar ability ▶ *vb* **6** to pour in a continuous flow: *rain streamed down her cheeks* **7** (of a crowd of people or traffic or a herd of animals) to move in unbroken succession **8** to send video or audio material over the internet so that the receiving system can play it almost simultaneously **9** to float freely or with a waving motion: *a flimsy pink dress that streamed out behind her* **10** *Brit & NZ* to group (schoolchildren) in streams > **streaming** *n* > **streamlet** *n*

> **stream** *n* **1** = river, brook, burn (*Scot*), beck, tributary, bayou, rivulet **2** = flow, current, rush, run, course, drift, surge, tide ▶ *vb* **6** = flow, run, pour, issue, flood, spill, cascade, gush **7** = rush, fly, speed, tear, flood, pour

streamer *n* **1** a person or thing that streams **2** a long coiled ribbon of coloured paper that unrolls when tossed **3** a long narrow flag

streamline *vb* **-lining, -lined 1** to improve (something) by removing the parts that are least useful or profitable **2** to make (an aircraft, boat, or vehicle) less resistant to flowing air or water by improving its shape > **streamlined** *adj*

street *n* **1** a public road that is usually lined with buildings, esp. in a town: *Sauchiehall Street* **2** the part of the road between the pavements, used by vehicles **3** the people living in a particular street **4 on the streets** homeless **5 right up one's street** *informal* just what one knows or likes best **6 streets ahead of** *informal* superior to or more advanced than

> **street** *n* **1** = road, lane, avenue, terrace, row, roadway

streetcar *n US & Canad* a tram

streetwise *adj* knowing how to survive or succeed in poor and often criminal sections of big cities

strength *n* **1** the state or quality of being physically or mentally strong **2** the ability to withstand great force, stress, or pressure **3** something regarded as valuable or a source of power: *his chief strength is rocketry* **4** potency or effectiveness, such as of a drink or drug **5** power to convince: *the strength of this argument* **6** degree of intensity or concentration of colour, light, sound, or flavour: *a medium-strength cheese* **7** the total number of people in a group: *at full strength; 50 000 men below strength* **8 go from strength to strength** to have ever-increasing success **9 on the strength of** on the basis of or relying upon

> **strength** *n* **1** = might, muscle, brawn; ≠ weakness **2** = toughness, soundness, robustness, sturdiness **3** = strong point, skill, asset, advantage, talent, forte, speciality; ≠ failing **4** = potency, effectiveness, efficacy **6** = force, power, intensity; ≠ weakness

strengthen *vb* to become stronger or make (something) stronger

> **strengthen** *vb* = fortify, harden, toughen, consolidate, stiffen, gee up, brace up; ≠ weaken

strenuous *adj* requiring or involving the use of great energy or effort > **strenuously** *adv*

streptococcus (strep-toe-kok-uss) *n, pl* **-cocci** (-**kok**-eye) a bacterium occurring in chains and including many species that cause disease

stress *n* **1** mental, emotional, or physical strain or tension **2** special emphasis or significance **3** emphasis placed upon a syllable by pronouncing it more loudly than those that surround it **4** *physics* force producing a change in shape or volume ▶ *vb* **5** to give emphasis to (a point or subject): *she stressed how difficult it had been* **6** to pronounce (a word or syllable) more loudly than those surrounding it > **stressful** *adj*

> **stress** *n* **1** = strain, pressure, worry, tension, burden, anxiety, trauma **2** = emphasis, significance, force, weight **3** = accent, beat, emphasis, accentuation ▶ *vb* **5** = emphasize, underline, dwell on **6** = place the emphasis on, emphasize, give emphasis to, lay emphasis upon

S

stressed or **stressed-out** adj informal suffering from anxiety or tension

stretch vb **1 stretch over** or **for** to extend or spread over (a specified distance): the flood barrier stretches for several miles **2** to draw out or extend (something) or to be drawn out or extended in length or area **3** to distort or lengthen (something) or to be distorted or lengthened permanently **4** to extend (the limbs or body), for example when one has just woken up **5** (often foll. by out or forward, etc.) to reach or hold out (a part of one's body) **6** to reach or suspend (a rope, etc.) from one place to another **7** to draw (something) tight; tighten **8** (usually foll. by over) to extend in time: a dinner which stretched over three consecutive evenings **9** to put a great strain upon (one's money or resources) **10** to make do with (limited resources): the Walkers decided to stretch their budget **11** to extend (someone) to the limit of his or her abilities **12** to extend (someone) to the limit of his or her tolerance **13 stretch a point** to make an exception not usually made ▸ n **14** the act of stretching **15** a large or continuous expanse or distance: this stretch of desert **16** extent in time **17** a term of imprisonment **18 at a stretch** chiefly Brit & NZ **A** with some difficulty; by making a special effort **B** at one time: for hours at a stretch they had no conversation ▸ adj **19** (of clothes) able to be stretched without permanently losing shape: a stretch suit ▸ **stretchy** adj

stretch vb **1** = extend, cover, spread, reach, put forth, unroll **2, 3** = expand **7** = pull, distend, strain, tighten, draw out, elongate **8** = last, continue, go on, carry on, reach (informal) ▸ n **15** = expanse, area, tract, spread, distance, extent **16** = period, time, spell, stint, term, space

stretcher n a frame covered with canvas, on which an ill or injured person is carried

strew vb **strewing**, **strewed**, **strewn** to scatter (things) over a surface

stricken adj badly affected by disease, pain, grief, etc.: flood-stricken areas

strict adj **1** severely correct in attention to behaviour or morality: a strict disciplinarian **2** following carefully and exactly a set of rules: she is a strict vegetarian **3** (of a rule or law) very precise and requiring total obedience: a strict code of practice **4** (of a meaning) exact: this is not, in the strictest sense, a biography **5** (of a punishment, etc.) harsh or severe **6** complete; absolute: strict obedience ▸ **strictly** adv ▸ **strictness** n

strict adj **1** = stern, firm, severe, harsh, authoritarian **4** = exact, accurate, precise, close, true, faithful, meticulous, scrupulous **5** = severe, harsh, stern, firm, stringent; ≠ easy-going **6** = absolute, total, utter

stricture n formal a severe criticism

stride n **1** a long step or pace **2** the length of

such a step **3** a striding walk **4** progress or development: he has made great strides in regaining his confidence **5** a regular pace or rate of progress: it put me off my stride **6 take something in one's stride** to do something without difficulty or effort ▸ vb **striding**, **strode**, **stridden 7** to walk with long steps or paces **8 stride over** or **across** to cross (over a space or an obstacle) with a stride

strident adj **1** (of a voice or sound) loud and harsh **2** loud, persistent, and forceful: a strident critic of the establishment ▸ **stridency** n

strife n angry or violent struggle; conflict

strife n = conflict, battle, clash, quarrel, friction, discord, dissension

strike vb **striking**, **struck 1** (of employees) to stop work collectively as a protest against working conditions, low pay, etc. **2** to hit (someone) **3** to cause (something) to come into sudden or violent contact with something **4 strike at** to attack (someone or something) **5** to cause (a match) to light by friction **6** to sound (a specific note) on a musical instrument **7** (of a clock) to indicate (a time) by the sound of a bell **8** to affect (someone) deeply in a particular way: he never struck me as the supportive type **9** to enter the mind of: a brilliant thought struck me **10** (of a poisonous snake) to injure by biting **11** past participle **struck** or **stricken** to change into (a different state): struck blind **12** to be noticed by; catch: the heavy smell of incense struck my nostrils **13** to arrive at (something) suddenly or unexpectedly: to strike on a solution **14** to afflict (someone) with a disease: he was struck with polio when he was six **15** to discover (a source of (gold, oil, etc.) **16** to reach (something) by agreement: to strike a deal **17** to take up (a posture or an attitude) **18** to take apart or pack up: to strike camp **19** to make (a coin) by stamping it **20 strike home** to achieve the desired effect **21 strike it rich** informal to have an unexpected financial success ▸ n **22** a stopping of work, as a protest against working conditions, low pay, etc.: a one-day strike **23** an act or instance of striking **24** a military attack, esp. an air attack on a target on land or at sea: a pre-emptive strike **25** baseball a pitched ball swung at and missed by the batter **26** tenpin bowling the knocking down of all the pins with one bowl **27** the discovery of a source of gold, oil, etc. ▸ See also **strike off**, **strike up**

strike vb **1** = walk out, down tools, revolt, mutiny **2** = hit, smack, thump, beat, knock, punch, hammer, slap **3** = collide with, hit, run into, bump into **8** = seem to, appear to, look to, give the impression to **9** = occur to, hit, come to, register (informal), dawn on or upon **14** = affect, touch, devastate (informal), overwhelm, leave a mark on ▸ n **22** = walkout, industrial action, mutiny, revolt, stop-work or stop-work meeting (Austral)

strike off *vb* to remove the name of (a doctor or lawyer who has done something wrong) from an official register, preventing him or her from practising again

striker *n* 1 a person who is on strike 2 *soccer* an attacking player

strike up *vb* 1 to begin (a conversation or friendship) 2 (of a band or an orchestra) to begin to play (a tune)

striking *adj* 1 attracting attention; impressive: *her striking appearance* 2 very noticeable: *a striking difference* ▸ **strikingly** *adv*

> **striking** *adj* 1 = impressive, dramatic, outstanding, noticeable, conspicuous, jaw-dropping; ≠ unimpressive

string *n* 1 thin cord or twine used for tying, hanging, or binding things 2 a group of objects threaded on a single strand: *a string of pearls* 3 a series of things or events: *a string of wins* 4 a tightly stretched wire or cord on a musical instrument, such as the guitar, violin, or piano, that produces sound when vibrated 5 **the strings** *music* A violins, violas, cellos, and double basses collectively B the section of an orchestra consisting of such instruments 6 a group of characters that can be treated as a unit by a computer program 7 **with no strings attached** (of an offer) without complications or conditions 8 **pull strings** *informal* to use one's power or influence, esp. secretly or unofficially ▸ *adj* 9 composed of stringlike strands woven in a large mesh: *a string bag* ▸ *vb* **stringing, strung** 10 to hang or stretch (something) from one point to another 11 to provide (something) with a string or strings 12 to thread (beads) on a string 13 to extend in a line or series: *towns strung out along the valley* ▸ **stringlike** *adj*

> **string** *n* 1 = cord, twine, fibre 3 = series, line, row, file, sequence, succession, procession

string along *vb informal* 1 **string along with** to accompany: *I'll string along with you* 2 to deceive (someone) over a period of time: *she had only been stringing him along*

stringed *adj* (of musical instruments) having strings

stringent (strin-jent) *adj* requiring strict attention to rules or detail: *all have particularly stringent environmental laws* ▸ **stringency** *n*

> **stringent** *adj* = strict, tough, rigorous, tight, severe, rigid, inflexible; ≠ lax

string up *vb informal* to kill (a person) by hanging

stringy *adj* **stringier, stringiest** 1 thin and rough: *stringy hair* 2 (of meat or other food) tough and fibrous

stringy-bark *n* an Australian eucalyptus with a fibrous bark

strip¹ *vb* **stripping, stripped** 1 to take (the covering or clothes) off (oneself, another person, or thing) 2 A to undress completely B to perform a striptease 3 to empty (a building) of all furniture 4 to take something away from (someone): *they were stripped of their possessions* 5 to remove (paint) from (a surface or furniture): *she stripped the plaster from the kitchen walls* 6 (often foll. by *down*) to dismantle (an engine or a mechanism) into individual parts ▸ *n* 7 the act or an instance of undressing or of performing a striptease

> **strip** *vb* 1, 2A = undress, disrobe, unclothe 4 = plunder, rob, loot, empty, sack, ransack, pillage, divest

strip² *n* 1 a long narrow piece of something 2 short for **airstrip** 3 *Brit, Austral & NZ* the clothes a sports team plays in

> **strip** *n* 1 = piece, shred, band, belt

strip cartoon *n* a sequence of drawings in a newspaper or magazine, telling an amusing story or an adventure

stripe *n* 1 a long band of colour that differs from the surrounding material 2 a chevron or band worn on a uniform to indicate rank ▸ *vb* **striping, striped** 3 to mark (something) with stripes ▸ **striped, stripy** or **stripey** *adj*

stripling *n* a teenage boy or young man

stripper *n* 1 a person who performs a striptease 2 a tool or liquid for removing paint or varnish

striptease *n* an entertainment in which a person gradually undresses to music

strive *vb* **striving, strove, striven** to make a great effort: *to strive for a peaceful settlement*

> **strive** *vb* = try, labour, struggle, attempt, toil, go all out (*informal*), bend over backwards (*informal*), do your best

strobe *n* short for **stroboscope**

stroboscope *n* an instrument producing a very bright flashing light which makes moving people appear stationary

strode *vb* the past tense of **stride**

stroke *vb* **stroking, stroked** 1 to touch or brush lightly or gently ▸ *n* 2 a light touch or caress with the fingers 3 *pathol* rupture of a blood vessel in the brain resulting in loss of consciousness, often followed by paralysis and damage to speech 4 a blow, knock, or hit 5 an action or occurrence of the kind specified: *a fantastic stroke of luck*; *a stroke of intuition* 6 A the striking of a clock B the hour registered by this: *at the stroke of twelve* 7 a mark made by a pen or paintbrush 8 the hitting of the ball in sports such as golf or cricket 9 any one of the repeated movements used by a swimmer 10 a particular style of swimming, such as the crawl 11 a single pull on the oars in rowing 12 **at a stroke** with one action 13 **not a stroke (of work)** no work at all

> **stroke** *vb* = caress, rub, fondle, pet ▸ *n* 3 = apoplexy, fit, seizure, attack, collapse 4 = blow, hit, knock, pat, rap, thump, swipe (*informal*)

S

stroll *vb* **1** to walk about in a leisurely manner ▸ *n* **2** a leisurely walk

> **stroll** *vb* = walk, ramble, amble, promenade, saunter ▸ *n* = walk, promenade, constitutional, ramble, breath of air

strong *adj* **stronger**, **strongest** **1** having physical power **2** not easily broken or injured; solid or robust **3** great in degree or intensity; not faint or feeble: *a strong voice; a strong smell of explosive* **4** (of arguments) supported by evidence; convincing **5** concentrated; not weak or diluted **6** having a powerful taste or smell: *strong perfume* **7** (of language) using swear words **8** (of a person) self-confident: *a strong personality* **9** committed or fervent: *a strong believer in free trade* **10** important or having a lot of power or influence: *a strong left-wing tendency within the university* **11** very competent at a particular activity: *they sent a very strong team to the Olympics* **12** containing or having a specified number: *the 700-strong workforce* **13** (of an accent) distinct and indicating where the speaker comes from **14** (of a relationship) stable and likely to last **15** having an extreme or drastic effect: *strong discipline* **16** (of a colour) very bright and intense **17** (of a wind, current, or earthquake) moving fast or intensely **18** (of an economy, an industry, a currency, etc.) growing, successful, or increasing in value ▸ *adv* **19 come on strong** *informal* **A** to show blatantly that one is sexually attracted to someone **B** to make a forceful or exaggerated impression **20 going strong** *informal* working or performing well; thriving > **strongly** *adv*

> **strong** *adj* **1** = powerful, muscular, tough, athletic, strapping, hardy, sturdy, burly; ≠ weak **2** = durable, substantial, sturdy, heavy-duty, well-built, hard-wearing; ≠ flimsy **9** = keen, deep, acute, fervent, zealous, vehement **13** = distinct, marked, clear, unmistakable; ≠ slight **15** = extreme, radical, drastic, strict, harsh, rigid, forceful, uncompromising **16** = bright, brilliant, dazzling, bold; ≠ dull **18** = fit, robust, lusty

stronghold *n* **1** an area in which a particular belief is shared by many people: *a Labour stronghold* **2** a place that is well defended; fortress

> **stronghold** *n* = bastion, fortress, bulwark

strongroom *n* a specially designed room in which valuables are locked for safety

strontium *n chem* a soft silvery-white metallic element: *the radioactive isotope* **strontium-90** *is used in nuclear power sources and is a hazardous nuclear fallout product. Symbol:* **Sr**

strop *n* a leather strap for sharpening razors

stroppy *adj* **-pier**, **-piest** *informal* bad-tempered or deliberately awkward

strove *vb* the past tense of **strive**

struck *vb* a past of **strike**

structural *adj* **1** of or having structure or a structure **2** of or forming part of the structure of a building **3** *chem* of or involving the arrangement of atoms in molecules: *a structural formula* > **structurally** *adv*

structuralism *n* an approach to social sciences and to literature which sees changes in the subject as caused and organized by a hidden set of universal rules > **structuralist** *n*, *adj*

structure *n* **1** something that has been built or organized **2** the way the individual parts of something are made, built, or organized into a whole **3** the pattern of interrelationships within an organization, society, etc. **4** an organized method of working, thinking, or behaving **5** *chem* the arrangement of atoms in a molecule of a chemical compound **6** *geol* the way in which a rock is made up of its component parts ▸ *vb* **-turing**, **-tured** **7** to arrange (something) into an organized system or pattern: *a structured school curriculum*

> **structure** *n* **1** = building, construction, erection (*formal*), edifice **2** = arrangement, form, make-up, design, organization, construction, formation, configuration ▸ *vb* = arrange, organize, design, shape, build up, assemble

strudel *n* a thin sheet of filled dough rolled up and baked: *apple strudel*

struggle *vb* **-gling**, **-gled** **1** to work or strive: *the old regime struggled for power; he struggled to keep the conversation flowing* **2** to move about violently in an attempt to escape from something restricting **3** to fight with someone, often for possession of something **4** to go or progress with difficulty **5 struggle on** to manage to do something with difficulty ▸ *n* **6** something requiring a lot of exertion or effort to achieve **7** a fight or battle **8 the struggle** *S African* the concerted opposition to apartheid > **struggling** *adj*

> **struggle** *vb* **1** = strive, labour, toil, work, strain, go all out (*informal*), give it your best shot (*informal*), exert yourself **3** = fight, battle, wrestle, grapple, compete, contend ▸ *n* **7** = fight, battle, conflict, clash, contest, brush, combat, tussle, biffo (*Austral slang*)

strum *vb* **strumming**, **strummed** **1** to play (a stringed instrument) by sweeping the thumb or a plectrum across the strings **2** to play (a tune) in this way

strumpet *n archaic* a prostitute or promiscuous woman

strung *vb* the past of **string**

strut *vb* **strutting**, **strutted** **1** to walk in a stiff proud way with head high and shoulders back; swagger ▸ *n* **2** a piece of wood or metal that forms part of the framework of a structure

> **strut** *vb* = swagger, parade, peacock, prance

strychnine (strik-neen) *n* a very poisonous drug formerly used in small quantities as a stimulant

stub *n* **1** a short piece remaining after something has been used: *a cigarette stub* **2** the section of a ticket or cheque which the purchaser keeps as a receipt ▸ *vb* **stubbing, stubbed 3** to strike (one's toe or foot) painfully against a hard surface **4 stub out** to put out (a cigarette or cigar) by pressing the end against a surface

stubble *n* **1** the short stalks left in a field where a crop has been harvested **2** the short bristly hair on the chin of a man who has not shaved for a while ▸ **stubbly** *adj*

stubborn *adj* **1** refusing to agree or give in **2** persistent and determined **3** difficult to handle, treat, or overcome: *the most stubborn dandruff* ▸ **stubbornly** *adv* ▸ **stubbornness** *n*

> **stubborn** *adj* **1, 2** = obstinate, dogged, inflexible, persistent, intractable, tenacious, recalcitrant, unyielding; ≠ compliant

stubby *adj* **-bier, -biest** short and broad

stucco *n* **1** plaster used for coating or decorating outside walls ▸ *vb* **-coing, -coed 2** to apply stucco to (a building)

stuck *vb* **1** the past of **stick²** ▸ *adj* **2** *informal* baffled by a problem or unable to find an answer to a question **3 be stuck on** *slang* to feel a strong attraction to; be infatuated with **4 get stuck in** *informal* to perform a task with determination

> **stuck** *adj* **2** = baffled, stumped, beaten

stuck-up *adj informal* proud or snobbish

stud¹ *n* **1** a small piece of metal attached to a surface for decoration **2** a fastener consisting of two discs at either end of a short bar, usually used with clothes **3** one of several small round objects attached to the sole of a football boot to give better grip ▸ *vb* **studding, studded 4** to decorate or cover (something) with or as if with studs: *apartment houses studded with satellite dishes*

stud² *n* **1** a male animal, esp. a stallion kept for breeding **2** Also: **stud farm** a place where animals are bred **3** the state of being kept for breeding purposes **4** *slang* a virile or sexually active man

student *n* **1** a person following a course of study in a school, college, or university **2** a person who makes a thorough study of a subject: *a keen student of opinion polls*

> **student** *n* **1** = undergraduate, scholar **2** = learner, trainee, apprentice, disciple

studied *adj* carefully practised or planned: *studied calm*

> **studied** *adj* = planned, deliberate, conscious, intentional, premeditated; ≠ unplanned

studio *n, pl* **-dios 1** a room in which an artist, photographer, or musician works **2** a room used to record television or radio programmes or to make films or records **3 studios** the premises of a radio, television, record, or film company

> **studio** *n* **1** = workshop, workroom, atelier

studio flat *n Brit* a flat with one main room and, usually, a small kitchen and bathroom. Also called: **studio apartment**

studious (styoo-dee-uss) *adj* **1** serious, thoughtful, and hard-working **2** precise, careful, or deliberate ▸ **studiously** *adv*

study *vb* **studies, studying, studied 1** to be engaged in the learning or understanding of (a subject) **2** to investigate or examine (something) by observation and research **3** to look at (something or someone) closely; scrutinize ▸ *n, pl* **studies 4** the act or process of studying **5** a room used for studying, reading, or writing **6** (*often pl*) work relating to a particular area of learning: *environmental studies* **7** an investigation and analysis of a particular subject **8** a paper or book produced as a result of study **9** a work of art, such as a drawing, done for practice or in preparation for another work **10** a musical composition designed to develop playing technique

> **study** *vb* **1** = learn, cram (*informal*), swot (up) (*Brit informal*), read up, mug up (*Brit slang*) **2** = contemplate, read, examine, consider, go into, pore over **3** = examine, survey, look at, scrutinize ▸ *n* **4** = learning, lessons, school work, reading, research, swotting (*Brit informal*) **7** = examination, investigation, analysis, consideration, inspection, scrutiny, contemplation **8** = piece of research, survey, report, review, inquiry, investigation

stuff *n* **1** substance or material **2** any collection of unnamed things **3** the raw material of something **4** subject matter, skill, etc.: *this journalist knew his stuff* **5** woollen fabric **6 do one's stuff** *informal* to do what is expected of one ▸ *vb* **7** to pack or fill (something) completely; cram **8** to force, shove, or squeeze (something somewhere): *I stuffed it in my briefcase* **9** to fill (food such as poultry or tomatoes) with a seasoned mixture **10** to fill (a dead animal's skin) with material so as to restore the shape of the live animal **11** *slang* to frustrate or defeat **12 get stuffed!** *Brit, Austral & NZ slang* an exclamation of anger or annoyance with someone **13 stuff oneself** *or* **one's face** to eat a large amount of food

> **stuff** *n* **2** = things, gear, possessions, effects, equipment, objects, tackle, kit **3** = substance, material, essence, matter ▸ *vb* **7** = cram, fill, pack, crowd **8** = shove, force, push, squeeze, jam, ram

stuffing *n* **1** a mixture of ingredients with which poultry or meat is stuffed before cooking **2** the material used to fill and give shape to soft toys, pillows, furniture, etc.; padding

> **stuffing** *n* **2** = wadding, filling, packing

S

stuffy *adj* **-ier**, **-iest** 1 lacking fresh air 2 old-fashioned and very formal: *an image of stuffy tradition* > **stuffiness** *n*

stumble *vb* **-bling**, **-bled** 1 to trip and almost fall while walking or running 2 to walk in an unsteady or unsure way 3 to make mistakes or hesitate in speech 4 **stumble across** *or* **on** *or* **upon** to encounter or discover (someone or something) by accident ▸ *n* 5 an act of stumbling

> **stumble** *vb* 1 = trip, fall, slip, reel, stagger, falter, lurch 2 = totter, reel, lurch, wobble 4 **stumble across** *or* **on something or someone** = discover, find, come across, chance upon

stumbling block *n* any obstacle that prevents something from taking place or progressing

stump *n* 1 the base of a tree trunk left standing after the tree has been cut down or has fallen 2 the part of something, such as a tooth or limb, that remains after a larger part has been removed 3 *cricket* any of three upright wooden sticks that, with two bails laid across them, form a wicket ▸ *vb* 4 to baffle or confuse (someone) 5 *cricket* to dismiss (a batsman) by breaking his or her wicket with the ball 6 *chiefly US & Canad* to campaign or canvass (an area), by political speech-making 7 to walk with heavy steps; trudge

> **stump** *n* 2 = tail end, end, remnant, remainder ▸ *vb* 4 = baffle, confuse, puzzle, bewilder, perplex, mystify, flummox, nonplus

stump up *vb Brit informal* to give (the money required)

stumpy *adj* **stumpier**, **stumpiest** short and thick like a stump; stubby

stun *vb* **stunning**, **stunned** 1 to shock or astonish (someone) so that he or she is unable to speak or act 2 (of a heavy blow or fall) to make (a person or an animal) unconscious

> **stun** *vb* 1 = overcome, shock, confuse, astonish, stagger, bewilder, astound, overpower 2 = daze, knock out, stupefy, numb, benumb

stung *vb* the past of **sting**

stunk *vb* a past of **stink**

stunning *adj informal* very attractive or impressive > **stunningly** *adv*

> **stunning** *adj* = wonderful, beautiful, impressive, striking, lovely, spectacular, marvellous, splendid; ≠ unimpressive

stunt¹ *vb* to prevent or slow down (the growth or development of a plant, animal, or person) > **stunted** *adj*

stunt² *n* 1 an acrobatic or dangerous piece of action in a film or television programme 2 anything spectacular or unusual done to gain publicity ▸ *adj* 3 of or relating to acrobatic or dangerous pieces of action in films or television programmes: *a stunt man*

> **stunt** *n* 2 = feat, act, trick, exploit, deed

stupefaction *n* the state of being unable to think clearly because of tiredness or boredom

stupefy *vb* **-pefies**, **-pefying**, **-pefied** 1 to make (someone) feel so bored and tired that he or she is unable to think clearly 2 to confuse or astound (someone) > **stupefying** *adj*

stupendous *adj* very large or impressive > **stupendously** *adv*

stupid *adj* 1 lacking in common sense or intelligence 2 trivial, silly, or childish: *we got into a stupid quarrel* 3 unable to think clearly; dazed: *stupid with tiredness* > **stupidity** *n* > **stupidly** *adv*

> **stupid** *adj* 1 = unintelligent, thick, dim (*informal*), dense; ≠ intelligent 2 = silly, foolish, daft (*informal*), rash, pointless, senseless, idiotic, fatuous; ≠ sensible 3 = senseless, dazed, groggy, insensate, semiconscious

stupor *n* a state of near unconsciousness in which a person is unable to behave normally or think clearly

sturdy *adj* **-dier**, **-diest** 1 (of a person) healthy, strong, and unlikely to tire or become injured 2 (of a piece of furniture, shoes, etc.) strongly built or made > **sturdily** *adv*

> **sturdy** *adj* 1 = robust, hardy, powerful, athletic, muscular, lusty, brawny; ≠ puny 2 = substantial, solid, durable, well-made, well-built; ≠ flimsy

sturgeon *n* a bony fish from which caviar is obtained

stutter *vb* 1 to speak (a word or phrase) with involuntary repetition of initial consonants ▸ *n* 2 the tendency to involuntarily repeat initial consonants while speaking > **stuttering** *n*

sty *n, pl* **sties** a pen in which pigs are kept

stye *or* **sty** *n, pl* **styes** *or* **sties** inflammation of a gland at the base of an eyelash

style *n* 1 a form of appearance, design, or production: *I like that style of dress* 2 the way in which something is done: *a new style of command* 3 elegance or refinement of manners and dress: *he has bags of style* 4 a distinctive manner of expression in words, music, painting, etc.: *a painting in the Expressionist style* 5 popular fashion in dress and looks: *the old ones had gone out of style* 6 a fashionable or showy way of life: *the newly rich could dine in style* 7 the particular kind of spelling, punctuation, and design followed by a book, journal, or publishing house 8 *botany* the stemlike part of a flower that bears the stigma ▸ *vb* **styling**, **styled** 9 to design, shape, or tailor: *neatly styled hair* 10 to name or call: *Walsh, who styled himself the Memory Man*

style n 1 = design, form, cut 2 = manner, way, method, approach, technique, mode 3 = elegance, taste, chic, flair (informal), polish, sophistication, panache, flamboyance, élan 5 = fashion, trend, mode, vogue, rage 6 = luxury, ease, comfort, elegance, grandeur, affluence ▸ vb 9 = design, cut, tailor, fashion, shape, arrange, adapt 10 = call, name, term, label, entitle, dub, designate

stylish adj smart, fashionable, and attracting attention > **stylishly** adv

stylish adj = smart, chic, fashionable, trendy (Brit informal), modish, dressy (informal), voguish, schmick (Austral informal), funky; ≠ scruffy

stylist n 1 a hairdresser who styles hair 2 a person who performs, writes, or acts with great attention to the particular style he or she employs

stylistic adj of the techniques used in creating or performing a work of art: there are many stylistic problems facing the performers of Baroque music > **stylistically** adv

stylus n a needle-like device in the pick-up arm of a record player that rests in the groove in the record and picks up the sound signals

stymie vb -mieing, -mied 1 to hinder or foil (someone): the President was stymied by a reluctant Congress ▸ n, pl -mies 2 golf (formerly) a situation in which an opponent's ball is blocking the line between the hole and the ball about to be played

styptic adj 1 used to stop bleeding: a styptic pencil ▸ n 2 a styptic drug

suave (swahv) adj (esp. of a man) smooth, confident, and sophisticated > **suavely** adv

sub n 1 short for **subeditor, submarine, subscription** or **substitute** 2 Brit informal an advance payment of wages or salary. Formal term: **subsistence allowance** ▸ vb **subbing, subbed** 3 to act as a substitute

sub- or before r **sur-** prefix 1 situated under or beneath: subterranean 2 secondary in rank; subordinate: sublieutenant 3 falling short of; less than or imperfectly: subarctic; subhuman 4 forming a subdivision or less important part: subcommittee

subaltern n a British army officer below the rank of captain

subatomic adj physics of, relating to, or being one of the particles making up an atom

subcommittee n a small committee consisting of members of a larger committee and which is set up to look into a particular matter

subconscious adj 1 happening or existing without one's awareness ▸ n 2 psychol the part of the mind that contains memories and motives of which one is not aware but which can influence one's behaviour > **subconsciously** adv

subcontinent n a large land mass that is a distinct part of a continent, such as India is of Asia

subcontract n 1 a secondary contract by which the main contractor for a job puts work out to another company ▸ vb 2 to let out (work) on a subcontract > **subcontractor** n

subcutaneous (sub-cute-ayn-ee-uss) adj med beneath the skin

subdivide vb -viding, -vided to divide (a part of something) into smaller parts > **subdivision** n

subdue vb -duing, -dued 1 to overcome and bring (a person or people) under control by persuasion or force 2 to make (feelings, colour, or lighting) less intense

subdue vb 1 = overcome, defeat, master, break, control, crush, conquer, tame 2 = moderate, suppress, soften, mellow, tone down, quieten down; ≠ arouse

subeditor n a person who checks and edits text for a newspaper or other publication

subject (sub-ject) n 1 the person, thing, or topic being dealt with or discussed 2 any branch of learning considered as a course of study 3 a person, object, idea, or scene portrayed in a work of art 4 grammar a word or phrase that represents the person or thing performing the action of the verb in a sentence; for example, the cat in the sentence The cat catches mice 5 a person or thing that undergoes an experiment or treatment 6 a person under the rule of a monarch or government: Zambian subjects ▸ adj 7 being under the rule of a monarch or government: a subject race 8 **subject to** A showing a tendency towards: they are expensive and subject to overruns in cost and time B exposed or vulnerable to: subject to ridicule C conditional upon: pay is subject to negotiation ▸ adv 9 **subject to** under the condition that something takes place: my visit was agreed subject to certain conditions ▸ vb (sub-ject) 10 **subject to** A to cause (someone) to experience (something unpleasant): they were subjected to beatings B to bring under the control or authority of: to subject a soldier to discipline > **subjection** n

subject n 1 = topic, question, issue, matter, point, business, affair, object 6 = citizen, resident, native, inhabitant, national ▸ adj 8A, 8B **subject to** = liable to, open to, exposed to, vulnerable to, prone to, susceptible to 8C **subject to** = dependent on, contingent on, controlled by, conditional on ▸ adv **subject to** = bound by ▸ vb **subject to** = put through, expose, submit, lay open

subjective adj 1 of or based on a person's emotions or prejudices ▸ n 2 grammar the grammatical case in certain languages that identifies the subject of a verb > **subjectively** adv

subjective adj = personal, prejudiced, biased, nonobjective; ≠ objective

S

sub judice (sub joo-diss-ee) *adj* before a court of law: *he declined to comment on the case saying it was sub judice*

subjugate *vb* **-gating, -gated** to bring (a group of people) under one's control ▸ **subjugation** *n*

subjunctive *grammar* ▸ *adj* **1** denoting a mood of verbs used when the content of the clause is being doubted, supposed, or feared true, for example *were* in the sentence *I'd be careful if I were you* ▸ *n* **2** the subjunctive mood

sublet *vb* **-letting, -let** to rent out (property which one is renting from someone else)

sublimate *vb* **-mating, -mated** *psychol* to direct the energy of (a strong desire, esp. a sexual one) into activities that are socially more acceptable ▸ **sublimation** *n*

sublime *adj* **1** causing deep emotions and feelings of wonder or joy **2** without equal; supreme **3** of great moral, artistic, or spiritual value ▸ *n* **4 the sublime** something that is sublime ▸ *vb* **-liming, -limed 5** *chem & physics* to change directly from a solid to a vapour without first melting ▸ **sublimely** *adv*

> **sublime** *adj* **1, 3** = noble, glorious, high, great, grand, elevated, lofty, exalted; ≠ lowly

subliminal *adj* resulting from or relating to mental processes of which the individual is not aware: *the subliminal message*

sub-machine-gun *n* a portable automatic or semiautomatic gun with a short barrel

submarine *n* **1** a vessel which can operate below the surface of the sea ▸ *adj* **2** existing or located below the surface of the sea: *submarine cables* ▸ **submariner** *n*

submerge *vb* **-merging, -merged 1** to put or go below the surface of water or another liquid **2** to involve totally: *she submerged herself in her work* ▸ **submersion** *n*

> **submerge** *vb* **1** = immerse, plunge, duck **2** = overwhelm, swamp, engulf, deluge

submission *n* **1** an act or instance of capitulation **2** the act of submitting (something) **3** something submitted, such as a proposal **4** the state in which someone has to accept the control of another person

> **submission** *n* **1** = surrender, yielding, giving in, cave-in (*informal*), capitulation **2** = presentation, handing in, entry, tendering **4** = compliance, obedience, meekness, resignation, deference, passivity, docility

submissive *adj* showing quiet obedience ▸ **submissively** *adv* ▸ **submissiveness** *n*

submit *vb* **-mitting, -mitted 1** to accept the will of another person or a superior force **2** to send (an application or proposal) to someone for judgment or consideration **3** to be voluntarily subjected (to medical or psychiatric treatment)

submit *vb* **1** = surrender, yield, give in, agree, endure, tolerate, comply, succumb **2** = present, hand in, tender, put forward, table (*Brit*), proffer

subordinate *adj* **1** of lesser rank or importance ▸ *n* **2** a person or thing that is of lesser rank or importance ▸ *vb* **-nating, -nated 3** (usually foll. by *to*) to regard (something) as less important than another: *the army's interests were subordinated to those of the air force* ▸ **subordination** *n*

> **subordinate** *adj* = inferior, lesser, lower, junior, subject, minor, secondary, dependent; ≠ superior ▸ *n* = inferior, junior, assistant, aide, second, attendant; ≠ superior

suborn *vb formal* to bribe or incite (a person) to commit a wrongful act

subpoena (sub-pee-na) *n* **1** a legal document requiring a person to appear before a court of law at a specified time ▸ *vb* **-naing, -naed 2** to summon (someone) with a subpoena

subprime *adj* **1** (of a loan) made to a borrower with a poor credit rating: *subprime mortgage* ▸ *n* **2** such a loan

subscribe *vb* **-scribing, -scribed 1** (usually foll. by *to*) to pay (money) as a contribution (to a charity, for a magazine, etc.) at regular intervals **2 subscribe to** to give support or approval to: *I do not subscribe to this view* ▸ **subscriber** *n*

> **subscribe** *vb* **1** = contribute to, give to, donate to **2** = support, advocate, endorse

subscription *n* **1** a payment for issues of a publication over a specified period of time **2** money paid or promised, such as to a charity, or the fund raised in this way **3** *Brit, Austral & NZ* the membership fees paid to a society **4** an advance order for a new product

> **subscription** *n* **3** = membership fee, dues, annual payment

subsection *n* any of the smaller parts into which a section may be divided

subsequent *adj* occurring after; succeeding ▸ **subsequently** *adv*

> **subsequent** *adj* = following, later, succeeding, after, successive, ensuing; ≠ previous

subservient *adj* **1** overeager to carry out someone else's wishes **2** of less importance or rank: *a loyal, subservient ally* ▸ **subservience** *n*

subside *vb* **-siding, -sided 1** to become less loud, excited, or violent **2** to sink to a lower level **3** (of the surface of the earth) to cave in; collapse ▸ **subsidence** *n*

> **subside** *vb* **1** = decrease, diminish, lessen, ease, wane, ebb, abate, slacken); ≠ increase **3** = collapse, sink, cave in, drop, lower, settle

subsidiary *n, pl* **-aries 1** Also called: **subsidiary company** a company which is at least half owned by another company **2** a person or thing that is of lesser importance ▸ *adj* **3** of lesser importance; subordinate

> **subsidiary** *adj* = secondary, lesser, subordinate, minor, supplementary, auxiliary, ancillary; ≠ main

subsidize *or* **-dise** *vb* **-dizing, -dized** *or* **-dising, -dised** to aid or support (an industry, a person, a public service, or a venture) with money

subsidy *n, pl* **-dies 1** financial aid supplied by a government, for example to industry, or for public welfare **2** any financial aid, grant, or contribution

> **subsidy** *n* = aid, help, support, grant, assistance, allowance

subsist *vb* **subsist on** to manage to live on: *to subsist on a diet of sausage rolls* › **subsistence** *n*

subsonic *adj* being or moving at a speed below that of sound

substance *n* **1** the basic matter of which a thing consists **2** a specific type of matter with definite or fairly definite chemical composition: *a fatty substance* **3** the essential meaning of a speech, thought, or written article **4** important or meaningful quality: *the only evidence of substance against him* **5** material possessions or wealth: *a woman of substance* **6 in substance** with regard to the most important points

> **substance** *n* **1** = material, body, stuff, fabric **3** = meaning, main point, gist, import, significance, essence **4** = importance, significance, concreteness **5** = wealth, means, property, assets, resources, estate

substantial *adj* **1** of a considerable size or value: *a substantial amount of money* **2** (of food or a meal) large and filling **3** solid or strong: *substantial brick pillars* **4** *formal* available to the senses; real: *substantial evidence* **5** of or relating to the basic material substance of a thing › **substantially** *adv*

> **substantial** *adj* **1** = big, significant, considerable, large, important, ample, sizable *or* sizeable; ≠ small

substantiate *vb* **-ating, -ated** to establish (a story) as genuine › **substantiation** *n*

substantive *n* **1** *grammar* a noun or pronoun used in place of a noun ▸ *adj* **2** having importance or significance: *substantive negotiations between management and staff* **3** of or being the essential element of a thing

substitute *vb* **-tuting, -tuted 1** (often foll. by *for*) to take the place of or put in place of another person or thing **2** *chem* to replace (an atom or group in a molecule) with (another atom or group) ▸ *n* **3** a person or thing that takes the place of another, such as a player who takes the place of a team-mate › **substitution** *n*

> **substitute** *vb* **1** = replace, exchange, swap, change, switch, interchange ▸ *n* = replacement, reserve, surrogate, deputy, sub, proxy, locum

subsume *vb* **-suming, -sumed** *formal* to include (something) under a larger classification or group: *an attempt to subsume fascism and communism under a general concept of totalitarianism*

subterfuge *n* a trick or deception used to achieve an objective

subterranean *adj* **1** found or operating below the surface of the earth **2** existing or working in a concealed or mysterious way: *the resistance movement worked largely by subterranean methods*

subtitle *n* **1 subtitles** *films* a written translation at the bottom of the picture in a film with foreign dialogue **2** a secondary title given to a book or play ▸ *vb* **-tling, -tled 3** to provide subtitles for (a film) or a subtitle for (a book or play)

subtle *adj* **1** not immediately obvious: *a subtle change in his views* **2** (of a colour, taste, or smell) delicate or faint: *the subtle aroma* **3** using shrewd and indirect methods to achieve an objective **4** having or requiring the ability to make fine distinctions: *a subtle argument* › **subtly** *adv*

> **subtle** *adj* **1,2** = faint, slight, implied, delicate, understated; ≠ obvious **3** = crafty, cunning, sly, shrewd, ingenious, devious, wily, artful; ≠ straightforward **4** = fine, minute, narrow, tenuous, hair-splitting

subtlety *n* **1** *pl* **-ties** a fine distinction **2** the state or quality of being subtle

> **subtlety** *n* **1** = fine point, refinement, sophistication, delicacy **2** = skill, ingenuity, cleverness, deviousness, craftiness, artfulness, slyness, wiliness

subtract *vb* **1** *maths* to take (one number or quantity) away from another **2** to remove (a part of something) from the whole › **subtraction** *n*

subtropical *adj* of the region lying between the tropics and temperate lands

suburb *n* a residential district on the outskirts of a city or town

suburban *adj* **1** of, in, or inhabiting a suburb **2** *derogatory* conventional and unexciting

suburbia *n* suburbs or the people living in them considered as a distinct community or class in society

subvention *n* *formal* a grant or subsidy, for example one from a government

subversion *n* the act or an instance of attempting to weaken or overthrow a government or an institution

subversive *adj* **1** intended or intending to weaken or overthrow a government or an institution ▸ *n* **2** a person engaged in subversive activities

> **subversive** *adj* = seditious, riotous, treasonous ▸ *n* = dissident, terrorist, saboteur, fifth columnist

S

subvert *vb* to bring about the downfall of (something existing by a system of law, such as a government)

subway *n* **1** *Brit & Austral* an underground passage for pedestrians to cross a road or railway **2** an underground railway

succeed *vb* **1** to achieve an aim **2** to turn out satisfactorily: *Grandfather's plan succeeded* **3** to do well in a specified field: *how to succeed in show biz* **4** to come next in order after (someone or something): *the first shock had been succeeded by a different kind of gloom* **5** to take over (a position) from (someone): *Henry VIII succeeded to the throne in 1509; he will be succeeded as president by his deputy* > **succeeding** *adj*

> **succeed** *vb* **1** = triumph, win, prevail **2** = work out, work, be successful **3** = make it (*informal*), do well, be successful, triumph, thrive, flourish, make good, prosper; ≠ fail **4** = follow, come after, follow after; ≠ precede **5** = take over from, assume the office of

success *n* **1** the achievement of something attempted **2** the attainment of wealth, fame, or position **3** a person or thing that is successful

> **success** *n* **1** = victory, triumph; ≠ failure **2** = prosperity, fortune, luck, fame **3** = hit (*informal*), winner, smash (*informal*), triumph, sensation; ≠ flop *informal*

successful *adj* **1** having a favourable outcome **2** having attained fame, wealth, or position > **successfully** *adv*

> **successful** *adj* **1** = triumphant, victorious, lucky, fortunate **2** = thriving, profitable, rewarding, booming, flourishing, fruitful; ≠ unprofitable

succession *n* **1** a number of people or things following one another in order **2** the act or right by which one person succeeds another in a position **3** **in succession** one after another: *the third time in succession*

> **succession** *n* **1** = series, run, sequence, course, order, train, chain, cycle **2** = taking over, assumption, inheritance, accession

successive *adj* following another or others without interruption: *eleven successive victories* > **successively** *adv*

> **successive** *adj* = consecutive, following, in succession

successor *n* a person or thing that follows another, esp. a person who takes over another's job or position

succinct *adj* brief and clear: *a succinct answer to this question* > **succinctly** *adv*

succour *or US* **succor** *n* **1** help in time of difficulty ▸ *vb* **2** to give aid to (someone in time of difficulty)

succulent *adj* **1** (of food) juicy and delicious **2** (of plants) having thick fleshy leaves or stems ▸ *n* **3** a plant that can exist in very dry conditions by using water stored in its fleshy tissues > **succulence** *n*

succumb *vb* **succumb to A** to give way to the force of or desire for (something) **B** to die of (a disease)

such *adj* **1** of the sort specified or understood: *such places* **2** so great or so much: *such a mess* ▸ *adv* **3** extremely: *such a powerful friend* ▸ *pron* **4** a person or thing of the sort specified or understood: *such is the law of the land; fruitcakes and puddings and such* **5** **as such** in itself or themselves: *the Nordic countries are not lifting sanctions as such* **6** **such as** for example: *other socialist groups, such as the Fabians*

suchlike *n* **1** such or similar things: *shampoos, talcs, and suchlike* ▸ *adj* **2** of such a kind; similar: *astrology and suchlike nonsense*

suck *vb* **1** to draw (a liquid) into the mouth through pursed lips **2** to take (something) into the mouth and moisten, dissolve, or roll it around with the tongue: *suck a mint* **3** to extract liquid from (a solid food): *he sat sucking orange segments* **4** to draw in (fluid) as if by sucking: *the mussel sucks in water* **5** to drink milk from (a mother's breast); suckle **6** (often foll. by *down* or *in*, *etc.*) to draw (a thing or person somewhere) with a powerful force **7** *slang* to be contemptible or disgusting ▸ *n* **8** a sucking

> **suck** *vb* **1** = drink, sip, draw **4** = take, draw, pull, extract

sucker *n* **1** *slang* a person who is easily deceived or swindled **2** *slang* a person who cannot resist something: *he's a sucker for fast cars* **3** *zool* a part of the body of certain animals that is used for sucking or sticking to a surface **4** a rubber cup-shaped device attached to objects allowing them to stick to a surface by suction **5** *botany* a strong shoot coming from a mature plant's root or the base of its main stem

suckle *vb* **-ling, -led** to give (a baby or young animal) milk from the breast or udder or (of a baby or young animal) to suck milk from its mother's breast or udder

suckling *n* a baby or young animal that is still sucking milk from its mother's breast or udder

suck up to *vb informal* to flatter (a person in authority) in order to get something, such as praise or promotion

sucrose (soo-kroze) *n chem* sugar

suction *n* **1** the act or process of sucking **2** the force produced by drawing air out of a space to make a vacuum that will suck in a substance from another space

sudden *adj* **1** occurring or performed quickly and without warning ▸ *n* **2** **all of a sudden** without warning; unexpectedly > **suddenly** *adv* > **suddenness** *n*

S

sudden *adj* = quick, rapid, unexpected, swift, hurried, abrupt, hasty; ≠ gradual

sudden death *n sport* an extra period of play to decide the winner of a tied competition: the first player or team to go into the lead is the winner

sudoku (soo-**doh**-koo) *n* a logic puzzle involving the insertion of numbers so that none is repeated in the same row, column, or internal square of a larger square

sudorific (syoo-dor-**if**-ik) *adj* **1** causing sweating ▸ *n* **2** a drug that causes sweating

suds *pl n* the bubbles on the surface of water in which soap or detergent has been dissolved; lather

sue *vb* **suing, sued** to start legal proceedings (against): *we want to sue the council; he sued for custody of the three children*

sue *vb* = take (someone) to court, prosecute, charge, summon, indict

suede *n* a leather with a fine velvet-like surface on one side

suet *n* a hard fat obtained from sheep and cattle and used for making pastry and puddings

suffer *vb* **1** to undergo or be subjected to (physical pain or mental distress) **2 suffer from** to be badly affected by (an illness): *he was suffering from flu* **3** to become worse in quality; deteriorate: *his work suffered during their divorce* **4** to tolerate: *he suffers no fools* **5** to be set at a disadvantage: *the strongest of them suffers by comparison* > **sufferer** *n* > **suffering** *n*

suffer *vb* **1** = be in pain, hurt, ache **4** = tolerate, stand, put up with (*informal*), bear, endure

sufferance *n* **on sufferance** tolerated with reluctance: *I was there on sufferance and all knew it*

suffice (suf-**fice**) *vb* **-ficing, -ficed 1** to be enough or satisfactory for a purpose **2 suffice it to say ...** it is enough to say ...: *suffice it to say that the overall result was very good*

suffice *vb* **1** = be enough, do, be sufficient, be adequate, serve, meet requirements, tick all the boxes

sufficiency *n, pl* **-cies** an adequate amount

sufficient *adj* enough to meet a need or purpose; adequate > **sufficiently** *adv*

sufficient *adj* = adequate, enough, ample, satisfactory; ≠ insufficient

suffix *grammar* ▸ *n* **1** a letter or letters added to the end of a word to form another word, such as *-s* and *-ness* in *dogs* and *softness* ▸ *vb* **2** to add (a letter or letters) to the end of a word to form another word

suffocate *vb* **-cating, -cated 1** to kill or die through lack of oxygen, such as by blockage of the air passage **2** to feel uncomfortable from heat and lack of air > **suffocating** *adj* > **suffocation** *n*

suffragan *n* a bishop appointed to assist an archbishop

suffrage *n* the right to vote in public elections

suffragette *n* (in Britain at the beginning of the 20th century) a woman who campaigned militantly for women to be given the right to vote in public elections

suffuse *vb* **-fusing, -fused** to spread through or over (something): *the dawn suffused the sky with a cold grey wash* > **suffusion** *n*

sugar *n* **1** a sweet carbohydrate, usually in the form of white or brown crystals, which is found in many plants and is used to sweeten food and drinks **2** *informal, chiefly US & Canad* a term of affection ▸ *vb* **3** to add sugar to (food or drink) to make it sweet **4** to cover with sugar: *sugared almonds* **5 sugar the pill** to make something unpleasant more tolerable by adding something pleasant > **sugared** *adj*

sugar beet *n* a beet grown for the sugar obtained from its roots

sugar cane *n* a tropical grass grown for the sugar obtained from its tall stout canes

sugar daddy *n* an elderly man who gives a young person money and gifts in return for their company

sugar glider *n* a common phalanger that glides from tree to tree feeding on insects and nectar

sugary *adj* **1** of, like, or containing sugar: *sugary snacks* **2** (of behaviour or language) very pleasant but probably not sincere: *sugary sentiment* > **sugariness** *n*

suggest *vb* **1** to put forward (a plan or an idea) for consideration: *he didn't suggest a meeting* **2** to bring (a person or thing) to the mind by the association of ideas: *a man whose very name suggests blandness* **3** to give a hint of: *her grey eyes suggesting a livelier mood than usual*

suggest *vb* **1** = recommend, propose, advise, advocate, prescribe **2** = bring to mind, evoke **3** = indicate

suggestible *adj* easily influenced by other people's ideas

suggestion *n* **1** something that is suggested **2** a hint or indication: *the entire castle gave no suggestion of period* **3** *psychol* the process whereby the presentation of an idea to a receptive individual leads to the acceptance of that idea

suggestion *n* **1** = recommendation, proposal, proposition, plan, motion **2** = hint, insinuation, intimation

suggestive *adj* **1** (of remarks or gestures) causing people to think of sex **2 suggestive of** communicating a hint of

suicidal *adj* **1** wanting to die by suicide **2** likely to lead to danger or death: *a suicidal attempt to rescue her son* **3** likely to destroy one's own career or future: *it would be suicidal for them to ignore public opinion*

suicide *n* **1** the act of killing oneself deliberately **2** a person who kills himself or herself intentionally **3** the self-inflicted ruin of one's own career or future: *such a cut would be political suicide*

suit *n* **1** a set of clothes of the same material designed to be worn together, usually a jacket with matching trousers or skirt **2** an outfit worn for a specific purpose: *a diving suit* **3** a legal action taken against someone; lawsuit **4** any of the four types of card in a pack of playing cards: spades, hearts, diamonds, or clubs **5** *slang* a business executive or white-collar worker **6 follow suit** to act in the same way as someone else **7 strong suit** *or* **strongest suit** something one excels in ▶ *vb* **8** to be fit or appropriate for: *that colour suits you* **9** to be acceptable to (someone) **10 suit oneself** to do what one wants without considering other people > **suited** *adj*

> **suit** *n* **2** = outfit, costume, ensemble, dress, clothing, habit **3** = lawsuit, case, trial, proceeding, cause, action, prosecution ▶ *vb* **8** = agree with, become, match, go with, harmonize with **9** = be acceptable to, please, satisfy, do, gratify

suitable *adj* appropriate for a particular function or occasion; proper > **suitability** *n* > **suitably** *adv*

> **suitable** *adj* = appropriate, right, fitting, fit, becoming, satisfactory, apt, befitting; ≠ inappropriate

suitcase *n* a large portable travelling case for clothing

suite *n* **1** a set of connected rooms in a hotel **2** a matching set of furniture, for example two armchairs and a settee **3** *music* a composition of several movements in the same key

> **suite** *n* **1** = rooms, apartment

suitor *n* **1** *old-fashioned* a man who wants to marry a woman **2** *law* a person who starts legal proceedings against someone; plaintiff

sulk *vb* **1** to be silent and moody as a way of showing anger or resentment: *I went home and sulked for two days* ▶ *n* **2** a mood in which one shows anger or resentment by being silent and moody: *he was just in a sulk*

sulky *adj* **sulkier**, **sulkiest** moody or silent because of anger or resentment > **sulkily** *adv* > **sulkiness** *n*

sullen *adj* unwilling to talk or be sociable; sulky > **sullenly** *adv* > **sullenness** *n*

sully *vb* **-lies**, **-lying**, **-lied** **1** to ruin (someone's reputation) **2** to spoil or make dirty: *the stream had been sullied by the smelter's pollution*

sulphate *or US* **sulfate** *n chem* a salt or ester of sulphuric acid

sulphide *or US* **sulfide** *n chem* a compound of sulphur with another element

sulphite *or US* **sulfite** *n chem* any salt or ester of sulphurous acid

sulphonamide *or US* **sulfonamide** (sulf-**on**-a-mide) *n pharmacol* any of a class of organic compounds that prevent the growth of bacteria

sulphur *or US* **sulfur** *n chem* a light yellow, highly inflammable, nonmetallic element used in the production of sulphuric acid, in the vulcanization of rubber, and in medicine. Symbol: **S** > **sulphuric** *or US* **sulfuric** *adj*

sultan *n* the sovereign of a Muslim country

sultana *n* **1** the dried fruit of a small white seedless grape **2** a sultan's wife, mother, daughter, or concubine

sultanate *n* **1** the territory ruled by a sultan **2** the office or rank of a sultan

sultry *adj* **-trier**, **-triest** **1** (of weather or climate) very hot and humid **2** suggesting hidden passion: *a sultry brunette*

sum *n* **1** the result of the addition of numbers or quantities **2** one or more columns or rows of numbers to be added, subtracted, multiplied, or divided **3** a quantity of money: *they can win enormous sums* **4 in sum** as a summary; in short: *in sum, it's been a bad week for the government* ▶ *adj* **5** complete or final: *the sum total* ▶ *vb* **summing**, **summed** **6** See **sum up**

> **sum** *n* **1** = total, aggregate **2** = calculation, figures, arithmetic, mathematics, maths (*Brit informal*), tally, math (*US informal*), arithmetical problem **3** = amount, quantity, volume

summarize *or* **-rise** *vb* **-rizing**, **-rized** *or* **-rising**, **-rised** to give a short account of (something)

> **summarize** *or* **-rise** *vb* = sum up, condense, encapsulate, epitomize, abridge, précis

summary *n*, *pl* **-maries** **1** a brief account giving the main points of something ▶ *adj* **2** performed quickly, without formality or attention to details: *a summary judgment* > **summarily** *adv*

> **summary** *n* = synopsis, résumé, précis, review, outline, rundown, abridgment

summation *n* **1** a summary of what has just been done or said **2** the process of working out a sum; addition **3** the result of such a process

summer *n* **1** the warmest season of the year, between spring and autumn **2** *literary* a time of youth, success, or happiness > **summery** *adj*

summerhouse *n* a small building in a garden, used for shade in the summer

summertime *n* the period or season of summer

summit *n* **1** the highest point or part of a mountain or hill **2** the highest possible degree or state; peak or climax: *the summit of success* **3** a meeting of heads of governments or other high officials

> **summit** *n* **1** = peak, top, tip, pinnacle, apex, head; ≠ base **2** = height, pinnacle, peak, zenith, acme; ≠ depths

S

summon vb **1** to order (someone) to come
2 to send for (someone) to appear in court
3 to call upon (someone) to do something: *the authorities had summoned the relatives to be available* **4** to convene (a meeting) **5** (often foll. by *up*) to call into action (one's strength, courage, etc.); muster

> **summon** vb **1, 3** = send for, call, bid, invite
> **5** = gather, muster, draw on

summons n, pl **-monses 1** a call or an order to attend a specified place at a specified time **2** an official order requiring a person to attend court, either to answer a charge or to give evidence ▸ vb **3** to order (someone) to appear in court: *three others had been summonsed for questioning*

sumo n the national style of wrestling of Japan, in which two contestants of great height and weight attempt to force each other out of the ring

sump n **1** a container in an internal-combustion engine into which oil can drain **2** same as **cesspool 3** *mining* a hollow at the bottom of a shaft where water collects

sumptuous adj magnificent and very expensive; splendid: *sumptuous decoration*

> **sumptuous** adj = luxurious, grand, superb, splendid, gorgeous, lavish, opulent; ≠ plain

sum up vb **1** to give a short account of (the main points of an argument, speech, or piece of writing) **2** to form a quick opinion of: *how well you have summed me up!*

sun n **1** the star that is the source of heat and light for the planets in the solar system. Related adjective: **solar 2** any star around which a system of planets revolves **3** the heat and light received from the sun; sunshine **4 catch the sun** to become slightly suntanned **5 under the sun** on earth; at all: *there are no free lunches under the sun* ▸ vb **sunning, sunned 6 sun oneself** to lie, sit, or walk in the sunshine on a warm day
> **sunless** adj

sunbathe vb **-bathing, -bathed** to lie or sit in the sunshine, in order to get a suntan
> **sunbather** n > **sunbathing** n

sunbeam n a ray of sunlight

sunburn n painful reddening of the skin caused by overexposure to the sun > **sunburnt** or **sunburned** adj

sundae n ice cream topped with a sweet sauce, nuts, whipped cream, and fruit

Sunday n the first day of the week and the Christian day of worship

Sunday school n a school for teaching children about Christianity, usually held in a church hall on Sunday

sundial n a device used for telling the time during the hours of sunlight, consisting of a pointer that casts a shadow onto a surface marked in hours

sundown n US sunset

sundries pl n several things of various sorts

sundry adj **1** several or various; miscellaneous
▸ pron **2 all and sundry** everybody

sunflower n **1** a very tall plant with large yellow flowers **2 sunflower seed oil** the oil extracted from sunflower seeds, used as a salad oil and in margarine

sung vb the past participle of **sing**

sunk vb a past participle of **sink**

sunken vb **1** a past participle of **sink** ▸ adj **2** (of a person's cheeks, eyes, or chest) curving inward due to old age or bad health **3** situated at a lower level than the surrounding or usual one: *the sunken garden* **4** situated under water; submerged: *sunken ships*

sunny adj **-nier, -niest 1** full of or lit up by sunshine **2** cheerful and happy

> **sunny** adj **1** = bright, clear, fine, radiant, sunlit, summery, unclouded; ≠ dull
> **2** = cheerful, happy, cheery, buoyant, joyful, light-hearted; ≠ gloomy

sunrise n **1** the daily appearance of the sun above the horizon **2** the time at which the sun rises

sunscreen n a cream or lotion applied to exposed skin to reduce the effect of the ultraviolet rays of the sun

sunset n **1** the daily disappearance of the sun below the horizon **2** the time at which the sun sets

> **sunset** n = nightfall, dusk, eventide, close of (the) day

sunshine n **1** the light and warmth from the sun **2** *Brit* a light-hearted term of address

sunspot n **1** *informal* a sunny holiday resort **2** a dark cool patch on the surface of the sun **3** *Austral* a small area of skin damage caused by exposure to the sun

sunstroke n a condition caused by spending too much time exposed to intensely hot sunlight, producing high fever and sometimes loss of consciousness

suntan n a brownish colouring of the skin caused by exposure to the sun or a sun lamp
> **suntanned** adj

sup vb **supping, supped 1** to take (liquid) by swallowing a little at a time ▸ n **2** a sip

super *informal* ▸ adj **1** very good or very nice: *they had a super holiday* ▸ n *Austral & NZ* **2** superannuation **3** superphosphate

super- *prefix* **1** above or over: *superscript* **2** outstanding: *superstar* **3** of greater size, extent, or quality: *supermarket*

superannuated adj **1** discharged with a pension, owing to age or illness **2** too old to be useful; obsolete

superannuation n **A** a regular payment made by an employee into a pension fund **B** the pension finally paid

S

superb *adj* extremely good or impressive
> **superbly** *adv*

> **superb** *adj* = splendid (*old-fashioned*), excellent, magnificent, fine, grand, superior, marvellous, world-class, booshit (*Austral slang*), exo (*Austral slang*), sik (*Austral slang*), rad (*informal*), phat (*slang*), schmick (*Austral informal*); ≠ inferior

superbug *n informal* a bacterium resistant to antibiotics

supercharger *n* a device that increases the power of an internal-combustion engine by forcing extra air into it

supercilious *adj* behaving in a superior and arrogant manner > **superciliously** *adv*
> **superciliousness** *n*

superconductivity *n physics* the ability of certain substances to conduct electric current with almost no resistance at very low temperatures > **superconducting** *adj*
> **superconductor** *n*

superficial *adj* 1 not careful or thorough: *a superficial analysis* 2 only outwardly apparent rather than genuine or actual: *those are merely superficial differences* 3 (of a person) lacking deep emotions or serious interests; shallow 4 of, near, or forming the surface: *the gash was superficial* > **superficiality** *n* > **superficially** *adv*

> **superficial** *adj* 1 = hasty, cursory, perfunctory, hurried, casual, sketchy, desultory, slapdash; ≠ thorough 3 = shallow, frivolous, empty-headed, silly, trivial; ≠ serious 4 = slight, surface, external, on the surface, exterior; ≠ profound

superfluous (soo-per-flew-uss) *adj* more than is sufficient or required > **superfluity** *n*

superfood *n* a food that is especially nutritious or otherwise beneficial to health

superhero *n, pl* -**roes** (in science fiction) a person who uses supernatural powers to fight against evil

superhuman *adj* beyond normal human ability or experience: *a superhuman effort*

superimpose *vb* -**posing**, -**posed** to set or place (something) on or over something else

superintend *vb* to supervise (a person or an activity)

superintendent *n* 1 a senior police officer 2 a person who directs and manages an organization or office

> **superintendent** *n* 2 = supervisor, director, manager, chief, governor, inspector, controller, overseer

superior *adj* 1 greater in quality, quantity, or usefulness 2 higher in rank, position, or status: *he was reprimanded by a superior officer* 3 believing oneself to be better than others 4 of very high quality or respectability: *superior merchandise* 5 *formal* placed higher up: *damage to the superior*

surface of the wing 6 *printing* (of a character) written or printed above the line ▸ *n* 7 a person of greater rank or status > **superiority** *n*

> **superior** *adj* 1 = better, higher, greater, grander, surpassing, unrivalled; ≠ inferior 3 = supercilious, patronizing, condescending, haughty, disdainful, lordly, lofty, pretentious 4 = first-class, excellent, first-rate, choice, exclusive, exceptional, de luxe, booshit (*Austral slang*), exo (*Austral slang*), sik (*Austral slang*), rad (*informal*), phat (*slang*), schmick (*Austral informal*); ≠ average ▸ *n* = boss, senior, director, manager, chief (*informal*), principal, supervisor, sherang (*Austral, NZ*); ≠ subordinate

superlative (soo-per-lat-iv) *adj* 1 of outstanding quality; supreme 2 *grammar* denoting the form of an adjective or adverb that expresses the highest degree of quality ▸ *n* 3 the highest quality 4 *grammar* the superlative form of an adjective or adverb

superman *or fem* **superwoman** *n, pl* -**men** *or* -**women** someone with great physical or mental powers

supermarket *n* a large self-service shop selling food and household goods

supermodel *n* a famous and highly-paid fashion model

supernatural *adj* 1 of or relating to things that cannot be explained by science, such as clairvoyance, ghosts, etc. ▸ *n* 2 **the supernatural** forces, occurrences, and beings that cannot be explained by science

> **supernatural** *adj* = paranormal, unearthly, uncanny, ghostly, psychic, mystic, miraculous, occult

supernova *n, pl* -**vae** *or* -**vas** a star that explodes and, for a few days, becomes one hundred million times brighter than the sun

supernumerary *adj* 1 exceeding the required or regular number; extra 2 employed as a substitute or assistant ▸ *n, pl* -**aries** 3 a person or thing that exceeds the required or regular number 4 a substitute or assistant 5 an actor who has no lines to say

superpower *n* a country of very great military and economic power, such as the US

superscript *printing* ▸ *adj* 1 (of a character) written or printed above the line ▸ *n* 2 a superscript character

supersede *vb* -**seding**, -**seded** 1 to take the place of (something old-fashioned or less appropriate): *cavalry was superseded by armoured vehicles* 2 to replace (someone) in function or office

supersize *adj also* **supersized** 1 larger than standard size ▸ *vb* -**sizes**, -**sizing**, -**sized** 2 to increase the size of (something, such as a standard portion of food)

supersonic *adj* being, having, or capable of a speed greater than the speed of sound

superstition *n* **1** irrational belief in magic and the powers that supposedly bring good luck or bad luck **2** a belief or practice based on this > **superstitious** *adj*

superstore *n* a large supermarket

superstructure *n* **1** any structure or concept built on something else **2** *naut* any structure above the main deck of a ship

supertax *n* an extra tax on incomes above a certain level

supervene *vb* **-vening, -vened** to happen as an unexpected development > **supervention** *n*

supervise *vb* **-vising, -vised 1** to direct the performance or operation of (an activity or a process) **2** to watch over (people) so as to ensure appropriate behaviour > **supervision** *n* > **supervisor** *n* > **supervisory** *adj*

> **supervise** *vb* **1** = oversee, run, manage, control, direct, handle, look after, superintend **2** = observe, guide, monitor, oversee, keep an eye on

supine (soo-pine) *adj formal* lying on one's back

supper *n* **1** an evening meal **2** a late evening snack

supplant *vb* to take the place of (someone or something)

supple *adj* **1** (of a person) moving and bending easily and gracefully **2** (of a material or object) soft and bending easily without breaking > **suppleness** *n*

supplement *n* **1** an addition designed to make something more adequate **2** a magazine distributed free with a newspaper **3** a section added to a publication to supply further information or correct errors **4** (of money) an additional payment to obtain special services ▶ *vb* **5** to provide an addition to (something), esp. in order to make up for an inadequacy: *she supplements her salary by renting her spare bedroom* > **supplementary** *adj*

> **supplement** *n* **2** = pull-out, insert **3** = appendix, add-on, postscript **4** = addition, extra ▶ *vb* = add to, reinforce, augment, extend

supplicant *n formal* a person who makes a humble request

supplication *n formal* a humble request for help

supply *vb* **-plies, -plying, -plied 1** to provide with something required: *Nigeria may supply them with oil* ▶ *n, pl* **-plies 2** the act of providing something **3** an amount available for use; stock: *electricity supply* **4** **supplies** food and equipment needed for a trip or military campaign **5** *econ* the amount of a commodity that producers are willing and able to offer for sale at a specified price: *supply and demand* **6** a person who acts as a temporary substitute ▶ *adj* **7** acting as a temporary substitute: *supply teachers* > **supplier** *n*

supply *vb* = provide, give, furnish, produce, stock, grant, contribute, yield ▶ *n* **3** = store, fund, stock, source, reserve, quantity, hoard, cache **4** = provisions, necessities, stores, food, materials, equipment, rations

support *vb* **1** to carry the weight of (a thing or person) **2** to provide the necessities of life for (a family or person) **3** to give practical or emotional help to (someone) **4** to give approval to (a cause, idea, or political party) **5** to take an active interest in and be loyal to (a particular football or other sports team) **6** to establish the truthfulness or accuracy of (a theory or statement) by providing new facts **7** to speak in a debate in favour of (a motion) **8** (in a concert) to perform earlier than (the main attraction) **9** *films & theatre* to play a less important role to (the leading actor) ▶ *n* **10** the act of supporting or the condition of being supported **11** a thing that bears the weight of an object from below **12** a person who gives someone practical or emotional help **13** the means of providing the necessities of life for a family or person **14** a band or entertainer not topping the bill > **supportive** *adj*

> **support** *vb* **1** = bear, carry, sustain, prop (up), reinforce, hold, brace, buttress **2** = provide for, maintain, look after, keep, fund, finance, sustain; ≠ live off **3** = help, back, champion, second, aid, defend, assist, side with; ≠ oppose **6** = bear out, confirm, verify, substantiate, corroborate; ≠ refute ▶ *n* **10** = furtherance, backing, promotion, assistance, encouragement; ≠ opposition **11** = prop, post, foundation, brace, pillar **12** = supporter, prop, mainstay, tower of strength, second, backer; ≠ antagonist **13** = upkeep, maintenance, keep, subsistence, sustenance

supporter *n* a person who supports a sports team, politician, etc.

> **supporter** *n* = follower, fan, advocate, friend, champion, sponsor, patron, helper; ≠ opponent

suppose *vb* **-posing, -posed 1** to presume (something) to be true without certain knowledge: *I suppose it will be in the papers* **2** to consider (something) as a possible suggestion for the sake of discussion: *suppose you're arrested on a misdemeanour* **3** (of a theory) to depend on the truth or existence of: *this scenario supposes that he would do so*

> **suppose** *vb* **1** = think, imagine, expect, assume, guess (*informal*), presume, conjecture **2** = imagine, consider, conjecture, postulate (*formal*), hypothesize

supposed *adj* **1** **supposed to** expected to: *spies aren't supposed to be nice* **2** presumed to be true without certain knowledge; doubtful: *the supposed wonders of drug therapy* > **supposedly** *adv*

> **supposed** *adj* **2** = presumed, alleged, professed, accepted, assumed

S

supposition n **1** an idea or a statement believed or assumed to be true **2** the act of supposing: *much of it is based on supposition*

suppository n, pl **-ries** med a medicine in solid form that is inserted into the vagina or rectum and left to dissolve

suppress vb **1** to put an end to (something) by physical or legal force **2** to prevent the circulation or publication of (information or books) **3** to hold (an emotion or a response) in check; restrain: *he could barely suppress a groan* **4** electronics to reduce or eliminate (interference) in a circuit ⊳ **suppression** n

> **suppress** vb **1** = stamp out, stop, check, crush, conquer, subdue, put an end to, overpower; ≠ encourage **3** = restrain, stifle, contain, silence, conceal, curb, repress, smother

suppurate vb **-rating, -rated** pathol (of a wound or sore) to produce or leak pus

supremacy n **1** supreme power; dominance **2** the state or quality of being superior

> **supremacy** n = domination, sovereignty, sway, mastery, primacy, predominance, supreme power

supreme adj **1** of highest status or power: *the Supreme Council* **2** of highest quality or importance: *a supreme player* **3** greatest in degree; extreme: *supreme happiness* ⊳ **supremely** adv

> **supreme** adj **1** = paramount, surpassing; ≠ least **2** = chief, leading, principal, highest, head, top, prime, foremost; ≠ lowest **3** = ultimate, highest, greatest

supremo n, pl **-mos** informal a person in overall authority

> **supremo** n = head, leader, boss (informal), director, master, governor, commander, principal

surcharge n **1** a charge in addition to the usual payment or tax **2** an excessive sum charged, often unlawfully ▸ vb **-charging, -charged** **3** to charge (someone) an additional sum or tax **4** to overcharge (someone) for something

surd maths ▸ n **1** an irrational number ▸ adj **2** of or relating to a surd

sure adj **1** free from doubt or uncertainty (in regard to a belief): *she was sure that she was still at home; I am sure he didn't mean it* **2 sure thing** having no doubt, such as of the occurrence of a future state or event: *sure of winning the point* **3** reliable or accurate: *a sure sign of dry rot* **4** bound inevitably (to be or do something); certain: *his aggressive style is sure to please the American fans* **5 sure of** or **about** happy to put one's trust in (someone): *I'm still not quite sure about her* **6 sure of oneself** confident in one's own abilities and opinions **7** not open to doubt: *sure proof* **8** bound to be or occur; inevitable: *victory is sure* **9** physically secure: *a sure footing*

10 be sure (usually foll. by to or and) be careful or certain (to do something): *be sure to label each jar* **11 for sure** without a doubt **12 make sure** to make certain: *make sure there is no-one in the car* **13 sure enough** informal in fact: *sure enough, this is happening* **14 to be sure** it has to be acknowledged; admittedly ▸ adv **15** informal, chiefly US & Canad without question; certainly: *it sure is bad news* ▸ interj **16** informal willingly; yes ⊳ **sureness** n

> **sure** adj **1** = certain, positive, decided, convinced, confident, assured, definite; ≠ uncertain **3** = reliable, accurate, dependable, undoubted, undeniable, foolproof, infallible, unerring; ≠ unreliable **4, 8** = inevitable, guaranteed, bound, assured, inescapable, nailed-on (slang); ≠ unsure

sure-footed adj **1** unlikely to fall, slip, or stumble **2** unlikely to make a mistake

surely adv **1** am I not right in thinking that?; I am sure that: *surely you can see that?* **2** without doubt: *without support they will surely fail* **3 slowly but surely** gradually but noticeably ▸ interj **4** chiefly US & Canad willingly; yes

> **surely** adv **1** = it must be the case that **2** = undoubtedly, certainly, definitely, without doubt, unquestionably, indubitably, doubtlessly

surety n, pl **-ties 1** a person who takes legal responsibility for the fulfilment of another's debt or obligation **2** security given as a guarantee that an obligation will be met

surf n **1** foam caused by waves breaking on the shore or on a reef ▸ vb **2** to take part in surfing **3** to move rapidly through a particular medium: *surfing the internet* **4** informal to be carried on top of something: *that guy's surfing the audience* ⊳ **surfer** n

surface n **1** the outside or top of an object **2** the size of such an area **3** material covering the surface of an object **4** the outward appearance as opposed to the real or hidden nature of something: *on the surface the idea seems attractive* **5** geom **A** the complete boundary of a solid figure **B** something that has length and breadth but no thickness **6** the uppermost level of the land or sea **7 come to the surface** to become apparent after being hidden ▸ vb **-facing, -faced 8** to become apparent or widely known **9** to rise to the surface of water **10** to give (an area) a particular kind of surface **11** informal to get up out of bed

> **surface** n **1** = covering, face, exterior, side, top, veneer **4** = facade ▸ vb **8** = appear, emerge, arise, come to light, crop up (informal), transpire, materialize **9** = emerge, come up, come to the surface

surfboard n a long narrow board used in surfing

surfeit n formal **1** an excessive amount **2** excessive eating or drinking **3** an uncomfortably full or sickened feeling caused by eating or drinking too much

surfing *n* the sport of riding towards shore on the crest of a wave by standing or lying on a surfboard

surge *n* **1** a sudden powerful increase: *a surge in spending* **2** a strong rolling movement of the sea **3** a heavy rolling motion or sound: *a great surge of people* ▸ *vb* **surging, surged 4** to move forward strongly and suddenly **5** to increase quickly and strongly **6** (of the sea) to rise or roll with a heavy swelling motion

> **surge** *n* **1** = rush, flood **2** = flow, wave, rush, roller, gush, outpouring **3** = wave, rush, storm, torrent, eruption ▸ *vb* **4** = rush, pour, rise, gush **6** = roll, rush, heave

surgeon *n* a medical doctor who specializes in surgery

surgery *n*, *pl* **-geries 1** medical treatment in which a person's body is cut open by a surgeon in order to treat or remove the problem part **2** *Brit* a place where, or time when, a doctor or dentist can be consulted **3** *Brit* a time when an MP or councillor can be consulted

surgical *adj* **1** involving or used in surgery **2** (of an action) performed with extreme precision: *a surgical air attack* > **surgically** *adv*

surly *adj* **-lier, -liest** bad-tempered and rude

surmise *vb* **-mising, -mised 1** to guess (something) from incomplete or uncertain evidence ▸ *n* **2** a conclusion based on incomplete or uncertain evidence

surmount *vb* **1** to overcome (a problem) **2** to be situated on top of (something): *the island is surmounted by a huge black castle* > **surmountable** *adj*

surname *n* a family name as opposed to a first or Christian name

surpass *vb* **1** to be greater in extent than or superior in achievement to (something or someone) **2 surpass oneself** *or* **expectations** to go beyond the limit of what was expected

> **surpass** *vb* **1** = outdo, beat, exceed, eclipse, excel, transcend, outstrip, outshine

surplice *n* a loose knee-length garment with wide sleeves, worn by members of the clergy and choristers

surplus *n* **1** a quantity or amount left over in excess of what is required **2** *accounting* an excess of income over spending ▸ *adj* **3** being in excess; extra: *surplus to requirements*

> **surplus** *n* **1** = excess, surfeit, ≠ shortage ▸ *adj* = extra, spare, excess, remaining, odd, superfluous, ≠ insufficient

surprise *n* **1** the act of taking someone unawares: *the element of surprise* **2** a sudden or unexpected event, gift, etc.: *this is a nice surprise* **3** the feeling of being surprised; astonishment: *to our great surprise* **4 take someone by surprise** to capture someone unexpectedly or catch

someone unprepared ▸ *adj* **5** causing surprise: *a surprise attack* ▸ *vb* **-prising, -prised 6** to cause (someone) to feel amazement or wonder **7** to come upon or discover (someone) unexpectedly or suddenly **8** to capture or attack (someone) suddenly and without warning **9 surprise into** to provoke (someone) to unintended action by a trick or deception > **surprised** *adj* > **surprising** *adj* > **surprisingly** *adv*

> **surprise** *n* **2** = shock, revelation, jolt, bombshell, eye-opener (*informal*) **3** = amazement, astonishment, wonder, incredulity ▸ *vb* **6** = amaze, astonish, stun, startle, stagger, take aback **7, 8** = catch unawares *or* off-guard, spring upon

surreal *adj* very strange or dreamlike; bizarre

surrealism *n* a movement in art and literature in the 1920s, involving the combination of images that would not normally be found together, as if in a dream > **surrealist** *n*, *adj* > **surrealistic** *adj*

surrender *vb* **1** to give oneself up physically to an enemy after defeat **2** to give (something) up to another, under pressure or on demand: *the rebels surrendered their arms* **3** to give (something) up voluntarily to another: *he was surrendering his own chance for the championship* **4** to give in to a temptation or an influence ▸ *n* **5** the act or instance of surrendering

> **surrender** *vb* **1, 4** = give in, yield, submit, give way, succumb, cave in (*informal*), capitulate; ≠ resist **2, 3** = give up, abandon, relinquish, yield, concede, part with, renounce, waive ▸ *n* = submission, cave-in (*informal*), capitulation, resignation, renunciation, relinquishment

surreptitious *adj* done in secret or without permission: *surreptitious moments of bliss* > **surreptitiously** *adv*

surrogate *n* **1** a person or thing acting as a substitute ▸ *adj* **2** acting as a substitute: *a surrogate father*

surrogate mother *n* a woman who gives birth to a child on behalf of a couple who cannot have a baby themselves, usually by artificial insemination > **surrogate motherhood** *or* **surrogacy** *n*

surround *vb* **1** to encircle or enclose (something or someone) **2** to exist around (someone or something): *the family members who surround him* ▸ *n* **3** *chiefly Brit* a border, such as the area of uncovered floor between the walls of a room and the carpet > **surrounding** *adj*

> **surround** *vb* **1** = enclose, ring, encircle, encompass, envelop, hem in

surroundings *pl n* the area and environment around a person, place, or thing

> **surroundings** *pl n* = environment, setting, background, location, milieu

surveillance *n* close observation of a person suspected of being a spy or a criminal

> **surveillance** *n* = observation, watch, scrutiny, supervision, inspection

survey *vb* **1** to view or consider (something) as a whole: *she surveyed her purchases anxiously* **2** to make a detailed map of (an area of land) by measuring or calculating distances and height **3** *Brit* to inspect (a building) to assess its condition and value **4** to make a detailed investigation of the behaviour, opinions, etc., of (a group of people) ▸ *n* **5** a detailed investigation of the behaviour, opinions, etc., of a group of people **6** the act of making a detailed map of an area of land by measuring or calculating distance and height **7** *Brit* an inspection of a building to assess its condition and value > **surveying** *n* > **surveyor** *n*

> **survey** *vb* **1** = look over, view, examine, observe, contemplate, inspect, eyeball (*slang*), scrutinize **2, 3** = measure, estimate, assess, appraise **4** = interview, question, poll, research, investigate ▸ *n* **5** = poll, study, research, review, inquiry, investigation **7** = valuation, estimate, assessment, appraisal

survival *n* **1** the condition of having survived something **2** a person or thing that continues to exist in the present despite being from an earlier time, such as a custom ▸ *adj* **3** of, relating to, or assisting the act of surviving: *survival suits*

survive *vb* **-viving, -vived 1 A** to continue to live or exist **B** to continue to live or exist after (a passage of time or a difficult or dangerous experience) **2** to live after the death of (another) > **survivor** *n*

> **survive** *vb* **1A** = remain alive, last, live on, endure **2** = live longer than, outlive, outlast

susceptibility *n, pl* **-ties 1** the quality or condition of being easily affected or influenced by something **2 susceptibilities** emotional feelings

susceptible *adj* **1 susceptible to A** giving in easily to: *susceptible to political pressure* **B** vulnerable to (a disease or injury): *susceptible to pneumonia* **2** easily affected emotionally; impressionable

> **susceptible** *adj* **2** = responsive, sensitive, receptive, impressionable, suggestible; ≠ unresponsive

sushi (soo-shee) *n* a Japanese dish consisting of small cakes of cold rice with a topping of raw fish

suspect *vb* **1** to believe (someone) to be guilty without having any proof **2** to think (something) to be false or doubtful: *he suspected her intent* **3** to believe (something) to be the case; think probable: *I suspect he had another reason* ▸ *n* **4** a person who is believed guilty of a specified offence ▸ *adj* **5** not to be trusted or relied upon: *her commitment to the cause has always been suspect*

suspect *vb* **2** = distrust, doubt, mistrust; ≠ trust **3** = believe, feel, guess, consider, suppose, speculate; ≠ know ▸ *adj* = dubious, doubtful, questionable, iffy (*informal*), shonky (*Austral, NZ informal*); ≠ innocent

suspend *vb* **1** to hang (something) from a high place **2** to cause (something) to remain floating or hanging: *a huge orange sun suspended above the horizon* **3** to cause (something) to stop temporarily: *the discussions have been suspended* **4** to remove (someone) temporarily from a job or position, usually as a punishment

> **suspend** *vb* **1, 2** = hang, attach, dangle **3** = postpone, put off, cease, interrupt, shelve, defer, cut short, discontinue; ≠ continue

suspenders *pl n* **A** elastic straps attached to a belt or corset, with fasteners for holding up women's stockings **B** similar fasteners attached to garters for holding up men's socks **2** *US & Canad* a pair of straps worn over the shoulders for holding up the trousers. Also called (*Brit*): **braces**

suspense *n* **1** a state of anxiety or uncertainty: *Sue and I stared at each other in suspense* **2** excitement felt at the approach of the climax of a book, film, or play: *action and suspense abound in this thriller* > **suspenseful** *adj*

suspension *n* **1** the delaying or stopping temporarily of something: *the suspension of the talks* **2** temporary removal from a job or position, usually as a punishment **3** the act of suspending or the state of being suspended **4** a system of springs and shock absorbers that supports the body of a vehicle **5** a device, usually a wire or spring, that suspends or supports something, such as the pendulum of a clock **6** *chem* a mixture in which fine solid or liquid particles are suspended in a fluid

> **suspension** *n* **1** = postponement, break, breaking off, interruption, abeyance, deferment, discontinuation

suspension bridge *n* a bridge suspended from cables that hang between two towers and are secured at both ends

suspicion *n* **1** the act or an instance of suspecting; belief without sure proof that something is wrong **2** a feeling of mistrust **3** a slight trace: *the merest suspicion of a threat* **4 above suspicion** not possibly guilty of anything, through having a good reputation **5 under suspicion** suspected of doing something wrong

> **suspicion** *n* **1** = idea, notion, hunch, guess, impression **2** = distrust, scepticism, mistrust, doubt, misgiving, qualm, wariness, dubiety **3** = trace, touch, hint, suggestion, shade, streak, tinge, soupçon (*French*)

suspicious *adj* **1** causing one to suspect something is wrong: *suspicious activities*

2 unwilling to trust: *I'm suspicious of his motives*
▸ **suspiciously** *adv*

suspicious *adj* **1** = suspect, dubious, questionable, doubtful, dodgy (*Brit, Austral, NZ informal*), fishy (*informal*), shonky (*Austral, NZ informal*); ≠ beyond suspicion **2** = distrustful, sceptical, doubtful, unbelieving, wary; ≠ trusting

suss out *vb Brit, Austral & NZ slang* to work out (a situation or a person's character), using one's intuition

sustain *vb* **1** to maintain or continue for a period of time: *I managed to sustain a conversation* **2** to keep up the strength or energy of (someone): *one mouthful of water to sustain him; the merest drop of comfort to sustain me* **3** to suffer (an injury or loss): *he sustained a spinal injury* **4** to support (something) from below **5** to support or agree with (a decision or statement): *objection sustained* ▸ **sustained** *adj*

sustain *vb* **1** = maintain, continue, keep up, prolong, protract **2** = keep alive, nourish, provide for **3** = suffer, experience, undergo, feel, bear, endure, withstand **4** = support, bear, uphold

sustenance *n* means of maintaining health or life; food and drink

suture (soo-tcher) *n surgery* a stitch made with catgut or silk thread, to join the edges of a wound together

SUV sport (*or* sports) utility vehicle: a car with off-road features such as four-wheel drive and raised ground clearance

suzerain *n* **1** a state or sovereign that has some degree of control over a dependent state **2** (formerly) a person who had power over many people ▸ **suzerainty** *n*

svelte *adj* attractively or gracefully slim; slender

SW 1 southwest(ern) **2** short wave

swab *n* **1** *med* a small piece of cotton wool used for applying medication or cleansing a wound ▸ *vb* **swabbing, swabbed 2** to clean or apply medication to (a wound) with a swab **3** to clean (the deck of a ship) with a mop

swaddle *vb* **-dling, -dled** to wrap (a baby) in swaddling clothes

swaddling clothes *pl n* long strips of cloth formerly wrapped round a newborn baby

swag *n* **1** *slang* stolen property **2** *Austral & NZ informal* (formerly) a swagman's pack containing personal belongings

swagger *vb* **1** to walk or behave in an arrogant manner ▸ *n* **2** an arrogant walk or manner

swagman *n, pl* **-men** *Austral & NZ informal* a labourer who carries his personal possessions in a pack while looking for work

swain *n archaic or poetic* **1** a male lover or admirer **2** a young man from the countryside

swallow¹ *vb* **1** to pass (food, drink, etc.) through the mouth and gullet to the stomach **2** *informal*

to believe (something) trustingly: *I was supposed to swallow the lie* **3** not to show: *I believe they should swallow their pride* **4** to make a gulping movement in the throat, such as when nervous **5** to put up with (an insult) without answering back **6 be swallowed up** to be taken into and made a part of something: *the old centre was being swallowed up by new estates* ▸ *n* **7** the act of swallowing **8** the amount swallowed at any single time; mouthful

swallow *vb* **1** = eat, consume, devour, swig (*informal*)

swallow² *n* a small migratory bird with long pointed wings and a forked tail

swam *vb* the past tense of **swim**

swamp *n* **1** an area of permanently waterlogged land; bog ▸ *vb* **2** *naut* to cause (a boat) to sink or fill with water **3** to overwhelm (a person or place) with more than can be dealt with or accommodated ▸ **swampy** *adj*

swamp *n* = bog, marsh, quagmire, slough, fen, mire, morass, pakihi (*NZ*), muskeg (*Canad*) ▸ *vb* **2** = flood, engulf, submerge, inundate **3** = overload, overwhelm, inundate

swan *n* **1** a large, usually white, water bird with a long neck ▸ *vb* **swanning, swanned 2 swan around** *or* **about** *informal* to wander about without purpose, but with an air of superiority

swank *informal* ▸ *vb* **1** to show off or boast ▸ *n* **2** showing off or boasting ▸ **swanky** *adj*

swanndri (swan-dry) *n trademark NZ* a weatherproof woollen shirt or jacket. Also called: **swannie**

swan song *n* the last public act of a person before retirement or death

swap *or* **swop** *vb* **swapping, swapped** *or* **swopping, swopped 1** to exchange (something) for something else ▸ *n* **2** an exchange

swap *or* **swop** *vb* = exchange, trade, switch, interchange, barter

sward *n* a stretch of turf or grass

swarm¹ *n* **1** a group of bees, led by a queen, that has left the hive to make a new home **2** a large mass of insects or other small animals **3** a moving mass of people ▸ *vb* **4** to move quickly and in large numbers **5** to be overrun: *the place is swarming with cops*

swarm *n* **2, 3** = multitude, crowd, mass, army, host, flock, herd, horde ▸ *vb* **4** = crowd, flock, throng, mass, stream **5** = teem, crawl, abound, bristle

swarm² *vb* **swarm up** to climb (a ladder or rope) by gripping it with the hands and feet: *the boys swarmed up the rigging*

swarthy *adj* **swarthier, swarthiest** having a dark complexion

swashbuckling *adj* having the exciting manner or behaviour of pirates, esp. those depicted in films ▸ **swashbuckler** *n*

S

swastika *n* **1** a primitive religious symbol in the shape of a Greek cross with the ends of the arms bent at right angles **2** this symbol with clockwise arms as the emblem of Nazi Germany

swat *vb* **swatting, swatted 1** to hit sharply: *swatting the ball with confidence* ▸ *n* **2** a sharp blow

swatch *n* **1** a sample of cloth **2** a collection of such samples

swath (swawth) *n* same as **swathe**

swathe *vb* **swathing, swathed 1** to wrap a bandage, garment, or piece of cloth around (a person or part of the body) ▸ *n* **2** a long strip of cloth wrapped around something **3** the width of one sweep of a scythe or of the blade of a mowing machine **4** the strip cut in one sweep **5** the quantity of cut crops left in one sweep **6** a long narrow strip of land

> **swathe** *vb* = wrap, drape, envelop, cloak, shroud, bundle up

sway *vb* **1** to swing to and fro: *red poppies swayed in the faint breeze* **2** to lean to one side and then the other: *entire rows swayed in time* **3** to be unable to decide between two or more opinions **4** to influence (someone) in his or her opinion or judgment ▸ *n* **5** power or influence **6** a swinging or leaning movement **7 hold sway** to have power or influence

> **sway** *vb* **1, 2** = move from side to side, rock, roll, swing, bend, lean **4** = influence, affect, guide, persuade, induce ▸ *n* **5** = power, control, influence, authority, clout (*informal*)

swear *vb* **swearing, swore, sworn 1** to use words considered obscene or blasphemous **2** to promise solemnly on oath; vow: *Sally and Peter swore to love and cherish each other* **3 swear by** to have complete confidence in (something) **4** to state (something) earnestly: *I swear he was all right* **5** to give evidence on oath in a law court

> **swear** *vb* **1** = curse, blaspheme, be foul-mouthed **2, 5** = vow, promise, testify, attest **4** = declare, assert, affirm

swear in *vb* to make (someone) take an oath when taking up an official position or entering the witness box to give evidence in court: *a new federal president was sworn in*

swearword *n* a word considered rude or blasphemous

sweat *n* **1** the salty liquid that comes out of the skin's pores during strenuous activity in excessive heat or when afraid **2** the state or condition of sweating: *he worked up a sweat* **3** *slang* hard work or effort: *climbing to the crest of Ward Hill was a sweat* **4 in a sweat** *informal* in a state of worry **5 no sweat** *slang* no problem ▸ *vb* **sweating, sweat** *or* **sweated 6** to have sweat come through the skin's pores, as a result of strenuous activity, excessive heat, nervousness, or fear **7** *informal* to suffer anxiety or distress **8 sweat blood** *informal* **A** to work very hard **B** to be filled with anxiety > **sweaty** *adj*

> **sweat** *n* **1** = perspiration ▸ *vb* **6** = perspire, glow **7** = worry, fret, agonize, torture yourself

sweatband *n* a piece of cloth tied around the forehead or around the wrist to absorb sweat during strenuous physical activity

sweater *n* a warm knitted piece of clothing covering the upper part of the body

sweatshirt *n* a long-sleeved casual top made of knitted cotton or cotton mixture

sweatshop *n* a workshop where employees work long hours in poor conditions for low pay

swede *n* a round root vegetable with a purplish-brown skin and yellow flesh

Swede *n* a person from Sweden

Swedish *adj* **1** of Sweden ▸ *n* **2** the language of Sweden

sweep *vb* **sweeping, swept 1** to clean (a floor or chimney) with a brush **2** (often foll. by *up*) to remove or collect (dirt or rubbish) with a brush **3** to move smoothly and quickly: *the car swept into the drive* **4** to spread rapidly across or through (a place): *fire swept through Southern California* **5** to move in a proud and majestic fashion: *the boss himself swept into the hall* **6** to direct (one's eyes, line of fire, etc.) over (a place or target) **7 sweep away** *or* **off** to overwhelm (someone) emotionally: *I've been swept away by my fears* **8** to brush or lightly touch (a surface): *the dress swept along the ground* **9** to clear away or get rid of (something) suddenly or forcefully: *these doubts were quickly swept aside; bridges have been swept away by the floods* **10** to stretch out gracefully or majestically, esp. in a wide circle: *the hills swept down into the green valley* **11** to win overwhelmingly: *the umbrella party which swept these elections* **12 sweep the board** to win every event or prize in a contest ▸ *n* **13** the act or an instance of sweeping **14** a swift or steady movement: *the wide sweep of the shoulders* **15** a wide expanse: *the whole sweep of the bay* **16** any curving line or contour, such as a driveway **17** short for **sweepstake 18** *chiefly Brit* same as **chimney sweep 19 make a clean sweep** to win an overwhelming victory

> **sweep** *vb* **1** = brush, clean **2** = clear, remove, brush, clean **3** = sail, pass, fly, tear, zoom, glide, skim ▸ *n* **14** = movement, move, swing, stroke **15** = extent, range, stretch, scope

sweeping *adj* **1** affecting many people to a great extent: *sweeping financial reforms* **2** (of a statement) making general assumptions about an issue without considering the details **3** decisive or overwhelming: *to suffer sweeping losses* **4** taking in a wide area: *a sweeping view of the area*

> **sweeping** *adj* **1** = wide-ranging, global, comprehensive, wide, broad, extensive, all-inclusive, all-embracing; ≠ limited **2** = indiscriminate, blanket, wholesale, exaggerated, overstated, unqualified

S

sweepstake *or esp US* **sweepstakes** *n* **1** a lottery in which the stakes of the participants make up the prize **2** a horse race involving such a lottery

sweet *adj* **1** tasting of or like sugar **2** kind and charming: *that was really sweet of you* **3** attractive and delightful: *a sweet child* **4** (of a sound) pleasant and tuneful: *sweet music* **5** (of wine) having a high sugar content; not dry **6** fresh, clear, and clean: *sweet water; sweet air* **7 sweet on someone** fond of or infatuated with someone ▸ *n Brit, Austral & NZ* **8** a shaped piece of confectionery consisting mainly of sugar **9** a dessert > **sweetly** *adv* > **sweetness** *n*

> **sweet** *adj* **1** = sugary, cloying, saccharine, icky (*informal*); ≠ sour **2** = charming, kind, agreeable; ≠ nasty **3** = delightful, appealing, cute, winning, engaging, lovable, likable *or* likeable; ≠ unpleasant **4** = melodious, musical, harmonious, mellow, dulcet; ≠ harsh **6** = fresh, clean, pure ▸ *n* **8** = confectionery, candy (*US*), lolly (*Austral*, NZ), bonbon **9** = dessert, pudding

sweetbread *n* the meat obtained from the pancreas of a calf or lamb

sweet corn *n* **1** a kind of maize with sweet yellow kernels, eaten as a vegetable when young **2** the sweet kernels removed from the maize cob, cooked as a vegetable

sweeten *vb* **1** to make (food or drink) sweet or sweeter **2** to be nice to (someone) in order to ensure cooperation **3** to make (an offer or a proposal) more acceptable

sweetener *n* **1** a sweetening agent that does not contain sugar **2** *Brit, Austral & NZ slang* an inducement offered to someone in order to persuade them to accept an offer or business deal

sweetheart *n* **1** an affectionate name to call someone **2** *old-fashioned* one's boyfriend or girlfriend **3** *informal* a lovable or generous person

> **sweetheart** *n* **1** = dearest, beloved, sweet, angel (*informal*), treasure, honey, dear, sweetie (*informal*) **2** = love, boyfriend *or* girlfriend, beloved, lover, darling

sweetmeat *n old-fashioned* a small delicacy preserved in sugar

sweet pea *n* a climbing plant with sweet-smelling pastel-coloured flowers

sweet potato *n* a root vegetable, grown in the tropics, with pinkish-brown skin and yellow flesh

sweet-talk *informal* ▸ *vb* **1** to persuade (someone) by flattery: *I thought I could sweet-talk you into teaching me* ▸ *n* **sweet talk** **2** insincere flattery intended to persuade

sweet tooth *n* a strong liking for sweet foods

swell *vb* **swelling, swelled, swollen** *or* **swelled** **1** (of a part of the body) to grow in size as a result of injury or infection: *his face swelled and became* pale **2** to increase in size as a result of being filled with air or liquid: *a balloon swells if you force in more air* **3** to grow or cause (something) to grow in size, numbers, amount, or degree: *Israel's population is swelling* **4** (of an emotion) to become more intense: *his anger swelled within him* **5** (of the seas) to rise in waves **6** (of a sound) to become gradually louder and then die away ▸ *n* **7** the waving movement of the surface of the open sea **8** an increase in size, numbers, amount, or degree **9** a bulge **10** *old-fashioned, informal* a person who is wealthy, upper class, and fashionably dressed **11** *music* an increase in sound followed by an immediate dying away ▸ *adj* **12** *slang, chiefly US* excellent or fine

> **swell** *vb* **2** = expand, increase, grow, rise, balloon, enlarge, bulge, dilate; ≠ shrink **3, 4** = increase, rise, grow, mount, expand, accelerate, escalate, multiply; ≠ decrease ▸ *n* **7** = wave, surge, billow

swelling *n* an enlargement of a part of the body as the result of injury or infection

> **swelling** *n* = enlargement, lump, bump, bulge, inflammation, protuberance, distension

swelter *vb* **1** to feel uncomfortable under extreme heat ▸ *n* **2** a hot and uncomfortable condition: *they left the city swelter for the beach*

sweltering *adj* uncomfortably hot: *a sweltering summer*

swept *vb* the past of **sweep**

swerve *vb* **swerving, swerved** **1** to turn aside from a course sharply or suddenly ▸ *n* **2** the act of swerving

swift *adj* **1** moving or able to move quickly; fast **2** happening or performed quickly or suddenly: *a swift glance this way* **3 swift to** prompt to (do something): *swift to retaliate* ▸ *n* **4** a small fast-flying insect-eating bird with long wings > **swiftly** *adv* > **swiftness** *n*

> **swift** *adj* **1** = fast, quick, rapid, hurried, speedy; ≠ slow **2** = quick, prompt, rapid

swig *informal* ▸ *n* **1** a large swallow or deep drink, esp. from a bottle ▸ *vb* **swigging, swigged** **2** to drink (some liquid) in large swallows, esp. from a bottle

swill *vb* **1** to drink large quantities of (an alcoholic drink) **2** (often foll. by *out*) *chiefly Brit & NZ* to rinse (something) in large amounts of water ▸ *n* **3** a liquid mixture containing waste food, fed to pigs **4** a deep drink, esp. of beer

swim *vb* **swimming, swam, swum** **1** to move along in water by movements of the arms and legs, or (in the case of fish) tail and fins **2** to cover (a stretch of water) in this way: *the first person to swim the Atlantic* **3** to float on a liquid: *flies swimming on the milk* **4** to be affected by dizziness: *his head was swimming* **5** (of the objects in someone's vision) to appear to spin or move around: *the faces*

S

of the nurses swam around her **6** (often foll. by *in* or *with*) to be covered or flooded with liquid: *a steak swimming in gravy* ▸ *n* **7** the act, an instance, or a period of swimming **8 in the swim** *informal* fashionable or active in social or political activities > **swimmer** *n* > **swimming** *n*

swimmingly *adv* successfully, effortlessly, or well: *everything went swimmingly*

swimming pool *n* a large hole in the ground, tiled and filled with water for swimming in

swindle *vb* **-dling, -dled 1** to cheat (someone) out of money **2** to obtain (money) from someone by fraud ▸ *n* **3** an instance of cheating someone out of money > **swindler** *n*

swine *n* **1** a mean or unpleasant person **2** *pl* **swine** same as **pig** > **swinish** *adj*

swine flu *n* a form of influenza occurring in swine caused by a virus capable of spreading to humans

swing *vb* **swinging, swung 1** to move backwards and forwards; sway **2** to pivot or cause (something) to pivot from a fixed point such as a hinge: *the door swung open* **3** to wave (a weapon, etc.) in a sweeping motion **4** to move in a sweeping curve: *the headlights swung along the street* **5** to alter one's opinion or mood suddenly **6** to hang so as to be able to turn freely **7** *old-fashioned slang* to be hanged: *you'll swing for this!* **8** *informal* to manipulate or influence successfully: *it may help to swing the election* **9** (often foll. by *at*) to hit out with a sweeping motion **10** *old-fashioned* to play (music) in the style of swing **11** *old-fashioned slang* to be lively and modern ▸ *n* **12** the act of swinging **13** a sweeping stroke or punch **14** a seat hanging from two chains or ropes on which a person may swing back and forth **15** popular dance music played by big bands in the 1930s and 1940s **16** *informal* the normal pace at which an activity, such as work, happens: *I'm into the swing of things now* **17** a sudden or extreme change, for example in some business activity or voting pattern **18 go with a swing** to go well; be successful **19 in full swing** at the height of activity

> **swing** *vb* **1** = sway, rock, wave, veer, oscillate **3** = brandish, wave, shake, flourish, wield, dangle **4** = turn, swivel, curve, rotate, pivot **6** = hang, dangle, suspend **9** = hit out, strike, swipe (*informal*), lash out at, slap ▸ *n* **12** = swaying, sway

swing by *vb informal* to go somewhere to pay a visit

swingeing (swin-jing) *adj chiefly Brit* severe or causing hardship: *swingeing spending cuts*

swipe *vb* **swiping, swiped 1** *informal* to try to hit (someone or something) with a sweeping blow: *he swiped at a boy who ran forward* **2** *slang* to steal (something) **3** to pass (a credit or debit card) through a machine which electronically interprets the information stored in the card **4** to activate a function on an electronic device

by moving one's finger across a touchscreen ▸ *n* **5** *informal* a hard blow

swipe card *n* a card with a magnetic strip that holds encoded information that can be interpreted when the card is passed through an electronic device

swirl *vb* **1** to turn round and round with a twisting motion ▸ *n* **2** a twisting or spinning motion **3** a twisting shape > **swirling** *adj*

> **swirl** *vb* = whirl, churn, spin, twist, eddy

swish *vb* **1** to move with or cause (something) to make a whistling or hissing sound ▸ *n* **2** a hissing or rustling sound or movement: *she turned with a swish of her skirt* ▸ *adj* **3** *informal, chiefly Brit, Austral & NZ* smart and fashionable

Swiss *adj* **1** of Switzerland ▸ *n, pl* **Swiss 2** a person from Switzerland

swiss roll *n* a sponge cake spread with jam or cream and rolled up

switch *n* **1** a device for opening or closing an electric circuit **2** a sudden quick change **3** an exchange or swap **4** a flexible rod or twig, used for punishment **5** *US & Canad* a pair of movable rails for diverting moving trains from one track to another ▸ *vb* **6** to change quickly and suddenly **7** to exchange (places) or swap (something for something else) **8** *chiefly US & Canad* to transfer (rolling stock) from one railway track to another ▸ See also **switch on**

> **switch** *n* **1** = control, button, lever, on/off device **2** = change, shift, reversal ▸ *vb* **6** = change, shift, divert, deviate **7** = exchange, swap, substitute

switchback *n* a steep mountain road, railway, or track which rises and falls sharply many times

switchboard *n* the place in a telephone exchange or office building where telephone calls are connected

switch on *vb* **1** to cause (a device) to operate by moving a switch or lever **2** *informal* to produce (a certain type of behaviour or emotion) suddenly or automatically: *she was good at switching on the charm*

swivel *vb* **-elling, -elled** *or US* **-eling, -eled 1** to turn on or swing round on a central point ▸ *n* **2** a coupling device which allows an attached object to turn freely

swizzle stick *n* a small stick used to stir cocktails

swollen *vb* **1** a past participle of **swell** ▸ *adj* **2** enlarged by swelling

> **swollen** *adj* = enlarged, bloated, inflamed, puffed up, distended

swoon *vb* **1** *literary* to faint because of shock or strong emotion **2** to be deeply affected by passion for (someone): *you've swooned over a string of rotten men* ▸ *n* **3** *literary* a faint > **swooning** *adj*

swoop *vb* **1** (usually foll. by *down*) to move quickly through the air in a downward curve:

an owl swooped down from its perch **2** (usually foll. by *on*) to move suddenly and quickly towards (a place) in order to attack, arrest, or question the people inside: *nine police cars and vans swooped on the premises* ▶ *n* **3** the act of swooping

swoop *vb* **1** = drop, plunge, dive, sweep, descend, pounce, stoop **2** = pounce, attack, charge, rush, descend

swop *vb* **swopping**, **swopped**, *n* same as **swap**
sword *n* **1** a weapon with a long sharp blade and a short handle **2 the sword A** military power **B** death; destruction: *we will put them to the sword* **3 cross swords** to have a disagreement with someone
swordfish *n, pl* **-fish** or **-fishes** a large fish with a very long upper jaw that resembles a sword
swordsman *n, pl* **-men** a person who is skilled in the use of a sword > **swordsmanship** *n*
swore *vb* the past tense of **swear**
sworn *vb* **1** the past participle of **swear** ▶ *adj* **2** bound by or as if by an oath: *a sworn enemy*
swot *informal* ▶ *vb* **swotting**, **swotted 1** (often foll. by *up*) to study (a subject) very hard, esp. for an exam; cram ▶ *n* **2** a person who works or studies hard
swum *vb* the past participle of **swim**
swung *vb* the past of **swing**
sybarite (sib-bar-ite) *n* **1** a lover of luxury and pleasure ▶ *adj* **2** luxurious or sensuous > **sybaritic** *adj*
sycamore *n* **1** a tree with five-pointed leaves and two-winged fruits **2** *US & Canad* an American plane tree
sycophant *n* a person who uses flattery to win favour from people with power or influence > **sycophancy** *n* > **sycophantic** *adj*
syllabic *adj* of or relating to syllables
syllable *n* **1** a part of a word which is pronounced as a unit, which contains a single vowel sound, and which may or may not contain consonants: for example, 'paper' has two syllables **2** the least mention: *without a syllable about what went on* **3 in words of one syllable** simply and plainly
syllabub *n Brit & Austral* a dessert made from milk or cream beaten with sugar, wine, and lemon juice
syllabus (sill-lab-buss) *n, pl* **-buses** or **-bi** (-bye) **A** the subjects studied for a particular course **B** a list of these subjects
syllogism *n* a form of reasoning consisting of two premises and a conclusion, for example *some temples are in ruins; all ruins are fascinating; so some temples are fascinating* > **syllogistic** *adj*
sylph *n* **1** a slender graceful girl or young woman **2** an imaginary creature believed to live in the air > **sylphlike** *adj*
sylvan or **silvan** *adj chiefly poetic* of or consisting of woods or forests
symbiosis *n* **1** *biol* a close association of two different animal or plant species living together

to their mutual benefit **2** a similar relationship between different individuals or groups: *the symbiosis of the coal and railway industries* > **symbiotic** *adj*
symbol *n* **1** something that represents or stands for something else, usually an object used to represent something abstract **2** a letter, figure, or sign used in mathematics, music, etc., to represent a quantity, operation, function, etc.

symbol *n* **1** = metaphor, image, sign, representation, token **2** = representation, sign, figure, mark, image, token, logo, badge

symbolic *adj* **1** of or relating to a symbol or symbols **2** being a symbol of something > **symbolically** *adv*

symbolic *adj* **1** = figurative, representative **2** = representative, emblematic, allegorical

symbolism *n* **1** the representation of something by the use of symbols **2** an art movement involving the use of symbols to express mystical or abstract ideas > **symbolist** *adj, n*
symbolize or **-lise** *vb* **-lizing**, **-lized** or **-lising**, **-lised 1** to be a symbol of (something) **2** to represent with a symbol > **symbolization** or **-lisation** *n*
symmetry *n, pl* **-tries 1** the state of having two halves that are mirror images of each other **2** beauty resulting from a balanced arrangement of parts > **symmetrical** *adj* > **symmetrically** *adv*
sympathetic *adj* **1** feeling or showing kindness and understanding **2** (of a person) likeable and appealing: *the film's only sympathetic character* **3 sympathetic to** showing agreement with or willing to lend support to: *sympathetic to the movement* > **sympathetically** *adv*

sympathetic *adj* **1** = caring, kind, understanding, concerned, interested, warm, pitying, supportive; ≠ uncaring

sympathize or **-thise** *vb* **-thizing**, **-thized** or **-thising**, **-thised** > **sympathize with A** to feel or express sympathy for: *I sympathized with this fear* **B** to agree with or support: *Pitt sympathized with these objectives* > **sympathizer** or **-thiser** *n*
sympathy *n, pl* **-thies 1** (often foll. by *for*) understanding of other people's problems; compassion **2 sympathy with** agreement with someone's feelings or interests: *we have every sympathy with how she felt* **3** (often *pl*) feelings of loyalty or support for an idea or a cause: *was this where her sympathies lay?* **4** mutual affection or understanding between two people or a person and an animal

sympathy *n* **1** = compassion, understanding, pity, commiseration, aroha (NZ); ≠ indifference **4** = affinity, agreement, rapport, fellow feeling; ≠ opposition

S

symphony n, pl **-nies** 1 a large-scale orchestral composition with several movements 2 an orchestral movement in a vocal work such as an oratorio 3 anything that has a pleasing arrangement of colours or shapes: *the garden was a symphony of coloured bunting* > **symphonic** adj

symposium n, pl **-sia** or **-siums** 1 a conference at which experts or academics discuss a particular subject 2 a collection of essays on a particular subject

symptom n 1 med a sign indicating the presence of an illness or disease 2 anything that is taken as an indication that something is wrong: *a growing symptom of grave social injustice* > **symptomatic** adj

symptom n 1 = sign, mark, indication, warning 2 = manifestation, sign, indication, mark, evidence, expression, proof, token

synagogue n a building for Jewish religious services and religious instruction

sync or **synch** films, television & computers informal ▸ vb 1 to synchronize ▸ n 2 synchronization: *the film and sound are in sync*

synchromesh adj 1 (of a gearbox) having a system of clutches that synchronizes the speeds of the gearwheels before they engage ▸ n 2 a gear system having these features

synchronize or **-nise** vb **-nizing, -nized** or **-nising, -nised** 1 (of two or more people) to perform (an action) at the same time: *a synchronized withdrawal of Allied forces* 2 to cause (two or more clocks or watches) to show the same time 3 films to match (the soundtrack and the action of a film) precisely > **synchronization** or **-nisation** n

synchronous adj occurring at the same time and rate > **synchrony** n

syncopate vb **-pating, -pated** music to stress the weak beats in (a rhythm or a piece of music) instead of the strong beats > **syncopation** n

syncope (sing-kop-ee) n 1 med a faint 2 linguistics the omission of sounds or letters from the middle of a word, as in *ne'er* for *never*

syndicate n 1 a group of people or firms organized to undertake a joint project 2 an association of individuals who control organized crime 3 a news agency that sells articles and photographs to a number of newspapers for simultaneous publication ▸ vb **-cating, -cated** 4 to sell (articles and photographs) to several newspapers for simultaneous publication 5 to form a syndicate of (people) > **syndication** n

syndrome n 1 med a combination of signs and symptoms that indicate a particular disease 2 a set of characteristics indicating the existence of a particular condition or problem

synergy n the potential ability for individuals or groups to be more successful working together than on their own

synod n a special church council which meets regularly to discuss church affairs

synonym n a word that means the same as another word, such as *bucket* and *pail*

synonymous adj 1 (often foll. by with) having the same meaning (as) 2 (foll. by with) closely associated (with): *a family whose name had been synonymous with fine jewellery*

synopsis (sin-op-siss) n, pl **-ses** (-seez) a brief review or outline of a subject; summary: *they have sent me a monthly synopsis of the plot*

syntax n the grammatical rules of a language and the way in which words are arranged to form phrases and sentences > **syntactic** or **syntactical** adj

synthesis (sinth-iss-siss) n, pl **-ses** (-seez) 1 the process of combining objects or ideas into a complex whole 2 the combination produced by such a process 3 chem the process of producing a compound by one or more chemical reactions, usually from simpler starting materials

synthesize or **-sise** vb **-sizing, -sized** or **-sising, -sised** 1 to combine (objects or ideas) into a complex whole 2 to produce (a compound) by synthesis

synthesizer n a keyboard instrument in which speech, music, or other sounds are produced electronically

synthetic adj 1 (of a substance or material) made artificially by chemical reaction 2 not sincere or genuine: *synthetic compassion* ▸ n 3 a synthetic substance or material > **synthetically** adv

synthetic adj 1 = artificial, fake, man-made; ≠ real

syphilis n a sexually transmitted disease that causes sores on the genitals and eventually on other parts of the body > **syphilitic** adj

syphon n, vb same as **siphon**

Syrian adj 1 of Syria ▸ n 2 a person from Syria

syringe n 1 med a device used for withdrawing or injecting fluids, consisting of a hollow cylinder of glass or plastic, a tightly fitting piston, and a hollow needle ▸ vb **-ringing, -ringed** 2 to wash out, inject, or spray with a syringe: *a harmless blue dye is syringed into the uterus*

syrup n 1 a solution of sugar dissolved in water and often flavoured with fruit juice: used for sweetening fruit, etc. 2 a thick sweet liquid food made from sugar or molasses: *maple syrup* 3 a liquid medicine containing a sugar solution: *cough syrup*

syrupy adj 1 (of a liquid) thick or sweet 2 excessively sentimental: *a soundtrack of syrupy violins*

system n 1 a method or set of methods for doing or organizing something: *a new system of production or distribution* 2 orderliness or routine; an ordered manner: *there is no system in his work* 3 the manner in which an institution or aspect of society has been arranged: *the Scottish legal* *system* **4 the system** the government and state regarded as exploiting, restricting, and repressing individuals **5** the manner in which the parts of something fit or function together; structure: *disruption of the earth's weather system* **6** any scheme or set of rules used to classify, explain, or calculate: *the Newtonian system of physics* **7** a network of communications, transportation, or distribution **8** *biol* an animal considered as a whole **9** *biol* a set of organs or structures that together perform some function: *the immune system* **10** one's physical or mental constitution: *the intrusion of the virus into my system; to get the hate out of my system* **11** an assembly of electronic or mechanical parts forming a self-contained unit: *an alarm system*

> **system** *n* **1** = method, practice, technique, procedure, routine **6** = arrangement, structure, organization, scheme, classification

systematic *adj* following a fixed plan and done in an efficient and methodical way: *a systematic approach to teaching* > **systematically** *adv*

> **systematic** *adj* = methodical, organized, efficient, orderly; ≠ unmethodical

systematize *or* **-tise** *vb* **-tizing, -tized** *or* **-tising, -tised** to arrange (information) in a system > **systematization** *or* **-tisation** *n*

systemic *adj biol* (of a poison, disease, etc.) affecting the entire animal or body > **systemically** *adv*

systole (siss-tol-ee) *n physiol* contraction of the heart, during which blood is pumped into the arteries > **systolic** *adj*

t *or* **T** *n, pl* **t's, T's** *or* **Ts** **1** the 20th letter of the English alphabet **2 to a T** ʌ in every detail: *that's her to a T* ʙ perfectly: *that dress suits you to a T*

t tonne(s)

T **1** *chem* tritium **2** tera-

t. **1** temperature **2** ton(s)

ta *interj Brit, Austral & NZ informal* thank you

TA (in Britain) Territorial Army

tab¹ *n* **1** a small flap of material, esp. one on a garment for decoration or for fastening to a button **2** any similar flap, such as a piece of paper attached to a file for identification **3** *chiefly US & Canad* a bill, esp. for a meal or drinks **4 keep tabs on** *informal* to keep a watchful eye on

tab² *n* short for **tabulator**

TAB (in Australia and New Zealand) Totalisator Agency Board: an agency for betting on horse and greyhound racing

tabard *n* **1** a sleeveless jacket, esp. one worn by a medieval knight over his armour **2** a short coat bearing the coat of arms of the sovereign, worn by a herald

Tabasco *n trademark* a very hot sauce made from capsicum peppers

tabby *n, pl* **-bies 1** a cat whose fur has dark stripes or wavy markings on a lighter background ▸ *adj* **2** having dark stripes or wavy markings on a lighter background

tabernacle *n* **1 the Tabernacle** *Bible* the portable sanctuary in which the ancient Israelites carried the Ark of the Covenant **2** any place of Christian worship that is not called a church **3** *RC Church* a receptacle in which the Blessed Sacrament is kept

tabla *n, pl* **-bla** *or* **-blas** one of a pair of Indian drums played with the hands

table *n* **1** a piece of furniture consisting of a flat top supported by legs: *a coffee table* **2** a set of facts or figures arranged in rows and columns: *a league table* **3** a group of people sitting round a table for a meal, game, etc.: *the whole table laughed* **4** *formal* the food provided at a meal or in a particular house: *he keeps a good table* **5 turn the tables** to cause a complete reversal of circumstances ▸ *vb* **-bling, -bled 6** *Brit & Austral* to submit (a motion) for discussion by a meeting **7** *US* to suspend discussion of (a proposal) indefinitely

> **table** *n* **1** = counter, bench, stand, board, surface, work surface **2** = list, chart, tabulation, record, roll, register, diagram, itemization ▸ *vb* **6** = submit, propose, put forward, move, suggest, enter, file, lodge

tableau | 860

tableau (tab-loh) *n, pl* **-leaux** (-loh) a silent motionless group of people arranged to represent a scene from history, legend, or literature

table d'hôte (tah-bla dote) *adj* **1** (of a meal) consisting of a set number of courses with a limited choice of dishes offered at a fixed price ▶ *n, pl* **tables d'hôte** (tah-bla dote) **2** a table d'hôte meal or menu

table football *n Brit* a game based on soccer, played on a table with sets of miniature human figures mounted on rods allowing them to be tilted or spun to strike the ball. US & Canad name: **foosball**

tableland *n* a flat area of high ground; plateau

tablespoon *n* **1** a spoon, larger than a dessertspoon, used for serving food **2** Also called: **tablespoonful** the amount contained in such a spoon **3** a unit of capacity used in cooking, equal to half a fluid ounce

tablet *n* **1** a pill consisting of a compressed medicinal substance **2** a flattish cake of some substance, such as soap **3** a slab of stone, wood, etc., used for writing on before the invention of paper **4** an inscribed piece of stone, wood, etc., that is fixed to a wall as a memorial: *a tablet in memory of those who died* **5** a handheld personal computer that is operated by touchscreen

table tennis *n* a game resembling a miniature form of tennis played on a table with bats and a small light ball

tabloid *n* a newspaper with fairly small pages, usually with many photographs and a concise and often sensational style

taboo or **tabu** *n, pl* **-boos** or **-bus** **1** a restriction or prohibition resulting from social or other conventions **2** a ritual prohibition, esp. of something that is considered holy or unclean ▶ *adj* **3** forbidden or disapproved of: *a taboo subject*

> **taboo** or **tabu** *n* = prohibition, ban, restriction, anathema, interdict, proscription, tapu (NZ) ▶ *adj* = forbidden, banned, prohibited, unacceptable, outlawed, anathema, proscribed, unmentionable; ≠ permitted

tabular *adj* arranged in parallel columns so as to form a table

tabulate *vb* **-lating, -lated** to arrange (information) in rows and columns > **tabulation** *n*

tabulator *n* a key on a typewriter or word processor that sets stops so that data can be arranged and presented in columns

tachograph *n* a device that measures the speed of a vehicle and the distance that it covers, and produces a record (**tachogram**) of its readings

tachometer *n* a device for measuring speed, esp. that of a revolving shaft

tacit (tass-it) *adj* understood or implied without actually being stated: *tacit support*

taciturn (tass-it-turn) *adj* habitually silent, reserved, or uncommunicative > **taciturnity** *n*

tack¹ *n* **1** a short sharp-pointed nail with a large flat head **2** Brit & NZ a long loose temporary stitch used in dressmaking ▶ *vb* **3** to fasten (something) with a tack or tacks: *the carpet needs to be tacked down* **4** Brit & NZ to sew (something) with long loose temporary stitches ▶ See also **tack on**

> **tack** *n* **1** = nail, pin, drawing pin ▶ *vb* **3** = fasten, fix, attach, pin, nail, affix

tack² *n* **1** *naut* the course of a boat sailing obliquely into the wind, expressed in terms of the side of the boat against which the wind is blowing: *on the port tack* **2** a course of action or a policy: *telling her to get off my back hadn't worked, so I took a different tack* ▶ *vb* **3** *naut* to steer (a boat) on a zigzag course, so as to make progress against the wind

tack³ *n* riding harness for horses, including saddles and bridles

tackies or **takkies** *pl n, sing* **tacky** *S African informal* tennis shoes or plimsolls

tackle *vb* **-ling, -led** **1** to deal with (a problem or task) in a determined way **2** to confront (someone) about something: *I intend to tackle both management and union on this issue* **3** to attack and fight (a person or animal) **4** *sport* to attempt to get the ball away from (an opposing player) ▶ **5** *sport* an attempt to get the ball away from an opposing player **6** the equipment required for a particular sport or occupation: *fishing tackle* **7** a set of ropes and pulleys for lifting heavy weights **8** *naut* the ropes and other rigging aboard a ship

> **tackle** *vb* **1** = undertake, attempt, embark upon, get stuck into (*informal*), have a go or stab at (*informal*) **4** = intercept, stop, challenge ▶ *n* **5** = block, challenge

tack on *vb* to attach or add (something) to something that is already complete: *an elegant mansion with a modern extension tacked on at the back*

> **tack on** *vb* **tack something onto something** = append (*formal*), add, attach, tag

tacky¹ *adj* **tackier, tackiest** slightly sticky > **tackiness** *n*

tacky² *adj* **tackier, tackiest** *informal* **1** vulgar and tasteless: *tacky commercialism* **2** shabby or shoddy: *tacky streets* > **tackiness** *n*

taco (tah-koh) *n, pl* **tacos** *Mexican cookery* a tortilla folded into a roll with a filling and usually fried

tact *n* **1** a sense of the best and most considerate way to deal with people so as not to upset them **2** skill in handling difficult situations > **tactful** *adj* > **tactfully** *adv* > **tactless** *adj* > **tactlessly** *adv* > **tactlessness** *n*

tactic *n* a move or method used to achieve an aim or task: *he has perfected dissent as a tactic to further his career*. See also **tactics**

tactic n = policy, approach, move, scheme, plans, method, manoeuvre, ploy

tactical adj **1** of or employing tactics: *a tactical advantage* **2** (of missiles, bombing, etc.) for use in limited military operations > **tactically** adv

tactical adj **1** = strategic, shrewd, smart, diplomatic, cunning; ≠ impolitic

tactics n **1** *military* the science of the detailed direction of forces in battle to achieve an aim or task ▸ pl n **2** the plans and methods used to achieve a particular short-term aim > **tactician** n

tactics pl n = strategy, campaigning, manoeuvres, generalship

tactile adj of or having a sense of touch: *the tactile sense*

tadpole n the aquatic larva of a frog or toad, which develops from a limbless tailed form with external gills into a form with internal gills, limbs, and a reduced tail

TAFE (in Australia) Technical and Further Education

taffeta n a thin shiny silk or rayon fabric used esp. for women's clothes

tag¹ n **1** a piece of paper, leather, etc., for attaching to something as a mark or label: *the price tag* **2** a point of metal or plastic at the end of a cord or lace **3** a brief trite quotation **4** an electronic device worn by a prisoner under house arrest so that his or her movements can be monitored **5** *slang* a graffito consisting of a nickname or personal symbol ▸ vb **tagging, tagged 6** to mark with a tag ▸ See also **tag along**

tag n **1** = label, tab, note, ticket, slip, identification, marker, flap ▸ vb = label, mark

tag² n **1** a children's game in which one player chases the others in an attempt to touch one of them, who will then become the chaser ▸ vb **tagging, tagged 2** to catch and touch (another child) in the game of tag. Also: **tig**

tag along vb to accompany someone, esp. when uninvited: *I tagged along behind the gang*

tagliatelle (tal-yat-tell-ee) n a form of pasta made in narrow strips

tail n **1** the rear part of an animal's body, usually forming a long thin flexible part attached to the trunk. Related adjective: **caudal 2** any long thin part projecting or hanging from the back or end of something: *the waiter produced menus from beneath the tail of his coat* **3** the last part: *the tail of the procession* **4** the rear part of an aircraft **5** *astron* the luminous stream of gas and dust particles driven from the head of a comet when it is close to the sun **6** *informal* a person employed to follow and spy upon another **7 turn tail** to run away **8 with one's tail between one's legs** completely defeated and demoralized ▸ adj **9** at the back:

tail feathers ▸ vb **10** *informal* to follow (someone) stealthily ▸ See also **tail off**, **tails** > **tailless** adj

tail n **1** = extremity, appendage, brush, rear end, hindquarters, hind part **2, 5** = train, end, trail, tailpiece **7 turn tail** = run away, flee, run off, retreat, cut and run, take to your heels ▸ vb = follow, track, shadow, trail, stalk

tailback n *Brit* a queue of traffic stretching back from an obstruction

tailboard n a removable or hinged rear board on a lorry or trailer

tail coat n a man's black coat which stops at the hips at the front and has a long back split into two below the waist

tail off or **tail away** vb **1** to decrease gradually: *orders tailed off* **2** (of someone's voice) to become gradually quieter and then silent

tailor n **1** a person who makes, repairs, or alters outer garments, esp. menswear. Related adjective: **sartorial** ▸ vb **2** to cut or style (a garment) to satisfy specific requirements **3** to adapt (something) so as to make it suitable: *activities are tailored to participants' capabilities* > **tailored** adj

tailor n = outfitter (*old-fashioned*), couturier, dressmaker, seamstress, clothier, costumier ▸ vb **3** = adapt, adjust, modify, style, fashion, shape, alter, mould

tailor-made adj **1** (of clothing) made by a tailor to fit exactly **2** perfect for a particular purpose: *I'm tailor-made for the role*

tailplane n a small horizontal wing at the tail of an aircraft to help keep it stable

tails pl n **1** *informal* same as **tail coat** ▸ interj, adv **2** with the side of a coin uppermost that does not have a portrait of a head on it

tailspin n **1** *aeronautics* same as **spin** (sense 10) **2** *informal* a state of confusion or panic

tailwind n a wind blowing from behind an aircraft or vehicle

taint vb **1** to spoil or contaminate by an undesirable quality: *tainted by corruption* ▸ n **2** a defect or flaw **3** a trace of contamination or infection > **tainted** adj

taint vb = spoil, ruin, contaminate, damage, stain, corrupt, pollute, tarnish; ≠ purify

taipan n a large poisonous Australian snake

take vb **taking, took, taken 1** to remove from a place, usually by grasping with the hand: *he took a fifty-dollar note from his wallet* **2** to accompany or escort: *he took me home* **3** to use as a means of transport: *we took a taxi* **4** to conduct or lead: *that road takes you to Preston* **5** to obtain possession of (something), often dishonestly: *they had taken everything most precious to us* **6** to seize or capture: *her husband had been taken by the rebels* **7** (in games such as chess or cards) to win or capture (a piece, trick, etc.) **8** to choose or select (something to use or buy): *I'll take the green one, please* **9** to put an end to: *he took his own life* **10** to require (time, resources, or ability): *this would have taken years to set up* **11** to use as a particular case: *take a friend of mine, for example* **12** to find and make use of (a seat, flat, etc.) **13** to accept the duties of: *the legitimate government will take office* **14** to receive in a specified way: *my mother took it calmly* **15** to receive and make use of: *she took the opportunity to splash her heated face* **16** to eat or drink: *all food substances are toxic if taken in excess* **17** to perform (an action, esp. a beneficial one): *she took a deep breath* **18** to accept (something that is offered or given): *she took a job as a waitress* **19** to put into effect: *taking military action simply* **20** to make (a photograph) **21** to write down or copy: *taking notes* **22** to work at or study: *taking painting lessons* **23** to do or sit (a test, exam, etc.) **24** to begin to experience or feel: *he took an interest in psychoanalysis* **25** to accept (responsibility, blame, or credit) **26** to accept as valid: *I take your point* **27** to stand up to or endure: *I can't take this harassment any more* **28** to wear a particular size of shoes or clothes: *what size of shoes do you take?* **29** to have a capacity of or room for: *the Concert Hall can take about 2500 people* **30** to ascertain by measuring: *she comes after breakfast to take her pulse and temperature* **31** to subtract or deduct: *take seven from eleven* **32** to aim or direct: *he took a few steps towards the door* **33** (of a shop, club, etc.) to make (a specified amount of money) from sales, tickets, etc.: *films that take no money at the box office* **34** to have or produce the intended effect: *the dye hasn't taken on your shoes* **35** (of seedlings) to start growing successfully **36 take account of** *or* **take into account** See **account** (sense 9) **37 take advantage of** See **advantage** (sense 4) **38 take care** See **care** (sense 10) **39 take care of** See **care** (sense 11) **40 take it** to assume or believe: *I take it that means they don't want to leave* **41 take part in** See **part** (sense 17) **42 take place** See **place** (sense 20) **43 take upon oneself** to assume the right or duty (to do something) **44 take your time** use as much time as you need ▸ *n* **45** *films & music* one of a series of recordings from which the best will be selected **46** *informal, chiefly US* a version or interpretation: *Minnelli's bleak take on the story* ▸ See also **take after** *etc.*

> **take** *vb* **1** = remove, draw, pull, fish, withdraw, extract **2** = accompany, lead, bring, guide, conduct, escort, convoy, usher **5** = steal, appropriate, pocket, pinch (*informal*), misappropriate, purloin; ≠ return **6** = capture, seize, take into custody, lay hold of; ≠ release **10** = require, need, involve, demand, call for, entail, necessitate **27** = tolerate, stand, bear, stomach, endure, abide, put up with (*informal*), withstand; ≠ avoid **29** = have room for, hold, contain, accommodate, accept

take after *vb* to resemble in appearance or character: *he takes after his grandfather*

take away *vb* **1** to remove or subtract: *the lymph glands are taken away and examined under a microscope* **2** to detract from or lessen the value of (something): *this does not take away from their achievement* ▸ *prep* **3** minus: *six take away two is four* ▸ *adj* **takeaway 4** *Brit, Austral & NZ* sold for consumption away from the premises: *takeaway food* ▸ *n* **takeaway** *Brit, Austral & NZ* **5** a shop or restaurant that sells such food **6** a meal sold for consumption away from the premises

take in *vb* **1** to understand: *I was too tired to take in all of what was being said* **2** *informal* to cheat or deceive: *don't be taken in by his charming manner* **3** to include: *this tour takes in the romance and history of Salzburg, Vienna, and Munich* **4** to receive into one's house: *his widowed mother lived by taking in boarders* **5** to make (clothing) smaller by altering the seams **6** to go to: *taking in a movie*

> **take in** *vb* **1 take something in** = understand, absorb, grasp, digest, comprehend, assimilate, get the hang of (*informal*) **2 take someone in** = deceive, fool, con (*informal*), trick, cheat, mislead, dupe, swindle, scam (*slang*)

take off *vb* **1** to remove (a garment) **2** (of an aircraft) to become airborne **3** *informal* to set out on a journey: *taking off for the Highlands* **4** *informal* to become successful or popular: *the record took off after being used in a film* **5** to deduct (an amount) from a price or total **6** to withdraw or put an end to: *the bus service has been taken off because of lack of demand* **7** *informal* to mimic (someone) ▸ *n* **takeoff 8** the act or process of making an aircraft airborne **9** *informal* an act of mimicry

> **take off** *vb* **2** = lift off, take to the air **3** = depart, go, leave, disappear, abscond, decamp, slope off **7 take someone off** = parody, imitate, mimic, mock, caricature, send up (*Brit informal*), lampoon, satirize

take over *vb* **1** to gain control or management of **2** to become responsible for (a job) after another person has stopped doing it: *I'll take over the driving if you want a break* **3 take over from** to become more successful or important than (something), and eventually replace it: *cars gradually took over from horses* ▸ *n* **takeover 4** the act of gaining control of a company by buying its shares **5** the act of seizing and taking control of something: *the rebel takeover in Ethiopia*

> **take over** *n* **takeover** = merger, coup, incorporation

take up *vb* **1** to occupy or fill (space or time): *looking after the baby takes up most of my time* **2** to adopt the study, practice, or activity of: *I took up architecture* **3** to shorten (a garment) **4** to accept (an offer): *I'd like to take up your offer of help* **5 take up on A** to accept what is offered by (someone): *I might just take you up on that offer* **B** to discuss (something) further with (someone): *I'd like*

to take you up on that last point **6 take up with**
A to discuss (an issue) with (someone): *take up the matter with the District Council more seriously* **B** to begin to be friendly and spend time with (someone): *he'd already taken up with the woman he would marry*

take up *vb* **1 take something up** = occupy, absorb, consume, use up, cover, fill, waste, squander **2 take something up** = start, begin, engage in, adopt, become involved in

taking *adj* charming, fascinating, or intriguing
takings *pl n* receipts; earnings
talc *or* **talcum** *n* **1** same as **talcum powder 2** a soft mineral, consisting of magnesium silicate, used in the manufacture of ceramics, paints, and talcum powder
talcum powder *n* a powder made of purified talc, usually scented, used to dry or perfume the body
tale *n* **1** a report, account, or story: *everyone had their own tale to tell about the flood* **2** a malicious piece of gossip **3 tell tales A** to tell fanciful lies **B** to report malicious stories or trivial complaints, esp. to someone in authority **4 tell a tale** to reveal something important **5 tell its own tale** to be self-evident

tale *n* **1** = story, narrative, anecdote, account, legend, saga, yarn (*informal*), fable

talent *n* **1** a natural ability to do something well: *the boy has a real talent for writing* **2** a person or people with such ability: *he is the major talent in Italian fashion* **3** *informal* people regarded as attractive or as potential sexual partners: *there's always lots of talent in that pub* **4** any of various ancient units of weight and money
> **talented** *adj*

talent *n* **1** = ability, gift, aptitude, capacity, genius, flair, knack

talisman *n, pl* **-mans** a stone or other small object, usually inscribed or carved, believed to protect the wearer from evil influences
> **talismanic** *adj*
talk *vb* **1** to express one's thoughts or feelings by means of spoken words **2** to exchange ideas or opinions about something: *they were talking about where they would go on holiday* **3** to give voice to; utter: *he was talking rubbish* **4** to discuss: *the political leaders were talking peace* **5** to reveal information: *she was ready to talk* **6** to be able to speak (a language or style) in conversation: *the ferry was full of people talking French* **7** to spread rumours or gossip **8** to be effective or persuasive: *money talks* **9** to get into a particular condition or state of mind by talking: *I had talked myself hoarse* **10 now you're talking** *informal* at last you're saying something agreeable **11 you can** *or* **can't talk** *informal* you are in no position to comment or criticize ▸ *n* **12** a speech or lecture: *a talk on local government reform* **13** an exchange of ideas or

thoughts: *we had a talk about our holiday plans* **14** idle chatter, gossip, or rumour **15** (*often pl*) a conference, discussion, or negotiation ▸ See also **talk back** > **talker** *n*

talk *vb* **1** = speak, chat, chatter, converse, communicate, natter, earbash (*Austral, NZ slang*) **2, 4** = discuss, confer, negotiate, parley, confabulate, korero (*NZ*) **5** = inform, grass (*Brit slang*), tell all, give the game away, blab, let the cat out of the bag ▸ *n* **12** = speech, lecture, presentation, report, address, discourse, sermon, symposium, whaikorero (*NZ*)

talkative *adj* given to talking a great deal
talkback *n NZ* a broadcast in which telephone comments or questions from the public are transmitted live
talk back *vb* to answer (someone) rudely or cheekily
talking-to *n informal* a scolding or telling-off

talking-to *n* = reprimand, lecture, rebuke, scolding, criticism, reproach, ticking-off (*informal*), dressing-down (*informal*); ≠ praise

tall *adj* **1** of greater than average height **2** having a specified height: *five feet tall*

tall *adj* **1** = lofty, big, giant, long-legged, lanky, leggy; ≠ short

tallboy *n Brit* a high chest of drawers made in two sections placed one on top of the other
tall order *n informal* a difficult or unreasonable request
tallow *n* a hard fatty animal fat used in making soap and candles
tall story *n informal* an unlikely and probably untrue tale
tally *vb* **-lies, -lying, -lied 1** to agree with or be consistent with something else: *this description didn't seem to me to tally with what we saw* **2** to keep score ▸ *n, pl* **-lies 3** any record of debit, credit, the score in a game, etc. **4** an identifying label or mark **5** a stick used (esp. formerly) as a record of the amount of a debt according to the notches cut in it

tally *vb* **1** = agree, match, accord, fit, square, coincide, correspond, conform; ≠ disagree ▸ *n* **3** = record, score, total, count, reckoning, running total

tally-ho *interj* the cry of a participant at a hunt when the quarry is sighted
Talmud *n Judaism* the primary source of Jewish religious law > **Talmudic** *adj* > **Talmudist** *n*
talon *n* a sharply hooked claw, such as that of a bird of prey
tamarind *n* a tropical evergreen tree with fruit whose acid pulp is used as a food and to make beverages and medicines
tamarisk *n* a tree or shrub of the Mediterranean region and S Asia, with scalelike leaves, slender branches, and feathery flower clusters

tambourine *n music* a percussion instrument consisting of a single drum skin stretched over a circular wooden frame with pairs of metal discs that jingle when it is struck or shaken

tame *adj* **1 A** (of an animal) changed by humans from a wild state into a domesticated state **B** (of an animal) not afraid of or aggressive towards humans **2** (of a person) tending to do what one is told without questioning or criticizing it **3** mild and unexciting: *the love scenes are fairly tame by modern standards* ▸ *vb* **taming, tamed 4** to make (an animal) tame; domesticate **5** to bring under control; make less extreme or dangerous: *many previously deadly diseases have been tamed by antibiotics*

> **tame** *adj* **1** = domesticated, docile, broken, gentle, obedient, amenable, tractable **2** = submissive, meek, compliant, subdued, manageable, obedient, docile, unresisting; ≠ stubborn **3** = unexciting, boring, dull, bland, uninspiring, humdrum, uninteresting, insipid; ≠ exciting ▸ *vb* **4** = domesticate, train, break in, house-train; ≠ make fiercer **5** = subdue, suppress, master, discipline, humble, conquer, subjugate; ≠ arouse

Tamil *n* **1** *pl* **-ils** *or* **-il** a member of a people of S India and Sri Lanka **2** the language of the Tamils ▸ *adj* **3** of the Tamils

tam-o'-shanter *n* a Scottish brimless woollen cap with a bobble in the centre

tamp *vb* to force or pack (something) down by tapping it several times: *he tamped the bowl of his pipe*

tamper *vb* (foll. by *with*) **1** to interfere or meddle with without permission: *someone has been tampering with the locks* **2** to attempt to influence someone, esp. by bribery: *an attempt to tamper with the jury*

tampon *n* an absorbent plug of cotton wool inserted into the vagina during menstruation

tan¹ *n* **1** a brown coloration of the skin caused by exposure to ultraviolet rays, esp. those of the sun ▸ *vb* **tanning, tanned 2** (of a person or his or her skin) to go brown after exposure to ultraviolet rays **3** to convert (a skin or hide) into leather by treating it with a tanning agent **4** *slang* to beat or flog ▸ *adj* **5** yellowish-brown

tan² *maths* tangent

tandem *n* **1** a bicycle with two sets of pedals and two saddles, arranged one behind the other for two riders **2 in tandem** together or in conjunction: *the two drugs work in tandem to combat the disease* ▸ *adv* **3** one behind the other: *Jim and Ruth arrived, riding tandem*

tandoor *n* a type of Indian clay oven

tandoori *adj* cooked in a tandoor: *tandoori chicken*

tang *n* **1** a strong sharp taste or smell: *we could already smell the tang of the distant sea* **2** a trace or hint of something: *there was a tang of cloves in the apple pie* **3** the pointed end of a tool, such as a knife or chisel, which fits into the handle > **tangy** *adj*

tangata whenua (tang-ah-tah fen-noo-ah) *pl n NZ* **1** the original Polynesian settlers in New Zealand **2** descendants of the original Polynesian settlers

tangent *n* **1** a line, curve, or plane that touches another curve or surface at one point but does not cross it **2** (in trigonometry) the ratio of the length of the opposite side to that of the adjacent side of a right-angled triangle **3 go off at a tangent** suddenly take a completely different line of thought or action ▸ *adj* **4** of or involving a tangent **5** touching at a single point

tangential *adj* **1** only having an indirect or superficial relevance: *Hitler's vegetarianism only has a tangential link with the policies of the Nazis* **2** of or being a tangent: *a street tangential to the market square* > **tangentially** *adv*

tangerine *n* **1** the small orange-like fruit, with a sweet juicy flesh, of an Asian tree ▸ *adj* **2** reddish-orange

tangible *adj* **1** able to be touched; material or physical **2** real or substantial: *tangible results* > **tangibility** *n* > **tangibly** *adv*

> **tangible** *adj* = definite, real, positive, material, actual, concrete, palpable, perceptible; ≠ intangible

tangle *n* **1** a confused or complicated mass of things, such as hair or fibres, knotted or coiled together: *a tangle of wires* **2** a complicated problem or situation ▸ *vb* **-gling, -gled 3** to twist (things, such as hair or fibres) together in a confused mass **4** to come into conflict: *the last thing she wanted was to tangle with the police* **5** to catch or trap in a net, ropes, etc.: *the string of the kite had got tangled in the branches* > **tangled** *adj*

> **tangle** *n* **1** = knot, twist, web, jungle, coil, entanglement **2** = mess, jam (*informal*), fix (*informal*), confusion, complication, mix-up, shambles, entanglement ▸ *vb* **3** = twist, knot, mat, coil, mesh, entangle, interweave, ravel; ≠ disentangle **4 tangle with someone** = come into conflict with, come up against, cross swords with, dispute with, contend with, contest with, lock horns with

tango *n*, *pl* **-gos 1** a Latin-American dance characterized by long gliding steps and sudden pauses **2** music for this dance ▸ *vb* **-going, -goed 3** to perform this dance

taniwha (tun-ee-fah) *n NZ* a mythical Māori monster that lives in rivers and lakes

tank *n* **1** a large container for storing liquids or gases **2** an armoured combat vehicle moving on tracks and armed with guns **3** Also called: **tankful** the quantity contained in a tank

tankard *n* a large one-handled beer-mug, sometimes fitted with a hinged lid

tanker *n* a ship or lorry for carrying liquid in bulk: *an oil tanker*

tannery *n*, *pl* **-neries** a place or building where skins and hides are tanned

tannin *n* a yellowish compound found in many plants, such as tea and grapes, and used in tanning and dyeing. Also called: **tannic acid**

Tannoy *n trademark Brit* a type of public-address system

tansy *n, pl* **-sies** a plant with yellow flowers in flat-topped clusters

tantalize *or* **-lise** *vb* **-lizing, -lized** *or* **-lising, -lised** to tease or make frustrated, for example by tormenting (someone) with the sight of something that he or she wants but cannot have › **tantalizing** *or* **-lising** *adj* › **tantalizingly** *or* **-lisingly** *adv*

tantalum *n chem* a hard greyish-white metallic element that resists corrosion. Symbol: **Ta**

tantamount *adj* **tantamount to** equivalent in effect to: *the raid was tantamount to a declaration of war*

tantrum *n* a childish outburst of bad temper

> **tantrum** *n* = outburst, temper, hysterics, fit, flare-up, foulie (*Austral slang*), hissy fit (*informal*), strop (*Brit informal*)

tap¹ *vb* **tapping, tapped 1** to knock lightly and usually repeatedly: *she tapped gently on the door* **2** to make a rhythmic sound with the hands or feet by lightly and repeatedly hitting a surface with them: *he was tapping one foot to the music* ▸ *n* **3** a light blow or knock, or the sound made by it **4** the metal piece attached to the toe or heel of a shoe used for tap-dancing

> **tap** *vb* = knock, strike, pat, rap, beat, touch, drum ▸ *n* **3** = knock, pat, rap, touch, drumming

tap² *n* **1** *Brit, Austral & NZ* a valve by which the flow of a liquid or gas from a pipe can be controlled. Usual US word: **faucet 2** a stopper to plug a cask or barrel **3** a concealed listening or recording device connected to a telephone **4** *med* the withdrawal of fluid from a bodily cavity: *a spinal tap* **5 on tap A** *informal* ready for use **B** (of drinks) on draught rather than in bottles ▸ *vb* **tapping, tapped 6** to listen in on (a telephone conversation) secretly by making an illegal connection **7** to obtain something useful or desirable from (something): *a new way of tapping the sun's energy* **8** to withdraw liquid from (something) as if through a tap: *to tap a cask of wine* **9** to cut into (a tree) and draw off sap from it **10** *Brit, Austral & NZ informal* to obtain (money or information) from (someone) **11** *informal* to make an illicit attempt to recruit (a player or employee bound by an existing contract)

> **tap** *n* **1** = valve, faucet (*US, Canad*), stopcock **5A on tap** = available, ready, standing by, to hand, on hand, at hand, in reserve **5B on tap** = on draught, cask-conditioned, from barrels, not bottled *or* canned ▸ *vb* **6** = listen in on, monitor, bug (*informal*), spy on, eavesdrop on, wiretap

tap-dancing *n* a style of dancing in which the performer wears shoes with metal plates at the heels and toes that make a rhythmic sound on the stage as he or she dances › **tap-dancer** *n* › **tap dance** *n*

tape *n* **1** a long thin strip of cotton or linen used for tying or fastening: *a parcel tied with pink tape* **2 A** short for **magnetic tape B** a spool or cassette containing magnetic tape, and used for recording or playing sound or video signals: *he put a tape into his stereo* **C** the music, speech, or pictures which have been recorded on a particular cassette or spool of magnetic tape **3** a narrow strip of plastic which has one side coated with an adhesive substance and is used to stick paper, etc., together: *sticky tape* **4** a string stretched across the track at the end of a race course **5** short for **tape measure** ▸ *vb* **taping, taped 6** Also: **tape-record** to record (speech, music, etc.) on magnetic tape **7** to bind or fasten with tape **8 have a person** *or* **situation taped** *Brit & Austral informal* to have full understanding and control of a person or situation

> **tape** *n* **1** = binding, strip, band, string, ribbon ▸ *vb* **6** = record, video, tape-record, make a recording of **7** = bind, secure, stick, seal, wrap

tape measure *n* a tape or length of metal marked off in centimetres or inches, used for measuring

taper *vb* **1** to become narrower towards one end **2 taper off** to become gradually less: *treatment should be tapered off gradually* ▸ *n* **3** a long thin fast-burning candle **4** a narrowing

tape recorder *n* an electrical device used for recording and reproducing sounds on magnetic tape

tapestry *n, pl* **-tries 1** a heavy woven fabric, often in the form of a picture, used for wall hangings or furnishings **2** a colourful and complicated situation that is made up of many different kinds of things: *the rich tapestry of Hindustani music*

tapeworm *n* a long flat parasitic worm that inhabits the intestines of vertebrates, including humans

tapioca *n* a beadlike starch made from cassava root, used in puddings

tapir (**tape**-er) *n* a piglike mammal of South and Central America and SE Asia, with a long snout, three-toed hind legs, and four-toed forelegs

tappet *n* a short steel rod in an engine which moves up and down transferring movement from one part of the machine to another

taproot *n* the main root of plants such as the dandelion, which grows straight down and bears smaller lateral roots

tar *n* **1** a dark sticky substance obtained by distilling organic matter such as coal, wood, or peat ▸ *vb* **tarring, tarred 2** to coat with tar **3 tar and feather** to cover (someone) with tar and feathers as a punishment **4 tarred with the same brush** having, or regarded as having, the same faults ▷ **tarry** *adj*

taramasalata *n* a creamy pale pink pâté, made from the eggs of fish, esp. smoked cod's roe, and served as an hors d'oeuvre

tarantella *n* **1** a peasant dance from S Italy **2** music for this dance

tarantula *n* **1** a large hairy spider of tropical America with a poisonous bite **2** a large hairy spider of S Europe

tardy *adj* **-dier, -diest 1** occurring later than it is expected to or than it should: *he spent the weekend writing tardy thank-you letters* **2** slow in progress, growth, etc.: *we made tardy progress across the ice* ▷ **tardily** *adv* ▷ **tardiness** *n*

tare *n* **1** any of various vetch plants of Eurasia and N Africa **2** *Bible* a weed, thought to be the darnel

target *n* **1** the object or person that a weapon, ball, etc., is aimed at: *the station was an easy target for an air attack* **2** an object at which an archer or marksman aims, usually a round flat surface marked with circles **3** a fixed goal or objective: *our sales figures are well below target* **4** a person or thing at which criticism or ridicule is directed: *the Chancellor has been the target of much of the criticism* ▸ *vb* **-geting, -geted 5** to direct: *an advertising campaign targeted at gay men* **6** to aim (a missile)

target *n* **1, 2** = mark, goal **3** = goal, aim, objective, end, mark, object, intention, ambition **4** = victim, butt, prey, scapegoat

tariff *n* **1 A** a tax levied by a government on imports or occasionally exports **B** a list of such taxes **2** a list of fixed prices, for example in a hotel **3** *chiefly Brit* a method of charging for services such as gas and electricity by setting a price per unit

tariff *n* **1A** = tax, duty, toll, levy, excise **2** = price list, schedule

Tarmac *n* **1** *trademark* a paving material made of crushed stone bound with a mixture of tar and bitumen, used for a road or airport runway **2 the tarmac** the area of an airport where planes wait and take off or land: *we had to wait for an hour on the tarmac* ▸ *vb* **tarmac, -macking, -macked 3** to apply Tarmac to (a surface)

tarn *n chiefly Brit* a small mountain lake

tarnish *vb* **1** (of a metal) to become stained or less bright, esp. by exposure to air or moisture **2** to damage or taint: *the affair could tarnish the reputation of the prime minister* ▸ *n* **3** a tarnished condition, surface, or film on a surface ▷ **tarnished** *adj*

tarnish *vb* **1** = stain, discolour, darken, blot, blemish; ≠ brighten **2** = damage, taint, blacken, sully, smirch; ≠ enhance ▸ *n* = stain, taint, discoloration, spot, blot, blemish

tarot (tarr-oh) *n* **1** a special pack of cards, now used mainly for fortune-telling **2** a card in a tarot pack with a distinctive symbolic design

tarpaulin *n* **1** a heavy waterproof canvas coated with tar, wax, or paint **2** a sheet of this canvas, used as a waterproof covering

tarragon *n* a European herb with narrow leaves, which are used as seasoning in cooking

tarry *vb* **-ries, -rying, -ried** *old-fashioned* **1** to delay or linger: *I have no plans to tarry longer than necessary* **2** to stay briefly: *most people tarried only a few hours before moving on*

tarsus *n, pl* **-si 1** the bones of the ankle and heel collectively **2** the corresponding part in other mammals and in amphibians and reptiles

tart¹ *n* **1** a pastry case, often having no top crust, with a sweet filling, such as jam or custard **2** *chiefly US* a small open pie with a fruit filling

tart *n* = pie, pastry, pasty, tartlet, patty

tart² *adj* **1** (of a flavour) sour or bitter **2** sharp and hurtful: *he made a rather tart comment* ▷ **tartly** *adv* ▷ **tartness** *n*

tart *adj* **1** = sharp, acid, sour, bitter, pungent, tangy, piquant, vinegary; ≠ sweet

tart³ *n informal* **1** a woman considered promiscuous **2** *old-fashioned* a prostitute. See also **tart up**

tartan *n* **1** a design of straight lines, crossing at right angles to give a chequered appearance, esp. one associated with a Scottish clan **2** a fabric with this design

tartar¹ *n* **1** a hard deposit on the teeth **2** a brownish-red substance deposited in a cask during the fermentation of wine

tartar² *n* a fearsome or formidable person

tartar sauce *or* **tartare sauce** *n* a mayonnaise sauce mixed with chopped herbs and capers, served with seafood

tartrazine (tar-traz-zeen) *n* an artificial yellow dye used as a food additive

tart up *vb Brit informal* **1** to decorate in a cheap and flashy way: *the shops were tarted up for Christmas* **2** to try to make (oneself) look smart and attractive

task *n* **1** a specific piece of work required to be done **2** an unpleasant or difficult job or duty **3 take to task** to criticize or rebuke

task *n* **1** = job, duty, assignment, exercise, mission, enterprise, undertaking, chore **3 take someone to task** = criticize, blame, censure, rebuke, reprimand, reproach, scold, tell off (*informal*)

task force *n* **1** a temporary grouping of military units formed to undertake a specific mission **2** any organization set up to carry out a continuing task

taskmaster *n* a person who enforces hard or continuous work

Tasmanian devil *n* a small flesh-eating marsupial of Tasmania

tassel *n* a tuft of loose threads secured by a knot or knob, used to decorate a cushion, piece of clothing, etc.

taste *n* **1** the sense by which the flavour of a substance is distinguished by the taste buds **2** the sensation experienced by means of the taste buds **3** a small amount eaten, sipped, or tried on the tongue **4** a brief experience of something: *a taste of the planter's life* **5** a liking for something: *a taste for puns* **6** the ability to appreciate what is beautiful and excellent: *she's got very good taste in clothes* **7** a person's typical preferences as displayed by what they choose to buy, enjoy, etc.: *the film was good but a bit violent for my taste* **8** the quality of not being offensive or bad-mannered: *that remark was in rather poor taste* ▸ *vb* **tasting, tasted** **9** to distinguish the taste of (a substance) by means of the taste buds: *I've got a stinking cold and can't taste anything* **10** to take a small amount of (a food or liquid) into the mouth, esp. in order to test the flavour **11** to have a flavour or taste as specified: *the pizza tastes delicious* **12** to have a brief experience of (something): *they have tasted democracy and they won't let go*

> **taste** *n* **2** = flavour, savour, relish, smack, tang; ≠ blandness **3** = bit, bite, mouthful, sample, dash, spoonful, morsel, titbit **5** = liking, preference, penchant, fondness, partiality, fancy, appetite, inclination; ≠ dislike **6** = refinement, style, judgment, discrimination, appreciation, elegance, sophistication, discernment; ≠ lack of judgment ▸ *vb* **9** = distinguish, perceive, discern, differentiate **10** = sample, try, test, sip, savour **11** = have a flavour of, smack of, savour of **12** = experience, know, undergo, partake of, encounter, meet with; ≠ miss

taste bud *n* any of the cells on the surface of the tongue, by means of which the sensation of taste is experienced

tasteful *adj* having or showing good social or aesthetic taste: *tasteful decor* > **tastefully** *adv*

tasteless *adj* **1** lacking in flavour: *the canteen serves cold, tasteless pizzas* **2** lacking social or aesthetic taste: *a room full of tasteless ornaments*; *a tasteless remark* > **tastelessly** *adv* > **tastelessness** *n*

tasty *adj* **tastier, tastiest** having a pleasant flavour

> **tasty** *adj* = delicious, luscious, palatable, delectable, savoury, full-flavoured, scrumptious (*informal*), appetizing, lekker (*S African slang*), yummo (*Austral slang*); ≠ bland

tat *n Brit* tatty or tasteless articles

tattered *adj* **1** ragged or torn: *a tattered old book* **2** wearing ragged or torn clothing: *the tattered refugees*

tattle *vb* **-tling, -tled** **1** to gossip or chatter ▸ *n* **2** gossip or chatter > **tattler** *n*

tattoo¹ *n, pl* **-toos** **1** a picture or design made on someone's body by pricking small holes in the skin and filling them with indelible dye ▸ *vb* **-tooing, -tooed** **2** to make pictures or designs on (a person's skin) by pricking and staining it with indelible colours > **tattooed** *adj* > **tattooist** *n*

tattoo² *n, pl* **-toos** **1** (formerly) a signal by drum or bugle ordering soldiers to return to their quarters **2** a military display or pageant **3** any drumming or tapping

tatty *adj* **-tier, -tiest** worn out, shabby, or unkempt

taught *vb* the past of **teach**

taunt *vb* **1** to tease or provoke (someone) with jeering remarks ▸ *n* **2** a jeering remark > **taunting** *adj*

> **taunt** *vb* = jeer, mock, tease, ridicule, provoke, insult, torment, deride ▸ *n* = jeer, dig, insult, ridicule, teasing, provocation, derision, sarcasm

taupe *adj* brownish-grey

taut *adj* **1** stretched tight: *the cable must be taut* **2** showing nervous strain: *he was looking taut and anxious* **3** (of a film or piece of writing) having no unnecessary or irrelevant details: *a taut thriller*

tauten *vb* to make or become taut

tautology *n, pl* **-gies** the use of words which merely repeat something already stated, as in *reverse back* > **tautological** *or* **tautologous** *adj*

tavern *n* **1** old-fashioned a pub **2** US, Canad, Austral & NZ a place licensed for the sale and consumption of alcoholic drink

> **tavern** *n* **1** = inn, bar, pub (*informal, chiefly Brit*), public house, beer parlour (*Canad*), beverage room (*Canad*), hostelry, alehouse (*archaic*)

tawdry *adj* **-drier, -driest** cheap, showy, and of poor quality: *tawdry Christmas decorations*

tawny *adj* brown to brownish-orange

tax *n* **1** a compulsory payment to a government to raise revenue, levied on income, property, or goods and services ▸ *vb* **2** to levy a tax on (people, companies, etc.) **3** to make heavy demands on: *the task taxed his ingenuity and patience* **4** **tax someone with** to accuse someone of: *he was taxed with parochialism and meanness* > **taxable** *adj* > **taxing** *adj*

> **tax** *n* = charge, duty, toll, levy, tariff, excise, tithe ▸ *vb* **2** = charge (*formal*), rate, assess **3** = strain, stretch, try, test, load, burden, exhaust, weaken

taxation *n* the levying of taxes or the condition of being taxed

tax-free *adj* not needing to have tax paid on it: *a tax-free lump sum*

taxi *n, pl* **taxis** **1** Also called: **cab, taxicab** a car that may be hired, along with its driver, to carry passengers to any specified destination ▸ *vb* **taxiing, taxied** **2** (of an aircraft) to move along the ground, esp. before takeoff and after landing

taxidermy *n* the art of preparing, stuffing, and mounting animal skins so that they have a lifelike appearance > **taxidermist** *n*

taxi rank *n* a place where taxis wait to be hired

taxonomy *n* **1** the branch of biology concerned with the classification of plants and animals into groups based on their similarities and differences **2** the science or practice of classification > **taxonomic** *adj* > **taxonomist** *n*

taxpayer *n* a person or organization that pays taxes

tax relief *n* a reduction in the amount of tax a person or company has to pay

tax return *n* a declaration of personal income used as a basis for assessing an individual's liability for taxation

TB tuberculosis

tba *or* **TBA** to be arranged

tbc *or* **TBC** to be confirmed

tbs. *or* **tbsp.** tablespoon(ful)

tea *n* **1 A** a drink made by infusing the dried chopped leaves of an Asian shrub in boiling water: *would you like a cup of tea?* **B** the dried chopped leaves of an Asian shrub used to make this drink: *could you get some tea at the grocer's?* **C** the Asian shrub on which these leaves grow **2** *Brit, Austral & NZ* the main evening meal **3** *chiefly Brit* a light meal eaten in mid-afternoon, usually consisting of tea and cakes, sometimes with sandwiches **4** a drink like tea made from other plants: *mint tea*

tea bag *n* a small bag containing tea leaves, infused in boiling water to make tea

teach *vb* **teaching**, **taught 1** to tell or show (someone) how to do something **2** to give instruction or lessons in (a subject) to (students) **3** to cause to learn or understand: *life has taught me to seize the day* **4 teach someone a lesson** to warn or punish someone: *a bully has to be taught a lesson* > **teachable** *adj*

> **teach** *vb* **1** = show, train **2** = instruct, train, coach, inform, educate, drill, tutor, enlighten

teacher *n* a person whose job is to teach others, esp. children

> **teacher** *n* = instructor, coach, tutor, guide, trainer, lecturer, mentor, educator

teaching *n* **1** the art or profession of a teacher **2 teachings** the ideas and principles taught by a person, school of thought, etc.: *the teachings of the Catholic Church*

tea cosy *n* a covering for a teapot to keep the contents hot

teak *n* the hard yellowish-brown wood of an Asian tree, used for furniture making

teal *n*, *pl* **teals** *or* **teal** a small freshwater duck related to the mallard

team *n* **1** a group of players forming one of the sides in a sporting contest **2** a group of people organized to work together: *a team of scientists* **3** two or more animals working together: *a sledge*

pulled by a team of dogs ▸ *vb* **4 team up with** to join with (someone) in order to work together **5 team with** to match (something) with something else: *navy skirts teamed with various coloured blouses*

> **team** *n* **1** = side, squad **2** = group, company, set, body, band, gang, line-up, bunch (*informal*)

teamster *n* **1** *US & Canad* a truck driver **2** (formerly) a driver of a team of horses

teamwork *n* the cooperative work done by a team

teapot *n* a container with a lid, spout, and handle, in which tea is made and from which it is served

tear¹ *n* **1** Also called: **teardrop** a drop of salty fluid appearing in and falling from the eye. Related adjective: **lacrimal, lachrymal, lacrymal 2 in tears** weeping

> **tear** *n* **2 in tears** = weeping, crying, sobbing, blubbering

tear² *vb* **tearing, tore, torn 1** to rip a hole in (something): *I tore my jumper on a nail* **2** to pull apart or to pieces: *eagles have powerful beaks for tearing flesh* **3** to hurry or rush **4** to remove or take by force: *the sacred things torn from the temples of Inca worshippers* **5 tear at someone's heartstrings** to cause someone distress or anguish **6** to injure (a muscle or ligament) by moving or twisting it violently ▸ *n* **7** a hole or split ▸ See also **tear away**

> **tear** *vb* **1** = rip, split, rend (*literary*), shred, rupture **2** = pull apart, claw, lacerate, mutilate, mangle, mangulate (*Austral slang*) **3** = rush, run, charge, race, fly, speed, dash, hurry ▸ *n* = hole, split, rip, rent, snag, rupture

tear away *vb* **1** to persuade (oneself or someone else) to leave: *she stood and watched, unable to tear herself away from the room* ▸ *n* **tearaway 2** *Brit* a wild or unruly person

tearful *adj* weeping or about to weep > **tearfully** *adv*

tear gas *n* a gas that stings the eyes and causes temporary blindness, used in warfare and to control riots

tear-jerker *n informal* an excessively sentimental film or book

tease *vb* **teasing, teased 1** to make fun of (someone) in a provocative and often playful manner **2** to arouse sexual desire in (someone) with no intention of satisfying it **3** to raise the nap of (a fabric) with a teasel ▸ *n* **4** a person who teases **5** a piece of teasing behaviour > **teasing** *adj*

> **tease** *vb* **1** = mock, provoke, torment, taunt, goad, pull someone's leg (*informal*), make fun of **2** = tantalize, lead on, flirt with, titillate

teasel, teazel *or* **teazle** *n* **1** a plant of Eurasia and N Africa, with prickly heads of yellow or purple flowers **2** the dried flower head of a teasel, used, esp. formerly, for raising the nap of cloth

tease out vb **1** to comb (hair, flax, or wool) so as to remove any tangles **2** to extract information with difficulty: *it's not easy to tease out the differences between anxiety and depression*

teaspoon n **1** a small spoon used for stirring tea or coffee **2** Also called: **teaspoonful** the amount contained in such a spoon **3** a unit of capacity used in cooking, etc., equal to 5 ml

teat n **1** the nipple of a breast or udder **2** something resembling a teat such as the rubber mouthpiece of a feeding bottle

tea towel or **tea cloth** n a towel for drying dishes

tea tree n a tree of Australia and New Zealand that yields an oil used as an antiseptic

tech n informal a technical college

techie or **techy** informal ▸ n **1** a person who is skilled in the use of technological devices, such as computers ▸ adj **2** of, relating to, or skilled in the use of such devices

technetium (tek-**neesh**-ee-um) n chem a silvery-grey metallic element, produced artificially, esp. by the fission of uranium. Symbol: **Tc**

technical adj **1** of or specializing in industrial, practical, or mechanical arts and applied sciences: *a technical school* **2** skilled in practical activities rather than abstract thinking **3** relating to a particular field of activity: *technical jargon* **4** according to the letter of the law: *a last-minute penalty awarded to the Irish for a technical offence* **5** showing technique: *technical perfection* ▸ **technically** adv

> **technical** adj **2** = scientific, technological, skilled, specialist, specialized, hi-tech or high-tech

technical college n Brit & Austral an institution for further education that provides courses in art and technical subjects

technicality n, pl **-ties** **1** a petty formal point arising from a strict interpretation of the law or a set of rules: *the case was dismissed on a legal technicality* **2** a detail of the method used to do something: *the technicalities of making a recording*

technician n a person skilled in a particular technical field: *oil technicians*

Technicolor n trademark a process of producing colour film for the cinema by superimposing synchronized films of the same scene, each having a different colour filter

technique n **1** a method or skill used for a particular task: *modern management techniques* **2** proficiency in a practical or mechanical skill: *he lacks the technique to be a good player*

> **technique** n **1** = method, way, system, approach, means, style, manner, procedure **2** = skill, performance, craft, touch, execution, artistry, craftsmanship, proficiency

techno n a type of very fast dance music, using electronic sounds and having a strong technological influence

technocracy n, pl **-cies** government by scientists, engineers, and other experts > **technocrat** n > **technocratic** adj

technology n, pl **-gies** **1** the application of practical or mechanical sciences to industry or commerce **2** the scientific methods or devices used in a particular field: *the latest aircraft technology* > **technological** adj > **technologist** n

tectonics n geol the study of the earth's crust and the forces that produce changes in it

teddy n, pl **-dies** short for **teddy bear**

teddy bear n a stuffed toy bear

tedious adj boring and uninteresting > **tediously** adv > **tediousness** n

> **tedious** adj = boring, dull, dreary, monotonous, drab, tiresome, laborious, humdrum; ≠ exciting

tedium n the state of being bored or the quality of being boring: *the tedium of a nine-to-five white-collar job*

tee n **1** a support for a golf ball, usually a small wooden or plastic peg, used when teeing off **2** an area on a golf course from which the first stroke of a hole is made **3** a mark used as a target in certain games such as curling and quoits ▸ See also **tee off**

teem[1] vb **teem with** to have a great number of: *the woods were teeming with snakes and bears*

teem[2] vb (of rain) to pour down in torrents

teenage adj **1** (of a person) aged between 13 and 19 **2** typical of or designed for people aged between 13 and 19: *teenage fashions*

teenager n a person between the ages of 13 and 19

> **teenager** n = youth, minor, adolescent, juvenile, girl, boy

teens pl n **1** the years of a person's life between the ages of 13 and 19 **2** all the numbers that end in -teen

tee off vb **teeing**, **teed** golf to hit (the ball) from a tee at the start of a hole

teepee n same as **tepee**

teeter vb to wobble or move unsteadily

teeth n **1** the plural of **tooth 2** the power to produce a desired effect: *resolution 672 had no teeth* **3 armed to the teeth** very heavily armed **4 get one's teeth into** to become engrossed in **5 in the teeth of** in spite of: *trying to run a business in the teeth of the recession*

teethe vb **teething**, **teethed** (of a baby) to grow his or her first teeth

teething troubles pl n problems arising during the early stages of a project

teetotal adj never drinking alcohol > **teetotaller** n

TEFL Teaching of English as a Foreign Language

Teflon n trademark a substance used for nonstick coatings on saucepans, etc.

tele- *combining form* **1** at or over a distance: *telecommunications* **2** television: *telegenic* **3** via telephone or television: *teleconference*

telecommunications *n* communications using electronic equipment, such as telephones, radio, and television

telegram *n* (formerly) a message transmitted by telegraph

telegraph *n* **1** (formerly) a system by which information could be transmitted over a distance, using electrical signals sent along a cable ▸ *vb* **2** (formerly) to send (a message) by telegraph **3** to give advance notice of (something), esp. unintentionally: *the twist in the plot was telegraphed long in advance* **4** *Canad informal* to cast (a vote) illegally by impersonating a registered voter › **telegraphist** *n* › **telegraphic** *adj*

telegraphy *n* (formerly) the science or use of a telegraph

telekinesis *n* movement of a body by thought or willpower, without the application of a physical force › **telekinetic** *adj*

telemarketing *n* another name for **telesales**

telemetry *n* the use of electronic devices to record or measure a distant event and transmit the data to a receiver › **telemetric** *adj*

teleology *n* **1** *philosophy* the doctrine that there is evidence of purpose or design in the universe **2** *biol* the belief that natural phenomena have a predetermined purpose and are not determined by mechanical laws › **teleological** *adj* › **teleologist** *n*

telepathy *n* the direct communication of thoughts and feelings between minds without the need to use normal means such as speech, writing, or touch › **telepathic** *adj* › **telepathically** *adv*

telephone *n* **1** a piece of equipment for transmitting speech, consisting of a microphone and receiver mounted on a handset: *the telephone was ringing* **2** the worldwide system of communications using telephones: *reports came in by telephone* ▸ *vb* **-phoning, -phoned** **3** to call or talk to (a person) by telephone ▸ *adj* **4** of or using a telephone: *a telephone call* › **telephonic** *adj*

telephone *n* **1** = phone, mobile, mobile phone *or (informal)* moby, cellphone *or* cellular phone (US), handset, landline, dog and bone (slang), iPhone (trademark), smartphone, Blackberry, camera phone, picture phone ▸ *vb* = call, phone, ring (chiefly Brit), dial

telephonist *n* a person who operates a telephone switchboard

telephony *n* a system of telecommunications for the transmission of speech or other sounds

telephoto lens *n* a lens fitted to a camera to produce a magnified image of a distant object

telesales *n* the selling of a commodity or service by telephone

telescope *n* **1** an optical instrument for making distant objects appear closer by use of a combination of lenses ▸ *vb* **-scoping, -scoped** **2** to shorten (something) while still keeping the important parts: *a hundred years of change has been telescoped into five years* › **telescopic** *adj*

telescope *n* = glass, scope (informal), spyglass ▸ *vb* = shorten, contract, compress, shrink, condense, abbreviate, abridge; ≠ lengthen

televise *vb* **-vising, -vised** to show (a programme or event) on television

television *n* **1** the system or process of producing a moving image with accompanying sound on a distant screen **2** Also called: **television set** a device for receiving broadcast signals and converting them into sound and pictures **3** the content of television programmes: *some people think that television is too violent nowadays* ▸ *adj* **4** of or relating to television: *a television interview* › **televisual** *adj*

television *n* **2** = TV, telly (Brit informal), small screen (informal), the box (Brit informal), the tube (slang)

telex *n* **1** an international communication service formerly used to send messages by teleprinter **2** a teleprinter used in such a service **3** a message sent by telex ▸ *vb* **4** to transmit (a message) by telex

tell *vb* **telling, told** **1** to make known in words; notify: *I told her what had happened* **2** to order or instruct (someone to do something): *he had been told to wait in the lobby* **3** to give an account (of an event or situation): *the President had been told of the developments* **4** to communicate by words: *he was woken at 5 am to be told the news* **5** to discover, distinguish, or discern: *she could tell that he was not sorry* **6** to have or produce an impact or effect: *the pressure had begun to tell on him* **7** *informal* to reveal secrets or gossip **8** **tell the time** to read the time from a clock **9** **you're telling me** *slang* I know that very well

tell *vb* **1** = inform, notify, state to, reveal to, express to, disclose to, proclaim to, divulge, flag up **2** = instruct, order, command, direct, bid **3** = describe, relate, recount, report, portray, depict, chronicle, narrate **5** = distinguish, discriminate, discern, differentiate, identify **6** = have or take effect, register (informal), weigh, count, take its toll, carry weight, make its presence felt

teller *n* **1** a narrator **2** a bank cashier **3** a person appointed to count votes

telling *adj* having a marked effect or impact: *to inflict telling damage on the enemy*

telling *adj* = effective, significant, considerable, marked, striking, powerful, impressive, influential; ≠ unimportant

tell off *vb informal* to reprimand or scold (someone) › **telling-off** *n*

tell off *vb* **tell someone off** = reprimand, rebuke, scold, lecture, censure, reproach, berate, chide

telltale *n* **1** a person who tells tales about others ▸ *adj* **2** giving away information: *examining the hands for telltale signs of age*

tellurium *n chem* a brittle silvery-white nonmetallic element. Symbol: **Te**

telly *n, pl* **-lies** *informal* short for **television**

temerity (tim-merr-it-tee) *n* boldness or audacity

temp *Brit informal* ▸ *n* **1** a person, esp. a secretary, employed on a temporary basis ▸ *vb* **2** to work as a temp

temp. 1 temperature **2** temporary

temper *n* **1** a sudden outburst of anger: *she stormed out in a temper* **2** a tendency to have sudden outbursts of anger: *you've got a temper all right* **3** a mental condition of moderation and calm: *he lost his temper* **4** a person's frame of mind: *he was in a bad temper* ▸ *vb* **5** to modify so as to make less extreme or more acceptable: *past militancy has been tempered with compassion and caring* **6** to reduce the brittleness of (a hardened metal) by reheating it and allowing it to cool **7** *music* to adjust the frequency differences between the notes of a scale on (a keyboard instrument)

temper *n* **1** = rage, fury, bad mood, passion, tantrum, foulie (*Austral slang*), hissy fit (*informal*), strop (*Brit informal*) **2** = irritability, irascibility, passion, resentment, petulance, surliness, hot-headedness; ≠ good humour **3** = self-control, composure, cool (*slang*), calmness, equanimity; ≠ anger **4** = frame of mind, nature, mind, mood, constitution, humour, temperament, disposition ▸ *vb* **5** = moderate, restrain, tone down, soften, soothe, lessen, mitigate, assuage; ≠ intensify **6** = strengthen, harden, toughen, anneal; ≠ soften

tempera *n* a painting medium for powdered pigments, consisting usually of egg yolk and water

temperament *n* a person's character or disposition

temperament *n* = nature, character, personality, make-up, constitution, bent, humour, temper

temperamental *adj* **1** (of a person) tending to be moody and have sudden outbursts of anger **2** *informal* working erratically and inconsistently; unreliable: *the temperamental microphone* **3** of or relating to a person's temperament: *we discussed temperamental and developmental differences* ▸ **temperamentally** *adv*

temperance *n* **1** restraint or moderation, esp. in yielding to one's appetites or desires **2** abstinence from alcoholic drink

temperate *adj* **1** of a climate which is never extremely hot or extremely cold **2** mild or moderate in quality or character: *try to be more temperate in your statements*

temperature *n* **1** the hotness or coldness of something, as measured on a scale that has one or more fixed reference points **2** *informal* an abnormally high body temperature **3** the strength of feeling among a group of people: *his remarks are likely to raise the political temperature considerably*

tempest *n literary* a violent wind or storm

tempestuous *adj* **1** violent or stormy **2** extremely emotional or passionate: *a tempestuous relationship* ▸ **tempestuously** *adv*

template *n* a wood or metal pattern, used to help cut out shapes accurately

temple¹ *n* a building or place used for the worship of a god or gods

temple *n* = shrine, church, sanctuary, house of God

temple² *n* the region on each side of the head in front of the ear and above the cheekbone

tempo (tem-po) *n, pl* **-pi** (-pee) *or* **-pos 1** rate or pace: *the slow tempo of change in an overwhelmingly rural country* **2** the speed at which a piece of music is played or meant to be played

temporal *adj* **1** of or relating to time **2** of secular as opposed to spiritual or religious affairs: *in the Middle Ages the Pope had temporal as well as spiritual power* **3** not permanent or eternal: *a temporal view of drugs as the No. 1 social problem*

temporary *adj* lasting only for a short time; not permanent: *temporary accommodation* ▸ **temporarily** *adv*

temporary *adj* = impermanent, transitory, brief, fleeting, interim, short-lived, momentary, ephemeral; ≠ permanent

temporize *or* **-rise** *vb* **-rizing, -rized** *or* **-rising, -rised 1** to delay, act evasively, or protract a negotiation in order to gain time or avoid making a decision: *'Well,' I temporized, 'I'll have to ask your mother'* **2** to adapt oneself to circumstances, as by temporary or apparent agreement

tempt *vb* **1** to entice (someone) to do something, esp. something morally wrong or unwise: *can I tempt you to have another whisky?* **2** to allure or attract: *she was tempted by the glamour of a modelling career* **3 be tempted** to want to do something while knowing it would be wrong or inappropriate to do so: *many youngsters are tempted to experiment with drugs* **4 tempt fate** or **providence** to take foolish or unnecessary risks ▸ **tempter** *or fem* **temptress** *n*

tempt *vb* **1** = entice, lure, lead on, invite, seduce, coax; ≠ discourage **2** = attract, allure

temptation *n* **1** the act of tempting or the state of being tempted **2** a person or thing that tempts

temptation *n* **1** = enticement, lure, inducement, pull, seduction, allurement, tantalization

tempting *adj* attractive or inviting: *it's tempting to say I told you so* > **temptingly** *adv*

> **tempting** *adj* = inviting, enticing, seductive, alluring, attractive, mouthwatering, appetizing; ≠ uninviting

ten *n* **1** the cardinal number that is the sum of one and nine **2** a numeral, 10 or X, representing this number **3** something representing or consisting of ten units ▸ *adj* **4** amounting to ten: *ten years* > **tenth** *adj*, *n*

tenable *adj* **1** able to be upheld or maintained: *a tenable strategy* **2** (of a job) intended to be held by a person for a particular length of time: *the post will be tenable for three years in the first instance* > **tenability** *n* > **tenably** *adv*

tenacious *adj* **1** holding firmly: *a tenacious grasp* **2** stubborn or persistent: *tenacious support* > **tenaciously** *adv* > **tenacity** *n*

tenancy *n*, *pl* **-cies** **1** the temporary possession or use of lands or property owned by someone else, in return for payment **2** the period of holding or occupying such property

tenant *n* **1** a person who pays rent for the use of land or property **2** any holder or occupant

> **tenant** *n* **1** = leaseholder, resident, renter, occupant, inhabitant, occupier, lodger, boarder

tench *n* a European freshwater game fish of the carp family

tend¹ *vb* to be inclined (to take a particular kind of action or to be in a particular condition) as a rule: *she tends to be rather absent-minded*

> **tend** *vb* = be inclined, be liable, have a tendency, be apt, be prone, lean, incline, gravitate

tend² *vb* **1** to take care of: *it is she who tends his wounds* **2** **tend to** to attend to: *excuse me, I have to tend to the other guests*

> **tend** *vb* **1** = take care of, look after, keep, attend, nurture, watch over; ≠ neglect

tendency *n*, *pl* **-cies** **1** an inclination to act in a particular way **2** the general course or drift of something **3** a faction, esp. within a political party

> **tendency** *n* **1** = inclination, leaning, liability, disposition, propensity, susceptibility, proclivity (*formal*), proneness

tendentious *adj* expressing a particular viewpoint or opinion, esp. a controversial one, in very strong terms: *a somewhat tendentious reading of French history* > **tendentiously** *adv*

tender¹ *adj* **1** (of cooked food) having softened and become easy to chew or cut **2** gentle and kind: *tender loving care* **3** vulnerable or sensitive: *at the tender age of 9* **4** painful when touched: *his wrist was swollen and tender* > **tenderly** *adv* > **tenderness** *n*

tender *adj* **2** = gentle, loving, kind, caring, sympathetic, affectionate, compassionate, considerate; ≠ harsh **3** = vulnerable, young, sensitive, raw, youthful, inexperienced, immature, impressionable; ≠ experienced **4** = sensitive, painful, sore, raw, bruised, inflamed

tender² *vb* **1** to present or offer: *he tendered his resignation* **2** to make a formal offer or estimate for a job or contract: *contractors tendering for government work* ▸ *n* **3** a formal offer to supply specified goods or services at a stated cost or rate: *the government invited tenders to run television and radio services* > **tenderer** *n* > **tendering** *n*

> **tender** *vb* **1** = offer, present, submit, give, propose, volunteer, hand in, put forward ▸ *n* = offer, bid, estimate, proposal, submission

tender³ *n* **1** a small boat that brings supplies to larger vessels in a port **2** a wagon attached to the rear of a steam locomotive that carries the fuel and water

tenderize *or* **-rise** *vb* **-rizing, -rized** *or* **-rising, -rised** to make (meat) tender, by pounding it or adding a substance to break down the fibres > **tenderizer** *or* **-riser** *n*

tendon *n* a band of tough tissue that attaches a muscle to a bone

tendril *n* a threadlike leaf or stem by which a climbing plant attaches itself to a support

tenement *n* a large building divided into several different flats

tenet (ten-nit) *n* a principle on which a belief or doctrine is based

tenner *n Brit, Austral & NZ informal* **1** a ten-pound or ten-dollar note **2** the sum of ten pounds or ten dollars: *it's worth a tenner at least*

tennessine *n chem* a synthetic radioactive element produced in small quantities. Symbol: **Ts**

tennis *n* a game played between two players or pairs of players who use a racket to hit a ball to and fro over a net on a rectangular court. See also **lawn tennis**, **table tennis**

tenon *n* a projecting end of a piece of wood, formed to fit into a corresponding slot in another piece

tenor *n* **1 A** the second highest male voice, between alto and baritone **B** a singer with such a voice **C** a saxophone, horn, or other musical instrument between the alto and bass **2** a general meaning or character: *it was clear from the tenor of the meeting that the manager's actions are very unpopular* ▸ *adj* **3** denoting a musical instrument between alto and baritone: *a tenor saxophone* **4** of or relating to the second highest male voice: *his voice lacks the range needed for the tenor role*

tenpin bowling *n* a game in which players try to knock over ten skittles by rolling a ball at them

tense¹ *adj* **1** having, showing, or causing mental or emotional strain: *the tense atmosphere* **2** stretched tight: *tense muscles* ▸ *vb* **tensing, tensed 3** Also: **tense up** to make or become tense ▸ **tensely** *adv* ▸ **tenseness** *n*

> **tense** *adj* **1** = nervous, edgy, strained, anxious, apprehensive, uptight (*informal*), on edge, jumpy, adrenalized; ≠ calm **2** = rigid, strained, taut, stretched, tight; ≠ relaxed ▸ *vb* = tighten, strain, brace, stretch, flex, stiffen; ≠ relax

tense² *n grammar* the form of a verb that indicates whether the action referred to in the sentence is located in the past, the present, or the future: *'ate' is the past tense of 'to eat'*

tensile *adj* of or relating to tension or being stretched: *The posts were linked by high tensile wire.*

tension *n* **1** a situation or condition of hostility, suspense, or uneasiness: *a renewed state of tension between old enemies* **2** mental or emotional strain: *nervous tension* **3** a force that stretches or the state or degree of being stretched tight: *keep tension on the line until the fish comes within range of the net* **4** *physics* a force that tends to produce an elongation of a body or structure **5** *physics* voltage, electromotive force, or potential difference

> **tension** *n* **1** = friction, hostility, unease, antagonism, antipathy, enmity; ≠ calmness **2** = strain, stress, nervousness, pressure, anxiety, unease, apprehension, suspense; ≠ calmness **3** = rigidity, tightness, stiffness, pressure, stress, stretching, tautness

tent *n* a portable shelter made of canvas or other fabric supported on poles, stretched out, and fastened to the ground by pegs and ropes

tentacle *n* **1** a flexible organ that grows near the mouth in many invertebrates and is used for feeding, grasping, etc. **2 tentacles** the unseen methods by which an organization or idea, esp. a sinister one, influences people and events: *the tentacles of the secret police* ▸ **tentacled** *adj*

tentative *adj* **1** provisional or unconfirmed: *a tentative agreement* **2** hesitant, uncertain, or cautious: *their rather tentative approach* ▸ **tentatively** *adv* ▸ **tentativeness** *n*

> **tentative** *adj* **1** = unconfirmed, provisional, indefinite, test, trial, pilot, preliminary, experimental; ≠ confirmed **2** = hesitant, cautious, uncertain, doubtful, faltering, unsure, timid, undecided; ≠ confident

tenterhooks *pl n* **on tenterhooks** in a state of tension or suspense

tenth *adj, n* See **ten**

tenuous *adj* insignificant or flimsy: *there is only the most tenuous evidence for it* ▸ **tenuously** *adv*

tenure *n* **1** the holding of an office or position **2** the length of time an office or position lasts **3** the holding of a teaching position at a university on a permanent basis **4** the legal right to live in a place or to use land or buildings for a period of time

tepee *or* **teepee** (**tee**-pee) *n* a cone-shaped tent of animal skins, formerly used by Native Americans

tepid *adj* **1** slightly warm **2** lacking enthusiasm: *tepid applause* ▸ **tepidity** *n* ▸ **tepidly** *adv*

tequila *n* a Mexican alcoholic spirit distilled from the agave plant

tercentenary *or* **tercentennial** *adj* **1** marking a 300th anniversary ▸ *n, pl* **-tenaries** *or* **-tennials 2** a 300th anniversary

term *n* **1** a word or expression, esp. one used in a specialized field of knowledge: *he coined the term 'inferiority complex'* **2** a period of time: *a four-year prison term* **3** one of the periods of the year when a school, university, or college is open or a lawcourt holds sessions **4** the period of pregnancy when childbirth is imminent **5** *maths* any distinct quantity making up a fraction or proportion, or contained in a sequence, series, etc. **6** *logic* any of the three subjects or predicates occurring in a syllogism **7 full term** the end of a specific period of time: *the agony of carrying the child to full term* ▸ *vb* **8** to name, call, or describe as being: *a musical style that could loosely be termed gospel*

> **term** *n* **1** = word, name, expression, title, label, phrase **2** = period, time, spell, while, season, interval, span, duration ▸ *vb* = call, name, label, style, entitle, tag, dub, designate

terminal *adj* **1** (of an illness) ending in death **2** situated at an end, terminus, or boundary: *the terminal joints of the fingers* **3** *informal* extreme or severe: *terminal boredom* ▸ *n* **4** a place where vehicles, passengers, or goods begin or end a journey: *the ferry terminal* **5** a point at which current enters or leaves an electrical device **6** *computers* a device, usually a keyboard and a visual display unit, having input/output links with a computer ▸ **terminally** *adv*

> **terminal** *adj* **1** = fatal, deadly, lethal, killing, mortal, incurable, inoperable, untreatable **2** = final, last, closing, finishing, concluding, ultimate, terminating; ≠ initial ▸ *n* **4** = terminus, station, depot (*US, Canad*), end of the line

terminate *vb* **-nating, -nated 1** to bring or come to an end: *his flying career was terminated by this crash* **2** to put an end to (a pregnancy) by inducing an abortion **3** (of the route of a train, bus, etc.) to stop at a particular place and not go any further: *this train terminates at Leicester* ▸ **termination** *n*

> **terminate** *vb* **1** = cease, end, close, finish; ≠ begin **2** = abort, end

terminology *n, pl* **-gies** the specialized words and expressions relating to a particular subject ▸ **terminological** *adj* ▸ **terminologist** *n*

terminus (term-in-nuss) *n, pl* **-ni** (-nye) *or*
-nuses the station or town at one end of a
railway line or bus route: *Vienna's Westbahnhof is
the terminus for trains to France*

termite *n* a whitish antlike insect of warm and
tropical regions that destroys timber

tern *n* a gull-like sea bird with a forked tail and
long narrow wings

ternary *adj* **1** consisting of three items or
groups of three items **2** *maths* (of a number
system) to the base three

Terpsichorean (turp-sick-or-**ee**-an) *adj often
facetious* of or relating to dancing

terrace *n* **1** a row of houses, usually identical
and joined together by common dividing walls,
or the street onto which they face **2** a paved
area alongside a building **3** a horizontal flat
area of ground, often one of a series in a slope
4 the terraces *or* **terracing** *Brit & NZ* a tiered area
in a stadium where spectators stand ▸ *vb*
-racing, -raced 5 to make into terraces

terracotta *n* **1** a hard unglazed brownish-red
earthenware used for pottery ▸ *adj* **2** made of
terracotta **3** brownish-orange

terra firma *n* the ground, as opposed to the
sea

terrain *n* an area of ground, esp. with reference
to its physical character: *mountainous terrain*

> **terrain** *n* = ground, country, land, landscape,
> topography, going

terrapin *n* a small turtle-like reptile of N
America that lives in fresh water and on land

terrarium *n* **1** an enclosed area or container
where small land animals are kept **2** a glass
container in which plants are grown

terrazzo *n, pl* **-zos** a floor made by setting
marble chips into a layer of mortar and
polishing the surface

terrestrial *adj* **1** of the planet earth **2** of the
land as opposed to the sea or air **3** (of animals
and plants) living or growing on the land
4 *television* denoting or using a signal sent over
land from a transmitter on land, rather than by
satellite

> **terrestrial** *adj* **1** = earthly, worldly, global

terrible *adj* **1** very serious or extreme: *war is a
terrible thing* **2** *informal* very bad, unpleasant, or
unsatisfactory: *terrible books* **3** causing fear
> **terribly** *adv*

> **terrible** *adj* **1** = serious, desperate, severe,
> extreme, dangerous, insufferable; ≠ mild
> **2** = bad, awful, dreadful, dire, abysmal, poor,
> rotten (*informal*); ≠ wonderful **3** = awful,
> shocking (*informal*), terrifying, horrible,
> dreadful, horrifying, fearful (*informal*),
> horrendous

terrier *n* any of several small active breeds of
dog, originally trained to hunt animals living
underground

terrific *adj* **1** very great or intense: *a terrific blow on
the head* **2** *informal* very good; excellent: *a terrific
book* > **terrifically** *adv*

> **terrific** *adj* **1** = intense, great, huge,
> enormous, tremendous (*informal*), fearful
> (*informal*), gigantic **2** = excellent, wonderful,
> brilliant, amazing, outstanding, superb
> (*old-fashioned*), fantastic, magnificent, booshit
> (*Austral slang*), exo (*Austral slang*), sik (*Austral
> slang*), ka pai (*NZ*), rad (*informal*), phat (*slang*),
> schmick (*Austral informal*); ≠ awful

terrify *vb* **-fies, -fying, -fied** to frighten greatly
> **terrified** *adj* > **terrifying** *adj* > **terrifyingly** *adv*

> **terrify** *vb* = frighten, scare, alarm, terrorize

terrine (terr-reen) *n* **1** an oval earthenware
cooking dish with a tightly fitting lid **2** the food
cooked or served in such a dish, esp. pâté

territorial *adj* **1** of or relating to a territory or
territories **2** of or concerned with the
ownership and control of an area of land or
water: *a territorial dispute* **3** (of an animal or bird)
establishing and defending an area which it
will not let other animals or birds into: *the baboon
is a territorial species* **4** of or relating to a territorial
army > **territorially** *adv* > **territoriality** *n*

Territorial Army *n* (in Britain) a reserve army,
known since 2014 as the **Army Reserve**, whose
members are not full-time soldiers but undergo
military training in their spare time so that
they can be called upon in an emergency

territory *n, pl* **-ries 1** any tract of land; district:
mountainous territory **2** the geographical area
under the control of a particular government:
the islands are Japanese territory **3** an area inhabited
and defended by a particular animal or pair of
animals **4** an area of knowledge or experience:
all this is familiar territory to readers of her recent novels
5 a country or region under the control of a
foreign country: *a French Overseas Territory*
6 a region of a country, esp. of a federal state,
that enjoys less autonomy and a lower status
than most constituent parts of the state

> **territory** *n* **1, 2** = district, area, land, region,
> country, zone, province, patch

terror *n* **1** very great fear, panic, or dread
2 a person or thing that inspires great dread
3 *Brit, Austral & NZ informal* a troublesome person,
esp. a child

> **terror** *n* **1** = fear, alarm, dread, fright, panic,
> anxiety **2** = nightmare, monster, bogeyman,
> devil, fiend, bugbear

terrorism *n* the systematic use of violence
and intimidation to achieve political ends
> **terrorist** *n, adj*

terrorize *or* **-rise** *vb* **-rizing, -rized** *or* **-rising,
-rised 1** to control or force (someone) to do
something by violence, fear, threats, etc.: *he was
terrorized into withdrawing his accusations* **2** to make

(someone) very frightened > **terrorization** or **-risation** n > **terrorizer** or **-riser** n

terry n a fabric covered on both sides with small uncut loops, used for towelling and nappies

terse adj 1 neatly brief and concise 2 curt or abrupt > **tersely** adv > **terseness** n

tertiary (tur-shar-ee) adj 1 third in degree, order, etc. 2 (of education) at university or college level 3 (of an industry) involving services, such as transport and financial services, as opposed to manufacture

Terylene n trademark a synthetic polyester fibre or fabric

tessellated adj paved or inlaid with a mosaic of small tiles

test vb 1 to try (something) out to ascertain its worth, safety, or endurance: the company has never tested its products on animals 2 to carry out an examination on (a substance, material, or system) in order to discover whether a particular substance, component, or feature is present: baby foods are regularly tested for pesticides 3 to put under severe strain: the long delay tested my patience 4 to achieve a result in a test which indicates the presence or absence of something: he tested positive for cocaine ▸ n 5 a method, practice, or examination designed to test a person or thing 6 a series of questions or problems designed to test a specific skill or knowledge: a spelling test 7 a chemical reaction or physical procedure for testing the composition or other qualities of a substance 8 sport short for **Test match** 9 **put to the test** to use (something) in order to gauge its usefulness or effectiveness > **testable** adj > **testing** adj

test vb 1 = check, investigate, assess, research, analyse, experiment with, try out, put something to the test, run something up the flagpole ▸ n 5, 6 = examination, paper, assessment, evaluation 7 = trial, research, check, investigation, analysis, assessment, examination, evaluation

testament n 1 something which provides proof of a fact about someone or something: the size of the audience was an immediate testament to his appeal 2 law a formal statement of how a person wants his or her property to be disposed of after his or her death: last will and testament > **testamentary** adj

testament n 1 = proof, evidence, testimony, witness, demonstration, tribute 2 = will, last wishes

Testament n either of the two main parts of the Bible, the Old Testament or the New Testament

testate law ▸ adj having left a legally valid will at death

test case n a legal action that serves as a precedent in deciding similar succeeding cases

testicle n either of the two male reproductive glands, in most mammals enclosed within the scrotum, that produce spermatozoa

testify vb -fies, -fying, -fied 1 law to declare or give evidence under oath, esp. in court 2 **testify to** to be evidence of: a piece of paper testifying to their educational qualifications

testify vb 1 = bear witness, state, swear, certify, assert, affirm, attest, corroborate; ≠ disprove

testimonial n 1 a recommendation of the character or worth of a person or thing 2 a tribute given for services or achievements ▸ adj 3 of a testimony or testimonial: a testimonial match

testimony n, pl -nies 1 a declaration of truth or fact 2 law evidence given by a witness, esp. in court under oath 3 evidence proving or supporting something: that they are still talking is a testimony to their 20-year friendship

testimony n 1, 2 = evidence, statement, submission, affidavit, deposition 3 = proof, evidence, demonstration, indication, support, manifestation, verification, corroboration

testis n, pl -tes same as **testicle**

Test match n (in various sports, esp. cricket) an international match, esp. one of a series

testosterone n a steroid male sex hormone secreted by the testes

test tube n a cylindrical round-bottomed glass tube open at one end, which is used in scientific experiments

test-tube baby n 1 a fetus that has developed from an ovum fertilized in an artificial womb 2 a baby conceived by artificial insemination

testy adj -tier, -tiest irritable or touchy > **testily** adv > **testiness** n

tetanus n an acute infectious disease in which toxins released from a bacterium cause muscular spasms and convulsions

tête-à-tête n, pl -têtes or -tête 1 a private conversation between two people ▸ adv 2 together in private: they dined tête-à-tête

tether n 1 a rope or chain for tying an animal to a fence, post, etc., so that it cannot move away from a particular place 2 **at the end of one's tether** at the limit of one's patience or endurance ▸ vb 3 to tie with a tether

tetrahedron (tet-ra-heed-ron) n, pl -drons or -dra a solid figure with four triangular plane faces > **tetrahedral** adj

tetralogy n, pl -gies a series of four related books, dramas, operas, etc.

Teutonic (tew-tonn-ik) adj 1 characteristic of or relating to the Germans 2 of the ancient Teutons

text n 1 the main body of a printed or written work as distinct from items such as notes or illustrations 2 any written material, such as words displayed on a visual display unit

3 the written version of the words of a speech, broadcast, or recording: *an advance text of the remarks the president will deliver tonight* **4** a short passage of the Bible used as a starting point for a sermon **5** a book required as part of a course of study: *shelves full of sociology texts* **6** short for **text message** ► *vb* **7** to send (a text message) by mobile phone **8** to contact (a person) by means of a text message

text *n* **1** = contents, words, content, wording, body, subject matter **2** = words, wording **3** = transcript, script

textbook *n* **1** a book of facts about a subject used by someone who is studying that subject ► *adj* **2** perfect or exemplary: *a textbook example of an emergency descent*

textile *n* **1** any fabric or cloth, esp. a woven one ► *adj* **2** of or relating to fabrics or their production: *the world textile market*

text message *n* **1** a message sent in text form, esp. by means of a mobile phone **2** a message appearing on a computer screen > **text messaging** *n*

textual *adj* of, based on, or relating to, a text or texts > **textually** *adv*

texture *n* **1** the structure, appearance, and feel of a substance: *curtains of many textures and colours* **2** the overall sound of a piece of music, resulting from the way the different instrumental parts in it are combined: *a big orchestra weaving rich textures* ► *vb* **-turing, -tured** **3** to give a distinctive texture to (something) > **textural** *adj*

texture *n* **1** = feel, consistency, structure, surface, tissue, grain

Thai *adj* **1** of Thailand ► *n* **2** *pl* **Thais** *or* **Thai** a person from Thailand **3** the main language of Thailand

thalidomide (thal-**lid**-oh-mide) *n* a drug formerly used as a sedative and hypnotic but withdrawn from use when found to cause abnormalities in developing fetuses

thallium *n chem* a soft highly toxic white metallic element. Symbol: **Tl**

than *conj, prep* **1** used to introduce the second element of a comparison, the first element of which expresses difference: *I'm less optimistic than I was at first* **2** used to state a number, quantity, or value in approximate terms by contrasting it with another number, quantity, or value: *temperatures lower than 25 degrees* **3** used after the adverbs *rather* and *sooner* to introduce a rejected alternative: *fruit is examined by hand, rather than by machine*

thane *n* **1** (in Anglo-Saxon England) a nobleman who held land from the king or from a superior nobleman in return for certain services **2** (in medieval Scotland) a person of rank holding land from the king

thank *vb* **1** to convey feelings of gratitude to: *he thanked the nursing staff for saving his life* **2** to hold

responsible: *he has his father to thank for his familiarity with the film world* **3 thank you** a polite response or expression of gratitude **4 thank goodness** *or* **thank heavens** *or* **thank God** an exclamation of relief

thank *vb* **1** = say thank you to, show your appreciation to

thankful *adj* grateful and appreciative > **thankfully** *adv*

thankless *adj* unrewarding or unappreciated: *she took on the thankless task of organizing the office Xmas lunch* > **thanklessly** *adv* > **thanklessness** *n*

thanks *pl n* **1** an expression of appreciation or gratitude **2 thanks to** because of: *the birth went very smoothly, thanks to the help of the GHQ medical officer* ► *interj* **3** *informal* an exclamation expressing gratitude

thanks *pl n* **1** = gratitude, appreciation, credit, recognition, acknowledgment, gratefulness **2 thanks to** = because of, through, due to, as a result of, owing to

that *adj* **1** used preceding a noun that has been mentioned or is already familiar: *he'd have to give up on that idea* **2** used preceding a noun that denotes something more remote: *that book on the top shelf* ► *pron* **3** used to denote something already mentioned or understood: *that's right* **4** used to denote a more remote person or thing: *is that him over there?* **5** used to introduce a restrictive relative clause: *a problem that has to be overcome* **6 and all that** *or* **and that** *informal* and similar or related things: *import cutting and all that* **7 that is** ᴀ to be precise ʙ in other words **8 that's that** there is no more to be said or done ► *conj* **9** used to introduce a noun clause: *he denied that the country was suffering from famine* **10** used, usually after *so*, to introduce a clause of purpose: *he turns his face away from her so that she shall not see his tears* **11** used to introduce a clause of result: *a scene so sickening and horrible that it is impossible to describe it* ► *adv* **12** Also: **all that** *informal* very or particularly: *the fines imposed have not been that large*

thatch *n* **1** Also called: **thatching** a roofing material that consists of straw or reeds **2** a roof made of such a material **3** a mass of thick untidy hair on someone's head ► *vb* **4** to cover with thatch > **thatched** *adj* > **thatcher** *n*

thaw *vb* **1** to melt or cause to melt: *snow thawing in the gutter* **2** (of frozen food) to become or cause to become unfrozen; defrost **3** (of weather) to be warm enough to cause ice or snow to melt: *it's not freezing, it's thawing again* **4** to become more relaxed or friendly: *only with Llewelyn did he thaw, let his defences down* ► *n* **5** the act or process of thawing **6** a spell of relatively warm weather, causing snow or ice to melt

thaw *vb* **1, 2** = melt, dissolve, soften, defrost, warm, liquefy, unfreeze; ≠ freeze

the *adj (definite article)* **1** used preceding a noun that has been previously specified or is a matter of common knowledge: *those involved in the search* **2** used to indicate a particular person or object: *the man called Frank turned to look at it* **3** used preceding certain nouns associated with one's culture, society, or community: *to comply with the law* **4** used preceding an adjective that is functioning as a collective noun: *the unemployed* **5** used preceding titles and certain proper nouns: *the Middle East* **6** used preceding an adjective or noun in certain names or titles: *Alexander the Great* **7** used preceding a noun to make it refer to its class as a whole: *cultivation of the coca plant* **8** used instead of *my, your, her,* etc., with parts of the body: *swelling of tissues in the brain* **9** the best or most remarkable: *it's THE place in town for good Mexican food*

theatre *or US* **theater** *n* **1** a building designed for the performance of plays, operas, etc. **2** a large room or hall with tiered seats for an audience: *a lecture theatre* **3** a room in a hospital equipped for surgical operations **4 the theatre** drama and acting in general **5** a region in which a war or conflict takes place: *a potential theatre of war close to Russian borders* **6** *US, Austral & NZ* same as **cinema** (sense 1)

theatrical *adj* **1** of or relating to the theatre or dramatic performances **2** exaggerated and affected in manner or behaviour > **theatricality** *n* > **theatrically** *adv*

> **theatrical** *adj* **1** = dramatic, stage, thespian **2** = exaggerated, dramatic, melodramatic, histrionic, affected, mannered, showy, ostentatious; ≠ natural

theatricals *pl n* dramatic performances, esp. as given by amateurs

thee *pron old-fashioned* the objective form of **thou**

theft *n* **1** the act or an instance of stealing: *he reported the theft of his passport* **2** the crime of stealing: *he had a number of convictions for theft*

> **theft** *n* = stealing, robbery, thieving, fraud, embezzlement, pilfering, larceny, purloining

their *adj* of or associated with them: *owning their own land; two girls on their way to school*

theirs *pron* **1** something or someone belonging to or associated with them: *it was his fault, not theirs* **2 of theirs** belonging to them

theism (thee-iz-zum) *n* **1** belief in one God as the creator of everything in the universe **2** belief in the existence of a God or gods > **theist** *n, adj* > **theistic** *adj*

them *pron (objective)* refers to things or people other than the speaker or people addressed: *I want you to give this to them*

theme *n* **1** the main idea or topic in a discussion or lecture **2** (in literature, music, or art) an idea, image, or motif, repeated or developed throughout a work or throughout an artist's career **3** *music* a group of notes forming a recognizable melodic unit, used as the basis of part or all of a composition **4** a short essay, esp. one set as an exercise for a student > **thematic** *adj* > **thematically** *adv*

> **theme** *n* **1** = subject, idea, topic, essence, subject matter, keynote, gist **2** = motif, leitmotif

theme park *n* an area planned as a leisure attraction in which all the displays and activities are based on a particular theme, story, or idea: *a Wild West theme park*

themselves *pron* **1 A** the reflexive form of *they* or *them*: *two men barricaded themselves into a cell* **B** used for emphasis: *among the targets were police officers themselves* **2** their normal or usual selves: *they don't seem themselves these days*

then *adv* **1** at that time: *he was then at the height of his sporting career* **2** after that: *let's eat first and then we can explore the town* **3** in that case: *then why did he work for you?* ► *pron* **4** that time: *since then the list of grievances has steadily grown* ► *adj* **5** existing or functioning at that time: *the then Defence Minister*

thence *adv formal* **1** from that place: *the train went south into Switzerland, and thence on to Italy* **2** for that reason; therefore

theocracy *n, pl* **-cies 1** government by a god or by priests **2** a community under such government > **theocrat** *n* > **theocratic** *adj* > **theocratically** *adv*

theodolite (thee-odd-oh-lite) *n* an instrument used in surveying for measuring horizontal and vertical angles

theologian *n* a person versed in the study of theology

theology *n, pl* **-gies 1** the systematic study of religions and religious beliefs **2** a specific system, form, or branch of this study: *Muslim theology* > **theological** *adj* > **theologically** *adv*

theorem *n* a proposition, esp. in maths, that can be proved by reasoning from the basic principles of a subject

theoretical *or* **theoretic** *adj* **1** based on or concerned with the ideas and abstract principles relating to a particular subject rather than its practical uses: *theoretical physics* **2** existing in theory but perhaps not in reality: *the secret service is under the theoretical control of the government* > **theoretically** *adv*

> **theoretical** *or* **theoretic** *adj* **1** = abstract, speculative; ≠ practical **2** = hypothetical, academic, notional, unproven, conjectural, nominal, postulatory

theorize *or* **-rise** *vb* **-rizing, -rized** *or* **-rising, -rised** to produce or use theories; speculate > **theorist** *n*

theory *n, pl* **-ries 1** a set of ideas, based on evidence and careful reasoning, which offers an explanation of how something works or why something happens, but has not been completely proved: *the theory of cosmology*

t

2 the ideas and abstract knowledge relating to something: *political theory* **3** an idea or opinion: *it's only a theory, admittedly, but I think it's worth pursuing* **4 in theory** in an ideal or hypothetical situation: *in theory, the tax is supposed to limit inflation*

> **theory** *n* **3** = belief, feeling, speculation, assumption, hunch, presumption, conjecture, surmise

theosophy *n* a religious or philosophical system claiming to be based on an intuitive insight into the divine nature › **theosophical** *adj* › **theosophist** *n*

therapeutic (ther-rap-**pew**-tik) *adj* of or relating to the treatment and cure of disease › **therapeutically** *adv*

> **therapeutic** *adj* = beneficial, healing, restorative, good, corrective, remedial, salutary, curative, ≠ harmful

therapeutics *n* the branch of medicine concerned with the treatment of disease

therapy *n, pl* -**pies** the treatment of physical, mental, or social disorders or disease › **therapist** *n*

> **therapy** *n* = remedy, treatment, cure, healing, method of healing

there *adv* **1** in, at, or to that place or position: *he won't be there* **2** in that respect: *you're right there* **3 there and then** immediately and without delay: *he walked out there and then* ▸ *adj* **4 not all there** *informal* mentally unbalanced or silly ▸ *pron* **5** that place: *to return from there* **6** used as a grammatical subject when the true subject follows the verb, esp. the verb 'to be': *there are no children in the house* **7 so there!** an exclamation, used esp. by children, that usually follows a declaration of refusal or defiance: *you can't come, so there!* **8 there you are** *or* **go** **A** an expression used when handing a person something **B** an exclamation of satisfaction or vindication ▸ *interj* **9** an expression of sympathy, for example when consoling a child: *there, there, pet!*

thereby *adv formal* by that means or consequently

therefore *adv* for that reason: *the training is long, and therefore expensive*

> **therefore** *adv* = consequently, so, thus, as a result, hence, accordingly, thence, ergo

thereupon *adv formal* immediately after that; at that point

therm *n Brit* a unit of heat equal to $1.055\,056 \times 10^8$ joules

thermal *adj* **1** of, caused by, or generating heat **2** hot or warm: *thermal springs* **3** (of garments) specially made so as to have exceptional heat-retaining qualities: *thermal underwear* ▸ *n* **4** a column of rising air caused by uneven heating of the land surface, and used by gliders and birds to gain height

thermodynamics *n* the branch of physical science concerned with the relationship between heat and other forms of energy

thermometer *n* an instrument used to measure temperature, esp. one in which a thin column of liquid, such as mercury, expands and contracts within a sealed tube marked with a temperature scale

thermonuclear *adj* **1** (of a nuclear reaction) involving a nuclear fusion reaction of a type which occurs at very high temperatures **2** (of a weapon) giving off energy as the result of a thermonuclear reaction **3** involving thermonuclear weapons

thermoplastic *adj* **1** (of a material, esp. a synthetic plastic) becoming soft when heated and rehardening on cooling ▸ *n* **2** a synthetic plastic or resin, such as polystyrene

Thermos *or* **Thermos flask** *n trademark* a type of stoppered vacuum flask used to preserve the temperature of its contents

thermosetting *adj* (of a material, esp. a synthetic plastic) hardening permanently after one application of heat and pressure

thermostat *n* a device which automatically regulates the temperature of central heating, an oven, etc., by switching it off or on when it reaches or drops below a particular temperature › **thermostatic** *adj* › **thermostatically** *adv*

thesaurus (thiss-**sore**-uss) *n, pl* -**ruses** *or* -**ri** a book containing lists of synonyms and related words

these *adj, pron* the plural of **this**

thesis (**theess**-siss) *n, pl* -**ses** (-seez) **1** a written work resulting from original research, esp. one submitted for a higher degree in a university **2** an opinion supported by reasoned argument: *it is the author's thesis that Britain has yet to come to terms with the loss of its Empire* **3** *logic* an unproved statement put forward as a premise in an argument

> **thesis** *n* **1** = dissertation, paper, treatise, essay, monograph **2** = proposition, theory, hypothesis, idea, view, opinion, proposal, contention

Thespian *n* **1** *often facetious* an actor ▸ *adj* **2** of or relating to drama and the theatre

they *pron* (*subjective*) **1** refers to people or things other than the speaker or people addressed: *they both giggled* **2** refers to people in general: *they say he adores children* **3** *informal* refers to an individual person whose gender is either not known or not regarded as important: *someone could have a nasty accident if they tripped over that* **4** refers to an individual person with a nonbinary gender identity who has chosen to be referred to in this way

thiamine *or* **thiamin** *n* vitamin B_1, a vitamin found in the outer coat of rice and other grains, a deficiency of which leads to nervous disorders and to beriberi

thick *adj* **1** having a relatively great distance between opposite surfaces: *thick slices* **2** having a specified distance between opposite surfaces: *fifty metres thick* **3** having a dense consistency: *thick fog* **4** consisting of a lot of things grouped closely together: *thick forest* **5** (of clothes) made of heavy cloth or wool: *a thick jumper* **6** *informal* stupid, slow, or insensitive **7** (of an accent) very noticeable: *each word was pronounced in a thick Dutch accent* **8** Also: **thick as thieves** *informal* very friendly **9 a bit thick** *Brit informal* unfair or unreasonable: *£2 an hour, that's a bit thick!* **10 thick with** **A** covered with a lot of: *glass panels thick with dust* **B** (of a voice) throaty and hard to make out: *his voice was thick with emotion* ▸ *adv* **11** in order to produce something thick: *the machine sliced the potatoes too thick* **12 lay it on thick** *informal* **A** to exaggerate a story **B** to flatter someone excessively **13 thick and fast** quickly and in large numbers: *theories were flying thick and fast* ▸ *n* **14 the thick** the most intense or active part: *in the thick of the fighting* **15 through thick and thin** in good times and bad > **thickly** *adv*

> **thick** *adj* **1** = bulky, broad, big, large, fat, solid, substantial, hefty; ≠ thin **2** = wide, across, deep, broad, in extent or diameter **3** = opaque, heavy, dense, impenetrable; ≠ runny **4** = crowded, full, covered, bursting, bristling, brimming; ≠ empty **5** = heavy, heavyweight, dense, chunky, bulky, woolly **6** = stupid, dense, dopey (*informal*), obtuse, brainless, dumb-ass (*informal*); ≠ clever **8** = friendly, close, intimate, familiar, pally (*informal*), devoted, inseparable; ≠ unfriendly

thicken *vb* **1** to make or become thick or thicker **2** to become more complicated: *the plot thickens* > **thickener** *n*

> **thicken** *vb* **1** = set, condense, congeal, clot, jell, coagulate; ≠ thin

thicket *n* a dense growth of small trees or shrubs
thickness *n* **1** the state or quality of being thick **2** the dimension through an object, as opposed to length or width **3** a layer: *several thicknesses of brown paper*
thickset *adj* **1** stocky in build **2** planted or placed close together
thief *n, pl* **thieves** a person who steals something from another > **thievish** *adj*

> **thief** *n* = robber, burglar, stealer, plunderer, shoplifter, embezzler, pickpocket, pilferer

thieve *vb* **thieving, thieved** to steal other people's possessions > **thieving** *adj*
thigh *n* the part of the human leg between the hip and the knee
thimble *n* a small metal or plastic cap used to protect the end of the finger from the needle when sewing
thin *adj* **thinner, thinnest 1** having a relatively small distance between opposite surfaces: *a thin mattress* **2** much narrower than it is long: *push a thin stick up the pipe in order to clear it* **3** (of a person or animal) having no excess body fat **4** made up of only a few, widely separated, people or things: *thin hair* **5** not dense: *a thin film of dust* **6** unconvincing because badly thought out or badly presented: *the evidence against him was extremely thin* **7** (of a voice) high-pitched and not very loud: *a thin squeaky voice* ▸ *adv* **8** in order to produce something thin: *roll the dough very thin* ▸ *vb* **thinning, thinned 9** to make or become thin or sparse > **thinly** *adv* > **thinness** *n*

> **thin** *adj* **2** = narrow, fine, attenuated; ≠ thick **3** = slim, spare, lean, slight, slender, skinny, skeletal, bony; ≠ fat **4** = wispy, thinning, sparse, scarce, scanty **5** = fine, delicate, flimsy, sheer, skimpy, gossamer, diaphanous, filmy; ≠ thick **6** = unconvincing, inadequate, feeble, poor, weak, superficial, lame, flimsy; ≠ convincing

thine *old-fashioned* ▸ *adj* **1** (*preceding a vowel*) of or associated with you (thou): *if thine eye offend thee, pluck it out!* ▸ *pron* **2** something belonging to you (thou): *the victory shall be thine*
thing *n* **1** any physical object that is not alive: *there are very few jobs left where people actually make things* **2** an object, fact, circumstance, or concept considered as being a separate entity: *that would be a terrible thing to do* **3** an object or entity that cannot or need not be precisely named: *squares and circles and things* **4** *informal* a person or animal: *pretty little thing, isn't she?* **5** a possession, article of clothing, etc.: *have you brought your swimming things?* **6** *informal* a preoccupation or obsession: *they have this thing about cleaning* **7 do one's own thing** to engage in an activity or mode of behaviour satisfying to one's personality **8 make a thing of** to exaggerate the importance of **9 the thing** the latest fashion

> **thing** *n* **5** = possessions, stuff, gear, belongings, effects, luggage, clobber (*Brit slang*), chattels **6** = obsession, liking, preoccupation, mania, fetish, fixation, soft spot, predilection

think *vb* **thinking, thought 1** to consider, judge, or believe: *I think that it is scandalous* **2** to make use of the mind, for example in order to make a decision: *I'll need to think about what I'm going to do* **3** to engage in conscious thought: *that made me think* **4** to be considerate enough or remember (to do something): *no other company had thought to bring high tech down to the user* **5 think much** or **a lot of** to have a favourable opinion of: *I don't think much of the new design* **6 think of** **A** to remember or recollect: *I couldn't think of your surname* **B** to conceive of or formulate: *for a long time he couldn't think of a response* **7 think twice** to consider something carefully before making a decision ▸ *n* **8** *informal* a careful open-minded assessment: *she had a long hard think* > **thinker** *n* ▸ See also **think up**

t

think vb 1 = judge, consider, estimate, reckon, deem, regard as 2, 3 = ponder, reflect, contemplate, deliberate, meditate, ruminate, cogitate, be lost in thought

thinking n 1 opinion or judgment: *contrary to all fashionable thinking* 2 the process of thought ▸ adj 3 using intelligent thought: *the thinking person's sport*

thinking n = reasoning, idea, view, position, theory, opinion, judgment, conjecture ▸ adj = thoughtful, intelligent, reasoning, rational, philosophical, reflective, contemplative, meditative

think-tank n informal a group of experts employed to study specific problems

think up vb to invent or devise

think up vb **think something up** = devise, create, come up with, invent, contrive, visualize, concoct, dream up

third adj 1 of or being number three in a series 2 rated, graded, or ranked below the second level 3 denoting the third from lowest forward gear in a motor vehicle ▸ n 4 one of three equal parts of something 5 the fraction equal to one divided by three ($1/3$) 6 the third from lowest forward gear in a motor vehicle 7 Brit an honours degree of the third and usually the lowest class 8 music the interval between one note and the note four semitones (**major third**) or three semitones (**minor third**) higher or lower than it ▸ adv 9 Also: **thirdly** in the third place

third degree n informal torture or bullying, esp. as used to extort confessions or information

third party n 1 a person who is involved in an event, legal proceeding, agreement, or other transaction only by chance or indirectly ▸ adj **third-party** 2 insurance providing protection against liability caused by accidental injury or death of other people: *third-party cover*

Third World n the developing countries of Africa, Asia, and Latin America collectively

thirst n 1 a desire to drink, accompanied by a feeling of dryness in the mouth and throat 2 a craving or yearning: *a thirst for knowledge* ▸ vb 3 to feel a thirst

thirst n 1 = dryness, thirstiness, drought 2 = craving, appetite, longing, desire, passion, yearning, hankering, keenness; ≠ aversion

thirsty adj **thirstier**, **thirstiest** 1 feeling a desire to drink 2 causing thirst: *morris dancing is thirsty work* 3 **thirsty for** feeling an eager desire for: *thirsty for information* > **thirstily** adv

thirteen n 1 the cardinal number that is the sum of ten and three 2 a numeral, 13 or XIII, representing this number 3 something representing or consisting of thirteen units ▸ adj 4 amounting to thirteen: *thirteen people* > **thirteenth** adj, n

thirty n, pl **-ties** 1 the cardinal number that is the product of ten and three 2 a numeral, 30 or XXX, representing this number 3 something representing or consisting of thirty units ▸ adj 4 amounting to thirty: *thirty miles* > **thirtieth** adj, n

this adj 1 used preceding a noun referring to something or someone that is closer: *on this side of the Channel* 2 used preceding a noun that has just been mentioned or is understood: *this text has two chief goals* 3 used to refer to something about to be mentioned: *NPR's Anne Garrels has this report* 4 used to refer to the present time or occasion: *this week's edition of the newspaper* 5 informal used instead of *a* or *the* in telling a story: *the film is about this couple who adopt a child* ▸ pron 6 used to denote a person or thing that is relatively close: *black coral like this* 7 used to denote something already mentioned or understood: *this didn't seem fair to me* 8 used to denote something about to be mentioned: *just say this: collect Standish from the top of the fire escape* 9 the present time or occasion: *after this it was impossible to talk to him about his feelings* 10 **this and that** various unspecified and trivial events or facts

thistle n a plant with prickly-edged leaves, dense flower heads, and feathery hairs on the seeds > **thistly** adj

thither adv formal to or towards that place

thong n 1 a thin strip of leather or other material 2 US, Canad & Austral same as **flip-flop** 3 a skimpy article of beachwear consisting of thin strips of leather or cloth attached to a piece of material that covers the genitals while leaving the buttocks bare

thorax (thaw-racks) n, pl **thoraxes** or **thoraces** (thaw-rass-seez) 1 the part of the human body enclosed by the ribs 2 the part of an insect's body between the head and abdomen > **thoracic** adj

thorn n 1 a sharp pointed woody projection from a stem or leaf 2 any of various trees or shrubs having thorns, esp. the hawthorn 3 a **thorn in one's side** or **flesh** a source of irritation: *he was sufficiently bright at school to become a thorn in the side of his maths teacher* > **thornless** adj

thorn n 1 = prickle, spike, spine, barb

thorny adj **thornier**, **thorniest** 1 covered with thorns 2 difficult or unpleasant: *a thorny issue*

thorough adj 1 carried out completely and carefully: *he needs a thorough checkup by the doctor* 2 (of a person) painstakingly careful: *he is very thorough if rather unimaginative* 3 great in extent or degree; utter: *a thorough disgrace* > **thoroughly** adv > **thoroughness** n

thorough adj 1, 3 = comprehensive, full, complete, sweeping, intensive, in-depth, exhaustive; ≠ cursory 2 = careful, conscientious, painstaking, efficient, meticulous, exhaustive, assiduous; ≠ careless

thoroughbred adj 1 obtained through successive generations of selective breeding: thoroughbred horses ▸ n 2 a pedigree animal, esp. a horse

thoroughfare n a way through from one place to another: the great thoroughfare from the Castle to the Palace of Holyrood

those adj, pron the plural of **that**

thou pron old-fashioned same as **you**: used when talking to one person

though conj 1 despite the fact that: he was smiling with relief and happiness though the tears still flowed down his cheeks ▸ adv 2 nevertheless or however: he can't dance – he sings well, though

> **though** conj = although, while, even if, even though, notwithstanding ▸ adv = nevertheless, still, however, yet, nonetheless, for all that, notwithstanding

thought vb 1 the past of **think** ▸ n 2 the act or process of thinking 3 a concept or idea 4 ideas typical of a particular time or place: the development of Western intellectual thought 5 detailed consideration: he appeared to give some sort of thought to the question 6 an intention, hope, or reason for doing something: his first thought was to call the guard and have the man arrested

> **thought** n 2 = thinking, consideration, reflection, deliberation, musing, meditation, rumination, cogitation 3 = opinion, view, idea, concept, notion, judgment 5 = consideration, study, attention, care, regard, scrutiny, heed 6 = hope, expectation, prospect, aspiration, anticipation

thoughtful adj 1 considerate in the treatment of other people 2 showing careful thought: a thoughtful and scholarly book 3 quiet, serious, and deep in thought ▸ **thoughtfully** adv ▸ **thoughtfulness** n

> **thoughtful** adj 1 = considerate, kind, caring, kindly, helpful, attentive, unselfish, solicitous; ≠ inconsiderate 3 = reflective, pensive, contemplative, meditative, serious, studious, deliberative, ruminative; ≠ shallow

thoughtless adj not considerate of the feelings of other people ▸ **thoughtlessly** adv ▸ **thoughtlessness** n

thousand n, pl **-sands** or **-sand** 1 the cardinal number that is the product of ten and one hundred 2 a numeral, 1000 or 10³, representing this number 3 a very large but unspecified number: thousands of bees swarmed out of the hive 4 something representing or consisting of 1000 units ▸ adj 5 amounting to a thousand: a thousand members ▸ **thousandth** adj, n

thrall n the state of being completely in the power of, or spellbound by, a person or thing: he was held in thrall by her almost supernatural beauty

thrash vb 1 to beat (someone), esp. with a stick or whip 2 to defeat totally: the All Blacks thrashed

England 24–3 3 to move about in a wild manner: his legs stuck and he fell sideways, thrashing about wildly 4 same as **thresh** ▸ n 5 informal a party ▸ See also **thrash out**

> **thrash** vb 1 = beat, wallop, whip, belt (informal), cane, flog, scourge, spank 2 = defeat, beat, crush, slaughter (informal), rout, trounce, run rings around (informal), wipe the floor with (informal) 3 = thresh, flail, jerk, writhe, toss and turn

thrashing n a severe beating

> **thrashing** n = beating, hiding (informal), belting (informal), whipping, flogging

thrash out vb to discuss (a problem or difficulty) fully in order to come to an agreement or decision about it: we must arrange a meeting to thrash out the details of the scheme

> **thrash out** vb thrash something out = settle, resolve, discuss, debate, solve, argue out, have out, talk over

thread n 1 a fine strand or fibre of some material 2 a fine cord of twisted yarns, esp. of cotton, used in sewing or weaving 3 something acting as the continuous link or theme of a whole: the thread of the story 4 the spiral ridge on a screw, bolt, or nut 5 a very small amount (of something): there was a thread of nervousness in his voice 6 a very thin seam of coal or vein of ore ▸ pl n **threads** 7 chiefly US slang clothes ▸ vb 8 to pass thread through the eye of (a needle) before sewing with it 9 to string together: plastic beads threaded on lengths of nylon line 10 to make (one's way) through a crowd of people or group of objects: she threaded and pushed her way through the crowds ▸ **threadlike** adj

> **thread** n 1,2 = strand, fibre, yarn, filament, line, string, twine 3 = theme, train of thought, direction, plot, drift, story line ▸ vb 10 = move, pass, ease, thrust, squeeze through, pick your way

threadbare adj 1 (of cloth, clothing, or a carpet) having the nap worn off so that the threads are exposed 2 having been used or expressed so often as to be no longer interesting: threadbare ideas 3 wearing shabby worn-out clothes

threat n 1 a declaration of an intention to inflict harm: they carried out their threat to kill the hostages 2 a strong possibility of something dangerous or unpleasant happening: the wet weather will bring a threat of flooding 3 a person or thing that is regarded as dangerous and likely to inflict harm: unemployment is a serious threat to the social order

> **threat** n 1 = threatening remark, menace 3 = danger, risk, hazard, menace, peril

threaten vb 1 to express a threat to (someone): he threatened John with the sack 2 to be a threat to:

he was worried about anything that might threaten the health of his child **3** to be a menacing indication of (something): *the early summer threatened drought* > **threatening** *adj* > **threateningly** *adv*

> **threaten** *vb* **1** = intimidate, bully, menace, terrorize, lean on (*slang*), pressurize, browbeat; ≠ defend **2** = endanger, jeopardize, put at risk, imperil, put in jeopardy, put on the line; ≠ protect

three *n* **1** the cardinal number that is the sum of one and two **2** a numeral, 3 or III, representing this number **3** something representing or consisting of three units ▸ *adj* **4** amounting to three: *three days*

three-dimensional *or* **3-D** *adj* **1** having three dimensions **2** lifelike or realistic: *all the characters are three-dimensional*

threesome *n* a group of three people

threnody *n, pl* **threnodies** *formal* a lament for the dead > **threnodic** *adj* > **threnodist** *n*

thresh *vb* **1** = beat (stalks of ripe corn, rice, etc.), either with a hand tool or by machine to separate the grain from the husks and straw **2 thresh about** to toss and turn

threshold *n* **1** the lower horizontal part of an entrance or doorway, esp. one made of stone or hardwood **2** any doorway or entrance: *he had never been over the threshold of a pub before* **3** the starting point of an experience, event, or venture: *she was on the threshold of a glorious career* **4** the point at which something begins to take effect or be noticeable: *the threshold for basic rate tax; he has a low boredom threshold*

> **threshold** *n* **1, 2** = entrance, doorway, door, doorstep **3** = start, beginning, opening, dawn (*literary*), verge, brink, outset, inception; ≠ end **4** = limit, margin, starting point, minimum

threw *vb* the past tense of **throw**

thrice *adv literary* **1** three times: *twice or thrice in a lifetime* **2** three times as big, much, etc.: *his vegetables are thrice the size of mine*

thrift *n* **1** wisdom and caution with money **2** a low-growing plant of Europe, W Asia, and North America, with narrow leaves and round heads of pink or white flowers > **thriftless** *adj*

> **thrift** *n* **1** = economy, prudence, frugality, saving, parsimony, carefulness, thriftiness; ≠ extravagance

thrifty *adj* **thriftier, thriftiest** not wasteful with money > **thriftily** *adv* > **thriftiness** *n*

thrill *n* **1** a sudden sensation of excitement and pleasure: *he felt a thrill of excitement* **2** a situation producing such a sensation: *all the thrills of rafting the meandering Dordogne* **3** a sudden trembling sensation caused by fear or emotional shock ▸ *vb* **4** to feel or cause to feel a thrill **5** to vibrate or quiver > **thrilling** *adj*

> **thrill** *n* **1** = pleasure, kick (*informal*), buzz (*slang*), high, stimulation, tingle, titillation; ≠ tedium ▸ *vb* **4** = excite, stimulate, arouse, move, stir, electrify, titillate, give someone a kick

thriller *n* a book, film, or play depicting crime, mystery, or espionage in an atmosphere of excitement and suspense

thrive *vb* **thriving, thrived** *or* **throve, thrived** *or* **thriven 1** to do well; be successful: *Munich has thrived as a centre of European commerce* **2** to grow strongly and vigorously: *the vine can thrive in the most unlikely soils*

> **thrive** *vb* = prosper, do well, flourish, increase, grow, develop, succeed, get on; ≠ decline

throat *n* **1** the passage from the mouth and nose to the stomach and lungs **2** the front part of the neck **3 at each other's throats** quarrelling or fighting with each other **4 cut one's own throat** to bring about one's own ruin **5 cut someone's throat** to kill someone **6 ram** *or* **force something down someone's throat** to insist that someone listen to or accept something **7 stick in one's throat** to be hard to accept: *his arrogance really sticks in my throat*

throaty *adj* **throatier, throatiest 1** hoarse and suggestive of a sore throat: *a throaty 40 fags-a-day bark* **2** deep, husky, or guttural: *she gives a deliciously throaty laugh*

throb *vb* **throbbing, throbbed 1** to pulsate or beat repeatedly, esp. with abnormally strong force: *her eardrums were throbbing with pain* **2** (of engines, drums, etc.) to have a strong rhythmic vibration or beat ▸ *n* **3** the act or sensation of throbbing: *he felt a throb of fear; the throb of the engines* > **throbbing** *adj, n*

> **throb** *vb* **1** = pulsate, pound, beat, pulse, thump, palpitate **2** = vibrate, pulsate, reverberate, shake, judder (*informal*) ▸ *n* = vibration, throbbing, reverberation, judder (*informal*), pulsation

throes *pl n* **1** violent pangs, pain, or convulsions: *an animal in its death throes* **2 in the throes of** struggling to cope with (something difficult or disruptive): *in the throes of a civil war*

thrombosis (throm-boh-siss) *n, pl* **-ses** (-seez) coagulation of the blood in the heart or in a blood vessel, forming a blood clot > **thrombotic** (throm-bot-ik) *adj*

throne *n* **1** the ceremonial seat occupied by a monarch or bishop on occasions of state **2** the rank or power of a monarch: *she came to the throne after her father was murdered*

throng *n* **1** a great number of people or things crowded together ▸ *vb* **2** to gather in or fill (a place) in large numbers: *streets thronged with shoppers*

> **throng** *n* = crowd, mob, horde, host, pack, mass, crush, swarm ▸ *vb* = pack, crowd; ≠ disperse

throstle *n poetic* a song thrush

throttle *n* **1** a device that controls the fuel-and-air mixture entering an engine ▸ *vb* **-tling, -tled 2** to kill or injure (someone) by squeezing his or her throat **3** to suppress or censor: *the government is trying to throttle dissent*

> **throttle** *vb* **2** = strangle, choke, garrotte, strangulate

through *prep* **1** going in at one side and coming out at the other side of: *he drove through the West of the city* **2** occupying or visiting several points scattered around in (an area): *a journey through the Scottish Highlands* **3** as a result of: *she retired through ill health* **4** during: *driving for five hours through the night* **5** for all of (a period): *it rained all through that summer* **6** *chiefly US* up to and including: *from Monday through Saturday* ▸ *adj* **7** finished: *I'm through with history* **8** having completed a specified amount of an activity: *he tried to stop the investigation halfway through* **9** (on a telephone line) connected **10** no longer able to function successfully in some specified capacity: *they are through, they haven't got a chance* **11** (of a train, plane flight, etc.) going directly to a place, so that passengers do not have to change: *the first ever through train between Singapore and Bangkok* ▸ *adv* **12** through a thing, place, or period of time: *the script gives up around halfway through* **13** extremely or absolutely: *I'm soaked through* **14 through and through** to the greatest possible extent: *the boards are rotten through and through*

> **through** *prep* **1** = via, by way of, by, between, past, from one side to the other of **3** = because of, by way of, by means of **4, 5** = during, throughout, for the duration of, in ▸ *adv* **14 through and through** = completely, totally, fully, thoroughly, entirely, altogether, wholly, utterly

throughout *prep* **1** through the whole of (a place or a period of time): *radio stations throughout the UK* ▸ *adv* **2** through the whole of a place or a period of time: *I led both races throughout*

> **throughout** *prep* = all over, everywhere in, through the whole of ▸ *adv* = all through, right through

throughput *n* the amount of material processed in a given period, esp. by a computer

throve *vb* a past tense of **thrive**

throw *vb* **throwing, threw, thrown 1** to hurl (something) through the air, esp. with a rapid motion of the arm **2** to put or move suddenly, carelessly, or violently: *she threw her arms round his neck* **3** to bring into a specified state or condition, esp. suddenly: *the invasion threw the region into turmoil* **4** to move (a switch or lever) so as to engage or disengage a mechanism **5** to cause (someone) to fall: *I'm riding the horse that threw me* **6 A** to tip (dice) out onto a flat surface **B** to obtain (a specified number) in this way:

one throws a 3 and the other throws a 5 **7** to shape (clay) on a potter's wheel **8** to give (a party) **9** *informal* to confuse or disconcert: *the question threw me* **10** to direct or cast (a look, light, etc.): *the lamp threw a shadow on the ceiling* **11** to project (the voice) so as to make it appear to come from somewhere else **12** *informal* to lose (a contest) deliberately **13 throw a punch** to strike, or attempt to strike, someone with one's fist **14 throw oneself at** to behave in a way which makes it clear that one is trying to win the affection of (someone) **15 throw oneself into** to involve oneself enthusiastically in **16 throw oneself on** to rely entirely upon (someone's goodwill, etc.): *the president threw himself on the mercy of the American people* ▸ *n* **17** the act or an instance of throwing **18** the distance thrown: *a throw of 90 metres* **19** (in sports such as wrestling or judo) a move which causes one's opponent to fall to the floor **20** a decorative blanket or cover **21 a throw** each: *we drank our way through a couple of bottles of claret at £12.50 a throw* ▸ See also **throwaway, throwback** *etc.*

> **throw** *vb* **1** = hurl, toss, fling, send, launch, cast, pitch, chuck (*informal*) **2** = toss, fling, chuck (*informal*), cast, hurl, sling (*informal*) **9** = confuse, baffle, faze, astonish, confound, disconcert, dumbfound ▸ *n* **1** = toss, pitch, fling, sling, lob (*informal*), heave

throwaway *adj* **1** said or done incidentally: *a throwaway line* **2** designed to be discarded after use: *throwaway cups* ▸ *vb* **throw away 3** to get rid of or discard: *try to recycle glass bottles instead of simply throwing them away* **4** to fail to make good use of: *she threw away the chance of a brilliant career when she got married*

throwback *n* **1** a person or thing that is like something that existed or was common long ago: *his ideas were a throwback to old colonial attitudes* **2** *informal* an occasion when someone is reminded of a past time ▸ *vb* **throw back 3** to remind someone of (something he or she said or did previously) in order to upset him or her: *he threw back at me everything I'd said the week before*

throw up *vb* **1** *informal* to vomit **2** to give up or abandon: *he would threaten to throw up his job* **3** to construct (a building or structure) hastily **4** to produce: *these links are throwing up fresh opportunities*

thrush¹ *n* any of a large group of songbirds, esp. one having a brown plumage with a spotted breast, such as the mistle thrush and song thrush

thrush² *n* **1** a fungal disease, esp. of infants, in which whitish spots form on the mouth, throat, and lips **2** a genital infection caused by the same fungus

thrust *vb* **thrusting, thrust 1** to push (someone or something) with force: *he took him by the arm and thrust him towards the door* **2** to force (someone) into some condition or situation: *unemployed people have been thrust into the front line of politics*

3 to force (one's way) through a crowd, forest, etc.: *Edward thrust his way towards them* **4** to stick out or up: *she thrust out her lower lip* ▸ *n* **5** a forceful drive, push, stab, or lunge: *the thrust of his spear* **6** a force, esp. one that produces motion **7** the propulsive force produced by the pressure of air and gas forced out of a jet engine or rocket engine **8** the essential or most forceful part: *the main thrust of the report* **9** *physics* a continuous pressure exerted by one part of an object against another **10** *informal* intellectual or emotional drive; forcefulness: *thanks to the ingenuity and enterprising thrust of this company*

> **thrust** *vb* **1** = push, force, shove, drive, plunge, jam, ram, propel ▸ *n* **5** = push, shove, poke, prod **6** = momentum, impetus, drive

thud *n* **1** a dull heavy sound **2** a blow or fall that causes such a sound ▸ *vb* **thudding**, **thudded** **3** to make or cause to make such a sound

thug *n* a tough and violent man, esp. a criminal > **thuggery** *n* > **thuggish** *adj*

> **thug** *n* = ruffian, hooligan, tough, heavy (*slang*), gangster, bully boy, bruiser (*informal*), tsotsi (*S African*)

thumb *n* **1** the short thick finger of the hand, set apart from the others **2** the part of a glove shaped to fit the thumb **3 all thumbs** very clumsy **4 thumbs down** an indication of refusal or disapproval **5 thumbs up** an indication of encouragement or approval **6 under someone's thumb** completely under someone else's control ▸ *vb* **7** to touch, mark, or move with the thumb: *he thumbed the volume switch to maximum* **8** to attempt to obtain (a lift in a motor vehicle) by signalling with the thumb: *he thumbed a lift to the station* **9 thumb one's nose at** to behave in a way that shows one's contempt or disregard for: *her mother had always thumbed her nose at convention* **10 thumb through** to flip the pages of (a book or magazine) in order to glance at the contents

thump *n* **1** the sound of something heavy hitting a comparatively soft surface **2** a heavy blow with the hand ▸ *vb* **3** to place (something) on or bang against (something) with a loud dull sound: *thumping the table is aggressive* **4** to hit or punch (someone): *stop that at once or I'll thump you!* **5** to throb or beat violently: *he could feel his heart thumping*

> **thump** *n* **1** = thud, crash, bang, clunk, thwack **2** = blow, knock, punch, rap, smack, clout (*informal*), whack, swipe (*informal*) ▸ *vb* **4** = strike, hit, punch, pound, beat, knock, smack, clout (*informal*)

thunder *n* **1** a loud cracking or deep rumbling noise caused by the rapid expansion of atmospheric gases that are suddenly heated by lightning **2** any loud booming sound: *the thunder of heavy gunfire* **3 steal someone's thunder** to lessen the effect of someone's idea or action by anticipating it ▸ *vb* **4** to make a loud noise like thunder: *an explosion thundered through the shaft* **5** to speak in a loud, angry manner: *'Get out of here this instant!' he thundered* **6** to move fast, heavily, and noisily: *a lorry thundered by* > **thundery** *adj*

> **thunder** *n* **2** = rumble, crash, boom, explosion ▸ *vb* **4** = rumble, crash, boom, roar, resound, reverberate, peal **5** = shout, roar, yell, bark, bellow

thunderbolt *n* **1** a flash of lightning accompanying thunder **2** something sudden and unexpected: *his career has been no thunderbolt* **3** *myth* a weapon thrown to earth by certain gods **4** *sport* a very fast-moving shot or serve

thunderclap *n* **1** a loud outburst of thunder **2** something as violent or unexpected as a clap of thunder

thunderous *adj* **1** resembling thunder in loudness: *thunderous applause* **2** threatening or angry: *a thunderous scowl*

thunderstruck *adj* amazed or shocked

Thursday *n* the fifth day of the week

thus *adv* **1** as a result or consequence: *the platforms provided a new floor and thus improved and enlarged the premises* **2** in this manner: *I sat thus for nearly half an hour* **3** to such a degree: *the competition has been almost bereft of surprise thus far*

> **thus** *adv* **1** = therefore, so, hence, consequently, accordingly, for this reason, ergo, on that account **2** = in this way, so, like this, as follows

thwack *vb* **1** to beat with something flat ▸ *n* **2 a** a blow with something flat **b** the sound made by it

thwart *vb* **1** to prevent or foil: *they inflicted such severe losses that they thwarted the invasion* ▸ *n* **2** the seat across a boat where the rower sits

> **thwart** *vb* = frustrate, foil, prevent, snooker, hinder, obstruct, outwit, stymie; ≠ assist

thy *adj old-fashioned* belonging to or associated in some way with you (thou): *love thy neighbour*

thyme (**time**) *n* a small shrub with white, pink, or red flowers and scented leaves used for seasoning food

thymus (**thigh**-muss) *n*, *pl* **-muses** *or* **-mi** (-my) *anatomy* a small gland situated near the base of the neck

thyroid *anatomy* ▸ *adj* **1** of or relating to the thyroid gland **2** of or relating to the largest cartilage of the larynx, which forms the Adam's apple in men ▸ *n* **3** the thyroid gland

thyroid gland *n anatomy* an endocrine gland that secretes hormones that control metabolism and body growth

thyself *pron old-fashioned* the reflexive form of **thou**

tiara *n* **1** a semicircular jewelled headdress worn by some women on formal occasions **2** the triple-tiered crown sometimes worn by the pope

tibia (tib-ee-a) *n, pl* **tibiae** (tib-ee-ee) *or* **tibias** the inner and thicker of the two bones of the human leg below the knee; shinbone ⊳ **tibial** *adj*

tic *n* a spasmodic muscular twitch

tick¹ *n* **1** a mark (✓) used to check off or indicate the correctness of something **2** a recurrent metallic tapping or clicking sound, such as that made by a clock **3** *informal* a moment or instant: *won't be a tick* ▸ *vb* **4** to mark or check with a tick **5** to produce a recurrent tapping sound or indicate by such a sound: *the clock ticked away* **6 what makes someone tick** *informal* the basic motivation of a person ▸ See also **tick off**, **tick over**

> **tick** *n* **1** = check mark, mark, line, stroke, dash **2** = click, tapping, clicking, ticktock **3** = moment, second, minute, flash, instant, twinkling, split second, trice ▸ *vb* **4** = mark, indicate, check off **5** = click, tap, ticktock

tick² *n* a small parasitic creature typically living on the skin of warm-blooded animals and feeding on the blood and tissues of their hosts: *a sheep tick*

tick³ *n Brit & NZ informal* account or credit: *a spending spree that was financed on tick*

ticket *n* **1** a printed piece of paper or cardboard showing that the holder is entitled to certain rights, such as travel on a train or bus or entry to a place of public entertainment **2** a label or tag attached to an article showing information such as its price and size **3** an official notification of a parking or traffic offence **4** the declared policy of a political party **5 that's (just) the ticket** *informal* that's the right or appropriate thing ▸ *vb* **-eting, -eted 6** to issue or attach a ticket or tickets to

> **ticket** *n* **1** = voucher, pass, coupon, card, slip, certificate, token, chit **2** = label, tag, marker, sticker, card, slip, tab, docket (*Brit*)

ticking *n* a strong cotton fabric, often striped, used esp. for mattress and pillow covers

tickle *vb* **-ling, -led 1** to touch or stroke (someone), so as to produce laughter or a twitching sensation **2** to itch or tingle **3** to amuse or please **4 tickled pink** *or* **to death** *informal* greatly pleased **5 tickle someone's fancy** to appeal to or amuse someone ▸ *n* **6** a sensation of light stroking or itching: *a tickle in the throat* **7** the act of tickling **8** *Canad* (in the Atlantic Provinces) a narrow strait

ticklish *adj* **1** sensitive to being tickled **2** delicate or difficult: *a ticklish problem*

tick off *vb* **1** to mark with a tick, esp. to show that an item on a list has been dealt with **2** *informal* to reprimand or scold (someone) ⊳ **ticking-off** *n*

tick over *vb* **1** (of an engine) to run at low speed with the transmission disengaged **2** to run smoothly without any major changes: *the business is just ticking over*

ticktack *n Brit & Austral* a system of sign language, mainly using the hands, by which bookmakers transmit their odds to each other at race courses

tidal *adj* **1** (of a river, lake, or sea) having tides **2** of or relating to tides: *a tidal surge*

tidal wave *n* **1** *not in technical use* same as **tsunami 2** an unusually large incoming wave, often caused by high winds and spring tides **3** a forceful and widespread movement in public opinion, action, etc.: *a tidal wave of scandals and embezzlement*

tiddler *n informal* **1** a very small fish, esp. a stickleback **2** a small child

tiddly¹ *adj* **-dlier, -dliest** *Brit* very small

tiddly² *adj* **-dlier, -dliest** *informal, chiefly Brit* slightly drunk

tiddlywinks *n* a game in which players try to flick discs of plastic into a cup

tide *n* **1** the alternate rise and fall of sea level caused by the gravitational pull of the sun and moon **2** the current caused by these changes in level: *I got caught by the tide and almost drowned* **3** a widespread tendency or movement: *the rising tide of nationalism* **4** *literary or old-fashioned* a season or time: *Yuletide*

> **tide** *n* **1, 2** = current, flow, stream, ebb, undertow, tideway **3** = course, direction, trend, movement, tendency, drift

tide over *vb* **tiding, tided** to help (someone) to get through a period of difficulty or distress: *they need some form of Social Security to tide them over*

tidings *pl n* information or news

tidy *adj* **-dier, -diest 1** neat and orderly **2** *Brit, Austral & NZ informal* quite large: *a tidy sum of money* ▸ *vb* **-dies, -dying, -died 3** to put (things) in their proper place; make neat: *I've tidied up the toys under the bed* ▸ *n, pl* **-dies 4** a small container for odds and ends ⊳ **tidily** *adv* ⊳ **tidiness** *n*

> **tidy** *adj* **1** = neat, orderly, clean, spruce, well-kept, well-ordered, shipshape; ≠ untidy **2** = considerable, large, substantial, goodly, healthy, generous, handsome, ample; ≠ small ▸ *vb* = neaten, straighten, order, clean, groom, spruce up; ≠ disorder

tie *vb* **tying, tied 1** to fasten or be fastened with string, rope, etc.: *a parcel tied with string* **2** to make a knot or bow in (something): *hang on while I tie my laces* **3** to restrict or limit: *they had children and were consequently tied to the school holidays* **4** to equal the score of a competitor or fellow candidate: *three players tied for second place* ▸ *n* **5** a long narrow piece of material worn, esp. by men, under the collar of a shirt, tied in a knot close to the throat with the ends hanging down the front **6** a bond or link: *he still has close ties to the town where he grew up* **7** a string, wire, etc., with which something is tied **8** *Brit sport* a match in a knockout competition: *whoever wins the tie will play Australia in the semi-finals* **9** ⒶⒶ a result in a match or competition in which the scores or times of some of the competitors are the same: *a tie for second place* **B** the match or competition in which the scores or results are equal **10** a regular commitment that limits a person's freedom: *it's a bit of a tie having to visit him every day* **11** something which supports or links parts of a structure **12** *US & Canad* a sleeper on a railway track **13** *music* a curved line connecting two notes of the same pitch indicating that the sound is to be prolonged for their joint time value

tie *vb* **1** = fasten, bind, join, link, connect, attach, knot; ≠ unfasten **3** = restrict, limit, confine, bind, restrain, hamper, hinder; ≠ free **4** = draw, be level, match, equal ▸ *n* **6** = bond, relationship, connection, commitment, liaison, allegiance, affiliation **7** = fastening, binding, link, bond, knot, cord, fetter, ligature **9** = draw, dead heat, deadlock, stalemate

tied *adj Brit* **1** (of a public house) allowed to sell beer from only one particular brewery **2** (of a house) rented out to the tenant for as long as he or she is employed by the owner

tier *n* one of a set of rows placed one above and behind the other, such as theatre seats

tier *n* = row, bank, layer, line, level, rank, storey, stratum

tiff *n* a minor quarrel

tiger *n* **1** a large Asian mammal of the cat family which has a tawny yellow coat with black stripes **2** a dynamic, forceful, or cruel person **3** a country, esp. in E Asia, that is achieving rapid economic growth

tiger lily *n* a lily of China and Japan with black-spotted orange flowers

tiger snake *n* a highly venomous brown-and-yellow Australian snake

tight *adj* **1** stretched or drawn taut: *loosening-up of tight muscles* **2** closely fitting: *wearing a jacket that was too tight for him* **3** made, fixed, or closed firmly and securely: *a tight band* **4** constructed so as to prevent the passage of water, air, etc.: *watertight*; *airtight* **5** cramped and allowing very little room for movement: *they squeezed him into the tight space* **6** unyielding or stringent: *tight security* **7** (of a situation) difficult or dangerous **8** allowing only the minimum time or money for doing something: *we have been working to a tight schedule* **9** *Brit, Austral & NZ informal* mean or miserly **10** (of a match or game) very close or even **11** *old-fashioned, informal* drunk **12** (of a corner or turn) turning through a large angle in a short distance: *the boat skidded round in a tight turn* ▸ *adv* **13** in a close, firm, or secure way: *they held each other tight* > **tightly** *adv* > **tightness** *n*

tight *adj* **1** = taut, stretched, rigid; ≠ slack **2** = close-fitting, narrow, cramped, snug, constricted, close; ≠ loose **3** = secure, firm, fast, fixed **9** = miserly, mean, stingy, grasping, parsimonious, niggardly, tightfisted; ≠ generous **10** = close, even, well-matched, hard-fought, evenly-balanced; ≠ uneven **11** = drunk, intoxicated, plastered (*slang*), under the influence (*informal*), tipsy, paralytic (*informal*), inebriated, out to it (*Austral, NZ slang*); ≠ sober

tighten *vb* to make or become tight or tighter

tighten *vb* = close, narrow, strengthen, squeeze, harden, constrict; ≠ slacken

tightrope *n* a rope stretched taut on which acrobats perform

tights *pl n* a one-piece clinging garment covering the body from the waist to the feet

tigress *n* **1** a female tiger **2** a fierce, cruel, or passionate woman

tiki (**tee**-kee) *n* a Māori greenstone neck ornament in the form of a fetus

tikka *adj Indian cookery* (of meat) marinated in spices and then dry-roasted: *chicken tikka*

tilde *n* a mark (˜) used in some languages to indicate that the letter over which it is placed is pronounced in a certain way, as in Spanish *señor*

tile *n* **1** a thin piece of ceramic, plastic, etc., used with others to cover a surface, such as a floor or wall **2** a rectangular block used as a playing piece in mah jong and other games **3 on the tiles** *informal* out having a good time and drinking a lot ▸ *vb* **tiling, tiled 4** to cover (a surface) with tiles > **tiled** *adj* > **tiler** *n*

tiling *n* **1** tiles collectively **2** something made of or surfaced with tiles

till[1] *conj, prep* same as **until**

till[2] *vb* to cultivate (land) for the raising of crops: *a constant round of sowing, tilling and harvesting* > **tillable** *adj* > **tiller** *n*

till *vb* = cultivate, dig, plough, work

till[3] *n* a box or drawer into which money taken from customers is put, now usually part of a cash register

till *n* = cash register, cash box

tillage *n* **1** the act, process, or art of tilling **2** tilled land

tiller *n naut* a handle used to turn the rudder when steering a boat

tilt *vb* **1** to move into a sloping position with one end or side higher than the other: *Dave tilted his chair back on two legs* **2** to move (part of the body) slightly upwards or to the side: *Marie tilted her head back* **3** to become more influenced by a particular idea or group: *the party is tilting more and more to the right* **4** to compete against someone in a jousting contest ▸ *n* **5** a slope or angle: *a tilt to one side* **6** the act of tilting **7 A** a jousting contest, esp. in medieval Europe **B** a thrust with a lance delivered during a medieval tournament **8** an attempt to win a contest: *a tilt at the world title* **9 at full tilt** at full speed or force

tilt *vb* **1** = slant, tip, slope, list, lean, heel, incline ▸ *n* **5** = slope, angle, inclination, list, pitch, incline, slant, camber **7a** = joust, fight, tournament, lists, combat, duel

timber *n* **1** wood as a building material **2** trees collectively **3** a wooden beam in the frame of a house, boat, etc. ▸ *adj* **4** made out of timber: *timber houses* **5** of or involved in the production or sale of wood as a building material: *a timber merchant* > **timbered** *adj* > **timbering** *n*

timber *n* **1** = wood, logs **3** = beams, boards, planks

timber line *n* the geographical limit beyond which trees will not grow

timbre (**tam**-bra) *n* the distinctive quality of sound produced by a particular voice or musical instrument

time *n* **1** the past, present, and future regarded as a continuous whole. Related adjective: **temporal 2** *physics* a quantity measuring duration, measured with reference to the rotation of the earth or from the vibrations of certain atoms **3** a specific point in time expressed in hours and minutes: *what time are you going?* **4** a system of reckoning for expressing time: *the deadline is 5:00 Eastern Time today* **5** an unspecified interval; a while: *some recover for a time and then relapse* **6** an instance or occasion: *when was the last time you saw it?* **7** a sufficient interval or period: *I need time to think* **8** an occasion or period of specified quality: *they'd had a lovely time* **9** a suitable moment: *the time has come to make peace* **10** a period or point marked by specific attributes or events: *in Victorian times* **11** *Brit* the time at which licensed premises are required by law to stop selling alcoholic drinks **12** the rate of pay for work done in normal working hours: *you get double time for working on a Sunday* **13** **a** the system of combining beats in music into successive groupings by which the rhythm of the music is established **b** a specific system having a specific number of beats in each grouping or bar: *duple time* **14** **against time** in an effort to complete something in a limited period **15 ahead of time** before the deadline **16 at one time a** once or formerly **b** simultaneously **17 at the same time a** simultaneously **b** nevertheless or however **18 at times** sometimes **19 beat time** to indicate the tempo of a piece of music by waving a baton, hand, etc. **20 do time** *informal* to serve a term in jail **21 for the time being** for the moment; temporarily **22 from time to time** at intervals; occasionally **23 have no time for** to have no patience with **24 in no time** very quickly **25 in one's own time a** outside paid working hours **b** at the speed of one's choice **26 in time a** early or at the appointed time: *he made it to the hospital in time for the baby's arrival* **b** eventually: *in time, the children of intelligent parents will come to dominate* **c** *music* at a correct metrical or rhythmic pulse **27 make time** to find an

opportunity **28 on time** at the expected or scheduled time **29 pass the time** to occupy oneself when there is nothing else to do: *they pass the time watching game shows on television* **30 pass the time of day** to have a short casual conversation (with someone) **31 time and again** frequently **32 time of one's life** a memorably enjoyable time **33 time out of mind** from long before anyone can remember ▸ *vb* **timing, timed 34** to measure the speed or duration of: *my Porsche was timed at 128 mph* **35** to set a time for: *the attack was timed for 6 am* **36** to do (something) at a suitable time: *her entry could not have been better timed* ▸ *adj* **37** operating automatically at or for a set time: *an electrical time switch* ▸ *interj* **38** the word called out by a publican signalling that it is closing time

time *n* **1, 5, 7, 25b** = period, term, space, stretch, spell, span, time frame, timeline **6, 9** = occasion, point, moment, stage, instance, point in time, juncture **10** = age, duration **13** = tempo, beat, rhythm, measure ▸ *vb* **35, 36** = schedule, set, plan, book, programme, set up, fix, arrange

time-honoured *adj* having been used or done for a long time and established by custom

timeless *adj* **1** unaffected by time or by changes in fashion, society, etc.: *the timeless appeal of tailored wool jackets* **2** eternal and everlasting: *the timeless universal reality behind all religions* > **timelessness** *n*

timeless *adj* = eternal, lasting, permanent, enduring, immortal, everlasting, ageless, changeless; ≠ temporary

timely *adj* **-lier, -liest,** *adv* at the right or an appropriate time

timely *adv* = opportune (*formal*), appropriate, well-timed, suitable, convenient, judicious, propitious, seasonable; ≠ untimely

timepiece *n* a device, such as a clock or watch, which measures and indicates time

timeserver *n* a person who changes his or her views in order to gain support or favour

time sharing *n* **1** a system of part ownership of a property for use as a holiday home whereby each participant owns the property for a particular period every year **2** a system by which users at different terminals of a computer can communicate with it at the same time

timetable *n* **1** a plan of the times when a job or activity should be done: *the timetable for the Royal Visit* **2** a list of departure and arrival times of trains or buses: *a timetable hung on the wall beside the ticket office* **3** a plan of the times when different subjects or classes are taught in a school or college: *a heavy timetable of lectures and practical classes* ▸ *vb* **-tabling, -tabled 4** to set a time when a particular thing should be done: *the meeting is timetabled for 3 o'clock*

timetable *n* **1** = schedule, programme, agenda, list, diary, calendar **3** = syllabus, course, curriculum, programme, teaching programme

timid *adj* **1** lacking courage or self-confidence: *a timid youth* **2** indicating shyness or fear: *a timid and embarrassed smile* > **timidity** *n* > **timidly** *adv*

timorous (tim-mor-uss) *adj literary* lacking courage or self-confidence: *a reclusive timorous creature* > **timorously** *adv*

timpani *or* **tympani** (tim-pan-ee) *pl n* a set of kettledrums > **timpanist** *or* **tympanist** *n*

tin *n* **1** a soft silvery-white metallic element. Symbol: **Sn 2** a sealed airtight metal container used for preserving and storing food or drink: *a cupboard full of packets and tins* **3** any metal container: *a tin of paint* **4** the contents of a tin **5** *Brit, Austral & NZ* galvanized iron, used to make roofs ▸ *vb* **tinning, tinned 6** to put (food) into tins

tincture *n* a medicine consisting of a small amount of a drug dissolved in alcohol

tinder *n* dry wood or other easily-burning material used to start a fire > **tindery** *adj*

tinderbox *n* (formerly) a small box for tinder, esp. one fitted with a flint and steel which could be used to make a spark

tine *n* a slender prong of a fork or a deer's antler > **tined** *adj*

ting *n* a high metallic sound such as that made by a small bell

tinge *n* **1** a slight tint or colouring: *his skin had an unhealthy greyish tinge* **2** a very small amount: *both goals had a tinge of fortune* ▸ *vb* **tingeing** *or* **tinging, tinged 3** to colour or tint faintly: *the sunset tinged the lake with pink* **4 tinged with** having a small amount of a particular quality: *the victory was tinged with sadness*

tinge *n* **1** = tint, colour, shade **2** = trace, bit, drop, touch, suggestion, dash, sprinkling, smattering ▸ *vb* **3** = tint, colour

tingle *vb* **-gling, -gled 1** to feel a mild prickling or stinging sensation, as from cold or excitement ▸ *n* **2** a mild prickling or stinging feeling > **tingling** *adj* > **tingly** *adj*

tinker *n* **1** (esp. formerly) a travelling mender of pots and pans **2** *Scot & Irish,* usually derogatory a traveller **3** a mischievous child ▸ *vb* **4 tinker with** to try to repair or improve (something) by making lots of minor adjustments

tinker *vb* = meddle, play, potter, fiddle (*informal*), dabble, mess about

tinkle *vb* **-kling, -kled 1** to ring with a high tinny sound like a small bell ▸ *n* **2** a high clear ringing sound **3** *Brit old-fashioned, informal* a telephone call > **tinkly** *adj*

tinned *adj* (of food) preserved by being sealed in a tin

tinny *adj* **-nier, -niest** (of a sound) high, thin, and metallic: *the tinny sound of a transistor radio*

tinpot *adj informal* worthless or unimportant: *a tinpot dictator*

tinsel *n* **1** a decoration consisting of a piece of metallic thread with thin strips of metal foil attached along its length **2** anything cheap, showy, and gaudy: *all their tinsel and show counts for nothing* ▸ *adj* **3** made of or decorated with tinsel **4** cheap, showy, and gaudy > **tinselly** *adj*

tint *n* **1** a shade of a colour, esp. a pale one: *his eyes had a yellow tint* **2** a colour that is softened by the addition of white: *a room decorated in pastel tints* **3** a dye for the hair ▸ *vb* **4** to give a tint to (something, such as hair)

tint *n* **1** = shade, colour, tone, hue **3** = dye, wash, rinse, tinge, tincture ▸ *vb* = dye, colour

tiny *adj* **tinier, tiniest** very small

tiny *adj* = small, little, minute, slight, miniature, negligible, microscopic, diminutive; ≠ huge

tip[1] *n* **1** a narrow or pointed end of something: *the northern tip of Japan* **2** a small piece attached to the end or bottom of something: *boot tips keep boots from getting scuffed* ▸ *vb* **tipping, tipped 3** to make or form a tip on: *the long strips that hang down are tipped with silver cones* > **tipped** *adj*

tip *n* **1** = end, point, head, extremity, sharp end, nib, prong ▸ *vb* = cap, top, crown, surmount (*formal*), finish

tip[2] *n* **1** an amount of money given to someone, such as a waiter, in return for service **2** a helpful hint or warning: *here are some sensible tips to help you avoid sunburn* **3** a piece of inside information, esp. in betting or investing ▸ *vb* **tipping, tipped 4** to give a tip to

tip *n* **1** = gratuity, gift, reward, present, sweetener (*informal*) **2, 3** = hint, suggestion, piece of advice, pointer, heads up (*US, Canad*) ▸ *vb* = reward, remunerate (*formal*), give a tip to, sweeten (*informal*)

tip[3] *vb* **tipping, tipped 1** to tilt: *he tipped back his chair* **2 tip over** to tilt so as to overturn or fall: *the box tipped over and the clothes in it spilled out* **3** *Brit* to dump (rubbish) **4** to pour out (the contents of a container): *he tipped the water from the basin down the sink* ▸ *n* **5** a rubbish dump

tip *vb* **3** = dump, empty, unload, pour out **4** = pour, drop, empty, dump, drain, discharge, unload, jettison ▸ *n* = dump, midden, rubbish heap, refuse heap

tipping point *n* a moment or event that marks a decisive change

tipple *vb* **-pling, -pled 1** to drink alcohol regularly, esp. in small quantities ▸ *n* **2** an alcoholic drink > **tippler** *n*

tipster *n* a person who sells tips to people betting on horse races or speculating on the stock market

tipsy *adj* **-sier, -siest** slightly drunk > **tipsiness** *n*

tiptoe *vb* **-toeing, -toed 1** to walk quietly with the heels off the ground ▸ *n* **2 on tiptoe** on the tips of the toes or on the ball of the foot and the toes: *I stood on tiptoe*

tiptop *adj, adv* of the highest quality or condition

tirade *n* a long angry speech or denunciation

tire *vb* **tiring, tired 1** to reduce the energy of, as by exertion: *she could still do things that would tire people half her age* **2** to become wearied or bored: *he simply stopped talking when he tired of my questions* > **tiring** *adj*

> **tire** *vb* **1** = exhaust, drain, fatigue, weary, wear out; ≠ refresh **2** = flag, become tired, fail

tired *adj* **1** weary or exhausted: *they were tired after their long journey* **2** bored with or no longer interested in something: *I'm tired of staying in watching TV every night* **3** having been used so often as to be no longer interesting: *you haven't fallen for that tired old line, have you?* > **tiredness** *n*

> **tired** *adj* **1** = exhausted, fatigued, weary, flagging, drained, sleepy, worn out, drowsy, tuckered out (*Austral, NZ informal*); ≠ energetic **2** = bored, fed up, weary, sick (*informal*), hoha (*NZ*); ≠ enthusiastic about **3** = hackneyed, stale, well-worn, old, corny (*slang*), threadbare, trite, clichéd; ≠ original

tireless *adj* energetic and determined: *a tireless worker for charity* > **tirelessly** *adv*

tiresome *adj* boring and irritating

tissue *n* **1** a group of cells in an animal or plant with a similar structure and function: *muscular tissue forms 42% of the body tissue* **2** a thin piece of soft absorbent paper used as a disposable handkerchief, towel, etc. **3** an interwoven series: *a tissue of lies*

tit[1] *n* any of various small European songbirds, such as the bluetit, that feed on insects and seeds

tit[2] *n* **1** *slang* a female breast **2** a teat or nipple

titanic *adj* having or requiring colossal strength: *a titanic struggle*

titanium *n chem* a strong white metallic element used in the manufacture of strong lightweight alloys, esp. aircraft parts. Symbol: Ti

titbit *or esp US* **tidbit** *n* **1** a tasty small piece of food **2** a pleasing scrap of scandal: *an interesting titbit of gossip*

tit-for-tat *adj* done in return or retaliation for a similar act: *a spate of tit-for-tat killings*

tithe *n* **1** one tenth of one's income or produce paid to the church as a tax **2** a tenth or very small part of anything: *he had accomplished only a tithe of his great dream* ▸ *vb* **tithing, tithed 3** to demand a tithe from **4** to pay a tithe or tithes > **tithable** *adj*

Titian (tish-un) *adj* (of hair) reddish-yellow

titillate *vb* **-lating, -lated** to arouse or excite pleasurably, esp. in a sexual way > **titillating** *adj* > **titillation** *n*

titivate *vb* **-vating, -vated** to make smarter or neater > **titivation** *n*

title *n* **1** the distinctive name of a book, film, record, etc.: *his first album bore the title 'Safe as Milk'* **2** a descriptive name or heading of a section of a book, speech, etc. **3** a book or periodical: *publishers were averaging a total of 500 new titles annually* **4** a name or epithet signifying rank, office, or function: *the job bears the title Assistant Divisional Administrator* **5** a formal designation, such as Mrs or Dr **6** *sport* a championship: *the Italians have won the title* **7** *law* the legal right to possession of property

> **title** *n* **4, 5** = name, designation, term, handle (*slang*), moniker or monicker (*slang*) **6** = championship, trophy, bays, crown, honour **7** = ownership, right, claim, privilege, entitlement, tenure, prerogative, freehold

titled *adj* having a title such as 'Lady' or 'Sir' which indicates a high social rank

title deed *n* a document containing evidence of a person's legal right or title to property, esp. a house or land

titter *vb* **1** to snigger, esp. derisively or in a suppressed way ▸ *n* **2** a suppressed laugh or snigger

tittle-tattle *n* **1** idle chat or gossip ▸ *vb* **-tattling, -tattled 2** to chatter or gossip

titular *adj* **1** in name only: *titular head of state* **2** of or having a title

tizzy *n, pl* **-zies** *informal* a state of confusion or excitement

TNT *n* 2,4,6-trinitrotoluene: a type of powerful explosive

to *prep* **1** used to indicate the destination of the subject or object of an action: *he went to the theatre* **2** used to introduce the indirect object of a verb: *talk to him* **3** used to introduce the infinitive of a verb: *I'm going to lie down* **4** as far as or until: *from September 11 to October 25* **5** used to indicate that two things have an equivalent value: *there are 16 ounces to the pound* **6** against or onto: *I put my ear to the door* **7** before the hour of: *17 minutes to midnight* **8** accompanied by: *dancing to a live band* **9** as compared with: *four goals to nil* **10** used to indicate a resulting condition: *burnt to death* **11** working for or employed by: *Chaplain to the Nigerian Chaplaincy in Britain* **12** in commemoration of: *a memorial to the victims of the disaster* ▸ *adv* **13** towards a closed position: *push the door to*

toad *n* **1** an amphibian which resembles a frog, but has a warty skin and spends more time on dry land **2** a loathsome person

toad-in-the-hole *n* a traditional British dish made of sausages baked in a batter

toadstool *n* any of various poisonous funguses consisting of a caplike top on a stem

toady *n, pl* **toadies 1** a person who flatters and ingratiates himself or herself in a fawning way: *a spineless political toady* ▸ *vb* **toadies, toadying, toadied 2** to fawn on and flatter (someone) > **toadyism** *n*

t

to and fro *adv, adj also* **to-and-fro 1** back and forth: *he moved his head to and fro as if dodging blows* **2** from one place to another then back again: *the ferry sailed to and fro across the river* ▸ **toing and froing** *n*

toast¹ *n* **1** sliced bread browned by exposure to heat ▸ *vb* **2** to brown (bread) under a grill or over a fire **3** to warm or be warmed: *toasting his feet at the fire*

> **toast** *vb* **2** = brown, grill, crisp, roast **3** = warm (up), heat (up), thaw, bring back to life

toast² *n* **1** a proposal of health or success given to a person or thing and marked by people raising glasses and drinking together **2** a person or thing that is honoured: *his success made him the toast of the British film industry* ▸ *vb* **3** to propose or drink a toast to (a person or thing)

> **toast** *n* **1** = tribute, compliment, salute, health, pledge, salutation (*formal*) **2** = favourite, celebrity, darling, talk, pet, focus of attention, hero *or* heroine, blue-eyed boy *or* girl (*Brit informal*) ▸ *vb* = drink to, honour, salute, drink (to) the health of

toaster *n* an electrical device for toasting bread

tobacco *n, pl* **-cos** *or* **-coes** an American plant with large leaves which are dried for smoking, or chewing, or made into snuff

tobacconist *n Brit & Austral* a person or shop that sells tobacco, cigarettes, pipes, etc.

toboggan *n* **1** a long narrow sledge used for sliding over snow and ice ▸ *vb* **2** to ride on a toboggan

toby jug *n chiefly Brit* a beer mug or jug in the form of a stout seated man wearing a three-cornered hat and smoking a pipe

toccata (tok-**kah**-ta) *n* a piece of fast music for the organ, harpsichord, or piano, usually in a rhythmically free style

today *n* **1** this day, as distinct from yesterday or tomorrow **2** the present age: *in today's world* ▸ *adv* **3** during or on this day: *I hope you're feeling better today* **4** nowadays: *this is one of the most reliable cars available today*

toddle *vb* **-dling, -dled 1** to walk with short unsteady steps, like a young child **2 toddle off** *humorous* to depart: *he toddled off to bed* ▸ *n* **3** the act or an instance of walking with short unsteady steps

toddler *n* a young child who has only just learned how to walk

toddy *n, pl* **-dies** a drink made from spirits, esp. whisky, hot water, sugar, and usually lemon juice

to-do *n, pl* **-dos** *Brit, Austral & NZ* a commotion, fuss, or quarrel

toe *n* **1** any one of the digits of the foot **2** the part of a shoe or sock covering the toes **3 on one's toes** alert **4 tread on someone's toes** to offend a person, esp. by trespassing on his or her

field of responsibility ▸ *vb* **toeing, toed 5** to touch or kick with the toe **6 toe the line** to conform to expected attitudes or standards

toff *n Brit slang* a well-dressed or upper-class person

toffee *n* **1** a sticky chewy sweet made by boiling sugar with water and butter **2 can't (do something) for toffee** *informal* is not competent or talented at (doing something): *she couldn't dance for toffee*

tofu *n* a food with a soft cheeselike consistency made from unfermented soya-bean curd

tog *n* unit for measuring the insulating power of duvets

toga (**toe**-ga) *n* a garment worn by citizens of ancient Rome, consisting of a piece of cloth draped around the body ▸ **togaed** *adj*

together *adv* **1** with cooperation between people or organizations: *we started a company together* **2** in or into contact with each other: *he clasped his hands together* **3** in or into one place: *the family gets together to talk* **4** at the same time: *'Disgusting,' said Julie and Alice together* **5** considered collectively: *the properties together were worth more as a unit* **6** *old-fashioned* continuously: *working for eight hours together* **7 together with** in addition to ▸ *adj* **8** *slang* self-possessed, competent, and well-organized

> **together** *adv* **1** = collectively, jointly, as one, with each other, in conjunction, side by side, mutually, in partnership; ≠ separately **4** = at the same time, simultaneously, concurrently, contemporaneously, at one fell swoop ▸ *adj* = self-possessed, composed, well-balanced, well-adjusted, grounded

toggle *n* **1** a bar-shaped button inserted through a loop for fastening coats, etc. **2** *computers* a key on a keyboard which, when pressed, will turn a function or feature on if it is currently off, and turn it off if it is currently on

toil *n* **1** hard or exhausting work: *hours of toil beneath the Catalan sun* ▸ *vb* **2** to work hard: *workers toiling in the fields to produce tea for westerners to drink* **3** to move slowly and with difficulty, for instance because of exhaustion or the steepness of a slope: *Joanna toiled up the steps to the church*

> **toil** *n* = hard work, effort, application, sweat, graft (*informal*), slog, exertion, drudgery; ≠ idleness ▸ *vb* **2** = labour, work, struggle, strive, sweat (*informal*), slave, graft (*informal*), slog **3** = struggle, trek, slog, trudge, fight your way, footslog

toilet *n* **1 A** a bowl fitted with a water-flushing device and connected to a drain, for receiving and disposing of urine and faeces **B** a room with such a fitment **2** *old-fashioned* the act of dressing and preparing oneself

> **toilet** *n* **1A** = lavatory, bathroom, loo (*Brit informal*), privy (*obsolete*), cloakroom (*Brit*),

urinal, latrine, washroom, dunny (*Austral, NZ old-fashioned, informal*), bogger (*Austral slang*), brasco (*Austral slang*) **1e** = bathroom, gents *or* ladies (*Brit informal*), privy, latrine, water closet, ladies' room, W.C.

toiletry *n, pl* **-ries** an object or cosmetic used in making up, dressing, etc.

toilet water *n* liquid perfume lighter than cologne

token *n* **1** a symbol, sign, or indication of something: *as a token of respect* **2** a gift voucher that can be used as payment for goods of a specified value **3** a metal or plastic disc, such as a substitute for currency for use in a slot machine **4 by the same token** in the same way as something mentioned previously ▸ *adj* **5** intended to create an impression but having no real importance: *as a token gesture of goodwill*

token *n* **1** = symbol, mark, sign, note, expression, indication, representation, badge ▸ *adj* = nominal, symbolic, minimal, hollow, superficial, perfunctory

tokenism *n* the practice of making only a token effort or doing no more than the minimum, esp. in order to comply with a law > **tokenist** *adj*

told *vb* the past of **tell**

tolerable *adj* **1** able to be put up with; bearable **2** *informal* fairly good > **tolerably** *adv*

tolerance *n* **1** the quality of accepting other people's rights to their own opinions, beliefs, or actions **2** capacity to endure something, esp. pain or hardship **3** the ability of a substance to withstand heat, stress, etc., without damage **4** *med* the capacity to endure the effects of a continued or increasing dose of a drug, poison, etc. **5** an acceptable degree of variation in a measurement or value: *the bodywork of the car is precision-engineered with a tolerance of 0.01 millimetres*

tolerance *n* **1** = broad-mindedness, indulgence, forbearance, permissiveness, open-mindedness; ≠ intolerance **2** = endurance, resistance, stamina, fortitude, resilience, toughness, staying power, hardiness **4** = resistance, immunity, resilience, non-susceptibility

tolerant *adj* **1** accepting of the beliefs, actions, etc., of other people **2 tolerant of** able to withstand (heat, stress, etc.) without damage

tolerant *adj* **1** = broad-minded, understanding, open-minded, catholic, long-suffering, permissive, forbearing, unprejudiced; ≠ intolerant

tolerate *vb* **-ating, -ated 1** to allow something to exist or happen, even though one does not approve of it: *you must learn to tolerate opinions other than your own* **2** to put up with (someone or something): *he found the pain hard to tolerate* > **toleration** *n*

tolerate *vb* **1** = allow, accept, permit, take, brook, put up with (*informal*), condone; ≠ forbid **2** = endure, stand, take, stomach, put up with (*informal*)

toll¹ *vb* **1** to ring (a bell) slowly and regularly **2** to announce by tolling: *the bells tolled the Queen's death* ▸ *n* **3** the slow regular ringing of a bell

toll *vb* **1** = ring, sound, strike, chime, knell, clang, peal ▸ *n* = ringing, chime, knell, clang, peal

toll² *n* **1** a charge for the use of certain roads and bridges: *the Skye Bridge toll* **2** loss or damage from a disaster: *the annual death toll on the roads is about 4500* **3 take a** *or* **its toll** to have a severe and damaging effect: *the continued stress had taken a toll on her health*

toll *n* **1** = charge, tax, fee, duty, payment, levy, tariff **2** = damage, cost, loss, roll, penalty, sum, number, roster

tom *n* **1** a male cat ▸ *adj* **2** (of an animal) male: *a tom turkey*

tomahawk *n* a fighting axe used by the Native Americans of N America

tomato *n, pl* **-toes 1** a red fleshy juicy fruit with many edible seeds, eaten in salads, as a vegetable, etc. **2** the plant, originally from South America, on which this fruit grows

tomb *n* **1** a place for the burial of a corpse **2** a monument over a grave **3 the tomb** *poetic* death

tomb *n* **1** = grave, vault, crypt, mausoleum, sarcophagus, catacomb, sepulchre

tombola *n Brit* a type of lottery, in which tickets are drawn from a revolving drum

tomboy *n* a girl who behaves or dresses in ways that are traditionally considered to be like a boy

tombstone *n* a gravestone

tome *n* a large heavy book

tomfoolery *n* foolish behaviour

Tommy gun *n* a type of light sub-machine-gun

tomorrow *n* **1** the day after today: *tomorrow's meeting has been cancelled* **2** the future: *the struggle to build a better tomorrow* ▸ *adv* **3** on the day after today: *the festival starts tomorrow* **4** at some time in the future: *they live today as millions more will live tomorrow*

tom-tom *n* a long narrow drum beaten with the hands

ton *n* **1** *Brit* a unit of weight equal to 2240 pounds or 1016.046 kilograms **2** *US & Canad* a unit of weight equal to 2000 pounds or 907.184 kilograms **3 come down on someone like a ton of bricks** to scold someone very severely ▸ *adv* **4 tons** a lot: *I've got tons of things to do before going on holiday*

tonal *adj* **1** *music* written in a key **2** of or relating to tone or tonality

tonality *n, pl* **-ties 1** *music* the presence of a musical key in a composition **2** the overall scheme of colours and tones in a painting

t

tone n **1** sound with reference to its pitch, timbre, or volume **2** US & Canad same as **note** (sense 6) **3** music an interval of two semitones, such as that between doh and ray in tonic sol-fa **4** the quality or character of a sound: *her tone was angry* **5** general aspect, quality, or style: *the tone of the conversation made him queasy* **6** high quality or style: *my car with its patches of rust lowered the tone of the neighbourhood* **7** the quality of a given colour, as modified by mixture with white or black; shade or tint **8** physiol the natural firmness of the tissues and normal functioning of bodily organs in health ▸ vb **toning**, **toned 9** to be of a matching or similar tone **10** to give a tone to or correct the tone of ▷ **toneless** adj ▷ **tonelessly** adv

> **tone** n **1, 4** = volume, timbre **5** = character, style, feel, air, spirit, attitude, manner, mood **7** = colour, shade, tint, tinge, hue ▸ vb **9** = harmonize, match, blend, suit, go well with

tone-deaf adj unable to distinguish subtle differences in musical pitch
tone down vb to moderate in tone: *I sensed some reserve in his manner, so I toned down my enthusiasm*

> **tone down** vb **tone something down** = moderate, temper, soften, restrain, subdue, play down

tongs pl n a tool for grasping or lifting, consisting of two long metal or wooden arms, joined with a hinge or flexible metal strip at one end
tongue n **1** a movable mass of muscular tissue attached to the floor of the mouth, used for tasting, eating, and speaking **2** a language, dialect, or idiom: *the Scots tongue* **3** the ability to speak: *taken aback, she could not find her tongue* **4** a manner of speaking: *a sharp tongue* **5** the tongue of certain animals used as food **6** a narrow strip of something that extends outwards: *a narrow tongue of flame* **7** a flap of leather on a shoe **8** the clapper of a bell **9** a projecting strip along an edge of a board that is made to fit a groove in another board **10 hold one's tongue** to keep quiet **11 on the tip of one's tongue** about to come to mind **12 with (one's) tongue in (one's) cheek** with insincere or ironical intent

> **tongue** n **2** = language, speech, dialect, parlance

tonic n **1** a medicine that improves the functioning of the body or increases the feeling of wellbeing **2** anything that enlivens or strengthens: *his dry humour was a stimulating tonic* **3** Also called: **tonic water** a carbonated beverage containing quinine and often mixed with alcoholic drinks: *gin and tonic* **4** music the first note of a major or minor scale and the tonal centre of a piece composed in a particular key ▸ adj **5** having an invigorating or refreshing effect: *a tonic bath* **6** music of the first note of a major or minor scale

> **tonic** n **1, 2** = stimulant, boost, pick-me-up (*informal*), fillip, shot in the arm (*informal*), restorative

tonic sol-fa n a method of teaching music, by which syllables are used as names for the notes of the major scale in any key
tonight n **1** the night or evening of this present day: *tonight's edition* ▸ adv **2** in or during the night or evening of this day: *I want to go out dancing tonight*
tonnage n **1** the capacity of a merchant ship expressed in tons **2** the weight of the cargo of a merchant ship **3** the total amount of shipping of a port or nation
tonne (tunn) n a unit of mass equal to 1000 kg or 2204.6 pounds
tonsil n either of two small oval lumps of spongy tissue situated one on each side of the back of the mouth ▷ **tonsillar** adj
tonsillectomy n, pl **-mies** surgical removal of the tonsils
tonsillitis n inflammation of the tonsils, causing a sore throat and fever
tonsure n **1 A** (in certain religions and monastic orders) the shaving of the head or the crown of the head only **B** the part of the head left bare by such shaving ▸ vb **-suring**, **-sured 2** to shave the head of ▷ **tonsured** adj
too adv **1** as well or also: *I'll miss you, too* **2** in or to an excessive degree: *it's too noisy in here* **3** extremely: *you're too kind* **4** US, Canad & Austral informal used to emphasize contradiction of a negative statement: *You didn't! – I did too!*

> **too** adv **1** = also, as well, further, in addition, moreover, besides, likewise, to boot **2** = excessively, very, extremely, overly, unduly, unreasonably, inordinately, immoderately

took vb the past tense of **take**
tool n **1 A** an implement, such as a hammer, saw, or spade, that is used by hand to help do a particular type of work **B** a power-driven instrument: *machine tool* **2** the cutting part of such an instrument **3** a person used to perform dishonourable or unpleasant tasks for another: *the government is acting as a tool of big business* **4** any object, skill, etc., used for a particular task or in a particular job: *a skilled therapist can use photographs as tools* ▸ vb **5** to work, cut, or form (something) with a tool

> **tool** n **1** = implement, device, appliance, machine, instrument, gadget, utensil, contraption (*informal*) **3** = puppet, creature, pawn, stooge (*slang*), minion, lackey, flunkey, hireling

toolbar n a row or column of buttons displayed on a computer screen, allowing the user to select a variety of functions
toot n **1** a short hooting sound ▸ vb **2** to give or cause to give a short blast, hoot, or whistle: *motorists tooted their car horns*

tooth *n*, *pl* **teeth 1** one of the bonelike projections in the jaws of most vertebrates that are used for biting, tearing, or chewing **2** one of the sharp projections on the edge of a comb, saw, zip, etc. **3 long in the tooth** old or ageing **4 a sweet tooth** a liking for sweet food **5 tooth and nail** with great vigour and determination: *the union would oppose compulsory redundancies tooth and nail* ▶ See also **teeth**

toothless *adj* **1** having no teeth **2** having no real power: *the proposed Commission will not be as toothless as scoffers suggest*

toothpaste *n* a paste used for cleaning the teeth, applied with a toothbrush

toothpick *n* a small wooden or plastic stick used for extracting pieces of food from between the teeth

top¹ *n* **1** the highest point or part of anything: *the top of the stairs* **2** the most important or successful position: *at the top of the agenda* **3** a lid or cap that fits onto one end of something, esp. to close it: *he unscrewed the top from a quart of ale* **4** the highest degree or point: *the two people at the top of the Party* **5** the most important person or people in an organization: *the top of the military establishment* **6** the loudest or highest pitch: *she cheered and sang at the top of her voice* **7** a garment, esp. for a woman, that extends from the shoulders to the waist or hips **8** the part of a plant that is above ground: *nettle tops* **9 off the top of one's head** without previous preparation or careful thought **10 on top of A** in addition to: *the average member of staff will get 25% on top of salary* **B** informal in complete control of: *we're on top of our costs and expenses and looking for other opportunities* **11 over the top A** lacking restraint or a sense of proportion: *you went over the top when you called her a religious maniac* **B** military over the edge of a trench ▶ *adj* **12** at, of, or being the top: *men still hold most of the top jobs in industry* ▶ *vb* **topping, topped 13** to put on top of (something): *top your salad with a mild dressing* **14** to reach or pass the top of **15** to be at the top of: *her biggest hit topped the charts for six weeks* **16** to exceed or surpass: *his estimated fortune tops £2 billion* **17 top and tail A** to trim off the ends of (fruit or vegetables) before cooking **B** to wash only a baby's face and bottom

> **top** *n* **1** = peak, summit, head, crown, height, ridge, brow, crest; ≠ **bottom 2** = first place, head, peak, lead, high point **3** = lid, cover, cap, plug, stopper, bung ▶ *adj* = prime, best, select, first-class, quality, choice, excellent, premier; ≠ lowest ▶ *vb* **13** = cover, garnish, finish, crown, cap **15** = lead, head, be at the top of, be first in **16** = surpass, better, beat, improve on, cap, exceed, eclipse, excel; ≠ not be as good as

top² *n* **1** a toy that is spun on its pointed base **2 sleep like a top** to sleep very soundly

topaz (toe-pazz) *n* a hard glassy yellow, pink, or colourless mineral used in making jewellery

top brass *pl n* the most important or high-ranking officials or leaders

topee *or* **topi** (toe-pee) *n*

top hat *n* a man's hat with a tall cylindrical crown and narrow brim, now only worn for some formal occasions

top-heavy *adj* unstable through being overloaded at the top

topiary (tope-yar-ee) *n* **1** the art of trimming trees or bushes into artificial decorative shapes **2** trees or bushes trimmed into decorative shapes ▶ *adj* **3** of or relating to topiary > **topiarist** *n*

topic *n* a subject of a speech, book, conversation, etc.

> **topic** *n* = subject, point, question, issue, matter, theme, subject matter

topical *adj* of or relating to current affairs > **topicality** *n* > **topically** *adv*

> **topical** *adj* = current, popular, contemporary, up-to-date, up-to-the-minute, newsworthy

topless *adj* of or relating to women wearing costumes that do not cover the breasts: *topless beaches*

topmost *adj* at or nearest the top

top-notch *adj informal* excellent or superb: *top-notch entertainment*

topography *n*, *pl* **-phies 1** the surface features of a region, such as its hills, valleys, or rivers: *the islands are fragile, with a topography constantly changed by wind and wave* **2** the study or description of such surface features **3** the representation of these features on a map > **topographer** *n* > **topographical** *adj*

topology *n* a branch of geometry describing the properties of a figure that are unaffected by continuous distortion > **topological** *adj*

topping *n* a sauce or garnish for food

topple *vb* **-pling, -pled 1** to fall over or cause (something) to fall over, esp. from a height: *he staggered back against the railing and toppled over into the river* **2** to overthrow or oust: *few believe the scandal will topple the government*

> **topple** *vb* **1** = knock over **2** = overthrow, overturn, bring down, oust, unseat, bring low

topsoil *n* the surface layer of soil

topsy-turvy *adj* **1** upside down **2** in a state of confusion ▶ *adv* **3** in a topsy-turvy manner

toque (toke) *n* a small round brimless hat

tor *n chiefly Brit* a high hill, esp. a bare rocky one

Torah *n* the whole body of traditional Jewish teaching, including the Oral Law

torch *n* **1** a small portable electric lamp powered by batteries **2** a wooden shaft dipped in wax or tallow and set alight **3** anything regarded as a source of enlightenment, guidance, etc.: *a torch of hope* **4 carry a torch for** to be in love with (someone), esp. unrequitedly ▶ *vb* **5** *informal* to deliberately set (a building) on fire

t

tore *vb* the past tense of **tear²**

toreador (torr-ee-a-dor) *n* a bullfighter, esp. one on horseback

torment *vb* **1** to cause (someone) great pain or suffering **2** to tease or pester (a person or animal) in an annoying or cruel way ▸ *n* **3** physical or mental pain **4** a source of pain or suffering › **tormentor** *n*

> **torment** *vb* **1** = torture, distress, rack, crucify; ≠ comfort **2** = tease, annoy, bother, irritate, harass, hassle (*informal*), pester, vex ▸ *n* **3** = suffering, distress, misery, pain, hell (*informal*), torture, agony, anguish; ≠ bliss

torn *vb* **1** the past participle of **tear²** ▸ *adj* **2** split or cut **3** divided or undecided, as in preference: *torn between two lovers*

> **torn** *adj* **2** = cut, split, rent, ripped, ragged, slit, lacerated **3** = undecided, uncertain, unsure, wavering, vacillating, in two minds (*informal*), irresolute

tornado *n*, *pl* **-dos** *or* **-does** a rapidly whirling column of air, usually characterized by a dark funnel-shaped cloud causing damage along its path

> **tornado** *n* = whirlwind, storm, hurricane, gale, cyclone, typhoon, tempest (*literary*), squall

torpedo *n*, *pl* **-does 1** a cylindrical self-propelled weapon carrying explosives that is launched from aircraft, ships, or submarines and follows an underwater path to hit its target ▸ *vb* **-doing**, **-doed 2** to attack or hit (a ship) with one or a number of torpedoes **3** to destroy or wreck: *the Prime Minister warned his party against torpedoing the bill*

torpid *adj* **1** sluggish or dull: *he has a rather torpid intellect* **2** (of a hibernating animal) dormant

torpor *n* drowsiness and apathy

torque (tork) *n* **1** a force that causes rotation around a central point such as an axle **2** an ancient Celtic necklace or armband made of twisted metal

torrent *n* **1** a fast or violent stream, esp. of water **2** a rapid flow of questions, abuse, etc.

torrential *adj* (of rain) very heavy

torrid *adj* **1** (of weather) so hot and dry as to parch or scorch **2** (of land) arid or parched **3** highly charged emotionally: *a torrid affair*

torsion *n* the twisting of a part by equal forces being applied at both ends but in opposite directions › **torsional** *adj*

torso *n*, *pl* **-sos 1** the trunk of the human body **2** a statue of a nude human trunk, esp. without the head or limbs

tort *n law* a civil wrong or injury, for which an action for damages may be brought

tortilla *n* (in Mexican cooking) a kind of thin pancake made from corn meal

tortoise *n* a land reptile with a heavy dome-shaped shell into which it can withdraw its head and legs

tortoiseshell *n* **1** the horny yellow-and-brown mottled shell of a sea turtle, used for making ornaments and jewellery **2** a domestic cat with black, cream, and brownish markings **3** a butterfly which has orange-brown wings with black markings ▸ *adj* **4** made of tortoiseshell

tortuous *adj* **1** twisted or winding: *a tortuous route* **2** devious or cunning: *months of tortuous negotiations*

torture *vb* **-turing**, **-tured 1** to cause (someone) extreme physical pain, esp. to extract information, etc.: *suspects were regularly tortured and murdered by the secret police* **2** to cause (someone) mental anguish ▸ *n* **3** physical or mental anguish **4** the practice of torturing a person **5** something which causes great mental distress: *she was going through the torture of a collapsing marriage* › **tortured** *adj* › **torturer** *n* › **torturous** *adj*

> **torture** *vb* **1** = torment, abuse, persecute, afflict, scourge, molest, crucify, mistreat; ≠ comfort **2** = distress, torment, worry, trouble, rack, afflict, harrow, inflict anguish on ▸ *n* **3** = agony, suffering, anguish, distress, torment, heartbreak; ≠ bliss **4** = ill-treatment, abuse, torment, persecution, maltreatment, harsh treatment

Tory *n*, *pl* **-ries 1** a member or supporter of the Conservative Party in Great Britain or Canada **2** *history* a member of the English political party that supported the Church and Crown and traditional political structures and opposed the Whigs ▸ *adj* **3** of or relating to a Tory or Tories › **Toryism** *n*

toss *vb* **1** to throw (something) lightly **2** to fling or be flung about, esp. in a violent way: *the salty sea breeze tossing the branches of the palms* **3** to coat (food) with a dressing by gentle stirring or mixing: *her technique for tossing Caesar salad* **4** (of a horse) to throw (its rider) **5** to move (one's head) suddenly backwards, as in impatience **6** to throw up (a coin) to decide between alternatives by guessing which side will land uppermost **7** **toss and turn** to be restless when trying to sleep ▸ *n* **8** the act or an instance of tossing **9** the act of deciding between alternatives by throwing up a coin and guessing which side will land uppermost: *Essex won the toss and decided to bat first* **10** **argue the toss** to waste time and energy arguing about an unimportant point **11** **not give a toss** *informal* not to care at all

> **toss** *vb* **1** = throw, pitch, hurl, fling, launch, cast, flip, sling (*informal*) **3** = shake **4** = throw, pitch, lob (*informal*) **7** = thrash (about), twitch, wriggle, squirm, writhe ▸ *n* **8** = throw, pitch, lob (*informal*)

toss up *vb* **1** to spin (a coin) in the air in order to decide between alternatives by guessing which side will land uppermost ▸ *n* **toss-up 2** an instance of tossing up a coin **3** *informal* an even chance or risk: *it's a toss-up whether prices will go up or down over the days ahead*

tot *n* **1** a very young child **2** a small drink of spirits

> **tot** *n* **1** = infant, child, baby, toddler, mite, littlie (*Austral informal*), ankle-biter (*Austral slang*), tacker (*Austral slang*) **2** = measure, shot (*informal*), finger, nip, slug, dram, snifter (*informal*)

total *n* **1** the whole, esp. regarded as the sum of a number of parts **2 in total** overall: *the company employs over 700 people in total* ▸ *adj* **3** complete: *a total ban on alcohol* **4** being or related to a total: *the total number of deaths* ▸ *vb* **-talling, -talled** or *US* **-taling, -taled 5** to amount to: *the firm's losses totalled more than $2 billion* **6** to add up: *purchases are totalled with a pencil and a notepad* ▸ **totally** *adv*

> **total** *n* **1** = sum, entirety, grand total, whole, aggregate, totality, full amount, sum total; ≠ part ▸ *adj* **3** = complete, absolute, utter, whole, entire, undivided, overarching, thoroughgoing; ≠ partial ▸ *vb* **5** = amount to, make, come to, reach, equal, run to, number, add up to **6** = add up, work out, compute, reckon, tot up; ≠ subtract

totalitarian *adj* **1** of a political system in which there is only one party, which allows no opposition and attempts to control everything: *a totalitarian state* ▸ *n* **2** a person who is in favour of totalitarian policies ▸ **totalitarianism** *n*

totality *n, pl* **-ties 1** the whole amount **2** the state of being total

totalizator, totalizer, totalisator or **totaliser** *n* a machine to operate a system of betting on a racecourse in which money is paid out to the winners in proportion to their stakes

tote¹ *vb* **toting, toted** *informal* **1** to carry or wear (a gun) **2** to haul or carry

tote² *n* **the tote** *trademark* short for **totalizator**

totem *n* **1** (esp. among Native Americans) an object or animal symbolizing a clan or family **2** a representation of such an object ▸ **totemic** *adj* ▸ **totemism** *n*

totem pole *n* a pole carved or painted with totemic figures set up by certain Native Americans as a tribal symbol

totter *vb* **1** to move in an unsteady manner **2** to sway or shake as if about to fall **3** to be failing, unstable, or precarious: *the world was tottering on the edge of war*

toucan *n* a tropical American fruit-eating bird with a large brightly coloured bill

touch *vb* **1** to cause or permit a part of the body to come into contact with (someone or something): *the baking tin is too hot to touch* **2** to tap, feel, or strike (someone or something): *he touched me on the shoulder* **3** to come or bring (something)

into contact with (something else): *the plane's wheels touched the runway* **4** to move or disturb by handling: *we shouldn't touch anything before the police arrive* **5** to have an effect on: *millions of people's lives had been touched by the music of the Beatles* **6** to produce an emotional response in: *the painful truth of it touched her* **7** to eat or drink: *she hardly ever touched alcohol* **8** to compare to in quality or attainment; equal or match: *nothing can touch them for scope and detail* **9** *Brit, Austral & NZ slang* to ask (someone) for a loan or gift of money **10** to fondle in a sexual manner: *I wouldn't let him touch me unless I was in the mood* **11** to strike, harm, or molest: *I never touched him!* **12 touch on** or **upon** to allude to briefly or in passing: *these two issues may be touched upon during the talks* ▸ *n* **13** the sense by which the texture and other qualities of objects can be experienced when they come in contact with a part of the body surface, esp. the tips of the fingers. Related adjective: **tactile 14** the feel or texture of an object as perceived by this sense: *she enjoyed the touch of the damp grass on her feet* **15** the act or an instance of something coming into contact with the body: *he remembered the touch of her hand* **16** a gentle push, tap, or caress: *the switch takes only the merest touch to operate* **17** a small amount; trace: *a touch of luxury* **18** a particular manner or style of doing something: *his songs always reveal his keen melodic touch* **19** a detail of some work: *final touches were now being put to the plans* **20** a slight attack: *a touch of dysentery* **21** (in sports such as football or rugby) the area outside the lines marking the side of the pitch: *he kicked the ball into touch* **22** the technique of fingering a keyboard instrument **23 a touch** slightly or marginally: *it's nice, but a touch expensive* **24 in touch A** regularly speaking to, writing to, or visiting someone **B** having up-to-date knowledge or understanding of a situation or trend **25 lose touch A** to gradually stop speaking to, writing to, or visiting someone **B** to stop having up-to-date knowledge or understanding of a situation or trend **26 out of touch A** no longer speaking to, writing to, or visiting someone **B** no longer having up-to-date knowledge or understanding of a situation or trend

> **touch** *vb* **1** = come into contact, meet, contact, border, graze, adjoin, be in contact, abut **2, 3** = tap **5** = affect, influence, inspire, impress **6** = move, stir, disturb **7** = consume, take, drink, eat, partake of **8** = match, rival, equal, compare with, parallel, hold a candle to (*informal*) **12 touch on something** = refer to, cover, raise, deal with, mention, bring in, speak of, hint at ▸ *n* **13** = feeling, handling, physical contact **16** = contact, push, stroke, brush, press, tap, poke, nudge **17** = bit, spot (*Brit*), trace, drop, dash, small amount, jot, smattering **18** = style, method, technique, way, manner, trademark

touch and go adj risky or critical: it was touch and go whether the mission would succeed

> **touch and go** adj = risky, close, near, critical, precarious, nerve-racking

touché (too-shay) interj 1 an acknowledgment that a remark or witty reply has been effective 2 an acknowledgment of a scoring hit in fencing

touched adj 1 moved to sympathy or emotion: I was touched by her understanding 2 informal slightly mad: she's a bit touched

touching adj 1 arousing tender feelings ▸ prep 2 relating to or concerning: she might talk about matters touching both of them

> **touching** adj = moving, affecting, sad, stirring, pathetic, poignant, emotive, pitiable

touchline n either of the lines marking the side of the playing area in certain games, such as rugby

touchscreen n a visual display unit screen that allows the user to give commands to the computer by touching parts of the screen instead of using the keyboard

touchstone n a standard by which judgment is made: this restaurant is the touchstone for genuine Italian cookery in Leeds

touch-type vb **-typing, -typed** to type without looking at the keyboard > **touch-typist** n

touchy adj **touchier, touchiest 1** easily upset or irritated: he is a touchy and quick-tempered man **2** requiring careful and tactful handling: a touchy subject > **touchiness** n

tough adj **1** strong and difficult to break, cut, or tear: this fabric is tough and water-resistant **2** (of meat or other food) difficult to cut and chew; not tender **3** physically or mentally strong and able to cope with hardship: a tough uncompromising woman, unwilling to take no for an answer **4** rough or violent: a tough and ruthless mercenary **5** strict and firm: the country's tough drugs laws **6** difficult or troublesome to do or deal with: a tough task **7 tough luck!** informal an expression of lack of sympathy for someone else's problems ▸ n **8** a rough, vicious, or violent person ▸ vb **9 tough it out** informal to endure a difficult situation until it improves: criticism of his performance has reinforced his desire to tough it out > **toughness** n

> **tough** adj **1** = resilient, hard, resistant, durable, strong, solid, rugged (US, Canad), sturdy; ≠ fragile **3** = hardy, strong, seasoned, strapping, vigorous, sturdy, stout; ≠ weak **4** = violent, rough, ruthless, pugnacious, hard-bitten **5** = strict, severe, stern, hard, firm, resolute, merciless, unbending; ≠ lenient **6** = hard, difficult, troublesome, uphill, strenuous, arduous, laborious ▸ n = ruffian, bully, thug, hooligan, bruiser (informal), roughneck (slang), tsotsi (S African)

toughen vb to make or become tough or tougher

toupee (too-pay) n a hairpiece worn by men to cover a bald place

tour n **1** an extended journey visiting places of interest along the route **2** a trip, by a band, theatre company, etc., to perform in several places **3** an overseas trip made by a cricket team, rugby team, etc., to play in several places **4** military a period of service, esp. in one place: the regiment has served several tours in Northern Ireland ▸ vb **5** to make a tour of (a place)

> **tour** n **1** = journey, expedition, excursion, trip, outing, jaunt, junket ▸ vb = visit, explore, go round, inspect, walk round, drive round, sightsee

tour de force n, pl **tours de force** a masterly or brilliant stroke or achievement

tourism n tourist travel, esp. when regarded as an industry

tourist n **1** a person who travels for pleasure, usually sightseeing and staying in hotels **2** a member of a sports team which is visiting a country to play a series of matches: the tourists were bowled out for 135 **3** the lowest class of accommodation on a passenger ship ▸ adj **4** of or relating to tourists or tourism: a popular tourist attraction **5** of the lowest class of accommodation on a passenger ship or aircraft

> **tourist** n **1** = traveller, voyager, tripper (Brit), globetrotter, holiday-maker, sightseer, excursionist

touristy adj informal, often derogatory full of tourists or tourist attractions

tournament n **1** a sporting competition in which contestants play a series of games to determine an overall winner **2** Also: **tourney** medieval history a contest in which mounted knights fought for a prize

> **tournament** n **1** = competition, meeting, event, series, contest

tourniquet (tour-nick-kay) n med a strip of cloth tied tightly round an arm or leg to stop bleeding from an artery

tout (rhymes with **shout**) vb **1** to seek (business, customers, etc.) or try to sell (goods), esp. in a persistent or direct manner: he went from door to door touting for business **2** to put forward or recommend (a person or thing) as a good or suitable example or candidate: the plant was once touted as a showcase factory ▸ n **3** a person who sells tickets for a heavily booked event at inflated prices

tow¹ vb **1** to pull or drag (a vehicle), esp. by means of a rope or cable ▸ n **2** the act or an instance of towing **3 in tow** informal in one's company or one's charge or under one's influence: she had a reporter and a photographer in tow **4 on tow** (of a vehicle) being towed

> **tow** vb = drag, draw, pull, haul, tug, yank, lug

tow² n fibres of hemp, flax, jute, etc., prepared for spinning

towards or US **toward** prep **1** in the direction of: *towards the lake* **2** with regard to: *hostility towards the President* **3** as a contribution to: *the profits will go towards three projects* **4** just before: *towards evening*

> **towards** or **toward** prep **1** = in the direction of, to, for, on the way to, en route for **2** = regarding, about, concerning, respecting, in relation to, with regard to, with respect to, apropos

towbar n a rigid metal bar attached to the back of a vehicle, from which a trailer or caravan can be towed

towel n **1** a piece of absorbent cloth or paper used for drying things ▸ vb **-elling, -elled** or US **-eling, -eled 2** to dry or wipe with a towel

towelling or US **toweling** n a soft, fairly thick fabric used to make towels and dressing gowns

tower n **1** a tall, usually square or circular structure, sometimes part of a larger building and usually built for a specific purpose **2 tower of strength** a person who supports or comforts someone else at a time of difficulty ▸ vb **3 tower over** to be much taller than: *sheer walls of limestone towered over us*

> **tower** n **1** = column, pillar, turret, belfry, steeple, obelisk

town n **1** a large group of houses, shops, factories, etc., smaller than a city and larger than a village. Related adjective: **urban 2** the nearest town or the chief town of an area: *people from town rarely went out to the farm* **3** the central area of a town where most of the shops and offices are: *we're going to a pub in town tonight* **4** the people of a town: *the town is split over the plans for a bypass* **5** built-up areas in general, as opposed to the countryside: *migration from the country to the town* **6 go to town** to make a supreme or unrestricted effort **7 on the town** visiting nightclubs, restaurants, etc.: *we had a night on the town to celebrate her promotion*

town hall n a large building in a town often containing the council offices and a hall for public meetings

township n **1** a small town **2** (in South Africa) a planned urban settlement of Black people or people of mixed racial descent **3** (in the US and Canada) a small unit of local government, often consisting of a town and the area surrounding it **4** (in Canada) a land-survey area, usually 36 square miles (93 square kilometres)

towpath n a path beside a canal or river, formerly used by horses pulling barges

toxaemia or US **toxemia** (tox-seem-ya) n **1** a form of blood poisoning caused by toxins released by bacteria at a wound or other site of infection **2** a condition in pregnant women characterized by high blood pressure > **toxaemic** or US **toxemic** adj

toxic adj **1** poisonous: *toxic fumes* **2** caused by poison: *toxic effects* > **toxicity** n

> **toxic** adj = poisonous, deadly, lethal, harmful, pernicious (formal), noxious, septic, pestilential; ≠ harmless

toxicology n the branch of science concerned with poisons and their effects > **toxicological** adj > **toxicologist** n

toxin n **1** any of various poisonous substances produced by microorganisms and causing certain diseases **2** any other poisonous substance of plant or animal origin

toy n **1** an object designed for children to play with, such as a doll or model car **2** an object that adults use for entertainment rather than for a serious purpose: *I do use my computer: it's not just a toy* ▸ adj **3** being an imitation or model of something for children to play with: *a toy aeroplane* **4** (of a dog) of a variety much smaller than is normal for that breed: *a toy poodle*

> **toy** n **1** = plaything, game, doll

toy-toy or **toyi-toyi** S African ▸ n **1** a dance expressing defiance and protest ▸ vb **2** to dance in this way

toy with vb **1** to consider an idea without being serious about it or being able to decide about it: *I've been toying with the idea of setting up my own firm* **2** to keep moving (an object) about with one's fingers, esp. when thinking about something else: *Jessica sat toying with her glass*

> **toy with** vb **1 toy with something** = play with, consider, trifle with, dally with, entertain the possibility of, amuse yourself with, think idly of

trace vb **tracing, traced 1** to locate or work out (the cause or source of something): *he traced the trouble to a faulty connection* **2** to find (something or someone that was missing): *the police were unable to trace her missing husband* **3** to discover or describe the progress or development of (something): *throughout the 19th century we can trace the development of more complex machinery* **4** to copy (a design, map, etc.) by putting a piece of transparent paper over it and following the lines which show through the paper with a pencil **5** to make the outline of (a shape or pattern): *his index finger was tracing circles on the arm of the chair* ▸ n **6** a mark, footprint, or other sign that shows that a person, animal, or thing has been in a particular place: *the police could find no trace of the missing van* **7** an amount of something so small that it is barely noticeable: *I detected a trace of jealousy in her voice* **8** a remnant of something: *traces of an Iron-Age fort remain visible* **9** a pattern made on a screen or a piece of paper by a device that is measuring or detecting something: *a baffling radar trace* > **traceable** adj

> **trace** vb **1** = search for, track, unearth, hunt down **2** = find, track (down), discover, detect, unearth, hunt down, ferret out, locate

t

3 = outline, sketch, draw **4** = copy, map, draft, outline, sketch, reproduce, draw over ▶ *n* **6** = track, trail, footstep, path, footprint, spoor, footmark, electronic footprint **7** = bit, drop, touch, shadow, suggestion, hint, suspicion, tinge **8** = remnant, sign, record, mark, evidence, indication, vestige, footprint, electronic footprint

trace element *n* a chemical element that occurs in very small amounts in soil, water, etc. and is essential for healthy growth

tracer *n* **1** a projectile that can be observed when in flight by the burning of chemical substances in its base **2** *med* an element or other substance introduced into the body to study metabolic processes

tracery *n*, *pl* **-eries 1** a pattern of interlacing lines, esp. one in a stained-glass window **2** any fine lacy pattern resembling this

traces *pl n* **1** the two side straps that connect a horse's harness to the vehicle being pulled **2 kick over the traces** to escape or defy control

trachea (track-**kee**-a) *n*, *pl* **-cheae** (-kee-ee) *anatomy & zool* the tube that carries inhaled air from the throat to the lungs

tracheotomy (track-ee-ot-a-mee) *n*, *pl* **-mies** surgical incision into the trachea, as performed when the air passage has been blocked

tracing *n* **1** a copy of something, such as a map, made by tracing **2** a line traced by a recording instrument

track *n* **1** a rough road or path: *a farm track* **2** the mark or trail left by something that has passed by: *the fox didn't leave any tracks* **3** a rail or pair of parallel rails on which a vehicle, such as a train, runs **4** a course for running or racing on: *a running track* **5** a separate song or piece of music on a recording: *Dolphy switches back to bass clarinet for the final track* **6** a course of action, thought, etc.: *I don't think you're on the right track at all* **7** an endless band on the wheels of a tank, bulldozer, etc. to enable it to move across rough ground **8 keep** or **lose track of** to follow or fail to follow the course or progress of **9 off the beaten track** in an isolated location: *the village where she lives is a bit off the beaten track* ▶ *vb* **10** to follow the trail of (a person or animal) **11** to follow the flight path of (a satellite, etc.) by picking up signals transmitted or reflected by it **12** *films* to follow (a moving object) while filming > **tracker** *n*

track *n* **1** = path, way, road, route, trail, pathway, footpath **2** = course, line, path, orbit, trajectory **3** = line, tramline ▶ *vb* **10** = follow, pursue, chase, trace, tail (*informal*), shadow, trail, stalk

track down *vb* to find (someone or something) by tracking or pursuing

track down *vb* **track something or someone down** = find, discover, trace, unearth, dig up, hunt down, sniff out, run to earth or ground

track event *n* a competition in athletics, such as sprinting, that takes place on a running track

track record *n informal* the past record of the accomplishments and failures of a person or organization

tracksuit *n* a warm loose-fitting suit worn by athletes, etc., esp. during training

tract[1] *n* **1** a large area, esp. of land: *an extensive tract of moorland* **2** *anatomy* a system of organs or glands that has a particular function: *the urinary tract*

tract *n* **1** = area, region, district, stretch, territory, extent, plot, expanse

tract[2] *n* a pamphlet, esp. a religious one

tract *n* = treatise, essay, booklet, pamphlet, dissertation, monograph, homily

tractable *adj formal* easy to control, manage, or deal with: *he could easily manage his tractable and worshipping younger brother* > **tractability** *n*

traction *n* **1** pulling, esp. by engine power: *the increased use of electric traction* **2** *med* the application of a steady pull on an injured limb using a system of weights and pulleys or splints: *he was in traction for weeks following the accident* **3** the grip that the wheels of a vehicle have on the ground: *four-wheel drive gives much better traction in wet or icy conditions* **4** the quality of being influential or popular: *her ideas are gaining traction with the public*

traction engine *n* a heavy steam-powered vehicle used, esp. formerly, for drawing heavy loads along roads or over rough ground

tractor *n* a motor vehicle with large rear wheels, used to pull heavy loads, esp. farm machinery

trade *n* **1** the buying and selling of goods and services **2** a person's job, esp. a craft requiring skill: *he's a plumber by trade* **3** the people and practices of an industry, craft, or business **4** amount of custom or commercial dealings: *a brisk trade in second-hand weapons* **5** a specified market or business: *the wool trade* **6 trades** the trade winds ▶ *vb* **trading, traded 7** to buy and sell (goods) **8** to exchange: *he traded a job in New York for a life as a cowboy* **9** to engage in trade **10** to deal or do business (with) > **tradable** or **tradeable** *adj* > **trader** *n* > **trading** *n*

trade *n* **1, 4** = commerce, business, transactions, dealing, exchange, traffic, truck, barter **2, 5** = job, employment, business, craft, profession, occupation, line of work, métier ▶ *vb* **7, 10** = deal, do business, traffic, truck, bargain, peddle, transact, cut a deal **8** = exchange, switch, swap, barter **9** = operate, run, deal, do business

trade-in *n* **1** a used article given in part payment for the purchase of a new article ▶ *vb* **trade in 2** to give (a used article) as part payment for a new article

trademark n **1 A** the name or other symbol used by a manufacturer to distinguish his or her products from those of competitors **B Registered Trademark** one that is officially registered and legally protected **2** any distinctive sign or mark of a person or thing: *the designer bars which have become the trademark of the city*

trade-off n an exchange, esp. as a compromise: *there is often a trade-off between manpower costs and computer costs*

tradesman or fem **tradeswoman** n, pl **-men** or **-women 1** a skilled worker, such as an electrician or painter **2** a shopkeeper

trade union or **trades union** n a society of workers formed to protect and improve their working conditions, pay, etc. > **trade unionism** or **trades unionism** n > **trade unionist** or **trades unionist** n

trade wind n a wind blowing steadily towards the equator either from the northeast in the N hemisphere or the southeast in the S hemisphere

tradition n **1** the handing down from generation to generation of customs, beliefs, etc. **2** the unwritten body of beliefs, customs, etc. handed down from generation to generation **3** a custom or practice of long standing **4 in the tradition of** having many features similar to those of a person or thing in the past: *a thriller writer in the tradition of Chandler*

> **tradition** n **1, 2** = customs, institution, ritual, folklore, lore, tikanga (NZ) **3** = established practice, custom, convention, habit, ritual

traditional adj of, relating to, or being a tradition > **traditionally** adv

> **traditional** adj = old-fashioned, old, established, conventional, usual, accustomed, customary, time-honoured; ≠ revolutionary

traduce vb **-ducing, -duced** formal to speak badly of (someone) > **traducement** n > **traducer** n

traffic n **1** the vehicles travelling on roads **2** the movement of vehicles or people in a particular place or for a particular purpose: *air traffic* **3** trade, esp. of an illicit kind: *drug traffic* **4** the exchange of ideas between people or organizations: *a lively traffic in ideas* ▶ vb **-ficking, -ficked 5** to carry on trade or business, esp. of an illicit kind: *he confessed to trafficking in gold and ivory* > **trafficker** n

> **traffic** n **1, 2** = transport, vehicles, transportation, freight **3** = trade, commerce, business, exchange, truck, dealings, peddling ▶ vb = trade, deal, exchange, bargain, do business, peddle, cut a deal, have dealings

traffic warden n Brit a person employed to supervise road traffic and report traffic offences

tragedian (traj-**jee**-dee-an) or fem **tragedienne** (traj-jee-dee-**enn**) n **1** an actor who specializes in tragic roles **2** a writer of tragedy

tragedy n, pl **-dies 1** a shocking or sad event **2** a serious play, film, or opera in which the main character is destroyed by a combination of a personal failing and adverse circumstances

> **tragedy** n **1** = disaster, catastrophe, misfortune, adversity, calamity; ≠ fortune

tragic adj **1** sad and distressing because it involves death or suffering: *she was blinded in a tragic accident* **2** of or like a tragedy: *a tragic hero* **3** sad or mournful: *a tragic melody* > **tragically** adv

> **tragic** adj **1** = distressing, sad, appalling, deadly, unfortunate, disastrous, dreadful, dire; ≠ fortunate **3** = sad, miserable, pathetic, mournful; ≠ happy

tragicomedy n, pl **-dies** a play or other written work having both comic and tragic elements > **tragicomic** adj

trail n **1** a rough path across open country or through a forest **2** a route along a series of roads or paths that has been specially planned to let people see or do particular things: *a nature trail through the woods* **3** a print, mark, or scent left by a person, animal, or object: *a trail of blood was found down three flights of stairs* **4** something that trails behind: *a vapour trail* **5** a sequence of results from an event: *a trail of mishaps* ▶ vb **6** to drag or stream along the ground or through the air behind someone or something: *part of her sari trailed behind her on the floor* **7** to lag behind (a person or thing): *Max had arrived as well, trailing behind the others* **8** to follow or hunt (an animal or person), usually secretly, by following the marks or tracks he, she, or it has made: *the police had trailed him the length and breadth of the country* **9** to be falling behind in a race, match or competition: *they trailed 2–1 at half-time* **10** to move wearily or slowly: *we spent the afternoon trailing round the shops*

> **trail** n **1** = path, track, route, way, course, road, pathway, footpath **3** = tracks, path, marks, wake, trace, scent, footprints, spoor **4** = wake, stream, tail ▶ vb **6** = drag, draw, pull, sweep, haul, tow, dangle, droop **7, 10** = lag, follow, drift, wander, linger, trudge, plod, meander **8** = follow, track, chase, pursue, dog, hunt, shadow, trace

trailer n **1** a road vehicle, usually two-wheeled, towed by a motor vehicle and used for carrying goods, transporting boats, etc.: *ahead of us was a tractor, drawing a trailer laden with dung* **2** the rear section of an articulated lorry **3** an extract or series of extracts from a film, TV, or radio programme, used to advertise it **4** US & Canad same as **caravan** (sense 1)

train vb **1** to instruct (someone) in a skill: *soldiers are trained to obey orders unquestioningly* **2** to learn the skills needed to do a particular job or activity: *she was training to be a computer programmer* **3** to do exercises and prepare for a specific purpose: *he was training for a marathon* **4** to focus on or aim at (something): *the warship kept its guns trained on the trawler* **5** to discipline (an animal) to obey commands or perform tricks **6** to tie or prune (a plant) so that it grows in a particular way: *he had trained the roses to grow up the wall* ▸ *n* **7** a line of railway coaches or wagons coupled together and drawn by a engine **8** a sequence or series: *following an earlier train of thought* **9** the long back section of a dress that trails along the floor **10 in its train** as a consequence: *economic mismanagement brought unemployment and inflation in its train* **11 in train** actually happening or being done: *the programme of reforms set in train by the new government* ▸ *adj* **12** of or by a train: *the long train journey North*

> **train** *vb* **1** = instruct, school, prepare, coach, teach, guide, educate, drill **3** = exercise, prepare, work out, practise, do exercise, get into shape **4** = aim, point, level, position, direct, focus, sight, zero in ▸ *n* **8** = sequence, series, chain, string, set, cycle, trail, succession

trainee *n* **1** a person undergoing training ▸ *adj* **2** (of a person) undergoing training: *a trainee journalist*

trainer *n* **1** a person who coaches a person or team in a sport **2** a person who trains racehorses **3** an aircraft used for training pilots **4** *Brit* a flat-soled sports shoe of the style used by athletes when training

> **trainer** *n* **1** = coach, manager, guide, adviser, tutor, instructor, counsellor, guru

traipse *informal* ▸ *vb* **traipsing, traipsed** **1** to walk heavily or tiredly ▸ *n* **2** a long or tiring walk

trait *n* a characteristic feature or quality of a person or thing

> **trait** *n* = characteristic, feature, quality, attribute, quirk, peculiarity, mannerism, idiosyncrasy

traitor *n* a person who betrays friends, country, a cause, etc. > **traitorous** *adj* > **traitress** *fem n*

> **traitor** *n* = betrayer, deserter, turncoat, renegade, defector, Judas, quisling, apostate, fizgig (*Austral slang*); ≠ loyalist

trajectory *n, pl* **-ries** the path described by an object moving in air or space, esp. the curved path of a projectile

tram *n* an electrically driven public transport vehicle that runs on rails laid into the road and takes its power from an overhead cable

tramlines *pl n* **1** the tracks on which a tram runs **2** the outer markings along the sides of a tennis or badminton court

tramp *vb* **1** to walk long and far; hike **2** to walk heavily or firmly across or through (a place): *she tramped slowly up the beach* ▸ *n* **3** a homeless person who travels about on foot, living by begging or doing casual work **4** a long hard walk; hike: *we*

went for a long tramp over the downs **5** the sound of heavy regular footsteps: *we could hear the tramp of the marching soldiers* **6** a small cargo ship that does not run on a regular schedule **7** *US, Canad, Austral & NZ derogatory slang* a woman considered promiscuous

> **tramp** *vb* = trudge, stump, toil, plod, traipse (*informal*) ▸ *n* **3** = vagrant, derelict, drifter, down-and-out, derro (*Austral slang*) **4** = hike, march, trek, ramble, slog **5** = tread, stamp, footstep, footfall

trample *vb* **-pling, -pled** **1** Also: **trample on** to tread on and crush: *three children were trampled to death when the crowd panicked and ran* **2 trample on** to treat (a person or his or her rights or feelings) with disregard or contempt

> **trample** *vb* **1** = stamp, crush, squash, tread, flatten, run over, walk over

trampoline *n* **1** a tough canvas sheet suspended by springs or cords from a frame, which acrobats, gymnasts, etc., bounce on ▸ *vb* **-lining, -lined** **2** to exercise on a trampoline

trance *n* **1** a hypnotic state resembling sleep in which a person is unable to move or act of his or her own will **2** a dazed or stunned state

> **trance** *n* = daze, dream, abstraction, rapture, reverie, stupor, unconsciousness

tranche (trahnsh) *n* an instalment or portion, esp. of a loan or share issue: *the new shares will be offered in four tranches around the world*

tranquil *adj* calm, peaceful, or quiet > **tranquilly** *adv*

tranquillity *or US sometimes* **tranquility** *n* a state of calmness or peace

tranquillize, -lise *or US* **tranquilize** *vb* **-lizing, -lized** *or* **-lising, -lised** **1** to make or become calm or calmer **2** to give (someone) a drug to make them calm or calmer > **tranquillization, -lisation** *or US* **tranquilization** *n* > **tranquillizing, -lising** *or US* **tranquilizing** *adj*

tranquillizer, -liser *or US* **tranquilizer** *n* a drug that calms someone experiencing anxiety, tension, etc.

trans *adj* short for **transgender**

trans- *prefix* **1** across, beyond, crossing, or on the other side of: *transnational* **2** changing thoroughly: *transliterate*

transact *vb* to do, conduct, or negotiate (a business deal)

transaction *n* **1** something that is transacted, esp. a business deal **2 transactions** the records of the proceedings of a society, etc.: *an article on land taken from the 'Transactions of the Royal Canadian Institute'*

> **transaction** *n* **1** = deal (*informal*), negotiation, business, enterprise, bargain, undertaking

transatlantic *adj* **1** on or from the other side of the Atlantic **2** crossing the Atlantic

transceiver *n* a device which transmits and receives radio or electronic signals

transcend *vb* 1 to go above or beyond what is expected or normal: *a vital party issue that transcends traditional party loyalties* 2 to overcome or be superior to: *to transcend all difficulties*

> **transcend** *vb* = surpass, exceed, go beyond, rise above, eclipse, excel, outstrip, outdo

transcendent *adj* 1 above or beyond what is expected or normal 2 *theol* (of God) having existence outside the created world
> **transcendence** *n*

transcendental *adj* 1 above or beyond what is expected or normal 2 *philosophy* based on intuition or innate belief rather than experience 3 supernatural or mystical > **transcendentally** *adv*

transcendentalism *n* any system of philosophy that seeks to discover the nature of reality by examining the processes of thought rather than the things thought about, or that emphasizes intuition as a means to knowledge > **transcendentalist** *n*, *adj*

transcribe *vb* **-scribing, -scribed** 1 to write, type, or print out (a text) fully from a speech or notes 2 to make an electrical recording of (a programme or speech) for a later broadcast 3 *music* to rewrite (a piece of music) for an instrument other than that originally intended > **transcriber** *n*

transcript *n* 1 a written, typed, or printed copy made by transcribing 2 *chiefly US & Canad* an official record of a student's school progress

> **transcript** *n* 1 = copy, record, manuscript, reproduction, duplicate, transcription

transducer *n* any device, such as a microphone or electric motor, that converts one form of energy into another

transept *n* either of the two shorter wings of a cross-shaped church

transfer *vb* **-ferring, -ferred** 1 to change or move from one thing, person, place, etc., to another: *he was transferred from prison to hospital* 2 to move (money or property) from the control of one person or organization to that of another: *the money has been transferred into your account* 3 (of a football club) to sell or release (a player) to another club: *he was transferred to Juventus for a world record fee* 4 to move (a drawing or design) from one surface to another ▸ *n* 5 the act, process, or system of transferring, or the state of being transferred 6 a person or thing that transfers or is transferred 7 a design or drawing that is transferred from one surface to another 8 the moving of (money or property) from the control of one person or organization to that of another > **transferable** or **transferrable** *adj* > **transference** *n*

> **transfer** *vb* 1 = move, transport, shift, relocate, transpose, change, download, upload ▸ *n* 5 = transference, move, handover, change, shift, transmission, translation, relocation

transfer station *n* NZ a depot where rubbish is sorted for recycling

transfiguration *n* a transfiguring or being transfigured

transfigure *vb* **-guring, -gured** 1 to change or cause to change in appearance 2 to become or cause to become more exalted

transfix *vb* **-fixing, -fixed** or **-fixt** 1 to make (someone) motionless, esp. with horror or shock: *they stood transfixed and revolted by what they saw* 2 to pierce (a person or animal) through with a pointed object: *the Pharaoh is shown transfixing enemies with arrows from a moving chariot*

transform *vb* 1 to change completely in form or function: *the last forty years have seen the country transformed from a peasant economy to a major industrial power* 2 to change so as to make better or more attractive: *most religions claim to be able to transform people's lives* 3 to convert (one form of energy) to another 4 *maths* to change the form of (an equation, expression, etc.) without changing its value 5 to change (an alternating current or voltage) using a transformer

> **transform** *vb* 1 = change, convert, alter, transmute 2 = make over, remodel, revolutionize

transformation *n* 1 a change or alteration, esp. a radical one 2 the act of transforming or the state of being transformed 3 *S African* a political slogan for demographic change in the power struggle

> **transformation** *n* 1, 2 = revolution, sea change

transformer *n* a device that transfers an alternating current from one circuit to one or more other circuits, usually with a change of voltage

transfuse *vb* **-fusing, -fused** 1 to inject (blood or other fluid) into a blood vessel 2 *literary* to transmit or instil

transfusion *n* 1 the injection of blood, blood plasma, etc., into the blood vessels of a patient 2 the act of transferring something: *a transfusion of new funds*

transgender *adj* having a gender identity that does not fully correspond to the gender assigned to one at birth

transgress *vb* *formal* 1 to break (a law or rule) 2 to overstep (a limit): *he had never before been known to transgress the very slowest of walks* > **transgression** *n* > **transgressor** *n*

transient *adj* 1 lasting for a short time only: *she had a number of transient relationships with fellow students* 2 (of a person) not remaining in a place for a long time: *the transient population of the inner city* ▸ *n* 3 a transient person or thing > **transience** *n*

transistor *n* 1 a semiconductor device used to amplify and control electric currents 2 *informal* a small portable radio containing transistors

t

transit n 1 the moving or carrying of goods or people from one place to another 2 a route or means of transport: *transit by road* 3 *astron* the apparent passage of a celestial body across the meridian 4 **in transit** while travelling or being taken from one place to another: *in transit the fruit can be damaged* ▸ adj 5 indicating a place or building where people wait or goods are kept between different stages of a journey: *a transit lounge for passengers who are changing planes*

> **transit** n 1 = movement, transfer, transport, passage, crossing, transportation, carriage, conveyance

transition n 1 the process of changing from one state or stage to another: *the transition from dictatorship to democracy* 2 *music* a movement from one key to another ▸ vb 3 to change from one state or stage to another 4 to undergo a process of changing from from one gender to another > **transitional** adj

> **transition** n 1 = change, passing, development, shift, conversion, alteration, progression, metamorphosis

transitive adj *grammar* denoting a verb that requires a direct object: *'to find' is a transitive verb*
transitory adj lasting only for a short time
translate vb **-lating, -lated** 1 **A** to change (something spoken or written in one language) into another **B** to be capable of being changed from one language into another: *puns do not translate well* 2 to express (something) in a different way, for instance by using a different measurement system or less technical language: *the temperature is 30° Celsius, or if we translate into Fahrenheit, 86°* 3 to transform or convert, for instance by putting an idea into practice: *cheap crops translate into lower feed prices* 4 to interpret the significance of (a gesture, action, etc.): *I gave him what I hoped would be translated as a thoughtful look* 5 to act as a translator: *I had to translate for a party of visiting Greeks* > **translatable** adj > **translator** n

> **translate** vb 1A = render, put, change, convert, interpret, decode, construe (*old-fashioned*), paraphrase

translation n 1 a piece of writing or speech that has been translated into another language 2 the act of translating something 3 the expression of something in a different way or form: *the book's plot was radically altered during its translation to film* 4 *maths* a transformation in which the origin of a coordinate system is moved to another position so that each axis retains the same direction > **translational** adj

> **translation** n 1 = interpretation, version, rendering, rendition, decoding, paraphrase

transliterate vb **-rating, -rated** to write or spell (a word, etc.) into corresponding letters of another alphabet > **transliteration** n
translucent adj allowing light to pass through, but not transparent > **translucency** or **translucence** n
transmigrate vb **-grating, -grated** (of a soul) to pass from one body into another at death > **transmigration** n
transmission n 1 the sending or passing of something, such as a message or disease from one place or person to another 2 something that is transmitted, esp. a radio or television broadcast 3 a system of shafts and gears that transmits power from the engine to the driving wheels of a motor vehicle

> **transmission** n 1 = transfer, spread, spreading, passing on, circulation, dispatch, relaying, mediation 2 = programme, broadcast, show, production, telecast, podcast

transmit vb **-mitting, -mitted** 1 to pass (something, such as a message or disease) from one place or person to another 2 **A** to send out (signals) by means of radio waves **B** to broadcast (a radio or television programme) 3 to allow the passage of (particles, energy, etc.): *water transmits sound better than air* 4 to transfer (a force, motion, etc.) from one part of a mechanical system to another: *the chain of the bike transmits the motion of the pedals to the rear wheel* > **transmittable** adj

> **transmit** vb 1 = pass on, carry, spread, send, bear, transfer, hand on, convey 2 = broadcast, televise, relay, air, radio, send out, disseminate, beam out, stream, podcast

transmitter n 1 a piece of equipment used for broadcasting radio or television programmes 2 a person or thing that transmits something
transmogrify vb **-fies, -fying, -fied** *humorous* to change or transform (someone or something) into a different shape or appearance, esp. a grotesque or bizarre one > **transmogrification** n
transmute vb **-muting, -muted** to change the form or nature of: *self-contempt is transmuted into hatred of others* > **transmutation** n
transom n 1 a horizontal bar across a window 2 a horizontal bar that separates a door from a window over it
transparency n, pl **-cies** 1 the state of being transparent 2 a positive photograph on transparent film, usually mounted in a frame or between glass plates, which can be viewed with the use of a slide projector
transparent adj 1 able to be seen through; clear 2 easy to understand or recognize; obvious: *transparent honesty* > **transparently** adv

> **transparent** adj 1 = clear, sheer, see-through, lucid, translucent, crystalline, limpid, diaphanous; ≠ opaque 2 = obvious, plain, patent, evident, explicit, manifest, recognizable, unambiguous; ≠ uncertain

t

transpire *vb* **-spiring, -spired 1** to come to light; become known **2** *not standard* to happen or occur **3** *physiol* to give off (water or vapour) through the pores of the skin, etc. **4** (of plants) to lose (water vapour) through the stomata > **transpiration** *n*

transplant *vb* **1** *surgery* to transfer (an organ or tissue) from one part of the body or from one person to another **2** to remove or transfer (esp. a plant) from one place to another ▸ *n* **3** *surgery* **A** the procedure involved in transferring an organ or tissue **B** the organ or tissue transplanted > **transplantation** *n*

> **transplant** *vb* **1** = implant, transfer, graft **2** = transfer, take, bring, carry, remove, transport, shift, convey

transport *vb* **1** to carry or move (people or goods) from one place to another, esp. over some distance **2** *history* to exile (a criminal) to a penal colony **3** to have a strong emotional effect on: *transported by joy* ▸ *n* **4** the business or system of transporting goods or people: *public transport* **5** *Brit* freight vehicles generally **6** a vehicle used to transport troops **7** a transporting or being transported **8** ecstasy or rapture: *transports of delight* > **transportable** *adj*

> **transport** *vb* **1** = convey, take, move, bring, send, carry, bear, transfer **2** = exile, banish, deport **3** = enrapture, move, delight, entrance, enchant, captivate, ravish ▸ *n* **4** = vehicle, transportation, conveyance (*old-fashioned*) **7** = transference, carrying, delivery, distribution, transportation, shipment, freight, haulage **8** = ecstasy, delight, heaven (*informal*), bliss, euphoria, rapture, enchantment, ravishment; ≠ despondency

transportation *n* **1** a means or system of transporting **2** the act of transporting or the state of being transported **3** *history* deportation to a penal colony

transporter *n* a large vehicle used for carrying cars from the factory to garages for sale

transpose *vb* **-posing, -posed 1** to change the order of (letters, words, or sentences) **2** *music* to play (notes, music, etc.) in a different key **3** *maths* to move (a term) from one side of an equation to the other with a corresponding reversal in sign: *transposing 3 in x - 3 = 6 gives x = 6 + 3* > **transposition** *n*

transsexual *or* **transexual** *n* **1** a person who believes that his or her true identity is of the opposite sex **2** a person who has had medical treatment to alter his or her sexual characteristics to those of the opposite sex

transubstantiation *n* *Christianity* the doctrine that the bread and wine consecrated in Communion changes into the substance of Christ's body and blood

transuranic (tranz-*yoor*-ran-ik) *adj chem* (of an element) having an atomic number greater than that of uranium

transverse *adj* crossing from side to side: *the transverse arches in the main hall of the college*

transvestite *n* a person, esp. a man, who seeks sexual pleasure from wearing clothes of the opposite sex > **transvestism** *n*

trap *n* **1** a device or hole in which something, esp. an animal, is caught: *a fox trap* **2** a plan for tricking a person into being caught unawares **3** a situation from which it is difficult to escape: *caught in the poverty trap* **4** a bend in a pipe that contains standing water to prevent the passage of gases **5** a boxlike stall in which greyhounds are enclosed before the start of a race **6** a device that hurls clay pigeons into the air to be fired at **7** See **trap door 8** a light two-wheeled carriage: *a pony and trap* **9** *Brit, Austral & NZ slang* the mouth: *shut your trap!* ▸ *vb* **trapping, trapped 10** to catch (an animal) in a trap **11** to catch (someone) by a trick: *the police trapped the drug dealers by posing as potential customers* **12** to hold or confine in an unpleasant situation from which it is difficult to escape: *trapped in the rubble of collapsed buildings*

> **trap** *n* **1** = snare, net, gin, pitfall, noose **2** = trick, set-up (*informal*), deception, ploy, ruse, trickery, subterfuge, stratagem ▸ *vb* **10** = catch, snare, ensnare, entrap, take, corner, bag, lay hold of **11** = capture, catch, arrest, seize, take, secure, collar (*informal*), apprehend

trap door *n* a hinged door in a ceiling, floor, or stage

trap-door spider *n* a spider that builds a silk-lined hole in the ground closed by a hinged door of earth and silk

trapeze *n* a horizontal bar suspended from two ropes, used by circus acrobats

trapezium *n, pl* **-ziums** *or* **-zia 1** a quadrilateral having two parallel sides of unequal length **2** *chiefly US & Canad* a quadrilateral having neither pair of sides parallel > **trapezial** *adj*

trapezoid (trap-piz-zoid) *n* **1** a quadrilateral having neither pair of sides parallel **2** *US & Canad* same as **trapezium** (sense 1)

trapper *n* a person who traps animals, esp. for their furs or skins

trappings *pl n* **1** the accessories that symbolize a condition, office, etc.: *the trappings of power* **2** a ceremonial harness for a horse or other animal

Trappist *n* a member of an order of Christian monks who follow a rule of strict silence

trash *n* **1** foolish ideas or talk; nonsense **2** *US, Canad, NZ & S African* unwanted objects; rubbish **3** *chiefly US, Canad & NZ* a worthless person or group of people ▸ *vb* **4** *slang* to attack or destroy maliciously: *we've never trashed a hotel room* > **trashy** *adj*

> **trash** *n* **1** = nonsense, rubbish, rot, drivel, twaddle, tripe (*informal*), moonshine, hogwash (*informal*), kak (*S African vulgar slang*), bizzo (*Austral slang*), bull's wool (*Austral, NZ slang*); ≠ sense **2** = litter, refuse, waste, rubbish, junk (*informal*), garbage (*chiefly US*), dross

trauma (traw-ma) *n* **1** *psychol* an emotional shock that may have long-lasting effects **2** *pathol* any bodily injury or wound › **traumatic** *adj* › **traumatically** *adv* › **traumatize** *or* **-ise** *vb*

> **trauma** *n* **1** = shock, suffering, pain, torture, ordeal, anguish **2** = injury, damage, hurt, wound, agony

travail *n literary* painful or exceptionally hard work

travel *vb* **-elling, -elled** *or US* **-eling, -eled 1** to go or move from one place to another **2** to go or journey through or across (an area, region, etc.): *Margaret travelled widely when she was in New Zealand* **3** to go at a specified speed or for a specified distance: *the car was travelling at 30 mph* **4** to go from place to place as a salesperson **5** (of perishable goods) to withstand a journey: *not all wines travel well* **6** (of light or sound) to be transmitted or carried from one place to another: *sound travels a long distance in these conditions* **7** (of a machine or part) to move in a fixed path **8** *informal* (of a vehicle) to move rapidly ▸ *n* **9** the act or a means of travelling: *air travel has changed the way people live* **10** a tour or journey: *his travels took him to Dublin* **11** the distance moved by a mechanical part, such as the stroke of a piston

> **travel** *vb* **1, 2** = go, journey, move, tour, progress, wander, trek, voyage ▸ *n*
> **10** = journey, wandering, expedition, globetrotting, tour, trip, voyage, excursion

traveller *or US* **traveler** *n* **1** a person who travels, esp. habitually **2** a travelling salesman or saleswoman **3** a member of a people with a nomadic lifestyle

> **traveller** *or* **traveler** *n* **1** = voyager, tourist, explorer, globetrotter, holiday-maker, wayfarer

travelogue *or US* **travelog** *n* a film or lecture on travels and travelling

traverse *vb* **-versing, -versed 1** to move over or back and forth over; cross: *he once traversed San Francisco harbour in a balloon* **2** to reach across **3** to walk, climb, or ski diagonally up or down a slope ▸ *n* **4** something being or lying across, such as a crossbar **5** the act or an instance of traversing or crossing **6** a path or road across ▸ *adj* **7** being or lying across › **traversal** *n*

travesty *n, pl* **-ties 1** a grotesque imitation or mockery: *a travesty of justice* ▸ *vb* **-ties, -tying, -tied 2** to make or be a travesty of

trawl *n* **1** a large net, usually in the shape of a sock or bag, dragged at deep levels behind a fishing boat ▸ *vb* **2** to fish using such a net

trawler *n* a ship used for trawling

tray *n* **1** a flat board of wood, plastic, or metal, usually with a rim, on which things can be carried **2** an open receptacle for office correspondence

treacherous *adj* **1** disloyal and untrustworthy: *he was cruel, treacherous, and unscrupulous* **2** unreliable or dangerous, esp. because of sudden changes: *the tides here can be very treacherous* › **treacherously** *adv*

treachery *n, pl* **-eries** the act or an instance of wilful betrayal

treacle *n* a thick dark syrup obtained during the refining of sugar › **treacly** *adj*

tread *vb* **treading, trod, trodden** *or* **trod 1** to set one's foot down on or in something: *he trod on some dog's dirt* **2** to crush or squash by treading (on): *treading on a biscuit* **3** to walk along (a path or road) **4** **tread carefully** *or* **warily** to proceed in a delicate or tactful manner **5** **tread water** to stay afloat in an upright position by moving the legs in a walking motion ▸ *n* **6** a way of walking or the sound of walking: *he walked, with a heavy tread, up the stairs* **7** the top surface of a step in a staircase **8** the pattern of grooves in the outer surface of a tyre that helps it grip the road **9** the part of a shoe that is generally in contact with the ground

> **tread** *vb* **1, 3** = step, walk, march, pace, stamp, stride, hike ▸ *n* **6** = step, walk, pace, stride, footstep, gait, footfall

treadle (tred-dl) *n* a lever operated by the foot to turn a wheel

treadmill *n* **1** (formerly) an apparatus turned by the weight of men or animals climbing steps on a revolving cylinder or wheel **2** a dreary routine: *they are chained to the treadmill of a job* **3** an exercise machine that consists of a continuous moving belt on which to walk or jog

treason *n* **1** betrayal of one's sovereign or country, esp. by attempting to overthrow the government **2** any treachery or betrayal › **treasonable** *adj* › **treasonous** *adj*

> **treason** *n* = disloyalty, mutiny, treachery, duplicity, perfidy (*literary*), lese-majesty, traitorousness; ≠ loyalty

treasure *n* **1** a collection of wealth, esp. in the form of money, precious metals, or gems **2** a valuable painting, ornament, or other object: *the museum has many art treasures* **3** *informal* a person who is highly valued: *she can turn her hand to anything, she's a perfect treasure* ▸ *vb* **-suring, -sured 4** to cherish (someone or something)

> **treasure** *n* **1** = riches, money, gold, fortune, wealth, valuables, jewels, cash **3** = angel, darling, jewel, gem, paragon, nonpareil
> ▸ *vb* = prize, value, esteem, adore, cherish, revere, hold dear, love

treasurer *n* a person appointed to look after the funds of a society or other organization

treasure-trove *n* *law* any articles, such as coins or valuable objects found hidden and without any evidence of ownership

treasury *n, pl* **-uries** 1 a storage place for treasure 2 the revenues or funds of a government or organization

> **treasury** *n* 1 = storehouse, bank, store, vault, hoard, cache, repository

Treasury *n* (in various countries) the government department in charge of finance

treat *vb* 1 to deal with or regard in a certain manner: *they treat each other abominably* 2 to attempt to cure or lessen the symptoms of (an illness or injury or a person experiencing it): *the drug is prescribed to treat asthma* 3 to subject to a chemical or industrial process: *the wood should be treated with a preservative* 4 to provide (someone) with something as a treat: *I'll treat you to an ice cream* 5 **treat of** to deal with (something) in writing or speaking: *this book treats of a most abstruse subject* ▸ *n* 6 a celebration, entertainment, gift, or meal given for or to someone and paid for by someone else 7 any delightful surprise or specially pleasant occasion > **treatable** *adj*

> **treat** *vb* 1 = behave towards, deal with, handle, act towards, use, consider, serve, manage 2 = take care of, minister to, attend to, give medical treatment to, doctor (*informal*), nurse, care for, prescribe medicine for 4 = provide, stand (*informal*), entertain, lay on, regale ▸ *n* 6 = entertainment, party, surprise, gift, celebration, feast, outing, excursion 7 = pleasure, delight, joy, thrill, satisfaction, enjoyment, source of pleasure, fun

treatise (**treat**-izz) *n* a formal piece of writing that deals systematically with a particular subject

treatment *n* 1 the medical or surgical care given to a patient 2 a way of handling a person or thing: *the party has had unfair treatment in the press*

> **treatment** *n* 1 = cure, remedy, medication, medicine 2 = handling, dealings with, behaviour towards, conduct towards, management, manipulation, action towards

treaty *n, pl* **-ties** 1 a formal written agreement between two or more states, such as an alliance or trade arrangement: *the Treaty of Rome established the Common Market* 2 an agreement between two parties concerning the purchase of property

> **treaty** *n* = agreement, pact, contract, alliance, convention, compact, covenant, entente

treble *adj* 1 three times as much or as many 2 of or denoting a soprano voice or part or a high-pitched instrument 3 of the highest range of musical notes: *these loudspeakers give excellent treble reproduction* ▸ *n* 4 a soprano voice or part or a high-pitched instrument ▸ *vb* **-bling, -bled** 5 to make or become three times as much or as many: *sales have trebled in three years* > **trebly** *adv*

tree *n* 1 any large woody perennial plant with a distinct trunk and usually having leaves and branches. Related adjective: **arboreal** 2 **at the top of the tree** in the highest position of a profession > **treeless** *adj*

tree kangaroo *n* a tree-living kangaroo of New Guinea and N Australia

tree surgery *n* the treatment of damaged trees by filling cavities, applying braces, etc. > **tree surgeon** *n*

trefoil (**tref**-foil) *n* 1 a plant, such as clover, with leaves divided into three smaller leaves 2 *archit* a carved ornament with a shape like such leaves > **trefoiled** *adj*

trek *n* 1 a long and often difficult journey, esp. on foot 2 *S African* a journey or stage of a journey, esp. a migration by ox wagon ▸ *vb* **trekking**, **trekked** 3 to make a trek

> **trek** *n* 1 = journey, hike, expedition, safari, march, odyssey ▸ *vb* = trudge, traipse (*informal*), footslog, slog

trellis *n* a frame made of vertical and horizontal strips of wood, esp. one used to support climbing plants > **trelliswork** *n*

tremble *vb* **-bling, -bled** 1 to shake with short slight movements: *her hands trembled uncontrollably; he felt the ground trembling beneath him* 2 to experience fear or anxiety: *his parents trembled with apprehension about his future* 3 (of the voice) to sound uncertain or unsteady, for instance through pain or emotion ▸ *n* 4 the act or an instance of trembling > **trembling** *adj*

> **tremble** *vb* 1, 3 = vibrate, shake, quake, wobble ▸ *n* = shake, shiver, quake (*informal*), shudder, wobble, tremor, quiver, vibration

tremendous *adj* 1 very large or impressive: *a tremendous amount of money* 2 very exciting or unusual: *a tremendous feeling of elation* 3 very good or pleasing: *my wife has given me tremendous support* > **tremendously** *adv*

> **tremendous** *adj* 1 = huge, great, enormous, terrific, formidable, immense, gigantic, colossal; ≠ tiny 3 = excellent, great, wonderful, brilliant, amazing, extraordinary, fantastic, marvellous, booshit (*Austral slang*), exo (*Austral slang*), sik (*Austral slang*), rad (*informal*), phat (*slang*), schmick (*Austral informal*); ≠ terrible

tremolo *n, pl* **-los** *music* 1 (in playing the violin or other stringed instrument) the rapid repetition of a note or notes to produce a trembling effect 2 (in singing) a fluctuation in pitch

tremor *n* 1 an involuntary shudder or vibration: *the slight tremor of excitement* 2 a minor earthquake

tremulous *adj literary* trembling, as from fear or excitement: *I managed a tremulous smile* > **tremulously** *adv*

trench *n* 1 a long narrow ditch in the ground, such as one for laying a pipe in 2 a long deep ditch used by soldiers for protection in a war: *my grandfather fought in the trenches in the First World War* ▸ *adj* **3** of or involving military trenches: *trench warfare*

> **trench** *n* = ditch, channel, drain, gutter, trough, furrow, excavation

trenchant *adj* **1** keen or incisive: *a trenchant screenplay* **2** vigorous and effective: *the prime minister's trenchant adoption of this issue* > **trenchancy** *n*

trench coat *n* a belted raincoat similar in style to a military officer's coat

trencher *n* *history* a wooden board on which food was served or cut

trencherman *n, pl* **-men** a person who enjoys food; hearty eater

trend *n* **1** general tendency or direction: *a trend towards flexible working hours* **2** fashionable style: *she set a trend for wearing lingerie as outer garments* ▸ *vb* **3** to take a certain trend **4** to be widely discussed on a social media site

> **trend** *n* **1** = tendency, swing, drift, inclination, current, direction, flow, leaning **2** = fashion, craze, fad (*informal*), mode, thing, style, rage, vogue

trendy *informal* ▸ *adj* **trendier, trendiest** **1** consciously fashionable: *a flat in Glasgow's trendy West End* ▸ *n, pl* **trendies 2** a trendy person: *a media trendy* > **trendily** *adv* > **trendiness** *n*

> **trendy** *adj* = fashionable, with it (*old-fashioned, informal*), stylish, in fashion, in vogue, modish, voguish, schmick (*Austral informal*), funky

trepidation *n formal* a state of fear or anxiety

trespass *vb* **1** to go onto somebody else's property without permission ▸ *n* **2** the act or an instance of trespassing **3** *old-fashioned* a sin or wrongdoing > **trespasser** *n*

trespass on *or* **trespass upon** *vb formal* to take unfair advantage of (someone's friendship, patience, etc.): *I won't trespass upon your hospitality any longer*

tresses *pl n* a woman's long flowing hair

trestle *n* **1** a support for one end of a table or beam, consisting of two rectangular frameworks or sets of legs which are joined at the top but not the bottom **2** Also called: **trestle table** a table consisting of a board supported by a trestle at each end

trevally (trih-**val**-lee) *n, pl* **-lies** *Austral & NZ* any of various food and game fishes

trews *pl n chiefly Brit* close-fitting trousers of tartan cloth

tri- *combining form* **1** three or thrice: *trilingual* **2** occurring every three: *triweekly*

triad *n* **1** a group of three **2** *music* a three-note chord consisting of a note and the third and fifth above it > **triadic** *adj*

Triad *n* a Chinese secret society involved in criminal activities, such as drug trafficking

trial *n* **1** *law* an investigation of a case in front of a judge to decide whether a person is innocent or guilty of a crime by questioning him or her and considering the evidence **2** the act or an instance of trying or proving; test or experiment: *the new drug is undergoing clinical trials* **3** an annoying or frustrating person or thing: *young children can be a great trial at times* **4** a motorcycling competition in which the skills of the riders are tested over rough ground **5 trials** a sporting competition for individual people or animals: *horse trials* **6 on trial A** undergoing trial, esp. before a court of law **B** being tested, for example before a commitment to purchase: *I only have the car out on trial* ▸ *adj* **7** on a temporary basis while being tried out or tested: *a trial run* ▸ *vb* **trialling, trialled 8** to test or make experimental use of: *the idea has been trialled in several schools*

> **trial** *n* **1** = hearing, case, court case, inquiry, tribunal, lawsuit, appeal, litigation **2** = test, experiment, evaluation, audition, dry run (*informal*), assessment, probation, appraisal

triangle *n* **1** a geometric figure with three sides and three angles **2** any object shaped like a triangle: *a triangle of streets running up from the river* **3** *music* a percussion instrument that consists of a metal bar bent into a triangular shape, played by striking it with a metal stick **4** any situation involving three people or points of view: *a torrid sex triangle* > **triangular** *adj*

tribalism *n* loyalty to a tribe, esp. as opposed to a modern political entity such as a state

tribe *n* **1** a group of families or clans believed to have a common ancestor **2** *informal* a group of people who do the same type of thing: *a tribe of German yachtsmen* > **tribal** *adj*

> **tribe** *n* **1** = race, people, family, clan, hapu (NZ), iwi (NZ)

tribulation *n* great distress: *the tribulations of a deserted wife*

tribunal *n* **1** a special court or committee that is appointed to deal with a particular problem: *an industrial tribunal investigating allegations of unfair dismissal* **2** a court of justice

> **tribunal** *n* = hearing, court, trial

tribune *n* **1** a person who upholds public rights **2** (in ancient Rome) an officer elected by the plebs to protect their interests

tributary *n, pl* **-taries 1** a stream or river that flows into a larger one: *Frankfurt lies on the River Main, a tributary of the Rhine* **2** a person, nation, or people that pays tribute ▸ *adj* **3** (of a stream or river) flowing into a larger stream **4** paying tribute: *Egypt was formerly a tributary province of the Turkish Empire*

tribute *n* **1** something given, done, or said as a mark of respect or admiration **2** a payment by one ruler or state to another, usually as an acknowledgment of submission **3** something that shows the merits of a particular quality of a person or thing: *the car's low fuel consumption is a tribute to the quality of its engine*

tribute *n* **1** = accolade, testimonial, eulogy, recognition, compliment, commendation, panegyric; ≠ criticism

tribute band *n* a rock or pop group that plays the music and copies the style of another, much more famous, group

trice *n* **in a trice** in a moment: *she was back in a trice*

triceps *n*, *pl* **-ceps** the muscle at the back of the upper arm

trichology (trick-**ol**-a-jee) *n* the branch of medicine concerned with the hair and its diseases > **trichologist** *n*

trick *n* **1** a deceitful or cunning action or plan: *she was willing to use any dirty trick to get what she wanted* **2** a joke or prank: *he loves playing tricks on his sister* **3** a clever way of doing something, learned from experience: *an old campers' trick is to use three thin blankets rather than one thick one* **4** an illusory or magical feat or device **5** a simple feat learned by an animal or person **6** a deceptive illusion: *a trick of the light* **7** a habit or mannerism: *she had a trick of saying 'oh dear'* **8** *cards* a batch of cards played in turn and won by the person playing the highest card **9 do the trick** *informal* to produce the desired result **10 how's tricks?** *slang* how are you? ▶ *vb* **11** to defraud, deceive, or cheat (someone) > **trickery** *n*

trick *n* **1** = deception, trap, fraud, manoeuvre, ploy, hoax, swindle, ruse, fastie (*Austral slang*) **2** = joke, stunt, spoof (*informal*), prank, practical joke, antic, jape, leg-pull (*Brit informal*) **3** = secret, skill, knack, hang (*informal*), technique, know-how (*informal*) **4** = sleight of hand, stunt, legerdemain **7** = mannerism, habit, characteristic, trait, quirk, peculiarity, foible, idiosyncrasy ▶ *vb* = deceive, trap, take someone in (*informal*), fool, cheat, con (*informal*), kid (*informal*), mislead, scam (*slang*)

trickle *vb* **-ling, -led 1** to flow or cause to flow in a thin stream or drops: *tears trickled down her cheeks* **2** to move slowly or in small groups: *voters trickled to the polls* ▶ *n* **3** a thin, irregular, or slow flow of something: *a trickle of blood*

trickle *vb* **1** = dribble, run, drop, stream, drip, ooze, seep, exude ▶ *n* = dribble, drip, seepage, thin stream

trickster *n* a person who deceives or plays tricks

tricky *adj* **trickier, trickiest 1** involving snags or difficulties: *a tricky task* **2** needing careful handling: *a tricky situation* **3** sly or wily: *a tricky customer* > **trickily** *adv* > **trickiness** *n*

tricky *adj* **1, 2** = difficult, sensitive, complicated, delicate, risky, hairy (*informal*), problematic, thorny; ≠ simple **3** = crafty, scheming, cunning, slippery, sly, devious, wily, artful; ≠ open

tricolour *or US* **tricolor** (trick-**kol**-or) *n* a flag with three equal stripes in different colours, esp. the French or Irish national flags

tricycle *n* a three-wheeled cycle > **tricyclist** *n*

trident *n* a three-pronged spear

triennial *adj* occurring every three years > **triennially** *adv*

trifle[1] *n* **1** a thing of little or no value or significance **2** *Brit, Austral & NZ* a cold dessert made of sponge cake spread with jam or fruit, soaked in sherry, covered with custard and cream **3 a trifle** to a small extent or degree; slightly: *he is a trifle eccentric*

trifle *n* **1** = knick-knack, toy, plaything, bauble, bagatelle

trifle[2] *vb* **trifling, trifled** > **trifle with** to treat (a person or his or her feelings) with disdain or disregard

trifling *adj* insignificant, petty, or frivolous: *a trifling misunderstanding*

trifling *adj* = insignificant, trivial, worthless, negligible, unimportant, paltry, measly; ≠ significant

trigger *n* **1** a small lever that releases a catch on a gun or machine **2** any event that sets a course of action in motion: *his murder was the trigger for a night of rioting* ▶ *vb* **3** Also: **trigger off** to set (an action or process) in motion: *various factors can trigger off a migraine*

trigger *vb* = bring about, start, cause, produce, generate, prompt, provoke, set off; ≠ prevent

trigger-happy *adj informal* too ready or willing to use guns or violence: *trigger-happy border guards*

trigonometry *n* the branch of mathematics concerned with the relations of sides and angles of triangles, which is used in surveying, navigation, etc.

trike *n informal* a tricycle

trilateral *adj* having three sides

trilby *n*, *pl* **-bies** a man's soft felt hat with an indented crown

trill *n* **1** *music* a rapid alternation between a note and the note above it **2** a shrill warbling sound made by some birds: *the canary's high trills* ▶ *vb* **3** (of a bird) to make a shrill warbling sound **4** (of a person) to talk or laugh in a high-pitched musical voice

trillion *n* **-lions** *or* **-lion 1** the number represented as one followed by twelve zeros (10^{12}); a million million **2** (in Britain, originally) the number represented as one followed by eighteen zeros (10^{18}); a million million million ▶ *adj* **3** amounting to a trillion: *a trillion dollars* > **trillionth** *n*, *adj*

trilobite (**trile**-oh-bite) *n* a small prehistoric marine arthropod, found as a fossil

trilogy (**trill**-a-jee) *n*, *pl* **-gies** a series of three books, plays, etc., which form a related group but are each complete works in themselves

t

trim *adj* **trimmer, trimmest** **1** neat and spruce in appearance: *trim lace curtains* **2** attractively slim: *his body was trim and athletic* ▶ *vb* **trimming, trimmed** **3** to make (something) neater by cutting it slightly without changing its basic shape: *his white beard was neatly trimmed* **4** to adorn or decorate (something, such as a garment) with lace, ribbons, etc.: *a cotton camisole neatly trimmed with lace* **5 A** to adjust the balance of (a ship or aircraft) by shifting cargo, etc. **B** to adjust (a ship's sails) to take advantage of the wind **6** to reduce or lower the size of: *the company has trimmed its pretax profits forecast by $2.3 million* **7** to alter (a plan or policy) by removing parts which seem unnecessary or unpopular: *the government would rather trim its policies than lose the election* **8 trim off** or **away** to cut so as to remove: *trim off most of the fat before cooking the meat* ▶ *n* **9** a decoration or adornment: *a black suit with scarlet trim* **10** the upholstery and decorative facings of a car's interior **11** good physical condition: *he had always kept himself in trim* **12** a haircut that neatens but does not alter the existing hairstyle

> **trim** *adj* **1** = neat, smart, tidy, spruce, dapper, natty (*informal*), well-groomed, shipshape; ≠ untidy **2** = slender, fit, slim, sleek, streamlined, shapely, svelte, willowy ▶ *vb* **3** = cut, crop, clip, shave, tidy, prune, pare, even up **4** = decorate, dress, array, adorn, ornament, embellish, deck out, beautify ▶ *n* **9** = decoration, edging, border, piping, trimming, frill, embellishment, adornment **11** = condition, health, shape (*informal*), fitness, wellness, fettle **12** = cut, crop, clipping, shave, pruning, shearing, tidying up

trimaran (trime-a-ran) *n* a boat with one smaller hull on each side of the main hull

trimming *n* **1** an extra piece added to a garment for decoration: *a pink nightie with lace trimming* **2 trimmings** usual or traditional accompaniments: *bacon and eggs with all the trimmings*

> **trimming** *n* **1** = decoration, edging, border, piping, frill, embellishment, adornment, ornamentation **2** = extras, accessories, ornaments, accompaniments, frills, trappings, paraphernalia

trinitrotoluene *n* the full name for **TNT**
trinity *n, pl* **-ties** a group of three people or things

> **trinity** *n* = threesome, trio, triad, triumvirate

Trinity *n Christianity* the union of three persons, the Father, Son, and Holy Spirit, in one God
trinket *n* a small or worthless ornament or piece of jewellery
trio *n, pl* **trios** **1** a group of three people or things **2** a group of three instrumentalists or singers **3** a piece of music for three performers

> **trio** *n* **1** = threesome, trinity, trilogy, triad, triumvirate

trip *n* **1** a journey to a place and back, esp. for pleasure: *they took a coach trip round the island* **2** a false step; stumble **3** the act of causing someone to stumble or fall by catching his or her foot with one's own **4** *informal* a hallucinogenic drug experience **5** a catch on a mechanism that acts as a switch ▶ *vb* **tripping, tripped** **6** Also: **trip up** to stumble or cause (someone) to stumble **7** Also: **trip up** to trap or catch (someone) in a mistake **8** to walk lightly and quickly, with a dancelike motion: *I could see Amelia tripping along beside him* **9** *informal* to experience the effects of a hallucinogenic drug

> **trip** *n* **1** = journey, outing, excursion, day out, run, drive, tour, spin (*informal*) **2** = stumble, fall, slip, misstep ▶ *vb* **6** = stumble, fall, fall over, slip, tumble, topple, stagger, misstep **7 trip someone up** = catch out, trap, wrongfoot **8** = skip, dance, hop, gambol

tripe *n* **1** the stomach lining of a cow or pig used as a food **2** *Brit, Austral & NZ informal* nonsense or rubbish
triple *adj* **1** made up of three parts or things: *a triple murder* **2** (of musical time or rhythm) having three beats in each bar **3** three times as great or as much: *a triple brandy* ▶ *vb* **-pling, -pled** **4** to make or become three times as much or as many: *the company has tripled its sales over the past five years* ▶ *n* **5** something that is, or contains, three times as much as normal **6** a group of three > **triply** *adv*

> **triple** *adj* **1** = three-way, threefold, tripartite **3** = treble, three times ▶ *vb* = treble, increase threefold

triple jump *n* an athletic event in which the competitor has to perform a hop, a step, and a jump in a continuous movement
triplet *n* **1** one of three children born at one birth **2** a group of three musical notes played in the time that two would normally take **3** a group or set of three similar things
triplicate *adj* **1** triple ▶ *vb* **-cating, -cated** **2** to multiply or be multiplied by three ▶ *n* **3 in triplicate** written out three times: *my request to interview the commander had to be made in triplicate* > **triplication** *n*
tripod (tripe-pod) *n* **1** a three-legged stand to which a camera can be attached to hold it steady **2** a three-legged stool, table, etc.
tripos (tripe-poss) *n Brit* the final honours degree examinations at Cambridge University
tripper *n chiefly Brit* a tourist
triptych (trip-tick) *n* a set of three pictures or panels, usually hinged together and often used as an altarpiece
trite *adj* (of a remark or idea) commonplace and unoriginal
tritium *n* a radioactive isotope of hydrogen. Symbol: **T**, ^{3}**H**
triumph *n* **1** the feeling of great happiness

resulting from a victory or major achievement **2** an outstanding success, achievement, or victory: *the concert was a musical triumph* **3** (in ancient Rome) a procession held in honour of a victorious general ▸ *vb* **4** to gain control or success: *triumphing over adversity* **5** to rejoice over a victory ▸ **triumphal** *adj*

> **triumph** *n* **1** = joy, pride, happiness, rejoicing, elation, jubilation, exultation **2** = success, victory, accomplishment, achievement, coup, feat, conquest, attainment; ≠ failure ▸ *vb* **4** = succeed, win, overcome, prevail, prosper, vanquish (*literary*); ≠ fail **5** = rejoice, celebrate, glory, revel, gloat, exult, crow

triumphant *adj* **1** feeling or displaying triumph: *her smile was triumphant* **2** celebrating a victory or success: *the general's triumphant tour round the city* ▸ **triumphantly** *adv*

> **triumphant** *adj* **1** = victorious, winning, successful, conquering; ≠ defeated **2** = celebratory, jubilant, proud, elated, exultant, cock-a-hoop (*old-fashioned*)

triumvirate (try-umm-vir-rit) *n* **1** a group of three people in joint control of something: *the triumvirate of great orchestras which dominates classical music in Europe* **2** (in ancient Rome) a board of three officials jointly responsible for some task

trivet (triv-vit) *n* **1** a three-legged stand for holding a pot, kettle, etc., over a fire **2** a short metal stand on which hot dishes are placed on a table

trivia *n* petty and unimportant things or details

trivial *adj* of little importance: *a trivial matter* ▸ **triviality** *n* ▸ **trivially** *adv*

> **trivial** *adj* = unimportant, small, minor, petty, meaningless, worthless, trifling, insignificant; ≠ important

trivialize *or* **-lise** *vb* **-lizing, -lized** *or* **-lising, -lised** to make (something) seem less important or complex than it is

trod *vb* the past tense and a past participle of **tread**

trodden *vb* a past participle of **tread**

troglodyte *n* a person who lives in a cave

troika *n* **1** a Russian coach or sleigh drawn by three horses abreast **2** a group of three people in authority: *a troika of European foreign ministers*

Trojan *adj* **1** of ancient Troy or its people ▸ *n* **2** a person from ancient Troy **3** a hard-working person

Trojan Horse *n* **1** *Greek myth* the huge wooden hollow figure of a horse used by the Greeks to enter Troy **2** a trap or trick intended to undermine an enemy

troll[1] *n* (in Scandinavian folklore) a supernatural dwarf or giant that dwells in a cave or mountain

troll[2] *vb* **1** to post deliberately provocative messages on an internet discussion board ▸ *n*

2 a person who posts deliberately provocative messages on an internet discussion board

trolley *n* **1** a small table on casters used for carrying food or drink **2** a wheeled cart or stand used for moving heavy items, such as shopping in a supermarket or luggage at a railway station **3** *Brit* See **trolley bus** **4** a device, such as a wheel that collects the current from an overhead wire, to drive the motor of an electric vehicle **5** *Brit & Austral* a low truck running on rails, used in factories, mines, etc.

trolley bus *n* a bus powered by electricity from two overhead wires but not running on rails

trollop *n derogatory* a woman who is considered promiscuous or slovenly

trombone *n* a brass musical instrument with a sliding tube which is moved in or out to alter the note played ▸ **trombonist** *n*

troop *n* **1** a large group: *a troop of dogs* **2 troops** soldiers: *troops have been maintaining an unusually high profile* **3** a subdivision of a cavalry armoured regiment **4** a large group of Scouts made up of several patrols ▸ *vb* **5** to move in a crowd: *we trooped into the room after her* **6** *military, chiefly Brit & Austral* to parade (a flag or banner) ceremonially: *trooping the colour*

> **troop** *n* **1** = group, company, team, body, unit, band, crowd, squad **3** = soldiers, men, armed forces, service personnel, army, soldiery ▸ *vb* **5** = flock, march, stream, swarm, throng, traipse (*informal*)

trooper *n* **1** a soldier in a cavalry regiment **2** *US & Austral* a mounted police officer **3** *US* a state police officer **4** a cavalry horse **5** *informal, chiefly Brit* a troopship

trope *n* **1** a word or expression used in a figurative sense **2** a recurring theme or idea

trophy *n, pl* **-phies 1** a cup, shield, etc., given as a prize **2** a memento of success, esp. one taken in war or hunting: *stuffed animal heads and other hunting trophies* ▸ *adj* **3** *informal* regarded as a highly desirable symbol of wealth or success: *a trophy wife*

> **trophy** *n* **1** = prize, cup, award, laurels **2** = souvenir, spoils, relic, memento, booty, keepsake

tropic *n* **1** either of the lines of latitude at about $23\frac{1}{2}°$N (**tropic of Cancer**) and $23\frac{1}{2}°$S (**tropic of Capricorn**) of the equator **2 the tropics** that part of the earth's surface between the tropics of Cancer and Capricorn: *the intense heat and humidity of the tropics*

tropical *adj* belonging to, typical of, or located in, the tropics: *tropical rainforests* ▸ **tropically** *adv*

> **tropical** *adj* = hot, stifling, steamy, torrid, sultry, sweltering; ≠ cold

trot *vb* **trotting, trotted 1** (of a horse) to move in a manner faster than a walk but slower than a gallop, in which diagonally opposite legs come down together **2** (of a person) to move fairly quickly, with small quick steps ▸ *n* **3** a medium-paced gait of a horse, in which diagonally opposite legs come down together **4** a steady brisk pace **5 on the trot** *informal* one after the other: *ten years on the trot* **6 the trots** *slang* diarrhoea

> **trot** *vb* **2** = run, jog, scamper, lope, canter
> ▸ *n* **4** = run, jog, lope, canter

troth (rhymes with **growth**) *n archaic* **1** a pledge of fidelity, esp. a betrothal **2 in troth** truly

trot out *vb informal* to repeat (old information or ideas) without fresh thought: *the government trots out the same excuse every time*

trotter *n* **1** the foot of a pig **2** a horse that is specially trained to trot fast

troubadour (troo-bad-oor) *n* a travelling poet and singer in S France or N Italy from the 11th to the 13th century who wrote chiefly on courtly love

trouble *n* **1** difficulties or problems: *I'd trouble finding somewhere to park* **2** a cause of distress, disturbance, or pain: *we must be sensitive to the troubles of other people* **3** disease or a problem with one's health: *ear trouble* **4** a state of disorder, ill-feeling, or unrest: *the police had orders to intervene at the first sign of trouble* **5** effort or exertion to do something: *they didn't even take the trouble to see the film before banning it* **6** a personal weakness or cause of annoyance: *his trouble is that he's constitutionally jealous* **7 in trouble A** likely to be punished for something one has done: *in trouble with the public prosecutor* **B** old-fashioned pregnant when not married **8 more trouble than it's worth** involving a lot of time or effort for very little reward: *making your own pasta is more trouble than it's worth* ▸ *vb* **-bling, -bled 9** to cause trouble to **10** to make an effort or exert oneself: *he dismissed the letters as forgeries without troubling to examine them* **11** to cause inconvenience or discomfort to: *sorry to trouble you!* ⊳ **troubled** *adj*

> **trouble** *n* **1** = bother, problems, concern, worry, stress, difficulty, anxiety, distress **2** = distress, problem, worry, pain, anxiety, grief, torment, sorrow; ≠ pleasure **3** = ailment, disease, failure, complaint, illness, disorder, defect, malfunction **4** = disorder, fighting, conflict, bother, unrest, disturbance, to-do (*informal*), furore, biffo (*Austral slang*), boilover (*Austral*); ≠ peace **5** = effort, work, thought, care, labour, pains, hassle (*informal*), inconvenience; ≠ convenience ▸ *vb* **9** = bother, worry, upset, disturb, distress, plague, pain, sadden; ≠ please **10** = take pains, take the time, make an effort, exert yourself; ≠ avoid **11** = inconvenience, disturb, burden, put out, impose upon, incommode; ≠ relieve

troubleshooter *n* a person employed to locate and deal with faults or problems ⊳ **troubleshooting** *n, adj*

troublesome *adj* causing trouble

> **troublesome** *adj* = disorderly, violent, turbulent, rebellious, unruly, rowdy, undisciplined, uncooperative; ≠ well-behaved

trough (troff) *n* **1** a long open container, esp. one for animals' food or water **2** a narrow channel between two waves or ridges **3** a low point in a pattern that has regular high and low points: *the trough of the slump in pupil numbers was in 1985* **4** *meteorol* a long narrow area of low pressure **5** a narrow channel or gutter

> **trough** *n* **1** = manger, water trough

trounce *vb* **trouncing, trounced** to defeat (someone) utterly

troupe (troop) *n* a company of actors or other performers

trouper *n* **1** a member of a troupe **2** an experienced person: *Bette plays a showbiz trouper*

trouser *adj* **1** of or relating to trousers: *trouser legs* ▸ *vb* **2** *Brit slang* to take (something, esp. money), often surreptitiously or unlawfully

trousers *pl n* a garment that covers the body from the waist to the ankles or knees with a separate tube-shaped section for each leg

trousseau (troo-so) *n, pl* **-seaux** (-so) the clothes, linen, and other possessions collected by a bride for her marriage

trout *n, pl* **trout** *or* **trouts** any of various game fishes related to the salmon and found chiefly in fresh water in northern regions

trowel *n* **1** a hand tool resembling a small spade with a curved blade, used by gardeners for lifting plants, etc. **2** a similar tool with a flat metal blade, used for spreading cement or plaster on a surface

troy weight *or* **troy** *n* a system of weights used for precious metals and gemstones in which one pound equals twelve ounces

truant *n* **1** a pupil who stays away from school without permission **2 play truant** to stay away from school without permission ▸ *adj* **3** being or relating to a truant: *a truant schoolkid* ⊳ **truancy** *n*

truce *n* a temporary agreement to stop fighting or quarrelling

> **truce** *n* = ceasefire, peace, moratorium, respite, lull, cessation, let-up (*informal*), armistice

truck¹ *n* **1** *Brit* a railway wagon for carrying freight **2** a large motor vehicle for transporting heavy loads **3** any wheeled vehicle used to move goods ▸ *vb* **4** *chiefly US* to transport goods in a truck

truck² *n* **1** *history* the payment of wages in goods rather than in money **2 have no truck with** to refuse to be involved with: *the opposition will have no truck with the planned cut in pensions*

trucker *n* a long-distance lorry driver

truculent (truck-yew-lent) *adj* defiantly aggressive or bad-tempered ⊳ **truculence** *n* ⊳ **truculently** *adv*

trudge *vb* **trudging, trudged 1** to walk or plod heavily or wearily ▸ *n* **2** a long tiring walk

true *adj* **truer, truest 1** in accordance with the truth or facts; factual: *not all of the stories about her are true* **2** real or genuine: *he didn't want to reveal his true feelings* **3** faithful and loyal: *a true friend* **4** accurate or precise: *he looked through the telescopic sight until he was convinced his aim was true* **5** (of a compass bearing) according to the earth's geographical rather than magnetic poles: *true north* **6 come true** to actually happen: *fortunately his gloomy prediction didn't come true* ▸ *n* **7 in** or **out of true** in or not in correct alignment ▸ *adv* **8** truthfully or rightly: *I'd like to move to Edinburgh, true, but I'd need to get a job there first*

> **true** *adj* **1** = correct, right, accurate, precise, factual, truthful, veracious; ≠ false **2** = actual, real, genuine, proper, authentic, dinkum (*Austral, NZ informal*), dinky-di (*Austral, NZ informal*) **3** = faithful, loyal, devoted, dedicated, steady, reliable, staunch, trustworthy; ≠ unfaithful **4** = exact, perfect, accurate, precise, spot-on (*Brit informal*), on target, unerring; ≠ inaccurate

truffle *n* **1** a round fungus which grows underground and is regarded as a delicacy **2** Also called: **rum truffle** a sweet flavoured with chocolate or rum

trug *n Brit* a long shallow basket for carrying garden tools, flowers, etc.

truism *n* a statement that is clearly true and well known

truly *adv* **1** in a true, just, or faithful manner **2** really: *a truly awful poem*

> **truly** *adv* **1** = faithfully, steadily, sincerely, staunchly, dutifully, loyally, devotedly **2** = genuinely, correctly, truthfully, rightly, precisely, exactly, legitimately, authentically; ≠ falsely

trump[1] *vb* **1** *cards* to beat a card by playing a card which belongs to a suit which outranks it **2** to outdo or surpass: *she trumped his news by announcing that she had been picked for the Olympic team*

trump[2] *n archaic, literary* **1** a trumpet or the sound produced by one **2 the last trump** the final trumpet call on the Day of Judgment

trumpet *n* **1** a valved brass musical instrument consisting of a narrow tube ending in a flare **2** a loud sound such as that of a trumpet: *the elephant gave a loud trumpet* **3 blow one's own trumpet** to boast about one's own skills or good qualities ▸ *vb* **-peting, -peted 4** to proclaim or state forcefully: *almost every one of the party's loudly trumpeted election claims is untrue* **5** (of an elephant) to make a loud cry ▸ **trumpeter** *n*

> **trumpet** *n* **1** = horn, clarion, bugle ▸ *vb* **4** = proclaim, advertise, tout (*informal*), announce, broadcast, shout from the rooftops; ≠ keep secret

truncate *vb* **-cating, -cated** to shorten by cutting ▸ **truncated** *adj* ▸ **truncation** *n*

truncheon *n chiefly Brit* a small club, esp one carried by a police officer

trundle *vb* **-dling, -dled** to move heavily on or as if on wheels: *a bus trundled along the drive*

trunk *n* **1** the main stem of a tree **2** a large strong case or box used to contain clothes when travelling and for storage **3** a person's body excluding the head, neck, and limbs; torso **4** the long nose of an elephant **5** *US* the boot of a car

> **trunk** *n* **1** = stem, stalk, bole **2** = chest, case, box, crate, coffer, casket **3** = body, torso **4** = snout, nose, proboscis

trunk call *n chiefly Brit & Austral* a long-distance telephone call

trunk road *n Brit* a main road, esp. one maintained by the central government

truss *vb* **1** to tie or bind (someone) up **2** to bind the wings and legs of (a fowl) before cooking ▸ *n* **3** *med* a device for holding a hernia in place **4** a framework of wood or metal used to support a roof, bridge, etc. **5** a cluster of flowers or fruit growing at the end of a single stalk

trust *vb* **1** to believe that (someone) is honest and means no harm: *my father warned me never to trust strangers* **2** to feel that (something) is safe and reliable: *I don't trust those new gadgets* **3** to entrust (someone) with important information or valuables: *she's not somebody I would trust with this sort of secret* **4** to believe that (someone) is likely to do something safely and reliably: *I wouldn't trust anyone else to look after my child properly* **5** to believe (a story, account, etc.) **6** to expect, hope, or suppose: *I trust you've made your brother welcome here* ▸ *n* **7** confidence in the truth, worth, reliability, etc., of a person or thing; faith: *he knew that his father had great trust in him* **8** the obligation of someone in a responsible position: *he was in a position of trust as her substitute father* **9 A** a legal arrangement whereby one person looks after property, money, etc., on another's behalf **B** property that is the subject of such an arrangement **10** (in England and Wales) a self-governing hospital, group of hospitals, or other body that operates as an independent commercial unit within the National Health Service **11** *chiefly US & Canad* a group of companies joined together to control the market for any commodity ▸ *adj* **12** of or relating to a trust or trusts: *trust status*

> **trust** *vb* **1, 2, 4, 5** = believe in, have faith in, depend on, count on, bank on, rely upon; ≠ distrust **3** = entrust, commit, assign, confide (*formal*), consign, put into the hands of, allow to look after, hand over **6** = expect, hope, suppose, assume, presume, surmise ▸ *n* **7** = confidence, credit, belief, faith, expectation, conviction, assurance, certainty; ≠ distrust

t

trustee *n* **1** a person who administers property on someone else's behalf **2** a member of a board that manages the affairs of an institution or organization

trustful *or* **trusting** *adj* characterized by a readiness to trust others > **trustfully** *or* **trustingly** *adv*

> **trustful** *or* **trusting** *adj* = unsuspecting, naive, gullible, unwary, credulous, unsuspicious; ≠ suspicious

trustworthy *adj* (of a person) honest, reliable, or dependable

trusty *adj* **trustier, trustiest 1** faithful or reliable: *his trusty steed* ▸ *n, pl* **trusties 2** a trustworthy convict to whom special privileges are granted

truth *n* **1** the quality of being true, genuine, or factual: *there is no truth in the allegations* **2** something that is true: *he finally learned the truth about his parents' marriage* **3** a proven or verified fact, principle, etc.: *some profound truths about biology have come to light*

> **truth** *n* **1** = truthfulness, fact, accuracy, precision, validity, legitimacy, veracity, genuineness; ≠ inaccuracy

truthful *adj* **1** telling the truth; honest **2** true; based on facts: *a truthful answer* > **truthfully** *adv* > **truthfulness** *n*

try *vb* **tries, trying, tried 1** to make an effort or attempt: *you must try to understand* **2** to sample or test (something) to see how enjoyable, good, or useful it is: *I tried smoking once but didn't like it* **3** to put strain or stress on (someone's patience) **4** to give pain, affliction, or vexation to: *sometimes when I've been sorely tried, my temper gets a little out of hand* **5 A** to investigate (a case) in a court of law **B** to hear evidence in order to determine the guilt or innocence of (a person) ▸ *n, pl* **tries 6** an attempt or effort **7** *rugby* a score made by placing the ball down behind the opposing team's goal line

> **try** *vb* **1** = attempt, seek, aim, strive, struggle, endeavour, have a go, make an effort **2** = experiment with, try out, put to the test, test, taste, examine, investigate, sample ▸ *n* **6** = attempt, go (*informal*), shot (*informal*), effort, crack (*informal*), stab (*informal*), bash (*informal*), whack (*informal*)

trying *adj* upsetting, difficult, or annoying

> **trying** *adj* = annoying, hard, taxing, difficult, tough, stressful, exasperating, tiresome; ≠ straightforward

tryst *n archaic or literary* **1** an arrangement to meet, esp. secretly **2** a meeting, esp. a secret one with a lover, or the place where such a meeting takes place

Ts tennessine

tsar *or* **czar** (zahr) *n* (until 1917) the emperor of Russia. Also: **tzar** > **tsarist** *or* **czarist** *n*

tsetse fly *or* **tzetze fly** (tset-see) *n* a bloodsucking African fly whose bite transmits disease, esp. sleeping sickness

T-shirt *or* **tee-shirt** *n* a short-sleeved casual shirt or top

tsp. teaspoon

T-square *n* a T-shaped ruler used for drawing horizontal lines and to support set squares when drawing vertical and inclined lines

tsunami *n* a large, often destructive, sea wave, usually caused by an earthquake under the sea

TT 1 teetotal **2** teetotaller **3** tuberculin-tested

tuatara (too-ah-tah-rah) *n* a large lizard-like New Zealand reptile

tub *n* **1** a low wide, usually round container **2** a small plastic or cardboard container for ice cream, etc. **3** *chiefly US* same as **bath** (sense 1) **4** Also called: **tubful** the amount a tub will hold **5** a slow and uncomfortable boat or ship

tuba (tube-a) *n* a low-pitched brass musical instrument with valves

tubby *adj* **-bier, -biest** (of a person) fat and short > **tubbiness** *n*

tube *n* **1** a long hollow cylindrical object, used for the passage of fluids or as a container **2** a flexible cylinder of soft metal or plastic closed with a cap, used to hold substances such as toothpaste **3** *anatomy* any hollow cylindrical structure: *the Fallopian tubes* **4 the Tube** *Brit trademark* the underground railway system in London **5** *slang, chiefly US* a television set > **tubeless** *adj*

tuber (tube-er) *n* a fleshy underground root of a plant such as a potato

tubercle (tube-er-kl) *n* **1** a small rounded swelling **2** any abnormal hard swelling, esp. one characteristic of tuberculosis

tubercular (tube-berk-yew-lar) *or* **tuberculous** *adj* **1** of or symptomatic of tuberculosis **2** of or relating to a tubercle

tuberculin (tube-berk-yew-lin) *n* a sterile liquid prepared from cultures of the tubercle bacillus and used in the diagnosis of tuberculosis

tuberculosis (tube-berk-yew-lohss-iss) *n* an infectious disease characterized by the formation of tubercles, esp. in the lungs

tuberous (tube-er-uss) *adj* (of plants) forming, bearing, or resembling a tuber or tubers

tubing (tube-ing) *n* **1** a length of tube **2** a system of tubes

tubular (tube-yew-lar) *adj* **1** having the shape of a tube or tubes **2** of or relating to a tube or tubing

TUC (in Britain and South Africa) Trades Union Congress

tuck *vb* **1** to push or fold into a small space or between two surfaces: *she tucked the letter into her handbag* **2** to thrust the loose ends or sides of (something) into a confining space, so as to make it neat and secure: *he tucked his shirt back into his trousers* **3** to make a tuck or tucks in (a garment)

▸ *n* **4** a pleat or fold in a part of a garment, usually stitched down **5** *Brit informal* food, esp. cakes and sweets

tuck *vb* **1, 2** = push, stick, stuff, slip, ease, insert, pop (*informal*) ▸ *n* **4** = fold, gather, pleat, pinch **5** = food, grub (*slang*), kai (*NZ informal*), nosh (*slang*)

tuck away *vb informal* **1** to eat (a large amount of food) **2** to store (something) in a safe place: *we knew he had some money tucked away somewhere* **3** to have a quiet, rarely disturbed or visited location: *the chapel is tucked away in a side street*

tucker *n* **1** a detachable yoke of lace, linen, etc., formerly worn over the breast of a low-cut dress **2** *Austral & NZ informal* food **3 one's best bib and tucker** *informal* one's best clothes

Tudor *adj* **1** of or in the reign of the English royal house ruling from 1485 to 1603 **2** denoting a style of architecture characterized by half-timbered houses: *a Tudor cottage*

Tuesday *n* the third day of the week

tufa (tew-fa) *n* a porous rock formed of calcium carbonate deposited from springs

tuffet *n* a small mound or low seat

tuft *n* a bunch of feathers, grass, hair, threads, etc., held together at the base ▸ **tufted** *adj* ▸ **tufty** *adj*

tug *vb* **tugging, tugged 1** to pull or drag with a sharp or powerful movement: *she tugged at my arm* **2** to tow (a ship or boat) by means of a tug ▸ *n* **3** a strong pull or jerk **4** Also called: **tugboat** a boat with a powerful engine, used for towing barges, ships, etc.

tug *vb* **1** = drag, pull, haul, tow, lug, heave, draw ▸ *n* **3** = pull, jerk, yank

tuition *n* **1** instruction, esp. that received individually or in a small group **2** the payment for instruction, esp. in colleges or universities

tuition *n* **1** = training, schooling, education, teaching, lessons, instruction, tutoring, tutelage (*formal*)

tulip *n* **1** a plant which produces bright cup-shaped flowers in spring **2** the flower or bulb

tulle (tewl) *n* a fine net fabric of silk, rayon, etc., used to make evening dresses

tumble *vb* **-bling, -bled 1** to fall or cause to fall, esp. awkwardly or violently: *chairs tumbled over* **2** to roll or twist, esp. in playing: *they rolled and tumbled as wild beasts* **3** to decrease in value suddenly: *interest rates tumbled* **4** to move in a quick and uncontrolled manner: *the crowd tumbled down the stairs* **5** to disturb, rumple, or toss around: *she was all tumbled by the fall* **6** to perform leaps or somersaults ▸ *n* **7** a fall, esp. an awkward or violent one: *he took a tumble down the stairs* **8** a somersault ▸ **tumbled** *adj*

tumble *vb* **1** = fall, drop, topple, plummet, stumble, flop ▸ *n* **7** = fall, drop, trip, plunge, spill (*informal*), stumble

tumbledown *adj* (of a building) falling to pieces; dilapidated

tumble dryer *or* **tumble drier** *n* an electrically-operated machine that dries wet laundry by rotating it in warmed air inside a metal drum

tumbler *n* **1 A** a flat-bottomed drinking glass with no handle or stem **B** the amount a tumbler will hold **2** a person who performs somersaults and other acrobatic feats **3** a part of the mechanism of a lock

tumble to *vb* to understand or become aware of: *how did he tumble to this?*

tumbril *n* a farm cart that tilts backwards to empty its load, which was used to take condemned prisoners to the guillotine during the French Revolution

tumescent (tew-mess-ent) *adj* swollen or becoming swollen

tummy *n, pl* **-mies** an informal or childish word for **stomach**

tumour *or US* **tumor** (tew-mer) *n pathol* **A** any abnormal swelling **B** a mass of tissue formed by a new growth of cells ▸ **tumorous** *adj*

tumour *or* **tumor** *n* **1B** = growth, cancer, swelling, lump, carcinoma (*pathol*), sarcoma (*med*)

tumult (tew-mult) *n* **1** a loud confused noise, such as one produced by a crowd **2** a state of confusion and excitement: *a tumult of emotions*

tumultuous (tew-mull-tew-uss) *adj* **1** exciting, confused, or turbulent: *this week's tumultuous events* **2** unruly, noisy, or excited: *a tumultuous welcome*

tumulus (tew-myew-luss) *n, pl* **-li** (-lie) *archaeol not in technical use* a burial mound

tun *n* a large beer cask

tuna (tune-a) *n, pl* **-na** *or* **-nas 1** a large marine spiny-finned fish **2** the flesh of this fish, often tinned for food

tundra *n* a vast treeless Arctic region with permanently frozen subsoil

tune *n* **1** a melody, esp. one for which harmony is not essential **2** the correct musical pitch: *many of the notes are out of tune* **3 call the tune** to be in control of the proceedings **4 change one's tune** to alter one's attitude or tone of speech **5 in** *or* **out of tune with** in or not in agreement or sympathy with: *in tune with public opinion* **6 to the tune of** *informal* to the amount or extent of ▸ *vb* **tuning, tuned 7** to adjust (a musical instrument) so each string, key, etc., produces the right note **8** to make small adjustments to (an engine, machine, etc.) to obtain the proper or desired performance **9** to adjust (a radio or television) to receive a particular station or programme: *the radio was tuned to the local station* ▸ **tuner** *n*

tune *n* **1** = melody, air, song, theme, strain(s), jingle, ditty, choon (*slang*) **2** = harmony, pitch, euphony ▸ *vb* **7** = tune up, adjust **8** = regulate, adapt, modulate, harmonize, attune, pitch

t

tuneful *adj* having a pleasant tune › **tunefully** *adv*

tune in *vb* **1** to adjust (a radio or television) to receive (a station or programme) **2 tuned in to** *slang* aware of or knowledgeable about: *tuned in to European cinema*

tuneless *adj* having no melody or tune

tungsten *n chem* a hard greyish-white metallic element. Symbol: **W**

tunic *n* **1** a close-fitting jacket forming part of some uniforms **2** a loose-fitting knee-length garment

tunnel *n* **1** an underground passageway, esp. one for trains or cars **2** any passage or channel through or under something: *the carpal tunnel* ▸ *vb* **-nelling, -nelled** *or US* **-neling, -neled 3** to make one's way through or under (something) by digging a tunnel: *ten men succeeded in tunnelling out of the prisoner-of-war camp* **4** to dig a tunnel (through or under something): *the idea of tunnelling under the English Channel had been around for a long time*

> **tunnel** *n* = passage, underpass, passageway, subway, channel, hole, shaft ▸ *vb* = dig, burrow, mine, bore, drill, excavate

tunny *n, pl* **-nies** *or* **-ny** same as **tuna**

tup *n chiefly Brit* a male sheep

turban *n* **1** a head-covering worn by a Muslim, Hindu, or Sikh man, consisting of a long piece of cloth wound round the head **2** any head-covering resembling this › **turbaned** *adj*

turbid *adj literary* (of water or air) full of mud or dirt, and frequently swirling around: *the turbid stream of the Loire* › **turbidity** *n*

turbine *n* a machine in which power is produced by a stream of water, air, etc., that pushes the blades of a wheel and causes it to rotate

turbot *n, pl* **-bot** *or* **-bots** a European flatfish, highly valued as a food fish

turbulence *n* **1** a state or condition of confusion, movement, or agitation **2** *meteorol* instability in the atmosphere causing gusty air currents

turbulent *adj* **1** involving a lot of sudden changes and conflicting elements: *the city has had a turbulent history* **2** (of people) wild and unruly: *a harsh mountain land inhabited by a score of turbulent tribes* **3** (of water or air) full of violent unpredictable currents: *the turbulent ocean*

> **turbulent** *adj* **3** = stormy, rough, raging, tempestuous, furious, foaming, agitated, tumultuous; ≠ calm

tureen *n* a large deep dish with a lid, used for serving soups

turf *n, pl* **turfs** *or* **turves 1** a layer of thick even grass with roots and soil attached: *a short turf rich in wild flowers* **2** a piece cut from this layer: *we spent the afternoon digging turves* **3** *informal* **A** the area where a person lives and feels at home: *my boyhood turf of east Cork* **B** a person's area of

knowledge or influence: *when Kate is at work, she's on her own turf* **4 the turf A** a track where horse races are run **B** horse racing as a sport or industry **5** same as **peat** ▸ *vb* **6** to cover (an area of ground) with pieces of turf

> **turf** *n* **1** = grass, sward **2** = sod **4B the turf** = horse-racing, the flat, racing

turf accountant *n Brit* same as **bookmaker**

turf out *vb informal* to throw (someone or something) out: *the residents fear a new landlord might push up rents and turf them out of their homes*

turgid (**tur**-jid) *adj* **1** (of language) pompous, boring, and hard to understand **2** (of water or mud) unpleasantly thick and brown › **turgidity** *n*

turkey *n, pl* **-keys** *or* **-key 1** a large bird of North America bred for its meat **2** *informal, chiefly US & Canad* something, esp. a theatrical production, that fails **3 cold turkey** *slang* a method of curing drug addiction by abrupt withdrawal of all doses **4 talk turkey** *informal, chiefly US & Canad* to discuss, esp. business, frankly and practically

Turkish *adj* **1** of Turkey ▸ *n* **2** the language of Turkey

Turkish bath *n* **1** a type of bath in which the bather sweats freely in hot dry air, is then washed, often massaged, and has a cold plunge or shower **2 Turkish baths** an establishment for such baths

Turkish delight *n* a jelly-like sweet flavoured with flower essences, usually cut into cubes and covered in icing sugar

turmeric *n* **1** a tropical Asian plant with yellow flowers and an aromatic underground stem **2** a yellow spice obtained from the root of this plant

turmoil *n* disorder, agitation, or confusion: *a period of political turmoil and uncertainty*

> **turmoil** *n* = confusion, disorder, chaos, upheaval, disarray, uproar, agitation, commotion; ≠ peace

turn *vb* **1** to move to face in another direction **2** to rotate or move round **3** to operate (a switch, key, etc.) by twisting it **4** to aim or point (something) in a particular direction: *they turned their guns on the crowd* **5** to change in course or direction: *the van turned right into Victoria Road* **6** (of a road, river, etc.) to have a bend or curve in it **7** to perform or do (something) with a rotating movement: *a small boy was turning somersaults* **8** to change so as to become: *he turned pale* **9** to reach, pass, or progress beyond in age, time, etc.: *she had just turned fourteen* **10** to find (a particular page) in a book: *turn to page 78* **11** to look at the other side of: *turning the pages of a book* **12** to shape (wood, metal, etc.) on a lathe **13** (of leaves) to change colour in autumn **14** to make or become sour: *the milk is starting to turn* **15** to affect or be affected with nausea or giddiness: *that would turn the strongest stomach* **16** (of the tide) to start coming in or going out **17 turn against** to stop liking (something or someone one previously liked): *people turned against her because she became so dictatorial* **18 turn into** to become or change into: *my mother turned our house into four apartments* **19 turn loose** to set (an animal or a person) free **20 turn someone's head** to affect someone mentally or emotionally **21 turn to A** to direct or apply (one's attention or thoughts) to **B** to stop doing or using one thing and start doing or using (another): *I turned to photography from writing* **c** to appeal or apply to (someone) for help, advice, etc. ▸ *n* **22** the act of turning **23** a movement of complete or partial rotation: *a turn of the dial* **24** a change of direction or position **25** same as **turning** (sense 1) **26** the right or opportunity to do something in an agreed order or succession: *it was her turn to play next* **27** a change in something that is happening or being done: *events took an unhappy turn* **28** a period of action, work, etc. **29** a short walk, ride, or excursion **30** natural inclination: *a liberal turn of mind* **31** distinctive form or style: *she'd a nice turn of phrase* **32** a deed that helps or hinders someone: *I'm trying to do you a good turn* **33** a twist, bend, or distortion in shape **34** a slight attack of an illness: *she's just having one of her turns* **35** *music* a melodic ornament that alternates the main note with the notes above and below it, beginning with the note above, in a variety of sequences **36** a short theatrical act: *tonight's star turn* **37** *informal* a shock or surprise: *you gave me rather a turn* **38 done to a turn** *informal* cooked perfectly **39 turn and turn about** one after another; alternately ▸ See also **turn down**, **turn in** *etc.* ▸ **turner** *n*

> **turn** *vb* **1** = change course, swing round, wheel round, veer, move, switch, shift, swerve **2** = rotate, spin, go round (and round), revolve, roll, circle, twist, spiral **8** = change, transform, shape, convert, alter, mould, remodel, mutate **12** = shape, form, fashion, cast, frame, mould, make **14** = make rancid, spoil, sour, taint ▸ *n* **22** = change of direction, shift, departure, deviation **24, 27** = direction, course, tack, tendency, drift **26** = opportunity, go, time, try, chance, crack (*informal*), stint **32** = deed, service, act, action, favour, gesture

turncoat *n* a person who deserts one cause or party to join an opposing one

turn down *vb* **1** to reduce (the volume, brightness, or temperature of something): *turn the heat down* **2** to reject or refuse: *the invitation was turned down* **3** to fold down (sheets, etc.)

> **turn down** *vb* **1 turn something down** = lower, soften, mute, lessen, muffle, quieten **2 turn something down** = refuse, decline, reject, spurn, rebuff, repudiate

turn in *vb informal* **1** to go to bed for the night **2** to hand in: *turning in my essay* **3** to hand (a suspect or criminal) over to the police: *his own brother turned him in*

> **turn in** *vb* **2 turn something in** = hand in, return, deliver, give up, hand over, submit, surrender, tender

turning *n* **1** a road, river, or path that turns off the main way **2** the point where such a way turns off **3** the process of turning objects on a lathe

> **turning** *n* **1** = bend, turn, curve **2** = turn-off, turn, junction, crossroads, side road, exit

turning point *n* a moment when a decisive change occurs

> **turning point** *n* = crossroads, change, crisis, crux, moment of truth, tipping point

turnip *n* a vegetable with a large yellow or white edible root

turn off *vb* **1** to leave (a road or path): *turning off the main road* **2** (of a road or path) to lead away from (another road or path): *a main street with alleys twisting and turning off it* **3** to cause (something) to stop operating by turning a knob, pushing a button, etc. **4** *informal* to cause disgust or disinterest in (someone): *keeping kids from getting turned off by mathematics* ▸ *n* **turn-off 5** a road or other way branching off from the main thoroughfare **6** *informal* a person or thing that causes dislike

> **turn off** *vb* **3 turn something off** = switch off, turn out, put out, stop, cut out, shut down, unplug, flick off

turn on *vb* **1** to cause (something) to operate by turning a knob, pushing a button, etc.: *turn on the radio, please* **2** to attack (someone), esp. without warning: *the Labrador turned on me* **3** *informal* to produce suddenly or automatically: *turning on that bland smile* **4** *slang* to arouse emotionally or sexually **5** to depend or hinge on: *the match turned on a contentious decision* ▸ *n* **turn-on 6** *slang* a person or thing that causes emotional or sexual arousal

> **turn on** *vb* **1 turn something on** = switch on, activate, start, start up, ignite, kick-start **4 turn someone on** = arouse, attract, excite, thrill, stimulate, please, titillate

turn out *vb* **1** to cause (something, esp. a light) to stop operating by moving a switch **2** to produce or create: *turning out two hits a year* **3** to force (someone) out of a place or position: *turned out of office* **4** to empty the contents of (something): *the police ordered him to turn out his pockets* **5** to be discovered or found (to be or do something): *he turned out to be a Finn* **6** to end up or result: *how interesting to see how it all turned out!* **7** to dress and groom: *she is always very well turned out* **8** to assemble or gather: *crowds turned out to see him* **9 turn out for** *informal* to make an appearance, esp. in a sporting competition: *he was asked to turn out for Liverpool* ▸ *n* **turnout**

10 a number of people attending an event: *there has been a high turnout of voters in elections in Bulgaria* **11** the quantity or amount produced

> **turn out** *n* **10 turnout** = attendance, crowd, audience, gate, assembly, congregation, number, throng

turn over *vb* **1** to change position, esp. so as to reverse top and bottom **2** to shift position, for instance by rolling onto one's side: *he turned over and went straight to sleep* **3** to consider carefully: *as I walked, I turned her story over* **4** to give (something) to someone who has a right to it or to the authorities: *the police ordered him to turn over the files to them* **5** (of an engine) to start or function correctly: *when he pressed the starter button, the engine turned over at once* **6** *slang* to rob: *the house had been turned over while they were out* ▸ **turnover 7** ᴀ the amount of business done by a company during a specified period ʙ the rate at which stock in trade is sold and replenished **8** a small pastry case filled with fruit or jam: *an apple turnover* **9** the number of workers employed by a firm in a given period to replace those who have left

> **turn over** *n* **7ᴀ turnover** = output, business, productivity **9 turnover** = movement, coming and going, change

turnpike *n* **1** *history* a barrier across a road to prevent vehicles or pedestrians passing until a charge (toll) had been paid **2** *US* a motorway for use of which a toll is charged

turnstile *n* a mechanical barrier with arms that are turned to admit one person at a time

turntable *n* **1** the circular platform in a record player that rotates the record while it is being played **2** a circular platform used for turning locomotives and cars

turn up *vb* **1** to arrive or appear: *few people turned up* **2** to find or discover or be found or discovered: *a medical checkup has only turned up a sinus infection* **3** to increase the flow, volume, etc., of: *he turned up the radio* ▸ *n* **turn-up 4** *Brit* the turned-up fold at the bottom of some trouser legs **5 a turn-up for the books** *informal* an unexpected happening

> **turn up** *vb* **1** = arrive, come, appear, show up (*informal*), attend, put in an appearance, show your face **2 turn something up** = find, reveal, discover, expose, disclose, unearth, dig up **3 turn something up** = increase, raise, boost, enhance, intensify, amplify

turpentine *n* **1** a strong-smelling colourless oil distilled from the resin of some coniferous trees, and used for thinning paint, for cleaning, and in medicine **2** a semisolid mixture of resin and oil obtained from various conifers, which is the main source of commercial turpentine **3** *not in technical use* any one of a number of thinners for paints and varnishes, consisting of fractions of petroleum

turps *n* short for **turpentine** (senses 1, 3)

turquoise *adj* **1** greenish-blue ▸ *n* **2** a greenish-blue precious stone

turret *n* **1** a small tower that projects from the wall of a building, esp. a castle **2** (on a tank or warship) a rotating structure on which guns are mounted **3** (on a machine tool) a turret-like steel structure with tools projecting from it that can be rotated to bring each tool to bear on the work › **turreted** *adj*

turtle *n* **1** an aquatic reptile with a flattened shell enclosing the body and flipper-like limbs adapted for swimming **2 turn turtle** (of a boat) to capsize

turtledove *n* an Old World dove noted for its soft cooing and devotion to its mate

turtleneck *n* a round high close-fitting neck on a sweater or a sweater with such a neck

tusk *n* a long pointed tooth in the elephant, walrus, and certain other mammals › **tusked** *adj*

tussle *n* **1** an energetic fight, struggle, or argument: *she resigned following a protracted boardroom tussle* ▸ *vb* **-sling, -sled 2** to fight or struggle energetically

tussock *n* a dense tuft of grass or other vegetation › **tussocky** *adj*

tutelage (tew-till-lij) *n formal* **1** instruction or guidance, esp. by a tutor **2** the state of being supervised by a guardian or tutor

tutelary (tew-till-lar-ee) *adj literary* **1** having the role of guardian or protector **2** of a guardian

tutor *n* **1** a teacher, usually one instructing individual pupils **2** (at a college or university) a member of staff responsible for the teaching and supervision of a certain number of students ▸ *vb* **3** to act as a tutor to (someone) › **tutorship** *n*

> **tutor** *n* **1** = teacher, coach, instructor, educator, guide, guardian, lecturer, guru ▸ *vb* = teach, educate, school, train, coach, guide, drill, instruct

tutorial *n* **1** a period of intensive tuition given by a tutor to an individual student or to a small group of students ▸ *adj* **2** of or relating to a tutor

tutu *n* a very short skirt worn by ballerinas, made of projecting layers of stiffened material

tuxedo *n, pl* **-dos** a dinner jacket

TV television

twaddle *n* **1** silly, trivial, or pretentious talk or writing ▸ *vb* **-dling, -dled 2** to talk or write in a silly or pretentious way

twang *n* **1** a sharp ringing sound produced by or as if by the plucking of a taut string **2** a strongly nasal quality in a person's speech: *a high-pitched Texas twang* ▸ *vb* **3** to make or cause to make a twang: *a bunch of angels twanging harps* › **twangy** *adj*

tweak *vb* **1** to twist or pinch with a sharp or sudden movement: *she tweaked his ear* **2** *informal* to make a minor alteration ▸ *n* **3** the act of tweaking **4** *informal* a minor alteration

tweed n 1 a thick woollen cloth produced originally in Scotland 2 **tweeds** a suit made of tweed

tweedy adj **tweedier, tweediest** 1 of, made of, or resembling tweed 2 showing a fondness for a hearty outdoor life, often associated with wearers of tweeds

tweet n 1 an imitation of the thin chirping sound made by small birds 2 a short message posted on the Twitter website ▸ vb 3 to make this sound 4 to post a short message on the Twitter website

tweeter n a loudspeaker used in high-fidelity systems for the reproduction of high audio frequencies

tweezers pl n a small pincer-like tool used for tasks such as handling small objects or plucking out hairs

twelfth adj 1 of or being number twelve in a series ▸ n 2 number twelve in a series 3 one of twelve equal parts of something

twelve n 1 the cardinal number that is the sum of ten and two 2 a numeral, 12 or XII, representing this number 3 something representing or consisting of twelve units ▸ adj 4 amounting to twelve: *twelve months*

twenty n, pl **-ties** 1 the cardinal number that is the product of ten and two 2 a numeral, 20 or XX, representing this number 3 something representing or consisting of twenty units ▸ adj 4 amounting to twenty: *twenty minutes* > **twentieth** adj, n

twenty-four-seven or **24/7** adv informal constantly or all the time: *consultants would no longer be available 24/7*

twerp or **twirp** n informal a silly, stupid, or contemptible person

twice adv 1 two times; on two occasions or in two cases: *I've met her only twice* 2 double in degree or quantity: *twice as big*

twiddle vb **-dling, -dled** 1 to twirl or fiddle, often in an idle way: *twiddling the knobs of a radio* 2 **twiddle one's thumbs** A to rotate one's thumbs around one another, when bored or impatient B to be bored, with nothing to do ▸ n 3 an unnecessary decoration, esp. a curly one

twig¹ n a small branch or shoot of a tree > **twiggy** adj

twig n = branch, stick, sprig, shoot, spray

twig² vb **twigging, twigged** informal to realize or understand: *I should have twigged it earlier*

twilight n 1 the soft dim light that occurs when the sun is just below the horizon after sunset 2 the period in which this light occurs: *soon after twilight we started marching again* 3 a period in which strength, importance, etc., is gradually declining: *the twilight of his political career* ▸ adj 4 of or relating to the period towards the end of the day: *the twilight shift* 5 of or being a period of decline: *he spent most of his twilight years working on a history of France* 6 denoting irregularity and obscurity: *a twilight existence* > **twilit** adj

twilight n 1 = half-light, gloom, dimness, semi-darkness 2 = dusk, evening, sunset, early evening, nightfall, sundown, gloaming (*Scot poetic*), close of day, evo (*Austral slang*); ≠ dawn

twill n a fabric woven to produce an effect of parallel diagonal lines or ribs in the cloth

twin n 1 one of a pair of people or animals conceived at the same time 2 one of a pair of people or things that are identical or very similar ▸ vb **twinning, twinned** 3 to pair or be paired together

twin n = double, counterpart, mate, match, fellow, clone, duplicate, lookalike ▸ vb = pair, match, join, couple, link, yoke

twine n 1 string or cord made by twisting fibres together ▸ vb **twining, twined** 2 to twist or wind together: *she twined the flowers into a garland* 3 **twine round** or **around** to twist or wind around: *she twined her arms around her neck*

twinge n 1 a sudden brief darting or stabbing pain 2 a sharp emotional pang: *a twinge of conscience*

twinkle vb **-kling, -kled** 1 to shine brightly and intermittently; sparkle 2 (of the eyes) to sparkle, esp. with amusement or delight ▸ n 3 a flickering brightness; sparkle

twinkle vb = sparkle, flash, shine, glitter, gleam, blink, flicker, shimmer ▸ n = sparkle, flash, spark, gleam, flicker, shimmer, glimmer

twirl vb 1 to move around rapidly and repeatedly in a circle 2 to twist, wind, or twiddle, often idly: *twirling the glass in her hand* ▸ n 3 a whirl or twist 4 a written flourish

twist vb 1 to turn one end or part while the other end or parts remain still or turn in the opposite direction: *never twist or wring woollen garments* 2 to distort or be distorted 3 to wind or twine: *the wire had been twisted twice* 4 to force or be forced out of the natural form or position: *I twisted my knee* 5 to change the meaning of; distort: *he'd twisted the truth to make himself look good* 6 to revolve or rotate: *he twisted the switch to turn the radio off* 7 to wrench with a turning action: *he twisted the wheel sharply* 8 to follow a winding course: *the road twisted as it climbed* 9 to dance the twist 10 **twist someone's arm** to persuade or coerce someone ▸ n 11 the act of twisting: *she gave a dainty little twist to her parasol* 12 something formed by or as if by twisting: *there's a twist in the cable* 13 a decisive change of direction, aim, meaning, or character: *the latest revelations give a new twist to the company's boardroom wranglings* 14 an unexpected development in a story, play, or film 15 a bend: *a twist of the mountain road* 16 a distortion of the original shape or form 17 a jerky pull, wrench, or turn 18 **the twist** a dance popular in the 1960s, in which dancers

vigorously twist the hips **19 round the twist**
slang mad or eccentric > **twisty** *adj*

twist *vb* **1** = coil, curl, wind, wrap, screw,
twirl **2** = distort, screw up, contort, mangle,
mangulate (*Austral slang*); ≠ straighten
3 = intertwine ▸ n **11, 17** = wind, turn, spin,
swivel, twirl **13** = development, emphasis,
variation, slant **14** = surprise, change, turn
(*informal*), development, revelation, reveal
15 = curve, turn, bend, loop, arc, kink, zigzag,
dog-leg

twisted *adj* (of a person) cruel or perverted
twister *n Brit* a swindling or dishonest
person
twit¹ *vb* **twitting, twitted** *Brit* to poke fun at
(someone)
twit² *n informal* a foolish or stupid person
twitch *vb* **1** (of a person or part of a person's
body) to move in a jerky spasmodic way: *his left
eyelid twitched involuntarily* **2** to pull (something)
with a quick jerky movement: *she twitched the
curtains shut* ▸ n **3** a sharp jerking movement,
esp. one caused by a nervous condition

twitch *vb* **1** = jerk, flutter, jump, squirm
2 = pull (at), tug (at), pluck (at), yank (at)
▸ n = jerk, tic, spasm, jump, flutter

twitter *vb* **1** (esp. of a bird) to utter a succession
of chirping sounds **2** to talk rapidly and
nervously in a high-pitched voice: *novelists who
twittered about how much they admired him* **3** to post a
short message on the Twitter website ▸ n **4** the
act or sound of twittering **5 in a twitter** in a
state of nervous excitement > **twitterer** *n*
> **twittering** *n* > **twittery** *adj*
Twitter *n trademark* a website where people can
post short messages
two *n* **1** the cardinal number that is the sum of
one and one **2** a numeral, 2 or II, representing
this number **3** something representing or
consisting of two units **4 in two** in or into two
parts: *cut the cake in two and take a bit each* **5 put
two and two together** to reach an obvious
conclusion by considering the evidence
available **6 that makes two of us** the same
applies to me ▸ *adj* **7** amounting to two: *two years*
two-edged *adj* **1** (of a remark) having both a
favourable and an unfavourable interpretation,
such as *she looks nice when she smiles* **2** (of a knife,
saw, etc.) having two cutting edges
two-faced *adj* deceitful or hypocritical: *he's a
two-faced liar and opportunist*
two-time *vb* **-timing, -timed** *informal* to deceive
(a lover) by having an affair with someone else
> **two-timer** *n*
tycoon *n* a businessperson of great wealth
and power

tycoon *n* = magnate, capitalist, baron,
industrialist, financier, fat cat (*slang*), mogul,
plutocrat

tyke *or* **tike** *n* **1** *Brit, Austral & NZ informal* a small
or cheeky child **2** *Brit dialect* a rough ill-
mannered person
type *n* **1** a kind, class, or category of things,
all of which have something in common
2 a subdivision of a particular class; sort: *it is more
alcoholic than most wines of this type* **3** the general
characteristics distinguishing a particular
group: *the old-fashioned type of nanny* **4** *informal*
a person, esp. of a specified kind: *a seagoing type*
5 a block with a raised character on it used for
printing **6** text printed from type; print ▸ *vb*
typing, typed 7 to write using a typewriter or
word processor **8** to be a symbol of or typify
9 to decide the type of; classify

type *n* **1, 2, 3** = kind, sort, class, variety, group,
order, style, species

typecast *vb* **-casting, -cast** to cast (an actors)
in the same kind of role continually
typewriter *n* a machine which prints a letter
or other character when the appropriate key is
pressed
typhoid fever *n* an acute infectious disease
characterized by high fever, spots, abdominal
pain, etc. It is spread by contaminated food or
water
typhoon *n* a violent tropical storm, esp. one in
the China Seas or W Pacific
typhus *n* an acute infectious disease
transmitted by lice or mites and characterized
by high fever, skin rash, and severe headache
typical *adj* **1** being or serving as a representative
example of a particular type; characteristic: *a
typical working day* **2** considered to be an example
of some undesirable trait: *it was typical that he
should start talking almost before he was inside the room*
> **typically** *adv*

typical *adj* **1** = archetypal, standard, model,
normal, stock, representative, usual, regular;
≠ unusual **2** = characteristic

typify *vb* **-fies, -fying, -fied 1** to be typical of or
characterize: *the beers made here typify all that is best
about the independent brewing sector* **2** to symbolize
or represent: *a number of dissident intellectuals,
typified by Andrei Sakharov*
typist *n* a person who types letters, reports, etc.,
esp. for a living
typography *n* **1** the art or craft of printing
2 the style or quality of printing and layout in a
book, magazine, etc. > **typographical** *adj*
> **typographically** *adv*
tyrannical *adj* of or like a tyrant; unjust and
oppressive
tyrannize *or* **-nise** *vb* **-nizing, -nized** *or* **-nising,
-nised** to rule or exercise power (over) in a cruel
or oppressive manner: *he dominated and tyrannized
his younger brother*
tyrannosaurus (tirr-ran-oh-**sore**-uss)
or **tyrannosaur** *n* a large two-footed
flesh-eating dinosaur common in North
America in Cretaceous times

tyranny *n, pl* **-nies 1 A** government by a tyrant **B** oppressive and unjust government by more than one person **2** the condition or state of being dominated or controlled by something that makes unpleasant or harsh demands: *the tyranny of fashion drives many people to diet* > **tyrannous** *adj*

> **tyranny** *n* **1B** = oppression, cruelty, dictatorship, authoritarianism, despotism, autocracy, absolutism, high-handedness

tyrant *n* **1** a person who governs oppressively, unjustly, and arbitrarily **2** any person who exercises authority in a tyrannical manner: *a domestic tyrant*

tyre *or US* **tire** *n* a ring of rubber, usually filled with air but sometimes solid, fitted round the rim of a wheel of a road vehicle to grip the road

Uu

ubiquitous (yew-**bik**-wit-uss) *adj* being or seeming to be everywhere at once > **ubiquity** *n*

> **ubiquitous** *adj* = ever-present, pervasive, omnipresent, everywhere, universal

udder *n* the large baglike milk-producing gland of cows, sheep, or goats, with two or more teats

UEFA Union of European Football Associations

UFO unidentified flying object

ugly *adj* **uglier, ugliest 1** so unattractive as to be unpleasant to look at **2** very unpleasant and involving violence or aggression: *an ugly incident in which one man was stabbed* **3** repulsive or displeasing: *ugly rumours* **4** bad-tempered or sullen: *an ugly mood* > **ugliness** *n*

> **ugly** *adj* **1** = unattractive, homely (*chiefly US*), plain, unsightly, unlovely, unprepossessing, ill-favoured; ≠ beautiful **2, 3** = unpleasant, shocking, terrible (*informal*), nasty, distasteful, horrid (*informal*), objectionable, disagreeable; ≠ pleasant **4** = bad-tempered, dangerous, menacing, sinister, baleful

UHF *radio* ultrahigh frequency

UHT ultra-heat-treated (milk or cream)

UK United Kingdom

ukulele *or* **ukelele** (yew-kal-**lay**-lee) *n* a small four-stringed guitar

ulcer *n* an open sore on the surface of the skin or a mucous membrane

> **ulcer** *n* = sore, abscess, peptic ulcer, gumboil

ulcerated *adj* made or becoming ulcerous > **ulceration** *n*

ulcerous *adj* of, like, or characterized by ulcers

ulna *n, pl* **-nae** *or* **-nas** the inner and longer of the two bones of the human forearm or of the forelimb in other vertebrates > **ulnar** *adj*

ulterior (ult-**ear**-ee-or) *adj* (of an aim, reason, etc.) concealed or hidden: *an ulterior motive*

ultimate *adj* **1** final in a series or process: *predictions about the ultimate destination of modern art* **2** highest, supreme, or unchallengeable: *he has the ultimate power to dismiss the Prime Minister* **3** fundamental or essential: *a believer in the ultimate goodness of people* **4** most extreme: *genocide is the ultimate abuse of human rights* **5** final or total: *she should be able to estimate the ultimate cost* ▸ *n* **6 the ultimate in** the best example of: *the ultimate in luxury holidays* > **ultimately** *adv*

> **ultimate** *adj* **1** = final, last, end **2** = supreme, highest, greatest, paramount, superlative **4** = worst, greatest, utmost, extreme

u

ultimatum (ult-im-may-tum) n a final warning to someone that they must agree to certain conditions or requirements, or else action will be taken against them: *Britain declared war after the Nazis rejected the ultimatum to withdraw from Poland*

ultra- prefix 1 beyond a specified extent, range, or limit: *ultrasonic* 2 extremely: *ultraleftist*

ultrahigh frequency n a radio frequency between 3000 and 300 megahertz

ultramarine n 1 a blue pigment originally made from lapis lazuli ▸ adj 2 vivid blue

ultrasonic adj of or producing sound waves with higher frequencies than humans can hear > **ultrasonically** adv

ultrasound n ultrasonic waves, used in echo sounding, medical diagnosis, and therapy

ultraviolet n 1 the part of the electromagnetic spectrum with wavelengths shorter than light but longer than X-rays ▸ adj 2 of or consisting of radiation lying in the ultraviolet: *ultraviolet light*

ululate (yewl-yew-late) vb **-lating, -lated** literary to howl or wail > **ululation** n

umber n 1 a type of dark brown earth containing ferric oxide (rust) ▸ adj 2 dark brown to reddish-brown

umbilical (um-bill-ik-kl) adj of or like the navel or the umbilical cord

umbilical cord n the long flexible cordlike structure that connects a fetus to the placenta

umbrage n **take umbrage** to take offence

umbrella n 1 a portable device used for protection against rain, consisting of a light canopy supported on a collapsible metal frame mounted on a central rod 2 a single organization, idea, etc., that contains or covers many different organizations or ideas 3 anything that has the effect of a protective screen or general cover: *under the umbrella of the Helsinki security conference* ▸ adj 4 containing or covering many different organizations, ideas, etc.: *an umbrella group of nationalists and anti-communists* > **umbrella-like** adj

umpire n 1 an official who ensures that the people taking part in a game follow the rules; referee ▸ vb **-piring, -pired** 2 to act as umpire in a game

umpire n = referee, judge, arbiter, arbitrator, umpie (*Austral slang*) ▸ vb = referee, judge, adjudicate, arbitrate

umpteen adj informal very many: *the centre of umpteen scandals* > **umpteenth** n, adj

UN United Nations

un-¹ prefix (*freely used with adjectives, participles, and their derivative adverbs and nouns: less frequently used with certain other nouns*) not; contrary to; opposite of: *uncertain; untidiness; unbelief; untruth*

un-² prefix 1 denoting reversal of an action or state: *uncover; untie* 2 denoting removal from, release, or deprivation: *unharness*

unable adj **unable to** not having the power, ability, or authority to; not able to

unable adj = incapable, powerless, unfit, impotent, unqualified, ineffectual; ≠ able

unaccountable adj 1 without any sensible explanation: *for some unaccountable reason I got on the wrong bus* 2 not having to justify or answer for one's actions to other people: *the secret service remains unaccountable to the public* > **unaccountably** adv

unadulterated adj 1 completely pure, with nothing added: *fresh unadulterated spring water* 2 (of an emotion) not mixed with anything else: *a look of unadulterated terror*

unanimous (yew-nan-im-uss) adj 1 in complete agreement 2 characterized by complete agreement: *unanimous approval* > **unanimity** n > **unanimously** adv

unanimous adj 1 = agreed, united, in agreement, harmonious, like-minded, of the same mind; ≠ divided 2 = united, common, concerted, solid, consistent, harmonious, undivided, congruent; ≠ split

unannounced adv without warning: *she turned up unannounced*

unarmed adj 1 not carrying any weapons: *they were shooting unarmed peasants* 2 not using any weapons: *unarmed combat*

unarmed adj 1 = defenceless, helpless, unprotected; ≠ armed

unassailable adj not able to be destroyed or overcome: *an unassailable lead*

unassuming adj modest or unpretentious

unaware adj 1 not aware or conscious: *unaware of my surroundings* ▸ adv 2 not standard same as **unawares**

unaware adj = ignorant, unconscious, oblivious, uninformed, unknowing, not in the loop (*informal*); ≠ aware

unawares adv 1 by surprise: *death had taken him unawares* 2 without knowing: *had he passed her, all unawares?*

unbalanced adj 1 lacking balance 2 mentally disturbed 3 biased; one-sided: *his unbalanced summing-up*

unbearable adj not able to be endured > **unbearably** adv

unbearable adj = intolerable, insufferable, too much (*informal*), unacceptable; ≠ tolerable

unbeknown adv (foll. by to) without the knowledge of (a person): *unbeknown to her family she had acquired modern ways*. Also (esp. Brit): **unbeknownst**

unbend vb **-bending, -bent** to become less strict or more informal in one's attitudes or behaviour

unbending adj rigid or inflexible: *an unbending routine*

unbidden adj literary not ordered or asked; voluntary or spontaneous: *unbidden thoughts came into Catherine's mind*

u

unborn *adj* not yet born

unborn *adj* = expected, awaited, embryonic

unbosom *vb* to relieve oneself of secrets or feelings by telling someone

unbridled *adj* (of feelings or behaviour) not restrained or controlled in any way: *unbridled passion*

unburden *vb* to relieve one's mind or oneself of a worry or trouble by telling someone about it

uncalled-for *adj* unnecessary or unwarranted: *uncalled-for comments*

uncanny *adj* 1 weird or mysterious: *an uncanny silence* 2 beyond what is normal: *an uncanny eye for detail* > **uncannily** *adv* > **uncanniness** *n*

unceremonious *adj* 1 relaxed and informal: *she greeted him with unceremonious friendliness* 2 abrupt or rude: *the answer was an unceremonious 'no'* > **unceremoniously** *adv*

uncertain *adj* 1 not able to be accurately known or predicted: *an uncertain future* 2 not definitely decided: *they are uncertain about the date* 3 not to be depended upon: *an uncertain career* 4 changeable: *an uncertain sky* > **uncertainty** *n*

uncertain *adj* 2 = unsure, undecided, vague, unclear, dubious, hazy, irresolute; ≠ sure

unchristian *or* **un-Christian** *adj* not in accordance with Christian principles

uncle *n* 1 a brother of one's father or mother 2 the husband of one's aunt 3 a child's term of address for a male friend of its parents 4 *slang* a pawnbroker

unclean *adj* lacking moral, spiritual, or physical cleanliness

uncomfortable *adj* 1 not physically relaxed: *he was forced to sit in an uncomfortable cross-legged position* 2 not comfortable to be in or use: *an uncomfortable chair* 3 causing discomfort or unease: *the uncomfortable truth* > **uncomfortably** *adv*

uncomfortable *adj* 2 = painful, awkward, rough 3 = uneasy, troubled, disturbed, embarrassed, awkward, discomfited; ≠ comfortable

uncommon *adj* 1 not happening or encountered often 2 in excess of what is normal: *an uncommon amount of powder*

uncommon *adj* 1 = rare, unusual, odd, novel, strange, peculiar, scarce, queer (*old-fashioned*); ≠ common 2 = extraordinary, remarkable, special, outstanding, distinctive, exceptional, notable; ≠ ordinary

uncommonly *adv* 1 in an unusual manner or degree 2 extremely: *an uncommonly good humour*

uncompromising *adj* not prepared to compromise; inflexible > **uncompromisingly** *adv*

uncompromising *adj* = inflexible, strict, rigid, firm, tough, inexorable, intransigent, unbending

unconcerned *adj* 1 not interested in something and not wanting to become involved 2 not worried or troubled > **unconcernedly** (un-kon-**sern**-id-lee) *adv*

unconditional *adj* without conditions or limitations: *an unconditional ceasefire* > **unconditionally** *adv*

unconditional *adj* = absolute, full, complete, total, positive (*informal*), entire, outright, unlimited; ≠ qualified

unconscionable *adj* 1 unscrupulous or unprincipled: *an unconscionable charmer* 2 excessive in amount or degree: *an unconscionable number of social obligations*

unconscious *adj* 1 unable to notice or respond to things which one would normally be aware of through the senses; insensible or comatose 2 not aware of one's actions or behaviour: *unconscious of his failure* 3 not realized or intended: *unconscious duplicity* 4 coming from or produced by the unconscious: *unconscious mental processes* ▶ *n* 5 *psychoanalysis* the part of the mind containing instincts, impulses, and ideas that are not available for direct examination > **unconsciously** *adv* > **unconsciousness** *n*

unconscious *adj* 1 = senseless, knocked out, out cold (*informal*), out, stunned, dazed, in a coma, stupefied; ≠ awake 2 = unaware, ignorant, oblivious, unknowing; ≠ aware 3 = unintentional, unwitting, inadvertent, accidental; ≠ intentional

uncooperative *adj* not willing to help other people with what they are trying to do

uncouth *adj* lacking in good manners, refinement, or grace

uncover *vb* 1 to remove the cover or top from 2 to reveal or disclose: *they have uncovered a plot to overthrow the government* > **uncovered** *adj*

uncover *vb* 1 = open, unveil, unwrap, show, strip, expose, bare, lay bare 2 = reveal, expose, disclose, divulge, make known; ≠ conceal

unction *n* 1 *chiefly RC Church & Eastern churches* the act of anointing with oil in sacramental ceremonies 2 oily charm 3 an ointment 4 anything soothing

unctuous *adj* pretending to be kind and concerned but obviously not sincere

undecided *adj* 1 not having made up one's mind 2 (of an issue or problem) not agreed or decided upon

undeniable *adj* 1 unquestionably true 2 of unquestionable excellence: *of undeniable character* > **undeniably** *adv*

under *prep* 1 directly below; on, to, or beneath the underside or base of: *under the bed* 2 less than: *in just under an hour* 3 lower in rank than: *under a general* 4 subject to the supervision, control, or influence of: *under communism for 45 years* 5 in or subject to certain circumstances or conditions:

u

the bridge is still under construction; under battle conditions **6** in (a specified category): he had filed Kafka's 'The Trial' under crime stories **7** known by: under their own names **8** planted with: a field under corn **9** powered by: under sail ▸ adv **10** below; to a position underneath

under prep **1** = below, beneath, underneath; ≠ over **3** = subordinate to, subject to, governed by, secondary to ▸ adv = below, down, beneath; ≠ up

under- prefix **1** below or beneath: underarm; underground **2** insufficient or insufficiently: underemployed **3** of lesser importance or lower rank: undersecretary **4** indicating secrecy or deception: underhand

underage adj below the required or standard age, usually below the legal age for voting or for drinking alcohol: underage sex

underarm adj **1** sport denoting a style of throwing, bowling, or serving in which the hand is swung below shoulder level **2** below the arm ▸ adv **3** in an underarm style

undercarriage n **1** the wheels, shock absorbers, and struts that support an aircraft on the ground and enable it to take off and land **2** the framework supporting the body of a vehicle

underclass n a class beneath the usual social scale consisting of the most disadvantaged people, such as the long-term unemployed

undercoat n **1** a coat of paint applied before the top coat **2** zool a layer of soft fur beneath the outer fur of animals such as the otter ▸ vb **3** to apply an undercoat to a surface

undercover adj done or acting in secret: an undercover investigation

undercover adj = secret, covert, private, hidden, concealed; ≠ open

undercurrent n **1** a current that is not apparent at the surface **2** an underlying opinion or emotion

undercut vb **-cutting, -cut 1** to charge less than a competitor in order to obtain trade **2** to undermine or render less effective: the latest fighting undercuts diplomatic attempts to find a peaceful solution **3** to cut away the under part of something

underdog n a person or team in a weak or underprivileged position

underdog n = weaker party, little fellow (informal), outsider

underdone adj insufficiently or lightly cooked

underestimate vb **-mating, -mated 1** to make too low an estimate of: the trust had underestimated the cost of work **2** to not be aware or take account of the full abilities or potential of: the police had underestimated him ▸ n **3** too low an estimate
> **underestimation** n

underestimate vb **1** = underrate, undervalue, belittle; ≠ overrate
2 = undervalue, understate, diminish, play down, minimize, downgrade, miscalculate, trivialize; ≠ overestimate

underfoot adv **1** underneath the feet; on the ground **2 trample** or **crush underfoot A** to damage or destroy by stepping on **B** to treat with contempt

undergarment n a garment worn under clothes

undergo vb **-goes, -going, -went, -gone** to experience, endure, or sustain: he underwent a three-hour operation

undergo vb = experience, go through, stand, suffer, bear, sustain, endure

undergraduate n a person studying in a university for a first degree

underground adv **1** below ground level: moles digging underground **2** secretly: several political parties had to operate underground for many years ▸ adj **3** beneath the ground: an underground bunker **4** secret; clandestine: an underground organization **5** (of art, film, music, etc.) avant-garde, experimental, or subversive ▸ n **6** a movement dedicated to overthrowing a government or occupation forces **7** (often preceded by the) an electric passenger railway operated in underground tunnels

underground adj **3** = subterranean, basement, lower-level, sunken, covered, buried, subterrestrial **4** = secret, covert, hidden, guerrilla, revolutionary, confidential, dissident, closet ▸ n **6 the underground** = the Resistance, partisans, freedom fighters **7 the underground** = the tube (Brit), the subway, the metro

undergrowth n small trees and bushes growing beneath taller trees in a wood or forest

underhand adj also **underhanded 1** sly, deceitful, and secretive **2** sport same as **underarm** ▸ adv **3** in an underhand manner or style

underlie vb **-lying, -lay, -lain 1** to lie or be placed under **2** to be the foundation, cause, or basis of: the basic unity which underlies all religion

underline vb **-lining, -lined 1** to put a line under **2** to emphasize

underline vb **1** = underscore, mark **2** = emphasize, stress, highlight, accentuate; ≠ minimize

underling n derogatory a subordinate

underlying adj **1** not obvious but detectable: the deeper and underlying aim of her travels **2** fundamental; basic: an underlying belief **3** lying under: the underlying layers of the skin

underlying adj **2** = fundamental, basic, prime, primary, elementary, intrinsic

undermine vb -mining, -mined 1 to weaken gradually or insidiously: *morphia had undermined his grasp of reality* 2 (of the sea or wind) to wear away the base of cliffs

> **undermine** vb 1 = weaken, sabotage, subvert, compromise, disable; ≠ reinforce

underneath prep 1 under or beneath: *a table underneath an olive tree* ▸ adv 2 under or beneath: *the chest of drawers was scratched underneath* ▸ adj 3 lower ▸ n 4 a lower part or surface

underpants pl n a man's undergarment covering the body from the waist or hips to the thighs

underpass n 1 a section of a road that passes under another road or a railway line 2 a subway for pedestrians

underpin vb -pinning, -pinned 1 to give strength or support to: *the principles that underpin his political convictions* 2 to support from beneath with a prop: *to underpin a wall* > **underpinning** n

underprivileged adj 1 lacking the rights and advantages of other members of society; deprived ▸ n 2 **the underprivileged** underprivileged people regarded as a group

underrate vb -rating, -rated to not be aware or take account of the full abilities or potential of > **underrated** adj

underseal n 1 a special coating applied to the underside of a motor vehicle to prevent corrosion ▸ vb 2 to apply such a coating to a motor vehicle

underside n the bottom or lower surface

understand vb -standing, -stood 1 to know and comprehend the nature or meaning of: *I understand what you are saying* 2 to know what is happening or why it is happening: *in order to understand the problems that can occur* 3 to assume, infer, or believe: *I understand he is based in this town* 4 to know how to translate or read: *don't you understand Russian?* 5 to be sympathetic to or compatible with: *she needed him to understand her completely* > **understandable** adj > **understandably** adv

> **understand** vb 1, 2 = comprehend, get, take in, perceive, grasp, see, follow, realize 3 = believe, gather, think, see, suppose, notice, assume, fancy

understanding n 1 the ability to learn, judge, or make decisions 2 personal opinion or interpretation of a subject: *my understanding of what he said* 3 a mutual agreement, usually an informal or private one ▸ adj 4 kind, sympathetic, or tolerant towards people

> **understanding** n 1 = perception, knowledge, grasp, sense, know-how (*informal*), judgment, awareness, appreciation; ≠ ignorance 2 = belief, view, opinion, impression, interpretation, feeling, idea, notion 3 = agreement, deal (*informal*), promise,

arrangement, accord, contract, bond, pledge; ≠ disagreement ▸ adj = sympathetic, kind, compassionate, considerate, patient, sensitive, tolerant; ≠ unsympathetic

understate vb -stating, -stated 1 to describe or portray something in restrained terms, often to obtain an ironic effect 2 to state that something, such as a number, is less than it is > **understatement** n

understudy n, pl -studies 1 an actor who studies a part so as to be able to replace the usual actor if necessary 2 anyone who is trained to take the place of another if necessary ▸ vb -studies, -studying, -studied 3 to act as an understudy to

undertake vb -taking, -took, -taken 1 to agree to or commit oneself to something or to do something: *I undertook the worst job in gardening* 2 to promise to do something

> **undertake** vb 2 = agree, promise, contract, guarantee, engage, pledge

undertaker n a person whose job is to look after the bodies of people who have died and to organize funerals

undertaking n 1 a task or enterprise 2 an agreement to do something 3 *informal* the practice of overtaking on an inner lane a vehicle which is travelling in an outer lane

> **undertaking** n 1 = task, business, operation, project, attempt, effort, affair, venture 2 = promise, commitment, pledge, word, vow, assurance

undertone n 1 a quiet tone of voice 2 something which suggests an underlying quality or feeling: *an undertone of anger*

undertow n a strong undercurrent flowing in a different direction from the surface current, such as in the sea

underwater adj 1 situated, occurring, or for use under the surface of the sea, a lake, or a river ▸ adv 2 beneath the surface of the sea, a lake, or a river

underwear n clothing worn under other garments, usually next to the skin

> **underwear** n = underclothes, lingerie, undies (*informal*), undergarments, underthings, broekies (*S African informal*), underdaks (*Austral slang*)

underworld n 1 criminals and their associates 2 *classical myth* the regions below the earth's surface regarded as the abode of the dead

> **underworld** n 1 = criminals, gangsters, organized crime, gangland (*informal*) 2 = nether world, Hades, nether regions

underwrite vb -writing, -wrote, -written 1 to accept financial responsibility for a commercial project or enterprise 2 to sign and issue an

u

insurance policy, thus accepting liability **3** to support › **underwriter** n

underwrite vb **1** = finance, back, fund, guarantee, sponsor, insure, ratify, subsidize

undesirable adj **1** not desirable or pleasant; objectionable ▸ n **2** a person considered undesirable

undesirable adj = unwanted, unwelcome, disagreeable, objectionable, unacceptable, unsuitable, unattractive, distasteful; ≠ desirable

undisclosed adj not made known or revealed: *the family business was sold for an undisclosed sum*

undo vb **-does, -doing, -did, -done 1** to open, unwrap or untie **2** to reverse the effects of: *all the work of the congress would be undone* **3** to cause the downfall of

undo vb **1** = open, unfasten, loose, untie, unbutton, disentangle **2** = reverse, cancel, offset, neutralize, invalidate, annul **3** = ruin, defeat, destroy, wreck, shatter, upset, undermine, overturn

undoing n **1** ruin; downfall **2** the cause of someone's downfall: *his confidence was his undoing*

undone¹ adj not done or completed; unfinished

undone adj = unfinished, left, neglected, omitted, unfulfilled, unperformed; ≠ finished

undone² adj **1** ruined; destroyed **2** unfastened; untied

undoubted adj beyond doubt; certain or indisputable › **undoubtedly** adv

undue adj greater than is reasonable; excessive: *undue attention*

undulate vb **-lating, -lated 1** to move gently and slowly from side to side or up and down **2** to have a wavy shape or appearance › **undulation** n

unduly adv excessively

undying adj never ending; eternal

unearth vb **1** to discover by searching **2** to dig up out of the earth

unearth vb **1** = discover, find, reveal, expose, uncover **2** = dig up, excavate, exhume, dredge up (*informal*)

unearthly adj **1** strange, unnatural, or eerie: *unearthly beauty* **2** ridiculous or unreasonable: *the unearthly hour of seven in the morning* › **unearthliness** n

unearthly adj **1** = eerie, strange, supernatural, ghostly, weird, phantom, uncanny, spooky (*informal*)

unease n **1** anxiety or nervousness: *my unease grew when she was not back by midnight* **2** dissatisfaction or tension: *unease about the government's handling of the affair*

uneasy adj **1** (of a person) anxious or apprehensive **2** (of a condition) precarious or insecure: *an uneasy peace* **3** (of a thought or feeling) disquieting › **uneasily** adv › **uneasiness** n

uneasy adj **1** = anxious, worried, troubled, nervous, disturbed, uncomfortable, edgy, perturbed; ≠ relaxed **2** = precarious, strained, uncomfortable, tense, awkward, shaky, insecure

unemployed adj **1** without paid employment; out of work **2** not being used; idle ▸ pl n **3** people who are out of work: *the long-term unemployed*

unemployed adj **1** = out of work, redundant, laid off, jobless, idle; ≠ working

unemployment n **1** the condition of being unemployed **2** the number of unemployed workers: *unemployment rose again last month*

unequivocal adj completely clear in meaning; unambiguous › **unequivocally** adv

unerring adj never mistaken; consistently accurate

unfailing adj continuous or reliable: *his unfailing enthusiasm* › **unfailingly** adv

unfair adj **1** unequal or unjust **2** dishonest or unethical › **unfairly** adv › **unfairness** n

unfair adj **1** = biased, prejudiced, unjust, one-sided, partial, partisan, bigoted **2** = unscrupulous, dishonest, unethical, wrongful, unsporting; ≠ ethical

unfaithful adj **1** having sex with someone other than one's regular partner **2** not true to a promise or vow › **unfaithfulness** n

unfeeling adj without sympathy; callous

unfit adj **1** unqualified for or incapable of a particular role or task: *an unfit mother; he was unfit to drive* **2** unsuitable: *this meat is unfit for human consumption* **3** in poor physical condition

unfit adj **1** = incapable, inadequate, incompetent, no good, useless (*informal*), unqualified; ≠ capable **2** = unsuitable, inadequate, useless, unsuited; ≠ suitable **3** = out of shape, feeble, unhealthy, flabby, in poor condition; ≠ healthy

unflappable adj informal (of a person) not easily upset › **unflappability** n

unfold vb **1** to open or spread out from a folded state **2** to reveal or be revealed: *a terrible truth unfolds* **3** to develop or be developed: *the novel unfolds through their recollections*

unfold vb **1** = open, spread out, undo, expand, unfurl, unwrap, unroll **2** = reveal, tell, present, show, disclose, uncover, divulge, make known

unfollow vb to stop following (a person) on a social networking site

unforgettable adj making such a strong impression that it is impossible to forget › **unforgettably** adv

unfortunate *adj* **1** caused or accompanied by bad luck: *an unfortunate coincidence* **2** having bad luck: *my unfortunate daughter* **3** regrettable or unsuitable: *an unfortunate choice of phrase* ▸ *n* **4** an unlucky person > **unfortunately** *adv*

unfortunate *adj* **1** = disastrous, calamitous, adverse, ill-fated; ≠ opportune **2** = unlucky, unhappy, doomed, cursed, unsuccessful, hapless, wretched; ≠ fortunate **3** = regrettable, deplorable, lamentable, unsuitable, unbecoming; ≠ becoming

unfounded *adj* (of ideas, fears, or allegations) not based on facts or evidence

unfrock *vb* to deprive (a person in holy orders) of the status of a priest

ungainly *adj* **-lier, -liest** lacking grace when moving > **ungainliness** *n*

ungodly *adj* **-lier, -liest** **1** wicked or sinful **2** *informal* unreasonable or outrageous: *at this ungodly hour* > **ungodliness** *n*

ungrateful *adj* not showing or offering thanks for a favour or compliment

unguarded *adj* **1** unprotected **2** open or frank: *one unguarded briefing* **3** incautious or careless: *an unguarded moment*

unhappy *adj* **-pier, -piest** **1** sad or depressed **2** unfortunate or wretched > **unhappily** *adv* > **unhappiness** *n*

unhappy *adj* **1** = sad, depressed, miserable, blue, melancholy, mournful, dejected, despondent; ≠ happy **2** = unlucky, unfortunate, hapless, cursed, wretched, ill-fated; ≠ fortunate

unhealthy *adj* **-healthier, -healthiest** **1** likely to cause illness or poor health: *unhealthy foods such as hamburger and chips* **2** not very fit or well **3** caused by or looking as if caused by poor health: *a thin unhealthy look about him* **4** morbid or unwholesome: *an unhealthy interest in computer fraud* > **unhealthiness** *n*

unhealthy *adj* **1** = harmful, detrimental, unwholesome, insanitary, insalubrious; ≠ beneficial **2** = sick, sickly, unwell, delicate, crook (*Austral, NZ informal*), ailing, frail, feeble, invalid; ≠ well

unhinge *vb* **-hinging, -hinged** to make a person mentally unbalanced > **unhinged** *adj*

uni *n* *Brit, Austral & NZ informal* short for **university**

uni- *combining form* of, consisting of, or having only one: *unilateral*

unicorn *n* a legendary creature resembling a white horse with one horn growing from its forehead

uniform *n* **1** a special identifying set of clothes for the members of an organization, such as soldiers ▸ *adj* **2** regular and even throughout: *the mixture must be beaten to a uniform consistency* **3** alike or like: *uniform green metal filing cabinets* > **uniformity** *n* > **uniformly** *adv*

uniform *n* = regalia, suit, livery, colours, habit ▸ *adj* **2** = consistent, unvarying, similar, even, same, matching, regular, constant; ≠ varying **3** = alike, similar, like, same, equal

unify *vb* **-fies, -fying, -fied** to make or become one; unite > **unification** *n*

unify *vb* = unite, join, combine, merge, consolidate, confederate, amalgamate; ≠ divide

unilateral *adj* made or done by only one person or group: *unilateral action* > **unilaterally** *adv* > **unilateralism** *n*

unimpeachable *adj* completely honest and reliable

uninterested *adj* having or showing no interest in someone or something

union *n* **1** the act of merging two or more things to become one, or the state of being merged in such a way **2** short for **trade union** **3** an association of individuals or groups for a common purpose: *the Scripture Union* **4** **A** an association or society: *the Students' union* **B** the buildings of such an organization **5** marriage or sexual intercourse **6** *maths* a set containing all the members of two given sets **7** (in 19th-century England) a workhouse maintained by a number of parishes ▸ *adj* **8** of a trade union

union *n* **1** = joining, uniting, unification, combination, coalition, merger, mixture, blend **3** = alliance, league, association, coalition, federation, confederacy

unionize *or* **-ise** *vb* **-izing, -ized** *or* **-ising, -ised** to organize workers into a trade union > **unionization** *or* **-isation** *n*

Union Jack *or* **Union flag** *n* the national flag of the United Kingdom, combining the crosses of Saint George, Saint Andrew, and Saint Patrick

unique (yew-neek) *adj* **1** being the only one of a particular type **2** **unique to** concerning or belonging to a particular person, thing, or group: *certain dishes are unique to this restaurant* **3** without equal or like **4** *informal* remarkable > **uniquely** *adv*

unique *adj* **1** = distinct, special, exclusive, peculiar, only, single, lone, solitary **3** = unparalleled, unmatched, unequalled, matchless, without equal

unisex *adj* designed for use by both men and women

unison *n* **1** **in unison** at the same time as another person or other people: *smiling and nodding in unison* **2** (usually preceded by *in*) complete agreement: *to act in unison* **3** *music* a style, technique, or passage in which all the performers sing or play the same notes at the same time

u

unit n 1 a single undivided entity or whole 2 a group or individual regarded as a basic element of a larger whole: *the clan was the basic unit of Highland society* 3 a mechanical part or small device that does a particular job: *a waste disposal unit* 4 a team of people that performs a specific function, and often also their buildings and equipment: *a combat unit* 5 a standard amount of a physical quantity, such as length or energy, used to express magnitudes of that quantity: *the year as a unit of time* 6 *maths* the digit or position immediately to the left of the decimal point 7 a piece of furniture designed to be fitted with other similar pieces: *bedroom units* 8 NZ a self-propelled railcar

unit n 1 = entity, whole, item, feature 2 = part, section, segment, class, element, component, constituent 4 = section, company, group, force, detail, division, cell, squad 5 = measure, quantity, measurement

Unitarian n 1 a person who believes that God is one being and rejects the Trinity ▸ *adj* 2 of Unitarians or Unitarianism > **Unitarianism** n
unitary *adj* 1 consisting of a single undivided whole: *a unitary state* 2 of a unit or units
unite *vb* **uniting, united** 1 to make or become an integrated whole: *conception occurs when a sperm unites with the egg* 2 to form an association or alliance: *the opposition parties united to fight against privatization* 3 to possess (a combination of qualities) at the same time: *he manages to unite charm and ruthlessness*

unite *vb* **1, 3** = join, link, combine, couple, blend, merge, unify, fuse; ≠ separate 2 = cooperate, ally, join forces, band, pool, collaborate; ≠ split

unit trust n an investment trust that issues units for public sale and invests the money in many different businesses
unity n, pl **-ties** 1 the state of being one 2 mutual agreement: *unity of intention* 3 the state of being a single thing that is composed of separate parts, organizations, etc.: *moves towards church unity* 4 *maths* the number or numeral one

unity n 1 = wholeness, integrity, oneness, union, entity, singleness; ≠ disunity 2 = agreement, accord, consensus, harmony, solidarity, unison, assent, concord; ≠ disagreement 3 = union, unification, coalition, federation, integration, confederation, amalgamation

universal *adj* 1 of or relating to everyone in the world or everyone in a particular place or society: *the introduction of universal primary education* 2 of, relating to, or affecting the entire world or universe: *the universal laws of physics* 3 true and relevant at all times and in all situations: *there may be no single universal solution* ▸ *n* 4 something which exists or is true in all places and all situations: *universals such as beauty and justice* > **universality** n > **universally** *adv*

universal *adj* 1 = widespread, general, common, whole, total, unlimited, overarching 2 = global, worldwide, international, pandemic

universe n 1 the whole of all existing matter, energy, and space 2 the world

universe n 1 = cosmos, space, creation, nature, heavens, macrocosm, all existence

university n, pl **-ties** 1 an institution of higher education with authority to award degrees 2 the buildings, members, staff, or campus of a university
unkempt *adj* 1 (of the hair) uncombed or dishevelled 2 untidy or slovenly: *an unkempt appearance*
unknown *adj* 1 not known, understood, or recognized 2 not famous: *a young and then unknown actor* 3 **unknown quantity** a person or thing whose action or effect is unknown or unpredictable ▸ *n* 4 an unknown person, quantity, or thing ▸ *adv* 5 **unknown to someone** without someone being aware: *unknown to him, the starboard engine had dropped off*

unknown *adj* 1 = strange, new, undiscovered, uncharted, unexplored, virgin, remote, alien 2 = obscure, humble, unfamiliar; ≠ famous

unleaded *adj* (of petrol) containing less tetraethyl lead, in order to reduce environmental pollution
unleash *vb* to set loose or cause (something bad): *to unleash war*
unless *conj* except under the circumstances that; except on the condition that: *you can't get in unless you can prove you're over eighteen*
unlike *adj* 1 not similar; different ▸ *prep* 2 not like or typical of: *unlike his brother, he could not control his weight* > **unlikeness** n

unlike *prep* = different from, dissimilar to, distinct from, unequal to; ≠ similar to

unlikely *adj* not likely; improbable > **unlikeliness** n

unlikely *adj* = improbable, doubtful, remote, slight, faint; ≠ probable

unload *vb* 1 to remove cargo from a ship, lorry, or plane 2 to express worries or problems by telling someone about them 3 to remove the ammunition from a gun

unload *vb* 1 = empty, clear, unpack, dump, discharge 2 = unburden

unmanned *adj* 1 having no personnel or crew: *the border posts were unmanned* 2 (of an aircraft or spacecraft) operated by automatic or remote control
unmask *vb* 1 to remove the mask or disguise from 2 to expose or reveal the true nature or character of

unmentionable *adj* unsuitable as a topic of conversation

unmistakable *or* **unmistakeable** *adj* clear or unambiguous > **unmistakably** *or* **unmistakeably** *adv*

unmitigated *adj* **1** not reduced or lessened in severity or intensity **2** total and complete: *unmitigated boredom*

unmoved *adj* not affected by emotion; indifferent

unnatural *adj* **1** strange and slightly frightening because it is not usual; abnormal: *an unnatural silence* **2** not in accordance with accepted standards of behaviour: *an unnatural relationship* **3** affected or forced: *a determined smile which seemed unnatural* **4** inhuman or monstrous: *unnatural evils* > **unnaturally** *adv*

> **unnatural** *adj* **1** = abnormal, odd, strange, unusual, extraordinary, perverted, queer (*old-fashioned*), irregular; ≠ normal **3** = false, forced, artificial, affected, stiff, feigned, stilted, insincere; ≠ genuine

unnerve *vb* **-nerving, -nerved** to cause to lose courage, confidence, or self-control: *he unnerves me* > **unnerving** *adj*

unnumbered *adj* **1** countless; too many to count **2** not counted or given a number

unorthodox *adj* **1** (of ideas, methods, etc.) unconventional and not generally accepted **2** (of a person) not conventional in beliefs, behaviour, etc.

unpack *vb* **1** to remove the packed contents of a case **2** to take something out of a packed container

unparalleled *adj* not equalled; supreme

unpick *vb* to undo the stitches of a piece of sewing

unpleasant *adj* not pleasant or agreeable > **unpleasantly** *adv* > **unpleasantness** *n*

> **unpleasant** *adj* = nasty, bad, horrid (*informal*), distasteful, displeasing, objectionable, disagreeable; ≠ nice

unprecedented *adj* never having happened before: *an unprecedented decision*

unprintable *adj* unsuitable for printing for reasons of obscenity, libel, or indecency

unprofessional *adj* not behaving according to the standards expected of a member of a particular profession

unqualified *adj* **1** lacking the necessary qualifications **2** having no conditions or limitations: *an unqualified denial* **3** total or complete: *unqualified admiration*

unravel *vb* **-velling, -velled** *or US* **-veling, -veled** **1** to separate something knitted or woven into individual strands **2** to become separated into individual strands **3** to explain or solve: *we unravelled the secrets*

> **unravel** *vb* **1** = undo, separate, disentangle, free, unwind, untangle **3** = solve, explain, work out, resolve, figure out (*informal*)

unreasonable *adj* **1** unfair and excessive: *an unreasonable request* **2** refusing to listen to reason > **unreasonably** *adv*

unremitting *adj* never slackening or stopping

unrequited *adj* (of love) not returned

unrest *n* **1** a rebellious state of discontent **2** an uneasy or troubled state

> **unrest** *n* = discontent, rebellion, protest, strife, agitation, discord, sedition, dissension; ≠ peace

unrivalled *or US* **unrivaled** *adj* having no equal; matchless

unroll *vb* **1** to open out or unwind: *I unrolled the map* **2** (of a series of events or period of time) to happen or be revealed or remembered one after the other

unruly *adj* **-lier, -liest** difficult to control or organize; disobedient or undisciplined > **unruliness** *n*

unsavoury *or US* **unsavory** *adj* objectionable or distasteful: *an unsavoury divorce*

unscathed *adj* not harmed or injured

unscrupulous *adj* prepared to act in a dishonest or immoral manner

unseat *vb* **1** to throw or displace from a seat or saddle **2** to depose from office or position

unsettled *adj* **1** lacking order or stability: *an unsettled time* **2** disturbed and restless: *your child will feel unsettled and insecure* **3** constantly changing or moving from place to place: *his wandering unsettled life* **4** (of an argument or dispute) not resolved **5** (of a debt or bill) not yet paid

> **unsettled** *adj* **1** = unstable, shaky, insecure, disorderly, unsteady **2** = restless, tense, shaken, confused, disturbed, anxious, agitated, flustered, adrenalized **3** = inconstant, changing, variable, uncertain

unsightly *adj* unpleasant to look at; ugly > **unsightliness** *n*

unsociable *adj* (of a person) not fond of the company of other people

unsocial *adj* **1** not fond of the company of other people **2** (of the hours of work of a job) falling outside the normal working day

unsound *adj* **1** unhealthy or unstable: *of unsound mind* **2** based on faulty ideas: *unsound judgment* **3** not firm: *unsound foundations* **4** not financially reliable: *his business plan was unsound*

unspeakable *adj* **1** incapable of expression in words: *unspeakable gratitude* **2** indescribably bad or evil: *unspeakable atrocities* > **unspeakably** *adv*

unstable *adj* **1** not firmly fixed and likely to wobble or fall: *an unstable pile of books* **2** likely to change suddenly and create difficulties or danger: *the unstable political climate* **3** (of a person) having abrupt changes of mood or behaviour **4** *chem & physics* readily decomposing

u

unstable *adj* 1 = insecure, shaky, precarious, unsettled, wobbly, tottering, unsteady 2 = changeable, volatile, unpredictable, variable, fluctuating, fitful, inconstant; ≠ constant 3 = unpredictable, irrational, erratic, inconsistent, temperamental, capricious, changeable; ≠ level-headed

unstinting *adj* generous and gladly given: *unstinting praise*

unsubscribe *vb* **-scribing, -scribed** to cancel a subscription, esp. to an online service

unsuitable *adj* not right or appropriate for a particular purpose

unsuited *adj* 1 not appropriate for a particular task or situation: *a likeable man unsuited to a military career* 2 (of a couple) having different personalities or tastes and unlikely to form a lasting relationship: *they are totally unsuited to each other*

unsung *adj* not appreciated or honoured: *an unsung hero*

unswerving *adj* not turning aside; constant

unsympathetic *adj* 1 not feeling or showing sympathy 2 unpleasant and unlikeable 3 (foll. by *to*) opposed or hostile to

unthinkable *adj* 1 so shocking or unpleasant that one cannot believe it to be true 2 unimaginable or inconceivable

unthinkable *adj* 1 = impossible, out of the question, inconceivable, absurd, unreasonable 2 = inconceivable, incredible, unimaginable

untidy *adj* **-dier, -diest** not neat; messy and disordered > **untidily** *adv* > **untidiness** *n*

untie *vb* **-tying, -tied** to unfasten or free something that is tied

until *conj* 1 up to a time that: *he lifted the wire until it was taut* 2 before (a time or event): *I won't speak to him until he apologizes* ▸ *prep* 3 (often preceded by *up*) in or throughout the period before: *up until then I'd never thought about having kids* 4 before: *Baker does not get to Israel until Sunday*

until *conj* 1 = till, up to, up till, up to the time, as late as ▸ *prep* 3 = till, up to, up till, up to the time, as late as 4 = before, up to, prior to, in advance of, previous to, pre-

untimely *adj* 1 occurring before the expected or normal time: *his untimely death* 2 inappropriate to the occasion or time: *an untimely idea to raise at the United Nations* > **untimeliness** *n*

unto *prep archaic* to

untold *adj* 1 incapable of description: *untold misery* 2 incalculably great in number or quantity: *untold millions* 3 not told

untold *adj* 1 = indescribable, unthinkable, unimaginable, undreamed of, unutterable, inexpressible 2 = countless, incalculable, innumerable, myriad, numberless, uncountable

untouchable *adj* 1 above criticism, suspicion or punishment 2 unable to be touched ▸ *n offensive* 3 a member of the lowest class in India

untoward *adj* 1 causing misfortune or annoyance 2 unfavourable: *untoward reactions* 3 out of the ordinary; out of the way: *nothing untoward had happened*

untrue *adj* 1 incorrect or false 2 disloyal or unfaithful

untrue *adj* 1 = false, lying, wrong, mistaken, incorrect, inaccurate, dishonest, deceptive; ≠ true 2 = unfaithful, disloyal, deceitful, treacherous, faithless, false, untrustworthy, inconstant; ≠ faithful

untruth *n* a statement that is not true; lie

unusual *adj* uncommon or extraordinary > **unusually** *adv*

unusual *adj* = rare, odd, strange, extraordinary, different, curious, queer (*old-fashioned*), uncommon; ≠ common

unutterable *adj* incapable of being expressed in words > **unutterably** *adv*

unvarnished *adj* not elaborated upon; plain: *an unvarnished account of literary life*

unveil *vb* 1 to ceremonially remove the cover from a new picture, statue, plaque, etc. 2 to make public a secret 3 to remove the veil from one's own or another person's face

unveiling *n* 1 a ceremony involving the removal of a veil covering a statue 2 the presentation of something for the first time

unwarranted *adj* not justified or necessary

unwieldy *adj* too heavy, large, or awkward to be easily handled

unwind *vb* **-winding, -wound** 1 to slacken, undo, or unravel: *Paul started to unwind the bandage* 2 to relax after a busy or tense time: *we go out to unwind after work*

unwitting *adj* 1 not intentional 2 not knowing or conscious > **unwittingly** *adv*

unwonted *adj* out of the ordinary; unusual

unworthy *adj* 1 not deserving or meriting: *a person deemed unworthy of membership* 2 (often foll. by *of*) beneath the level considered befitting (to): *unworthy of a prime minister* 3 lacking merit or value > **unworthiness** *n*

unwrap *vb* **-wrapping, -wrapped** to remove the wrapping from something or (of something wrapped) to have the covering removed

unwritten *adj* 1 not printed or in writing 2 operating only through custom: *an unwritten code of conduct*

unzip *vb* **-zipping, -zipped** 1 to unfasten the zip of a garment or (of a zip or a garment with a zip) to become unfastened 2 to open (a data file that has been compressed)

up *prep* 1 indicating movement to a higher position: *go up the stairs* 2 at a higher or further level or position in or on: *a shop up the road* ▸ *adv* 3 to an upward, higher, or erect position: *the men*

u

straightened up from their digging **4** indicating readiness for an activity: *up and about* **5** indicating intensity or completion of an action: *he tore up the cheque* **6** to the place referred to or where the speaker is: *a man came up to me* **7** **A** to a more important place: *up to the city* **B** to a more northerly place: *pensioners who were going up to Norway* **c** to or at university **8** above the horizon: *the sun came up* **9** appearing for trial: *up before the judge* **10** having gained: *ten pounds up on the deal* **11** higher in price: *beer has gone up again* **12** **all up with someone** *informal* over or hopeless for someone **13** **something's up** *informal* something strange is happening **14** **up against** having to cope with: *look what we're up against now* **15** **up for** being a candidate or applicant for: *he's up for the job* **16** **up to** **A** occupied with; scheming: *she's up to no good* **B** dependent upon: *the decision is up to you* **c** equal to or capable of: *are you up to playing in the final?* **D** as far as: *up to his neck in mud* **E** as many as: *up to two years' credit* **F** comparable with: *not up to my usual standard* **17** **what's up?** *informal* **A** what is the matter? **B** what is happening? ▸ *adj* **18** of a high or higher position **19** out of bed: *aren't you up yet?* **20** (of a period of time) over or completed: *the examiner announced that their time was up* **21** of or relating to a train going to a more important place: *the up platform* ▸ *vb* **upping, upped 22** to increase or raise **23** **up and** *informal* to do something suddenly: *he upped and left her* ▸ *n* **24** a high point: *when the ups come along you have to enjoy them* **25** **on the up and up** **A** *Brit, Austral & NZ* on an upward trend: *our firm's on the up and up* **B** *US* trustworthy or honest

upbeat *adj* **1** *informal* cheerful and optimistic: *the upbeat atmosphere of a thriving metropolis* ▸ *n* **2** *music* **A** an unaccented beat **B** the upward gesture of a conductor's baton indicating this

> **upbeat** *adj* = cheerful, positive, optimistic, encouraging, hopeful, cheery

upbraid *vb* to scold or reproach
upbringing *n* the education of a person during his or her formative years

> **upbringing** *n* = education, training, rearing, raising

update *vb* **-dating, -dated 1** to bring up to date **2** inform; relay the most recent information to

> **update** *vb* **1** = bring up to date, improve, correct, renew, revise, upgrade, amend, overhaul, refresh

upend *vb* to turn or set or become turned or set on end
upfront *adj* **1** open and frank **2** (of money) paid at the beginning of a business arrangement ▸ *adv* **up front 3** at the front; (in sport) in attack: *Liverpool's strikers dominated up front* **4** at the beginning of a business arrangement; in advance: *we charge up front*

upgrade *vb* **-grading, -graded 1** to promote a person or job to a higher rank **2** to raise in value, importance, or esteem

> **upgrade** *vb* **1** = promote, raise, advance, boost, move up, elevate, kick upstairs (*informal*), give promotion to; ≠ demote **2** = improve, better, update, reform, add to, enhance, refurbish, renovate

upheaval *n* a strong, sudden, or violent disturbance

> **upheaval** *n* = disturbance, revolution, disorder, turmoil, disruption

uphill *adj* **1** sloping or leading upwards **2** requiring a great deal of effort: *an uphill struggle* ▸ *adv* **3** up a slope ▸ *n* **4** *S African* a difficulty

> **uphill** *adj* **1** = ascending, rising, upward, mounting, climbing; ≠ descending **2** = arduous, hard, taxing, difficult, tough, exhausting, gruelling, strenuous

uphold *vb* **-holding, -held 1** to maintain or defend against opposition **2** to give moral support to ▸ **upholder** *n*

> **uphold** *vb* **1** = confirm, endorse **2** = support, back, defend, aid, champion, maintain, promote, sustain

upholster *vb* to fit chairs or sofas with padding, springs, and covering ▸ **upholstered** *adj* ▸ **upholsterer** *n*
upholstery *n* the padding, springs, and covering of a chair or sofa
upkeep *n* **1** the act or process of keeping something in good repair **2** the cost of maintenance
upland *adj* of or in an area of high or relatively high ground: *an upland wilderness*
uplands *pl n* an area of high or relatively high ground: *the uplands of Nepal*
uplift *vb* **1** to raise or lift up **2** to raise morally or spiritually **3** *Scot* to collect or pick up ▸ *n* **4** the act or process of bettering moral, social, or cultural conditions ▸ *adj* **5** (of a bra) designed to lift and support the breasts ▸ **uplifting** *adj*

> **uplift** *vb* **2** = improve, better, raise, advance, inspire, refine, edify ▸ *n* = improvement, enlightenment, advancement, refinement, enhancement, enrichment, edification

upload *vb* **1** to transfer (data or a program) from one computer's memory into that of another ▸ *n* **2** a file transferred in such a way
upon *prep* **1** on **2** up and on: *they climbed upon his lap for comfort*
upper *adj* **1** higher or highest in physical position, wealth, rank, or status **2** **Upper** *geol* denoting the late part of a period or formation: *Upper Cretaceous* ▸ *n* **3** the part of a shoe above the sole **4** **on one's uppers** *Brit, Austral & NZ* very poor; penniless

> **upper** *adj* **1** = topmost, top; ≠ bottom

u

upper-case *adj* denoting capital letters as used in printed or typed matter

upper class *n* **1** the highest social class; aristocracy ▸ *adj* **upper-class 2** of the upper class

> **upper class** *adj* **upper-class** = aristocratic, noble, high-class, patrician, blue-blooded, highborn (*old-fashioned*)

upper crust *n Brit, Austral & NZ informal* the upper class

upper hand *n* the position of control: *the hardliners have gained the upper hand*

uppermost *adj* **1** highest in position, power, or importance ▸ *adv* **2** in or into the highest place or position

uppish *adj Brit informal* uppity

uppity *adj informal* snobbish, arrogant, or presumptuous

upright *adj* **1** vertical or erect **2** honest or just ▸ *adv* **3** vertically or in an erect position ▸ *n* **4** a vertical support, such as a post **5** the state of being vertical ▸ **uprightness** *n*

> **upright** *adj* **1** = vertical, straight, standing up, erect, perpendicular, bolt upright; ≠ horizontal **2** = honest, good, principled, just, ethical, honourable, righteous, conscientious; ≠ dishonourable

uprising *n* a revolt or rebellion

> **uprising** *n* = rebellion, rising, revolution, revolt, disturbance, mutiny, insurrection, insurgence

uproar *n* **1** a commotion or disturbance characterized by loud noise and confusion **2** angry public criticism or debates: *the decision to close the railway led to an uproar*

> **uproar** *n* **1** = commotion, noise, racket, riot, turmoil, mayhem, din, pandemonium **2** = protest, outrage, complaint, objection, fuss, stink (*informal*), outcry, furore

uproarious *adj* **1** very funny **2** (of laughter) loud and boisterous

uproot *vb* **1** to pull up by or as if by the roots **2** to displace (a person or people) from their native or usual surroundings **3** to remove or destroy utterly: *we must uproot all remnants of feudalism*

ups and downs *pl n* alternating periods of good and bad luck or high and low spirits

upscale *informal* ▸ *adj* (up-skale) **1** of or for the upper end of an economic or social scale; upmarket ▸ *vb* (up-skale) **-scaling, -scaled 2** to increase the scale of

upset *adj* **1** emotionally or physically disturbed or distressed ▸ *vb* **-setting, -set 2** to turn or tip over **3** to disrupt the normal state or progress of: *bad weather upset their plans* **4** to disturb mentally or emotionally **5** to make physically ill: *it still seems to upset my stomach* ▸ *n* **6** an unexpected defeat or reversal, as in a contest or plans

7 a disturbance or disorder of the emotions, mind, or body ▸ **upsetting** *adj*

> **upset** *adj* = distressed, shaken, disturbed, worried, troubled, hurt, bothered, unhappy ▸ *vb* **2** = tip over, overturn, capsize, knock over, spill **3** = mess up, spoil, disturb, change, confuse, disorder, unsettle, disorganize **4** = distress, trouble, disturb, worry, alarm, bother, grieve, agitate ▸ *n* **6** = reversal, shake-up (*informal*), defeat **7** = illness, complaint, disorder, bug (*informal*), sickness, malady

upshot *n* the final result or conclusion; outcome

upside down *adj* **1** with the bottom where the top would normally be; inverted **2** *informal* confused or jumbled ▸ *adv* **3** in an inverted fashion **4** in a chaotic manner or into a chaotic state: *recent events have turned many people's lives upside down*

> **upside down** *adj* **1** = inverted, overturned, upturned **2** = confused, disordered, chaotic, muddled, topsy-turvy, higgledy-piggledy (*informal*) ▸ *adv* = wrong side up

upstage *adv* **1** on, at, or to the rear of the stage ▸ *adj* **2** at the back half of the stage ▸ *vb* **-staging, -staged 3** to move upstage of another actor, forcing him or her to turn away from the audience **4** *informal* to draw attention to oneself and away from someone else

upstairs *adv* **1** to or on an upper floor of a building **2** *informal* to or into a higher rank or office ▸ *n* **3** an upper floor ▸ *adj* **4** situated on an upper floor: *an upstairs bedroom*

upstanding *adj* **1** of good character **2** upright and vigorous in build

upstart *n* a person who has risen suddenly to a position of power and behaves arrogantly

upstream *adv, adj* in or towards the higher part of a stream; against the current

upsurge *n* a rapid rise or swell

uptake *n* **1 quick** or **slow on the uptake** *informal* quick or slow to understand or learn **2** the use or consumption of something by a machine or part of the body: *the uptake of oxygen into the blood*

uptight *adj informal* **1** nervously tense, irritable, or angry **2** unable to express one's feelings

up-to-date *adj* modern or fashionable: *an up-to-date kitchen*

> **up-to-date** *adj* = modern, fashionable, trendy (*Brit informal*), current, stylish, in vogue, up-to-the-minute; ≠ out-of-date

upturn *n* **1** an upward trend or improvement ▸ *vb* **2** to turn or cause to turn over or upside down

upward *adj* **1** directed or moving towards a higher place or level ▸ *adv also* **upwards 2** from a lower to a higher place, level, or condition **3 upward** or **upwards of** more than (the stated figure): *a crowd estimated at upward of one hundred thousand people*

uranium (yew-rain-ee-um) *n* *chem* a radioactive silvery-white metallic element of the actinide series. It is used chiefly as a source of nuclear energy by fission of the radioisotope **uranium** 235. Symbol: **U**

Uranus *n* 1 *Greek myth* a god; the personification of the sky 2 the seventh planet from the sun

urban *adj* 1 of or living in a city or town 2 relating to modern pop music of African-American origin, such as hip-hop

> **urban** *adj* 1 = civic, city, town, metropolitan, municipal, dorp (*S African*)

urbane *adj* polite, elegant, and sophisticated in manner

urbanity *n* the quality of being urbane

urbanize *or* **-nise** *vb* **-nizing, -nized** *or* **-nising, -nised** to make a rural area more industrialized and urban > **urbanization** *or* **-nisation** *n*

urchin *n* 1 a mischievous child 2 See **sea urchin**

Urdu (oor-doo) *n* an Indic language of the Indo-European family which is an official language of Pakistan and is also spoken in India

urethra (yew-reeth-ra) *n* the tube that in most mammals carries urine from the bladder out of the body

urge *n* 1 a strong impulse, inner drive, or yearning ▶ *vb* **urging, urged** 2 to plead with or press someone to do something: *he urged his readers to do the same* 3 to advocate earnestly and persistently: *I have long urged this change* 4 (often foll. by *on*) to force or hasten onwards: *something very powerful urged him on*

> **urge** *n* = impulse, longing, wish, desire, drive, yearning, itch (*informal*), thirst; ≠ reluctance ▶ *vb* 2 = beg, exhort (*formal*), plead, implore, beseech, entreat 3 = advocate, recommend, advise, support, counsel; ≠ discourage

urgent *adj* 1 requiring speedy action or attention: *an urgent inquiry* 2 earnest and forceful: *she heard loud urgent voices in the corridor* > **urgency** *n* > **urgently** *adv*

> **urgent** *adj* 1 = crucial (*informal*), desperate, pressing, great, important, crying, critical, immediate; ≠ unimportant

urinal *n* 1 a sanitary fitting, used by men for urination 2 a room containing urinals

urinary *adj* *anatomy* of urine or the organs that secrete and pass urine

urinate *vb* **-nating, -nated** to excrete urine > **urination** *n*

urine *n* the pale yellow fluid excreted by the kidneys, containing waste products from the blood. It is stored in the bladder and discharged through the urethra

URL uniform resource locator: a standardized address of a location on the internet

urn *n* 1 a vaselike container, usually with a foot and a rounded body 2 a vase used as a container for the ashes of the dead 3 a large metal container, with a tap, used for making and holding tea or coffee

ursine *adj* of or like a bear

us *pron* (*objective*) 1 refers to the speaker or writer and another person or other people: *the bond between us* 2 refers to all people or people in general: *this table shows us the tides* 3 *informal* me: *give us a kiss!* 4 *formal* same as **me**: used by monarchs

US *or* **U.S.** United States

USA *or* **U.S.A.** United States of America

usable *adj* able to be used > **usability** *n*

usage *n* 1 regular or constant use: *a move to reduce pesticide usage* 2 the way in which a word is actually used in a language 3 a particular meaning or use that a word can have

> **usage** *n* 1 = use, operation, employment, running, control, management, handling

USB Universal Serial Bus: a standard for connection sockets on computers and other electronic equipment

USB drive *n* *computers* a small portable data storage device with a USB connection

use *vb* **using, used** 1 to put into service or action; employ for a given purpose: *use a garden fork to mix them together* 2 to choose or employ regularly: *what sort of toothpaste do you use?* 3 to take advantage of; exploit: *I used Jason and he used me* 4 to consume or expend: *a manufacturing plant uses 1000 tonnes of steel a month* ▶ *n* 5 the act or fact of using or being used: *large-scale use of pesticides* 6 the ability or permission to use 7 need or opportunity to use: *the Colombian government had no use for them* 8 usefulness or advantage: *there is no use in complaining* 9 the purpose for which something is used 10 **have no use for** A to have no need of B to have a contemptuous dislike for 11 **make use of** A to employ; use B to exploit (a person) > **user** *n*

> **use** *vb* 1 = employ, utilize, work, apply, operate, exercise, practise, resort to 3 = take advantage of, exploit, manipulate 4 = consume, exhaust, spend, run through, expend ▶ *n* 5 = usage, employment, operation, application 7, 9 = purpose, end, reason, object 8 = good, point, help, service, value, benefit, profit, advantage

use-by date *n* the date on packaged food after which it should not be sold

used *adj* second-hand: *it was a used car*

> **used** *adj* = second-hand, cast-off, nearly new, shopsoiled, preloved (*informal*); ≠ new

used to *adj* 1 accustomed to: *I am used to being a medical guinea pig* ▶ *vb* 2 used as an auxiliary to express habitual or accustomed actions or states taking place in the past but not continuing to be the case in the present: *he used to vanish into his studio for days*

> **used to** *adj* = accustomed to, familiar with

u

useful adj 1 able to be used advantageously or for several purposes 2 informal commendable or capable: a useful hurdler > **usefully** adv > **usefulness** n

> **useful** adj 1 = helpful, effective, valuable, practical, profitable, worthwhile, beneficial, fruitful; ≠ useless

useless adj 1 having no practical use 2 informal ineffectual, weak, or stupid: I'm useless at most things > **uselessly** adv > **uselessness** n

> **useless** adj 1 = pointless, futile, vain; ≠ worthwhile 2 = worthless, valueless, impractical, fruitless, unproductive, ineffectual, unsuitable; ≠ useful

user-friendly adj easy to familiarize oneself with, understand, and use

username n computers a name that someone uses for identification purposes when logging onto a computer or certain computer applications

usher n 1 an official who shows people to their seats, as in a church 2 a person who acts as doorkeeper in a court of law ▶ vb 3 to conduct or escort 4 (foll. by in) to happen immediately before something or cause it to happen; herald: the French Revolution ushered in a new age

> **usher** n = attendant, guide, doorman, escort, doorkeeper ▶ vb 3 = escort, lead, direct, guide, conduct

usherette n a woman assistant in a cinema, who shows people to their seats

USSR Union of Soviet Socialist Republics: a former state in E Europe and N Asia, covering the area now composed of Russia, Ukraine, Kazakhstan, and a number of smaller states

usual adj 1 of the most normal, frequent, or regular type: the usual assortment of stories 2 ordinary or commonplace events: the dirt was nothing out of the usual 3 **as usual** as happens normally 4 **the usual** informal the habitual or usual drink > **usually** adv

> **usual** adj = normal, customary, regular, general, common, standard, ordinary, typical; ≠ unusual

usurp (yewz-**zurp**) vb to seize a position or power without authority > **usurpation** n > **usurper** n

usury (yewz-yoor-ree) n, pl **-ries** old-fashioned 1 the practice of loaning money at an exorbitant rate of interest 2 an unlawfully high rate of interest > **usurer** n

ute n Austral & NZ informal a utility truck

utensil n a tool or container for practical use: cooking utensils

uterine adj of or affecting the womb

uterus (yew-ter-russ) n, pl **uteri** (yew-ter-rye) anatomy a hollow muscular organ in the pelvic cavity of female mammals, which houses the developing fetus; womb

utilitarian adj 1 useful rather than beautiful 2 of utilitarianism ▶ n 3 an advocate of utilitarianism

utilitarianism n ethics the doctrine that the right thing to do is that which brings about the greatest good for the greatest number

utility n, pl **-ties** 1 usefulness 2 something useful 3 a public service, such as water or electricity ▶ adj 4 designed for use rather than beauty: utility fabrics

> **utility** n 1 = usefulness, benefit, convenience, practicality, efficacy, serviceableness

utility room n a room with equipment for domestic work like washing and ironing

utility truck n Austral & NZ a small truck with an open body and low sides

utilize or **-lise** vb **-lizing**, **-lized** or **-lising**, **-lised** to make practical or worthwhile use of > **utilization** or **-lisation** n

> **utilize** or **-lise** vb = use, employ, deploy, take advantage of, make use of, put to use, bring into play, avail yourself of

utmost adj 1 of the greatest possible degree or amount: the utmost seriousness 2 at the furthest limit: the utmost point ▶ n 3 the greatest possible degree or amount: I was doing my utmost to comply

> **utmost** adj 1 = greatest, highest, maximum, supreme, paramount, pre-eminent 2 = farthest, extreme, last, final ▶ n = best, greatest, maximum, highest, hardest

Utopia (yew-**tope**-ee-a) n any real or imaginary society, place, or state considered to be perfect or ideal > **Utopian** adj

utter¹ vb 1 to express something in sounds or words: she hadn't uttered a single word 2 criminal law to put counterfeit money or forged cheques into circulation

> **utter** vb 1 = say, state, speak, voice, express, deliver, declare, mouth

utter² adj total or absolute: utter amazement > **utterly** adv

> **utter** adj = absolute, complete, total, sheer, outright, thorough, downright (derogatory), unmitigated

utterance n 1 something expressed in speech or writing 2 the expression in words of ideas, thoughts, or feelings

uttermost adj, n same as **utmost**

U-turn n 1 a turn, made by a vehicle, in the shape of a U, resulting in a reversal of direction 2 a complete change in policy

UV ultraviolet

uvula (yew-view-la) n the small fleshy part of the soft palate that hangs in the back of the throat > **uvular** adj

uxorious (ux-or-ee-uss) adj excessively fond of or dependent on one's wife

u

Vv

V 1 *chem* vanadium **2** volt **3** the Roman numeral for five

v. 1 verb **2** verse **3** versus **4** volume

vacancy *n*, *pl* **-cies 1** an unoccupied job or position: *he had heard of a vacancy for a librarian* **2** an unoccupied room in a hotel or guesthouse: *the last hotel we tried had a vacancy* **3** the state of being unoccupied

> **vacancy** *n* **1** = opening, job, post, place, position, role, situation, opportunity **2** = room, space, available accommodation, unoccupied room

vacant *adj* **1** (of a toilet, room, etc.) unoccupied or not being used: *I sat down in a vacant chair* **2** (of a job or position) unfilled at the present time **3** having or suggesting a lack of interest or understanding: *he sat there staring at me with a vacant look* **4** (of a period of time) not set aside for any particular activity: *two slots in his programme have been left vacant* > **vacantly** *adv*

> **vacant** *adj* **1** = empty, free, available, abandoned, deserted, for sale, on the market, void; ≠ occupied **2** = unfilled, unoccupied; ≠ taken **3** = blank, vague, dreamy, empty, abstracted, idle, vacuous, inane; ≠ thoughtful

vacate *vb* **-cating, -cated 1** to cause (something) to be empty by leaving: *do you wish us to vacate the room?* **2** to give up (a job or position)

vacation *n* **1** *Brit & S African* a time of the year when the universities or law courts are closed **2** *US, Canad & Austral* same as **holiday** (sense 2)

vaccinate *vb* **-nating, -nated** to give (someone) a vaccine, usually by injection, in order to protect them against a disease: *children vaccinated against meningitis* > **vaccination** *n*

vaccine *n* **1** *med* a substance made from the germs that cause a disease which is given to people to prevent them getting the disease **2** *computers* a piece of software that detects and removes computer viruses from a system

vacillate (vass-ill-late) *vb* **-lating, -lated** to keep changing one's mind or opinions about something: *he vacillated between republican and monarchist sentiments* > **vacillation** *n*

vacuity *n* an absence of intelligent thought or ideas: *I suggested to one of his advisers that his vacuity was a handicap in these debates*

vacuous *adj* **1** lacking in intelligent ideas **2** showing no sign of intelligence or understanding: *her smile was vacuous but without malice*

vacuum *n*, *pl* **vacuums** or **vacua 1** a space which contains no air or other gas **2** a vacant place or position that needs to be filled by someone or something else: *the army moved in to fill the power vacuum* **3** short for **vacuum cleaner ▸** *vb* **4** to clean (something) with a vacuum cleaner

> **vacuum** *n* **1** = emptiness, space, void, gap, nothingness, vacuity **2** = gap, lack, absence, space, deficiency, void

vacuum cleaner *n* an electric machine which sucks up dust and dirt from carpets and upholstery > **vacuum cleaning** *n*

vacuum flask *n* a double-walled flask with a vacuum between the walls that keeps drinks hot or cold

vacuum-packed *adj* (of food) packed in an airtight container in order to preserve freshness

vagabond *n* a person who travels from place to place and has no fixed home or job

vagary (vaig-a-ree) *n*, *pl* **-garies** an unpredictable change in a situation or in someone's behaviour: *I was unused to the vagaries of the retailer's world*

vagina (vaj-jine-a) *n* the passage in most female mammals that extends from the neck of the womb to the external genitals > **vaginal** *adj*

vagrant (vaig-rant) *n* **1** a person who moves from place to place and has no regular home or job ▸ *adj* **2** wandering about > **vagrancy** *n*

vague *adj* **1** not expressed or explained clearly: *he thought of his instructions, so vague and imprecise* **2** deliberately withholding information: *she was rather vague about the whole deal* **3** (of a sound or shape) unable to be heard or seen clearly: *he heard some vague sound from downstairs* **4** (of a person) not concentrating or thinking clearly: *she was mumbling to herself in a vague way* **5** not clearly established or known: *it was a vague rumour which would fade away and be forgotten* > **vaguely** *adv* > **vagueness** *n*

> **vague** *adj* **1** = unclear, indefinite, hazy, confused, loose, uncertain, unsure, superficial; ≠ clear **2** = imprecise, unspecified, generalized, rough, loose, ambiguous, hazy, equivocal **3** = indistinct, unclear, faint, hazy, indeterminate, nebulous, ill-defined; ≠ distinct **4** = absent-minded, distracted, vacant, preoccupied, oblivious, inattentive

vain *adj* **1** excessively proud of one's appearance or achievements **2** senseless or unsuccessful: *he made a vain attempt to lighten the atmosphere* ▸ **3 in vain** without achieving the desired effects or results: *the old man searched in vain for his son* > **vainly** *adv*

> **vain** *adj* **1** = conceited, narcissistic, proud, arrogant, swaggering, egotistical, self-important; ≠ modest **2** = futile, useless, pointless, unsuccessful, idle, worthless, senseless, fruitless; ≠ successful ▸ *n* **in vain** = useless, to no avail, unsuccessful, fruitless, vain

V

vainglorious *adj* boastful or proud: *his vainglorious posturing had earned him numerous powerful enemies*

valance (val-lenss) *n* a short piece of decorative material hung round the edge of a bed or above a window

vale *n literary* a valley

valediction (val-lid-dik-shun) *n* a farewell speech > **valedictory** *adj*

valence (vale-enss) *n chem* the ability of atoms and chemical groups to form compounds

valency *or esp US & Canad* **valence** *n, pl* **-cies** *or* **-ces** *chem* the number of atoms of hydrogen that an atom or chemical group is able to combine with in forming compounds

valentine *n* **1** a card sent, often anonymously, as an expression of love on Saint Valentine's Day, February 14 **2** the person to whom one sends such a card

valerian *n* a plant with small white or pinkish flowers and a medicinal root

valet *n* **1** a male servant employed to look after another man ▸ *vb* **-eting, -eted 2** to act as a valet (for) **3** to clean the bodywork and interior of (a car) as a professional service

valetudinarian (val-lit-yew-din-air-ee-an) *n* **1** a person who is chronically sick **2** a person who continually worries about his or her health > **valetudinarianism** *n*

valiant *adj* very brave: *it was a valiant attempt to rescue the struggling victim* > **valiantly** *adv*

valid *adj* **1** based on sound reasoning: *I think that's a very valid question* **2** legally acceptable: *she must produce a valid driving licence* **3** important or serious enough to say or do: *religious broadcasting has a valid purpose* > **validity** *n*

> **valid** *adj* **1** = sound, good, reasonable, telling, convincing, rational, logical, viable; ≠ unfounded **2** = legal, official, legitimate, genuine, authentic, lawful, bona fide; ≠ invalid

validate *vb* **-dating, -dated 1** to prove (a claim or statement) to be true or correct **2** to give legal force or official confirmation to > **validation** *n*

valise (val-leez) *n old-fashioned* a small suitcase

Valium *n trademark* a drug used as a tranquilliser

valley *n* a long stretch of land between hills, often with a river flowing through it

> **valley** *n* = hollow, dale, glen, vale, depression, dell

valour *or US* **valor** *n literary* great bravery, esp. in battle > **valorous** *adj*

valuable *adj* **1** worth a large amount of money: *his house was furnished with valuable antique furniture* **2** of great use or importance: *the investigations will provide valuable information* ▸ *n* **3** **valuables** valuable articles of personal property, such as jewellery

> **valuable** *adj* **1** = precious, expensive, costly, dear, high-priced, priceless, irreplaceable; ≠ worthless **2** = useful, important, profitable, worthwhile, beneficial, helpful; ≠ useless ▸ *n* = treasures, prized possessions, precious items, heirlooms, personal effects, costly articles

valuation *n* **1** a formal assessment of how much something is worth: *they will arrange a valuation on your house* **2** the price arrived at by the process of valuing

value *n* **1** the desirability of something, often in terms of its usefulness or exchangeability **2** an amount of money considered to be a fair exchange for something: *scrap metal with a value of £100* **3** something worth the money it cost: *the set meal was great value* **4 values** the moral principles and beliefs of a person or group **5** *maths* a particular number or quantity represented by a figure or symbol ▸ *vb* **-uing, -ued 6** to assess the worth or desirability of (something) **7** to hold (someone or something) in high regard > **valued** *adj* > **valueless** *adj* > **valuer** *n*

> **value** *n* **1** = importance, benefit, worth, merit, point, service, sense, profit; ≠ worthlessness **2** = cost, price, worth, rate, market price, face value, asking price, selling price **4** = principles, morals, ethics, mores, standards of behaviour, (moral) standards ▸ *vb* **6** = evaluate, price, estimate, rate, cost, assess, set at, appraise **7** = appreciate, rate (*slang*), prize, regard highly, respect, admire, treasure, esteem; ≠ undervalue

value-added tax *n Brit & S African* See **VAT**

value judgment *n* a personal opinion about something based on an individual's beliefs and not on facts which can be checked or proved

valve *n* **1** a part attached to a pipe or tube which controls the flow of gas or liquid **2** *anatomy* a small flap in a hollow organ, such as the heart, that controls the flow and direction of blood **3** a closed tube through which electrons move in a vacuum **4** *zool* one of the hinged shells of an oyster or clam **5** *music* a device on some brass instruments by which the effective length of the tube may be varied

valvular *adj* of or relating to valves: *valvular heart disease*

vamp¹ *informal* ▸ *n* **1** a sexually attractive woman who seduces men ▸ *vb* **2** (of a woman) to seduce (a man)

vamp² *vb* **vamp up** to make (a story, piece of music, etc.) seem new by inventing additional parts

vampire *n* (in European folklore) a corpse that rises nightly from its grave to drink the blood of living people

vampire bat *n* a bat of Central and South America that feeds on the blood of birds and mammals

van¹ n 1 a road vehicle with a roof and no side windows used to transport goods 2 Brit a closed railway wagon used to transport luggage, goods, or mail

van² n short for **vanguard**

vanadium n chem a silvery-white metallic element used to toughen steel. Symbol: **V**

vandal n someone who deliberately causes damage to personal or public property > **vandalism** n

vandalize or **-lise** vb **-lizing, -lized** or **-lising, -lised** to cause damage to (personal or public property) deliberately

vane n one of the blades forming part of the wheel of a windmill, a screw propeller, etc.

vanguard n 1 the leading division or units of an army 2 the most advanced group or position in scientific research, a movement, etc.: a distinguished architect in the vanguard of her profession

vanilla n 1 a flavouring for food such as ice cream, which comes from the pods of a tropical plant 2 a flavouring extract prepared from the beans of this plant and used in cooking ▸ adj 3 flavoured with vanilla: vanilla essence 4 slang ordinary or conventional: a vanilla kind of guy

vanish vb 1 to disappear suddenly: the choppers vanished from radar screens at dawn yesterday 2 to cease to exist: the old landmarks had vanished

> **vanish** vb 1 = disappear, dissolve, evaporate, fade away, melt away, evanesce (formal); ≠ appear 2 = die out, disappear, pass away, end, fade, dwindle, cease to exist, become extinct

vanity n 1 a feeling of pride about one's appearance or ability 2 pl **-ties** something about which one is vain: it's one of my vanities that I can guess scents

> **vanity** n 1 = pride, arrogance, conceit, narcissism, egotism, conceitedness; ≠ modesty

vanquish vb literary to defeat (someone) in a battle, contest, or argument

vantage n a state, position, or opportunity offering advantage

vape vb **vaping, vaped** informal to inhale vapour from an e-cigarette

vapid adj dull and uninteresting: their publications were vapid and amateurish > **vapidity** n

vapor n US same as **vapour**

vaporize or **-rise** vb **-rizing, -rized** or **-rising, -rised** (of a liquid or solid) to change into vapour > **vaporization** or **-risation** n

vaporous adj resembling or full of vapour

vapour or US **vapor** n 1 a mass of tiny drops of water or other liquids in the air, which appear as a mist 2 the gaseous form of a substance that is usually a liquid or a solid 3 **the vapours** old-fashioned a feeling of faintness, dizziness, and depression

VAR video assistant referee: an official at a football match who examines important incidents using video replay equipment

variable adj 1 likely to change at any time: variable weather 2 maths having a range of possible values ▸ n 3 something that is subject to variation 4 maths an expression that can be assigned any of a set of values > **variability** n > **variably** adv

> **variable** adj 1 = changeable, unstable, fluctuating, shifting, flexible, uneven, temperamental, unsteady; ≠ constant

variant adj 1 differing from a standard or type: variant spellings ▸ n 2 something that differs from a standard or type

> **variant** adj = different, alternative, modified, divergent ▸ n = variation, form, version, development, alternative, adaptation, revision, modification

variation n 1 something presented in a slightly different form: his books are all variations on a basic theme 2 a change in level, amount, or quantity: there was a variation in the figures 3 music the repetition of a simple tune with the addition of new harmonies or a change in rhythm: Variations on a Hussar's Song

> **variation** n 1 = alternative, variety, modification, departure, innovation, variant 2 = variety, change, deviation, difference, diversity, diversion (Brit), novelty; ≠ uniformity

varicose veins pl n veins, usually in the legs, which have become knotted, swollen, and sometimes painful

varied adj of different types, sizes, or quantities: these young men and women would be of varied backgrounds

> **varied** adj = different, mixed, various, diverse, assorted, miscellaneous, sundry, motley; ≠ unvarying

variegated adj having patches or streaks of different colours: variegated holly > **variegation** n

variety n, pl **-ties** 1 the state of being diverse or various 2 different things of the same kind: I'm cooking the mince with a variety of vegetables 3 a particular type of something in the same general category: this variety of pear is extremely juicy 4 taxonomy a race whose distinct characters do not justify classification as a separate species 5 a type of entertainment consisting of short unrelated acts, such as singing, dancing, and comedy

> **variety** n 1 = diversity, change, variation, difference, diversification, heterogeneity, multifariousness; ≠ uniformity 2 = range, selection, assortment, mix, collection, line-up, mixture, array 3 = type, sort, kind, class, brand, species, breed, strain

various adj 1 several different: there are various possible answers to this question 2 of different kinds:

V

the causes of high blood pressure are various and complicated > **variously** *adv*

> **various** *adj* **1** = many, numerous, countless, several, abundant, innumerable, sundry, profuse **2** = different, assorted, miscellaneous, varied, distinct, diverse, disparate, sundry; ≠ similar

varnish *n* **1** a liquid painted onto a surface to give it a hard glossy finish **2** a smooth surface, coated with or as if with varnish **3** an artificial, superficial, or deceptively pleasing manner or appearance: *those who aspired to become civil servants acquired a varnish of university education* **4** chiefly Brit short for **nail varnish** ▸ *vb* **5** to apply varnish to **6** to try to make (something unpleasant) appear more attractive: *when did we start equivocating, camouflaging, varnishing the truth?*

> **varnish** *n* **1** = lacquer, polish, glaze, gloss
> ▸ *vb* **5** = lacquer, polish, glaze, gloss

varsity *n, pl* **-ties** old-fashioned or informal short for **university**

vary *vb* **varies, varying, varied** **1** to change in appearance, character, or form **2** to be different or cause to be different: *the age of appearance of underarm and body hair varies greatly from person to person* **3** to give variety to: *you can vary the type of exercise you do* **4** to change in accordance with another variable: *an individual's calorie requirement varies with age, sex, and physical activity* > **varying** *adj*

> **vary** *vb* **2** = differ, be different, be dissimilar, disagree, diverge **3** = alternate **4** = change, shift, swing, alter, fluctuate, oscillate, seesaw

vascular *adj biol & anatomy* of or relating to the vessels that conduct and circulate body fluids such as blood or sap

vas deferens *n, pl* **vasa deferentia** *anatomy* either of the two ducts that convey sperm from the testicles to the penis

vase *n* a glass or pottery jar used as an ornament or for holding cut flowers

vasectomy *n, pl* **-mies** surgical removal of all or part of the vas deferens as a method of contraception

Vaseline *n trademark* petroleum jelly, used as an ointment or a lubricant

vassal *n* **1** (in feudal society) a man who gave military service to a lord in return for protection and often land **2** a person, nation, or state dominated by another > **vassalage** *n*

vast *adj* unusually large in size, degree, or number > **vastly** *adv* > **vastness** *n*

> **vast** *adj* = huge, massive, enormous, great, wide, immense, gigantic, monumental (*informal*); ≠ tiny

vat *n* a large container for holding or storing liquids

VAT (in Britain and S Africa) value-added tax: a tax levied on the difference between the cost of

materials and the selling price of a commodity or service

Vatican *n* **1** the Pope's palace, in Rome **2** the authority of the Pope

vaudeville *n* variety entertainment consisting of short acts such as song-and-dance routines and comic turns

vault¹ *n* **1** a secure room where money and other valuables are stored safely **2** an underground burial chamber **3** an arched structure that forms a roof or ceiling **4** a cellar for storing wine

> **vault** *n* **1** = strongroom, repository, depository **2** = crypt, tomb, catacomb, cellar, mausoleum, charnel house, undercroft

vault² *vb* **1** to jump over (something) by resting one's hands on it or by using a long pole ▸ *n* **2** the act of vaulting > **vaulter** *n*

> **vault** *vb* = jump, spring, leap, clear, bound, hurdle

vaulted *adj* being or having an arched roof: *an atmospheric vaulted dining room*

vaunt *vb* **1** to describe or display (one's success or possessions) boastfully ▸ *n* **2** a boast > **vaunted** *adj*

VC **1** Vice Chancellor **2** Victoria Cross **3** *history* Vietcong: the Communist-led guerrilla force of South Vietnam

VD venereal disease

VDU visual display unit

veal *n* the meat from a calf, used as food

vector *n* **1** *maths* a variable quantity, such as force, that has magnitude and direction **2** *pathol* an animal, usually an insect, that carries a disease-producing microorganism from person to person

veer *vb* **1** to change direction suddenly: *the plane veered off the runway and careered through the perimeter fence* **2** to change from one position or opinion to another: *her feelings veered from tenderness to sudden spurts of genuine love* ▸ *n* **3** a change of course or direction

> **veer** *vb* **1** = change direction, turn, swerve, shift, sheer, change course

vegan (*vee*-gan) *n* a person who does not eat meat, fish, or any animal products such as cheese, butter, etc.

vegetable *n* **1** a plant, such as potato or cauliflower, with parts that are used as food **2** *offensive* someone who is unable to move or think, as a result of brain damage ▸ *adj* **3** of or like plants or vegetables

vegetarian *n* **1** a person who does not eat meat or fish ▸ *adj* **2** excluding meat and fish: *a vegetarian diet* > **vegetarianism** *n*

vegetate *vb* **-tating, -tated** to live in a dull and boring way with no mental stimulation

vegetation *n* plant life as a whole

veg out *vb* **vegges, vegging, vegged** *slang* to relax in a passive way

vehement adj 1 expressing strong feelings or opinions 2 (of actions or gestures) performed with great force or energy > **vehemence** n > **vehemently** adv

vehicle n 1 a machine such as a bus or car for transporting people or goods 2 something used to achieve a particular purpose or as a means of expression: *the newspaper was a vehicle for explaining government policies* 3 *pharmacol* an inactive substance mixed with the active ingredient in a medicine 4 a liquid, such as oil, in which a pigment is mixed before it is applied to a surface > **vehicular** adj

vehicle n 1 = conveyance (*old-fashioned*), machine, motor vehicle 2 = medium, means, channel, mechanism, organ, apparatus

veil n 1 a piece of thin cloth, usually as part of a hat or headdress, used to cover a woman's face 2 something that conceals the truth: *a veil of secrecy* 3 **take the veil** to become a nun ▸ vb 4 to cover or conceal with or as if with a veil

veil n 1 = mask, cover, shroud, film, curtain, cloak 2 = screen, mask, disguise, blind ▸ vb = cover, screen, hide, mask, shield, disguise, conceal, obscure; ≠ reveal

veiled adj (of a comment or remark) presented in a disguised form: *it was a thinly veiled criticism*

veiled adj = disguised, implied, hinted at, covert, masked, concealed, suppressed

vein n 1 any of the tubes that carry blood to the heart 2 a thin line in a leaf or in an insect's wing 3 a clearly defined layer of ore or mineral in rock 4 an irregular streak of colour in marble, wood, or cheese 5 a distinctive trait or quality in speech or writing: *critics have exposed a strong vein of moralism in the poem* 6 a temporary mood: *we're in a very humorous vein tonight* > **veined** adj

vein n 1 = blood vessel 3 = seam, layer, stratum, course, current, bed, deposit, streak 6 = mood, style, note, tone, mode, temper, tenor

Velcro n *trademark* a type of fastening consisting of one piece of fabric with tiny hooked threads and another with a coarse surface that sticks to it

veld or **veldt** n the open country of South Africa including landscapes which are grassy, bushy, or thinly forested

veldskoen or **velskoen** (felt-skoon) n *S African* a sturdy ankle boot

vellum n 1 a fine calf, kid, or lamb parchment 2 a strong good-quality paper that resembles this

velocity (vel-loss-it-ee) n, pl **-ties** the speed at which something is moving in a particular direction

velocity n = speed, pace, rapidity, quickness, swiftness

velour or **velours** (vel-loor) n a silk or cotton cloth similar to velvet

velvet n 1 a fabric with a thick close soft pile on one side 2 the furry covering of the newly formed antlers of a deer ▸ adj 3 made of velvet 4 soft or smooth like velvet 5 **an iron fist** or **hand in a velvet glove** determination concealed by a gentle manner > **velvety** adj

velveteen n a cotton fabric that resembles velvet

venal (vee-nal) adj 1 willing to accept bribes in return for acting dishonestly: *venal politicians* 2 associated with corruption or bribery: *venal greed* > **venality** n

vend vb to sell (goods)

vendetta n 1 a long-lasting quarrel between people or organizations in which they attempt to harm each other: *it's an inexplicable vendetta against the firm and its directors* 2 a private feud between families in which members of one family kill members of the other family in revenge for earlier murders

vending machine n a machine that automatically dispenses food, drinks, etc. when money is inserted

vendor n 1 a person who sells goods such as newspapers or hamburgers from a stall or cart 2 *chiefly law* a person who sells property

veneer n 1 a thin layer of wood or plastic used to cover the surface of something made of cheaper material 2 a deceptive but convincing appearance: *nobody penetrated his veneer of modest charm*

venerable adj 1 (of a person) entitled to respect because of great age or wisdom 2 (of an object) impressive because it is old or important historically 3 *RC Church* a title given to a dead person who is going to be declared a saint 4 *Church of England* a title given to an archdeacon

venerate vb **-ating, -ated** to hold (someone) in deep respect > **venerator** n

veneration n a feeling of awe or great respect: *George Gershwin is worthy of the veneration accorded his classical counterparts*

venereal disease n a disease, such as syphilis, transmitted by sexual intercourse

Venetian adj 1 of Venice, a port in NE Italy ▸ n 2 a person from Venice

Venetian blind n a window blind made of thin horizontal slats

vengeance n 1 the act of killing, injuring, or harming someone for revenge 2 **with a vengeance** to a much greater extent or with much greater force than expected: *my career was beginning to take off with a vengeance*

vengeance n 1 = revenge, retaliation, reprisal, retribution, requital; ≠ forgiveness

vengeful adj wanting revenge

venial (veen-ee-al) adj easily excused or forgiven: *venial sins*

venison n the flesh of a deer, used as food

venom n 1 a feeling of great bitterness or anger towards someone 2 the poison that certain snakes and scorpions inject when they bite or sting > **venomous** adj > **venomously** adv

venous (vee-nuss) adj of or relating to veins

vent[1] n 1 a small opening in something through which fresh air can enter and fumes can be released 2 the shaft of a volcano through which lava and gases erupt 3 the anal opening of a bird or other small animal 4 **give vent to** to release (an emotion) in an outburst: *she gave vent to her misery and loneliness* ► vb 5 to release or express freely: *consumers vented their anger on the group by boycotting its products* 6 to make vents in

> **vent** n 1 = outlet, opening, aperture, duct, orifice ► vb 5 = express, release, voice, air, discharge, utter, emit, pour out; ≠ hold back

vent[2] n a vertical slit in the lower hem of a jacket

ventilate vb -lating, -lated 1 to let fresh air into (a room or building) 2 to discuss (ideas or feelings) openly: *people need a safe place to ventilate their feelings* > **ventilation** n

ventilator n an opening or device, such as a fan, used to let fresh air into a room or building

ventral adj relating to the front part of the body > **ventrally** adv

ventricle n anatomy 1 a chamber of the heart that pumps blood to the arteries 2 any one of the four main cavities of the brain > **ventricular** adj

ventriloquism n the ability to speak without moving the lips so that the words appear to come from another person or from another part of the room > **ventriloquist** n

venture n 1 a project or activity that is risky or of uncertain outcome 2 a business operation in which there is the risk of loss as well as the opportunity for profit ► vb -turing, -tured 3 to do something that involves risk or danger: *I thought it wise to venture into foreign trade* 4 to dare to express (an opinion) 5 to go to an unknown or dangerous place 6 to dare (to do something): *you have asked me so often to come to your place that I ventured to drop in* > **venturer** n

> **venture** n 1 = undertaking, project, enterprise, campaign, risk, operation, activity, scheme ► vb 4 = put forward, volunteer 5 = go, travel, journey, set out, wander, stray, plunge into, rove 6 = dare, presume, have the courage to, be brave enough, hazard, go out on a limb (*informal*), take the liberty, go so far as

venturesome adj willing to take risks

venue n a place where an organized gathering, such as a concert or a sporting event, is held

Venus n 1 the Roman goddess of love 2 the planet second nearest to the sun

veracious adj habitually truthful

veracity n 1 habitual truthfulness 2 accuracy

verandah or **veranda** n 1 an open porch

attached to a house 2 NZ a continuous overhead canopy outside shops that gives shelter to pedestrians

verb n a word that is used to indicate the occurrence or performance of an action or the existence of a state, for example *run, make,* or *do*

verbal adj 1 of or relating to words: *verbal skills* 2 spoken rather than written: *a verbal agreement* 3 *grammar* of or relating to a verb > **verbally** adv

> **verbal** adj 2 = spoken, oral, word-of-mouth, unwritten

verbalize or **-lise** vb -lizing, -lized or -lising, -lised to express (an idea or feeling) in words

verbatim (verb-bait-im) adv 1 using exactly the same words: *I'll repeat it verbatim* ► adj 2 using exactly the same words: *a verbatim account*

verbena n a plant with red, white, or purple sweet-smelling flowers

verbiage n the excessive use of words

verbose (verb-bohss) adj using more words than is necessary > **verbosity** n

verdant adj literary covered with green vegetation

verdict n 1 the decision made by a jury about the guilt or innocence of a defendant 2 an opinion formed after examining the facts

> **verdict** n = decision, finding, judgment, opinion, sentence, conclusion, conviction, adjudication

verdigris (ver-dig-reess) n a green or bluish coating which forms on copper, brass, or bronze that has been exposed to damp

verdure n literary flourishing green vegetation

verge n 1 a grass border along a road 2 **on the verge of** having almost reached (a point or condition) 3 an edge or rim ► vb **verging, verged** 4 **verge on** to be near to: *she was verging on hysteria*

> **verge** n 3 = border, edge, margin, limit, boundary, threshold, brim ► vb **verge on something** = come near to, approach, border on, resemble, incline to, be similar to, touch on, be more or less

verger n chiefly Church of England 1 a church official who acts as caretaker 2 an official who carries the rod of office before a bishop or dean in ceremonies and processions

verify vb -fies, -fying, -fied 1 to check the truth of (something) by investigation 2 to prove (something) to be true > **verifiable** adj > **verification** n

> **verify** vb 1 = check, make sure, examine, monitor, inspect 2 = confirm, prove, substantiate, support, validate, bear out, corroborate, authenticate; ≠ disprove

verily adv literary truly: *for verily, this was their destiny*

verisimilitude n the appearance of truth or reality

veritable adj rightly called; real: a veritable mine of information > **veritably** adv

verity n, pl **-ties** a true statement or principle

vermicelli (ver-me-**chell**-ee) n **1** very fine strands of pasta, used in soups **2** tiny chocolate strands used as a topping for cakes or ice cream

vermiform adj shaped like a worm

vermiform appendix n anatomy same as **appendix**

vermilion adj **1** orange-red ▸ n **2** mercuric sulphide, used as an orange-red pigment; cinnabar

vermin pl n **1** small animals collectively, such as insects and rodents, that spread disease and damage crops **2** unpleasant people > **verminous** adj

vermouth (ver-**muth**) n a wine flavoured with herbs

vernacular (ver-**nak**-yew-lar) n **1** the commonly spoken language or dialect of a particular people or place ▸ adj **2** in or using the vernacular

vernal adj of or occurring in spring > **vernally** adv

vernier (ver-nee-er) n a small movable scale in certain measuring instruments such as theodolites, used to obtain a fractional reading of one of the divisions on the main scale

veronica n a plant with small blue, pink, or white flowers

verruca (ver-**roo**-ka) n pathol a wart, usually on the sole of the foot

versatile adj having many different skills or uses > **versatility** n

versatile adj = adaptable, flexible, all-round, resourceful, multifaceted; ≠ unadaptable

verse n **1** a division of a poem or song **2** poetry as distinct from prose **3** one of the short sections into which chapters of the books of the Bible are divided **4** a poem

version n **1** a form of something, such as a piece of writing, with some differences from other forms **2** an account of something from a certain point of view: so far there's been no official version of the incident **3** an adaptation, for example of a book or play into a film

version n **1** = form, variety, variant, sort, class, design, style, model **2** = account, report, description, record, reading, story, view, understanding **3** = adaptation, edition, interpretation, form, copy, rendering, reproduction, portrayal

verso n, pl **-sos 1** the left-hand page of a book **2** the back of a sheet of printed paper

versus prep **1** (in a sporting competition or lawsuit) against **2** in opposition to or in contrast with: peace versus war

vertebra (ver-**tib**-bra) n, pl **-brae** (-bree) one of the bony segments of the spinal column > **vertebral** adj

vertebrate n **1** an animal with a backbone, such as a fish, amphibian, reptile, bird, or mammal ▸ adj **2** having a backbone

vertex (ver-tex) n, pl **-tices** (-tiss-seez) **1** the highest point **2** maths **a** the point on a geometric figure where the sides form an angle **b** the highest point of a triangle

vertical adj **1** at right angles to the horizon: the vertical cliff **2** straight up and down: a vertical cut **3** econ of or relating to associated or consecutive, though not identical, stages of industrial activity: the purchase of a chain of travel agents by a leading tour operator will increase vertical integration in the holiday industry ▸ n **4** a vertical line or direction > **vertically** adv

vertical adj **1, 2** = upright, sheer, perpendicular, straight (up and down), erect, plumb, on end, precipitous, vertiginous; ≠ horizontal

vertiginous adj producing dizziness

vertigo n pathol a sensation of dizziness felt because one's balance is disturbed, sometimes experienced when looking down from a high place

vervain n a plant with long slender spikes of purple, blue, or white flowers

verve n great enthusiasm or liveliness

very adv **1** used to add emphasis to adjectives and adverbs that are able to be graded: I'm very happy; he'll be home very soon ▸ adj **2** used with nouns to give emphasis or exaggerated intensity: the very end of his visit; the very thing I need

very adv = extremely, highly, greatly, really, deeply, unusually, profoundly, decidedly ▸ adj = exact, precise, selfsame

vesicle n biol **1** a small sac or cavity, esp. one filled with fluid **2** a blister

vespers n an evening service in some Christian churches

vessel n **1** a ship or large boat **2** an object used as a container for liquid **3** biol a tubular structure in animals and plants that carries body fluids, such as blood and sap

vessel n **1** = ship, boat, craft **2** = container, receptacle, can, bowl, tank, pot, drum, barrel

vest n **1** Brit an undergarment covering the top half of the body **2** US, Canad & Austral a waistcoat ▸ vb **3 vest in** to settle (power or property) on: by the power vested in me, I pronounce you married **4 vest with** to bestow on: the sponsorship has vested these matches with a new interest

vest vb **3 vest in something or someone** = place, invest, entrust, settle, confer, endow, bestow, consign **4 vest with something** = endow with, entrust with

vested interest n **1** a strong personal interest someone has in a matter because he or she might benefit from it **2** property law an existing

V

right to the immediate or future possession of property

vestibule *n* a small entrance hall

vestige (vest-ij) *n* **1** a small amount or trace **2** *biol* an organ or part that is a small nonfunctional remnant of a functional organ in an ancestor

vestigial (vest-ij-ee-al) *adj* remaining after a larger or more important thing has gone: *a strong seam of vestigial belief*

vestments *pl n* **1** ceremonial clothes worn by the clergy at religious services **2** robes that show authority or rank

vestry *n, pl* **-tries** a room in a church used as an office by the priest or minister

vet¹ *n* **1** short for **veterinary surgeon** ▸ *vb* **vetting, vetted 2** to make a careful check of (a person or document) for suitability: *guests have to be vetted and vouched for*

> **vet** *n* = veterinary surgeon, veterinarian (US), animal doctor ▸ *vb* = check, examine, investigate, review, appraise, scrutinize

vet² *n US, Canad, Austral & NZ* short for **veteran**

vetch *n* **1** a climbing plant with blue or purple flowers **2** the beanlike fruit of the vetch, used as fodder

veteran *n* **1** a person who has given long service in some capacity **2** a soldier who has seen a lot of active service **3** a person who has served in the military forces ▸ *adj* **4** long-serving: *the veteran American politician*

> **veteran** *n* **1** = old hand, past master, warhorse (*informal*), old stager; ≠ novice ▸ *adj* = long-serving, seasoned, experienced, old, established, qualified, mature, practised

veterinarian *n US, Canad & Austral* a veterinary surgeon

veterinary *adj* relating to veterinary science

veterinary surgeon *n Brit* a person qualified to practise veterinary medicine

veto (vee-toe) *n, pl* **-toes 1** the power to prevent legislation or action proposed by others: *no single state has a veto* **2** the exercise of this power ▸ *vb* **-toing, -toed 3** to refuse consent to (a proposal, such as a government bill) **4** to prohibit or forbid: *the minister vetoed the appointments*

> **veto** *n* = ban, dismissal, rejection, vetoing, boycott, embargo, prohibiting, prohibition; ≠ ratification ▸ *vb* = ban, block, reject, rule out, turn down, forbid, boycott, prohibit; ≠ pass

vex *vb* to cause (someone) to feel annoyance or irritation > **vexing** *adj* > **vexation** *n*

vexatious *adj* vexing

VHF *or* **vhf** *radio* very high frequency

via *prep* **1** by way of; through: *they fled to London via Crete* **2** by means of: *we keep in touch via email*

viable *adj* **1** able to be put into practice: *the party has failed to propose a viable alternative* **2** (of seeds or eggs) capable of growth

3 (of a fetus) sufficiently developed to survive outside the uterus > **viability** *n*

> **viable** *adj* **1** = workable, practical, feasible, suitable, realistic, operational, applicable, usable; ≠ unworkable

viaduct *n* a bridge for carrying a road or railway across a valley

Viagra *n trademark* a drug that allows increased blood flow into the penis, used to treat impotence in men

vial *n* same as **phial**

viands *pl n old-fashioned* food

vibes *pl n informal* **1** the emotional reactions between people **2** the atmosphere of a place **3** short for **vibraphone**

vibrant (vibe-rant) *adj* **1** full of energy and enthusiasm **2** (of a voice) rich and full of emotion **3** (of a colour) strong and bright > **vibrancy** *n*

> **vibrant** *adj* **1** = energetic, dynamic, sparkling, vivid, spirited, storming, alive, vigorous **3** = vivid, bright, brilliant, intense, clear, rich, glowing

vibraphone *n* a musical instrument with metal bars that resonate electronically when hit

vibrate *vb* **-brating, -brated 1** to move backwards and forwards rapidly **2** to have or produce a quivering or echoing sound **3** *physics* to undergo or cause to undergo vibration > **vibratory** *adj*

vibration *n* **1** a vibrating **2** *physics* **A** a periodic motion about an equilibrium position, such as in the production of sound **B** a single cycle of such a motion

vibrato *n, pl* **-tos** *music* a slight rapid fluctuation in the pitch of a note

vibrator *n* a device for producing a vibratory motion, used for massage or as a sex aid

Vic. Victoria (Australian state)

vicar *n* **1** *Church of England* a priest who is in charge of a parish **2** *RC Church* a church officer acting as deputy to a bishop > **vicarial** *adj*

vicarage *n* the house where a vicar lives

vicarious (vik-air-ee-uss) *adj* **1** felt indirectly by imagining what another person experiences: *vicarious satisfaction* **2** undergone or done as the substitute for another: *vicarious adventures* **3** delegated: *vicarious power* > **vicariously** *adv*

vice¹ *n* **1** an immoral or evil habit or action: *greed is only one of their vices* **2** a habit regarded as a weakness in someone's character: *his only vice is an obsession with gadgets* **3** criminal activities involving sex, drugs, or gambling

> **vice** *n* **1, 2** = fault, failing, weakness, limitation, defect, deficiency, flaw, shortcoming; ≠ good point **3** = wickedness, evil, corruption, sin, depravity, immorality, iniquity, turpitude (*formal*); ≠ virtue

vice² or US **vise** n a tool with a pair of jaws for holding an object while work is done on it

vice³ adj serving in the place of; being next in importance to: *the vice captain*

vice chancellor n the chief executive or administrator at a number of universities

vice president n an officer ranking immediately below a president and serving as his or her deputy ▷ **vice-presidency** n

viceregal adj 1 of a viceroy 2 *chiefly Austral & NZ* of a governor or governor general

viceroy n a governor of a colony or country who represents the monarch

vice versa adv the other way round: *there were attacks on northerners by southerners and vice versa*

> **vice versa** adv = the other way round, conversely, in reverse, contrariwise

vicinity (viss-in-it-ee) n the area immediately surrounding a place

vicious adj 1 cruel or violent: *vicious attacks* 2 forceful or ferocious: *she gave the chair a vicious jerk* 3 intended to cause hurt or distress: *vicious letters* 4 (of an animal) fierce or hostile ▷ **viciously** adv ▷ **viciousness** n

> **vicious** adj 1, 4 = savage, brutal, violent, cruel, ferocious, barbarous; ≠ gentle 3 = malicious, vindictive, spiteful, mean, cruel, venomous

vicious circle n a situation in which an attempt to resolve one problem creates new problems that re-create the original one

vicissitudes (viss-iss-it-yewds) pl n changes in circumstance or fortune

victim n 1 a person or thing that suffers harm or death 2 a person who is tricked or swindled 3 a living person or animal sacrificed in a religious rite

> **victim** n 1 = casualty, sufferer, fatality; ≠ survivor

victimize or **-mise** vb **-mizing, -mized** or **-mising, -mised** to punish or discriminate against (someone) selectively or unfairly ▷ **victimization** or **-misation** n

victor n 1 a person or nation that has defeated an enemy in war 2 the winner of a contest or struggle

> **victor** n = winner, champion, conqueror, vanquisher, prizewinner; ≠ loser

Victoria Cross n the highest decoration for bravery in battle awarded to the British and Commonwealth armed forces

Victoria Day n the Monday preceding May 24: observed in Canada as a national holiday

Victorian adj 1 of or in the reign of Queen Victoria of Great Britain and Ireland (1837–1901) 2 characterized by prudery or hypocrisy 3 of or relating to Victoria (the state or any of the cities) ▷ n 4 a person who lived during the reign of

Queen Victoria 5 an inhabitant of Victoria (the state or any of the cities)

victorious adj 1 having defeated an enemy or opponent: *the victorious allies* 2 of or characterized by victory: *a victorious smile*

> **victorious** adj 1 = winning, successful, triumphant, first, champion, conquering, vanquishing, prizewinning; ≠ losing

victory n, pl **-ries** 1 the winning of a war or battle 2 success attained in a contest or struggle

> **victory** n = win, success, triumph, conquest, walkover (*informal*); ≠ defeat

victuals (vit-tals) pl n *old-fashioned* food and drink

vicuna (vik-kew-na) n 1 a S American mammal like the llama 2 the fine cloth made from its wool

video n, pl **-os** 1 the recording and broadcasting of moving images using digital technology or (esp. formerly) video tape 2 a recording of moving images 3 short for **video cassette** 4 short for **video cassette recorder** ▶ vb **videoing, videoed** 5 to record (moving images) ▶ adj 6 relating to or used in recording moving images

video cassette n a cassette containing video tape

video cassette recorder n a device for recording and playing back television programmes and films

video tape n 1 magnetic tape used mainly for recording the video-frequency signals of a television programme or film ▶ vb **video-tape, -taping, -taped** 2 to record (a film or programme) on video tape

vie vb **vying, vied** to compete (with someone): *the sisters vied with each other to care for her*

> **vie** vb = compete, struggle, contend, strive

Vietnamese adj 1 of Vietnam ▶ n 2 pl **-ese** a person from Vietnam 3 the language of Vietnam

view n 1 opinion, judgment, or belief: *in my view that doesn't really work* 2 an understanding of or outlook on something: *a specific view of human history* 3 everything that can be seen from a particular place or in a particular direction: *there was a beautiful view from the window* 4 vision or sight, esp. range of vision: *as they turned into the drive, the house came into view* 5 a picture of a scene 6 the act of seeing or observing 7 **in view of** taking into consideration 8 **on view** exhibited to the public 9 **take a dim** or **poor view of** to regard (something) unfavourably 10 **with a view to** with the intention of ▶ vb 11 to consider in a specified manner: *they viewed the visit with hardly disguised apprehension* 12 to examine or inspect (a house or flat) carefully with a view to buying it 13 to look at 14 to watch (television, videos, etc.)

V

view n **1** = opinion, belief, feeling, attitude, impression, conviction, point of view, sentiment **3** = scene, picture, sight, prospect, perspective, landscape, outlook, spectacle **4** = vision, sight, visibility, perspective, eyeshot ▶ vb **11** = regard, see, consider, perceive, treat, estimate, reckon, deem

viewer n a person who views something, esp. television

viewer n = watcher, observer, spectator, onlooker

viewfinder n a device on a camera that lets the user see what will be included in the photograph

vigil (vij-ill) n **1** a night-time period of staying awake to look after a sick person, pray, etc. **2** RC Church & Church of England the eve of certain major festivals

vigilance n careful attention

vigilant adj on the watch for trouble or danger

vigilante (vij-ill-ant-ee) n a person who takes it upon himself or herself to enforce the law

vignette (vin-yet) n **1** a short description of the typical features of something **2** a small decorative illustration in a book **3** a photograph or drawing with edges that are shaded off

vigorous adj **1** having physical or mental energy **2** displaying or performed with vigour: vigorous exercise > **vigorously** adv

vigorous adj **1** = spirited, lively, energetic, active, dynamic, animated, forceful, feisty (informal); ≠ lethargic **2** = strenuous, energetic, arduous, hard, taxing, active, rigorous

vigour or US **vigor** n **1** physical or mental energy: the vigour of his invective astonished MPs **2** strong healthy growth

vigour or **vigor** n **1** = energy, vitality, power, spirit, strength, animation, verve, gusto; ≠ weakness

Viking n any of the Scandinavians who raided by sea most of N and W Europe from the 8th to the 11th centuries

vile adj **1** morally wicked: a vile regime **2** disgusting: the vile smell of the room **3** unpleasant or bad: I had a vile day at work > **vilely** adv > **vileness** n

vile adj **1** = wicked, evil, corrupt, perverted, degenerate, depraved, nefarious; ≠ honourable **2** = disgusting, foul, revolting, offensive, nasty, sickening, horrid (informal), repulsive, yucko (Austral slang); ≠ pleasant

vilify (vill-if-fie) vb **-fies, -fying, -fied** to speak very badly of (someone) > **vilification** n

villa n **1** a large house with gardens **2** Brit a house rented to holiday-makers

village n **1** a small group of houses in a country area **2** the inhabitants of such a community > **villager** n

villain n **1** a wicked or evil person **2** the main wicked character in a novel or play

villain n **1** = evildoer, criminal, rogue, scoundrel (old-fashioned), wretch, reprobate, miscreant, blackguard, wrong 'un (slang) **2** = baddy (informal), antihero; ≠ hero

villainous adj of or like a villain

villainy n, pl **-lainies** evil or vicious behaviour

villein (vill-an) n (in medieval Europe) a peasant who was directly subject to his lord, to whom he paid dues and services in return for his land > **villeinage** n

vinaigrette n salad dressing made from oil and vinegar with seasonings

vindicate vb **-cating, -cated 1** to clear (someone) of guilt or suspicion **2** to provide justification for: the arrests may vindicate the strong-arm tactics > **vindication** n

vindicate vb **1** = clear, acquit, exonerate, absolve, let off the hook, exculpate; ≠ condemn **2** = support, defend, excuse, justify

vindictive adj **1** maliciously seeking revenge **2** characterized by spite or ill will > **vindictively** adv > **vindictiveness** n

vine n **1** a plant, such as the grapevine, with long flexible stems that climb by clinging to a support **2** the stem of such a plant > **viny** adj

vinegar n **1** a sour-tasting liquid made by fermentation of beer, wine, or cider, used for salad dressing or for pickling **2** bad temper or spitefulness: the vinegar in her pen is often a welcome seasoning to duller news > **vinegary** adj

vineyard (vinn-yard) n an area of land where grapes are grown

vino (vee-noh) n, pl **-nos** informal wine

vintage n **1** the wine obtained from a particular harvest of grapes **2** the harvest from which such a wine is obtained **3** a time of origin: an open-necked shirt of uncertain vintage ▶ adj **4** (of wine) of an outstandingly good year **5** representative of the best and most typical: a vintage Saint Laurent dress

vintage n **1, 2** = harvest ▶ adj **4** = high-quality, best, prime, quality, choice, select, superior **5** = classic, old, veteran, historic, heritage, enduring, antique, timeless

vintage car n a car built between 1919 and 1930

vintner n a wine merchant

vinyl (vine-ill) n **1** any of various strong plastics made by the polymerization of vinyl compounds, such as PVC **2** musical records produced on vinyl discs ▶ adj **3** chem of or containing the monovalent group of atoms CH_2CH-: vinyl chloride **4** of or made of vinyl: vinyl tiles

viol (vie-oll) n a stringed musical instrument that preceded the violin

viola[1] (vee-oh-la) n a bowed stringed instrument of the violin family, slightly larger and lower in pitch than the violin

viola² (vie-ol-la) *n* a variety of pansy

violate *vb* **-lating, -lated 1** to break (a law or agreement): *he violated export laws* **2** to disturb rudely or improperly: *these men who were violating her privacy* **3** to treat (a sacred place) disrespectfully **4** to rape > **violation** *n* > **violator** *n*

> **violate** *vb* **1** = break, infringe, disobey, transgress, ignore, defy, disregard, flout; ≠ obey **2** = invade, infringe on, disturb, upset, shatter, disrupt, impinge on, encroach on **3** = desecrate, profane, defile, abuse, pollute, deface, dishonour, vandalize; ≠ honour **4** = rape, sexually assault, abuse

violence *n* **1** the use of physical force, usually intended to cause injury or destruction **2** great force or strength in action, feeling, or expression

> **violence** *n* **1** = brutality, bloodshed, savagery, fighting, terrorism **2** = force, power, strength, might, ferocity, forcefulness, powerfulness

violent *adj* **1** using or involving physical force with the intention of causing injury or destruction: *violent clashes with government supporters* **2** very intense: *I took a violent dislike to him* **3** sudden and forceful: *a violent explosion* > **violently** *adv*

> **violent** *adj* **1** = brutal, aggressive, savage, wild, fierce, bullying, cruel, vicious; ≠ gentle **2** = passionate, uncontrollable, unrestrained

violet *n* **1** a plant with bluish-purple flowers ▸ *adj* **2** bluish-purple

violin *n* a musical instrument, the highest member of the violin family, with four strings played with a bow

violinist *n* a person who plays the violin

VIP very important person

viper *n* a type of poisonous snake

virago (vir-**rah**-go) *n, pl* **-goes** *or* **-gos** *archaic* an aggressive woman

viral (**vie**-ral) *adj* **1** of or caused by a virus ▸ *adv* **2 go viral** (of an image, video, story, etc.) to spread quickly and widely among internet users ▸ *n* **3** an image, video, story, etc. that is spread quickly and widely via the internet

virgin *n* **1** a person who has never had sexual intercourse **2** a person who is inexperienced in a specified field: *a ski virgin* ▸ *adj* **3** not having had sexual intercourse **4** fresh and unused: *he found a scrap of virgin paper in a sea of memoranda* **5** not yet cultivated, explored, or exploited by people: *virgin territory*

> **virgin** *n* **1** = maiden (*archaic, literary*), girl (*archaic*) ▸ *adj* **3** = pure, chaste, immaculate, virginal, vestal, uncorrupted, undefiled; ≠ corrupted

virginal¹ *adj* **1** like a virgin **2** extremely pure or fresh

virginal² *n* an early keyboard instrument like a small harpsichord

virginity *n* the condition or fact of being a virgin

virile *adj* **1** having the traditional male characteristics of physical strength and a high sex drive **2** forceful and energetic: *a virile Highland fling* > **virility** *n*

virology *n* the branch of medicine concerned with the study of viruses > **virological** *adj*

virtual *adj* **1** having the effect but not the appearance or form of: *the investigation has now come to a virtual standstill* **2** *computers* designed so as to extend the potential of a finite system beyond its immediate limits: *virtual memory* **3** of or relating to virtual reality

> **virtual** *adj* **1** = practical, essential, in all but name

virtually *adv* almost or nearly: *he is virtually a prisoner in his own palace*

> **virtually** *adv* = practically, almost, nearly, in effect, in essence, as good as, in all but name

virtual reality *n* a computer-generated environment that seems real to the user

virtue *n* **1** moral goodness **2** a positive moral quality: *the virtue of humility* **3** an advantage or benefit: *the added virtue of being harmless* **4** chastity, esp. in women **5 by virtue of** by reason of; because of: *they escaped execution by virtue of their high rank*

> **virtue** *n* **1** = goodness, integrity, worth, morality, righteousness, probity (*formal*), rectitude, incorruptibility; ≠ vice **2** = merit, strength, asset, plus (*informal*), attribute, good point, strong point; ≠ failing **3** = advantage, benefit, merit, credit, usefulness, efficacy

virtuoso *n, pl* **-si** *or* **-sos 1** a person with exceptional musical skill **2** a person with exceptional skill in any area ▸ *adj* **3** showing exceptional skill or brilliance: *a virtuoso performance* > **virtuosity** *n*

virtuous *adj* morally good > **virtuously** *adv*

virulent (**vir**-yew-lent) *adj* **1** extremely bitter or hostile **2** **A** (of a microorganism) very infectious **B** (of a disease) having a violent effect **3** extremely poisonous or harmful: *the most virulent poison known to humanity* > **virulence** *n*

virus *n* **1** a microorganism that is smaller than a bacterium and can cause disease in humans, animals, or plants **2** *informal* a disease caused by a virus **3** *computers* an unsanctioned and self-replicating program which, when activated, corrupts a computer's data and disables its operating system

visa *n* an official stamp in a passport permitting its holder to travel into or through the country of the government issuing it

visage (**viz**-zij) *n chiefly literary* **1** face **2** appearance

vis-à-vis (veez-ah-**vee**) *prep* in relation to

V

viscera (viss-er-a) *pl n anatomy* the large internal organs of the body collectively

visceral *adj* **1** of or affecting the viscera **2** instinctive rather than rational: *visceral hatred of the neighbours*

viscid (viss-id) *adj* sticky

viscose *n* **1** a sticky solution obtained by dissolving cellulose **2** rayon made from this material

viscosity *n, pl* **-ties 1** the state of being viscous **2** *physics* the extent to which a fluid resists a tendency to flow

viscount (vie-count) *n* (in the British Isles) a nobleman ranking below an earl and above a baron > **viscountcy** *n*

viscountess (vie-count-iss) *n* **1** a woman holding the rank of viscount **2** the wife or widow of a viscount

viscous *adj* (of liquids) thick and sticky

vise *n US* same as **vice²**

visibility *n* **1** the range or clarity of vision: *visibility was good, despite rain* **2** the condition of being visible

visible *adj* **1** able to be seen **2** able to be perceived by the mind: *a visible and flagrant act of aggression* > **visibly** *adv*

> **visible** *adj* = perceptible, observable, clear, apparent, evident, manifest, in view, discernible; ≠ invisible

vision *n* **1** the ability to see **2** a vivid mental image produced by the imagination: *I kept having visions of her getting lost* **3** a hallucination caused by divine inspiration, madness, or drugs: *visions of angels* **4** great perception of future developments: *what he had instead of charisma was vision* **5** the image on a television screen **6** a person or thing of extraordinary beauty

> **vision** *n* **1** = sight, seeing, eyesight, view, perception **2** = image, idea, dream, plans, hopes, prospect, ideal, concept **3** = hallucination, illusion, apparition, revelation, delusion, mirage, chimera **4** = foresight, imagination, perception, insight, awareness, inspiration, innovation, creativity

visionary *adj* **1** showing foresight: *a visionary leader* **2** idealistic but impractical **3** given to having visions **4** of or like visions ▸ *n, pl* **-naries 5** a visionary person

> **visionary** *adj* **2** = idealistic, romantic, unrealistic, utopian, speculative, impractical, unworkable, quixotic; ≠ realistic **3** = prophetic, mystical, predictive, oracular, sibylline ▸ *n* = idealist, romantic, dreamer, daydreamer; ≠ realist

visit *vb* **-siting, -sited 1** to go or come to see (a person or place) **2** to stay with (someone) as a guest **3** *old-fashioned* (of a disease or disaster) to afflict **4** **visit on** *or* **upon** to inflict (punishment)

on **5** **visit with** *US informal* to chat with (someone) ▸ *n* **6** the act or an instance of visiting **7** a professional or official call **8** a stay as a guest

> **visit** *vb* **1** = call on, drop in on (*informal*), stop by, look up, go see (*US*), swing by (*informal*) **2** = stay at, stay with, spend time with ▸ *n* **6** = call, social call **8** = trip, stop, stay, break, tour, holiday, vacation, stopover

visitation *n* **1** an official visit or inspection **2** a punishment or reward from heaven **3** an appearance of a supernatural being

visitor *n* a person who visits a person or place

> **visitor** *n* = guest, caller, company, manu(w)hiri (*NZ*)

visor (vize-or) *n* **1** a transparent flap on a helmet that can be pulled down to protect the face **2** a small movable screen attached above the windscreen in a vehicle, used as protection against the glare of the sun **3** a peak on a cap

vista *n* **1** an extensive view **2** a wide range of possibilities or future events: *the vista of opportunity*

> **vista** *n* **1** = view, scene, prospect, landscape, panorama, perspective

visual *adj* **1** done by or used in seeing **2** capable of being seen > **visually** *adv*

> **visual** *adj* **1** = optical, optic, ocular **2** = observable, visible, perceptible, discernible; ≠ imperceptible

visual display unit *n computers* a device with a screen for displaying data held in a computer

visualize *or* **-lise** *vb* **-lizing, -lized** *or* **-lising, -lised** to form a mental image of (something not at that moment visible) > **visualization** *or* **-lisation** *n*

vital *adj* **1** essential or highly important: *marriage isn't such a vital part of his life* **2** energetic or lively: *the epitome of vital youthful manhood* **3** necessary to maintain life: *the vital organs* ▸ *n* **4** **vitals** the bodily organs, such as the brain and heart, that are necessary to maintain life > **vitally** *adv*

> **vital** *adj* **1** = essential, important, necessary, key, basic, significant, critical, crucial (*informal*); ≠ unnecessary **2** = lively, vigorous, energetic, spirited, dynamic, animated, vibrant, vivacious; ≠ lethargic

vitality *n* physical or mental energy

> **vitality** *n* = energy, vivacity, life, strength, animation, vigour, exuberance, liveliness; ≠ lethargy

vital statistics *pl n* **1** population statistics, such as the numbers of births, marriages, and deaths **2** *informal* the measurements of a woman's bust, waist, and hips

vitamin *n* one of a group of substances that occur naturally in certain foods and are essential for normal health and growth

vitiate (vish-ee-ate) *vb* **-ating, -ated 1** to spoil or weaken the effectiveness of (something) **2** to destroy the legal effect of (a contract) > **vitiation** *n*

viticulture *n* the cultivation of grapevines

vitreous *adj* **1** of or like glass **2** of or relating to the vitreous humour

vitreous humour *or* **vitreous body** *n* a transparent gelatinous substance that fills the eyeball between the lens and the retina

vitriol *n* **1** language expressing bitterness and hatred **2** sulphuric acid

vitriolic *adj* (of language) severely bitter or harsh

vituperative (vite-tyew-pra-tiv) *adj* bitterly abusive > **vituperation** *n*

viva[1] *interj* long live (a specified person or thing)

viva[2] *Brit* ▸ *n* **1** an examination in the form of an interview ▸ *vb* **vivaing, vivaed 2** to examine (a candidate) in a spoken interview

vivace (viv-vah-chee) *adj music* to be performed in a lively manner

vivacious *adj* full of energy and enthusiasm

vivacity *n* the quality of being vivacious

viva voce (vive-a voh-chee) *adv, adj* **1** by word of mouth ▸ *n* **2** same as **viva**[2] (sense 1)

vivid *adj* **1** very bright: *a vivid blue sky* **2** very clear and detailed: *vivid memories* **3** easily forming lifelike images: *a vivid imagination* > **vividly** *adv* > **vividness** *n*

> **vivid** *adj* **1** = bright, brilliant, intense, clear, rich, glowing, colourful; ≠ dull **2** = clear, detailed, realistic, telling, moving, affecting, arresting, powerful; ≠ vague

vivisection *n* the performing of experiments on living animals, involving cutting into or dissecting the body > **vivisectionist** *n*

vixen *n* **1** a female fox **2** *Brit, Austral & NZ informal, derogatory* a spiteful woman

viz *adv* namely: used to specify items: *I had only one object, viz, to win the trophy*

vizier (viz-**zeer**) *n* a high official in certain Muslim countries

vizor *n* same as **visor**

vocabulary *n, pl* **-laries 1** all the words that a person knows **2** all the words contained in a language **3** the specialist terms used in a given subject **4** a list of words in another language with their translations **5** a range of symbols or techniques as used in any of the arts or crafts: *the building's vocabulary of materials, textures, and tones*

> **vocabulary** *n* **1, 2** = language, words, lexicon **4** = wordbook, dictionary, glossary, lexicon

vocal *adj* **1** of or relating to the voice: *vocal pitch* **2** expressing one's opinions clearly and openly: *a vocal minority with racist views* ▸ *n* **3 vocals** the singing part of a piece of jazz or pop music > **vocally** *adv*

> **vocal** *adj* **1** = spoken, voiced, uttered, oral, said **2** = outspoken, frank, forthright, strident, vociferous, articulate, expressive, eloquent; ≠ quiet

vocal cords *pl n* either of two pairs of membranous folds in the larynx, of which the lower pair can be made to vibrate and produce sound by forcing air from the lungs over them

vocalist *n* a singer with a pop group

vocalize *or* **-lise** *vb* **-lizing, -lized** *or* **-lising, -lised 1** to express with or use the voice **2** to make vocal or articulate: *vocalize your discontent* **3** *phonetics* to articulate (a speech sound) with voice > **vocalization** *or* **-lisation** *n*

vocation *n* **1** a specified profession or trade **2 A** a special urge to a particular calling or career, esp. a religious one **B** such a calling or career

> **vocation** *n* **1** = profession, calling, job, trade, career, mission, pursuit

vocational *adj* directed towards a particular profession or trade: *vocational training*

vociferous *adj* loud and forceful: *a vociferous minority* > **vociferously** *adv*

VOD video on demand: a system that allows a television viewer to select content and view it at a time of his or her own choosing

vodka *n* a clear alcoholic spirit originating in Russia, made from potatoes or grain

voetsak *or* **voetsek** (**foot**-sak) *interj S African offensive, informal* an expression of dismissal or rejection

vogue *n* **1** the popular style at a given time **2 in vogue** fashionable ▸ *adj* **3** fashionable: *a vogue word* > **voguish** *adj*

> **vogue** *n* **1** = fashion, trend, craze, style, mode, passing fancy, dernier cri (*French*)

voice *n* **1** the sound made by the vibration of the vocal cords, esp. when modified by the tongue and mouth **2** a distinctive tone of the speech sounds characteristic of a particular person: *he can recognize her voice* **3** the ability to speak or sing: *he had at last found his voice* **4** the condition or quality of a person's voice: *her voice was kind* **5** the musical sound of a singing voice: *what I have is a good voice and a great love of lyrics* **6** the expression of feeling or opinion: *there was a chorus of dissenting voices* **7** a right to express an opinion: *the party should now move towards a system which will give every member an equal voice* **8** *grammar* a category of the verb that expresses whether it is active or passive **9** *phonetics* the sound characterizing the articulation of several speech sounds, that is produced when the vocal cords are vibrated by the breath **10 with one voice** unanimously ▸ *vb* **voicing, voiced 11** to express verbally: *anyone with an objection has a chance to voice it* **12** to articulate (a speech sound) with voice

> **voice** *n* **1** = tone, sound, articulation **3** = utterance **6** = opinion, will, feeling, wish, desire **7** = say, view, vote, comment, input ▸ *vb* **11** = express, declare, air, raise, reveal, mention, mouth, pronounce

V

voiceless *adj* **1** without a voice **2** *phonetics* articulated without accompanying vibration of the vocal cords, for example 'p' in English

voice mail *n* an electronic system for the transfer and storage of telephone messages, which can then be dealt with by the user at his or her convenience

voice-over *n* the voice of an unseen commentator heard during a film

void *n* **1** a feeling or condition of loneliness or deprivation **2** an empty space or area ▸ *adj* **3** having no official value or authority, because the terms have been broken or have not been fulfilled: *the race was declared void and rerun* **4** *old-fashioned or literary* empty: *behold, the tomb is void!* **5 void of** devoid of or without: *the fact of being punished becomes void of all moral significance* ▸ *vb* **6** to make ineffective or invalid **7** to empty **8** to discharge the contents of (the bowels or bladder)

> **void** *n* **1** = gap, space, lack, hole, emptiness **2** = emptiness, space, vacuum, oblivion, blankness, nullity, vacuity ▸ *adj* **3** = invalid, null and void, inoperative, useless, ineffective, worthless ▸ *vb* **6** = invalidate, nullify, cancel, withdraw, reverse, undo, repeal, quash

voile (**voyl**) *n* a light semitransparent dress fabric

vol. volume

volatile (**voll**-a-tile) *adj* **1** (of circumstances) liable to sudden change **2** (of people) liable to sudden changes of mood and behaviour **3** (of a substance) changing quickly from a solid or liquid form to a vapour > **volatility** *n*

> **volatile** *adj* **1** = changeable, shifting, variable, unsettled, unstable, explosive, unreliable, unsteady; ≠ stable **2** = temperamental, erratic, mercurial, up and down (*informal*), fickle, overemotional; ≠ calm

vol-au-vent (**voll**-oh-von) *n* a very light puff pastry case with a savoury filling

volcanic *adj* **1** of or relating to volcanoes: *volcanic ash* **2** displaying sudden violence or anger: *their boisterous and often volcanic behaviour*

volcano *n, pl* **-noes** *or* **-nos** **1** an opening in the earth's crust from which molten lava, ashes, dust, and gases are ejected from below the earth's surface **2** a mountain formed from volcanic material ejected from a vent

vole *n* a small rodent with a stocky body and a short tail

volition *n* **1** the ability to decide things for oneself **2 of one's own volition** through one's own choice > **volitional** *adj*

volley *n* **1** the simultaneous firing of several weapons **2** the bullets fired **3** a burst of questions or critical comments **4** *sport* a stroke or kick at a moving ball before it hits the ground ▸ *vb* **5** to fire (weapons) in a volley **6** *sport* to hit or kick (a moving ball) before it hits the ground

> **volley** *n* **1** = barrage, blast, burst, shower, hail, bombardment, salvo, fusillade

volleyball *n* a game in which two teams hit a large ball backwards and forwards over a high net with their hands

volt *n* the SI unit of electric potential; the potential difference between two points on a conductor carrying a current of 1 ampere, when the power dissipated between these points is 1 watt

voltage *n* an electromotive force or potential difference expressed in volts

volte-face (volt-**fass**) *n, pl* **volte-face** a reversal of opinion

voltmeter *n* an instrument for measuring voltage

voluble *adj* talking easily and at length > **volubility** *n* > **volubly** *adv*

volume *n* **1** the magnitude of the three-dimensional space enclosed within or occupied by something **2** an amount or total: *the volume of trade between the two countries; the volume of military traffic* **3** loudness of sound **4** the control on a radio, etc. for adjusting the loudness of sound **5** a book: *a slim volume* **6** one of several books that make up a series **7** a set of issues of a magazine over a specified period

> **volume** *n* **1** = capacity, size, mass, extent, proportions, dimensions, bulk, measurements **2** = amount, quantity, level, body, total, measure, degree, mass **3** = loudness, sound, amplification **5, 6** = book, work, title, opus, publication, manual, tome, treatise

volumetric *adj* of or using measurement by volume: *a simple volumetric measurement*

voluminous *adj* **1** (of clothes) large and roomy **2** (of writings) extensive and detailed

voluntary *adj* **1** done or undertaken by free choice: *voluntary repatriation* **2** done or maintained without payment: *voluntary work* **3** (of muscles) having their action controlled by the will ▸ *n, pl* **-taries** **4** *music* a composition, usually for organ, played at the beginning or end of a church service > **voluntarily** *adv*

> **voluntary** *adj* **1** = intentional, deliberate, planned, calculated, wilful; ≠ unintentional **2** = unpaid, free, willing, pro bono (*law*)

volunteer *n* **1** a person who offers voluntarily to do something **2** a person who freely undertakes military service ▸ *vb* **3** to offer (oneself or one's services) by choice and without being forced **4** to enlist voluntarily for military service **5** to give (information) willingly **6** to offer the services of (another person)

> **volunteer** *vb* **3** = offer, step forward; ≠ refuse

voluptuary *n, pl* **-aries** a person devoted to luxury and sensual pleasures

voluptuous *adj* **1** (of a woman) sexually alluring because of the fullness of her figure

2 pleasing to the senses: *voluptuous yellow peaches*
> **voluptuously** *adv* > **voluptuousness** *n*

volute *n* a spiral or twisting shape or object, such as a carved spiral scroll on an Ionic capital

vomit *vb* **-iting, -ited 1** to eject (the contents of the stomach) through the mouth **2** to eject or be ejected forcefully ► *n* **3** the partly digested food and drink ejected in vomiting

> **vomit** *vb* **1** = be sick, throw up (*informal*), spew, chuck (*Austral, NZ informal*), heave (*slang*), retch

voodoo *n* **1** a religion involving ancestor worship and witchcraft, practised by some people in the West Indies, esp. in Haiti ► *adj* **2** of or relating to voodoo: *a voodoo curse*

voracious *adj* **1** eating or craving great quantities of food **2** very eager or insatiable in some activity: *a voracious collector* > **voraciously** *adv* > **voracity** *n*

vortex (vor-tex) *n, pl* **-tices** (-tiss-seez) **1** a whirling mass or motion, such as a whirlpool or whirlwind **2** a situation which draws people into it against their will: *the vortex of other people's problems* > **vortical** *adj*

vote *n* **1** a choice made by a participant in a shared decision, esp. in electing a candidate **2** the right to vote **3** the total number of votes cast **4** the opinion of a group of people as determined by voting: *the draft should be put to the vote at a meeting of the Council* **5** a body of votes or voters collectively: *the youth vote* ► *vb* **voting, voted 6** to make a choice by vote **7** to authorize or allow by voting: *the organizing committee voted itself controversial new powers* **8** to declare oneself as being (something or in favour of something) by voting: *I've always voted Labour* **9** *informal* to declare by common opinion: *he was voted hotelier of the year for the third time*

> **vote** *n* **1** = poll, election, ballot, referendum, popular vote, plebiscite, straw poll, show of hands ► *vb* **6** = cast your vote

voter *n* a person who can or does vote

votive *adj* done or given to fulfil a vow

vouch *vb* **vouch for A** to give personal assurance about: *I can vouch for the man, he's a relative by marriage* **B** to give supporting evidence for or be proof of: *his presence alone vouches for the political nature of the trip*

voucher *n* **1** a ticket or card used instead of money to buy specified goods: *a gift voucher* **2** a document recording a financial transaction

> **voucher** *n* **1** = ticket, token, coupon, pass, slip, chit, docket

vouchsafe *vb* **-safing, -safed 1** *old-fashioned* to give or grant: *she has powers vouchsafed to few* **2** to offer assurances about; guarantee: *he absolutely vouchsafed your integrity*

vow *n* **1** a solemn and binding promise **2 take vows** to enter a religious order and commit oneself to its rule of life by the vows of poverty,

chastity, and obedience ► *vb* **3** to promise or decide solemnly: *she vowed to fight on; I solemnly vowed that some day I would return to live in Europe*

> **vow** *n* **1** = promise, commitment, pledge, oath, profession, avowal ► *vb* = promise, pledge, swear, commit, engage, affirm, avow, bind yourself

vowel *n* **A** a voiced speech sound made with the mouth open and the stream of breath unobstructed by the tongue, teeth, or lips, for example *a* or *e* **B** a letter representing this

vox pop *n Brit* interviews with members of the public on a radio or television programme

vox populi *n* public opinion

voyage *n* **1** a long journey by sea or in space ► *vb* **-aging, -aged 2** to go on a voyage: *in this story he voyages to Ireland* > **voyager** *n*

> **voyage** *n* = journey, trip, passage, expedition, crossing, sail, cruise, excursion ► *vb* = travel, journey, tour, cruise, steam, take a trip, go on an expedition

voyeur *n* a person who obtains sexual pleasure from watching people undressing or having sexual intercourse > **voyeurism** *n* > **voyeuristic** *adj*

vs versus

V-sign *n* **1** (in Britain and Australia) an offensive gesture made by sticking up the index and middle fingers with the palm of the hand inwards **2** a similar gesture with the palm outwards meaning victory or peace

VSO (in Britain) Voluntary Service Overseas

VSOP very special (*or* superior) old pale: used of brandy or port

VTOL vertical takeoff and landing

vulcanize *or* **-nise** *vb* **-nizing, -nized** *or* **-nising, -nised** to treat (rubber) with sulphur under heat and pressure to improve elasticity and strength > **vulcanization** *or* **-nisation** *n*

vulgar *adj* **1** showing lack of good taste, decency, or refinement: *vulgar tabloid sensationalism* **2** denoting a form of a language spoken by the ordinary people, rather than the literary form > **vulgarly** *adv*

> **vulgar** *adj* **1** = tasteless, common; ≠ tasteful

vulgar fraction *n* same as **simple fraction**

vulgarian *n* a vulgar person, usually one who is rich

vulgarity *n, pl* **-ties 1** the condition of being vulgar **2** a vulgar action or phrase

Vulgate *n* the fourth-century Latin version of the Bible

vulnerable *adj* **1** able to be physically or emotionally hurt **2** easily influenced or tempted **3** *military* exposed to attack **4** financially weak and likely to fail: *this company could be vulnerable in a prolonged economic slump* **5** *bridge* (of a side that has won one game towards rubber) subject to increased bonuses or penalties > **vulnerability** *n*

V

vulpine *adj* **1** of or like a fox **2** clever and cunning

vulture *n* **1** a very large bird of prey that feeds on flesh of dead animals **2** a person who profits from the misfortune and weakness of others

vulva *n* the external genitals of human females

vuvuzela *n* S *African* an elongated plastic instrument that football fans blow to make a loud trumpeting noise

vying *vb* the present participle of **vie**

W **1** *chem* tungsten **2** watt **3** West(ern)

WA **1** Washington (state) **2** Western Australia

wacky *adj* **wackier, wackiest** *slang* odd, eccentric, or slightly crazy: *a wacky idea* > **wackiness** *n*

wad *n* **1** a small mass of soft material, such as cotton wool, used for packing or stuffing **2** a roll or bundle of banknotes or papers

wadding *n* a soft material used for padding or stuffing

waddle *vb* **-dling, -dled 1** to walk with short steps, rocking slightly from side to side ▸ *n* **2** a swaying walk

waddy *n, pl* **-dies** a heavy wooden club used by Australian Aborigines

wade *vb* **wading, waded 1** to walk slowly and with difficulty through water or mud **2 wade in** *or* **into** to begin doing (something) in an energetic way: *wading into the fray* **3 wade through** to proceed with difficulty through: *a stack of literature to wade through*

wader *n* a long-legged bird, such as the heron or stork, that lives near water and feeds on fish. Also called: **wading bird**

wadi (wod-dee) *n, pl* **-dies** a river in N Africa or Arabia, which is dry except in the rainy season

wafer *n* **1** a thin crisp sweetened biscuit, often served with ice cream **2** *Christianity* a round thin piece of unleavened bread used at Communion **3** *electronics* a small thin slice of germanium or silicon that is separated into numerous individual components or circuits

waffle¹ *n* a square crisp pancake with a gridlike pattern

waffle² *informal, chiefly Brit, Austral & NZ* ▸ *vb* **-fling, -fled 1** to speak or write in a vague and wordy manner ▸ *n* **2** vague and wordy speech or writing

waft *vb* **1** to move gently through the air as if being carried by the wind: *the scent of summer flowers gently wafting through my window* ▸ *n* **2** a scent carried on the air

wag¹ *vb* **wagging, wagged 1** to move rapidly and repeatedly from side to side or up and down: *Franklin wagged his tail* ▸ *n* **2** an instance of wagging

wag² *n old-fashioned* a humorous or witty person

Wag *n informal* the wife or girlfriend of a famous sportsperson

wage *n* **1** Also: **wages** the money paid in return for a person's work, esp. when paid weekly or daily rather than monthly: *a campaign for higher wages* ▸ *vb* **waging**, **waged** **2** to engage in (a campaign or war)

> **wage** *n* = payment, pay, remuneration, fee, reward, income, allowance, recompense
> ▸ *vb* = engage in, conduct, pursue, carry on, undertake, practise, prosecute, proceed with

wager *n* **1** a bet on the outcome of an event or activity ▸ *vb* **2** to bet (something, esp. money) on the outcome of an event or activity

waggle *vb* **-gling**, **-gled** to move with a rapid shaking or wobbling motion

wagon *or* **waggon** *n* **1** a four-wheeled vehicle used for carrying heavy loads, sometimes pulled by a horse or tractor **2** an open railway freight truck **3** a lorry **4** **on the wagon** *informal* abstaining from alcoholic drink > **wagoner** *or* **waggoner** *n*

wagtail *n* a small songbird of Eurasia and Africa with a very long tail that wags up and down when it walks

wahoo *n* a large food and game fish of tropical seas

waif *n* a person, esp. a child, who is, or who looks as if he or she might be, homeless or neglected

wail *vb* **1** to utter a prolonged high-pitched cry of pain or sorrow ▸ *n* **2** a prolonged high-pitched cry of pain or sorrow > **wailing** *n*, *adj*

> **wail** *vb* = cry, weep, grieve, lament, howl, bawl, yowl ▸ *n* = cry, moan, howl, lament, yowl

wain *n poetic* a farm cart

wainscot *n* a wooden covering on the lower half of the walls of a room. Also: **wainscoting**

waist *n* **1** *anatomy* the narrow part of the body between the ribs and the hips **2** the part of a garment covering the waist

waistband *n* a band of material sewn onto the waist of a garment to strengthen it

waistcoat *n* a sleeveless upper garment which buttons up the front and is usually worn by men over a shirt and under a jacket

waistline *n* **1** an imaginary line around the body at the narrowest part of the waist **2** the place where the upper and lower part of a garment are joined together

wait *vb* **1** to stay in one place or remain inactive in expectation of something: *the delegates have to wait for a reply* **2** to be temporarily delayed: *the celebrations can wait* **3** (of a thing) to be ready or be in store: *waiting for her on the library table was the latest Jilly Cooper novel* ▸ *n* **4** the act or a period of waiting **5** **lie in wait for** **A** to prepare an ambush for **B** to be ready or be in store for

wait *vb* **1** = stay, remain, stop, pause, rest, linger, loiter, tarry; ≠ go **2** = be postponed, be suspended, be delayed, be put off, be put back, be deferred, be put on hold (*informal*), be shelved ▸ *n* **4** = delay, gap, pause, interval, stay, rest, halt, hold-up

Waitangi Day *n* February 6, the national day of New Zealand commemorating the Treaty Of Waitangi in 1840

waiter *n* a person, esp. a man, who serves people with food and drink in a restaurant

> **waiter** *n* = attendant, server, flunkey, steward, servant

waitress *n* **1** a woman who serves people with food and drink in a restaurant ▸ *vb* **2** to work as a waitress

> **waitress** *n* = attendant, server, stewardess, servant

waive *vb* **waiving**, **waived** to refrain from enforcing or claiming (a rule or right)

> **waive** *vb* = give up, relinquish, renounce, forsake, drop, abandon, set aside, dispense with; ≠ claim

waiver *n* the act or an instance of voluntary giving up a claim or right

waka *n* NZ a Māori canoe

wake¹ *vb* **waking**, **woke**, **woken** **1** Also: **wake up** to become conscious again or bring (someone) to consciousness again after a sleep **2** **wake up** to make (someone) more alert after a period of inactivity **3** **wake up to** to become aware of: *the world did not wake up to this tragedy until many people had died* **4** **waking hours** the time when a person is awake: *he often used his waking hours to write music* ▸ *n* **5** a watch or vigil held over the body of a dead person during the night before burial

> **wake** *vb* **1** = awake, stir, awaken, come to, arise, get up, rouse, get out of bed; ≠ fall asleep ▸ *n* = vigil, watch, funeral, deathwatch, tangi (NZ)

wake² *n* **1** the track left by a ship moving through water **2** **in the wake of** following soon after: *the arrests come in the wake of the assassination*

> **wake** *n* **1** = slipstream, wash, trail, backwash, train, track, waves, path **2** **in the wake of** = in the aftermath of, following, because of, as a result of, on account of, as a consequence of

wakeful *adj* **1** unable to sleep **2** without sleep: *wakeful nights* **3** alert: *wakeful readiness* > **wakefulness** *n*

waken *vb* to become conscious again or bring (someone) to consciousness again after a sleep

walk *vb* **1** to move on foot at a moderate rate with at least one foot always on the ground **2** to pass through, on, or over on foot: *to walk a short distance* **3** to walk somewhere with

W

(a person or a dog) **4 walking on air** very happy and excited **5 walk the streets** to wander about, esp. when looking for work or when homeless ▸ *n* **6** a short journey on foot, usually for pleasure **7** the action of walking rather than running **8** a manner of walking: *a proud slow walk* **9** a place or route for walking **10 walk of life** social position or profession: *people from all walks of life were drawn to her* ▸ See also **walk into**, **walk out** *etc.* > **walker** *n*

walk *vb* **1** = travel on foot **2** = stride, stroll, go, move, step, march, pace, hike **3** = escort, take, see, show, partner, guide, conduct, accompany ▸ *n* **6** = stroll, hike, ramble, march, trek, trudge, promenade, saunter **8** = gait, step, bearing, carriage, tread **9** = path, footpath (*Austral, NZ*), track, way, road, lane, trail, avenue, berm (*NZ*) **10 walk of life** = area, calling, business, line, trade, class, field, career

walkabout *n* **1** an occasion when royalty, politicians, or other celebrities walk among and meet the public **2 go walkabout** *Austral* **A** to wander through the bush as a nomad **B** *informal* to be lost or misplaced **C** *informal* to lose one's concentration

walkie-talkie *n* a small combined radio transmitter and receiver that can be carried around by one person

walking stick *n* a stick or cane carried in the hand to assist walking

walk into *vb* to encounter unexpectedly: *the troop reinforcements had walked into a trap*

walk out *vb* **1** to leave suddenly and without explanation, usually in anger **2** (of workers) to go on strike **3 walk out on** *informal* to abandon or desert ▸ *n* **walkout 4** a strike by workers

walkover *n* **1** *informal* an easy victory ▸ *vb* **walk over 2** to mistreat or bully; take advantage of: *if you don't make your mark early, people will walk all over you*

wall *n* **1** a vertical structure made of stone, brick, or wood, with a length and height much greater than its thickness, used to enclose, divide, or support. Related adjective: **mural 2** anything that suggests a wall in function or effect: *a wall of elm trees; a wall of suspicion* **3** *anatomy* any lining or membrane that encloses a bodily cavity or structure: *cell walls* **4 drive someone up the wall** *slang* to make someone angry or irritated **5 go to the wall** *informal* to be financially ruined **6 have one's back to the wall** *informal* to be in a very difficult situation, with no obvious way out of it ▸ *vb* **7** to surround or enclose (an area) with a wall **8 wall in** *or* **up** to enclose (someone or something) completely in a room or place > **walled** *adj*

wall *n* **1** = partition, screen, barrier, enclosure **2** = barrier, obstacle, barricade, obstruction, check, bar, fence, impediment

wallaby *n, pl* **-bies** a marsupial of Australia and New Guinea that resembles a small kangaroo

wallaroo *n* a large stocky Australian kangaroo of rocky regions

wallet *n* a small folding case, usually of leather, for holding paper money and credit cards

wallet *n* = purse, pocketbook, pouch, case, holder, moneybag, e-wallet *or* eWallet

walleye *n* a North American pikeperch with large opaque eyes

wallflower *n* **1** a plant grown for its clusters of yellow, orange, red, or purple fragrant flowers **2** *informal* a person who does not get involved in dancing or talking at a social event because they are shy

wallop *informal* ▸ *vb* **1** to hit hard ▸ *n* **2** a hard blow

walloping *informal* ▸ *n* **1** a severe physical beating ▸ *adj* **2** large or great: *a walloping amount of sodium*

wallow *vb* **1** to indulge oneself in some emotion: *they wallow in self-pity* **2** to lie or roll about in mud or water for pleasure ▸ *n* **3** the act or an instance of wallowing **4** a muddy place where animals wallow

wallpaper *n* **1** a printed or embossed paper for covering the walls of a room ▸ *vb* **2** to cover (walls) with wallpaper

wally *n, pl* **-lies** *Brit slang* a stupid or foolish person

walnut *n* **1** an edible nut with a hard, wrinkled, light brown shell **2** a tree on which walnuts grow **3** the light brown wood of a walnut tree, used for making furniture

walrus *n, pl* **-ruses** *or* **-rus** a mammal of cold northern seas, with two tusks that hang down from the upper jaw, tough thick skin, and coarse whiskers

waltz *n* **1** a ballroom dance in triple time in which couples spin round as they progress round the room **2** music for this dance ▸ *vb* **3** to dance a waltz **4** *informal* to move in a relaxed and confident way: *he waltzed over to her table to say hello*

wampum (**wom**-pum) *n* (formerly) money used by Native Americans of N America, made of shells strung or woven together

wan (rhymes with **swan**) *adj* **wanner, wannest** very pale, as a result of illness or unhappiness > **wanly** *adv*

WAN *computers* wide area network

wand *n* **1** a rod supposed to have magical properties, used to perform conjuring tricks or casting spells **2** a hand-held electronic device which is pointed at or passed over an item to read the data stored there

wander *vb* **1** to walk about in a place without any definite purpose or destination **2** (often foll. by *off*) to leave a place where one is supposed to stay: *kids wander off* **3** (of the mind) to lose concentration ▸ *n* **4** the act or an instance of wandering > **wanderer** *n* > **wandering** *adj, n*

W

wander *vb* **1** = roam, walk, drift, stroll, range, stray, ramble, prowl ▸ *n* = excursion, walk, stroll, cruise, ramble, meander, promenade, mosey (*informal*)

wanderlust *n* a great desire to travel

wane *vb* **waning, waned 1** to decrease gradually in size, strength, or power: *the influence of the extremists is waning* **2** (of the moon) to show a gradually decreasing area of brightness from full moon until new moon ▸ *n* **3 on the wane** decreasing in size, strength, or power: *his fame was on the wane* > **waning** *adj*

wane *vb* **1** = decline, weaken, diminish, fail, fade, decrease, dwindle, lessen; ≠ grow **2** = diminish, decrease, dwindle; ≠ wax

wangle *vb* **-gling, -gled** *informal* to get (something) by cunning or devious methods: *I've wangled you both an invitation*

want *vb* **1** to feel a need or longing for: *I want a job* **2** to wish or desire (to do something): *we did not want to get involved* **3** *Brit, Austral & NZ* to have need of or require (doing or being something): *what will you do when it wants cleaning?* **4** should or ought (to do something): *the last person you want to hire is someone who is desperate for a job* **5 want for** to be lacking or deficient in: *they were convinced I was wealthy and wanted for nothing* ▸ *n* **6** something that is needed, desired, or lacked: *attempts to satisfy a number of wants* **7** a lack, shortage, or absence: *for want of opportunity* **8 in want of** needing or lacking: *the Chinese peasant farmer may be in want of a roof, a job, a doctor nearby*

want *vb* **1** = wish for, desire, long for, crave, covet, hope for, yearn for, thirst for; ≠ have **3** = need, demand, require, call for **4** = should, need, must, ought **5** = lack, need, require, miss ▸ *n* **6** = wish, will, need, desire, requirement, longing, appetite, craving **7** = lack, need, absence, shortage, deficiency, famine, scarcity, dearth; ≠ abundance

wanted *adj* being searched for by the police in connection with a crime that has been committed

wanting *adj* **1** lacking: *I would be wanting in charity if I did not explain the terms* **2** not meeting requirements or expectations: *she compares herself to her sister and finds herself wanting*

wanting *adj* **1** = lacking, missing, absent, incomplete, short, shy; ≠ complete **2** = deficient, poor, inadequate, insufficient, faulty, defective, imperfect, unsound, bodger or bodgie (*Austral slang*); ≠ adequate

wanton *adj* **1** without motive, provocation, or justification: *sheer wanton destruction* **2** (of a person) maliciously and unnecessarily cruel **3** *old-fashioned, derogatory* (of a woman) sexually unrestrained or immodest ▸ *n* **4** *old-fashioned, derogatory* a sexually unrestrained or immodest woman

WAP *n* Wireless Application Protocol: a system that allows mobile phone users to access the internet and other information services

wapiti (wop-pit-tee) *n, pl* **-tis** a large North American deer, now also found in New Zealand

war *n* **1** open armed conflict between two or more countries or groups: *this international situation led to war* **2** a particular armed conflict: *the American war in Vietnam* **3** any conflict or contest: *a trade war* **4 have been in the wars** *informal* to look as if one has been in a fight ▸ *adj* **5** relating to war or a war: *the war effort; a war correspondent* ▸ *vb* **warring, warred 6** to conduct a war > **warring** *adj*

war *n* **1** = conflict, drive, attack, fighting, fight, operation, battle, movement; ≠ peace **2, 3** = campaign, drive, attack, operation, movement, push (*informal*), mission, offensive, cyberwar ▸ *vb* = fight, battle, clash, wage war, campaign, combat, do battle, take up arms; ≠ make peace

waratah *n* an Australian shrub with crimson flowers

warble *vb* **-bling, -bled** to sing in a high-pitched trilling voice

warbler *n* any of various small songbirds

war crime *n* a crime committed in wartime in violation of the accepted customs, such as ill-treatment of prisoners > **war criminal** *n*

ward *n* **1** a room in a hospital for patients requiring similar kinds of care: *the maternity ward* **2** one of the districts into which a town, parish, or other area is divided for administration or elections **3** Also called: **ward of court** *law* a person, esp. a child whose parents are dead, who is placed under the control or protection of a guardian or of a court ▸ See also **ward off** > **wardship** *n*

ward *n* **1** = room, department, unit, quarter, division, section, apartment (*US*), cubicle **2** = district, constituency, area, division, zone, parish, precinct **3** = dependant, charge, pupil, minor, protégé

warden *n* **1** a person who is in charge of a building, such as a youth hostel, and its occupants **2** a public official who is responsible for the enforcement of certain regulations: *a game warden* **3** the chief officer in charge of a prison

warden *n* **1** = steward, guardian, administrator, superintendent (*US*), caretaker, curator, custodian **2** = ranger, keeper, guardian, protector, custodian, official **3** = governor, head, leader, director, manager, chief, executive, commander

warder *or fem* **wardress** *n chiefly Brit* a prison officer

ward off *vb* to prevent (something unpleasant) from happening or from causing harm: *to ward off the pangs of hunger; to ward off cancer cells*

W

ward off *vb* **ward something off** = avert, fend off, stave off, avoid, frustrate, deflect, repel

wardrobe *n* **1** a tall cupboard, with a rail or hooks on which to hang clothes **2** the total collection of articles of clothing belonging to one person: *your autumn wardrobe* **3** the collection of costumes belonging to a theatre or theatrical company

wardrobe *n* **1** = clothes cupboard, cupboard, closet (*US*), cabinet **2** = clothes, apparel (*old-fashioned*), attire

wardroom *n* the quarters assigned to the officers of a warship, apart from the captain

ware *n* articles of the same kind or material: *crystal ware*

warehouse *n* a place where goods are stored prior to their sale or distribution

warehouse *n* = store, depot, storehouse, repository, depository, stockroom

warfare *n* **1** the act of conducting a war **2** a violent or intense conflict of any kind: *class warfare*

warfare *n* = war, fighting, battle, conflict, combat, hostilities, enmity; ≠ peace

warhead *n* the front section of a missile or projectile that contains explosives

warlike *adj* **1** of or relating to war: *warlike stores and equipment* **2** hostile and eager to have a war: *a warlike nation*

warlock *n* a man who practises black magic

warm *adj* **1** feeling or having a moderate degree of heat: *warm clothing* **2** giving heat: *warm clothing* **3** (of colours) predominantly red or yellow in tone **4** kindly or affectionate: *warm embraces* **5** *informal* near to finding a hidden object or guessing facts, for example in a children's game ▸ *vb* **6** to make warm **7 warm to** **A** to become fonder of: *I warmed to him when he defended me* **B** to become more excited or enthusiastic about: *he had warmed to his theme* ▸ See also **warm up** › **warmly** *adv* › **warmness** *n*

warm *adj* **1** = balmy, mild, temperate, pleasant, fine, bright, sunny, agreeable; ≠ cool **2** = thermal, winter, thick, chunky, woolly; ≠ cool **3** = mellow, relaxing, pleasant, agreeable, restful **4** = affable, kindly, friendly, affectionate, loving, tender, amicable, cordial; ≠ unfriendly **5** = near, close, hot, near to the truth ▸ *vb* **6** = warm up, heat, thaw (out), heat up; ≠ cool down

warmonger *n* a person who encourages warlike ideas or advocates war › **warmongering** *n*

warmth *n* **1** the state of being warm **2** affection or cordiality: *the warmth of their friendship*

warmth *n* **1** = heat, snugness, warmness, comfort, homeliness, hotness; ≠ coolness **2** = affection, feeling, love, goodwill, kindness, tenderness, cordiality, kindliness; ≠ hostility

warm up *vb* **1** to make or become warm or warmer **2** to prepare for a race, sporting contest, or exercise routine by doing gentle exercises immediately beforehand **3** (of an engine or machine) to be started and left running until the working temperature is reached **4** to become more lively: *wait until things warm up* **5** to reheat (food that has already been cooked) ▸ *n* **warm-up** **6** a preparatory exercise routine

warm up *vb* **1, 5 warm something or someone up** = heat, thaw, heat up

warn *vb* **1** to make (someone) aware of a possible danger or problem **2** to inform (someone) in advance: *you'd better warn your girlfriend that you'll be working at the weekend* **3 warn off** to advise (someone) to go away or not to do something

warn *vb* **1, 2** = notify, tell, remind, inform, alert, tip off, give notice, make someone aware

warning *n* **1** a hint, threat, or advance notice of a possible danger or problem **2** advice not to do something ▸ *adj* **3** giving or serving as a warning: *warning signs* › **warningly** *adv*

warning *n* **1** = notice, notification, sign, alarm, announcement, alert, tip-off (*informal*), heads up (*US, Canad*) **2** = caution, information, advice, injunction, notification

warp *vb* **1** (esp. of wooden objects) to be twisted out of shape, for example by heat or damp **2** to distort or influence in a negative way: *love warps judgment* ▸ *n* **3** a fault or an irregularity in the shape or surface of an object **4** a fault or deviation in someone's character **5** the yarns arranged lengthways on a loom through which the weft yarns are woven › **warped** *adj*

warp *vb* **1** = distort, bend, twist, buckle, deform, disfigure, contort, malform **2** = pervert, twist, corrupt, degrade, deprave, debase, debauch, lead astray ▸ *n* **3** = twist, bend, defect, flaw, distortion, imperfection, kink, contortion

warrant *n* **1** an official authorization for some action or decision: *Scotland Yard today issued a warrant for the arrest of this man* **2** a document that certifies or guarantees something, such as a receipt or licence ▸ *vb* **3** to make necessary: *we've no hard evidence to warrant a murder investigation*

warrant *n* **1** = authorization, permit, licence, permission, authority, sanction ▸ *vb* = call for, demand, require, merit, rate, earn, deserve, permit

warrant officer *n* an officer in certain armed services with a rank between those of commissioned and noncommissioned officers

warranty *n, pl* **-ties** a guarantee or assurance that goods meet a specified standard or that the facts in a legal document are as stated

W

warranty *n* = guarantee, promise, contract, bond, pledge, certificate, assurance, covenant

warren *n* **1** a series of interconnected underground tunnels in which rabbits live **2** an overcrowded building or area of a city with many narrow passages or streets: *a mountainous concrete warren of apartments*

warrigal *Austral* ▸ *n* **1** a dingo ▸ *adj* **2** wild

warrior *n* a person who is engaged in or experienced in war

warrior *n* = soldier, combatant, fighter, gladiator, trooper, man-at-arms (*history*)

warship *n* a ship designed for naval warfare

wart *n* **1** a firm abnormal growth on the skin caused by a virus **2 warts and all** including faults: *she loves him warts and all* > **warty** *adj*

wary (ware-ree) *adj* **warier**, **wariest** cautious or on one's guard: *be wary of hitchhikers* > **warily** *adv* > **wariness** *n*

wary *adj* = suspicious, sceptical, guarded, distrustful, chary; ≠ careless

was *vb* (with 'I', 'he', 'she', 'it', or a singular noun as subject) the past tense of **be**

wash *vb* **1** to clean (oneself, part of one's body, or a thing) with soap or detergent and water **2** (of a garment or fabric) to be capable of being washed without damage or loss of colour **3** to move or be moved in a particular direction by water: *houses may be washed away in floods* **4** (of waves) to flow or sweep against or over (a surface or object), often with a lapping sound **5** *informal* to be acceptable or believable: *that excuse won't wash* ▸ *n* **6** the act or process of washing **7** all the clothes, etc. to be washed together on one occasion **8** a thin layer of paint or ink: *a pale wash of blue* **9** the disturbance in the air or water produced at the rear of an aircraft, boat, or other moving object: *we were hit by the wash of a large vessel* **10 come out in the wash** *informal* to become known or apparent in the course of time ▸ See also **wash out**, **wash up** > **washable** *adj*

wash *vb* **1** = clean, scrub, sponge, rinse, scour, cleanse **5** = be plausible, stand up, hold up, pass muster, hold water, stick, carry weight, be convincing ▸ *n* **6** = laundering, cleaning, clean, cleansing **8** = coat, film, covering, layer, coating, overlay **9** = backwash, slipstream, path, trail, train, track, waves, aftermath

washer *n* **1** a flat ring of rubber, felt, or metal used to provide a seal under a nut or bolt or in a tap or valve **2** *informal* a washing machine **3** a person who washes things, esp. as a job: *chief cook and bottle washer* **4** *Austral* a small piece of towelling cloth used to wash the face

washing *n* all the clothes, etc. to be washed together on one occasion

washing-up *n* the act of washing used dishes and cutlery after a meal

wash out *vb* **1** Also: **wash off** to remove or be removed by washing: *the rain washes the red dye out of the cap* **2** to wash the inside of (a container) ▸ *n* **washout 3** a total failure or disaster **4** NZ a part of a road or railway washed away by floodwaters

wash up *vb* **1** to wash used dishes and cutlery after a meal **2** *US & Canad* to wash one's face and hands

wasp *n* a common stinging insect with a slender black-and-yellow striped body

waspish *adj* bad-tempered or spiteful: *waspish comments*

wastage *n* **1** the act of wasting something or the state of being wasted: *wastage of raw materials* **2** reduction in the size of a workforce by retirement, redundancy, etc.

waste *vb* **wasting**, **wasted 1** to use up thoughtlessly, carelessly, or unsuccessfully **2** to fail to take advantage of: *let's not waste an opportunity to see the children* **3 be wasted on** to be too good for; not be appreciated by: *fine brandy is wasted on you* **4 waste away** to lose one's strength or health: *wasting away from unrequited love* ▸ *n* **5** the act of wasting something or the state of being wasted: *a waste of time* **6** something that is left over because it is in excess of requirements **7** rubbish: *toxic waste* **8** *physiol* matter discharged from the body as faeces or urine **9 wastes** a region that is wild or uncultivated ▸ *adj* **10** rejected as being useless, unwanted, or worthless: *waste products* **11** not cultivated or productive: *waste ground* **12** *physiol* discharged from the body as faeces or urine: *waste matter* **13 lay waste** or **lay waste to** to devastate or destroy: *the Bikini atoll, laid waste by nuclear tests*

waste *vb* **1, 2** = squander, throw away, blow (*slang*), lavish, misuse, dissipate, fritter away; ≠ save **4 waste away** = decline, dwindle, wither, fade, crumble, decay, wane, wear out ▸ *n* **5** = squandering, misuse, extravagance, frittering away, dissipation, wastefulness, prodigality; ≠ saving **7** = rubbish, refuse, debris, scrap, litter, garbage (*chiefly US*), trash (*chiefly US, Canad*), leftovers **9** = desert, wilderness, wasteland ▸ *adj* **10** = unwanted, useless, worthless, unused, leftover, superfluous, unusable, supernumerary; ≠ necessary **11** = uncultivated, wild, bare, barren, empty, desolate, unproductive, uninhabited; ≠ cultivated

wasteful *adj* causing waste: *wasteful expenditure* > **wastefully** *adv*

wastepaper basket *n* a container for paper discarded after use

waster *n informal* a lazy or worthless person

watch *vb* **1** to look at or observe closely and attentively **2** to look after (a child or a pet) **3** to maintain a careful interest in or control over: *it reminds me to watch my diet* **4 watch for** to be keenly alert to or cautious about: *the vigilant night watchman hired to watch for thieves* **5 watch it!** be careful! ▸ *n* **6** a small portable timepiece worn strapped to the wrist or in a waistcoat pocket **7** the act or an instance of watching **8** *naut* any of the periods, usually of four hours, during which part of a ship's crew are on duty **9 keep a close watch on** to maintain a careful interest in or control over: *he keeps a close watch on party opinion* **10 keep watch** to be keenly alert to danger; keep guard **11 on the watch** on the lookout ▸ **watcher** *n*

> **watch** *vb* **1** = look at, observe, regard, eye, see, view, contemplate, eyeball (*slang*) **2** = guard, keep, mind, protect, tend, look after, shelter, take care of ▸ *n* **6** = wristwatch, timepiece, chronometer **7** = guard, surveillance, observation, vigil, lookout

watchable *adj* interesting, enjoyable, or entertaining: *watchable films*
watchdog *n* **1** a dog kept to guard property **2** a person or group that acts as a guard against inefficiency or illegality

> **watchdog** *n* **1** = guard dog **2** = guardian, monitor, protector, custodian, scrutineer

watchful *adj* **1** carefully observing everything that happens **2 under the watchful eye of** being closely observed by > **watchfully** *adv* > **watchfulness** *n*
watchman *n, pl* **-men** a man employed to guard buildings or property
watchword *n* a slogan or motto: *quality, not quantity, is the watchword*
water *n* **1** a clear colourless tasteless liquid that is essential for plant and animal life, that falls as rain, and forms seas, rivers, and lakes. Related adjectives: **aquatic, aqueous 2** any area of this liquid, such as a sea, river, or lake **3** the surface of such an area of water: *four-fifths of an iceberg's mass lie below water* **4** the level of the tide: *at high water* **5** *physiol* **A** any fluid discharged from the body, such as sweat, urine, or tears **B** the fluid surrounding a fetus in the womb **6 hold water** (of an argument or idea) to be believable or reasonable **7 of the first water** of the highest quality or the most extreme degree: *he's a scoundrel of the first water* **8 pass water** to urinate **9 water under the bridge** events that are past and done with ▸ *vb* **10** to moisten or soak with water: *keep greenhouse plants well watered* **11** to give (an animal) water to drink **12** (of the eyes) to fill with tears: *our eyes were watering from the fumes* **13** (of the mouth) to fill with saliva in anticipation of food ▸ See also **water down** > **waterless** *adj*

> **water** *n* **1** = liquid, H$_2$O, wai (*NZ*) **2** = sea, main, waves, ocean, depths, briny (*informal*) ▸ *vb* **10** = sprinkle, spray, soak, irrigate, hose, dampen, drench, douse, fertigate (*Austral*) **12** = get wet, cry, weep, become wet, exude water

water buffalo *n* a large black oxlike draught animal of S Asia, with long backward-curving horns
water closet *n old-fashioned* a toilet. Abbrev: **WC**
watercolour *or US* **watercolor** *n* **1** a kind of paint that is applied with water rather than oil **2** a painting done in watercolours
watercourse *n* the channel or bed of a river or stream
watercress *n* a plant that grows in ponds and streams, with strong-tasting leaves that are used in salads and as a garnish
water down *vb* **1** to weaken (a drink or food) with water **2** to make (a story, plan, or proposal) weaker and less controversial > **watered-down** *adj*

> **water down** *vb* **1 water something down** = dilute, weaken, water, doctor, thin

waterfall *n* a cascade of falling water where there is a vertical or almost vertical step in a river

> **waterfall** *n* = cascade, fall, cataract

waterfront *n* the area of a town or city next to an area of water, such as a harbour or dockyard
water lily *n* a plant with large leaves and showy flowers that float on the surface of an area of water
watermark *n* **1** a mark impressed on paper during manufacture, visible when the paper is held up to the light **2** a line marking the level reached by an area of water
watermelon *n* a large round melon with a hard green rind and sweet watery reddish flesh
water polo *n* a game played in water by two teams of seven swimmers in which each side tries to throw a ball into the opponents' goal
waterproof *adj* **1** not allowing water to pass through: *waterproof trousers* ▸ *n* **2** *chiefly Brit* a waterproof garment, such as a raincoat ▸ *vb* **3** to make waterproof: *the bridge is having its deck waterproofed*
watershed *n* **1** the dividing line between two adjacent river systems, such as a ridge **2** an important period or factor that serves as a dividing line: *a watershed in history*
watersider *n NZ* a person employed to load and unload ships
watertight *adj* **1** not letting water through: *watertight compartments* **2** without loopholes or weak points: *a watertight system*
water wheel *n* a large wheel with vanes set across its rim, which is turned by flowing water to drive machinery
watery *adj* **1** of, like, or containing water: *a watery discharge* **2** (of eyes) filled with tears **3** insipid, thin, or weak: *a watery sun had appeared*

W

watt (wott) *n* the SI unit of power, equal to the power dissipated by a current of 1 ampere flowing across a potential difference of 1 volt

wattage *n* the amount of electrical power, expressed in watts, that an appliance uses or generates

wattle (wott-tl) *n* **1** a frame of rods or stakes interwoven with twigs or branches used to make fences **2** a loose fold of brightly coloured skin hanging from the throat of certain birds and lizards **3** an Australian acacia tree with dense golden, yellow or cream flowers ▸ *adj* **4** made of, formed by, or covered with wattle: *a wattle fence*

wave *vb* **waving**, **waved 1** to move (one's hand) to and fro as a greeting **2** to direct (someone) to move in a particular direction by waving: *I waved him on* **3** to hold (something) up and move it from side to side in order to attract attention **4** to move freely to and fro: *flowers waving in the wind* ▸ *n* **5** one of a sequence of ridges or undulations that moves across the surface of the sea or a lake **6** a curve in the hair **7** a sudden rise in the frequency or intensity of something: *a wave of sympathy* **8** a widespread movement that advances in a body: *a new wave of refugees* **9** a prolonged spell of some particular type of weather: *a heat wave* **10** the act or an instance of waving **11** *physics* an energy-carrying disturbance travelling through a medium or space by a series of vibrations without any overall movement of matter **12 make waves** to cause trouble

wave *vb* **1** = signal, sign, gesture, gesticulate **2** = guide, point, direct, indicate, signal, motion, gesture, nod **3** = brandish, swing, flourish, wag, shake **4** = flutter, flap, stir, shake, swing, wag, oscillate ▸ *n* **5** = ripple, breaker, swell, ridge, roller, billow **7** = outbreak, rash, upsurge, flood, surge, groundswell **8** = stream, flood, surge, spate, current, flow, rush, tide **10** = gesture, sign, signal, indication, gesticulation

wavelength *n* **1** *physics* the distance between two points of the same phase in consecutive cycles of a wave **2** the wavelength of the carrier wave used by a particular broadcasting station **3 on the same wavelength** *informal* having similar views, feelings, or thoughts

waver *vb* **1** to hesitate between possibilities; be indecisive **2** to swing from one thing to another: *she wavered between annoyance and civility* **3** (of a voice or stare) to become unsteady **4** to move back and forth or one way and another: *the barrel of the gun began to waver* > **wavering** *adj*

waver *vb* **1, 2** = hesitate, dither (*chiefly Brit*), vacillate, falter, fluctuate, seesaw, hum and haw; ≠ be decisive **4** = flicker, shake, tremble, wobble, quiver, totter

wavy *adj* **wavier**, **waviest** having curves: *wavy hair*; *a wavy line*

wax¹ *n* **1** a solid fatty or oily substance used for making candles and polish, which softens and melts when heated **2** *physiol* a brownish-yellow waxy substance secreted by glands in the ear ▸ *vb* **3** to coat or polish with wax > **waxed** *adj* > **waxy** *adj*

wax² *vb* **1** to increase gradually in size, strength, or power: *trading has waxed and waned with the economic cycle* **2** (of the moon) to show a gradually increasing area of brightness from new moon until full moon **3** to become: *he waxed eloquent on the disadvantages of marriage*

wax *vb* **1** = increase, grow, develop, expand, swell, enlarge, magnify; ≠ wane **2** = become fuller, enlarge

waxen *adj* **1** resembling wax in colour or texture: *his face was waxen and pale* **2** made of, treated with, or covered with wax: *a waxen image*

waxwork *n* a life-size lifelike wax figure of a famous person

way *n* **1** a manner, method, or means: *a new way of life*; *a tactful way of finding out* **2** a characteristic style or manner: *we are all special in our own way* **3 ways** habits or customs: *he had a liking for British ways* **4** an aspect or detail of something: *the tourist industry is in many ways a success story* **5** a choice or option, for example in a vote: *he thought it could go either way* **6** a route or direction: *the shortest way home* **7** a journey: *you could buy a magazine to read on the way* **8** distance: *they are a long way from Paris* **9** space or room for movement or activity: *you won't be in his way* **10 by the way** incidentally: *by the way, I've decided to leave* **11 by way of A** serving as: *by way of explanation* **B** by the route of: *I went by way of my family home* **12 get one's own way** to have things exactly as one wants them to be **13 give way A** to collapse or break **B** to yield or concede: *I tried to make him understand but he did not give way an inch* **14 give way to A** to be replaced by: *my first feelings of dismay have given way to comparative complacency* **B** to show (an emotion) unrestrainedly **c** to slow down or stop when driving to let (another driver) pass **15 go out of one's way** to take considerable trouble: *he had gone out of his way to reassure me* **16 have it both ways** to enjoy two things that would normally be mutually exclusive **17 in a bad way** *informal* in a poor state of health or a poor financial state **18 in a way** in some respects **19 in no way** not at all **20 make one's way** to proceed or go: *he decided to make his way back in the dark* **21 on the way out** *informal* becoming unfashionable **22 out of the way A** removed or dealt with so as to be no longer a hindrance **B** remote **23 under way** having started moving or making progress ▸ *adv* **24** *informal* far or by far: *that is way out of line*

way *n* **1** = method, means, system, process, technique, manner, procedure, mode **2** = manner, style, fashion, mode **3** = custom, manner, habit, style, practice, nature,

W

personality, wont, tikanga (NZ) **6** = route, direction, course, road, path **7** = journey, approach, passage **8** = distance, length, stretch

wayfarer *n old-fashioned* a traveller

waylay *vb* **-laying, -laid** **1** to lie in wait for and attack **2** to intercept (someone) unexpectedly

wayside *adj* **1** *old-fashioned* situated by the side of a road: *wayside shrines* ▸ *n* **2** **fall by the wayside** to be unsuccessful or stop being successful: *thousands of new diets are dreamed up yearly – many fall by the wayside*

wayward *adj* erratic, selfish, or stubborn › **waywardness** *n*

> **wayward** *adj* = erratic, unruly, unmanageable, unpredictable, capricious, ungovernable, inconstant; ≠ obedient

WC *or* **wc** *n* a toilet

we *pron* (*used as the subject of a verb*) **1** the speaker or writer and another person or other people: *we arrived in Calais* **2** all people or people in general: *it's an unfair world we live in* **3** *formal* same as **I**: used by monarchs and editors

weak *adj* **1** lacking in physical or mental strength **2** (of a part of the body) not functioning as well as is normal: *a weak heart* **3** liable to collapse or break: *weak bridges* **4** lacking in importance, influence, or strength: *a weak government* **5** (of a currency or shares) falling in price or characterized by falling prices **6** lacking in moral strength; easily influenced **7** not convincing: *weak arguments* **8** lacking strength or power: *his voice was weak* **9** not having a strong flavour: *weak coffee* › **weakly** *adv*

> **weak** *adj* **1** = feeble, frail, debilitated, fragile, sickly, puny, unsteady, infirm; ≠ strong **3** = fragile, brittle, flimsy, fine, delicate, frail, dainty, breakable **4** = unsafe, exposed, vulnerable, helpless, unprotected, defenceless, unguarded; ≠ secure **7** = unconvincing, unsatisfactory, lame, flimsy, pathetic; ≠ convincing **9** = tasteless, thin, diluted, watery, runny, insipid; ≠ strong

weaken *vb* to become or make weak or weaker

> **weaken** *vb* = reduce, undermine, moderate, diminish, lessen, sap; ≠ boost

weakling *n derogatory* a person who is considered lacking in physical or mental strength

weakness *n* **1** the state of being weak **2** a failing in a person's character: *his weakness is his impetuosity* **3** a self-indulgent liking: *a weakness for gin*

> **weakness** *n* **1** = frailty, fatigue, exhaustion, fragility, infirmity, feebleness, decrepitude; ≠ strength **2** = failing, fault, defect, deficiency, flaw, shortcoming, blemish, imperfection; ≠ strong point **3** = liking, appetite, penchant,

soft spot, passion, inclination, fondness, partiality; ≠ aversion

weal *n* a raised mark on the skin produced by a blow

wealth *n* **1** the state of being rich **2** a large amount of money and valuable material possessions: *redistribution of wealth* **3** a great amount or number: *a wealth of detail*

> **wealth** *n* **1** = riches, fortune, prosperity, affluence, money, opulence; ≠ poverty **2** = property, capital, fortune **3** = abundance, plenty, richness, profusion, fullness, cornucopia, copiousness; ≠ lack

wealthy *adj* **wealthier, wealthiest** **1** having a large amount of money and valuable material possessions **2** **wealthy in** having a great amount or number of: *a continent exceptionally wealthy in minerals*

> **wealthy** *adj* **1** = rich, prosperous, affluent, well-off, flush (*informal*), opulent, well-heeled (*informal*), well-to-do, minted (*Brit slang*); ≠ poor

wean *vb* **1** to start giving (a baby or young mammal) food other than its mother's milk **2** to cause (oneself or someone else) to give up a former habit: *they are unable to wean themselves from the tobacco habit* › **weaning** *n*

weapon *n* **1** an object used in fighting, such as a knife or gun **2** anything used to get the better of an opponent: *having a sense of humour is a weapon of self-defence*

weaponry *n* weapons regarded collectively

wear *vb* **wearing, wore, worn** **1** to carry or have (a garment or jewellery) on one's body as clothing or ornament **2** to have (a particular facial expression): *she wore a scowl of frank antagonism* **3** to style (the hair) in a particular way: *she wears her hair in a braid* **4** to deteriorate or cause to deteriorate by constant use or action **5** *informal* to accept: *he won't be given a top job – the Party wouldn't wear it* **6** **wear thin** to lessen or become weaker: *his patience began to wear thin* **7** **wear well** to remain in good condition for a long time ▸ *n* **8** clothes that are suitable for a particular time or purpose: *evening wear; beach wear* **9** deterioration from constant or normal use **10** the quality of resisting the effects of constant use ▸ See also **wear off** › **wearer** *n*

> **wear** *vb* **1** = be dressed in, have on, sport (*informal*), put on **2** = show, present, bear, display, assume, put on, exhibit **4** = deteriorate, fray, wear thin ▸ *n* **8** = clothes, things, dress, gear (*informal*), attire, costume, garments, apparel (*old-fashioned*) **9** = damage, wear and tear, erosion, deterioration, attrition, corrosion, abrasion; ≠ repair

wearable *adj* **1** (of a garment) comfortable and practical **2** (of an electronic device) designed to be worn on the body

W

wearisome *adj* causing fatigue and irritation

wear off *vb* to have a gradual decrease in effect or intensity: *the novelty began to wear off*

> **wear off** *vb* = subside, disappear, fade, diminish, decrease, dwindle, wane, peter out

wear on *vb* (of time) to pass slowly

weary *adj* **-rier, -riest** 1 very tired; lacking energy 2 caused by or suggestive of weariness: *he managed a weary smile* 3 causing exhaustion: *a long weary struggle* 4 **weary of** discontented or bored with: *he was weary of the war* ▸ *vb* **-ries, -rying, -ried** 5 to make weary 6 **weary of** to become discontented or bored with: *he seems to have wearied of her possessiveness* > **wearily** *adv* > **weariness** *n* > **wearying** *adj*

> **weary** *adj* 1 = tired, exhausted, drained, worn out, done in (*informal*), flagging, fatigued, sleepy, clapped out (*Austral, NZ informal*); ≠ energetic 3 = tiring, arduous, tiresome, laborious, wearisome; ≠ refreshing ▸ *vb* 6 = grow tired, tire, become bored

weasel *n, pl* **-sels** *or* **-sel** 1 a small meat-eating mammal with reddish-brown fur, a long body and neck, and short legs 2 *informal* a sly or treacherous person

weather *n* 1 the day-to-day atmospheric conditions, such as temperature, cloudiness, and rainfall, affecting a specific place 2 **make heavy weather of** *informal* to carry out (a task) with great difficulty or needless effort 3 **under the weather** *informal* feeling slightly ill ▸ *vb* 4 to undergo or cause to undergo changes, such as discoloration, due to the action of the weather 5 to come safely through (a storm, problem, or difficulty)

> **weather** *n* 1 = climate, conditions, temperature, forecast, outlook, meteorological conditions, elements ▸ *vb* 5 = withstand, stand, survive, overcome, resist, brave, endure, come through; ≠ surrender to

weather-beaten *adj* 1 tanned by exposure to the weather: *a crumpled weather-beaten face* 2 worn or damaged as a result of exposure to the weather

weave *vb* **weaving, wove** *or* **weaved, woven** *or* **weaved** 1 to form (a fabric) by interlacing yarn on a loom 2 to make (a garment or a blanket) by this process 3 to construct (a basket or fence) by interlacing cane or twigs 4 to compose (a story or plan) by combining separate elements into a whole 5 to move from side to side while going forward: *to weave in and out of lanes* 6 **get weaving** *informal* to hurry ▸ *n* 7 the structure or pattern of a woven fabric: *the rough weave of the cloth* > **weaver** *n* > **weaving** *n*

> **weave** *vb* 1 = knit, intertwine, plait, braid, entwine, interlace 4 = create, tell, recount, narrate, build, relate, make up, spin (*informal*) 5 = zigzag, wind, crisscross

web *n* 1 a mesh of fine tough threads built by a spider to trap insects 2 anything that is intricately formed or complex: *a web of relationships* 3 a membrane connecting the toes of some water birds and water-dwelling animals such as frogs 4 **the web** (*often cap*) short for **World Wide Web** ▸ *adj* 5 of or situated on the World Wide Web: *a web server; web pages* > **webbed** *adj*

> **web** *n* 1 = cobweb, spider's web 2 = tangle, network

Web 2.0 *n* the internet viewed as a medium in which interactive experience plays a more important role than simply accessing information

webbing *n* a strong fabric that is woven in strips and used under springs in upholstery or for straps

webcam *n* a camera that transmits still or moving images over the internet

webcast *n* a broadcast of an event over the internet

weblog *n* a person's online journal

webmail *n* an email system that allows account holders to access mail via an internet site rather than by downloading it onto a computer

website *n* a group of connected pages on the World Wide Web situated under a single domain name

wed *vb* **wedding, wedded** *or* **wed** 1 *old-fashioned* to take (a person) as a husband or wife; marry 2 to unite closely: *to wed folklore and magic*

> **wed** *vb* 1 = get married to, be united to; ≠ divorce 2 = unite, combine, join, link, ally, blend, merge, interweave; ≠ divide

wedding *n* 1 a marriage ceremony 2 a special wedding anniversary, esp. the 25th (**silver wedding**) or 50th (**golden wedding**)

> **wedding** *n* 1 = marriage, nuptials, wedding ceremony, marriage service, wedding service

wedge *n* 1 a block of solid material, esp. wood or metal, that is shaped like a narrow V in cross section and can be pushed or driven between two objects or parts of an object in order to split or secure them 2 a slice shaped like a wedge: *a wedge of quiche* 3 *golf* a club with a wedge-shaped face, used for bunker or pitch shots 4 **drive a wedge between** to cause a split between (people or groups) 5 **the thin end of the wedge** anything unimportant in itself that implies the start of something much larger ▸ *vb* **wedging, wedged** 6 to secure (something) with a wedge 7 to squeeze into a narrow space: *a book wedged between the bed and the table*

> **wedge** *n* 1, 2 = block, lump, chunk ▸ *vb* 7 = squeeze, force, lodge, jam, crowd, stuff, pack, thrust

W

wedge-tailed eagle *n* a large brown Australian eagle with a wedge-shaped tail

wedlock *n* **1** the state of being married **2 born out of wedlock** born when one's parents are not legally married

Wednesday *n* the fourth day of the week

wee¹ *adj Brit, Austral & NZ* small or short

wee² *informal* ▸ *n* **1** an instance of urinating ▸ *vb* **weeing, weed 2** to urinate. Also: **wee-wee**

weed *n* **1** any plant that grows wild and profusely, esp. among cultivated plants **2** *slang* **A** marijuana **B the weed** or **the evil weed** tobacco **3** *informal* a thin weak person ▸ *vb* **4** to remove weeds from (a garden)

weed out *vb* to separate out, remove, or eliminate (an unwanted element): *to weed out the thugs*

weedy *adj* **weedier, weediest 1** *informal* thin or weak: *sick and weedy children* **2** full of weeds: *weedy patches of garden*

week *n* **1** a period of seven consecutive days, esp. one beginning with Sunday **2** a period of seven consecutive days from a specified day: *a week from today* **3** the period of time within a week that is spent at work

weekday *n* any day of the week other than Saturday or Sunday

weekend *n* Saturday and Sunday

weekly *adj* **1** happening once a week or every week: *a weekly column* **2** determined or calculated by the week: *weekly earnings* ▸ *adv* **3** once a week or every week: *report to the police weekly* ▸ *n, pl* **-lies 4** a newspaper or magazine issued every week

weep *vb* **weeping, wept 1** to shed tears; cry **2** to ooze liquid: *the skin cracked and wept; the label is weeping black ink in the rain* ▸ *n* **3** a spell of weeping: *together we had a good weep*

> **weep** *vb* **1** = cry, shed tears, sob, whimper, mourn, lament, blubber, snivel; ≠ rejoice

weeping willow *n* a willow tree with graceful drooping branches

weepy *informal* ▸ *adj* **weepier, weepiest 1** liable or tending to weep ▸ *n, pl* **weepies 2** a sentimental film or book

weevil *n* a beetle with a long snout that feeds on plants

weft *n* the yarns woven across the width of the fabric through the lengthways warp yarns

weigh *vb* **1** to have weight as specified: *the tree weighs nearly three tons* **2** to measure the weight of **3** to consider carefully: *the President now has to weigh his options* **4** to be influential: *the authorities did not enter my mind or weigh with me* **5 weigh anchor** to raise a ship's anchor **6 weigh out** to measure out by weight

> **weigh** *vb* **1** = have a weight of, tip the scales at (*informal*) **3** = consider, examine, contemplate, evaluate, ponder, think over, reflect upon, meditate upon **4** = matter, carry weight, count

weighbridge *n* a machine for weighing vehicles by means of a metal plate set into a road

weight *n* **1** the heaviness of an object, substance, or person **2** *physics* the vertical force experienced by a mass as a result of gravitation **3 A** a system of units used to express weight: *metric weight* **B** a unit used to measure weight: *the kilogram is the weight used in the metric system* **4 A** an object of known heaviness used for weighing objects, substances, or people **B** an object of known heaviness used in weight training or weightlifting to strengthen the muscles **5** any heavy load: *with a weight of fish on their backs* **6** force, importance, or influence: *they want their words to carry weight* **7** an oppressive force: *the weight of expectation* **8 pull one's weight** *informal* to do one's full share of a task **9 throw one's weight about** *informal* to act in an aggressive authoritarian manner ▸ *vb* **10** to add weight to; make heavier **11** to slant (a system) so that it favours one side rather than another

> **weight** *n* **1** = heaviness, mass, poundage, load, tonnage **6** = importance, force, power, value, authority, influence, impact, import (*formal*), mana (NZ) ▸ *vb* **10** = load **11** = bias, load, slant, unbalance

weightless *adj* **1** seeming to have very little weight or no weight at all **2** seeming not to be affected by gravity, as in the case of astronauts in an orbiting spacecraft › **weightlessness** *n*

weighty *adj* **weightier, weightiest 1** important or serious: *weighty matters* **2** very heavy

weir *n* **1** a low dam that is built across a river to divert the water or control its flow **2** a fencelike trap built across a stream for catching fish in

weird *adj* **1** strange or bizarre **2** suggestive of the supernatural; uncanny › **weirdly** *adv* › **weirdness** *n*

> **weird** *adj* **1** = bizarre, odd, strange, unusual, queer (*old-fashioned*), unnatural, creepy (*informal*), freakish; ≠ ordinary **2** = strange, odd, unusual, bizarre, mysterious, queer (*old-fashioned*), eerie, unnatural; ≠ normal

weirdo *n, pl* **-dos** *informal* a person whose behaviour or dress is considered bizarre or eccentric

welch *vb* same as **welsh**

welcome *vb* **-coming, -comed 1** to greet the arrival of (a guest) cordially **2** to receive or accept (something) gladly: *I would welcome a chance to speak to him* ▸ *n* **3** the act of greeting or receiving someone or something in a specified manner: *the President was given a warm welcome* ▸ *adj* **4** gladly received or admitted: *I wouldn't want to stay where I'm not welcome* **5** encouraged or invited: *you are welcome to join us at one of our social events* **6** bringing pleasure: *a welcome change* **7 you're welcome** an expression used to acknowledge someone's thanks › **welcoming** *adj*

W

welcome *vb* **1** = greet, meet, receive, embrace, hail, karanga (NZ), mihi (NZ), haeremai (NZ); ≠ reject **2** = accept gladly, appreciate, embrace, approve of, be pleased by, give the thumbs up to (*informal*), be glad about, express pleasure *or* satisfaction at ▸ *n* = greeting, welcoming, reception, acceptance, hail, hospitality, salutation (*formal*), haeremai (NZ); ≠ rejection ▸ *adj* **4** = wanted; ≠ unwanted **5** = free **6** = pleasing, appreciated, acceptable, pleasant, desirable, refreshing, delightful, gratifying; ≠ unpleasant

weld *vb* **1** to join (two pieces of metal or plastic) by softening with heat and hammering or by fusion **2** to unite closely: *the diverse ethnic groups had been welded together by the anti-Fascist cause* ▸ *n* **3** a joint formed by welding > **welder** *n*

weld *vb* **1** = join, link, bond, bind, connect, fuse, solder **2** = unite, combine, blend, unify, fuse

welfare *n* **1** health, happiness, prosperity, and general wellbeing **2** financial and other assistance given, usually by the government, to people in need

welfare *n* **1** = wellbeing, good, interest, health, security, benefit, safety, protection **2** = state benefit, support, benefits, pensions, dole (*slang*), social security, unemployment benefit, state benefits, pogey (*Canad*)

welfare state *n* a system in which the government undertakes responsibility for the wellbeing of its population, through unemployment insurance, retirement pensions, and other social-security measures

well¹ *adv* **better, best 1** satisfactorily or pleasingly: *well proportioned* **2** skilfully: *I played well for the last six holes* **3** thoroughly: *make sure the chicken is well cooked* **4** comfortably or prosperously: *he has lived well from his various nautical exploits* **5** suitably or fittingly: *you can't very well refuse* **6** intimately: *darling Robert, I know him so well* **7** favourably: *it will go down very well with all the people who support him* **8** by a considerable margin: *well over half; she left well before tea* **9** very likely: *the claim may well be true* **10** *informal* extremely: *well cool* **11 all very well** used ironically to express discontent or annoyance: *that's all very well, but I'm left to pick up the pieces* **12 as well A** in addition **B** with equal effect: used to express indifference or reluctance: *I might as well go out* **13 as well as** in addition to **14 just as well** fortunate or appropriate: *it's just as well I didn't spend all my money* ▸ *adj* **15** in good health: *I'm not feeling well* **16** satisfactory or acceptable: *all was well in the aircraft* ▸ *interj* **17 A** an expression of surprise, indignation, or reproof: *well, what a cheek!* **B** an expression of anticipation in waiting for an answer or remark: *well, what do you think?*

well *adv* **1** = satisfactorily, nicely, smoothly, successfully, pleasantly, splendidly, agreeably; ≠ badly **2** = skilfully, expertly, adeptly, professionally, correctly, properly, efficiently, adequately; ≠ badly **3** = thoroughly, completely, fully, carefully, effectively, efficiently, rigorously **4** = prosperously, comfortably, splendidly, in comfort, in (the lap of) luxury, without hardship **5** = decently, right, kindly, fittingly, fairly, properly, politely, suitably; ≠ unfairly **6** = intimately, deeply, fully, profoundly; ≠ slightly **7** = favourably, highly, kindly, warmly, enthusiastically, approvingly, admiringly, with admiration; ≠ unfavourably **8** = considerably, easily, very much, significantly, substantially, markedly **9** = possibly, probably, certainly, reasonably, conceivably, justifiably **10** = fully, highly, greatly, amply, very much, thoroughly, considerably, substantially ▸ *adj* **15** = healthy, sound, fit, blooming, in fine fettle, in good condition; ≠ ill **16** = satisfactory, right, fine, pleasing, proper, thriving; ≠ unsatisfactory

well² *n* **1** a hole or shaft bored into the earth to tap a supply of water, oil, or gas **2** an open shaft through the floors of a building, used for a staircase ▸ *vb* **3** to flow upwards or outwards: *tears welled up into my eyes*

well *n* **1** = hole, bore, pit, shaft ▸ *vb* = flow, spring, pour, jet, surge, gush, spurt, spout

well-being *n* the state of being contented and healthy: *a sense of well-being*

well-disposed *adj* inclined to be sympathetic, kindly, or friendly towards a person or idea

well-heeled *adj informal* wealthy

wellies *pl n Brit, NZ & Austral informal* Wellington boots

Wellington boots *or* **wellingtons** *pl n* long rubber boots, worn in wet or muddy conditions

well-meaning *adj* having or indicating good intentions, usually with unfortunate results

well-spoken *adj* having a clear, articulate, and socially acceptable accent and way of speaking

well-worn *adj* **1** (of a word or phrase) having lost its meaning or force through being overused **2** having been used so much as to show signs of wear: *well-worn leather*

welsh *or* **welch** *vb* **welsh on** to fail to pay (a debt) or fulfil (an obligation)

Welsh *adj* **1** of Wales ▸ *n* **2** a Celtic language spoken in some parts of Wales ▸ *pl n* **3 the Welsh** the people of Wales

Welsh rarebit *n* melted cheese, sometimes mixed with milk or seasonings, served on hot toast. Also called: **Welsh rabbit**

welt *n* **1** a raised mark on the skin produced by a blow **2** a raised or strengthened seam in a garment

welter *n* a confused mass or jumble: *a welter of facts*

W

welterweight *n* a professional boxer weighing up to 147 pounds (66.5 kg) or an amateur boxer weighing up to 67 kg

wen *n pathol* a cyst on the scalp

wench *n old-fashioned* **1** a girl or young woman **2** a prostitute or female servant

wend *vb* to make (one's way) in a particular direction: *it's time to wend our way back home*

went *vb* the past tense of **go**

wept *vb* the past of **weep**

were *vb* the form of the past tense of **be**: used after *we, you, they,* or a plural noun, or as a subjunctive in conditional sentences

we're we are

weren't were not

werewolf *n, pl* **-wolves** (in folklore) a person who can turn into a wolf

west *n* **1** one of the four cardinal points of the compass, at 270° clockwise from north; the direction along a line of latitude towards the sunset **2 the west** any area lying in or towards the west ▸ *adj* **3** situated in, moving towards, or facing the west **4** (esp. of the wind) from the west ▸ *adv* **5** in, to, or towards the west

West *n* **1 the West** **A** the western part of the world contrasted historically and culturally with the East **B** (esp. formerly) the non-Communist countries of Europe and America contrasted with the Communist states of the East ▸ *adj* **2** of or denoting the western part of a country or region

westerly *adj* **1** of or in the west ▸ *adv, adj* **2** towards the west **3** from the west: *a westerly wind*

western *adj* **1** situated in or towards the west **2** facing or moving towards the west **3** (*sometimes cap*) of or characteristic of the west or West ▸ *n* **4** a film or book about cowboys in the western states of the US in the 19th century > **westernmost** *adj*

Western *adj* (esp. formerly) of or characteristic of the Americas and the parts of Europe not under Communist rule

westernize *or* **-nise** *vb* **-nizing, -nized** *or* **-nising, -nised** to influence or make familiar with the customs or practices of the West > **westernization** *or* **-nisation** *n*

westward *adj, adv also* **westwards** **1** towards the west ▸ *n* **2** the westward part or direction

wet *adj* **wetter, wettest** **1** moistened, covered, or soaked with water or some other liquid **2** not yet dry or solid: *wet paint* **3** rainy: *the weather was cold and wet* **4** *Brit & NZ informal* feeble or foolish **5 wet behind the ears** *informal* immature or inexperienced ▸ *n* **6** rainy weather **7** *Brit informal* a feeble or foolish person ▸ *vb* **wetting, wet** *or* **wetted** **8** to make wet: *wet the brush before applying the paint* **9** to urinate in (one's clothes or bed) **10 wet oneself** to urinate in one's clothes > **wetly** *adv* > **wetness** *n*

wet *adj* **1** = damp, soaking, saturated, moist, watery, soggy, sodden, waterlogged; ≠ dry **3** = rainy, damp, drizzly, showery, raining, pouring, drizzling, teeming; ≠ sunny **4** = feeble, soft, weak, ineffectual, weedy (*informal*), spineless, effete, timorous ▸ *n* **6** = rain, drizzle; ≠ fine weather ▸ *vb* **8** = moisten, spray, dampen, water, soak, saturate, douse, irrigate, fertigate (*Austral*); ≠ dry

wet blanket *n informal* a person whose low spirits or lack of enthusiasm have a depressing effect on others

wetland *n* an area of marshy land

wet nurse *n* (esp. formerly) a woman hired to breast-feed another woman's baby

wet room *n* a type of waterproofed room with a drain in the floor often serving as an open-plan shower

wet suit *n* a close-fitting rubber suit used by skin-divers and yachtsmen to retain body heat

whack *vb* **1** to hit hard: *that lad whacked him over the head with a bottle* **2** (usually foll. by in or on) *informal* to put something onto or into (something else) with force or abandon: *whack on some sunscreen* ▸ *n* **3** a hard blow or the sound of one: *a whack with a blunt instrument* **4** *informal* a share: *he took his whack of that money* **5 have a whack** to make an attempt **6 out of whack** *informal* out of order or out of condition: *my body is just a little out of whack*

whack *vb* **1** = strike, hit, belt (*informal*), bang, smack, thrash, thump, swipe (*informal*) ▸ *n* **3** = blow, hit, stroke, belt (*informal*), bang, smack, thump, swipe (*informal*) **4** = share, part, cut (*informal*), bit, portion, quota

whacked *adj informal* completely exhausted

whacking *n* **1** *old-fashioned* a severe beating ▸ *adv* **2** *Brit, Austral & NZ informal* extremely: *a whacking great elm*

whale *n* **1** a very large fishlike sea mammal that breathes through a blowhole on the top of its head **2 have a whale of a time** *informal* to enjoy oneself very much

whaler *n* **1** a ship used for hunting whales **2** a person whose job is to hunt whales

whaling *n* the activity of hunting and killing whales for food or oil

wharf *n, pl* **wharves** *or* **wharfs** a platform along the side of a waterfront for docking, loading, and unloading ships

wharf *n* = dock, pier, berth, quay, jetty, landing stage

wharfie *n Austral & NZ* a dock labourer

what *pron* **1** used in requesting further information about the identity or categorization of something: *what was he wearing?*; *I knew what would happen* **2** the person, thing, people, or things that: *all was not what it seemed* **3** used in

exclamations to add emphasis: *what a creep!*
4 what for? for what reason? **5 what have you**
other similar or related things: *qualifications,
interests, profession, what have you* ▸ *adj* **6** used with
a noun in requesting further information about
the identity or categorization of something:
what difference can it make now? **7** to any degree or
in any amount: *they provided what financial support
they could*

whatever *pron* **1** everything or anything that:
I can handle whatever comes up **2** no matter what:
whatever you do, keep your temper **3** *informal* other
similar or related things: *a block of wood, rock, or
whatever* **4** an intensive form of *what*, used in
questions: *whatever gave you that impression?* ▸ *adj*
5 an intensive form of *what*: *I can take whatever
actions I deem necessary* **6** at all: *there is no foundation
whatever for such opinions* ▸ *interj* **7** an expression of
indifference

whatnot *n informal* other similar or related
things: *groceries, wines, and whatnot*

whatsoever *adj* at all: used for emphasis after
a noun phrase that uses words such as *none* or
any: *there is nothing whatsoever wrong with your heart;
it can be used at any time and under any circumstances
whatsoever*

wheat *n* **1** a kind of grain used in making flour
and pasta **2** the plant from which this grain is
obtained

wheatear *n* a small northern songbird with a
white rump

wheaten *adj* made from the grain or flour of
wheat: *wheaten bread*

wheedle *vb* **-dling, -dled** **1** to try to persuade
(someone) by coaxing or flattery: *wheedling you
into giving them their way* **2** to obtain (something)
in this way: *she wheedled money out of him*
▷ **wheedling** *adj, n*

wheel *n* **1** a circular object mounted on a shaft
around which it can turn, fixed under vehicles
to enable them to move **2** anything like a wheel
in shape or function: *the steering wheel; a spinning
wheel* **3** something that is repeated in cycles: *the
wheel of fashion would turn, and the clothes would be
back in style* **4** or **behind the wheel** driving a
vehicle ▸ *vb* **5** to push (a bicycle, wheelchair, or
pram) along **6** to turn in a circle **7 wheel and
deal** to operate shrewdly and sometimes
unscrupulously in order to advance one's own
interests **8 wheel round** to change direction or
turn round suddenly

> **wheel** *n* **1, 2** = disc, ring, hoop ▸ *vb* **5** = push,
> trundle, roll **6** = turn, swing, spin, revolve,
> rotate, whirl, swivel

wheelbarrow *n* a shallow open box for
carrying small loads, with a wheel at the front
and two handles

wheelbase *n* the distance between the front
and back axles of a motor vehicle

wheelchair *n* a special chair on large wheels,
for use by people who cannot walk properly

wheel clamp *n* a device fixed onto one wheel
of an illegally parked car to prevent the car
being driven off

wheeze *vb* **wheezing, wheezed** **1** to breathe
with a rasping or whistling sound ▸ *n* **2** a
wheezing breath or sound **3** *Brit old-fashioned
slang* a trick or plan: *a money-making wheeze*
▷ **wheezy** *adj*

whelk *n* an edible sea creature with a strong
snail-like shell

whelp *n* **1** a young wolf or dog **2** *offensive* a youth
▸ *vb* **3** (of an animal) to give birth

when *adv* **1** at what time?: *when are they leaving?*
▸ *conj* **2** at the time at which: *he was twenty when
the war started* **3** although: *he drives when he could
walk* **4** considering the fact that: *how did you pass
the exam when you hadn't studied for it?* ▸ *pron* **5** at
which time: *she's at the age when girls get interested
in boys*

whence *conj old-fashioned or poetic* from what
place, cause, or origin: *he would then ask them
whence they came*

whenever *conj* **1** at every or any time that:
*the filly was trained to stop whenever a jockey used a
whip* ▸ *adv* **2** no matter when: *I am eager to come
whenever you suggest* **3** *informal* at an unknown
or unspecified time: *the 16th, 17th, or whenever*
4 an intensive form of *when*, used in
questions: *if we can't exercise restraint now,
whenever can we?*

where *adv* **1** in, at, or to what place, point, or
position?: *where are we going?; I know where he found
it* ▸ *pron* **2** in, at, or to which place: *he found a
sandwich bar where he could get a snack* ▸ *conj* **3** in the
place at which: *he should have stayed where he was
doing well*

whereabouts *pl n* **1** the place, esp. the
approximate place, where a person or thing is:
the whereabouts of the president are unknown ▸ *adv*
2 approximately where: *whereabouts will you go?*

> **whereabouts** *pl n* = position, situation,
> site, location

whereas *conj* but by contrast: *she was crazy about
him, whereas for him it was just another affair*

whereby *pron* by or because of which: *the process
whereby pests become resistant to pesticides*

wherefore *n* **1 the whys and wherefores** the
reasons or explanation: *the whys and wherefores of
the war* ▸ *conj* **2** *old-fashioned, formal* for which
reason

whereupon *conj* at which point: *they sentenced
him to death, whereupon he fainted*

wherever *pron* **1** at, in, or to every place or point
which: *I got a wonderful reception wherever I went*
▸ *conj* **2** in, to, or at whatever place: *wherever they
went, the conditions were harsh* ▸ *adv* **3** no matter
where: *we're going to find him, wherever he is*
4 *informal* at, in, or to an unknown or unspecified
place: *the jungles of Borneo or wherever* **5** an
intensive form of *where*, used in questions:
wherever have you been?

W

wherewithal *n* **the wherewithal** the necessary funds, resources, or equipment: *the wherewithal for making chemical weapons*

whet *vb* **whetting, whetted 1 whet someone's appetite** to increase someone's desire for or interest in something: *she gave him just enough information to whet his appetite* **2** old-fashioned to sharpen (a knife or other tool)

whether *conj* **1** used to introduce an indirect question: *he asked him whether he had seen the hunter* **2** used to introduce a clause expressing doubt or choice: *you are entitled to the assistance of a lawyer, whether or not you can afford one; we learn from experience, whether good or bad*

whetstone *n* a stone used for sharpening knives or other tools

whey (**way**) *n* the watery liquid that separates from the curd when milk is clotted, for example in making cheese

which *adj* **1** used with a noun in requesting that the particular thing being referred to is further identified or distinguished: *which way had he gone?; a questionnaire to find out which shops local consumers use* **2** any out of several: *you have to choose which goods and services you want* ▸ *pron* **3** used in requesting that the particular thing being referred to is further identified or distinguished: *which of these occupations would be suitable for you?* **4** used in relative clauses referring to a thing rather than a person: *a discovery which could have lasting effects* **5** and that: *her books were all over the dining table, which meant we had to eat in the kitchen*

whichever *adj* **1** any out of several: *choose whichever line you feel more comfortable with* **2** no matter which: *whichever bridge you take, pause mid-stream for a look up and down the river* ▸ *pron* **3** any one or ones out of several: *delete whichever is inapplicable* **4** no matter which one or ones: *whichever you choose, you must be consistent throughout*

whiff *n* **1** a passing odour: *I got a whiff of her perfume* **2** a trace or hint: *the first whiff of jealousy*

whiff *n* **1** = smell, hint, scent, sniff, aroma, odour

Whig *n* **1** a member of a British political party of the 18th–19th centuries that sought limited political and social reform and provided the core of the Liberal Party ▸ *adj* **2** of or relating to Whigs › **Whiggism** *n*

while *conj* **1** at the same time that: *anti-inflammatory remedies may be used to alleviate the condition while background factors are investigated* **2** at some point during the time that: *her father had died while she was gone* **3** although or whereas: *while she tossed and turned, he fell into a dreamless sleep* ▸ *n* **4** a period of time: *I'd like to stay a while*

while away *vb* **whiling, whiled** to pass (time) idly but pleasantly

whilst *conj* chiefly Brit same as **while**

whim *n* a sudden, passing, and often fanciful idea

whim *n* = impulse, caprice, fancy, urge, notion

whimper *vb* **1** to cry, complain, or say (something) in a whining plaintive way ▸ *n* **2** a soft plaintive whine

whimsical *adj* unusual, playful, and fanciful: *a whimsical story* › **whimsically** *adv*

whimsy *n* **1** *pl* **-sies** a fanciful or playful idea: *they thought sparing the rod a foolish whimsy* **2** capricious or playful behaviour: *sudden flights of whimsy*

whin *n* chiefly Brit same as **gorse**

whine *n* **1** a long high-pitched plaintive cry or moan **2** a peevish complaint ▸ *vb* **whining, whined 3** to whinge or complain **4** to issue a long high-pitched moan › **whiner** *n* › **whining** *adj, n*

whine *n* **1** = cry, moan, sob, wail, whimper **2** = complaint, moan (*informal*), grumble, grouse, gripe (*informal*), whinge (*informal*), grouch (*informal*) ▸ *vb* **3** = complain, grumble, gripe (*informal*), whinge (*informal*), moan, grouse, grizzle (*informal, chiefly Brit*), grouch (*informal*) **4** = cry, sob, wail, whimper, sniffle, snivel, moan

whinge Brit, Austral & NZ informal ▸ *vb* **whingeing, whinged 1** to complain in a moaning manner ▸ *n* **2** a complaint › **whinger** *n*

whinny *vb* **-nies, -nying, -nied 1** (of a horse) to neigh softly or gently ▸ *n, pl* **-nies 2** a gentle or low-pitched neigh

whip *n* **1** a piece of leather or rope attached at one end to a stiff handle, used for hitting people or animals **2 a** a member of a political party who is responsible for urging members to attend Parliament to vote on an important issue **b** a notice sent to members of a political party by the whip, urging them to attend Parliament to vote in a particular way on an important issue **3** a dessert made from egg whites or cream beaten stiff: *raspberry whip* ▸ *vb* **whipping, whipped 4** to hit with a whip **5** to hit sharply: *strands of hair whipped across her cheeks* **6** informal to move or go quickly and suddenly: *machine-gun bullets whipped past him* **7** to beat (cream or eggs) with a whisk or fork until frothy or stiff **8** to rouse (someone) into a particular condition: *politicians have whipped themselves into a panic about never-ending recession* **9** informal to steal (something) ▸ *See also* **whip-round** › **whipping** *n*

whip *n* **1** = lash, cane, birch, crop, scourge, cat-o'-nine-tails ▸ *vb* **4** = lash, cane, flog, beat, strap, thrash, birch, scourge **6** = dash, shoot, fly, tear, rush, dive, dart, whisk **7** = whisk, beat, mix vigorously, stir vigorously **8** = incite, drive, stir, spur, work up, get going, agitate, inflame

whip bird *n* Austral a bird with a whistle ending in a note like the crack of a whip

whiplash injury *n* an injury to the neck resulting from the head being suddenly thrust forward and then snapped back, for example in a car crash

whippet *n* a small slender dog similar to a greyhound

whip-round *n informal* an impromptu collection of money

whir *n*, *vb* **whirring**, **whirred** same as **whirr**

whirl *vb* **1** to spin or turn round very fast **2** to seem to spin from dizziness or confusion: *my mind whirled with half-formed thoughts* ▸ *n* **3** the act or an instance of whirling: *he grasps her by the waist and gives her a whirl* **4** a round of intense activity: *the social whirl of Paris* **5** a confused state: *my thoughts are in a whirl* **6 give something a whirl** *informal* to try something new

> **whirl** *vb* **1** = spin, turn, twist, rotate, twirl **2** = feel dizzy, swim, spin, reel, go round ▸ *n* **3** = revolution, turn, roll, spin, twist, swirl, rotation, twirl **4** = bustle, round, series, succession, flurry, merry-go-round **5** = confusion, daze, dither (*chiefly Brit*), giddiness

whirlpool *n* a powerful circular current of water, into which objects floating nearby are drawn

whirlwind *n* **1** a column of air whirling violently upwards in a spiral ▸ *adj* **2** done or happening much more quickly than usual: *a whirlwind tour of France*

whirr *or* **whir** *n* **1** a prolonged soft whizz or buzz: *the whirr of the fax machine* ▸ *vb* **whirring**, **whirred 2** to produce a prolonged soft whizz or buzz > **whirring** *n*, *adj*

whisk *vb* **1** to move or take somewhere swiftly: *I was whisked away in a police car* **2** to brush away lightly: *the waiter whisked the crumbs away with a napkin* **3** to beat (cream or eggs) with a whisk or fork until frothy or stiff ▸ *n* **4** the act or an instance of whisking: *a whisk of a scaly tail* **5** a utensil for beating cream or eggs until frothy or stiff

> **whisk** *vb* **2** = flick, whip, sweep, brush **3** = beat, mix vigorously, stir vigorously, whip, fluff up ▸ *n* **4** = flick, sweep, brush, whip **5** = beater, mixer, blender

whisker *n* **1** any of the long stiff hairs that grow out from the sides of the mouth of a cat or other mammal **2** any of the hairs growing on a man's face, esp. on the cheeks or chin **3 by a whisker** by a very small distance or amount: *we missed him by a whisker* > **whiskered** *or* **whiskery** *adj*

whiskey *n* Irish or American whisky

whisky *n*, *pl* **-kies** a strong alcoholic drink made by distilling fermented cereals

whisper *vb* **1** to speak or say (something) very softly, using the breath instead of the vocal cords **2** to make a low soft rustling sound: *the leaves whispered* ▸ *n* **3** a low soft voice: *her voice sank to a whisper* **4** *informal* a rumour: *I just picked up a whisper on this killing* **5** a low soft rustling sound: *a whisper of breeze in the shrubbery* > **whispered** *adj*

> **whisper** *vb* **1** = murmur, breathe; ≠ shout **2** = rustle, sigh, hiss, swish ▸ *n* **3** = murmur, mutter, mumble, undertone **4** = rumour, report, gossip, goss (*informal*), innuendo, insinuation **5** = rustle, sigh, hiss, swish

whist *n* a card game for two pairs of players

whistle *vb* **-tling**, **-tled 1** to produce a shrill sound by forcing breath between pursed lips **2** to produce (a tune) by making a series of such sounds **3** to signal (to) by whistling or blowing a whistle: *the doorman whistled a cruising cab* **4** to move with a whistling sound: *a shell whistled through the upper air* **5** (of a kettle or train) to produce a shrill sound caused by steam being forced through a small opening **6** (of a bird) to give a shrill cry **7 whistle in the dark** to try to keep up one's confidence in spite of being afraid ▸ *n* **8** the act or sound of whistling: *he gave a whistle of astonishment* **9** a metal instrument that is blown down its end to produce a tune, signal, or alarm: *he played the tin whistle*; *the referee's whistle* **10** a device in a kettle or a train that makes a shrill sound by means of steam under pressure **11 blow the whistle on** *informal* to reveal and put a stop to (wrongdoing or a wrongdoer): *to blow the whistle on corrupt top-level officials* **12 wet one's whistle** *informal* to have a drink

whit *n* **not a whit** not at all: *it does not matter a whit*

white *adj* **1** having no hue, owing to the reflection of all or almost all light; of the colour of snow **2** pale, because of illness, fear, shock, or another emotion: *white with rage* **3** (of hair) having lost its colour, usually from age **4** (of coffee or tea) with milk or cream **5** (of wine) made from pale grapes or from black grapes separated from their skins **6** denoting flour, or bread made from flour, that has had part of the grain removed ▸ *n* **7** the lightest colour; the colour of snow **8** the clear fluid that surrounds the yolk of an egg **9** *anatomy* the white part of the eyeball **10** anything white, such as white paint or white clothing: *a room decorated all in white* > **whiteness** *n* > **whitish** *adj*

> **white** *adj* **2** = pale, wan, pasty, pallid, ashen

W

White *n* **1** a member of a light-skinned race ▸ *adj* **2** of or relating to a White or Whites

whitebait *n* **1** the young of herrings, sprats, or pilchards, cooked and eaten whole **2** any of various small silvery fishes of Australia and New Zealand and of North American coastal regions of the Pacific

white-collar *adj* denoting workers employed in professional and clerical occupations

> **white-collar** *adj* = clerical, professional, salaried, nonmanual

white elephant *n* a possession that is unwanted by its owner

white flag *n* a signal of surrender or to request a truce

white goods *pl n* large household appliances, such as refrigerators and cookers

white-hot *adj* **1** at such a high temperature that white light is produced **2** *informal* in a state of intense emotion: *white-hot agony*

white lie *n* a small lie, usually told to avoid hurting someone's feelings

whiten *vb* to make or become white or whiter ▷ **whitener** *n* ▷ **whitening** *n*

white paper *n* an official government report which sets out the government's policy on a specific matter

whitewash *n* **1** a mixture of lime or chalk in water, for whitening walls and other surfaces **2** an attempt to conceal the unpleasant truth: *the report was a whitewash* ▶ *vb* **3** to cover with whitewash **4** to conceal the unpleasant truth about ▷ **whitewashed** *adj*

whither *conj old-fashioned or poetic* to what place or for what purpose: *they knew not whither they went*

whiting (white-ing) *n* **1** a white-fleshed food fish of European seas **2** *Austral* any of several marine food fishes

Whitsun *n* **1** short for **Whitsuntide** ▶ *adj* **2** of Whit Sunday or Whitsuntide

Whit Sunday *n* the seventh Sunday after Easter

Whitsuntide *n* the week that begins with Whit Sunday

whittle *vb* **-tling, -tled 1** to make (an object) by cutting or shaving pieces from (a piece of wood) with a small knife **2 whittle down** *or* **away** to reduce in size or effectiveness gradually: *my self-confidence had been whittled away to almost nothing*

> **whittle** *vb* **1** = carve, cut, hew (*old-fashioned*), shape, trim, shave, pare **2 whittle something away** = undermine, reduce, consume, erode, eat away, wear away, cut down, cut, decrease, prune, scale down

whizz *or* **whiz** *vb* **whizzing, whizzed 1** to move with a loud humming or buzzing sound: *the bullets whizzed overhead* **2** *informal* to move or go quickly: *the wind surfers fairly whizzed along the water* ▶ *n, pl* **whizzes 3** a loud humming or buzzing sound **4** *informal* a person who is extremely good at something: *he's a whizz on finance* **5** *slang* amphetamine

whizz kid *or* **whiz kid** *n informal* a person who is outstandingly able and successful for his or her age

who *pron* **1** which person: *who are you?; he didn't know who had started it* **2** used at the beginning of a relative clause referring to a person or people already mentioned: *he is a man who can effect change*

whodunnit *or* **whodunit** (hoo-dun-nit) *n informal* a novel, play, or film about the solving of a murder mystery

whoever *pron* **1** the person or people who: *whoever bought it for you has to make the claim* **2** no matter who: *I pity him, whoever he is* **3** *informal* other similar or related people or person: *your best friend, your neighbours, or whoever* **4** an intensive form of *who*, used in questions: *whoever thought of such a thing?*

whole *adj* **1** constituting or referring to all of something: *I'd spent my whole allowance by Saturday afternoon* **2** unbroken or undamaged ▶ *adv* **3** in an undivided or unbroken piece: *truffles are cooked whole* **4** *informal* completely or entirely: *a whole new theory of treatment* ▶ *n* **5** all there is of a thing: *the whole of my salary* **6** a collection of parts viewed together as a unit: *taking Great Britain as a whole* **7 on the whole A** taking all things into consideration: *on the whole he has worked about one year out of twelve* **B** in general: *on the whole they were not successful* ▷ **wholeness** *n*

> **whole** *adj* **1** = complete, full, total, entire, uncut, undivided, unabridged; ≠ partial **2** = undamaged, intact, unscathed, unbroken, untouched, unharmed, in one piece; ≠ damaged ▶ *n* **6** = unit, ensemble, entirety, totality; ≠ part **7A on the whole** = all in all, altogether, all things considered, by and large **7B on the whole** = generally, in general, as a rule, chiefly, mainly, mostly, principally, on average

wholefood *n* **1** food that has been refined or processed as little as possible ▶ *adj* **2** of or relating to wholefood: *a wholefood diet*

wholehearted *adj* done or given with total sincerity or enthusiasm: *wholehearted support* ▷ **wholeheartedly** *adv*

wholemeal *adj Brit & Austral* **1** (of flour) made from the entire wheat kernel **2** made from wholemeal flour: *wholemeal bread*

whole number *n maths* a number that does not contain a fraction, such as 0, 1, or 2

wholesale *n* **1** the business of selling goods in large quantities and at lower prices to retailers for resale ▶ *adj* **2** relating to such business: *wholesale prices* **3** extensive or indiscriminate: *the wholesale destruction of forests* ▶ *adv* **4** by or through the wholesale business: *we buy beef wholesale* **5** extensively or indiscriminately: *buffalo were slaughtered wholesale* ▷ **wholesaler** *n*

> **wholesale** *adj* **3** = extensive, total, mass, sweeping, broad, comprehensive, wide-ranging, blanket; ≠ limited ▶ *adv* **5** = extensively, comprehensively, across the board, indiscriminately

wholesome *adj* **1** physically beneficial: *wholesome food* **2** morally beneficial: *a wholesome attitude of the mind*

wholly *adv* completely or totally

> **wholly** *adv* = completely, totally, perfectly, fully, entirely, altogether, thoroughly, utterly; ≠ partly

W

whom *pron* the objective form of *who: whom will you tell?; he was devoted to his wife, whom he married in 1960*

whoop *vb* **1** to cry out in excitement or joy **2 whoop it up** *informal* to indulge in a noisy celebration ▸ *n* **3** a loud cry of excitement or joy

whoopee *old-fashioned, informal* ▸ *interj* **1** an exclamation of joy or excitement ▸ *n* **2 make whoopee** A to indulge in a noisy celebration B to make love

whopper *n informal* **1** an unusually large or impressive example of something: *Deauville's beach is a whopper* **2** a big lie

whopping *informal* ▸ *adj* **1** unusually large: *a whopping 40 per cent* ▸ *adv* **2** extremely: *it's a whopping great gamble*

whore (**hore**) *n* a prostitute or promiscuous woman: often a term of abuse

> **whore** *n* = prostitute, streetwalker, call girl

whorl *n* **1** *botany* a circular arrangement of leaves or flowers round the stem of a plant **2** *zool* a single turn in a spiral shell **3** anything shaped like a coil

whose *pron* **1** of whom? belonging to whom?: used in direct and indirect questions: *whose idea was it?; I wondered whose it was* **2** of whom or of which: used as a relative pronoun: *Gran had sympathy for anybody whose life had gone wrong*

why *adv* **1** for what reason?: *why did he marry her?; she avoided asking him why he was there* ▸ *pron* **2** for or because of which: *you can think of all kinds of reasons why you should not believe it* ▸ *n, pl* **whys 3 the whys and wherefores** See **wherefore** (sense 1) ▸ *interj* **4** an exclamation of surprise, indignation, or impatience: *why, I listen to you on the radio twice a week*

wick *n* **1** a cord through the middle of a candle, through which the fuel reaches the flame **2 get on someone's wick** *Brit & Austral slang* to annoy someone

wicked *adj* **1** morally bad: *the wicked queen in 'Snow White'* **2** playfully mischievous or roguish: *let's be wicked and go skinny-dipping* **3** dangerous or unpleasant: *there was a wicked cut over his eye* **4** *slang* very good ▸ **wickedly** *adv* ▸ **wickedness** *n*

wicker *adj* made of wickerwork: *a wicker chair*

wickerwork *n* a material consisting of slender flexible twigs woven together

wicket *n cricket* **1** either of two sets of three stumps stuck in the ground with two wooden bails resting on top, at which the batsman stands **2** the playing space between these **3** the act or instance of a batsman being got out

wide *adj* **1** having a great extent from side to side: *the wide main street* **2** having a specified extent from side to side: *three metres wide* **3** covering or including many different things: *a wide range of services* **4** covering a large distance or extent: *the proposal was voted down by a wide margin* **5** (of eyes) opened fully ▸ *adv* **6** to a large or full extent: *he swung the door wide* **7 far and wide**

See **far** (sense 7) ▸ *n* **8** *cricket* a ball bowled outside the batsman's reach, which scores a run for the batting side ▸ **widely** *adv*

> **wide** *adj* **1** = spacious, broad, extensive, roomy, commodious; ≠ confined **3** = broad, extensive, wide-ranging, large, sweeping, vast, immense, expansive; ≠ restricted **4** = large, broad, vast, immense **5** = expanded, dilated, distended; ≠ shut ▸ *adv* **6** = fully, completely; ≠ partly

widen *vb* to make or become wide or wider

> **widen** *vb* = broaden, expand, enlarge, dilate, spread, extend, stretch; ≠ narrow

widescreen *adj* (of a television set) having a screen whose width is much greater than its height

widespread *adj* affecting an extensive area or a large number of people: *widespread damage; widespread public support*

> **widespread** *adj* = common, general, popular, broad, extensive, universal, far-reaching, pervasive; ≠ limited

widgeon *n* same as **wigeon**

widget *n* **1** *informal* any small device, the name of which is unknown or forgotten **2** a small device in a beer can which, when the can is opened, releases nitrogen gas into the beer, giving it a head **3** (in the graphical user interface of a computer or mobile phone) an element of interaction, such as a scroll bar or button

widow *n* a woman whose spouse has died and who has not remarried ▸ **widowhood** *n*

widowed *adj* denoting a person whose spouse has died and who has not remarried

widower *n* a man whose spouse has died and who has not remarried

width *n* **1** the extent or measurement of something from side to side **2** the distance across a rectangular swimming bath, as opposed to its length

> **width** *n* **1** = breadth, extent, span, scope, diameter, compass, thickness, girth

wield *vb* **1** to handle or use (a weapon or tool) **2** to exert or maintain (power or influence)

> **wield** *vb* **1** = brandish, flourish, manipulate, swing, use, manage, handle, employ **2** = exert, maintain, exercise, have, possess

wife *n, pl* **wives** the woman to whom a person is married ▸ **wifely** *adj*

> **wife** *n* = spouse, partner, mate, bride, better half (*humorous*), vrou (*S African*), wahine (NZ), wifey (*informal*)

Wi-Fi *n trademark* a system of wireless access to the internet

wig *n* an artificial head of hair

W

wigeon or **widgeon** n a wild marshland duck

wiggle vb **-gling, -gled 1** to move with jerky movements from side to side or up and down: *she wiggled her toes in the cool water* ▸ n **2** a wiggling movement or walk

wigwam n a Native American's tent, made of animal skins

wiki computers ▸ n **1** a website, or page within one, whose content can be edited freely by anyone with access to a web browser ▸ adj **2** of or relating to the software which facilitates such open editing: *wiki technology*

wild adj **1** (of animals or birds) living in natural surroundings; not domesticated or tame **2** (of plants) growing in a natural state; not cultivated **3** uninhabited and desolate: *wild country* **4** living in a savage or uncivilized way: *a wild mountain man* **5** lacking restraint or control: *a wild party* **6** stormy or violent: *a wild windy October morning* **7** in a state of extreme emotional intensity: *wild with excitement* **8** without reason or substance: *wild accusations* **9 wild about** *informal* very enthusiastic about: *his colleagues aren't all that wild about him* ▸ adv **10 run wild** to behave without restraint: *she was allowed to run completely wild* ▸ n **11 the wild** a free natural state of living: *creatures of the wild* **12 the wilds** a desolate or uninhabited region: *the wilds of Africa* > **wildly** adv ▸ **wildness** n

> **wild** adj **1** = untamed, fierce, savage, ferocious, unbroken, feral, undomesticated, free, warrigal (*Austral literary*); ≠ tame **2** = uncultivated, natural; ≠ cultivated **4** = uncivilized, fierce, savage, primitive, ferocious, barbaric, brutish, barbarous; ≠ civilized **5** = uncontrolled, disorderly, turbulent, wayward, unruly, rowdy, unfettered, riotous; ≠ calm **6** = stormy, violent, rough, raging, choppy, tempestuous, blustery **7** = excited, crazy (*informal*), enthusiastic, raving, hysterical; ≠ unenthusiastic ▸ n **12 the wilds** = wilderness, desert, wasteland, middle of nowhere (*informal*), backwoods, back of beyond (*informal*)

wildcat n, pl **-cats** or **-cat 1** a wild European cat that looks like a domesticated cat but is larger and has a bushy tail **2** *informal* a quick-tempered person ▸ adj **3** *chiefly US* risky and financially unsound: *a wildcat operation*

wildcat strike n a strike begun by workers spontaneously or without union approval

wildebeest n, pl **-beests** or **-beest** same as **gnu**

wilderness n **1** a wild uninhabited uncultivated region **2** a confused mass or tangle: *a wilderness of long grass and wild flowers* **3** a state of being no longer in a prominent position: *a long spell in the political wilderness*

> **wilderness** n **1** = wilds, desert, wasteland, uncultivated region

wildfire n **spread like wildfire** to spread very quickly or uncontrollably

wild-goose chase n a search that has little or no chance of success

wildlife n wild animals and plants collectively

wiles pl n artful or seductive tricks or ploys

wilful or US **willful** adj **1** determined to do things in one's own way: *a wilful and insubordinate child* **2** deliberate and intentional: *wilful misconduct* > **wilfully** adv

will[1] vb, past tense **would 1** used as an auxiliary to make the future tense: *he will go on trial on October 7* **2** to express resolution: *they will not consider giving up territories* **3** to express a polite request: *will you please calm Mummy and Daddy down* **4** to express ability: *many essential oils will protect clothing from moths* **5** to express probability or expectation: *his followers will be relieved to hear that* **6** to express customary practice: *boys will be boys!* **7** to express desire: *go in very small steps, if you will*

will[2] n **1** a strong determination: *a fierce will to survive* **2** desire or wish: *a referendum to determine the will of the people* **3** a document setting out a person's wishes regarding the disposal of his or her property after death **4 at will** when and as one chooses: *customers can withdraw money at will* ▸ vb **willing, willed 5** to try to make (something) happen by wishing very hard for it: *she willed herself not to cry* **6** to wish or desire: *if he wills it, we will meet again* **7** to leave (property) in one's will: *the farm had been willed to her*

> **will** n **1** = determination, drive, purpose, commitment, resolution, resolve, spine, backbone **2** = wish, mind, desire, intention, fancy, preference, inclination **3** = testament, bequest(s), last wishes, last will and testament ▸ vb **6** = wish, want, prefer, desire, see fit **7** = bequeath, give, leave, transfer, gift, hand on, pass on, confer

willing adj **1** favourably disposed or inclined: *I'm willing to hear what you have to say* **2** keen and obliging: *willing volunteers* > **willingly** adv > **willingness** n

> **willing** adj **1** = inclined, prepared, consenting, agreeable, compliant, amenable; ≠ unwilling **2** = ready, game (*informal*); ≠ reluctant

will-o'-the-wisp n **1** someone or something that is elusive or deceptively alluring: *their freedom was just a will-o'-the-wisp* **2** a pale light that is sometimes seen over marshy ground at night

willow n a tree that grows near water, with thin flexible branches used in weaving baskets and wood used for making cricket bats

willowy adj slender and graceful

willpower n strong self-disciplined determination to do something

willy-nilly adv **1** in a haphazard fashion; indiscriminately: *spending taxpayers' money willy-nilly* **2** whether desired or not

W

willy wagtail *n Austral* a black-and-white flycatcher

willy-willy *n Austral* a small tropical dust storm

wilt *vb* **1** (of a flower or plant) to become limp or drooping **2** (of a person) to lose strength or confidence

> **wilt** *vb* **1** = droop, wither, sag, shrivel
> **2** = weaken, languish, droop

wily *adj* **wilier, wiliest** sly or crafty

wimp *informal* ▸ *n* **1** a feeble ineffective person ▸ *vb* **2 wimp out of** to fail to do (something) through lack of courage > **wimpish** *or* **wimpy** *adj*

wimple *n* a piece of cloth draped round the head to frame the face, worn by women in the Middle Ages and now by some nuns

win *vb* **winning, won 1** to achieve first place in (a competition or race) **2** to gain (a prize or first place) in a competition or race **3** to gain victory in (a battle, argument, or struggle) **4** to gain (sympathy, approval, or support) ▸ *n* **5** *informal* a success, victory, or triumph: *three consecutive wins* ▸ See also **win over** > **winnable** *adj*

> **win** *vb* **1, 3** = be victorious in, succeed in, prevail in, come first in, be the victor in; ≠ lose **2, 4** = gain, get, land (*informal*), achieve, earn, secure, obtain, acquire; ≠ forfeit ▸ *n* = victory, success, triumph, conquest; ≠ defeat

wince *vb* **wincing, winced 1** to draw back slightly, as if in sudden pain ▸ *n* **2** the act of wincing

> **wince** *vb* = flinch, start, shrink, cringe, quail, recoil, cower, draw back ▸ *n* = flinch, start, cringe

winch *n* **1** a lifting or hauling device consisting of a rope or chain wound round a barrel or drum ▸ *vb* **2** to haul or lift using a winch: *two men were winched to safety by a helicopter*

wind¹ (rhymes with *pinned*) *n* **1** a current of air moving across the earth's surface **2** a trend or force: *the chill wind of change* **3** the power to breathe normally, esp. during or after physical exercise: *if you feel tired during the exercise, persevere – you'll soon get a second wind* **4** gas in the stomach or intestines **5** *informal* foolish or empty talk: *political language is designed to give an appearance of solidity to pure wind* **6 break wind** to release intestinal gas through the anus **7 get wind of** *informal* to find out about: *the media finally got wind of her disappearance* ▸ *adj* **8** *music* of or relating to wind instruments: *the wind section* ▸ *vb* **winding, winded 9** to cause (someone) to be short of breath: *he fell with a thud that left him winded* **10** to cause (a baby) to bring up wind after feeding > **windless** *adj*

> **wind** *n* **1** = air, blast, hurricane, breeze, draught, gust, zephyr **3** = breath, puff, respiration **4** = flatulence, gas **5** = nonsense, talk, boasting, hot air, babble, bluster,
> humbug, twaddle (*informal*), bizzo (*Austral slang*), bull's wool (*Austral, NZ slang*) **7 get wind of something** = hear about, learn of, find out about, become aware of, be told about, be informed of, be made aware of, hear tell of

wind² (rhymes with *pined*) *vb* **winding, wound 1** to twist (something flexible) round some object: *a sweatband was wound round his head* **2** to tighten the spring of (a clock or watch) by turning a key or knob **3** to follow a twisting course: *a narrow path wound through the shrubbery* ▸ See also **wind up** > **winding** *adj, n*

> **wind** *vb* **1** = wrap, twist, reel, curl, loop, coil **3** = meander, turn, bend, twist, curve, snake, ramble, twist and turn

windfall *n* **1** a piece of unexpected good fortune, esp. financial gain **2** a fruit blown off a tree by the wind

> **windfall** *n* **1** = godsend, find, jackpot, bonanza, manna from heaven; ≠ misfortune

wind farm *n* a large group of wind-driven generators for electricity supply

wind instrument *n* a musical instrument, such as a flute, that is played by having air blown into it

windlass *n* a machine for lifting heavy objects by winding a rope or chain round a barrel or drum driven by a motor

windmill *n* **1** a building containing machinery for grinding corn or for pumping, driven by sails that are turned by the wind **2** *Brit* a toy consisting of a stick with plastic vanes attached, which revolve in the wind

window *n* **1** an opening in a building or a vehicle containing glass within a framework, which lets in light and enables people to see in or out **2** the display area behind a glass window in a shop **3** a transparent area in an envelope which reveals the address on the letter inside **4** an area on a computer screen that can be manipulated separately from the rest of the display area, for example so that two or more files can be displayed at the same time **5** a period of unbooked time in a diary or schedule

window-dressing *n* **1** the art of arranging goods in shop windows in such a way as to attract customers **2** an attempt to make something seem better than it is by stressing only its attractive features: *do you think that the president's calling for an investigation is window-dressing, or do you think he actually means to do something?* > **window-dresser** *n*

window-shopping *n* looking at goods in shop windows without intending to buy anything

windpipe *n* a nontechnical name for **trachea**

windscreen *n Brit, Austral & NZ* the sheet of glass that forms the front window of a motor vehicle

W

windscreen wiper *n Brit, Austral & NZ* an electrically operated blade with a rubber edge that wipes a windscreen clear of rain

windsock *n* a cloth cone mounted on a mast, used esp. at airports to indicate the direction of the wind

windsurfing *n* the sport of riding on water using a surfboard steered and propelled by an attached sail > **windsurfer** *n*

wind up *vb* **1** to bring to a conclusion: *we want to wind this conflict up as quickly as possible* **2** *informal* to dissolve (a company) and divide its assets among creditors **3** to tighten the spring of (a clockwork mechanism) by turning a key or knob **4** to move (a car window) upwards by turning a handle **5** *informal* to end up: *to wind up in the hospital* **6** *informal* to make nervous or tense: *as crisis after crisis broke, I became increasingly wound up* **7** *Brit, Austral & NZ slang* to tease or annoy: *that really used to wind my old man up something rotten* ▸ *adj* **wind-up 8** operated by clockwork: *a wind-up toy* ▸ *n* **wind-up 9** a light-hearted hoax **10** the finish

wind up *vb* **1 wind something up** = end, finish, settle, conclude, tie up, wrap up, finalize **2 wind something up** = close down, close, dissolve, terminate, put something into liquidation **5** = end up, be left, finish up, fetch up (*informal*), land up **6 wind someone up** = irritate, excite, anger, annoy, exasperate, nettle, work someone up, pique **7 wind someone up** = tease, kid (*informal*), have someone on (*informal*), annoy, rag (*informal*), rib (*informal*), josh (*informal*), vex

windward *chiefly naut* ▸ *adj* **1** of or in the direction from which the wind blows ▸ *n* **2** the windward direction ▸ *adv* **3** towards the wind

windy *adj* **windier, windiest 1** denoting a time or conditions in which there is a strong wind: *a windy day* **2** exposed to the wind: *the windy graveyard* **3** long-winded or pompous: *his speeches are long and windy* **4** *old-fashioned slang* frightened

windy *adj* **1** = breezy, wild, stormy, windswept, blustery, gusty, squally, blowy; ≠ calm

wine *n* **1** **A** an alcoholic drink produced by the fermenting of grapes with water and sugar **B** an alcoholic drink produced in this way from other fruits or flowers: *dandelion wine* ▸ *adj* **2** dark purplish-red ▸ *vb* **wining, wined 3 wine and dine** to entertain (someone) with wine and fine food

wing *n* **1** one of the limbs or organs of a bird, bat, or insect that are used for flying **2** one of the two winglike supporting parts of an aircraft **3** a projecting part of a building: *converting the unused east wing into a suitable habitation* **4** a faction or group within a political party or other organization: *the youth wing of the African National Congress* **5** *Brit* the part of a car body surrounding the wheels **6** *sport* **A** either of the two sides of the pitch near the touchline **B** same as **winger**

7 wings *theatre* the space offstage to the right or left of the acting area **8 in the wings** ready to step in when needed **9 on the wing** flying **10 spread one's wings** to make fuller use of one's abilities by trying new experiences: *he increasingly spread his wings abroad* **11 take someone under one's wing** to look after someone **12 take wing** to fly away ▸ *vb* **13** to fly: *a lone bird winging its way from the island* **14** to move through the air: *sending a shower of loose gravel winging towards the house* **15** to shoot or wound in the wing or arm **16** to provide with wings > **winged** *adj* > **wingless** *adj*

wing *n* **4** = faction, group, arm, section, branch ▸ *vb* **13** = fly, soar, glide, take wing **15** = wound, hit, clip

winger *n sport* a player positioned on a wing

wink *vb* **1** to close and open one eye quickly as a signal **2** (of a light) to shine brightly and intermittently; twinkle ▸ *n* **3** the act or an instance of winking, esp. as a signal **4** a twinkling of light **5** *informal* the smallest amount of sleep: *I didn't sleep a wink last night* **6 tip someone the wink** *Brit, Austral & NZ informal* to give someone a hint or warning

wink *vb* **1** = blink, bat, flutter **2** = twinkle, flash, shine, sparkle, gleam, shimmer, glimmer ▸ *n* **3** = blink, flutter

winkle *n* **1** an edible shellfish with a spirally coiled shell ▸ *vb* **-kling, -kled 2 winkle out** *informal, chiefly Brit* **A** to obtain (information) from someone who is not willing to provide it: *try to winkle the real problem out of them* **B** to coax or force out: *he somehow managed to winkle him out of his room*

winner *n* **1** a person or thing that wins **2** *informal* a person or thing that seems sure to be successful

winner *n* **1** = victor, champion, master, champ (*informal*), conqueror, prizewinner; ≠ loser

winning *adj* **1** gaining victory: *the winning side* **2** charming or attractive: *her winning smiles*

winning *adj* **1** = victorious, first, top, successful, unbeaten, conquering, triumphant, undefeated **2** = charming, pleasing, attractive, engaging, cute, disarming, enchanting, endearing; ≠ unpleasant

winnings *pl n* the money won in a competition or in gambling

winnings *pl n* = spoils, profits, gains, prize, proceeds, takings

winnow *vb* **1** to separate (grain) from (chaff) by a current of air **2** (often foll. by *out*) to separate out (an unwanted element): *the committee will need to winnow out the nonsense*

W

win over *vb* to gain the support or consent of: *his robust performance won over his critics*

> **win over** *vb* **win someone over or round**
> = convince, influence, persuade, convert, sway, prevail upon, bring or talk round

winsome *adj literary* charming or attractive: *a winsome smile*

winter *n* **1** the coldest season of the year, between autumn and spring ▸ *vb* **2** to spend the winter in a specified place: *wintering in Rome*

winter sports *pl n* sports held on snow or ice, such as skiing and skating

wintry *adj* **-trier, -triest 1** of or characteristic of winter: *a cold wintry day* **2** cold or unfriendly: *a wintry smile*

win-win *adj* guaranteeing a favourable outcome for everyone involved: *a win-win situation for NATO*

wipe *vb* **wiping, wiped 1** to rub (a surface or object) lightly with a cloth or the hand, in order to remove dirt or liquid from it **2** to remove by wiping: *she made a futile attempt to wipe away her tears* **3** to erase a recording from (a video or audio tape) ▸ *n* **4** the act or an instance of wiping: *a quick wipe*

> **wipe** *vb* **1** = clean, polish, brush, rub, sponge, mop, swab **2** = erase, remove ▸ *n* = rub, brush

wipe out *vb* to destroy or get rid of completely: *a hail storm wipes out a wheat crop in five minutes*

> **wipe out** *vb* **wipe something or someone out** = destroy, massacre, erase, eradicate, obliterate, annihilate, exterminate, expunge (*formal*)

wire *n* **1** a slender flexible strand of metal **2** a length of this used to carry electric current in a circuit **3** a long continuous piece of wire or cable connecting points in a telephone or telegraph system **4** *old-fashioned, informal* a telegram ▸ *vb* **wiring, wired 5** to fasten with wire **6** to equip (an electrical system, circuit, or component) with wires **7** *informal* to send a telegram to **8** to send by telegraph: *they wired the money for a train ticket*

wire-haired *adj* (of a dog) having a rough wiry coat

wireless *n* **1** *old-fashioned* same as **radio** ▸ *adj* **2** *computers* communicating without connecting wires: *wireless application protocol*

wiring *n* the network of wires used in an electrical system, device, or circuit

wiry *adj* **wirier, wiriest 1** (of a person) slim but strong **2** coarse and stiff: *wiry grass*

wisdom *n* **1** the ability to use one's experience and knowledge to make sensible decisions or judgments **2** accumulated knowledge or learning: *the wisdom of Asia and of Africa*

> **wisdom** *n* **1** = understanding, learning, knowledge, intelligence, judgment, insight, enlightenment, erudition; ≠ foolishness

wisdom tooth *n* any of the four molar teeth, one at the back of each side of the jaw, that are the last of the permanent teeth to come through

wise[1] *adj* **1** possessing or showing wisdom: *a wise move* **2 none the wiser** knowing no more than before: *I left the conference none the wiser* **3 wise to** *informal* aware of or informed about: *they'll get wise to our system; he put him wise to the rumour* > **wisely** *adv*

> **wise** *adj* **1** = sage, clever, intelligent, sensible, enlightened, discerning, perceptive, erudite, grounded; ≠ foolish

wise[2] *n old-fashioned* way, manner, or respect: *in no wise*

-wise *suffix* forming adverbs **1** indicating direction or manner: *crabwise* **2** with reference to: *moneywise*

wiseacre *n* a person who wishes to seem wise

wisecrack *informal* ▸ *n* **1** a clever, amusing, sometimes unkind, remark ▸ *vb* **2** to make such remarks > **wisecracking** *adj*

wish *vb* **1** to want or desire (something impossible or improbable): *he wished he'd kept quiet* **2** to desire or prefer to be or do something: *the next person who wished to speak* **3** to feel or express a hope concerning the welfare, health, or success of: *we wished him well* **4** to greet as specified: *I wished her a Merry Christmas* ▸ *n* **5** a desire, often for something impossible or improbable: *a desperate wish to succeed as a professional artist* **6** something desired or wished for: *your wishes will come true* **7** the expression of a hope for someone's welfare, health, or success: *give him our best wishes*

> **wish** *vb* **2** = want, feel, choose, please, desire, think fit ▸ *n* **5** = desire, want, hope, urge, intention, fancy (*informal*), ambition, yen (*informal*); ≠ aversion

wishbone *n* the V-shaped bone above the breastbone of a chicken or turkey

wishful *adj* desirous or longing: *she seemed wishful of prolonging the discussion*

wishy-washy *adj informal* lacking in character, force, or colour

wisp *n* **1** a thin, delicate, or filmy piece or streak: *little wisps of cloud* **2** a small untidy bundle, tuft, or strand: *a wisp of hair* **3** a slight trace: *a wisp of a smile*

wispy *adj* **wispier, wispiest** thin, fine, or delicate: *grey wispy hair*

wisteria *n* a climbing plant with large drooping clusters of blue, purple, or white flowers

wistful *adj* sadly wishing for something lost or unobtainable > **wistfully** *adv* > **wistfulness** *n*

wit *n* **1** the ability to use words or ideas in a clever, amusing, and imaginative way **2** a person possessing this ability **3** practical intelligence: *do credit me with some wit*

W

wit n 1 = humour, quips, banter, puns, repartee, wordplay, witticisms, badinage; ≠ seriousness 2 = humorist, card (*informal*), comedian, wag, joker, dag (*NZ informal*) 3 = cleverness, sense, brains, wisdom, common sense, intellect, ingenuity, acumen; ≠ stupidity

witch n 1 (in former times) a woman believed to possess evil magic powers 2 a person who practises magic or sorcery, esp. black magic 3 *derogatory* an ugly or wicked old woman

witch n 1 = enchantress, magician, hag, crone, sorceress, Wiccan

witchcraft n the use of magic, esp. for evil purposes

witchcraft n = magic, voodoo, wizardry, black magic, enchantment, occultism, sorcery, Wicca, makutu (*NZ*)

witch doctor n a man in certain tribal societies who is believed to possess magical powers, which can be used to cure sickness or to harm people

witchetty grub n a wood-boring edible Australian caterpillar

witch-hunt n a rigorous campaign to expose and discredit people considered to hold unorthodox views on the pretext of safeguarding the public welfare

with prep 1 accompanying; in the company of: *the captain called to the sergeant to come with him* 2 using; by means of: *unlocking the padlock with a key* 3 possessing or having: *a woman with black hair; the patient with angina* 4 concerning or regarding: *be gentle with me* 5 in a manner characterized by: *I know you will handle it with discretion* 6 as a result of: *his voice was hoarse with nervousness* 7 following the line of thought of: *are you with me so far?* 8 having the same opinions as; supporting: *are you with us or against us?*

withdraw vb **-drawing, -drew, -drawn** 1 to take out or remove: *he withdrew an envelope from his pocket* 2 to remove (money) from a bank account or savings account 3 to leave one place to go to another, usually quieter, place: *he withdrew into his bedroom* 4 (of troops) to leave or be pulled back from the battleground 5 to take back (a statement) formally 6 **withdraw from** to give up: *they withdrew from the competition*

withdraw vb 1 = remove, take off, pull out, extract, take away, pull back, draw out, draw back 2 = take out, extract, draw out

withdrawal n 1 the act or an instance of withdrawing 2 the period that a drug addict goes through after stopping using drugs, during which he or she may experience symptoms such as tremors, sweating, and vomiting ▸ adj 3 of or relating to withdrawal from an addictive drug: *withdrawal symptoms*

withdrawal n 1 = removal, ending, stopping, taking away, abolition, elimination, cancellation, termination

withdrawn vb 1 the past participle of **withdraw** ▸ adj 2 extremely reserved or shy

withdrawn adj = uncommunicative, reserved, retiring, distant, shy, taciturn, introverted, unforthcoming; ≠ outgoing

wither vb 1 to make or become dried up or shrivelled: *the leaves had withered but not fallen* 2 to fade or waste: *deprived of the nerve supply the muscles wither* 3 to humiliate (someone) with a scornful look or remark ▸ **withered** adj

wither vb 1 = wilt, decline, decay, disintegrate, perish, shrivel; ≠ flourish 2 = waste, decline, shrivel; ≠ increase

withering adj (of a look or remark) extremely scornful

withering adj = scornful, devastating, humiliating, snubbing, hurtful, mortifying

withers pl n the highest part of the back of a horse, between the shoulders

withhold vb **-holding, -held** to keep back (information or money)

withhold vb = keep secret, refuse, hide, reserve, retain, conceal, suppress, hold back; ≠ reveal

within prep 1 in or inside: *within the hospital grounds* 2 before (a period of time) has passed: *within a month* 3 not beyond: *within the confines of a low budget; he positioned a low table within her reach* ▸ adv 4 *formal* inside or internally: *a glimpse of what was hidden within*

without prep 1 not accompanied by: *I can't imagine going through life without him* 2 not using: *our Jeep drove without lights* 3 not possessing or having: *four months without a job; a lot of them came across the border without shoes* 4 in a manner showing a lack of: *without reverence* 5 while not or after not: *she sat without speaking for some while* ▸ adv 6 *formal* outside: *seated on the graveyard without*

withstand vb **-standing, -stood** to resist and endure successfully: *our ability to withstand stress*

withstand vb = resist, suffer, bear, sustain, oppose, cope with, endure, tolerate, stand up to; ≠ give in to

witless adj 1 *formal* lacking intelligence or sense 2 **scared witless** extremely frightened

witness n 1 a person who has seen or can give first-hand evidence of some event: *the only witness to a killing* 2 a person who gives evidence in a court of law: *a witness for the defence* 3 a person who confirms the genuineness of a document or signature by adding his or her own signature 4 evidence proving or supporting something: *the Church of England, that historic witness to the power of the Christian faith* 5 **bear witness to** to be evidence or proof of: *the high turn-out bore witness to the popularity of the contest* ▶ *vb* **6** to see, be present at, or know at first hand: *I have witnessed many motor-racing accidents* **7** to be the scene or setting of: *the 1970s witnessed an enormous increase in international lending* **8** to confirm the genuineness of (a document or signature) by adding one's own signature **9 witness to** *formal* to confirm: *our aim is to witness to the fact of the empty tomb*

> **witness** *n* **1** = observer, viewer, spectator, looker-on, watcher, onlooker, eyewitness, bystander **2** = testifier ▶ *vb* **6** = see, view, watch, note, notice, observe, perceive **8** = countersign, sign, endorse, validate

witter *vb chiefly Brit informal* to chatter or babble pointlessly or at unnecessary length
witticism *n* a witty remark
wittingly *adv* intentionally and knowingly
witty *adj* **-tier, -tiest** clever and amusing
> **wittily** *adv*

> **witty** *adj* = humorous, funny, clever, amusing, sparkling, whimsical, droll, piquant; ≠ dull

wives *n* the plural of **wife**
wizard *n* **1** a man in fairy tales who has magic powers **2** a person who is outstandingly gifted in some specified field: *a financial wizard*

> **wizard** *n* **1** = magician, witch, shaman, sorcerer, occultist, magus, conjuror, warlock, tohunga (NZ)

wizardry *n* **1** magic or sorcery **2** outstanding skill or accomplishment in some specified field: *technological wizardry*
wizened (**wiz**-zend) *adj* shrivelled, wrinkled, or dried up with age
WMD *n* weapon(s) of mass destruction
woad *n* a blue dye obtained from a European plant, used by the ancient Britons as a body dye
wobbegong *n* an Australian shark with brown-and-white skin
wobble *vb* **-bling, -bled 1** to move or sway unsteadily **2** to shake: *she was having difficulty in controlling her voice, which wobbled about* ▶ *n* **3** a wobbling movement or sound

> **wobble** *vb* **1** = shake, rock, sway, tremble, teeter, totter **2** = tremble, shake ▶ *n* = unsteadiness, shake, tremble

wobbly *adj* **-blier, -bliest 1** unsteady **2** trembling ▶ *n* **3 throw a wobbly** *Brit slang* to become suddenly angry or upset
wodge *n informal* a thick lump or chunk: *my wodge of Kleenex was a sodden ball*
woe *n* **1** *literary* intense grief **2 woes** misfortunes or problems: *economic woes* **3 woe betide someone** someone will or would experience misfortune: *woe betide anyone who got in his way*

> **woe** *n* **1** = misery, distress, grief, agony, gloom, sadness, sorrow, anguish; ≠ happiness **2** = problem, grief, misery, sorrow

woebegone *adj* sad in appearance
woeful *adj* **1** extremely sad **2** pitiful or deplorable: *a woeful lack of understanding*
> **woefully** *adv*
wok *n* a large bowl-shaped metal Chinese cooking pot, used for stir-frying
woke *vb* the past tense of **wake¹** ▶ *adj informal* alert to social and political injustice
woken *vb* the past participle of **wake¹**
wold *n* a large area of high open rolling country
wolf *n, pl* **wolves 1** a predatory doglike wild animal which hunts in packs **2** *old-fashioned, informal* a man who habitually tries to seduce women **3 cry wolf** to give false alarms repeatedly: *if you cry wolf too often, people will take no notice* ▶ *vb* **4 wolf down** to eat quickly or greedily: *they will wolf down kidneys but refuse tongue*
wolf whistle *n* **1** a whistle expressing admiration of a person's appearance ▶ *vb* **wolf-whistle, -whistling, -whistled 2** to produce such a whistle
wolverine *n* a large meat-eating mammal of Eurasia and North America with very thick dark fur
woman *n, pl* **women 1** an adult female human being **2** adult female human beings collectively: *the very image of woman pared of the trappings of 'femininity'* **3** an adult female human being with qualities associated with the female, such as tenderness or maternalism: *she's more woman than you know* **4** a female servant or domestic help **5** *informal* a wife or girlfriend ▶ *adj* **6** female: *a woman doctor*

> **woman** *n* **1** = lady, girl, female (*sometimes derogatory*), sheila (*Austral, NZ informal*), vrou (*S African*), adult female, femme, wahine (NZ); ≠ man

womanhood *n* **1** the state of being a woman: *young girls approaching womanhood* **2** women collectively: *Asian womanhood*
womanish *adj* (of a man) looking or behaving like a woman
womanizer *or* **-niser** *n* a man who has casual affairs with many women
womanizing *or* **-nising** *n* (of a man) the practice of indulging in casual affairs with women
womanly *adj* possessing qualities generally regarded as typical of, or appropriate to, a woman

> **womanly** *adj* = feminine, motherly, female, matronly, ladylike

womb *n* the nontechnical name for **uterus**
wombat *n* a furry heavily-built plant-eating Australian marsupial
Women's Liberation *n* a movement promoting the removal of inequalities based upon the assumption that men are superior to women. Also called: **women's lib**
won *vb* the past of **win**

W

wonder *vb* **1** to think about something with curiosity or doubt: *I wonder why she did that* **2** to be amazed: *I did wonder at her leaving valuable china on the shelves* ▸ *n* **3** something that causes surprise or awe: *it's a wonder she isn't speechless with fright* **4** the feeling of surprise or awe caused by something strange: *the wonder of travel* **5 do** or **work wonders** to achieve spectacularly good results **6 no** or **small wonder** it is not surprising: *no wonder you're going broke* ▸ *adj* **7** causing surprise or awe because of spectacular results achieved: *a new wonder drug for treating migraine* > **wonderingly** *adv* > **wonderment** *n*

wonder *vb* **1** = think, question, puzzle, speculate, query, ponder, meditate, conjecture **2** = be amazed, stare, marvel, be astonished, gape ▸ *n* **3** = phenomenon, sight, miracle, spectacle, curiosity, marvel, prodigy, rarity **4** = amazement, surprise, admiration, awe, fascination, astonishment, bewilderment, wonderment

wonderful *adj* **1** extremely fine; excellent: *I've been offered a wonderful job* **2** causing surprise, amazement, or awe: *a strange and wonderful phenomenon* > **wonderfully** *adv*

wonderful *adj* **1** = excellent, great (*informal*), brilliant, outstanding, superb, fantastic (*informal*), tremendous, magnificent, booshit (*Austral slang*), exo (*Austral slang*), sik (*Austral slang*), rad (*informal*), phat (*slang*), schmick (*Austral informal*); ≠ terrible **2** = remarkable, amazing, extraordinary, incredible (*informal*), astonishing, staggering, startling, phenomenal; ≠ ordinary

wondrous *adj old-fashioned or literary* causing surprise or awe; marvellous

wonky *adj* **-kier, -kiest** *Brit, Austral & NZ slang* **1** shaky or unsteady: *wonky wheelbarrows; wonky knees* **2** insecure or unreliable: *his marriage is looking a bit wonky*

wont (rhymes with **don't**) *old-fashioned* ▸ *adj* **1** accustomed: *most murderers, his police friends were wont to say, were male* ▸ *n* **2** a usual practice: *she waded straight in, as was her wont*

won't will not

woo *vb* **wooing, wooed 1** to coax or urge: *it will woo people back into the kitchen* **2** *old-fashioned* to attempt to gain the love of (a person) > **wooing** *n*

woo *vb* **2** = court, pursue

wood *n* **1** the hard fibrous substance beneath the bark in trees and shrubs, which is used in building and carpentry and as fuel. Related adjective: **ligneous 2** an area of trees growing together that is smaller than a forest: *a track leading into a wood*. Related adjective: **sylvan 3** *golf* a long-shafted club with a wooden head ▸ *adj* **4** made of, using, or for use with wood: *wood fires*

wood *n* **1** = timber, planks, planking, lumber (*US*) **2** = woodland, forest, grove, thicket, copse, coppice, bushland

woodbine *n* a wild honeysuckle with sweet-smelling yellow flowers

woodcock *n* a large game bird with a long straight bill

woodcut *n* a print made from a block of wood with a design cut into it

wooded *adj* covered with woods or trees

wooded *adj* = tree-covered, forested, timbered, sylvan (*poetic*), tree-clad

wooden *adj* **1** made of wood **2** lacking spirit or animation: *the man's expression became wooden* > **woodenly** *adv*

wooden *adj* **1** = made of wood, timber, woody, ligneous **2** = expressionless, lifeless, deadpan, unresponsive

woodland *n* **1** land that is mostly covered with woods or trees ▸ *adj* **2** living in woods: *woodland birds*

woodlouse *n, pl* **-lice** a very small grey creature with many legs that lives in damp places

woodpecker *n* a bird with a strong beak with which it bores into trees for insects

woodwind *music* ▸ *adj* **1** of or denoting a type of wind instrument, such as the oboe ▸ *n* **2** the woodwind instruments of an orchestra

woodworm *n* **1** a beetle larva that bores into wooden furniture or beams **2** the damage caused to wood by these larvae

woody *adj* **woodier, woodiest 1** (of a plant) having a very hard stem **2** (of an area) covered with woods or trees

woof¹ *n* same as **weft**

woof² *n* an imitation of the bark of a dog

woofer *n* a loudspeaker used in high-fidelity systems for the reproduction of low audio frequencies

wool *n* **1** the soft curly hair of sheep and some other animals **2** yarn spun from this, used in weaving and knitting **3** cloth made from this yarn **4 pull the wool over someone's eyes** to deceive someone

wool *n* **1** = fleece, hair, coat **2** = yarn

woollen *or US* **woolen** *adj* **1** made of wool or of a mixture of wool and another material **2** relating to wool: *woollen mills* ▸ *n* **3 woollens** woollen clothes, esp. knitted ones

woolly *or US* **wooly** *adj* **-lier, -liest 1** made of or like wool **2** confused or indistinct: *woolly ideas* ▸ *n, pl* **-lies 3** a woollen garment, such as a sweater

woomera *n* a notched stick used by Australian Aborigines to aid the propulsion of a spear

woozy *adj* **woozier, wooziest** *informal* feeling slightly dizzy

wop-wops *pl n NZ informal* remote rural areas

word *n* 1 the smallest single meaningful unit of speech or writing. Related adjective: **lexical** 2 a brief conversation: *I would like a word with you* 3 a brief statement: *a word of warning* 4 news or information: *let me know if you get word of my wife* 5 a solemn promise: *he had given his word as a rabbi* 6 a command or order: *he had only to say the word and they'd hang him* 7 computers a set of bits used to store, transmit, or operate upon an item of information in a computer 8 **by word of mouth** by spoken rather than by written means: *their reputation spreads by word of mouth* 9 **in a word** briefly or in short: *in a word, we've won* 10 **my word!** Also: **upon my word!** *old-fashioned* an exclamation of surprise or amazement 11 **take someone at his** *or* **her word** to accept that someone really means what he or she says: *they're willing to take him at his word when he says he'll change* 12 **take someone's word for it** to believe what someone says 13 **the last word** the closing remark of a conversation or argument, often regarded as settling an issue 14 **the last word in** the finest example of: *the last word in comfort* 15 **word for word** using exactly the same words: *he repeated almost word for word what had been said* 16 **word of honour** a solemn promise ▸ *vb* 17 to state in words: *the questions have to be carefully worded*

> **word** *n* 1 = term, name, expression 2 = chat, tête-à-tête, talk, discussion, consultation, confab (*informal*), heart-to-heart, powwow (*informal*) 3 = comment, remark, utterance 4 = message, news, report, information, notice, intelligence, dispatch, communiqué, heads up (*US, Canad*) 5 = promise, guarantee, pledge, vow, assurance, oath 6 = command, order, decree, bidding, mandate ▸ *vb* = express, say, state, put, phrase, utter, couch, formulate

wording *n* the way in which words are used to express something: *the exact wording of the regulation has still not been worked out*

> **wording** *n* = phraseology, words, language, phrasing, terminology

word processing *n* the creation, organization, and storage of text on a computer or word processor

word processor *n* a computer program or electronic machine for the creation, organization, and storage of text entered from a keyboard and providing a means for printing out such text

wordy *adj* **wordier**, **wordiest** using too many words, esp. long words: *wordy explanations*

wore *vb* the past tense of **wear**

work *n* 1 physical or mental effort directed to doing or making something 2 paid employment at a job, trade, or profession 3 duties or tasks: *I had to delegate as much work as I could* 4 something done or made as a result of effort: *a work by a major artist* 5 the place where a person is employed: *accidents at work* 6 physics old-fashioned the transfer of energy occurring when a force is applied to move a body 7 **at work** working or in action: *the social forces at work in society* ▸ *adj* 8 of or for work: *work experience* ▸ *vb* 9 to do work; labour: *no-one worked harder than Arnold* 10 to be employed: *she worked as a waitress* 11 to make (a person or animal) labour 12 to operate (a machine or a piece of equipment) 13 (of a machine or a piece of equipment) to function, esp. effectively: *he doesn't have to know how things work* 14 (of a plan or system) to be successful 15 to cultivate (land) 16 to move gradually into a specific condition or position: *he picked up the shovel, worked it under the ice, and levered* 17 to make (one's) way with effort: *he worked his way to the top* 18 *informal* to manipulate to one's own advantage: *they could see an angle and they'd know how to work it*

> **work** *n* 1 = effort, industry, labour, sweat, toil, exertion, drudgery, elbow grease (*facetious*); ≠ leisure 2 = employment, business, job, trade, duty, profession, occupation, livelihood; ≠ play 3 = task, jobs, projects, commissions, duties, assignments, chores, yakka (*Austral, NZ informal*) 4 = creation, piece, production, opus, achievement, composition, handiwork ▸ *vb* 9 = labour, sweat, slave, toil, slog (away), drudge, peg away, exert yourself; ≠ relax 10 = be employed, be in work 12 = operate, use, move, control, drive, manage, handle, manipulate 13 = function, go, run, operate, be in working order; ≠ be out of order 14 = succeed, work out, pay off (*informal*), be successful, be effective, do the trick (*informal*), do the business (*informal*), get results 15 = cultivate, farm, dig, till, plough

workable *adj* 1 able to operate efficiently: *a workable solution* 2 able to be used: *a workable mine*

workaholic *n* a person who is obsessed with work

worker *n* 1 a person who works in a specified way: *a hard worker* 2 a person who works at a specific job: *a government worker* 3 an employee, as opposed to an employer 4 a sterile female bee, ant, or wasp, that works for the colony

> **worker** *n* 2 = employee, hand, labourer, workman *or* woman *or* person, craftsman *or* woman *or* person, artisan, tradesperson

workhorse *n* a person or thing that does a lot of work, esp. dull or routine work: *this plane is the workhorse of most short-haul airlines*

workhouse *n* (formerly, in England) a public institution where very poor people did work in return for food and accommodation

working class *n* 1 the social group that consists of people who earn wages, esp. as manual workers ▸ *adj* **working-class** 2 of or relating to the working class: *a working-class neighbourhood*

W

working party *n* a committee established to investigate a problem

workman *n, pl* **-men** a man who is employed to do manual work

> **workman** *n* = labourer, hand, worker, employee, mechanic, operative, craftsman *or* woman *or* person, artisan

workmanship *n* the degree of skill with which an object is made: *shoddy workmanship*

workshop *n* **1** a room or building where manufacturing or other manual work is carried on **2** a group of people engaged in intensive study or work in a creative or practical field: *a writers' workshop*

> **workshop** *n* **1** = factory, plant, mill

worktop *n* a surface in a kitchen, usually the top of a fitted kitchen unit, which is used for food preparation. Also: **work surface**

work-to-rule *n* a form of industrial action in which employees keep strictly to their employers' rules, with the result of reducing the work rate

world *n* **1** the earth as a planet **2** the human race; people generally: *providing food for the world* **3** any planet or moon, esp. one that might be inhabited **4** a particular group of countries or period of history, or its inhabitants: *the Arab world*; *the post-Cold War world* **5** an area, sphere, or realm considered as a complete environment: *the art world*; *the world of nature* **6** the total circumstances and experience of a person that make up his or her life: *there may not ever be a place for us in your world* **7 bring into the world** to deliver or give birth to (a baby) **8 come into the world** to be born **9 for all the world** exactly or very much: *they looked for all the world like a pair of newly-weds* **10 in the world** used to emphasize a statement: *she didn't have a worry in the world* **11 man** or **woman of the world** a man or woman who is experienced in social or public life **12 worlds apart** very different from each other: *this man and I are worlds apart* ▸ *adj* **13** of or concerning the entire world: *the world championship*

> **world** *n* **1** = earth, planet, globe **2** = humankind, mankind, man, everyone, the public, everybody, humanity **5** = sphere, area, field, environment, realm, domain

worldly *adj* **-lier, -liest 1** not spiritual; earthly or temporal: *as a simple monk he had no interest in politics and other worldly affairs* **2** of or relating to material things: *all his worldly goods* **3** wise in the ways of the world; sophisticated: *a suave, worldly, charming Frenchman* ▸ **worldliness** *n*

> **worldly** *adj* **1** = earthly, physical, secular, terrestrial, temporal, profane; ≠ spiritual **3** = worldly-wise, knowing, experienced, sophisticated, cosmopolitan, urbane, blasé; ≠ naive

world-weary *adj* no longer finding pleasure in life

World Wide Web *n computers* a vast network of hypertext files, stored on computers throughout the world, that can provide a computer user with information on a huge variety of subjects

worm *n* **1** a small invertebrate animal with a long thin body and no limbs **2** an insect larva that looks like a worm **3** a despicable or weak person **4** a slight trace: *a worm of doubt* **5** a shaft on which a spiral thread has been cut, for example in a gear arrangement in which such a shaft drives a toothed wheel **6** *computers* a type of virus ▸ *vb* **7** to rid (an animal) of worms in its intestines **8 worm one's way A** to go or move slowly and with difficulty: *I had to worm my way out sideways from the bench* **B** to get oneself into a certain situation or position gradually: *worming your way into my good books* **9 worm out of** to obtain (information) from someone who is not willing to provide it: *it took me weeks to worm the facts out of him*

worm-eaten *adj* eaten into by worms: *worm-eaten beams*

wormwood *n* a plant from which a bitter oil formerly used in making absinthe is obtained

wormy *adj* **wormier, wormiest** infested with or eaten by worms

worn *vb* **1** the past participle of **wear** ▸ *adj* **2** showing signs of long use or wear: *the worn soles of his boots* **3** looking tired and ill: *that worn pain-creased face*

> **worn** *adj* **2** = ragged, frayed, shabby, tattered, tatty (*Brit*), threadbare, the worse for wear

worried *adj* concerned and anxious about things that may happen > **worriedly** *adv*

> **worried** *adj* = anxious, concerned, troubled, afraid, frightened, nervous, tense, uneasy; ≠ unworried

worry *vb* **-ries, -rying, -ried 1** to be or cause to be anxious or uneasy **2** to annoy or bother: *don't worry yourself with the details* **3** (of a dog) to frighten (sheep or other animals) by chasing and trying to bite them **4 worry away at** to struggle with or work on (a problem) ▸ *n, pl* **-ries 5** a state or feeling of anxiety: *he was beside himself with worry* **6** a cause for anxiety: *having a premature baby is much less of a worry these days* > **worrier** *n*

> **worry** *vb* **1** = be anxious, be concerned, be worried, obsess, brood, fret, agonize, get in a lather (*informal*); ≠ be unconcerned **2** = trouble, upset, bother, disturb, annoy, unsettle, pester, vex; ≠ soothe ▸ *n* **5** = anxiety, concern, fear, trouble, unease, apprehension, misgiving, trepidation (*formal*); ≠ peace of mind **6** = problem, care, trouble, bother, hassle (*informal*)

worrying *adj* causing concern and anxiety

worse *adj* **1** the comparative of **bad 2 none the worse for** not harmed by (adverse events or circumstances) **3 the worse for wear** *informal* in a poor condition; not at one's best: *returning the worse for wear from the pub* ▸ *n* **4 for the worse** into a worse condition: *taking a turn for the worse* ▸ *adv* **5** the comparative of **badly 6 worse off** in a worse condition, esp. financially

worsen *vb* to make or become worse > **worsening** *adj, n*

> **worsen** *vb* = deteriorate, decline, sink, decay, get worse, degenerate, go downhill (*informal*); ≠ improve

worship *vb* **-shipping, -shipped** *or US* **-shiping, -shiped 1** to show profound religious devotion to (one's god), for example by praying **2** to have intense love and admiration for (a person) ▸ *n* **3** religious adoration or devotion **4** formal expression of religious adoration, for example by praying **5** intense love or devotion to a person > **worshipper** *n*

> **worship** *vb* **1** = revere, praise, honour, adore, glorify, exalt, pray to, venerate; ≠ dishonour **2** = love, adore, idolize, put on a pedestal; ≠ despise ▸ *n* **3, 5** = reverence, praise, regard, respect, honour, glory, devotion, adulation

Worship *n* **Your** *or* **His** *or* **Her Worship** *chiefly Brit* a title for a mayor or magistrate

worshipful *adj* feeling or showing reverence or adoration

worst *adj, adv* **1** the superlative of **bad** or **badly** ▸ *n* **2** the least good or the most terrible person, thing, or part: *the worst is yet to come* **3 at one's worst** in the worst condition or aspect of a thing or person: *the British male is at his worst in July and August* **4 at worst** in the least favourable interpretation or conditions: *all the questions should ideally be answered 'no', or at worst 'sometimes'* ▸ *vb* **5** *old-fashioned* to defeat or beat

worsted (**wooss**-tid) *n* a close-textured woollen fabric used to make jackets and trousers

worth *prep* **1** having a value of: *the fire destroyed property worth $200 million* **2** worthy of; meriting or justifying: *if a job is worth doing, it's worth doing well* **3 worth one's weight in gold** extremely useful or helpful; very highly valued **4 worth one's while** worthy of spending one's time or effort on something: *they needed a wage of at least £40 a week to make it worth their while returning to work* ▸ *n* **5** monetary value: *the corporation's net worth* **6** high quality; value: *the submarine proved its military worth during the Second World War* **7** the amount of something that can be bought for a specified price: *$10 billion worth of property*

> **worth** *n* **5** = value, price, rate, cost, estimate, valuation; ≠ worthlessness **6** = merit, value, quality, importance, excellence, goodness, worthiness; ≠ unworthiness

worthless *adj* **1** without value or usefulness: *worthless junk bonds* **2** without merit: *he sees himself as a worthless creature* > **worthlessness** *n*

worthless *adj* **1** = valueless, rubbishy, negligible; ≠ valuable **2** = good-for-nothing, vile, despicable, contemptible; ≠ honourable

worthwhile *adj* sufficiently important, rewarding, or valuable to justify spending time or effort on it

> **worthwhile** *adj* = useful, valuable, helpful, profitable, productive, beneficial, meaningful, constructive; ≠ useless

worthy *adj* **-thier, -thiest 1** deserving of admiration or respect: *motives which were less than worthy* **2 worthy of** deserving of: *he would practise extra hard to be worthy of such an honour* ▸ *n, pl* **-thies 3** *often facetious* an important person > **worthily** *adv* > **worthiness** *n*

> **worthy** *adj* **1** = praiseworthy, deserving, valuable, worthwhile, admirable, virtuous, creditable, laudable; ≠ disreputable

would *vb* **1** used as an auxiliary to form the past tense or subjunctive mood of **will**[1]: *he asked if she would marry him; that would be delightful* **2** to express a polite offer or request: *would you like some lunch?* **3** to describe a habitual past action: *sometimes at lunch time I would choose a painting to go and see*

would-be *adj* wanting or pretending to be: *would-be brides*

> **would-be** *adj* = budding, self-styled, wannabe (*informal*), unfulfilled, self-appointed

wouldn't would not

wound[1] *n* **1** an injury to the body such as a cut or a gunshot injury **2** an injury to one's feelings or reputation ▸ *vb* **3** to cause an injury to the body or feelings of > **wounding** *adj*

> **wound** *n* **1** = injury, cut, hurt, trauma (*pathol*), gash, lesion, laceration **2** = trauma, offence, slight, insult ▸ *vb* = injure, cut, wing, hurt, pierce, gash, lacerate

wound[2] *vb* the past of **wind**[2]

wove *vb* a past tense of **weave**

woven *vb* a past participle of **weave**

wow *interj* **1** an exclamation of admiration or amazement ▸ *n* **2** *slang* a person or thing that is amazingly successful: *he would be an absolute wow on the chat shows* ▸ *vb* **3** *slang* to be a great success with: *the new Disney film wowed festival audiences*

wowser *n Austral & NZ slang* **1** a fanatically puritanical person **2** a teetotaller

wpm words per minute

wraith *n literary* a ghost > **wraithlike** *adj*

wrangle *vb* **-gling, -gled 1** to argue noisily or angrily ▸ *n* **2** a noisy or angry argument

> **wrangle** *vb* = argue, fight, row, dispute, disagree, contend, quarrel, squabble ▸ *n* = argument, row, dispute, quarrel, squabble, bickering, tiff, altercation

W

wrap *vb* **wrapping, wrapped 1** to fold a covering round (something) and fasten it securely: *a small package wrapped in brown paper* **2** to fold or wind (something) round a person or thing: *she wrapped a handkerchief around her bleeding palm* **3** to fold, wind, or coil: *she wrapped her arms around her mother* **4** to complete the filming of (a motion picture or television programme) ▸ *n* **5** *old-fashioned* a garment worn wrapped round the shoulders **6** (in the filming of a motion picture or television programme) the end of a day's filming or the completion of filming **7** a type of sandwich consisting of filling rolled up in a flour tortilla **8** *Brit slang* a small packet of an illegal drug in powder form: *a wrap of heroin* **9 keep something under wraps** to keep something secret

> **wrap** *vb* **1** = cover, enclose, shroud, swathe, encase, enfold, bundle up; ≠ unpack **2, 3** = bind, swathe; ≠ unwind ▸ *n* **5** = cloak, cape, stole, mantle (*archaic*), shawl

wrapper *n* a paper, foil, or plastic cover in which a product is wrapped: *a single sweet wrapper*

wrapping *n* a piece of paper, foil, or other material used to wrap something in

wrap up *vb* **1** to fold paper, cloth, or other material round (something) **2** to put warm clothes on: *remember to wrap up warmly on cold or windy days* **3** *informal* to finish or settle: *he will need 60 to 90 days to wrap up his current business dealings* **4** *slang* to stop talking **5 wrapped up in** giving all one's attention to: *wrapped up in her new baby*

> **wrap up** *vb* **1 wrap something up** = giftwrap, pack, package, bundle up **3 wrap something up** = end, conclude, wind up, terminate, finish off, round off, polish off

wrasse *n* a brightly coloured sea fish

wrath (roth) *n old-fashioned or literary* intense anger > **wrathful** *adj*

> **wrath** *n* = anger, rage, temper, fury, resentment, indignation, ire, displeasure; ≠ satisfaction

wreak *vb* **1 wreak havoc** to cause chaos or damage: *this Australian sun will wreak havoc with your complexions* **2 wreak vengeance on** to take revenge on

wreath *n, pl* **wreaths 1** a ring of flowers or leaves, placed on a grave as a memorial or worn on the head as a garland or a mark of honour **2** anything circular or spiral: *a wreath of smoke*

wreck *vb* **1** to break, spoil, or destroy completely **2** to cause the accidental sinking or destruction of (a ship) at sea ▸ *n* **3** something that has been destroyed or badly damaged, such as a crashed car or aircraft **4** a ship that has been sunk or destroyed at sea **5** a person in a poor mental or physical state

> **wreck** *vb* **1** = destroy, break, smash, ruin, devastate, shatter, spoil, demolish, kennet (*Austral slang*), jeff (*Austral slang*); ≠ build ▸ *n* **4** = shipwreck, hulk

wreckage *n* the remains of something that has been destroyed or badly damaged, such as a crashed car or aircraft

wrecker *n* **1** a person who destroys or badly damages something: *a marriage wrecker* **2** (formerly) a person who lured ships onto rocks in order to plunder them **3** *chiefly US, Canad & NZ* a person whose job is to demolish buildings or dismantle cars **4** *US & Canad* a breakdown van

wren *n* a very small brown songbird

Wren *n informal* (formerly, in Britain and certain other nations) a member of the former Women's Royal Naval Service

wrench *vb* **1** to twist or pull (something) violently, for example to remove it from something to which it is attached: *he grabbed the cable and wrenched it out of the wall socket* **2** to move or twist away with a sudden violent effort: *she wrenched free of his embrace* **3** to injure (a limb or joint) by a sudden twist ▸ *n* **4** a violent twist or pull **5** an injury to a limb or joint, caused by twisting it **6** a feeling of sadness experienced on leaving a person or place: *it would be a wrench to leave Essex after all these years* **7** a spanner with adjustable jaws

> **wrench** *vb* **1** = twist, force, pull, tear, rip, tug, jerk, yank **3** = sprain, strain, rick ▸ *n* **4** = twist, pull, rip, tug, jerk, yank **5** = sprain, strain, twist **6** = blow, shock, upheaval, pang **7** = spanner, adjustable spanner

wrest *vb* **1** to take (something) away from someone with a violent pull or twist **2** to seize forcibly by violent or unlawful means: *she must begin to wrest control of the army and the police*

wrestle *vb* **-tling, -tled 1** to fight (someone) by grappling and trying to throw or pin him or her to the ground, often as a sport **2 wrestle with** to struggle hard with (a person, problem, or thing): *I wrestled with my conscience* > **wrestler** *n*

> **wrestle** *vb* **1** = fight, battle, struggle, combat, grapple, tussle, scuffle

wrestling *n* a sport in which each contestant tries to overcome the other either by throwing or pinning him or her to the ground or by forcing a submission

wretch *n old-fashioned* **1** a despicable person **2** a person pitied for his or her misfortune

wretched (retch-id) *adj* **1** in poor or pitiful circumstances: *a vast wretched slum* **2** feeling very unhappy **3** of poor quality: *the wretched state of the cabbages* **4** *informal* undesirable or displeasing: *what a wretched muddle* > **wretchedly** *adv* > **wretchedness** *n*

wriggle *vb* **-gling, -gled 1** to twist and turn with quick movements: *he wriggled on the hard seat*

2 to move along by twisting and turning
3 wriggle out of to avoid (doing something that one does not want to do): *he wriggled out of donating blood* ▸ *n* **4** a wriggling movement or action

wring *vb* **wringing, wrung 1** Also: **wring out** to squeeze water from (a cloth or clothing) by twisting it tightly **2** to twist (a neck) violently **3** to clasp and twist (one's hands) in anguish **4** to grip (someone's hand) vigorously in greeting **5** to obtain by forceful means: *to wring concessions from the army* **6 wring someone's heart** to make someone feel sorrow or pity

wrinkle *n* **1** a slight ridge in the smoothness of a surface, such as a crease in the skin as a result of age ▸ *vb* **-kling, -kled 2** to develop or cause to develop wrinkles > **wrinkled** or **wrinkly** *adj*

> **wrinkle** *n* = line, fold, crease, furrow, crow's-foot, corrugation ▸ *vb* = crease, gather, fold, crumple, furrow, rumple, pucker, corrugate; ≠ smooth

wrist *n* **1** the joint between the forearm and the hand **2** the part of a sleeve that covers the wrist

wristwatch *n* a watch worn strapped round the wrist

writ *n* a formal legal document ordering a person to do or not to do something

> **writ** *n* = summons, document, decree, indictment, court order, subpoena, arraignment

write *vb* **writing, wrote, written 1** to draw or mark (words, letters, or numbers) on paper or a blackboard with a pen, pencil, or chalk **2** to describe or record (something) in writing: *he began to write his memoirs* **3** to be an author: *he still taught writing, but he didn't write* **4** to write a letter to or correspond regularly with someone: *don't forget to write!* **5** *informal, chiefly US & Canad* to write a letter to (someone): *I wrote him several times* **6** to say or communicate in a letter or a book: *in a recent letter a friend wrote that everything costs more in Russia now* **7** to fill in the details for (a cheque or document) **8** *computers* to record (data) in a storage device **9 write down** to record in writing: *write it down if you find it too embarrassing to talk about*

> **write** *vb* **1** = record, scribble, inscribe, set down, jot down **2** = compose, draft, pen, draw up **4** = correspond, get in touch, keep in touch, write a letter, drop a line, drop a note, email *or* e-mail

writer *n* **1** a person whose job is writing; author **2** the person who has written something specified: *the writer of this letter is pretty dangerous*

> **writer** *n* **1** = author, novelist, hack, scribbler, scribe, wordsmith, penpusher

writhe *vb* **writhing, writhed** to twist or squirm in pain: *writhing in agony*

writing *n* **1** something that has been written: *the writing on the outer flap was faint* **2** written form: *permission in writing* **3** short for **handwriting** **4** a kind or style of writing: *creative writing* **5** the work of a writer: *Wilde never mentioned chess in his writing*

> **writing** *n* **3** = script, hand, printing, fist (*informal*), scribble, handwriting, scrawl, calligraphy

wrong *adj* **1** not correct or accurate: *the wrong answers* **2** acting or judging in error; mistaken: *do correct me if I'm wrong* **3** not in accordance with correct or conventional rules or standards; immoral: *this group argues that even gently slapping a child is wrong* **4** not intended or appropriate: *I ordered the wrong things; you've picked the wrong time to ask such questions* **5** being a problem or trouble: *come on, I know when something's wrong* **6** not functioning properly: *there's something wrong with the temperature sensor* **7** denoting the side of cloth that is worn facing inwards ▸ *adv* **8** in a wrong manner: *I guessed wrong* **9 get someone wrong** to misunderstand someone: *don't get me wrong, I'm not making threats* **10 get something wrong** to make a mistake about something: *he had got his body language wrong* **11 go wrong A** to turn out badly or not as intended **B** to make a mistake **C** (of a machine) to stop functioning properly: *pilots must be able to react instantly if the automatic equipment suddenly goes wrong* ▸ *n* **12** something bad, immoral, or unjust: *how can such a wrong be redressed?* **13 in the wrong** mistaken or guilty ▸ *vb* **14** to treat (someone) unjustly **15** to think or speak unfairly of (someone) > **wrongly** *adv*

> **wrong** *adj* **1, 2** = incorrect, mistaken, false, inaccurate, untrue, erroneous, wide of the mark, fallacious **3** = bad, criminal, illegal, evil, unlawful, immoral, unjust, dishonest; ≠ moral **4** = inappropriate, incorrect, unsuitable, unacceptable, undesirable, incongruous, unseemly, unbecoming; ≠ correct **5** = amiss, faulty, unsatisfactory, not right, defective, awry **6** = defective, faulty, awry, askew ▸ *adv* **8** = incorrectly, badly, wrongly, mistakenly, erroneously, inaccurately; ≠ correctly ▸ *n* **12** = offence, injury, crime, error, sin, injustice, misdeed, transgression; ≠ good deed ▸ *vb* **14** = mistreat, abuse, hurt, harm, cheat, take advantage of, oppress, malign; ≠ treat well

wrongdoing *n* immoral or illegal behaviour > **wrongdoer** *n*

wrongful *adj* unjust or illegal: *wrongful imprisonment* > **wrongfully** *adv*

wrote *vb* the past tense of **write**

wrought (rawt) *vb* **1** *old-fashioned* a past of **work** ▸ *adj* **2** *metallurgy* shaped by hammering or beating: *wrought copper and brass*

wrought iron *n* a pure form of iron with a low carbon content, often used for decorative work

W

wrung *vb* the past of **wring**

wry *adj* **wrier, wriest** *or* **wryer, wryest 1** drily humorous; sardonic: *wry amusement* **2** (of a facial expression) produced by twisting one's features to denote amusement or displeasure: *a small wry smile twisted the corner of his mouth* ⟩ **wryly** *adv*

wt. weight

WWW World Wide Web

wych-elm *or* **witch-elm** *n* a Eurasian elm with long pointed leaves

X 1 indicating an error, a choice, or a kiss **2** indicating an unknown, unspecified, or variable factor, person, or thing: *Miss X* **3** the Roman numeral for ten **4** (formerly) indicating a film that may not be publicly shown to anyone under 18: since 1982 replaced by symbol 18

xenon *n chem* a colourless odourless gas found in minute quantities in the air. Symbol: **Xe**

xenophobia (zen-oh-**fobe**-ee-a) *n* hatred or fear of foreigners or strangers ⟩ **xenophobic** *adj*

Xerox (**zeer**-ox) *n trademark* **1** a machine for copying printed material **2** a copy made by a Xerox machine ▸ *vb* **3** to produce a copy of (a document) using such a machine

Xmas (**eks**-mass) *n informal* short for **Christmas**

XML extensible markup language: a computer language used in text formatting

X-ray *or* **x-ray** *n* **1** a stream of electromagnetic radiation of short wavelength that can pass through some solid materials **2** a picture produced by exposing photographic film to X-rays: used in medicine as a diagnostic aid, since parts of the body, such as bones, absorb X-rays and so appear as opaque areas on the picture ▸ *vb* **3** to photograph, treat, or examine using X-rays

> **X-ray** *or* **x-ray** *n* **2** = radiograph, X-ray image

xylem (**zile**-em) *n botany* a plant tissue that conducts water and mineral salts from the roots to all other parts

xylophone (**zile**-oh-fone) *n music* a percussion instrument consisting of a set of wooden bars played with hammers ⟩ **xylophonist** *n*

Yy

ya *interj S African* yes

yabby *n, pl* **-bies** *Austral* **1** a small freshwater crayfish **2** a marine prawn used as bait

yacht (yott) *n* **1** a large boat with sails or an engine, used for racing or pleasure cruising ▸ *vb* **2** to sail or cruise in a yacht > **yachting** *n, adj*

yachtsman *or fem* **yachtswoman** *n, pl* **-men** *or* **-women** a person who sails a yacht

yak¹ *n* a Tibetan ox with long shaggy hair

yak² *slang* ▸ *n* **1** noisy, continuous, and trivial talk ▸ *vb* **yakking, yakked 2** to talk continuously about unimportant matters

yakka *n Austral & NZ informal* work

yam *n* **1** a twining plant of tropical and subtropical regions, cultivated for its starchy roots, which are eaten as a vegetable **2** the sweet potato

yank *vb* **1** to pull (someone or something) with a sharp movement: *I yanked myself out of the water* ▸ *n* **2** a sudden pull or jerk

> **yank** *vb* = pull, tug, jerk, seize, snatch, pluck, hitch, wrench ▸ *n* = pull, tug, jerk, snatch, hitch, wrench, tweak

Yank *n slang* a person from the United States

Yankee *n* **1** *slang* same as **Yank 2** a person from the Northern United States ▸ *adj* **3** of or characteristic of Yankees

yap *vb* **yapping, yapped 1** to bark with a high-pitched sound **2** *informal* to talk at length in an annoying or stupid way ▸ *n* **3** a high-pitched bark **4** *slang* annoying or stupid speech > **yappy** *adj*

yard¹ *n* **1** a unit of length equal to 3 feet (0.9144 metre) **2** *naut* a spar slung across a ship's mast to extend the sail

yard² *n* **1** a piece of enclosed ground, often adjoining or surrounded by a building or buildings **2** an enclosed or open area where a particular type of work is done: *a shipbuilding yard* **3** *US, Canad & Austral* the garden of a house **4** *US & Canad* the winter pasture of deer, moose, and similar animals

yardstick *n* **1** a measure or standard used for comparison: *there's no yardstick for judging a problem of this sort* **2** a graduated measuring stick one yard long

yarmulke (yar-mull-ka) *n* a skullcap worn by Jewish men

yarn *n* **1** a continuous twisted strand of natural or synthetic fibres, used for knitting or making cloth **2** *informal* a long involved story **3 spin a yarn** *informal* to tell such a story

yarn *n* **1** = thread, fibre, cotton, wool **2** = story, tale, anecdote, account, narrative, fable, reminiscence, urban myth

yashmak *n* a veil worn by some Muslim women to cover the face in public

yaw *vb* **1** (of an aircraft or ship) to turn to one side or from side to side while moving ▸ *n* **2** the act or movement of yawing

yawl *n* **1** a two-masted sailing boat **2** a ship's small boat

yawn *vb* **1** to open one's mouth wide and take in air deeply, often when sleepy or bored **2** to be open wide as if threatening to engulf someone or something: *the doorway yawned blackly open at the end of the hall* ▸ *n* **3** the act or an instance of yawning > **yawning** *adj*

yd yard (measure)

ye (yee) *pron old-fashioned or dialect* you

year *n* **1** the time taken for the earth to make one revolution around the sun, about 365 days **2** the twelve months from January 1 to December 31 **3** a period of twelve months from any specified date **4** a specific period of time, usually occupying a definite part or parts of a twelve-month period, used for some particular activity: *the financial year* **5** a group of people who have started an academic course at the same time **6 year in, year out** regularly or monotonously, over a long period **7 years A** a long time: *the legal case could take years to resolve* **B** age, usually old age: *a man of his years*

yearling *n* an animal that is between one and two years old

yearly *adj* **1** occurring, done, or appearing once a year or every year **2** lasting or valid for a year: *the yearly cycle* ▸ *adv* **3** once a year

> **yearly** *adj* **1** = annual, each year, every year, once a year ▸ *adv* = annually, every year, by the year, once a year, per annum

yearn *vb* **1** to have an intense desire or longing: *he often yearned for life in a country town* **2** to feel tenderness or affection: *I yearn for you* > **yearning** *n, adj*

> **yearn** *vb* **1** = long, desire, hunger, ache, crave, covet, itch, hanker after

yeast *n* a yellowish fungus used in fermenting alcoholic drinks and in raising dough for bread > **yeasty** *adj*

yebo *interj S African informal* yes

yell *vb* **1** to shout, scream, or cheer in a loud or piercing way ▸ *n* **2** a loud piercing cry of pain, anger, or fear

> **yell** *vb* = scream, shout, cry out, howl, call out, wail, shriek, screech; ≠ whisper ▸ *n* = scream, cry, shout, roar, howl, shriek, whoop, screech; ≠ whisper

yellow *n* **1** the colour of a lemon or an egg yolk **2** anything yellow, such as yellow clothing or yellow paint: *painted in yellow* ▸ *adj* **3** of the colour yellow; of the colour of a lemon or an egg yolk **4** *informal* cowardly or afraid **5** having a yellowish complexion ▸ *vb* **6** to make or become yellow or yellower ⊳ **yellowish** or **yellowy** *adj*

> **yellow** *n* **1** = lemon, gold, amber

yellow fever *n* an acute infectious tropical disease causing fever and jaundice, caused by certain mosquitoes

yellowhammer *n* a European songbird with a yellowish head and body

Yellow Pages *pl n trademark* a telephone directory that lists businesses under the headings of the type of business or service they provide

yelp *vb* **1** to utter a sharp or high-pitched cry of pain ▸ *n* **2** a sharp or high-pitched cry of pain

yen¹ *n, pl* **yen** the standard monetary unit of Japan

yen² *informal* ▸ *n* **1** a longing or desire ▸ *vb* **yenning, yenned 2** to have a longing

> **yen** *n* = longing, desire, craving, yearning, passion, hunger, ache, itch

yeoman (yo-man) *n, pl* **-men** *history* a farmer owning and farming his own land

yeoman of the guard *n* a member of the ceremonial bodyguard (**Yeomen of the Guard**) of the British monarch

yes *interj* **1** used to express consent, agreement, or approval, or to answer when one is addressed **2** used to signal someone to speak or keep speaking, enter a room, or do something ▸ *n* **3** an answer or vote of *yes* **4** a person who answers or votes *yes*

yes man *n* a person who always agrees with his or her superior in order to gain favour

yesterday *n* **1** the day before today **2** the recent past ▸ *adv* **3** on or during the day before today **4** in the recent past

yet *conj* **1** nevertheless or still: *I'm too tired to work, yet I have to go on* ▸ *adv* **2** up until then or now: *this may be her most rewarding book yet* **3** still: *yet more work to do* **4** now (as contrasted with later): *not ready for that yet* **5** eventually in spite of everything: *I'll break your spirit yet!* **6 as yet** up until then or now

> **yet** *conj* = nevertheless, still, however, for all that, notwithstanding, just the same, be that as it may ▸ *adv* **2** = so far, until now, up to now, still, as yet, even now, thus far, up till now **3** = still, in addition, besides, to boot, into the bargain **4** = now, right now, just now, so soon

yeti *n* same as **abominable snowman**

yew *n* an evergreen tree with needle-like leaves, red berries, and fine-grained elastic wood

Yiddish *n* **1** a language derived from High German, spoken by Jews in Europe and elsewhere by Jewish emigrants, and usually written in the Hebrew alphabet ▸ *adj* **2** of this language

yield *vb* **1** to produce or bear **2** to give as a return: *some of his policies have yielded large savings* **3** to give up control of; surrender **4** to give way, submit, or surrender, through force or persuasion: *the players finally yielded to the weather* **5** to agree (to): *governments too weak to say no repeatedly yielded to petitions for charters* **6** to grant or allow: *to yield right of way* ▸ *n* **7** the amount produced

> **yield** *vb* **1, 2** = produce, give, provide, return, supply, bear, net, earn; ≠ use up **3** = relinquish, resign, hand over, surrender, turn over, make over, give over, bequeath; ≠ retain **4** = bow, submit, give in, surrender, succumb, cave in (*informal*), capitulate ▸ *n* = produce, crop, harvest, output; ≠ loss

yielding *adj* **1** compliant or submissive **2** soft or flexible: *he landed on a yielding surface rather than rock or board*

> **yielding** *adj* **1** = submissive, obedient, compliant, docile, flexible, accommodating, pliant, acquiescent; ≠ obstinate **2** = soft, pliable, springy, elastic, supple, spongy, unresisting

YMCA Young Men's Christian Association

yob or **yobbo** *n, pl* **yobs** or **yobbos** *Brit, Austral & NZ slang* a bad-mannered aggressive youth ⊳ **yobbish** *adj*

> **yob** or **yobbo** *n* = thug, hooligan, lout, hoon (*Austral, NZ informal*), ruffian, roughneck (*slang*), tsotsi (*S African*), cougan (*Austral slang*), scozza (*Austral slang*), bogan (*Austral slang*)

yodel *vb* **-delling, -delled** or *US* **-deling, -deled 1** to sing with abrupt changes back and forth between the normal voice and falsetto, as in folk songs of the Swiss Alps ▸ *n* **2** the act or sound of yodelling ⊳ **yodeller** or *US* **yodeler** *n*

yoga *n* **1** a Hindu system of philosophy aiming at spiritual, mental, and physical wellbeing by means of deep meditation, prescribed postures, and controlled breathing **2** a system of exercising involving such meditation, postures, and breathing

yogi *n* a person who practises or is a master of yoga

yogurt or **yoghurt** *n* a slightly sour custard-like food made from milk curdled by bacteria, often sweetened and flavoured with fruit

yoke *n, pl* **yokes** or **yoke 1** a wooden frame with a bar put across the necks of two animals to hold them together so that they can be worked as a team **2** a pair of animals joined by a yoke **3** a frame fitting over a person's shoulders for carrying buckets **4** an oppressive force or burden: *people are still suffering under the yoke of slavery* **5** a fitted part of a garment to which a fuller part is attached ▸ *vb* **yoking, yoked 6** to put a yoke on **7** to unite or link

y

yokel n derogatory a person who lives in the country, esp. one who appears simple and old-fashioned

yolk n the yellow part in the middle of an egg that provides food for the developing embryo

Yom Kippur n an annual Jewish holiday celebrated as a day of fasting, with prayers of penitence

yonder adv 1 over there ▸ adj 2 situated over there: a tree at yonder waterfall

yonks pl n informal a very long time: he must have been planning this for yonks

yore n of yore a long time ago: in days of yore

Yorkshire pudding n a baked pudding made from a batter of flour, eggs, and milk, often served with roast beef

you pron 1 (refers to) the person or people addressed: can I get you a drink? 2 (refers to) an unspecified person or people in general: just keep it simple and you can't go wrong ▸ n 3 informal the personality of the person being addressed: that hat isn't really you

young adj 1 having lived or existed for a relatively short time 2 having qualities associated with youth: their innovative approach and young attitude appealed to him 3 of or relating to youth: he'd been a terrorist himself in France in his young days 4 of a group representing the younger members of a larger organization: Young Conservatives ▸ n 5 young people in general: that never seems very important to the young 6 offspring, esp. young animals: a deer suckling her young > **youngish** adj

young adj 1 = immature, juvenile, youthful, little, green, junior, infant, adolescent; ≠ old ▸ n 6 = offspring, baby, litter, family, issue, brood, progeny; ≠ parent

youngster n a young person

youngster n = youth, girl, boy, kid (informal), lad, teenager, juvenile, lass

your adj 1 of, belonging to, or associated with you: ask your doctor to make the necessary calls 2 of, belonging to, or associated with an unspecified person or people in general: it is not right to take another baby to replace your own 3 informal used to indicate all things or people of a certain type: these characters are not your average housebreakers

yours pron 1 something belonging to you: my reputation is better than yours 2 your family: a blessed Christmas to you and yours 3 used in closing phrases at the end of a letter: yours sincerely; yours faithfully 4 of yours belonging to you: that husband of yours

yourself pron, pl -selves 1 A the reflexive form of you B used for emphasis: you've stated publicly that you yourself use drugs 2 your normal self: you're not yourself today

youth n 1 the period between childhood and maturity 2 the quality or condition of being young, immature, or inexperienced: his youth told against him in the contest 3 a young man or boy

4 young people collectively: there is still hope for today's youth 5 the freshness, vigour, or vitality associated with being young

youth n 1 = immaturity, adolescence, boyhood or girlhood, salad days; ≠ old age 3 = boy, lad, youngster, kid (informal), teenager, young man, adolescent, teen (informal); ≠ adult

youth club n a club that provides leisure activities for young people

youthful adj 1 vigorous or active: the intermediate section was won by a youthful grandmother 2 of, relating to, possessing, or associated with youth: youthful good looks > **youthfully** adv > **youthfulness** n

youthful adj 2 = young, juvenile, childish, immature, boyish, girlish; ≠ elderly

youth hostel n an inexpensive lodging place for young people travelling cheaply

yowl vb 1 to produce a loud mournful wail or cry ▸ n 2 a wail or howl

yo-yo n, pl -yos 1 a toy consisting of a spool attached to a string, the end of which is held while it is repeatedly spun out and reeled in ▸ vb **yo-yoing, yo-yoed** 2 to change repeatedly from one position to another

yttrium (it-ree-um) n chem a silvery metallic element used in various alloys and in lasers. Symbol: **Y**

yucca n a tropical plant with spiky leaves and white flowers

yucky or **yukky** adj **yuckier, yuckiest** or **yukkier, yukkiest** slang disgusting or nasty

Yule n literary or old-fashioned Christmas or the Christmas season: Yuletide

yuppie n 1 a young highly-paid professional person, esp. one who has a fashionable way of life ▸ adj 2 typical of or reflecting the values of yuppies: a yuppie accessory

YWCA Young Women's Christian Association

y

Zz

zany (zane-ee) *adj* **zanier**, **zaniest** comical in an endearing way

zap *vb* **zapping**, **zapped** *slang* **1** to kill, esp. by shooting **2** to change television channels rapidly by remote control **3** to move quickly

zeal *n* great enthusiasm or eagerness, esp. for a religious movement

> **zeal** *n* = enthusiasm, passion, zest, spirit, verve, fervour, eagerness, gusto; ≠ apathy

zealot (zel-lot) *n* a fanatic or an extreme enthusiast > **zealotry** *n*

zealous (zel-luss) *adj* extremely eager or enthusiastic > **zealously** *adv*

zebra *n, pl* **-ras** *or* **-ra** a black-and-white striped African animal of the horse family

zebra crossing *n Brit* a pedestrian crossing marked by broad black and white stripes: once on the crossing the pedestrian has right of way

zebu (zee-boo) *n* a domesticated ox of Africa and Asia, with a humped back and long horns

Zen *n* a Japanese form of Buddhism that concentrates on learning through meditation and intuition

zenith *n* **1** the point in the sky directly above an observer **2** the highest or most successful point of anything: *he was at the zenith of his military career* > **zenithal** *adj*

zephyr (zef-fer) *n* a soft gentle breeze

Zeppelin *n* a large cylindrical rigid German airship of the early 20th century

zero *n, pl* **-ros** *or* **-roes** **1** the cardinal number between +1 and -1 **2** the symbol, 0, representing this number **3** the line or point on a scale of measurement from which the graduations commence **4** the lowest point or degree: *my credibility is down to zero* **5** nothing or nil **6** the temperature, pressure, etc., that registers a reading of zero on a scale ▸ *adj* **7** amounting to zero: *zero inflation* **8** *meteorol* (of visibility) limited to a very short distance ▸ *vb* **-roing, -roed** **9** to adjust (an instrument or scale) so as to read zero

> **zero** *n* **1** = nought, nothing (*informal*), nil **4** = rock bottom, the bottom, an all-time low, a nadir, as low as you can get

zero in on *vb* **1** to aim a weapon at (a target) **2** to concentrate one's attention on

zest *n* **1** invigorating or keen excitement or enjoyment: *she has a zest for life and a quick intellect* **2** added interest, flavour, or charm: *he said that she would provide a new zest for his government* **3** the peel of an orange or lemon, used as flavouring > **zestful** *adj*

zigzag *n* **1** a line or course having sharp turns in alternating directions ▸ *adj* **2** formed in or proceeding in a zigzag ▸ *adv* **3** in a zigzag manner ▸ *vb* **-zagging, -zagged** **4** to move in a zigzag

zinc *n chem* a brittle bluish-white metallic element that is used in alloys such as brass, to form a protective coating on metals, and in battery electrodes. Symbol: **Zn**

zing *n* **1** *informal* the quality in something that makes it lively or interesting **2** a short high-pitched buzzing sound, like the sound of a bullet or vibrating string

Zionism *n* a political movement for the establishment and support of a national homeland for Jews in what is now Israel > **Zionist** *n, adj*

zip *n* **1** Also called: **zip fastener** a fastener with two parallel rows of metal or plastic teeth, one on either side of a closure, which are interlocked by a sliding tab **2** *informal* energy or vigour **3** a short sharp whizzing sound, like the sound of a passing bullet ▸ *vb* **zipping, zipped** **4** (often foll. by *up*) to fasten with a zip **5** to move with a sharp whizzing sound: *bullets zipped and ricocheted all around us* **6** to hurry or rush **7** to compress (a data file) prior to transmission

> **zip** *n* **2** = energy, drive, vigour, verve, zest, gusto, liveliness; ≠ lethargy ▸ *vb* **5, 6** = speed, shoot, fly, flash, zoom, whizz (*informal*)

zipline *or* **zipwire** *n* a cable mechanism used for transportation across a river, gorge, etc.

zircon *n mineralogy* a hard mineral consisting of zirconium silicate, used as a gemstone and in industry

zirconium *n chem* a greyish-white metallic element, occurring chiefly in zircon, that is exceptionally corrosion-resistant. Symbol: **Zr**

zither *n* a musical instrument consisting of numerous strings stretched over a flat box and plucked to produce notes > **zitherist** *n*

zodiac *n* **1** an imaginary belt in the sky within which the sun, moon, and planets appear to move, and which is divided into 12 equal areas called **signs of the zodiac**, each named after the constellation which once lay in it **2** *astrol* a diagram, usually circular, representing this belt > **zodiacal** *adj*

zombie *or* **zombi** *n, pl* **-bies** *or* **-bis** **1** a person who appears to be lifeless, apathetic, or totally lacking in independent judgment **2** a corpse brought to life by witchcraft

zone *n* **1** a region, area, or section characterized by some distinctive feature or quality: *a demilitarized zone* **2** *geog* one of the divisions of the earth's surface according to temperature **3** a section on a transport route **4** *maths* a portion of a sphere between two parallel lines intersecting

Z

the sphere **5** NZ a catchment area for a specific school ▸ *vb* **zoning**, **zoned 6** to divide (a place) into zones for different uses or activities › **zonal** *adj* › **zoning** *n*

> **zone** *n* **1** = area, region, section, sector, district, territory, belt, sphere

zoo *n, pl* **zoos** a place where live animals are kept, studied, bred, and exhibited to the public

zoological garden *n* the formal term for **zoo**

zoology *n* the study of animals, including their classification, structure, physiology, and history › **zoological** *adj* › **zoologist** *n*

zoom *vb* **1** to move very rapidly: *the first rocket zoomed into the sky* **2** to increase or rise rapidly: *stocks zoomed on the American exchange* **3** to move with or make a continuous buzzing or humming sound ▸ *n* **4** the sound or act of zooming **5** a zoom lens

> **zoom** *vb* **1** = speed, shoot, fly, rush, flash, dash, whizz (*informal*), hurtle

zoom lens *n* a lens system that can make the details of a picture larger or smaller while keeping the picture in focus

zucchini (zoo-**keen**-ee) *n, pl* **-ni** *or* **-nis** *chiefly US, Canad & Austral* a courgette

Zulu *n* **1** *pl* **-lus** *or* **-lu** a member of a people of Southern Africa **2** the language of this people

Zumba *n trademark* a system of exercises performed to Latin American dance music

zygote *n* the cell resulting from the union of an ovum and a spermatozoon

Z